CHILD AND
ADOLESCENT PSYCHIATRY
MODERN APPROACHES

He who does not doubt, does not investigate,
and he who does not investigate does not perceive,
and he who does not perceive remains in
blindness and error.

Al-Ghazali (1058—1111)

CHILD AND ADOLESCENT PSYCHIATRY

MODERN APPROACHES

EDITED BY

MICHAEL RUTTER
CBE, MD, FRCP, FRCPsych, FRS
Professor of Psychiatry and Honorary Director
MRC Child Psychiatry Unit
Institute of Psychiatry, London

ERIC TAYLOR
FRCP, FRCPsych
Professor of Developmental Neuropsychiatry
Department of Child and Adolescent Psychiatry
Institute of Psychiatry, London

LIONEL HERSOV
MD, FRCP, FRCPsych, DPM
Formerly Professor of Psychiatry and Pediatrics
University of Massachusetts Medical School

THIRD EDITION

b

Blackwell
Science

© 1976, 1985, 1994 by
Blackwell Science Ltd
Editorial Offices:
Osney Mead, Oxford OX2 0EL
25 John Street, London WC1N 2BL
23 Ainslie Place, Edinburgh EH3 6AJ
238 Main Street, Cambridge
   Massachusetts 02142, USA
54 University Street, Carlton
   Victoria 3053, Australia

Other Editorial Offices:
Arnette Blackwell SA
1, rue de Lille
75007 Paris
France

Blackwell Wissenschafts-Verlag GmbH
Kurfürstendamm 57
10707 Berlin,
Germany

Blackwell MZV
Feldgasse 13
A-1238 Wien
Austria

First published 1976
Second edition 1985
Reprinted as paperback 1987, 1990, 1991
Third edition 1994
Reprinted 1995

Set by Setrite Typesetters Ltd, Hong Kong
Printed and bound in Great Britain
by The Bath Press, Bath, Avon

DISTRIBUTORS

Marston Book Services Ltd
PO Box 87
Oxford OX2 0DT
(*Orders*: Tel: 01865 791155
        Fax: 01865 791927
        Telex: 837515)

North America
Blackwell Science, Inc.
238 Main Street
Cambridge, MA 02142
(*Orders*: Tel 800 215–1000
        617 876–7000
        Fax: 617 492–5263)

Australia
Blackwell Science Pty Ltd
54 University Street
Carlton, Victoria 3053
(*Orders*: Tel: 03 347–5552)

A catalogue record for this title
is available from the British Library

ISBN 0–632–02822–X

Library of Congress
Cataloging in Publication Data

Child and adolescent psychiatry:
modern approaches/edited by
   Michael Rutter, Eric Taylor, Lionel Hersov.
   — 3rd ed.
              p.   cm.
      Includes bibliographical references
      and index.
      ISBN 0–632–02822–X
      1. Child psychiatry.
   2. Adolescent psychiatry.
   I. Rutter, Michael. II. Taylor, Eric A.
   III. Hersov, L.A. (Lionel Abraham)
      [DNLM: 1. Adolescent Behavior.
   2. Child Development Disorders.
   3. Mental Disorders — in adolescence.
   4. Mental Disorders — in infancy
   & childhood.   WS 350 C53503 1994]
   RJ499.C486   1994
   618.92'89 — dc20

Contents

Contributors

Adrian Angold BSc, MB BS, MRCPsych
Developmental Epidemiology Program, Department of Psychiatry, Duke University Medical Center, Durham, NC 27710, USA

Anthony Bailey BSc, MB BS, MRCPsych, DCH
MRC Child Psychiatry Unit, Institute of Psychiatry, De Crespigny Park, London SE5 8AF

Arnon Bentovim MB BS, DPM, FRCPsych
Department of Psychological Medicine, The Hospitals for Sick Children, Great Ormond Street, London WC1N 3JH

Michael Berger BA, Dip Psych (London), PhD
Department of Clinical Psychology (Child and Adolescent Service), St George's Hospital, Blackshaw Road, London SW17 0QT

Colin D. Binnie MD, MA, BChir
Department of Clinical Neurophysiology, The Maudsley Hospital, Denmark Hill, London SE5 8AZ

D.V.M. Bishop MA, MPhil, DPhil
MRC Applied Psychology Unit, 15 Chaucer Road, Cambridge CB2 2EF

Dora Black MB, FRCPsych, DPM
Department of Child and Adolescent Psychiatry, The Royal Free Hospital, Pond Street, Hampstead, London NW3 2QG

Patrick Bolton BSc, MB BS, MRCPsych
University of Cambridge, Section of Developmental Psychiatry, Douglas House, 18b Trumpington Road, Cambridge CB2 4AH

Stewart Boyd MB ChB, MD
Department of Clinical Neurophysiology, The Hospitals for Sick Children, Great Ormond Street, London WC1N 3JH

Rachel M.A. Brown MB BS, MPhil, MRCPsych
Department of Child and Family Psychiatry, South-West Herts Health Authority, 180 Hempstead Road, Watford, Herts WD1 3LG; and Developmental Psychopathology Research Unit, The Tavistock Clinic, and University College Hospital School of Medicine

Maria Callias BA, BA (Hons), MA, MSc
Departments of Psychology and of Child and Adolescent Psychiatry, Institute of Psychiatry, De Crespigny Park, London SE5 8AF

Dennis P. Cantwell BS, MD
Neuropsychiatric Institute and Hospital Center for the Health Sciences, UCLA, 760 Westwood Plaza, Los Angeles, CA 90024-1759, USA

Donald J. Cohen MD
Child Study Center, Yale University School of Medicine, New Haven, CT 06510-8009, USA

Antony D. Cox MA, MB, MPhil, FRCP, FRCPsych
Guy's and St Thomas's Medical and Dental School, Division of Psychiatry, Section of Child and Adolescent Psychiatry, Bloomfield Clinic, Guy's Hospital, St Thomas Street, London SE1 9RT

Felton Earls MD
Harvard School of Public Health, Harvard Medical School, Judge Baker Children's Center, 295 Longwood Avenue, Boston, MA 02115, USA

Robert N. Emde MD
Department of Psychiatry, University of Colorado Health Sciences Center, 4200 East Ninth Avenue, Denver, CO 80262, USA

D. Mary Eminson MA, MB ChB, MRCPsych
Department of Child and Adolescent Psychiatry, Royal Manchester Children's Hospital, Hospital Road, Pendlebury, Manchester M27 1HA

Michael Farrell BM, BCh, BAO, MRCP, MRCPsych
National Addiction Centre, The Maudsley Hospital, Denmark Hill, London SE5 8AZ

Jonathan Flint BM, BCh, MRCPsych
MRC Molecular Haematology Unit, Institute of Molecular Medicine, John Radcliffe Hospital, Oxford OX3 9DU

Norman Garmezy PhD
University of Minnesota, Department of Psychology, Elliott Hall, 75 East River Road, Minneapolis, MN 55455, USA

M. Elena Garralda MD, MPhil, FRCPsych, DPM
Department of Child and Adolescent Psychiatry, St Mary's Hospital
Medical School, Horace Joules Hall, Central Middlesex Hospital, Park
Royal, London NW10 7NS

Robert Goodman MA, BM BCh, MRCP, MRCPsych
Department of Child and Adolescent Psychiatry, Institute of
Psychiatry, De Crespigny Park, London SE5 8AF

Gill Gorell Barnes MA, MSc
The Tavistock Clinic, 120 Belsize Lane, London NW3 5BA

Irving I. Gottesman BS, PhD, MRCPsych (Assoc)
Department of Psychology, Gilmer Hall, University of Virginia,
Charlottesville, VA 22901, USA

Philip Graham FRCP, FRCPsych
Institute of Child Health, Behavioural Sciences Unit, 30 Guilford
Street, London WC1N 1EH

Richard Green MD, JD
Neuropsychiatric Institute and Hospital Center for the Health
Sciences, UCLA, 760 Westwood Plaza, Los Angeles, CA 90024-1759,
USA

Richard Harrington MD, MPhil, MRCPsych
Department of Child and Adolescent Psychiatry, Royal Manchester
Children's Hospital, Hospital Road, Pendlebury, Manchester M27
1HA

Martin Herbert MA (Natal), PhD (London), FBPsS, CPsychol
Exeter Community Health Trust, Royal Devon and Exeter Hospital,
and Psychology Department, University of Exeter, Exeter EX4 4QG

Lionel Hersov MD, FRCP, FRCPsych, DPM
Royal Free Hospital Medical School, and Tavistock Clinic, Pond Street,
London NW3 2QG

Jonathan Hill BA, MB BChir, MRCP, MRCPsych
Department of Child and Adolescent Psychiatry, Royal Liverpool
Children's Hospital, Alder Hey, Eaton Road, Liverpool L12 2AP

Peter D. Hill MA, MB BChir, MRCP, FRCPsych
Department of Psychiatry, St George's Hospital Medical School,
Cranmer Terrace, London SW17 0RE

Peter Hindley BSc, MB BS, MRCPsych
Deaf Children & Family Team, Springfield Hospital, 61 Glenburnie
Road, London, SW17 7DJ; and Department of Mental Health
Sciences, St George's Hospital Medical School, Cranmer Terrace,
London SW17 0RE

Alison E. Hipwell BSc, PhD
Winnicott Research Unit, University of Cambridge, Fenners, Gresham
Road, Cambridge CB1 2ES

Anthony Holland BSc, MB BS, MRCP, MRCPsych
University of Cambridge, Section of Developmental Psychiatry,
Douglas House, 18b Trumpington Road, Cambridge CB2 4AH

Patricia Howlin BA, MSc, PhD
Department of Psychology, St George's Hospital Medical School,
Cranmer Terrace, London SW17 0RE

Hugh Jenkins BA, BPhil, CQSW, DIPFT
Institute of Family Therapy (London), 43 New Cavendish Street,
London W1M 7RG; and Institute of Psychiatry, De Crespigny Park,
London, SE5 8AF

Philip C. Kendall PhD, ABPP
Division of Clinical Psychology, Temple University, Weiss Hall,
Philadelphia, PA 19122, USA

Rachel G. Klein PhD
Columbia University, College of Physicians and Surgeons; and
Department of Psychology, New York State Psychiatric Institute, 722
West 168th Street, New York, NY 10032, USA

R. Channi Kumar MD, PhD, MPhil, FRCPsych
Department of Psychiatry, Institute of Psychiatry, De Crespigny Park,
London SE5 8AF

Bryan Lask MB BS, MPhil, MRCS, LRCP, FRCPsych
Department of Psychological Medicine, The Hospitals for Sick
Children, Great Ormond Street, London WC1N 3JH

Judith Lask BA, MSc, CQSW, ADFT
Belgrave Department of Child and Family Psychiatry, King's College
Hospital, Denmark Hill, London SE5 9RS

James F. Leckman MD
Child Study Center, Yale University School of Medicine, New Haven,
CT 06510-8009, USA

Henrietta Leonard MD
Child Psychiatry Branch, Department of Health and Human Services,
NIMH Building 10, Room 6N240, 9000 Rockville Pike, Bethesda,
MA 20892, USA

John Lochman PhD
Medical Psychology, Duke University Medical Center, Box 2906,
Durham, NC 27710, USA

Catherine Lord PhD
Department of Psychiatry, University of Chicago, 5841 S. Maryland
Avenue, Chicago, IL 60637, USA

Ann S. Masten PhD
Institute of Child Development, University of Minnesota, 51 East
River Road, Minneapolis, MN 55455, USA

Barbara Maughan BA, MSc
MRC Child Psychiatry Unit, Institute of Psychiatry, De Crespigny
Park, London SE5 8AF

Peter McGuffin MB ChB, FRCP, FRCPsych, DPM
Department of Psychological Medicine, University of Wales, School of
Medicine, Heath Park, Cardiff CF4 4XN

David A. Mrazek MD, FRCPsych
Department of Psychiatry, Children's National Medical Center; and
Departments of Psychiatry, Behavioral Sciences, and Pediatrics, The
George Washington University School of Medicine, 111 Michigan
Avenue NW, Washington DC 20010-2970, USA

Glynis Murphy BA, MSc, PhD
Department of Psychology, Institute of Psychiatry, De Crespigny Park,
London SE5 8AF

A.R. Nicol BSc, MB BS, MPhil, FRCP, FRCPsych
Department of Psychiatry, University of Leicester, Westcotes House,
Westcotes Drive, Leicester LE3 0QU

William Ll. Parry-Jones MA, MD, FRCP, FRCPsych, DPM
Department of Child and Adolescent Psychiatry, University of
Glasgow, and Department of Child and Adolescent Psychiatry, Royal
Hospital for Sick Children, Yorkhill, Glasgow G3 8SJ

David S. Pellegrini PhD
3222 N Street NW, Suite 325, Washington DC 20007, USA

John Piacentini PhD
Columbia University, College of Physicians and Surgeons, New York
State Psychiatric Institute, 722 West 168th Street, New York, NY
10032, USA

Judith L. Rapoport MD
Child Psychiatry Branch, Department of Health and Human Services,
NIMH Building 10, Room 6N240, 9000 Rockville Pike, Bethesda,
MA 20892, USA

Alan Rushton BA, CQSW
Social Work Department, Maudsley Hospital, 101 Denmark Hill,
London SE5 8AZ

Sir Michael Rutter CBE, MD, FRCP, FRCPsych, FRS
MRC Child Psychiatry Unit, Institute of Psychiatry, De Crespigny
Park, London SE5 8AF; and Honorary Consultant Psychiatrist,
Bethlem Royal and Maudsley Hospital, Denmark Hill, London SE5
8AZ

Stephen Scott BSc, MB BChir, DCH, MRCP, MRCPsych
Department of Child and Adolescent Psychiatry, Institute of
Psychiatry, De Crespigny Park, London SE5 8AF

David Shaffer MB BS, FRCP, FRCPsych
Columbia University, College of Physicians and Surgeons, New York
State Psychiatric Institute, 722 West 168th Street, New York, NY
10032, USA

Carol Sheldrick MA, MPhil, MRCP, FRCPsych
Children's Department, Maudsley Hospital, Denmark Hill, London
SE5 8AZ

Emily Simonoff BA, MD(US), MCRPsych
MRC Child Psychiatry Unit, Institute of Psychiatry, De Crespigny
Park, London SE5 8AF

David Skuse FRCP, FRCPsych
Behavioural Sciences Unit, Institute of Child Health, University of
London, 30 Guilford Street, London WC1N 1EH

Marjorie Smith PhD, CPsychol
Thomas Coram Research Unit, Institute of Education 27/28 Woburn
Square, London WC1H 0AA

Derek Steinberg MB BS, MPhil, DPM, FRCPsych
Adolescent Service, Ticehurst House Hospital, Ticehurst, Wadhurst,
E. Sussex TN5 7HU

Hans-Christoph Steinhausen MD, PhD
Department of Child and Adolescent Psychiatry, University of Zurich,
Freiestrasse 15, Ch 8028 Zurich, Switzerland

Susan Swedo MD
Child Psychiatry Branch, Department of Health and Human Services,
NIMH Building 10, Room 6N240, 9000 Rockville Pike, Bethesda, MA
20892, USA

David C. Taylor MB BS, DPM, MD, FRCP, FRCPsych
Department of Child and Adolescent Psychiatry, Royal Manchester
Children's Hospital, Hospital Road, Pendlebury, Manchester M27
1HA

Eric Taylor FRCP, FRCPsych
MRC Child Psychiatry Unit, Institute of Psychiatry, De Crespigny
Park, London SE5 8AF; and Bethlem Royal and Maudsley Hospital,
Denmark Hill, London SE5 8AZ

Chris Thompson MB BS, BSc, MPhil, MD, FRCPsych
Department of Psychiatry, University of Southampton, Royal South
Hants Hospital, Graham Road, Southampton SO9 4PE

Judith Trowell MB BS, DPM, DCH, FRCPsych
Child and Family Department, Tavistock Centre, The Tavistock Clinic,
120 Belsize Lane, London NW3 5BA

Deborah Viney BSc
Department of Psychiatry, University of Southampton, Royal South
Hants Hospital, Graham Road, Southampton SO9 4PE

John Scott Werry MD
Department of Psychiatry and Behavioural Science, University of
Auckland, Auckland, New Zealand

Pamela Westwell BSc
Department of Psychiatry, University of Southampton, Royal South
Hants Hospital, Graham Road, Southampton SO9 4PE

Stephen Wolkind MB BS, MD, FRCPsych, DPM
Children's Department, Maudsley Hospital, Denmark Hill, London
SE5 8AZ

William Yule MA, DipPsychol, PhD, FBPsS
Department of Psychology, Institute of Psychiatry, De Crespigny Park,
London SE5 8AF

Charles H. Zeanah MD
Division of Infant, Child and Adolescent Psychiatry, LSU School of
Medicine, 1542 Tulane Avenue, New Orleans, LA 70112-2822 USA

Preface to the Third Edition

There have been considerable professional changes since the second edition of this work: these are reflected in this new edition. Most fundamentally, the volume of scientific work has increased greatly. The book has therefore been completely rewritten. Previous contributors have provided new and re-conceptualized accounts, and a range of new contributors has been brought in to provide a fresh approach. Some of the new authors are internationally eminent authorities; others are from a new generation of clinical scientists on whose work the future of the subject will depend. All of them are engaged in clinical work and have tried to present sound practice as well as a guide to current knowledge and future development. The increasingly international and interdisciplinary authorship reflects not only the global nature of the challenges we face, but also the growing consensus that allows workers from differing clinical and academic traditions to communicate effectively.

The increasing complexity of the scientific work makes a clinical synthesis both harder and more important. Many chapters take a historical approach to outlining why current ideas are in the form they are. The limitations of knowledge are also addressed, to help practitioners to a critical understanding. We hope that the book will provide not only a snapshot of current knowledge and practice but also a perspective on the future developments that can be anticipated. The subject is in rapid change and we have tried to achieve a picture of a moving process of clinical and scientific development.

Several trends can be discerned in the development of the subject. The place of theory is altering: the grand developmental theories of Freud, Piaget and social learning no longer directly generate the clinical and scientific hypotheses in the way that they once did. Correspondingly, this edition no longer includes outlines of the theories as separate chapters; rather, the chapters about disorders include the major developmental ideas about their origin; and the chapters about influences on psychopathology treat their subjects, for the most part, within a developmental framework. This organization seems more in keeping with the increasingly influential approach of developmental psychopathology; the discipline that brings developmental thinking to the task of explaining the origins and course of individual psychological disorders.

The questions raised by this approach are about the factors leading to variations in the main developmental lines and so to differences between individuals. The interplay between nature and nurture becomes the chief thing to investigate rather than a polar opposition of influences. This does not imply that all disorders are determined by the operation of the same influences that shape normal development: on the contrary, some disorders described in this book — such as autism — present qualitative differences from normal development. Rather, the developmental approach concentrates attention upon the continuities and discontinuities between normal and pathological development and the reasons for them; and is therefore directly relevant to the clinician trying to understand the pathogenesis of an individual's disorder and the ways that it may be possible to promote healthy psychological development. A systematic account of developmental concepts and findings relevant to clinical work is provided in a companion volume (Rutter & Hay 1994).

A richer appreciation of the role of biological factors in the origin of psychological disorders is apparent from many of the chapters. The evidence is sometimes contradictory still, for example when new techniques of imaging brain function are applied; often it gives a pointer to the understanding that we can expect from the future rather than the grounds for consensus now. Nevertheless, the rise of behavioural and molecular genetics is altering the way that we conceive of disorders, as several chapters indicate — including those on autism, Gilles de la Tourette's syndrome, schizophrenia and obsessive — compulsive disorders, and the consideration of behavioural phenotypes of genetic disorders. Genetic studies will make it easier to determine the ways in which psychosocial influences have their effects; the coming together of biological and psychological approaches is a theme of several of the chapters.

The relationship between childhood disorders and the abnormalities of adult life has been attracting substantial investigation. Necessarily, such studies have a long gestation. Nevertheless, findings on continuities and discontinuities between childhood and adult life are already having an impact upon the way that we think about children's disorders; and these are reflected in chapters on the conduct disorders and on disturbances of personality.

The classification of mental disorders is improving in clarity and validity. The period of time since the last edition has seen the formulation of the 10th revision of the World Health

Organisation's classification of diseases, and the DSM-III-R and DSM-IV versions of the American Psychiatric Association's diagnostic and statistical manual. It is encouraging that the American and international schemes are converging, and this book draws on both. The enterprise of classification is crucial for clinical work and teaching, and indeed there has been an improved conceptualization of the issues involved in diagnosis and classification. The book therefore begins with a general consideration before going on to the methods for assessment of children and adolescents.

Clinical as well as scientific changes drive some of the alterations in this latest edition. The involvement of the mental health professions in the consequences of child maltreatment has called for an expanded cover, as has the increasing variety of ways in which psychiatry interacts with the paediatric disciplines. Psychiatric involvement with infants has been expanding, and separate chapters are now provided for the disorders of attachment, the consequences of parental illness, and the disorders of eating and sleeping. The AIDS pandemic has made a separate chapter essential. Sadly, there has been a fragmentation in some areas of the mental health disciplines that ought to work together. The sections on assessment and treatment have therefore included explicit consideration of the relationships between disciplines; and have striven to bear in mind the constraints on practice that may arise, and to be useful to practitioners in areas where support services are underdeveloped as well as those with the benefits of comprehensive services in child health, education and social work.

Advances in therapy also continue: not least in the introduction of a widening range of techniques. A fuller coverage of the issues raised in treatment has therefore been provided. Not only are treatments such as cognitive therapy, social problem-solving and parent training included separately, but the chapters on longer-established therapies emphasize the breadth of approach and the range of technique that increasingly characterize good practice. Evidence from trials provides more of the basis for therapists' actions. As knowledge about the development of disorders deepens, so we can hope that the future will bring fuller understanding about the means by which effective interventions can be deployed to have a lasting effect upon psychological development.

ACKNOWLEDGEMENTS

The production of a book such as this is a complex undertaking, and involves a team too large for everyone to be named. Thanks in particular go to Vicky Murray for her efficiency in translating the manuscripts into the printed page, and to Caroline Sheard for her professionalism in preparing the index. Expert referees who commented on chapters were very helpful, but must remain anonymous. The checking and organization of manuscripts involved many people, especially Verity Corbett, together with Toyin Adigun-Saka, Angela Mullins, Adele Summers, Ann Hagell, Matthew Lawrence, and Joy Maxwell. Catherine Buckley marshalled the process with good humour as well as dedication. We are grateful to all.

Michael Rutter
Eric Taylor
Lionel Hersov

Preface to the First Edition

These are exciting times for anyone working in the field of child psychiatry. A wider understanding of child development now throws a clearer light on deviations from the normal pattern; knowledge of the nature and causes of psychiatric disorders in childhood is steadily increasing; new and effective methods of treatment are evolving; and clinical and education services for children with mental disorders are growing in scope and sophistication. The first academic departments of child psychiatry in the United Kingdom are now established to meet the needs for teaching and research and to add to the existing body of knowledge. A serious concern to raise training standards in the specialty has led to recommendations on the range of content of training and a national exercise to visit and appraise all training schemes is under way.

For these reasons the time seemed ripe for a new and different textbook of child psychiatry. Our aim has been to provide an accurate and comprehensive account of the current state of knowledge through the integration of research approaches and findings with the understanding that comes from clinical experience and practice. Each chapter scrutinizes existing information and emphasizes areas of growth and fresh ideas on a particular topic in a rigorous and critical fashion, but also in practical vein to help clinicians meet the needs of individual children and their families.

In planning the book we had to decide how to choose authors of individual chapters. Obviously we wanted colleagues who had made important contributions in their fields of interest and who could write with authority and knowledge. We were fortunate in our choice and we are deeply indebted to all of them. We also decided that it would be appropriate to invite contributions from those who had worked at The Bethlem Royal and The Maudsley Hospital or its closely associated postgraduate medical school, The Institute of Psychiatry. Over the years 'The Maudsley' has played a major role in training psychiatrists from all parts of the world and members of its staff have been among the leaders in both research and clinical practice. The fact that we have all worked at the same institution has produced some similarities: a firm acceptance of the value of interdisciplinary collaboration; an intense interest in new ideas and creative thinking; a commitment to the integration of academic and clinical approaches; a concern for empirical findings; and a belief in the benefits that follow from open discussion between people who hold differing views. As all of us work with children we have a common concern with developmental theories and with the process of development. However, as will also be apparent, we do not share any single theoretical viewpoint. A variety of theoretical approaches are represented in the chapters which also reflect a differing emphasis on biological, sociocultural, behavioural and psychodynamic aetiologies and formulations.

It is also fitting that this book should be based on The Joint Hospital as it has played such an important part in the development of child psychiatry. Children with psychiatric disorders were first seen at The Bethlehem Royal Hospital as long ago as 1800 and Henry Maudsley was unusual among the psychiatrists of his day in appreciating the importance of psychiatric disorders arising in childhood. In his *Physiology and Pathology of Mind*, published in 1867, he included a 34-page chapter on 'Insanity of early life'. The Maudsley Hospital first opened its doors just over half a century ago, children have always been included among its patients and the Children's Department became firmly established during those early years. Since then, and especially with the first British academic appointment in child psychiatry at the Institute of Psychiatry in the 1950s, it has trained many child psychiatrists who now practise in all parts of the globe.

The book is organized into five sections. The first eight chapters review different influences on psychological development in childhood and are followed by three that discuss the foremost developmental theories. A third section describes some of the crucial issues in clinical assessment and the fourth deals systematically with the various clinical syndromes and their treatment. The final section comprises six chapters that bring together knowledge on some of the main therapeutic approaches. We have sought to include most of the topics and issues that are central to modern child psychiatry, but there has been no attempt to cover all known syndromes and symptoms. Instead, the focus has been on concepts and methods with special emphasis on those areas where development of new ideas or knowledge has been greatest.

We hope that the book's contents will be of interest and use to all those professionally concerned with the care, study and treatment of children with psychiatric disorders. We will be satisfied if, in the words of Sir Aubrey Lewis, it also helps the psychiatrist in training to acquire 'reasoning and understanding' and fits him 'to combine the scientific and humane temper in his studies as the psychiatrist needs to'.

M. Rutter
L. Hersov

PART 1
CLINICAL ASSESSMENT

Chapter 1
Classification: Conceptual Issues and Substantive Findings

Dennis P. Cantwell & Michael Rutter

Classification constitutes a means of ordering information, of grouping phenomena and of providing a language by which to communicate with other people (Rutter *et al.*, 1975a; Achenbach, 1985; Rutter & Gould, 1985; Cantwell & Baker, 1991). As such, it is not only basic to all forms of scientific enquiry, but also it reflects a general human tendency to use differentiating concepts in order to make sense of the world. Thus, by the age of 3 or 4 years, children have acquired quite firm notions of which behaviours and activities are male and female. They are not deterred by the arbitrariness of such classifications, by the degree of overlap or by the dimensional nature of many of the distinctions. Similarly, objects are described as blue or red in disregard of the dimensional character of the colour spectrum. In the same way, classification terms are used all the time in our everyday conversations: 'You will recognize George easily; he's short, fat and has a bushy moustache.' Of course, all such classifications are only partial descriptions; doubtless George is distinctive in numerous other ways and indeed he is unique in the particular individual pattern of all his characteristics. Nevertheless, for some purpose, it is useful to select just a few features by which to pick him out.

In other words, a tendency to classify is part of the human condition and the use of classificatory terms is basic to all forms of communication. The questions, therefore, do not focus on whether or not to classify (because all language necessarily includes some form of classification), but rather on the scientific justifications for particular classificatory strategies and decisions and on the practical consequences of the use of specific systems of classification or of particular diagnostic categories.

It is important to bear in mind these general considerations regarding classification when considering psychiatric classifications. Because medical classifications were first developed as a means of grouping causes of death (Rutter *et al.*, 1975a), there is a tendency to assume that psychiatric classifications must imply the existence of disease entities and that there is some 'natural' 'correct' scheme waiting to be discovered, if only we could undertake the 'right' research needed to find out what it is. However, as well argued by Jaspers (1962), this is clearly not the case. There is a need to classify patterns of psychological disturbance, personality characteristics, levels of adaptive functioning and types of psychosocial situations, just

as much as we need to classify 'illnesses'. Moreover, this applies throughout the whole of medicine and not just to psychiatry, as Scadding (1980, 1982) made explicit. Thus, in internal medicine, for many purposes, it may be at least as important to classify the level of respiratory function as to differentiate between bronchitis and emphysema, or to determine whether a cancer is at stage 1 or stage 4, as to categorize its type. There is no one universally correct scheme. Rather, it is necessary to examine the validity and value of classificatory schemes in relation to the specific purposes for which they are devised.

HISTORY OF CHILD PSYCHIATRIC CLASSIFICATIONS

Although the classification of mental illnesses had much earlier origins, modern empirically based schemes started with Kraepelin's use of outcome differences to differentiate between schizophrenia and manic-depressive disorder (see Cantwell & Baker, 1991; Mattison & Hooper, 1992). The more broadranging 'official' psychiatric classifications of the *Diagnostic and Statistical Manual* (DSM-I; American Psychiatric Association, 1952) and *International Classification of Diseases*, 8th revision (ICD-8; World Health Organization, 1967) covered quite a wide range of disorders in adult life but included no more than a few token categories applying to childhood. Anna Freud's (1965) developmental profile, based on psychoanalytic concepts, was the first system to focus extensively on childhood disorders. This was closely followed by the scheme proposed by the Group for the Advancement of Psychiatry (1966), which was supposedly descriptive, but heavily influenced by psychoanalytic thinking. The field trials undertaken by the World Health Organization in preparation for ICD-9 (World Health Organization, 1978) quickly showed that there was little agreement among psychiatrists regarding theoretical concepts, but fairly good agreement on broadly defined simple phenomenological diagnoses (Rutter *et al.*, 1969). Similar findings were evident in numerous other investigations and, following the pioneering work by the Washington University group of psychiatrists (Feighner *et al.*, 1972), it came to be accepted that psychiatric classifications needed to be based on patterns of symptomatology, rather than on theories that lacked empirical substantiation. Without a doubt, this constituted a major advance in that it led the way to diagnostic schemes that could be used in the same manner by different clinicians and different researchers. The American Psychiatric Association's (1980) scheme, DSM-III, was the first 'official' classification to follow this approach in its setting down of specific 'rules' and criteria for each classification category, but the current World Health Organization (1992) scheme, ICD-10, has adopted much the same format, as have the later American Psychiatric Association schemes (1987, in press), DSM-III-R and DSM-IV.

One very important benefit of this change in principles has been the much greater ease of comparison across research reports and clinical papers. However, four major weaknesses have tended to be overlooked. Firstly, only a very limited operationalization of diagnostic criteria has been achieved (Cantwell, 1988). It is all very well to specify that such and such a diagnosis requires the presence of, say, three out of five specified symptoms. However, much of the operationalization is spurious unless the diagnostic instrument is specified and the criteria for severity made absolutely explicit. The importance of this caveat is indicated by the wildly different general population lifetime prevalence rates for major depression (supposedly diagnosed using the same DSM-III criteria) in different studies (McGuffin et al., in press).

Secondly, the rejection of theory as a basis for classification has sometimes led to an assumption that diagnoses should be based only on cross-sectional patterns of symptomatology without regard to concept, aetiology, course or outcome (Waterhouse et al., 1992). Clearly, this is not only misguided but also a complete misunderstanding of the Feighner et al. (1972) approach. Their key paper emphasized the importance of diagnostic distinctions by means of laboratory studies, follow-up and family history data. Cantwell (1975) made the same points in extending the approach to child psychiatric disorders. As Rutter (1965, 1978; Rutter & Gould, 1985) noted, it is not enough to show that diagnoses differ in symptomatology; rather the distinctions must be validated by criteria that are external to the symptomatology and shown to have clinical meaning and utility.

Thirdly, there is a danger in assuming that diagnostic problems have been resolved once an agreed set of criteria has been established. That is not so for two rather different reasons: first, as already noted, external validation is necessary; and second, all behavioural measures (even the best) include systematic bias and random error as well as reflecting the constructs they are supposed to tap (Rutter & Pickles, 1990). Ordinarily, this means that multiple sources of measurement are desirable and that statistical techniques to combine them in error-free fashion are required.

Fourthly, there are huge differences between diagnoses in the extent to which there is empirical substantiation of their validity. In no case is their validity fully established and in some instances there are very few, if any, validating data. For most, the evidence provides partial support, albeit sometimes strong, but uncertainty remains on key details. This issue is discussed more fully below.

CONCEPTS OF DISORDER

Before turning to validating criteria and to the prevailing 'official' classifications, it is necessary to consider what is involved in concepts of child psychiatric disorder. Several rather different issues need to be discussed.

Dimensions or categories

One important distinction is that between a dimensional or categorical approach. On the whole, psychologists have tended to prefer the former (Achenbach & Edelbrock, 1978; Quay, 1986), both because it has statistical advantages and because most psychiatric categories have parallels in continuously distributed 'normal' traits. Thus, in child psychiatry there are at least surface similarities between major depression and 'normal' feelings of misery and despair; between conduct disorder and 'normal' disruptive behaviour; and between anorexia nervosa and 'normal' adolescent dieting and dissatisfaction with body shape (Rutter & Sandberg, 1985). By contrast, all psychiatric classifications have used categories that imply meaningful differences between normality and 'disorder'. Accordingly, we need to consider which is to be preferred.

It is crucial to appreciate that this has to be discussed on two quite different bases: (1) the practical advantages of each approach; and (2) the scientific validity of qualitative distinctions between normality and disorder. The issues involved in these two bases are quite different.

Klein and Riso (in press) have succinctly summarized some of the main practical advantages and disadvantages of dimensional and categorical classification models. Categorical schemes have four main merits: (1) a single diagnostic term provides a more efficient, simple summary of a large quantity of information; (2) everyday concepts tend to be categorical even when the basic construct is dimensional (this is obvious, as already noted, with respect to colours, but it also applies to numerous other characteristics); (3) most clinical decisions are categorical in nature (e.g. whether to give a particular treatment, whether to operate or whether to discontinue clinic attendance) so that even if a dimensional classification scheme was to be employed clinically, it would be necessary for many purposes to impose arbitrary cut-offs, so converting it into a categorical format; and (4) a categorical system facilitates the discovery of rare qualitatively distinct and discrete disease entities. In many situations, these advantages outweigh the very substantial strengths of dimensional systems with their preservation of more information, (usually) greater reliability, greater statistical power and the avoidance of distortions arising from error and bias surmounting arbitrary categorical cut-off points.

However, Klein and Riso (in press) also made the very important observation that categorical systems lose most of their practical advantages if the omission of hierarchical exclusionary rules results in a high degree of comorbidity. Clearly, that is the situation with DSM-III-R (Caron & Rutter, 1991) and it is likely to be so also with DSM-IV.

A further point is that, even when disorders are based on a continuously distributed underlying liability, they may nevertheless function as a category because the clinical implications change above a certain threshold (Rutter *et al.*, in press). Thus, it is clear that blood pressure is a continuously distributed variable with a steady increase in morbid risk as blood pressure levels rise; nevertheless, above a certain point, secondary pathological changes occur (so-called malignant hypertension), with a consequent dramatic increase in mortality (Sleight, 1988). Similarly, it is likely that many cases of epilepsy are based on a continuously distributed convulsive liability. Despite this, treatment implications change once a person begins to suffer from recurrent convulsions; it is useful therefore to consider epilepsy as a categorical disorder. Within child psychiatry, epidemiological data show that overall symptom counts are continuously distributed and that high counts meeting usually accepted diagnostic criteria result in absurdly high rates of disorder (Bird *et al.*, 1990; Weissman *et al.*, 1990). Accordingly, it has come to be appreciated that it may be advantageous to define disorder in terms of impaired social functioning rather than symptom counts alone (Rutter *et al.*, 1970; Rutter, 1989b). Similarly, the evidence that severe conduct disorders have a generally poor prognosis with a substantially elevated rate of personality disorder in adult life suggests that it may be useful in practice to consider them as a clinical disorder regardless of aetiological continuity or discontinuity with normal variations in disruptive behaviour (Zoccolillo *et al.*, 1992; Rutter *et al.*, in press).

For all these practical reasons, it is likely that psychiatric classification will continue to be based on categories rather than dimensions. Nevertheless, it is most important to address the scientific issue of whether or not such categorical disorders are aetiologically continuous with normal variations in comparable characteristics.

Qualitative or quantitative differences

A variety of statistical approaches have been employed in order to determine whether disorders show continuity or discontinuity with normality (Grayson, 1987; Klein & Riso, in press). These include tests for bimodality in the distribution of symptoms, cluster analyses, mixture analyses, latent class analyses and tests for nonlinearity in the relationship with some external variable. Each of these methods is heavily dependent on the appropriate choice of variables and each is highly susceptible to a host of biases and psychometric artefacts. Tests for bimodality are particularly problematic in these respects and have been superseded by other methods that incorporate some test of whether or not the two populations function differently in relation to some external validating criterion (Kendell, 1982, 1989). A particularly elegant example of this approach is provided by DeFries and Fulker's (1988) development of multiple regression techniques to compare individual and group familiality in order to test for genetic continuity/discontinuity between disorders and continuously distributed dimensions. In essence, the method seeks to detect

nonlinearity in regression to the mean. Thus, for example, severe mental retardation is obviously *dis*continuous with mild retardation and normal intelligence because the siblings of severely retarded individuals show a normal distribution of intelligence rather than the partial regression to the mean that would be expected if they constituted an extreme extension of the normal distribution (Plomin *et al.*, 1991). In this case, we know that there is indeed discontinuity because, for example, chromosomal anomalies (as with Down's syndrome) play a major role in severe retardation whereas they do not do so with respect to normal variations in intelligence. Recently, this method has been applied to specific reading retardation with findings that are inconclusive but suggest discontinuity (De Fries & Gillis, 1991). Unfortunately, the technique lacks power unless samples are very large, it is very dependent on the most appropriate choice of variables and it is better at ruling out continuity than discontinuity.

Quite apart from the statistical concerns that need to be addressed in testing for continuities/discontinuities between disorders and normality, several conceptual issues also have to be borne in mind (Rutter *et al.*, in press). Firstly, the finding that a trait functions dimensionally in many respects by no means rules out the existence of qualitatively discrete categories that are biologically discontinuous with the normally distributed dimension. This is clearly the case with respect to intelligence quotient (IQ). In terms of its correlations with educational attainment, IQ functions as a dimension throughout the whole of its range from severe retardation to superior intelligence (Rutter & Madge, 1976). Despite this, severe retardation is biologically distinct from both mild retardation and normality in terms of its association with markedly reduced fecundity and life expectancy. Accordingly, the finding that conduct problems seem to function dimensionally in terms of their association with drug use (i.e. the more conduct problems there are, the greater the risk of drug use; Robins & McEvoy, 1990) does not necessarily mean that there cannot be a qualitatively distinct category of conduct disorder as well.

Secondly, it must be assumed that most categories will vary in their severity and, therefore, can readily be dimensionalized. This variation is apparent in extreme degree even with single major gene disorders such as neurofibromatosis or tuberous sclerosis. Therefore it may be expected that psychiatric disorders will also vary in severity and, because most normal dimensions extend into the normal range, there can be no reliance on bimodal distributions for the detection of discontinuous psychopathological categories.

A third, related issue is that any empirical test for discrete categories of disorder must avoid any presumption that they should be defined solely in terms of severity. Medical analogies indicate that most categorical disorders are differentiated from their relevant parallel dimension because of some distinctive pattern of features, rather than because any one feature falls on the extreme of a dimension. For example, Magnusson and Bergman (1988, 1990) found that aggression in childhood predicted both adult criminality and alcohol abuse, suggesting the appropriateness of a dimensional concept. However, further analyses focusing on patterns showed that the prediction was accounted for by the subgroup of boys (13% of the total population) with multiple problems. When this multiproblem group was removed from the sample, aggression ceased to have any link with other types of adult outcome — suggesting that the multiproblem group might constitute a meaningfully distinct disorder category.

Discreteness of diagnostic categories

The question of whether there is a meaningful boundary between normality and disorder is paralleled by the further question of whether or not the disorders themselves are discrete and separate from one another (Klein & Riso, in press). In medicine as a whole, discreteness tends to be implicit in disease constructs. This makes sense with those that have a single main cause and a specific pathophysiology, but it is not so obvious that this is so with multifactorial chronic diseases such as chronic bronchitis or osteoarthritis or atherosclerosis (Whitbeck, 1977). In psychiatry, too, it is by no means evident that discreteness is to be expected between conditions such as dysthymia, anxiety states, adjustment reactions and the milder variety of major depression. Kendell (1975) has argued that discreteness should be defined in terms of a point of rarity between the two disorders; that is, the admixture should be less common than the 'pure' syndromes and no more frequent than that expected by chance. Clearly that does not apply to most child psychiatric disorders, because comorbidity has been found to be very common (Caron & Rutter, 1991); however, the high degree of overlap may reflect inadequate conceptualization of the disorders as well as overlapping risk factors and other considerations. Probably, the crucial issue is whether the causes and correlates of the two conditions are different (see Caron & Rutter, 1991 and Klein and Riso, in press, for research implications).

Aetiology

Throughout medicine, aetiology plays a key role in decisions on how to classify disorders/diseases. That is because it is desirable that diagnostic categories should have a meaningful unity that reflects a common pathological mechanism with treatment implications. Although there are numerous effective treatments that were developed without any knowledge about the cause of disorders, nevertheless an understanding of aetiological mechanisms constitutes the single best means of developing effective prevention and treatment strategies (Kendell, 1989). It is for this practical (rather than theoretical) reason that aetiology tends to be accorded priority in classification, once it is known. Should the same apply in psychiatry? Once more, several different conceptual issues need to be kept in mind.

Firstly, there are several examples of important major risk factors that lead to a range of quite different disorders through diverse mechanisms. For example, smoking predisposes to lung cancer, coronary artery disease, chronic bronchitis and osteoporosis (to mention but four out of a longer list of sequelae), but it does so through quite different causal mechanisms. It would make no sense to group these together as smoking diseases because their clinical implications are quite different. Of course, to an important extent, this is because the cause has been conceptualized too broadly and greater tightness would be achieved if it were reconceptualized in terms of, say, tar carcinogens, nicotine and carbon monoxide. Still, the point remains that, ordinarily, the key consideration concerns the aetiological mechanisms, rather than the risk factor or agent.

This is a common situation in child psychiatry. For example, numerous studies have shown that the children of parents with a depressive disorder have an increased risk for a wide range of disorders (Rutter, 1989a, 1990). This could well be the case because a heterogeneous mixture of mechanisms are involved. Thus, major depressive disorders involve a substantial genetic component (McGuffin *et al.*, in press), and hence the risk for depression in the children may be genetically mediated in part. However, severe depression may also interfere with parenting to a serious degree and hence predispose to attachment disorders (Radke-Yarrow *et al.*, 1985). Also, there is a strong association between depression and family discord (Gotlib & Hooley, 1988) and the discord is likely to create an increased risk for conduct disorders (Rutter & Quinton, 1984). If aetiological considerations are to play any role in classification it will be crucial to proceed from the identification of broad risk factors to the delineations of specific risk mechanisms.

A second consideration is that, even when there is a single basic aetiological mechanism, there may be diverse clinical consequences associated with quite different patterns of symptomatology with different prognoses. Thus, for example, the clinical implications of primary tuberculosis differ from those of tuberculous meningitis or pulmonary tuberculosis; similarly those of a gumma, tabes dorsalis and general paralysis of the insane differ in spite of their common origins in a syphilitic infection. The various consequences of acquired immunodeficiency syndrome (AIDS) provide a more modern example. These variations may stem from the organ involved, the stage of the disease or the nature of the bodily reaction but, in each case, the clinical importance of the differences requires their separate classification. On the other hand, the treatment implications of the common underlying cause also require that this constitutes a key element in the classification. In psychiatry, the varied consequences of alcoholism or brain trauma constitute examples of this kind. The clinical implications of delirium and of dementia are quite different but it is also important that they both constitute direct organic reactions.

The converse situation, a common outcome from different causal mechanisms, is also quite common. Thus, there are several genetically distinct but clinically similar varieties of retinitis pigmentosa which (amongst other varieties) may represent an autosomal dominant or a sex-linked recessive disorder. Similarly, Down's syndrome may be the result of a new mutation or, less commonly, an inherited translocation. The distinction is crucial for genetic counselling, but the common clinical picture is more important in terms of the implications for the affected individual. More broadly, it is clear that, in psychiatry, it is common for similar clinical presentations (such as mental retardation or dementia) to derive from different aetiological processes and to represent a final common pathway for diverse causal processes (Klein & Riso, in press). Also it is evident that many causal mechanisms involve a chain of multiple indirect or direct steps or links (see, for example, that proposed by Brown and his colleagues, 1986, for depressive disorders).

Of course, most conditions in medicine do not have a single cause; multifactorial causation is much more common. That is so even with infectious diseases because a person's liability to succumb to infections is greatly influenced by, for example, nutritional status, age and concurrent disease. The reason why the bacterial or viral origin is given precedence is that, unlike these other risk factors, it is a specific cause (the tubercle bacillus causes tuberculosis but not measles) and it is a necessary one (not every one exposed to streptococci develops a streptococcal infection, but such an infection cannot develop in the absence of the streptococcus). The need to include aetiology in classificatory distinctions principally arises when there is a cause that is specific or necessary or both; however, it need not be the only cause.

However, with many multifactorial diseases there is no one specific or necessary, or even main, cause so far as is known and, hence, no aetiological feature to form an organizing basis for classification. It should be added that, following from these considerations, disorders may be discrete at one level (such as aetiology or pathophysiology), but not at others (e.g. clinical syndrome). Which should take precedence in classification needs to be decided on what is most important for the specific purposes of that classification, and not on some general theoretical principle.

The implications of these several concepts and considerations for child psychiatry is that the acquisition of knowledge on aetiology is very likely to shape classification decisions in the future, but it will not necessarily, or even often, lead to decisions based only on cause. Nevertheless, in so far as causes prove to be specific or necessary, they will be important for diagnosis. That is where advances in psychiatric genetics over the next decade may be particularly important. Some genes are pleiotropic in their behavioural consequences (Plomin, 1991) but it is probable that others will prove to be much more specific (see below) and some may be necessary elements in multifactorial determination (even though they will account for only some half or less of the overall variance). Such genes will, and should, lead to changes in diagnosis and classification, even though it is most unlikely that more than a tiny handful of child psychiatric disorders will prove to be due to a single major gene. The reason why theoretically based psychiatric classifications were abandoned in the recent past was not because theory is irrelevant, but rather because the prevailing theories lacked empirical support, with a resulting widespread disagreement on which theory to adopt.

VALIDATING CRITERIA

As noted by Feighner *et al.* (1972), Cantwell (1975), Rutter (1965, 1978) and Rutter and Gould (1985), amongst others, the validity of psychiatric categories must be established by determining their differential association with a range of external criteria. The chief criteria that have been employed in child and adolescent psychiatry, together with their main findings, may be summarized briefly.

Statistical grouping of symptoms

There is a substantial literature on the use of multivariate statistical techniques, such as factor analysis or cluster analysis, to derive diagnostic dimensions and categories through findings on symptom patterning (Achenbach & Edelbrock, 1978; Quay, 1986; Klein & Riso, in press). The findings show broad groupings that approximate to the main categories in the prevailing psychiatric classifications. The techniques are useful in exploring the nature of symptom patterns but, despite the psychometric sophistication of these methods, it is doubtful if they contribute much to decisions on classification. There are four main limitations to most of the standard techniques as they have been employed. Firstly, they provide only internal analyses without reference to external validating criteria (although this need not be so); secondly, they have tended to be limited to questionnaire data (which are necessarily rather crude); thirdly, they are of limited value in identifying uncommon syndromes; and fourthly, even random data may generate clusters and there are no independent criteria to decide how many clusters there should be. However, there are ways of overcoming some of these limitations — see, for example, Magnusson and Bergman (1988), described above.

Epidemiological data

Age trends are most useful in separating off those disorders that show a marked rise in incidence during the adolescent age period, such as anorexia nervosa, schizophrenia, major depression, and drug misuse (Rutter, 1990) and those with an onset in the first few years of life, such as autism, hyperkinetic disorders, and the developmental speech and language disorders (see Chapters 32 and 33). The early-onset group seem likely to reflect some abnormality in the developmental process. The 'point of rarity' in age of onset between autism and schizophrenia (extremely few cases of either begin in middle childhood) was one of the key reasons for separating these two conditions two decades ago (Rutter, 1972). However, the reasons for the rise in incidence during adolescence for several disorders remain uncertain and it is unlikely that the mechanisms are the same for all the conditions. Nevertheless, the finding that major depressive disorders rise in frequency over the teenage years (Angold & Rutter, 1992; also see Chapter 19), whereas anxiety disorders probably do not (although the evidence on this point is less satisfactory — Rutter & Garmezy, 1983) suggests the possible validity of the distinction between these two classes of emotional disorder.

There are also important differences between disorders in sex ratio. Almost all the early-onset disorders associated with abnormalities of the developmental process (autism, hyperkinetic disorder, developmental disorders of speech and language) are much commoner in boys than in girls; the same applies to multiple chronic tics and reading retardation. In addition, however, conduct disorders are also much more frequent in males and it is not at all obvious that this is likely to be for the same reasons, although that possibility cannot be firmly ruled out (Gualtieri & Hicks, 1985; Taylor & Rutter, 1985). The one neurodevelopmental disorder that stands out in having a totally different sex ratio is Rett's syndrome, which is confined (or almost confined) to girls. The meaning of this sex ratio is not yet known but it is likely to reflect the causal mechanism and it is so distinctive that it justifies a separate classification for this condition. By contrast with most developmental disorders (other than Rett's syndrome), major depression (after early/mid-adolescence) and anorexia nervosa are much more frequent in females.

Long-term course

Several disorders stand out in terms of their high degree of consistency across a long time span extending from childhood into adult life. In some ways, this consistency is most striking in relation to depressive disorders because of the very high frequency with which depression shows an admixture with a wide range of other symptomatology. In spite of this admixture, the long-term follow-up into the early 30s by Harrington *et al.* (1990) showed that depressive disorders in childhood were followed by a much increased risk for major affective disorders in adult life, but not for any other psychiatric condition. The finding provides strong evidence for the discreteness and distinctiveness of major depressive disorders. The adult outcome of conduct disorders in childhood is also distinctive in terms of the high likelihood of personality disorder (especially, but not exclusively, of the antisocial type) and pervasive social malfunction (Robins, 1991; Zoccolillo *et al.*, 1992; Rutter *et al.*, in press). This poor outcome seems particularly likely when the disorder is of unusually early onset, associated with hyperactivity/inattention and poor peer relationships, when it arises in the context of family discord and disorganization and (possibly) when it is accompanied by low physiological reactivity. However, these findings also raise queries about the separateness or communality of this variety of early-onset severe conduct disorder and hyperkinetic/attention deficit disorder.

Obsessional disorders constitute another group that stands out in terms of the relatively high consistency over time of this type of symptomatology (see Chapter 25). However, there is much more variation in the extent to which there is continuing

or recurrent social impairment; also there tends to be variability in the patterns of associated symptomatology (Zeitlin, 1986).

Autism shows a very high persistence into adult life with scarcely any individuals showing fully normal social functioning (see Chapter 33). However, it also stands out from other psychiatric disorders in terms of the finding that a quarter to a third of individuals develop epileptic attacks, with a particular tendency to do so in late adolescence or early adult life. It differs from specific developmental language disorders (SDLD) in its long-term course by virtue of the strong association between language impairment and social outcome (in autism but not SDLD; see Rutter *et al.*, 1992) and by continuing patterns of stereotyped behaviour and pragmatic and other language abnormalities. Within the broader field of pervasive developmental disorders, Rett's syndrome stands out because of its highly characteristic course with loss of purposive hand movements, development of microcephaly, a plateau in cognitive development, early onset of epileptic seizures and neuromuscular impairment (see Chapters 11 and 33).

Schizophrenic disorders, too, tend to continue or recur with the same broad diagnostic pattern (Eggers, 1978; Werry *et al.*, 1991; see also Chapter 34). However, there is no temporal consistency in the subtype of schizophrenia. Also, during the adolescent age period there is considerable two-way change between the diagnoses of manic-depressive psychosis and schizophrenia (Zeitlin, 1986; Werry *et al.*, 1991). The phenomenon requires further systematic study with larger samples but it is possible that the inconsistency is more a reflection of diagnostic difficulties during this age period than lack of discreteness of these diagnoses. Nevertheless, there is continuing uncertainty over the nosological meaning of mixed schizoaffective disorders (Eggers, 1989).

SDLDs show an interesting pattern over time in that there is a marked disjunction between those that clear up by age 5 and those that continue after that age (Rutter & Mawhood, 1991; see Chapter 32). The former group show no significant sequelae in the school-age years whereas the latter exhibit an increased rate of scholastic and social difficulties. It seems that even some quite severe instances of language delay constitute essentially normal, albeit extreme, variations of the normal distribution, whereas others constitute disorders with a substantial degree of persistence.

Specific reading retardation, too, shows a relatively high degree of persistence into adult life, with continuing cognitive deficits (and usually spelling difficulties) even when reading has improved substantially (see Chapter 36). What does change is the association with psychiatric disorder, which is strong in childhood but weak in adult life. As already noted, the long-term course of severe mental retardation is distinctive in terms not only of the persisting severe social impairment in adult life, but more particularly with respect to the marked reduction in fecundity and life expectancy (see Chapter 35).

Early studies suggested that, by contrast with their marked educational difficulties during the period of schooling, individuals with mild mental retardation tended to be absorbed into the general population in adult life, usually holding unskilled jobs, marrying, raising families and generally appearing relatively unremarkable (Tizard, 1974). However, Richardson and Koller's (1992) systematic follow-up of Aberdeen children suggests that this picture is much too optimistic. In their study, although a minority were functioning well, the majority showed degrees of social impairment. This outcome was decisively better than that for severely retarded children but it was evident that most mildly retarded individuals exhibited some continuing disorder.

There are very few data on even the short-term outcome of anxiety disorders during childhood and adolescence (Keller *et al.*, 1992; Last *et al.*, 1992), and even fewer on adult outcome (see Chapter 20). It seems that, by and large, when disorders persist into adult life (and they may do so more frequently than realized hitherto; Quinton *et al.*, 1990), they continue to take the form of some kind of emotional disturbance, usually involving anxiety, but sometimes depressive in type. However, as is the case in adult life (Greer & Cawley, 1966), there is little consistency in the details of symptom pattern, casting some doubt on the nosological validity of subcategories (Cantwell & Baker, 1988a, 1989).

The limited follow-up data on anorexia nervosa arising in childhood/adolescence suggest that eating problems of one sort or another persist in quite a high proportion of individuals in spite of a general tendency to improvement; many also experience dysthymia and/or depressive disorders (see Chapter 24).

Genetic findings

Genetic data are relevant to classification only in so far as they discriminate between supposedly separate psychiatric disorders. It is the specificity of the genetic contribution, and not the overall level of heritability as such, that justifies nosological distinctions. Unfortunately, relatively few genetic studies provide adequate evidence on this point. It is also crucial that the research both measures and takes into account the extent to which the family background includes a genetic risk for more than one disorder. To the extent that there is a multiple risk, it will obscure genetic discreteness. Also, it is important to appreciate that genetic data may be very informative on the boundaries of diagnostic categories — a key area of uncertainty with respect to most psychiatric diagnoses (Rutter, 1990).

In the adult field, the research into schizophrenia provides a useful model of what can be achieved (but also shows the difficulties). Because of the limitations in any one genetic strategy, it is highly desirable to combine twin, family and adoptee strategies whenever possible. The findings show a diagnostic specificity in the associations between schizophrenia in the proband and an increased risk of schizophrenia in relatives. The risk extends to schizotypal and paranoid personality disorders but not to other psychiatric conditions (Kendler & Gruenberg, 1984). Also, there is little within-family consistency in the subtype of schizophrenia. The data

mainly apply to schizophrenia in adults but it seems likely that the findings may be extrapolated to cases with an onset in adolescence or earlier (Werry, 1992a).

There is a similar diagnostic specificity to the familial loading associated with major affective disorders and in this case it is known that this applies to those with an onset in the preadult years (Harrington *et al.*, 1993). Both the twin and family data indicate that the genetic component is greater in the case of bipolar and serious unipolar disorders (McGuffin & Katz, 1986) but there is uncertainty on whether there is genetic continuity between bipolar and strictly unipolar conditions.

Genetic data for anxiety disorders in childhood are sparse (Rutter *et al.*, 1990) but the available findings for both children and adults (Andrews *et al.*, 1990; Kendler *et al.*, 1992a) provide only limited support for the distinctions made between different subcategories of anxiety disorder.

Autism stands out among all child psychiatric disorders in the extent to which it is strongly genetic (Rutter, 1991a; Rutter *et al.*, in press; see also Chapter 33). Both twin and family data indicate that the phenotype probably extends to include a combination of social and specific cognitive deficits (probably including circumscribed interests and rigidities of behaviour) that does not follow within the traditional diagnostic boundaries of autism. However, there is no increased familial loading for schizophrenia, underlining the discreteness of these two conditions. Recent reports have argued for connections between autism and Tourette's syndrome, anorexia nervosa and manic-depressive disorder, but these remain to be confirmed or refuted (Rutter *et al.*, in press).

Twin data suggest an important genetic component to anorexia nervosa (but much less so to bulimia nervosa) and, like family data (Strober & Katz, 1987), do not support a genetic connection with affective disorder in spite of the fact that depressive symptomatology is often associated with anorexia (Treasure & Holland, 1991). The family genetic data, in conjunction with twin findings, suggest that Tourette's syndrome, chronic multiple tics and some cases of obsessional disorder may constitute different manifestations of the same genetically determined disorder (see Chapter 26). The findings require replication but, if confirmed, would suggest that the diagnostic criteria and boundaries may need to be revised.

Psychosocial risk factors

There is extensive evidence documenting relatively strong associations between psychosocial stresses and adversities of various links and psychiatric disorder in childhood and adolescence (see Chapter 12). Moreover, at least with some adversities, there are grounds for supposing that the associations represent environmental causative influences (Rutter 1985, 1991b), even though many supposedly environmental factors include a genetic component (Plomin & Bergeman, 1991). However, with a few exceptions, there is rather little diagnostic specificity to the associations. On the whole, family discord and disruption tend to be associated with conduct disorders and delinquency, rather than with emotional and affective disorders. This relative differentiation is generally supportive of the distinction between these two broad groups of disorders but it does not lead to any clear and specific nosological specifications.

The two possible exceptions concern the connection between grossly abnormal parenting patterns, such as those implicit in child abuse or an institutional upbringing, and attachment disorders (see Chapter 28); and the connection between severe acute stress and posttraumatic stress disorders (see Chapter 22). In both instances, the findings are suggestive, rather than definitive. Thus, although it has already been demonstrated that abnormal parenting is indeed associated with distinctive disturbances in attachment behaviour, the strength and specificity of the associations remain uncertain and the clinical implications are only poorly understood. Similarly, it is evident that the experience of very severe stress is associated with some distinctive symptomatic features but stress is also associated with other patterns of disorder and it is not known whether the apparently stress-specific symptoms define a distinctive disorder with a characteristic course or, rather, add a particular behavioural 'colouring' to a mixed bag of disorders. The specificity of so-called adjustment reactions has even weaker empirical support (see Chapter 21).

Neuropsychological patterns

Autism stands out as the disorder with the nearest approach to a diagnosis-specific pattern of cognitive deficits (see Chapter 33). Many important questions remain unanswered (see Baron-Cohen et al., 1993), but it is evident already that the pattern of deficit in mentalizing (or theory of mind) abilities and in pragmatic and prosodic language features clearly differentiates autism from (nonautistic) mental retardation and SDLDs, and probably from other psychiatric disorders as well.

Hyperkinetic disorders are differentiated from conduct disorders in terms of the presence of attentional deficits and impulsivity (although uncertainty remains on just what these mean in neurophysiological terms), and the frequency with which there is associated neurodevelopmental retardation and mild cognitive deficits. These differences are sufficiently robust to warrant the separation of hyperkinetic and conduct disorders, but the hope that the former might be defined by reference to a specific kind of attentional dysfunction has yet to be realized (see Chapter 17).

Schizophrenia, too, is associated with attentional problems, albeit, apparently, of a somewhat different kind: neuropsychological comparisons of specific reading retardation and other types of learning disability are few but the findings from studies by Rourke (1985) show important differences between reading and mathematical disorders (see Chapter 36).

Biological investigations

There is a very substantial literature documenting a wide range of biological investigations in many different psychiatric disorders, as noted in other chapters in this volume dealing with specific syndromes. Some of the findings are interesting and potentially informative but, so far, few have shown much diagnostic specificity. There were high hopes for the dexamethasone suppression test in relation to depression but, although there are indeed associations suggesting some possibly specific physiological process, there are far too many false positives and negatives (especially in childhood) for findings to be used to validate diagnosis (see Chapter 19). Moreover, there are some puzzling age differences in the biological findings in depression; for example, the high cortisol levels usually found with major depression in adult life are less evident in childhood.

Laboratory findings in other syndromes are not yet at a stage where they do much to validate diagnostic distinctions.

The abnormal magnetic resonance imaging findings recently reported in some cases of developmental language disorders (Plante et al., 1991) substantiate the view that some instances of severe language delay represent a qualitatively distinct disorder rather than a normal variation, but otherwise remain some way from showing a distinctive type of structural abnormality.

Drug response

It might be thought that pharmacological specific drug responses would do much to validate differentiations between different diagnostic categories in child and adolescent psychiatry. Unfortunately, they are of very limited help in that connection, for several different reasons: (1) many drugs have a wide range of pharmacological actions so that it is scarcely surprising that their benefits extend across a diverse range of disorders (as, for example, with the effects of tricyclics on depression, enuresis and hyperkinetic disorders); (2) some disorders respond to a variety of drugs with pharmacological effects that are not identical (thus, schizophrenia tends to respond to major tranquillizers but the effective drugs have several different pharmacological consequences); and (3) many drugs have effects that target symptoms rather than disorders (see Chapter 51).

The main features of drug effects that aid nosological distinctions may be summarized as follows. Firstly, autism stands out as different from schizophrenia in not usually having a markedly beneficial response to major tranquillizers (see Chapter 33). Secondly, of all conditions, schizophrenia does respond most consistently to these drugs, the regular taking of which has a marked effect in preventing relapses (see Chapter 34). Thirdly, the (short-term) beneficial response of obsessional disorders to clomipramine (which is greater than the response to other tricyclics) argues for a modest degree of diagnostic specificity (see Chapter 25). Fourthly, the finding that the beneficial response to stimulants in children with disruptive behaviour disorders is proportional to the initial level of hyperactivity, together with the absence of high anxiety (Taylor et al., 1987; Pliszka, 1989), has implications for the definition of hyperkinetic disorder (however, see Livingston et al., 1992 for a failure to replicate the latter effect). Fifthly, the benefits of lithium in the treatment of bipolar affective disorder (see Chapter 19) might be thought to have some diagnostic implications: however the apparent benefits of lithium in the treatment of other disorders (see Chapter 51) and the resistance of some bipolar disorders to lithium markedly diminish the diagnostic weight that can be attached to lithium responsiveness.

VALIDITY OF CHILD/ADOLESCENT PSYCHIATRIC DISORDERS

During the last decade, research findings (as briefly and selectively summarized above) have provided an increasing body of evidence supporting the validity of some of the broad diagnostic distinctions within the field of child and adolescent psychiatric disorders (see also Werry, 1992b). In particular, combinations of research strategies have shown the distinctiveness of depressive disorders, schizophrenia, hyperkinetic disorders, conduct disorders, autism, Rett's syndrome, severe mental retardation, mild mental retardation, specific developmental disorders of language, Tourette's syndrome, obsessional disorders and anorexia nervosa. As discussed in greater detail in individual chapters, that does not mean that all diagnostic issues regarding these disorders have been resolved. That is far from the case. Thus, although the validity of autism has been well-established, and although the differentiation from Rett's syndrome is clear, there is continuing uncertainty on the extent to which other differentiations within the group of pervasive developmental disorders (such as with Asperger's syndrome and disintegrative disorders) are justified (see Chapter 33). Similarly, although there are well-demonstrated differences between hyperkinetic disorder (as narrowly defined) and conduct disorder, it remains uncertain whether the former is a distinct syndrome or rather a distinctive variety of conduct disorder characterized by the presence of hyperactivity as a risk factor (see Chapters 17 and 18). Equally, the meaning and boundaries of the overlap between Tourette's syndrome and obsessional disorder have yet to be established (see Chapters 25 and 26). These issues are very important ones and their resolution in the years to come is likely to have substantial clinical implications. Nevertheless, despite these continuing diagnostic and classificatory uncertainties, it is clearly evident that differentiation between the main diagnostic categories has major clinical meaning already.

Of course, both ICD-10 (World Health Organization, 1992) and DSM-IV (American Psychiatric Association, in press) include many psychiatric categories that have far weaker empirical validation. That is reasonable on the grounds that a clinically useful classification must provide adequate coverage of all common and all clinically important disorders. Stengel (1959) succinctly summarized the need by noting that classification categories should be jointly exhaustive and mutually exclusive. The real question is how best to meet this aim when adequate data on validation are lacking. One extreme solution would be to group all invalidated disorders together under

some general portmanteau heading such as other or unclassified disorders. The inevitable result would be that this residual group would be both large and extremely heterogeneous. At the other extreme, an alternative solution would be to provide separate categories for any disorders that a substantial proportion of clinicians think *might* be meaningful. The unavoidable consequence of this approach would be an extremely large number of diagnostic categories. Because, by the nature of their origins, both DSM-IV and ICD-10 are consensus schemes, they approximate to the latter approach with a very large number of codes. Not surprisingly, studies of both classification systems have shown that many of these diagnostic differentiations have poor interrater reliability, as well as weak validity (Rutter *et al.*, 1988), and it is all too easy to point to limitations in the schemes (Rutter & Shaffer, 1980). What is not quite so easy is to decide what would be the best solution.

One basic question is whether it is preferable to adopt a 'lumping' or 'splitting' strategy; that is, when the evidence is uncertain, is it better to use a broad diagnostic grouping or to prefer finer diagnostic distinctions? At first sight, that seems a perfectly straightforward choice that should be open to empirical testing, but a moment's thought indicates that the matter is rather more complicated than it seems (Rutter & Schopler, 1992). Two main issues require consideration. Firstly, there is the need to decide on the most appropriate starting point. Autism provides a convenient illustration of the dilemma. Most of the evidence validating that diagnosis derives from studies using fairly narrow criteria (Rutter & Schopler, 1988), rather than the broad approach advocated by Wing and Gould (1979) which includes many profoundly retarded children. Is it, therefore, better to keep the latter separate (under some term such as atypical autism) on the grounds that we lack good evidence that they represent the same basic condition as traditional autism; or, rather, should autism and atypical autism be pooled on the grounds that we lack good evidence that they are different? It is not self-evident which is to be preferred when the real problem is the lack of good evidence pointing unequivocally in either direction.

The second concern is whether a 'lumping' or 'splitting' approach is most likely to advance knowledge. The key consideration in that connection is that, unless research uses and tests the validity of these uncertain diagnostic distinctions, it will not be possible to find out whether or not the differentiations are valid (Rutter & Schopler, 1992). Accordingly, it seems desirable to include some weakly validated diagnostic categories in any classification scheme in order to facilitate the nosological research that is required to enable classificatory decisions in the future to have a stronger empirical basis than is possible today.

In that connection, of course, it will be important to test hypotheses that argue for very broad groupings, as well as to find subdivisions. Thus Crow (1990) has put forward a unitary view of psychosis in which schizophrenia and manic-depressive disorders are supposed to be variants of the same condition; Comings and Comings (1990) have suggested that autism and Tourette's syndrome reflect the same genotype;

and Gillberg (1992) has put forward an even broader grouping of empathy disorders, including anorexia nervosa, obsessive-compulsive disorder, paranoid disorder and Tourette's syndrome, as well as autism. We do not find the evidence in favour of these broad groupings at all persuasive but, nevertheless, research must address the possibility that, if validating criteria point in that direction, quite radical reconceptualizations of diagnosis may be required. Even so, it would not be helpful to have a large-scale proliferation of poorly substantiated categories and the question of how to decide which to include and which to reject remains.

Several approaches have been suggested. Thus, Werry *et al.* (1987) have argued for an embargo on change on the grounds that there is a need to test the validity of existing classifications thoroughly before we create new systems. They pointed out that such testing of DSM-III had not been undertaken before the quite major changes of DSM-III-R were introduced. We are certainly sympathetic to the plea to avoid unsubstantiated frequent alterations to psychiatric classifications. However, the weakness of that position is that many of the classificatory distinctions in DSM-III lacked an empirical backing at the time and still do. Accordingly, there is no particular advantage in sticking to those aspects of a system that are self-evidently weak. The approach adopted in planning for DSM-IV has been to undertake systematic reviews of the available research findings in order to decide whether diagnostic criteria and groupings should be retained or altered. All too frequently, it is obvious that crucial data are lacking but certainly there has been a serious attempt to base decisions on such empirical evidence as is available. Because ICD-10 sought to adopt a comparable approach, and because it was appreciated that it was highly desirable for everyone to use the same system (or at least to use systems that were translatable one into the other), the criteria for individual child psychiatric diagnostic categories in DSM-IV and ICD-10 are closely similar and often identical.

An alternative approach is to stick with strictly behavioural groupings, ignoring all evidence on differences related to aetiology, course or other nonbehavioural features. Thus, both Waterhouse *et al.* (1992) and Steffenburg and Gillberg (1989) have argued the position in relation to autism. Indeed, the latter have proposed that it is high time that autism be regarded as an administrative label (p. 75). On this basis, they pooled Rett's syndrome and autism. For the reasons already given, we do not agree with that position. There is abundant evidence of the scientific validity of the diagnosis of autism (Rutter & Schopler, 1988) and it is important that diagnostic distinctions be scientifically and clinically meaningful. Of course, the mere demonstration that a distinctive clinical syndrome has multiple aetiologies is definitely *not* a sufficient reason to split up the syndrome according to cause if it is otherwise coherent. However, when evidence indicates that the syndrome is not as behaviourally homogeneous as supposed hitherto, and that the behavioural differences are associated with a quite different course and set of correlates, it is time to split up the original broad group. Thus, the behavioural

differences between autism and Rett's syndrome, the extremely different sex ratio, and the quite different clinical course constitute the rationale for separating these two syndromes (Rutter & Schopler, 1992).

Both DSM-IV and ICD-10 have taken a pragmatic approach to this problem. Thus, where there are categories that are phenomenologically distinctive, which cannot readily be included in existing broad diagnostic groupings, and where there are therapeutic or prognostic implications, specific diagnostic codes have been included. Thus, this has been the rationale for the provision of categories for elective mutism (see Chapter 32), enuresis (see Chapter 29), and reactive attachment disorders (see Chapter 28). The same has applied to specific symptoms of particular clinical importance, such as pica (see Chapter 27), with its attendant risk of lead intoxication, and self-injury, with its risk of brain injury in severe cases (see Chapter 35).

There has been a greater problem in deciding how far broad diagnostic categories should be subdivided. Thus, there are umpteen subcategories of affective disorder, and of anxiety disorder, in both DSM-IV and ICD-10. Some of these are reasonably well validated. Nevertheless, it is quite clear that many of the subdivisions are unreliable and many, too, lack demonstrated validity. Clinicians tend to like to make many subtle differentiations between syndromes but, as they cannot agree on the basis for the differentiations, and as the distinctions seem to lack much meaning, it would appear preferable for the number of subdivisions to be substantially reduced.

There is one particular classificatory issue that needs highlighting and that concerns the decision of whether or not to group disorders arising in childhood separately from apparently comparable disorders with an onset in adult life (Rutter *et al.*, 1975a). At one time, this separation applied to several major diagnostic categories, but as evidence on the coherence of diagnoses across age groups accumulated, the distinctions have been given up. Thus, the separate classification of childhood schizophrenia has been abandoned as a result of the lack of empirical justification for its differentiation from schizophrenia arising in adult life (Rutter, 1972; Werry, 1992a; see Chapter 34). Similarly, although there are differences between major depressive disorders in childhood and adult life (see Chapter 19), the similarities and the continuities between the two (with the one frequently being followed by the other; Harrington *et al.*, 1990) have led to a unitary classification across age groups. The one major exception concerns anxiety disorders where both ICD-10 and DSM-IV have separate categories for those with an onset that seems to be specific to childhood, although the basis for the differentiation is not the same in the two schemes (see Chapter 20). The justification for these separations rests on rather flimsy evidence and research to test their validity is greatly needed. However, the bringing together in both DSM-IV and ICD-10 of the adult category of generalized anxiety disorder and the child category of overanxious disorder has reduced the separation in a way that is probably advantageous.

Diagnostic reliability

Over the last decade, much attention has been paid to the interrater reliability of psychiatric diagnoses (Rutter *et al.*, 1988; Rey *et al.*, 1989). The general conclusion has been that the reliability of most major psychiatric categories has been acceptably high (with kappa values in the region of 0.6 to 0.7 or better), but that the reliability of subcategories tends to be less satisfactory. However, that summary statement conceals as much as it reveals in that a more detailed study of the findings brings out several other crucial considerations. Firstly, it is apparent that researchers who have been trained to make diagnostic distinctions in a standardized way tend to be much more reliable than even quite experienced clinicians. For example, Prendergast *et al.* (1988) found that researchers achieved kappa values of 0.83, 0.80 and 0.74 for the DSM-III categories of attention deficit disorder, conduct disorder and emotional disorder; the comparable figures for US clinicians were 0.30, 0.27 and 0.27. It is evident that good diagnostic reliabilities can be obtained but, equally, it is clear that it cannot be assumed that they are typical of what is achieved in ordinary clinical practice.

Secondly, the particular data sources used make a big impact on findings. From the Isle of Wight studies onwards (Rutter *et al.*, 1970; Rutter, 1989b), numerous investigations have shown the relatively weak agreement between reports from parents, teachers and the young people themselves (see Chapters 3 and 4). Accordingly, it must be expected that there will be poor reliability between clinicians who rely on different sources of information, or who weight their value in different ways.

Thirdly, although precise diagnostic rules tend to improve reliability, if they are to do so they must be explicit not only on which symptoms are required for a diagnosis but also on how such symptoms should be judged to be present (in terms of frequency, severity, data sources etc.). Fourthly, relatively small changes in diagnostic rules can make quite a big difference to the frequency with which a diagnosis is made (see, for example Kendler *et al.*, 1992b, for an illustration of this in relation to major depressive disorders in adults).

Fifthly, although in general broader diagnostic groupings tend to be more reliable than narrow ones, this is far from a universal finding; the reliability depends more on the clarity and lack of ambiguity in diagnostic rules than on the narrowness or breadth of the diagnosis *per se*. For example, most studies have found separation anxiety disorders to have a higher interrater reliability than the overall group of anxiety disorders (Rey *et al.*, 1989, report a mean across studies of 0.74 compared with 0.58). Sixthly, in view of the high rate of comorbidity with most child psychiatric disorders (Caron & Rutter, 1991), good reliability will be dependent on consistency and agreement on how diagnoses should be made does not necessarily mean that even well-trained clinicians will follow such rules (see Cantwell, 1988). For all these reasons, just because two groups of investigators both state in their scientific papers that they have applied DSM-IV or ICD-10 (or any other) criteria, it cannot be assumed that they have made the diagnoses comparably.

ORGANIZATION OF CLASSIFICATION

Logical consistency

Most reviews of the principles that should underlie psychiatric classification systems have argued for the need for logical consistency, so that the system is based on a constant set of principles with a clear set of precise rules (see, for example, Werry, 1972; Cromwell *et al.*, 1975). Manifestly, neither DSM-IV nor ICD-10 has a consistent logic. Thus, on the whole, aetiology does not constitute a basis for the grouping of disorders. However, there are exceptions to this avoidance of causal groupings; the organic groupings which includes dementia and acute confusional or delirious states; the substance abuse disorders, posttraumatic stress disorders, and adjustment disorder.

Of course, the use of aetiology for the classification of some disorders, but not others, is not necessarily illogical. The approach could be said to be consistent if aetiology constituted the basis whenever it was known, but not otherwise. However, that is not what is done. Thus, there is strong evidence for organic aetiologies in the case of both schizophrenia (see Chapter 34) and autism (see Chapter 33), but neither are included in the organic disorders section of the classification. Similarly, there is good evidence for the role of acute and chronic stresses in a wide range of psychiatric disorders, arising in both childhood and adult life (Brown & Harris, 1989; Goodyer, 1990; see also Chapter 21), yet they are not classified as stress disorders.

Nevertheless, the use of aetiology in some categories but not others should not be rejected on this ground because there are at least two other possible justifications, each of which provides a logic. Firstly, there is a difference between conditions in which the aetiological factor used to classify is necessary, sufficient and specific and those where it is just contributory and nonspecific. Thus, the role of organic factors in both acute confusional/delirious states and dementia is direct, linked to a particular clinical syndrome, and invariant (that is, the disorders cannot arise in the absence of the organic factor, although other influences may contribute to the causal process). Manifestly, that is not the case with the wide range of psychiatric disorders that may arise after, say, a severe head injury (Rutter *et al.*, 1983). The causal influence of organic brain damage in these disorders is not in doubt but it plays a role in conjunction with psychosocial factors; its influence is neither necessary nor sufficient, and the effects are far from diagnosis-specific. That is a completely different state of affairs to that which applies to dementia. At present, it is not known which of these two extreme alternatives (or some intermediate position) applies to schizophrenia or autism and, therefore, it is reasonable to classify both separately from the organic disorders for the moment, even though it is known that organic factors predominate in aetiology.

The situation regarding posttraumatic stress disorders and adjustment disorder could be viewed as somewhat parallel, except that the supporting empirical evidence is far weaker, especially with respect to adjustment reactions (see Chapter 21). There may be value in having a diagnostic category for mild transient disorders but, as Hill points out, these do not show a strong, necessary or specific connection with stressful experiences. The situation with posttraumatic stress disorders is somewhat different, at least in the case of very severe unusual stress (such as shipwrecks or volcanoes), in that the connection with the stress is much more direct, and there is an association with certain relatively specific symptom features (see Chapter 22). The doubts lie in the extent to which the disorders overlap in characteristics with a broad range of psychiatric conditions and the uncertainty regarding a consistent clinical course.

The second, rather different, justification for the use of aetiology, in some parts of the classification system, but not others, is that public health considerations may mean that there is a need to highlight a particular aetiology. Thus, it could be argued that this is so with substance abuse disorders where the role of the drug has important implications for preventive policies. Similarly, it might be suggested that the same applies to posttraumatic disorders because of the need for an appreciation that severe and unusual acutely stressful experiences can lead to a socially handicapping psychiatric disorder in previously healthy individuals in the absence of other risk factors. This is indeed an important consideration; there is a difficulty, however, if the concept is extended to less severe stresses when the combination with other risk factors is much more important.

Neurological or psychiatric disorder

A further classification issue concerns 'territorial' disputes on whether a particular disorder should be classified under neurological or psychiatric syndromes. Sometimes, it is assumed that once an emotional or behavioural or cognitive disorder has been shown to have an organic basis, it should be removed from psychiatry, on the grounds that the speciality deals only with disorders of the mind, and not the brain. We reject that view completely. There are two main reasons why this dualistic mind−brain dichotomy should not be applied to classification (Rutter & Schopler, 1992). Firstly, it is seriously misleading to suppose that there can be workings of the mind that are unconnected with the brain. Thus, it is known that there are neural changes that accompany forms of learning (Horn, 1990). Of course, there is a real difference between intrinsic brain abnormalities that *cause* mental malfunction and neural alterations that *accompany* environmental effects of one sort or another. Nevertheless, the dichotomy is far from clear-cut. Consider, for example, the evidence that genetic influences play a role (sometimes weak, sometimes strong) in virtually all psychiatric disorders (see Chapter 9). This must involve some type of biological substrate. It could be suggested that there are important distinctions between the inheritance of

diseases, the inheritance of specific risk factors, and the inheritance of continuously distributed traits that play an indirect role in multifactorial causation. However, these distinctions are not absolute and do not lend themselves to any kind of subdivision of disorders into those of the brain and those of the mind.

The second reason why this subdivision is unhelpful is that classifications do not represent some eternal 'natural' truth; rather they are devised on the basis of empirical research findings to meet some practical need. In the planning of services, it may be as important to diagnose and code the nature of the presenting clinical problem as it is to note the aetiology. Thus, psychiatric classifications have always included categories for dementia and severe mental retardation in spite of the fact that there is virtually always some underlying causal brain disease or damage. Where these brain disorders constitute a meaningful diagnostic category, they are separately coded in the appropriate section of the medical classification. For example, when severe mental retardation is associated with cerebral palsy, Down's syndrome or the fragile X anomaly, these conditions are separately coded in addition to the presenting clinical problem of severe retardation. This is desirable because not everyone with these conditions shows the same type or degree of clinical problem. Practical considerations require that *both* the retardation and the medical condition should be classified.

Should this practice of double coding (which applies to both DSM-IV and ICD-10) apply generally? There can be no unequivocal correct answer to that question; the decision should be decided on the basis of the information that is needed with respect to the purpose of the classification. The situation, perhaps, in which double coding is least needed is when there is an invariant, or at least highly consistent, relationship between the brain condition and the psychiatric disorder. To a considerable extent, this seems to apply to Alzheimer's disease and dementia, and to Rett's syndrome and pervasive developmental disorder, to take examples from opposite ends of the age spectrum. Nevertheless, in both cases, the psychiatric disorder is separately classified in ICD-10 and DSM-IV because it is useful in the planning and monitoring of clinical services and because the patients with these disorders frequently present to psychiatric services.

Multiaxial systems

It follows from these considerations that, with complicated disorders, it may often be necessary to code several different facets of a condition. Thus, in order to cater for aetiological factors, as well as the form of the clinical disorder, it is necessary that the classification system include a means of coding abnormal psychological situations and medical conditions, in addition to the psychiatric syndrome. During the World Health Organization field trials for ICD-9, it became clear at an early stage that this need was met more by means of a multiaxial than a multicategory organization of the system (Rutter *et al.*, 1969, 1975a; Tarjan *et al.*, 1972). There are three main reasons for this preference. Firstly, these different elements refer to facets that are conceptually quite different and not alternatives. It is meaningful to ask whether the diagnosis is schizophrenia or mania, but not whether it is cerebral palsy or mental retardation. Secondly, it was found that, even when psychiatrists agreed well on their diagnostic formulations, they varied greatly in their use of multiple categories. Some tended to diagnose only the facet that reflected the main clinical problem from the perspective of the service which the patient attended, whereas others frequently coded multiple facets. Thirdly, despite this variation, the provision to code multiple facets of a clinical problem, including aetiological factors, fitted better with most clinicians' approach to diagnostic formulations. Accordingly, child psychiatrists all over the world came to favour a multiaxial system of classification. DSM-III (American Psychiatric Association, 1980) became the first 'official' classification to adopt such a system (a major conceptual strength of DSM-III — Cantwell & Baker, 1988b), and ICD-9, although not multiaxial in design, included a multiaxial version for child psychiatric purposes (Rutter *et al.*, 1975b). DSM-III-R, DSM-IV and ICD-10 have all followed suit.

In fact, multiaxial systems are no more than a logical development of traditional multicategory systems, in which specific modifications have been introduced to deal with the needs noted above. They have three main distinguishing features; (1) a set number of axes, each of which has a conceptual unity that differentiates it from the other axes; (2) a rule that there must be a coding on each and every axis in all cases; and (3) the provision of a 'no abnormality' code on each axis (in order to allow the second feature to operate). The statistical handling of the classification is eased by the operation of a rule that there must be only one code per axis (as was the case with the multiaxial version of ICD-9), but this also has disadvantages and is not a necessary feature of multiaxial systems (multiple codings are allowed in both DSM-IV and ICD-10).

In setting up a multiaxial system, a key decision concerns the choice of the number of axes and the basis of their conceptual organization. Obviously, there need to be axes for clinical psychiatric syndromes, for physical (medical) disorders, and for psychosocial adversities and stressors and these are included in both DSM-IV and the multiaxial system of ICD-10. DSM-III-R used severity of stressors as the organizing construct for the psychosocial axis and did not differentiate according to type or chronicity. Rutter and Shaffer (1980) noted the limitations stemming from a focus only on severity, a lack of detailed rules or guidelines and a failure to make use of the available empirical findings. DSM-IV differs from DSM-III-R in dealing with psychosocial features in terms of different areas of problems — such as educational or housing or economic.

The ICD-10 scheme (Van Goor-Lambo *et al.*, 1990) is ambitious in its attempt to provide a more discriminating differentiation with rather specific guidelines on the features to be used in rating. The main psychosocial categories are: abnormal intrafamilial relationships; familial mental disorder or handicaps; inadequate or distorted intrafamilial communication; abnormal qualities of upbringing; abnormal immediate environment; acute life events; and societal stressors, each of which has finer subdivisions. There is still a need for systematic evaluation of this axis, but it seems to have promise in view of its having been planned on the basis of research findings. What is clear already, however, is that information requirements of the psychosocial classifications are substantial and, if reliable and valid coding is to be achieved, it will be important that the clinical assessment includes an adequate systematic evaluation of the child's psychosocial circumstances.

Epidemiological studies have been consistent in indicating the importance of assessing children's level of adaptive functioning, as well as their pattern of symptomatology (Bird *et al.*, 1990; Weissman *et al.*, 1990) and both DMS-IV and ICD-10 have an axis for this purpose (in the latter case this involves an addition since ICD-9). The Global Assessment Scale, developed by Endicott & Spitzer (1978), and adopted for children (C-GAS) by Shaffer *et al.* (1983), constitutes the basis for both axes. This has been found to work reasonably well in practice but it is more difficult to apply to preschool children. Also, the C-GAS suffers from its inclusion of some symptoms in the criteria for adaptive functioning — an unfortunate confound. The ICD-10 scheme has removed this confound but is otherwise closely comparable with DSM-IV. In spite of its fairly satisfactory performance in practice, little is known on the measurement qualities of this axis and these need further study.

One of the main issues that led to the development of a multiaxial version of the ICD-9 was the need to discourage clinicians from viewing autism and mental retardation as alternative diagnoses (Rutter *et al.*, 1969). Clearly, they are not alternatives as they are based on quite different constructs — behavioural pattern in the case of autism and cognitive level in the case of mental retardation. Furthermore, as already noted, clinicians varied in whether they chose to focus their diagnoses on the behavioural pattern or the cognitive level, a variation that led to artefactual unreliability. The placement of mental retardation (or intellectual level) on a separate axis in the multiaxial version of ICD-10 (World Health Organization, in press) has helped to resolve both these problems.

Two further issues on the organization of axes remain to be considered: the placements of specific developmental disorders (of speech and language, reading, etc.) and of pervasive developmental disorders (autism, atypical autism, etc.). The difficulties involved in these decisions are reflected in the to-and-fro changes between DSM-III, DSM-III-R and DSM-IV in how they are dealt with (Cantwell & Baker, 1991). In that both comprise disorders of development, it might seem obvious that they should be placed together with mental retardation on one axis of developmental disorders. However, there are good practical reasons why that is not the best option (Rutter & Schopler, 1992). The key issue concerns the most helpful mix of information for research and clinical purposes. Thus, the presence or absence of mental retardation is the single most important prognostic factor in autism (see Chapter 33) and it is important that this item be recorded routinely; this argues for the two diagnoses to be placed on separate axes. It is also relevant that pervasive developmental disorders are conceptualized and diagnosed on the basis of behavioural deviance and not cognitive level. It is, therefore, appropriate that they should be included in the axis of clinical psychiatric syndromes and that is the approach adopted in DSM-IV and ICD-10.

The situation with respect to specific developmental disorders is somewhat more complicated. Because, in some respects, it is reasonable to consider developmental delay in specific cognitive functions as part of the differential diagnosis from general mental retardation, there is something to be said for having both on the same axis. However, psychiatrists concerned with mental retardation have noted that it is quite possible for someone to have both general retardation and specific cognitive deficits much more severe than, and out of keeping with, their overall mental age. Because the recognition of this combination of general and specific deficits is clinically important, it was argued that the two should be on separate axes and this option was followed in the clinical version of ICD-10. Of course, multiple diagnoses using DSM-IV allow this to be recorded and, although the ways of handling the issue differ between DSM-IV and ICD-10, the basic concepts are similar.

Comorbidity

Epidemiological and clinical studies have been consistent in showing a very high level of comorbidity. It is usual for a child with one diagnosis to have at least one other diagnosis as well, and often several (Caron & Rutter, 1991). There are many different ways in which this comorbidity may come about (Caron & Rutter, 1991; Klein & Riso, in press). It may be artefactual, the co-occurrence being a consequence of a single disorder having a complex pattern of symptomatology, which appears to span two disorders but which actually reflects just one. Alternatively, it may arise through two disorders sharing the same set of risk factors or through overlap between two different sets of risk variables. Another possibility is that one disorder creates a risk for another and yet another alternative is that the comorbid combination constitutes a distinctive syndrome in its own right. An example of the latter, which is classified separately in both ICD-10 and DSM-IV, is schizo-affective disorder. However, there are other instances where there is evidence suggesting that the presence of comorbidity changes the meaning of the two disorders that make up the comorbid combination. For example, the comorbid combination of depression plus conduct disorder seems to differ from 'pure' depression with respect to adult outcome (the risk of adult depression *not* being raised — Harrington *et al.*, 1991), a lower familial loading for affective disorder (Puig-Antich *et al.*, 1989) and a lack of increase in frequency over the adolescent age period (Angold & Rutter, 1992). The findings require replication and it would be premature to conclude

that this comorbid syndrome is a meaningfully separate disorder. The important thing is to appreciate that this is a real possibility. ICD-10 provides a separate code to enable the possibility to be tested; DSM-IV does not, on the grounds that the supporting evidence is, as yet, insufficient to justify it. Either position is justifiable but a consequence of the DSM-IV approach is that studies of depression will need to note, and pay special attention to, the comorbid combination in order to determine whether or not it has a special meaning. Another possible example of a meaningful comorbid pattern is provided by the combination of hyperactivity and anxiety, because the co-occurrence of anxiety has been found in several (but not all) studies to be associated with a worse response to stimulant medication than that ordinarily found with hyperkinetic/attention deficit disorder (see above).

The diagnostic criteria for child psychiatric disorders in DSM-IV and ICD-10 are very closely similar (unlike those for DSM-III or DSM-III-R and ICD-9). Nevertheless, to some extent, the philosophy underlying the two systems differs with respect to their approach to comorbidity (Rutter, 1988). In both, multiple diagnosis is possible, but it is likely to occur more commonly with DSM-IV than ICD-10 in its clinical version (the research version has rules that closely parallel those in DSM-IV and, hence, is likely to give rise to similar patterns of comorbidity). In ICD-10, the clinician is expected to choose the diagnosis that most closely matches the symptom pattern shown by each patient. The assumption, as in the rest of medicine, is that ordinarily a mixed clinical picture is more likely to represent a slightly atypical manifestation of one disorder than the co-occurrence of two entirely separate conditions. It is up to clinicians to use their skills to decide which condition that is likely to be. Only if it is clear that there are two truly independent conditions will a double diagnosis be made. By sharp contrast, with DSM-IV, the clinician simply follows the sets of rules for each diagnosis in the fashion specified in the rules and codes every diagnosis for which the rules are met. Because mixed clinical pictures are common in psychiatry, it is inevitable that multiple diagnoses will be frequent.

Each approach has its own logic and its own set of advantages and disadvantages. ICD-10 treats psychiatric disorders like other medical conditions and, if this approach is correct, the assumption about mixed clinical pictures usually (but not always) representing just one condition is probably also correct. The problems with this approach are twofold. First, there is the query on the parallel between mental and physical disorders. Do most psychiatric conditions represent discrete conditions of the kind implied by medical diagnoses? It is quite likely that some (such as, perhaps, schizophrenia, autism and bipolar affective disorders) do, but does this apply to all? (It is not so obvious that it does to, say, anxiety and conduct disorders that blend more into the borders of normality.) Second, there is the shortage of sound empirical evidence required to decide on just how mixed clinical pictures *should* be diagnosed. Accordingly, there is a danger that the wrong hierarchical rules will be employed. DSM-IV has a contrasting set of pluses and minuses. Its approach should avoid the difficulty of deciding on the hierarchies when evidence is thin, although in practice (like DSM-III-R), it includes more hierarchies than usually appreciated and some appear weak on both logic and empirical support (Rutter, 1988). For example, if a generalized anxiety disorder is present in conjunction with specific separation anxiety, it is assumed that these represent two separate and independent conditions, rather than that the specific fear is part of the broader anxiety disorder. Also, as Klein and Riso (in press) have pointed out, many of the advantages of a categorical system are lost when comorbidity is common and, if it is assumed that this represents reality, it is not clear why a dimensional system is not adopted.

We note these advantages and disadvantages that apply to both DSM-IV and ICD-10, not to choose between them (because both involve substantial problems), but rather to point out the need for research designed to elucidate the meaning of different patterns of comorbidity and the mechanism involved.

LABELLING AND ADMINISTRATIVE USE OF DIAGNOSES

Over the years, periodic concern has been expressed over the labelling effects of diagnoses (see Hobbs, 1975; Rutter & Shaffer, 1980; Rutter & Gould, 1985). It has been recognized that, whatever our intentions, there are ways in which the terms used to classify disorders carry implicit messages. Thus, at one time, some psychologists were concerned that calling a classification system psychiatric implied that the disorders needed to be treated by psychiatrists, and that including specific learning disorders in such a system meant that they were due to some form of mental illness. Also, people have been bothered that the particular words used may be perceived as derogatory. Thus, in the field of mental retardation, it has come to be unacceptable to use terms such as idiot, imbecile and mental deficiency, which were at one time standard descriptors. Indeed, currently in the UK there is an expectation that the proper term should be learning difficulty (see Chapter 60), a term that creates potential confusion because it fails to differentiate between mental retardation and specific learning disorders affecting language, reading or spelling. The difficulty with this never-ending chase for a nonderogatory term is that each of the discarded terms acquired its derogatory connotation through its application to mental retardation, not the other way round. Although it is undesirable, it is an unfortunate fact of life that many people have a negative attitude to mental retardation whatever term is used.

These concerns seem to suggest that labels necessarily have negative effects but, of course, the consequences may also be positive. For example, many years ago, Clausen and Yarrow (1955) found that families often found it easier to cope with disturbed behaviour in a spouse or parent when it was diagnosed as a mental illness. Instead of seeing the person as having become inexplicably difficult and unpleasant towards the family, the recognition that this was the result of a disorder outside the person's control made it both more understandable and more acceptable. Similarly, studies of teachers have shown that some respond positively to children labelled as low achievers because they appreciate that they need extra help (Brophy & Good, 1974). Diagnoses may serve as 'passports' providing access to services (see Chapter 63); thus, some clinicians have wanted as wide as possible a diagnosis of autism in order that the maximum number of children may be eligible to receive skilled help (Rutter & Schopler, 1992).

As we indicated in our introduction to this chapter, classification is a necessary element in all human communication, as well as being basic to all scientific endeavours. In itself it is neither beneficial nor harmful but it is important that classification systems should be constructed, and used, in a way that facilitates benefit. Four main points need to be made. Firstly, diagnoses apply to disorders and not to people. It is offensive to suggest that children are merely vehicles of disorder and, scientifically it implies a fixity of disorder that is out of keeping with the evidence. Secondly, a diagnostic term, or even a multiaxial set of codings, cannot provide a sufficient summary of all that is clinically important. Classificatory terms provide a handy summary for communication but, in clinical practice, they need to be supplemented by diagnostic formulations that bring out what is individual and special in the problems presented by the particular patient (see Chapter 2 for a discussion of this need). Thirdly, it is a mistake to equate diagnoses with administrative actions or particular service (in spite of the fact that this is an intrinsic part of US practice). They provide a useful general guide but not all children with a particular diagnosis require the same treatment or the same service. It is necessary that services should be tailored to individual needs rather than provided on the basis of diagnostic pigeon-holing. Fourthly, if appropriate action is to be taken to help children with a psychiatric disorder, it is important that clinical reports (to parents, teachers, primary care physicians and others) should go beyond specification of the diagnosis to indicate what the term means with respect to the problems of this particular child and what should be done to help the child overcome his or her difficulties or cope with his or her handicap.

CONCLUSIONS

In looking back on the ways in which psychiatric classifications have changed over the last 40 years, several key features seem to have particularly important implications for the advances that may be anticipated in the years to come. At first, theoretical concepts dominated classification systems, with consequent chaos and confusion because the theories lacked empirical justification and because there was widespread disagreement on which theory should be preferred. This approach was replaced by an atheoretical classification based on behavioural constellations. In its purest form, this was reflected in schemes based on factor analyses of symptoms, the diagnoses being derived from the factor structure found. In psychiatry, this led for a while to a tendency to base diagnoses only on cross-sectional symptom patterns without regard to validating findings. The approach carried the advantage of facilitating good reliability, but the danger of landing up with diagnoses that carried little scientific meaning or clinical utility. There is now a much greater appreciation of the need to focus on validation and, moreover, to use multiple validating criteria.

Five main features are likely to facilitate advances in the future. Firstly, there is the appreciation that it is necessary to use more than cross-sectional behavioural patterns in order to make a diagnosis. Thus, it may be desirable to take into account age or mode of onset, the absence as well as presence of particular symptoms, pervasiveness across situations or results of special investigations. Secondly, advances in biological investigations (perhaps especially genetics) and better data on continuities/discontinuities between child and adult psychopathology are both likely to increase the power of validating research strategies. Up to now, studies of diagnosis have tended to place main reliance on the extent of agreement between particular sets of diagnostic criteria and clinical judgement (which provides a most unsatisfactory criterion, even if it is the best that is available for many diagnoses now). Thirdly, improved statistical techniques allow a much more satisfactory testing of diagnostic criteria and constructs (Klein & Riso, in press).

Two warrant particular mention. Receiver operator curves provide a good means of deciding the point at which optimal sensitivity and specificity are achieved in relation to some specified external criterion (Hsiao *et al.*, 1989). Latent trait and class analyses provide a good way of specifying the construct in a fashion that goes well beyond factor structure; for example, it could be specified as the symptom combination that provides the highest heritability, or the greatest continuity with some disorder in adult life, or the best response to a particular drug, or the greatest agreement with some investigation abnormality. It also allows a probabilistic approach to patterns of symptomatology that avoids the inevitable error inherent in arbitrary thresholds (Rutter & Pickles, 1990; Zoccolillo *et al.*, 1992).

Fourthly, it is now clear that it is important to take comorbid patterns into account and to investigate the mechanisms underlying them. Finally, it has come to be realized that the requirements of clinical and research classifications are not the same (Rutter & Schopler, 1992). Thus, for research purposes it may often be advantageous to seek relatively narrow, 'pure' diagnoses, without being concerned that the consequence is a relatively high rate of undiagnosed cases; this would, however, not be acceptable for most clinical purposes. Although it is clear that there remain huge areas of ignorance and uncertainty regarding the classification of child psychiatric disorders, it is also evident that it has a more satisfactory empirical basis than was the case at the time when ICD-9 and DSM-III were introduced, and there is a sound expectation of important advances in knowledge in the years ahead.

REFERENCES

Achenbach T.M. (1985) *Assessment and Taxonomy of Child and Adolescent Psychopathology.* Sage, Beverly Hills.

Achenbach T.M. & Edelbrock C.S. (1978) The classification of child psychopathology: a review and analysis of empirical efforts. *Psychological Bulletin,* **85,** 1275–1301.

American Psychiatric Association (1952) *Diagnostic and Statistical Manual, Mental Disorders.* American Psychiatric Association, Washington DC.

American Psychiatric Association (1980) *Diagnostic and Statistical Manual of Mental Disorders,* 3rd edn. American Psychiatric Association, Washington, DC.

American Psychiatric Association (1987) *Diagnostic and Statistical Manual of Mental Disorders,* 3rd edn revised. American Psychiatric Association, Washington, DC.

American Psychiatric Association (1994) *Diagnostic and Statistical Manual of Mental Disorders,* 4th edn (DSM-IV). American Psychiatric Association, Washington, DC.

Andrews G., Stewart G., Allen R. & Henderson A.S. (1990) The genetics of six neurotic disorders: a twin study. *Journal of Affective Disorders,* **19,** 23–29.

Angold A. & Rutter M. (1992) Effects of age and pubertal status on depression in a large clinical sample. *Development and Psychopathology,* **4,** 5–28.

Baron-Cohen S., Tager-Flusberg H. & Cohen D. (eds) (1993) *Understanding Other Minds: Perspectives from Autism.* Oxford University Press, Oxford.

Bird H.R., Yager T.J., Staghezza B., Gould M.S., Canino G. & Rubio-Stipec M. (1990) Impairment in the epidemiological measurement of childhood psychopathology in the community. *Journal of the American Academy of Child and Adolescent Psychiatry,* **29,** 796–803.

Brophy J.E. & Good T.L. (1974) *Teacher–Student Relationships: Causes and Consequences.* Holt, Rinehard & Winston, New York.

Brown G.W. & Harris T.O. (1989) Depression. In: Brown G.W. & Harris T.O. (eds) *Life Events and Illness,* pp. 49–93. Unwin Hyman, London; New York: Guilford Press.

Brown G.W., Harris T.O. & Bifulco A. (1986) Long-term effects of early loss of parent. In: Rutter M., Izard C.E. & Read P.B. (eds) *Depression in Young People: Developmental and Clinical Perspectives,* pp. 251–296. Guilford Press, New York.

Cantwell D.P. (1975) A model for the investigation of psychiatric disorders of childhood: its application in genetic studies of the hyperkinetic syndrome. In: Anthony E.J. (ed) *Explorations in Child Psychiatry,* pp. 57–59. Plenum Press, New York.

Cantwell D. (1988) DSM-III studies. In: Rutter M., Tuma A.H. & Lann I.S. (eds) *Assessment and Diagnosis in Child Psychopathology,* pp. 3–36. Guilford Press, New York.

Cantwell D. & Baker L. (1988a) Anxiety disorders in children with communication disorders: correlates and outcome. *Journal of Anxiety Disorders,* **2,** 135–146.

Cantwell D. & Baker L. (1988b) Issues in the classification of child and adolescent psychopathology. *Journal of the American Academy of Child and Adolescent Psychiatry,* **27,** 521–533.

Cantwell D. & Baker L. (1989) Stability and natural history of DSM-III childhood diagnoses. *Journal of the American Academy of Child and Adolescent Psychiatry,* **28,** 691–700.

Cantwell D.P. & Baker L. (1991) Psychiatric classification. In: Michels R., Cooper A.M., Guze S.B., Judd L.L., Klerman G.L., Solnit A.J., Stunkard A.J. & Wilner P.J. (eds) *Psychiatry* (revised edition). J.B. Lippincott, Philadelphia.

Caron C. & Rutter M. (1991) Comorbidity in child psychopathology: concepts, issues and research strategies. *Journal of Child Psychology and Psychiatry,* **32,** 1064–1080.

Clausen J.A. & Yarrow M.R. (1955) Paths to the mental hospital. *Journal of Social Issues*, 11, 25–32.

Comings D.E. & Comings B.G. (1990) Clinical and genetic relationships between autism-pervasive developmental disorder and Tourette syndrome: a study of 19 cases. *American Journal of Human Genetics*, 39, 180–191.

Cromwell R.L., Blashfield R.K. & Strauss J.S. (1975) Criteria for classification systems. In: Hobbs N. (ed) *Issues in the Classification of Children*, pp. 4–25. Jossey-Bass, San Francisco.

Crow T.J. (1990) The continuum of psychosis and its genetic origin. *British Journal of Psychiatry*, 156, 788–787.

DeFries J.C. & Fulker D.W. (1988) Multiple regression analysis of twin data: etiology of deviant scores versus individual differences. *Acta Geneticae Medicae et Gemellologiae*, 37, 205–216.

DeFries J.C. & Gillis J.J. (1991) Etiology of reading deficits in learning disabilities: quantitative genetic analysis. In: Orbzut J.E. & Hynd G.W. (eds) *Neuropsychological Foundations of Learning Disabilities. A Handbook of Issues, Methods, and Practice.* Academic Press, New York.

Eggers C. (1978) Course and prognosis of childhood schizophrenia. *Journal of Autism and Childhood Schizophrenia*, 8, 21–35.

Eggers C. (1989) Schizo-affective psychoses in childhood: a follow-up study. *Journal of Autism and Developmental Disorders*, 19, 327–342.

Endicott J. & Spitzer R.L. (1978) A diagnostic interview: the schedule for affective disorders and schizophrenia. *Archives of General Psychiatry*, 35, 773–782.

Feighner J., Robins E., Guze S.B., Woodruff R.A., Winokur G. & Munoz R. (1972) Diagnostic criteria for use in psychiatric research. *Archives of General Psychiatry*, 26, 57–63.

Freud A. (1965) *Normality and Pathology in Childhood.* International Universities Press, New York.

Gillberg C.L. (1992) Autism and autistic-like conditions: sub-classes among disorders of empathy. *Journal of Child Psychology and Psychiatry*, 33, 813–842.

Goodyer I.M. (1990) *Life Experiences, Development and Childhood Psychopathology.* Wiley, Chichester.

Gotlib I.H. & Hooley J.M. (1988). Depression and marital distress: current status and future directions. In: Duck S. (ed) *Handbook of Personal Relationships: Theory, Research and Interventions*, pp. 543–570. Wiley, Chichester.

Grayson D.A. (1987) Can categorical and dimensional views of psychiatric illness be distinguished? *British Journal of Psychiatry*, 151, 355–361.

Greer H.S. & Cawley R.H. (1966) *Some Observations on the Natural History of Neurotic Illness.* Mervyn Archdall Medical Monograph no. 3. Australian Medical Association, Sydney.

Group for the Advancement of Psychiatry (1966) *Psychopathological Disorders in Childhood: Theoretical Considerations and a Proposed Classification* (research report no. 62), pp. 229–230. Group for the Advancement of Psychiatry, New York.

Gualtieri T. & Hicks R.E. (1985) An immunoreactive theory of selective male affliction. *Behavioral and Brain Sciences*, 8, 427–441.

Harrington R., Fudge H., Rutter M., Pickles A. & Hill J. (1990) Adult outcome of childhood and adolescent depression. I. Psychiatric status. *Archives of General Psychiatry*, 47, 465–473.

Harrington R., Fudge H., Rutter M., Pickles A. & Hill J. (1991) Adult outcomes of childhood and adolescent depression. II. Links with antisocial disorder. *Journal of the American Academy of Child and Adolescent Psychiatry*, 30, 434–439.

Harrington R., Fudge H., Rutter M., Bredenkamp D., Groothues C. & Pridham J. (1993) Child and adult depression: a test of continuities with family study data. *British Journal of Psychiatry*, 162, 627–633.

Hobbs N. (1975) *Issues in the Classification of Children.* Jossey-Bass, San Francisco.

Horn G. (1990) Neural bases of recognition memory investigated through an analysis of imprinting. *Philosophical Transaction of the Royal Society*, 329, 133–142.

Hsiao J.K., Bartko J.J. & Potter W.Z. (1989) Diagnosing diagnoses: receiver operating characteristic methods and psychiatry. *Archives of General Psychiatry*, 46, 664–667.

Jaspers K. (1962) *General Psychopathology.* Translated by Hoening J. & Hamilton M.W. University Press, Manchester.

Keller M.B., Lavori P.W., Wunder J., Beardslee W.R., Schwartz C.E. & Roth J. (1992) Chronic course of anxiety disorders in children and adolescents. *Journal of the American Academy of Child and Adolescent Psychiatry*, 31, 595–599.

Kendell R.E. (1975) *The Role of Diagnosis.* Blackwell Scientific Publications, Oxford.

Kendell R.E. (1982) The choice of diagnostic criteria for biological research. *Archives of General Psychiatry*, 39, 1334–1339.

Kendell R.E. (1989) Clinical validity. *Psychological Medicine*, 19, 45–55.

Kendler K.S. & Gruenberg A.M. (1984) An independent analysis of the Danish adoption study of schizophrenia. VI: The relationship between psychiatric disorders as defined by DSM-III in the relatives and adoptees. *Archives of General Psychiatry*, 41, 555–564.

Kendler K.S., Neale M.C., Kessler R.C., Heath A.C. & Eaves L.J. (1992a) Generalized anxiety disorder in women. *Archives of General Psychiatry*, 49, 267–272.

Kendler K.S., Neale M.C., Kessler R.C., Heath A.C. & Eaves L.J. (1992b) A population-based twin study of major depression in women: the impact of varying definitions of illness. *Archives of General Psychiatry*, 49, 257–266.

Klein D.N. & Riso L.P. (1993) Psychiatric disorders: Problems of boundaries and comorbidity. In: Costello C.G. (ed) *Basic Issues in Psychopathology*, pp. 19–66. Guilford Press, New York.

Last C.G., Perrin S., Hersen M. & Kazdin A.E. (1992) DSM-III-R anxiety disorders in children: sociodemographic and clinical characteristics. *Journal of the American Academy of Child and Adolescent Psychiatry*, 31, 1070–1076.

Livingston R.L., Dykman R.A. & Ackerman P.T. (1992) Psychiatric comorbidity and response to two doses of methylphenidate in children with attention deficit disorder. *Journal of Child and Adolescent Psychopharmacology*, 2, 115–122.

McGuffin P. & Katz R. (1986) Nature, nurture and affective disorder. In: Deakin J.F.W. (ed) *The Biology of Depression.* Gaskell Press, London.

McGuffin P., Katz R., Rutherford J., Watkins S., Farmer A.E. & Gottesman I.I. (1993) Twin studies as vital indicators of phenotypes in molecular genetic research. In: Bouchard Jr. T.J. & Propping P. (eds) *Twins as a Tool of Behavioral Genetics*, pp. 243–256. Wiley, Chichester.

Magnusson D. & Bergman L.R. (1988) Individual and variable-based approaches to longitudinal research on early risk factors. In: Rutter M. (ed) *Studies of Psychosocial Risk: The Power of Longitudinal Data*, pp. 45–61. Cambridge University Press, Cambridge.

Magnusson D. & Bergman L.R. (1990) A pattern approach to the study of pathways from childhood to adulthood. In: Robins L. & Rutter M. (eds) *Straight and Devious Pathways from Childhood to Adulthood.* Cambridge University Press, New York.

Mattison R.E. & Hooper S.R. (1992) The history of modern classification of child and adolescent psychiatric disorders: an overview. In: Hooper S.R., Hynd G.W. & Mattison R.E. (eds) *Assessment and Diagnosis of Child and Adolescent Psychiatric Disorders. Volume 1: Psychiatric Disorders.* Lawrence Erlbaum Publishers, Hillsdale, NJ.

Plante E., Swisher L. & Vance R. (1991) MRI findings in boys with specific language impairment. *Brain and Language*, 41, 52–66.

Pliszka S.R. (1989) Effects of anxiety on cognition, behavior, and stimulant response in ADHD. *Journal of the American Academy of Child and Adolescent Psychiatry*, 28, 882–887.

Plomin R. (1991) Genetic risk and psychosocial disorders: links between the normal and abnormal. In: Rutter M. & Casaer P. (eds) *Biological Risk Factors for Psychosocial Disorders*, pp. 101–138. Cambridge University Press, Cambridge.

Plomin R. & Bergeman C.S. (1991) The nature of nurture: genetic influence on 'environmental' measures. *Behavioral and Brain Sciences*, **14**, 373–386.

Plomin R., Rende R. & Rutter M. (1991) Quantitative genetics and developmental psychopathology. In: Cicchetti D. & Toth S.L. (eds) *Internalizing and Externalizing Expressions of Dysfunction: Rochester Symposium on Developmental Psychopathology*, Vol. 2, pp. 155–202. Lawrence Erlbaum Associates, Hillsdale, NJ.

Prendergast M., Taylor E., Rapoport J.L., Bartko J., Donnelly M., Zametkin A., Ahearn M.B., Dunn G. & Wieselberg H.M. (1988) The diagnosis of childhood hyperactivity: a U.S.–U.K. cross-national study of DSM-III and ICD-9. *Journal of Child Psychology and Psychiatry*, **29**, 289–300.

Puig-Antich J., Goetz D., Davies M., Kaplan T., Davies S., Ostrow L., Asnis L., Twomey J., Lyengar S. & Ryan N.D. (1989) A controlled family history study of prepubertal major depressive disorder. *Archives of General Psychiatry*, **46**, 406–418.

Quay H.C̆. (1986) A critical analysis of DSM-III as a taxonomy of psychopathology in childhood and adolescence. In: Millon T. & Klerman G.L. (eds) *Contemporary Directions in Psychopathology: Towards the DSM-IV*, pp. 151–165. Guilford Press, New York.

Quinton D., Rutter M. & Gulliver L. (1990) Continuities in psychiatric disorders from childhood to adulthood in the children of psychiatric patients. In: Robins L. & Rutter M. (eds) *Straight and Devious Pathways from Childhood to Adulthood*, pp. 259–278. Cambridge University Press, New York.

Radke-Yarrow M., Cummings E.M., Kuczynski L. & Chapman M. (1985) Patterns of attachment in two and three year old normal families and families with parental depression. *Child Development*, **56**, 884–893.

Rey J.M., Plapp J.M. & Stewart G.W. (1989) Reliability of psychiatric diagnosis in referred adolescents. *Journal of Child Psychology and Psychiatry*, **30**, 879–888.

Richardson S. & Koller H. (1992) Vulnerability and resilience in adults who were classified as mildly mentally handicapped in childhood. In: Tizard B. & Varma V. (eds) *Vulnerability and Resilience in Human Development*, pp. 102–122. Jessica Kingsley Publishers, London.

Robins L.N. (1991) Conduct disorder. *Journal of Child Psychology and Psychiatry*, **32**, 193–212.

Robins L. & McEvoy L. (1990) Conduct problems as predictors of substance abuse. In: Robins L. & Rutter M. (eds) *Straight and Devious Pathways from Childhood to Adulthood*, pp. 182–204. Cambridge University Press, New York.

Rourke B.P. (1985) *Neuropsychology of Learning Disabilities: Essentials of Sub-Type Analysis*. Guilford Press, New York.

Rutter M. (1965) Classification and categorization in child psychiatry. *Journal of Child Psychology and Psychiatry*, **6**, 71–83.

Rutter M. (1972) Childhood schizophrenia reconsidered. *Journal of Autism and Childhood Schizophrenia*, **2**, 315–337.

Rutter M. (1978) Diagnostic validity in child psychiatry. *Advances in Biological Psychiatry*, **2**, 2–22.

Rutter M. (1985) Family and school influences on behavioural development. *Journal of Child Psychology and Psychiatry*, **26**, 349–368.

Rutter M. (1988) DSM-III-R: a postscript. In: Rutter M., Tuma A.H. & Lann I.S. (eds) *Assessment and Diagnosis in Child Psychopathology*, pp. 453–464. Guilford Press, New York.

Rutter M. (1989a) Psychiatric disorder in parents as a risk factor for children. In: Shaffer D., Philips I. & Enzer N.B. (eds) *Prevention of Mental Disorders, Alcohol and Other Drug Use in Children and Adolescents*. OSAP Prevention Monograph 2, pp. 157–189. Office for Substance Abuse Prevention, US Department of Health and Human Services, Rockville, Md.

Rutter M. (1989b) Isle of Wight revisited: twenty-five years of child psychiatric epidemiology. *Journal of the American Academy of Child and Adolescent Psychiatry*, **28**, 633–653.

Rutter M. (1990) Commentary: some focus and process considerations regarding effects of parental depression on children. *Developmental Psychology*, **26**, 60–67.

Rutter M. (1991a) Autism as a genetic disorder. In: McGuffin P. & Murray R. (eds) *The New Genetics of Mental Illness*, pp. 225–244. Butterworth-Heinemann, Oxford.

Rutter M. (1991b) A fresh look at 'maternal deprivation'. In: Bateson P. (ed) *The Development and Integration of Behaviour*, pp. 331–374. Cambridge University Press, Cambridge.

Rutter M. & Garmezy N. (1983) Developmental psychopathology. In: Hetherington E.M. (ed) *Socialization, Personality, and Social Development, vol. 4, Mussen's Handbook of Child Psychology*, pp. 775–911. Wiley, New York.

Rutter M. & Gould M. (1985) Classification. In: Rutter M. & Hersov L. (eds) *Child and Adolescent Psychiatry: Modern Approaches*, 2nd edn, pp. 304–431. Blackwell Scientific Publications, Oxford.

Rutter M. & Madge N. (1976) *Cycles of Disadvantage: A Review of Research*. Heinemann Educational, London.

Rutter M. & Mawhood L. (1991) The long-term psychosocial sequelae of specific developmental disorders of speech and language. In: Rutter M. & Casaer P. (eds) *Biological Risk Factors for Psychosocial Disorders*, pp. 233–259. Cambridge University Press, Cambridge.

Rutter M. & Pickles A. (1990) Improving the quality of psychiatric data: classification, cause and course. In: Magnusson D. & Bergman L.R. (eds) *Data Quality in Longitudinal Research*, pp. 32–57. Cambridge University Press, Cambridge.

Rutter M. & Quinton D. (1984) Parental psychiatric disorder: effects on children. *Psychological Medicine*, **14**, 853–880.

Rutter M. & Sandberg S. (1985) Epidemiology of child psychiatric disorder: methodological issues and some substantive findings. *Child Psychiatry and Human Development*, **15**, 209–233.

Rutter M. & Schopler E. (1988) Autism and pervasive developmental disorders. In: Rutter M., Tuma A.H. & Lann I.S. (eds) *Assessment and Diagnosis in Child Psychopathology*, pp. 408–434. Guilford Press, New York.

Rutter M. & Schopler E. (1992) Classification of pervasive developmental disorders: some concepts and practical considerations. *Journal of Autism and Developmental Disorders*, **22**, 459–482.

Rutter M. & Shaffer D. (1980) DMS-III: a step forward or back in terms of the classification of child psychiatric disorders? *Journal of the American Academy of Child Psychiatry*, **19**, 371–394.

Rutter M., Lebovici S., Eisenberg L., Sneznevskij A.V., Sadoun R., Brooke E. & Lin T.-Y. (1969) A triaxial classification of mental disorders in childhood. *Journal of Child Psychology and Psychiatry*, **10**, 41–61.

Rutter M., Tizard J. & Whitmore K. (eds) (1970) *Education, Health and Behaviour*. Longmans, London (Reprinted, 1981, Krieger, Melbourne, FL.).

Rutter M., Shaffer D. & Shepherd M. (1975a) *A Multiaxial Classification of Child Psychiatric Disorders*. World Health Organization, Geneva.

Rutter M., Shaffer D. & Sturge C. (1975b) *A Guide to a Multiaxial Classification Scheme for Psychiatric Disorders in Childhood and Adolescence*. Institute of Psychiatry, London.

Rutter M., Chadwick O. & Shaffer D. (1983) Head injury. In: Rutter M. (ed) *Developmental Neuropsychiatry*, pp. 83–111. Guilford Press, New York.

Rutter M., Tuma A.H. & Lann I.S. (eds) (1988) *Assessment and Diagnosis in Child Psychopathology*. Guilford Press, New York.

Rutter M., Macdonald H., Le Couteur A., Harrington R., Bolton P. &

Bailey A. (1990) Genetic factors in child psychiatric disorders. II. Empirical findings. *Journal of Child Psychology and Psychiatry*, **31**, 39–83.

Rutter M., Mawhood L. & Howlin P. (1992) Language delay and social development. In: Fletcher P. & Hall D. (eds) *Specific Speech and Language Disorders in Children*, pp. 63–78. Whurr Publishers, London.

Rutter M., Harrington R., Quinton D. & Pickles A. (in press) Adult outcome of depressive and conduct disorders in childhood. In: Ketterlinus R. & Lamb M. (eds) *Adolescent Problem Behaviors*. Lawrence Erlbaum Associates, Hillsdale, NJ.

Scadding J.G. (1980) The concepts of disease: a response. *Psychological Medicine*, **20**, 425–427.

Scadding J.G. (1982) What is a case? Book review. *Psychological Medicine*, **12**, 207–208.

Shaffer D., Gould M.S., Brasic J., Ambrosini P., Fisher P., Bird H. & Aluwahlia S. (1983) A children's global assessment scale (C-GAS). *Archives of General Psychiatry*, **40**, 1228–1231.

Sleight P. (1988) Essential hypertension. In: Weatherall D.J., Ledingham J.G.G. & Warrell D.A. (eds) *Oxford Textbook of Medicine*, 2nd edn, pp. 13.360–13.382. Oxford University Press, Oxford.

Steffenburg S. & Gillberg C. (1989) The etiology of autism. In: Gillberg C. (ed) *Diagnosis and Treatment of Autism*, pp. 63–82. Plenum Press, New York.

Stengel E. (1959) Classification of mental disorders. *Bulletin of the World Health Organization*, **21**, 601–663.

Strober M. & Katz J.L. (1987) Do eating disorders and affective disorders share a common etiology? A dissenting opinion. *International Journal of Eating Disorders*, **6**, 171–180.

Tarjan M.D., Tizard J., Rutter M., Begab M., Brooke E., de la Cruz F., Lin T-Y., Montenegro H., Strotzka H. & Sartorius N. (1972) Classification and mental retardation: issues arising in the fifth WHO seminar on psychiatric diagnosis, classification and statistics. *American Journal of Psychiatry*, **128** (suppl.), 34–45.

Taylor E. & Rutter M. (1985) Sex differences in neurodevelopmental and psychiatric disorders: one explanation or many? *Behavioral and Brain Sciences*, **8**, 460.

Taylor E., Schachar R., Thorley G., Wieselberg H.M., Everitt B. & Rutter M. (1987) Which boys respond to stimulant medication? A controlled trial of methylphenidate in boys with disruptive behaviour. *Psychological Medicine*, **17**, 121–143.

Tizard J. (1974) Longitudinal studies: problems and findings. In: Clarke A.M. & Clarke A.D.B. (eds) *Mental Deficiency: The Changing Outlook*, pp. 223–256. Methuen, London.

Treasure J.L. & Holland A.J. (1991) Genes and the aetiology of eating disorders. In: McGuffin P. & Murray R. (eds) *The New Genetics of Mental Illness*, pp. 198–211. Butterworth-Heinemann, Oxford.

Van Goor-Lambo G., Orley J., Poutska F. & Rutter M. (1990) Classification of abnormal psychosocial situations: preliminary report of a revision of a WHO scheme. *Journal of Child Psychology and Psychiatry*, **31**, 229–241.

Waterhouse L., Wing L., Spitzer R. & Siegel B. (1992) Pervasive developmental disorders: from DSM-III to DSM-III-R. *Journal of Autism and Developmental Disorders*, **22**, 525–549.

Weissman M., Warner V. & Fendrich M. (1990) Applying impairment criteria to children's psychiatric diagnosis. *Journal of the American Academy of Child and Adolescent Psychiatry*, **29**, 789–796.

Werry J. (1972) Diagnosis for psychopharmacological studies in children. *Psychopharmacological Bulletin*, **9** (suppl.), 89–96.

Werry J. (1992a) Child and adolescent (early-onset) schizophrenia: a review in the light of DSM-III-R. *Journal of Autism and Developmental Disorders*, **22**, 601–624.

Werry J.S (1992b) Child psychiatric disorders: are they classifiable? *British Journal of Psychiatry*, **161**, 472–480.

Werry J.S., Reeves J.C. & Elkind G.S. (1987) Attention deficit, conduct, oppositional, and anxiety disorders in children: I. A review of research on differentiating characteristics. *Journal of the American Academy of Child Psychiatry*, **26**, 133–143.

Werry J.S., McClellan J.M. & Chard L. (1991) Childhood and adolescent schizophrenic, bipolar, and schizoaffective disorders: a clinical and outcome study. *Journal of the American Academy of Child and Adolescent Psychiatry*, **30**, 457–465.

Whitbeck C. (1977) Causation in medicine: the disease entity model. *Philosophy of Science*, **44**, 619–637.

Wing L. & Gould J. (1979) Severe impairments of social interaction and associated abnormalities in children: epidemiology and classification. *Journal of Autism and Developmental Disorders*, **9**, 11–30.

World Health Organization (1967) *International Classification of Diseases: Manual of the International Statistical Classification of Diseases, Injuries and Causes of Death*, 8th revision. World Health Organization, Geneva.

World Health Organization (1978) *Mental Disorders: Glossary and Guide to their Classification in Accordance with the Ninth Revision of the International Classification of Diseases*. World Health Organization, Geneva.

World Health Organization (1992) *ICD-10: The ICD-10 Classification of Mental and Behavioural Disorders: Clinical Descriptions and Diagnostic Guidelines*. World Health Organization, Geneva.

World Health Organization (in press) *Multi-axial Version of ICD-10: Prepared for Use by Clinicians Dealing with Child and Adolescent Psychiatric Disorders*. Cambridge University Press, Cambridge.

Zeitlin H. (1986) *The Natural History of Psychiatric Disorder in Childhood*. Institute of Psychiatry/Maudsley Monograph no. 29. Oxford University Press, Oxford.

Zoccolillo M., Pickles A., Quinton D. & Rutter M. (1992) The outcome of conduct disorder: implications for defining adult personality disorder and conduct disorder. *Psychological Medicine*, **22**, 971–986.

Chapter 2
Diagnostic Appraisal

Antony D. Cox

INTRODUCTION

Cantwell (1988) described the way in which the diagnostic process can be conceptualized as answering a number of questions:

1 Does the child have any type of psychiatric disorder?

2 If there is a disorder, does the clinical picture fit that of a recognized clinical syndrome?

3 What are the various roots of that disorder in terms of intrapsychic, family, sociocultural and biological factors; and what are the relative strengths of each of these root causes in this particular patient?

4 What forces are maintaining the problem?

5 What forces are facilitating the child's normal development?

6 What are the strengths and competencies of the child and of the family?

7 Untreated, what is the likely outcome of the child's disorder(s)?

8 Is intervention necessary in this case?

9 What types of intervention are most likely to be effective?

The process should develop hypotheses about whether there is a problem relevant to a psychiatric service and, if there is, hypotheses about its nature and aetiology should constitute a basis for intervention. However it is necessary first to understand why the psychiatric service has been contacted; that is, the context of the referral and the characteristics of the referral process. The appraisal of referral and referred problem needs to be done in such a way that engagement in treatment can be achieved. The understanding of the nature of the problem and its aetiology and the impact of any intervention then need to be continuously reevaluated, so that initial hypotheses and plans are revised accordingly (Nurcombe & Gallagher, 1986).

Diagnostic appraisal is essentially a joint activity shared amongst professionals and the child and family (Nurcombe & Gallagher, 1986). As such, the process of assessment has the potential for altering the perceptions, attitudes and feelings of those involved. Thus, there is a therapeutic aspect to diagnostic appraisal which cannot be separated functionally from intervention, although it is helpful conceptually to distinguish assessment goals and procedures.

THE CONTEXT OF ASSESSMENT

There are many reasons why children are referred to psychiatric clinics and multiple factors play a part in the process. These need to be understood if there is to be an appropriate service response. There is usually a professional referrer mediating between the family and the clinic, and usually the parents play a greater role in negotiating referral than does the child. Therefore the referral may reflect concerns in the referrer or agency or in the parents and family, rather than the child. It is rare for the child to complain directly to the psychiatric services.

While the great majority of children who are referred have some form of psychiatric disorder, the presence of disorder is rarely a *sufficient* reason for referral. If it were, all children with a disorder would get to attend a clinic and numerous studies have shown that this is far from the case (Rutter *et al.*, 1970; Garralda & Bailey, 1986).

Referral is influenced by a number of factors. Firstly, there is the degree of awareness that there is a problem. Thus, it is quite common for adolescents to experience marked feelings of misery and distress without adults realizing it (Rutter *et al.*, 1976; Angold *et al.*, 1987; Weissman *et al.*, 1987). It is also a matter of recognizing that particular symptoms mean that there is a problem. Many parents of children with obvious psychiatric disorders do not appreciate either the meaning or severity of their children's difficulties (Rutter *et al.*, 1970; Stern *et al.*, 1990). They may feel that the child is merely 'naughty' or 'not trying' or that the child will 'grow out of it' if left alone. These views and attitudes tend to vary from week to week (Graham & Rutter, 1968) and are often influenced by particular events or crises. No notice may be taken of a desperately unhappy child until she runs away from home or swallows her mother's pills. An aggressive child may be tolerated at school until he hits or threatens the teacher, and then what was a minor discipline problem becomes a 'real' disorder warranting psychiatric referral.

Secondly, the family or referral agency requires knowledge of the help available and how to access it. Misconceptions are not uncommon amongst professionals as well as the general public (Oke & Mayer, 1991).

Thirdly, there is the attitude of the family to the problem, which may be influenced by concurrent factors, so that to some extent the reasons for referral may lie in the parents or in the family rather than the child. Thus, Shepherd *et al.* (1971) compared children attending clinics and those not attending; the children in both cases had roughly comparable disorders. It was found that, compared with the mothers of children with psychiatric disorder who were *not* attending clinics, the clinic mothers were more likely to have suffered nervous complaints themselves and to be worried about their children. In addition, more of the clinic mothers came from broken homes.

Fourthly, there is the question of the attitude of the family to referral to a psychiatric service and it is clear that there are families who are resistant to such referral (Cottrell *et al.*, 1988).

Fifthly, the family or agency system that has been containing the problem may change or break down, precipitating referral. For example, a health visitor or social worker who has been supporting a family may be leaving the agency and know that there is no one to replace him or her.

Sixthly, the impetus for referral may come primarily for reasons other than disorder in the child, for example where one parent wishes to influence the extent to which a separated parent has access. In a comparable way, a marked increase in referrals from a particular school may reflect rising tensions and insecurity among the staff (Rutter, 1975). Although the referred children may all have psychiatric problems, the fact that they have all been referred to the clinic at the same time may have as much to do with the school's circumstances as with the individual children's problems.

Seventhly, the initiative for referral may come from beyond the family and those in most direct contact. For example, a court may request assessment or reassessment of suspected child abuse or care arrangements.

For all these reasons, the diagnostic appraisal must focus on the social context and manner of referral as well as on the child. This means that it is necessary to understand the dynamics of the process of referral. Who is concerned about the child? *Why* are they concerned? Why are they concerned *now* rather than at some other time?

In the same way that referral may spring from different sources, Kanner (1957) has described how symptoms can serve several rather different functions. First, they constitute an 'admission ticket' to the clinic, indicating that there is a problem to be studied. Second, they may be a signal that something is wrong within the child. Third, they may act as a safety valve, as when rebellion and defiance are used as a response to an intolerable situation. Fourth, they may be a means of solving problems, as when a child copes with anxiety about school by complaining of a belly-ache and going to bed. Fifth, the symptom constitutes a nuisance, as when fighting and aggressive behaviour at school cause annoyance to teachers. To these may be added a sixth, where the child's disturbance serves some role in the family, as when a child's noncompliant behaviour unites parents whose marriage is in danger of breaking. The diagnostic evaluation must include an appraisal of what the symptoms mean in each referral: not only in psychiatric terms but also in terms of their meaning to the particular child, to his or her family and to the referral agent.

PRINCIPLES UNDERLYING ASSESSMENT

Diagnostic appraisal needs to be based on what is known about child development and child psychiatric disorders.

Developmental process

A developmental approach to diagnostic assessment is necessary for several rather different reasons (Rutter & Garmezy, 1983). Firstly, children behave differently at different ages and the clinician needs to know the range of behaviours expected at each age to judge what is normal and abnormal. Secondly, in order to assess the severity of psychiatric disturbance, it is useful to consider how far there has been interference with the normal course of psychological development (Rutter, 1975; Achenbach, 1990). Just as the milestones of sitting, standing and walking provide a guide to motor development, so there are comparable indices of social and psychological development. Thus, children develop emotional bonds and attachments that initiate the process of socialization (Rutter, 1980a; Bretherton & Waters, 1985; Lamb *et al.*, 1991); also they move from solitary to parallel to cooperative play and then develop friendships which deepen and persist to an increasing extent with maturity (Hartup, 1983; Dunn & McGuire, 1992). Psychosexual development similarly goes through predictable stages (Rutter, 1980b). Thirdly, different phases of development are associated with different stresses and different susceptibilities and these must also be taken into account (Rutter, 1981, 1989a). For example, the toddler age period is the time when children are most likely to be adversely affected by hospital admission or separation experiences, and adolescence is the time when depressive mood swings are most common (Rutter, 1986; Kashani & Sherman, 1988; Cooper & Goodyer, (in press); Kolvin *et al.*, 1991). Fourthly, if clinicians are to understand how problems have arisen, they must understand the processes that underlie both normal and abnormal development, and the extent to which they are similar or different (Rutter & Garmezy, 1983; Rutter, 1987; Robins & Rutter, 1990).

In understanding these processes, the principles and concepts of development that derive from the study of normal development and psychopathology (Rutter, 1989a) have direct application to assessment because they point to the type of data that may be relevant, sources from which they may need to be obtained and the manner in which they can be interpreted. Firstly, humans are social beings and social development is related to interactions and transactions with the social environment. It is not just individuals' capacities that are important but also the content of emotions and relationships. Secondly, the timing of experiences influences impact because of the stage of neurodevelopment and the individual's psychological capacities that are emerging, and also because of the relevance of happenings that are felt in their specific context, including the response of others. Thirdly, intrinsic and extrinsic factors interweave and both are crucial.

Fourthly, it can be expected that there will be continuities and discontinuities in outward behaviour, but if they are to be understood it is necessary to seek for evidence of continuity and discontinuity in underlying factors and processes both in the individual and in his or her environment. For example, continuity in behaviour may 'have a fragile dependency on consistency in the environment' and particular behaviours may reflect different psychological processes at different ages (Hinde, 1988). Conversely, behaviours may change their form but nevertheless still be manifestations of the same basic process: the psychological processes may display greater continuity than the overt behaviour. Hinde (1988) argued for aggregate measures in research in order that psychological processes may be inferred. His principle is just as germane in clinical practice.

Fifthly, it is insufficient to know that major life events and transitions, such as starting school and leaving home, have occurred. Detail about the context, and about how the changes have been negotiated and experienced, is required. It is important to understand individual differences in the meaning of such transitions and responses to them.

Sixthly, increasingly research has drawn attention to the need to evaluate protective factors as well as risk factors. Finally it is necessary to disentangle direct and indirect effects and the 'chaining' of events, capacities and behaviours. 'Bad' experiences tend to increase the risk of other bad experiences both directly by altering opportunities, and also indirectly by changing self-perceptions, attitudes and behaviours. Outcome may be mediated or moderated by other concurrent or antecedent factors (Silbereisen & Walper, 1988). For example, maternal warmth has been shown to protect 6-year-olds from the effects of peer rejection (Patterson *et al.*, 1989). These principles and concepts should influence both the gathering and interpretation of data during assessment.

Epidemiology

Epidemiological studies indicate that over the course of 1 year some 5–15% of 9–10-year-old children suffer from emotional or behavioural disorders of sufficient severity to handicap them in their everyday life (Rutter *et al.*, 1970; Graham, 1979; Yule, 1980; Costello, 1989; Rutter, 1989b; Brandenburg *et al.*, 1990; Offord & Fleming, 1991). The figures for preschool children are of the same order, while those for adolescents are somewhat higher. Prevalence is greater where measures of impairment are less exacting (e.g. Verhulst *et al.*, 1985 — 26%), and lower where they are more stringent (Rutter *et al.*, 1970). The rates are lowest where the criterion of need for treatment is included (e.g. Vikan, 1985 — 5%). While there are more boys with disorders in the 4–11-year-old age group, girls predominate amongst 12–16-year-olds (Offord *et al.*, 1987). This means that psychiatric disorders in childhood are very common, but that their identification depends on the criteria

employed, in particular the extent of personal and social impairment.

Isolated problems such as fears, tantrums or nightmares are very much more common than psychiatric disorders. Thus, Lapouse and Monk (1958, 1959) found that one-third of 6–12-year-old children experience nightmares and one-half had multiple fears. Numerous other epidemiological studies of the general population have shown the same thing (Shepherd *et al.*, 1971; Tuddenham *et al.*, 1974; Graham, 1979; Yule, 1980; see reviews by Rutter, 1989b, Offord & Fleming, 1991). However such isolated problems rarely merit a diagnosis of psychiatric disorder. Generally speaking, the greater the number of symptoms, the more likely the child is to have a clinically significant psychiatric disorder (Glidewell *et al.*, 1957; Rutter *et al.*, 1970, 1975) and for each symptom, the more severe it is and the more frequently it occurs, the greater is the likelihood of psychiatric disorder (Glidewell *et al.*, 1957; Shepherd *et al.*, 1971; Rutter *et al.*, 1976). Some behaviours are much better indicators of disorder than others. Thus, so-called neurotic traits of childhood are very poor psychiatric indicators, whereas poor peer relations are not only a good indicator of current disorder (Rutter *et al.*, 1970; Hartup, 1983; Dunn & McGuire, 1992), but also a predictor of persisting disorder (Hartup, 1989; Dunn & McGuire, 1992).

However, even in the case of clear disorders with multiple symptoms, the same epidemiological investigations show that usually no sharp line can be drawn between normality and psychiatric disorder. Many normal children have transient minor problems of a type that, appropriately, might be regarded as psychiatric disorder if the disturbance was more severe and more persistent. In short, most psychiatric conditions differ *quantitatively* from normal in terms of severity, persistence and social impairment, but minor variations of the same behaviour can be found in many essentially normal children. Only a few psychiatric conditions in childhood constitute diseases or illnesses that differ *qualitatively* from normality.

Although transient isolated difficulties may be no more than temporary exaggerations of widely distributed reaction patterns, the 5–15% of the general population with psychiatric disorder with functional impairment have persistent disorders associated with appreciable personal suffering and are often accompanied by serious difficulties of other kinds, such as poor scholastic attainment (Rutter *et al.*, 1970). Indeed, the assessment of the severity of functional impairment is a crucial aspect of diagnostic appraisal and Rutter (1975) has listed four useful criteria: (1) the amount of personal suffering; (2) the extent of restriction of social activities; (3) the degree of interference with normal psychological development; and (4) the effects of the child's behaviour on others.

Other information needed to make a judgement regarding the presence of psychiatric disorder in childhood includes (Shepherd *et al.*, 1971): (1) the frequency or intensity of the problem; (2) the abnormality of the behaviour in relation to age and sex norms; (3) the number of other abnormal behaviours; (4) the duration and type of disturbance; (5) attitudes to the problem; and (6) the circumstances in which the behaviour occurs. To these may be added the need to take into account sociocultural norms and to look for significant changes over time in behaviour and development.

Other epidemiological findings draw attention to the situational nature of much behaviour in children and to major factors either in the child or in its environment that need to be taken into account in assessment and the development of a full diagnostic formulation.

A widespread epidemiological finding is that there is only moderate agreement between different informants when reporting on the *same* child (e.g. Shepherd *et al.*, 1971; Rutter *et al.*, 1976, 1970; Achenbach *et al.*, 1987; Verhulst *et al.*, 1987; Offord *et al.*, 1989; Rutter, 1989b; Offord & Fleming, 1991). There appear to be three main reasons for these discrepancies. Firstly, people vary in their access to information. This most obviously arises with children's anxiety, fears and depression when, to a considerable extent, parents have to rely on what their children happen to tell them about their inner feelings. Not surprisingly, parent–child agreement is relatively poor on these items (Rutter *et al.*, 1976; Weissman *et al.*, 1980; Kazdin *et al.*, 1983; Edelbrock *et al.*, 1986; Angold *et al.*, 1987; Weissman *et al.*, 1987). The same issue arises with children's peer relationships because so many peer interactions take place away from the family. There is no adequate substitute for an interview with the child to obtain data on both these aspects of functioning (see Chapter 4). However, parental perceptions should always be elicited in addition. Often it is informative to talk about these matters in a conjoint family interview (see Chapter 5), where there is an opportunity to discuss and consider the meaning of discrepancies between accounts. The same principles apply to the need to gain good data from the school setting and this may require a visit combining observation of the child in class or playground and an interview with the child's teachers.

Secondly, people vary in their perceptions and evaluations of behaviour (Routh, 1990). What appears pathological overactivity to one person may seem only natural exuberance to another (Stern *et al.*, 1990). This emphasizes the need to obtain accurate and detailed descriptions of what the child *actually* did on particular occasions. Generalizations and value judgements are poor misleading substitutes. Parents should always be asked for a systematic account of one or more recent examples of the behaviour in question. Thirdly, it is quite common for disorders to be partially, or even entirely, specific to certain situations (Rutter *et al.*, 1970; Offord *et al.*, 1989; Rutter, 1989b; Offord & Fleming, 1991). Children may be aggressive and disruptive at home but not at all at school; or fearful and anxious when away from the family but never with their parents. This is not just an artefact of differences between observers, because single observers often report that children behave in strikingly different ways in different situations. Moreover, the situation-specificity for some behaviours (such as activity level) has been confirmed with objective mechanical measurements (Rutter, 1983) and the indepen-

dent influence of school and family factors has been demonstrated (Rutter *et al.*, 1979; Maughan, 1988).

The finding that disorders often show relative situation-specificity has three important implications. Firstly, it means that information must always be sought from several sources (Achenbach *et al.*, 1987; Routh, 1990); in practice this means the child, the parents, and the school as a minimum. This is essential in order to determine whether some situations are more likely than others to elicit emotional and behavioural disturbance. Of course, if the evidence suggests the importance of situational effects, matters should not be left there. Rather, it is necessary to go on to delineate the particular characteristics of situations that appear protective and of those that predispose to disturbance. The need to identify such characteristics also carries implications for the structuring of the initial diagnostic assessment. Much can be learned from the observation of the child in different circumstances during the same first clinic attendance — in a conjoint interview with the family, in an interview on his or her own, and in the more structured task-setting of psychological testing (see Chapter 7). The opportunity should be taken to compare and contrast behaviour in these various settings.

Secondly, it is a general feature of psychological measurement that multimethod repeated measurements are more reliable than assessments that rely on a single measurement of any kind. If the aim is to study consistency in a person's behaviour over time, it is desirable to use measures that average responses across situations (Epstein, 1979). In general, disorders that are pervasive over situations are also more likely to be persistent over time (Rutter & Garmezy, 1983). The distinction between pervasive and situational disorders tends to carry important diagnostic and prognostic implications.

Thirdly, the presence of situation-specificity implies that disorder must be regarded in interactional terms. That is to say, the problem lies in the interaction between a child and its environment and not just within the child. This conclusion has crucial consequences for both diagnostic formulations and treatment plans. For the most part, disorders cannot be viewed simply as disease states or the result of intrapsychic conflict alone. The essence of psychiatric disorders in childhood lies also in the importance of interpersonal interactions and of the social context. Therapeutic interventions must be planned accordingly.

Of course, that does not mean that factors within the child are unimportant, for that is far from the case. Nor does it necessarily mean that disorders are best classified in interactional terms. Whereas there is good evidence that diagnoses based on phenomenology have good validity in conveying clinically useful information (see Chapter 1), such evidence is so far lacking for family or interactional systems of classification. However, epidemiological studies (Rutter, 1989b) do indicate the strong associations between child psychiatric disorder and both family relationships and interactions and also school and community influences (see Chapter 12). Furthermore, family variables have been shown to relate to the course of delinquency (Farrington, 1988; Robins, 1991) and other psychiatric conditions (Richman *et al.*, 1982; Goodyer, 1990; Quinton *et al.*, 1990; Zeitlin, 1990).

Epidemiological findings point to other major areas requiring assessment, both within the child and in the environment (Rutter, 1989b; Offord & Fleming, 1991). These include the physical health of the child, including particularly the presence and absence of chronic health problems and hospitalization (see Chapters 39 and 42), brain dysfunction (see Chapter 11), temperament, IQ, learning disorders and educational competence (see Chapters 35 and 36), social class and ethnic grouping.

Research has also drawn attention to the importance of protective factors, and it can be particularly helpful to evaluate these in planning intervention strategies. Within the child, above-average IQ and easy temperament are important (Rutter, 1985; Masten, 1989). Within the family cohesiveness (Masten, 1989), a good relationship with one parent (Jenkins & Smith, 1990) and a resilient mother who adopts problem-solving approaches (Kolvin *et al.*, 1990) protect. Outside the home, relationships with friends and other relatives and good experiences in school and elsewhere (Jenkins & Smith, 1990; Rutter *et al.*, 1990) have been found to reduce the likelihood of development of child psychiatric disorders and the risk of involvement in future unsatisfactory relationships.

DIAGNOSTIC FORMULATION

Diagnosis involves picking out the key features of the psychiatric disorder, and classification means a grouping and labelling of the disorder according to the denominators that it has in common with other similar conditions (Rutter, 1975). It is a useful thing to do, both because it narrows down the field in terms of causes, treatment and prognosis, and because it provides a shorthand language of communication with other professionals (see Chapter 1). However, by definition, it necessarily provides a crude grouping that disregards all that is unique about the child. A further process of diagnostic formulation is required to bring out the qualities that are different and distinctive about the individual child and family. The formulation puts forward hypotheses about the biological or psychological mechanisms that might be operating, about the underlying causes and precipitants of the disorder in *this* child, about the factors leading to a continuation of the disorder and about the potential strengths and ameliorating factors that could be used in formulating a treatment plan. In doing so, it is useful to distinguish factors in the child and in the environment and to discriminate between predisposing, precipitating and maintaining or perpetuating factors (Nurcombe & Gallagher, 1986). Thus, low intelligence may be a predisposing factor, specific life events may precipitate a disorder and a particular pattern of family interaction may maintain it. However, it is particularly important to make hypotheses about processes in a fashion that guides intervention. A formulation should also include statements about further investigations, data gathering from other informants or by other means that might modify hypotheses, the short- and long-term interven-

tions that are planned and prognosis. Finally, there can be benefit in establishing operationally defined treatment goals jointly with the child, parents or family (Nurcombe & Gallagher, 1986): in other words, statements about goals that indicate how it could be known that desired changes have occurred.

If this process is to take place during the initial diagnostic appraisal, it is essential that a problem-solving approach be followed in processing the referral and gathering information. It is quite inadequate merely to collect a lot of facts in the hope that some sense will come of them when they are all put together. Rather, from the very first moment of receiving a referral, the clinician must be formulating hypotheses to be tested. For example, in school refusal the mode and context of the referral may point to who is concerned about the child's nonattendance and therefore motivated to help resolve the problem. The refusal may arise amongst other things as a result of fear of school, separation anxiety, a general social withdrawal or a combination of these. If the possible mechanisms are to be differentiated, it will be necessary to gather appropriate information (Rutter, 1975). Information on what the child is like when he is not in school will help to determine whether there is general social withdrawal (such as with a depressive disorder). If he is cheerful and lively then this would make withdrawal unlikely, whereas if he is withdrawn, miserable, and lacking in interest, that would support such a hypothesis. Information on whether the school refusal varies with the school situation or school curriculum will help to determine whether the refusal is associated with anxiety about happenings at school. Similarly, information on whether the school refusal varies according to what is happening at home (i.e. is worse when the father is out of work or the mother is ill, or has an onset associated with the mother starting a job outside the home) will point to the importance or otherwise of anxieties about the home or family. The possibility of separation anxiety may be assessed by asking about separations unconnected with school (such as when the parents go out at night or when the child stays with friends or relatives). In short, the interviewing and observations need to be specifically tailored to the issues relevant to each child's problems as well as systematically covering a range of possible difficulties and situations.

Much the same points arise with respect to individual items of behaviour (Rutter, 1975). The therapist must understand the meaning and function of each behaviour, and this requires an analysis of the various factors in the child and in the environment that either increase or decrease the likelihood of the behaviour occurring (Gross, 1984). As Anna Freud (1966) pointed out, apparently similar behaviours may have quite different meanings and serve different functions; these must be taken into account when planning treatments. She gave the example of temper tantrums, which may be no more than a normal motor outlet for ill-controlled emotions in a young child, an aggressive-destructive outburst, or an anxiety attack that builds up to panic. These may be differentiated by examining the associated behaviours and by a functional analysis of the prior circumstances including the state of the child (physically, cognitively and emotionally), the precipitants and contingencies of each key behaviour (Gross, 1984). By prior circumstances is meant the more long-lasting conditions that play a part in determining behaviour, for example, the lack of communication skills that increase the likelihood of frustration tantrums in the child with a language handicap; or the mother's depression that increases the child's insecurity and that contributes to maladaptive patterns of mother−child interaction. The first example emphasizes the need to evaluate a child's cognitive state including language development. By precipitants is meant the happenings that immediately precede the problem behaviours and that seem to trigger them off (e.g. the unexpected contact with a dog that leads to panic and a tantrum in the child with a severe dog phobia). These must be understood in context. By contingencies is meant what immediately *follows* the behaviour, in circumstances where the behaviour seems to bring about a predictable response (such as the parental attention that regularly comes to the child whose tantrums have an attention-seeking component). Again, the process of diagnostic appraisal must be focused and purposeful so that sufficient information is obtained on the key problems, in order for their meaning and function to be determined.

This chapter has outlined some of the main concepts and principles that underline the process of diagnostic appraisal. It is evident that systematic and detailed factual information is required on various aspects of the child's genetic constitution, cognitive and physical state and behaviour, and on patterns of family life and relationships. In addition, the initial interviews must be designed to assess cognitions, feelings, attitudes and emotions, which have to be observed as well as reported. Finally, as the diagnostic appraisal will usually lead on to some form of treatment, the process must establish relationships with the child and family and provide a *modus operandi* for subsequent therapeutic interventions. This means that the therapist must establish trust and give confidence but must also provide feedback so that the family members are helped to look at the problem and to negotiate the roles that may be valuable to them in therapy.

INFORMATION GATHERING: SOURCES, SETTINGS AND METHODS

Adequate diagnostic appraisal requires information not just from the child and family. It is apparent that data may need to be gathered from a variety of sources and settings and by a variety of means (Achenbach *et al.*, 1987; Cox, 1989; Routh 1990), often over a period of time. These include (Angold, 1989) self-report questionnaires, interviews, observation and formal psychological testing.

To these may be added diaries, which are a way of placing someone other than the assessing professional in the position of observer (Patterson, 1982; Trickett & Kuczynski, 1986), and medical investigations. Settings include not only school and home but other places where the child has significant interactions, for example youth clubs, or where a child has contact with a separated parent. Sources of information and settings have to be considered separately and in combination. Thus, different information may be obtained by an interview in the clinic with the child alone, as opposed to with her parents, or by observing her during psychometric testing in contrast to the school playground. Variations in what is obtained can be influenced by the mental state and role of the person reporting and his or her relationship to the child (Routh, 1990). For example, depressed mothers tend to rate their children as more disturbed than direct observation indicates (Griest *et al.*, 1980). There is evidence that teachers are less sensitive than parents in picking up children's emotional distress (Wolfe *et al.*, 1987).

In considering means or methods, it is not just a question of what is done, but how it is done. How can refer both to structure and style, so that an interview may be structured or semistructured; it can be delivered by an interviewer with a warm or neutral style (see Chapters 3 and 4). Both can influence the information obtained and the collaboration established.

In deriving a diagnostic formulation the data from the various sources need to be critically evaluated, the weight attributed ranging according to such factors as the nature of the symptoms, or hypothesized diagnosis, and the age of the child (Routh, 1990).

Both psychological testing (see Chapter 7) and medical examination (see Chapter 6) also constitute key elements in diagnostic appraisal. Psychological testing may be informative in assessing the meaning of key behaviours, in evaluating specific and general delays in development (see Chapters 32 and 35), and in diagnosing specific learning disorders (see Chapter 36). Although psychometry need not constitute an element in all diagnostic assessments, consideration of possibly relevant cognitive impairments should be routine, because of their relatively strong association with psychiatric disorder in childhood and adolescence. Whenever clinical evaluation suggests their possible presence, there should be discussion with a clinical or educational psychologist colleague on how to proceed, and ordinarily systematic testing will be required (see Chapter 7).

It should also be routine to consider the possible presence of neurodevelopmental impairment or somatic disease (see Chapter 6), as either may be associated with psychiatric disorder (see Chapters 11 and 39). Obviously, their likely relevance varies according to the type of psychiatric problem but the possibility that they may have played a role should be considered in all cases. The implications for physical examinations and for special investigations are discussed by Bailey (see Chapter 6).

The contribution of observation to diagnostic appraisal

Observation of parents and children is fundamental to diagnostic appraisal. First, it contributes to formal diagnosis: indeed it is crucial in the diagnosis of certain specific disorders, such as autism, hyperkinetic syndrome and schizophrenia, because professional skills are needed to elicit or appraise certain phenomenology. Second, it provides data relevant to the understanding of disorders, for instance suggesting contingent factors relevant to their onset and maintenance that may not have been obvious to those directly involved. In this respect, it may be more productive than interviewing that is oriented to formal diagnosis (Reid *et al.*, 1988). Third, it is helpful in the evaluation of intervention where independent assessment is needed. Observation is of particular importance for obtaining data not readily reported, such as the behaviour of young children, who may not give verbal accounts themselves, and for a description of more or less complex sequences of behaviour that cannot be reported accurately. Qualitative aspects of parent–child interaction are also less readily obtained by parental report (Cox, 1975). Observations have greater objectivity and by virtue of being direct may give a more valid indication of change than the reports of involved observers.

The principles of observation for both research and clinical purposes have been outlined by Reid *et al.* (1988). In considering approaches to observation it is helpful to identify the observer, the setting, who is being observed, the measures employed, the method of data-gathering and the method of recording. All can influence the information obtained, whether the aim is clinical assessment or research. The observer may be an involved adult or child, for example a parent or teacher, or an independent observer such as a professional. Observation may take place in standardized or naturalistic settings. Standardized settings include laboratories and analogue settings such as rooms furnished as a family's living room. Naturalistic settings include the home or classroom. Rooms in clinics fall somewhere between the two, so that there may be some attempt at standardization of equipment and personnel but not to the rigorous level applied in a laboratory setting. Those observed almost invariably include the child alone or with a variety of children or adults with whom they customarily interact. These range from peers and siblings or the whole family to parents and teachers. Clinically it is important to make selections according to the nature of the problems assessed. For example, it is necessary to observe contact between a separated parent and the child when there is interpersonal conflict over the contact.

The approach to measurement may be more or less structured. Thus, in clinical practice, observation in the course of interviewing is often relatively unstructured, while the semi-structured interviews, for example, the K-SADS, ISC and CAPA (Kiddie-Schedule for Affective Disorders and Schizophrenia, Interview Schedule for Children, and Child and Adolescent Psychiatric Assessment), all include observational items (see Chapters 3 and 4). Fully structured approaches may be *ad hoc* or employ a standardized instrument. *Ad hoc* but structured approaches are described in a number of texts, for example, Barton and Ascione (1984). Such structured approaches are usually based on a functional behavioural analysis. Standardized instruments have the value that findings can be generalized, but usually they require considerable training and may not be designed to focus on the particular

aspects of behaviour or interaction under consideration.

Observational data may be obtained by direct observation with paper and pencil, or by scoring audio or video tapes. The latter have the advantage that more time can be taken to score them, but the disadvantage of providing a limited data set (for example, the camera may be pointing in the wrong direction) and there is some loss of definition, particularly with regard to emotional data. Various methods of recording can be employed; these range from continuous narrative recording which may nevertheless be structured to focus on particular aspects of behaviour (Barton & Ascione, 1984); recording of the frequency of particular items of behaviour throughout a given period of time; interval sampling, recording the occurrence or nonoccurrence of behaviour in equal time intervals, or event sampling where detailed recording is triggered by selected events. The items of behavioural interaction that it is intended to measure can also vary considerably. For example, there can be ratings of the quality of behaviour of individuals or dyads or families. Counts of behaviours are usually related to a particular duration of time, and the proportion of given behavioural events per unit time or as a proportion of all events can be calculated.

Standardized observational systems have usually been developed in research contexts but may be useful clinically. For example, there is a direct observation method linked to the Child Behavior Checklist (CBCL; Achenbach & Edelbrock, 1983) — the Direct Observation Form (Reed & Edelbrock, 1983). This has been shown to relate to the parent and teacher assessment of the child on the CBCL and Teacher Report Form (Achenbach & Edelbrock, 1986), but in a rather nonspecific fashion (McConaughy *et al.*, 1988). Observations relevant to specific symptoms incorporated in various semi-structured interviews (K-SADS, ISC, CAPA) contribute to the establishment of specific diagnoses such as schizophrenia. Other standardized approaches are available for certain specific disorders such as, for example, autism (see Chapter 33), hyperkinetic syndrome (see Chapter 17), childhood depression (see Chapter 19) and anxiety (see Chapter 20). All these techniques have clinical application in particular circumstances.

There are also standardized observational systems employed to assess family or parent–child interaction (see Chapter 5). Rating systems include the Beavers Interaction Scale I (BIS-I; Beavers & Voeller, 1983; Green *et al.*, 1985), the Oregon Observer Impressions of Problem Solving (Forgatch *et al.*, 1984), the Parent–Child Interaction Evaluation Scale (Santrock & Warshak, 1979), Tool-Use Task (Pianta *et al.*, 1989) and the Ward Play Situation (Sroufe *et al.*, 1985). All these approaches require extensive observer training and involve parents and children interacting over a task in a clinic or laboratory setting. Items rated tend to be global, such as warmth, hostility, empathy, or discipline, and therefore provide little information about process.

Reid *et al.* (1988) reviewed a number of more detailed observational systems employed in research, including the Dyadic Parent–Child Interaction Coding System (Robinson &

Eyberg, 1981) and the Oregon Family Interaction System (Reid, 1978). These two approaches have been particularly concerned with oppositional, conduct and aggressive behaviour in children and both have been found to be useful in assessing the effectiveness of intervention. Again the time taken to train and the problem of observer drift (Reid *et al.*, 1988) tend to make these approaches unsatisfactory for translation into most clinical settings. However the Home Observation for Measurement of the Environment (HOME; Elardo & Bradley, 1981), which combines observation in the home with a semistructured interview with the mother, probably requires less training than many other observational approaches and has been found to have significant concurrent and predictive validity, for example predicting children's IQ scores and success in school (Bradley *et al.*, 1988, 1989).

In summary, there is now a wide range of both rating scales and observational systems for assessing parent—child and family interaction, but there are few in widespread clinical usage. The HOME and the Oregon Family Interaction Coding System (FICS) are probably the most frequently used. However, tailor-made methods of observational assessment are often used clinically. The targeted behaviours or interactions require careful selection, particularly if parents are being used as the observers, as is most economically and very often appropriately the case (Reid *et al.*, 1988). Diaries or score sheets need to be constructed for the specific needs in individual cases. Simplicity and good operational definitions are required. Antecedent events and actions, and consequences, including parental action, are commonly recorded, together with other contingencies or descriptions of behaviour that may seem particularly relevant. Observations are also helpful in evaluating progress where intervention is aimed to improve the quality of parent—child relationships (Cox *et al.*, 1990, 1991). Measures that involve an interactional component have generally been found to be more discriminating than those that count the behaviour of one party or the other. It is therefore usually helpful to pick categories that are intrinsically interactional such as 'mother ignores child approach' or 'mother criticizes distressed child'. It is important to pick some categories thought to reflect positive aspects of parent—child interaction that need to be enhanced, as for example parents' facilitations of children's accomplishment of a task (Cox *et al.*, 1992).

Other data

Comprehensive diagnostic appraisal requires direct assessment of the child's developmental, physical and mental status. The evaluation of the child's mental state is essential; physical examination, psychometry and special medical investigations will be required when indicated. These are discussed elsewhere (see Chapters 6 and 7).

Because children often behave differently in different situations (see above), it will nearly always be necessary to obtain an account of the child's behaviour, attainments, attitudes and relationships at school. In the first instance, this may be gathered by asking the school for a report. Usually the information will be more focused and relevant if the school knows the particular questions and issues on which data are required. In addition to free comment by teachers, it is sometimes useful to have more standardized (but necessarily less individualized) information in the form of a behavioural questionnaire. The Rutter B[2] or Teacher scale (Rutter, 1967, 1976; Rutter *et al.*, 1970, 1975, 1981) has been shown to have satisfactory reliability and validity as a screening instrument for use with the teachers of school-age children. Behar and Stringfield (1974) have produced an adaptation of the scale for use with kindergarten children (see also Behar, 1971). In the same age group the Behaviour Screening Questionnaire is widely used and has interview and checklist versions for teachers (Richman *et al.*, 1982). Several teacher questionnaires with satisfactory reliability and validity have been developed in the US; of these, probably the most useful are the Quay and Peterson Behaviour Problem Checklist (Quay, 1977), the Conners Teacher Rating Scale (Conners, 1969; Goyette *et al.*, 1978) and the Teacher Report Form (Achenbach & Edelbrock, 1986). Each of these, like the Rutter and Richman scales, has parallel versions for completion by parents. Teacher and parent questionnaires have the advantage that they obtain systematic information on a specified list of behaviours and that the total score provides a handy, rough-and-ready, measure of the overall level of disturbance. However, like other screening instruments, they provide only a rather crude differentiation regarding the type of disorder and are not suitable tools to use for individual diagnosis.

School information is always valuable, but is essential if the child shows problems at school. Fuller information is best obtained through personal contact (by telephone or interview) with the teachers who know the child best, and the head or senior teacher responsible for the staff directly involved with the child. The object is not just to gather data on the child's behaviour and educational attainment, but to understand the school's point of view and perception of the situation, to discover teachers' attitudes and responses to the child, to appreciate the nature of the school environment, to assess the qualities of the child's interactions with staff and pupils and to establish the basis for the school's collaboration with therapy if this seems appropriate. Such information and cooperation is vital if there is concern about school attendance, educational difficulties or problems in relationships between the child and staff or peers. Detailed discussion is required about for example the school's response to attendance and bullying, and arrangements for special educational support. The principles and issues are closely similar to those already discussed in relation to parents and families and, as with the home, observations are sometimes needed in addition to interviews.

Depending on circumstances, other sources of data may also need to be tapped. The family doctor may have useful information on the process of referral, on family circumstances, on past treatment and on current medication that has not been included in the referral letter. Similarly, social services may already have had contact with the family. The same applies to health visitors, education welfare workers, and a variety of voluntary agencies. With parental permission, contacts can be used to gain these professionals' perception of the problem and clarify any collaboration in treatment, as well as to obtain information on the referral problem.

Choice and ordering of modes of assessment

Every type of assessment in every setting could be advocated. Economy and the need to sustain cooperation make selection necessary. In making the selection it is helpful to bear in mind (Cox, 1983) the following:

1 Certain assessments are crucial for certain problems, for instance an individual interview with a family member who may be psychotic or depressed or who has been thought to be abused.

2 Assessment teams function better if they have systematic methods. These give experience that enables the behaviour to be compared and its significance to be assessed, and it also gives confidence to team members. However, there are dangers if the assessment methods are too narrowly focused. For example, if a clinic specializes in the assessment and treatment of particular child psychiatric conditions, and uses assessment methods geared for those particular conditions, then there is a danger that comorbidity and other factors relevant to aetiology may be missed.

3 If a particular therapy is envisaged, assessment in that mode is usually indicated.

4 If the trust of family members is to be won, information must not be sought without their permission, the limits of confidentiality need to be established and a child or adolescent may best be seen before or with his or her parents.

There is evidence that therapeutic contact is better sustained where clinics employ a flexible approach, in which a variety or combination of treatment methods is employed after initial assessment. Continued attendance is more likely also if individual contacts follow a family assessment than if a family assessment follows individual interviews with parents and child (Cox, 1988). This suggests that when a family assessment and/or family therapy is intended, first contact should be with the whole family. Individual assessment interviews with parents and child, psychological testing and neurological screening or other medical investigations can follow on another occasion if appropriate and more readily acceptable to the family.

REFERENCES

Achenbach T.M. (1990) Conceptualization of developmental psychopathology. In: Lewis M. & Miller S.M. (eds) *Handbook of Developmental Psychopathology*, pp. 3–14. Plenum, New York.

Achenbach T.M. & Edelbrock C.S. (1983) *Manual for the Child Behavior Checklist and Revised Child Behavior Profile*. University of Vermont, Department of Psychiatry, Burlington, VT.

Achenbach T.M. & Edelbrock C.S. (1986) *Manual for the Child Behavior Profile*. University of Vermont, Department of Psychiatry, Burlington, VT.

Achenbach T.M., McConaughy S.H. & Howell C.T. (1987) Child-adolescent behavioral and emotional problems. Implications of cross informant correlations for situation specificity. *Psychological Bulletin*, **101**, 213–232.

Angold A. (1989) Structured assessments of psychopathology in children and adolescents. In: Thompson C. (ed) *The Instruments of Psychiatric Research*, pp. 271–304. Wiley, Chichester.

Angold A., Weissman M.M., John K., Merikangas K.R., Prusoff B.A., Wickramaratne I., Gammon G.P. & Warner V. (1987) Parent and child reports of depressive symptoms in children at low and high risk of depression. *Journal of Child Psychology and Psychiatry*, **28**, 901–909.

Barton E.J. & Ascione F.R. (1984) Direct observation. In: Ollendick T.H. & Hersen M. (eds) *Child Behavioral Assessment: Principles and Procedures*, pp. 166–194. Pergamon, New York.

Beavers W. & Voeller M. (1983) Family models: comparing and contrasting the Olson circumplex model with the Beavers systems model. *Family Process*, **22**, 85–98.

Behar L.B. (1971) The pre-school behavior questionnaire. *Journal of Abnormal Child Psychology*, **5**, 265–275.

Behar L. & Stringfield S. (1974) A behavior rating scale for the pre-school child. *Developmental Psychology*, **10**, 601–610.

Bradley R., Caldwell B. & Rock S. (1988) Home environment and school performance: a ten year follow-up. *Child Development*, **59**, 852–867.

Bradley R., Caldwell B., Rock S., Bonnard K.E., Gray C., Hammond M.A., Mitchell S., Siegel L., Ramey C.T., Gottfried A.W. & Johnson D.L. (1989) Home environment and cognitive development in the first 3 years of life: a collaborative study involving six sites and three ethnic groups in North America. *Developmental Psychology*, **25**, 217–235.

Brandenburg N.A., Friedman R.M., Silver S.F. (1990) The epidemiology of childhood psychiatric disorders: prevalence findings from recent studies. *Journal of the American Academy of Child and Adolescent Psychiatry*, **29**, 76–83.

Bretherton I. & Waters E. (eds) (1985) Growing Points of Attachment Theory and Research. *Monographs of the Society for Research in Child Development*, serial no. 209, **50**, nos. 1–2.

Cantwell D.P. (1988) DSM-III studies. In: Rutter M., Tuma A.H. & Lann I.S. (eds) *Assessment and Diagnosis in Child Psychopathology*, pp. 3–36. Fulton, London.

Conners C.K. (1969) A teacher-rating scale for use in drug studies with children. *American Journal of Psychiatry*, **124**, 884–888.

Cooper P.J. & Goodyer I. (in press) A community study of depression in adolescent girls: I: Estimates of symptom and symptom-prevalence. *British Journal of Psychiatry*.

Costello E.J. (1989) Developments in child psychiatric epidemiology. *Journal of the American Academy of Child and Adolescent Psychiatry*, **28**, 836–841.

Cottrell D., Hill P., Walk D., Dearnaly J. & Ierotheou A. (1988) Factors influencing non-attendance at child psychiatry out-patient appointments. *British Journal of Psychiatry*, **152**, 201–204.

Cox A. (1975) The assessment of parental behaviour. *Journal of Child Psychology and Psychiatry*, **16**, 255–259.

Cox A. (1983) Clinical assessment of the emotionally disturbed child and his family. In: Russell G.F.M. & Hersov L. (eds) *Handbook of Psychiatry, 4: The Neuroses and Personality Disorders*, pp. 68–71. Cambridge University Press, Cambridge.

Cox A. (1988) The assessment of child psychiatric disturbance. Maudsley Bequest lecture presented to Autumn Quarterly Meeting of the Royal College of Psychiatrists.

Cox A. (1989) Classification in child psychiatry: a critique of approaches based on parental questionnaires. In: Schmidt M.H. & Remschmidt H. (eds) *Needs and Prospects of Child and Adolescent*

Psychiatry, pp. 93—97. Hogrefe & Huber, Toronto.

Cox A.D., Pound A., Mills M., Puckering C. & Owen A.L. (1990) *Evaluation of a Home Visiting and Befriending Scheme for Young Mothers: Newpin.* Final Report to Dept of Health 1990.

Cox A.D., Pound A., Mills M., Puckering C. & Owen A.L. (1991) Evaluation of a home visiting and befriending scheme for young mothers: Newpin. *Journal of the Royal Society of Medicine*, **84**, 217—220.

Cox A., Pound A. & Puckering C. (1992) Newpin: a befriending scheme and therapeutic network for carers of young children. In: Gibbons J. (ed) *The Children Act 1989 and Family Support: Principles into Practice*, pp. 37—47. Her Majesty's Stationery Office, London.

Dunn J. & McGuire S. (1992) Sibling and peer relationships in childhood. *Journal of Child Psychology and Psychiatry*, **33**, 67—105.

Edelbrock C., Costello S.A., Dulcan M.K., Conover M.C. & Kalas R. (1986) Parent—child agreement on child psychiatric symptoms assessed via structured interview. *Journal of Child Psychology and Psychiatry*, **27**, 181—190.

Elardo R. & Bradley R. (1981) The home observation for measurement of the environment (HOME) scale: a review of research. *Developmental Review*, **1**, 113—145.

Epstein S. (1979) The stability of behaviour: I. On predicting most of the people most of the time. *Journal of Personality and Social Psychology*, **37**, 1097—1126.

Farrington D.P. (1988) Studying changes within individuals: the causes of offending. In: Rutter M. (ed) *Studies of Psychosocial Risk: The Power of Longitudinal Data*, pp. 158—183. Cambridge University Press, Cambridge.

Forgatch M., Fetrow R. & Lathrop M. (1984) SPI-F1 Coder Impressions. Unpublished assessment instrument, Oregon Social Learning Centre.

Freud A. (1966) *Normality and Pathology in Childhood*. Hogarth Press, London.

Garralda M.E. & Bailey D. (1986) Children with psychiatric disorders in primary care. *Journal of Child Psychology and Psychiatry*, **27**, 611—624.

Glidewell J.C., Mensh I.N. & Gildea M.C.L. (1957) Behaviour symptoms in children and degree of sickness. *American Journal of Psychiatry*, **114**, 47—53.

Goodyer I. (1990) Family relationships, life events and childhood psychopathology. *Journal of Child Psychology and Psychiatry*, **31**, 161—192.

Goodyer I. & Cooper P.J. (1991) A community study of depression in adolescent girls: the characteristics of identified disorder. Paper given at European Society for Child & Adolescent Psychiatry Congress, London, September 1991.

Goyette A.U., Conners C.K. & Ulrich R.F. (1978) Normative data on revised Conners' parent and teacher rating scales. *Journal of Abnormal Child Psychology*, **6**, 221—236.

Graham P. (1979) Epidemiological studies. In: Quay H.C. & Werry J. (eds) *Psychopathological Disorders of Childhood*, 2nd edn, pp. 185—209. Wiley, New York.

Graham P. & Rutter M. (1968) The reliability and validity of the psychiatric assessment of the child. II: Interview with the parent. *British Journal of Psychiatry*, **114**, 581—592.

Green R.G., Kolevzon M.S. & Vosler N.R. (1985) The Beavers—Timberlawn model of family competence and the circumplex model of family adaptability and cohesion: separate, but equal? *Family Process*, **24**, 385—408.

Griest D.L., Forehand R., Wells K.C. & McMahon R.J. (1980) An examination of differences between non-clinic and behaviour-problem clinic-referred children and their mothers. *Journal of Abnormal Psychology*, **89**, 497—500.

Gross A.M. (1984) Behavioral interviewing. In: Ollendick H. & Hersen M. (eds) *Child Behavioural Assessment: Principles and Procedures*, pp. 61—79. Pergamon, New York.

Hartup W.W. (1983) Peer relations. In: Hetherington E.M. (ed) *Socialization, Personality and Social Development: Vol. 4, Mussen's Handbook of Child Psychology*, 4th edn, pp. 103—196. Wiley, New York.

Hartup W.W. (1989) Social relationships and their developmental significance. In: Luszcz M.A. & Nettelbeck T. (eds) *Psychological Development: Perspectives across the Life-Span*, pp. 3—14. Elsevier, Amsterdam.

Hinde R. (1988) Continuities and discontinuities: conceptual issues and methodological considerations. In: Rutter M. (ed) *Studies of Psychosocial Risk: The Power of Longitudinal Data*, pp. 367—383. Cambridge University Press, Cambridge.

Jenkins J.M. & Smith M.A. (1990) Factors protecting children living in disharmonious homes: maternal reports. *Journal of the American Academy of Child and Adolescent Psychiatry*, **29**, 60—69.

Kanner L. (1957) *Child Psychiatry*, 3rd edn. Charles C. Thomas, Springfield, Ill.

Kashani J.H. & Sherman D.D. (1988) Childhood depression: epidemiology, etiological models and treatment implications. *Integrative Psychiatry*, **6**, 1—8.

Kazdin A.E., French N.H., Unis A.S. & Esvelot-Dawson K. (1983) Assessment of depression: correspondence of child and parent ratings. *Journal of the American Academy of Child Psychiatry*, **22**, 157—164.

Kolvin I., Charles G., Nicholson R., Fleeting M. & Fundudis T. (1990) Factors in prevention: inner-city deprivation. In: Goldberg D. & Tantam D. (eds) *The Public Health Impact of Mental Disorder*, pp. 115—123. Hogrefe & Huber, Toronto.

Kolvin I., Barrett M.L., Bhate S.R., Berney T.P., Famuyiwa O.O., Fundudis T. & Tyrer S. (1991) The Newcastle child depression project: diagnosis and classification of depression. *British Journal of Psychiatry;* **159** (suppl. 11), 9—21.

Lamb M.E., Nash A., Teti D.M. & Bornstein M.H. (1991) Infancy. In: Lewis M. (ed) *Child and Adolescent Psychiatry: A Comprehensive Textbook*, pp. 222—256. Williams & Wilkins, Baltimore.

Lapouse R. & Monk M. (1958) An epidemiological study of behaviour characteristics in children. *American Journal of Public Health*, **48**, 1134—1144.

Lapouse R. & Monk M. (1959) Fears and worries in a representative sample of children. *American Journal of Orthopsychiatry*, **29**, 803—818.

McConaughy S.H., Achenbach T.M. & Gent C.L. (1988) Multiaxial emperically based assessment: parent, teacher, observational, cognitive and personality correlates of child behaviour profile types for 6- to 11-year-old boys. *Journal of Abnormal Child Psychology*, **16**, 485—509.

Masten A.S. (1989) Resilience in development: implications of the study of successful adaptation for developmental psychopathology. In: Cicchetti D. (ed) *The Emergence of a Discipline: Rochester Symposium on Developmental Psychopathology*, vol. I, pp. 261—294. Erlbaum, Hillsdale, Nj.

Maughan B. (1988) School experiences as risk/protective factors. In: Rutter M. (ed) *Studies of Psychosocial Risk: The Power of Longitudinal Data*, pp. 200—220. Cambridge University Press, Cambridge.

Nurcombe B. & Gallagher R.M. (1986) *The Clinical Process in Psychiatry*. Cambridge University Press, Cambridge.

Offord D.R. & Fleming J.E. (1991) Epidemiology. In: Lewis M. (ed) *Child and Adolescent Psychiatry: A Comprehensive Textbook*, pp. 1156—1168. Williams & Wilkins, Baltimore.

Offord D.R., Boyle M.H., Szatmari P., Rae-Grant N.I., Links P.S., Cadman D.T., Byles J.A., Crawford J.W., Blum H.M., Byrne C., Thomas H. & Woodward C.A. (1987) Ontario child health study, II. Six month prevalence of disorder and rates of service utilization.

Archives of General Psychiatry, **44**, 832—836.

Offord D.R., Boyle M.H. & Racine I. (1989) Ontario child health study: correlates of disorder. *Journal of the American Academy of Child and Adolescent Psychiatry*, **28**, 856—860.

Oke S. & Mayer R. (1991) Referrals to child psychiatry — a survey of staff attitudes. *Archives of Disease in Childhood*, **66**, 862—865.

Patterson G.R. (1982) *Coercive Family Process*. Castalia, Eugene, Or.

Patterson C.J., Cohn D.A. & Kao B.T. (1989) Maternal warmth as a protective factor against risks associated with peer rejection among children. *Development and Psychopathology*, **1**, 21—38.

Pianta R., Sroufe L. & Egeland B. (1989) Continuity and discontinuity in maternal sensitivity at 6, 24, and 42 months in a high-risk sample. *Child Development*, **60**, 437—481.

Quay H.C. (1977) Measuring dimensions of deviant behaviour: the behaviour problem checklist. *Journal of Abnormal Child Psychology*, **5**, 277—289.

Quinton D., Rutter M. & Gulliver I. (1990) Continuities in psychiatric disorders from childhood to adulthood in the children of psychiatric patients. In: Robins L. & Rutter M. (eds) *Straight and Devious Pathways from Childhood to Adulthood*, pp. 259—278. Cambridge University Press, Cambridge.

Reed M.L. & Edelbrock L.S. (1983) Reliability and validity of the direct observation form of the child behavior checklist. *Journal of Abnormal Child Psychology*, **II**, 521—530.

Reid J.B. (ed) (1978) *A Social Learning Approach to Family Intervention, Vol. II: Observation in Work Settings*. Castalia, Eugene, Or.

Reid J.B., Baldwin D.V., Patterson G.R. & Dishion T.S. (1988) Observations in the assessment of childhood disorders. In: Rutter M., Tuma A.H. & Lann I.S. (eds) *Assessment and Diagnosis in Child Psychopathology*, pp. 156—195. Fulton, London.

Richman M., Stevenson J. & Graham P. (1982) *Pre-school to School: A Behavioural Study*. Academic Press, London.

Robins L. (1991) Conduct disorder. *Journal of Child Psychology and Psychiatry*, **32**, 193—212.

Robins L. & Rutter M. (eds) (1990) *Straight and Devious Pathways from Childhood to Adulthood*. Cambridge University Press, Cambridge.

Robinson E.A. & Eyberg S.M. (1981) The dyadic parent—child coding system: standardization and validation. *Journal of Consulting and Clinical Psychology*, **49**, 245—250.

Routh D.K. (1990) Taxonomy in developmental psychopathology: consider the source. In: Lewis M. & Miller S.M. (eds) *Handbook of Developmental Psychopathology*, pp. 53—62. Plenum, New York.

Rutter M. (1967) A children's behaviour questionnaire for completion by teachers: preliminary findings. *Journal of Child Psychology and Psychiatry*, **8**, 1—11.

Rutter M. (1975) *Helping Troubled Children*. Penguin, Harmondsworth.

Rutter M. (1976) Prospective studies to investigate behaviour change. In: Strauss J.S., Babigian H.M. & Roff M. (eds) *Methods of Longitudinal Research in Psychopathology*, pp. 223—248. Plenum, New York.

Rutter M. (1980a) Attachment and development of social relationships. In: Rutter M. (ed) *Scientific Foundations of Developmental Psychiatry*, pp. 267—279. Heinemann Medical, London.

Rutter M. (1980b) Psychosexual development. In: Rutter M. (ed) *Scientific Foundations of Developmental Psychiatry*, pp. 322—339. Heinemann Medical, London.

Rutter M. (1981) Stress, coping and development: some issues and some questions. *Journal of Child Psychology and Psychiatry*, **22**, 323—356.

Rutter M. (1983) Behavioural studies: questions and findings on the concept of a distinctive syndrome. In: Rutter M. (ed) *Developmental Neuropsychiatry*, pp. 259—279. Guilford Press, New York.

Rutter M. (1985) Resilience in the face of adversity: protective factors and resilience to psychiatric disorder. *British Journal of Psychiatry*, **147**, 598—611.

Rutter M. (1986) The developmental psychopathology of depression: issues and perspectives. In: Rutter M., Izard C.E. & Reed P.B. (eds) *Depression in Young People: Developmental and Clinical Perspectives*, pp. 3—30. Guilford, New York.

Rutter M. (1987) Continuities and discontinuities from infancy. In: Osofsky J. (ed) *Handbook of Infant Development*, 2nd edn, pp. 1256—1296. Wiley, New York.

Rutter M. (1989a) Pathways from childhood to adult life. *Journal of Child Psychology and Psychiatry*, **30**, 23—51.

Rutter M. (1989b) Isle of Wight revisited: twenty-five years of child psychiatric epidemiology. *Journal of the American Academy of Child and Adolescent Psychiatry*, **28**, 633—653.

Rutter M. & Garmezy N. (1983) Developmental psychopathology. In: Hetherington E.M. (ed) *Socialisation, Personality and Social Development: Vol. 4. Mussen's Handbook of Child Psychology*, 4th edn, pp. 775—911. Wiley, New York.

Rutter M., Cox A., Tuplin C., Berger M. & Yule W. (1975) Attainment and adjustment in two geographical areas. I. The prevalence of psychiatric disorder. *British Journal of Psychiatry*, **126**, 493—509.

Rutter M., Graham P., Chadwick D. & Yule W. (1976) Adolescent turmoil: fact or fiction? *Journal of Child Psychology and Psychiatry*, **17**, 35—56.

Rutter M., Maughan B., Mortimore P., Ouston J. & Smith A. (1979) *Fifteen Thousand Hours: Secondary Schools and their Effects on Children*. Open Books, London.

Rutter M., Tizard J. & Whitmore K. (eds) (1970) *Education, Health and Behaviour*, Longmans, London. (Reprinted, 1981, Krieger, Melbourne, Fl.).

Rutter M., Quinton D. & Hill J. (1990) Adult outcome of institution-reared children: males and females compared. In: Robins L. & Rutter M. (eds) *Straight and Devious Pathways from Childhood to Adulthood*, pp. 135—157. Cambridge University Press, Cambridge.

Santrock J. & Warshak R. (1979) Father custody and social development in boys and girls. *Journal of Social Issues*, **35**, 112—125.

Shepherd M., Oppenheim B., & Mitchell, S. (1971) *Childhood Behaviour and Mental Health*. University of London Press, London.

Silbereisen R.K. & Walper S. (1988) A person—process—context approach. In: Rutter M. (ed) *Studies in Psychosocial Risk: The Power of Longitudinal Data*, pp. 96—113. Cambridge University Press, Cambridge.

Sroufe L.A., Jacobvitz J., Mangelsdorf S., De Angelo E. & Ward M.J. (1985) Generational boundary dissolution between mothers and their pre-school children: a relationship systems approach. *Child Development*, **56**, 317—325.

Stern G., Cotterell D. & Holmes S. (1990) Patterns of attendance of child psychiatry out-patients with special reference to Asian families. *British Journal of Psychiatry*, **156**, 384—387.

Trickett P. & Kuczynski L. (1986) Children's misbehaviours and parental discipline strategies in abusive and non-abusive families. *Developmental Psychology*, **22**, 115—123.

Tuddenham R.D., Brooks J. & Milkovich L. (1974) Mothers' reports of behaviour of ten year olds: relationships with sex, ethnicity and mother's education. *Developmental Psychology*, **10**, 959—995.

Verhulst F.C., Berden G.F.G., Sanders-Woudstra J.A.R. (1985) Mental health in Dutch children. II. *Acta Psychiatrica Scandinavica*, **72**, 1—44.

Verhulst F.C., Althaus M. & Berden G.E.M.G. (1987) The child assessment schedule: parent—child agreement and validity measures. *Journal of Child Psychology and Psychiatry*, **28**, 455—466.

Vikan A. (1985) Psychiatric epidemiology in a sample of 1510 ten-year old children. I. *Journal of Child Psychology and Psychiatry*, **76**, 55—75.

Weissman M.M., Orvaschel H. & Padian N. (1980) Children's symptoms and social functioning self-report scales: comparison of mothers' and children's reports. *Journal of Nervous and Mental Disease*, **168**, 736—740.

Weissman M.M., Wickramaratine P., Warner V., John K., Prusoff B.A., Merikangas K.R. & Gammon G.D. (1987) Assessing psychiatric disorders in children: discrepancies between mothers' and children's reports. *Archives of General Psychiatry*, **44**, 747—753.

Wolfe V.V., Finch A.J., Saylor C.F., Blount R.L., Pallmeyer T.P. & Carek D.J. (1987) Negative affectivity in children: a multi-trait—multi-method investigation. *Journal of Consulting and Clinical Psychology*, **55**, 245—250.

Yule W. (1980) The epidemiology of child psychopathology. In: Lahey B.B. & Kazdin A.E. (eds) *Advances in Clinical Child Psychology*, vol. 4, pp. 1—51. Plenum, New York.

Zeitlin H. (1990) Current interests in child—adult psychopathological continuities. *Journal of Child Psychology and Psychiatry*, **31**, 671—679.

Chapter 3
Interviews with Parents

Antony D. Cox

There is a very extensive research literature on the skills involved in interviewing (see Richardson *et al.*, 1965; Cannell & Kahn, 1968, for good reviews). Although most of the research has been concerned with interviews in settings and with purposes very different from those in clinical psychiatry, many of the findings are relevant. Interviewing, both diagnostic and therapeutic, is the chief tool-in-trade of the psychiatrist and above all it is the skill that every psychiatrist must possess (Shea & Mezzich, 1988). There are serious problems to be overcome if interviews are to provide accurate unbiased information (Yarrow, 1963; Yarrow *et al.*, 1968; Young *et al.*, 1987), but several studies have shown that skilled interviewing with parents can give rise to reliable and valid measures of child psychiatric disorder (Graham & Rutter, 1968; Rutter *et al.*, 1975), of the marriage (Quinton *et al.*, 1976) and of many aspects of family life and relationships (Brown & Rutter, 1966; Rutter & Brown, 1966). The relevant skills and techniques are most conveniently described under the different purposes of the interview, but before proceeding to examine interviewing styles in clinical interviews in more detail, it is important to emphasize the collaborative nature of the interview process (Nurcombe & Gallagher, 1986). In a child mental health setting the professional seeks a range of information about presenting problems and underlying issues. He or she aims to engage parents in assessment and treatment if appropriate. Parents may seek a diagnosis or specific advice, and may not be sophisticated about engagement in a therapeutic process. There is evidence that adult patients want doctors to listen, to be competent, caring and thorough (Nurcombe & Gallagher, 1986). Parents in a child mental health setting often feel guilty or responsible for their child's developmental, emotional or behavioural difficulties. The interviewer needs to be sensitive to these issues. Information is valueless if there is no collaboration in treatment. Parents are vital to any therapeutic endeavour with children. The interview process can enable parents to see experiences in a new light: the interviewer should be aware of the value of shared understanding between professional and parent.

These considerations indicate that it is usually appropriate for the interviewer to begin by encouraging parents to express their concerns and why they have come to the clinic when they have. It is useful to explore what they wish to get from the consultation. However the interviewer will usually need to move to more detailed and systematic questioning if there is to be an appropriately broad-based understanding of the problems (Cox & Rutter, 1985).

Specific issues concerning interviewing approaches will be considered in more detail, but the essence of the process is a dialogue in which the parents explore their concerns and perspectives using frameworks provided by the interviewer. A central issue concerns the extent to which the professional imposes structure on the interchange. Clinicians vary in their preferred style, but there is evidence that approaches may usefully be varied according to the character of the parents, the nature of the problem addressed and the stage of the interview. Certain techniques are helpful in eliciting parents' extended accounts of the main presenting problems — other approaches are required to obtain additional broad-ranging or detailed material and to elicit feelings.

INFORMATION GATHERING: GENERAL CONSIDERATIONS

The general considerations underlying diagnostic appraisal (see Chapter 2) indicate that the interviewer requires a framework of potentially relevant data when exploring the presented problems, whether they concern the child's symptomatology or the family relationships and circumstances. The range of types of data that contribute to a diagnostic appraisal includes the development of the index child and his or her mental and physical status; the family structure and function; home, school and out-of-school circumstances, activities and influences, and life events and chronic difficulties experienced by the index child or family.

The data within this framework need to be explored according to certain general principles. Firstly, as in all diagnostic assessment, enquiry should proceed within a hypotheses-testing framework (see Chapter 2). The interviewer continually develops and tests hypotheses during the interview concerning the nature of the problems and the processes relevant to their aetiology. Secondly, and at the same time, the quality of data needs to be evaluated. For example, the general accuracy of a particular informant's account or the likely validity of particular data requires assessment. Retrospective and third-hand information can be expected to be less accurate. Thirdly, a developmental perspective should be adopted with a focus on course, transitions, repetitions, continuities and discontinuities (Rutter, 1989). Development should be considered in all its aspects in relation to the individual family members, particularly the index child. But the family should also be viewed as a whole in terms of life-stage, the demands on the child and parents and the resources that they have to meet them. Timing and the relationship between events, actions and mental states need to be explored. Fourthly, enquiry should be broad-based, for example covering a full range of potential symptomatology, not just those spontaneously presented; covering activities in school and out of school as well as at home and covering social development as well as physical development. Fifthly, the interviewer needs to evaluate the quality of relationships surrounding the index child and family. To do so it is valuable not only to observe interaction and learn how various individuals perceive each other but also to gain information about the nature, frequency and quality of shared experiences. Sixthly, events, behaviours and states of mind must be explored in detail in order to understand the individual experiences and how they have come about. This involves comprehending the context of events both historically and concurrently, and the manner in which individuals respond. A problem-solving perspective is useful (Lesser, 1985; Gask *et al.*, 1991). If a family member is presented with a challenge, is it identified? What communication occurs? What feelings are expressed? What roles are adopted or assigned? What options for action are considered and who implements them? What was the outcome, and was it monitored?

ELICITING INFORMATION ABOUT BEHAVIOUR, EVENTS AND SITUATIONS

Initial clinical approaches

Widely differing recommendations have been made about the best way to obtain accurate and meaningful information. Some writers have suggested a non-directive technique designed to encourage the informant to talk on the issues that he or she thinks are important (Deutsch, 1939; Gill *et al.*, 1954; Lisansky, 1969). The assumption is that the informant's thought processes and mental associations will naturally lead to the most clinically significant material. Others have advocated a series of standard questions followed by non-specific probes but no cross-examination (Spitzer *et al.*, 1964, 1970). Yet others have argued that there must be both systematic coverage of all relevant areas and flexible probing and specific cross-questioning to get an accurate picture of actual behaviour (Wing *et al.*, 1967). In any assessment of the relative merits and demerits of these contrasting approaches, attention must be paid to the goals of the interview and the range of information obtained, its accuracy and its clinical pertinence.

In the initial interview with the parents, the task should not be entirely defined by the professional. There is now a substantial literature on the importance of patient-centredness and mutual participation by doctor and patient in primary health care (e.g. Frankel & Beckman, 1989; Butler *et al.*, 1992). Litwak (1956) has pointed out that the interviewer's use of words may be different from that of the informant. These considerations have implications for the order in which various techniques are used. If interviewers lead straight into systematic specific questioning without learning the language and viewpoint of the parent, they may get misleading answers. It is likely, too, that if the parents cannot start by putting the problem in their own terms, they may feel that they have not been understood. This is likely to affect both their preparedness to give certain information and their desire to cooperate in therapy.

Data from different medical settings support the need for an open listening stance by the interviewer at the outset. Stiles *et al.* (1979) showed that in initial medical consultations, patients were more satisfied if doctors first encouraged them to tell their story in their own way. In the same setting patient-centredness has been linked to patient satisfaction (Stewart, 1984), knowledge about illness and compliance with medical recommendations (Carter *et al.*, 1982). Practitioners in the community (Goldberg & Huxley, 1980) were more effective in identifying psychiatric disorders if they started with a more open enquiry and then focused down. In the same setting it has been suggested that a sharing approach is probably more relevant to psychological issues or psychological aspects of physical problems (Savage & Armstrong, 1990). It is important to note that in their initial interviews, medical students' errors included focusing prematurely on a particular topic (Maguire & Rutter, 1976).

Cox and colleagues were the first investigators to have systematically studied interview techniques in the clinical setting of a child psychiatric clinic. Their first study was a naturalistic examination of interviews by psychiatrists in training (Cox *et al.*, 1981a; Hopkinson *et al.*, 1981; Rutter & Cox, 1981). They made video tape recordings of the first interviews with the parents of children newly referred to the clinic. Interviewer behaviour and informant responses were assessed in several different ways, all shown to have satisfactory inter-rater reliability. Frequency counts were made of different types of interviewer statement or question and also of specified interviewer nonverbal behaviours. In addition, systematic assessments were made of both verbal and nonverbal sequences of interaction between psychiatrist and parent. These interview variables were then related to measures of the range and extent of emotional feelings expressed by the parent. In terms of the child's behaviour and development, systematic questioning did not add much to the range of problems reported but it elicited much more detailed information, particularly about symptoms and the child's development. The parents tended to give quite full data on family life and relationships without extensive probing by the interviewer.

These findings were subject to more rigorous examination by a clinical experimental study (Cox *et al.*, 1981b,c; Rutter *et al.*, 1981). The mothers of newly referred children were interviewed twice, 2 weeks apart. On each occasion, one of two experienced trained interviewers used a different technique selected from four that were compared. Each technique combined a verbally active or inactive approach to factual material with a verbally active and responsive, or inactive, approach to the expression of feelings. The findings of the initial study were confirmed. The major benefit gained from the active probing method for facts was in the much better detail and depth of data on child symptoms. Mothers spontaneously talked quite fully about family matters including their own and their spouse's mental health. However, there were important differences between mothers. A few had a strong preference for being questioned actively and a few preferred to tell the story in their own words. There was no relationship between the quality of factual information obtained and the degree of emotional expression by the parents, nor did active probing for factual material prevent adequate expression of feeling. It is evident that systematic questioning is definitely superior to free reporting when it comes to obtaining full and detailed factual information about children's symptoms, but that parents spontaneously give a significant amount of data about the index problem and the family. It is therefore appropriate to encourage parents to talk freely at the outset of the interview.

During parents' extended free reporting it is important that interviewers are aware that they can influence what the parents say simply by virtue of when they show interest or encouragement (Truax, 1966, 1968; Cox & Rutter, 1985). By the way they listen, by the model set and by what they say, interviewers can make clear to the parents the kind of information they want (Cannell & Axelrod, 1956; Krasner, 1958; Gelder, 1968; McGinnies, 1970; Goldstein, 1971; Heilbron, 1971; Marlatt, 1972; Matarazzo & Weins, 1972). It is wise to use this influence knowingly in a way that minimizes bias, rather than run unknowingly the risk of unconscious selective distortion.

Systematic questioning

When the goal is to explore a predefined field, systematic questioning is usually superior to less structured approaches. The studies of Cox and his colleagues, referred to above, indicate that this may be required after parents' initial spontaneous reports. Research in other settings gives support to this view. For example, Marquis *et al.* (1972a) examined experimentally people's reports of what they had just seen in a short film. Specific detailed structured questions produced very much fuller information than did free reporting. Clinical studies with a similar preset focus have produced broadly comparable findings. Saghir (1971) compared a highly structured interview with a more traditional freestyle (but not undirected) interview in terms of their efficiency in assessing the present mental state of adult psychiatric patients. The structured interview produced much more extensive information. In a community epidemiological study Graham and Rutter (1968) compared parents' spontaneous reports of their

child's behaviour with the results of systematic questioning. The latter gave rise to fuller information that showed superior reliability (as indicated by the correlation between interviews by different people 1 month apart in time).

However, how interviewers go about questioning is also important, both during the phase of more spontaneous report and later during any systematic enquiries. First they need to have a clear idea of what they are looking for and what is important. This has been shown in studies of medical students' errors in medical assessment interviews (Maguire & Rutter, 1976) and in the assessment of the presence or absence of psychiatric disorders by general practitioners (Goldberg & Huxley, 1980). Rutter and Cox (Cox *et al.*, 1981a; Rutter & Cox, 1981) found that the experienced interviewers in their experimental study were far more efficient in obtaining factual information than the trainee psychiatrists: they needed many fewer probes to obtain good-quality data. It may be inferred that they were more sure of their goals. Second, open questions — those that expect an extended answer and give the floor to the parent — are important, particularly at the start of an interview or when any new area is entered. Closed questions need to be kept for the purpose of eliciting specific details that have not emerged spontaneously. A related technique is to ask for examples of behaviour and then obtain blow-by-blow accounts of what happened. This is a valuable method which was used more by experienced interviewers than inexperienced interviewers in the studies by Cox and Rutter. However, a variety of examples are needed because the behaviour of both children and their parents tends to vary according to context (Grusec & Kuejymski, 1980). Iwata *et al.* (1982) have shown that interviewing techniques of these kinds can be improved by systematic training.

Third, when going on to systematic questioning, flexible supplementary probing will often be required to clarify the meaning of initial answers (Guest, 1947; Shapiro & Eberhart, 1947; Wyatt & Campbell, 1950). Failure of clarification has been noted as a common deficiency in interviewing techniques in several different studies (Maguire & Rutter, 1976; Goldberg & Huxley, 1980; Maguire *et al.*, 1989). However, the way clarification is done needs to be modified to suit different informants and different situations. It has been found that short, simple questions lead to more accurate reporting of recent health events by poorly educated informants than do long, complex questions (Marquis *et al.*, 1972b). Social reinforcement of answers (saying things such as 'Mm-mm, we're interested in that') also improved accuracy of reporting by less-educated informants. However, in both cases, the reverse applied to more-educated informants.

A related aspect of clarification is the need to differentiate between what in fact happened and what the informant felt about what happened. General questions such as 'How much does your husband help at home?' are unsatisfactory because there is an ambiguity as to whether opinions, attitudes or descriptions are being asked for (Brown & Rutter, 1966). Hoffman (1957, 1960) has suggested that the request for specific details of particular recent events leads to more dispassionate reporting. It seems that a focus on the cognitive task of remembering what actually happened helps to divest the event of much of its emotional meaning. The interviewing methods of Brown and Rutter (Brown & Rutter, 1966; Rutter & Brown, 1966) that use this approach confirm that the technique provides a good differentiation between events and attitudes about the events.

Fourth, multiple choice, leading and 'yes—no' questions all carry the danger of reducing accuracy (Cahalan *et al.*, 1947; Marquis *et al.*, 1972a). Multiple choice questions (e.g. 'Does he have tantrums once a week or twice a week?') may present alternatives that are not applicable, or that do not cover the appropriate area. Cox and Rutter's research, however, suggests that, if well-chosen, a choice need not necessarily lead to bias and may be a useful technique for prompting informants to give frequencies or dates (Cox *et al.*, 1981a). Probably it is wise to choose widely differing alternatives in order to avoid the effects of suggestion (e.g. 'Were the tantrums several times a day or just once every few months?'). 'Yes—no' questions also limit the range of answers and present the additional problem that some people have a general tendency to answer 'yes' or 'no' to most questions (Couch & Kemiston, 1960). Leading questions carry the danger of suggesting wrong answers. Although the biasing effect of certain kinds of leading questions may have been exaggerated (Dohrenwend & Richardson, 1964), a negatively phrased leading question about an unexplored item (e.g. 'He doesn't wet the bed, does he?') is clearly unsatisfactory. Impersonal leading questions (e.g. 'Was there a ...?') are also more likely to lead to inaccurate answers than are personal questions (e.g. 'Did you see a ...?'), presumably because the former requests an opinion whereas the latter emphasizes the informant's role as an observer (Burtt & Gaskill, 1932). Leading questions are really only desirable as a means of providing feedback that the interviewer has understood, as checks on information just given, or as a means of enquiring into areas where there may be underreporting because of embarrassment (Richardson *et al.*, 1965; Brandt, 1972). Thus, it may be preferable to ask 'How often do you and your husband disagree about what time Johnny comes in at night?' rather than 'Do you and your husband ever disagree ...?', in order to indicate acceptance of the fact that married couples often do disagree.

It should be emphasized, however, that it is not sufficient for the interviewer to give the parent a chance to talk and then to question relentlessly. All the available evidence points to the importance of picking up cues as an important component in more experienced and more effective interviewing (Rutter & Maguire, 1976; Goldberg & Huxley, 1980; Cox *et al.*, 1981a).

The assessment of children's symptomatology: clinical considerations deriving from research instruments

The approach underlying the assessment of symptoms in the Child and Adolescent Psychiatric Assessment (CAPA; Angold, 1989) has value in clinical practice.

Severity of symptomatology is approached in a detailed fashion. Firstly, impact of symptoms or incapacity is treated separately from intensity. Secondly, intensity is separated from frequency of symptoms and duration of bouts of symptoms. Thus, incapacity, intensity, frequency and duration of bouts are all discriminable facets of severity. The criteria for intensity are different for different types of symptoms. The first group of symptoms consists of those intrapsychic phenomena which are normal when present in lesser degree (such as worrying). For these items the symptom's intensity is evaluated according to three dimensions:

1 Intrusiveness into other mental activities (as for instance in the case of worries intruding into other thoughts).
2 Lack of modifiability or controllability: the child's inability to modify the phenomena by action, thought, behaviour or environmental manipulation (as when a miserable boy cheers himself up by going out to play football with his friends).
3 Generalization or the degree to which symptomatic thoughts or emotions are present across a range of activities that may be quite unrelated to the content of the symptom (as in the case of the child who feels afraid of parental separation in situations where separation is not threatened).

The second group of symptoms comprises those where there is a qualitative difference that defines the features as abnormal whenever it occurs, regardless of the level of intensity. This applies to psychotic phenomena, but there are various other symptoms when the same approach is appropriate because the presence of the feature at any intensity is of clinical importance. For example, this applies to uncommon conduct symptoms (such as fire-setting or running away from home), to developmental abnormalities that are unusual in the age group (such as enuresis) and to certain other disturbances (such as derealization and depersonalization).

The third group of symptoms comprise disturbances of conduct that are abnormal only when they are intense. This applies for example to items such as disobedience and temper tantrums. Here it was found necessary to specify a minimum frequency combined with the requirement of generalization across activities in order to set a threshold. The fourth group of symptoms is intermediate between the last two groups, in that they are common but not universally acceptable at low intensity in the same way as intrapsychic phenomena or the third group of conduct disturbances. In this fourth group are items such as stealing and tics. Apart from psychotic phenomena and some relatively unusual intrapsychic phenomena, most of the symptoms in groups 2—4 are externalizing or behavioural symptoms. They differ in terms of the threshold that can be considered abnormal, ranging from those in group 2 which are abnormal in any circumstance to those in group 3 which are only considered abnormal at higher intensity. For these behavioural symptoms, generalization and controllability are relevant in considering significance, but intrusiveness into mental activities is not. The additional intensity criterion, responsiveness to admonition, is therefore included. Frequency is also relevant. Further important discriminations in considering significance are the directedness of the behaviour, whether it is towards objects or particular persons, and whether it occurs when the child is solitary or accompanied by others. Not all criteria are applied to every symptom since they are not always appropriate. In addition to the intensity rating there is an overall incapacity rating concerned with the loss of functional capacity, the degree of such loss and whether it is characterized by disturbance in relationships due to withdrawal or discord. Which symptom areas contribute to which losses of capacity is recorded.

Retrospective recall

Certain well-defined items such as period of gestation, birth weight, age when the child walked and serious illnesses are recalled fairly accurately. Speech milestones tend to be reported as earlier than they were (Hart *et al.*, 1978). *Whether* something occurred is better remembered than *when* it occurred (Quinton, 1988), although recall including recall of sequences of events is better if respondents are asked to relate events to major life changes such as entering school (Robins, 1988). Major events that carry some importance for the individual are more likely to be recalled than are minor happenings; thus, prolonged hospital admissions or those involving surgery are more likely to be remembered than overnight or very brief stops in hospital (Cannell *et al.*, 1961).

It is likely that events that make a strong emotional impact are better recalled than those that were effectively neutral or at least of lesser meaning at the time (Cannell, 1977). Thus, parents are likely to remember if the children were ever placed in foster care but they may not remember separations that resulted from holiday visits to relatives or friends. On the other hand, in some circumstances, threatening events, unpleasant experiences or situations giving rise to anxiety tend to be underreported or less easily remembered (Janis, 1958; Cannell *et al.*, 1961; Goddard *et al.*, 1961; Lishman, 1974; Steele *et al.*, 1980). Reactions to previous adverse experiences may be reported differently over periods as short as 2 weeks (Steele *et al.*, 1980). Retrospective recall of interpersonal relationships, child-rearing practices, more subtle aspects of behaviour and sequences of events is particularly subject to systematic bias. For example, Wolkind and Coleman (1983) found that currently anxious or depressed women reported more childhood parental marital problems than women who had been previously depressed but were now well. However this finding was not replicated when the recall of siblings with and without psychiatric problems was compared. At 30–50 years after the events there was good agreement not only for number of homes and schools lived in and attended, but also parental marital disputes (Robins *et al.*, 1985). It is suggested that bias is less where the time between potential cause and outcome is great (Robins, 1988). On the whole, there is a tendency to distort accounts of the past to coincide more with current feelings and attitudes, with stereotypes of behaviour or with prevailing views on child-rearing (Robins, 1963; Chess *et al.*, 1966; Yarrow *et al.*, 1970; Robins, 1988). One study found a tendency for mothers to overesti-

mate their husbands' periods away from home and to underestimate their children's emotional and behavioural difficulties during their preschool years (Yarrow *et al.*, 1970). These tendencies must be borne in mind when interpreting retrospective information.

ELICITING EMOTIONS AND FEELINGS

It will always be valuable to understand parents' feelings about what they are describing, whether it is the index child, others in the family or particular life experiences. Information about feelings is a vital component of diagnostic appraisal. Emotions are probably most validly assessed while the parent is giving an account of events or behaviours. Direct enquiry may well produce a response modulated by social desirability.

Almost all writers on interviewing have emphasized the need to establish rapport if satisfactory communication is to be established for both feelings and factual material. Rapport is an ill-defined term but it includes the notion that the informant trusts the interviewer so that there is mutual understanding and cooperation (Vontress, 1971; Brown, 1972). Sometimes it has been assumed that this means maximum informality on the part of the interviewer, but probably this is wrong (Hyman *et al.*, 1954). Undue informality orients the informant to a social rather than a task orientation. This may inhibit emotional expression because individuals do not usually reveal intimate details at a first social meeting (Miller, 1952). There is a possibility of distortion in that informants may express only attitudes consonant with the interviewer's expectations so as not to disturb the friendly interchange (Hyman *et al.*, 1954; Ulrich & Trumbo, 1965). In addition, parents may perceive very informal behaviour as dissonant with the professional role and so be disconcerted (Argyle, 1969). How far these biases actually occur is not known, but it is evident that maximum informality does not necessarily aid rapport and the expression of emotion.

In a professional interview setting, empathy refers to a sensitivity to people's feelings, together with an ability to communicate understanding in a language well-attuned to the feelings. It tends to be associated with warmth (Shapiro, 1969) and a warm tone of voice and responsive facial expression are probably important in leading an informant to feel understood (Shapiro J.G., 1968; Shapiro D.A., 1969; English & Jelenevsky, 1971). Both empathy and warmth contribute to the development of rapport and have been shown to increase self-exploration in psychotherapy (Truax & Carkhuff, 1967). However, although at least *some* warmth is necessary in interviewing, a variety of findings suggest that *very high* levels of warmth or of behaviours associated with warmth may be disadvantageous.

Warmth may be conveyed by tone of voice, smiling, nodding and brief expressions of interest or approval (Reece & Whitman, 1961; Heller, 1968; Strong *et al.*, 1971; Breed, 1972). These behaviours, together with eye contact and physical proximity, tend to indicate a positive evaluation (Mehrabian, 1971) and may encourage emotional expression

(Heller *et al.*, 1966; Flanders, 1968; Argyle, 1969; Matarazzo & Wiens, 1972). On the other hand, high rates of indiscriminate smiling and nodding tend to cause informants to stop talking, perhaps because they suggest that the interviewer has heard enough or understood everything (Heller, 1968), which may lead some informants to withdraw. Furthermore, people vary in the intimacy or social distance that they like to maintain (Argyle, 1969). When two people interact it seems that they tend to adjust their behaviour to achieve an emotional equilibrium at a level of intimacy that suits them both. Accordingly, it is probably best for the interviewer to maintain an intermediate level of warmth at first and then modify it according to the individual informant's responses. This means not sitting too close (Patterson, 1968; Boucher, 1972; Dinges & Oetting, 1972) or too far away — say about 1.5 metres. Sitting diagonally probably avoids the competitive ethos of direct facing and also the undue intimacy of being side by side (Cook, 1970). It also allows sensitive adjustment of eye to eye gaze. Sitting behind a desk is not conducive to patient relaxation (White, 1953) and an emphasis on authority probably produces too much social distance and so discourages free emotional expression. The evidence is circumstantial and incomplete but, apart from avoiding extremes, it seems that the degree of warmth or closeness is probably not a crucial variable in eliciting emotions. Empathy may be more important.

The findings from the naturalistic and experimental clinical interviewing studies by Cox and his colleagues (Cox *et al.*, 1981a,b,c; Hopkinson *et al.*, 1981; Rutter & Cox, 1981; Rutter *et al.*, 1981) showed which interviewing styles and techniques were most successful in eliciting expressions of emotions from informants. The results emphasized the wide range of approaches that could serve to encourage emotional expression. Firstly, informants tended to express more feelings in interviews in which the clinician listened, was attentive and responsive, and talked less. Similarly, emotions (or reports of emotive matters such as marital discord or mental disturbance) were more likely to be expressed following open rather than closed questions. Thus, it seemed advantageous to ask questions requiring an extended answer (e.g. 'What did you do when she became aggressive?') rather than one answerable by 'yes' or 'no' or some specific brief response (e.g. 'Did you smack her when she was aggressive to you?' or 'Who disciplined her?'). It seems that an excessive and constricting focus on a series of objective facts may convey the message that the interviewer is not concerned with emotions and attitudes. Conversely, a more open approach allows informants to express the feelings engendered by what happened.

Secondly, the interviewer may encourage informants to show and to speak about their emotions by the manner of his or her response when they do so. Thus, further emotional expression is more likely following expressions of sympathy or reflective interpretations of feelings.

Alternatively, emotions may be elicited by direct enquiries about feelings, attitudes or emotional responses. This means that, provided the appropriate questions are asked, an active directive interview style may be effective in tapping emotions as well as in gleaning factual data. It is more likely to be so, however, if combined with a sensitivity to emotional cues and some form of appropriate response to the informant's emotional expressions.

In a second experimental study, Cox *et al.* (1988) explored further the effect of different styles of interviewing on the eliciting of parents' feelings. Two interview styles, designed to differ in the extent of their use of active feeling-oriented techniques, but similar in their use of active fact-oriented techniques, were compared in initial diagnostic interviews with 16 mothers of children referred to a child psychiatric clinic. The design was similar to the first experimental study, except that only two styles were compared, since mothers had the same approach to facts with both styles but a different one for feelings. The verbally active approach to facts incorporated in both styles led to a similar range and quality of factual data in the two conditions. In the style using an active approach to feelings as well as facts, expressions of sympathy, reflection of feeling and questions about feelings were used more often and, as in the first study, these techniques were much more often immediately followed by expressions of emotions whatever the interview style. Overall more feelings were expressed with the active feeling style but the difference was not apparent in the first 15 minutes. Certain types of feeling are of particular diagnostic importance, such as negative feelings about spouse, child or self. The different styles did not elicit different amounts of these types of feelings.

Strong correlations were found between pairs of interviews with the same mother in the amount of feelings expressed, and also between the use of the prescribed feeling techniques and the amount of expressed emotion. Since these results suggested an informant effect, the impact of the style in the latter part of the interview, depending on the mother's level of emotional expressiveness in the first 15 minutes, was analysed. The approach employing more active feeling techniques tended to sustain a high rate of emotional expression in high expressers or to increase it in low expressers. The more passive verbal approach to feelings kept low expressers' rates lower and reduced rates in most of the high expressers. A change from passive to active feeling style always led to sustained or increased rates of expression; a change from active to passive feeling style usually decreased the rate.

Pairs of interviews were compared to see which style detected types of feelings that the other failed to detect. The active feeling style performed significantly better in this comparison. There were also interesting context effects: mothers more often expressed negative feelings about themselves after the interviewer reflected feelings with a sympathetic tone, while criticism of respondents' spouses was most often expressed after a request for information about sensitive data. Positive feelings were more often expressed after other feelings, rather than at the beginning of an utterance, emphasizing the importance of encouraging sufficiently long utterances. Finally, the feeling techniques, whether prescribed or not, tended to facilitate the expression of feeling, while structuring statements, clarifications, multiple choice and closed questions tended to inhibit the expression of emotions.

It seems that some information about feelings will emerge from initial interviews with parents no matter what the interviewer does. This is probably true of all initial medical consultations, despite quite marked differences between informants in the extent to which they express feelings (Butler *et al.*, 1992; Campion *et al.*, 1992). The setting, the informant's expectations and an attentive, interested interviewer will likely produce a considerable amount of relevant data on both facts and feelings; these factors were not varied in the studies described. They are relevant to the techniques employed and may have overriding importance for what is reported or expressed. Nevertheless, it appears that many different techniques are relevant to facilitating emotional expression and obtaining sensitive data. These include asking about feelings, reflecting feelings, expressing sympathy, open questioning, questioning about sensitive material and encouraging longer utterances, which are more likely to occur if interviewers talk less. Since passive or nonspecific methods appear quite effective, there may be a case for using active methods more sparingly, since maximum revelation of feelings on first contact is probably not optimum. However, interviewers need to be aware of differences between informants — more persistence with feeling techniques may be needed with less expressive interviewees. There are limits to how much people can alter their interviewing techniques, but since there are several ways of achieving similar ends, there may be methods to suit most interviewers and most clients (Cox, 1989a).

From the diagnostic point of view, of course, the balance of feelings or the presence of particular types may be more important than the overall amount of emotional expression. In this connection, it may be relevant that expressions of sympathy and reflective interpretations were most effective in eliciting parental distress or depression. By the nature of things, reflections frequently involve warmth and sympathy and may therefore be reinforcing (Adams *et al.*, 1962a,b; Noblin *et al.*, 1963). On the other hand, this is often not the case with challenging interpretations or confrontations (Hopkinson *et al.*, 1981). This is in keeping with evidence from psychotherapy which suggests that interpretations that are too dissonant or that provoke too strong an emotional response may inhibit the expressions of feelings (Kanfer *et al.*, 1960; Pope & Siegman, 1965; Bierman, 1969). Anderson (1968) found that confrontations given by warm, empathic interviewers increased adult patients' self-exploration, but those given by less warm and less empathic interviewers did not do so.

Combining techniques

It is sometimes feared that the techniques most suitable for eliciting facts make it very difficult to elicit feelings, and vice versa. Fortunately, the evidence shows that this is not the case, although rather different approaches are needed for the two. The available evidence suggests that the overall needs of the diagnostic appraisal are likely to be best met by an approach in which open questions with minimal cross-examination are used at the start of the interview, in order to obtain the informant's perception of the problem and to gauge his or her style of language and interaction. This needs to be followed by a systematic coverage of a broader range of topics and by detailed questioning on all key areas. Specific examples of actual recent behaviour are to be preferred to informant generalizations, and on the whole negative-leading, multiple choice and yes—no questions should be avoided. Although some closed questions are helpful, there should be a preponderance of open enquiries. The interviewer should be sympathetic, reflective, understanding and encouraging, also empathic and warm, but not over-intimate or intrusive. A moderate degree of activity and directiveness is desirable, but the interviewer should not interrupt or talk excessively; neither should he or she be very passive. The structure of the interview needs to be sufficiently flexible for the interviewer to respond to the cues given by informants and to meet their emotional needs, while at the same time ensuring a systematic coverage of important topics.

The interview has been described as a 'conversation with a purpose' (Bingham & Moore, 1924), a definition that emphasizes the need for the interviewer to have the objectives clearly in mind and to manage the interview in order to reach those objectives. This requires specific skills (Menninger, 1962) and somewhat different approaches may be needed for different people. However, while retaining flexibility and individuality, there is a need for the diagnostic interview to present comparable stimuli to all informants, otherwise their responses cannot be compared (Balint & Balint, 1961). The interview serves as a standard stimulus for eliciting emotions and attitudes (Chapple, 1953; Balint & Balint, 1961; Rutter & Brown, 1966), as well as a means of enquiring for information.

ASSESSING FAMILY LIFE AND RELATIONSHIPS

Rutter and Brown (1966; Brown & Rutter, 1966) have shown that, with the use of these interviewing techniques, sensitive, reliable and valid measures of quite subtle aspects of family life and relationships can be obtained from a single interview with one parent. A methodological study was undertaken with 30 families, in all of which there were children of school age or younger. For each family there were separate interviews by different interviewers with the father, the mother and the two parents together. There was good interrater reliability and reasonable agreement between husband and wife for most measures of family activities (participation in household tasks, leisure activities, parent—child interaction etc.). However, care and skill were needed in questioning if attitudinal biases in reporting were to be avoided. In addition, it was necessary to enquire specifically into each aspect of family interaction if information on an adequate range of family behaviours was to be obtained.

High interrater reliability was achieved on measures of feelings such as warmth, criticism, dissatisfaction and hostility.

Furthermore, the feelings expressed by a mother when talking about her husband when interviewed on her own agreed well with the feelings shown towards him when he was present in a separate and independent conjoint interview. However, training in the recognition of emotions as well as in interviewing was needed. By the use of tape recordings and group discussions, interviewers were taught to recognize differences in tone of voice as shown in the speed, pitch and intensity of speech. Emotional meaning and the nature of social relationships (Argyle, 1969) are conveyed in vocal as well as verbal aspects of speech (Starkweather, 1956; Alpert *et al.*, 1963; Kramer, 1963), in facial expression (Ekman *et al.*, 1972) and in gesture (Reece & Whitman, 1961). Clinicians need to acquire skills in observing these phenomena and to apply these observational skills during diagnostic interviews. Noting the emotional reactions of informants is as crucial an aspect of interviewing as listening to what they say.

Quinton *et al.* (1976) have also shown that an interview with one marriage partner can be used to make reliable and valid judgements of the marriage relationship that predict well later marital discord, divorce and separation. Indeed, more may be obtained about some aspects of the marriage from individual partners than by joint interviews (Haines *et al.*, 1981). Evaluations of the marriage are very important in the diagnostic appraisal because of the relatively strong associations between marital disharmony and psychiatric disorder in the children. In order to assess the marriage, it is not enough to ask people how they get on together or whether they are satisfied with the marriage. Rather, attention needs to be paid to items such as the frequency and severity of quarrelling and bickering, the amount of expressed affection and concern and the presence or absence of overt tension in the relationship. Lengthy interviewing is not required (Vaughn & Leff, 1976) but it is necessary to ask about irritability, quarrelling and separations and to obtain enough discussion about family activities and about the behaviour of both husband and wife to elicit feelings and attitudes about the marriage (Quinton *et al.*, 1976). Additionally, information should be sought on the extent to which the children are present during, and drawn into, family quarrels (Quinton & Rutter, 1985).

A great deal of information about family life and relationships can be obtained from a simple interview with one parent, and indeed, this is possibly the best and most efficient means of assessing many aspects of family life and relationships. However, it is important to note those aspects that cannot adequately be assessed in this way. Firstly, reports by one parent about the emotions and feelings of the other have only weak validity (Becker, 1960; Brown & Rutter, 1966; Rutter & Brown, 1966). This finding alone is enough to indicate the need to interview *both* parents of children referred to psychiatric clinics. Secondly, people have great difficulty in reporting accurately even quite crude aspects of communication and decision-making (Kenkel & Hoffman, 1956; Kenkel, 1957; Brown & Rutter, 1966). If these features of family interaction are to be evaluated (and they show some association with child psychiatric disorder), some type of conjoint family interview is required (see Chapter 5). Thirdly, although parents can give accurate reports of the duration and types of parent–child interaction, they are much less accurate about its timing and sequences of interaction (Douglas *et al.*, 1968). If knowledge on sequences is required, as it may well be if there is to be understanding of what is going wrong in parent–child interactions, there is no substitute for some form of observation either in the home or the clinic (see Maccoby & Martin, 1983).

INTERVIEWING CHILDREN WITH AND WITHOUT PARENTS

Some aspects of family relationships can be expected to be more effectively assessed by observation during family interviews. Such aspects include communication patterns, the emotional tone employed during communication, responsivity, alliances between family members and modes of mutual influence, including discipline, control and authority (Kinston *et al.*, 1979, 1987; Kinston & Loader, 1988). Beliefs and knowledge about events impinging on the family, and whether and how they are shared, can also be obtained in this context, but if family members are seen together, certain information may be kept back by some participants. There is only one systematic unpublished study that has compared the data emerging from initial family assessment interviews and those conducted with parents and their adolescent child separately (Eminson, 1988). This study involved newly referred outpatients to an adolescent unit. Whole family interviews were contrasted with individual patient and parent interviews. All families received both modes of assessment with a 1–3-week gap, being randomly assigned to initial family or individual modes. Neither technique had an advantage in identifying the range of problems or symptoms shown by the adolescent, but individual interviews obtained good-quality data on specific symptoms significantly more often. Information on past symptoms did not differ according to the interview conditions, but the account of the adolescent's development was better with the individual interviews. There were no order effects, but as is common with repeated assessment, problems emerged in one session which did not in the other. Idiosyncratic information with particular significance was reported with equal frequency, and on relatively gross measures of family relationships there was no difference between the two methods. The results point to the need for other justifications for initial family assessment than getting information. One justification may be that what is significant for engagement and intervention is not the information derived at initial assessment, but the manner and context in which it is obtained.

STANDARDIZED PARENTAL INTERVIEWS AND QUESTIONNAIRES

Many interviews and questionnaires have been developed for use with parents in research settings and they are increasingly used clinically, partly because of concerns about the reliability and validity of unsubstantiated clinical interviews (Robins, 1985, 1989; Young *et al.*, 1987).

Since there are now many standardized interview measures and questionnaires, only a selection of the best known and most frequently used will be considered. Reviews of these instruments are to be found in Kovacs (1986), Gutterman *et al.* (1987), Barkley (1988), Edelbrock and Costello (1988), and Angold (1989). Since questionnaires for adults about children are like highly structured interviews they are also included and will be referred to as questionnaires.

If instruments are to be selected for particular clinical purposes it is necessary to put the use of standardized instruments into context and consider their characteristics.

First, standardized interviews and questionnaires can be considered to be a subset of psychological tests and they are therefore systematic procedures for obtaining information about psychological functioning and describing it with the aid of a numerical scale or category system. They are concerned with quantification and measurement and therefore with assessment with respect to either a criterion or norms (see Chapter 7). Clinically one may be interested in both. Norm-based assessment in which there is comparison with a criterion group is relevant for the detection of the presence or absence of disorder and the discrimination of types of disorder. Criterion-based assessment, in which an individual's status is compared with a criterion, may be particularly relevant in looking at response to treatment in a specific case where there is interest in change in a particular targeted behaviour, e.g. the frequency of stealing.

Second, it must always be remembered that assessment has both a purpose and a context (Angold, 1989). This has to be remembered not only in selecting questionnaires for use but also when applying them. It is not enough to know the purpose for which a questionnaire was constructed, the context in which it has been used and its mode of administration — one must also consider how those facets match with proposed use and where the assessment fits in with other assessments. Is the information being tapped in several ways? What happens for example if a questionnaire designed to screen for psychiatric problems is used to assess change in response to a specific treatment programme for an individual child?

Third, it must be remembered that the content and form of questionnaires necessarily reflect a theory or at least a perspective. For example, if the view is held that depressive symptomatology in children is essentially similar to that in adults, this will be reflected in the construction of any questionnaire to assess depression in children. There will be differences in structure depending on whether a behaviour is seen as qualitatively different from normal or on a continuum.

Related to the issue of underlying theory or perspective are questions about whether the perspective of those who construct or administer a particular questionnaire have a set of assumptions in common with the informants to whom the questionnaires are applied. Although this consideration is particularly appropriate to checklists and rating scales (Cairns & Green, 1979), the issue of shared assumptions is also relevant to semistructured interviews (Barkley, 1988). It is partly because of the difficulty of checking these assumptions in fixed worded questionnaires or checklists that semistructured interviews are favoured for certain purposes (Rutter & Tuma, 1988; Angold, 1989). This highlights the need to consider the characteristics of standardized parental instruments in more detail.

Firstly, there is the format of the instrument. Formats vary from questionnaires with fixed wording and only yes or no alternative responses to semistructured interviews (Edelbrock & Costello, 1988). Table 3.1 contrasts some of the features that distinguish highly structured checklists or interviews and semistructured interviews.

Secondly, the number of items in the interview or questionnaire and the time taken to administer them may influence choice. Thirdly, there is the scaling of responses and whether there is a glossary — if there are very limited response options and fixed wording, no glossary is required, but if the responses are open-ended then one is necessary. Fourthly, it is necessary to consider the informant, whether parent, child, teacher, peer or professional staff, and whether there are versions available for different informants. This may make it possible to have more exact comparisons between the views of different people and also assist in the making of diagnoses on the basis of multiple sources of information (Reich & Earls, 1987; McConaughy *et al.*, 1988). Fifthly, there is the mode of administration: whether self-administered or by an interviewer, and whether the interviewer needs to be trained or not. Sixth,

Table 3.1 Contrasting features of highly structured and semi-structured interviews

	Fixed word questionnaire	Semi-structured interviews
1 Form of question	Fixed	Initial probes may be specified: follow-up not
2 Intent of question on schedule	To be standard stimulus	To orient informant and direct interviewer
3 Use of glossary	Not required	Essential
4 Ratings from observation of informant	No	May be
5 Administration	By lay person	By trained person or professional
6 Training of person administering	Minimal	Extensive
7 Judgement required to score	Nil	Considerable
8 Duration	Medium	Long
9 Cost	Low	High

consideration must be given to the information yield, whether this is of symptoms, diagnoses or measures of adaptive functioning. Finally, sensitivity, specificity, reliability and validity are important since they help the clinician to judge what weight to put on the measure used. How good is the instrument at determining the presence or absence of psychiatric disorder or at contributing to the assignment of a particular diagnosis? Good interrater reliability is needed for semistructured instruments which require interviewer training and judgement. Such reliability may need to be established within any given clinical setting, whereas this will not be necessary for instruments, designed to be administered by lay persons, that have been standardized on general population and clinical samples, although different cut-offs may need to be used in different populations (Achenbach *et al.*, 1989). In research studies interinformant reliability is often referred to but clinically differences need to be heeded rather than dismissed. It cannot be expected that individuals who have a different experience of the subject in different situations will make similar ratings. Furthermore, if informants appear to make different judgements because they have different attitudes, this may be highly relevant.

Clinical applications of standardized parental interviews and questionnaires

As already indicated, the purposes for which questionnaires may have been constructed may be quite different from the uses to which they are put and this translation of function may be justified or not. Sometimes modifications to questionnaires have been made in order to make them more appropriate to, for example, a clinical rather than a research context or clinic populations as opposed to the general population. However, most of those who have constructed interviews and questionnaires have been interested in research and it is therefore not surprising that it is more often that an instrument which has been developed for research use is then applied clinically. Table 3.2 lists uses of questionnaires and gives some examples.

Firstly, questionnaires have been devised to screen general populations for the presence or absence of psychological or psychiatric disorder. Angold (1989), reviewing these scales, concluded that the revised Behavioural Problem Checklist and the revised Conners scale are satisfactory for screening for conduct disorder and hyperactivity, although there is more psychometric information on the Conners scale. The Child Behaviour Checklist (CBCL), which is much longer, may be more satisfactory if emotional disorders are a real focus of interest. However the comparison of computer and standard administration of both the Rutter A^2 Parent Scale and CBCL point to somewhat better sensitivity in detection of disorder for the Rutter (80 versus 73%) and little difference in specificity (70 versus 72%; Berg *et al.*, 1992).

For young children the Richman Behaviour Screening Questionnaire or the paper and pencil version of it, the Behaviour Checklist which can be used by parents, nursery

Table 3.2 Uses of Questionnaires

(a) Screening general population

For presence/absence of disorder
1 Semi-structured interview
e.g. Behaviour Screening Questionnaire: BSQ (Richman & Graham, 1971)
2 Highly structured interview
e.g. Diagnostic Interview Schedule for Children: DISC (Costello *et al.*, 1982, 1984)
   Diagnostic Interview for Children and Adolescents: DICA (Herjanic & Reich 1982)
3 Checklist
e.g. Rutter 'A' and 'B' Scales for parents and teachers (Rutter 1967, Rutter *et al.*, 1970; Berg *et al.*, 1992)
   Child Behaviour Checklist: CBCL (Achenbach & Edelbrock 1981, 1983)
   Behaviour Problem Checklist (Quay, 1977; Quay & Peterson, 1983, 1984)
   Conners Parent & Teacher Rating Scales (Conners, 1969; 1973; Goyette *et al.*, 1978)

For specific disorders or syndromes
1 Highly structured interviews
e.g. DISC, DICA
2 Checklists,
e.g. Conners Parent and Teachers Rating Scales
   Mood and Feelings Questionnaire (MFQ) (Costello & Angold, 1988)
   Children's Depression Inventory (CDI) (Kovacs, 1982a)
   Revised Children's Manifest Anxiety Scale
   RCMAS (Reynolds & Paget, 1981, 1983)

(b) Screening clinical populations for particular disorders or syndromes
1 Highly structured interviews,
e.g. DISC and DICA
2 Checklists
e.g. Conners Scales
   Eyberg Behaviour Inventory (Eyberg, 1980; Eyberg & Robinson, 1983)
   Depression Self-Rating Scale (Birleson, 1981)

(c) To obtain diagnoses or diagnostic profiles in clinical populations
1 Semi-structured interviews
e.g. Child Assessment Schedule: CAS (Hodges *et al.*, 1982)
   Interview Schedule for Children: ISC (Kovacs, 1982b)
   Kiddie — SADS — Schedule for Affective Disorders and Schizophrenia (Puig-Antich and Chambers 1978)
   Child and Adolescent Psychiatric Assessment: CAPA (Angold, 1989)
2 Highly structured interviews
e.g. DICA, DISC
3 Checklists
e.g. CBCL

(d) To tap experiences and social adjustments
e.g. Revised Vineland Social Adjustment Scales
   Social Adjustment Inventory for Children and Adolescents: SAICA (John *et al.*, 1987)
   Life Events Questionnaires (Goodyer *et al.*, 1985; Goodyer 1990)

teachers or health visitors, has quite reasonable sensitivity and specificity (Edelbrock & Costello, 1988). It is sensitivity rather than specificity that is required in primary health care to ensure most problems are detected, although it is wasteful to spend clinical time evaluating false positives.

Secondly, questionnaires may be used to screen general populations for specific disorders or syndromes. The Diagnostic Interview Schedule for Children (DISC) and Diagnostic Interview for Children and Adolescents (DICA) questionnaires were designed for epidemiological use and to generate DSM-III diagnoses. In practice, agreement between clinicians and the questionnaires has not always been good (Robins, 1985; Carlson *et al.*, 1987; Weinstein *et al.*, 1989). Both tend to generate far more symptoms and diagnoses than do clinicians (Breslau, 1987; Welner *et al.*, 1987; Weinstein *et al.*, 1989). Although the rating scales or checklists listed above and those for specific disorders can also be used to screen general populations for particular types of problem, such screening is not usually appropriate in clinical practice.

Within the clinic it is not relevant to screen for the presence or absence of problems. It is the job of clinicians to assess whether the assumed presence of a problem is substantive or not and understand why referral has come about. What may be helpful is screening for specific problems and it is here that the questionnaires focused on depression, anxiety, conduct problems and hyperactivity may be useful. Although the DISC and DICA could be seen as potentially useful for this purpose, it has been indicated above that there is some doubt about whether they discriminate in clinically appropriate ways and they take longer to administer than the more focused instruments.

There have been a number of attempts to devise semistructured interviews to obtain reliable and valid diagnoses in clinical samples and these have evident utility (see Table 3.2). The main problem for clinical use of all these instruments is their length and heavy focus on symptomatology, so that much further assessment is required to develop a full formulation. However they have value in complex cases and when assessing inpatients. The best worked out approach using checklists to generate diagnoses in clinical populations is Achenbach's Child Behavior Checklist (Achenbach, 1989). This aims not only to generate empirically based diagnoses but also provides a social competence profile. This means that, like the four semistructured interviews listed in Table 3.2, it aims to do a fuller and more detailed evaluation of the child in addition to producing diagnoses. However there are significant problems in using questionnaires to generate diagnoses, particularly if they tap only one data source and do not cover the full range of child psychiatric problems (Cox, 1989b).

All the major semistructured interviews, the Kiddie-SADS, the CAS, and the ISC and the CAPA have parent and child versions. This is also true for the DICA and DISC, the highly structured interviews. In contrast, checklists or rating scales often have parent and teacher versions, this being true for Conners', Achenbach's and Rutter's scales.

Two other major purposes for which interviews or checklists

have been devised should be mentioned and these concern experiences and social adjustment.

Clinical advantages of questionnaires and checklists are firstly that they provide systematic data collection. Those with a broad base, such as the CBCL, are useful in picking up comorbidity since they can ensure that a wide range of symptoms is covered. Affective symptoms may be neglected when the referred problem is a disorder of conduct (Anderson *et al.*, 1987; Fleming & Offord, 1990; Williams *et al.*, 1990; Harrington *et al.*, 1991; Sawyer *et al.*, 1991).

Secondly, checklists can be economical because they can be filled out by subjects or parents or teachers without using clinic time. If the provisos about source of information and quality of data are kept in mind, then they can provide useful leads. Life events questionnaires and those of social adjustment can be similarly useful.

Thirdly, there is evidence that subjects and patients may report data in response to a written or computerized version of questionnaires which they would not report face to face (Carr *et al.*, 1983; Greist *et al.*, 1987; Wyndowe, 1987; Blouin *et al.*, 1988; Sawyer *et al.*, 1991).

Fourthly, self-report questionnaires can function as self-monitoring questionnaires or instruments.

Fifthly, questionnaires can be valuable in assessing change. This may be true even if use is made of one of the instruments devised for more general use, such as the CBCL. However, one of those designed to focus on the particular problems concerned can be expected to be more sensitive. The various Conners Parent and Teacher Rating Scales are known to be sensitive in this respect with regard to hyperactivity, including assessment of response to both drugs and behavioural programmes. The same is true of the Werry–Weiss–Peters Activity Rating Scale (Werry & Sprague, 1970; Routh *et al.*, 1974), which was also devised to evaluate treatment in hyperactive children. For conduct disorder, the Eyberg Child Behaviour Inventory has been found to be treatment-sensitive. It is not clear whether the parent version of the Child Depression Inventory is similarly useful (Costello & Angold, 1988).

Finally, it is important to emphasize the training value of the use of standardized interviews and questionnaires. Once people have used such instruments on a number of occasions, they begin to build into their usual clinical repertoire a more suitably broad scope of assessment and a range of approaches to doing such assessment. There can be similar value in primary health care or with staff in nurseries or children's homes. Here, questionnaires can be used to alert staff to a discriminating approach to the observation of behaviour. Individual items can be used as a basis for discussion and debate between staff about the significance of rating in a particular way.

ESTABLISHING A THERAPEUTIC RELATIONSHIP

Firstly, contact between the mental health professionals and the child and family usually occurs in a clinic so it is important to understand influences affecting attendance. Kourany *et al.* (1990) have reviewed factors associated with appointment failures and these include socioeconomic status, length of waiting time between initial contact with the clinic and the scheduled initial appointment, referral source, history of previous treatment, clinical characteristics, distance from the clinic and demographic characteristics including age, sex and race. Results have often been conflicting so that some studies have found that there is a significant association between waiting time for the initial appointment and a failure of attendance (Raynes & Warren, 1971; Wolkon, 1972) and others have not (Gould *et al.*, 1970; Lowman *et al.*, 1984). Attendance is less likely if parents are against the referral (Eminson, 1986; Cottrell *et al.*, 1988).

A study by Stern *et al.* (1990) examining patterns of attendance of Asian families at a UK child psychiatry outpatient clinic emphasized the importance of parents' perception of problems and the perceived relevance of mental health services. The authors concluded that their lower rate of attendance was due to the local Asian population's perception of unwanted behaviour in children as being due to 'badness', physical illness or the activity of spirits, so that there was no expectation that psychiatric help might be useful. Also there was a greater tolerance of a wider range of behaviour, particularly amongst preschool children, so that parents were less concerned about behaviour identified by referrers as problematic.

A wide variety of studies reviewed by Kourany *et al.* (1990) and others (Skuse, 1975; Churven, 1978; Brockless, 1990) indicate that contacts between the clinic and families prior to the first appointment promote attendance. For example, research interviews conducted prior to initial assessment in order to explore families' responses to family therapy led to better attendances in one study (Churven, 1978). It may be inferred that the research interview clarified what was to be expected. Mathai and Markantonakis (1990) who also examined this question concluded that interim contact helps to deal with resistance and misunderstandings, whatever method is used. They themselves employed both a family data questionnaire and telephone contact. Various methods have been advocated as a means of induction into different types of treatment (e.g. Bessell, 1971; Feusterheim, 1972). Little is known about their effectiveness, but there is some suggestion that preparation for psychotherapy may increase its effectiveness (Bierman, 1969; Goldstein, 1971; Heilbron, 1971). It seems desirable that clients should be given some guidance on what is expected of them in therapy.

Less is known about the value of different styles and techniques in preparing families for therapy once contact has been established. Within the initial interview four main factors have been found to be relevant to continuance in therapy: therapist activity, congruence between family expectations and therapist response, giving clients the opportunity to influence the consultation and, in family therapy, the presence of the father. Thus, contrary to some teaching, the balance of

evidence suggests that most patients prefer their therapists to be active and directive rather than passive (Lennard & Bernstein, 1960; Heller, 1968; Bierman, 1969; Matarazzo & Wiens, 1972; Shapiro & Budman, 1973). This is particularly so with unsophisticated clients (Heilbron, 1971). One study of admission interviews with psychiatric inpatients showed them to be less anxious when the interviewer used structured questioning rather than just open encouragements to talk (Dibner, 1958). Heller (1968) suggested that active directive interviewers are better liked because they give their respondents more clues on how to behave. Verbally active techniques also promote better subsequent attendance for treatment (Lennard & Bernstein, 1960; Heilbron, 1971; Shapiro & Budman, 1973).

The initiation of treatment involves some kind of agreement or contract between the therapist and patient. This needs to take account of the patient's attitudes and views of the problem as well as the clinician's evaluation. In a study of adult patients, it was found that continuance in therapy after initial interview was better when clinicians were perceived to give feedback to patients that their messages were received, and when the content of clinicians' responses was perceived as relevant to the patients' own definitions of the content appropriate to be discussed in treatment (Duehn & Proctor, 1977). In medical consultations, patients were more satisfied if they could tell their history in their own words at first, with the doctor later providing objective feedback of his or her assessment of that information (Stiles *et al.*, 1979). Where doctor and patient share opinions patients comply better with medical recommendations (Carter *et al.*, 1982). These results point to the value of congruence between what happens in the assessment and what the parents or patients expect.

Roter (1989) conducted a metaanalysis of 41 observational studies of medical interviews where there was assessment of outcome variables: heightened patient satisfaction, recall of information given by the doctor and compliance. In combination with a review of relevant literature, she concluded that information-giving by the physician to the patient was most strongly related to patient compliance and satisfaction. There was a weaker relationship between doctors' socioemotional responses such as partnership building and positive talk, although these were related to satisfaction. She suggested that doctor information-giving can be viewed as enhancing patient power and increasing their ability to participate actively in the therapeutic process, while question-asking by the physician, although important for problem-solving from the point of view of the doctor, may have little value to the patient (Waitzkin, 1985). A previous study (Roter *et al.*, 1987) found a positive association between patient satisfaction and the opportunity to ask questions. These findings from general medicine emphasize that, while data from psychotherapists suggest that active therapists may better sustain therapeutic relationships, those who give parents and children opportunities to influence the data-gathering process and the future therapeutic interaction may also sustain involvement.

Several studies conclude that there is a higher chance of the family continuing in treatment where the father has come to the initial session (Heubeck *et al.*, 1986).

In a study in a child psychiatry setting, Kazdin (1990) found that children of families who terminated treatment early evinced a greater number of symptoms of conduct disorder or delinquent behaviour and lower educational/occupational status and level of income. They also showed greater stress from parent—child interactions, parent role functioning and life events. Mothers who terminated treatment found their children less able to adjust to changes in their environment, less acceptable and attractive and more unhappy and depressed. The mothers reported greater dissatisfaction with themselves and less emotional closeness to their children. The majority of children in this study had conduct or oppositional disorders. Kazdin pointed out that there are several inter-related steps that can be identified in the referral and treatment process, including never seeking treatment and, among those referred, seeking treatment but not arriving for evaluation, and receiving an initial evaluation but not beginning treatment, starting treatment and terminating it early, middle or late, and completing treatment. He pointed out that there is still much to be learned in this area.

The early therapeutic studies of Truax and Carkhuff (1967) with adults suggested that warmth, empathy and understanding facilitated therapy and, presumably for this reason, might be valuable too in the diagnostic interview. However, the results of more recent studies have been less clear-cut (Mitchell *et al.*, 1977), with particular uncertainty regarding their application to work with children (Kolvin *et al.*, 1981).

REFERENCES

Achenbach T.M. (1989) Internalising disorders. Subtyping based on parental questionnaires. In: Schmidt M. & Remschmidt H. (eds) *Needs and Prospects of Child and Adolescent Psychiatry*, pp. 83—92.

Achenbach T.M. & Edelbrock C.S. (1981) Behavioral problems and competencies reported by parents of normal and disturbed children aged four through sixteen. *Monographs of the Society for Research in Child Development*, **46**, 1.

Achenbach T.M. & Edelbrock C.S. (1983) *Manual for the Child Behavior Checklist and Revised Child Behavior Profile*. University of Vermont, Dept of Psychiatry, Burlington.

Achenbach T.M., Bird H.R., Canino G., Phares V., Gould M.S. & Rubio-Stipec M. (1989) Epidemiological comparisons of Puerto Ricans and US mainland children: parent, teacher and self-reports. *Journal of the American Academy of Child and Adolescent Psychiatry*, **29**, 84—93.

Adams H.E., Butler J. & Noblin C.D. (1962a) Effects of psychoanalytically derived interpretations: a verbal conditioning paradigm. *Psychological Reports*, **10**, 691—694.

Adams H.E., Noblin C.D., Butler J.R. & Timmons E.O. (1962b) The differential effect of psychoanalytically derived interpretations and verbal conditioning in schizophrenics. *Psychological Reports*, **11**, 195—198.

Alpert M., Kurtzberg R.L. & Friedhoff A.J. (1963) Transient voice changes associated with emotional stimuli. *Archives of General Psychiatry*, **8**, 362—365.

Anderson S.C. (1968) Effects of confrontation by high-and-low functioning therapists. *Journal of Counseling Psychology*, **15**, 411—416.

Anderson J.C., Williams S., McGee R. & Silva P.A. (1987) DSM-III disorders in a large sample of pre-adolescent children: prevalence in a large sample from the general population. *Archives of General Psychiatry*, **44**, 69—76.

Angold A. (1989) Structured assessments of psychopathology in children and adolescents. In: Thompson C. (ed) *The Instruments of Psychiatric Research*, pp. 271—304. Wiley, Chichester.

Argyle M. (1969) *Social Interaction*. Methuen, London.

Balint M. & Balint E. (1961) *Psychotherapeutic Techniques in Medicine*. Tavistock Publications, London.

Barkley R.A. (1988) Child Behavior rating scales and checklists. In: Rutter M., Tuma A.H. & Lann I.S. (eds) *Assessment and Diagnosis in Child Psychopathology*, pp. 113—155. Fulton, London.

Becker W.C. (1960) The relationships of factors in parental ratings of self and each other to the behavior of kindergarten children as rated by mothers, fathers, and teacher. *Journal of Consulting Psychology*, **24**, 507—527.

Berg I., Lucas C. & McGuire R. (1992) Measurement of behaviour difficulties in children using standard scales administered to mothers by computer: reliability and validity. *European Child and Adolescent Psychiatry*, **1**, 14—23.

Bessell R. (1971) *Interviewing and Counselling*. Batsford, London.

Bierman R. (1969) Dimensions of interpersonal facilitation in psychotherapy and child development. *Psychological Bulletin*, **72**, 338—352.

Bingham M.V. & Moore B.V. (1924) *How to Interview*. Harper, New York.

Birleson P. (1981) The validity of depressive disorder in childhood and the development of a self-rating scale: a research report. *Journal of Child Psychology and Psychiatry*, **22**, 73—88.

Blouin A.G., Perez E.L. & Blouin J.H. (1988). Computerized administration of the Diagnostic Interview Schedule. *Psychiatry Research*, **23**, 335—344.

Boucher M.L. (1972) Effect of seating distance on interpersonal attraction in an interview situation. *Journal of Consulting and Clinical Psychology*, **38**, 15—19.

Brandt R.M. (1972) *Studying Behaviour in Natural Settings*. Holt Rinehart & Winston, New York.

Breed G. (1972) The effect of intimacy: reciprocity or retreat? *British Journal of Social and Clinical Psychology*, **11**, 135—142.

Breslau N. (1987) Inquiring about the bizarre: false positives in Diagnostic Interview Schedule for Children (DISC) ascertainment of obsessions, compulsions and psychotic symptoms. *Journal of the American Academy of Child and Adolescent Psychiatry*, **26**, 639—644.

Brockless J. (1990) The effects of telephone contact/prompting on subsequent attendance at initial appointments at a hospital department of child and adolescent psychiatry. *Newsletter of the Association for Child Psychology and Psychiatry*, **12**, 5—8.

Brown B.M. (1972) The multiple techniques of broad spectrum psychotherapy. In: Lazarus A.A. (ed) *Clinical Behaviour Therapy*, pp. 174—226. Brunner/Mazel, New York.

Brown G.W. & Rutter M. (1966) The measurement of family activities and relationships; a methodological study. *Human Relations*, **19**, 241—263.

Burtt H.E. & Gaskill H.V. (1932) Suggestibility and the form of the question. *Journal of Applied Psychology*, **16**, 358—373.

Butler N., Campion P. & Cox A. (1992) Exploration of doctor and patient agendas in general practice consultations I. *Methods, Social Science and Medicine*, **35**, 1145—1155.

Cahalan D., Tamulonis V. & Verner H. (1947) Interviewer bias involved in certain types of opinion survey questions. *International Journal of Opinion and Attitude Research*, **1**, 63—77.

Cairns R.B. & Green J.A. (1979) How to assess personality and social patterns: observations or ratings? In: Cairns R.B. (ed) *The Analysis of Social Interactions*, pp. 209—226. Erlbaum, Hillsdale, NJ.

Campion P.D., Butler N.M. & Cox A.D. (1992) Principle agendas of doctors and patients in general practice consultations. *Family Practice*, **9**, 181–190.

Cannell C.F. (1977) A summary of studies of interviewing methodology. *Vital and Health Statistics*, **69**, 1–78.

Cannell C.F. & Axelrod M. (1956) The respondent reports on the interview. *American Journal of Sociology*, **62**, 177–181.

Cannell C.F. & Kahn R.L. (1968) Interviewing. In: Lindzey G. & Aronson F. (eds) *Handbook of Social Psychology*, vol. 2, 2nd edn, pp. 526–595. Addison-Wesley, Cambridge, MA.

Cannell C.F., Fisher G. & Bakker T. (1961) Reporting of hospitalization in the health interview survey. Health Statistics, series D, no. 4 (reprinted in *Vital and Health Statistics*, 1965, series 2, no. 6). US Dept of Health, Education & Welfare, Public Health Service, Washington.

Carlson G.A., Kashani J.H., Thomas M. de F., Vaidya A. & Daniel A.E. (1987) Comparisons of two structured interviews on a psychiatrically hospitalized population of children. *Journal of the American Academy of Child and Adolescent Psychiatry*, **26**, 645–648.

Carr A.C., Ghosh A. & Ancill R.J. (1983) Can a computer take a psychiatric history? *Psychological Medicine*, **13**, 151–158.

Carter W.B., Inui T.S., Kukull W. & Haigh V. (1982) Outcome-based doctor–patient interaction analysis: II. Identifying effective provider and patient behaviour. *Medical Care*, **20**, 550–566.

Chapple E.D. (1953) The standard experimental (stress) interview as used in interaction chronograph investigations. *Human Organization*, **12**, 23–32.

Chess S., Thomas A. & Birch H.G. (1966) Distortions in developmental reporting made by parents of behaviorally disturbed children. *Journal of the American Academy of Child Psychiatry*, **5**, 226–234.

Churven P.G. (1978) Parental attitudes to family assessment in a child psychiatry setting. *Journal of Child Psychology and Psychiatry*, **19**, 33–41.

Conners C.K. (1969) A teacher rating scale for use in drug studies with children. *American Journal of Psychiatry*, **126**, 884–888.

Conners C.K. (1973) Rating scales for use in drug studies with children. *Psychopharmacology Bulletin* Special Issue, 24–84.

Cook M. (1970) Experiments on orientation and proxemics. *Human Relations*, **23**, 66–76.

Costello E.J. & Angold A. (1988) Scales to assess child and adolescent depression: checklists, screens and nets. *Journal of the American Academy of Child and Adolescent Psychiatry*, **27**, 726–737.

Costello A.J., Edelbrock C., Kalas R., Kessler M.D. & Klaric S.N. (1982) The NIMH Diagnostic Interview Schedule for Children (DISC) Unpublished interview schedule Department of Psychiatry, University of Pittsburg.

Costello A.J., Edelbrock C., Dulcan M.K., Kalas R. & Klaric S.H. (1984) *Development and Testing of the NIMH Diagnostic Interview Schedule for Children in a Clinic Population*. Final report (contract no. RFP-DB-81-0027). Center for Epidemiological Studies, National Institute for Mental Health, Rockville, MD.

Cottrell D., Hill P., Walk D., Dearnaly J. & Ierotheou A. (1988) Factors influencing non-attendance at child psychiatry outpatient appointments. *British Journal of Psychiatry*, **152**, 201–204.

Couch A. & Kemiston K. (1960) Yeasayers and naysayers. *Journal of Abnormal Social Psychology*, **60**, 151–174.

Cox A. (1989a) Eliciting patients' feelings. In: Stewart M. & Roter D. (eds) *Communicating with Medical Patients*, pp. 99–106. Sage, London.

Cox A.D. (1989b) Classification in child psychiatry: a critique of approaches based on parental questionnaires. In: Schmidt M. & Remschmidt H. (eds) *Needs and Prospects of Child and Adolescent Psychiatry*, pp. 93–97. Hogrefe & Huber, Toronto.

Cox A. & Rutter M. (1985) Diagnostic appraisal and interviewing. In: Rutter M. & Hersov L. (eds) *Child and Adolescent Psychiatry: Modern Approaches*, (2nd ed) pp. 233–248. Blackwell Scientific Publications, Oxford.

Cox A., Hopkinson K.F. & Rutter M. (1981a) Psychiatric interview techniques. II. Naturalistic study: eliciting factual information. *British Journal of Psychiatry*, **138**, 283–291.

Cox A., Rutter M. & Holbrook D. (1981b) Psychiatric interviewing techniques. V. Experimental study: eliciting factual information. *British Journal of Psychiatry*, **139**, 29–37.

Cox A., Holbrook D. & Rutter M. (1981c) Psychiatric interviewing techniques. VI. Experimental study: eliciting feelings. *British Journal of Psychiatry*, **139**, 144–152.

Cox A., Rutter M. & Holbrook D. (1988) Psychiatric interviewing techniques: a second experimental study: eliciting feelings. *British Journal of Psychiatry*, **152**, 64–72.

Deutsch F. (1939) The associative anamnesis. *Psychoanalytic Quarterly*, **8**, 354–381.

Dibner A.A. (1958) Ambiguity and anxiety. *Journal of Abnormal Social Psychology*, **56**, 165–174.

Dinges N.G. & Oetting E.R. (1972) Interaction distance and anxiety in the counselling dyad. *Journal of Counseling Psychology*, **19**, 146–149.

Dohrenwend B.S. & Richardson S.A. (1964) A use for leading questions in research interviewing. *Human Organization*, **23**, 76–77.

Douglas J.W.B., Lawson A., Cooper J.E. & Cooper E. (1968) Family interaction and the activities of young children. *Journal of Child Psychology and Psychiatry*, **9**, 157–171.

Duehn W.D. & Proctor E.K. (1977) Initial clinical interaction and premature discontinuance in treatment. *American Journal of Orthopsychiatry*, **47**, 284–290.

Edelbrock C. & Costello A. (1988) Structured psychiatric interviews for children. In: Rutter M., Tuma A.H. & Lann I.S. (eds) *Assessment and Diagnosis in Child Psychopathology*, pp. 87–112. Fulton, London.

Ekman P., Friesen W.V. & Ellsworth P. (1972) *Emotion in the Human Face: Guidelines for Research and an Integration of Findings*. Pergamon, New York.

Eminson M. (1986) Clinic refusers — a brief study of non-attendance at an out-patient clinic for adolescents. *Newsletter of the Association of Child Psychology and Psychiatry*, **8**, 23–26.

Eminson M. (1988) A comparison of data obtained from initial individual and family interviews with adolescents and their parents. Paper presented to Annual Residential Conference of the Child & Adolescent Psychiatry Section of the Royal College of Psychiatrists, Sheffield, September 1988.

English R.W. & Jelenevsky S. (1971) Counsellor behavior as judged under audio, visual and audiovisual communication conditions. *Journal of Counseling Psychology*, **18**, 509–513.

Eyberg S. (1980) Eyberg child behavior inventory. *Journal of Clinical Child Psychology*, **9**, 22–28.

Eyberg S. & Robinson E.A. (1983) Conduct problem behavior: standardisations of a behaviour rating scale with adolescents. *Journal of Clinical Child Psychology*, **12**, 347–354.

Feusterheim H. (1972) The initial interview. In: Lazarus A.A. (ed) *Clinical Behaviour Therapy*, pp. 22–40. Butterworths, London.

Flanders J.P. (1968) A review of research on imitative behaviour. *Psychological Bulletin*, **69**, 316–337.

Fleming J.E. & Offord D. (1990) Epidemiology of childhood depressive disorders: critical review. *Journal of the American Academy of Child and Adolescent Psychiatry*, **29**, 571–580.

Frankel R. & Beckman A. (1989) Evaluating the patient's primary problem(s). In: Stewart M. & Roter D. (eds) *Communicating with Medical Patients*, pp. 86–98, Sage, London.

Gask L., Boardman J. & Standart S. (1991) Teaching communication skills: a problem-based approach. *Postgraduate Education for General Practice*, **2**, 7–15.

Gelder M.G. (1968) Verbal conditioning, as a measure of interpersonal influence in psychiatric interviews. *British Journal of Social and Clinical Psychology*, **7**, 194–209.

Gill M., Newman R. & Redlich F.C. (1954) *The Initial Interview in Psychiatric Practice*. International Universities Press, New York.

Goddard K.E., Broder A. & Wenar C. (1961) Reliability of pediatric histories: a preliminary report. *Pediatrics*, **28**, 1011–1018.

Goldberg D. & Huxley P. (1980) *Mental Illness in the Community: The Pathway to Psychiatric Care*. Tavistock Publications, London.

Goldstein A.P. (1971) *Psychotherapeutic Attraction*. Pergamon, Oxford.

Goodyer J. (1990) Annotation: recent life events and psychiatric disorder in school age children. *Journal of Child Psychology and Psychiatry*, **31**, 839–848.

Goodyer I.M., Kolvin I. & Gatzanis S. (1985) Recent undesirable life events and psychiatric disorder in childhood and adolescence. *British Journal of Psychiatry*, **147**, 517–523.

Gould R.L., Paulson L. & Daniel-Epps L. (1970) Patients who flirt with treatment: the silent population. *American Journal of Clinical Psychiatry*, **39**, 494–497.

Goyette C.H., Conners C.K. & Ulrich R.F. (1978) Normative data on revised Conners parent and teacher rating scales. *Journal of Abnormal Child Psychology*, **6**, 221–236.

Graham P. & Rutter M. (1968) The reliability and validity of the psychiatric assessment of the child. II: Interview with the parent. *British Journal of Psychiatry*, **114**, 581–592.

Greist J.H., Klein M.H., Erdman H.P., Bires J.K., Bass S.M., Machtinger M.S.W. & Kresge D.G. (1987) Comparison of computer- and interview-administered versions of the Diagnostic Interview Schedule. *Hospital and Community Psychiatry*, **38**, 1304–1311.

Grusec J. & Kuejymski L. (1980) Direction of effective socialization: a comparison of parent's versus child's behaviour as determinants of disciplinary techniques. *Developmental Psychology*, **16**, 1–9.

Guest L. (1947) A study of interviewer competence. *International Journal of Opinion and Attitude Research*, **1**, 1730.

Gutterman E.M., O'Brien J.D. & Young J.G. (1987) Structured diagnostic interviews for children and adolescents: current status and future directions. *Journal of the American Academy of Child and Adolescent Psychiatry*, **26**, 621–630.

Haines G.J., Jensen B.J., Wise E. & Sherman D. (1981) The marital intake interview: a multimethod criterion validity assessment. *Journal of Consulting and Clinical Psychology*, **49**, 379–387.

Harrington R., Fudge H., Rutter M., Pickles A. & Hill J. (1991) Adult outcomes of childhood and adolescent depression: II links with antisocial disorders. *Journal of the American Academy of Child and Adolescent Psychiatry*, **30**, 434–439.

Hart H., Bax M. & Jenkins S. (1978) The value of developmental history. *Developmental Medicine and Child Neurology*, **20**, 442–452.

Heilbron A.B. (1971) Female preference for therapist initial interview style as a function of 'client' and therapist social role variables. *Journal of Counseling Psychology*, **18**, 285–291.

Heller K. (1968) Ambiguity in the interview interaction. In: Shlien J.M. (ed) *Research in Psychotherapy*, vol. III, pp. 242–259. American Psychological Association, Washington DC.

Heller K., David J.D. & Myers R.A. (1966) The effect of interviewer style in a standardised interview. *Journal of Consulting Psychology*, **30**, 501–508.

Herjanic B. & Reich W. (1982) Development of a structured psychiatric interview for children: agreement between child and parent on individual symptoms. *Journal of Abnormal Child Psychology*, **10**, 307–324.

Heubeck B., Watson J. & Russell G. (1986) Father involvement and family therapy. In: Lamb M.E. (ed) *The Father's Role: Applied Perspectives*. Wiley, New York.

Hodges K., Kline J., Stern L., Cytryn L. & McKnew D. (1982) The development of a child assessment interview for research and clinical use. *Journal of Abnormal Child Psychology*, **10**, 173–189.

Hoffman M.L. (1957) An interview method for obtaining descriptions of parent–child interaction. *Merrill-Palmer Quarterly*, **4**, 76–83.

Hoffman M. (1960) Power assertion by the parent and its impact on the child. *Child Development*, **31**, 129–143.

Hopkinson K.F., Cox A. & Rutter M. (1981) Psychiatric interviewing techniques. III: Naturalistic study: eliciting feelings. *British Journal of Psychiatry*, **138**, 406–415.

Hyman H.H., Cobb W.J., Feldman J.J., Hart C.W. & Steinber C.H. (1954) *Interviewing in Social Research*. University of Chicago Press, Chicago.

Iwata B.A., Wong S.E., Riordan M.M., Dorsey M.F. & Lau M.M. (1982) Assessment and training of clinical interviewing skills: analogue analysis and field replication. *Journal of Applied Behavior Analysis*, **15**, 191–203.

Janis I.L. (1958) *Psychological Stress*. Wiley, New York.

John K., Gammon D., Prusoff B.A. & Warner V. (1987) The Social Adjustment Inventory for Children and Adolescents (SAICA): testing of a new semi-structured interview. *Journal of the American Academy of Child and Adolescent Psychiatry*, **26**, 898–916.

Kanfer F.H., Philips J.S., Matarazzo J.D. & Saslow G. (1960) Experimental modification of interviewer content in standardized interviews. *Journal of Consulting Psychology*, **24**, 528–536.

Kazdin A.E. (1990) Premature termination from treatment among children referred for antisocial behaviour. *Journal of Child Psychology and Psychiatry*, **31**, 415–425.

Kenkel W.F. (1957) Influence differentiation in family decision-making. *Sociology and Society Research*, **42**, 18–25.

Kenkel W.F. & Hoffman D.K. (1956) Real and conceived roles in family decision-making. *Marriage and Family Living*, **18**, 311–316.

Kinston W. & Loader P. (1988) The family task interview; a tool for clinical research in family interaction. *Journal of Marital and Family Therapy*, **14**, 67–87.

Kinston W., Loader P. & Stratford J. (1979) Clinical assessment of family interactions: a reliability study. *Journal of Family Therapy*, **1**, 291–312.

Kinston W., Loader P. & Miller L. (1987) Quantifying the clinical assessment of family health. *Journal of Marital and Family Therapy* **13**, 49–67.

Kolvin E., Garside R.F., Nichol A.R., Macmillan A., Wolstenholme F. & Leitch I.M. (1981) *Help Starts Here: The Maladjusted Child in the Ordinary School*. Tavistock Publications, London.

Kourany R.F.C., Garber J. & Tornusciolo G. (1990) Improving first appointment attendance rates in child psychiatry outpatient clinics. *Journal of the American Academy of Child and Adolescent Psychiatry*, **29**, 657–660.

Kovacs M. (1982a) The Children's Depression Inventory. Unpublished manuscript, University of Pittsburgh.

Kovacs M. (1982b) The interview Schedule for Children (ISC). Unpublished interview schedule, Dept. of Psychiatry, University of Pittsburgh.

Kovacs M. (1986) A developmental perspective on methods and measures in the assessment of depressive disorders: the clinical interview. In: Rutter M., Izard C.E. & Read P.B. (eds) *Depression in Young People: Developmental and Clinical Perspectives*, pp. 435–465. Guilford, New York.

Kramer E. (1963) Judgement of personal characteristics and emotions from non-verbal properties of speech. *Psychological Bulletin*, **60**, 408–420.

Krasner L. (1958) Studies of the conditioning of verbal behaviour. *Psychological Bulletin*, **55**, 148–170.

Lennard H.L. & Bernstein A. (1960) *The Anatomy of Psychotherapy*. Columbia University Press, New York.

Lesser A.L. (1985) Problem-based interviewing in general practice: a model. *Medical Education*, **19**, 299–304.

Lisansky E.T. (1969) History-taking and interviewing. *Modern Treatment*, 656–687.

Lishman W.A. (1974) The speed of recall of pleasant and unpleasant experiences. *Psychological Medicine*, **4**, 212–218.

Litwak E. (1956) A classification of biased questions. *American Journal of Sociology*, **62**, 182–186.

Lowman R.L., DeLange W.H., Roberts T.K. & Brady C.P. (1984) Users and teasers: failure to follow through with initial mental health services inquiries in a child and family treatment centre. *Journal of Comparative Psychology*, **12**, 253–261.

McConaughy S.M., Achenbach T.M. & Gent C.L. (1988) Multiaxial empirically based assessment: parent, teacher, observational, cognitive, and personality correlates of child behaviour profile types for 6–11 year old boys. *Journal of Abnormal Child Psychology*, **16**, 485–509.

McGinnies E. (1970) *Social Behaviour: A Functional Analysis*. Houghton Mifflin, Boston, MA.

Maccoby E.E. & Martin J.A. (1983) Socialization in the context of the family: parent–child interaction. In: Hetherington E.M. (ed) *Socialization, Personality, and Social Development*, vol. 4, *Mussen's Handbook of Child Psychology*, 4th edn, pp. 1–101. Wiley, New York.

Maguire G.P. & Rutter D.R. (1976) History-taking for medical students: I. Deficiencies in performance. *Lancet*, **ii**, 556–558.

Maguire P., Fairburn S. & Fletcher C. (1989) Consultation skills of young doctors — benefits of undergraduate feedback training in interviewing. In: Stewart M. & Roter D. (eds) *Communicating with Medical Patients*, pp. 124–137, Sage, London.

Marlatt G.A. (1972) Task, structure and experimental modification of verbal behaviour. *Psychological Bulletin*, **78**, 335–350.

Marquis K.H., Marshall J. & Oskamp S. (1972a) Testimony validity as a function of question form, atmosphere, and item difficulty. *Journal of Applied Social Psychology*, **2**, 167–186.

Marquis K.H., Cannell C.F. & Laurent A. (1972b) Reporting health events in household interviews: effects of reinforcement, question length and reinterviewers. *Vital and Health Statistics*, series 2, no. 45. US Dept of Health, Education & Welfare, Rockville, Md.

Matarazzo J. & Wiens A.N. (1972) *The Interview: Research on its Anatomy and Structure*. Aldine, Chicago.

Mathai J. & Markantonakis A. (1990) Improving initial attendance to a child and family psychiatric clinic. *Psychological Bulletin of the Royal College of Psychiatry*, **14**, 151–152.

Mehrabian A. (1971) Non-verbal communication. In: Cole J.K. (ed) *Nebraska Symposium on Motivation*, vol. 19, pp. 107–161. University of Nebraska Press, Lincoln, Nebraska.

Menninger K.A. (1962) *A Manual for Psychiatric Case Study*. Grune & Stratton, New York.

Miller S.M. (1952) The participant observer and 'over-rapport'. *American Sociological Review*, **17**, 97–99.

Mitchell K.M., Bozarth J.D. & Krouft C.C. (1977) A reappraisal of the therapeutic effectiveness of accurate empathy, non-possessive warmth and genuineness. In: Gurman A.S. & Razin A.M. (eds) *Effective Psychotherapy: A Handbook of Research*, pp. 482–502. Pergamon, Oxford.

Noblin C.D., Timmons E.O. & Reynard M.C. (1963) Psychoanalytic interpretations as verbal reinforcers: importance of interpretation content. *Journal of Clinical Psychology*, **19**, 479–481.

Nurcombe B. & Gallagher R.M. (1986) *The Clinical Process in Psychiatry*. Cambridge University Press, Cambridge.

Patterson M. (1968) Spatial factors in social interaction. *Human Relations*, **21**, 351–361.

Pope B. & Siegman A.W. (1965) Interviewer specificity and topical focus in relation to interviewer productivity. *Journal of Verbal Learning and Verbal Behaviour*, **4**, 188–192.

Puig-Antich J. & Chambers W. (1978) The Schedule for Affective Disorders and Schizophrenia for school aged children. Unpublished interview schedule, New York State Psychiatric Institute.

Quay H.C. (1977) Measuring dimensions of deviant behavior: the behavior problem checklist. *Journal of Abnormal Child Psychology*, **5**, 277–289.

Quay H.C. & Peterson D.R. (1983) Interim manual for the Revised Behavior Problem Checklist. Unpublished manuscript. University of Miami.

Quay H.C. & Peterson D.R. (1984) Appendix 1 to the Interim manual for the Revised Behavior Problem Checklist. Unpublished manuscript, University of Miami.

Quinton D. (1988) Longitudinal approaches to intergenerational studies: definition, design and use. In: Rutter M. (ed) *Studies of Psychosocial Risk: the Power of Longitudinal Data*, pp. 272–284. Cambridge University Press, Cambridge.

Quinton D. & Rutter M. (1985) Parenting behaviour of mothers raised 'in care'. In: Nicol A.R. (ed) *Longitudinal Studies in Child Psychology and Psychiatry: Practical Lessons from Research Experience*, pp. 157–201. Wiley, Chichester.

Quinton D., Rutter M. & Rowlands O. (1976) An evaluation of an interview assessment of marriage. *Psychological Medicine*, **6**, 577–586.

Raynes A.E. & Warren G. (1971) Some characteristics of 'dropouts' at first contact with a psychiatric clinic. *Community Mental Health Journal*, **7**, 144–150.

Reece M.M. & Whitman R.N. (1961) Warmth and expressive movements. *Psychological Reports*, **8**, 76.

Reich W. & Earls F. (1987) Rules for making psychiatric diagnoses in children on the basis of multiple sources of information; preliminary strategies. *Journal of Abnormal Child Psychology*, **15**, 601–616.

Reynolds C.R. & Paget K.D. (1981) Factor analysis of the Revised Children's Manifest Anxiety Scale for whites, blacks, males and females with a national normative sample. *Journal of Clinical Consulting Psychology*, **49**, 352–359.

Reynolds L.R. & Paget K.D. (1983) National normative and reliability data for the Revised Children's Manifest Anxiety Scale. *School Psychological Review*, **12**, 324–336.

Richardson S.A., Dohrenwend B. & Klein D. (1965) *Interviewing*. Basic Books, New York.

Richman N. & Graham P. (1971) A behavioural screening questionnaire for use with three-year old children: preliminary findings. *Journal of Child Psychology and Psychiatry*, **12**, 5–33.

Richman M., Stevenson J. & Graham P. (1982) Pre-school to school: a behavioural study. Academic Press, London.

Robins L. (1963) The accuracy of parental recall of aspects of child development and child-rearing practice. *Journal of Abnormal Social Psychology*, **66**, 261–270.

Robins L.N. (1985) Epidemiology: reflections on testing the validity of psychiatric interviews. *Archives of General psychiatry*, **42**, 918–924.

Robins L.N. (1988) Data gathering and data analysis for prospective and retrospective studies. In: Rutter M. (ed) *Studies of Psychosocial Risk: The Power of Longitudinal Data*, pp. 315–324. Cambridge University Press, Cambridge.

Robins L.N. (1989) Diagnostic grammar and assessment: translating criteria into questions. *Psychological Medicine*, **19**, 57–68.

Robins L.N., Schoenberg S.P., Holmes S.J., Ratcliff K.S., Benham A. & Works J. (1985) Early home environment and retrospective recall: a test of concordance between siblings with and without psychiatric disorders. *American Journal of Orthopsychiatry*, **55**, 27–41.

Roter D. (1989) Which facets of communication have strong effects on outcome — a meta-analysis. In: Stewart M. & Roter D. (eds) *Communicating with Medical Patients*, pp. 183–196. Sage, London.

Roter D.L., Hall J.A. & Katz N.R. (1987) Relations between physicians' behaviour and analogue patients' satisfaction, recall, and impressions. *Medical Care*, **25**, 135–154.

Routh D.K., Schroeder L.S. & O'Tuama L. (1974) The development of activity level in children. *Developmental Psychology*, **10**, 163–168.

Rutter D.R. & Maguire G.P. (1976) History-taking for medical students: II. Evaluation of a training programme. *Lancet*, **ii**, 538–560.

Rutter M. (1967) A children's behaviour questionnaire for completion by teachers: preliminary findings. *Journal of Child Psychology and Psychiatry*, **8**, 1–11.

Rutter M. (1989) Pathways from childhood to adult life. *Journal of Child Psychology and Psychiatry*, **30**, 23–51.

Rutter M. & Brown G.W. (1966) The reliability and validity of measures of family life and relationships in families containing a psychiatric patient. *Social Psychiatry*, **1**, 38–53.

Rutter M. & Cox A. (1981) Psychiatric interviewing techniques: I. Methods and measures. *British Journal of Psychiatry*, **138**, 273–282.

Rutter M. & Tuma A.H. (1988) Diagnosis and classification: some outstanding issues. In: Rutter M., Tuma A.H. & Lann I.S. (eds) *Assessment and Diagnosis in Child Psychopathology*, pp. 437–452. Fulton, London.

Rutter M., Cox A., Tupling C., Berger M. & Yule W. (1975) Attainment and adjustment in two geographical areas. I. The prevalence of psychiatric disorder. *British Journal of Psychiatry*, **126**, 493–509.

Rutter M., Cox A., Egert S., Holbrook D. & Everitt B. (1981) Psychiatric interviewing techniques V: Experimental study: eliciting information. *British Journal of Psychiatry*, **139**, 29–37.

Rutter M., Tizard J. & Whitmore K. (eds) (1970) *Education, Health and Behaviour*. Longmans, London (Reprinted, 1981, Krieger, Melbourne, Fl.).

Saghir M.T. (1971) A comparison of some aspects of structured and unstructured psychiatric interviews. *American Journal of Psychiatry*, **128**, 180–184.

Savage R. & Armstrong D. (1990) Effect of a general practitioner's consulting style on patients' satisfaction: controlled study. *British Medical Journal*, **301**, 968–970.

Sawyer M.G., Sarris A. & Baghurst P. (1991) The use of a computer assisted interview to administer the Child Behaviour Checklist in a child psychiatry service. *Journal of the American Academy of Child and Adolescent Psychiatry*, **30**, 674–681.

Shapiro D.A. (1969) Empathy warmth and genuineness in psychotherapy. *British Journal of Social and Clinical Psychology*, **8**, 350–361.

Shapiro J.G. (1968) Relationship between visual and auditory cues of therapeutic effectiveness. *Journal of Clinical Psychology*, **24**, 236–239.

Shapiro R.J. & Budman S.H. (1973) Defection, termination and continuation in family and individual therapy. *Family Process*, **12**, 55–67.

Shapiro S. & Eberhart J. (1947) Interviewer differences in an intensive interview survey. *International Journal of Opinion and Attitude Research*, **1**, 1–17.

Shea S.C. & Mezzich J.E. (1988) Contemporary psychiatric interviewing. *Psychiatry*, **51**, 385–397.

Skuse D.H. (1975) Attitudes to the psychiatric outpatient clinic. *British Medical Journal*, **iii**, 469–471.

Spitzer R.L., Fleiss J.L., Burdock E.I. & Hardesty A.A. (1964) The mental status schedule; rationale, reliability and validity. *Comprehensive Psychiatry*, **5**, 384–395.

Spitzer R.L., Endicott J., Fleiss J.L. & Cohen J. (1970) The psychiatric status schedule. *Archives of General Psychiatry*, **23**, 41–55.

Starkweather J.A. (1956) Content-free speech as a source of information about the speaker. *Journal of Abnormal Social Psychology*, **52**, 394–402.

Steele G.P., Henderson S. & Duncan-Jones P. (1980) The reliability of reporting adverse experiences. *Psychological Medicine*, **10**, 301–306.

Stern G., Cottrell D. & Holmes J. (1990) Patterns of attendance of child psychiatry out-patients with specific reference to Asian families. *British Journal of Psychiatry*, **156**, 384–387.

Stewart M. (1984) What is a successful doctor–patient interview? A study of interactions and outcomes. *Social Science and Medicine*, **19**, 167–175.

Stiles W.B., Puttman S.M., Wolf M.H. & Sherman A.J. (1979) Interaction exchange structure and patient satisfaction with medical interviews. *Medical Care*, **17**, 667–681.

Strong S.R., Taylor R.G., Bratton J.C. & Loper R.G. (1971) Non-verbal behaviour and perceived counsellor characteristics. *Journal of Counselling and Psychology*, **18**, 554–567.

Truax C.B. (1966) Reinforcement and non-reinforcement in Rogerian psychotherapy. *Journal of Abnormal Psychology*, **71**, 1–9.

Truax C.B. (1968) Therapist interpersonal reinforcement of client-self-exploration and therapeutic outcome in group psychotherapy. *Journal of Counseling Psychology*, **15**, 225–231.

Truax C.B. & Carkhuff R.R. (1967) *Towards Effective Counselling and Psychotherapy: Training and Practice*. Aldine, Chicago.

Ulrich L. & Trumbo D. (1965) The selection interview since 1949. *Psychological Bulletin*, **63**, 100–116.

Vaughn C. & Leff J. (1976) The measurement of expressed emotion in families of psychiatric patients. *British Journal of Social and Clinical Psychology*, **15**, 157–165.

Vontress C.E. (1971) Racial differences: impediments to rapport. *Journal of Counseling Psychology*, **18**, 7–13.

Waitzkin H. (1985) Information giving in medical care. *Journal of Health and Social Behaviour*, **26**, 81–101.

Weinstein S.R., Stone K., Noam G.G., Grimes K. & Schwab-Stone M. (1989) Comparison of DISC with clinicians' DSM-III diagnoses in psychiatric inpatients. *Journal of the American Academy of Child and Adolescent Psychiatry*, **28**, 53–60.

Welner Z., Reich W., Herjanic B., Jung K.G. & Amado H. (1987) Reliability, validity and parent–child agreement studies of the Diagnostic Interview for Children & Adolescents (DICA). *Journal of the American Academy of Child and Adolescent Psychiatry*, **26**, 649–653.

Werry J.S. & Sprague R.L. (1970) Hyperactivity. In: Costello C.G. (ed) *Symptoms of Psychopathology*, pp. 397–417. Wiley: New York.

White A.G. (1953) The patient sits down: a clinical note. *Psychosomatic Medicine*, **15**, 256–257.

Williams S., Anderson J., McGee R. & Silva P.A. (1990) Risk factors for behavioral and emotional disorder in pre-adolescent children. *Journal of the American Academy of Child Psychiatry*, **29**, 413–419.

Wing J.K., Birley J.L.T., Cooper J.E., Graham P. & Isaacs A.D. (1967) Reliability of a procedure for measuring and classifying 'present psychiatric state'. *British Journal of Psychiatry*, **113**, 499–515.

Wolkind S.N. & Coleman E.Z. (1983) Adult psychiatric disorder and childhood experiences: the validity of retrospective data. *British Journal of Psychiatry*, **143**, 188–191.

Wolkon G.H. (1972) Crisis theory, the application for treatment and dependancy. *Comprehensive Psychiatry*, **13**, 459–464.

Wyatt D. & Campbell D. (1950) A study of interview bias as related to interviewers' expectations and own opinions. *International Journal of Opinion and Attitude Research*, **4**, 77–83.

Wyndowe J. (1987) The microcomputerized Diagnostic Interview Schedule: clinical use in an outpatient setting. *Canadian Journal of Psychiatry*, **32**, 93–99.

Yarrow M.R. (1963) Problems of methods in parent–child research. *Child Development*, **324**, 215–226.

Yarrow M.R., Campbell J.D. & Burton R.V. (1968) Child rearing: an enquiry into research and methods. Jossey-Bass, San Francisco.

Yarrow M.R., Campbell J.D. & Burton R.V. (1970) recollections of childhood: a study of retrospective methods. *Monographs of the Society for Research in Child Development*, **35**, No. 5.

Young J.G., O'Brien J.D., Gutterman E.M. & Cohen P. (1987) Research on the clinical interview. *Journal of the American Academy of Child and Adolescent Psychiatry*, **26**, 613–620.

Chapter 4
Clinical Interviewing with Children and Adolescents

Adrian Angold

THE PURPOSES OF THE DIAGNOSTIC INTERVIEW

The clinical interview is the primary diagnostic tool in child and adolescent psychiatry, as in the rest of clinical medicine. Its first purpose is to collect information that will assist in the tasks of making a diagnosis and formulating and implementing a treatment plan. With the official adoption of a phenomenologically based psychiatric nosology in the US, and the introduction and increasingly widespread use of structured interviews, the diagnostic process has become more consistent over the last decade or so. Phenomenological diagnosis requires that information be collected in a coherent and consistent fashion, and thus sets the predominant style of the interview. The basic format is one of sensitive guidance by the clinician, rather than a free format in which the child is encouraged to play or free-associate. The clinician guides, organizes and structures the collection of information in a way that is sensitive to the child's problems and concerns. This approach is very different from that of the nondirective interviewer who attempts to act as a sympathetic observer or sounding board and interprets the material presented by the child. It has been shown that even supposedly nondirective interviews are more clinical-directed than was once thought (Traux, 1966, 1968), because the use of 'uh huhs' and the timing of reflections on what the patient has said serve as strong indicators of the clinician's real interests.

However, a good interview also aims to achieve several other objectives apart from discovering the facts about a patient. A diagnostic interview is often the initial contact between child and clinician, and then it is the first step in establishing a treatment alliance with the clinical team. The same clinician may be the child's psychotherapist later on, so the diagnostic interview also represents a first step in the formation of a therapeutic relationship. All too frequently the initial diagnostic assessment is the only contact an individual or family has with the clinical team, because many never return for treatment. With this in mind, it is important to avoid increasing the barriers to future treatment-seeking by providing a good experience of psychiatric services. For all these reasons, and because of the need to ask about emotionally sensitive material, the clinician should approach the task of collecting information in such a way as to assure the child

of a genuine interest in his or her problems and sympathy with his or her difficulties. Under the best circumstances, the product of such an interview is not just a lot of relevant information, but also the child's having a sense that something important about him or her has been understood by someone who cares and is willing (and perhaps able) to help. The child's behaviour in the interview is another important source of diagnostic information. Thus, the art of good clinical interviewing lies in the ability to combine the efficient collection of reported information, an observant eye and the projection of interest and concern about the child's problems.

CHILDREN'S MEMORY: A LIMITING FACTOR?

It has been widely believed that children's memory limitations place severe constraints on what can be learned from questioning them directly (Goodman, 1984; Ross *et al.*, 1987). However, the empirical literature on the subject has been slow to expand because early findings indicated that there were rather few differences even between quite young children and adults on mnemonic tasks. Interest in this question has now been renewed, at least in part because of the increasing use of children's testimony in cases of suspected abuse. This 'real world' motivation for research has also led to studies that have attempted to use more realistic experiments, rather than highly artificial laboratory paradigms.

Though much remains to be done, a number of fairly consistent themes emerge from this work. First, from the age of 3 until the teenage years, there is an increase in the amount of information provided in free-recall situations. However, though younger children provide less information, they are no less accurate in their recall than older children and adults. Second, when structured, and especially forced-choice question formats are used, younger children (and especially 3–6-year-olds) can usually provide more information (Bjorklund, 1987; Bjorklund & Muir, 1988; Dent, 1991; Ornstein *et al.*, 1991). However, they are also more likely to provide erroneous information, although the absolute magnitude of this effect is rather small after the age of 6 (Dent & Stephenson, 1979). Third, while the youngest age groups are more likely to incorporate erroneous material introduced through repeated questioning, suggestion and leading questions than older children (Loftus, 1979; Cohen & Harnick, 1980; Siegal *et al.*, 1988), this effect is probably more marked in relation to peripheral details than to the central features of a situation or experience (see Hedderman, 1987; Zaragoza, 1987 for reviews; Dodd & Bradshaw, 1980; Yuille, 1980; Ceci *et al.*, 1987). It also seems that recall errors are not evenly distributed across recalled material, since Dent and her co-workers (Dent & Stephenson, 1979; Dent, 1991) found that, in recalling filmed events, children made more errors about the appearance of people and things than about the sequence of events portrayed. Furthermore, there is impressionistic evidence that children in the most 'suggestible' age groups may often be aware that they do not really remember the suggested material but included it because they thought they were being asked to. Such material is apparently likely to be offered rather tentatively, and rarely with the sort of elaboration that may accompany accurately recalled information (Goodman *et al.*, 1987). Fourth, though it is possible to demonstrate increased rates of forgetting in younger children through formal memory tests (Brainerd *et al.*, 1990; Ornstein *et al.*, 1992), it seems that rates of forgetting are not markedly different, at least from the age of 6 to adulthood. Fifth, even 3-year-olds have been shown to be capable of remembering some events that occurred as much as a year before the interview (see Pillemer & White, 1989 for a review). Sixth, in both adults and children, there is a tendency to conflate memories of repeated events into 'scripts' that provide a generalized memory of such events (Nelson *et al.*, 1983; Saywitz, 1987), incorporating features from a number of specific instances. Again, children under the age of 6 may have more difficulty in reporting details of specific instances of such repeated events, and are likely to describe their script memories, but confirmation that this is so awaits studies of recall of material that is equally enscripted at different ages. Seventh, young children respond poorly when asked to perform tasks that are beyond their cognitive capacities, or asked questions using words they do not understand (Dale *et al.*, 1978).

All in all, these findings strongly refute the notion that children's recall is subject to biases that invalidate the child as an informant about the facts of his or her experience. By the age of 6–8, the recall abilities of children do not seem to be dramatically different from those of adults. However, the results do point to the need to avoid leading questions, and indicate that the use of free recall, at least as a first step, is likely to lead to the most accurate accounts, though with 3–6-year-olds these accounts can be expected to be very sketchy. In clinical practice it is quite appropriate to use direct questions about past experiences, emotional states and behaviours from an early age. However, with the youngest children particular care is needed to avoid leading questions. When the interviewer is unsure how much reliance can be placed on a particular piece of information, asking the child how sure she is, and checking what she thought was being demanded of her may clarify the situation. It is also important to ensure that the child pays attention to what is being asked and understands

the questions. Research with both adults and children also teaches us not to place too much reliance on the precision of long-term recall (longer than about 3–4 months). The process of script formation means that, while a general picture of repeated events may be available, the specifics of each individual event are likely to be unreliable. Even a general outline of the past history can be diagnostically important, so this in no way undermines the status of this aspect of the clinical history. Much information may be lost in long-term recall, but there is little evidence that events are commonly invented. The past history is, therefore, an insensitive tool, but positive reports of past symptomatology can usually be relied upon.

RESEARCH ON DIAGNOSTIC INTERVIEWING IN CHILDREN

There is now quite a substantial body of literature on the psychometric properties of diagnostic interviews with children and adolescents, which outlines quite well both the strengths and limitations of various approaches to such interviews (see Edelbrock & Costello, 1988; and Angold, 1989 for reviews). In the first place, it should be noted that structured interviews were originally developed because researchers were aware that clinicians unaided by such instruments tended to operate in an idiosyncratic fashion, and to adopt inefficient decision rules in coming to a diagnosis. It was also apparent that there was a tendency to focus on a particular set of problems without giving adequate weight to an exploration of the full range of symptomatology. Both of these problems are typical of unstructured medical decision-making in general. Other general human information-processing characteristics that may endanger the diagnostic process include illusory correlation (Chapman & Chapman, 1967), in which the expectation that a correlation between two phenomena exists leads to the imputation of the presence of a second phenomenon from the observed presence of the first. On the other hand, people appear to have great difficulty identifying correlations when they really do exist in the phenomena that they are observing (Chapman & Chapman, 1971). Thus the observation that a child had made a suicide attempt might lead a clinician who believes that such actions are related to depression to assume that the child must be depressed, and to interpret any hint of sadness as confirming these suppositions. This latter tendency to weight information that fits in with expectations is also called the confirmatory bias (Tversky & Kahnemann, 1974). Its corollary is that information that does not fit in with expectations tends to be ignored (thus our clinician might fail to take a careful history of behaviour problems, which would be a serious mistake, since suicidality is also strongly related to conduct problems). The representativeness heuristic (Tversky & Kahnemann, 1974) may also bias clinical judgements when a child has the characteristics of a particular group (say, children with conduct disorder), leading the clinician to impute to the child other characteristics of conduct-disordered children that actually do not apply to that individual (see

Achenbach, 1985 for a basic introduction to the application of decision-making analysis to the assessment of psychopathology and Weinstein & Fineberg, 1980; Dawes, 1988; Sox *et al.*, 1988, for more advanced treatments). That these effects occur in ordinary clinical practice is indicated by Costello's (1982) examination of diagnostic case conferences at a major child psychiatric center (described in Cantwell, 1988). Shaffer and his co-workers (1992) have also recently documented the very poor test−retest reliability of clinician diagnoses, while Bird *et al.* (1992) found that clinicians were less likely to assign certain comorbid diagnoses than a computer algorithm incorporating the DSM-III diagnostic rules when both made diagnoses based on the same information.

Two basic strategies were adopted from the adult interviewing literature in an attempt to overcome these problems. The first approach, which we may call the respondent-based interview (also sometimes known as a fully structured or highly structured interview), depends upon a fully specified set of questions, from which the interviewer should not deviate. The Diagnostic Interview Schedule for Children (DISC; Costello *et al.*, 1984) and the Diagnostic Interview for Children and Adolescents (DICA; Herjanic & Campbell, 1977) are the best-known examples of such interviews for children. The interviewer is required only to know the rules governing when questions should be asked, and is then expected to follow the interview schedule verbatim. Thus the task of deciding whether a symptom is present or not falls upon the interviewee, who must interpret the question and then respond to it as he or she thinks is appropriate. Such an interview requires relatively little training to produce proficient interviewers, and so nonclinician interviewers can be used. One knows exactly what has been asked of each child, and can be sure that the questioning has been consistent from one subject to the next. However, this approach also has certain weaknesses. In particular, it has proven difficult to achieve test−retest reliability with the DISC in children under the age of 10 and, even in adolescents, accounts of emotional disorders tend to be unreliable (Edelbrock *et al.*, 1985; Schwab-Stone *et al.*, 1989), though the DICA has fared better in this respect (Herjanic & Reich, 1982). The reliabilities of parent reports, however, are usually quite satisfactory. There is a deeper underlying problem that may, in part, explain some of these findings, in that we cannot be sure that what each child believes a question to mean was what the developers of the interview intended it to mean. This problem has been documented with unusual symptoms that most children never experience, such as obsessive-compulsive or psychotic symptoms. Such symptoms are greatly overreported (Breslau, 1987). When clinicians reviewed what the children said, it was obvious that what was being reported was not obsessions or psychosis. However, if an unstructured clinician review is added to the diagnostic process, one no longer knows exactly what factors went into the final rating, and one great advantage of the respondent-based interview is lost.

The second approach to clinical interviewing may be termed the interviewer-based interview (also sometimes called a semi-structured interview). The best-known example here is the Kiddie-Schedule for Affective Disorders and Schizophrenia (K-SADS; Puig-Antich & Chambers, 1978), which is also available in a lifetime version which makes much less detailed symptom ratings (the K-SADS-E; Orvaschel *et al.*, 1982). Other examples are the Interview Schedule for Children (ISC; Kovacs, 1983), the Child Assessment Schedule (CAS; Hodges *et al.*, 1981), and the Child and Adolescent Psychiatric Assessment (CAPA; Angold *et al.*, 1987, 1991b). In these interviews, key questions are provided for guidance, but the interviewer is expected to ask whatever questions are necessary in order to determine whether a particular symptom is present or not. Usually, some guidance is also given as to what rules should be used in order to make this decision. This approach is much closer to the usual clinical approach, but it ensures that all the material that should be covered is covered. The second strength lies in the fact that a clinically based judgement of the presence of a symptom is being made − it is up to the interviewer to decide whether a symptom is present, not the child. Clearly such an approach places increased demands upon the interviewer, which, in turn, increases the amount of training required. The K-SADS, the ISC and the CAS were specifically designed for use by clinicians, and most clinicians find them much more pleasant to use than respondent-based interviews. The CAPA was designed for use by either clinical or lay interviewers, and has an extensive glossary of symptom definitions to allow nonclinicians to make judgements about symptoms that conform to clinical standards (Angold *et al.*, 1987, 1991b). The K-SADS has not been proven to have good test−retest reliability and no such reliability data are available for the ISC. The CAS and the CAPA both appear to have good psychometric properties (Hodges *et al.*, 1989; Angold *et al.*, 1991a).

Most clinicians in training find that learning how to conduct an interviewer-based interview improves their interviewing skills and provides useful experience that they can call upon in their ordinary practice. Though the reliability coefficients of structured interviews are often not as high as one would like, they are universally better than those achieved by unstructured clinical interviews. The research community has more or less abandoned the unstructured interview as a viable diagnostic technique, and one might ask why a method that is inadequate for research should be considered appropriate for clinical purposes. Many major centres now incorporate structured interviews into their basic diagnostic work-up, and it seems likely that this trend will continue. It may be that the days of unstructured clinical diagnostic interviews in child and adolescent psychiatry are numbered. However, there are also dangers to routinizing the diagnostic process. Long lists of unvarying questions tend to result in boredom and annoyance in both the interviewer and the interviewee, and that can hardly help in establishing a treatment alliance. Careful attention and skill are still required from the clinician in detecting and sorting out conflicting statements, and observing when children seem to be skirting important issues or showing signs of discomfort or anxiety. Though structured interview techniques have many advantages, they will aid the clinical process only when used skilfully and sensitively.

Research on these interviews has also provided some important information about diagnostic interviewing in general. First, reports from parents and children do not agree very highly, even in relation to what might be thought to be reasonably observable events. In particular, children are usually better informants about their own internal states than their parents, and they know more about their covert antisocial activities and substance use than their parents. Thus there is a move away from requiring adult confirmation of children's reports and towards giving such reports equal status in the diagnostic equation (see Angold *et al.*, 1987 for a review).

Second, research with structured interviews has also emphasized that the most visible problems may not be the child's only problems, and thereby focused attention on comorbidity (Angold & Costello, in press). In particular it has reminded us that many children whose teachers or parents have noticed that they are ill-behaved are also depressed or anxious, while many depressed or anxious children have overt or covert behaviour problems that may not have come to the attention of adults. In the clinical arena, these findings point to the necessity of addressing a wide range of problems that may not have been noted as reasons for referral, in much the same way as is usual in the review of systems embodied in the time-honoured general medical history. This is a time-consuming task, but it must be undertaken if a full clinical picture is to emerge.

Third, the development of structured interviews has led to some hard thinking and research about the best ways to ask questions if the aims of the clinical interview are to be achieved, and the next section discusses some of the major implications of this work.

INTERVIEWING STYLE

Open questions and closed questions

The distinction between open and closed questions is not absolute, but open questions are those that offer the chance to provide a wide range of answers or free-recall descriptions of phenomena, while closed questions call for one of a limited set of responses. For example, an open question response to being told by a child that he had received a bad school report might be 'How did you feel about your bad grades?', whereas 'Did your bad grades make you feel unhappy?' would be a closed question. If a child had just admitted to stealing, responding with 'Tell me more about that' involves an open question, whereas 'What did you steal?' is a closed question. Basically, closed questions call for a yes−no answer or a date, frequency, duration or other quite specific piece of information, whereas open questions give the opportunity for the child to provide a description of his behaviour or feelings, which might or might not involve sadness.

The work of Rutter and Cox and their colleagues offers some direct guidance on the best ways to use these different sorts of questions with adults, and in the light of the literature on children's memory cited above, there is little reason not to use a similar approach with children. In general, most factual information was collected when a systematic approach that relied heavily on open questions was used. Furthermore, this approach was also conducive to parental expressions of emotion, since it involved less talking on the part of the interviewer and gave more time for parents to discuss their concerns. On the other hand, a noninterventionist approach resulted in the provision of less relevant information, while challenging interpretations and a confrontational style proved less effective in eliciting emotions (Cox *et al.*, 1981a,b,c; Hopkinson, *et al.*, 1981; Rutter & Cox, 1981; Rutter *et al.*, 1981). This is not to say that closed questions do not have an important place in the clinical interview, but they should be used to fill in the gaps in the information provided in response to open questions, or to clarify confusion, rather than constituting the basic approach. Sometimes it seems as though it might be quicker to ask a set of specific questions (especially when working through a set of diagnostic criteria). However, this is rarely the case. If open questions are well-thought-out, a child will often provide much of the necessary information spontaneously, so that only one or two follow-up questions need be asked. Thus open questions may actually save time, and simultaneously avoid a barrage of closed questions that may seem to the child to reflect the clinician's needs more than his own.

Leading questions

Leading questions are sometimes confused with closed questions, but whereas the latter are a necessary part of interviewing technique, leading questions have almost no place at all in psychiatric interviewing, for the simple reason that one can never believe the answer to such a question, especially in the case of young children. A leading question is one that directly suggests its answer. For example, to return to the boy with the problems at school, a response like 'I expect that made you feel pretty unhappy, didn't it?' places the child in the position of having to disagree with the interviewer if he really did not care about his grades. We have already noted that young children may be prone to respond with what they believe is being demanded of them, so we can expect agreement, even if the child was in fact angry or completely unconcerned. On the other hand, such a question provides a golden opportunity for an oppositional adolescent to demonstrate how wide of the mark the interviewer was, regardless of his actual feelings about school.

Double and multiple questions

A double question asks about two different things at the same time. Consider the question 'When you got your school report, were you worried, or angry, or didn't you care?' Such a question will often draw an answer like 'yes' or 'no', but one cannot tell what that answer refers to — it could refer to any combination of worrying, anger or insouciance. The operation of the recency effect means that it is quite likely that the response refers to the last part of the question. But the only way to be sure is to ask specific questions about worrying, anger and not caring. Since this could have been done in the first place, the multiple question has only served to waste time. Double and multiple questions also place an increased load on the cognitive capacities of the interviewee, because she must remember several options in order to choose among them. Thus double and multiple questions join leading questions as major interviewing sins.

Though multiple questions cause problems, the same cannot be said of redundant questions; that is, single questions that contain two presentations of the same item, as in 'Did you feel angry about your report? ... Did it make you angry at all?' The adult survey literature (Cannell *et al.*, 1973) suggests that such redundancy can actually be helpful, and the same may be true in interviewing children, though this issue does not seem to have been studied specifically.

Multiple choice questions

Multiple choice questions are a subset of closed questions that have a place when regular open and closed questions fail to provide an adequate answer. For instance, if one asks about the frequency of temper tantrums, and the child says she 'doesn't know', a question like 'well, is it every day, once a week or once a month?' can be helpful. However, such multiple choice questions may not include the proper range of choices. What is the right answer if tantrums actually occur only a couple of times a year, or if they occur many times a day? It is usually necessary to ask a supplementary question or two to clarify these points, so multiple choice questions are relatively inefficient, though they may be the only way to get the necessary information. They also have a second drawback in that, like multiple questions, they require the child to hold the available choices in memory before selecting amongst them. It has already been noted that the multiple choice format leads to the reporting of more incorrect information in younger children.

Inappropriately worded questions

In most circumstances it is best to use simple words and short sentences. It is also important to be on the alert for possible misunderstanding. Here again the open question approach, with its emphasis on getting the child to describe her experiences and behaviour, helps to ensure that both interviewer and interviewee are talking about the same thing. On the other hand, it is important to avoid the appearance of condescension with intelligent adolescents, who may be all too ready to take umbrage.

ORGANIZING THE INTERVIEW

So far, we have examined some basic interviewing techniques, and the next question is how to organize these into a coherent interview.

Beginning the interview

The first task is to get the child into a conducive situation; that is, somewhere quiet, private and undistracting. The presence of large numbers of interesting toys should be avoided.

The child often does not know why he is talking to the interviewer, since his parents may have told him that he is going to the dentist, or some other fiction. The first step, then, is to clarify why the child thinks he is seeing you, and to allay fears that injections or extractions are just around the corner. Even if the child has a reasonable notion of where he is, his ideas about why he is there may differ dramatically from the actual reasons for referral. The next step is to explain why you think he is there, to explain the purpose of the interview and to give a brief description of what it will be like.

Since an immediate barrage of questions about emotionally loaded topics is likely to be very off-putting, it is usually best to begin with some questions that allow the child to describe his family situation, the things he enjoys doing and is good at, and what his social life is like. If the child is aware that he has problems, a brief description of how he sees those problems can be helpful also. By this point, both the child and the interviewer should have a fairly good idea of what to expect from one another, so the interviewer can formulate a plan for the rest of the interview. If it has become clear that some topics are a source of discomfort or avoidance, it is best to steer away from these at the start, and to begin with less threatening material, allowing a sense of trust to develop. On the other hand, some children are keen to get right down to a description of what bothers them most. In either case, following the child's leads and exploring his problems in the order in which they come up is a good strategy. However, in being sensitive to the child's ordering of the material, it is important not to allow the interview to become incoherent. Once a topic (such as symptoms of depression) has been begun, it is usually best to continue with it until all the necessary information has been collected. Otherwise it is very likely that important questions will be forgotten in jumping from topic to topic. There is nothing wrong with telling the child that you will come back to a different topic later (so long as you do).

Those just beginning work in child and adolescent psychiatry usually do not know what all the relevant symptoms are, and here the use of a simple checklist (for the interviewer, not the child) based on the DSM or ICD criteria can be very helpful. However, these criteria give no guidance as to how to turn them into suitable questions, and familiarity with a good structured interview helps to fill this gap. If the child has previously completed a symptom checklist, it is a good idea to have looked it over before starting the interview. However, it is vital that the diagnostic criteria are not allowed to become a straitjacket for the interview. It is all too easy to emerge with more or less accurate diagnoses but little idea of what the child is actually like. A lot goes into good treatment planning besides the diagnosis.

Common child psychopathology is divided into two broad domains: emotional and behavioural disorders, and in the next two sections we will discuss some general principles of rating symptoms in these areas.

Emotional disorders

The central distinctions to be made here are between mood and affect, thoughts, behaviour and impairments secondary to the first three. The distinction between moods and thoughts is the most difficult to maintain in practice, largely because English does not clearly distinguish between them in everyday speech. For instance, it is usual to ask whether someone 'felt' guilty rather than whether she 'had guilty thoughts', though the latter is more accurate. When interviewing one must use everyday language, but it is important to be clear that while 'feeling guilty' may be evidence of a depressive disorder, it is not the same thing as depressed mood. It is quite possible to have an overdeveloped sense of guilt without depressed mood and vice versa. Thus some common questions like 'Did you feel bad about that?' must be treated with caution, because an affirmative response could refer either to a mood state — as in, 'that made me feel unhappy' — or a cognitive state — as in, 'that induced the thought that I had done something bad or wrong'. Similarly, worrying (a cognitive symptom) must be distinguished from anxiety (a mood state). While, at first, these distinctions may seem to be splitting psychopathological hairs, they are diagnostically important, and of direct relevance to treatment (consider, for example, cognitive therapy for depression, which focuses directly on thought processes, rather than the mood state itself).

When is an emotional 'symptom' abnormal?

One problem with emotional symptoms is that they are often extremes of normal emotions. This represents no problem when someone reports that she has been depressed all day, every day, for 2 months, and that before that she was of a cheerful disposition. Unfortunately, things are not always so simple. In the absence of a detailed epidemiological literature describing how much time the average child spends feeling depressed, or worrying, it is necessary to have some general rules of thumb for deciding what is abnormal:

1 Look for changes in state or failure to make normal developmental progress. A description of a marked change in state, especially if it is of relatively acute onset, is strong evidence for the pathological status of a symptom. However, it has to be said that in developmental psychopathology, acute onsets are the exception, rather than the rule. Symptoms may also have begun years before the child presents for help. However, if care is taken to get adequate descriptions, and the child is encouraged to think hard about whether and when a change

occurred, it is usually possible to determine whether a symptom represents a change from some previous state.

Some symptoms represent the inappropriate continuation of a state that is normal in earlier life. Separation anxiety is the paradigmatic example here. The majority of children show separation and stranger anxiety in their second year, and many are unhappy about leaving their parents on first going to school. However, much more independence is expected of teenagers, and a 12-year-old who wishes to sleep with her parents, because she is afraid to sleep alone, is distinctly abnormal.

2 How long do bouts of the symptom last, and how often do they occur? Most people worry or feel depressed sometimes, but these are evanescent phenomena. They are only symptomatic when present for an inordinate amount of time. Once again, we lack data on how much worrying is normal, but can determine how much time (average length of bout of worrying × number of bouts per week) has been spent worrying and make a common-sense judgement about whether this is pathological.

3 Is the symptom intrusive into other thoughts and activities? A symptom that disappears as soon as something comes along to take an individual's mind off it is unlikely to be of psychopathological import, so it is important to ask whether symptoms intrude into, or interfere with, other activities. Thus worrying that interferes with concentrating on schoolwork represents a problem, whereas worries that disappear as soon as there is a job to be done probably do not.

4 Is the symptom controllable? If a child can get rid of a symptom by thinking about, or doing, something else, then one can usually be fairly sure that it is not psychopathologically significant. Obviously intrusiveness and uncontrollability are very closely related ideas and, in general, both will be reported in relation to important symptoms.

5 Is the symptom generalized across more than one activity? A symptom that is restricted to a single activity (such as worrying about a maths test just before the test, but only then) is usually not a marker for a clinically relevant problem. In the case of specific phobias, a child who is frightened of dogs only when a dog is barking at her is unlikely to encounter many problems, while the child who is afraid of dogs whenever she is out in the street, regardless of the presence of a dog, can be regarded as being symptomatic.

Behavioural problems

An overlapping set of considerations is of primary relevance for behaviour problems. Some undesirable behaviours are normal (such as disobedience or lying) when they occur at low frequency, and should only be regarded as symptoms when they occur often. In such cases, frequency, controllability and generalization are relevant, but bout duration and intrusiveness are not. Once again, we do not know how often the average 8-year-old is disobedient, but we do know that the average mother issues a command statement to her 2-year-old about once every 2 minutes, so questioning about controllability requires the added dimension of response to admonition. Here, two levels of nonresponse may be discerned: some children simply do not do as they are told, while others actively challenge their admonisher (for instance by swearing at, or hitting, a teacher).

It is also worth noting that clinical experience indicates that many children with marked attentional and activity problems are poor reporters of their behaviour in this respect. It is not uncommon for such children to report that they are not fidgety and have no difficulty remaining seated when told to do so, despite the fact that they have spent most of the interview wandering around the office, in the face of repeated requests that they should sit down. They may also seem to be unaware of their social skills defects, so it is important to get detailed descriptions of how they interact with their reported 'best friends'.

Some other dimensions of behaviour problems are also relevant for certain symptoms:

1 In what situations did the behaviour occur? Three general settings may be distinguished: (1) home; (2) school; and (3) elsewhere. Determining where problematic behaviour occurs has important treatment implications, and also seems to have some prognostic importance, in that pervasively disturbed children appear to have more persistent problems and to do worse in young adulthood.

2 Was the child usually alone or in company when performing antisocial acts? This distinction corresponds to the DSM-III-R categories of solitary and socialized conduct problems (it should be noted, however, that the ICD-10 system makes this distinction not on whether the child committed offences alone or with others, but on the basis of the quality of his social relationships in general).

3 Who was the victim of the antisocial acts? Here distinctions may be made between: (1) community property (as in vandalizing park benches); (2) the property of individuals not known to the child (as in shoplifting); and (3) the property of individuals known to the child (as in stealing from mother's purse).

Many types of antisocial acts are considered abnormal whenever they occur (armed robbery, for instance), and are not at all uncommon in some psychiatric settings (such as substance abuse treatment programmes), so it is important to ask teenagers about these sorts of activities. In many areas, it is also common for teenagers, and even younger children, to carry weapons, and to use them, so it is often worth asking about this as well.

Symptoms of psychosis

Children and adolescents may manifest all the symptoms characteristic of adult psychotic disorders. Childhood schizophrenia and psychotic depression and mania are uncommon, but both become more common in adolescence. In childhood, especially, great care must be taken in establishing the presence of delusions and hallucinations, since a number of other phenomena can easily be confused with these very serious symptoms. In particular, hypnogogic hallucinations (vivid true hallucinations occurring when falling asleep) and hypnopompic hallucinations (vivid true hallucinations occurring on waking up) are normal phenomena. In general, hallucinations occurring only when the child is in bed should not be regarded as being evidence of psychotic disorders, even if the child insists that he was not falling asleep or waking up when they occurred. Care also needs to be taken not to mistake eidetic imagery, imaginary companions, elaborated fantasies, perceptual illusions, seizure phenomena, drug-induced experiences, subcultural beliefs and hallucinations accompanying toxic encephalopathies for manifestations of the functional psychoses.

Déjà vu, *jamais vu*, derealization and depersonalization are states that most people experience from time to time, but when severe and prolonged are symptomatic of mental disorder. Once again, it is important to get a clear description of the phenomena, and to pay particular attention to how often they occur and how long they last. Derealization and depersonalization are also common effects of certain drugs (such as cannabis and LSD) and the possibility of drug use should be investigated when these states are reported. Premonitions of events are also often described by quite normal people, and should only be regarded as being psychotic phenomena when they clearly fall outside the normal range of experiences for the cultural group to which the child belongs. In most cases, consideration of the overall clinical picture will ensure that these phenomena are interpreted appropriately.

Impairment of psychosocial functioning

Psychiatric disorders impact on a person's ability to function at her highest level in the psychosocial environment, and it is vital to assess the degree to which such functioning is impaired. Here the main areas of concern are school (or work) performance and behaviour, peer relationships, social and spare-time activities and relationships within the family. Relying solely on symptom ratings and DSM-III for diagnosis has been found to lead to ridiculously high rates of diagnosis in epidemiological studies using respondent-based interviews and one strategy for producing more sensible estimates has been to require some degree of psychosocial impairment to be present if a diagnosis is to be made (Bird *et al.*, 1988). In clinical settings, most patients have some degree of impairment, so the issue of severity looms larger there.

Two approaches have been adopted to the measurement of impairment. The first is to consider the patient's overall level of functioning, by combining information about symptomatology and psychosocial impairment into a single rating. The Children's Global Assessment Scale (Shaffer *et al.*, 1983; Bird *et al.*, 1987) is the best example here. This instrument, based on DSM-III-R axis V, provides a simple, reliable scale with the ratings keyed to descriptive sentences, and can be coded after all the information about the child has been gathered. The K-SADS adopts a somewhat different approach by including aspects of psychosocial functioning in a number of the ratings of specific symptoms (Chambers *et al.*, 1985). The strength of this combined technique is that it provides an overall clinical summary of how 'disturbed' the child is, and it is widely used in both clinical practice and research. On the other hand, because symptoms and psychosocial impairments are conflated in the ratings, it is impossible to look at each dimension separately.

An alternative approach is provided by the CAPA, which calls for separate ratings of psychosocial impairment secondary to psychiatric symptomatology in a number of domains. (The DISC also calls for coding of a limited range of codings of psychosocial impairment and treatment in relation to each diagnostic area.) In this case, the symptom ratings are separated out from the impairment ratings and the contributions of particular symptom areas to the overall degree of impairment are assessed. This can be helpful with children with multiple problems, since it gives an idea of which areas of symptomatology are most responsible for any psychosocial difficulties, and this may help in deciding where to begin as far as treatment is concerned.

A third useful measure is the Social Adjustment Inventory for Children and Adolescents (SAICA; John *et al.*, 1987), a 20-minute interview schedule that includes ratings of a number of psychosocial problems. However, it also includes items that are ordinarily regarded as conduct problems, and usually covered in the exploration of symptomatology. For use as a clinical aid, it is quite possible to use the nonsymptom items alone, though the usual scoring system does not adopt this approach.

SPECIAL INTERVIEWING SITUATIONS

Children with limited understanding: the young and the mentally retarded

Any interview is an exercise in verbal skills, and it is important to be sensitive to verbal limitations in those being interviewed. As we have already noted, young children are unlikely to provide much information in a free-recall setting, and the same is true of the mentally retarded. These groups also have shorter attention spans, and usually cannot be expected to sit for 2 hours of interview without breaks. However, they may well be the only available sources of information about their inner lives. The temptation is to ask a lot of closed questions, and that often leads to the use of leading questions in order to make it easier for the individual to respond. These groups are particularly likely to respond to such questioning by supposing that they are expected to agree with the interviewer, and mistakenly trying to oblige in this way. While there may be no way around the need to ask greater numbers of closed questions, every attempt should be made to get as good descriptions as possible of the phenomena that the child is referring to, so as to avoid confusion. It is also important to try to check that the words that the child is using to describe his inner world are being used in the same way that we would use them. Thus a 4-year-old's 'worry' might be our 'frightened' or 'depressed'.

It can be helpful to find situations in which one can be fairly sure that a child was feeling a particular emotion (like sadness), and then ask whether the feeling they are talking about now is the same as that. In fact, this problem is not qualitatively different from the general issue of making sure that both parties in the interview mean the same thing, but it is quantitatively more demanding.

There have been few studies of the best ways to collect reliable diagnostic information from preschool children, but a promising approach developed by Martini *et al.* (1990) uses pictures to facilitate self-reports of depression in children in an instrument called the Preschool Symptom Self-Report (PRESS), and initial data support its usefulness for assessing depression.

Additional tools may also be helpful in getting descriptions of events that occurred, thus using play-like materials, such as puppets, or toy houses, or photographs of individuals involved in events may be useful. Drawing is also a time-honoured modality in child psychiatry, and can be useful here. The aim is to provide a focus for cognitively reconstructing the situation to be remembered. However, it is important to recognize that the aim, in this case, is to help the child to remember, and not to make interpretations. However, the degree to which these aids generate misleading as well as accurate information has not been adequately tested (King & Yuille, 1987).

The investigation of abuse

Now that greater attention is being paid to the problems of physical and sexual abuse, an increased load has been placed upon the clinical interview, and a new set of demands are being made on the 'evidence' we collect. The ordinary standard for clinical evidence is the best diagnostic formulation that can be made from the information available. This is rather different from the legal standards of 'a preponderance of the evidence' or 'beyond a reasonable doubt', though it is clearly closer to the former. In collecting material that may be called into evidence it is particularly important that leading questions or other suggestive strategies should be avoided, since, in some well-publicized cases, such material has led to children's testimony being rejected (Cole & Loftus, 1987). On the other hand, in dealing with issues that may be frightening or embarrassing, or about which the child may have been threatened should she ever reveal what happened, there is naturally a wish to make it as easy as possible to give a full description. Furthermore, since most young children lack an adequate anatomical vocabulary to describe sexual abuse, the use of anatomically correct dolls to allow children to demonstrate what happened has become fashionable. However, some have argued that such dolls (with their obvious protuberances and orifices) themselves suggest certain forms of play that may then be misinterpreted as evidence of sexual abuse (King & Yuille, 1987). On the other hand, case reviews of sexual abuse records have suggested that fabrications of stories of sexual abuse are rare and that when they occur, such fabrications have usually been started by an adult, (Jones, 1985).

The final answers to the best way to collect evidence of abuse are still some way off, but, at present, an acceptable approach seems to be to use ordinary good interviewing strategies as far as possible and to supplement these with descriptions using anatomically correct dolls when necessary, always bearing in mind that the child must understand that one is asking what actually happened rather than what you can do with these dolls. Since the claim that evidence of abuse was obtained by the use of leading questions and techniques that relied on the children's supposed suggestibility is almost certain to be made in court, it is important to be sure that this was not the case, and the best way of doing this is to record (preferably on video tape) exactly what happened in the interview. When this is not possible, it is important to record both the questions asked and the answers obtained (see Ornstein *et al.*, 1992, for a helpful discussion of the implications of memory development research for children's testimony, and Ross *et al.*, 1987 and Leippe & Romanczyk, 1987, on jurors' reactions to child witnesses).

Children who 'don't know'

All child psychiatric clinicians have been faced with children who resolutely 'don't know'. In such cases, persistence can make a huge difference, particularly with information about duration, frequency and the timing of symptom onsets. It may also be the case that a child really does not know how to answer a particular question like 'How have you been feeling lately?' because he is unfamiliar with describing his feelings. In such a case, more focused questions (such as 'Have you been feeling miserable?') can help a lot by providing a series of categories that the child can use to describe his feelings. Thus the ubiquitous 'boredom' of adolescence may be reducible to a number of more sharply focused states, when a framework for more accurate descriptions is offered.

Though there have been concerns about the accuracy with which children and adolescents can date events and the onsets of symptoms in their lives, there is little evidence that after the age of 8 they are any worse than adults at this task. The adult literature suggests that it is easier to recall that something happened than when it happened, and major events are more likely to be remembered than minor events. The work of Cannell and his colleagues in relation to the Household Survey (Cannell *et al.*, 1973) suggests high rates of forgetting of minor health problems (like headaches) over periods as short as 1 week, and substantial underreporting of even major events by 1 year. The adult psychiatric literature indicates that the test–retest reliability of lifetime diagnoses of psychiatric disorders using the SADS is quite good (Andreasen *et al.*, 1981; Keller *et al.*, 1981). Only the K-SADS-E collects lifetime psychiatric histories from children. However, two studies (Orvaschel *et al.*, 1982; Fendrich *et al.*, 1990) have found that the kappas for child reports of known depressive episodes reported on between 6 months and 2 years later were around 0.6. Fendrich *et al.* (1990) also present evidence of reasonable stability for diagnoses of conduct disorder, atten-

tion deficit disorder and substance abuse, but poor stability for anxiety diagnoses. However, it is important to remember that the usual form of instability is failure to recall a previous episode; few symptoms are invented. On the other hand the use of scripts means that a series of events may be conflated into a single memory, so very accurate dating may not be attainable. Recent work in the survey literature suggests that attempts to decompose such memories into a series of more specific instances can be surprisingly successful. Likewise, tying the onsets of symptoms to events, such as birthdays and school semesters, can also lead to finer-grained dating than seemed possible at the beginning of the interview. It is usually possible at least to determine the age by which a symptom was definitely present, which is certainly better than nothing. In general, the further back in time one goes, the more information is lost, though for events of major significance, the degree of decrement after the first year may be small. It is also important to remember that in adults, for most memories, there is a 'brought-forward' effect, by which events are remembered as having happened more recently than was the case (though there are exceptions to this rule — as in the case of memories for certain developmental milestones in one's children; Hart *et al.*, 1978), and there is no reason to suppose that this is not the case in children also. In fact, the situation may be more complicated than this in children since it has been found that the age at which children and adolescents were interviewed about their depressive psychopathology had a significant effect on the rates at which they reported depressive symptoms and the reported timing of their first episodes and worst episodes of dysphoria, with girls around the age of 16 reporting earlier episodes than either younger or older girls (Angold *et al.*, 1991). This age group also reported a higher level of current symptoms, so it may be that the finding from adults that being currently depressed increases the chance of reporting a previous depression holds in children as well. As long as these caveats are borne in mind, a lifetime history is well worth taking, but it must be remembered that negative responses are not as reliable as positive ones.

The psychodynamic interview

Psychodynamic psychotherapy uses an interview format as its central modality; however, the aims of such interviews are rather different from those of the diagnostic clinical interview. The emphasis is not on collecting 'facts' in an efficient manner, but on engaging the child in an exploration of his or her own inner world and attempting to understand how that world combines fantasy and reality in relation to experience and behaviour. It is therefore usual for the therapist to be much less active and to allow the child to play and draw quite freely. The therapist provides interpretations that represent attempts to understand the meaning of the child's experiences within the framework of psychodynamic theory. This is not the place to explore the intricacies of psychodynamic technique, but it should be borne in mind that these differences in aim and practice mean that a psychodynamically oriented interview is unlikely to provide the best means of collecting the information necessary to make a phenomenological diagnosis; that is not its purpose. On the other hand, though the phenomenological interview may not be the best method for psychoanalysis, it is important that a sense of trust and understanding be generated in such interviews, so as not to compromise later psychodynamic work. Many of the techniques involved in a good phenomenological interview may be seen as laying the groundwork for psychodynamic therapy and there is no reason to see the two as being in opposition (see Chapter 54 for a discussion of some further aspects of psychodynamic psychotherapy).

Projective testing

The aim of projective testing is to provide a child with an ambiguous stimulus, and then to use the responses to indicate underlying problems. At the simple end of the spectrum, children have been asked for years what their three magic wishes would be, and it has been shown that the magic wishes of psychiatrically referred children differ in content from those of normal controls (Winkley, 1982) in frequently containing wishes related to real problems. However, it has not been shown that these same problems could not have been uncovered by simply asking the child about his problems in a straightforward way. And herein lies the issue with projective testing in general. In a thorough review of the literature on the subject, Gittelman-Klein (1978) concluded that there was no evidence that such testing revealed any information that was either not already known to the clinicians before testing or could not have been discovered by the simpler means of asking about it directly. On the other hand, if the aim is to explore a child's fantasy life, particularly as part of psychodynamically oriented play therapy or psychotherapy, then projective techniques clearly have an important part to play, and Winnicott's (1971) famous interactive squiggle game and talking about drawings can certainly serve to initiate and maintain psychotherapeutic interactions.

OBSERVATIONS OF BEHAVIOUR

Observation of the child's behaviour is a central focus of the diagnostic interview. Indeed, with some very disturbed children, it may contribute the most significant material. A number of dimensions should be considered, including separation responses, physical appearance, motor behaviour, form and content of speech, the quality of social interactions, affective behaviour, level of consciousness and developmental level.

Separation responses

The younger the child, the more likely he is to protest against separation from parents, so the interviewer may also need to engage parents in helping the child to separate, and this provides an opportunity to observe parental responses too. During the interview a child will often become more anxious at times, and ask to see his parents. If this anxiety seems likely to disrupt the interview, then a quick visit to the parents will usually settle things down for a while. Sometimes the level of anxiety is such that a child simply cannot be interviewed when the parents are absent, in which case there is no alternative to conducting the interview with them in the room. On the other hand, some children who have experienced multiple caregivers will separate with undue ease, and may end up trying to sit on the interviewer's knee and shower him or her with kisses. A firm but friendly attempt to get the child to adopt more suitable seating usually has the desired effect.

Physical appearance

The physical appearance of the child may provide indications of abuse (e.g. bruising) or neglect (such as dirty, ill-fitting clothes or signs of malnourishment). Signs of genetic abnormalities (such as low-set ears) or other deformities should also be looked for (see Chapter 6). Sometimes oddities of dress, hairstyle or make-up may be helpful in identifying deviant subculture membership, or even psychosis.

Motor behaviour

A number of motor abnormalities that may have psychiatric significance may be observed. The most common example is the restlessness, fidgetiness and distractibility of hyperactivity, which needs to be distinguished from manic motor excitement. Depression may be accompanied by motor slowness and underactivity, and in very rare cases primary obsessional slowness may occur in severe obsessive-compulsive disorder. Obsessive-compulsive disorders may manifest as compulsive acts or rituals (which must be distinguished from motor stereotypies, tics and mannerisms). Potentially self-injurious behaviour such as head-banging or self-biting may occur (usually in mentally retarded subjects), and catatonic states may still very occasionally be observed. The clinician should also be on the alert for medication-induced movement disorders (such as the tremor of lithium intoxication or the choreoathetoid movements of tardive dyskinesia).

Form of speech

Speech disorders, such as stuttering, cluttering and articulation defects, should be noted if they occur, since they may require specialist treatment. A number of psychiatric disorders also produce abnormalities in the form of speech, such as the low-volume mumbling of some socially anxious or depressed individuals, the slowness of speech of psychomotor retardation, manic pressure of speech, and the prosodic abnormalities that may occur in some psychotic states or autism. Vocal tics may occur alone or in combination with motor tics. The assessment of children with serious developmental impairment (which may involve a failure to develop language) is considered in Chapter 33.

Content of speech

A range of speech content abnormalities may be observed including the neologisms, incoherence and poverty of content that may occur in schizophrenia, and manic flight of ideas. Unusual grammatical forms (such as the pronominal inversions of autistic children) may occur, and verbal stereotypies and the occurrence of self-directed speech should also be watched for.

Social interaction

An interview is a social interaction, and can provide a good deal of information about a child's social abilities. Both verbal and nonverbal social functioning should be considered.

How readily does the child provide information? Does the child engage in normal reciprocal social communication with good articulation of both verbal and nonverbal interchanges? Are the child's overtures and responses appropriate to the interview situation or is the child overly withdrawn, overly friendly or socially inappropriate or odd? Is the pattern of eye contact unusual in any way? Does the child maintain an appropriate social distance? Is the child unusually disinhibited, aggressive or oppositional during the interview? Is there unusual preoccupation with idiosyncratic special interests? What is the overall quality of the rapport between the interviewer and the child?

Affective behaviour

Though many children are shy, anxious or sullen at the beginning of an interview, most warm up after a little while and it then becomes possible to detemine whether there are signs of affective dysfunction.

Does the child smile and laugh appropriately and show a normal range of facial expressions and emotional responses? Are there any signs of overly expansive mood? Is the predominant facial expression one of sadness or anxiety? Are there any visible signs of autonomic disturbance, such as sweating or hyperventilation? Is the child frequently tearful, irritable, suspicious or perplexed? Is affective behaviour appropriate to the material being discussed, and does the child show a full range of affective responses? Is the child's mood abnormally labile?

Level of consciousness

In most circumstances, clouding of consciousness will be obvious. However, on rare occasions, previously unrecognized *absences* may be spotted by a careful interviewer.

Developmental level

A full developmental assessment requires expertly administered standardized testing, but a brief evaluation of a child's verbal, reading, writing, mathematical and drawing abilities can indicate the presence of obvious delays or deficits.

CONCLUSIONS

The self-report diagnostic interview has now been shown to be as important a component of a full diagnostic work-up in child psychiatry as it is in adult psychiatry. The child can no longer be dismissed as a primary source of diagnostic information on grounds of mnemonic deficiency or unreliability. Structured interviewing techniques have been found to improve the quality of information collected from children and adolescents, and are becoming ever more widely used in clinical settings. However, much work remains to be done in improving the current state of the art of child psychiatric interviewing. In particular, standardized reliable procedures for coding observed behavioural abnormalities are not available for general clinical use, and interview procedures for children under the age of 8 are not well worked out. Researchers are beginning to turn their attention to developing interview procedures with younger children, and it seems likely that these will involve mnemonic aids such as drawings, puppets and story completion tasks. If the pace of interview development seen during the last decade keeps up, the next 10 years may see these gaps filled and psychiatric diagnosis at a level of psychometric excellence rivalling that of the assessment of developmental level and intelligence.

ACKNOWLEDGEMENTS

I would like to thank Peter Ornstein, PhD, for his helpful comments on my brief review of research on children's memory. This work was supported in part by the William T. Grant Foundation and the Leon Lowenstein Foundation.

REFERENCES

Achenbach T.M. (1985) *Assessment and Taxonomy of Child and Adolescent Psychopathology.* London: Sage Publications.

Andreasen N.C., Grove W.M., Shapiro R.W., Keller M.B., Hirschfeld R.M.A. & McDonald-Scott P. (1981) Reliability of lifetime diagnosis: a multicenter collaborative perspective. *Archives of General Psychiatry,* **38**, 400–405.

Angold A. (1989) Structured assessments of psychopathology in children and adolescents. In: Thompson C. (ed) *The Instruments of Psychiatric Research,* pp. 271–304. John Wiley, Chichester.

Angold A. & Costello E.J. (in press) Depressive co-morbidity in children and adolescents: meanings and mechanisms. *American Journal of Psychiatry.*

Angold A., Burns B.J., Shugart M., Lochman J., Magruder-Habib K. & Looney J. (1991a June). *Psychiatric comorbidity and service use in adolescent substance abusers.* Paper presented at the annual meeting of the Society for Research in Child and Adolescent Psychiatry, Zandvoort, Holland.

Angold A., Cox A., Prendergast M. & Rutter M. (1987, 1991b) *The Child and Adolescent Psychiatric Assessment (CAPA).* This unpublished interview can be obtained through the Developmental Epidemiology Program, Duke University Medical Center, Box 3454, Durham, North Carolina, 27710, USA.

Angold A., Weissman M., John K., Wickramaratne P. & Prusoff B. (1991c) The effects of age and sex on depression ratings in children and adolescents. *Journal of the American Academy of Child and*

Adolescent Psychiatry, **30**, 67−72.

Bird H.R., Canino G., Rubio-Stipec M. & Ribera J.C. (1987) Further measures of the psychometric properties of the children's global assessment scale. *Archives of General Psychiatry*, **44**, 821−824.

Bird H.R., Canino G., Rubio-Stipec M., Gould M., Ribera J., Sesman M., Woodbury M., Huertas-Goldman A, P Pagan A., Sanchez-Lacay A. & Moscoso M. (1988) Estimates of the prevalence of childhood maladjustment in a community survey in Puerto Rico: the use of combined measures. *Archives of General Psychiatry*, **45**, 1120−1126.

Bird H.R., Gould M.S. & Staghezza B.M. (1992, February). Patterns of diagnostic comorbidity in a community sample of children aged 9 through 16 years. Talk presented at the annual meeting of the Society for Research in Child and Adolescent Psychopathology, Sarasota, Florida.

Bjorklund D.F. (1987) How age changes in knowledge base contribute to the development of children's memory: an interpretive review. *Developmental Review*, **7**, 93−130.

Bjorklund D.F. & Muir J.E. (1988) Children's development of free recall memory: remembering on their own. *Annals of Child Development*, **5**, 79−123.

Brainerd C.J., Reyna V.F., Howe M.L. & Kingma J. (1990) The development of forgetting and reminiscence. *Monographs of the Society for Research in Child Development*, serial no. 222, vol. 55, nos. 3−4.

Breslau N. (1987) Inquiring about the bizarre: false positives in Diagnostic Interview Schedule for Children (DISC) ascertainment of obsessions, compulsions, and psychotic symptoms. *Journal of the American Academy of Child and Adolescent Psychiatry*, **26**, 639−644.

Cannell C.F., Marquis K.H. & Laurent A. (1973) A summary of studies of interviewing methodology. In: *Vital and Health Statistics*, series 2, no. 69. US Department of Health, Education, and Welfare publication (HRA)77−1343. National Center for Health Statistics.

Cantwell D.P. (1988) DSM-III studies. In: Rutter M., Tuma A.H. & Lann I.S. (eds) *Assessment and Diagnosis in Child Psychopathology*, pp. 3−36. Guilford Press, New York.

Ceci S.J., Ross D.F. & Toglia M.P. (1987) Suggestibility of children's memory: psycholegal implications. *Journal of Experimental Psychology: General*, **116**, 38−49.

Chambers W.J., Puig-Antich J., Hirsch M., Paez P., Ambrosini P.J., Tabrizi M.A. & Davies M. (1985) The assessment of affective disorders in children and adolescents by semi-structured interview: test−retest reliability of the schedule for affective disorders and schizophrenia for school-age children, present episode version. *Archives of General Psychiatry*, **42**, 696−702.

Chapman L.J. & Chapman J.P. (1967) Genesis of popular but erroneous psychodiagnostic observations. *Journal of Abnormal Psychology*, **74**, 271−280.

Chapman L.J. & Chapman J.P. (1971) Associatively based illusory correlation as a source of psychodiagnostic folklore. In: Goodstein L.D. & Lanyon R.I. (eds) *Readings in Personality Assessment*. John Wiley, New York.

Cohen R.L. & Harnick M.A. (1980) The susceptibility of child witnesses to suggestion. *Law and Human Behavior*, **4**, 201−210.

Cole C.B. & Loftus E.F. (1987) The memory of children. In: Ceci S.J., Toglia M.P. & Ross D.F. (eds) *Children's Eyewitness Memory*, pp. 178−208. Springer-Verlag, New York.

Costello E.J. (1982, October). Clinical decision making in child psychiatry. Paper presented at the 29th Meeting of the American Academy of Child Psychiatry, Washington, DC.

Costello A.J., Edelbrock C.S., Dulcan M.K., Kalas R. & Klaric S.H. (1984) *The NIMH Diagnostic Interview Schedule for Children (DISC): Final Report*. National Institute of Mental Health, Bethesda, MD.

Cox A., Hopkinson K.F., & Rutter M. (1981a) Psychiatric interview techniques. II. Naturalistic study: eliciting factual information. *British Journal of Psychiatry*, **139**, 29−37.

Cox A., Rutter M. & Holbrook D. (1981b) Psychiatric interview techniques. V. Experimental study: eliciting factual information. *British Journal of Psychiatry*, **139**, 29−37.

Cox A., Holbrook D. & Rutter M. (1981c) Psychiatric interviewing techniques. VI. Experimental study: eliciting feelings *British Journal of Psychiatry*, **139**, 144−156.

Dale P.S., Loftus E.F. & Rathban L. (1978) The influence of the form of the question on the eyewitness testimony of preschool children. *Journal of Psycholinguistic Research*, **7**, 269−277.

Dawes R.M. (1988) *Rational Choice in an Uncertain World*. Harcourt Brace Jovanovich, New York.

Dent H.R. (1991) Experimental studies of interviewing child witnesses. In: Doris J. (ed) *The Suggestibility of Children's Recollections*, pp. 138−146. American Psychological Association, Washington, DC.

Dent H.R. & Stephenson G.M. (1979) An experimental study of the effectiveness of different techniques of questioning child witnesses. *British Journal of Social and Clinical Psychology*, **18**, 41−51.

Dodd D.H. & Bradshaw J.M. (1980) Leading questions and memory: pragmatic constraints. *Journal of Verbal Learning and Verbal Behavior*, **19**, 695−704.

Edelbrock C. & Costello A.J. (1988) Structured psychiatric interviews for children. In: Rutter M., Tuma A.H. & Lann I.S. (eds) *Assessment and Diagnosis in Child Psychopathology*, pp. 87−407. Guilford Press, New York.

Edelbrock C., Costello A.J., Dulcan M.K., Kalas R. & Conover N.C. (1985) Age differences in the reliability of the psychiatric interview of the child. *Child Development*, **56**, 265−275.

Fendrich M., Weissman M., Warner V., Mufson L. (1990) Two-year recall of lifetime diagnoses in offspring at high and low risk for major depression. *Archives of General Psychiatry*, **47**, 1121−1127.

Gittelman-Klein R. (1978) Validity of projective tests for psychodiagnosis in children. In: Spitzen R.L., Klein D.F. (eds) *Critical Issues in Psychiatric Diagnosis*. Raven Press, New York.

Goodman G.S. (1984) Children's testimony in historical perspective. *Journal of Social Issues*, **40**, 9−31.

Goodman G.S., Aman C. & Hirschman J. (1987) Child sexual and physical abuse: children's testimony. In: Ceci S.J., Toglia M.P. & Ross D.F. (eds) *Children's Eyewitness Memory*, pp. 1−23. Springer-Verlag, New York.

Hart H., Bax M. & Jenkins S. (1978) The value of a developmental history. *Developmental Medicine and Child Neurology*, **20**, 442−452.

Hedderman C. (1987) *Children's Evidence: The Need for Corroboration*. Research and Planning Unit paper no. 41. Home Office, London.

Herjanic B. & Campbell W. (1977) Differentiating psychiatrically disturbed children on the basis of a structured interview. *Journal of Abnormal Child Psychology*, **5**, 127−134.

Herjanic B. & Reich W. (1982) Development of a structured psychiatric interview for children: agreement between child and parent on individual symptoms. *Journal of Abnormal Child Psychology*, **10**, 307−324.

Hodges K., Klein J., Fitch P., McKnew D. & Cytryn L. (1981) The child assessment schedule. *Catalog of Selected Documents in Psychology*, **11**, 56.

Hodges K., Cools J., McKnew D. (1989) Test−retest reliability of a clinical research interview for children: the child assessment schedule. *Psychological Assessment*, **1**, 317−322.

Hopkinson K.F., Cox A. & Rutter M. (1981) Psychiatric interviewing techniques. III. Naturalistic study. Eliciting feelings. *British Journal of Psychiatry*, **138**, 406−415.

John K., Gammon G.D., Prusoff B.A. & Warner V. (1987) The social adjustment inventory for children and adolescents (SAICA): testing a new semi-structured interview. *Journal of the American Academy of Child and Adolescent Psychiatry*, **26**, 898−911.

Jones D.P.H. (1985, November). Reliable and fictitious accounts of sexual abuse in children. Paper presented at the Seventh National

Conference on Child Abuse and Neglect, Chicago, Ill.

Keller M.B., Lavori P.W., McDonald-Scott P., Scheftner W.A., Andreasen N.C., Shapiro R.W. & Croughan J. (1981) Reliability of lifetime diagnosis and symptoms in patients with a current psychiatric disorder. *Journal of Psychiatry Research*, **16**, 229–240.

King M. & Yuille J.C. (1987) Suggestibility and the child witness. In: Ceci S.J., Toglia M.P. & Ross D.F. (eds) *Children's Eyewitness Memory*, pp. 24–35. Springer-Verlag, New York.

Kovacs M. (1983) The children's depression inventory: a self-rated depression scale for school-aged youngsters. This unpublished document can be obtained through the Western Psychiatric Institute and Clinic, Department of Psychiatry, University of Pittsburgh School of Medicine, 3811 O'Hara Street, Pittsburgh, Pennsylvania, 15213–2593, USA.

Leippe M.R. & Romanczyk A. (1987) Children on the witness stand: a communication/persuasion analysis of jurors' reactions to child witnesses. In: Ceci S.J., Toglia M.P. & Ross D.F. (eds) *Children's Eyewitness Memory*, pp. 155–177. Springer-Verlag, New York.

Loftus E.F. (1979) *Eyewitness Testimony*. Harvard University Press, Cambridge, MA.

Martini D.R., Strayhorn J.M. & Puig-Antich J. (1990) A symptom self-report measure for preschool children. *Journal of the American Academy of Child and Adolescent Psychiatry*, **29**, 594–600.

Nelson K., Fivush R., Hudson J. & Lucariello J. (1983) Scripts and the development of memory. In: Chi M.T.H. (ed) *Trends in Memory Development Research. Contributions to Human Development*, vol. 9. S. Karger, Basel.

Ornstein P.A., Gordon B.N. & Larus D.M. (1992) Children's memory for a personally experienced event: implications for testimony. *Applied Cognitive Psychology*, **6**, 49–60.

Ornstein P.A., Larus D.M. & Clubb P.A. (1991) Understanding children's testimony: implications of research on the development of memory. In: Vasta R. (ed) *Annals of Child Development* vol. 8, pp. 145–176. Jessica Kingsley, London.

Orvaschel H., Puig-Antich J., Chambers M.D., Tabrizi M.A. & Johnson R. (1982) Retrospective assessment of prepubertal major depression with the Kiddie-SADS-E. *Journal of the American Academy of Child Psychiatry*, **4**, 392–397.

Pillemer D.B. & White S.H. (1989) Childhood events recalled by children and adults. *Advances in Child Development and Behavior*, **21**, 297–340.

Puig-Antich J. & Chambers W. (1978) The schedule for affective disorders and schizophrenia for school-aged children. This unpublished interview schedule can be obtained through the New York State Psychiatric Institute, 722 West 168 Street, New York, New York, 10032, USA.

Ross D.F., Miller B.S. & Moran P.B. (1987) The child in the eyes of the jury: assessing mock jurors' perceptions of the child witness. In: Ceci S.J., Toglia M.P. & Ross D.F. (eds) *Children's Eyewitness Memory*, pp. 142–154. Springer-Verlag, New York.

Rutter M. & Cox A. (1981) Psychiatric interviewing techniques: I. Methods and measures. *British Journal of Psychiatry*, **138**, 273–282.

Rutter M., Cox A., Egert S., Holbrook D. & Everitt B. (1981) Psychiatric interviewing techniques. V: Experimental study: eliciting information. *British Journal of Psychiatry*, **139**, 29–37.

Saywitz K.J. (1987) Children's testimony: age-related patterns of memory errors. In: Ceci S.J., Toglia M.P. & Ross D.F. (eds) *Children's Eyewitness Memory*, pp. 6–52. Springer-Verlag, New York.

Schwab-Stone M., Fennelly B., Fischer D., Briggs M., Raymond L., Crowther B. & Figueroa K. (1989, October). Issues in structured diagnostic interviewing of children ages 6–11 years. Paper presented at the annual meeting of the Ameircan Academy of Child and Adolescent Psychiatry, New York, NY.

Shaffer D., Gould M.S., Brasic J., Ambrosini P., Fisher P., Bird H. & Aluwahlia S. (1983) A children's global assessment scale (CGAS). *Archives of General Psychiatry*, **40**, 1228–1231.

Shaffer D., Schwab-Stone M., Fisher P., Piacentini J., Davies M., Bird H. & Hoven C. (1992, February). Development and status of the Diagnostic Interview Schedule for children (DISC). Talk presented at the annual meeting of the Society for Research in Child and Adolescent Psychopathology, Sarasota, Florida.

Siegal M., Waters L.J. & Dinwiddy L.S. (1988) Misleading children: causal attributions for inconsistency under repeated questioning. *Journal of Experimental Child Psychology*, **45**, 438–456.

Sox H.C., Blatt M.A., Higgins M.C., & Marton K.I. (1988) *Medical Decision Making*. Butterworth, Boston.

Traux C.B. (1966) Reinforcement and non-reinforcement in Rogerian psychotherapy. *Journal of Abnormal Psychology*, **71**, 1–9.

Traux C.B. (1968) Therapist interpersonal reinforcement of client-self-exploration and therapeutic outcome in group psychotherapy. *Journal of Counseling Psychology*, **15**, 225–231.

Tversky A. & Kahnemann D. (1974) Judgement under uncertainty: heuristics and biases. *Science*, **185**, 1124–1131.

Weinstein M.C. & Fineberg H.V. (1980) *Clinical Decision Analysis*. W.B. Saunders, Philadelphia.

Winkley L. (1982) The implications of children's wishes — research note. *Journal of Child Psychology and Psychiatry*, **23**, 477–483.

Winnicott D.W. (1971) *Therapeutic Consultations in Child Psychiatry*. Hogarth Press, London.

Yuille J.C. (1980) A critical examination of the psychological and practical implications of eyewitness research. *Law and Human Behavior*, **4**, 335–345.

Zaragoza M.S. (1987) Memory, suggestibility, and eyewitness testimony in children and adults. In: Ceci S.J., Toglia M.P. & Ross D.F. (eds) *Children's Eyewitness Memory*, pp. 53–78. Springer-Verlag, New York.

Chapter 5
Family Interviewing:
Issues of Theory and Practice

Hugh Jenkins

INTRODUCTION

This chapter identifies some of the issues related to family interviewing in assessment and treatment, and notes some of the advantages of conjoint family interviewing in mental health practice. By seeing the whole family as part of a standard procedure 'one may considerably improve the effectiveness and economy of clinical work, even in instances where family therapy as such is not contemplated. Information is developed rapidly and in appropriate multi-dimensional complexity; scapegoating of the identified patient is reduced; family systems resistances are made visible, and strategies for coping with them are initiated from the outset ... [and] ... substantial benefits can accrue to the patient, his family, and the therapeutic enterprise when this procedure is used.' (Franklin & Prosky, 1973, p. 29.)

The primary tool of the mental health clinician is the spoken word. A range of techniques, including family sculpting, role play, genograms whether used diagnostically or as part of clinical work, and family drawings, may form an integral part of this process. The assessment interview may be supplemented by formal psychological testing (see Chapter 7), or other investigations such as neurological or physical screening (see Chapter 6). Written reports from other professionals will often be needed. None of these can supersede assessment and clinical interviews. However, clinicians are frequently unclear about the purpose of different types of interview and too often employing agencies confuse means and ends. The key questions are: who should be interviewed, by whom, and for what purpose?

If an interview is to ascertain an individual's mental state, to what extent should other significant family members be involved? If an interview is to discover whether sexual abuse has occurred, often referred to as a disclosure interview, who else should be seen, when and by whom? In what way is such an interview different from an ordinary assessment or an ongoing therapeutic interview? Where such interviews take place will alter the meaning of the interview. One that is conducted in a social services agency under the auspices of child protection work or for the provision of resources will differ significantly from one conducted in a department of child and adolescent psychiatry. If the interview is to assess developmental delay in a child, family-focused interviewing will differ from that which sets out to understand how the behaviours of family members make it difficult for the individual child not to behave in distressing or unacceptable ways.

If interviewers, irrespective of theoretical orientation, choose only to see an individual, their interventions will still affect the whole family or social group. The conjoint family interview enables the clinician to perceive the whole. At the same time this broader perspective should not distract the interviewer from evaluating the more detailed qualities of the individual's behaviour and internal world (Nichols, 1987).

This chapter will refer to the background to family interviewing since the 1950s, followed by a comment on the recent literature on family interviewing methods. This should be read in conjunction with Chapter 55 on family therapy. It will cover the different purposes of interviewing whole families when working within a systemic framework. The different reasons for seeing the whole family include its value as a diagnostic tool, the first family interview as part of the process of treatment, and the ongoing interview in therapy. The final section introduces some techniques and clinical issues for a conjoint family interview model in treatment.

HISTORICAL BACKGROUND

When a group begins to see familiar material differently, it requires what Kuhn (1970) calls a paradigm shift. This was necessary in introducing a family systemic framework into the mental health field when the dominant model was an individual one. Although it would no longer be possible to think of the individual in isolation, more traditional methods of thinking and practice have remained powerful organizers of mental health and social care systems.

In the wider scientific community, the shift that began to occur in people's thinking was influenced by the science of cybernetics (Wiener, 1948) and of general systems theory (von Bertalanffy, 1968). It is a tenet of systems thinkers that the whole cannot be understood by the arithmetical addition of information from different parts. In human behaviour all events occur in contexts of place and time, and behavioural patterns tend to be repetitive or circular (Gorell Barnes, 1985).

The ideas that emerged from Bateson's group in the 1950s and 1960s (Bateson, 1973; 1980) were influential in the field of family systems thinking. Jackson (1965a,b) began systematically to interview and treat whole families. He highlighted the shift from a linear to a circular way of viewing behaviours:

> One important concept ignored by [a linear] theory is that of feedback, which proposes that information about event B impinges on event A, which then affects B, etc., in a circle of events which modify each other. Since psychological 'events' seldom occur only once . . . this circular model is often more appropriate than one which artificially abstracts such events from the intricate time sequence in which they occur (Jackson, 1965a, p. 5).

From a research aspect, Haley focused on the problems of describing complexity in relationships in the field of family study:

> The problem is no longer how to characterize and classify these individuals; it is how to describe and classify the habitual patterns of responsive behaviour exchanged by intimates. . . . With this focus, the 'cause' of why someone does what he does is shifting from inside him to the context in which he lives (Haley, 1967, p. 12).

A problem related to this shift in perspective is of the data becoming more 'soft'. In effect, the focus of attention is to the spaces in between individuals (interactional perspective), rather than the spaces within (intrapsychic perspective) and the discrete behaviours of psychiatric or behavioural phenomena. Interviewing methods had to account for the complexity of working both with more than one person present in the room and in the mind of the clinician. This complexity makes it difficult for research to progress much beyond descriptions of individuals and dyads, even though as early as 1956, Ackerman and Behrens began to think in terms of family diagnosis (Ackerman & Behrens, 1956).

DEFINING A FAMILY INTERVIEW

It is not the number of people present that transforms an individual interview into a family interview. The difference is how the clinician thinks about the nature of the problem, how it evolved, how its presence is maintained in a particular context and the implications for change on the wider social context. 'Family therapy operates on the theoretical assumption that man is part of his context and that individual changes require a change in the reciprocal relationship of man in his context' (Minuchin, 1979, p. 6). In the UK, a group of clinicians and researchers experimented with ways of describing family interaction, and of interviewing families for clinical and research purposes (Bentovim & Kinston, 1978, 1991; Kinston & Bentovim, 1978; Loader *et al.*, 1981; Stratford *et al.*, 1982). Their early thinking on the use of structured tasks in the interview was influenced by the early work of Watzlawick (1966).

FAMILY INFLUENCES ON PSYCHOPATHOLOGY

There is an abundance of empirical evidence that experiences in the family constitute an important influence on children's psychological development and play a major role in the causation of psychological disorder (see Chapter 12; Rutter, 1991; Dunn, in press). Accordingly, it is clear that any adequate diagnostic appraisal must include a systematic evaluation of family functioning. The key questions then are not whether this should be done but rather which elements of family interaction are most important to assess, and how this is best achieved. In that connection, several research findings are pertinent. Firstly, of all family features, family discord, disorganization and disruption show the strongest associations with psychiatric disorder. Secondly, however, to a substantial extent, the psychiatric risks stem more from the specific interpersonal relationships experienced by the individual child than from the overall family atmosphere. This is evident from both quantitative behaviour genetic analyses that can separate shared from nonshared environmental effects (Plomin & Daniels, 1987) and detailed clinical-style interview studies (e.g. Buchanan *et al.*, 1991; Jenkins & Smith, 1991). Thirdly, people's relationships show quite complicated reciprocal patterns (Hinde & Stevenson-Hinde, 1988). It is seriously misleading to think of individuals as generally warm, critical, hostile or dominant. Of course, there are consistencies in affective style that generalize across relationships but so, too, people interact in *different* ways with different people as a result of feelings of rivalry, rejection and lack of satisfaction. Thus, mothers sometimes develop a smotheringly close relationship with one of their children as a way of compensating for a loveless marriage (Engfer, 1988), and first-born girls with an unusually close relationship with their mothers are particularly likely to develop a negative relationship with their younger siblings (Dunn & Kendrick, 1982). The clear implication is that it is necessary to assess individual dyadic relationships and not just overall family emotional qualities. Because relationships show complementarity, as well as generalization, it follows that it is important to evaluate the overall pattern of family relationships and not just those that impinge directly on the child. This was evident in Levy's (1943) pioneering studies of maternal overprotection 50 years ago, as well as in more modern family investigations.

There is more uncertainty on the range of family qualities that are relevant to the cause or course of psychiatric disorder. However, it seems that deviant communication patterns, as well as affective style, may be important (Doane *et al.*, 1981; Valone *et al.*, 1983; Noller & Fitzpatrick, 1990). It should be added that it is not enough to measure the family features that carry a major psychiatric risk. If therapeutic interventions are to be planned on a rational empirical basis, it is also necessary to determine how the maladaptive patterns of relationships and of communication developed and how they are maintained. That is no easy task. Rutter (1989) highlighted the complexity of the challenges in relation to family assessment and intervention; and early pioneers in the family field struggled with the problems involved in seeking to classify health in family terms (Lewis *et al.*, 1976).

Nevertheless, despite the difficulties, there has been considerable progress in the development of reliable and valid measures of family features (Wilkinson, 1987; Jacob & Tennenbaum, 1988). Brown and Rutter were among the first investigators to develop sound standardized interview measures of family relationships and patterns of family inter-action (Brown & Rutter, 1966; Rutter & Brown, 1966). These were found to predict later marriage breakdown (Quinton et al., 1976) as well as the course of psychiatric disorder (Brown et al., 1962; Leff & Vaughn, 1981, 1985; Szmukler et al., 1985, 1987; Vostanis et al., 1992). There has been a particular focus on negative expressed emotion (Leff & Vaughn, 1985) and family discord (Quinton et al., 1976) but it has proved possible to assess a wider range of family features reliably. In addition to these more clinical interview measures, there are many questionnaire, observational and other assess-ment techniques (Jacob & Tennenbaum, 1988; Akister & Stevenson-Hinde, 1991; Akister et al., 1993).

INDIVIDUAL AND CONJOINT FAMILY INTERVIEWS: PROS AND CONS

Given the need to assess family functioning, it is necessary to consider whether this is best done through separate individual interviews with different family members or through a con-joint interview with the whole family together. There have been surprisingly few systematic comparisons of these two interview approaches but a few broad conclusions are possible. First, findings have been consistent in showing that individual interview measures of relationships show generally good validity as evident in husband–wife agreement, agreement with emotions as shown directly in conjoint interviews, and predictions to both psychopathology and family functioning as assessed later (Brown & Rutter, 1966; Rutter & Brown, 1966; Quinton et al., 1976; Jacob & Tennenbaum, 1988). Indeed, individual interviews may even be superior to conjoint family interviews as a means of differentiating marriages under stress (Haynes et al., 1981). On the other hand, conjoint interviews appear clearly better for the assessment of communication (Haynes et al., 1981). Although not adequately put to the test, it is clear that individual interviews are very inefficient for the delineation of detailed family patterns of most kinds and are particularly unsatisfactory for the assess-ment of the dynamics of ongoing interactions between family members. In short, individual interviews are good at the detection of family psychopathology but probably much less good at the assessment of how this arises and is maintained. That constitutes the main objective of family interviews. It cannot be claimed that the validity of measures of these more subtle dynamic features is well-established but the initial findings from systematic research assessments are promising (Jacob & Tennenbaum, 1988; Kinston & Loader, 1988; Noller & Fitzpatrick, 1990). Because conjoint family interviews are probably superior for the detection of family interactions that may be important for therapeutic planning, it seems desirable that a brief conjoint interview should form at least a part of nearly all diagnostic assessments.

Of course, an adequate diagnostic appraisal also requires the gathering of good-quality factual information of various types about the child and about the family (see Chapters 2 and 4). Such data as are available indicate that individual interviews tend to be superior for this purpose (Eminson & Cox, described in Chapter 3 on interviews with parents; Haynes et al., 1981). Probably this superiority arises for two rather separate reasons: firstly, systematic detailed questioning produces better information than more open-ended approaches that are reliant on the views of the informant about what is important (see Chapter 3); and, secondly, the presence of other family members may inhibit certain sorts of disclosures. Nevertheless, all studies of family interviews have shown that they provide a rich source of information and they may well be better than individual interviews for the assessment of family attitudes and values regarding problem behaviour. Still, their limitations mean that many clinicians regard it as important, at least for some types of referral, to include an individual interview as part of the overall diagnostic appraisal.

A third concern is whether families prefer a family or individual interview. It seems that there is considerable vari-ation in preferences with no clear favouring of either style. Probably it is easier to move from a family appraisal to an individual one, when that is required, rather than the reverse, but there is limited evidence on this point.

ASSESSMENT AND DIAGNOSIS

In all clinical approaches there is a close overlapping connec-tion between assessment and treatment (see Chapters 2 and 4), but the two are particularly closely intertwined in family therapy. Inevitably the practitioner's theoretical framework about the nature of symptom formation and of therapeutic change will influence therapeutic decisions (Frosh, 1991). In terms of the ICD classificatory system, the major component from a systems basis is axis 5 (van Goor-Lambo et al., 1990). Once the clinician begins to think interactionally, an interest in the contexts in which psychiatric and behavioural sympto-matology occur and the relationships between psychological ability as set against achievement will also take on different meanings. Medical conditions will be significant, especially depending on the ways in which family members deal with illness or handicap (Bloch, 1989). Family transactional styles significantly affect both coping strategies and therapeutic out-come. From a family systems perspective, failure to undertake a comprehensive family interview assessment will result in insufficient information being available about the meaning of the problem(s) presented and the likely strengths which can be mobilized from within the family and wider family/social network.

EARLY EXPERIMENTS WITH STRUCTURED FAMILY INTERVIEWS

In 1966 Watzlawick described a structured whole-family inter-view protocol intended to reduce the length of therapy. The brief therapy approaches associated with the Mental Research Institute in Palo Alto developed out of these early ideas. The aim was to identify the levels of information outside family members' awareness where the interviewer is interested more in process than in content. The structured format was designed to create situations that would reveal different communication levels and hence provide an understanding of the family's dynamics and patterns of interaction. In this format, family members first completed tasks individually with the interviewer, and then in the whole-family context (see Watzlawick, 1966).

This represented an attempt to use tasks with the whole family in order to elicit information about family communication patterns and problem-solving skills. The significant conceptual shift was to an interest in patterns of interaction between family members, and the ways in which families jointly construct their realities. The focus of treatment that followed was on how to interrupt those interactional patterns that appeared maladaptive.

A more comprehensive project, both in scope and reporting, was provided by Goldstein *et al.* (1968). These researchers used a semistructured interview format, together with a wider range of assessment procedures than Watzlawick. Their aim was to 'study social influence and coping styles in families of disturbed adolescents' (p. 250), assessing the extent to which parental figures use deviant means of influencing or controlling their children, and how children develop dysfunctional methods for dealing with parental pressures. Information from this project allowed an analysis of data from the perspectives of 'affectional patterns, communication patterns and role relationships and reversals within the family' (p. 234). By recording all the individual, dyadic and triadic (parent–parent–child) interviews, they were able to play back and compare statements made in each family configuration. The format was structured in that there was a sequence of five sessions, each with varying tasks, and semistructured, for example, in that specific cue statements for each family had to be elicited because 'problems uniform in content are often not comparable in their emotional significance for different families' (pp. 236–237). This work showed how much could be obtained from a structured family assessment. Even so, problems remain on decisions on what is acceptable as hard empirical data and how to deal with complexity in coding relationship variables (Loader *et al.*, 1980; Bloch, 1989; Jenkins, 1990a).

Whom to see, and when

The decision about whom to see will be determined largely by the clinician's theoretical framework and the agency context. The individual and the particular contexts must both be addressed. For the clinician who holds a systemic perspective, it is possible to work with the individual, various subgroups and the whole family (Hoffman, 1985). It is a matter of conceptualizing processes and behaviours at a number of different levels of abstraction, of being clear about the tasks to be undertaken and then deciding what are the best strategies for achieving them.

A formal developmental history, emphasizing clear chronological factual information, may be given most economically by one or both parents. How one parent relates the story and how the other responds nonverbally as well as verbally will be critical in assessing levels of mutual support and agreement; how feelings of blame or guilt are mediated; and styles for dealing with conflict. If the aim is to assess family functioning and coping strategies, it will be uneconomical of time and effort for the referred child and siblings, with any other actively involved relatives, to be absent. A child who appears alert in an individual interview may appear sad or depressed in the family context or vice versa. Siblings may be solicitous or resentful, especially if, for example, a developmentally delayed child consumes most of their parents' energies. Equally the marital relationship may suffer as the price of high investment in parenting tasks. A nonhandicapped child may be the silent sufferer whose own developmental needs are neglected; or that child may have established strong relationships with another family member to compensate for his or her unmet needs. This is discussed further in the section on assessing relationships.

Just as the context of the clinical interview room or home visit will affect family functioning and provide different pictures, so the presence or absence of family members will influence the nature of the information available to the interviewer. If the aim of the clinician is to obtain an individual's 'story', it would seem that it is necessary to see that individual alone. There are however often practical difficulties in starting with only one family member if others are likely to be involved later, because a privileged relationship between clinician and individual may develop and potentially cloud subsequent contacts with other family members, especially where communication patterns are highly disturbed. It is easier to work later with subgroups if the initial contact starts with all concerned. Reconvening the whole family becomes easier. To date, no formal studies have been undertaken comparing drop-out rates from treatment depending on whether work begins with the whole family or only one member. However, clinical experience would seem to indicate this tendency. Nonattendance where everyone involved has been invited is information for the therapist about family dilemmas or possible resistance (Anderson & Stewart, 1983). There are however, exceptions to this statement. In forensic, sexual abuse disclosure work, or other serious abuses of power in relationships, individual interviews will be indicated.

One of the difficulties in mental health work is to define what information is required. Bateson (1973b) suggested that information is the difference that makes a difference. Confusion arises between obtaining information and factual data such as names, dates of birth, onset of illnesses or problems, none of which in itself is likely to be new to the informants. In the family interview the clinician seeks to understand the interactional patterns between people, the meanings ascribed to events, and how the same event may have significantly different meanings for different family members. The important new information may be the realization for the first time about the pain or hurt that a family member has been carrying for years. It is not enough to know that maternal grandmother died 5 years ago and that the mother shortly after had her first episode of depression or the child started to display behavioural problems. Mother's loss may have been father's release. The important questions then become: 'How did your husband support you at that time?' or 'How did your child learn about grandmother's death? Who had time for her/him when you were so upset?' It may be the first time that the husband learns that his wife felt he was not supportive, or that she felt she could not tell him how she felt, not knowing if he would cope. Sensitive interviewing, perhaps using interventive questioning (Tomm, 1987, 1988), will reveal a picture of how support is given and received; intimacy is negotiated; children are able to be part of the family at difficult times, or are relied on more than the spouse/partner. The clinician can assess who should be involved at different stages of treatment, whether the emphasis should be to strengthen parental functioning by working separately with them first, or with all the family members conjointly. Where there are high levels of family disorganization and chaos (Minuchin & Montalvo, 1967; Minuchin *et al.*, 1967; Patterson, 1982) separate work with family subgroups may be indicated.

Assessing relationships

Relationships can be understood by those involved, each describing individually how they perceive their part and the part that others play. Inevitably, this will only provide one aspect of the picture. A conjoint family approach is a powerful and more direct way of evaluating how family members interact. Relationships can be much better understood by observation than by report. The following vignettes indicate how this may be done.

A parent may say that their child will not leave her or him to go to school. If the clinician then asks the parent to have the child leave the interview and wait in the waiting room while the parent talks with the clinician, he may observe the parent 'overreassuring' the child that there is no need to worry, and of course the child can always come in again if at all upset. This sort of interaction highlights how the cues given by the parent amount almost to an 'instruction' to worry. The clinician can use this interaction to inquire how the parent communicates with the child before going to school, whether in fact the sequences observed in the interview room are isomorphic with the home situation. Why the parent feels anxious may relate to the parent's own early life experiences, current events, feeling depressed, or feeling unsupported by the other parent, and these issues may need to be explored by the clinician. Bateson *et al.* (1973) reported similar communication patterns. In order better to assess relationships the clinician may ask one parent to have a child undertake something quite simple rather than describe what happens at home. The extent to which the other parent allows the parent

to do this, or interrupts the parent will provide information about relationships between the three people concerned. Such a simple task can reveal the family's structural organization, communication patterns and denied relationships most effectively. This forms the basis of much of Minuchin's structural work with families (Minuchin, 1974).

Children who have suffered considerable emotional and material deprivation frequently have difficulty making significant attachments (Bowlby, 1969, 1977). In conjoint sessions the clinician will observe the extent to which the child discriminates between him or her as a stranger and family members. He or she will observe, and therefore will not have to ask, how the parent(s) deal(s) with requests for attention, whether the child behaves as though he or she expects his or her request to be responded to and the extent to which the parent is able to attend to the child's needs while following what else is happening in the room.

In referrals involving developmental delay it can be useful to have a parent leave the room at a prearranged time in order to observe the child's responses and then to return later to see how the child and parent greet each other. Some autistic children, for example, seem not to differentiate between different adults. The autistic child may not register the disappearance and reappearance of the parent, although the parent shows concern about leaving the child. The important and sometimes difficult work that is then needed is to help the parent(s) accept the child's limitations and to learn to relate in such a way that the child can best appreciate its surroundings. Parents who come hoping for a confirmation that their child is not as handicapped as they have been led to believe need sensitive help in what can be a mourning process for the perfect child that never was (Jenkins, 1986).

The clinician must develop ways to enact at least in part the dilemmas that the family brings in relation to their child. Just by starting: 'If you were at home now, and you wanted your child to leave the room while we talk/sit quietly for a moment/ talk with one of its parents/stay here while you go out' the clinician can begin to create a situation where the presenting problem is brought directly into the room, available for observation and the beginnings of the change process. When parents say: 'We've already tried this/he won't do it here because it's artificial,' the clinician must find ways of saying that this is still important, and it is not the same but is to help the clinician. Different approaches to these clinical dilemmas are discussed in greater detail in Chapter 55.

GUIDELINES FOR
A FAMILY DIAGNOSTIC
INTERVIEW

Conjoint family interviewing may not be the method of treatment in a mental health service and on occasion conjoint family interviewing will clearly be contraindicated, as in child sexual abuse where the alleged perpetrator is a family member and denies or does not take responsibility for the abuse (Jenkins, 1989a), or where violence to an individual as a result is likely. However, in other instances, an initial conjoint family diagnostic interview is strongly recommended (Franklin & Prosky, 1973). Family members may be more readily reengaged as part of treatment when they have been part of the initial assessment process (Jenkins & Asen, 1992).

The short diagnostic family interview

The short diagnostic family interview format, used as one element of a battery of assessment procedures, is necessarily limited in its aims. It provides the initial contact with the family, followed by formal history-taking and psychological assessments. Despite its brevity (10–15 minutes), it can provide considerable information, especially at the level of process information of which family members are not directly aware. All family members attending are seen by the primary clinician, and after introducing the structure of the whole assessment process, the interviewer works to create a climate that enables family members to demonstrate rather than report their ways of interacting and of coping with each other, and also begins to ascertain what are their beliefs as to the nature of the difficulties. The clinician does not set out specifically to change the family, although the experience inevitably will impact on them. At a surface level, the interviewer elicits information from family members. Even so, the style and structure of the questions will 'introduce new information' into the family system (Tomm, 1987, 1988). In the guidelines to the interviewer, the following explanations are given.

Demonstrate means to show through their behaviour the ways that family members communicate with each other and with the therapist(s), how they as a social unit are organized, and how they organize others.

Report means that what people say they do or believe is often different from the ways in which they communicate non-verbally to one another.

Beliefs mean that each person will have a view about the problem(s) and what they believe should be done about it, as well as the reasons why they think the difficulties arose in the first place. Therapy frequently involves working with the differences between the patient's views and the understanding or beliefs that the therapist holds about the nature of the problems, and how to solve them.

Clinicians often think in terms of obtaining information, and then making a diagnosis. This results in an early emphasis on obtaining facts. This is important when tracing the development of an illness, although even here the clinician will be looking for patterns. The interviewer must focus on the 'process' of interaction in the family diagnostic interview. The interviewer's task is to elicit behaviour that provides indications about how family members deal with their worries and each other, what the family structure is, and what are the typical family communication patterns. Verification is not the primary task. The interviewer's task is firstly, to facilitate interaction and secondly, to observe what happens, without aiming to provide interpretations to the family.

In order that the interviewer does not become too central, some simple question formats are suggested. They draw particularly on the work of Palazzoli *et al.* (1980a), Penn (1982, 1985) Boscolo *et al.* (1987), Campbell and Draper (1985), Cecchin (1987), Tomm (1987, 1988) and Campbell *et al.* (1989). This style is referred to broadly as circular questioning, or interventive interviewing (Tomm, 1987). Even a question such as: 'Who would be the best person to begin telling me why you came here today?' or 'What would your husband say if I asked him why you have brought your son/daughter here today?' will begin to elicit information as family members respond or listen. With younger children, as well as adolescents, it may be useful to find out when, how and from whom they learnt about the appointment. From this, more general questions can be generated about how children are communicated to and by whom, how conflict is dealt with and how competing interests are met.

The nonverbal messages as one person speaks will often be more important for understanding structure and family patterns than what is said. The interviewer also must ensure that no single person is allowed to hold the floor for too long. A lengthy account by one person can be politely and firmly interrupted by a question such as: 'How would your wife/husband/son/daughter see the problem compared to how you have been describing it?' This can then be verified, even by asking a third party: 'How do you think your mother/father/brother would differ in how she/he viewed the problem?' This technique allows the interviewer to bring other people in quite naturally. A question such as: 'Would your partner/child agree?' or 'Your partner/child looks as though he/she might have a different view' allows the interviewer to deal simultaneously with process and content issues. As the interviewer becomes engaged in the questioning process, subsequent questions will naturally suggest themselves.

It is important that the interviewer adopts a neutral stance. The question 'Who does it most affect when *Y* does this?' allows the interviewer to explore the interpersonal consequences of individual behaviours from which patterns begin to be observable. After the diagnostic interview, the interviewer should go through the following checklist:

1 What are the patterns of affect in this family?

2 (a) What are the various attitudes towards the problem?
  (b) Who is the family expert on the problem?
  (c) Who is most worried about the problem?
  (d) How is worry shown in this family?

3 (a) What is the individual life cycle stage for the patient?
  (b) What are the main current life cycle stages for the operative family system? (Usually at least three generations.)
  (c) How is the family negotiating current transition stages?

4 Identify the presenting family structure in terms of:
  (a) Subsystem boundaries.
  (b) Hierarchies.
  (c) Coalitions.

5 Communication patterns/styles:

(a) Who speaks for whom?

(b) Congruence of verbal/nonverbal communication?

6 Family style(s) for dealing with conflict.

7 (a) Why was this referral made at this point in the family's history?

(b) In what sense is the referred problem a solution?

8 Who does the interviewer wish had also been present at the interview?

Assessment of individual symptomatology begun with an interactionally focused interview gives a different meaning to the more specific data relating to that person. The interviewer will think differently about individual material. An expanded mental set makes a wider range of treatment options available when making decisions about whom to involve in treatment. This brief family interview protocol includes elements of the longer first family interview which is described below.

The first interview as the start of treatment

The family diagnostic interview that is part of a multifaceted assessment process and the first interview as an integral part of treatment will have different foci. Most family therapy primers include guidelines for conducting a first interview (Franklin & Prosky, 1973; Haley, 1976; de Shazer, 1982; Gorell Barnes, 1984; Burnham, 1986; Stratton *et al.*, 1990). Haley stated: 'If therapy is to end properly, it must begin properly — by negotiating a solvable problem and discovering the social situation that makes the problem necessary. The act of therapy begins with the way the problem is examined.' (Haley, 1976, p. 9.) His first interview model listed five stages: (1) the social stage; (2) the problem definition stage; (3) the interaction stage where family members are encouraged by the clinician to interact directly with each other about the problem; (4) a definition of desired changes; and (5) ending the interview, usually with a simple task.

The format outlined here is a basic protocol used for both training and clinical purposes. It was developed initially for training professionals who do not necessarily wish to become family therapists, but who need a range of interviewing skills. The format draws on ideas from a number of schools of family therapy. This highlights how different therapeutic models can be integrated. A narrow adherence to a single model is inevitably inhibiting (Jenkins, 1985). The format is completed by observers on a nine-page protocol behind a one-way screen, or by the interviewer before seeing the family for the preinterview information, and then after the family has left.

The information available to the clinician before the first family meeting may be sparse, although there is always more than is first apparent. Before the family is seen, the front sheet is completed with basic biodata, together with the names of the interviewer and observers if present. The next item is the customer. This draws on the thinking of the brief therapy model of the Mental Research Institute in Palo Alto (Watzlawick *et al.*, 1974; Fisch *et al.*, 1982). The customer is the person who has identified the need for change or help. Usually this is not the same as the referred person. The customer may be someone who both feels concerned about the situation and also feels relatively powerless to effect change and therefore seeks an ally as part of the referral process. Next is the referrer's beliefs about the problem(s). The referrer and the customer may also be different people. The referrer's position in the system must always be carefully respected if assessment and therapy are to be effective (Palazzoli *et al.*, 1980b). Names of other agencies and their beliefs about the difficulties, if known, are noted. This information allows for views about the difficulties from a number of perspectives. Such discrepancies will provide information about the process of referral, and the attempted solutions of those, both family and professionals, involved so far. This helps the clinician think beyond the problem individual in isolation.

Based on this information, the clinician makes one or more initial hypotheses that serve as an attempt to link the information so far in a systemic manner (see Chapter 2). The symptoms described as the problem are linked to the context(s) in which they occur (Papp, 1983). Family therapy attempts to intervene in the feedback loop between the problem and the context in which the problem is located. This perspective helps the clinician focus as much on process as on content. The importance of developing hypotheses was emphasized in the early work of Palazzoli and her team (Palazzoli *et al.*, 1980a; Cecchin, 1987), and also by Jenkins and Cowley (1985). However, as Stratton and colleagues (1990) emphasized, hypotheses are to help the therapist orient his or her thinking and interventions, and should not be treated as truths. They help questioning become more focused.

Information is immediately available to clinicians as they meet the family for the first time. Who sits close to whom is potential 'soft' information. A parent who sits outside the family circle, or the child between two parents, may be communicating something about the family's structure, its alliances and coalitions. On the interview format, a note is made of the seating plan, which may change during the session or from one to the next. The interviewer will also note the absence of someone important, such as a parent, a child or other family member.

It is important that clinicians maintain their focus on the individual while working with the whole family (Nichols, 1987), just as when working with individuals it is important to hold a family or systemic perspective (Jenkins, 1989b; Jenkins & Asen, 1992). The interviewer must take account of how each person presents him- or herself in terms of affect, dress and posture, and must obtain a statement from each person about his or her views as to the nature of the problem. Different views are important information, as are the reactions to statements by others. Since problems do not develop in a vacuum, the clinician should inquire about the circumstances associated with the onset of difficulties. Life events in terms of trauma to the individual or the family or in a wider socio-economic context may be related to the onset of problems. However, why difficulties arise and what helps perpetuate them will not necessarily be the same (Lask & Lask, 1981). It is also important early on to learn what the family have done in their attempts to resolve their problems. This may extend from nothing to extreme punishments, threat, rejection or the involvement of a whole host of professional agencies. It is also important to know what other helping agencies have done in their attempts to intervene. This stems from the belief that the attempted solutions often become as much the problem as the referred problems themselves (Watzlawick *et al.*, 1967, 1974). At this stage, an attempt should be made to obtain some definition of the family's expectations for help. Those responses will relate to each person's views about the nature of the problem and will save the clinician from later being unable to satisfy the family, as well as agreeing achievable goals.

As interviewers build up a mental map of the family, they should not become too preoccupied with a here-and-now focus, as this will result in too restricted a focus in serious psychopathology. Clinicians should keep an open mind early on, before deciding whether to stay present-oriented throughout treatment.

In this respect a psychodynamic framework is useful in relating past experiences to the present (Malan 1979; Casement, 1988). Dare (Pincus & Dare, 1978; Dare, 1988) has made links between psychodynamic theories and family therapy, further developed by Bentovim and Kinston (1991). A number of clinicians have developed models for working with the family from a transgenerational perspective (Boszormenyi-Nagy & Spark, 1973; Byng-Hall, 1973, 1988; Bowen, 1978; Lieberman, 1979a,b,c; Friedman *et al.*, 1988). The technique most usually associated with this perspective is the drawing of genograms (see below).

When interviewing the whole family, the process of taking a genogram fulfils a number of important functions. The current family is quickly contextualized in relation to the wider family and the family life cycle (McGoldrick & Gerson, 1989). Young children or adolescents can be engaged effectively in what is happening and be encouraged to find out about family members, their stories, or forgotten events. Children can learn quite dramatically, perhaps for the first time, about issues that have worried parents for years, or secrets that have had a negative organizing effect on the family related to past events, losses or illnesses. Engaging children in family interviewing is often difficult for clinicians, especially if they rely on words and abstract thinking (Dare & Lindsey, 1979; O'Brien & Loudon, 1985; Zilbach, 1986; Jenkins, 1989c). Whether drawing a genogram with the family is lengthy or brief will depend on clinical judgement about where to focus the family's thinking. The value of engaging all in the room in the process cannot be overestimated (Jenkins & Donnelly, 1983) and the genogram becomes simultaneously part of assessment and treatment.

Information relating to present and past physical and psychiatric illnesses can quite naturally be elicited at this stage, both while constructing a genogram and by simple direct questioning. This may make it possible to understand some of the belief systems that organize the family to act in one way more than another. Beliefs about physical or psychiatric illness,

depression and death will influence how family members relate and negotiate family life cycle stages, based on gender, culture, religious beliefs, who takes after whom, or what happens in the family at particular ages.

Related to family history, the clinician must take account of the current life cycle stages of family members (Solomon, 1973; Carter & McGoldrick, 1980, 1989; Jenkins, 1983; Combrinck-Graham, 1985), both in terms of normative tasks and the particular difficulties that the family is experiencing in negotiating life cycle transitions. These are frequently to do with negotiating intimacy and interpersonal distance manifested by how a parent allows or encourages autonomy in a child or adolescent. Clinicians will be helped if by now they are thinking more in terms of the dilemmas that the family is facing, rather than of a series of problems to be overcome. A framework around dilemmas introduces more easily the possibility of choices.

In the first family interview the therapist and observers can only come to what is an impressionistic evaluation along the five dimensions of hostility, critical comments, emotional overinvolvement, warmth and supportive comments (Vaughn & Leff, 1976). A focus on these five facets helps identify both individual attitudes towards others in the family and different alliances and coalitions. It is clinically useful in pinpointing where most difficulty is likely to be experienced in bringing about change, while highlighting where most change needs to occur.

A family life cycle framework and impressionistic expressed emotion evaluation leads easily into focusing on the clarity of intergenerational boundaries within the family (Minuchin *et al.*, 1967, 1978; Minuchin, 1974; Aponte & Van Deusen, 1981; Minuchin & Fishman, 1981). Structural family therapy pays particular attention to the quality of the boundaries between individuals and different subgroupings. Inevitably, value judgements are involved in deciding whether alliances across generations are adaptive or maladaptive. This provides the clinician with an important understanding of the family's organization and structure. A series of diagrams can be drawn from this, representing the key dyadic and triadic relationships.

Much of the material gathered through the interviewing process so far has a static quality. The clinician must also identify the main significant repetitive behavioural sequences of interaction between family members. Breunlin and Schwartz (1986) described sequencing of behaviour at four different levels. More explicit focus is given to this in the protocol for ongoing interview recording in second and subsequent interviews described below. At this stage the clinician needs to identify patterns of verbal and nonverbal behaviour that appear characteristic of the family's ways of dealing with issues such as intimacy, difference, conflict, upset, depression and enjoyment. This includes those who are significantly not involved in the process. The different levels of patterning in therapeutic work are just as relevant as content.

From the information gained so far the clinician attempts to abstract what are the family rules. Family rules may be thought of as the underlying principles that organize behaviour. The early pioneers in family therapy were particularly interested in this concept (Jackson, 1965a,b). Jackson also described them as norms, as a setting or baseline on which family behaviour is measured. By focusing on rules, the clinician further identifies patterns over time and begins to develop a conceptual perspective on the dilemmas with which the family is struggling. From this, the clinician moves to yet another level of abstraction, that of beliefs. Put as a question, it would be: What are the beliefs held in this family about *X* or *Y* from which such rule-governed behaviour follows? The belief system level is one that is not within the immediate conscious awareness of the family, any more than are the rules. The belief system level is therefore all the more powerful because it is correspondingly difficult to challenge. The work of Palazzoli (Palazzoli *et al.*, 1980a,b,) and related developments (Boscolo *et al.*, 1987; Cecchin, 1987) pay particular attention to the family belief system as the necessary conceptual level for therapeutic change to occur. The protocol addresses the question of disadvantages of change. There are often secondary gains for the family from the difficulties presented. A behavioural problem in a child may allow the mother to remain intensely involved. In the context of a relatively absent father, the behavioural difficulties may bring the father more actively into the arena of child care, which the mother would apparently want. However, there may also be losses. Father's greater involvement in child care may result in the mother feeling she has a less important role. A feared crisis precipitated by improvement might be: (1) the mother loses the special closeness with the child; or (2) the parents find themselves dealing much more directly with each other, and marital problems surface around issues of intimacy. Asking the question about the fears of improvement enables the clinician to deal directly with such issues and to understand the function of the problems as part of maintaining the stability in the family, despite the stress caused. Problems both draw attention to the need for change and the possible dangers inherent in such change.

In addition to what happens with the family in the room, the clinician must pay attention to external factors affecting the family's ability to cope. Without this, the best therapeutic work will founder. Therefore an assessment of external factors affecting the family's ability to cope should also be made, whether by direct questioning or by observation (John, 1963; Minuchin & Montalvo, 1967; Minuchin *et al.*, 1967; Hoffman & Long, 1969; Tonge *et al.*, 1975; Kingston, 1977, 1979; Jenkins, 1990b). Socioeconomic factors, housing, health services, employment, transport and recreational facilities are all organizing factors for families and sources of potential stress.

The clinicians' behaviour is another important dimension of the family interview. They must observe themselves as part of the process and be aware of how they are organized by the family's responses (Hoffman, 1985; Casement, 1988). The interview protocol provides for the observers to identify attempts by the clinician to make change-inducing interventions, followed by the response(s) of the family, followed by the clinician's response(s) in turn. By listing series of at least three interaction sequences, patterning between the clinician and family members can be identified. This helps the clinician work with the family in ways which will intensify their preferred ways of dealing with stress (Jenkins, 1989d), and also provides possible indications of how the family has tended to deal with professionals in the past.

The first interview begins with the clinician formulating an initial hypothesis, based on preinterview information. It is important to review the initial hypothesis in the light of information from the session. The clinician relates symptomatic behaviour to the significant systems, with perhaps particular reference to the stability/change dilemma of the particular family. The practice of reformulating the hypothesis ensures that clinical work remains focused throughout treatment.

Classification

Classification of behaviour remains a difficult subject which exercises the minds of clinician and researcher alike (Rutter, 1976). The classification of families remains a particularly difficult area (Brown & Rutter, 1966; Frances *et al.*, 1984). Attempts have been made to classify families, usually by the symptom of the index patient (Wynne *et al.*, 1958; Minuchin *et al.*, 1978; Loader *et al.*, 1980). While not part of the direct interviewing process, the ICD classification (see Chapter 1) helps highlight areas of strength and difficulty. Axes 1–4 are as important as axis 5, which deals with the psychosocial situation. From a family interviewing perspective, the clinician may be tempted to treat axes 1–4 as contexts for axis 5, whereas in more individually oriented interviewing and assessment formats, axis 5 tends to be seen as a context for the previous four. It is not a question of either/or, but rather of a whole perspective. Having been a Cinderella category, axis 5 has been given more salience (van Goor-Lambo *et al.*, 1990).

Endings

Ending the interview is important. Emphasis throughout is on defining areas of difficulty and on goals for change. In completing the protocol, a decision needs to be made on whether further evaluation is required, whether of the family or of individuals, and whether by psychometric testing, physical examination, individual interview or other means. On the basis of this a decision should be made whether the team can offer a formal start to treatment; should refer on; or that there is no need for ongoing work. A decision should be made about who should be involved in treatment, from those who attended, from absent family members and possibly other professionals. In order to avoid unfocused therapy, it is important to determine both short-term aims of treatment, which may be as limited as engaging an absent member for the next meeting, and long-term goals, by which it will be possible to measure outcome and agree on closure (Jenkins, 1980). An estimate of duration and frequency of sessions is important.

These decisions, although simple, are essential in keeping professional activity focused. The final decisions relate to the message or task given to the family, and what should be said to the referrer and any other agencies involved (Palazzoli *et al.*, 1978; Jenkins, 1987; Allman *et al.*, 1992).

Although apparently long, the protocol can be completed during the course of a session by observers behind the screen with relatively little time for familiarization. As a result, clinicians quickly begin to think systemically and to observe patterned behaviour quite differently from individually focused models. Without a team, the protocol helps organize the clinician in planning for the interview and is relatively simple to complete at the end of the session.

SECOND AND SUBSEQUENT INTERVIEWS

A similar protocol is used for second and subsequent interviews. As before, the work done before the interview starts is important. With reference to the first or previous sessions and the message or tasks given then, the clinician lists the given problems. These may differ from the those given in the original referral. At the very minimum, the clinician will formulate them differently. With no reformulation of the problem(s) the clinician is probably beginning to see the difficulties only in the same ways as the family and therefore will not be introducing any significant difference to the family. The clinician reviews any new information received since the previous meeting, and attempts to identify the significant patterns so far, including his or her own behaviours and responses. It is important to identify the family's characteristic ways of dealing with issues. It is also useful if the clinician can begin to identify his or her part in those patterned responses. This helps identify how treatment may hinder change. Clinicians use this information to formulate one or more provisional hypotheses. This discipline forces them to stay 'light on their feet' with respect to realities for the family and themselves. They then identify what are likely to be the provisional therapeutic foci for the session, and the probable difficulties in achieving them. This is both from the point of view of the predictable responses from the family and from their knowledge of their own vulnerabilities in working with particular types of problem. In this way clinicians will be thinking from both inside and outside the family — an important stance to adopt for effective therapy. If clinicians are unaware of likely areas of becoming stuck, it is all the more certain that this will happen (Treacher & Carpenter, 1982; Carpenter *et al.*, 1983).

From the first moments of the session, clinicians must use their powers of observation to see what changes have taken place. They will note any change in seating arrangements and whether that seems significant. They will ask the family for feedback on any tasks given (Jenkins, 1987), and note whether their observations match the family's reports. They will register whether the family volunteers important new information about the past, present or future. As they engage with the family they must now pay particular attention to different levels of patterning (Breunlin & Schwartz, 1986). This will be partly gained by observation, since families cannot readily comment on their own processes, and partly by report from the family. The four levels of patterning are:

First level: this is patterned behaviour that the clinician observes over brief time spells within the session between individuals, including him- or herself.

Second level: these are elicited from accounts by family members of what happens over days/weeks in the family's life.

Third level: these are reported over months/years within the family's current life history.

Fourth level: these are reported or evident over generations in the family's life history.

A brief case vignette will highlight this. A 16-year-old girl was seen with her family for reported depression and general misery. It was possible to see how she and the family interacted with each other, but difficult to have a sense of why they had so much difficulty in coping, since everyone seemed committed. Patterned behaviour within the session could be identified, as could what took place between meetings. This still did not help to understand what the daughter's depression meant to the family or to her. On further inquiry, and on asking what was happening to the mother when she was 16, it was discovered that the mother had been depressed when about the same age, and so had the maternal grandmother. Of even more interest, each had also been brought to the same psychiatric outpatient service. Here were three generations of patterning in terms of bringing adolescent daughters for psychiatric help at the same developmental stage. This family used outside services to help with some of the rituals of adolescent independence for girls, although not boys. When the clinician obtained this three-generational information, the slightly puzzling although well-meaning behaviour of the family began to make sense. The girl learnt for the first time of her mother's and her maternal grandmother's similar difficulties, thereby normalizing some of the dilemmas she and the family were facing. The opportunity to discuss this openly helped both daughter and mother begin to deal with the issues of independence and autonomy in a different way, and for the mother–daughter relationship to be less polarized. It is in ways such as this that history can be important in how families negotiate their current dilemmas.

During the session, clinicians note significant alliances among family members, and between them and family members. They also note any new information arising during the session. They should be able, either during the session or in consultation with the team, to devise either a new provisional hypothesis or to refine the one they have been testing through questioning. An appropriate message or task should be devised from this, and thought given as to whether other agencies need to be contacted.

As any message or task is given to the family, the therapist observes how different family members receive the message, and must be ready to modify it in the light of immediate feedback. The family members' responses become the beginning stage for the clinician to think about issues for the next session. It is important for the clinician to think of each session as part of a larger whole. Treatment then becomes a constant feedback process between clinician and family, clinician and team, clinician, team and family.

Techniques in family interviewing

So far the emphasis has been on the verbal aspect of family interviewing. Sometimes the clinician needs alternative pathways to reach the family and introduce useful differences.

The genogram, as discussed above, along with its variants, is one of the most useful techniques (Lieberman, 1979a,b; Duhl, 1981; Friedman *et al.*, 1988; McGoldrick & Gerson, 1989). It allows the clinician to gain a clear overview of the family over three and sometimes four or even five generations either in a relatively short time, or in greater depth over a number of interviews. When the clinician is working with even quite young children and with adolescents, the genogram can engage them powerfully in treatment. Not infrequently, new information about the family's history emerges, linked to earlier marriages, children who did not survive, relatives who have never been talked about, or 'forgotten' events. Of particular importance, this offers the opportunity to reveal patterns over generations which may be important in terms of inherited physical vulnerabilities, psychiatric histories, or perhaps how males or females have left the family in the past. The very process of objectifying emotive material on paper in a collaborative way can be a first important step in the family's healing. It is important that the clinician does not take over from the family in eagerness to obtain the information. The genogram is also useful in work with individuals from a transgenerational perspective (Lieberman, 1979a; Jenkins & Asen, 1992).

Family drawing is an effective technique that adapts well to systemic work with families (Jenkins & Donnelly, 1983). This can be used diagnostically early on in treatment, or later if the therapist feels stuck and needs to find a way of generating flexibility into the clinical work. Burns (1990) described a variant on the theme of drawing. His work within the framework of individual psychodynamic work readily adapts to family- and couple-oriented work. Family work with younger patients requires even greater flexibility. The techniques described by O'Brien and Loudon (1985) are particularly helpful.

One of the techniques early associated with family therapy and conjoint work is sculpting (Duhl *et al.*, 1973; Papp *et al.*, 1973; Jefferson, 1978; Hearn & Lawrence, 1985). In this, the therapist helps family members represent aspects of family relationships, using fellow family members as statues, to make a statement about the family in relation to a particular issue or period of the family's life. The power is in the immediacy of impact. It allows each family member to have a voice and a view that does not have to be correct as regards other members' views. It is the way that the individual construes the issue that is important. Very young children can be as correct as adults. The therapist organizes the session so that no one is allowed to challenge whether the statement is right or wrong. The sculpt may be about a time in the past, the present, or how it might be in the future. It is important that an opportunity is given to allow everyone to comment on the experience in an open and nondefensive manner. Frequently such a shared experience will bring family members together where much talking will not. It is shared by everyone and can be referred to throughout subsequent therapy.

The writing of letters, which are not necessarily sent, has proved to be a powerful tool in individual systemic work, in couple therapy and for parents with children who are struggling to make sense of their confusing earlier experiences. Adolescents who are no longer in contact with their families have found this helpful. Although an apparently simple task, it is one that frequently calls forth strong emotions, and should only be used with care when there is a good therapeutic relationship between patient and therapist. The patient may write 'to and from himself', thereby experiencing both perspectives (Jenkins, 1989a).

Such techniques seem to help the individual and the family gain some measure of control over their dilemmas or problems, both by externalizing them and by developing interactional coping strategies. In this respect there are clearly similarities in thinking and practice with gestalt work and psychodrama (Compernolle, 1981), and with Tomm's modification of the Japanese Kan-No-Mushi (Tomm *et al.*, 1990).

Clinical issues for family interviews in practice

The conjoint family interview is not an end in itself. It is not somehow superior to individual interviewing. There will be times when it is advisable to see individuals alone, or couples, or other subgroupings of the family. Sometimes the whole family will not be available. At others, conjoint interviewing will be contraindicated (Jenkins, 1989a). The advantages of working whenever possible with the whole family include the opportunity to work directly with the people concerned; that problems of projection, transference and countertransference, which are powerful factors in individual psychodynamic work, can be dealt with more directly in conjoint work; and it is easier to test out what people say or feel directly with those concerned. Work with the whole family allows the clinician to work faster than with a single individual and it is possible to work with more than one problem at the same time, since frequently difficulties experienced by different family members are related.

One of the difficulties for those with a more traditional individually oriented training is to believe that enough information can be obtained this way to undertake effective treatment. The question here becomes: For what purposes is information gathered? Once that is clear, clinicians can decide how they should go about gathering it. Some information gathered in the interactional context of the family could not be obtained from individual interviewing, since it is outside the awareness of the participants. Other information, of a more intimate nature, may better be obtained by an individual interview or when only certain members of the family are present. Reticence about asking particular kinds of questions in front of the whole family may be related more to the uncertainty of the clinician than of the family. Children often know much more than adult family members suppose they know and the real secret is that everyone knows that everyone knows.

There is always the danger in work with the family group that the individual's needs are ignored (Nichols, 1987). The indications for individual interviews might include working with adolescents on their own as part of treatment, replicating thereby some of the necessary processes of individuation from the family. If clinicians do not bear in mind the implications from a systemic perspective of the adolescent leaving home, they may be surprised at the resistances shown by family members at the least signs of independence. Separate interviews with partners may be necessary when dealing with secrets such as extramarital affairs as a first step to finding ways of addressing this with the couple. Secrets can well be powerful organizers in families that render the therapist impotent (Pincus & Dare, 1978; Karpel, 1980; Feinstein, 1981). It is also important in instances of developmental delay that full and proper assessment is made of the individual's history and development. Even so, failure to involve the family actively may both miss out on possible strengths and, where there are siblings, miss the silent sufferers where attention of the parents is focused primarily on the needs of the handicapped child, or where as a result the marital relationship suffers.

Whatever style clinicians adopt in working with families as opposed to individuals, they will have to be much more active than in individual work (Dare, 1988). The clinician who does not develop these skills will also not have the necessary skills to meet the needs of child and adolescent psychiatry in the 1990s. The most difficult initial shift is from a linear cause-and-effect model to one that pays attention to feedback, recursiveness, pattern and organization. The change needs to occur at the level of conceptualization so that the clinician's framework for practice alters, and within this framework the clinician will feel comfortable working with individuals, couples, families and larger groups (Hoffman, 1985). Without this, it will be almost immaterial whether clinicians see the whole family or not. At the same time, they must continue to bring to bear all that they know about individual development and functioning.

Inevitably the debate will continue about the most appropriate and effective way to interview children and adolescents. Nevertheless, a systemic perspective should always inform the thinking of the clinician. Even so, the separate interviewing of subgroups of the family such as adolescents and parents to reflect life cycle developmental issues should always be a possibility. Individual assessments (apart from medical or psychological examinations) should be undertaken by the same clinician who sees the whole family. Where this does not happen, sufficient time for discussion and sharing of work

is essential to avoid the professional splitting which easily replicates the splits in the family. Finally, depending on where the assessment and treatment process begins, the clinician will see different phenomena, influenced strongly by the theoretical framework(s) used (Scheflen, 1978). The first step is to make explicit those frameworks so that informed discussion will result in coherent decision-making.

ACKNOWLEDGEMENTS

I am grateful to both Christine Groothues and Michael Rutter for helpful suggestions about some relevant research findings.

REFERENCES

Ackerman N.W. & Behrens M.L. (1956) A study of family diagnosis. *American Journal of Orthopsychiatry*, **26**, 66–78.

Akister J. & Stevenson-Hinde J. (1991) Identifying families at risk: exploring the potential of the McMaster Family Assessment Device. *Journal of Family Therapy*, **13**, 411–422.

Akister J., Meekings E. & Stevenson-Hinde J. (1993) The spouse subsystem in the family context: couple interaction categories. *Journal of Family Therapy*, **15**, 1–21.

Allman P., Bloch P. & Sharpe M. (1992) The end of session message in systemic family therapy. *Journal of Family Therapy*, **14**, 69–85.

Anderson C.M. & Stewart S. (1983) *Mastering Resistance: A Practical Guide*. Guilford Press, New York.

Aponte H.J. & Van Deusen J.M. (1981) Structural family therapy. In: Gurman A.S. & Kniskern D.P. (eds) *Handbook of Family Therapy*, pp. 310–360. Brunner/Mazel, New York.

Bateson G. (1973a) A theory of play and fantasy. In: Bateson G. (ed) *Steps to an Ecology of Mind*, pp. 150–166. Paladin Books, London.

Bateson G. (1973b) The cybernetics of 'Self': a theory of alcoholism. In: Bateson G. (ed) *Steps to an Ecology of Mind*, pp. 280–308. Paladin Books, London.

Bateson G. (1980) *Mind and Nature*. Fontana, Glasgow.

Bateson G., Jackson D.D., Haley J. & Weakland J.H. (1973) Towards a theory of schizophrenia. In: Bateson G. (ed) *Steps to an Ecology of Mind*, pp. 173–198. Paladin Books, London.

Bentovim A. & Kinston W. (1978) Brief focal family therapy when the child is the referred patient. I. Clinical. *Journal of Child Psychology and Psychiatry*, **19**, 1–12.

Bentovim A. & Kinston W. (1991) Focal family therapy: linking systems theory with psychodynamic understanding. In: Gurman A.S. & Kniskern D.P. (eds) *Handbook of Family Therapy*, 2nd edn, pp. 284–324. Brunner/Mazel, New York.

Bloch D.A. (1989) The dual optic: researchers and therapists. *Family Systems Medicine*, **7**, 115–119.

Boscolo L., Cecchin G., Hoffman L. & Penn P. (1987) *Milan Systemic Family Therapy: Conversations in Theory and Practice*. Basic Books, New York.

Boszormenyi-Nagy I. & Spark G.M. (1973) *Invisible Loyalties*. Harper & Row, Hagerstown. Reprinted (1984) Brunner/Mazel, New York.

Bowen M. (1978) *Family Therapy in Clinical Practice*. Jason Aronson, New York.

Bowlby J. (1969) *Attachment and Loss. Vol. 1 Attachment*. Hogarth Press, London.

Bowlby J. (1977) The making and breaking of affectual bonds. *British Journal of Psychiatry*, **130**, 201–210.

Breunlin D.C. & Schwartz R.C. (1986) Sequences: toward a common denominator of family therapy. *Family Process*, **25**, 67–87.

Brown G.W., Monck E.M., Carstairs G.M. & Wing J.K. (1962) The influence of family life on the course of schizophrenic illness. *British Journal of Preventative Medicine*, **16**, 355–368.

Brown G.W. & Rutter M. (1966) The measurement of family activities and relationships. *Human Relations*, **19**, 241–263.

Buchanan C.M., Maccoby E. & Dornbusch S.M. (1991) Caught between parents: adolescents' experience in divorced homes. *Child Development*, **62**, 1008–1029.

Burnham J. (1986) *Family Therapy*. Tavistock, London.

Burns R.C. (1990) *Family Centred Circle Drawings*. Brunner/Mazel, New York.

Byng-Hall J. (1973) Family myths as defence in conjoint family therapy. *British Journal of Medical Psychology*, **46**, 239–250.

Byng-Hall J. (1988) Scripts and legends in families and family therapy. *Family Process*, **27**, 167–179.

Campbell D. & Draper R. (eds) (1985) *Applications of Systemic Family Therapy: The Milan Approach*. Grune & Stratton, London.

Campbell D., Draper R. & Huffington C. (1989) *Second Thoughts on the Theory and Practice of the Milan Approach to Family Therapy*. D.C. Associates, London.

Carpenter J., Treacher A., Jenkins H. & O'Reilly P. (1983) 'Oh no! Not the Smiths again!' An exploration of how to identify and overcome stuckness in family therapy. Part II. Stuckness in the therapeutic and supervisory systems. *Journal of Family Therapy*, **5**, 81–96.

Carter E. & McGoldrick M. (eds) (1980) *The Family Life Cycle: A Framework for Family Therapy*. Gardner Press, New York.

Carter B. & McGoldrick M. (eds) (1989) *The Changing Family Life Cycle: A Framework for Family Therapy*. Allyn & Bacon, Boston.

Casement P. (1988) *On Learning from the Patient*. Routledge, London.

Cecchin G. (1987) Hypothesising, circularity, and neutrality revisited: an invitation to curiosity. *Family Process*, **26**, 405–413.

Combrinck-Graham L. (1985) A developmental model for family systems. *Family Process*, **24**, 139–150.

Compernolle T. (1981) Moreno J.L.: An unrecognized pioneer of family therapy. *Family Process*, **20**, 405–413.

Dare C. (1988) Psychoanalytic family therapy. In: Street E. & Dryden W. (eds) *Family Therapy in Britain*, pp. 23–50. Open University Press, Milton Keynes.

Dare C. & Lindsey C. (1979) Children in family therapy. *Journal of Family Therapy*, **1**, 253–269.

de Shazer S. (1982) *Patterns of Brief Family Therapy: An Ecosystemic Approach*. Guilford Press, New York.

Doane J.A., West K.L., Goldstein M.J., Rodnick E.H. & Jones J.E. (1981) Parental communication deviance and affective style. *Archives of General Psychiatry*, **38**, 679–685.

Duhl F.J. (1981) The use of the chronological chart in general systems family therapy. *Journal of Marital and Family Therapy*, **7**, 361–373.

Duhl F.J., Kanttor D. & Duhl B.S. (1973) Learning, space and action in family therapy. In: Bloch D. (ed) *Techniques of Family Psychotherapy: A Primer*, pp. 47–63. Grune & Stratton, New York.

Dunn J. (in press) Family influences. In: Rutter M. & Hay D. (eds) *Development through Life: A Handbook for Clinicians*. Blackwell Scientific Publications, Oxford.

Dunn J. & Kendrick C. (1982) *Siblings: Love, Envy and Understanding*. Blackwell, Oxford.

Engfer A. (1988) The interrelatedness of marriage and the mother–child relationship. In: Hinde R.A. & Stevenson-Hinde J. (eds) *Relationships Within Families: Mutual References*, pp. 104–118. Clarendon Press, Oxford.

Feinstein H.M. (1981) Family therapy for the historian? the case of William James. *Family Process*, **20**, 97–107.

Fisch R., Weakland J.H. & Segal L. (1982) *The Tactics of Change*. Jossey Bass, San Francisco.

Frances A., Clarkin J.F. & Perry S. (1984) DSM III and family therapy. *American Journal of Psychiatry*, **141**, 406–409.

Franklin P. & Prosky P. (1973) A standardized interview. In: Bloch D. (ed) *Techniques of Family Psychotherapy: A Primer*, pp. 29–37. Grune & Stratton, New York.

Friedman H., Rohrbaugh M. & Krakauer S. (1988) The time–line genogram: highlighting temporal aspects of family relationships. *Family Process*, **27**, 293–303.

Frosh S. (1991) The semantics of therapeutic change. *Journal of Family Therapy*, **13**, 171–186.

Goldstein M.J., Judd L.L., Rodnick E.H., Alkire A. & Gouild E. (1968) A method for studying social influence and coping patterns with families of disturbed adolescents. *Journal of Nervous and Mental Disease*, **147**, 233–251.

Gorell Barnes G. (1984) *Working with Families*. MacMillan, Houndmills, Basingstoke.

Gorell Barnes G. (1985) Systems theory and family therapy. In: Rutter M. & Hersov L. (eds) *Child and Adolescent Psychiatry*, 2nd edn, pp. 216–229. Blackwell Scientific Publications, Oxford.

Haley J. (1967) Toward a theory of pathological systems. In: Zuk G. & Boszormneyi-Nagy I. (eds) *Family Therapy and Disturbed Families*, pp. 11–27. Science and Behavior Books, Palo Alto.

Haley J. (1976) *Problem-Solving Therapy*. Jossey Bass, New York.

Haynes S.N., Jensen B.J., Wise E. & Sherman D. (1981) The marital intake interview: a multimethod criterion validity assessment. *Journal of Consulting and Clinical Psychology*, **49**, 379–387.

Hearn J. & Lawrence M. (1985) Family sculpting: II. Some practical examples. *Journal of Family Therapy*, **7**, 113–131.

Hinde R. & Stevenson-Hinde J. (eds) (1988) *Relationships Within Families: Mutual Influences*. Clarendon Press, Oxford.

Hoffman L. (1985) Beyond power and control: toward a 'second order' family systems therapy. *Family Systems Medicine*, **3**, 381–396.

Hoffman L. & Long L. (1969) A systems dilemma. *Family Process*, **8**, 211–234.

Jackson D.D. (1965a) The study of the family. *Family Process*, **4**, 1–20.

Jackson D.D. (1965b) Family rules: marital quid pro quo. *Archives of General Psychiatry*, **12**, 589–594.

Jacob T. & Tennenbaum D.L. (1988) Family assessment methods. In: Rutter M., Tuma A.H. & Lann I. (eds) *Assessment and Diagnosis in Child Psychopathology*, pp. 196–231. Guilford Press, New York.

Jefferson C. (1978) Some notes on the use of family sculpture in family therapy. *Family Process*, **17**, 69–76.

Jenkins H. (1980) Paradox: a pivotal point in therapy. *Journal of Family Therapy*, **2**, 339–356.

Jenkins H. (1983) A life cycle framework in the treatment of under-organized families. *Journal of Family Therapy*, **5**, 359–377.

Jenkins H. (1985) Orthodoxy in family therapy practice as servant or tyrant. *Journal of Family Therapy*, **7**, 19–30.

Jenkins H. (1986) Loss: bereavement, illness, and other factors. In: Horobin G. (ed) *The Family: Client or Context?* pp. 97–120. Kogan Page, London.

Jenkins H. (1987) Task-setting in family therapy. *Practice*, **1**, 363–373.

Jenkins H. (1989a) Family therapy and child sexual abuse: a treatment of choice? *Psihoterapija* [Yugoslavia], **18**, 1–11.

Jenkins H. (1989b) Family therapy with one person: a systemic framework for treating individuals. *Psihoterapija* [Yugoslavia], **19**, 61–74.

Jenkins H. (1989c) The therapist in a 'foreign land'. Family therapy with young children. *Psihoterapija* [Yugoslavia], **19**, 37–48.

Jenkins H. (1989d) Precipitating crises in families: patterns which connect. *Journal of Family Therapy*, **II**, 99–109.

Jenkins H. (1990a) Annotation: family therapy — developments in thinking and practice. *Journal of Child Psychology and Psychiatry*, **31**, 1015–1026.

Jenkins H. (1990b) Poverty, state and the family: a challenge for family therapy. *Contemporary Family Therapy*, **12**, 311–325.

Jenkins H. & Asen K. (1992) Family therapy without the family: a framework for systemic practice. *Journal of Family Therapy*, **14**, 1–14.

Jenkins H. & Cowley J. (1985) Adolescents in crisis: on hypothesising with minimal information. *British Journal of Social Work*, **15**, 351–362.

Jenkins H. & Donnelly M. (1983) The therapist's responsibility: a systemic approach to mobilizing family creativity. *Journal of Family Therapy*, **5**, 199–218.

Jenkins J.M. & Smith M.A. (1991) Marital disharmony and children's behaviour problems: aspects of a poor marriage that affect children adversely. *Journal of Child Psychology and Psychiatry*, **32**, 793–810.

John V.P. (1963) The intellectual development of slum children: some preliminary findings. *American Journal of Orthopsychiatry*, **33**, 813–822.

Karpel M.A. (1980) 'Family secrets'. I. Conceptual and ethical issues in the relational context. II. Ethical and practical considerations in therapeutic management. *Family Process*, **19**, 295–306.

Kingston P. (1977) Family therapy and material aid. *Family Service Units Quarterly*, December, 1–22.

Kingston P. (1979) The social context of family therapy. In: Walrond-Skinner S. (ed) *Family and Marital Psychotherapy: A Critical Approach*. RKP, London.

Kinston W. & Bentovim A. (1978) Brief focal family therapy when the child is the referred patient. II. Methodology and results. *Journal of Child Psychology and Psychiatry*, **19**, 119–143.

Kinston W. & Loader P. (1988) The family task interview: a tool for clinical research in family interaction. *Journal of Marital and Family Therapy*, **14**, 67–87.

Kuhn T. (1970) *The Structure of Scientific Revolutions*. The University of Chicago Press, Chicago.

Lask J. & Lask B. (1981) *Child Psychiatry and Social Work*. Tavistock, London.

Leff J. & Vaughn C. (1981) The role of maintenance therapy and relatives' expressed emotion in relapse of schizophrenia: a two year follow-up. *British Journal of Psychiatry*, **139**, 102–104.

Leff J. & Vaughn C. (1985) *Expressed Emotion in Families*. Guilford Press, New York.

Levy D.M. (1943) *Maternal Over-Protection*. Columbia University Press, New York.

Lewis J.M., Beavers W.R., Gossett J.T. & Phillips V.A. (1976) *No Single Thread: Psychological Health in Family Systems*. Brunner/Mazel, New York.

Lieberman S. (1979a) *Transgenerational Family Therapy*. Croom Helm, London.

Lieberman S. (1979b) Transgenerational analysis: the genogram as a technique in family therapy. *Journal of Family Therapy*, **1**, 51–64.

Lieberman S. (1979c) A transgenerational theory. *Journal of Family Therapy*, **1**, 347–360.

Loader P., Kinston W. & Stratford J. (1980) Is there a 'psychosomatogenic' family? *Journal of Family Therapy*, **2**, 311–326.

Loader P., Burck C., Kinston W. & Bentovim A. (1981) A method for organizing the clinical description of family interaction: the 'Family Interaction Summary Format'. *Australian Journal of Family Therapy*, **2**, 131–141.

McGoldrick M. & Gerson R. (1989) Genograms and the family life cycle. In: Carter B. & McGoldrick M. (eds) *The Changing Family Life Cycle: A Framework for Family Therapy*, 2nd edn, pp. 164–189. Allyn and Bacon, Boston.

Malan D.H. (1979) *Individual Psychotherapy and the Science of Psychodynamics*. Butterworths, London.

Minuchin S. (1974) *Families and Family Therapy*. Tavistock, London.

Minuchin S. (1979) Constructing a therapeutic reality. In: Kaufman E. & Kaufmann P.N. (eds) *Family Therapy of Drug and Alcohol Abuse*, pp. 5–18. Gardner Press, New York.

Minuchin S. & Fishman H.C. (1981) *Family Therapy Techniques*. Harvard University Press, Cambridge, MA.

Minuchin S. & Montalvo B. (1967) Techniques for working with disorganised low socioeconomic families. *Psychiatry*, **37**, 880–887.

Minuchin S., Montalvo B., Guerney B.C., Rosman B.L. & Schumer F. (1967) *Families of the Slums*. Basic Books, New York.

Minuchin S., Rosman B. & Baker L. (1978) *Psychosomatic Families: Anorexia Nervosa in Context*. Harvard University Press, Cambridge, MA.

Nichols M. (1987) *The Self in the System: Expanding the Limits of Family Therapy*. Brunner/Mazel, New York.

Noller P. & Fitzpatrick M.A. (1990) Marital communications in the eighties. *Journal of Marriage and the Family*, **52**, 832–843.

O'Brien A. & Loudon P. (1985) Redressing the balance — involving children in family therapy. *Journal of Family Therapy*, **7**, 81–98.

Palazzoli M.S., Cecchin G., Prata G. & Boscolo L. (1978) *Paradox and Counterparadox*. Jason Aronson, New York.

Palazzoli M.S., Boscolo L., Cecchin G. & Prata G. (1980a) Hypothesising-circularity-neutrality: three guidelines for the conductor of the session. *Family Process*, **19**, 3–12.

Palazzoli M.S., Boscolo L., Cecchin G. & Prata G. (1980b) The problem of the referring person. *Journal of Marital and Family Therapy*, **6**, 3–9.

Papp P. (1983) *The Process of Change*. Guilford Press, New York.

Papp P., Silverstein O. & Carter E. (1973) Family sculpting in preventive work with 'well' families. *Family Process*, **12**, 197–212.

Patterson G. (1982) *Coercive Family Process*, Castalia Publishing, Oregon.

Penn P. (1982) Circular questions. *Family Process*, **21**, 267–280.

Penn P. (1985) Feed forward: future questions, future maps. *Family Process*, **24**, 299–310.

Pincus L. & Dare C. (1978) *Secrets in the Family*. Faber, London.

Plomin R. & Daniels D. (1987) Why are children in the same family so different from one another? *Behavioral and Brain Sciences*, **10**, 1–15.

Quinton D., Rutter M. & Rowlands O. (1976) An evaluation of an interview assessment of marriage. *Psychological Medicine*, **6**, 557–586.

Rutter M. (1976) Classification. In: Rutter M. & Hersov L. (eds) *Child Psychiatry: Modern Approaches*, pp. 359–384. Blackwell Scientific Publications, Oxford.

Rutter M. (1989) What does family therapy need from research? Institute of Psychiatry, London. Research Conference, Family Research and Family Therapy: Marriage, Cohabitation or divorce? 20–21 April 1989. London.

Rutter M. (1991) A fresh look at 'maternal deprivation.' In: Bateson P. (ed) *The Development and Integration of Behaviour*, pp. 331–374. Cambridge University Press, Cambridge.

Rutter M. & Brown G.W. (1966) The reliability and validity of measures of family life and relationships in families containing a psychiatric patient. *Social Psychiatry*, **1**, 38–53.

Scheflen A.E. (1978) Susan smiled: On explanation in family therapy. *Family Process*, **17**, 59–68.

Slipp S. & Kressel K. (1978) Difficulties in family therapy evaluation. *Family Process*, **17**, 409–422.

Solomon M.A. (1973) A developmental, conceptual premise for family therapy. *Family Process*, **12**, 179–188.

Stratford J., Burck C. & Kinston W. (1982) The influence of context on the assesement of family interaction in a clinical study. *Journal of Family Therapy*, **4**, 359–371.

Stratton P., Preston-Shoot M. & Hanks H. (1990) *Family Therapy: Training and Practice*. Venture Press, Birmingham.

Szmukler G., Eisler I., Russell G.F.M. & Dare C. (1985) Anorexia nervosa, parental 'expressed emotion' and dropping out of treatment. *British Journal of Psychiatry*, **147**, 265–271.

Szmukler G., Berkowitz R., Eisler I., Leff J. & Dare C. (1987) Expressed emotion in individual and family settings: a comparative study. *British Journal of Psychiatry*, **151**, 174–178.

Tomm K. (1987) Interventive interviewing. Part 1 & 2. *Family Process*, **26**, 3–13; 165–183.

Tomm K. (1988) Interventive interviewing. Part 3. *Family Process*, **27**, 1–15.

Tomm K., Suzuki K. & Suzuki K. (1990) The Kan-No-Mushi: An inner externalization that enables compromise? *Australian and New Zealand Journal of Family Therapy*, **11**, 104–107.

Tonge W.L., James D.S. & Hillam S.M. (1975) *Families without Hope: a Controlled Study of 33 Problem Families*. Headley, London.

Treacher A. & Carpenter J. (1982) 'Oh no! Not the Smiths again!' An exploration of how to identify and overcome 'stuckness' in family therapy. Part I: Stuckness involving the contextual and technical aspects of therapy. *Journal of Family Therapy*, **4**, 285–305.

Valone K., Norton J.P., Goldstein M.J. & Doane J. (1983) Parental expressed emotion and affective style in an adolescent sample at risk for schizophrenia spectrum disorders. *Journal of Abnormal Psychology*, **92**, 399–407.

van Goor-Lambo G., Orley J., Poustka F. & Rutter M. (1990) Classification of abnormal psychosocial situations: preliminary report of a revision of a WHO scheme. *Journal of Child Psychology and Psychiatry*, **31**, 229–241.

Vaughn C. & Leff J. (1976) The measurement of expressed emotion in the families of psychiatric patients. *British Journal of Social and Clinical Psychology*, **15**, 157–165.

von Bertalanffy L. (1968) *General Systems Theory*. Penguin, Harmondsworth.

Vostanis P., Burnham J. & Harris Q. (1992) Changes of expressed emotion in systemic family therapy. *Journal of Family Therapy*, **14**, 15–27.

Watzlawick P. (1966) A structured family interview. *Family Process*, **5**, 256–271.

Watzlawick P., Beavin J. & Jackson D. (1967) *Pragmatics of Human Communication*. Norton, New York.

Watzlawick P., Weakland J. & Fisch R. (1974) *Change: Principles of Problem Formation and Problem Resolution*. Norton, New York.

Wiener N. (1948) Cybernetics. *Scientific American*, **179**, 14–18.

Wilkinson I. (1987) Family assessment: a review. *Journal of Family Therapy*, **9**, 367–380.

Wynne L.C., Ryckoff I.M., Day J. & Hirsch S.I. (1958) Pseudo-mutuality in the family relations of schizophrenics. *Psychiatry*, **21**, 205–220.

Zilbach J.J. (1986) *Young Children in Family Therapy*. Brunner/Mazel, New York.

Chapter 6
Physical Examination and Medical Investigations

Anthony Bailey

INTRODUCTION

Most child psychiatrists would probably agree that a detailed history and mental state are essential for accurate diagnosis. This apparent unanimity contrasts with the widely differing attitudes to the role of the physical examination: in some departments all children are physically examined, whereas others have neither the appropriate equipment nor facilities. Similarly, the medical investigation of particular disorders can vary widely — a phenomenon that reflects different interpretations of empirical research findings. The aim of this chapter is to outline how a relevant history, physical examination and appropriate medical investigations can make a useful contribution to the management of young people and their families. Each of these areas is discussed in turn, and the commoner clinical presentations dealt with individually.

There are several reasons for including a medical assessment as part of the routine diagnostic process. Foremost is that psychiatric disorders can have recognizable physical causes, and a wide range of aetiological mechanisms need to be considered: disorders may be caused by drugs, prescribed or otherwise; by ingestion of toxins, such as lead; by infectious processes, such as acquired immunodeficiency syndrome (AIDS) or as sequelae of meningitis or encephalitis; by head injury; by perinatal brain damage; by abnormal hormone secretion; and as a consequence of many different genetic disorders.

A further reason for examining young people is to monitor their physical development and health, especially in populations at high risk. There are also specific reasons why psychiatrists should be interested in growth and physical health. Mildly abnormal growth may not in itself merit investigation, but in conjunction with developmental or behavioural abnormalities it may point to the presence of an underlying disorder. Various psychiatric conditions, such as anorexia nervosa or drug abuse, may cause growth impairment and disease. Physical disorders, such as renal, hepatic or thyroid disease, may need to be excluded before drug treatment can be commenced, and it may also be necessary to monitor patients for physical side-effects during such treatment.

ORGANIZATIONAL ISSUES

The need to examine and test children raises a number of organizational issues. Of course, appropriate examination equipment and a satisfactory environment in which to conduct a physical examination are both required. In addition to the usual medical examination equipment, the following are needed: a weighing scale, a fixed rule for measuring height, a tape measure, and a vision testing chart (a Snellen-type chart that can be used at 3 metres is the most practical). The room where the examination is to be conducted should be warm and well-lit, free of interruptions, and should provide privacy for undressing.

When patients have not been referred by a doctor, a particularly thorough history is necessary as behavioural change secondary to a physical disorder may have been misinterpreted as psychological in origin. Conversely, when patients are referred by their own doctors or specialists, the unnecessary repetition of examinations or investigations should be avoided, as should the assumption that particular disorders have been excluded when they have not. In this respect good communication between medical staff and familiarity with the practice of nonpsychiatric colleagues are important; where matters are ambiguous, a telephone call or letter before the patient is seen may clarify what has already been done.

The practice of child and adolescent psychiatry is multidisciplinary. Young people are often seen by nonmedical professionals, especially if a walk-in clinic is available, or the referral information suggests a psychological aetiology. In these circumstances medical staff have two roles: to educate nonmedical colleagues and to examine children when requested. Colleagues should be aware of the different types of relationship between physical and psychological disorders, of the need to take a relevant history, and of the features of the history that should arouse diagnostic suspicion. Observation of the patient and following this through with pertinent questions should be encouraged. All staff can learn to measure height, weight and head circumference; if these measurements are always performed, then an opportunity is provided for observing the growth and physical health of young people.

The skills of interviewing are developed and maintained through constant use, and the ability to identify the pathological depends on a wide experience of normal variation. Physical examination skills similarly need to be maintained; if they are lost, then so is one of the specialist contributions of medical staff.

HISTORY TAKING

The history of the disorder, the young person's medical and developmental history and the family history may provide clues to the presence, and possibly the nature, of organic factors. Without a satisfactory history the physical examination may become a routine, rather than a focused search for signs to confirm or refute differential diagnoses. Aspects of the history relevant to all disorders are dealt with here; those relevant to particular disorders are discussed below.

The correct identification of an organic aetiology often requires considerable diagnostic acumen on the part of the clinician. Important clues include an atypical history of the disorder, such as a lack of psychosocial precipitants or stressors, the presence of physical symptoms, or unusual symptoms such as visual hallucinations or disturbance of gait (Rivinus *et al.*, 1975). It is helpful to record previous clinical opinions about the nature of the disorder, as these may influence the parents' current account. The brief cognitive assessment that forms part of a comprehensive mental state examination may also reveal unsuspected abnormalities.

Taking a detailed personal history is helpful for a number of reasons. Firstly, parents may not spontaneously mention events of real aetiological significance. Secondly, parents may have forgotten to describe abnormalities, such as floppiness, weakness or clumsiness, that have improved with time. Thirdly, parents may not volunteer information about corrective operations, for instance for deformities or squints. Finally, parents may omit to mention events which they previously believed to be of aetiological significance, and which influenced their attitude towards the child.

The nature of the presenting problem, environmental characteristics and the age of the young person will determine how much emphasis, if any, is placed upon various aspects of the history; an outline of a full history follows. The history will usually start with an account of the pregnancy, in order to establish whether there were any adverse environmental influences or significant events. Several specific points should be enquired about. There may have been either long-standing or acute maternal illnesses during the pregnancy; if so, a description should be obtained of symptomatology, timing, diagnosis and any medication taken. Enquiry should also be made about exposure to radiation and toxins, the amount of alcohol consumed and the use of nonprescribed drugs, and vaginal bleeding up to the second stage of delivery should be enquired about directly.

The birth history should include the baby's original presentation, any fetal distress or prolonged rupture of membranes, the mode of delivery and presentation, gestational age and birth weight. Neonatal problems to enquire about include severe respiratory distress syndrome, severe jaundice, severe infections and neurological problems such as intracranial infarction or haemorrhage, convulsions, floppiness and meningitis.

The parents should also be asked about the following post-neonatal events: fits, meningitis or encephalitis, head injuries, severe infections and recent viral illnesses. The nature and duration of any treatment should be recorded. Surgical procedures and any transfusion of blood products should be noted. The parents or guardians should also be asked whether the child has ever been the victim of physical or sexual abuse.

Reviewing symptomatology in each of the bodily systems, with particular emphasis upon neurological abnormalities, may be helpful. Dietary habits should be noted, especially pica in the handicapped, and past episodes of malnutrition recorded. Where appropriate, the young person should be asked about drug and alcohol intake and unprotected sexual contact. Foreign travel and any accompanying illnesses should be recorded.

The developmental history records the timing, the pattern of acquisition, and any loss of motor or language skills; difficulties with hearing or vision should also be recorded (a useful brief description of normal development is provided by Sheridan, 1975). If there is a history of developmental difficulties, social development should also be noted.

A thorough family history can make a useful contribution to the diagnostic process by alerting the interviewer to the existence of possible medical aetiologies. The link may be obvious, as in the case of a sibling with an identical syndrome of mental handicap of known genetic aetiology, or more subtle, as in the case of a girl with an apparent anxiety disorder whose mother has a history of thyroid disease. A pedigree should be drawn of first- and second-degree relatives, and all the mother's pregnancies and their outcomes recorded. The parents should be asked if they are related. If there have been previous stillbirths or neonatal deaths, and the referred child has mental handicap, developmental regression or evidence of a neurological disorder, then postmortem findings may be informative. The parents should be systematically questioned about whether relatives have an identical or related psychiatric disorder to that of the proband, and whether there is a history of medical disorders in other family members. It is helpful to enquire directly about the presence of mental handicap, epilepsy and developmental delays.

Finally the clinician should note any abnormalities in the appearance or behaviour of the parents or siblings as occasionally these may provide useful pointers to an organic diagnosis in the patient.

THE PHYSICAL EXAMINATION

Introduction

Because the physical examination forms part of a diagnostic process, the clinician should formulate answers to the following questions before beginning the examination: What organic conditions, if any, are suggested by the history or observations? What organic conditions might cause this clinical picture and should be excluded? What conditions might a person of this age be vulnerable to in his or her environment?

It is helpful to consider the physical examination as comprising two processes: physical inspection and physical testing. Inspection (or observation) requires neither special equipment nor an examination room and can begin the moment the patient is first seen. An abnormal facial appearance is often most striking during the initial minutes of an interview, and nonmedical staff may realize that a patient's appearance is unusual, even if the nature of the abnormality cannot be identified. Other abnormalities may also be noted prior to the examination. Attention should be paid to whether the patient looks well or ill, obese or underfed, well-cared-for or unkempt; build and the relative proportions of body and limbs; gait, stair-climbing and rising from a chair; the presence of abnormal movements such as tremor, tics or dystonia (more rarely, chorea or athetosis); excessive perspiration; poor coordination or articulation; and problems with vision or hearing. If abnormalities are observed during the interview, then relevant details can be quickly focused upon that may either save time or indicate the need for a full physical examination.

Measurement and nutrition

Height, weight and head circumference should be plotted at the beginning of the examination because deviation from normal, particularly of the head circumference, may not be apparent until measured. Ideally these measurements should be recorded on percentile charts appropriate for the population or ethnic group of origin of the child, but in practice the charts of Tanner are most widely available (Tanner & Whitehouse, 1976). If a child is referred for assessment of developmental delay or possible regression, then obtaining previous measurements may be informative.

A number of disorders that may present with developmental abnormalities or behavioural disturbance are associated with abnormalities of growth. Tall stature is usually either constitutional or associated with obesity. However, excessive growth may be a feature of a number of genetic disorders: chromosomal abnormalities include Klinefelter's syndrome (Mandoki *et al.*, 1991), 47 XYY and 48 XXYY; nonchromosomal disorders include neurofibromatosis and homocystinuria (Nyhan, 1984). Children with cerebral gigantism (Soto's syndrome) are usually large at birth, remain above the 97th percentile, and their head circumference is usually increased. Children with thyrotoxicosis tend to be in the upper percentiles for height (Fisher, 1987).

Worldwide, malnutrition is the commonest cause of growth retardation, frequently exacerbated by hookworm disease. Where these are not factors, short stature is usually constitutional and is relatively common in handicapped children (Pryor & Thelander, 1967). Severe retardation of growth is seen in children with trisomy 21, and girls with Turner's syndrome are usually short and stocky. A number of less common congenital syndromes are also characterized by short stature and mental handicap (Smith & Jones, 1988). Children

with intrauterine growth retardation usually grow at a normal rate but their height deviates significantly from the norm; the child with fetal alcohol syndrome may also have a characteristic facial appearance (Smith & Jones, 1988). Hormonal abnormalities are less frequent causes of short stature than chronic illness. Nonorganic failure to thrive and psychosocial dwarfism are disorders of infancy in which psychosocial factors are thought to contribute to poor growth (Woolston, 1983; and see Chapter 27).

Obesity in children is usually caused by a combination of excessive calorie intake and insufficient exercise; however, it is also a feature of a number of congenital and acquired syndromes, many of which are characterized by hypogonadism and delayed puberty. Some of the congenital syndromes include major malformations that aid in their identification (Smith & Jones, 1988), whereas others, such as the syndromes of Klinefelter and Prader–Willi (Butler, 1990), are more subtle in their manifestations.

Small head size may be a familial or ethnic trait, and may be proportionate to short height; however, proportionate smallness should not be assumed in a child who is physically or neurologically abnormal (Carey, 1987). Differentiating between prenatal and postnatal onset of microcephaly depends upon obtaining the newborn head circumference and as many postnatal measurements as possible. To establish the cause of microcephaly, a systematic search for structural defects and dysmorphic features should be undertaken, which is dealt with below.

Large head size may also be a normal variant or familial trait (Lorber & Priestley, 1981). Pathological increase in head circumference can result from hydrocephalus (which may be arrested), space-occupying lesions, Soto's syndrome and the fragile X anomaly. Megalencephaly can also be a feature of neurofibromatosis, various degenerative disorders and the mucopolysaccharidoses. There is preliminary evidence that some cases of autism are also associated with megalencephaly or macrocephaly (Bailey *et al.*, 1993).

Assessment of the physical changes — in pubic hair, the male genitalia and the female breasts — that accompany puberty forms part of a full medical examination and is recorded using the rating scales of Marshall and Tanner (1969, 1970). A brief synopsis is included on the Tanner growth charts for each sex (Tanner & Whitehouse, 1976). There are considerable individual differences in the timing of these changes, but they are precocious when seen before 8 years in girls or 9 years in boys; and delayed if not visible before 13 years in girls or 14 years in boys (Kelch, 1987). Although the differential diagnosis of disorders of pubertal timing is complex, some causes may be seen by the child psychiatrist. Precocious puberty may occur in children who have had meningitis or encephalitis, and also in those with tuberous sclerosis or neurofibromatosis. In some children with hypothyroidism, puberty is precocious: more usually it is delayed. Anorexia nervosa and drug abuse also delay sexual maturation, and delayed or incomplete puberty is a feature of the syndromes of Turner, Klinefelter and Prader–Willi.

Growing children are particularly vulnerable to vitamin and mineral deficiencies — a problem not confined to the developing world. Iron deficiency in childhood is not uncommon, and young people should be examined for evidence of anaemia; deficiency should be suspected if there is a history of pica or the ingestion of excessive quantities of ice (Oski, 1979). Because vitamin A deficiency is a major public health problem in many areas of the world, the conjunctiva should be examined for xerosis and Bitot's spots where dietary deficiency is endemic. Vitamin D deficiency can affect children in high latitudes, particularly those of West Indian or Asian origin (Harris *et al.*, 1983). It can also occur in children receiving long-term treatment with anticonvulsants, especially phenobarbitone and phenytoin; vigilance for the signs of rickets is necessary in these groups.

In many parts of the world infectious diseases are endemic, and many young people seen in clinics will harbour infections. These require treatment in their own right, and, rarely may present with psychiatric symptoms. Numerically the most important diseases are malaria, tuberculosis and infections with helminths.

Medical examination

When young people are to have a physical examination that requires undressing, it is important to have established a good rapport. A parent should be encouraged to accompany younger children. Older children and adolescents of opposite sex to the examiner should be accompanied by a chaperone; this is also a sensible precaution for both sexes if there is any suspicion of sexual abuse. If a specialist examination for sexual abuse is thought to be necessary, then this should be performed by an appropriately trained individual.

Although the examination of adults may be performed in a relatively invariant manner, this is often an unsuccessful strategy with young children. It is usually necessary to be opportunistic, and the examiner who is also able to turn a physical examination into a series of games is frequently rewarded by a cooperative child. Finger and glove puppets can be useful accomplices when examining eye movements and the visual fields. At any age, cooperation is more likely if only the area to be examined is undressed at any one time. Any part of the examination that is potentially painful, or may be construed as threatening, should be left until last. If there is any suspicion of abnormality, then the examination must be thorough enough to differentiate between pathology and normal variation.

Several psychiatric syndromes of childhood are associated with an increased number of minor congenital anomalies (Firestone & Peters, 1983; Pomeroy *et al.*, 1988). These are of no serious medical consequence in themselves, but appear to be useful indicators of altered morphogenesis (Marden *et al.*, 1964), and may provide clues to the presence of a specific pattern of malformation. Most are thought to arise from abnormal patterns of growth during the first trimester of pregnancy (Smith & Jones, 1988). Although some anomalies are familial traits, the presence of three or more different anomalies in newborns is extremely uncommon (Marden *et al.*, 1964). The anomalies are not specific to particular developmental disorders; however, a brief search for such anomalies serves several purposes. Firstly, the presence of several anomalies indicates the need to consider whether the child has a recognizable syndrome, although this will not usually be the case. Secondly, the presence of anomalies may be helpful when interpreting the significance of other clinical information — an issue that is dealt with below. Lastly, the identification of abnormalities in structure and form is an essential skill when the clinician has to assess children with mental handicap and regression. Studies examining the prevalence of minor anomalies have usually used the scale devised by Waldrop and Halverson (1971); Largo *et al.* (1989) provide a more extensive list of anomalies.

Although patients' mental states are often examined whenever they are seen, the repetition of a physical examination is an unusual occurrence. Nevertheless, if a disorder is resistant to appropriate treatment, the diagnosis remains uncertain, or the clinical picture is deteriorating, then a further physical examination may detect important signs that have either recently appeared or whose significance was initially overlooked.

Patients may refuse an examination for a variety of reasons, and the response to such a refusal needs to be flexible. Refusal can be a focus for work with the family, or it may be more appropriate for an examination to be conducted by the patient's own doctor. A thorough examination of an acutely disturbed adolescent may need to be postponed until there has been an improvement in the mental state, although organic causes of acute behavioural disturbance need to be excluded quickly.

INVESTIGATIONS

Medical investigations are part of a process to confirm or refute competing diagnoses; their selection should be based on knowledge about the possible aetiologies for a behavioural syndrome and the information available from the history and examination. Of course the clinician's knowledge base needs constant revision: new aetiological factors — such as fragile X and human immunodeficiency virus (HIV) — continue to be identified, and the aetiological role of known factors may be thrown into doubt by new findings. Similarly, technological advances may alter the threshold for testing for different disorders.

Patients may not have appropriate investigations for a variety of reasons. If an adequate family history is not obtained then a range of possible genetic disorders may be overlooked. Failure to observe or appreciate the significance of physical signs may also lead to the omission of relevant examinations. Finally, the physician may simply overlook a test that should be routine for a particular presentation. Overinvestigation of patients by psychiatrists is probably a relatively infrequent occurrence. The debate about appropriate investigations for individuals with autism is dealt with below.

If the history of physical examination suggests an organic aetiology, then investigations should be ordered in a logical manner relating both to the amount of information that can be gained from an investigation, and the relative likelihood of different disorders. The choice and order of investigations are also influenced by the relative prevalence of genetic and environmental influences in the local population; for this reason there is not always a universal scheme for the investigation of particular disorders. Similarly, when faced with a change in behaviour in a mentally handicapped individual, it is usually necessary to set a lower threshold for investigation, as important information from a history may not be available. A deterioration in any patient's condition may require a review of the working diagnosis and consideration of whether further investigations are merited.

The molecular genetic investigation of psychiatric disorders is likely to become increasingly important in the future, as such approaches can simultaneously identify a specific marker for a disorder and the aetiological abnormality. Genes have already been identified for conditions such as fragile X syndrome (Verkerk *et al.*, 1991), Huntington's chorea (Huntington's Disease Collaborative Research Group, 1993) and X-linked adrenoleukodystrophy (Mosser *et al.*, 1993). In the immediate future these techniques will be confined to single gene disorders, and are likely to have their greatest impact on the assessment of mental handicap and developmental regression. The identification of the fragile X gene should enable affected individuals to be more accurately, cheaply and quickly identified than using traditional cytogenetic methods (although cytogenetic techniques still have a role in certain cases). In the more distant future, molecular genetic screening for inherited disorders may be more economical than conducting the equivalent unrelated biochemical tests.

Neuroimaging has improved greatly over the last decade. There has been continuing development of computer tomography (CT) and the clinical application of magnetic resonance imaging (MRI) has enabled very high-resolution imaging of the nervous system in any plane without radiation exposure (Armstrong & Keevil, 1991a,b). MRI provides superior visualization of neuronal migration abnormalities (Barkovich *et al.*, 1988), inflammatory and demyelinating white-matter diseases (Miller *et al.*, 1990) and leukomalacia (De Vries *et al.*, 1989); however, calcification is not visualized.

Although structural imaging is a powerful technique, there are no psychiatric disorders that are consistently associated with specific structural abnormalities. Clinical use should be restricted to cases where there is electroencephalographic (EEG) evidence of focal abnormality, or the following are suspected: structural developmental abnormalities; the sequelae of perinatal anoxia, hypercapnoea, or acidosis; degenerative diseases; or tumours. Although at present there are no clinical indications for using positron emission tomography (PET) (Bench *et al.*, 1990), single photon emission computed tomography (SPECT) (Costa & Ell, 1991) or magnetic resonance functional imaging (Belliveau *et al.*, 1991) for the investigation of childhood psychiatric disorders, the use of these methodologies to study the neural basis of cognitive functions may produce future diagnostic applications.

INTERPRETATION

During the assessment process decisions about what to ask, look for, or do are influenced by the interpretation of previously acquired information; correct interpretation requires knowledge about individual disorders and aetiological mechanisms. Two particular pitfalls in interpreting the history deserve especial mention: assuming from the apparent absence of a family history that genetic factors are not involved; and automatically assuming a causal role for obstetric factors. It is sometimes argued that genetic factors are implicated only in patients with a relevant family history. Steffenburg (1991) and Gillberg (1992) have taken this stance with regard to autism whilst others have split the population of schizophrenic individuals into those with and without a family history (see Chapter 34). However, there are a number of reasons why genetically determined disorders may not produce an informative pedigree. First, most patients with autosomal recessive disorders are born to unaffected heterozygous parents, and in a small family may have no affected siblings. Secondly, in autosomal dominant conditions individuals may be only mildly affected as a consequence of variable expressivity, or appear normal because of lack of penetrance or not having passed through the age of risk. Thirdly, in multifactorial or oligogenic disorders, the recurrence risk for relatives, although greater than the population base rate, may still be so low that no affected relatives are seen in an individual family. Fourthly, genetically determined disorders may arise *de novo*, either as new single gene mutations or as chromosomal disorders. Finally, nonpaternity may confound attempts to identify affected relatives. Because the lack of a relevant family history does not necessarily exclude a genetic disorder, clinicians must rely upon their knowledge about possible aetiologies when deciding how intensively to search for nongenetic factors, and when giving advice about recurrence risks.

The presence of other adverse factors can act as a powerful draw away from a genetic diagnosis. Obstetric and perinatal complications are not uncommon, and parents or other clinicians may view these as aetiological factors. This may be a correct interpretation when, for instance, a history of intraventricular haemorrhage or evidence of periventricular leukomalacia provides evidence of brain damage. Nevertheless, a history of obstetric or perinatal complications does not imply that brain damage necessarily occurred, even if it is associated with a psychiatric disorder. That is because severe perinatal complications appear to account for only a few cases of abnormal postnatal development (Nelson & Ellenberg, 1986), and genetically abnormal fetuses appear to be at higher risk for obstetric complications (Rantakallio & Von Wendt, 1985; Bailey *et al.*, 1991). Recording the presence of minor congenital anomalies has been a useful research strategy for recognizing less than optimal intrauterine development. Their significance in individual cases is less certain, but if a poor obstetric history is not accompanied by focal neurological signs or abnormal scan findings, then the presence of three or more minor anomalies may indicate that obstetric hazards were secondary to abnormal development.

A related issue arises in the interpretation of impaired motor coordination and motor delays — so-called soft signs (Tupper, 1987). Focal neurological signs are indicative of some form of localized abnormality in brain functioning. Although problems with motor coordination may be secondary to cerebellar abnormalities, most children with minor motor problems or delays do not have cerebellar signs. On balance it seems unlikely that these minor abnormalities are usually the consequence of brain damage. In the careful study of Largo *et al.* (1989), the neurodevelopmental outcome of preterm infants was related to the number of minor congenital anomalies, birth weight and gestational age, but not to the pregnancy optimality score. In a study of hyperactive children by Taylor (1986), developmental delays were a better predictor of outcome than perinatal adversities. It seems more likely that both minor problems of motor coordination and obstetric hazards are manifestations of abnormal development. Soft signs by themselves should not be taken as evidence of brain damage, and unless they are accompanied by focal neurological signs, localized EEG abnormalities or psychometric evidence of localized abnormality, they are not sufficient justification for CT or MRI.

The interpretation of structural imaging findings may also be difficult. Abnormalities such as periventricular leukomalacia or the white matter changes of demyelination are the outcome of identifiable pathologies and may bear a close relationship to clinical findings. Other abnormalities, such as nonprogressive ventricular dilatation or small areas of cortical abnormality, are not obviously related either to particular pathologies or to clinical features or syndromes. Unless characteristic of an anoxic or haemorrhagic process, scan abnormalities should not, without other evidence, be attributed to obstetric or perinatal events. When not associated with localizing clinical features, structural abnormalities may represent sequelae of abnormal brain development, rather than the cause of the clinical syndrome. That being said, the site of an abnormality probably influences the clinical interpretation; so that while few would argue that mild ventricular dilatation is the cause of a disorder, an abnormality localized to a temporal or frontal lobe is probably more frequently interpreted in this way. At present clinicians must rely on knowledge about individual disorders when interpreting scan abnormalities; in syndromes which are under a high degree of genetic control and are not associated with pathognomonic scan abnormalities, such as autism, minor abnormalities are unlikely to be of aetiological significance. However, if children show markedly atypical or partial behavioural syndromes, aetiological factors may be different, and scan abnormalities may not be so easily dismissed.

CLINICAL PRESENTATIONS

Disorders of conduct and emotion

These disorders are very common and usually are not attributable to medical aetiologies, so several factors need to be taken into account when deciding whether a full physical examination is required. The most important is the history: if the presentation of the disorder is atypical, or the personal, medical or family history is suggestive of a possible organic aetiology, then a physical examination is necessary. A second consideration is the environment of the young person: if physical ill health or malnutrition is common in the population, or the child lives in a socially disadvantaged area, or there is concern about the quality of parenting or possible abuse, then a physical examination is also necessary. Finally, if any abnormalities are observed during the interview (or there is suspicion of hearing loss), or the height, weight or head circumference is outside the normal range, then an examination should also be undertaken. If there are no indications for a full examination this should be recorded in the notes; when the case is reviewed the necessity for an examination or investigations may be reconsidered.

The routine investigation of all psychiatric patients does not appear to be justified: Gabel and Hsu (1986) studied 100 adolescents who required hospitalization for psychiatric disorders and, even in these severe cases, found that routine tests did not alter diagnostic classifications.

Behavioural change and psychosis

A wide variety of organic aetiologies may produce a change in behaviour or psychosis, and their manifestations may be protean: change may be insidious or rapid, severity may range from mild to psychosis, and cognitive functions may be preserved, or acutely or chronically impaired. For these reasons the focus here is on the clinical features of organic disorders that may present with behavioural change or psychosis, rather than on particular behavioural presentations. This section is also laid out according to the nature of the underlying aetiology; reference to a classification of diseases is a useful aid in the approach to diagnosis. Many of the disorders dealt with are rare, but they all serve to illustrate how disparate items of clinical information may help to identify an organic aetiology.

Because depression, mania and schizophrenia are rare before puberty, a marked change in the behaviour of a prepubertal child in the absence of environmental stressors ought to arouse suspicion of either an organic disorder, or physical or sexual abuse. Similarly a history of declining school performance may indicate declining cognitive skills. Establishing what the child can and cannot do in a variety of environmental situations compared with the premorbid state is important, as an apparent decline may only represent unrealistic parental expectations.

History

Changes in behaviour that bear a close temporal relationship to a severe head injury are unlikely to present diagnostic difficulty. Chronic subdural haematomas are very rare in children over the age of 1 year, but they may be caused by trauma without concussion.

In the UK it is unusual for a young person with a postnatally acquired cerebral infection to present to a psychiatrist. If there is a history of recent ill health and possible confusion, then a thorough cognitive assessment is necessary. Worldwide several different cerebral infections may present with behavioural change or cognitive decline. Where tuberculosis is endemic, a change in temperament of a child with a primary complex should arouse suspicion of tuberculous meningitis. Many parasitic organisms invade the central nervous system, producing focal seizures, signs of space-occupying lesions, encephalopathies or behavioural change. These include hydatid cyst disease, malaria, schistosomiasis, tapeworms, toxocariasis and trichinosis.

HIV infection may be acquired postnatally by transfusion with contaminated blood or its products; through the use of contaminated needles; or by sexual contact, including sexual abuse (Gutman *et al.*, 1991). In adults a decline in cognitive, behavioural and motor function may be the only clinical manifestation of infection (Navia *et al.*, 1986). Increasingly the disorder needs to be considered in the differential diagnosis of young people exposed to known risk factors (see Chapter 40).

There is continuing dispute about the existence of postviral myeloencephalopathies. Nevertheless, following convalescence from infectious mononucleosis, some patients do experience marked fatigue which may last for months. Other neurological postinfective manifestations include headache and symptoms of anxiety or depression. A haematological diagnosis may not have been made at the time of the primary infection; where appropriate, patients should be asked about a history of prolonged fever, sore throat and posterior cervical lymphadenopathy.

Affective-psychic seizures may present to the psychiatrist rather than to the paediatrician, as they may not be accompanied by significant changes in consciousness. In young children there is usually an initial impression of panic: the child runs to an adult for help, often with a plagued facial expression, and may cling and scream fearfully. In older children the picture is usually more complex: there may be an ill-defined unpleasant sensation welling up from the abdomen and tightening of the throat, or vague feelings related to the alimentary tract, or to the head or abdomen as a whole (Aicardi, 1986). Visual and auditory hallucinations and illusions can occur and may be accompanied by fear; there may also be subtle changes in cognition without loss of consciousness. Seizures can be activated by emotional stress. Several features of the history are helpful in differentiating these seizures from other behavioural phenomena. Firstly, they are usually of brief duration, lasting 90–110 seconds. Secondly, they are frequently accompanied by motor automatisms and autonomic changes. Thirdly, it is rare for there not to be a brief period of confusion or drowsiness following the seizure, although careful questioning may be required to elicit this history from informants.

The clinical diagnosis may occasionally be forthcoming during the interview; for instance, a change in mental state associated with prescribed drugs, such as steroids, or associated with illicit drug taking. The identification of nonprescribed drug use is important because the young person may need help with a wide range of problems associated with drug taking (DHSS, 1984). The drug user who injects may contract a variety of infectious diseases, either directly from injection or as a result of the lifestyle that often accompanies misuse; the possibility of infection with hepatitis, sexually transmitted disease or HIV needs to be considered in young people with a history of drug and alcohol abuse.

A review of bodily symptoms may reveal informative symptoms. A history of increased appetite, fatigability and palpitations in individuals with an apparent anxiety disorder or declining school performance may signify thyrotoxicosis. This is most frequently the result of Graves' disease, and less often Hashimoto's thyroiditis; both disorders have a genetic basis and predominantly affect girls. An attack of acute intermittent porphyria may be accompanied by a wide variety of psychiatric symptoms, including hallucinations and delusions. The patient is usually postpubertal and there is usually a history of colicky abdominal pain which may be accompanied by constipation, nausea or vomiting. Postpubertal girls should be asked the date of their last menstrual period, as behavioural change may be secondary to pregnancy and its concealment.

Mental state examination

An acute brain syndrome with impairments in consciousness, thinking and memory and disturbances of perception, emotion and motor behaviour requires an intensive search to identify the organic aetiology. The psychiatrist is unlikely to see cases where impairments of consciousness predominate. However, cognitive impairments should not be overlooked in young people presenting with hallucinations or irrational behaviour. A chronic brain syndrome may be suggested by a history of schooling difficulties or cognitive decline; a complete cognitive assessment is necessary.

Physical examination

If a change in behaviour is acute the patient's temperature should be taken: the majority of acute infections of the nervous system will be accompanied by a pyrexia.

Abnormalities of movement may have been noticed prior to

the physical examination. Rapid movements are characteristic of thyrotoxicosis. Rheumatic fever may also present with behavioural disturbance and chorea in the absence of joint, skin or heart manifestations (Bender, 1942). The choreiform movements are exaggerated by emotion but diminish during sleep.

A diagnosis of a psychiatric disorder is initially made in nearly a quarter of adolescents with Wilson's disease (Walshe & Yealland, 1992). The earliest symptoms are usually dysarthria or difficulty with the hands. The upper lip may be retracted (risus sardonicus), facial expression is frequently lacking and the patient may drool. Usually the neurological picture is dominated by dystonia, which may be asymmetrical, and choreic or athetoid movements. The eyes should be examined for Kayser–Fleischer rings, a brown-green discoloration in the limbic area of the cornea; these are not always full circles and may be visible without a slitlamp. Hepatomegaly or splenomegaly may also be found.

Evidence of intravenous or subcutaneous drug injection may be found in the form of needle tracks, abscesses, areas of hyperpigmentation or scar tissue from healed abscesses. Long-term stigmata of oral or nasal ingestion of drugs are minimal, with the exception of inhalation of solvents from a bag which may produce a circumoral rash. The physical examination may provide some information about which drugs have been abused. Phencyclidine (PCP) intoxication is accompanied by pupillary constriction, hypersalivation and nystagmus; whereas LSD abuse may be accompanied by pupillary dilatation, tachycardia, hyperthermia and piloerection. Recognition of intoxication is important as phenothiazines are contraindicated when the intoxicant has anticholinergic properties, since fatal tachycardia and hypotension may be induced (Schonberg *et al.*, 1987). Amphetamine abuse may be accompanied by dilated pupils, hypertension, tachycardia and blanched mucous membranes.

A skin lesion, in the form of a photosensitive skin rash in a characteristic butterfly distribution over the nose and cheeks, is also a feature of systemic lupus erythematosus. Nervous system involvement with personality disturbances and psychosis may be a prominent or isolated feature of this disorder, which predominantly affects females and may be accompanied by arthritis.

Thyrotoxicosis may be accompanied by tachycardia, an overactive precordium, gallop rhythms, a fine tremor and increased perspiration.

Patients with acute intermittent porphyria develop a peripheral neuropathy characterized by flaccid paresis with pain or paraesthesia; they frequently have a tachycardia and many are hypertensive. The early neurological findings in AIDS include gait ataxia — which may be mild — hyperreflexia and weakness of the lower limbs. Where infection is endemic, late congenital syphilis may present with congenital paresis; a search should be made for Hutchinson's teeth, interstitial keratitis, eighth nerve deafness, Clutton's joints and rhagades.

Genetic progressive neurological disorders are rare; however, dementia is sometimes an early feature and may be manifested as behavioural disturbance. Abnormalities of gait are a feature of several disorders; early ataxia may be detected on testing tandem walk. X-linked adrenoleukodystrophy affects only boys who usually present between the ages of 5 and 9 with a change in behaviour and difficulty with school work; with an adolescent presentation progression is slower. Difficulties with seeing precede the gait disturbance, which is usually associated with spasticity. Problems with memory and language gradually become apparent and the patient's speech may be noted to be dysarthric. In patients with overt signs of adrenal failure increased skin pigmentation may be noted in skin folds. Juvenile-onset metachromatic leukodystrophy may also present with emotional or schooling difficulties. In addition to ataxia, the examiner may detect nystagmus, hypertonia and intention tremor.

Investigations — general approach

Although diseases do not always present in a textbook manner, there will often be clues from the history or examination that point to a particular organic diagnosis. In a nonacute situation, there is no justification for requesting a battery of investigations in the hope that something might turn up: tests should be requested on the basis of clinical information, and there may be no indication for any investigations. Initially some organic aetiologies may not be associated with obvious diagnostic clues, such as mental state changes secondary to cerebral tumours or abnormal serum calcium levels. However, these disorders are very uncommon, and in the case of tumours, localizing signs or symptoms of raised intracranial pressure will eventually develop which should not be ignored. If hormonal abnormalities are suspected, then serum calcium as well as thyroid function should be checked.

When young people present with a severe change in behaviour or psychosis there are several reasons for routinely investigating to detect organic factors. Most importantly the disorder may be unnecessarily perpetuated either by the patient's actions, such as continuing to take drugs, or by failing to treat a remediable condition. Additionally, many patients will require medication and for several reasons routine investigations should be conducted as soon as possible. Firstly, symptomatology may be suppressed by medication, with the result that appropriate investigations are unnecessarily delayed. Secondly, hepatic and renal impairment should be excluded before treatment with drugs that are metabolized and excreted by these organs. Finally, adequate thyroid functioning should be ascertained prior to administration of lithium.

The initial investigation of behavioural change or psychosis should include a full blood count and erythrocyte sedimentation rate; urea and electrolytes; calcium and phosphate; alkaline phosphatase, aspartate transaminase and albumin; thyroxine and thyroid-stimulating hormone; a routine urinalysis; and a urine toxicology screen (although hallucinogens will not be detected by urinalysis). Because multiple drug abuse is common (Clayton, 1986), urine testing should not be restricted to the reported drug of abuse. A presumptive positive screen should be followed by a standard reference procedure (Stewart, 1982). Serological tests for syphilis should be conducted where congenital syphilis is common, and in young people who may have been exposed to sexual abuse.

Investigations — specific disorders

In Wilson's disease serum ceruloplasmin levels and total serum copper levels are usually low, with decreased ceruloplasmin-bound copper and increased albumin-bound copper. A 24-hour urine collection may reveal increased urinary copper excretion. Slit-lamp examination of the cornea for Kayser–Fleischer rings should be conducted by a qualified ophthalmologist. Asymptomatic siblings of an affected patient should be tested for the disorder.

During an attack of acute intermittent porphyria urinary porphobilinogen excretion is increased; if patients present late in an attack it may be necessary to conduct a quantitative estimate of porphobilinogen and faecal porphyrins to confirm the diagnosis (Elder, 1987). Acute rheumatic fever is usually accompanied by a rise in the erythrocyte sedimentation rate. Group A streptococcus may be isolated from the patient and titres of antibodies of specific streptococcal antigens may be elevated. The antinuclear antibody test is positive in virtually all patients with systemic lupus erythematosus (Melsin & Rothfield, 1968). The investigation of young people with suspected affective-psychic seizures is dealt with in Chapter 11.

Vitamin B_{12} and folate deficiency are uncommon prior to adulthood; moreover there is little evidence to suggest that folate deficiency is associated with mental state changes in childhood. Dietary deficiency of vitamin B_{12} may occur in strict vegetarians, and malabsorption of the vitamins may occur with bowel disorders and infestations: pernicious anaemia is a similar disorder in children and adults. Anticonvulsant medication, particularly phenytoin, may interfere with intestinal absorption of folate (De Gruchy, 1975). Estimating serum levels of these vitamins will be most helpful in the above high-risk groups; those with early haematological findings, such as hypersegmented neutrophils; and those with the neurological findings of B_{12} deficiency (paraesthesiae, sensory deficits, loss of tendon reflexes and mental state changes).

The investigation of the progressive neurological disorders is beyond the scope of this chapter. Although in some individuals the history or examination may be diagnostic or helpful in guiding investigations, in others a systematic series of investigations will be required, and liaison with a paediatric neurologist is necessary.

Somatic symptoms and hysteria

Somatic complaints may present in a number of guises (see Chapter 39). The focus here is on school refusal, but the underlying principles apply to all presentations.

In school refusal, symptoms are most commonly referred to the gastrointestinal system, but may also include malaise, headaches and fainting. The history is most important in differentiating organic from psychosomatic cases. Firstly, it is important to establish that there really is a fear of either going to school or of being ill at school; this may require a wide-ranging discussion of all aspects of attendance at school. Secondly, a detailed description of the physical symptomatology is needed to decide whether it is characteristic of a recognizable disorder — remote causes of abdominal pain should not be forgotten, such as affective-psychic seizures, migraine, referred pain and lead poisoning. Thirdly, the timing of the symptoms needs to be ascertained; symptoms that only occur on weekday mornings are more likely to be functional than pain that is continuous or disturbs sleep. Lastly, the patient should be asked about relevant associated symptoms that might suggest an organic condition. In the case of abdominal pain these would include a change in bowel habit, blood in the stool, painful defecation and alleviation of the pain by eating.

During the physical examination the clinician should attempt to elicit physical signs and note whether growth and pubertal status are appropriate for the child's age. If the history and examination suggest a psychosomatic disorder, then investigations are probably not warranted. In warm countries infections with intestinal helminths are common, particularly ascariasis, and these may cause abdominal pain. In such areas it is probably sensible to examine the stools of all children presenting in this way, although in some infestation may be coincidental.

Hysterical conversion reactions most commonly present with abnormalities of gait and posture, blindness, deafness or aphonia. Organic disorders must be detected when signs are minimal, and disorders recognized in which the signs, although obvious, have been misinterpreted as psychological in origin. Many disorders with minimal or nonspecific signs will only be detected following suitable investigation and rare disorders will often be amongst the differential diagnoses.

Abnormalities of movement are easily misinterpreted as hysterical in origin. Many of these are rare (Marsden, 1986); however, a relatively common disorder is dystonia — a syndrome of sustained muscle contraction frequently causing twisting and repetitive movements or abnormal posture (Fahn, 1988). Dystonia may be idiopathic or a consequence of a variety of conditions (Calne & Lang, 1988). Agonist and antagonist muscles are simultaneously active and the movements may be exacerbated by fatigue, stress or emotional states. The disorder may be focal, segmental, generalized, involve noncontiguous body parts, or affect one-half of the body. Common manifestations of focal dystonia are torticollis, writer's cramp, blepharospasm, oromandibular dystonia and dysphonia. Gait disturbances may also occur; a common presentation is an equinovarus posture of the foot as soon as walking is attempted.

The need for physical investigation should be considered individually for each case (see Chapter 39). A planned approach to investigation, with all the relevant tests being completed as quickly as possible, is greatly preferable to piecemeal testing over weeks or months.

Anorexia and bulimia

Although these diagnoses are usually apparent from the history, the conviction with which the morbid ideas are held may be expressed most openly during a physical examination. The purpose of the examination is to measure the patient's current weight, height and head circumference; assess pubertal status; note the extent of emaciation in patients with weight loss; and to document the complications of malnutrition, vomiting, purging and medication abuse. The examination provides information on which to base a decision about the necessity of inpatient treatment. Moreover, explaining about observed complications may be helpful when emphasizing the seriousness of the condition to the parents, and is also an important part of helping the patient to understand the disorder.

Weight loss is usually obvious on the limbs, buttocks and breasts and there may be dependent oedema. Fine lanugo hair is often visible on the back, the limbs, the side of the face and the upper lip. In premenarchal anorexia there may be signs of pubertal arrest with no evidence of breast budding and only scanty pubic hair (Russell, 1983). The extremities are usually cold, the pulse slow and the blood pressure low. Individuals who induce vomiting may have scarring over the dorsum of the hand (Russell, 1979) and a round face from parotid gland enlargement; buccal tears may be visible in the mouth, and dental enamel and dentine may have been eroded by gastric acid. If water and metabolic homeostasis is severely disturbed, the patient may be dehydrated and application of a venepuncture cuff can produce tetany.

Endocrine and metabolic disturbances can accompany severe weight loss, vomiting, purging and excessive exercise. Initial assessment should include a full blood count with red cell indices; urea and electrolytes; calcium and phosphate; liver function tests and plasma proteins; plasma lipids and cholesterol; and follicle-stimulating hormone and luteinizing hormone levels. Further aspects are considered in Chapter 24.

Autism

Autism is considered separately from mental handicap because genetic influences predominate and recognizable medical aetiologies are relatively uncommon; consequently less comprehensive investigation is required, although this view is not universally supported. Gillberg (1990, 1992) has argued for a series of investigations on all cases that is both more exhaustive than advocated below for mental handicap, and unrelated to the clinical findings. Because unnecessary investigations are wasteful and stressful — CT or MRI, using general anaesthetic if necessary, and lumbar puncture are advocated by Gillberg — the data supporting these recommendations are briefly examined.

Gillberg (1992) and Steffenburg (1991) group cases of autism into a very small (<10%) familial category, who have affected relatives, and a variety of other groups, including a large group (34–37%) with medical syndromes. The categorization of cases as familial or sporadic on the basis of a family history can, as discussed above, be misleading. The findings from all three epidemiological twin studies of autism (Folstein & Rutter, 1977; Steffenburg et al., 1989; Bailey et al., 1991) suggest that the heritability of autism is very high (a conclusion supported by the singleton data), indicating that even cases without a family history are most likely under strong genetic control. Moreover, the incidence of possible medical aetiologies was low in all these series. Many medical disorders identified by Gillberg and coworkers are either of uncertain significance, or have not been observed by other workers. In the case of some disorders, such as neurofibromatosis, it appears that the association with autism is no greater than that expected by chance (Mouridsen et al., 1992). Particularly strong claims were initially made for the role of fragile X in autism: 16% of Swedish cases were reported to have the anomaly (Blomquist et al., 1985). A rate of 7% is currently reported (Gillberg, 1992), and the two studies that have used both a standardized diagnostic instrument and rigorous cytogenetic criteria report rates of 2.7% (Piven et al., 1991) and 1.6% (Bailey et al., 1993). A wide variety of structural abnormalities have been documented in scanning studies (Bailey, 1993); however, the heterogeneity of the findings, taken in conjunction with the genetic data, suggests that these are probably consequences rather than causes of autism.

The data do not support the notion of a sizeable group of nongenetic patients with medical aetiologies. Of course some patients will have a recognizable aetiology and a thorough history and a detailed examination (as outlined below) should always be conducted. In the absence of clinical indicators of a medical syndrome, investigations can, at present, be confined to the disorders which have been most frequently associated with the syndrome: chromosome karyotyping, with a cytogenetic or molecular genetic search for the fragile X anomaly in both males and females (see Chapter 10); and an EEG if seizures are suspected (see Chapter 8). Handicapped children with mental handicap and only a partial or atypical syndrome of autism should be investigated as outlined below.

Mental handicap and developmental regression

Introduction

Establishing the cause of these disorders permits a better assessment of prognosis, alerts the clinician to likely complications, and enables families to be counselled about likely recurrence risks. Although a thorough history and examination may not result in an immediate diagnosis, they will enable either suitable investigations to be initiated or an appropriate referral to be made. Close cooperation with paediatric neurologists, clinical geneticists and the clinical chemistry laboratory will often be required. A full neurological examination is usually necessary and a standard text should be consulted for details (for instance, Paine & Oppe, 1966).

The approach here is to indicate those physical abnormalities that are easily seen, providing they are looked for, and whose detection does not require special skills or complicated procedures. The phenotypic characteristics of many disorders become increasingly apparent with development; for instance, the characteristic facies of the fragile X syndrome is most obvious after puberty (Fryns, 1989). Regular photographic records of patients can be a helpful means of recognizing that an identifiable phenotype is emerging; anthropometric definitions of dysmorphic facial signs whose indices can be calculated from photographs are available (Stengel-Rutkowski *et al.*, 1984).

If an aetiology is identified and optimal care is to be provided, then the child should be seen by a doctor with experience of the disorder. As new aetiologies are identified and diagnostic testing improves, clinicians should consider reexamining and testing young people under their care, as the number of new specific diagnoses may be surprisingly high (Asthana *et al.*, 1990). This is especially important when disorders are genetically determined, as relatives can also be tested.

Mental handicap is frequently accompanied by sensory impairments (Ellis, 1986; Kropka & Williams, 1986) and all individuals should have audiometry and a thorough assessment of visual acuity.

History

It is important to differentiate between static disorders and the predominantly genetically determined progressive disorders that may be associated with high recurrence risks. Regression is obvious when previously acquired skills, such as language, are lost. Sometimes a slowing or plateau in the rate of acquisition of new skills may precede frank loss of skills; this will only be recognized if a detailed developmental history is taken. In a young child, recognizing the type of disorder may not be possible at a single assessment; in these circumstances accurate measures of psychological and physical development should be obtained at an initial visit in order to establish the developmental trajectory over the coming months.

A thorough history may indicate the presence of possible prenatal, perinatal or postnatal aetiologies (see the section on history taking, above). Prenatal influences may not be immediately obvious, as in the case of children with mental retardation and microcephaly (resulting from elevated intrauterine phenylalanine levels) born to women with phenylketonuria who were treated with dietary restriction during childhood (Levy & Waisbren, 1983). Even if there is no significant history of maternal infection during pregnancy, congenital infection should be suspected if there is a history of intrauterine growth retardation or prematurity or a history of neonatal jaundice, hepatosplenomegaly, purpura or rashes. The various aetiological agents are frequently clinically indistinguishable, producing microcephaly, eye signs (such as retinopathy, cataracts, corneal scarring and microphthalmia), hearing impairment and cerebral palsy.

If a history of perinatal adversity is accompanied by con-genital anomalies, then perinatal insults may have affected an abnormal individual. If mental handicap appears to be the result of kernicterus, and there is no history of rhesus or ABO incompatibility, glucose-6-phosphate dehydrogenase deficiency should have been excluded: further episodes of haemolysis may be precipitated by a variety of chemicals and drugs.

Physical examination

Useful information may already have been gained from measurement of height, weight and head circumference. Postnatal onset of microcephaly is associated with a number of chromosomal and malformation syndromes and metabolic disorders (Carey, 1987); physical findings to support these diagnoses may be apparent. Girls with Rett's syndrome (Hagberg *et al.*, 1983) show deceleration of head growth and lose communicative skills and purposeful hand use. Secondary microcephaly is a reported feature of HIV infection acquired by vertical infection (Falloon *et al.*, 1989).

The skin should be examined for evidence of phakomatoses (Vinken & Bruyn, 1972). In neurofibromatosis, café-au-lait spots — oval pigmented macules with their long axis parallel to a cutaneous nerve — may appear during infancy; common moles and axillary freckles may also be seen. The earliest skin lesion in tuberous sclerosis is the depigmented, ash leaf-shaped macule; it is more easily seen under a Wood's ultra-violet light. Fibroangiomatous naevi may not be apparent until 4—7 years of age and occur principally in the nasolabial folds and on the cheeks.

The skin should also be examined for hypo- or hyperpigmentation and naevi, looseness or oedema, absent or excessive facial or body hair, telangiectases, and haemangiomata, which are found in the distribution of the ophthalmic branch of the trigeminal nerve in Sturge—Weber syndrome (Smith & Jones, 1988). A malar flush is usually seen in homocystinuria and a photosensitive eruption is common in Hartnup disease.

The shape of the skull should be noted and the forehead examined for prominent supraorbital ridges or frontal bossing. The examiner should consider whether the face is particularly round, broad, triangular or flat and note any excessive subcutaneous tissue or coarseness. The jaw may be unusually prominent or receding and there may be malar or maxillary hypoplasia. The ears should be examined for signs of malformation, abnormal vertical position or posterior rotation. Examination of the hair may reveal displacement of the parietal whorl, unusual hair loss, or altered form or brittleness of the hairs.

The examiner should consider whether the nose is particularly short, small or unusually prominent, and also note whether the nostrils are properly formed, or are hypoplastic or anteverted. The nasal bridge may be unusually low, high or prominent, and both the nasal bridge and nasal root may be unusually broad.

Eye abnormalities are found in association with all the major chromosomal aberrations, with many inborn errors of metabolism and with congenital infections. During embryonic development the eyes move medially; many syndromes and diseases are associated with an increased distance between the orbits — hyperteleorism — or, less commonly, a decreased distance — hypoteleorism. Many facial features may produce the appearance of hyperteleorism; when the abnormality is suspected, interpupillary distance can be measured and compared with published norms (Smith & Jones, 1988). The slant and length of the palpebral fissures should be assessed, any prominence or retraction of the eyeballs noted, and the eyes examined for congenital ptosis. The medial canthi may be laterally displaced and epicanthal folds may be observed.

The sclera should be inspected for abnormal pigmentation and the cornea for abnormal size, clouding, opacity or deposits. Defects, unusual patterning or coloration of the iris may also be noted. Brushfield's spots may be seen in both Klinefelter's and Down's syndromes, and Lisch's nodules — pigmented hamartomas of the iris — are seen in the majority of patients with neurofibromatosis.

A thorough fundoscopic examination of the eye requires pupillary dilation. Whether this is a worthwhile procedure must be decided on the basis of the fundal findings without mydriasis, and the abnormalities detected in the remainder of the examination. A darkened room will normally ensure a reasonable view. Cataracts may be noted and the retina should be examined for abnormal pigmentation, chorioretinitis and the macular changes seen in storage diseases, i.e. a cherry-red spot or grey coloration. The optic nerve should be examined for atrophy.

The overall size and shape of the mouth, lips and philtrum should be assessed. Inside the mouth, the size of the tongue and any irregularities in its shape and the presence of frenula should be noted. The height and width of the palate can also be assessed and the alveolar ridges examined for hypertrophy and lead lines. The examiner should consider whether the right number of teeth are present in the right position and whether their form or size is abnormal.

The length of the neck should be noted and any abnormal formation of the thorax, such as pectus excavatum or carinatum. The spine should be examined for evidence of scoliosis, kyphosis, vertebral defects and sacral dimples.

The examiner should consider whether the limbs are in proportion to body size and look for fixed deformities of the joints; any joint hyperextensibility should also be recorded. The hands and feet should be carefully examined, paying attention to their overall size, absence or duplication of any fingers or toes or their partial fusion. The examiner may also assess whether the fingers or thumb are unusually long or short and whether there is metacarpal or metatarsal hypoplasia. The thumb and big toe should be inspected to determine if they are unusually broad, and the examiner should determine if any digits are either bent or permanently flexed. The pattern of creases on the fingers, palms and soles should be checked and the nails examined for unusual formation, in particular hypoplasia or hyperconvexity.

A thorough examination of the bodily systems is necessary, with particular attention paid to the presence of heart murmurs, hepatosplenomegaly, and anomalies or hyperplasia or hypoplasia of the external genitalia.

Investigations

Although information from the history and physical examination may be insufficient to make a clinical diagnosis and order confirmatory investigations, it may indicate either when in development an abnormality arose, or the likely nature of the aetiology. The order and type of investigations should be guided by this information.

Different laboratory tests are available for detecting some abnormalities. If assessment of mental handicap is a substantial part of the clinician's work, then it is helpful to review the limitations of the tests that are used with laboratory staff. Many tests require fresh specimens, and advice should always be sought on the optimal time and manner of specimen collection and transportation. Some laboratories advise that specimens for a metabolic screen be collected after the metabolic challenge provided by a meal, such as a breakfast of milk and cereal.

Children with a history or signs of prenatal infection can be tested for immunological evidence of the common aetiological agents: toxoplasmosis, rubella, cytomegalovirus, herpes simplex and syphilis — the so-called TORCHES screen. These tests are usually most informative when conducted early in life, prior to postnatal infection or vaccination, although the serological tests for syphilis will usually not have been affected by postnatal infection. The sequelae of many congenital infections are very variable; for instance, the outcome of congenital rubella infection is strongly influenced by the stage of pregnancy at which infection occurs (Miller *et al.*, 1982), and ranges from abortion, stillbirth or multiple anomalies to normal infants. Moreover, many individuals with congenital infections may be asymptomatic at birth, with mental retardation or neurological abnormalities, such as seizures, sensorineural hearing loss, microcephaly or motor problems appearing at a later date.

Laboratory methods include indirect fluorescence (IFA), indirect haemagglutination (IHA) and enzyme-linked immunosorbent assay (ELISA). For syphilis the Venereal Disease Research Laboratory test (VDRL) and rapid plasma reagin (RPR) flocculation test are nontreponemal antigen tests. If these are positive, then a sensitive and specific treponemal antigen test such as the treponemal antibody absorption test (FTA-ABS) should be performed. In congenital Toxoplasmosis there may be considerable intracranial pathology, but calcification of cysts will only be seen on CT scanning or plain skull X-ray. HIV testing should be considered when the child is at risk (see Chapter 40).

Children with congenital anomalies and malformations, or those with abnormal growth or head circumference not attributable to another cause, should have chromosomal karyotyping of sufficient resolution to detect microdeletions. Karyotyping should also have been performed on individuals with a recognizable chromosomal syndrome, such as trisomy 21: if the chromosomal imbalance is the result of an inherited translocation, then other family members may be at increased risk of having affected children. The fragile X syndrome is a common cause of X-linked mental retardation (Webb, 1989); the chromosomal abnormality has been detected by growing cells in specially adapted media, but it is now possible to use molecular genetic techniques to detect the mutation (Verkerk *et al.*, 1991). There is considerable variability in the physical phenotype, and checklists of physical and behavioural features have been devised to improve the detection of individuals likely to manifest the anomaly (Laing *et al.*, 1991). If karyotyping is uninformative, individuals with congenital anomalies should also be tested for metabolic disorders. Children with either unexplained skull shape or abnormal head circumference should be investigated by CT or MRI.

In individuals without a recognizable syndrome, and with no evidence of prenatal, perinatal or postnatal aetiologies, metabolic abnormalities should be searched for. If the course of the disorder is progressive, or there is clinical evidence of a particular disorder, but screening tests are negative, then further investigation should be conducted by a centre with expertise in inborn errors of metabolism and progressive neurological disorders. Many metabolic disorders present either early in infancy or with an acute illness. Outlined here are first-line tests for stable disorders that the majority of laboratories are able to perform.

Much information may be gained from a straightforward analysis of a urine specimen (Borden, 1984). The sample should be examined for unusual colour, odour or sediment; tested for protein, glucose, ketones and occult blood; and the specific gravity and pH measured. The amino acid and sugar composition of the sample should be qualitatively determined by chromatography, and these results interpreted relative to a urinary creatinine estimation. Many laboratories will also test qualitatively for phenylalanine metabolites, and cystine and homocystine. The urine should be examined for metachromatic granules and tested for the presence of mucopolysaccharides. If the Lesch–Nyhan syndrome (hypoxanthineguanine phosphoribosyltransferase deficiency) is suspected in boys, then uric acid should be measured in the urine; prior to puberty this is a more sensitive test than plasma uric acid estimation (Simmonds, 1987).

Haematological investigations include a full blood count with red cell indices, and microscopic examination of a blood film; vacuolated lymphocytes may be apparent in the GM1 gangliosidosis, and metachromatic inclusions observed in leukocytes in the mucopolysaccharidoses (Watts & Gibbs, 1986). Biochemical investigations on blood include measurement of thyroxine, thyroid-stimulating hormone, calcium and phosphate, and plasma amino acid chromatography. In those areas where lead remains an environmental hazard, serum levels should be estimated.

It is not sensible to test every child for all possible biochemical abnormalities. The physician is dependent upon the laboratory to recommend further investigations on the basis of initial results; but equally, investigations must be guided by the clinical findings. This is particularly true for the lysosomal storage diseases; specific assays for many of the enzymes are available, but these are expensive determinations and are not warranted as a first-line investigation unless the history or examination is indicative of a storage disorder.

There may be little in the way of history, or few clinical signs to indicate a possible aetiology. At some research centres such children may receive intensive investigations. This may not be a practical proposition elsewhere, and a more restricted set of investigations may be all that is possible to exclude either treatable disorders or those with genetic implications. Scott (Chapter 35) describes one such approach. Tests for syphilis, a metabolic screen of urine and blood and a full blood count are neither particularly difficult nor expensive procedures to perform. Because the fragile X anomaly is common and likely to affect relatives, and its phenotype difficult to identify prepubertally, DNA analysis for this disorder should also be conducted where it is available. As the yield from chromosome analysis in individuals without dysmorphic features is usually low, and chromosomal anomalies are only rarely associated with increased risk to relatives (Harper, 1988), routine chromosomal analysis is probably not warranted without clinical indications.

REFERENCES

Aicardi M.D. (1986) *Epilepsy in Children. The International Review of Child Neurology.* Raven Press, New York.

Armstrong P. & Keevil S.F. (1991a) Magnetic resonance imaging-1: basic principles of image production. *British Medical Journal*, **303**, 35–40.

Armstrong P. & Keevil S.F. (1991b) Magnetic resonance imaging-2: clinical uses. *British Medical Journal*, **303**, 105–109.

Asthana J.C., Sinha S., Haslam J.S. & Kingston H.M. (1990) Survey of adolescents with severe intellectual handicap. *Archives of Diseases in Childhood*, **65**, 1133–1136.

Bailey A. (1993) The biology of autism. *Psychological Medicine*, **23**, 1, 7–12.

Bailey A., Luthert P., Bolton, P., Le Couteur A., Rutter M. & Harding B. (1993) Autism is associated with megalencephaly (Letter). *The Lancet*, **341**, 1225–1226.

Bailey A., Bolton P., Butler L., Le Couteur A., Murphy M., Scott S., Webb T. & Rutter M. (1991) Prevalence of the fragile X anomaly amongst autistic twins and singletons. *Journal of Child Psychology and Psychiatry*.

Bailey A., Le Couteur A., Rutter M., Pickles A., Yuzda E., Schmidt D. & Gottesman I. (1991) Obstetric and neurodevelopmental data from the British Twin Study of Autism. Paper presented at the Second World Congress on Psychiatric Genetics, London, August 1991.

Barkovich A.J., Chuang S.H. & Norman D. (1988) MR of neuronal migration anomalies. *American Journal of Radiology*, **150**, 179–187.

Belliveau J.W., Kennedy D.N., McKinstry R.C., Buchbinder B.R., Weisskoff R.M., Cohen M.S., Vevea J.M., Brady T.J. & Rosen B.R. (1991) Functional mapping of the human visual cortex by magnetic resonance imaging. *Science*, **254**, 716–719.

Bench C.J., Dolan R.J., Friston K.J. & Frackowiak R.S.J. (1990) Positron emission tomography in the study of brain metabolism in psychiatric and neuropsychiatric disorders. *British Journal of Psy-*

chiatry, **157** (suppl. 9), 82–95.

Bender L. (1942) Post-encephalitic behavior disorders in childhood. In: Neal J.B. (ed) *Encephalitis: A Clinical Study*. Grune & Stratton, New York.

Blomquist H.K., Bohman M., Edvinsson S., Gillberg C., Gustavson K., Holmgren G. & Wahlström J. (1985) Frequency of the fragile X syndrome in infantile autism. *Clinical Genetics*, **27**, 113–117.

Borden M. (1984) Screening for metabolic disease. In: Nyhan W.L. (ed) *Abnormalities in Amino Acid Metabolism in Clinical Medicine*, pp. 408–418. Appleton-Century-Crofts, Norwalk, CT.

Butler M.G. (1990) Prader–Willi syndrome: current understanding of cause and diagnosis. *American Journal of Medical Genetics*, **35**, 319–332.

Calne D.B. & Lang A.E. (1988) Secondary dystonia. In: Fahn S., Marsden D. & Calne D.B. (eds) *Advances in Neurology*, **50**, 33. Raven Press, New York.

Carey J.C. (1987) Microcephaly. In: Rudolph A.M., Hoffman J.I.E. & Axelrod S. (eds) *Pediatrics*. Appleton & Lange, Norwalk, Ct.

Clayton R.R. (1986) Multiple drug use. *Recent Developments in Alcoholism*, **4**, 7–38.

Costa D.C. & Ell P.J. (1991) *Brain Blood Flow in Neurology and Psychiatry*. Churchill Livingstone, Edinburgh.

DHSS (1984) *Guidelines of Good Clinical Practice in the Treatment of Drug Misuse. Report of the Medical Working Group on Drug Dependence*. DHSS, London.

De Gruchy G.C. (1975) *Drug Induced Blood Disorders*. Blackwell Scientific Publications, Oxford.

De Vries L.S., Dubowitz L.M.S., Pennock J.M. & Bydder G.M. (1989) Extensive cystic leucomalacia: correlation of cranial ultrasound, magnetic resonance imaging and clinical findings in sequential studies. *Clinical Radiology*, **40**, 158–166.

Elder G.H. (1987) The porphyrias. In: Holton J.B. (ed) *The Inherited Metabolic Diseases*, pp. 256–284. Churchill Livingstone, Edinburgh.

Ellis D. (1986) The epidemiology of visual impairment in people with a mental handicap. In: Ellis D. (ed) *Sensory Impairments in Mentally Handicapped People*. College-Hill, San Diego.

Fahn S. (1988) Concept and classification of dystonia. In: Fahn S., Marsden D. & Calne D.B. (eds) *Advances in Neurology*, vol. 50: *Dystonia*, pp. 1–8. Raven Press, New York.

Falloon J., Eddy J., Wiener L. & Pizzo P.A. (1989) Human immunodeficiency virus infection in children. *Journal of Pediatrics*, **114**, 1–30.

Firestone P. & Peters S. (1983) Minor physical anomalies and behavior in children: a review. *Journal of Autism and Developmental Disorders*, **13**, 411–473.

Fisher D. (1987) The thyroid. In: Rudolph A.M., Hoffman J.I.E. & Axelrod S. (eds) *Pediatrics*. Appleton & Lange, Norwalk, CT.

Folstein S. & Rutter M. (1977) Genetic influences and infantile autism. *Nature*, **265**, 726–728.

Fryns J-P. (1989) X-linked mental retardation and the fragile X syndrome: a clinical approach. In: Davies K.E. (ed) *The Fragile X Syndrome*, pp. 1–40. Oxford University Press, Oxford.

Gabel S. & Hsu L.K.G. (1986) Routine laboratory tests in adolescent psychiatric inpatients: their value in making psychiatric diagnoses and in detecting medical disorders. *Journal of the American Academy of Child Psychiatry*, **25**, 113–119.

Gillberg C. (1990) Medical work-up in children with autism and Asperger syndrome. *Brain Dysfunction*, **3**, 249–260.

Gillberg C. (1992) Autism and autisticlike conditions. *Journal of Child Psychology and Psychiatry*, **33**, 813–842.

Gutman L.T., St Claire K.K., Weedy C., Herman-Giddens M.E., Lane B.A., Niemeyer J.G. & McKinney R.E. (1991) Human immunodeficiency virus transmission by child sexual abuse. *American Journal of Diseases of Childhood*, **145**, 137–141.

Hagberg B., Aicardi J., Dias K. & Ramos O. (1983) A progressive syndrome of autism, dementia, ataxia, and loss of purposeful hand use in girls: Rett's syndrome: report of 35 cases. *Annals of Neurology*, **14**, 471–479.

Harper P.S. (1988) *Practical Genetic Counselling*. Butterworth-Heinemann, Oxford.

Harris R.J., Armstrong D., Ali R. & Loynes A. (1983) Nutritional survey of Bangladeshi children aged under 5 years in the London borough of Tower Hamlets. *Archives of Diseases in Childhood*, **58**, 428–432.

Huntington's Disease Collaborative Research Group. (1993) A novel gene containing a trinucleotide repeat that is expanded and unstable on Huntington's disease chromosomes. *Cell*, **72**, 971–983.

Kelch R.P. (1987) Disorders of pubertal maturation. In: Rudolph A.M., Hoffman J.I.E. & Axelrod S. (eds) *Pediatrics*. Appleton & Lange, Norwalk, CT.

Kropka B.I. & Williams C. (1986) The epidemiology of hearing impairment in people with a mental handicap. In: Ellis D. (ed) *Sensory Impairments in Mentally Handicapped People*. College-Hill Press, San Diego.

Laing S., Partinton M. & Robinson Turner G. (1991) Clinical screening score for the fragile X (Martin-Bell) syndrome. *American Journal of Medical Genetics*, **38**, 2–3, 256–259.

Largo R.H., Pfister D., Molinari L., Kundu S., Lipp A. & Duc G. (1989) Significance of prenatal, perinatal and postnatal factors in the development of AGA preterm infants at five to seven years. *Developmental Medicine and Child Neurology*, **31**, 440–456.

Levy H.L. & Waisbren S.E. (1983) Effects of untreated maternal phenylketonuria and hyperphenylalaninemia on the fetus. *New England Journal of Medicine*, **309**, 1269–1274.

Lorber J. & Priestley B.L. (1981) Children with large heads: a practical approach to diagnosis in 557 children, with special reference to 109 children with megalencephaly. *Developmental Medicine and Child Neurology*, **23**, 494–504.

Mandoki M.W., Sumner G.S., Hoffman R.P. & Riconda D.L. (1991) A review of Klinefelter's syndrome in children and adolescents. *Journal of the American Academy of Child and Adolescent Psychiatry*, **30**, 167–172.

Marden P.M., Smith D.W. & McDonald M.J. (1964) Congenital anomalies in the newborn infant, including minor variations. *Journal of Pediatrics*, **64**, 357–371.

Marsden C.D. (1986) Hysteria: a neurologist's view. *Psychological Medicine*, **16**, 277–288.

Marshall W.A. & Tanner J.M. (1969) Variations in the pattern of pubertal changes in girls. *Archives of Diseases in Childhood*, **44**, 291–303.

Marshall W.A. & Tanner J.M. (1970) Variations in the pattern of pubertal changes in boys. *Archives of Diseases in Childhood*, **45**, 13–23.

Melsin A.G. & Rothfield N. (1968) Systemic lupus erythematosus in childhood: analysis of 42 cases with comparative data in 200 adults followed concurrently. *Paediatrics*, **42**, 37–49.

Miller E., Cradock-Watson J.E. & Pollock T.M. (1982) Consequences of confirmed maternal rubella at successive stages of pregnancy. *Lancet*, **2**, 781–784.

Miller D.H., Robb S.A., Ormerod I.E., Pohl K.R., MacManus D.G., Kendall B.E., Moseley I.F. & McDonald W.I. (1990) Magnetic resonance imaging of inflammatory and demyelinating white-matter diseases of childhood. *Developmental Medicine and Child Neurology*, **32**, 97–107.

Mosser J., Dovar A., Sarde C., Kioschis P., Feil R., Moser H., Poustka A., Mandel J. & Aubourg P. (1993) Putative X-linked adrenoleukodystrophy gene shares unexpected homology with ABC transporters. *Nature*, **361**, 726–730.

Mouridsen S.E., Andersen L.B., Sorensen S.A., Rich B. & Isager T. (1992). Neurofibromatosis in infantile autism and other types of childhood psychoses. *Acta Paedopsychiatrica*, **55**, 15−18.

Navia B.A., Jordan B.D. & Price R.W. (1986) The AIDS dementia complex: I. Clinical features. *Annals of Neurology*, **19**, 517−524.

Nelson K.B., & Ellenberg J.H. (1986) Antecedents of cerebral palsy. I: multivariate analysis of risks. *New England Journal of Medicine*, **315**, 81−86.

Nyhan W.I. (1984) *Abnormalities in Amino Acid Metabolism in Clinical Medicine*. Appleton-Century-Crofts, Norwalk, CT.

Oski F.A. (1979) The nonhematologic manifestations of iron deficiency. *American Journal of Diseases in Childhood*, **133**, 315−322.

Paine R.S. & Oppe T.E. (1966) Neurological examination of children. *Clinics in Developmental Medicine*, vol. 20/21.

Piven J., Gayle J., Landa R., Wzorek M. & Folstein S. (1991) The prevalence of fragile X in a sample of autistic individuals diagnosed using a standardized interview. *Journal of the American Academy of Child and Adolescent Psychiatry*, **30**, 825−830.

Pomeroy J.C., Sprafkin J. & Gadow K.D. (1988) Minor physical anomalies as a biologic marker for behavior disorders. *Journal of the American Academy of Child and Adolescent Psychiatry*, **27**, 466−473.

Pryor H.B. & Thelander H.E. (1967) Growth deviations in handicapped children. *Clinical Pediatrics*, **6**, 501.

Rantakallio P. & Von Wendt L. (1985) Risk factors for mental retardation. *Archives of Diseases in Childhood*, **60**, 946−952.

Rivinus T.M., Jamison D.L., Graham P.J. (1975) Childhood organic neurological disease presenting as psychiatric disorder. *Archives of Diseases in Childhood*, **50**, 115−119.

Russell G.F.M. (1979) Bulimia nervosa: an ominous variant of anorexia nervosa. *Psychological Medicine*, **9**, 429−448.

Russell G.F.M. (1983) Delayed puberty due to anorexia of early onset. In: Darby P.L., Garfinkel P.E., Garner D.M. & Coscina D.V. (eds) *Anorexia Nervosa: Recent Developments in Research*, pp. 331−342. Alan R. Liss, New York.

Schonberg S.K., Litt I.F. & Cohen M.I. (1987) Drug abuse. In: Rudolph A.M., Hoffman J.I.E. & Axelrod S. (eds) *Pediatrics*. Appleton & Lange, Norwalk, CT.

Sheridan M.D. (1975) *From Birth to Five Years*, 3rd edn. NFER-Nelson, Windsor.

Simmonds H.A. (1987) Purine and pyrimidine disorders. In: Holton J.B. (ed) *The Inherited Metabolic Diseases*, pp. 215−255. Churchill Livingstone, Edinburgh.

Smith D.W. & Jones K.L. (1988) *Smith's Recognisable Patterns of Human Malformation*. Saunders, Philadelphia.

Steffenburg S. (1991) Neuropsychiatric assessment of children with autism: a population-based study. *Developmental Medicine and Child Neurology*, **33**, 495−511.

Steffenburg S., Gillberg C., Hellgren L., Andersson L., Gillberg I.C., Jacobsson G. & Bohman M. (1989) A twin study of autism in Denmark, Finland, Iceland, Norway and Sweden. *Journal of Child Psychology and Psychiatry*, **30**, 405−416.

Stengel-Rutkowski S., Schimanek P. & Wernheimer A. (1984) Anthropometric definitions of dysmorphic facial signs. *Human Genetics*, **67**, 272−295.

Stewart D.C. (1982) The use of the clinical laboratory in the diagnosis and treatment of substance abuse. *Paediatric Annals*, **11**, 669−682.

Tanner J.M. & Whitehouse R.H. (1976) Clinical longitudinal standards for height, weight, height velocity, weight velocity, and the stages of puberty. *Archives of Diseases in Childhood*, **51**, 170−179.

Taylor E.A. (1986) Causes and development of hyperactive behaviour. In: Taylor E. (ed) *The Overactive Child. Clinics in Developmental Medicine*, vol. 97. Mackeith Press, London.

Tupper D.E. (ed) (1987) *Soft Neurological Signs*. Grune & Stratton, New York.

Verkerk A., Pieretti M., Sutcliffe J., Fu Y., Kuhl D., Pizzuti A., Reiner O., Richards S., Victoria M., Zhang F., Eussen B., Van Ommen G., Blonden L., Riggins G., Chastain J., Kunst C., Galjaard H., Caskey C., Nelson D., Oostra B. & Warren S. (1991) Identification of a gene (FMR-1) containing a CGG repeat coincident with a breakpoint cluster region exhibiting length variation in fragile X syndrome. *Cell*, **65**, 905−914.

Vinken P.J. & Bruyn G.W. (1972) The phakomatoses. *Handbook of Clinical Neurology*, vol. 14. North-Holland, Amsterdam.

Waldrop M. & Halverson C. (1971) In: Hellmuth J. (ed) *Exceptional Infant: Studies in Abnormalities*, pp. 343−381. Brunner/Mazel, New York.

Walshe J.M. & Yealland M. (1992) Wilson's disease: the problem of delayed diagnosis. *Journal of Neurology, Neurosurgery, and Psychiatry*, **55**, 692−696.

Watts R.W.E. & Gibbs D.A. (1986) *Lysosomal Storage Diseases: Biochemical and Clinical Aspects*, pp. 43−118. Taylor & Francis, London.

Webb T. (1989) The epidemiology of the fragile X syndrome. In: Davies K.E. (ed) *The Fragile X Syndrome*, pp. 40−55. Oxford University Press, Oxford.

Woolston J.L. (1983) Eating disorders in infancy and early childhood. *Journal of the American Academy of Child Psychiatry*, **22**, 114−121.

Chapter 7
Psychological Tests and Assessment

Michael Berger

INTRODUCTION

Why test?

In dealing with the complexity of psychological and psychiatric disorders, clinicians rely on experience and judgement to gather and organize the information necessary for diagnosis and treatment. The core clinical processes — gathering and organizing information, developing an understanding of the problems and decision-making — can be substantially enhanced through the use of psychological tests.

Tests are procedures for measuring individual differences in psychological characteristics. Their use has a special place in clinical practice with children and young people. It is in this early phase of life when abilities and characteristics are emerging rapidly that unusual or uneven development may first be manifest, with potentially major implications for child and family. Mental and behavioural development inconsistent with age, sociocultural expectations and demands can be significant factors in the aetiology of childhood disorders, and can have important implications for management and treatment. Although clinical judgement can be adequate for assessing the many facets of development, it is well-recognized that judgements may not cover a sufficiently comprehensive or differentiated range of behaviour and skills, leading to inaccurate or incomplete conclusions. Clinical judgements are also most vulnerable to error in borderline circumstances. Psychological tests can quickly, objectively and systematically provide much of the necessary information, thereby complementing clinical opinion.

Psychological tests possess a number of features that enable them to fulfil these important clinical functions. To begin with, they use specially selected tasks that focus on the characteristics of interest. Substantial effort goes into selecting and refining items to ensure they measure coherent characteristics relevant to the intended use of the test, whether these are cognitive competence, comprehension, depressive symptomatology or motor development. Secondly, standardized administration and scoring reduce the influence of subjectivity. When clinicians make judgements about psychological characteristics, the grounds on which the judgements are made can vary between clinicians and the same clinician may vary over time. This lack of consistency creates problems, such as making communication difficult, that can be surmounted by explicit and replicable test procedures. Thirdly, tests quantify skills or other characteristics, enabling individual differences to be highlighted. Fourthly, several items are used to sample a characteristic and special rules are used to determine the length of testing (for example, only end testing following three successive failures), reducing the influence of chance factors. Finally, by relating scores to data from comparison groups, it is possible to know the extent of deviation from expectation. The standard of reference to which an individual can be compared is the whole population on which normative values have been obtained, so the database is vastly larger than any one clinician's individual experience.

These advantages can be illustrated by considering the investigation of a child referred because of language delay. Parental reports of language skills are important for giving a general picture of the child's development and linguistic competence. However, their views can be distorted by several factors: they are familiar with the child and the home environment and can guess what the child wants because of contextual cues. Also, they provide inadvertent cues in communicating, through gesture or eye-pointing. Parents may also modify their own communication with the child, unaware that they are successively adapting it to the level of the child. Such factors can lead to an overestimate of the child's skills. Finally, parents are not trained to make the sorts of precise observations that characterize clinical investigation, so that they may not be able to provide answers to detailed clinical questions. Consequently, information from parental interview has important but circumscribed value. Experienced clinicians can get more appropriate information from the child during the interview, but even then variations in investigation procedure, if not intraclinician, are still likely between clinicians, making for inconsistencies in diagnosis.

Psychological tests begin by putting all children to be tested into a less familiar and more homogeneous setting, devoid of clues other than those needed for the test. All are asked the same questions in the same way and several attempts are made to ensure that failure is not due to chance. Comprehensive samples of behaviour are taken and at the end of the session, a measure of the skills is provided, enabling a quantitative assessment of any departures from expectation. This is particularly helpful in borderline cases where clinicians may feel most uncertainty.

There are further advantages to testing. Test data can make

other clinical information more comprehensible. The child who presents with moderate language delay and immature behaviour may through testing be revealed to be someone with more global deficits. The language difficulty thereby emerges as a nonspecific disorder, again with differential implications for diagnosis and management. The converse may also hold: a child with suspected global delay may through testing be shown to have significant age-appropriate skills.

Psychological test scores can have important prognostic implications, especially with regard to intellectual functioning (Berger & Yule, 1985; Culbertson & Gyurke, 1990). There is a substantial empirical literature linking test scores to a wide variety of behaviours and outcomes. With access to test scores, clinicians are able to base judgements on evidence from empirical studies, thereby providing stronger grounds for decisions.

The usefulness of psychological tests goes well beyond intellectual assessment. Apart from procedures to quantify and explore educational accomplishments, tests can tap areas of functioning not as easily, comprehensively or economically accessible by other means. Self-concept, depressive symptomatology and other sensitive areas may sometimes be more easily elucidated through self-report questionnaires than by direct questioning. Test scores can also be related to normative data, enabling an assessment of the severity or extent of problems.

Through the opportunities they provide for observation and the scores they yield, tests stimulate alternative hypotheses and explanations, adding to the creative dimension of practice. Further, some tests are designed to differentiate among abilities and processes (auditory contrasted with visual memory), and this is also of importance in clinical practice, for instance in characterizing neuropsychological dysfunctions and in making more refined discriminations. Test scores can further provide the baseline for the assessment of deterioration or for monitoring progress in treatment. Finally, it is worth noting the importance of test data in clinical research either for matching purposes or for providing the main indices in projects. There are thus many good reasons for using tests (Berger & Yule, 1985), particularly in clinical practice with children and young people.

Testing as a technical skill

Most psychological tests are fairly simple to use, with manuals providing clear instructions so that administration and scoring are essentially technical skills readily acquired. These skills on their own are not sufficient for clinical practice. The proper interpretation of test scores requires an understanding of the theories, principles and techniques of measurement, a knowledge of the related research literature and the empirically justifiable interpretations of scores from particular tests. This needs to be complemented by a knowledge of the issues and techniques that are central to individual test score interpretation. This information must be integrated with knowledge of development and developmental psychopathology to produce

interpretations that are relevant to the reasons for testing. This skill base characterizes the tester and distinguishes him or her from a technician simply trained to give a test and report the results.

THE NATURE OF PSYCHOLOGICAL TESTS

Standardization

The idea of standardization is critical in psychological measurement. By specifying, and therefore controlling content and procedures for administration and scoring, errors are greatly reduced, leading to coherent measurement, interpretation and communication.

A *psychological test* can be more formally defined as 'any systematic procedure for observing a person's behaviour and describing it with the aid of a numerical scale or category system' (Cronbach, 1970). A procedure that is rule-based (systematic) can be classed as a *standardized test*. A standard interview which yields a categorical conclusion (e.g. depressed/mildly depressed/not depressed) would be covered by the definition.

This definition encourages clinicians to regard their activities as akin to, if not the equivalent of, testing and therefore subject to the same quality standards for psychological tests published by the American Educational Research Association & American Psychological Association National Council on Measurement in Education (1985), for instance.

Test content

Tests are devised to provoke specific forms of behaviour — physical actions or reports of thoughts and feelings. Some tests are nonprovocative and rely instead on naturally occurring events. Behaviours are selected that can be quantified. The interest is not the overt behaviours as such but what they reveal about some underlying characteristic or process.

Single tasks (complete a three-piece inset puzzle or answer yes or no to a questionnaire item) are termed items. Groups of items constitute a *test*. The English version of the Peabody Picture Vocabulary Test (Dunn & Dunn, 1981) is a test with homogeneous content comprising sets of four pictures, one of which corresponds to a word given by the tester, the task being to identify the correct picture. If there are different types of grouped items making up the test, each group is called a *subtest*, with several subtests combined constituting a *battery*. Batteries are occasionally comprised of sets of subtests to form *subscales*. The Wechsler Intelligence Scales (Wechsler, 1974, 1990, 1992) consist of subtests organized into two subscales, verbal and performance.

Measurement and scaling

Summation of the item performance produces the raw score, for instance, total words correctly defined from the list of 20. To become meaningful, raw scores must be compared with a standard, the performance of a specially selected group on the same tasks. Or it could be the performance of an individual on the tasks on a previous occasion, for instance tic frequency before medication. Psychological measurement, like other measurement, is comparative. The criterion against which test performance is compared is called the *test norms* and the procedure a *norm-referenced test*.

Norms are derived from testing samples from a population, the nature of the sample depending on the intended range of use of the test. One criterion of test quality is the adequacy of normative sampling.

Test scores should correspond in magnitude with the characteristic being measured: the higher the score, or the better the performance, the more the characteristic. The process used to assign numbers to levels of performance is called *scaling*. The purposes of scaling are to ensure that different scores on tests are closely linked with performance differences and that the magnitude of the test score accurately reflects the magnitude of the characteristic. A good introduction to the scaling of psychological tests is provided by Reckase (1990).

Types of score

For some purposes it is important to know how an individual's functioning compares with that of similar individuals. Does a child have the same competence in understanding complex sentences as others of her age (because of suspected language difficulties)?

To answer such questions the test is given to selected criterion groups, for instance a representative sample of the population of children at each of several age levels. Average scores and standard deviations are computed for each age group. The score obtained by any individual on the test can then be compared with the average of the group and characterized as average, above or below average — the same as or above or below that of the comparison group, respectively. The comparison can be refined by introducing units which then place the score so many units above or below the average. The common practice is to compute the distance from the average in intervals or steps of standard deviation units. Such scores are known as *deviation scores*.

The average score and variability (standard deviation) can vary at different ages. To avoid the difficulties of interpretation this might produce, the means and standard deviations are set at arbitrary but useful values. Most commonly the average is set at 100 and the standard deviation at 15. Hence, an IQ of 115 indicates that the individual obtained a score 1 s.d. above the mean. Another common measure is the T-score, set with a mean of 50 and a standard deviation of 10. Scores transformed in this way are called *standard scores*.

Scores can be expressed in terms of age equivalence. Mental age, reading age, language age and the like, depending on the test given, are examples of this. Age scores indicate the achievement of a level of performance equivalent to that of individuals with the same chronological age as the testees's test age. A reading age of 10 years indicates the same score on the test

obtained by 10-year-olds. Test ages are useful for communication, for instance with parents or teachers.

The *percentile* is another transformation. These range from 0 to 100 and indicate the percentage of comparable individuals obtaining a similar score or less than the testee.

Numbers derived from psychological tests increase in intervals of 1 (110, 111, 112 etc.), and the average IQ for a group may be 93.5. Such characteristics give these scores an aura of precision they do not merit. No well-informed test user would argue that there was a real difference in intelligence between two individuals with IQs of 85 and 86, or even 95 and 100 (but see Jensen, 1969 for a discussion of why a difference between populations with mean IQs of 95 and 100 is significant). Nor for strong technical reasons can it be argued that someone with an IQ of 100 is twice as intelligent as someone with an IQ of 50.

Setting the average score on a test at 100 leads to a confusion with percentages. The critical point is that scores vary above and below 100 (or 50 in the case of T-scores) and it is the score deviation from this midpoint that provides the main basis for measurement and interpretation.

Types of test

Two types of standardized test, norm-referenced and criterion-referenced, are distinguished on the basis of the criterion used for comparison. As already indicated, norm-referenced procedures use data from some normative group for comparison. Criterion-referenced tests are those in which the items represent 'achievements' (Kiernan, 1985) or skills to be attained. The criterion-referenced test samples the individual's skills and is a systematic way of discovering whether certain skills are present. Such tests are particularly useful in mainstream and special educational settings where teachers might for instance be interested in testing which of their pupils have mastered subtraction. They can also have utility in clinical practice in assessing children with handicaps and in treatment programmes. Despite serious limitations in some published and criterion-referenced tests (Katz & Slomka, 1990), they continue to find use in assessing competencies and in computer-based education programmes.

Norm and criterion-referenced tests are not always easy to distinguish and some criterion-referenced tests can also be normative (Katz & Slomka, 1990).

Selecting tests: reliabilities and validities

The decision to use a particular test depends on the likelihood that it will provide information relevant to the purpose of testing. Various criteria, such as the representativeness of the sample, reliability and validity, are important considerations.

Reliability refers to accuracy, the extent to which the test is free from error. Tests are never completely error-free, but vary in their proneness to various types of error. During test development and subsequently, studies are undertaken of the extent to which scores are stable over time or subject to scorer and administration or other errors. On the basis of such reliability studies, conclusions are drawn about the acceptability of the test for clinical purposes. One way of using information from reliability studies is to derive the standard error of measurement. This index is used to qualify the accuracy of the test scores in terms of their margins of error (Dudek, 1979).

Studies of tests in different contexts and circumstances have discovered that reliability can vary for a number of reasons. Hence, no test is now regarded as reliable or unreliable in any absolute sense. Rather, it is recognized that it may only be reliable in some circumstances (for instance, when given by trained practitioners).

The ultimate question in testing is what scores mean or what interpretations are permissible. Their meaning or interpretation depends on evidence that they measure what they are supposed to measure and how well they do so; that is, their *validities* (Anastasi, 1982, 1986; Golden *et al.*, 1990).

A fundamental problem in testing is that performance (and hence the score) is an amalgam of many influences, only some of which may be the characteristic of interest. Scores on tests of language development or motor coordination may be influenced by poor attention. Test validation is concerned with accumulating evidence that a test of a particular attribute measures that attribute and little else. Without this purity, it is difficult to know what a test or subtest score potentially means. (Potential meaning is emphasized because, despite the strength of evidence for what a test measures, it is always possible, particularly in clinical settings, for an individual's score to represent the operation of impurities — for instance, distractability can interfere with performance on a timed task, the final score reflecting the ability distorted by the effects of distractions.)

Indices of test validity vary. Consequently, there is a concern about the applicability of validation studies. If a low score on a test means poor spatial ability in one study, will a low score mean the same thing if someone from a different cultural group is tested? *Validity generalization* is a concept that refers to the grounds for 'applying validity evidence obtained in one or more situations to other similar situations' (American Psychological Association, 1985, pp. 94−95).

Differential prediction — the issue of test bias

An important aspect of validity generalization concerns the interpretation of tests in different cultural groups. Originally, this question manifested under the heading of culture fairness, test bias or test fairness, the concern being the extent to which psychological tests discriminated against minority group members (Puente, 1989). Jones and Applebaum (1989) suggest the term *differential prediction* to cover these concerns, because it implies determining whether or not the same criteria are applicable across different demographic groups or groups with different prior experiences, in making test-based decisions and predictions. Bias can arise from several sources, including inappropriate content and normative samples, examiner and

language bias and inequitable social consequences (Reynolds & Brown, 1984). The core issue is whether or not it is justifiable to interpret test scores irrespective of cultural, racial, ethnic and even social class characteristics.

Clinicians must assess the quality and applicability of data before tests are interpreted. With an ongoing awareness of the possible influence of cultural factors, including those stemming from race and ethnicity, individual assessment should be able to take into account potential test biases.

THE INTERPRETATION OF PSYCHOLOGICAL TEST SCORES

The central role of theory in test interpretation

All tests are theory-dependent: selection of items, structuring the test and scoring reflect how the author, consciously or inadvertently, thinks about what is measured and how. Otherwise, selection of items and their organization would be random.

There are many examples of this in other realms, but intelligence testing provides a striking illustration of the theory dependence of tests. In the early attempts to measure intelligence reaction speed tasks were used because it was believed that intelligence was a matter of speed of sensory processes. Subsequently, intelligence came to be regarded as concerned with higher-level conceptual processes and the nature of the test content changed to involve reasoning and problem solving (Berger, 1982).

Decisions and descriptive interpretations

Test data can be used in two main ways, for empirically based decisions and for descriptive interpretations (Cronbach, 1971). Decisions involve interpretations which enable a choice between alternative courses of action. Streaming children into ability bands and then placing them in different classes or deciding on alternative treatment regimes on the basis of test scores illustrates the use of tests for decisions. The challenge is to show empirically that better outcomes can be achieved by using test scores to allocate individuals to different academic streams. This is a complex task because of the need to operationalize 'better outcomes', a concept that is itself multifaceted (including educational, emotional and social outcomes, immediate and long-term), and each of these will in turn require valid indices. (The concepts of screening efficiency and sensitivity, among others — see Ireton (1990) — are aspects of test decision technology that are well-developed in personnel selection and occupational psychology.)

Statistical interpretations (such as 'average' or 'below average') use normative data as a basis for decisions, and are circumscribed in meaning. No reference need be made to the psychological attributes that the test is supposed to measure. Their utility depends on evidence that individuals with scores at particular levels show specific outcomes in other areas of their lives. For instance, individuals with very low scores on

IQ tests tend to function poorly in other aspects of their lives, both concurrently and later, as well as performing poorly on similar tests administered later (Berger & Yule, 1985; Culbertson & Gyurke, 1990).

Descriptive or psychological interpretations take the form 'He is mentally handicapped' or 'She is an introvert' or 'She has poor spatial ability'. These are statements about people or their characteristics that assume a direct link between the score and the concept, that an IQ is an index of intelligence or a reading age measures reading competence. As Cronbach (1971) puts it, 'A description is more than an adjectival phrase; it pulls behind it a whole train of implications. To say a child is mentally retarded is to call up a great number of expectations about what he will do in response to certain demands' (p. 448). Such interpretations are common in clinical practice and especially in neuropsychological assessment where tests are used to identify specific cognitive deficits.

Descriptive interpretations can be very difficult to justify. Firstly, current tests of intelligence are not securely grounded in accepted theory. The psychometric theories, on which most tests are based, have only limited correspondence with more recent thinking about human intelligence based on information theory or the ideas and work of Sternberg (Kail & Pellegrino, 1985). Given this theoretical heterogeneity, it is difficult to claim that IQ scores are measures of intelligence. Proper measures of intelligence will emerge over time only in the context of theory testing and refinement, itself a process which will involve ever-increasing refinement of measuring procedures.

The second difficulty with descriptive interpretations is the lack of specificity in many tests, i.e. the extent to which they fall short of the ideal of being pure measures of psychological characteristics, uncontaminated by error and the influence of other abilities. For instance, the Object Assembly subtest of the Wechsler Intelligence Scale for Children — Revised (WISC-R) requires the assembly of pieces to create a two-dimensional representation of an everyday object, much like a cut-out puzzle. While it could be argued that this task reflects the operation of spatial abilities, based on the surface features of the task, Kaufman (1979) shows it to be one of the subtests with inadequate specificity (p. 114). Scores on this subtest should therefore not be interpreted in any way that suggests it measures particular abilities. Studies of the subtests of the WISC-R, carried out by Kaufman (1979) led him to conclude that although it was possible to interpret some of the subtests in terms of their unique characteristics, 'it is more justifiable to stress the likelihood that a child's performance on most WISC-R subtests is due to abilities shared with other subtests than to focus on uniqueness' (p. 114). Overenthusiastic interpretation of specific abilities or deficits on the basis of individual subtest scores is therefore unscientific.

It needs to be noted that even if a test has high specificity, the score of an individual can nevertheless be a consequence of other factors: a high score due to training or a low score due to impulsiveness.

The cultural context

One of the hazards of test interpretation is the extent to which there has been deliberate or inadvertent tutoring. When first designed, tests utilized tasks that were unfamiliar. Now, many educational or other toys widely available are identical to test items. Further, the use of tests for selective education has meant that some children will have been specifically tutored to perform such tasks. Also, in children's educational television programmes such as *Sesame Street*, tasks found in tests can be seen being posed and tutored to correct responding. Consequently, test results may be influenced by deliberate or inadvertent tutoring and this has to be borne in mind as a possible factor in test interpretation.

Diagnostic testing

The potential value of tests as diagnostic instruments has long been recognized (Garfield, 1974). Possible applications include the identification of broad syndromes of psychiatric and personality disorder and brain damage; or the identification of assets or deficits in cognitive abilities, reading, memory, or other specific processes, especially in neuropsychological testing.

Diagnostic testing is based on a variety of techniques:

1 An extreme score (on tests of ability, motor coordination, reading or on a subtest of a battery) can be indicative of either a deficit or an outstanding ability.
2 A difference between scores on two tests or subtests may do likewise.
3 The pattern or profile of test scores may match that of an already 'diagnosed' or criterion group.
4 A change in score (increase or decrease) or the absence of change on repeated testing could have diagnostic implications, for instance in detecting deterioration.
5 Wide variability in a set of scores may also indicate dysfunction.

While these patterns appear dissimilar, they have common features, the most important being that diagnosis is based on some form of difference between scores.

The interpretation of even a single score depends on a difference, that between the most likely score (the average for the testee's age) and the obtained score. All score patterns or differences pose particular difficulties in interpretation and require special procedures to ensure that they do not simply reflect the operation of chance (Payne & Jones, 1957; Rosen, 1966; Silverstein, 1981; 1989; Sattler, 1982; Payne, 1989). Further, even when differences are found to be reliable (non-chance), they can exist in the normal population with substantial frequency, as has been found in studies of the WISC-R Verbal and Performance Scale differences (Kaufman, 1979, p. 50), for instance. Because they can be common, differences may not on their own have diagnostic import. A further issue is the identification of the criteria against which the meaning of difference scores are to be checked or validated. For instance, clinical judgements or diagnoses as criteria are themselves often unreliable, particularly in the borderline range where the utility of diagnostic tests is likely to be greatest.

Finally, tests should select individuals more efficiently than would happen by chance, determined by the base rates or normal frequency of occurrence in the population, and do so in ways that minimize wrong decisions (Ireton, 1990).

Practical implications

The issues in diagnostic testing have been emphasized, not to belittle its value, but to stress the need for skilled and cautious interpretation. The decision to undertake formal testing normally arises following and in the context of a comprehensive systematic clinical history. Testing should not be a routine procedure, but should stem directly from uncertainties and unanswered questions in the history. Diagnostic testing is a way of checking such hypotheses and in the process may lead to new hypotheses. Further, a cardinal principle in the use of test information is that it should never on its own be taken as some absolute truth. As noted earlier, test information is part of the totality of clinical information. It needs to make sense in that context. Provided the statistical criteria for diagnosis are respected, within a context of hypothesis investigation, diagnostic testing can make an important contribution to clinical practice.

PSYCHOLOGICAL TESTING IN CLINICAL PRACTICE

A clear statement of the problem

Requests for psychological assessment must give reasons for testing. Referrals such as 'What is the child's level of intelligence?' or 'Has she adjusted to her new school?' are illustrations of referral questions that can lead to unhelpful answers. Adjustment is a very general concept. It can imply coping with the academic demands of school, or with relationships with peers and teachers, or adaptation to being away from a parent or all of these. Test procedures could be used to respond to any of these questions, for example by setting up direct observation in the classroom or systematically interviewing the individuals involved or using teacher rating scales. The information from these procedures could turn out to be irrelevant if the originating questions were unclear. The task for the psychologist is to ensure he or she has understood the referral in a way that does not distort the intentions of the referrer.

Availability of tests

Once the nature of the problem is clear, a decision can be taken as to the most appropriate assessment method. Frequently, the solution lies in familiar procedures. On occasion it may necessitate consulting compendia such as the *Mental Measurements Yearbooks* (Buros, 1985) or have recourse to the research literature to identify a methodology and normative

data. (The single case study described later illustrates the approach.)

Suitability of tests

Although many tests are available, the decision to select a particular test rests on an appraisal of the test as an instrument likely to yield information relevant to the purpose of testing. Criteria to use in evaluating tests have been drawn up by various organizations, and include the *Standards for Educational and Psychological Testing* published by the American Educational Research Association, the American Psychological Association, the National Council on Measurement in Education (1985) and other bodies. There are also regular reviews of common tests and many aspects of testing that can be drawn upon in evaluating a test.

The selection of a particular approach sometimes presents special problems. There are many tests of ability and educational attainment and a range of procedures for other areas such as language. An index of general ability can be obtained from the Binet Test (Thorndike *et al.*, 1989), the McCarthy, Wechsler and Bayley Scales (see Culbertson & Gyurke, 1990 or Perlman & Kaufman, 1990 for recent descriptive evaluations), as well as the British Ability Scales (Elliott *et al.*, 1983) and the Vineland Adaptive Behaviour Scales (Cicchetti & Sparrow, 1990). Sometimes the choice is determined by special circumstances, such as a child whose behaviour is so limited or noncompliant that a conventional procedure has to be forgone and replaced by parent or teacher interviews. Where such special circumstances do not apply, there are psychometric grounds for selecting a procedure. These are derived from studies of the test reliabilities and validities and from assessments of the appropriateness or otherwise of the normative data. Many tests that could be used are normed in the US and use, for instance, with UK or other populations could result in inappropriate interpretations.

Other considerations also need to be taken into account. Direct measures of behaviours such as activity or impulsiveness pose special problems due to the tendency for there to be low intercorrelations between measures of the same phenomenon. Changes in one index of activity will not necessarily be reflected by changes monitored using a different procedure or with indices based on direct observation or interview (Whalen, 1989).

Selection of tests

The decision to test and the selection of a procedure depend on the nature of the clinical problem, the clarity with which it is identified and communicated, and the availability of suitable procedures. Ultimately, it must be the clinical question that determines the procedure to be used and it is the tester who decides this.

The interdependence of clinical problem and choice of test can be illustrated by a common referral problem, such as difficulties in school. These difficulties can arise for a variety of reasons and standardized tests can be given to eliminate certain hypotheses or support others. Thus a test of general abilities and reading might be given to exclude the possibility of a mismatch between the teacher's expectations and the child's level of functioning. Or, during the course of a clinical interview, it appears that the individual is phobic. A systematic schedule surveying a range of childhood fears can be administered to uncover other specific fears.

Sometimes there is a need to monitor progress. Will medication alter levels of activity or improve concentration? Is remedial teaching leading to improved skill? Is the frequency of tantrums changing as a result of the management programme? Such questions indicate the use of criterion-referenced measures based on normed tests or on specially devised procedures, for instance, a record system for counting tantrum frequency.

Influences on test performance

Psychological testing is intrusive and engenders reactions in the testee. Commonly the test requires the testee to do things and in the process of doing, the individual learns and experiences the demands of the test and situation. These demands can also produce derivative effects — anxiety about being tested, elation at success or unhappiness and reduced motivation following failure as well as learning how to do the test. Because these are behavioural effects, they can distort the test score and undermine the purpose of testing. Some influences on test score and performance are considered next.

How children respond to testing will depend on the requirements of the test procedure (e.g. whether or not answers can be probed); on test format (e.g. reading prose passages or single words as tests or reading accuracy); test length (longer tests being more prone to fatigue effects or the effect of poor concentration); the appearance and style of the tester and the physical setting (e.g. the presence of distracting extraneous noise). In certain instances, test difficulty can be very important, for instance if early on items are failed, there could be a lowering of motivation.

Scores can incorrectly represent the characteristic being measured through *floor* and *ceiling* effects. Most tests are designed to cover a specific ability range. Floor effects occur when the ability of the individual is below the lowest score obtainable on the test — the test overestimates ability. Ceiling effects arise when the ability is above the maximum score on the test — the score underestimates ability.

Special considerations

Many of the points made in the preceding paragraphs apply to testing generally. Testing children poses several special problems.

The tester has to recognize that behaviour is being sampled at a period of rapid development in an individual who may not be able to understand what is required or to communicate what is known because test instructions do not always allow

ready flexibility. The younger the child, the more considerations regarding communication must be taken into account. A detailed knowledge of child development, its disorders, and the role and influence of family, school and society on individual development is also essential. This knowledge guides the preparation of the setting and the selection of procedures to be used and it provides a basis for understanding the meaning of children's behaviour and hence aids the evaluation of test results.

Because of the rapid rates at which certain abilities develop, skills may emerge in a short space of time; such changes can alter the outcome on repeated testing. It is also possible for one test to sample a particular area of skill in such a way that competence cannot be demonstrated whereas an alternative approach is able to demonstrate the capability of the child. Comprehension, for instance, can be tested in a number of ways. One test may require the child to verbalize responses, whereas another may simply require pointing at an object. Both are legitimate approaches. However, the child who is shy may produce substantially different results when tested on these two tests.

Tests developed for use with nonhandicapped children are likely to yield inappropriate conclusions when applied to those who are handicapped. Special care has to be exercised to ensure that their particular disabilities do not place them at a disadvantage. Even seemingly trivial occurrences such as having left spectacles at home or a hearing aid set at a suboptimal volume may have a profound impact on test outcome. Tests should be carefully chosen for each individual child, taking into account his or her difficulties. Occasionally, standardized procedures will have to be modified. This leads to changed reliabilities and validities. The tester then has to balance limitations on interpretations against gains from the modified test.

Incomplete testing

Incomplete testing is a special form of modified testing that requires careful interpretation. Autistic children, among others, usually complete only parts of the Merrill–Palmer test (Stutsman, 1948) or several subtests of the WISC-III (UK). Apart from problems of reliability, interpretations have then to be restricted in several ways. Major secular changes mean that test ages, specially those on the Merrill–Palmer, may not correspond accurately to the current chronological age equivalents. Interpretations may need to be restricted to the statistical: the results can be used as indices of the differential levels at which the child can perform a class of cognitive tasks. Scores should not be given their usual labels (MA — Mental Age or IQ, for example) unless it is made quite explicit that the IQ is based on an incomplete or nonstandard administration of the test and potentially misleading norms. Among the reasons for this sanction is that some scores have a variety of implications that may not hold if they are based on nonstandard procedures or if they are used to generalize about atypical individuals. A child with language difficulties who is successful on some of the items passed by children aged 36 months on a test of language comprehension cannot be said necessarily to have a comprehension age of 36 months, with all that this implies about the linguistic capabilities of children of this age; to make such an interpretation would require other forms of evidence. For example, how many nonlanguage-handicapped children in the population of the same age pass as few items as the child tested? Does evidence from other sources, such as parental report, indicate that the child's breadth of understanding is consistent with what one would anticipate from studies of the language development of 3-year-olds? Evidence of this type can then be used to determine the sorts of generalization that are permissible.

It is worth distinguishing between children who refuse to be tested — deliberate noncompliance — and those whose behaviour and handicaps make them difficult to test. Clark and Rutter (1979) describe a rare instance of the former, a negativistic autistic child who became amenable to testing when he was allowed to say what the answer was, rather than point to the correct solution. There is no doubt that some children are difficult to test and that for a given tester, procedure, circumstances and number of attempts, the statement that the child is 'untestable' may hold. However, children are not tested with the purpose of getting a test score. They are tested as part of the process of assessment, of which the score is but one element. Testing is a tactic in the strategies of assessment and, with the problem clearly articulated, an answer can be arrived at in different ways. If the tester cannot wait to get a test result or is unsatisfied with partial testing, direct observation and structured interviews with parents and teachers can be used. The Vineland Adaptive Behaviour Scales (Sparrow *et al.*, 1984) are one form of interview procedure that could contribute the desired information.

The observations made by the tester, and those recounted by others, can be related to the tester's knowledge of child development to reach an estimate of developmental level if this is what is required. Such knowledge should also be used to guide the selection of questions that will be put to informants. For example, it is possible to formulate questions on language and social development guided by the findings of current research in these areas. As this information is not as yet incorporated in standardized tests, such questions should be posed if the assessment is in any way concerned with these aspects of functioning, irrespective of whether or not full testing was accomplished.

Children from different cultural groups

It was noted earlier that there is no consistent information on the question of test bias. Nevertheless, testing children from different backgrounds, racial and ethnic groups requires careful consideration. Developmental and behavioural expectations may differ, as may the life experiences of children from different backgrounds, even though brought up in a common broader society. Further, parental interpretations of behaviour can differ and there are likely to be obvious differences in

language usage between cultures. Even within a language such as English, there are important variants. For instance, the Wechsler Scales needed to be translated from American English to British English before they could be used in the UK. In Scotland, local samples have been used to renorm the tests. Despite these changes, it is still possible that some items are misplaced because of cultural differences. The WISC-III (UK) has been specially adapted from the US version for use in the UK.

For these and other reasons, when individuals from different backgrounds are tested, the examiner must understand, actively identify and if appropriate attempt to take account of cultural factors in making interpretations.

The role of observation

With standardized tests, the test situation and tasks tend to be constant. Hence, individual differences in performance become more apparent to an experienced tester, and these observations can be valuable sources of relevant clinical hypotheses.

Using a standardized procedure, a clinically experienced tester with knowledge of development and its disorders may also be able to detect abnormalities — for example, in motor coordination or social responsiveness — that might not have been seen in other circumstances. Further, by careful observation of the style and content of the answers, and by *ad hoc* investigations when testing is completed, other information relevant to understanding a child's performance can be obtained. For example, the errors made may be a function of impulsive answering, or they may be rule-governed. Clark and Rutter (1979) were able to demonstrate that some autistic children made systematic errors in their responses to tests; even though the answers were wrong, there was clear evidence of a consistent strategy.

In sum, careful observation during testing serves at least three important functions. Firstly, it provides information that is helpful in understanding why a particular score or pattern of performance arose. Secondly, it is a source of hypotheses that may be important in leading to an understanding of why the child was referred. In this regard, observations as hypotheses can illuminate characteristics of children's style of approach to problems as well as their reactions to new situations and to failure. Finally, and perhaps most crucially, observation provides a basis for an evaluation of the findings and the decision as to whether or not they should be used (see below).

Test adequacy and data adequacy

It is important to distinguish between the adequacy of a test and the adequacy of the test data obtained during an individual examination. Formal test reviews and evaluations provide a general guide to the test as a psychometric instrument. Even the best test may not produce accurate or interpretable test results for an individual. Normally, test evaluations are based on data from large groups in which individual idiosyncracies are assumed to be averaged out. The score from an individual testee is more immediately open to the effects of anxiety, administration and scoring errors and the like. Children with motor coordination difficulties, for instance, having to do spatial tasks that also need good motor control, may produce low scores because it takes them longer to complete the task. What is being measured in this instance is not their spatial skills but their motor speed, hence the scores may not be interpretable.

While it is always important to give the child the benefit of the doubt, low scores should not be dismissed because of anxiety during testing. An alternative hypothesis could be that poor abilities have led to the child being anxious in situations that require the exercise of such abilities. In the final analysis, test scores should always be checked against nontest or other test indicators of the characteristic. It is for such reasons that the tester must be able to observe testing and the associated behaviours. If necessary test scores must be disregarded if there are reasons to believe that the data are of poor quality as a result of excessive anxiety or other influence.

On occasion test results may need to be disregarded in favour of information from other sources. Parents may insist that test results are wrong, pointing to examples of everyday behaviour as evidence for their views, for instance, sentences, memory recall, problem solving or constructional skills that suggest levels well in advance of test results. Such differences can arise for a variety of reasons, to do with the testing or the contrary observations, and their resolution depends on the time available for further investigation. There could for instance be some advantage to visiting the child at home to observe the way in which everyday events are dealt with. This observation could be guided by a schedule such as the Vineland Adaptive Behaviours Scales (Sparrow *et al.*, 1984). It would be particularly important not to base judgements on what could be well-practised skills, although these can give an idea of minimal level. Some attempts should be made to observe the child facing new challenges, if necessary introducing them in order to observe how they are responded to. Qualitative indicators, such as exploratory behaviour or curiosity, can at certain ages also give a guide to the way a child is developing.

Social interactions and play can be important sources of information. Engaging in reciprocal play, the ability to follow complex conversations or respond to complex instructions and produce long interactive sentences can be markers for estimating abilities, depending on age. Complexity of play and the creation of novel and detailed objects such as with Lego or similar materials or in drawings can also be good indicators of competencies, provided they do not come across as routinized. The evidence should be cumulative, not based on a single instance of a skill, and should be as extensive as possible.

Being realistic

The ideals of testing cannot always be satisfied in clinical practice. However, the tester who is aware of the limitations of tests is in a position to qualify the findings effectively. Steps must be taken to ensure that the results are seen in their full context. Firstly, detailed and systematic observations of behaviour should be made and recorded in the test report so that sources of unreliability are known. Secondly, all nonstandard procedures should be reported. Finally, a concerted effort should be made to obtain independent confirmation of test results. This can be achieved partly by relating what was seen in the test situation to information given by parents and others, and partly by comparing test scores with other developmental data. An attempt should be made at the same time to confirm that the behaviour seen during testing was typical of the child in other situations. Relevant discrepancies should be investigated. Testing should not be regarded as complete while unresolved discrepancies remain.

APPROACHES TO TESTING CHILDREN WITH DEVELOPMENTAL, EMOTIONAL AND BEHAVIOURAL PROBLEMS

Most child psychological, psychiatric or developmental disorders have some, or an abundance of, specific tests that quantify their characteristics.

In general, where questions relate to abilities, specific or general, or where some exploratory testing is indicated, a comprehensive test battery such as the Wechsler Scales is a good starting point for testing. Such tests sample a range of different abilities across a wide age and ability spectrum and enable observations of the child's behaviour when confronted with different tasks. They allow differentiation of verbal and nonverbal skills which can be useful when dealing with children with, or suspected of having, a language or other specific disorder. Another advantage is that they allow conversion of test scores into age norms, useful for communication to nonprofessional audiences. Most tests of this type have somewhat similar content. More recent batteries are accompanied by statistical tables or procedures that enable proper differentiation of strengths and weakness by excluding chance variations. A number of batteries also have microcomputer scoring and report outline packages (see later), one of the benefits of which is the rapid identification of statistically reliable differences between the subtests. Which particular battery is chosen will depend on the variety of consideration discussed earlier.

Completion of tests such as the Wechsler Scales presupposes an ability to understand the instructions and/or a willingness to respond through speech. Where compliance with these requirements cannot be obtained, it is possible to use tests that require only manual pointing, or in the case of children with severe movement disorders, eye pointing or some other form of communication. The Peabody Picture Vocabulary Test (Dunn & Dunn, 1981) or its equivalent, the British Picture Vocabulary Test (Dunn *et al.*, 1982) can be used as a means of indexing comprehension and getting a level for verbal skills.

A number of tasks that require motor responses to produce scores are sometimes confounded by complex verbal instructions, so that poor performance may be due to verbal difficulties and not poor motor or spatial skills. In these circumstances, there are a number of tasks the nature of which seems to be implicit in the task, not requiring verbal mediation. Raven's Coloured Progressive Matrices (Raven, 1956), the Seguin and other form boards and inset puzzles seem to have this property. The main problems with such tasks is that they have also influenced the design of toys and many children are practised in their use. Consequently, the main inference that can be drawn from successful completion may be that the individual can learn and generalize the skills required to perform such tasks.

Certain tests, such as the Merrill—Palmer (Stutsman, 1948), although normed many years ago, have a number of advantages when other tests are not producing scoreable responses. For instance, they contain several simple form-board tasks such as the Seguin Board. The Snijders-Oomen Non-Verbal Intelligence Scale (Snijders & Snijders-Oomen, 1976), a test developed initially for deaf children, is also useful when dealing with children who may not understand verbal instructions and has the advantage of versions for individuals from 2 to 17 years of age.

Some tests are particularly disadvantageous when used with children with suspected or actual language disorders. Versions of the Stanford—Binet (Thorndike *et al.*, 1989) lead to a single general ability score weighted in favour of verbal skills so that language-disordered children may score lower on such a test than on others which are more evenly balanced and allow separate abilities to be identified. In general, batteries that allow only one global score should be avoided when testing children suspected of having specific disabilities.

INVESTIGATION OF SINGLE CASES: A CONTEXT FOR TESTING

Clinical practice is distinguished by its focus on the individual. One approach widely accepted (Hersen & Barlow, 1976) is that proposed by Shapiro (1957, 1970). Its essence lies in the formulation and testing of hypotheses relevant to clinical needs. The hypotheses should be based on research findings and testing should be guided by the same considerations of design and measurement that operate in research. That is, wherever possible, clinical problems should be conceptualized as research problems.

Clinicians do not normally have the opportunity to continue individual investigations to the point where they can attach a high degree of confidence in the outcome. In addition, there are unresolved methodological and technical limitations. The statistical testing of outcomes constitutes a major difficulty (Kazdin & Tuma, 1982).

Clinical and developmental research provides an abundant source of hypotheses and of designs for individual investigations (Hersen & Barlow, 1976). There are statistical procedures to analyse data from such investigations (Payne & Jones, 1957). However, most can be used only when the characteristics of the individual closely match those of subjects used in the research samples; moreover, the assumptions required in the use of most statistical tests are rarely met when applied to the individual case.

Some features of single case study are illustrated in the following example.

RM, a 10-year-old boy, was originally referred to the clinic because of reading, spelling and writing difficulties. Following a full psychiatric, psychological and neurological assessment, it was decided to provide him with remedial reading as part of the treatment for his difficulties. During the initial assessments, it had emerged that in addition to being specifically retarded in reading, RM also showed a number of motor coordination difficulties, a not uncommon finding in specifically retarded readers (Rutter *et al.*, 1970).

In the course of remedial reading, it was observed that while RM was reading one line of prose he appeared to be picking up words or parts of words from lines above and below the line he was reading. A brief unsystematic test was carried out. This consisted of using a mask to cover all of the printed page except for a small area just large enough to expose 6—8 letters on a single line. The use of this mask led to an improvement in his reading accuracy.

A number of hypotheses were advanced to account for this. One of these was that RM had not yet learned the left—right scanning that seems necessary in the initial stages of learning to read. A related hypothesis was that immaturity or a defect in his eye-movement control (possibly associated with his other motor difficulties) was interfering with scanning skill. In view of the implications for treatment, it was decided to investigate his eye movements in greater detail.

A number of studies (Abercrombie *et al.*, 1963) have shown important differences in the eye movements of cerebral-palsied and normal children. There are also several procedures available for detailed recording of eye movements (as opposed to eye fixation). Shackel's (1967) procedure (electrooculography) was chosen in the present instance. It uses specially designed cup-electrodes placed around the eyes and linked to a polygraph. RM was tested using a number of the fixation and tracking tasks described by Abercrombie *et al.* (1963). The polygraph records revealed a degree of impairment relative to comparable normal children, but not of the severity encountered in cerebral-palsied children.

Had the records shown no sign of impairment, treatment would have consisted of gradually increasing the size of the slot in the mask and then, at a later stage, getting RM to use his finger to guide his eyes along the printed sentence. As his skill improved the use of pointing would be gradually faded out. However, because there were indications of some motor difficulty, the treatment regime included the procedures described above as well as practice using other visual tracking tasks in an attempt to improve the skills.

The case of RM is intended to convey something of the

nature or style of approach that can be adopted in clinical work. Although the problems and procedures may be somewhat unusual, the underlying approach is not. At the present time, behavioural assessment is the most common example of this approach.

This style of investigation is strongly influenced by the considerations that guide scientific research. A systematic approach to the investigation of individual cases, in which tests are used as a means of hypothesis testing, is an important beginning. It is in this framework that psychological tests can demonstrate their value.

Individual investigations of this type are not intended to provide the answers being sought in what is commonly called research, although obviously they can stimulate such studies. Also, given the demands of the clinical setting, there is a limit to the amount of time that can be devoted to intensive studies. It is possible to generate many more hypotheses that can be tested and the opportunity to follow through even one or two in any depth is restricted. For each individual, some order of priority has to be set up in relation to both clinical needs and feasibility. Nevertheless, the style of the approach to individual investigations is now well-articulated and can serve to improve clinical practice.

NEUROPSYCHOLOGICAL ASSESSMENT

In the past, neuropsychological testing was especially concerned with the diagnosis of brain damage. Adult neuropsychology grew from such roots (Goldstein, 1990) and similar concerns, sometimes expressed as the diagnosis of cerebral dysfunction or minimal brain damage, characterized early approaches in child neuropsychology (Taylor & Fletcher, 1990). This orientation remains in the adult field, but extended by an increased emphasis on localization and the identification of specific disorders and defects. Sophisticated brain imaging technology now available, coupled with the greater stability of structure and function of the adult brain (Goldstein, 1990), has facilitated the development of adult neuropsychology. Neuropsychological assessment of children has progressed differently. The rapid development of the child brain makes it difficult to establish brain–behaviour relationships; where brain disease has been identified, the effects tend to be more diffuse; distinctive syndromes are rare in children and the consequent trend has been for child neuropsychology to take different pathways (Taylor & Fletcher, 1990). The detection of brain damage in children was also one of the areas in which diagnostic testing showed some of its more severe limitations (Herbert, 1964, 1974; Werry, 1972; Chadwick & Rutter, 1983).

In one sense, all tests are neuropsychological in that they require involvement of the central nervous system in order to be carried out. Consequently, expositions of child neuropsychological testing can verge on the overinclusive. Taylor (1988), for instance, states that 'any test that neuropsychologists or others are willing to use to make CNS inferences qualifies as neuropsychological'.

Neuropsychological tests consist of tasks aimed at tapping specific functions such as the Rivermead Behavioural Memory Test (Wilson *et al.*, 1991), or comprehensive batteries, of which there are several, the most well-known being the Halstead–Reitan Batteries for Children and the Luria–Nebraska Neuropsychological Battery (Hynd *et al.*, 1986; Taylor & Fletcher, 1990). A number of other batteries or tests, particularly the Wechsler Intelligence Scales, are usually administered as part of the assessment. Taylor (1988) notes that, despite variability in content, most neuropsychological batteries incorporate procedures to cover somatosensory and motor skills, language and auditory processing, visual–spatial and constructional skills, memory and learning abilities, attention and psychomotor efficiency and abstract reasoning and problem solving.

In their review of the Halstead–Reitan battery, Hynd *et al.* (1986) state that it is fairly good at differentiating normal from brain-injured children and those with learning disabilities. There is some evidence that suggests the battery can identify localized lesions but using it with individuals for this purpose or for anything other than broad classification goes beyond available evidence. Research with the Luria–Nebraska points towards 'cautious use of the test', perhaps in a more limited way than the Halstead–Reitan (Hynd *et al.*, 1986, p. 62).

While proponents of neuropsychological testing with children seem clear that broad differentiations can be made between children with and without brain damage, and those with and without learning difficulties (Taylor, 1988), it is equally clear that their measurement procedures are at best crude. For instance, Taylor and Fletcher (1990) indicate that it remains difficult to apportion the effects of multiple influences on test performances such as controlling for attention and language in tests of memory. Part of the problem is that many of the theories and concepts fundamental to refining neuropsychological tests are themselves at an elementary stage of evolution. Theories of memory and its development in children remain (Gregg, 1986) with little yet to provide an empirically based differentiated framework for the comprehensive assessment of memory. An examination of the developmental literature fairly soon reveals that memory is not a homogeneous phenomenon either within or across ages. Dempster (1985) presents evidence for major improvements in short-term memory performance from early to middle childhood. Apart from such obvious dichotomies as auditory, visual, olfactory and kinaesthetic memory, and the short- and long-term memory combinations of these, there are such phenomena as memory for the time of past events (Friedman, 1991). The field is further complicated by other aspects of children's memory, including metamemory (which encompasses the development of an awareness of memory phenomena such as remembering and forgetting), and memory strategies (Flavell, 1985).

Apart from validity issues inherent in the above, it is reported that neuropsychological tests have other major psychometric limitations. Among the more significant are the absence of adequate reliability and normative data and, as Taylor (1988) goes on to note, interpretation is based 'more on intuition than on empirical data'.

Taylor and Fletcher (1990), recognizing these difficulties, point out that child neuropsychologists are just as interested in the systematic analysis of behaviour—behaviour relationships, for example, the language correlates of reading disability, partly motivated by the belief that in the longer term, this could lead to uncovering central nervous system mechanisms. While this is a justifiable stance, it does not avoid some of the issues already identified, for instance, the dependence of language tests on an adequate theory and conceptual framework for language development and the extent to which such tests are influenced by attention or memory difficulties.

On the basis of the present evidence, therefore, it seems appropriate to conclude, as previously (Berger, 1985), that child neuropsychological tests, in so far as they focus on uncovering behaviour—brain relationships (structure and process), or for describing behaviour—behaviour relationships, continue to be usable in a restricted sense, mainly as sources of hypotheses that need further investigation in the framework of the clinical history and individual case methodology.

DIAGNOSTIC-PRESCRIPTIVE APPROACHES

Diagnostic testing would be of reduced relevance if it did not have implications for interventions. Prescriptive interventions are those that aim to overcome the difficulties identified in testing. The approach can presuppose that the deficit or features identified in testing — for instance, perceptual problems — are in some way responsible for a more general difficulty, such as reading or language disorder.

Education is one of the main contexts for the diagnostic-prescriptive approach where tests are used to identify poor performance in academic attainment, skill assets and deficits. While the tests are able to identify areas of difficulty, they are as yet unable to inform the user how to teach (Ysseldyke, 1987). Other attempts to establish diagnostic-prescriptive approaches, such as the Frostig Test and its associated remedial package (Frostig *et al.*, 1964) involving diagnosis of perceptual disorders, have proved singularly unsuccessful (Ysseldyke & Mirkin, 1982).

PROJECTIVE TECHNIQUES

A number of theories of personality development and of psychopathology accept, implicitly or explicitly, the projective hypothesis: that the way an individual perceives and interprets various experiences reflects some basic, deeper or underlying characteristics of his or her intellect, emotions or psychopathology. The outside world, as it were, is a screen on to which his or her 'psychic' characteristics are projected (Anastasi, 1982). In its more psychodynamic form, the hypothesis proposes that these projections reflect the unconscious conflicts and motivations of the individual. Numerous clinical procedures have been devised to elicit verbal and nonverbal interpretations from clients, that are assumed to reveal these conflicts, needs and striving, as well as other aspects of personality and psychopathology.

Devices range from abstract symmetric inkblots (Rorschach) to drawings depicting people in situations or relationships that are ambiguous but none the less provocative, as is the case with the Thematic Apperception Test (TAT; Murray, 1938). (The term provocative is used in the sense of channelling or guiding the nature of what is produced. Rorschach ink-blots are in this sense perhaps less provocative than a TAT card picturing two women, one older than the other, in drab clothing, or than the incomplete sentence 'I like my father . . .'. Similarly, providing the child with a set of family dolls invites one class of behaviours rather than being open-ended or neutral.) There are theoretical reasons for selecting the classes of responses to provoke and these influence interpretation.

Procedures for children include children or animals depicted in situations that might, on theoretical grounds, be expected to reveal unconscious anxieties or other special internal states. They are devised to engage children at an appropriate developmental level. Play techniques (and therapy), using toys, sand trays, drawings and the like are in part an attempt to exploit the projective hypothesis without necessarily requiring the child to verbalize: the information sought by the clinician is to be found in the arrangement of the materials or in the drawings. Koppitz (1982) describes briefly but uncritically procedures used with children. Anastasi (1982) examines fewer procedures, but provides useful evaluations as well as a discussion of the more general issues.

The literature on projective procedures is both extensive and varied, reflecting their value for many clinicians and the critical reactions of those who have carried out psychometric evaluations. The divisive issues include the veracity of the projective hypothesis, the reliabilities and validities of individual techniques, and even whether it is appropriate to evaluate them using conventional psychometric criteria, hence their being called techniques rather than tests. In general, when evaluated by such criteria, the large majority are found to be deficient (Anastasi, 1982).

Some authors (e.g. Goldstein, 1990) point to a general decline in the use of projective procedures. One exception is the use of Exner's Comprehensive System for the Rorschach (Erdberg, 1990), a systematic approach utilizing conventional psychometric criteria in its development. This approach is for adults rather than children. There is however an increase in empirical research on projective procedures for children. Tharinger and Stark (1990), for instance, describe qualitative and quantitative approaches to the differentiation of children with mood and anxiety disorders using the Draw-a-Person and Kinetic Family Drawing procedures, with the qualitative approach proving more accurate. The review of the assessment of object relations using projective procedures prepared by Stricker and Healey (1991) includes studies involving children.

The decision to use projective techniques as such, rather than to encourage rapport, for instance, depends on the inclinations of the clinician. The divide is substantial; behaviourally oriented texts on assessment do not even list projective procedures in their indexes.

Perception is now generally regarded as an active, constructive process depending not only on the objective nature of the stimulus material, but on the past experience, knowledge and expectations. When people respond to projective stimuli, particularly those of an overtly provocative nature, they *may* be telling us about their fantasies, preoccupations, expectations, experiences and views of the world. The issue is not whether they are doing so, but how we understand and use this information.

The controversies surrounding the use of projective procedures cannot be avoided or resolved by labelling them techniques rather than tests. The issues are in many ways similar to those that surround the use of diagnostic instruments or the use of tests in general. The use of projective techniques, and all tests, becomes questionable when they are regarded as the endpoint of assessment, as a sort of ultimate truth, requiring no further corroboration. Knowledge of disorders is not yet such that we can disregard the possible contribution of projective or, more aptly, open-ended procedures. Whether or not they are clinically productive with the individual case, and for what, has yet to be determined.

BEHAVIOURAL ASSESSMENT

The establishment of behaviour therapy as a major part of clinical practice has entailed a number of important changes in the conceptualization of disorders, assessment, treatment and treatment evaluation. The central task of behavioural assessment is to identify functional relationships between presenting problems and cognitive and environmental influences. This involves a search for antecedent, concurrent, contextual and consequential associations that influence clinical problems. The approach derives from Skinner's (1974) experimental technique, functional analysis, although in its current form it is theoretically, conceptually and technically much more diverse (Bellack & Hersen, 1988; Ollendick & Greene, 1990; Martin, 1991). This diversity stems from an increasing awareness of the importance of cognitive psychology and the realization that the problems of people are more complex than are the behaviours of rats and pigeons.

The traditional foci of psychological assessment (such as IQ measurement or personality elucidation) were seen by some psychologists as essentially irrelevant in the search for functional relationships or ways of modifying behaviours. In addition, there have been protracted debates on the theoretical and empirical status of enduring personality traits and their influence on behaviour across situations (Anastasi, 1986). The behaviourally oriented have tended to regard their role as minimal. These individual difference variables have now come to be recognized as important. Mash and Terdal (1981) state that the influence of personality traits (or of internal mental events) on behaviour is not at issue: what matters are those characteristics relevant to the purpose of the assessment that

can be reliably measured (p. 10); that is, the functional significance of individual characteristics.

Behavioural assessment was very dependent on direct, naturalistic observation for its data, and this together with a commitment to evaluation led eventually to detailed, psychometrically focused evaluations of observation as a data-gathering technique. The weaknesses of observation measures (Johnson & Bolstad, 1973; Mitchell, 1979; Barton & Ascione, 1984), together with an increasing awareness of instrument specificity (the finding that several instruments intended to measure the same phenomenon intercorrelate poorly), have contributed to the use of a wider range of techniques (multi-method assessment; Nay, 1979) for data gathering. Ollendick and Greene (1990) describe a wide range of standardized procedures including behavioural interviews, self-report and self-monitoring procedures, rating scales and even projective techniques instead of or as a supplement to direct observation. It is worth pointing out here the concern expressed by Morris *et al.* (1991) that little attempt has been made to establish the construct validity of a large number of instruments used in the clinical assessment of children.

Clinicians working within the behavioural framework accept the potential functional significance of marital discord, temperament, biological dysfunctions and self-concept and the like in the genesis and maintenance of disorder. The task of assessment is to isolate and where possible deal with those that are currently influential. It is worth noting too that attempts to provide credible evidence for the efficacy of interventions stimulated the development and appraisal of a series of treatment research designs suitable for use with individuals (Hersen & Barlow, 1976; Ollendick & Hersen, 1984).

The theoretical context of behavioural assessment admits the inclusion of a broader range of perspectives both as a way of conceptualizing disorders and for developing assessment procedures (Ollendick & Greene, 1990). It retains a strong emphasis on empirical methods and the psychometric adequacy of its procedures for gathering information. The major theoretical shifts have been both general (encompassing ecological system theory), and specific (in its acceptance of the central role of affect and cognition in behaviour and its disorders). Many of these changes represent a major departure from the constraints of Skinnerian analysis and its applications in clinical settings.

In recent years, more attention has been given to the behavioural assessment of diverse childhood disorders (Mash & Terdal, 1981; Ollendick & Hersen, 1984) and to considering the implications of a developmental perspective (Ollendick & King, 1991). Although current behavioural assessment appears more eclectic than it seemed in the past, the continuing emphasis on psychometric adequacy and empirical evidence introduces a degree of constraint on what is allowed to influence clinical practice, the approach being seen as having to fall within the compass of experimental psychology and empirical clinical research.

COMPUTER-BASED TESTING AND TEST INTERPRETATION

The availability of powerful but inexpensive desk-top and portable computers is beginning to have a major impact on psychological testing. Their main advantages are speed, flexibility, consistency and the near simultaneous collection of different response characteristics — for instance, being able to record response speed and accuracy. The major use to which computers are being put at present is in test administration — allowing tighter presentation, immediate scoring, rapid report generation and the option for tailored testing.

Tailored testing involves using response information such as the pattern of correct and incorrect answers gathered during testing to select further items for administration. Items that are easy for the testee are skipped and more items at the individual's skill level can be used for finer differentiation of abilities. Computerizing the process enables item selection to take place rapidly during testing.

More restricted programs are available, particularly those that convert the raw test scores, compute various indices and generate tentative reports suggesting possible interpretations of score patterns. Several such programs are available for children, including a number that score and interpret the Wechsler Scales for preschoolers and older children. Provided the raw scores are correctly allocated and summed by the human tester (a major potential source of error), further computer data conversion is virtually error-free (whereas the human process is again error-prone).

Many paper-and-pencil tests and diagnostic systems are now also available in computer-administered form for use by children, parents and teachers as the respondents. Achenbach's Child Behavior Checklists for very young and for older children, the Children's State—Trait Anxiety Inventory developed by Spielberger, Parent and Teacher versions of the Conners Behaviour Rating Scales as well as psychiatric and developmental history diagnostic interviews are among the many procedures that are available in computer versions (see, for example, the Stoloff & Couch (1988) directory of software). Further, because of the standardization of computer systems, it has also become possible to obtain copies of computerized research instruments and normative data for clinic use.

There are important limitations to computer-based tests and report generators. Certain types of tasks cannot be given via computer and there are limitations to the range of responses (such as extensive verbal reports) that can be tapped, at least currently.

Computer-generated reports cannot take account of behaviour during testing and moderate reports accordingly. Further, the interpretations they offer are built into the software and are thus simply mechanistic translations of research findings, so that the adequacy of the interpretation depends on the adequacy of the associated research and the recency of the information. Unless regularly updated, the software for report generation quickly becomes outdated. Responsible programmers insert clear warnings about such limitations in the reports produced by computer. While there will always be a need for regular updating, increasingly sophisticated programs are likely to be developed, involving the use of so-called expert systems and neural network software that may overcome some of the limitations that currently exist in combining multiple sources of information.

Despite the many advances that have occurred, several fundamental requirements remain common to computer and manual testing: the need for proper evaluation of the procedure and appropriate norms. It cannot for instance be assumed that normative data are equally appropriate for manual and computer versions of a test. Equally, it cannot be assumed that validity data retain their interpretative characteristics when transferred from one medium to the other. Such issues, like much else in psychological testing, remain matters for empirical resolution. The evidence to date is that psychometrically, computerized tests (not just those for children) are not the equivalent of more traditional procedures and that in personality assessment, there is strong evidence of nonequivalence (Honaker & Fowler, 1990). Also, the validity of computer-based interpretative reports has been questioned by many (Guastello & Rieke, 1990).

The British Psychological Society (1984) and the American Psychological Association (1986) have both published guidelines for the development and use of computer-based tests and interpretations.

CONCLUDING REMARKS

Psychological testing has a history of varying popularity, with particular concerns arising because of the ways in which they have been abused, because of a belief that important human characteristics are not measurable or that what is measured is of little relevance in the real world.

While tests have been abused, and will probably continue to be so, it is only through an educated understanding of tests and testing that the abuses can be curtailed and their impact minimized. Hopefully, this chapter goes some way towards doing this. However, the intention was not to protect against abuse so much as to counter beliefs that tests have little if anything to contribute to clinical practice. On the contrary, psychological tests, properly used and interpreted, can and do make a substantial contribution to clinical practice with children and young people. They do this in a variety of ways, provided they are properly understood and are seen not as an alternative to other clinical skills but as ways of complementing them.

REFERENCES

Abercrombie M.L.J., Davis J.R. & Shackel B. (1963) Pilot study of aversion movements of the eyes in cerebral-palsied and other children. *Vision Research*, **3**, 135—153.

American Educational Research Association, American Psychological

Association, National Council on Measurement in Education (1985) *Standards for Educational and Psychological Testing*. American Psychological Association, Washington, DC.

American Psychological Association (1986) *Guidelines for Computer Based Tests and Interpretations*. American Psychological Association, Washington, DC.

Anastasi A. (1982) *Psychological Testing*, 5th edn. Macmillan, New York.

Anastasi A. (1986) Evolving concepts of test validation. *Annual Review of Psychology*, **37**, 1–15.

Barton E.J. & Ascione F.R. (1984) Direct observation. In: Ollendick T.H. & Hersen M. (eds) *Child Behavioral Assessment*. Pergamon Press, New York.

Bellack A.S. & Hersen M. (1988) In: Hersen M. & Bellack A.S. (eds) *Behavioral Assessment: A Practical Handbook*, 3rd edn. Pergamon Press, New York.

Berger M. (1982) The scientific approach to intelligence: an overview of its history with special reference to mental speed. In: Eyseneck H.J. (ed) *A Model for Intelligence*, pp. 13–43. Springer-Verlag, Berlin.

Berger M. (1985) Psychological assessment and testing. In: Rutter M. & Hersov L. (eds) *Child and Adolescent Psychiatry*, (2nd edn), pp. 264–279. Blackwell Scientific Publications, Oxford.

Berger M. & Yule W. (1985) IQ tests and assessment. In: Clarke A.M., Clarke A.D.B. (eds) *Mental Deficiency: The Changing Outlook*, 4th edn, pp. 53–96. Methuen, London.

British Psychological Society (1984) Note on the computerization of printed psychological tests and questionnaires. *Bulletin of the British Psychological Society*, **37**, 416–417.

Buros O.K. (ed) (1985) *Ninth Mental Measurements Yearbook*. Gryphon, Highland Park, NJ.

Chadwick O. & Rutter M. (1983) Neuropsychological assessment. In: Rutter M. (ed) *Developmental Neuropsychiatry*, pp. 181–212. Guilford Press, New York.

Cicchetti D.V. & Sparrow S.S. (1990) Assessment of adaptive behavior in young children. In: Johnson J.H. & Goldman J. (eds) *Development Assessment in Clinical Child Psychology*, pp. 173–196. Pergamon Press, New York.

Clark P. & Rutter M (1979) Task difficulty and task performance in autistic children. *Journal of Child Psychology and Psychiatry*, **20**, 271–285.

Cronbach L.J. (1970) *Essentials of Psychological Testing*, 3rd edn. Harper & Row, New York.

Cronbach L.J. (1971) Test validation. In: Thorndike R.L. (ed) *Educational Measurement*, 2nd edn, pp. 443–507. American Council on Education, Washington, DC.

Culbertson J.L. & Gyurke J. (1990) Assessment of cognitive and motor development in infancy and childhood. In: Johnson J.H. & Goldman J. (eds) *Developmental Assessment in Clinical Psychology*, pp. 100–131. Pergamon Press, New York.

Dempster F.N. (1985) Short-term memory development in childhood and adolescence. In: Brainerd D.J. & Pressley M. (eds) *Basic Processes in Memory Development*. Springer-Verlag, New York.

Dudek F.J. (1979) The continuing misinterpretation of the standard error of measurement. *Psychological Bulletin*, **86**, 335–337.

Dunn L. & Dunn L. (1981) *Peabody Picture Vocabulary Test — Revised*. American Guidance Services, Circle Pines.

Dunn L.M., Dunn L.M., Whetton C. & Pintilie D. (1982) *The British Picture Vocabulary Scale*. NFER-Nelson, Windsor.

Elliott C., Murray D.J. & Pearson L. (1983) *The British Ability Scales (New Edition)*. National Foundation for Educational Research/Nelson, Windsor.

Erdberg P. (1990) Rorschach assessment, In: Goldstein G. & Hersen M. (eds) *Handbook of Psychological Assessment*, 2nd edn, pp. 387–402. Pergamon Press, New York.

Flavell J.H. (1985) *Cognitive Development*, 2nd edn. Prentice Hall, New Jersey.

Friedman W.J. (1991) The development of children's memory for time of past events. *Child Development*, **62**, 139–155.

Frostig M., Lefever D.W. & Whittlesey J. (1964) *The Marianne Frostig Developmental Test of Visual Perception*. Consulting Psychologists Press, Palo Alto.

Garfield S.L. (1974) *Clinical Psychology*. Aldine, Chicago.

Glasser A.J. & Zimmerman I.L. (1967) *Clinical Interpretations of the WISC*. Grune & Stratton, New York.

Golden C., Sawicki R.F. & Franzen M. (1990) Test construction. In: Goldstein G. & Hersen M. (eds) *Handbook of Psychological Assessment*, 2nd edn, pp. 21–40. Pergamon Press, New York.

Goldstein G. (1990) Comprehensive neuropsychological assessment batteries. In: Goldstein G. & Hersen M. (eds) *Handbook of Psychological Assessment*, 2nd edn, pp. 21–40. Pergamon Press, New York.

Goldstein G. & Hersen M. (1990) Historical perspectives. In: Goldstein G. & Hersen M. (eds) *Handbook of Psychological Assessment*, 2nd edn, pp. 3–20. Pergamon Press, New York.

Gregg V.H. (1986) *Introduction to Human Memory*. Routledge & Kegan Paul, London.

Guastello S.J. & Rieke M.L. (1990) The Barnum effect and validity of computer-based test interpretations: the human resource development report. *Psychological Assessment*, **2**, 186–190.

Herbert M. (1964) The concept and testing of brain-damage in children: a review. *Journal of Child Psychology and Psychiatry*, **5**, 197–216.

Herbert M. (1974) *Emotional Problems of Development in Children*. Academic Press, London.

Hersen M. & Barlow F.S. (1976) *Single Case Experimental Designs: Strategies for Studying Behaviour Change*. Pergamon Press, New York.

Honaker L.M. & Fowler R.D. (1990) Computer assisted psychological assessment. In: Goldstein G. & Hersen M. (eds) *Handbook of Psychological Assessment*, 2nd edn, pp. 521–546. Pergamon Press, New York.

Hynd G.W., Snow J. & Becker M.G. (1986) Neuropsychological assessment in clinical child psychology. In: Lahey B. & Kazdin A.E. (eds) *Advances in Clinical Child Psychology*, vol. 9, pp. 35–86. Plenum Press, New York.

Ireton H. (1990) Developmental screening measures. In: Johnson J.H. & Goldman J. (eds) *Developmental Assessment in Clinical Child Psychology*, pp. 78–99. Pergamon Press, New York.

Jensen A.R. (1969) *Bias in Mental Testing*. Methuen, London.

Johnson S.M. & Bolstad O.D. (1973) Methodological issues in naturalistic observation: some problems and solutions for field research. In: Hamerlynck L.A., Handy L.C. & Mash E.J. (eds) *Behaviour Change: Methodology, Concepts and Practice*. Research Press, Champaign.

Jones L.V. & Applebaum M.I. (1989) Psychometric methods. *Annual Review of Psychology*. **40**, 107–115.

Kail R. & Pellegrino J.W. (1985) *Human Intelligence: Perspectives and Prospects*. W.H. Freeman, New York.

Katz L.J. & Slomka G.T. (1990) Achievement testing. In: Goldstein G. & Hersen M. (eds) *Handbook of Psychological Assessment*, 2nd edn, pp. 123–147. Pergamon Press, New York.

Kaufman A.S. (1979) *Intelligent Testing With the WISC-R*. Wiley, New York.

Kazdin A.E. & Tuma A.H. (eds) (1982) *New Directions in the Methodology of Social and Behavioural Sciences: Single Case Research Designs*. no. 13. Jossey-Bass, San Francisco.

Kiernan C. (1985) Criterion-referenced tests. In: Hogg J. & Raynes N.V. (eds) *Assessment in Mental Handicap: A Guide to Assessment Practices, Tests and Checklists*, pp. 158–189. Croom-Helm, Kent.

Koppitz E.M. (1982) Personality assessment in schools. In: Reynolds C.R. & Gutkin T.B. (eds) *The Handbook of School Psychology*, pp. 273–295. Wiley, New York.

Lumsden J. (1976) Test theory. *Annual Review of Psychology*, **27**, 251–280.

Martin P.R. (1991) Theoretical and empirical foundations of behavior therapy. In: Martin P.R. (ed) *Handbook of Behaviour Therapy and Behavioral Science*, pp. 1–12. Pergamon Press, New York.

Mash E.J. & Terdal L.G. (1981) Behavioral assessment of psychological disturbance. In: Mash E.J. & Terdal L.G. (eds) *Behavioral Assessment of Childhood Disorders*, pp. 3–76. Guilford Press, New York.

Mitchell S.K. (1979) Interobserver agreement, reliability and generalizability of data collected in observational studies. *Psychological Bulletin*, **86**, 376–390.

Morris R.J., Bergan J.R. & Fulginiti J.V. (1991) Structural equation modelling in clinical assessment research with children. *Journal of Consulting and Clinical Psychology*, **59**, 371–379.

Murray H.A. (1938) *Explorations in Personality*. Oxford University Press, New York.

Nay W.R. (1979) *Multimethod Clinical Assessment*. Gardner Press, New York.

Ollendick T.H. & Greene R. (1990) Behavioral assessment of children. In: Goldstein G. & Hersen M. (eds) *Handbook of Psychological Assessment*, 2nd edn, pp. 403–422. Pergamon Press, New York.

Ollendick T.H. & Hersen M. (1984) An overview of child behavioral assessment. In: Ollendick T.H. & Hersen M. (eds) *Child Behavioral Assessment: Principles and Procedures*, pp. 3–19. Pergamon Press, New York.

Ollendick T.H. & King N.J. (1991) Developmental factors in child behavioral assessment. In: Martin P.R. (ed) *Handbook of Behaviour Therapy and Behavioral Science*, pp. 57–72. Pergamon Press, New York.

Payne R.W. (1989) Reliability theory and clinial psychology. *Journal of Clinical Psychology*, **45**, 351–353.

Payne R.W. & Jones H.G. (1957) Statistics for the investigation of individual cases. *Journal of Clinical Psychology*, **13**, 115–121.

Perlman M. & Kaufman A.S. Assessment of child intelligence. In: Goldstein G. & Hersen M. (eds) *Handbook of Psychological Assessment*, 2nd edn, pp. 59–78. Pergamon Press, New York.

Puente A.E. (1989) Psychological assessement of minority group members. In: Goldstein G. & Hersen M. (eds) *Handbook of Psychological Assessment*, 2nd edn, pp. 505–520. Pergamon Press, New York.

Raven J. (1956) *Guide to Using the Coloured Progressive Matrices*. H.K. Lewis, London.

Reckase M.D. (1990) Scaling techniques. In: Goldstein G. & Hersen M. (eds) *Handbook of Psychological Assessment*, 2nd edn, pp. 41–56. Pergamon Press, New York.

Reynolds C.R. & Brown R.T. (1984) Bias in mental testing. In: Reynolds C.R. & Brown R.T. (eds) *Perspectives on Bias in Mental Testing*. Plenum Press, New York.

Rosen A. (1966) Stability of the new MMPI scales and statistical procedures for evaluating changes and differences in psychiatric patients. *Journal of Consulting Psychology*, **30**, 142–145.

Rutter M., Graham P. & Yule W. (1970) *A Neuropsychiatric Study in Childhood*. Clinics in Developmental Medicine, 35/36. Heinemann/Spastics International Medical Publications, London.

Sattler J.M. (1982) *Assessment of Children's Intelligence and Special Abilities*, 2nd edn. Allyn & Bacon, Boston, MA.

Shackel B. (1967) Electrocculography. In: Venables P.H. & Martin I. (eds) *Manual of Psychophysiological Methods*. North Holland, Amsterdam.

Shapiro M.B. (1957) Experimental method in the psychological description of the individual psychiatric patient. *International Journal of Social Psychiatry*, **3**, 89–103.

Shapiro M.B. (1970) The intensive investigation of the single case: an inductive-deductive approach. In: Mittler P. (ed) *The Psychological Assessment of Mental and Physical Handicap*, pp. 645–666. Methuen, London.

Silverstein A.B. (1981) Reliability and abnormality of test score differences. *Journal of Clinical Psychology*, **37**, 392–394.

Silverstein A.B. (1989) Reliability and abnormality of scaled-score ranges. *Journal of Clinical Psychology*, **45**, 926–929.

Skinner B.F. (1974) *About Behaviorism*. Knopf, New York.

Snijders J.Th. & Snijders-Oomen N. (1976) *Snijders-Oomen Non-verbal Intelligence Scale S.O.N 2 1/2–7*. H.D. Tjeenk Willink, Groningen.

Sparrow S., Balla D. & Cicchetti D. (1984) *Vineland Adaptive Behavior Scale*. American Guidance Service, Circle Pines, MN.

Stoloff M.L. & Couch J.V. (1988) *Computer Use in Psychology: A Directory of Software*, 2nd edn. American Psychological Association, Washington, DC.

Stricker G. & Healey B.J. (1991) Projective assessment of object relations. *Psychological Assessment*, **2**, 219–230.

Stutsman R. (1948) *Guide for Administering the Merrill-Palmer Scale of Mental Tests*. Harcourt, Brace & World, New York.

Taylor H.G. (1988) Neuropsychological testing: relevance for assessing children's learning disabilities. *Journal of Consulting and Clinical Psychology*, **56**, 795–800.

Taylor H.G. & Fletcher J.M. (1990) Neuropsychological assessment of children. In: Goldstein G. & Hersen M. (eds) *Handbook of Psychological Assessment*, 2nd edn, pp. 387–402. Pergamon Press, New York.

Tharinger D.J. & Stark K. (1990) A qualitative versus quantitative approach to evaluating the draw-a-person and kinetic family drawing: a study of mood-and anxiety-disorder children. *Psychological Assessment*, **4**, 365–375.

Thorndike R.L., Hagen E. & Sattler J. (1989) *Standford-Binet Intelligence Scale*, 4th edn. NFER-Nelson, Windsor.

Wechsler D. (1974) *Manual for the Wechsler Intelligence Scale for Children — Revised*. Psychological Corporation, New York.

Wechsler D. (1990) *Manual for the Wechsler Preschool and Primary Scale of Intelligence — Revised (British Amendments)*. The Psychological Corporation, Kent.

Wechsler D. (1992) *Manual for the Wechsler Intelligence Scale for Children — Third UK Edition (WISC-III UK)*. Psychological Corporation, Kent.

Werry J.S. (1972) Organic factors in childhood psychopathology. In: Quay H.A. & Werry J.S.. (eds) *Psychopathological Disorders of Children*, pp. 234–272. Wiley, New York.

Whalen C.K. (1989) Attention deficit and hyperactivity disorders. In: Ollendick T.H. & Hersen M. (eds) *Child Behavioral Assessment: Principles and Procedures*, pp. 171–196. Pergamon Press, New York.

Wilson B., Ivani-Chalian R. & Aldrich F. (1991) *The Rivermead Behavioural Memory Test for Children aged 5 to 10 Years*. Thames Valley Test Company, Bury St. Edmonds.

Ysseldyke J.E. (1987) Diagnostic-prescriptive teaching: the search for aptitude-treatment interactions. In: Mann L. & Sabatino D.A. (eds) *The First Review of Special Education*, vol. 1, pp. 5–32. JSE Press, Philadelphia.

Ysseldyke J.E. & Mirkin P.K. (1982) The use of assessment information to plan instructional interventions: a review of the research. In: Reynolds C.R. & Gutkin T.B. (eds) *The Handbook of School Psychology*, pp. 395–409. Wiley, New York.

Chapter 8
Clinical Neurophysiology

Colin D. Binnie & Stewart Boyd

INTRODUCTION

As a noninvasive, inexpensive and repeatable means of assessing cerebral function, the electroencephalogram (EEG) can prove an invaluable diagnostic aid in child psychiatry. Nevertheless, paediatric electroencephalography presents many complexities, not least because of the changes in the EEG occurring throughout childhood and adolescence due to maturation.

Clinicians need to understand about neurophysiological investigations to the point where they can consult productively and use the resulting information wisely. The commonest clinical needs are the detection of possible brain disease, localization of a neurological abnormality, finding out whether a patient has seizures, assessment of the nature of a seizure disorder, and determining whether sensory pathways are intact in children with possible impairment of hearing or vision.

The commonest single reason for requesting an EEG is probably to detect cerebral abnormality in a child, when changes in mental state or behaviour have raised the possibility of an organic cause. It is therefore important to appreciate that there is often no clear boundary between the normal and the pathological; and that the sensitivity and specificity of differing EEG abnormalities vary greatly as indices of underlying brain disease.

The areas of child psychiatry in which the EEG is of most value are epilepsy and the various cerebral degenerative diseases. More questionable is its utility as a 'soft' sign of cerebral dysfunction in a much wider range of disorders.

Evoked potentials (EPs) elicited by sensory stimulation serve two clinical purposes: as an aid to assessing sensory function, for instance to test hearing in children with communication difficulties, and as a means of detecting and sometimes identifying cerebral disease involving the afferent pathways in the brainstem and white matter and projection areas.

STANDARD CLINICAL NEUROPHYSIOLOGICAL TECHNIQUES IN CHILDREN

The EEG

Origin of the EEG

The EEG is a recording of cerebral electrical activity from the scalp. It mainly comprises the averaged synchronous post-synaptic potentials from radially oriented cortical neurons. EPs are similarly recorded from the scalp when a brief sequence of synchronous neuronal events is elicited by a sudden, transitory stimulus. Various other transient EEG phenomena, both normal and pathological, also owe their synchronicity to a triggering event. However, the ongoing activity of the spontaneous EEG is rhythmic in character, reflecting synchronous oscillatory processes involving many neurons.

Several sources of rhythmic neuronal activity are known. Individual neurons or groups of interconnected cells can display rhythmic discharge. There also exist anatomically discrete pacemakers, or distributed systems of interacting neurons (see Steriade *et al.*, 1990, for review). Rhythmic activity may be suppressed, for instance by brainstem projections, which desynchronize the EEG (increased frequency and reduced amplitude) during arousal. Conversely, deafferentation during sleep promotes synchrony, reflected in increased EEG amplitude and reduced frequency, and by an increase of synchronous transients such as spikes.

Recording the EEG

Like other bioelectrical signals, such as the electrocardiogram (ECG) the EEG is picked up by electrodes and amplified to drive a display, usually a chart recorder. The signal is smaller than the ECG, of the order of $10-200\,\mu V$. Consequently the recording is more liable to artefacts, from biological sources such as the eyes and scalp muscles, and from electrical interference. These can be reduced by meticulous technique. Electrode preparation and application are crucial. Low, stable electrode potentials and contact resistances reduce susceptibility to physical interference, and the promotion of cooperation and relaxation in the subject helps to minimize biological artefact. These may be difficult to achieve in children, especially infants and those who are mentally handicapped or disturbed. The importance of skill on the part of the technologist is reflected in the difference between the technical quality of children's EEGs obtained in routine departments and those recorded in specialized paediatric units.

Sometimes it is impossible to obtain an EEG without sedation or even anaesthesia, and it is then necessary to consider whether the clinical value of the investigation justifies such measures. Preschool children will usually take a sedative antihistamine syrup, for instance trimeprazine 2–4 mg/kg, and older patients can be sedated with short-acting barbiturates, e.g. quinalbarbitone 100–150 mg. Before the last resort of general anaesthesia, which precludes a waking EEG, intramuscular droperidol may be tried.

Normal EEG phenomena in childhood and adolescence

For descriptive purposes, continuous ongoing activity is distinguished from transients. Ongoing EEG activities are classified into four frequency bands: delta, below 4 c/s; theta, from 4 up to 8 c/s; alpha, from 8 c/s up to 14; and beta, from 14 c/s upwards. The EEG changes from birth, throughout childhood and adolescence, stabilizing as the adult pattern at about 22 years. We shall first describe the mature EEG and then consider how this develops.

The main feature of the waking, adult EEG is usually the alpha rhythm: alpha frequency activity, at about 9–10 c/s, with an amplitude of 50–100 µV seen symmetrically at the back of the head. The alpha rhythm is best developed in quiet wakefulness with closed eyes; it is attenuated by eye opening and disappears in drowsiness. Beta activity, usually at about 18–25 c/s, is of lower amplitude, usually some 10–20 µV, again symmetrical, and most prominent over the frontal regions. Theta activity may be inconspicuous but is always present, generally with a bitemporal maximum, increasing in drowsiness. Particularly in young adults, theta activity of half the alpha frequency may be seen posteriorly intermixed with the alpha rhythm and showing a similar response to eye opening (this is the slow alpha variant). Delta activity is not usually obvious in the mature waking EEG.

Changes in sleep are classified into five stages, by a system described by Dement and Kleitman (1957). In drowsiness (stage I) the alpha rhythm is replaced by theta and/or beta activity; slow lateral eye movements appear. Auditory stimuli elicit sharp transients at the vertex. In stage II, delta activity appears, beta activity increases further and spindle-shaped bursts of sigma activity at about 14 c/s appear with a frontal preponderance. Arousal now produces more complicated waveforms near the vertex, typically K-complexes: a sharp wave, a delta wave and a sigma burst. Stages III and IV are distinguished by increasing amounts of delta activity, and a possible disappearance of sigma in stage IV. After the first 90 minutes of sleep, episodes occur in which the EEG is of low amplitude, resembling stage I, but accompanied by rapid

lateral eye movements, seen as oculographic artefacts, which give this stage the name of REM sleep. REM appears to accompany dreaming.

The EEG of the full-term waking newborn consists mainly of diffuse activity in the delta range with amplitudes of 50–100 µV. Two sleep patterns may be distinguished. In quiet sleep, bursts of delta activity are separated by 6–10 second periods of relatively low amplitude (*tracé alternant*), whereas in active sleep, probably corresponding to adult REM, continuous delta activity is seen with ripples of superimposed faster rhythms.

The first year of life sees a gradual increase in EEG frequency and the emergence of a responsive posterior theta rhythm which reaches about 6 c/s by 12 months and will attain a low alpha frequency of about 8 c/s by the age of 3 years. From 3 to 12 months a Rolandic rhythm of 6–7 c/s is seen. A transitional state between waking and sleep appears at about 6 months, with dominant theta activity. From this time the classical sleep stages are distinguishable and much the same criteria apply as in adults. Sigma activity appears at about 2 months and vertex sharp transients and K-complexes in the middle of the first year.

In early childhood the alpha rhythm gradually emerges, increasing in frequency and responsiveness, but its frequency shows considerable variability, both between subjects and between published normative series. A dominant frequency of 8–9 c/s may be expected by the age of 5 years, but underlying the alpha rhythm large amounts of theta and delta activity remain. The theta activity takes on the characteristics of a slow alpha variant and the delta becomes intermittent and focal over the posterior temporal regions. The further evolution of the waking EEG through late childhood and adolescence involves quantitative rather than qualitative change. The slow alpha variant and posterior delta activity become more limited in extent and less in amount, the posterior slow waves usually disappearing entirely by the age of 22 years, and slow alpha variant a few years later. Drowsiness in early childhood produces an EEG dominated by theta activity with a frontal maximum, a picture which can easily be misinterpreted as abnormal if the reduced level of arousal is not recognized. Slow activity in sleep shows a posterior maximum up to 3 years of age; thereafter non-REM sleep patterns are not unlike those of adults. REM sleep is characterized by persisting slow activity to the age of 5 years but resembles the mature pattern thereafter.

Pathological EEG phenomena

The EEG changes with age and state of awareness, but a further source of intersubject variance is simply that the EEGs of individuals differ considerably one from another. To some extent EEG characteristics are genetically determined. There are greater similarities between the records of monozygotic than between dizygotic twins, both on visual assessment (Lennox *et al.*, 1945) and using quantitative measures (Dümermuth, 1968; Stassen *et al.*, 1988). These similarities extend to changes on hyperventilation and in sleep (Vogel, 1958). Various unusual or arguably abnormal EEG features (see below) also have a genetic component (Doose & Gerken, 1973).

Clinical EEG interpretation is based on subjective judgements which are complicated by the difficulty of defining normality at different ages. Maturation is accompanied by a reduction of the slower components, whereas drowsiness and cerebral dysfunction both produce slowing; thus it may be difficult to distinguish between the effects of immaturity, drowsiness and pathology. Currency has been given to statements to the effect that some 15% of normal children have abnormal EEGs. This merely reflects a general lack of familiarity with the range of EEG findings in normal children who may show various atypical patterns. Some of these are common, others rare, but they are not to be regarded as evidence of cerebral dysfunction or pathology. Conversely, changes within the normal range may be pathological for the individual concerned.

Another important consideration is that the EEG reflects cerebral function, and structural abnormality is manifest only in functional changes. Cerebral dysfunction produces in the EEG a rather limited range of abnormal phenomena, of uncertain pathophysiology.

Ongoing activities

Amplitude reduction. The most unequivocal sign of cerebral dysfunction is reduction in amplitude of normal activities. This may result from neuronal loss and from suppression of neuronal activity by toxic or metabolic factors. Extreme amplitude reduction is therefore found in brain death, after barbiturate overdose, during profound surgical hypothermia, in the terminal stages of various dementias, and immediately after a convulsive seizure. Amplitude reduction may also result from impaired conduction from the cortex to the scalp, for instance due to an intervening subdural haematoma. Reduction in EEG amplitude may occur at the onset of an epileptic seizure (an electrodecremental event), involving yet another mechanism, desynchronization of neuronal activity.

Some healthy adolescents constitutionally have low-amplitude EEGs and other children exhibit a marked voltage reduction when anxious or hyperaroused, thus minor amplitude reduction may be not recognizable as abnormal unless also asymmetrical. An asymmetry greater than 50% in normal activities will generally reflect disease on the side where the amplitude is less.

Slowing. An increase in slower components of the EEG is seen in many cerebral disorders. Minor changes in ongoing frequencies may be recognized as pathological only if they are also asymmetrical. As low-frequency activity may reflect cerebral dysfunction, it might be expected to be of greater amplitude over the more disturbed hemisphere; however, the opposite will be found if the underlying pathology also leads to amplitude reduction. Slowing is a nonspecific ab-

normality which can reflect various pathological processes including cerebral hypoxia, oedema, raised intracranial pressure, cerebral inflammatory or degenerative processes, and intoxications.

Excess beta activity. The amount of beta activity varies greatly between children. Beta activity is moreover increased in spontaneous drowsiness and by many sedative drugs, notably barbiturates and benzodiazepines. Excess beta activity is rarely pathological, but if very prominent may raise the possibility that the patient is consuming nonprescribed drugs.

Altered responsiveness. When the postcentral dominant rhythm is slowed it often shows a reduced responsiveness to eye opening or alerting. However, some normal subjects exhibit only minimal alpha blocking, and most will show reduced reactivity when drowsy. Thus poor responsiveness cannot reliably be regarded as pathological unless it is also asymmetrical (less response on the more abnormal side), or is seen in a subject whose EEG was previously responsive in the same behavioural state.

Localized abnormalities

Amplitude reduction and slowing may be bilateral or asymmetrical. Essentially similar disturbances can be more localized. Amplitude reduction over a small area may involve all components of the EEG or selectively the higher frequencies. Global reduction of amplitude generally reflects gross hypofunction or destruction of underlying cortical neurons.

Localized slow activities, apart from so-called rhythms at a distance (see below), generally reflect structural abnormality in the underlying cortex. Note that it is not cerebral lesions, but dysfunctional neurons, which generate abnormal EEG activity; thus slowing may be seen around the periphery of a space-occupying lesion but not over its centre where amplitude reduction may be detected. Localized slowing may present as abnormal activity in the lower alpha, theta or delta ranges or combinations of these.

Another important category of abnormal phenomena which may be localized, epileptiform activity, is considered in a later section.

Rhythms at a distance

Structurally normal cortex may generate abnormal activities in response to altered afferents from deep structures; these are termed rhythms at a distance.

FIRDA. Frontal intermittent rhythmic delta activity (FIRDA) occurs over the frontal regions, usually bilateral and synchronous. The frequency is 1.5–2.5 c/s, and the waveform typically sinusoidal. The rhythmic bursts typically last 2–5 seconds. It is dependent on arousal level, being absent in the fully alert subject and below stage I of sleep. FIRDA can occur in metabolic and toxic disorders, status epilepticus, and occasionally postictally, and in association with abnormalities of the diencephalon. It may thus for instance occur with thalamic tumours and with obstruction of the aqueduct. However, the most common pathological correlate of FIRDA is diffuse disease involving grey and white matter (Gloor *et al.*, 1968).

Bitemporal theta activity. In early drowsiness theta activity may increase over the temporal regions but in various states causing pathological drowsiness bilateral rhythmic temporal or frontotemporal theta activity occurs. It occurs under much the same circumstances as FIRDA. It must not be confused with the very prominent frontotemporal theta activity of drowsiness seen in preschool children.

Posterior slow activity. As noted above, posterior temporal slow activity is a normal finding in the young, disappearing in the early 20s. Posterior temporal slow waves may exceed the norm for the child's age, as a nonspecific abnormality after such cerebral insults as trauma, cerebrovascular accidents and severe hypoglycaemia. The slow activity may be of greater amplitude on the side of greater cerebral abnormality, but in general it shares with maturational posterior temporal slow activity a tendency to predominate over the nondominant hemisphere. Sometimes there is evidence of brainstem dysfunction as the immediate cause of posterior slow activity.

Very slow delta waves (of more than 1 second duration) are sometimes seen over the occipital regions, particularly in children, in association with mass lesions in the posterior fossa, and also with haemorrhage from the vertebrobasilar system.

Rhythmic, usually bilateral, posterior slow activity at about 3 c/s is seen in some children with absence seizures. It may represent a variant of spike-and-wave activity (see below), as on overbreathing it often acquires a notched waveform and spreads more widely before being replaced by typical generalized spike-and-wave discharges.

Epileptiform activity

Cerebral electrical activity changes during epileptic seizures and becomes characteristically spiky. Waves of sharp outline standing out from the background rhythms and lasting less than 70 ms are spikes. Those lasting 70–200 ms are termed sharp waves. Spikes are often followed by delta waves to form spike-and-wave complexes, which may occur in runs as spike-and-wave activity. Any of these can be generalized or focal.

Sharp waveforms occur in the interictal state, between overt seizures, in most people with epilepsy. Similar phenomena are also found in some patients with other cerebral disorders without seizures. There is no agreement as to a suitable collective term to describe this category of phenomena, but epileptiform activity, used here, acknowledges the association with epilepsy underlying the concept, whilst stressing that the term refers to the waveform, not a diagnosis.

Interpretative difficulties are increased by the occurrence in normal subjects of various sharp waveforms, unrelated to epilepsy. The most important of these in paediatrics are 6 c/s and 14 c/s positive spikes which occur in short bursts at these two distinctive frequencies. At the focus the spike components are positive — a distinctive feature as most spikes are negative. Positive spikes occur in 20–30% of adolescents and young adults during drowsiness and light sleep. An increased incidence has been claimed in conditions ranging from behaviour disorders to allergies, but they contribute nothing to the diagnosis of epilepsy. These and other spiky phenomena which are normal or of little diagnostic significance are distinguishable by characteristic morphology, topography or circumstances of occurrence.

Periodicity

Various pathological EEG phenomena occur at more or less constant intervals. The most dramatic example is provided by stereotyped complexes of slow waves, spikes and sharp waves occurring every 10–20 seconds in subacute sclerosing panencephalitis. Periodic phenomena appear in various conditions; if these have any common feature, it is probably diffuse dysfunction of both white and grey matter.

Other transients

Triphasic complexes comprise three waves of alternating polarity, some or all of which lie in the delta range. Typically the first and third components are frontonegative but the whole complex spreads across the head from front to back with a small time lag. This phenomenon is a sign of severe diffuse cerebral dysfunction, usually associated with metabolic disorder and typically with hepatic encephalopathy.

Paroxysmal lateralized epileptiform discharges (PLEDs) are stereotyped sharp waves or complexes of sharp waves repeating at intervals of about a second. They generally show a localized maximum but appear widely over one hemisphere. Occasionally the phenomenon is bilateral, although usually asynchronous. PLEDs are seen in a variety of conditions both acute and chronic, but always associated with localized structural disease and possibly more generalized cerebral dysfunction; examples include rapidly growing tumours, cerebrovascular accidents, herpes simplex encephalitis, cerebral abscess and following head injury.

Activation procedures

Various measures may be used to activate the EEG to increase the yield of clinically significant findings.

Hyperventilation, probably by reducing cerebral blood flow, slows the EEG, especially in the young. Children from the age of 3 years can be persuaded to overbreathe, if necessary with the help of a toy windmill. Background rhythms are slowed, posterior slow activity increases, and rhythmic bifrontal delta activity appears. Various abnormalities may be increased, epileptiform activity in particular, and generalized spike-and-wave discharges may occur, notably in children with absences. Bifrontal delta activity on overbreathing in young people is normal, but often misinterpreted, sometimes resulting in unnecessary administration of antiepileptic drugs.

Flashes elicit visual evoked potentials (see below). Repetitive flashes at 4–30/s or more produce a rhythmic response termed photic following. In some people, most of whom have epilepsy, generalized epileptiform discharges are elicited by flicker at certain frequencies, most readily at 18/s. Between these extremes, other anomalous responses may be observed, some of which are genetically determined but of little clinical significance. Some confusion has resulted in the literature from some authors attaching the term photosensitivity to all anomalous photic responses, and others confining it to the triggering of generalized spike-and-wave activity (the photo-convulsive response of Bickford *et al.*, 1952). However defined, photosensitivity is considerably more common in children than in adults. Some 20% of children with epilepsy show a photoconvulsive response. The diagnostic specificity of this phenomenon is disputed; various authors have reported photosensitivity in as many as 15% of normal children but have generally failed clearly to distinguish between photo-convulsive and other anomalous responses.

Photosensitivity in a child with epilepsy has practical significance. Firstly, it lends support to the classification of the epilepsy as idiopathic and may encourage screening of siblings for possible seizure disorders. More importantly, some 50% of photosensitive patients with epilepsy have no spontaneous seizures, all attacks being precipitated by visual stimuli. Thus seizure control may be achieved without drugs, by practical measures to avoid provocative stimuli. Further, some 30% of children with photosensitive epilepsy use visual stimuli to induce seizures. The most easily recognized manoeuvre is to wave the outspread fingers of one hand in front of the eyes while staring at a bright light. However, the majority of children use a more subtle method, involving a slow eye closure with lid fluttering, itself easily mistaken for a seizure or a tic. EEG and video monitoring in a well-lit room may be required to establish the occurrence of self-induction, and should be considered in any therapy-resistant photosensitive child.

Sleep has a profound effect on epilepsy: many seizure types show a marked dependence on the sleep–wake cycle. In general, epileptiform activity occurs more readily in sleep than in waking, particularly focal discharges. Recording of the EEG during sleep, induced if necessary by sedative drugs, therefore plays an important role in the diagnostic EEG investigation of epilepsy.

Evoked potentials

General aspects of evoked potentials, methods of recording, terminology

EPs are responses to stimulation. An abrupt stimulus, such as a click, produces a synchronous volley in the afferent pathways of the cord and/or brainstem and thalamic radiations, followed by a more complex sequence of events when the signal reaches the specific and nonspecific cortical projection areas. These phenomena have a fairly constant time course following each stimulus, whereas the waves of the ongoing EEG occur randomly in time. Therefore if the average of the signals following repeated stimulus presentations is calculated, the random activity tends to zero and the constant response to the stimulus is unmasked. Registration of EPs thus requires a special recorder containing a computer to average signals, and control the stimulators.

EPs consist of a sequence of waves, or components, identified by their latency and polarity. Normative values are published, but minor differences in technique and instrumentation result in substantial differences between laboratories; every department should obtain its own local reference data — a difficult achievement in paediatric practice, as different norms apply to each age group.

Auditory EPs

Auditory EPs are divided into early, middle latency and late. The early components, arising from the VIIIth nerve, cochlear nucleus and brainstem pathways, are termed brainstem auditory evoked potentials (BAEPs). They are elicited by a click and, being of low amplitude, may be detected only after many stimuli; difficult children will often need sedation. The BAEPs are designated by the Roman numerals I–VII and occur within 10 ms after the stimulus. BAEPs are recorded between bilateral mastoid or earlobe electrodes and the vertex. Wave I arises from the peripheral part of the ipsilateral cochlear nerve and may persist even when the brainstem or the proximal part of the nerve is damaged. Wave II is often inconspicuous and originates in the proximal part of the nerve and the cochlear nucleus. The other components arise in the brainstem and are recorded remotely from the vertex. The most robust is wave V which persists close to the subjective auditory threshold and can be used for audiometry. Waves I, III and V are present at birth. The latencies of BAEPs are the most stable of all EPs within and between subjects but diminish with maturation, virtually attaining the adult values by 3 years of age. Conduction velocity in the brainstem is assessed by measurement of the peak to peak latencies of waves I–III or I–V (the latter is typically about 4 ms).

Middle latency auditory evoked potentials (MLAEPs) occur in the 10–50 ms after the stimulus. Five waves are distinguished, of which only those at 16–20 and 27–33 ms are sufficiently consistent to be of clinical value. Asymmetries may provide evidence of hemisphere lesions.

Long latency auditory evoked potentials (LLAEPs) comprise a negative wave at about 100 ms and a 180 ms latency positive component. Their amplitude and latency are unstable, as they are influenced by vigilance, cognitive processes and drugs. Formerly they were used for audiometric testing, but have been superseded by BAEPs. However, abnormal or absent LLAEPs may offer evidence of hemispheric lesions.

Visual evoked potentials

Visual stimuli, flashes of light or reversing black and white patterns, elicit potentials both from the retina (the electroretinogram) and from the cortex (visual evoked potentials, VEPs).

The electroretinogram (ERG) to white flash is characterized by two waves, a and b. The a-wave arises from the receptor layers of the retina, and is followed by the b-wave which probably originates in the Müller cells. Some small, faster waves appear superimposed upon the b-wave, the oscillatory potentials. Later components, the c- and d-waves are of little clinical significance. By changing the intensity and colour of the flash or the state of light adaptation, it is possible to distinguish rod and cone components of the ERG. Ideally, electroretinography requires corneal electrodes; these are not tolerated by children, so supraorbital electrodes are used. Paediatric ERG is therefore rather crude, and may be limited to establishing whether a response is present, as a check on retinal function which greatly aids the interpretation of abnormal VEPs. If necessary, the examination can be performed under general anaesthesia.

The flash ERG is detectable after the first week of life, but is smaller and of greater latency than in adults. The mature pattern is attained, however, by the age of 1–2 years.

The VEPs to a diffuse flash of light comprise up to seven waves, within 250 ms of the stimulus, of which the most consistent are N70, P100 and P160. The intersubject variation of latency and amplitude is considerable. For clinical purposes, absence of response and interocular asymmetries of latency or amplitude are considered. In infants the earliest wave is positive at 170–190 ms, followed by a negative one at 220–240 ms. An adult waveform is attained by 4–6 years but the P100 still has a latency of 110–130 ms.

Flash-induced VEPs are simple to elicit and suitable for less cooperative patients. Responses to patterned stimuli may appear more physiological than those elicited by diffuse flash, and indeed pattern VEPs generally prove of greater clinical value when there is reasonably good cooperation. For routine purposes the stimulus used is the sudden reversal of the black and white squares of a chessboard. The pattern VEPs comprise three main waves: N75, P100 and N145, of which P100 is the most prominent. Pattern VEP studies require good cooperation and ocular fixation by the subject and are difficult before the age of 6 years, by which time the potentials resemble those of adults. Only limited normative data are available for infancy and early childhood. Latencies are much greater than in adults.

Somatosensory evoked potentials

Somatosensory evoked potentials (SEPs) are elicited by electrical shocks applied to peripheral nerves. The ascending impulses can be traced along the limbs, the brachial plexus and spinal cord to the cortex. In the present context only cortical potentials are relevant, and for simplicity only latencies from median nerve stimulation will be cited.

The first short latency cortical potentials comprise a parietal N20–P27 complex, and the frontocentral P22 and N30 potentials; all are recorded contralateral to the stimulus, but the N30 often extends to the ipsilateral frontal area. Responses to right- or left-sided stimuli are of equal amplitude and latency, and asymmetries reflect pathology of the underlying pathways. The short-latency SEPs include two later components, the P45 and N60 potentials, neither of which is studied for clinical purposes.

Auditory and visual EPs show a reduction in latency from infancy to adulthood, with increasing conduction velocity due to myelination and increase in fibre diameter. However, in the case of SEPs a second factor comes into play — the lengthening of the neural pathways with growth, delaying and desynchronizing the afferent volleys. In the preschool period the net effect is a reduction in latency; thereafter latencies again increase and the waveforms are widened. Comparison of the findings to normative values is simplified by correcting latencies for limb length or height, but again it is essential that each laboratory collects its own set of reference data.

Event-related potentials

The EPs described above are generated as a direct consequence of a stimulus. However, there are some, termed event-related potentials (ERPs), which are associated with endogenous or cognitive events. These include potentials preceding a voluntary movement, the Bereitschaftspotential, and potentials evoked when a stimulus is omitted from a regular series of stimuli. In psychiatry special attention has been directed to the P300, a positive wave with a latency of 250–450 ms, related to decision-making or recognition of a stimulus relevant to a particular task. For a review see Picton (1988), and for details of maturation of ERPs, see Picton et al. (1984).

Selection and interpretation of clinical neurophysiological tests in a clinical setting

Clinical neurophysiological investigations have been used in psychiatric disorders ever since the introduction of EEGs, although clinicians have often found it difficult to relate the findings to the specific clinical context. However, with a better understanding of the significance of particular EEG findings and the development of newer techniques such as EPs, combined neurophysiological investigations now offer improved prospects of obtaining clinically meaningful data. Nevertheless, it is important to understand the strengths and limitations of particular investigations. For example, many clinicians request visual or auditory EPs in the expectation that they will reveal whether the child 'sees' or 'hears'. Although conventional EP testing can indicate whether the pathways are functioning appropriately, it will not determine what use the child is able to make of the sensory information.

To take two extreme cases, an infant may have normal short-latency EP findings yet not respond normally due to severe impairment of cortical activity, while a bright child with a severe visual pathway problem and grossly impaired EP findings may have learned ploys of head movement etc. which allow the child to use residual visual function to the full.

Discussion in this chapter will focus on conventional clinical neurophysiological investigations since quantitative methods have often failed to fulfil their promise and have not entered routine practice (Nuwer, 1988a,b).

Selection and interpretation of such investigations should be considered as a continuing clinical process of reappraisal between clinicians and neurophysiologists (Table 8.1).

If the diagnosis is secure, then neurophysiological investigations are not relevant.

When there are specific questions relating to aspects of management, such as episodic alterations in behaviour, then appropriately selected neurophysiological investigations may help clarify the nature of the problem, within the limitations of the tests as described above. Prior discussion with the clinical neurophysiologist will facilitate the selection of relevant tests.

When the diagnosis is in doubt, and particularly where there is concern about regression, then investigations at an early stage may suggest the nature of the problem. Investigations in clinical neurophysiology should not be undertaken on a purely speculative basis, but there may be clinical hints which will repay further consideration if supported by neurophysiological findings. Since Batten's disease (see below) is the commonest neurodegenerative (central nervous system) disease, it is useful to combine flash ERG/VEP studies with EEG recording.

If there is continuing clinical uncertainty, then repeating the investigations after an interval, determined by the tempo of the clinical condition, may indicate whether the process is progressive.

SPECIAL TECHNIQUES

Long-term EEG monitoring

There are serious limitations to the routine EEG investigation of known or possible epilepsy. The clinical and electrophysiological manifestations of epilepsy are intermittent: a single routine recording may fail to show epileptiform activity, which may indeed occur only during seizures. The relevance of interictal discharges to specific clinical events may be uncertain: spikes in the EEG of a mentally handicapped child with episodes of aggressive behaviour do not indicate that these attacks are epileptic. Finally, clinical and electrophysiological observations of seizures in the EEG laboratory offer little guide as to their frequency and significance in daily life. These problems can be addressed by long-term monitoring of EEG and behaviour. Two methods are available: continuous EEG recording by telemetry with behavioural observation by video recording, and ambulatory monitoring of the EEG in the patient's everyday environment with a portable cassette recorder. These technologies are not alternatives and have different applications.

Telemetry

Routine EEG recording limits the patient's activity and will not be tolerated by a lively child for much more than an hour. Moreover limiting activity may prevent the observation of subtle ictal phenomena, or the effects of behaviour and environment on seizures. Greater mobility is achieved by telemetering the EEG through a long, flexible cable, or by a radio link.

Simultaneous video recording is important. Subtle clinical and electrophysiological ictal events are often identifiable only by comparison of EEG and behaviour. Thus a momentary arrest of activity may be shown to be a seizure because it consistently coincides with an EEG change. Conversely, apparent subclinical discharges may prove to be ictal because of associated but inconspicuous clinical events.

Some misunderstanding surrounds the significance of the negative ictal EEG. All epileptic seizures involve abnormal neuronal discharge, but this may not be recorded from the scalp. Ictal EEG changes may be entirely absent or consist, not of epileptiform activity, but rather of a minor change in ongoing rhythms. Some seizure types, as absences, are consistently accompanied by epileptiform activity. Some are usually associated with other changes, for instance bitemporal theta activity during a complex partial seizure. Simple partial seizures, particularly with psychic or viscerosensory symptoms, often produce no EEG change. Interpretation of an apparently negative ictal EEG depends on the nature of the seizure and correlation in time of EEG and behaviour to detect subtle changes.

Table 8.1 Stages in the selection and interpretation of clinical neurophysiological investigations

What is the clinical question?
↓
Which investigations are appropriate?
↓
Is there an abnormality?
↓
What does this mean in the clinical context?
↓
Which further investigations might be helpful?
↓
Does the combination of findings suggest a particular diagnosis or process?
↓
Will repeat investigations help?
↓
At what interval?

Ambulatory monitoring

Ambulatory cassette recorders permit recording outside the EEG laboratory. Each cassette runs for 24 hours between technical checks. Recording quality is inferior to that of telemetry, and this increases the difficulty of distinguishing EEG activity from artefact, which may be abundant in an actively moving child. There are also difficulties in synchronizing the recording with behaviour.

Ambulatory monitoring is no substitute for telemetry, for instance for detecting subtle seizures or deciding whether particular events are epileptic. However, it is invaluable for investigating a known EEG phenomenon in a particular situation, for instance to determine the frequency of absence seizures during school.

Brain mapping

As the EEG and EPs are distributed over a three-dimensional surface and change with time, ideally they should be presented using a five-dimensional display system. As this is not practical they are usually demonstrated in two dimensions as voltage/time curves. However, by adopting a stylized two-dimensional scalp outline and sacrificing information about changes in time, the distribution of the electrical field can be displayed as an isopotential contour map. This can highlight features of both EEGs and EPs which are not easily recognized in conventional displays. Mapping has, for instance, shown that the negative Rolandic spike of benign childhood epilepsy is typically accompanied by a midfrontal positive wave — an unusual distribution, as dipoles are rarely recognizable in the scalp EEG. Minor variations in the topography of this phenomenon appear to be clinically significant (Van Der Meij *et al.*, 1992). The technique depends critically on the skill of the user who must first identify those momentary, salient features of field distribution which justify closer inspection.

Mapping is also applied to quantitative results of EEG analysis, for instance, the total electrical power or the ratio between the amounts of activities in two frequency bands. Temporal information is again lost, as the analysis presents a time average of some EEG feature over one or more epochs, typically of many seconds. This user-friendly way of presenting quantitative information is fraught with problems. The values plotted at each site represent not the cerebral activity of that region, but the difference between the electrode and a reference. For instance, if the reference is obtained jointly from both ears and the patient has a temporal delta focus, a map may show maximum delta power in the contralateral central region. Any but the most sophisticated user, who hardly needs the help of mapping, is likely to interpret the map as showing an abnormality incorrectly localized and over the wrong hemisphere.

Interest in this long-established technique has been recently increased by developments in computer graphics. There is great appeal in the apparent demystification of the EEG and EPs by the substitution of simple coloured maps for long and complex chart tracings. Unfortunately, the appeal is greatest to those who least understand it. It must be hoped that the present misuse of this potentially valuable technique will prove a temporary aberration (Binnie & MacGillivray, 1992).

EEG FINDINGS IN PSYCHIATRIC DISORDERS

Autism

Clinical neurophysiological abnormalities have been reported more often in autism than in any other psychiatric condition in childhood (Small, 1987), but usually simply as evidence of an organic basis for the condition. The criteria for definition of autism, degrees of severity at the time of testing, EEG recording conditions (sleep or wakefulness), and the EEG abnormalities described have all varied widely. This complicates interpretation of the findings, but slow activity or discharges, generalized or in a variable focal distribution, will be found in around 30–40%. There is a relationship between IQ and the likelihood of finding EEG abnormalities: the more severely affected children are more likely to show changes.

Musumeci *et al.* (1988) found centrotemporal spikes in 5 of 12 men with fragile X syndrome, suggesting a significant association which might be diagnostically helpful and not simply related to the occurrence of seizures. However, focal, particularly centrotemporal, spikes are found in children with many different conditions; Wisniewski *et al.* (1991) calculated that the prevalence in autistic children did not exceed that seen in other patient populations. The diagnostic and pathophysiological significance of these findings remains very uncertain.

Routine EEG investigation of the autistic child does not seem warranted. Gillberg and colleagues suggested that at least some children may have complex partial seizures, affecting behaviour (Gillberg & Schaumann, 1983, Olsson *et al.*, 1988) but there is no real evidence that seizures in autism are especially likely to take this form. Seizures in autism need to be investigated as in any other child. Identification of persistent EEG foci with changes during episodic behaviour disturbances should identify children who might respond to anticonvulsant treatment.

EP studies, particularly of the auditory system, have been widely used to test various hypotheses concerning putative defects in acquisition and/or processing of sensory information. Between a third and a half of autistic patients show impairment of function in the auditory pathways, particularly through the upper brainstem (Thivierge *et al.*, 1990; Wisniewski *et al.*, 1991). However, it remains difficult to assess the clinical relevance of this finding and routine BAEP studies are not indicated.

Grillon *et al.* (1989) examined MLAEPs (and BAEPs) in 8 nonretarded autistic subjects and found no alterations. Buchwald *et al.* (1992) believe that the reductions found in the P1 component in drowsiness and sleep in 11 young autistic adults represent alterations in the reticular activating system. However, it appears that all MLAEPs in children are rather inconstantly recordable under the age of 8 years (Suzuki *et al.*, 1983, Kraus *et al.*, 1985), which would complicate interpretation of findings in young autistic children.

Schizophrenia

No constant EEG abnormalities have been reported in schizophrenia during childhood. Although polygraphic sleep studies have suggested that there is reduced REM latency in schizophrenic patients, the results have been variable and this may be accounted for, in part, by methodological problems and the effects of treatment (Thaker *et al.*, 1990). There are therefore no indications for routine clinical neurophysiological studies.

Attention deficit disorders

Interpretation of neurophysiological findings in these disorders is complicated by differences in both clinical classification and methodology. There are no specific indications for conventional neurophysiological studies.

SPECIFIC LEARNING DISORDERS

Clinical neurophysiological findings have been used by various groups to support organic models of dyslexia and other less well-defined disorders. Conners (1978) noted that while many studies had reported EEG abnormalities in dyslexic children, the nature of these abnormalities varied between the different studies and that strict definitions of dyslexia were not used. It is worth bearing these strictures in mind when considering subsequent claims for more subtle abnormalities which often depend on finding differences between the patient and normal populations using increasingly complex statistical measures. Some studies have used small numbers of subjects and a few have not incorporated a control group.

Reading disorders

There is as yet no consensus despite numerous studies of dyslexics as to whether there are characteristic features in the EEG. For example, many EEG investigations of dyslexia have shown coherence differences between the two hemispheres, but methodological difficulties (French & Beaumont, 1984) were not always appreciated in the older studies. Galin *et al.* (1992) have reviewed criteria for selection and methods in this difficult area of research, stressing the importance of examining dyslexic and normal readers during both silent and oral reading.

Dysphasia

Acquired dysphasia
(Landau–Kleffner syndrome)

Landau and Kleffner (1957) described 6 children (including

siblings) with acquired dysphasia who had discharges in their EEGs and who improved with anticonvulsant treatment. An association between a prompt improvement in the EEG with treatment and a satisfactory clinical outcome continues to be reported (Lerman *et al.*, 1991), but individual cases may be left with language deficits (van Dongen *et al.*, 1989).

The nature of the relationship between the discharges and the dysphasia is much debated. The two main hypotheses are that the discharges and the dysphasia are epiphenomena related to a single underlying cause, or that the dysphasia is a direct consequence of focal discharges. On reviewing the condition, Deonna (1991) cited the absence of structural pathology and improvement with anticonvulsant treatment in favour of the latter explanation, a view supported by magnetoencephalographic studies (Paetau *et al.*, 1991). Cole *et al.* (1988) reported that EEG discharges were generalized, bilateral, multifocal or with shifting predominance, but with a mainly temporal distribution in 85% of cases, and unilateral and again predominantly temporal in the remaining 15%.

Although Landau and Kleffner defined their syndrome (q.v.) as one of acquired dysphasia, other evidence (Maccario *et al.*, 1982) suggested that it may also present as developmental dysphasia. Presentation of each form in a pair of monozygotic twins (Echenne, 1990) lends strong support to this view.

Developmental language disorders

In common with many disorders, estimates of the prevalence of EEG abnormalities in children with developmental language disorders is complicated by the fact that the condition is heterogeneous and that children are much more likely to have an EEG if seizures are suspected. In a survey of 237 dysphasic children without evidence of autism, Tuchman *et al.* (1991) found that EEGs had been carried out on all 19 with epilepsy but on only 66 (30%) without seizures. EEG abnormalities, mainly epileptiform changes, were found in 63% of those with seizures and 20% of those without. Both the proportion and the type of EEG changes were similar to those seen in a comparison group of 314 children with autism.

Such findings make it difficult to devise definitive guidelines for identifying children with language disorders who might benefit from anticonvulsant medication, particularly as marked variability in abundance and distribution of discharges in serial sleep records has been emphasized (Deonna, 1991). However, most patients with the Landau–Kleffner syndrome show continuous temporal or bitemporal discharges during sleep at some stage. It would therefore seem reasonable to consider the diagnosis in those children where the EEG during sleep shows frequent or continuous discharges predominantly in the temporal regions, and to adopt a more sceptical approach when the discharges are only sporadic and mainly extratemporal. In patients in whom speech disturbance is clearly episodic (and occurring several times per week), ictal recording may be warranted.

Although early reports emphasized the occurrence of BAEP abnormalities, these are much less apparent when clearly organic disorders are excluded.

CLINICAL NEUROPHYSIOLOGICAL INVESTIGATIONS IN MENTAL HANDICAP

Associations between particular conditions and neurophysiological findings have usually been of more immediate clinical assistance than efforts to define the nature of changes related to mental handicap. Many children with mental handicap have normal EEGs; in most others, abnormalities are nonspecific and inconstant. In a small number of conditions neurophysiological findings are sufficiently distinctive and consistently associated to suggest the diagnosis. Unusual neurophysiological features shared by retarded sibs can also be used to help delineate a recognizable syndrome (Baraitser & Winter, 1992).

Chromosomal abnormalities

Down's syndrome

Infantile spasms are not uncommon in Down's syndrome (Gregoriades & Pampiglione, 1966) and the EEG features are similar to those associated with other conditions. The notion that other forms of seizures are rare in children with Down's syndrome has been discarded; Guerrini *et al.* (1990) suggested that reflex seizures are common (20% of their series) in children with Down's syndrome and epilepsy and speculated that this might be related to increased cortical excitability. The risks of neurological deficit due to cervicomedullary compression seem to be less than originally feared, but in those cases where further investigation seems warranted, SEPs are a useful component of the assessment (Pueschel *et al.*, 1987).

Angelman's syndrome

The EEG in Angelman's syndrome shows a distinctive pattern consisting of three different elements (Table 8.2) found in variable proportions in the same or in serial records (Boyd *et al.*, 1988). These EEG changes are not present at birth but develop in the first year of life (Bower & Jeavons, 1967) and are present during both wakefulness and sleep. The abnormalities are most striking in the younger children, and the amplitude of these changes tends to decrease with age, though this is not invariable.

Table 8.2 EEG abnormalities in Angelman's syndrome. (More than one is usually present)

1 Persistent rhythmic 4–6 c/s activities, often reaching more than 200 µV, not associated with drowsiness.
2 Prolonged runs of rhythmic 2–3 c/s activity reaching 200–500 µV, often more prominent anteriorly and sometimes associated with discharges forming ill-defined spike-and-wave complexes.
3 Spikes mixed with 3–4 c/s components reaching 200 µV or more, mainly posteriorly and facilitated by or only seen during eye closure.

The EEG changes have been interpreted as epileptiform, with children receiving large doses of anticonvulsants without benefit. However, EEGs taken during periods when they appear 'out of touch' may show features of nonconvulsive status epilepticus. More intensive anticonvulsant treatment at these times restores both alertness and the distinctive EEG features. By contrast, no striking EEG changes are seen in Prader–Willi syndrome, the other condition associated with mental handicap and a similar chromosome deletion. Conventional clinical EP investigations have not shown clinically useful changes in either condition.

Rett's syndrome

There is a clustering of EEG features in Rett's syndrome which may evolve with the clinical stages of the disease (Glaze *et al.*, 1985). EEG development is normal until about 18 months of age, when there is often loss of sleep spindles and normal rhythmic activities. Discharges appear, solely or especially during sleep (Hagberg *et al.*, 1983), mostly over the parasagittal and centrotemporal regions whether or not clinical seizures have occurred (Robb *et al.*, 1989; Aldrich *et al.*, 1990). In the later stages, repetitive bursts of slow components are seen during sleep (Hagne *et al.*, 1989), but in our own experience this is rather variable. In some girls, discharges are related to obsessive finger tapping and can also be elicited by passive finger tapping by the EEG technician during recording. It was found in a third of the cases seen by Robb *et al.* (1989).

Episodic hyperventilation and apnoea during waking, sometimes leading to cyanosis or even to loss of consciousness (Lugaresi *et al.*, 1985), has also been studied; Elian & Rudolf, (1991) found bursts of high-amplitude slow waves associated with apnoea and faster activities during hyperventilation or normal breathing. Although the breathing pattern is normal during sleep, Nomura *et al.* (1984) found abnormalities of tonic and phasic components of sleep and of incremental increase in REM sleep with increasing age.

EPs showed variable abnormalities in 9 girls aged 10–12 years investigated by Bader *et al.* (1989a,b).

Neuronal migration defects

The reported frequency of neuronal migration defects in children with varying degrees of mental handicap and/or epilepsy has increased with improved diagnostic imaging. Lissencephaly, the most severe of these abnormalities, has been shown to be associated with striking patterns of high-amplitude rhythmic activity in the EEG. Gastaut *et al.* (1987) found this pattern in 13 of 15 cases with proven lissencephaly and concluded that, below the age of 1 year, it was virtually specific for this malformation. They speculate that this appearance may be related to different orientation of the cortical neurons. In older children, widespread slow activity may be the only feature (Hakamada *et al.*, 1979).

Type 2 lissencephaly, with hydrocephalus, is associated with eye defects (Borardier *et al.*, 1984) and congenital muscular dystrophy (Heyer *et al.*, 1986) and clinical neurophysiological investigations, including ERG and EMG, are helpful.

NEUROLOGICAL DISORDERS WITH PSYCHIATRIC CONSEQUENCES

Epilepsy

The EEG and the classification of the epilepsies

Epileptic disorders are described in terms of syndromes, and within the general framework of a classification of the epilepsies (ILAE Commission on Terminology and Classification, 1989). The classification distinguishes generalized epilepsies, in which seizures apparently arise in both hemispheres, and partial (or localization-related) epilepsies in which seizure onset is in a circumscribed cortical area. A division is also made between symptomatic epilepsies in patients with structural brain disease, cryptogenic epilepsies in which the pathology is presumed but unproven, and idiopathic epilepsies arising in an intact brain. These criteria are reflected in the EEG. In idiopathic generalized epilepsies both ictal and interictal discharges are generalized, often with a frontal emphasis, as typified by the bilateral spike-and-wave activity in absences. Partial epilepsies are accompanied by focal discharges, both at seizure onset and in the interictal state. These are not, however, necessarily detectable in the scalp EEG (see the section on pathological EEG phenomena, above). Both partial seizures and focal discharges may spread to involve homologous regions of both hemispheres, or become generalized. In some patients, the secondarily generalized phenomena may dominate the picture and the underlying focal elements pass undetected. In symptomatic generalized epilepsies, both multifocal and generalized interictal discharges are usually found, against a diffusely abnormal background, reflecting the generalized cerebral pathology.

EEG features of epilepsy syndromes of childhood and adolescence

Many epileptic syndromes are described in childhood and all present characteristic EEG features. Those seen in the neonatal period will not be considered here.

West's syndrome (infantile spasms) is typically associated with a chaotic EEG pattern termed hypsarrhythmia, characterized by diffuse high-voltage irregular slow waves with multifocal sharp waves and spikes. During seizures there is usually a reduction of amplitude, often with the appearance of fast activity, preceded by an initial high-voltage slow wave with or without a spike. In some instances the ictal EEG consists of high-amplitude slow waves and spikes. In many patients this condition subsequently evolves into the Lennox–Gastaut syndrome.

Febrile convulsions are seizures, usually tonic–clonic, occurring with fever. Postictal slowing of background activity reflects the length of the seizure, but except where gross cerebral pathology is present, the EEG is of little value for predicting the subsequent development of epilepsy.

The Lennox–Gastaut syndrome is a form of symptomatic or cryptogenic generalized epilepsy presenting in mid-childhood and characterized by atonic and axial tonic seizures, atypical absences, myoclonic jerks and generalized tonic–clonic as well as partial seizures. The EEG is grossly abnormal with features of symptomatic generalized epilepsy, but in particular slow spike-and-wave EEG activity (at less than 2.5 c/s) is among the diagnostic criteria of the syndrome.

Benign myoclonic epilepsy in infancy presents after 6 months of age with single generalized myoclonic seizures. The waking EEG contains occasional spike-and-wave discharges, increasing during sleep.

By contrast, severe myoclonic epilepsy in infancy is characterized by generalized clonic and myoclonic seizures, partial seizures and atypical absences. The EEG is normal initially but later develops fast generalized spike-and-wave discharges and focal abnormalities.

Myoclonic astatic epilepsy of early childhood is a form of idiopathic generalized epilepsy presenting in, or soon after, late infancy, usually with generalized tonic–clonic seizures. The interictal EEG is initially normal or contains excess theta activity. Later myoclonic jerks and astatic fits develop and the EEG shows irregular fast spike-and-wave activity. Many patients are photosensitive.

Absence seizures occur in various forms of idiopathic generalized epilepsy. Childhood absence epilepsy appears at 6–7 years, with various types of absence seizure, but without myoclonus. The EEG shows classical 3 c/s spike-and-wave activity against a normal background. Despite very frequent seizures, prognosis is good; three-quarters of the patients become seizure-free, but the remainder continue to suffer absences or develop tonic–clonic seizures at puberty or in early adult life.

Epilepsy with myoclonic absences differs from the above in that the seizures are accompanied by myoclonus and the prognosis is less favourable, with respect to response to treatment, subsequent development of other seizure types, and mental deterioration. The EEG findings are similar to those in childhood absence epilepsy.

Juvenile absence epilepsy presents at puberty. The seizures are generally less frequent than in the childhood syndrome, but most of the patients also develop tonic–clonic seizures. All types of absence seizure occur. The EEG shows spike-and-wave activity, typically slightly faster than 3 c/s.

Benign partial epilepsy of childhood with Rolandic spikes is characterized by focal seizures with somatosensory symptoms, mainly during sleep. Prognosis for seizure control and for eventual remission is good. The EEG shows frequent centro-temporal spikes or sharp waves of high amplitude (sometimes exceeding 300 μV) often followed by a slow wave. Twenty per cent of patients also show generalized spikes and waves or polyspikes and waves which are activated during slow wave and REM sleep. A liability to Rolandic spikes has a genetic component and many children with this EEG abnormality have no overt seizures.

Benign partial epilepsy of childhood with occipital foci is accompanied by interictal posterior temporal occipital spike-and-wave activity or sharp waves. The seizures are characterized by visual symptoms, nausea and vomiting and occasionally hemiconvulsions.

Electrical status epilepticus during slow sleep is a condition which is probably underdiagnosed, presenting as a progressive neuropsychological deterioration, affecting language and memory in particular. Various types of seizure may occur and these are often mainly nocturnal. Prolonged sleep EEG recording is required to recognize the syndrome: spike-and-wave activity is present during the greater part of slow wave sleep. The condition is self-limiting, but the prognosis for psychological function is poor.

A similar condition, often accompanied by electrical status epilepticus during slow sleep is the Landau−Kleffner syndrome. Again there is cognitive deterioration, particularly affecting language, but epilepsy occurs in only two-thirds of the patients and is rarely severe. The EEG shows diffuse, or focal, usually bilateral spike-and-wave discharges, in waking and marked activation during sleep. This syndrome is considered more fully above.

Chronic progressive epilepsia continua of childhood may be due either to a discrete cerebral lesion or to more diffuse Rasmussen's encephalitis. In the former case focal EEG discharges occur against a normal background. In Rasmussen's syndrome there is a marked diffuse abnormality of background activity and often bilateral discharges; the encephalitic process is usually unilateral and the EEG is asymmetrical, but progressive destruction of one hemisphere may reduce all EEG activities, so that the discharges are paradoxically of greater amplitude on the unaffected side.

Juvenile myoclonic epilepsy is due to a known genetic defect involving chromosome 6. It presents with irregular bilateral myoclonic jerks, generally worst within an hour of waking. The EEG shows both ictal and interictal irregular, fast multiple spike-and-wave discharges; many patients are photosensitive. Later tonic−clonic seizures may appear. Medication is effective but often needs to be prolonged.

Another syndrome of adolescence continuing into adulthood is epilepsy with generalized tonic−clonic seizures on awakening. The background EEG activity is often abnormal and various types of generalized spike-and-wave discharges occur.

The progressive myoclonic epilepsies of childhood and adolescence include various unrelated disorders with the common clinical features of myoclonus, other types of seizure, progressive mental deterioration and variable neurological symptoms. Various specific neurodegenerative conditions fall in this group, and some have characteristic EEG features. However, in general the EEG shows bursts of spikes, spike-and-wave activity and multiple spikes and slow waves, with slowing of ongoing activity and disruption of sleep patterns.

EEG investigation of children with epilepsy

It is a truism that epilepsy is a clinical diagnosis, to which the EEG can add only confirmatory evidence. In general the EEG is of greater value in identifying syndromes than for establishing, or excluding, epilepsy. Thus, slow spike-and-wave activity is among the diagnostic criteria of the Lennox−Gastaut syndrome, and (without an adequate history) benign childhood epilepsy is often first identified by the EEG finding of Rolandic spikes. If in a particular clinical context the EEG excludes the only plausible syndrome, another diagnosis should be considered. For instance, if a child reported to be inattentive overbreathes for 3 minutes hard enough to produce EEG slowing, and does not exhibit spike-and-wave activity, active absence epilepsy can be excluded, and some other explanation should be sought.

Using the EEG as a screening test for epilepsy without adequate clinical evidence is rarely helpful, particularly in children with 'soft' signs of organic cerebral disease. Thus, only an ictal EEG will establish an epileptic basis for episodic behavioural disturbances in a handicapped, presumably brain-damaged child; interictal epileptiform discharges are without diagnostic significance in this context.

Some scenarios will be briefly considered:

1 Routine investigation of newly diagnosed epilepsy. The EEG may help to identify the syndrome, with implications for management and prognosis. Significant, unexpected findings sometimes arise — photosensitivity, or frequent unrecognized seizures, for instance. If a waking record does not provide the information required, a sleep tracing should always be obtained; this increases the yield of abnormal findings, especially in partial epilepsies, and may be crucial to early identification of benign childhood epilepsy or electrical status epilepticus during slow sleep.

2 Screening of children with an increased risk or doubtful evidence of epilepsy. Abnormal findings should be interpreted cautiously. Spiky EEG phenomena unrelated to epilepsy (6 and 14 c/s positive spikes, for instance) should be ignored. Rolandic spikes, photosensitivity and generalized spike-and-wave activity may reflect a genetic liability, rather than an active seizure disorder. However, such findings justify further enquiry, which may, for instance, reveal previously unrecognized ictal events related to visual stimuli: myoclonus in proximity to a television set, self-inducing behaviour, etc.

During apparently subclinical EEG discharges, unexpected ictal events may be detected. If the child sits upright with outstretched arms during recording, momentary loss of muscle tone may be shown to accompany the discharges. Psychological tests administered under EEG monitoring often detect transitory cognitive impairment associated with seemingly subclinical discharges. These findings may have clinical implications in a child with learning difficulties; in any case, such events are technically epileptic seizures.

3 Investigation of episodic abnormal behaviour. The only reliable method of establishing that a particular episodic behaviour is epileptic is by demonstrating ictal EEG changes.

This applies equally to children with known epilepsy and to those without. The dangers of misinterpreting an interictal EEG abnormality in this context were noted above. The practicalities of capturing an ictal EEG depend on the frequency, nature and circumstances of occurrence of the episodes (see the section on long-term EEG monitoring, above). It must be recognized, however, that even intensive monitoring may not solve the problem. If the seizures are infrequent they are unlikely to be captured at all, and if of certain types, may not produce ictal EEG changes. Referral for EEG investigation of episodic behavioural disorder should be selective and not viewed as a panacea for this common problem.

Neurodegenerative disease

Clinical neurophysiological findings can help identify individuals who may be suffering from a neurodegenerative disease, as a number of distinctive patterns have been associated with various conditions (Boyd & Harden, 1991). They may also suggest that the child does *not* have a neurodegenerative disorder by demonstrating some other process leading to a decline in behaviour or performance, notably nonconvulsive status epilepticus.

Subacute sclerosing panencephalitis

The association between subacute sclerosing panencephalitis and periodic complexes in the EEG is probably one of the best known electroclinical associations. Despite this, cases are still missed, often due to a failure to consider the condition. This may be because of an unusual presentation such as visual disturbance (8.75% of a series of 80 children; Pampiglione & Harden, 1986) or because behavioural disturbances or fits initially suggest other conditions. The EEG complexes themselves may not be striking or their significance may be dismissed because of the presence of normal activities, including alpha rhythm.

Cerebral lipoidoses

Batten's disease (ceroid lipofuscinosis) is the most important of this group of disorders. Distinctive neurophysiological findings in the different forms have been useful in helping to identify affected children. In the juvenile form, the child presents at around 5–6 years of age with visual symptoms and may be referred to the psychiatrist if no ophthalmic cause is found. By this time the ERG is usually absent and the flash VEP is poorly formed or absent. The EEG shows runs of sharp waves and slower components at around 2 c/s in about 50% of cases.

Variant forms of this group of disorders are not infrequent and Santavuori *et al.* (1991) have emphasized the wider spectrum of clinical presentation. In one personal case, a girl presenting with a progressive dementia without any other clinical features was eventually shown to have Batten's disease on biopsy following the unexpected finding of a small ERG.

Leukodystrophies

Behavioural abnormalities in boys with adrenoleukodystrophy are well-known, but visual symptoms often predominate. Affected boys are often able to cooperate with measurement of the pattern-reversal VEP, which usually shows increased latency of P100. However, this finding is not invariable even in clinically advancing cases and though the BAEPs are often affected, EP changes seem to be consistently less marked than in other forms of leukodystrophy (Pitt *et al.*, 1991).

Sleep disorders

Sleep disorders in children have been characterized as both underdiagnosed and undertreated (Stores, 1990). A comprehensive classification of diagnostic criteria, including neurophysiological findings, was published in 1990 (Thorpy, 1990). Technical aspects of making polysomnographic recordings in infants, children and adolescents have also been reviewed (Guilleminault & Philip, 1992; Hoppenbrouwers, 1992; Keenan, 1992). However, most of these disorders, including night terrors (Guilleminault & Silvestri, 1982), are rarely associated with seizures or with EEG abnormalities. Different disorders may be associated with particular phases of sleep (see Table 8.3).

Epileptic disorders manifesting as abnormal movements during sleep (especially frontal lobe seizures) are also difficult to recognize (Stores *et al.*, 1991) and often have to be considered in the differential diagnosis, e.g. the case for nocturnal paroxysmal dystonia as a nonepileptic condition has been challenged (Meierkord *et al.*, 1992).

A summary of polysomnographic and EEG findings in sleep disorders seen mainly in childhood and adolescence is shown in Table 8.3.

FUTURE DEVELOPMENTS

The history of clinical neurophysiological investigations in psychiatry and psychology has been one of high hopes succeeded by disappointment as each technique in turn proved unable to sustain the expectations placed upon it. It is to be hoped that some of the lessons have now been learnt, and that the importance of careful definition of the type of disorder being investigated and equally careful patient selection will lead to much greater progress. The experience with EEG and latterly EPs should be borne in mind when considering the claims of topographic mapping and ERPs. The need to establish reliable norms, and proper caution in establishing the limits and strengths of any new technique, is fundamental.

Conventional techniques, used carefully and in combination both with each other and with other methods of investigation, are still capable of providing valuable insights into psychological processes both in normal children and in those with psychiatric disease. This is likely to be enhanced by improved applications of the powerful mathematical tools provided by digital signal processing, though the importance of ensuring

Table 8.3 Electroencephalogram (EEG) and polysomnographic features in some sleep disorders of infancy, childhood and adolescence (after Thorpy, 1990). See text for epileptic and mental disorders

Disorder	Typical age of onset	Polysomnographic features	EEG features
DYSSOMNIAS			
Intrinsic sleep disorders			
Idiopathic insomnia (childhood-onset insomnia)	Birth	Sleep spindles may be poorly formed and somnograms difficult to score. Long periods of REM sleep without eye movements	Varied, minor nonspecific abnormalities are common
Narcolepsy	Second decade. Peak incidence 14 years	Short sleep latency. Sleep-onset REM can be associated with hypnogogic hallucinations	Often features of drowsiness. Eye opening may increase alpha activity
Recurrent hypersomnia (Kleine–Levin syndrome)	Adolescence	High sleep efficiency. Reduced stage 3 and 4 sleep	Low-voltage slow activity or diffuse alpha activity
Idiopathic hypersomnia (NREM narcolepsy)	Adolescence	Normal	Normal
Obstructive sleep apnoea	Any age	Complex and varied. Some have initial central apnoea followed by obstruction (mixed type). Short sleep latency; occasionally sleep-onset REM	Normal
Central alveolar hypoventilation	Idiopathic; adolescence Acquired: any age	Periods of oxygen desaturation worse in REM sleep. Frequent arousals, body movements	Normal
Restless legs syndrome	Any age (mostly in middle age)	Sustained tonic EMG activity alternates between legs, occurs in antagonistic muscles during flexion and extension of legs	Normal (wake) EMG and nerve conduction studies usual in young subjects
Extrinsic sleep disorders			
Adjustment sleep disorder (transient psychological insomnia)	Any age	Very variable	Normal
Limit-setting sleep disorder (childhood insomnia)	2–3 years variable	Normal	Normal
Sleep-onset association disorder	6 months	Normal	Normal
Food allergy insomnia (food intolerance)	In first to second year	Frequent arousals. No preceding EEG change	Normal
Nocturnal eating (drinking) syndrome	6 months	Normal except for increased waking	Normal
Stimulant-dependent sleep disorder (stimulant sleep suppression)	Adolescence	↑ Sleep and REM latency. ↓ Total sleep and REM time. Rebound on stimulant withdrawal; MSLT may then resemble narcolepsy	Normal
Circadian rhythm sleep disorders			
Irregular sleep–wake pattern	Variable	Paucity of information	↓ Sleep spindles and K-complexes ± changes associated with underlying cerebral condition
Delayed sleep phase syndrome	Adolescence	↑ Sleep latency. Some ↓ REM latency	Normal
Non-24-hour sleep–wake syndrome	Variable. Usually blind infant/child	Paucity of information	↓ Sleep spindles and K-complexes ± changes associated with any underlying cerebral problem

Continued on p. 124

Table 8.3 *Continued*

Disorder	Typical age of onset	Polysomnographic features	EEG features
PARASOMNIAS *Arousal disorders*			
Confusional arousals (sleep drunkenness)	<5 years	Arousals from slow wave sleep, especially first third of night	Slow activity during episode, otherwise normal
Sleepwalking	4–8 years	Begins in stage 3 or 4 sleep	Normal*
Sleep terrors (night terrors)	Childhood	Especially in stage 3 or 4 sleep	Normal*
Sleep–wake transition disorders			
Rhythmic movement disorder (head-banging, body-rocking)	Usually <1year	Episodes in drowsiness or (mainly) light sleep	Normal*
Parasomnias usually associated with REM sleep			
Nightmares	Any age 3–6 years	Abrupt awakening from REM sleep. ↑ REM duration and density	Normal
Sleep paralysis	Adolescence	Loss of tone, ↓ EMG activity, H reflex studies; ↓ anterior horn cell excitability as in REM sleep	Slow activity and/or pendular eye movements during episode
Other parasomnias			
Bruxism (tooth grinding)	10–20 years	↑ Masseter and temporalis activity; stage 2 sleep	Normal
Sleep enuresis	Primary from infancy Secondary any age	Episodes in all sleep stages, also wakefulness	Occasionally associated with epilepsy — discharges may be found
Nocturnal paroxysmal dystonia	Variable	Episodes mainly in stage 2, but also in stage 3 or 4 sleep. EEG desynchronization; no discharges	Normal*
Infant sleep apnoea (apparent life-threatening event)	First days to weeks of life	Usually no abnormalities. Prematures; AS > QS	*Rarely* associated with localized discharges†
Benign neonatal sleep myoclonus	First week of life	EMG bursts lasting 40–30 ms, usually in QS	Normal*
Psychiatric sleep disorders			
Psychosis	Adolescence	Very variable	(See text)
Mood disorders (depressive disorder)	Childhood and adolescence	Typically ↓ delta and ↑ REM sleep. Short REM latency. ↑ density REM. Findings in children and adolescents less marked, c.f. adults	Normal
Anxiety disorder	Any age	Mild changes. ↑ Sleep latency, ↑ stage 1 and 2 sleep	Normal

AS, Active sleep; EMG, electromyogram; QS, quiet sleep; MSLT, multiple sleep latency test; NREM, non-rapid eye movement; REM, rapid eye movement.
* Normal: Useful contribution by excluding other conditions in differential diagnosis.
† Watanabe *et al.* (1982).

that the signals obtained from the patient are of the highest quality must never be forgotten. The recent upsurge in intra-operative neurophysiological monitoring will afford great opportunities for research and is likely to refine our understanding of the correct interpretation of standard investigations.

In addition, it will be possible to activate specific pathways and study their function with much greater accuracy. Examples of this include stimulation of central motor pathways (see Rothwell *et al.*, 1991 for a review) — there are as yet no specific clinical indications. The ability to study small myelinated and unmyelinated nerve fibre pathways selectively, using various laser techniques, may improve understanding of nociception (Bromm & Treede, 1991).

Clinical applications of biomagnetic recordings have moved closer with the development of multichannel magnetometers, and combined EEG and MEG (magnetoencephalographic) studies are proposed (Mauguière, 1992), though widespread clinical use of the technique still seems some way off.

Rather than being superseded by other techniques, it seems more likely that clinical neurophysiological investigations will continue to provide unique information on the function of the nervous system. While new techniques of data collection and manipulation may prove useful, cross-reference to other investigations and other methods of studying the nervous system are also likely to be fruitful. As a consequence, the quality and relevance of this information seem likely to improve markedly due to improvements in its interpretation and in our confidence concerning its clinical and biological significance.

REFERENCES

Aldrich M.S., Garofalo E.A. & Drury I. (1990) Epileptiform abnormalities during sleep in Rett syndrome. *Electroencephalography and Clinical Neurophysiology*, **75**, 365–370.

Bader G.G., Witt-Engerstrom I. & Hagberg B. (1989a) Neurophysiological findings in the Rett syndrome: I: EMG, conduction velocity, EEG and somatosensory evoked potential studies. *Brain and Development*, **11**, 102–109.

Bader G.G., Witt-Engerstrom I. & Hagberg B. (1989b) Neurophysiological findings in the Rett syndrome: II: Visual and auditory brainstem, middle and late evoked responses. *Brain and Development*, **11**, 110–114.

Baraitser M. & Winter R. (1992) *The London Neurology Database*. Oxford University Press, Oxford.

Bickford R.G., Sem-Jacobsen C.W., White P.T. & Daly D. (1952) Some observations on the mechanism of photic and photo-metrazol activation. *Electroencephalography and Clinical Neurophysiology*, **4**, 275–282.

Binnie C.D. & MacGillivray B.B. (1992) Brain mapping — a useful tool or a dangerous toy? *Journal of Neurology, Neurosurgery and Psychiatry*, **55**, 527–529.

Borardier C., Aicardi J. & Goutieres F. (1984) Congenital hydrocephalus and eye abnormalities with severe developmental brain defects: Warburg's syndrome. *Annals of Neurology*, **16**, 60–65.

Bower B.D. & Jeavons P.M. (1967). The 'happy puppet' syndrome. *Archives of Disease in Childhood*, **42**, 298–302.

Boyd S.G. & Harden A. (1991). Clinical neurophysiology of the central nervous system. In: Brett E.M. (ed) *Paediatric Neurology*, pp. 717–795. Churchill Livingstone, Edinburgh.

Boyd S., Harden A. & Patton M.A. (1988) The EEG in the early diagnosis of the Angelman (happy puppet) syndrome. *European Journal of Paediatrics*, **147**, 508–513.

Bromm B. & Treede R.D. (1991) Laser-evoked potentials in the assessment of cutaneous pain sensitivity in normal subjects and patients. *Revue Neurologique (Paris)*, **147**, 625–643.

Buchwald J.S. & Erwin R., van Lancker D., Guthrie D., Schwafel J. & Tanguay P. (1992) Midlatency auditory evoked responses: P1 abnormalities in adult autistic subjects. *Electroencephalography and Clinical Neurophysiology*, **84**, 164–171.

Cole A.J., Andermann F., Taylor L., Olivier A., Rasmussen T., Robitaille Y. & Spire J.P. (1988) The Landau–Kleffner syndrome of acquired epileptic aphasia: unusual clinical outcome, surgical experience, and absence of encephalitis. *Neurology*, **38**, 31–38.

Conners C.K. (1978) Critical review of 'electroencephalographic and neurophysiological studies in dyslexia'. In: Benton A.L. & Pearl D. (eds) *Dyslexia: An Appraisal of Current Knowledge*, pp. 251–264. Oxford University Press, New York.

Dement W. & Kleitman N. (1957) Cyclic variations in EEG during sleep and their relation to eye movements, body motility, and dreaming. *Electroencephalography and Clinical Neurophysiology*, **9**, 673–690.

Deonna T.W. (1991) Acquired epileptiform aphasia in children (Landau–Kleffner syndrome). *Journal of Clinical Neurophysiology*, **8**, 288–298.

Doose H. & Gerken H. (1973) On the genetics of EEG-anomalies in childhood: IV. Photoconvulsive reaction. *Neuropaediatrie*, **4**, 162–171.

Dümermuth G. (1968) Variance spectra of electroencephalograms in twins — a contribution to the problem of quantification of EEG background activity in childhood. In: Kellaway P. & Petersén I. (eds) *Clinical Electroencephalography of Children*, pp. 119–154. Almquist and Wiksell, Stockholm.

Echenne B. (1990) Les formes sévères de retard de langage chez l'enfant. *Revue Internationale de Pediatrie*, **201**, 5–11.

Elian M. & Rudolf N. de M. (1991) EEG and respiration in Rett syndrome. *Acta Neurologica Scandinavica*, **83**, 123–128.

French C.C. & Beaumont J.G. (1984). A critical review of EEG coherence studies of hemisphere function. *International Journal of Psychophysiology*, **1**, 241–254.

Galin D., Raz J., Fein G., Johnstone J., Herron J. & Yingling C. (1992) EEG spectra in dyslexic and normal readers during normal and silent reading. *Electroencephalography and Clinical Neurophysiology*, **82**, 87–101.

Gastaut H., Pinsard N., Raybaud C.L., Aicardi J. & Zifkin B. (1987) Lissencephaly (agyria-pachygyria): clinical findings and serial EEG studies. *Developmental Medicine and Child Neurology*, **29**, 167–180.

Gillberg C. & Schaumann H. (1983) Epilepsy presenting as infantile autism? Two case studies. *Neuropediatrics*, **14**, 206–212.

Glaze D.G., Frost J.D., el Hibri H.Y. & Percy A.K. (1985) Rett's syndrome: polygraphic electroencephalographic-video characterization of sleep and respiratory patterns during sleep and wakefulness. *Annals of Neurology*, **18**, 417–418.

Gloor P., Kalabay O. & Giard N. (1968) The electroencephalogram in diffuse encephalopathies: electroencephalographic correlates of grey and white matter lesions. *Brain*, **91**, 779–802.

Gregoriades A. & Pampiglione G. (1966) Seizures in children with Down's syndrome. *Electroencephalography and Clinical Neurophysiology*, **21**, 307.

Grillon C., Courchesne E. & Akshoomoff N. (1989) Brainstem and middle latency auditory evoked potentials in autism and developmental language disorder. *Journal of Autism and Developmental Disorders*, **19**, 255–269.

Guerrini R., Genton P., Bureau M., Dravet C. & Roger J. (1990) Reflex seizures are frequent in patients with Down's syndrome and epilepsy. *Epilepsia*, **31**, 406–417.

Guilleminault C. & Philip P. (1992) Polygraphic investigation of respiration during sleep in infants and children. *Journal of Clinical Neurophysiology*, **9**, 48–55.

Guilleminault C. & Silvestri R. (1982) Disorders of arousal and epilepsy during sleep. In: Sterman M.B., Shouse M.N. & Passouant P. (eds) *Sleep and Epilepsy*, pp. 513–529. Academic Press, New York.

Hagberg B., Aicardi J., Dias K. & Ramos O. (1983) A progressive syndrome of autism, dementia and loss of purposeful hand use in girls: Rett's syndrome: a report of 35 cases. *Annals of Neurology*, **14**, 471–479.

Hagne I., Witt-Engerström I. & Hagberg B. (1989) EEG development in Rett syndrome. A study of 30 cases. *Electroencephalography and Clinical Neurophysiology*, **72**, 1–6.

Hakamada S., Watanabe K., Hara K. & Miyazaki S. (1979) The evolution of electroencephalographic features in lissencephaly syndrome. *Brain and Development*, **1**, 277–283.

Heyer R., Ehrich J., Goebel H.H., Christen H.J. & Hanefeld F. (1986) Congenital muscular dystrophy with cerebral and ocular malformation (cerebro-oculo-muscular syndrome). *Brain and Development*, **8**, 614–619.

Hoppenbrouwers T. (1992) Polysomnography in newborns and young infants: sleep architecture. *Journal of Clinical Neurophysiology*, **9**, 32–47.

ILAE Commission on Terminology and Classification (1989) Proposal for a revised classification of epilepsies and epileptic syndromes. *Epilepsia*, **30**, 389–399.

Keenan S.A. (1992) Polysomnography: technical aspects in adolescents and adults. *Journal of Clinical Neurophysiology*, **9**, 21–31.

Kraus N., Smith D.I., Reed N.I., Stein I.K. & Cartlee C. (1985) Auditory middle latency responses in children: effect of age and diagnostic category. *Electroencephalography and Clinical Neurophysiology*, **62**, 343–359.

Landau W.M. & Kleffner F.R. (1957) Syndrome of acquired aphasia with convulsive disorder. *Neurology*, **7**, 523–530.

Lennox W.G., Gibbs E.L. & Gibbs F.A. (1945) The brain wave pattern, an hereditary trait. Evidence from 74 'normal' pairs of twins. *Journal of Heredity*, **36**, 233–243.

Lerman P., Lerman-Sagie T. & Kivity S. (1991) Effect of early corticosteroid therapy for Landau–Kleffner syndrome. *Developmental Medicine and Child Neurology*, **33**, 257–260.

Lugaresi E., Cirignotta F. & Montagna P. (1985) Abnormal breathing in the Rett syndrome. *Brain and Development*, **7**, 329–333.

Maccario M., Hefferen S.J., Keblusek S.J. & Lipinski K.A. (1982) Developmental dysphasia and electroencephalographic abnormalities. *Developmental Medicine and Child Neurology*, **24**, 141–155.

Mauguière F. (1992) A consensus statement on relative merits of EEG and MEG. *Electroencephalography and Clinical Neurophysiology*, **82**, 317–319.

Meierkord H., Fish D.R., Smith S.J.M., Scott C.A., Shorvon S.D. & Marsden C.D. (1992) Is nocturnal paroxysmal dystonia a form of frontal lobe epilepsy? *Movement Disorders*, **7**, 38–42.

Musumeci S.A., Colonognola R.M., Ferri R., Gigli G.L., Petrella M.A., Sanfilippo S., Bergonzi P. & Tassinari C.A. (1988) Fragile-X syndrome: a particular epileptogenic EEG pattern. *Epilepsia*, **29**, 41–47.

Nomura Y., Segawa M., & Hasegawa M. (1984) Rett syndrome: clinical studies and pathophysiological consideration. *Brain and Development*, **6**, 475–486.

Nuwer M.R. (1988a) Quantitative EEG: I. Techniques and problems of frequency analysis and topographic mapping. *Journal of Clinical Neurophysiology*, **5**, 1–44.

Nuwer M.R. (1988b) Quantitative EEG: II. Frequency analysis and topographic mapping in clinical settings. *Journal of Clinical Neurophysiology*, **5**, 45–86.

Olsson I., Steffenburg S. & Gillberg C. (1988) Epilepsy in autism and autisticlike conditions. *Archives of Neurology*, **45**, 666–668.

Paetau R., Kajola M., Korkman M., Hamalainen M., Granstrom M.L. & Hari R. (1991) Landau–Kleffner syndrome: epileptic activity in the auditory cortex. *Neuroreport*, **2**, 201–204.

Pampiglione G. & Harden A. (1986) SSPE: neurophysiological findings in 80 cases. In: Bergamini F., Defanti C.A. & Ferrante P. (eds) *Subacute Sclerosing Panencephalitis: A Reappraisal*, pp. 98–105. Elsevier, Amsterdam.

Picton T.W. (ed) (1988) Human event related potentials. *EEG Handbook (revised series vol. 3)*. Elsevier Science, Amsterdam.

Picton T.W., Stuss D.T., Champagne S.C. & Nelson R.P. (1984) The effects of age on human event-related potentials. *Psychophysiology*, **21**, 312–325.

Pitt M.C., Esquivel E. & Boyd S.G. (1991) BAEP findings in X-linked adrenoleucodystrophy. *Electroencephalography and Clinical Neurophysiology*, **79**, 57P.

Pueschel S.M., Findley T.W., Furia J., Gallagher P.L., Scolla F.H. & Penzullo J.C. (1987) Atlantoaxial instability in Down syndrome: roentgenographic, neurologic and somatosensory evoked potential studies. *Journal of Pediatrics*, **110**, 512–521.

Robb S.A., Harden A. & Boyd S.G. (1989) Rett syndrome: an EEG study in 52 girls. *Neuropediatrics*, **20**, 192–195.

Rothwell J.C., Thompson P.D., Day B.L., Boyd S.G. & Marsden C.D. (1991) Stimulation of the human motor cortex through the scalp. *Experimental Physiology*, **76**, 159–200.

Santavuori P., Rapola J., Nuutila A., Raininko R., Lappi M., Launes J., Herva R. & Sainio K. (1991) The spectrum of Jansky–Bielschowsky disease. *Neuropediatrics*, **22**, 92–96.

Small J.G. (1987) Psychiatric disorders and EEG. In: Niedermayer E. (ed) *Electroencephalography. Basic Principles, Clinical Applications and Related Fields*, 2nd edn, pp. 526–527. Urban & Schwarzenburg, Baltimore.

Stassen H.H., Lykken D.T., Propping P. & Bomben G. (1988) Genetic determination of the human EEG. *Human Genetics*, **80**, 165–176.

Steriade M., Gloor P., Llinas R.R., Lopes da Silva F.H. & Mesulam M.-M. (1990) Basic mechanisms of cerebral rhythmic activities. *Electroencephalography and Clinical Neurophysiology*, **76**, 481–508.

Stores G. Sleep disorders in children. (1990) *British Medical Journal*, **301**, 351–352.

Stores G., Zaiwalla Z. & Bergel N. (1991) Frontal lobe complex partial seizures in children: a form of epilepsy at particular risk of misdiagnosis. *Developmental Medicine and Child Neurology*, **33**, 998–1009.

Suzuki T., Hirabayashi M. & Kobayashi K. (1983) Auditory middle latency responses in young children. *British Journal of Audiology*, **17**, 5–9.

Thaker G.K., Wagman A.M. & Tamminga C.A. (1990) Sleep polygraphy in schizophrenia: methodological issues. *Biological Psychiatry*, **28**, 240–246.

Thivierge J., Bedard C., Cote R. & Maziade M. (1990) Brainstem auditory evoked responses and subcortical abnormalities in autism. *American Journal of Psychiatry*, **147**, 1609–1613.

Thorpy M.J. (ed) (1990) *International Classification of Sleep Disorders. Diagnostic and Coding Manual*. American Sleep Disorders Association, Rochester.

Tuchman R.F., Rapin I. & Shinnar S. (1991) Autistic and dysphasic children. II: epilepsy. *Pediatrics*, **88**, 1219–1225.

Van Der Meij W., Van Huffelen A.L., Wieneke G.H. & Willemse T. (1992) Sequential EEG mapping may differentiate 'epileptic' from 'non-epileptic' Rolandic spikes. *Electroencephalography and Clinical Neurophysiology*, **82**, 408–414.

van Dongen H.R., Meulstee J., Blauw-van Mourik M. & van Harskamp F. (1989) Landau–Kleffner syndrome: a case study with a fourteen-year follow-up. *European Neurology*, **29**, 109–114.

Vogel F. (1958) *Über die Erblichkeit des normalen EEG. Zwillinguntersuchungen*. Thieme, Stuttgart.

Watanabe K., Hara K., Hakamada S., Negoro T., Sugiura M., Matsumoto A. & Maehara M. (1982) Seizures with apnea in children. *Pediatrics*, **79**, 87–90.

Wisniewski KE, Segan SM, Miezejeski CM, Sersen EA & Rudelli RD (1991) The fragile (X) syndrome: neurological, electrophysiological and neuropathological abnormalities. *American Journal of Medical Genetics*, **38**, 476–480.

PART 2
INFLUENCES ON
PSYCHOPATHOLOGY

Chapter 9
Genetic Influences on Normal and Abnormal Development

Emily Simonoff, Peter McGuffin & Irving I. Gottesman

In the last two decades, we have witnessed a transformation in the techniques available for studying genetics. Along with this has come an increasing awareness that genetic mechanisms that appear simple at the molecular level may result in both complex and widespread behavioural changes at the phenotypic level. Within both adult and child psychiatry, there has been a growing appreciation that an understanding of genetic influences is important to an integrative, multifactorial approach to the aetiology and treatment of disorders. Such an appreciation has derived in large part from the many advances in genetics. Many of the most publicized advances have been in molecular genetics, where a host of new techniques has made it possible to identify the location of genes involved in disease, to examine the structure, expression and function of genes at a molecular level, and to look at changes in gene expression at different ages (see McGuffin, 1987; Weatherall, 1991; Whatley & Owen, 1991, for a review). These techniques have led to the identification of the genes involved in a number of medical conditions, including cystic fibrosis, Duchenne and Becker muscular dystrophy and Friedreich's ataxia (McKusick, 1992). Such advances have also indicated the complexity of the underlying nature of various conditions. For example, in phenylketonuria (PKU) and cystic fibrosis, both Mendelian recessive disorders, over 50 different mutations have been identified for each (Beaudet, 1990; Eisensmith & Woo, 1992). Among other things, these findings will have important effects on the feasibility of screening for carrier status of such conditions. In addition, recent advances have led to the elucidation of novel mechanisms of disease. For example, an understanding of the molecular biology of the fragile X syndrome has helped to explain the observed puzzle that individuals known by their family history to carry the gene were sometimes unaffected (Davies, 1991; Yu *et al.*, 1991).

Within psychiatric genetics, this has led to a desire to discover single gene aetiologies for a number of conditions, including schizophrenia, manic depression, Tourette's syndrome and Alzheimer's disease. The hope is that identification of single genes causing disorder, or genes having a major effect on the disorder, would lead to a better understanding of the pathogenesis of the disorder with more focused treatment and, possibly, gene therapy. However, with the notable exceptions of some cases of early-onset Alzheimer's disease

(Goate *et al.*, 1991) and Huntington's disease, none of the putative linkages has withstood replication, leading scientists to reevaluate the genetic mechanism underlying such conditions (Risch, 1990d).

Alongside the molecular genetic revolution, if somewhat trailing it, has been the development of new statistical techniques, aimed primarily at helping to determine whether molecular genetic–disease associations are likely to be true relationships or the artefactual result of multiple testing (e.g. Ott, 1985; Weeks & Lange, 1988; Clerget-Darpoux, 1991). Important advances have been made in techniques to help determine whether only one or more genes are involved in a condition (Risch, 1990a), using the relative risk to relatives of probands with the condition compared to the general population. The number of genes involved in any disorder has important implications both for the strategy used and the sample sizes planned. Other strategies, e.g. the affected sib-pair method and variants thereof (Lange, 1986; Bishop & Williamson, 1990; Risch, 1990c,d), and allelic association (Edwards, 1980) have been tested to see under what conditions of inheritance they are most powerful (e.g. Cox *et al.*, 1988; Goldin & Gershon, 1988; Gershon *et al.*, 1989; Majunder, 1989). Ways of testing for genetic heterogeneity in both modes of inheritance and across loci have also been worked out (Risch, 1988).

There have also been developments in behavioural genetics. Perhaps the most important shift has been the appreciation that trying to understand behaviour in terms of the relative importance of heredity compared to environment (nature versus nurture) is a false distinction; for virtually all behaviours, both play a role, and what is important is how they act together. Thus, genetic designs have taken increasing interest in obtaining measures of the environment and examining how these function in relation to genetic liability (e.g. Plomin *et al.*, 1988a; Kendler *et al.*, 1991). For example, Kendler *et al.* (1991) suggested from a twin study of adult women that genetic and/or familial environmental influences on symptoms of depression have a greater effect on women who have experienced stressful life events than those who have not. Theoretical work has focused on the changes over time of the relative importance of genetic and environmental influences and the ways in which these changes might operate (Scarr & McCartney, 1983; Eaves *et al.*, 1986). Techniques that allow more complex models of the way in which genetic and environmental influences operate have been developed (Heath *et al.*, 1989). Behaviour genetic studies are no longer viewed as an end in themselves but rather as a tool in understanding how such influences on traits and conditions operate and as a method in addressing other questions regarding the traits which have arisen at the phenotypic level, such as the spectrum of the phenotype (Folstein & Rutter, 1977; Bolton & Rutter, 1990) and the nature of comorbidity between disorders (Caron & Rutter, 1990).

In general, genetic advances in child psychiatry have lagged behind those in adult psychiatry. Rutter *et al.* (1990) suggested that this may in part reflect a general tendency of child psychiatrists to see genetic influences as having effects on individuals that cannot be modified. The authors point out, using the example of PKU, that an understanding of genetic influences may be necessary to target environmental treatment appropriately. Child psychiatrists have perhaps assumed that family risk factors, such as parental psychiatric disorder and deprivation, act primarily as environmental risk factors. While it is likely that such influences do exert an important environmental effect, the possibility that such factors are also operating to increase genetic risk should be considered. Thus, criminality in parents has been shown to be a risk factor for conduct disorder, and early work assumed that this acted through the environment (Rutter, 1978). However, given the strong continuity between childhood conduct disorder and adult criminality (Robins, 1984; Robins & McEvoy, 1990) and the genetic contribution to the latter (McGuffin & Gottesman, 1985), it is entirely possible that part of the risk is conferred genetically. In designing powerful interventions, an understanding of how such influences interact may provide valuable leverage.

STRATEGIES AND CAUSAL MODELS

A variety of techniques have been used to examine the role of genetic influences on behaviour and disorders. In some cases, different strategies are addressing the same question. For example, twin and adoption studies both aim to determine the extent to which family resemblance is genetic, while linkage and sib-pair analysis both try to identify gene locations in single gene or oligogenic disorders. As each strategy has its own strengths and weaknesses, it is important to look across not only individual studies but also methods for comparability of results.

Twin studies

Twin studies as a group have perhaps been the most influential single design in determining the relative importance of genetic and environmental influences on behavioural traits and psychopathology. The classical twin design compares identical or monozygotic (MZ) twins with nonidentical or dizygotic (DZ) twins. The comparison rests on the fact that MZ twins share all their genes whereas DZ twins share only half their genes and

it is assumed that they share their environment to the same extent. Thus, the difference between the similarity of MZ and DZ twins is a reflection of the relative roles of genetic and environmental influences; the larger the difference, the greater the role of genetic influences. The extent to which the total variance is accounted for by additive genetic variance, that is, the heritability, can be estimated by twice the difference between MZ and DZ correlations (Table 9.1). Twin studies have been widely used because of the relative frequency of twins; approximately 1 in 80 births produces twins. Rates of dizygotic twinning are associated with increased maternal age, with various infertility treatments and show considerable geographical variation (Little & Thompson, 1988). Such effects are not seen on the rate of MZ twinning. As average maternal age has decreased and infertility treatments have increased in recent years, these two trends have acted in opposite directions on the rates of DZ twinning.

A number of critical assumptions underlie the validity of the twin design. Firstly, it is necessary to discriminate accurately between MZ and DZ twins. Zygosity determination, in the past, has been carried out either by questionnaires or by blood typing. Questionnaires correctly assign zygosity in about 90% of instances (Cederlof *et al.*, 1961; Martin & Martin, 1975; Goldsmith, 1991) when compared with results from blood typing which is 95–99% accurate (Lykken, 1978; Wilson, 1980). Some groups are now using DNA fingerprinting, which is theoretically 100% correct in its assignment of zygosity, although early laboratory problems suggest caution should be used until such techniques are validated against conventional blood typing (E. Bryan, unpublished observations). For most purposes the accuracy of zygosity determination by questionnaire or blood typing is sufficient, often with less measurement error involved than that associated with the traits being studied.

Secondly, it is also assumed that MZ twins share all their genes while DZ twins *on average* share only half. This is correct for all practical purposes. However, there may be a variety of postfertilization genetic changes rendering MZ twins genetically discordant. The best documented is that of X chromosome

Table 9.1 Extracting meaning from twin and adoptee correlations: estimates of additive genetic, shared environmental and nonshared environmental influences

Using MZ and DZ twins
Broad-sense heritability: $2(r_{MZ} - r_{DZ})$
Shared environment: $2(r_{DZ}) - r_{MZ}$
Nonshared environment: $1 - r_{MZ}$
Using twins reared apart
Broad-sense heritability: r_{MZA}
Shared environment: $r_{MZT} - r_{MZA}$
Using adoptees
Additive genetic: $2(r_{offspring-biological\ parent})$
Shared environment: $r_{offspring-adoptive\ parent}$

DZ, Dizygotic; MZ, monozygotic; MZA, monozygotic twins reared apart; MZT, monozygotic twins reared together.

inactivation which appears to occur randomly in each cell of females during fetal development and may lead to differences in the extent to which the paternal and maternal X chromosomes are expressed. Cases of female MZ twins discordant for Duchenne muscular dystrophy (Burn *et al.*, 1986; Richards *et al.*, 1990) and red−green colour blindness (Jorgensen *et al.*, 1992) have been explained as being caused by predominant inactivation of the chromosome with the affected genotype in one twin and inactivation of the normal chromosome in the other (affected) twin. However, such extreme effects are likely to occur in a very small minority of female pairs and are only important if genes on the X chromosome contribute to the trait under examination.

A third premiss in twin studies is that MZ and DZ twins share their environment to the same extent — the so-called equal environments assumption. Critics have pointed out that parents and others are more likely to treat MZ twins, who look alike, more similarly than DZ twins. Hence, MZ twins are more likely to be dressed in the same clothes by their parents and to share their bedroom than DZ twins (Smith, 1965; Scarr, 1968; Loehlin & Nichols, 1976). MZ twins are also more likely to share the same friends and to be involved in the same activities out of school (Smith, 1965) and mothers are more likely to rate them as being of the same level of social maturity (Scarr, 1968). One concern has been that parents are more likely to treat MZ twins more similarly than DZ pairs because of their knowledge that they are identical. However, several studies have examined parental ratings of personality and behaviour in cases where the parents' belief about the twins' zygosity was shown to be incorrect and have shown that these intrapair correlations were more similar to true as opposed to perceived zygosity (Scarr, 1968; Scarr & Carter Saltzman, 1979; Goodman & Stevenson, 1989). In a study where twins and nontwin siblings rated their perceptions of their home environment, MZ twins gave more similar ratings of their parents' degree of acceptance−rejection (but not of twin restrictiveness−permissiveness), suggesting that they may experience a more similar environment in some respects (Rowe, 1983). In this case, one must consider the possibility that MZ twins may *rate* more similarly than DZ twins or nontwin siblings. More generally, it is important to test whether the aspects of the environment that appear more similar in MZ twins are likely to influence the trait(s) of interest. It is unclear that dressing alike or sharing the same bedroom will make twins more prone to concordance for behavioural traits or disorders. Thus Morris-Yates *et al.* (1990) showed that, while some aspects of the environment that were imposed on twins were more similar for MZ than DZ pairs, this did not relate to the degree of within-pair similarity in personality. The question also arises as to whether greater similarities in the environments of MZ twins occur because of greater resemblance in their behaviour, due to genetic effects on that behaviour. The distinction is between environments that are *imposed upon* the twins, either because of their physical similarity or beliefs about their zygosity, and those that the twins *elicit* because their behaviour, which is genetically influ-

enced, leads to greater similarity in their choice of environment and the response they evoke in others. Thus, Lytton (1977) confirmed that mothers are more likely to behave in a similar manner toward MZ than DZ twins but only when the parental behaviour is in response to the twins. In examining changes in MZ twin similarity during the transition from adolescence to adulthood, Kaprio *et al.* (1990) found an effect of cohabitation and frequency of contact on resemblance for alcohol consumption and neuroticism but not for extroversion scores as measured on the Eysenck Personality Inventory, highlighting the fact that shared environments will have different effects on different behaviours.

A fourth assumption is that the results of twin studies can be generalized to the much larger singleton population. For this to be the case, twins should be fully comparable to singletons regarding the trait under examination. There are a number of differences between twins and singletons which may invalidate this assumption for various traits. Regarding obstetric factors, twins are more likely to experience pregnancy complications including maternal hypertension and pre-eclampsia, to be premature and of low birth weight for gestational age, and to have perinatal complications with increased mortality and low Apgar scores (Campbell & MacGillivray, 1988; Campbell & Samphler, 1988; MacGillivray & Campbell, 1988). Twins are also more prone to certain congenital anomalies, both minor (Myrianthopoulos & Melnick, 1977) and major (Little & Bryan, 1988). In their development, language acquisition is commonly delayed compared to singletons and the rate of specific reading retardation is increased, perhaps more so in MZ twins (Mittler, 1970; Hay *et al.*, 1984, 1987). Overall, the verbal IQ of twins is about four points lower than singletons (see Rutter & Redshaw, 1991, for a review). It is uncertain whether the effects on verbal skills are due to the increased rate of biological hazards experienced by twins or to the psychosocial adversity of having to share adult attention with a co-twin at certain stages in development. Two studies that examine the verbal IQs of twins reared as singletons because of the neonatal death of the co-twin arrive at different results. Record *et al.* (1970) found the verbal IQ as measured on the 11+ examination of the singleton twins comparable to that of the general population (and increased over the twins reared with their co-twin), whereas Myrianthopoulos *et al.* (1976) showed that IQs of singleton twins at 4 and 7 years were equivalent to those in twin pairs. Childhood psychopathology in twins compared to singletons has been little studied; however, one study from the National Child Development Survey suggested a slightly higher rate of conduct disorder in twins (M. Ghodsian, unpublished observations; see discussion in Rutter & Redshaw, 1991); this finding was supported by a comparison of twin and singleton child psychiatric cases where twins were more likely to have a diagnosis of conduct disorder, with a relative reduction in rates of emotional disorder, compared to singletons (Simonoff, 1992). The differences between twins and singletons appear, for the most part, to be minor and for many behaviours and traits, it is reasonable to generalize from twins to singletons. In cases where twins do differ from singletons, there may be differences in the aetiology or factors influencing the trait and such generalization may be inappropriate.

There are a few further technical considerations in twin studies. Classical twin designs can only estimate three separate influences on individual traits, usually genetic, shared environmental and nonshared environmental influences. Without other types of relatives, it is not possible to take account of more influences in any one model. Hence, traits where more influences, such as nonadditive genetic variance, e.g. dominance, play an important role may be misrepresented in these models. Classical twin designs also assume that there has been no assortative mating between the twins' parents. While extended twin designs can take account of assortative mating, classical twin studies which neglect this feature may produce a falsely elevated DZ correlation and hence a lowered estimate of the effect of genetic influences.

Special types of twin studies

There are a number of variants on the twin design. The use of twins separated in early life and reared apart allows the disentanglement of genetic and environmental influences and addresses the concern that MZ twins may share their environment to a greater extent than DZ pairs. The correlation between MZ twins reared apart (MZA) represents the degree of genetic influence on the trait, provided that the environments in which the twins have been raised are not correlated, and this design has been used either on its own or in comparison with MZ twins reared together (MZT) to study a host of traits, including intelligence and personality (Shields, 1962; Tellegren *et al.*, 1988; Bouchard *et al.*, 1990). The difference between the correlation for MZT and MZA represents an estimate of the shared environment and, as such, serves as a useful check against the results from classical twin and adoption studies.

Another variant is the study of the offspring of twins (Eaves *et al.*, 1978). The design takes advantage of the fact that the offspring of MZ co-twins are genetically half sibs but environmentally cousins. The critical comparison is between the similarity of the MZ twin parent and his/her offspring on the one hand and the similarity of that parent to the offspring of his/her co-twin on the other hand. The addition of such information helps in explaining the potentially important effects of assortative mating, cultural inheritance (the transmission of environmental influences from parents to their children), to test whether dominance (interactions between alleles) and epistasis (interactions among genes) are present and whether there are sex-specific transgenerational effects (Eaves *et al.*, 1978).

Another research strategy has been to select pairs of MZ twins that are discordant for the condition in question to look for differences in environmental exposure that might explain the discordance. The co-twin control design, as it has been called, has been used in studies of schizophrenia, both in looking for experiential differences between the twins (Lewis

et al., 1987) and in attempting to find brain abnormalities that are causally associated with the condition (Reveley *et al.*, 1987; Suddath *et al.*, 1990). A variant on this design has been used in studying disorders where the offspring of MZ twins discordant for disorder have been followed into adult life to compare the rates at which they manifest the condition (Gottesman & Bertelsen, 1989; Kringlen & Cramer, 1989). The design rests on the fact that offspring of such discordant twins receive, on average, the same proportion of pathogenic genes but differ in their environmental risk, in particular, in being exposed to an ill parent. Hence, if the rate of disorder in offspring of affected versus unaffected twins is the same, this is highly suggestive of genetic influences, which need not be expressed to be transmitted (reduced penetrance; see below).

Adoption studies

Adoption studies have provided important evidence for the relative influences of genes and environment on a host of behavioural traits and areas of psychopathology. The utility of adoption designs derives from the fact that genetic and (shared) environmental influences, which are confounded in family studies, are separated. A number of variants on the adoption paradigm have been used, of which the most common are the adoptees' study, the adoptees' family study and cross-fostering analyses. The *adoptees' study* starts with affected biological parents and compares the rates of disorder in their adopted offspring with that in adopted offspring of unaffected, control parents. The *adoptees' family study* begins with affected adoptees and compares the rates of disorder in their biological and adoptive relatives. *Cross-fostering studies* compare adopted offspring with unaffected biological parents raised by affected adoptive parents with adopted offspring of affected biological parents raised by unaffected adoptive parents. There are a number of variants of adoption studies, including the adoptive sibling design and parent–offspring designs (see Rutter *et al.*, 1990). As shown in Table 9.1, the correlation between adopted offspring and their biological parents reflects the genetic influences on the trait (as parents and offspring share half of their genes, the correlation represents half of the additive genetic variance). The correlation between adoptive parents and their adopted offspring, with whom they share no genes, is due to environmental influences shared between the parent and child (which may be less than those shared by twins or siblings).

The complete dissociation of genes and environment in the adoption studies is based on a number of assumptions underlying the adoption design (Cadoret, 1986). The first is that the biological and adoptive parents are uncorrelated for the relevant trait, or for characteristics which may affect that trait. Selective placement has been demonstrated in several studies (Leahy, 1932; Bohman & Sigvardsson, 1980). Secondly, there may be a relationship between the biological parents' status and pre- or perinatal hazards, such as the effects of maternal smoking or alcohol consumption, that influence offspring status at a later point. Thirdly, a systematic relationship may exist between pre- and perinatal environmental influences and later postnatal experiences. Thus, adoption agencies might wait longer to place children with pre- and perinatal adversities until they have a clearer understanding of what effect these will have on the child, (e.g. Bohman & Sigvardsson, 1980). Fourthly, there is the amount of knowledge the adoptive parents have regarding the biological parents. Such information could bias their expectations of and behaviour towards their adopted children. There has been variation between agencies and over time on the amount of information given to parents. Finally, there is the effect of adoption itself. The rate of psychiatric referrals is higher than expected in adoptees (Goldberg & Wolkind, 1992; see also Chapter 11). While this has not been systematically studied and may reflect the genetic effects of biological parental status and of environmental adversity, it raises the possibility that adoption itself is an adversity which predisposes to psychopathology. It should also be borne in mind that, in at least some samples, biological parents whose children were adopted may differ from the general population. While this has not been the case in all samples (e.g. the Colorado Adoption Project; Plomin *et al.*, 1988a), it has been demonstrated in others (e.g. the Swedish adoption sample; Bohman & Sigvardsson, 1980).

Family studies

Although twin and adoption studies are invaluable in their ability to separate out the contributions of genetic and environmental influences, they are less helpful in providing information about the mode of transmission. Studying the rates and patterns of affection in individuals of varying degrees of relatedness to the proband gives important information as to whether transmission is likely to be due to one single major locus or whether multiple genes are involved (Risch, 1990a, 1990b). Risch has demonstrated that if the relative risk of being affected decreases by more than twofold when going from first- to second- to third-degree relatives, then more than one gene must be involved. Family studies are also crucial in studying rare disorders, where it may be difficult to find sufficient numbers affected with rare disorders for a powerful genetic design.

Family studies derive their strength from comparing the correlations for a given trait among individuals with different degrees of relatedness (e.g. first- and second-degree) and different types of relationships (e.g parent—offspring and siblings). However, many studies only include first-degree relatives and it is therefore impossible to distinguish between genetic and environmental influences. When the nature of the potential environmental transmission is specified, this can then be tested if the appropriate control groups are used. Thus Rutter (1966) studied psychiatric disorder in children of parents with varying psychiatric conditions to see whether the risk and type (e.g. conduct versus emotional disorder) of disorder were specific to the nature of the parental disorder. In general, the findings suggested that the primary risk for childhood disorder was conferred by discordant marital and family relationships which were seen in all the various parental conditions; this pattern is highly suggestive of an environmental risk.

A particular problem for family studies of child psychiatric disorders is acquiring accurate information from adult family members that is relevant to their child psychiatric status. Many disorders remit or may change in nature over time, so that there are few conditions where adult status is a reliable indicator of a particular child psychiatric disorder. An alternative strategy is to gather retrospective information from adults on their child psychiatric status. The validity of such information has been little studied but there is some indication that adults' recollections of their childhoods are better for aspects that reflect the predominant behaviour of themselves and others compared with specific items of behaviour or for particular times at which events occurred (D. Quinton, unpublished observations). Gaining retrospective information in family studies would be further complicated if it were necessary to use the family history method in which family members are asked to consider whether individuals within the pedigree have suffered with various symptoms and disorders. It is clear that this method is less sensitive, particularly for disorders where the outward manifestations may be subtle (Thompson *et al.*, 1982), and it is likely that the accuracy of the method would be further undermined both by the longer periods of recollection required and by the fact that family members may not have known each other in childhood. It is clear that reliance cannot be placed on a child psychiatric attendance, because of altering diagnostic conceptualizations over time and place (Prendergast *et al.*, 1988), but also, more importantly, because many children with psychiatric disorders do not present to services (Offord *et al.*, 1987; Rutter *et al.*, 1970).

Assortative mating

Assortative mating refers to population-wide, nonrandom selection of a mate and its consequences upon the genetic make-up of the offspring from that mating. Assortative mating may be homotypic (mating based on the same trait) or heterotypic (mating based on a different trait). Furthermore, the correlation may be positive (attraction of like individuals) or negative (attraction of opposites). There is evidence for homotypic-positive assortative mating for a number of sociodemographic variables including age, social class, ethnic background and religion, for physical features including height, hair colour and eye colour (Vandenberg, 1972), and for intelligence (Johnson *et al.*, 1976; Mascie-Taylor & Vandenberg, 1988). There remains controversy over whether assortative mating for personality traits exists, as the results of different studies are contradictory; however, there is a suggestion that those couples who are unhappily married are more likely to differ in personality than are happily married couples (Cattell & Nesselroade, 1967), although it is uncertain whether this is cause or consequence of marital disharmony. Furthermore, many of these relationships are not strong, with spousal correlations in the region of 0.1 to 0.3.

Assortative mating may occur because of attraction to others based on observable characteristics (phenotypic assortment) or because individuals from certain social backgrounds are more likely to meet others from similar backgrounds (social homogamy). Few investigators have examined the relative roles of these two mechanisms of assortment; however, both a family study approach (Rao *et al.*, 1976) and twin-spouse design (Heath & Eaves, 1985) can be used to estimate the importance of the two mechanisms. The distinction may be important genetically; if assortment occurs simply because individuals come from the same social background, the genetic effects may be trivial. However, if mating occurs because of phenotypic similarity on traits that are genetically influenced, spouses will tend to share genes for those traits and their offspring will be more similar to each other than would be expected under random mating. Assortative mating will also cause an increase in the observed parent−offspring correlation. In adoption paradigms, under phenotypic assortment, where the correlation between biological parent and offspring is assumed to be wholly genetic, assortative mating will inflate the estimate of genetic effects. The effect in twin studies will be to decrease the estimates of genetic effects; this is because the DZ twin correlation will be increased, as they share more than half their genes, while the MZ correlation is not increased, because they already share all their genes. Linkage studies commonly require families where the inheritance of the disorder is unilineal. However, if heterotypic assortative mating occurs, the phenotype in the offspring may not be easily or correctly categorized, and incorrect phenotyping of the offspring may lead to inaccuracies in the results of linkage studies.

Many studies fail to differentiate between increased rates of psychiatric disorder in spouses of psychiatric patients and true assortative mating: an affected individual mating with another affected person. However, there is broad general support for increased rates of alcohol abuse in spouses of alcoholics (Rimmer & Winokur, 1972; Beckman, 1975; Hall *et al.*, 1983a,b; Jacob & Bremer, 1986). The evidence for increased rates of depression among spouses of depressed probands has been mixed with some studies (Gershon *et al.*, 1973; Dunner *et al.*, 1976; Baron *et al.*, 1981; Merikangas, 1984) suggesting the rate may be increased, but others finding no convincing evidence of such an effect (Gershon *et al.*, 1975; Negri *et al.*, 1979). Mednick and colleagues (Kirkegaard-Sorensen & Mednick, 1975; Parnas, 1988) have suggested that heterotypic assortative mating occurs in schizophrenic women who are more likely to mate with antisocial men.

BASIC PRINCIPLES

Genetics and epidemiology

In studying both behavioural traits and disorders, it is essential to have an understanding of the epidemiology of the trait before carrying out genetic analyses. While it is quite possible to explore the molecular genetic basis of rare and well-defined conditions with relatively little understanding of the epidemiology of the disorder, problems arise for child psychiatric disorders. For many conditions, the discrimination between the normal range and disorder is far from clear. Conduct disorder and depression are good examples in which alternative conceptualizations may lead to quite different inclusions. Even when a conceptual framework is accepted, relatively minor changes in the definition, for example, in the number of symptoms required, can lead to marked changes in the prevalence rates (e.g. McGuffin *et al.*, 1991; Kendler *et al.*, 1992).

It is also important to consider age and sex trends. Many child psychiatric disorders show a preponderance of one sex affected over the other. For example, boys are approximately three times more commonly affected with pervasive developmental disorders, including autism and hyperkinesis. A number of the specific developmental disorders, such as enuresis, language and reading disorders, tics and Tourette's syndrome, also show a male preponderance, as do oppositional and conduct disorders. On the other hand, depressive disorders are probably more common in girls, particularly in the post-pubertal years. Age trends are also an important characteristic of a number of conditions. Perhaps most striking are the increased rates of depressive symptoms and disorders reported by girls during the teenage years (see Chapter 19). Other conditions appear to be considerably more common during a limited age period, so that simple phobias of animals peak in early to middle childhood (Marks, 1987). Although it is unclear to what extent such sex and age differences are due to genetic or environmental factors, it will be necessary to identify the factors involved in causing the unequal sex distribution and changes over age before we can claim to understand the mechanisms involved in the disorders. It is likely that the role of genetic and environmental factors will differ across disorders.

An understanding of base rates is important in determining whether or not conditions are familial. In autism, the rate of recurrence in sibs is so low (approximately 3%) that for many years it was not recognized that this was very much increased (approximately 100-fold) over the general population. In contrast, while depression has been frequently observed to run in families, many studies, e.g. Kendler *et al.* (1992), also show high base rates — up to 30% — which need to be taken into account. Older studies have taken a difference in the MZ and DZ concordance rates to be indicative of genetic influences; the authors demonstrated that the translation of such a difference into genetic effects depends on the base rate as well as the concordances. This has been demonstrated graphically by Gottesman (Gottesman & Carey, 1983; LaBuda *et al.* 1993) in relation to twin studies. Base rates in conjunction with proband concordance rates can be translated into tetrachoric correlations, correlations that assume that the observed differentiation of classes (affected versus not affected) is due to an underlying liability. For any individual concordance rate, the correlation becomes higher as the base rate becomes lower. This can be seen in Table 9.2, in the comparison between hypothetical disorders A and B; in the rarer disorder

Table 9.2 Probandwise twin concordances, base rates and resulting correlations and heritabilities

Disorder	Base rate	Concordance		r_{MZ}	r_{DZ}	Heritability
		MZ	DZ			
A*	0.1%	50%	30%	0.92	0.82	0.20
B*	5.0%	50%	30%	0.80	0.58	0.44
C*	0.1%	18%	2%	0.72	0.34	0.76
D*	5.0%	50%	20%	0.80	0.42	0.76
Autism†	0.03%	72%	3%	0.96	0.48	0.98
DSM-III-R depression‡	31%	48%	42%	0.44	0.19	0.50

DZ, Dizygotic; MZ, monozygotic, Heritabilities are calculated as $2(r_{MZ}-r_{DZ})$.
* From La Buda *et al.*, 1993.
† From Rutter (1991).
‡ From Kendler *et al.* (1992).

(A), both the MZ and DZ correlations are higher. In this case, the effect is to reduce heritability, but this would not necessarily occur. For low base rates, even low concordances for both MZ and DZ twins may translate to substantial heritabilities (disorder C), while strikingly different concordances with different base rates may give the same heritability (disorders C and D). For very rare disorders, such as autism, even very low concordances, such as the 3% for DZ twins, give correlations close to 0.5. In contrast, where the base rates are almost as high as the concordances, as in the Virginia twin study of depression in women (Kendler *et al.*, 1992), correlations are low. Such effects are also relevant in family studies.

Single gene inheritance

In general, disorders that have been shown to be caused by a faulty single gene appear to be discrete. In psychiatry, examples of known single-gene disorders include PKU, Huntington's disease and tuberous sclerosis. Transmission of phenotypes due to single genes is associated with several well-recognized patterns of inheritance within families, which are described in most textbooks of medical genetics. However, these predictable patterns of inheritance may be affected by several phenomena. The first is reduced or incomplete penetrance, in which an individual carrying the genotype for the disorder does not demonstrate the phenotype. The assumption is that other genetic or environmental factors affect expression of the phenotype. A related effect is that of variable expression where individuals with the same genotype show different phenotypic expression. Examples include that of neurofibromatosis where some individuals are minimally affected with a few café-au-lait spots, whereas others show multiple skin tumours, and tuberous sclerosis in which some individuals demonstrate only a few skin lesions while others have epilepsy and severe mental retardation. The notion of variable

expression is employed in psychiatry for a number of disorders, including schizophrenia, Tourette's disorder and autism. Kendler (1988) has shown, for example, that schizotypal and schizoid personality disorders occur at a higher rate in relatives of schizophrenics compared with controls. In Tourette's syndrome, increased rates of obsessive-compulsive disorder have been observed (Pauls *et al.*, 1991), and in autism, MZ co-twins have shown a spectrum of cognitive and social disabilities that fall within the same spectrum as autism, but which are not severe enough to meet criteria for autism (Folstein & Rutter, 1977; Rutter, 1991).

Fitness refers to the phenomenon where individuals with certain phenotypes may be more or less likely to reproduce, thus altering the likelihood that the disease allele will be transmitted to offspring. Reduced fitness has been demonstrated for schizophrenia (see Gottesman, 1991, for a review) and it is rare for autistic individuals even to marry (Bolton & Rutter, 1990). Reduced fitness will decrease the chances of observing transmission from one generation to the next, if it is present. *Stoppage* refers to the limitation of family size because of having an affected child. In practice, this usually applies to severely handicapping conditions with an onset in early childhood, when parents are making decisions about family size. Stoppage has been proposed to occur in families with an autistic child (Jones & Szatmari, 1988). The effect of stoppage will be to decrease the number of families in which more than one sib is affected, thus reducing the likelihood that a pattern of Mendelian inheritance will be observable. It is possible to look for the effects of reduced fitness and stoppage and to take them into account in deciding whether Mendelian inheritance is likely.

Both reduced fitness and stoppage lead to selection, by decreasing vertical transmission and reducing the number of individuals in the next generation who carry the faulty gene. Ordinarily, selection will reduce the prevalence of the disorder over successive generations, but there are two situations in which this does not occur. One is where there is heterozygote advantage, that is, where a selective *advantage* is conferred on individuals who are heterozygous for the disease gene. Thus, heterozygotes for haemoglobin S, an abnormal variant produced in sickle cell anaemia, are more resistant to malaria in infancy and childhood, explaining the high frequency of the gene in African populations where malaria is prevalent (Kaback, 1990). A second effect that cancels out selection is a high rate of new mutations, as has been demonstrated for tuberous sclerosis (Harper, 1988). Finally, disorders caused by multiple genes take much longer to be selected out, because selection must operate on each gene (Risch, 1990d).

It can be seen that these influences may alter the patterns of familial aggregation for single-gene conditions. Thus, segregation analyses of some conditions that had not previously been thought to be explicable by single genes have suggested that this might be possible. A case in point is Tourette's disorder, where segregation analysis has demonstrated that the inheritance is compatible with a single gene with reduced penetrance of the phenotype and variable expression, including obsessive-compulsive disorder (Pauls & Leckman, 1986). Similar arguments have been made for other disorders, such as schizophrenia. Just as we have seen how a number of influences may distort the apparent mode of inheritance in truly Mendelian conditions, we must be aware that it is possible to simulate Mendelism (McGuffin & Huckle, 1990). In some cases (e.g. Sherrington *et al.*, 1988), the pedigrees were selected because of an apparent Mendelian pattern of inheritance. It is important to be aware that some families will show a high recurrence rate by chance or through polygenic mechanisms (McGue & Gottesman, 1989). Secondly, it is important to decide whether the assumptions that have been made regarding the extent of the phenotype, or the degree of variable expression, are clinically valid. A number of tests may be employed, but examining the disorders seen in MZ co-twins compared to an appropriate control group demonstrates the degree of variable expression due to genetic and shared environmental influences. Thirdly, the estimates of penetrance should also be examined. Once again, a useful yardstick is the rate of affected MZ co-twins. Under the assumption of a single-gene model, the penetrance rate should equal the MZ concordance. It should be noted that most disorders known to be due to single-gene defects show high penetrance rates, usually greater than 95%. Thus, caution should be used in inferring single-gene inheritance when high rates of reduced penetrance are impugned and where these rates and/or those of variable expression differ greatly from the MZ concordance rates.

Polygenic and multifactorial inheritance

The need for alternative models of inheritance comes from two sources. Firstly, there are the traits that are continuously distributed and for which there are genetic influences. Height and weight are both instances of such traits; in child psychiatry, intelligence and temperament are more relevant examples. For each of these traits, the role of genetic influences has been well-documented for the normal distribution of the trait, and thus the model of inheritance must be able to account for a continuously distributed phenotype. While such traits must be, in the first instance, conceptualized as continuous, this does not mean that elements that are discontinuously distributed do not contribute. For example, there are rare single-gene disorders that cause both short stature (e.g. the various chondrodysplasias) and exceptional height (e.g. Marfan's syndrome). The contribution of such genes to the overall distribution is minimal, because of the rarity of the affected genotypes, but their effect on individuals is striking. The situation is similar for severe mental handicap, where a number of medical conditions are found.

Alternative models of inheritance have also been required for disorders whose inheritance is not readily explicable by single-gene patterns. Thus, despite the effects influencing single-gene inheritance mentioned above, there are conditions in which there is evidence of genetic influence from twin and/or adoption studies, but where the pattern is inconsistent with Mendelian inheritance (Smith, 1971). Usually a number of features are observed. First, the fall-off in the rate of affected individuals when moving from first-degree (e.g. parents, siblings, offspring) to second-degree relatives (e.g. grandparents/children, avuncular relationships) is greater than would be expected under single gene inheritance. Secondly, such conditions frequently show sex differences in base rates that do not conform to Mendelian patterns of X-linked transmission. Thirdly, there may be differences in the rate of affected relatives depending upon whether the proband is of the more or less frequently affected sex; for example, in pyloric stenosis, which affects males more commonly than females, female probands have on average more affected relatives than do male probands (Carter, 1976). For such conditions, the action of multiple genes has been hypothesized. In many cases, hypothetical multiple gene disorders are very much more common than single-gene disorders. Medical examples include coronary artery disease and diabetes, which contrast with cystic fibrosis, the most common autosomal recessive disorder in the US and Western Europe, which has a population prevalence of only 0.05% (Harper, 1988). In psychiatry, the disorders of known single-gene aetiologies are among the rarest conditions.

There are two steps involved in understanding how multiple genes might cause such aggregation. Firstly, multiple genes acting equally and additively, as described in the polygenic model, will produce a variety of phenotypes which will rapidly approach a distribution that is indistinguishable from a normal one. This is illustrated in Figure 9.1, where the action of one, two and three loci is shown, respectively, in which the one allele of each gene carries a hypothetical value of -1 and the other allele a value of 1. As the number of individual genes (loci) involved increases, so does the extent of variation in the phenotype. This normal distribution of phenotypes has been used to explain the genetic contribution to continuous traits. Environmental influences may further modify the distribution of phenotypes; the joint operation of multiple genes and environment is referred to as multifactorial inheritance.

The second step involves assuming than an apparently discrete trait or disorder is due to an underlying continuous distribution of liability to the trait, but that the trait is only manifest above a certain level or threshold. Such a model was used by Falconer (1965, 1967) to describe the genetics of common familial disorders such as diabetes where the underlying distribution of *liability* was hypothesized to be related to continuously distributed blood sugar levels. Individuals with blood sugar levels above a certain threshold will be diabetic. Shortly thereafter Gottesman and Shields (1967) proposed a similar mechanism to explain the genetics of schizophrenia; in this case, however, there was no direct measure of liability. Such models are tremendously attractive for psychiatric disorders because of their ability not only to describe observed familial aggregation but also to explain the patterns of sex differences. Variations on the model allow for different thresholds, which may reflect the severity of the disorder or the sex of the individual. It is also possible to assume sex-dependent

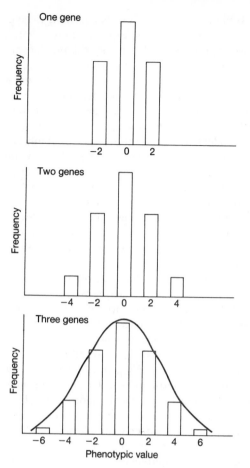

Fig. 9.1 Range and distribution of phenotypes for a trait determined by one, two and three genes, each with two alleles, respectively. With three genes, the distribution is approximately normal.

differences in liability to the disorder (see Reich *et al.*, 1972; Cloninger *et al.*, 1978 and McGuffin & Gottesman, 1985 for a fuller discussion of various models). Each of these models makes clear predictions which can be tested against the available data.

One of the potential objections to the multifactorial threshold theory is that the notion of underlying liability must be assumed. This is particularly a problem in the behavioural sciences where biological markers are currently less available, because of our limited understanding of the pathophysiology, and the difficulties in making direct measurements relevant to brain function. We can use psychological measures that are normally distributed to define the underlying distribution of liability, for example, symptoms of depression for depressive disorder, schizoid traits for schizophrenia, and so forth. Alternatively, we can look for biological markers of disorder, perhaps a measure of certain neurotransmitter levels or of brain receptors. The more closely the measure is related to the aetiology of the disorder, the better the model will fit the observed data. Thus, it is possible to test hypotheses about underlying liability.

Because polygenic and multifactorial models assume (underlying) continuous variation, we conceive of genetic and environmental influences in terms of the amount of variance each explains. Variation due to genetic influences is termed heritability and that due to environment is sometimes referred to as environmentality. In summary, the polygenic or multifactorial model provides an alternative conceptualization of genetic mechanisms which is highly attractive because of its ability to explain observed patterns of disorder in families but which is also, for many disorders, not yet proven. It should be noted that genetic effects can make individuals in the same family *different*, as well as more similar. In single-gene disorders, those with the disease gene(s) are affected, or different from other family members. The same applies to conditions or traits where multiple genes are involved; although individuals in the same family have a greater chance of sharing the same genes, if they have different genes, they may differ for the trait under examination.

Segregation analysis

In segregation analysis (which involves the statistical examination of rates and patterns of disorder in family members), the aim is to infer which mode of transmission of a trait best explains the observed pattern of affected versus unaffected individuals. This is best performed as a two-stage process where first a drawing of the pedigree or a set of pedigrees is inspected to see whether or not the segregation of the trait corresponds to some obvious pattern. At the second stage, formal statistical testing of the segregation ratios is then carried out. Regular phenotypes (Morton, 1982) are those that show simple Mendelian segregation and such patterns will generally be clear when the pedigrees are first inspected. For example, a trait that is passed regularly from one generation to the next, with no skipped generations, no difference in sex distribution and an average ratio of affecteds to unaffecteds of 1:1 in sibships, would be typical of an autosomal dominant inheritance. After inspecting the pedigree data and deciding that it exhibited these characteristics, one would then proceed to confirm this statistically by checking the male:female ratio in sibship. In this case, one would not expect a significant deviation (tested by a chi-square goodness of fit test) from 1:1; any significant deviation would argue against the hypothesized mode of inheritance.

However, the great majority of childhood psychiatric disorders showing familial aggregation (and the majority of common familial disorders generally) are characterized by more complex distribution of affected individuals. For such traits, referred to by Morton (1982) as irregular phenotypes, statistical analysis is necessarily more complex. The statistical analysis of such disorders requires complex segregation analysis. Although the details are complicated, the general principles are fairly straightforward.

We have already discussed the polygenic or multifactorial model, in which liability to a continuously distributed trait is determined by multiple genes, or genes acting in concert with environmental influences. However, it is possible that a single locus of major effect either acting on its own or together with polygenic or familial environmental factors contributes to liability (Reich *et al.*, 1972). That a major locus alone may result in a phenotype with an irregular pattern of transmission may initially seem like a contradiction in terms to readers brought up on traditional Mendelian genetics, and so it is worthwhile just briefly to consider the so-called two allele general single major locus (sml) model.

Let us postulate a genetic locus at which there are two alternative genes (alleles) A_1 and A_2. There are then three possible combinations of genotypes: A_1A_1, A_1A_2, and A_2A_2. Suppose that A_2 is a mutant of disease allele. There are then different probabilities of manifesting the disease associated with each of the three genotypes. For a typical dominant, the probabilities manifesting the disorder (or penetrances) will be 0, 1 and 1 for individual types A_1A_1, A_1A_2 and A_2A_2 respectively. For a typical recessive the corresponding penetrances would be 0, 0 and 1 respectively. However, suppose that occasional phenocopies of the disorder arise in individuals not carrying the disease allele (i.e. the penetrance of A_1A_1 is greater than 0) and also various environmental factors to which individuals are exposed influence the A_1A_2 and A_2A_2 genotypes. Both phenomena will affect penetrances, so they are no longer 0 and 1. The pattern of affected to nonaffected individuals would then differ from that expected from Mendelian segregation ratios. In addition to the three penetrances, a fourth parameter, q, the gene frequency of A_2, defines the general sml model.

We are now in a position to consider the most popular approach currently to complex segregation analysis, which is based on the mixed model of Morton and MacLean (1974). Here it is postulated that liability to develop the disorder is given by a combination of a major gene effect, a polygenic effect and a residual environmental component. It may be seen that this is effectively a combination of the multifactorial threshold model and the sml model. The mixed model approach uses information from whole pedigrees and a computer program incorporating the model is used iteratively to find the best fit to the available data (Lalouel *et al.*, 1983). Usually a hierarchical strategy is adopted. That is, we first attempt to fit the full mixed model comprising both major genes and multi-factorial components and then progress to fit reduced models, for example, either the multifactorial component alone or the single-gene component alone. If a reduced model is found to fit just as well as the full mixed model then the simpler model is selected on grounds of parsimony. Similarly, we might then go to examine the fit of simpler versions of the single model, for example, with parameters constrained to their Mendelian values.

A further check on the plausibility of major gene transmission is to carry out tests of transmission probabilities (Elston & Stewart, 1971); namely, that the probabilities of parents transmitting the allele A_1 to their offspring are 1, 0.5 and 0 for parents of the types A_1A_1, A_1A_2 and A_2A_2 respectively. Therefore, if there is evidence for an sml effect resulting

from mixed model analysis, it is then possible to go on to test for deviation from Mendelian expectations by iterating on the transmission probabilities. Essentially, this provides an alternative conceptualization of the same issues regarding Mendelian transmission as the Morton and MacLean models. For example, Rice *et al.* (1987) carried out a mixed model analysis of the transmission of the affective disorder in families ascertained through probands with bipolar illness. They found that a mixed model was superior to multifactorial inheritance but did not offer any appreciable advantage over an sml model. Thus, on grounds of parsimony, the sml model would be favoured. However, when they went on to analyse their data further by exploring the transmission probabilities, the best fit was achieved with a model where these deviated from Mendelian expectations, casting doubt on the hypothesis that all familial bipolar disorder can be explained on the basis of a single major gene.

Although most attention has focused on either polygenic or sml models, it is worth considering whether most common familial diseases may actually turn out to be oligogenic, i.e. to result from the combined effects of a small number of genes with or without environmental contributors. In practice, using purely statistical approaches, it is difficult to distinguish between the action of a few genes (say four or five), each having a modest contribution to liability, and many genes, each adding a small effect. Furthermore, it has been argued that nonadditive interactions between genes (epistasis) are probably present in oligogenic disorders (Risch, 1990a) and that such a model is the most likely explanation of the transmission of schizophrenia.

In summary, complex segregation analysis is a potentially powerful tool which, if used carefully, can provide important insights into the transmission of genetic disorders and is a useful preliminary to linkage studies, where the defining parameters of a major locus must be estimated (see below). However, if approached without proper circumspection, segregation analysis can also be misleading. It is important to be aware that genetic transmission, even with Mendelian-like segregation, can be simulated by traits that are predominantly environmental (Edwards, 1960; McGuffin & Huckle, 1990).

Structural equation modelling

An important advance in the past 10−15 years has been the use of structural equation models to estimate the effects of genetic and environmental influences (Loehlin, 1987; Heath *et al.*, 1989; Neale *et al.*, 1989). The technique is based on path analysis, and, like complex segregation analysis, uses iterative computer algorithms to find the best estimates for the various parameters that define a model. However, whereas in segregation analysis we ask questions such as, Is there a major gene effect? and explore models defined in terms of gene frequency, penetrance values, etc., in structural equations models, an attempt is made to explore the correlational architecture of a familial trait. Thus, the questions asked may include: How much of the variance is explained by additive genetic effects? How much is explained by nonadditive genetic effects? Does shared environment have a role and, if so, how much of a role?

Structural equation modelling has a number of advantages. Firstly, not only can the approach give estimates of genetic and environmental effects; it can also give information on how well a particular model explains the data. Secondly, parameters (e.g. additive genetic or common environmental effects) can be added or dropped to test whether their contribution to the model is important in explaining the data. Again, as with segregation analysis, the model that gives an acceptable fit to the data with the fewest parameters is generally selected on grounds of parsimony. For example, we might begin with a full model that includes additive genetic, shared and nonshared environmental effects. However, if the role of shared environmental influences appears to be small, and a reduced model that does not include shared environmental influences provides a fit that is not significantly worse than the full model, then this reduced, more parsimonious model is accepted.

A third advantage is that groups can be compared to see whether there are differences in the best parameter estimates. This approach can be used for a number of different purposes. In examining sex differences, a frequent question is whether it is correct to assume the same underlying genetic and environmental influences for males and females. By comparing models where such influences are constrained to be the same for the two sexes with models where they are allowed to differ, it is possible to address this question. The same technique can be used to compare across other groupings. This can be done for samples ascertained in different ways, where it would be desirable to merge the data if appropriate. Conversely, specified subgroups can be selected on the basis of different genetic and environmental influences. For example, one might want to examine whether the genetic and environmental influences on conduct disorder are the same when hyperactivity is present and absent (because of the documented comorbidity of hyperactivity and conduct disorder; Taylor *et al.*, 1986, and because of the genetic contribution to questionnaire measures of hyperactivity; Goodman & Stevenson, 1989). If the model-fitting indicated that a better fit was obtained when the groups were separate, this would suggest that the genetic and environmental influences differed within that subgroup. Fourthly, with sufficient data, many more influences can be estimated at once, allowing the maximum benefit from extended genetic designs. In such instances, effects such as dominance, assortative mating and the transmission of environmental effects can be examined and taken into account.

For classical twin designs, parameter estimates are usually very similar to those obtained through the use of correlations. For example, in a recent twin study of autism, the tetrachoric correlations in liability for MZ and DZ twins were calculated to be 0.965 and 0.479 respectively, when the DZ twin correlation was based on the sibling concordance (Rutter, 1991). Using the method described by Gottesman and Carey (1985), estimates of the variance due to additive genetic, shared environmental and nonshared environmental influences were 96, 0.5 and 3.5%, respectively. Model-fitting parameter estimates of the same variables were 96.4, 0.1 and 3.5%, respectively. Not surprisingly, when a model that dropped shared environment was fitted, it revealed that this influence did not contribute to the fit of the model and that the variance in the data could be explained satisfactorily with additive genetic and nonshared environmental parameters.

A related useful method is the multiple regression analysis of genetic data described by DeFries and colleagues (DeFries & Fulker, 1985; LaBuda *et al.*, 1986). The technique is particularly appropriate for samples in which probands have been selected because of deviance on a trait that is continuously measured, such as reading disability or low intelligence. The technique not only measures heritability, through partial regression coefficients, but it can also compare different groups, such as the reading-disabled, with those of normal reading ability, to see whether the degree of heritability is the same in both groups. The new modelling techniques have many advantages and are now preferred in behaviour genetic analyses.

Linkage, association and molecular genetics

So far in our discussion we have dealt almost exclusively with genetic analysis at the level of symptoms, signs and measurable psychological traits. One of the major problems for the genetic study of childhood disorders is a lack of biochemical or physiological measures lying a step nearer the genotype on the complicated pathway between abnormal genes and abnormal behaviour. The discovery of a biochemical basis for an inherited disorder (e.g. showing an excess of phenylalanine in the blood of children with PKU) has been the usual starting point for unravelling the genetics of inborn errors and other simply inherited genetic disorders. However, recent spectacular advances in mapping the human genome have allowed the development of a radically different approach to understanding the molecular basis of inherited disease even when there is no clear prior knowledge about the biochemical abnormalities (Strachan, 1992). In this strategy, called positional cloning, the aim is to find linkage between genetic markers and the gene(s) — locus (or loci) — responsible for the disease and thence to use a variety of molecular genetic techniques to identify the disease gene itself. Once the gene has been identified, it is then possible to study its DNA sequence and structure, and infer what protein the mutant gene makes or fails to make. At this point, it may be possible to derive both diagnostic tests and rational treatment (Davies & Read, 1991).

Genetic linkage was recognized long before the advent of molecular genetics. Linkage can be inferred when alleles at two loci fail to obey Mendel's law of independent assortment. For example, a doubly heterozygous parent of the type $A_1A_2B_1B_2$ whose partner is homozygous at both loci, $A_1A_1B_1B_1$, will, in the absence of linkage, have offspring of the types $A_1A_1B_1B_1$, $A_1A_1B_1B_2$, $A_1A_2B_1B_1$ and $A_1A_2B_1B_2$ with equal probabilities. This is because during meiosis in the germline cells of the double heterozygote parent, the alleles at the two loci will, half of the time, remain together and, half of the time, cross over (or recombine), providing that the loci are on different chromosomes or are far apart on the same chromosome. Let us suppose however that the two loci are actually close together on the same chromosome. Thus if the doubly heterozygous parent has A_1 and B_1 on the same chromosome (and A_2 and B_2 on the other member of the homologous, or paired chromosome), offspring of the type $A_1A_2B_1B_2$ and $A_1A_1B_1B_1$ (nonrecombinants) will outnumber offspring of the types $A_1A_2B_1B_1$, $A_1A_1B_1B_2$ (recombinants). When there is complete linkage, these will be the only possibilities. The number of nonrecombinant offspring divided by the total number of offspring is called the recombination fraction and it has a maximum value of 0.5 since in independent assortment the average numbers of recombinant and nonrecombinant offspring are equal. Within certain limits, the size of the recombination fraction is roughly proportional to the physical distance between the two loci, so that for loci very close together the recombination fraction approaches 0. Thus the task of linkage analysis is to detect recombination fractions of less than 0.5 and to estimate their size.

In experimental plants and animals, the detection of linkage and estimation of recombination is relatively straightforward because the necessary matings can readily be carried out. However, with human beings, the genetic researcher is not in such a fortunate position and needs to have recourse to more complicated statistics. The usual method is to apply a method called lod score analysis (Morton, 1982). Lod (logarithm of the odds) scores use odds ratios to compare the likelihood of linkage (a recombination fraction less than 0.5) to the likelihood of no linkage (a recombination fraction equal to 0.5) based on the observed proportions of genotypes. By convention, a lod score of 3 or greater (odds in favour of linkage of 1000:1) is considered proof of linkage while lod scores of -2 or less (odds against linkage of 100:1) generally constitutes evidence against linkage, and intermediate lod scores are inconclusive.

Obviously linkage analysis is most straightforward when dealing with a pair of traits that have simple Mendelian modes of transmission and it was this for which the lod score method was originally devised. However, it is possible to carry out linkage analysis where one of the traits (referred to as the main trait, for example, a disease) shows an irregular pattern of transmission, provided that some assumptions can be made about the penetrance values and gene frequency and that the second trait fulfils the criteria for a genetic marker. This is a simply inherited character that has a known mode of transmission and is polymorphic (i.e. there are two or more alleles, each with a gene frequency of at least 1%). Genetic markers used in studies of diseases have in most cases been mapped to precise chromosomal locations. Other recent developments of linkage analysis include multipoint methods where it is possible to study the cosegregation of a main trait and two or more

genetic markers providing that the location of the markers relative to each other is already known (Ott, 1985). Multipoint linkage gives more precise information about the location of the gene for trait under examination.

As we have mentioned, the main reason that linkage analysis has assumed enormous importance recently in medical genetics has been the rapid increase in the number of genetic markers available and the breathtaking pace of developments in using linkage and other techniques to map the human genome. Until the beginning of the 1980s, the range of markers available for linkage studies of disease was comparatively small. These included ABO and other red blood cell groups, certain red cell enzymes, a variety of protein polymorphisms found in the blood, the human leukocyte antigen (HLA) system and polymorphisms resulting from differences in banding patterns on chromosomes. Even with good collaboration between several laboratories it was difficult to study more than about 25–30 of these polymorphisms in relationship to a disease, leaving the vast majority of the genome uncovered in search for linkage. However, the introduction of the first generation of DNA polymorphisms (Botstein *et al.*, 1980), so-called restriction fragment length polymorphisms (RFLPs), had a near revolutionary effect. RFLPs exist because of variations in DNA sequences. Some such variations result in changes in the specific sites at which a type of bacterially derived enzyme, called restriction endonucleases, cut DNA. This results in a variation in fragment lengths after DNA has been cut (digested) using a restriction enzyme, and these fragments of different size can be separated, using electrophoresis, where the distance that each migrates on a gel is inversely related to its size. Fragments containing a particular DNA sequence can be identified using a radioactive-labelled probe consisting of a homologous DNA sequence in an ingenious set of procedures known as Southern blot analysis (Southern, 1975). More recently, a variety of new techniques have been developed which greatly increase our ability to detect DNA variation. These include the polymerase chain reaction (PCR) which allows many copies of a short sequence of DNA to be made from small samples that have not been previously purified, making it easier to study, both in determining linkage and also determining the actual DNA sequence.

The success of genetic linkage studies in psychiatric disorders (or any other common familial disease where the mode of inheritance is unknown) depends upon the correctness of three assumptions. Firstly, it assumes that a major gene is involved in the transmission of at least some forms of the disorder; secondly, that, at least within families containing two or more affected individuals, homogeneity can be assumed and, thirdly, that even if the mode of transmission is not known precisely, it can be specified approximately. In practice, researchers tend to try to maximize the chances that these assumptions are correct by concentrating on multiplex families with multiply affected individuals, in which several members are affected, and by adopting an exploratory approach where several plausible models of transmission and, often, several definitions of the disorder are explored. Unfortunately, such an exploratory strategy introduces the additional problem, familiar in statistics, of multiple testing. That is, if several tests of linkage between a marker and disease are carried out rather than just one, the confidence that may be placed in a 'significant' finding is reduced, because the probability of a chance positive result increases with the number of tests. Disappointingly, recent claims of linkage in adult disorders, for example, between markers on chromosome 11 and manic depression (Egeland *et al.*, 1987) and between markers on chromosome 5 and schizophrenia (Sherrington *et al.*, 1988) have not been supported (Kelsoe *et al.*, 1989; McGuffin *et al.*, 1990). While there may be several reasons for such contradictory results, it is likely that multiple testing was one contributor to the initial positive lod scores.

All of the findings just discussed are examples of researchers focusing on a favoured region of the genome. However, such attempts to obtain short-cuts to finding disease genes are, as we have seen, not always successful. It then becomes necessary to mount a systematic search throughout the entire genome. As this is a costly exercise in time and resources, it usually requires multicentre collaboration and, at present, collaborations are underway both in Europe and North America attempting to discover genes of major effect in adult psychiatric disorders such as schizophrenia and manic depression. Despite recent widespread enthusiasm, the whole issue of performing linkage studies in psychiatric disorders with unknown modes of transmission remains controversial. Some authors have urged caution because of the statistical problems (Sturt & McGuffin, 1985; Clerget-Darpoux, 1991; Edwards, 1991) but others have put forward more radical objections on the basis that most common variations in behaviour, normal or abnormal, are unlikely to result from single genes of large effect (Plomin, 1990). This argument largely follows from animal studies where heritabilities for behavioural characteristics rarely exceed 50% and where most evidence points to the involvement of several (perhaps many) genes, each of comparatively small effect. Most continuously distributed human behaviours (e.g. IQ, personality) also have heritabilities of around 50% or less and are most likely to be polygenic (or possibly oligogenic). The point becomes more debatable for abnormal behaviours but here again there are persuasive arguments that conditions such as schizophrenia will in a great majority of cases turn out to be polygenic rather than involve genes of large effect (Gottesman, 1991). The question then arises: does molecular genetics still have anything to offer?

This general problem is by no means limited to psychiatric genetics and some of the most encouraging evidence that molecular genetics can help resolve polygenic systems comes from areas of research that at first sight seem remote. Plant geneticists interested in crop yield have for many years studied quantitative traits. Recently attention has turned to using genetic markers to locate so-called quantitative trait loci (QTLs). QTLs refer to genetic markers that are associated with normally distributed traits, or traits whose liability is normally distributed. Each locus generally contributes a small amount,

e.g. 5–10%, to the variance of that distribution. This work has implicated genetic loci responsible for small amounts of variation in the qualities of the fruit of tomatoes (Patterson *et al.*, 1988), and in semiquantitative traits such as hypertension in the rat (Hilbert *et al.*, 1991) and nonobese diabetes in mice (Todd *et al.*, 1991).

Again, the impossibility of breeding experiments means that the search for QTLs in human beings is more complicated. However, one comparatively simple strategy is to carry out association studies where populations rather than families are studied. The basic aim in an association study is to detect differences in allele frequencies for a particular marker between a sample of subjects with the disorder and either healthy controls or a sample representative of the general population. Allelic association (Edwards, 1991) between a marker and a disease or other trait can arise for three main reasons. The first of these is that the marker locus itself plays some causative role in the disease or trait. This is sometimes referred to as pleiotropy, when the same gene has two or more apparently different effects. Secondly, the marker itself may have no direct role but may be very closely linked to a gene that does; so close, in fact, that the allelic association is undisturbed over many generations of recombination. This situation is known as linkage disequilibrium. However, the third cause of association is of less interest. This is called stratification and most commonly arises from a recent (in genetic terms) admixture of populations. Suppose, for example, we were to carry out an association study between cannabis smoking and markers of the HLA system in South London. Cannabis use is frequent but is more popular among some subcultures than others. For example, it may be more common among people of Afro-Caribbean than of British ancestry. However, Afro-Caribbeans and white Europeans have rather different distributions of HLA types. Therefore, if we were to compare cannabis users and noncannabis users without controlling for ethnic differences, we might find an HLA–cannabis-use association and make a false inference that cannabis smoking is somehow genetically influenced.

Another disadvantage of association studies is that misleading false-positive results can arise because of the statistical problem, mentioned earlier, of multiple testing. Paradoxically, the most valuable markers are those that are highly polymorphic, having many alleles, but having many alleles then necessitates many tests for allelic association. A further difficulty is that association is a 'short-sighted' strategy. That is, negative results may arise either because the marker being tested is in completely the wrong region of the genome or because it is roughly in the right region, but not nearly close enough to a trait locus to detect association. As mentioned above, linkage disequilibrium only arises when loci are very close together and this usually means a recombination fraction of 0.01 or less. Linkage strategies by contrast may detect recombination fractions of 0.2 or slightly over in human beings. On the other hand, a corollary of their short-sightedness is that association studies can detect genes of small effect. Thus, one of the oldest and best established associations in human disease is between blood group O and predisposition to duodenal ulcer, but the association only accounts for about 1% of the variance in liability to develop this order (Edwards, 1965). Similarly, HLA associations have been established with many diseases but the amount of variance explained is comparatively small (McGuffin & Buckland, 1990). Because of this potential to detect genes of small effect and despite the difficulties, attention is once again turning to association strategies in studies of psychiatric and other common familial disorders. Recently, it has become possible to detect the effect of single genes in disorders thought to be multifactorial. For example, a recent study of coronary artery disease has suggested a role for the gene for angiotensin-converting enzyme, a protein important in hypertension and vascular tone. Coronary artery disease is generally conceptualized as a disorder involving both a number of genes and environmental influences. However, individuals usually thought to be at low risk of heart disease were three times more likely to suffer a myocardial infarction if they carried a sequence thought to be tightly linked (through association; Cambien *et al.*, 1992) with a particular form of the enzyme. At present most work is focusing on candidate genes, whose location and function are known, such as genes coding for neuroreceptors or other proteins which might plausibly be involved in the pathogenesis of psychiatric disorders. However, it is an interesting speculation that a systematic scan of the entire genome using association may become feasible in the foreseeable future (Owen, 1992). This would require a total of about 1500 markers roughly evenly spaced throughout the genome.

ENVIRONMENTAL INFLUENCES

Genetic studies, both behavioural and molecular, are just as important for what they can say about the role of environmental effects as what they say about genes. Phenotypes are always influenced by the environment. Even for single-gene disorders, environmental influences are important; for metabolic conditions, such as PKU and other aminoacidurias, the treatment consists of dietary manipulation to avoid commonly ingested amino acids. For other conditions, environmental agents are a prerequisite for the manifestation of the disorder; for example, a genetic predisposition to alcohol abuse will have no effect on the phenotype in a society where alcohol is not available. It is helpful to partition environmental effects into shared, or familial, and nonshared, or individual, effects. Nonshared environment reflects those effects that are uncorrelated between individuals, and hence make people less like each other. Shared environment refers to those aspects of the environment that are shared by individuals in a way that makes them more similar to each other. Thus, such effects not only need to impinge on both individuals but also to increase their resemblance. Shared effects may come from within the family or from the wider environment, including peers, school and exposure to environmental agents. Thus, while it is possible to note whether observable environments are shared or not, this does not tell us whether they are experienced in the

same way by different people and whether the shared experiences make those individuals more similar to each other. There are a number of reasons why apparently shared environments may not make individuals more similar. First, there may be individual characteristics, such as age and sex, that lead people to be differentially affected. Hospital admission, for example, appears to have the greatest deleterious effect between 6 months and 4 years of age (Schaffer & Callender, 1959). Secondly, an event affecting an entire family may have different meanings for various members. Thus, parental divorce will have a different effect on the child who is close to the departing parent compared to the child who had a conflictual relationship with that parent. Thirdly, it is possible that relatively small differences in parental treatment of siblings is more important than the absolute treatment they give. Rowe (1983) showed that twins and siblings may give different ratings of parental treatment, depending on whether they are rating parental treatment of themselves or their siblings. Such differences would be missed if parents were asked to give an overall rating of the way in which they treated their children.

One of the findings of twin and adoption studies that have partitioned environmental effects into shared and nonshared influences has been the considerably greater influence of nonshared environment, especially for personality traits but also for intelligence (see Plomin & Daniels, 1987, for a review). The relative unimportance of shared environment is somewhat surprising but, again, it should be remembered that influences relating to the family need not be shared by siblings. Another concern is that measurement error will be included in the estimates of nonshared environment, making nonshared environment appear more important, and genetic and shared environment less important. Another potential confound is that of nonadditive genetic influences. The genetic effects of dominance and epistasis will lower the DZ correlation (because DZ twins will share less than half of a *combination* of genes) while the MZ correlation remains constant. If nonadditive genetic influences are not taken into account, the data will appear to show a lack of influence of shared environment. As discussed previously, it is necessary to measure the trait in individuals of several different degrees of relatedness, e.g. twins and their parents, to be able to incorporate both nonadditive genetic influences and shared environment into a single model.

Several further points have been raised by Goodman (1991), who suggested that random, or chance, factors in development can lead to differences in individuals with the same genetic make-up and may appear to behave as nonshared environment. Such influences have been postulated in handedness and fit well to the observed data (Annett, 1985). In addition, Goodman suggested that siblings may either become more like each other, or more different, and that the relative importance of these two influences may change over time. Many genetic models ignore the possibility that the behaviour of one individual will influence others nearby, causing them to be more similar or more different from each other. Eaves (1976) has referred to such effects as cooperation and competition, respectively, and has demonstrated the effect they will have on data. Not only will the correlations between twins increase under cooperation, mimicking shared environment, and decrease under competition, looking like nonadditive genetic variance, there will also be systematic effects on the variances and covariances which can be tested to try to discriminate these influences. Carey (1986) has explored how foster/adopted sibships can be incorporated into such models. While such influences seem highly plausible, studies that measure them directly are needed, along with methods that will account for both individual differences and group trends in whether identifying or polarizing influences predominate. In summary, while some current research suggests a minor role for shared environmental influences, these studies may underestimate their importance and such findings do not assess the mechanisms that underlie whether individuals are similar or dissimilar.

Gene–environment interaction

Gene–environment interaction refers to a joint, nonadditive effect of genotype with environment. The concept should not be confused with the notion of interactionism which refers to the idea that genes and environment act together to form the phenotype; this is implicit in any model that incorporates both genetic and environmental influences. Rather, gene–environment interaction refers to the case where genotypes combined with different environments (or vice versa) produce nonlinear changes in the phenotype. A straightforward example of this would be the effect of placing an individual with the PKU phenotype on a phenylalanine-free diet; the effect on phenylalanine levels of such a diet is dramatically different for affected and nonaffected individuals.

Wahlsten (1990) has noted the relative infrequency with which gene–environment interaction has been detected in humans. He argued that the methods used, particularly in behaviour genetic studies, may not be the most sensitive to picking up such interactions. However, there is a more basic problem in human studies, namely that for virtually all the behaviours we are interested in, we cannot specify the genotype. It is entirely possible that many gene–environment interactions depend on a specific environmental alteration that relates to a particular genotype. Hence, it we lumped PKU with all other forms of severe mental retardation and then looked for an effect of reduced dietary phenylalanine, we would probably miss it.

The advent of molecular genetic techniques that allow specification of individuals' genotypes at particular loci involved in the phenotypic expression of a trait will undoubtedly increase the power to detect genotype–environment interaction. This has been seen in the case of the apolipoprotein E gene and dietary intake of cholesterol (Xu *et al.*, 1990), where, in a Finnish population known for high cholesterol levels, 15% of the phenotypic variance in cholesterol levels was due to apolipoprotein E variation on the high-cholesterol basal diet, but no significant effect of variation at that locus

could be found on the low-cholesterol intervention diet. This also illustrates the point, made by Wahlsten (1990), that genotype–environment interaction is most likely to be detected when the variations in genotype and/or environment are great, as in the case of a diet in which cholesterol intake is purposely kept very low.

A further difficulty in detecting gene–environment interaction in behaviour genetic studies is that, in twin and family studies, individuals will share a large proportion of their genes. Hence, the likelihood of having enough variation in genotypes (as well as environments) is not great. Adoption studies are better suited than twin or family studies for the detection of gene–environment interaction (Plomin *et al.*, 1977) because the sources of genetic and environmental variation are not confounded. To date, little evidence has been found for gene–environment interaction in adoption studies of normal development where the range of behaviours examined have generally fallen well within the normal range rather than representing extremes or disorder (Plomin *et al.*, 1977; Plomin & DeFries, 1985). However, we should note from the examples above just how important it is to be able to specify the genotype, the environmental manipulation and the phenotype measured.

Some suggestion of gene–environment interaction for a human trait comes from adoption studies on adult criminality. Hutchings and Mednick (1975) found that in Danish adoptees whose biological father was 'known to the police' but whose adoptive father had no criminal record, the rate of criminality was 24%. It was thus clearly higher than the rate of criminality in adoptees whose adopting but not biological father had a criminal record, which, at 12%, was little higher than the rate (11%) in adoptees where neither adopting nor biological father had a history of criminality. Thus, genes appeared to exert an effect in the absence of criminality in the home environment, while the reverse effect, that of home environment in the absence of the relevant genes, was not observed. However, where both adopting and biological fathers had criminal records, the rate of criminality in adoptees was highest of all, at 36%. This suggests an interaction effect, although a subsequent analysis did not find it to be significant (Cloninger *et al.*, 1982). Similarly, Cloninger *et al.* (1982) found, in a study of male Swedish adoptees, that placement in a home of low social status increased the risk of petty criminality where the biological father had been criminal, but had no effect if the biological father had no police record. This was supported by Cadoret *et al.* (1983), who demonstrated an interaction between having a biological parent with a criminal record and being adopted later than usual: the combination of factors led to a higher rate of antisocial personality in the adopted offspring than would be expected from an additive effect of the influences. Using logistic regression models to test an interaction, both Cadoret *et al.* (1983) and Tienari *et al.* (1990) found evidence of such effects in adoptive samples looking at depression and schizophrenia, respectively. Thus, for depressive symptoms, there was an interaction effect between age at adoption and affective illness in a biological parent and for schizophrenia; a significant interaction was demonstrated between schizophrenia in a biological parent and a measure of the adoptive family's psychological health.

Kendler and Eaves (1986) explored the effects on risk to relatives under varying models of the joint action of genes and environment. The classical model, as described under multifactorial inheritance, assumes that genes and environment act additively and independently. In the first instance, they examined how the risk to relatives would be affected under such a model in which there were three possible environmental conditions — a random environment, an environment predisposing to the condition and an environment protective for the condition — and three genotypes (a single gene with two alleles producing three genotypes, A_1A_1, A_1A_2 and A_2A_2). In this model, each genotype confers a separate liability for expressing the condition. They confirmed an increased risk for relatives of probands compared to the general population under all environmental conditions. When both probands and relatives were classified according to the environmental conditions, the highest risk in relatives occurred when the proband developed the condition in a protective environment and the relative was in a predisposing environment. This is because a proband developing the condition in a protective environment is relatively more likely to have the most vulnerable genotype and therefore their relatives are also more likely also to have this genotype. However, all genotypes are more likely to express the condition in a predisposing environment so the highest risk will be for relatives with the vulnerable genotype in a predisposing environment. This is exactly what is expected under the multifactorial model previously described. However, when gene−environment interaction is postulated, the results are rather different. Here, the risk to relatives is greatest in the group in which the proband exhibited the condition in a predisposing environment. This is because individuals who exhibit the condition in the predisposing environment, under gene−environment interaction, are more likely to have a sensitive genotype which, in turn, is more likely than the insensitive genotype to demonstrate the condition in the predisposing environment. We can see from these examples how different mechanisms underlying phenotypic expression can change the pattern of recurrence in relatives.

Gene−environment correlation

Gene−environment correlation refers to a nonrandom association between the genotype of the individual and the environment. To the extent that genes influence our behaviour, which in turn affects how we interact with others and use our environment, this is axiomatic. There are a variety of different ways in which gene−environment correlation may occur. Firstly, there is the transmission of environments from parents to children. The phenomenon is generally called cultural transmission (Cavalli-Sforza & Feldman, 1973) and refers to the fact that there are elements of the environment that parents make available to and share with their children, including such varying experiences as the neighbourhood in

which they live, the number and type of books and other commodities in the home, the degree of warmth expressed and the amount of autonomy for individual family members. However, to the extent that each of these is a reflection of parental behaviour, and to the extent that this parental behaviour is in part genetically mediated, cultural transmission is also a form of gene−environment correlation in families of biologically related individuals. Plomin *et al.* (1977) distinguish three types of gene−environment correlation. Passive gene−environment correlation is that which is imposed on the individual by others, or which is independent of that person. In families of biologically related individuals, this will be a positive correlation because of the shared genes of parents and children. For example, the musical parent is more likely to expose his or her child to a musical environment but is also more likely to have a child whose genotype predisposes him or her to be musical. Reactive gene−environment correlation refers to alterations in the environment caused by the reactions of others to the phenotype (and therefore to the genotype) of the individual. Thus, the parents who note their child playing the piano will spontaneously arrange music lessons for him or her, thereby promoting his or her talent. The third type of gene−environment correlation is active, in which the individual seeks out certain environments. Our musical child will spend more time practising the piano and improve his or her skill. The authors make the point that genotype−environment correlation can be negative as well as positive, particularly in cases where individuals are selected out for specific environmental treatments. One example would be special school programmes for children of lower ability. Another example would be, in the case of adoption, where parents and children will not share their genes and, furthermore, adopted children frequently have parents with personality and psychiatric disturbance while adoptive parents are selected to be supernormal, so their genotypes may be negatively rather than randomly correlated. The important point is that, in many instances, genes and environment will not coexist randomly but rather will relate to each other in ways that may influence the phenotype.

One way of looking at this is to measure the roles of genetic influences on measures of the environment (Plomin & Bergaman, 1991). Clearly, the environment is not influenced directly by genetic factors; rather, people's behaviour, which is genetically influenced, affects their environment, both in what actually occurs and also (probably) in how they rate it. Plomin and Bergaman suggested that there are a number of generally consistent findings. Parental warmth to children, as measured in a variety of ways from observational studies in infancy through contemporaneous self-ratings in adolescence to retrospective recollections in middle age, shows substantial genetic influence, while parental control does not. This finding is of particular interest in that the evidence for juvenile delinquency and conduct disorder suggests an important role for shared environment (McGuffin & Gottesman, 1985), and that parental control may well be a relevant influence. A further surprising finding was that genetic effects appear to influence life events. This provides indirect support for a controversial finding from a previous family study of adult depression in which the experience (or perhaps the reporting) of threatening life events was found to be familial (McGuffin *et al.*, 1988). However, Kendler *et al.* (1991) found that genetic influence was greater for those classified *a priori* as independent rather than dependent. This perhaps suggests that controllable events are associated with the genetic determination of certain personality traits or behavioural styles.

Kendler and Eaves (1986) have examined the effects of a particular type of gene–environment correlation, namely that of genetic control over exposure to an environment, which predisposes to a trait or illness. In their model, different genotypes vary in the extent to which individuals are exposed to the predisposing environment; however, once exposed, the risk of developing the condition is the same for all genotypes. They point out how such a mechanism could appear to be misinterpreted as due to differing penetrances for the various genotypes if the mediating role of environment were not noted. As in the gene–environment interaction model, but not that of independent additive action, relatives of probands who demonstrated the trait in the context of the predisposing environment have a greater risk of being affected. In this case, this is because such probands, and therefore their relatives, are more likely to have the genotype causing exposure to the predisposing environment. It is possible that this mechanism will apply to some disorders where predisposition is related to life events, such as the milder forms of depression (McGuffin *et al.*, 1988; Kendler, 1991). Under this model and not the others, however, the risk of demonstrating the condition is indexed almost entirely by whether or not the individual has been exposed to the relevant environment. It is important to note that, unless the relevant environment is measured, it would appear that the disorder itself was genetically influenced, rather than exposure to the environment. Such mechanisms of gene–environment action could have important implications for intervention. Because, for virtually all behaviours, both genes and environment are important, it makes no sense to think of a disorder as either genetic or environmental.

Scarr and McCartney (1983) amplified the role of gene–environment correlation, suggesting both that the importance of such relationships increases with age and that there is a developmental pattern in which passive gene–environment correlations are most important in infants and younger children but decrease in prominence with age, while reactive and then active gene–environment correlations come in with increasing age and play a greater role as the individual develops. The notion of passive gene–environment correlation could be termed imposed environment since the gene–environment correlation occurs because biological parents and their offspring share genes; however, adoptive and stepparents do not share genes with their offspring but the passive transmission of environment still occurs. This theory predicts that related individuals will become more similar over time and that unrelated people sharing the same environment (such as adoptees) and twin sibs or parents will become less

similar over time. This does not imply that the environment is unimportant but rather that the environment is at least in part selected by behaviours that are genetically influenced. This is consistent with the data presented by Plomin and Bergaman (1991), indicating the role of genetic influences on environmental measures. Thus, in understanding gene–environment action, it is important not only to obtain relevant measures of the environment but also to examine changes over time.

Continuity versus change over time

There are several facets of the question of continuity versus change over time. Firstly, there is the problem of taking account of changes in the observed phenotype that occur as a result of normal development. This is exemplified in the study of temperament where theory suggests that a number of dimensions of behavioural style underpin the manner in which people behave across situations and across ages; however, this style is often measured, particularly in children, by obtaining examples of how people behave in various situations. The difficulty arises because the details of behaviour, and the situations that are appropriate, change with age. Another area in which this occurs is in oppositional and conduct disorder and antisocial personality, where there are strong continuities between the three but where the behaviours involved in each are different. It is unclear whether the continuity represents an underlying trait that remains constant throughout the individual's life but is expressed by different behaviours at various ages or whether some other mechanism is operating, e.g. each behavioural disorder conferring a risk for the next, or each disorder exposing the individual to environmental risks which promote continuity, to name just two other possibilities.

A second problem is the changes that occur in prevalence rates over age for many of the behaviours of interest. These are particularly problematic for genetic designs that rely on the comparison of individuals of different ages and for studies using continuous measures because it is often uncertain whether different scores at different ages relate to true changes or result from some artefact. Thirdly, while longitudinal or cohort-sequential studies are optimal, much of the conclusions about stability derive from comparing cross-sectional studies on different populations where the relative influence of genetic and environmental influences may differ for reasons other than the age of the cohort. Fourthly, the measures used at different ages vary not only in their item composition but also in their theoretical underpinnings. Thus, in the study of temperament and personality, the tendency (with some exceptions, e.g. Plomin *et al.*, 1988b) has been to use measures of temperament in infancy and childhood and personality in adult life that have different theoretical backgrounds and dimensions of behaviour.

We need to bear in mind that continuity or change at a phenotypic level tell us very little about the change in underlying genetic or environmental influences. Thus, while some single-gene disorders are present at birth (such as PKU), others (such as Huntington's disease) present much later in life. We also know that genes 'switch on' and 'off' during the lifespan. Hence genetic influences need not be associated with continuity, nor environmental ones with change (Fig. 9.2).

Despite these difficulties, there is a tentative suggestion of consistency in development, when examining studies of intelligence, temperament/personality and psychopathology, with all suggesting that the role of genetic influences increases with time. Plomin (1986) reviewed the studies of intelligence at different ages and showed a sharp decrease in nonshared environment from infancy to childhood, a moderate increase in heritability from infancy to adolescence, followed by a more gradual increase in adult life and a small decrease in shared environment from childhood onwards. The Louisville Twin Study obtained temperament measures from twins from birth to 9 years (Wilson, 1985). Interestingly, shortly after birth, many of the DZ correlations were higher than those of the MZ twins. One possible explanation would be the effect of the twin transfusion syndrome, leading to greater birth weight discrepancies in the MZ pairs. From 3 months on, the study showed decreases in the DZ correlations over time, with relative constancy in the MZ correlations, reducing the estimate of shared environment with a corresponding increase in the heritability. A similar picture is seen in this study for IQ, where, again, heritability increases because the DZ correlation decreases.

The literature on psychopathology is sparse. However, McGuffin and Gottesman's (1985) review of twin studies of conduct disorder and antisocial personality suggested that the importance of shared environmental influences decreases with age. In line with this, the Swedish adoption study which examined adopted boys at 15, 18 and 21 years (Bohman & Sigvardsson, 1978, 1980; Cloninger *et al.*, 1981) showed the boys to become increasingly like their biological parents with age.

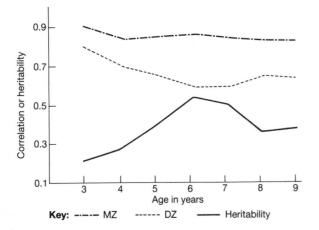

Fig. 9.2 Changes in the heritability of IQ during childhood. Longitudinal data from the Louisville Twin Study showing decreasing dizygotic (DZ) correlations, with monozygotic (MZ) correlations remaining constant. Based on data from Wilson (1985).

The way forward

The next two decades promise to be even more exciting than the last two in terms of advances in the genetics of behaviour and psychiatric conditions. With the sophisticated and powerful armamentarium of molecular genetics, advances that are of relevance for child psychiatry are almost certain. However, there is still much groundwork to be done. For many child psychiatric conditions, it is not clear whether genetic influences play a role or, if so, what modes of transmission are likely. In addition, many disorders are probably genetically heterogeneous, with both phenocopies and different genetic aetiologies. For example, it seems likely that there are many routes into conduct disorder, including those through reading difficulties, consequences of hyperactivity, family adversities, parental psychiatric disorder and sociocultural influences such as exposure to a delinquent peer group. It is necessary to differentiate the various pathways into what may appear to be a homogeneous condition at its endpoint.

For almost all child psychiatric disorders, basic research into the extent of genetic influences and their nature is necessary. We have witnessed, in the last 5 years, an overwhelming enthusiasm for searching for single genes of major influence in adult psychiatric disorders. However, it should be noted that the only cases in which linkage results have been confirmed (some cases of early-onset Alzheimer's disease and Huntington's disease) are ones in which the mode of inheritance appeared Mendelian from simple inspection of the pedigrees. It is our view that most of the genetic influences in child psychiatric disorders will not be of a sml type. In none of these conditions is there evidence of a classic Mendelian pattern of familial aggregation. This does not exclude the possibility that there will be rare families in which a single major gene gives rise to behaviour which would be classified as a particular disorder. However, if this does occur, we expect it will account for a very small minority of cases. It should be borne in mind that current evidence suggests that autism is transmitted by several genes (Rutter, 1991). The importance of this is that autism could be considered the most likely child psychiatric candidate for a single major gene, based on its high heritability and its rarity in the population.

When molecular genetic strategies can be employed in child psychiatric conditions, it is likely that for many disorders designs will need to take into account the action of multiple genes, either in oligogenic or polygenic models, with the influence of environmental factors. As such, the techniques for detecting genes of smaller effect will be applicable and, along with this, the large sample sizes required for detection of genes of small effect. To acquire sufficiently large samples, collaborative efforts to identify and recruit patients meeting the criteria for specific subgroups of diagnostic entities will be necessary. While there are instances when large pedigrees with multiply affected individuals may be helpful in molecular genetics, this is unlikely to be often the case in child psychiatry.

It cannot be left to molecular genetic techniques to define the phenotype; phenotypic misclassification of individuals generally reduces the power of linkage and related studies to detect true findings (Baron *et al.*, 1990). A number of tools must be used in disentangling the aetiological subgroups of disorder. Along with prospective, longitudinal studies, behaviour genetic strategies that decompose the total diagnostic group into subgroups defined according to theoretical distinctions in aetiology and then examine the extent to which the relative importance of genetic and environmental influences differ both in degree and in pattern across the classification can shed light on the distinctions which need to be made at an endophenotypic level. Subgroups can also be defined according to operational criteria to help shed light on which criteria are likely to be genetically mediated (McGuffin *et al.*, 1984). Progress will involve a boot-strapping operation between genetic studies and other strategies, including epidemiological and high-risk samples, both longitudinal and cross-sectional, and using a variety of measurement techniques including psychiatric, psychological, neurobiological and neurophysiological, to gain a better definition of the phenotype.

As our understanding increases, of how genetic risks operate there will be a greater demand for genetic counselling. At present, families with relatives affected with a severely disabling disorder, such as autism, are beginning to consider the risks of having similarly affected children. At the moment, genetic advice is based on empirical recurrence risks that have not taken into account a number of potentially relevant factors, such as the degree of family loading and whether the individual is affected with a broader phenotype, or milder variant. In the long term, the aim should be to be able to identify at-risk individuals by their genotype.

It would be a mistake, however, to see the sole aim of genetic research on normal and abnormal behavioural development as identifying the genes responsible. Although this is likely to be valuable, both in furthering our understanding of the relationship between brain function and behaviour and also possibly in developing gene therapy for extremely deviant cases, it is necessary to bear in mind the extent to which most behaviours show substantial environmental influence and that, in many cases, it is likely that genetic influences will act through the environment. Therefore, it is essential that genetic studies of all sorts continue to include measures of the environment. In addition, these measures will need to become more subtle and studies will need to be designed in ways that allow testing of the various mechanisms by which genes and environment influence behaviour. Genetic studies over the next two decades will inform us not only about disorders but about normal development and how genes and environment act together.

REFERENCES

Annett M. (1985) *Left, Right, Hand and Brain: The Right Shift Theory.* Lawrence Erlbaum, Hillsdale, NJ.

Baron M., Mandlewicz J., Gruen R., Asnis L. & Fieve R.R. (1981) Assortative mating in the effective disorders. *Journal of Affective Disorders*, **3**, 167–171.

Baron M., Endicott J. & Ott J. (1990) Genetic linkage and mental illness: limitations and prospects. *British Journal of Psychiatry*, **157**, 645–665.

Beaudet A.L. (1990) Invited editorial: carrier screening for cystic fibrosis. *American Journal of Human Genetics*, **47**, 603–605.

Beckman L.J. (1975) Women alcoholics: a review of social and psychological studies. *Journal of Studies on Alcohol*, **36**, 797–824.

Bishop D.T. & Williamson J.A. (1990) The powers of identity by state methods for linkage analysis. *American Journal of Human Genetics*, **45**, 254–265.

Bohman M. & Sigvardsson S. (1978) An 18-year, prospective, longitudinal study of adopted boys. In: Anthony E.J. & Koupernik C.C. (eds) *The Child in his Family*, pp. 473–486. Krieger, Huntington, NY.

Bohman M. & Sigvardsson S. (1980) A prospective longitudinal study of children registered for adoption. A 15-year follow-up. *Acta Psychiatrica Scandinavica*, **61**, 339–353.

Bolton P. & Rutter M. (1990) Genetic influences in autism. *International Review of Psychiatry*, **2**, 67–80.

Botstein D., White R., Skocnick M. & Davis R.W. (1980) Construction of a genetic linkage map in man using restriction fragment polymorphisms. *American Journal of Human Genetics*, **32**, 314–331.

Bouchard T.J., Lykken D.T., McGue M., Segal N.L. & Tellegren A. (1990) Sources of human psychological differences: the Minnesota study of twins reared apart. *Science*, **250**, 223–228.

Burn J., Povey S., Boyd Y., Munro E.A., West L., Harper K. & Thomas D. (1986) Duchenne muscular dystrophy in one of monozygotic twin girls. *Journal of Medical Genetics*, **23**, 494–500.

Cadoret R.J. (1986) Adoption studies: historical and methodological critique. *Psychiatric Developments*, **1**, 45–64.

Cadoret R.J., Cain C.A. & Crowe R.R. (1983) Evidence for gene–environment interaction in the development of adolescent antisocial behavior. *Behavior Genetics*, **13**, 301–310.

Cambien F., Poirier O., Lecerf L., Evans A., Cambou J.-A., Arveiler D., Luc G., Bard J.-M., Bara L., Ricard S., Tiret L., Amouyel P., Alhenc-Gelas F. & Soubrier F. (1992) Deletion polymorphism in the gene for angiotensin-converting enzyme is a potent risk factor for myocardial infarction. *Nature*, **359**, 641–644.

Campbell D.M. & MacGillivray I. (1988) Outcome of twin pregnancies. In: MacGillivray I., Campbell D.M. & Thompson B. (eds) *Twinning and Twins*, pp. 179–206. Wiley, Chichester.

Campbell D.M. & Samphler M. (1988) Birth weight standards for twins. In: MacGillivray I.M., Campbell D.M. & Thompson B. (eds) *Twinning and Twins*, pp. 161–178. Wiley, Chichester.

Carey G. (1986) Sibling imitation and contrast effects. *Behavior Genetics*, **16**, 319–341.

Caron C. & Rutter M. (1990) Comorbidity in child psychopathology: concepts, issues and research strategies. *Journal of Child Psychology and Psychiatry*, **32**, 1063–1081.

Carter C.O. (1976) Genetics of common single malformations. *British Medical Bulletin*, **32**, 21–26.

Cattell R.B. & Nesselroade J.R. (1967) Likeness and completeness theories examined by sixteen personality factors measured on stably and unstably married couples. *Journal of Personality and Social Psychology*, **7**, 351–361.

Cavalli-Sforza L.L. & Feldman M.W. (1973) Cultural versus biological inheritance: phenotypic transmission from parents to children (a theory of the effect of parental phenotypes on children's phenotypes). *American Journal of Human Genetics*, **25**, 618–637.

Cederlof R., Frieberg L., Johnson E. & Kaij L. (1961) Studies on similarity diagnosis in twins with the aid of mailed questionnaires. *Acta Genetica*, **11**, 338–362.

Clerget-Darpoux F. (1991) The uses and misuses of linkage analysis in neuropsychiatric disorder. In: McGuffin P. & Murray R. (eds) *The New Genetics of Mental Illness*, pp. 44–57. Butterworth-Heinemann, Oxford.

Cloninger C.R., Christiansen K.O., Reich T. & Gottesman I.I. (1978) Implications of sex differences in the prevalence of ASP, alcoholism and criminality for familial transmission. *Archives of General Psychiatry*, **35**, 941–951.

Cloninger C.R., Bohman M. & Sigvardsson S. (1981) Inheritance of alcohol abuse: cross-fostering analysis of adopted men. *Archives of General Psychiatry*, **38**, 861–868.

Cloninger C.R., Sigvardsson S., Bohman M. & van Knorring A.L. (1982) Predisposition to petty criminality in Swedish adoptees: II. Cross-fostering analysis of gene–environment interaction. *Archives of General Psychiatry*, **39**, 1242–1247.

Cox N.L., Hodge S.E., Marazita M.L., Spence M.A. & Kidd K.K. (1988) Some effects of selection strategies on linkage analysis. *Genetic Epidemiology*, **5**, 269–277.

Davies K. (1991) Breaking the fragile X. *Nature*, **351**, 439–440.

Davies K. & Read A.P. (1991) *Molecular Basis of Inherited Disease*, 2nd edn. Oxford University Press, Oxford.

DeFries J.C. & Fulker D.W. (1985) Multiple regression analysis of twin data. *Behavior Genetics*, **15**, 467–473.

Dunner D.L., Fleiss J.L., Addonizio G. & Fieve R.R. (1976) Assortative mating in primary affective disorder. *Biological Psychiatry*, **11**, 43–51.

Eaves L.J. (1976) A model of sibling effects in man. *Heredity*, **36**, 206–214.

Eaves L.J., Hart K., Young P.A. & Martin N.G. (1978) Model-fitting approaches to the analysis of human behaviour. *Heredity*, **41**, 249–320.

Eaves L.J., Long J. & Heath A.C. (1986) A theory of developmental change in quantitative phenotypes applied to cognitive development. *Behavior Genetics*, **16**, 143–162.

Edwards J.H. (1960) The simulation of Mendelism. *Acta Geneticae*, **10**, 63–70.

Edwards J.H. (1965) The meaning of the association between blood groups and disease. *Annals of Human Genetics*, **29**, 77–83.

Edwards J.H. (1980) Allelic association in man. In: Eriksson A.W. (ed) *Population Structure and Genetic Disorders*, pp. 239–255. Academic Press, London.

Edwards J.H. (1991) The formal problems of linkage. In: McGuffin P. & Murray R. (eds) *The New Genetics of Mental Illness*, pp. 58–70. Butterworth-Heinemann, Oxford.

Egeland J.A., Gerhard D.S., Pauls D.L., Sussex J.N. & Kidd K. (1987) Bipolar affective disorders linked to DNA markers on chromosome 11. *Nature*, **325**, 783–787.

Eisensmith B.C. & Woo S.L.C. (1992) Molecular basis of phenylketonuria-alaneniao: mutations and polymorphisms in the human phenylalanine hydroxylase gene. *Human Mutation*, **1**, 13–23.

Elston R.C. & Stewart J. (1971) A general model for the genetic analysis of pedigree data. *Human Heredity*, **21**, 523–542.

Falconer D.S. (1965) The inheritance of liability to certain diseases examined from the incidence among relatives. *Annals of Human Genetics*, **29**, 51–76.

Falconer D.S. (1967) The inheritance of liability to diseases with variable age of onset with particular reference to diabetes mellitus. *Annals of Human Genetics (London)*, **34**, 31–38.

Folstein S. & Rutter M. (1977) Infantile autism: a genetic study of 21 twin pairs. *Journal of Child Psychology and Psychiatry*, **18**, 297–321.

Gershon E.S., Dunner D.L., Stuart L. & Goodwin F.K. (1973) Assortative mating in the affective disorders. *Biological Psychiatry*, **7**, 63–74.

Gershon E.S., Mark A., Cohen N., Bellzon N., Baron M. & Knobe K.E. (1975) Transmitted factors in the morbid risk of affective disorders – a controlled study. *Journal of Psychiatric Research*, **12**, 283–299.

Gershon E.S., Martinez M., Goldin L., Gelerher J. & Silver J. (1989) Detection of marker associations in to a dominant disease gene in

genetically complex and heterogenous diseases. *American Journal of Human Genetics*, **45**, 578–585.

Goate A., Chartier-Halin M.-C., Mullan M., Brown J., Crawford F., Fidani L., Giuffra L., Haynes A., Irving N. & Jamer L. (1991) Segregation of a missense mutation in the amyloid precursor protein gene with familial Alzheimer's disease. *Nature*, **349**, 704–706.

Goldberg D. & Wolkind S.N. (1992) Patterns of psychiatric disorder in adopted girls: a research note. *Journal of Child Psychology and Psychiatry*, **33**, 935–940.

Goldin L. & Gershon E.S. (1988) Power of the affected sib-pair method for heterogeneous disorders. *Genetic Epidemiology*, **5**, 35–42.

Goldsmith H.H. (1991) A zygosity questionnaire for young twins: a research note. *Behavior Genetics*, **21**, 257–270.

Goodman R. (1991) Growing together and growing apart: the non-genetic influences on children in the same family. In: McGuffin A. & Murray R.M. (eds) *The New Genetics of Mental Illness*, pp. 212–224. Butterworth-Heinemann, Oxford.

Goodman R. & Stevenson J. (1989) A twin study of hyperactivity — II. The aetiological role of genes, family relationships and perinatal adversity. *Journal of Child Psychology and Psychiatry*, **30**, 691–709.

Gottesman I.I. (1991) *Schizophrenia Genesis*. W.H. Freeman, New York.

Gottesman I.I. & Bertelsen A. (1989) Confirming unexpressed genotypes for schizophrenia. Results in the offspring of Fischer's Danish identical and fraternal discordant twins. *Archives of General Psychiatry*, **46**, 867–872.

Gottesman I.I. & Carey G. (1983) Extracting meaning and direction from twin data. *Psychiatric Development*, **1**, 35–50.

Gottesman I.I. & Shields J. (1967) A polygenic theory of schizophrenia. *Proceedings of the National Academy of Sciences*, **58**, 199–205.

Hall R.L., Hesselbrock V.M. & Stabenau J.R. (1983a) Familial distribution of alcohol use. I. Assortative mating in the parents of alcoholics. *Behavior Genetics*, **13**, 361–372.

Hall R.L., Hesselbrock V.M. & Stabenau J.R. (1983b) Familial distribution of alcohol use. II. Assortative mating of alcoholic probands. *Behavior Genetics*, **13**, 373–382.

Harper P.S. (1988) *Practical Genetic Counselling*. Butterworth-Heinemann, Oxford.

Harrington R., Rutter M., Fudge H., Bredenkamp D. & Groothues C. (submitted) Age and sex trends in depressive symptomatology: comparison with self-recorded anxiety, fears, eating attitudes and behavioral problems.

Hay D.A., Collett S.M., Johnston C.J. & Prior M. (1984) The high incidence of reading disability in twin boys and its implications for genetic analysis. *Acta Geneticae Medicae et Gemellologicae*, **33**, 223–236.

Hay D.A., Prior M., Collett S. & Williams M. (1987) Speech and language development in preschool twins. *Acta Geneticae Medicae et Gemellogicae*, **36**, 213–223.

Heath A.C. & Eaves L.J. (1985) Resolving the effects of phenotype and social background on mate selection. *Behavior Genetics*, **15**, 15–30.

Heath A.C., Neale M.C., Hewitt J.L., Eaves L.J. & Fulker D.W. (1989) Testing structural equation models for twin data using LISREL. *Behavior Genetics*, **19**, 9–35.

Hersov L. (1992) Adoption and fostering. In: Rutter M. & Hersov L. (eds) *Child and Adolescent Psychiatry: Modern Approaches*, 2nd edn, pp. 101–117. Blackwell Scientific Publications, Oxford.

Hilbert P., Lindpainter K., Beckmann J.S., Serikawa T., Soubrier F., Dubay C., Cartwright P., De Gouyon B., Julier C., Takahasi S., Vincent M., Gauteri D., Georges M. & Lathrop G.M. (1991) Chromosomal mapping of two genetic loci associated with blood pressure regulation in hereditary hypertensive rats. *Nature*, **353**, 521–529.

Hutchings B. & Mednick S.A. (1975) Registered criminality in the adoptive and biological parents of registered male criminal adoptees. In: Fieve R.R., Rosenthal D. & Brill H. (eds) *Genetic Research in Psychiatry*, pp. 105–116. Johns Hopkins University Press, Baltimore.

Jacob T. & Bremer D.A. (1986) Assortative mating among men and women alcoholics. *Journal of Studies on Alcohol*, **47**, 219–222.

Johnson R.C., DeFries J.C., Wilson J.R., McClearn G.E., Vandenberg S.G., Ashton G.C., Mi M.P. & Rashad M.N. (1976) Assortative mating for specific cognitive abilities in two ethnic groups. *Human Biology*, **48**, 343–352.

Jones M.B. & Szatmari P. (1988) Stoppage rules and the genetics of autism. *Journal of Autism and Developmental Disorders*, **18**, 31–41.

Jorgensen A.L., Philip J., Raskind W.H., Matsushita M., Christensen B., Dreyer V. & Motulsky A.G. (1992) Different patterns of X inactivation in MZ twins discordant for red-green colour vision deficiency. *American Journal of Human Genetics*, **51**, 291–298.

Kaback M.M. (1990) Heterozygostic screening. In: Emery A.E.H. & Rimon D.L. (eds) *Principles and Practice of Medical Genetics*, 2nd edn, pp. 1951–1958. Churchill Livingstone, Edinburgh.

Kaprio J., Koskenvuo M. & Rose R.J. (1990) Change in cohabitation and intrapair similarity of monozygotic (MZ) cotwins for alcohol use, extraversion and neuroticism. *Behavior Genetics*, **20**, 265–276.

Kelsoe J.R., Ginns E.I., Egeland J.A., Gerhard D.S., Goldstein A.M., Bale S.J., Pauls D.J., Long R.T., Kidd K.K., Conte C., Housman D.E. & Paul S.M. (1989) Re-evaluation of the linkage relationship between chromosome 11p loci and the gene for bipolar affective disorder in the Old Order Amish. *Nature*, **342**, 238–243.

Kendler K.S. (1988) Familial aggregation of schizophrenia and schizophrenia spectrum disorders. *Archives of General Psychiatry*, **45**, 377–383.

Kendler K.S. & Eaves L.J. (1986) Models for the joint effect of genotype and environment on liability to psychiatric illness. *American Journal of Psychiatry*, **143**, 179–189.

Kendler K.S., Neale M.C., Heath A.C., Kessler R.C. & Eaves L.J. (1991) Life events and depressive symptoms: a twin study perspective. In: McGuffin P. & Murray R. (eds) *The New Genetics of Mental Illness*, pp. 146–164. Butterworth-Heinemann, Oxford.

Kendler K.S., Neale M.C., Kessler R.C., Heath A.C. & Eaves L.J. (1992) A population-based twin study of major depression in women: the impact of varying definitions of illness. *Archives of General Psychiatry*, **49**, 257–266.

Kirkegaard-Sorensen L. & Mednick S.A. (1975) Registered criminality in children at high risk for schizophrenia. *Journal of Abnormal Psychology*, **84**, 197–204.

Kringlen E. & Cramer G. (1989) Offspring of monozygotic twins discordant for schizophrenia. *Archives of General Psychiatry*, **46**, 873–877.

La Buda M.C., Gottesman I.I. & Pauls D.L. (1993) The usefulness of twin studies for exploring the etiology of child and adolescent psychiatric disorders. *American Journal of Medical Genetics*, **48**, 47–59.

LaBuda M., Defries J.C. & Fulker D.W. (1986) Multiple regression analysis of twin data obtained from selected samples. *Genetic Epidemiology*, **3**, 425–433.

Lalouel J.M., Rao D.C., Morton M.E. & Elston R.N. (1983) A unified model for complex segregation analysis. *American Journal of Human Genetics*, **35**, 816–826.

Lange K. (1986) Cohabitation, convergence and environmental covariances. *American Journal of Medical Genetics*, **24**, 483–491.

Leahy A.M. (1932) A study of certain selective factors influencing prediction of the mental status of adoptive children in nature–nurture research. *Journal of Genetic Psychology*, **41**, 294–329.

Lewis S.W., Chitkara B., Reveley A.M. & Murray R.M. (1987) Family history and birth weight in monozygotic twins discordant for psychosis. *Acta Geneticae Medicae et Gemellologicae*, **36**, 267–273.

Little J. & Bryan E.M. (1988) Congenital anomalies. In: MacGillivray I.M., Campbell D.M. & Thompson B. (eds) *Twinning and Twins*, pp. 207–240. Wiley, Chichester.

Little J. & Thompson B. (1988) Descriptive epidemiology. In: MacGillivray I.M., Campbell D.M. & Thompson B. (eds) *Twinning and Twins*, pp. 37–66. Wiley, Chichester.

Loehlin J.C. (1987) *Latent Variable Models. An Introduction to Factor, Path and Structural Analysis*. Lawrence Erlbaum, Hillsdale, NJ.

Loehlin J.C. & Nichols R.C. (1976) *Heredity, Environment and Personality*. University of Texas Press, Austin.

Lykken D.T. (1978) The diagnosis of zygosity in twins. *Behavior Genetics*, **8**, 437–443.

Lytton H. (1977) Do parents create or respond to differences in their twins? *Developmental Psychology*, **13**, 456–459.

MacGillivray I. & Campbell D.M. (1988) Management of twin pregnancies. In: MacGillivray I., Campbell D.M. & Thompson B. (eds) *Twinning and Twins*, pp. 143–160. Wiley, Chichester.

McGue M. & Gottesman I.I. (1989) Genetic linkage in schizophrenia: perspectives from genetic epidemiology. *Schizophrenia Bulletin*, **15**, 453–464.

McGuffin P. (1987) The new genetics and childhood psychiatric disorders. *Journal of Child Psychology and Psychiatry*, **28**, 215–222.

McGuffin P. & Buckland P. (1990) Major genes, minor genes and molecular neurobiology of mental illness: a comment on 'Quantitative trait loci and psychopharmacology' by Plomin, McClearn and Gora-Maslak. *Journal of Psychopharmacology*, **5**, 18–22.

McGuffin P. & Gottesman I.I. (1985) Genetic influences on normal and abnormal development. In: Rutter M. & Hersov L. (eds) *Child and Adolescent Psychiatry: Modern Approaches*, pp. 17–34. Blackwell Scientific Publications, Oxford.

McGuffin P. & Huckle P. (1990) Simulation of Mendelism revisited: the recessive gene for attending medical school. *American Journal of Human Genetics*, **46**, 994–999.

McGuffin P., Farmer A.E., Gottesman I.I., Murray R.M. & Reveley A.M. (1984) Twin concordance for operationally defined schizophrenia. Confirmation of familiality and heritability. *Archives of General Psychiatry*, **41**, 541–547.

McGuffin P., Katz R. & Bebbington P. (1988) The Camberwell collaborative depression study: III. Depression and adversity in the relatives of depressed probands. *British Journal of Psychiatry*, **152**, 775–782.

McGuffin P., Sargeant M.P., Hett G., Tidmarsh S., Whatley S. & Marchbanks R.M. (1990) Exclusion of a schizophrenia susceptibility gene for the chromosome 5q11–q13 region: New data and a reanalysis of previous reports. *American Journal of Human Genetics*, **47**, 524–535.

McGuffin P., Katz R. & Rutherford J. (1991) Nature, nurture and depression: a twin study. *Psychological Medicine*, **21**, 329–335.

McKusick V.A. (1992) *Mendelian Inheritance in Man*, 9th edn. Johns Hopkins University Press, Baltimore.

Majunder P.P. (1989) Strategies and sample size considerations for mapping a two-locus in to autosomal recessive disorders. *American Journal of Human Genetics*, **45**, 412–423.

Marks I. (1987) The development of normal fears: a review. *Journal of Child Psychology and Psychiatry*, **28**, 667–698.

Martin N.G. & Martin P.G. (1975) The inheritance of scholastic abilities in a sample of twins. I. Ascertainment of the sample and diagnosis of zygosity. *Annals of Human Genetics*, **39**, 213–218.

Mascie-Taylor C.G.N. & Vandenberg S.G. (1988) Assortative mating for IQ and personality due to propinquity and personal preference. *Behavior Genetics*, **18**, 339–345.

Merikangas K.R. (1984) Divorce and assortative mating among depressed patients. *American Journal of Psychiatry*, **141**, 74–76.

Mittler P. (1970) Biological and social aspects of language development in twins. *Developmental Medicine and Child Neurology*, **12**, 741–747.

Morris-Yates A., Andrews G., Howie P. & Henderson S. (1990) Twins: a test of the equal environments assumption. *Acta Psychiatrica Scandinavica*, **81**, 322–326.

Morton N.E. (1982) *Outline of Genetic Epidemiology*. Karger, Basel.

Morton N.E. & MacLean C.J. (1974) Analysis of family resemblance. III. Complex segregation of quantitative traits. *American Journal of Human Genetics*, **26**, 489–503.

Myrianthopoulos N.C. & Melnick M. (1977) Malformations in monozygotic twins: a possible explanation of environmental influence on the developmental genetic clock. In: Innoye E. & Nishimira H. (eds) *Gene–environment Interactions in Common Diseases*. University Park Press, Tokyo.

Myrianthopoulos N.C., Nichols P.L. & Broman S. (1976) Intellectual development of twins — comparison with singletons. *Acta Geneticae Medicae et Gemellologicae*, **26**, 376–380.

Neale M.C. & Stevenson J. (1989) Rater bias in the EASI temperament scales: a twin study. *Journal of Personality and Social Psychology*, **56**, 446–455.

Neale M.C., Heath A.C., Hewitt J.K., Eaves L.J. & Fulker D.W. (1989) Fitting genetic models with LISREL: hypothesis testing. *Behavior Genetics*, **19**, 37–49.

Negri F., Melica A.M., Zuliani R. & Smeraldi E. (1979) Assortative mating and affective disorders. *Journal of Affective Disorders*, **1**, 247–253.

Offord D.R., Boyle M.H., Szatmari P., Rae-Grant N.L., Links P.S., Cadman P.T., Byles J.A., Crawford J.W., Munroe Blum H., Byme C., Thomas H. & Woodward C.A. (1987) Ontario child health study II. Six month prevalence of disorders and rates of service utilization. *Archives of General Psychiatry*, **44**, 832–838.

Ott J. (1985) *Analysis of Human Genetic Linkage*. Johns Hopkins University Press, Baltimore.

Owen M.J. (1992) Will schizophrenia become a graveyard for molecular geneticists? *Psychological Medicine*, **22**, 289–293.

Parnas J. (1988) Assortative mating in schizophrenia: results from the Copenhagen high-risk study. *Psychiatry*, **51**, 58–64.

Patterson A.H., Lander E.S., Hewitt J.D., Peterson S., Lincoln S.E. & Tanksley S.D. (1988) Resolution of quantitative traits into Mendelian factors by using a complete linkage map of restriction fragment length polymorphisms. *Nature*, **335**, 721–726.

Pauls D.L. & Leckman J.F. (1986) The inheritance of Gilles de la Tourette syndrome and associated behaviors: evidence for autosomal dominant transmission. *New England Journal of Medicine*, **315**, 993–997.

Pauls D.L., Reymond C.L., Stevenson J.M. & Leckman J.F. (1991) A family study of Gilles de la Tourette syndrome. *American Journal of Human Genetics*, **48**, 154–163.

Plomin R. (1986) *Development, Genetics and Psychology*. Lawrence Erlbaum, Hillsdale, NJ.

Plomin R. (1990) The role of inheritance in behavior. *Science*, **248**, 183–188.

Plomin R. & Bergaman C.S. (1991) The nature of nurture: genetic influences on environmental measures. *Behavioral and Brain Sciences*, **14**, 373–427.

Plomin R. & Daniels D. (1987) Why are children in the same family so different from one another? *Behavioral and Brain Sciences*, **10**, 1–60.

Plomin R. & Defries J.C. (1985) *Origins of Individual Differences in Infancy: The Colorado Adoption Project*. Academic Press, New York.

Plomin R., Defries J.C. & Loehlin J.C. (1977) Genotype–environment interaction and correlation in the analysis of human behaviour.

Psychological Bulletin, **84**, 309–322.

Plomin R., DeFries J.C. & Fulker D.W. (1988a) *Nature and Nurture during Infancy and Early Childhood*. Cambridge University Press, Cambridge.

Plomin R., Pedersen N.L., McClearn G.E., Nesselroade N.R. & Bergeman C.S. (1988b) EAS temperaments during the last half of the life span: twins reared apart and twins reared together. *Psychology and Aging*, **3**, 43–50.

Prendergast M., Taylor E., Rappoport J.L., Bartko J., Donnelly M., Zametkin A., Ahearn M.B., Dunn G. & Wieselberg H.M. (1988) The diagnosis of childhood hyperactivity. A US–UK cross-national study. *Journal of Child Psychology and Psychiatry*, **29**, 289–300.

Rao D.C., Morton N.E. & Yee S. (1976) Resolution of cultural and biological inheritance by path analysis. *American Journal of Human Genetics*, **28**, 228–242.

Record R.G., McKeown T. & Edwards J.H. (1970) An investigation of the differences in measured intelligence between twins and single births. *Annals of Human Genetics, London*, **3**, 11–20.

Reich T., Cloninger C.R., Wette R. & James J. (1972) The use of multiple thresholds and segregation analysis in analysing the phenotypic heterogeneity of multifactorial traits. *Annals of Human Genetics*, **36**, 163–186.

Reveley M.A., Reveley A.M. & Baldy R. (1987) Left cerebral hemisphere hypodensity in discordant schizophrenic twins: a controlled study. *Archives of General Psychiatry*, **44**, 625–632.

Rice J., Reich T., Andreasen N.C., Endicott J., Van Eerdewegh M., Fishman R., Hirshfeld R.M.A. & Kierman G.L. (1987) The familial transmission of bipolar illness. *Archives of General Psychiatry*, **44**, 441–447.

Richards C.S., Watkins S.C., Hoffman E.P., Schneider N.R., Milssark I.W., Katz K.S., Cook J.D., Kunkel L.M. & Cortada J.M. (1990) Skewed inactivation in a female MZ twin results in Duchenne muscular dystrophy. *American Journal of Human Genetics*, **46**, 672–681.

Rimmer J. & Winokur G. (1972) The spouses of alcoholics: an example of assortative mating. *Diseases of the Nervous System*, **33**, 509–511.

Risch N. (1988) A new statistical test for linkage heterogeneity. *American Journal of Human Genetics*, **45**, 353–364.

Risch N. (1990a) Linkage strategies for genetically complex traits. I: Multilocus models. *American Journal of Human Genetics*, **46**, 222–228.

Risch N. (1990b) Linkage strategies for genetically complex traits. II: The power of affected relative pairs. *American Journal of Human Genetics*, **46**, 229–241.

Risch N. (1990c) Linkage strategies for genetically complex traits. III: The effect of marker polymorphism analysis on affected relative pairs. *American Journal of Human Genetics*, **46**, 242–253.

Risch N. (1990d) Genetic linkage and complex diseases, with special reference to psychiatric disorders. *Genetic Epidemiology*, **7**, 3–16.

Robins L.N. (1984) Sturdy childhood predictors of adult outcomes: replications from longitudinal studies. *Psychological Medicine*, **8**, 611–622.

Robins L.N. & McEvoy L.C. (1990) Conduct problems and predictors of substance abuse. In: Robins L.N. & Rutter M. (eds) *Straight and Devious Pathways from Childhood to Adulthood*, pp. 182–204. Cambridge University Press, Cambridge.

Rowe D.C. (1983) Biological analysis of family environment: a study of twins and singleton sibling kinships. *Child Development*, **54**, 416–423.

Rutter M. (1966) *Children of Sick Parents: An Environmental and Psychiatric Study*. Institute of Psychiatry Maudsley Monographs No. 16. Oxford University Press, London.

Rutter M. (1978) Family, area and school influences in the genesis of conduct disorders. In: Hersov L.A., Berger M. & Shaffer D. (eds) *Aggression and Antisocial Behaviours in Childhood and Adolescence*, pp. 95–114. Pergamon Press, Oxford.

Rutter M. (1989) Psychiatric disorder in parents as a risk factor for children. In Shaffer D., Philips I. & Enzer M.B.S. (eds) *Assessment of Mental Disorder, Alcohol and Other Drug Use in Childhood and Adolescence*, pp. 137–159. OSAP Press Monograph 2. Office for Substance Abuse Prevention, US Department of Health and Human Services, Rockfield, MD.

Rutter M. (1991) Autism as a genetic disorder. In: McGuffin P. & Murray R.M. (eds) *The New Genetics of Mental Illness*, pp. 225–244. Butterworth-Heinemann, Oxford.

Rutter M. & Redshaw J. (1991) Growing up as a twin: twin–singleton differences in psychosocial development. *Journal of Child Psychology and Psychiatry*, **32**, 885–896.

Rutter M., Bolton P., Harrington R., Le Couteur A., Macdonald H. & Simonoff E. (1990) Genetic factors in child psychiatric disorders — I. A review of research strategies. *Journal of Child Psychology and Psychiatry*, **31**, 3–38.

Rutter M., Tizzard J. & Whitmore K. (eds) (1970) *Education, Health and Behaviour*. Longman, London. (Reprinted Krieger, Melbourne, Fl., 1981.)

Scarr S. (1968) Environmental bias in twin studies. *Eugenics Quarterly*, **15**, 34–40.

Scarr S. & Carter-Saltzman L. (1979) Twin method: defense of a critical assumption. *Behavior Genetics*, **9**, 527–542.

Scarr S. & McCartney K. (1983) How people create their own environments: a theory of genotype–environment effects. *Child Development*, **54**, 424–435.

Schaffer H.R. & Callender W.M. (1959) Psychological effects of hospitalization during infancy. *Pediatrics*, **24**, 528–539.

Sherrington R.S., Brynjonson H.P., Porter M., Dudleston K., Barraclough B., Wasmuth J., Dobbs M. & Gurling H. (1988) Localization of a susceptibility for schizophrenia on chromosome 5. *Nature*, **536**, 164–167.

Shields J. (1962) *Monozygotic Twins Brought Up Apart and Brought Up Together*. Oxford University Press, London.

Simonoff E. (1992) A comparison of twins and singletons with child psychiatric disorders: an item sheet study. *Journal of Child Psychology and Psychiatry*, **33**, 1319–1332.

Smith C. (1971) Discriminating between different modes of inheritance in genetic disease. *Clinical Genetics*, **2**, 303–314.

Smith R.T. (1965) A comparison of socioenvironmental factors in monozygote and dizygotic twins, testing an assumption. In: Vandenberg S.G. (ed) *Methods and Goals in Human Behavior Genetics*, pp. 45–61. Academic Press, New York.

Southern E.M. (1975) Detection of specific sequences among DNA fragments separated by gel eletrophoresis. *Journal of Molecular Biology*, **98**, 503–517.

Strachan T. (1992) *The Human Genome*. Bios Scientific Publishers, Oxford.

Sturt E. & McGuffin P. (1985) Can linkage and marker association resolve the genetic aetiology of psychiatric disorders: review and argument (editorial). *Psychological Medicine*, **15**, 455–462.

Suddath R.L., Christison G.W., Torrey F., Casanova M.F. & Weinberger D.R. (1990) Anatomic abnormalities in the brains of monozygotic twins discordant for schizophrenia. *New England Journal of Medicine*, **322**, 789–794.

Taylor E., Schachar R., Thorley G. & Wieselberg M. (1986) Conduct disorder and hyperactivity I. Separation of hyperactivity and antisocial behaviour in British child psychiatric patients. *British Journal of Psychiatry*, **149**, 760–767.

Tellegren A., Lykken D.T., Bouchard T.J., Wilcox K.J., Segal N.L. & Rich S. (1988) Personality similarity in twins reared apart and together. *Journal of Personality and Social Psychology*, **54**, 1031–1039.

Thompson W.D., Orvaschel H., Prusoff B.A. & Kidd K.K. (1982) An evaluation of the family history method for ascertaining psychiatric disorders. *Archives of General Psychiatry*, **39**, 53–58.

Tienari F., Lahti I., Sorri A., Narrala M., Moring J., Kaleva M., Walberg K.E. & Wynne L.C. (1990) Adopted away offspring of schizophrenics and controls: the Finnish adoptive family study of schizophrenia. In: Robins L.N. & Rutter M. (eds) *Straight and Devious Pathways from Childhood to Adulthood*, pp. 365–379. Cambridge University Press, Cambridge.

Todd R.D., O'Malley K.L., Parsian A., Simpson S.G. & DePaulo J.R. (1991) Bipolar affective disorder and alleles of the tyrosine hydroxylase locus. Presented at the 2nd World Congress on Psychiatric Genetics, London.

Vandenberg S.G. (1972) Assortative mating, or who marries whom? *Behavior Genetics*, **2**, 127–157.

Wahlsten D. (1990) Insensitivity of the analysis of variance to heredity–environment interaction. *Behavioral and Brain Sciences*, **13**, 109–161.

Weatherall D.J. (1991) *The New Genetics and Clinical Practice*, 3rd edn. Oxford University Press, Oxford.

Weeks D.E. & Lange K. (1988) The affected pedigree-member method for linkage analysis. *American Journal of Human Genetics*, **42**, 315–326.

Whatley S.A. & Owen M.J. (1991) The cell, molecular biology and the new genetics. In: McGuffin P. & Murray R. (eds) *The New Genetics of Mental Illness*, pp. 1–26. Butterworth-Heinemann, Oxford.

Wilson R.S. (1980) Bloodtyping and twin zygosity. Reassessment and extension. *Acta Geneticae Medicae et Gemellologicae*, **29**, 103–120.

Wilson R.S. (1985) The Louisville twin study: developmental syndromes in behavior. *Child Development*, **56**, 298–316.

Xu C.F., Boerwinkle E., Tikkanen N.J., Huttunen J.K., Humphries S.E. & Talmud P.J. (1990) Genetic variation at the apolipoprotein gene loci contribute to responses of plasma lipids to dietary change. *Genetic Epidemiology*, **7**, 261–275.

Yu S., Pritchard M., Kremer E., Lynch M., Nancarrow J., Baker E., Holman K., Mulley J.C., Warren S.T., Schlessinger D., Sutherland G.R. & Richards R.I. (1991) Fragile X genotype characterised by an unstable region of DNA. *Science*, **252**, 1179–1181.

Chapter 10
Chromosomal Abnormalities

Patrick Bolton & Anthony Holland

INTRODUCTION

Early prevalence studies of chromosomal abnormalties in liveborn children found about 0.6% to have some kind of anomaly (Hook & Hamerton, 1977). However, this figure underestimated the true prevalence rate because it was based on studies using cytogenetic procedures that may have missed small structural abnormalities (Hook *et al.*, 1989). Estimates that take the likelihood of the missing anomalies into account suggest that approximately 1% of all newborns have a chromosomal abnormality (Jacobs, 1990). Many of these abnormalities increase the vulnerability to psychiatric or developmental disorder (Lamont *et al.*, 1986) and, as a result, child psychiatrists and psychologists can expect to see children with these conditions in clinical practice. This chapter outlines the developments in cytogenetics that paved the way for identification of chromosomal abnormalities; the aetiology of these conditions; the related biological mechanisms; and the current knowledge regarding the characteristic features and approaches to treatment.

There are a host of different types of chromosomal abnormality and many have an extensive literature on their manifestations. In addition, chromosomal disorders may result in or be associated with spontaneous abortion, stillbirth or death in early infancy. Consequently, the aim of this chapter is not a comprehensive account of all the different types of abnormality, but rather a description of the common disorders that may be encountered in clinical practice and also, when necessary, a discussion of one or two rare disorders that illustrate important features or mechanism.

Descriptions of the chromosomal abnormalities found in association with specific psychiatric and developmental syndromes can be found in the chapters dealing with these disorders. Detailed descriptions of all the different types of anomaly (including those not covered here) may be found in Emery and Rimoin (1983), Vogel and Motulsky (1986) and Evans *et al.* (1990).

CYTOGENETICS

Although the study of abnormalities in plant and animal chromosomes was well-established in the early part of this century, the identification of human chromosomal anomalies has been surprisingly recent. In 1956 the human chromosome complement was first identified (Levan, 1956), although even then there was uncertainty regarding the exact number of chromosomes. Hence, it was 1959 before the presence of trisomy 21 in Down's syndrome was reported (Lejeune *et al.*, 1959). By the late 1950s it was established that there were 22 pairs of autosomes and one pair of sex chromosomes: females have two X chromosomes (46,XX) and males one X and one Y (46,XY).

During the 1970s and 1980s, techniques for staining chromosomes to demonstrate their characteristic banding patterns were developed. Figure 10.1 illustrates the commonest banding technique using Giemsa (G) banding (ISCN (The Information System for Human Cytogenetic Nomenclature), 1978, 1981). Consequently, structural (as opposed to numerical) chromosomal abnormalities, involving small deletions and rearrangements, were identified. Further advances have resulted in the identification of ever smaller deletions and anomalies. Indeed, the latest procedures have

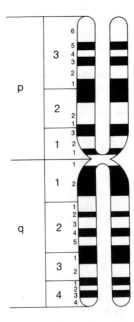

Fig. 10.1 Diagram of Geimsa stained chromosome illustrating the characteristic banding pattern and the system of chromosome nomenclature.

permitted the localization of submicroscopic defects and obscured the distinctions between molecular and cytogenetics.

Over the same period, a new group of abnormalities were also identified, following the observation that certain structural features called fragile sites manifested themselves following the culture of cells in special conditions that stressed the integrity of the chromosomes (Sutherland, 1977). The discovery of these fragile sites has led to developments in the understanding of cancer genetics and the identification of an important form of heritable mental retardation, termed the fragile X syndrome.

Chromosome morphology and nomenclature

In parallel with the improved techniques for examining chromosomes there have been advances in the description and classification of chromosomes as well as knowledge of their structure. It was agreed at the Paris Conference in 1971 (Paris Conference, 1972) that human chromosomes should be classified according to their size and the position of the centromere (the point at which the arms of dividing chromosomes, called chromatids, join). Thus, human chromosomes were allocated to five groups (A−E), numbered 1−22 (the autosomes), leaving X and Y (the sex chromosomes). In each chromosome the short arm was labelled p and the long arm q (Figure 10.1).

The location of chromosomal abnormalities (deletions, breakpoints etc.) can, therefore, be described in terms of the number of the chromosome involved (1−22), the arm it is situated on (p or q) and the band in which it is positioned. Additional or absent chromosomal material can be described in a shorthand way by the use of + and − signs, respectively. For example, 46,XY 18q− denotes the karyotype of a male with a shortened long arm of chromosome 18. With sophisti-

cated high-resolution banding, it is now possible to delineate the type of structural abnormality with considerable precision. For example, the location of the fragile X site is now known to be in band Xq27.3, indicating that the anomaly occurs in a specific band on the long arm of the X chromosome.

Chromosomes are most commonly viewed during the stage of cell division known as metaphase (Figure 10.2). They are made up of deoxyribonucleic acid (DNA) and low molecular weight proteins, mainly histone. The DNA consists of two complementary strands of nucleotides with purine (adenine and guanine) and pyrimidine (cytosine and thymine) bases making up the coding sequences for protein specification. Structurally, DNA is tightly coiled and complexly folded, although the extent of coiling and folding varies during the cell cycle. Chromosomes are easiest to visualize during metaphase when the DNA is condensed and tightly coiled in preparation for cell division. They are, however, longest and least condensed during the interphase of cell division and examination at this time can be a useful means of determining the order of markers stuck (hybridized) to the DNA — see Conclusions and future developments, below.

A number of different models have been suggested to explain the changing structure of chromosomes during the cell cycle, but as yet there is uncertainty regarding the exact nature of the molecular structures involved (Schulz-Schaeffer, 1980).

There are two forms of cell division: somatic cell division (termed mitosis) which occurs during tissue growth or repair, and germ cell division (termed meiosis) which finally produces ova and spermatozoa by reducing the number of chromosomes from the diploid number (46, i.e. 22 pairs of chromosomes and the sex chromosomes) to the haploid number (23 chromosomes), so that when fertilization takes place one set of chromosomes from each parent combine to make up the

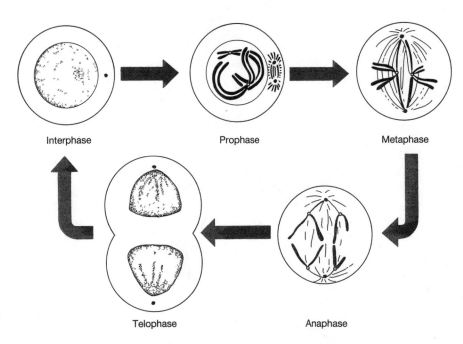

Fig. 10.2 The phases of mitosis. Reproduced with permission from the figure (courtesy of Buselmaier) appearing in Vogel & Motulsky (1986).

zygote (fertilized egg). During meiotic cell division another important event occurs that leads to variation in the genetic make-up of the chromosomes. This process is termed crossing over or recombination and takes place before the stage of cell division when the chromosome pairs are pulled apart to the poles of the cell (Figure 10.3). It leads to genetic material from one chromosome exchanging with the other member of the pair and results in the independent assortment of genes.

CHROMOSOME ABNORMALITIES

Many chromosomal abnormalities seem to originate at the time of cell division, either through a failure of the chromosomes to separate properly (resulting in abnormalities of chromosome number), or through problems during recombination (for example, unequal lengths of chromosome pairs crossing over, which may produce deletions, rearrangements and inversions (Schulz-Schaeffer, 1980).

Chromosome abnormalities are classified according to whether there is an abnormality of number or structure, and whether the autosomes or the sex chromosomes are affected. These are listed in Figure 10.4 with examples of specific syndromes.

The rate of chromosomal abnormality in recognizable miscarriages (50%), stillbirths (6%) and liveborn children (0.5−1%) clearly indicates that many of these conditions predispose to spontaneous abortion and fetal death (Vogel & Motulsky, 1986; Jacobs, 1990) and as a result some anomalies are rarely if ever seen in liveborn children. Moreover, it is unclear precisely what range of chromosomal abnormalities occurs in humans because it is estimated that about 50% of pregnancies may miscarry in the 2 weeks immediately following conception and prior to the recognition of pregnancy (Sperling, 1984). Hence, abnormalities that always lead to very early abortion may never be identified. This may be the reason why polyploidies, which are well-recognized in plants, are not described in humans.

The types of chromosomal abnormality found in abortuses, stillbirths and liveborn children are shown in Table 10.1. It is apparent that certain types of anomaly are more likely to miscarry than others and that, consequently, the prevalence rates of specific chromosomal abnormalities found in liveborns do not reflect the true likelihood of each abnormality occurring. The data in Table 10.1 show that structural abnormalities are associated with the lowest risk of miscarriage, followed by the trisomies and then X chromosomal disorders. The least

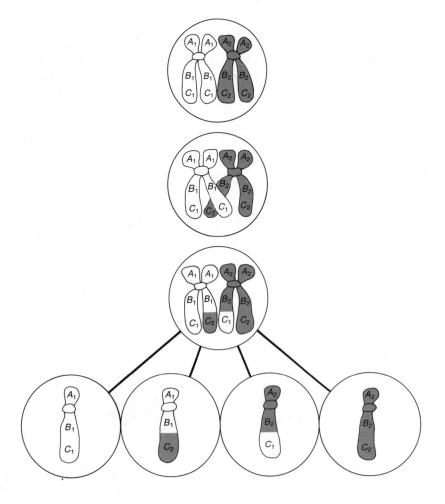

Fig. 10.3 A schematic representation of 'crossing over' during meiosis. Note how genetic material is exchanged between the homologous chromosome pair.

Type of disorder	Example		Outcome
Numerical			
Polyploid	Triploidy	69 chromosomes	Lethal
Aneuploid	Trisomy of chromosome 21		Down's syndrome
	Monosomy of X chromosome		Turner's syndrome
	47 chromosomes (XXY)		Klinefelter's syndrome
Structural			
Deletion	Terminal deletion 5p		Cri du chat syndrome
	Interstitial deletion 11p	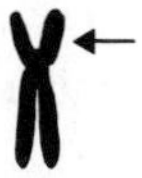	Found in Wilms's tumour
Inversion	Pericentric inversion 9		Normal phenotype
Duplication	Isochromosome X (fusion of long arms with loss of short arms)		Infertility in females
Ring chromosome	Ring chromosome 18		Mental retardation syndrome
Fragile site	Fragile X		Mental retardation syndrome
Translocation	Reciprocal		Balanced translocations cause no abnormality. Unbalanced translocations cause spontaneous abortions or syndromes of multiple physical and mental handicaps
	Robertsonian		

Fig. 10.4 Types of chromosomal abnormality. Adapted with permission from Kingston (1989).

viable conceptuses are the triploidies and tetraploidies. The risk of miscarriage within each of these broad groupings also varies according to the type of structural abnormality, chromosome involved and number of additional chromosomes. For example, in newborns, trisomy 21 is much more common than trisomy 18, 8, 9 and 22 and, similarly, abnormalities involving an extra X chromosome (producing XXY or XXX karyotypes) are much more common than anomalies involving two or more additional X chromosomes. The biological factors responsible for the variations in prevalence and viability are poorly understood, so it should be borne in mind that

liveborn children with chromosome anomalies may represent atypical genetic subgroups.

Abnormalities in the number of chromosomes

Abnormalities in the number of human chromosomes seem to be confined to extra or missing chromosomes of a single pair, a phenomenon termed aneuploidy. The commonest abnormalities of number are, therefore, monosomies (one chromosome of a pair is missing, e.g. XO genotype) or trisomies where there is an additional chromosome (e.g. trisomy 21

Table 10.1 Types of chromosomal abnormality found in abortuses, stillbirths and liveborn children

Population	Abnormality (%)						Total abnormal
	45,X	Trisomic	Triploid	Tetraploid	Structural	Other	
Spontaneous abortions	8.6	26.8	7.3	2.5	2.0	0.7	47.9
Stillbirths	0.25	3.8	0.6	—	0.4	0.6	5.65
Live births	<0.01	0.30	—	—	0.25†	0.02	0.57
All clinically recognized pregnancies*	1.30	4.31	1.10	0.38	0.76	0.15	8.0
Probability of survival to birth (%)	0.3	5.8	0	0	27	11.5	6

* Assuming 15% spontaneous abortion, 1% stillbirth.·
† Uncorrected for banding.

where there is an extra copy of chromosome 21). As mentioned previously, abnormalities in chromosome number may arise during meiosis, through failure of a chromosome pair to separate to opposite poles of the cell (technically termed nondisjunction) or through loss of a chromosome (supposedly due to anaphase lagging; Vogel & Motulsky, 1986). These abnormalities lead to the production of a germ cell without a chromosome (nullisomic cell) or with an additional one (disomic cell) and, following fertilization, a zygote with either a missing (monosomic) or an additional chromosome (trisomic).

Sometimes, abnormalities in chromosome separation occur during the mitotic division of stem cells and when this happens early in blastogenesis (the 2−8-cell stage of embryogenesis), normal and abnormal stem cells may develop. As a result, only the progeny of the anomalous stem cell exhibit abnormality, rather than all cells — leading to a phenomenon termed mosaicism. The proportion of aberrant and normal cells depends on how early in blastogenesis the anomaly occurs.

Occasionally, another form of chromosal anomaly, called uniparental disomy, takes place. This abnormality arises when both homologues of a chromosome pair originate from the same parent. As a result, the total number of chromosomes is normal, but both chromosomes of one pair are inherited from just one of the parents. It probably results from the union of a nullisomic (no chromosomes) with a disomic (two sets of chromosomes) cell, although other mechanisms may also lead to the anomaly (Engel & DeLozier-Blanchet, 1991). Uniparental disomy may go completely unnoticed or it may lead to abnormalities through one of several mechanisms. Firstly, it can be the basis for a child being affected by a recessive disorder despite the fact that only one parent has the recessive gene (the child inherits duplicate copies of the chromosome with the recessive abnormality). Secondly, it can lead to male-to-male transmission of an X-linked condition when the son of an affected father inherits both X and Y chromosomes from the father. Thirdly, when uniparental disomy involves a region that is subject to imprinting, phenotypic expression may be altered (see the section on biological mechanisms, below).

Abnormalities of chromosome structure

Chromosomes may break during cell division and give rise to a number of structural abnormalities. For example, the broken ends of chromosomes may reunite incorrectly and produce a balanced or unbalanced translocation. The term balanced translocation is used to describe the situation where the overall amount of chromosomal material is normal (e.g. when part of one arm of chromosome 8 sticks on to the X chromosome and part of the X on to the missing segment of chromosome 8), and the term unbalanced translocation when the overall amount of chromosomal material is abnormal. Translocations may be reciprocal between chromosomes (i.e. an exchange of chromosomal material) and Robertsonian, whereby most of an acrocentric chromosome (chromosome with centromere near the ends) becomes attached to most of another acrocentric.

Other types of structural abnormality include duplications (a repeated and duplicate segment), inversions (a rotated segment) and deletions (a missing segment).

Fragile sites

The latest class of chromosomal abnormalities to be described are termed fragile sites. The term simply refers to gaps or breaks seen on chromosomes when they are examined under the microscope, following the use of cell culture procedures that in some way induce the chromosomal fragility. There are various kinds of fragile site, classified according to the cell culture technique required to induce them (folic acid-sensitive; bromo-deoxy-uridine-sensitive etc.), their prevalence and heritability (common sites or rare heritable sites) and their location (Sutherland & Hecht, 1985). Fragile X is an example of a folate-sensitive, rare heritable site located at Xq27.3. It is particularly important because of its association with physical abnormalities and intellectual and developmental impairments; see the section on phenotypes of sex chromosome anomalies, below.

The aetiology of chromosomal abnormalities

A number of factors have been found to be associated with increased rates of chromosomal abnormality, although the mechanisms are unclear (Vogel & Motulsky, 1986). For example, the association between aneuploidy and increasing maternal age has been extensively studied, particularly in Down's syndrome. Thus, Down's syndrome births increase from approximately 1 in 700 for mothers aged 30, to 1 in 50 for mothers aged 43 (Vogel & Motulsky, 1986). From these investigations, it is apparent that the effect is predominantly related to maternal age and not the correlated paternal age, although inconsistent and small effects have been reported for paternal age.

It is also well-recognized from the follow-up of people exposed to ionizing radiation from medical evaluation, treatment or nuclear war and catastrophe that radiation induces abnormalities in the somatic cells of these individuals. The issue with regard to the germ cell lines and the offspring of people exposed to radiation is not so clear. It is apparent that the rate of chromosomal translocation is increased, but not (or probably not) Robertsonian translocation. The evidence concerning aneuploidy and deletions is rather more complex. It appears that aneuploidy following exposure to radiation whilst in the early stages or just before pregnancy is a risk, but it is not certain if there is any risk to offspring conceived some time after the exposure or how much any effects are dose-dependent (Vogel & Motulsky, 1986). In the case of deletions, the view has been that radiation exposure plays no or only a minor role. However, there is increasing evidence to suggest that what were regarded as radiation-induced gene mutations may, in fact, be microdeletions, so firm conclusions are not possible.

Biological mechanisms

The mechanisms by which chromosomal anomalies lead to abnormal phenotypes are ill-understood. In the case of structural anomalies like small deletions, many aspects of phenotypic expression are often attributed to the reduction in products from the deleted gene. For more major abnormalities (e.g. aneuploidies) processes are more difficult to identify. The fact that specific syndromes (Down's, Turner's, Klinefelter's etc.) are associated with particular types of aneuploidy suggests that the genes located on the absent or additional chromosome directly determine the phenotype. Indeed, with the recent advances made in mapping the human genome, it has become apparent that specific chromosomal regions are critical for the development of key phenotypic features. For example, the mental retardation and physical features of Down's syndrome (facial characteristics, hand anomalies and heart defects) are determined by the extra copy of a relatively small segment of chromosome 21: 21q 22.1–22.3 (Opitz & Gilbert-Barness, 1990). Thus, a Down's phenotype can result from all the different types of abnormality that lead to duplication of this region of chromosome 21 (translocations etc.). Apparently,

therefore, it is the excess of genetic products from this region that leads to the core features of Down's syndrome, although no specific genes have yet been identified (Stewart *et al.*, 1989).

The overall phenotype and the precise blend of features, although largely due to the involvement of these critical regions, also stem from the disruption to segments outside these locations. For example, duplications confined to the proximal part of 21q have been shown to affect mental development (Park *et al.*, 1987) and, supposedly, therefore, genes in this region also contribute to the clinical picture in trisomy 21. Likewise, the mapping of a gene implicated in Alzheimer's disease to 21q21 suggests that Alzheimer-like brain changes may not be characteristic of Down's syndrome deriving from circumscribed duplications of 21q22 (Epstein, 1990).

Although specific syndromes are associated with particular aneuploidies, many phenotypic features are shared between syndromes. For example, mental retardation is a feature of almost all the autosomal aneuploidies and can also be found in the sex chromosomal abnormalities. Similarly, many of the same congenital anomalies are seen in a wide range of different chromosomal conditions. The overlap in phenotypic manifestations of aneuploidy syndromes could conceivably derive from the multiple determination of developmental processes. Thus, although the functions of different genes, enzymes and proteins are disturbed in the separate syndromes, the conditions might share features because the developmental pathway for the common symptom or sign is disrupted, albeit in different ways. Alternatively, it has been proposed that similarities in symptomatology may be a consequence of nonspecific developmental instability and the disruption of the key developmental stages subserving the emergence of particular structures and functions (Shapiro, 1983; Opitz & Gilbert-Barness, 1990). This proposition derives from the Waddington—Shapiro model of developmental biology whereby developmental pathways are considered to be canalized or buffered, so as to bring about one definite end-result despite minor variations in conditions during the course of development (Thom, 1989). It is hypothesized that aneuploidy syndromes are associated with poor buffering and developmental instability, hence the emergence of structures is arrested or incomplete, leaving atavisms and vestigia. These remnants of developmental processes then constitute the basis for the similarities between different syndromes. The proponents of this explanation argue that the instability in the developmental system is reflected in a general increase in the variance of phenotypic expression and that this, in turn, leads to the loss of familial resemblance that so characterizes aneuploidy (Opitz & Gilbert-Barness, 1990). If proven to be correct, this explanation would throw some light on the nature of the earliest stages of normal development. However, as Epstein points out, if aneuploidy is solely associated with a generalized disturbance of developmental homeostasis, it would not be possible to distinguish one aneuploidy syndrome from another (Epstein, 1990). It is clear that any coherent answer regarding the ways in which aneuploidies may disrupt development is some way off, but the eventual explanation will need to account for both specific and general effects.

Aside from the mechanisms responsible for similarities and differences in the manifestations of aneuploidy syndromes and the increase in variance of their developmental outcome, there are also questions concerning the biological basis for variability in phenotypic expression within syndromes associated with chromosomal abnormalities. Such variation is a noteworthy feature of many chromosomal abnormalities and is evident, for example, in the degree of intellectual impairment accompanying Klinefelter's (XXY), Turner's (XO) or Down's (trisomy 21) syndrome. Presumably, variable expression is partly related to the same factors that operate in unaffected individuals and due, therefore, to stochastic, environmental and other genetic factors that impinge on, but do not obscure, the overall pattern of abnormalities (Epstein, 1990). Nevertheless, there are a few special mechanisms that do require further consideration.

Atypical presentations may, in fact, be due to subtle differences in the type of chromosomal abnormality. Thus, an unusual clinical picture found in some deletion syndromes may be the result of a larger deletion at the molecular level even though microscopically the deletions look similar. In fact, it is sometimes the identification of individuals with coexistent syndromes, one of which is recognized as being due to a deletion or specific genetic defect, that points the way to the identification of the genetic basis for the other syndrome. The recognition of these so-called contiguous gene syndromes has primarily been of importance in identifying the genetic basis of particular medical syndromes, although more recently the same phenomenon has been proposed as the basis for the mental retardation seen in some cases of alpha-thalassaemia (Lamb *et al.*, 1989). In these cases, the coexistence of the conditions appears to be due to deletions in 16p13.3 (Wilkie *et al.*, 1990). However, these examples do not represent variable expression *per se*; rather they are phenomena that may mimic variable expression if the boundaries of the syndrome are ill-defined.

Mosaicism

True phenotypic variation may, in some instances, be a consequence of mosaicism (i.e. only a proportion of the cells developed the abnormality). This is well-recognized and usually obvious in Down's syndrome and sex chromosome anomalies, but the mosaic lines may sometimes be difficult to identify in blood and may only be manifest in other tissues. Indeed, this differential expression of mosaicism may in itself influence the nature of the expression. For example, it has been suggested that a mosaic line that predominantly expresses itself in nervous tissue may exert its major effect on neurodevelopment. Whether this mechanism is, in fact, important in modifying symptomatology requires further study.

X inactivation

In abnormalities of the sex chromosomes, another process may operate in influencing expression. This is the result of the normal dosage compensation mechanism of X inactivation, first described by Mary Lyon in 1961 and termed Lyonization. In essence, this process randomly switches off one of the female X chromosomes in individual cells, to ensure that males and females have the same dose of X gene product. The phenomenon is thought to be effective in inactivating the extra X chromosomes found in Klinefelter's and other multiple X chromosome variants. It can influence the outcome of certain chromosomal abnormalities in two ways. Firstly, in females with X chromosome anomalies (e.g. fragile X syndrome), disproportionately more of the normal or abnormal X chromosomes may be inactivated. As a result, the individual is more or less affected. This mechanism is thought to account for the few cases of identical fragile X female twins with different or discordant phenotypes (Tuckerman *et al.*, 1985). Secondly, in translocations between the X chromosome and an autosome, it has been proposed that inactivation may spread from the X chromosome down the translocated part of the autosome, leading to an absence or reduction of the gene product from this part of the genome. As a consequence, the individual may show features of an autosomal deletion, despite the fact that the translocation is balanced. The corollary of this is that the translocated part of the X chromosome may also now escape inactivation. It is unclear whether this mechanism does, in fact, operate to any significant extent because it appears that in X:autosome translocations some early embryogenic process generally inactivates the normal X, leaving the translocated X active (Mandel *et al.*, 1992).

Imprinting

Another recently identified phenomenon, called imprinting, influences chromosomal function, the expression of inherited traits and, hence, the manifestations of chromosomal abnormalities. The term refers to the differential expression of genes according to the sex of the parent from which they have been inherited (Hall, 1990). Although this differential expression is stable over an individual's lifetime, it may be altered by passage through to the next generation. As such, it can lead to inheritance patterns that do not at first appear to fit in with Mendelian genetics. In the female, the process is thought to begin during oogenesis with the erasure of the previously inherited imprint, probably through loss of DNA methylation, and end, prior to the maturation of the oocyte, with the reestablishment of an imprint. In the male, erasure of the imprint also begins in gametogenesis, but although a partial imprint emerges during spermatogenesis, this is erased again in early embryogenesis (Chaillet *et al.*, 1991). Therefore, chromosomes can acquire an imprint when they pass through females, but lose this after passing through males. As such, genes can differ functionally according to whether they stem from mother or father. The experimental creation of mice with duplicate sets of maternally and paternally derived chromosomes has shown that this process has important influences on development (Sapienza, 1990), and recent evidence has suggested that imprinting may be an important factor in the formation of human tumours (Wilms tumour, retinoblastoma) as well as the phenotypic expression of some human chromosomal abnormalities (Hall, 1990). Its influence on the phenotypic expression of human chromosomal disorders is best illustrated by considering the Prader–Willi and Angelman syndromes. These two conditions are quite distinct: Prader–Willi is characterized by obesity, hyperphagia, short stature and mental retardation, whereas individuals with Angelman syndrome have severe mental retardation, unusual facies, a happy sociable mood, ataxic gait and jerky movements. In a proportion of cases with either syndrome, apparently similar deletions of 15q11–13 have been identified. In Prader–Willi syndrome, however, the chromosome 15 containing the deletion appears to be inherited from the father, whereas in Angelman's the deletion seems to be on the maternally inherited chromosome. Imprinting has been proposed as the mechanism accounting for the different phenotypes and has also been mooted as the explanation for the finding in Huntington's disease that early juvenile onset occurs after inheritance has taken place through the male line (Laird, 1990). The role of imprinting in other deletion syndromes is considered further in an annotation by Punnett and Zakai (1990), who suggested that phenotypic abnormalities derive from the loss of one allele coupled with the effects of imprinting.

Uniparental disomy

Another way in which imprinting may be associated with developmental disorders is through uniparental disomy. In uniparental disomy the fetus inherits two chromosomes from the same parent (e.g. both chromosome 15s from the mother or father) — see Engel and DeLozier-Blanchet (1991) for a review. It has been shown that some of the nondeletion cases of Prader–Willi and Angelman syndromes result from uniparental disomy for chromosome 15, with uniparental maternal disomy leading to Prader–Willi and uniparental paternal disomy to Angelman syndrome (Malcolm *et al.*, 1991).

It is not known how frequently uniparental disomy occurs, but it has also been shown to underlie some cases of atypical cystic fibrosis characterized by unusually short stature (Hall, 1990) and the phenotypic manifestations of human triploidies according to whether the extra haploid set of chromosomes are maternally or parentally derived.

Amplified repeat sequences

Another mechanism that may influence phenotypic expression has been identified through the molecular genetic investigation of the fragile X syndrome, myotonic dystrophy and spinal bulbar spastic paraplegia. These disorders are characterized by abnormally amplified trinucleotide repeat sequences. The length of the repeat sequence has been found to change following passage through the generations and in some instances the severity of affliction seems to be associated with the length of trinucleotide repeat. Thus, fragile X subjects with a short repeat sequence are usually unaffected or only mildly afflicted, whereas those with long sequences are more severely handicapped. It seems that the length of the repeat sequence is related to the methylation status of the chromosomal region and, hence, to the expression of genes from this location (Davies, 1992).

Late effects

It must also be pointed out that the effects of chromosomal abnormalities are not confined to early development, rather effects may develop in adult life (as occurs in the premature onset of Alzheimer-type dementia in Down's syndrome and the macroorchidism and facial characteristics associated with fragile X) or only reveal themselves at a later age when a normal phase of development would usually begin (the amenorrhoea associated with Turner's syndrome would constitute one such example). Thus, variation in phenotypic manifestations may reflect a normal developmental component to expression.

Obstetric complications

Phenotypic expression is probably also influenced by untoward events during pregnancy and birth. However, it is not yet known whether obstetric complications in children with chromosomal abnormalities have the same effects as those found in children without clear evidence of genetic or chromosomal abnormality. It is quite possible, for example, that obstetric hazards have more deleterious effects when the developing nervous system is already compromised, but no evidence is yet available to address this issue. There is, nevertheless, some evidence to suggest that obstetric complications may be more common during the pregnancy and birth of children with genetic and chromosomal abnormalities, so the issue may have particular importance. The increased rate of complications is evident in the well-documented elevation in miscarriages amongst chromosomally abnormal fetuses (see Table 10.1) as well as the increased rates of threatened abortion (Boué *et al.*, 1980), low birth weight (Smith & McKeown, 1955) and prematurity (Parker, 1950) in pregnancies of Down's syndrome children. However, accurate prevalence figures regarding the type of complications experienced by liveborn infants with these conditions are scarce, even though obstetricians recognize that birth complications may pose problems in the clinical management of these pregnancies. Moreover, apart from a few straightforward examples, it is often unclear why conceptuses with these abnormalities should be prone to obstetric complications. In all probability it reflects impairments in placental function as well as the fetal contribution to the maintenance of normal pregnancy, but the specifics of the involved mechanisms are not understood.

The association between chromosomal or genetic abnormalities and obstetric hazards complicates the interpretation of data that demonstrate associations between obstetric hazard and later psychosocial adjustment, because the causal relationship cannot be specified without additional information. The issue can best be illustrated by considering cerebral palsy and autism. Obstetric complications are well-known to be associated with both these conditions, but there is uncertainty whether the complications cause the impairment, derive from it or are due to some third factor. Thus, for a long time, it was thought that pregnancy and birth complications caused cerebral palsy, but, more recently, it has been proposed that these complications may be the consequence of abnormality in the fetus, rather than a cause of the disorder (Caesar *et al.*, 1991). This view emerged following the realization that the prevalence of cerebral palsy remained fairly constant despite marked temporal and geographic variation in the rate of obstetric complications and following the identification of increased rates of minor congenital anomalies (which derive from disturbances very early in fetal development and indicate that the fetus was abnormal prior to the experience of birth hazards) in infants with cerebral palsy (Miller, 1989; Nelson & Ellenberg, 1986). The findings raise the possibility that fetal abnormality may predispose to obstetric complications. Similar issues have emerged in autism, where an association between obstetric suboptimality and familial loading for the related phenotype suggest that the complications may also stem from abnormality in the fetus (Bolton *et al.*, submitted). Clearly, further work is required before these issues can be resolved, but clarification of the nature of the interrelationships would be useful in determining the way in which obstetric complications determine later intellectual and psychosocial function both within normal populations and within vulnerable groups (Caesar *et al.*, 1991).

Other considerations

Quite apart from these special influences, it should also be stressed that sex and individual differences will be influencing phenotypic expression as they do for many forms of developmental psychopathology. Thus, the background effect of the genetic complement and the particular strengths and vulnerabilities of males and females will contribute to the overall picture and eventual outcome.

Furthermore, any developmental course will, to a significant extent, be influenced and determined by various environmental factors. Thus, the child's psychological adjustment and the family's adaptation will determine outcome. Moreover, manipulation of environments may provide one method of treatment. For example, dietary intervention in children with Prader—Willi syndrome obviously influences the eventual degree of obesity, but in addition, educational achievement in individuals with sex chromosome anomalies may be improved by manipulation of the home and family environment (Bender *et al.*, 1987).

PHENOTYPES OF SEX CHROMOSOME ANOMALIES

Early investigations of unrepresentative samples of liveborn children and adults with sex chromosomal abnormalities suggested that psychiatric disturbance, criminality and mental retardation were unusually common. However, with the advent of prospective, long-term follow-up studies on consecutive series of cases identified through systematic cytogenetic examination of newborn children, views on the range of phenotypic expression have changed substantially. The picture that has emerged from these studies has, by and large, shown that a remarkable range of outcomes are possible and that in many instances problems may be almost absent or very mild.

Sex chromosome abnormalities, e.g. Kleinfelter's syndrome (47,XXY) and 47,XYY syndrome, Turner's syndrome (45,X) and 47,XXX, occur in approximately 2.5 per 1000 of the population. The presence of an abnormal number of sex chromosomes has a less deleterious effect than anomalies in the number of autosomes and consequently are much the commonest kinds of numerical abnormality. However, syndromes involving more than just one additional sex chromosome are much rarer (e.g. XXXX, XXYY etc.) and more likely to produce severe developmental abnormalities.

The amount of research into the behavioural characteristics of individuals with sex chromosome abnormalities increased dramatically following the early reports of aggressive, violent and criminal behaviour in XYY males. Subsequent research has shown that these conclusions were somewhat misleading because of the highly selected and unrepresentative nature of the samples investigated. These experiences show how important it is to carry out prospective long-term follow-up studies to clarify developmental processes (Schiavi *et al.*, 1984; Walzer, 1985). The longitudinal research on the development of children with sex chromosomal abnormalities has recently been summarized (Evans *et al.*, 1990).

One enduring and intriguing finding of the research into sex chromosomal anomalies has been the importance of the X chromosome in cognitive function and development. Several studies have shown that XO (Turner's syndrome) females are prone to a visuospatial deficit, whereas individuals with extra X chromosomes seem to be at increased risk of language-related cognitive disorders. The basis of these cognitive impairments has yet to be clarified (Pembrey, 1991), but its elucidation may prove helpful in identifying the determinants of cognitive disorders in people with a normal chromosomal complement (Walzer, 1985).

Klinefelter's syndrome (47,XXY)

Klinefelter's syndrome was first described in 1942 (Klinefelter *et al.*, 1942) on the basis of endocrinological findings. The identification of the underlying sex chromosomal abnormality, characterized by 47,XXY or mosaic patterns (46,XY/47,XXY) only came following the development of methods for examining the chromosomes. It is now known to be the result of meiotic nondisjunction during gametogenesis and seems to occur more commonly in offspring of older women (Carothers & Fillippi, 1988). Otherwise, aetiology is unknown. The anomaly is estimated to occur in 1 in 500 to 1 in 1000 liveborn males — two-thirds of whom are predominantly of the 47,XXY variety. The phenotypic features have recently been reviewed (Mandoki *et al.*, 1991).

Major and minor congenital abnormalities occur more commonly in individuals with Klinefelter's syndrome than in their siblings. At birth, their mean height and weight fall within the normal range, but their head circumference tends to be smaller and remains so. With advancing age, height increases above normal as does height velocity. Testicular development, follicle-stimulating hormone (FSH) and luteinizing hormone (LH) levels are normal prior to puberty, but during puberty hypogonadism develops, along with a plateau in testosterone levels and elevation of FSH and LH. Motor development usually proceeds normally, although a tendency to clumsiness and poor gross motor coordination has been observed.

Speech development is frequently delayed compared with siblings and there may be articulation problems and word-finding difficulties. It has been suggested that these language problems relate to auditory memory and rate-processing deficits (Graham *et al.*, 1988). On tests of intellectual functioning, people with Klinefelter's syndrome have, in comparison with siblings and controls, a decreased verbal IQ, which may result in a depressed full-scale score. Nevertheless, it appears that less than 20% have an IQ below 90 and performance scores have not been found to be significantly reduced, indicating that there is not a predisposition to mental retardation. The majority show problems in educational performance, with most series reporting difficulties in more than 60% of subjects compared with a rate of 25% or thereabouts of controls. The difficulties mainly centre on reading and spelling skills and are associated with oral language difficulties.

The data on other aspects of development are less clear, partly because in many of the prospective studies the subjects have not grown into adulthood. However, it is now evident that Klinefelter's syndrome does not predispose to criminality once intelligence and parental socioeconomic status are controlled for (Schiavi *et al.*, 1984). Temperamentally, the reports indicate that individuals are quiet, sensitive, passive and introverted with a susceptibility to anxiety. Scores on the Rutter parent questionnaire in the Edinburgh series showed an elevation in neuroticism (Ratcliffe, in press). Temper tantrums, solitariness and poor peer relationships have also been noted and these, as well as the educational problems, may require referral to psychiatric or school psychological services.

There have been some investigations of the possible basis for the variation in expression found in Klinefelter's. Thus, the parental origin of the extra chromosome has been examined to see if expression is different when the additional X comes from the father or mother. The results of the initial studies suggest, however, that equal proportions of cases have paternally or maternally derived extra chromosomes and that phenotypes are not obviously different (Harvey *et al.*, 1990).

Treatment

The role of testosterone therapy in Klinefelter's is not well-established. Intramuscular injections of testosterone cypionate (100–200 mg) during adolescence have been reported as improving mood, zeal and concentration (Sorensen *et al.*, 1981) but others have failed to replicate this effect (Stewart *et al.*, 1990). However, the study by Stewart and colleagues did not use the most appropriate therapeutic regime, as there is some evidence to indicate that effects may only be produced when injections are given at least fortnightly (Nielsen & Sorensen, 1988). At present, testosterone treatment is recommended from about 12 years of age, but new forms of androgen therapy are still being developed and evaluated (Winter, 1990).

XYY males

In systematic investigations of newborn populations, XYY occurs in approximately 1 in 1000 live births. Physically, males with XYY are of normal size at birth, but during childhood height velocity is significantly increased and, as a result, subjects tend to be tall. Head circumference is average and the other aspects of the childhood phase of physical development appear to be normal, although there have been reports of awkwardness and clumsiness. Puberty has its onset some 6 months or so later than usual but otherwise proceeds normally (Ratcliffe *et al.*, 1990; Robinson *et al.*, 1990).

IQ tests indicate that scores fall within the average range but are less than the scores of sibs and control populations. Speech and language development shows a good deal of clinical diversity with evidence of articulation problems, in addition to receptive and expressive language difficulties, all of which can be associated with reading and spelling deficits necessitating remedial help and special educational provision (Walzer *et al.*, 1990). In the Edinburgh series, speech was delayed in one-third and reading retardation requiring remedial teaching was evident in 54%. Numerical ability, by contrast, was slightly above the level of the control group (Ratcliffe *et al.*, 1990; Ratcliffe, in press). However, multiple regression analysis of the Edinburgh data, using IQ scores, father's occupation and mother's educational level as dependent variables, revealed that the reading scores were explained by these factors without the need for additional mediators (Ratcliffe, in press).

Behaviour problems in childhood have been reported (Ratcliffe *et al.*, 1982) and the more recent Edinburgh reports suggest that temper tantrums may be especially problematic — occurring in up to 86% (Ratcliffe, in press). During childhood, scores on the Rutter parent questionnaire showed the XYY children to have elevated scores both overall and on the antisocial items compared with controls (Ratcliffe, in press). In addition, social withdrawal, solitariness, carelessness of social rules and unpopularity with peers are often noted. Occasionally, misery and unhappiness develop and may require antidepressant medication. About half of the children were referred to a psychiatrist (compared with 9.1% of controls) and most seemed to benefit from traditional forms of treatment and remedial help (Ratcliffe *et al.*, 1990). However, it is still unclear to what extent these difficulties are the direct consequence of the XYY chromosomal abnormality, as the rate of marital breakdown and maternal psychiatric illness in the Edinburgh series was some three times higher in the parents of XYY children than in controls (Ratcliffe, in press).

Early reports suggested that XYY males were aggressive, violent and prone to criminal acts because the anomaly was commonly found in inmates of penal institutions (Jacobs *et al.*, 1965). It is not clear why this overrepresentation in prisons occurred, but it does not seem to be related to the increased height of XYY men, as has been suggested (Hook & Healy, 1977). Recent investigations do not support the view that aggression and violence are associated with an XYY chromosomal complement (Schiavi *et al.*, 1984), so some other factors associated with incarceration must be operating.

Studies of the sexual behaviour of XYY males indicate that they are no different from controls during childhood. Nevertheless, in adult life they are less likely to have stable sexual relationships and, if they are in such relationships, to have less satisfying, less frequent sexual intercourse. Masturbation and unconventional sexual pursuits (fetishism, voyeurism, exhibitionism and sadomasochism) are reportedly more common than in controls. In addition, the sense of gender role is said to be weaker and XYY males less often report a sense of 'self acceptance' (Schiavi, 1988).

Turner's syndrome (45,X) and its variants

Henry Turner first described this syndrome in 1938 (Turner, 1938). It is a consequence of a chromosomal aberration in which all or part of the X chromosome is missing in some or all cells. Classically, it is characterized by short stature, sexual infantilism, webbed neck, cubitus valgus and gonadal dysgenesis, although the diagnosis should be considered in infants with lymphoedema or young women with short stature, primary and secondary, amenorrhoea (Hall & Gilchrist, 1990).

Turner's syndrome occurs in 1 of 4000−10 000 live births (incidence of approximately 1 in 2500 female births). These rates may vary according to geography, time and season (Robinson *et al.*, 1990). About 50% of cases are due to the complete loss of the X chromosome and 30−40% from mosaicism, with the 45,X/46,XX mosaic occurring 2−3 times more commonly than the 45,X/46,XY variant. The presence of the Y chromosome is important as these individuals seem to be prone to developing gonadoblastoma. The remaining 10−20% of Turner's syndrome cases are due either to an isochromosome (duplication of one arm of the X chromosome with loss of the other) or, very rarely, an X autosome translocation (Dorus *et al.*, 1979). The current evidence indicates

that the paternal X chromosome is more often lost, although the mechanism accounting for this is not known (Hassold *et al.*, 1990). Only about 1% of XO conceptuses survive to birth — a finding that has led to the suggestion that only those with some degree of mosaicism, albeit undetectable in 50% of cases, is present in those that do survive.

Embryonic lethality and Turner's syndrome are thought to be due to monosomy for a gene or genes common to both X and Y chromosome. These genes would be expected to be expressed in both the active and inactive X chromosome of females (Ferguson-Smith, 1965). Recent evidence from an investigation of the reason for the different rates of viability in human and mice XO conceptuses (which are viable, fertile and normal anatomically) suggests that the difference may, in part, be related to the genes ZFX (zinc finger protein gene — possibly involved in transcription) and RPS4X (ribosomal encoding protein S4 gene) with their corresponding Y chromosome forms ZFY and RPS4Y (Ashworth *et al.*, 1991). These genes seem to be X and Y chromosome homologues and escape normal X inactivation in humans but not in mice. The expression of these genes in XO mice is similar, therefore, to that found in mice with normal karyotypes, because the region incorporating these genes is normally inactivated in one of the sex chromosomes. Hence, the XO mouse conceptus is viable and normal. By contrast, the XO human conceptus is monosomic for the genes in this region as normally these escape X inactivation. It is thought that the loss of these gene products leads to the fetus being nonviable or developing Turner's syndrome (Ashworth *et al.*, 1991).

The physical concomitants of Turner's syndrome have recently been reviewed (Hall & Gilchrist, 1990) and include short stature, gonadal dysgenesis, lymphoedema, hypoplastic nipples, prominent and anomalous ears, high arched palate, short and webbed neck, cubitus valgus, short fourth metacarpal, nail hypoplasia, excessive naevi, renal anomalies, cardiac malformations (coarctation of the aorta) and hearing impairment. The presence of these features roughly correlates with the absence or deletion of the short arm of the X chromosome, whereas absence of the long arm of the X chromosome is thought to contribute to the gonadal dysgenesis. There is also a rough correlation between the degree of mosaicism and the severity of affliction. The phenotype does not seem to correlate with the parental origin of the X chromosome (Hassold *et al.*, 1990).

Mental retardation usually occurs only in conjunction with other additional chromosomal abnormality (Sybert *et al.*, 1980) and its prevalence is either not increased or only slightly so. Problems in the conceptualization of spatial relations and numeracy appear to be associated and difficulties with perceptuomotor organization and fine motor coordination have been reported.

Studies of psychosocial development suggest that socializing, the establishment of friendships and intimate heterosexual relationships are problematic compared to women with other causes of short stature. Various psychiatric disorders have been reported in individuals with Turner's syndrome, but it is still unclear whether there is any special susceptibility or association.

Treatment

Gonadal dysgenesis with the loss of oocytes and fibrotic streaks in the ovaries develops *in utero* and progresses following birth. Consequently, high levels of gonadotrophins may be evident in the first few years of life, then disappear during the normal period of hypothalamic damping between 3 and 8 years and reappear at the time of puberty. Spontaneous onset of puberty occurs in only 5–15% and in the rest replacement hormone therapy should be considered, beginning with a small dose of oestrogen for a year or two and then instigating oestrogen and progesterone cycles and continuing until the 40s. Some investigators have begun to evaluate treatments for the short stature that commonly accompanies Turner's syndrome and have tried growth hormone and oestrogen for this purpose. As yet, the value of these treatments has not been adequately assessed (Dean, 1990). Treatments otherwise should be aimed at any concomitant disorder and should employ the interventions shown to be of most value in these conditions.

XXX Females

XXX occurs in around 1 in 1000 liveborns. Early neuromotor development may be delayed and these children are often thought to be awkward and clumsy. Specific tests of neuromotor function confirm that there are neuromotor impairments on the Bruininks–Oseretsky test of motor proficiency (Robinson *et al.*, 1990). Females with this chromosome complement tend to be tall. Puberty usually begins at the normal age and gonadotrophins are normal in level. Several women have given birth to children and the chromosome complement in these offspring has been normal.

Intellectual performance is lower than average with a mean score in the 80–90 range and is significantly below that of controls, particularly on the verbal score. Speech and language development are frequently delayed and speech therapy is often required. Later, problems in reading, spelling and arithmetic may arise and need special help.

Socioemotional development has been reported as immature, with shyness being a frequent feature (Robinson *et al.*, 1990). Psychiatric disorders (including DSM-III diagnoses of depression, conduct disorder, psychosomatization and undersocialization) have also been noted, although again the mechanisms producing these conditions are not known (Robinson *et al.*, 1990).

Treatment is aimed at fostering development and the alleviation of symptoms, through educational and behavioural programmes and psychiatric treatment.

Fragile X

The gap or break at Xq27.3 that represents fragile X is induced by culturing cells in conditions of abnormal thymidine metab-

olism. It was first described in association with mental retardation in 1969 by Lubs. However, it was not reported again until 1977 because laboratories inadvertently abandoned the culture protocols responsible for induction (Sutherland, 1977). Diagnosis has until recently been made following chromosome culture and the microscopic examination of at least 100 cells. Some 3–4% of X chromosomes have to exhibit the anomaly before the diagnosis can be confirmed with any certainty and care has to be taken to ensure that the anomaly is not due to the common fragile site located nearby in band Xq27.2 (Sutherland & Baker, 1990; Bolton *et al.*, 1992). Molecular genetic approaches to diagnosis have now, however, been developed and these are proving to be simpler to perform and especially helpful in identifying carriers of the premutation (Verkerk *et al.*, 1991).

Fragile X is the principal X-linked mental retardation syndrome and the commonest heritable form of mental retardation yet identified. It ranks as second only to Down's syndrome as a chromosomal cause of mental handicap and, on the basis of cytogenetic data, has been estimated to have a population prevalence of 0.75 per 1000 males and 1.8 per 1000 females (Webb *et al.*, 1986). Since the early years of its discovery, it has been known to display an unusual manner of inheritance, with some pedigrees showing transmission through an apparently unaffected male, in contravention of the classic X-linked pattern. Moreover, both affected and unaffected carrier females have been identified and the penetrance of the gene seems to change according to its passage through the generations, apparently in relationship to the process of oogenesis. Recently, large tri-nucleotide repeat sequences have been found upstream of the FMRI (fragile X mental retardation gene) in affected and carrier individuals (Verkerk *et al.*, 1991; Yu *et al.*, 1991). Hence, although the precise nature of the mutation and the mechanism responsible for the mental retardation are still to be fully elucidated, diagnostic procedures have improved considerably using DNA techniques. It is also evident that these long repeat sequences increase in length with passage through carrier females.

The physical features of fragile X are minimal during childhood, but become more pronounced with age and the onset of puberty. Males often develop macroorchidism in puberty, and the facial characteristics, consisting of a large head with high forehead, prominent ears, mid facial hypoplasia and prognathism, also become more evident. Connective tissue abnormalities result in joint laxity and, occasionally, mitral valve prolapse. Epilepsy, reported in up to 23% of patients, is usually of the *grand mal* type, responds well to treatment and may cease during adolescence (Wisniewski *et al.*, 1991). The electroencephalogram (EEG) frequently shows focal spike-and-wave discharges in centrotemporal regions and a pattern similar to the benign epilepsy of childhood with Rolandic spikes (Musumeci *et al.*, 1991). This pattern may be found even in subjects who do not have a clinical seizure disorder (Musumeci *et al.*, 1991).

The degree of associated mental retardation varies in males from profound to normal, with most falling in the moderate range. The same range of intellectual impairment occurs in female carriers, although many more fall within the average range. Sometimes, only specific learning difficulties (reading, arithmetic etc.) are evident. Other studies of psychological function have suggested that sequential processing, short-term memory and arithmetic ability are areas of weakness (Kemper *et al.*, 1988). Speech has been described clinically as litanic, cluttered and jocular, but these terms are not well-defined or researched. Language studies have, however, shown that individuals with fragile X show abnormalities in speech due both to developmental delay and deviance, with immature expressive syntax as well as perseverative language (Sudhalter *et al.*, 1991). In a similar investigation Ferrier and colleagues found corresponding disabilities (Ferrier *et al.*, 1991).

Social development and behaviour in the fragile X syndrome have also been found abnormal. Social anxiety and shyness seem to be the main features and are associated with gaze avoidance (Cohen *et al.*, 1988). It may, in part, be these impairments in social interaction that led to early reports of high rates of autism in fragile X populations and vice versa. More recent investigations suggest that 5% or less of individuals with autism have fragile X (Bolton & Rutter, 1990; Bailey *et al.*, 1993), a rate probably no different to that found in populations of nonautistic mentally handicapped individuals. Similarly, the rate of autism in fragile X-positive males has been reported as no higher than that in fragile X-negative mentally retarded controls (Einfeld *et al.*, 1989). These findings suggest that the association between autism and fragile X may be mediated through their common link with mental retardation. However, there are two reasons for caution in accepting this conclusion: firstly, autism in fragile X-positive males of average intellectual ability has been reported and secondly, the neurobiological correlates of mental retardation with and without autism are quite different (Down's syndrome and cerebral palsy are rarely associated with autism; Rutter, 1988), a finding that suggests there must be some special reason for the association between autism and fragile X which may eventually prove enlightening (Bolton *et al.*, 1992).

Several reports have also indicated that hyperactivity is a frequent feature of the child with fragile X, although systematic study with appropriate comparison groups is lacking.

Investigations of fragile X female carriers (Reiss *et al.*, 1988, 1991; Reiss & Freund, 1990) have shown that social impairments, features of schizotypy, chronic affective disorder and posterior fossa abnormalities (posterior cerebellar vermis and fourth ventricle) are more common than in appropriately matched controls and that the occurrence of these within families is related to the pattern of inheritance (Reiss *et al.*, 1991).

There is some evidence to suggest that the phenotypic features found in female carriers are related to the pattern of X chromosome inactivation: the fragile X chromosome in affected females is more often found to be active than inactive and vice versa (Wilhelm *et al.*, 1988; Rosenberg *et al.*, 1991).

Treatment

There have been numerous anecdotal reports on the value of a wide variety of drug treatments in fragile X (folic acid, methylphenidate, major tranquillizers, etc.) but very few proper trials. Those that have been completed show no benefits or only very limited improvements in the nonspecific behavioural components of the disorder. In many respects, this is not, of course, surprising with a developmental disorder of this type.

It appears that there is some success with the drug treatment of concurrent hyperactivity using folic acid (Giannapoulu *et al.*, 1991), but this requires more detailed investigation. The evaluation of other, nonmedicinal forms of treatments is practically nonexistent but there are no particular reasons to doubt that the behavioural treatments and educational provisions found to be of value in the management of people with autism or mental retardation should be any less effective in individuals with fragile X.

PHENOTYPES OF AUTOSOMAL ABNORMALITIES

Additional autosomes often result in a nonviable fetus but three syndromes are described; Patau's (trisomy 13), Edward's (trisomy 18) and Down's syndrome (trisomy 21). The first two are rare and result in severe congenital malformation as well as shortened life span; consequently, they will not be considered in this chapter. Similarly, many structural abnormalities are uncommon and usually present in genetics clinics, so these also are not reported here. Instead, described in this section are the abnormalities with rather better delineated behavioural phenotypes and the conditions which best illustrate the phenomena of microscopic deletions and contiguous gene syndromes.

Prior, however, to a consideration of the specific syndromes, one general point concerning the phenotypes associated with structural anomalies should be made. In balanced translocations, the carrier is usually unaffected (Nielsen & Krag-Olsen, 1981), as the person concerned has a normal complement of genetic material (albeit in an unusual form). However, when the translocation is unbalanced the fetus inherits too little or too much genetic material. This can lead to a spontaneous miscarriage or the child having major abnormalities.

Down's syndrome

This syndrome is perhaps the best-known disorder associated with impaired intellectual development and mental handicap. It affects approximately 1 in 600 births and is most commonly (95% of cases) due to the *de novo* inheritance of an extra chromosome 21 (trisomy 21) following chromosomal nondisjunction (see the section on chromosome morphology and nomenclature, above). As the risk of nondisjunction increases with maternal age, it is now the practice in the UK to offer prenatal chromosomal examination of the fetus to mothers 35–37 years and over. A small percentage of people have Down's syndrome due to an unbalanced chromosomal translocation. The translocation may be inherited and consequently its presence is important because it leads to a substantial and different recurrence risk compared with trisomy 21. Consequently, genetic advice to these families is different.

Although chromosome 21 is the smallest chromosome, the presence of trisomy 21 has a marked effect on the development and differentiation of many of the organ systems in the body. For example, congenital cardiac abnormalities occur in a third of Down's syndrome babies and are a significant cause of early death. Sensory impairments are frequent and the incidence of respiratory disorders and leukaemia is also increased. Characteristically, there is a particular facial appearance, a reduced frontooccipital diameter of the skull and short stature. Impairment of intellectual development is highly likely and the majority of people with Down's syndrome will have some degree of mental handicap.

The development of the central nervous system has been shown to be markedly impaired. Abnormalities have been reported in the normal progression of neuronal migration and growth and also in later differentiation. For example, in the neocortex there is dysgenesis of the small granular layer of cells (Wisniewski *et al.*, 1985), the cerebellum is poorly formed (Crome *et al.*, 1966) and although early dendritic development appears normal this process is arrested early in postnatal life (Takashima *et al.*, 1981). It is thought that early abnormalities of brain structure have a particularly marked effect on pre- and postnatal brain development. Brain weight of people with Down's syndrome is not markedly reduced compared to non-Down's syndrome children at birth but there is a clear decrease in the expected weight by 2 years of age (Benda, 1971), and brain volume is only slightly decreased at birth but fails to increase as expected in the first 2–4 years of life (Roche, 1966).

There has been a considerable interest in the emotional and intellectual development of children with Down's syndrome and studies have shown a wide variation in ability, suggesting that other influences, possibly environmental, have an impact on the future intellectual achievements and social functioning of the child (Wishart, 1987).

Treatment

A wide variety of medical treatments may be required for the physical disorders found in Down's syndrome, but these will not be considered here.

With the improvement in attitudes towards people with mental handicap, the move away from institutional care and the greater emphasis on early intervention, it has become clear that people with Down's syndrome are capable of developing skills sufficient to allow them a considerable degree of independence in later life (Centerwall & Certerwall, 1960; Carr, 1975).

It was considered particularly promising, therefore, when studies of the effectiveness of early intervention programmes on the development of children with Down's syndrome suggested that such intervention was beneficial (Duffy & Wishart, 1987). However, it is less clear whether any gains are maintained in the long term and, therefore, there has been an increasing emphasis on the need for parents to learn appropriate skills in order that they can continue to stimulate their child (Halpern, 1984; Sloper *et al.*, 1986).

Prader–Willi syndrome

In 1956 Prader and colleagues described a group of Swiss children with severe muscle hypotonia at birth, similar facial appearance, obesity and learning difficulties. Laurance (1967) in the UK reported the case histories of 6 children and later described 24 adults (Laurance *et al.*, 1981) all with a similar disorder, which has now come to be known as the Prader–Willi syndrome. In addition to the characteristics listed in these reports, other features of the syndrome have been identified, including excessive daytime sleepiness, skin picking and temper tantrums (Clarke *et al.*, 1989). Obesity may develop as early as 2 years of age and is associated with an apparently insatiable appetite (Zipf & Bernston, 1987; Holland, 1991). The prevalence is estimated to be about 13–20/100 000 depending on the diagnostic criteria employed (Åkefeldt *et al.*, 1991). Modern cytogenetic analysis has demonstrated a deletion of part of the proximal long arm of chromosome 15 (15qll–13) in over half those studied cytogenetically and this is usually found to be on the paternally inherited chromosome (Ledbetter *et al.*, 1981; Trent *et al.*, 1991).

Some cases without a chromosome 15 deletion may be due to uniparental maternal disomy (Nichols *et al.*, 1989) — see the section on biological mechanisms, above. The combination of endocrine disturbance, short stature and an eating disorder suggests that there is a hypothalamic abnormality but there have been no good postmortem studies to confirm whether this is the case. However, there appears to be an abnormality of the normal feedback mechanism which results in loss of hunger following food intake (Holland, 1991) and therefore eating continues.

Treatment

The observed overeating behaviour in people with this syndrome can result in severe obesity and is associated with an increased mortality. Families often have to resort to total control of food intake by locking food away and controlling the diet. Whilst it is usually possible for carers to control food intake during childhood, this becomes more difficult as the person becomes older and more independent. A number of different treatment strategies have been tried including behavioural programmes (Thompson *et al.*, 1980; Caldwell *et al.*, 1986), the use of appetite suppressants (e.g. fenfluramine; Selikowitz *et al.*, 1990), and also surgical procedures, including stomach bypass and stapling. None have been universally successful, although fenfluramine has been said to be beneficial in some cases, and a behavioural approach can help the person acquire some external control over his or her eating behaviour.

Angelman syndrome

In 1965 Angelman described 3 children with mental retardation, profound speech delay, ataxic gait, unusual jerky movements (likened to those of a puppet on a string) and unprovoked paroxysms of laughter. Initially, the condition was known as the happy puppet syndrome but it is now eponymously named (Angelman, 1965).

It is a rare disorder with only 150 cases or so currently described in the literature and with an incidence estimated at 1 in 20 000 (Clayton-Smith & Pembrey, 1992). The syndrome is associated with a deletion of 15q11–15q13 in about 50% of cases and, by contrast with Prader–Willi syndrome, this is usually found on the maternally inherited chromosome. A few cases seem to be due to uniparental paternal disomy — see the section on biological mechanisms, above (Williams *et al.*, 1989; Malcolm *et al.*, 1991; Clayton-Smith & Pembrey, 1992). In some families siblings have developed the same syndrome (Willems *et al.*, 1987) but the reasons for the recurrence are not known.

Abnormalities in development are present from early on, but the diagnosis is often not made until early or middle childhood when the typical picture is most evident. The earliest features to emerge (apart from general developmental delay) seem to be jerky movements, ataxia and EEG abnormalities. Three patterns of EEG abnormality have been described: persistent rhythmic 4–6 c/s high-amplitude activity; prolonged runs of rhythmic 2–3 c/s 200–500 μV activity; and spikes mixed with 3–4 c/s components of 200 μV or more (Boyd *et al.*, 1988). The outbursts of laughter usually appear between 16 months and 3 years of age.

Neuroimaging studies have usually not identified any abnormalities, although cerebral atrophy has sometimes been present. There has been one report of cerebellar atrophy, but after the onset of seizures (Williams & Frias, 1982), and one report of a subarachnoid cyst in the left sylvian fissure with temporal dysgenesis, a finding that was interpreted as indicating early disturbances in embryogenesis (Van Lierde *et al.*, 1990). Treatment is currently symptomatic.

Contiguous gene syndromes

Deletions may lead to contiguous gene syndromes (Schmickel, 1986) whereby the resultant phenotype is due to the effects of the removal of one copy of a number of different genes located on the missing part of the chromosome. Examples of such syndromes include Miller–Dieker (Van Tuinen *et al.*, 1988; Dobyns *et al.*, 1991), Langer–Giedion, DiGeorge, Beckwith–Wiedemann and Alagille syndromes, as well as the AGR triad (aniridia, genitourinary malformations and mental retardation). The hallmark of these conditions is the variation in expression according to the extent of the associated deletion — a feature that indicates how the deletion of several genes underlies the eventual mix of symptoms and signs.

DIAGNOSIS

Diagnosis in all of the chromosomal abnormalities ultimately depends on the use of the appropriate cytogenetic or molecular genetic investigation. However, a good clinical and family history and careful examination are helpful in determining the likelihood of finding an anomaly as this varies according to the presentation. Clinical algorithms have been developed as aids to the decision making about investigations, but these often need to be modified according to the specific requirements of the clinic and the facilities available (S. Scott, personal observations). In clinical practice the presence of a chromosomal abnormality may be suspected because of the characteristic appearance (phenotype) of the person, the presence of multiple congenital abnormalities, general developmental delay or a family history of abnormality. Sometimes, however, manifestations may be very mild, as for example in a person with Klinefelter's syndrome, who may only be identified because of investigations for infertility. Similarly, short stature or amenorrhoea may be the only signs of Turner's syndrome (Hall & Gilchrist, 1990). If there are strong grounds for suspecting the presence of a chromosomal abnormality because of the clinical picture, but the karyotype is normal, examination of other cell lines (e.g. skin fibroblasts) should be considered to rule out the presence of mosaicism.

GENETIC COUNSELLING AND PRENATAL DIAGNOSIS

The great majority of chromosomal disorders have a low risk of recurrence (Harper, 1988). The actual level of risk depends on the type of anomaly, with certain conditions (e.g. fragile X; translocation Down's) having a considerable risk of recurrence. For other kinds of abnormality (e.g. inversions) the risk is not well-established. For all at-risk families, counselling by a clinical geneticist is advisable.

Prenatal diagnosis is now an integral part of genetic counselling in many circumstances. For pregnancies at risk for chromosomal abnormality, due to family history of disorder, maternal age or exposure to a possible mutagen, there are now a number of possible prenatal diagnostic procedures. To begin with, there are a forever increasing number of maternal blood and urine investigations that can pick up the presence of biochemical or metabolic abnormalities. As yet, however, these tests are of limited value in the diagnosis of chromosomal disorders with only Down's syndrome associated with any detectable abnormalities (human chorionic gonadotrophin, oestradiol and alpha-fetoprotein levels). Instead, it is necessary to use a more direct technique for examining the conceptus.

Chorionic villus sampling (a sample from the chorion of the placenta) is now possible between the eighth and 11th week of pregnancy and prior to the safe use of amniocentesis. This technique therefore has the advantage of reaching a diagnosis at a stage when abortion may be easier and less traumatic. Against this advantage must be put the elevated risk of miscarriage as a result of the procedure (this varies from centre to centre). To counter this drawback, some centres are now beginning to try amniocentesis at around the 12th week of pregnancy. As yet, however, it is unclear how useful and safe this procedure is. It can be anticipated that diagnosis using molecular genetic probes on chorionic villus or amniocentesis samples will become much more prevalent. For example, with the identification of abnormalities in the DNA at the fragile X locus, new and more accurate tests for fragile X are now possible. Similarly, new molecular genetic procedures for identifying trisomy 21, following amniocentesis or chorionic villus sampling, hold the promise of more rapid diagnosis and less of a wait for concerned parents (Bryndorf *et al.*, 1992).

Amniocentesis is a well-established procedure with known hazards. It is still the most commonly used prenatal diagnostic technique for chromosomal anomalies and will continue to be of value for diagnosis in later pregnancy (after the 12th week).

Another diagnostic procedure uses ultrasound scans to identify any physical anomalies suggestive of chromosomal abnormality. For example, certain nervous system, limb or abdominal abnormalities (gastroschisis, omphaloceles, diaphragmatic hernias, duodenal atresia and renal malformations) may suggest a diagnosis of chromosomal disorder (Hirata *et al.*, 1990).

As a consequence, centres are now counselling families with the benefit of information obtained from the combined use of chorionic villus sampling, amniocentesis and ultrasound diagnosis. Results so far suggest that the parents' decision to terminate the pregnancy, in instances where the chorionic villus sampling or amniocentesis result has not clearly identified a serious abnormality, is strongly influenced by the finding of abnormality on ultrasound (Drugan *et al.*, 1990).

CONCLUSIONS AND FUTURE DEVELOPMENTS

It is evident that recently, developments in genetics have led to substantial gains in our ability to diagnose and study chromosomal disorders. The evidence so far suggests that certain chromosomal anomalies can give rise to rather distinctive forms of behavioural disturbance. Broadly, these findings support the notion of behavioural phenotypy (see also Chapters 11 and 37) and suggest that certain aspects of abnormal behaviour are under fairly strong genetic control. It is also apparent, however, that much of the cognitive and behavioural disturbance reported in children with chromosomal abnormalities is nonspecific. Nevertheless, the results suggest that further study of representative samples of people with chromosomal anomalies will provide important information on developmental psychopathology.

It is also clear that further genetic advances are imminent and that the combined application of the powerful new molecular and cytogenetic techniques to the study of human behaviour will enable far more detailed investigations of the nature of the genetic contribution to development and developmental psychopathology. In this respect, several key developments can shortly be anticipated.

Firstly, advances in staining techniques and the examination of chromosomes at different stages of the cell cycle will lead to increased resolution in mapping chromosomes. For example, one of the most recent techniques, called fluorescence *in situ* hybridization (FISH), hybridizes fluorescent DNA probes on to chromosomes, so that the location and order of particular genes and DNA sequences can be identified rapidly and easily. The procedure also allows for the identification of deletions and microdeletions and the mapping of the extent and boundaries of any structural anomaly. Currently, FISH gives a resolution of about 50 kb (50 000 bp of DNA) when it is used during the interphase stage of the cell cycle (see the section on chromosome morphology and nomenclature) and, consequently, rivals other procedures (pulse field gel electrophoresis and genetic linkage approaches) used for gene mapping (Ferguson-Smith, 1991).

It is also now possible for fluorescently stained chromosomes in fluid suspensions to be sorted automatically and allocated to their respective groups and pairs. As a result, large numbers of the same chromosome can be grouped together and studied. The procedure produces fairly accurate estimates of chromosome length and consequently allows for the automated measurement of additional and missing chromosomal material (duplications and deletions respectively) as well as the mapping of genes to particular chromosomes. With the advent of these new techniques automated testing of large epidemiological series of newborns will become much more practicable and hence pave the way for further studies.

These improvements in approaches to diagnosis will also lead to better prenatal diagnosis. This is the case for fragile X diagnosis, where the use of the new molecular genetic approaches to diagnosis have been introduced, but improvements in the ability to diagnose other conditions and an increased use of automated procedures will follow. It is also apparent that preimplantation diagnosis (the most recent early diagnostic technique) will become more widespread. Here, the chromosomes of the fertilized egg are examined, once the blastocyst has reached the 6−8-cell stage, by removal of one of the cells. Examination to determine the sex of the developing embryo is then possible and for sex-linked conditions blastocysts of the at-risk sex can be discarded whilst low-risk blastocysts can be implanted in the uterus. The technique will also allow for the identification of specific chromosomal and genetic disorders by the use of molecular genetic probes. It is a new procedure that is not currently available outside a few centres. As a result of these developments, the need and scope of genetic counselling will become greater and its practice more complex.

Secondly, it is likely that new chromosomal abnormalities will be identified as the basis for some developmental disorders, particularly syndromes associated with mental retardation and multiple congenital anomalies, such as Rubenstein-Taybi and deLange syndromes.

Thirdly, new genetic processes will be identified. For example, it is just beginning to emerge that myotonic dystrophy, X-linked spinobulbar muscular atrophy and fragile X have similar molecular genetic mechanisms of inheritance, with amplification across the generations of trinucleotide repeat sequences (Davies, 1992). Studies that have examined the interrelationship between the size of the amplified sequence and the form of phenotypic expression have suggested that, for some disorders at least, the severity of affliction may be correlated with the length of the trinucleotide repeat sequence (Davies, 1992). This may represent a novel form of inheritance that could account for phenomena like genetic anticipation (earlier age of onset as the mutation passes through the generations). Similarly, further research into the nature and effects of imprinting should help clarify this enigmatic phenomenon and its influence on phenotypic expression.

Finally, the identification of chromosomal abnormalities that confer vulnerability to later developmental psychopathology will help to identify mechanisms important in normal development and facilitate the development of rational, effective therapeutic interventions.

REFERENCES

Åkefeldt A., Gillberg C. & Larsson C. (1991) Prader–Willi syndrome in a Swedish rural country: epidemiological aspects. *Developmental Medicine and Child Neurology* 33, 715–721.

Angelman H. (1965) 'Puppet' children: a report on three cases. *Developmental Medicine and Child Neurology*, 7, 681–688.

Ashworth A., Rastan S., Lovell-Badge R. & Kay G. (1991) X-chromosome inactivation may explain the difference in viability of XO humans and mice. *Nature*, 351, 406–408.

Bailey A.J., Bolton P., Butler L., LeCouteur A., Murphy M., Scott S., Webb T. & Rutter M. (1993) Prevalence of the fragile X anomaly amongst autistic twins and singletons. *Journal of Child Psychology and Psychiatry*, 34, 673–688.

Benda C.A. (1971) Mongolism. In: Menken J. (ed) *Pathology of the Nervous System*, vol. 2. pp. 1361–1371, McGraw-Hill, New York.

Bender B.G., Linden M.G. & Robinson A. (1987) Environment and developmental risk in children with sex chromosome abnormalities. *Journal of the American Academy of Child and Adolescent Psychiatry*, 26, 499–503.

Bolton P. & Rutter M. (1990) Genetic influence in autism. *International Review of Psychiatry*, 2, 67–80.

Bolton P., Pickles A., Butler L., Summers D., Webb T., Lord C., LeCouteur A., Bailey A. & Rutter M. (1992) Fragile X in families multiplex for autism and related phenotypes: prevalence and criteria for cytogenic diagnosis. *Psychiatric Genetics*, 2, 277–300.

Bolton P., Macdonald H., Pickles A., Rios P., Goode S., Crowson M., Bailey A. & Rutter M. (submitted) A case control family history study of autism.

Boué J., Morer I. & Vigual P. (1980) Essai de definition d'un coefficient de risque d'anomalie chromosomique en debut de grossesse. *Journal de Génétique Humaine*, 28, 149–154.

Boyd S.G., Harden A. & Patton M.A. (1988) The EEG in early diagnosis of Angelman's (happy puppet) syndrome. *European Journal of Paediatrics*, 147, 508–513.

Bryndorf T., Christensen B., Philip J., Hansen W., Yokobata K., Nga Bui & Gaiser C. (1992) New rapid test for prenatal of trisomy 21 (Down's syndrome): preliminary report. *British Medical Journal*, 6481, 1536–1539.

Caesar P., de Vries L. & Marlow N. (1991) Prenatal and perinatal risk factors for psychosocial development. In: Rutter M. & Casaer P. (eds) *Biological Risk Factors For Psychosocial Disorders*, pp. 139–174. Cambridge University Press, Cambridge.

Caldwell M.L., Taylor R. & Blume S. (1986) An investigation of the use of preferred and non-preferred food as a reinforcer to increase activity of individuals with Prader–Willi syndrome. *Journal of Mental Deficiency Research*, 30, 347–354.

Carothers A.D. & Fillippi G. (1988) Klinefelter's syndrome in Sardinia and Scotland: comparative studies of parental age and other aetiological factors in 47,XYY. *Human Genetics*, 81, 71–75.

Carr J. (1975) *Young Children with Down's Syndrome*. Butterworth, London.

Centerwall D.J. & Centerwall W.R. (1960) A study of children with mongolism reared in the home compared to those reared away from home. *Paediatrics*, 25, 678–685.

Chaillet J.R., Vogt T.F., Beier D.R. & Leder P. (1991) Parental-specific methylation of an imprinted transgene is established during gametogenesis and progressively changes during embryogenesis. *Cell*, 66, 77–83.

Clarke D.J., Waters J. & Corbett J.A. (1989) Adults with Prader–Willi syndrome: abnormalities of sleep and behaviour. *Journal of the Royal Society of Medicine*, 82, 21–24.

Clayton-Smith J. & Pembrey M. (1992) Angelman syndrome. *Journal of Medical Genetics*, 29, 412–415.

Cohen I.L., Fisch G., Sudhalter V., Wolf-Schein E., Hanson D., Hagerman R., Jenkins E. & Brown W. (1988) Social gaze, social avoidance, and repetitive behaviour in fragile X males: a controlled study. *American Journal on Mental Retardation*, 92, 436–446.

Crome L., Cowie V. & Slater E. (1966) A statistical note on cerebellar and brain-stem weight in mongolism. *Journal of Mental Deficiency Research*, 10, 69–72.

Davies K.E. (1992) The costs of instability. *Nature*, 356, 15.

Dean H. (1990) Growth hormone therapy in girls with Turner syndrome. In: Evans J.A., Hamerton J.L. & Robinson A. (eds) *Children and Young Adults with Sex Chromosome Aneuploidy: Follow-up, Clinical, and Molecular Studies*. Proceedings of the 5th International Workshop on Sex Chromosome Anomalies held at Minaki, Ontario, Canada, June 7–10, 1989. Birth Defects: Original article series, No. 26, pp. 229–235. March of Dimes Foundation, New York.

Dobyns W.B., Curry C.J.R., Hoyme E., Turlington L. & Ledbetter D.H. (1991) Clinical and molecular diagnosis of Miller–Dieker syndrome. *American Journal of Human Genetics*, 48, 584–594.

Dorus E., Amarose A.P., Tredway D.R., Reale F.R., Hatch R. & Serrano L.F. (1979) A reciprocal translocation (X;11) in a female with gonadal dysgenesis. *Clinical Genetics*, 16, 253–259.

Drugan A., Greb A., Johnson M.P., Krivchenia E.L., Uhlmann W.R., Moghissi K.S. & Evans M.I. (1990) Determinants of parental decisions to abort for chromosome abnormalities. *Prenatal Diagnosis*, 10, 483–490.

Duffy L. & Wishart J.G. (1987) A comparison of two procedures for teaching discrimination to Down's syndrome and normal children. *British Journal of Educational Psychology*, 57, 265–278.

Einfeld S.L., Maloney H. & Hall W. (1989) Autism is not associated with the fragile-X syndrome. *American Journal of Medical Genetics*, 34, 187–193.

Emery H. & Rimoin D.L. (1983) *Principles and Practice of Medical Genetics*. Churchill Livingstone, Edinburgh.

Engel E. & DeLozier-Blanchet D. (1991) Uniparental disomy, isodisomy, and imprinting: probable effects in man and strategies for their detection. *American Journal of Medical Genetics*, 40, 432–439.

Epstein C.J. (1990) The consequences of chromosome imbalance. *American Journal of Medical Genetics*, **7** (suppl.), 31–37.

Evans J., Hamerton J. & Robinson A. (eds) (1990) Children and young adults with sex chromosome aneuploidy. *Birth Defects: Original Article Series*, **26**, 4. March of Dimes Foundation, New York.

Ferguson-Smith M.A. (1965) Karyotype–phenotype correlations in gonadal dysgenesis and their bearing on the pathogenesis of malformation. *Journal of Medical Genetics*, **2**, 142–155.

Ferguson-Smith M.A. (1991) Invited editorial: putting the genetics back into cytogenetics. *American Journal of Human Genetics*, **48**, 179–182.

Ferrier L.J., Bashir A.S., Meryash D.L., Johnston J. & Wolff P. (1991) Conversational skills of individuals with fragile-X syndrome: a comparison with autism and Down's syndrome. *Developmental Medicine and Child Neurology*, **33**, 776–788.

Giannapoulu I., Turk J. & Gath A. (1991) Folic acid as a treatment for hyperactivity in children with the fragile X syndrome. In: *European Society for Child and Adolescent Psychiatry: Conference Abstracts*, pp. 74–75. Pergamon, Oxford.

Graham J.H., Bashir A.S., Stark R.E., Silbert A. & Walzer S. (1988) Oral and written language abilities of XXY boys: implications for anticipatory guidance. *Pediatrics*, **81**, 795–806.

Hall J.G. (1990) Genomic imprinting: review and relevance to human diseases. *American Journal of Human Genetics*, **46**, 857–873.

Hall J.G. & Gilchrist D.M. (1990) Turner syndrome and its variants. *Pediatric Clinics of North America*, **37**, 1421–1440.

Halpern R. (1984) Lack of effects for home-based early intervention? Some possible explanations. *American Journal of Orthopsychiatry*, **54**, 33–42.

Harper P.S. (1988) *Practical Genetic Counselling*. Wright, Butterworth, London.

Harvey J., Jacobs P.A., Hassold T. & Pettay D. (1990) The parental origin of 47,XXY males. In: Evans J.A., Hamerton J.L. & Robinson A. (eds) *Children and Young Adults with Sex Chromosome Aneuploidy: Follow-up, Clinical, and Molecular Studies*. Proceedings of the 5th International Workshop on Sex Chromosome Anomalies held at Minaki, Ontario, Canada, June 7–10, 1989. Birth Defects: Original article series, No. 26, pp. 289–297. March of Dimes Foundation, New York.

Hassold T., Arnovitz K., Jacobs P.A., May K. & Robinson D. (1990) The parental origin of the missing or additional chromosome in 45,X and 47,XXX females. In: Evans J.A., Hamerton J.L. & Robinson A. (eds) *Children and Young Adults with Sex Chromosome Aneuploidy: Follow-up, Clinical, and Molecular Studies*. Proceedings of the 5th International Workshop on Sex Chromosome Anomalies held at Minaki, Ontario, Canada, June 7–10, 1989. Birth Defects: Original article series, No. 26, pp. 297–305. March of Dimes Foundation, New York.

Hirata G.I., Medearis A.L. & Platt L.D. (1990) Fetal abdominal abnormalities associated with genetic syndromes. *Clinics in Perinatology*, **17**, No. 3, Part I: Fetal Dysmorphology pp. 675–702.

Holland A.J. (1991) Learning disability and psychiatric/behavioural disorders: a genetic perspective. In: McGuffin P. & Murray R. (eds) *The New Genetics of Mental Illness*, pp. 245–258. Butterworth-Heinemann, Oxford.

Hook E.B. & Hamerton J.L. (1977) The frequency of chromosomal abnormalities detected in consecutive new-born studies. In: Hook E.B. & Porter I.H. (eds) *Population Cytogenetics*, pp. 63–79. Academic Press, New York.

Hook E.B. & Healy K.M. (1977) Height and seriousness of crime in XYY men. *Journal of Medical Genetics*, **14**, 10–12.

Hook E.B., Healy N.P. & Willey A.M. (1989) How much difference does chromosome banding make? *Annals of Human Genetics*, **53**, 237–242.

ISCN (1978) An international system for human cytogenetic nomenclature. *Birth Defects Original Article Series*, **XIV**, 18.

ISCN (1981) An international system for human cytogenetic nomenclature: high resolution banding. *Birth Defects Original Article Series*, **XVII**, 5.

Jacobs P.A. (1990) Review: The role of chromosome abnormalities in reproductive failure. *Reproduction Nutrition Development* (suppl. 1), 63s–74s.

Jacobs P.A., Brunton M., Melville M., Brittain R. & McClermont W. (1965) Aggressive behaviour, mental subnormality and the XYY male. *Nature*, **208**, 1351–1352.

Kemper M.B., Hagerman R.J. & Altshul-Stark D. (1988) Cognitive profiles of boys with the fragile X syndrome. *American Journal of Medical Genetics*, **30**, 191–200.

Kingston H. (1989) *ABC of Clinical Genetics*. British Medical Association, London.

Klinefelter H.F., Reifenstein E.C. & Albright F. (1942) Syndrome characterized by gynaecomastia aspermatogenesis without A-Leydigism and increased excretion of follicle stimulating hormone. *Journal of Clinical Endocrinology Metabolism*, **2**, 615–627.

Laird C.D. (1990) Proposed genetic basis of Huntington's disease. *Trends in Genetics*, **6**, 242–247.

Lamb J., Wilkey A.D.M., Harris P.C., Buckle V.J., Lindenbaum R.H., Barten N.J., Reeders S.T. & Higgs D.R. (1989) Detection of break points in sub-microscopic chromosomal translocation illustrating an important mechanism for genetic disease. *Lancet*, **2**, 819–824.

Lamont M.A., Dennis N.R. & Seebright M. (1986) Chromosome abnormalities in pupils attending ESN/M schools. *Archives of Disease in Childhood*, **61**, 223–226.

Laurance B.M. (1967) Hypotonia, mental retardation, obesity, and cryptorchidism associated with dwarfism and diabetes in children. *Archives of Disease in Childhood*, **42**, 126–139.

Laurance B.M., Brito A. & Wilkinson J. (1981) Prader–Willi syndrome after age 15 years. *Archives of Disease in Childhood*, **56**, 181–186.

Ledbetter D.H., Riccardi V.M., Airhart S.D., Strobel R.J., Keenan B.S. & Crawford J.D. (1981) Deletions of chromosome 15 as a cause of Prader–Willi syndrome. *New England Journal of Medicine*, **304**, 325–328.

Lejeune J., Gautier M. & Turpin R. (1959) Etude des chromosomes somatiques de neuf enfants mongoliens. *Comptes Rendus de l'Académie des Sciences (Sér D) (Paris)*, **248**, 1721–1722.

Levan A. (1956) Chromosome studies in some human tumours and tissues of normal origin, grown *in vivo* and *in vitro* at the Sloan-Kettering Institute. *Cancer*, **9**, 648–663.

Lubs H.A. (1969) A marker X chromosome. *American Journal of Human Genetics*, **21**, 231–244.

Malcolm S., Clayton-Smith J., Nichols M., Robb S., Webb T., Armour J.A.L., Jeffreys A.J. & Pembrey M.E. (1991) Uniparental paternal disomy in Angelman's syndrome. *Lancet*, **337**, 694–697.

Mandel J.-L., Monaco A., Nelson D., Schlessinger D. & Huntington W. (1992) Genome analysis and the human X chromosome. *Science*, **258**, 103–109.

Mandoki M.W., Sumner G.A., Hoffman R.P. & Riconda D.L. (1991) A review of Klinefelter's syndrome in children and adolescents. *Journal of the American Academy of Child and Adolescent Psychiatry*, **30**, 167–172.

Miller G. (1989) Minor congenital anomalies and ataxic cerebral palsy. *Archives of Diseases in Childhood*, **64**, 557–562.

Musumeci S.A., Ferri R., Elia R.M., Bergonzi P. & Tassinari C.A. (1991) Epilepsy and fragile X syndrome: a follow-up study. *American Journal of Medical Genetics*, **38**, 511–513.

Nelson K. & Ellenberg J. (1986) Antecedents of cerebral palsy: multivariate analysis of risk. *New England Journal of Medicine*, **315**, 81–86.

Nichols R.D., Knoll J.H.M., Butler M.G., Karam S. & Lalande M. (1989) Genetic imprinting suggested by maternal heterodisomy in non-deletion Prader–Willi syndrome. *Nature*, **342**, 281–285.

Nielsen J. & Krag-Olsen B. (1981) Follow-up of 32 children with autosomal translocations found among 11,148 consecutively new-born children from 1969 to 1974. *Clinical Genetics*, **20**, 48–54.

Nielsen J. & Sorensen K. (1988) Follow-up of 30 Klinefelter males treated with testosterone. *Clinical Genetics*, **33**, 262–269.

Opitz J.M. & Gilbert-Barness E.F. (1990) Reflections on the pathogenesis of Down syndrome. *American Journal of Medical Genetics* **7** (suppl.), 38–51.

Paris Conference (1972) Standardization in human cytogenetics. *Cytogenetics*, **11**, 317–362.

Park J.D., Wurster-Hill D.H., Andrews P.A., Colley W.C. & Graham J.M. Jr (1987) Free proximal trisomy 21 without the Down syndrome. *Clinical Genetics*, **32**, 342–348.

Parker G.F. (1950) Incidence of mongoloid imbecility in new born infants; 10 yr study covering 27 931 livebirths. *Journal of Paediatrics*, **36**, 493–494.

Pembrey M. (1991) Chromosomal abnormalities. In: Rutter M. & Casaer P. (eds) *Biological Risk Factors For Psychosocial Disorders*. Cambridge University Press, Cambridge.

Prader A., Labhart A. & Willi H. (1956) Ein Syndrom von Adipositas Kleinwuchs, Kryptorchismus and Oligophrenie nach myatonieartigem Zustand in Neugeborenalter. *Schweizerische Medizinische Wochenschrift*, **86**, 1260–1261.

Punnett H.H. & Zakai E.H. (1990) Old syndromes and new cytogenetics. *Developmental Medicine and Child Neurology*, **32**, 820–831.

Ratcliffe S.G. (1994) The psychological and psychiatric consequences of sex chromosomal abnormalities in children based on population studies. In: Poustka F. (ed) *Basic Approaches to Genetic and Molecular Etiological Developmental Psychiatry*, Quintessenz, Berlin.

Ratcliffe S.G., Tierney I., Nshaho J., Smith L., Springbett A. & Callan S. (1982) The Edinburgh study of growth and development of children with sex chromosome abnormalities. In: Stewart D.A. (ed) Birth Defects: Original article series **18**(4), 41–60. March of Dimes Foundation, New York.

Ratcliffe S.G., Butler G.E. & Jones M. (1990) Edinburgh study of growth and development of children with sex chromosome abnormalities. IV. In: Evans J.A., Hamerton J.L. & Robinson A. (eds) *Children and Young Adults with Sex Chromosome Aneuploidy: Follow-up, Clinical, and Molecular Studies.* Proceedings of the 5th International Workshop on Sex Chromosome Anomalies held at Minaki, Ontario, Canada, June 7–10, 1989. Birth Defects: Original article series, No. 26(4), pp. 1–45. March of Dimes Foundation, New York.

Reiss A.L. & Freund L. (1990) Review: Fragile X syndrome. *Biological Psychiatry*, **27**, 223–240.

Reiss A.L., Hagerman R.J., Vinogradov S., Abrams M. & King R. (1988) Psychiatric disability in female carriers of the fragile X chromosome. *Archives of General Psychiatry*, **45**, 25–30.

Reiss A.L., Freund L., Tseng, J.E. & Joshi P.K. (1991) Neuroanatomy in fragile X females: the posterior fossa. *American Journal of Human Genetics*, **49**, 279–288.

Robinson A., Bender B.G., Linden M.G. & Salbenblatt J.A. (1990) Sex chromosome aneuploidy: the Denver prospective study. In: Evans J.A., Hamerton J.L. & Robinson A. (eds) *Children and Young Adults with Sex Chromosome Aneuploidy: Follow-up, Clinical, and Molecular Studies.* Proceedings of the 5th International Workshop on Sex Chromosome Anomalies held at Minaki, Ontario, Canada, June 7–10, 1989. Birth Defects: Original article series, No. 26(4), pp. 59–117. March of Dimes Foundation, New York.

Roche A.F. (1966) The cranium in mongolism. *Acta Neurologica Scandinavica*, **42**, 62–78.

Rosenberg C., Vianna-Morgante A.M., Otto P.A. & Navajas L. (1991) Effect of X inactivation on fragile X frequency and mental retardation. *American Journal of Medical Genetics*, **38**, 421–424.

Rutter M. (1988) Biological basis of autism: implications for intervention. In: Menolascino F.J. & Stark J.A. (eds) *Preventative and Curative Interventions in Mental Retardation*, pp. 265–294. Brookes Publishing, Baltimore.

Sapienza C. (1990) Parental imprinting of genes. *Scientific American*, **263**, 26–32.

Schiavi R.C. (1988) Sex chromosome anomalies, hormones, and sexuality. *Archives of General Psychiatry*, **45**, 19–24.

Schiavi R.C., Theilgaard A., Owen D.R. & White D. (1984) Sex chromosome anomalies, hormones and aggressivity. *Archives of General Psychiatry*, **41**, 93–99.

Schmickel R.D. (1986) Contiguous gene syndromes: a component of recognizable syndromes. *Journal of Paediatrics*, **109**, 231–231.

Schulz-Schaeffer J. (1980) *Cytogenetics: Plants. Animals. Humans.* Springer-Verlag, New York.

Selikowitz M., Sunman J., Prendergast A. & Wright S. (1990) Fenfluramine in Prader–Willi syndrome: a double blind placebo controlled trial. *Archives of Disease in Childhood*, **65**, 112–114.

Shapiro B.L. (1983) Down syndrome – a disruption of homeostasis. *American Journal of Medical Genetics*, **14**, 241–269.

Sloper P., Glenn S.M. & Cuningham C.C. (1986) The effect of intensity of training on sensori-motor development in infants with Down's syndrome. *Journal of Mental Deficiency Research*, **30**, 149–162.

Smith A. & McKeown T. (1955) Pre-natal growth of mongoloid defectives. *Archives of Disease in Childhood*, **30**, 257–259.

Sorensen K., Sorensen A.M. & Nielsen J. (1981) Social and psychological development of adolescents with Klinefelter's syndrome. In: Schmid W. & Nielson J. (eds) *Human Behaviour and Genetics*, pp. 45–64. Biomedical Press, New York.

Sperling K. (1984) Frequency and origin of chromosomal abnormalities in man. In: Obe B. (ed) *Mutation in Man*, pp. 128–146. Springer, Berlin.

Stewart G.D., Van Keuren M.L., Galt J., Kurachi S., Buraczynska M.J. & Kurnit D.M. (1989) Molecular structure of human chromosome 21. *Annual Review of Genetics*, **23**, 409–423.

Stewart D.A., Bailey J.D. Netley C.T. & Park E. (1990) Growth, development, and behavioral outcome from mid-adolescence to adulthood in subjects with chromosome aneuploidy: the Toronto study. In: Evans J.A., Hamerton J.L. & Robinson A. (eds) *Children and Young Adults with Sex Chromosome Aneuploidy: Follow-up, Clinical, and Molecular Studies.* Proceedings of the 5th International Workshop on Sex Chromosome Anomalies held at Minaki, Ontario, Canada, June 7–10, 1989. Birth Defects: Original article series, No. 26(4), pp. 131–189. March of Dimes Foundation, New York.

Sudhalter V., Scarborough H.S., & Cohen I.L. (1991) Syntactic delay and pragmatic deviance in the language of fragile X males. *American Journal of Medical Genetics*, **38**, 493–497.

Sutherland G.R. (1977) Fragile sites on human chromosomes: demonstration of their dependence on the type of tissue culture medium. *Science*, **197**, 265–266.

Sutherland G.R. & Baker E. (1990) The common fragile site in band q27 of the human X chromosome is not coincident with the fragile X. *Clinical Genetics*, **37**, 167–172.

Sutherland G.R. & Hecht F. (1985) *Fragile Sites on Human Chromosomes.* Oxford University Press, New York.

Sybert V.P., Reed S.D. & Hall J.G. (1980) Mental retardation in the Turner syndrome. *American Journal of Human Genetics*, **32**, 131A.

Takashima S., Becker L., Armstrong D. & Chan F. (1981) Abnormal neuronal development in visual cortex of the human fetus and infant with Down's syndrome: a quantitative and qualitative golgi study. *Brain Research*, **225**, 1–21.

Thom R. (1989) An inventory of Waddington concepts. In: Goodwin

B. & Saunders P. (eds) *Theoretical Biology: Epigenetic and Evolutionary Order from Complex Systems*, pp. 1−7. Edinburgh University Press, Edinburgh.

Thompson T., Kodluboy S. & Heston L. (1980) Behavioural treatment of obesity in Prader−Willi syndrome. *Behaviour Therapy*, **11**, 588−593.

Trent R.J., Volpato F., Smith A., Lindeman R., Wong M.-K., Warne K.T. & Haan E. (1991) Molecular and cytogenetic studies of the Prader−Willi syndrome. *Journal of Medical Genetics*, **28**, 649−654.

Tuckerman E., Webb T. & Bundey S.E. (1985) Frequency and replication status of the fragile X, fra(X) (q27−28), in a pair of monozygotic twins of markedly differing intelligence. *Journal of Medical Genetics*, **22**, 85−91.

Turner H.H. (1938) A syndrome of infantilism, congenital webbed neck and cubitus valgus. *Endocrinology*, **23**, 566−578.

Van Lierde A., Atza M.G., Giardino D. & Viani F. (1990) Angelman's syndrome in the first year of life. *Developmental Medicine and Child Neurology*, **32**, 1005−1021.

Van Tuinen T., Dobyns W.B., Rich D.C., Summers K.M., Robinson T.K., Nakamura Y. & Ledbetter D.H. (1988) Molecular detection of microscopic and submicroscopic deletions associated with Miller−Dieker syndrome. *American Journal of Human Genetics*, **43**, 587−596.

Verkerk A., Pieretti M., Sutcliffe J., Ying-Hui F., Kuhl D., Pizzuti A., Reiner O., Richards S., Victoria M., Fuping Z., Eussen B., van Ommen G.-J., Blonden L., Riggins G., Chastain J., Kunst C., Galjaard H., Caskey T., Nelson D., Oostra B. & Warren S. (1991) Identification of a gene (FMR-1) containing a CGG repeat coincident with a breakpoint cluster region exhibiting length variation in fragile X syndrome. *Cell*, **65**, 905−914.

Vogel F. & Motulsky A.G. (1986) *Human Genetics: Problems and Approaches*, 2nd edn. Springer Verlag, Berlin.

Walzer S. (1985) Annotation: X chromosome abnormalities and cognitive development: implications for understanding normal human development. *Journal of Child Psychology and Psychiatry*, **26**, 177−184.

Walzer S., Bashir A.S. & Silvert A.R. (1990) Cognitive and behavioural factors in the learning disabilities of 47,XXY and 47,XYY boys. In: Evans J.A., Hamerton J.L. & Robinson A. (eds) *Children and Young Adults with Sex Chromosome Aneuploidy: Follow-up, Clinical, and Molecular Studies*. Proceedings of the 5th International Workshop on Sex Chromosome Anomalies held at Minaki, Ontario, Canada, June 7−10, 1989. Birth Defects: Original article series, No. 26(4), pp. 45−59. March of Dimes Foundation, New York.

Webb T.P., Bundey S., Thake A. & Todd J. (1986) The frequency of the fragile X chromosome among the schoolchildren in Coventry.

Journal of Medical Genetics, **23**, 396−399.

Wilhelm D., Froster-Iskenius U., Paul J. & Schwinger E. (1988) Fra(X) frequency on the active X-chromosome and phenotype in heterozygous carriers of the fra(X) form of mental retardation. *American Journal of Medical Genetics*, **30**, 407−415.

Wilkie A.D.M., Buckle V.J., Harris P.C., Lamb J., Barton N.J., Reeders S.T., Lindenbaum R.H. & Higgs D.R. (1990) Clinical features and molecular analysis of the thalassaemia/mental retardation syndromes. I cases due to deletions involving chromosome band 16p13,3. *American Journal of Human Genetics*, **46**, 1112−1126.

Willems P.J., Dijkstra J., Brouwer O.F. & Smit G.P.A. (1987) Recurrence risk in the Angelman ('happy puppet') syndrome. *American Journal of Medical Genetics*, **27**, 773−780.

Williams C.A. & Frias J.I. (1982) The Angelman ('happy puppet') syndrome. *American Journal of Medical Genetics*, **11**, 453−460.

Williams C.A., Gray B.A., Hendrickson J.E., Stone J.W. & Cantu E.S. (1989) Incidence of 15q deletions in the Angelman syndrome: a survey of twelve affected persons. *American Journal of Medical Genetics*, **32**, 339−345.

Winter J.S.D. (1990) Androgen therapy in Klinefelter syndrome during adolescence. In: Evans J.A., Hamerton J.L. & Robinson A. (eds) *Children and Young Adults with Sex Chromosome Aneuploidy: Follow-up, Clinical, and Molecular Studies*. Proceedings of the 5th International Workshop on Sex Chromosome Anomalies held at Minaki, Ontario, Canada, June 7−10, 1989. Birth Defects: Original article series, No. 26(4), pp. 235−247.

Wishart J.G. (1987) Performance of young non-retarded children and children with Down syndrome on Piagetian infant search tasks. *American Journal of Mental Deficiency*, **92**, 167−177.

Wisniewski K.E., Wisniewski H.M. & Wen G.Y. (1985) Occurrence of neuropathological changes and dementia of Alzheimer's disease in Down's syndrome. *Annals of Neurology*, **17**, 278−282.

Wisniewski K.E., Segan S.M., Miezejeski C.M., Sersen E.A. & Rudelli R. (1991) The Fra(X) syndrome: neurological, electrophysiological, and neuropathological abnormalities. *American Journal of Medical Genetics*, **38**, 476−480.

Yu S., Pritchard M., Kremer E., Lynch M., Nancarrow J., Baker K., Holman J.C., Mulley S., Warren S., Schlessinger G., Sutherland G. & Richards R. (1991) Fragile X genotype characterized by an unstable region of DNA. *Science*, **252**, 1179−1181.

Zipf W.B. & Bernston G.G. (1987) Characteristics of abnormal food-intake patterns in children with Prader−Willi syndrome and study of effects of naloxone. *American Journal of Clinical Nutrition*, **46**, 277−281.

Chapter 11
Brain Disorders

Robert Goodman

This chapter focuses on the psychiatric consequences of childhood brain disorders, including epilepsy. Readers are warned in advance that this chapter offers no more than a few glimpses of the interesting but largely unexplored territory that has variously been called organic child psychiatry, paediatric behavioural neurology and developmental neuropsychiatry. Our current knowledge of the childhood links between brain and behavioural disorders is extremely sketchy, partly because of limitations in the 'parent' disciplines of child psychiatry and paediatric neurology. Readers who are only too well aware of how little is known about the classification, aetiology, course and management of child psychiatric disorders may be surprised to learn that the situation is no better for most of the common neurological disorders of childhood. The classification of seizure disorders has changed repeatedly, and the existence and nosological status of many named syndromes (such as the Lennox–Gastaut syndrome) remain controversial. The classification of cerebral palsy is also problematic. Everyone agrees that cerebral palsy should be thought of as a group of disorders rather than a single disorder, but there is much less agreement about what to include under the rubric, or how to subclassify the varieties of cerebral palsy. In these areas, paediatric neurology has lagged at least two decades behind child psychiatry in the use of epidemiological samples and multivariate statistics to refine clinical classification. Cerebral palsy also exemplifies many of the uncertainties in paediatric neurology about aetiology, course and management. What causes cerebral palsy? What becomes of cerebral-palsied children when they grow up? Is conductive education a more effective treatment package than less intensive alternatives? None of these questions can be answered satisfactorily at present. This dismal account of the state of paediatric neurology is not the whole story of course. In some areas, much has already been learned and progress is rapid. This is true, for example, of the biochemistry and molecular genetics of many neurodegenerative and neuromuscular disorders. Most of these disorders are rare, however, and advances in the assessment and management of common neurological and neurosurgical problems are less impressive. In this context, it is bound to be difficult to make sense of the links between brain and behavioural problems in childhood. Given the crude and changing classifications of both psychiatric disorders and cerebral palsy, how can we sensibly examine the psychiatric correlates of cerebral palsy? Given the recent delineation of a distinctive variety of epilepsy, benign epilepsy of childhood with Rolandic spikes (BECRS), that is common and causes remarkably few problems (Aicardi, 1986), how should we interpret older studies that examined the psychiatric correlates of childhood epilepsy without separating out this group of children? These difficulties are not mentioned to discourage readers, but to put them on their guard against simplistic conclusions drawn from inadequate data.

BRAIN DAMAGE?

Although this chapter is entitled Brain Disorders, its predecessor in the previous edition was entitled Brain Damage. The change is more than a switch to a less emotive synonym. The term damage suggests that the brain was developing normally until something happened to damage it. This is accurate in some instances: athetoid cerebral palsy following rhesus haemolytic disease; hydrocephalus following tuberculous meningitis; epilepsy following a penetrating head injury; and so on. In other instances, however, brain development may have been abnormal from the beginning, rather than proceeding normally until derailed by some insult. Brain abnormalities can be due to inherited disorders, new mutations and chromosomal aberrations. The power of language is such that an ill-chosen term, such as brain damage, can seriously distort clinical and scientific reasoning. Once children with cerebral palsy or mental retardation are labelled as brain-damaged, parents and researchers tend to assume that the cause must be some insult, such as a difficult birth, and the possible role of genetically or chromosomally determined malformations tends to be forgotten. As far as the common brain disorders in childhood are concerned, we do not even know if acquired or intrinsic aetiologies are more important.

Another disadvantage of the term brain damage is that it suggests permanence to anyone who has been taught that the brain cannot regenerate lost or damaged parts. This connotation of irreversibility is potentially misleading. For example, children do commonly grow out of epilepsy (Aicardi, 1986) and may even grow out of cerebral palsy (Taudorf *et al.*, 1986). In some instances, reversible brain disorders may arise not from fixed abnormalities of neuronal organization but from delayed or precocious neuronal maturation. It is plausible but unproven, for instance, that transient childhood epilepsy reflects temporarily delayed development of inhibitory neurotransmitter systems (or prematurely accelerated development of excitatory systems). Once again, damage is too narrow a concept to embrace all possible brain disorders.

BIRTH DAMAGE

The best known brain damage theories are those that emphasize birth damage. Generations of medical students have been taught that cerebral palsy, mental retardation and epilepsy are commonly due to perinatal complications. This view is almost certainly false. Obstetric and neonatal complications are common but are generally innocuous. Thus in one study based on detailed records, over half the *normal* controls had experienced one such complication (Jacobsen & Kinney, 1980).

Even severe perinatal complications are usually harmless. In the best prospective study of cerebral palsy, for example, children who had an Apgar score of 3 or less at 5 minutes after birth were roughly 30 times more likely to be neurologically normal at the age of 7 than to have cerebral palsy (Freeman & Nelson, 1988). The same study showed that only 21% of children with cerebral palsy had at least one of three markers suggestive of birth asphyxia (Nelson & Ellenberg, 1986). Even among the cerebral-palsied children who did experience birth asphyxia, many had congenital malformations or microcephaly at birth, suggesting that these fetuses were already abnormal before labour began (Nelson & Ellenberg, 1986). This suggestion is reinforced by Miller's (1989) study of ataxic cerebral palsy: 25 patients had multiple minor congenital anomalies, suggesting that development had already gone awry in the first half of pregnancy, and 64% of these also experienced perinatal or early postnatal complications.

Since the fetus is an active participant in the delivery process, and not simply a passive passenger who is expelled when his or her time is up, it is not surprising that an abnormal fetus is particularly liable to an abnormal birth (see also Chapter 10). It is possible that perinatal complications compound whatever damage has already occurred prenatally (just as labour may compound the existing damage in spina bifida (Luthy *et al.*, 1991)). Alternatively, perinatal complications may simply be harmless markers for an abnormal fetus. This harmless marker possibility is supported by findings that cerebral palsy rates have been fairly steady over the recent past, despite major advances in perinatal management and a dramatic fall in perinatal mortality (Paneth & Kiely, 1984). If perinatal complications commonly converted normal or vulnerable fetuses into cerebral-palsied children, improvements in obstetrics and neonatal paediatrics should have resulted in a clear fall in the rate of cerebral palsy — and this does not seem to have occurred.

Although this account has focused on the extent to which birth complications are largely irrelevant to cerebral palsy (probably accounting for fewer than 10% of cases (Nelson & Ellenberg, 1986)), similar considerations may apply to mental handicap. Thus Rantakallio and von Wendt (1985) described a high rate of perinatal complications in children whose mental handicap was genetic or chromosomal in origin. Had the prenatal origin not been established in these cases, it is easy to imagine that the perinatal complications would have been blamed for the mental handicap. For epilepsy too, prenatal risk factors seem far more important than perinatal risk factors (Wallace, 1992).

These new views on the relationship between birth complications and brain damage are clearly relevant to obstetricians, paediatricians and their lawyers. The findings also carry two important lessons for child psychiatrists. Firstly, neurological theories about aetiology are as error-prone as psychiatric theories — psychiatrists should not be too willing to take neurological theories on trust simply because neurology is a high-status discipline. Secondly, if birth complications are not common causes of overt brain disorders such as cerebral palsy, it is even less likely that birth complications commonly result in minimal brain damage manifesting solely in behavioural or learning difficulties. Child psychiatrists who make detailed enquiries about obstetric and neonatal complications will often elicit positive histories from the parents of their patients (as they would from the parents of normal children). This information may be clinically useful, e.g. when it reveals that the father blames the mother for their child's behavioural problems because she chose to have an epidural and this made a forceps delivery necessary. It is important that child psychiatrists do not fall into the same sort of trap, pinning the blame on birth complications without scientific justification. Although it is theoretically possible that birth complications sometimes cause covert brain damage that is manifest only in the psychiatric domain, there is no reason to suppose that this sort of causal link is at all common (Goodman, 1993). By contrast, the combination of birth complications and psychiatric problems will often occur by chance since both are common in the general population.

HOW TO RECOGNIZE A HARDWARE DEFECT

If a computer is not working properly, three sorts of explanation need to be considered: the computer is being used inappropriately; there is a software problem in the way the computer has been programmed; or there is a hardware fault in the electronic circuits. Though the analogy is crude, three similar sorts of explanation need to be considered, singly or in combination, for a child's psychiatric problems: the child's social world is making inappropriate demands on him or her; the child has learned or internalized maladaptive ways of being in the world; or the child has an abnormal brain. This is an oversimplification, of course, but it is a useful starting point. Parents and professionals have a shared interest in establishing how far a child's problems can be attributed to underlying hardware defects in the child's brain — the issue is potentially relevant to further investigations, referral to a paediatrician or paediatric neurologist, prognosis and treatment (not to mention the question of blame). There are several sorts of pointers to a hardware defect. Some of these pointers are persuasive while others are best ignored. In a rough and ready sort of way, it is worth distinguishing between six sorts of pointers:

1 Brain abnormalities are most convincingly inferred from the sorts of evidence acquired in a standard neurological assessment, e.g. a clear-cut history of seizures, the signs of a spastic diplegia, an unequivocally abnormal electroencephalogram (EEG), or a focal lesion on computed tomography (CT) or magnetic resonance imaging (MRI) scanning.

2 Less weight can be placed on 'soft' neurological signs (mostly reflecting immature motor development), abnormal neuropsychological profiles, or abnormalities of derived neurophysiological measures. In each case, abnormalities add extra weight to the suspicion that something is wrong with the child, but these abnormalities do not prove that the something is the child's brain (see Goodman, 1993).

3 Brain abnormalities may also be inferred from a history of exposure to the sorts of insults that can damage the brain, e.g. a head injury, an encephalitic illness, or high-dose cranial irradiation. There are several potential problems with this sort of inference. Firstly, some members of a high-risk group may escape unscathed. Secondly, changes in behaviour after a potential brain insult may be mediated by maladaptive parental responses (such as overprotectiveness or inconsistent discipline) rather than by biological damage. After mild head injuries, for example, the increased rate of child psychiatric disorders seems to owe more to disrupted parenting than to acquired brain damage (Hjern & Nylander, 1964). Finally, when risk factors for brain injury are associated with psychiatric problems, it may be unclear what is cause and what is effect. For example, it is equally plausible *a priori* that head injury leads to hyperactivity, that hyperactivity and impulsiveness lead to head injury, or that some third factor, such as psychosocial disadvantage, independently predisposes a child to both head injury and hyperactivity.

4 There is accumulating evidence that genetic factors play an important role in at least some child psychiatric disorders (Rutter *et al.*, 1990). Although this genetic liability may be mediated by an inherited hardware fault in the child's brain, this is not necessarily the case. In a prejudiced society, for example, genes for skin pigmentation, short stature or adiposity may be risk factors for peer rejection, low self-esteem and secondary behavioural problems that have nothing to do with brain abnormalities.

5 When a child develops psychiatric problems despite apparently favourable home and school circumstances, it is tempting to suppose that the child's problems are biological in origin. This is a very weak argument. Until relatively recently, this sort of argument led to the consequences of child sexual abuse being attributed to constitutional factors in the child. Absence of proof of psychosocial causation is not proof of absence.

6 The presence of a specific behavioural syndrome is sometimes taken as suggestive or even sufficient evidence that the child has an abnormal brain. This is rarely warranted since few behavioural syndromes are commonly associated with

independent evidence of underlying brain abnormalities — the exceptions being progressive dementia, severe mental retardation and perhaps autism. Inferring minimal brain damage or minimal cerebral dysfunction from common child psychiatric problems is currently no more than an exercise in faulty reasoning. Thus, although it is true, as described later in this chapter, that neurologically impaired children are particularly prone to hyperactivity, it does not necessarily follow that all hyperactive children have brain damage. (Consider the logic of: people with strokes are prone to limp, so anyone with a limp must be suffering from a stroke or a 'minimal stroke'.)

Given the potential difficulties in deciding whether or not a child does have a hardware defect, the following sections on the links between brain and behavioural problems are based on studies of children with the best-authenticated brain abnormalities (as established by the first set of criteria on the preceding list).

BRAIN DISORDERS INCREASE THE RISK OF CHILD PSYCHIATRIC DISORDERS

Although clinicians have long suspected that brain–behaviour links were important in childhood, the evidence was suggestive but not conclusive until relatively recently. Clinic series (e.g. Still, 1902; Ounsted, 1955) reported a high rate of behavioural problems in children with brain disorders, but these sorts of studies left three key questions unanswered. Firstly, how common were similar behavioural problems in the general child population? Secondly, even if psychiatric problems were commoner in neurology clinics than in the general population, was this simply because children with a mixture of neurological and psychiatric problems were particularly likely to be referred to a specialist clinic? Thirdly, even if the problem of referral bias could be overcome, and representative samples of children with brain disorders could be shown to have a high rate of psychiatric problems, would this reflect specific brain–behaviour links, or would it simply reflect the impact of any disabling or stigmatizing disorder, whether affecting the brain, skin, heart or any other organ?

All three of these key questions were tackled in the neuropsychiatric part of the Isle of Wight study (Rutter *et al.*, 1970a). Standardized assessments were used to establish the rates of psychiatric disorder in four representative groups of children from a single geographical area: children with cerebral palsy or other evidence of structural brain disorders; children with idiopathic epilepsy; children with physical disorders not involving the brain (e.g. deafness, blindness, diabetes); and children free from physical disorders. Children with severe mental handicap were not included in any of these groups. The results of that study provided the first firm evidence for strong brain–behaviour links in childhood. As summarized in Table 11.1, the rate of psychiatric disorder was substantially higher in children with brain disorders than in children who were free of physical problems, or in children with physical problems not affecting the brain. Similar links

Table 11.1 Prevalence on the Isle of Wight of psychiatric disorder in children with and without brain disorder (from Rutter *et al.*, 1970a)

Group	Prevalence of psychiatric disorder
Population sample	7%
Nonbrain disorder	12%
Uncomplicated epilepsy	29%
Structural brain disorder (IQ > 50)	44%

were found between brain disorders and specific reading retardation. Since the study was epidemiological rather than clinic-based, the clear association between brain and behavioural disorders cannot have been due to a referral bias. The finding that cerebral disorders carried a much higher psychiatric risk than noncerebral disorders strongly suggested direct brain–behaviour links in addition to the risks attendant on any chronic or stigmatizing disorder. This conclusion was supported by a separate study (Seidel *et al.*, 1975) that compared children who had cerebral disorders with a matched group of children disabled by other disorders (mainly musculoskeletal). The children with cerebral disorders were twice as likely to have psychiatric problems, even though children with an IQ of under 70 were excluded from both groups, and the two groups were well-matched for social background and degree of physical incapacity.

Although the evidence that brain abnormalities increase the risk of child psychiatric disorders is persuasive, it is important to remember not only that many children with brain disorders are free from psychiatric problems, but also that the great majority of children with psychiatric problems are free from overt brain disorders. On the Isle of Wight, for example, 65% of the children with cerebral palsy or epilepsy had no psychiatric disorder, and fewer than 10% of the children with psychiatric disorders also had brain disorders (as judged by the presence of epilepsy, severe mental retardation, cerebral palsy and related disorders).

Different brain disorders increase psychiatric risk to different extents. As shown in Table 11.1, the Isle of Wight study showed that structural brain disorders had more impact on psychiatric risk than did uncomplicated epilepsy. In this same study, psychiatric disorder was commoner among children with structural brain disorders plus epilepsy (58% affected) than among children with structural brain disorders but no epilepsy (38% affected). Among the children with uncomplicated epilepsy, psychiatric risk varied with the type of seizure, with temporal lobe seizures carrying the greatest risk — a conclusion that has both been supported and challenged by subsequent studies (see below).

AT RISK FOR WHICH PSYCHIATRIC DISORDERS?

There is a long-running controversy about the extent to which brain disorders are specific risk factors for particular sorts of psychiatric problems, as opposed to nonspecific risk factors for all types of psychiatric problems. Once again, the results of the Isle of Wight neuropsychiatric study (Rutter *et al.*, 1970a) are particularly instructive because the sample was epidemiological rather than clinic-based. Table 11.2 summarizes the Isle of Wight findings on the types of psychiatric disorder in children with and without brain disorders. Among the neurologically intact children who had psychiatric disorders, over 98% had either a conduct or an emotional disorder, or a mixture of the two. These were also the commonest disorders among the children who had both neurological and psychiatric disorders. In other words, if a child with a brain disorder develops a psychiatric disorder too, that disorder is typically a run-of-the-mill psychiatric disorder and not a specific 'brain damage' syndrome. This being so, brain disorders can be seen as nonspecific risk factors for a wide range of child psychiatric disorders. It is not the case, however, that brain disorders increase the risk of all psychiatric problems to the same extent. As can be seen in Table 11.2, hyperkinesis was particularly overrepresented among children with cerebral palsy or epilepsy on the Isle of Wight. Thus while the overall prevalence of psychiatric disorders was about seven times higher in children with brain disorders than in neurologically intact children, the prevalence of hyperkinesis was

Table 11.2 Diagnostic breakdown of psychiatrically disordered children on the Isle of Wight with and without brain disorders (from Rutter *et al.*, 1970a)

Psychiatrically disordered children with:	Diagnosis				
	Conduct disorder	Emotional disorder	Mixed disorder	Hyperkinesis	PDD and other
No neurological disorder (*n* = 111)	37%	38%	23%	1%	1%
Uncomplicated epilepsy (*n* = 18)	33%	44%	17%	6%	0%
Structural brain abnormality IQ > 50 (*n* = 16)	19%	25%	25%	19%	12%

PDD, Pervasive developmental disorder, e.g. autism.

about 90 times higher. This suggests that neurological factors do have some influence on the type of psychiatric disorder — a conclusion that is reinforced by numerous studies reporting associations between particular brain abnormalities and specific psychiatric disorders, e.g. between tuberous sclerosis and pervasive developmental disorders (Hunt & Dennis, 1987; Hunt & Shepherd, 1993), between Sydenham's chorea and obsessive-compulsive disorder (Swedo *et al.*, 1989), between developmental abnormalities of the left temporal lobe and adult schizophrenia (Taylor, 1975; Ounsted *et al.*, 1987), and between hemiplegic (but not diplegic) cerebral palsy and hyperkinesis (Ingram, 1955). When the neurological disorder is genetic, as in the case of tuberous sclerosis, the associated psychiatric problems are increasingly referred to as part of the behavioural phenotype of the underlying genetic disorder (see Chapter 37) — a term that would be misleading if it were taken to refer to an invariable link rather than some degree of statistical association. To summarize, brain–behaviour links show partial specificity: brain disorders are not entirely non-specific risk factors, increasing the likelihood of all psychiatric problems to the same degree; nor, for the most part, are they highly specific risk factors, increasing the likelihood of just one or two psychiatric disorders and having no effect on the rates of the others.

LEFT HEMISPHERE VERSUS RIGHT HEMISPHERE SYNDROMES?

Since asymmetrical specialization of the two cerebral hemispheres is evident in early childhood and even in prenatal life (see Goodman, in press), it is plausible that purely left-sided and purely right-sided brain disorders have different psychiatric manifestations. Consider the following line of argument. Language processing in children (as in adults) is normally particularly dependent on the left hemisphere (Goodman, in press). Perhaps as a result, reading problems may be commoner with left-sided rather than right-sided brain disorders (Galaburda *et al.*, 1985). In ordinary children, reading problems are often associated with conduct disorder (Rutter *et al.*, 1970b). Pulling these strands together, it is plausible that left-sided brain disorders are especially likely to lead to conduct problems via language and reading difficulties. Conversely, given the evidence suggesting that the right hemisphere is particularly specialized in emotional processing, at least in adults (Ross, 1985), children with right-sided brain disorders may be especially prone to emotional rather than conduct disorders. These hypotheses receive some support from Sollee and Kindlon's (1987) small clinic-based study showing that unilateral damage to the dominant (usually left) hemisphere resulted in more externalizing than internalizing symptomatology, while damage to the other hemisphere had the opposite effect. A similar trend was evident in preliminary data on a large epidemiological study of childhood hemiplegia, though the effect fell well short of statistical significance (Goodman, 1991).

Adult lesions of the right hemisphere have been linked with problems in nonverbal communication (Ross, 1985), and similar problems have been reported in small clinic-based studies of children with right hemisphere lesions (Weintraub & Mesulam, 1983; Voeller, 1986). Judging from brief case histories, some of these children with right hemisphere deficit syndrome may have pervasive developmental disorders akin to Asperger's syndrome. Before concluding that autistic symptomatology is particularly characteristic of right hemisphere disorders, it is worth noting that no such effect was evident in the study of hemiplegia mentioned above — with autistic features being evident in some children with left hemisphere lesions as well as some children with right hemisphere lesions (Goodman, 1991).

Reported links between lateralized brain abnormalities and hyperactivity are equally inconclusive. Thus Voeller (1986) described a high rate of hyperactivity in children with right-sided lesions, whereas Stores (1977) reported that boys (but not girls) were more likely to be hyperactive if they had left-sided epileptic foci. In both studies, conclusions were based on small and possibly unrepresentative samples. The rate of hyperactivity was not influenced by the laterality of lesion in several large studies of children with brain disorders (Ingram, 1955, 1956; Ounsted, 1955; Rutter *et al.*, 1970a, 1983).

At present, then, there are only unconfirmed hints that brain lesions have side-specific effects on the pattern of child psychiatric disorder. The relevance of lateralized abnormalities in the EEG is even less clear. EEGs obtained from the same child on different occasions can differ markedly from one another (Kaufman *et al.*, 1980), so little weight can be placed on inferences drawn from a single EEG recording. Even when the side of origin of seizures is clear, as in the case of epilepsy associated with unilateral brain lesions, the impact of seizures on psychological development may be unrelated to laterality. In the study by Vargha-Khadem and colleagues (1992) of the cognitive consequences of childhood hemiplegia, coexistent epilepsy was strongly associated with deficits in IQ and memory but the laterality of the lesion (and, presumably, of the epileptic focus) made no difference to the cognitive sequelae. It is not yet clear whether the side of origin of epileptic discharges is equally unimportant as far as child psychiatric sequelae are concerned. There is one well-established instance of a late psychiatric consequence of childhood epilepsy that is greatly influenced by the laterality of the epileptic focus: adult-onset schizophrenia is much commoner after early lesions of the left rather than right temporal lobe (Taylor, 1975; Ounsted *et al.*, 1987). Future studies may yet demonstrate equally clear laterality effects for some aspects of childhood psychopathology.

HOW DO NEUROLOGICAL AND NONNEUROLOGICAL RISK FACTORS INTERACT?

As described in the rest of this volume, a multitude of psychosocial and genetic factors influence a child's liability to psychiatric disorders. How do these 'ordinary' risk factors interact with neurological risk factors? The first point to note is that children with brain disorders can be affected by ordinary risk factors. In the Isle of Wight study, for example, children with brain disorders were more likely to have a psychiatric problem if they also came from a broken home or had an emotionally disturbed mother (Rutter *et al.*, 1970a). The most likely explanation for this finding is that parental discord or distress resulted in child psychiatric problems, though it is also possible that neurologically determined behavioural problems in the child had an adverse impact on the parents' marriage and mental state. The direction of causality is clearer in Rutter *et al.*'s (1983) prospective study of childhood head injuries. Although the severity of head injury was the most powerful single predictor of whether a child would develop a psychiatric problem, ordinary risk factors were also influential. Thus, considering just children with severe head injuries, new psychiatric disorders developed in 60% of children who also experienced high levels of psychosocial adversity, but only in 14% of the children who experienced low levels of psychosocial adversity. In this instance, the child's behavioural problems could not have created the psychosocial adversity because the presence or absence of adversity predated both the head injury and the psychiatric problem.

In one instance, brain disorders do seem to override an ordinary risk factor for child psychiatric problems. Among prepubertal children without neurological problems, boys are at considerably greater psychiatric risk than girls (e.g. Rutter *et al.*, 1975). This male vulnerability is not evident in children with brain disorders. Thus psychiatric disorder was equally common in the two sexes in the Isle of Wight sample of children with brain disorders (Rutter *et al.*, 1970a), and in the sample of children followed prospectively after a severe head injury (Rutter *et al.*, 1983). Similarly, the rate of autism in tuberous sclerosis seems to be roughly equal in boys and girls (Hunt & Shepherd, 1993).

If brain abnormalities and ordinary risk factors (other than male sex) do both increase a child's liability to psychiatric problems, it is important to consider whether neurological and nonneurological risk factors act independently or synergistically. For the sake of clarity, it is worth distinguishing between vulnerability and separate paths models, though hybrid models are certainly plausible. According to the vulnerability model, neurological abnormalities are relatively or totally innocuous on their own, but amplify the effects of any coexistent nonneurological risk factors. Thus Rutter *et al.* (1970a) suggest that the 'effect of brain dysfunction is largely to render the child more liable to react adversely to the stresses and strains which may impair the development of any child' (pp. 208–209). By contrast, the separate paths model (e.g. Breslau, 1990) suggests that there are at least two independent routes into psychiatric disorder: a neurological route that is unaffected by the presence or absence of additional psychosocial or genetic adversity; and one or more nonneurological routes that are unaffected by the presence or absence of brain abnormalities. In statistical terms, the vulnerability model predicts a significant additive interaction between neurological and nonneurological risk factors, whereas the separate paths model variables predict separate main effects without an interaction. To date, the evidence favours separate paths (Breslau, 1990), but the evidence is based on such weak measures of psychopathology that it would be premature to write off the notion that brain abnormalities sometimes act as risk multipliers rather than as risks in themselves (Goodman, 1993).

Our current understanding of the interaction of neurological and ordinary risk factors suggests two lessons for clinicians. Firstly, since children with brain disorders are not immune to ordinary risk factors, the rate of psychiatric problems in this high-risk group could be reduced by tackling coexistent risk factors, such as parental discord or inadequate supervision. Secondly, if there is any truth in the separate paths model, some children with brain disorders will develop psychiatric problems even in the most favourable of environments. Clinicians who bear this in mind will often be able to reassure parents and teachers who blame themselves for not having done enough to prevent the emergence of psychiatric problems. Families and schools who are doing a good-enough job with an extremely challenging group of children deserve to feel admired rather than blamed.

WHAT ARE THE MEDIATING LINKS?

Establishing that children with brain disorders have strikingly high rates of psychiatric problems should be the beginning rather than the end of neuropsychiatric inquiry. All too often, however, neuropsychiatrists have been content to call a halt to their inquiries once they have demonstrated that brain–behaviour links exist. This is particularly unfortunate since a better understanding of the mediating mechanisms would be of great theoretical and practical interest. From a theoretical point of view, the links between brain and behavioural disorders in childhood potentially provide a unique window on the biological determinants of psychological development. From a practical point of view, we need to know much more about mediating processes if we are to prevent or treat psychiatric disorders in neurologically impaired children. Imagine, for example, that the main reason brain disorder X leads to psychiatric problems is because it results in specific learning problems that engender marked frustration with schooling, leading on to defiant and disruptive behaviour in class. Imagine also that brain disorder Y leads to psychiatric problems largely as a result of inducing parental overprotectiveness and inconsistent discipline. To be as effective as possible, preventive efforts should mainly be school-based for disorder X but home-based for disorder Y. There are a multitude of possible links between neurological and psychiatric problems, and until we know how to identify the major links for any particular child or group of children, we will misdirect much of our preventive and curative effort.

Given the current dearth of relevant studies, this account of the mediating processes has had to be based largely on clinical plausibility. Before considering the ways in which brain disorders may result in psychiatric problems, it is worth re-iterating that just because a child has both neurological and psychiatric problems, it does not necessarily follow that the neurological problems caused the psychiatric problems. It is possible that the two sets of problems are a coincidence, e.g. the child's psychiatric problems may be attributable to parental discord that is unrelated to the child's brain disorder. Alternatively, the two sets of problems may reflect a common origin, e.g. the child's head injury and conduct disorder may both be attributable to inadequate parental supervision. In many cases, though, the child's brain disorder will have played some direct or indirect part in the origin of the concomitant psychiatric problems. For the sake of clarity, it is helpful to distinguish between the organic and psychosocial consequences of a brain disorder (Fig. 11.1), acknowledging that these consequences are often intimately interrelated and that the distinction is sometimes impossible in practice.

The organic consequences of a brain disorder may be evident in the physical, psychoeducational and neurobehavioural domains. Physical disabilities, ranging from easy fatigability to lack of independent mobility, may have an indirect impact on psychological well-being, e.g. by influencing self-esteem or peer relationships. In many cases, the treatments of physical problems have their own psychological costs. Children may spend many hours each week in physiotherapy (sacrificing play time and occasioning 'I don't want to' battles), and some children experience repeated hospital admissions, with their attendant separations and disruptions.

Specific learning problems and below-average intelligence are common psychoeducational consequences of brain abnormalities (e.g. Rutter *et al.*, 1970a). This probably reflects a direct link between brain disorders and impaired cognitive processing, though the situation is sometimes aggravated by

restricted educational opportunities, lower expectations and lengthy absences from school for therapy or operations. For children with epilepsy, cognitive and scholastic skills can be disrupted not only by their clinical and subclinical seizures, but also by the effects of their anticonvulsant medication (see below).

The evidence that brain disorders lead directly to some types of childhood psychopathology is largely circumstantial. Firstly, there are adult parallels for direct brain–behaviour links (Lishman, 1987), and even some animal models (e.g. Robinson, 1979). Secondly, various medications have an adverse impact on children's behaviour, e.g. barbiturates on activity and attention control (Ounsted, 1955). Thirdly, organic links seem to provide the best explanation for the wide variety of specific neuropsychiatric associations in childhood, such as the association between Prader–Willi syndrome and characteristic sleep and appetite problems (Cassidy, 1984), or the association between Lesch–Nyhan syndrome and severe self-injury (Christie *et al.*, 1982).

Brain disorders can lead to a multitude of adverse psychosocial consequences. Physical disabilities can result in teasing, poor self-image and reduced opportunities for peer interaction. Repeated hospitalizations may disrupt friendships and predispose to behavioural disorders, perhaps as a result of repeated separations from family (see Chapter 12). Specific learning problems and low intelligence are associated with a much higher rate of psychiatric problems in children with brain disorders, just as they are in ordinary children (Rutter *et al.*, 1970a). There are several possible reasons for this association, including the frustration engendered by school failure, and its impact on self-esteem. If brain abnormalities do have organic neurobehavioural consequences, such as hyperkinesis or an impaired ability to decipher social and

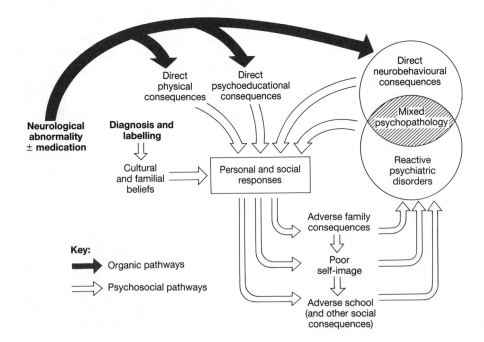

Fig. 11.1 A simplified representation of organic and psychosocial pathways from brain to behavioural abnormalities.

emotional cues, then these organic consequences may, in turn, have adverse effects on family relationships and friendship patterns. The beliefs and attitudes of the family and the wider social world also have a major impact. Parents, teachers and peers respond to a neurologically impaired child in the light of their beliefs and prejudices about brain-damaged children. These beliefs influence the likelihood of overprotection, peer rejection, and unrealistic expectations. Beliefs can also interfere with parents' abilities to set limits to unacceptable behaviours. This can happen, for example, if parents assume that all bad behaviour is neurologically driven and beyond the child's control, or if they fear that any reproof will trigger off an epileptic seizure and further damage the child's brain. Family relationships can be disrupted for other reasons as well. Sibling rivalry, for example, can be fuelled by the resentment of disabled children who see themselves being overtaken by younger siblings, or by the resentment of non-disabled siblings who feel they are missing out on parental attention. These are only a few of the many possible psychosocial pathways from brain disorders to child psychiatric problems. Others are well-described, with a wealth of case histories, in Taylor's (1989) account of the psychosocial consequences of childhood epilepsy.

It is one thing to describe a mixture of organic and psychosocial pathways from neurological abnormalities to psychiatric disorder, and it is quite another thing to establish the importance of any given pathway in practice. There are disappointingly few good studies in this area, but relevant research strategies can be summarized fairly briefly (with a more detailed account being available in Goodman, 1993). If we want to establish whether factor X (e.g. marital breakdown, self-esteem, friendships) is an important mediating link between neurological and psychiatric disorders in childhood, several research strategies are available. The most basic strategy (and one that is sometimes overlooked) is to establish whether factor X is commoner in a representative sample of children with some particular brain disorder than in the general child population. Thus several studies suggest that the parents of children with chronic physical disorders are *not* at increased risk of marital breakdown (e.g. Sabbeth & Leventhal, 1984), making it most unlikely that the high rate of psychiatric disorder in neurologically impaired children can be attributed to a high rate of marital breakdown brought on by the strains of looking after a disabled child.

If factor X is commoner in a neurologically impaired group, the next step is to examine whether factor X predicts which neurologically impaired children will also develop a psychiatric problem. Once again, the answers may be surprising. There is no convincing evidence, for example, that a high level of physical disability increases the risk of psychiatric problems within a neurologically impaired group (Rutter *et al.*, 1970a; Seidel *et al.*, 1975). By contrast, not only are specific reading retardation and low IQ particularly common among children with brain disorders, but these children with additional learning problems are at considerably greater psychiatric risk (Rutter *et al.*, 1970a). When factor X does predict psychiatric

risk, multivariate statistical techniques can be used to quantify the possible importance of X as a mediating factor (e.g. Breslau, 1985). It is important to remember, however, that even strong associations are not proof of causation. The presence of factor X may be a consequence rather than a cause of psychiatric disorder, or some third factor may independently increase both X and psychiatric disorder (so that X is a marker for the mediating process rather than the mediator itself).

Longitudinal studies and intervention studies are invaluable research strategies for investigating the causal mechanisms underlying cross-sectional associations — though this potential has hardly been tapped in developmental neuropsychiatry to date.

THE PSYCHIATRIC CONSEQUENCES OF SPECIFIC BRAIN DISORDERS

Turning from the general to the particular, the following sections review a range of childhood brain disorders from a psychiatric perspective. It is obviously impossible to cover the whole of paediatric neurology and neurosurgery in a few pages; disorders have been selected on the basis of frequency, severity or particular relevance to child psychiatry. The main clinical features of each disorder are reviewed along with the psychiatric consequences. Readers who want to learn more about specific aspects of paediatric neurology are recommended to turn to Aicardi (1992), Brett (1991) or Menkes (1990) for succinct, readable, and well-referenced accounts.

Regression

A variety of dementing disorders present in childhood with an insidious loss of skills, often accompanied by rather nonspecific psychiatric problems. Child psychiatrists have a key role to play in recognizing these disorders at an early stage so that the child can be referred to a paediatric neurologist for detailed assessment. In disorders such as Wilson's disease where there is a specific treatment, delayed diagnosis and treatment can result in unnecessary and irreversible damage. In most childhood dementias there is no specific treatment — but that does not mean that delayed diagnosis is trivial. Until the organic basis is recognized, the child's problems may be blamed on his or her laziness, or on parental mishandling, causing unnecessary anguish and subsequent guilt or anger. Occasionally, prompt diagnosis and genetic counselling would have averted the birth of a second affected child. Finally, once the diagnosis has been made, a child psychiatrist may be able to offer useful help to the child, the parents, and the siblings — and this help is much more likely to be accepted if the child psychiatrist referred the case on for physical investigation at any early stage.

Although desirable, prompt recognition of a dementing disorder is undoubtedly difficult. Normal development often involves some degree of 'two steps forward, one step back'; many children revert to more babyish ways when physically ill or under stress; and almost any child psychiatric disorder can interfere with concentration or application at school, leading to a falling off in classroom performance. Even when there is a marked loss of skills in several areas, the cause may be psychosocial rather than organic. For example, Brown and Perkins (1989) described child sexual abuse presenting with marked regression. The presence of psychosocial or organic risk factors can sometimes be misleading in individual cases. For example, the victims of sexual abuse and the offspring of prostitutes or drug addicts are clearly at psychiatric risk for psychosocial reasons, but they are also at risk of human immunodeficiency virus (HIV) infection and its associated dementia (see Chapter 40). Conversely, since the children of patients with Huntington's disease have a 50% chance of carrying the gene themselves, psychiatric problems in these children could be due to early-onset Huntington's disease — but the problems could also be due to the abuse, neglect and disorganization that are common in affected families (Dewhurst *et al.*, 1970; Folstein *et al.*, 1983). In practice, an organic cause needs to be considered (and appropriate referrals or investigations initiated) when the child meets one or more of the following three criteria:

1 Progressive loss of well-established linguistic, academic, or self-help skills — with performance being well below previous levels even when the child seems content, motivated and not preoccupied. Psychometric testing is sometimes helpful, particularly if repeated measures are available (Lobascher & Cavanagh, 1980).

2 Emergence of other features suggestive of a brain disorder, such as seizures, evidence of visual impairment, tremor or postural disturbance.

3 Risk factors for relevant genetic or infectious diseases, e.g. father with Huntington's disease, mother with acquired immunodeficiency syndrome.

Clinicians who make a practice of reviewing their initial diagnostic formulation at regular intervals will be less likely to miss insidiously progressive disorders that initially present with apparently straightforward psychiatric symptoms. The dementing disorders that are most likely to present to child psychiatrists are described below.

Batten's disease

Batten's disease (which is also known as neuronal ceroid lipofuscinosis) refers to a group of related disorders, all of which are autosomal recessive. Child psychiatrists are most likely to encounter children with the juvenile form, which usually presents with visual failure aged 5–7, and which does not generally result in obvious dementia for a further few years. If no cause is initially found for the visual failure, the child may be referred for psychiatric assessment of 'hysterical' blindness. Alternatively, if the visual impairment is attributed to a nonprogressive cause, psychiatric referral may occur several years later when deteriorating school work and non-specific behavioural problems (such as disruptive and aggressive behaviour) are mistakenly attributed to the psychological consequences of blindness or family stresses. Seizures may

occur fairly early in the disorder, but the emergence of hard neurological signs is usually a late feature. Exceptionally, dementia and seizures may be the presenting features without any visual failure (Scully *et al.*, 1978). The electroretinogram and EEG are suggestive, and rectal biopsy is usually diagnostic.

Wilson's disease

Wilson's disease is an autosomal recessive disorder of copper metabolism. As a rule of thumb, children presenting before the age of 10 do so with progressive liver failure, whereas children presenting after the age of 10 do so with neurological features, insidious dementia or nonspecific emotional or behavioural problems. Early neurological features include extrapyramidal and cerebellar signs. Dystonic movements and postures can be bizarre, unilateral and exacerbated by stress, so misdiagnosis as conversion hysteria is all too easy. The child's writing may change to a crabbed Parkinsonian style, or may provide evidence of involuntary jerks of the pen. Urinary copper is high, while plasma copper and caeruloplasmin are both low. Ophthalmological examination with a slit lamp may reveal the pathognomonic Kayser–Fleischer ring on the iris. Liver biopsy is necessary in doubtful cases. The disorder can be treated successfully by copper chelation, and earlier treatment results in a better outcome.

Huntington's disease

Huntington's disease is an autosomal dominant disorder that typically presents with chorea and dementia in mid-adult life. The abnormal gene, on the short arm of chromosome 4, includes an excessively high number of trinucleotide repeats (The Huntington's Disease Research Group, 1993). The disorder has its onset before 14 years of age in about 5% of cases, with early-onset cases more often having an affected father than an affected mother. Chorea may occur but a rigid Parkinsonian picture is more common. Epilepsy is an early feature in a substantial minority. The first presentation may be with disturbed or withdrawn behaviour, with loss of interest in games and lessons. These psychiatric features are particularly difficult to interpret in the context of the marked psychosocial disturbance that is common in families where one parent has Huntington's disease (Dewhurst *et al.*, 1970). The child's fear of developing the same disease may also be important. Just as a positive family history does not make the diagnosis, a negative family history does not rule out the diagnosis since the presence of affected relatives may be concealed, may be masked by misdiagnosis, or may be inapparent due to nonpaternity. CT or MRI scanning may demonstrate caudate atrophy, and positron emission tomography scans may show caudate hypometabolism. Now that the gene has been identified genetic testing is likely to become the primary diagnostic tool. Harper and Clarke (1990) have discussed some of the ethical issues involved in predictive DNA testing of asymptomatic children with affected relatives.

Adrenoleukodystrophy

Adrenoleukodystrophy is an X-linked recessive disorder. The most characteristic presentation is a combination of adrenal insufficiency, progressive dementia and neurological features. Even within the same family, however, the presentation can be very variable, with adrenal failure predominating in some affected boys, and with dementia and neurological features predominating in others. Problems with restlessness, poor coordination, disruptiveness and deteriorating school progress are often the earliest manifestations. Psychotic symptoms may also be prominent (Corbett *et al.*, 1977). Unequivocal neurological abnormalities usually begin at 5–9 years of age, with pyramidal and extrapyramidal signs, convulsions, deafness or visual failure (sometimes due to cortical blindness). If present, severe adrenal failure results in diarrhoea, vomiting, hypotension and pigmentation. Subtle adrenocortical insufficiency may only be evident from the results of an adrenocorticotrophic hormone challenge. A leukodystrophy with occipital predominance is often evident on CT scan. The combination of leukodystrophy and adrenal failure is pathognomonic. The diagnosis can be confirmed by high plasma levels of saturated very long chain fatty acids.

Juvenile-onset metachromatic leukodystrophy

Juvenile-onset metachromatic leukodystrophy is an autosomal recessive disorder with an onset at 6–10 years of age. It often presents insidiously with cognitive decline, deteriorating school performance, and the emergence of oppositional, aggressive or antisocial behaviours. As the disorder progresses, the dementia worsens, Parkinsonian signs emerge, and fits may occur. Optic atrophy and visual failure are late signs. The presence of metachromatic material in the urine can be a reliable test, but the definitive diagnosis is based on markedly reduced arylsulphatase A activity in white cells or cultured fibroblasts.

Subacute sclerosing panencephalitis

Subacute sclerosing panencephalitis is a slow virus infection caused by measles virus. It is much commoner after wild type measles (particularly if contracted during infancy) than after immunization with live attenuated measles virus. Boys are affected five times more often than girls. Onset is between 5 and 15 years, usually starting with insidious intellectual deterioration and personality change. The emergent behaviours range from irritability to withdrawal, and from defiance to inappropriate affection. Myoclonic jerks without interruption of consciousness begin several months later. Initially these jerks are infrequent and lead to occasional episodes of the child falling or staggering backwards. As the disorder progresses, the jerks become increasingly evident as shock-like movements affect the head or the whole body, recurring every 5–20 seconds (accompanied by characteristic periodic complexes on the EEG). These myoclonic jerks are accentuated

by excitement or loud noises, and are absent in sleep. The serum and cerebrospinal fluid levels of measles antibodies are markedly elevated.

HIV encephalopathy

HIV encephalopathy may now be the commonest cause of childhood dementia worldwide. Some congenitally infected children make slow developmental progress, others reach a developmental plateau and fail to advance further, and yet others suffer from a true dementia, with loss of early-acquired skills. The neurological and psychiatric features of congenital and acquired HIV infections are described in Chapter 40.

Pervasive developmental disorders

Pervasive developmental disorders may present with regression, involving the loss of established skills in the domains of communication, social interaction and play — sometimes accompanied by general intellectual deterioration. Regression is always present at the start of disintegrative disorder. In addition, a substantial minority of autistic children also come to medical attention after losing skills in the second year of life (e.g. Kurita, 1985). Cases of regressive-onset autism are particularly likely to be referred to paediatric neurologists to rule out progressive neurodegenerative disorders. Clinical features supporting a pervasive developmental disorder rather than a neurodegenerative disorder include the presence of subtle abnormalities in communication, social interaction or play *prior* to the episode of regression; the absence of abnormalities on neurological examination and investigation; and a resumption of developmental progress and new learning in the months following the regression. The pervasive developmental disorders are described in Chapter 33.

Rett's syndrome

Rett's syndrome is a progressive neurological disorder that only affects girls (see also Chapter 33). The cause is unknown. Development progresses normally for the first 7–18 months, followed first by a phase of developmental stagnation, and then by a rapid period of skill loss, commonly accompanied by screaming attacks. The girl is left with a mental age of about 6–9 months, and remains at this level for years. Hand use is limited and the hands are characteristically held close to the chest in the midline with prominent hand-washing or hand-to-mouth stereotypies. Mobility is impaired, ranging from an inability to stand at worst, to satisfactory walking but ataxic running at best. Other features of Rett's syndrome include episodic hyperventilation; episodic laughter, which is often unprovoked; an evolving microcephaly, with a head circumference that is normal at birth but typically below the third centile by the age of 3 years (due to unusually slow head growth); seizures and EEG abnormalities in some girls; and slow neurological deterioration with rigidity and loss of mobility. Although Hagberg *et al.* (1983) described the disorder as a dementia with autistic features, Olsson and Rett (1987) suggest that the similarity with autism is more apparent than real, with most affected girls showing a level of social interest, communication and play that is appropriate to their very low mental age. In any case, child psychiatrists do need to keep Rett's syndrome in mind when assessing a girl with possible autistic features — either as a differential diagnosis for autism, or as a possible cause of autism.

Epilepsy

Convulsions are the commonest problem encountered in paediatric neurology. Of the many paediatric accounts of childhood epilepsy, two can be particularly recommended: O'Donohoe (1985) for a clear introduction, and Aicardi (1986) for a more detailed and densely referenced account. References are only provided in this section for topics that are not well-covered in the main paediatric texts.

At least 1 child in 200 experiences repeated epileptic seizures without a detectable extracerebral cause — the usual definition of epilepsy. This definition excludes children who have hypo-glycaemic seizures due to their diabetes, or children who have anoxic seizures due to faints or breath-holding attacks. The definition also excludes the 3% of preschool children who have one or more convulsions provoked by febrile illnesses — these febrile convulsions are generally benign, with about 98% of affected individuals *not* developing true epilepsy. Distinguishing epilepsy from other sorts of paroxysmal disorders (such as faints and parasomnias) can be surprisingly difficult, and misdiagnoses are all too common in both directions. Stores (1985) has summarized the clinical and EEG evaluation of seizures and seizure-like disorders, and has more recently reviewed possible confusions between sleep disorders and epilepsy (Stores, 1991).

Psychiatrists may be asked to help distinguish between true seizures and pseudoseizures. This is not an easy task, particularly since most children with pseudoseizures do also suffer from true seizures, since emotional stresses can precipitate true seizures, and since many children with true epilepsy have psychiatric problems as well. Possible pointers to pseudo-seizures include: they occur when the child is being observed but not when the child is alone; the onset is gradual rather than sudden; the paroxysm involves quivering or uncontrolled flailing rather than true clonus; there are theatrical semi-purposive movements accompanied by loud screaming or shouting; painful stimuli are actively avoided during an attack and serious injury does not occur; the offset is sudden with an immediate return to an alert and responsive state; and the EEG does not show any paroxysmal discharge during an episode. All these observations are easier to make when the child is assessed with combined EEG and video monitoring. None of the pointers is infallible, however, and some sorts of true seizures (most notably frontal lobe seizures) are easily mistaken for pseudoseizures. Williams *et al.* (1978), Holmes *et al.* (1980), and Goodyer (1985) have written helpful accounts of the assessment and management of pseudoseizures.

The classification of epileptic seizures and syndromes has changed repeatedly over recent decades. In the current (1981) classification of the International League Against Epilepsy (ILAE), the most basic distinction in seizure type is between generalized and partial seizures (Commission on Classification and Terminology of the International League Against Epilepsy, 1981). Generalized seizures are bilaterally symmetrical and the first clinical symptoms do not suggest a focal onset. Examples of generalized seizures include generalized tonic–clonic seizures (*grand mal*), absence seizures (*petit mal*), atypical absences, tonic seizures, atonic seizures and myoclonic seizures. In partial seizures, the first clinical symptoms do indicate activation of a relatively localized group of neurons, accompanied by a correspondingly localized EEG discharge. Partial seizures are further subclassified as simple or complex. In ILAE's 1969 classification (Gastaut, 1970), partial seizures were described as simple when symptoms just involved elementary sensory or motor functions, and as complex when symptoms involved 'higher functions' (e.g. *déjà vu*, forced thinking). In ILAE's 1981 revision, however, the definition was radically changed: partial seizures are described as simple if full consciousness is retained (even if the symptoms involve higher functions), and as complex if consciousness is impaired (even if the symptoms do not involve higher functions). Either sort of partial seizure can evolve into generalized tonic–clonic seizures. Changes in classification make it difficult to compare studies conducted at different times. Thus studies of psychomotor epilepsy, temporal lobe epilepsy, complex partial seizures (1969 definition), and complex partial seizures (1981 definition) have investigated overlapping but not identical groups of subjects, making it hard to integrate the findings of different eras.

The link between epilepsy and cognitive impairment is complex and controversial. Some of the complexities are illustrated by findings from the National Collaborative Perinatal Project, which followed a large representative sample of children from before birth until 7 years of age (Ellenberg *et al.*, 1986). When tested at 7, the children who had experienced one or more nonfebrile seizures had an average IQ about 10 points lower than the sample average. When children with seizures were compared with siblings who had never had seizures, the difference was much less marked (4 points), and even this nonsignificant difference disappeared when the case–sibling comparisons were restricted to cases who appeared neurologically normal prior to the onset of seizures. When cases whose seizures began after the age of 4 were compared with carefully matched controls, there was no evidence that the onset of seizures led to a fall in IQ by age 7. The results of this study suggest that the average IQ of children with seizures is reduced not because of the seizures themselves but because seizures are often markers either for other neurological abnormalities or for adverse family factors, whether social or genetic.

Although the conclusion that seizures have no direct effect

on IQ probably applies to the large number of epileptic children who have relatively few seizures and respond well to standard treatment, intellectual deterioration as a result of epilepsy may occur among the smaller number of children with frequent treatment-resistant seizures (Rodin, 1989). Whatever the doubts on this issue, other community and clinic-based studies do support the National Collaborative Perinatal Project conclusion that children whose epilepsy is associated with other neurological abnormalities have a significantly lower mean IQ than children with idiopathic epilepsy (e.g. Rutter *et al.*, 1970a; Bourgeois *et al.*, 1983). Clinic studies also suggest that cognitive impairment is associated with frequent seizures, multiple seizure types, early onset and chronicity (Corbett & Trimble, 1983; Farwell *et al.*, 1985; Seidenberg *et al.*, 1986). Two other factors are potentially relevant to cognitive impairments in children with epilepsy. Firstly, subclinical seizure discharges in the EEG are sometimes associated with significant impairments in cognitive processing (Binnie *et al.*, 1990; see Chapter 8). Secondly, anticonvulsant medications may also impair cognition: phenobarbitone and phenytoin are the worst offenders, while carbamazepine and sodium valproate seem less harmful, particularly when they are used singly (see Cull & Trimble, 1989). Although most studies of cognition and epilepsy have focused on IQ, there is good evidence that children with seizures have a high rate of specific learning problems (Rutter *et al.*, 1970a; Seidenberg *et al.*, 1986). In the Isle of Wight study, for example, children with idiopathic epilepsy had specific reading retardation almost three times more than children without physical disorders (Rutter *et al.*, 1970a). By definition, these children were at least 2 years behind in their reading *after allowing for their IQ* (see Chapter 36 for a discussion of this approach).

Epilepsy in childhood is a powerful risk factor for emotional and behavioural disorders. In the Isle of Wight study (Rutter *et al.*, 1970a), 29% of 63 children with idiopathic epilepsy had a psychiatric disorder — four times the rate in children without physical disorders, and over twice the rate in children with physical disorders not affecting the brain (Table 11.1). Similarly, Mellor *et al.* (1974) reported on the basis of a questionnaire study that 27% of 308 schoolchildren with epilepsy had a behavioural disorder, as compared with 15% of controls. Though children with epilepsy have a high rate of psychiatric problems, the nature of these problems is not particularly distinctive (with a few rare exceptions, as described below). On the Isle of Wight over 90% of the epileptic children who had a psychiatric problem had either a conduct or an emotional disorder, or a mixture of the two (Table 11.2; Rutter *et al.*, 1970a).

What factors predict which children with epilepsy develop a psychiatric disorder? One powerful predictor is the presence or absence of associated neurological abnormalities. In the Isle of Wight study, for example, psychiatric disorders were twice as common among epileptic children when there were additional neurological problems (Rutter *et al.*, 1970a). Similarly, in Ounsted *et al.*'s (1966) study of temporal lobe epilepsy (TLE), the rate of hyperkinesis was several times commoner if

the TLE was secondary to a known brain insult rather than idiopathic. It is possible that many of the other predictors of psychopathology — such as frequency of seizures or presence of cognitive impairment — are primarily markers for the extensiveness of underlying brain abnormalities. The other predictors can be divided into seizure factors, medication, cognitive factors, social factors and family factors.

Possible seizure factors include type and frequency of seizures, and age of onset. As described below, TLE may be associated with a particularly high rate of psychiatric disorder, though the matter remains somewhat controversial. Stores (1977) reported that boys (but not girls) with TLE had more behavioural problems if the focus was in the left rather than the right hemisphere, but Camfield *et al.* (1984) did not find any laterality effect. The existence of a link between frequent seizures and more psychopathology is also controversial — Pond and Bidwell (1960) and Hermann *et al.* (1989) found evidence for such a link but Berg *et al.* (1984) did not. Early onset of seizures may also be a risk factor (Pond & Bidwell, 1960).

Choice of medication probably also influences psychopathology, though the evidence is surprisingly weak (Taylor, 1991). Phenobarbitone has been linked to a variety of behavioural problems, including aggression and hyperactivity (Ounsted, 1955). Vigabatrin, which is increasingly used for refractory epilepsy, also seems particularly likely to result in agitation, aggression or hyperactivity — side-effects that are often reduced or abolished by lowering the dose (Luna *et al.*, 1989). Polytherapy (i.e. treatment with two or more anticonvulsants at the same time) may also increase psychiatric risk (Hermann *et al.*, 1989).

Cognitive predictors of psychopathology include impaired neuropsychological functioning (Hermann, 1982) and specific reading retardation (Rutter *et al.*, 1970a). One possible social predictor is the extent to which the child is rejected or stigmatized as a result of community prejudices about epilepsy. While there can be no doubt that such prejudices are common (British Office of Health Economics, 1971), Rutter *et al.*'s (1970a) study suggests that peer rejection is more often a consequence rather than a cause of psychiatric problems in children with epilepsy. The link with family factors is well-illustrated by Grunberg and Pond's (1957) study of epileptic children with and without conduct disorders. The children with conduct disorders were much more likely to have been exposed to marital friction, disrupted care, and parental hostility or neglect, i.e. the same sorts of adverse family factors that are associated with conduct disorders in nonepileptic children too. Parental separation or divorce has also been linked to more psychopathology in children with epilepsy (Hermann *et al.*, 1989). Epilepsy does not render children immune to adverse family factors, but neither does it necessarily accentuate their vulnerability to these factors. (Our current ignorance of the interaction of neurological and psychosocial risk factors is reviewed in an earlier section of this chapter.) Finally, it is worth noting that a child's epilepsy can affect the psychological well-being and coping style of other family members (Hoare, 1987), and these effects potentially influence the course of the child's own development.

Although child psychiatrists assess and treat children with all varieties of epilepsy, some epileptic syndromes have behavioural correlates that are particularly relevant to psychiatrists, and these are described below.

Temporal lobe epilepsy

TLE generally involves a mixture of complex partial seizures and generalized tonic–clonic seizures, combined with EEG evidence of a temporal lobe origin. The onset (aura) of seizures may involve a rising epigastric feeling or fear. *Déjà vu*, forced thinking and other distortions of higher functions are rare in young children. In Ounsted *et al.*'s (1966, 1987) longitudinal clinic-based study of 100 children with TLE, only 15% were wholly free from psychological problems in childhood, and almost half had catastrophic rage outbursts, or hyperkinesis, or both. Rutter *et al.*'s (1970a) epidemiological study and Hoare's (1984) clinic-based study also found that children with TLE were at particularly high psychiatric risk (though the number of subjects in the epidemiological sample was small). By contrast, Whitman *et al.*'s (1982) clinic-based comparison of children with TLE and primary generalized epilepsy suggested that the two groups of children had comparable levels of psychopathology once suitable allowance had been made for confounding factors. This controversy is unlikely to be resolved without a large epidemiological study. From a psychiatric perspective, three reported features of TLE are of particular note. Firstly, TLE is a risk factor for a schizophrenia-like psychosis in adult life (Davison & Bagley, 1969; Ounsted *et al.*, 1987), particularly when the TLE arises from the left hemisphere (Taylor, 1975; Perez *et al.*, 1985; Ounsted *et al.*, 1987). In Ounsted *et al.*'s (1987) series, 10% of the children with TLE subsequently developed a psychosis. Secondly, boys whose TLE persists through puberty are particularly likely to be sexually indifferent during adulthood, and to remain unmarried (Taylor, 1969; Ounsted *et al.*, 1987). Finally, despite everything, many children with TLE and psychiatric problems grow up to be well-adjusted adults (Ounsted *et al.*, 1987).

Frontal lobe epilepsy

Frontal lobe epilepsy is primarily of interest to child psychiatrists because the seizures are easily misdiagnosed as pseudoseizures or sleep disorders (Stores *et al.*, 1991). Complex partial seizures arising from the frontal lobe can be very bizarre, with odd movements, postures and vocalizations. Possible features include rocking from side to side, thrashing about, making cycling movements of the legs, punching into the air, turning to one side, arching backwards, squealing, screaming or swearing. Seizures may occur primarily or exclusively during sleep. Other clinical features that make these episodes hard to recognize as true seizures include short duration (generally under a minute), absence of tonic–clonic movements and abrupt termination with prompt return of

responsiveness. To make matters worse, the EEG recorded between or even during seizures may be unhelpful. Combined video and EEG monitoring can be extremely useful in doubtful cases (Stores *et al.*, 1991).

Infantile spasms

Infantile spasms often have psychiatric sequelae. In a typical case, runs of brief jack-knife spasms begin at about 6 months of age, accompanied by developmental regression and a hypsarrhythmic EEG. A cause, such as tuberous sclerosis or a major brain malformation, can be identified in most cases. Children with no identifiable cause have a better prognosis. Most affected children are severely mentally handicapped. In a large follow-up study, Riikonen and Amnell (1981) found that serious psychiatric sequelae were common: autism was diagnosed in 12% of the sample and hyperkinesis in 23% (with considerable overlap between the two diagnoses). Using similar diagnostic criteria, Hunt and colleagues have reported considerably higher rates of autism and hyperkinesis among children whose infantile spasms were due to tuberous sclerosis (Hunt & Dennis, 1987; Hunt & Shepherd, 1993). Child psychiatrists should always enquire about infantile spasms when assessing mentally handicapped children with autistic or hyperkinetic features. When there is a history of infantile spasms, the child should be examined particularly thoroughly for the skin signs of tuberous sclerosis — a disorder that may have important genetic implications for the family.

Lennox–Gastaut syndrome

Lennox–Gastaut syndrome accounts for about 3–10% of childhood epilepsy. The syndrome is briefly reviewed in Brown and Livingston (1985) and Livingston (1988), and reviewed in more detail in Aicardi (1986) and Beaumanoir (1985a). Although there are doubts about the nosological validity of the syndrome, both because of its heterogeneity and because typical Lennox–Gastaut syndrome grades off into a wide range of atypical variants and other syndromes, most paediatric neurologists find Lennox–Gastaut syndrome a useful diagnostic category. Its onset is typically between the age of 1 and 7 years, with 'stare, jerk, and fall' epilepsy, involving frequent myoclonic, tonic, and atonic seizures, as well as atypical absences. Generalized tonic–clonic and partial seizures may also occur. EEG accompaniments include diffuse and irregular episodes of slow spike wave that are more prominent in non-REM sleep (see Chapter 8). The great majority of affected individuals are mentally handicapped. In most cases, slow development and neurological abnormalities (including infantile spasms) were evident prior to the onset of Lennox–Gastaut syndrome. In a significant minority, however, early development was normal, with cognitive deterioration at the onset of Lennox–Gastaut syndrome resulting in acquired mental handicap. Incapacitating seizures often persist despite medication, and many affected children need helmets to prevent them being injured by their frequent drop attacks.

Although neurological accounts mention problems with social responsiveness, attention, and aggression, there have been no systematic studies of psychiatric aspects of Lennox–Gastaut syndrome. One feature of the disorder that may bring a child to psychiatric attention is a tendency to prolonged episodes of minor status. During such an episode, which may last for weeks, the child can still engage in a variety of everyday activities but may appear 'switched off', socially unresponsive, aggressive, less articulate than normal, and unusually wobbly, with minor twitching of the face and hands. If the organic basis for the episode is not recognized, the deterioration may be attributed to psychological or social factors, leading to psychiatric referral.

Landau–Kleffner syndrome

Landau–Kleffner syndrome is also discussed in Chapters 8 and 32. In a typical case, a child of between 3 and 9 years of age loses receptive and expressive language skills, either suddenly or gradually. This acquired aphasia is accompanied by EEG changes, involving paroxysmal discharges that affect both hemispheres, often independently. The EEG abnormalities may be most prominent during non-REM sleep. Seizures occur in approximately 70% of cases, usually starting about the same time as the aphasia, and taking the form of generalized or simple partial seizures that are infrequent and mainly nocturnal. Seizures cease by adulthood, but the prognosis for language recovery is far more variable. It is uncertain whether the likelihood of language recovery is increased by vigorous anticonvulsant treatment designed to suppress EEG abnormalities. Neurological features of Landau–Kleffner syndrome are reviewed by Beaumanoir (1985b) and Gordon (1990). Perplexity, anxiety and tantrums are common at the time of onset. In the longer term, affected children do not show autistic impairments in social interactions, but often show some degree of hyperactivity. More marked psychiatric problems have been described in what may be a related disorder, namely epilepsy with continuous spikes and waves during slow sleep (also known as electrical status epilepticus during sleep) — a condition in which the onset of seizures is accompanied by a loss of language and other cognitive skills (Tassinari *et al.*, 1985; Hirsch *et al.*, 1990).

Cerebral palsy

Cerebral palsy refers to a heterogeneous group of congenital and early-acquired brain disorders that meet three criteria. Firstly, the disorders are chronic rather than transient. Secondly, the underlying brain lesions are static, though the clinical manifestations may change as the child grows up. This criterion rules out progressive neurodegenerative conditions or brain tumours. Thirdly, the clinical manifestations include abnormalities of motor function. These motor defects are often accompanied by other clinical manifestations of brain abnormalities, including epilepsy, learning problems and sensory impairments. The American term static encephalopathy

is roughly equivalent to cerebral palsy except that motor involvement is not obligatory. The subclassification of cerebral palsy is based on the type and distribution of motor problems (though no one scheme is entirely satisfactory). Spasticity is usually the dominant motor problem, affecting just one side of the body in spastic hemiplegia; affecting both legs to a severe extent and both arms to a mild extent in spastic diplegia; and affecting all four limbs severely in spastic quadriplegia (which is also known as tetraplegia or double hemiplegia). Less commonly, the motor problems are dominated by ataxia, or by dyskinesia (athetosis). The aetiology of cerebral palsy is largely unknown, though there are some recognized associations, e.g. between severe rhesus disease and athetosis, between cerebrovascular accidents and hemiplegia, and between a variety of severe generalized brain insults and quadriplegia. Heredity seems particularly relevant to ataxia. Prematurity is an important risk factor for diplegia (and, to a lesser extent, for others varieties of cerebral palsy as well).

In the Isle of Wight study (Rutter *et al.*, 1970a), psychiatric problems were evident in almost half of the children with cerebral palsy or related disorders (Table 11.1). The likelihood of psychiatric problems was significantly increased by two common accompaniments of cerebral palsy, namely low intelligence and specific reading retardation. When the child with cerebral palsy also had seizures, the rate of psychiatric disorder was higher (58% versus 38%), though this difference fell short of statistical significance. The type of psychiatric disorder was not particularly distinctive, though there was a hint that hyperkinesis was disproportionately common (Table 11.2). Ingram's (1955) large epidemiological study also suggested a link between cerebral palsy and hyperkinesis (with this link being most evident for hemiplegic and ataxic cerebral palsy). Autistic features are uncommon but not unknown among children with cerebral palsy. Preliminary data on a large series of hemiplegic children suggested that between 2% and 5% of the sample had significant autistic features (Goodman, 1991).

Head injury

The nature and consequences of children's head injuries are well-reviewed in a chapter by Rutter *et al.* (1983) and in a book edited by Johnson *et al.* (1989). Interested readers are advised to turn to these sources for more detailed accounts and further references. Head injuries are major causes of hospitalization, severe disability and death in childhood. It is useful to distinguish between open head injuries, which typically involve localized brain damage due to a penetrating injury, and closed head injuries, which typically involve widespread bilateral damage due to acceleration/deceleration and rotation injuries secondary to a road traffic accident or a fall. Closed head injuries are commoner, are much more likely to result in prolonged unconsciousness and posttraumatic amnesia and are less likely to result in epilepsy.

The victims are not a random cross-section of children. For example, children who are male, hyperkinetic or of below-average intelligence are more likely to sustain head injuries (particularly mild head injuries), as are children who are poorly supervised because of parental illness or depression. In other words, child psychiatric problems may be antecedents rather than consequences of head injury, or may reflect third factors (such as lack of parental supervision) that independently increase the risk of psychiatric disorder and head injury. This has made it particularly hard to determine if mild head injuries cause psychiatric disorders or cognitive deficits. The Institute of Psychiatry studies (Rutter *et al.*, 1983) suggested that mild injuries are innocuous, but doubts persist (Middleton, 1989).

By contrast, there is no longer any doubt that severe head injuries often result in cognitive impairments and psychiatric problems. Closed head injuries that result in at least 2 weeks of posttraumatic amnesia commonly result in impaired performance on a wide range of cognitive tests (affecting visuomotor and visuospatial tasks somewhat more than verbal tasks). Cognitive recovery may be partial or complete. Catch-up is fastest in the first year after injury, but may continue at a slower pace thereafter. Open head injuries also result in cognitive impairments, with performance IQ being more affected than verbal IQ whatever the laterality or locus of injury. Damage before the age of 5 years may result in faster but less complete recovery, with persisting impairments in scholastic attainments.

The short-term psychiatric sequelae of severe head injuries are well-summarized by Hill (1989). Three overlapping phases may be evident: an early phase of confusion, regression, or denial; a middle phase of demanding and arrogant behaviour or listlessness and depression; and a final phase of gradual accommodation to disability.

In the longer term, psychiatric disorders are evident in roughly half of the survivors of severe closed or open head injuries (Rutter *et al.*, 1983; Lehmkuhl & Thoma, 1990). Within this group, the risk of psychiatric disorder is not related to age, sex or locus of injury, is only weakly related to the severity of the injury, and is best predicted by preinjury characteristics, social adversity and parental handling. Children who had minor emotional or behavioural symptoms prior to injury are at greater psychiatric risk than children whose preinjury behaviour was normal. Coexistent psychosocial adversities — such as maternal depression, paternal criminality or overcrowding — further increase the child's psychiatric risk. This risk is probably also increased when parents respond to the injury by becoming overprotective and reluctant to discipline their child.

Although the psychiatric disorders of head-injured children mostly involve the sorts of emotional and conduct problems that dominate ordinary child psychiatric practice, severe closed head injury can result in a distinctive syndrome of social disinhibition (resembling an adult frontal lobe syndrome). These disinhibited children are unduly outspoken, ask embarrasing questions, make very personal comments, and get undressed in inappropriate contexts. They may also be forgetful, overtalkative, impulsive or careless about their own cleanliness and appearance. The localization of an open head injury has little if any impact on psychiatric symptomatology; hints that depression is particularly linked with right anterior or left posterior damage have yet to be confirmed.

THE PROGNOSIS OF PSYCHIATRIC PROBLEMS IN CHILDREN WITH BRAIN DISORDERS

Is the prognosis of a psychiatric disorder worse if the child also has a brain disorder? Clinicians and parents often suppose so, and this pessimism may be self-fulfilling if it leads to inappropriately low expectations and therapeutic nihilism. The pessimism has more to do with theoretical expectations than empirical evidence. If a damaged brain cannot mend, it seems to follow that associated psychiatric problems cannot mend either. This is faulty reasoning. Firstly, the association between brain and behavioural disorders is sometimes simply a coincidence. For example, the child's psychiatric disorder may reflect parental quarrels that have nothing to do with the child's neurological problems; if the quarrels resolve, so may the child's psychiatric disorder. Secondly, even when the psychiatric disorder is secondary to the child's brain disorder, the causal chain may be indirect and easy to interrupt. For instance, if a boy with epilepsy develops a conduct disorder, the mediating link may be the parents' fear that he will have a fit if they discipline him in any way. Helping the parents to reinstate appropriate discipline may cure the conduct disorder. Thirdly, even when psychiatric problems are direct consequences of the brain disorder, the psychiatric problems may still be temporary (just as some children with fixed brain lesions have seizures for a few months or years and then grow out of them). Finally, as noted earlier in the chapter, brain disorders do not necessarily arise from irreversible brain damage. On theoretical grounds, then, there is no reason to suppose that psychiatric disorders are bound to be persistent just because the child also has a brain disorder.

There is little empirical evidence on prognosis because there have been so few longitudinal neuropsychiatric studies. In the Institute of Psychiatry study of children with closed head injuries (Brown *et al.*, 1981), psychiatric disorders attributable to head injury were somewhat more persistent than psychiatric disorders that were not attributable to head injury, but the difference was not statistically significant. Breslau and Marshall (1985) used a brief screening inventory to assess the stability of psychiatric problems over the course of 5 years in a group of children with a mixture of brain disorders, and in a comparison group of children with cystic fibrosis. Judging from this limited assessment, psychiatric problems were more likely to persist in the children with brain disorders — a persistence that was only partially explained by coexistent mental handicap. This evidence for persistence needs to be set against the more optimistic findings of Ounsted *et al.* (1987) who followed up 100 children with temporal lobe epilepsy for over 20 years. Although 85% of the sample had some psychological problems during childhood, the adult outcome was surprisingly good. When severe mental handicap was excluded, 70% of the survivors were entirely free of psychiatric disorder in adult life.

Individuals can grow into as well as out of the psychiatric consequences of childhood brain disorders. For example, a child who initially adjusts well to an acquired hemiplegia may subsequently become increasingly depressed as recovery slows down and the implications of lifelong disability sink in. Brain maturation may also be relevant. It is possible, for example, that some psychiatric consequences of head injury do not emerge until the child reaches the age when damaged late-maturing cortex normally comes 'on line' (see Goodman, 1989).

THE PREVENTION AND TREATMENT OF PSYCHIATRIC PROBLEMS IN CHILDREN WITH BRAIN DISORDERS

Because children with brain disorders commonly develop psychiatric problems, and because combined physical and psychiatric problems impose a severe burden on parents and teachers, children with brain disorders seem an obvious target for interventions designed to prevent psychiatric problems. Unfortunately, few such studies have been conducted. Hjern and Nylander (1964) found that head-injured children were significantly less likely to develop psychiatric problems if their parents had been counselled that the sequelae of head injury were generally transient, and that head-injured children benefit from a graded reintroduction to all normal activities. Lewis *et al.* (1990, 1991) compared two educational programmes for children with epilepsy and their parents. Families were randomly allocated either to lecture sessions followed by question-and-answer periods, or to a specially devised series of parent and child groups. The group counselling approach was more likely to reduce parental anxiety and foster children's self-perceptions of social competency. Though the gains were modest, this study does demonstrate the feasibility of randomized controlled trials of preventive interventions.

The psychiatric problems of children with brain disorders can be treated in just the same ways as the psychiatric problems of neurologically intact children. Biological treatments are neither more nor less useful than in ordinary child psychiatric practice. There is no empirical basis, for example, for treating a child's conduct disorder with carbamazepine rather than with behavioural therapy or parent management training simply because the child also has a brain disorder. Individual, family and school-based treatment approaches can all be helpful. As far as drug treatment is concerned, five points are worth emphasizing. Firstly, the indications for, and choice of, psychotropic medication differs little from standard practice (see Chapter 51). Secondly, epilepsy is not a strong contra-indication to using neuroleptics or antidepressants even though these drugs may increase seizure frequency. In practice, an increase in seizure frequency is rarely a major problem, and can often be countered by adjusting the dose of anti-convulsant. Of the commonly used neuroleptics, pimozide, thioridazine and haloperidol probably have less effect on

seizure threshold than chlorpromazine (Lishman, 1987). Thirdly, although brain disorders are often mentioned as a risk factor for neuroleptic-induced tardive dyskinesias, the evidence is decidedly weak (Kane & Smith, 1982). Fourthly, stimulant medication can be very helpful for hyperkinetic children who also have a neurological problem, though the risk of a dysphoric reaction to stimulants may be higher than in other hyperkinetic children (Ounsted, 1955; Ingram, 1956). Dexamphetamine is the stimulant of choice for hyperkinetic children with epilepsy since it raises seizure threshold while methylphenidate lowers it (see Chapter 51). Finally, when children with epilepsy develop behavioural problems, changing their anticonvulsant regime can sometimes help. Behavioural problems may improve dramatically, for example, if toxic levels of phenytoin are reduced, or if phenobarbitone is replaced by carbamazepine. Proposed changes in anticonvulsant medication should obviously be discussed with the child's paediatrician.

REFERENCES

Aicardi J. (1986) *Epilepsy in children.* Raven Press, London.

Aicardi J. (1992) *Diseases of the Nervous System in Children. Clinics in Developmental Medicine no 115/118.* Mac Keith Press, London.

Beaumanoir A. (1985a) The Lennox−Gastaut syndrome. In: Roger J., Dravet C., Bureau M., Dreifuss F.E. & Wolf P. (eds) *Epileptic Syndromes in Infancy, Childhood and Adolescence*, pp. 89−99. John Libbey, London.

Beaumanoir A. (1985b) The Landau−Kleffner syndrome. In: Roger J., Dravet C., Bureau M., Dreifuss F.E. & Wolf P. (eds) *Epileptic Syndromes in Infancy, Childhood and Adolescence*, pp. 181−191. John Libbey, London.

Berg R.A., Bolter J.F., Ch'ien L.T. & Cummins J. (1984) A standardized assessment of emotionality in children suffering from epilepsy. *International Journal of Clinical Neuropsychology*, **4**, 247−248.

Binnie C.D., Channon S. & Marston D. (1990) Learning disabilities in epilepsy: neurophysiological aspects. *Epilepsia*, **31** (suppl. 4), S2−S60.

Bourgeois B.F.D., Prensky A.L., Palkes H.S., Talent B.K. & Busch S.G. (1983) Intelligence in epilepsy: a prospective study in children. *Annals of Neurology*, **14**, 438−444.

Breslau N. (1985) Psychiatric disorder in children with physical disabilities. *Journal of the American Academy of Child Psychiatry*, **24**, 87−94.

Breslau N. (1990) Does brain dysfunction increase children's vulnerability to environmetal stress? *Archives of General Psychiatry*, **47**, 15−20.

Breslau N. & Marshall I.A. (1985) Psychological disturbance in children with physical disabilities: continuity and change in a 5-year follow up. *Journal of Abnormal Child Psychology*, **13**, 199−216.

Brett E.M. (ed) (1991) *Paediatric Neurology*, 2nd edn. Churchill Livingstone, Edinburgh.

British Office of Health Economics (1971) *Epilepsy in Society.* Office of Health Economics, London.

Brown J.K. & Livingston J. (1985) The malignant epilepsies of childhood: West's syndrome and the Lennox−Gastaut syndrome. In: Ross E. & Reynolds E. (eds) *Paediatric Perspectives on Epilepsy*, pp. 29−39. John Wiley, Chichester.

Brown R.M.A.. & Perkins M.J. (1989) Child sexual abuse presenting as organic disease. *British Medical Journal*, **299**, 614−615.

Brown G., Chadwick O., Shaffer D., Rutter M. & Traub M. (1981) A prospective study of children with head injuries: III Psychiatric sequelae. *Psychological Medicine*, **11**, 63–78.

Camfield P.R., Gates R., Ronen G., Camfield C., Ferguson A. & MacDonald W. (1984) Comparison of cognitive ability, personality profile, and school success in epileptic children with pure right versus left temporal lobe EEG foci. *Annals of Neurology*, **15**, 122–126.

Cassidy S.B. (1984) Prader–Willi syndrome. *Current Problems in Pediatrics*, **14**, 1–55.

Christie R., Bay C., Kaufman I.A., Bakay B., Borden M. & Nyhan W.L. (1982) Lesch–Nyhan disease: clinical experience with 19 patients. *Developmental Medicine and Child Neurology*, **24**, 293–306.

Commission on Classification and Terminology of the International League Against Epilepsy (1981) Proposal for revised clinical and electroencephalographic classification of epileptic seizures. *Epilepsia*, **22**, 489–501.

Corbett J.A. & Trimble M.R. (1983) Epilepsy and anticonvulsant medication. In: Rutter M. (ed) *Developmental Neuropsychiatry*, pp. 112–129. Churchill Livingstone, Edinburgh.

Corbett J., Harris R., Taylor E. & Trimble M. (1977) Progressive disintegrative psychosis of childhood. *Journal of Child Psychology and Psychiatry*, **18**, 211–219.

Cull A. & Trimble M.R. (1989) Effects of anticonvulsant medications on cognitive functioning in children with epilepsy. In: Hermann B.P. & Seidenberg M. (eds) *Childhood Epilepsies: Neuropsychological, Psychosocial and Interventions Aspects*, pp. 83–103. John Wiley, Chichester.

Davison K. & Bagley C.R. (1969) Schizophrenia-like psychoses associated with organic disorders of the central nervous system: a review of the literature. *British Journal of Psychiatry, Special Publication No. 4*. pp. 113–184.

Dewhurst K., Oliver J.E. & McKnight A.L. (1970) Socio-psychiatric consequences of Huntington's disease. *British Journal of Psychiatry*, **116**, 255–258.

Ellenberg J.H. Hirtz D.G. & Nelson D.B. (1986) Do seizures in children cause intellectual deterioration? *New England Journal of Medicine*, **314**, 1085–1088.

Farwell J.R., Dodrill C.B. & Batzel L.W. (1985) Neuropsychological abilities of children with epilepsy. *Epilepsia*, **26**, 395–400.

Folstein S.E., Franz M.L., Jensen B.A., Chase G.A. & Folstein M.F. (1983) Conduct disorder and affective disorder among the offspring of patients with Huntington's disease. *Psychological Medicine*, **13**, 45–52.

Freeman J.M. & Nelson K.B. (1988) Intrapartum asphyxia and cerebral palsy. *Pediatrics*, **82**, 240–249.

Galaburda A.M., Sherman G.F., Rosen G.D., Aboitz F. & Geschwind N. (1985) Developmental dyslexia: four consecutive patients with cortical anomalies. *Annals of Neurology*, **18**, 222–233.

Gastaut H. (1970) Clinical and electroencephalographical classification of epileptic seizures. *Epilepsia*, **11**, 102–113.

Goodman R. (1989) Limits of cerebral plasticity. In: Johnson D.A., Uttley D. & Wyke M. (eds) *Children's Head Injury: Who Cares?* pp. 12–22. Taylor & Francis, London.

Goodman R. (1991) The right hemisphere and child psychiatric disorder. Paper presented at the Winter Meeting of the British Neuropsychiatry Association, London, January, 1991.

Goodman R. (1993) Brain abnormalities and psychological development. In: Hay D.F. & Angold A. (eds) *Precursors, Causes and Psychopathology*, pp. 51–85. John Wiley, Chichester.

Goodman R. (1994) Brain development. In: Rutter M. & Hay D.F. (eds) *Development Through Life: A Handbook for Clinicians*, pp. 49–78. Blackwell Scientific Publications, Oxford.

Goodyer I.M. (1985) Epileptic and pseudoepileptic seizures in childhood and adolescence. *Journal of the American Academy of Child Psychiatry*, **24**, 3–8.

Gordon N. (1990) Acquired aphasia in childhood: the Landau–Kleffner syndrome. *Developmental Medicine and Child Neurology*, **32**, 270–274.

Grunberg F. & Pond D.A. (1957) Conduct disorders in epileptic children. *Journal of Neurology, Neurosurgery and Psychiatry*, **20**, 65–68.

Hagberg G., Aicardi J., Dias K. & Ramos O. (1983) A progressive syndrome of autism, dementia, ataxia, and loss of purposeful hand use in girls: Rett's syndrome: report of 35 cases. *Annals of Neurology*, **14**, 471–479.

Harper P.S. & Clarke A. (1990) Should we test children for adult genetic diseases? *Lancet*, **i**, 1205–1206.

Hermann B.P. (1982) Neuropsychological functioning and psychopathology in children with epilepsy. *Epilepsia*, **23**, 545–554.

Hermann B.P., Whitman S. & Dell J. (1989) Correlates of behaviour problems and social competence in children with epilepsy, aged 6–11. In: Hermann B. & Seidenberg M. (eds) *Childhood Epilepsies: Neuropsychological, Psychosocial and Intervention Aspects*, pp. 143–157. John Wiley, Chichester.

Hill P. (1989) Psychiatric aspects of children's head injury. In: Johnson D.A., Uttley D. & Wyke M. (1989) *Children's Head Injury: Who Cares?* pp. 134–146. Taylor & Francis, London.

Hirsch E., Marescaux C., Maquet P., Metz-Lutz M.N., Kiesmann M., Salmon E., Franck G. & Kurtz D. (1990) Landau–Kleffner syndrome: a clinical and EEG study of five cases. *Epilepsia*, **31**, 756–767.

Hjern B. & Nylander I. (1964) Acute head injuries in children: traumatology, therapy and prognosis. *Acta Paediatrica Scandinavica*, (suppl 152), 1–37.

Hoare P. (1984) The development of psychiatric disorder among school children with epilepsy. *Developmental Medicine and Child Neurology*, **26**, 3–13.

Hoare P. (1987) Children with epilepsy and their families. *Journal of Child Psychology and Psychiatry*, **28**, 651–655.

Holmes G., Sackellares J.C., McKiernan J., Ragland M. & Dreifuss F.E. (1980) Evaluation of childhood pseudoseizures using EEG telemetry and video tape monitoring. *Journal of Pediatrics*, **97**, 554–558.

Hunt A. & Dennis J. (1987) Psychiatric disorder among children with tuberous sclerosis. *Developmental Medicine and Child Neurology*, **29**, 190–198.

Hunt A. & Shepherd C. (1993) A prevalence study of autism in tuberous sclerosis. *Journal of Autism and Developmental Disorders*, **23**, 323–339.

Huntington's Disease Collaborative Research Group (1993) A novel gene containing a trinucleotide repeat that is expanded and unstable on Huntington's Disease chromosomes. *Cell*, **72**, 971–983.

Ingram T.T.S. (1955) A study of cerebral palsy in the childhood population of Edinburgh. *Archives of Disease in Childhood*, **30**, 85–98.

Ingram T.T.S. (1956) A characteristic form of overactive behaviour in brain damaged children. *Journal of Mental Science*, **102**, 550–558.

Jacobsen B. & Kinney D.K. (1980) Perinatal complications in adopted and non-adopted schizophrenics and their controls: preliminary results. *Acta Psychiatrica Scandinavica*. (suppl 285), 337–346.

Johnson D.A., Uttley D. & Wyke M.A. (1989) *Children's Head Injury: Who Cares?* Taylor & Francis, London.

Kane J.M. & Smith J.M. (1982) Tardive dyskinesia. *Archives of General Psychiatry*, **39**, 473–491.

Kaufman K.R., Harris R. & Shaffer D. (1980) Problems in the categorization of child and adolescent EEGs. *Journal of Child Psychology and Psychiatry*, **21**, 333–342.

Kurita H. (1985) Infantile autism with speech loss before the age of thirty months. *Journal of the American Academy of Child Psychiatry*, **24**, 191–196.

Lehmkuhl M. & Thoma W. (1990) Development in children after severe head injury. In: Rothenberger A. (ed) *Brain and Behavior in*

Child Psychiatry, pp. 267–282. Springer-Verlag, Berlin.

Lewis M.A., Salas I., de la Sota A., Chiofalo N. & Leake B. (1990) Randomized trial of a program to enhance the competencies of children with epilepsy. *Epilepsia*, **31**, 101–109.

Lewis M.A., Hatton C.L., Salas I., Leake B. & Chiofalo N. (1991) Impact of the children's epilepsy program on parents. *Epilepsia*, **32**, 365–374.

Lishman W.A. (1987) *Organic Psychiatry: The Psychological Consequences of Cerebral Disorder*, 2nd edn. Blackwell Scientific Publications, Oxford.

Livingston J.H. (1988) The Lennox–Gastaut syndrome. *Developmental Medicine and Child Neurology*, **30**, 536–549.

Lobascher M.E. & Cavanagh N.P.C. (1980) Patterns of intellectual change in the dementing school child. *Child: Care, Health and Development*, **6**, 255–265.

Luna D., Dulac O., Pajot N. & Beaumont D. (1989) Vigabatrin in the treatment of childhood epilepsies: a single-blind placebo-controlled study. *Epilepsia*, **30**, 430–437.

Luthy D.A., Wardinsky R., Shurtleff D.B., Hollenbach K.S., Hickok D.E., Nyberg D.A. & Benedetti T.J. (1991) Cesarean section before the onset of labor and subsequent motor function in infants with meningomyelocele diagnosed antenatally. *New England Journal of Medicine*, **324**, 662–666.

Mellor D.H., Lowit I. & Hall D.J. (1974) Are epileptic children behaviourally different from other children? In: Harris P. & Mawdsley C. (eds) *Proceeding of the Hans Berger Centenary Symposium*, pp. 313–316. Churchill Livingstone, Edinburgh.

Menkes J.H. (1990) *Textbook of Child Neurology*, 4th edn. Lea & Febinger, Philadelphia.

Middleton J. (1989) Annotation: thinking about head injuries in children. *Journal of Child Psychology and Psychiatry*, **30**, 663–670.

Miller G. (1989) Minor congenital anomalies and ataxic cerebral palsy. *Archives of Disease in Childhood*, **64**, 557–562.

Nelson K.B. & Ellenberg J.H. (1986) Antecedents of cerebral palsy: multivariate analysis of risk. *New England Journal of Medicine*, **315**, 81–86.

O'Donohoe N.V. (1985) *Epilepsies of Childhood*, 2nd edn. Butterworths, London.

Olsson B. & Rett A. (1987) Autism and Rett syndrome: behavioural investigations and differential diagnosis. *Developmental Medicine and Child Neurology*, **29**, 429–441.

Ounsted C. (1955) The hyperkinetic syndrome in epileptic children. *Lancet*, **ii**, 303–11.

Ounsted C., Lindsay J. & Norman R. (1966) *Biological Factors in Temporal Lobe Epilepsy*. Clinics in Developmental Medicine no 22. S.I.M.P./Heinemann, London.

Ounsted C., Lindsay J. & Richards P. (1987) *Temporal Lobe Epilepsy 1948–1986: A Biographical Study*. Clinics in Developmental Medicine No. 103. Mac Keith Press/Blackwell Scientific Publications, Oxford.

Paneth N. & Kiely P. (1984) The frequency of cerebral palsy: a review of population studies in industrialised nations since 1950. In: Stanley F. & Alberman E. (eds) *The Epidemiology of the Cerebral Palsies*, pp. 46–56. S.I.M.P./Blackwell Scientific Publications, Oxford.

Perez M.M., Trimble M.R., Murray N.M.F. & Reider I. (1985) Epileptic psychosis: an evaluation of PSE profiles. *Bristish Journal of Psychiatry*, **146**, 155–163.

Pond D.A. & Bidwell B.H. (1960) A survey of epilepsy in the general practices — II. Social and psychological aspects. *Epilepsia*, **1**, 285–299.

Rantakallio P. & von Wendt L. (1985) Risk factors for mental retardation. *Archives of Disease in Childhood*, **60**, 946–952.

Riikonen R. & Amnell G. (1981) Psychiatric disorders in children with earlier infantile spasms. *Developmental Medicine and Child Neurology*, **23**, 747–760.

Robinson R.G. (1979) Differential behavioral and biochemical effects of right and left hemispheric cerebral infarction in the rat. *Science*, **205**, 707–710.

Rodin E. (1989) Prognosis of cognitive functions in children with epilepsy. In: Hermann B.P. & Seidenberg M. (eds) *Childhood Epilepsies: Neuropsychological, Psychosocial and Intervention Aspects*, pp. 33–50. John Wiley, Chichester.

Ross E.D. (1985) Modulation of affect and nonverbal communication by the right hemisphere. In: Mesulam M.-M. (ed) *Principles of Behavioral Neurology*, pp. 239–257. Davis, Philadelphia.

Rutter M., Graham P. & Yule W. (1970a) *A Neuropsychiatric Study in Childhood. Clinics in Developmental Medicine nos 35/36*. S.I.M.P./ Heinemann, London.

Rutter M., Tizard J. & Whitmore K. (1970b) *Education, Health and Behaviour*. Longman, London.

Rutter M., Cox A., Tupling C., Berger M. & Yule W. (1975) Attainment and adjustment in two geographical areas — I. The prevalence of psychiatric disorder. *British Journal of Psychiatry*, **126**, 493–509.

Rutter M., Chadwick O. & Shaffer D. (1983) Head injury. In: Rutter M. (ed) *Developmental Neuropsychiatry*, pp. 83–111. Churchill Livingstone, Edinburgh.

Rutter M., MacDonald H., LeCouteur A., Harrington R., Bolton P. & Bailey A. (1990) Genetic factors in child psychiatric disorders — II. empirical findings. *Journal of Child Psychology and Psychiatry*, **31**, 39–83.

Sabbeth B.F. & Leventhal J.M. (1984) Marital adjustment to chronic childhood illness: a critique of the literature. *Pediatrics*, **73**, 762–768.

Scully R.E., Galdabini J.J. & McNeely B.U. (1978) Case records of the Massachusetts General Hospital, case 29–1978. *New England Journal of Medicine*, **299**, 189–194.

Seidel U.P., Chadwick O.F.D. & Rutter M. (1975) Psychological disorders in crippled children. A comparative study of children with and without brain damage. *Developmental Medicine and Child Neurology*, **17**, 563–573.

Seidenberg M., Beck N., Geisser M., Giordani B., Sackellares J.C., Berent S., Dreifuss F.E. & Boll T.J. (1986) Academic achievement of children with epilepsy. *Epilepsia*, **27**, 753–759.

Sollee N.D. & Kindlon D.J. (1987) Lateralized brain injury and behavior problems in children. *Journal of Abnormal Child Psychology*, **15**, 479–490.

Still G.F. (1902) Some abnormal psychical conditions in children. *Lancet*, **i**, 1008–1012, 1077–1082, 1163–1168.

Stores G. (1977) Behavior disturbance and type of epilepsy in children attending ordinary school. In: Penry J.K. (ed) *Epilepsy: The Eighth International Symposium*, pp. 245–249. Raven Press, New York.

Stores G. (1985) Clinical and EEG evaluation of seizures and seizure-like disorders. *Journal of the American Academy of Child Psychiatry*, **24**, 10–16.

Stores G. (1991) Confusions concerning sleep disorders and the epilepsies in children and adolescents. *British Journal of Psychiatry*, **158**, 1–7.

Stores G., Zaiwalla A. & Bergel N. (1991) Frontal lobe complex partial seizures in children: a form of epilepsy at particular risk of misdiagnosis. *Developmental Medicine and Child Neurology*, **33**, 998–1009.

Swedo S.E., Rapoport J.L., Cheslow D.L., Leonard H.L., Ayoub E.M., Hosier D.M. & Wald E.R. (1989) High prevalence of obsessive-compulsive symptoms in patients with Sydenham's chorea. *American Journal of Psychiatry*, **146**, 246–249.

Tassinari C.A., Bureau M., Dravet C., Dalla Bernardina B. & Roger J. (1985) Epilepsy with continous spikes and waves during slow sleep. In: Roger J., Dravet C., Bureau M., Dreifuss F.E. & Wolf P. (eds) *Epileptic Syndromes in Infancy, Childhood and Adolescence*, pp. 194–204. John Libbey, London.

Taudorf K., Hansen F.J. & Melchior J.C. (1986) Spontaneous remission of cerebral palsy. *Neuropediatrics*, **17**, 19–22.

Taylor D.C. (1969) Sexual behaviour and temporal lobe epilepsy. *Archives of Neurology*, **21**, 510−516.

Taylor D.C. (1975) Factors influencing the occurrence of schizophrenia-like psychosis in patients with temporal lobe epilepsy. *Psychological Medicine*, **5**, 249−254.

Taylor D.C. (1989) Psychosocial components of childhood epilepsy. In: Hermann B.P. & Seidenberg M. *Childhood Epilepsies: Neuropsychological, Psychosocial and Interventions Aspects*, pp. 119−142. John Wiley, Chichester.

Taylor E. (1991) Developmental neuropsychiatry. *Journal of Child Psychology and Psychiatry*, **32**, 3−47.

Vargha-Khadem F., Isaacs E., van der Werf S., Robb S. & Wilson J. (1992) Development of intelligence and memory in children with hemiplegic cerebral palsy: the deleterious consequences of early seizures. *Brain*, **115**, 315−329.

Voeller K.K.S. (1986) Right-hemisphere deficit syndrome in children. *American Journal of Psychiatry*, **143**, 1004−1009.

Wallace S.J. (1992) Prenatal and perinatal risk factors for epilepsy. In: Pedley T.A. & Meldrum B.S. (eds) *Recent Advances in Epilepsy, no. 5*, pp. 91−108. Churchill Livingstone, Edinburgh.

Weintraub S. & Mesulam M-M. (1983) Developmental learning disabilities of the right hemisphere: emotional, interpersonal and cognitive components. *Archives of Neurology*, **40**, 463−468.

Whitman S., Hermann B.P., Black R.B. & Chhabria S. (1982) Psychopathology and seizure type in children with epilepsy. *Psychological Medicine*, **12**, 843−853.

Williams D.T., Spiegel H. & Mostofsky D.I. (1978) Neurogenic and hysterical seizures in children and adolescents: differential diagnostic and therapeutic considerations. *American Journal of Psychiatry*, **135**, 82−86.

Chapter 12
Chronic Adversities

Norman Garmezy & Ann S. Masten

INTRODUCTION

A long historical association binds adverse experiences or circumstances to psychopathology. In 1541, Sir Thomas Elyot, a member of Parliament and a 'student of medicine' (whose mentor was physician to Henry VIII), published a book, *The Castel of Health*, in which he wrote of the causes of the 'hevynesse of mynde' (i.e. depression) including 'the death of chylderne ... the loss of goodes and authorite' and the 'repulse of promotion' (Hunter & Macalpine, 1963, pp. 8—9). Although these medieval experiences went undefined, their counterparts are evident today as specific stressors often listed in life events schedules (Dohrenwend & Dohrenwend, 1974, 1984; Johnson, 1986; Snyder & Ford, 1987) as bereavement, unemployment, income loss and job demotion (Wheaton, 1990). Thus, for at least four centuries, such stressful life experiences have been viewed as direct aetiological agents of disorder.

More recently, speculations about direct causes have given way to research on adversities as risk factors that are predictors of negative outcomes that often suggest causal processes. Moreover, interest has grown in the potential significance of studying variability in individuals who, despite exposure to shared risk status, differ dramatically in outcome, suggesting differences in actual level of risk, individual patterns of vulnerability, or the operation of protective processes (Rolf *et al.*, 1990; Rutter, 1990b; Masten *et al.*, 1990). Adversities also have been examined as possible potentiators of disorder in already vulnerable individuals (Garmezy, 1985b; Masten & Garmezy, 1985; Rutter, 1979, 1990b).

Acute vs. chronic adversities

Chapter 22 focuses on acute traumatic experiences. The focus of this chapter is on chronic adversities. Acute stressors typically imply sudden or rapid onset, and fearfulness which is often of brief duration marked by a single severe peak of intensity. Traumatic events are so intense that individual functioning is expected to falter because coping resources are overwhelmed. Chronic adversities, in contrast, usually imply gradual or indeterminate onset, moderate to high intensity, and long duration. However, the distinction between acute and chronic adversities is not always clear.

Classification can become much more difficult when: (1) acute stressors are repeated; (2) when acute stressors precipitate chronic adversities; or (3) when chronic adversities lead to acute crises. For example, sexual assault of a child by a parent often is a long-term pattern of behaviour that constitutes a severe, chronic adversity for the child. Similarly, although the death of a parent may be an acute event, the loss is enduring. Moreover, the death of a parent may result in inadequate care if the caregiving role of that parent is not replaced. Finally, chronic adversities, such as interparental conflict, can be punctuated by acute crisis events wherein an intense episode of violence may occur in the context of an ongoing sense of threat and almost continuous conflict which may be of moderate intensity.

When acute stressors do not result in chronic adversities, the expectation is that the effects will decline as a function of time. Acute stressors that do not damage the organism and that do not produce chronic adversities may not have substantial long-term effects on the mental health of children (Masten *et al.*, 1990). Chronic adversities, on the other hand, are characterized by the possibility of accumulating effects. Moreover, individuals are not expected to adapt and recover so long as the stressful conditions continue.

The classification of an experience as an acute or chronic adversity implies that most individuals would be affected in some way by such an experience. None the less, it is important to recognize, for both types of adversities, that variations in response and adaptation are likely to occur. Not all cases of the same event or situation are equivalent: most are unique in the exact nature of the threat posed to an individual. Similarly, individuals differ in their vulnerabilities and potential for adaptation with respect to different experiences. Vulnerabilities refer to individual susceptibilities that potentiate the effects of a stressor while protective factors refer to qualities of the individual or environment that buffer the individual in some way with respect to the stressor, either by reducing exposure itself or the effects of exposure.

Forms of chronic adversity

There is a wide variety of experiences that can be viewed as chronic adversities, many of which reflect biological disadvantage, physical handicaps, or severe and intense family problems which may pose threats to the lives of family members. In many instances, these stressors are combinatorial and cumulative, often resulting in long-term disadvantage to children. Some are rooted in child attributes, others reside within family members, particularly parents, while others reflect limitations induced by low socioeconomic status. For the latter the adversity is to be found in the social climate of a dangerous neighbourhood, or a larger community under threat.

Chronic adversities inhabit a broad domain of settings and contexts that provide constraints on the authors of a single chapter. Given the primacy of the family in most societies for rearing and protecting children, for providing caregiving, sustenance and socialization of the child, it is not surprising that many studies have focused on the family as the source, mediator or protector of the young against adverse experiences. Space limitations and the salience of the family in research on chronic adversities have led the authors to select several family-based adversities as the focus for this chapter. Specifically, the emphasis is on the effects of: (1) cumulative risk, often characterized by psychosocial disadvantage in the family; (2) the consequences for the child of mentally disordered parentage; (3) bereavement; and (4) the effects on children of divorce and discord. Physical and sexual abuse of children in recent years has become the focus of intense research and treatment activities (Cicchetti & Carlson, 1989; Ammerman & Herson, 1990). Consequently, maltreatment of children is the subject of two separate chapters in this book (see Chapters 13 and 14). The present chapter concludes with overviewing sections on: (1) resilience and protective processes in chronic adversity; and (2) research issues and future directions.

Cumulative risk and development

Risk factors often co-occur and this is particularly so for chronic adversities. Death of a parent, divorce or mental illness in a parent, for example, are not isolated events. They are experiences with complex, long-term consequences that frequently occur in the context of multiple additional risk factors. Moreover, major chronic adversities sometimes co-occur, such as psychiatric disorder in a parent that is followed by divorce or death. Poverty often accompanies these experiences. Similarly, economic hardship can lead to additional adversities such as moving to dangerous neighbourhoods or heightened interparental conflict.

Three important programmes of research have demonstrated the profound effects of cumulative disadvantage and adversity on children. Rutter and his colleagues, in a series of studies, have shown the synergistic effects of multiple risk factors (Rutter, 1978, 1979, 1984, 1985, 1987). Investigators identified a set of six variables, reflecting chronic familial adversities, that cumulatively proved to be significantly associated with psychiatric disorder in the offspring: (1) severe marital discord; (2) low social status; (3) overcrowding or large family size; (4) paternal criminality; (5) maternal

psychiatric disorder; and (6) the placement of a child in the care of local authority. A child with only one of these risk factors fared almost as well as did children with none. The presence of two risk factors increased the probability of disorder fourfold. Among children with four or more risk factors, 21% had manifest psychiatric disorder, in contrast to only 6% with two or three risk factors.

Kolvin and his colleagues (1988a,b,c) have reported comparable results in the longitudinal Newcastle Thousand Family Study of risk and protective factors and their influence on the development of criminality. Cumulative indicators, in part, paralleled the Rutter *et al.* investigation: (1) marital instability; (2) parental illness; (3) poor domestic and physical care of the children and home; (4) dependence on state or community for subsistence; (5) overcrowded housing; and (6) poor mothering ability. Follow-up studies of criminal records of the offspring revealed a marked relationship between heightened risk exposure and rate of offending. A single deprivation was associated with a 29% rate of later criminality; two criteria increased the rate to 69%. Parental illness alone carried the lowermost risk; poor mothering, overcrowding and marital disruption were the most powerful indicators of the adversity core.

The Newcastle study also demonstrated the dynamic nature of cumulative risk. When deprivation increased over time, the subsequent rate of offending increased; when deprivation decreased, subsequent criminality rates decreased.

Protective factors associated with nondelinquent outcomes among the deprived group were also examined in the Newcastle study. During the first 5 years of life, these included good mothering, good maternal health and employment of the breadwinner. Apparently, protective child characteristics included healthy physical development and being elder-born. By age 10–11, intellectual functioning and school achievement emerged as salient protective factors, as did good parental supervision and belonging to positive youth clubs.

In a third research programme illustrating cumulative risk, Sameroff *et al.* (1982; Sameroff & Seifer 1983, 1990) studied the effects of 10 familial risk factors on the offspring born to schizophrenic mothers: (1) a prior history of mental illness in the mother; (2) high maternal anxiety; (3) mother's rigidity in attitudes, beliefs and values with regard to her child's development; (4) few positive maternal interactions that would foster a child's development; (5) unskilled occupational status of the head of the household; (6) minimal maternal education; (7) disadvantaged minority status; (8) reduced family support; (9) stressful life events in the family; and (10) large family size. These offspring were observed intensively in infancy, early childhood, and in preadolescence. At the age of 4, measures of intelligence and adaptive functioning led the investigators to conclude that each of the 10 familial factors in effect cost the child the equivalent of 4 IQ points relative to the development of normal children. In this study, too, cumulative risk effects were noted in the deprived children, leading to decrements in fundamental competencies necessary for successful adaptation in later years. Thus, when the children were 13 years old, a follow-up investigation suggested that the continuity of a negative family and social environment pattern was reflected in a lack of environmental support for the child, restricted parenting, limited opportunities for the child's development and additional supporting evidence for the observation that the larger the cumulation of risk factors, the greater the negative influence on the child's cognitive and social/emotional development.

PARENTAL MENTAL DISORDER AND ITS INFLUENCE ON OFFSPRING

The cumulative risks studied by Rutter, Kolvin and Sameroff included parental psychiatric disorders, which contributed to the prediction of maladaptation in subsets of children reared in high-risk families. There is also a broadly based literature focused primarily on the effects of specific parental mental disorders. As in most efforts at presumed disaggregation, however, the emphasis on a single risk factor often camouflages common consequences of mentally disordered parentage, including poverty, job insecurity or unemployment, welfare status, marital instability, severe marital discord and negative rearing practices.

For example, from a genetic perspective, children born to a schizophrenic parent have an elevated and specific risk for developing this disorder during their lifetime — approximately 8–10 times the risk found in the general population (Gottesman & Shields, 1972, 1982). During childhood, however, the risk associated with parental schizophrenia appears to have a more general cast, similar to risks associated with other severe mental disorders in parents. The severity of the parent's illness and the level of associated psychosocial disadvantage consistently emerge as strong predictors of problem behaviours among the offspring (Sameroff & Seifer, 1983, 1990; Goldstein & Tuma, 1987).

Comorbidity is another issue related to the specificity of effects of parental mental disorder on children. Recent data suggest that the usual procedure of studying specific single parental disorders in isolation may be unwise and misleading because of the frequency of comorbidity in psychiatric disorders (Boyd *et al.*, 1984; Robins & Regier, 1991; Rutter *et al.*, 1990a,b). Evidence for this phenomenon began to appear in the 1970s and has accelerated markedly in the 1980s and 1990s. Using data drawn from the Epidemiological Catchment Area Study (US), Robins *et al.* (1991) provided an interesting validation of earlier findings. In this sample, 60% of the patients diagnosed with a single disorder had at least two other psychiatric disorders during their lifetime. Among those disorders with the highest rates of comorbidity (>90%) were antisocial personality and schizophrenia. Comorbidity is similarly striking in the diagnoses of child psychiatric inpatients (Rutter, 1990a,b).

The prevalence of comorbidity has explicit implications for the sections that follow: (1) problems of children of disordered parents may be misattributed to a specific mental disorder when, in fact, comorbidity may be a relevant consideration in interpreting parental effects; and (2) similarities in the behaviour patterns of children across different parental disorders may reflect either diagnostic comorbidity or the generalized effects of inadequate or malignant parenting; interrelatedness between parent disorder and child functioning may not be a function of a specific psychiatric disorder in the parent presumed to be the focus of study, but rather the presence of additional disorders in the parent or the co-sharing of risk factors that mark many troubled families. These include genetic and biological influences as well as those provided by negative psychosocial and psychological similarities: family discord, poor parenting, economic distress, poverty, unemployment, welfare status and overcrowding in inadequate housing situations. These are some of the shared and overlapping factors that can affect and generate comparabilities in children's adaptations despite specific diagnoses that have been assigned to ill parents.

With these cautions in mind, two specific literatures concerning parental disorder will be examined: antisocial disorder and depression. A significant empirical literature on children has emerged for each of these classes of disorder in parents.

Delinquency, criminality and antisocial disorder

The literature on delinquency and criminality is voluminous and diverse with regard to outcomes (e.g. McCord & McCord, 1959; Glueck & Glueck, 1962, 1968; West & Farrington, 1973; McCord, 1979; West, 1982; Rutter & Giller, 1983). It is helpful, therefore, to review the results of a metaanalysis of multiple studies of the factors that characterize the lives of children of criminal parents reported by Loeber and Stouthamer-Loeber (1986). Their superb analysis of a broad band of studies of parent–child relationships for these high-risk children reveals the operation of four major characteristics: (1) a repetitive pattern of conflict between parent and child; (2) neglect, as reflected in: (a) a lack of parental supervision; (b) an incapacity to exert discipline in the home (cf. Patterson, 1982); and (c) a lack of active parental responsivity to children's antisocial acts; (3) the manifestation of deviant familial values such as drug and alcohol abuse, and the modelling of antisocial behaviour by parents; and (4) a family climate of pronounced discord and conflict that ranges from quarrels to hostile, abusive acts and family violence. These factors, accompanied by poor academic performance, markedly influence the likelihood of male delinquency in families that share these attributes (Loeber & Dishion, 1983).

To a large extent the factors that appear central to the prediction of delinquency are rooted in familial and psychosocial factors, although increasingly, biogenetic influences have been brought into the predictive equation (Trasler, 1987). Loeber & Stouthamer-Loeber join Rutter and Giller (1983) in concluding that, although the evidence is scanty, there is a relatively weak hereditary influence for juvenile delinquency while a stronger one may exist for recidivist behaviour that extends into adult life (see Chapters 9 and 18). Generally lacking are studies that separate the effects of heredity and social influences. However, behaviour geneticists are beginning to examine potential factors that may account for behavioural variability within family sibships by the introduction of concepts such as 'shared and non-shared environmental (family) variance' (Plomin & Daniels, 1987).

Risk and protective factors in delinquency

The description of the Newcastle Thousand Family Study (Kolvin *et al.*, 1988a,b,c) cited earlier is prototypic of the orientation of many of the research programmes that have focused on the origins of delinquency and crime. Examples of such significant studies include: Robins's (1966) *Deviant Children Grown Up*; McCord and McCord's (1959) longitudinal study of the *Origins of Crime*; West's (1982) volume on *Delinquency: Its Roots, Careers, and Prospects*; West and Farrington's (1973) summary of *Who Becomes Delinquent?*, and Patterson's (1982; Patterson & Capaldi, 1990) theoretical/clinical research on delinquent behaviour utilizing social learning theory and practice to modify coercive family processes that undermine the mother−child relationship. Patterson's work also provides a research model for the measurement of parental behaviours that can serve to exacerbate children's delinquent acts. The theoretical formulation of the acquisition of such acts and a treatment programme based on the same model is unique in research on delinquency aimed at substituting prosocial behaviours for aggressive antisocial actions.

Certain common factors can be extracted from these various studies of the roots and correlates of conduct and antisocial disorders in children and adolescents. These factors reflect: (1) risk elements that provide a potential developmental progression toward delinquency and criminal behaviour, and (2) protective factors that serve to contain, overcome and substitute prosocial behaviours for deviant ones (Rutter & Giller, 1983). Risk factors for delinquencies implicate genetics, physiological processes (e.g. hyperactivity, impaired avoidance learning etc.), educational failure (school drop-out, low IQ), community elements (delinquent gang membership, overcrowded slum housing, high crime neighbourhood, drug availability) and above all negative family patterns (paternal criminality, broken home, family discord, lax parental behaviour, early separation from parent; large sibship housed in limited space).

Protective factors that appear to diminish the likelihood of delinquent acts include work (adequate job opportunities), educational opportunities (school attendance, positive peer group influence, school leadership, demands for achievement, positive efforts by teachers), community (available social services, low neighbourhood delinquency rates, movement away from high delinquency areas) and family (cohesiveness, maternal and paternal love, consistent discipline, parental supervision, positive parental marital relationship, home ownership, parental stability). Research efforts emphasizing positive adaptation of children and families in neighbourhoods marked by high delinquency rates have unfortunately been in small supply.

Children of depressed parents

Over a span of more than two decades, the output of studies of children born to schizophrenic parents dominated the at-risk literature. In the mid 1980s, studies of depressed parents and their offspring began to appear, providing a new entry into studies of children of mentally disordered parents. These investigations were preceded a quarter of a century earlier by Rutter's study (1966), *Children of Sick Parents*, in which he examined the impact of parental depression, among other disorders. In an article published the same year, Perris (1966) evaluated developmental precursors to depression by focusing on the reconstruction of the early histories of 1435 bipolar and 150 unipolar depressive patients. These early case contents revealed the presence of family conflict, single parenting and parental loss in the early years of the lives of many of these adult patients. Perris found that the earlier the patient's age at the onset of symptoms, the more negative was the patient's early rearing conditions. In a subgroup whose onset was 10 years earlier than the rest of the group, unfavourable home and rearing conditions prevailed, whereas later-onset patients reported fewer such adversities. This covariation of adverse rearing conditions and early age of onset of depression may have reflected the consequences of cumulative stress on these children or the shared genetic vulnerability of parent and child, or some combination of the two. Rutter (1990a) has pointed to the multiple complexities that invite caution in the interpretation of parental depression effects on children.

Multiple symptoms in a parent may reach into the heart of family functioning. The depressed mother typically involves herself less and less with family members, including her children. Communication with other family members is reduced and responsibilities are neglected, resulting in friction between and among family members. She may resent her role and yet be guilt-ridden about her neglect. In turn there may be compensatory efforts at overprotectiveness or of marked withdrawal from her children and spouse, distancing herself from the family members and often overtly rejecting them (Weissman *et al.*, 1972). In older children, these behaviours may be misunderstood and invoke resentment; in the younger child, confusion and distress may follow. The effect of her behaviour on the family does not escape the disturbed mother. One report has indicated that 68% of depressed parents were aware of their ineffectual parenting (Orvaschel, 1983).

It is evident from this catalogue of behaviours that depression in parents can exert a profound effect on children. Thus, the depressed parent has become the selection base for studying the development of adaptive and maladaptive patterns of behaviour in the offspring of such emotionally disabled caregivers. A secondary method, as indicated earlier, has been the use of the follow-back method to examine the family history of adults now suffering from an affective disorder. This method, however, has many limitations generated by faulty recall, motivated forgetting and the absence of effective records for validating events during the early years of childhood and adolescence.

Research studies of school-aged children of depressed mothers describe them as shy, isolated and withdrawn. Orvaschel (1983), in a review of 13 research programmes, reported that interviews with depressed mothers and their children affirmed that the offspring in comparison with the children of control parents showed evidence of maladaptation in school, at home, with their siblings and with their peers. Their behaviours were described as destructive, defiant, withdrawn, uncooperative, impatient, belligerent, and socially isolated (pp. 187–188).

Noting the limitations in these earlier studies of the children of depressed mothers, Orvaschel called for greater care in selecting and identifying cases, the necessity of comparison (via other parental illnesses) and control groups, attention to factors such as age, sex and presenting symptoms, the use of multiple informants located in school, community and employment settings, and the need for longer-term longitudinal studies.

Orvaschel suggested a revised emphasis in risk research, namely that the search not be directed solely to establish a continuity of disorder from parent to child, but also that attention be given to including children who appear to be 'pathology-resistant' accompanied by data on buffering factors that may play a role in their escape from disorder. She noted that a comparison of psychiatrically ill children with those seemingly resistant to the disorder might in time provide insight both into the nature of protective factors, and those vulnerability indices that may be subject to modification.

The more recent portrait of children at risk for depression has emphasized the presence of dysfunctional behaviours in many offspring of depressed parents — deficiencies which reflect a composite of the judgements of parents, teachers and clinicians. Included among these deficits are evidence of both externalizing and internalizing symptoms (the correlates of which remain unmapped), poor academic performance, social incompetence, lowered physical health status, clinical diagnoses which affirm a precursor behaviour pattern of affective disorder including depressive contents, hypomanic behaviour and other possible early indicators of future unipolar or bipolar disorder. Some children exhibit conduct-disordered behaviour and signs of attention deficit disorder, which may reflect the possible intrusion of comorbidity elements. In another domain, attachment behaviour studies reveal patterns of insecurity in the child's relationship to the depressed mother.

A major research programme by Hammen and her associates, focused on children of depressed parents, has added to our knowledge of this relationship (Hammen *et al.*, 1987, 1990, 1991; Conrad & Hammen, 1989; Gordon *et al.*, 1989; Hammen, 1993). Four family groups were compared: (1) unipolar and (2) bipolar affective disorder; (3) a chronic illness parent group; and (4) a nonpsychiatric normal parent group. A variety of measures were used in the comparative analysis: psychosocial family variables, diagnostic assessment of the offspring, including depressive cognition, the interpersonal relationships between mother and child, etc. Follow-up accounts were secured at half-year intervals over a 3-year span. Among the many findings are these: children of unipolar mothers relative to the three other groups have higher lifetime rates of major depression, greater impairment in social functioning, worse school performance, and a more negative self-concept, sufficient to constitute a potential vulnerability factor for future depression.

In addition, powerful genetic factors appear operative given the high proportion (88%) of unipolar women whose parents and siblings also exhibited psychopathology. However, negative interactions of mother and child within this group pointed to the chronicity of contemporary stressors that further exacerbated this predisposition. Further, the unipolar mother had directed her recurrent anger not only to her child but also to friends, family members, teachers and others. This anger, Hammen reported, was unique to the unipolar mothers and was not evident among mothers in the three comparison groups.

Hammen noted that symptom expression in unipolar mothers and their children had a mutual timing of depressive episodes, but this was not uniform for all children in the family. Nonshared environmental influences (Plomin & Daniels, 1987), reflected in a small group of 10 families, suggest that discordant behavioural patterns in the affectively disordered child were not characteristic of the unaffected sibling.

Hammen observed that cumulative stressors paralleled the earlier cited studies of Rutter, Kolvin and Sameroff. Among her cited multiple resilience factors (the obverse of which she perceived to be risk factors) were: (1) self-concept; (2) paternal diagnosis; (3) presence of father in the home; (4) current maternal mood; (5) level of maternal chronic stress; (6) the offspring's social competence; and (7) academic performance. The data revealed a striking decline in the affective diagnostic ratings of the children as a function of the number of evident protective factors. This finding confirms the evocative power of risk/resilience elements in the manifestation of, or freedom from, parental psychopathology.

Other attributes characterizing children of depressed parents reported by investigators include deficits in social interaction, a lack of empathy, an inability to assist others, a low threshold for distress, and a negative concept of the self. In an excellent review, Downey and Coyne (1990) noted that these behavioural patterns need not implicate an underlying substrate for depression, but may be related to the failure to develop a pattern of multiple competencies that characterize healthy children at different age levels. Such a failure requires more systematic age-related developmental studies of children who are at risk for depression by virtue of manifest parental affective disorders.

In summarizing the current status of these at-risk children, Downey and Coyne wrote:

> Children of depressed parents show heightened rates of general problems in adjustment, putative markers at risk

for depression, and clinical depression. Difficulties are found even in infancy. They emerge in peer, teacher, and observer reports as well as in self- and parent reports. The general adjustment problems shown by children of depressed parents include social and academic difficulties at school and internalizing and externalizing behavior problems. In showing these problems, they resemble other children who experience the stress and disruption that accompany serious parental psychiatric or medical illness [p. 59].

Given the absence of necessary control groups in many of these early studies of children at risk for depression, it has not been known whether these behaviours reflect generalized deficiencies in parenting or more specific effects of depression. The literature on children at risk for schizophrenia (Watt *et al.*, 1984) suggests that these deficiencies are probably not specific solely to depression, but rather the outcome of deficiencies within the more general context of families at risk.

Downey and Coyne's hesitancy about the specificity view is contained in three caveats that they set forth.

1 Researchers have reported disagreements between mother and child as to the emotional status of the child.

2 The 'at-risk' studies cited in the literature typically review the constrast between children of depressed and normal parents. Multiple comparison groups are needed that would incorporate children at risk for other mental disorders, other medical problem groups, and disadvantaged children and their families as well.

3 A more systematic study of different age groupings of children presumed to be at risk for depression is needed. This may highlight critical stages for the preemergence of disorder in the child. However, it is necessary to separate two issues: firstly, whether such behaviours are true precursors to adult depression which would require adequate longitudinal studies; and, secondly, whether such behaviours are a more generalized response to the stressfulness of the immediate family environment and/or to a broader external environment.

Another caveat warrants attention. Generally, the dependent variable under study in this area of risk research has been focused primarily on the adaptational qualities of the at-risk child and the nature of suggested diagnoses. What has been neglected is the creation of new studies that would utilize a greater breadth of psychological and biological variables. This would require incorporating not only mood states but cognitive, psychophysiological and neuropsychological studies as well as those descriptive of manifest competencies in both at-risk and control children and their parents. This would broaden knowledge of internal and external risk and protective factors that could provide a more effective canvas for portraying the developmental status of the at-risk child. Further, it could serve to bring to attention two groups: those at-risk children who may in time develop an affective disorder, as well as those who would be manifestly adaptive in the face of multiple stressors associated with parental depression.

BEREAVEMENT: THE TRAUMA OF PARENTAL DEATH

One of the most profound stressors a child ever has to face is the partial dissolution of a family through the death of a parent. In 1984, it was estimated that 3.7% of American children under age 18 had lost a parent (Masterman & Reams, 1988). Earlier US data had suggested that an estimated 5.2% of children younger than age 18 had lost either parent by death; 3.5% were paternal orphans, 1.5% maternal orphans and 0.1% full orphans (Critelli, 1983). Recent data indicate that approximately 1.5 million children in the US live with one parent, the other parent being deceased (Silverman & Worden, 1992).

Clinical observations of grief in children are discussed in Chapters 21 and 45. The comparatively sparse empirical literature on bereavement in relation to psychopathology is reviewed here.

The consequences of bereavement have been accorded little empirical attention in light of the comparatively large numbers of children who experience the death of a parent. Many of the studies of bereaved children have focused on clinical populations that provide limited generalizability or have other methodological weaknesses. There are only a few controlled or longitudinal studies of children who experience parental death. Developmental studies, contrasting outcomes among different age groups, are almost nonexistent.

Bereavement could be expected to affect children in multiple ways: through the loss of a primary attachment figure in young children; through the normal grief process; through diminished caregiving that ensues; or through other effects of death on the surviving parent (Rutter, 1966; Bowlby, 1980). Age-related effects would be expected, in terms of the perception and comprehension of unfolding events, and the effects of altered caregiving. For example, young infants and pre-schoolers may be buffered from full comprehension of the event but vulnerable to the loss of attachment figure and alterations in the quality of care. Older children, on the other hand, may be painfully aware of the situation but have wider networks of social support and less dependence on a single parent for care.

The role of cognitive development in the effect of parental death is clearly important in terms of comprehending the abstractions that accompany the concept of death — its universality, inevitability and, above all, its irreversibility. Unfortunately, there are few longitudinal data that examine these age-related patterns (Speece & Brent, 1984). Cross-sectional data suggest that at about 5–7 years of age, children acquire some understanding of the universality, finality and biological characteristics of death. Experiences with death in relatives and peers appear to be related to a more realistic appraisal of death (Reilly *et al.*, 1983). Such experience and exposure may be powerful teachers and by age 8 many children do have a comprehension of death's irreversibility (often abetted by death of a pet). Hence parental loss even at this young age may generate fear, anxiety and depression in more knowledgeable and experienced youngsters (Garmezy, 1986).

Even in the young child, the staying power of a memory of a parent's death may be an extended one, with consequences that are evident in behavioural changes. In his classic trilogy, *Attachment and Loss*, Bowlby (1969, 1973, 1980) devoted the contents of the final volume to *Loss, Sadness and Depression* (1980). He concluded that a sense of loss in the young child is not short-lived but recurrent and marked by continued distress. Bowlby viewed the understated grief in a very young child as the result of a phasing of the grief response — initially protest followed by a quietude that may be deceptive, in which the child's muteness cloaks the internalized sense of loss that the child continues to feel (Freud & Burlingham, 1943). It was Bowlby's (1980) view that the perceptive observer can see the 'persistent orientation to the lost mother [that] is evident even in younger children' (p. 11).

Nevertheless, despite the ubiquity of grieving, there are critical ages in which loss brings great suffering to the child (Garmezy, 1986). The period of 10–14 years of age has been viewed as a particularly vulnerable age period which for some children may be the precursor to chronicity. This period may provide the seed ground for later depression in adulthood if that later period is marked by additional stressors that can heighten despair and a sense of failure (Brown *et al.*, 1977, 1986; Brown & Harris, 1978).

One of the few longitudinal studies of bereavement followed a small sample of 25 preadolescent children who represented all the children from 7 kibbutzim in Israel who lost a father in the October (1973) War (Elizur & Kaffman, 1982, 1983; Kaffman & Elizur, 1983). This sample is particularly interesting because the children lived in a kibbutz, thus bereavement was not complicated by loss of home or income. Most children showed strong emotional grief reactions, with prolonged crying and sadness. There followed a great variety of responses, ranging from increased fears to aggressiveness. Preschoolers showed more denial of the finality of death and more separation anxiety behaviours. Older children showed more restlessness, aggression, and exemplary behaviour, the latter somewhat surprising to the investigators (Kaffman & Elizur, 1983). Follow-up after 18 and 42 months indicated high levels of disturbance among the children that fluctuated over time. Although a control group was absent, rates of emotional and behavioural problems were higher than reported for kibbutzim children in other epidemiological studies. Adjustment disorder was the most common diagnosis assigned and few sex differences were observed.

At 6 months after bereavement, a number of current and preexisting family variables predicted child problems, including suppression of grief by the mother, previous separation or loss experiences, marital discord and a negative relationship between father and child. By 42 months, these had faded to nonsignificance. More salient in later assessments were the quality of the mother–child relationship and the presence of a surrogate father. Children with previous behaviour problems seemed to be particularly vulnerable, although

these children had complicated histories of family risk that made it difficult to attribute even new problems to bereavement (Elizur & Kaffman, 1983).

Though sparse, the literature on bereaved children documents a variety of short-term problems that often follow the loss. These include crying and sadness, sleep disturbances and school-related problems. Age is related to the occurrence of some symptoms, young children evidencing more bed-wetting and tantrums, while problems with academic achievement are more salient for older children.

Van Eerdewegh and her associates (1982, 1985) conducted a year-long prospective study of 105 bereaved children, aged 2–17. The widowed spouse served as the informant of the child's adaptation at 1 month and 13 months following the parental death. A marked dysphoria in the children tended to disappear over time, but there was a longer-time retention of a minor depression, bed-wetting in the younger children and impaired school performance in the older ones. Adolescent boys who had lost their fathers showed signs of primary or secondary depression, somatic anxiety reactions and problem behaviour in school. Since the surviving parent alone provided these data, the investigators suggest a variety of additional contents needed in future studies of bereaved children: (1) a comparison group of children exposed to divorce or marital separation; (2) the effect of changes in the family's socioeconomic status resulting from the loss of the parent; (3) the effect on children produced by the degree of distress and disorder evidenced by the widowed spouse; and (4) the quality of the marital relationship prior to the parental death. To these suggestions can be added the need for direct evaluations of bereaved children's efforts to adapt to the loss of a parent with attention to the comparative status of boys and girls at different ages. This latter suggestion is necessary given the indications that older girls do show more depression and more internalizing symptoms, in contrast to the more typical externalizing behaviours of boys following bereavement, as reported by Kranzler *et al.* (1990).

The long-term effects of childhood bereavement have received little research attention, except for the important series of studies conducted by Brown and his colleagues (Brown & Harris, 1978; Brown & Prudo, 1981; Brown *et al.*, 1986; Harris *et al.*, 1990). In a research programme marked by a series of studies employing different samples, these investigators have linked the death or separation of a mother in childhood to factors influencing the onset of depression in adult women who had been subjected to such a loss.

In seeking to validate that early loss of the mother contributes to adult depression in women, Brown *et al.* (1977) have considered three elements: (1) vulnerability factors that create a sensitivity for responsiveness to the provoking agents, but do not directly play a role in the onset of the disorder if these agents are absent; (2) provoking agents that are involved in producing the disorder at some point in the life span; and (3) symptom formation factors that can determine the form and severity of the depression, but are not causative agents in the disorder.

There are three common features of the vulnerability factors that have been associated with the low self-esteem that characterized the depressed women: (1) a lack of intimacy or a confiding relationship, particularly with the husband; (2) the presence of three or more children in the home, all under 14 years of age; and (3) the lack of a full-time or part-time job that the mother could hold. Brown and Harris have argued that the presence of these three factors in the lives of women in their adulthood, given the context of the early death of their mothers, generated a sense of failure, a self-derogation in their inability to meet their aspirations as mother and wife, with a resultant low level of self-esteem — all of which were conducive to the onset of depression. This research also has pointed to protective factors for bereavement in childhood. Closer examination of the circumstances following bereavement indicated that the quality of child care following maternal loss was a critical element. Good care appeared in part to compensate for the loss and to serve as a moderator with respect to vulnerability for adult depression. In adulthood, additional current protective factors were observed. Women who had a loving spousal relationship, employment opportunities as a partial escape from household duties and lessened demands of younger children were less likely to become depressed following a triggering event.

The study of bereavement as a great universal stressor for children requires systematic attention to the effects of parental death as a function of the child's age and the nature of available supports and stressors in the contemporary environment. Even in the carefully prepared, systematic research programme of Brown and his associates there has been a neglect of the normative development of children under the stress of parental loss. As in all cases of serious traumas, variability in adaptation can be anticipated for children who lose their parents. Contained within the database of the Brown *et al.* studies is clear evidence that variation in competence and effectance exists within the cohorts that have been studied. Comparative studies of successful and unsuccessful adaptation of children grown to adulthood who have had to cope with the death of a parent warrant continued research.

A recent article by Kendler *et al.* (1992), focused on a genetic epidemiologic perspective, provides a new dimension to the study of childhood parental loss and specific forms of subsequent adult psychopathology. Using a population-based registry these investigators examined the relationship between parental loss prior to age 17 and the presence of adult psychiatric disorders in 1018 pairs of female twins. Adult psychopathology varied as a function of: (1) loss induced by death as opposed to loss due to separation; (2) the gender of the deceased parent; and (3) the specific forms of psychopathology evident in the subject sample.

Parental separation increased the offspring's risk for major depression and generalized anxiety disorder. Panic disorder was associated with parental death as well as with maternal (not paternal) separation. Phobias too were associated with parental death.

What is the basis for the demonstrated association between early parental loss and the type of subsequent adult psychiatric disorders? Kendler and his colleagues (1992) suggested a variety of potential causative elements. Possible forms of mediation incorporate both sociopsychological and genetic factors. On the one hand, parental separation may be mediated not by parental loss but rather by exposure to the parental discord that often precedes divorce or by the poor parental care that follows. But genetic factors too may be mediators predisposing a parent to poor mental adaptation, poor health in the parental generation or to genetic liability to disorder in the offspring generation. Although the complexity that inheres in explanatory hypotheses is evident, the virtue of the Kendler *et al.* study is that it opens a new line of potential investigations to parental bereavement and its consequences for children.

DIVORCE AND INTERPARENTAL CONFLICT

Divorce has become one of the most common life events experienced by children. Although divorce rates have been generally increasing for more than a century in the US, there was a sharp increase in the late 1960s and 1970s before rates stabilized in the 1980s (Norton & Moorman, 1987; Hernandez, 1988). Divorce rates have shown similar increases in European countries over the course of the past century (Boh *et al.*, 1989). In the US, more than half of women born in the postwar baby boom who marry will divorce. From 1972 to 1982, more than a million children a year experienced divorces in the US (Norton & Moorman, 1987).

Divorce is a dynamic and complex process (Kurdek, 1981; Emery, 1988; Kitson & Morgan, 1990; Wallerstein, 1991). A cumulation of potential stressors typically accompany the singular events of separation and divorce, including changes in income or social status, conflict between parents and children, diminished parenting, parental distress or disorder, moving and children changing schools. Remarriage is common; about 70–75% of divorced women in the US remarry (Norton & Moorman, 1987). Thus, many children must also face new relationships with romantic partners of the parents, and stepsiblings. Further, since a third of these marriages also end in divorce, children are often subjected to multiple changes in the family configuration (Glick, 1979).

Longitudinal studies of divorce

One of the key questions in the study of marital disruption as a stressor is whether the problems children exhibit following divorce actually precede the separation. Studies limited to assessments after divorce has occurred are uninformative on this question. One study drew on two longitudinal data sets to examine whether the problems of divorced children preceded the separation (Cherlin *et al.*, 1991). Data from the British National Child Development study indicated that children of divorced families had more behaviour problems at age 11. However, for boys, controlling for the level of child and family problems at age 7 reduced the differences between boys from divorced and intact families to a negligible level. For girls, significant differences remained in achievement and teacher ratings of behaviour problems even when preexisting child behaviour and family problems were controlled. Data from the US National Survey of children, on the other hand, revealed few differences between girls from divorced families and girls in intact families. In contrast, results for boys were similar to the British sample, suggesting that a large part of the differences found for boys following divorce could be attributed to preexisting differences in the child and family. Data from a Berkeley, California cohort followed since age 3 by Jeanne and Jack Block also suggested that boys in families that would subsequently divorce already had more externalizing problems years prior to the separation. Girls seemed less affected prior to divorce in this study (Block *et al.*, 1986).

Most of the subjects in these three sets of data experienced divorce in childhood or early adolescence. These findings may not hold for older adolescents who have undergone the same experience. Results from one of the few prospective studies of adolescent males showed increases in substance abuse and decreases in psychological well-being following divorce (Doherty & Needle, 1991). Adolescent girls in divorced families already had a lower state of psychological well-being than nondivorced peers before the divorce. These investigators suggested that adolescent females may be quite sensitive to the strains of family life that precede divorce.

Studies that begin with assessments that follow separation or divorce pose limitations for causal analyses, but these studies may provide clues to individual and family differences that may function as risk or protective factors in the context of divorce. Again, longitudinal data are the most informative.

The Virginia Longitudinal Study of Divorce and Remarriage (Hetherington *et al.*, 1982, 1985) followed a sample of white, middle-class families with a 4-year-old child for 6 years following divorce. Considerable distress and dysfunction were observed in both the children and their parents over the first year. Boys appeared to have the most difficulty, as evidenced by aggressive, noncompliant behaviour and troubled mother—son relationships. Substantial improvements were noted during the second year, although boys still had significantly more problems than nondivorced boys. The behaviour of divorced girls was much like their nondivorced counterparts. Compared to children in highly conflicted nondivorced families, divorced children initially were worse off, but at the 2-year follow-up, they were better adjusted than children remaining in high-conflict marriages. After 6 years, boys living with mothers who had not remarried continued to have more externalizing symptoms than did girls in similar families or nondivorced children. At follow-up, the majority of the original divorced sample in the Virginia study had remarried. Boys and girls in recently remarried families had significant externalizing problems on a number of measures. Girls in stepfamilies also appeared on some measures to have more internalizing symptoms and less social competence than nondivorced or nonremarried girls. After 2 years of remarriage,

behaviour appeared to improve for both boys and girls.

A subsequent longitudinal study of remarriage suggested that young adolescents may have more difficulty adjusting to remarriage (Hetherington & Clingempeel, 1992). Three groups of young adolescents were followed for more than 2 years. At each assessment, adolescents from both remarried and divorced families generally had more problems and lower competence than adolescents from nondivorced families. Very little improvement occurred in adolescent behaviour or their relationships with stepfathers over the 2 years of the study, suggesting that a parent's remarriage may be difficult for both boys and girls in early adolescence. In contrast to the Virginia study of younger children, gender differences did not emerge; both boys and girls in the divorced group exhibited more problems than nondivorced adolescents.

Data on the role of gender in divorce have been inconsistent. A number of studies have found boys to have more externalizing problems than girls following divorce (Demo & Acock, 1988; Emery, 1988; Hetherington, 1989). While this gender difference may precede divorce to some degree, other factors also appear to be important. Custody arrangements may play a role (Santrock & Warshak, 1979). For example, Peterson and Zill (1986), in a national US sample of 1400 12—16-year-olds, found that divorced boys in the custody of mothers were more disruptive and aggressive and more depressed than boys in the custody of fathers. Moreover, in the infrequent situation of girls placed in the custody of fathers, they too showed more externalizing symptoms and depressed mood than did girls in the custody of mothers. Residing with a parenting figure of the same sex may be an important influence on child behaviour following divorce. Alternatively, the quality of the relationship with the same-sex parent may be the key factor, both before and after divorce.

Much of the speculation concerning the difficulties of divorced sons living with their mothers has focused on the mother—son relationship and the challenge of disciplining sons who may be more likely to react with noncompliance and aggression to diminished parenting or the stress of loss. Data from the Virginia study of Hetherington and Clingempeel (1992) suggested that mother—son relationships were often characterized by patterns that Patterson (1982) has described as coercive cycles. This transactional pattern is thought to arise from inept discipline that contributes to negative transactions between parent and child, leading to increased noncompliance in the child and escalating aggression over time. Patterson and his colleagues have presented data supportive of this pattern in recently divorced mothers and their 6—8-year-old sons (Forgatch *et al.*, 1988).

The data supporting gender differences following divorce are stronger for younger children. However, not all major studies of divorce have found gender differences, even in younger children. A large longitudinal study of a New Zealand birth cohort found antisocial problems subsequent to divorce in both boys and girls at age 6 (Fergusson *et al.*, 1986). This study indicated a main effect for sex — boys had higher scores on aggressive/antisocial behavior overall — but once this difference was accounted for, the relation of divorce to child behaviour was similar for both boys and girls.

Developmental differences

Emery noted in 1982 that there were surprisingly few studies of differential developmental effects in divorce or marital discord. More than a decade later, there continues to be a paucity of developmental studies. Many studies focus on one age group or utilize measures insensitive to developmental differences. Findings relevant to age differences, for the most part, do not present a consistent picture (Hetherington *et al.*, 1989). An exception is the study of how children perceive and reason about divorce, which is consistent with normative social-cognitive development (Kurdek, 1986). Whether these differences influence vulnerability to psychopathology in children, however, is not clear.

The longitudinal study of Wallerstein and her colleagues still provides the richest source of clinically descriptive data about age differences, although the study focused on a clinic sample of well-educated parents and lacked a comparison group (Wallerstein & Kelly, 1980; Wallerstein *et al.*, 1988). For example, preschoolers initially showed great distress, expressed in typical ways for their age, such as loss of toileting skills, being demanding, crying and intense separation anxiety. However, after 10 years, those who were preschoolers at the time of separation, now adolescents, appeared to be faring better than children who had been older at the time of the separation. Initially quite vulnerable to diminished parenting, the preschool cohort seems to have been buffered by their age, protected by their limited ability to process and to remember many negative aspects of the divorce.

Interparental conflict and child maladjustment

The level of conflict between parents before and after divorce has been linked strongly to child maladjustment (Demo & Acock, 1988; Emery, 1982, 1988). Longitudinal studies have found that continuing conflict between divorced parents is associated with worse outcomes for children (e.g. Johnson *et al.*, 1987; Wallerstein *et al.*, 1988; Hetherington, 1989).

In the Berkeley longitudinal study, additional analyses of families who would divorce revealed more marital tension as well as more parenting problems long before the time of divorce as well as after the separation (Block *et al.*, 1988). More conflict was reported by mothers and fathers with sons in families that would divorce. After divorce, and consistent with other reports, mothers appeared to have warmer relations with daughters and to have lost control over sons. Given the associations that have been found among conflict, divorce and child maladjustment, it is reasonable to ask whether separation and other aspects of divorce contribute any more to child psychopathology than do marital discord and associated parenting problems.

Studies of discord in intact marriages consistently indicate elevated rates of antisocial behaviour in children, particularly boys (Emery, 1982). Children who witness violence between parents but are not themselves direct victims have elevated rates of both externalizing and internalizing symptoms (Emery, 1989). Witnessing extreme violence can also trigger symptoms of posttraumatic stress disorder in children (Masten *et al.*, 1990). Even very young children exposed to angry interchanges simulated in the laboratory show distress, suggesting the possibility of direct emotional effects on children of witnessing parental conflict (Cummings, 1987; Cummings *et al.*, 1985). Among older children, a number of other processes have been suggested by which conflict may influence children, including direct effects of modelling aggression or a diminution of parenting quality by distressed or angry parents, and other alterations in the quality of life that may be caused by disturbed parents. The role of parental psychopathology in the associations found between divorce or discord and child maladjustment must also be considered.

Parental psychopathology, divorce and interparental conflict

Psychopathology in parents has been linked to marital problems (Emery, 1982; Lahey *et al.*, 1988) as well as to risk for psychopathology in their children, as discussed previously in this chapter (Rutter & Quinton, 1987). This raises a number of problems in seeking to separate genetic and environmental risk factors for psychopathology in children exposed to divorce or marital conflict. Parents with antisocial personality disorders may tend to have marital problems, and also manifest harsh and inconsistent parenting. Their children may be genetically vulnerable to aggressive or impulsive behaviour and at the same time they are being exposed to family violence and ineffective parenting. The result may be a confluence of divorce, discord, poor parenting, and difficulty in managing conduct-disordered children. Sorting out cause and effect in such a scenario is very difficult. Surprisingly few studies of divorced children have even assessed parental disorder as a first step in sorting out the role of parent psychopathology.

Two studies suggest that parental antisocial disorder may play a role in the externalizing symptoms often reported in children of divorce (Lahey *et al.*, 1988; Capaldi & Patterson, 1991). For example, Capaldi and Patterson (1991) followed a sample of more than 200 boys (aged 9–11) from fourth to sixth grade, drawn from an area in which there was a high risk for antisocial behaviour. The number of marital transitions had a strong linear relation to antisocial behaviour in boys. However, causal modelling indicated that this linkage could be accounted for by antisocial behaviour in the mothers, which was strongly related to the number of marital changes. Moreover, the effect of antisocial mothers was mediated by their ineffective parenting as reflected in poor supervision and low involvement.

Such studies suggest that antisocial disorder in parents may play a role in the externalizing symptoms of boys who have experienced divorce and discord, particularly as mediated by poor-quality parenting. Genetic vulnerability transmitted from parent to child may also be involved. Additional studies are needed to clarify if this linkage holds for lower-risk samples and for girls and to sort out precisely how the risk factor operates. Parental alcoholism may also be a relevant factor, as alcoholism is associated with antisocial personality disorder, family violence, parenting problems, and child maladjustment (Russell *et al.*, 1985).

Divorce also has been linked to depression in parents (e.g. Lewinsohn *et al.*, 1988), which is associated with parenting difficulties (Downey & Coyne, 1990; Rutter, 1990a). Moreover, as discussed in a previous section, children of depressed parents have elevated risk for general adjustment problems and depression (Downey & Coyne, 1990). Thus, the same questions that are raised for antisocial parents arise in seeking to understand the linkage of parental depression, divorce, diminished parenting and child psychopathology.

In this connection, discord has received more attention than divorce. Studies reviewed by Downey and Coyne (1990) led these authors to suggest the interesting possibility of differential effects of parental depression and discord in families with a depressed parent. Their review suggests that discord is associated with externalizing symptoms in children while parental depression may be uniquely related to children's depression.

One study has analysed family risk factors, including divorce, before and after, controlling for parental depression (Fendrich *et al.*, 1990). Children (aged 6–23) of depressed parents had experienced more divorced but they did not have higher rates of major depression than did the comparison children of nondepressed parents. Divorce was significantly related to conduct disorder in children before and after parental depression was considered. In contrast, major depression and anxiety disorders in children were not related to divorce. It is interesting to note that despite the careful differentiation of effects in terms of childhood disorders, the role of comorbidity in parents, most notably the role of concurrent antisocial personality disorder, was not considered in this study.

Clearly, additional research is needed to examine the possible role of parental depression in the functioning of their children when discord or divorce is also present. Research has suggested that children may respond to increases in the depression of their mothers and that mothers may respond to their children's behaviour by becoming more depressed (Hetherington, 1989; Hammen *et al.*, 1990, 1991). A question for further research is whether divorce or discord indirectly increases the specific risk for childhood depression by triggering or exacerbating depression in mothers. It is also conceivable that preexisting depression in a parent increases marital discord which then increases obnoxious behaviour in children which, in turn, contributes to the parent's depression. Closer attention to patterns of psychopathology in both parents and children, especially over time, will be important in establishing differential patterns of risk in children from families with interparental conflict or divorce.

Protective factors in divorce and discord

Several studies have suggested that a good relationship with one of the parents is associated with better outcomes in children from divorced families (Emery, 1982). The Virginia study, for example, indicated that in this mother-custody sample, a good relationship with the mother appeared to buffer the effects of a negative relationship with the father. However, the buffering effect appeared only when the relationship with the mother was exceptionally good (Hetherington *et al.*, 1979). Modest ameliorative effects of parent–child relationships also were found in a large cross-sectional study of divorce (Peterson & Zill, 1986). Similar results have been obtained in studies of discord that report on the protective effects of a good relationship (Emery, 1982; Rutter, 1990a).

Few data are available on the possible protective role of siblings, peers, schools and adults other than parents. A recent US study suggested that perceived support of other adults, as well as mothers, was related to better functioning in an urban sample of fourth- and sixth-graders from divorced families (Cowen *et al.*, 1990). The Virginia study (Hetherington, 1989) found that grandparents served as a stress buffer for children only when the grandparent lived in the home. Nevertheless one study of 9–12-year-old children in London suggested that a good relationship with an adult outside the family (usually a grandparent) was protective in children whose parents had a disharmonious marriage (Jenkins & Smith, 1990). The London study also found the quality of sibling relationships moderated the relation of marital quality to child symptoms. Children in poor marriages with poor sibling relationships appeared much worse off than did other groups. Child friendships, at least as reported by their parents, did not appear to function as a vulnerability or protective factor for this London sample, although the Virginia study suggested that having a single friend was helpful to older divorced children. Wallerstein's (1985) clinical data also suggested that siblings helped each other cope with divorce.

It is unlikely that any of these protective effects are unique to divorce or discord. The Virginia study, for example, found that structured, positive school environments were beneficial to children from divorced, remarried and high-conflict married families. Moreover, these protective factors are reported to obtain for a wide variety of situations in childhood (Masten *et al.*, 1990). None the less, the protective processes implicated in studies of divorce and interparental conflict suggest that there is likely to be differential protection among siblings in the same family.

Gender differences in studies of divorce and discord, as well as protective effects of a child's relationships, suggest the likelihood of nonshared influences on siblings in the same household. Differential effects of divorce and interparental conflict among siblings have not been consistently explored. Research is needed on the nonshared effects of these adversities on siblings (Plomin & Daniels, 1987).

RESILIENCE IN ADVERSITY: COMPENSATORY AND PROTECTIVE PROCESSES

The primary orientation of this chapter to this point has been the focus on risk factors that enhance maladaptive behaviours in children exposed to familial and environmental stressors. This has been the traditional orientation in stress research. Over the past decade, however, an alternative view emphasizing positive adaptations to stressful circumstances has begun to come to prominence. This focus on resilience (or stress-resistance) looks to individual and environmental protective factors that enable persons to respond to obstacles and adversities in a socially consonant, productive manner.

The validity of this area of research has been supported by case studies, clinical research and experimental studies (Werner & Smith, 1982, 1992; Beardslee *et al.*, 1983; Garmezy & Rutter, 1983; Garmezy, 1985b, 1987; Rutter, 1985; Anthony & Cohler, 1987; Farber & Egeland, 1987; Masten, 1989; Werner, 1989; Masten *et al.*, 1990; Luther & Zigler, 1991).

Of these ventures, the most salient in terms of longitudinal data on resilience has been the more than 30 years of evaluations that Werner and her associates have conducted with 505 individuals born during 1955 on the Hawaiian Island of Kauai (Werner *et al.*, 1971; Werner & Smith, 1977, 1982, 1992). This significant study has provided a wealth of data focused initially on a birth cohort of children, many of whom were born and reared under conditions of poverty and disadvantage.

Initial results of this longitudinal study demonstrated the significance of prenatal care in reducing the overall risk of perinatal complications. Results also demonstrated the influence of higher socioeconomic status as a moderator of risk when perinatal complications did occur.

In the third volume of their pioneering work, Werner and Smith (1982) focused on approximately one-third of the original cohort, who were followed from the prenatal period into their early 30s. This subset was designated as a high-risk group by virtue of their having been born into poverty, primarily to parents who were either semiskilled or unskilled plantation workers. For this group adversities were cumulative. Initially there were the perinatal stressors that some infants had endured to a moderate or severe extent. Further, in many instances the family life of this cohort was marked by a persistently disorganized family environment evidenced in some cases by discord, divorce, parental alcoholism or mental illness. Werner and Smith (1982) noted among this sub-cohort, who had been exposed to a significant cumulation of stressors that implicated four or more risk factors by age 2, two-thirds developed serious problems. By age 10, some developed learning problems while others, by age 18, had delinquency records or mental disorder problems. Among the female members, a number of them had become pregnant by age 18.

Despite these disadvantaged rearing circumstances, Werner and Smith noted that 1 of 3 high-risk children (10% of the original cohort) grew into competent young adults, as reflected in school success, their management of home and social life, and their search for post-schooling opportunities.

In summarizing the characteristics of this subset of resilient young adults the investigators set forth three forms of protec-

tive factors that differentiated them from other high-risk nonachieving counterparts. Firstly, there were the dispositional attributes of the individual, some undoubtedly rooted in temperament characteristics, others possibly acquired through learning and experience. Examples were activity level, sociability, intelligence, capacity for problem-solving and competencies in social and academic spheres. Secondly, there were strengths within the family that were utilized in creating and sustaining affectional ties, while providing emotional and cognitive support to the children when under stress. The picture elicited is one of a positive bonding that characterized these disadvantaged families. Thirdly, there were available to these children external social supports that were provided by significant others. These could be individuals, but also there were present institutions within the community such as the school, the church, or other affiliative and helping groups. The nature of these support groups provided an enhancement of the individual's competencies that added to his or her sense of self-worth and the formation of an internal locus of control (Lefcourt *et al.*, 1984). Such inner strengths in times of distress served to sustain the individual, to reinforce the self-image of competence and capability and, by doing so, to enhance the individual's vision of goals and the sense of efficacy needed to achieve these desired ends.

Many of the qualities of the resilient group in this study suggest that some of these children were exposed to less cumulative risk and more resources than their less successful contemporaries who shared some of the same risk factors. In other words, compensatory factors may have outweighed the risk. Other qualities of children and their rearing environments suggest vulnerability and/or protective factors, where the risk for the children was amplified or reduced by a variety of dispositional, relational or circumstantial variables.

These protective elements housed in child, family and community reflect the contents of protective factors that have been reported by numerous investigators (e.g. Hetherington *et al.*, 1979; Bleuler, 1984; Peterson & Zill, 1986; Anthony, 1987; Fisher *et al.*, 1987; Musick *et al.*, 1987; Seifer & Sameroff, 1987; Worland *et al.*, 1987; Kolvin *et al.*, 1988a). The basic issue for research is one of delineating the processes that may underlie these resiliency elements in the presence or aftermath of adverse life experiences. Few investigators have attempted to hypothesize and test what type of processes may underlie the attributes listed above, or other so-called protective factors (Rutter, 1990b).

Intensive case studies, often a starting point in science, have provided some clues about possible processes. For example, Radke-Yarrow and Sherman (1990) have studied 4 children of parents with affective disorders who were maintaining their competence. These children appeared to garner the best of whatever resources were available to the family, in part because the child possessed a quality that was valued by the parents and others. This match seemed to provide an ongoing source of self-esteem, building experiences as well as greater adult attention to the child by a parent who felt 'rewarded' by the child for doing so. The attributes were individualized: for one child, the good fortune of being born a boy seemed to make a difference in his family; in another case, of a young girl whose sisters were anaemic, physical health and hardiness appeared to play a role in protecting the child from negative interactions with her mother. Maintaining a good relationship with a parent may reflect in part this type of goodness of fit in which a positive pattern of transactions is established between child and parent. Under adverse conditions, as when the mother has a serious mental illness, the scarce resource of positive parent attention may subsequently be provided by an older child in the family whose desirable attributes may be furthered by such a responsible role (Bleuler, 1984).

Parents are one of nature's multifaceted buffer systems for human development. When there is substantial, enduring interference in basic parental care, one would expect developmental problems. Chronic adversities appear to work much of their harm through their effects on the caregiving/socialization system. Severe, enduring stressors have the potential to erode the effectiveness and protective capacity of any parent. However, even one effective parent in a household appears to compensate for a disabled parent (e.g. Fisher *et al.*, 1987). When key elements of the parenting role are preserved, whether through one healthy parent, or intermittently good parenting by a disturbed parent or alternative parental figures, there appears to be less risk for disturbed behaviour in the children. Examples of key elements include affection, consistent discipline and supervision, all expressed in ways appropriate to the child and evident even in stressful contexts.

There are many other ways that parents may buffer children from adversity. They may actively avert or reduce exposure to stressful experiences. They may model competent behaviour or serve as a source of information and guidance. Effective parents will also teach their children how to recognize and avoid specific dangers in their environment.

Intellectual skills are also ubiquitous in studies of children who show competence or avoid deviance despite chronic adversity. This finding may reflect the central role of learning and problem-solving in human adaptation as well as the importance of academic achievement as a conduit for rewards in modern society. However, IQ could additionally be a marker variable, standing in for many unmeasured correlates, such as an undamaged central nervous system, reflective thinking or maternal competence. IQ might also be a partial marker for the capacity to identify an environment that is conducive to one's own competence, actively to seek and acquire better care or varied role models, and to seek and locate an adaptive niche (Scarr & McCartney, 1983).

As indicated throughout this chapter, social supports outside the family have been implicated as protective factors for a wide variety of adversities and children (Cohen & Wills, 1985; Hobfall, 1986; Eckenrode, 1991). An interesting question for this group of protective factors is the degree to which these supports reflect the appealing qualities or talents of the individual in seeking or eliciting social supports from peers, neighbours, teachers, therapists, religious leaders and other community resources. Such factors are also influenced by the degree to which the opportunities are available, the proactive role of the supporters, or the goodness of fit between child and helper provide the support context. Newcomb (1990) has argued that 'a social support network is constructed throughout life in a reciprocal developmental manner between personal characteristics and social contacts' (p. 54). Social support networks are ubiquitous over the life course, and multiple factors influence their creation. These may include specific needs, abilities and interests of the interacting parties. The sustaining power of such networks also varies depending upon the mutual satisfaction derived by the participants. Regardless of how it may arise, the construct of social support may cover a multitude of processes, analogous to the multifaceted ways in which parents function as protective factors.

Broad protective factors such as good intellectual skills or connectedness to competent parenting figures undoubtedly capture many different processes that vary across individuals and situations. What appears to be the same protective factor could result from different processes. One of the most important questions for further research is whether there are particular processes that ameliorate specific outcomes of adversity, even across different adversities. For example, while various stressors may place boys at risk for disruptive/aggressive behaviour, consistent discipline and strict monitoring may specifically contain the development of antisocial behaviours. At the same time, these parenting qualities may temper a risk for depression. A more specific understanding of such protective processes, their utilization and acceptance within families, would facilitate prevention and intervention efforts.

RESEARCH ISSUES AND FUTURE DIRECTIONS

There are many difficulties in drawing conclusions about the role of chronic adversities in childhood psychopathology. In addition to a diverse and scattered body of data, there are a number of challenging aspects to research in this area: (1) the paucity of prospective data that documents the level of child or family problems prior to the onset of adversity; (2) the difficulty of separating chronic adversities from parent personality problems and individual vulnerabilities; (3) the tendency of adversities to be nonrandomly distributed in the population; (4) the tendency of adversities to co-occur or pile up over time; (5) the role of individual perceptions or appraisals in experiencing adversity; (6) the issue of specificity of adversity and its effects; and (7) the transactional influence of children and parents on each other over time.

The need for prospective research

One of the thorniest problems with research on chronic adversities is the difficulty of obtaining information prior to the onset of the adversity, especially when the onset is indeterminate. The importance of this issue was illustrated by studies of divorce discussed earlier in this chapter, revealing that some of the problems that have been attributed to divorce may precede the separation, particularly for boys. These studies also suggest that parental dysfunction and discord, which sometimes lead to divorce, influence child behaviour in multiple ways. It is usually impossible to determine how an individual child has been affected when the onset of adversity cannot be determined and may precede even the birth of the child. Studies of divorce, criminality and economic hardship illustrate how investigators effectively can take advantage of large longitudinal data sets, such as the New Zealand cohort (e.g. Fergusson *et al.*, 1986), the Newcastle Thousand Family Study (e.g. Kolvin *et al.*, 1988a,b,c), the British National Child Development study (e.g. Cherlin *et al.*, 1991) and the US National Surveys of Children (e.g. Peterson & Zill, 1986; Cherlin *et al.*, 1991). Such data sets may offer the best opportunity to examine the effects of more common adversities while controlling for preexisting symptoms in both parent and child.

Studies of shared and nonshared environments in siblings also offer an important avenue for further research in this confounded situation (Plomin & Daniels, 1987). Data from the longitudinal Cambridge Sibling Study indicate that 69% of adverse life events and experiences over a 3-year period were not shared by a sibling either because the event more directly involved one child (e.g. a school transition) or because there was a differential impact (Beardsall & Dunn, 1992). Further investigations of differential parenting and experiences that siblings do not share may clarify some of the processes by which parental dysfunction and conflict affect development.

The confounding of chronic adversities, parent pathology and genetic vulnerability

Many of the adversities experienced by children result from the behaviour or circumstances of their parents. Negative life experiences can result directly or indirectly from symptoms or psychopathology in a parent. A biological child in such a family not only shares the parents' genes, but also is exposed to both the symptoms of the disorder and the family behaviour that may derive from the symptoms. Many studies of chronic adversity assume that child problems result from the adversities children experience rather than the genetic transmission of vulnerability or some combination of the two. Sorting out the effects of psychosocial adversity in relation to genetic vulnerability is almost impossible in this situation without a reliable marker of vulnerability or research designs that allow for estimates of heritability (e.g. twin and adoption designs). However, it would be a helpful start if more investigators assessed the psychopathology of the parents as well as their behaviours and seemingly relevant family life events.

The nonrandom distribution of adversities

A related problem for research is the fact that chronic adversities are not randomly distributed in the population. For example, economic disadvantage covaries with some forms of physical and mental illness in parents and child maltreatment. Minority children in a given society may experience discrimination, a more extreme poverty, worse schools, and exposure to more frequent violence in dangerous neighbourhoods. Investigators must be cautious in attributing to a specific adversity that which is actually the result of unmeasured, correlated adversities.

The pile-up of adversities

Similarly, adversities tend to co-occur in time. The timing of an adversity with respect to what else is going on in an individual's life may be an important moderator of its effects. Studies of cumulative risk, discussed above, illustrate how combined adversities may have synergistic effects. These studies emphasize again the importance of studying the context for adversity, both with respect to timing and other life circumstances.

The role of cognitive appraisal

Another type of difficulty faced by investigators in this area is the central role of human cognition in the perception and interpretation of chronic adversities. Appraisal is clearly crucial to the phenomenon of adversity (Lazarus & Folkman, 1984) but extraordinarily difficult to assess, especially in young children. Young children may be protected in some ways from purely psychosocial adversity by limitations in their cognitive capacities to apprehend and remember adversities such as bereavement or wartime atrocities. Infants are buffered from many psychosocial adversities by their lack of comprehension. On the other hand, infants and young children are highly vulnerable to the diminished care that may accompany or result from bereavement, war or marital conflict. Infants and toddlers may also be very attuned to the emotional cues of distressed or frightened parents (Walden & Baxter, 1989).

Human appraisal systems are complex and strongly influenced by development. Clinical observations suggest that as a person develops, appraisals of ongoing and past adversities change and undergo reexamination and reinterpretation from new perspectives. Very little research has been done to examine systematically the role of appraisal in chronic adversities. This is an area for further research by investigators well-versed in normative child development as well as psychopathological and psychosocial influences on adverse events.

Specificity issues

In regard to the specificity of the role of adversity in development, gains have been made, but there is still much to be learned. Studies that allow for analysis of comorbidity in both parent and child have been the most informative on the specificity of adversity with respect to a particular disorder in children. Thus, it appears that a depressive episode in a parent may contribute to an ensuing episode in a child (Hammen *et al.*, 1991). Shared vulnerability may play a role. But this effect stands apart from the generalized risk for maladjustment in children with mentally ill parents.

Many studies of family adversity do not allow for any but the most general conclusions about elevated risk for maladjustment in children. In some cases, in fact, psychosocial adversities may have quite general effects. However, until research designs include multifaceted assessments of both the nature of the adversity and the nature of the effects, little will be learned about specific effects of particular adversities, how risk works, or whether the risk is general, specific or both, and which aspects most influence child functioning. Studies of psychosocial adversity need to undergo a period of refinement characterized by finer-grained analyses of adversities and outcomes.

Transactional influences

Transactional models (e.g. Sameroff & Chandler, 1975) have become popular in theorizing about development. However, research with transactional designs and analysis has lagged behind theory. Studies of psychosocial adversity have tended to focus on parent-to-child effects and less on child-to-parent or ongoing mutual shaping of parent and child behaviour. None the less, data from a few telling studies suggest that bidirectional influences are important for an understanding of adversity in the family (e.g. Hetherington, 1989; Capaldi & Patterson, 1991; Hammen *et al.*, 1991). Children who respond to perceived threats from the environment (whether the precipitant be violence, 'nattering', or distress in a parent) by annoying or demanding behaviours may further erode the quality of their own caregiving environment through their effects on parent mood and behaviour. In the refinement stage called for above, it will be important to examine the sequencing of parent and child behaviour over time in the context of family adversity.

CONCLUSIONS

Chronic adversities provide an entryway into the exploration of the effects of stress on development. Yet these complex stressors have taken a back seat to the more dramatic visage presented by manifestly acute stressful experiences. Nevertheless, in terms of long-term developmental consequences the influence of such adversities is more powerful than are the acute stressors, however dramatic their content.

Both for the clinician and the researcher, it is important to seek to disaggregate this core of adversity in an attempt to understand its composition and the differential power these constituents may play in development. Central to such a task would be the careful delineation of component risk factors that make for the adversity, and those protective factors in person, biology, environment, and culture that enable individuals to overcome disadvantage.

ACKNOWLEDGEMENTS

The authors are grateful for the support provided by the following funding institutions: the National Institute of Mental Health, the William T. Grant Foundation, the John D. & Catherine T. MacArthur Foundation, The Minnesota Center for Research on Disability Studies and the Graduate School, University of Minnesota.

REFERENCES

Ammerman R.T. & Herson M. (1990) *Children at Risk: an Evaluation of Factors Contributing to Child Abuse and Neglect*. Plenum Press, New York.

Anthony E.J. (1987) Risk, vulnerability and resilience: an overview. In: Anthony E.J. & Cohler B.J. (eds) *The Invulnerable Child*, pp. 3–48. Guilford Press, New York.

Anthony E.J. & Cohler B.J. (1987) *The Invulnerable Child*. Guilford Press, New York.

Beardsall L. & Dunn J. (1992) Adversities in childhood: siblings' experience, and their relations to self-esteem. *Journal of Child Psychology and Psychiatry*, **33**, 349–359.

Beardslee W.R., Bemperad J., Keller M.B. & Klerman G.L. (1983) Children of parents with major affective disorder: a review. *American Journal of Psychiatry*, **140**, 825–832.

Bleuler M. (1984) Different forms of childhood stress and patterns of adult psychiatric outcome. In: Watt N.F., Anthony E.J., Wynne L.C. & Rolf J.E. (eds) *Children at Risk for Schizophrenia: A Longitudinal Perspective*, pp. 537–542. Cambridge University Press, Cambridge.

Block J.H., Block J. & Gjerde P.F. (1986) The personality of children prior to divorce: a prospective study. *Child Development*, **57**, 827–840.

Block J., Block J.H. & Gjerde P.F. (1988) Parental functioning and the home environment in families of divorce: prospective and concurrent analyses. *Journal of the American Academy of Child and Adolescent Psychiatry*, **27**, 207–213.

Boh K., Bak M., Clason C., Pankratova M., Qvortrup J., Sgritta G.B. & Waerness K. (1989) *Changing Patterns of European Family Life: A Comparative Analysis of 14 European Countries*. Routledge, London.

Bowlby J. (1969) *Attachment and Loss: Attachment*, vol. 2. Basic Books, New York.

Bowlby J. (1973) *Attachment and Loss: Separation*, vol. 2. Basic Books, New York.

Bowlby J. (1980) *Attachment and Loss: Loss, Sadness and Depression*, vol. 3. Basic Books, New York.

Boyd J.H., Burke J.D., Gruenberg E., Holzer C.E., Rae D.S., George L.K., Karno M., Stoltaman R., McEvoy L. & Nestadt G. (1984) Exclusion criteria for DSM-III: a study of co-occurrence of hierarchy-free syndromes. *Archives of General Psychiatry*, **41**, 983–989.

Brown G.W. & Harris T. (1978) *Social Origins of Depression: A Study of Psychiatric Disorder in Women*. The Free Press, New York.

Brown G.W. & Prudo R. (1981) Psychiatric disorder in a rural and urban population: aetiology of depression. *Psychological Medicine*, **11**, 581–599.

Brown G.W., Harris T.O. & Bifulco A. (1986) Long term effects of early loss of a parent. In: Rutter M., Izard C.E. & Read P.B. (eds) *Depression in Young People: Developmental and Clinical Perspectives*, pp. 251–296. Guilford Press, New York.

Brown G.W., Harris T. & Copeland J.R. (1977) Depression and loss. *British Journal of Psychiatry*, **112**, 1043–1048.

Capaldi D.M. & Patterson G.R. (1991) Relation of parental transitions to boys' adjustment problems: I. A linear hypothesis. II. Mothers at risk for transitions and unskilled parenting. *Developmental Psychology*, **27**, 489–504.

Cherlin A.J., Furstenberg F.F. Jr., Chase-Lansdale P.L., Kiernan K.E., Robins P.K., Morrison D.R. & Teitler J.O. (1991) Longitudinal studies of divorce on children in Great Britain and the United States. *Science*, **252**, 1386–1389.

Cicchetti D. & Carlson V. (eds) (1989) *Child Maltreatment*. Cambridge University Press, Cambridge.

Cohen S. & Wills T.A. (1985) Stress, social support, and the buffering hypothesis. *Psychological Bulletin*, **98**, 310–357.

Conrad M. & Hammen C. (1989) Role of maternal depression in perceptions of child maladjustment. *Journal of Consulting and Clinical Psychology*, **57**, 663–667.

Cowen E.L., Pedro-Carroll J.L. & Alpert-Gillis L.J. (1990) Relationships between support and adjustment among children of divorce. *Journal of Child Psychology and Psychiatry*, **31**, 727–735.

Critelli R. (1983) Parental death in childhood: a review of the literature. In: Schowalter J.E., Patterson P.R., Tallmer M., Kutscher A., Gullo S.V. & Peretz D. (eds) *The Child and Death*, pp. 89–103. Columbia University Press, New York.

Cummings E.M. (1987) Coping with background anger in early childhood. *Child Development*, **58**, 976–984.

Cummings E.M., Iannotti R.J. & Zahn-Waxler C. (1985) Influence of conflict between adults on the emotions and aggression of young children. *Developmental Psychology*, **21**, 495–507.

Demo D.H. & Acock A.C. (1988) The impact of divorce on children. *Journal of Marriage and the Family*, **50**, 619–648.

Doherty W.J. & Needle R.H. (1991) Psychological adjustment and substance abuse among adolescents before and after a parental divorce. *Child Development*, **62**, 328–337.

Dohrenwend B.S. & Dohrenwend B.P. (eds) (1974) *Stressful Life Events: Their Nature and Effects*. Wiley, New York.

Dohrenwend B.S. & Dohrenwend B.P. (eds) (1984) *Stressful Life Events and Their Contexts*. Rutgers University Press, New Brunswick, NJ.

Downey G. & Coyne J.C. (1990) Children of depressed parents: an integrative review. *Psychological Bulletin*, **108**, 50–76.

Eckenrode J. (ed) (1991) *The Social Context of Coping*. Plenum Press, New York.

Elizur E. & Kaffman M. (1982) Children's bereavement reactions following death of the father, vol. 2. *Journal of the American Academy of Child Psychiatry*, **21**, 474–480.

Elizur E. & Kaffman M. (1983) Factors influencing the severity of childhood bereavement reactions. *American Journal of Orthopsychiatry*, **53**, 668–676.

Emery R.E. (1982) Interparental conflict and the children of discord and divorce. *Psychological Bulletin*, **92**, 310–330.

Emery R.E. (1988) *Marriage, Divorce, and Children's Adjustment*. Sage, Newbury Park, CA.

Emery R.E. (1989) Family violence. *American Psychologist*, **44**, 321–328.

Farber E.A. & Egeland B. (1987) Invulnerability among abused and neglected children. In: Anthony E.J. & Cohler B.J. (eds) *The Invulnerable Child*, pp. 253–288. Guilford Press, New York.

Fendrich M., Warner V. & Weissman M.M. (1990) Family risk factors, parental depression, and psychopathology in offspring. *Developmental Psychology*, **26**, 40–50.

Fergusson D.M., Dimond M.E. & Horwood L.J. (1986) Childhood family placement history and behaviour problems in 6-year-old children. *Journal of Child Psychology and Psychiatry*, **27**, 213–226.

Fisher L., Kokes R.F., Cole R.E., Perkins P.M. & Wynne L.C. (1987) Competent children at risk: a study of well-functioning offspring of disturbed parents. In: Anthony E.J. & Cohler B.J. (eds) *The Invulnerable Child*, pp. 211–228. Guilford Press, New York.

Forgatch M.S., Patterson G.R. & Skinner M.L. (1988) A mediational model for the effect of divorce on antisocial behavior in boys. In:

Hetherington E.M. & Arasteh J.D. (eds) *Impact of Divorce, Single Parenting, and Stepparenting on Children*, pp. 135–154. Lawrence Erlbaum, Hillsdale, NJ.

Freud A. & Burlingham D. (1943) *War and Children*. International Universities Press, New York.

Garmezy N. (1985a) Developmental aspects of children's reaction to separation and loss. In: Rutter M., Izard C. & Read P. (eds) *Depression in Young Children: Developmental Perspectives*, pp. 297–323. Guilford Press, New York.

Garmezy N. (1985b) Stress-resistant children: the search for protective factors. *Journal of Child Psychology and Psychiatry*, **4** (suppl.), 213–233.

Garmezy N. (1986) Developmental aspects of children's responses to the stress of separation and loss. In: Rutter M., Izard C.E. & Read P.B. (eds) *Depression in Young People: Developmental and Clinical Perspectives*, pp. 297–323. Guilford press, New York.

Garmezy N. (1987) Stress, competence and development: continuities in the study of schizophrenic adults, children vulnerable to psychopathology, and the search for stress-resistant children. *American Journal of Orthopsychiatry*, **57**, 159–174.

Garmezy N. & Rutter M. (eds) (1983) *Stress, Coping and Development in Children*. McGraw-Hill, New York.

Glick T.C. (1979) Children of divorced parent in demographic perspective. *Journal of Social Issues*, **35**, 170–182.

Glueck S. & Glueck E. (1962) *Family Environment and Delinquency*. Houghton Mifflin, Boston, MA.

Glueck S. & Glueck E. (1968) *Delinquents and Non-Delinquents in Perspective*. Harvard University Press, Cambridge, MA.

Goldstein M.J. & Tuma A.H. (1987) High-risk research. *Schizophrenia Bulletin*, **13**, 369–531.

Gordon D., Burge D., Hammen C., Adrian C., Jaenicke C. & Hiroto D. (1989) Observations of interactions of depressed women with their children. *American Journal of Psychiatry*, **146**, 50–55.

Gottesman I.I. & Shields J. (1972) *Schizophrenia and Genetics*. Academic Press, New York.

Gottesman I.I. & Shields J. (1982) *Schizophrenia: The Epigenetic Puzzle*. Cambridge University Press, New York.

Hammen C. (1993) The family-environmental context of depression. In: Cicchetti D. & Toth S. (eds) *Rochester Symposium on Developmental Psychopathology*, vol. 4, 251–281. Erlbaum, Hillsdale, NJ.

Hammen C., Adrian C., Gordon D., Burge D., Jaenicke C. & Hiroto D. (1987) Children of depressed mothers: maternal strain and symptom predictors of dysfunction. *Journal of Abnormal Psychology*, **96**, 190–198.

Hammen C., Burge D. & Stansbury K. (1990) Relationship of mother and child variables to child outcomes in a high-risk sample: a causal modeling analysis. *Developmental Psychology*, **26**, 24–30.

Hammen C., Burge D. & Adrian C. (1991) Timing of mother and child depression in a longitudinal study of children at risk. *Journal of Consulting and Clinical Psychology*, **59**, 341–345.

Harris T., Brown G.W. & Bifulco A. (1990) Loss of parent in childhood and adult psychiatric disorder: a tentative overall model. *Development and Psychopathology*, **2**, 311–328.

Hernandez D.J. (1988) Demographic trends and the living arrangements of children. In: Hetherington E.M. & Arasteh J.D. (eds) *Impact of Divorce, Single Parenting and Stepparenting on Children*, pp. 3–22. Lawrence Erlbaum, Hillsdale, NJ.

Hetherington E.M. (1989) Coping with family transitions: Winners, losers, and survivors. *Child Development*, **60**, 1–14.

Hetherington E.M. & Clingempeel W.G. (1992) Coping with marital transitions: a family systems perspective. *Monographs of the Society for Research in Child Development*, **57**, 2–3.

Hetherington E.M., Cox M. & Cox R. (1979) Family interaction and the social, emotional and cognitive development of children following divorce. In: Vaughn V. & Brazelton T. (eds) *The Family:*

Setting Priorities, pp. 89–128. Science and Medicine, New York.

Hetherington E.M., Cox M. & Cox R. (1982) Effects of divorce on parents and children. In: Lamb M. (ed) *Nontraditional Families*, pp. 233–288. Erlbaum, Hillsdale, NJ.

Hetherington E.M., Cox M. & Cox R. (1985) Long-term effects of divorce and remarriage on the adjustment of children. *Journal of the American Academy of Child Psychiatry*, **24**, 518–530.

Hetherington E.M., Stanley-Hagan M. & Anderson E.R. (1989) Marital transitions: a child's perspective. *American Psychologist*, **44**, 303–312.

Hobfoll S.E. (ed) (1986) *Stress, Social Support and Women*. Hemisphere, Washington.

Hunter R. & Macalpine I. (1963) *Three Hundred Years of Psychiatry 1538–1860*. Oxford University Press, London. (excerpted Sir Thomas Elyot, *The Control of Health*).

Jenkins J.M. & Smith M.A. (1990) Factors protecting children living in disharmonious homes: maternal reports. *Journal of the American Academy of Child and Adolescent Psychiatry*, **29**, 60–69.

Johnson J.H. (1986) *Life Events as Stressors in Childhood and Adolescence*. Sage, Newbury Park, CA.

Johnson J., Gonzalez R. & Campbell L.E.G. (1987) Ongoing post-divorce conflict and child disturbance. *Journal of Abnormal Child Psychology*, **15**, 493–509.

Kaffman M. & Elizur E. (1983) Bereavement responses of kibbutz and non-kibbutz children following the death of the father. *Journal of Child Psychology and Psychiatry*, **24**, 435–442.

Kendler K.S., Neale M.C., Kessler R.C., Heath A.C. & Eaves L.J. (1992) Childhood parental loss and adult psychopathology in women. *Archives of General Psychiatry*, **49**, 109–116.

Kitson G.C. & Morgan L.A. (1990) The multiple consequences of divorce: a decade review. *Journal of Marriage and the Family*, **52**, 913–924.

Kolvin I., Miller F.J.W., Fleeting M. & Kolvin P.A. (1988a) Risk/protective factors for offending with particular reference to deprivation. In: Rutter M. (ed) *Studies of Psychosocial Risk: The Power of Longitudinal Data*, pp. 77–95. Cambridge University Press, Cambridge.

Kolvin I., Miller F.J.W., Scott D.McI., Gatznis S.R.M. & Fleeting M. (1988b) *Adversity and Destiny: Explorations in the Transmission of Deprivation — Newcastle Thousand Families Study*. Gower, Aldershot.

Kolvin I., Miller F.J.W., Fleeting M. & Kolvin P.A. (1988c) Social and parenting factors affecting criminal offence rates (findings from the Newcastle Thousand Families Study, 1947–1980). *British Journal of Psychiatry*, **152**, 80–90.

Kranzler E.M., Shaffer D., Wasserman G. & Davies M. (1990) Early childhood bereavement. *Journal of the American Academy of Child and Adolescent Psychiatry*, **29**, 513–520.

Kurdek A. (1981) An integrative perspective on children's divorce adjustment. *American Psychologist*, **36**, 856–866.

Kurdek L.A. (1986) Children's reasoning about parental divorce. In: Ashmore R.D. & Brodzinsky D.M. (eds) *Thinking About the Family: Views of Parents and Children*. Erlbaum, Hillsdale, NJ.

Lahey B.B., Hartdagen S.E., Frick P.J., McBurnett K., Connor R. & Hynd G.W. (1988) Conduct disorder: parsing the confounded relation to parental divorce and antisocial personality. *Journal of Abnormal Psychology*, **97**, 334–337.

Lazarus R.S. & Folkman S. (1984) *Stress, Appraisal and Coping*. Springer, New York.

Lefcourt H.M., Martin R.A. & Saleh W.E. (1984) Locus of control and social support: interactive moderators of stress. *Journal of Personality and Social Psychology*, **47**, 378–389.

Lewinsohn P.M., Hoberman H.M. & Rosenbaum M. (1988) A prospective study of risk factors for unipolar depression. *Journal of Abnormal Psychology*, **97**, 251–264.

Loeber R. & Dishion T.J. (1983) Early predictors of male delinquency:

a review. *Psychological Bulletin*, **94**, 68–99.

Loeber R. & Stouthamer-Loeber M. (1986) Family factors as correlates and predictors of juvenile conduct problems and delinquency. In: Tonry M. & Morris N. (eds) *Crime and Justice: An Annual Review of Research*, vol. 7. University of Chicago Press, Chicago, IL.

Luthar S.S. & Zigler E. (1991) Vulnerability and competence: a review of research on resilience in childhood. *American Journal of Orthopsychiatry*, **61**, 6–22.

McCord J. (1979) Some child-rearing antecedents of criminal behavior in adult men. *Journal of Personality and Social Psychology*, **37**, 1477–1486.

McCord W. & McCord J. (1959) *Origins of Crime*. Columbia University Press, New York.

Masten A. (1989) Resilience in development: implications of the study of successful adaptation for developmental psychopathology. In: Cicchetti D. (ed) *Rochester Symposium on Developmental Psychopathology*, pp. 261–294. Erlbaum, Hillsdale, NJ.

Masten A. & Garmezy N. (1985) Risk, vulnerability and protective factors in developmental psychopathology. In: Lahey B.B. & Kazdin A.E. (eds) *Advances in Clinical Child Psychology*, vol. 8, pp. 1–52. Plenum Press, New York.

Masten A.S., Best K.M. & Garmezy N. (1990) Resilience and development: contributions from the study of children who overcome adversity. *Development and Psychopathology*, **2**, 425–444.

Masterman S.H. & Reams R. (1988) Support groups for bereaved preschool and school-age children. *American Journal of Orthopsychiatry*, **58**, 562–570.

Musick J.S., Stott F.M., Spencer K.K., Goldman J. & Cohler B.J. (1987) Maternal factors related to vulnerability and resilience in young children at risk. In: Anthony E.J. & Cohler B.J. (eds) *The Invulnerable Child*, pp. 229–252. Guilford Press, New York.

Newcomb M.D. (1990) Social support and personal characteristics: a developmental and interactional perspective. *Journal of Social and Clinical Psychology*, **9**, 54–68.

Norton A.J. & Moorman J.E. (1987) Current trends in marriage and divorce among American women. *Journal of Marriage and the Family*, **49**, 3–14.

Orvaschel H. (1983) Maternal depression and child dysfunction: children at risk. In: Lahey B.B. & Kazdin A.E. (eds) *Advances in Clinical Psychology*, vol. 6, pp. 169–197. Plenum Press, New York.

Patterson G.R. (1982) *Coercive Family Processes*, vol. 2. Castalia Eugene, OR.

Patterson G.R. & Capaldi D.M. (1990) A mediational model for boys' depressive moods. In: Rolf J., Masten A.S., Cicchetti D. Nuechterlein K.H. & Weintraub S. (eds) *Risk and Protective Factors in the Development of Psychopathology*, pp. 141–163. Cambridge University Press, New York.

Perris C. (1966) A study of biopolar (M-D) and unipolar recurrent depressive psychosis II. Childhood environment and precipitating factors. *Acta Psychiatrica Scandinavica* (suppl. 194), 45–57.

Peterson J.L. & Zill N. (1986) Marital disruption, parent–child relationships, and behavior problems in children. *Journal of Marriage and the Family*, **48**, 295–307.

Plomin R. & Daniels D. (1987) Why are children in the same family so different from one another? *The Behavioral and Brain Sciences*, **10**, 1–16, 44–49.

Radke-Yarrow M. & Sherman T. (1990). Hard growing: children who survive. In: Rolf J.E., Masten A., Cicchetti D., Nuechterlein K. & Weintraub S. (eds) *Risk and Protective Factors in the Development of Psychopathology*, pp. 97–119. Cambridge University Press, New York.

Reilly T.P., Hasazi J.E. & Bond L.A. (1983) Children's conceptions of death and personal morality. *Journal of Pediatric Psychology*, **8**, 21–31.

Robins L.N. & Regier D.A. (eds) (1991) *Psychiatric Disorders in America*. The Free Press, New York.

Robins L.N., Locke B.Z. & Regier D.A. (1991) An overview of psychiatric disorders in America. In: Robins L.N. & Regier D.A. (eds) *Psychiatric Disorders in America: The Epidemiological Catchment Area Study*, pp. 328–366. The Free Press, New York.

Robins N. (1966) *Deviant Children Grown Up*. Williams & Wilkins Baltimore, MD.

Rolf J., Masten A.S., Cicchetti D., Nuechterlein K.H. & Weintraub S. (eds) (1990) *Risk and Protective Factors in the Development of Psychopathology*. Cambridge University Press, Cambridge.

Russell M., Henderson C. & Blume S.B. (1985) *Children of Alcoholics: A Review of the Literature*. Children of Alcoholics Foundation, New York.

Rutter M. (1966) *Children of Sick Parents: An Environmental and Psychiatric Study*. Oxford University Press, Oxford.

Rutter M. (1978) Family, area and school influences in the genesis of conduct disorders. In: Hersov L.A., Berger M. & Schaffer D. (eds) *Aggression and Anti-Social Behavior in Childhood and Adolescence*, pp. 95–113. Pergamon Press, Oxford.

Rutter M. (1979) Protective factors in children's responses to stress and disadvantage. In: Kent M.W. & Rolf J.E. (eds) *Primary Prevention in Psychopathology: Social Competence in Children*, vol. 3, pp. 49–74. University Press of New England, Hanover, NH.

Rutter M. (1984) Psychopathology and development. I. Childhood antecedents of adult psychiatric disorder. *Australian and New Zealand Journal of Psychiatry*, **18**, 225–234.

Rutter M. (1985) Resilience in the face of adversity: protective factors and resistance to psychiatric disorder. *British Journal of Psychiatry*, **147**, 598–611.

Rutter M. (1987) Psychosocial resilience and protective mechanisms. *American Journal of Orthopsychiatry*, **57**, 316–331.

Rutter M. (1990a) Commentary: Some focus and process considerations regarding effects of parental depression on children. *Developmental Psychology*, **26**, 60–67.

Rutter M. (1990b) Psychosocial resilience and protective mechanisms. In: Rolf J., Masten A.S., Cicchetti D., Nuechterlein K.H. & Weintraub S. (eds) *Risk and Protective Factors in the Development of Psychopathology*, pp. 181–214. Cambridge University Press, Cambridge.

Rutter M. & Giller H. (1983) *Juvenile Delinquency*. Penguin Books, Harmondsworth.

Rutter M. & Quinton D. (1987) Parental mental illness as a risk factor for psychiatric disorders in childhood. In: Magnusson D. & Ohman A. (eds) *Psychopathology: An Interactional Perspective*, pp. 199–219. Academic Press, Orlando.

Rutter M., Bolton P., Harrington R., LeCouteur A., MacDonald H. & Simonoff E. (1990a) Genetic factors in child psychiatric disorders. I. A review of research strategies. *Journal of Child Psychology and Psychiatry*, **31**, 3–37.

Rutter M., MacDonald H., LeCouteur A., Harrington R., Bolton P. & Bailey A. (1990b) Genetic factors in child psychiatric disorders. II. Empirical findings. *Journal of Child Psychology and Psychiatry*, **31**, 39–83.

Sameroff A.J. & Chandler M.J. (1975) Reproductive risk and the continuum of caretaking casualty. In: Horowitz F.D., Hetherington M., Scarr-Salapatek S. & Siegel G. (eds) *Review of Child Development Research*, vol. 4, pp. 187–244. University of Chicago Press, Chicago, IL.

Sameroff A.J. & Seifer R. (1983) Familial risk and child competence. *Child Development*, **36**, 413–424.

Sameroff A.J. & Seifer R. (1990) Early contributors to developmental risk. In: Rolf J., Masten A.S., Cicchetti D., Nuechterlein K.H. & Weintraub S. (eds) *Risk and Protective Factors in the Development of Psychopathology*, pp. 52–66. Cambridge University Press, Cambridge.

Sameroff A.J., Seifer R. & Zax M. (1982) Early development of children at risk for emotional disorder. *Monographs of the Society for Research in Child Development*, **47**(7), 1–82.

Santrock J.W. & Warshak R.A. (1979) Father custody and social development in boys and girls. *Journal of Social Issues*, **35**, 112–125.

Scarr S. & McCartney K. (1983) How people make their own environments: a theory of genotype–environment effects. *Child Development*, **54**, 424–435.

Seifer R. & Sameroff A.J. (1987) Multiple determinants of risk and invulnerability. In: Anthony E.J. & Cohler B.J. (eds) *The Invulnerable Child*, pp. 51–69. Guilford Press, New York.

Silverman P.R. & Worden J.W. (1992) Children's reactions in the early months after the death of a parent. *American Journal of Orthopsychiatry*, **62**, 93–104.

Snyder C.R. & Ford C.E. (1987) *Coping with Negative Life Events*. Plenum Press, New York.

Speece M.W. & Brent S.B. (1984) Children's understanding of death: a review of three components of a death concept. *Child Development*, **55**, 1671–1686.

Trasler G. (1987) Biogenetic factors. In: Quay H.C. (ed) *Handbook of Juvenile Delinquency*, pp. 184–215. John Wiley, New York.

Van Eerdewegh M.M., Bier M.D., Parrilla R.H. & Clayton P.C. (1982) The bereaved child. *British Journal of Psychiatry*, **140**, 23–29.

Van Eerdewegh M.M., Clayton P.J. & Van Eerdewegh P. (1985) The bereaved child: variables influencing early psychopathology. *British Journal of Psychiatry*, **147**, 188–194.

Walden T.A. & Baxter A. (1989) The effects of contextual age on social referencing. *Child Development*, **60**, 1511–1518.

Wallerstein J.S. (1985) Children of divorce: preliminary report of a ten-year follow-up of older children and adolescents. *Journal of the American Academy of Child Psychiatry*, **24**, 545–553.

Wallerstein J.S. (1991) The long-term effects of divorce on children: a review. *Journal of the American Academy of Child and Adolescent Psychiatry*, **30**, 349–360.

Wallerstein J.S. & Kelly J.B. (1980) *Surviving the Breakup: How Children and Parents Cope with Divorce*. Basic Books, New York.

Wallerstein J.S., Corbin S.B. & Lewis J.M. (1988) Children of divorce: a 10-year study. In: Hetherington E.M. & Arasteh J.D. (eds) *Impact of Divorce, Single Parenting, and Stepparenting on Children*, pp. 197–214. Lawrence Erlbaum, Hillsdale, NJ.

Watt N.F., Anthony E.J., Wynne L.C. & Rolf J.E. (1984) *Children at Risk for Schizophrenia: A Longitudinal Perspective*. Cambridge University Press, Cambridge.

Weissman M.M., Paykel E.S. & Klerman G.L. (1972) The depressed woman as a mother. *Social Psychiatry*, **7**, 98–108.

Werner E.E. (1989) High-risk children in young adulthood: A longitudinal study from birth to 32 years. *American Journal of Orthopsychiatry*, **59**, 72–81.

Werner E.E. & Smith R.S. (1977) *Kauai's Children Come of Age*. University of Hawaii Press, Honolulu, Hawaii.

Werner E.E. & Smith R.S. (1982) *Vulnerable but Invincible: A Study of Resilient Children*. McGraw-Hill, New York.

Werner E.E. & Smith R.S. (1992) *Overcoming the Odds; High Risk Children from Birth to Adulthood*. Cornell University Press, Ithaca, NY.

Werner E.E., Bierman J.M. & French F.E. (1971) *The Children of Kauai*. University of Hawaii Press, Honolulu, Hawaii.

West D.J. (1982) *Delinquency: Its Roots, Careers and Prospects*. Harvard University Press, Cambridge, MA.

West D.J. & Farrington D.P. (1973) *Who Becomes Delinquent?* Heinemann Educational Books, London.

Wheaton B. (1990) Where work and family meet: stress across social roles. In: Eckenrode J. & Gore S. (eds) *Stress Between Work and Family*, pp. 153–174. Plenum Press, New York.

Worland J., Weeks D.G. & Jones C.L. (1987) Predicting mental health in children at risk. In: Anthony E.J. & Cohler B.J. (eds) *The invulnerable Child*, pp. 185–210. Guilford Press, New York.

Chapter 13
Physical and Emotional Maltreatment

David Skuse & Arnon Bentovim

DEFINITIONAL ISSUES

Definitions of child abuse inevitably vary according to the uses for which they have been devised. There will be differences of emphasis between definitions that are intended for legal purposes, clinical diagnostic purposes or to suit the needs of a research study. Cultural relativity may be a significant issue, for certain behaviours that are construed as abusive by some cultures or subcultures will not be regarded in the same light by others. Definitions of abusive behaviours that are essentially acts of commission may need to be distinguished from neglectful caretaking, which is characterized by acts of omission. The extent to which account should be taken of the intention of the perpetrator, in arriving at a comprehensive definition of abuse and neglect, is a contentious point. How culpable is the perpetrator when the consequences of the abuse for the child were far more serious than might have been envisaged when the act was committed? Few parents expect brain damage to result from shaking a child (Eager *et al.*, 1985; Showers, 1992). Severe burns may be caused by minimal exposure of an infant's skin to hot water, and the seriousness of the injury is not immediately apparent (Watkins *et al.*, 1985). Developmental trends in relation to appropriate parental behaviours should also be taken into account. Behaviours that would be construed as abusive or neglectful for a child in infancy will be very different from those that indicate maltreatment of an adolescent.

A recent example of a legal definition of abuse can be found in the Children Act of England and Wales (White *et al.*, 1990) which states: 'the primary justification for the State to initiate proceedings seeking compulsory powers is actual or likely harm to the child, where harm includes both ill-treatment (which includes sexual abuse and non-physical ill-treatment such as emotional abuse) and the impairment of health or development, *health* meaning physical or mental health, and *development* meaning physical, intellectual, emotional, social or behavioural development'. In the US proposed changes to statutes and judicial standards aimed at rectifying the vagueness of existing legal definitions have been resisted by the judiciary because of the very restrictions imposed by the criterion of harm, where such harm is defined as observable and serious consequences to the child (see Giovannoni, 1989). Medical definitions arouse least controversy when the focus

is upon diagnostic features compatible with the physical abuse of children. Certain physical signs, such as those of burning, slapping, pinching or characteristic bone fractures, are now well-recognized by many, if not by most physicians (Meadow, 1989a). But the symptoms of emotional abuse or long-standing neglect may not be so obvious; they may be ambiguous and controversial. If psychological symptoms merit clinical significance in virtue of their supposed aetiology we should be able to demonstrate, through empirical research, the specificity of that causal relationship. Unfortunately, whereas we can infer from radiological evidence of metaphyseal or epiphyseal fractures in an infant that those injuries were very likely to have been caused by trauma, and are probably nonaccidental (e.g. Worlock *et al.*, 1986), we do not find many patterns of psychological or behavioural symptoms that possess the same specificity. Finkelhor and Korbin (1988) suggested that emotional abuse comprises rejection (chronic denigration), social isolation, terrorizing by threatened abandonment, chronic deprivation of attention, corruption by exposure to deviant child care practices and 'adultifying', by which they mean persistently making age-inappropriate demands upon the child. Physical neglect is defined as the deprivation or nonprovision of necessary and societally available resources due to proximate and proscribed human actions that create the risk of permanent impairment to development or functioning. This emphasis on acts by the perpetrator has been made by others (e.g. Garbarino & Garbarino, 1986; Hart & Brassard, 1987) but an alternative view is that parental behaviour alone is an inadequate predictor of psychological harm. Instead, child outcome must be taken into account, as a more appropriate and relevant variable (Aber & Zigler, 1981).

Certainly it is no answer to construct idiosyncratic definitions for the purposes of research into emotional abuse and neglect. The definitions must have utility outside the research setting. One way of approaching a solution could be to identify more clearly exactly which elements in the child's experiences are causally linked to a detriment outcome. If it could be demonstrated that similar psychological detriment results from a whole range of abusive experiences it should be possible to distinguish the core elements of that abuse. If it could be shown, for example, that a variable termed victimization, the engendering of a sense of powerlessness and exploitation in the victim, was a feature common to a range of physical, emotional and sexual abuses, and that the outcome in all those cases was a similar measurable deficit in social cognitive development or behavioural adjustment, then the definition of abuse ought to incorporate those elements of the abusive behaviour.

CULTURAL INFLUENCES

Contemporary evidence suggests the incidence of child abuse is increasing (Cohn, 1983), but if we take a historical perspective on the subject it is arguable that, at least in developed western societies, the treatment of children is far less neglectful of their welfare than it was in times past (deMause, 1976; Zigler & Hall, 1989). The modern history of child advocacy began in the US with the case of Mary Ellen, an 8-year-old who was chained, starved and beaten by her adoptive parents (Lazoritz, 1990). Widespread publicity about this case led to the founding of the Society for the Prevention of Cruelty to Children in 1875. Subsequently, in the UK the National Society for the Prevention of Cruelty to Children was founded in 1884. However, the concerns of the public and of medical practitioners were confined to relatively overt and severe cases of abuse and neglect until quite recently. The modern history of child abuse and neglect began with the recognition of the relatively subtle consequences of physical abuse, manifested by healing fractures, as highlighted by the observations of Caffey (1946) and other radiologists (e.g. Wooley & Evans, 1955). The implications of their observations were not fully realized until the early 1960s when Henry Kempe and his colleagues (Kempe *et al.*, 1962) coined the term 'the battered child syndrome' and the full culpability of parents in the aetiology of certain characteristic injuries of their children was appreciated.

Because the first such cases were described in the US it was inevitable that questions would be raised as to whether the phenomenon had cultural specificity. The growing international literature on this subject makes it quite clear that gross physical abuse is of course found throughout the world (Korbin, 1991) but there is still the question of the extent to which certain sorts of abuse are always damaging to a child's psychological development and the extent to which there is cultural specificity. Our consideration of this subject will take a focused viewpoint; some forms of detriment to children's welfare such as malnutrition, war and abandonment will not be discussed.

Cross-cultural variability in child-rearing beliefs and behaviours is so great that it would be difficult, although probably not impossible, to define a framework of acceptable child-rearing practices that would be universally applicable. Korbin (1981, 1987a, 1987b) has attempted to clarify this matter by discriminating between cultural differences in child-rearing practices and beliefs, idiosyncratic departures from broad cultural norms and societally induced harm. Within the first category are practices that are acceptable within a culture but that are considered abusive by outsiders. Turnbull (1961)

gave a fascinating account of conflict in societal attitudes towards harsh child-rearing practices in Zaire. In that country, the Bantu believed their sons would not be adequately prepared for manhood if they did not undergo a painful and harsh initiation rite during adolescence. Their 'Mbuti neighbours did not hold with such practices and were accordingly regarded by the Bantu as neglectful of their sons' welfare. In time, the 'Mbuti people came to adopt a watered-down version of the Bantu initiation practices.

Secular trends in western societies' attitudes towards the deliberate infliction of physical pain go in the opposite direction to the 'Mbuti and Bantu initiation rites. For example, until just 20 years or so ago, corporal punishment was ubiquitous in both state-funded and independent schools in the UK (Benthall, 1991). It has now been abolished in state schools there, although in the US in the late 1980s it was estimated that 2–3 million acts of corporal punishment per year were still being carried out (Hyman, 1987). Evidence on the long-term consequences of such socially sanctioned abuse upon psychological development is scanty (see Hyman, 1987); indeed it would have been argued not so long ago that the practice had a formative influence on the cultural identity of the British ruling class (Benthall, 1991). Cultural relativity also exists for the severity of physical punishments tolerated within the domestic environment, as demonstrated by a cross-cultural comparison study between Sweden and the US (see Somander & Rammer, 1991). Approximately 4% of all children between 3 and 17 years in both countries were abused at least once a year, by a parent, so severely that they risked being physically injured. However, punishment by hitting with an object was more acceptable in American society than in Sweden. Nevertheless, in the 10 years between the first and second national surveys of family violence in the US, there was a 24% decrease in the proportion of parents who said they would use severe violence against their children (Gelles & Straus, 1987).

Certain societal conditions themselves make for maltreatment. The consequences of such conditions, their adverse effects upon child development, may not be appreciated at the time, or may be ignored. A striking example in recent years was the restriction on hospital visiting by parents of young children. In the mid 1950s the Royal Hospital for Sick Children in Bristol instructed parents to visit no more than one at a time, for a maximum of 4 hours each day if their child was under 3 years or 2 hours a day for older children. They were advised: 'don't worry if he cries when you leave; it's normal'. The adverse long-term consequences for behaviour of repeated hospital admissions under such a policy have been reviewed by Quinton and Rutter (1976). Similarly, we nowadays appreciate the long-term consequences of an upbringing within a poor-quality institution, in which little personal attention is given to children (Skuse, 1992). Although rarely found within western Europe and the US, very poor-quality child care, with foreseeable detrimental consequences, is still a feature of foundling homes, crèches and similar institutions within the Middle East (Hakimi-Manesh *et al.*, 1984), in eastern Europe (especially Romania; McKinley, 1991) and in Russia (Zdanska-Brincken *et al.*, 1983; Chernova, 1990).

FORMS OF ABUSE

The categorization of forms of abuse is inevitably somewhat arbitrary when considered from the point of view of psychological welfare. Physical abuse may not only have immediate and long-term somatic consequences but may also directly or indirectly affect psychological development. Shaking is a frequent cause of brain damage in infants (Frank *et al.*, 1985). Extensive burn injuries may cause permanent physical deformity, with the concomitant risk to emotional and behavioural adjustment. Other forms of abuse, that do not cause physical injury directly, may nevertheless by direct or indirect means influence somatic development. Malnutrition, due to neglect, can cause stunting and impair cognitive and psychomotor development (Grantham-McGregor, 1987). In some children emotional abuse interferes with the neurohumoral control of skeletal growth (Stanhope *et al.*, 1988; Skuse *et al.*, 1992). Sexual abuse can have profound short- and long-term effects upon social and emotional adjustment and may be a precursor to serious mental illness (see Chapter 14), Münchausen syndrome by proxy or factitious illness, deliberate suffocation and the recently described phenomenon of fetal abuse of an unborn child by a substance-abusing pregnant mother may all impair psychological development one way or another.

Physical abuse, within western cultures, usually presents with some form of injury. A decision must then be made about whether that injury was accidental or nonaccidental. Speight (1989) described pointers to the diagnosis of nonaccidental injury. None is pathognomonic, nor does the absence of any item exclude the diagnosis. Firstly, there is a delay in seeking or failure to seek medical help. Secondly, an account of the 'accident' that is vague, lacking in detail and which varies with each telling is suggestive; innocent incidents are related in vivid ways that ring true. Thirdly, an account of the incident that is not compatible with the injury observed provides an important pointer. Fourthly, there is parental affect that is abnormal and does not reflect the degree of concern and anxiety one would expect in circumstances following a genuine accident. Abusing parents tend to be preoccupied with their own problems. Fifthly, there are other aspects of the parents' demeanour that give cause for concern, including hostility, the rebuttal of accusations that have not explicitly been made, attempts to leave (with or without the injured child) before medical investigations are complete. Sixthly, there is an appearance of the child and the interaction with the parents that gives cause for concern; many abused children look sad, withdrawn and frightened. In some cases they show frozen watchfulness. Finally, the child may say something to arouse suspicion.

Considerable experience has now been accumulated by paediatricians concerning the diagnostic characteristics associated with forms of nonaccidental injury, including fractures (Kleinman, 1987), head injuries (Billmire & Myers, 1985), burns and scalds (Hobbs, 1986) and patterns of bruising.

Deliberate poisoning is perhaps unusual, and is especially difficult to detect because accidental poisoning is so common in young children. Meadow (1989b) considered that deliberate poisoning mainly occurs in children below the age of 2 years and may present in any one of four ways. In the first, the presentation is exactly the same as if the child had ingested the substance accidentally and is rushed to hospital by the parent. In the second, the child presents with inexplicable symptoms and signs without a history of poisoning. In the third, the child presents with a recurrent unexplained illness that has features compatible with poisoning, such as recurrent episodes of drowsiness or hyperventilation. There is an overlap here with Münchausen syndrome by proxy or factitious illness. Finally, the child may be moribund or have died by the time medical attention is sought.

In recent years a number of reports of deliberate suffocation of children has been published (e.g. Southall *et al.*, 1987). The commonest form is smothering in which the abuser, usually the child's mother, uses a pillow or similar object to cause mechanical obstruction to the child's airways. The condition usually presents in infancy, either as an alleged apnoeic attack or, in the most serious cases, as an apparent cot death or sudden infant death syndrome (SIDS). The differential diagnosis in cases in which the child survives will have to be determined by specialist investigations in hospital (Meadow, 1990). It has been estimated that about 10% of all cases of SIDS are due to suffocation (Emery & Taylor, 1986); in such cases there is a substantially increased risk to the siblings of the victims. A recent study by Newlands and Emery (1991) showed a far higher than expected rate of SIDS among the siblings of children whose names appeared on a child protection register, over a 4-year period. In southern Derbyshire the rate of SIDS deaths was 3.1 per 1000 children at risk, whereas 1 in 30 of the children on the register had a sibling whose death was registered as due to that condition.

Münchausen syndrome by proxy is now a well-known phenomenon, which was first described in 1977 by Meadow. In this case, the parent, almost invariably the mother, fabricates illness in her child or children and presents the problem to doctors. The child is usually persistently brought for medical investigations, yet acute symptoms and the signs of illness cease when the child is separated from the presenting parent, who denies having any knowledge of the aetiology of the disorder (Rosenberg, 1987). There is a strong tendency for other children in these families to be, or have been, similarly afflicted. Bools *et al.* (1992) found 39% of siblings from a large series of patients had themselves been subject to fabricated illness, and 1 in 10 had died in mysterious circumstances. Comorbidity is a major problem; it is highly likely that affected children will have had more than one fabricated illness; failure to thrive and nonaccidental injuries are also commonly associated (Bools *et al.*, 1992). Forms of fabricated illness in this extraordinary condition include, most frequently, smotherings, poisonings, seizures, apparent bleeding from a variety of orifices, skin rashes and other lesions, pyrexias and hypertension (see Meadow, 1989c).

Emotional abuse and neglect of children may take many forms, from a lack of care for their physical needs, through a failure to provide consistent love and nurture, to overt hostility and rejection. Emotional abuse is rarely the sole reason for seeking child protection through legal action yet evidence is accumulating that its long-term consequences upon social, emotional, cognitive and behavioural development may be far-reaching and profound. Characteristic features include the habitual verbal harassment of a child by disparagement, criticism, threat and ridicule and the inversion of love; by verbal and nonverbal means, rejection and withdrawal are substituted.

Neglect comprises both a lack of physical caretaking and supervision and a failure to fulfil the developmental needs of the child in terms of cognitive stimulation. Although direct observations of parenting may raise suspicions about the presence of emotional abuse or neglect, the diagnosis is usually suggested by its consequences for the child in terms of emotional and behavioural adjustment. All abuse entails some emotional ill-treatment. There is often accompanying physical or sexual abuse. However, even without signs of physical or sexual maltreatment and disclosure of specific abusive activities, it is sometimes still possible to recognize characteristic groups of features that demand further investigation (Skuse, 1993). Current knowledge on emotional abuse and neglect does not yet allow us causally to link specific patterns of maltreatment to particular delays and disorders. The symptoms we regard as suspicious may not be invariably indicative of abuse and neglect. Nevertheless, it is important to recognize that the cessation of emotional abuse and its substitution by sensitive care, often in an alternative family, is usually followed by rapid and dramatic improvement in developmental attainments, behaviour and socioemotional adjustment (Skuse, 1988, 1992). In this sense, the diagnosis can be validated in retrospect.

EPIDEMIOLOGY

Four per cent of children up to the age of 12 are brought to the attention of professional agencies (Social Services Departments or the National Society for the Prevention of Cruelty to Children) because of suspected abuse each year. In England, in 1988, 3.5 per 1000 children below the age of 18 years were on Child Protection Registers, and more than a quarter of these were in the care of local authorities (Browne & Saqi, 1987). About 1 in 4 of those on Child Protection Registers had suffered physical abuse, and 1 in 8 neglect. The largest proportion — one-third — were subjects of grave concern, a term that often indicates another child in the family is known to have been abused. In the US the 1986 National Incidence and Prevalence Study of the National Center on Child Abuse and Neglect estimated that 25.2 per 1000 children had been maltreated in that year (US Department of Health and Human Services, 1988), of whom about two-thirds were cases of

neglect and just over a quarter were of physical abuse. We do not know exactly what the mortality from child abuse is in the UK; it is at least 1 in every 100 000 but it may be greater. In the US homicide accounts for more than 4000 deaths each year among children under 6 years of age (Council on Scientific Affairs, 1985).

The incidence of alleged cases of abuse is likely to be substantially higher in countries that have a system of mandatory reporting. By 1967 all the states of the US had passed child abuse reporting laws that require specified professionals likely to come into contact with children to report suspected abuse and neglect to child-protective agencies. Yet even where mandatory reporting legislation exists, a substantial minority of child abuse and neglect cases known to professionals are not registered (Zellman, 1990).

Available figures on the incidence of child abuse are undoubtedly underestimates for three main reasons (Zigler & Hall, 1989). Firstly, there is often failure to detect the signs and symptoms that are indicative of abuse, especially if these are psychological rather than physical in nature. Secondly, even if the signs and symptoms are recognized it may not be realized that they result from abuse. Thirdly, even if the true aetiology is suspected, the case may not be reported and so cannot enter into any official statistics. An interesting account of how an extension of mandatory reporting from doctors to school workers was introduced into New South Wales, Australia, emphasizes the importance of training staff to recognize potential cases, whilst acknowledging the dangers of inaccurate ascertainment (Lamond, 1989).

Within a given society, some simple demographic variables define groups who are at substantially higher risk of being abused than others. Studies have consistently demonstrated that there is a significant association between socioeconomic status and child maltreatment, although the interpretation of these figures must take into account the probability that official statistics reflect biased samples (Trickett *et al.*, 1991).

Within the epidemiological literature on abuse, relatively little has been written about the impact of physical abuse and neglect upon adolescents (Powers *et al.*, 1988). Yet a national study of incidence of child abuse in the US (US Department of Health and Human Services, 1988) reported that adolescents accounted for 47% of alleged cases, the great majority of which were substantiated upon investigation. A potentially important finding is that adolescent abuse is rather less likely to be reported to the protective services than are cases of abuse involving other age groups.

Reviewing the available literature, Garbarino (1989) drew the following conclusions. Firstly, the incidence of adolescent maltreatment equals or exceeds the incidence of maltreatment of younger children. Secondly, all forms of abuse and neglect may be encountered, but psychological and sexual abuse predominates. Thirdly, females are more likely to be abused as they pass through adolescence than during earlier childhood, whereas boys are more at risk at a younger age (e.g. Powers *et al.*, 1988). Fourthly, it is uncertain whether a substantial proportion of maltreatment cases involving adolescents have their onset at that time, or whether many are simply the continuance of abusive and neglectful patterns of parenting that began many years previously. There are conflicting findings on this matter. For example, Pelcovitz *et al.* (1984) reported 50% of adolescent onset but Berdie *et al.* (1983) concluded that only 23% commenced in adolescence. Fifthly, unlike the majority of families known to abuse younger children, those who are identified as maltreating their adolescent offspring are not predominantly socioeconomically disadvantaged (Garbarino *et al.*, 1986; Vondra, 1986). Sixthly, families with adolescents containing stepparents are at a higher risk of maltreating them than families in which both parents are biologically related to their children. For example, Farber and Joseph (1985) reported that only 30% of adolescents in their study were living with both biological parents. The mechanisms underlying this observation are not known, and it must be borne in mind that children whose parents have separated will have suffered traumas that those with an intact family have not. Families who are at risk for adolescent maltreatment may have other difficulties too, which have been summarized by Pelcovitz *et al.* (1984) as parenting styles that are either authoritarian or overindulgent.

DEVELOPMENTAL CONSEQUENCES

The effects of maltreatment on development during early childhood may manifest in both physical and psychological sequelae. The focus here will be on the latter set of disorders, although where there are integral links between physical and mental manifestations of abuse, as in disorders of growth, these will be discussed in some detail. It is the psychological aspects of maltreatment that are at the core of negative developmental outcomes (Claussen & Crittenden, 1991) and the psychological consequences of abuse that are often the most profound and enduring (see Garbarino & Vondra, 1987).

Until quite recently the few scientific studies of the effects of maltreatment were largely atheoretical (Aber & Cicchetti, 1984; Aber & Allen, 1987; Cicchetti *et al.*, 1987). However, in order to achieve an understanding of the causal relationship between abuse and its consequences we need to be guided by a developmental perspective. It would be an oversimplification to think of aetiological influences in terms of main effects (e.g. Parke & Collmer, 1975), because adverse outcomes must be related to a dynamic process of maladaptation in which both parenting and child behaviour exert evolving influences upon one another (Cicchetti, 1989). Domains of adaptive functioning should bear a theoretical relationship to the nature of risk to which the child is exposed. According to this organizational perspective (e.g. Rieder & Cicchetti, 1989), healthy development results from specific attainments within each age period. For example, a secure attachment in infancy facilitates autonomous functioning during toddlerhood and peer relationships in later childhood (e.g. Waters & Sroufe, 1983).

The effects of maltreatment have been well summarized by Aber *et al.* (1989).

Considering first socioemotional development, attachment theory suggests that children's expectations of adult availability and responsiveness are generalizations, developed during infancy and toddlerhood through interaction with their primary attachment figures (Crittenden & Ainsworth, 1989). Relationships with novel adults, encountered in child care settings and schools, are linked to children's expectations about adult availability and responsiveness which have been carried forward by means of internal representational models. These influence both the construction of new relationships and the ability to explore and cope with the demands of new and stressful situations (Bowlby, 1980; Main & Weston, 1981; Sroufe & Fleeson, 1986). Research has shown that histories of early insecure, especially disorganized or disoriented attachments, such as are associated with situations of neglect and abuse (Carlson *et al.*, 1989), can distort the child's subsequent relationships with unfamiliar adults outside the home, leading to abnormal patterns of social interaction (Sroufe *et al.*, 1983).

Prosocial behaviour is often disrupted in preschool children who have been subject to abuse. They may avoid people who make friendly overtures toward them, respond angrily or in other aversive ways to same-age peers (Main, 1980), unlike toddlers from socioeconomically disadvantaged backgrounds who have not been abused, who respond with concern, empathy and sadness to peer distress (Main & George, 1985). Abused preschool children can also be abusive to adults with whom they come into contact in daycare settings, (e.g. Klimes-Dougan & Kistner, 1990). In other words, their behavioural style shows a strong resemblance to that observed among abusive parents (e.g. Howes & Eldridge, 1985; Wolfe, 1985). Paradoxically, there is some evidence that within this preschool age group there is a tendency for abused children to rate themselves highly on peer acceptance, although this is in stark contrast to the opinions of their parents and teachers (Vondra *et al.*, 1990).

The socioemotional adjustment of school-age children may also be adversely affected by an early history of maltreatment. Regardless of the abuse they have suffered, there is a tendency for self-esteem to be depressed (Oates *et al.*, 1984; Kazdin *et al.*, 1985), behaviour to be more withdrawn or more aggressive (Straker & Jacobson, 1981) and peer relations to be impaired (Jacobson & Straker, 1982; Kaufman & Cicchetti, 1989). Attempts in recent years to try and draw specific cause-and-effect links between histories of neglect, emotional abuse and physical abuse and outcomes have less practical value than might be expected, probably because most children have been subjected to more than one form of maltreatment. No doubt there are substantial interactions between these variables, which serve to exacerbate the children's difficulties. However, one example of the limited evidence for abuse-behaviour specificity comes from a number of sources that suggest that being nominated as aggressive by one's peers is likely to be indicative of a history of physical rather than other forms of abuse (see Kohlberg *et al.*, 1984).

Overall, children who have been subjected to the most severe maltreatment, and have experienced a combination of neglect, emotional and physical abuse, suffer the greatest detriment to their socioemotional development. They experience problems with self-esteem, ego control and ego resiliency (Egeland *et al.*, 1983; Cicchetti & Olsen, 1991). A substantial minority of formerly neglected and abused children develop depressive disorders of clinical significance before puberty (Kaufman, 1991). A 10-year follow-up of formerly physically abused children has recently been completed in the UK (Gibbons *et al.*, 1992). Although there was no evidence, at a mean age of 11 years, for an excess of depressive symptomatology (Birleson, 1981), both teachers and parents rated formerly abused children more highly on a broad measure of behavioural and emotional maladjustment (Rutter, 1983).

Until the past few years little was known about the effects of early maltreatment upon children's social cognitive development. In other words, how they construct, interpret and structure their social world, what understanding they have of other's emotions, what attributions they ascribe to the behaviour of others, how they justify their own behaviour and how their moral judgements compare with those of nonmaltreated children (Smetana & Kelly, 1989). There is relatively little literature on this subject; it may be considered briefly under the broad headings of how maltreated children conceive of persons *qua* persons, social relations and social systems, including moral knowledge and social role-taking.

Investigations of the attributional style that is associated with a history of physical punishment have found affected children tend to take responsibility for their punishment, but beyond that only subtle differences distinguish abused from nonabused subjects (Herzberger *et al.*, 1981). However, Barahal *et al.* (1981) found that abused children were significantly less able to identify and label the emotional states of others, were less able to describe social and interpersonal causes of specific emotions and were less able to understand social roles than nonabused children. Interpretation of the findings of studies such as this must take into account potential group differences in intelligence and socioeconomic status. Differences between abused and nonabused children in respect of moral evaluations — a subject that has received very little attention — suggests that they do not differ when background variables are taken into account (Smetana *et al.*, 1984).

The detrimental impact of abuse and neglect upon cognitive development is well-recognized. Studies have consistently found that maltreated children usually score lower than expected on cognitive tests and demonstrate poorer school achievements than demographically matched peers (Hoffman-Plotkin & Twentyman, 1984). Intellectual impairments might result from a variety of sources. For example, many maltreated children are raised in social environments that are typified by a low degree of reciprocity, low rates of verbal interaction, limited playful exchanges and a lack of harmony (e.g. Wasserman *et al.*, 1983; Herrenkohl *et al.*, 1984). Occasionally adverse outcomes may result from neurological damage due to head injury or from inadequate nutrition. On the other hand, studies on the effects of other risk factors such as perinatal stress (Werner & Smith, 1982) and maternal mental

illness (e.g. Sameroff & Seifer, 1983) suggest that socioeconomic status also has a prominent role in determining the outcome of intellectual development. Accordingly, it has been necessary to attempt to distinguish the deleterious consequences of an upbringing in relative social deprivation from the direct effects of abuse and neglect. One way of approaching this task is to elucidate the mechanisms that link abuse and neglect with poor cognitive functioning. One strong possibility is that abused and neglected children lack motivation during testing, and this may account for their poor performance (Aber & Allen, 1987). To date, studies have merely confirmed that the two sets of variables are so closely related that it is a very difficult task to separate them. For example, Zigler and Butterfield (1968) proposed that socially deprived subjects may in general be unduly cautious and inhibited in the presence of unfamiliar adults, thereby compromising their ability to learn at school. Older maltreated children do show a relatively high incidence of language delay and deviation (e.g. Vondra *et al.*, 1990); compared to normative data, or to nonabused children of similar intelligence, they score significantly less well on standardized language tests and also on the verbal scales of intelligence tests (e.g. Blager & Martin, 1976; Oates *et al.*, 1984; Gibbons *et al.*, 1992). Methodological deficiencies in earlier studies, which made it impossible to conclude that observed scores resulted from abuse and neglect, rather than the broader effects of an upbringing in socially disadvantageous circumstances (Aber & Cicchetti, 1984), were addressed by Coster *et al.* (1989). They found that delays in syntactic development, vocabulary usage, functional communication and discourse in the language of maltreated children at the age of 30 months were most saliently related to their mother's concurrent style of communication.

In conclusion, cognitive competence is usually found to be impaired in maltreated children but it is often difficult to differentiate the adverse effects of abuse and neglect from the impact of an upbringing in socially disadvantageous circumstances. The two sources of detriment may be additive, or one may potentiate the effects of the other (Kaufman & Cicchetti, 1989; Vondra *et al.*, 1990). The interpersonal processes that provide a link between home experience and cognitive, motivational and self-perception differences between maltreated and nonmaltreated socioeconomically disadvantaged children have yet to be firmly established.

On the basis of evidence to date, it can merely be concluded that the home environments of maltreated children probably exert an adverse influence on their intellectual performance by providing care that fails to nurture their socioemotional development. Consequently ability to learn and ability to perform up to potential are inhibited (e.g. Giblin *et al.*, 1984; Tramontana *et al.*, 1988; Trickett & Susman, 1988).

In terms of the behavioural consequences of an upbringing in an abusive household upon younger children, the processes that lead to disorders of adjustment are rather better understood, due in large measure to the careful work of Patterson and his colleagues (Patterson, 1982; Patterson *et al.*, 1989). Their home observation methodology provided convincing evidence that parenting styles characterized by explosiveness, irritability and threats tend to train children in the use of aggressive behaviour. Children generalize this aggressive interpersonal style to interactions with peers and teachers at school (e.g. Patterson *et al.*, 1989; Simons *et al.*, 1991). Abusive families differ from nonabusive families in their handling of the 5–10% of parent–child interactions that are negative (Reid, 1984). Nonabusive families are able to conclude such potentially conflictual situations relatively quickly, but abusive families are ineffective in their attempts to provide control. Consequently members become enmeshed in escalating conflicts.

A survey among runaway and homeless youths in New York State during 1986–1987 found that the majority were girls between 15 and 16 years of age, of whom 60% claimed to have been physically abused by their families, 42% to have suffered emotional abuse, 48% neglect and 21% sexual abuse (Powers & Eckenrode, 1990). Biological mothers were the usual perpetrators of maltreatment (63%), followed next in frequency by biological fathers (45%). Factors that are frequently found to be associated with suicide attempts (e.g. conduct disorder, substance abuse, family discord; Shaffer *et al.*, 1988) are also characteristics commonly encountered amongst adolescent victims of abuse (e.g. Cavaiola & Schiff, 1989; Singer & Petchers, 1989; Power *et al.*, 1990). The consequences of abuse upon adolescent adjustment may be severe, and a causal relationship between abuse and attempted or completed suicide has been hypothesized (e.g. Farber *et al.*, 1984; Deykin *et al.*, 1985; Rotherham, 1987).

Finally, a link does seem to exist between history of victimization in childhood and subsequent antisocial, aggressive acts (Lewis *et al.*, 1989). The question of intergenerational transmission is discussed briefly below. Here we consider the evidence that there are continuities between the two phenomena within the life span of an individual (e.g. Garbarino & Plantz, 1986). Probably the best data on this subject come from an extraordinarily comprehensive study by Dodge *et al.* (1990) in which four hypotheses were addressed: (1) that the experience of severe physical harm in early childhood would increase a child's risk of later chronic aggressive behaviour, above and beyond the risk that accrued from related environmental and temperamental characteristics; (2) that such experiences would predict the later development of biased and deficient patterns in the processing of social information; (3) that such biased and deficient patterns would predict the occurrence of chronic aggressive behaviour; and (4) that social information-processing patterns would mediate the relationship between early physical harm and later aggression. The design entailed the longitudinal study of 309 4-year-old children from a range of socioeconomic backgrounds. Both home- and school-based measures were obtained and a wide range of observational and interview techniques were employed. Substantial support for the prior hypotheses was found.

Other data on the long-term effects of early maltreatment upon behaviour come from a small number of sources, anec-dotal and small-scale reports of violent homicidal offenders in clinical or penal institutions. Rosenbaum and Bennett (1986) and Sendi and Blomgren (1975) suggested that physical, sexual and/or psychological abuse can be found exceptionally commonly in their early childhood histories. Secondly, there are both prospective (Bolton *et al.*, 1977; Alfaro, 1981; McCord, 1983) and retrospective (Glueck & Glueck, 1950; Lewis & Shanok, 1977; Alfaro, 1981; Mouzakitis, 1981; Wick, 1981; Kratcoski, 1982) studies of the association between abuse and neglect and subsequent delinquency. The findings of these studies are not consistent, but they suggest that the risk is increased in the order of two to three times, compared with what would be expected on the basis of comparison data on nonabused adolescents.

Abuse and neglect may also have an adverse influence on children's physical growth. When this manifests in infancy the main effect is upon weight gain, and the condition is known as failure to thrive (FTT) or nonorganic failure to thrive (NOFT), to distinguish it from situations where the impaired growth results primarily from an organic disease or disorder. In later childhood, especially over the age of 3 years or so, the condition manifests as stunted linear growth and is variously known as abuse dwarfism or psychosocial dwarfism (e.g. Green *et al.*, 1984). These disorders are often confused with one another, but they should be differentiated on the grounds of distinct aetiologies, signs and symptoms, and prognoses.

The term failure to thrive is a symptom, and a presenting problem, that should be defined simply in terms of poor weight gain (Skuse, 1989a). In all cases of NOFT, and in many cases of FTT associated with organic disease, the proximate aetiology is insufficient nutrition (Frank & Zeisel, 1988). Because inadequate nutrition is the endpoint of an interaction involving a whole range of variables, it is exceptionally difficult to define the contributions made by each one of them. However, it is often, although not always, the case that NOFT arises within the context of deviant patterns of parent–child interaction which are specially prominent during feeding (Skuse *et al.*, 1992).

The earliest reports of NOFT reflected a presumption that the condition resulted from deprivation, and terms such as hospitalism, anaclitic depression and institutional syndrome were employed as synonyms (Spitz, 1945; Bowlby, 1951; Provence & Lipton, 1962). Whilst problems may well result from an upbringing in severely depriving and deleterious circumstances, it is fallacious to conclude that cases of FTT must, therefore, have been subjected to equivalent adversity. Accordingly, the importance of NOFT as a manifestation of abusive and neglectful childrearing practices has probably been overstated (Koel, 1969). A recent epidemiological study of a socioeconomically disadvantaged inner city area identified all cases of failure to thrive in the first year of life within one calendar year's birth cohort of 2607 children (Skuse *et al.*, 1992). Four years later all entries on the Child Protection Register of social service departments covering this area were matched to the original age–sex register. Infants who had been diagnosed NOFT were at approximately six times increased risk of subsequent abuse and/or neglect than those who had not failed to thrive; about 1 in 12 cases had been abused or neglected by 4 years of age, and their names had been entered on to the Register, for reasons other than the growth problem (Skuse *et al.*, 1992).

The impairment of linear growth in conditions of severe abuse and neglect is the hallmark of psychosocial short stature. The disorder has been recognized for many years (Talbot *et al.*, 1947) and several collections of case histories have been published (for review, see Green *et al.*, 1984, 1987). The diagnosis is rarely made before the age of 2 years (Blizzard & Bulatovic, 1992) and should be reserved for children with dysfunctional growth hormone secretion in which there is no significant element of associated malnutrition. The incidence of the condition is uncertain because there have been no epidemiological surveys that have systematically investigated this matter. Following gross and comprehensive maltreatment in which emotional and sexual abuse predominate, the children present with characteristic signs and symptoms. Physical signs include stunting, immature body proportions and near-normal weight for height, often with microcephaly (Marks *et al.*, 1978). Symptoms can be considered under four broad headings: (1) disorders of biological rhythms; (2) disorders of self-regulation; (3) disorders of mood; and (4) disorders of social relationships. Relevant biological rhythms include sleep, appetite and growth hormone release. Sleep is disrupted with frequent wakings and night wanderings, often in search of food. Active rapid eye movement sleep may be increased and stage 3 and 4 nonrapid eye movement sleep decreased (Taylor & Brook, 1986). Appetite is disturbed, normal hunger and satiety rhythms are lost, and there is an apparent inability to achieve satiation. Consequently these children habitually take food which they have been forbidden, steal food from their peers and — given the opportunity — gorge themselves until they vomit. Growth hormone release shows a diminished pulse amplitude (Stanhope *et al.*, 1988), meaning that the cumulated 24-hour circulating levels of the hormone are severely curtailed. Disordered self-regulation means deviant patterns of defecation, urination and attention. It is not uncommon to encounter a history that goes far beyond simple encopresis and enuresis to encompass features in which those bodily functions have acquired the quality of aggressive acts. Deliberate urination over other's belongings and the concealment of faeces or soiled clothes in public places are typical. Attention span is almost invariably brief. Receptive and expressive language skills are impaired; the children also have poor nonverbal skills and poor practical reasoning abilities (see Skuse *et al.*, 1990). At school they underfunction, and may require special education for moderate learning difficulties. Mood is almost invariably characterized by depression and poor self-esteem. Social relationships are always severely impaired; these children are disliked by virtually everybody with whom they come into contact, including siblings, peers, and schoolteachers as well as their parents. External validation for the condition comes from

a fairly well-recognized aetiology, in terms primarily of emotional abuse (which may be a necessary criterion) but the condition is often associated with physical abuse and sexual abuse too. The natural history is less well-documented. The growth problem often commences as failure to thrive in infancy but most cases of NOFT do not progress to psychosocial short stature (see Dowdney *et al.*, 1987). A cardinal feature is the potential for reversibility of all symptoms when the child is removed from the abusing environment (Money *et al.*, 1983; Skuse, 1989b, 1992). The rate of change in mental growth seems to run parallel to that of physical development, and is reflected by a progressive increase in intelligence. The bizarre behavioural features are usually lost within a few weeks of the child being taken into a caring and nurturing family, but if they persist for months or years the possibility that the abuse is also persisting should be considered. The increase in height velocity is often dramatic, and pathognomonic. Children's stature catches up to a trajectory far closer to their genetic potential.

Further data on the association between growth retardation, intellectual performance and catch-up growth in a large sample of abused and neglected children have been provided by Taitz and his colleagues (King & Taitz, 1985; Taitz & King, 1988a,b).

RISK FACTORS

In recent years there have been increasingly sophisticated attempts to combine environmental, social and personal components that are known to contribute to child abuse into theoretical frameworks that allegedly have some predictive value. Belsky's (1980) ecological model, which draws on Bronfenbrenner's (1979) approach to the study of child development, has been especially influential. This posits an integrated series of interactions between ontogenic factors measured at various levels. The most proximal to the child is the so-called microsystem, which comprises the child's own characteristics and immediate environment. The next most proximal is the exosystem, which includes social factors that impinge on the family at risk of abuse. Finally, there is the macrosystem, or the larger cultural fabric which comprises broad societal attitudes to violence and related matters. At each level of this complex interacting system variables known to be associated with increased risk are entered.

Inherent in the way this model operates is the premise that certain characteristics of the abuser may predispose him or her to engage in abusive behaviour. That individual's style of parenting will in turn reflect his or her own developmental history, knowledge of childrearing, mental state and social milieu. One way of approaching the question of which are the important antecedents of child abuse is to examine factors that are associated with a broader range of parenting difficulties (Rutter, 1989a). Evidence suggests that there is little specificity about the antecedents of abusive behaviour as such; it may more accurately be considered an aspect of parenting failure in the broader sense. Accordingly, when considering relevant risk factors, and how they operate, it may be useful to outline those aspects of parenting that make for satisfactory nonabusive relationships.

Firstly, there are basic parenting skills that are used in the day-to-day management of child behaviour and that promote development (Maccoby & Martin, 1983; Rutter, 1983). The children of those who lack such skills may be at higher risk of neglect or abuse, but the evidence on this matter is scanty. Women brought up in institutions would have had relatively little opportunity to learn such skills by observation, but they would also have been subject to a variety of other deprivations and distortions of early experience (Rutter, 1983; Quinton & Rutter, 1988). Similarly, although mentally retarded parents may be regarded as another population at risk, the evidence on rates of abuse and neglect among their children is not clear-cut (Dowdney & Skuse, 1993). Other characteristics that are believed to be relevant include the parent's psychological maturity (Newberger & Cook, 1983; Ross & Zigler, 1983). Comparisons of teenage and older mothers have come up with consistent findings; young mothers in general have less desirable childrearing attitudes and have less realistic expectations for their infant's development than do older mothers (Belsky & Vondra, 1989). Their actual parenting practices are less adaptive to their children's welfare (Levine *et al.*, 1984). Of course, parents learn from the experience of bringing up their firstborn child and for that reason we might expect that second or subsequent-born children would be less at risk of abuse or neglect by such vulnerable subjects. However, in general, abused children tend to come from large families and the smallest percentage of abusing families are those with just one child (Light, 1973; Zigler, 1976).

The contribution made by attributional processes to parenting style, and consequently the risk of abuse, has become a matter of increasing interest in recent years. By attributions we mean beliefs about the causes of child behaviours and of care-giving outcomes (Bugental *et al.*, 1989). Clinical analyses of the personalities of child-abusing parents provide support for the role of such processes in shaping parenting practices (Rosenberg & Reppucci, 1983). Larrance and Twentyman (1983) noted that abusive mothers made more stable and global attributions for their children's negative behaviour, and less stable, global attributions for their positive behaviours. In other words, they had a tendency to adopt rigid, so-called categorical conceptions of their child's personal characteristics (Sameroff & Feil, 1985) in which the offspring's disposition is perceived to possess enduring negative attributes, such as stubbornness and irritability. Common behaviours, such as crying, may be perceived negatively and increase the risk of abuse. Abusive or potentially abusive parents seem to respond to cries of a certain pitch more aversively than comparisons (Crowe & Zeskind, 1992). Abusive parents appear to perceive that they themselves have very little power to control care-giving outcomes, whereas their children have a great deal of power. Bugental and Shennum (1984) found that parents who assigned high importance to external, unstable events (luck) and low importance to internal stable factors (their own ability) as causes of care-giving success were particularly reactive to aversive and unresponsive children. Where the child posed an interpersonal problem and the environment provided few clues as to what would be a reasonable or appropriate response, adults at high risk of abuse were guided in their response primarily by negative attributes. That these theoretical models of predisposition to abusive behaviour have practical importance has been explored by Bugental *et al.* (1989) and Sylvester (1990).

The contribution made by poor mental health depends upon the nature and aetiology of that condition. Families in which the parent is suffering from a major psychotic illness such as schizophrenia may not differ from controls in the amount of time spent with their infants, or the adequacy of the biological care they provide, but there are quantifiable differences in psychological aspects of the nurturance they provide (Walker & Emory, 1983; Sameroff *et al.*, 1984). The children of schizophrenic parents may not be at higher risk of abuse or neglect but they do have higher rates of psychiatric disturbance (especially borderline and personality disorders) than do children of affectively disordered parents, or those of normal controls (Erlenmeyer-Kimling & Cornblatt, 1987; Weintraub, 1987).

Rather more attention has been paid to the risks attributable to depressive disorders (Downey & Coyne, 1990; Rutter, 1990). Retrospective reports suggest the association between parental depression and depressive disorders in their adult children is mediated largely by harsh and unfair parenting practices and such parenting is also believed to have aetiological significance for some cases of depression in childhood (Burbach & Borduin, 1986). However, the issue is complicated by the fact that unhappy maladjusted children may reciprocate their parent's behaviour in the sense that difficulties beget difficulties, irritability and negative exchanges being initiated by both parties. Accordingly, the independent contribution made by the parent's depressive illness *per se* to the children's later maladjustment is hard to determine (Hammen *et al.*, 1987; Radke-Yarrow *et al.*, 1991). Furthermore, because there is, on the whole, little specificity between the presence of mental disorder in a parent and the risk to the child, the construction of explanatory models is complex (Downey & Coyne, 1990; Rutter, 1990). For example, some of the association between depression and both parenting problems and child maladjustment may be spurious, with the same interpersonal factors (for example, marital discord) that produce depression in mothers also producing parenting and child problems.

The importance of viewing parenting difficulties within a broader social context was emphasized by Rutter (1989b). Risks may be increased in circumstances where there is excessive stress, or when dealing with an especially difficult child, or if the parent lacks effective social supports (Crnic *et al.*, 1983; Belsky, 1984). When assessing risk it is important to bear in mind that these factors in turn reflect personality strengths and weaknesses, and the ability to elicit and attract support (Cohen & Syme, 1985; Rutter, 1985).

Certain characteristics of children themselves may put them at increased risk of being abused, and a number of these have been recognized for some years. Perinatal factors, such as low birth weight and prematurity (Lynch & Roberts, 1982; Benedict & White, 1985), are relevant, possibly because such infants function within a narrower band of optimal arousal (Field, 1993). Consequently, they might be regarded as having more difficult temperaments and dispositions than the average infant (Power *et al.*, 1990). An aversive cry, especially if related to neurological disorders, may be a significant source of parental stress and a substantial contributory factor (Frodi, 1981; Donovan & Leavitt, 1985). Coercive and oppositional behaviour in older abused children may put them at increased risk (Wolfe & Mosk, 1983; Lahey *et al.*, 1984), although it is difficult to determine the direction of cause and effect (Lorber *et al.*, 1984; Dowdney & Pickles, 1991). Boys may be subject to different abusive experiences than girls (Agathonos *et al.*, 1982). In countries where girls are less valued than boys they may be relatively neglected, both in terms of nutrition (McKee, 1984) and medical care (Korbin, 1991).

Children with chronic illnesses or disabilities, including mental and physical handicaps, also tend to place high emotional, physical, economic and social demands upon their families (Ammerman *et al.*, 1988). Early studies suggested that such children were at higher risk of maltreatment, but an inadequate account was taken of the fact that the disability could either have antedated or be a consequence of the abuse (Ammerman *et al.*, 1989). Although children suffering from chronic mental and physical handicaps may indeed be over-represented among the population of abused children, studies to date have been flawed methodologically (White *et al.*, 1987) and no coherent theoretical model has been proposed to account for the alleged increased degree of risk (Westcott, 1991).

A number of studies have demonstrated a significant association between socioeconomic circumstances and child maltreatment, such that abuse occurs more frequently among lower socioeconomic status families (Straus & Gelles, 1986). Relevant variables have been reported to include a lack of social supports, such as an extended family (Polansky *et al.*, 1985; Gaudin & Polansky, 1986), high stress levels within the family (Browne, 1986), and recent adverse life events (Justice *et al.*, 1985). The quality of the marital relationship also exerts an important influence, although this may be indirect, rather than directly acting upon parenting style (Belsky & Vondra, 1989).

Little research has focused on the processes that could account for the relationship between socioeconomic status and abuse rates, although one possibility is the known association between lower socioeconomic status and greater use of authoritarian punishment, lower parental involvement and nurturance, and a lack of emphasis on independence (Gecas, 1979). Trickett *et al.* (1991) found strong support for the hypothesis that, even within lower socioeconomic status homes, abusing households can be distinguished from non-abusing homes of similar social status. Relevant factors include heightened conflict, disciplinary techniques that exert undue control and are punitive (Wolfe, 1985; Trickett & Kuczynski, 1986), as well as rather striking differences in their emotional climate.

A picture thus emerges of worried parents with little enjoyment of parenting, little satisfaction with and expressed affection for their child, isolation from the wider community and a lack of encouragement for the development of autonomy and independence in their child. Yet these abusing parents also expect high standards of achievement.

Society's own attitude to the abuse of children may well be relevant. When Sweden introduced legislation prohibiting parents from physically punishing their children, the aim was not primarily to institute a series of prosecutions for a common parenting practice but to change the climate of opinion toward corporal punishment so as to make it less acceptable to society at large (Commission on Children's Rights, 1978). Perhaps societal attitudes towards violence and societal expectations about what is appropriate discipline at home and at school are of considerable importance (Zigler & Hall, 1989). So long as violence is portrayed by the media for its entertainment value (Friedrich-Cofer & Huston, 1986) and corporal punishment within the home is the rule rather than the exception (e.g. Straus *et al.*, 1980), the use of physical force as either a method of behavioural control or as an expression of anger and frustration may seem to be condoned by society (for review, see Widom, 1989).

Although being abused as a child is not a necessary or sufficient cause of becoming an abusive parent, the way in which adults conceptualize their childhood contributes significantly to the way in which they view and practice childrearing (Altemeier *et al.*, 1982; Egeland & Jakobvitz, 1984; Main & Goldwyn, 1984; Kaufman & Zigler, 1987). Both professional child care workers and indeed the general public tend to assume that harsh parenting styles are transmitted across generations, but several researchers have noted significant limitations in the data cited in support of that relationship (Kaufman & Zigler, 1987; Burgess & Youngblade, 1988). Research during the 1960s and early 1970s suggested a strong association between engaging in abusive parenting and having been a victim of maltreatment (Kempe *et al.*, 1962; Fontana, 1968; Silver *et al.*, 1969; Green *et al.*, 1974). Recent studies, using greater methodological rigour, have found only a modest association between a history of harsh and abusive parenting and current parenting practices in the next generation (Herrenkohl *et al.*, 1983; Straus, 1983; Egeland *et al.*, 1987; Rutter, 1989b).

Speculation about the processes that mediate intergenerational effects are often couched in terms of social learning theory (Burgess, 1979; Gelles & Straus, 1979; Straus, 1983; Burgess & Youngblade, 1988). Researchers sharing this perspective believe that harsh parenting influences the next generation through a process of modelling and reinforcement. However, opinions are diverse about what exactly is learned;

whether, for example, severe coercive measures are part of normal parenting (Straus *et al.*, 1980), those who have experienced such parenting simply going on to use harsh parenting methods with their own children in an unthinking way (Simons *et al.*, 1991), or whether the abused individual develops a consciously applied set of rules or normative beliefs (Bandura, 1986) concerning the desirability or perhaps even the necessity of strict physical discipline as an approach to childrearing.

As discussed, Patterson and his colleagues (Patterson, 1982; Patterson *et al.*, 1989) have provided convincing evidence that parenting style characterized by explosiveness and irritability and threats tends to train a child in the use of aggressive behaviour and an aggressive approach to social interactions in general could be transmitted across generations (Burgess & Youngblade, 1988) as a result of hostile parenting practices (Elder *et al.*, 1986; Caspi & Elder, 1988; Simons *et al.*, 1991).

Gender factors may be important in determining harsh and abusive parenting styles, yet most studies exclude fathers (Biller & Solomon, 1986; Wolfe, 1987). This is strange, because fathers are involved in a substantial proportion of violent parenting incidents (Straus *et al.*, 1980) and because the causal mechanisms at work may differ by gender of parent. A recent study by Simons *et al.* (1991) showed that grandparents who had engaged in aggressive parenting produced present-day parents who were likely to use similar parenting practices but the effect was stronger for mothers than for fathers, regardless of the gender of their children.

In summary, the major determinants of parenting behaviour will be the personality and psychological well-being of that individual, his or her own experience of parenting practices, the characteristics of the child, socioeconomic influences and contextual sources of stress and support. The role played by broader societal influences has not yet been established. Parental competence is multiply determined and consequently is buffered against threats from any single source (Belsky & Vondra, 1989).

INTERVENTION

Educational and therapeutic approaches to the subject of child abuse may be considered at the primary, secondary and tertiary levels. By primary prevention we refer to the means by which abuse and neglect are averted entirely. This approach might be initiated by parentcraft classes in schools, for prospective parents during the antenatal period, or for vulnerable high-risk groups such as teenage parents. Other techniques which would fall within the ambit of primary prevention include the initiation of legislation which reflects society's attitude towards proscribed childrearing practices.

Secondary prevention refers to the engagement of families who have already abused with a view to forestalling further abusive episodes, involving either the affected individuals or their siblings. Under this heading we will consider issues pertinent to rehabilitation. By tertiary prevention we refer

specifically to the importance of targeting parents, or potential parents, who were themselves victims of abuse and who are believed to be at especial risk of acting in ways detrimental to the mental and physical welfare of their own children.

Primary prevention

Gelles and Cornell (1985) suggested, apparently in a utopian frame of mind, that effective primary prevention of family violence might be enacted by 'the elimination of norms that legitimate and glorify violence in society and the family, such as the use of violence as a form of media entertainment; that stresses such as poverty and inequality of opportunity should be abolished; that families should be incorporated into a network of kin and community, to reduce social isolation; that the sexist characteristics of society should be changed by educational development, and that families should be taught alternatives to violence as a means of controlling their children's behaviour'.

Because no single causal influence can explain maltreatment, preventive interventions that proceed on the assumption that by dealing with one or two obvious risk factors, a significant reduction in risk will ensue, are unlikely to be successful. For example, a lack of social support is associated with high risk in some groups. Yet, intervention aimed at broadening and strengthening social networks fails because parents at risk for maltreatment often lack the social skills to take advantage of the social supports made available to them, and because their social isolation may be more of a symptom than a cause of their maltreating behaviour (Olds & Henderson, 1989).

Parent education classes for new parents may have benefits for those who are most motivated to attend, but probably make little impact upon those families who are at highest risk because of their apathy or antipathy towards such facilities. Similarly, one might argue that a reduction in unemployment could play an important role in the primary prevention of abuse and neglect, in view of the known association between these phenomena (Jones & McCurdy, 1992). However, macroeconomic forces determine unemployment levels in ways that seem well beyond even the scope of governments to control; all that can be hoped is that high-risk families might be assisted on a case-by-case basis. Indeed, society-wide secular changes are such that the number of individuals at risk may be increasing rather than reducing.

Primary prevention strategies have been reviewed by Gough (1989); chief among them was home visitation (Gray *et al.*, 1979; Siegel *et al.*, 1980; Lealman *et al.*, 1983), which has been proposed as a potent means of preventing child maltreatment (Kempe, 1976; Olds, 1981, 1982, 1983). A comprehensive home visitation service was rigorously evaluated by Olds and Henderson (1989), choosing as their at-risk sample first-time mothers who were in their teens, and/or single parents, and/or of low socioeconomic status, and enrolling them in the second trimester of pregnancy. The aim of the home visitation was to provide both educational and social support simultaneously. In view of the intensity of the intervention, sample size in each of the four treatment groups was relatively small. Nevertheless over the first 2 years of the children's lives a strong, although statistically nonsignificant, trend was found for fewer confirmed reports of abuse and neglect in the case group families who were visited regularly by a nurse.

In the UK, nonprofessional social support is sometimes provided by volunteers in the community as in programmes such as Homestart (van der Eyken, 1982) and Newpin (Cox *et al.*, 1991). Trained but nonprofessional peers assist parents in practical tasks, providing emotional support and a sounding board. Despite the enthusiasm of the subjects of such interventions for the services provided, it has proved difficult to demonstrate that substantial benefits accrue when the projects are evaluated with the aid of comparison groups.

Over the past decade or so numerous efforts have been made to compile checklists which, when used antenatally, would allow the identification of families at especially high risk of maltreating their children. Not unreasonably, it has been argued that any preventive strategy should aim to use resources efficiently, and the first step would be to distinguish those most in need. For example, Kempe and Kempe (1978) compiled a set of characteristics of abusing families for which they claimed 76% accuracy, from observations made during the first 24 hours after birth. They subsequently suggested screening for potential abusers should be a routine part of all obstetric and postnatal care (Dean *et al.*, 1978). Unfortunately, such screening tests are unlikely to find wide acceptance for the simple reason that abuse is a relatively rare phenomenon; that is to say, it has a very low prevalence. Any screening instrument will fail to perform efficiently in such circumstances. Even if it were possible to design a checklist that had 95% sensitivity and specificity, it would lose positive predictive value and gain negative predictive value as prevalence falls. Accordingly, it can be shown that if the prevalence of the condition of interest is, say, 0.5% then the predictive value of a positive result with such an exceptional instrument would be just 9% (Sackett *et al.*, 1985). Exactly in line with expectations, Browne and Saqi (1987) carried out a prospective study on over 4000 births in the south of England. They found 6.8% (965) were high-risk families, as identified by their screening instrument. Over the next 2 years, 106 (0.74%) of the original cohort were subject to case conference proceedings for suspected abuse, of whom just over two-thirds had earlier been identified as high-risk. The positive predictive value of their screening instrument was thus 7.5%. In the US Altemeier *et al.* (1979) devised a comprehensive screening interview which was given to 1400 expectant mothers, of whom 19.5% were consequently considered to be at high risk. When those children were 21–48-months-old, Tennessee state records were searched for reports of abuse with injury or failure to thrive (Altemeier *et al.*, 1982, 1984). From the data presented, the interview can be shown to have a sensitivity of 44% and a specificity of 81%, in its ability to predict abuse of the target child. Given the very low prevalence

of that outcome (just 1.3%) this translates into a positive predictive value of 3%. Refining the criteria associated with risk is unlikely to improve matters; the poor practical performance of screening instruments for child abuse is related to a statistical, not a design, problem.

Secondary prevention

Secondary prevention refers to interventions that are designed to work with families who have already abused one child and who are believed to be at high risk of doing so again. A variety of techniques has been employed, but distinctions are not usually made between approaches that would be suitable for physical abuse, emotional abuse or neglect.

In general the success of treatment is likely to be influenced by the following considerations, which are based upon frameworks of assessment proposed by Bentovim *et al.* (1987) and Kempe and Goldbloom (1987). The issues that require assessment are firstly, when confronted with failure to provide adequate care, what degree of responsibility do parents take for the state of the child? How aware are they of the need to change their behaviour? Secondly, what evidence is there that family members can put the needs of the child before their own? To what extent do they adopt an attitude that blames the victim for his or her own abuse? Thirdly, to what extent is there a recognition by the parents that, if relevant, they should accept help for long-standing personal, marital or relationship problems, including states of psychiatric disorder and drug or alcohol abuse? Fourthly, to what extent are they willing to cooperate with professionals in the process of treatment? Fifthly, to what extent do the parents show a potential for change, flexibility, and a willingness to try and find different approaches to problem-solving within a time scale that is appropriate for their child? Finally, to what extent are professional resources to treat the problem available? On the basis of responses to these key questions the prospect of a successful outcome of intervention can be rated in the following terms:

Hopeful when family members acknowledge their role and responsibility for the abused status of the child, do not blame the child, and are willing to work on problems. In addition there is appropriate agency support.

Doubtful when there is uncertainty as to whether the adults in question do take responsibility for the abuse. Some attribution of responsibility to the child may be evident, together with limited acknowledgement of their need to change, either at a personal or at a family-wide level.

Hopeless is a term applied to situations where the parents do not begin to acknowledge their role in perpetrating abuse or neglect. There may be denial, blaming of professionals or intense anger, together with a feeling of being scapegoated and blamed for the child's condition. Other major problems may coexist, including alcoholism, psychiatric illness, and a long-standing history of violence. Even if professional resources exist, there is little hope of any cooperation.

Application of these guidelines within the context of treatment programmes may allow a reasonably successful prediction of outcome. Asen *et al.* (1989) used such an approach to differentiate families into risk categories; 30% were assigned into the hopeless category and rehabilitation was not attempted. However, of those who were rehabilitated because of their hopeful status, just 3% were reabused. A complementary approach, by which the progress of families actually during treatment can be monitored, was proposed by Smith and Rachman (1984). Their aim was to select target problems on which the family was prepared to work and which the clinician felt were reasonable short-term goals. There was then a brief period of work with the family and, depending on the outcome of this initial phase, plans could then be made for a further intervention phase, or for termination of treatment. The point is that the decision could be made on the basis of evidence, rather than merely a subjective professional opinion. If treatment were to be continued, it could be planned as a series of focused interventions graded as to difficulty, with continuing regular interdisciplinary reviews of progress (Gilgun, 1988; Nicol *et al.*, 1988). If either of these approaches to intervention with abusing families were to be widely implemented, scarce resources would not be wasted on families unable to change at a rate necessary for the welfare of their own children (Jones, 1987).

Specific techniques of secondary prevention of physical abuse are now considered. Within the past 15 years, interventions based on learning theory emerged as potentially useful modes of treatment (Ammerman, 1989; Azar & Siegel, 1990), based on the presumption that five broad areas of disturbance are at the root of abusive parental behaviours across all periods of childhood. These are: (1) maladaptive interpretive processes, including unrealistic expectations of child behaviour and capabilities, poor problem-solving skills, and negative interpretations of (attributions for) child behaviour; (2) poor parenting strategies; (3) poor impulse control; (4) difficulty coping with stress; and (5) deficient social skills.

Given the crucial role that cognitions play in producing aggression under stress (Averill, 1983), cognitive work may be a useful prerequisite to other approaches to treatment. Application of parent-training techniques in community-based programmes has produced mixed evidence of success (Lutzker *et al.*, 1984; Szykula & Fleischman, 1985). Barth *et al.* (1983) provided examples of cognitive behavioural approaches to self-control training that may be of value for parents of infants and toddlers (Sanders, 1978; St James-Roberts, 1989). Others have attempted to promote positive and responsive parent–infant interaction (Wolfe *et al.*, 1988), using feedback during home observations to increase parental responsiveness and sensitivity to that child (Olds *et al.*, 1986). Education in safety practices may be important (Tertinger *et al.*, 1984). In families with older children, developmental education, cognitive restructuring and problem-solving training have been used to shift negative biases, challenge unrealistic expectations of child behaviour and increase parents' ability to generate and select alternative nonabusive responses (Dawson *et al.*, 1986; Azar, 1989). Other important strategies include anger-control

training (Novaco, 1975), stress-management training and relaxation techniques. Although most evaluations have been in the form of single case studies (Isaacs, 1982; Azar & Wolfe, 1989), there are encouraging signs that such techniques really are effective in changing parental behaviours. However, alterations in the children's contribution to interactions as a result of these interventions is less clear.

Finally, despite estimates that a high proportion of abusive incidents involve adolescents (Garbarino, 1989), there is almost no literature on interventions with abusing parents of adolescent children. Azar and Siegel (1990) suggest targets during this period might include improving communication and negotiation strategies, cognitive restructuring to decrease unrealistic expectations regarding adolescent behaviour and misinterpretations of developmentally normal responses, anger-control training, and training contingency management techniques.

Interventions with families who are seriously neglectful of their child's welfare have received less attention than those who have been responsible for overt acts of physical or sexual abuse. An interesting series of interventions has been described by Lutzker (1990), involving referrals for neglect to an Illinois department of child and family services (Lutzker *et al.*, 1984). The focus of work was upon personal cleanliness, nutrition, home safety and cleanliness demonstrations of affect during parent–child interaction, improved physical health and cognitive stimulation.

Unfortunately, despite all the optimism about the success of individual case studies, or small-scale research studies aimed at the secondary prevention of child abuse, the broad picture is not encouraging. Whereas individually tailored approaches may be effective, there is as yet no evidence for the success of treatment efforts in general. In an extensive review of 89 treatment programmes in the US, involving 3253 families, Cohn and Daro (1987) found one-third or more of parents continued to mistreat their children whilst in treatment and over half the families treated were considered likely to continue to mistreat their children following termination of treatment. The implication of this grim prospect is that greater care should now be given to the identification of families who are likely to be successful in the course of treatment or rehabilitation; British studies that have attempted in recent years to intervene with relatively unselected samples have produced similarly pessimistic findings (Smith & Rachman, 1984; Nicol *et al.*, 1988).

FUTURE DIRECTIONS FOR RESEARCH

To date, much research on child abuse has been methodologically flawed and limited in its generalizability, scientific validity and, ultimately, in its relevance for policy (Widom, 1989). If future research is to rectify these deficiencies it will have to take into account the following points.

Firstly, the design of any study that aims to investigate child abuse and neglect should be linked closely to prior hypotheses. Rarely have these been made explicit, but broadly speaking they fall into two main categories: hypotheses on the potential aetiological influences upon abuse and neglect, and hypotheses on the outcome of childhood maltreatment. A sound approach to these issues entails rigorous attention to the strategy and tactics of relevant methodology. For many purposes the prospective case-comparison design would be appropriate, with power estimates of adequate sample size undertaken beforehand.

Secondly, it is important to bear in mind that criteria for child abuse and neglect vary widely. There is a strong tendency for psychological and physical maltreatment to be confounded in most studies, although there are major methodological difficulties inherent in differentiating their effects because of co-occurrence. Nevertheless there is a need to distinguish a history of neglect from that of overt abuse. Treating these experiences as equivalent or inextricably linked, or studying only one or other form of abuse, may obscure important differences in their consequences.

A few years ago one of the greatest challenges facing clinicians was the identification and appraisal of sexual abuse among children. The fruits of the considerable efforts put into understanding this subject are summarized in Chapter 14. Now, an even greater challenge will be to define and consequently identify the scope of emotional abuse. Where the nature of the abusive experience and its consequences upon development are likely to be purely psychological, legal sanctions for child protection can prove hard to apply. Clarification of this subject will greatly assist those concerned with child protection.

We also need to be aware, both in research and in clinical practice, that the outcome of physical and emotional maltreatment is very likely to be influenced by the nature and severity of the abuse or neglect, by the age of the children at which the abuse occurred (Rutter, 1983), the characteristics of the perpetrator (Adam-Tucker, 1982), the characteristics of the child, including his or her level of intelligence (Frodi & Smetana, 1984) and the abused child's perception of his or her experiences as a victim (Herzberger *et al.*, 1981). Not all children will react to those experiences in the same way; we do need to understand more about the role played by so-called protective and vulnerability factors in developmental psychopathology (Rutter, 1989a).

We have already emphasized the need to undertake more prospective studies of children who are either at exceptionally high risk of abuse, or who have actually been abused. There is a danger that conclusions about risk and other matters solely upon the basis of retrospective recall by victims of abuse may be misleading, because of systematic distortions in their perception of earlier events (see Femina *et al.*, 1990). When we plan such studies we should bear in mind the choice of appropriate comparison groups that enhances our ability to draw conclusions about variables that predispose to, or are apparent consequences of abuse and neglect. Confounding by such characteristics as poverty, unemployment, parental alcoholism, drug dependence and other aspects of suboptimal social and family functioning can be a major problem,

especially when considering risk in relationship to socio-economic status. These issues were elegantly addressed by the study by Dodge *et al.* (1990) on the long-term consequences of early maltreatment.

For a whole variety of reasons, samples of abused children that have been intensively studied are almost inevitably unrepresentative of the generality of similarly maltreated subjects, because of potential distortions at a number of different levels. These range from biases in the identification of cases within a community to selective recruitment into clinical programmes and treatment centres. Not infrequently, sample sizes are far too small to possess adequate power for conventional statistical analysis but this may simply reflect difficulties in recruitment. We need to consider new approaches; for example, more intensive investigations of children and their families that are designed to be hypothesis-generating, rather than just applying conventional measures in an unthinking stereotypical fashion. Novel approaches to statistical analysis may also be employed, with a view to data exploration as opposed to the sterile search for statistical significance.

Finally, there is the thorny issue of prevention. Is it conceivable that, through education, the provision of resources targeted at those most at risk, or through structured changes in society at large, the incidence of child maltreatment might be reduced? In some respects the signs are encouraging. Certainly, institutionalized physical punishment (as applied, for example, within schools) is on the way out in Europe, as a consequence of legislation. Perhaps, over the next decade or so, we shall see the wider application of legislation aimed, as in Sweden, at discouraging parental physical chastisement of their children. Emotional abuse and neglect might possibly be reduced through increasing understanding, by education, among potential parents, of relevant issues in child development. As the average family size shrinks and so children have far less opportunity than formerly to observe and interact with infants and toddlers, formal instruction on these matters becomes increasingly desirable. Finally, despite the ubiquitous emphasis upon the dependent preschool child, in the literature on physical and emotional maltreatment let us not forget the vulnerable adolescent.

REFERENCES

Aber J.L. & Allen J.P. (1987) The effects of maltreatment on young children's socioemotional development: an attachment theory perspective. *Developmental Psychology*, **23**, 406−414.

Aber J.L. & Cicchetti D. (1984) Socioemotional development in maltreated children: an empirical and theoretical analysis. In: Fitzgerald J., Lester B. & Yogman M. (eds) *Theory and Research in Behavioral Pediatrics, vol. II.* Plenum, New York.

Aber J.L. & Zigler E. (1981) Developmental considerations in the definition of child maltreatment. *New Directions for Child Development*, **11**, 1−29.

Aber J.L., Allen J.P., Carlson V. & Cicchetti D. (1989) The effects of maltreatment on development during early childhood: recent studies and their theoretical, clinical and policy implications. In: Cicchetti D. & Carlson V. (eds) *Child Maltreatment. Theory and Research on the Causes and Consequences of Child Abuse and Neglect,* pp. 579–619. Cambridge University Press, New York.

Adam-Tucker C. (1982) Proximate effects of sexual abuse in childhood: a report on 28 children. *American Journal of Psychiatry*, **13**, 1252–1256.

Agathonos H., Stathacopoulou N., Adams H. & Nakou S. (1982) Child abuse and neglect in Greece: sociomedical aspects. *Child Abuse and Neglect*, **6**, 307–311.

Alfaro J.D. (1981) Report on the relationship between child abuse and neglect and later socially deviant behavior. In: Hunner R.J. & Walker Y.E. (eds) *Exploring the Relationship between Child Abuse and Delinquency*. Allanheld, Osman, Montclair, NJ.

Altemeier W., Vietze P.M., Sherrod K.B., Sandler H.M. & Falsey S. & O'Connor S. (1979) Prediction of child maltreatment during pregnancy. *Journal of the American Academy of Child Psychiatry*, **18**, 205–218.

Altemeier W., O'Connor S., Vietze P., Sandler H. & Sherrod K. (1982) Antecedents of child abuse. *Journal of Pediatrics*, **100**, 823–829.

Altemeier W., O'Connor S., Vietze P., Sandler H. & Sherrod K. (1984) Prediction of child abuse: a prospective study of feasibility. *Child Abuse and Neglect*, **8**, 393–400.

Ammerman R.T. (1989) Child abuse and neglect. In: Hersen M. (ed) *Innovations in Child Behavior Therapy*, pp. 353–394. Springer, New York.

Ammerman R.T., van Hassels V.B. & Hemem M. (1988) Abuse and neglect in handicapped children: a critical review. *Journal of Family Violence*, **3**, 53–72.

Ammerman R.T., van Hasselt V.B., Hersen M., McGonigle J.J. & Lubetsky M.J. (1989) Abuse and neglect in psychiatrically hospitalized multihandicapped children. *Child Abuse and Neglect*, **13**, 335–344.

Asen K., George R., Piper R. & Stevens A. (1989) A systems approach to child abuse: management and treatment issues. *Child Abuse and Neglect*, **13**, 45–88.

Averill J.R. (1983) Studies of anger and aggression. Implications for theories of emotion. *American Psychologist*, **38**, 1145–1160.

Azar S.T. (1989) Training parents of abused children. In: Schaefer C.E. & Briesmiester J.M. (eds) *Handbook of Parenting Training: Parents as Cotherapists for Children's Behavior Problems*, pp. 414–441. John Wiley, New York.

Azar S.T. & Siegel B.R. (1990) Behavioral treatment of child abuse: a developmental perspective. *Behavior Modification*, **14**, 279–300.

Azar S.T. & Wolfe D.A. (1989) Child abuse and neglect. In: Mash E.J. & Barkley R.A. (eds) *Treatment of Childhood Disorders*, pp. 451–489. Guilford, New York.

Bandura A. (1986) *Social Foundations of Thought and Action*. Prentice-Hall, Englewood Cliffs, NJ.

Barahal R., Waterman J. & Martin H.P. (1981) The social cognitive development of abused children. *Journal of Consulting and Clinical Psychology*, **49**, 508–516.

Barth R.P., Blythe B.J., Schinke S.P. & Schilling R.F. (1983) Self-control training with maltreating parents. *Child Welfare*, **62**, 313–324.

Belsky J. (1980) Child maltreatment: an ecological integration. *American Psychologist*, **35**, 320–335.

Belsky J. (1984) The determinants of parenting: a process model. *Child Development*, **55**, 83–96.

Belsky J. & Vondra J. (1989) Lessons from child abuse: the determinants of parenting. In: Cicchetti D. & Carlson V. (eds) *Child Maltreatment. Theory and Research on the Causes and Consequences of Child Abuse and Neglect*, pp. 153–202. Cambridge University Press, New York.

Benedict M.I. & White R.B. (1985) Selected perinatal factors and child abuse. *American Journal of Public Health*, **75**, 780–781.

Benthall J. (1991) Invisible wounds: corporal punishment in British schools as a form of ritual. *Child Abuse and Neglect*, **15**, 377–388.

Bentovim A., Elton A. & Tranter M. (1987) Prognosis for rehabilitation after abuse. *Adoption and Fostering*, **11**, 26–31.

Berdie J., Berdie M., Wexler S. & Fisher B. (1983) *An Empirical Study of Families Involved in Adolescent Maltreatment*. URSA Institute, San Francisco.

Biller H.B. & Solomon R.S. (1986) *Child Maltreatment and Paternal Deprivation: A Manifesto for Research, Prevention and Treatment*. Lexington, Lexington, MA.

Billmire M.E. & Myers P.A. (1985) Serious head injury in infants: accident or abuse? *Pediatrics*, **75**, 340–342.

Birleson P. (1981) The validity of depressive disorder in childhood and the development of a self-rating scale: a research report. *Journal of Child Psychology and Psychiatry*, **22**, 73–88.

Blager F. & Martin H.P. (1976) Speech and language of abused children. In: Martin H.P. (ed) *The Abused Child*. Ballinger, Cambridge, MA.

Blizzard R.M. & Bulatovic A. Psychological short stature: a syndrome with many variables. In: *Ballière's Clinical Endocrinology and Metabolism*, vol. 6, No. 3, July 1993, pp. 687–712. Ballière Tindall, London.

Bolton F.G., Reich J.W. & Gutierres S.E. (1977) Delinquency patterns in maltreated children and siblings. *Victimology*, **2**, 349–357.

Bools C.N., Neale B.A. & Meadow S.R. (1992) Co-morbidity associated with fabricated illness (Munchausen syndrome by proxy). *Archives of Disease in Childhood*, **67**, 77–79.

Bowlby J. (1951) Maternal care and mental health. *Bulletin of the World Health Organization*, **31**, 355–533.

Bowlby J. (1980) *Attachment and Loss, vol. 3: Loss, sadness and depression*. Basic Books, New York.

Bronfenbrenner U. (1979) *The Ecology of Human Development: Experiments by Nature and Design*. Harvard University Press, Cambridge, MA.

Browne D.H. (1986) The role of stress in the commission of subsequent acts of child abuse and neglect. *Journal of Family Violence*, **1**, 289–297.

Browne K. & Saqi S. (1987) Parent–child interaction in abusing families and its possible causes and consequences. In: Maher P. (ed) *Child Abuse: The Educational Perspective*. Basil Blackwell, Oxford.

Bugental D.B. & Shennum W.A. (1984) 'Difficult' children as elicitors and targets of adult communication patterns: at attributional–behavioral transactional analysis. *Monographs of the Society for Research in Child Development*, **49** (Serial No. 205, 1).

Bugental D.B., Blue J. & Cruzcosa M. (1989) Perceived control over caregiving outcomes: implications for child abuse. *Developmental Psychology*, **25**, 532–539.

Burbach D. & Borduin C. (1986) Parent–child relations and the etiology of depression: a review of methods and findings. *Clinical Psychology Review*, **6**, 133–153.

Burgess R.L. (1979) Project interact: a study of patterns of interaction inabusive, neglectful and control families. *Child Abuse and Neglect*, **3**, 781–791.

Burgess R. & Youngblade L. (1988) The intergenerational transmission of abusive parental practices: a social interactional analysis. In: Gelles R., Hotaling G., Finkelhor D. & Straus M. (eds) *New Directions in Family Violence Research*. Sage, Beverly Hills, CA.

Caffey J. (1946) Multiple fractures in the long bones of infants suffering from chronic subdural hematoma. *American Journal of Roentgenology*, **56**, 163–173.

Carlson V., Cicchetti D., Barnett D. & Braunwald K. (1989) Disorganized/disoriented attachment relationships in maltreated infants. *Developmental Psychology*, **25**, 525–531.

Caspi A. & Elder G.H. Jr (1988) Emergent family patterns: the intergenerational construction of problem behavior and relationships. In: Hinde R.A. & Stevenson-Hinde J. (eds) *Relationships within*

Families: Mutual Influences, Oxford University Press, pp. 218–240. New York.

Cavaiola A.A. & Schiff M. (1989) Self-esteem in abused chemically dependent adolescents. *Child Abuse and Neglect*, **13**, 327–334.

Chernova T.V. (1990) Morbidity and physical development of children's homes residents. *Sovetskoe Zdravookhranenie*, **7**, 34–36.

Cicchetti D. (1989) How research on child maltreatment has informed the study of child development: perspectives from developmental psychopathology. In: Cicchetti D. & Carlson V. (eds) *Child Maltreatment. Theory and Research on the Causes and Consequences of Child Abuse and Neglect*. pp. 377–431. Cambridge University Press, New York.

Cicchetti D. & Olsen K. (1991) The developmental psychopathology of child maltreatment. In: Lewis M. & Miller S. (eds) *Handbook of Developmental Psychopathology*. pp. 261–279. Plenum, New York.

Cicchetti D., Carlson V., Braunwald K. & Aber J.L. (1987). The sequelae of child maltreatment. In: Gelles R.J. & Lancaster J.B. (eds) *Child Abuse and Neglect: Biosocial Dimensions*, pp. 277–298. Aldine, Hawthorne, NY.

Claussen A.H. & Crittenden P.M. (1991) Physical and psychological maltreatment: relations among types of maltreatment. *Child Abuse and Neglect*, **15**, 5–18.

Cohen S. & Syme L.S. (1985) *Social Support and Health*. Academic Press, New York.

Cohn A.H. (1983) *An Approach to Preventing Child Abuse*. National Committee for the Prevention of Child Abuse, Chicago.

Cohn A.H. & Daro D. (1987) Is treatment too late: what ten years of evaluative research tells us. *Child Abuse and Neglect*, **11**, 433–442.

Commission on Children's Rights (1978) *Barnesratt: On forbud not aga*. Swedish Department of Justice, Stockholm.

Coster W.J., Gersten M.S., Beeghly M. & Cicchetti D. (1989) Communicative functioning in maltreated toddlers. *Developmental Psychology*, **25**, 1020–1029.

Council on Scientific Affairs (1985) see American Medical Association Diagnostic and Treatment Guidelines concerning child sexual abuse and neglect in *Journal of the American Medical Association*, **254**, 796–800.

Cox A.D., Pound A., Mills M., Puckering C. & Owen A.L. (1991) Evaluation of a home visiting and befriending scheme for young mothers: NEWPIN. *Journal of the Royal Society of Medicine*, **84**, 217–220.

Crittenden P.M. & Ainsworth M.D.S. (1989) Child maltreatment and attachment theory. In: Cicchetti D. & Carlson V. (eds) *Child Maltreatment. Theory and Research on the Causes and Consequences of Child Abuse and Neglect*, pp. 432–463. Cambridge University Press, New York.

Crnic K., Greenbert M.T., Ragozin A., Robinson N. & Basham R. (1983) Effects of stress and social support on mothers and premature and full-term infants. *Child Development*, **54**, 209–217.

Crowe H.P. & Zeskind P.S. (1992) Psychophysiological and perceptual responses to infant cries varying in pitch: comparison of adults with low and high scores on the child abuse potential inventory. *Child Abuse and Neglect*, **16**, 19–29.

Dawson B., de Armas A., McGrath M.L. & Kelly J.A. (1986) Cognitive problem solving training to improve the child-care judgment of child neglectful parents. *Journal of Family Violence*, **1**, 209–221.

Dean J.G., MacQueen I.G., Mitchell R.G. & Kempe C.H. (1978) Health visitor's role in prediction of early childhood injuries and failure to thrive. *Child Abuse and Neglect*, **2**, 1–17.

deMause L. (1976) *The History of Childhood*. Souvenir Press, London.

Deykin E., Alpert J. & McNamara J. (1985) A pilot study of the effect of exposure to child abuse or neglect on adolescent suicidal behavior. *American Journal of Psychiatry*, **142**, 1299–1303.

Dodge K.A., Bates J.E. & Pettit G.S. (1990) Mechanisms in the cycle of violence. *Science*, **250**, 1678–1683.

Donovan W.L. & Leavitt L.A. (1985) Physiologic assessment of mother–infant attachment. *Journal of the American Academy of Child Psychiatry*, **24**, 65–70.

Dowdney L. & Pickles A. (1991) Expression of negative affect within disciplinary encounters: is there dyadic reciprocity? *Developmental Psychology*, **27**, 606–617.

Dowdney L. & Skuse D. (1993) Parenting provided by mentally retarded adults. *Journal of Child Psychology and Psychiatry Annual Research Review*, **34**, 25–47.

Dowdney L., Skuse D., Heptinstall E., Puckering C. & Zur-Szpiro S. (1987) Growth retardation and developmental delay amongst innercity infants. *Journal of Child Psychology and Psychiatry*, **28**, 529–541.

Downey G. & Coyne J.C. (1990) Children of depressed parents: an integrative review. *Psychological Bulletin*, **108**, 50–76.

Eager B.A., Whelan-Williams S. & Brooks W.G. (1985) The abuse of infants by manual shaking: medical social and legal issues. *Journal of the Florida Medical Association*, **72**, 503–507.

Egeland B., Sroufe L.A. & Erickson M.F. (1983) Developmental consequences of different patterns of maltreatment. *Child Abuse and Neglect*, **7**, 459–469.

Egeland B., Jacobvitz D. & Papatola K. (1987) Intergenerational continuity of abuse. In: Gelles R.J. & Lancaster J.B. (eds) *Child Abuse and Neglect: Biosocial Dimensions*, pp. 255–276. Aldine de Gruyter, New York.

Elder G.H., Caspi A. & Downey G. (1986) Problem behavior and family relationships: life course and intergenerational themes. In: Sorensen A., Weinert F. & Sherrod L. (eds) *Human Development and the Life Course: Multidisciplinary Perspectives*, pp. 293–340. Lawrence Erlbaum, Hillsdale, NJ.

Emery J.L. & Taylor E.M. (1986) Letter to the editor. *New England Journal of Medicine*, **315**, 1676.

Erlenmeyer-Kimling L. & Cornblatt B. (1987) The New York High-Risk Project: a follow-up report. *Schizophrenia Bulletin*, **13**, 451–461.

Farber E. & Joseph J. (1985) The maltreated adolescent: patterns of physical abuse. *Child Abuse and Neglect*, **9**, 201–206.

Farber E., McCoard W.D., Kinast C. & Falkner D. (1984) Violence in the families of adolescent runaways. *Child Abuse and Neglect*, **8**, 295–300.

Femina D.D., Yaeger C.A. & Lewis D.O. (1990) Child abuse: adolescent records versus adult recall. *Child Abuse and Neglect*, **14**, 227–231.

Field T.M. (1993) Enhancing parent sensitivity. In: Anastasion N.J. & Harel S. (eds) *At Risk Infants: Interventions, Families and Research*, pp. 81–89. Paul H. Brooks Publishing Company, Baltimore, MD.

Finkelhor D. & Korbin J. (1988) Child abuse as an international issue. *Child Abuse and Neglect*, **12**, 2–24.

Fontana V.J. (1968) Further reflections on maltreatment of children. *New York State Journal of Medicine*, **68**, 2214–2215.

Frank D.A. & Zeisel S.H. (1988) Failure to thrive. *Pediatric Clinics of North America*, **35**, 1187–1207.

Frank Y., Zimmerman R. & Leeds N. (1985) Neurological manifestations in abused children who have been shaken. *Developmental Medicine and Child Neurology*, **27**, 312–316.

Friedrich-Cofer L. & Huston A.C. (1986) Television violence and aggression: the debate continues. *Psychological Bulletin*, **100**, 364–371.

Frodi A. (1981) Contribution of infant characteristics to child abuse. *American Journal of Mental Deficiency*, **85**, 341–349.

Frodi A. & Smetana J. (1984) Abused, neglected, and nonmaltreated preschoolers' ability to discriminate emotions in others: the effects of IQ. *Child Abuse and Neglect*, **8**, 459–465.

Garbarino J. (1989) Troubled youth, troubled families: the dynamics of adolescent maltreatment. In: Cicchetti D. & Carlson V. (eds) *Child Maltreatment. Theory and Research on the Causes and Consequences of*

Child Abuse and Neglect, pp. 685–706. Cambridge University Press, New York.

Garbarino J. & Garbarino A.C. (1986) *Emotional Maltreatment of Children*. National Committee for the Prevention of Child Abuse, Chicago, IL.

Garbarino J. & Plantz M.C. (1986) Child abuse and juvenile delinquency: what are the links? In: Garbarino J., Schellenbach C., Sebes J. and Associates (eds) *Troubled Youth, Troubled Families*. Aldine, New York.

Garbarino J. & Vondra J. (1987) Psychological maltreatment: issues and perspectives. In: Brassard M., Germain B. & Hart S. (eds) *Psychological Maltreatment of Children and Youth*. Pergamon, New York.

Garbarino J., Guttman E. & Seeley J.W. (1986) *The Psychologically Battered Child*. Jossey-Bass, San Francisco.

Gaudin J.M. & Polansky N.A. (1986) Social distancing of neglectful families. *Children and Youth Services Review*, **8**, 1–12.

Gecas V. (1979) The influence of social class on socialization. In: Burr W. (ed) *Contemporary Theories about the Family*, vol. 1, pp. 365–401. Free Press, New York.

Gelles R.J. & Cornell C.P. (1985) *Intimate Violence in Families. Family Studies Text Services*, vol. 2, Sage, Beverly Hills.

Gelles R. & Straus M. (1979) Determinants of violence in the family: toward a theoretical integration. In: Burr W., Hill R., Nye F. & Reiss I. (eds) *Contemporary Theories about the Family*, Free Press, New York.

Gelles R.J. & Straus M. (1987) The comparison of severe abuse 1975 to 1985. *Journal of Interpersonal Violence*, **2**, 212–222.

Gibbons J.S., Gallagher B. & Bell C. (1992) *First Draft — Report of the Family Health and Development Project: A Follow-up of Physically Abused Children*. Social Work Development Unit, University of East Anglia.

Giblin P.T., Starr R.H. Jr & Agronow S.J. (1984) Affective behavior of abused and control children: comparisons of parent–child interactions and the influence of home environment variables. *Journal of Genetic Psychology*, **144**, 69–82.

Gilgun J.F. (1988) Decision-making in interdisciplinary treatment teams. *Child Abuse and Neglect*, **12**, 231–239.

Giovannoni J. (1989) Definitional issues in child maltreatment. In: Cicchetti D. & Carlson V. (eds) *Child Maltreatment. Theory and Research on the Causes and Consequences of Child Abuse and Neglect*, pp. 3–37. Cambridge University Press, New York.

Glueck S. & Glueck E. (1950) *Unraveling Juvenile Delinquency*. Cambridge University Press, Cambridge.

Gough D. (1989) Approaches to child abuse prevention. In: Browne K., Davies C. & Stratton P. (eds) *Early Prediction and Prevention of Child Abuse*, pp. 107–120. Willey, Chichester.

Grantham-McGregor S. (1987) Field studies in early nutrition and later achievement. In: Dobbing J. (ed) *Early Nutrition and Later Achievement*, pp. 128–174. Academic Press, London.

Gray J., Cutler C., Dean J. & Kempe C. (1979) Prediction and prevention of child abuse and neglect. *Journal of Social Issues*, **35**, 127–139.

Green A.H., Gaines R.W. & Sandgrund A. (1974) Child abuse: a pathological syndrome of family interaction. *American Journal of Psychiatry*, **131**, 882–886.

Green W.H., Campbell M. & David R. (1984) Psychosocial dwarfism: a critical review of the evidence. *Journal of the American Academy of Child and Adolescent Psychiatry*, **23**, 39–48.

Green W.H., Deutsch S.I. & Campbell M. (1987) Psychosocial dwarfism: psychological and etiological considerations. In: Nemeroff C.B. & Loosen P.T. (eds) *Handbook of Psychoneuroendocrinology*, pp. 109–142. Guilford Press, New York.

Hakimi-Manesh Y., Mojdehi H. & Tashakkori A. (1984) Effects of environmental enrichment on the mental and psychomotor development of orphanage children. *Journal of Child Psychology and Psychiatry*, **25**, 643–650.

Hammen C., Gordon D., Burge D., Adrian C., Jaenicke C. & Hiroto G. (1987) Maternal affective disorders, illness and stress: risk for children's psychopathology. *American Journal of Psychiatry*, **144**, 736–741.

Hart S.N. & Brassard M.R. (1987) A major threat to children's mental health: psychological maltreatment. *American Psychologist*, **42**, 160–165.

Herrenkohl E., Herrenkohl R. & Toedtler L. (1983) Perspectives on the intergenerational transmission of abuse. In: Finkelhor D., Gelles R., Hotaling G. & Straus M. (eds) *The Darkside of Families: Current Family Violence Research*. Sage, Beverly Hills, CA.

Herrenkohl E.C., Herrenkohl R.C., Toedter L. & Yanushevski M. (1984) Parent–child interactions in abusive and nonabusive families. *Journal of the American Academy of Child Psychiatry*, **23**, 641–648.

Herzberger S.D., Potts D.A. & Dillon M. (1981) Abusive and nonabusive parental treatment from the child's perspective. *Journal of Consulting and Clinical Psychology*, **49**, 81–90.

Hobbs C.J. (1986) When are burns not accidental? *Archives of Disease in Childhood*, **61**, 357–361.

Hoffman-Plotkin D. & Twentyman C.T. (1984) A multimodal assessment of behavioral and cognitive deficits in abused and neglected preschoolers. *Child Development*, **55**, 794–802.

Howes C. & Eldridge R. (1985) Responses of abused, neglected, and non-maltreated children to the behaviors of their peers. *Journal of Applied Developmental Psychology*, **6**, 261–270.

Hyman I.A. (1987) Psychological correlates of corporal punishment. In: Brassard M.R., Germain R. & Hart S.N. (eds) *Psychological Maltreatment of Children and Youth*, pp. 59–68. Pergamon Press, Oxford.

Isaacs C.D. (1982) Treatment of child abuse: a review of the behavioural interventions. *Journal of Applied Behavioural Analysis*, **15**, 273–294.

Jacobson R.S. & Straker G. (1982) Peer group interaction of physically abused children. *Child Abuse and Neglect*, **6**, 321–327.

Jones D. (1987) The untreatable family. *Child Abuse and Neglect*, **11**, 409–420.

Jones E.D. & McCurdy K. (1992) The links between types of maltreatment and demographic characteristics of children. *Child Abuse and Neglect*, **16**, 201–215.

Justice B., Calvert A. & Justice R. (1985) Factors mediating child abuse as a response to stress. *Child Abuse and Neglect*, **9**, 365–372.

Kaufman J. (1991) Depressive disorders in maltreated children. *Journal of the American Academy of Child and Adolescent Psychiatry*, **30**, 257–265.

Kaufman J. & Cicchetti D. (1989) Effects of maltreatment on school-age children's socioemotional development: assessments in a day-camp setting. *Developmental Psychology*, **25**, 516–524.

Kaufman J. & Zigler E. (1987) Do abused children become abusive parents? *American Journal of Orthopsychiatry*, **57**, 186–191.

Kazdin A.E., Moser J. & Bell R. (1985) Depressive symptoms among physically abused and psychiatrically disturbed children. *Journal of Abnormal Psychology*, **94**, 298–307.

Kempe C. (1976) Approaches to preventing child abuse: the health visitor concept. *American Journal of Diseases of Children*, **130**, 941–947.

Kempe R.S. & Goldbloom R.B. (1987) Malnutrition and growth retardation (failure to thrive) in the context of child abuse and neglect. In: Helfer R.E. & Kempe R.S. (eds) *The Battered Child*, 4th edn. University of Chicago Press, Chicago.

Kempe R. & Kempe C.H. (1978) *Child Abuse*. Fontana/Open Books, London.

Kempe C.H., Silverman F.N., Steele B.F., Droegemueller W. & Silver H.K. (1962) The battered child syndrome. *Journal of the American Medical Association*, **181**, 4–11.

King J.M. & Taitz L.S. (1985) Catch up growth following abuse.

Archives of Disease in Childhood, **60**, 1152—1154.

Kleinman P.K. (1987) *Diagnostic Imaging of Child Abuse.* Williams & Wilkins, Baltimore.

Klimes-Dougan B. & Kistner J. (1990) Physically abused preschoolers' responses to peers' distress. *Developmental Psychology*, **26**, 599—602.

Koel B.S. (1969) Failure to thrive and fatal injury as a continuum. *American Journal of Diseases of Children*, **118**, 565—567.

Kohlberg L., Ricks D. & Snarey J. (1984) Childhood depression as a predictor of adaptation in adulthood. *Genetic Psychology Monographs*, **110**, 91—172.

Korbin J. (ed) (1981) *Child Abuse and Neglect: Cross-cultural Perspectives.* University of California Press, Berkeley.

Korbin J. (1987a) Child abuse and neglect: the cultural context. In: Helfer R. & Kempe R. (eds) *The Battered Child*, 4th edn, pp. 23—41. University of Chicago Press, Chicago.

Korbin J. (1987b) Child sexual abuse: implications from the cross-cultural record. In: Schoper-Hughes N. (ed) *Child Survival: Anthropological Perspectives on the Treatment and Maltreatment of Children*, pp. 247—265. Reidel, Dordrecht, Holland.

Korbin J.E. (1991) Cross-cultural perspectives and research directions for the 21st century. *Child Abuse and Neglect*, **15**, 67—77.

Kratcoski P.C. (1982) Child abuse and violence against the family. *Child Welfare*, **61**, 435—444.

Lahey B.B., Conger R.D., Atkeson B.M. & Treiber F.A. (1984) Parenting behavior and emotional status of physically abusive mothers. *Journal of Consulting and Clinical Psychology*, **52**, 1062—1071.

Lamond D.A.P. (1989) The impact of mandatory reporting legislation on reporting behaviour. *Child Abuse and Neglect*, **13**, 471—480.

Larrance D.T. & Twentyman C.T. (1983) Maternal attributions and child abuse. *Journal of Abnormal Psychology*, **92**, 449—457.

Lazoritz S. (1990) Whatever happened to Mary Ellen? *Child Abuse and Neglect*, **14**, 143—149.

Lealman G.T., Phillips J.M., Haigh D., Stone J., Ord-Smith C. & Stone J. (1983) Prediction and prevention of child abuse — an empty hope? *Lancet*, **1**, 1423—1424.

Levine L., Coll C. & Oh W. (1984) Determinants of mother—infant interaction in adolescent mothers. Paper presented at the International Conference on Infant Studies, New York, April, 1984.

Lewis D.L., Mallouh C. & Webb V. (1989) Child abuse, delinquency, and violent criminality. In: Cicchetti D. & Carlson V. (eds) *Child Maltreatment. Theory and Research on the Causes and Consequences of Child Abuse and Neglect*, pp. 707—721. Cambridge University Press, New York.

Lewis D.O. & Shanok S.S. (1977) Medical histories of delinquent and non-delinquent children: an epidemiological study. *American Journal of Psychiatry*, **134**, 1020—1025.

Light R. (1973) Abused and neglected children in America: a study of alternative policies. *Harvard Educational Review*, **43**, 556—598.

Lorber R., Felton D.K. & Reid J.B. (1984) A social learning approach to the reduction of coercive processes in child abusive families: a molecular analysis. *Advances in Behavior Research and Therapy*, **6**, 29—45.

Lutzker J.R. (1990) Behavioural treatment of child neglect. *Behavior Modification*, **14**, 301—315.

Lutzker J.R. & Rice J.M. (1984) Project 12-ways: measuring outcome of a large in-home service for treatment and prevention of child abuse and neglect. *Child Abuse and Neglect*, **8**, 519—524.

Lynch M.A. & Roberts J. (1982) *Consequences of Child Abuse.* Academic Press, London.

McCord J. (1983) A 40 year perspective of effects of child abuse and neglect. *Child Abuse and Neglect*, **7**, 265—270.

McKee L. (1984) Sex differentials in survivorship and customary treatment of infants and children. *Medical Anthropology*, **8**, 91—108.

McKinley I. (1991) Letter from Romania. *Archives of Disease in Child-hood*, **66**, 1258—1259.

Maccoby E. & Martin J. (1983) Socialization in the context of the family: parent—child interaction. In: Hetherington E.M. (ed) *Handbook of Child Psychology, vol. 4: Socialization, Personality and Social Development.* Wiley, New York.

Main M. (1980) Abusive and rejecting infants. In: Frude N. (ed) *The Understanding and Prevention of Child Abuse: Psychological Approaches*, pp. 19—38. Concord Press, London.

Main M. & George C. (1985) Responses of abused and disadvantaged toddlers to distress in age mates: a study in the day care setting. *Developmental Psychology*, **21**, 407—412.

Main M. & Goldwyn R. (1984) Predicting rejection of her infant from mother's representation of her own experience: implications for the abused-abusing intergenerational cycle. *Child Abuse and Neglect*, **8**, 203—217.

Main M. & Weston D. (1981) The quality of toddler's relationship to mother and father. Related to conflict behavior and the readiness to establish a new relationship. *Child Development*, **52**, 932—940.

Marks H.G., Borns P., Steg N.L., Stine S.B., Stroud H.H. & Vates T.S. (1978) Catch-up brain growth — demonstration by CAT scan. *Journal of Pediatrics*, **93**, 254—257.

Meadow R. (1977) Munchausen syndrome by proxy. The hinterland of child abuse. *Lancet*, **ii**, 343—345.

Meadow R. (1989a) Epidemiology. In: Meadow R. (ed) *ABC of Child Abuse*, pp. 1—4. British Medical Association, London.

Meadow R. (1989b) Poisoning. *ABC of Child Abuse*, pp. 19—20. British Medical Association, London.

Meadow R. (1989c) Munchausen syndrome by proxy. *ABC of Child Abuse*, pp. 37—39. British Medical Association, London.

Meadow R. (1990) Suffocation, recurrent apnea, and sudden infant death. *Journal of Pediatrics*, **117**, 351—357.

Money J., Annecillo C. & Kelley J.F. (1983) Growth of intelligence: failure and catchup associated respectively with abuse and rescue in the syndrome of abuse dwarfism. *Psychoneuroendocrinology*, **8**, 309—319.

Mouzakitis C.M. (1981) An inquiry into the problem of child abuse and juvenile delinquency. In: Hunner R.J. & Walker Y.E. (eds) *Exploring the Relationship between Child Abuse and Delinquency*, pp. 220—232. Allanheld, Osmun, Montclair, NJ.

Newberger E.M. & Cook S. (1983) Parental awareness and child abuse: a cognitive-developmental analysis of urban and rural samples. *American Journal of Orthopsychiatry*, **53**, 512—524.

Newlands M. & Emery J.S. (1991) Child abuse and cot deaths. *Child Abuse and Neglect*, **15**, 275—278.

Nicol A.R., Smith J., Kay B., Hall D., Barlow J. & Wiliams B. (1988) A focussed casework approach to the treatment of child abuse: a controlled comparison. *Journal of Child Psychology and Psychiatry*, **29**, 703—711.

Novaco R.W. (1975) *Anger Control: The Development and Evaluation of an Experimental Treatment.* Heath/Lexington Books, Lexington, MA.

Oates R.K., Peacock A. & Forrest D. (1984) The development of abused children. *Developmental Medicine and Child Neurology*, **26**, 649—656.

Olds D. (1981) Improving formal services for mothers and children. In: Garbarino J. & Stocking S. (eds) *Protecting Children from Abuse and Neglect: Developing and Maintaining Effective Support System for Families.* Jossey-Bass, San Francisco.

Olds D. (1982) The prenatal/early infancy project: an ecological approach to prevention of developmental disabilities. In: Belsky J. (ed) *In the Beginning.* Columbia University Press, New York.

Olds D. (1983) An intervention program for high-risk families. In: Hoekelman R. (ed) *Minimizing High-risk Parenting.* Harwal, Media, PA.

Olds D.L. & Henderson C.R. Jr (1989) The prevention of maltreatment. In: Cicchetti D. & Carlson V. (eds) *Child Maltreatment. Theory and Research on the Causes and Consequences of Child Abuse and Neglect*, pp. 722–763. Cambridge University Press, New York.

Olds D.L., Henderson C.R., Camberlin R. & Tatelbaum R. (1986) Preventing child abuse and neglect: randomised trial of nurse home visitation. *Pediatrics*, **78**, 65–78.

Parke R.D. & Collmer C.W. (1975) Child abuse: an interdisciplinary analysis. In: Hetherington E.M. (ed) *Review of Child Development Research*, pp. 509–591. University of Chicago Press, Chicago.

Patterson G.R. (1982) *Coercive Family Process*. Castalia, Eugene, OR.

Patterson G.R., DeBaryshe B.D. & Ramsay E. (1989) A developmental perspective on antisocial behavior. *American Psychologist*, **44**, 329–335.

Pelcovitz D., Kaplan S., Samit C., Krieger R. & Cornelius P. (1984) Adolescent abuse: family structure and implications for treatment. *Journal of Child Psychiatry*, **23**, 85–90.

Polansky N.A., Gaudin J.M., Ammons P.W. & Davis K.B. (1985) The psychological ecology of the neglectful mother. *Child Abuse and Neglect*, **9**, 265–275.

Power T.G., Gershenhorn S. & Stafford D. (1990) Maternal perceptions of infant difficultness: the influence of maternal attitudes and attributions. *Infant Behavior and Development*, **13**, 421–437.

Powers J.L. & Eckenrode J. (1990) Maltreatment among runaway and homeless youths. *Child Abuse and Neglect*, **14**, 87–98.

Powers, J.L., Eckenrode J. & Jaklitsch B. (1988) The maltreatment of adolescents. *Child Abuse and Neglect*, **12**, 189–199.

Provence S. & Lipton R.C. (1962) *Infants in Institutions*. International Universities Press, New York.

Quinton D. & Rutter M. (1976) Early hospital admissions and later disturbances of behaviour. *Developmental Medicine and Child Neurology*, **18**, 447–450.

Quinton D. & Rutter M. (1988) *Parenting Breakdown: The Making and Breaking of Intergenerational Links*. Avebury, Aldershot.

Radke-Yarrow M., Richters J. & Wilson W.E. (1991) Child development in a network of relationships. In: Hinde R. & Stevenson-Hinde J. (eds) *Individuals in a Network of Relationships*. Cambridge University Press, Cambridge.

Reid J. (1984) Social interactional patterns in families of abused and non-abused children. In: Waxler C. & Radke-Yarrow M. (eds) *Social and Biological Origins of Altruism and Aggression*. Cambridge University Press, Cambridge.

Rieder C. & Cicchetti D. (1989) An organizational perspective on cognitive control functioning and cognitive-affective balance in maltreated children. *Developmental Psychology*, **25**, 382–393.

Rosenbaum M. & Bennett B. (1986) Homicide and depression. *American Journal of Psychiatry*, **143**, 367–370.

Rosenberg D.A. (1987) Web of deceit: a literature review of Munchausen syndrome by proxy. *Child Abuse and Neglect*, **11**, 547–564.

Rosenberg M.S. & Reppucci N.D. (1983) Abusive mothers: perceptions of their own and their children's behavior. *Consulting Psychology*, **51**, 674–682.

Ross C.D. & Zigler E. (1983) Treatment issues in child abuse. *Journal of the American Academy of Child Psychiatry*, **22**, 305–308.

Rotherham M.J. (1987) Evaluation of imminent danger for suicide among youth. *American Journal of Orthopsychiatry*, **57**, 102–110.

Rutter M. (1983) Stress coping and development: some issues and some questions. In: Garmezy N. & Rutter M. (eds) *Stress, Coping and Development in Young Children*, pp. 1–41. McGraw Hill, New York.

Rutter M. (1985) Resilience in the face of adversity: protective factors and resistance to psychiatric disorder. *British Journal of Psychiatry*, **147**, 598–611.

Rutter M. (1989a) Pathways from childhood to adult life. *Journal of Child Psychology and Psychiatry*, **30**, 23–51.

Rutter M. (1989b) Intergenerational continuities and discontinuities. In: Cicchetti D. & Carlson V. (eds) *Child Maltreatment. Theory and Research on the Causes and Consequences of Child Abuse and Neglect*. pp. 317–348. Cambridge University Press, New York.

Rutter M. (1990) Commentary: Some focus and process considerations regarding effects of parental depression on children. *Developmental Psychology*, **26**, 60–67.

Rutter M., Quinton D. & Liddle C. (1983) Parenting in two generations: looking backwards and looking forwards. In: Madge N. (ed) *Families At Risk*, pp. 60–98. Heinemann Educational, London.

Sackett D.L., Haynes R.B. & Tugwell P. (1985) *Clinical Epidemiology: A Basic Science for Clinical Medicine*. Little, Brewer, Boston.

St James Roberts I. (1989) Persistent crying in infancy. *Journal of Child Psychology and Psychiatry*, **30**, 189–196.

Sameroff A.J. & Feil L.A. (1985) Parental concepts of development. In: Sigel I.E. (ed) *Parental Belief Systems: The Psychological Consequences for Children*. Lawrence Erlbaum, New Jersey.

Sameroff A.J. & Seifer R. (1983) Familial risk and child competence. *Child Development*, **54**, 1254–1268.

Sameroff A.J., Barocas R. & Seifer R. (1984) The early development of children born to mentally-ill women. In: Watt N.F., Anthony E.J., Wynne L.C. & Rolf J. (eds) *Children at Risk for Schizophrenia: A Longitudinal Perspective*. Cambridge University Press, New York.

Sanders R.W. (1978) Systematic desensitization in the treatment of child abuse. *American Journal of Psychiatry*, **135**, 483–484.

Sendi I.B. & Blomgren P.G. (1975) A comparative study of predictive criteria in the predisposition of homicidal adolescents. *American Journal of Psychiatry*, **132**, 423–427.

Shaffer D., Garland A., Gould M., Fisher P. & Trautman P. (1988) Preventing teenage suicide: a critical review. *Journal of the American Academy of Child and Adolescent Psychiatry*, **27**, 675–687.

Showers J. (1992) Don't shake the baby: the effectiveness of a prevention program. *Child Abuse and Neglect*, **16**, 11–18.

Siegel E., Bauman K.E., Schaefer E.S., Saunders M.M. & Ingram D.D. (1980) Hospital and home support during infancy: impact on maternal attachment, child abuse and neglect, and health care utilisation. *Pediatrics*, **66**, 183–190.

Silver L.B., Dublin C.C. & Lourie R.S. (1969) Does violence breed violence? Contributions from a study of the child abuse syndrome. *American Journal of Psychiatry*, **126**, 152–155.

Simons R.L., Whitbeck L.B., Conger R.D. & Chyi-In W. (1991) Intergenerational transmission of harsh parenting. *Developmental Psychology*, **27**, 159–171.

Singer M.I. & Petchers M.K. (1989) The relationship between sexual abuse and substance among psychiatrically hospitalized adolescents. *Child Abuse and Neglect*, **13**, 319–325.

Skuse D. (1988) Extreme deprivation in early childhood. In: Mogford K. & Bishop D. (eds) *Language Development in Exceptional Circumstances*, pp. 29–46. Churchill Livingstone, London.

Skuse D. (1989a) Emotional abuse and delay in growth. In: Meadow R. (ed) *ABC of Child Abuse*, pp. 26–28. British Medical Association, London.

Skuse D. (1989b) Emotional abuse and neglect. In: Meadow R. (ed) *ABC of Child Abuse*, pp. 23–25. British Medical Association, London.

Skuse D. (1992) The relationship between deprivation, physical growth and the impaired development of language. In: Fletcher P. & Hall D. (eds) *Specific Speech and Language Disorders in Children: Correlates, Characteristics and Outcomes*, pp. 29–50. Whurr Publishers, London.

Skuse D. (1993) Epidemiological and definitional issues in failure to thrive. In: Woolston J. (ed). *Child and Adolescent Psychiatric Clinics of North America*, pp. 37–59. Saunders, Philadelphia.

Skuse D., Wolke D. & Reilly S. (1990) How commonly are failing to thrive' infants abused or neglected? Presentation at the British

Paediatric Association Annual Conference, University of Warwick, April.

Skuse D., Wolke D. & Reilly S. (1992) Failure to thrive. Clinical and developmental aspects. In: Remschmidt H. & Schmidt M. (eds) *Child and Youth Psychiatry, European Perspectives. Vol. II: Developmental Psychopathology*, pp. 46–71. Hans Huber, Stuttgart.

Smetana J.G. & Kelly M. (1989) Social cognition in maltreated children. In: Cicchetti D. & Carlson V. (eds) *Child Maltreatment. Theory and Research on the Causes and Consequences of Child Abuse and Neglect*, pp. 620–646. Cambridge University Press, New York.

Smetana J.G., Kelly M. & Twentyman C.T. (1984) Abused, neglected, and non maltreated children's conceptions of moral and social-conventional transgressions. *Child Development*, **55**, 277–287.

Smith J.E. & Rachman S.J. (1984) Non-accidental injury to children. Part II. A controlled evaluation of a behavioural management programme. *Behavior Research and Therapy*, **22**, 349–366.

Somander L.K.H. & Rammer L.M. (1991) Intra- and extrafamilial child homicide in Sweden 1971–1980. *Child Abuse and Neglect*, **15**, 45–55.

Southall D.P., Stebbens V.A., Rees S.V., Lang M.H. & Warner J.O. (1987) Apnoeic episodes induced by smothering: two cases identified by covert video surveillance. *British Medical Journal*, **294**, 1637–1641.

Speight N. (1989) Non-accidental injury. *British Medical Journal*, **298**, 879–882.

Spitz R.A. (1945) Hospitalism: an inquiry into the genesis of psychiatric conditions in early childhood. *Psychoanalytic Study of the Child*, **1**, 55–74.

Sroufe L.A. & Fleeson J. (1986) Attachment and the construction of relationships. In: Hartup W. & Rubin Z. (eds) *Relationships and Development*, pp. 51–71. Cambridge University Press, New York.

Sroufe L.A., Fox N. & Pancake V. (1983) Attachment and dependency in developmental perspective. *Child Development*, **55**, 17–29.

Stanhope R., Adlard P., Hamill G., Jones J., Skuse D. & Preece M.A. (1988) Physiological growth hormone (GH) secretion during the recovery from psychosocial dwarfism: a case report. *Clinical Endocrinology*, **28**, 335–339.

Straker G. & Jacobson R.S. (1981) Aggression, emotional adjustment and empathy in the abused child. *Developmental Psychology*, **17**, 762–765.

Straus M. (1983) Ordinary violence, child abuse, and wife beating: what do they have in common? In: Finkelhor D., Gelles R., Hotaling G. & Straus M. (eds) *The Darkside of Families: Current Family Violence Research*. Sage, Beverly Hills, CA.

Straus M.A. & Gelles R.J. (1986) Change in family violence from 1975–1985. *Journal of Marriage and the Family*, **48**, 465–479.

Straus M., Gelles R. & Steinmetz S. (1980) *Behind Closed Doors: Violence in the American Family*. Anchor/Doubleday, Garden City, NY.

Sylvester J. (1990) Attributions of parents who abuse their children. PhD dissertation. University of Leeds.

Szykula S.A. & Fleischman M.J. (1985) Reducing out of home placements of abused children: two controlled field studies. *Child Abuse and Neglect*, **9**, 277–283.

Taitz L.S. & King J.M. (1988a) Growth patterns in child abuse. *Acta Paediatrica Scandinavica*, **343**, 62–72.

Taitz L.S. & King J.M. (1988b) A profile of abuse. *Archives of Disease in Childhood*, **63**, 1026–1031.

Talbot N.B., Sobel E.H., Burke B.S., Lindemann E. & Kaufman S.B. (1947) Dwarfism in healthy children: its possible relation to emotional, nutritional and endocrine disturbances. *New England Journal of Medicine*, **236**, 783–793.

Taylor B.J. & Brook C.G.D. (1986) Sleep EEG in growth disorders. *Archives of Disease in Childhood*, **61**, 754–760.

Tertinger D.A., Greene B.F. & Lutzker J.R. (1984) Home safety: development and validation of one component of an ecobehavioural treatment programme for abused and neglected children. *Journal of Applied Behavioral Analysis*, **17**, 159–174.

Tramontana M.G., Hooper S.R. & Selzer S.C. (1988) Research on the preschool prediction of later academic achievement: a review. *Developmental Review*, **8**, 89–146.

Trickett P.K. & Kuczynski L. (1986) Children's misbehaviors and parental discipline strategies in abusive and nonabusive families. *Developmental Psychology*, **22**, 115–123.

Trickett P.K. & Susman E.J. (1988) Parental perceptions of child-rearing practices in physically abusive and nonabusive families. *Developmental Psychology*, **24**, 270–276.

Trickett P.K., Aber J.L., Carlson V. & Cicchetti D. (1991) Relationship of socioeconomic status to the etiology and developmental sequelae of physical child abuse. *Developmental Psychology*, **27**, 148–158.

Turnbull C. (1961) *The Forest People: A Study of the People of the Congo*. Simon and Schuster, New York.

United States Department of Health and Human Services (1988) *Study Findings: Study of the National Incidence and Prevalence of Child Abuse and Neglect*, pp. 5–8. US Department of Health and Human Services, Washington DC.

van der Eyken W. (1982) *Home Start. A Four Year Evaluation*. Home Start Consultancy, Leicester.

Vondra J. (1986) The socioeconomic context of parenting. Unpublished masters thesis. Pennsylvania State University.

Vondra J.I., Barnett D. & Cicchetti D. (1990) Self-concept, motivation and competence among preschoolers from maltreating and comparison families. *Child Abuse and Neglect*, **14**, 525–540.

Walker E. & Emory E. (1983) Infants at risk for psychopathology: offspring of schizophrenic parents. *Child Development*, **54**, 1269–1285.

Wasserman G., Green A. & Allen R. (1983) Going beyond abuse: maladaptive patterns of interaction in abusing mother–infant pairs. *Journal of the American Academy of Child Psychiatry*, **22**, 245–252.

Waters E. & Sroufe L.A. (1983) Social competence as a developmental construct. *Developmental Review*, **3**, 79–97.

Watkins A.H., Gagan R.J. & Cupoli J.H. (1985) Child abuse by burning. *Journal of the Florida Medical Association*, **72**, 497–502.

Weintraub S. (1987) Risk factors in schizophrenia: the Stony Brook high-risk project. *Schizophrenia Bulletin*, **13**, 439–449.

Werner E.E. & Smith R.S. (1982) *Vulnerable but Invincible: A Longitudinal Study of Resilient Children and Youth*. McGraw-Hill, New York.

Westcott H. (1991) The abuse of disabled children: a review of the literature. *Child Care, Health and Development*, **17**, 243–258.

White R., Benedict M.I., Wulff L. & Kelley M. (1987) Physical disabilities as risk factors for child maltreatment. *American Journal of Orthopsychiatry*, **57**, 93–101.

White R., Carr P. & Lowe N. (1990) *A Guide to the Children Act, 1989*. Butterworths, London.

Wick S.C. (1981) Child abuse as a causation of juvenile delinquency in central Texas. In: Hunner R.J. & Walker Y.E. (eds) *Exploring the Relationship between Child Abuse and Delinquency*, pp. 233–239. Allanheld Osmun, Montclair, NJ.

Widom C.S. (1989) Does violence beget violence? A critical examination of the literature. *Psychological Bulletin*, **106**, 3–28.

Wolfe D.A. (1985) Child-abusive parents: an empirical review and analysis. *Psychological Bulletin*, **97**, 462–482.

Wolfe D.A. (1987) *Child Abuse: Implications for Child Development*. Sage, Newbury Park, CA.

Wolfe D.A. & Mosk M.D. (1983) Behavioural comparisons of children from abusive and distressed families. *Journal of Consulting and Clinical Psychology*, **51**, 702–708.

Wolfe D.A., Edwards B., Manion I. & Koverola C. (1988) Early intervention for parents at risk of child abuse and neglect: a preliminary investigation. *Journal of Consulting and Clinical Psychology,* **56**, 40–47.

Wooley P. & Evans W. (1955) Significance of skeletal lesions in infants resembling those of traumatic origin. *Journal of the American Medical Association,* **158**, 539–543.

Worlock P., Stower M. & Barbor P. (1986) Patterns of fractures of accidental and non-accidental injury in children: a comparative study. *British Medical Journal,* **293**, 100–102.

Zdanska-Brincken M., Grodzka K., Kurniewicz-Witczakowa R., Szilagyi-Pagowska I., Antoszewska A. & Kopczynska-Sirkorska J. (1983) Level and characteristics of the psychosomatic development of children from nurseries. *Problemy Medycyny Wieku Rozwojowego,* **12**, 7–26.

Zellman G.L. (1990) Child abuse reporting and failure to report among mandated reporters. *Journal of Interpersonal Violence,* **5**, 3–22.

Zigler E. (1976) Controlling child abuse in America: an effort doomed to failure. In: Adamovics D. (ed) *Proceedings of the First National Conference on Child Abuse and Neglect.* Department of Health, Education, and Welfare, Washington, DC.

Zigler E. & Butterfield E.C. (1968) Motivational aspects of changes in IQ test performance of culturally deprived nursery school children. *Child Development,* **39**, 1–14.

Zigler E. & Hall N.W. (1989) Physical child abuse in America: past, present, and future. In: Cicchetti D. & Carlson V. (eds) *Child Maltreatment. Theory and Research on the Causes and Consequences of Child Abuse and Neglect,* pp. 38–75. Cambridge University Press, New York.

Chapter 14
Sexual Abuse

Marjorie Smith & Arnon Bentovim

The general climate of increasing openness about sex and sexuality that started in the 1960s has had an impact on families and children. It has meant that children have been exposed to much more information on sex and sexual topics. Some of this is through education both in and out of school; children in most western societies receive some form of sex education as part of their schooling, but there is also more openness about sex and sexuality in the media, and children are exposed to this too. However, the attitudes about children and sexuality still reflect some past attitudes, and are inconsistent and contradictory in some respects (Yates, 1991).

Historically, attitudes towards children and sexuality have been repressive. In the 17th century there was a spread of sexual repression throughout Europe following the religious teachings of John Calvin, and any form of bodily lust or public expression of sexuality by adults was seen as shameful. Until the 20th century many parents took action to prevent any expressions of sexuality in children, and extreme steps, including the use of mechanical contraptions, were taken to prevent children's self-abuse, as masturbation was called.

The view that normal children were asexual was challenged by several medical writers before Freud, but it was not until the publication of Freud's (1905) essay on infantile sexuality that these ideas became more widely known. The essay presented a theory of human development that proposed that the development of sexuality was part of normal development, and proceeded through stages from birth onwards.

Attitudes have changed to the extent that most parents now regard some sexual behaviour by their children as part of normal development, and it is acknowledged by professionals that sexual play or sexually exploratory behaviour is normal, at least in young children (Rutter, 1971). Masturbation is an example of one of the behaviours that most parents now see as normal, and although most parents discourage or try to distract their children from doing this at least in public, only a few punish their children for masturbating (Gagnon, 1985; Smith & Grocke, 1993). There has been less change in attitudes relating to children as innocent, and to be protected from any matters of sex or sexuality. Parents who do not talk about sexuality or sex with their children often give as their reason the wish to preserve the child's innocence. This attitude implies that it is reasonable to expect children to move easily from an asexual childhood to a fully sexual adulthood (Yates, 1991).

Despite the persistence of these attitudes, and professional advice, such as that of Spock (1976), advising parents against sexual openness in the family, there has been a trend towards more expression of emotion and less anxiety about nudity within the family. A recent detailed interview study on normal sexual behaviour in families carried out in England (Smith & Grocke, 1993) found that most mothers reported enjoying close physical contact with their children, and that both parents hugged and kissed their children, although fathers did this less often than mothers. More than half the children (aged 4–16 years) regularly or frequently saw both their parents naked, although this became less common as the children got older. Children were less likely to see their father naked than their mother, and less likely to see a stepparent (mostly stepfathers) naked. Most children had bathed with both their parents (usually separately!), although for the large majority of children this practice had stopped before they were 5 years of age. Over two-thirds of children were reported to have come into their parents' bed at least weekly, at some point in their lives. Rosenfeld and colleagues (1982, 1984, 1987) have carried out a similar survey in the US, and although there were methodological differences that make direct comparison difficult, the results appear to be broadly comparable.

Some general points on family sexuality are apparent from the relatively small amount of information available. It is clear that in any population there is a range of different behaviours that are seen as normal, but that within a family unit there is an association between different behaviours (Friedrich *et al.*, 1991; Smith & Grocke, 1993). That is to say that, to a certain extent, behaviour in one area, such as family nudity, will predict behaviour in other aspects of family life, such as children getting into the parental bed or tolerance of sexual behaviour in children. In western societies, where the available research has been carried out, there are differences in the patterns of behaviour that are associated with socioeconomic status of the family, in the direction of more openness about sexuality in families of higher socioeconomic status. These differences were evident in the US in data collected in the 1950s (Elias & Gebhard, 1969) and in the UK in the 1960s (Newson & Newson, 1969). More recent evidence suggests that class differences are still apparent (Smith & Grocke, 1993).

There is little published information on cultural differences in normal sexual behaviours in families, but such evidence as there is suggests that there are definite cultural differences in what is deemed acceptable and normal. For example, Singer *et al.* (1978) reported on the suppression of all sexuality in traditional Chinese families. Olson (1981) commented that Turkish mothers regard it as a positive and motherly action to kiss and praise the genitals of young children. It is probable that this latter practice would not be judged as normal in many other countries. Korbin (1981) pointed to the importance of avoiding taking an ethnocentric position on the limits of normal behaviours. Within cultures, it appears that most families are relatively confident of the boundaries between normal and abusive sexual behaviours towards children, and operate within them (this may not be the case for physical abuse where parents seem much less certain of the boundaries between normal and abusive behaviour — see Chapter 13).

Skynner (1982), taking a systems approach to family functioning, described the role of the family in providing a model for the sexual development of the child. In an optimal situation a balance is achieved between over- and underreaction to the child's sexual initiatives. Parental prudishness or complete denial of sexuality in the child may suppress the development of normal sexuality. On the other hand, normal sexual development may also be disrupted by a lack of appropriate boundaries, leading to sexual abuse or incest. There are different theoretical views on the association between sexual behaviour within families and child sexual abuse, with both openness and restrictive behaviour seen as risk factors for sexual exploitation (Finkelhor, 1979); there is little evidence in support of either view.

THE HISTORY OF CHILD SEXUAL ABUSE

Although the sexual abuse of children has undoubtedly occurred for centuries, it was not seen as a child health or welfare problem until recently. In the mid-1970s the problem of child sexual abuse became apparent in the US, with a sudden rise in the number of reported cases. This was followed some years later by a similar surge in reporting of cases of sexual abuse in the UK and in Canada. In the UK, cases of sexual abuse have only been registered for 8 years. Reports of abuse in nonwestern countries are only just beginning to appear (Haffejee, 1991; Ho & Kwok, 1991).

It is not clear why the rates of sexual abuse appeared to rise at such a meteoric rate. On the whole the evidence is towards greater ease of disclosure, and greater sensitivity by professionals to the possibility of abuse, rather than a real change in the prevalence of abuse. Professionals dealing with children are more aware of what to look for as suspicious signs, although there are few, if any (differential) symptoms that are indicative of abuse having occurred (Hibbard *et al.*, 1988; Beitchman *et al.*, 1991). Retrospective studies of the prevalence of sexual abuse do not show any great difference between rates in older women and those in younger women (Wyatt & Peters, 1986b; Anderson *et al.*, 1993). Indeed in one study (Wyatt, 1985) prevalence rates were lower in women aged 18−26 years of

age than in women aged over 27 years of age. The feminist movement has been an important factor in the increase of disclosures of sexual abuse, and the generally greater openness about sexuality may also be a contributory factor.

DEFINITIONS OF CHILD ABUSE

The term child sexual abuse is widely used by professionals from a number of different disciplines, and by lay people, with the assumption that they are talking about the same phenomenon (Haugaard & Reppucci, 1988). Yet professionals from different groups differ in their definitions of abusive behaviours (Haugaard & Reppucci, 1988) and there are differences between the public and professional viewpoints (Finkelhor & Redfield, 1984). Several general definitions are often cited. One of these is that of Schechter and Roberge (1976) who defined sexual abuse as 'the involvement of dependent, developmentally immature children and adolescents in sexual activities that they do not fully comprehend, and to which they are unable to give informed consent, and that violate the social taboos of family roles'. Some definitions concentrate on sexual gratification as the central element of the abuse. For example, Baker and Duncan (1985) provided the following definition: 'A child (anyone under sixteen years) is sexually abused when another person, who is sexually mature, involves the child in any activity which the other person expects to lead to their sexual arousal.'

Finkelhor and Korbin (1988) provided a more comprehensive definition: 'Sexual abuse has been defined as any sexual contact between an adult and a sexually immature (sexual maturity is socially as well as physiologically defined) child for the purposes of the adult's sexual gratification; or any sexual contact to a child made by the use of force, threat, or deceit to secure the child's participation; or sexual contact to which a child is incapable of consenting by virtue of age or power differentials and the nature of the relationship with the adult.' As they point out, this definition covers sexual experiences between the child and her or his parents or carers, but it also covers sexual acts involving children where the child is involved for monetary gain, such as pornography involving children or child prostitution. They also make clear that it excludes actions that, although they may broadly be classified as sexual, are not for the adult's sexual gratification. An example they give is the practice in some cultures of soothing the young child by stroking its genitals.

Some definitions of abuse (such as that above) have excluded abuse by adolescents or peers, but there has been a shift towards definitions that include this as a form of sexual abuse (it is interesting that despite the recent attention and interest in bullying, there does not appear to have been a similar move to include abuse by adolescents and children in definitions of physical abuse). Finkelhor and Hotaling (1984) suggested that a definition should include 'sexual contact that occurs as a result of force, threat, deceit, while unconscious or through exploitation of an authority relationship, no matter what the age of the partner'. Sorrenti-Little *et al.* (1984)

argued that the definition of abuse should be related to the outcome: that is, that abuse should be construed as an act that has a significant likelihood of resulting in harm, or distortion or impairment of a young person's mental health development. Taking this definition, child sexual abuse consists of, at least, unwanted physical contact with the child's genital area or breasts (Bagley, 1990).

The term incest is often used to describe intrafamilial sexual abuse, but it is not always correctly used, as it has a precise meaning in the law, where its origin was in the prevention of genetic disorders of consanguinity. In the correct legal definition, the term incest applies to vaginal intercourse between a male and a female whom the offender knows to be his daughter, granddaughter, sister or mother. It does not cover abuses by stepfathers or adoptive fathers, or actions other than vaginal intercourse.

How does the public define sexual abuse?

Public definitions of sexually abusive behaviour, to a certain extent, determine how people behave, and the behaviours that are reported to the authorities. At the core of the definition is the concept of sexual acts involving a child. Finkelhor (1984) identified a number of variables that are relevant to the definition of sexual abuse, and to assessment of its seriousness. These were: the age of the victim; the age of the perpetrator (and the difference in age between victim and perpetrator); the relationship between the victim and the perpetrator (sexual acts occurring within the family may be seen as more abusive than those occurring outside the family); sex of the victim (sexual acts involving boys may be seen as less serious); sex of the perpetrator; the nature of the sexual act; consent (the degree to which the child was willing, or resisting); consequence (the outcome, in terms of the effect on the child — is an act seen as more abusive if the outcome is negative?); and the sex of the respondent (do men see sexual acts against children as less serious than women?).

Finkelhor and Redfield (1984) used a series of vignettes that systematically varied these categories to assess parental ratings of the abusiveness and seriousness of different acts. The age of the perpetrator and the nature of the sexual act were found to be the most important determinants of ratings of abusiveness. Sexual acts committed by adults over the age of 25 were more likely to be rated as 'definitely sexual abuse' than those committed by perpetrators aged under 20, and parents were much more likely to rate acts involving sexual intercourse or attempted intercourse as abusive than acts involving fondling, exhibitionism or voyeurism. Although less important, the extent to which the child objected or was passively compliant was taken into account in parents' ratings for all ages of children, with acts that were strenuously objected to rated as more serious than those not objected to, or (for older children) agreed to or suggested. The age of the child was relevant, but not in a linear way, as parents considered that acts were less abusive when they involved very young or adolescent children. In terms of the relationship of the perpetrator and

victim, father—daughter, mother—son and male relative—girl combinations were rated significantly more abusive than other combinations. On the whole there was little differentiation between other combinations (including intrafamilial and extrafamilial relationships) but abuses involving women as perpetrators were rated the least abusive. Men and women rated the relationships differently: men tended to rate vignettes involving older women as less serious than women did, but situations occurring outside the family as more serious. The consequences of the act constituted the least important variable in this experiment. Overall ratings of abusiveness made by men were significantly lower than the ratings by women, although the pattern of responses was relatively similar (for instance, men did not see abuses against boys as more or less serious than abuse against girls), suggesting that in general men see sexual abuse as less serious than women.

THE NATURE OF CHILD SEXUAL ABUSE

Types of sexual abuse

Most definitions of child sexual abuse do not specify the nature of the sexually abusive act; these range from exhibitionism or gentle fondling to forced penetrative acts. Mrazek (1980) suggested a division of sexual acts into exposure, molestation, sexual intercourse and rape. Peters *et al.* (1986) separated the sexually abusive acts involving contact (all behaviours that involve intercourse, oral or anal sex, and fondling of breasts or genitals) from noncontact abuse (exhibitionism, exposure to pornography and solicitation to engage in sexual activity). Others (e.g. Research Team, 1990; Monck *et al.*, 1993) have divided sexual acts into penetrative or nonpenetrative, thus distinguishing oral, anal or vaginal intercourse, and digital or object penetration from masturbation, fondling or exhibitionism.

The definition of abuse employed will determine to some extent the types of sexual act reported as most commonly perpetrated on children, but population studies suggest that exhibitionism and inappropriate fondling or touching are the most common forms of abuse, usually followed by masturbation and penetrative acts (Finkelhor, 1979; Baker & Duncan, 1985; Kelly *et al.*, 1991; Martin *et al.*, 1993). In the Baker and Duncan survey (1985) just over half (51%) of those who reported abusive experiences had experienced noncontact abuse, and only 5% had experienced anal or vaginal intercourse. Studies of clinical populations suggest that cases of abuse that come to clinical attention are likely to be more severe, with penetrative sexual acts more commonly reported (Bentovim *et al.*, 1987; Research Team, 1990; Monck *et al.*, 1993). Penetrative acts were the most common form of abuse for over half the sample investigated by Monck and colleagues (1993), and sexual intercourse was the second most frequent experience (after inappropriate fondling) recorded in the Northern Ireland Incidence study (Research Team, 1990). Many children who come to clinical notice have experienced multiple forms of sexual abuse (Grant, 1984; Bentovim *et al.*,

1987; Research Team, 1990; Monck *et al.*, 1993) and a higher proportion than in community surveys have been abused by more than one person (9% in the Northern Ireland study had experienced multiple abusers; 20% of the children abused within the family studied by Monck *et al.* had also been abused by someone else). Masturbation and anal intercourse are more common abuses against boys than girls. In the Northern Ireland incidence study, 42% of boys experienced anal intercourse or attempted anal intercourse versus 7% of girls (Research Team, 1990).

Age

Children of all ages are abused. Both clinical and nonclinical prevalence studies suggest that there is a peak onset, with the first abuse most commonly occurring between the ages of 8 and 12 years, although there are some indications that this peak may occur earlier in boys (Bentovim *et al.*, 1987; Research Team, 1990; Monck *et al.*, 1993). Finkelhor and Baron (1986) pooled data from a number of studies, and demonstrated an increase in the risk of onset of abuse for girls at 6—7 years of age, and a more marked increase in the rate at 10 years of age.

WHO ABUSES?

Gender

Most abuse is committed by men. Some 5—15% of abuse is perpetrated by women (Mrazek *et al.*, 1983; Faller, 1990; Research Team, 1990; Kelly *et al.*, 1991), with more recent studies suggesting higher rates than earlier studies. Women are more likely to abuse boys than girls. Finkelhor and Russell (1984), reviewing the data on women as perpetrators, suggest that they may be responsible for up to 20% of the abuse of boys. In a reanalysis of data from the American National Incidence study, Finkelhor and Russell (1984) calculated that 14% of abuse against boys and 6% of abuse against girls is perpetrated by women acting alone. Women are more often involved as co-abusers, acting with men, but figures relating to women in this context are complicated by failure to identify the role of the women — some may not be involved in sexual contact with the child, or may be acting under duress (Finkelhor & Russell, 1984). The percentages are higher in clinical studies than in community prevalence studies; this implies that abuse by women may be more likely to come to professional attention, but other data suggest abuses by women may be less likely to be reported, or indeed recognized as abuse (Finkelhor & Russell, 1984). Female abusers are more likely to commit single offences (Russell, 1986; Faller, 1990).

Extrafamilial versus intrafamilial abuse: relationship with the victim

Much of the sexual abuse that comes to professional attention is perpetrated within the family or household, although there is wide variation between studies in the proportion. Bentovim

et al. (1987) found that 75% of the cases seen clinically had been abused within the household, predominantly by fathers (46%) or stepfathers (27%). The Northern Ireland incidence study (Research Team, 1990) found that although 85% of the children knew their abuser, only 31% of children had been abused within the household, and 54% had been abused by a known person not living in the home. Five per cent were abused by a stranger. Most other clinical studies show a proportion somewhere between these two (e.g. Mrazek *et al.*, 1983; Pierce & Pierce, 1985; Hobbs & Wynne, 1987).

In clinical samples, intrafamilial abuse is most commonly perpetrated by fathers, but stepfathers are overrepresented in the abuse statistics, and have been identified as a risk factor for sexual abuse (Gruber & Jones, 1983; Finkelhor, 1984, 1986; Russell, 1984). A girl living in a stepfather household is at six times the risk of being abused as a girl living with her biological father; the abuse by stepfathers also tends to be more serious (Russell, 1984). Finkelhor (1980) noted that girls in stepfather households were also at greater risk of being abused by men other than the stepfather. However, Finkelhor (1986) cautioned that most of the stepfather data were collected some time ago, when the situation was more atypical than it is now and the findings may no longer apply.

Intrafamilial abuse is overrepresented in clinical studies, and stranger abuse is underrepresented. Nonclinical studies indicate that extrafamilial abuse either by an acquaintance or a stranger may constitute between 30 and 50% of cases of sexual contact between children and adults (Finkelhor, 1986; Anderson *et al.*, 1993) and a higher percentage if unwanted noncontact sexual experiences are included (Baker & Duncan, 1985; Kelly *et al.*, 1991). There are differences between clinical and nonclinical studies in the pattern of intrafamilial abuse. Sibling abuse is relatively uncommon in clinical studies, but in community studies it is at least as common as abuse by fathers (Finkelhor, 1979; Kelly *et al.*, 1991; Anderson *et al.*, 1993).

Both clinical and community studies agree on the proportion of abuse that is perpetrated outside the family, but by individuals who are known to the child. These are most frequently neighbours, friends of the family, peers or other people such as teachers, babysitters or club leaders, who are trusted to have contact with the child alone.

It is apparent from clinical studies, but more markedly so from prevalence studies, that there are gender differences in the pattern of intra- and extrafamilial abuse. Girls are more likely to be abused intrafamilially, and boys more likely to be abused by strangers (Haugaard & Reppucci, 1988; Faller, 1989; Research Team, 1990; Kelly *et al.*, 1991).

Differences between clinic and community studies in the proportions of intra- and extrafamilial abuse partially reflect the definitions employed. Community studies have tended to include noncontact and other 'less serious' forms of abuse, which do not usually come to professional attention. Most noncontact abuse is termed exhibitionism, but possibly it is better described as 'flashing' (e.g. Kelly *et al.*, 1991). This single-incident stranger action, although unwanted and unsettling, may also be experienced very differently from exhibitionism by a known person, in a situation from which the child cannot escape. Intrafamilial abuse may be more likely to come to professional attention, either because it is more serious in type, or in its consequences, involving, as it does in most cases, a breach of trust. Extrafamilial abuse is more likely to be a single incident, whereas intrafamilial abuse is more likely to be an ongoing or repeated phenomenon, and this (independently of any effect that this may have on symptom development) may increase the probability of disclosure, and professional attention. Families may find it easier to cope with a child who has experienced abuse outside the family, and may be less likely to ask for professional help. Finally, in retrospective studies, people may find it easier to disclose isolated extrafamilial incidents than long-standing familial abuse.

Margolin (1991) found that over three-quarters (84%) of extrafamilial abuse by unrelated caregivers was committed by men, and occurred over the whole range of caretaking arrangements, with no discernible pattern. Most of the female perpetrators were adolescents, with an average age of 17 years, and the majority of abuses took place during regular caretaking arrangements, such as babysitting, where the female had been selected by the parents, and paid for her services. Kouramy *et al.* (1979) have also described the phenomenon of sexual experimentation by adolescents while babysitting. Two other types of extrafamilial abuse warrant special mention: sex rings and ritual abuse.

Sex rings

The label sex ring has been used to describe an adult perpetrator or perpetrators simultaneously involved with several children, who are aware of each other's participation in sexual activity. They were first described in the US (Burgess *et al.*, 1981) but have since been identified in the UK (Wild & Wynne, 1986; Wild, 1989). They are characterized by repeated abuse of multiple victims by a paedophile. The abuser is nearly always male, and may be a family friend or acquaintance, but institutional sex rings, such as in schools or children's homes, have also been described. The abuse usually takes place in the adult's home, and several children may be present or involved simultaneously. Perpetrators are usually involved directly in sexual activity with the children, but sex rings have also been used to generate child pornography that then may be traded with other paedophiles, sometimes on a commercial scale, or used to blackmail children into continuing membership of the ring (Wild, 1987). Children in the ring may be bribed to recruit with money or goods, or simply rewarded in this way. Children who have run away from home or are truanting from school may be bribed into membership of a ring, in order to get a place to stay. Child prostitution is closely linked with sex rings and 'rent boy' activities.

The scale of the problem is unknown. Police investigations in the UK have revealed as many as 160 rings. Wild's (1989) survey of one city in Northern England with a population of nearly 750 000 identified 31 child sex rings during a 2-year period, involving 47 male perpetrators and 334 children. This represented nearly 5% of all cases of child sexual abuse reported to the police during that time. The large majority (89%) of the victims were girls, and their mean age was 12.2 years. The relatively small number of boys involved were slightly younger on average (9.9 years), but the age range was from 4 to 15 years for both genders. Sexual activity reported by children involved fondling and masturbation in almost every one of the rings, oral intercourse in two-thirds of the rings, and anal or vaginal intercourse in one-third.

In North America, Burgess *et al.* (1984) found more middle-class boys involved in sex rings, with child pornography more commonly involved, but these differences in findings are probably due to the methods of ascertainment of the rings.

Ritual abuse

In recent years there have been concerns about the involvement of children in ritual abuse (Jones, 1991; Jonker & Jonker-Bakker, 1991; Lanning, 1991; Putnam, 1991; Young *et al.*, 1991). Satanism, for instance, reverses ethical values, and thus promotes the idea that children need not be protected, and rules against sexual activities with children can be disregarded. There have been controversies both about whether ritual abuse occurs at all, and its extent. Ritual activities may be used as ways of silencing children.

Age of perpetrators

During the last decade it has been increasingly recognized that there are many adolescents who abuse younger children, both within and outside their families. Russell (1983) urged that unwanted sexual experiences with children or adolescents should be included in studies of abuse. If the age differential in the definition of abuse is dropped, it is clear from prevalence studies that a lot of unwanted sexual experiences are perpetrated by peers or young people (Haugaard & Tilly, 1988; Kelly *et al.*, 1991). In studies that have excluded noncoercive experiences with peers, between a quarter and a half of all reported abuses have been committed by children or young people aged under 18 (Davis & Leitenberg, 1987; Kelly *et al.*, 1991; Anderson *et al.*, 1993). Despite this, the problem of child or teenage perpetrators, some of whom have been victims of sexual abuse themselves, has only recently attracted clinical attention (Fehrenbach *et al.*, 1986; Cantwell, 1988; Johnson, 1988, 1989; Bentovim, 1991a). One interesting gender difference is suggested by some studies of adolescent perpetrators: Russell (1986) and Faller (1990) found that the majority of adolescent perpetrators committing single offences were female, and this links in with the data of Kouramy *et al.* (1979) on sexual exploration by adolescent babysitters.

INCIDENCE OF CHILD SEXUAL ABUSE

The incidence of child sexual abuse is defined as the proportion of a population who have experienced it at any time during childhood. Most studies (Hamilton, 1929; Kinsey *et al.*, 1953; Landis, 1956; Finkelhor, 1979, 1984; Fritz *et al.*, 1981; Kercher & McShane, 1984; Baker & Duncan, 1985; Bagley & Ramsay, 1986; Fromuth, 1986; Fromuth & Burkhart, 1987; Siegeal *et al.*, 1987; Kelly *et al.*, 1991; Anderson *et al.*, 1993) are based on retrospective recall by adults; most stem from the US, but there are some from Canada, the UK and New Zealand. There is wide variation — from 6 to 62% in females, and 3 to 31% in males — in quoted rates (Finkelhor, 1986). It is clear that both methodological issues and differences in definitions contribute to the variations in reported levels of sexual abuse (Wyatt & Peters, 1986a,b; Haugaard & Reppucci, 1988; Kelly *et al.*, 1991; Martin *et al.*, 1993).

The influence of definitions on prevalence rates

The detail of the definition with respect to factors such as the upper age limit for child sexual abuse, the types of sexual experiences included or excluded, and the inclusion or exclusion of experiences with adolescents or peers has a profound impact on prevalence rates (Finkelhor, 1979, 1984; Wyatt & Peters, 1986a; Fromuth & Burkhart, 1987; Haugaard & Emery, 1989; Kelly *et al.*, 1991). Wyatt and Peters (1986a) investigated four studies carried out in the US and showed, by recalculating prevalence rates with new criteria, that where the methodologies were similar, as was the case in two of the studies, differences in reported prevalence rates could be almost entirely explained by differences in definitions.

Kelly *et al.* (1991), in their survey of further education students aged 16 to 21, analysed the same data set of students' reports of unwanted sexual experiences, employing nine different definitions of increasing severity that had been used by other researchers. The least restrictive definitions (mostly exhibitionism or touching) produced a rate of 59% for women and 27% for men, compared with rates of 4 and 2% respectively using the most restrictive definition. The biggest drop in rates resulted from the exclusion of noncontact abuse. Reported rates of over 50% for women (Russell, 1983; Baker & Duncan, 1985) have all included noncontact abuse. In general, the highest rates for women are between 20 and 30% if noncontact abuse is excluded.

The influence of methodology on incidence rates

Many incidence studies have features likely to result in bias. The rate of refusal or nonresponse in prevalence studies on this sensitive topic tends to be high — for example, 36% of women invited to do so did not take part in Russell's (1983) survey. It is not clear in which direction this bias will operate. People who have been abused may refuse because their experiences were too painful; conversely, those who have not been abused may see it as irrelevant to cooperate. Several samples have been restricted to women (e.g. Russell, 1983; Wyatt, 1985; Bagley & Ramsay, 1986; Anderson *et al.*, 1993), which restricts generalizability. Others have relied on volunteers (e.g. Kinsey *et al.*, 1953) or students (e.g. Landis, 1956;

Finkelhor, 1979; Fritz *et al.*, 1981: Fromuth, 1986; Fromuth & Burkhart, 1987; Kelly *et al.*, 1991). It appears that the greatest effect on rates comes from methods of data collection, and from the framing of questions on abusive experiences. Wyatt and Peters (1986b) examined these influences in four studies in the US, reporting rates of abuse ranging from 15 to 62%. In the two studies showing markedly lower rates, data were collected by questionnaire, using broad general questions covering all sexual experiences. In the other two studies with higher rates, the data were obtained by face-to-face interview, by means of specific questions about different sorts of possible sexual experiences. Wyatt and Peters suggested that the use of these more behaviourally specific questions may aid the subject's recall of abusive experiences, by clarifying the nature of the experiences being enquired about, and at the same time triggering memories that might not be retrieved by a more general question.

The effects of sampling biases, of underreporting due to the sensitive nature of the topic, or of denial of abuse remain uncertain. At a best estimate, it appears that between 15 and 30% of women will have been subjected to an unwanted experience of sexual contact at some time during childhood, and probably twice this number will have experienced an unwanted sexual experience not involving contact. This latter category will include some experiences that, although unwanted, would not necessarily be deemed abusive by those who experienced them.

Gender differences in incidence

All studies have shown higher rates of abuse against girls than against boys. Some clinical studies have suggested very low rates of abuse against boys, with abuse against girls about nine or 10 times as common as abuse against boys (Spencer & Dunklee, 1986). Most recent clinical studies suggest a female to male ratio of about 4 or 5 : 1 (e.g. The American Humane Association national incidence survey, cited by Finkelhor, 1986; Research Team, 1990; Monck *et al.*, 1993). Nonclinical studies suggest that the difference in rates of abuse between boys and girls is rather less, with a ratio of 2 or 3 : 1. Finkelhor (1986), reviewing the eight random community samples for which data were available at that time, calculated that 71% of victims were female, and 29% male — a ratio of 2.5 : 1. Although the rates for males are lower, it appears that relatively more of the abuse involves sexual contact (Kelly *et al.*, 1991).

The difference in the gender ratios between clinical and nonclinical studies suggests that abuses against boys are less likely to be reported, and therefore that clinical studies have underrepresented the problem. Recent studies suggest that relatively more cases of abuse against boys are being disclosed or identified now. It has been suggested that the homosexual nature of most abuse against boys and the macho image of sexual contacts between mature women and adolescent boys has played a part in the underreporting of abuse of males.

Although data are beginning to accumulate (Johnson &

Shrier, 1985; Spencer & Dunklee, 1986; Reinhart, 1987), much less is known about male victims of abuse than about female victims.

Ethnic differences in incidence

Clinical studies from the US suggested that rates of abuse were higher in Americans of Afro-Carribean descent than in white Americans (Peters, 1976), but subsequent surveys have found no significant differences in rates of sexual abuse between black and white women (Kercher & McShane, 1984; Wyatt, 1985; Kelly *et al.*, 1991). Apart from a few isolated reports (Russell, 1986; Carter & Parker, 1991), there is little information on other minority ethnic groups.

Socioeconomic differences

The strong association between low socioeconomic status and nonsexual child abuse (e.g. Straus *et al.*, 1980) is not so evident in cases of sexual abuse. There is a downward socioeconomic bias in cases of sexual abuse coming to clinical attention (Bentovim *et al.*, 1987; Research Team, 1990; Monck *et al.*, 1993) but it is less marked than with other forms of abuse (Finkelhor, 1984; Wolfe, 1987). The lower social status is a feature of reported cases and is probably due to a number of factors, such as greater contact with social and other statutory support services, differences in thresholds for suspicion, and differences in acceptability of different behaviours in different social class groups. Families where cases of sexual abuse are reported appear to have higher levels of family stress and disruption before disclosure (Friedrich *et al.*, 1988), and these other factors may serve to bring the sexual abuse to professional attention. Community studies of women indicate broadly comparable rates of abuse in all social groups (Russell, 1986), but the few available data suggest that sexually abused boys may be more likely to come from socially disadvantaged or disrupted families (Finkelhor, 1984).

Relationship with physical abuse

The possible links between physical and sexual abuse remain uncertain. Aggressive behaviour involving either physical or psychological coercion or threat is commonly involved in sexual abuse (Wyatt, 1985), but aggression unconnected with manipulation is less common, and it is usually supposed that sexual and physical abuse tend not to occur together. This view is based on the supposition that there are important differences in the family dynamics in physically abusing and sexually abusing families. Some sexual abuse, however, expresses a hostile or sadistic impulse towards the child. Faller (1990) described this exception to the general pattern, in terms of sexual abuse perpetrated by people whose primary motivation is that they hate children, where the abuse may be both physical and sexual, with the intention of terrorizing the child.

Recent estimates from studies in the US and UK suggest somewhat higher rates of co-occurrence, with between 15 and 25% of sexually abused children also physically abused (Finkelhor, 1984; Hobbs & Wynne, 1987; Monck *et al.*, 1993). This may be especially the case in boys (Finkelhor, 1984).

To some extent, co-occurrence is dependent on reporting; children registered for sexual abuse may not also be registered for physical abuse, even where this has taken place.

THE EFFECTS OF SEXUAL ABUSE

An understanding of the consequences of sexual abuse and of factors that influence children's reactions is important for both assessment and therapeutic planning. It is important to be aware of the mechanisms involved in adverse reactions and in effective coping in order to facilitate the latter.

Investigations of the effects of child sexual abuse

In any investigation of the effects of child sexual abuse, it is necessary to separate the effects of abuse *per se* from other preexisting or concurrent influences (such as family discord or disadvantage) and from the consequences of disclosure, assessment processes or treatment. A second need concerns the choice of an appropriate control group for comparison (Dempster & Roberts, 1991). Thirdly, it is necessary to take account of possible bias in the group of subjects investigated. For obvious reasons, research is limited to disclosed cases, and these are likely to differ from undisclosed cases. Finally, reporting bias needs to be considered; many studies have relied on reports from caring parents, or from professionals involved with the children, such as teachers or social workers. These people are likely to know about the abuse, and this may have a profound effect on their perceptions or reporting.

Some limitations are inherent in the different types of study. Clinical samples provide complete and detailed clinical descriptions of behaviour of victims of abuse. The lack of any comparison group means that it will not be possible to determine either the level of risk or the sequelae specifically due to abuse. The study of risk and protective factors will also be problematical. Clinical groups may also include an unduly high proportion with adverse consequences. For instance, the study by Monck *et al.* (1993) that looked at a series of 98 children referred to a sexual abuse treatment project showed that those children who received treatment were more disturbed than those who did not. This was not accounted for by failure to offer treatment, but by refusal of those with responsibility for the children who felt that the treatment was not necessary. Herman *et al.* (1986) also noted that women in treatment who had experienced abuse seemed more traumatized than women in the community who had been abused.

Clinical studies, however, have served to highlight important areas for investigation in systematic comparisons of victim groups with others. It is only recently that a reliable measure of traumatic effect has been developed (Orvaschel, quoted by Deblinger *et al.*, 1990). Until now, a variety of instruments have been used to measure levels of disturbance, and these may be more sensitive to some broader family risk factors than to the specific trauma of abuse itself. Comparative studies allow a systematic evaluation of the factors associated with the abusive situation, and with the characteristics of the individuals involved, that relate most strongly to adverse sequelae. However, their power to do this is reliant both on the most appropriate choice of comparison group and on analyses that can identify individual differences in response. Thus, Conte and Schuerman's (1987) comparison of behavioural symptoms following sexual abuse suffered from the fact that, on average, the comparison group were less disadvantaged, with higher incomes, higher parental education, more intact marriages and fewer overall stresses.

Effects of abuse: clinical and empirical studies

The majority of clinical accounts (e.g. Bentovim *et al.*, 1987) indicate that, for most victims, there are a variety of negative consequences of abuse, often lasting for many years (Beitchman *et al.*, 1992). These include emotional disturbances (such as somatic complaints, sleep difficulties, nightmares and self-destructive behaviour), and also aggression, sometimes associated with sexual activities with both younger and older individuals. Detrimental effects on the sexuality of adolescents and adults occur. However, positive adjustments, sometimes after initial difficulties, have also been reported (Yorukoglu & Kemph, 1966; Bernard, 1981; Sandfort, 1984). Clinical experience suggests that what may feel emotionally satisfying at one stage in development may be felt as an abuse at a later stage (for example, if eroticized needs have been created). The possible sequelae of sexual abuse will be considered in terms of: (1) sexualizing effects; (2) emotional effects; (3) depressed mood; (4) anxiety; (5) behavioural effects; and (6) specific effects of sex rings and ritual abuse.

Sexualizing effects

Probably, heightened sexual activities, both during childhood and later on in adult life, constitute the most specific response to sexual abuse. Yates (1982) and De Young (1984) reported hypersexual and sexually provocative behaviour as a consequence of having been eroticized by abuse. James and Nasjheti (1983), Bentovim and Boston (1988) and Kohan *et al.* (1987) described a series of children showing sexual behaviour, initiating sexual contact with adults, or with other younger children, being involved in sexual play with others and behaving in a seductive way towards staff in inpatient units. A number of recent studies (Friedrich *et al.*, 1988; Gale *et al.*, 1988; Gomes-Schwartz *et al.*, 1990; Monck *et al.*, 1993) have all reported higher levels of sexualized behaviour in sexually abused children.

Friedrich (1988) used a specific standardized measure of sexual behaviour, and Monck *et al.* (1993) asked mothers and caretakers about overt sexual behaviour; both noted that the most persistent sexualized behaviour (often intensive public masturbation) occurred in younger children. The role of sexual abuse in the genesis of sexually delinquent behaviour has been intensely debated. Abel *et al.* (1987) and Watkins and Bentovim (1992) noted that a sexually abusive orientation often begins during adolescence and that a cycle of deviant fantasies, masturbation and sexual activities is shaped by inappropriate early sexual experiences (Ryan, 1989). Studies in special populations, such as prostitutes, suggest that abused girls may engage in intensive sexual activities during adolescence (James & Meyerding, 1977; Silbert & Pines, 1981). Equally, there may be a marked inhibiting effect on the development of sexual activities and sexual responses (Finkelhor, 1979).

Boys who experience homosexual abuse commonly show confusion and anxiety over their sexual identity (Rogers & Terry, 1984). This seems to stem from their concerns over the reason for their selection as victims. They fear that homosexual qualities were recognized in them by the abuser, or that their inadequate resistance to the abuse meant that there was a likelihood of them having some homosexual orientation. A number of reports support an increased likelihood of homosexual preference in later life (Finkelhor, 1984; Johnson & Shrier, 1985; Krug, 1989; Singer, 1989) but not all do (Becker, 1988; Fromuth & Burkhart, 1989).

Thus, although there may be a variety of different explanations for inappropriate sexual activity in childhood and adolescence, the most common, particularly amongst younger children, may well be as a response to being sexually abused. Such behaviours would certainly require appropriate investigation and treatment, because of the persistence and development of an inappropriate sexual orientation.

Emotional effects

A sense of guilt and responsibility for the abuse experienced is reported by many victims in clinical studies (for example, Byrne & Valdiserri, 1982; Gelinas, 1983; Summit, 1983). It was suggested that this arose in older children because they believed that they could or should have stopped the abuse if they had wished to. Those children who experienced a physical response or who enjoyed the increased attention and warmth may feel guilty that they must have wanted the abuse to occur. If, during an investigation or a criminal prosecution, the child is portrayed as seductive, or as a willing participant, a sense of guilt increases. Distress on the mother's part, or if a father has to separate from the family, or is imprisoned, can also increase guilt (Giarretto, 1981).

Victims often experience a sense of powerlessness (Finkelhor & Browne, 1985) in response to their inability to stop repeated invasions of their body, or to control what happens to them. Many victims are described as experiencing a sense of loss: loss of the family if the child is placed in foster care, or if the mother chooses to support the perpetrator rather than the victim. A sense of isolation is often described, including isolation from peers, fears of being recognized as a victim of sexual abuse, or isolation from siblings because of a fear of rejection when a parent with whom the sibling had a good relationship had to leave home. Victimization may also lead to difficulty in trusting, with major concerns about relating to the opposite sex, although older adolescent girls may show the opposite effects, in a too rapid clinging to partners who may be unsuitable.

Depressed mood

Depressed mood, often associated with anger, is also commonly described in clinical samples (Gelinas, 1983; Bentovim & Boston, 1988). Victims often express a helplessness and hopelessness, with anger that is often pervasive and directed towards the abuser, other family members or the social service agencies. There may be differences between boys and girls on the target of the anger (Watkins & Bentovim, 1992); there is some impression that boys abused by their fathers are angry with their fathers, but girls are also angry with their mothers.

Monck et al. (1993) used the Children's Depression Inventory (Kovacs & Beck, 1977) to assess mood. High scores were common on the somatic symptoms, such as disturbance of sleep and appetite, fatigue and general worries about their own health, and nearly a quarter of sexually abused youngsters (24%) expressed strong worries about the future, with high scores on the fear that 'bad things will happen'. There was a significant tendency for children who were more depressed to be more likely to report lower self-esteem. High scores on the Children's Depression Inventory were given by 26% of the children; in an unselected nonclinical population only 10% would be expected (Kovacs & Beck, 1977). Self-esteem measures observed in the same study (Monck et al., 1993) indicated that the lowest self-image was concerned with body image and peer relationships.

Anxiety effects

Anxiety is expressed through increased fearfulness, somatic complaints, changes in sleep patterns and nightmares (Adams-Tucker, 1982; Bentovim & Boston, 1988). These symptoms are frequently associated with posttraumatic effects. Those noted as associated with sexual abuse are flashbacks of experiences, reenactments associated with reminders of the context or individuals, withdrawal from situations or contexts where abuse has occurred, startle reactions and hypervigilance associated with hyperarousal (Goodwin, 1985; Kiser et al., 1988; McLeer et al., 1988; Wolfe et al., 1989). Intrusive thoughts related to the event and abuse-specific fears may differentiate children who have been abused from other children with psychiatric problems. In only one study, using standardized structured interviews of children, did the children appear as generally fearful as a psychiatric population (Runyon et al., 1988).

A number of studies of adults (Briere & Runtz, 1988; Mullen et al., 1988; Finkelhor et al., 1989; Siegel et al., 1990; Bifulco et al., 1991) have demonstrated a convincing link between traumatic events, particularly sexual abuse in childhood, and subsequent affective and phobic disorders in the adult life of women, and on self-esteem, mood regulation, sexuality and marital satisfaction in women. Studies of men who have been abused in childhood (Briere et al., 1988; Dimock, 1988; Briere & Runtz, 1989; Cavaiola & Schiff, 1989; Krug, 1989) have also shown a greater prevalence of depression, suicidal feelings, low self-esteem, anxiety disorders and relationship problems. Such studies indicate the importance of diagnosis and preventive work in childhood and adolescence.

Behavioural effects

The most common behaviour reactions described in boys who have been sexually abused is the development of aggressive behaviour, such as bullying, chronic disobedience and anti-social acts. Rogers and Terry (1984) suggested that this was a way of reestablishing masculinity. Girls have been described as having a far higher level of suicidal thoughts and activities (Herman, 1981; Adams-Tucker, 1982; Gomes-Schwartz et al., 1990). Self-mutilation, burning with cigarettes, cutting wrists, and anorectic responses are commonly described clinically. These reactions are postulated to be attempts by the victim to make themselves less attractive or tempting or to blot out memories, particularly those of any erotic nature, with self-inflicted pain. In recent investigations, children have been assessed directly, or by a parent or teacher rating, or by self-report (e.g. Conte & Schuerman, 1987; Tong et al., 1987; Conte & Berliner, 1988; Cohen & Mannarino, 1988; Friedrich et al., 1988, 1991; White et al., 1988; Einbender & Friedrich, 1989; Wolfe et al., 1989; Gomes-Schwartz et al., 1990; Monck et al., 1993). Abused children as a group differ behaviourally from nonabused children, but they show somewhat less psychopathology than psychiatrically disturbed populations. Monck et al. (1993), however, found teachers' scores on behaviour ratings to be much the same as those found by Rutter (1967) for a group of children referred to a psychiatric clinic. The abused children appeared a distressed and difficult group (more fidgety, more likely to be disliked, rated as solitary, unhappy or worried, significantly more restless, disobedient, fearful, bullying and having more somatic symptoms than the psychiatric clinic sample).

Mothers' or carers' reports of symptoms were higher in the conduct problem area, with irritability, aggression, misery and fears most frequently noted by mothers. The children's self-report of symptomatology was higher than in a community population of preadolescent school children (Smith & Jenkins, 1991) and the items most frequently reported by children were depression or misery, stomach aches, headaches, sleep problems, restlessness and fears and phobias. In the study by Monck et al. (1993), as in other studies, a number of children were reported to have few or no symptoms.

Specific effects of sex rings and ritual abuse

The effects of, and feelings of responsibility for, being involved in a sex ring can be widespread, and highly confusing for young people's sense of identity, and large-scale intervention may be needed (Burgess *et al.*, 1984). There may be conflicts between the need to await the outcome of criminal proceedings before offering therapeutic work, or to meet with traumatic effects in a primary way. Burgess (1984) examined children involved in sex rings and found that those involved for over a year and those who had been involved in pornography had the most negative symptoms. Children's knowledge that there may be a permanent record of their activities and that pictures of themselves may appear in magazines and be seen by people they knew may be a cause for a continuing high level of anxiety after exploitation had stopped (Mulvey & Haugaard, 1986).

Jones (1991) has indicated three main concerns expressed by clinicians in relation to ritual abuse. Firstly, the embedding of child sexual abuse within a powerful belief system, especially deviant ones such as Satanism, can create significant and long-lasting distortion of the victim's attitudes, beliefs, allegiances and fundamental personality structure to such a degree that adaptive recovery is very difficult. Secondly, the combination of child sexual abuse with premeditated and sadistic activities appears to result in more serious psychological effects. Thirdly, child sexual abuse accompanied by extreme degradation and demeaning of the victim provides a major concern because it seems to have the most devastating consequences for the victim's sense of self-esteem.

In assessing the effects of abuse it may be preferable to define abuse partly in terms of context (Jones, 1991). For example, it may be relevant whether more than one family member is being abused; whether it is ritual or ring abuse; whether there is concurrent abuse by the same perpetrator or perpetrators; and whether in addition to sexual abuse, there is extensive physical or emotional abuse.

COPING WITH ABUSE EXPERIENCES

Positive coping

Some studies (Fritz *et al.*, 1981) report a considerable number of abused individuals who voice few concerns about their experiences. Finkelhor (1979) stated that 33% of respondents viewed the abuse as neutral or positive. Constantine (1981) felt that children who were sexually knowledgeable and comprehended the activity seemed to be less affected. Monck *et al.*'s study (1993) indicated that for 16% of children the experiences had usually been pleasurable, and 13% believed it was a normal part of family life. It may be that some children are especially resilient to unpleasant experiences, or the aversiveness of the experience does not achieve dramatic levels. They may have developed coping skills, such as choosing and using good confidants, or come from supportive environments, and this may make them able to handle abusive experiences with a minimum of distress.

Berliner (1991) pointed out that what appears to be good coping may be accounted for by dissociative responses and, at a later date, for example, at later stages of development or key stress periods such as during pregnancy, there may be a triggering of negative responses.

Negative coping

The effects of trauma may well give rise to forms of coping that permit the individual to reduce or avoid the anxiety attendant to remembering stressful events, but that have negative effects generally. These may include dissociation, deletion responses, amnesia and multiple personality development (Kluft, 1985). Self-destructive attitudes, such as self-hate, anxieties about appearance and poor body image, that are reported by some abused children (Monck *et al.*, 1993), are also common to anorectic patients. In recent years it has been evident that there has been a higher than expected rate of sexual abuse in anorectic and bulimic patients (Palmer *et al.*, 1990; Lask & Bryant-Waugh, 1992). Hall *et al.* (1989) estimated that half of the patients admitted to an eating disorders unit had a history of childhood sexual abuse. It has been suggested that posttraumatic phenomena, such as avoidance of oral reminders, control of intake and appetite, may play a part in the genesis of anorectic symptoms as a way of coping with traumatic effects. Lask *et al.* (1991) also described a pervasive refusal syndrome, that appears to be a way of attempting totally to regress in order to reduce the internal discomfort at some level. Not only does the memory of the actual abuse produce discomfort, but explaining why it happened and what it means may cause psychological distress.

With all the above sections on the sequelae of sexual abuse, it is necessary to bear in mind (as noted above) that in almost all cases the data are not of a kind that enable any accurate estimate of the extent of risk associated with sexual abuse. That there are important risks (especially from more severe abuse) is not in doubt, but the high incidence of abuse in the general population carries the clear implication that many individuals must escape seriously handicapping sequelae.

FACTORS INFLUENCING THE EFFECTS OF CHILD SEXUAL ABUSE

Systematic attempts have now been made to examine the differential effects of various abusive situations, and the relationships between the abuse and other variables.

Child characteristics

Age of onset of abuse

Findings have been equivocal about the influence on later adjustment of the child's age when first sexually abused. Some suggest that younger children may be more affected than older ones (Meiselman, 1978; MacVicar, 1979; Gomes-Schwartz *et al.*, 1990) but others have shown no age effect (Finkelhor, 1979; Tsai *et al.*, 1979; Russell, 1984).

Previous stressful experiences

Ruch and Chandler (1982) reported that those with stressful experiences prior to abuse were more traumatized by their sexual assault than those without such (undefined) stresses. Previous functional difficulties and previous pathological family relationships (MacVicar, 1979; Conte & Schuerman, 1987) have both been found to be associated with a worse outcome.

Physical violence and coercion

Abusive experiences that are coercive, or which involve the use of force, seem particularly likely to result in negative consequences in both the short and long term. Finkelhor (1979), Russell (1984), Fromuth (1986) and Haugaard and Tilly (1988) in college students noted greater feelings of traumatization when coercion or physical violence was used.

Duration and penetrative nature of abuse

Abuse of longer-term duration and penetrative abuse have been associated with more traumatic effects (Russell, 1984; Monck et al., 1993). Mannarino et al. (1992) noted penetrative abuse as a factor associated with more negative effects at follow-up, but not at diagnosis. In general, the fact that children who come to clinical attention are more likely to have experienced penetrative abuse suggests that the effects are greater.

The age of, and relationship with, the perpetrator

The specific relationship with the perpetrator has also been associated with the severity of effects, but in many cases this may be attributable to differences in the abuse characteristics. For example, Gomes-Schwartz et al. (1990) showed that those abused by biological parents were less seriously affected than those abused by stepparents, but this may have been accounted for by the fact that stepfather abuse tended to be more serious. Similarly, differences in the impact of sibling abuse and extra-familial abuse may be at least partly attributable to the fact that sibling abuse is more serious, and more likely to involve penetration, to be of long duration, and to involve the use of coercion (Russell, 1984). There is some evidence (Kiser et al., 1988) that abuse by another child or adolescent may cause less negative effects than abuse by a parent, because of the differences in authority. Johnson (1988, 1989) and Johnson and Berry (1989) reported that the main effect of sexual abuse by other children appeared to be a triggering of sexual activities in the victims.

Events subsequent to abuse

Psychological disturbances following abuse may be a consequence of the abuse itself, but may stem from the detection process or from the events that follow disclosure. Some symptoms may diminish because abuse has ended, whereas others may increase or change as a result of subsequent events. Physical trauma and sexually transmitted disease may begin to repair, but other posttraumatic states, such as sleeplessness, anxiety and depression, may increase. Other factors such as court appearances may also have a role. Goodman et al. (1992) found that children who had to testify in criminal court showed greater behavioural disturbance, both during and after the trial, than children who did not, and felt that this was in part due to the lack of systematic preparation of the child and outdated legal practices. Monck et al. (1993) noted that a third (36%) of mothers were not supportive of their children after disclosure of abuse and maintained this position up to the time of referral to a treatment agency. Schultz (1973), Adams-Tucker (1982), Rogers and Terry (1984), Conte and Schuerman (1987), and Gomes-Schwartz et al. (1990) all agreed that negative responses by mothers tend to worsen the child's trauma. Monck et al.'s (1993) study indicated that there was a strong association between whether children were believed by their mothers and their positive self-esteem. Mothers who disbelieved their older abused girls had a higher self-regard and were more likely to choose to remain with the perpetrator and reject the child. Conversely, mothers who believed that abuse had occurred tended to feel badly about themselves, presumably feeling a sense of responsibility for the abuse, and this was reflected in the child's own state. Other studies indicate that victims feel better if perpetrators take responsibility for their abusive actions.

Conclusion

Characteristics associated with outcome include the age of child, the particular form of abuse, long duration, coercion and violence. Evidence about the effects of age at first abuse and the relationship with the perpetrator is less clear. What is striking is that both the quality of relationships within the family before abuse is reported, and in particular the response of a parent who should be supportive — the mother — have a profound effect on whether the abuse itself will have serious and persistent effects, or whether there will be the possibility of recovery. It is extremely important for the future mental health and well-being of the child to ensure that she or he is in a protective and supportive context following diagnosis.

MODELS TO ACCOUNT FOR THE DELETERIOUS EFFECTS OF SEXUAL ABUSE

A variety of different theories have been put forward to account for the deleterious effect of abuse. These include family systemic effects that contribute to the distress associated with abuse. Madonna et al. (1991) carried out a controlled study looking at family interactions within families where sexual abuse had occurred. They noted significantly more interactional dysfunction in families with an abused child than in psychiatric clinic families where abuse had not occurred. Families were characterized by rigid belief systems, dysfunctional parental coalitions, parental neglect, emotional unavailability and the inability to nurture autonomy in family members. Family members were told how to act, feel and think, they were constricted in mood, and tended to avoid or obscure conflict. Such findings support the family contextual explanation for the negative effects of abuse. Monck *et al.* (1993) also studied the parents of children who were abused, and noted the high proportion who reported having been abused themselves, or who described a predominant sense of dissatisfaction in childhood, and few happy memories, contributing to marital dysfunction and discord.

Such factors are seen as having an important role in men's development of a paedophilic orientation towards children. Finkelhor (1984) reviewed the literature on why perpetrators abuse children, asking the following questions: (1) Why does a person find relating sexually to a child emotionally gratifying and congruent? (2) Why is a person capable of being sexually aroused by a child? (3) Why is a person blocked in his or her efforts to obtain sexual and emotional gratification from more normatively approved sources? and (4) Why is a person not deterred by conventional social inhibitions from sexual relationships with a child? Explanations focus on the specific effects of being involved in sexual activities, such as through sexual stimulation, or learning inappropriate ways to gain warmth, intimacy or power.

Summit (1983) described the child sexual abuse accommodation syndrome to account for the child's view of her- or himself being responsible for the adult's abusive actions towards him- or herself, and the posttraumatic effects and traumagenic dynamics (Finkelhor & Browne, 1985). Terr (1991) introduced the notion of a type II posttraumatic state to account for the effects of repeated traumatic experiences. These include the sense of futility, lack of hope in the future and rage, also noted by Monck *et al.* (1993) to be associated with long-standing abuse.

INVESTIGATION OF CHILDREN FOR SEXUAL ABUSE

Recognition of sexual abuse depends upon a child's account of her or his experiences, and less frequently on physical findings. Thus the child's account is of prime importance. The assessment of possible cases involving child sexual abuse has come under scrutiny in all countries where the problem of child sexual abuse is being increasingly recognized and addressed. To achieve an adequate assessment, it is essential that high-quality multidisciplinary working practices are developed, in which interviews with children fit in with other parts of the multidisciplinary process of assessment. Interviews with children are supplemented by enquiries in other areas of the child's life, including family life. Child interviews have to be conducted within the context of available research on the memory ability of young children, the child as a witness, questions of how suggestible children are, and what is the normative language and knowledge of sexuality (see Chapter 4). Sexual abuse may be one of a number of possible considerations and decisions have to be made as to when screening is appropriate, and when a full-scale investigation of sexual abuse is appropriate. These issues have been extensively reviewed (e.g. Leventhal *et al.*, 1987; Davis *et al.*, 1988; Vizard, 1991; Jones, 1992; UK: Home Office and Department of Health, 1992).

Presentation

The most common mode of presentation is through the direct statement of the child (Conte & Berliner, 1988). Monck *et al.* (1993) indicated that 47% of presentations came through direct telling. The first person told is frequently another child of a similar age, then a parent or trusted adult. Increasingly children use telephone helplines anonymously, and it is essential that appropriate advice is given, for the child to talk to a trusted adult. A change in behaviour is another common presentation; for example, the development of sexualized patterns of behaviour in school or at home. Physical illness is another not uncommon presentation, for example, the presence of venereal disease in prepubescent children. Some children present with physical evidence of an assault or rape, and frequent urinary tract infections without clear physical cause, or enuresis and encopresis, may raise the question of child sexual abuse. In older adolescents sexual abuse may also present through pregnancy, overdosing, running away, or through the abuse of other children.

The role of the caretaking parent is important in disclosure as well as in what happens after disclosure. Lawson and Chaffin (1992) found that disclosure of abuse in children who presented with sexually transmitted disease was strongly associated with the attitude of their mother: children whose mother accepted the possibility that their child might have been abused were more than three times as likely to disclose abuse than those whose caretaker denied the possibility.

The Royal College of Physicians (1991) advised a physical examination of the anus and external genitalia of children in cases of suspected abuse, as a valuable approach to assessment. The examination may be carried out before an investigative interview if the concern has arisen through presentation with physical symptoms. Children will often begin to talk about their experiences in the context of a sympathetic examination. Alternatively the physical examination can be carried out after the initial interview if the presentation is on the basis of the child's statements or behaviour. Issues of consent to examination need to be carefully worked out, particularly with older children.

It is essential that such examinations are carried out by experienced trained paediatricians or by physicians with forensic training (for example, police surgeons) or preferably jointly, using the approach recommended by the Royal College of Physicians (1991) on, for example, the optimal position for the child to be examined in, the use of colposcopy and photographic recording.

There has been a singular lack of established norms for

genital appearance for both boys and girls, but these are now being established. The only certain physical signs of sexual abuse are the presence of semen, or sexually transmitted disease. Because of rapid recovery of physical effects, a negative physical examination does not rule out the occurrence of abuse. In a well-validated series of children who had been abused, less than 40% showed physical signs of abuse (Royal College of Physicians, 1991).

INVESTIGATION AND THE COGNITIVE CAPACITIES OF CHILDREN

It is now established that the long-term capacity of children to remember past events is as good as that of adults. Children below the age of 5 recall less detail than older children or adults (Goodman & Helgson, 1985), but in general children recall less well because their understanding of the world is not so well-developed at earlier ages, and they may not have a sufficient grasp of language to be able to relate the events. However, even young prelanguage children who have experienced events that made an impact upon them remember those events accurately when they were 3 or 4 years old, and used current language to relate the facts (Todd & Perlmutter, 1980). Memory for events of central importance to children, and their capacity to place them directly in temporal order, is surprisingly well-developed, even for very young children (Gelman, 1978).

Younger children can be susceptible to influence by the authority of an interviewer, and may have some problems in distinguishing their own thoughts and dreams from what actually did happen. There is great controversy about the introduction of anatomical dolls as an aid for younger children to describe their experiences, but Vizard's (1991) review of the use of dolls indicates that children who are abused may well demonstrate more sexual activities when presented with the dolls, and their use does not force younger children into being more suggestive than when dolls without such features are used. Props and cues that suggest a context are aids to memories, but there is concern in ensuring that questions and ways of facilitating children's memories should not unduly suggest the responses in an overly leading or pressured way (Jones, 1992).

Screening and level of concern

Decisions need to be made as to whether a full investigative interview should be carried out, or a screening interview. Distinctions need to be made between high levels of concern, for example, children with physical findings together with highly sexualized patterns of behaviour; and lower levels of concern, such as a child with anorectic patterns, onset of enuresis, encopresis, or other physical symptoms that may be effects of abuse.

For mental health professionals, there is a distinction to be made between the assessment of the extent of psychological ill-effects on a child as a consequence of abuse, in order to plan a comprehensive intervention, and investigation into the possibility of abuse, for example, with very young children, or children with learning disabilities or overt disturbance (Royal College of Psychiatrists, 1988). Jones (1992) argued that, generally speaking, child mental health professionals do not interview well children who are free from disturbance, in order to see if they have been abused, whereas social workers and police officers may well be required to interview psychologically well children to see if the child requires protection or if a crime has been committed. Nevertheless, we suggest that mental health professionals also have a protective task, and their skills with children may be appropriately used to interview any child where abuse is a concern.

Screening interviews

It is essential that such interviews be carried out with the child alone, because it would not be reasonable to expect a child, in a family context, to reveal abusive experiences that often have been carried out in an atmosphere of threat. There often needs to be a general discussion about sleeping, bathing arrangements, privacy, discipline, application of creams and medications, or other worries and concerns that a child may have about particular people or places (Jones, 1992; Tranter, 1993). Enquiries about secrets, whom children would speak to if they did have any worries, anything they have not been able to tell somebody about, and whether anybody had hurt or touched the child in a way that she or he did not like, may all be appropriate. Lanktree *et al.* (1991) noted that the proportion of positive reports of child sexual abuse obtained at interview increased from 7 to 31% when team members were trained to ask a number of specific screening questions.

Investigative interviews

Investigative interviews may well be planned, or carried out jointly, with police or social work colleagues. It is advantageous to video-tape interviews as a result of the acceptance in several countries of their use in court, instead of the child having to give evidence (UK: Home Office and Department of Health, 1992). Vizard (1991) reviewed a variety of structured approaches to interviewing children, with and without anatomical dolls, and with a variety of open-ended, closed and facilitative questioning and tasks. Wiseman *et al.* (1992) found that professionals' abilities to recognize abuse from interviews became more reliable with experience. Yuille (1988) developed an approach to validity by looking for idiosyncratic features of an interview; that is, those statements and activities indicating a level of knowledge and experiences outside the bounds of what would be expected for the child's particular stage of development and knowledge.

The majority of interviews use a structured approach that includes making a rapport with the child, giving children the opportunity to tell their own story of what has occurred to them, and using a variety of facilitatory techniques to help overcome the secrecy and anxiety that accompany the revelation of abuse (Vizard, 1991; Jones, 1992). It is essential that no investigative interview of a child should be conducted without full consultation and collaboration with protection agencies to ensure that an appropriate response can be planned if the child was to reveal an abusive experience. The Cleveland report (Butler-Sloss, 1988) distinguished between those primary investigations that are the responsibility of the police/social work team, and second-stage interviews with children with a variety of learning and communication disabilities, and behavioural disturbance. These may require highly skilled trained interviewers, including mental health professionals, and the use of facilitatory methods that may give rise to problems of interpretation and challenge in court. The process of validation can involve mental health professionals in a multidisciplinary review of the evidence of interviews, examinations and family assessments. Jones and McGraw (1987), Jones and Seig (1988), and McGraw and Smith (1992) have reviewed the characteristics of children's accounts that seemed to distinguish between reliable and false statements, particularly in the highly contentious field of allegations associated with marital breakdown and separation. For example, reliable reports appeared to be those describing experiences that clearly confused and puzzled the child, but which were clear to those who understand the way that adults involve and develop abusive activities with children, whereas statements in which use of language forms was more reminiscent of adults than children in their descriptions of abuse, were more likely to be false.

Interviews with parents and family assessment

It is essential for there to be sufficient interviews and physical examination of children where abuse is suspected to be able to make a diagnosis with enough authority to be able to protect a child if necessary. This requires the use of strategy meetings, multidisciplinary conferences, or appropriate strategy to achieve such goals. Local practices indicate that interviews with parents or alleged abusers are carried out initially by the protection/criminal police/social work team. A mental health investigation may then be called for to assess the degree of risk or dangerousness of the offender, the supportiveness of the mother and the treatment needs of the child (Bentovim, 1991b).

TREATMENT

It is usual to think of treatment as occurring over a period of time and in a sequence of stages: (1) the period of disclosure; (2) work during a period of family separation — separation of the abused child from the abuser, in a context of protection; (3) a rehabilitation phase; and (4) working towards a new family for those children where rehabilitation is not possible.

The disclosure phase

The disclosure process is a complex one because it involves recognition of abuse, assessment of the impact of abuse on the child, assessment of the protective capacity of the nonabusive parent and a risk assessment of the offender if they are a family member. There needs to be extensive consultation between professionals; the use of case conferences to bring together information; professional networking to make decisions both within the child care legal context and the criminal context; and decisions about the need for statutory action to protect, prosecute or make longer-term treatment plans (Law of Great Britain, 1989; UK: Department of Health, 1989; UK: Home Office and others, 1991).

Depending on the assessment of the extent of abuse, the degree of protection and support provided by the nonabusive parent(s) and the degree of responsibility taken by the alleged offender, decisions have to be made about where the child should live. There is very considerable turmoil following the diagnosis of sexual abuse and the Cleveland inquiry (Butler-Sloss, 1988) pointed to the importance of good interagency working and interdisciplinary practice to ensure minimum disruption to a child's life. Gomes-Schwartz *et al.* (1990) noted that initially 79% of children were placed with family members, whereas Monck *et al.* (1993) indicated that initially only 53% of children lived with family members because so many parents were not supportive.

As well as assessing the offending parent or family member during this phase it is also essential to carry out a full family assessment. This should involve looking at the factors described by Madonna *et al.* (1991) and Furniss (1991) with respect to the unavailability of parents, the degree of parental and marital conflict, patterns of secrecy and boundary confusion, the ability of the families to put children's needs first, and the presence of other associated longer-term emotional or physical abuse. An essential task during this phase is the breaking of the taboo of secrecy about sexual matters that often occurs within the family. In families where there is major denial of the possibility of abuse, then children who may be placed in alternative contexts such as foster homes or children's homes need the opportunity to share the nature of their abusive experience.

The ability of an offender to acknowledge at an early stage his (or her) responsibility may be helpful in beginning to reverse the child's guilt and self-blame, which appear to play such an important part in maintaining emotional and behavioural symptoms. A variety of approaches have been put forward to facilitate the treatment and processing of the traumatic experiences of abused children, and for working with offenders. These include the use of statutory orders ensuring ongoing protection and support, statutory provision of treatment for children and parental counselling (Law of Great Britain, 1989). An alternative is the use of diversionary approaches within the criminal procedures in the US or, in the UK, probation orders with treatment for prosecuted offenders.

Work during separation

Protection of the child from ongoing abuse implies physical separation from the offender, if a parental figure, but when the abuser is an older child it may be possible to provide a protective context within the family for a younger child. There may be separation from both parents if there is rejection of the child and denial of abuse.

To deal with the effects of sexualization, emotional ill-effects, depression, anxiety and behavioural problems, a variety of approaches — cognitive, behavioural, psycho-dynamic and systems — have been advocated (Haugaard & Reppucci, 1988). Berliner and Wheeler (1987) emphasized the importance of processing both the emotional and cognitive effects of sexual abuse.

Emotional processing

The specific emotional effects associated with posttraumatic stress and the associated depressed affect require processing of fear-producing experiences by exposure to the memories of abusive acts (Berliner & Wheeler, 1987; Berliner, 1991; Kiser et al., 1991). This means that the child victim will be expected to talk about abuse in therapy. Repeated exposure to the memories in the safe and supportive therapy environment is designed to decondition the effect of associations. Initially, some distress is inevitable and, if not observed, could raise the possibility that a child may be continuing to dissociate from the emotional content. Recollection of all aspects of the experience is necessary to identify the stimuli that evoke abuse associations. This is particularly complicated where there has been multiple abuse over an extended period. Episodes may be forgotten or repressed, or the elements of different experiences mixed up and confused. Berliner (1991) suggested listing everything such as places, sounds, or smells, that reminds the child of the abuse or that causes anxiety. Strategies for managing fear and anxiety are used to increase the child's sense of self-efficacy and control, learning to reduce physical sensations by employing systematic relaxation, controlled breathing, cognitive approaches, thought-stopping, reassuring self-statements, covert rehearsal and cognitive restructuring. This can be helpfully linked with work with the parent, including expression of anger, teaching specific behavioural management skills and prevention training (Deblinger et al., 1990).

Structured group work that influences cognitive understanding of the experience and promotes spontaneous psychological support can help achieve some of the tasks of emotional processing (MacFarlane et al., 1986; Bentovim et al., 1988; Berliner, 1991). Groups are topic-led in relationship to the age and stage of development of the children. Varying types of activities achieve set goals, for example, role play, tasks involving drawing, story-telling, observing videos and flash cards. Fostering altruism and sharing in communication, enjoyment and humour all have a normalizing effect on what can seem extreme experiences. Self-assertion skills and facilitating the expression of a range of feelings can be helpful in group work.

Cognitive processing

This addresses the way in which the child understands the abusive experiences (Berliner & Wheeler, 1987; Bentovim et al., 1988). There needs to be direct attribution of responsibilities made in family meetings, individual work and in group work, and directly by offenders, protective parents and other family members. This issue often needs to be gone over a number of times and in various contexts. The issue of self-blame needs to be addressed and explanations given about the offender's behaviour, mother's responses and work on the concept of ownership, competency and coping. It is necessary to reduce vulnerability to susequent abuse through teaching understanding of abusive cycles, helping to develop telling skills, role play of assertive and social skills and communication training. Formal and informal therapeutic relationships with careworkers as well as specific therapeutic work can foster trust and positive esteem. It is essential to develop a way of working that is direct and supportive. The silence of the nondirective approach may foster avoidance and may, to the child, be reminiscent of the silence of the abusive context, although at a later stage such an approach may be helpful.

Dealing with sexualization and sexualized behaviour

To deal with sexualization effects, children need to think appropriately about sexuality, to understand arousal and orgasmic responses, to have an adequate understanding of sexual issues relative to age, and to find ways of meeting sexual needs in acceptable ways, relative to age and state of development (Berliner, 1991). Work needs to be done both in family contexts, for example on dealing with masturbation, and direct confrontation within groups when inappropriate sexual ways of behaving are demonstrated. A variety of methods may be necessary to review, and teach older children age-appropriate basic sexual knowledge discussing consent, mutuality and readiness for sexual activities (MacFarlane et al., 1986). With younger children it is important to sort out the limits of appropriate and inappropriate touching, appropriate exposure in relationship to age, gender and the differences between strangers, peers, close and distant family members. There are a variety of ways of pursuing these through tasks, and through parent/caretaker work to reinforce modesty. Caution needs to be exercised in relation to the gender of the caretaker, and scrupulous care taken over physical contact in foster and community care settings.

One of the major concerns is the danger of sexually abused children, particularly boys, becoming abusers. It is essential therefore to pursue the issue of the potentially abusive cycles that children are already involved in with their peers, or with younger children (Johnson & Berry, 1989).

Seriously affected children

Children and young people with a profound mood disturbance, suicidal behaviour, mutilation, or serious anorectic symptoms may require placement in inpatient and longer-term therapeutic communities. An extensive programme of therapeutic activities to improve self-esteem, as well as deal with specific effects, is needed. The revealing and processing of traumatic experiences are often necessary as part of a general therapeutic programme.

Family work

The issue of whether a mother has resolved her dilemmas about supporting her children versus her own needs for a partner has an important effect on whether the relationship between the mother and abused child can improve and be repaired. If the family factors described by Madonna *et al.* (1991) are affecting the capacity of the mother to parent her child, specific parent–child work may need to be planned to achieve such goals. Parent groups may be particularly helpful for mothers sharing the sense of loss and bereavement associated with discovery of what may have been long-standing abusive acts by their partners, or other children (Bentovim, 1991b). Siblings often need support over this phase of separation, because they may reveal the fact of their own abuse when a sibling has disclosed, or they may be extremely angry with the child who has disclosed abuse because it may have led to separation from a parent.

Although meetings with offenders can help reverse misconceptions and beliefs, any work with the family as a total group must be seen to be limited because there may be no possibility of working together during an interim period between sessions. Protective parents need a good deal of help to cope with and understand the emotional responses, the sexualization and behavioural patterns of their abused children. There is probably a broad need for educational facilities, whether in groups or in written or other forms to assist this task. Exploring a mother's own history of abuse, and the way in which such experiences may have hindered the perception of her own child's abuse is important, as well as helping the development of understanding of the way in which a family context developed when offending could take place in a context of secrecy.

Work with nonfamily caretakers

Foster carers, residential workers and community support workers need educational information about the responses of children to abuse, and need to be helped to find ways of supporting children. Again the use of supportive groups may assist this process. Work on developing rules for appropriate physical contact and on reducing confusion for children may be essential to reduce the vulnerability of children to further abuse (Elton, 1988).

Work with offending behaviour

Models and settings

There are a number of models of comprehensive approaches to treatment, including work with offenders — such as the Giarretto model (1981), adapted by Bentovim *et al.* (1988). This attempts to treat all members of the family (including abusers) as part of the same programme. The alternative model is where a number of specialist agencies work together, e.g. a probation/forensic psychiatric service treating offenders (Wolfe, 1987; Berliner, 1991; Mezey *et al.*, 1991; Wyre, 1989), integrating their work with social work and child psychiatric services. Through liaison and networking, a comprehensive approach can be offered.

Basic work with offenders: with offending behaviour

A variety of approaches have been described for working with offending behaviour in young people or adults; these include psychodynamic (Glasser, 1990) and cognitive behavioural (Salter, 1988), and the combination of various approaches including development of social skills approaches (Abel *et al.*, 1987). It is essential that there is an adequate assessment of dangerousness so that it can be determined whether residential settings are needed or whether treatment in the community is safe (Ryan *et al.*, 1987; National Children's Home, 1992). The common issues in a number of programmes are the importance of taking adequate responsibility for offending behaviour, understanding the particular cycle of offending behaviour for the individual, learning preventive skills in the future, having sensitivity to and understanding of the victim's response, and connecting abusing behaviour with personal experiences of abuse.

Marshall and Eccles' (1991) review of the effectiveness of treatment approaches indicated that cognitive behavioural approaches that look at the triggering and maintenance of abusive patterns of behaviour and attempt to alter the pattern of abuse are beginning to show some treatment effectiveness, although further follow-up is needed to ascertain whether there will be long-term effectiveness.

The rehabilitation phase of treatment

This is the phase in which, having completed appropriate work in separation contexts, contact can be increased between abusers and other family members, including the children they have abused, providing there is genuine agreement by all parties that this is in the child's interests. A series of rules needs to be established relating to contact, where the mother has the major responsibility for care. This is the period of the most extensive family work (Bentovim, 1991b), involving a concern to develop appropriate communication skills, and to think about future stress points. The need for longer-term individual and marital work for family members may emerge for those families where rehabilitation is a possibility. In the process of working towards reconciliation, some parents may decide to separate permanently (Bentovim *et al.*, 1988).

LONGER-TERM PLACEMENT

In a significant number of children, because of the parents' initial disbelief and failure to take responsibility, or through longer-term failure to be involved in a treatment programme, long-term alternative care may be required. Foster or adoptive families who accept sexually abused children may need extensive help to deal with sexualized behaviour, to adopt clear rules of contact, and to ensure that the child's confusion between normal affection and sexual contact can be avoided by clear house rules.

EVALUATION OF TREATMENT

Despite the increasing number of treatment approaches currently described in the literature, the empirical testing of the effectiveness of these approaches is in its infancy, and there are few systematic or controlled accounts of the effect of treatment of victimized children and their families. There is a dearth of follow-up studies using empirical measures to evaluate the effect of time on the traumatic effects of sexual abuse. Mannarino *et al.* (1992) recently published a follow-up study that compared progress over time of sexually abused children with a psychiatrically disturbed population and a normal population. What was striking was that the children's own account of their state showed no significant differences over time when comparisons between abused and nonabused children were made, although a 'sleeper' effect of the emergence of more distress amongst children who experienced penetration was noted. Parents noted more significant differences in their children's state, but there were few differences between the sexually abused and psychiatrically disturbed children on empirical measures.

An early study by Kroth (1979) of the Giarretto approach used a multiple cross-sectional approach to assess children and families at different stages of the uniform treatment approach. They claimed striking improvement, with a high rate (up to 80%) of family rehabilitation. Neither standardized outcome measures nor independent accounts of whether children had been reabused at follow-up were used. This early study has not been repeated or replicated and the value of the Giarretto approach, which is popular in the US, remains uncertain.

Bentovim *et al.* (1988) used professional reports to follow up a group of sexually abused children over a 3–4-year period. An improvement in children's emotional and behavioural symptoms, as well as a lessening in sexualized behaviour, was described by professionals who knew the children well. It was noted, however, that the proportion of families who achieved rehabilitation of the children with the original offenders was very small; only 15% of the abused children were living in their original families. About 25% were living in foster homes or children's homes over a long period, and a

further 20% (mostly in their late teens) were living independently. It is likely that some of the reported differences in rehabilitation rate reflect variations in how families come to treatment. Thus, in some countries diversion from prosecution or imprisonment may be achieved by entering a treatment programme. There is very little published research on the effects of diversion programmes in which offenders can chose treatment instead of prosecution. However, Becker (1991) indicated a considerable scepticism about the value of this approach amongst clinicians, because of the difficulty in imposing strong treatment conditions in these circumstances. There is also an impression that young people collaborate more effectively with treatment programmes if strict conditions are laid down.

The Tufts study (Gomes-Schwartz *et al.*, 1990) showed comparable results to Bentovim *et al.* (1988). A total of 150 children were followed for an 18-month period, and the effects of a crisis management approach to treatment was assessed. Many of the children had been removed from their homes in order to ensure adequate protection, and there were high levels of denial of abuse by perpetrators and of disbelief by their parents. Gomes-Schwartz *et al.* (1990) considered that participation in a treatment programme helped children recover from the emotional stress of victimization. However, a number of children showed more in the way of symptoms and little improvement after treatment. Worst effects were noted amongst those who had been living in disorganized home environments, and who had been subjected to major turmoil as a result of the disclosure of sexual abuse. Changes in living accommodation, such as moving between foster homes or children's homes, may have a disruptive effect on some children.

Monck *et al.* (1993) undertook a systematic comparison, with a 1-year follow-up, of the effects of adding group therapy to the basic protection and family work provided for sexually abused children at a psychiatric clinic. In the treated group as a whole, there was an overall significant improvement during the 1-year follow-up with a lessening in depressive symptoms. Although on mothers' ratings there was an overall lessening in symptoms, a proportion of children continued with the same level of symptoms or worsened. Clinicians' ratings showed a significant improvement in children's symptoms over time, this being greater among those who participated in group work programmes. Other findings, however, failed to show any additional benefits accruing from group treatment. The contradictory findings on group treatment may reflect the clinicians' lack of blindness, or their better appreciation of subtle changes in behaviour. Also, variations in children's responses to group treatment may reflect the impact of parental denial and disbelief about aspects of the abuse. This does not provide a supportive context for children to describe what have often been long-term abusive experiences. Nevertheless, some children expressed relief at having talked about their abuse, although a subgroup wished they had not spoken, and felt that the group had been less supportive than their original family context. Most mothers responded very positively to the opportunities of being in a group with other parents in similar situations, and children also appreciated the opportunity of sharing with other children.

Friedrich *et al.* (1992) assessed outcome of psychotherapy with sexually abused boys; success was described using a combination of group, individual parent training and family therapy.

THE PREVENTION OF CHILD SEXUAL ABUSE

One of the most striking facts about child sexual abuse is the hidden nature of the experience for children and families, and one of the most important approaches to prevention must be the diagnosis of child sexual abuse, and the treatment of those individuals who have offended against children and may go on to develop a more extensive offending pattern in the community. Programmes to treat children who have been abused and who are becoming abusers in their own right constitute an important focus for prevention (Johnson & Berry, 1989; Ryan, 1989). Finkelhor (1986) pointed to the value of prevention programmes aimed at parents and professionals involved with children. Programmes may help parents to identify signs that their children are being abused and to react in a constructive manner. Prevention programmes aimed at teachers, paediatricians, police and nursery workers can provide information that will allow these professionals to detect abuse and respond constructively.

There is an enthusiastic acceptance of preventive programmes to help younger children to protect themselves against abusive action by adults, both inside and outside the family, but as Wurtele *et al.* (1991) commented, the empirical validation of these programmes has been limited. This has not prevented development and implementation, because subjective evaluations are often positive. Cohn and Daro (1987) argued that, unless predisposing conditions and risk factors have been altered considerably, the likelihood for abuse remains high, even in children who have developed some self-protective skills.

It remains uncertain how long children retain information about whom to talk to, what is appropriate or inappropriate behaviour, and how to apply these ideas to day-to-day life. A considerable percentage (between 35 and 50%) of children were worried or scared when exposed to a Spiderman prevention comic, perhaps feeling that they might be abused (Garbarino, 1987). More recently, effective programmes have shifted away from stressing abstract concepts such as good versus bad touch, and have emphasized building skills in such areas as assertive behaviour, decision-making and communication (Daro, 1991). The introduction in a number of countries of telephone helplines for children indicates the need for a confidential context in which children can talk about distressing experiences in their lives. A significant proportion of such calls from older children are concerned with sexual abuse, and although many children are resistant to seeking a safe adult to confide in, at least in a number of cases the process of revealing current abusive experiences can begin.

REFERENCES

Abel G.G., Becker J.V., Mittelman M., Cunningham-Rathier J., Rouleau J. & Murphy W. (1987) Self-reported sex crimes in non-incarcerated paraphilias. *Journal of Interpersonal Violence*, **2**, 3–35.

Adams-Tucker C. (1982) Proximate effects of sexual abuse in childhood: a report on 28 children. *American Journal of Psychiatry*, **139**, 1252–1256.

Anderson J.C., Martin J.L., Mullen P.E., Romans S.E. & Herbison, G.P. (1993) The prevalence of sexual abuse experiences in a community sample of women. *Journal of the American Academy of Child and Adolescent Psychiatry*, **32(5)** (in press).

Bagley C.R. (1990) Measuring child sexual abuse and its long term psychological outcomes: a review of some British and Canadian studies of victims and their families. Paper presented at the Sixth International Congress on Child Abuse, Hamburg, September, 1990.

Bagley C. & Ramsay R. (1986) Sexual abuse in childhood: psycho-social outcomes and implications for social work practice. *Journal of Social Work and Human Sexuality*, **4**, 33–47.

Baker A.W. & Duncan S.P. (1985) Child sexual abuse: a study of prevalence in Great Britain. *Child Abuse and Neglect*, **9**, 457–467.

Becker J.V. (1988) The effects of child sexual abuse on adolescent sexual offenders. In: Wyatt G.E. & Powell G.J. (eds) *Lasting Effects of Child Sexual Abuse*, pp. 193–207. Sage, Beverly Hills, CA.

Becker J. (1991) Working with perpetrators. In: Murray K. & Gough D.A. (eds) *Interviewing in Child Sexual Abuse*. Scottish Academic.

Beitchman J.H., Zucker K.J., Hood J.E., da Costa G.A. & Akman D. (1991) A review of the short-term effects of child sexual abuse. *Child Abuse and Neglect*, **15**, 537–556.

Beitchman J.H., Zucker K.J., Hood J.E., da Costa G.A., Akman D. & Cassavia E. (1992) A review of the long-term effects of child sexual abuse. *Child Abuse and Neglect*, **16**, 101–118.

Bentovim A. (1991a) Children and young people as abusers. In: Hollows A. & Armstrong H. (eds) *Children and Young People as Abusers: An Agenda for Action*. National Children's Bureau, London.

Bentovim A. (1991b) Clinical work with families in which sexual abuse has occurred. In: Hollin C.R. & Howells K. (eds) *Clinical Approaches to Sex Offenders and their Victims*, pp. 179–208. John Wiley, Chichester.

Bentovim A. & Boston P. (1988) Sexual abuse — basic issues — characteristics of children and families. In: Bentovim A., Elton A., Hildebrand J., Tranter M. & Vizard E. (eds) *Child Sexual Abuse within the Family: Assessment and Treatment*, pp. 16–39. John Wright, London.

Bentovim A., Boston P. & van Elburg A. (1987) Child sexual abuse — children and families referred to a treatment project and the effects of intervention. *British Medical Journal*, **295**, 1453–1457.

Bentovim A., van Elburg A. & Boston P. (1988) The results of treatment. In: Bentovim A., Elton A., Hildebrand J., Tranter M. & Vizard E. (eds) *Child Sexual Abuse within the Family: Assessment and Treatment*, pp. 252–268. John Wright, London.

Berliner L. (1991) Clinical work with sexually abused children. In: Hollin C.R. & Howells K. (eds) *Clinical Approaches to Sex Offenders and their Victims*, pp. 209–228. John Wiley, Chichester,

Berliner J. & Wheeler J.R. (1987) Treating the effects of sexual abuse on children. *Journal of Interpersonal Violences*, **2**, 415–434.

Bernard F. (1981) A study of pedophiliac relationships. In: Constantine L.M. & Martinson F.M. (eds) *Children and Sex: New Findings, New Perspective*, Little, Brown, Boston.

Bifulco A., Brown G.W. & Alder Z. (1991) Early sexual abuse and depression in adult life. *British Journal of Psychiatry*, **159**, 115–122.

Briere J. & Runtz M. (1988) Symptomatology associated with childhood sexual victimization in a nonclinical adult sample. *Child Abuse and Neglect*, **12**, 51–59.

Briere J. & Runtz M. (1989) University males' sexual interest in children: predicting potential indices of 'pedophilia' in a nonforensic sample. *Child Abuse and Neglect*, **13**, 65−75.

Briere J., Evans D., Runtz M. & Wall T. (1988) Symptomatology in men who were molested as children: a comparison study. *American Journal of Orthopsychiatry*, **58**, 457−461.

Burgess A.W. (ed) (1984) *Child Pornography and Sex Rings*. Lexington Books, Lexington, MA.

Burgess A.W., Groth A.N. & McCausland M.P. (1981) Child sex initiation rings. *American Journal of Orthopsychiatry*, **51**, 110−119.

Burgess A.W., Hartman C.R., McCausland M.P. & Powers P. (1984) Response patterns in children and adolescents exploited through sex rings and pornography. *American Journal of Psychiatry*, **141**, 656−662.

Butler-Sloss Lord Justice E. (1988) *Report of the Inquiry into Child Abuse in Cleveland (1987)*. HMSO, London.

Byrne J.P. & Valdiserri E.V. (1982) Victims of childhood sexual abuse: a follow-up study of a non-compliant population. *Hospital and Community Psychiatry*, **33**, 938−940.

Cantwell H.B. (1988) Child sexual abuse: very young perpetrators. *Child Abuse and Neglect*, **12**, 579−582.

Carter I. & Parker L.J. (1991) Intrafamilial sexual abuse in American Indian families. In: Patton M.Q. (ed) *Family Sexual Abuse*, pp. 106−117. Sage, London.

Cavaiola A.A. & Schiff M. (1989) Self-esteem in abused chemically dependent adolescents. *Child Abuse and Neglect*, **13**, 327−334.

Cohen J.A. & Mannarino A.P. (1988) Psychological symptoms in sexually abused girls. *Child Abuse and Neglect*, **12**, 571−577.

Cohn A.H. & Daro D. (1987) Is treatment too late: what ten years of evaluative research tell us. *Child Abuse and Neglect*, **11**, 433−442.

Constantine L. (1981) The effects of early sexual experience: a review and synthesis of research. In: Constantine L.M. & Martinson F.M. (eds) *Children and Sex: New Findings, New Perspectives*, pp. 217−244. Little, Brown, Boston.

Conte J. & Berliner L. (1988) The impact of sexual abuse on children: the empirical findings. In: Walter L. (ed) *Handbook on Sexual Abuse of Children: Assessment and Treatment Issues*, pp. 72−93. Springer, New York.

Conte J.R. & Schuerman J.R. (1987) Factors associated with an increased impact of child sexual abuse. *Child Abuse and Neglect*, **11**, 201−211.

Daro D. (1991) Child sexual abuse prevention: separating fact from fiction. *Child Abuse and Neglect* **15**, 1−4.

Davis G.E. & Leitenberg H. (1987) Adolescent sex offenders. *Psychological Bulletin*, **101**, 417−427.

Davis G.N., Stephenson-Robb Y. & Flin R. (1988) The reliability of children's testimony. *International Legal Practitioner*, **13**, 95−103.

Deblinger E., McLeer S.V. & Henry D. (1990) Cognitive behavioral treatment for sexually abused children suffering from post-traumatic stress: preliminary findings. *Journal of American Academy of Child and Adolescent Psychiatry*, **29**, 747−752.

Dempster H.L. & Roberts J. (1991) Child sexual abuse research: a methodological quagmire. *Child Abuse and Neglect*, **15**, 593−595.

De Young M. (1984) *Sexual Victimization of Children*. McFarland, Jefferson, NC.

Dimock P.T. (1988) Adult males sexually abused as children. *Journal of Interpersonal Violence*, **3**, 203−221.

Einbender A. & Friedrich W. (1989) The psychological functioning and behavior of sexually abused girls. *Journal of Clinical and Consulting Psychology*, **57**, 155−157.

Elias J. & Gebhard P. (1969) Sexuality and sexual learning in childhood. *Phi Delta Kappan*, **50**, 401−405.

Elton A. (1988) Working with substitute carers. In: Bentovim A., Elton A., Hildebrand J., Tranter M. & Vizard E. (eds) *Child Sexual Abuse within the Family: Assessment and Treatment*, pp. 238−251. John Wright, London.

Faller K.C. (1989) Characteristics of a clinical sample of sexually abused children: how boy and girl victims differ. *Child Abuse and Neglect*, **13**, 281−291.

Faller K.C. (1990) *Understanding Child Sexual Maltreatment*. Sage, London.

Fehrenbach P.A., Smith W., Monastersky C. & Deisher R.W. (1986) Adolescent sexual offenders: offender and offence characteristics. *American Journal of Orthopsychiatry*, **56**, 225−233.

Finkelhor D. (1979) *Sexually Victimised Children*. Free Press, New York.

Finkelhor D. (1980) Risk factors in the sexual victimisation of children. *Child Abuse and Neglect*, **4**, 265−273.

Finkelhor D. (1984) *Child Sexual Abuse: New Theory and Research*. Free Press, New York.

Finkelhor D. (1986) *A Sourcebook on Child Sexual Abuse*. Sage, Beverly Hills, CA.

Finkelhor D. & Baron L. (1986) High-risk children. In: Finkelhor D. (ed) *A Sourcebook on Child Sexual Abuse*, pp. 61−88. Sage, Beverly Hills, CA.

Finkelhor D. & Browne A. (1985) The traumatic impact of child sexual abuse. *American Journal of Orthopsychiatry*, **55**, 530−541.

Finkelhor D. & Hotaling G.T. (1984) Sexual abuse in the National Incidence Study of Child Abuse and Neglect: an appraisal. *Child Abuse and Neglect*, **8**, 23−33.

Finkelhor D. & Korbin J. (1988) Child abuse as an international issue. *Child Abuse and Neglect*, **12**, 3−23.

Finkelhor D. & Redfield D. (1984) How the public defines sexual abuse. In: Finkelhor D. (ed) *Child Sexual Abuse: New Theory and Research*, pp. 107−133. Free Press, New York.

Finkelhor D. & Russell D. (1984) Women as perpetrators. In: Finkelhor D. (ed) *Child Sexual Abuse: New Theory and Research*, pp. 171−187. Free Press, New York.

Finkelhor D., Hotaling G.T., Lewis A. & Smith C. (1989) Sexual abuse and its relationship to later sexual satisfaction, marital status, religion and attitudes. *Journal of Interpersonal Violence*, **4**, 379−399.

Freud S. (1905) *Three Essays on the Theory of Sexuality*. Standard Edition 7 Strachey J. (ed). Hogarth Press and the Institute of Psychoanalysis, London. 1953.

Friedrich W.N. (1988) Behaviour problems in sexually abused children: an adaptational perspective. In: Wyatt G.E. & Powell, G.J. (eds) *Lasting Effects of Child Sexual Abuse*, pp. 171−191. Sage, Beverly Hills.

Friedrich W.N., Beilke R.L. & Urquiza A.J. (1988) Behavior problems in young sexually abused boys: a comparison study. *Journal of Interpersonal Violence*, **3**, 21−28.

Friedrich W.N., Grambsch P., Broughton D., Kuiper J. & Beilke R.L. (1991) Normative sexual behavior in children. *Paediatrics*, **88**, 456−464.

Friedrich W.N., Luecke W.J., Beilke R.L. & Place V. (1992) Psychotherapy outcome of sexually abused boys. *Journal of Interpersonal Violence*, **7**, 396−409.

Fritz G.S., Stoll K. & Wagner N.A. (1981) A comparison of males and females who were sexually molested as children. *Journal of Sex and Marital Therapy*, **7**, 54−59.

Fromuth M.E. (1986) The relationship of childhood sexual abuse with later psychological and sexual adjustment in a sample of college women. *Child Abuse and Neglect*, **10**, 5−15.

Fromuth M. & Burkhart B. (1987) Childhood sexual victimisation among college men: definitional and methodological issues. *Violence and Victims*, **2**, 241−253.

Fromuth M.E. & Burkhart B.R. (1989) Long term psychological correlates of childhood sexual abuse in two samples of college men. *Child Abuse and Neglect*, **13**, 533−542.

Furniss T. (1991) *The Multiprofessional Handbook of Child Sexual Abuse.* Routledge, London.

Gagnon J.H. (1985) Attitudes and responses of parents to pre-adolescent masturbation. *Archives of Sexual Behaviour,* **14,** 451–466.

Gale J., Thompson R.J., Moran T. & Sack W.H. (1988) Sexual abuse in young children: its clinical presentation and characteristic patterns. *Child Abuse and Neglect,* **12,** 163–170.

Garbarino J. (1987) Children's response to a sexual abuse prevention program: a study of the Spiderman comic. *Child Abuse and Neglect,* **11,** 143–148.

Gelinas D.J. (1983) The persisting negative effects of incest. *Psychiatry,* **46,** 312–332.

Gelman R. (1978) Cognitive development. *Annual Review of Psychology,* **29,** 297–332.

Giarretto H.A. (1981) A comprehensive child sexual abuse treatment program. In: Mrazek P.B. & Kempe C.H. (eds) *Sexually Abused Children and Their Families.* Pergamon Press, Oxford.

Glasser M. (1990) Psychodynamic approaches to working with sex offenders. In: Bluglass R. & Bowden R. (eds) *Principles and Practice of Forensic Psychiatry.* Churchill Livingstone, Edinburgh.

Gomes-Schwartz B., Horowitz J.M. & Cardarelli A. (1990) *Child Sexual Abuse: The Initial Effects.* Sage, Beverly Hills, CA.

Goodman G.S. & Helgson V.S. (1985) Child sexual assault: children's memory and the law. *University of Miami Law Review,* **40,** 181–208.

Goodman G.S., Taub E.P., Jones D.P.H., England P., Port L.K., Rudy L. & Prado L. (1992) Testifying in criminal court: emotional effects on child sexual assault victims. *Monographs of the Society for Research in Child Development,* **57(5),** pp. 1–161, serial no. 229.

Goodwin J. (1985) Post-traumatic symptoms in incest victims. In: Eth S. & Pynoos R.S. (eds) *Post-Traumatic Stress Disorder in Children.* American Psychiatric Association, Los Angeles.

Grant L.J. (1984) Assessment of child sexual abuse: eighteen months experience at the child protection center. *American Journal of Obstetrics and Gynecology,* **148,** 617–620.

Gruber K. & Jones, R. (1983) Identifying determinants of risk of sexual victimisation of youth. *Child Abuse and Neglect,* **7,** 17–24.

Haffejee I.E. (1991) Sexual abuse of Indian (Asian) children in South Africa: first report in a community undergoing cultural change. *Child Abuse and Neglect,* **15,** 147–151.

Hall R., Tice L., Beresford T., Wooley B. & Klassen A. (1989) Sexual abuse in patients with anorexia nervosa and bulimia. *Psychosomatics,* **30,** 73–79.

Hamilton G.V. (1929) *A Research in Marriage.* Albert and Charles Boni, New York.

Haugaard J. & Emery R. (1989) Methodological issues in child sexual abuse research. *Child Abuse and Neglect,* **13,** 89–100.

Haugaard J. & Reppucci N.D. (1988) *The Sexual Abuse of Children.* Jossey-Bass, London.

Haugaard J. & Tilly C. (1988) Characteristics predicting children's responses to sexual encounters with other children. *Child Abuse and Neglect,* **12,** 209–218.

Herman J. (1981) *Father Daughter Incest.* Harvard University Press, Cambridge, MA.

Herman J., Russell D.E.H. & Trocki K. (1986) Long term effects of incestuous abuse in childhood. *American Journal of Psychiatry,* **143,** 1293–1296.

Hibbard R.A., Brack C.J., Rauch S. & Orr D.P. (1988) Abuse, feelings, and health behaviors in a student population. *American Journal of Diseases of Children,* **142,** 326–330.

Ho T-P., & Kwok W-M. (1991) Child sexual abuse in Hong Kong. *Child Abuse and Neglect,* **15,** 597–600.

Hobbs, C.J. & Wynne J.M. (1987) Child sexual abuse — an increasing rate of diagnosis. *Lancet,* **II,** 837–841.

James J. & Meyerding J. (1977) Early sexual experience as a factor in prostitution. *Archives of Sexual Behavior,* **7,** 31–42.

James B. & Nasjheti, M. (1983) *Treating Sexually Abused Children and their Families.* Consulting Psychologists Press, Palo Alto, CA.

Johnson R.L. & Shrier D.K. (1985) Sexual victimization of boys. *Journal of Adolescent Health Care,* **6,** 372–376.

Johnson T.C. (1988) Child perpetrators — children who molest other children: preliminary findings. *Child Abuse and Neglect,* **12,** 219–229.

Johnson T.C. (1989) Female child perpetrators: children who molest other children. *Child Abuse and Neglect,* **13,** 571–585.

Johnson T.C. & Berry C. (1989) Children who molest — a treatment program. *Journal of Interpersonal Violence,* **4,** 185–203.

Jones D.P.H. (1991) Ritualism and child sexual abuse. *Child Abuse and Neglect,* **15,** 163–170.

Jones D. (1992) *Interviewing Children who have been Sexually Abused,* 4th edn. Royal College of Psychiatrists/Gaskell Press, London.

Jones D.P.H. & McGraw J.M. (1987) Reliable and fictitious accounts of sexual abuse to children. *Journal of Interpersonal Violence,* **2,** 27–45.

Jones D.P.H. & Seig A. (1988) Child sexual abuse allegations in custody or visitation disputes: a report of 20 cases. In: Nicholson E.B. & Bulkley J. (eds) *Sexual Abuse Allegation in Custody and Visitation Disputes.* American Bar Association, Washington, DC.

Jonker F. & Jonker-Bakker P. (1991) Experiences with ritualist child sexual abuse: a case study from the Netherlands. *Child Abuse and Neglect,* **15,** 191–196.

Kelly L., Regan L. & Burton S. (1991) *An Exploratory Study of the Prevalence of Sexual Abuse in a Sample of 16–21 Year Olds.* Polytechnic of North London, London.

Kercher G. & McShane M. (1984) The prevalence of child sexual abuse victimization in an adult sample of Texas residents. *Child Abuse and Neglect,* **8,** 495–502.

Kinsey A.C., Pomeroy W.B., Martin C.E. & Gebhard P.H. (1953) *Sexual Behavior in the Human Female.* W.B. Saunders, Philadelphia.

Kiser L.J., Ackerman B.J., Brown E., Edwards N.B., McColgan E., Pugh, R. & Pruitt D.B. (1988) Post-traumatic stress disorder in young chidren: a reaction to purported sexual abuse. *Journal of the American Academy of Child and Adolescent Psychiatry,* **27,** 645–649.

Kiser L.J., Heston J., Millsap P.A. & Pruitt D.B. (1991) Physical and sexual abuse in childhood: relationship with post-traumatic stress disorder. *Journal of the American Academy of Child and Adolescent Psychiatry,* **30,** 776–783.

Kluft R.P. (1985) Childhood multiple personality disorder: predictors, clinical findings and treatment results. In: Kluft R. (ed) *Childhood Antecedents of Multiple Personality.* American Psychiatric Press, Washington, DC.

Kohan M.J., Pothier P. & Norbeck J.S. (1987) Hospitalized children with a history of sexual abuse: incidence and care issues. *American Journal of Orthopsychiatry,* **57,** 258–264.

Korbin J. (1981) Culturally appropriate definitions of child abuse and neglect. In: Korbin J. (ed) *Child Abuse and Neglect: Cross-cultural Perspectives,* pp. 3–5. University of California Press, Berkeley, CA.

Kouramy R.F.C., Martin J.E. & Armstrong S.H. (1979) Sexual experimentation by adolescents while babysitting. *Adolescence,* **14,** 283–288.

Kovacs M. & Beck A.T. (1977) An empirical clinical approach towards a definition of childhood depression. In: Schulterbrandt, J.G. & Raskin A. (eds) *Depression in Childhood: Diagnosis, Treatment and Conceptual Models,* Raven, New York.

Kroth J.V. (1979) *Child Sexual Abuse: Analysis of a Family Therapy Approach.* Charles C. Thomas, Springfield, IL.

Krug R.S. (1989) Adult male report of childhood sexual abuse by mothers: case descriptions, motivations and long term consequences. *Child Abuse and Neglect,* **13,** 111–119.

Landis J. (1956) Experiences of 500 children with adult sexual deviants. *Psychiatric Quarterly Supplement*, **30**, 91–109.

Lanktree C., Briere J. & Zaidi L. (1991) Incidence and impact of sexual abuse in a child outpatient sample: the role of direct enquiry. *Child Abuse and Neglect*, **15**, 447–453.

Lanning K.V. (1991) Ritual abuse: a law enforcement view or perspective. *Child Abuse and Neglect*, **15**, 171–173.

Lask B. & Bryant-Waugh R. (1992) Early-onset anorexia nervosa and related eating disorders. *Journal of Child Psychology and Psychiatry*, **33**, 281–300.

Lask B., Britten C., Kroll L., Magagna J. & Tranter M. (1991) Children with pervasive refusal. *Archives of Disease in Childhood*, **66**, 866–869.

Law of Great Britain (1989) *Children Act (1989)*. HMSO, London.

Lawson L. & Chaffin M. (1992) False negatives in sexual abuse disclosure interviews: incidence and influence of caretaker's belief in abuse in cases of accidental abuse discovery by diagnosis of STD. *Journal of Interpersonal Violence*, **7**, 532–542.

Leventhal J.M., Bentovim A., Elton A., Tranter M. & Read L. (1987) What to ask when sexual abuse is suspected. *Archives of Disease in Childhood*, **62**, 1118–1195.

MacFarlane K., Waterman J., Conerly S., Damon L., Durfee M. & Long S. (eds) (1986) *Sexual Abuse of Young Children: Evaluation and Treatment*. Guilford Press, New York.

McGraw J.M. & Smith H. (1992) Child sexual abuse allegations amidst divorce and custody proceedings: refining the validation process. *Journal of Child Sexual Abuse*, **1**, 49–62.

McLeer S.V., Deblinger E., Atkins M.S., Foa E.B. & Ralphe D.L. (1988) Post-traumatic stress disorder in sexually abused children. *Journal of the American Academy of Child and Adolescent Psychiatry*, **27**, 650–654.

MacVicar K. (1979) Psychotherapeutic issues in the treatment of sexually abused girls. *Journal of the American Academy of Child Psychiatry*, **18**, 342–353.

Madonna P., van Scoyk, S. & Jones D.P.H. (1991) Family interaction within incest and non-incest families. *American Journal of Psychiatry*, **148**, 46–49.

Mannarino, A.P., Cohen J.A., Smith J.A. & Moore-Motily S. (1992) Six and twelve month follow-up of sexually abused girls. *Journal of Interpersonal Violence*, **6**, 494–511.

Margolin L. (1991) Child sexual abuse by nonrelated caregivers. *Child Abuse and Neglect*, **15**, 213–221.

Marshall W. & Eccles A. (1991) Issues in clinical practice with sex offenders. *Journal of Interpersonal Violence*, **6**, 68–93.

Martin J.L., Anderson J.C., Romans-Clarkson S.E., Mullen P.E. & O'Shea M. (1993) Asking about child sexual abuse: methodological implications of a two stage study. *Child Abuse and Neglect* (in press).

Meiselman K. (1978) *Incest: A Psychological Study of Causes and Effects with Treatment Recommendations*. Jossey-Bass, San Francisco.

Mezey G., Vizard E., Hawks C. & Austin R. (1991) A community treatment programme for convicted child sex offenders: a preliminary report. *Journal of Forensic Psychiatry*, **2**, 11–25.

Monck E., Bentovim A., Goodall G., Hyde C., Lwin R. & Sharland E. (1993) *Child Sexual Abuse: A Descriptive and Treatment Study*. Her Majesty's Stationery Office, London (in preparation).

Mrazek P. (1980) Sexual abuse of children. *Journal of Child Psychology and Psychiatry*, **21**, 91.

Mrazek P., Lynch M.A. & Bentovim A. (1983) Sexual abuse of children in the United Kingdom. *Child Abuse and Neglect*, **7**, 147–153.

Mullen P.E., Romans S.E., Walton V.A. & Herbison G.P. (1988) Impact of sexual and physical abuse on women's mental health. *Lancet*, **(i)**, 841–845.

Mulvey E.P. & Haugaard J.J. (1986) *Report of the Surgeon General's Workshop on Pornography and Public Health*. Public Health Service, Washington, DC.

National Children's Home (1992) *Working Party Report on Services for Children and Young People who Offend*. National Children's Home, London.

Newson J. & Newson E. (1969) *Four Years Old in an Urban Community*. George Allen and Unwin, London.

Olson E. (1981) Socioeconomic and psychocultural contexts of child abuse and neglect in Turkey. In: Korbin J. (ed) *Child Abuse and Neglect: Cross-cultural Perspectives*, pp. 96–119. University of California Press, Berkeley, CA.

Palmer R., Oppenheimer R., Dignon A., Chaloner D. & Howells K. (1990) Childhood sexual experience with adults reported by women with eating disorders. *British Journal of Psychiatry*, **156**, 699–703.

Peters J.J. (1976) Children who are victims of sexual assault, and the psychology of offenders. *American Journal of Psychotherapy*, **30**, 395–421.

Peters S.D., Wyatt G.E. & Finkelhor D. (1986) Prevalence. In: Finkelhor D. (ed) *A Sourcebook on Child Sexual Abuse*, pp. 15–59. Sage, Beverly Hills, CA.

Pierce R. & Pierce L. (1985) The sexually abused child: a comparison of male and female victims. *Child Abuse and Neglect*, **9**, 191–199.

Putnam F.W. (1991) The Satanic ritual abuse controversy. *Child Abuse and Neglect*, **15**, 175–179.

Reinhart M. (1987) Sexually abused boys. *Child Abuse and Neglect*, **11**, 229–235.

Research Team (1990) *Child Sexual Abuse in Northern Ireland: A Research Study of Incidence*. Greystone, Antrim, Northern Ireland.

Rogers C.N. & Terry T. (1984) Clinical interventions with boy victims of sexual abuse. In: Stuart I.R. & Greer J.R. (eds) *Victims of Sexual Aggression: Treatment of Children, Women and Men*, Van Nostrand Reinhold, New York.

Rosenfeld A.A., O'Reilly Wenegrat A., Haavik D.K., Wenegrat B.G. & Smith C.R. (1982) Sleeping patterns in upper-middle class families when the child awakens ill or frightened. *Archives of General Psychiatry*, **39**, 943–947.

Rosenfeld A.A., Siegel-Gorelick B., Haavik D., Duryea M., Wenegrat A., Martin J. & Bailey R. (1984) Parental perceptions of children's modesty: a cross-sectional survey of ages 2–10 years. *Psychiatry*, **47**, 351–365.

Rosenfeld A.A., Siegel B. & Bailey R. (1987) Familial bathing patterns: implications for cases of alleged molestation and for pediatric practice. *Pediatrics*, **79**, 224–229.

Royal College of Physicians (1991) *Physical Signs of Sexual Abuse in Children*. Royal College of Physicians, London.

Royal College of Psychiatrists (1988) Child psychiatric perspectives on the assessment and management of sexually maltreated children. *Psychiatric Bulletin of the Royal College of Psychiatrists*, **12**, 534–540.

Ruch L. & Chandler S. (1982) The crisis impact of sexual assault on three victim groups: adult rape victims, child rape victims and incest victims. *Journal of Social Service Research*, **5**, 83–100.

Runyon D., Everson M., Edolsohn G., Hunter W. & Coulter M. (1988) Impact of legal intervention on sexually abused children. *Journal of Pediatrics*, **113**, 647–653.

Russell D.E.H. (1983) The incidence of prevalence of intrafamilial and extrafamilial sexual abuse of female children. *Child Abuse and Neglect*, **7**, 133–146.

Russell D.E.H. (1984) The prevalence and seriousness of incestuous abuse: stepfathers vs. biological fathers. *Child Abuse and Neglect*, **8**, 15–22.

Russell D.E.H. (1986) *The Secret Trauma: Incest in the Lives of Girls and Women*. Basic Books, New York.

Rutter M. (1967) A children's behaviour checklist for completion by teachers: preliminary findings. *Journal of Child Psychology and Psychiatry*, **8**, 1–11.

Rutter M. (1971) Normal psychosexual development. *Journal of Child*

Psychology and Psychiatry, **11**, 259−283.

Ryan G. (1989) Victim to victimizer: rethinking victim treatment. *Journal of Interpersonal Violence*, **4**, 325−341.

Ryan G., Lane S., Davis J. & Isaac C. (1987) Juvenile sex offenders: development and correction. *Child Abuse and Neglect*, **11**, 385−395.

Salter A.C. (ed) (1988) *Treating Child Sex Offenders and their Victims: A Practical Guide*, Sage, Beverly Hills, CA.

Sandfort T.G. (1984) Sex in pedophiliac relationships: an empirical investigation among a non-representative group of boys. *Journal of Sex Research*, **20**, 123−142.

Schechter M.D. & Roberge L. (1976) Sexual exploitation. In: Helfer R.E. & Kempe C.H. (eds) *Child Abuse and Neglect: the Family and the Community*, pp. 127−142. Ballinger, Cambridge, MA.

Schultz L.G. (1973) The child sex victim: social, psychological and legal perspectives. *Child Welfare*, **52**, 147−157.

Siegel J.M., Sorenson S.B., Golding J.M., Burnham M.A. & Stein J.A. (1987) The prevalence of childhood sexual assault: the Los Angeles epidemiologic catchment area project. *American Journal of Epidemiology*, **126**, 1141−1153.

Siegel J.M., Golding J.M., Stein J.A., Burnham M.A. & Sorenson S.B. (1990) Reactions to sexual assault: a community study. *Journal of Interpersonal Violence*, **5**, 229−246.

Silbert M.H. & Pines A.M. (1981) Sexual child abuse as an antecedent to prostitution. *Child Abuse and Neglect*, **5**, 407−411.

Singer K.I. (1989) Group work with men who experienced incest in childhood. *American Journal of Orthopsychiatry*, **59**, 468−472.

Singer K., Ney P.G. & Lieh-Mak F. (1978) A cultural perspective on child psychiatric disorders. *Comprehensive Psychiatry*, **19**, 533−540.

Skynner R. (1982) Frameworks for viewing the family as a system. In: Bentovim A., Gorrell-Barnes G. & Cooklin A. (eds) *Family Therapy 1*, pp. 3−35. Academic Press, London.

Smith M.A. & Grocke M. (1993) *Normal Family Sexuality and Sexual Knowledge in Children*, Royal College of Psychiatrists/Gaskell Press, London (in preparation).

Smith M.A. & Jenkins J.M. (1991) The effects of marital disharmony on pre-pubertal children. *Journal of Abnormal Child Psychology*, **19**, 625−644.

Sorrenti-Little L., Bagley C. & Robertson R. (1984) An operational defition of the long-term harmfulness of sexual relations with peers and adults by young children. *Journal of the Canadian Association for Young Children*, **9**, 46−57.

Spencer M.J. & Dunklee P. (1986) Sexual abuse of boys. *Pediatrics*, **78**, 133−138.

Spock B. (1976) *Baby and Child Care*. Pocket Books, New York.

Straus M.A., Gelles R. & Steinmetz S. (1980) *Behind Closed Doors: Violence in the American Family*. Anchor Press, New York.

Summit R.C. (1983) The child sexual abuse accommodation syndrome. *Child Abuse and Neglect*, **7**, 177−193.

Terr L. (1991) Childhood traumas: an outline and overview. *American Journal of Psychiatry*, **148**, 10−20.

Todd C.M. & Perlmutter M. (1980) Reality recalled by preschool children. In: Perlmutter M. (ed) *Children's Memory: New Directions in Child Development*, vol. 10, pp. 69−86. Jossey Bass, San Francisco, CA.

Tong L., Oates K. & McDowell H. (1987) Personality development following sexual abuse. *Child Abuse and Neglect*, **11**, 371−383.

Tranter M. (1993) Assessment. In: Lask B. & Bryant-Waugh R. (eds) *Childhood Onset of Anorexia Nervosa and Related Eating Disorders*, pp. 109−125. Lawrence Erlbaum Associates, Hove.

Tsai M., Feldman-Summers S. & Edgar M. (1979) Childhood molestation: variables related to differential impacts of psychosexual

functioning in adult women. *Journal of Abnormal Psychology*, **88**, 407−417.

UK: Department of Health (1989) *An Introduction to the Children Act 1989*. Her Majesty's Stationery Office, London.

UK: Home Office and Department of Health (1992) *Memorandum to Good Practice in Interviewing Children who may be Suspected of being Sexually Abused*. Her Majesty's Stationery Office, London.

UK (Home Office, Department of Health, Department of Education, & Welsh Office) (1991) *Working Together Under the Children Act, 1989*. Her Majesty's Stationery Office, London.

Vizard E. (1991) Interviewing children suspected of being sexually abused: a review of theory and practice. In: Hollin C.R. & Howells K. (eds) *Clinical Approaches to Sex Offenders and their Victims*, pp. 117−148. John Wiley, Chichester.

Watkins B. & Bentovim A. (1992) The sexual abuse of male children and adolescents: a review of current research. *Journal of Child Psychiatry and Psychology*, **33**, 197−249.

White S., Halpin B., Strom G. & Santelli G. (1988) Behavioral comparisons of young sexually abused, neglected and non-referred children. *Journal of Clinical Child Pyschology*, **17**, 53−61.

Wild N.J. (1987) Child sex rings in context. *Child Abuse Review*, **1**, 7−9.

Wild N.J. (1989) Prevalence of child sex rings. *Pediatrics*, **83**, 553−558.

Wild N.J. & Wynne J.M. (1986) Child sex rings. *British Medical Journal*, **293**, 183−185.

Wiseman M., Vizard E., Bentovim A. & Leventhal J.M. (1992) Reliability of videotaped interviews with children suspected of being sexually abused. *British Medical Journal*, **304**, 1089−1091.

Wolfe D.A. (1987) *Child Abuse: Implications for Child Development and Psychopathology*. Sage, London.

Wolfe V.V., Gentile C. & Wolfe D.A. (1989) The impact of sexual abuse on children: a PTSD formulation. *Behavior Therapy*, **20**, 215−228.

Wurtele S.K., Currien L.L., Gillespie E.I. & Franklin C.F. (1991) The efficacy of a parent-implemented program for teaching preschoolers personal safety skills. *Behaviour Therapy*, **22**, 69−83.

Wyatt G.E. (1985) The sexual abuse of Afro-American and white-American women in childhood. *Child Abuse and Neglect*, **9**, 507−519.

Wyatt G.E. & Peters S.D. (1986a) Issues in the definition of child sexual abuse in prevalence research. *Child Abuse and Neglect*, **10**, 231−240.

Wyatt G.E. & Peters S.D. (1986b) Methodological considerations in research on the prevalence of child sexual abuse. *Child Abuse and Neglect*, **10**, 241−251.

Wyre R. (1989) Protecting children: treatment for offenders. Paper presented at NACRO Conference on Preventing Child Abuse — Problems and Prospects in Dealing with Offenders. London, September 1989.

Yates A.Y. (1982) Children eroticized by incest. *American Journal of Psychiatry*, **139**, 482−485.

Yates A. (1991) Childhood sexuality. In: Lewis M. (ed) *Child Psychiatry*, pp. 195−215. Williams & Wilkins, Baltimore, MA.

Yorukoglu A. & Kemph J.P. (1966) Children not severely damaged by incest with a parent. *Journal of the American Academy of Child and Adolescent Psychiatry*, **5**, 111−124.

Young W.C., Sachs R.G., Braun B.G. & Watkins R.T. (1991) Patients reporting ritual abuse in childhood: a clinical syndrome. Report of 37 cases. *Child Abuse and Neglect*, **15**, 181−189.

Yuille J.C. (1988) The systematic assessment of children's testimony. *Canadian Psychology*, **29**, 247−262.

Chapter 15
Residential and Foster Family Care

Stephen Wolkind & Alan Rushton

INTRODUCTION

The two major forms of out-of-home care provided by the public child care services are residential care (also referred to as children's homes, institutional care or group care) and foster family care (or boarding out). National differences in terminology can be confusing. In North America the term foster care is used to cover both placement in children's homes and placement in families whereas in the UK it is used only to refer to the latter. This chapter will confine itself to children who are placed in these settings because their families are not able to care for them, or because of abuse, or because the troublesome behaviour of the child makes him or her in need of care and control. These three groups have been called the volunteereds, the victims and the villains (Packman *et al.*, 1986). The special circumstances of children living away from home in hospitals, child psychiatric inpatient units, boarding and special schools and institutions for juvenile offenders are not covered here.

There have been major difficulties for public agencies and for researchers in collecting meaningful data on the number of children in different forms of public care, the length of their placements and the relation between placement aims and outcome. However, the most recent British study confirmed that the majority of admissions are short-term. There is a steep rise in discharges from care within the first weeks and months but, following this period, the 'leaving care curve' flattens out and a substantial minority remain in care on a long-term basis (Rowe *et al.*, 1989). Measured by national statistical returns, the number of children in care rose to a peak of 99 000 in England and Wales in 1975. There was then a dramatic decrease to about 60 000 in 1990. Although there have been changes in the general population of children during this period the number in care as a rate per 1000 still fell from 7.70 in 1979 to 5.69 in 1989 (Department of Health, 1991a). This reflects the wish of social service departments to reduce admission into care as a means of protecting children and also to contain the costs of residential care.

Over the last decade, the number of children placed in local authority residential establishments has declined by 60% (Department of Health, 1991b). The numbers fostered, however, have remained stable (about 35 000), thereby constituting an increasing *proportion* of placements.

Similar trends are evident in the US where efforts have been made to introduce family preservation programmes designed to avoid the need for placement away from home. The number of children currently living in out-of-home care in the US has been estimated at 300 000 (Tatara, 1988), which gives a similar proportion to the UK of about 5 per 1000.

CIRCUMSTANCES THAT GIVE RISE TO OUT-OF-HOME PLACEMENT

Children come to be looked after by the child welfare system by a number of routes, but largely as a result of parents asking for temporary help or where children are removed because they have been or are at risk of neglect or abuse. It is important to differentiate between children admitted to care because their parents need short-term help and those admitted for longer periods because of abuse, neglect, chronic social difficulties or severe behavioural problems. The first group is by far the larger, the main reason for admission being parental ill-health. They are predominantly infants and young children as compared to the second group, a high proportion of whom are adolescents (Millham *et al.*, 1986). The two groups do, however, share more in common than might be suspected. Although the use of state facilities is clearly a reasonable step for a family facing temporary crisis, such families differ from others in a similar situation who find an informal solution to the difficulty. Schaffer and Schaffer (1968) demonstrated that, compared with a control group, families whose children were admitted to care while their mothers were in hospital for a confinement were more isolated and less able to rely on extended family and neighbours, and were generally more deprived.

A recent English survey (Bebbington & Miles, 1989) showed that deprivation continues to be the main factor separating children in care from those not in care. The single greatest risk factor associated with reception into care was living with only one parent. Other factors included: living in crowded accommodation, a head of household who was receiving state financial benefits, a mother under 21, living in a poor neighbourhood and being of mixed-race parentage. In relation to this last risk factor, it is not clear whether being of mixed race constitutes a stress in itself or whether it is an indicator of other aspects of social adversity. It is well-known that stresses involved in these living situations put children at higher risk for health and developmental problems (Yule & Raynes, 1972; Wolkind

252

& Rutter, 1973; Lambert *et al.*, 1977; Bamford & Wolkind, 1988).

Many factors influence the choice of type of placement, including the child's characteristics, especially age. The closure of children's homes has meant that most younger children are now fostered, while residential care is mostly used for adolescents who cannot or who do not wish to be placed with families. Other influences on the type of placement include the wide variation in local authority activity in recruiting foster carers, the level of financial support for fostering as well as the extent of social work involvement and quality of decision-making. Political views have been as influential as research evidence on which forms of care are preferred for which children. It should be remembered, however, that there may be no sharp distinction between foster and residential care in terms of the child's experience. Foster care has been shown to be more child-centred in general but not all placements are so, and some residential settings achieve warm, stimulating, child-centred care (Colton, 1989). Those who study child care environments should be aware both of the common features and of where distinctions exist.

Residential and foster care are fundamentally social work responsibilities but the topic is important to other professionals because children in care are known to be a vulnerable group requiring a variety of assessment and treatment services. As they develop beyond childhood, some are likely to suffer poor mental health and need adult psychiatric services. The needs of these groups are best served by mutidisciplinary investigation and intervention.

RESIDENTIAL GROUP CARE

Historical background

Bullock (1991) pointed out that in the UK residential care is available for only two groups, the very advantaged or the very disadvantaged. For the former group their residential facilities, the English public schools, have a very long history, with Winchester having been established in 1382 and Eton in 1440. Parker (1988) traced the development of residential care for the disadvantaged and showed how our present range of children's homes evolved from the workhouse system for paupers of the early 19th century. A key feature of this system was that its very nature should act as a deterrence to those seeking admission. The stigma attached to residence was deliberately encouraged and, even within the workhouses, classifications of increasing stigma were found. This attitude underpinned all residential facilites, including those for the destitute, mentally ill or physically handicapped. Parker saw the philosophy of this system continuing until the 1930s when the separation of unemployment relief and residential care began, a process which only finally ended in the UK in 1948.

There existed one exception to this general rule. From the 1860s onwards, running alongside this approach there developed a new theme of rescue and of giving children a fresh start. A great variety of orphanages, reformatories and industrial schools were set up by charities and religious groups for this purpose. Although Parker (1988) acknowledged the role of compassion and social conscience in these moves, he considered that this was of less importance than the fear of large numbers of children neither working nor in compulsory education and the threat they were thought to pose to the stability of society. This historical background, reinforced by Dickens's descriptions of Dotheboys Hall and the experiences of Oliver Twist, helped to form public attitudes to the residential care of children in the UK over the past 50 years. On the one hand the threat of the children's home could be used as an alternative to the bogey man by parents of noncompliant children. On the other hand the image of the orphanage run by a respected and compassionate charity such as Barnardos remained and, indeed, still retains a powerfully sentimental and positive image.

An account of the advantages and disadvantages of residential care was prepared in 1929 by Elias Trotzkey, director of a Chicago orphanage (Trotzkey, 1974). In this he reviewed the history of residential care throughout the world. He described the first recognizable orphanage as being that established by August Francke in Germany in 1695. In the US the first institution was established in 1729 in New Orleans, to shelter children orphaned through the Indian massacres. Thenceforth the development was similar to that in the UK, with public almshouses of very poor quality being gradually replaced in the second half of the 19th century by charitable homes with an educative function. A massive growth in state provision took place, however, between 1890 and 1903 when, coinciding with the increased immigration from Europe, 400 new orphanages were opened. Bakwin (1949) suggested that the mortality rate in some of these homes was terrifyingly high.

During much of this century a sharp distinction was drawn between children admitted to residential care because of their own difficult behaviour or unruliness and those admitted because their emotional and physical needs could not be met by their parents. In the UK the former entered approved schools designed for their education and the treatment of their delinquency, the latter went into the children's homes that were the direct descendants of the early orphanages. The formal distinction in the UK was deliberately blurred in the 1969 Children and Young Person Act with all establishments becoming 'community homes'. Underlying this change was an attempt to see both groups as suffering the same adverse circumstances, but merely showing different responses to these. Approved schools ceased to exist as such in 1974 and many that became 'community homes with education' have since closed (Parker, 1988). Although one can respect the sentiment that the needs of the 'bad' child are identical to those of the 'sad' child, the loss of the distinction has led to difficulties. The variety of tasks facing the care workers in any one home can be so great that this can pose real problems (Berridge, 1985). It can also lead to major problems in interpreting research findings.

Effects of group care

Almost any discussion on group care starts by seeing it as a problem. Sinclair (1988), examining the entire residential field, including provision for ill, handicapped and elderly people as well as that for children, considered that there are four main criticisms of traditional group care. Firstly, he argued that any residential facility is not a place where a resident can be expected to lead a normal or reasonable life as measured by the general standards of society. In the child care field the comparisons of group and foster care made by Colton (1988) certainly support that argument. Secondly, very few individuals actually wish to enter residential care. While this is probably true in general, we have seen that there is good evidence that some adolescents positively do wish to be cared for in group homes. Thirdly, a damning criticism is that traditional forms of group care have been proved to be ineffective in reaching their goals. He used as a telling example its failure to reform delinquents (see Chapter 56). Fourthly, he pointed to the very high and growing cost of residential care. This may not, however, be the full story for children. The cost of good-quality specialist foster care may be almost as high as that for residential care when one adds in the hidden costs of support services, advertising and training campaigns and respite care schemes (Davies & Knapp, 1988).

Sinclair accepted that these criticisms were justly applied to traditional residential care but that recent changes within the system must be acknowledged. The size of homes and the number of residents within homes continue to fall and they are now far less isolated from the community. Most children in residential care leave the homes to receive their schooling in ordinary mainstream schools. The homes are now more likely to be part of an integrated network of services. Within them there is a greater focus on normalizing the residents' experiences. Different residential facilities are available for different purposes and there are greater checks to ensure that the individual needs and rights of each resident are respected. Sinclair also felt that the economic arguments have been one-sided, ignoring some adverse consequences of the reduction of residential provision. For children, he considered that this includes more adolescents entering prison and some children remaining far too long in grossly unsatisfying home situations. It is unfortunate, however that much of the debate on residential care has been conducted upon ideological lines rather than as a response to empirical data (Fulcher & Ainsworth, 1985). In the UK, evidence of severe child abuse within the residential system (Levy & Kahan, 1991) will strengthen the case of those opposed to institutional care in any form.

A more positive view can, however, be found. In 1974 Wolins brought together a series of accounts of successful group care, demonstrating how in certain circumstances a children's home or similar institution could provide a very satisfactory environment for some children, including some who needed help to overcome earlier adverse experiences. We shall consider these settings when we look at those factors that determine the outcome for children in residential care. The best way to examine the positive and negative aspects of group care is to look at the development of children brought up in and discharged from the system. A problem that has been extensively debated is the extent to which any deficits seen are due to the residential experience itself or to the reasons that led to the child requiring this form of care. This debate has been of very great importance in understanding the effects of early experience on later development (e.g. Rutter, 1981). In essence it is clear that, for most children, the admission to group care is only one facet of a life marked by many other disadvantages and it is often difficult to disentangle the different effects of these.

Although this is of considerable theoretical significance, in practical terms it is more important to accept that these children have multiple disadvantages. The key issue then becomes whether residential care, a largely state-run service, staffed by professionals, can help those children admitted to it to achieve a more satisfactory development or whether it is to be considered as one more adverse factor in their lives adding to their difficulties. To some extent, the latter has been thought to be the case. van Goor-Lambo *et al.* (1990), in revising the psychosocial axis of *ICD-9*, saw institutional upbringing as a possible aetiological factor for disturbance, one that needs to be distinguished from the situation where it is the child's disturbance that leads to the admission to care. This accords with the memories of young adults, who had been brought up in care, of predominantly negative experiences (Kahan, 1979).

The psychological development of children in residential care

An examination of the data on how children who are or have been in residential care function will be a starting point to determining what are the actual effects of the group experience. Interest in this question began in the 1930s and 1940s. These early descriptions were mainly of children resident in large barrack-like children's homes. Prevalence rates were not given, but the impression is of a large proportion, if not most of the children showing patterns of severe disturbance. There were some differences but the general pattern described by different authors was remarkably similar. Various terms were used to describe the alarming pictures seen, such as 'affect hunger' (Levy, 1937), 'affectionless psychopathy' (Bender & Yarnell, 1941) and the 'institutional syndrome' (Goldfarb, 1949). There were a number of key features of this picture. The children were aggressive, inattentive and had many habit disturbances. Most striking, however, were the gross abnormalities they showed in relationships. This was best seen in their approach to unfamiliar adults where they demonstrated a shallow overfriendliness. Accompanying this picture of severe disturbance was a very poor level of cognitive ability and educational attainments.

Later studies tended to start by looking at rates of disorder, and in most cases these were in the range of 50–60%, with equally high rates being obtained from care staff and from teachers in the children's schools (e.g. Wolkind, 1974a; Yule & Raynes, 1972). These studies were predominantly carried out on children in large long-stay homes and we have little information on rates of disorder amongst children in small family group homes. It is also striking that the patterns of disorder found in these studies and indeed in others performed during the 1950s (e.g. Pringle, 1961) were very similar to those found amongst children in the community. The diagnostic differences have tended to be relatively minor (Pillay *et al.*, 1989). Wolkind (1974a), for example, found a range of different disorders. Both he and Pringle noted that many of the children showed individual features of the earlier described institutional syndromes, but these did not appear to cluster together in the same children. Nevertheless, it is evident that very high rates of psychiatric disorder are found amongst children in residential care in industrialized societies. Certain other situations should, however, first be mentioned.

Residential care for the under-5s is now a rarity in western countries — a case where research findings have influenced public policy. In other societies, natural or manmade disasters have led to an increase in the numbers of residential nurseries. Little research has been done on their progress. Hakimi-Manesh *et al.* (1984), however, described a group of infants aged 4–13 months resident in an Iranian institution. They demonstrated a picture seen in some very early studies with the children's mental and motor abilities declining over time. They also showed how relatively minimal intervention with increased stimulation could arrest this deterioration. Bagenholm and Kristiansson (1987) described the health and psychological development of a group of children being cared for in a large Ethiopian children's village. Alarming pictures of children in residential care in certain east European countries, such as Romania, are now emerging. The exceptions to the poor outcome as documented by Wolins (1974) are predominantly institutions such as the Israeli kibbutzim positively believed in by the participating families or the Austrian Kindersdorf staffed by adults committed to the institution and sharing a common belief. Such child care arrangements have, however, become much less common over the last 20 years.

Concern has also been expressed over the health of children in residential care. It has been suggested that with many different carers remediable conditions may be overlooked (Department of Health, 1991a,b,c). The educational attainments of children in residential care have also been noted to be depressingly poor (Jackson, 1987). It must be emphasized, however, that two factors suggest that we must be careful in generalizing from these findings and assuming that residential care is bad *per se*. The majority of studies are confined to young children and very few give any information on the quality of care offered to the children.

The picture painted above suggests that in most spheres of functioning children in residential care do less well on average than those in the population as a whole. The various studies demonstrating this also show clearly the great variation that is seen within the residential group. Some children show appallingly poor functioning in all areas; others appear to do

remarkably well. Part of this variation can be explained by factors such as the child's age at admission, experiences before and after admission and the quality of the care offered (Rutter, 1981). These factors, however, only explain part of the variation and individual responses to stress and other experiences are crucial (e.g. Garmezy, 1984). The importance of temperamental and other genetic factors in determining the outcome has however been little studied. It seems that boys are more likely than girls to show disturbance after short-term admission to care (Wolkind & Rutter, 1973), perhaps reflecting boys' greater vulnerability generally to adverse life events. With long-term care, however, no sex differences are found (Yule & Raynes, 1972; Wolkind, 1974b).

Children and adults
who have been in residential care

With some exceptions, most outcome studies have used the wider category of being 'in care' rather than in residential care. In practice, with most of the studies having been done on children who left care in the 1970s or earlier, the majority had been in children's homes, with only relatively few in foster care. Depressingly, almost all point to a poor outcome. Although there is a great deal of heterogeneity, with some individuals doing extremely well, a high proportion show evidence of severe psychosocial maladjustment. Rather different patterns are seen for each sex, though both share a poor level of educational achievement (St Claire & Osborne 1987).

Mapstone (1969) looked at the 340 children from the 15 000 in the 1958 British National Child Development Study who had at some time before the age of 7 been in care. A third were doing badly in terms of psychological adjustment — a figure three times higher than that in the general population. The discrepancy widened by the time the children reached the age of 11 (Essen *et al.*, 1976; Lambert *et al.*, 1977). Wolkind and Rutter (1973) studied the 2% of 11–12-year-old children in a large community sample who had been in care before the age of 5. Although the overall rate of psychiatric disorder was very high, there was a marked sex difference, with almost all the boys affected and few of the girls. The disorder amongst boys was predominantly of conduct. This study demonstrated well the difficulty in attempting to disentangle the effects of group care from other factors such as those which led to the admission and those which followed discharge. In addition to their experience of care, the index children differed from the remainder in the quality of family life they were experiencing. They were far more likely to be living in families characterized by parental disharmony. This issue will be explored further below.

Studies of adults who have been in residential care show a consistent picture of high rates of psychosocial difficulties, with different patterns for males and females. For young men the major problem area is with the law. Ferguson (1966) found high rates of convictions and imprisonment among young men who had, as children, been in residential care in Glasgow during the 1940s and 1950s. Twenty years later,

Minty and Ashcroft (1987) found a very similar picture in Manchester. More recently, informal surveys in London suggest that young men who have been in care are very overrepresented amongst male prostitutes and homeless beggars (Stein, 1991). For women the major area of difficulty is in parenthood. Wolkind (1977) found, in a large sample of primiparous women in a deprived London borough, that those who had been in care were far more likely than the remainder to have entered their pregnancy unmarried and in their teens — a circumstance that would be expected to predict greater rates of difficulties for both themselves and their children (Baldwin & Cain, 1980). Quinton and Rutter (1984) examined in detail 81 women who as children had all been resident in a large residential unit. Here too single early pregnancy was common, as was relatively rapid reconception. Although some of the women did well, the rate of difficulties in parenting was significantly higher than in a control group. Almost one-fifth had their own children taken into care by a local authority — an experience not seen amongst the controls. In some of the women the parenting difficulties were part of a much wider picture of maladjustment, with a quarter showing definite evidence of a personality disorder and many exhibiting depression.

Specificity of the effects of residential care

In looking at these findings amongst children and adults who had previously been in residential care, the main question that arises is the extent to which it is the care experience itself that causes the later difficulties or whether this is merely an index of other experiences that are more relevant. The findings of Wolkind and Rutter (1973) quoted above would suggest the latter. Most of the excess of disturbance among the ex-care group could be accounted for by the associated family factors. Further support for this comes from the study of Minty and Ashcroft (1987). Although they found that having been in care was associated with a high rate of later conviction, within the care group they obtained an apparently paradoxical finding. Length of stay in care was inversely related to the chance of a conviction. This can be intrepreted as suggesting that it was the environment pre- and postcare that increased the chances of criminality and that the time spent in residential care actually offered some protection. For antisocial disorder and criminality among men, this indeed seemed to be the case and family factors rather than the admission were the key causes. For women it seemed very likely that the same causal pattern explained some but not all of the later parenting difficulties. A direct care effect seems possible as prolonged periods in care at a young age are related to antisocial disorder in girls but not in boys (Wolkind & Rutter, 1973; Wolkind, 1974b).

The findings on educational attainments are conflicting. Using data from a large cohort of children born in the UK in 1970, St Claire and Osborne (1987) examined the possible effects of residential care, controlling for previous social deprivation. A small additional deficit was associated with being in care. Heath *et al.* (1989) found, however, that children in *long-*

term care did no worse than children receiving social work help within their own homes, and Garnett (1990) reported children brought up in care doing better than those admitted during adolescence. There may, however, be a specific effect of the length of time a child spends in residential care and a child's ability to later catch up on any deficits. Tizard and Hodges (1978) found that the IQ of children adopted from institutions before the age of 4 increased considerably after placement. For those adopted after that age, little improvement occurred.

One behavioural characteristic does however appear to be directly linked to an *early* experience of residential care. Disinhibited overfriendliness, possibly similar to the 'affect hunger' described by Levy (1937), was found by Wolkind (1974a) to be virtually confined to those children admitted to residential care before the age of 2 (see Chapter 28). Tizard and Hodges (1978) described a similar pattern in their sample of children in a residential nursery. Their work also shows clearly the limitations in providing satisfactory residential care for very young children. They described the nurseries as being well-designed and run and with the children receiving a great deal of stimulation. The cognitive deficits were minimal compared to those in the early accounts. The social deficits in contrast, were very similar.

The mechanism of group care effects

It seems that very few of the negative outcomes for children in residential care can be directly attributed to that care itself. The exception, disinhibition, is very probably due to a child being deprived of the opportunity to develop enduring secure attachments (Rutter, 1981; see Chapter 28). Although mainly described in institutionalized children, even this is not totally specific and is very similar to the picture seen found in some children from poorly functioning disorganized families, showing patterns of avoidant attachment to their caretakers (Bretherton & Waters, 1985). It should also be noted that the presence of indiscriminate overfriendliness in children in residential care does not necessarily preclude the later development of secure and satisfying relationships in new families (Hodges & Tizard, 1989). As yet we cannot explain why the children in Hodges and Tizard's study with more than 4 years in residential care did not catch up intellectually after subsequent family placement. There may well be some form of critical period for the effects of additional stimulation. What is also unclear is whether group care might have other relatively subtle effects on psychological development. There have been controversies over whether a kibbutz upbringing in Israel is associated with a particular form of personality (Bronfenbrenner, 1979). Terwogt *et al.* (1990) suggested that institutionalized children are slower than others in developing a mature understanding of other people's emotions and are less attentive to their own, but far more work is required in this area.

With group care itself being apparently so little implicated in explaining the overall poor outcome, it is necessary to return to a point made earlier in this chapter. The question must be not what are the direct adverse effects of group care, but rather why cannot this system of child rearing, set up to give some of the most deprived children in any community a chance to overcome their deprivation, succeed? One remarkably neglected area is that of the quality of care in any particular home. Tizard (1975) developed a methodology to examine the extent to which the regime of a children's home could meet the fundamental needs of a child. It is disappointing, however, to see how little has been done in this field since then, possibly because of a quite unreal view that such homes were now a thing of the past and would soon be extinct. One exception is the work of Colton (1988) who used this approach to look at differences between individual homes and also at the differences and similarities between residential and foster care. A minority of residential units produced a child-centred style of care very similar to that found in foster homes. Unfortunately we cannot as yet relate this to the outcome for the children.

For group care as a whole there remain many problems. One area of great concern has been the fast turnover of staff, with children having to relate to very large numbers of adults (Tizard, 1975). The remarkably small proportion of staff who have received any form of training to deal with some of the most difficult children in the community remains very worrying (Department of Health, 1991b). There are many exciting if unevaluated examples of good practice in group care (e.g. Fulcher & Ainsworth, 1985), but all require highly trained and motivated staff. There is little known about what makes a successful child care worker. Some attempts have been made to describe personality traits associated with effectiveness (e.g. Wasmund & Tate, 1989), but information is very limited. What is known, however, is that it is possible for the staff of children's homes to develop very idiosyncratic and ultimately highly damaging forms of child care (Levy & Kahan, 1991). Some of these practices certainly constitute forms of child abuse. In addition there has been growing recognition of how children admitted to group care because they had experienced physical and sexual abuse in their own families can be reabused by staff or older children (Kelleher, 1987; Newbern; 1989; Nunno & Motz, 1989).

The future of residential care

Despite numerous and repeated predictions of the imminent demise of residential care and the justified concerns about its shortcomings, group care will continue for the foreseeable future to be provided for children. What is crucial is that lessons are learned both from what goes wrong and from examples of good practice. Its future role will need to be carefully defined and safeguards established to protect its residents. There appears to be general agreement that residential care should not be used merely as a way of providing care for the child with no family, although this may well continue to be necessary in developing countries. The more clearly the purpose of any particular unit is defined, the more likely that unit is to succeed in its tasks (Parker, 1988). An example that

appears to be demonstrating this are those units designed to help adolescents prepare for independent living (Kroner, 1989). Although unevaluated, residential units that can admit parents with their children may well prove to have an important part to play (e.g. Dydyk *et al.*, 1989). The experiment of the Israeli kibbutzim, although now no longer ideologically in favour, has demonstrated how a combination of group and family care can well meet the needs of children in a particular society (Beit-Hallahmi & Rabin, 1977). What will also be important is that group care is not seen as an isolated system cut off from other facilities for children, but rather as part of an integrated network of services. It should be available to meet the needs of a particular time and should allow easy transition for the child to and from day care (Hamm, 1989) and should be linked to fostering and even adoption services (Nothmann, 1979). The educational needs of the child in group care must never be forgotten. Academic success, however limited, may be a crucial factor preventing a child slipping into a state of psychosocial maladjustment (Rutter & Quinton, 1984). For some very disturbed children better results may be obtained from units where the child's educational needs may be met within the residential setting rather than in the community. Attempts are being made to evaluate the effectiveness of these 'therapeutic communities' (Fitzgerald, 1990).

A great danger for children in residential care is the gradual loss of contact with family and other important individuals from their preadmission community. There is a tendency for contacts slowly to diminish over time so that by the time the child is discharged from care these are virtually ended (Millham *et al.*, 1986). Despite this, Millham and his colleagues found that most children drifted back to their families and presumably tried to reestablish contact with them. In addition there is some evidence that *regular*, but not necessarily frequent, contact with important adults from outside the home is associated with a better adjustment within it (Pringle, 1961). Virtually nothing is known, however, on the optimal level of contact and how it is possible to determine when a given level carries more advantages than disadvantages for the child.

Leaving care

In most countries children being looked after in state-provided residential care remain the responsibility of public authorities until they are between the ages of 16 and 18. Increasing attention is being paid to the significance in young people's lives of this major transition from a highly protected environment to one where they may have virtually no supports and have to fend for themselves. Quinton and Rutter (1988) showed how the events that immediately follow discharge from care can set in motion a series of steps that can determine the individual's long-term psychosocial adjustment. Thus, for example, if early unplanned pregnancy can be avoided, a young woman's chances of achieving a better long-term set of relationships may be considerably enhanced. Stein and Carey (1986) provided vivid and distressing accounts by young people describing their attempts to cope with the transition. Some have spoken of the process as being suddenly 'kicked out' (Stein, 1991). The 1989 Children Act lays great stress on the need for social service departments to take a number of steps to help the leavers. These include aftercare services that can offer counselling as well as practical and financial aid (Department of Health, 1991a,c). Smit (1991) reviewed the situation throughout Europe and suggests that a stress model both helps explain the process and provides ideas for lessening its negative potential.

FOSTER FAMILY CARE

Historical background

Foster care as a means of supporting children who cannot live with their own parents is found in all societies and notably at times of human disaster. However, the formality and concepts, of fostering arrangements vary with different conditions being attached to the arrangement, the most significant being the degree of separation from birth parents. Historically, adoption has been accorded social approval as a means of caring for parentless children or perhaps for acquiring heirs (see Chapter 16). The term foster care, by contrast, has come to be associated with the recent development of the public child care system and with payment to the alternative parents for providing a service to deprived children on behalf of the state or welfare agency. Its origins have been traced to the child indenture system in Poor Law England and in North America to religious charities who 'rescued' children from undesirable circumstances and transferred them to 'wholesome and upright' families away from the city (Wiltse, 1985).

Foster care was formalized in the UK in the 18th century (Heywood, 1978). The current legal framework derives from the 1948 Children's Act based on the Curtis Committee's recommendations that foster family care was to be preferred to residential care for deprived children. The increasing need to oversee the fostering process is evident in further government legislation and stricter regulations and guidance to promote not just the stability of placements but the quality of the new family relationships and the child's psychological, educational and medical status.

As the disadvantages of residential care became clearer and hopes were pinned instead on adoption as a better form of substitute care, a large number of children, nevertheless, still remained in indeterminate foster care. The classic study by Maas and Engler (1959) in the US showed that foster care, having begun as a temporary arrangement, became, for more than half the children they studied, the basic mode of care for their whole childhood and very few went on to be adopted or to be returned home.

Studies both in the UK and the US brought to light the disturbingly high number of children who, if not returned home quickly, remained in foster care without a clear plan for their future (Rowe & Lambert, 1973; Fanshel & Shinn, 1978). The term limbo was fittingly used to describe the condition of

these children who waited in an intermediate state for a decision to be made about them.

Foster care might more accurately have been termed serial family care, for a large proportion of these children were moved from family to family several times. This lack of stability aroused concern that the children would suffer from poor self-confidence and lack personal relationship skills.

The child welfare system was clearly failing large numbers of foster children and this prompted a call to establish the child's right to satisfactory care by the state. The permanence planning movement in the US (Maluccio *et al.*, 1986) began to reform social work practice and sought to remove obstacles to achieving permanent placements (Downs, 1981).

Although security of placement and the child's safety remain the primary concern, further requirements, such as matching foster parent and child for class, religion, cultural, linguistic and racial background, have been made to minimize the social dislocation for the child in substitute care. The need to help the child to resolve problems over past experiences, to acknowledge personal and racial identity issues and to maintain contact with relatives where appropriate is now central to ensuring a satisfactory placement.

The major shift in fostering policy has been to try to avoid precipitate and indetermine placements and to substitute clearer aims and expectations for the placement, with the goal of providing a stable environment for the child until a permanent home can be found.

Varieties of foster family care

It is important to keep in mind the variety of experiences included within foster family care. For example, children may be placed at different ages, be admitted to foster family care for different reasons and for different lengths of time, with or without their siblings and with or without continuing contact with birth parents and relatives. The point of stressing this variety is that the child's experience of these arrangements is more likely to predict later adjustment than a simple variable such as length of time in care itself.

The following diverse range of placements differ in length and function: a major difference is whether the aim is for return home. These categories will merge, however, and the children may experience many status changes over time.

Short-term care can include placement in an emergency, pre-arranged respite care, placement with the intention of rapid progress to adoption and placement of an adolescent as a bridge to independence.

Medium-term care can include placement on a temporary basis, where rehabilitation is planned, and specialist fostering placements where a period of assessment or treatment is designed to assist in a permanent care plan.

Long-term care can include permanent foster family care through to independence, but without legal adoption intended, and permanent placement with the possibility of subsequent adoption by the new family.

The foster families

Foster families tend to be larger and the foster parents older than average families and they are more likely to be at the lower end of the social class scale. These differences in family environment complicate attempts to compare foster with other, especially adopted, children. New recruitment policies have tried to broaden the spectrum of race, class and sexual orientation of foster parents but Bebbington and Miles (1990) argued that foster family characteristics have not differed greatly over time. However, the task has changed in that fewer children are now deliberately placed with a view to long-term fostering.

The selection and approval of foster parents is largely based on the agencies' views of the applicants' personal suitability to foster. However, few attempts have been made to establish whether foster parental characteristics predict placement outcome. Cautley's study (1980) attempted to distinguish promising from less promising applicants but was not able to predict from the information available at assessment which foster parents would ask for their child to be removed.

It would be unwise to judge that an adverse background should in itself indicate rejection. Dando and Minty (1987) found that even parents with disrupted or unhappy childhoods could make excellent foster parents and they thought these personal experiences may have contributed to their capacity to identify with deprived children.

Doelling and Johnson (1990) approached the question of identifying successful fostering by studying placements that had lasted for 7 years and attempting to measure the temperament of the foster mother and foster child and to relate this to placement outcome. They found a mismatch between an inflexible mother and a negative-mood child predicted poorer placement outcome. However, it was not clear whether it was the mother's temperament itself that was being revealed or perhaps a negative reaction to a particular foster child. Further clarification of what is being measured is necessary before such findings can be employed to guide placement decisions.

Recruiting foster carers of suitable characteristics is one concern but they also have to be found in sufficient numbers and there are likely to be limits to how many foster parents any community can provide. Bebbington and Miles (1990) produced rates of potential foster parents by geographical area and concluded that areas with the greatest need for placements, like the inner cities, had the lowest prospects of recruitment.

Now that the aim of foster parenting is moving away from the notion of a replacement for the birth parents and towards the concept of a team of professionals and nonprofessionals working together towards rehabilitation or permanent substitute care, more understanding and tolerance are demanded of foster parents, with recognition that foster parenting is a skilled task. This requires that the relationship between social workers and experienced foster parents is sensitively understood and managed (Rushton, 1989) and that appropriate training is offered. There have been few attempts to evaluate the outcome of foster parent training programmes and no particular training model has so far been demonstrated to be superior (Lee & Holland, 1991).

THE PSYCHOLOGICAL DEVELOPMENT OF CHILDREN IN FOSTER FAMILY CARE

Clearly these dissimilar parenting arrangements may have a variety of consequences for a child's development, but the research that has been undertaken has not covered the range of alternatives, and all too often it has been of poor quality Publication is scattered, with much in social welfare publications rather than scientific child development journals. The international literature was surveyed in 1967 (Dinnage & Pringle, 1967) and updated in 1978 (Prosser, 1978). Murray's (1984) review examined recent American studies and Triseliotis (1989) conducted the most recent research review on foster care outcomes. Studies tend either to be concerned with the psychiatric status of the foster child (Theis, 1924; Hopkins & Haines, 1931; Weinstein, 1960; Williams, 1961) or with foster care as a type of provision for children.

Rates of behaviour disorder in foster children

The Rutter A Scale (Rutter *et al.*, 1970) has frequently been used as a standardized measure of the level of disturbance in foster children but rarely with the benefit of a comparison group (Thorpe, 1980; Keane, 1983; Rowe *et al.*, 1984). Between 29% and 38% of samples have shown significant disturbance. However, there are difficulties in aggregating these findings because of variations in the ages of the children at placement and at assessment and in the reasons for children going into foster placements. When compared with inner city children (Rutter *et al.*, 1975) or children placed with the intention of adoption (Rushton *et al.*, 1988), permanently placed foster children show a greater level of behavioural disturbance. American findings confirm this picture (Fein *et al.*, 1990).

Rowe *et al.* (1984) found that foster children have a higher incidence of temper tantrums, enuresis, lack of concentration, destructiveness and stealing. However, assessment by means of questionnaires originally designed as screening instruments has limitations and would be improved by atttempts to measure more complex concepts such as social functioning, identity and self-esteem.

Roy (1983) compared children in foster family placement with those in small-scale children's homes and found restless and inattentive behaviour to be higher in both groups when followed up between 5 and 8 years. More problems of task and social behaviour were found in the institutional group.

D. Holbrook's (unpublished) interview-based study compared two groups — a long-term fostered and an adoptive group — with a control group of children living with their birth parents. She found that the foster children's scores were markedly lower on self-esteem. They also had more conduct and peer relationship problems, were doing less well academically and felt negatively about their foster care status.

This accumulating evidence contributed to a dampening of enthusiasm for long-term foster care, although it has proved difficult to determine which specific aspects of foster care are responsible for the generally poorer psychosocial functioning. Evidence that long-term foster children have higher rates of maladjustment than adoptive children in spite of stable family placement is open to several explanations. The quality of care may be different or those not selected for adoption may be more disturbed initially, but the view currently favoured is that the children feel a reduced sense of permanence and sense of belonging compared with the legal security of adoption and that this is manifested in increased problems.

Although it is important to recognize the common disturbances of foster children, the effect these have on the placement is likely to depend more on the relationship that develops between the child and new family.

The health and educational status of foster children

Concern has been expressed that foster children have poorer health (Bamford & Wolkind, 1988) and poorer educational attainment (Essen *et al.*, 1976; Aldgate, 1990) than the general population. A current study is comparing the educational attainment of children in stable, long-term placements with children from the same schools in contact with social services (Heath *et al.*, 1989). Initial findings show that both groups have below-average levels of attainment and it will be important to develop a better understanding of the links between a sense of permanence and scholastic achievement so that educational potential can be fully realized.

OUTCOMES OF FOSTER FAMILY CARE

Children coming into temporary care for a few weeks before returning home constitute the largest group in foster care. Such placements are generally successful but not often researched. Berridge and Cleaver's study (1987) showed that only 10% of 156 short-term placements broke down over 8 weeks — a relatively successful policy. Foster care designed to assist in a short-term crisis can frequently be beneficial (Fisher *et al.*, 1986) but some of these placements may drift into long-term arrangements rather than disrupt, or lead to repeated short-term admissions. Rowe reported that medium-term placements intended to change behaviour, relationships or family circumstances have not been shown to be very successful in achieving their aims (Rowe *et al.*, 1989).

Long-term foster care has commanded more research attention. Three British studies in the 1960s deserve special mention for identifying worryingly high breakdown rates, leading to disillusion with this form of care. Trasler (1960) found a 40% failure rate over a 3-year period. The majority of

the failed placements occurred in the first 2 years and Trasler identified the child's behaviour resulting from previous rejection as a major cause of breakdown, together with unreasonable expectations on the part of the foster parents. Those children placed between the ages of 7 and 13 had a significantly higher chance of breakdown.

Parker's (1966) study has been one of the most influential. This was a retrospective study of 209 children in long-stay foster placements where nearly half (48%) broke down over a 5-year period. Parker attempted to establish variations in fostering outcome and to examine which factors proved predictive. Placements of older children and those with behaviour problems were less successful, as were those where the foster parents' own children were very young or close in age to the foster child. This finding, that the presence of another child of the same age constitutes a risk factor, has been replicated in many studies and must be regarded as one of few items of secure knowledge with clear practice implications.

However, this research brought only small advances in understanding the processes that led to breakdown. For example, it is still not clear which aspects of having another child of similar age in the family predict failure. It would be a reasonable supposition that jealousy and rivalry play a part and that foster parents will put the needs of their own unhappy children first, but these and other processes have not been investigated in detail. Although it has been found that breakdown frequently occurred 12–18 months after placement, the reasons for this have not been established. A reasonable hypothesis is that this is a critical time for foster parents to assess if any improvement is being made in the child's level of difficulty and whether a satisfactory fresh attachment is growing. Small-scale studies are beginning to examine disrupted placements in more detail to this end (Aldgate & Hawley, 1986).

Further studies have confirmed the pattern of disruption and drift. George's (1970) study of 128 children found that high breakdown rates (40% failing over 5 years) were still continuing. Fanshel and Shinn (1978), in their 5-year prospective study of 624 foster children in New York, found that 36% of the sample were still in indeterminate care at the end of 5 years.

These attempts to identify predictors of breakdown were based on fairly limited information. It is hoped that data on the relational processes among the newly constituted families will yield better understanding of the failing placements. However, such studies have rarely been attempted. Nor has there been an attempt to assess the impact of the detailed components of social work and other professional services in sustaining the placement. Berridge and Cleaver (1987) have collected the most recent data on fostering breakdowns in the UK. Although the breakdown rate remained disappointingly high in one local authority (42% within 3 years), it was lower than expected in another (21%). Contrasting agency practices may have contributed to these differences.

Rowe *et al.* (1984) conducted a major study of the well-being of long-term foster children and reported positively on the placements when there remained a strong bond with birth families, although the majority of the placements did not include parental contact. This study maintains concern about the nature of long term foster care. Even children who had been living with their foster parents for between 3 and 10 years were more disturbed than those of the general population and adopted children. The authors concluded that foster care provides 'an insecure base for children to recover from earlier traumas or achieve their best development' (p. 84).

A more recent study by Rowe and her colleagues (Rowe *et al.* 1989) examined 4615 foster placements across six local authorities, this time excluding stable long-term placements. They found that the rhetoric of permanence has still to be turned into reality. Emergency placements were still common; there were many short-term admissions, returns home and moves between placements. Clearly, recommendations have resulted from research and guidelines for better practice have followed, but studies of agency practice still seem to show patterns of case management and decision-making that fall short of serving the child's best interests.

Follow-up studies of foster children

A major concern of foster care research has been to establish whether children who have experienced a period of foster care, often preceded by disadvantage and disruption, are likely to have more adjustment problems in adolescence and adulthood. Theis (1924) conducted the earliest foster care follow-up study comprising a group of 18-year-olds who had grown up in long-term foster homes; some of them had been adopted. It was found that those placed early fared better.

Fanshel and Shinn's (1978) study is one of the few with an adequate design: that is, a prospective, longitudinal examination of a well-defined population. They followed up after 5 years children still in foster care and found that behavioural problems as a reason for placement did not predict behavioural difficulty 5 years later. The suggestion is that a stable setting and good-quality care may have helped diminish the earlier problems.

There are few follow-up studies of foster children into adulthood using adequate comparison groups and results have not been entirely consistent. Meier (1965) interviewed 61 former long-term foster children at the age of 28–32 and found they were largely indistinguishable from the ordinary population and did not repeat the pattern of their parents. However, the incidence of marital breakdown and illegitimacy was higher than among the general population and women fared worse, having poorer levels of confidence. Festinger (1983) found that children who had lived mainly in a single, stable placement had moderately good outcomes in young adulthood and those with multiple placements had poorer outcomes (Fanshel *et al.*, 1990). Triseliotis (1980), in his Scottish follow-up study, found that the educational achievements of ex-foster children were poor and linked this to the low aspirations the foster parents had of their foster children

in contrast to adoptive parents. The aspirations of contemporary foster parents may be greater.

Triseliotis and Russell (1984) chose a design that permitted the comparison of the long-term outcome of foster, adoptive and residential environments, although the findings are limited by the low rate of successful follow-up. Over half of the foster children were very happy with the care they received and the quality of relationship between them and their foster families but, in contrast to the adopted group, they felt anxiety about the impermanency of the placement and less comfortable with their foster child status. Whether or not children felt positively about having been fostered seemed to depend, not surprisingly, upon the extent to which they felt genuinely cared for.

Bohman's studies (1971, 1990) offer the best data on fostering outcomes. His Swedish comparative study followed up a sample of 203 children placed permanently in foster homes at several points throughout childhood and young adulthood. It might have been expected that the children would have progressed well. The foster homes, although less advantaged than adoptive homes, were stable, the children were placed permanently from infancy and 70% were subsequently adopted by the foster parents. However, at 11 years, a greater proportion of foster children than classroom controls or adopted children were found to be maladjusted and failing at school. This proportion increased at the age of 15 and problems persisted, on selected indicators, into adulthood. It was true that the children placed in foster care were more likely to have a background of parental criminality and alcohol abuse, raising the possibility that inherited factors may have played some part in accounting for the negative outcome. Also, absence of these factors may have contributed to the adoption decision. Bohman concluded, however, that lack of security in the first years of the placement may have been the factor that distinguished fostering outcomes from the largely favourable adoption outcomes due to interference with the development of a close parent–child relationship.

CURRENT ISSUES IN PLACEMENT POLICY

A major development in fostering practice has been the need to consider placement requirements in addition to providing secure family life. The following sections consider current thinking and placement practice and the status of relevant research.

Foster family placements for adolescents

One bold development of the last 15 years has been specialist fostering projects pioneering the placement of difficult adolescents in foster families, even for short periods of time before they leave care. One such project has been evaluated with promising results (Yelloly, 1979; Hazel, 1981; Kent Family Placement Service, 1985; Fenyo *et al.*, 1989). However, there is often great variation in the provision of these schemes from area to area.

Downes (1988) examined the nature of the interaction of difficult adolescents with their foster families in her interview-based study of 23 time-limited placements. She reported that tackling the normal psychosocial tasks of adolescence could be affected both by the adolescent's attachment history and by the capacity of the foster family to assist in this developmental process.

The key question remains whether family placements, even for disturbed adolescents, produce better long-term outcomes than residential options. Such a study has yet to be done with carefully matched samples and a long enough follow-up period.

Sibling placements

Research on siblings has so far focused on biological rather than substitute families. The current view that it is desirable to keep siblings together wherever possible means that this is now a very common but underinvestigated form of placement. Findings on whether single or sibling placements are to be preferred have so far been contradictory. One study of permanent placements showed that, although outcome was better for children in sibling groups, this could be accounted for by singly placed children being more disturbed (Rushton *et al.*, 1989).

Same-race and transracial placements

The policy of arranging same-race placements has been the focus of major differences of opinion in fostering policy. Even more heated controversy has attached to transracial adoption (see Chapter 16), probably because of the finality of that arrangement. It has been argued that several factors have resulted in black children being disproportionately represented in the child care system: poverty and racism, the unavailability of support from relatives, the lack of cultural understanding of predominantly white social service agencies and inadequate efforts to rehabilitate these children or to recruit black substitute families for them. These black children have frequently been placed with white foster parents and separated from their ethnic origins. Early investigation into the fostering of black children showed that white foster carers were encouraging the children to identify with white rather than black people (Jenkins, 1963). Alarm at this process, raised particularly by black professionals and in the light of the unhappy testimony of some black children who had grown up in care, prompted a shift in policy to recruiting same-race placements wherever possible. It is also considered unwise to move black children from urban to rural areas where they could find themselves caught between conflicting cultures and have difficulty relating to the community from which they originated.

There has been a sharp decrease in the number of new transracial placements as a consequences but placement decisions have been particularly contentious when race has been held to be the most salient consideration. If white foster parents wish to adopt their black or mixed-parentage foster child, the agency may not support this transracial placement and the child could then be moved to one which is racially matched. Also, in circumstances where a suitable placement does not materialize, a black child may remain without a permanent home, forcing the arguments for permanence and the arguments for same-race placements sharply into conflict.

Matching a placement for race will depend upon how children are classified. Children of diverse backgrounds may be grouped together as black because they are seen in this way by white society and will have common experiences that are best dealt with by placement in black families. This means of classification is challenged by Tizard and Phoenix (1989), who argue that treating black people as a homogenous group denies the immense cultural diversity within the black community and also the mediating effects of social class, gender and generation. The Tizard and Phoenix paper, although primarily about adoption, has brought greater conceptual clarity to a debate which has often reduced the understanding of complex psychological functioning to simplistic notions about race and identity.

There is little research evidence to settle these questions. Properly conducted studies comparing the outcome of racially matched and racially different placements have yet to be undertaken. However, it is unlikely that race-matching in itself will protect against the overall risk of disruption when placing older, disturbed children.

Contact with birth families

It has been argued that continued contact between foster children and birth families increases the chance of rehabilitation or, if the children remain in placement, helps them to cope with feelings of rejection and learn about their origins and offers the possibility of adult support on leaving care (Holman, 1975).

It is important to know under what circumstances it is desirable to adopt this inclusive fostering model and with what frequency of contact. A number of studies have tackled the question of the impact of regular contact with the birth parents on the child and the placement. Fanshel (1975) reported that parental visiting was the best single predictor of the child's discharge from care but was not able to demonstrate empirically that contact benefited children still in foster care at the 5-year follow-up. Visiting was often stressful for the parties involved.

More recent British studies have also claimed that contact with birth families is associated with better outcomes (Millham *et al.*, 1986; Berridge & Cleaver, 1987; Thoburn & Rowe, 1988). However, research has yet to be designed that places the effect of contact as the central question. The data pertinent to this question are sparse and so far no particular conclusion can be justified with any certainty. It is important to take account of the fact that contact can take many forms and is likely to have quite a different effect depending on the nature and context of the contact, the child's age, the type of placement, the attitude of the birth parents to the placement and changes in the child's perspective over time. All these aspects need more careful assessment and measurement. Cumulative findings may lean in the direction of the benefits of contact but the strength of the association found is usually weak and a causal link is by no means established. The evidence certainly does not support maintaining sporadic or distressing contact with birth parents when there is no likelihood of the child returning home. More definite conclusions that can be drawn from these studies are that opportunities for preserving contact are not pursued often enough, but when they are, it is most desirable that contact arrangements have careful social work management over time.

Abused children and abuse in foster care

There is little research on subsequent abuse in foster care but it is a question of growing importance. Attention is currently being drawn to abuse by foster fathers, abuse by formerly abused foster children and abuse by a child of the foster family. One study of 290 cases of reported abuse during out-of-home care showed that equal frequency of abuse was reported in foster and residential care but the paper specifically draws attention to the frequency of natural, older male children of the foster family as perpetrators of sexual abuse of foster children (Rosenthal *et al.*, 1991).

Data on the care of sexually abused children are beginning to emerge. One study (Lie & McMurty, 1991) found that a group of sexually abused children placed in foster care and compared with a matched group of children in care for other reasons remained in foster care on average for 2 years less than the matched comparisons. They concluded that sexually abused children are not necessarily ill-served by foster care arrangements, although less than half had left care for a planned placement by the end of the study.

Evaluating family foster care services

Little is known about the types of professional intervention that achieve effective support of foster placements and the optimum functioning of the foster child. Studies have mostly been concerned with the evaluation of projects designed to find permanent homes for children in indeterminate foster care. The Oregon Project (Lahti, 1982) aimed to work aggressively towards either rehabilitation or permanent substitute care by means of trained caseworkers using behavioural contracting and encouraging greater involvement with birth parents. Lahti demonstrated that the project had greater success in achieving permanence than the routine service. Adoption was the most secure and long-term fostering the least stable of all the placement arrangements. This study also showed that the child's sense of permanence, more than legal status, was associated with positive outcome. In the Alameda Project (Stein & Gambrill, 1977), a controlled comparison of focused decision-making methods was found to be superior to the regular foster care service in the country. Some 21% of the children in the experimental group remained in long-term foster care, as against 60% of the control group children.

These findings were influential in stressing the importance of continuity of care to children and in beginning to identify the type of professional intervention likely to secure it. However, research has not so far identified which specific aspects of intervention are associated with positive outcome (Rushton, 1989). More precise description and categorization of social work and other professional interventions are necessary in order to reveal selective effects on outcome.

CONCLUSION

During the 1960s and 1970s there were many claims that 'the family was dead' and that this was no bad thing (Cooper, 1972). This examination of how difficult it is for the state to provide adequate care for those children who cannot be cared for by their own families is one of the strongest counterarguments. Although some children do well in both foster and group care, the high rates of psychiatric disorder and of later psychosocial difficulties are extremely worrying. Perhaps the most hopeful way of moving forward is to get away from a starting point of a particular set of child care facilities or philosophies and insisting that it is the needs of the individual child that will determine what will be provided.

In defining those needs, child mental health professionals have an important role to play. An awareness of this seems to have been present since the early days of child psychiatry. In 1932, Maskey described how he worked in a child care setting. He offered direct treatment to individual children and consultation to staff members. Since then this appears to have remained the general pattern, probably with most emphasis on the second activity, despite any clear evidence, a lack of its effectiveness (e.g. Mannino & Shore, 1975). What must be ensured is that new developments in assessment and treatment in child psychiatry are not denied to this population because of their special status. The whole spectrum of psychiatric disorders will be seen and appropriate treatment must be available. The fact of a child being outside of its family of origin will, of course be important and it is good to see that attempts are being made to adapt techniques for use in this setting. Boston and Szur (1983) have described this with individual psychotherapy and Sholevar (1980) with family therapy. The development of this work and its evaluation should be a major task for all those responsible for organizing child psychiatric services.

REFERENCES

Aldgate J. (1990) Foster children at school: success or failure? *Adoption and Fostering*, **14**, 38–49.

Aldgate J. & Hawley D. (1986) *Recollections of Disruption: a Study of Foster Care Breakdowns*. National Foster Care Association, London.

Bagenholm G. & Kristiansson B. (1987) Child health in a large-scale Ethiopian institution II. Psychosomatic health. *Ethiopian Medical Journal*, **25**, 9–14.

Bakwin H. (1949) Emotional deprivation in infants. *Journal of Paediatrics*, **35**, 512.

Baldwin W. & Cain V.S. (1980) The children of teenage parents. *Family Planning Perspectives*, **12**, 34−43.

Bamford F. & Wolkind S. (1988) *The Physical and Mental Health of Children in Care: Research Needs*. Economic and Social Research Council, London.

Bebbington A. & Miles J. (1989) The background of children who enter local authority care. *British Journal of Social Work*, **19**, 349−368.

Bebbington A. & Miles J. (1990) The supply of foster families for children in care. *British Journal of Social Work*, **20**, 283−307.

Beit-Hallahmi B. & Rabin A.I. (1977) The kibbutz as a social experiment and as a child rearing laboratory. *American Psychologist*, **32**, 532−541.

Bender L. & Yarnell H. (1941) An observation nursery; a study of 250 children on the psychiatric division of Bellevue hospital. *American Journal of Psychiatry*, **97**, 1158−1174.

Berridge D. (1985) *Children's Homes*. Basil Blackwell, Oxford.

Berridge D. & Cleaver H. (1987) *Foster Home Breakdown*. Basil Blackwell, Oxford.

Bohman M. (1971) A comparative study of adopted children, foster children and in their biological environment born after undesired pregnancies. *Acta Paediatrica Scandinavica* (suppl. 221), 1−38.

Bohman M. (1990) Outcome in adoption: lessons from longitudinal studies. In: Brodzinsky D. & Schechter M. (eds) *The Psychology of Adoption*, pp. 93−106. Oxford University Press, Oxford.

Boston M. & Szur R. (1983) *Psychotherapy with Severely Deprived Children*. Routledge & Kegan Paul, London.

Bretherton I. & Waters E. (1985) Growing points of attachment theory and research. *Monographs for the Society for Research in Child Development*, **50**, 1−2. Serial No 209.

Bronfenbrenner U. (1979) *The Ecology of Human Development*. Harvard University Press, Cambridge, MA.

Bullock R. (1991) Residential care for children. Issues and developments. In: Hellinckx W., Broekaert E., Vanden Berge, A. & Colton M. (eds) *Innovations in Residential Care*. Acco, Leuven.

Cautley P. (1980) *New Foster Parents: The First Experience*. Human Sciences Press, New York.

Colton M. (1988) Dimensions of foster and residential care practice. *Journal of Child Psychology and Psychiatry* **29**, 589−600.

Colton M. (1989) Foster and residential children's perceptions of their social environments. *British Journal of Social Work*, **19**, 217−233.

Cooper D. (1972). *The Death of the Family*. Penguin, Harmondsworth.

Dando I. & Minty B. (1987) What makes good foster parents? *British Journal of Social Work*, **17**, 383−399.

Davies B. & Knapp M. (1988) Costs and residential social care. In: Sinclair I. (ed) *Residential Care: The Research Reviewed*, pp. 293−378. HMSO, London.

Department of Health (1991a) *Children in Care of Local Authorities*. HMSO, London.

Department of Health (1991b) *Children in the Public Care: A Review of Residential Child Care*. HMSO, London.

Department of Health (1991c) *Patterns and Outcomes in Child Placement*. HMSO, London.

Dinnage R. & Pringle M. (1967) *Foster Home Care: Facts and Fallacies*. Longmans, London.

Doelling J. & Johnson J. (1990) Predicting success in foster placement: the contribution of parent−child temperament characteristics. *American Journal of Orthopsychiatry*, **60**, 585−593.

Downes C. (1988) Foster families for adolescents: the healing potential of time-limited placements. *British Journal of Social Work*, **18**, 437−487.

Downs S. (1981) *Foster Care Reform in the 1970s: Final Report of the Permanency Planning Dissemination Project*. Regional Research Insitute for Human Sciences, Portland State University, Oregon.

Dydyk B.J., French G., Gertsman C., Morrison N. & O'Neill I. (1989) Admitting whole families: an alternative to residential care. *Canadian Journal of Psychiatry*, **34**, 694−699.

Essen J., Lambert L. & Head J. (1976) School attainment of children who have been in care. *Child Care, Health and Development*, **2**, 339−351.

Fanshel D. (1975) Parental visiting of children in foster care: key to discharge? *Social Services Review*, **49**, 493−514.

Fanshel D. & Shinn E. (1978) *Children in Foster Care; a Longitudinal Study*. Columbia University Press, New York.

Fanshel D., Finch S. & Grundy J. (1990) *Foster Children in a Life Course Perspective*. Columbia University Press, New York.

Fein E., Maluccio A. & Kluger M. (1990) *No More Partings, an Examination of Long Term Foster Care*. Child Welfare League of America, New York.

Fenyo A., Knapp M. & Baines B. (1989) Foster care breakdown: a study of a special teenage fostering scheme. In: Hudson J. & Galaway B. (eds) *The State as Parent*. Kluwer Academic Publishers, Dordrecht.

Ferguson T. (1966) *Children in Care and After*. Oxford University Press, Oxford.

Festinger T. (1983) *No-one Ever Asked Us. . . . A Postcript to Foster Care*. Columbia University Press, New York.

Fisher M., Marsh P., Phillips D. & Sainsbury E. (1986) *In and Out of Care: The Experiences of Children, Parents and Social Workers*. Batsford, London.

Fitzgerald J. (1990) *The Hurt and the Healing*. Charterhouse Group, London.

Fulcher L.C. & Ainsworth F. (eds) (1985) *Group Care Practice with Children*. Tavistock, London.

Garmezy N. (1984) Stress resistant children. In: Stevenson J.E. (ed) *Recent Research in Developmental Psychopathology*. Pergamon Press, London.

Garnett L. (1990) Leaving care for independence: a follow up study to the Placement Outcomes Project. Report to the Department of Health. Quoted in Department of Health 1991 *Patterns and Outcomes in Child Placement*. HMSO, London.

George V. (1970) *Foster Care: Theory and Practice*. Routledge & Kegan Paul, London.

Goldfarb W. (1949) Rorschach test differences between family-reared, institution-reared and schizophrenic children. *American Journal of Orthopsychiatry*, **1**, 624−633.

Hakimi-Manesh Y., Mojdehi H. & Tashakkori A. (1984) Effects of environmental enrichment on the mental and psychomotor development of orphanage children. *Journal of Child Psychology and Psychiatry*, **25**, 643−650.

Hamm J. (1989) Intensive day treatment provides an alternative to residential care. *Child Today*, **18**, 11−15.

Hazel N. (1981) *A Bridge to Independence*. Blackwell, Oxford.

Heath A., Colton M. & Aldgate J. (1989) Educational progress of children in and out of care. *British Journal of Social Work*, **19**, 447−460.

Heywood J. (1978) *Children in Care*. Routledge & Kegan Paul, London.

Hodges J. & Tizard B. (1989) IQ and behavioural adjustment of ex-institutional adolescents. *Journal of Child Psychology and Psychiatry*, **30**, 63−75.

Holman R. (1975) The place of fostering in social work. *British Journal of Social Work*, **5**, 3−29.

Hopkins C. & Haines A. (1931) A study of one hundred problem children for whom foster care was advised. *American Journal of Orthopsychiatry*, **I**, 107−128.

Jackson S. (1987) *The Education of Children in Care*. Bristol Papers in Applied Social Studies, University of Bristol, Bristol.

Jenkins R. (1963) The fostering of coloured children. *Case Conference*, **10**, 129–134.

Kahan B. (1979) *Growing up in Care*. Blackwell, Oxford.

Keane A. (1983) Behaviour problems among long term foster children. *Adoption and Fostering*, **7**, 53–62.

Kelleher M.E. (1987) Investigating institutional abuse: a post substantiation model. *Child Welfare*, **66**, 343–351.

Kent Family Placement Service (1985) *10 years on: 1975 to 1985 Reviewed*. Kent Family Placement Service, Kent.

Kroner M.J. (1989) Living arrangement options for young people preparing for independent living. *Child Welfare*, **67**, 547–561.

Lahti J. (1982) A follow-up study of foster children in permanent placements. *Social Service Review*, **56**, 556–571.

Lambert L., Essen J. & Head J. (1977) Variations in behaviour ratings of children who have been in care. *Journal of Child Psychology and Psychiatry*, **18**, 335–346.

Lee J. & Holland T. (1991) Evaluating the effectiveness of foster parent training. *Research on Social Work Practice*, **1**, 162–174.

Levy D.M. (1937) Primary affect hunger. *American Journal of Psychiatry* **94**, 643–652.

Levy A. & Kahan B. (1991) *The Pindown Experience and the Protection of Children*. Staffordshire County Council.

Lie G.-L. & McMurty S. (1991) Foster care for sexually abused children: a comparative study. *Child Abuse and Neglect*, **15**, 111–121.

Maas H. & Engler R. (1959) *Children in Need of Parents*. Columbia University Press, New York.

Maluccio A., Fein E. & Olmstead K. (1986) *Permanency Planning for Children: Concepts and Methods*. Tavistock Publications, London.

Mannino F. & Shore M. (1975) The effects of consultation: a review of empirical studies. *American Journal of Community Psychology*, **3**, 1–21.

Mapstone E. (1969) Children in care. *Concern*, **3**, 23–28.

Maskey O.B. (1932) Psychiatry in the children's institution. *American Journal of Orthopsychiatry*, **1**, 25–34.

Meier E.G. (1965) Current circumstances of former foster children. *Child Welfare*, **44**, 196–206.

Millham S., Bullock R., Hosie K. & Little M. (1986) *Lost in Care: the Problems of Maintaining Links between Children in Care and their Families*. Gower, Aldershot.

Minty E.B. & Ashcroft C. (1987) *Child Care and Adult Crime*. Manchester University Press, Manchester.

Murray L. (1984) A review of selected foster care-adoption research from 1978 to mid 1982. *Child Welfare*, **58**, 113–124.

Newbern V.B. (1989) Sexual victimization of child and adolescent patients. *Image. Journal of the Nurse School*, **21**, 10–13.

Nothmann R. (1979) Adoption and fostering in the context of other child care and family provisions. In: Wolkind S. (ed) *Medical Aspects of Adoption and Foster Care*. Heinemann Medical, London.

Nunno M.A. & Motz J.K. (1989) The development of an effective response to the abuse of children in out-of-home care. *Child Abuse and Neglect*, **12**, 521–529.

Packman J., Randall J. & Jacques N. (1986) *Who Needs Care? Social Work Decisions about Children*, Basil Blackwell, Oxford.

Parker R. (1966) *Decision in Child Care: A Study of Prediction in Fostering*. Allen & Unwin. London.

Parker R.A. (1988) A historical background. In: Sinclair I. (ed) *Residential Care. The Research Reviewed*, pp. 1–38. HMSO, London.

Pillay A.L., Vawda N.B. & Pollock L.R. (1989) Secondary enuresis in institutionalized conduct-disordered children. *Psychological Report*, **64**, 624–626.

Pringle M.L.M. (1961) Emotional adjustment in children in care. Part 1; A firm friend outside. *Child Care*, **15**, 5–12.

Prosser H. (1978) *Perspectives on Foster Care*. NFER, Windsor, Berkshire.

Quinton D. & Rutter M. (1984) Parents with children in care: current circumstances and parenting skills. *Journal of Child Psychology and Psychiatry*, **25**, 211–230.

Quinton D. & Rutter M. (1988) *Parenting Breakdown: The Making and Breaking of Inter-generational Links*. Studies in Deprivation and Disadvantage. Avebury, Aldershot.

Rosenthal J., Motz J., Edmonson D. & Groze V. (1991) A descriptive study of abuse and neglect in out-of-home-placement. *Child Abuse and Neglect*, **15**, 249–260.

Rowe J. & Lambert L. (1973) *Children who Wait*. Association of British Adoption and Fostering Agencies, London.

Rowe J., Cain H., Hundleby M. & Keane A. (1984) *Long Term Foster Care*. Batsford. London.

Rowe J., Hundleby M. & Garnett L. (1989) *Child care Now: a Study of Placement Patterns*. Research Series 6. British Agencies for Adoption and Fostering, London.

Roy P. (1983) Is continuity enough? Substitute care and socialisation. Paper presented at the Spring Scientific Meeting, Child and Adolescent Psychiatry Specialist Section, Royal College of Psychiatrists. London, March.

Rushton A. (1989) Post-placement services for foster and adoptive parents. *Journal of Child Psychology and Psychiatry*, **30**, 197–204.

Rushton A., Treseder J. & Quinton D. (1988) *New Parents for Older Children* Discussion series no. 10. British Agencies for Adoption and Fostering, London.

Rushton A., Treseder J. & Quinton D. (1989) Sibling groups in permanent placements. *Adoption and Fostering*, **13**, 5–11.

Rutter M. (1981) *Maternal Deprivation Re-assessed*. Penguin, Harmondsworth.

Rutter M. & Quinton D. (1984) Long term follow up of women institutionalized in childhood: factors promoting good functioning in later life. *British Journal of Developmental Psychology*, **18**, 225–234.

Rutter M. Tizard J. & Whitmore K. (eds) (1970) *Education, Health and Behaviour*. Longman, London.

Rutter M., Cox A., Tupling C., Berger M. & Yule W. (1975) Attainment and adjustment in two geographical areas 1. The prevalence of psychiatric disorder. *British Journal of Psychiatry*, **126**, 493–509.

St Claire L. & Osborne A.F. (1987) The ability and behaviour of children who have been 'in care' or separated from their parents. *Early Child Development and Care*, Special Issue No. **28**, (3).

Schaffer H.R. & Schaffer E.B. (1968) *Child Care and the Family: A Study of Short-Term Admission to Care*. Occasional Papers on Social Administration, no 25 Bell, London.

Sholevar P.G. (1980) Families of institutionalized children. In: Sholevar P.G. (ed) *Emotional Disorders in Children and Adolescents: Medical and Psychological Approaches to Treatment*. MTP, Lancaster.

Sinclair I. (1988) Common issues. In: Sinclair I. (ed) *Residential Care: The Research Reviewed*, pp. 39–56. HMSO, London.

Smit M. (1991) Leaving residential care. A stressful experience. In: Hellinckx W., Broekaert E., Vanden Berge A. & Colton M. (eds) *Innovations in Residential Care*. Acco, Leuven.

Stein M. (1991) *Leaving Care and the 1989 Children Act*. First Key, Leeds.

Stein M. & Carey K. (1986) *Leaving Care*. Basil Blackwell, Oxford.

Stein T. & Gambrill E. (1977) Facilitating decision-making in foster care: the Alameda project. *Social Services Review*, **51**, 502–513.

Tatara T. (1988) *Characteristics of Children in Substitute Care*. American Public Welfare Association, Washington, DC.

Terwogt M.M., Schene J. & Koops W. (1990) Concepts of emotion in institutionalized children. *Journal of Child Psychology and Psychiatry*, **31**, 1131–1143.

Theis S. van S. (1924) *How Foster Children Turn Out*. State Charities Association, New York.

Thoburn J. & Rowe J. (1988) Research: a snapshot of permanent family placement. *Adoption and Fostering*, **12**, 29–34.

Thorpe R. (1980) The experience of parents and children living apart. In: Triseliotis J.P. (ed) *New Developments in Foster Care and Adoption*. Routledge & Kegan Paul, London.

Tizard J. (1975) Quality of residential care for retarded children. In: Tizard J., Sinclair I. & Clarke R.V.G. (eds) *Varieties of Residential Experience*. Routledge & Kegan Paul, London.

Tizard B. & Hodges J. (1978) The effects of early institutional rearing on the development of eight year old children. *Journal of Child Psychology and Psychiatry*, **19**, 99–118.

Tizard B. & Phoenix A. (1989) Black identity and transracial adoption. *New Community*, **15**, 427–437.

Trasler G. (1960) *In Place of Parents: A Study of Foster Care*, Routledge, London.

Triseliotis J. (1980) *Growing up in Foster Care and After*. Social Science Research Council, London.

Triseliotis J. (1989) Foster care outcomes: a review of key research findings. *Adoption and Fostering*, **13**, 5–17.

Triseliotis J. & Russell J. (1984) *Hard to Place: The Outcome of Adoption and Residential Care*. Heinemann Educational Books, London.

Trotzkey E.L. (1974) Institutional care and placing out: the place of each in the care of dependent children. Report prepared for Marks Nathan Jewish Orphan Home. Republished in Wolins M. (ed) *Successful Group Care*, Aldine, Chicago.

van Goor-Lambo G., Orley J., Poustka F. & Rutter M. (1990) Classification of abnormal psychosocial situations; preliminary report of a revision of a WHO scheme. *Journal of Child Psychology and Psychiatry*, **31**, 229–241.

Wasmund W.C. & Tate T.F. (1989) Personality and performance; attributes of effective residential child care workers. *Child Welfare*, **67**, 291–299.

Weinstein E. (1960) *The Self Image of the Foster Child*. Russell Sage Foundation, New York.

Williams J. (1961) Children who break down in foster homes: a psychological study of patterns of personality growth in grossly deprived children. *Journal of Child Psychology and Psychiatry*, **2**, 5–20.

Wiltse K.T. (1985) Foster care: an overview. In: Laird J. & Hartman A. (eds) *A Handbook of Child Welfare: Context, Knowledge and Practice*, pp. 565–584. Free Press, New York.

Wolins M. (ed) (1974) *Successful Group Care*. Aldine, Chicago.

Wolkind S.N. (1974a) The components of 'affectionless psychopathy' in institutionalized children. *Journal of Child Psychology and Psychiatry*, **15**, 215–220.

Wolkind S.N. (1974b) Sex differences in the aetiology of antisocial disorders in children in long-term residential care. *British Journal of Psychiatry*, **125**, 125–130.

Wolkind S.N. (1977) Women who have been 'in care' — psychological and social status during pregnancy. *Journal of Child Psychology and Psychiatry*, **18**, 179–182.

Wolkind S.N. & Rutter M. (1973) Children who have been 'in care': an epidemiological study. *Journal of Child Psychology and Psychiatry*, **14**, 97–105.

Yelloly M. (1979) *Independent Evaluation of 25 Placements*. Kent County Social Services Department, Kent.

Yule W. & Raynes N. (1972) Behaviour characteristics of children in residential care in relation to indices of separation. *Journal of Child Psychology and Psychiatry*, **13**, 249–258.

Chapter 16
Adoption

Lionel Hersov

INTRODUCTION

The practice of adoption has its origin in the beginning of human society. The Babylonian code of Hammurabi, the oldest written set of laws (2250 BC), includes a section on adoption dealing with some of the legal issues that still concern us today (Benet, 1976): 'If a man takes a child in his name, adopt and rear him as a son, the grown-up son may not be demanded back' (cited in Sorosky *et al.*, 1984, p. 25). Such ancient civilizations as the Egyptian, Chinese, Indian and Roman practised adoption as it was among several possible ways of providing an heir, safeguarding the succession of wealthy families by property inheritance, as well as ensuring the continuity of ancestral worship.

Adoption has only recently become a recognized practice in western society and it was in the US, with its egalitarian ideas, that modern adoption practice developed. Historians and legal scholars concur that the American law on adoption emerged in the middle of the 19th century with the passage in 1851 of the Massachussetts statute 'An Act to Provide for the Adoption of Children' (Kawashima, 1981/1982). The Act is agreed to be the first general law of adoption in the US and UK. It was aimed at the *welfare* of children, in contrast to the traditional adoption systems which existed in different societies outside the common law. There are obvious differences between the 1851 law and current adoption laws, but in both, the child's welfare and adopting parent's rights are safeguarded.

This chapter aims to help readers understand why parents adopt, the changing trends in adoption practice, assessment of suitability for adoption, the adoption of children with mental and physical handicap, psychological and social development and psychiatric disorder in adopted children and other factors such as age at adoption, interracial adoption, adoption disruption and clinical issues in adoption.

THE ADOPTION ARRANGEMENT

Adoption involves a triangular relationship between the natural parents, the child and the adopting parents serving these parties through different functions (Sorosky *et al.*, 1984). The interests of each may differ widely. The child's welfare is enhanced by a better upbringing and a superior education when compared with what the natural parents can often provide. Parental burdens may be eased and their hopes for their child realized in a more congenial family environment with better stimulation, wider experience and vocational choice. The reasons and motives of the adopting parents are more varied: a desire to perpetuate their family and pass on their family traditions in more tangible form, satisfaction in rearing a child, often in addition to their own, to make the lives of an infertile couple more lively and meaningful by including a child (Kawashima, 1981/1982).

Each year many thousands of children are adopted. The majority are illegitimate births but increasing numbers result from legal termination of biological parents' rights because of abuse or neglect. Other children become available for adoption because of parental death, abandonment or voluntary relinquishment by parents. Also, increasing numbers of foreign-born children are being adopted.

CHANGING TRENDS IN ADOPTION PRACTICE

Since the 1920s, until fairly recently, adoption was seen primarily as a service for childless couples. As has been pointed out (Tizard, 1977), adoption is now seen as a *form of child care*, one of several ways of bringing up children whose parents are unable to do so, or simply will not look after them. As a result, different criteria now exist for placement. Earlier on, proof of infertility was required, the racial origins and health of the child were closely examined, and attempts were made to match infant and couple. At present, any child in need can be considered for adoption, whatever his or her colour, family history, state of health or handicap and level of intelligence. Placement today does not necessarily reproduce the pattern of family life that was attempted by earlier adoptions. Adoption is seen as a way of purposefully influencing the circumstances of a child's life by removing children from adverse environments and placing them in families likely to advance their intelligence and social and emotional development.

The current pattern of adoption is very different from that of 25 years ago. The number of legal adoptions in the UK rose steadily over the 10 years from 1958 to a peak in 1968 (Home Office, 1972). Since then, there has been a steady decline with a drop of over 50% between 1976 and 1982 (Office of Population Censuses and Surveys, 1987). The number of adoptions by natural parents and stepparents has risen considerably, probably reflecting higher rates of divorce and remarriage. Over the last decade or so, the main changes in the age distribution have been a general decline in the proportion of children adopted under 2 years of age and an increase in children aged 10 and over, with a particularly sharp increase for children aged 15–17 years. In 1981 50% of adoptions in the UK were of children aged 5–14 years.

The data on adoption in the US are similar in many respects. A peak was reached in 1970 (Adoption Factbook, 1985). The proportion of adoptions by related individuals also steadily increased until they made up nearly two-thirds of all adoptions in 1982. Between 1951 and 1975 the percentage of independent adoptions declined substantially, while those by public and private agencies more than doubled (Barth & Berry, 1988). There was also a steady increase in foreign-born adoptions from 1979 to 1984 (Adoption Factbook, 1985). A recent national health survey suggested that there are approximately 1.3 million adopted children under 18 years of age or roughly 3% of the child population (Zill, 1985). Nearly two-thirds of all adoptions are related or intrafamilial. Since 1980, more older children and those with special needs are entering adoptive placements. In California the percentage of older-child adoptions rose nearly 10-fold in 10 years from 1970 to 1980 (Barth & Berry, 1988). The latest adoption statistics from the US by the National Council for Adoption showed that about 97% of babies born to unmarried women were kept by the mother (Adoption Factbook, 1989).

Adoption and fostering

There is still much discussion about the indications for placing a child for adoption or in long-term fostering. Adcock (1980) took the view that serious consideration should be given to adoption if, after being taken into care, the child has a need to remain in long-term care and has not had consistent and affectionate relationships with his or her parents before he or she came into care. Another indication would be that if the child came into care when very young and she or he then remains in care with only sporadic or no parental contact, serious consideration should be given to the possibility of adoption.

The breakdown rate in fostering has been estimated to be as high as 50%, so that foster children appear to be more at risk in terms of security, stability and continuity. Triseliotis and Hill (1990) looked at outcome in the current personal and social circumstances of adults and older children who as children were adopted, fostered with a family or cared for in residential institutions. The attrition rate in the sample was high, so the findings must be regarded with caution. Their evidence points to the relative security in family-type placements as compared with long-term residential care. Although long-term foster care has its satisfactions, 'its ambiguous status gives rise to an element of insecurity not found in adoption' (p. 120). These authors also claim that those children growing up adopted, even if placed when older, appear in adulthood to

have a stronger sense of self and function more adequately at the personal, social and economic level, compared to those formerly fostered (Triseliotis & Hill, 1990). They maintain that adoption has a greater potential for reversing earlier adverse experiences than foster or residential care. Adoption gave a feeling of permanence for life and a sense of belonging to those who experienced it, as opposed to the sense of anxiety and uncertainty in those in foster care. Abuse is also less likely in adoption and higher rates of abuse are predictable in foster and group care (Barth & Berry, 1988).

Some factors influencing adoption practice

There are approximately 1 million teenage pregnancies annually in the US, with 600 000 resulting in live births (McCluskey, 1983). These teenage parents represent only 6% of their age group. Teenage pregnancy is still considerably higher in the US than in the great majority of other developed countries (Westoff et al., 1983; Hayes, 1987). Even if the rates in whites only are taken into account, the US rates are very much higher than most, almost certainly due to the difference in availability and use of contraception (Jones et al., 1985). There is general concern over the rise in the number of abortions, the rising proportion of illegitimate births and the high rates of adolescent premarital pregnancy with birth occurring after marriage (Chilman, 1983). The social and psychological circumstances in which such pregnancies occur are extremely important in deciding what to advise. The main alternatives are therapeutic abortion, carrying to term and delivery (during which marriage may occur, often to another adolescent), placement for adoption after delivery and finally the setting up of a one-parent family.

Several factors have contributed to the situation whereby fewer babies can be offered for adoption in the UK and US. Greater use of contraception and an increasing number of legal abortions is one. The changing attitude to illegitimacy and unmarried parenthood is another; there is now a greater acceptance of single parenthood, including a negative feeling towards pregnant adolescents who are considering adoption. There is also peer pressure upon adolescents to keep their babies, which makes it difficult to reach a thoughtful decision. Now only around 4–6% of babies of unmarried mothers are given up, and white women are more likely to place their infants than black women (Deykin et al., 1984; Resnick, 1984). However, many of the infants and children born to teenagers are relinquished voluntarily or involuntarily later in infancy or early childhood when they prove more troublesome than expected, or when the mothers are unable to manage them. Such children make up the large numbers of 'special needs' children.

There is also the traditional role of the extended family in raising black children, which amounts to informal adoption, so that placing a child in either foster care or adoption outside the family violates the values of many black families and placement for adoption only occurs where there is no alternative.

Relinquishing an infant for adoption

Up till recently, relatively little attention has been paid to the mothers who relinquish their children for adoption. It is assumed that having made the decision, the women will put the experience behind them and go on with their lives. In the more open environment of the last two decades, many of these mothers have begun to express their feelings of sorrow, regret and anger arising from their decision (Rynearson, 1982; Deykin *et al.*, 1984). A growing number of women have, in recent years, formed several support groups in the UK and US. Many insist that, if it were not for insensitive handling and coercion, together with lack of family support, they would have been able to bring up their children (Brodzinsky, 1990).

Various studies have been carried out looking at the adjustment of women following the relinquishment of their children (Burnell & Norfleet, 1979; Rynearson, 1982; Deykin *et al.*, 1984; Sorosky *et al.*, 1984; Winkler & van Keppel, 1984). There are many methodological problems in these studies, including sampling biases, lack of control groups and questionable measures, so that generalizations are hazardous. It is suggested that many women experience a severe sense of loss on relinquishing their infants and that, in some, the effects were long-lasting. Many others go through the experience differently, apparently without severe reactions. Are there protective factors that lead to the better outcome? More research is needed.

Open adoption

There is increasing interest in and discussion about so-called open or inclusive adoption in which birth parents retain contact with their child after adoption, especially when older children are adopted, while the adoptive parents have permanent responsibility for care, custody and control (Borgman, 1982). Many older children find it very difficult, if not impossible, suddenly to wipe out years of relationships and shared experience. Trying to do so may lead to considerable conflict with loss of feelings of security and self-esteem.

In these circumstances, it is argued, it is better to set up an open adoption where the child and biological family have rights of association and perhaps other rights such as inheritance and use of the family surname (Borgman, 1982). The child is shielded from the anxiety and guilt of having to choose between his/her biological and adoptive family.

Some adoption workers have argued for totally open adoption with personal exchange of information. Contact between the two families is encouraged from before the child's birth and throughout the child's life. It is also argued that more children would be given up for adoption if mothers could have more choice in the placement and later continuing contact with the adopting families and the child (Samuels, 1990). Some adoption agencies in the US act as intermediaries to exchange information that is kept in confidential files (Samuels, 1990). Clearly more needs to be known about the process generally and studies carried out of the consequences of open adoption before broad changes in practice are made.

Searching in adoption

The movement for opening sealed records in the US began in 1954, but came to the fore in 1973 (Samuels, 1990). Sorosky *et al.* (1984) were the first to report on the long-term effects of relinquishing an infant on the birth parents, and the needs of adult adoptees to make contact with their birth parents. They argued that major changes were needed in adoption practice as reunions became more frequent and searching more sophisticated. Birth parents have formed support and search groups in their desire for reunion with their children.

Researchers disagree as to whether adoptive children who search have more psychological problems than those who do not. Sorosky *et al.* (1984), Day and Leeding (1980), and Haimes and Timms (1985) did not find that searchers are necessarily psychologically disturbed. Others have found that problems in relationships with adoptive parents lead to a search for birth families (Triseliotis, 1973; Feigelman & Silverman, 1983; Aumend & Barrett, 1984). It appears that although the desire to search for origins and birth parents has become more acceptable, relatively fewer people than might have been expected to do so have actively sought face-to-face meetings. Humphrey and Humphrey (1988) found that more women than men replied to a questionnaire sent to adult adoptees who felt the need to search for their origins, and more women than men reported unhappy experiences in their adoptive family. Twice as many women as men had decided in their childhood to try and find their natural mother. More women than men mentioned the need for medical information for the sake of their children and more women had taken their search as far as meeting their natural mother or other relatives. On an adoption stress inventory women scored more highly than men on items that focused on anxiety about personal identity. The authors concluded that 'adoptees have a healthy curiosity about their origins and a need for full perinatal history in order to complete their sense of self' (p. 111).

Single adoptive parents

In the past, adoption agencies regarded single-parent adoptions as placements of last resort, when the child's only options were foster care or institutionalization (Simon & Altstein, 1987). 'Special needs' children were most often made available for this kind of placement. Since 1971 the number of lone parent families has risen by 77%, reaching a total of about 1 million in 1986 (Haskey, 1989). Only a small minority of families with dependent children (1%) are headed by a lone father, with this proportion remaining fairly constant since the early 1970s. The rise in the numbers of single-parent families headed by never married women is partly due to the growing trend for extramarital childbearing, but also reflects the decreasing proportion of out-of-wedlock births that are subsequently adopted (Estaugh & Wheatley, 1990).

Accurate data are not easily available on single-parent adoptions, but these appear to be increasing. Also, the increase in numbers of 'special needs' children available for adoption leads to the necessity of recruiting special groups of parents. In the US there appear to be two broad groups of single-parent adoptions: black working-class or lower middle-class women and white upper-class professional women (Samuels, 1990). Many of the upper-class women are in their 30s and work in traditional female occupations such as teaching, social work and nursing (Simon & Altstein, 1987). There is said to be no difference in the assessment and screening of single parents from that of other adoptive parents, but the lack of adoptable physically healthy infants makes it largely impossible for single parents to obtain such infants. Single parents are still continuing to adopt foreign-born children, even though some foreign countries may be reluctant to allow this (Samuels, 1990). The opinion is from clinical experience and quality of life measures that children adopted by single parents appear in no way adversely affected by their experience (Kadushin, 1970; Shireman & Johnson, 1976), but more effective research is needed.

Homosexual and lesbian parents

Much of the research in child development is carried out on children in traditional heterosexual nuclear families. Views have been expressed that upbringing in alternatives to the traditional family may lead to deviant behaviour and harm development generally (Hetherington & Deur, 1971). Increasingly however, children in western society grow up in single-parent families, in communities, lesbian or gay families or other alternatives to the usual arrangement. There is much debate about the suitability of lesbian and gay women and men to foster or adopt children. There is only anecdotal evidence and virtually no published studies on gay and lesbian foster and adoptive parents. Practice varies in different countries and among different adoption agencies. There is the possibility that more lesbian and gay foster and adoptive parenting exists than is believed because they do not disclose their sexual orientation at interview and are assumed to be heterosexual.

There are very few studies that can help to decide whether childbearing by a lesbian or gay couple is detrimental to the child's development. Golombok *et al.* (1983) compared 27 school-age children reared in 27 lesbian households with 38 school-age children reared in 27 heterosexual single-parent households with respect to their psychosexual development and their emotions, behaviour and relationships using systematic standardized interviews and parent and teacher questionnaires. The two groups did not differ in terms of their gender identity, sex role behaviour or sexual orientation on most measures. Psychiatric problems were more frequent in the single-parent group. The conclusion was that rearing in a lesbian household *per se* did not lead to atypical psychosexual

development or constitute a psychiatric risk factor. Other less adequate and some uncontrolled studies (Green, 1978; Hoeffer, 1981; Kirkpatrick *et al.*, 1981) indicate that such children usually develop an appropriate psychosexual identity and a typical heterosexual orientation. There are no reported studies of the development of sexual identity of children of gay fathers, but it is unlikely that the findings would differ appreciably from those reported for the children of lesbian mothers. Much more research is needed to clarify the issue. Green *et al.* (1986) studied aspects of the psychosexual and psychosocial development of prepubescent children aged 3–11 years living with their mothers. A group of 50 currently homosexual women and their 56 children were compared with a matched group of 40 heterosexual women and their 48 children. A variety of test questionnaires and interviews assessed the effects on children's sexual identity development of living in a father-absent household with either a heterosexual or a homosexual mother. No significant differences were found between the two types of households for boys, and few significant differences for girls. Concerns that being raised by a homosexual mother might produce sexual identity conflict and peer group stigmatization were not supported by the research findings.

However, the data refer almost entirely to children who spent their first few years in a heterosexual household and little is known so far about outcome at or after puberty. Kleber *et al.* (1986) reviewing the literature on the impact of parental homosexuality in child custody cases failed to find evidence on the detrimental effects of parenting by homosexuals on child development. The data available so far are modest in amount and the inferences from it should be made with caution. However, the available evidence has been well-reviewed by Patterson (1992).

Alternatives to adoption

Now that the traditional form of adoption of an infant by an infertile couple is beset by obstacles, many have turned to artificial insemination by donor as a means of beginning a family. It is difficult to determine the number of childless marriages resulting from male infertility. Hull *et al.* (1985) estimated that at least one couple in six living in a defined geographical area would require specialized advice about infertility and concluded that 'sperm defects or dysfunction were the most commonly defined cause of infertility (24%) and led to a poor chance of pregnancy (0–27%) without donor insemination' (p. 1695).

The impact of male infertility can be quite devastating at first, and at present, adoption does not provide an easy solution to the problem (Humphrey & Humphrey, 1988). Donor insemination has become a more realistic solution where male infertility is the reason for childlessness. These authors point out that husbands and wives stress the psychological advantages of going through pregnancy and childbirth and that they can then be sure of a genetic link on at least one side of the family.

There are other newer trends in human reproduction, including *in vitro* fertilization and surrogacy, in which a fertile woman volunteers to conceive and carry a child for the benefit of an infertile couple who intend to bring it up as their own. Both profit and altruism enter into the decision. A new variant is discussed by Humphrey and Humphrey (1988), where a woman and her husband provide the embryo through *in vitro* fertilization; the embryo is then implanted into the uterus of a host mother to carry to term on their behalf. No doubt different techniques and procedures will evolve in the future.

Interracial adoption

Interracial adoption is a recent event. After World War II American soldiers and their families began to adopt large numbers of children from Asia (Silverman & Feigelman, 1990), including Japanese and Chinese children. During the early 1950s the next stage of renewed activity in interracial and intercountry adoption followed the Korean War, and Weil (1984) reported over 38 000 adoptions of Korean children during the period 1953–1984. The Vietnam War and its aftermath led to numbers of Asian interracial adoptions. Hispanic children have been adopted in increasing numbers from South and Central America (Weil, 1984). Native American children were adopted in the late 1950s and close to 700 were placed, most interracially, before these efforts were given up due to Native Indian opposition (Silverman & Feigelman, 1990).

Another form of interracial adoption and fostering is the placement of black children in white homes. In the early 1960s such adoptions began to expand throughout the US and reached a peak in 1971, with over 12 000 such adoptions being recorded (Silverman & Weitzman, 1986). Following opposition to such placements, the numbers dwindled. There are still issues not yet settled about interracial adoption, since in many countries concern has been expressed about the ethics and politics of such action, with charges that nonwhite families and children are being exploited by the white majority with detrimental effects on the development of children.

Gill and Jackson (1983), in the UK, examined the lives and experiences of 36 interracially adopted children who had reached adolescence. Using criteria of family relationships, peer-group relationships, level of self-esteem and behaviour disorder, they concluded that only a small number of adoptions could be regarded as problematic, namely 6 children (17%) of the group, and in only 1 case were there indications of breakdown in the adoption. The remainder would be regarded as definitely successful, in keeping with other findings (Grow & Shapiro, 1974; Simon & Altstein, 1987; Altstein & Simon, 1991).

The reasons for this successful outcome were regarded as arising from the parents' commitment to caring for the child and making him/her part of their family and the early age of placement, so that the child grew up entirely in a white world, with consistent messages and definitions about his or her racial background. An important factor was the social class of families (mainly I and II). This meant that the majority were able to live far removed from the racially mixed areas of large cities, in communities where racial tension was unlikely to be a factor, and where good schools were available.

The authors comment that the large majority of families made little attempt to give their adopted children a sense of racial pride or awareness of their racial origin. The children saw themselves as 'white' in all but skin colour and had little knowledge or experience of their counterparts growing up in a black community. Their coping mechanisms appeared to depend on a denial up till then of their racial background.

Gill and Jackson (1983) believed that it is vitally important for every effort to be made to find black homes for black children, whenever possible, and that more black families should be encouraged to adopt. These authors were also concerned that there will be problems for a black child in developing a sense of racial identity in a white family; tensions will arise between making a child fully part of the family, while highlighting the differences. Also, the social class influences will mean that children will be unlikely to have significant contacts with the black community.

Tizard and Phoenix (1989) in a critical appraisal of these issues review studies on racial identity in children, identity conflict, self-esteem and the concept of a positive black identity. They concluded on the evidence that both interracially adopted and other young black children often have ambivalent attitudes toward their race. Furthermore, mixed-race children living with their own parents, especially those in multiracial areas, may be satisfied with an 'intermediate' identity, rather than a black racial identity. Self-esteem and mental health do not appear to be necessarily tied to attitudes to race, and there is such a variety of modern black British lifestyles that the notion of a black culture is not convincing. Positive black identity is an oversimplification, failing to take into account the way in which black children and parents describe themselves. The equation of positive black identity with positive identity cannot be supported on the basis of existing research, because it neglects other important social identities, such as gender, social class, occupation, peer and neighbourhood groupings. These authors did not consider that the race of the adoptive parents should necessarily override other considerations in determining placement. The Department of Health has issued guidance to directors of Social Services in the UK on this issue (Department of Health, 1990), stating that 'a child's ethnic origin, cultural background and religion are important factors; it may be taken as a guiding principle of good practice that, other things being equal, and in the great majority of cases, placement with a family of similar ethnic origin and religion is most likely to meet a child's needs as fully as possible and to safeguard his or her welfare most effectively' (p. 3). They also add that circumstances might arise where placement with a family of different ethnic origin may offer the best chance for a particular child.

Intercountry adoption

Adopting children from other countries is a relatively new phenomenon (Weil, 1984). As indicated earlier, it began after the end of World War II, involving children from Germany, Greece, and the Baltic states who were placed for adoption in other European countries and the US (Tizard, 1991). Later, orphans from the Korean and Vietnam Wars were adopted, overseas and Korean orphans continued to be the main source until the 1980s (Hoksbergen, 1991). Earlier on, the adoptive families usually had their own children, often taking several overseas children from different countries. Later on, childless couples from the west began seeking children who were now poverty victims rather than war victims (Tizard, 1991). There is no reliable evidence on the scale of intercountry adoption, but the largest number is in the US where the numbers doubled over 6 years from 1981 to 1987 (Tizard, 1991).

The majority of studies looking at the outcome of intercountry adoption in terms of the satisfaction of the adopting couple and the development of children are from Europe and there are not all that many of them. The most recent come from Holland and Norway (Altstein & Simon, 1991).

A large-scale Dutch study by Verhulst *et al.* (1990a,b) assessed 2148 international adoptees aged 10–15 years whose age of placement varied from a few days to 10 years. Using a behaviour checklist, the parents reported more behaviour problems in adopted children compared with nonadopted children, although the difference was not very great, mainly due to a minority of 12–15-year-old boys (23% compared to 10% in the comparison group) who had particularly high problem scores. The major problems were stealing, lying, truanting and hyperactivity. The older the children at placement, the greater the chance that problems would be reported by parents. Children placed after the age of 2 years showed a sharp rise in problems. Adopted children scored less than controls in their social and academic functioning, but were reported to be more active in nonsports activities and to function somewhat better than controls in sports and nonsports activities. Verhulst *et al.* (1990c) also used a clinical interview to assess 132 14-year-old adoptees and their parents, selected on the basis of the checklist scores. A prevalence rate of 28% psychiatric disorder was somewhat higher than in other general population studies. The behaviour of the adopted children diagnosed as having a psychiatric disorder was particularly characterized by antisocial behaviour, poor relationships and problems of affect. The problem scores for the 200 children from European countries were similar to those of Asian and Latin American children. Tizard (1991) drew the conclusion from this that the behaviour problems cannot be attributed to racism.

Verhulst *et al.* (1990a,b) found that the proportions of children in special schools and who had to repeat classes were larger in the adopted group, especially among the later adopted, although the numbers were small. Other studies (Hoksbergen, 1991) have found good to above average school performance in adopted children who were adopted in early life.

Andresen (1991) used the Rutter Scales for teachers and parents (Rutter, 1967, 1970a) to assess behavioural and emotional adjustment in 151 12–13-year-old internationally adopted children, drawn from an adoption register in Norway. The majority of adopted children were found to be well-adjusted, but the adopted children as a group scored higher on the full scale and the hyperactive subscale of the measures than a control group. Boys scored higher than girls on both scales and age at adoption was not related to outcome.

Tizard (1991), on the basis of her review of the literature, concluded that 75% of international adoptions appear, by most criteria, to be successful and the rate of serious breakdown is small. Hoksbergen (1991) estimated in Holland that around 5–6% of intercountry adoptees enter residential care at some time. A quarter return home, but the remainder remain in care. This is in line with earlier figures showing that adopted children are overrepresented in populations referred to child psychiatric services.

ASSESSMENT OF SUITABILITY FOR ADOPTION

The assessment of infants for adoption includes not only the detection of severe subnormality, neurological defects, congenital anomalies and other features that may impede physical and psychological development, but also some attempt at the prediction of whether the infant has a normal potential for later development. Illingworth (1968) claimed that only a very small number (3.4%) out of the 156 infants he had originally assessed at 6–10 months were reclassified on terms of broad groupings on later intellectual assessment at age 6–7 years. Rutter (1970b) argued that, in spite of consistencies and meaning in psychological development, the level of prediction that can be made at 6 months is very poor, and no useful predictions of psychological characteristics within the normal range can be made. Some crude differentiation in terms of level of intelligence (normal, mildly subnormal or severely subnormal) is possible in the first year of life, but an appreciable number will be seriously misclassified. Important aspects of cognitive and emotional growth only develop in the second year of life and are strongly influenced by the sort of environment experienced by the infant and young child. There is little connection between the tangible criteria of age, religion and socioeconomic circumstances, as often used by adoption agencies, and later outcome in terms of the children's emotional stability. There has been little research evaluation of different methods of selection, and so there is no way of telling which is the most effective for the purpose. Although the better agencies used trained caseworkers to carry out a series of careful interviews designed to assess motivation to adopt, marital stability, love of children etc., these qualities are not defined, nor is any special attention given to the assessment of personality disorder or psychiatric illness, although there is now a large body of data on the factors in family life and the qualities in parents that give rise to psychiatric disorder in childhood or later life (Rutter, 1981, 1985, 1989; Quinton *et al.*, 1984).

PLACEMENT OF CHILDREN WITH MENTAL AND PHYSICAL HANDICAP

Until about 40 years ago most adoption agencies considered children with various mental defects as not adoptable; the emphasis was on placing the mentally and physically healthy (usually white) infant. Then, as today, the majority of prospective adopters preferred an infant who had been assessed as healthy and potentially normal in development and with a good hereditary background. There is now change towards a broader definition of an adoptable child, which includes those with medical conditions, provided a family can be found that will accept the 'imperfect' child with his or her mental and physical disabilities. The desirable goal of placement in early infancy is often difficult to achieve with such children as they are held in foster or institutional care until a preplacement medical evaluation can be completed. Illingworth (1968) stated that an experienced paediatrician should be able to diagnose a definitely abnormal infant at the age of 6 months, but in some cases it is fair to the prospective adopters to postpone the decision until 10 months of age if there are still doubts about the infant's health and future development.

Wolkind and Kozurak (1983), in their follow-up of 108 adopted children who had been deemed hard to place for medical reasons, found that in the great majority of cases the adopting parents regarded the adoption as successful. Nevertheless, behavioural problems were relatively common — especially in children with severe physical handicaps, those adopted from institutions rather than foster homes, and those in families experiencing marital difficulties.

Special care is needed to explain to couples who prepare to adopt a handicapped infant or child the size, nature and extent of the medical, social and psychological problems that may confront them. The combined help of a paediatrician and experienced medical social worker may be necessary to explain the range and limits of the child's developmental potential and to allay anxiety. In this way, some misconceptions arising out of ignorance can be avoided and the confidence gained can be reinforced by later paediatric consultation, if necessary. Although the severely handicapped child makes great demands upon the parents' time and the family's stability, it is more often the concomitant emotional disturbance that poses the greater problem of management (Knight, 1970, 1971).

Children with physical disorders face difficulties in terms of limitations of normal activity, lack of important formative experiences and negative self-image, as well as the parental reactions that the handicap induces. The rate of psychiatric disorder in children with physical disorder is somewhat greater than in the general population, and for children with neuro-epileptic conditions, the rate is three or four times that in the general population (Rutter *et al.*, 1970). In discussion with prospective adopters of handicapped children, particular emphasis must be given to the possibility of transient emotional disturbance and frank psychiatric disorder at different stages of development. In this way and by offering help later if needed, there is the possibility of early prevention of problems. Knight (1971) has also written on the difficult problem of placement for adoption in families with an already severely handicapped child. She argued that each application should be treated on its individual merits, but that in almost all instances, the decision will be taken against placement.

The situation where one prospective adopter suffers from a physical disability or has a psychiatric disorder poses equal problems in selection. Numerous studies (Rutter, 1989) have shown that there is a strong association between chronic parental mental illness and psychiatric disorder in children, but not all parental illnesses affect children's development. The seriousness of the parental psychiatric disorder does not seem as important as the presence of family discord and the involvement of the child in the symptoms of parental disorder. Rutter (1971) found that when parents have a long-standing disorder of personality, there is likely to be generalized family disharmony and this is associated with behaviour disorders in the children. Hersov (1973) discussed the implications for adoption practice of knowledge about the self-limiting nature and good response to treatment of some psychiatric disorders in adults. A history of such illness should not necessarily debar a parent or parents from being considered as prospective adopters.

AGE AT ADOPTION

Another issue in adoption theory and practice has been the age of adoption. Late adoption has long been thought of as a second best, or to be avoided for several reasons, but partly because there has been a strongly held belief that early rearing experiences are critically important for later development. It has also been said that adoption placements are best made before the age of 6 months, i.e. before the infant develops focused attachments (Yarrow & Klein, 1980).

However, studies by Tizard (1977), Hodges and Tizard (1989a,b) and others have shown that older children can be successfully adopted. Triseliotis and Russell's (1984) follow-up study of late adopted children, i.e. settled into their adoptive families between the ages of 2 and 8 years, also showed that the majority had a good outcome and that the rate of psychosocial problems, both in child and adult life, was below that of institution-reared children but above that in the general population. These and other data may increase the temptation to use adoption as an outlet for the children of the most disadvantaged. However, this must be thought about most carefully.

It is also true that hard-to-place and handicapped children are being found homes and families in greater numbers than before, but a great deal more preparation for the adoption of older children is needed than is often provided. Some children have strong ties with their families, in spite of the way they have been treated and do not wish to be adopted. Others need unhurried preparation and a graded introduction to their prospective families. These obviously should be chosen with care, as well as being given adequate preparation for dealing with an older child with a past experience of failed fostering. In a situation like this love is not enough, for the children may have many problems with authority, are often grossly insecure, with poor impulse control, as well as sometimes having a diagnosable psychiatric disorder. They are also often attention-seeking with poor peer relationships (Hodges & Tizard, 1989b).

PSYCHOLOGICAL DEVELOPMENT AND PSYCHIATRIC DISORDER

Any service dealing with children and adolescents, whether in hospital or in the community, is bound to have adopted children referred. Questions have arisen about the psychological development of adopted children and whether adopted children are overrepresented in clinical populations; whether there are distinctive biological social and emotional factors which differentiate adopted children and their families from natural families; and whether it is these differences that are responsible for the apparent increase in referral of adopted children for inpatient and outpatient treatment.

Adoption and psychological development

Tizard and her colleagues (Tizard, 1977) assessed 30 adopted children and 23 children restored to their natural parents, all of whom had spent the first 2−7 years of their life in an institution. Most had left between the ages of 2 and 4 years but a smaller group were adopted, fostered or returned to a parent after the age of $4\frac{1}{2}$ years. All were illegitimate and had been admitted before the age of 4 months; boys outnumbered girls by 3 : 1. One-third were of mixed race. The children were first assessed on a variety of measures at $4\frac{1}{2}$ years and again at 8 years, and comparisons were made between those adopted, those fostered, those restored to natural parents and those who remained in institutions. At $4\frac{1}{2}$ years (Tizard & Rees, 1975) the adopted children showed significantly fewer problems and more satisfactory development than institutional children. They formed attachments to their adoptive parents more easily but in one-third the parents were concerned at their overfriendliness to strangers. At 8 years, the adoptive parents did not describe any greater number of problems than did parents of home-reared children, the only problems being overfriendliness and attention-seeking. A small minority described difficult or unusual behaviour but more restored than adopted children were bullies, had a variety of nervous habits, were described as overfriendly to strangers and two-thirds had been referred to a psychiatrist or doctor because of their behaviour as compared with 5% of adopted children. In general, adopted children were in a more stable situation, had fewer emotional problems, and were intellectually and academically superior to the fostered, institutional or natural children, in spite of the fact that one-half were rated by their teachers as causing moderate or severe problems at school. Tizard (1977) discussed the social policy implications of her own and other findings, especially the finding that later adoption can be successful, contrary to conventional beliefs.

The original sample was followed up again at 8 years and 16 years. It was found that by the age of 8 the majority of adopted children and some of the restored children had formed close attachments to their parents despite the lack of early attachments in institutions (Tizard & Hodges, 1978). The children adopted before $4\frac{1}{2}$ years old scored well above the average, and above restored and later-placed children, in IQ and reading attainment (see also Dumaret, 1985). Teachers observed that more ex-institutional children showed problems, notably attention-seeking behaviour, restlessness, disobedience and poor peer relationships.

At 16 years (Hodges & Tizard, 1989a), these particular difficulties had lessened but teachers still reported that they showed more problems at school than either of their comparison groups in that they tended to be restless and distractible, quarrelsome with peers, unstable and resentful if corrected by adults. It appeared that adopted adolescents now showed various sorts of behaviour indicative of anxiety more often than their comparisons. Further study of family relationships at age 16 (Hodges & Tizard, 1989b) showed relationships to be satisfactory for most adopted adolescents and their families, unlike the restored group where attachments between parents and adolescents were fewer, less affection was displayed by both parents and adolescents to each other and the youngsters had particularly great difficulty with their siblings. Although the indiscriminate overfriendliness of their early years (Tizard & Hodges, 1978) no longer seemed a problem at 16 years, the institutional adolescents were still more often oriented towards adult attention and approval than comparison adolescents (Hodges & Tizard, 1989b). They were more likely to have difficulties in peer relationships and less likely to have a special friend at an age when peer relationships are generally considered important. Others have described identity conflicts during adolescence (Sorosky *et al.*, 1975).

The authors concluded that their studies supply evidence that children who are deprived early in life of close and lasting attachments to adults can make these attachments later, provided they are placed in a family which will nurture such attachments. Despite these attachments, certain differences and difficulties in family relationships are still evident in adolescence and appear to have their origins in the early experience of institutional care. They may have implications for future adult relationships.

Psychiatric disorder in adopted children

The earlier clinical studies in the US in the 1950s showed an overrepresentation of adoptees referred to private and hospital services who were likely to show aggressive and antisocial problems and learning difficulties. Conduct disorder was more often found than emotional disorder and boys were more affected than girls. More recent studies have also shown a higher frequency of adoptees in specialist clinics (Deutsch *et al.*, 1982), and a higher rate of adolescent adoptees with eating disorders, behavioural disturbance, and lower academic achievement referred to a psychiatric hospital (Holden, 1991). In both studies referral bias must be taken into account.

Although it seems true that the majority of adoptions turn

out well and that cognitive abilities of adopted and nonadopted children do not differ, studies in the US, France, Sweden and England suggest that a somewhat higher proportion of adoptees have problems. The National Child Development Study (Seglow *et al.*, 1972) found that adopted children differed little from legitimate children at age 7 years, but by 11 years, especially when their more favoured social situation had been taken into account, their adjustment had deteriorated. The Swedish study (Bohman, 1970) showed behavioural problems as rated by teachers to be more common in adopted boys who were more disturbed than controls at age 11 years, but the differences then decreased during adolescence. Maughan and Pickles (1990), following up the population in the National Child Development Study into adolescence and adulthood, found that the apparent deterioration between 7 and 11 years did not continue into adolescence. The adoptees' disturbed adjustment peaked around the time of the 11-year contact and was much less marked in adolescence. This was regarded as a period of increased vulnerability for adoptees because of concerns about identity, but there were still higher rates of emotional problems and anxiety in the adopted group, compared with the legitimate group.

The general conclusion that emerges from these and other studies is that adoptees are at a slightly greater risk of psychiatric disorder in clinical studies. When a longitudinal prospective study (Plomin & De Fries, 1985) was carried out in matched adoptive and control families, there were *few* differences at about 2 years after the beginning of the study. There were some minor differences between adopted and control infants and toddlers in terms of adjustment but the adoptees generally displayed more favourable adjustment. The conclusion was that prediction of individual outcomes of early adoption cannot be made with sufficient certainty to be useful in predicting success or forecasting problems and that there were no important differences between adopted and control infants and their families at this early stage.

There are broader and separate issues about the possible effects on adopted children of the characteristics of their adoptive parents and the circumstances in which they live. There is the general finding that as a group, older adopted children have IQ scores and scholastic attainments as good as those in the general population, and substantially better than might have been expected on the basis of their biological background (Lambert & Streather, 1980; Scarr, 1981). It seems clear that this is due to the fact that, in general, adoptive parents tend to be rather better educated and of higher socioeconomic status than average for the population. It appears that adopted children's cognitive performance is responsive to their rearing environment, which tends to be above average, and adoptees perform well because they have benefited from the environment in which they were reared. This also applies to interracial adoptions. Scarr and Weinberg (1976, 1978, 1983) found that black children adopted by white parents had a mean IQ of 110, some 20 points above comparable children reared in the black community (although some 6 points below the natural children in the white adopting

families). The families were restudied 10 years after the initial research (Weinberg *et al.*, 1992). Despite the tendency for IQ test performance to decline in the sample, there were no differences between the transracial adoptees and the biological offspring of the adoptive parents in changes from time 1 to time 2. The results support the original finding that being reared in the culture of the tests and the culture of the schools benefits children's IQ scores and school achievements.

Lambert and Streather (1980), discussing comparable findings in their own outcome study of illegitimate and adopted children, remark that it may be that it is not necessarily adoption *per se* that is good for the children, but rather the combination of factors associated with: (1) social class and materially comfortable homes; (2) older adopting parents who are more likely to be settled in homes and jobs; and (3) family size, since adopting families tend to be smaller — the majority are two-child families but a large number are one-child families.

The question should be asked whether the same pattern of effects applies to personality differences and the prevalence and outcome of psychiatric disorder. The evidence on this is variable and more limited than with intellectual development. Adoptees have a rate of psychiatric disorder that is above that in the general population (Von Knorring, 1983), although certainly it is not as great as was originally claimed in the 1950s and 1960s. The early studies of selected clinical populations were invalidated by their lack of adequate comparison groups and failure to control for socioeconomic features (Shaw, 1984). Several studies show that in the UK, US and Canada, adopted children are referred to social and psychiatric services with about twice the frequency of the general population, but this difference may reflect patterns of referral as well as increased rates of disturbance (Jerome, 1986; Kotsopoulus *et al.*, 1988).

Studies from hospital populations

A number of studies, mainly in the US, on adopted adolescents undergoing hospital or residential care for psychiatric disorder, have looked at frequency of adoption in hospitalized adolescents (Senior & Himadi, 1985; Fullerton *et al.*, 1986; Piersma, 1987; McRoy *et al.*, 1988; Rogeness *et al.*, 1988; Hajal *et al.*, 1988; Wun Jung Kim *et al.*, 1988).

These studies all show that a higher percentage of adopted adolescents are found in hospital populations than are found in outpatient samples. The frequency of adoptees in these hospitals has ranged from 2.9 to 21.2% of consecutive admissions, as against estimates of 3% of adoptees under 18 years of age in the general population (Zill, 1985). There are many possible reasons for the excess of admissions, including hospital admission policies, socioeconomic status of families, whether a public or private hospital, the rate in the population of adopted adolescents in the catchment area, differences in diagnostic practice and treatment planning. Some of the studies are weak in terms of control groups, data about the age at adoption, reasons for adoption, family size and presence of other adopted or nonadopted children in the family, and whether the adoptions were extrafamilial or intrafamilial, i.e. by a related family member or not.

The studies show that adoptees display a wide range of psychiatric disorders which differ in some aspects from those found in other groups of nonadopted patients. Adoptees show more externalizing disorders (Achenbach & Edelbrock, 1983) with behaviour directed outward to the environment such as adjustment, conduct, oppositional and antisocial disorders. Where the diagnosis of personality disorder was made, there was a higher frequency in adopted adolescents due to an increased frequency of this diagnosis in girls (Rogeness *et al.*, 1986). Some studies reported an excess of runaway behaviour in adopted adolescents, with themes of abandonment and heightened depressive affect emerging during observation and treatment (Fullerton *et al.*, 1986). Sometimes the adoption broke down during hospital admission and the youngsters did not return to their adoptive families at the completion of treatment.

One study in the US predicted that there would be higher rates of extrafamilial adoptions among children and adolescents admitted to psychiatric hospitals, as well as among juvenile offenders attending court (Wun Jung Kim *et al.*, 1988). The prediction was correct for hospital admissions, but a significant underrepresentation of adopted adolescents was found among juvenile offenders. The same socioeconomic factors influencing admission rates to psychiatric hospitals may be operating in that middle and upper middle class families were overrepresented in the samples. Such families may seek psychiatric help earlier so that their children may possibly be protected from contact with the juvenile court system by referral to outpatient and inpatient hospital services first (Wun Jung Kim *et al.*, 1988).

Goldberg and Wolkind (1992) found that over a 15-year period adopted children were overrepresented in a hospital psychiatric clinic population. The excess was seen in all age groups with no rise in referrals at adolescence. Adopted girls were more likely than other girls to have conduct disorders and were more likely than nonadopted girls with the same disorder to be taken into care and to be given inpatient treatment.

Excess of referrals to clinics and hospital

Many reasons have been put forward to explain the excess of disturbance in adopted children referred to clinics and hospitals. These include:

1 Biological and social factors related to the pregnancy and perinatal experience in children born illegitimately to mothers coming from disadvantaged homes, such as inadequate prenatal medical care, poor nutrition, drug and alcohol abuse, mental illness in the mother and father (Crellin *et al.*, 1971; Seglow *et al.*, 1972).

2 Experiences prior to final placement in an adoptive family, including the transition from foster care to adoptive home after attachments have been made (Yarrow & Klein, 1980).

3 Interference with the formation of normal attachments in early life with later effects on personality and relationships. However, a study of attachment in adopted children placed as young infants (Singer *et al.*, 1985) found no differences between adopted and nonadopted children in the frequency of 'strange situation' attachment classifications, and concluded that insecure family attachment was unlikely to explain problems in middle childhood and adolescence.

4 Adoption after an early infancy and childhood spent in an institution with problems in adapting to family life.

5 The social stigma surrounding adoption (Kirk, 1964, 1981).

6 Problems over identity in adolescence arising from confusion and uncertainly over unknown origins (Sants, 1964; Humphrey & Humphrey, 1986).

7 The suggestion that adoptees are at higher risk for genetic factors leading to increased psychopathology. Genetic factors have been implicated in antisocial behaviour, criminality, alcoholism and some psychiatric disorders (Mednick *et al.*, 1983; Bohman & Sigvardsson, 1985). There is a high rate of unmarried mothers among the biological mothers of nonrelated adoptees (Seglow *et al.*, 1972). With pregnancy effects controlled, these mothers score highly on measures of psychopathology and there is possible genetic transmission of psychopathology to the children (Bohman, 1978; Loehlin *et al.*, 1982).

8 Difficulties arising from the 'telling' process affecting family relationships.

'TELLING' IN ADOPTION

One of the issues facing parents who have adopted infants is when, what and how to tell children initially about being adopted, and then how to manage the later, and often persistent, questions that the child asks. It has been suggested that the vulnerability of some adopted children to psychological and academic problems had to do with inappropriate or clumsy telling. Most authorities are quite insistent about the need for early 'telling', i.e. between 2 and 4 years, starting with the simplest facts and providing additional information as the child grows and comes to understand and adjust to its unique family situation (Mech, 1973). However, there are still deep differences of opinion about when and how to 'tell' (Macintyre & Donovan, 1990).

Tizard (1977) observed that young children often show mixed feelings in response to statements that they were specially chosen, or that their biological parents had not brought them up. Holbrook (1984), in her study of 11−13-year-old adopted and fostered children, found there were marked individual differences in the kind of information the children wanted. It was striking that parents wishing to shield their children from potentially hurtful truths sometimes shied away from discussion, when the children would welcome it. Many parents waited for the child to take the initiative, whereas the same children said they would prefer their parents to take the lead. It is clear that false explanations about adoption or the biological parents are resented by adoptees, who find out the truth when they are older, but there is no clear association between parent's willingness to communicate the facts and adoption outcome (Triseliotis, 1973).

Schwartz (1975) provided guidelines to paediatricians involved in potential early intervention in problems arising in adopting families. He found in 44 adoptive families that pre-school children, because of their egocentric thinking and self-centred view of the world, find statements about being 'chosen' very positive and only rarely react with concern, negative responses or questions about this information. During middle childhood, or the stage of concrete operational thinking, the earliest level of information is no longer sufficient for the children who can now think more logically and appraise information more realistically. The child also develops differ-ent perceptions about being adopted and therefore different from other children, within or outside the family. They have many new and unanswered questions in spite of having been told earlier, but parents may not appreciate the need for additional information in keeping with the new develop-mental level. The older child may want to know what its parents look like, but not necessarily their names. When adolescent, they want to know their parents' level of education as well as their work, their abilities and what sort of person they are. In late adolescence and adulthood, they can be interested in the medical history of their natural parents, especially when their own marriage is likely. This may pre-cipitate attempts to search for and find their natural parents (Triseliotis, 1973).

Brodzinsky *et al.* (1984a) studied 200 adopted and non-adopted children ranging in age from 4 to 13 years. They were first interviewed to evaluate their understanding about their adoptive family experiences, and then given a Q-Sort task to assess their perception of the appropriateness of the motives underlying adoption. Six levels of understanding were ident-ified, as well as the children's beliefs about adoption. Clear developmental changes were found in children's knowledge about adoptive family relationships and in the awareness of motives for adoption. Most preschool children are unlikely to understand much about adoption, even when told about it by their parents and referring to themselves as adopted. By 6 years of age, most children do differentiate between birth and adoption as alternative paths to parenthood. They also appreci-ate the *permanence* of adoptive family relationships. Between 8 and 11 years, their conception of adoption broadens in terms of appreciation of the uniqueness of the family and what this entails (Brodzinsky *et al.*, 1986).

For some children between 8 and 11 years, this increase in knowledge gives rise to anxiety about the permanence of place in the family. Data from the above study showed that much of the child's fantasy life is focused on the biological parents' potential for reclaiming the child, and so disrupting adoptive family life. These finds are of particular interest because the period of 8–11 years is the time when disturbance increases in adopted children (Bohman, 1970; Lambert & Streather, 1980; Maughan & Pickles, 1990), and it is also the time when many adopted children are referred for psychiatric

assessment. It may be a vulnerable period in which anxiety, uncertainty and associated problems become manifest. As children grow older, their uncertainty diminishes and they come to recognize the legal process of transfer of parental rights to adoptive parents. However, problems over identity may arise anew during mid-adolescence, another period of vulnerability, and Maughan and Pickles (1990) found higher rates of anxiety and emotional problems among adoptees at age 16 years. Brodzinsky *et al.* (1984a) found that adopted children moved from more positive attribution about adoption in the early school years to more negative positions by late childhood and early adolescence, and this may have something to do with increased disturbance during this age period.

These studies have important implications for adoption practice, particularly the advice given to parents about 'telling'. They question a central assumption, i.e. that 'telling' before 5 years of age gives a child a basic understanding of its unique position in the family, as well as establishing a trusting relationship and sense of self-confidence. We have to ask whether preschool children really understand their adoptive status. Others have found that parents far too often overesti-mate the child's knowledge and unrealistically assume that there is no further need for disclosure and discussion as the child grows older (Raynor, 1980; Holbrook, 1984). The devel-opmental aspect should be stressed in advice to parents, for if this is handled effectively, it may well forestall some of the later problems of behaviour and relationships that arise during late childhood and adolescence (Brodzinsky *et al.*, 1984a).

ADOPTION DISRUPTION

In recent years, more older children and those with special needs are being placed for adoption. Many studies have shown that adoption disruption increases with age at adoption. 'Dis-ruption' is preferred to 'failed adoption' and is defined as all placements that ended with the return of the child to the agency (Barth, 1988). The outcome in adoption results from a complex number of factors and no single characteristic of a child, family or adoption practice is a reliable guide to predicting the outcome at placement. Certain features suggest a risk of disruption. Children with a previous adoptive place-ment, older children, children with problems of behaviour or relationships, children adopted without financial subsidy and adoptive mothers with higher education were found signifi-cantly more often in disrupted placements (Barth, 1988; Barth & Berry, 1988). Sibling adoptive placements in homes with no other children are unlikely to disrupt. Only 10% of placements disrupted after an average time of 18 months, and this compares well with the figure of 9% in British studies (Fitzgerald, 1990).

Both the above studies support the conclusions of earlier studies that the amount and type of information and preplace-ment preparation are crucial to a successful outcome. The views of families and social workers differ widely about the amount and quality of information given to a family. When not informed in advance, families had particular difficulty adjusting to children who had been sexually abused or who had serious behaviour problems.

Families that adopted children who differed considerably from what they had hoped for had more difficult placements, but the difficulties could be ameliorated by providing more and accurate information. Families with the highest-risk placements reported receiving the least accurate information. Families who reported receiving realistic information were overrepresented in the group with placements predicted to disrupt, but which did not (Barth & Berry, 1988). Fewer than half of the families reported getting adequate information about their child's psychological, dental, medical, educational and neurological background, birth history and early childhood development, and few postplacement services were offered and these were generally insufficient to prevent disruption.

CLINICAL ISSUES IN ADOPTION

A child and adolescent psychiatrist may be asked to help with the assessment of deviant emotional and intellectual development in young people who are being placed for adoption; to give a prediction about the likelihood of later mental disorder in a child, where there is a history of functional psychosis or personality disorder in the natural parents (Shields, 1975; Sameroff & Zax, 1979); or to assess the long-term prognosis for emotional development and psychiatric disorder in children who have been in institutions for the early part of their lives and are now being offered for adoption. With the changing pattern of adoption, it is now not uncommon for physically handicapped children, who have a somewhat increased risk of psychiatric disorder, to be considered for adoption. The psychiatrist may also be involved in legal cases in litigation over refusal by a mother to part with her child, or in issues over applications by foster parents to adopt. In addition, the human, personal, social and psychological elements in adoption are encountered in day-to-day work in psychiatric practice with adults and children, and a psychiatrist can be a member of an adoption case committee or consult for an agency placing children for adoption.

Chess (1969), a very experienced child psychiatrist, took the line that the problems that occur between parents and adopted children are identical to those that occur, given the same personalities and circumstances, if the children were not adopted. She attributed many of the problems to the fact that adults tend to assume that what bothers them also bothers their children, so that adopting parents project their own uncertainties on to their children. She did not regard adoption in itself as a potential source of difficulty, but thought it could be of great significance to some parents and children as a secondary and complicating factor, but almost never as the nucleus of the difficulty. It may become a source of stress in adolescence, particularly when doubts about identity and security boil up into intense conflicts with parents and compensatory fantasy about natural parents.

Clinical experience points to the importance of the adoptive situation in children and adolescents referred for psychiatric help, and adoptive families seek treatment from mental health facilities and social agencies with the same range of problems and concerns that worry other families. It is possible that many clinicians are unaware or unresponsive to the fact of adoption, when it emerges among their patients, noting it only as historical data. A clinician may encounter a patient whose mother was adopted, or an adult adoptee, the man or woman who relinquished a child, the adoptive family looking for help for an adopted child, or for some kind of family stress. They may see adults and adolescents and young people who are troubled by issues over searching, or a family who have adopted an older child, or one with special needs. A family may identify adoption as a source of concern or may apparently disregard it. Many therapeutic approaches may be used depending on the nature of the problem or the therapist's orientation.

Treatment approaches are much influenced by psychoanalytical theory, focused on the intrapsychic life of the child or adoptee (Brinich, 1980; Kernberg, 1985–1986; Nickman, 1985). According to Hodges (1984), adopted children face a particular set of difficulties in their development centring around two questions which appeared particularly important in the treatment material: firstly, *Who* were my first parents; what were they like? and secondly, *Why* did they give me up? The child develops theories about adoption in an attempt to answer the first question, blending what he or she has been told with fantasies related to psychosexual development. The second question relates to feelings of self-worth, self-esteem, rejection and loss. How to deal with these issues is the task of therapy.

In adolescence, particular stresses influence the adoption of the adolescent adoptee (Mackie, 1982). There are conflicts over sexuality, control by parents, and sense of loss. The history in such cases is a troublefree childhood with the sudden onset of problem behaviour, such as gross verbal aggression, stealing, running away, deterioration in school performance and failure in one of the tasks of adolescence, namely the establishment of an effective identity and personal sense of security (Sorosky *et al.*, 1975).

Nickman (1985) stressed the finding in therapy that adoptees have a need to mourn several kinds of loss, such as the disruption of existing attachments, particularly in children placed after 6 months; status loss arising from being physically different from adoptive parents, and the sense of loss from being relinquished and its effects on self-esteem, as mentioned earlier (Hodges, 1984).

As adoption has an effect on all members of a family, it is not surprising that themes relating to this emerge to influence a family's intrapersonal and interpersonal adaptation, requiring work with the whole family (Hartman & Laird, 1990). The older adopted children may already have had several years of life experience before placement, some of which may have been painful, if not traumatic, such as neglect or physical or sexual abuse. Families may deny the relevance of adoption to the problems, but these authors feel it should always be evaluated and explained. Particular issues are the myth of the 'bad seed' and hereditary taint leading to the antisocial behaviour displayed; the adoption story of being 'chosen' and the importance of the telling, retelling and reconstruction of the adoption story for the particular family.

CONCLUSIONS

With the change in traditional assumptions and concepts in adoption practice, it is more realistic to think of a spectrum of resources for children in need which include adoption, fostering with a view to adoption, long- and short-term fostering and residential care. The demand for these will continue along with the hope that improvements in forming welfare policy will reduce the need for substitute family care.

Interracial adoption, intercountry adoption and finding families for hard-to-place children have become popular. There has been a fall-off in interracial adoption of black children, in spite of successful outcome using the usual criteria, because of concern that the experience may not necessarily leave black or coloured children with the appropriate sense of identity, but only further studies will clarify this.

There is no single reason why adopted children are over-represented in clinical populations. In view of the data on multifactorial causation of child and adolescent psychiatric disorder, this should come as no surprise. The data from adoption studies show the importance of genetic factors in the major disorders, but the commoner problems result from interactional factors and intervention should take this into account.

As older children and those with special needs are increasingly placed for adoption, they will take a central place in permanency planning. This population is more prone to adoption disruption and psychiatric disorder, given the circumstances mentioned earlier. The severity of some disorders mean that both they and their adoptive parents may require particular clinical intervention. Further study is needed to understand better the factors leading to disruption, as well as the provision of improved adoption programmes and practice, including postplacement support.

The difficulties in obtaining an infant for adoption have meant that many couples have turned to artificial insemination or other methods as a means of beginning a family. This practice will no doubt expand as newer methods become available. It is difficult to predict what effect this will have on future adoption practice, for there will always be a demand for families for older and hard-to-place children.

ACKNOWLEDGEMENTS

Portions of this chapter are adapted from 'Aspects of Adoption' published in the *Journal of Child Psychology and Psychiatry* Vol. 31 No. 4 pp. 493–510 1990, reproduced with permission of the publishers.

REFERENCES

Achenbach T.M. & Edelbrock C. (1983) *Manual for the Child Behavior Checklist and Revised Child Behavior Profile.* Burlington University Associates in Psychiatry, Burlington, VT, USA.

Adcock M. (1980) Dilemmas in planning long-term care. In: Triseliotis J. (ed) *New Developments in Foster Care and Adoption*, pp. 7–21. Routledge & Kegan Paul, London.

Adoption Factbook (1985) *United States Data, Issues, Regulations and Resources.* National Committee for Adoption, Washington, DC.

Adoption Factbook (1989) *United States Data, Issues, Regulations and Resources.* National Committee for Adoption, Washington, DC.

Altstein H. & Simon R.J. (1991) *Intercountry Adoption: A Multinational Perspective.* Praeger, New York.

Andresen I.K. (1991) Behavioral and school adjustment of 12–13 year old internationally adopted children in Norway. Research note. *Journal of Child Psychology and Psychiatry*, **33**, 427–439.

Aumend S.A. & Barrett M.C. (1984) Self-concept and attitudes toward adoption: a comparison of searching and non-searching adult adoptees. *Child Welfare*, **63**, 251–259.

Barth R.P. (1988) Disruption in older child adoptions. *Public Welfare*, **6**, 23–44.

Barth R.P. & Berry M. (1988) *Adoption and Disruption. Rates, Risks, and Responses.* Aldine De Gruyter, New York.

Benet M.K. (1976) *The Politics of Adoption.* Free Press, New York.

Bohman M. (1970) *Adopted Children and their Families.* Proprius, Stockholm, Sweden.

Bohman M. (1978) An eighteen-year prospective longitudinal study of adopted boys. In: Anthony E.J. & Chiland C. (eds) *The Child in his Family: Vulnerable Children*, pp. 473–486. Wiley, New York.

Bohman M. & Sigvardsson S. (1985) A prospective longitudinal study of adoption. In: Nicol A.R. (ed) *Longitudinal Studies in Child Psychology and Psychiatry*, pp. 137–155. Wiley, Chichester.

Borgman R. (1982) The consequences of open and closed adoption for older children. *Child Welfare*, **61**, 217–226.

Brinich P.M. (1980) Some potential effects of adoption on self and object representations. *Psychoanalytical Study of the Child*, **35**, 107–133.

Brodzinsky A.B. (1990) Surrendering an infant for adoption: the birthmother experience. In: Brodzinsky D.M. & Schechter M.D. (eds) *The Psychology of Adoption*, pp. 295–315. Oxford University Press, Oxford.

Brodzinsky D.M. (1987) Adjustment to adoption — a psychosocial perspective. *Clinical Psychology Review*, **7**, 25–47.

Brodzinsky D.M., Singer L.M. & Braff A.M. (1984a) Children's understanding of adoption. *Child Development*, **55**, 869–878.

Brodzinsky D.M., Schechter D.E., Braff A.M. & Singer L.M. (1984b) Psychological and academic adjustment in adopted children. *Journal of Consulting and Clinical Psychology*, **51**, 588–591.

Brodzinsky D.M., Schechter D.E. & Brodzinsky A.B. (1986) Children's knowledge of adoption: developmental changes and implications for adjustment. In: Ashmore R.D. & Brodzinsky D.M. (eds) *Thinking about the Family: Views of Parents and Children*, pp. 205–232. Lawrence Erlbaum, Hillsdale, NJ.

Burnell G. & Norfleet M. (1979) Women who place their children for adoption. *Parent Counselling and Health Education*, **16**, 169–176.

Chess S. (1969) *An Introduction to Child Psychiatry*, 2nd edn. Grune & Stratton, New York.

Chilman C.S. (1983) *Adolescent Sexuality in a Changing American Society: Social and Psychological Perspectives for the Human Resources Profession*, 2nd edn. Wiley, New York.

Crellin E., Kellmer Pringle M.L. & West P. (1971) *Born Illegitimate Social and Educational Implications.* NFER, Windsor.

Day C. & Leeding A. (1980) *Access to Birth Records.* Association of

British Adoption and Fostering Agencies, London.

Department of Health Social Services Inspectorate (1990) *Issues of Race and Culture in the Family Placement of Children.* C1. (90)2. London.

Deutsch C.K., Swanson J.M., Burell J.H., Cantwell D.P., Weinberg F. & Barem M. (1982) Overrepresentation of adoptees in children with attention deficit disorder. *Behavioural Genetics,* **12,** 231–237.

Deykin E.Y., Lee C., Campbell P.H. & Patti P. (1984) The post-adoption experience of surrendering parents. *American Journal of Orthopsychiatry,* **54,** 271–280.

Dumaret A. (1985) I.Q. Scholastic performance and behavior of girls raised in contrasting environments. *Journal of Child Psychology and Psychiatry,* **4,** 553–580.

Estaugh V. & Wheatley J. (1990) *Family Planning and Well-being.* Occasional Papers No. 12. Family Policy Study Centre, London.

Feigelman W. & Silverman A.R. (1983) *Chosen Children: New Patterns of Adoptive Relationships.* Praeger, New York.

Fitzgerald J. (1990) *Understanding Disruption,* 2nd edn. British Agencies for Adoption and Fostering, London.

Fullerton C.S., Goodrich W. & Berman L.B. (1986) Adoption predicts psychiatric treatment resistances in hospitalized adolescents. *Journal of the American Academy of Child and Adolescent Psychiatry,* **25,** 542–551.

Gill O. & Jackson B. (1983) *Adoption and Race.* Batsford, London.

Goldberg D. & Wolkind S. (1992) Patterns of psychiatric disorder in adopted girls. A research note. *Journal of Child Psychology and Psychiatry,* **33,** 945–950.

Golombok S., Spencer A. & Rutter M. (1983) Children in lesbian and single-parent households. Psychosexual and psychiatric appraisal. *Journal of Child Psychology and Psychiatry,* **24,** 551–572.

Green R. (1978) Sexual identity of 37 children raised by homosexual or transsexual parents. *American Journal of Psychiatry,* **135,** 692–697.

Green R., Mandel J.B., Hotvedt M.E., Gray J. & Smith L. (1986) Lesbian mothers and their children: a comparison with solo parent heterosexual mothers and their children. *Archive of Sexual Behaviour,* **15,** 167–184.

Grow L.J. & Shapiro O. (1974) *Black Children, White Parents: A Study of Transracial Adoption.* Child Welfare League of America, New York.

Haimes E.V. & Timms N.W. (1985) *Adoption Identity and Social Policy. The Search for Distant Relatives.* Gower, Aldershot.

Hajal F., Catenaccio R. & Hyler I. (1988) Adopted adolescents in the psychiatric hospital and their families. Paper presented at the Annual Meeting of the American Academy of Child and Adolescent Psychiatry. Seattle, WA, October 1988.

Hartman A. & Laird J. (1990) Family treatment after adoption: common themes. In: Brodzinsky D.M. & Schechter M.D. (eds) *The Psychology of Adoption,* pp. 221–239. Oxford University Press, New York.

Haskey J. (1989) One-parent families and their children in Great Britain: numbers and characteristics. In: *Population Trends,* 55. Her Majesty's Stationery Office, London.

Hayes C.D. (1987) *Risking the Future. Adolescent Sexuality, Pregnancy and Childbearing,* vol. 1. National Academy Press, Washington, DC.

Hersov L.A. (1973) The psychiatrist and modern adoption practice. *Child Adoption,* **71,** 17–31.

Hetherington E.M. & Deur J.L. (1971) The effects of father absence on child development. *Young Children,* **26,** 233–248.

Hodges J. (1984) The crucial questions: adopted children in psycho-analytical treatment. *Child Psychotherapy,* **10,** 47–56.

Hodges J. & Tizard B. (1989a) I.Q. and behavioral adjustment of ex-institutional adolescents. *Journal of Child Psychology and Psychiatry,* **30,** 53–75.

Hodges J. & Tizard B. (1989b) Social and family relationships of ex-institutional adults. *Journal of Child Psychology and Psychiatry,* **30,** 77–97.

Hoeffer B. (1981) Children's acquisition of sex role behavior in lesbian-mother families. *American Journal of Orthopsychiatry,* **5,** 536–544.

Hoksbergen R.A.C. (1991) Intercountry adoption coming of age in the Netherlands: basic issues, trends and developments. In: Altstein H. & Simon R.J. (eds) *Intercountry Adoption: A Multinational Perspective,* pp. 141–158. Praeger, New York.

Holbrook D. (1984) *Knowledge of Origins, Self-esteem and Family Ties of Long-term Fostered and Adopted Children.* Report to the Holden Trust:

Holden N. (1991) Adoption and eating disorders: a high-risk group? *British Journal of Psychiatry,* **15,** 829–833.

Home Office (1972) *Report of the Departmental Committee on the Adoption of Children.* Chairmen: His Honour Judge F.A. Stockdale and Sir William Houghton. Home Office: Scottish Education Department Cmnd 5107. Her Majesty's Stationery Office, London.

Hull M.G.R., Glazener C.M.A., Kelly N.J., Conway D.I., Foster F.A., Hinton R.A., Coulson C., Lambert P.A., Watt E.M. & Desai K.M. (1985) Population study of causes, treatment and outcome of infertility. *British Medical Journal,* **291,** 1693–1697.

Humphrey M. & Humphrey H. (1986) A fresh look at genealogical bewilderment. *British Journal of Medical Psychology,* **59,** 133–140.

Humphrey M. & Humphrey H. (1988) *Families with a Difference: Varieties of Surrogate Parenthood.* Routledge, London.

Illingworth R. (1968) Assessment for adoption. In: *Genetic and Psychological Aspects of Adoption.* The Association of British Adoption Agencies. The University Press: Aberdeen.

Jerome L. (1986) Overrepresentation of adopted children attending a children's mental health center. *Canadian Journal of Psychiatry,* **31,** 526–531.

Jones E.F., Forrest J.D., Goldman N., Henshaw S.K., Lincoln R., Rosoff J.I., Westoff C.F. & Wulf D. (1985) Teenage Pregnancy in developed countries: determinants and policy implications. *Family Planning Perspectives,* **17,** 53–63.

Kadushin A. (1970) Single parent adoptions: an overview and some relevant research. *Social Service Review,* **44,** 263–274.

Kawashima Y. (1981/1982) Adoption in early America. *American Journal of Family Law,* **20,** 677–696.

Kernberg P.F. (1985–1986) Child analysis with a severely disturbed adopted child. *International Journal of Psychoanalytic Psychotherapy,* **II,** 277–299.

Kirk H.D. (1964) *Shared Fate: A Theory of Adoption and Mental Health.* Collier Macmillan, London.

Kirk H.J.D. (1981) *Adoptive Kinship.* Butterworths, Toronto, Canada.

Kirkpatrick M., Smith C. & Roy R. (1981) Lesbian mothers and their children: a comparative survey. *American Journal of Orthopsychiatry,* **51,** 545–551.

Kleber D., Howell R. & Tibbits-Kleber A. (1986) The impact of parental homosexuality in child custody cases: a review of the literature. *Bulletin of the American Academy of Psychiatric Law,* **14,** 81–87.

Knight I. (1970) Placing the handicapped child. *Child Adoption,* **62,** 27–35.

Knight I. (1971) Placement of children into families with a seriously handicapped child. *Child Adoption,* **63,** 56–59.

Kotsopoulos S., Côté A., Joseph L., Pentland N., Stavraki C., Sheahan P. & Oke L. (1988) Psychiatric disorders in adopted children: a controlled study. *American Journal of Orthopsychiatry,* **58,** 608–612.

Lambert L. & Streather J. (1980) *Children in Changing Families: A Study of Adoption.* Macmillan, London.

Loehlin J.C., Willerman L. & Horn J.M. (1982) Personality differences between unwed mothers and their adopted-away offspring. *Journal of Personality and Social Psychology,* **42,** 1080–1099.

Macintyre J.C. & Donovan D.M. (1990) Debate forum. Children should be told of their adoption before they ask. *Journal of the American Academy of Child and Adolescent Psychiatry,* **29,** 828–833.

McRoy R.G., Grotevant H.D. & Zurcher L.A. (1988) *The Development of Emotional Disturbance in Adopted Adolescents.* Praeger, New York.

Mackie A.J. (1982) Families of adopted adolescents. *Journal of Adolescence*, **5**, 167−178.

Maughan B. & Pickles A. (1990) Adopted and illegitimate children growing up. In: Robins L.N. & Rutter M. (eds) *Straight and Devious Pathways from Childhood to Adulthood*, pp. 36−61. Cambridge University Press, Cambridge.

McCluskey K.A. (1983) Adolescent pregnancy and parenthood: Implications for development. In: Callahan E.J. & McCluskey K.A. (eds) *Life-Span Developmental Psychology: nonnormative life events*, pp. 69−113. Academic Press, New York.

Mech E.Y. (1973) Adoption: a policy perspective. In: Caldwell B. & Picciuti H. (eds) *Review of Child Development Research*, vol. 3, pp. 467−508. University of Chicago Press, Chicago, IL.

Mednick S.A., Moffitt T.E., Pollock V., Talovic S., Gabrielli W.F. & Van Dusenk T. (1983) The inheritance of human deviance. In: Magnusson D. & Allen V. (eds) *Human Development: An International Perspective*, pp. 221−242. Academic Press, New York.

Nickman S.L. (1985) Losses in adoption: the need for dialogue. *Psychoanalytic Study of the Child*, **40**, 365−398.

Office of Population Censuses and Surveys (1987) *Adoptions in England and Wales ratified during 1985 and 1986.* Reference FM3.87/1. Her Majesty's Stationery Office, London.

Patterson C.J. (1992) Children of lesbian and gay parents. *Child Development*, **63**, 1025−1042.

Piersma H.L. (1987) Adopted children and inpatient psychiatric treatment: a retrospective study. *Psychiatric Hospital*, **18**, 153−158.

Plomin R. & DeFries J.C. (1985) *Origins of Individual Differences in Infancy. The Colorado Adoption Project.* Academic Press, New York.

Quinton D., Rutter M. & Liddle C. (1984) Institutional rearing, parenting difficulties and marital support. *Psychological Medicine*, **14**, 107−124.

Raynor L. (1980) *The Adopted Child Comes of Age.* George Allen and Unwin, London.

Resnick M.D. (1984) Studying adolescent mothers' decision making about adoption and parenting. *Social Work*, **29**, 5−10.

Rogeness G.A., Hope S.K., Macedo C.A., Fischer, C. & Harms W.A. (1988) Psychopathology in hospitalised adopted children. *Journal of the American Academy of Child and Adolescent Psychiatry*, **27**, 628−631.

Rutter M. (1967) A children's behaviour questionnaire for completion by teachers: preliminary findings. *Journal of Child Psychology and Psychiatry*, **8**, 1−11.

Rutter M. (1970a) Appendix 6. A children's behaviour questionnaire for completion by parents. In: Rutter M., Tizard J. & Whitmore K. (eds) *Education, Health and Behaviour*, pp. 412−418. Longman, London.

Rutter M. (1970b) Psychological development: predictions from infancy. *Journal of Child Psychology and Psychiatry*, **12**, 223−260.

Rutter M. (1971) Parent−child separation: psychological effects on the children. *Journal of Child Psychology and Psychiatry*, **11**, 49−62.

Rutter M. (1981) *Maternal Deprivation Reassessed*, 2nd edn. Penguin, Harmondsworth.

Rutter M. (1985) Family and school influences on behavioral development. *Journal of Child Psychology and Psychiatry*, **26**, 683−704.

Rutter M. (1989) Psychiatric disorder in parents as a risk factor for children. In: Shaffer D., Phillips I. & Enzer N.B. (eds) *Prevention of Mental Disorders, Alcohol and Other Drug Use in Children and Adolescents*, pp. 157−189. OSAP Prevention Monograph-2. DHHS, Rockville MA.

Rutter M., Tizard J. & Whitmore K. (eds) (1970) *Education, Health and Behaviour.* Longman, London. (Reprinted 1981 Krieger Melbourne, FL.)

Rynearson E.K. (1982) Relinquishment and its maternal complications. *American Journal of Psychiatry*, **139**, 338−340.

Sameroff A. & Zax M. (1979) The child of psychotic parents. In: Wolkind S. (ed) *Medical Aspects of Adoption and Foster Care.* Clinics in Developmental Medicine, no 74, pp. 42−48. Heinemann Medical, London.

Samuels S.C. (1990) *Ideal Adoption: A Comprehensive Guide to Forming an Adoptive Family.* Insight Books, New York.

Sants H.J. (1964) Genealogical bewilderment in children with substitute parents. *British Journal of Medical Psychology*, **37**, 133−141.

Scarr S. (1981) *Race, Social Class and Individual Differences: New Studies of Old Problems.* Lawrence Erlbaum, Hillsdale, NJ.

Scarr S. & Weinberg R.A. (1976) I.Q. test performance of black children adopted by white families. *American Psychologist*, **31**, 726−739.

Scarr S. & Weinberg R.A. (1978) The influence of 'family background' on intellectual attainment. *American Sociological Review*, **43**, 674−692.

Scarr S. & Weinberg R. (1983) The Minnesota Adoption Studies. Genetic differences and malleability. *Child Development*, **54**, 260−267.

Schwartz E.M. (1975) Problems after adoption: some guidelines for paediatrician involvement. *Journal of Paediatrics*, **87**, 991−994.

Seglow J., Pringle M.K. & Wedge P. (1972) *Growing up Adopted.* NFER, Windsor.

Senior M. & Himadi E. (1985) Emotionally disturbed and adopted inpatient adolescents. *Child Psychiatry and Human Development*, **15**, 189−197.

Shaw M. (1984) Growing up adopted. In: Bean P. (ed) *Adoption: Essays in Social Policy, Law and Sociology.* Tavistock, London.

Shields J. (1975) Schizophrenia, genetics and adoption. *Child Adoption*, **2**, 19−24.

Shireman J. & Johnson P. (1976) Single persons as adoptive parents. *Social Service Review*, **50**, 103−116.

Silverman A.R. & Feigelman W. (1990) Adjustment in interracial adoptees: an overview. In: Brodzinsky D.M. & Schechter M.D. (eds) *The Psychology of Adoption*, pp. 187−200. Oxford University Press, Oxford.

Silverman A. & Weitzman R. (1986) Non-relative adoption in the United States. In: Hoksbergen R.A.C. (ed) *Adoption in Worldwide Perspective: A Review of Programs, Politics and Legislation in 14 Countries.* Swets and Zeitlinger, Lisse, Netherlands.

Simon R.J. & Altstein H. (1987) *Transracial Adoptees and their Families.* Praeger, New York.

Singer L.M., Brodzinsky D.M., Ramsay D., Steir M. & Waters E. (1985) Mother−infant attachment in adoptive families. *Child Development*, **56**, 1543−1551.

Sorosky A.D., Baran A. & Pannor R. (1975) Identity conflicts in adoptees. *American Journal of Orthopsychiatry*, **45**, 18−27.

Sorosky A.D., Baran A. & Pannor R. (1984) *The Adoption Triangle.* AnchorBook, New York.

Tizard B. (1977) *Adoption: A Second Chance.* Open Books, London.

Tizard B. (1991) Intercountry adoption: a review of the evidence. *Journal of Child Psychology and Psychiatry*, **32**, 743−756.

Tizard B. & Hodges J. (1978) The effect of early institutional rearing on the development of eight-year-old children. *Journal of Child Psychology and Psychiatry*, **19**, 99−188.

Tizard B. & Phoenix A. (1989) Black identity and transracial adoption. *New Community*, **15**, 427−437.

Tizard B. & Rees J. (1975) The effect of early institutional rearing on the behaviour problems and affectional relationships of four-year-old children. *Journal of Child Psychology and Psychiatry*, **16**, 61−73.

Triseliotis J. (1970) *Evaluation of Adoption Policy and Practice.* University of Edinburgh, Edinburgh.

Triseliotis J. (1973) *In Search of Origins: The Experiences of Adopted People.* Routledge & Kegan Paul, London.

Triseliotis J. & Hill M. (1990) Contrasting adoption, foster care and residential rearing. In: Brodzinsky D.M. & Schechter M.D. (eds) *The Psychology of Adoption*, pp. 107–120. Oxford University Press, New York.

Triseliotis J. & Russell J. (1984) *Hard to Place: The Outcome of Late Adoptions and Residential Care*. Heinemann, London.

Verhulst F.C., Althaus M. & Versluis-Den Bieman H. (1990a) Problem behavior in international adoptees. I, An epidemiological study. *Journal of the American Academy of Child and Adolescent Psychiatry*, **29**, 94–103.

Verhulst F.C., Althaus M. & Versluis-Den Bieman H. (1990b) Problem behavior in international adoptees. II, Age at placement. *Journal of the American Academy of Child and Adolescent Psychiatry*, **29**, 104–111.

Verhulst F.C., Versluis-Den Bieman H., Van Der Emde J., Berden G.F.M.G. & Sanders-Woudstra J.A.R. (1990c) Problem behavior in international adoptees. III, Diagnosis of child psychiatric disorders. *Journal of the American Academy of Child and Adolescent Psychiatry*, **29**, 420–428.

Von Knorring A.L. (1983) *Adoption Studies on Psychiatric Illness. Epidemiological, Environmental and Genetic Aspects*. Ume University Medical Dissertations (New Series) no 101. Sweden.

Weil R.H. (1984) International adoption: the quiet migration. *International Migration Review*, **18**, 280–281.

Weinberg R., Scarr S. & Waldman E.D. (1993) The Minnesota trans-racial adoption study. A follow-up of I.Q. test performance of adolescence. *Intelligence*, (in press).

Westoff C.F., Calot G. & Foster A.D. (1983) Teenage fertility in developed nations (1971–1980). *Family Planning Perspective*, **15**, 105.

Winkler R. & van Keppel M. (1984) *Relinquishing Mothers in Adoption: Their Long-term Adjustment*. Monograph no 13. Institute of Family Studies, Melbourne.

Wolkind S. & Kozurak A. (1983) Children with special needs: a review of children with medical problems placed by the Adoption Resource Exchange from 1974–77. Report to the (UK) Department of Health and Social Security, London.

Wun Jung Kim, Davenport C., Joseph J.M., Zrull J. & Woolford E. (1988) Psychiatric disorder and juvenile delinquency in adopted children and adolescents. *Journal of the American Academy of Child and Adolescent Psychiatry*, **27**, 111–115.

Yarrow L.J. & Klein R.P. (1980) Environmental discontinuity associated with transition from foster to adoptive homes. *International Journal of Behaviour and Development*, **3**, 311–322.

Zill N. (1985) Behaviour and learning problems among adopted children. Findings from a U.S. National Survey of Child Health. Paper presented at the bi-annual meeting of The Society for Research in Child Development. Toronto, Canada.

PART 3
CLINICAL SYNDROMES

Chapter 17
Syndromes of Attention Deficit and Overactivity

Eric Taylor

Severe degrees of inattentive and restless behaviour put children's psychological development at risk. Accordingly, all the major schemes of classification include a disorder that is characterized by distractibility and overactivity. These traits are very common reasons for referral to child psychiatric services in all developed countries, yet they elicit great differences in how they are conceptualized and treated. Clinicians must therefore synthesize a confusingly varied literature.

HISTORY

Nineteenth century psychiatry in both England and France recognized severe overactivity as a symptom of disorder in handicapped children (Ireland, 1877; Bourneville, 1897). Frederic Still, who pioneered paediatrics in the UK, elaborated the description of 'abnormal psychical conditions' in children and the concept of deficit in moral control (Still, 1902). A deficit in sustained attention, neurological abnormalities including choreiform movements, minor congenital anomalies, restlessness, fidgetiness, aggression, rule-breaking and destructiveness: all were adumbrated in this account and attributed to an organic and constitutional aetiology.

Ideologies such as Social Darwinism seized upon minimal brain dysfunction as the cause of a wide range of childhood symptoms, often without rigorous consideration of alternative explanations (Schachar, 1986). The pandemics of encephalitis that followed the Great War caused both a wave of children with psychiatric disabilities attributable to brain disease (Kahn & Cohen, 1934) and a habit of diagnostic thinking that was ready to attribute disability to brain disease even when the clinical evidence was very scanty. The pitfalls in this were known at the time: for instance, Levin (1938) made a careful clinical study of more than 200 restless children and a comparison with normally active controls and found that only very severe restlessness was linked with lesions of the brain. Milder degrees of restlessness were associated rather with parenting problems. Nevertheless, neurological theories of aetiology won increasing support.

Bradley's (1937) observation of the unexpected effect of amphetamine on hyperactivity and other behavioural problems provided an important practical reason for making a physically based diagnosis. Strauss's writings in the 1940s broadened the idea still further, to the point where hyper-activity, in the absence of a family history of subnormality, came to be considered as sufficient evidence for a diagnosis of brain damage (Strauss & Lehtinen, 1947). The influential writings of Laufer *et al.* (1957) ensured a frequent and increasing diagnostic practice among paediatricians in the US. Both the diagnosis of attention deficit disorders and the prescription of sympathomimetic central nervous stimulants became very common indeed during the 1960s and 1970s.

In the UK and France, by contrast, the diagnosis and the treatment both remained rather rare events. Both stayed much more closely tied to overt neurological conditions such as epilepsy (Ounsted, 1955) and cerebral palsy (Ingram, 1956). In both countries the dominant theories of children's disorders stressed psychological aetiologies, and this may have restricted the use of a diagnostic concept of hyperactivity, for which the implications were of physical cause and treatment.

In other European countries there was a diversity of practice (Sergeant & Steinhausen, 1992), ranging from public concern about high rates in parts of Germany to a virtual absence of hyperactivity in the Netherlands — but a corresponding readiness to diagnose 'minimal brain dysfunction' (MBD) (Verberg, 1986).

The 1970s and 1980s saw the arrival of explicit diagnostic criteria and a rapid growth of research. Intensive biological, experimental, psychological and psychopharmacological investigations made attention deficit the childhood condition most written about and most cited in *Index Medicus*. Epidemiological research has tested ideas about aetiology and course. An increasing appreciation of the heterogeneity of the problems subsumed within the diagnosis has led to reappraisal of the components of the disorder. Even so, cultural differences remain and the history of thinking about these behaviours in the past still shackles the range of therapeutic efforts in the present.

RECOGNITION OF HYPERACTIVITY

Behavioural components

In this chapter hyperactivity will be used as a term for an enduring disposition to behave in a restless, inattentive, distractible and disorganized fashion. It therefore refers to qualitative changes, not simply moving about more than most children. Several overlapping concepts are applied to describe the different aspects of this sort of behaviour: attention deficit, overactivity and impulsiveness. They need to be defined for clarity, but the distinctions do not imply that they are known to be separate or that they are deep pathological processes, of which a 'true' definition could be obtained.

Attention deficit can refer to a behavioural trait, a pattern of test performance, or a hypothesized deficit in a psychological process. These different meanings need to be kept clear — indeed, it is unfortunate that the same word is used for all of them because it can blur the imporant distinctions.

The behavioural sense is the one on which psychiatric diagnosis is based. The behaviours involved are those of orienting only briefly to tasks imposed by adults, changing activities rapidly when spontaneous choice is allowed, orienting towards irrelevant aspects of the environment, and playing for brief periods only. Direct observations, as well as the reports of parents and teachers, confirm that these behaviours are much more common in children who have received a diagnosis of hyperactivity than in normal controls or children with other disorders of behaviour (Milich *et al.*, 1982; Taylor, 1986a).

Overactivity means an excess of movements. While the idea is simple, there is a wide range of activity in the normal population and no very clear point at which activity level becomes excessive. Overactivity can refer to an increased tempo of normal activities, an increase in purposeless, minor movements that are irrelevant to the task in hand (fidgeting), or an amount of movement of the whole body that is excessive for the situation (restlessness). Direct observations and mechanical recordings of leg and trunk movements have indeed shown an excess in children with diagnosed hyperactivity, so there is some validity in the use of the idea (Milich *et al.*, 1982; Porrino *et al.*, 1983; Taylor *et al.*, 1991). The excess of movements is there even when hyperactive children are in bed and asleep (Porrino *et al.*, 1983), so it is unlikely to be secondary to attention deficit.

Impulsiveness means acting without reflecting. In different contexts this may imply getting into dangerous situations because of recklessness, thoughtless rule-breaking or impetuously acting out of turn when with other children (Stewart *et al.*, 1966). These behaviours are seen in children with hyperactivity; but they are also found in excess in nonhyperactive children who are oppositional or aggressive (Taylor *et al.*, 1991). In principle, children can break rules, and get into danger, and act out of turn for other reasons than thoughtlessness. They may act from bravado or anger or nihilism. It is therefore not clear yet how to define behavioural impulsiveness in an unambiguous way. Accordingly, opinions differ about which behaviours should be part of the definition of hyperactivity.

All these styles of behaviour are present to some degree in many normal children. Scores based on rating scales are continuously distributed in the population (Taylor *et al.*, 1991). Clinical recognition of an affected individual therefore needs to be based upon a firm idea of what is expected of children at that age and of that developmental level. Research definitions need either to be based upon explicit criteria of what is normative for different ages and developmental levels, or else to use a standard set of measures that are then corrected statistically for age and IQ.

Situational factors

The recognition and measurement of the components of hyperactivity are complicated by the frequent finding that a child who is hyperactive at home may show no trace of the behaviour at school or when observed at a clinic; and that children whose behaviour at school is inattentive, impulsive and overactive are sometimes described by their parents as perfectly normal. The correlation between teacher and parent ratings in epidemiological studies is usually significant but always small (Sandberg 1986). This can be seen as a *source* effect reflecting the imperfect reporting of parents and teachers: the child is the same, but raters vary. The low agreement between raters can also be seen as a *situation* effect: the child behaves differently in different settings. Situation specificity is not complete, for parent and teacher ratings both predict objective activity measures (Taylor *et al.*, 1991). Nevertheless, some situation effect is probable. The correlation between two teachers' ratings (0.6) or two parents' ratings (0.6) is higher than that between teacher and parent (0.3; Achenbach *et al.*, 1987). It is even possible that home hyperactivity and school hyperactivity are quite different functional patterns, representing two traits, not one — though this is improbable in that they both predict the same kinds of cognitive and neurodevelopmental impairment (Taylor *et al.*, 1986).

This situation specificity needs to be dealt with explicitly in assessing the presence of hyperactivity. One solution is simply to add the teacher and parent ratings together — but this oversimplifies the concept. It is not necessarily correct that there is a single dimension. Rather, any single measure can be composed of an underlying dimension of hyperactivity, source error, bias and situational effects. Investigators have therefore begun to use structural equation modelling to estimate the latent dimension of hyperactivity (Fergusson *et al.*, 1991). There are many technical difficulties, but the approach has the great merit of making explicit the assumptions behind the method. Another approach is to give one source priority: the DSM-III definition was based primarily upon teacher's accounts. This has the merit of clarity, but the disadvantage of being arbitrary and possibly invalid. A third approach, adopted in the ICD-10 scheme, is to require that hyperactivity is pervasive (i.e. present in more than one situation) before it is recognized as a diagnosis. This has the merit of yielding a valid definition (Schachar *et al.*, 1981, Taylor *et al.*, 1991). However, it may lead to underrecognition of the problem and the Ontario Survey has suggested that pervasiveness is not a necessary condition of a valid definition (Szatmari *et al.*, 1989). A clear solution waits upon a deeper understanding of the nature of situational specificity.

Measures and instruments

Rating scales by parents and teachers have been widely used as standardized measures (Barkley, 1988). Conners, Classroom Rating Scale was originally developed for measuring outcome in drug trials (Conners, 1969), but has since been used in epidemiological surveys and cross-cultural studies. Goyette *et al.* (1978) provided some psychometric data and reliability information came from Taylor and Sandberg (1984). A parent scale is also available. There have been several editions and revisions of the scales, which can be confusing. In particular, investigators often use the abbreviated version of the scale (Conners, 1973) as though it were a measure of hyperactivity: in fact it contains items from other factors as well, especially that of defiance. The Child Behavior Checklist (Achenbach & Edelbrock, 1983) has also been used extensively, translated into several languages, and used as the basis for a programme of research about classification. It contains a broad-band factor of externalizing disruptive behaviour and, within that, a rather less stable narrow-band factor of hyperactive behaviour. Validation of this instrument has been by association with referral for clinical assessment, which is neither an independent nor an unambiguous criterion. Rutter's A2 and B2 scales for parents and teachers both contain a factor of hyperactivity, but it consists only of three items. In spite of this, they have proved competent to predict later developmental course (Schachar *et al.*, 1981) and independent clinical assessment (Taylor *et al.*, 1991) — partly because the cut-off is based on high scores from both sources. The internal reliability of the teacher's hyperactivity factor was satisfactory, and increased only slightly by adding further items.

Questionnaires have only a modest agreement with one another: different scales identify different groups as hyperactive (Holborow *et al.*, 1984). Each scale must be considered as subject to a large amount of error variance, as well as the 'true' variance that is accounted for by the trait in the child. Accordingly, the scales are reasonable as group measures when fairly large numbers of subjects are available, but they are not very satisfactory ways of identifying individuals as hyperactive.

Interviews with parents and teachers can improve the precision of recognizing hyperactivity by ensuring that the respondent is describing what the investigator intends and by making explicit what severity of problem must be present for the problem to be identified. These techniques are the foundation of clinical diagnosis and can also reach the reliability needed for research purposes (Taylor *et al.*, 1986). Interviews with children should not only elicit children's self-ratings but also take the opportunity to assess how children behave in a standardized interview situation. Ethological observations of children in diagnostic interviews have supported the validity of a trained interviewer's judgements of overactivity, restlessness and social disinhibition (Dienske *et al.*, 1985; Luk *et al.*, 1987).

Direct observations of children in their natural settings — including classrooms — allow for great clarity about the presence of the behavioural changes of hyperactivity. Schachar *et al.* (1986) have described a detailed classroom observation scheme that validated teacher ratings of deviance and also showed the limitations of teacher's ratings in making distinctions between different types of deviance. Methods such as this are expensive to apply, and carry a risk of recording unrepresentative samples of behaviour unless they are repeated. Their main place in clinical practice comes when there is a clash of information from two sources about a child and a diagnostic doubt can only be resolved by going to see.

Diagnostic definitions

Research has not yet established whether hyperactivity should be considered as a disorder or a risk. The risk idea implies that there is a continuum; that it affects psychological development adversely at all levels of severity including those that fall short of abnormality. The disorder concept implies a more qualitative change in some children, so that only those above a threshold are vulnerable to later problems in social adjustment. It is clear (see above) that rated hyperactivity is on a continuum of severity. It is much less clear whether there is a continuum of risk, for longitudinal studies have not spoken definitely about the prediction of later disorder. Schachar *et al.* (1981) used an epidemiological sample of children followed up from age 10 to 14, and concluded that pervasive hyperactivity was a strong predictor that conduct disorder would persist, whereas situation-specific hyperactivity was not a significant risk. This could favour a disorder, but a much larger study would be needed to establish whether those with milder degrees of hyperactivity were free of risk. Mannuzza *et al.* (1988) found little adversity in the outcome of those who had been hyperactive but fell short of a full diagnosis. The disorder was predictive, not the dimension. Taylor *et al.* (1991) charted different levels of hyperactivity against the criterion of developmental impairment: only at the highest level of severity was there an increase in clumsiness, language delay and perinatal adversity.

The idea of a disorder also implies that it compromises later development even without the additional presence of other problems, while a risk factor might affect later development only if it is combined with other problems. Magnusson and Bergman (1990) found, in a follow-up of aggressive and disruptive boys, that a poor prognosis was found only in those with an early onset, the presence of hyperactivity, and poor peer relationships. This called into question whether aggression without these extra problems should be seen as a disorder of development; by the same token it raised the issue of whether hyperactivity is a significant hazard for development if it occurs without aggression or problems with peers (see the section on comorbidity, below).

In the absence of conclusive developmental evidence, both dimensional and categorical approaches to classifying hyperactivity are in use. In practice, categorical approaches are much more common, for even advocates of a dimensional ordering of problems tend to apply an arbitrary cut-off on that dimension to identify a hyperactive group.

Diagnostic criteria in the major schemes have varied. In DSM-III there was a category of attention deficit disorder (ADD), defined by the presence of inattentive and impulsive behaviour, especially as seen at school. It was further divided into those with the symptoms of motor overactivity as well (ADDH) and those without (American Psychiatric Association, 1980). In DSM-III-R the category of attention deficit without hyperactivity was dropped, and the resulting group renamed attention deficit—hyperactivity disorder (ADHD) (American Psychiatric Association, 1987). DSM-IV has reintroduced the distinction and now has subtypes of ADHD according to whether the predominant symptoms are inattentiveness, overactivity/impulsiveness, or mixed. Symptoms must be pervasive over situations.

The World Health Organization scheme has also evolved over time. ICD-9 included a condition of hyperkinetic syndrome, defined by 'extreme' overactivity and inability to attend; and, unlike DSM required all other disorders to be absent if the diagnosis was to be made (World Health Organization, 1978). ICD-10 proposed a category of hyperkinetic disorder, whose characteristics were severe, and pervasive inattentiveness together with less extreme exclusionary criteria: the absence of pervasive developmental and affective disorders (World Health Organization, 1988).

ICD-10 has more explicit criteria than ICD-9, and will probably identify rather more children (Steinhausen & Erdin, 1991). The DSM and ICD schemes appear to be moving towards greater harmony.

ICD-10 and DSM-IV are very similar in the behaviours that are considered to be the basis for the diagnosis. They vary, however, in the rules for weighting them. Impulsiveness and hyperactivity are pooled in DSM-IV. In ICD-10, impulsiveness and hyperactivity are considered separately, so that impulsive behaviours cannot by themselves amount to grounds for the diagnosis and inattentive restlessness must also be present. Hyperkinetic disorder should resemble the mixed subtype of ADHD. The DSM-IV definition therefore picks up a more common, and perhaps less distinctive, pattern.

The differences between schemes do not arise from deep disagreements about the fundamental constructs. It is common ground, for instance, that impulsiveness and hyperactivity are often associated. It may well turn out that impulsiveness constitutes a key aspect of the basic concept; ICD-10 is neutral on this point. The reluctance to make impulsive behaviours a sufficient ground for the diagnosis stems from the likelihood that behavioural ratings of impulsiveness tap a much wider range of behaviours than those likely to contribute to the definition of the core disorder. The requirement for pervasiveness of hyperactivity to be present as well comes about because this has worked reasonably well in generating a discriminatively valid diagnosis. The nature of the fundamental construct still has to be established by research.

RELATED CONDITIONS

Several other conditions can present with hyperactivity and need to be considered in differential diagnosis. Autism can be associated with hyperactive behaviour, as can depression, mania and schizophrenia; but in all these the features of the primary condition will make the true diagnosis plain (see the section on comorbidity, below).

Hyperkinesis with stereotypies

Severe hyperactivity may be encountered in some intellectually retarded children who do not have an autistic pattern of social or communication impairment. In some of them, the symptom pattern is similar to that outlined above and the diagnosis of hyperkinetic disorder need not be withheld. In others, the presentation is dominated by repetitive and stereotyped behaviours rather than by flitting from one activity to another. Clinical experience suggests that amphetamine-type drugs are unlikely to be helpful in such children, and, in some trials of stimulants in populations of intellectually retarded children with hyperactivity, the response has been poor (Aman & Singh, 1982). Not very much is known about this group of children. On the face of it, their stereotyped overactivity is more reminiscent of some animal models, such as those produced by an excess of amphetamine or a deficiency of serotonin, than it is of hyperkinetic disorder. ICD-10 provides a tentative category of hyperkinesis with stereotypies to allow them to be considered separately. It is classified with the pervasive developmental disorders.

Attention deficit without overactivity

Some children show the behaviours of attention deficit without being overactive or impulsive. They may even be rather passive and inert in their manner, but do not sustain their attention on play or schoolwork. In the DSM-III scheme they were a separate group. Rather little research was forthcoming about them, and such as there was did not encourage the idea, probably because most of them only just failed to meet hyperactivity criteria and should have been seen as mildly hyperactive. Lahey *et al.* (1987) found that a clinically referred group who were inattentive but not overactive tended to be rather anxious and introverted. The category was dropped from DSM-III-R, does not figure in ICD-10, and accounts for few referrals to psychiatric services. However, paediatricians working in developmental assessment centres have continued to recognize such problems. Epidemiological studies, too, have consistently found such a group with a prevalence of about 1% in primary school populations (Anderson *et al.*, 1987; Szatmari *et al.*, 1989; Taylor *et al.*, 1991). Taylor *et al.* (1991) examined the group with detailed interview methods and psychometric testing. It was characterized by low IQ and low socioeconomic status. While the children scored poorly on tests of attention, this was only to the degree expected from their lowered IQ. Short-term follow-up suggested that they were not at risk for behaviour disorders. They seemed to represent a cognitively impaired group that had escaped major behaviour complications. On the evidence so far, they are not a part of the hyperkinetic disorders.

Attachment disorders

Some children from disrupted family backgrounds show a rather characteristic type of social interaction (see Chapter 28). Their first contacts with a new person are overaffectionate and unreserved, but they do not develop relationships with any depth or trust. They are often rather changeable in their interests and brief in their activities, so hyperactivity is a part of their symptomatology, though it is seldom severe. When this full picture is present then the implication is strong that the behaviour results from the privation. Accordingly, it is classed in ICD-10 as a form of attachment disorder.

COMORBIDITY

Conduct disorder

Most children referred for help because of disruptive behaviour show both hyperactivity and antisocial conduct. Even in epidemiological studies the overlap is great. Hinshaw's (1987) review of rating scale studies found a considerable consensus that hyperactivity and conduct disorder are separate factors, but also that there is a high correlation between them (the median correlation in all reported studies is 0.6). Fergusson *et al.* (1991), using an approach to modelling latent dimensions, agreed on separate factors, but estimated an even higher correlation of 0.9. These very high figures could in part be due to the weaknesses of questionnaire scales. Halo effects are likely to be at their greatest when the rater has a long-standing relationship with the child; and the emphasis on teacher rating scales in the studies may exaggerate the association since the classroom's demands for order and quiet are likely to ensure that hyperactive behaviour is also seen as antisocial and rule-breaking. Lower, though still significant, correlations were found for factors extracted from chart ratings (0.3; Loney *et al.*, 1978) or from standardized interviews (0.4; Taylor *et al.*, 1986).

The association is so great that some reviewers consider that hyperactivity and conduct disorder are in truth the same problem under different names (Shaffer & Greenhill, 1979; Prior & Sanson, 1986; Quay, 1986). Indeed, studies based on the DSM-III diagnoses have failed to find discriminative validity; the two conditions generally have the same correlates (Koriath *et al.*, 1985; Reeves *et al.*, 1987). This is a serious weakness of the DSM-III definitions, and may also be a problem in DSM-IV. More satisfactory measures do suggest that there are differential associations: interview measures and rating scales in epidemiological samples find that hyperactivity is associated with developmental delays in motor, language and cognitive skills, whereas conduct disorder is not (McGee *et al.*, 1984a,b; Szatmari *et al.*, 1990; Taylor *et al.*,

1992). Clinically based studies have argued not only for this pattern but also for an association between conduct disorder and family adversity that does not apply to hyperactivity (Taylor *et al.*, 1986; Biederman *et al.*, 1987; Schachar & Wachsmuth, 1990).

If the two problems are distinct, why should there be so much comorbidity between them? The comorbid group, displaying both problems, is similar to the hyperactive group in its neurodevelopmental associations (McGee *et al.*, 1984a; Taylor *et al.*, 1991). It is just as likely to respond to stimulant medication (Taylor *et al.*, 1987). It also has a poor outcome by comparison with either the conduct disorder group (Schachar *et al.*, 1981; Magnusson, 1988; Farrington *et al.*, 1990) or hyperactivity alone (August *et al.*, 1983; Barkley *et al.*, 1990). This does not mean that it is a separate entity in its own right. The comorbid group is also more seriously affected — more conduct-disordered than those with conduct disorder, more hyperactive than the hyperactive (Taylor *et al.*, 1991).

The reason for comorbidity is clearer when considered developmentally. Children with both problems usually began with hyperactivity (Barkley *et al.*, 1990). Hyperactive children, without conduct disorder, were identified from a community sample of 7- and 8-year-olds by Taylor *et al.* (1991) and studied again at a mean of 9 months later. They were at increased risk for conduct disorder as well as for hyperactivity when compared with normal controls; indeed, some were classified as nonhyperactive conduct disorder at follow-up. By contrast, those with conduct disorder at the age of 7 were not at risk for hyperactivity, but only for conduct disorder. In short, hyperactivity is one of the routes into conduct disorder. Family adversity may help to determine whether the route is followed.

Emotional disorder

The comorbidity between hyperactivity and emotional symptoms is not strong, and has been little studied; but it exists. In a questionnaire survey of the whole population of 7- and 8-year-old boys in a school system, hyperactivity carried a relative risk of 1.3 for a high score on a scale of emotional symptoms (Taylor *et al.*, 1991). Clinical series have also described the overlap: children with both ADDH and emotional disorders may have a more severe disorder, for comorbid children tend to show higher levels of hyperactivity and learning disorder than do children with ADDH only (Livingston *et al.*, 1990).

Longitudinal studies are needed to clarify how far emotional disorder leads to hyperactive behaviour (e.g. through agitation), how far it is a result of being hyperactive and suffering the consequent reactions of others, and how far they share common causes. One route has been suggested by a follow-up of children, from the Perinatal Collaborative Survey, who still had minor neurological signs at the age of 7 years (and high rates of hyperactive–impulsive behaviour, Shaffer *et al.*, 1983). In late adolescence they had lower IQs than normal controls and were more likely to show an affective disorder. Anxiety and depression may be complications of neurodevelopmental delay.

On the other hand, a little evidence indicates that the comorbid group may be rather different from those with hyperactivity alone. In a cluster analytic study of children referred because of disruptive behaviour, those with anxious and depressive symptoms came out as a separate cluster that showed little evidence of neurological or cognitive impairment, had a later onset, and were unlikely to respond to stimulants (Taylor *et al.*, 1986). This suggested the possibility of a distinct aetiology from hyperkinetic disorder. Current knowledge only allows the issues to be put: more research will be needed to show the pathways involved. In the meantime, clinicians will need to be alert for signs of emotional disorder, and not to assume that they are simply one aspect of a unitary disorder of hyperactivity.

Pervasive developmental disorder

Children with autism not infrequently show hyperactive behaviour, but autistic symptoms are rare in the hyperactive. Diagnostic schemes contain rules to ensure that those with both problems are diagnosed as autistic. This reflects an implicit belief that there is a hierarchy of diagnoses in which autism stands higher.

Although we know little of the determinants of hyperactivity in autism, the longitudinal course suggests that it may mean something rather different from hyperactivity in more normal children. A follow-up study of autism identified a group of young people who reversed their pattern: as they passed through adolescence their overactivity gave way to an inert passivity (Rutter & Lockyer, 1967). There is nothing comparable to be expected in the adult outcome of children with hyperkinetic disorder or ADDH (Weiss & Hechtman, 1986). The effect of stimulants, too, may be rather different in children with autism and hyperactivity (see Chapter 51). Clinically, it is common to encounter acute withdrawal and depression in such children. Practically, much caution is needed; theoretically, the comorbid condition is autism and the symptom of hyperactivity is part of it.

In summary, there are several types of comorbidity and the reasons for overlap with other conditions vary with the condition. The association with conduct disorder is so strong that researchers must always take it into account, and clinicians must be wary in their interpretation of the literature lest they base their management of hyperactivity on findings that were wholly attributable to conduct disorder. In current evidence, it is sound to recognize hyperactivity as a disorder in which conduct disorder may be either present or absent; but future evidence could change this. If longitudinal studies indicate that hyperactivity without conduct disorder is not a risk for later development, then the disorder to recognize will be the combination of hyperactivity and conduct disorder.

EPIDEMIOLOGY

Prevalence

The prevalence rate in various studies depends critically upon the definition of what constitutes a case. The most widely repeated figure is the 3–5% suggested by the DSM manual (American Psychiatric Association, 1980, 1987); but this is an estimate based on the experience of clinicians rather than on any empirical data. When the diagnosis of ADDH is made with standardized structured interviews to parent or teacher then the prevalence is very much higher: 14% according to Shekim *et al.* (1985), reaching 19% in primary-school-age boys; 17% in the primary school boys investigated by Taylor *et al.* (1991). Studies based on rating scales also give high rates, but in the absence of a validated cut-off point on the scales the exact rates have little meaning. One should, however, note particularly the 19% rate in the primary school boys whom Szatmari *et al.* (1989) studied with questionnaires because cut-off points were taken on the basis of giving the same rate as a psychiatrist's DSM diagnosis.

These rates are all very high — indeed, they are high enough to suggest that the diagnosis is unmanageably overinclusive. Perhaps this is why the DSM categorizations have generally been lacking in discriminative validity. The ICD definition of hyperkinetic disorder has also been studied and — as expected from the definition — has a lower prevalence: 1.7% in a population of primary school boys (Taylor *et al.*, 1991). One can also calculate a figure for a similar group from the study of MBD with hyperkinesis reported by Gillberg *et al.* (1983): it is similar, at 1.3%. After making allowance for gender differences and geographical variation, these figures would imply a point prevalence of about 1 in 200 for hyperkinetic disorder in the whole population of children.

Epidemiological studies have also identified populations with striking differences in prevalence. This could be a very helpful finding: the reasons for the differences could throw light on the causes of the disorder, and the study of hyperactivity in low-risk populations could be a good strategy for identifying causative agents. Geographical and gender differences need particular attention.

Geographical differences

The enormous variation in practice in different parts of the world can scarcely be paralleled in the rest of modern medicine. The most striking variations appear when one considers the administrative prevalence — the rate with which the diagnosis is made in routine clinical practice. In the US, two surveys suggested that more than 1 child in every 100 was receiving a physician's diagnosis and treatment accordingly — usually with stimulant drugs (Lambert *et al.*, 1978; Bosco & Robin, 1980). By contrast, in an inner city population in London, UK, the 10-year period prevalence from a comprehensive case register was only 1 in 2000 of the nonretarded child population (Camberwell Register, cited in Taylor & Sandberg, 1984).

The lower figures in the UK reflect chiefly differences in diagnostic practice. There is no such difference when questionnaire ratings are used to define cases (Taylor, 1987). Prendergast *et al.* (1988) studied diagnostic practice directly by presenting a set of case histories and video tapes of children to panels of clinicians in the US and the UK. The panels used both the DSM-III and the ICD-9 manuals. When the single-diagnosis ICD-9 scheme was in use, then the British diagnosticians identified far fewer cases of hyperkinesis. When multiple diagnoses were allowed in the DSM-III scheme, then British clinicians identified the same number of cases. The difference therefore lay, not in the recognition of symptomatology, but in the way that comorbidity is considered.

There may also be a difference between the US and the UK in the way that children are referred to clinics. Even though questionnaire ratings are similar in population samples from both sides of the Atlantic, they differ in clinically referred populations: at a UK clinic the children had lower scores for hyperactivity and higher scores for emotional disorder, by comparison with US figures (Taylor, 1987).

Different reasons generate the variations between UK and Chinese populations. One of the replicated findings from cross-cultural questionnaire ratings is a high rate of hyperactivity in China and Hong Kong (Shen *et al.*, 1985; Luk & Leung, 1989): nearly three times as many Chinese as English boys scored above the cut-off on the Conners and the Rutter scales. This is of course out of line with the stereotype of Chinese children as docile and well-controlled in their classrooms; and indeed more detailed assessments of the children indicate that the 'hyperactive' Chinese are a good deal less active and more attentive than their English counterparts. The reason for the disparity appears to lie in the great importance of school success in the Chinese culture, an intolerance of relatively minor degrees of disruptive behaviour, and consequently a greater readiness of the raters to identify children as hyperactive. The social construction of deviance is emphasized by these findings, and should give pause to all those attempting to overinterpret the findings of rating scales.

Different reasons again underlie the geographical differences that are to be found between urban and rural areas. Questionnaire scales suggested that pervasive hyperactivity was approximately three times as common in an inner city area of London as it had been in the Isle of Wight survey (Schachar *et al.*, 1981; Taylor *et al.*, 1991), but some of the difference could have come from the separation of these surveys in time as well as in space. The Ontario Child Health Study has confirmed that hyperactivity identified by questionnaires is more common in the cities than in the country; indeed, the difference was greater for hyperactivity than for other childhood conditions (Boyle *et al.*, 1987). The reasons for this are suggested by the findings in a very different culture. In mainland China there was a reverse differential, with higher rates of hyperactivity in the deprived mountain areas than in a suburban region or in Beijing itself (Shen *et al.*, 1985). Presumably therefore the urban–rural differences do not result from the city environment itself but from the greater rates of psychosocial disadvantage that, in western cultures, are to be found there. While this does not rule out genetic explanations, because drifts of population could in theory account for the findings, it is likely that there is an environmental contribution to the observed prevalence rates.

Gender differences

Hyperactivity is less common in girls than in boys. Ross and Ross (1982) provided a review of the prevalence of ADDH in US clinics and suggested a male to female ratio of about 4:1. In systematically gathered data from a UK clinic, the gender ratio for the hyperkinetic syndrome was similar (3.6:1); but this ratio fell markedly to 1.9:1 when considering only children with mental retardation (Taylor, 1986b). Questionnaire studies in the general population yield figures that vary greatly with no very satisfactory explanation for the variation, from about 2.5:1 in the recent large-scale studies from Ontario and London (Boyle *et al.*, 1987; Taylor *et al.*, 1992); to figures of 5:1 in the Dunedin study (McGee *et al.*, 1987) and 10:1 in an Australian study (Glow, 1981). The disagreements presumably reflect the lack of precision in the rating scales commonly employed.

Probably there are several reasons for the greater vulnerability of boys. Adults are often more tolerant of hyperactivity in girls than in boys, at least before school age (Battle & Lacey, 1972). This could lead to some underidentification of girls, but is unlikely to account for gender differences since girls identified as hyperactive are in fact considerably less active on objective measures than are affected boys (Taylor *et al.*, 1992). When hyperactive girls and hyperactive boys are directly compared, then some evidence suggests that the girls are even more likely to show neurodevelopmental delays in language, cognitive and motor skills (Kashani *et al.*, 1979; Berry *et al.*, 1985; Taylor *et al.*, 1992). Indeed, in the study of clinically referred children with hyperkinetic syndrome reported by James and Taylor (1990), the distribution of cognitive skills was markedly different. Boys had a bimodal distribution of IQ scores, there being a population of normal IQ and a separate population with a mean IQ of about 70. In girls, only the 'retarded' population could be found. The greater concentration of neurodevelopmental abnormalities suggests that they are part of the cause, and that more abnormality needs to be present in a girl before the disorder is expressed in behaviour. Once the hyperactivity is manifest in a girl, however, then her outlook is very like that of an affected boy: she is equally likely to develop comorbid conduct disorder and her short-term course is very similar (Szatmari *et al.*, 1989; Taylor *et al.*, 1992).

FACTORS RELEVANT TO AETIOLOGY

Intensive research has been in progress for decades to clarify the aetiology of hyperactive behaviours. Many associations have been found, and some of them will be summarized below. Most associations have been found in case-control studies where the cases are from specialized clinics and the controls are from the general population. The use of over-extended diagnostic definitions and the high rates of comorbidity (see above) mean that in many cases the specificity of findings is in doubt: it is not clear whether an observed change in a group of children with hyperactivity stems from their hyperactivity, or their other symptomatology, or accompanying difficulties in learning, or motivational changes, or the fact of referral to a clinic. The reliance upon cross-sectional studies means that the pathogenetic importance of any given association is often in doubt. The heterogeneous groups studied and the small size of the associations that are typically found make it uncertain whether a possible cause is truly of small effect or whether it has a large effect within a subgroup of cases. The lack of replicability in clinically categorized groups makes it difficult to interpret clashes of evidence. This last problem is fundamental, for inconsistencies in the biological findings about hyperactivity are very common (Ferguson & Rapoport, 1983). It is very hard to determine whether a clash of results between two laboratories reflects differences in the children that they are studying or requires a more fundamental explanation.

As will be seen, inconsistencies in the biological findings are more marked than in the psychological. The same contrast applies in the investigation of autism (see Chapter 33). It may of course be the case that ultimately the best level of explanation will be that of biological brain function; but that is not the case yet. It might equally well turn out that the key level for the identification of disorder is that of altered psychological processes, and that biological mechanisms are complex and heterogeneous. The point matters to clinicians, for it would be naively reductionist to decide that a biological association of disorder is somehow more fundamental than a psychological, and that biological tests will necessarily take precedence in investigation and formulation.

This summary of an extensive literature is deliberately selective. It emphasizes areas of enquiry where associations have been relatively consistent or have appeared in epidemiological as well as clinical populations, where findings are specific to hyperactivity rather than merely to deviance in behaviour, and where observed results can be related to theory about the nature of any underlying impairment.

Neuropsychological tests

Attention deficit

Hyperactive children perform poorly on tests that require sustained and organized concentration (see reviews by Douglas, 1988, and Sergeant, 1988). The tests that have shown impairment include those that are intended to measure the maintenance of vigilance over a lengthy period (such as the Continuous Performance Test; Rosvold et al., 1956), the inhibition of overrapid and thoughtless responding (the Matching Familiar Figures Test; Kagan et al., 1964), the allo-

cation of processing capacity in line with changing task demands (Sergeant & Scholten, 1985), and the maintenance of readiness to respond (reaction time tests with varying delays after a preparatory signal; Sonuga-Barke & Taylor, 1992). All these are, in a sense, useful general tests for the impairment of attention and all are close to the intuitive idea of what is meant by an attention deficit.

In spite of the widespread finding of impairment on tests, there is considerable doubt about whether attention deficit is in fact a valid way of describing the cognitive impairments of children with inattentive behaviour. For one thing, all these tests can be affected by unrelated factors such as motivation and the general willingness to engage in laboratory tests. For another, several reviewers have argued that the impairment of test scores is a nonspecific accompaniment of many types of disturbance in behaviour and learning, not just of hyperactivity (e.g. Prior & Sanson, 1986; McGee & Share, 1988). Another doubt comes from the fact that impairment can also be seen in a number of tests that are not particularly intended to assess attention — such as short-term memory (the Digit Span Test; Taylor et al., 1991), speed of response (serial and choice reaction time tests; Sykes et al., 1973), new learning (Paired Associate Learning Tests; Swanson & Kinsbourne, 1976), and even tachistocopically presented tests that were originally designed to avoid effects of attention (McIntyre et al., 1978). The specificity and the experimental analysis of cognitive impairment therefore need particular consideration.

Recent studies have shown that poor test performance in primary school children is relatively specific to the behaviours of hyperactivity (Schachar, 1991). Hyperactivity in population-based samples is correlated with reduced scores; nonhyperactive conduct disorder is not; the association is clearest at severe degrees of hyperactivity (McGee et al., 1984a; Sergeant, 1988; Szatmari et al., 1989; Taylor et al., 1991). The reduction in scores is found in a wide variety of tests and indeed the IQ is reduced in hyperactive children in most of these studies. However, some abnormalities are still to be found even after IQ has been controlled for by analysis of covariance.

One may conclude that the link between hyperactivity and cognitive impairment is specific but weak, but that it becomes much stronger when the condition under scrutiny is strictly defined. Most of the experimental analyses have been carried out on the broader group defined by questionnaire scales as showing the presence of hyperactive behaviour. They have tried to alter the parameters of stimulus presentation or response requirement in order to seek an experimental manipulation that could define an attention deficit.

Most attempts to control the experimental presentation of tests in this way have concluded that the deficit is at a rather high 'executive' level and does not involve a breakdown of any one of the steps of processing information. For example, the deficit is manifest in tests lasting a few seconds just as it is in those lasting for 10 minutes or more (Taylor et al., 1991) or even in tests lasting for several hours (van der Meere &

Sergeant, 1988). The problem is therefore unlikely to be one of sustaining attention over time. Neither is it likely to be a problem of selecting one source of attention from others, as would be implied by the idea of distractibility, for the addition of irrelevant information to test stimuli does not worsen performance disproportionately in children with hyperactivity (Douglas & Peters, 1979; Sergeant & Scholten, 1985). Some have suggested that the deficit lies in an excessive breadth of attention, so that performance on incidental tests should be improved to the same extent as performance on a central test is reduced. The evidence is contradictory here. One investigation did find a shift of attention from what is centrally relevant to what is peripheral (Ceci & Tishman, 1984), but the majority of studies investigating this possibility have not found it (Douglas & Peters, 1979; Taylor *et al.*, 1991). In a similar way, there have been failed attempts to implicate encoding, search and decision stages of processing information (Sergeant & Scholten, 1985) and overall attentional capacity (Schachar & Logan, 1990a).

Sergeant (1988) has reviewed this literature from the point of view of information-processing theory. He has concluded that none of the early stages of information processing is likely to be impaired in pervasive hyperactivity. However, there is some evidence of abnormalities at the later stages of response selection and enaction — as witnessed, for example, by a disproportionate effect on hyperactive children of making the response incompatible with the stimulus (van der Meere *et al.*, 1989).

Douglas (1988) has reviewed the literature from the related standpoint of cognitive psychology. The experiments carried out in this tradition are difficult to interpret in any simple information-processing model. However, they do bear witness to the complexity of the deficit. Experimenter effects are very strong, as are other details of the way that an experiment is set up. The conclusion is that the deficit in performance is the result of very high-level control processes of self-regulation and inhibition rather than failure in elementary steps of perception and attention. This conclusion is quite compatible with that of Sergeant (above), for these control processes would be one of the possible explanations for abnormalities at the response end of the chain of events that lead to action.

The research evidence is not yet conclusive, but seems to be converging on the notion that attention deficit is a misnomer for the problems of children who behave in an inattentive, restless fashion. The problem rather is to do with the way that children regulate their responsiveness.

Impulsiveness has therefore become a key construct for understanding the cognitive changes. This refers to a reduced ability or willingness to inhibit inappropriate actions and to wait for a delayed consequence. It is important to recognize that this is not necessarily the same thing as the intrusive behaviours (acting out of turn) that clinicians would describe as impulsive. As considered above, behavioural ratings of impulsiveness include all sorts of activity, and the issue of whether they are in truth founded upon impulsiveness in the

cognitive sense is an unanswered empirical question. Just as in the case of attention, one must not assume that the behaviours bearing that name necessarily have any close connection with the altered neurophysiological process.

The best-known way of testing the cognitive idea of impulsiveness is through Kagan's Matching Familiar Figures test (cited above). In conditions of uncertainty, impulsive children make rapid and inaccurate responses; in the theory, they are inaccurate because they are too rapid. The analysis applies well in some epidemiological research. Not only are hyperactive children unduly quick in their response, but accuracy falls as they take less time to do it (Fuhrman & Kendall, 1986; Taylor *et al.*, 1991). In clinical research, the analysis has not always worked very well. In some studies, especially of pervasive hyperactivity where there is likely to be a high rate of developmental disorders, children with hyperactivity have proved to be less accurate but no faster in their responses than clinically referred controls (Sandberg *et al.*, 1978; Firestone & Martin, 1979). The likely reason for this comes from the high rate of other developmental disabilities in these series. Such children are likely to have slower reactions because their processing time takes longer. Many studies have shown that they have slow reactions when they are told to go quickly (Sergeant, 1988). Their responses may therefore be premature, even when they take the same amount of time as ordinary children. Their usual tendency is still to take less time in inspecting new material than most children do; when this is prevented by the experimenter's controlling the amount of time that they spend looking at a visual test, then their performance is no worse than anybody else's (Sonuga-Barke *et al.*, 1992a).

Schachar and Logan (1990b) have directly tested the idea that children with hyperactivity are less able to inhibit a response than others, and found that the prediction holds for children with the serious problem of hyperkinetic disorder (not for those with ADDH). Rapport *et al.* (1986) tied this more closely to the obtaining of reward with the finding that children with hyperactivity were more likely to respond for a small immediate reward than for a large delayed one. Sonuga-Barke *et al.* (1992b) made a systematic examination of the effects of delay and size of incentive on children's choices. In one sense, they confirmed the impulsiveness of children with pervasive hyperactivity: under some circumstances they were indeed maladaptive in responding too quickly and not waiting for a reward. But they did not have a fixed inability to withhold responses: under some circumstances, when the total amount of time they had to wait was controlled, then they were no more impulsive than ordinary children. Their impulsiveness appeared when they could use it to control the total amount of time that they had to spend in waiting: it was an aversion to delay rather than a failure of control.

These analyses suggest how children may learn best in school and elsewhere. Successful teaching is not a matter of excluding irrelevant stimuli (though it makes good sense to highlight what is relevant and avoid attractive distractors during the teaching). Rather, it is a matter of keeping children applied to the task in hand and ensuring that they orient to and explore the material from which they are supposed to be learning.

OTHER DEVELOPMENTAL DELAYS

Hyperkinetic disorder is quite strongly associated with a range of abnormalities in psychological and motor development (Gillberg *et al.*, 1983; Taylor *et al.*, 1986). The typical abnormalities found in school-age children are reduced verbal and performance IQ, immature articulation of speech, a history of language delay in earlier development, and poor motor coordination in skilled tasks with marked overflow movements from one side of the body to the other and impersistence in sustained acts. Such abnormalities have not generally been found in studies of children with ADDH (Reeves *et al.*, 1987; Werry *et al.*, 1987).

It is not yet possible to go further and assert that neurodevelopmental immaturity is the cause of hyperactive behaviour. For one thing, cohort studies focusing on children with motor and language delays have not indicated that hyperkinesis is a very characteristic outcome. The rates were increased in children who were studied because they had signs of neurological immaturity (Nichols & Chen, 1981) but the association was quite weak, there were other kinds of psychopathology as well, and developmental factors other than the presence of 'soft' signs predicted much of the behavioural outcome.

Another difficulty for the neurological immaturity theory comes from the general rejection of a unitary condition of minor neurological dysfunction. MBD has collapsed as an explanatory theory because of the failure of its supposed components to be associated with one another in the same children (Schmidt *et al.*, 1987) and the failure of the condition to support coherent biological or prognostic findings. The heir to the idea could be the DAMP (disorders of attention, motor and perception) proposed by Gillberg *et al.* (1983), but the objections levelled against MBD are equally strong against DAMP unless and until new evidence validates the concept.

Another weakness in the view that would attribute hyperactivity directly to delay in neurological development is the very early onset, implying that children are recognizably different at an early stage rather than prolonging a normal early stage to an inappropriate point. Furthermore, a good response to stimulant medication is not a function of developmental level but of attention and activity (Taylor *et al.*, 1987). Further still, pure attention deficit uncomplicated by hyperactivity has already been seen to have different antecedents to hyperactivity, yet a similar pattern of developmental and cognitive delays. Possibly, therefore, one should think of the inattentive style of behaviour as being the basic pathology and leading to a delay in the learning of motor, language and other cognitive skills. Developmental research will be needed before clinicians can be secure about making any judgements of differential diagnosis or prognosis on the basis of the child's neurodevelopmental state.

NEUROBIOLOGICAL ASSOCIATIONS

Genetic influences

Twin studies have indicated a genetic component in hyperactivity. Monozygotic twins have been known for some time to be more concordant than dizygotic twins for several temperamental dimensions, including activity (Buss & Plomin, 1975; Torgersen & Kringlen, 1978). Goodman and Stevenson (1989) have analysed teacher and parent questionnaire ratings on a large sample of twins from the general population; they concluded that pervasive hyperactivity shows more concordance in monozygotic twins than dizygotic. This could not be accounted for by the greater physical similarity of the monozygotic, for the finding still held when considering cases where parents were mistaken about their children's zygosity. Large nongenetic effects were also to be found.

Even these large series of twins include few who could be expected to show a clinically diagnosable disorder. We do not yet know the genetic contribution to the disorder, nor do we know very much about just what is inherited. The study by Goodman and Stevenson suggested that pervasive hyperactivity in the probands was accompanied by pervasive or school-based hyperactivity in the co-twins, suggesting that home-specific problems might have a rather different basis. The inheritance of attention deficit is not known, nor whether it segregates with hyperactive behaviour in the way that must be expected if inattentiveness is indeed to be seen as a fundamental pathology. (Alberts-Corush *et al.*, 1986, argued for increased inattentiveness in the relatives of hyperactive children, but could not allow for sampling problems.)

An older literature comparing relatives of different degrees of relatedness has been reviewed elsewhere (Taylor, 1986b). Full siblings of hyperactive children are more likely than half-siblings to be hyperactive themselves (Safer, 1973). Biological parents who are living with their own hyperactive children are more likely to have had behavioural problems than the adoptive parents of hyperactive children — but this could reflect some other factor such as the selection of problem-free people as adopters (Cantwell, 1975). The adopted-away offspring of psychiatric patients are particularly likely to be hyperkinetic (Cunningham *et al.*, 1975). A complex set of findings from a Scandinavian register-based study suggested that the link between hyperactivity in children and antisocial behaviour in their parents was partly genetic (Bohman *et al.*, 1982). This is circumstantial evidence, but it all points in the same direction towards a genetically inherited basis, without saying exactly what that basis is.

The inherited basis might be rather nonspecific. Studies of psychopathology in the parents of children with hyperactivity have shown an increase in antisocial behaviours, which is very similar to the increased rate in the parents of antisocial children (Stewart *et al.*, 1980; Biederman *et al.*, 1986; Schachar & Wachsmuth, 1990). Schachar (1991) suggested that this is all due to the presence of comorbid antisocial disorder in the hyperactive children, and that hyperactivity in itself has no association with parental psychopathology; but epidemiological findings suggest that even children with a pure pattern of hyperactivity have an increased likelihood that their parents will show psychopathology (Szatmari *et al.*, 1989). The argument is complex and not yet resolved: there may well be several mechanisms through which behaviour disorders in parents may be transmitted to their children, and some parental depression is probably the result of caring for a difficult child. The genetic contribution may need to be disentangled from a mixture of other influences, so more research here is greatly needed.

Imaging of brain structure and function

No evidence of structural damage in the brains of children with hyperactivity has yet appeared. Imaging techniques, however, can also be applied to detect alterations of function, either those of altered blood flow in parts of the brain or localized changes in metabolic rate (see Chapter 6). Two single-photon emission studies have been reported from Denmark; children with attention deficit disorder were characterized by underperfusion of the frontal areas of the brain (Lou *et al.*, 1984) and the striatum (Lou *et al.*, 1989). In both studies this was in contrast to different areas being hypoperfused in other disorders of learning. A positron emission tomographic study has been reported from Washington, not indeed on hyperactive children themselves but upon those of their parents who still show behavioural disturbance in adult life (Zametkin *et al.*, 1990). It described a reduced uptake of glucose in several areas of the cerebral cortex, including especially the frontal region.

These are exciting findings; they do not yet constitute a biological marker for the condition. The specificity of the findings is not yet known and we do not know whether any abnormalities result from the details of the psychological experiment that is carried out. They could, for example, be seen in normal people who are not engaged in or interested by the task in hand. Accordingly, they remain a research procedure and do not yet enter into the clinical evaluation.

Neurochemical measures

Neurotransmitter changes in hyperactivity are made very likely by the rapid and marked effect of amphetamines and related drugs upon the symptoms. A rather scattered set of research studies has not yet prompted a general agreement. The clearest pattern of findings stems from the investigations that have examined the urinary levels of metabolites of the catecholamine neurotransmitter noradrenaline. Shekim *et al.* (1979), Shen and Wang (1984) and Zametkin *et al.* (1984) have concurred in finding a reduction in the excretion of metabolites of noradrenaline. The specificity and significance of the finding are in doubt still; it has perhaps been followed up less than it might have been because of the equally robust finding that amphetamine-type medication reduces the excretion of noradrenaline metabolites even further (Shekim

et al., 1979; Shen & Wang, 1984; Zametkin *et al.*, 1984). While this may seem like a rather paradoxical effect of amphetamines, it should not be taken to dismiss the noradrenaline hypothesis. It may point to further complications: perhaps amphetamine has an action in stimulating a second messenger that in turn inhibits noradrenaline release, or perhaps an effect on presynaptic inhibitory receptors is linked to therapeutic effectiveness.

A dopamine hypothesis has been very popular, partly because of the existence of animal models in which stereotactic or chemical destruction of ascending dopaminergic nerve cell bodies produces an amphetamine-sensitive syndrome of overactivity. However, there are many animal models that do not implicate dopamine, including depletion of cerebral noradrenaline (Shaywitz *et al.*, 1982), prefrontal lesions (Jacobsen, 1935) and an isolated upbringing (Robbins & Sahakian, 1979). All these produce an overactive animal with learning difficulties that are reversed by amphetamine. The pharmacological effect may well not be related to the cause of the hyperactivity. Direct measures of dopamine metabolites have not produced evidence of abnormality in children with hyperactivity (Wender *et al.*, 1971; Shetty & Chase, 1976; Shaywitz *et al.*, 1977). The enzyme dopamine beta hydroxylase has been reported as reduced in subgroups of hyperactive children, including those with minor congenital anomalies (Rapoport *et al.*, 1974) and those who show conduct disorder as well (Bowden *et al.*, 1988): indeed, the finding may be linked primarily to conduct disorder rather than hyperactivity (Rogeness *et al.*, 1982).

In summary, children with hyperactive behaviour are likely to repay future neurochemical research. The work so far suggests that noradrenaline changes are to be found, but has not yet identified a pathogenesis involving this or any other neurotransmitter. The future work will have to pay stronger attention to good neurochemical method (including dietary control), to examine the possibility of heterogeneity, and to link chemical findings to sound clinical descriptions so as to determine which syndrome, or which component of disorder, generates the association.

Electrophysiological studies

Several neurophysiological measures have suggested that hyperactive children react less to stimuli than do other children of the same age. Resting levels of autonomic nervous system activity are probably unchanged but the heart rate, the skin conductance response, the blocking of the alpha rhythm of the electroencephalogram (EEG) and the average evoked EEG response all show a diminished reaction to novel stimuli and to stimuli that should have signal value (Taylor, 1986b).

The specificity of the finding is in considerable doubt, since diminished physiological responsiveness also characterizes children with learning disorders (e.g. Maxwell *et al.*, 1974) and unsocialized aggression (Delamater & Lahey, 1983). All these conditions tend to occur together in the same children, and it is not clear which of them, or which component of disorder, is responsible. It could be that diminished physiological responsiveness is part of the construct of hyperactivity and its presence in other conditions reflects how often hyperactivity is encountered in them. It could also turn out to be characteristic of unsocialized aggression. In fact, in one of the few studies to examine the clinical correlates of autonomic unresponsiveness within a group of hyperactive children, neither of these behaviour patterns was related to electrodermal or finger pulse volume changes; rather, the association was between autonomic change and signs of neurological incoordination (Conners, 1975). This would be compatible with a different explanatory model, in which physiological unresponsiveness is part of a neurodevelopmental risk factor with widespread and relatively nonspecific behavioural consequences.

A fourth kind of explanation of the physiological findings would be that high responsiveness represents a protective factor — either against disruptive behaviour in general, or hyperactivity in particular. The finding of diminished responsiveness in children with hyperactivity would then reflect their lack of a protective factor and the consequently unrestrained play of pathogenic forces.

The data we have now do not allow for a good test of these different causal mechanisms. Clinical considerations make it important that they are tested, because understanding the developmental mechanisms involved would make intervention fruitful. At present, no effect of underresponsiveness on the course of clinical disorder has been shown; so again an initially promising finding has not yet been translated into a useful clinical investigation.

ASSOCIATIONS WITH NEUROLOGICAL ILLNESS AND INJURY

Neonatal disease and injury

ADDH and milder degrees of hyperactive behaviour do not show any association with obstetric abnormalities in clinic surveys. On the other hand, the more severe hyperkinetic syndrome of childhood has an increased chance of occurring in a child with a previous history of perinatal problems (Gillberg *et al.*, 1983; Taylor *et al.*, 1991). These problems are not accounted for by social disadvantage of the parents, but neither are they necessarily the cause of the hyperactivity. Most of the risk factors identified in both studies were rather minor, such as a seizure or jitteriness in the neonatal period, or evidence of hypoxia in a neonate after an unremarkable delivery.

Cohort studies focusing on the later outcome of children with birth complications suggest that hyperactive and impulsive behaviour in childhood is a little more common than in children born normally, but that the prediction is quite weak and not specific to hyperactivity (Neligan *et al.*, 1976; Nichols & Chen, 1981). Maternal smoking in pregnancy, low fetal heart rate during labour and a small head circumference at birth are the strongest of the early factors. They all seem to bear witness to a very early onset of the disorder rather than to any damaging effect around the time of birth.

Associations with neurological illness

Brain disease with localizing neurological signs is uncommon in children with ADDH and is excluded from most research series. By contrast, the more severe hyperkinetic disorder is disproportionately common in children with damaged brains: not only is it, like other psychiatric disorders, more common than in normal controls, but also it accounts for a higher proportion of all the diagnoses that are made (Rutter *et al.*, 1970; Thorley, 1984a). Some of this association, at least, can probably be explained by the prior association with intellectual retardation. Jenkins and Stable (1971) drew severely hyperkinetic cases from a register of people with mental subnormality and compared them with matched cases from the same register matched for age; they found higher rates of cerebral palsy and other structural lesions in those with hyperkinesis, and also more retardation on a global measure of development. Thorley (1984a) took this further, also using a case register of children referred for psychiatric assessment, from which he was able to take controls who were matched for IQ as well as for chronological age: he found no increase in the rate of structural brain damage.

Several individual diseases have been thought by clinicians to be causes of hyperactivity. Infantile hemiplegia, ataxic cerebral palsy, phenylketonuria, and some mucopolysaccharidoses have a reputation for generating wildly overactive behaviour. More systematic and controlled descriptions of some conditions such as the fragile X chromosome anomaly, idiopathic infantile hypercalcaemia, fetal alcohol syndrome, generalized resistance to thyroid hormone, congenital hypothyroidism and tuberous sclerosis have suggested that hyperactive and inattentive behaviour is part of the behavioural phenotype (see Chapter 37). However, some caution is in order: controls are not always adequate, the coexistence of intellectual retardation is not always adequately allowed for, and the description of hyperactivity is not always very precise, so that it may include many forms of disruptive behaviour. For all these reasons the study of congenital neurological abnormalities has not yet generated strong brain–behaviour correlations that could illuminate the nature of brain alterations in hyperkinesis.

Brain disease that is acquired in later childhood is an occasional cause of late-onset hyperactivity. Sydenham's chorea is by far the commonest; indeed, the sudden appearance of hyperactive behaviour in a previously normal child is most often due to rheumatic fever and is not always correctly diagnosed. Thyrotoxicosis is supposed to present with hyperactive behaviour, but in practice tiredness is much more characteristic.

Epilepsy is often associated with hyperactive behaviour, but not inevitably or specifically. The mechanisms are often complex (Taylor, 1991). The effects of frequent seizures can be devastating to the ability to attend and control one's activity.

The underlying brain damage may be producing behavioural symptoms in its own right. The psychological effect of having fits and being stigmatized can of itself produce a wide range of behavioural symptoms. Anticonvulsant medication can produce hyperactive behaviour and impairment of cognitive performance — especially when anticonvulsant levels are high and folate levels are low. A child with poorly controlled fits, intellectual impairment, and who is taking anticonvulsants, will therefore present a diagnostic challenge. It can be very helpful to make systematic changes to the dosage of anticonvulsants, with monitoring of behavioural cognitive and blood changes, to disentangle the web of causality before embarking upon specific treatments for hyperactivity.

Toxic and allergic factors

Acute lead poisoning produces a severe encephalopathy and those children who recover very often show a hyperkinetic disorder. Chronic exposure to lead may cause an increase in tissue concentrations of lead without any definite neurological signs. Several surveys of children from the general population have shown a correlation between blood or dentine lead and behaviour problems (Taylor, 1991). Although this has usually been studied with the belief that hyperactivity is the main outcome (Needleman *et al.*, 1979), this is a matter of tradition rather than empirical knowledge. Thomson *et al.* (1989) found that the aggressive and antisocial items of the Rutter Scale were more closely related to lead levels than were the other items; Needleman *et al.* (1979) found that the item of overactivity on their behavioural scale was one of the few that was not related to lead level. While it is probable that lead does have deleterious effects upon behaviour, the mechanism is not yet known: it may be as a result of the minor cognitive impairment that is also to be found.

Effects of diet on hyperactivity have been intensively sought since Feingold's (1975) suggestion that food dyes and preservatives caused genetic changes whose effect was to make children become intolerant to those same substances and therefore to suffer in their behaviour and their learning abilities. Double-blind trials of the effects of food dyes did not sustain either this hypothesis or the weaker form of it, that removing food additives from the diet would improve hyperactivity (Mattes & Gittleman, 1981). Single case studies, however, indicated that a very few individual children could indeed be helped by this form of diet (Weiss *et al.*, 1980).

More recently, investigators have returned to an older hypothesis, that behaviour might be disturbed by any of a wide range of foods to which a child might become intolerant (Trites *et al.*, 1980). Radical exclusion diets, followed by the serial reintroduction of different foods one at a time, allow the particular foods affecting an individual child to be identified. Blind challenge with the target foods can then be shown to worsen behaviour and psychological test performance (Egger *et al.*, 1985; Carter *et al.*, in press). The commonest foodstuffs to worsen behaviour in this way include cows' milk, wheat flour, food dyes, and citrus fruits, among others. Trial of a diet excluding this limited range of food, against a control diet, has also given significantly positive results (Kaplan *et al.*, 1989). The practical value of this treatment approach is still limited, because it is not clear which children will respond and the regime is very arduous. Indeed, a community survey suggested that the vast majority of children whose parents believe them to be intolerant of food are not — or not, at least, when the food is given in blind challenge conditions (Young *et al.*, 1987).

It would be very helpful to the clinician to be able to identify the children for whom it would be useful to explore the possibility of food intolerance. None of the trials has suggested that diet responders are characterized by any specific psychiatric pattern, and a wide range of disruptive and emotional problems have been the targets. It may well be that the hyperactivity of the child is not the chief target but that (for instance) tempers and irritability are just as likely, or unlikely, to respond. The trial by Carter *et al.* suggested that the children responding would have been identified by enquiry about food, not about behaviour. A beneficial effect of eliminating specific foods was more probable when parents had previously noted a specific intolerance or craving for a food. Knowledge of the physical basis of food sensitivity might allow for a predictive test; but so far there is none.

ASSOCIATIONS WITH PSYCHOSOCIAL FACTORS

Researchers have given less attention to the psychological environment than they have to the working of the brain. Nevertheless, a number of associations are known that could have aetiological importance.

Social adversity

The external disadvantages that affect family life should be distinguished from the alterations of personal relationships that they may cause. Poverty, bad housing and low socio-economic status have been investigated several times but their role is still uncertain. In some surveys there has been no association at all (Goyette *et al.*, 1978; Campbell & Redfering, 1979; Szatmari *et al.*, 1989; Taylor *et al.*, 1991). Pervasive hyperactivity has been linked with lower social class (Schachar *et al.*, 1981) but this could be due to the effect of coexisting conduct disorder.

Institutional upbringing is associated with inattentive and impulsive behaviour (Tizard & Hodges, 1978; Roy, 1983). This is not likely to reflect material disadvantage, for the children's homes studied were on the whole reasonably well-provided. Rather, the experience of changing caretakers and the lack of opportunity for stable attachments seem to be at the heart of the problem. Children who have grown up in this way are particularly likely to be inattentive in their classrooms, even after they have been adopted into a family home and their other psychological problems have improved. Some such children will show a clear attachment disorder, and should be diagnosed as such even if inattentiveness and overactivity are present too. For others, the chief problem is hyperactivity and we do not yet know whether this should be seen as part of a hyperkinetic disorder or a partial form of attachment disorder. The safest diagnostic practice is therefore to categorize on the basis of whatever symptomatology is predominant.

Family relationships

Adversity in close personal relationships has a robust association with hyperactive behaviour. Hyperactivity is more common in children from families characterized by marital discord (Brandon, 1971), hostile parent–child relationships (Battle & Lacey, 1972; Tallmadge & Barkley, 1983), parents who sought a termination of the pregnancy (Matejccek *et al.*, 1985) and discordant family life (Gillberg *et al.*, 1983). These studies do not allow for the likely presence of conduct disorder as well; but poor coping and critical emotion from parents were characteristic of hyperactivity, even allowing for conduct disorder in the study by Taylor *et al.* (1991). In the last study, adverse family relationships were associated with the persistence of disorder over time: their developmental role may be the maintenance rather than the initiation of disorder.

DEVELOPMENTAL COURSE

From birth to school entry

Infants vary greatly in their activity levels, but individual differences are not very stable over time. Indeed, one study suggested an inversion in the intensity of behaviour between the ages of 3 days and 2½ years (Bell *et al.*, 1971). The neonates with highest frequency and speed of behaviours became the toddlers with least vigour and lowest responsiveness.

In the preschool period overactivity is a very common complaint made by parents. It is often hard to evaluate because activity is very high in normal children, there are few demands upon sustained concentration, and so it is difficult to determine whether the complaint is a valid comment on a deviation of development or whether it reflects a parent's reduced tolerance of a developmentally unremarkable level of demandingness. Sometimes 'hyperactivity' is used by caretakers to refer to quite different problems from those in this chapter — such as sleeplessness and oppositionality. Careful history-taking is needed.

Nevertheless, the complaint of overactivity should not be ignored. At the age of 3 years it is a good predictor of the presence of conduct disorder in later childhood (Stevenson *et al.*, 1985; Campbell, 1987). After the age of 3 the normal course of development involves a reduction of the general level of activity in some settings but not others (Routh, 1980). Starting at school makes prolonged attention more necessary. Some children — especially the most intelligent — cope with this transition well and meet all the requirements even if they are still distressingly uncontrolled at home. The persistence of unmodulated and inattentive behaviour beyond this age

becomes more and more of a problem as schooling proceeds. It carries risks for failing to learn, and other children are antagonized and begin to withdraw from them.

School age to adolescence

Hyperactivity, as noted under the section on comorbidity, above, is a risk factor for outcome in later childhood even when one allows for the presence of conduct disorder. The major outcome is the development of aggressive and antisocial behaviour and delinquency (Riddle & Rapoport, 1976; Hoy *et al.*, 1978; Satterfield *et al.*, 1982; August *et al.*, 1983; Barkley *et al.*, 1990). Affected children also tend to remain inattentive and impulsive, become isolated and unpopular among their peers, and do not achieve academically as they should (Hechtman *et al.*, 1984). They have several routes into an antisocial adjustment: for some, it is the direct continuation of their reckless and demanding attempts to satisfy the wishes of the moment; for others, it is a reaction to their poor opinion of themselves; for others again, it reflects an absence of other skills in getting their own way. Some find that they are exploited by other children and become the 'fall guy' in group offending; others develop a view of the world in which they are victimized by everyone else, and react with the aggression of one who is under attack.

Hyperactivity, then is one of the routes into conduct disorder. Even when conduct disorder has developed, hyperactivity is still a predictor of a more antisocial outcome (Schachar *et al.*, 1981; Farrington *et al.*, 1990). Its developmental importance is therefore not confined to acting as an entry route into conduct disorder; it also modulates the course of the antisocial. This may be partly because it increases the impact of conduct disorder on other people and therefore the vicious cycle of angry, untrusting and coercive relationships. Indeed, Gittelman and her colleagues (1985) have described a follow-up into early adult life of children previously diagnosed as showing ADDH: only those in whom attention deficit symptoms had persisted were at risk for an adult DSM diagnosis. This may be pointing to a severe developmental impact of hyperactivity, or to a poor-prognosis subgroup in which hyperactivity is particularly marked. A longitudinal study of boys by Magnusson and Bergman (1990) has already been cited — the suggestion was that an antisocial adolescent outcome was predicted, not simply by hyperactivity, but by a constellation of features of which hyperactivity was one and which also included poor peer relationships and early onset.

We do not yet know the mediating pathways involved. It is possible that the mechanism is the continuation of a hyperactivity disorder — in which case the key to treatment should be the meticulous and prolonged control of the symptoms. However, against this notion is the clear finding of a very poor outcome in series of children who have been thoroughly treated at famous clinics specializing in the management of hyperactivity (Barkley *et al.*, 1990). Accordingly, it is also possible that the risk is mediated through other factors such as self-esteem or the critical reactions of other people. A poor outcome in hyperactive children is predicted not only by severity of symptomatology and the presence of conduct disorder but also by discordant family relationships, depression in mothers and antisocial fathers (Weiss & Hechtman, 1986; Lambert, 1988; Wallander, 1988; Barkley *et al.*, 1990; Taylor *et al.*, 1991).

Outcome in adult life

The stormy course in adolescence can sometimes be followed by a relatively happy adult adjustment. For example, Thorley (1984b) followed a group of children, who had been identified from clinical records as hyperactive, over a 15-year period to their early adult life. The worst of the outcome had been during their adolescence. Then, they were even more at risk than a group of children referred at the same time for psychiatric help, usually because of conduct disorder. They were more likely to be expelled from school, to be the subjects of psychiatric treatment, to suffer multiple accidents and to have fits. But, by the time they were in their adult life, their outcome was little worse than that of the psychiatric controls and was more determined by their intelligence, social class and aggression than by just how hyperactive they had been as children.

A comparable picture comes from the Montreal cohort, on which most of our knowledge is based (Weiss & Hechtman, 1986). Many children grow out of their hyperactivity and escape disablement. Those who do not avoid the risk are likely to show an explosive or an immature kind of personality, and this risk is mediated as much or more by aggression and family relationships as by the original degree of hyperactivity.

Both these follow-up studies may be optimistic. Attrition of the cohorts may well remove those who have the worst outcome, and their initial selection ensured that they had all been treated. The Montreal studies have excluded some of the worst-outcome cases, such as those with brain damage and intellectual retardation. A briefly described follow-up study by Menkes *et al.* (1967) is still noteworthy for its high rates of institutionalization encountered in adult life. Nevertheless, they make it reasonable for clinicians to advise patients and their families that there is a fair chance of a good eventual outcome provided that the worst traps in development can be avoided.

TREATMENT

Many of the general principles of treatment follow from the view of psychopathology outlined above. Comorbidity is frequent, there are many complications, and other types of adversity are part of the cause and may need intervention in their own right. The course is determined by more than just the presence and degree of hyperactivity. Therefore, management must be comprehensive. Biological, family, school and peer contributions need to be assessed. The aggression, learning abilities and emotional life of affected children need full evaluation.

The overriding goal of treatment is to foster normal development. All treatments must be judged ultimately for their ability to give protection against the risks for long-term psychological development. To approach this goal, there are several aims: to reduce hyperactivity, treat coexisting disorders, prevent or treat disorders of conduct, promote academic and social learning, improve emotional adjustment and self-esteem and relieve family distress. The balance of these will be different for individual children, but all must be considered.

Reduction of hyperactivity

Medication

The most powerful treatment available is medication with central nervous stimulants such as dexamphetamine and methylphenidate. Scores of controlled trials have been unanimous in showing that such drugs produce a large fall in hyperactive behaviour (see Chapter 51). Adverse effects of medication are seldom severe; the main contraindications are the presence of tic disorders, heart disease and autism, and even these are not absolute.

The short-term action of drugs is not paradoxical or unique to hyperactive children. Normal children show a similar reduction in activity level and enhancement of attentive behaviour (Rapoport *et al.*, 1978). The various animal models of hyperactivity mentioned above are disparate in their brain lesions but unified in that they all respond to amphetamines. Apparently, therefore, the action is not the reversal of the underlying cause of hyperactivity. This conclusion is reinforced by the predictive studies of which children will respond best in a group of children with disruptive behaviour. Taylor *et al.* (1987) found the main predictors to be high levels of hyperactivity, poor scores on psychometric measures of attention, and the absence of symptoms of anxiety; when these were allowed for, then neither neurodevelopmental delays nor family adversity were related to the outcome of treatment. One should therefore consider children as candidates for stimulant drug treatment on the basis of their symptomatology, not on the aetiological formulation.

The impact of stimulants on development is still unclear. Controlled trials typically last for a few weeks only, a few months at the very most. Treatment, however, is often maintained for years and certainly the risks from the disorder appear over a period of several years. The uncertainty about long-term effects is the main reason for controversy about the place of medication in therapy. There are two poles of the debate. The first points to the large effects on hyperactivity and the range of effects on related problems (see Chapter 51), and takes them as presumptive reasons for continuing therapy in the longer term unless and until sound empirical evidence proves it ineffective. The opposite pole is the view most commonly held in the UK — that there is no evidence for long-term benefit and therefore no reason for prescribing unless and until sound empirical evidence shows that the treatment works. Jacobvitz *et al.* (1990) recently reviewed the issue but could not resolve the problems.

The evidence usually cited comes from the follow-up of children who were or were not given medication during their childhood, or from those who had a short duration of therapy compared with those who persisted in therapy for longer. Some studies suggest a better outcome in those who take treatment for longer (Satterfield *et al.*, 1982), some a marginal improvement in self-esteem in those who have had medication in the past (Hechtman *et al.*, 1984), some no improvement at all (Charles & Schain, 1981). None of them really contribute, because of the difficulty of comparing groups that have been set up opportunistically rather than experimentally. Those who have stopped treatment early or never been given it may well be those with a better prognosis anyway, and therefore bias the results against showing a true effect of drug. Alternatively, those who do not persist with treatment may be those with the least supportive families and the least benefit from the treatment, thus exaggerating treatment effects.

The controlled studies so far allow only for limited conclusions. When children stop taking medication after a period of years then some but not all show a worsening of symptoms (Sleator *et al.*, 1974). It seems unlikely that pharmacological tolerance to the drug develops. Those who have been in treatment for a few months lose the benefit of medication soon after it is stopped (Brown *et al.*, 1986). Harmful effects of medication in encouraging external attributions and loss of personal responsibility have not been found, even though they have been looked for (Horn *et al.*, 1991).

Clinicians should keep strongly in mind the studies of course cited above. If hyperactivity is not a sufficient reason for a poor outcome, then antihyperactivity therapies of any kind may well not be sufficient to improve the eventual outcome. The suppression of hyperactivity is only a means to a goal, not an end in itself, so medication should be seen as an adjunct to other therapies. Drug treatment may well need to be prolonged over years. It should be monitored throughout this time with occasional periods off medication to assess the continuing effectiveness of suppressing the target symptom of hyperactivity. A long-term trial would be ethically acceptable. Until its results appear, clinical experience suggests that long-term medication does indeed have a place in the management of severely hyperactive individuals (see Chapter 51 for further consideration of the practicalities of therapy).

Diet

Dietary treatment should still be seen as experimental. The evidence (see above) supports the idea that parents who have seen a change in their child's behaviour due to particular foods are often right. The most helpful therapeutic position is often to be frank in explaining the scientific uncertainties and

supportive in assisting the efforts of parents. Useful support includes the monitoring of changes as the diet is altered, advice on the foods most likely to upset children and the ways of avoiding them, and identification of other ways of helping the child's development. It is still all too common for parents to find that diet is ineffective, and therefore to abandon therapeutic efforts on the grounds that hyperactivity cannot be the cause of the bad behaviour. If parents have not found any particular foods that upset the child, and still have not done so when their attention is directed to the possibility, then it is unlikely that the imposition of radical exclusion diets will produce any benefit.

Behavioural modification

Behaviour therapy is useful for many affected children (Yule, 1986). The goal should not be just the reduction of activity, but rather the promotion of attentive and controlled behaviour. Many of the systematic trials of behavioural techniques have been directed to the control of associated problems such as antisocial behaviour (see Chapter 50). Inattention and restlessness can also be the main targets. Operant conditioning of children's attention, parent and teacher training to assist them in applying operant techniques, and self-control cognitive therapies have all been used.

The value of cognitive therapy is questionable (Gittelman-Klein & Abikoff, 1989). Effects can certainly be produced upon laboratory tests measuring impulsiveness, but the difficulty has been to show any translation of these effects into the real world. Hyperactive children are often limited by not applying skills that they already have, so skills learning is not necessarily going to be a good treatment in itself. There may need to be much more attention to the role of concerned adults in maintaining children's application. Self-control is the ultimate goal, but it has eluded attempts to teach it quickly and directly.

Operant conditioning may be particularly relevant because of the emphasis on rapid and clear reinforcement of gradual approximations of desirable behaviours (see Chapter 50). If the delay characteristics of a task are important determinants of performance, as suggested above, then very swift feedback may help to avoid some of the impairment of attention deficit. It is tempting to suppose that the effects of drugs should be to render children more open to the helpful actions of psychological programmes. However, there is little empirical support for this. Horn *et al.* (1991) have described an additive effect of stimulants, parent training and self-control therapies. All had some effect, but they did not potentiate each other. This is in keeping with some other findings. For example, Wolraich *et al.* (1978) compared the effects of methylphenidate (in a comparison with placebo) and behaviour management in an experimental classroom (in a reversal design). Both had effects, but they did not interact. Indeed, there was a strong suggestion that the different treatments affected rather different aspects of behaviour. Methylphenidate reduced fidgeting and off-task behaviour; behaviour therapy improved output and behaviour in group settings. Gittelman-Klein *et al.* (1980) found that methylphenidate was a more potent treatment than a contingency management programme on behavioural problems, but there was still an effect of the behavioural approach.

The lessons seem to be that operant techniques are useful, whether or not children are on medication. They may be less powerful than medication — or perhaps it would be fairer to say that they are slower than medication in their effects, for of course the comparisons with medication have all been made upon the basis of short-term trials. They are also more generally applicable than stimulants: for instance, they are of value in children with severe intellectual retardation in whom medication is often of very limited value. The physical hazards of medication have to be set against the greater immediate power. Many clinicians will come to the conclusion that mild degrees of hyperactivity (including most of those meeting the DSM-IV criteria) are best managed in the first instance with behavioural approaches as the specific treatment to back up general advice. Medication will then be reserved for those who do not respond. More severe degrees of hyperactivity (including most of those meeting the ICD-10 criteria) can be expected to need medication — indeed, it may be needed from the start to counteract gloomy attitudes of helplessness. One important interaction between medication and psychological programmes is that some children may only be acceptable to schemes of psychological therapy if their wilder symptoms are treated physically.

Treatment of associated disorders

The short-term benefits of stimulants include a helpful action on several of the other psychological problems often seen in the hyperactive. Improvements have been reported for defiant antisocial behaviour (Taylor *et al.*, 1987; Barkley *et al.*, 1989; Hinshaw *et al.*, 1989), quality of interactions with other children (Whalen *et al.*, 1989), hostility and lack of warmth in parent–child interactions (Schachar *et al.*, 1987), and academic productivity (Douglas *et al.*, 1988). Probably all these benefits stem from the reduction of hyperactivity. Some at least of these associated problems may start to reappear again as treatment continues (Kupietz *et al.*, 1988).

The improvement in associated problems seldom amounts to 'normalization'; in all the above studies, medicated children were still worse off than normal children.

The principles of treating associated disorders are not different from those of treating the same problems when they are not combined with hyperactivity. However, the greater salience of any problem when it is present in a very active, noticeable and troublesome child may call for greater persistence and more supportive input from therapists. The general advice given may also need to be modified. An attitude of despair and therapeutic nihilism can easily develop around a child with multiple problems and lead to neglect of easily remediable problems that do not seem central. Parents may,

for example, dismiss advice on management techniques on the grounds that they have been tried before and do not work. This may well be the case, but if the central problems of hyperactive behaviour have been reduced by appropriate treatment or the passage of time then approaches such as contingency management may now be well worth another try. Counselling approaches, such as family therapy for the treatment of coexistent emotional problems, may also need some modification because of the presence of a medically recognized disorder. It brings both opportunities, e.g. for the relief of parental guilt by an external attribution of the cause, and difficulties, e.g. the reluctance of some families to entertain the notion that their own actions may have effects for good or for ill. It can be very helpful to use the initial detailed assessment as a way of emphasizing the effects that parental and teacher actions have already had and therefore the scope for work in the future.

Promotion of learning

This should always be explicitly considered. Classroom learning may require adjustment of curriculum to the needs of the child with a previously unrecognized disability, or a review of provision when special needs have already been recognized. Two approaches seem to follow from the basic research done so far. The first is the emphasis on short periods of one-to-one learning. The dependence of achievement in test performance on the details of the experimenter's involvement emphasizes how much can be done by a person who will be tactful and patient in maintaining the child's attention on a task and highlighting the relevant aspects of the task in hand. Such a person need not be a qualified teacher but will need training in the job.

The second classroom approach derives from the trials that have been done already. Teachers having to cope with children with hyperkinetic disorder should have experience and training in the techniques of behaviour modification. These recommendations can be met in both specialized units and mainstream classes with extra resources, and which is chosen will be a matter of local provision and parental choice. Educational systems all need to recognize attention deficit as a category of special need and think much more explicitly about how it should be met.

Social learning with other children normally proceeds much less formally. We do not yet know how to instil the abilities that lead to popularity and acceptance. Dodge's *et al.*'s (1987) models of social information processing illustrate how one might think about the peer problems of the hyperactive and how children might be taught better to recognize the nature of social problems, generate solutions and alter their reactions in the light of the reaction. However, it is still not clear that the main problem is in fact a lack of knowledge and skills; it might come much more directly from the aversive qualities of hyperactivity itself. Since the social skill programmes available now are not of proven value, one should not distort educational experience in order to make room for such groups. Peer groups supervised by adults may be a better way of allowing children to experiment in situations where the worst consequences of ineptness are mitigated and where adults can quickly point out to them their successes and their failures.

Promotion of emotional adjustment

The beginning of coping with a handicap is recognizing and understanding it. This should be a prime goal of clinicians' initial contacts with children and their families. Families will already have explanations in terms of easily reversible physical disease or else of personal failure and even ingratitude. The conveying of the professional's knowledge about the condition and the attitude of respecting the child's struggle against impairment can help all family members.

Alternative sources of self-esteem need searching out. Physical achievement is often as barred to affected children as academic success. Individual counselling can be useful here but should not be offered as a treatment for hyperactivity as it is unlikely to help. Negative attitudes from parents are common (see above) and can be matched by rejection from teachers. Both educational explanations and family-based counselling have a place in modifying overcritical reactions.

Relieving family distress

This should be a goal in itself as well as a means of helping children to adjust. When it fails, then family breakdown can result. Severe hyperkinesis remains one of the commonest reasons for which intellectually retarded children have to enter institutional care. Respite care and links with other families can help to reduce the rate of the worst outcomes. When alternative care has to be found, then professional foster care or small home-like settings should be able to contain even the most severely affected. Large institutions such as hospitals are to be avoided for they tend to make worse the isolation and the aimlessness to which severe hyperkinesis predisposes.

CONCLUSIONS

The last 10 years have seen advances in the clinical understanding of problems presenting with disturbances of activity and attention. The variety of subgroups is better recognized, the epidemiology is clearer and the cognitive impairments more understood. The persistence of symptoms of hyperactivity into adolescence and adult life has been much better recognized, and treatment programmes are accordingly taking on a more realistic time scale that can cater for continuing handicap and the recurrence of crises. The limitations as well as the value of stimulant medication have become clearer. The stage is set for a more fundamental understanding of biological mechanisms that predispose to hyperactivity and the psychosocial factors that maintain it. In the meanwhile, a range of treatments needs to be used. This calls for good cooperation between professionals from different disciplines, and training schemes should therefore ensure that the theory and practice of all relevant approaches are thoroughly taught.

REFERENCES

Achenbach T.M. & Edelbrock C.S. (1983) *Manual for the Child Behavior Checklist and Behavior Profile.* University of Vermont, Burlington.

Achenbach T.A., McConaughy S.H. & Howell C.T. (1987) Child/ adolescent behavioural and emotional problems: implications of cross-informant correlations for situational specificity. *Psychological Bulletin,* **101**, 213–232.

Alberts-Corush J., Firestone P. & Goodman J.T. (1986) Attention and impulsivity characteristics of the biological and adoptive parents of hyperactive and normal control children. *American Journal of Orthopsychiatry,* **56**, 413–423.

Aman M.E. & Singh N.N. (1982) Methylphenidate in severely retarded residents and the clinical significance of stereotypic behavior. *Applied Research in Mental Retardation,* **3**, 345–358.

American Psychiatric Association (1980) *Diagnostic and Statistical Manual of Mental Disorders,* (3rd edn). American Psychiatric Association, Washington, DC.

American Psychiatric Association (1987) *Diagnostic and Statistical Manual of Mental Disorders,* 3rd revised edn. American Psychiatric Association, Washington, DC.

Anderson J.C., McGee R. & Silva P.A. (1987) DSM-III disorders in preadolescent children. Prevalence in a large sample from the general population. *Archives of General Psychiatry,* **44**, 69–76.

August G.J., Stewart M.A. & Holmes C.S. (1983) A four-year follow-up of hyperactive boys with and without conduct disorder. *British Journal of Psychiatry,* **143**, 192–198.

Barkley R.A. (1988) Child behavior rating scales and checklists. In: Rutter M., Tuma A.H. & Lunn I.S. (eds) *Assessment and Diagnosis in Child Psychopathology,* pp. 113–155. Guilford Press, New York.

Barkley R.A., McMurray M.B., Edelbrock C.S. & Robbins K. (1989) The response of aggressive and nonaggressive ADHD children to two doses of methylphenidate. *Journal of the American Academy of Child and Adolescent Psychiatry,* **28**, 873–881.

Barkley R.A., Fischer M., Edelbrock C.S. & Smallish L. (1990) The adolescent outcome of hyperactive children diagnosed by research criteria: I. An 8-year prospective follow-up study. *Journal of the American Academy of Child and Adolescent Psychiatry,* **29**, 546–557.

Battle E.S. & Lacey B. (1972) A context for hyperactivity in children over time. *Child Development,* **43**, 757–773.

Bell R.Q., Weller G.M. & Waldrop M.F. (1971) Newborn and preschooler: organisation of behavior and relations between periods. *Monographs of the Society for Research in Child Development,* **36**, 1–145.

Berry C.A., Shaywitz S.E. & Shaywitz B.A. (1985) Girls with attention deficit disorder: a silent minority? A report on behavioral and cognitive characteristics. *Pediatrics,* **76**, 801–809.

Biederman J., Munir K., Knee D., Habelow W., Armentano M., Autor S., Hodge S.K. & Waternaux C. (1986) A family study of patients with attention deficit disorder and normal controls. *Journal of Psychiatric Research,* **20**, 263–274.

Biederman J., Munir K. & Knee D. (1987) Conduct and oppositional disorder in clinically referred children with attention deficit disorder: a controlled family study. *Journal of the American Academy of Child and Adolescent Psychiatry,* **26**, 724–727.

Bohman M., Cloninger C.R., Sigvardsson S. & von Knorring A.-L. (1982) Predisposition of petty criminality in Swedish adoptees: 1. Genetic and environmental heterogeneity. *Archives of General Psychiatry,* **29**, 1233–1241.

Bosco J.J. & Robin S.S. (1980) Hyperkinesis: prevalence and treatment. In: Whalen C.K. & Henker B. (eds) *Hyperactive Children: The Social Ecology of Identification and Treatment*, pp. 173–190. Academic Press, New York.

Bourneville E. (1897) *Le Traitement Medico-pedagogique des Différentes Formes de l'Idiocie*. Alcan, Paris.

Bowden C.L., Deutsch C.K. & Swanson J.M. (1988) Plasma dopamine-B-hydroxylase and platelet monoamine oxidase in attention deficit disorder and conduct disorder. *Journal of the American Academy of Child and Adolescent Psychiatry*, **27**, 171–174.

Boyle M.H., Offord D.R., Hofmann H.G., Catlin G.P., Byles J.A., Cadman D.T., Crawford J.W., Links P.S., Rae-Grant N.I. & Szatmari P. (1987) Ontario Child Health Study: I. Methodology; II. Six-month prevalence of disorder and rates of service utilisation. *Archives of General Psychiatry*, **44**, 826–836.

Bradley C. (1937) The behavior of children receiving benzedrine. *American Journal of Psychiatry*, **94**, 557–585.

Brandon S. (1971) Overactivity in childhood. *Journal of Psychosomatic Research*, **15**, 411–415.

Brown R.T., Borden K.A., Wynne M.E., Schleser R. & Clingerman S.R. (1986) Methylphenidate and cognitive therapy with ADD children: a methodological reconsideration. *Journal of Abnormal Child Psychology*, **14**, 481–497.

Buss A.H. & Plomin R. (1975) *A Temperament Theory of Personality Development*. Wiley, New York.

Campbell S.B. (1987) Parent-referred problem three-year-olds: developmental changes in symptoms. *Journal of Child Psychology and Psychiatry*, **28**, 835–845.

Campbell E.S. & Redfering D.L. (1979) Relationships among environmental and demographic variables and teacher-rated hyperactivity. *Journal of Abnormal Child Psychology*, **1**, 77–81.

Cantwell D. (1975) Genetic studies of hyperactive children: psychiatric illness in biologic and adopting parents. In: Fieve R., Rosenthal D. & Brill H. (eds) *Genetic Research in Psychiatry*, pp. 273–280. Johns Hopkins University Press, Baltimore.

Carter C.M., Urbanowicz M., Hemsley R., Mantilla L., Strobel S., Graham P.J. & Taylor E. (1993) Effects of a few-food diet in attention deficit disorder. *Archives of Disease in Childhood*, **69**, 564–568.

Ceci S.J. & Tishman J. (1984) Hyperactivity and incidental memory: evidence for attentional diffusion. *Child Development*, **55**, 2192–2203.

Charles L. & Schain R. (1981) A four-year follow-up study of the effects of methylphenidate on the behavior and academic achievement of hyperactive children. *Journal of Abnormal Child Psychology*, **9**, 495–505.

Conners C.K. (1969) A teacher rating scale for use in drug studies with children. *American Journal of Psychiatry*, **126**, 884–888.

Conners C.K. (1973) Rating scales for use in drug studies with children. *Psychopharmacology Bulletin*: Special issue on Pharmacotherapy of Children.

Conners C.K. (1975) Minimal brain dysfunction and psychopathology in children. In: Davids A. (ed) *Child Personality and Psychopathology: Current Topics*, vol. 2, pp. 137–169. Wiley, New York.

Cunningham L., Cadoret R., Loftus R. & Edwards J.E. (1975) Studies of adoptees from psychiatrically disturbed biological parents. *British Journal of Psychiatry*, **126**, 534–539.

Delamater A.M. & Lahey B.B. (1983) Physiological correlates of conduct problems and anxiety in hyperactive and learning-disabled children. *Journal of Abnormal Child Psychology*, **11**, 85–100.

Dienske H., de Jonge G. & Sanders-Woudstra J.A.R. (1985) Quantitative criteria for attention and activity in child psychiatric patients. *Journal of Child Psychology and Psychiatry*, **26**, 895–916.

Dodge K.A., Pettit G.S. & Braun M.M. (1987) Social competence in children. *Monographs of the Society for Research in Child Development*, **51**, no. 2.

Douglas V.I. (1988) Cognitive deficits in children with attention deficit disorder with hyperactivity. In: Bloomingdale L.M. & Sergeant J. (eds) *Attention Deficit Disorder — Criteria, Cognition, Intervention*, pp. 65–81. Pergamon, New York.

Douglas V.I. & Peters K.G. (1979) Toward a clearer definition of the attentional deficit of hyperactive children. In: Hale E.A. & Lewis M. (eds) *Attention and the Development of Cognitive Skills*, pp. 173–247. Plenum, New York.

Douglas V.I., Barr R.G., Amin K, O'Neill M.E. & Britton B.G. (1988) Dosage effects and individual responsivity to methylphenidate in attention deficit disorder. *Journal of Child Psychology and Psychiatry*, **29**, 453–475.

Egger J., Carter C.M., Graham P.J., Gumley D. & Soothill J.F. (1985) Controlled trial of oligoantigenic treatment in the hyperkinetic syndrome. *Lancet*, **i**, 540–545.

Farrington D.P., Loeber R. & van Kammen W.B. (1990) Long-term criminal outcomes of hyperactivity-impulsivity-attention deficit and conduct problems in childhood. In: Robins L.N. & Rutter M. (eds) *Straight and Devious Pathways from Childhood to Adulthood*, pp. 62–81. Cambridge University Press, Cambridge.

Feingold B.F. (1975) Hyperkinesis and learning disabilities linked to artificial food flavors and colors. *American Journal of Nursing*, **75**, 797–803.

Ferguson H.B. & Rapoport J.L. (1983) Nosological issues and biological validation. In: Rutter M. (ed.) *Developmental Neuropsychiatry*, pp. 369–384. Guilford Press, New York.

Fergusson D.M., Horwood L.J. & Lloyd M. (1991) Confirmatory factor models of attention deficit and conduct disorder. *Journal of Child Psychology and Psychiatry*, **32**, 257–274.

Firestone P. & Martin J.E. (1979) An analysis of the hyperactive syndrome: a comparison of hyperactive, behavior problem, asthmatic and normal children. *Journal of Abnormal Child Psychology*, **7**, 261–273.

Fuhrman M.J. & Kendall P.C. (1986) Cognitive tempo and behavioral adjustment in children. *Cognitive Therapy and Research*, **10**, 45–50.

Gillberg C., Carlstrom G. & Rasmussen P. (1983) Hyperkinetic disorders in children with perceptual, motor and attentional deficits. *Journal of Child Psychology and Psychiatry*, **24**, 233–246.

Gittelman-Klein R. & Abikoff H. (1989) The role of psychostimulants and psychosocial treatments in hyperkinesis. In: Sagvolden T. & Archer T. (eds) *Attention Deficit Disorder. Clinical and Basic Research*, pp. 167–180. Lawrence Erlbaum, Hillsdale, NJ.

Gittelman-Klein R., Abikoff H., Pollack E., Klein D.F., Katz S. & Mattes J. (1980) A controlled trial of behavior modification and methylphenidate in hyperactive children. In: Whalen C.K. & Henker B. (eds) *Hyperactive Children: The Social Ecology of Identification and Treatment*, pp. 221–246. Academic Press, New York.

Gittelman R., Mannuzza S., Shenker R. & Bonagura N. (1985) Hyperactive boys almost grown up. I. Psychiatric status. *Archives of General Psychiatry*, **42**, 937–947.

Glow R.A. (1981) Cross-validity and normative data on the Conners' Parent and Teacher Rating Scales. In: Gadow K.D. & Loney J. (eds) *The Psychosocial Aspects of Drug Treatment for Hyperactivity*, pp. 107–150. Westview Press, Boulder, CO.

Goodman R. & Stevenson J. (1989) A twin study of hyperactivity: I. An examination of hyperactivity scores and categories derived from Rutter Teacher and Parent Questionnaires. II. The aetiological role of genes, family relationships, and perinatal adversity. *Journal of Child Psychology and Psychiatry*, **30**, 671–710.

Goyette C.H., Conners C.K. & Ulrich R.F. (1978) Normative data on revised Conners' parent and teacher rating scales. *Journal of Abnormal Child Psychology*, **6**, 221–236.

Hechtman L., Weiss G. & Perlman T. (1984) Young adult outcome of hyperactive children who received long-term stimulant treatment.

Journal of the American Academy of Child Psychiatry, **23**, 261–269.

Hinshaw S.P. (1987) On the distinction between attentional deficits/hyperactivity and conduct problems/aggression in child psychopathology. *Psychological Bulletin*, **101**, 443–463.

Hinshaw S.P., Henker B., Whalen C.K., Ernhardt D. & Dunnington R.E. Jr (1989) Aggressive, prosocial, and nonsocial behavior in hyperactive boys: dose effects of methylphenidate in naturalistic settings. *Journal of Consulting and Clinical Psychology*, **57**, 636–643.

Holborow P.L., Berry P. & Elkins J. (1984). Prevalence of hyperkinesis: a comparison of three rating scales. *Journal of Learning Disabilities*, **17**, 411–417.

Horn W.F., Ialongo N.S., Pascoe J.M., Greenberg G., Packard T., Lopez M., Wagner A. & Puttler L. (1991) Additive effects of psychostimulants, parent training, and self-control therapy with ADHD children. *Journal of the American Academy of Child and Adolescent Psychiatry*, **30**, 233–240.

Hoy E., Weiss G., Minde K. & Cohen N. (1978) The hyperactive child at adolescence: cognitive, emotional, and social functioning. *Journal of Abnormal Child Psychology*, **6**, 311–324.

Ingram T.T.S. (1956) A characteristic form of overactive behaviour in brain damaged children. *Journal of Mental Science*, **102**, 550–558.

Ireland W.H. (1877) *On Idiocy and Imbecility*. Churchill, London.

Jacobsen C.F. (1935) Functions of the frontal association area in primates. *Archives of Neurology and Psychiatry*, **33**, 558–569.

Jacobvitz D., Sroufe L.A., Stewart M. & Leffert N. (1990) Treatment of attentional and hyperactivity problems in children with sympathomimetic drugs: a comprehensive review. *Journal of the American Academy of Child and Adolescent Psychiatry*, **29**, 677–688.

James A. & Taylor E. (1990) Sex differences in the hyperkinetic syndrome of childhood. *Journal of Child Psychology and Psychiatry*, **31**, 437–446.

Jenkins R.L. & Stable G. (1971) Special characteristics of retarded children rated as severely hyperactive. *Child Psychiatry and Human Development*, **2**, 26–31.

Kagan J., Rosman B.L., Day D., Albert J. & Philips W. (1964) Information processing in the child: significance of analytic and reflective attitudes. *Psychological Monographs*, **78**, (I, No. 578).

Kahn E. & Cohen L.H. (1934) Organic drivenness: a brain-stem syndrome and an experience with case reports. *New England Journal of Medicine*, **210**, 748–756.

Kaplan B.J., McNicol J., Conte R.A. & Moghadam H.K. (1989) Dietary replacement in preschool-aged hyperactive boys. *Pediatrics*, **83**, 7–17.

Kashani J., Chapel J.L., Ellis J. & Shekim W.O. (1979) Hyperactive girls. *Journal of Operational Psychiatry*, **10**, 146–148.

Koriath U., Gualtieri C.T., van Bourgondien M.E., Quade D. & Werry J.S. (1985) Construct validity of clinical diagnosis in pediatric psychiatry: relationship among measures. *Journal of the American Academy of Child Psychiatry*, **24**, 429–436.

Kupietz S.S., Winsberg B.G., Richardson E., Maitinsky S. & Mendell N. (1988) Effects of methylphenidate dosage in hyperactive reading-disabled children: I. Behavior and cognitive performance effects. *Journal of the American Academy of Child and Adolescent Psychiatry*, **27**, 70–77.

Lahey B.B., Schaughency E.A., Hynd G.W., Carlson C.L. & Nieves N. (1987) Attention deficit disorder with and without hyperactivity: comparison of behavioural characteristics of clinic-referred children. *Journal of the American Academy of Child and Adolescent Psychiatry*, **26**, 718–723.

Lambert N.M. (1988) Adolescent outcomes for hyperactive children: perspectives on general and specific patterns of childhood risk for adolescent, educational, social and mental health problems. *American Psychologist*, **43**, 786–799.

Lambert N.M., Sandoval J. & Sassone D. (1978) Prevalence of hyper-

activity in elementary school children as a function of social system definers. *American Journal of Orthopsychiatry*, **48**, 446–463.

Laufer M., Denhoff E. & Solomons G. (1957) Hyperkinetic impulse disorder in children's behavior problems. *Psychosomatic Medicine*, **19**, 38–49.

Levin P.M. (1938) Restlessness in children. *Archives of Neurology and Psychiatry*, **39**, 764–770.

Livingston R.L., Dykman R.A., Ackerman P.T. (1990) The frequency and significance of additional self-reported psychiatric diagnoses in children with attention deficit disorder. *Journal of Abnormal Child Psychology*, **18**, 465–478.

Loney J., Langhorne J. & Paternite C. (1978) An empirical basis for subgrouping the hyperkinetic/minimal brain dysfunction syndrome. *Journal of Abnormal Psychology*, **87**, 431–441.

Lou H.C., Henriksen L. & Bruhn P. (1984) Focal cerebral hypoperfusion in children with dysphasia and/or attention deficit disorder. *Archives of Neurology*, **41**, 825–829.

Lou H.C., Henriksen L., Bruhn P., Borner H. & Nielsen J.B. (1989) Striatal dysfunction in attention deficit and hyperkinetic disorder. *Archives of Neurology*, **46**, 48–52.

Luk S.-L. & Leung P.W.L. (1989) Conners' teacher's rating scale — a validity study in Hong Kong. *Journal of Child Psychology and Psychiatry*, **30**, 785–794.

Luk S.-L., Thorley G. & Taylor E. (1987) Gross overactivity: a study by direct observation. *Journal of Psychopathology and Behavioral Assessment*, **9**, 173–182.

McGee R. & Share D.L. (1988) Attention deficit disorder-hyperactivity and academic failure: which comes first and what should be treated? *Journal of the American Academy of Child and Adolescent Psychiatry*, **27**, 318–325.

McGee R., Williams S. & Silva P.A. (1984a) Behavioral and developmental characteristics of aggressive, hyperactive and aggressive-hyperactive boys. *Journal of the American Academy of Child Psychiatry*, **23**, 270–279.

McGee R., Williams S. & Silva P.A. (1984b) Background characteristics of aggressive, hyperactive and aggressive-hyperactive boys. *Journal of the American Academy of Child and Adolescent Psychiatry*, **23**, 280–284.

McGee R., Williams S. & Silva P.A. (1987) A comparison of girls and boys with teacher-identified problems of attention. *Journal of the American Academy of Child and Adolescent Psychiatry*, **26**, 711–717.

McIntyre C.W., Blackwell S.L. & Denton C.L. (1978) Effect of noise distractibility on the spans of apprehension of hyperactive boys. *Journal of Abnormal Child Psychology*, **6**, 483–492.

Magnusson D. (1988) Individual development in an interactional perspective. In: Magnusson D. (ed) *Paths Through Life*, vol. 1. Lawrence Erlbaum, Hillsdale, NJ.

Magnusson D. & Bergman L.R. (1990) A pattern approach to the study of pathways from childhood to adulthood. In: Robins L. & Rutter M. (eds) *Straight and Devious Pathways from Childhood to Adulthood*, pp. 101–115. Cambridge University Press, Cambridge.

Mannuzza S., Gittelman-Klein R., Bonagura N., Horowitz Konig P. & Shenker R. (1988) Hyperactive boys almost grown up. II. Status of subjects without a mental disorder. *Archives of General Psychiatry*, **45**, 13–18.

Matejccek Z., Dytrych Z. & Schuller V. (1985) Follow-up study of children born to women denied abortion. In: Porter R. & O'Connor M. (eds) *Abortion: Medical Progress and Social Implications*. Ciba Foundation Symposium 115. Pitman, London.

Mattes J.A. & Gittleman R. (1981) Effects of artificial food colorings in children with hyperactive symptoms. *Archives of General Psychiatry*, **38**, 714–718.

Maxwell A.E., Fenwick P.B.C., Fenton G.W. & Dallimore J. (1974) Reading ability and brain function: a simple statistical model. *Psycho-

logical Medicine, **4**, 274−280.

Menkes M., Rowe J. & Menkes J. (1967) A 25-year followup study on the hyperactive child with minimal brain dysfunction. *Pediatrics*, **39**, 393−399.

Milich R., Loney J. & Landau S. (1982) The independent dimensions of hyperactivity and aggression: a validation with playroom observation data. *Journal of Abnormal Psychology*, **91**, 183−198.

Needleman H.L., Gunnoe C., Leviton A., Reed R., Peresie H., Maher C. & Barratt P. (1979) Deficits in psychologic and classroom performance of children with elevated dentine lead levels. *New England Journal of Medicine*, **300**, 689−695.

Neligan G.A., Kolvin I., Scott D.McL. & Garside R.F. (1976) *Born Too Soon or Born Too Small*. Clinics in Developmental Medicine no. 61. S.I.M.P./Heinemann, London.

Nichols P. & Chen T.-C. (1981) *Minimal Brain Dysfunction: A Prospective Study*. Erlbaum, Hillsdale, NJ.

Ounsted C. (1955) The hyperkinetic syndrome in epileptic children. *Lancet*, **ii**, 303−311.

Porrino L.J., Rapoport J.L., Behar D., Sceery W., Ismond D. & Bunney W.E. (1983) A naturalistic assessment of the motor activity of hyperactive boys: I. Comparison with normal controls. *Archives of General Psychiatry*, **40**, 681−687.

Prendergast M., Taylor E., Rapoport J.L., Bartko J., Donnelly M., Zametkin A., Ahearn M.B., Dunn G. & Wieselberg H.M. (1988) The diagnosis of childhood hyperactivity: A U.S.−U.K. cross-national study of DSM-III and ICD-9. *Journal of Child Psychology and Psychiatry*, **29**, 289−300.

Prior M. & Sanson A. (1986) Attention deficit disorder with hyperactivity: a critique. *Journal of Child Psychology and Psychiatry*, **27**, 307−319.

Quay H.C. (1986) A critical analysis of DSM-III as a taxonomy of psychopathology in childhood and adolescence. In: Millon T. & Klerman G.L. (eds) *Contemporary Directions in Psychopathology Toward the DSM-IV*. Guilford, New York.

Rapoport J.L., Quinn P.O. & Lamprecht F. (1974) Minor physical anomalies and plasma dopamine-beta-hydroxylase activity in hyperactive boys. *American Journal of Psychiatry*, **131**, 386−389.

Rapoport J.L., Buchsbaum M., Weingartner H., Zahn T., Ludlow C. & Mikkelsen E. (1978) Dextroamphetamine: behavioral and cognitive effects in normal prepubertal boys. *Science*, **199**, 560−563.

Rapport M.D., Tucker S.B., DuPaul G.J., Merlo M. & Stoner G. (1986) Hyperactivity and frustration: the influence of control over and size of rewards in delaying gratification. *Journal of Abnormal Child Psychology*, **14**, 191−204.

Reeves J.C., Werry J.S., Elkind G.S. & Zametkin A. (1987) Attention deficit, conduct, oppositional, and anxiety disorders in children: II. Clinical characteristics. *Journal of the American Academy of Child and Adolescent Psychiatry*, **26**, 144−155.

Riddle K.D. & Rapoport J.L. (1976) A 2-year follow-up of 72 hyperactive boys. *Journal of Nervous and Mental Diseases*, **162**, 126−134.

Robbins T.W. & Sahakian B.J. (1979) 'Paradoxical' effects of psychomotor stimulant drugs in hyperactive children from the standpoint of behavioural pharmacology. *Neuropharmacology*, **18**, 931−950.

Rogeness G.A., Hernandez J.M., Macedo C.A. & Mitchell E.L. (1982) Biochemical differences in children with conduct disorder socialised and undersocialised. *American Journal of Psychiatry*, **139**, 307−311.

Ross D.M. & Ross S.A. (1982) *Hyperactivity: Current Issues, Research and Theory*. Wiley, New York.

Rosvold H.E., Mirsky A.F., Sarason I., Bransome E.D. Jr & Beck L.H. (1956) A continuous performance test of brain damage. *Journal of Consulting Psychology*, **20**, 343−350.

Routh D.K. (1980) Developmental and social aspects of hyperactivity. In: Whalen C.K. & Henker B. (eds) *Hyperactive Children: The Social Ecology of Identification and Treatment*, pp. 55−74. Academic Press, New York.

Roy P. (1983) Is continuity enough? Substitute care and socialisation. Paper presented at the 1983 Spring Scientific Meeting, Child and Adolescent Psychiatry Specialist Section, Royal College of Psychiatrists, London.

Rutter M. & Lockyer L. (1967) A five- to fifteen-year follow-up study of infantile psychosis. *British Journal of Psychiatry*, **113**, 1169−1182.

Rutter M., Graham P. & Yule W. (1970) *A Neuropsychiatric Study in Childhood*. Clinics in Developmental Medicine, nos. 35/36. S.I.M.P./Heinemann, London.

Safer D.J. (1973) A familial factor in minimal brain dysfunction. *Behavior Genetics*, **3**, 175−186.

Sandberg S. (1986) Overactivity: behaviour or syndrome? In: Taylor E. (ed) *The Overactive Child*, pp. 41−72. MacKeith Press/Blackwell, London.

Sandberg S., Rutter M. & Taylor E. (1978) Hyperkinetic disorder in psychiatric clinic attenders. *Developmental Medicine and Child Neurology*, **20**, 279−299.

Satterfield J., Hoppe C.M. & Schell A.M. (1982) A prospective study of delinquency in 100 adolescent boys with attention deficit disorder and 88 normal adolescent boys. *American Journal of Psychiatry*, **139**, 795−798.

Schachar R.J. (1986) Hyperkinetic syndrome: historical development of the concept. In: Taylor E.A. (ed) *The Overactive Child*. Clinics in Developmental Medicine no. 97. MacKeith Press/Blackwell, London.

Schachar R.J. (1991) Childhood hyperactivity. *Journal of Child Psychology and Psychiatry*, **32**, 155−191.

Schachar R. & Logan G.D. (1990a) Are hyperactive children deficient in attentional capacity? *Journal of Abnormal Child Psychology*, **18**, 493−513.

Schachar R. & Logan G.D. (1990b) Impulsivity and inhibitory control in development and psychopathology. *Developmental Psychology*, **26**, 1−11.

Schachar R. & Wachsmuth R. (1990) Hyperactivity and parental psychopathology. *Journal of Child Psychology and Psychiatry*, **31**, 381−392.

Schachar R.J., Rutter M. & Smith A. (1981) The characteristics of situationally and pervasively hyperactive children: implications for syndrome definition. *Journal of Child Psychology and Psychiatry*, **22**, 375−392.

Schachar R., Sandberg S. & Rutter M. (1986) Agreement between teachers' ratings and observations of hyperactivity, inattentiveness, and defiance. *Journal of Abnormal Child Psychology*, **14**, 331−345.

Schachar R., Taylor E., Wieselberg M., Thorley G. & Rutter M. (1987) Changes in family function and relationships in children who respond to methylphenidate. *Journal of the American Academy of Child and Adolescent Psychiatry*, **26**, 728−732.

Schmidt M.H., Esser G., Allehoff W., Geisel B., Laught M. & Woerner W. (1987) Evaluating the significance of minimal brain dysfunction − results of an epidemiological study. *Journal of Child Psychology and Psychiatry*, **28**, 803−821.

Sergeant J. (1988) From DSM-III attentional deficit disorder to functional defects. In: Bloomingdale L.M. & Sergeant J. (eds) *Attention Deficit Disorder: Criteria, Cognition, Intervention*. Pergamon Press, Oxford.

Sergeant J.A. & Scholten C.A. (1985) On data limitations in hyperactivity. *Journal of Child Psychology and Psychiatry*, **26**, 111−124.

Sergeant J. & Steinhausen H.-C. (1992) European perspectives on hyperkinetic disorder. *European Journal of Child Psychiatry*, **1**, 34−41.

Shaffer D. & Greenhill L. (1979) A critical note on the predictive validity of 'the hyperkinetic syndrome'. *Journal of Child Psychology and Psychiatry*, **20**, 61−72.

Shaffer D., O'Connor P.A., Shafer S.Q. & Prupis S. (1983) Neurological 'soft signs': their origins and significance for behavior. In: Rutter M. (ed) *Developmental Neuropsychiatry*, pp. 144–180. Guilford, New York.

Shaywitz B.A., Cohen D.J. & Bowers M.B. Jr (1977) CSF amine metabolites in children with minimal brain dysfunction (MBD): evidence for involvement of brain dopamine. *Journal of Pediatrics*, **90**, 67–71.

Shaywitz B.A., Hunt R.D., Jatlow P., Cohen D.J., Young J.G., Pierce R.N., Anderson E.M. & Shaywitz B.A. (1982) Psychopharmacology of attention deficit disorder. *Pediatrics*, **69**, 688–684.

Shekim W.O., Dekirmenjian H. & Chapel J.L. (1979) Urinary MHPG excretion in minimal brain dysfunction and its modification by d-amphetamine. *American Journal of Psychiatry*, **136**, 667–671.

Shekim W.O., Kashani J., Beck N., Cantwell D., Martin J., Rosenberg J. & Costello A. (1985) The prevalence of attention deficit disorders in a rural midwestern community sample of nine-year-old children. *Journal of the American Academy of Child Psychiatry*, **24**, 765–770.

Shen Y. & Wang Y. (1984) Urinary 3-methoxy-4-hydroxphenyl-glycol sulfate excretion in seventy-three school children with minimal brain dysfunction syndrome. *Biological Psychiatry*, **19**, 861–877.

Shen Y.-C., Wong Y.-F. & Yang X.-L. (1985) An epidemiological investigation of minimal brain dysfunction in six elementary schools in Beijing. *Journal of Child Psychology and Psychiatry*, **26**, 777–788.

Shetty T. & Chase T.N. (1976) Central monoamines and hyperkinesis of childhood. *Neurology*, **26**, 1000–1002.

Sleator E., Neumann H. & Sprague R. (1974) Hyperactive children: a continuous long term placebo controlled follow-up. *Journal of the American Medical Association*, **229**, 316–317.

Sonuga-Barke E.J.S. & Taylor E. (1992) The effect of delay on hyperactive and non-hyperactive children's response times: research note. *Journal of Child Psychology and Psychiatry*, **33**, 1091–1096.

Sonuga-Barke E.J.S., Taylor E. & Heptinstall E. (1992a) Hyperactivity and delay aversion: II. The effects of self versus externally imposed stimulus presentation periods on memory. *Journal of Child Psychology and Psychiatry*, **33**, 399–410.

Sonuga-Barke E.J.S., Taylor E., Sembi S. & Smith J. (1992b) Hyperactivity and delay aversion: I. The effect of delay on choice. *Journal of Child Psychology and Psychiatry*, **33**, 387–398.

Steinhausen H.-C. & Erdin (1991) A comparison of ICD-9 and ICD-10 diagnoses of child and adolescent psychiatric disorders. *Journal of Child Psychology and Psychiatry*, **32**, 909–920.

Stevenson J., Richman N. & Graham P. (1985) Behaviour problems and language abilities at three years and behavioural deviance at eight years. *Journal of Child Psychology and Psychiatry*, **26**, 215–230.

Stewart M.A., Pitts F.N., Craig A.G. & Dieruf W. (1966) The hyperactive child syndrome. *American Journal of Orthopsychiatry*, **36**, 861–867.

Stewart M.A., deBlois C.S. & Cummings C. (1980) Psychiatric disorder in the parents of hyperactive boys and those with conduct disorder. *Journal of Child Psychology and Psychiatry*, **21**, 283–292.

Still G.F. (1902) The Coulstonian lectures on some abnormal psychical conditions in children. *Lancet*, **i**, 1008–1012.

Strauss A. & Lehtinen L. (1947) *Psychopathology and Education of the Brain-Injured Child*. Grune & Stratton, New York.

Swanson J. & Kinsbourne M. (1976) Stimulant related state-dependent learning in hyperactive children. *Science*, **192**, 1354–1356.

Sykes D.H., Douglas V.I. & Morgenstern G. (1973) Sustained attention in hyperactive children. *Journal of Child Psychology and Psychiatry*, **14**, 213–220.

Szatmari P., Offord D.R. & Boyle M.H. (1989) Ontario Child Health Study: prevalence of attention deficit disorder with hyperactivity. *Journal of Child Psychology and Psychiatry*, **30**, 219–230.

Szatmari P., Offord D.R., Siegel L.S., Finlayson M.A.J. & Tuff L. (1990) The clinical significance of neurocognitive impairments among children with psychiatric disorders: diagnosis and situational specificity. *Journal of Child Psychology and Psychiatry*, **31**, 287–299.

Tallmadge J. & Barkley R.A. (1983) The interactions of hyperactive and normal boys with their fathers and mothers. *Journal of Abnormal Child Psychology*, **11**, 565–579.

Taylor E. (1986a) Attention deficit. In: Taylor E. (ed) *The Overactive Child*, pp. 73–106. MacKeith Press/Blackwell, Oxford.

Taylor E. (1986b) The causes and development of hyperactive behaviour. In: Taylor E. (ed) *The Overactive Child*, pp. 118–160. MacKeith Press/Blackwell, Oxford.

Taylor E. (1987) Cultural differences in hyperactivity. *Advances in Developmental and Behavioural Pediatrics*, **8**, 125–150.

Taylor E. (1991) Developmental neuropsychiatry. *Annual Research Review, Journal of Child Psychology and Psychiatry*, **32**, 3–47.

Taylor E. & Sandberg S. (1984) Hyperactive behavior in English schoolchildren: a questionnaire survey. *Journal of Abnormal Child Psychology*, **12**, 143–156.

Taylor E., Schachar R., Thorley G. & Wieselberg M. (1986) Conduct disorder and hyperactivity. *British Journal of Psychiatry*, **149**, 760–767.

Taylor E., Schachar R., Thorley G., Wieselberg M., Everitt B. & Rutter M. (1987) Which boys respond to stimulant medication? A controlled trial of methylphenidate in boys with disruptive behaviour. *Psychological Medicine*, **17**, 121–143.

Taylor E., Sandberg S., Thorley G. & Giles S. (1991) *The Epidemiology of Childhood Hyperactivity*, Maudsley monographs no. 33. Oxford University Press, Oxford.

Taylor E., Heptinstall E., Sonuga-Barke E., Sandberg S. & Bowyer J. (1992) Gender differences in the associations of hyperactivity and conduct disorder: *Final Report to The Wellcome Trust*. Available from MRC Child Psychiatry Unit, London.

Thomson G.O.B., Raab G.M., Hepburn W.S., Hunter R., Fulton M. & Laxon D.P.H. (1989) Blood-lead levels and children's behaviour — results from the Edinburgh Lead Study. *Journal of Child Psychology and Psychiatry*, **30**, 515–528.

Thorley G. (1984a) Hyperkinetic syndrome of childhood: clinical characteristics. *British Journal of Psychiatry*, **144**, 16–24.

Thorley G. (1984b) *Clinical Characteristics and Outcome of Hyperactive Children*. Ph.D. thesis, University of London.

Tizard B. & Hodges J. (1978) The effect of early institutional rearing on the development of eight year old children. *Journal of Child Psychology and Psychiatry*, **19**, 99–118.

Torgersen A.M. & Kringlen E. (1978) Genetic aspects of temperamental differences in infants: their cause as shown through twin studies. *Journal of the American Academy of Child Psychiatry*, **17**, 433–444.

Trites R.L., Tryphonas H. & Ferguson H.B. (1980) Diet treatment for hyperactive children with food allergies. In: Knights R.M. & Bakker D. (eds) *Treatment of Hyperactive and Learning Disordered Children*. University Park Press, Baltimore.

van der Meere J. & Sergeant J. (1988) Focused attention in pervasively hyperactive children. *Journal of Abnormal Child Psychology*, **16**, 627–639.

van der Meere J., van Baal M. & Sergeant J. (1989) The additive factor method: a differential diagnostic tool in hyperactivity and learning disability. *Journal of Abnormal Child Psychology*, **17**, 409–422.

Verberg G.M. (1986) *The Effects of Psychopharmacological Agents — Especially Stimulants — In Hyperactive Children. Including Some Remarks on the Use of the MBD Concept*. Kanters, Amsterdam.

Wallander J.L. (1988) The relationship between attention problems in childhood and antisocial behaviour eight years later. *Journal of Child Psychology and Psychiatry*, **29**, 53–61.

Weiss G. & Hechtman L.T. (1986) *Hyperactive Children Grown Up*.

Guilford Press, New York.

Weiss B., Williams J.H., Margen S., Abrams B., Caan B., Citron L., Cox C., McKibben J., Ogar D. & Schultz S. (1980) Behavioral response to artificial food colors. *Science*, **207**, 1487–1489.

Wender P., Epstein R.S., Kopin I.J. & Gordon E.K. (1971) Urinary monoamine metabolites in children with minimal brain dysfunction. *American Journal of Psychiatry*, **127**, 1411–1415.

Werry J.S., Reeves J.C. & Elkind G.S. (1987) Attention deficit, conduct, oppositional and anxiety disorders in children. I. A review of research on differentiating characteristics. *Journal of the American Academy of Child and Adolescent Psychiatry*, **26**, 133–143.

Whalen C.K., Henker B., Buhrmester D., Hinshaw S.P., Huber A. & Laski K. (1989). Does stimulant medication improve the peer status of hyperactive children? *Journal of Consulting and Clinical Psychology*, **57**, 545–549.

Wolraich M., Drummond T., Salomon M., O'Brien M. & Sivage C. (1978) Effects of methylphenidate alone and in combination with behavior modification procedures on the behavior and academic performance of hyperactive children. *Journal of Abnormal Child Psychology*, **6**, 149–161.

World Health Organization (1978) *International Classification of Diseases*, 9th edn. WHO, Geneva.

World Health Organization (1988) *I.C.D.-10: 1988 Draft of Chapter V. Categories F00-F99. Mental, Behavioural and Developmental Disorders.* WHO Division of Mental Health, Geneva.

Young E., Patel S., Stoneham M., Rona R. & Wilkinson J.D. (1987) The prevalence of reaction to food additives in a survey population. *Journal of the Royal College of Physicians of London*, **21**, 241–247.

Yule W. (1986) Behavioural treatments. In: Taylor E. (ed) *The Overactive Child. Clinics in Developmental Medicine no. 97*, pp. 219–235. MacKeith Press/Blackwell, Oxford.

Zametkin A.J., Karoum F., Rapoport J.L. *et al.* (1984) Phenylethylamine excretion in attention deficit disorder. *Journal of the American Academy of Child Psychiatry*, **23**, 310–314.

Zametkin A.J., Nordahl T.E., Gross M., King A.C., Semple W.E., Rumsey J., Hamburger S. & Cohen R.M. (1990) Cerebral glucose metabolism in adults with hyperactivity of childhood onset. *New England Journal of Medicine*, **323**, 1361–1366.

Chapter 18
Oppositional-Defiant and Conduct Disorders

Felton Earls

Two closely related syndromes of childhood and adolescence, oppositional-defiant disorder and conduct disorder, are reviewed in this chapter. A cardinal feature of these disorders, one that distinguishes them from most other psychiatric conditions, is the unremitting display of annoying, destructive, dangerous and even illegal behaviour. At the core of these disorders is an unresolved question about the nature of the child's insensitivity to others and what may appear to be a diminished capacity to learn from experience. As a result, in defining them greater emphasis is given to the impact of such behaviour on others than on the personal distress or discomfort of the individual child. Both juvenile justice and child mental health agencies have assumed the responsibility for helping parents to manage the rearing and guidance of these children. Furthermore, the concepts used to define and explain antisocial behaviour in these two service sectors are similar. In many cases the same child is termed a delinquent because of behaviour defined as illegal, and diagnosed as having a conduct disorder because the same behaviour is recognized as a symptom of a psychiatric syndrome.

HISTORICAL CONSIDERATIONS

Psychologists and psychiatrists have traditionally viewed the significance of antisocial behaviour in children from two perspectives. The first is derived from experience with adult patients thought to have a substantial defect in character formation. The social and moral deficiencies of these individuals typically result in a host of problems that are reflected in their interpersonal relationships, occupations and involvement in community life. The term psychopathic personality has been widely used over the past century to capture the clinical characteristics of this disorder. The second approach derives from the considerable experience gained in working with delinquent youths. A prevalent assumption has been that such children are reacting with antisocial behaviour to harsh circumstances experienced in their families and communities. This assumption has supported the belief that the childhood manifestations of 'psychopathic' behaviour should be more remediable than the adult form.

With the establishment of clinics attached to juvenile courts and the ascendancy of the mental hygiene movement, tension emerged between those who regarded delinquent youths as budding psychopaths and those who believed their behaviour to be reactive to adverse circumstances. This distinction became deeply rooted and richly chronicled as the discipline of child psychiatry was conceived towards the middle of this century (Levy, 1952a).

William Healy, an obstetrician and founder of the first juvenile court clinics in Chicago and Boston, described delinquents as having a 'psychic constitutional deficiency' (Healy & Bronner, 1926). He stressed the importance of finding both physical and mental defects in patients. This combination of deficiencies supported his belief that the behaviour of these youths was of a hereditary nature. The English psychologist Cyril Burt (1925), working at the same time as Healy, published a monumental treatise also recognizing the multiple biological and social insults contributing to delinquency, but stopped short of placing primary emphasis on hereditary causes.

As psychoanalytic ideas gained prominence, the concept of a poorly developed superego became a popular approach that attracted a great deal of speculation and some interesting therapeutic approaches (Aichorn, 1935; Johnson & Szurek, 1952), although there is little concrete evidence to support their success.

Cleckley's monograph, *The Mask of Sanity* (1941), provided detailed clinical descriptions and a comprehensive assessment of both the constitutional and the psychodynamic theories of the psychopath. After reviewing the characteristics of his own patients, many of whom were outwardly successful in some professional endeavour, he arrived at his own list of cardinal features: 1 an absent sense of responsibility; 2 refusal to accept blame for wrongdoing; 3 an absent sense of shame, humiliation, regret; 4 lying and cheating; 5 a failure to learn from experience; 6 a marked self-centredness that interferes with the capacity to love; 7 poverty of affect; 8 a lack of insight; 9 alcoholic indulgences; 10 sexual peculiarities; and 11 lack of goal-directedness resulting in a chaotic lifestyle.

In considering the causes of psychopathy, he admitted to being on soft ground. He believed, as did Healy and Burt, that both hereditary and environmental influences were important, but was careful to note that not all cases exhibited these behaviours at young ages, and that some psychopaths came from undeniably 'good stock'. However, he believed that the defect was deep-seated and used the term emotional dementia to describe the apparent absence of personal insight and responsibility in the lives of the patients he treated.

While Cleckley's work was having a significant impact on efforts to classify this disorder, clinicians working with children were endeavouring to understand the origins of behavioural syndromes that were conceivably linked to adult psychopathy. One of the most influential members of this group was John Bowlby. In one of his early studies of delinquent boys, Bowlby devised a system consisting of six types, the most common of which were the affectionless character, the hyperthymic character and the depressive character. As will be seen in a subsequent section, this subtyping is similar to the major classes of conduct disorder currently adopted in the ICD-10 (World Health Organization, 1992).

Bowlby (1944) was particularly interested in the affectionless character for reasons revealed in this quotation:

> It is my hope that the Affectionless Characters will be studied in great detail in the future, for I believe that they form the real hard core of the problem of recidivism. There can be no doubt that they are essentially delinquent characters, which is not true of the other characters discussed in this paper. The Depressed, Circular, Hyperthymic, and Schizoid all had counterparts among the controls. We can get a Depressive who does not steal as well as one who does, we can find a law-abiding Hyperthymic as well as his antisocial brother. I am doubtful, however, whether the law-abiding Affectionless Character exists [p. 39].

His intense interest in the developmental antecedents of this group, whose early histories are marked by 'prolonged separations from their mothers and foster-mothers', became the inspiration for his subsequent work on attachment (Bowlby, 1969; Ainsworth *et al.*, 1978).

Although the multiple determinants of delinquency and psychopathy acknowledged in the work of Burt and Cleckley have not led to the isolation of specific causal factors, the work of Robins (1966) provided a grasp of its natural history. By tracing the adult outcomes of children who were initially seen in a child guidance clinic, a convincing link was established between childhood conduct problems and antisocial personality disorder, a constellation of problems that were similar to the descriptions provided by Cleckley. This important study has been replicated in several different samples and the findings remain some of the most secure in modern psychiatry (Robins, 1978). Recognition of this fact has been of enormous value in underscoring both the seriousness and chronicity of antisocial disorders (Loeber & LeBlanc, 1990).

CLASSIFICATION

As the profession moved beyond court clinics into community and medical settings, as younger children were seen in these contexts, and as psychodynamic principles began to prosper in the minds of many psychiatrists, a more benign and developmental perspective began to replace notions of constitutional inferiority. It was in these contexts that new diagnostic concepts evolved. Firstly conduct disorder, and later oppositional disorder, were introduced into the lexicon of child psychiatrists as diagnostic categories that underscored the reality that not all antisocial children were delinquent. This restricted the use of the term delinquency to a legal definition. Conduct disorder, on the other hand, was reserved for the clinical condition in which a pattern of antisocial behaviour was present which may or may not have involved officially documented occasions of misconduct.

Although the first version of the DSM (American Psychiatric Association, 1952) included a category for adults termed sociopathic personality: antisocial reaction, no mention was made of a similar or premonitory form of this disorder in children. This absence occurred despite the successful efforts of Hewitt and Jenkins (1946) to distinguish unsocialized and socialized aggressiveness in children in clinical samples. With the publication of DSM-II (American Psychiatric Association, 1968), three subtypes of the conduct disorder were recognized: (1) unsocialized, aggressive reaction of childhood: (2) group delinquent reaction; and (3) runaway reaction.

Around the same time that DSM-II was published, the Group for the Advancement of Psychiatry (1966) also published a classification system. This system provided fairly elaborate descriptions of antisocial disorders, categorizing them as aberrations of personality. Oppositional disorder was considered a close approximation to the passive-aggressive personality. For conduct disorder the term tension-discharge disorder was advised and two subtypes described: impulse-ridden and neurotic personality disorder. Children with the first type were characterized by severe deprivation in early childhood and marked immaturity of psychological defences (denial and projection). The neurotic group was thought to be more mature, as evidenced by their capacity to show anxiety, guilt or remorse. Their antisocial behaviour reflected an underlying neurotic conflict which was believed to reveal itself symbolically in their actions. Use of the term tension-discharge reflected 'a conceptual recognition of the central tendency of these two groups. . .to discharge, rather than delay or inhibit, impulses unacceptable to the larger society'.

Since then, two major systems of classifying psychiatric disorders have been refined by independent teams: the DSM of the American Psychiatric Association and the ICD of the World Health Organization (1978, 1992). An increasing level of interaction between these two committees in recent years is facilitating a convergence of definitions. Both now include definitions of oppositional-defiant and conduct disorders. Table 18.1 provides a summary of the symptoms used to define these disorders in the two systems. What follows is a summary of the way in which these systems have been defined.

Oppositional disorders

DSM-III (American Psychiatric Association, 1980) offered the first definition of oppositional disorder as part of an official nomenclature. It isolated a cluster of six symptoms character-

Table 18.1 Classification of oppositional and conduct disorder

DSM-III	DSM-III-R	ICD-9	ICD-10 and DSM-IV
Oppositional disorder (at 2 least of 5) Violations of rules Tantrums Argumentativeness Stubbornness Provocative behaviour	*Oppositional-defiant disorder* (at least 5 of 9) Defiant Argues with adults Tantrums Annoying Blames others Touchy Angry/resentful Spiteful Uses obscene language		*Oppositional-defiant and conduct disorders* Tantrums Argues with adults Defiant Annoying Blames others Touchy Angry/resentful Spiteful/vindictive Lying Initiates fights Uses weapons
*Conduct disorder** *Socialized* (no more than 1 for undersocialized, 2 or more for socialized) One or more friends Extends self for no immediate advantage Feels guilt/remorse Avoids blaming others Shares concerns for welfare of others *Aggressive* (at least 1 of 2) Violence against property or persons Theft *Nonaggressive* (at least 1 of 4) Violation of rules Runaway Lying Stealing	*Conduct disorder†* (at least 3 of 13) Truant Lying Stealing Runaway Destructive Fire-starting Burglary Robbery Initiates fights Uses weapons Forces sex Cruel to animals Cruel to people	*Unsocialized conduct disorder* Defiant Disobedient Aggressive Destructive Tantrums Lying Quarrelsome Teasing Bullying Disturbed relationships	Stays out late Cruel to animals Cruel to people Destructive Fire-setting Stealing Truant Runaway Robbery/mugging Forces sex Bullying Burglary

* 4 types are recognized: Undersocialized-Aggressive; Undersocialized-Nonaggressive; Socialized-Aggressive; and Socialized-Nonaggressive.
† 3 subtypes are recognized: Group; Solitary; and Undifferentiated. The degree of the disorder is estimated as mild, moderate or severe based on the number of symptoms and/or their seriousness.

izing the resistant, uncooperative and defiant child. To meet diagnostic criteria, the child must manifest a minimum of three of these six symptoms. No age criterion was given. In the revision of this manual, DSM-III-R (American Psychiatric Association, 1987), the list of symptoms was expanded to 10. Three of the original symptoms remained and six new ones were added. The result was to define a disorder that included not only problems a parent might object to, but ones that would lead to peer unpopularity as well.

ICD-9 (WHO, 1978) did not include oppositional disorder among its categories, but ICD-10 has done so. In keeping with the original plan to make ICD-10 and DSM-IV identical, the same list of symptoms and diagnostic criteria for oppositional-defiant and conduct disorders were adopted. The basis for this decision was the inclination to view oppositional disorder as a milder and developmentally related form of conduct disorder. Recent data provide support for this notion (Schachar & Wachsmuth, 1990; Frick *et al.*, 1991a; Loeber *et al.*, 1991b). The list of 23 symptoms is shown in Table 18.1. The first eight represent the category of oppositional-defiant disorder, the diagnostic criterion requiring the presence of at least four of these eight. An issue not addressed in either system is the possibility that the behaviours represented by this category reflect temperamental characteristics rather than symptoms of a disorder (Earls, 1981). It is in this connection that Levy's important analysis (1952b) distinguishing normative and deviant forms of negativism is pertinent.

Conduct disorders

Rather substantial changes occurred between DSM-III and DSM-III-R in the definitions of conduct disorder. Out of a list of 17 possible symptoms, DSM-III divided conduct disorder into four types. Preserving the distinction made by Hewitt and Jenkins (1946), aggressive and nonaggressive forms were recognized, as were unsocialized and socialized. These characteristics are conceptualized as distinct axes permitting four combinations: (1) unsocialized-aggressive; (2) socialized-aggressive; (3) unsocialized-nonaggressive; and (4) socialized-nonaggressive. The diagnosis of aggressive or nonaggressive manifestations is made on the basis of the presence of at least one symptom in the appropriate cell, as long as it has existed for 6 months or longer. To be considered socialized, two of the five characteristics indicating good socialization must be present. As shown in Table 18.1, these qualities relate to the capacities for empathy, guilt, remorse and the demonstration of lasting and valued friendships. It is the relative absence of these qualities that earmark the unsocialized child.

DSM-III-R simplified the diagnosis by attempting to emphasize a core group of symptoms representing a single disorder. By doing so, the significance of the subtyping created in DSM-III was minimized. None the less, subcategorical distinctions were still made. The terms 'solitary' and 'group' appear to be quite consistent with the unsocialized-aggressive and socialized-aggressive varieties included in DSM-III. In addition, DSM-III-R allowed for an undifferentiated form of conduct disorder. The criteria for establishing the presence of the diagnosis in DSM-III-R were more stringent: three symptoms rather than one were required. The duration criterion of 6 months and the absence of an age of onset requirement remained unchanged.

In reviewing Table 18.1, changes in criterion symptoms between the two systems can be seen. Substance abuse was dropped (it had been a 'violation of rules') and several new symptoms appeared, among them cruelty to animals or people and weapons use. Each of these changes should raise the threshold for making the diagnosis. In fact, Lahey *et al.* (1990), applying different criteria to the data collected on the same clinical sample of children, found a pronounced reduction in the number of cases of conduct disorder defined when the DSM-III-R diagnostic criteria as opposed to DSM-III criteria were used. Just over half (56%) of the children defined as having a conduct disorder by DSM-III met criteria on DSM-III-R. The proportional decrease was somewhat less prominent for oppositional disorder.

Of equal importance in this study was the demonstration of enhanced validity of the DSM-III-R diagnosis. The greater probability of police contacts and school suspensions was predicted by the number of conduct disorder symptoms present. The strength of this relationship was enhanced by the higher threshold in DSM-III-R.

Although the manual continued to note the importance of age-appropriate socialization, operationalization of the socialized/unsocialized distinction that was included in DSM-III was also missing. Thus the behavioural manifestations of the disorder are emphasized over those aspects of character and moral development that appear to represent the precursors of psychopathy.

Both ICD-9 and ICD-10 include socialized and unsocialized types of conduct disorder, although the concept of socialized has been widened so that ICD-10 recognizes an individual as socialized if he or she is integrated into either a deviant or a nondeviant peer network. As shown in Table 18.1, several minor symptoms indicative of oppositional behaviour, such as teasing, disturbed relationships and quarrelsomeness, were deleted from the ICD-9. These were replaced in ICD-10 by a more severe cluster of symptoms that include cruelty to animals or people, sexual coercion, robbery, firesetting and running away. ICD-10 also requires that at least two of these symptoms be present and that they exist for a period of no less than 6 months. Similar to the shift in DSM, the changes produced between the two versions of ICD raise the threshold of clinical severity.

Both ICD-10 (World Health Organization 1992) and DSM-IV (American Psychiatric Association, in press) require the presence of at least three of 15 symptoms from the list shown in Table 18.1 (numbers 9–23). Subcategorization is made based on the presence of definitely poor peer relations. In addition, severity is graded as mild, moderate or severe and is based on the number and seriousness of symptoms present. A new feature of both systems is the recommendation that the age of onset be specified as part of the diagnosis. Childhood onset type is distinguished from adolescent onset type by the appearance of at least one conduct problem prior to the age of 10. Assuming the developmental link between conduct disorder and oppositional disorder, it stands to reason that some children will present with an admixture of features from both categories. The integration of a common list of symptoms which has become a feature of both DSM-IV and ICD-10 permits an improved description of children in a transitional state between the two disorders.

So far, conduct and oppositional disorders have been discussed as categorical entities with membership established on the basis of specific inclusion and exclusion criteria. This approach is necessary in clinical work since treatment decisions require it. Another approach to definition and classification in child psychiatry has been to assume that these disorders represent statistical departures from normal behaviour (see Chapter 1). If the categorical approach is fuelled by assumptions about the nature of a disorder, the statistical approach rests on a tradition which avoids, or at least minimizes, such assumptions.

Despite their conceptual differences, considerable overlap exists between them in practice (Edelbrock & Costello, 1988). The strategy used in the statistical approach is for an investigator to assemble an array of symptoms and problematic behaviours, each of which is graded in terms of severity. To standardize such instruments large samples of key informants are administered questionnaires. Mathematical methods are then used to determine how symptoms aggregate into recognizable patterns. Many instruments have been devised for this purpose over the years. Two of the most widely used in current research are the Child Behavior Checklist (CBCL); Achenbach et al., 1989), and the Revised Behavior Problem Checklist (RBPC; Quay, 1983). The two methods include nearly the same number of items (38 and 39), but the CBCL makes none of the distinctions (i.e. socialized, unsocialized, oppositional) discussed so far. The RBPC, on the other hand, lists two separate factors, conduct disorder and socialized aggression. The items composing these scales are shown in Table 18.2. The important distinction between the categorical and statistical approaches is that the statistical approach permits one to judge the degree to which an antisocial behaviour exists, while the categorical approach assigns children to membership in a diagnostic grouping.

PREVALENCE AND CORRELATES

One of the first investigations to estimate the prevalence of conduct disorder in the general population was the Isle of Wight study (Rutter et al., 1970). Given an overall rate of 4.2% among 10–11-year-olds, the rate in boys was four times higher than the rate in girls: 6.2% compared to 1.6%. Conduct disorder was found to be by far the most common disorder in males, accounting for about three-quarters of all disorders in this group. When similar methods were used in a relatively poor area of London, the rate of conduct disorder doubled (Rutter et al., 1975).

More recently, the Ontario Child Health Survey has provided a comprehensive picture of conduct disorder in the general population (Offord et al., 1987, 1991). In this study of children, covering the ages between 4 and 16 and sampled throughout the province of Ontario, a diagnostic method was produced that conformed to criteria established in DSM-III. For younger children (4–11), scales were used to rate both parent- and teacher-reported symptoms, while for adolescents (12–16), parent and self-report data were collected (teacher data were found to be unreliable). Care was taken to measure the accuracy of the scales prior to launching the project.

The prevalence of individual symptoms varied in a number of ways. As expected, the frequency of symptoms of lesser seriousness declined with age while those of a more serious nature increased with age. Predictably, males exceeded females in prevalence for most symptoms. For all 15 symptoms surveyed, adolescents reported more symptoms than did their parents and this was especially true for the more serious symptoms such as vandalism, threats to hurt someone and cruelty to animals. Among younger children, parents and teachers varied considerably in their reporting patterns.

The overall rate of conduct disorder, 5.5%, was similar to the rate reported 25 years earlier in the Isle of Wight study.

Table 18.2 Items composing antisocial scales in the Revised Behavior Problem Checklist (RBPC) and the Child Behavior Checklist (CBCL)

Revised Behavior Problem Checklist	Child Behavior Checklist
Scale I. Conduct disorder	*Aggressive*
Seeks attention; shows-off	Argues
Disruptive; annoys and bothers others	Defiant
Fights	Bragging
Has temper tantrums	Fidgets
Disobedient; difficult to control	Cruelty
Uncooperative in group situations	Demands attention
Negative; tends to do the opposite of what is requested	Destroys own things
	Destroys others' things
Impertinent; talks back	Disobedient at school
Irritable; hot-tempered; easily angered	Disturbs others
Argues; quarrels	Poor peer relations
Sulks and pouts	Lacks guilt
Persists and nags; can't take no for an answer	Jealous
	Feels persecuted
Tries to dominate others; bullies, threatens	Fights
Picks at other children as a way of getting attention; seems to want to relate but doesn't know how	Bad friends
	Impulsive
	Lying, cheating
Brags and boasts	Not liked
Teases others	Talks out of turn
Selfish; won't share; always takes the biggest pieces	Attacks people
	Disrupts class
Not liked by others; is a loner because of aggressive behavior	Screams
	Acts irresponsibly
Cannot stand to wait; wants everything right now	Shows off
	Explosive
Refuses to take directions; won't do as told	Easily frustrated
Blames others; denies own mistakes	Steals
Deliberately cruel to others	Stubborn
	Moody
Scale II. Socialized aggression	Sulks
Stays out late	Suspicious
Steals in company with others	Swearing
Belongs to a gang	Talks too much
Loyal to delinquent friends	Teases
Truant from school, usually in company with others	Temper tantrums
	Threatens
Has bad companions, ones who are always in some kind of trouble	Loud
Uses drugs in company with others	
Steals from people outside the home	
Freely admits disrespect for moral values and laws	
Is part of a group that rejects school activities such as team sports, clubs, projects to help others	
Cheats	
Seeks company of older, more experienced companions	
Will lie to protect his friends	
Uses alcohol in company with others	
Admires and seeks to associate with rougher peers	
Runs away; is truant from home	
Openly admires people who operate outside the law	

The male to female ratio was also similar: 8.2% for males and 2.8% for females; however, geographical area differences were not found. The urban rate was just slightly higher than the rural rate: 5.6% compared to 5.2%. There was an unexpected reversal in the relationship of area differences to age. For both sexes, younger children in urban areas had a higher rate, but rural adolescents had higher rates than urban adolescents. The investigators interpreted these findings as showing the importance of socioeconomic status. The effect of geographical area was diminished when the degree of poverty in the different contexts was taken into account.

The amount of agreement between any pair of informants was so slight as not to exceed that expected by chance alone. Thus, fewer than 10% of males had a pervasively defined disorder and not a single case was found in young females. The proportion of cases defined by both parents and adolescents increased slightly at the older age level, but it still left over 80% of males and 90% of females with a disorder defined by only one informant. An interesting and perhaps unanticipated result was the large number of cases of conduct disorder found among the younger children that were defined only by teachers (80%). Offord and colleagues (1991) suggested that this finding reflects the fact that conduct disorder is highly conditioned by school settings. This reasoning, however, may not extend to the findings with the older group, since self-reported symptoms cannot be regarded as suggesting situation specificity.

The findings of these two studies are in agreement with others that have examined oppositional and conduct problems in the general population (Earls, 1985; Costello, 1989). One of the most consistent findings is a sex ratio of about 4:1. On close examination, however, there is some evidence of a narrowing of this ratio in official reports of delinquency (Rutter & Giller, 1983). This should not be an unexpected development in view of changing patterns of female socialization.

The correlates of conduct disorder reported in the Ontario study are quite similar to those of other studies. The three most significant risk factors exerting independent effects on conduct disorder were family dysfunction (relative odds = 3.1), parental mental illness (relative odds = 2.2) and low income. Low income had its effect on children aged 4–11 (relative odds = 3.7), but not on adolescents. These factors resemble the six described by Rutter (1978) as general indicators of psychosocial adversity: (1) low socioeconomic status; (2) criminality of the father; (3) overcrowding; (4) maternal neurosis; (5) chronic marital discord; and (6) institutional care. These indicators were incorporated in a longitudinal study of child psychiatric disorder in Mannheim (Blantz *et al.*, 1991). The findings of this project confirm that, for boys, as the number of these adverse conditions accumulate, the risk of conduct disorders increases proportionately.

Throughout the age range covered, those with conduct disorder were more likely to have impairments as reflected in school underachievement and interpersonal problems. At the younger age level, 62% were thought to be in need of inter-vention compared to 8% without conduct disorder; in adolescence, similar figures were 74 and 44%. These findings provide a source of external validity for the method of selecting children with conduct disorder. This result becomes all the more important given the marginal indices of agreement between the method and the independent evaluations of psychiatrists.

NATURAL HISTORY: PATTERNS OF ESCALATION AND DECLINE

The classic study by Robins (1966) on the natural history of conduct disorder showed that nearly half the children with this diagnosis go on to develop antisocial personality disorder as adults. Broadly defined, this finding is consistent with many other studies demonstrating the stability of aggressive behaviour (Olweus, 1979; Loeber, 1982; Rutter & Giller, 1983). While evidence for the continuity of symptoms in adolescence is of principal concern, it is noteworthy that in the majority of studies less than half the children defined as aggressive, antisocial or delinquent at one age, as in the Robins study, are found to warrant such diagnoses at follow-up (Loeber, 1990). Thus many children appear to escape such a negative outcome. However, the Robins study (1966) indicated that many children who did not warrant a diagnosis of antisocial personality disorder showed a wide range of other psychiatric disturbances, from alcoholism to schizophrenia. More recently, Zoccolillo *et al.* (1992), in a longitudinal study of adults who had spent much of their childhoods in foster care, demonstrated that the great majority experienced a variety of social problems as adults. By enlarging the range of outcomes beyond the criteria established for personality disorder to include multiple areas of adult social dysfunction, greater coherence between the childhood and adult manifestations of antisocial behaviour was found. Thus it is important to consider a range of psychiatric and nonpsychiatric problems in studying the transition of conduct problems from adolescence to adulthood.

A study by Robins and Price (1991) gives evidence that conduct disorder may predict adult substance abuse about as efficiently as it predicts adult antisocial behaviour. Although the results were based on retrospective reports of adults and should be regarded somewhat cautiously, they showed that the relationship between conduct disorder and substance abuse is mediated by its relationship to adult antisocial behaviour. As the number of childhood symptoms increased from two to five, the probability of one or both of these disorders increased proportionately. However, because of known sex differences in the prevalence of these disorders, the possibility exists that for each sex there are distinctive pathways to them. In fact, for females, conduct disorder predicted depression and anxiety disorders more strongly than it did antisocial behaviour and substance abuse. This alternative pathway, possibly more important in females than in males, suggests that conduct disorder may be more strongly linked to depression than substance abuse since the presence of both conduct disorder and depression may then result in substance abuse through efforts at self-medication.

Two studies demonstrate the seriousness of conduct disorder in terms of premature death. Yeager and Lewis (1990) in a 7-year follow-up study of 118 incarcerated delinquents found that the rate of death for this group was 58 times the expected rate. Of the 7 individuals who died, 6 male and 1 female, all were from violent causes. The investigators were not able to find factors that distinguished those who died from the larger group of offenders. Rydelius (1988), following a larger sample in Sweden ($n = 1056$; 832 males and 224 females) over a longer interval, found that 13% of males and 10% of females died. These rates were also severalfold higher than expected. Nearly 90% of males and 80% of females died of 'sudden, violent causes' between the ages of 28 and 42. These studies only capture the most dramatic form of injury. It is probable that many more are seriously, but nonfatally, injured and suffer other causes of ill health including sexually transmitted diseases and acquired immunodeficiency syndrome (Stiffman & Earls, 1990).

A number of approaches have been taken to describe the progression of symptoms associated with conduct disorder and delinquency. Loeber and LeBlanc (1990) proposed that the overall pattern be divided into periods of activation, aggravation and desistance. This notion conforms to the well-established age−crime curve. However, a single curve made up of cross-sectional data does not disclose individual patterns of offending. For example, a study of a Philadelphia cohort showed that a small proportion of all boys who had contact with juvenile authorities by age 18 accounted for a disproportionately high number of all arrests (Wolfgang *et al.*, 1972). Thirty-five per cent of boys reported at least one juvenile contact, but only about one-fifth were chronic offenders (defined as four or more arrests). The majority of boys had just one or two contacts. The presumption is that the chronic offenders represent a distinct subgroup.

The age of onset is the most consistently examined characteristic marking the activation of a pattern of antisocial behaviour. Many studies have found early age of onset to be related to more serious and persistent antisocial behaviour (Glueck & Glueck, 1940; Robins, 1966; Loeber & Dishion, 1983). Tolan (1987), separating delinquent youths into early- (under 12) and later-onset groups, found that the earlier-onset group reported $3\frac{1}{2}$ times the rate of self-reported delinquency as the later-onset group. Other studies tracing onset back as far as the preschool period have also found a higher rate of antisocial behaviour (Loeber *et al.*, 1990a). These findings and others indicate that early activation is related to a more aggravated course than later onset (Farrington *et al.*, 1990).

The 'stepping stone' hypothesis is helpful in examining how symptoms are linked sequentially (Farrington, 1990). This hypothesis suggests that minor antisocial behaviours are followed by more serious ones. Thus one might expect to see a sequence beginning with larceny or shoplifting and proceeding to petty theft, burglary, motor vehicle theft, robbery, fraud

and assault. Since each step represents a heightened risk for punishment, it should be expected that fewer and fewer individuals will remain on the ladder. Farrington (1991) provided data from his London study to show that oppositional behaviour in preadolescents predicted convictions in early adolescence. Once a youth had been convicted, this fact became the best predictor for subsequent convictions. However, the contextual factors linked to persistence appeared to change with age. At the earliest ages, inadequate parental discipline and school failure combined with economic adversity and family criminality as predictors of juvenile convictions. These latter two factors remained predictors of adult convictions, but they were considerably strengthened by the addition of low occupational status and poor marital quality. The study emphasized factors that predict progression, but not those features associated with desistance.

A sample of normal and delinquent adolescents studied by LeBlanc *et al.* (1991) indicated that both groups showed different patterns of stability, escalation and decline. Twenty-nine per cent of the normal group showed stable delinquent activity on a self-report questionnaire compared to 48% of the delinquents. But 32% of the normals and 24% of the delinquents progressed to a more serious level, whereas 31% of normal subjects and 20% of delinquents remitted to lesser infractions. Small groups in both samples reported no delinquent acts at both points in time.

RISK MECHANISMS

This section considers some of the ways in which the risk factors described in the previous section may produce oppositional and conduct disorders. The discussion reviews what is known about cognitive, emotional and biological factors that operate early in life and which could plausibly assume an aetiological role.

Many of the correlates listed in the previous section are concentrated on family dysfunction and parental deviance, but as suggested in both the epidemiological and clinical studies mentioned above, this is not the complete picture. For it is specifically in the presence of low socioeconomic status that these characteristics appear to gain much of their strength as predictors. Thus, one mechanism to explore is the nature of the contextual influences associated with low socioeconomic status that relate to the particular virulence of these risk factors.

Community factors

Sociological studies of geographic differences have shown that urban areas typically experience the highest rates of delinquency. The fact that this was not shown in the Ontario Child Health Study suggests a possible subtle distinction between delinquency and conduct disorder. It may be that a higher tolerance exists for antisocial behaviour in rural areas as opposed to the more densely populated city areas and this results in a lower probability for arrest in the former. Yet within cities characterized by high crime there is typically marked variation by neighbourhood, with rates varying by as much as a factor of five (Rutter & Giller, 1983). Even in high-delinquency neighbourhoods there is often considerable variation by block areas (Shaw & MacKay, 1942; Sampson, 1985). High-delinquency neighbourhoods are depicted as areas which are socially fragmented, overcrowded and inhabited by poor and disenfranchised families. They are places that harbour a wide range of social problems including high rates of adult crime, substance use, infant mortality, low birth weight and child maltreatment. What is less well-understood is the relationship between these environmental conditions and family functioning (Sampson, 1991). Not all families residing in such places suffer these pathologies and most children are not delinquent. The strategies used by families to cope successfully with such adversity are an understudied area. By the same token, the way these social insults impinge on families that do exhibit such pathologies is not so evident. Thus the question of how neighbourhood improvements would lead to reduced rates of antisocial behaviour is far from clear. Yet the magnitude of differences in rates of delinquency within the same urban area can be so great as to demand attention (Rutter, 1978).

Family environment

By whatever means these ecological influences exert their effect, we know from follow-up studies that the impact of socioeconomic disadvantage and parental dysfunction has long-lasting negative effects (West & Farrington, 1977; Farrington, 1978). Unlike studies that first measure antisocial behaviour in school-age children or adolescents, the Newcastle Thousand Family Study established this pattern of combined risk for delinquency in early childhood. In this study the family environment and parental characteristics were assessed in the first 5 years of life and outcomes measured repeatedly over a 30-year period (Kolvin *et al.*, 1988). Combining both juvenile and adult offences, the overall rate of officially recorded criminality was 31% for males and 6% for females. Based on the family's socioeconomic status, assessed when the children were age 5, the distribution of male offenders was especially dramatic. Only 5% came from social classes I and II, whereas 26% were from social class III and 42% from social classes IV and V. Beyond the effects of social stratification, however, were profound effects of parental neglect (termed poor domestic and physical care of the child) and poor quality of parenting. Although these were the most pressing risk conditions, all the environmental factors examined showed a significant relationship to delinquency and crime. These conditions included large sibships, marital disruption and parental mental illness. As the number of these factors accumulated in a family, the likelihood that a child would begin a career of delinquency and crime early and persist for many years increased proportionately. For males, the rate of offending increased fourfold, from 17% for individuals with none of the risk factors to 66% for individuals with three or more of them.

Overall, these results generally agree with those of McCord (1979) and Stattin and Klackenberg-Larsson (1990). All three studies provide evidence supporting the enduring effects of adverse maternal characteristics. The findings of these long-term studies are consistent with those found when studying conduct disorder in children and adolescents. The fact that official records rather than self-reports were used implies that the cases selected as delinquent were serious.

Studies by several authors (Carmen *et al.*, 1987; Lane & Davis, 1987; Widom, 1989) that went beyond home environment characteristics to explore the effects of overt harm to the child demonstrated a strong association between such physical abuse and neglect in childhood, and delinquency and adult crime in later years. It was shown that about a quarter of the abused or neglected children became delinquent — a rate double that in nonabused controls. However, while the significance of abuse as a risk factor was considerable, the majority of children with such experiences did not show such outcomes. These dual findings produce something of a paradox in deciding where to focus a research strategy. It is of obvious importance to treatment and prevention research to understand in sufficient detail those collaborating factors which, in combination with abuse, cause delinquency. Alternatively, if most children experiencing abuse are somehow protected from adverse outcomes, it would be of value to know what these buffering factors and mechanisms are since they might help target interventions for unprotected children.

Parental psychopathology

The importance of psychiatric disorder in parents has been underscored in several clinical studies (Morris *et al.*, 1956; Robins, 1966; Stewart *et al.*, 1979; Lahey *et al.*, 1988). One of the strongest relationships these authors discovered was between alcoholism and antisocial personality in the father, in combination with low socioeconomic status and unsocialized conduct disorder in the child (Earls *et al.*, 1988). Stewart *et al.* (1979) showed that this relationship existed for children with conduct disorder, but not for those with hyperactivity which was unassociated with aggressive behaviour. However, since most of the fathers studied were married to women who also reported various forms of psychopathology, it was not possible to ascribe the effects of mental disorder in the children directly to the father.

In a more recent set of studies, psychopathology in the mother has been the focus of inquiry (Frick *et al.*, 1989; Lahey *et al.*, 1989). Recognizing the significant correlation between marital conflict, low socioeconomic status and personality disorder, these investigators found both conduct disorder and marital conflict to be associated with maternal antisocial characteristics, as measured with the Minnesota Multiphasic Personality Inventory. Socioeconomic status was not related to marital conflict, but was associated with maternal personality. Although the personality adjustment of fathers was not among the measures included in this study, the findings demonstrated that maternal antisocial personality has a direct effect on the childhood conduct disorder, perhaps even more powerfully than the father's. How to interpret this relationship in causal terms is open to question. Is it through the production of a disorganized rearing environment, as suggested by the Kolvin *et al.*, (1988) study or are both the mother's and the child's deviant personality genetically mediated?

Psychosocial factors in the child

It is important to consider the child's contribution to the quality of the relationship with the parent. The child who is difficult to manage, displays frequent temper outbursts and fails to respond to discipline may indeed facilitate the disorganization of his or her own environment by eliciting maladaptive parental behaviour, or increasing the strain on a marginally good marriage. The process by which both parent and child contribute to an escalating cycle of coercive interactions is at the core of the Oregon Social Learning Center's theory about the origins of conduct disorder (Patterson *et al.*, 1989; Reid & Patterson, 1989).

Recent developments in the application of social learning theory to the study of aggressive behaviour have advanced the idea that biased attributions of hostility towards others represent a central mechanism in stabilizing antisocial behaviour (Dodge, 1980). In a set of experiments involving school-age boys, it was demonstrated that such biases occur specifically when aggressive children believe that a provocation is being directed towards them (Dodge & Frame, 1982). A model of social cognition was developed in which five components were postulated: (1) the encoding of social cues; (2) interpretation of cues; (3) search for response to the incoming information; (4) making a decision of how to respond; and (5) enacting a response. Slaby and Guerra (1988) elaborated this model by demonstrating first, in delinquent and normal adolescents, and then in younger school-age children, that the content of children's thoughts and beliefs about social encounters was also important (Guerra & Slaby, 1989). Highly aggressive children adopted an orientation to perceive the world in more hostile terms than nonaggressive children. When given a set of hypothetical vignettes in which they were asked to describe how to respond to potentially conflictual situations, aggressive boys not only perceived hostility in others more readily, but generated fewer alternatives to physical confrontation and reported less dissatisfaction with their aggressive solutions than boys who were nominated by their teachers to be less aggressive.

Dodge *et al.* (1990) carried this work a step further by examining the relationship between physical abuse in infancy and aggressive behaviour at age 6. In a community-based sample of 4- and 5-year-old children, they tested the assumption that abuse led to social cognitive deficits of the type described in their earlier work. On finding the expected relationship, they then followed the sample over a short interval to predict high aggressivity. While diagnoses of conduct disorder were not included in this study, many children had scores on the CBCL that placed them in a clinical range. Of added interest was the finding that abused girls and some abused boys reacted to abusive experiences not with aggressive but with internalizing symptoms. Interestingly, these children were not found to have social cognitive deficits. The authors interpret their finding to be consistent with both attachment and social learning theories. Insecure attachment would produce an internal working model of poor self-esteem and diminished social competence. According to social learning theory, if confrontational behaviour is approved and rewarded, this reinforcement strengthens the behaviour and makes it a preferred strategy on encountering conflictual situations.

We might ask if these social cognitive deficits bear any relation to the low verbal intelligence and reading retardation that have been consistently demonstrated as a correlate of conduct disorder and delinquency (Sturge, 1982; Huesmann *et al.*, 1984; Walsh *et al.*, 1987; Moffitt, 1990b). This association could be produced by any one of three plausible connections. Firstly, antisocial behaviour could cause school underachievement, with low intelligence as an outcome. However, Richman *et al.*'s (1982) demonstration that aggressive behaviour and low intelligence were associated as early as age 3 argues against this hypothesis. Secondly, cognitive deficits in language might cause children to respond to their inadequate school achievement with antisocial behaviour. A third approach posits that both low verbal intelligence and antisocial behaviour are caused by an additional background factor.

Schonfeld *et al.* (1988) examined these competing hypotheses with data from the US Collaborative Perinatal Study. This project collected information on the neurological, family and psychological characteristics of a large sample of children born in the early 1960s and followed over four waves of data collection to age 17. The findings support the existence of a third factor, most likely to be of a social or cultural nature, that forecasts both low verbal scores and conduct disorder. The pattern of intelligence test results suggests that the deficit exists in areas influenced by the cultural environment of the family. This is more likely to impact vocabulary subtest scores, but not spatial or performance scores. Taking the position that the language environment is a critical determinant of both social competence and verbal skill (Damon, 1977), the cognitive deficits described in the work on attribution biases in aggressive children could be the product of social and cultural disadvantage. Low verbal intelligence might then be considered simply an indicator of a more pervasive deficit in social reasoning as well as in educational preparedness. In the Schonfeld *et al.* (1988) study the background factor described as influencing both verbal intelligence and antisocial behaviour was thought to be parental psychopathology. This global measure of parental dysfunction was believed to reflect a general impoverishment of the home environment, the results of which are consistent with those from Kolvin and colleagues (Kolvin *et al.*, 1988).

Psychologists have not as yet evolved a consistent approach to studying moral development. The work on social cognitive development, with its focus on behaviour, occupies one of at least three traditions in this area. It happens to be the one which has attracted the most rigorous research. Other researchers have emphasized either the role of emotions (Hoffman, 1982; Kagan, 1984) or the role of reasoning capacity (Kohlberg, 1976; Walker, 1988) in studying moral development. We do not understand well enough what the personal and familial characteristics are that foster high moral standards, nor do we know what goes wrong in the apparent breakdown of such standards in the child with conduct disorder. Have such children not been taught, or have they not learned to acknowledge the rights and feelings of others? What should we expect in terms of the development of moral emotions and behaviours in children at different ages? Evidence exists that children as young as 3 recognize and appropriately respond to moral infractions (Sanderson & Siegal, 1988; Smetana & Braeges, 1990). The paucity of research in this area represents a major barrier towards understanding an important developmental mechanism that may underpin the production and maintenance of antisocial behaviour.

Factors intrinsic to the child

To this point the discussion of risk mechanisms has concentrated on environmental factors as a source of stress and disadvantage and as the context in which learning may take place that might produce antisocial behaviour in children. However, not all children in such environments develop conduct disorder, and it has already been suggested that some children contribute to the circumstances in which they might appear to be victims. This requires a search for factors that set some children apart from others as being vulnerable to environmental risks.

It is appropriate to begin this search with a most obvious correlate of conduct disorder, male gender. In studies of young children it appears to be the case that boys are more likely than girls to respond with behaviour problems that may represent the early precursors of oppositional and conduct disturbances (Richman et al., 1982; Earls & Jung, 1987). Why is this so? Are there important exceptions to this rule? Is it reasonable to assume that the constitutional differences between the sexes are reflected in some types of behavioural differences (Earls, 1987)? Is it that males have a predisposition to respond to adversity with greater degrees of aggressiveness than females? Or, on the other hand, is it because boys and girls are socialized with different expectations about what constitutes appropriate behaviour and so their learning experiences are made to be distinctive?

One potential way to resolve the issue of biological proclivities is to consider sex as something other than a dichotomous variable. Evidence supporting the possible significance of testosterone on aggression has been reviewed in several places (Mattsson et al., 1980; Dabbs et al., 1991) and duplication of the Y chromosome may be associated with criminality (see Chapter 10 for discussion of the evidence on this point). This suggests that males do vary to some extent in the biological indicators that have been linked to aggressive behaviour.

There are only rare exceptions to the customary finding that males are markedly overrepresented among children receiving the diagnosis of conduct disorder. One such exception is from Rutter et al. (1974) who found that London girls of West Indian parents had a rate of conduct disorder that was similar to that of boys. However, this discovery might be explained as a cultural distinction because of the relative dominance of women in West Indian societies. Also, if girls were being raised to take on major responsibilities as breadwinners and heads of households, this could make them subject to harsher and less tolerant parental rearing tactics. If this explanation is correct, one would expect to see an increase in conduct disorders among girls in any society that made a deliberate effort to socialize them into roles that were traditionally assumed by males (Earls, 1982).

An alternative suggestion is that girls simply have different ways of expressing deviancy, and the process subserving this difference is culturally determined. Precocious sexual behaviour is one overt manifestation of a conduct disturbance which carries greater salience in females than in males (Robins, 1986). In this connection a number of investigators have examined the role that early onset of puberty may play in the genesis of female adolescent behavioural and emotional problems (Susman et al., 1987; Brooks-Gunn & Reiter, 1990).

One assumption is that the development of conduct disorder might be facilitated by the more rapid biological maturation of females who become recruited into older and potentially more deviant peer networks. Evidence in support of this hypothesis was reported by Caspi et al. (1993) based on findings from a New Zealand sample. Underscoring the importance of contextual influences, the results indicate that conduct disorder was more frequent among girls in mixed-sex schools, but not among those in same-sex schools. In examining secular trends in delinquency, it is apparent that a greater rise has occurred in female than male rates. The result has been a sizeable reduction in the sex ratio. Rutter and Giller (1983), reporting on rates in the UK, for example, describe a reduction in the male to female ratio of 10.79 : 1 in 1957 to 4.97 : 1 in 1977.

Implicating temperament as a risk factor for conduct disorder is contingent on the capacity to show that temperament is stable and predates the onset of oppositional and conduct disorder. Although this remains a popular idea, the evidence is still incomplete (Graham et al., 1973; Earls, 1981; Maziade et al., 1990; Chess & Thomas, 1991). Two orientations characterize approaches in this area. Some investigators acknowledge that temperament is fundamentally an interactive concept and is thus validly evaluated on the basis of how others view the child (Bates, 1980). Others view temperament as the phenotypic expression of a genotype. Prominent among the latter are studies of temperament in twins and those using an adoption design (Torgersen & Kringlen, 1978; Plomin & De-Fries, 1983). One notable and surprising result in some of this work is that impulsivity, a trait long believed to be one of the most salient features representing a risk for conduct disorder, has proved very difficult to measure (Buss & Plomin, 1984).

Kagan and Snidman (1991), using a biobehavioural

approach, have described uninhibited as opposed to inhibited children as those characterized by a lack of fear and high degrees of approach and sociable interaction. These children also have a physiological profile marked by low heart rate and a relatively low level of circulating cortisol. It is this profile that conforms to the theory of underarousal of central adrenergic function in the brain (Gray *et al.*, 1983; Quay, 1984; Gray, 1987). Children with such a vulnerability may be prone to acquire conduct disorder in circumstances marked by high family stress. However, other authors have implicated the parasympathetic system and high vagal tone as the basis of low arousability (Raine *et al.*, 1990). Indeed, both systems are no doubt involved, a factor that makes attributing a causal role to autonomic functions more difficult.

There are no twin or adoption studies so far reporting on oppositional or conduct disorder as currently conceptualized, thus estimates of heritability must be estimated from studies of adult antisocial disorder and from other sources which offer suggestive evidence at best (Crowe, 1974; Jary & Stewart, 1985). Nevertheless, several twin studies have been conducted over the past century that consistently demonstrate higher concordance for monozygotic over dyzygotic twins in criminal behaviour (Christiansen, 1977a,b). Adoption and cross-fostering studies represent an improvement over the twin design and these, too, have consistently indicated a significant heritable component in criminal behaviour. For example, Mednick *et al.* (1986) report from a Danish adoption study that biological fathers and male adoptees have much higher rates of criminality than adoptive fathers. How consistently this relationship might hold for delinquent behaviour and for conduct disorder is unknown. Some support for the relevance of this finding to conduct disorder is that the level of chronicity in male adoptees is associated with recidivism in their biological fathers. An important addition to this literature is the finding that a heritable contribution to adult criminality appears more clearly established than to conduct disorder and delinquency (DiLalla & Gottesman, 1989).

Assuming that a heritable component exists, the enlisting of candidate genes and an analysis of what products these genes produce must eventually be advanced. One type of exploration that might contribute to the resolution of this issue regards functions of the central nervous system. Many of these physiological processes may be under a degree of genetic control. One such profile, associated with the uninhibited temperament, is reflected in sluggishness of the autonomic nervous system. The characteristics of this underarousal are low heart rate, decreased amplitude and slow recovery of skin conductance, and excessive slow wave activity in the electroencephalogram (Raine, 1988; Raine *et al.*, 1990).

Other plausible indicators of a physiological basis for antisocial behaviour relate to central neurotransmitter systems, dietary or metabolic influences and the effects of gonadal hormones (Rogeness *et al.*, 1982, 1984, 1986; Linnoila *et al.*, 1983; Virkkunen & Penttinen, 1984; Virkkunen *et al.*, 1989; Kruesi *et al.*, 1990). Unfortunately, none of these features has been as well-replicated as those biological aspects associated with autonomic nervous functioning. Stoff *et al.* (1989) showed that elevated levels of platelet monoamine oxidase were associated with impulsivity in boys with conduct disorder. However, another group of investigators found the opposite: low levels of platelet monoamine oxidase and plasma dopamine beta-hydroxylase characterized the profiles of boys with both attentional and conduct disorders, but not those with attentional disorders only (Bowden *et al.*, 1988). A more recent strategy has been to examine imipramine-binding sites in platelets as a marker of the functioning of serotoninergic systems (Stoff *et al.*, 1987; Birmaher *et al.*, 1990). The results implicate this system in impulsive and aggressive behaviour. The unknown relationship of these peripheral measures to central functioning should be kept in mind.

Until more direct methods are available to evaluate brain activity during cognitive functioning, neuropsychological measures offer a useful approach. A variety of studies have described the cognitive deficits that are associated with delinquency and, by implication, conduct disorder. Some investigators have suggested that impaired frontal lobe functions produce many of the deficits seen in chronic offenders, such as the inability to plan, to redirect potentially harmful behaviour, and to learn from negative consequences of their actions (Pontius, 1972, 1976; Luria, 1973; Moffitt & Henry, 1991). Yeudall *et al.* (1982) employed an extensive battery of neuropsychological tests to examine delinquents and nondelinquents. The vast majority of delinquents had some abnormality on tests measuring such executive functions in contrast to only 11% of nondelinquents. These investigators interpreted their results to suggest that frontal lobe functions may be more important than the decreased verbal skills so commonly found in other studies. However, not all studies have reported deficits that implicate the anterior cerebral areas. After controlling for social class, Karniski *et a*. (1982) found that 18% of delinquents and 4% of nondelinquents had deficits in visual processing and auditory-language functions, but not in motor or temporal sequencing skills. Still other work has shown that in violently aggressive children seizures were present with signs of substantive brain damage (Lewis *et al.*, 1979, 1987). Spellacy (1977, 1978) observed that neuropsychological deficits appeared to be more characteristic of delinquents than personality factors, as measured with the Minnesota Multiphasic Personality Inventory.

These case-control studies appear to have inspired few prospective studies to determine if neuropsychological deficits fúnction as true risk factors. Taken collectively, it is not clear what factors should be highlighted for hypothesis testing. Much of the literature suggests poor impulse control as a common characteristic that may account for a wide range of cognitive deficits revealed by these tests. Prospective studies could determine if deficits existed prior to the onset of conduct disorder. If this proved to be the case, a related question would pertain to the capacity of these tests to discriminate chronic delinquents (and children with conduct disorder) from delinquents with transient, short-lived careers. The work of Denno (1989) illustrates the value of such prospective work. In this study violent juveniles could not be discriminated from controls who were matched for race and socioeconomic class on measures of intelligence and achievement.

Aside from genetic factors, a host of environmental insults could contribute to the cognitive deficits detected on neuropsychological measures. These include, but are not limited to, prenatal exposure to alcohol and drugs, absorption of heavy metals such as lead, injury to and infections of the developing brain.

Exposure to lead has been one of the more exhaustively investigated biological risk factors and there is now convincing evidence that even at low levels of accumulation, it contributes to lowered performance on cognitive tests and to behaviour problems (Needleman *et al.*, 1979; 1990; Fergusson *et al.*, 1988a,b).

A coherent account of the neuropsychological mechanisms associated with conduct disorder cannot be derived from the evidence reviewed. Even when contextual factors are carefully controlled, it is difficult to establish the independent contributions that such handicaps of early development may make towards bringing about aggressive and antisocial behaviour.

DIAGNOSTIC ASSESSMENT

Clinicians faced with the evaluation of a child with oppositional or conduct disorder should view the diagnosis as only one component of an overall process. Attention to the child's behaviour and personal qualities should be considered in relation to the family, school and community contexts. In addition, it is necessary to distinguish transient from chronic patterns, reactive from habitual manifestations of deviance, and the number and types of settings in which antisocial behaviour is expressed. The complete assessment should consider all these aspects when deciding how to treat the child. Beyond the need to establish the presence of a diagnosis, the purpose of the evaluation is to decide whether or not intervention is warranted, and if so, what its intensity and duration should be. In developing a treatment plan it is essential to have a concept of how the major areas of dysfunction are to be targeted.

Structuring the evaluation carefully is essential. It is preferable to interview the child separately from interviews with parents or other significant adults. Since the nature of conduct disturbances are such that they are more likely to be of concern to others than to the patient, such children are prone to view themselves as victims of adult authority. Indeed, the clinic contact may all too readily be perceived as punishment for the conflict generated at home or school. To counteract this tendency, it is wise to establish direct contact with the child. Although parents and children have closer agreement on symptoms of conduct disorder than other types of disorders, including oppositional disorders, it remains the case that children have a unique perspective in reporting on their own peer relations, patterns of substance abuse, emotional symptoms and details about their antisocial and delinquent behaviour.

A significant proportion of children with oppositional and conduct problems have a pattern of symptoms that is not limited to these diagnostic categories (Bukstein *et al.*, 1989; Szatmari *et al.*, 1989; Walker *et al.*, 1991). As a first step in assessment, the various manifestations of antisocial behaviour must be recorded along with other symptom areas. Particular attention should be directed to anxious, hyperactive, attentional, impulse control, somatic and depressive symptoms and to symptoms associated with substance use. Although it is possible to concentrate on particular patterns of antisocial symptoms, differentiating, for example, between children who are primarily aggressive from those exhibiting covert symptoms, this distinction appears to be of little prognostic significance (Loeber & Schmaling, 1985). The number of symptoms is a better indicator of seriousness than the pattern at any point in time (Robins & Wish, 1977; Robins & Ratcliff, 1980). Nevertheless, evaluation of a child's personality and peer relations is of great importance in terms of understanding the nature of the child's disturbance. Some research has shown peer unpopularity to be an unstable feature among aggressive children (Cairns & Cairns, 1991), thus more weight should be given to personality than to peer acceptance and the number of friends. The types of activities engaged in with peers and their apparent behavioural norms are important since these factors may represent important indicators of the potential for escalation (Elliott *et al.*, 1985).

The pattern of symptoms becomes more significant when evaluating the presence of disorders other than oppositional and conduct disorders. As demonstrated in several studies, children with symptoms of attention deficit hyperactivity disorder and conduct disorder are at greater risk for poor outcomes than children with either disorder alone (Stewart *et al.*, 1981; McGee *et al.*, 1984; Gittelman *et al.*, 1985; Moffitt, 1990a; Mannuzza *et al.*, 1991). Moreover, this combination of cognitive impairment and antisocial behaviour may act synergistically (Loeber *et al.*, 1990a; Frick *et al.*, 1991b). Children with conduct and anxiety symptoms, on the other hand, are less likely to have police contacts and to be perceived by their peers as bullies than conduct-disordered children without anxiety symptoms (Walker *et al.*, 1991). The assumption is that the presence of anxiety acts as a 'braking system' on the seriousness of antisocial behaviour.

Conduct disorder appears to be more closely related to substance abuse than other psychiatric disorders. The association covers alcohol and several types of drugs, including stimulants, depressants, inhalants, opiates and cocaine (Kandel *et al.*, 1978; Elliott *et al.*, 1989; Greenbaum *et al.*, 1991; Milin *et al.*, 1991). In a large group of seriously delinquent youths, Weisz *et al.* (1991) found that substance abuse predicted the escalation of violent behaviour.

The diverse nature of antisocial symptoms makes it essential to obtain the reports of parents as well as teachers. While children and parents agree to a fair extent on symptoms of conduct disorder, greater degrees of disagreement are found when inquiring about attentional, impulse control and oppositional symptoms. On analysing these patterns of agreement and disagreement, Loeber *et al.* (1990b, 1991a) found that parents and teachers reported more symptoms of attention deficit hyperactivity disorder and oppositional behaviour than did children. Information from parents was found to be more useful in predicting police contacts than the two other sources. Both parents and teachers predicted placement in special classes better than children. The three informants were about equally good in predicting school suspensions, however.

It is of obvious significance to have a means of resolving disagreement as part of the diagnostic assessment and it is likely that many clinicians use the 'best estimate' procedure in doing so (Leckman *et al.*, 1982). Reich and Earls (1987) described a procedure for systematically evaluating parent and child information derived from parallel, but separately administered, diagnostic interviews, which may be useful in clinical practice.

Because the pattern of symptoms in conduct disorder follows a developmental trend to become more diverse over time, it is essential to establish a history of antisocial behaviour at the time the clinical assessment is made. A number of studies have shown that symptoms may become prominent in the preschool period, creating a noticeable pressure on parental authority and control (Campbell & Ewing, 1990; White *et al.*, 1990; Tremblay *et al.*, 1991). Early onset may be an indicator of persistence simply because it reflects a degree of skill and control acquired by the child in adapting to its environment. As Patterson *et al.* (1989) adroitly put it, the child can become both victim and architect of a maladaptive lifestyle in which investment in aggressive behaviour is paramount.

The evaluation should include a search for diagnosable and possibly treatable diseases of the central nervous system. In addition to a neurological examination, the history should include a detailed review of head injuries, especially those associated with a loss of consciousness, infectious diseases involving the brain and seizures. It is essential to inquire specifically about exposure to sources of lead contamination. Often young children will have had lead levels determined in the past, and if so a record of the actual level should be ascertained.

A neuropsychological assessment is a critically important component to the overall evaluation. Measures of intellectual capacity, language development, reading and arithmetic skills should be included to evaluate school performance and intelligence and the extent to which one predicts the other. It is worth emphasizing that careful attention to performance in these areas is important at all ages, including adolescence. The presence of above-average intellectual functioning and achievement should be considered as a good prognostic sign (White *et al.*, 1989).

School records are a valuable source of information beyond their contribution to the evaluation of academic performance. Information on behaviour problems, absenteeism, truancy, reasons for parent conferences and extracurricular activities may all be helpful in completing a picture of the child. Review of such records prior to contacting the school may also assist in preparing for an efficient use of time with school personnel.

Once these multiple sources of information are at hand, a differential diagnosis can be entertained. Other disorders may be of primary or secondary importance relative to symptoms of oppositional and conduct disorders. Among the diagnoses to consider are psychoses, seizure disorders, mental retardation, specific developmental disorders, attention-deficit disorders, substance abuse, posttraumatic stress disorder as well as other anxiety disorders, and major depressive disorder.

Conduct disorders, and to a lesser extent oppositional disorders, are often associated with impairments in the areas of family and peer relations, and school and job performance. These should be carefully assessed since they may have implications for the type of treatment. In judging the seriousness of behavioural disturbance, attention must also be given to patterns of risk-taking. Frequency of fighting and the types of injuries sustained in such conflicts, the possession and use of weapons, patterns of offending and co-offending, gang membership, use of drugs, and the use of coercion in sexual encounters are the areas of inquiry that will help determine severity.

As a final step in determining the prognosis of these disorders, two considerations should be added to knowledge about the severity of the symptom pattern. These are the degree to which the individual manifests a restricted range of reasoning about interpersonal relationships and conflict negotiation, and the degree of support provided by immediate family members. The inability to view social encounters as events that require thinking about the feelings and rights of others and the consequences of one's actions in these regards may well represent the most profound problem associated with conduct disorder (Joffe *et al.*, 1990). The child's lack of sensitivity to other family members may make parents feel a sense of futility about helping the child. This, in turn, may serve to justify their withdrawal of support and care. Of course, these problems exist in a nexus which it is usually impossible to disentangle during a clinical evaluation. More important than understanding the dynamics of such predicaments is the need to acknowledge their presence as a complicating factor towards recovery.

Another way to evaluate the family in this regard is in relation to the resources available to them that might be mobilized to support an antisocial child. Much has been made of the role of family conflict and harsh rearing conditions as risk factors in the development of conduct disorder. If these conditions are present, the treatment plan must undoubtedly address efforts to reduce the level of disharmony in the home or the child's exposure to it. But at the same time, the presence of a caring adult within the family or in the community should not be missed (Jenkins & Smith, 1990).

TREATMENT

The clinician is well-advised to consider conduct disturbances as chronic childhood conditions when making treatment decisions. Decisions on what treatment or combination of treatments is to be used and on what level of intervention (i.e.

outpatient, inpatient, residential) to apply these techniques are necessary. Treatment approaches may target the individual child or adolescent, the parents, the family as a whole, or they may aim to marshall the recreational and educational resources of the community in which the child lives. Assuming that oppositional disorder is a milder form of conduct disorder, what follows in this section applies to both conditions, with appropriate adjustments in the intensity, duration and breadth of intervention.

In general, therapeutic techniques that target the individual child are insufficient and attention should be given to the contextual influences of family and peer relations, school adjustment, and the social and economic welfare of the immediate family and neighbourhood circumstances (Wells *et al.*, 1980; Lipsey, 1992). This is a complex demand that requires that the clinician work closely with a variety of other professionals, including teachers, psychologists and social workers. While the psychiatrist will usually be called on to focus treatment on the child, it is wise not to conceive of this component as the primary or most effective one.

Treatment approaches include community-based models of intervention, family treatment, parent training, and a variety of interventions focusing on the individual child or adolescent. The strength of community-based treatment is that it avoids stigmatizing a disturbed child by integrating him or her into settings with normal children (Fleischman & Szykula, 1981). The focus of intervention is on skill acquisition and prosocial behaviour. Games, crafts, sports and discussion groups can be superimposed on the ongoing activities of a community centre. One of the best-known evaluations of this approach was carried out by Feldman *et al.* (1983) in St Louis. The programme involved the assignment of children with conduct disorder to treatment and control conditions in a local community centre. The treatment group was provided a number of skill-promoting activities. Because such programmes typically avoid reliance on highly trained professionals to deliver the intervention, characteristics of persons selected as treatment providers were carefully weighed. Positive results were observed immediately following the end of the intervention and at 1-year follow-up. The success of treatment appeared to be influenced by two cardinal factors. Firstly, the previous experience and personal maturity of providers was important. Secondly, exposure to nondeviant peers in group settings was an essential component of a good outcome. A further benefit of the community-based approach, aside from the avoidance of labelling, is that the intervention can be applied to large groups of children.

A variety of family therapy techniques have been developed, but few have been systematically evaluated. Alexander and Parsons (1973) provide one of the few examples of an evaluation that demonstrates beneficial effects over the short term. In general, these approaches attempt to alter maladaptive patterns of interaction and communication among family members. The patterns involve lack of support, scapegoating and isolation of particular members. A great deal of emphasis has been placed on training in these techniques, but this has not been balanced by an interest in careful evaluation. Considering the expense and laboriousness of this method, the omission of evaluation studies represents a serious impediment.

The systematic training of parents to become more effective in managing difficult child behaviour has become one of the most widely used approaches. A considerable body of theory and numerous evaluation studies pointing out the efficacy of this treatment modality support its popularity (Baum & Forehand, 1981; Patterson *et al.*, 1982; Kazdin, 1985, 1987). Parent management training focuses on noxious behaviours such as temper outbursts and destructiveness as well as lower-intensity problems such as noncompliance, arguing and teasing. The method instructs parents to use positive reinforcement for prosocial behaviour and mild, nonviolent punishment (e.g. time out, withdrawal of privileges) for infractions on a daily basis. Brief interventions that are planned for only a few months appear not to be as effective as programmes that provide 50 or more total hours of intervention (Kazdin, 1985). The technique seems to be especially appropriate for parents of preadolescents, although its efficacy for parents of adolescents has not been clearly established. The ready availability of teaching material and manuals increases the attractiveness of this method. However, two major factors should be kept in mind when using it. Firstly, parents must be highly motivated to comply with treatment and to make the effort to generalize what is learned in therapy sessions to multiple situations in which they encounter the resistant and aggressive behaviour of their children (Lochman *et al.*, 1984). They must be committed to a high degree of monitoring the child and have a readiness to intervene promptly. Secondly, in some cases the child's level of defiance may escalate so quickly as to exceed the parents' tolerance. Few opportunities for positive interaction may be perceived by some parents and the child's acquisition of new response patterns may seem to materialize too slowly given the parents' expectations.

An approach that has gained prominence over the past decade relates to enhancing the child's capacity to recognize and solve conflictual situations (Kendall & Braswell, 1985). The approach accents strengthening the social reasoning capacities and interpersonal sensitivity of children with oppositional and conduct symptoms. The method usually involves a highly active process in which the therapist aims to help the child restructure certain simulated or real events involving conflict. Such encounters are broken down and analysed by components with the objective of developing a variety of alternative solutions. Through the use of role-playing, reciting of stories and reports of real-life encounters, the child gradually increases his or her repertoire of nonviolent, socially appropriate responses. A variety of attractive manuals exist and many therapists effectively incorporate the use of video taping of social encounters in treatment sessions (Platt *et al.*, 1974). Obviously, the approach requires a cooperative patient. A particular value of this approach is that it has been proven effective with seriously disturbed older adolescents (Guerra & Slaby, 1990).

Both parent management training and social problem-solving share a number of attractive features, as outlined. Therapist training is not elaborate and the use of less highly trained providers may be an important issue in cost-containment. The fact that both methods require the active role of parents enhances the prospects for a positive and enduring outcome. The two techniques have been carefully codified and the strategies by which to judge their efficacy are well-established. Recognizing their complementarity, Kazdin *et al.* (1987) combined these methods in planning a treatment programme for an inpatient sample and compared their outcomes with a control group that received a nonspecific intervention. The results were encouraging in showing that improvements in the combined treatment group were still present 1 year after termination.

Use of medications does not have an established place in the ensemble of treatment approaches for oppositional and conduct disorders. When conditions that are more routinely treated with psychoactive drugs coexist with conduct disorder, the use of these agents may improve the conduct symptoms as well as the targeted symptoms. Thus the use of stimulants and antidepressants can conceivably have a place in overall treatment strategies. On the other hand, a few investigators have supported the use of major tranquillizers, such as haloperidol, and lithium for extreme varieties of aggressive behaviour (Campbell *et al.*, 1984). While these drugs may have some benefit in the context of institutional care, they have not been shown to be beneficial in natural settings.

As suggested above, a single treatment approach is seldom warranted and indeed there is good reason to believe that combinations of approaches are maximally beneficial. This necessitates that careful attention be given to orchestrating the various components of an intervention. The decision of which one to use will usually rest on the degree of severity or dangerousness of the individual's symptoms, the types of impairments and the degree of family and community support available. Oppositional disorder, by its nature, would nearly always be treated on an outpatient basis or in a community setting. The majority of children with conduct disorder can also be managed just as well in such noninstitutional settings.

None the less, conduct disorder is one of the leading reasons for admission to child psychiatric inpatient units and to residential treatment centres (Kashani & Cantwell, 1983). Admission of these children to inpatient units can be based on the need to undergo detailed differential diagnosis, to establish the presence of other psychiatric disorders, and for immediate control of aggressive behaviour or threats of such behaviour. The inpatient setting also affords the psychiatrist an opportunity for more extensive observation of the child and for composing a multifaceted intervention with a higher degree of control than is possible on an outpatient basis. An appropriate use of inpatient admission might involve a child who has not made progress as an outpatient or in whom a more exhaustive evaluation or treatment programme seems warranted. Residential treatment is usually reserved for children who are so seriously disturbed that they require intensive,

long-term management. A comprehensive evaluation during a short-term hospital stay is preferred prior to admitting a child to such a facility. It is worth noting that in many areas residential treatment centres also include day treatment programmes, which make it possible for children with such extreme needs to live at home.

PREVENTION

The chronicity and relatively high prevalence of conduct disorder combined with its refractoriness to treatment methods and high societal costs make it a prime candidate for primary prevention. It has become increasingly clear that prevention efforts must be concentrated in the first decade of life and probably in the first 5 years to offset the production of this disorder (Earls, 1989; Price *et al.*, 1989). However, it is far from obvious what to emphasize in a prevention campaign since the risk factors represent such a complex configuration of environmental and personal factors (Walter *et al.*, 1991).

Public health approaches to prevention generally work in one of two ways. Either the environment harbouring the risk conditions is improved, or the personal resources and competence of children to deal with such conditions are strengthened. In evaluating what has been done to prevent conduct disorder, we must again widen the margins of inquiry to include aggressive and delinquent behaviour that may not conform to a particular clustering of problems that we acknowledge as the psychiatric disorder. Offord (1987, 1989) has supplied a balanced account of prevention efforts in this area, and provided a rationale for the design of experiments based on the analysis of risk factors from the Ontario Child Health Study (Boyle & Offord, 1989). Most of the effort has been given to community and school-based experiments to prevent conduct problems, and less to strategies that target individuals at high risk.

One of the most important community-based experiments was carried out in an area of public housing in Ottawa, Canada (Offord & Jones, 1983; Jones & Offord, 1989). A comprehensive programme of nonacademic skill development for boys between 5 and 15 years was established in one of two comparable areas. In the area receiving the intervention, the number of police and fire calls was reduced, as was the frequency of vandalism over a 3-year period. At the same time evidence was amassed to show that the children actually achieved new levels of athletic and physical skills. A cost analysis demonstrated that the money saved by government agencies far exceeded the programme's expenditures. A caveat worth noting is that the benefits were limited to nonacademic areas. There was little evidence that the results generalized to areas of school performance or social skills.

School-based interventions have been popular for a number of years but have produced varying degrees of success in prevention (Gottfredson, 1987). Recently, Hawkins *et al.* (1991) combined parent and teacher training programmes to promote social skill development in first-graders. The intervention, carried out over the first 2 years of primary school, significantly reduced the level of aggressive behaviour for white students, but not for black students. While the possibility of biased teacher ratings cannot be discounted, it is conceivable that the level of risk in black children was beyond the level of impact of this experiment. Nevertheless, the results are broadly similar to the Newcastle experiment in which group therapy and behaviour modification produced improvements in behavioural outcomes in children in primary school (Kolvin *et al.*, 1981).

The nationwide effort in Norway to reduce the level of interpersonal violence among schoolchildren is unique in its scope (Olweus, 1991). The intervention was initiated by the Ministry of Education in the wake of an outbreak of completed suicides among boys who had apparently been victimized by peers. The endeavour involved mobilizing all the resources of the school system to educate teachers, administrators, parents and students in understanding the nature and seriousness of the aggressor–victim relationship. The programme was designed as a quasiexperiment in which results were assessed in a time-lagged fashion, permitting an estimate to be made about the size of the intervention effect in the absence of a control group. Judged by this standard the effort was not only remarkably successful in reducing the level of violence, but in diminishing antisocial behaviour in the school environment as well.

Prevention experiments that target preschool children should conceivably have a more powerful impact than those that start later (McGuire & Earls, 1991). Some evidence that this approach might work to reduce the prevalence of conduct disorder was obtained in the US Headstart Program. Though this effort was designed as an educational enrichment programme for poor children, one follow-up study indicated that reduction in officially recorded delinquency was achieved in the experimental group (Schweinhart & Weikart, 1983). To date, pre-school experiments explicitly designed to reduce the rate of conduct problems have not been conducted, but the evidence derived from studies such as those must be regarded as promising.

The Montreal Prevention Experiment is a prime example of a high-risk design (Tremblay *et al.*, 1990). In this study of kindergarten boys, all from low-income families, positive screening for oppositional and aggressive behaviour was performed prior to randomly assigning the subjects to one of three groups: experimental, control and placebo (these subjects were observed frequently but did not receive an intervention). The 2-year programme of intervention included parent management training, social skills development for children, and a television-viewing training curriculum for both parents and children. Follow-up at 3 years postintervention demonstrated lower levels of grade retention, and less fighting and delinquent behaviour in the experimental group. The study is now tracking subjects into their adolescent years to observe if these promising results endure.

Robins and Earls (1986) suggested an approach that selects children at extremely high risk for conduct disorder for enrolment in an intervention programme beginning shortly after birth. Infants born to women known to have personality disorders would be randomly assigned to an intervention that included a high-quality day care programme. In the first year the programme would aim to stimulate language, social and physical skill development in the children and provide good health care, while providing support to the family and specific training in management skills to parents. The programme would continue such a developmentally graded curriculum until the children reached school age. The outcomes measured in such an experiment, conduct problems and academic readiness, could be estimated by the time the children reached school age.

CONCLUSIONS

Throughout this chapter oppositional defiant and conduct disorders have been discussed as if they were dimensions of the same condition. Delinquency has been considered as closely aligned to, and in many cases merely an administrative definition for, children with one or both of these conditions. These disturbances tend to remain stable once they appear in middle childhood, although the actual behaviours composing the diagnostic picture become increasingly diverse and serious as children move into the adolescent years. The multiple pathways of growth and desistance are currently being studied by a number of investigators and it is already apparent that most adults who have had a conduct disorder in childhood continue to show significant indications of social dysfunction, even when they do not warrant a psychiatric diagnosis. The symptom pattern and developmental course of the disorder do not fit comfortably into a diagnostic class. There continues to be concern that it is better reflected as a dimensional index of social and behavioural problems than as a disease category.

Although the problems subsumed under the psychiatric definitions of oppositional and conduct disorder have been a major preoccupation of the child mental health, educational and juvenile justice systems for many decades, and despite the considerable energy of many researchers in this field, much still eludes us. The simple idea that persistent patterns of antisocial behaviour reflect an underdeveloped or deviantly developed conscience has somehow not been reconciled in modern psychology and psychiatry. To advance knowledge, improved concepts, interdisciplinary research, and a considerable investment of human resources is needed. The combination of individual and contextual risk factors and the early onset of the disorder make it difficult to unravel causal pathways. Both prospective, longitudinal studies that begin early in life and well-designed efforts at prevention are needed for progress to occur (Tonry *et al.*, 1990).

REFERENCES

Achenbach T.M., Connors C.K., Quay H.C., Verhulst F.C. & Howell C.T. (1989) Replication of empirically derived syndromes as a basis for taxonomy of child/adolescent psychopathology. *Journal of Abnormal Child Psychology*, **17**, 299–323.

Aichorn A. (1935) *Wayward Youth*. Viking Press, New York.

Ainsworth M.D.S., Blehar M.C., Waters E. & Wall S. (1978) *Patterns of Attachment, A Psychological Study of the Strange Situation*. Lawrence Erlbaum, Hillsdale, NJ.

Alexander J.F. & Parsons B.V. (1973) Short-term behavioral intervention with delinquent families: impact on family process and recidivism. *Journal of Abnormal Psychology*, **81**, 219–225.

American Psychiatric Association (1952) *Diagnostic and Statistical Manual of Mental Disorders (DSM-I)*. American Psychiatric Association, Washington, DC.

American Psychiatric Association (1968) *Diagnostic and Statistical Manual of Mental Disorders (DSM-II)*. American Psychiatric Association, Washington, DC.

American Psychiatric Association (1980) *Diagnostic and Statistical Manual of Mental Disorders (DSM-III)*. American Psychiatric Association, Washington, DC.

American Psychiatric Association (1987) *Diagnostic and Statistical Manual of Mental Disorders (DSM-III-R)*, 3rd edn revised. American Psychiatric Association, Washington, DC.

American Psychiatric Association (1994) *Diagnostic and Statistical Manual of Mental Disorders, 4th edn — DSM-IV*. American Psychiatric Association, Washington, DC.

Bates J. (1980) The concept of difficult temperament. *Merrill-Palmer Quarterly*, **26**, 299–319.

Baum C.G. & Forehand R. (1981) Long-term follow-up assessment of parent training by use of multiple outcome measures. *Behavior Therapy*, **12**, 643–652.

Birmaher B., Stanley M., Greenhill L., Twomey J., Gavrilescu A. & Rabinovich H. (1990) Platelet imipramine binding in children and adolescents with impulsive behavior. *Journal of the American Academy of Child and Adolescent Psychiatry*, **29(6)**, 914–918.

Blantz B., Schmidt M.H. & Esser G. (1991) Familial adversities and child psychiatric disorders. *Journal of Child Psychology and Psychiatry*, **32**, 939–950.

Bowden C.L., Deutsch C.K. & Swanson J.M. (1988) Plasma dopamine-β-hydroxylase and platelet monoamine oxidase in attention deficit disorder and conduct disorder. *Journal of the American Academy of Child and Adolescent Psychiatry*, **27(2)**, 171–174.

Bowlby J. (1944) Forty-four juvenile thieves: their characters and home-life. *International Journal of Psychoanalysis*, **25**, 1–57.

Bowlby J. (1969) *Attachment*. Basic Books, New York.

Boyle M.H. & Offord D.R. (1989) Primary prevention of conduct disorder: issues and prospects. *Journal of the American Academy of Child and Adolescent Psychiatry*, **29(2)**, 227–233.

Brooks-Gunn J. & Reiter E.O. (1990) The role of pubertal processes. In: Feldman S.S. & Elliott G.R. (eds) *At the Threshold*, pp. 16–53. Harvard University Press, Cambridge, MA.

Bukstein O.G., Brent D.A. & Kaminer Y. (1989) Comorbidity of substance abuse and other psychiatric disorders in adolescents. *American Journal of Psychiatry*, **146**, 1131–1141.

Burt C. (1925) *The Young Delinquent*. D. Appleton, New York.

Buss A.H. & Plomin R. (1984) *Temperament: Early Developing Personality Traits*. Lawrence Erlbaum, Hillsdale, NJ.

Cairns R.B. & Cairns B.D. (1991) Social cognition and social networks: a developmental perspective. In: Pepler D.J. & Rubin K.H. (eds) *The Development and Treatment of Childhood Aggression*, pp. 249–278. Lawrence Erlbaum, Hillsdale, NJ.

Campbell S.B. & Ewing L.J. (1990) Follow-up of hard-to-manage preschoolers: adjustment at age 9 and predictors of continuing symptoms. *Journal of Child Psychology and Psychiatry*, **31(6)**, 871–889.

Campbell M., Small A.M., Green W.H., Jennings S.J., Perry R., Bennett W.G. & Anderson L. (1984) Behavioral efficacy of haloperidol and lithium carbonate. *Archives of General Psychiatry*, **41**, 650–656.

Carmen E., Rieker P.P. & Mills T. (1987) Victims of violence and psychiatric illness. *American Journal of Psychiatry*, **141**, 378–383.

Caspi A., Lynam D., Moffitt T.E. & Silva P.A. (1993) Unraveling girls' delinquency: biological, dispositional, and contextual contributions to adolescent misbehavior. *Developmental Psychology*, **29**, 19–30.

Chess S. & Thomas A. (1991) Temperament. In: Lewis M. (ed) *Child and Adolescent Psychiatry. A Comprehensive Textbook*, pp. 145–159. Williams & Wilkins, Baltimore.

Christiansen K.O. (1977a) A review of studies of criminality among twins. In: Mednick S.A. & Christiansen K.O. (eds) *Biosocial Bases of Criminal Behavior*, pp. 75–88. Gardner Press, New York.

Christiansen K.O. (1977b) A preliminary study of criminality among twins. In: Mednick S.A. & Christiansen K.O. (eds) *Biosocial Bases of Criminal Behavior*, pp. 89–103. Gardner Press, New York.

Cleckley H. (1941) *The Mask of Sanity*. C.V. Mosby, St Louis.

Costello E. (1989) Developments in child psychiatric epidemiology. *Journal of the American Academy of Child and Adolescent Psychiatry*, **28(6)**, 836–841.

Crowe R.R. (1974) An adoption study of antisocial personality. *Archives of General Psychiatry*, **31**, 785–791.

Dabbs J.M., Jurkovic G.J. & Frady R.L. (1991) Salivary testosterone and cortisol among late adolescent male offenders. *Journal of Abnormal Child Psychology*, **19(4)**, 469–478.

Damon W. (1977) *The Social World of the Child*, p. 66. Jossey-Bass, San Francisco.

Denno D.J. (1989) *Biology, Crime and Violence: New Evidence*. Cambridge University Press, Cambridge.

DiLalla L.F. & Gottesman I.I. (1989) Heterogeneity of causes for delinquency and criminality: lifespan perspectives. *Development and Psychopathology*, **1(4)**, 339–349.

Dodge K.A. (1980) Social cognition and children's aggressive behavior. *Child Development*, **51**, 162–170.

Dodge K.A. & Frame C.L. (1982) Social cognitive biases and deficits in aggressive boys. *Child Development*, **53**, 620–635.

Dodge K.A., Bates J.E. & Pettit G.S. (1990) Mechanisms in the cycle of violence. *Science*, **250**, 1678–1683.

Earls F. (1981) Temperament characteristics and behavior problems in three-year-old children. *Journal of Nervous and Mental Disease*, **169**, 367–373.

Earls F. (1982) Cultural and national differences in the epidemiology of behavior problems of preschool children. *Culture, Medicine and Psychiatry*, **6**, 45–56.

Earls F. (1985) Epidemiology of psychiatric disorders in children and adolescents. In: Cavenar J.O. (ed) *Psychiatry*, Vol. 3, pp. 1–30. J.B. Lippincott, Philadelphia.

Earls F. (1987) Sex differences in psychiatric disorders: origins and developmental influences. *Psychiatric Developments*, **1**, 1–23.

Earls F. (1989) Epidemiology and child psychiatry: entering the second phase. *American Journal of Orthopsychiatry*, **59(2)**, 279–283.

Earls F. & Jung K.G. (1987) Temperament and home environment characteristics as causal factors in the early development of childhood psychopathology. *Journal of the American Academy of Child and Adolescent Psychiatry*, **26(4)**, 491–498.

Earls F., Reich W., Jung K. & Cloninger C.R. (1988) Psychopathology in children of alcoholic and antisocial parents. *Alcoholism: Clinical and Experimental Research*, **12**, 481–487.

Edelbrock C. & Costello A.J. (1988) Convergence between statistically derived behavior problem syndromes and child psychiatric diagnoses. *Journal of Abnormal Child Psychology*, **16**, 219–232.

Elliott D.S., Huizinga D. & Ageton S.S. (1985) *Explaining Delinquency and Drug Use*. Sage, Newbury Park, CA.

Elliott D.S., Huizinga D. & Menard S. (1989) *Multiple Problem Youth: Delinquency, Substance Use, and Mental Health Problems*. Springer-Verlag, New York.

Farrington D.P. (1978) The family background of aggressive youths. In: Hersov L.A., Berger M. & Shaffer D. (eds) *Aggression and Antisocial Behaviour in Childhood and Adolescence*, pp. 73–93. Pergamon Press, Oxford.

Farrington D.P. (1990) Implications of criminal career research for the prevention of offending. *Journal of Adolescence*, **13**, 93–113.

Farrington D.P. (1991) Antisocial personality from childhood to adulthood. *The Psychologist: Bulletin of the British Psychological Society*, **4**, 389–394.

Farrington D.P., Loeber R., Elliott D.S., Hawkins J.D., Kandel D.B., Klein M.W., McCord J., Rowe D.C. & Tremblay R.E. (1990) Advancing knowledge about the onset of delinquency and crime. In: Lahey B.B. & Kazdin A.E. (eds) *Advances in Clinical Child Psychology*, vol. 13, pp. 283–342. Plenum Press, New York.

Feldman R.A., Caplinger T.E. & Wodarski J.S. (1983) *The St. Louis Conundrum: The Effective Treatment of Antisocial Youths*. Prentice-Hall, Englewood Cliffs, NJ.

Fergusson D.M., Fergusson J.E., Horwood L.J. & Kinzett N.G. (1988a) A longitudinal study of dentine lead levels, intelligence, school performance and behaviour. Part II. Dentine lead and cognitive ability. *Journal of Child Psychology and Psychiatry*, **29(6)**, 793–809.

Fergusson D.M., Fergusson J.E., Horwood L.J. & Kinzett N.G. (1988b) A longitudinal study of dentine lead levels, intelligence, school performance and behaviour. Part III. Dentine lead levels and attention/activity. *Journal of Child Psychology and Psychiatry* **29(6)**, 811–824.

Fleischman M.J. & Szykula S.A. (1981) A community setting replication of a social learning treatment for aggressive children. *Behavior Therapy*, **12**, 115–122.

Frick P.J., Lahey B.B., Hartdagen S. & Hynd G.W. (1989) Conduct problems in boys: relations to maternal personality, marital satisfaction, and socioeconomic status. *Journal of Clinical Child Psychology*, **18(2)**, 114–120.

Frick P.J., Lahey B.B., Loeber R., Stouthamer-Lahey M., Green S., Hart E.L. & Christ M.A.G. (1991a) Oppositional defiant disorder and conduct disorder in boys: patterns of behavioral covariation. *Journal of Clinical Child Psychology*, **20(2)**, 202–208.

Frick P.J., Kamphaus R.W., Lahey B.B., Loeber R., Christ M.A.G., Hart E.L. & Tannenbaum L.E. (1991b) Academic underachievement and the disruptive behavior disorders. *Journal of Consulting and Clinical Psychology*, **59(2)**, 289–294.

Gittelman R., Mannuzza S., Shenker R. & Bonagura N. (1985) Hyperactive boys almost grown up, I: psychiatric status. *Archives of General Psychiatry*, **42**, 937–947.

Glueck S. & Glueck E. (1940) *Juvenile Delinquents Grown Up*. Commonwealth Fund, New York.

Gottfredson D.C. (1987) An empirical test of school-based environmental and individual interventions to reduce the risk of delinquent behavior. *Criminology*, **24**, 705–731.

Graham P., Rutter M. & George S. (1973) Temperamental characteristics as predictors of behavior disorders in children. *American Journal of Orthopsychiatry*, **43**, 328–339.

Gray J.A. (1987) *The Psychology of Fear and Stress*, 2nd edn. Cambridge University Press, Cambridge.

Gray J.A., Owen S., Davis N. & Tsaltas E. (1983) Psychological and physiological relations between anxiety and impulsivity. In: Zuckerman M. (ed) *Biological Bases of Sensation Seeking, Impulsivity and Anxiety*, pp. 181–217. Erlbaum, Hillsdale, NJ.

Greenbaum P.E., Prange M.E., Friedman R.M. & Silver S.E. (1991) Substance abuse prevalence and comorbidity with other psychiatric disorders among adolescents with severe emotional disturbances. *Journal of the American Academy of Child and Adolescent Psychiatry*, **30(4)**, 575–583.

Group for the Advancement of Psychiatry (1966) Psychopathological disorders in childhood: theoretical considerations and a proposed classification (report no. 62). Group for the Advancement of Psychiatry, New York.

Guerra N.G. & Slaby R.G. (1989) Evaluative factors in social problem solving by aggressive boys. *Journal of Abnormal Child Psychology*, **17(3)**, 277–289.

Guerra N.G. & Slaby R.G. (1990) Cognitive mediators of aggression in adolescent offenders: 2. Intervention. *Developmental Psychology*, **26(2)**, 269–277.

Hawkins J.D., Von Cleve E. & Catalano R.F. (1991) Reducing early childhood aggression: results of a primary prevention program. *Journal of the American Academy of Child and Adolescent Psychiatry*, **30(2)**, 208–217.

Healy W. (1917) *Mental Conflicts and Misconduct*. Little, Brown, Boston.

Healy W. & Bronner A.F. (1926) *Delinquents and Criminals, Their Making and Unmaking. Studies in Two American Cities*. MacMillan, New York.

Hewitt L.E. & Jenkins R.L. (1946) *Fundamental Patterns of Maladjustment: The Dynamics of Their Origins*. State of Illinois, Springfield, IL.

Hoffman M. (1982) Affect and moral development. In: Cichetti D. & Hesse P. (eds) *New Directions for Child Development: Emotional Development*, vol. 16, pp. 83–103. Jossey-Bass, San Francisco.

Huesmann L.R., Eron L.D., Lefkowitz M.M. & Walder L.O. (1984) Stability of aggression over time and generations. *Developmental Psychology*, **20**, 1120–1134.

Jary M.L. & Stewart M.A. (1985) Psychiatric disorder in the parents of adopted children with aggressive conduct disorder. *Neuropsychobiology*, **13**, 7–11.

Jenkins J.M. & Smith, M.A. (1990) Factors protecting children in disharmonious homes. *American Academy of Child and Adolescent Psychiatry*, **29**, 60–69.

Joffe R.D., Dobson K.S., Fine S., Marriage K. & Haley G. (1990) Social problem-solving in depressed, conduct-disordered and normal adolescents. *Journal of Abnormal Child Psychology*, **18(5)**, 565–575.

Johnson A.M. & Szurek S.A. (1952) The genesis of antisocial acting-out in children and adolescents. *Psychoanalytic Quarterly*, **21**, 323–343.

Jones M.B. & Offord D.R. (1989) Reduction of antisocial behavior in poor children by nonschool skill-development. *Journal of Child Psychology and Psychiatry*, **30(5)**, 737–750.

Kagan J. (1984) *The Nature of the Child*. Basic Books, New York.

Kagan J. & Snidman N. (1991) Temperamental factors in human development. *American Psychologist*, **46**, 856–862.

Kandel D., Kessler R.C. & Margulies R.Z. (1978) Antecedents of adolescent initiation into stages of drug use: a developmental analysis. In: Kandel D.B. (ed) *Longitudinal Research and Drug Use: Empirical Findings and Methodological Issues*, pp. 73–98. Hemisphere, Washington, DC.

Karniski W.M., Levine M.D., Clarke S., Palfrey J.S. & Meltzer L.J. (1982) A study of neurodevelopmental findings in early adolescent delinquents. *Journal of Adolescent Health Care*, **3**, 151–159.

Kashani J.H. & Cantwell D.P. (1983) Characteristics of children admitted to inpatient community mental health center. *Archives of General Psychiatry*, **40**, 397–400.

Kazdin A.E. (1985) *Treatment of Antisocial Behavior in Children and Adolescents*. Dorsey, Homewood, IL.

Kazdin A.E. (1987) Current treatments. In: Kazdin, A.E. (ed) *Conduct Disorders in Childhood and Adolescence*, pp. 73–95. Sage Publications, Newbury Park, CA.

Kazdin A.E., Esveldt-Dawson K., French N.H. & Unis A.S. (1987) Effects of parent management training and problem-solving skills training combined in the treatment of antisocial child behavior. *Journal of the American Academy of Child and Adolescent Psychiatry*, **26(3)**, 416–424.

Kendall P.C. & Braswell L. (1985) *Cognitive-Behavioral Therapy for Impulsive Children*. Guilford, New York.

Kohlberg L. (1976) Moral stages and moralization: the cognitive developmental approach. In: Lickona T. (ed) *Handbook of Socialization Theory and Research*, pp. 347–480. Rand McNally, Chicago.

Kolvin I., Garside R.F., Nicol A.R., MacMillen A., Wolstenhome F. & Leitch I.M. (1981) *Help Starts Here: The Maladjusted Child in the Ordinary School*. Tavistock Publications, New York.

Kolvin F.J., Miller J.W., Fleeting M. & Kolvin P.A. (1988) Social and parenting factors affecting criminal-offence rates. Findings from the Newcastle thousand family study (1947–1980). *British Journal of Psychiatry*, **152**, 80–90.

Kruesi M.J.P., Rapoport J.L., Hamburger S., Hibbs E., Potter W.Z., Lenane M. & Brown G.L. (1990) Cerebrospinal fluid monoamine metabolites, aggression, and impulsivity in disruptive behavior disorders of children and adolescents. *Archives of General Psychiatry*, **47**, 419–426.

Lahey B.B., Piacentini J.C., McBurnett K., Stone P., Hartdagen S.E. & Hynd G.W. (1988) Psychopathology in the parents of children with conduct disorder and hyperactivity. *Journal of the American Academy of Child and Adolescent Psychiatry*, **27**, 163–170.

Lahey B.B., Russo M.F., Walker J.L. & Piacentini J.C. (1989) Personality characteristics of the mothers of children with disruptive behavior disorders. *Journal of Consulting and Clinical Psychology*, **57(4)**, 512–515.

Lahey B.B., Loeber R., Stouthamer-Loeber M., Christ M.A.G., Green S., Russo M.F., Frick P.J. & Dulcan M. (1990) Comparison of DSM-III and DSM-III-R diagnoses for prepubertal children: changes in prevalence and validity. *Journal of the American Academy of Child and Adolescent Psychiatry*, **29(4)**, 620–626.

Lane T.W. & Davis G.E. (1987) Child maltreatment and juvenile delinquency: does a relationship exist? In: Burchard J.D. & Burchard S.N. (eds) *Prevention of Delinquent Behavior. Primary Prevention of Psychopathology*, pp. 122–138. Sage, Newbury Park, CA.

LeBlanc M., Cote G. & Loeber R. (1991) Temporal paths in delinquency: stability, regression and progression analyzed with panel data from an adolescent and a delinquent male sample. *Canadian Journal of Criminology*, **January**, 23–44.

Leckman J.F., Sholomskas D., Thompson W.D., Belanger A. & Weissman M.M. (1982) Best estimate of lifetime psychiatric diagnosis. A methodological study. *Archives of General Psychiatry*, **39**, 879–883.

Levy D.M. (1952a) Critical evaluation of the present state of child psychiatry. *American Journal of Psychiatry*, **108**, 481–490.

Levy D.M. (1952b) Oppositional syndromes and oppositional behavior. In: Hach P.H. & Zubin J. (eds) *Psychopathology of Childhood*, pp. 204–226. Grune & Stratton, New York.

Lewis D.O., Shanok S., Pincus J. & Glaser G.H. (1979) Violent juvenile delinquents: psychiatric, neurological, psychological and abuse factors. *Journal of the American Academy of Child Psychiatry*, **18**, 307–319.

Lewis D.O., Pincus J.H., Lovely R., Spitzer E. & Moy E. (1987) Biopsychosocial characteristics of matched samples of delinquents and nondelinquents. *Journal of the Academy of Child and Adolescent Psychiatry*, **26**, 744–752.

Links P.S. (1983) Community surveys of the prevalence of childhood psychiatric disorders: a review. *Child Development*, **54**, 531–584.

Linnoila M., Virkkunen M., Scheinin M., Nuutila A., Rimon R. & Goodwin F.K. (1983) Low cerebrospinal fluid 5-hydroxyindoleacetic acid differentiates impulsive from non-impulsive violent behavior. *Life Sciences*, **33**, 2609–2614.

Lipsey M.W. (1992) Juvenile delinquency treatment: a meta-analytic inquiry into the variability of effects. In: Cook T.D., Cooper H., Cordray D.S., Hartmann H., Hedges L.V., Light R.J., Louis T.A. & Mosteller F. (eds) *Meta-Analysis for Explanation: A Casebook*. Russell Sage Foundation, New York.

Lochman J.E., Burch P.R., Curry J.F. & Lampron L.B. (1984) Treatment and generalization effects of cognitive-behavioral and goal-setting interventions with aggressive boys. *Journal of Consulting and Clinical Psychology*, **52**, 915–916.

Loeber R. (1982) The stability of antisocial and delinquent child behavior: a review. *Child Development*, **53**, 1431–1446.

Loeber R. (1990) Development and risk factors of juvenile antisocial behavior and delinquency. *Clinical Psychology Review*, **10**, 1–41.

Loeber R. & Dishion T.J. (1983) Early predictors of male delinquency: a review. *Psychological Bulletin*, **94**, 68–99.

Loeber R. & LeBlanc M. (1990) Toward a developmental criminology. In: Tonry M. & Morris N. (eds) *Crime and Justice: A Review of Research*, pp. 375–473. University of Chicago Press, Chicago, IL.

Loeber R. & Schmaling K.B. (1985) Empirical evidence for overt and covert patterns of antisocial conduct problems: a meta-analysis. *Journal of Abnormal Child Psychology*, **13**, 337–352.

Loeber R., Brinthaupt V.P. & Green S.M. (1990a) Attention deficits, impulsivity, and hyperactivity with or without conduct problems: relationships to delinquency and unique contextual factors. In: McMahon R.J. & Peters R.DeV. (eds) *Behavior Disorders of Adolescence. Research, Intervention and Policy in Clinical and School Settings*, pp. 39–61. Plenum Press, New York.

Loeber R., Green S.M. & Lahey B.B. (1990b) Mental health professionals' perception of the utility of children, mothers, and teachers as informants on childhood psychopathology. *Journal of Clinical Child Psychology*, **19**, 136–143.

Loeber R., Green S.M., Lahey B.B. & Stouthamer-Loeber M. (1991a) Differences and similarities between children, mothers, and teachers as informants on disruptive child behavior. *Journal of Abnormal Child Psychology*, **19(1)**, 75–95.

Loeber R., Lahey B.B. & Thomas C. (1991b) Diagnostic conundrum of oppositional defiant disorder and conduct disorder. *Journal of Abnormal Psychology*, **100(3)**, 379–390.

Luria A.R. (1973) *The Working Brain*. Penguin Books, London.

McCord J. (1979) Some child-rearing antecedents of criminal behaviour in adult men. *Journal of Personality and Social Psychology*, **37**, 1477–1486.

McGee R., Williams S. & Silva P.A. (1984) Behavioral and developmental characteristics of aggressive, hyperactive, and aggressive-hyperactive boys. *Journal of the American Academy of Child Psychiatry*, **23**, 270–279.

McGuire J. & Earls F. (1991) Prevention of psychiatric disorders in early childhood. *Journal of Child Psychology and Psychiatry*, **32(1)**, 129–154.

Mannuzza S., Klein R.G., Bonagura N., Malloy P., Giampino T.L. & Addalli K.A. (1991) Hyperactive boys almost grown up, V: Replication of psychiatric status. *Archives of General Psychiatry*, **48**, 77–83.

Mattsson A., Schalling D., Olweus D., Low H. & Svensson J. (1980) Plasma testosterone, aggressive behavior and personality dimensions in young male delinquents. *Journal of the American Academy of Child Psychiatry*, **19**, 476–490.

Maziade M., Caron C., Côté R., Boutin P. & Thivierge J. (1990) Extreme temperament and diagnosis. A study in a psychiatric sample of consecutive children. *Archives of General Psychiatry*, **47**, 477–484.

Mednick S.A., Moffitt T.E., Pollock V., Talovic S. & Gabvielli W. (1986) The inheritance of human deviance. In: Olweus D. & Yarrow M.R. (eds) *Development of Antisocial and Prosocial Behavior*. Academic Press, New York.

Milin R., Halikas J.A., Meller J.E. & Morse C. (1991) Psychopathology among substance abusing juvenile offenders. *Journal of the American Academy of Child and Adolescent Psychiatry*, **30(4)**, 569–574.

Moffitt T.E. (1990a) Juvenile delinquency and attention deficit disorder: boys' developmental trajectories from age 3 to age 15. *Child*

Development, **61**, 893–910.

Moffitt T.E. (1990b) The neuropsychology of delinquency: a critical review of theory and research. In: Morris N. & Tonry M. (eds) *Crime and Justice: An Annual Review of Research*, vol. 12, pp. 99–169. University of Chicago Press, Chicago.

Moffitt T.E. & Henry B. (1991) Neuropsychological studies of juvenile delinquency and juvenile violence. In: Milner J.S. (ed) *Neuropsychology of Aggression*, pp. 67–91. Kluwer Academic Publishers, Boston.

Morris H.H., Escoll P.J. & Wexler R. (1956) Aggressive behavior disorders of childhood, a follow-up study. *American Journal of Psychiatry*, **112**, 991–997.

Needleman H.L., Gunnoe C., Leviton A., Reed R., Peresie H., Maher C. & Barrett P. (1979) Deficits in psychologic and classroom performance of children with elevated dentine lead levels. *New England Journal of Medicine*, **300(13)**, 689–695.

Needleman H.L., Schell A., Bellinger D., Leviton A. & Allred E.N. (1990) The long-term effects of exposure to low doses of lead in childhood. An 11-year follow-up report. *New England Journal of Medicine*, **322(2)**, 83–88.

Offord D.R. (1987) Prevention of behavioral and emotional disorders in children. *Journal of Child Psychology and Psychiatry*, **28(1)**, 9–19.

Offord D.R. (1989) Conduct disorders: risk factors and prevention. In: Shaffer D., Philips I., Enzer N.B. & Silverman M.M. (eds) *Prevention of Mental Disorders, Alcohol and Other Drug Use in Children and Adolescents*, pp. 273–307. OSAP Prevention Monograph-2. US Department of Health and Human Services, Rockville, MD.

Offord D.R. & Jones M.B. (1983) Skill development: a community intervention program for the prevention of antisocial behavior. In: Guze S.B., Earls F. & Barrett J.E. (eds) *Childhood Psychopathology and Development*. Raven Press, New York.

Offord D.R., Boyle M.H., Szatmari P., Rae-Grant N.I., Links P.S., Cadman D.T., Byles J.A., Crawford J.W., Blum H.M., Byrne C., Thomas H. & Woodward C.A. (1987) Ontario Child Health Study: I. Six-month prevalence of disorder and service utilization. *Archives of General Psychiatry*, **44**, 832–836.

Offord D.R., Boyle M.C. & Racine Y.A. (1991) The epidemiology of antisocial behavior in childhood and adolescence. In: Pepler D.J. & Rubin K.H. (eds) *The Development and Treatment of Childhood Aggression*, pp. 31–54. Lawrence Erlbaum, Hillsdale, NJ.

Olweus D. (1979) Stability of aggressive reaction patterns in males: a review. *Psychological Bulletin*, **86**, 852–875.

Olweus D. (1991) Bully/victim problems among schoolchildren: basic facts and effects of a school based intervention program. In: Pepler D.J. & Rubin K.H. (eds) *The Development and Treatment of Childhood Aggression*, pp. 411–448. Lawrence Erlbaum, Hillsdale, NJ.

Patterson G.R., Chamberlain P. & Reid J.B. (1982) A comparative evaluation of a parent-training program. *Behavior Therapy*, **13**, 638–650.

Patterson G.R., DeBarysh B.D. & Ramsey E. (1989) A developmental perspective on antisocial behavior. *American Psychologist*, **44**, 329–335.

Platt N.J., Spivack G., Altman N., Altman D. & Peizer S. (1974) Adolescent problem solving thinking. *Journal of Consulting and Clinical Psychology*, **47**, 787–793.

Plomin R. & DeFries J.C. (1983) The Colorado adoption project. *Child Development*, **54**, 276–289.

Pontius A.A. (1972) Neurological aspects in some type of delinquency, especially among juveniles: toward a neurological model of ethical action. *Adolescence*, **7**, 289–308.

Pontius A.A. (1976) Frontal lobe system maturational lag in juvenile delinquents shown in narratives test. *Adolescence*, **11**, 509–518.

Price R.H., Cowen E.L., Lorion R.P. & Ramos-McKay J. (1989) The search for effective prevention programs: what we learned along the way. *American Journal of Orthopsychiatry*, **59**, 49–58.

Quay HC. (1983) A dimensional approach to children's behavior disorder: the Revised Behavior Problem Checklist. *School Psychology Review*, **12**, 244–249.

Quay H.C. (1988) The behavioral reward and inhibition system in childhood behavior disorder. In: Bloomingdale L.M. (ed) *Attention Deficit Disorder*, pp. 176–186. Spectrum Press, New York.

Raine A. (1988) Antisocial behaviour and social psychophysiology. In: Wagner H.L. (ed) *Social Psychophysiology and Emotion: Theory and Clinical Applications*, pp. 231–250. John Wiley, New York.

Raine A., Venables P.H. & Mark W. (1990) Relationships between central and autonomic measures of arousal at age 15 years and criminality at age 24 years. *Archives of General Psychiatry*, **47**, 1003–1007.

Reich W. & Earls F. (1987) Rules for making psychiatric diagnoses in children on the basis of multiple sources of information: preliminary strategies. *Journal of Abnormal Child Psychology*, **15(4)**, 601–616.

Reid J.B. & Patterson G.R. (1989) The development of antisocial behaviour patterns in childhood and adolescence. *European Journal of Personality*, **3**, 107–119.

Richman N., Stevenson J. & Graham P.J. (1982) *Pre-school to School: A Behavioural Study*. Academic Press, London.

Robins L.N. (1966) *Deviant Children Grown Up*. Williams & Wilkins, Baltimore.

Robins L.N. (1978) Sturdy childhood predictors of adult antisocial behavior: replications from longitudinal studies. *Psychological Medicine*, **8**, 611–622.

Robins L.N. (1986) The consequences of conduct disorder in girls. In: Olweus D. & Yarrow M.R. (eds) *Development of Antisocial and Prosocial Behavior*, pp. 385–414. Academic Press, New York.

Robins L.N. & Earls F. (1986) A program for preventing antisocial behavior for high-risk infants and preschoolers: a research prospectus. In: Hough R.L., Gongla P.A., Brown V.B. & Goldston S.E. (eds) *Psychiatric Epidemiology and Prevention: The Possibilities*, pp. 73–83. Neuropsychiatric Institute, University of California, Los Angeles.

Robins L.N. & Price R.K. (1991) Adult disorders predicted by childhood conduct problems: results from the NIMH Epidemiologic Catchment Area project. *Psychiatry*, **54**, 116–132.

Robins L.N. & Ratcliff K.S. (1980) Childhood conduct disorders and later arrest. In: Robins L.N., Clayton P.J. & Wing J.K. (eds) *The Social Consequences of Psychiatric Illness*, pp. 248–263. Brunner/Mazel, New York.

Robins L.N. & Wish E. (1977) Childhood deviance as a developmental process: a study of 223 urban black men from birth to 18. *Social Forces*, **56**, 448–473.

Rogeness G.A., Hernandez J.M., Macedo C.A. & Mitchell E.L. (1982) Biochemical differences in children with conduct disorder socialized and undersocialized. *American Journal of Psychiatry*, **139**, 307–311.

Rogeness G.A., Hernandez J.M., Macedo C.A., Mitchell E.L., Amrung S.A. & Harris W.R. (1984) Clinical characteristics of emotionally disturbed boys with very low activities of dopamine-β-hydroxylase. *Journal of the American Academy of Child and Adolescent Psychiatry*, **23**, 203–208.

Rogeness G.A., Hernandez J.M., Macedo C.A., Mitchell E.L., Amrung S.A. & Hoppe S.K. (1986) Near-zero plasma dopamine-β-hydroxylase and conduct disorder in emotionally disturbed boys. *Journal of the American Academy of Child Psychiatry*, **25**, 521–527.

Rutter M. (1978) Family, area, and school influences in the genesis of conduct disorders. In: Hersov L.A. & Berger M. (eds) *Aggression and Anti-social Behaviour in Childhood and Adolescence*, pp. 95–114. Pergamon, London.

Rutter M. (1989) Annotation: child psychiatric disorders in ICD-10. *Journal of Child Psychology and Psychiatry*, **30**, 499–513.

Rutter M. & Giller H. (1983) *Juvenile Delinquency, Trends and Perspectives*.

Guilford Press, New York.

Rutter M., Tizard J. & Whitmore K. (1970) *Education, Health and Behaviour*. Longmans, London.

Rutter M., Yule W., Berger M., Yule B., Morton J. & Bagley C. (1974) Children of West Indian immigrants: I. Rates of behavioural deviance and of psychiatric disorder. *Journal of Child Psychology and Psychiatry*, **15**, 241–262.

Rutter M., Cox A., Tupling C., Berger M. & Yule W. (1975) Attainment and adjustment in two geographical areas: I. Prevalence of psychiatric disorder. *British Journal of Psychiatry*, **126**, 493–509.

Rydelius P.A. (1988) The development of antisocial behaviour and sudden violent death. *Acta Psychiatrica Scandinavica*, **77**, 398–403.

Sampson R. (1985) Neighborhood and crime: the structural determinants of personal victimization. *Journal of Research on Crime and Delinquency*, **22**, 7–40.

Sampson R.J. (1992) Family management and child development: insights from social disorganization theory. In: McCord J. (ed) *Facts, Framerworks and Forecasts: Advances in Criminological Theory*, vol. 3, pp. 63–93. Transaction Publishers, New Brunswick, NJ & London.

Sanderson J.A. & Siegal M. (1988) Conceptions of moral and social rules in rejected and nonrejected preschoolers. *Journal of Clinical Child Psychology*, **17(1)**, 66–72.

Schachar R. & Wachsmuth R. (1990) Oppositional disorder in children: a validation study comparing conduct disorder, oppositional disorder and normal control children. *Journal of Child Psychology and Psychiatry*, **31(7)**, 1089–1102.

Schonfeld I.S., Shaffer D., O'Connor P. & Portnoy S. (1988) Conduct disorder and cognitive functioning: testing three causal hypotheses. *Child Development*, **59**, 993–1007.

Schweinhart L.J. & Weikart D.P. (1983) The effects of the Perry Preschool Program on youths through age 15 — a summary. In: Grotberg E.H. (ed) *As the Twig is Bent: Lasting Effects of Preschool Programs*, pp. 71–101. Lawrence Erlbaum, Hillsdale, NJ.

Shaffer D., Campbell M., Cantwell D., Bradley S., Carlson G., Cohen D., Denckla M., Frances A., Garfinkel B., Klein R., Pincus H., Spitzer R.L., Volkmar F. & Widiger T. (1989) Child and adolescent psychiatric disorders in DSM-IV: issues facing the work group. *Journal of the American Academy of Child and Adolescent Psychiatry*, **28**, 830–835.

Shaw C.R. & MacKay H.D. (1942) *Juvenile Delinquency and Urban Areas*. University of Chicago, Chicago, IL.

Slaby R.G. & Guerra N.G. (1988) Cognitive mediators of aggression in adolescent offenders: 1. Assessment. *Developmental Psychology*, **24(4)**, 580–588.

Smetana J.G. & Braeges J.L. (1990) The development of toddlers' moral and conventional judgements. *Merrill-Palmer Quarterly*, **36(3)**, 329–346.

Spellacy F. (1977) Neuropsychological differences between violent and nonviolent adolescents. *Journal of Clinical Psychology*, **33(4)**, 966–969.

Spellacy F. (1978) Neuropsychological discrimination between violent and nonviolent men. *Journal of Clinical Psychology*, **34(1)**, 49–52.

Stattin H. & Klackenberg-Larsson I. (1990) The relationship between maternal attributes in the early life of the child and the child's future criminal behavior. *Development and Psychopathology*, **2**, 99–111.

Stewart M.A., DeBlois C.S. & Cummings C. (1979) Psychiatric disorder in the parents of hyperactive boys and those with conduct disorder. *Journal of Child Psychology and Psychiatry*, **21**, 283–292.

Stewart M.A., Cummings C., Singer S. & DeBlois C.S. (1981) The overlap between hyperactive and unsocialized aggressive children. *Journal of Child Psychology and Psychiatry*, **22**, 35–45.

Stiffman A.R. & Earls F. (1990) Behavioral risks for HIV infection in adolescent medical patients. *Pediatrics*, **85**, 303–310.

Stoff D.M., Pollack L., Vitiello B., Behar D. & Bridger W.H. (1987) Reduction of 3-H-imipramine binding sites on platelets of conduct disordered children. *Neuropsychopharmacology*, **155**, 62.

Stoff D.M., Friedman E., Pollock L., Vitiello B., Kendall P.C. & Bridger W.H. (1989) Elevated platelet MAO is related to impulsivity in disruptive behavior disorders. *Journal of the American Academy of Child and Adolescent Psychiatry*, **28(5)**, 754–760.

Sturge C. (1982) Reading retardation and antisocial behaviour. *Journal of Child Psychology and Psychiatry*, **23**, 21–31.

Susman E.J., Inoff-Germain G., Nottelmann E.D., Loriaux D.L., Cutler G.B. & Chrousos G.P. (1987) Hormones, emotional dispositions, and aggressive attributes in young adolescents. *Child Development*, **58**, 1114–1134.

Szatmari P., Boyle M. & Offord D.R. (1989) ADDH and conduct disorder: degree of diagnostic overlap and differences among correlates. *Journal of the American Academy of Child and Adolescent Psychiatry*, **28**, 865–872.

Tolan P.H. (1987) Implications of age of onset for delinquency risk. *Journal of Abnormal Child Psychology*, **15(1)**, 47–65.

Tonry M., Ohlin L. & Farrington D. (1990) *Human Development and Criminal Behavior: New Ways of Advancing Knowledge*. Springer-Verlag, New York.

Torgersen A.M. & Kringlen E. (1978) Genetic aspects of temperamental differences in infants. *Journal of the American Academy of Child Psychiatry*, **17**, 433–434.

Tremblay R.E., McCord J., Boileau H., LeBlanc M., Gagnon C., Charlebois P. & Larivée S. (1990) The Montréal experiment: school adjustment and self-reported delinquency after three years of follow-up. Paper presented at the Annual Meeting of the American Society of Criminology, Baltimore, MD.

Tremblay R.E., Loeber R., Gagnon C., Charlebois P., Larivee S. & LeBlanc M. (1991) Disruptive boys with stable and unstable high fighting behavior patterns during junior elementary school. *Journal of Abnormal Child Psychology*, **19(3)**, 285–299.

Virkkunen M. & Penttinen H. (1984) Serum cholesterol in aggressive conduct disorder: a preliminary study. *Biological Psychiatry*, **19(3)**, 435–439.

Virkkunen M., DeJong J., Bartko J., Goodwin F.K. & Linnoila M. (1989) Relationship of psychobiological variables to recidivism in violent offenders and impulsive fire setters. *Archives of General Psychiatry*, **46**, 600–603.

Walker L.J. (1988) The development of moral reasoning. *Annals of Child Development*, **5**, 33–78.

Walker L.J., Lahey B.B., Russo M.F., Frick P.J., Christ M.A.G., McBurnett K., Loeber R., Stouthamer-Loeber M. & Green S.M. (1991) Anxiety, inhibition, and conduct disorder in children: I. Relations to social impairment. *Journal of the American Academy of Child and Adolescent Psychiatry*, **30(2)**, 187–191.

Walsh A., Petee T.A. & Beyer J.A. (1987) Intellectual imbalance and delinquency: comparing high verbal and high performance IQ delinquents. *Criminal Justice and Behavior*, **14(3)**, 370–379.

Walter H.J., Vaughn R.D. & Cohall A.T. (1991) Risk factors for substance use among high school students: implications for prevention. *Journal of the American Academy of Child and Adolescent Psychiatry*, **30(4)**, 556–562.

Weisz J.R., Martin S.L., Walter B.R. & Fernandez G.A. (1991) Differential prediction of young adult arrests for property and personal crimes: findings of a cohort follow-up study of violent boys from North Carolina's Willie M Program. *Journal of Child Psychology and Psychiatry*, **32**, 783–792.

Wells K.C., Forehand R. & Griest D.L. (1980) Generality of treatment effects from treated to untreated behaviors resulting from a parent training program. *Journal of Clinical Child Psychology*, **9**, 217–219.

West D.J. & Farrington D.P. (1977) *The Delinquent Way of Life*. Heinemann, London.

White J.L., Moffitt T.E. & Silva P.A. (1989) A prospective replication of the protective effects of IQ in subjects at high risk for juvenile delinquency. *Journal of Clinical and Consulting Psychology*, **57**, 719–724.

White J.L., Moffitt T.E., Earls F., Robins L. & Silva P.A. (1990) How early can we tell? Predictors of childhood conduct disorder and adolescent delinquency. *Criminology*, **28(4)**, 507–533.

Widom C.S. (1989) The cycle of violence. *Science*, **244**, 160–166.

Wolfgang M.E., Figlio R.M. & Sellin T. (1972) *Delinquency in a Birth Cohort*. University of Chicago Press, Chicago.

World Health Organization (1978) *Mental Disorders: Glossary and Guide to Their Classification in Accordance with the Ninth Revision of the International Classification of Diseases*. World Health Organization, Geneva.

World Health Organization (1992) *The ICD-10 Classification of Mental and Behavioral Disorders: Clinical Descriptions and Diagnostic Guidelines*. World Health Organization, Geneva.

Yeager C.A. & Lewis D.O. (1990) Mortality in a group of formerly incarcerated juvenile delinquents. *American Journal of Psychiatry*, **147(5)**, 612–614.

Yeudall L.T., Fromm-Auch D. & Davies P. (1982) Neuropsychological impairment of persistent delinquency. *Journal of Nervous and Mental Disease*, **170(5)**, 257–265.

Zoccolillo M., Pickles A., Quinton D., & Rutter M. (1992) The outcome of childhood conduct disorder: implications for defining adult personality disorder and conduct disorder. *Psychological Medicine*, **22**, 971–986.

Chapter 19
Affective Disorders

Richard Harrington

DEPRESSIVE DISORDERS

Concepts of depression

Sadness is part of the normal range of emotional reactions. The symptom of depression, however, is not synonymous with sadness or unhappiness. Although unhappiness is a prominent component of the depressive mood state, the negative mood of depression may be represented more by features such as emotional emptiness or a feeling of flatness (Hamilton, 1982). The symptom of depression occurs in many different psychiatric disorders and may also be found in some physical conditions.

In the present chapter we are concerned neither with normal unhappiness nor with the single symptom of depression, but rather with those syndromes known as depressive disorders. The term syndrome implies more than just an isolated symptom; it requires the combination with other symptoms to form a symptom complex. In most classification systems, the syndrome of depression is defined by the combination of depressed mood with certain associated symptoms, particularly a negative style of thinking, loss of enjoyment, and somatic symptoms such as loss of energy and reduced sleep. For instance, in DSM-IV (American Psychiatric Association, in press) the diagnosis of major depressive episode requires at least four accessory symptoms.

It will be appreciated that to define the syndrome of depression in terms of numbers of symptoms only may give rise to error. For example, one person with many minor symptoms causing no impairment may be seen as suffering from the depressive syndrome, while another whose few symptoms cause much impairment may not be so regarded. Accordingly, most diagnostic systems include additional criteria that are intended to sharpen the differentiation between depressive symptoms and the disorder of depression. For instance, the DSM-IV definition of major depressive episode requires that symptoms have been present during the same 2-week period and that there is impairment.

Concepts of depression in children

The idea that children can develop conditions that are the same as these depressive disorders of adults has been contro-versial (Rutter, 1986a; Harrington, 1989). Indeed, until recently it was widely believed that depressive disorders could not occur in childhood or that if they did occur then they took a 'masked' form, being expressed through symptoms such as delinquency or phobias. However, the use of symptom-oriented, personal interviews with children has now led to widespread recognition that disorders resembling adult depression can and do occur in childhood. Indeed, in DSM-IV the criteria for prepubertal, adolescent and adult depression are identical.

It might therefore be thought that the controversy surrounding the concept of depression in childhood has been resolved. This is not the case. Many uncertainties remain. Some of these uncertainties apply to depressive disorders across the age span. For example, at no age is it clear where the line should be drawn between clinical depressive disorder and normal feelings of sadness that occur in the context of adversity. Similarly, the boundary between affective disorders and other psychiatric conditions is uncertain (Andreasen, 1982).

However, perhaps more importantly the strategy of applying unmodified adult criteria to children has been criticized because it ignores developmental research on age changes in the frequency and expression of affective phenomena. Three developmental issues are especially relevant here. Firstly, as we shall see later, there are substantial age differences in the occurrence of most forms of affective phenomena (Rutter, 1986b; Angold, 1988a,b). Secondly, children differ from adults in their ability to experience some of the cognitive features said to characterize adult depression, such as guilt (Rutter, 1986a). Thirdly, the valid application of adult criteria to children requires not only that they are capable of experiencing depression, but also that they can report it accurately (Rutter, 1986a). It seems that young children have limitations in this last respect, frequently confusing emotions such as sadness and anger (Kovacs, 1986).

These difficulties have led several investigators to suggest that it might be better to identify *age-appropriate* symptoms of depression that take into account the child's level of functioning in the various cognitive and affective domains (Carlson & Garber, 1986; Cicchetti & Schneider-Rosen, 1986; Harrington, 1991). Carlson and Garber (1986), for example, have proposed that current diagnostic systems such as DSM could be revised to take into account developmental differences. Their classification scheme proposes that depression in children could be conceptualized as having a basic similarity with adult-onset depression, but with some age-specific features.

Some support for this idea came from the Maudsley follow-up of depressed child and adolescent patients (Harrington *et al.*, 1990; Harrington, 1991). Depression in adulthood was best predicted by adult-like depressive symptoms, but age-specific symptoms such as school refusal were powerful discriminators between depressed and nondepressed children (Harrington, 1991). Clearly, then, developmental approaches to the diagnosis and classification of affective conditions among the young require more investigation, though they are going to be difficult to define.

Subclassification of affective disorder

A variety of different techniques have been used to subclassify affective disorders, including mathematical approaches, family history and response to treatment. The result has been a large number of competing classification schemes (Andreasen, 1982; Farmer & McGuffin, 1989). In this chapter only the two main ones will be considered: DSM-IV and ICD-10 (World Health Organization, 1992).

DSM-IV

DSM-IV differentiates between mood disorders in which there may or may not have been episodes of mania (bipolar disorders and depressive disorders respectively). The current state of major depressive disorder (MDD) is characterized further according to other features such as the presence of psychotic symptoms or melancholia. Psychotic is used to mean delusions or hallucinations. Melancholic subtype refers to a major depressive episode in which symptoms such as loss of interest, lack of reactivity to pleasurable stimuli and significant anorexia occur. The course of the main mood disorders may also be specified according to such features as rapidity of cycling and seasonal pattern.

The other principal depressive disorder is in DSM-IV is dysthymia. The diagnosis of dysthymic disorder applies to long-standing (1 year for children and adolescents) mood disorders characterized by mild depressive symptoms. Cyclothymic disorder is diagnosed when there are also chronic hypomanic episodes.

ICD-10

Like DSM-IV, ICD-10 makes an explicit distinction between unipolar and bipolar disorders and ICD-10 also distinguishes between milder forms of affective disorder (classified under neurotic disorders, stress-related disorders and mood disorder), and severe affective disorders, which are mostly included under mood disorders. There are diagnostic guidelines that attempt to provide an explicit specification of the concepts that underlie each disorder. These indicate the number and balance of symptoms usually required before a diagnosis can be made. They also give an indication of the level of knowledge represented in each category.

In line with DSM-IV, depressive disorders that can occur at any age are not separately categorized when they happen to occur in children. Bipolar disorder, for example, is classified in the same ICD-10 category regardless of age of onset. There is, however, a separate childhood category for mixed disorders characterized by both conduct disorder and depression (depressive conduct disorder). ICD continues to be different from DSM in its use of such combination categories.

Nosological validity of subdivisions

The distinction between unipolar and bipolar disorders is probably the best established of the subdivisions within the affective disorders, being supported by several different lines of evidence, most notably the family genetic findings (see Perris, 1982; Rutter *et al.*, 1990a).

Studies of response to treatment have tended to show that the presence of melancholic features predicts a better response to electroconvulsive treatment (ECT; Scott, 1989) and possibly to tricyclic antidepressants (Paykel, 1989). However, the family history findings have been contradictory (Leckman *et al.*, 1984; Andreasen *et al.*, 1986). The nosological validity of major depression with psychotic features has been supported by data from several sources (Schatzberg & Rothschild, 1992), especially from longitudinal studies, which have generally shown that the prognosis of patients with psychotic features is worse than that of those with nonpsychotic major depression (e.g. Johnson *et al.*, 1991).

Subclassification of childhood affective disorders

Since affective disorders in young people are now grouped together with those arising in other age periods, it might be thought that they should be subtyped in the same way. This would not be ideal. The most successful subclassification of adult affective disorders is based on the presence or absence of manic episodes but mania is rare in childhood. Moreover, the young child's difficulties in recalling past events may limit the reliability of subcategories that depend on historical data (e.g. recurrent depressive disorder in ICD-10).

However, attempts to develop a subclassification of affective disorders that would be more suitable for use with younger age groups are at an early stage. Indeed, most of the early mathematical studies did not even identify a depressive factor (Quay, 1979) and more recently Nurcombe *et al.* (1989) have reported that a 'nuclear' depressive disorder is less prevalent than is currently assumed. Their multivariate analyses of an inpatient sample appeared to show that only a small number of subjects had a categorically distinct depressive disorder. In the remainder, depression seemed to be distributed along a dimension.

It should be borne in mind, however, that these studies were mostly based on questionnaire ratings completed by parents. We shall see later that such ratings are a relatively crude way of assessing depressive phenomena. In fact, two recent studies in which symptom data were obtained by detailed face-to-face interviews have suggested that depressive disorders among the young can be subdivided into distinct subgroups (Ryan *et al.*, 1987; Kolvin *et al.*, 1991, 1992). Both studies applied principal components analysis, a statistical technique that divides patients into groups based on similarities of symptoms between individuals, to psychiatric samples containing children and adolescents previously diagnosed as having major depression. The results were striking in showing agreement between the studies on the presence of three clinically interpretable factors: an endogenous factor (symptoms such as loss of enjoyment, decreased weight and psychomotor retardation): a negative cognitions factor (symptoms such as negative self-image and suicidal ideation) and an anxiety factor. Ryan *et al.* (1987) also identified a disturbed conduct factor and an appetite—weight factor, but neither of these was found by Kolvin and his colleagues (1991).

Of course, the way in which symptoms cluster together is only one guideline for a useful classification system. It is also necessary to explore the utility of other validators, such as outcome, correlates and response to treatment. As yet, few investigators have attempted to subclassify affective disorders among the young in terms of these features. However, one subcategory, *depressive conduct disorder*, has been investigated by several different kinds of research strategy and the preliminary findings indicate that it may represent a distinct subgroup. Thus, in comparison with depressed children who do not have conduct problems, children who meet criteria for both depressive disorder and conduct disorder seem to have *lower* rates of depressive disorder when followed into adulthood (Harrington *et al.*, 1991), lower rates of depression among relatives (Puig-Antich *et al.*, 1989), a worse prognosis in terms of substance abuse (Caron *et al.*, submitted), a worse response to imipramine (Hughes *et al.*, 1990) and greater variability of mood (Costello *et al.*, 1991). In addition, Angold and Rutter (1992) reported that comorbid disorders constituted the only form of depression that did not show a rise with age.

Most of these studies were based on relatively small numbers and therefore require replication. Nevertheless, it is noteworthy that these different forms of enquiry all produced similar findings. Depression seems to have a different meaning when it occurs in conjunction with conduct disorder.

Epidemiology

Prevalence in community samples

Uncertainties surrounding the concept of depression in young people and unstandardized methods of assessment led to huge variability in the rates of depressive disorder that were found in early studies (Angold, 1988a). Recent epidemiological surveys have also had methodological problems (Verhulst & Koot, 1992) such as in sampling (Fleming & Offord, 1990),

and there have been differences between them in the types of prevalence rates reported, in the definition of caseness, and in the way in which data from subjects and parents have been combined (Brandenburg *et al.*, 1990). Nevertheless, the use of similar diagnostic criteria together with more comparable methods of data collection has led to greater consistency in estimates of the prevalence of depressive disorders among *preadolescents*, with the majority of 'current' rates (variously defined, but all within the year prior to interview) in the range from 0.5 to 2.5% (Kashani *et al.*, 1983; Anderson *et al.*, 1987; Fleming *et al.*, 1989; Velez *et al.*, 1989). Epidemiological studies of *adolescents* have generally reported higher prevalences, with current rates of major depression ranging from 2.0 to 8.0% (Kashani *et al.*, 1987; Velez *et al.*, 1989; McGee *et al.*, 1990; Whitaker *et al.*, 1990; Roberts *et al.*, 1991; Cooper & Goodyer, 1993).

Age trends and sex differences

Studies that have examined both preadolescents and adolescents have confirmed that there is an increase in rates of depression with age (Rutter *et al.*, 1970, 1976; Fleming *et al.*, 1989; Velez *et al.*, 1989; McGee *et al.*, 1992). There are also strong age trends for depression-related conditions such as suicide, which shows a huge rise over the adolescent years (McClure, 1984, 1988) and parasuicide (Sellar *et al.*, 1990). However, parasuicide differs from suicide in reaching a peak in early adulthood rather than in middle age.

Interestingly, it seems that among depressed children the sex ratio is about equal (Kashani *et al.*, 1983; Fleming *et al.*, 1989; Velez *et al.*, 1989) or there is a male preponderance (Anderson *et al.*, 1987), but that by adolescence the female preponderance found in adult depression (Weissman & Klerman, 1977) becomes evident (Kashani *et al.*, 1987; McGee *et al.*, 1990). The numbers of depressed cases found in community samples have been too small to allow accurate estimates of the age at which this switch of sex ratio occurs. However, data from other sources such as clinical samples have suggested that the switch begins at around the age of 10 years, with rates of depression increasing steadily in both boys and girls, but with the increase being more marked in girls (Zeitlin, 1986; Weissman *et al.*, 1987; Angold & Rutter, 1992).

Possible explanations for these age trends and sex differences (reviewed by Rutter, 1991) include an increase in risk factors (e.g. hormonal changes, genetic factors, increased adverse life events), a decline in protective factors (e.g. loss of social support, changes in the ability to experience depressive cognitions) and measurement artefacts.

Secular trends

It has been suggested that major depression is becoming more common both among young adults (Klerman, 1988) and among children (Ryan *et al.*, 1992). The evidence for these suggestions comes mostly from retrospective accounts of age at onset that have been obtained from subjects who have been ascertained in cross-sectional studies. Such accounts may be biased by the tendency for informants to be more likely to forget episodes when they have happened a long time before. Indeed, Giuffra and Risch (1991) showed that quite small rates of forgetting could explain the cohort effects. Nevertheless, an overall review of findings does suggest a possible increase in the rate of depressive disorders over the last generation (Fombonne, in press).

Also, recall artefacts could not account for the recent rise in rates of suicide among young males that has been described in both North America (Shaffer, 1988) and the UK (Hawton, 1992). In England and Wales, suicide is now the second most common cause of death among young people aged 15–24 years (Office of Population Census and Surveys, 1990). Psychological 'autopsy' studies have reported that many young suicides had a depressive disorder prior to death (reviewed by Marttunen *et al.*, 1991). Of course, other factors (such as unemployment — see Pritchard, 1992) may be important in these secular trends for suicide, but they do support the idea that depression may be on the increase among the young.

Clinical studies

Several studies have reported that depressive disorders may be quite common among children referred for evaluation in mental health settings. Thus, Carlson and Cantwell (1980) found that 60% of referred children had depressive symptoms, 49% had a depressive syndrome and 28% had an affective disorder. Similarly, Kolvin *et al.* (1991) estimated that 1 in 3 outpatients at a child psychiatric department had significant depression and 1 in 4 had major depression.

Overlap with other conditions

Many clinicians will find it surprising that these prevalence estimates for major depression among referred children were so high. However, it should be noted that these diagnoses were made without a diagnostic hierarchy. In other words, although these children met the criteria for major depression, many of them had other diagnoses as well. Indeed, it seems that most children who meet research criteria for depressive disorder are given some other primary diagnosis by the clinicians involved in their care (Harrington *et al.*, 1990). This overlap of depression and other psychiatric diagnoses has been one of the most consistent findings from research in referred populations, where an association has been found with conditions as diverse as conduct disorder (Marriage *et al.*, 1986; Harrington *et al.*, 1991), anxiety states (Bernstein & Garfinkel, 1986, 1988; Puig-Antich & Rabinovich, 1986; Mitchell *et al.*, 1988), learning problems (Forness, 1988), drug use (Greenbaum *et al.*, 1991; Millin *et al.*, 1991), hyperactivity (Bierderman *et al.*, 1991), anorexia nervosa (Lask & Bryant-Waugh, 1992) and school refusal (Bernstein, 1991).

Of course, apparent comorbidity between psychiatric disorders in clinical samples may be artefactual, as a result of referral biases. However, the epidemiological data confirm that the co-occurrence of depression and other conditions far exceeds that expected by chance (Caron & Rutter, 1991). Anderson *et al.* (1987), for example, found that of 14 children (aged 11 years) with depressive disorders, 11 had at least one other psychiatric condition as well. Indeed 8 of the 14 children had depression and an anxiety disorder and an attention deficit disorder and a conduct disorder! Reexamination of this sample 4 years later showed that once again affective disorders had the greatest degree of comorbidity (McGee *et al.*, 1990). Adolescents with depressive disorders seem to be more likely to have an additional psychiatric condition than depressed adults (Rohde *et al.*, 1991).

DSM-IV and ICD-10 take different approaches to the overlap between depression and other child psychiatric problems. In the DSM, there is no separate category for conditions characterized by two problems. Rather, it is assumed that comorbidity between depression and other psychiatric conditions represents the co-occurrence of separate disorders. By contrast, in ICD-10 the expectation is that just one disorder will be diagnosed. Here, the assumption is that a mixed clinical picture is more likely to mean a single disorder with varied manifestations than two different disorders that happen to occur in the same individual at the same time.

It is not yet clear which approach is to be preferred, but it seems likely that the meaning of the mixed state differs according to the type of comorbid diagnosis. Thus, as described earlier, there is evidence that when depression occurs in conjunction with conduct disorder it is associated with a different course and family background. The implication is that depression is in some sense secondary to the conduct disorder or that the two disorders are separately determined. By contrast, when depression occurs with an anxiety disorder, its prognosis is unaffected (Kovacs *et al.*, 1989) and the familial aggregation of depressive disorders is not significantly different from when depression is 'pure' (Puig-Antich *et al.*, 1989; Mufson *et al.*, 1992). Thus, although anxiety may signal a more severe type of disorder (Bernstein, 1991) and tends to precede the depression (Brady & Kendall, 1992), on present evidence it is unlikely that it indicates a qualitatively different form of depressive condition.

Finally, it should be borne in mind that depressive disorders may present not only with nondepressive psychiatric symptoms like anxiety but also with somatic complaints such as recurrent abdominal pain (Garber *et al.*, 1990). McCauley *et al.* (1991), for instance, reported that 70% of children with a diagnosis of depression had significant somatic complaints. So, children who present with unexplained physical symptoms require careful mental state examination to ensure that depression is not overlooked. Conversely, it should be remembered that physical conditions such as inflammatory bowel disease (P. Burke *et al.*, 1990) or endocrine disorders may be associated with significant depression.

Aetiology

Genetic influences

Genetic factors have been shown to account for about 80% of the variance in the liability to bipolar illness in adults (McGuffin & Katz, 1986) but probably play a less substantial, though still significant, role in unipolar depressive conditions (McGuffin, 1991; Kendler *et al.*, 1992). Interest in the genetics of depressive disorders arising in childhood has been stimulated by data from several different types of studies. Firstly, a number of studies of depressed adults have reported that earlier age of onset was associated with an increased familial loading for depressive disorder. For example, in the Yale family study (Weissman *et al.*, 1984) the risk was particularly great when the depression in the parent was of early onset (Weissman *et al.*, 1988). Secondly, both cross-sectional and longitudinal studies of the children of depressed parents have found that they have greater than expected rates of depression (Beardslee *et al.*, 1983; Weissman *et al.*, 1992). However, the risk seems to be nonspecific to the extent that nondepressive problems (such as substance abuse or behavioural difficulties) are increased as well (Weissman *et al.*, 1987; Radke-Yarrow *et al.*, 1992).

Thirdly, several investigators have reported high rates of affective disorders among relatives of depressed child probands (Livingston *et al.*, 1985; Dwyer & Delong, 1987; Mitchell *et al.*, 1989; Puig-Antich *et al.*, 1989; Kutcher & Marton, 1991). Many of these studies lacked adequate control groups, so again it is not clear whether the risk was specific for depression (Rutter *et al.*, 1990a,b). Better matching was achieved by Harrington *et al.* (1993) who found that the lifetime prevalence of depressive disorder in the relatives of depressed children was double that in the relatives of closely matched non-depressed controls. These findings suggest that there is specificity in the familial links between child and adult depression.

Of course, it does not necessarily follow that the continuities are mediated genetically. Perhaps specific familial aggregation occurs because certain kinds of adversity are familial. Indeed, Goodyer *et al.* (1993) reported that the families of depressed adolescent girls seemed to become 'life event-prone' as a result of parental psychopathology. Family studies cannot effectively discriminate between genetic and environmental mediation and we must therefore wait for the results of twin studies before reaching definite conclusions on the relative contributions of genes and environments. Genetic studies will need to consider not only the possibility of direct genetic influences on mood regulatory systems but also the ways in which there may be indirect genetic effects, as when individuals create their own experience (Scarr, 1992). There is evidence, for instance, that child characteristics can elicit negative parental reactions, which in turn increase the risk for psychopathology in the child (Cook *et al.*, 1991).

Psychosocial influences

Three types of research strategy provide information on the role of psychosocial influences in juvenile depressive disorders. 'Top-down' approaches, in which the impact of parental depression on children is studied, have shown that there are a number of ways in which depression in a parent can influence the environment of the child (Rutter, 1990). There may, for example, be a direct impact of depressive symptoms, reduced mother–child interaction (Stein *et al.*, 1991), and/or an association with family discord (Rutter & Quinton, 1984). Any one of these factors could lead to psychiatric disorder in offspring, though it is important to note that the paths may be bidirectional, to the extent that the characteristics of the child could contribute to parental depression (Dodge, 1990).

The second strategy, the 'bottom-up' approach, starts with depressed children and examines their psychosocial environments. Here, it is helpful to distinguish between three kinds of risk factor: acute life events, chronic adversities and vulnerability factors. Research in samples of young women has suggested that acute life events or chronic difficulties often precede the onset of depressive disorder (Brown & Harris, 1978). However, to explain why only some women who experience such provoking agents develop depression, Brown and Harris suggested that other factors (such as early loss) made some women more vulnerable than others. These vulnerability factors are usually conceived as only raising the risk of depression in the presence of a provoking agent.

Research on the psychosocial correlates of childhood depression is at an early stage and there are a number of reasons for thinking that a straightforward downward extension of these models developed with adult cases will not be adequate. For instance, many acute life stresses in childhood arise in the context of chronic adversities (e.g. divorce often follows prolonged family discord) so acute life events may need to be conceptualized as one class of social adversity, rather than as something different (Sandberg *et al.*, in press). Indeed, the finding that depression in young people tends to be recurrent (see later) suggests that the child's experiences of adversity over time are just as important as the precipitants of a single episode.

In addition, Brown *et al.*'s (1986) studies of parental loss suggest that the risk for psychiatric disorder stems from the deficient parental care that follows the loss rather than from the loss *per se*. So, it will also be important to study the circumstances surrounding adversity as well as the adversity itself (Rutter & Sandberg, 1992). For instance, Goodyer *et al.* (1988) found that the onset of emotional disorders in children was associated not only with undesirable life events but also with maternal distress and poor maternal confiding relationships. They suggested that some children become exposed to adversity because mothers are less able to protect them. Similarly, Wilde *et al.* (1992) found that in depressed young people acute life events often occurred in the context of long-standing problems.

The relationship between stress and the type of emotional disorder that occurs in the child appears to be nonspecific. Thus, in the presence of acute adversity it seems that children are equally likely to become anxious as they are to become depressed (Goodyer *et al.*, 1988). Similar findings have been reported in respect of the role of life events (Berney *et al.*, 1991) and maternal expressed emotion (Schwartz *et al.*, 1990). Research in adults had suggested that 'exit' events (such as loss) may be specifically linked with depression (Paykel, 1982) but in children the available data suggest that early 'exit' experiences predispose to anxiety as well as depressive disorders (Goodyer & Altham, 1991).

The third type of strategy involves the study of children who have experienced a specific event. Depressive symptoms have been found in association with many types of adverse life experiences, including divorce (Wallerstein & Kelly, 1980; Aro & Palosaari, 1992; see also Chapter 12), disasters (Yule *et al.*, 1990; see also Chapter 22), and being in a concentration camp (Kinzie *et al.*, 1989). Recently bereaved preschoolers often have depressive symptoms (Kranzler *et al.*, 1990) and Weller *et al.* (1991) reported that around one-third of bereaved prepubertal children met criteria for depressive disorder. These children had less guilt and less often made a suicidal attempt than nonbereaved children with major depression.

Depressive symptoms have also been found in association with both physical abuse (Allen & Tarnowski, 1989; see also Chapter 13) and sexual abuse (Goldston *et al.*, 1989; see also Chapter 14). Depressive disorders have been estimated to occur in about 20% of maltreated children (Famularo *et al.*, 1992). Studies of adults who said they had been sexually abused as children have reported a link with depressive disorder (Bifulco *et al.*, 1991) but the methodological issues involved in such retrospective studies (Briere, 1992) make it difficult to interpret the results. Studies of children who have been sexually abused have generally found low rates of depressive disorder (Sirles *et al.*, 1989).

The responses of children to many other kinds of adverse experiences have been studied. Little will be gained by considering all of these different adversities here. Suffice to say, that although levels of depressive symptoms are often quite high in such children, on current evidence it seems that most young people who experience adversity will not develop a depressive disorder. Furthermore, those who do develop a mental illness seem just as likely to develop a nondepressive condition as a depressive one (viz. the study of Stoddard *et al.* (1989) on burned children).

Of course, all this does not mean that adverse experiences are not important in the aetiology of childhood depressive disorders. Many important risk factors in general medicine (e.g. smoking) are relatively nonspecific and associated with a low absolute risk of any single disorder. None the less, the low rate of depressive disorder in young people who have experienced adversity reminds us both that some young people can be very resilient to stress and that there is a need to look for additional factors that may increase the child's vulnerability.

Psychological mechanisms

We also need to know about the mechanisms by which these external stressors lead to the internal mood state of depression. Many psychological models have been devised to explain these links, but perhaps the most influential among investigators of childhood depression has been the idea of learned helplessness. Seligman and his co-workers observed that dogs exposed to uncontrollable electric shocks failed subsequently either to learn the response to terminate the shock or to initiate as many escape attempts. In human terms, there was an expectation of helplessness that was generalized to the new situation (Seligman & Peterson, 1986). Subsequently, the notion of learned helplessness has been reformulated within an attributional framework (Abramson *et al.*, 1978). It is asserted that the expectation of uncontrollable adverse events leads to depression, but only if the person attributes them to internal, stable and global causes. For example, 'I failed the exam because I am useless'. The reformulated learned helplessness theory (now the hopelessness theory — see Abramson *et al.*, 1989) has many similarities with the so-called cognitive theories of depression. Beck (1976), for example, saw depressed people as characterized by a negative cognitive set: they have a negative view of themselves, of the world and of the future.

The occurrence of such cognitions has been documented in several cross-sectional studies of depressed children (McCauley *et al.*, 1988; Meyer *et al.*, 1989; Kendall *et al.*, 1990), whose distorted style of processing self-evaluative information distinguishes them from children with other psychiatric disorders (Kendall, 1992). In addition, it seems that negative cognitions such as self-criticism can be remarkably stable (Koestner *et al.*, 1991) and several longitudinal studies have shown that they may precede depressive symptoms (Seligman & Peterson, 1986; Reinherz *et al.*, 1989; Nolen-Hoeksema *et al.*, 1992). However, different results have been obtained with depressive disorders. Thus, in a study that included the offspring of women with affective disorders, Hammen *et al.* (1988) found that depression at follow-up was best predicted by initial symptoms and life events but not by negative attributions. Similarly, Asarnow and Bates (1988) found that inpatient children whose depressive disorder had remitted did not show negative attributional patterns. The latter findings suggest that negative attributional style is a state-dependent symptom of depressive disorder rather than a trait-like predisposition.

Another psychological construct, low social competence, has also been seen as important in the aetiology of depression in young people (Cole, 1991). There is evidence of an association between perceived incompetence and depressive symptoms (Adams & Adams, 1991) and competence theories do offer an explanation for the sex differences in depressive symptoms that appear during adolescence (Wilson & Cairns, 1988). Patterson and Stoolmiller (1991) reported that rejection by peers was an important correlate of depressed mood in preadolescent boys from at-risk families and it may be that peer and/or parental rejection mediates the link between antisocial behaviour and depression in young people (Patterson & Capaldi, 1990).

Finally, it should be noted that many of the psychological constructs discussed above show developmental changes. For instance, from the age of 7 years children begin to shift from the view that task performance skills are specific, to a conception of general abilities that are both global and stable (Dweck & Elliot, 1983). These changes may explain the age trends in the prevalence of depression that were described earlier.

Biological mechanisms

The amine hypothesis continues to be influential in attempts to understand the pathophysiology of affective disorders. The hypothesis proposes that depression results from hypoactivity of monoamine reward systems (Deakin & Crow, 1986). This idea arose from the observations that drugs that deplete monoamines can cause depression and that drugs such as imipramine that inhibit monoamine reuptake have an antidepressant effect.

Several studies of young people with depressive disorders have reported abnormalities of the biological markers that are thought to reflect the activity of these systems (reviewed by Rogeness et al., 1992, and Yaylayan et al., 1992). For instance, it seems that some depressed youngsters do not show the suppression of cortisol secretion that usually occurs when dexamethasone is administered (Casat & Powell, 1988). Abnormalities of neuroendocrine response have also been found during other challenge tests, such as the thyroid-releasing hormone test (Kutcher et al., 1991) and in the secretion of growth hormone after hypoglycaemia (Puig-Antich et al., 1981) or clonidine (Jensen & Garfinkel, 1990). Sleep encephalography may also be abnormal (Emslie et al., 1990; Kutcher et al., 1992).

However, there have been difficulties in replicating these positive findings. Thus, for instance, the results of other sleep studies have been negative (Goetz et al., 1991). Moreover, the specificity of these measures for depressive disorder is low. For example, many child patients who are not depressed will have a positive Dexamethasone Suppression Test (DST; Tyrer et al., 1991) and it seems that the specificity of the DST for major depression in children is lower than for adults (Ferguson & Bawden, 1988). In addition, the main pillar on which the amine hypothesis has been based is the response of depressed adults to drugs that alter cerebral amine metabolism (Charney et al., 1991). We shall see later that depressed young people do not show the same responses to antidepressants as their adult counterparts.

There are several possible explanations for these biological differences between child and adult depressions. It could be that early-onset depressions represent a different kind of condition altogether. However, this seems unlikely because family studies and longitudinal studies have found strong links between child and adult depressive disorders. Alternatively, it is possible that there are developmental differences in the balance between different neuroregulatory systems. In other words, the variation in psychobiological responses with age may simply be a reflection of maturational differences in biology and not a result of differences in the nature of depression. So, for instance, the failure consistently to demonstrate in prepubertal depression the kinds of sleep abnormalities that have been found in adults (see Benca et al., 1992) could be due to age differences in the nature of sleep (Puig-Antich, 1986).

The importance of these developmental differences is further underlined by the age and sex trends in the prevalence of depressive disorders that were reviewed earlier. Indeed, it may be that the biological changes of puberty lead to the increase in rates of depressive disorder during adolescence. However, the size of the association between depression and indices of these changes such as hormone levels appears to be small (reviewed by Buchanan et al., 1992). Moreover, research on hormone–depression relationships among the young has mostly been concerned with depressive affect rather than depressive disorder. In addition, some studies have failed to find an independent contribution of puberty to the rise in depressive disorder in adolescence once age was controlled for (Angold & Rutter, 1992).

It should also be borne in mind that early-onset depressive conditions are likely to be biologically heterogeneous. Goodyer et al. (1991a), for example, reported that while some depressed subjects showed very abnormal basal cortisol levels, others showed cortisol levels that were well within the normal range. Similarly, Giles et al. (1992) suggested that sleep electro-encephalogram abnormalities were much more likely to occur when depressed children had both a family history of depression and a parent with sleep abnormalities. Thus a negative finding in one sample may not necessarily generalize to another. Indeed, the results of studies of biological markers differ according to whether the subjects were in- or outpatients at the time of the assessment (Goetz et al., 1991; Birmaher et al., 1992a).

Assessment

Assessment of depression in young people should start with a thorough evaluation of depressive symptomatology. This will mean interviewing the child alone. It is not enough to rely on accounts obtained from the parents since they may not notice depression in their children (Angold et al., 1987; Barrett et al., 1991) and may not even be aware of suicidal attempts (Walker et al., 1990). Indeed, it is now common practice to obtain information from several sources. Children usually give a better account of symptoms related to internal experience whereas parents are likely to be better informants on overt behavioural difficulties. Accounts from children and parents can be supplemented by information from other sources, such as teachers (Hoier & Kerr, 1988), peers (Lefkowitz & Tesiny, 1980) and/or direct observations (Kazdin et al., 1985).

Although the interviewing of multiple informants may yield much useful information, the diagnosis of depressive disorder in young people can still be very difficult. Efforts to improve the reliability and validity of the diagnosis have been focused on two areas: the development of standardized assessment instruments, and biological tests.

A number of factors need to be considered in selecting an instrument to assess depression among the young (Harrington & Shariff, 1992). In choosing between the *questionnaires* that are available, it is especially important that the user has a clear idea of what the scale is going to be used for (Costello & Angold, 1988). For example, questionnaires that are good discriminators between depressed and nondepressed children may be ineffective as measures of change during treatment. In clinical settings, self-report questionnaires provide a convenient way of screening for symptoms that are not part of the presenting complaint, and may be useful for measuring treatment response. They are especially helpful in monitoring subjective feelings. In research settings, questionnaires have been used both as a primary source of data and as a screening instrument to select subjects for further in-depth interviews. Unfortunately, many depression questionnaires have low specificity for depressive disorder. This means that if they are used as screens in a two-stage survey then time-consuming second-stage interviews will have to be conducted with several false positives to generate one case of major depression (Garrison *et al.*, 1991; Roberts *et al.*, 1991). Some of the new questionnaires that cover most of the symptoms of major depression, such as the Mood and Feelings Questionnaire (Angold *et al.*, 1987b) may be more efficient, but that has yet to be determined.

Several *standardized interviews* have been devised for use with children and many of them will generate depressive diagnoses (see Edelbrock & Costello, 1988; Kazdin, 1990). These instruments have led to important advances in the assessment of juvenile depression and as a result structured psychiatric interviews are being used more and more as diagnostic tools in clinical settings. Nevertheless, there are several unresolved difficulties. Firstly, although interrater reliability has been reasonable (Costello, 1986), test–retest reliability has been less good and affective symptoms are particularly unstable in the younger age groups (Chambers *et al.*, 1985; Edelbrock *et al.*, 1985). Secondly, there is often low agreement between parent and child on depressive features (see above) and it is still not clear how information from different sources should be combined. Indeed, some investigators suggest that the two sources of data should be kept separate as each is likely to have validity. When it is necessary to combine sources into a best estimate, the simple rule of counting a symptom as positive if it is acknowledged as positive by either the parent or the child seems to work as well as more complicated statistical procedures (Bird *et al.*, 1992).

In addition to questionnaires and interviews, a variety of *other measures* exist for the assessment of depression among the young. These include pictorial self-report measures for use with preschool children (Martini *et al.*, 1990) and time-sampling techniques in which children and adolescents report their moods on an hour-to-hour basis (Larson *et al.*, 1990).

The second development has been the use of *psychobio-logical measures* as markers of depressive disorder. Probably the best known of these is the DST (see above). Unfortunately, several recent studies have shown that in both children and adolescents the DST is a poor discriminator between depressed and nondepressed cases (Tyrer *et al.*, 1991; Birmaher *et al.*, 1992a). Moreover, its results are influenced by many other factors, such as weight loss (Cowen & Wood, 1991). As a result, few clinicians place great reliance on its findings. It may be, however, that the mechanisms involved in early-onset depressions do not influence cortisol regulation. Indeed, one study of depressed adolescents found that cortisol secretory profiles were relatively normal but that there were abnormalities of nocturnal growth hormone secretion (Kutcher *et al.*, 1991). Perhaps, then, other psychobiological tests will prove to be more specific.

Although the accurate diagnosis of depressive disorder is an important part of clinical management, it should also be noted that the assessment of depression in young people only starts with the diagnosis, not stops with it. Depressed children usually have multiple problems, such as educational failure (Forness, 1988), impaired psychosocial functioning (Puig-Antich *et al.*, 1985), and comorbid psychiatric disorders. Moreover they tend to come from families with high rates of psychopathology (see above) and may have experienced adverse life events (Goodyer, 1990), including maltreatment (Kaufman, 1991). All these problems need to be identified and the causes of each assessed.

Treatment

Initial management

The initial management of depressed children therefore depends greatly on the nature of the problems identified during the assessment procedure. The assessment may indicate that the reaction of the child is appropriate for the situation in which he or she finds him- or herself. In such a case, and if the depression is mild, a sensible approach can consist of regular meetings, sympathetic discussions with the child and the parents, and encouraging support. These simple interventions, especially if combined with measures designed to alleviate stress, are often followed by an improvement in mood. In other cases, particularly those with severe depression or suicidal ideation, a more focused form of treatment is indicated, and it may occasionally be necessary to admit such children to hospital.

Wherever treatment is carried out, it should be tailored to the needs of the individual child, rather than prescribed as a standard package. The multiple problems of the depressed child make it especially important that the goals of treatment are precisely formulated and that a realistic contract with the child and family is established. Reduction of depression is a legitimate focus of treatment but should not distract from the treatment of other problems such as impaired peer relationships, which may play a part in maintaining depression (Goodyer *et al.*, 1991b). Multiple treatment approaches are needed.

Treatment of depression in adults

Since depressive disorders in young people are now diagnosed using adult criteria, it is appropriate to consider briefly the findings from the large literature on the treatment of depression in adults. The most extensively studied of these treatments have been the tricyclic antidepressants (TCAs), which have been evaluated in many comparative trials against placebo. The results have been impressive, with three-quarters of these trials showing that the drug was superior (Elkins & Rapoport, 1983). It seems that the best results occur in depressions of moderate severity. Severe psychotic depressions do not respond well to TCAs (Schatzberg, 1992). Such disorders do better with ECT (Scott, 1989), though the beneficial effects of ECT do not seem to persist beyond a few months (Buchan *et al.*, 1992).

There is a growing literature on the efficacy of psychological treatments in the less severe forms of adult depression. Thus, several studies have reported that interpersonal psychotherapy (IPT) was of value (Paykel, 1989). Cognitive-behavioural therapy (CBT) has been evaluated in several comparative trials with drug therapy (Dobson, 1989), which have generally found that the two were equally effective on symptom measures. However, these trials may have undersampled patients who would have responded to antidepressants (Hollon *et al.*, 1991). Indeed, the most systematic of the recent studies (the National Institute of Mental Health study) found that cognitive therapy was less effective than drugs, especially in moderately severe depression (Elkin *et al.*, 1989).

It is important to note that there has been increasing recognition of the need to develop treatments to prevent relapse, as depressive disorders in adults tend to follow a recurrent course (Guze & Freedman, 1991). Maintenance treatments can include both medication (Kupfer, 1992), and psychological therapies such as IPT (Frank *et al.*, 1991). Strategies to recognize and treat relapses at an early stage are also being developed (Kupfer, 1992).

Psychological treatment of depression in young people

Similar psychological interventions have been used in the treatment of depressed young people. Most of the trials have fulfilled present-day requirements (see Kendall & Morris, 1991) regarding randomization, control groups, manualization of treatments and the use of appropriate tests of clinical as well as statistical significance. However, sample sizes have generally been rather small, durations of follow-up short, and none have studied the prevention of relapse.

Nevertheless, several psychological therapies show promise. The most extensively studied has been CBT (see Chapter 49), which has been evaluated in several investigations of depressed young people selected from schools (Butler *et al.*, 1980; Reynolds & Coats, 1986; Stark *et al.*, 1987; Kahn *et al.*, 1990). Reynolds and Coats (1986) found that both CBT and relaxation were superior to a waiting list control condition in adolescents

with high depression questionnaire scores. Stark *et al.* (1987) found that children having self-control therapy or a behavioural problem-solving therapy reported significantly less depressive symptomatology than children on the waiting list. Since children in these studies improved not only with cognitive interventions but also with other psychological treatments, the question arises as to the specificity of the mechanisms leading to improvement. However, Stark (1990) reported that depressed adolescents did better with a cognitive intervention than with nondirective counselling. This finding argues for the operation of a specific therapeutic mechanism.

None of these studies included young people who had been diagnosed as having a depressive disorder. Lewinsohn *et al.* (1990), however, found that group-based CBT produced significant improvement among adolescents with dysthymia or major depression who had been recruited through adverts, health professionals or schools. To date, the only forms of psychological therapy that have been systematically evaluated in clinical cases with depressive disorders are social skills training and therapeutic support. Fine *et al.* (1991) compared group-based versions of these treatments in adolescent outpatients with major depression or dysthymia. Those having therapeutic support did better posttreatment than subjects in the social skills group, though the differences did not persist to follow-up. Incidentally, it is worth noting that the effect size in this comparison of two active therapies was much smaller than that found in the school-based studies cited above, in which comparisons were made with waiting list controls. The implication is that in clinical settings, where it is necessary to use active therapies, larger samples are going to be needed to demonstrate an effect.

Since depressed children often come from families in which there are substantial problems, it is usually necessary to undertake family work of one kind or another (see Chapter 55). At the very least, parents will benefit from information about the nature of depression and the prospects for recovery. Some therapists advocate the active involvement of parents in CBT (Stark *et al.*, 1991) but Lewinsohn *et al.* (1990) found that parental groups did not significantly enhance their cognitive-behavioural package. There have been no systematic studies in which the family rather than the depressed child was the focus of treatment, although there are anecdotal accounts of the benefits of this approach (Oster & Caro, 1990).

Several other psychological therapies have been advocated for depression in young people, of which perhaps the most promising is IPT (Mufson *et al.*, 1993). Moreau *et al.* (1991) pointed out that there are a number of features of IPT that may make it especially suitable for the treatment of depressed adolescents, such as its focus on life transitions. Certainly, there is a need to explore further approaches that can be used in one-to-one sessions. Most of the psychological treatment studies published so far have concerned group interventions, but these may not be practical in clinics where the number of depressed cases is small.

All in all, these initial studies suggest that focused and planned psychological therapies may be of benefit in aiding recovery from mild depressive conditions. However, we need to know more about which therapy is appropriate for which patient with which problem. In particular, much more data are needed on the efficacy of psychological treatments with young people who have moderate or severe depressive disorders. We also need information on the ability of treatment to prevent relapse since, as we see later, depressive disorders among the young resemble their adult counterparts in their tendency to recur.

Tricyclic antidepressants

Medication has been more extensively evaluated in clinical depressive disorders than psychological treatments, although it has to be said that compared with the large literature on adult depression there have been relatively few systematic drug studies (see Chapter 51). There were promising results from early trials, with most reporting that the TCAs were an effective treatment for depressed children (Petti, 1983). However, the findings of these studies were limited by issues such as diagnostic heterogeneity and a lack of appropriate controls.

The results from recent double-blind controlled trials have been less encouraging. Amongst the most thorough was the study of Puig-Antich et al. (1987), in which imipramine was compared with placebo in prepubertal children with major depression. The proportion of subjects who responded was very similar in the two groups (56 versus 68% respectively), but any other finding would have been difficult given this high rate of response to placebo. Geller et al. (1992) tackled this issue by admitting 6−12-year-olds with major depression to a 2-week placebo washout phase before the main trial, so that placebo responders could be excluded. Yet, in spite of the fact that their study also had the benefit of a 'fixed plasma level design' (Geller et al., 1986), there was again no significant difference in the rate of response between treatment (nortriptyline) and placebo.

Of course, it could be that this lack of response to TCAs was the result of biological heterogeneity. Indeed, Preskorn et al. (1987) reported that superiority of imipramine over placebo was particularly marked in dexamethasone-nonsuppressing children. Hughes et al. (1990) found that prepubertal children with depression and an anxiety disorder had higher response rates to imipramine than children with depression and conduct disorder. Clearly, then, more work is needed to identify the characteristics of children who are likely to respond to antidepressants.

To turn to the treatment of adolescent major depression, the small number of systematic studies of the efficacy of TCAs have been unable to show either superiority over placebo or a consistent relationship between plasma level and response (Geller, 1991). Thus, placebo-controlled trials of amitriptyline (Kramer & Feiguine, 1983), nortriptyline (Geller et al., 1990) and desipramine (Boulos et al., 1991) have all produced negative results. Ryan et al. (1986) gave a fixed, weight-adjusted dose of imipramine in adolescent depression, but failed to find a plasma level−response relationship. Only 44%

were rated as significantly improved. Strober et al. (1990a) found an even lower response rate (one-third) in adolescent inpatients with nondelusional major depression treated with imipramine in an open design. Several investigators have therefore augmented TCA treatment with lithium. The results of early uncontrolled trials have been promising (Ryan et al., 1988; Strober et al., 1992) but confirmation in controlled designs is needed.

Why is it that the TCAs seem to be less efficacious in the treatment of major depression in young people than in the similar condition when it occurs in adults? A variety of different types of explanations have been put forward (reviewed by Ryan, 1990; Strober, in press). It could be, for example, that developmental variations in the rate of elimination of psychotropics (see Geller, 1991) make it harder to get the dosage right in children/adolescents than in adults. Or, it is possible that juvenile depression, though phenotypically similar to adult depression, differs in some important respect that might affect drug responsiveness. For instance, perhaps early-onset depressive disorders are more severe. Alternatively, it has been suggested that young people differ from adults both in the relative balance of the cerebral neurotransmitters on which antidepressants are thought to act (Strober et al., 1990a) and in the hormonal milieu of the brain (Ryan et al., 1986).

It is, however, important to remember that research on the clinical utility of antidepressants in juvenile depressive conditions is necessarily at an early stage, if only because of the relatively recent identification of depressive disorders among the young using standardized methods of assessment. It could be that the next wave of controlled studies will provide more pointers on which depressed young people are likely to respond to TCAs. In the meantime, it would seem best to restrict the use of these drugs to patients with severe depression, and to those who fail to respond to other forms of treatment. The administration of TCAs to children can be difficult, especially in centres that do not have easy access to a laboratory that can measure plasma levels. Side-effects, though usually minor (Petti, 1983), can include effects on the cardiovascular system (Bartels et al., 1991) so there needs to be regular monitoring of pulse, blood pressure and the electrocardiograph (Ryan, 1992). While reports of sudden death in children who received doses of TCAs that were probably within the therapeutic range have caused appropriate concern (Riddle et al., 1991; Tingelstad, 1991), it should also be borne in mind that the TCAs are very toxic in overdose (Henry, 1992). The decision to prescribe them should not, therefore, be taken lightly.

Other physical treatments

These concerns about the potential toxicity of the TCAs, together with doubts about their efficacy, suggest that other physical treatments deserve closer scrutiny. Monoamine oxidase inhibitors (MAOIs) were reported in an early controlled trial to be beneficial in prepubertal depression

(Frommer, 1967) but it is difficult to interpret the results of this study because the MAOI was combined with chlordiazepoxide. Moreover, the old irreversible MAOIs can cause hypertension after the ingestion of foods containing tyramine, so patients taking them need to be on a special diet. Nevertheless, there has recently been renewed interest in the use of MAOIs for depression in young people. Ryan (1990) reported an open study in which more than 50% of depressed adolescents were thought to have made a good response. However, 5 were discontinued from medication because of poor dietary compliance. Ryan (1990) therefore suggested that these drugs should not be used in adolescents who are unlikely to comply with the necessary dietary restrictions.

The new reversible MAOIs such as moclobemide, which seems to have a low risk of hypertensive crises (Burkard *et al.*, 1989) and is well-tolerated by most adult patients (Guelfi *et al.*, 1992), could prove to be more suitable for young people. However, they have yet to be systematically evaluated in this age group. Early results with another new antidepressant, fluoxetine, have not been encouraging (Simeon *et al.*, 1990).

Severe depressions in young people may respond to ECT. The giving of ECT to children naturally raises concerns about long-term cognitive effects. However, recent research in adults has shown that modern ECT techniques such as nondominant placement and brief pulse stimuli are associated with less memory impairment than the older methods (Weiner & Coffey, 1991). In addition, brain imaging studies have found no evidence that ECT produces structural brain changes (Coffey *et al.*, 1991). The available data suggest that ECT given to young people is not associated with substantial long-term effects on cognitive performance (Bertagnoli & Borchardt, 1990) although further research on this issue is required. Other physical treatments that have been used in childhood depressive disorders include light therapy (Sonis, 1992) and thyroid hormone (Alessi, 1991).

Outcome of depressive disorder in childhood and adolescence

In considering studies of the natural history of depressive disorder in young people, it is immediately apparent that many authors use different definitions of recovery and relapse. For example, for some investigators the definition of recovery has included states in which there was persistence of some subclinical symptoms (Kovacs *et al.*, 1984a), whereas for others it was defined as 'no mental state abnormalities' whatsoever (Goodyer *et al.*, 1991b). Moreover, it seems that there is only moderate agreement between different informants on the classification of recovery (Goodyer *et al.*, 1991b).

The problems of defining recovery are formidable enough but a further difficulty in the interpretation of follow-ups of depressed children arises from the fact that few studies have taken account of the overlap with nondepressive symptoms. It is therefore unclear how much the outcome of childhood depression is the result of the earlier depression and how much it relates to the comorbid psychiatric problems.

Risk of a subsequent episode in childhood

It is necessary, then, to be cautious in interpreting the follow-ups published so far, especially as many of them have been based on cases seen in hospitals, thus limiting the range of severity. Nevertheless, one conclusion seems reasonably secure: by comparison with nondepressed subjects, young people diagnosed as depressed are more likely to have subsequent episodes of depression. Thus, studies of preadolescent children meeting DSM-III criteria for depression have shown that depression in childhood often recurs (Kovacs *et al.*, 1984b; Asarnow *et al.*, 1988; McGee & Williams, 1988). For example, Kovacs *et al.* (1984b) found that about 70% of child patients with a major depressive disorder had another episode within 5 years.

Adult outcomes

None of these studies has yet extended beyond mid-adolescence, but a similarly high rate of subsequent psychiatric morbidity has been reported in follow-up studies of depressed adolescents that have extended into late adolescence or early adult life (Strober & Carlson, 1982; Kandel & Davies, 1986; Garber *et al.*, 1988). These studies have suggested both that self-ratings of depression in adolescent community samples predict similar problems in early adulthood (Kandel & Davies, 1986) and that adolescent patients with depressive disorders are at high risk of subsequent major affective disturbance (Strober & Carlson, 1982; Garber *et al.*, 1988). Although the findings of these studies are limited by issues such as the uncertainty regarding the connection between depression questionnaire scores and clinical depressive disorder (Kandel & Davies, 1986) and high rates of sample attrition (Garber *et al.*, 1988), they clearly suggest that adolescents with depression are at increased risk of depression in early adulthood.

Moving still further into adult life, Harrington *et al.* (1990) followed up 63 depressed children and adolescents on average 18 years after their initial contact. The depressed group was four times more likely to have an episode of depression after the age of 17 years than a control group who had been matched on a large number of variables, including nondepressive symptoms. This increased risk was maintained well into adulthood and was associated with significantly increased rates of attending psychiatric services and of using medication as compared to the controls. Depressed children were no more likely than control children to suffer nondepressive disorders in adulthood, suggesting that the risk for adult depression was specific and unrelated to comorbidity with other psychiatric problems. Zeitlin (1986), in a study of child psychiatric patients who attended the same hospital as adults, also found strong continuities for depression.

Predictors and mechanisms of continuity

Little is known about predictors of continuity. The characteristics of the index episode appear to be important to the extent that children with DSM-III 'double depression' (major depression and dysthymic disorder) have a worse short-term outcome than children with major depression alone (Kovacs *et al.*, 1984b; Asarnow *et al.*, 1988). Continuity to adulthood is best predicted by a severe adult-like depressive presentation and, interestingly, by the absence of conduct disorder (Harrington *et al.*, 1990, 1991). However, neither anxiety disorder nor conduct disorder seems to influence the short-term outcome (Kovacs *et al.*, 1988, 1989). Two studies have found that older depressed children have a worse prognosis than younger ones (Kovacs *et al.*, 1989; Harrington *et al.*, 1990).

Although it is often assumed that continuity of depression is mainly due to the direct persistence of the initial disorder or of premorbid psychological and/or biological vulnerabilities to depression, it should be borne in mind that other mechanisms may also be involved. Perhaps, for example, continuity stems from the persistence of adverse environments. Asarnow *et al.* (1993), for instance, found that inpatients with depressive disorders who returned to families in which there were high levels of expressed emotion were much less likely to recover than depressed children returning to homes with low expressed emotion. Of course, this last finding could be confounded by the presence of parental depression. However, Hammen *et al.*, (1991) found a close temporal relationship between maternal depression and a recurrence of depression in the child, supporting the idea of an environmentally mediated mechanism.

Alternatively, it could be that individuals are changed in one way or another by the first episode so that they become more vulnerable to subsequent problems. This notion, often referred to as *scarring*, is attracting a good deal of attention from investigators of the psychological (Rohde *et al.*, 1990) and neurobiological (Post, 1992) processes that may be involved in the relapsing and remitting course of depression in adults. The idea is important because it suggests that much greater attention should be paid to the recognition and treatment of the first episode of depression. Since late adolescence is an important period for the onset of adult depressive disorders (K.C. Burke *et al.*, 1990), the implication is that child and adolescent psychiatry could have a role in the prevention of depression in adulthood.

Risk of other adverse outcomes

The impact of juvenile depression on other aspects of adult outcome is unclear. Several investigators have reported an association with subsequent social dysfunction (Kandel & Davies, 1986; Garber *et al.*, 1988) and/or impaired cognitive development (Kovacs & Goldston, 1991) but it is uncertain whether this was a function of the initial depression or of the associated nondepressive symptoms. Harrington *et al.* (1991) found that juvenile depression seemed to have little direct impact on social functioning in adulthood whereas comorbid conduct disorder was a strong predictor of subsequent social difficulties. Clearly, it is important to disentangle the effects of early depressive disorder from the effects of comorbid disorders.

Depressed young people are at risk of suicidal behaviour (Myers *et al.*, 1991; Andrews & Lewinsohn, 1992). In the follow-up of Harrington *et al.* (1990), all 3 deaths in the depressed group were due to 'unnatural causes', of which 2 were definite suicides. Similarly, in a preliminary communication from a longitudinal study of the depressed children and adolescents initially studied by the Puig-Antich *et al.* group, Rao *et al.* (1993) reported that 7 had committed suicide. Little is known about the factors that predict which depressed young person is most at risk of suicidal behaviour, but the risk indicators probably include previous suicidality, suicidal ideation, hopelessness, comorbid problems such as substance abuse and anger, easy access to the method, and lack of social support (reviewed by Pfeffer, 1992).

Recovery from the index episode

It is important to distinguish between the risk of recurrence which, as described above, seems to be quite high, and the prognosis for the index attack. Indeed, the available data suggest that the majority of children with major depression will recover within 2 years. For example, Kovacs *et al.* (1984a) reported that the cumulative probability of recovery from major depression by 1 year after onset was 74% and by 2 years was 92%. This study included many subjects who had had previous emotional-behavioural problems and some form of treatment. However, very similar results were reported by Keller *et al.* (1988) in a retrospective study of time to recovery from first episode of major depression in young people who had mostly not received treatment (Keller *et al.*, 1991). The probability of recovery for adolescent inpatients with major depression also appears to be about 90% by 2 years (Strober *et al.*, 1993), though those with long-standing depressions recover less quickly than those whose presentation was acute (Shain *et al.*, 1991).

It seems, then, that most young people with major depressive disorder will recover to a significant extent but that a majority of those who recover will relapse.

BIPOLAR DISORDERS

Different views have been put forward about the prevalence of manic-depressive illness in children. Anthony and Scott (1960) applied a set of 10 criteria derived from the literature on manic depression in adults to published reports of children and found only 3 cases. However, these criteria were very stringent and included features that are not usually included in the criteria for bipolar disorder in adults, such as a positive family history. Retrospective studies of the age of onset of bipolar disorders ascertained in adulthood have noted that about one-fifth had an onset before the age of 19 years (Perris, 1966; Winokur *et al.*, 1969).

Carlson (1990) has systematically reviewed the literature on the phenomenology of mania in children and adolescents. In older children (9−12 years) aberrations in thought content such as grandiosity and paranoia are common whereas irritability and emotional lability are common in younger children. Hyperactivity, pressure of speech and distractibility are common in both age groups. Strober *et al.* (1989) suggested that prepubertal bipolar children have an illness characterized by frequent cycles of brief duration in which dysphoria and hypomania are intermixed; with the onset of puberty the cyclical extremes of depression and mania occur.

The diagnosis of manic disorders in young people can be very difficult (Bowring & Kovacs, 1992). Clearly, there are some superficial similarities between hypomania and hyperactivity. However, follow-ups of hyperactive children have not found an excess of affective disorders (Gittelman *et al.*, 1985). Strober *et al.* (1989) considered that the child with bipolar illness has a more pronounced shift in mood than the hyperactive child, activity tends to be more goal-directed, and there may be delusions or hallucinations. The distinction between bipolar illness and schizophrenia can also be a problem. Werry *et al.* (1991) reported that over half of bipolar adolescents were misdiagnosed as schizophrenic when first seen. Patients with schizophrenia manifested more abnormal personalities and had a lower level of adaptive functioning before the illness. However, symptomatology during the index episode was quite similar (Werry *et al.*, 1991). Zeitlin (1986) found few differences in presenting symptomatology between children subsequently diagnosed as schizophrenic or manic-depressive in adulthood.

As described earlier, manic-depressive illness in adults seems to have a substantial genetic component. The mode of inheritance is unclear (McGuffin & Sargeant, 1991). Several early studies reported linkage findings suggestive of single major gene inheritance, but these findings have not been replicated (Baron *et al.*, 1990). Family studies of adolescent probands with bipolar disorders support the idea that genetic factors may be important. Strober *et al.* (1988) found major affective disorder in 30% of the first-degree relatives of bipolar probands compared with 4% of those of schizophrenic probands. The familial loading for major affective disorder was greater when the bipolar disorder in the proband was preceded by symptoms before the age of 12 years (though these symptoms consisted mostly of hyperactivity or conduct disturbance). These rates are above those usually found in family studies of adults with bipolar disorder and several other studies have reported that an earlier age of onset was associated with an increased familial loading for depression (reviewed by Strober, 1992). It remains to be seen whether these findings reflect genetic or environmental mediation.

Information on the treatment of bipolar disorders arising in adolescence is largely derived from studies of adults. Neuroleptics continue to be the most commonly used treatment for acute mania. Other drugs such as lithium, valproate (Pope *et al.*, 1991) and carbamazepine (Small *et al.*, 1991) may also be effective, but they usually need to be augmented with major tranquillizers. Surprisingly little is known about the drug treatment of the depressed phase of bipolar disorder (Prien & Potter, 1990) and it should be borne in mind that TCAs and MAOIs may cause hypomanic reactions in susceptible patients. For this reason, lithium may be the best first-line treatment in acute bipolar depression, with TCAs and MAOIs kept in reserve for those cases who fail to respond (see the review by Prien & Potter, 1990). Lithium is still the treatment of choice for the prevention of relapse in adults. Anticonvulsants may be useful alternatives to lithium in refractory bipolar illness (Post, 1991) or when rapid cycling occurs (Post *et al.*, 1990).

Data from naturalistic studies support the idea that lithium reduces the risk of further episodes of illness in adolescents with bipolar disorder (Strober *et al.*, 1990b). There is, however, some evidence that adolescents with bipolar disorder who have had an onset of psychiatric problems before puberty show a relatively worse response to lithium (Strober *et al.*, 1988).

It is unclear whether there is a difference in the course of bipolar illness when it arises early in life (Strober *et al.*, 1989). Carlson *et al.* (1977) compared bipolar patients with an onset at around the age of 16 years with later-onset bipolars and found no significant difference in episode frequency. Werry *et al.* (1991) reported that the outcome of bipolar disorder arising in adolescence seemed to be better than early-onset schizophrenia. However, compliance with treatment was poor in one-third of cases, so active follow-up is required. The strongest predictor of future functioning was premorbid adjustment (Werry & McClellan, 1992).

SUMMARY AND CONCLUSIONS

Since the first edition of this volume, great progress has been made in the definition and measurement of affective conditions among the young. As a result, there is now much greater consistency in the findings from epidemiological studies, which have generally shown that depressive disorders do occur in children, with a sharp increase in rates during adolescence. These early-onset depressive conditions constitute a substantial problem. They are associated with considerable impairment of psychosocial functioning and in severe cases there is a high risk of recurrence, with vulnerability extending into adult life.

Early-onset affective conditions are likely to be heterogeneous with regard to cause. A few cases, such as the bipolar conditions, probably result from genetic inheritance, and a few from severe adversity. However, in the majority it is likely that there is an interaction between multiple causes.

Data from several different kinds of studies, particularly the longitudinal and family genetic data, support the nosological validity of the concept of depressive disorder among the young. Nevertheless, classification remains a problem. It is becoming clear that the majority of cases of early-onset depressive disorder also meet the criteria for one or more nondepressive diagnoses, especially anxiety and conduct disorders. On present evidence it would appear that disorders characterized by depression and conduct disorder should be separated from other forms of early-onset depression. The presence of an anxiety disorder seems to signal a more severe form of depression rather than a qualitatively distinct condition.

The multiple problems that are found among depressed children mean that management should be based on a detailed assessment of the child and the family, rather than on the psychiatric diagnosis as such. Depressed children have multiple problems that require a range of therapeutic interventions, including physical, psychological and social treatments. Unfortunately, it must be conceded that the efficacy of these treatments in clinical samples remains to be conclusively demonstrated. Depressed young people therefore require repeated assessment and long-term strategies for management.

ACKNOWLEDGEMENTS

The author's research on childhood depression has been supported by the MacArthur Foundation and the Mental Health Foundation. Portions of this chapter are based on an annotation in the *Journal of Child Psychology and Psychiatry*, with the permission of the publishers.

REFERENCES

Abramson L.Y., Seligman M.E.P. & Teasdale J.D. (1978) Learned helplessness in humans: critique and reformulation. *Journal of Abnormal Psychology*, **87**, 49–74.

Abramson L.Y., Metalsky G.I. & Alloy L.B. (1989) Hopelessness depression: a theory-based subtype of depression. *Psychological Review*, **96**, 358–372.

Adams M. & Adams J. (1991) Life events, depression, and perceived problem solving alternatives in adolescents. *Journal of Child Psychology and Psychiatry*, **32**, 811–820.

Alessi N.E. (1991) Refractory childhood depressive disorders from a pharmacotherapeutic perspective. In: Amsterdam J.D. (ed) *Advances in Neuropsychiatry and Psychopharmacology, Volume 2: Refractory Depression*, pp. 53–63. Rave Press, New York.

Allen D.M. & Tarnowski K.J. (1989) Depressive characteristics of physically abused children. *Journal of Abnormal Child Psychology*, **17**, 1–11.

American Psychiatric Association (1994) *Diagnostic and Statistical Manual of Mental Disorders — DSM-IV* (4th edn). American Psychiatric Association, Washington, DC.

Anderson J.C., Williams S., McGee R. & Silva P.A. (1987) DSM-III disorders in preadolescent children: prevalence in a large sample from the general population. *Archives of General Psychiatry*, **44**, 69–76.

Andreasen N.C. (1982) Concepts, diagnosis and classification. In: Paykel E.S. (ed) *Handbook of Affective Disorders*, pp. 24–44. Churchill Livingstone, Edinburgh.

Andreasen N.C., Scheftner W., Reich T., Hirschfeld R.M.A., Endicott J. & Keller M.B. (1986) The validation of the concept of endogenous depression. A family study approach. *Archives of General Psychiatry*, **43**, 246–251.

Andrews J.A. & Lewinsohn P.M. (1992) Suicidal attempts among older adolescents: prevalence and co-occurrence with psychiatric disorders. *Journal of the American Academy of Child and Adolescent Psychiatry*, **31**, 655–662.

Angold A. (1988a) Childhood and adolescent depression. I. Epidemiological and aetiological aspects. *British Journal of Psychiatry*, **152**, 601–617.

Angold A. (1988b) Childhood and adolescent depression. II. Research in clinical populations. *British Journal of Psychiatry*, **153**, 476–492.

Angold A. & Rutter M. (1992) Effects of age and pubertal status on depression in a large clinical sample. *Development and Psychopathology*, **4**, 5–28.

Angold A., Weissmann M.M., John K., Merikangas K.R., Prusoff P., Wickramaratne G., Gammon G.D. & Warner V. (1987a) Parent and child reports of depressive symptoms in children at low and high risk of depression. *Journal of Child Psychology and Psychiatry*, **28**, 901–915.

Angold A., Costello E.J., Pickles A., Winder F. & Silver A. (1987b) The development of a questionnaire for use in epidemiological studies of depression in children and adolescents. Institute of Psychiatry, London University.

Anthony J. & Scott P. (1960) Manic-depressive psychosis in childhood. *Journal of Child Psychology and Psychiatry*, **1**, 53–72.

Aro H.M. & Palosaari U.K. (1992) Parental divorce, adolescence, and transition to young adulthood: a follow-up study. *American Journal of Orthopsychiatry*, **62**, 421–429.

Asarnow J.R. & Bates S. (1988) Depression in child psychiatric inpatients: cognitive and attributional patterns. *Journal of Abnormal Child Psychology*, **16**, 601–615.

Asarnow J.R., Goldstein M.J., Carlson G.A., Perdue S., Bates S. & Keller J. (1988) Childhood-onset depressive disorders. A follow-up study of rates of rehospitalization and out-of-home placement among child psychiatric inpatients. *Journal of Affective Disorders*, **15**, 245–253.

Asarnow J.R., Goldstein M.J., Tompson M. & Guthrie D. (1993) One-year outcomes of depressive disorders in child psychiatric inpatients: evaluation of the prognostic power of a brief measure of expressed emotion. *Journal of Child Psychology and Psychiatry*, **34**, 129–138.

Baron M., Endicott J. & Ott J. (1990) Genetic linkage in mental illness. Limitations and prospects. *British Journal of Psychiatry*, **157**, 645–655.

Barrett M.L., Berney T.P., Bhate S., Famuyiwa O., Fundudis T., Kolvin I. & Tyrer S. (1991) Diagnosing childhood depression: who should be interviewed — parent or child? The Newcastle Child Depression Project. *British Journal of Psychiatry*, **159** (suppl. 11), 22–27.

Bartels M.G., Varley C.K., Mitchell J. & Stamm S.J. (1991) Pediatric cardiovascular effects of imipramine and desipramine. *Journal of the American Academy of Child and Adolescent Psychiatry*, **30**, 100–103.

Beardslee W.R., Bemporad J., Keller M.B. & Klerman G.L. (1983) Children of parents with major affective disorder: a review. *American Journal of Psychiatry*, **140**, 825–832.

Beck A.T. (1976) *Cognitive Therapy and the Emotional Disorders*. International Universities Press, New York.

Benca R.M., Obermeyer W.H., Thisted R.A. & Gillin C. (1992) Sleep and psychiatric disorders: a meta-analysis. *Archives of General Psychiatry*, **49**, 651–668.

Berney T.P., Bhate S.R., Kolvin I., Famuyiwa O., Barrett M.L., Fundudis T. & Tyrer S.P. (1991) The context of childhood depression. The Newcastle Childhood Depression Project. *British Journal of Psychiatry*, **159** (suppl. 11), 28–35.

Bernstein G.A. (1991) Comorbidity and severity of anxiety and depressive disorders in a clinic population. *Journal of the American Academy of Child and Adolescent Psychiatry*, **30**, 43–50.

Bernstein G.A. & Garfinkel B.D. (1986) School phobia: the overlap of affective and anxiety disorders. *Journal of the American Academy of Child Psychiatry*, **25**, 235–241.

Bernstein G.A. & Garfinkel B.D. (1988) Pedigrees, functioning, and psychopathology in families of school phobic children. *American Journal of Psychiatry*, **145**, 70–74.

Bertagnoli M.W. & Borchardt C.M. (1990) A review of ECT for children and adolescents. *Journal of the American Academy of Child and Adolescent Psychiatry*, **29**, 302–307.

Biederman J., Newcorn J. & Sprich S. (1991) Comorbidity of attention deficit hyperactivity disorder with conduct, depressive, anxiety, and other disorders. *American Journal of Psychiatry*, **148**, 564–577.

Bifulco A., Brown G.W. & Adler Z. (1991) Early sexual abuse and clinical depression in adult life. *British Journal of Psychiatry*, **159**, 115–122.

Bird H.R., Gould M.S. & Staghezza B. (1992) Aggregating data from multiple informants in child psychiatry epidemiological research. *Journal of the American Academy of Child and Adolescent Psychiatry*, **31**, 78–85.

Birmaher B., Ryan N.D., Dahl R., Rabinovich H., Ambrosini P., Williamson D.E., Novacenko H., Nelson B., Sing Lo E. & Puig-Antich J. (1992a) Dexamethasone suppression test in children with major depressive disorder. *Journal of the American Academy of Child and Adolescent Psychiatry*, **31**, 291–297.

Birmaher B., Dahl R.E., Ryan N.D., Rabinovich H., Ambrosini P., Al-Shabbout M., Novacenko H., Nelson B. & Puig-Antich J. (1992b) The dexamethasone suppression test in adolescent outpatients with major depressive disorder. *American Journal of Psychiatry*, **149**, 1040–1045.

Boulos C., Kutcher S., Marton P., Simeon J., Ferguson B. & Roberts N. (1991) Response to desipramine treatment in adolescent major depression. *Psychopharmacology Bulletin*, **27**, 59–65.

Bowring M.A. & Kovacs M. (1992) Difficulties in diagnosing manic disorders among children and adolescents. *Journal of the American Academy of Child and Adolescent Psychiatry*, **31**, 611–614.

Brady E.U. & Kendall P.C. (1992) Comorbidity of anxiety and depression in children and adolescents. *Psychological Bulletin*, **111**, 244–255.

Brandenburg N.A, Friedman R.M. & Silver S.E. (1990) The epidemiology of childhood psychiatric disorders: prevalence findings from recent studies. *Journal of the American Academy of Child and Adolescent Psychiatry*, **29**, 76–83.

Briere J. (1992) Methodological issues in the study of sexual abuse effects. *Journal of Consulting and Clinical Psychology*, **60**, 196–203.

Brown G.W. & Harris T. (1978) *Social Origins of Depression*. Tavistock Publications, London.

Brown G.W., Harris T.O. & Bifulco A. (1986) Long-term effects of early loss of parent. In: Rutter M., Izard C.E. & Read P.B. (eds) *Depression in Young People: Clinical and Developmental Perspectives*, pp. 251–296. Guilford Press, New York.

Buchan H., Johnstone E., McPherson K., Palmer, R.L., Crow T.J. & Brandon S. (1992) Who benefits from electroconvulsive therapy? Combined results of the Leicester and Northwick Park trials. *British Journal of Psychiatry*, **160**, 355–359.

Buchanan C.M., Eccles J.S. & Becker J.B. (1992) Are adolescents the victims of raging hormones: evidence for activational effects of hormones on moods and behavior at adolescence. *Psychology Bulletin*, **111**, 62–107.

Burkard W.P., Prada M.D., Keller H.H., Kettler R. & Haefely W. (1989) Pre-clinical pharmacology of moclobemide. A review of published studies. *British Journal of Psychiatry*, **155** (suppl. 6), 84–88.

Burke K.C., Burke J.D., Regier D.A. & Rae D.S. (1990) Age at onset of selected mental disorders in five community populations. *Archives of General Psychiatry*, **47**, 511–518.

Burke P., Kochoshis S.A., Chandra R., Whiteway M. & Sauer J. (1990) Determinants of depression in recent onset pediatric inflammatory bowel disease. *Journal of the American Academy of Child and Adolescent Psychiatry*, **29**, 608–610.

Butler L., Miezitis S., Friedman R. & Cole E. (1980) The effect of two school-based intervention programs on depressive symptoms in preadolescents. *American Education Research Journal*, **17**, 111–119.

Carlson G.A. (1990) Child and adolescent mania — diagnostic considerations. *Journal of Child Psychology and Psychiatry*, **31**, 331–341.

Carlson G.A. & Cantwell D.P. (1980) A survey of depressive symptoms, syndrome and disorder in a child psychiatric population. *Journal of Child Psychology and Psychiatry*, **21**, 19–25.

Carlson G.A. & Garber J. (1986) Developmental issues in the classification of depression in children. In: Rutter M., Izard C.E. & Read P.B. (eds) *Depression in Young People: Developmental and Clinical Perspectives*, pp. 399–434. Guilford Press, New York.

Carlson G.A., Davenport Y.B. & Jamison K. (1977) A comparison of outcome in adolescent and late onset bipolar manic depressive illness. *American Journal of Psychiatry*, **134**, 919–922.

Caron C. & Rutter M. (1991) Comorbidity in child psychopathology: concepts, issues and research strategies. *Journal of Child Psychology and Psychiatry*, **32**, 1063–1080.

Caron C., Wickramaratne P., Warner V., Weissman M. & Merette C. (submitted) A search for pathways to comorbidity of major depression and conduct disorder.

Casat C.D. & Powell K. (1988) The dexamethasone suppression test in children and adolescents with major depressive disorder: a review. *Journal of Clinical Psychiatry*, **49**, 390–393.

Chambers W., Puig-Antich J., Hirsch M., Paez P., Ambrosini P.J., Tabrizi M.A. & Davies M. (1985) The assessment of affective disorders in children and adolescents by semi-structured interview: test-retest reliability of the K-SADS-P. *Archives of General Psychiatry*, **42**, 696–702.

Charney D.S., Delgado P.L., Southwick S.M., Krystal J.H., Price L.H. & Heninger G.R. (1991) Current hypotheses of the mechanism of antidepressant treatments: implications for the treatment of refractory depression. In: Amsterdam J.D. (ed) *Advances in Neuropsychiatry and Psychopharmacology, Vol. 2: Refractory Depression*, pp. 23–40. Raven Press, New York.

Cicchetti D. & Schneider-Rosen K. (1986) An organizational approach to childhood depression. In: Rutter M., Izard C.E. & Read P.B. (eds) *Depression in Young People: Developmental and Clinical Perspectives*, pp. 71–134. Guilford Press, New York.

Coffey C.E., Weiner R.D., Djang W.T., Figiel G.S., Soady S.A.R., Patterson L.J., Holt P.D., Spritzer C.E. & Wilkinson W.E. (1991) Brain anatomic effects of electroconvulsive therapy. A prospective magnetic resonance imaging study. *Archives of General Psychiatry*, **48**, 1013–1021.

Cole D.A. (1991) Preliminary support for a competency-based model of depression in children. *Journal of Abnormal Psychology*, **100**, 181–190.

Cook W.L., Kenny D.A. & Goldstein M.J. (1991) Parental affective style risk and the family system: a social relations model analysis. *Journal of Abnormal Psychology*, **100**, 492–501.

Cooper P.J. & Goodyer I. (1993) A community study of depression in adolescent girls. I: estimates of symptom and syndrome prevalence. *British Journal of Psychiatry*, **163**, 369–374.

Costello A.J. (1986) Assessment and diagnosis of affective disorders in children. *Journal of Child Psychology and Psychiatry*, **27**, 565–574.

Costello E.J. & Angold A. (1988) Scales to assess child and adolescent depression: checklists, screens and nets. *Journal of the American Academy of Child and Adolescent Psychiatry*, **27**, 726–737.

Costello E.J., Benjamin R., Angold A. & Silver D. (1991) Mood variability in adolescents: a study of depressed, nondepressed and comorbid patients. *Journal of Affective Disorders*, **23**, 199–212.

Cowen P.J. & Wood A.J. (1991) Biological markers of depression. *Psychological Medicine*, **21**, 831–836.

Deakin J.F.W. & Crow T.J. (1986) Monoamines, rewards and punishments — the anatomy and physiology of the affective disorders. In: Deakin J.F.W. (ed) *The Biology of Depression*, pp. 1–25. Royal College of Psychiatrists, London.

Dobson K.S. (1989) A meta-analysis of the efficacy of cognitive therapy for depression. *Journal of Consulting and Clinical Psychology*, **57**, 414–419.

Dodge K.A. (1990) Developmental psychopathology in children of depressed mothers. *Developmental Psychology*, **26**, 3–6.

Dweck C.S. & Elliot E.S. (1983) Achievement motivation. In: Hetherington E.M. (ed) *Socialization, Personality, and Social Development*, vol. 4, *Mussen's Handbook of Child Psychology*, 4th edn, pp. 643–691. Wiley, New York.

Dwyer J.T. & Delong G.R. (1987) A family history study of twenty probands with childhood manic-depressive illness. *Journal of the American Academy of Child and Adolescent Psychiatry*, **26**, 176–180.

Edelbrock C.S. & Costello A.J. (1988) Structured psychiatric interviews for children. In: Rutter M., Tuma A.H. & Lann I.S. (eds) *Assessment and Diagnosis in Child Psychopathology*, pp. 87–112. Guilford Press, New York.

Edelbrock C., Costello A.J., Dulcan M.K., Kalas R. & Conover N.C. (1985) Age differences in the reliability of the psychiatric interview with the child. *Child Development*, **56**, 265–275.

Elkin I., Shea T., Watkins J.T., Imber S.D., Sotsky S.M., Collins J.F., Glass D.R., Pilkonis P.A., Leber W.R., Docherty J.P., Fiester S.J. & Parloff M.B. (1989) National Institute of Mental Health treatment of depression collaborative research programme: general effectiveness of treatments. *Archives of General Psychiatry*, **46**, 971–982.

Elkins R. & Rapoport J.L. (1983) Psychopharmacology of adult and childhood depression: an overview. In: Cantwell D.P. & Carlson G.A. (eds) *Affective Disorders in Childhood and Adolescence*, pp. 363–374. MTP Press, Lancaster.

Emslie G.J., Rush A.J., Weinberg W.A., Rintelmann J.W. & Roffwarg H.P. (1990) Children with major depression show reduced rapid eye movement latencies. *Archives of General Psychiatry*, **47**, 119–124.

Famularo R., Kinscherff R. & Fenton T. (1992) Psychiatric diagnoses of maltreated children: preliminary findings. *Journal of the American Academy of Child and Adolescent Psychiatry*, **31**, 863–867.

Farmer A. & McGuffin P. (1989) The classification of the depressions. Contemporary confusion revisited. *British Journal of Psychiatry*, **155**, 437–443.

Ferguson H.B. & Bawden H.N. (1988). Psychobiological measures. In: Rutter M., Tuma A.H. & Lann I.S. (eds) *Assessment and Diagnosis in Child Psychopathology*, pp. 232–263. Guilford Press, New York.

Fine S., Forth A., Gilbert M. & Haley G. (1991) Group therapy for adolescent depressive disorder: a comparison of social skills and therapeutic support. *Journal of the American Academy of Child and Adolescent Psychiatry*, **30**, 79–85.

Fleming J. & Offord D.R. (1990) Epidemiology of childhood depressive disorders: a critical review. *Journal of the American Academy of Child and Adolescent Psychiatry*, **29**, 571–580.

Fleming J.E., Offord D.R. & Boyle M.H. (1989) Prevalence of childhood and adolescent depression in the community: Ontario child health study. *British Journal of Psychiatry*, **155**, 647–654.

Fombonne E. (in press) In: Rutter M. & Smith D. (eds) *Psychosocial Disorders in Young People: Time Trends and their Origins*. Wiley, Chichester.

Forness S.R. (1988) School characteristics of children and adolescents with depression. In: Rutherford R.B., Nelson C.M. & Forness S.R. (eds) *Bases of Severe Behavioural Disorders in Children and Youth*, pp. 177–203. Little, Brown, Boston, MA.

Frank E., Kupfer D.J., Wager E.F., McEachran A.B. & Cornes C. (1991) Efficacy of interpersonal psychotherapy as a maintenance treatment of recurrent depression. *Archives of General Psychiatry*, **48**, 1053–1059.

Frommer E.A. (1967) Treatment of childhood depression with antidepressant drugs. *British Medical Journal*, **1**, 729–732.

Garber J., Kriss M.R., Koch M. & Lindholm L. (1988) Recurrent depression in adolescents: a follow-up study. *Journal of the American Academy of Child Psychiatry*, **27**, 49–54.

Garber J., Zeman J. & Walker L.S. (1990) Recurrent abdominal pain in children: psychiatric diagnoses and parental psychopathology. *Journal of the American Academy of Child and Adolescent Psychiatry*, **29**, 648–656.

Garrison C.Z., Addy C.L., Jackson K.L., McKeown R.E. & Waller J.L. (1991) The CES-D as a screen for depression and other psychiatric disorders in adolescents. *Journal of the American Academy of Child and Adolescent Psychiatry*, **30**, 636–641.

Geller B. (1991) Psychopharmacology of children and adolescents: pharmacokinetics and relationships of plasma/serum levels to response. *Psychopharmacology Bulletin*, **27**, 401–409.

Geller B., Cooper T.B., Chestnut E.C., Anker J.A. & Schluchter M.D. (1986) Preliminary data on the relationship between nortriptyline plasma level and response in depressed children. *American Journal of Psychiatry*, **143**, 1283–1286.

Geller B., Cooper T.B., Graham D.L., Marsteller F.A. & Bryant D.M. (1990) Double-blind placebo-controlled study of nortriptyline in depressed adolescents using a 'fixed plasma level' design. *Psychopharmacology Bulletin*, **26**, 85–90.

Geller B., Cooper T.B., Graham D.L., Fetner H.H., Marsteller F.A. & Wells J.M., (1992) Pharmacokinetically designed double-blind placebo-controlled study of nortriptyline in 6- to 12-year-olds with major depressive disorder. *Journal of the American Academy of Child and Adolescent Psychiatry*, **31**, 34–44.

Giles D.E., Roffwarg H.P., Dahl R.E. & Kupfer D.J. (1992) Electro-encephalographic sleep abnormalities in depressed children: a hypothesis. *Psychiatry Research*, **41**, 53–63.

Gittelman R., Mannuzza S., Shenker R. & Bonagura N. (1985) Hyperactive boys almost grown up. I: Psychiatric status. *Archives of General Psychiatry*, **42**, 937–947.

Giuffra L.A. & Risch N. (1991) Forgetting and the cohort effect: a simulation study. *Abstracts of the Second World Congress on Psychiatric Genetics*, p. 41. Cambridge.

Goetz R.R., Puig-Antich J., Dahl R.E., Ryan N.D., Asnis G.M., Rabinovich H. & Nelson B. (1991) EEG sleep of young adults with major depression: a controlled study. *Journal of Affective Disorders*, **22**, 91–100.

Goldston D.B., Turnquist D.C. & Knutson J.F. (1989) Presenting problems of sexually abused girls receiving psychiatric services. *Journal of Abnormal Psychology*, **98**, 314–317.

Goodyer I.M. (1990) *Life Experiences, Development and Childhood Psychopathology*. Wiley, Chichester.

Goodyer I.M. & Altham P.M.E. (1991) Lifetime exit events and recent social and family adversities in anxious and depressed school-age children and adolescents — II. *Journal of Affective Disorders*, **21**, 229–238.

Goodyer I.M., Wright C. & Altham P.M.E. (1988) Maternal adversity and recent stressful life events in anxious and depressed children. *Journal of Child Psychology and Psychiatry*, **29**, 651–667.

Goodyer I., Herbert J., Moor S. & Altham P. (1991a) Cortisol hypersecretion in depressed school-aged children and adolescents. *Psychiatry Research*, **37**, 237–244.

Goodyer I.M., Germany E., Gowrusankur J. & Altham P. (1991b) Social influences on the course of anxious and depressive disorders in school-age children. *British Journal of Psychiatry*, **158**, 676–684.

Goodyer I.M., Cooper P.J., Vize C. & Ashby L. (1993) Depression in 11 to 16 year old girls: the role of past parental psychopathology and exposure to recent life events. *Journal of Child Psychology and Psychiatry*, **34**, 1103–1115.

Greenbaum P.E., Prange M.E., Friedman R.M. & Silver S.E. (1991) Substance abuse prevalence and comorbidity with other psychiatric disorders among adolescents with severe emotional disturbance. *Journal of the American Academy of Child Psychiatry*, **30**, 575–583.

Guelfi J.D., Payan C., Fermanian J., Pedarriosse A.M. & Manfredi R. (1992) Moclobemide versus clomipramine in endogenous depression. A double-blind randomized clinical trial. *British Journal of Psychiatry*, **160**, 519–524.

Guze B.H. & Freedman D.X. (1991) Psychiatry (commentary). *Journal of the American Medical Association*, **265**, 3164–3165.

Hamilton M. (1982) Symptoms and assessment of depression. In: Payke E. (ed) *Handbook of Affective Disorders*, pp. 3–11. Churchill Livingstone, Edinburgh.

Hammen C., Adrian C. & Hiroto D. (1988) A longitudinal test of the attributional vulnerability model in children at risk for depression. *British Journal of Clinical Psychology*, **27**, 37–46.

Hammen C., Burge D. & Adrian C. (1991) Timing of mother and child depression in a longitudinal study of children at risk. *Journal of Consulting and Clinical Psychology*, **59**, 341–345.

Harrington R.C. (1989) Childhood and adolescent depression: recent developments. *Current Opinion in Psychiatry*, **2**, 480–483.

Harrington R.C. (1991) Do we need different criteria to diagnose depression in children? Paper presented at the Ninth meeting of the European Society for Child and Adolescent Psychiatry.

Harrington R.C. & Shariff A. (1992) Choosing an instrument to assess depression in young people. *Newsletter of the Association of Child Psychology and Psychiatry*, **14**, 279–282.

Harrington R.C., Fudge H., Rutter M., Pickles A. & Hill J. (1990) Adult outcomes of childhood and adolescent depression: I. Psychiatric status. *Archives of General Psychiatry*, **47**, 465–473.

Harrington R.C., Fudge H., Rutter M., Pickles A. & Hill J. (1991) Adult outcomes of childhood and adolescent depression: II. Risk for antisocial disorders. *Journal of the American Academy of Child and Adolescent Psychiatry*, **30**, 434–439.

Harrington R.C., Fudge H., Rutter M., Bredenkamp D., Groothues C. & Pridham J. (1993) Child and adult depression: a test of continuities with data from a family study. *British Journal of Psychiatry*, **162**, 627–633.

Hawton K. (1992) By their own young hand. *British Medical Journal*, **304**, 1000.

Henry J.A. (1992) The safety of antidepressants. *British Journal of Psychiatry*, **160**, 439–441.

Hoier T.S. & Kerr M.M. (1988) Extrafamilial information sources in the study of childhood depression. *Journal of the American Academy of Child and Adolescent Psychiatry*, **27**, 21–33.

Hollon S.D., Shelton R.C. & Loosen P.T. (1991) Cognitive therapy and pharmacotherapy for depression. *Journal of Consulting and Clinical Psychology*, **59**, 88–99.

Hughes C.W., Preskorn S.H., Weller E., Weller R., Hassanein R. & Tucker S. (1990) The effect of concomitant disorders in childhood depression on predicting clinical response. *Psychopharmacology Bulletin*, **26**, 235–238.

Jensen J.B. & Garfinkel B.D. (1990) Growth hormone dysregulation in children with major depressive disorder. *Journal of the American Academy of Child and Adolescent Psychiatry*, **29**, 295–301.

Johnson J., Horwarth E. & Weissman M.M. (1991) The validity of major depression with psychotic features based on a community study. *Archives of General Psychiatry*, **48**, 1075–1081.

Kahn J.S., Kehle T.J., Jenson W.R. & Clark E. (1990) Comparison of cognitive-behavioural, relaxation, and self-modeling interventions for depression among middle-school students. *School Psychology Review*, **19**, 196–211.

Kandel D.B. & Davies M. (1986) Adult sequelae of adolescent depressive symptoms. *Archives of General Psychiatry*, **43**, 255–262.

Kashani J.H., McGee R., Clarkson S., Anderson J., Walton L., Williams S., Silva P., Robins A., Cytryn M. & McKnew D. (1983) Depression in a sample of 9-year-old children: prevalence and associated characteristics. *Archives of General Psychiatry*, **40**, 1217–1223.

Kashani J.H., Beck N.C., Hoeper E.W., Fallahi C., Corcoran C.M., McAllister J.A., Rosenberg T.K. & Reid J.C. (1987) Psychiatric disorders in a community sample of adolescents. *American Journal of Psychiatry*, **144**, 584–589.

Kaufman J. (1991) Depressive disorders in maltreated children. *Journal of the American Academy of Child Psychiatry*, **30**, 257–265.

Kazdin A.E. (1990) Childhood depression. *Journal of Child Psychology and Psychiatry*, **31**, 121–160.

Kazdin A.E., Esveldt-Dawson K., Sherick R.B. & Colbus D. (1985) Assessment of overt behavior and childhood depression among psychiatrically disturbed children. *Journal of Consulting and Clinical Psychology*, **53**, 201–210.

Keller M.B., Beardslee W., Lavori P.W., Wunder J., Drs D.L. & Samuelson H. (1988) Course of major depression in non-referred adolescents: a retrospective study. *Journal of Affective Disorders*, **15**, 235–243.

Keller M.B., Lavori P.W., Beardslee W.R., Wunder J. & Ryan N. (1991) Depression in children and adolescents: new data on 'under-treatment' and a literature review on the efficacy of available treatments. *Journal of Affective Disorders*, **21**, 163–171.

Kendall P.C. (1992) Healthy thinking. *Behavioral Therapy*, **23**, 1–11.

Kendall P.C. & Morris R.J. (1991) Child therapy: issues and recommendations. *Journal of Consulting and Clinical Psychology*, **59**, 777–784.

Kendall P.C., Stark K.D. & Adam T. (1990) Cognitive deficit or cognitive distortion in childhood depression. *Journal of Abnormal Child Psychology*, **18**, 255–270.

Kendler K.S., Neale M.C., Kessler R.C., Heath A.C. & Eaves L.J. (1992) A population-based twin study of major depression in women. The impact of varying definitions of illness. *Archives of General Psychiatry*, **49**, 257–266.

Kinzie J.D., Sack W., Angell R., Clarke G. & Ben R. (1989) A three-year follow-up of Cambodian young people traumatized as children. *Journal of the American Academy of Child and Adolescent Psychiatry*, **28**, 501–504.

Klerman G.L. (1988) The current age of youthful melancholia: evidence for increase in depression among adolescents and young adults. *British Journal of Psychiatry*, **152**, 4–14.

Koestner R., Zuroff D.C. & Powers T.A. (1991) Family origins of adolescent self-criticism and its continuity into adulthood. *Journal of Abnormal Psychology*, **100**, 191–197.

Kolvin I., Barrett M.L., Bhate S.R., Berney T.P., Famuyiwa O., Fundudis T. & Tyrer S. (1991) The Newcastle Child Depression Project: diagnosis and classification of depression. *British Journal of Psychiatry*, **159** (suppl. 11), 9–21.

Kolvin I., Berney T.P., Barrett L.M. & Bhate S. (1992) Development and evaluation of a diagnostic algorithm for depression in childhood. *European Child and Adolescent Psychiatry*, **1**, 119–129.

Kovacs M. (1986) A developmental perspective on methods and measures in the assessment of depressive disorders: the clinical interview. In: Rutter M., Izard C.E. & Read P.B. (eds) *Depression in Young People: Developmental and Clinical Perspectives*, pp. 435–468. Guilford Press, New York.

Kovacs M. & Goldston D. (1991) Cognitive and social cognitive development of depressed children and adolescents. *Journal of the*

American Academy of Child and Adolescent Psychiatry, **30**, 388–392.

Kovacs M., Feinberg T.L., Crouse-Novak M.A., Paulauskas S.L. & Finkelstein R. (1984a) Depressive disorders in childhood. I. A longitudinal prospective study of characteristics and recovery. *Archives of General Psychiatry*, **41**, 229–237.

Kovacs M., Feinberg T.L., Crouse-Novak M.A., Paulauskas S.L. Pollock M. & Finkelstein R. (1984b) Depressive disorders in childhood. II. A longitudinal study of the risk for a subsequent major depression. *Archives of General Psychiatry*, **41**, 643–649.

Kovacs M., Paulauskas S., Gatsonis C. & Richards C. (1988) Depressive disorders in childhood. III. A longitudinal study of comorbidity with and risk for conduct disorders. *Journal of Affective Disorders*, **15**, 205–217.

Kovacs M., Gatsonis C., Paulauskas S. & Richards C. (1989) Depressive disorders in childhood. IV. A longitudinal study of comorbidity with and risk for anxiety disorders. *Archives of General Psychiatry*, **46**, 776–782.

Kramer A.D. & Feiguine R.J. (1983) Clinical effects of amitriptyline in adolescent depression: a pilot study. *Journal of the American Academy of Child and Adolescent Psychiatry*, **20**, 636–644.

Kranzler E.M., Shaffer D., Wasserman G. & Davies M. (1990) Early childhood bereavement. *Journal of the American Academy of Child and Adolescent Psychiatry*, **29**, 513–520.

Kupfer D. (1992) Maintenance treatment in recurrent depression: current and future directions. *British Journal of Psychiatry*, **161**, 309–316.

Kutcher S. & Marton P. (1991) Affective disorders in first degree relatives of adolescent onset bipolars, unipolars, and normal controls. *Journal of the American Academy of Child and Adolescent Psychiatry*, **30**, 75–78.

Kutcher S., Malkin D., Silverberg J., Marton P., Williamson P., Malkin A., Szalai J. & Katic M. (1991) Nocturnal cortisol, thyroid stimulating hormone, and growth hormone secretory profiles in depressed adolescents. *Journal of the American Academy of Child and Adolescent Psychiatry*, **30**, 407–414.

Kutcher S., Williamson P., Marton P. & Szalai J. (1992) REM latency in endogenously depressed adolescents. *British Journal of Psychiatry*, **161**, 399–402.

Larson R.W., Raffaelli M., Richards M.H., Ham M. & Jewell L. (1990) Ecology of depression in late childhood and early adolescence: a profile of daily states and activities. *Journal of Abnormal Psychology*, **99**, 92–102.

Lask B. & Bryant-Waugh R. (1992) Early-onset anorexia nervosa and related eating disorders. *Journal of Child Psychology and Psychiatry*, **33**, 281–300.

Leckman J.F., Weissman M.M., Prusoff B.A., Caruso K.A., Merikangas K.R., Pauls D.L. & Kidd K.K. (1984) Subtypes of depression. Family study perspective. *Archives of General Psychiatry*, **41**, 833–838.

Lefkowitz M.M. & Tesiny E.P. (1980) Assessment of childhood depression. *Journal of Consulting and Clinical Psychology*, **48**, 43–50.

Lewinsohn P.M., Clarke G.N., Hops H. & Andrews J. (1990) Cognitive-behavioral treatment for depressed adolescents. *Behavior Therapy*, **21**, 385–401.

Livingston R., Nugent H., Rader L. & Smith G.R. (1985) Family histories of depressed and severely anxious children. *American Journal of Psychiatry*, **142**, 1497–1499.

McCauley E., Mitchell J.R., Burke P. & Moss S. (1988) Cognitive attributes of depression in children and adolescents. *Journal of Consulting and Clinical Psychology*, **56**, 903–908.

McCauley E., Carlson G.A. & Calderon R. (1991) The role of somatic complaints in the diagnosis of depression in children and adolescents. *Journal of the American Academy of Child Psychiatry*, **30**, 631–635.

McClure G.M.G. (1984) Trends in suicide rate for England and Wales 1975–1980. *British Journal of Psychiatry*, **144**, 119–126.

McClure G.M.G. (1988) Suicide in children in England and Wales. *Journal of Child Psychology and Psychiatry*, **29**, 345–349.

McGee R. & Williams S. (1988) A longitudinal study of depression in nine-year-old children. *Journal of the American Academy of Child and Adolescent Psychiatry*, **27**, 342–348.

McGee R., Feehan M., Williams S., Partridge F., Silva P.A. & Kelly J. (1990) DSM-III disorders in a large sample of adolescents. *Journal of the American Academy of Child Psychiatry*, **29**, 611–619.

McGee R., Feehan M., Williams S. & Anderson J. (1992) DSM-III disorders from age 11 to age 15 years. *Journal of the American Academy of Child and Adolescent Psychiatry*, **31**, 50–59.

McGuffin P. (1991) Genetic models of madness. In: McGuffin P. & Murray R. (eds) *The New Genetics of Mental Illness*, pp. 27–43. Butterworth-Heinemann, Oxford.

McGuffin P. & Katz R. (1986) Nature, nurture and affective disorder. In: Deakin J.F.W. (ed) *The Biology of Depression*, pp. 26–52. Royal College of Psychiatrists, London.

McGuffin P. & Sargeant M.P. (1991) Genetic markers and affective disorder. In: McGuffin P. & Murray R. (eds) *The New Genetics of Mental Illness*, pp. 165–181. Butterworth-Heinemann, Oxford.

Marriage K., Fine S., Moretti M. & Haley G. (1986) Relationship between depression and conduct disorder in children and adolescents. *Journal of the American Academy of Child Psychiatry*, **25**, 687–691.

Martini D.R., Strayhorn J.M. & Puig-Antich J. (1990) A symptom self-report measure for preschool children. *Journal of the American Academy of Child and Adolescent Psychiatry*, **29**, 594–600.

Marttunen M.J., Aro H.M., Henriksson M.M. & Lonnqvist J.K. (1991) Mental disorders in adolescent suicide. DSM-III-R axes I and II diagnoses in suicides among 13- to 19-year-olds in Finland. *Archives of General Psychiatry*, **48**, 834–839.

Meyer N.E., Dyck D.G. & Petrinack R.J. (1989) Cognitive appraisal and attributional correlates of depressive symptoms in children. *Journal of Abnormal Child Psychology*, **17**, 325–336.

Milin R., Halikas J.A., Meller J.E. & Morse C. (1991) Psychopathology among substance abusing juvenile offenders. *Journal of the American Academy of Child Psychiatry*, **30**, 569–574.

Mitchell J., McCauley E., Burke P.M. & Moss S.J. (1988) Phenomenology of depression in children and adolescents. *Journal of the American Academy of Child and Adolescent Psychiatry*, **27**, 12–20.

Mitchell J., McCauley E., Burke P., Calderon R. & Schloredt K. (1989) Psychopathology in parents of depressed children and adolescents. *Journal of the American Academy of Child and Adolescent Psychiatry*, **28**, 352–357.

Moreau D., Mufson L., Weissman M.M. & Klerman G.L. (1991) Interpersonal psychotherapy for adolescent depression: description of modification and preliminary application. *Journal of the American Academy of Child and Adolescent Psychiatry*, **30**, 642–651.

Mufson L., Weissman M.M. & Warner V. (1992) Depression and anxiety in parents and children: a direct interview study. *Journal of Anxiety Disorders*, **6**, 1–13.

Mufson L., Moreau D., Weissman M.M. & Klerman G.L. (1993) *Interpersonal Psychotherapy for Depressed Adolescents*. Guilford Press, New York.

Myers K., McCauley E., Calderon R. & Treder R. (1991) The 3-year longitudinal course of suicidality and predictive factors for subsequent suicidality in youths with major depressive disorder. *Journal of the American Academy of Child and Adolescent Psychiatry*, **30**, 804–810.

Nolen-Hoeksema S., Girgus J.S. & Seligman M.E.P. (1992) Predictors and consequences of childhood depressive symptoms: a 5-year longitudinal study. *Journal of Abnormal Psychology*, **101**, 405–422.

Nurcombe B., Seifer R., Scioli A., Tramontana M.G., Grapentine W.L.

& Beauchesne H.C. (1989) Is major depressive disorder in adolescence a distinct diagnostic entitity? *Journal of the American Academy of Child and Adolescent Psychiatry*, **28**, 333–342.

Office of Population Census and Surveys (1990) *1990 Mortality Statistics, Cause: England and Wales.* Series DH 2, no. 17. HMSO, London.

Oster G.D. & Caro J.E. (1990) *Understanding and Treating Depressed Adolescents and their Families.* Wiley, New York.

Patterson G.R. & Capaldi D.M. (1990) A mediational model for boys' depressed mood. In: Rolf J., Masten A.S., Cicchetti D., Nuechterlein K.H. & Weintraub S. (eds) *Risk and Protective Factors in the Development of Psychopathology*, pp. 141–163. Cambridge University Press, Cambridge.

Patterson G.R. & Stoolmiller M. (1991) Replications of a dual failure model for boys' depressed mood. *Journal of Consulting and Clinical Psychology*, **59**, 491–498.

Paykel E.S. (1982) Life events and early environment. In: Paykel E.S. (ed) *Handbook of Affective Disorders*, pp. 146–161. Churchill Livingstone, Edinburgh.

Paykel E.S. (1989) Treatment of depression: the relevance of research for clinical practice. *British Journal of Psychiatry*, **155**, 754–763.

Perris C. (1966) A study of bipolar (manic-depressive) and unipolar recurrent depressive psychoses. *Acta Psychiatrica Scandinavica*, (suppl. 194), 9–189.

Perris C. (1982) The distinction between bipolar and unipolar affective disorders. In: Paykel E.S. (ed) *Handbook of Affective Disorders*, pp. 45–58. Churchill Livingstone, Edinburgh.

Petti T.A. (1983) Imipramine in the treatment of depressed children. In: Cantwell D.P. & Carlson G.A. (eds) *Affective Disorders in Childhood and Adolescence: An Update*, pp. 375–415. MTP Press, Lancaster.

Pfeffer C.R. (1992) Relationship between depression and suicidal behaviour. In: Shafii M. & Shafii S.L. (eds) *Clinical Guide to Depression in Children and Adolescents*, pp. 115–126. American Psychiatric Press, Washington.

Pope H.G., McElroy S.L., Keck P.E. & Hudson J.I. (1991) Valproate in the treatment of acute mania. A placebo-controlled study. *Archives of General Psychiatry*, **48**, 62–68.

Post R.M. (1991) Anticonvulsants as adjuncts or alternatives to lithium in refractory bipolar illness. In: Amsterdam J.D. (ed) *Advances in Neuropsychiatry and Psychopharmacology, vol. 2: Refractory Depression*, pp. 155–165. Raven Press, New York.

Post R.M. (1992) Transduction of psychosocial stress into the neurobiology of recurrent affective disorder. *American Journal of Psychiatry*, **149**, 999–1010.

Post R.M., Kramlinger K.G., Altshuler L.L., Ketter T. & Denicoff K. (1990) Treatment of rapid cycling bipolar illness. *Psychopharmacology Bulletin*, **26**, 37–47.

Preskorn S.H., Weller E.B., Hughes C.W., Weller R.A. & Bolte K. (1987) Depression in prepubertal children: dexamethasone non-suppression predicts differential response to imipramine vs. placebo. *Psychopharmacology Bulletin*, **23**, 128–133.

Prien R.F. & Potter W.Z. (1990) NIMH workshop report on treatment of bipolar disorder. *Psychopharmacology Bulletin*, **26**, 409–427.

Pritchard C. (1992) Is there a link between suicide in young men and unemployment? A comparison of the UK with other European community countries. *British Journal of Psychiatry*, **160**, 750–756.

Puig-Antich J. (1986) Psychobiological markers: effects of age and puberty. In: Rutter M., Izard C.E. & Read P.B. (eds) *Depression in Young People: Developmental and Clinical Perspectives*, pp. 341–382. Guilford Press, New York.

Puig-Antich J. & Rabinovich H. (1986) Relationship between affective and anxiety disorders in childhood. In: Gittelman R. (ed) *Anxiety Disorders of Childhood*, pp. 136–156. Guilford Press, New York.

Puig-Antich J., Tabrizi M.A., Davies M., Chambers W., Halpern F. & Sachar E.J. (1981) Prepubertal endogenous major depressives hypo-

secrete growth hormone in response to insulin-induced hypoglycaemia. *Journal of Biological Psychiatry*, **16**, 801–818.

Puig-Antich J., Lukens E., Davies M., Goetz D., Brennan-Quattrock J. & Todak G. (1985) Psychosocial functioning in prepubertal major depressive disorders. I. Interpersonal relationships during the depressive episode. *Archives of General Psychiatry*, **42**, 500–507.

Puig-Antich J., Perel J.M., Lupatkin W., Chambers W.J., Tabrizi M.A., King J., Goetz R., Davies M. & Stiller R.L. (1987) Imipramine in prepubertal major depressive disorders. *Archives of General Psychiatry*, **44**, 81–89.

Puig-Antich J., Goetz D., Davies M., Kaplan T., Davies S., Ostrow L., Asnis L., Twomey J., Iyengar S. & Ryan N.D. (1989) A controlled family history study of prepubertal major depressive disorder. *Archives of General Psychiatry*, **46**, 406–418.

Quay H.C. (1979) Classification. In: Quay H.C. & Werry J.S. (eds) *Psychopathological Disorders of Childhood*, 2nd edn, pp. 1–42. Wiley, New York.

Radke-Yarrow M., Nottelmann E., Martinez P., Fox M.B. & Belmont B. (1992) Young children of affectively ill parents: a longitudinal study of psychosocial development. *Journal of the American Academy of Child Psychiatry*, **31**, 68–77.

Rao U., Weissman M., Martin J.A. & Hammond R.W. (1993) Childhood depression and risk of suicide: preliminary report of a longitudinal study. *Journal of the American Academy of Child and Adolescent Psychiatry*, **32**, 21–27.

Reinherz H.Z., Stewart-Berghauer G., Pakiz B., Frost A.K., Moeykens B.A. & Holmes W.M. (1989) The relationship of early risk and current mediators to depressive symptomatology in adolescence. *Journal of the American Academy of Child and Adolescent Psychiatry*, **28**, 942–947.

Reynolds W.M. & Coats K.I. (1986) A comparison of cognitive-behavioural therapy and relaxation training for the treatment of depression in adolescents. *Journal of Consulting and Clinical Psychology*, **54**, 653–660.

Riddle M.A., Nelson J.C., Kleinman C.S., Rasmusson A., Leckman J.F., King R.A. & Cohen D.J. (1991) Sudden death in children receiving norpramin: a review of three reported cases and commentary. *Journal of the American Academy of Child and Adolescent Psychiatry*, **30**, 104–108.

Roberts R.E., Lewinsohn P.M. & Seeley J.R. (1991) Screening for adolescent depression: a comparison of depression scales. *Journal of the American Academy of Child and Adolescent Psychiatry*, **30**, 58–66.

Rogeness G.A., Javors M.A. & Pliszka S.R. (1992) Neurochemistry and child and adolescent psychiatry. *Journal of the American Academy of Child and Adolescent Psychiatry*, **31**, 765–781.

Rohde P., Lewinsohn P.M. & Seeley J.R. (1990) Are people changed by the experience of having an episode of depression? A further test of the scar hypothesis. *Journal of Abnormal Psychology*, **99**, 264–271.

Rohde P., Lewinsohn P.M. & Seeley J.R. (1991) Comorbidity of unipolar depression: II. Comorbidity with other mental disorders in adolescents and adults. *Journal of Abnormal Psychology*, **100**, 214–222.

Rutter M. (1986a) Depressive feelings, cognitions, and disorders: a research postscript. In: Rutter M., Izard C.E. & Read P.B. (eds) *Depression in Young People: Developmental and Clinical Perspectives*, pp. 491–519. Guilford Press, New York.

Rutter M. (1986b) The developmental psychopathology of depression: issues and perspectives. In: Rutter M., Izard C.E. & Read P.B. (eds) *Depression in Young People: Developmental and Clinical Perspectives*, pp. 3–32. Guilford Press, New York.

Rutter M. (1990) Commentary: some focus and process considerations regarding effects of parental depression on children. *Developmental Psychology*, **26**, 60–67.

Rutter M. (1991) Age changes in depressive disorders: some developmental considerations. In: Garber J. & Dodge K.A. (eds) *The Development of Emotion Regulation and Dysregulation*, pp. 273–300. Cambridge University Press, Cambridge.

Rutter M. & Quinton D. (1984) Parental psychiatric disorder: effects on children. *Psychological Medicine*, **14**, 853–880.

Rutter M. & Sandberg S. (1992) Psychosocial stressors: concepts, causes and effects. *European Child and Adolescent Psychiatry*, **1**, 3–13.

Rutter M., Tizard J. & Whitmore K. (1970) *Education, Health, and Behaviour*. Longmans, London.

Rutter M., Graham P., Chadwick O.F. & Yule W. (1976) Adolescent turmoil: fact or fiction? *Journal of Child Psychology and Psychiatry*, **17**, 35–56.

Rutter M., Macdonald H., Le Couteur A., Harrington R.C., Bolton P. & Bailey A. (1990a) Genetic factors in child psychiatric disorders — II. Empirical findings. *Journal of Child Psychology and Psychiatry*, **31**, 39–83.

Rutter M., Bolton P., Harrington R.C., Le Couteur A., Macdonald H. & Simonoff E. (1990b) Genetic factors in child psychiatric disorders — I. A review of research strategies. *Journal of Child Psychology and Psychiatry*, **31**, 3–37.

Ryan N.D. (1990) Pharmacotherapy of adolescent major depression: beyond TCAs. *Psychopharmacology Bulletin*, **26**, 75–79.

Ryan N.D. (1992) Pharmacological treatment of major depression. In: Shafii M. & Shafii S.L. (eds) *Clinical Guide to Depression in Children and Adolescents*, pp. 219–232. American Psychiatric Press, Washington.

Ryan N.D., Puig-Antich J., Cooper T., Rabinovich H., Ambrosini P., Davies M., King J., Torres D. & Fried J. (1986) Imipramine in adolescent major depression: plasma level and clinical response. *Acta Psychiatrica Scandinavica*, **73**, 275–288.

Ryan N.D., Puig-Antich J., Ambrosini P., Rabinovich H., Robinson D., Nelson B., Iyengar S. & Twomey J. (1987) The clinical picture of major depression in children and adolescents. *Archives of General Psychiatry*, **44**, 854–861.

Ryan N.D., Meyer V., Dachille S., Mazzie D. & Puig-Antich J. (1988) Lithium antidepressant augmentation in TCA-refractory depression in adolescents. *Journal of the American Academy of Child and Adolescent Psychiatry*, **27**, 371–376.

Ryan N.D., Williamson D.E., Iyengar S., Orvaschel H., Reich T., Dahl R.E. & Puig-Antich J. (1992) A secular increase in child and adolescent onset affective disorder. *Journal of the American Academy of Child and Adolescent Psychiatry*, **31**, 600–605.

Sandberg S., Rutter M., Champion L., Drinnan D., Giles S., McGuinness D., Nicholls J., Owen A. & Prior V. Assessment of psychosocial experiences in childhood: methodological issues and some illustrative findings. *Journal of Child Psychology and Psychiatry* (in press).

Scarr S. (1992) Developmental theories for the 1990s: development and individual differences. *Child Development*, **63**, 1–19.

Schatzberg A.F. (1992) Recent developments in the acute somatic treatment of major depression. *Journal of Clinical Psychiatry*, **53** (suppl. 3), 20–25.

Schatzberg A.F. & Rothschild A.J. (1992) Psychotic (delusional) major depression: should it be included as a distinct syndrome in DSM-IV? *American Journal of Psychiatry*, **149**, 733–745.

Schwartz C.E., Dorer D.J., Beardslee W.R., Lavori P.W. & Keller M.B. (1990) Maternal expressed emotion and parental affective disorder: risk for childhood depressive disorder, substance abuse, or conduct disorder. *Journal of Psychiatric Research*, **24**, 231–250.

Scott A.I.F. (1989) Which depressed patients will respond to electroconvulsive therapy? The search for biological predictors of recovery. *British Journal of Psychiatry*, **154**, 8–17.

Seligman M.E.P. & Peterson C. (1986) A learned helplessness perspective on childhood depression: theory and research. In: Rutter M.,

Izard C.E. & Read P.B. (eds) *Depression in Young People: Developmental and Clinical Perspectives*, pp. 223–250. Guilford Press, New York.

Sellar C., Hawton K. & Goldacre M.J. (1990) Self-poisoning in adolescents. Hospital admissions and deaths in the Oxford region 1980–85. *British Journal of Psychiatry*, **156**, 866–870.

Shaffer D. (1988) The epidemiology of teen suicide: an examination of risk factors. *Journal of Clinical Psychiatry*, **9** (suppl.), 36–41.

Shain B.N., King C.A., Naylor M. & Alessi N. (1991) Chronic depression and hospital course in adolescents. *Journal of the American Academy of Child and Adolescent Psychiatry*, **30**, 428–433.

Simeon J.G., Dinicola V.F., Ferguson H.B. & Copping W. (1990) Adolescent depression: a placebo-controlled fluoxetine treatment study and follow-up. *Progress in Neuro-Psychopharmacology and Biological Psychiatry*, **14**, 791–795.

Sirles E.A., Smith J.A. & Kusama H. (1989) Psychiatric status of intrafamilial child sexual abuse victims. *Journal of the American Academy of Child and Adolescent Psychiatry*, **28**, 225–229.

Small J.G., Klapper M.H., Milstein V., Kellams J.J., Miller M.J., Marhenke J.D. & Small I.F. (1991) Carbamazepine compared with lithium in the treatment of mania. *Archives of General Psychiatry*, **48**, 915–921.

Sonis W.A. (1992) Chronobiology of seasonal mood disorders. In: Shafii M. & Shafii S.L. (eds) *Clinical Guide to Depression in Children and Adolescents*, pp. 89–114. American Psychiatric Press, Washington.

Stark K.D. (1990) *Childhood Depression: School-based Intervention*. Guilford, New York.

Stark K.D., Reynolds W.M. & Kaslow N. (1987) A comparison of the relative efficacy of self-control therapy and a behavioural problem-solving therapy for depression in children. *Journal of Abnormal Child Psychology*, **15**, 91–113.

Stark K.D., Rouse L.W. & Livingston R. (1991) Treatment of depression during childhood and adolescence: cognitive behavioural procedures for the individual and family. In: Kendall P.C. (ed) *Child and Adolescent Therapy: Cognitive-Behavioural Procedures*, pp. 165–206. Guilford, New York.

Stein A., Gath D.H., Bucher J., Bond A., Day A. & Cooper P.J. (1991) The relationship between post-natal depression and mother–child interaction. *British Journal of Psychiatry*, **158**, 46–52.

Stoddard F.J., Norman D.K., Murphy J.M. & Beardslee W.R. (1989) Psychiatric outcome of burned children and adolescents. *Journal of the American Academy of Child and Adolescent Psychiatry*, **28**, 589–595.

Strober M. (in press) The pharmacotherapy of depressive illness in adolescence: III. Diagnostic and conceptual issues in studies of tricyclic drugs. *Journal of Child Adolescence and Psychopharmacology*, (in press).

Strober M. (1992) Relevance of early age-of-onset in genetic studies of bipolar affective disorder. *Journal of the American Academy of Child and Adolescent Psychiatry*, **31**, 606–610.

Strober M. & Carlson G. (1982) Bipolar illness in adolescents with major depression: clinical, genetic and psychopharmacologic predictors in a three- to four-year prospective follow-up investigation. *Archives of General Psychiatry*, **39**, 549–555.

Strober M., Morrell W., Burroughs J., Lampert C., Danforth H. & Freeman R. (1988) A family study of bipolar I disorder in adolescence: early onset of symptoms linked to increased familial loading and lithium resistance. *Journal of Affective Disorders*, **15**, 255–268.

Strober M., Hanna G. & McCracken J. (1989) Bipolar disorder. In: Last C.G. & Hersen M. (eds) *Handbook of Child Psychiatric Diagnosis*, pp. 299–316. Wiley, New York.

Strober M., Freeman R. & Rigali J. (1990a) The pharmacotherapy of depressive illness in adolescence: I. An open label trial of imipramine. *Psychopharmacology Bulletin*, **26**, 80–84.

Strober M., Morrell W., Lampert C. & Burroughs J. (1990b) Relapse following discontinuation of lithium maintenance therapy in adolescents with bipolar I illness: a naturalistic study. *American Journal of Psychiatry*, **147**, 457–461.

Strober M., Freeman R., Rigali J., Schmidt S. & Diamond R. (1992) The pharmacotherapy of depressive illness in adolescence: II. Effects of lithium augmentation in nonresponders to imipramine. *Journal of the American Academy of Child and Adolescent Psychiatry*, **31**, 16–20.

Strober M., Lampert C., Schmidt S. & Morrell W. (1993) The course of major depressive disorder in adolescents. I. Recovery and risk of manic switching in a 24-month prospective, naturalistic follow-up of psychotic and nonpsychotic subtypes. *Journal of the American Academy of Child and Adolescent Psychiatry*, **32**, 34–42.

Tingelstad J.B. (1991) The cardiotoxicity of the tricyclics. *Journal of the American Academy of Child Psychiatry*, **30**, 845–846.

Tyrer S.P., Barrett M.L., Berney T.P., Bhate S., Watson M.J., Fundudis T. & Kolvin I. (1991) The dexamethasone suppression test in children: lack of an association with diagnosis. *British Journal of Psychiatry*, **159** (suppl. 11), 41–48.

Velez C.N., Johnson J. & Cohen P. (1989) A longitudinal analysis of selected risk factors for childhood psychopathology. *Journal of the American Academy of Child and Adolescent Psychiatry*, **28**, 861–864.

Verhulst F.C. & Koot H.M. (1992) *Child Psychiatric Epidemiology, Concepts, Methods, and Findings*. Sage Publications, London.

Walker M., Moreau D. & Weissman M.M. (1990) Parents' awareness of children's suicide attempts. *American Journal of Psychiatry*, **147**, 1364–1366.

Wallerstein J.S. & Kelly J.B. (1980) *Surviving the Breakup: How Children and Parents cope with Divorce*. Grant McIntyre, London.

Weiner R.D. & Coffey C.E. (1991) Electroconvulsive therapy in the United States. *Psychopharmacology Bulletin*, **27**, 9–15.

Weissman M.M. & Klerman G.L. (1977) Sex differences and the epidemiology of depression. *Archives of General Psychiatry*, **34**, 98–111.

Weissman M.M., Wickramaratne P., Merikangas K.R., Leckman J.F., Prusoff B.A., Caruso K.A., Kidd K.K. & Gammon G.D. (1984) Onset of major depression in early adulthood: increased familial loading and specificity. *Archives of General Psychiatry*, **41**, 1136–1143.

Weissman M.M., Gammon D., John K., Merikangas K.R., Warner V., Prusoff B.A. & Sholomskas D. (1987) Children of depressed parents: increased psychopathology and early onset of major depression. *Archives of General Psychiatry*, **44**, 847–853.

Weissman M.M., Warner V., Wickramaratne P., & Prusoff B.A. (1988) Early-onset major depression in parents and their children. *Journal of Affective Disorders*, **15**, 269–277.

Weissman M.M., Fendrich M., Warner V. & Wickramaratne P. (1992) Incidence of psychiatric disorder in offspring at high and low risk for depression. *Journal of the American Academy of Child and Adolescent Psychiatry*, **31**, 640–648.

Weller R.A., Weller E.B., Fristad M.A. & Bowes J.M. (1991) Depression in recently bereaved prepubertal children. *American Journal of Psychiatry*, **148**, 1536–1540.

Werry J.S. & McClellan J.M. (1992) Predicting outcome in child and adolescent (early onset) schizophrenia and bipolar disorder. *Journal of the American Academy of Child and Adolescent Psychiatry*, **31**, 147–150.

Werry J.S., McClellan J.M. & Chard L. (1991) Childhood and adolescent schizophrenic, bipolar, and schizoaffective disorders: a clinical and outcome study. *Journal of the American Academy of Child and Adolescent Psychiatry*, **30**, 457–465.

Whitaker A., Johnson J., Shaffer D., Rapoport J.L., Kalikow K., Walsh B.T., Davies M., Braiman S. & Dolinsky A. (1990) Uncommon troubles in young people: prevalence estimates of selected psychiatric disorders in a nonreferred adolescent population. *Archives of General Psychiatry*, **47**, 487–496.

Wilde E.J., Kienhorst I.C.W.M., Diekstra R.F.W. & Wolters W.H.G. (1992) The relationship between adolescent suicidal behaviour and life events in childhood and adolescence. *American Journal of Psychiatry*, **149**, 45–51.

Wilson R. & Cairns B. (1988) Sex-role attributes, perceived competence and the development of depression in adolescence. *Journal of Child Psychology and Psychiatry*, **29**, 635–650.

Winokur G., Clayton P.J. & Reich T. (1969) *Manic Depressive Illness*. Mosby, St Louis.

World Health Organization (1992) *The ICD-10 Classification of Mental and Behavioural Disorders. Clinical Descriptions and Diagnostic Guidelines*. World Health Organization, Geneva.

Yaylayan S., Weller E.B. & Weller R.A. (1992) Neurobiology of depression. In: Shafii M. & Shafii S.L. (eds) *Clinical Guide to Depression in Children and Adolescents*, pp. 65–88. American Psychiatric Press, Washington.

Yule W., Udwin O. & Murdoch K. (1990) The 'Jupiter' sinking: effects on children's fears, depression and anxiety. *Journal of Child Psychology and Psychiatry*, **31**, 1051–1061.

Zeitlin H. (1986) *The Natural History of Psychiatric Disorder in Children*. Maudsley monograph 29. Oxford University Press, Oxford.

Chapter 20
Anxiety Disorders

Rachel G. Klein

DEVELOPMENTAL PATTERNS OF CHILDHOOD FEARS AND ANXIETY

Whether one agrees or not that childhood anxiety is inevitable because of the nature of human psychology, social experiences or biology, it is evident that it is extremely prevalent, if not universal. In itself, it does not represent a deviant phenomenon, and its expression over time has been well-described (Hersov, 1985; Campbell, 1986; Marks, 1987). Anxiety follows an identifiable evolution that parallels other aspects of growth. In infancy, sensory experiences predominate and are the major source of fear, such as loud sounds, or sudden loss of physical support (Bronson, 1968, 1970, 1972; Ball & Tronick, 1971). As cognitive development proceeds during the first year of life and the infant acquires object constancy, fear of strangers and distress upon the caretaker's departure emerge and separation anxiety appears (Schaffer & Emerson, 1964; Ainsworth, 1967; Stayton & Ainsworth, 1973; Lewis & Brooks, 1974). New fears appear in early childhood: animals, the dark, and imaginary beasts and creatures (Jersild & Holmes, 1935; Maurer, 1965; Bauer, 1976, 1980). Concerns about performance are reported to begin in late childhood (Bauer, 1980), whereas interpersonal, social anxiety does so in early adolescence (Marks & Gelder, 1966; Öst, 1987). This developmental sequence should be viewed as modal, and exceptions are bound to occur. The Piagetan model of cognitive development has been invoked as explanatory of the age-related changes in anxiety-provoking situations, from undifferentiated to specific, on to abstract sources (Bauer, 1976, 1980). There is little doubt that cognitive abilities, such as memory and understanding of complex social interactions, are necessary for many forms of anxiety, such as performance or interpersonal anxiety. However, it is less clear that these developmental features, though necessary, are sufficient explanatory principles. In contrast, for example, ethological theory would view age differences in propensities to specific anxiety responses as reflecting, at least in part, the differential threat that stimuli pose at various ages in the course of development.

Importantly, the same age pattern is reflected to a large extent in the onset of pathological and age-appropriate manifestations of respective anxieties. Phobias of animals frequently have their onset in childhood, severe performance anxiety in late childhood, and social anxiety in adolescence (Marks &

Gelder, 1966; Öst, 1987). Therefore, there is congruence between the developmental timing of the normal and abnormal forms of these affective states. Exceptionally, the onset of maladaptive separation anxiety does not fit this pattern. The peak age in community and clinical samples is reported in late childhood rather than infancy (Gittelman, 1986; Bird *et al.*, 1988; Last *et al.*, 1992). As described by Bowlby (1973), separation leads to a three-part sequential emotional response. The immediate reaction to separation in infants is protest (crying, pleading, etc.). If ineffectual in reuniting the infant to the mother, despair (withdrawal, sadness) follows. Finally, if the child remains separated, detachment occurs (indifference to the mother's return). Each is viewed as playing an important instrumental role. Protest signals to the mother (or caretaker) that the child is in difficulty and guides her search for him or her. If protest has failed to lead to the mother's return, despair economizes the child's energy until he or she is found. Ultimately, if never found by the parent, detachment enables the surviving abandoned child to form new attachments and prepares him or her for successful adoption. The pattern has been well-documented in humans and subhuman primates (detachment is not a regular phase of the separation response in nonhumans, especially when adoption is not a feature of the species). In addition, nonhumans without previous separation experiences show marked variability in the severity of their reaction to separation. The interindividual variability in normal separation anxiety and its cross-species regularity have fostered the hypothesis that this functional system is likely unlearned and under genetic control (Suomi, 1986).

As children's cognitive resources evolve, capacity for anticipating events becomes an established mental operation. It has the marked value of enabling preparatory behaviours required for increasingly complex task demands. Affectively, it has the unfortunate consequence of causing discomfort at the expectation of future unpleasant events. Normal and abnormal anxiety are coupled with anticipatory anxiety, becoming progressively more salient with age.

It has been suggested that the onset of anxieties may differ developmentally between the genders, with girls having earlier onsets than boys (Abe & Masui, 1981). However, the evidence on this point is contradictory. Problematically, means of assessing fear are inconsistent. Some studies use direct questions (Angelino *et al.*, 1956; Maurer, 1965; Bauer, 1976; Abe &

Masui, 1981), whereas others rely on self-ratings on paper and pencil scales (Croake, 1967; Bamber, 1974; Ollendick *et al.*, 1985).

While it is true that age is associated with the development of various fear reactions, and that these are considered normal at certain times, it would be erroneous to assume that they are modal at any age, or occur in most children during specific phases of development. For example, in laboratory studies, most infants display positive responses to strangers (Ricciuti, 1974; Sroufe *et al.*, 1974), and most do not respond with fear to separation (Ricciuti, 1974). Moreover, developmentally appropriate fears can be influenced by their context, which includes maternal behaviour. It would be simplistic to view children's fears as a function of age exclusively.

Developmental patterns have been viewed as critical to the definition of psychopathology in children (Rutter, 1988). This model has practical implications and has influenced psychiatric nomenclature. For example, the ICD-10 (World Health Organization, 1989) limits diagnoses of separation anxiety and social sensitivity to cases with an onset *before* the age of 6. Presumably, the assumption is that syndromes with later onsets have different diagnostic significance. However, empirical evidence bearing on the question is lacking.

THE ORIGINS OF ANXIETY

It is not possible to do justice to the multiple theories concerning the origins of anxiety, nor to their complexities. Some are noted briefly because of their influential roles on clinical practice or research.

Prior to the early 20th century, childhood anxiety was largely ignored; when noted, its sole purpose was to elaborate on adult psychopathology (Klein & Last, 1989). It was Freud's (1953) psychodynamic postulations that heralded modern theories of childhood anxiety. For the first time, anxiety in early life was not only important in itself, but also a key factor in understanding mental function and psychopathology throughout the age range. It is beyond the scope of the chapter to review Freud's and others' views; we merely summarize briefly some major distinguishing conceptual features.

According to Freud, anxiety is activated initially by external events that trigger internal anxiety linked to unconscious wishes of libidinal or aggressive nature, or most often their combination. This formulation is the basis for the widely prevalent notion of the symbolic representation of anxiety; namely, that the manifest symptoms are distortions of unconscious unacceptable wishes. (Therefrom the dictum that every fear hides a wish.) The distortions serve the purpose of disguising the true nature of these wishes. Important features in this theory (features that will be discarded by other psychological theories) include the notion that anxiety has internal origins, and that it is the result of unconscious psychological conflict.

Subsequent non-Freudian psychological theories of childhood anxiety challenged the notion of unconscious internal states. Rather, they emphasized early social relationships,

proposing the mother–child relationship as prototypical. A related theory holds that the parent, usually the mother, transfers her own anxiety to the child (i.e. Eisenberg, 1958). Reasons vary, but usually serve the mother's psychological needs. This model focuses on the mother's internal state, and views the child as the unwitting victim. This dyadic theory of childhood anxiety had a major impact on child psychiatric practice. Treatment of the child served the purpose of helping him or her be less vulnerable to the anxiogenic parent.

The deemphasis of organismic or internal characteristics in anxiety was carried to its full import by learning theorists. Although some, such as Pavlov, 1927 and Eysenck, 1967, proposed individual differences in vulnerability to anxiety stemming from biological characteristics under genetic control, learning theorists who had most influence on clinical practice posited that classical and instrumental conditioning principles were sufficient to account for any anxiety state (Mowrer, 1939, 1960). Phobic avoidance is reinforced by reducing subjective anxiety, and is thereby maintained. Treatments that follow this model are consistent with the view that maladaptive associations and their behavioural consequences require corrective experiences.

Cognitive developmental views also have influenced theories of anxiety in children. With time, children develop increasingly stable and organized cognitive representations or schemas of their environment and experience. Schemas play a dynamic role in regulating the child's behaviour and information processing, and their disruption causes anxiety (Kagan, 1974). Ordinarily, unpleasant stimuli lead to adaptive behaviour. However, cognitive distortions prevent normal affective or behavioural responses. Ensuing dysfunction causes inaccurate and relatively rigid schema that, in turn, induce a variety of symptoms, including anxiety (Beck & Emery, 1985). In this model, affective input does not differ in normal and abnormal anxiety. What distinguishes the two is the manner in which it is interpreted. Anxiety symptoms vary as a function of the cognitive distortions which, according to some, can be identified in children (Kendall & Chansky, 1991). Anxious schemata may remain latent until triggered by stresses (Clark & Beck, 1989). This argument uses the concept of unconscious affect potential. Cognitive theory does not account well for the specificity of the distortions, or for their striking consistency across individuals, as evidenced by the regularity in types of fears. It is difficult to believe that documented childhood fears reflect the limits of cognitive resources at any age. Furthermore, the theory fails to deal adequately with the vast animal literature concerning variability in fear reactions.

The psychological views, psychoanalytic (Freudian and non-Freudian), learning, and cognitive theories differ sharply in their identification of the processes that activate anxiety, but they share the notion that anxiety is a unitary emotion with similar psychological mechanisms underlying normal and pathological states. In all these models, anxiety varies in severity, but not in its fundamental nature.

Another influential view of anxiety has roots in the 19th century, from the writings of Charles Darwin which largely were ignored until recently. Emotions are adaptive consequences of evolutionary processes resultant from natural selection. Like fear, these are protective of naturally occurring danger, and also regulate social bonds — both key features of adaptation that maximize survival, and in turn reproduction (Darwin, 1965). This ethological model discounts the role of internal conflict, of unconscious wishes, of subtle aspects of mother—child interaction in the origin of anxiety responses. The model set the stage for investigations that documented the principle of preparedness for learning, namely, that there are preferential predispositions for acquiring certain avoidant behaviours over others. This point emphasizes the differential effect of various experiences and rejects the learning theory tenet of the equipotentiality of stimuli in their ability to elicit anxiety (Seligman & Hager, 1972; Marks, 1987). Thus, it is very difficult to condition fears of certain objects (such as opera glasses), but it is easy of others, such as animals. (Obviously, the latter are natural threats in the course of human evolution, whereas the former are not.)

Darwin's conjectures about the role of innate emotions in the formation of social bonds are also echoed in modern theories of attachment as well as in the related view that the normal distress experienced by children at separation from the attachment figure serves the important purpose of maintaining bonding.

It is apparent that ethological views of human behaviour are quite capable of accounting for normal, adaptive anxiety. It is less obvious that they inform on human pathological forms. This model is congruent with the view that normal and pathological anxiety may be qualitatively distinct in some fashion. Such theories of anxiety have been advanced.

The development of antianxiety agents, specifically benzodiazepines, has stimulated neurophysiological theories of anxiety regulation. Gray, the main protagonist, argues for the presence of a neural behavioural inhibitory system, which causes subjective anxiety when activated by specific experiences (Gray, 1982, 1987). The behavioural consequences consist of reduced motor behaviour and increases in arousal and vigilance. These are in part mediated through changes in the autonomic system controlled by a central inhibitory system. Each structure of this system regulates distinct components of anxiety responses. As is true of all biological regulatory mechanisms, individual differences are the rule, and some individuals have relatively more active inhibitory systems than others. Anxiolytic drugs exert their effect by dampening the system through monoamine structures in different brain centres. Exposure therapy is effective through the well-known mechanism of habituation (in this instance of septohippocampal activity; Gray, 1982). Gray's model of inhibition has a parallel in the views of Kagan who argues for temperamental differences in behavioural inhibition, as defined by reticence to approach unfamiliar situations and reluctance to engage in risk-taking behaviour. In ordinary parlance, these children are described as shy. The notion that temperament is an appropriate behavioural construct to account for inhibited behaviours is supported by a series of elegant developmental studies

of normal children that document moderate but significant stability of such behaviours from infancy through mid-childhood (Garcia-Coll *et al.*, 1984; Kagan *et al.*, 1984, 1988; Reznick *et al.*, 1986). Behavioural inhibition has been found to be associated with sympathetic activity such as reduced heart rate variability, pupillary dilation and increased noradrenaline levels. Significant continuity has been found in heart rate function; moreover, physiological findings correlate with behavioural inhibition at all ages. Strikingly, the stability of behavioural inhibition is predicted by earlier heart rate (Kagan *et al.*, 1988). Inhibited temperament is said to result from innate, genetically determined biological regulation. A report that socially reticent behaviour is relatively stable in monkeys supports this view (Higley *et al.*, 1984; quoted in Suomi, 1986). Specifically, inhibition is said to be the result of lowered limbic activity thresholds (in the amygdala and hypothalamus), consistent with increased activity of the sympathetic nervous system (Kagan *et al.*, 1987, 1988).

This model posits a relationship between temperamental inhibition and anxiety disorders. To examine this issue, the children of the original cohorts studied by Kagan and co-workers at 21 months of age, as well as their parents and siblings, were assessed for the presence of anxiety disorders. Increased rates of anxiety disorders were found in the inhibited children and relatives compared to the uninhibited group (Hirshfeld *et al.*, 1992; Rosenbaum *et al.*, 1991). Social anxiety disorders seemed especially salient. In a related study, behavioural inhibition was evaluated in the offspring of adult patients with panic disorders, mood disorders and controls (Rosenbaum *et al.*, 1988). As predicted, children of adults with panic disorder showed greater behavioural inhibition than those of normal subjects. However, they did not differ from children of parents with mood disorders. These studies give support to a link between temperamental inhibition and anxiety disorders. Whether this link is exclusive to the anxiety disorders is less clear. It may be that behavioural inhibition is an early marker of emotional dysregulation, of which anxiety is only one eventual consequence.

In spite of seeming similarities, there are basic differences between Gray's and Kagan's views, leaving aside the divergences in their neuroanatomical models. Gray's theory derives from an enormous experimental literature on animal responses to benzodiazepines and on brain ablation studies, usually done with rats. However, it is not clear that shyness and social reticence respond to these compounds. The potential usefulness of a model based on animal studies is a direct function of the match between the animal behaviour and human function. It seems inevitable that equivalence is relatively limited between experimentally induced anxiety in rats and the manifold expressions of human anxiety. Furthermore, the model does not address developmental patterns.

A developmental approach to the study of anxiety has been pursued by Suomi and colleagues in higher primates (Suomi, 1986). Their extensive research has specified situations with high potential for anxiety, established that there is considerable variation in individuals' responses to experimentally controlled provocative situations, has noted specific physiological correlates of anxious behaviour, and, importantly, has identified environmental conditions that maintain anxiety (Marks, 1987). Primate research has shown also that elevated anxiety is not a generalized response; rather, it has situational specificity. Each finding has clear relevance to an understanding of anxiety in young humans. With regard to environmental factors, repeated maternal separations, inadequate infant call and unstable social environments are predictive of high stress reaction in young monkeys (Suomi, 1987). Drawing parallels with human development is most tempting. It is a great advantage that animal research is able to manipulate interpersonal conditions that, in humans, can be studied only through naturalistic observations. The latter are difficult to interpret, and often misleading, since any environmental stress is a complex phenomenon with multiple antecedents, such as parental illness, poverty, etc., and it is rarely possible to disentangle their effect. The experimental studies conducted with primates have been critical in illustrating that environmental circumstances can maintain anxiety, and that they interact with propensity for anxiety, or inhibited temperament (Suomi, 1987). In this vein, Kagan *et al.* (1988) have argued that the expression of behavioural inhibition in some is the result of the action of chronic environmental stress on innate temperamental disposition. In others, chronic environmental stress suffices. However, the environmental features that are critical to the occurrence and maintenance of anxiety in humans are not known. Bowlby (1973) has pointed to rejecting mothers as a key provocation to severity of sustained distress after separation. This relationship, now conceived as insecure attachment in the child, is viewed as an important influence in the equation accounting for individual differences in separation anxiety.

Genetics of childhood anxiety disorders

That level of anxiety is under some genetic control is suggested by several reports (Plomin & Rowe, 1979; Stevenson *et al.*, 1992). In a twin study of children from 8 to 18 who completed the Fear Survey for Children (Stevenson *et al.*, 1992), the authors did not find greater heritability for extreme scores. Unfortunately, the clinical significance of scale scores is unclear, and it is not possible to equate them with anxiety diagnoses.

Family studies in adults have indicated that the presence of anxiety disorders confers an increased risk for these disorders among relatives. Familial aggregation has been noted, for panic disorder (Crowe *et al.*, 1983; Torgersen, 1983; Noyes *et al.*, 1987), simple phobias (Fyer *et al.*, 1990b), social phobia (Fyer *et al.*, 1993) and generalized anxiety (Noyes *et al.*, 1987, Kendler *et al.*, 1992). The family studies of adult anxiety disorders argue against the notion that it is a general nonspecific susceptibility to anxiety that is transmitted (regardless of the mechanism) and in favour of specificity in the transmission of anxiety disorders (Torgersen, 1990). Research on this point is limited in the childhood anxiety disorders.

The only large family study to date of children with anxiety disorders found that anxiety disorders were more prevalent in their relatives compared to those of children with attention deficit disorder with hyperactivity disorder (ADDH) and normal controls (Last *et al.*, 1991). However, some of the results are difficult to reconcile with familial models of anxiety disorder. Firstly, siblings of the three diagnostic groups (anxiety, ADDH and normals) did not differ in prevalence of anxiety disorders. Secondly, mothers of anxious and ADDH children reported indistinguishable rates of anxiety disorders in themselves — both significantly higher than the rate in mothers of normals. It may be that anxiety disorders are more likely to be reported by mothers whose children are undergoing psychiatric care, regardless of the nature of the child's disorder. The impact of children's clinical status is not known. It is possible that it may not be irrelevant to self-reports of some maternal psychopathology, such as anxiety.

Distinction between normal and pathological anxiety

Defining the boundaries between extremes of normal behaviour and psychopathology is a dilemma that pervades all psychiatry. In the very extreme, the diagnostic decision is straightforward (as in mental retardation, for example), but with milder forms, the defining point for caseness is often ambiguous. A few symptoms escape this definitional conundrum by virtue of being deviant no matter their severity, such as delusional beliefs or hallucinations. But even in these cases, some childlike fantasies may resemble these invariably abnormal states, leading to diagnostic confusion. It is especially problematic to establish the limits between normal behaviour and pathology for anxiety since many childhood anxieties are not only common, but they may also play an adaptive role in human development, signalling that action is required to ensure safety. It is often believed that because a characteristic is distributed along a unimodal curve, and gauged along a continuum, the extremes of the distribution represent a severe expression of the trait, rather than a distinct state. A telling recent example is the interpretation that dyslexia is not a disorder because of these measurement properties (Shaywitz *et al.*, 1992). This view fails to acknowledge that unimodal distributions may be comprised of distinct entities (Murphy, 1964; see also Chapter 1). Therefore, the mere fact that anxiety falls on a continuum of severity does not preclude the presence of qualitatively distinct disorders at the extremes. Anxiety may become symptomatic at any age when it prevents or limits developmentally appropriate adaptive behaviour. What are the standards for diagnostic decisions? A useful rule of thumb is the child's ability to recover from anxiety, and to remain anxiety-free when the provoking situation is absent. For example, in a separation paradigm, it is not usually deviant for a young child to respond with distress to the parent's departure. What are no longer unremarkable are: (1) the inability to recover promptly once the separation is effected (if proper care is available to the child); (2) compromised functioning during normal separation experiences, and (3) concerns about future separations and vigilance or even avoidance of activities potentially associated with separation. Therefore, inflexibility of affective response is an important pathological indicator. In addition, the degree of distress and dysfunction influences diagnostic standards. It is difficult to specify guidelines since these vary with age, as well as with cultural and familial standards. A useful rule of thumb is to judge the child's ability to participate in expected, age-appropriate social and academic activities. If none is compromised, it is difficult to argue for the presence of an anxiety disorder; rather, fearful traits or temperament need to be considered. Finally, the timing of the symptoms influences diagnostic decisions. For example, moderate reactions to separation in a young child would not lead to a diagnosis of separation anxiety disorder whereas they might in an adolescent. Therefore, when the occurrence of anxiety symptoms is desynchronized developmentally, subjective distress is relatively more diagnostically informative, and impairment may be less so. In brief, three clinical features impinge on the definition of pathological anxiety. Two of these, distress and dysfunction, vary in importance as a function of developmental stage. The third, symptomatic inflexibility, is diagnostically important regardless of age (Klein, 1978).

These broad clinical standards are similar to those advanced by Marks (1969) for the definition of a phobia. In addition, Marks believed that age or stage specificity rules out the presence of a phobia. This point is problematic. If a child displays extreme, impairing, inflexible fear responses at a stage during which the fear is considered developmentally normal, should it be considered normal? Most would think not. In fact, the ICD-10 has taken the opposite view.

As long as signs and symptoms are the exclusive basis for establishing the presence of psychiatric disorders, it is unlikely that a completely satisfactory resolution of the definitional problems of pathology will be reached. One might argue that longitudinal research will provide answers by identifying specific symptom patterns and thresholds that have long-term significance. Indeed, such evidence is informative, but not regularly conclusive. Even if recovery were a common ultimate outcome, it would not follow that the syndrome in question did not represent a discrete disorder. Until our understanding of childhood mental disorders is more precise, common sense will have to prevail. Two major epidemiological studies have reported that the rates of all psychiatric disorders in children are markedly reduced by requiring functional impairment (Bird *et al.*, 1990; Weissman *et al.*, 1990). This result is hardly surprising, and one might well ask why definite diagnoses should be given to traits that resemble symptoms but do not lead to distress or dysfunction. The answers to such questions require empirical data that are lacking.

DIAGNOSIS OF ANXIETY DISORDERS

Historically, anxiety disorders have been conceptualized as variants of the nonspecific class of childhood emotional or neurotic disorders which encompassed anxiety, depressive, hysterical and obsessional disorders, and whose main clinical significance was their distinction from conduct and psychotic disorders (Rutter *et al.*, 1969; Anthony, 1975; Hersov, 1985). The field has shifted towards greater diagnostic refinement. Childhood depressive and anxiety disorders are distinguished, as are various anxiety syndromes (American Psychiatric Association, 1987).

As noted, phobias, separation anxiety and social anxiety are major types of anxiety. The nomenclature provides specific diagnoses for each. The ICD-10 and DSM-IV have very similar approaches to the classification of anxiety disorders, but differ in several ways.

Some historical notes on DSM-III anxiety disorders

History is informative, and places issues in perspective. By excluding the obsessive-compulsive disorders from the present review of anxiety disorders (see Chapter 25), the implicit message is given that obsessive-compulsive disorder is not part and parcel of the overall class of anxiety disorders. The rationale for its inclusion as an anxiety disorder in the DSM-III (American Psychiatric Association, 1980) relates to the organizational principles of the DSM-III. DSM-III was designed to provide groupings of syndromes reflecting a common clinical construct. However, obsessive-compulsive disorder did not fit readily in any grouping, and was clearly inappropriate for most. The anxiety disorders provided the least incongruous locus for it. The rationale was that individuals with obsessive-compulsive disorder were often highly anxious, especially if rituals were interfered with. Problematically, anxiety is a salient feature associated with numerous psychiatric disorders of childhood and adulthood, and the empirical evidence does not support the hypothesis that obsessive-compulsive disorder is related to the anxiety disorders (see Chapter 25).

What of the other anxiety disorders? Separation anxiety had been described in children by many clinicians of varying schools of thought, and there was little doubt that it represented an acknowledged clinical phenomenon. Researcher clinicians on the DSM-III Task Force were able to rely on experience and the literature to generate a description and diagnostic criteria for the condition.

Avoidant disorder was introduced in the DSM-III, in part to eliminate the confusion inherent in the diagnosis of withdrawing reaction in the DSM-II (American Psychiatric Association, 1968). Withdrawing reaction included the clinical concepts of shy, anxious social reticence as well as indifference to social interaction (i.e. schizoid adjustment). Although these two symptomatic patterns are manifested behaviourally by social avoidance, they represent markedly different syndromes. The introduction of avoidant disorder was intended to provide a diagnostic distinction that had been ignored hitherto. The clinical concept was straightforward and captured the notion of severe shyness in children who were capable of and interested in social relationships. Because of marked phenomenological similarities between avoidant and social phobia disorders, the DSM-IV has combined the two conditions.

What about overanxious disorder? Werry (1991) rightly has raised questions regarding its diagnostic items in view of their poor face validity. Although the DSM-III Task Force was cognizant of the fact that some children might experience nonspecific anxiety symptoms, no clinical base or literature existed. Therefore, the disorder was essentially made up *de novo*; it was invented. Committee members were not critical of its clinical content since no clear picture of the disorder was held. The disorder was targeted for removal in the DSM-III-R because its vagueness had become apparent, and it did not appear to have been clarified in the ensuing time. At the last moment, it was retained because of a petition by an investigator whose ongoing investigations addressed the validity of overanxious disorder. The creation of a mental disorder is not unique to overanxious disorder. The same process accounted for the inclusion of generalized anxiety disorder (as well as others beyond our interest here). It is entertaining to witness the degree to which such syndromes have generated uncritical acceptance, and even endorsement (see Werry, 1991). It is likely that, had the committee appreciated fully the enormous impact the new nomenclature was to have, and the massive research investment it would generate, a less permissive attitude might have prevailed. In fact, scrutiny of the diagnostic criteria for overanxious disorder reveals its ambiguities (American Psychiatric Association, 1991) — these do not require sophisticated, costly investigations to become apparent. Firstly, the initial two diagnostic criteria (the child is overconcerned (1) about future events, and (2) the appropriateness of his or her past behaviour) imply that concern is not about past or present events, only future ones; however, worries about the appropriateness of one's behaviour are only for the past, not the present or future. Do these clinical descriptions make good clinical sense? Secondly, concern about future events reflects anticipatory anxiety which is common to all anxiety disorders of certain severity (the same lack of specificity applies to other criteria, such as need for reassurance and feelings of tension). Thirdly, there is much content overlap between avoidant and social phobia disorders. These comments do not argue that there may not be children with admixtures of anxious symptomatology that do not constitute an integrated anxiety syndrome, such as separation or social anxiety. However, the provision of a disorder in the absence of articulated, replicable clinical observations is bound to create confusion. Overanxious disorder in DSM-IV has been combined with generalized anxiety disorder which focuses on overconcerns not reflected in other anxiety disorders, such as worries about untoward events.

Panic disorder was recognized as a distinct adult anxiety disorder in the DSM-III, based on the work of Klein who also posited a developmental relationship between childhood separation anxiety disorder and adolescent or adult panic disorder (Klein, 1964, 1981). Although young children displayed panic reactions, they did not present with spontaneous, unprovoked panic attacks, the hallmark of panic disorder (Gittelman-Klein & Klein, 1973). A number of case reports have appeared challenging the claim that panic disorder does not occur in preadolescence (Herskowitz, 1986; Biederman, 1987; Alessi & Magen, 1988; Ballenger *et al.*, 1989; Last & Strauss, 1989; Moreau *et al.*, 1989; Black & Robbins, 1990; Vitiello *et al.*, 1990; Klein *et al.*, 1992a). Age of onset of panic attacks was established retrospectively in half the cases (Herskowitz, 1986; Last & Strauss, 1989; Black & Robbins, 1990; Klein *et al.*, 1992a). In a study of adults with panic disorder, only 1.7% reported experiencing panic attacks before age 13, and only one instance of unequivocal childhood panic disorder was identified (Klein *et al.*, 1992a). Historical reports are certainly suggestive, but they fall short of being conclusive since they may be subject to retrospective distortions. Further, it is not easy to establish spontaneity of panic attacks retrospectively, or to distinguish other forms of severe anxiety from panic attacks. Confirmation of panic disorder in young children requires contemporary observations.

Concerns regarding the independence of children's panic attacks from other anxieties are raised by the fact that all but one of the reported cases with an onset in preadolescence also had separation anxiety disorder (in the exceptional case, the presence of separation anxiety disorder is not addressed; Ballenger *et al.*, 1989). The only study to date of offspring of adults with panic disorder has not found any child with panic disorder (McClellan *et al.*, 1990). Our ongoing study has also failed to detect a single child with panic disorder (R.C. Klein, S. Mannuzza & R.J. Kramer unpublished observations). Other studies of high-risk children are in process and should provide clarification of the occurrence of panic disorder in children.

Whether panic disorder occurs at all in preadolescents is still an unresolved issue, but it seems clear that if it does, it is very rare. It has been suggested that, in keeping with the cognitive model of anxiety, children may lack the cognitive resources for misinterpreting somatic experiences in a catastrophic fashion and therefore do not have panic attacks (Nelles & Barlow, 1988). This conjecture seems unlikely, since panic reactions associated with terror occur in children. It is the sudden, unprovoked aspect of panic that seems to be missing in childhood, not the catastrophic reaction. At the same time, it is possible that true panic attacks have age-related clinical variants.

ICD-10 and the DSM-IV

Separation anxiety disorder

A major and important difference between the ICD-10 and DSM-IV is that the ICD requires an onset before age 6. It is not clear how a child with an onset of separation anxiety after age 6 would be diagnosed. Furthermore, two syndromes with identical presentation at age 10, for example, would receive different diagnoses if one had begun recently and the other had occurred for the first time 4 years earlier, regardless of whether it had continued uninterrupted or remitted. This diagnostic standard appears based on a developmental model of pathological anxiety, rather than on empirical data.

Social anxiety disorder

ICD-10 includes social anxiety disorder that is equivalent to dysfunction reflected in the DSM-III-R avoidant disorder. In the DSM-IV, this disorder is combined with the adult diagnosis of social phobia.

Overanxious/generalized anxiety disorder

The DSM-IV has eliminated overanxious disorder, which was the childhood variant of generalized anxiety disorder. Instead, children may receive a diagnosis of generalized anxiety disorder, as is the case in ICD-10.

Phobic disorder

The ICD-10 includes a phobic disorder of childhood. Its essential clinical features are the equivalent of the simple phobia disorder of the DSM-IV. There are three crucial distinctions. One is the ICD requirement that the onset occur at a time when the fear is developmentally phase-appropriate, to distinguish it from the adult diagnosis, since it is likely that phobias that are exaggerations of age-appropriate fears may differ from those that occur at other developmental points (M. Rutter, personal communication). However, standards for determination of age-appropriateness are not clear. Secondly, diffuse anxiety and anxiety related to other situations may not be present. Therefore, the diagnosis cannot be given as a comorbid anxiety disorder. Thirdly, the occurrence of personality disturbance rules out the disorder but clinical standards for establishing the presence of disturbance of personality are not plain.

The ICD has narrowed the application of specific childhood anxiety disorders to those that are exaggerations of normal developmental phenomena, since other anxiety syndromes in children should be diagnosed from disorders listed in the general section of the classification.

ASSESSMENT OF ANXIETY DISORDERS

The quantification of anxiety has a long history dating back to the development of factor analytic techniques, which in turn gave impetus to personality questionnaires. However, these early measures were never adapted for use in clinical populations (Klein, 1988). The current methodology for the assessment of childhood anxiety disorders includes rating scales and direct interviews. The scales are all designed to quantify level or type of anxiety. However, as the review will indicate, their usefulness is limited and they cannot be said to contribute meaningfully to the clinical situation.

Self-rating anxiety scales

A few paper-and-pencil measures derived from adult scales are designed to obtain self-perceptions of anxiety in children. The first, the Children's Manifest Anxiety Scale (a modified version of the Manifest Anxiety Scale; Taylor, 1953; Castaneda *et al.*, 1956; Finch *et al.*, 1974) was in turn revised based on factor analytic studies (Reynolds & Richmond, 1978, 1979, 1985). It has the unique feature of providing a lie scale, but its validity is questionable (Roberts *et al.*, 1989).

Spielberger and colleagues (1970) devised a scale for adults derived from a two-part model of anxiety, one tapping stable, consistent tendencies (traits), and the other reflecting situational temporary reactions (states; the State–Trait Anxiety Inventory; Spielberger *et al.*, 1970). A child version was adapted subsequently, the State–Trait Anxiety Inventory for Children (STAIC; Spielberger, 1973).

The Wolpe–Lang Fear Survey (Wolpe & Lang, 1964) was modified for use in children, and became the Fear Survey Schedule for Children (Scherer & Nakamura, 1968). It was revised to apply to children below age 9 (Ollendick, 1983a), and to update its content (Gullone & King, 1992). A scale designed to assess anxiety related to negative social evaluation in adults (Watson & Friend, 1969) has been modified for use in children (Social Anxiety Scale for Children; LaGreca *et al.*, 1988). The short-term reliability (1 or 2 weeks) of these scales has been found to be satisfactory (Ollendick, 1983a; Wisniewski *et al.*, 1987; LaGreca *et al.*, 1988; Gullone & King, 1992; LaGreca & Stone, 1993).

Concurrent validity for the Revised Children's Manifest Anxiety Scale has been inferred from correlational studies with the trait anxiety score of the STAIC (Reynolds, 1980). In contrast, only moderate relationships have been obtained between the Fear Survey Schedule for Children and the STAIC and the Revised Children's Manifest Anxiety Scale (Ollendick, 1983a; Gullone & King, 1992). Similarly moderate to low associates have been reported between the Social Anxiety Scale for Children and the Manifest Anxiety Scale (La Greca *et al.*, 1988).

Evidence for the diagnostic validity of self-rating scales is limited, and not encouraging. Although higher scale ratings have been obtained in children with anxiety disorders compared to normal subjects (Miller *et al.*, 1971; Ollendick, 1983a; Beidel & Turner, 1988; Sylvester *et al.*, 1988; Perrin & Last, 1992), this finding has not been consistent (Beidel & Turner, 1988; Strauss *et al.*, 1988; Sylvester *et al.*, 1988; Perrin & Last, 1992). Moreover, when differences between normal and anxious children occur, there is large overlap between the groups, rendering the scales poor means for the identification of affected children.

The minimum psychometric requirement, that the self-rated anxiety scales reliably distinguish anxious from normal children, is only partially met. The more meaningful clinical goal, that scale scores discriminate across clinical groups, is clearly not met (Saylor *et al.*, 1984; Beidel & Turner, 1988; Strauss *et al.*, 1988; Sylvester *et al.*, 1988; Perrin & Last, 1992). Although some claim that self-ratings can distinguish the affects of anxiety and depression in children (Izard & Blumberg, 1985), reviews of the adult literature document the poor discriminative ability of such scales (Dobson, 1985; Finch *et al.*, 1989; Dobson & Cheung, 1990). Attempts to show that anxious children rate themselves differently from other psychiatric groups have been unsuccessful, and the scales cannot be viewed as valid diagnostic indicators, as has been claimed (Finch & Rogers, 1984).

The hope remains that self-rating anxiety scales will be sensitive to treatment effects. Unless this expectation turns out to be the case, it will be difficult indeed to find any meaningful clinical or scientific use for these measures.

Parent- and teacher-rated anxiety scales

Anxiety factor scores are included in several parent scales, such as the Louisville Behavior Checklist (Miller *et al.*, 1971) elaborated into the Louisville Fear Survey (Miller *et al.*, 1972), the Personality Inventory for Children (PIC; Lachar, 1982), and the Child Behavior Checklist (CBCL; Achenbach, 1978; Achenbach & Edelbrock, 1979). Their item content was not designed to sample domains corresponding to nosological concepts of anxiety. The most widely used parent scale, the CBCL, does not have an anxiety factor at all ages. Furthermore, the content of the anxiety factor varies between boys and girls. Since epidemiological studies do not indicate sex differences in types of childhood anxiety, the discrepancies in the CBCL suggest that the item content may fail to capture relevant aspects of children's anxious symptomatology. It is also conceivable that parents are poor, invalid informants for assessing children's anxiety. Scores on the CBCL for offspring of adults with anxiety disorders were higher than the scale norms in a study which used the standardization sample as controls — a methodologically questionable procedure (Silverman *et al.*, 1988). Results indicate convergent validity for scale identification of problems, since a correlation of 0.67 was obtained between the CBCL and interview results (the nature of the problems correlated is not specified).

Regardless of the reason for the unusual factor structure of the parental CBCL, its ability to assess anxiety for both genders at all ages is limited by the peculiarities of its factorial structure. Reliability of parental ratings of anxiety has not been reported.

The PIC has been found to distinguish between anxious and normal children, but not between anxious and depressed cases (Sylvester *et al.*, 1988).

As disappointing as the results are with child and parent anxiety scales, the picture seems even worse with regard to teacher scales. Although the test–retest reliability of the anxiety scores of the teacher CBCL appear to be satisfactory (Achenbach & Edelbrock, 1979), teachers' ability to identify anxious children is questionable. A group of children referred for the most part by schools because of severe anxiety received low scores on a scale with extensive coverage for anxiety (Klein *et al.*, 1992b). The merits of the anxiety factors of various teacher rating scales have not been examined, but there appears to be little basis for optimism.

Clinical interviews

The inclusion of diagnostic criteria in DSM-III (American Psychiatric Association, 1980) gave impetus to the development of clinical interviews designed to elicit diagnostic information. Several are in general use, and the studies summarized in this chapter almost always utilize one of these interview schedules. The Schedule for Affective Disorders and Schizophrenia for School-Age Children (Kiddie-SADS, or K-SADS; Chambers *et al.*, 1985; Ambrosini *et al.*, 1989; J. Puig-Antich & W.J. Chambers, unpublished observations), the Diagnostic Interview for Children and Adolescents (DICA; Herjanic & Reich, 1982; Welner *et al.*, 1987; Reich *et al.*, 1992a,b), the Diagnostic Interview Schedule for Children (DISC; Costello *et al.*, 1985), the Child Assessment Schedule (CAS; Hodges *et al.*, 1982a,b, 1989) and the Interview Schedule for Children (ISC; Kovacs, 1985) are omnibus interviews that include DSM-III-R childhood anxiety disorders. However, their coverage of the adult anxiety disorders is partial. This omission is important since the onset of adult anxiety disorders is frequently in childhood (Christie *et al.*, 1988; Burke *et al.*, 1990). Therefore, the results obtained reflect only a partial picture of anxiety disorders in youth. An interview specific to anxiety disorders, the Anxiety Disorders Interview Schedule for Children (ADIS; Silverman & Nelles, 1988; Silverman, 1991) provides inquiry for all anxiety disorders. It is still in the investigative stage.

Two other interviews are undergoing testing. One, a new version of the DISC for use in epidemiological studies (NIMH, 1991) includes detailed inquiry about all anxiety disorders. The Child and Adolescent Psychiatric Assessment (CAPA; A. Angold, A. Cox, M. Prendergast, M. Rutter & E. Simonoff, unpublished observations), designed for clinicians, elicits symptoms of all anxiety disorders over a 3-month period. The methodology of clinical interviewing is in the process of active development, and is likely to lead to improvements in the assessment of anxiety disorders.

The clinical interviews are helpful in providing systematic, comprehensive coverage of symptomatic status and, as such, may be a useful resource to clinicians. There is a plethora of interview schedules for children, but little to facilitate determination of their relative merit. The K-SADS, the least structured, has been compared to the highly structured DICA and DISC. In 30 inpatients, the K-SADS and DICA yielded markedly different rates of separation anxiety disorders (9 versus 26%, respectively; Carlson *et al.*, 1987). Best-estimate clinical diagnoses of anxiety disorders had much better concordance with the K-SADS than the DICA. Therefore, it would seem that the K-SADS was more valid. In an epidemiological sample, the K-SADS and DISC yielded very poor agreement for the anxiety disorders (kappa values 0–0.38; Cohen *et al.*, 1987).

Only one outpatient study has contrasted the K-SADS with another clinical interviews, the CAS. Only moderate agreement was obtained for anxiety disorders (kappa = 0.54; Hodges *et al.*, 1987). However, interviews were conducted by non-clinicians, so that results fail to address the issue of comparability of two clinical interviews.

The scant information on the relative performance of interview schedules does not support the expectation that they are equivalent clinical assessments, and that the consequences of selection are trivial to the determination of anxiety disorders. In view of this interview variance, the issue of validity becomes salient. Which of the available procedures yields the most accurate estimate of anxiety disorders? The only suggestion so far is that the *DICA* may overdiagnose these conditions.

It is routine clinical diagnostic practice to obtain information from the child and a parent, and most interviews provide a version for each. Great variation in reporting has been found between these informants, especially for anxiety symptoms. However, no empirical data exist to indicate which source yields more valid information for the identification of anxiety disorders (Klein, 1991).

The review of the assessment literature points to problematic results generated by rating scales. As a result, the empirical findings reviewed in the chapter exclude reports that have relied on scale scores to evaluate anxiety in children (e.g. Macaulay & Kleinknecht, 1989; Bowen *et al.*, 1990; Bradley *et al.*, 1990). The contents of the chapter are restricted to clinical data generated by interview with children and/or parents.

Diagnostic reliability of anxiety disorders

There is ample evidence that specially trained clinicians in research settings can obtain satisfactory reliability for at least some anxiety diagnoses (Table 20.1) (Chambers *et al.*, 1985; Last *et al.*, 1987a, 1991; Welner *et al.*, 1987; Silverman & Nelles, 1988; Ambrosini *et al.*, 1989). Epidemiological studies also indicate adequate interrater agreement for any anxiety disorders (kappa values of 0.70 or over), but do not report reliability of specific subdiagnoses (Anderson *et al.*, 1987; Benjamin *et al.*, 1990).

A different picture emerges from reliability studies conducted outside research settings. In an interesting exercise, a total of 134 clinicians (clinical psychologists and child psy-

Table 20.1 Interrater reliability of DSM-III childhood anxiety disorders

Study	Sample/setting	n	Ages (years)	Raters	Method	Anxiety disorders (kappa values) Any	SAD	OAD	SP	AD	Other disorders*
Strober *et al.* (1981)	Adolescent inpatients	95	12−17	2 clinicians	SADS Joint interviews	0.47	NR	NR	NR	NR	0.64−1.0
Werry *et al.* (1983a,b)	Outpatient clinic	195	2−17	2 clinicians	Clinical conference	NR	0.72	0.65	0.27	0.05	0.05−0.96
Rey *et al.* (1989)	Adolescent inpatients	393	12−17	2 senior clinicians	Complete chart review	0.82	0.80	0.14	0.57	0.39	0.36−1.0
Anderson *et al.* (1987)	Community cases	792	11	Lay interviewers	DISC	0.70†	NR	NR	NR	NR	NR
Silverman and Nelles (1988)	1 Offspring of anxious adults 2 Anxiety clinic	51	6−18	6 clinicians	ADIS with child and parent	NR	NR	0.54	1.0	NR	
Mezzich *et al.* (1985)	Case histories	27	2−15	134 clinicians	Clinical diagnosis	0.20	NR	NR	NR	NR	0.01−0.96
Ambrosini *et al.* (1989)	1 Outpatient clinic 2 Depression clinic	25	6−18	Clinicians	K-SADS Video tapes	NR	0.85	0.85	0.64	NR	0.80−0.88
Last *et al.* (1991)	Relatives of children 1 with anxiety disorders 2 with other disorders 3 without disorders (normals)	1178	Adults	Clinicians	K-SADS Audio tapes	0.95	0.91	0.93	NR	0.89	0.92−0.99

SAD, Separation anxiety disorder; OAD, overanxious disorder; SP, simple phobia; AD, avoidant disorder; SADS, Schedule for Affective Disorders and Schizophrenia; DISC, Diagnostic Interview Schedule for Children; ADIS, Anxiety Disorders Interview Schedule for Children; K-SADS, Schedule for Affective Disorders and Schizophrenia for School-age Children; NR, not reported.
* Range of kappa values for other DSM-III disorders assessed in study.
† Anxiety and affective disorders combined.

chiatrists), randomly selected from professional rosters, diagnosed several of 27 case histories (Mezzich *et al.*, 1985). The reliability across DSM-III anxiety disorders was very poor (kappa = 0.20), in spite of the advantage of having provided identical written clinical material to clinicians. (Results are not presented for specific anxiety diagnoses.) Other disorders fared much better, indicating that the poor agreement was selective. At the same time, reliability was even worse for many other conditions. These results indicate that the provision of clinical diagnostic criteria falls far short of ensuring consensus among clinicians.

More encouraging results were obtained in two reliability studies from clinical settings in New Zealand and Australia. In the first, based on case presentations at clinical rounds in an inpatient setting, two clinicians made DSM-III diagnoses (Werry *et al.*, 1983a,b). Moderate to satisfactory reliability was found for separation anxiety and overanxious disorders, but very poor agreement for avoidant disorder (see Table 20.1). In another study, charts of adolescents referred to an inpatient setting were reviewed independently by two clinicians (Rey *et al.*, 1989). Reliability was good for only one anxiety disorder — separation anxiety (kappa = 0.80), and moderate for simple phobia (kappa = 0.57). Other anxiety disorders had poor agreement (avoidant, kappa = 0.39; overanxious, kappa = 0.14).

A critical point is the stability of diagnosis over time (test–retest reliability). Short-term test–retest reliability is essential to establish that anxiety symptoms elicited reflect a relatively enduring rather than an ephemeral momentary condition that is unpredictably elicited. Test–retest reliability values for anxiety disorders, over short intervals, have ranged from 0.29 to 0.82. Separation anxiety disorder appears more consistently reliable than other anxiety disorders as shown in Table 20.2. Inquiry for a lifetime history of anxiety disorders over a 2-year interval yielded very poor consistency of recall by parents as well as children (kappa = 0.25 and −0.07, respectively; Fendrich *et al.*, 1991). In contrast, parental recall of major depressive disorders was excellent. These findings do not foster confidence regarding the validity of lifetime anxiety diagnoses, even when the parent is the informant. It remains possible that the problem lies in the instruments, rather than on recall of anxiety symptoms *per se*. Results from a controlled follow-up study into adulthood of children with separation anxiety disorder suggest that this may be the case. Retrospective childhood diagnoses of separation anxiety disorder were made by 'blind' interviewers in 76% of the cases, compared to 6% in hyperactive children and 2% in community controls (Klein & Mannuzza, 1991a) using a specially developed clinical interview (S. Mannuzza & R.G. Klein, unpublished observations). Until the measurement issue is resolved, it is not possible to determine whether stability of reporting is a realistic goal for anxiety disorders in children.

EPIDEMIOLOGY OF CHILDHOOD ANXIETY DISORDERS

Unexpectedly, epidemiological studies have observed high rates of anxiety disorders in children and adolescents, as well as in adults (Christie *et al.*, 1988). Anxiety disorders frequently have been the most prevalent diagnoses in community inter-

Table 20.2 Test–retest reliability of DSM-III childhood anxiety disorders

Study	Sample/setting	n	Ages (years)	Raters	Method	Interval	Anxiety disorders (kappa values)				
							Any	SAD	OAD	SP	AD
Canino *et al.* (1987)	1 Clinic referrals 2 Community cases	91	4–16	Child psychiatrists	DISC Current	0 day– 10 weeks	0.53	0.51	0.35	NR	NR
Chambers *et al.* (1985)	1 Outpatient clinic 2 Depression clinic 3 Inpatient clinic	52	6–17	Clinicians and raters	K-SADS Current	Up to 72 hours	0.24	0.53	0.29*	0.38	NR
Last *et al.* (1987a)	Anxiety clinic	91	5–18	Clinicians	ISC Current	A few hours	NR	0.81	0.82	NR	NR
Welner *et al.* (1987)	Inpatient unit	27	7–17	Lay interviewers	DICA-C	1–7 days	0.76	NR	NR	NR	NR
Hodges *et al.* (1989)	Inpatient unit	32	6–12	Clinicians	CAS	1–10 days	0.72	0.56	0.38	NR	NR
Fendrich *et al.* (1991)	Offspring of: 1 depressed adults 2 normal adults	59	6–16	Interviewers	K-SADS Lifetime	2 years	0.25† −0.07‡	NR	NR	NR	NR

SAD, Separation anxiety disorder; OAD, overanxious disorder; SP, simple phobia; AD, avoidant disorder; DISC, Diagnostic Interview Schedule for Children; K-SADS, Schedule for Affective Disorders and Schizophrenia for School-age Children; ISC, Interview Schedule for Children; DICA, Diagnostic Interview for Children and Adolescents; CAS, Child Assessment Schedule; NR, not reported.
* Generalized anxiety.
† Parent reliability.
‡ Child reliability.

Table 20.3 Rates of DSM-III anxiety disorders in the community based on diagnostic interviews

Study*	Site	n	Ages (years)	Time frame	Source	Instrument	Anxiety disorder (percentages)					
							Any	SAD	OAD	SP	AD	ScP
Bird *et al.* (1988)	Puerto Rico	777	4–16	12 months	C,P	DISC	NR	3.5	NR	2.3	NR	NR
Anderson *et al.* (1987)	New Zealand	782	11	12 months	C	DISC	7.5	3.5	2.9	2.4	NR	0.9
Kashani and Orvaschel (1988)	US	150	14–16	6 months	C,P	DICA	8.7	4.1	NR	9.1	NR	NR
Velez *et al.* (1989)	US	320	9–12	12 months	P,C	DISC	NR	25.6	19.1	NR	NR	NR
		456	13–18	12 months	P,C	DISC	NR	6.8	12.7	NR	NR	NR
Benjamin *et al.* (1990)	US	789	7–11	12 months	C,P	DISC	5.4	4.1	4.6	9.1	1.6	1.0
McGee *et al.* (1990)	New Zealand	962	15	Present†	C		NR	2.0	5.9	3.6	NR	1.1

* In chronological order
SAD, separation anxiety disorder; OAD, overanxious disorder; SP, simple phobia; AD, avoidant disorder; ScP, social phobia; C, interviews with child; P, interviews with parent; DISC, Diagnostic Interview Schedule for Children; DICA, Diagnostic Interview for Children and Adolescents; NR, not reported.
† Specific time frame not specified.

view surveys (see Table 20.3 for population rates). Interest in childhood anxiety has been heightened by reports that early onset characterizes adult anxiety disorders (Christie *et al.*, 1988; Burke *et al.*, 1990). The median age of onset for any anxiety disorder was reported to be 16 (Christie *et al.*, 1988), and 12 for social or simple phobias (Bourdon *et al.*, 1988). These findings suggest a childhood onset in about half of adults with an anxiety disorder, and raise the possibility of a strong link between childhood and adult anxiety disorders. In spite of their elevated frequency in the general population, childhood anxiety disorders are not highly prevalent among clinic attendees (Gittelman, 1986); perhaps, in part, because anxiety disorders may be less disabling than other childhood conditions (Werry *et al.*, 1987). Certainly, the discrepancy between the population and clinic rates of anxiety disorders suggests that such may be the case. Addressing this issue, a community study of children between ages 7 and 11 examined impairment in children with anxiety or behaviour disorders during the past year, and normals (no psychiatric diagnosis in past year; Benjamin *et al.*, 1990). Overall dysfunction did not differ between children with anxiety disorders and those with behaviour disorders; and both groups differed from normals to the same degree. These findings seem to indicate that anxiety disorders are not less 'serious' than behaviour disorders. In addition, teachers viewed children with anxiety disorders as significantly worse than normals on measures of academic, social and learning ability. However, the absolute level of impairment was low in all clinical groups, and the diagnosed community cases may not have captured the equivalents of clinical populations.

COMORBIDITY

The development of the DSM-III had a major influence in modifying established diagnostic practice which typically consisted of an overall diagnosis, with multiple diagnoses being the exception rather than the rule. Since the advent of the DSM-III, which facilitated multiple diagnoses, clinical studies have reported high rates of comorbidity in children with anxiety disorders. Two types of comorbidity, each with its own diagnostic implications, are reviewed: the co-occurrence of multiple anxiety disorders, and the co-occurrence of anxiety disorders with other conditions.

Comorbidity among anxiety disorders

The legitimacy of the multiplicity of anxiety disorders has been questioned (Rutter & Shaffer, 1980). If the conditions co-occurred regularly, it would be unlikely that they represented specific discrete illnesses. The pertinent literature consists of clinical and epidemiological studies.

Clinical studies

It is well-known that clinical samples are bound to generate inflated rates of comorbidity (Caron & Rutter, 1991). However, they may be useful by generating heuristic hypotheses about the nature of the comorbidity, and by fostering more rigorous, pointed investigations than would be likely otherwise.

Clinical studies have reported high comorbidity across anxiety disorders (50% or more; Bernstein & Garfinkel, 1986; Last *et al.*, 1987a,c, 1992; Strauss *et al.*, 1988). The DSM-III-R overanxious disorder seems to be the one most frequently associated with multiple anxiety diagnoses. Some of the estimates are based on very small (*n* = 16), highly selected treatment-refractory cases (Bernstein & Garfinkel, 1986). Others report on larger, less biased groups, but it is not clear that these represent independent studies, or whether they are multiple reports of overlapping samples (Last *et al.*, 1987a,c; Strauss *et al.*, 1988). The clinical database on comorbidity of anxiety disorders is limited, and estimates of rates in clinical settings are unclear.

Epidemiological studies

Community cases, unbiased by clinical factors that impinge on treatment referrals, are important informative sources of comorbidity. Benjamin and co-workers (1990) examined the 1-year prevalence of anxiety disorders in community cases between 7 and 11 years of age. Relying on children's self-reports ($n = 300$), they found that 50% of those with overanxious disorder also had separation anxiety disorder; of those with a separation anxiety disorder, 27% had an overanxious disorder and 33% had simple phobias.

A New Zealand study of 15-year-olds found that 17% of those with an anxiety disorder received more than one anxiety diagnosis (McGee *et al.*, 1990). In a small US community sample, multiple anxiety disorders occurred in 38% of those with an anxiety disorder (Kashani & Orvaschel, 1988). Other epidemiological studies do not report rates of comorbidity across anxiety disorders (Anderson *et al.*, 1987; Bird *et al.*, 1988).

From the epidemiological evidence, multiple anxiety disorders appear frequent, and comorbidity rates appear to exceed chance expectations. This finding raises questions regarding their distinctiveness.

Ages of onset in comorbid anxiety disorders

The respective ages of onset of the overlapping anxiety disorders have not been reported. In a small clinical sample of children selected for separation anxiety disorder ($n = 21$), overanxious disorder co-occurred in 29% of patients, but its onset never preceded that of the separation anxiety disorder (Klein *et al.*, 1992b). This chronological sequence raises the possibility that, at times, symptoms subsumed in overanxious disorder simply may be complications of a specific anxiety diagnosis, and may represent a severity dimension rather than additional discrete disorder. In a large clinical sample ($n = 188$), almost all with an overanxious disorder ($n = 49$) also had another comorbid anxiety which began after the onset of the overanxious disorder in half the cases (Last *et al.*, 1992). These findings do not support the notion that overanxious disorder symptoms are nonspecific complications of other disorders.

Diagnostic overlap in comorbid anxiety disorders

Also problematic for a clear understanding of comorbidity of anxiety disorders is the lack of knowledge concerning the boundaries of these disorders. For example, many children with separation anxiety disorders have a fear of the dark.

Some investigators may interpret this fear as a feature consistent with separation anxiety (the child feels more vulnerable in situations where dangers are not immediately perceptible); others may view a fear of the dark as an additional simple phobia, since the symptom is not a defining criterion of separation anxiety disorder. Rates of comorbidity will vary greatly depending on the conventions applied to overlapping syndromal presentations. To some extent, the DSM-III and DSM-III-R nomenclatures foster multiple diagnoses by providing discrete, seemingly unique symptom lists for each anxiety disorder. These fail to communicate the important clinical phenomenon that associated features of one syndrome may be identical to the primary signs of another syndrome. It is difficult to include appropriate clinical caveats in a diagnostic manual, since their exact nature is not well-understood. At the same time, one cannot escape the suspicion that at least some of the comorbidity is likely due to an overzealous (and perhaps overly mechanical) application of diagnostic criteria that fails to distinguish the proverbial forest from the trees. Finally, it is not clear that dysfunction and impairment are required to the same degree across investigators, since standards for establishing the presence of diagnoses are almost never provided. This important issue is bound to influence estimates of comorbidity.

Furthermore, the diagnostic criteria of overanxious disorder in DSM-III and DSM-III-R lacked descriptive syndromal specificity. This feature as well is bound to increase comorbidity across childhood anxiety disorders.

Comorbidity of anxiety disorders with other disorders

Complicating a straightforward interpretation of comorbidity is the inability to assume that anxiety disorders that coexist with other psychopathology are the same clinical phenomena (biologically, etiologically, etc.) as those that occur in 'pure' form (Fyer *et al.*, 1990a), and it remains to be demonstrated that they represent the same clinical entities. As in the case of comorbidity within anxiety disorders, comorbidity between different psychopathology may suggest unwarranted diagnostic distinctions, and points to the possibility that varying co-occurring syndromes may reflect a single underlying disorder, or represent different clinical phases of the same disorder over time. Clinical, epidemiological and family studies have generated informative data. (Longitudinal studies also would contribute to our understanding of comorbidity, but these are virtually nonexistent.)

Clinical studies

Several studies of children with anxiety disorders have noted a frequent co-occurrence of major depressive disorder (from 30 to 80%; Bernstein & Garfinkel, 1986; Last *et al.*, 1987c; 1992; Strauss *et al.*, 1988), whereas two other small investigations failed to obtain similar findings (Hershberg *et al.*, 1982; Klein *et al.*, 1992b). Problematically, discrepant results call into question consistency across studies in standards for clinical diagnoses of depression, and in the clinical compositions of samples.

In contrast to the inconsistent rates of depression in children selected for anxiety disorders, there is almost unanimous agreement that the rate of anxiety disorders far exceeds chance expectation among children selected for major depressive disorder (Hershberg *et al.*, 1982; Ryan *et al.*, 1986; Boulos *et al.*, 1991; Geller *et al.*, 1990; Klein, 1990). The observation that when anxiety and depression co-occur, onset of the anxiety syndrome typically precedes that of the affective disorder (Kovacs *et al.*, 1989; Klein, 1990) has implications regarding the developmental relationship between the two affects.

Clinical reports are inconsistent with regard to comorbidity of other disorders, such as conduct disorder or ADDH, among children selected for anxiety disorders. Last *et al.*, (1987c, 1992) reported approximate rates of behaviour disorders of 20%. Others have found very few behaviour disorders among anxiety disorders (Bernstein & Garfinkel, 1986; Klein *et al.*, 1992b). In contrast, clinical studies of children identified because of ADDH have noted a surprisingly high prevalence of anxiety disorders (Livingston *et al.*, 1990; Shekim *et al.*, 1985; Pliszka, 1989; Livingston *et al.*, 1990), with some exceptions (Munir *et al.*, 1987). It has even been suggested that ADDH combined with anxiety disorders represents a distinct clinical subgroup of ADDH (Pliszka, 1989).

Epidemiological studies

An extensive New Zealand study of 11-year-olds reported a 17% rate of depression among children with anxiety disorders. Interpretation of this finding is complicated by the fact that every case of anxiety with depression also had a conduct/oppositional disorder (Anderson *et al.*, 1987). The same New Zealand study of 15-year-olds found a 14% comorbid rate of depression with anxiety disorders (McGee *et al.*, 1992). In contrast to the findings in 11-year-olds, concurrent conduct disorders were extremely rare in the 15-year-old cohort. If children and adolescents with a depressive disorder are selected, rates of comorbid anxiety were very elevated, but differed between childhood and adolescence; 71 and 33%, respectively. The contrasting pattern of comorbidity between anxiety and depression at two phases of development suggests that it may have different significance at each stage. Possible distinctions between child and adolescent depression are suggested as well by the only adequate follow-up study to date of depressed children, which found differential predictive significance for child and adolescent depression (Harrington *et al.*, 1990; see Chapter 19).

In the Puerto Rican population, the 6-month prevalence of patients with anxiety disorders who also had an affective disorders was 23% (Bird *et al.*, 1988; Table 20.1). Among the depressed children, 31% had an anxiety disorder — a comorbidity rate that does not differ from that of depression in anxious youngsters. No age contrast is indicated.

The most recent US study by Benjamin *et al.* (1990) found a significant association between depression and anxiety over the previous year, accounted for by the boys exclusively. Among girls, the relative rates for depression in anxiety versus nonanxiety cases were 2.5 and 0.8%, whereas in boys they were 10.5 versus 0.8%.

Epidemiological studies suggest age- as well as sex-related differences in comorbidity between anxiety and depression. As noted, the age differences in the rate of coexisting anxiety and depression are consistent with follow-up as well as prevalence studies of child and adolescent depression. Gender differences require replication.

Consistent with clinical reports, epidemiological studies have reported a beyond-chance aggregation of anxiety and behaviour disorders (Shekim *et al.*, 1985; Anderson *et al.*, 1987; Kashani *et al.*, 1987; Bird *et al.*, 1988; Benjamin *et al.*, 1990; McGee *et al.*, 1990).

Family studies

Family studies have used two strategies: firstly, the examination of offspring of anxious or depressed adults, and secondly, the study of relatives of anxious or depressed children. Depressed mothers have reported increased rates of separation anxiety disorder in their children compared to controls (10 versus 0%, respectively; Weissman *et al.*, 1984b). Further examination of the data revealed that the co-occurrence of panic attacks in the depressed mothers was the key clinical characteristic conferring risk for separation anxiety disorder to the children (36 versus 0% of separation anxiety disorder in offspring of mothers with depression plus panic disorder versus pure depression; Weissman *et al.*, 1984a). The children were interviewed 6 years later (Weissman *et al.*, 1987). The self-reports of psychopathology failed to replicate previous findings based on the parents' interviews; the children of depressed and normal parents no longer differed in frequency of lifetime anxiety disorder (37 versus 27%). Furthermore, only a trend for an excess of self-reported anxiety disorders was found in the offspring of depressed probands with panic disorder compared to other groups (Mufson *et al.*, 1992). This study failed to replicate the previously observed link between children's separation anxiety disorder and parental panic disorder in the same sample. The results obtained from parental and self-reports differ markedly. Relying on parents, a DSM-III diagnosis was made in 8% of children of normal adults, in 21% of children of parents with depression but no panic attacks, and in 28% of children of adults with comorbid panic and depressive disorders (Weissman *et al.*, 1984b). In the same samples, using self-reports, the respective rates for any DSM-III diagnosis were 50% (normals; Weissman *et al.*, 1987), 68% (depression without panic), and 83% (depression plus panic disorder; Mufson *et al.*, 1992). Thus, the studies differ markedly in frequency of diagnosis in the same cases. The introduction of child interviews would seem unlikely to alter rates of psychopathology to the extent reported. These discrepancies make it difficult to integrate the two data sets and to reconcile the results.

However, a link between depression and anxiety is suggested by the findings that in a 2-year follow-up of the cohort, new cases of anxiety disorders had occurred exclusively among offspring of the depressed women (11 versus 0% in controls; Weissman *et al.*, 1992).

Another community study found that major depressive disorder in mothers conferred an increased risk of overanxious disorder in their children compared to those of normal subjects (Breslau *et al.*, 1986). This relationship is all the more striking since generalized anxiety in the mothers did not influence the rate of anxiety in the children (11 and 12% of overanxious disorder in the high-risk and control children). Thus, a specific relationship between depression and anxiety was noted.

The rate of lifetime anxiety disorders was obtained from parent and child interviews in a well-documented sample of recurrent unipolar depressed patients and community controls. No difference in frequency of anxiety disorder was found between the two groups (20 versus 9% in the high-risk and control groups; Orvaschel *et al.*, 1988).

Another study of offspring of depressed women (unipolar and bipolar) did not observe higher rates of lifetime prevalence of anxiety disorders in their children compared to those of normal controls, except if the children of the two affective disorders were combined (Hammen *et al.*, 1990).

In a further offspring study, lifetime diagnoses were generated based on interviews with children and their parents who consisted of (1) patients with panic disorder; (2) patients with major depressive disorders; and (3) normals (McClellan *et al.*, 1990). The frequency of anxiety disorders was greater in the children of depressed parents than in those of controls (27 versus 6%), but the two clinical groups did not differ.

Several models of specific relationships between anxiety and depression in children were examined by comparing psychiatric disorders in the offspring of adult outpatients (Biederman *et al.*, 1991a). Compared to children of 'pure' depressives, those of parents with panic disorders had more anxiety disorders regardless of comorbid depression in the parents. The results suggest that depression *per se* is not linked to childhood anxiety. However, the number of children in some groups is small, and it is difficult to reach firm conclusions regarding negative results.

Only one study so far has reported on a sizeable group of relatives of anxious children (Last *et al.*, 1991). Anxiety disorders in children were not associated with major depressive disorders in first-degree relatives. These results are not congruent with a postulated relationship between depression and anxiety. In a previous smaller study, these investigators failed to find a higher preponderance of affective disorders in mothers of anxious children compared to mothers of behaviour disorders (Last *et al.*, 1987b).

A sprinkling of family studies have reported concordance between anxiety and behaviour disorders. Thus, McClellan *et al.* (1990) and Biederman *et al.* (1991a) diagnosed attention deficit disorder more often in children of adults with panic disorder (15 and 25%) than in controls (4 and 6%; problems in subject selection limit generalizations from the proband/ normal contrasts in one report — Biederman *et al.*, 1991a).

Similarly, attention deficit disorder in boys as well as girls was reported to confer a significant risk for anxiety disorders in their relatives (Biederman *et al.*, 1991b; Faraone *et al.*, 1991).

Two other family studies of children with ADDH have failed to find elevated rates of anxiety disorders in parents or siblings of probands compared to those of controls (Mannuzza *et al.*, 1991a; Klein & Mannuzza, 1990).

If attention deficit disorders were associated with anxiety disorders, it would be reasonable to expect the two to aggregate in the natural history of children with attention deficit disorder. Contrary to this expectation, follow-up studies of children with attention deficit disorder which have included systematic assessments of anxiety disorders have failed to find an excess of anxiety disorders in the children's long-term course (Mannuzza & Gittelman, 1984; Gittelman *et al.*, 1985; Weiss *et al.*, 1985; Klein & Mannuzza, 1991; Mannuzza *et al.*, 1991b; 1993).

Distinctions among childhood anxiety disorders

Perhaps the most compelling evidence supporting the distinctiveness of anxiety disorders is their differential timing for onset. Developmental differences in onset have been shown for specific phobias, social anxiety and panic disorder. Therefore, this discriminating criterion applies to these conditions, but not to the rest of the anxiety diagnoses. Other data regarding antecedents and correlates are too limited to contribute to an assessment of validity (Gittelman, 1986). A recent study reports significant differentiation on self-ratings and pulse rate between social phobic and normal children, but little difference between the latter and overanxious children (Beidel, 1991). Therefore, the diagnostic validity of overanxious disorder is called into question. However, small groups were studied, so that negative findings are inconclusive. Also, the comprehensiveness and relevance of validating measures is problematic in any such study. There is the possibility that relevant, discriminating variables are not examined. In the absence of clear hypotheses concerning the specific nature of disorders, it is difficult to design investigations that provide a critical test of diagnostic validity. Therefore, the lack of discrimination between disorders may be difficult to interpret unless contrasts rest on clearly formulated predictions.

Stability of childhood anxiety disorders

The significance of a clinical condition is determined by multiple factors, one of which is long-term consistency. All other things being equal, it follows that disorders that affect function over extended time carry relatively greater concern than transient, self-limited conditions. Little is known about the course of childhood anxiety disorders, although clinical observations suggest that they frequently remit, but may recur. The New Zealand epidemiological study examined the stability of internalizing disorders between ages 11 and 15 without specific reference to anxiety disorders (McGee *et al.*, 1992). Internalizing disorders had significant stability in girls, but not in boys.

There is indirect evidence suggesting a specific relationship between childhood separation anxiety and adult panic disorder (Gittelman & Klein, 1984; Klein & Klein, 1988). However, results are not unanimous. It is relevant to note that studies that have failed to find a relative excess of childhood separation anxiety among adults with panic disorder have relied on self-rating scales to assess childhood separation anxiety (e.g. Thyer *et al.*, 1985, 1986; van der Molen *et al.*, 1989). In view of the poor performance of these measures, they cannot be viewed as satisfactory means of obtaining subtle historic diagnostic information. The postulated link between childhood separation anxiety disorder and adult panic disorder was not supported by findings from the family study of children with anxiety disorders (Last *et al.*, 1991). Contrary to the hypothesis, the first-degree relatives of children with separation anxiety had lower rates of panic disorder than relatives of children with overanxious disorder. This investigation is unique in finding distinct features in overanxious disorder compared to other childhood anxiety disorders.

Longitudinal studies have reported on children with school phobia, or on 'neurotic' children, but diagnostic characteristics are unspecified. Moreover, assessment of outcome rarely includes diagnostic status and often relies on methods that are no longer viewed as adequate for evaluating functional status. Table 20.4 summarizes these studies. A small 4 year follow-up study of children with language and anxiety disorders found little consistency over time in psychopathology; about a third of the initially anxious children developed a behaviour disorder (Cantwell & Baker, 1989). At follow-up, half of the anxiety diagnoses differed from the initial ones. The unusual shift from anxiety to behaviour disorders suggests that children with both anxiety and language disorders may not be typical of other anxiety disorders in childhood, and raises the issue of syndromal equivalence between pure and comorbid cases.

The adult diagnostic status of children with separation anxiety disorder who also had school phobia (Gittelman-Klein

Table 20.4 Long-term clinical outcome of school-phobic children*

Author	*n*	Original number	Number of years	Method	Controls	Results
Outpatients						
Rodriguez *et al.* (1959)	41	?	1–7	Telephone and mail	No	1 30% still not in school 2 30% moderate to severe impairment 3 3 schizophrenic 4 Better outcome in *Ss* below 11
Coolidge *et al.* (1964)	49	66	9	Open-ended interview	No	1 60% with adjustment problems 2 20% with serious problems

Waldron (1976)	24	35	10	Interview	Yes: 18 neurotics 20 normals	1 Phobics versus neurotics: no difference
						2 Patients versus normals:
						  (a) more neurotic than controls
						  (b) worse work and social adjustment

Baker and Wills (1979)	67	71	6	Questionnaire	No	1 20% never back in school 2 Work history overall OK 3 Treatment response not related to long-term outcome
Inpatients						
Warren (1965)	16	16	6	Interview	No	44% with phobic symptoms (unspecified)
Berg *et al.* (1976)	100	125	3	Interview	No	1 50% poor school attendance 2 50% other problems 3 5 with agoraphobia 4 IQ inversely related to outcome
Weiss and Burke (1970)	9	14	6	Interview	No	1 Overall function OK 2 93% with serious neurosis
Roberts (1975)	56	131	5–18	Questionnaire	No	1 100% with significant anxiety 2 25% with separation anxiety 3 Over 50% poor school attendance 4 Age of onset not predictive
Boreham (1983)	54	67	≥2	Questionnaire	No	1 22% some agoraphobia 2 6% agoraphobia 3 No salient mood or social problems

* In chronological order.

& Klein, 1973, 1980) was compared to that of community controls (Klein, 1990). This follow-up study does not address the validity of various childhood anxiety disorders, but bears on the relationship between childhood separation anxiety disorder and adult anxiety disorders. Panic disorder was the only disorder that was significantly elevated in the index cases (7 versus 0%). No other anxiety disorder differentiated between the child separation anxiety and control groups. The results support a relationship between childhood separation anxiety and adult panic disorder. However, the adult disorder seems to be an infrequent sequela of the childhood condition. Yet, it is possible that the presence of childhood anxiety may influence the course of adult panic disorder. The onset of panic disorder seems earlier among cases with childhood separation anxiety disorder than among others (Gittelman & Klein, 1985; Yeragani *et al.*, 1989). In addition, among adults with panic disorder who had made a serious suicide attempt, more were likely to have had childhood phobias than non-suicidal cases (Noyes *et al.*, 1991). In view of the negative results obtained in the family study of anxious children (Last *et al.*, 1991), unambiguous conclusions are precluded regarding a diagnostical relationship between anxiety disorders at different developmental periods (i.e. between separation anxiety and panic disorders).

VALIDITY OF CHILDHOOD ANXIETY DISORDERS

The distinction between childhood anxiety disorders and other types of psychopathology such as behaviour disorders and pervasive developmental disorders is well-established. Diagnostic validity of the anxiety disorders concerns their differentiation from major depressive disorders, and from each other. As with all psychiatric disorders, the diagnostic validity is inferred from patterns of treatment response, familial concordance, natural history, antecedents and correlates (Rutter & Gould, 1985). As noted in the treatment review, little therapeutic research has been conducted, and the data do not further our understanding of the diagnostic distinctions pertinent to childhood anxiety disorders.

Childhood anxiety disorders and major depressive disorders

The literature review of comorbidity between childhood anxiety and depression indicates that family studies have yielded conflicting results concerning the intergenerational relationships between anxiety and depression (Weissman *et al.*, 1984a,b; Breslau *et al.*, 1986; Puig-Antich & Rabinovich, 1986; Orvaschel *et al.*, 1988; Hammen *et al.*, 1990; McClellan *et al.*, 1990; Biederman *et al.*, 1991a; Last *et al.*, 1991; Mufson *et al.*, 1992). A small study of the relatives of anxious and depressed inpatient children (atypical clinical populations) did not find differences in parental psychopathology between the two diagnostic groups. Nonpathological controls were not included (Livingston *et al.*, 1985). Another small study con-

trasting offspring of adults with anxiety or dysthymic disorders combined obsessive-compulsive and agoraphobic disorders, thereby confounding results (Turner *et al.*, 1987).

In a follow-up study designed to contrast the natural history of depressive and anxiety disorders in adolescents, no difference in the rate of recovery was noted within a 1-year period between the two clinical groups (Goodyer *et al.*, 1991). As with other similar negative studies, sample sizes are problematically small for confident inferences.

A follow-up into adulthood of children with separation anxiety disorder found only a trend for a higher rate of lifetime major depression in the childhood anxiety group compared to controls (Klein, 1990). In sum, the weight of the evidence favours retaining diagnostic distinctions between childhood depression and anxiety.

TREATMENT OF CHILDHOOD ANXIETY DISORDERS

Treatments have been influenced greatly by theoretical models of anxiety. Psychoanalytic views have led to active developments of individual psychotherapy that relies on psychodynamic interpretations (Lewis, 1986). Cognitive theorists have developed interventions aimed at correcting misinterpretations and distortions (Kendall *et al.*, 1988; Kane & Kendall, 1989). Learning theorists have elaborated several behavioural treatments designed to reduce anxiety in children (*in vivo* desensitization, contingency management, flooding, modelling). The clinical procedures inherent in each approach have been described well (Morris & Kratochwill, 1983; Ollendick, 1983b; Siegel & Ridley-Johnson, 1985; Foa *et al.*, 1989). However, almost all the reports consist of case studies. Biologically oriented practitioners have utilized psychotropic medications (Klein & Last, 1989; Kutcher *et al.*, 1992).

Psychotherapeutic treatments

Only two comparative trials of psychotherapy in childhood anxiety disorders have been identified: the first dates back to the early 1970s (Miller *et al.*, 1972), and the second did not use random treatment assignment (Blagg & Yule, 1984).

Unselected outpatients with an anxiety disorder, most with school phobia, were assigned for 6 weeks to focused behavioural treatment, or to individual insight-oriented psychotherapy, or a waiting list control (Miller *et al.*, 1972). Compared to controls, children who received either form of psychotherapy were rated as significantly more improved by their mothers who did not differentiate the outcome of the two psychotherapies. In contrast, the clinicians' improvement estimates did not differ across the three conditions.

In vivo flooding (average of 2.5 weeks), inpatient care (average of 45 weeks), and home tutoring with psychotherapy (average 72 weeks) were compared in school-phobic children in clinical care. The rate of return to school was strikingly better for the children who received flooding compared with the other two groups. Unfortunately, confidence in the relative merit of each intervention is limited by the lack of randomization to treatment. Nevertheless, the outcome encourages the use of brief vigorous behavioural approaches to treat school phobia prior to the implementation of extended, costly and disruptive treatments. Moreover, the very low rate of improvement (10%) in those who received home instruction and psychotherapy does not engender positive expectations for the efficacy of this therapeutic regimen.

Pharmacotherapy

The view, largely derived from psychoanalytic theory, that anxiety was the underlying kingpin of all psychopathology, led to trials of diverse compounds (neuroleptics, stimulants and antihistamines) in a wide range of childhood disorders with the hope that an array of symptoms would improve by reducing anxiety. The logic of the reasoning is flawless, since one could expect richly varied improvements by treating the ubiquitously provocative symptom; however, the premise from which the practice evolved is less than probable. The literature that followed this vein is outdated (Gittelman-Klein, 1978; Gittelman & Koplewicz, 1986). Currently, the most likely compounds for the management of childhood anxiety disorders are high-potency benzodiazepines (e.g. alprazolam and clonazepam) and tricyclics (see also Chapter 51). In addition, a more recent agent from a different chemical class, fluoxetine, is in testing. Although tolerance to benzodiazepines can occur, it has not been reported in children.

The concept of anxiety is insufficiently precise to guide treatment with medication. Yet, the bulk of the literature does not pertain to well-defined diagnostic groups. Three placebo-controlled trials have examined the efficacy of a tricyclic in children with school phobia or separation anxiety disorder. One reported significant efficacy for moderately high doses of imipramine on a variety of behavioural and emotional outcomes in children with separation anxiety (Gittelman-Klein & Klein, 1971, 1980). In contrast, clomipramine in low doses was not found to be effective in a similar clinical population (Berney *et al.*, 1981). Finally, a recent trial of imipramine failed to replicate previously reported positive results (Klein *et al.*, 1992b). Therefore, the clinical efficacy of tricyclic treatment in separation anxiety disorder is not established.

Alprazolam was reported to be superior to a placebo in 8–16-year-olds with overanxious and avoidant disorders who served as their own controls (Simeon & Ferguson, 1987). However, the lack of randomized treatment periods limits the generalizability of the results. A subsequent parallel group design in similar clinical cases failed to indicate efficacy for low doses of alprazolam (Simeon *et al.*, 1992). Alprazolam was reported to be helpful for the alleviation of acute anxiety in a small group of children with cancer (Pfefferbaum *et al.*, 1987). Other high-potency benzodiazepines have been tried, such as clonazepam, but no controlled studies have been reported (Kutcher *et al.*, 1992).

Clinical management

There is no body of knowledge that documents the effectiveness of any treatment in childhood anxiety disorders (except for obsessive-compulsive disorder, discussed in Chapter 25). Yet clinicians cannot await the scientific verdict to care for children who seek treatment. Based on clinical experience, the use of behavioural treatments is rational since many children improve rapidly when it is implemented. These approaches are often combined, and an admixture of exposure, relaxation and reinforcement is likely. There is no evidence that the specific procedures are key to inducing change (Carlson *et al.*, 1986; Shaffer, 1986; Friedman & Ollendick, 1989). If behavioural interventions yield unsatifactory results, clinical expediency may lead also to a medication trial. Clinical experience suggests that even when medication appears effective in reducing anxiety, it is rare that other therapeutic efforts involving the child, parent and at times the school become superfluous. These are still necessary to help the child overcome phobic adaptation, and to assist the family and the school in managing a difficult situation more constructively. Unfortunately, the optimal means of achieving these goals remain undocumented.

A key clinical feature that influences treatment is the episodicity of anxiety states. Unlike most child and adolescent psychopathology that has a chronic course without a clear, definable onset, anxiety disorders may occur abruptly, and unexpectedly, in well-functioning children. In addition, children with anxiety disorders differ from those with other disorders because of their subjective distress. Unlike other ill children, many anxious children and teenagers are visibly in pain, aware of their altered emotional state and desirous of help. Children's altered functioning and their discomfort usually cause great stress in families, and affect parent–child as well as conjugal relationships. Anxiety-ridden children often become dependent and demanding. As examples, children who develop separation anxiety may for the first time demand to be taken to school or to sleep near their parents. Children who are overanxious about their schoolwork often exact much time from parents for assistance with school assignments. Families, not unusually, react with combinations of guilt, fear, sorrow, puzzlement, helplessness, anger and resentment. Alternatively, they may overrespond to the child's anxiety with their own anguish, and may overinvolve themselves in their child's life, or may simply overaccommodate the child and ignore the problem. At times parents vacillate from one type of response to another, and come for treatment demoralized by the conviction that they have 'tried everything'.

Because of these clinical features, the care of anxiety disorders typically requires active involvement with the family. The degree of parental involvement depends on the child's age and the nature of the child's difficulties (Kutcher *et al.*, 1992).

A common response by parents to their child's anxiety consists of overextensive discussions consisting of parental querying as to why the child is fearful. This approach has the effect of reinforcing the child's sense of helplessness since no sensible explanation is possible. Sometimes children with anxiety disorders develop artful explanations for their problems, but they are rarely justified, and fail to help the child overcome the handicap.

A major concern for many anxious children is to retain control over their activities in order to avoid exposure to anxiety-provoking situations. In such cases it is usual for parents to have been manipulated into a helpless, ineffectual role. Some parents feel, either through their own anxiety or misguided desire to help, that accommodating the child's wishes is appropriate and caring. Yet enabling children to avoid feared situations is conterproductive. The treating clinician has the challenge to alter such parental behaviours and to help parents understand that assuming a less indulgent stance is likely to enhance recovery.

In brief, clinicians need to assist parents to alter their means of handling what is admittedly a difficult and often painful situation. Doing so is not only a relief to parents, but also helps reverse ineffectual parental behaviour and induce parental responses that should facilitate the child's progress.

SUMMARY

Because anxiety has normal adaptive forms through development, the identification of pathology may pose difficulty in ambiguous cases. Inflexibility of affect is suggested as a key feature of symptomatic anxiety.

The multiple theories of anxiety in children have generated differing approaches to treatment. Very few systematic studies have been conducted, and no intervention has documented efficacy for the management of anxiety disorders in children.

Rating scales completed by children or informants have not been shown to have satisfactory validity for the identification or quantification of childhood anxiety disorders. The several interview schedules available differ in rates of anxiety disorders generated, but their relative merits are not known. Diagnostic interrater reliability is inconsistent; it is markedly superior among specialists than clinicians. Test–retest reliability for anxiety disorders is moderate.

Intergenerational studies have produced inconsistent results regarding links between anxiety and depression and attention deficit disorders.

The only adequate study of relatives of children with anxiety disorders indicates an increased risk for anxiety disorders in the relatives, and no increase in siblings (both genders combined). There seems to be little specificity of familial concordance for anxiety disorder since no differences in rates of anxiety disorders were obtained between relatives of anxious and behaviour-disordered children. In contrast, support for the distinction between overanxious (generalized anxiety) and other childhood anxiety disorders is suggested from differential rates of familial risks. So far, no longitudinal study has reported on the differential outcome of various childhood anxiety disorders. One longitudinal study suggests a relation-ship between childhood separation anxiety disorder and adult panic disorder. However, the evidence on this point is not consistent. No body of data supports the validity of the sub-diagnoses of childhood anxiety disorders, but differing onset ages imply distinct syndromes in the case of specific phobias, social phobia and panic disorder.

REFERENCES

Abe K. & Masui T. (1981) Age-sex trends of phobic and anxiety symptoms in adolescents. *British Journal of Psychiatry*, **138**, 297–302.

Achenbach T.M. (1978) The child behaviour profile: 1. Boys aged 6–11. *Journal of Consulting and Clinical Psychology*, **46**, 478–488.

Achenbach T.M. & Edelbrock C.S. (1979) The child behavior profile: 2. Boys aged 12–16 and girls aged 6–11 and 12–16. *Journal of Consulting and Clinical Psychology*, **47**, 223–233.

Ainsworth M.D.S. (1967) *Infancy in Uganda: Infant Care and the Growth of Love.* Johns Hopkins Press, Baltimore, MD.

Alessi N.E. & Magen J. (1988) Panic disorder in psychiatrically hospitalized children. *American Journal of Psychiatry*, **145**, 1450–1452.

Ambrosini P.J., Metz C., Prabucki K. & Lee J. (1989) Videotape reliability of the third revised edition of the K-SADS. *Journal of the American Academy of Child and Adolescent Psychiatry*, **28**, 723–728.

American Psychiatric Association (1968) *Diagnostic and Statistical Manual of Mental Disorders*, 2nd edn. American Psychiatric Association, Washington, DC.

American Psychiatric Association (1980) *Diagnostic and Statistical Manual of Mental Disorders*, 3rd edn. American Psychiatric Association, Washington, DC.

American Psychiatric Association (1987) *Diagnostic and Statistical Manual of Mental Disorders*, 3rd edn revised. American Psychiatric Association, Washington, DC.

American Psychiatric Association (1994) *Diagnostic and Statistical Manual of Mental Disorders*, 4th edn, DSM-IV. American Psychiatric Association, Washington, DC.

Anderson J.C., Williams S., McGee R. & Silva P.A. (1987) DSM-III disorders in preadolescent children: prevalence in a large sample from the general population. *Archives of General Psychiatry*, **44**, 69–76.

Angelino H., Dollins J. & Mech E.V. (1956) Trends in the 'fears and worries' of school children as related to socio-economic status and age. *Journal of Genetic Psychology*, **89**, 263–276.

Anthony E.J. (1975) Neurotic disorders. In: Freedman A., Kaplan H.I. & Sadock B.J. (eds) *Comprehensive Textbook of Psychiatry*, vol. II, pp. 2143–2160. Williams & Wilkins, Baltimore, MD.

Baker H. & Wills U. (1979) School phobic children at work. *British Journal of Psychiatry*, **135**, 561–564.

Ball W. & Tronick E. (1971) Infant responses to impending collision: optical and real. *Science*, **171**, 818–820.

Ballenger J.C., Carek D.J., Steele J.J. & Cornish-McTighe D. (1989) Three cases of panic disorder with agoraphobia in children. *American Journal of Psychiatry*, **146**, 922–924.

Bamber J.H. (1974) The fears of adolescents. *Journal of Genetic Psychology*, **125**, 127–140.

Bauer D. (1976) An exploratory study of developmental changes in children's fears. *Journal of Child Psychology and Psychiatry*, **17**, 69–74.

Bauer D. (1980) Childhood fears in developmental perspective. In: Hersov L. & Berg I. (eds) *Out of School*, pp. 189–208. John Wiley, London.

Beck A.T. & Emery G. (1985) *Anxiety Disorders and Phobias: A Cognitive Perspective.* Basic Books, New York.

Beidel D.C. (1991) Social phobia and overanxious disorder in school-age children. *Journal of the American Academy of Child and Adolescent Psychiatry*, **30**, 545—552.

Beidel D.C. & Turner S.M. (1988) Comorbidity of test anxiety and other anxiety disorders in children. *Journal of Abnormal Child Psychology*, **16**, 275—287.

Benjamin R.S., Costello E.J. & Warren M. (1990) Anxiety disorders in a pediatric sample. *Journal of Anxiety Disorders*, **4**, 293—316.

Berg I., Butler A. & Hall G. (1976) The outcome of adolescent school phobia. *British Journal of Psychiatry*, **128**, 80—85.

Berney T., Kolvin I., Bhate S.R., Garside R.F., Jeans J., Kay B. & Scarth L. (1981) School phobia: a therapeutic trial with clomipramine and short-term outcome. *British Journal of Psychiatry*, **138**, 110—118.

Bernstein G.A. & Garfinkel B.D. (1986) School phobia: the overlap of affective and anxiety disorders. *Journal of American the Academy of Child Psychiatry*, **25**, 235—241.

Biederman J. (1987) Clonazepam in the treatment of prepubertal children with panic-like symptoms. *Journal of Clinical Psychiatry*, **48**, 38—41.

Biederman J., Rosenbaum J.F., Bolduc E.A., Faraone S.V. & Hirshfeld D.R. (1991a) A high risk study of young children of parents with panic disorder and agoraphobia with and without comorbid major depression. *Psychiatric Research*, **37**, 333—348.

Biederman J., Faraone SV., Keenan K., Steingard R. & Tsuang M.T. (1991b) Familial association between attention deficit disorder and anxiety disorders. *American Journal of Psychiatry*, **148**, 251—256.

Bird H.R., Canino G., Rubio-Stipec M., Gould M.S., Ribera J., Sesman M., Woodbury M., Huertas-Goldman S., Pagan A., Sanchez-Lacay A. & Moscoso M. (1988) Estimates of the prevalence of childhood maladjustment in a community survey in Puerto Rico. *Archives of General Psychiatry*, **45**, 1120—1126.

Bird H.R., Yager T.J., Staghezza B., Gould M.S., Canino G. & Rubio-Stipec M. (1990) Impairment in the epidemiological measurement of childhood psychopathology in the community. *Journal of the American Academy of Child and Adolescent Psychiatry*, **29**, 796—803.

Black B. & Robbins D.R. (1990) Panic disorder in children and adolescents. *Journal of the American Academy of Child and Adolescent Psychiatry*, **29**, 36—44.

Blagg N.R. & Yule W. (1984) The behavioural treatment of school refusal — a comparative study. *Behavioural Research Therapy*, **22**, 119—127.

Boreham J. (1983) A follow-up study of 54 persistent school refusers. *Association for Child Psychology and Psychiatry News*, **15**, 8—14.

Boulos C., Kutcher S., Marton P., Simeon J., Ferguson B. & Roberts N. (1990) Response to desipiamine treatment in adolescent major depression. *Psychopharmacology Bulletin* 1991, **27**, 59—65.

Bourdon K.H., Boyd J.H., Rae D.S., Burns B.J., Thompson J.W. & Locke B.Z. (1988) Gender differences in phobias: results of the ECA Community Survey. *Journal of Anxiety Disorders*, **2**, 227—241.

Bowen R.C., Offord D.R. & Boyle M.H.(1990) The prevalence of overanxious disorder and separation anxious disorder: results from the Ontario child health study. *Journal of the American Academy of Child and Adolescent Psychiatry*, **29**, 753—758.

Bowlby J. (1973) *Attachment and Loss. Vol. 2, Separation: Anxiety and Anger*. Basic Books, New York.

Bradley S., Wachsmuth R., Swinson R. & Hnatko G. (1990) A pilot study of panic attacks in a child and adolescent psychiatric population. *Canadian Journal of Psychiatry*, **35**, 526—528.

Breslau N., Davis G.C. & Prabucki K. (1986) Searching for evidence on the validity of generalized anxiety disorder: psychopathology in children of anxious mothers. *Psychiatric Research*, **20**, 285—297.

Bronson G.W. (1968) The development of fear in man and other animals. *Child Development*, **39**, 409—432.

Bronson G.W. (1970) Fear of visual novelty: developmental patterns in males and females. *Developmental Psychology*, **2**, 33—40.

Bronson G.W. (1972) Infants' reactions to unfamiliar persons and novel objects. *Monographs of the Society for Research in Child Development*, **37**, (3, serial no 148).

Burke K.C., Burke J.D., Regier D.A. & Rae D.S. (1990) Age at onset of selected mental disorders in five community populations. *Archives of General Psychiatry*, **47**, 511—518.

Campbell S.B. (1986) Developmental issues in childhood anxiety. In: Gittelman R. (ed) *Anxiety Disorders of Childhood*, pp. 24—57. Guilford Press, New York.

Canino G.J., Bird H.R., Rubio-Stipec M., Woodbury M.A., Ribera J.C., Huertas S.E. & Sesman M.J. (1987) Reliability of child diagnosis in a Hispanic sample. *Journal of the American Academy of Child and Adolescent Psychiatry*, **26**, 560—565.

Cantwell D.P. & Baker L. (1989) Stability and natural history of DSM-III childhood diagnoses. *Journal of the American Academy of Child and Adolescent Psychiatry*, **28**, 691—700.

Carlson C.L., Figueroa R.G. & Lahey B.B. (1986) Behavior therapy for childhood anxiety disorders. In: Gittelman R. (ed) *Anxiety Disorders of Childhood*, pp. 204—232. Guilford Press, New York.

Carlson G.A., Kashani J.H., Thomas M.D.F., Vaidya A. & Daniel A.E. (1987) Comparison of two structured interviews on a psychiatrically hospitalized population of children. *Journal of the American Academy of Child and Adolescent Psychiatry*, **26**, 645—648.

Caron C. & Rutter M. (1991) Comorbidity in child psychopathology: concepts, issues and research strategies. *Journal of Child Psychology and Psychiatry*, **32**, 1063—1080.

Castaneda A., McCandless B.R. & Palermo D.S. (1956) The children's form of the Manifest Anxiety Scale. *Child Development*, **27**, 317—326.

Chambers W.J., Puig-Antich J., Hirsch M., Paez P., Ambrosini P.J., Tabrizi M.A. & Davies M. (1985) The assessment of affective disorders in children and adolescents by semi-structured interview. *Archives of General Psychiatry*, **42**, 696—702.

Christie K.A., Burke J.D. Jr, Regier D.A., Rae D.S., Boyd J.H. & Locke B.Z. (1988) Epidemiologic evidence for early onset of mental disorders and higher risk of drug abuse in young adults. *American Journal of Psychiatry*, **145**, 971—975.

Clark D.A. & Beck A.T. (1989) Cognitive theory and therapy of anxiety and depression. In: Kendall P.C. & Watson D. (eds) *Anxiety and Depression: Distinctive and Overlapping Features*, pp. 379—411. Academic Press, New York.

Cohen P., O'Connor P., Lewis S., Velez N. & Malachowski B. (1987) Comparison of DISC and K-SADS-P interviews of an epidemiological sample of children. *Journal of the American Academy of Child and Adolescent Psychiatry*, **26**, 662—667.

Coolidge J.C., Brodie R.D. & Feeney B. (1964) A ten-year follow-up study of sixty-six school children. *American Journal of Orthopsychiatry*, **34**, 675—684.

Costello E.J., Edelbrock C.S. & Costello A.J. (1985) Validity of the NIMH diagnostic interview schedule for children: a comparison between psychiatric referrals and pediatric referrals. *Journal of Abnormal Child Psychology*, **13**, 579—595.

Croake J.W. (1967) Adolescent fear. *Adolescent*, **2**, 459—468.

Crowe R.R., Noyes R., Pauls D.L. & Slymen D. (1983) A family study of panic disorder. *Achives of General Psychiatry*, **48**, 1065—1069.

Darwin C. (1965) *The Expression of Emotions in Men and Animals*. University of Chicago Press, Chicago.

Dobson K.S. (1985) The relationship between anxiety and depression. *Clinics Psychology Review*, **5**, 307—324.

Dobson K.S. & Cheung E. (1990) Relationship between anxiety and depression: conceptual and methodological issues. In: Maser J.D. & Cloninger C.R. (eds) *Comorbidity of Mood and Anxiety Disorders*, pp. 611—632. American Psychiatric Press, Washington, D.C.

Eisenberg L. (1958) A study in the communication of anxiety. *American Journal of Psychiatry*, **114**, 712−718.

Eysenck H.J. (1967) *The Biological Basis of Personality*. Springfield, MA.

Faraone S.V., Biederman J., Keenan K. & Tsuang M.T. (1991) A family-genetic study for girls with DSM-III attention deficit disorder. *American Journal Psychiatry*, **148**, 112−117.

Fendrich M., Weissmann M.M. & Warner V. (1991) Longitudinal assessment of major depression and anxiety disorders in children. *Journal of the American Academy of Child and Adolescent Psychiatry*, **30**, 38−42.

Finch A.J. Jr & Rogers T.R. (1984) Self-report instruments. In: Ollendick T.H. & Hersen M. (eds) *Child Behavioral Assessment: Principles and Procedures*, pp. 106−123. Pergamon Press, New York.

Finch A.J., Kendall P.C. & Montgomery L.E. (1974) Multidimensionality of anxiety in children: factor structure of the Children's Manifest Anxiety Scale. *Journal of Abnormal Child Psychology*, **2**, 331−336.

Finch A.J. Jr, Lipovsky J.A. & Casat C.D. (1989) Anxiety and depression in children and adolescents: negative affectivity or separate constructs? In: Kendall P.C. & Watson D. (eds) *Anxiety and Depression: Distinctive and Overlapping Features*, pp. 171−202. Academic Press, New York.

Foa E.B., Rothbaum B.O. & Kozak M.J. (1989) Behavioral treatments for anxiety and depression. In: Kendall P.C. & Watson D. (eds) *Anxiety and Depression*, pp. 413−454. Academic Press, New York.

Freud S. (1953) *Collected papers*. Jones E. (ed). Hogarth Press, London.

Friedman A.G. & Ollendick T.H. (1989) Treatment programs for severe night-time fears: a methodological note. *Journal of Behavioral Therapy and Experimental Psychiatry*, **20**, 171−178.

Fyer A.J., Liebowitz M.R. & Klein D.F. (1990a) Treatment trials, comorbidity, and syndromal complexity. In: Maser J.D. & Cloninger C.R. (eds) *Comorbidity of Mood and Anxiety Disorders*, pp. 669−679. American Psychiatric Press, Washington D.C.

Fyer A.J., Mannuzza S., Gallops M.S., Martin L.Y., Aaronson C., Gorman J.M., Liebowitz M.R. & Klein D.F. (1990b) Familial transmission of simple phobias and fears. *Archives of General Psychiatry*, **47**, 252−256.

Fyer A.J., Mannuzza S., Chapman T.F., Liebowitz M.R. & Klein D.F. (1993) A direct interview family study of social phobia. *Archives of General Psychiatry*, **50**, 286−293.

Garcia-Coll C., Kagan J. & Reznick J.S. (1984) Behavioral inhibition in young children. *Child Development*, **55**, 1005−1019.

Geller B., Cooper T.B., Graham D.L., Marsteller F.A. & Bryant D.M. (1990) Double-blind placebo controlled study of nortriptyline in depressed adolescents using a 'fixed plasma level' design. *Psychopharmacology Bulletin*, **26**, 85−90.

Gittelman R. (1986) Childhood anxiety disorders: Correlates and outcome. In: Gittelman R. (ed) *Anxiety Disorders of Childhood*, pp. 101−125. Guilford Press, New York.

Gittelman R. & Klein D.F. (1984) Relationship between separation anxiety and panic and agoraphobic disorders. *Psychopathology*, **17**, 56−65.

Gittelman R. & Klein D.F. (1985) Childhood separation anxiety and adult agoraphobia. In: Tuma A.H. & Maser J.D. (eds) *Anxiety and the Anxiety Disorders*, pp. 389−402. Laurence Erlbaum, Hillsdale, NJ.

Gittelman R. & Koplewicz H.S. (1986) Pharmacotherapy of childhood anxiety disorders. In: Gittelman R. (ed) *Anxiety Disorders of Childhood*, pp. 188−203. Guilford Press, New York.

Gittelman R., Mannuzza S., Shenker R. & Bonagura N. (1985) Hyperactive boys almost grown-up: I. Psychiatric status. *Archives of General Psychiatry*, **42**, 937−947.

Gittelman-Klein R. (1978) Psychopharmacological treatment of anxiety disorders, mood disorders, and Tourette's disorder in children. In: Lipton M.A., DiMascio A. & Killam K.F. (eds) *Psycho-*

pharmacology: A Generation of Progress, pp. 1471−1480. Raven Press, New York.

Gittelman-Klein R. & Klein D.F. (1971) Controlled imipramine treatment of school phobia. Archives of General Psychiatry, **25**, 204−207.

Gittelman-Klein R. & Klein D.F. (1973) School phobia: diagnostic considerations in the light of imipramine effects. *Journal Nervous and Mental Disease* **156**, 199−215.

Gittelman-Klein R. & Klein D.F. (1980) Separation anxiety in school refusal and its treatment with drugs. In: Hersov L. & Berg I. (eds) *Out of School*, pp. 321−341. John Wiley, London.

Goodyer I., Germany E., Gowrusankur J. & Altham P. (1991) Social influences on the course of anxious and depressive disorders in school-age children. *British Journal of Psychiatry*, **158**, 676−684.

Gray J.A. (1982) *The Neuropsychology of Anxiety: An Enquiry into the Functions of the Septo-hippocampal System*. Oxford University Press, New York.

Gray J.A. (1987) *The Psychology of Fear and Stress*, 2nd edn. Cambridge University Press, Cambridge.

Gullone E. & King N.J. (1992) Psychometric evaluation of a revised fear schedule for children and adolescents. *Journal of Child Psychology and Psychiatry*, **33**, 987−998.

Hammen C., Burge D., Burney E. & Adrian C. (1990) Longitudinal study of diagnoses in children of women with unipolar and bipolar affective disorder. *Archives of General Psychiatry*, **47**, 1112−1117.

Harrington R., Fudge H., Rutter M., Pickles A. & Hill A. (1990) Adult outcomes of childhood and adolescent depression. I. Psychiatric status. *Archives of General Psychiatry*, **47**, 465−473.

Herjanic B. & Reich W. (1982) Development of a structured psychiatric interview for children: agreement between child and parent on individual symptoms. *Journal of Abnormal Child Psychology*, **10**, 307−324.

Hershberg S.G., Carlson G.A., Cantwell D.P. & Strober M. (1982) Anxiety and depressive disorders in psychiatrically disturbed children. *Journal of Clinical Psychiatry*, **43**, 358−361.

Herskowitz J. (1986) Neurologic presentations of panic disorder in childhood and adolescence. *Developmental Medicine and Child Neurology*, **28**, 617−623.

Hersov L. (1985) Emotional disorders. In: Rutter M. & Hersov L. (eds) *Child and Adolescent Psychiatry. Modern Approaches*, 2nd edn, pp. 368−381. Blackwell Scientific Publications, London.

Higley J.D., Suomi S.J. & Delizio R.D. (1984) Continuity of social separation behaviors from infancy to adolescence. Paper presented at the seventh meeting of the American Society of Primatologists, Arcata, CA. August 1984 (Quoted in Suomi S.J., 1986.)

Hodges K., Kline J., Stern L., Cytryn L. & McKnew D. (1982a) The development of a child assessment interview for research and clinical use. *Journal of Abnormal Child Psychology*, **10**, 173−189.

Hirshfeld D.R., Rosenbaum J.F., Biederman J., Bolduc E.A., Faraone S.V., Snidman N., Reznick J.S. & Kagan J. (1992) Stable behavioral inhibition and its association with anxiety disorder. *Journal of the American Academy of Child and Adolescent Psychiatry*, **31**, 103−111.

Hodges K., McKnew D., Cytryn L., Stern L. & Kline J. (1982b) The Child Assessment Schedule (CAS) diagnostic interview: a report on reliability and validity. *Journal of the American Academy of Child Psychiatry*, **21**, 468−473.

Hodges K., McKnew D., Burbach D.J. & Roebuck L. (1987) Diagnostic concordance between the Child Assessment Schedule (CAS) and the Schedule for Affective Disorders and Schizophrenia for school-age Children (K-SADS) in an outpatient sample using lay interviewers. *Journal of the American Academy of Child and Adolescent Psychiatry*, **26**, 654−661.

Hodges K., Cools J. & Mcknew D. (1989) Test-retest reliability of a clinical research interview for children: the child assessment schedule. *Journal of Consulting and Clinical Psychology*, **1**, 317–322.

Izard C.E. & Blumberg S.H. (1985) Emotion theory and the role of emotions in anxiety in children and adults. In: Tuma A.H. & Maser J.D. (eds) *Anxiety and the Anxiety Disorders*, pp. 109–129. Erlbaum Associates, Hillsdale, NJ.

Jersild A.T. & Holmes F.G. (1935) Children's fears. *Child Development Monographs*, no 20, pp. 1–358.

Kagan J. (1974) Discrepancy, temperament and infant distress. In: Lewis M. & Rosenblum L.A. (eds) *The Origins of Fear*, pp. 229–248. Wiley, New York.

Kagan J., Reznick J.S., Clarke C. & Snidman N. (1984) Behavioral inhibition to the unfamiliar. *Child Development*, **55**, 2212–2225.

Kagan J., Reznick J.S. & Snidman N. (1987) The physiology and psychology of behavioral inhibition in children. *Child Development*, **58**, 1459–1473.

Kagan J., Reznick J.S. & Snidman N. (1988) Biological bases of childhood shyness. *Science*, **240**, 167–171.

Kane M.T. & Kendall P.C. (1989) Anxiety disorders in children: a multiple-baseline evaluation of a cognitive-behavioral treatment. *Behavioral Therapy*, **20**, 499–508.

Kashani J.H. & Orvaschel H. (1988) Anxiety disorders in mid-adolescence: a community sample. *American Journal of Psychiatry*, **145**, 960–964.

Kashani J.H., Niels C.B., Hoeper E.W., Fallahi C., Corcoran C.M., McAllister J.A., Rosenberg T.K. & Reid J.C. (1987) Psychiatric disorders in a community sample of adolescents. *American Journal of Psychiatry*, **144**, 584–589.

Kendall P.C. & Chansky T.E. (1991) Considering cognition in anxiety-disordered children. *Journal of Anxiety Disorders*, **5**, 167–185.

Kendall P.C., Howard B.L. & Epps J. (1988) The anxious child: cognitive-behavioral treatment strategies. *Behavioral Modification*, **12**, 281–310.

Kendler K.S., Neale M.C., Kessler R.C., Heath A.C. & Eaves L.J. (1992) Generalized anxiety disorder in women. A population-based twin study. *Archives of General Psychiatry*, **49**, 267–272.

Klein D.F. (1964) Delineation of two drug-responsive anxiety syndromes. *Psychopharmacologia*, **5**, 397–408.

Klein D.F. (1978) A proposed definition of mental illness. In: Spitzer R.L. & Klein D.F. (eds) *Critical Issues in Psychiatric Diagnosis*, pp. 41–71. Raven Press, New York.

Klein D.F. (1981) Anxiety reconceptualized. In: Klein D.F. & Rabkin J.G. (eds) *Anxiety: New Research and Changing Concepts*, pp. 235–262. Raven Press, New York.

Klein R.G. (1988) Childhood anxiety disorders. In: Kestenbaum C.J. & Williams D.T. (eds) *Clinical Assessment of Children and Adolescents*, pp. 722–742. New York University Press, New York.

Klein R.G. (1990) Prospective follow-up of childhood disorders: Separation anxiety disorder. Paper presented at the seventh Conference on Recent Advances in Psychiatry, Rouffach, France, September 28, 1990.

Klein R.G. (1991) Parent–child agreement in clinical assessment of anxiety and other psychopathology: a review. *Journal of Anxiety Disorders*, **5**, 187–198.

Klein R.G. & Klein D.F. (1988) Adult anxiety disorders and childhood separation anxiety. In: Roth M., Noyes R. & Burrows G.D. (eds) *Handbook of Anxiety. Vol. I. Biological, Clinical and Cultural Perspectives*, pp. 213–229. Elsevier Science Publishers, Amsterdam.

Klein R.G. & Last C.G. (1989) *Anxiety Disorders in Children*. Sage Publications, Newbury Park, CA.

Klein R.G. & Mannuzza S. (1990) Psychiatric family history in ADHD. Paper presented at the Annual Meeting of the American Academy of Child and Adolescent Psychiatry, Chicago, IL, October 24–28, 1990.

Klein R.G. & Mannuzza S. (1991a) Retrospective self-reports of child-

hood separation anxiety and ADHD. Paper presented at the Annual Meeting of the American Academy of Child and Adolescent Psychiatry, San Francisco, CA, October 16–20, 1991.

Klein R.G. & Mannuzza S. (1991b) Long-term outcome of hyperactive children: a review. *Journal of the American Academy of Child and Adolescent Psychiatry*, **30**, 383–387.

Klein D.F., Mannuzza S., Chapman T. & Fyer A.J. (1992a) Child panic revisited. *Journal of the American Academy of Child and Adolescent Psychiatry*, **31**, 112–114.

Klein R.G., Koplewicz H.S. & Kanner A. (1992b) Imipramine treatment of children with separation anxiety disorder. *Journal of the American Academy of Child and Adolescent Psychiatry*, **31**, 21–28.

Kovacs M. (1985) The Interview Schedule for Children (ISC). *Psychopharmacology Bulletin* **21**, 991–994.

Kovacs M., Gatsonis C., Paulauskas S. & Richards C. (1989) Depressive disorders in childhood. IV. A longitudinal study of comorbidity with a risk for anxiety disorders. *Archives of General Psychiatry*, **46**, 776–782.

Kutcher S., Reiter S., Gardner D. & Klein R.G. (1992) The pharmacotherapy of anxiety disorders in children and adolescents. *Psychiatric Clinics of North America*, **15**, 41–67.

Lachar D. (1982) *Personality Inventory for Children (PIC) Revised Format Manual Supplement*. Western Psychological Services, Los Angeles, CA.

LaGreca A.M., Dandes S.K., Nick P., Shaw K. & Stone W.L. (1988) Development of the Social Anxiety Scale for children: reliability and concurrent validity. *Journal of Clinical Child Psychology*, **17**, 84–91.

LaGreca A.M. & Stone W. (1993) Social anxiety scale for children — revised: factor structure and concurrent validity. *Journal of Clinical Child Psychology*, **22**, 17–27.

Last C.G. & Strauss C.C. (1989) Panic disorder in children and adolescents. *Journal of Anxiety Disorders*, **3**, 87–95.

Last C.G., Hersen M., Kazdin A.E., Finkelstein R. & Strauss C.C. (1987a) Comparison of DSM-III separation anxiety and overanxious disorders: demographic characteristics and patterns of comorbidity. *Journal of the American Academy of Child and Adolescent Psychiatry*, **26**, 527–531.

Last C.G., Hersen M., Kazdin A.E., Francis G. & Grubb H.J. (1987b) Psychiatric illness in the mothers of anxious children. *American Journal of Psychiatry*, **144**, 1580–1583.

Last C.G., Strauss C.C. & Francis G. (1987c) Comorbidity among childhood anxiety disorders. *Journal of Nervous and Mental Disease*, **175**, 726–730.

Last C.G., Hersen M., Kazdin A., Orvaschel H. & Perrin S. (1991) Anxiety disorders in children and their families. *Archives of General Psychiatry*, **48**, 928–934.

Last C.G., Perrin S., Hersen M. & Kazdin A.E. (1992) DSM-III-R anxiety disorders in children: sociodemographic and clinical characteristics *Journal of the American Academy of Child and Adolescent Psychiatry*, **31**, 1070–1076.

Lewis M. (1986) Principles of intensive individual psychoanalytic psychotherapy for childhood anxiety disorders. In: Gittelman R. (ed) *Anxiety Disorders of Childhood*, pp. 233–255. Guilford Press, New York.

Lewis M. & Brooks J. (1974) Self, other, and fear: infants' reactions to people. In: Lewis M. & Rosenblum L.A. (eds) *The Origins of Behavior: The Origins of Fear*, vol. 2. Wiley, New York.

Livingston R., Nugent H., Rader L. & Smith G.R. (1985) Family histories of depressed and severely anxious children. *American Journal of Psychiatry*, **142**, 1497–1499.

Livingston R.L., Dykman R.A. & Ackerman P.T. (1990) The frequency and significance of additional self-reported psychiatric diagnoses in children with attention deficit disorder. *Journal of Abnormal Child*

Psychology, **18**, 465–478.

Macaulay J.L. & Kleinknecht R.A (1989) Panic and panic attacks in adolescents. *Journal of Anxiety Disorders*, **3**, 221–241.

McClellan J.M., Rubert M.P., Reichler R.J. & Sylvester C.E. (1990) Attention deficit disorder in children at risk for anxiety and depression. *Journal of the American Academy of Child and Adolescent Psychiatry*, **29**, 534–539.

McGee R., Feehan M., Williams S., Partridge F., Silva P.A. & Kelly J. (1990) DSM-III disorders in a large sample of adolescents. *Journal of the American Academy of Child and Adolescent Psychiatry*, **29**, 611–619.

McGee R., Feehan M., Williams S. & Anderson J. (1992) DSM-III disorders from age 11 to age 15. *Journal of the American Academy of Child and Adolescent Psychiatry*, **31**, 50–59.

Mannuza S. & Gittelman R. (1984) The adolescent outcome of hyperactive girls. *Psychiatry Research*, **13**, 19–29.

Mannuzza S., Klein R.G. & Addalli K.A. (1991a) Young adult mental status of hyperactive boys and their brothers: a prospective follow-up study. *Journal of the American Academy of Child and Adolescent Psychiatry*, **30**, 383–387.

Mannuzza S., Klein R.G., Bonagura N., Malloy P., Giampino T.L. & Addalli K.A. (1991b) Hyperactive boys almost grown up: V. Replication of psychiatric status. *Archives of General Psychiatry*, **48**, 77–83.

Mannuzza S., Klein R.G., Bessler A., Malloy P. & LaPadula M. (1993) Adult outcome of hyperactive boys: I. Educational achievement occupational rank, and psychiatric status. *Archives of General Psychiatry*, **50**, 565–576.

Marks I.M. (1969) *Fears and Phobias*. American Press, New York.

Marks I. (1987) The development of normal fear: a review. *Journal of Child Psychology and Psychiatry*, **28**, 667–697.

Marks I.M. & Gelder M.G. (1966) Different ages of onset in varieties of phobia. *American Journal of Psychiatry*, **123**, 218–221.

Maurer A. (1965) What children fear. *Journal of Genetic Psychology*. **106**, 265–277.

Mezzich A.C., Mezzich J.E. & Coffman G.A. (1985) Reliability of DSM-III vs. DSM-II in child psychopathology. *Journal of the American Academy of Child Psychiatry*, **24**, 273–280.

Miller L.C., Barrett C.L., Hampe E. & Noble H. (1971) Revised anxiety scales for the Louisville Behavior Check List. *Psychological Report*, **29**, 503–511.

Miller L.C., Barrett C.L., Hampe E. & Noble H. (1972) Factor structure of childhood fears. *Journal of Consultory and Clinical Psychology*, **39**, 264–268.

Moreau D.L., Weissman M. & Warner V. (1989) Panic disorder in children at high risk for depression. *American Journal of Psychiatry*, **146**, 1059–1060.

Morris R.J. & Kratochwill T.R. (1983) *Treating Children's Fears and Phobias*. Pergamon Press, New York.

Mowrer O.H. (1939) Stimulus response theory of anxiety. *Psychological Review*, **46**, 553–565.

Mowrer O.H. (1960) *Learning Theory and Behavior*. John Wiley, New York.

Mufson L., Weissman M.M. & Warner V. (1992) Depression and anxiety in parents and children: a direct interview study. *Journal of Anxiety Disorders*, **6**, 1–13.

Munir K., Biederman J. & Knee D. (1987) Psychiatric comorbidity in patients with attention deficit disorder: a controlled study. *Journal of the American Academy of Child and Adolescent Psychiatry*, **26**, 844–848.

Murphy E.A. (1964) One cause? Many causes? The argument from the bimodal distribution. *Journal of Chronic Diseases*, **17**, 301–324.

National Institute of Mental Health. (1991) *The NIMH Diagnostic Interview Schedule for Children*. National Institute of Mental Health, Rockville, MD.

Nelles W.B. & Barlow D.H. (1988) Do children panic? *Clinics in*

Psychological Review, **8**, 359–372.

Noyes R. Jr, Clarkson C., Crowe R.R., Yates W.R. & McChesney C.M. (1987) A family study of generalized anxiety disorder. *American Journal of Psychiatry*, **144**, 1019–1024.

Noyes R. Jr, Christiansen J., Clancy J., Garvey M.J., Suelzer M. & Anderson D.J. (1991) Predictors of serious suicide attempts among patients with panic disorder. *Comprehensive Psychiatry*, **32**, 261–267.

Ollendick T.H. (1983a) Reliability and validity of the revised Fear Survey Schedule for Children (FSSC-R). *Behavioral Research Therapy*, **21**, 685–692.

Ollendick T.H. (1983b) Anxiety-based disorders. In: Hersen M. (ed) *The Practice of Outpatient Behavior Therapy: A Clinician's Handbook*, pp. 273–305. Plenum Press, New York.

Ollendick T.H., Matson J.L. & Helsel W.J. (1985) Fears in children and adolescents: normative data. *Behavioral Research Therapy*, **23**, 465–467.

Orvaschel H., Walsh-Allis G. & Ye W. (1988) Psychopathology in children of parents with recurrent depression. *Journal of Abnormal Child Psychology*, **16**, 17–28.

Öst L.-G. (1987) Age of onset in different phobias. *Journal of Abnormal Psychology*, **96**, 223–229.

Pavlov I.P. (1927) *Conditioned Reflexes*. Oxford Press, London.

Perrin S. & Last C.G. (1992) Do childhood anxiety measures measure anxiety? *Journal of Abnormal Psychology*, **20**, 567–578.

Pfefferbaum B., Overall J.E., Boren H.A., Frankel L.S., Sullivan M.P. & Johnson K. (1987) Alprazolam in the treatment of anticipatory and acute situational anxiety in children with cancer. *Journal of the American Academy of Child and Adolescent Psychiatry*, **26**, 532–535.

Pliszka S.R. (1989) Effect of anxiety on cognition, behavior, and stimulant response in ADHD. *Journal of the American Academy of Child and Adolescent Psychiatry*, **26**, 532–535.

Pliszka S.R. (1989) Effect of anxiety on cognition, behavior and stimulant response in ADHD. *Journal of the American Academy of Child and Adolescent Psychiatry*, **28**, 882–887.

Plomin R. & Rowe D.C. (1979) Genetic and environmental etiology of social behavior in infancy. *Developmental Psychology*, **15**, 62–72.

Puig-Antich J. & Rabinovich H. (1986) Relationship between affective and anxiety disorders in childhood. In: Gittelman R. (ed) *Anxiety Disorders of Childhood* pp. 136–156. Guilford Press, New York.

Reich W., Shayka J.J. & Taibleson C. (1992a) Diagnostic Interview for Children and Adolescents (DICA-R-A): adolescent version: DSM-III-R version. Washington University, St. Louis, MO.

Reich W., Shayka J.J. & Taibleson C. (1992b) Diagnostic Interview for Children and Adolescents (DICA-R-C): child version: DSM-III-R version.

Rey J.M., Plapp J.M. & Stewart G.W. (1989) Reliability of psychiatric diagnosis in referred adolescents. *Journal of Child Psychology and Psychiatry*, **30**, 879–888.

Reynolds C.R. (1980) Concurrent validity of what I think and feel: the revised Children's Manifest Anxiety Scale. *Journal of Consultory and Clinical Psychology*, **48**, 774–775.

Reynolds C.R. & Richmond B.O. (1978) What I think and feel: a revised measure of children's manifest anxiety. *Journal of Abnormal Child Psychology*, **6**, 271–280.

Reynolds C.R. & Richmond B.O. (1979) Factor structure and construct validity of 'What I think and feel': the revised Children's Manifest Anxiety Scale. *Journal of Personality Assessment*, **43**, 281–283.

Reynolds C.R. & Richmond B.O. (1985) *Revised Children's Manifest Anxiety Scale: Manual*. Western Psychological Services, Los Angeles, CA.

Reznick J.S., Kagan J., Snidman N., Gersten M., Bask K. & Rosenberg A. (1986) Inhibited and uninhibited children: a follow-up study. *Child Development*, **57**, 660–680.

Ricciuti H.N. (1974) Fear and the development of social attachments in the first year of life. In: Lewis M. & Rosenblum L.A. (eds) *The Origins of Fear*, pp. 73–106. Wiley, New York.

Roberts M. (1975) Persistent school refusal among children and adolescents. In: Wirt R.D., Winokur G. & Roff M. (eds) *Life History Research in Psychopathology*, vol. 4, pp. 79–108. University of Minnesota Press, Minneapolis.

Roberts N., Vargo B. & Ferguson H.B. (1989) Measurement of anxiety and depression in children and adolescents. *Psychiatric Clinics of North America*, **12**, 837–861.

Rodriguez A., Rodriguez M. & Eisenberg L. (1959) The Outcome of school phobia: a follow-up study based on 41 cases. *American Journal of Psychiatry*, **116**, 540–544.

Rosenbaum J.F., Biederman J., Gersten M., Hirshfeld D.R., Meminger S.R., Herman J.B., Kagan J., Reznick J.S. & Snidman N. (1988) Behavioral inhibition in children of parents with panic disorder and agoraphobia. *Archives of General Psychiatry*, **45** 463–470.

Rosenbaum J.F., Biederman J., Hirshfeld D.R., Bolduc E.A., Faraone S.V., Kagan J., Snidman N. & Reznick J.S. (1991) Further evidence of an association between behavioral inhibition and anxiety disorders: results from a family study of children from a non-clinical sample. *Journal of Psychiatric Research*, **25**, 49–65.

Rutter M. (1988) Epidemiological approaches to developmental psychopathology. *Archives of General Psychiatry*, **45**, 486–495.

Rutter M. & Gould M. (1985) Classification. In: Rutter M. & Hersov L. (eds) *Child and Adolescent Psychiatry. Modern Approaches, 2nd edn*, pp. 304–321. Blackwell Scientific Publications, London.

Rutter M. & Shaffer D. (1980) DSM-III: a step forward or back in terms of the classification of child psychiatric disorders? *Journal of the Academy of Child and Adolescent Psychiatry*, **19**, 371–394.

Rutter M., Lebovici S., Eisenberg L., Sneznevskij A.V., Sadoun R., Brooke E. & Lin T.-Y. (1969) A tri-axial classification of mental disorders in childhood: an international study. *Journal of Child Psychology and Psychiatry*, **10**, 41–61.

Ryan N.D., Puig-Antich J., Cooper T., Rabinovich H., Ambrosini P., Davies M., King J., Torres D. & Fried J. (1986) Imipramine in adolescent major depression: plasma level and clinical response. *Acta Psychiatrica Scandinavica*, **73**, 275–288.

Saylor C.F., Finch A.J. Jr, Spirito A. & Bennett B. (1984) The Children's Depression Inventory: a systematic evaluation of psychometric properties. *Journal of Consulting and Clinical Psychology* **52**, 955–967.

Schaffer H.R. & Emerson P.E. (1964) The development of social attachments in infancy. *Monographs of the Society for Research in Child Development* **29**, 1–77 (3, serial no 94).

Scherer M.W. & Nakamura C.Y. (1968) A Fear Survey Schedule for Children (FSS-FC): a factor analytic comparison with manifest anxiety (CMAS). *Behavioral Research Therapy*, **6**, 173–182.

Seligman M.E.P. & Hager J.L (1972) *Biological Boundaries of Learning*. Prentice-Hall, Englewood Cliffs, NJ.

Shaffer D. (1986) Learning theories of anxiety. In: Gittelman R. (ed) *Anxiety Disorders of Childhood*, pp. 157–167. Guilford Press, New York.

Shaywitz S.E., Escobar M.D., Shaywitz B.A., Fletcher J.M. & Makuch R. (1992) Evidence that dyslexia may represent the lower tail of a normal distribution of reading ability. *New England Journal of Medicine*, **326**, 145–150.

Shekim W.O., Kashani J., Beck N., Cantwell D.P., Martin J., Rosenberg J. & Costello A. (1985) The prevalence of attention deficit disorders in a rural midwestern community sample of nine-year-old children. *Journal of American Academy of Child Psychiatry*, **24**, 765–770.

Siegel L.J. & Ridley-Johnson R. (1985) Anxiety disorders of childhood and adolescence. In: Bornstein P.H. & Kazdin A.E. (eds) *Handbook of Clinical Behavior Therapy with Children*, pp. 266–308. Dorsey Press, Homewood, IL.

Silverman W.K. (1991) Diagnostic reliability of anxiety disorders in children using structured interviews. *Journal of Anxiety Disorders*, **5**, 105–124.

Silverman W.K. & Nelles W.B. (1988) The Anxiety Disorders Interview Schedule for children. *Journal of the American Academy of Child and Adolescent Psychiatry*, **27**, 772–778.

Silverman W.K., Cerny J.A., Nelles W.B. & Burke A.E. (1988) Behavior problems in children of parents with anxiety disorders. *Journal of the American Academy of Child and Adolescent Psychiatry*, **27**, 779–784.

Simeon J.G. & Ferguson H.B. (1987) Alprazolam effects in children with anxiety disorders. *Canadian Journal of Psychiatry*, **32**, 570–574.

Simeon J.G., Ferguson H.B., Knott V., Roberts N., Gauthier B., Dubois C. & Wiggins D. Clinical, cognitive and neurophysiological effects of alprazolam in children and adolescents with overanxious and avoidant disorders. *Journal of the American Academy of Child and Adolescent Psychiatry*, **31**, 29–33.

Spielberger C.D. (1973) *State-Trait Anxiety Inventory for Children*. Consulting Psychologists Press, Palo Alto, CA.

Spielberger C.D., Gorsuch R.L. & Lushene R.E. (1970) *STAI Manual for the State-Trait Anxiety Inventory*. Consulting Psychologists Press, Palo Alto, CA.

Sroufe L.A., Waters E. & Matas L. (1974) Contextual determinants of infant affective response. In: Lewis M. & Rosenblum L.A. (eds) *The Origins of Fear*, pp. 49–72. John Wiley, New York.

Stayton D.J. & Ainsworth M.D.S. (1973) Individual differences in infant responses to brief everyday separations as related to other infant and maternal behaviors. *Developmental Psychology*, **9**, 226–235.

Stevenson J., Batten N. & Cherner M. (1992) Fears and fearfulness in children and adolescents: a genetic analysis of twin data. *Journal of Child Psychology and Psychiatry*, **33**, 977–985.

Strauss C.C., Last C.G., Hersen M. & Kazdin A.E. (1988) Association between anxiety and depression in children and adolescents with anxiety disorders. *Journal of Abnormal Psychology*, **16**, 57–68.

Strober M., Green J. & Carlson G. (1981) Reliability of psychiatric diagnosis in hospitalized adolescents. *Archives of General Psychiatry*, **38**, 141–145.

Suomi S.J. (1986) Anxiety-like disorders in young nonhuman primates. In: Gittelman R. (ed) *Anxiety Disorders of Childhood*, pp. 1–23. Guilford Press, New York.

Suomi S.J. (1987) Genetic and maternal contributions to individual differences in rhesus monkey behavioral development. In: Krasnegor N.A., Blass E.M., Hofer M.A. & Smotherman W.P. (eds) *Perinatal Development*, pp. 397–419. Academic Press, New York.

Sylvester C.E., Hyde T.S. & Reichler R.J. (1988) Clinical psychopathology among children of adults with panic disorder. In: Dunner D.L., Gershon E.S. & Barrett J.E. (eds) *Relatives at Risk for Mental Disorder*, pp. 87–102. Raven Press, New York.

Taylor J.A. (1953) A personality scale of manifest anxiety. *Journal of Abnormal Social Psychology*, **48**, 285–290.

Thyer B.A., Nesse R.M., Cameron O.G. & Curtis G.C. (1985) Agoraphobia: a test of the separation anxiety hypothesis. *Behavioral Research Therapy*, **23**, 75–78.

Thyer B.A., Nesse R.M., Curtis G.E. & Cameron O.G. (1986) Panic disorder: a test of the separation anxiety hypothesis. *Behavioral Research Therapy*, **24**, 209–211.

Torgersen S. (1983) Genetic factors in anxiety disorders. *Archives of General Psychiatry*, **40**, 1085–1089.

Torgersen S. (1990) Genetics of anxiety and its clinical implications. In: Burrows G.D., Roth M. & Noyes R. Jr. (eds) *Handbook of Anxiety*, vol. 3: *Neurobiology of Anxiety*, pp. 381–406. Elsevier Science Publishers, Holland.

Turner S.M., Beidel D.C. & Costello A. (1987) Psychopathology in the offspring of anxiety disorders patients. *Journal of Consulting and Clinical Psychology*, **55**, 229–235.

Van der Molen G.M., Van den Hout M.A., Van Dieren A.C. & Griez E. (1989) Childhood separation anxiety and adult-onset panic disorders. *Journal of Anxiety Disorders*, **3**, 97–106.

Velez C.N., Johnson J. & Cohen P. (1989) A longitudinal analysis of selected risk factors for childhood psychopathology. *Journal of the American Academy of Child and Adolescent Psychiatry*, **28**, 861–864.

Vitiello B., Behar D., Wolfson S. & McLeer S.V. (1990) Diagnosis of panic disorder in prepubertal children. *Journal of the American Academy of Child and Adolescent Psychiatry*, **29**, 782–784.

Waldron S. (1976) The significance of childhood neurosis for adult mental health: a follow-up study. *American Journal of Psychiatry*, **133**, 532–538.

Warren W. (1965) A study of adolescent psychiatric inpatients and the outcome six or more years later. I. Clinical histories and hospital findings. *Journal of Child Psychology and Psychiatry*, **6**, 1–17.

Watson D. & Friend M. (1969) Measurement of social-evaluative anxiety. *Journal of Consulting and Clinical Psychology*, **33**, 448–457.

Weiss M. & Burke A. (1970) A 5- to 10-year follow-up of hospitalized school phobic children and adolescents. *American Journal of Ortho-Psychiatry*, **40**, 672–676.

Weiss G., Hechtman L.T., Milroy T. & Perlman T. (1985) Psychiatric status of hyperactives as adults: a controlled prospective 15-year follow-up of 63 hyperactive children. *Journal of the American Academy of Child Psychiatry*, **24**, 211–220.

Weissman M.M., Leckman J.F., Merikangas K.R., Gammon G.D. & Prusoff B.A. (1984a) Depression and anxiety disorders in parents and children. *Archives of General Psychiatry*, **41**, 845–852.

Weissman M.M., Prusoff B.A., Gammon G.D., Merikangas K.R., Leckman J.F. & Kidd K.K. (1984b) Psychopathology in the children (ages 6–18) of depressed and normal parents. *Journal of the American Academy of Child Psychiatry*, **23**, 78–84.

Weissman M.M., Gammon G.D., John K., Merikangas K.R., Warner V., Prusoff B.A. & Sholomskas D. (1987) Children of depressed parents. *Archives of General Psychiatry*, **44**, 847–853.

Weissman M.M., Warner V. & Fendrich M. (1990) Applying impair-ment criteria to children's psychiatric diagnosis. *Journal of the American Academy of Child and Adolescent Psychiatry*, **29**, 789–795.

Weissman M.M., Fendrich M., Warner V. & Wickramaratne P. (1992) Incidence of psychiatric disorder in offspring at high and low risk for depression. *Journal of the American Academy of Child and Adolescent Psychiatry*, **31**, 640–648.

Welner Z., Reich W., Herjanic B., Jung K.G. & Amado H. (1987) Reliability, validity, and parent–child agreement studies of the Diagnostic Interview for Children and Adolescents (DICA). *Journal of the American Academy of Child and Adolescent Psychiatry*, **26**, 649–653.

Werry J.S. (1991) Overanxious disorder: a review of its taxonomic properties. *Journal of the American Academy of Child and Adolescent Psychiatry*, **30**, 533–544.

Werry J.S., Methven R.J., Fitzpatrick J. & Dixon H. (1983a) The DSM-III diagnoses of New Zealand children. In: Spitzer R.L., Williams J.B.W. & Skodol A.E. (eds) *International Perspectives on DSM-III*, pp. 291–307. American Psychiatric Press, Washington, DC.

Werry J.S., Methven R.J., Fitzpatrick J. & Dixon H. (1983b) the interrater reliability of DSM III in children. *Journal of Abnormal Child Psychology*, **11**, 341–354.

Werry J.S., Reeves J.C. & Elkind G.S. (1987) Attention deficit, conduct, oppositional, and anxiety disorders in children: I. A review of research on differentiating characteristics. *Journal of the American Academy of Child and Adolescent Psychiatry*, **26**, 133–143.

World Health Organization (1989) *International Classification of Diseases*, 10th revision: draft of chapter 5: Mental, behavioral and developmental disorders: diagnostic criteria for research. WHO, Geneva.

Wisniewski J.J., Genshaft J.L., Mulick J.A. & Coury D.L. (1987) Test-retest reliability of the Revised Children's Manifest Anxiety Scale. *Perceptual and Motor Skills*, **65**, 67–70.

Wolpe J. & Lang P.J. (1964) A fear survey schedule for use in behavior therapy. *Behavioral Research Therapy*, **2**, 27–30.

Yeragani V.K., Meiri P.C., Balon R., Patel H. & Pohl R. (1989) History of separation anxiety in patients with panic disorder and depression and normal controls. *Acta Psychiatrica Scandinavica*, **79**, 550–556.

Chapter 21
Adjustment Disorders

Peter D. Hill

The concept of a group of childhood psychiatric disorders, separately recognizable as a response to identifiable adverse circumstances, has a long history that reflects the development of ideas through the whole of 20th century psychiatry. The strong influence of psychodynamic theory on the child guidance and mental hygiene movements in the first half of the century created an early appreciation of the role of stressful life circumstances and events upon psychological health, particularly through the effects of personal experience on the development of the mind. Subsequently the psychobiological approach of Adolf Meyer (1866–1950) emphasized the use of a life chart in assessing the impact of life events and life changes in the aetiology of psychiatric disorder, especially when conceptualized as failed adaptation. The experience of military psychiatrists in the Second World War lent strength to the notion that emotional pathology or deviant behaviour could be precipitated by combat stress and the concept of a category of psychiatric disorder which was primarily a reaction to stress and social adversity was well-established by the postwar period. The dominant metaphor for understanding the relation of psychological dysfunction to stressors throughout the 1950s was psychoanalytic, a model that incorporated its own ideas of personal development. Certain aspects of psychological development were associated with intrapsychic conflict which itself required adaptation and this could be maladaptive so that personal growth came to be seen as an additional source of stress-related disorder. Adjustment as a dynamic process precipitated by psychosocial stressors, external and internal, could be perverse.

The subsequent partial eclipse of psychoanalysis by empirical science did nothing to weaken the idea that psychosocial adversity might be a potent contributor to the causes of psychiatric disorder. Indeed, if anything there was an extension to a more specifically social model and the general assumption that acute and chronic social stressors associated with relationships, life circumstances and specific experiences are of powerful aetiological importance for child and adolescent psychiatric disorder, as has subsequently been amply buttressed by empirical findings (see Chapter 12; Cox, 1992, Hill, 1992).

Coupled with such an approach that emphasized an interaction between social stressors and maladaptive responses was, during the years following the Second World War, a general reluctance to apply categorical psychiatric diagnoses, especially to the young (for example, see review by Weiner, 1982). This was a phenomenon that was particularly marked in the US where the largely equivalent diagnostic terms of adjustment reaction or transient situational (personality) disturbance, terms used in DSM-I and II, were the commonest diagnoses in American child psychiatric practice at that time (Rosen *et al.*, 1964). Part of the reason for this was their nonspecificity, part because of a belief that disturbances of behaviour and emotion in the young were brief, not serious and could be easily related either to observable stressors or inferred developmental turmoil, especially in adolescence (Weiner and Del Gaudio, 1976).

Thus, DSM-I (American Psychiatric Association, 1952) provided only two categories of childhood psychiatric disorder: adjustment reaction and childhood schizophrenia. Adjustment reaction, subcategorized by age group and separated from gross stress reaction, was included under the general heading of transient personality disorder. In contrast to gross stress reaction (a diagnosis only to be made for reactions to extreme physical or emotional stressors), adjustment reactions were 'superficial maladjustments' to 'difficult situations or newly experienced environmental factors' when no 'underlying personality defects or chronic patterns' were clinically evident.

An early recognition that the hedonic quality of a reaction is no guide to its status as healthy or unhealthy was illustrated by the Group for the Advancement of Psychiatry's (1966) proposal of a category of healthy responses which would include emotional and behavioural reactions to stress (such as anxiety caused by separation from an attachment figure in infancy). These might initially appear abnormal but are actually normal. This concept was not subsequently developed in DSM-II (American Psychiatric Association, 1968) but the diagnostic category of adjustment reaction was preserved under an altered general heading of transient situational disturbance (rather than disorder). The term was to be applied to 'transient disorders of any severity (including those of psychotic proportions) that occur in individuals without any apparent underlying mental disorders and that represent an acute reaction to overwhelming environmental stress'.

If symptoms persisted after the identified stressor was removed, another psychiatric diagnosis was to be made. The diagnosis continued to be popular with American child and adolescent psychiatrists (Cerreto and Tuma, 1977), although Fard *et al.* (1979) criticized its over-inclusive and vague application in the practice of adolescent psychiatry. In DSM-III (American Psychiatric Association, 1980), the term adjustment *disorder* first appeared and was subcategorized by symptom rather than by age group, an approach preserved in DSM-III-R (American Psychiatric Association, 1987). The third editions of the manual introduced changes in criteria that represented significant conceptual shifts. Thus, the maladaptive reaction ('impairment in social or occupational functioning or symptoms that are in excess of a normal and expected reaction') had to occur within 3 months of the onset of the identified stressor and persist no longer than 6 months after exposure to it, identical limits being applied for adults and children. The diagnosis could not represent an exacerbation of another mental disorder. The symptomatic subcategorization reflected a stated notion that the clinical subtypes are 'partial syndromes of specific disorders'. In other words, adjustment disorder with depressed mood, the full diagnostic criteria for major depression would not be met. Psychotic reactions could not now be included. Axis IV allowed the severity of the psychosocial stress to be quantified.

Very similar principles apply to the draft version of DSM-IV (*American Psychiatric Association*, in press). The idea of maladaptive reaction is replaced by the simpler 'emotional or behavioral symptoms in response to an identifiable stressor' though there is a complicated rule about duration. For the diagnosis to be made, symptoms must arise within 3 months of the onset of the stressor and not last longer than 6 months after its termination. A rider instructs specification into acute and chronic subtypes according to whether symptoms last less or more than 6 months. There is a specific exclusion of bereavement as a cause of symptoms. The list of types is pruned to five and one unspecified (see Table 21.1).

The ICD has included a category of adjustment reaction, at least since its Eighth Revision (World Health Organization, 1965). In this revision, adjustment reaction of adolescence was included within the major coding of transient situational disturbance, whereas adjustment reactions of infancy or childhood were subsumed under the heading of behaviour disorders of childhood. In the Ninth Revision (World Health organization, 1974), adjustment reactions were considered conceptually homologous irrespective of developmental status.

The glossary described 'mild or transient disorders lasting longer than acute stress reactions which can occur in individuals of any age without any apparent pre-existing mental disorder [and] are relatively circumscribed or situation specific, are generally reversible, and usually last only a few months. They are usually closely related in time to stresses .... In children [they] are associated with no significant distortion of development.'

ICD-10 includes two main categories of reaction to severe stress: acute stress reaction (with a subcategory of post-traumatic stress disorder; PTSD) and adjustment *disorder* (World Health Organization, 1992). The latter is divided further into six main subcategories defined symptomatically, an extension of the previous revision. At each level of classification there is provision for 'other' categories (Table 21.2). The diagnoses can be made at any age.

The concept in ICD-10 parallels that informing the DSM-IV diagnosis. Thus the 'subjective distress and emotional disturbance, usually interfering with social functioning and performance' arises 'in the period of adaptation to a significant life change or to the consequences of a stressful life event'. There are contradictory statements about individual vulnerability. The clearest reads: 'individual predisposition or vulnerability plays a greater role in the risk of occurrence and the shaping of adjustment disorders than in [other stress related conditions] ... but it is nevertheless assumed that the condition would not have arisen without the stressor'. The implication might be drawn that the vulnerability falls short of overt previous psychopathology. 'None of the symptoms is of sufficient severity or prominence in its own right to justify a more specific diagnosis.' Stressors should be more than minor and the onset of the disorder is 'usually' within 1 month of the occurrence of the stressful event, 'significant life change leading to continued unpleasant life circumstances', or life crisis. A period of more than 3 months between stressor and symptom onset indicates that the disorder should be classified differently. For most reactions, the duration of symptoms will not normally exceed 6 months (brief and prolonged depressive reactions have maximum limits of 1 month and 2 years respectively) and if it does, the diagnosis should be changed to a more specific category. Bereavement reactions are qualified considerably. The identified stressor event or situation can be coded with a separate Z code.

Although this is intended to be a category that can be applied to all age groups, some comments in the diagnostic guidelines apply specifically to children. The subcategory 'with

Table 21.1 DSM-IV adjustment disorder

Adjustment disorder	
309.24	With anxiety
309.0	With depressed mood
309.3	With disturbance of conduct
309.4	With mixed disturbance of emotions and conduct
309.28	With mixed anxiety and depressed mood
309.9	Unspecified

Acute if symptoms persist >6 months
Chronic if symptoms persist >6 months

Table 21.2 ICD-10 Adjustment disorder subcategories

F43.20	Brief depressive reaction
F43.21	Prolonged depressive reaction
F43.22	Mixed anxiety and depressive reaction
F43.23	With predominant disturbance of other emotions
F43.24	With predominant disturbance of conduct
F43.25	With predominant disturbance of emotions and conduct
F43.28	Other specified

predominant disturbance of other emotions ... should be used for reactions in children in which regressive behaviour such as bed-wetting or thumb-sucking are also present'. Later in the guidelines an adolescent grief reaction resulting in aggressive or dissocial behaviour is given as an instance of the subcategory 'with predominant disturbance of conduct'. Separation anxiety is specifically excluded but 'hospitalism' in children is included.

In parallel with these alterations and refinements of the terms connected with an idea of maladaptation provoked by stress or challenge is the progressive exploration of the role of psychosocial adversity in the genesis of other psychiatric diagnoses. Thus there is now, for example, widespread confirmation of the importance of family relationship disturbances and disrupted parenting associated with conduct disorder, increasing evidence that overwhelmingly unpleasant experiences link with the anxiety reaction known as PTSD (see Chapter 22) and acceptance that early institutional rearing can cause disturbed personality functioning (Hodges & Tizard, 1989). In other words, the impact of adversity is now recognized to be relevant to a number of other psychiatric conditions so that the concept of adjustment disorder has shrunk to describing a mild, short-lived and nonspecific reaction to an adversity that is itself circumscribed in duration.

In the ICD clinical description, the points are made that there is commonly a plurality of emotional symptoms and that there needs to be a careful evaluation of relationships between form, content and severity, previous personality and the stressor. This is the kernel of the concept which, in both classification schemes has four, possibly five components:

1 Distress or disturbance of functioning that is beyond a normal range or is maladaptive.
2 Psychopathology less severe than a major category diagnosis would require.
3 An identifiable stressor that is an event or onset of change in circumstances occurring within a maximum of 3 months prior to onset of the disorder, which is of significant but not exceptional severity and a necessary condition for the condition arising.
4 Relatively short duration.
5 Not an exacerbation of previously identified psychopathology.

SOME PROBLEMS WITH THE CURRENT DEFINITIONS

Before examining empirical findings in any great detail, several logical problems immediately arise from the definitions proposed in the classificatory systems.

Rules for distinction from major disorders

The presence of a psychiatric disorder in childhood hinges in part upon the threshold criteria of impaired functioning or significant suffering, either or both of which can be applied to deviant emotional, behavioural or developmental signs and symptoms (see Chapters 1, 2 and 4). Effectively, these criteria provide cut-offs from a range of difficulty or distress that can be seen in normal children. Their application has the effect of identifying the presence of disorder according to a dichotomous rule; disorder is either present or absent and this presumably applies as much to adjustment disorder as to any other psychiatric disorder. Certainly impairment of or interference with functioning is specified in both classificatory systems. It is clear from the above history that adjustment disorders are conceptualized as milder than major category disorders. The implication is that the diagnosis of a major category disorder would require not just an impairment/significant suffering criterion but more severe psychopathology than an adjustment disorder, yet there are not always consistent rules specifying how this might be quantified. Where there are such rules they do not always leave room for adjustment disorder. Consider, for instance, the criteria for 'depressive episode, mild severity' in ICD-10 (which presumably is a major category diagnosis and therefore something from which an adjustment reaction would be distinguished by being less severe). These are minimal so that an individual would fulfil the criteria by manifesting anhedonia, increased fatiguability, loss of self-confidence and disturbed sleep for about 2 weeks. To specify that the psychopathology of an adjustment reaction should fall short of this is to identify a remarkably dilute disorder of mind. In research practice, this distinction from a major category disorder is often ignored and a dimensional approach using symptomatology is adopted, as witnessed by the widespread practice of including adjustment disorder (depressed type) along with dysthymic disorder and major depressive disorder when investigating depression in childhood.

Aetiological presumption

Adjustment disorder has the odd distinction of possessing no characteristic psychopathology. Its nature is defined by its relationship to a stressor. The fact that a particular psychiatric disorder is understood always to be caused by a putative stressor sits awkwardly with any attempt by a diagnostic scheme to be atheoretical. There is a clear statement in ICD-10 that the disorder is caused by a particular identified stressor ('a direct consequence of the acute stress or continued trauma. The stressful event or the continuing unpleasant circumstances are the primary and over-riding causal factor and the disorder would not have occurred without its impact'), yet existing knowledge suggests very strongly that most childhood psychiatric disorder is multifactorially determined by complex interactional and transactional mechanisms (Woolston, 1988). The interplay of individual vulnerability, precipitating stressors and maintaining factors in a variety of disorders is well-documented, yet there is a danger that the existence of the adjustment disorder taxon may perpetuate the lay myth that psychiatric disorders in childhood are commonly or typically reactions to single stressors ('life changes or life events' in ICD terminology or the 'identifiable stressor' of DSM). Rutter and

Sandberg (1992) point out that chronic adversities usually exist in combination and an adverse experience occurring in isolation is usually not pathogenic. In a particular case, the aetiological contribution of chronic stressors may be proportionally greater but masked by a recent dramatic acute event; the straw on the camel's back, yet it is this event that forms the base from which are drawn the time limits specified in the diagnostic rules.

In any case the association between apparent stressor and reaction will necessarily be based on *post hoc* reasoning. It will rest upon a clinical judgement as to how closely the stressor relates to the behaviour or emotional disorder in terms of form and content or in temporal proximity. Effectively a *verstehende* concept applies in that the type of stressor and the content of the psychopathology must be understood by the observer to be semantically related. Yet when an attempt is made to link disorder with life events, it is apparent that the association between type of event and type of disorder is very weak (Goodyer *et al.*, 1985) and even extreme stressors do not consistently produce predictable types of reactions such as posttraumatic stress disorder (Breslau & Davis, 1987). There is an obvious possibility that any association is coincidental and spurious, particularly if meaning is understood predominantly in relation to a metaphorical system of psychic functioning such as a psychoanalytic model.

On closer examination of the manner in which the terms adjustment reaction and adjustment disorder have developed, it appears that there is an implication that the affected child's reaction is abnormal. This may be judged in at least three different ways.

Firstly, there is the criterion of quality, in that normal grief would not be included but uncontrolled outbursts of aggressive behaviour following bereavement might be.

Secondly, a quantitative aspect can emerge. For instance, the extent to which tearfulness and avoidance of school as a response to bullying at school might be described as an adjustment disorder will depend upon an evaluation of proportionality in the child's response.

There is an implicit assumption that normal patterns of adjustment to stressors are sufficiently well-defined for a normality to be identifiable by the above criteria, yet this is not necessarily so. For instance, with respect to qualitative abnormalities in bereavement reactions (the example cited in ICD-10), Kranzler (1990) demonstrated that better studies of grief in children reveal that aspects of the bereavement response previously considered pathological may be seen in most bereaved children, as is the case in adults (Vargas *et al.*, 1989). Frequency and intensity of symptoms or chronicity would be a better indicator of abnormality rather than presence or absence of particular features. Yet estimating the normal intensity or duration of responses to adverse events is not straightforward and may indeed be beyond many psychiatrists (Malt, 1986). For instance, in the bullying example above this would involve an extensive knowledge of how the stressor impinges upon the individual child in terms of the child's attributions or previous sensitization. A more general appeal

to empirical data may help but little because of the influence of development and context. With respect to children's reactions to divorce, responses are known to alter by age and sex, according to the quality of previous family relationships and to continuing features of relationships between the parents and between parents and children (Arnold and Carnahan, 1990). Given so many qualifications, specification of a normal reaction becomes difficult in terms of description.

Thirdly, it may be determined that the child's reaction is maladaptive, placing the child at risk or at an avoidable disadvantage as in repeated acts of deliberate self-harm. Yet these may ultimately prove beneficial if they recruit help in resolving the child's predicament. There is a difficulty in moving beyond the descriptive to evaluating the cost to the child since this may alter according to whether short-term or long-term benefits are considered.

Time criteria

The use of a maximum time (1 month in ICD-10 and 3 months in DSM-IV) allowable between stressful event and onset of symptoms implies a simple notion of causality akin to the direct impact of a specific experience upon the individual. This might be true for adults, yet the situation with children is likely to be different because of the various kinds of mechanism which can operate indirectly (see below).

In life events studies, events considered to be possible aetiological factors are by no means confined to the 4 weeks before the onset of disorder, though they do tend to cluster in the 16 weeks prior to onset (Goodyer, 1990b), suggesting direct aetiological relevance but not confined to the time scale specified for adjustment disorder. Whether there is a subtype of psychiatric disorder specifically associated with immediate precipitant life events is not a question that has been addressed in life event work.

Moreover, the stressors recognized as psychopathogenic in child psychiatry are usually associated with difficulties in family relationships which are notoriously chronic. This is apparently acknowledged in the ICD-10 guidance which differentiates between 'an exceptionally stressful life event producing an acute stress reaction [and] a significant life change leading to continued unpleasant circumstances which result in an adjustment disorder', yet the diagnostic guidelines for adjustment disorder mention both stressful life events and significant life changes so that the confusion as to whether suffering and maladaptive behaviour are responses to an event or a process is unresolved. The common factor would seem to be adaptation and its pathology rather than the manner of impact. An event can wreak psychopathological havoc by the overwhelming effect of its associated emotional impact: fear, sense of loss or anger. It may also shock by revealing a new world-view which contains the previously unaccounted for: betrayal, cruelty, or displacement from a favoured position. A change in life circumstances (such as parental divorce) can include any of these at its inception but go on to require adaptation in the sense of new ways of coping and relating to the altered circumstances. Some apparent events, such as the birth of a younger sibling, may be initiators of continuing processes with wider changes in parental–child relationships (Dunn & Kendrick, 1982) and the definitions of adjustment disorder reflect this by rolling both such adversities into one, yet the time criterion is principally relevant to a specific event. Even when an event is considered, as in the ICD-10 description of posttraumatic stress disorder, it is recognized that there can be a delayed onset of up to several months. With this in mind, the use of a 1-month limit between event or onset of life change and disorder is again questionable.

There is also a presumption that there is a single onset of the disorder which enables easy assessment of the interval between event or initiation of life change and subsequent psychopathology. Yet Rutter and Sandberg (1992) cited a study in process that suggested that it was more likely than not that psychiatric disorders in childhood have multiple onsets or times of worsening.

Earlier versions of DSM indicated a relatively brief duration but DSM-IV has avoided this constraint by tying onset of the disorder to within 3 months of the *onset* of the stressor, subsequently allowing symptoms to persist for up to 6 months after the *termination* of the stressor. This means that the chronic subtype (symptom duration more than 6 months) could notionally last for years in contrast to the ICD-10 rules which still state a maximum duration of 6 months for all but prolonged depressive reaction. The DSM-IV position is helpful in the familiar example of the child who is bullied at school but does not disclose this and who manifests anxious misery with a range of somatic complaints that lead to sporadic attendance and social withdrawal for the better part of a year yet which disappear when the bullying is stopped. The pivotal concept of adaptation pathology is evidenced here by prompt symptom resolution but the time course would, certainly under ICD-10 and the older DSM-III-R rules, exclude a diagnosis of adjustment disorder.

The nature of vulnerability

Exploration of children's response to stress reveals a complex picture. Whilst at first sight it should be possible to make a number of statements about which factors make a particular child vulnerable to a particular stressor, there are at least three complicating factors:

1 Individual variables in children that affect their susceptibility have often been studied separately and, although social psychiatric research has explored the interactive effects of mainly chronic adversities applied to groups of children, the manner in which they combine in the individual child (which is likely often to be multiplicative rather than simply arithmetical) has been less systematically explored.

2 Children live with parents whose reaction to an event will usually be part of the context of that event for the child. Indeed, their reaction may be more stressful to the child than the direct impact of the event.

3 The child may, through various mechanisms, influence the event in question and either maintain it or magnify its impact through the manner of his or her adaptation.

Following from this, it would be an oversimplification to assume that vulnerability is a property of the individual child. It appears to be a function of the interplay of variables within and external to the child and goes beyond the phrase 'individual predisposition' in ICD-10.

THE USE OF THE TERM

One might ask why, given its rather unsatisfactory conceptual status, the diagnostic category survives. One explanation is that effectively it is a waste-basket term applied to a residuum of patients who have psychiatric problems that are hard to characterize except in terms of their apparent response to stress. This was the impression noted by Looney and Gunderson (1978) in a study of late teenagers and young adults. It may be an issue that particularly applies to the young (or to their psychiatrists); certainly the diagnosis of adjustment disorder is made more frequently in children and adolescents than in adults (Hillard *et al.*, 1987; Mezzich *et al.*, 1989). Fard *et al.* (1978) noted that among studies of disordered adolescents that use strict diagnostic criteria derived from adult psychiatric practice, the proportion of undiagnosed subjects in an adolescent population is greater than among adults. For instance, Hudgens (1971) found that 22% of a sample of adolescent patients could not be classified by the criteria of Feighner's *et al.* (1972) as having 'one of the established [psychiatric] syndromes' which did not include adjustment disorder. On follow-up of the undiagnosable group, it was possible to differentiate between two subgroups: one with irritable reactivity, depressive affect and domestic misbehaviour, often in response to stress, who did well, in contrast to a group with psychotic symptoms who did badly. The authors did not use the term adjustment disorder (or reaction) for the former group but the similarities are clear. This sits easily with the implication in the DSM-IV criteria that adjustment disorder is, in part, a diagnosis by exclusion; the disturbance does not meet the criteria for any other specific disorder.

A further possibility derives from the observation that there is a tendency for clinicians actually to use simpler aetiological models than they profess to employ (Goldberg, 1970; Fisch *et al.*, 1981) so that they intuitively favour a category that suggests a straightforward stress-reaction model based on linear causality. As an extension of this, it is easy to see how a psychoanalytically oriented psychiatrist would in any case tend to see many psychiatric disorders in terms of the activities of unconscious defence mechanisms in response to stressors. Times when or settings where psychoanalytic practice was influential would also be those in which a diagnosis specifying a link between stressor and psychopathology would be preferred. Some evidence that this is so is provided by the extensive use of the term adjustment reaction in the US in the 1950s and 1960s referred to above, yet the practice clearly continued into the 1970s, as shown by Sowder's nationwide survey of 441 000 children and teenagers seen in most of the hospital psychiatric services in the US in 1975 (Sowder *et al.*, 1981). Of this total population, 44% received the diagnosis of adjustment reaction (DSM-III). As recently as the mid 1980s, adjustment disorder was found to be the most common diagnosis at admission of adolescents to North American psychiatric hospitals (Faulstich *et al.*, 1986).

In contrast, the diagnosis of adjustment disorder or reaction is unusual in the UK and an unpublished postal survey of all senior child and adolescent psychiatrists conducted by the author in a Health Service Region in southern England whilst writing this chapter revealed that 53% of 40 child psychiatrists never used either diagnosis. Of those who did, the ICD-9 term adjustment reaction was preferred by the vast majority. Several respondents made unelicited comments that they found the notion particularly helpful in connection with children with divorcing parents; yet others bemoaned the vagueness of the terms.

In a larger study, Setterburg *et al.* (1991) surveyed American child psychiatrists and reported that the diagnosis was more frequently used by those who were psychodynamically trained, older, and in office rather than hospital practice. Some 55% of those surveyed stated that they employed the diagnosis specifically in order to avoid stigmatization of the patient. The authors also commented that the diagnosis retained its popularity because of the way in which its non-specific wording maintained a degree of confidentiality as to the exact nature of the psychopathology and did not prejudice subsequent life insurance application.

Given such revelations about diagnostic practice, this latter study does not breed confidence in the published literature on the condition. Particularly tragically for any author who wishes to draw on published empirical findings, it reveals that 58% of those psychiatrists circulated said they did not observe the DSM-III-R time criteria in making the diagnosis. Furthermore, 52% of the psychiatrists used the term adjustment disorder to describe mild conditions, often unrelated to stressors, that did not meet DSM-III-R diagnostic criteria for specific syndromes (instead of coding the correct NOS category).

EMPIRICAL EXPLORATIONS

Little that is useful has been written about adjustment disorders. Noshpitz and Coddington (1990), editors of a book on *Stressors and the Adjustment Disorders*, have commented, somewhat plaintively: 'one author after another was unable to accept an assignment to write about some aspect of adjustment disorder. The explanation offered was always the same, namely, that there was so little literature about the syndrome.'

More accurately, there is an appreciable volume of published work over the last three decades but little of it reliable. Bearing in mind the apparently erratic way in which the diagnosis has often been made, considerable caution has to be applied in interpreting what is written. The bulk of articles use the term to refer to nonpsychotic disorder in children and adolescents who come from troubled homes and have been subjected to chronic multiple stressors over a protracted period.

Alternatively, adolescents are described who exhibit drug misuse or conduct problems which are understood to arise from difficulties in handling developmental challenges. Almost certainly, such young people would not be classified as having adjustment disorders by modern classificatory schemes.

Nevertheless it is possible to use the literature to explore some issues around adjustment reaction or adjustment disorder (taken synonymously) and these are treated separately below.

WHAT FORM DOES ADJUSTMENT DISORDER PREDOMINANTLY TAKE?

Given that there are no defining psychopathological characteristics by which adjustment disorder is diagnosed, it is necessary to turn to described clinical samples or examples provided by authorities. There is very little guidance in recent literature, although earlier studies such as those by Andreasen (see below) provide a glimpse of what psychopathology was typically present in the 1970s. More recently, Andreasen and Black (1991; pp. 384–385) have implied that symptoms of anxiety and sadness associated with deliberate self-harm such as an overdose would be more typical of adjustment disorder in an adult, whereas acting out or behaviour abnormalities would be more typical manifestations in adolescence. In European and American studies of deliberate self-harm involving adolescents and young adults, adjustment disorder is typically diagnosed in only about 10–15% (Fowler *et al.*, 1986, Runeson, 1989), which suggests that the association with self-harm is not particularly strong in this age group, although in an Australian study of all age groups with a marked predominance of adults, the diagnosis of adjustment disorder was indeed the most frequently made (McGrath, 1989).

HOW FREQUENTLY IS ADJUSTMENT DISORDER DIAGNOSED?

Because of the shift in diagnostic criteria, only recent studies can be used to determine the answer. Unfortunately, most modern whole-population studies use diagnostic categories that do not include adjustment disorder. An exception is the general population study of 4–16-year-olds in Puerto Rico using DSM-III criteria which gave a prevalence rate for definite adjustment disorder of 4.2% within a total prevalence rate for psychiatric morbidity of 17.9%, i.e. about one-quarter of all cases (Bird *et al.*, 1989). Curiously, adjustment disorders in this population showed no relationship with the number of life events or family dysfunction, nor with age or sex.

Within clinic populations, not dissimilar percentage figures are suggested for the prevalence of adjustment disorder by recent criteria. For instance, in studies around Pittsburgh, Doan and Petti (1989) found a rate of 7% among child patients attending day-units and Mezzich *et al.* (1989) a rate of 16% among all under-18s seen for evaluation at the Western

Psychiatric Institute. In selected clinical populations, rates of adjustment disorder are high — 42% of adolescents seen in a psychiatric emergency clinic (Hillard *et al.*, 1987) and, using DSM-II criteria, rates of between 24 and 66% for children seen in various primary care settings (Jacobson *et al.*, 1980). Steinhausen and Erdin (1991a) examined the distribution of diagnoses in a Zurich child clinic population during epochs when ICD-9 and ICD-10 were each applied. There was no reason to think that there was any change in the types of patients seen over time. According to ICD-9 criteria, 20% of children received a diagnosis of adjustment reaction, whereas by ICD-10 rules, 5.9% were diagnosed as having adjustment disorder. The authors considered that this was a result of new (and tighter) diagnostic criteria overturning previous habits established under the influence of psychodynamic theory but hazard no guesses as to which category erstwhile adjustment reactions would now be assigned. It would probably not be acute stress reaction as the proportion of cases given that diagnosis did not change significantly, but inspection of their data suggests it might be conduct disorder.

In the author's own survey referred to above, in which respondents variously used ICD-9 and ICD-10 criteria, only one clinician estimated having applied the term to more than 10% of child patients seen in the past year (she suggested 20%). The mean percentage of patients receiving diagnoses of adjustment reaction or disorder from clinicians who used the terms at all was 6% and this fell to 2.5% if all 40 clinicians were included. If this is representative, then it is unsurprising that there is no recent UK literature on adjustment reaction/ disorder.

HOW RELIABLY IS THE DIAGNOSIS MADE?

The answer seems to be that it depends upon which set of criteria are used. A number of studies demonstrate inter-reliability ratings which are consistently low when DSM-III criteria are used with children and adolescents (Williams & Spitzer, 1980; Werry *et al.*, 1983; Canino *et al.*, 1987; Rey *et al.*, 1989). Rey *et al.* (1989) calculate a mean value for Cohen's kappa of 0.41 across studies, the lowest for any DSM-III diagnosis apart from attention deficit disorder without hyperactivity. According to ICD criteria, only poor interrater reliability was obtained by Gould *et al.* (1988) and Remschmidt (1988) using ICD-9 criteria but Steinhausen and Erdin (1991b) found a high interrater agreement of 82% for the diagnosis using ICD-10 criteria applied to a written vignette. In view of the small number of vignettes (5) used in the latter study, this may be an unrepresentative finding.

THE VALIDITY OF THE DIAGNOSIS

From examination of the literature, two sources of empirical information as to the validity of the concept emerge. One is the predictive power of the diagnosis compared with other diagnoses as revealed on follow-up. The other is whether follow-up studies suggest that it breeds true to type.

According to the criteria contained in the major classificatory systems, the identification of an acute, recent stressor and the establishment of a direct relationship to the continuance of disorder, a good prognosis would be predicted on general grounds. Indeed it is sometimes said that is why clinicians wish to retain the term. However, actual outcomes are not consistently so benign.

Although carried out before DSM-III, it is instructive to examine the widely cited study carried out by Andreason and her colleagues (Andreason & Wasek, 1980; Andreason & Hoenk, 1982) because of its origins in a sound academic centre. The records of all adolescents and adults receiving the diagnosis of adjustment reaction when seen at the University of Iowa Department of Psychiatry ('a centre with a rather biological orientation', in the authors' own words) over a 4-year period (1971—1974) were studied in detail. There were about 200 in each age group, of which nearly one-half of the adolescents and somewhat less than one-third of the adults were inpatients. Only 5% of all inpatients received the diagnosis but, although the diagnostic rate among outpatients could not be similarly assessed, it was thought that it would have been higher. The requirements for the diagnosis were unclear; by inference, DSM-II criteria were used. However, the fact that nearly half of the adolescents had been ill for a year or more suggests that the 'transient' descriptor contained in the DSM-II definition of adjustment reaction would have been frequently ignored. Nor is there a comparison group of other diagnoses in the study, so it is difficult to know how specific were the characteristics of adolescents with adjustment reactions compared to those receiving other diagnoses. Nevertheless, the study provides a snapshot of how the diagnosis was applied to American teenagers in the 1970s.

With respect to the adolescents with adjustment reactions, there was a nonsignificant small excess of girls. In any study including inpatients, gender ratios may be influenced by the number of beds available if wards for boys and girls are separate but for whatever reason, the sex difference in this population was small, something echoed in the life events literature. For instance, Goodyer *et al.* (1986) found no effect for age or sex on the association between adverse life events and psychiatric disorder in school-age children, even though girls seemed to experience more in the way of negative life events and daily hassles than boys (Kanner *et al.*, 1991). Most teenagers in the Iowa study displayed behavioural problems, particularly drug abuse, truancy, running away, temper outbursts, chronic rule violations and academic underachievement. This was a quite different picture from that revealed by the adults with adjustment reactions in the same study, who were considerably more likely to be female and had predominantly (87%) depressive symptoms. Among the adolescents, depressive symptomatology was present in nearly two-thirds: dysphoric mood, suicidal thoughts or behaviour, and tearfulness being the commonest, and the authors comment that some of the patients 'would probably have met DSM-III criteria for major depressive disorder'. Anxiety symptoms were less prevalent, being reported by one-quarter of adolescents, and a similar proportion complained of psycho-physiological symptoms.

Exploration of the stressors acting on adolescents with the diagnosis indicated that few were overwhelming and most had been present for a year or more. School problems, parental rejection, parental divorce and drug or alcohol abuse by the adolescent themselves were the commonest identified stressors.

In their discussion, the authors recognized that, in contrast to the DSM-II characteristics 'the disorder was not transient, the reaction not acute, and the stress not overwhelming'. Yet the frequent use of the diagnosis suggested to them that it fulfilled some nosological need. It appeared that patients received little medication, psychotherapy being presumed to be the treatment of choice.

Following a random selection of about one-third of the original sample, 50 teenagers were eventually located and agreed to follow-up 5 years later. Standardized interview instruments were used and just under one-half of initial cases were found to be well and employed with no intervening problem since discharge. The remaining 56% had received diagnoses such as schizophrenia, bipolar disorder, major depressive disorder, antisocial personality, alcoholism and drug abuse. This is reminiscent of both the study on undiagnosable disorder in adolescents mentioned above (Fard *et al.*, 1978), which found about two-thirds to be psychiatrically ill or dead from suicide on follow-up, and that of Looney and Gunderson (1978) on older teenagers and young adults which found just under half to have been readmitted to hospital or prematurely discharged from the Navy on psychiatric grounds. Within the latter group, half eventually received diagnoses of personality disorder and the remainder were diagnosed as having neuroses or psychoses. In the Andreason and Hoenk (1982) study, the outcome for adults similarly followed up was much better, with virtually no serious mental illness or personality disorder detected, though 2 had killed themselves. Although none of the above studies used tight diagnostic criteria, the implication is that about half of adolescents diagnosed as having adjustment reactions in the pre-DSM-III era will be found to have more serious mental pathology on follow-up. This might relate to the allegedly overinclusive use of the term 'adjustment reaction' in American adolescent inpatient units recorded contemporaneously by Robins *et al.* (1982), though this is unlikely to be true of the Iowa study in which the diagnosis seems to have been used relatively sparingly.

The use of more recent and tighter diagnostic criteria (DSM-III) does not necessarily alter the uncertainty about prognosis. Cantwell and Baker (1989) carried out a 4-year follow-up of children seen at a speech and language clinic with a psychiatric disorder rate of about 50%. The diagnosis of adjustment disorder made in 19 children was the least stable (0%) of all diagnoses made and the recovery rate was remarkably low, at 26%. There was no correspondence between the type of symptoms exhibited initially and those on follow-up. In other words, adjustment disorder with disturbance of conduct did not develop into conduct disorder. Some of the rediagnoses appeared to represent reappraisal of a comorbid condition such as attention deficit disorder but there was no support for the notions that adjustment disorder indicated a benign prognosis nor a stable diagnostic category, breeding true.

IS ADJUSTMENT DISORDER A SYNONYM FOR MILD SPECIFIC DISORDER?

One question that might reasonably be posed is whether young people with a diagnosis of adjustment disorder are actually ill. They might be relatively invulnerable to stressors that produce specific disorders in others. Alternatively they might be highly vulnerable to minor stress. A third possibility is that they might be just as ill but recover more quickly. The separate coding of stressor severity on axis IV of DSM-III allows some exploration of this. Fabrega *et al.* (1987) surveyed patients of all ages (including those under 19) seen at a university centre with a structured approach to diagnosis and found that patients with adjustment disorder (DSM-III) had higher stressor severity scores than patients with specific psychiatric diagnoses or patients who received a V code (no psychiatric disorder) entry only. The difficulty here is that the same clinical panel entered the ratings on all axes so the possibility of a halo effect operating is very high. Interestingly, the highest level of social functioning during the previous year was at a lower average level among those diagnosed as having an adjustment disorder than among the V code group, suggesting that the patients with adjustment disorders were not functioning in an especially healthy manner before developing the condition. The study suggests that, premorbidly, they were neither conspicuously healthy nor exquisitely vulnerable to trivial stressors; they appeared to be a group with moderate levels of psychopathology who had been exposed to appreciable stress.

Raters using the Children's Global Assessment Scale regard case histories of children with an adjustment reaction (ICD-9) as indicating a rather less severe disorder than other major category disorders (Steinhausen, 1987). Correspondingly, Khan (1988) found that the thyrotrophin-releasing hormone stimulation test was abnormal in only 17% of adolescents with adjustment disorders, compared to 37% of those with major depression and 21% of those with conduct disorders.

If it is the case that adjustment disorder as currently diagnosed equates with mild or moderate illness, then what should emerge is that adjustment disorders would have a prognosis intermediate between health and major diagnoses and that they would breed true. Studies on the prognosis of affective symptomatology in childhood and adolescence usually combine diagnosis such as major affective disorder, dysthymic disorder and adjustment disorder with depressed mood. Unfortunately, the separate outcome for each diagnostic subgroup is not usually given. An exception is the study by Kovacs and Gatsonis (1989) which followed up children with some form of depressive symptomatology (DSM-III criteria for the above groups) and matched, nondepressed clinic controls.

The children with adjustment disorder took less time to recover than did those with major depressive disorder (median time 6.2 months compared with 9.5 months) and a very much lower likelihood (0.09 compared with 0.72) of a new episode of major depression, or indeed any other psychiatric disorder, developing during follow-up.

The implication is that, although a diagnosis of adjustment disorder is no guarantee of a rapid recovery and good prognosis thereafter, a group of children so diagnosed will do better than those with a major-category psychiatric disorder. They will be appreciably ill and be previously neither robust paragons of mental health nor remarkably vulnerable.

RELEVANCE OF THE TIME CONSTRAINT

Before the draft version of DSM-IV appeared, both DSM-III-R and ICD-10 specified a 6-month maximum duration after which reclassification is required, though it is not explained why such a time is selected. Clearly this constraint is often neglected, as admitted by a majority of those psychiatrists surveyed by Setterburg *et al.* (1991) and is apparent from data published by academically respectable institutions. An instance of this is contained in the Kovacs and Gatsonis (1989) study wherein the *mean* time for recovery following diagnosis was 6.2 months. It may be that the diagnosing clinicians were aware that the time course of children's response to stress can be protracted and that they were responding to the idea of an adjustment disorder rather than the diagnostic rules.

Furthermore, there is the issue not just of what the time course of understandable reactive distress might be, but whether this can be related to a definition of disorder. If one takes bereavement as the paradigm for a stressor which can lead to an adjustment reaction, then it is instructive to note that in Fristad *et al.*'s (1989) study, one-third of children were at their *most* distressed at 6 months after the death, though by 13 months matters had subsided somewhat. Making a distinction between mourning symptoms and behavioural disturbance, Kaffman and Elizur (1983) noted that, although mourning symptoms decreased after the first year, the highest rate of behavioural disturbance was in the second year of bereavement and a high rate of disturbance persisted for $3\frac{1}{2}$ years. Those who were disturbed the longest were not necessarily those who were the most upset initially. This echoes the finding of Rutter (1966) that bereaved children were most likely to be referred to psychiatric services more than 5 years after bereavement.

One interpretation of such findings is that children's response to a stressor is not only their own distress at the experience but is also mediated through the reactions of their carers. For instance, Van Eerdewegh *et al.* (1985) demonstrated a relationship between the amount of parental psychopathology and the child's emotional and behavioural status following bereavement. With this in mind, it is probable that the time limitations set for adults might not be appropriate for children dependent on carers who are also affected by similar life stresses.

RELATIONS BETWEEN STRESSORS AND DISORDER

Various authors have commented on the difficulty of specifying and quantifying stressors and their relation to psychopathology (Fabrega & Mezzich, 1987). Although not specifically concerned with adjustment disorder, the literature on life events and major-category psychiatric disorder in children and adolescents raises pertinent issues relevant to the relationship between stressful events and disorder. For instance, Goodyer (1990b, p. 194) estimated that each year an average school-age child will experience approximately three life events that are independent of any psychiatric disorder he or she may have. However, only about one-quarter of children will experience severely adverse life events and it would seem to be these that are principally relevant to aetiology. In two studies on clinic populations, about two-thirds of child psychiatric patients with emotional and conduct disorders (major-category diagnoses) had experienced a moderate to severe life event in the year before developing symptoms (Goodyer *et al.*, 1985, 1988), a significant but not very strong association. In this work, a stressful life event raised the relative risk of developing emotional or conduct disorder by three to six times.

Not all studies produce a clear association between life events and psychopathology. McFarlane (1988) was unable to show that subsequent adverse life events contributed to psychopathology following an Australian bushfire. Even when the impact of the disaster was taken into account, only a minority of children who experienced it developed psychiatric pathology, a similar finding to Goodyer's group examining less dramatic events. Conversely, a substantial minority of new child psychiatric patients will have experienced no serious adverse life events recently. In the formulation of an individual case, the possibility of falsely assuming a connection between a discrete life event and the onset of a disorder seems appreciable.

The provoking effect of an event is most usually in the context of chronic adversity, although it can be shown that acute events and chronic processes have separate effects (Goodyer, 1990a). In favour of a direct link between life event and disorder is the finding that events recalled for the 12 months prior to onset of disorder showed a progressive tendency to occur as the onset of disorder was approached, with 71% of child patients experiencing an event in the 6 months before onset and 49% in the most recent 16 weeks before disorder appeared (Goodyer *et al.*, 1987). One issue is whether there is any difference, other than degree, between instances of major category diagnoses that are apparently precipitated by adverse life events and adjustment disorders. Steinhausen and Erdin (1992) found adjustment disorders to have a relatively high rate of preceding acute life events recorded on the proposed ICD-10 psychosocial axis compared with other ICD-10 disorders but, as the authors pointed out, the same raters coded both clinical and psychosocial axes so the possibility of an effect of preconceived notions remains. There is not much on which to base a theory of how types of event relate to particular diagnoses. On the basis of his experience, Goodyer (1990b) tentatively proposed that exit events are relatively more likely to be associated with severe anxious and depressive disorders', but the sample suggesting such a conclusion was small. This general lack of demonstrated connection between type of event and type of psychopathology, as well as the frequent delay between event and appearance of symptoms, has been explained by McFarlane (1987) on the basis of the impact of undesirable life events being through their effect upon the mental state of the child's parents, a theme pursued below when the effects of specific stressors are noted.

IDENTIFYING STRESSORS

There is little disagreement as to what constitutes stressful situations for children. Garmezy and Rutter (1983) suggested that they could be classified into five categories: (1) loss; (2) chronically disturbed relationships; (3) events that change the family status quo; (4) events that require social adaptation; and (5) acute traumatic events. This system allows for coverage of most agreed stressful situations and resonates satisfactorily with the way in which childhood stressors have been explored in the literature but a categorical approach to classifying stressors does not necessarily parallel categorical boundaries when it comes to the mechanisms involved. Parental divorce with a single assault by one parent on the other which was witnessed by their child could be represented by any of the above categories.

An alternative approach, which may have more value in the assessment of an individual case, is to plot contributions from three variables on a three-dimensional grid. One variable is the amount of threatened or actual loss, particularly as applied to relationships and self-image. A second is the amount of anxiety as caused by various perceived threats — to life, limb, self-concept or reputation. The third is the amount of adaptation required in the way of new skills or new understandings. Even stresses to do with straightforward developmental challenges such as starting school will have contributions from all three components and the balance between all three will alter as the situation is progressively experienced. Transitions with relationships are likely to have major contributions from all three. There is the possibility of forcing this into a categorical classification, for instance a notional type A stressor with a predominance of adaptational demands with comparatively little in the way of major anxiety or loss, a type B with predominant aspects of loss, and a type C with predominant aspects of anxiety.

Even without further exploring the way in which children's reactions to a stressor can vary according to individual and contextual differences, the concept of classifying adjustment problems by stressor appears shaky. Nevertheless, this is the way in which the literature has usually approached the problem and the principal identified stressors associated with adjustment disorder are considered below (other than those dealt with in Chapter 22).

Death of a parent

In contrast to earlier studies which relied upon parental report, interview studies of bereaved children reveal that psychological disturbance akin to adult grief can be identified in children who have suffered the death of a parent (Fristad *et al.*, 1989; Weller *et al.*, 1989; Kranzler, 1990). Moreover, this can be directly related to feelings of sadness and loss when thinking about the parent and is not just derived from perceived changes in their social situation or a response to their surviving parent's mood state (Kranzler *et al.*, 1990). Symptoms of anxiety and depression predominate with probably relatively more anxiety than would be expected among adults. Many bereaved children, although sad, will not be ill with their unhappiness but an appreciable minority (40% in Kranzler *et al.*'s (1990) study of 3–6-year-olds) will experience emotional distress that reaches clinical criterion level on the Achenbach Child Behavior Checklist. By and large, the children with the most severe initial reactions are those who show the most protracted disturbance (Kaffman & Elizur, 1983). Generally speaking the levels of distress have begun to subside after 1 year, though behavioural disturbance peaks during the second year. The implication is that, because of the current time limits included in the diagnostic guidelines, an adjustment disorder could not be differentiated from normal grief by duration of symptoms.

Although the death of a parent can be regarded as a discrete event, it can set in train a number of potential adversities. Death of the father in particular often means a lowering of family income, possibly a move of house and, if so, move to a new school and loss of friends. Most importantly, the ultimate psychological adjustment of the child is compromised if the same event has an adverse emotional effect on a caregiver, in this instance protracted grieving or depression in the surviving parent. The duration of the child's psychological disturbance is related to the mental state of the surviving caregiver (Goodyer, 1990a). This is well-recognized in life events research and complicates the simple idea that an event exerts an impact upon a child through the experience of the event. Refuge in the concept of 'significant life change leading to continued unpleasant life circumstances' becomes inevitable but calls into question the validity of a diagnostic cut-off at 6 months' duration since the persistence is related in part to elements outside the child.

Divorce

In spite of psychiatrists' apparent predilection for using a diagnosis of adjustment disorder to account for children's disorder associated with parental divorce, it is doubtful whether most divorces could be regarded as the kind of circumscribed event or onset of changed circumstances which the time criterion in the diagnostic rules for adjustment disorder reflects. The actual divorce can occur on a defined date but is likely to follow a period of discordant marital relationships and disorder in the child can be shown often to arise from the marital strain and discord which typically precedes the actual divorce (Block *et al.*, 1986, 1988), so that using divorce as a timeable, specific event for the purposes of making a diagnosis of adjustment reaction under current rules would be misleading. The divorce may be followed by further interparental acrimony, parental distress or illness, moves of house and school, loss of family income, compromised relationships with either parent and parental remarriage (see, for example, Arnold and Carnahan (1990) who discuss 14 different stressors related to parental divorce that can affect children's emotions and behaviour). There is no suggestion that an improvement in a child's mental state is normally to be expected within the 6 months following the actual divorce; indeed symptomatology lasting years is common (Wallerstein & Kelly, 1980; Hetherington *et al.*, 1985; Wallerstein 1985, 1987). Once again, the influence of parental mental state is substantial: parental adjustment had a predictive strength on children's adjustment 4 years after divorce in Guidubaldi and Perry's (1985) follow-up study. It seems more appropriate to include divorce in a category of potential chronic stressors involving disadvantage or strained relationships rather than an independent or initiating event which may precipitate an adjustment reaction as currently defined. It would be wrong to consider divorce as necessarily pathogenic; there are children whose healthy development can be accelerated by the experience (Hetherington, 1989).

Birth of a sibling

Like divorce, this appears to be a life event with a number of possible pathogenic and development-promoting mechanisms not amenable to simple summary by a single motivational explanation such as jealousy. The birth may not be the critical initiating event. Nadelman and Begun (1982) found that some of the children in their study showed emotional and behavioural disturbances that started during the mother's pregnancy and improved after the birth of the sibling. Where a mother is admitted to hospital for an appreciable period for hypertension control or the actual delivery, distress related to separation may be seen which subsides following the return of the mother after the birth (Field & Reite, 1984).

The most thorough study in the field suggests that the key mechanisms are related to changes in the mother–child relationship (Dunn & Kendrick, 1982; Dunn, 1988) so that the amount of positive, playful attention paid to the firstborn diminishes and the number of maternal negative or controlling comments increases after the birth of a younger sibling, coming to dominate the conversations between mother and child. Nearly all firstborn children were difficult, demanding and defiant when their mother attended to the new baby. Although demanding behaviour tended to subside with time, emotional symptoms such as fears, moodiness and worries had actually increased by 14 months after the birth, flouting the 6-month adjustment threshold. The source of stress for the older children seems to be the alteration in their relationship with their mother rather more than, say, resentment at the arrival of the

newcomer, and the implication from the data is that it is the mother's behaviour (her rates of initiating games, conversations and suggesting new activities) which is the determining element in this change of relationship. It does not entirely follow from diversion of caregiving towards the new baby but can also arise from the mother feeling tired and depressed.

Two other relevant findings emerge from Dunn and Kendrick's work. Rather more than half of the elder siblings showed some signs of being more 'grown-up' in areas such as independence in self-care or language, suggesting that the birth of a sibling is by no means necessarily entirely adverse and can, as divorce may for some adolescents (Wallerstein & Kelly, 1980), act as a developmental stimulus. To make an inferential leap in judging an emotional disturbance to be a consequence of a recent sibling birth may be misleading unless the content of the child's disturbance supports such a link; there may be other reasons.

The second finding is that the differing signs of regression such as baby talk, wanting to be fed, loss of recently acquired skills etc. did not act in concert in data analysis and there was no support for a unitary concept of regression; different aspects showed different patterns of association with such variables as quality of relationship with mother. This calls into question the guidance given in ICD-10 which directs that the presence of 'regressive behaviour such as bed wetting or thumb-sucking' (neither of which might be judged to be usually indicative of regression) should lead to a subcategory of adjustment disorder with predominant disturbance of other emotions (F43.23).

Acquired physical illness or injury

By current definition it is impossible to display an adjustment disorder to a chronic illness, present from birth. This is not to say that children with such illnesses do not develop problems of adjusting to disability or physical suffering since they clearly do, as when an adolescent with established diabetes comes to a realization that their condition is lifelong and may cause blindness or lead to amputation. Yet the chance of being able to relate this to an identifiable external event, rather than an internal cognitive change, is slim.

There is no lack of clinical observation illustrating how children respond to the various stressors involved in becoming ill or injured. Prugh and Eckhardt (1980) provided a three-stage model for adjustment: (1) *impact*, in which the child exhibits either defensive denial of the seriousness of his or her condition or lapses into profound helplessness; (2) *recoil*, as the child becomes less preoccupied with self and tries to exert control over the situation by demanding, arrogant behaviour which may flip into listless misery; and (3) *restitution*, characterized by positive accommodation to the fact of the injury or illness. This is not a model that has been rigorously tested and is subject to the usual criticisms of stage models; yet it has some face validity and makes the point that apparently maladaptive behaviour can be understood within an overall framework of progressive adaptation. What is unknown is the extent to which it is exhibited by children and to what extent, for instance, bloody-mindedness in the recoil stage should be regarded as pathological and how much a necessary evil, like inflammation around a recent surgical incision.

Rather similarly, the age-appropriate attributions made by young children about illnesses or injuries can seem, for instance, like depressive symptoms should such children state that they are ill as a punishment for misdeeds, or resemble a phobic reaction if they are fearful about dressings being removed. In both instances the child's response may be normal for age but initially impress as pathological and lead to an inappropriate diagnosis of adjustment disorder. Nevertheless, even with tight criteria, rates of adjustment disorder seem likely to be high in association with acute onset of chronic illness, as in the rate of 30% among children with recently diagnosed diabetes reported by Kovacs *et al.* (1985).

A number of young children admitted to hospital in circumstances where their parents cannot visit will develop variants of the acute separation reaction (Rutter, 1981) which has a characteristic sequence of stages. In hospital, it will be compounded by other elements such as anxiety induced by surroundings and procedures, the reason for the admission and medication. To dignify such a reaction, which combines distortion of early attachments with reactions to disease, pain and strange surroundings, with a single term hospitalism is an oversimplification, yet it is preserved in ICD-10 guidelines as an instance of a condition to be included within adjustment disorder.

Developmental challenges

It is apparent from reading the older literature that the diagnosis of adjustment reaction originally derived from an approach that understood much psychiatric disorder as deviant development resulting from the overwhelming of normal intrapsychic processes by either external stressors (often chronic) or by demands for integrative maturation imposed by developmental processes. The habit persists, though the notion of developmental challenges nowadays emphasizes externally imposed demands such as changes of school as well as internal ones involving the resolution of contradictory emotions or wishes. Certainly some aspects of maturation are often at some emotional cost — the toddler learning to cope with separations from an attachment figure, the first attendance at school, the first sexualized peer relationship etc. — and it is unsurprising that adolescence, which has a large number of developmental, transitive challenges within its compass, is characterized by moderately high rates of minor psychological pathology (see, for example, Rutter *et al.*, 1976). Yet such psychopathology is usually nonhandicapping and whether its severity is sufficient to qualify a psychiatric diagnosis depends almost entirely on the testimony of the teenagers themselves, a controversial practice in young teenagers whose scale of reference may, through inexperience, lack calibration with general expectations of emotional range and thus be unreliable.

Although it seems plausible that some psychiatric disorder arises out of failure to cope adequately with new understandings and feelings arising purely from maturation or developmental changes in the individual's own body (some aspects of Crisp's (1980) theory of the genesis of anorexia nervosa represent this), the diagnosis of adjustment disorder according to contemporary rules is most likely to be made when an external stressor can be identified which poses a challenge to the child's coping. This may be quite appropriate because an imposed dichotomy between internal, developmental challenges and external threats or challenges may be false. A stressor may be either a positive challenge or a deficiency of support. Developmental tasks tend to include responses to events which are likely to be experienced by most children at particular ages. This implies that there will exist family and social support systems to guide children through such challenges and the failure of a child to cope may mean not just that the child is individually vulnerable but that support systems were unavailable or not employed, perhaps because of parental idiosyncracy. Maladaptation might therefore derive from sources or deficiencies outside the individual child in spite of the putative stressors precipitating the condition being loosely termed developmental in origin, with the connotation that such stressors are internal.

THE DISTINCTION BETWEEN ACUTE STRESS REACTION AND POSTTRAUMATIC STRESS DISORDER

Within ICD-10, the concept of acute stress reaction is a brief (hours or days) emotional reaction to a traumatic experience such as a natural catastrophe, multiple bereavement or accident. Psychopathologically there is an initial state of 'daze' with narrowing of attention and disorientation and any of a variety of transient emotional symptoms. There is little likelihood of this being confused nosologically or clinically with an adjustment disorder.

The distinction from PTSD presents more problems. A definable clinical picture has been recognized (see Chapter 22), whereas adjustment disorders by definition have no distinct psychopathology. Theoretically, the distinction might be made on the grounds of the stressor — PTSD arising in response to an event 'exceptionally threatening or catastrophic' (ICD-10) or involving 'actual or threatened death or serious injury' (DSM-IV) compared with stressors 'within the range of common experience' in adjustment disorder. However, not all children exposed to catastrophic events develop PTSD and some appear to develop reactions that might be diagnosable as adjustment disorder (Earls *et al.*, 1988). Conversely, trauma far short of the catastrophic, such as dog bite, can produce PTSD (author's case). The empirical study of children's responses to acute trauma is not sufficiently complete for the boundaries of a category of PTSD in childhood to be defined solely by type of trauma.

Indeed, there may be a spectrum rather than a category boundary between adjustment disorder and PTSD since evidence from various studies (Pynoos *et al.*, 1987; Nader *et al.*,

1990; Udwin, 1993; Yule, 1990) suggests parallel gradients of exposure to the threat and the strength of emotional reaction to the trauma, of which PTSD is the most severe. This is not to say that PTSD is not a useful concept; rather that it should not be conceptualized too rigidly by premature closure on the relationship between its form, the child's developmental level, and the type of traumatic stressor.

ASSESSMENT

A conventional child psychiatric assessment is as much required for the diagnosis of an adjustment disorder as any other psychiatric condition. It would seem particularly important to interview the individual child to obtain quantification of the impact of supposed adversity for various reasons. Firstly, parents may be unaware of experiences such as bullying, which is characteristically kept secret by its victims. Secondly, the parents may conceal an adversity which implicates them, sexual abuse being a case in point. Thirdly, an apparently moderate stressor may be severe for the child in question because of idiosyncratic personal elements such as previous sensitization. Fourthly, skilled interviewers who know what questions to ask may reveal symptoms which would otherwise remain undisclosed (Frederick, 1985).

In related vein, it may be only the child who can reveal the timing of onset of private symptoms. This should not mean that only the child can provide information; life events interviews have shown how the best data are derived from combining parental and child accounts (Monck & Dobbs, 1985). Certainly, parental mental state must be assessed, given the evidence that this may be the maintaining factor in responses to a number of stressors (see above).

Careful formulation of the mechanisms involved in the genesis and maintenance of disorder must include specification as to how the child has attempted to cope with the stressor or new life circumstances as well as to what extent his or her efforts have contributed to exacerbating their impact. There would seem to be some advantage in documenting how previous stresses and life transitions have been successfully managed since this may indicate a logical approach to treatment (see below).

If ICD-10 guidelines are followed, a reassessment at 6 months is mandatory to examine whether redesignation to a major category diagnosis is required.

PREVENTION

Although there are no solid data on prevention of adjustment disorders as such, the evidence that preparation by discussion, explanation, visiting and provision of mitigating circumstances will minimize the distress of young children in hospital with minimal contact with their parents (Ferguson, 1979; Wolfer & Visintainer, 1979). This suggests that predictable changes in life circumstances can be constructively prepared for. Otherwise, the recommendations for prevention follow rather diffuse lines: reducing the number of stressors (such as divorce) through mental health education or social support systems, building self-esteem and educating children about how to cope with predictable stressors such as examinations. These are untested and, in current formulation, probably too diffuse to be testable.

TREATMENT

There are no data on treatment choice or effectiveness for adjustment disorders as currently defined. At first glance, an approach combining environmental manipulation with individual or family counselling which hinged upon removing or minimizing the stressor situation whilst supporting the child and family in constructive adaptation would seem appropriate. There is some evidence from related areas such as bereavement counselling (Black & Urbanowicz, 1987) that this is likely to prove helpful but the suggestion is speculative.

If it were possible to identify how children's coping strategies related to immunity from stress-related psychiatric disorder then this would provide a basis on which to use a more educative model which could build coping mechanisms. However, most of the work on invulnerability documents personality characteristics rather than coping skills (Garmezy, 1985; Rutter, 1985; Rae-Grant *et al.*, 1989). Attempts to explore the deployment of coping skills and vulnerability to disorder have not yet yielded sufficient positive results on which to build to treatments (see Jenkins *et al.* (1989) for a well-executed but ultimately disappointing instance). Although there is a little indirect evidence that cognitive therapies might assist children with a depressive reaction (Leon *et al.*, 1980), the power and permanence of current cognitive and social problem-solving approaches is questionable when these are used in major category disorders (Webster-Stratton, 1991). There is the possibility that they may prove fruitful with milder psychopathology but mild does not always mean more easily treated (as with the old categories of neurotic versus psychotic depression).

CONCLUSIONS

The existence of a disorder category that has no defining psychopathology and is defined with reference to a specified time relationship with a putative aetiological factor that is nonspecific and inconsistently pathogenic is extraordinary. It is not a concept that has spawned useful research. Clearly there is a wish among many clinical psychiatrists that the idea of adjustment disorder be retained but there is also evidence that their reasons for so doing are not scientifically derived (though J.H. Newcorn & J. Strain, having reviewed the academic literature, believe the concept can be retained provided that new wording of criteria can be adopted (personal communication)). The establishment of social psychiatric concepts of risk, adversity, life events and vulnerability coupled with increasingly fruitful work on coping, resilience and perpetuating mechanisms, combined in complex but analysable explanatory models, ought to remove the need for the rather simple-minded concept of linear causality which underpins the notion of an adjustment disorder. The relationship between life events and major-category psychiatric disorders in childhood and adolescence is becoming better understood as something which is complex and not to be reduced to simple models of reaction.

The logic of the arguments above leads to a conclusion that adjustment disorder, as currently defined, is an anomaly, perhaps representing a failure of psychiatrists themselves to adjust their classifications in the face of accumulating evidence of the relevance of adversity as aetiologically relevant in a number of the psychiatric disorders of the young. Is there, nevertheless a need for a similar term? There are two possibilities.

Firstly, various authorities have proposed (Campbell, 1990, p. 73; Graham, 1991) that in children aged under 5 there is a recognizable condition that can be termed an adjustment disorder with 'widespread disturbance of behaviour, especially in the areas of activity, control and aggression ... more prominent in some situations than others ... and may be more apparent with one parent than the other' (Graham, 1991, p. 70). Graham's description depicts a familiar enough picture but is unsupported by epidemiological findings that would delineate the boundaries of the condition, nor does it make it clear what the behaviour is an adjustment to. The general view taken is that it may either be critical, rejecting, remote or unstimulating parental behaviour as a primary feature, or that it may arise secondarily from a poor fit between temperament (or mild developmental delay) and parental personality. The latter is a position taken by Chess and Thomas (1984, p. 53) with respect to their celebrated follow-up study. In this, they asserted that adjustment reaction accounted for some 89% of the psychiatric diagnoses among preschool children.

The principal argument is that fitting the nonspecific disorders shown by young children into diagnostic categories designed for older children is unrewarding and that a term is needed pending further delineation of disorder categories in this age group. Disorganization of behaviour may itself be a feature of substantial immaturity, as in the disorganization subcategory of attachment behaviour, so that a pleomorphic presentation could itself be a characteristic. However there is no necessary reason to select adjustment disorder as a label because it is psychopathologically nonspecific. The general absence of a clear precipitant and the comparatively poor prognosis of preschool behaviour problems indicate that adjustment disorder as defined in the major classification schemes would not apply to the problems of these children. They may well need to be a term to describe disorganized behaviour in preschool children but it should usually not be adjustment disorder.

Secondly, there is the possible need for a subclinical category to account formally for mild emotional and behavioural reactions to stressors. This is the sense of the current definitions which aim to delineate a mild disorder but these become illogical because it is treated as a psychiatric disorder, being

above threshold for severity of impairment or suffering. Once such a threshold has been crossed, differentiation from other sorts of disorder in terms of typical psychopathology, duration or relationship to stressors becomes tortuous. It would be preferable to reframe the concept as one of adaptation reaction. This would be a subdisorder category analogous to a V code, a descriptive term for a temporary disturbance of emotion, behaviour, relationships or learning secondary to identifiable adversity or stress. The conceptual parallel is with bereavement, sprained ankle or superficial burn: situations in which the reaction to insult itself causes symptoms which can temporarily interfere with ordinary functioning without seriously disrupting it. Individuals with such reactions would be seen in medical services (e.g. following overdoses precipitated by temporary mental distress: Andreasen & Black (1991; p. 384)) and their condition needs recording, yet such a condition need not be regarded as equivalent in severity to being ill or seriously injured. This would lead to the notion of an adaptation *reaction* (rather than disorder): a condition less severe than an illness and not listed within a set of disorders in a classification scheme, yet of clinical significance and therefore something for which a descriptive category needs to persist.

REFERENCES

American Psychiatric Association (1952) *Diagnostic and Statistical Manual of Mental Disorders*, 1st edn. American Psychiatric Press, Washington DC.

American Psychiatric Association (1968) *Diagnostic and Statistical Manual of Mental Disorders*, 2nd edn. American Psychiatric Press, Washington DC.

American Psychiatric Association (1980) *Diagnostic and Statistical Manual of Mental Disorders*, 3rd edn. American Psychiatric Press, Washington DC.

American Psychiatric Association (1987) *Diagnostic and Statistical Manual of Mental Disorders*, 3rd edn, revised. American Psychiatric Press, Washington DC.

American Psychiatric Association (1994) *Diagnostic and Statistical Manual of Mental Disorders*, 4th edn (DSM-IV). American Psychiatric Association, Washington DC.

Andreasen N.C. & Black D.W. (1991) *Introductory Textbook of Psychiatry*, pp. 383–389. American Psychiatric Press, Washington DC.

Andreason N.C. & Hoenk P.R. (1982) The predictive value of adjustment disorders: A follow-up study. *American Journal of Psychiatry*, **139**, 584–590.

Andreason N.C. & Wasek P. (1980) Adjustment disorders in adolescents and adults. *Archives of General Psychiatry*, **37**, 1166–1170.

Arnold L.E. & Carnahan J.A. (1990) Child divorce stress. In: Arnold L.E. (ed) *Childhood Stress*, pp. 373–403. John Wiley, New York.

Bird H.R., Gould M.S., Yager T., Staghezza M.P.H. & Canino G. (1989) Risk factors for maladjustment in Puerto Rican children. *Journal of the American Academy of Child and Adolescent Psychiatry*, **28**, 847–850.

Black D. & Urbanowicz M. (1987) Family intervention with bereaved children. *Journal of Child Psychology and Psychiatry*, **28**, 467–476.

Block J.H., Block J. & Gjerde P.F. (1986) The personality of children prior to divorce: a prospective study. *Child Development*, **57**, 827–840.

Block J., Block J.H. & Gjerde P.F. (1988) Parental functioning and the home environment in families of divorce: prospective and concurrent analyses. *Journal of the American Academy of Child and Adolescent*

Psychiatry, **27**, 207–213.

Breslau N. & Davis G.C. (1987) Post-traumatic stress disorder: the stressor criterion. *Journal of Nervous and Mental Disease*, **175**, 255–264.

Campbell S.B. (1990) *Behavior Problems in Preschool Children*. Guilford Press, New York.

Canino G., Bird H.R., Rubio-Stipec M., Woodbury M.A., Ribera J.C., Huertas S.E. & Sesman M.J. (1987) Reliability of a child diagnosis in a Hispanic sample. *Journal of the American Academy of Child and Adolescent Psychiatry*, **26**, 560–565.

Cantwell, D.P. and Baker L. (1989) Stability and natural history of DSM-III childhood diagnoses. *Journal of the American Academy of Child and Adolescent Psychiatry*, **28**, 691–700.

Cerreto M.C. & Tuma J.M. (1977) Distribution of DSM-II diagnoses in a child psychiatric setting. *Journal of Abnormal Child Psychology*, **5**, 147–153.

Chess S. & Thomas A. (1984) *Origins and Evolution of Behaviour Disorders from Infancy to Adult Life*. Harvard University Press, Cambridge, MA.

Cox A.D. (1993) Social factors in child psychiatric disorder. In: Bhugra D. & Leff J. (eds) *Principles of Social Psychiatry*, pp. 202–233. Blackwell Scientific Publications, Oxford.

Crisp A.H. (1980) *Anorexia Nervosa: Let Me Be*. Academic Press, London.

Doan R.J. & Petti T.A. (1989) Clinical and demographic characteristics of child and adolescent partial hospital patients. *Journal of the American Academy of Child and Adolescent Psychiatry*, **28**, 66–69.

Dunn J. (1988) Connections between relationships: implications of research on mothers and siblings. In: Hinde R. & Stevenson-Hinde J. (eds) *Relationships within Families: Mutual Influences*, pp. 168–180. Oxford University Press, Oxford.

Dunn J. & Kendrick C. (1982) *Siblings: Love, Envy and Understanding*. Cambridge University Press, Cambridge MA.

Earls F., Smith E., Reich W. & Jung K.G. (1988) Investigating psychopathological consequences of a disaster in children: a pilot study incorporating a structured diagnostic interview. *Journal of the American Academy of Child and Adolescent Psychiatry*, **27**, 90–95.

Fabrega H. & Mezzich J. (1987) Adjustment disorder and psychiatric practice: cultural and historical aspects. *Psychiatry*, **50**, 31–49.

Fabrega H., Mezzich J.E. & Mezzich A.C. (1987) Adjustment disorder as a marginal or transitional illness category in DSM-III. *Archives of General Psychiatry*, **44**, 567–572.

Fard F., Hudgens R.W. & Welner A. (1978) Undiagnosed psychiatric illness in adolescents: a prospective study and seven-year follow-up. *Archives of General Psychiatry*, **35**, 279–282.

Faulstich M.E., Moore J.R., Carey M.P., Ruggiero L. & Gresham F. (1986) Prevalence of DSM-III conduct and adjustment disorders for adolescent psychiatric in-patients. *Adolescence*, **21**, 333–337.

Feighner J.P., Robins E., Guze S.B., Woodruff R.A., Winokur G. & Munoz R. (1972) Diagnostic criteria for use in psychiatric research. *Archives of General Psychiatry*, **26**, 57–63.

Ferguson B.F. (1979) Preparing young children for hospitalisation. *Pediatrics*, **64**, 656–664.

Field T. & Reite M. (1984) Children's responses to separation from mother during the birth of another child. *Child Development*, **55**, 1308–1316.

Fisch H.-U., Hammond K.R., Joyce C.R.B. & O'Reilly M. (1981) An experimental study of the clinical judgement of general physicians in evaluating and prescribing for depression. *British Journal of Psychiatry*, **138**, 100–109.

Fowler R.C., Rich C.L. & Young D. (1986) San Diego suicide study II. Substance abuse in young cases. *Archives of General Psychiatry*, **43**, 962–965.

Frederick C.J. (1985) Children traumatized by catastrophic situations.

In: Eth S. & Pynoos R. (eds) *Post Traumatic Stress Disorder in Children*, pp. 73–99. American Psychiatric Press, Washington DC.

Fristad M., Weller E., Weller R. & Grosshans B. (1989) Children's bereavement during the first year post-parental death. *Scientific Proceedings of the Annual Meeting of the American Academy of Child and Adolescent Psychiatry*, **5**, 62–63.

Garmezy N. (1985) Stress-resistant children: the search for protective factors. In: Stevenson J. (ed) *Aspects of Current Child Psychiatry Research*. Journal of Child Psychiatry and Psychology Book Supplement No. 4. Pergamon, Oxford.

Garmezy N. & Rutter M. (Eds) (1983) *Stress, Coping and Development*. McGraw-Hill, New York.

Goldberg L.R. (1970) Man versus model of man: a rationale, plus some evidence, for a method of improving on clinical inference. *Psychological Bulletin*, **73**, 422–432.

Goodyer I. (1990a) Family relationships, life events and childhood psychopathology. *Journal of Child Psychology and Psychiatry Annual Research Review*, **31**, 161–192.

Goodyer I. (1990b) *Life Experiences, Development and Childhood Psychopathology*. John Wiley, Chichester.

Goodyer I., Kolvin I. & Gatzanis S. (1985) Recent undesirable life events and psychiatric disorders of childhood and adolescence. *British Journal of Psychiatry*, **47**, 517–523.

Goodyer I., Kolvin I. & Gatzanis S. (1986) Do age and sex influence the association between recent life events and psychiatric disorders in children and adolescents? A controlled enquiry. *Journal of Child Psychology and Psychiatry*, **27**, 681–687.

Goodyer I., Kolvin I. & Gatzanis S. (1987) The impact of recent life events in psychiatric disorders of childhood and adolescence. *British Journal of Psychiatry*, **151**, 179–185.

Goodyer I., Wright C. & Altham P.M.E. (1988) Maternal adversity and recent stressful life events in anxious and depressed children. *Journal of Child Psychology and Psychiatry*, **29**, 651–669.

Gould M.S., Rutter M., Shaffer D. & Sturge C. (1988) UK/WHO Study of ICD-9. In: Rutter M., Tuma A.H. & Lann I.S. (eds) *Assessment and Diagnosis in Child Psychopathology*, pp. 37–65. Guilford Press, New York.

Graham P. (1991) *Child Psychiatry: A Developmental Approach*. Oxford University Press, Oxford.

Group for the Advancement of Psychiatry (1966) *Psychopathological Disorders in Childhood: Theoretical Considerations and a Proposed Classification*. GAP Report No. 62. Jason Aronson, New York.

Guidubaldi J. & Perry J.D. (1985) Divorce and mental health sequelae for children: a two-year follow-up of a nationwide sample. *Journal of the American Academy of Child and Adolescent Psychiatry*, **24**, 531–537.

Hetherington E.M. (1989) Coping with family transitions: winners, losers and survivors. *Child Development*, **60**, 1–14.

Hetherington E.M., Cox M. & Cox R. (1985) Long-term effects of divorce and remarriage on the adjustment of children. *Journal of the American Academy of Child Psychiatry*, **24**, 518–530.

Hill P. (1993) Adolescent psychiatry. In: Bhugra D. & Leff J. (eds) *Principles of Social Psychiatry*, pp. 234–248. Blackwell Scientific Publications, Oxford.

Hillard J.R., Slomowitz M. & Levi L.S. (1987) A retrospective study of adolescents' visits to a general hospital psychiatric emergency service. *American Journal of Psychiatry*, **144**, 432–436.

Hodges J. & Tizard B. (1989) Social and family relationships of ex-institutional adolescents. *Journal of Child Psychology and Psychiatry*, **30**, 77–97.

Hudgens R.W. (1971) Use of the term 'undiagnosed psychiatric disorder'. *British Journal of Psychiatry*, **119**, 529–532.

Jacobson A.M., Goldberg I.D., Burns B.J., Hoeper E.W., Hankin J.R. & Hewitt K. (1980) Diagnosed mental disorder in children and use of health services in four organized health care settings. *American Journal of Psychiatry*, **137**, 559–565.

Jenkins J.M., Smith M.A. & Graham P.J. (1989) Coping with parental quarrels. *Journal of the American Academy of Child and Adolescent Psychiatry*, **28**, 182–189.

Kaffman M. & Elizur E. (1983) Bereavement responses of kibbutz and non-kibbutz children following the death of a father. *Journal of Child Psychology and Psychiatry*, **24**, 435–442.

Kanner A.D., Feldman S., Weinberger D.A. & Ford M.E. (1991) Uplifts, hassles and adaptational outcomes in early adolescents. In: Monat A. & Lazarus R.S. (eds) *Stress and Coping: an Anthology*, pp. 158–179. Columbia University Press, New York.

Khan A.U. (1988) Sensitivity and specificity of TRH stimulation test in depressed and nondepressed adolescents. *Psychiatry Research*, **25**, 11–17.

Kovacs M. & Gatsonis C. (1989) Stability and change in childhood-onset depressive disorders: longitudinal course as a diagnostic validator. In: Robins L.N. & Barrett J.E. (eds) *The Validity of Psychiatric Diagnosis*, pp. 57–73. Raven Press, New York.

Kovacs M., Feinberg T., Paulaskas S., Finkelstein R., Pollock M., Crouse-Novak M. (1985) Initial coping responses and psychosocial characteristics of children with insulin-resistant diabetes mellitus. *Journal of Pediatrics*, **106**, 827–834.

Kranzler E. (1990) Parent death in childhood. In: Arnold L.E. (ed) *Childhood Stress*, pp. 405–421. Wiley Interscience, New York.

Kranzler E.M., Shaffer D., Wasserman G. & Davies M. (1990) Early child bereavement. *Journal of the American Academy of Child and Adolescent Psychiatry*, **29**, 513–520.

Leon G.R., Kendall P.C. & Garber J. (1980) Depression in children: parent, child and teacher perspectives. *Journal of Abnormal Child Psychology*, **8**, 221–235.

Looney J.G. & Gunderson E. (1978) Transient situational disturbances: course and outcome. *American Journal of Psychiatry*, **135**, 660–663.

McFarlane A.C. (1987) Family functioning and overprotection following a natural disaster: the longitudinal effects of post-traumatic morbidity. *Australian and New Zealand Journal of Psychiatry*, **21**, 210–218.

McFarlane A.C. (1988) Recent life events and psychiatric disorder in children: the interaction with preceding extreme adversity. *Journal of Child Psychology and Psychiatry*, **29**, 677–690.

McGrath J. (1989) A survey of deliberate self-poisoning. *Medical Journal of Australia*, **150**, 317–324.

Malt U.C. (1986) Five years of experience with the DSM-III system in clinical work and research: some concluding remarks. *Acta Psychiatrica Scandinavica Supplement*, **328**, 76–84.

Mezzich J.E., Fabrega H., Coffman G.A. & Haley R. (1989) DSM-III disorders in a large sample of psychiatric patients: frequency and specificity of diagnoses. *American Journal of Psychiatry*, **146**, 212–219.

Monck E. & Dobbs R. (1985) Measuring life events in an adolescent population: methodological issues and related findings. *Psychological Medicine*, **15**, 841–850.

Nadelman L. & Begun A. (1982) The effect of the newborn on the older sibling. In: Lamb M.E. & Sutton-Smith B. (eds) *Sibling Relationships*. Lawrence Erlbaum, Hillsdale, NJ.

Nader K., Pynoos R.S., Fairbanks L. & Frederick C. (1990) Children's PTSD reactions one year after a sniper attack at their school. *American Journal of Psychiatry*, **147**, 1526–1530.

Noshpitz J.D. & Coddington R.D. (eds) (1990) *Stressors and the Adjustment Disorders*, p. 535. Wiley, New York.

Prugh D.G. & Eckhardt L.O. (1980) Stages and phases in the response of children and adolescents to illness and injury. *Advances in Behavioral Pediatrics*, **1**, 181–194.

Pynoos R., Frederick C., Nader K., Arroyo W., Steinberg A., Eth S.,

Nunez F. & Fairbanks L. (1987) Life threat and posttraumatic stress in school-age children. *Archives of General Psychiatry*, **44**, 1057–1063.

Rae-Grant N., Thomas H., Offord D.R. & Boyle M.H. (1989) Risk, protective factors, and the prevalence of behavioral and emotional disorders in children and adolescents. *Journal of the American Academy of Child and Adolescent Psychiatry*, **28**, 262–268.

Remschmidt H. (1988) German study of ICD-9. In: Rutter M., Tuma A.H. & Lann I.S. (eds) *Assessment and Diagnosis in Child Psychopathology*, pp. 66–83. Guilford Press, New York.

Rey J.M., Plapp J.M. & Stewart G.W. (1989) Reliability of psychiatric diagnosis in referred adolescents. *Journal of Child Psychology and Psychiatry*, **30**, 879–888.

Robins D.R., Alessi N.E., Cook S.C., Poznanski E.O. & Yanchyshyn G.W. (1982) The use of the research diagnostic criteria for depression in adolescent psychiatric inpatients. *Journal of the American Academy of Child Psychiatry*, **21**, 251–255.

Rosen B.M., Bahn A.K. & Kramer M. (1964) Demographic and diagnostic characteristics of psychiatric clinic out-patients in the USA, 1961. *American Journal of Orthopsychiatry*, **34**, 122–136.

Runeson B. (1989) Mental disorder in youth suicide. *Acta Psychiatrica Scandinavica*, **79**, 490–497.

Rutter M. (1966) *Children of Sick Parents*. Maudsley Monograph No. 16. Oxford University Press, Oxford.

Rutter M. (1981) *Maternal Deprivation Reassessed*, 2nd edn. Penguin, Harmondsworth.

Rutter M. (1985) Resilience in the face of adversity. *British Journal of Psychiatry*, **147**, 598–611.

Rutter M. & Sandberg S. (1992) Psychosocial stressors: concepts, causes and effects. *European Child and Adolescent Psychiatry*, **1**, 3–13.

Rutter M., Graham P., Chadwick O. & Yule W. (1976) Adolescent turmoil: fact or fiction? *Journal of Child Psychology and Psychiatry*, **22**, 375–392.

Setterburg S.R., Ernst M., Rao U., Campbell M., Carlson G., Shaffer D. & Staghezza B.M. (1991) Child psychiatrists' views of DSM-II-R: a survey of usage and opinions. *Journal of the American Academy of Child and Adolescent Psychiatry*, **30**, 652–658.

Sowder R.J., Burt M.R., Rosenstein M.J. & Milazzo-Sayre L.J. (1981) *Use of Psychiatric Facilities by Children and Youth, United States 1975*. Mental Health Service System Reports, no. 6. US Government Printing Office, Washington, DC.

Steinhausen H.-C. (1987) Global assessment of child psychopathology. *Journal of the American Academy of Child and Adolescent Psychiatry*, **26**, 203–206.

Steinhausen H.-C. & Erdin A. (1991a) A comparison of ICD-9 and ICD-10 diagnoses of child and adolescent psychiatric disorders. *Journal of Child Psychology and Psychiatry*, **32**, 909–920.

Steinhausen H.-C. & Erdin A. (1991b) The inter-rater reliability of child and adolescent psychiatric disorders in the ICD-10. *Journal of Child Psychology and Psychiatry*, **32**, 921–928.

Steinhausen H.-C. & Erdin A. (1992) Abnormal psychosocial situations and ICD-10 diagnoses in children and adolescents attending a psychiatric service. *Journal of Child Psychology and Psychiatry*, **33**, 731–740.

Udwin O. (1993) Children's reactions to traumatic events. *Journal of Child Psychology and Psychiatry*, **34**, 115–127.

Van Eerdewegh M.M., Clayton P.J. & Van Eerdewegh P. (1985) The bereaved child: factors influencing early psychopathology. *British Journal of Psychiatry*, **147**, 188–194.

Vargas L.A., Loya F. & Hodde-Vargas J. (1989) Exploring the multidimensional aspects of grief reactions. *American Journal of Psychiatry*, **146**, 1484–1488.

Wallerstein J.S. (1985) Children of divorce: preliminary report of a ten-year follow-up of older children and adolescents. *Journal of the American Academy of Child Psychiatry*, **24**, 545–553.

Wallerstein J.S. (1987) Children of divorce: report of a 10-year follow-up of early latency-age children. *American Journal of Orthopsychiatry*, **57**, 199–211.

Wallerstein J.S. & Kelly J. (1980) *Surviving the Breakup*. Grant McIntyre, London.

Webster-Stratton C. (1991) Strategies for helping families with conduct disordered children. *Journal of Child Psychology and Psychiatry*, **32**, 1047–1062.

Weiner I.B. (1982) *Child and Adolescent Psychopathology*, pp. 44–52. John Wiley, Chichester.

Weiner I.B. & Del Gaudio A.C. (1976) Psychopathology in adolescence: an epidemiological study. *Archives of General Psychiatry*, **33**, 187–193.

Weller E., Fristad M. & Weller R. (1989) Adolescent bereavement post parental death. *Scientific Proceedings of the American Academy of Child Psychiatry*, **5**, 63.

Werry J.S., Methven J., Fitzpatrick J. & Dixon H. (1983) The inter-rater reliability of DSM-III in children. *Journal of Abnormal Child Psychology*, **11**, 341–354.

Williams J.B.W. & Spitzer R.L. (1980) DSM-III field trials: inter-rater reliability and list of project staff and participants. Appendix F. In: *Diagnostic and Statistical Manual of Mental Disorders*, 3rd edn. American Psychiatric Association, Washington DC.

Wolfer J.A. & Visintainer M.A. (1979) Prehospital psychological preparation for tonsillectomy patients: effects on children's and parents' adjustment. *Pediatrics*, **64**, 646–655.

Woolston J.L. (1988) Theoretical considerations of the adjustment disorders. *Journal of the American Academy of Child and Adolescent Psychiatry*, **27**, 280–287.

World Health Organization (1965) *Manual of the International Statistical Classification of Diseases, Injuries, and Causes of Death*, 8th edn. World Health Organization, Geneva.

World Health Organization (1974) *Manual of the International Statistical Classification of Diseases, Injuries, and Causes of Death*, 9th edn. World Health Organization, Geneva.

World Health Organization (1992) *The ICD-10 Classification of Mental and Behavioural Disorders: Clinical Descriptions and Diagnostic Guidelines*. World Health Organization, Geneva.

Yule W. (1990) Work with children following disasters. In: Herbert M. (ed) *Clinical Child Psychology: Theory and Practice*. John Wiley, Chichester.

Chapter 22
Posttraumatic Stress Disorders

William Yule

Both the major systems of psychiatric classification, ICD-10 (World Health Organization, 1992) and DSM-IV (American Psychiatric Association, 1987) have been recently revised and each has, in differing ways, reflected the increased awareness that major stressors can cause serious morbidity. Both systems now acknowledge that children may suffer from posttraumatic stress disorder (PTSD), but each reflects the paucity of methodologically sound studies in their vague descriptions of how major stressors may affect children of widely differing ages.

The question for child psychiatry is whether severe acute stresses, as opposed to chronic ones linked to social adversity, carry a substantial increased risk of psychiatric sequelae. If so, what sort of stressors carry such increased risk? What are the commonest psychological sequelae? Do these vary according to stressor, according to developmental level? What is the role of the family in moderating the reactions? Are there other known risk and protective factors? Indeed, is PTSD truly a separate disorder or is it merely a variant of other well-recognized disorders such as anxiety, phobias or depression? Finally, what is currently known about intervention?

THE CONCEPT OF POSTTRAUMATIC STRESS DISORDER

The concept of PTSD was first developed in relation to studies of adult reactions to major stress. Following the Second World War, there was far better understanding of the psychological nature of so-called battle fatigue, and as the dramatic and long-lasting psychological effects of the Vietnam War began to be recognized, it came to be appreciated that three major groups of symptoms — (1) distressing recurring recollections of the traumatic event; (2) avoidance of stimuli associated with the trauma; and (3) a range of signs of increased physiological arousal — seemed to form a coherent syndrome. That came to be labelled PTSD (Horowitz, 1976; American Psychiatric Association, 1980).

The introduction of the category and its first operationalization in DSM-III (American Psychiatric Association, 1980) sparked a great deal of research, as well as controversy. PTSD was classified as an anxiety disorder, but many argued that it should be included as a dissociative disorder. It was increasingly described as 'a normal reaction to an abnormal situation', and so, logically, it was queried whether it should be regarded as a psychiatric disorder at all (O'Donohue & Eliot, 1992).

Although DSM is a predominantly phenomenological classification, the diagnosis of PTSD involves a putative aetiology — experience of a traumatic event outside the range of usual human experience. This requirement has been helpful in focusing attention on emotional reactions following major trauma, but the criteria for which stressors are outside the range of usual human experience are not adequately operationalized. Presumably 'usual' is not meant to be defined statistically on the basis of community prevalence, because exposure to atrocity is usual in some urban wars. Similarly, probably a sixth to a third of women experience some form of sexual abuse by the time they are aged 18 (see Chapter 14). Does this mean that sexual abuse cannot precipitate PTSD because it is so common (O'Donohue & Eliot, 1992)? By contrast, relatively few children experience the death of a parent during their growing years. This is a clearly stressful experience (see Chapters 45 and 12) but it tends to be viewed as normal and therefore not a cause of PTSD, although it can give rise to depression. Thus, there is a need to consider more fully what sorts of acute, severe stressors give rise to posttraumatic disorders, irrespective of the frequency of occurrence of the stressors, and to determine whether different types of stressor give rise to different types of pathology.

Results from studies of adults have shown that PTSD, although predominantly characterized by anxiety, differs from other anxiety disorders in important ways. Thus, Foa *et al.* (1989) showed that the trauma giving rise to PTSD violated more of the patients' safety assumptions than did events giving rise to other forms of anxiety. There was a much greater generalization of fear responses in the PTSD groups, and, unlike other anxious patients, they reported far more frequent reexperiencing of the traumatic event. Indeed, it is this internal, subjective experience that seems most to mark out PTSD from other disorders (Jones & Barlow, 1992).

It may be concluded that the symptomatology of PTSD differs in key respects from that of other psychiatric disorders. Taken together with its close temporal association with some severe acute stress, this has important implications for treatment (see below). This constitutes a justification for a separate diagnostic grouping. Nevertheless, it has to be admitted that the separateness, or otherwise, of PTSD on other criteria has yet to be determined. Thus, for example, it is not known whether PTSD differs from adjustment disorders, or from other emotional disorders precipitated by some stresses, in degree or kind. Similarly, there is no evidence on whether genetic factors play a role in vulnerability to PTSD or, if they do, whether they are coterminous with those that predispose to anxiety disorders, or to affective conditions. These and other questions relevant to diagnosis remain to be tackled.

Having attempted to operationalize the category of PTSD, questions were raised as to whether there is a spectrum of PTSD (Kolb, 1988). It soon became clear that, while many patients met the criteria listed in DSM-III, some showed many, but insufficient, symptoms to meet full criteria. Even with the revision to the criteria (American Psychiatric Association, 1987), this is still the case and some researchers and clinicians are arguing for an additional grouping to be recognized — disorders of extreme stress not otherwise specified (DESNOS; Herman, 1992). To some extent, this category is being sought to encompass the complex symptomatology shown by people who have been incarcerated or otherwise suffered repeated traumatization, as in cases of child sexual abuse. To that extent, the distinction between PTSD and DESNOS is similar to the distinction drawn by Terr (1991) between her type I and type II PTSD in children (see later).

There is good evidence that exposure to severe, acute stress does increase psychiatric morbidity. Raphael (1986) reviewed results from many different studies of different types of disaster using different definitions of psychopathology. She concluded that 1 year after the disaster, some 30–40% of survivors showed significant impairment. This level of morbidity reduced only slowly over the following 5 years.

A more recent review incorporating sophisticated meta-analytic techniques also concluded that major disasters gave rise to increases in psychopathology (Rubonis & Bickman, 1991). Their review of 31 published studies that had sufficient published data for inclusion concluded that anxiety disorders and increased alcohol use were commoner that depression following a trauma. Strangely, they did not mention the prevalence of PTSD. A comparison of the prevalence of disorder in survivors with appropriate controls showed a 17% increase in psychopathology among survivors. However, effects varied significantly across different studies; accordingly caution must be used in generalizing from this result. These authors warn that the more rigorous the study, the lower the estimate of pathology. The studies with standard measures reported lower rates than those that did not, with interview methods yielding lower rates than questionnaires. The meta-analysis confirmed that women were more vulnerable than men. Disasters involving a high number of deaths gave rise to higher levels of distress in survivors. Unfortunately, 9 of the 31 studies reviewed were of the Three Mile Island nuclear accident which might have been disastrous, but fortunately was not. The inclusion of so many studies of the one incident may account for their unusual conclusion that natural disasters gave rise to more psychopathology than manmade disasters, a point returned to below.

In summary, the recognition of PTSD as a separate category of psychiatric disorder in adults has been found to be very meaningful and productive. PTSD is similar to but different from other anxiety disorders, particularly in the reexperiencing of the traumatic incident. The first attempts to operationalize the disorder in DSM-III and DSM-R have been useful, but still require revision. It is not clear whether there is a spectrum of posttraumatic reactions, nor whether there is a distinct type that follows from repeated traumatization. It is clear that major stress leads to an increase in psychopathology, but there is disagreement about the type of stressor that leads to particular types of reactions.

CURRENT PSYCHIATRIC CLASSIFICATIONS: DSM-IV AND ICD-10

DSM-IV (American Psychiatric Association, in press)

In DSM-III-R (American Psychiatric Association, 1987) *Posttraumatic Stress Disorder* was described as follows:

> The essential feature of this disorder is the development of characteristic symptoms following a psychologically distressing event that is outside the range of usual human experience (i.e. outside the range of such common experiences as simple bereavement, chronic illness, business losses, and marital conflict). The stressor producing this syndrome would be markedy distressing to almost anyone, and is usually experienced with intense fear, terror, and helplessness. The characteristic symptoms involve re-experiencing the traumatic event, avoidance of stimuli associated with the event or numbing of general responsiveness, and increased arousal. The diagnosis is not made if the disturbance lasts less than one month. (p. 247)

DSM-III-R went on to note that PTSD can occur during childhood. Children may refuse to talk about the trauma, but they may well remember it vividly. They especially may show a marked change in orientation to the future, and they may show a variety of physical symptoms such as stomach aches or headaches.

There is no information on prevalence, sex ratio or familial pattern in this disorder.

In DSM-IV, PTSD is classified as an anxiety disorder. It is pertinent to note that the requirements for meeting a diagnosis of PTSD changed considerably between its introduction in 1980 and the current revision in 1987. In particular, the revised definition does not acknowledge the presence of 'survivor guilt', whether it be guilt over the fact of surviving when many have died, guilt over not doing enough to help others in the crisis, or guilt over what was done to survive. These subjective feelings still remain prominent among adults and children who present with PTSD.

Although not part of the definition, DSM-IV requires specification on whether the disorder is *acute* or *chronic* (duration less, or more, than 3 months) and on whether the onset was *delayed* (at least 6 months after the event). The distinction between acute and chronic subtypes was always arbitrary and no data have been produced to warrant the distinction. That some posttraumatic stress reactions appear to have a delay in onset seems reasonably established in the case of Vietnam veterans, but one must distinguish between delay in onset and delay in recognition of the disorder, especially in children and adolescents where the diagnosis has not been much used until recently.

ICD-10 (World Health Organization, 1992)

Reaction to severe stress and adjustment disorders are also defined within ICD-10. It is noted that:

> This category differs from others in that it includes disorders identifiable not only on grounds of symptomatology and course but also on the basis of one or other of two causative influences — an exceptionally stressful life event producing an acute stress reaction, or a significant life change leading to continued unpleasant circumstances that result in an adjustment disorder.
>
> The disorders brought together here are thought to arise always as a direct consequence of the acute severe stress or continued trauma, [unlike more transient reactions to lesser life events].

Acute stress reaction

Acute stress reaction develops in individuals without prior problems, and usually subsides within hours or days. When symptoms persist longer, a change in diagnosis is probably required.

Posttraumatic stress disorder

PTSD '. . . arises as a delayed or protracted response to a stressful event or situation . . . of an exceptionally threatening or catastrophic nature, which is likely to cause pervasive distress in almost everyone.' Predisposing personality traits or prior history are neither sufficient nor necessary to explain the onset of PTSD. ICD-10 lists similar symptoms to those in DSM-IV, again emphasizing the repetitive intrusive memories, stating that:

> Conspicuous emotional detachment, numbing of feeling, and avoidance of stimuli that might arouse recollections of the trauma are often present but are not essential for the diagnosis. The autonomic disturbances, mood disorder, and behavioural abnormalities all contribute to the diagnosis but not are of prime importance.

Thus, ICD places most emphasis on the troublesome reexperiencing phenomena and much less emphasis on the emotional numbing which has proven difficult to elicit in many adults and also proved difficult to define in children and adolescents. It should also be noted that ICD states that PTSD should normally be diagnosed only when it arises within 6 months of a major trauma.

Adjustment disorder

ICD-10 also recognizes a category of adjustment disorder that is characterized by 'states of subjective distress and emotional disturbance, usually interfering with social functioning and performance, arising in the period of adaptation to a significant life change or a stressful life event'. Individual vulnerability is seen as important, but the disorder would not have occurred without the stressor (see Chapter 21).

Undoubtedly, the recognition of PTSD as a separate category of adjustment/anxiety disorder by DSM-III constituted a major step in focusing attention on the vexed question of why only some people persist in having major dysfunction after experiencing a severe stressor. Once described, the question was asked to what extent children and young people react with the same or similar symptoms, and indeed what is the developmental progression of reactions to major stressors.

As is inevitable with classificatory schemes that have to be agreed by committees in advance of complete evidence, the two schemes place differing emphases on different signs. It is far from clear that the signs included in either scheme represent all the reactions people display to stress. These issues have important implications for future studies as they caution against too mechanistic application of the diagnostic algorithms, particularly in research studies.

POSTTRAUMATIC STRESS DISORDER IN CHILDREN

The main problem when applying the working criteria of either DSM or ICD to disorders shown by children and adolescents after experiencing a major trauma is that the criteria were not developed on the basis of studies of young people. Do the same symptoms manifest? Do they manifest differently at different ages? Do they cluster differently? Are any absent in younger children? Are there symptoms shown by children that do not manifest in adults? Only careful descriptive studies of representative groups of traumatized children studied over periods of time can establish the natural history of the disorder in children. Such studies have yet to be done systematically and, when they are, it will be important that the investigators keep an open mind about the range of symptoms studied and do not merely enquire about symptoms that are already incorporated in the official classifications. A flavour of how major stressors affect children can, however, be obtained from a number of published studies.

Following the Aberfan disaster of 21 October 1966, in which a huge coal tip slid down a mountainside killing 116 children and 28 adults, Lacey (1972) reported how 56 children presented at the local child guidance clinic over the following 4 years:

> Symptoms varied but the commonest were sleeping difficulties, nervousness, lack of friends, unwillingness to go to school or out to play, instability and enuresis. Some of the children too, had shown some of these symptoms before the disaster, but they were said to be very much

worse after it. Broadly speaking, the children who were most affected were those with other anxiety creating situations in their backgrounds. (Lacey, 1972, p. 259)

Some anxious parents became overprotective of their children. Fears of the dark and nightmares caused sleep problems. Bad weather upset the children, as a period of bad weather had preceded the tip slide. Children rarely spoke spontaneously of their experiences. Three children played games of burying in the sand.

Unfortunately, no systematic studies were undertaken of the effects of this major disaster. Even so, Lacey identified a number of the themes that are still pertinent today. The reactions were seen as predominantly related to anxiety. Some children with prior difficulties were at greater risk. The families' reactions mediated the course of the disorder. There was repetitive play in some children. And above all, she noted that children rarely spoke spontaneously of their experiences.

Following my experience of assessing and working with child and adolescent survivors of the capsize of the Herald of Free Enterprise car ferry (Yule & Williams, 1990) and those from the sinking of the cruise ship, Jupiter (Yule *et al.*, 1990; Yule, 1992), I noted the following common reactions.

Most children were troubled by repetitive, intrusive thoughts about the accident. Such thoughts could occur at any time, but particularly when the children were otherwise quiet, as when they were trying to drop off to sleep. At other times, the thoughts and vivid recollections were triggered off by reminders in their environment. Vivid flashbacks were not uncommon. Sleep disturbances were very common, particularly in the first few weeks. Fears of the dark and bad dreams, nightmares and waking through the night were widespread. Separation difficulties were frequent, even among teenagers. For the first few days, children often did not want to let their parents out of their sight, even reverting to sleeping in the parental bed. Many children became much more irritable and angry than previously, both with parents and peers. Although child survivors experienced a pressure to talk about their experiences, paradoxically they also found it very difficult to talk with their parents and peers. Often they did not want to upset the adults, and so many parents were not aware of the full extent of their children's suffering. Peers sometimes held back from asking what happened in case they upset the child further; the survivor often felt this as a rejection.

Children reported a number of cognitive changes. Many experienced difficulties in concentration, especially in school work. Others reported memory problems, both in mastering new material and in remembering old skills such as reading music. They became very alert to danger in their environment, being adversely affected by reports of other disasters. Survivors learned that life is very fragile. This could lead to a loss of faith in the future or a sense of foreshortened future. Their priorities changed. Some felt that they should live each day to the full and not plan far ahead. Others realized they had been over-concerned with materialistic or petty matters and resolved to rethink their values. Not surprisingly, many developed fears associated with specific aspects of their experiences. They avoided situations that they associated with the disaster. Many experienced 'survivor guilt' — about surviving when others died; about thinking they should have done more to help others; about what they themselves did to survive.

Adolescent survivors reported significantly high rates of depression, some becoming clinically depressed, having suicidal thoughts and taking overdoses in the year after a disaster. A significant number became very anxious after accidents, although the appearance of panic attacks was sometimes considerably delayed. When children had been bereaved, they sometimes needed bereavement counselling.

In summary, children and adolescents surviving a life-threatening disaster showed most of the same range of symptoms as reported in adults. There may be considerable comorbidity with depression, generalized anxiety or pathological grief reactions.

Effects on younger children

Very young children may show all sorts of regressive behaviour or antisocial behaviour. Parents may avoid talking to the child about what happened. However, it is possible to get children as young as 4–6 years old to describe vividly what they had experienced, much to their parents' surprise.

A number of the preschool children who survived the sinking of the Herald were reported by their parents and teachers as being involved in repetitive play or drawings involving themes about the ship. Some preschool boys became aggressive and antisocial both at home and at school. In all cases, their parents knew they were still upset thinking about the ferry, but they could never talk about it to anyone.

Very young children have only limited understanding of the life-threatening nature of disasters. Even so, we know from other studies of the concepts of death and dying that some preschool children have very adult concepts of these. It is important that we remember the range of individual differences in cognitive awareness when discussing (or not discussing) the effects of disasters with children. It is always a good strategy to get children to repeat back to you what you have tried to explain. That way, any muddles or misunderstandings are quickly revealed and can be corrected.

As young children's understanding develops, they will need to go back over the troubling events so that they can make better sense of them from their more advanced level of understanding.

Thus, clinical experience demonstrates that many children and adolescents present with symptoms of anxiety, depression and stress following major life-threatening disasters. The list of problems presented above is remarkably similar to the symptoms subsumed under the category of PTSD, but there are some differences.

Like others (Frederick, 1985) it was difficult to elicit evidence of emotional numbing in children and adolescents. In contrast, many showed evidence of survivor guilt, no longer one of the DSM-IV criteria. Above all, it was surprising how easy it was to get children to give graphic accounts of what had happened to them and just how distressing the reexperiencing in thoughts and images was. Often, children had not confided this to parents or teachers, so inevitably the latter would underestimate the extent and nature of the children's distress.

PROBLEMS DEFINING STRESS

Stress is one of those concepts that is widely used in everyday life, but that eludes precise definition. In general, people feel under stress when the demands made on them exceed their capacity to meet those demands.

Objective versus subjective measure of stressor

Garmezy and Masten (1990) considered that the concept of stress '... implicates four factors: (1) the presence of a manifest stimulus event; (2) the event is one capable of modifying the organism's physiological and psychological equilibrium; (3) the disequilibrium is reflected in a state of arousal marked by neuropsychological, cognitive and emotional consequences for the individual; (4) these changes, in turn, disrupt the adaptation of the person' (pp. 462−3). The individual responds to stress by coping, but how one copes is determined by an appraisal of what the demands are and whether one is able to meet these. Thus, increasingly it is recognized that whatever the objective, stimulus properties of a stressor, the individual's coping will be affected by how that individual appraises the threat. Hence, there has been an increased interest in cognitive coping strategies and attributional processes (Joseph *et al.*, 1991, 1993).

Given the individual differences in reaction to objectively similar stimuli or stressors, it will never prove possible to predict precisely how many children will react adversely to a particular event. But a better understanding of the range and nature of reactions to different life events will help improve the predictions.

The study of life events in adults has established that some single life events, such as bereavement, are fairly consistently associated with psychiatric disorder (Paykel, 1974). Parallel studies of life events in children (Coddington, 1972a,b; Monaghan *et al.*, 1979; Yeaworth *et al.*, 1980) have usually used life event scores. They have face validity and predictions based on the sum of a variety of life events are stronger than those based on single events within the normal everyday range. They are easily administered to large groups and so open the way to better epidemiological studies, free of biases inherent in most clinic-referred samples. However, they are limited in that it is impossible to judge the quality and personal meaning of a particular event for an individual child from a simple questionnaire (Goodyer, 1990); accordingly semistructured interviews are to be preferred.

Children's exposure to stressful events is related both to psychological disturbance and physical disorders (cf. Garmezy & Rutter, 1985; Goodyer, 1990, for reviews). However, the cross-sectional and retrospective nature of most enquiries raises the issues of the direction of causality and the nature of the processes involved. In two separate studies of children diagnosed as having a psychiatric disorder, it was found that moderately severe undesirable life events occurred in between 60 and 70% of new cases in the year prior to the onset of the disorders (Goodyer *et al.*, 1985, 1988). Recent stresses were seen as probably provoking new episodes of disorder, but the authors also point to the fact that many children experiencing apparently similar stressors did not break down.

Thus, there is a need for careful, prospective studies of groups of children exposed to particular stressors. The study of children who survive disasters affords one important opportunity to investigate the effects of major stressors on psychological adjustment.

Implications for severe acute stressors

Generally, it can be assumed that children who are the victims of a large-scale disaster are an unselected group. This provides an opportunity to assess the dose-response relationship between stressor and sequelae, as well as to examine risk and protective factors such as age, sex and family support. However, as the previous section cautions, one has to differentiate the objective level of threat from the subjectively perceived level of threat. For example, in the California school sniper attack, Pynoos *et al.* (1987) demonstrated a strong relationship between the distance from the sniper and later psychopathology, with some individual differences such as the boy who had left early to play football, leaving his sister in the line of fire. Not surprisingly, although he was in a safe area, he experienced considerable posttraumatic stress.

The implication of this is that studies of the effects of severe acute stressors will have to use specially developed semistructured interviews to tease out the unique aspects of the particular disaster for each individual survivor, whilst at the same time incorporating sufficient standard measures to permit comparisons with other studies of disasters. Standard life event schedules are unlikely to discriminate between survivors and controls when the schedule has no or few items related to the particular disaster. However, they may be very important in examining the claim that children who have survived disasters experience an increase in life events in the subsequent years. In any follow-up, life event schedules should be incorporated to check whether the then current levels of pathology relate more to the original trauma or to the intervening events.

Dose−response relationship

One of the key concepts in PTSD is that anyone can develop the disorder, irrespective of prior vulnerabilities, provided the stressor is sufficiently great. There is, therefore, considerable interest in whether there is any evidence for a dose−response relationship between stressor and pathology.

In his study of the effects of a paint factory explosion on factory workers in Norway, Weisaeth (1983) demonstrated that workers who were at the centre of the explosion developed considerably higher levels of distress than those at the periphery, with lowest levels being recorded by those at home at the time. There are four published studies that bear on this point in relation to children.

California school sniper

Pynoos and his colleagues have undertaken among the most systematic studies of children suffering a variety of trauma, ranging from witnessing a parent being murdered or raped, to themselves surviving an attack from a sniper in their school playground (Pynoos & Eth, 1986; Pynoos et al., 1987; Pynoos & Nader, 1988). To avoid the weaknesses of previous studies, they sampled 159 children with an average age of 9 years (14.5% of those attending the school) who were exposed to a sniper attack on the school in which one child and a passer-by were killed and 13 other children were injured. Many children were trapped in the playground under gunfire and others were trapped in classrooms. Many were separated from siblings and, of course, parents. The siege lasted a number of hours.

Approximately 1 month after the event, nearly 40% of the children were found to have moderate to severe PTSD on the Frederick and Pynoos (1988) Post Traumatic Stress Reaction Index. There was a very strong relationship between exposure and later effects in that those children who were trapped in the playground scored much higher than those who had left the vicinity of the school before the attack or were not in school that day.

Fourteen months later, Nader et al. (1991) reported that 74% of the most severely exposed children in the playground still reported moderate to severe levels of PTSD, whereas only 19% of the unexposed children reported any PTSD. Earlier PTSD Reaction Index scores were strongly related to those obtained at follow-up. Only among the less exposed children did greater knowledge of the victim increase the strength of the emotional reaction to the trauma. In other words, the level of exposure to the life-threatening trauma was more important than other factors such as knowledge of the victim. In this study, the moderating effects of families' reactions were not reported but the strength of the relationships noted challenges McFarlane's (1987) claim that most effects are mediated by parental reaction.

Sinking of the Jupiter

Five months after the sinking of the cruise ship *Jupiter* with over 400 British schoolchildren on board, Yule et al. (1990) studied self-reported fears, anxiety and depression in a party of 24 adolescent girls from one school. Compared to girls who wanted to go on the cruise (but did not get a place), other girls in the same school who expressed no interest in the cruise (but may have been upset by subsequent events) and controls from a similar school elsewhere, a subjective exposure–response effect was found for depression and anxiety, but not reported fears.

Armenian earthquake

Pynoos et al. (in press) used the Post Traumatic Stress Reaction Index in translation in three groups of children in Armenia — one from a town at the epicentre where buildings were totally demolished; one from a town at the periphery of the devastation; and one control group from outside the affected area. There was a clear exposure–effect relationship, with the most exposed children reporting highest scores.

South Carolina Hurricane Hugo (1989)

Lonigan et al. (1991) received self-report data from 5687 children and adolescents aged 9–19 years exposed to Hurricane Hugo in 1989. The subjects completed the Revised Children's Manifest Anxiety Scale (Reynolds & Richmond, 1978) and a self-completed version of the Frederick Reaction Index for Children (Frederick, 1985).

Degree of exposure was significantly associated with increased scores on both anxiety and stress reactions. Girls scored significantly higher than boys on both scales. The proportion with PTSD, as categorized on their total Stress Reaction Index Scores, was 5% in the no exposure group, 10% in the mild, 16% in the moderate and 29% in the high exposure group. The average anxiety scores for the hurricane survivors were much lower than those obtained from the 334 survivors of the Jupiter sinking (Yule, 1992), suggesting that the hurricane was less of a direct threat to the children.

The findings from these studies strongly suggest that within a single disaster, there is a strong relationship between degree of exposure to the stressor and subsequent adjustment. However, subjective factors also play a role. Studies of adult survivors find that high levels of pathology are related to the belief that the survivors were going to die during the incident, as well as to the experience of seeing dead and mutilated bodies (Williams et al., 1993). Similar findings are emerging from the study of the most severely affected children assessed individually after the sinking of the Jupiter (Yule et al., 1992).

Physiological versus psychological reactions

Reactions to major stress have both physiological and psychological components. Any major life-threatening experience may activate primitive flight/fight/freeze mechanisms. In some individuals following some threats, these reactions seem to get stuck. The trauma is then relived at all levels — behavioural, emotional, physiological and neuroendocrinological. The reactions involve many systems, including the release of noradrenaline from the locus coeruleus and endogenous opiates in the septohippocampal system (van der Kolk et al., 1985; Goodyer, 1990). A better understanding of these mechanisms may lead to better targeted pharmacological therapy that may, in turn, prevent chronic reactions. For the present, the main point to emphasize is that massive threat can lead to changes that may remain over many years, as demonstrated by Ornitz and Pynoos (1989) in their study of a persisting startle reaction in a child with PTSD.

This was shown in a different way by Suomi (1991) in his studies of the effects of enforced separation of young monkeys from their mothers. Although the well-documented distress apparently settled reasonably soon after reunion, neuro-chemical changes remained and the monkeys remained highly reactive to later threats. This raises the question of the long-term effects of major stressors on human adaptation systems and whether, even after apparent recovery, the systems remain more vulnerable than previously to future stress.

SIGNIFICANT INDIVIDUAL STRESSORS

Having established that children and adolescents can develop posttraumatic reactions after various stressors, and that there is some evidence that the severity of the stressor is related to the subsequent level of psychopathology, we now ask whether different types of stressors give rise either to different levels or different types of psychopathology. Unfortunately, the database is too weak to answer these important questions with confidence.

In presenting the following review, studies have been grouped according to the nature of the disaster. In general, findings from adult studies suggest that natural disasters produce less emotional problems than technological ones; that accidental man-made accidents have less serious sequelae than those where deliberate actions cause the harm. Acts of deliberate violence, particularly child physical and sexual abuse, may have the worst outcome (Raphael, 1986; Hodgkinson & Stewart, 1991).

War

UNICEF estimated that 80% of the victims of military action are women and children (Lee, 1991). During World War II, some attempts were made to chart the effects of the conflict on children. The major findings are summarized by Garmezy and Rutter (1985) and Goodyer (1990). Studies of the effects of the evacuation of large numbers of British children from towns to the supposedly safer countryside seemed to conclude that separation from parents was probably more damaging psychologically than remaining in high-risk areas. What has only recently come to light in direct testimony is that many of the evacuees were cruelly treated, even to the extent of experiencing physical and sexual abuse (Wicks, 1988). It was not fashionable to enquire into such matters in the 1940s.

Recent studies of the effects of local wars on children are reviewed elsewhere (Macksoud, in press; Macksoud *et al.*, 1992). N. Richman, A. Ratilal and A. Aly (1990, personal communication) reported on 50 Mozambican children aged 7–15 years who had been brutalized by kidnapping or witnessing murder or other atrocities. Forty of the children suffered psychological symptoms related to the war; 25%

were markedly affected. While such children may well require specialist psychological services to help them readjust, what is really needed is a political solution to end such wars. While, rightly, people emphasize that many children are resilient in the face of continuing armed struggles, this view may be misused to avoid studying the effects of war. Partisan and patriotic fervour seems to hold sway over humanitarian and scientific interests in such long-standing battle grounds as Northern Ireland and Israel (see Garmezy & Rutter, 1985, for a review).

Israeli children who experienced terrorist attacks at first hand during the continuing Arab–Israeli conflicts developed high rates of anxiety (Ayalon, 1983) and a manual for use in alleviating the children's distress has been developed (Ayalon, 1988). In the Lebanese civil war, 273 of 840 children aged 9–13 were found to have PTSD (Saigh, 1989). The levels of PTSD were similar regardless of whether the route of traumatization was direct, through observation or other indirect means (Saigh, 1991). Such emotional effects of war can last a number of years. Six years after fleeing Cambodia and the Pol Pot regime, 50% of adolescent refugees met the criteria for PTSD (Kinzie *et al.*, 1986). At a 5-year follow-up, there was some evidence that the level of posttraumatic stress symptoms was beginning to fall (Sack, 1990).

Thus, there can be little doubt that children are emotionally affected by war in all its forms. Those in the front line or who experience atrocities at first hand have a high — 25–50% — risk of developing PTSD.

Disasters

Estimates of the rates of PTSD in child survivors of natural disasters range from about 10 to 100% depending on the nature of the disaster, the degree of life threat to the children, the measures taken and the time that has elapsed between the occurrence and the study. Of 179 children aged 2–15 years who were examined 2 years after the Buffalo Creek dam disaster, 37% received probable PTSD diagnoses (Green *et al.*, 1991). These diagnoses were made retrospectively on records that did not include systematic data from questioning the children about recurring thoughts and images of the disaster, so the 37% prevalence estimate may be very conservative. After a tornado in Vicksburg, Mississipi, 56 out of 183 children (30%) showed mild to severe reactions, and many children played 'tornado games' (Bloch *et al.*, 1956). A small study of the effects of the 1989 San Francisco earthquake in 22 children aged 10–12 years (Bradburn, 1991), some 6–8 months after the event, used the Post Traumatic Stress Reaction Index. Six children (27%) had moderate PTSD and 8 (36%) had mild PTSD; none had severe PTSD. Distance from the collapsed highway was positively correlated to scores on the PTSD Index. Separation from parents and the degree of perceived parental distress were not related to the scores. Having previously experienced severe traumas such as witnessing murder did not relate to the stress scores.

Five young children were studied after a power boat

ploughed into spectators at a regatta in Pittsburgh (Martini *et al.*, 1990). On the PTSD Reaction Index, 4 of the 5 children aged 3−9 years reported scores that indicated they suffered PTSD, but only 3 satisfied DSM-III-R criteria. Parents and children disagreed on the reporting of symptoms, but even 3-year-olds could provide detailed information on their own reactions.

One of the problems in estimating prevalence rates is that it is difficult to examine all the survivors and considerable doubt often exists about the representativeness of those reported on. Parry Jones (1991) studied the effects of the Pan Am disaster on children in the Scottish town of Lockerbie, where 8 adults and 3 children living in the town were killed by debris. One year later, 54 children were individually assessed, and even later, a further 67 were assessed. No examples of delayed reactions were found. Over half reported intrusive thoughts, and a third had traumatic dreams. Two-thirds showed evidence of loss of skills, this being slightly commoner among younger children. Sleep disturbance was present in 80% and half reported increased irritability and difficulties in concentration. Over half showed evidence of altered mood and anxiety symptoms. Of the first 54 examined, 9 presented with brief adjustment reactions while the remaining 45 met ICD criteria for psychiatric diagnoses. Thirty-six (66%) met criteria for PTSD. Teachers grossly underestimated levels of psychopathology among the children. Twenty-one of the children aged 8−17 years completed the Horowitz Impact of Events Scale, scoring an average of 24.8. This is lower than children who survived the Jupiter sinking (Yule, 1992) and considerably lower than the scores of the survivors of the Herald of Free Enterprise (Yule & Williams, 1990).

Following the collapse of a pedestrian skywalk, school children who were either on the walkway at the time or who witnessed the accident from the school playground were studied. Seventeen children (11%) were still noticeably upset 4−6 weeks later; 7 months later, only 3 children were mildly upset (Blom, 1986).

From this it can be seen that some studies predate the operationalizing of PTSD, and even recent studies have not always examined children individually in order to be able to make reliable diagnoses. With that caveat in mind, it can still be concluded that considerable psychopathology arises in the wake of a disaster and so mental health services for children need to plan their response.

Differences between disasters

Judged from the responses to standardized measures, it appears that children who survived the capsize of the Herald of Free Enterprise (Yule & Williams, 1990) fared worse than the adolescents who survived the sinking of the Jupiter (Yule, 1992), who did worse than children who survived the explosion at Lockerbie (Parry Jones, 1991) or those who survived Hurricane Hugo (Lonigan *et al.*, 1991).

This fits reasonably with Rachman's (1980) theory of emotional processing, a term he used to describe how people must adjust to the major threats experienced in traumas and disasters. Poor emotional processing was evidenced by '. . . the persistence or return of intrusive signs of emotional activity (such as obsessions, nightmares, pressure of talk, phobias, inappropriate expressions of emotion that are out of context or out of proportion, or simply out of time). Indirect signs may include an inability to concentrate on the task at hand, excessive restlessness, irritability.' Such a characterization of poor emotional processing is closely similar to the symptoms of PTSD. Fortunately, Rachman noted, '. . . most people successfully process the overwhelming majority of the disturbing events that occur in their lives' (p. 56), but here we are considering their reactions to major stressors.

He considered that there were four groups of factors that increased the risk of difficulties in emotional processing: factors of (1) state; (2) personality; (3) stimulus; and (4) associated activity. When survivors are highly aroused, suffer sleeplessness and are tired, they will have greater difficulties in processing the emotions aroused by the disaster. Where the disaster is sudden, intense, dangerous (involves considerable loss of life), unpredictable, uncontrollable and involves exposure to fears that are prepared in Seligman's (1971) sense, then Rachman predicted the difficulties in emotional processing and hence the prevalence of PTSD will be greater.

The children on the Herald of Free Enterprise experienced a disaster that happened within 45 seconds (sudden), was intense and lasted for up to 2 hours before they were rescued, was unexpected and totally out of their control. They saw people panicking and dying around them. They often realized their own lives were in danger. The disaster evoked prepared fears of the cold, the dark and of drowning. The Jupiter took 45 minutes to sink, and although only four people died in that tragedy, many of the surviving adolescents saw the dead bodies of the seamen killed during the rescue. Although there was no warning of the Lockerbie disaster, children reported seeing many dead bodies during the aftermath. Note that the individual assessments took place later than those in the two shipping disasters, and this may be an important consideration. Hurricane Hugo was expected and caused damage to property without injuring or killing many people.

Thus, the use of standard measures permits easier comparison across studies. Rachman's (1980) list of stimulus characteristics of the trauma shows promise in relating to the subsequent level of pathology. As such, it should be of value to those who have to set up emergency services after catastrophes.

Effects on school work

Given that poor concentration and difficulties with new learning are said to be characteristic of PTSD, one might expect that children's schoolwork would suffer after a disaster. Martin and Little (1986) investigated this following a tornado in Wichita Falls in April 1979. A study of school records on three samples of children — 30 9−10-year-olds who reported significant losses during the tornado; 30 who were present but did not suffer loss; and 16 who only joined the school system 2 years after the disaster — failed to show any meaningful differences across the groups. The authors speculated that this may be because the community pulled together in the face of adversity and because when children had to be relocated in new schools, the new teachers were instructed to take time to discuss the children's traumatic experiences.

Adolescents' academic performances was found to be adversely affected in the only study to date to measure this directly from school records. Girls who survived the sinking of the Jupiter were above average in attainment during the 3 years prior to the cruise, but their attainment plummeted significantly to merely average levels 1 year after the accident. Two years after the accident, in their GCSE results, the survivors still performed less well than expected, although the difference was no longer as marked (Tsui, 1990).

Thus, the experience of a major disaster can have an adverse effect on scholastic attainment. If this occurs at a crucial examination time, there may well be long-term consequences. Schools must plan ahead with mental health and social services to ensure that any effects of a major crisis are minimized (Yule & Gold, 1993).

Developmental considerations

Clinically, there seems to be a major consensus that preschool children react differently to major stressful experiences. Developmentally, one would expect this, as the child's ability to process information cognitively and emotionally are crucial to adjustment. Traumatized children aged over 28 months often have excellent verbal memory of what happened to them and their accounts were very accurate. Visual memories seemed particularly 'burned in' to memory, and these gave rise to the behavioural reenactments that were present in most of those under 28 months of age as well (Terr, 1988). Many young children repeatedly draw pictures of what they experienced or act it out in their play, but what is not clear is whether this repetitive behaviour is the precursor to the reexperiencing reported by adults. If so, at what age does it change to the adult form? If not, what purpose does it serve? Many assume that it is a manifestation of the child's attempt to regain mastery over the environment and his or her feelings.

It is still not clear whether younger children are at greater risk than older ones from the effects of a disaster. It is tempting to conclude that they are protected both by the presence of their families and their cognitive inability to be aware of the risks. However, Terr's (1988) findings remind us not to be complacent about even preverbal children's memories, and the bulk of the studies to date have not asked the children themselves how they have reacted. Even so, Sullivan *et al.*'s (1991) study holds out hope that, in the wake of a hurricane at least, few preschool children manifest clinically significant disorders.

Gender differences

There are conflicting findings on whether gender is a risk factor, but in general, females seem more vulnerable to the effects of disasters than males (Lonigan *et al.*, 1991; Gibbs, 1989; Yule, 1992). However, following the Yom Kippur war, Milgram and Milgram (1976) reported increased anxiety in boys but not in girls, and Burke *et al.* (1982, 1986) found different effects of gender at different ages.

Predictors of distress

In the Buffalo Creek study, the strongest predictor of PTSD was threat to the life of the child, although the adjustment of the parents and a rating of family atmosphere also contributed to the prediction (Green *et al.*, 1991).

In the studies of the effects of the Australian bush fires, McFarlane (1987) investigated family reactions and functioning and their relationship to children's adjustment, and found that at the 8-month follow-up, the families showed increased levels of conflict, irritability and withdrawal, with maternal overprotection being quite common. The adjustment of the parents themselves was an important determinant of the adjustment of the children. In particular, McFarlane commented that '. . . families who did not share their immediate reactions to disaster may have had more trouble with their long-term adjustment . . . and experienced a greater degree of estrangement'. Equally important, the child's reactions to the fire affected the adjustment of the family, emphasizing the reciprocal interactions among members of a family system.

Family strengths and family reactions to the disaster can, therefore, be seen as important mediating and moderating factors to be taken into account by both clinicians and researchers in trying to understand the development and maintenance of posttraumatic stress reactions.

Longer-term course

Very few systematic follow-up studies have been reported, and, as was noted earlier, one has to interpret prevalence estimates with care, depending on the time that has elapsed between the accident and the study.

In the immediate aftermath of the Australian bush fire at 2 months, the children were rated as less disturbed than a comparison group studied elsewhere on Rutter's screening scales (McFarlane, 1987; McFarlane *et al.*, 1987). However, by 8 months, both parents and teachers reported significant increases in the numbers of children at high risk of psychiatric disorder and these high rates were maintained at 26 months. In fact, close inspection of the data shows that teachers lagged behind parents in reporting problems and overall the study demonstrated a consistent increase in reported morbidity from 8 months after the disaster. McFarlane *et al.* (1987) concluded that the delayed recognition of problems suggests that many problems do not spontaneously resolve.

Children who survived the Herald of Free Enterprise capsize completed Horowitz's Revised Impact of Events Scale (Horowitz *et al.*, 1979). Children as young as 8 years found the scale meaningful and on that basis it was concluded that the children scored higher than adult patients attending Horowitz's clinic for treatment. At 12–15 months post-accident, the children repeated their ratings and it was found that the overall level had scarcely dropped.

Adolescents who survived the Jupiter sinking were screened for impact of events, anxiety and depression at 10 days and 5 months after the accident. At 10 days, they scored as high as adult traumatized groups on the Impact of Events Scale, and this score remained steady over the first 5 months. Initially, they were no more anxious than other girls of their age, although they were significantly more depressed. At 5 months, their scores on both anxiety and depression had increased significantly (Yule & Udwin, 1991).

However, children do improve over time. Following an Israeli school bus crash, high levels of acute stress reactions during the first week dropped markedly over the following 9 months, although initial levels predicted later ones ($r = +0.51$). The degree of distress was more closely related to knowing the children who were killed than to which coach the respondents were on (Milgram *et al.*, 1988).

Thus, there is evidence that the initial levels of distress following a disaster are strongly related to later levels. The more severe the trauma, the more likely it is that effects will last for 6 months to a year and more. The course of post-traumatic symptoms such as intrusive reexperiencing and avoidance of feelings follows a different time course than symptoms of depression and anxiety, both of which increase over the first 6 months postdisaster. Moderating variables such as familiarity with victims and family reactions seem to have stronger effects in less serious incidents, again suggesting that the severity of the stressor is the most powerful factor in determining the severity of later psychopathology.

Deliberate attacks and witness to violence

Studies of the effects of different stressors on adults conclude that where the trauma is deliberately perpetrated, the ensuing distress is greater. Children are both subjected to deliberate attacks and often witness violence directed to others, notably their parents.

Witness to familicide

There have been few published accounts of children's reactions to seeing one parent murder the other (Schetky, 1978; Pruett, 1979; Malmquist, 1986). Black and Kaplan (1988) initially reported on 28 children of 14 families in which the father had killed the mother, often in front of the children. Later, they described over 80 cases in which they were able to undertake full diagnostic examinations in 30 cases (Black *et al.*, 1991). Nearly all the children who witnessed the killing developed PTSD. With their mothers dead and their fathers taken into custody, the children were often placed temporarily with grandparents, themselves shocked and grieving. In most cases, the children's needs were overlooked — they could not discuss what happened with their new caretakers, nor could they begin to grieve properly. Issues of custody and access were often not addressed and the children were left in limbo. No one helped the children to make sense of what was witnessed — indeed, too often no one discussed what had happened at all.

Pynoos and Eth (1986) described a technique of interviewing children as soon as practicable after the event to assist the child and the remaining family to function more effectively. The main value lies not so much in the specific details of their approach — although the value of this is considerable for anyone forced unexpectedly to deal with such a situation — but rather in emphasizing that children do want and need to share their thoughts, feelings and fears with an adult outside the immediate social network. Their experience is that most children gain a great sense of relief when taken through the incident in detail.

The Chowchilla kidnap

Terr (1979, 1983) worked with children who were kidnapped in a school bus and imprisoned underground for 27 hours. All the children were badly affected and, despite help, remained affected over 4 years later. Terr's studies were influential in focusing on such phenomena as distortions in time perception, reenactment of the trauma in play, and sense of foreshortened future.

Physical and sexual abuse

Abuse differs from disasters in that frequently the abusive acts are repeated and often take place in the context of other adversities: not surprisingly, the effects are manifold (see Chapters 14 and 13). Nevertheless, many abused children suffer PTSD (Frederick, 1985; Goodwin, 1988). Wolfe *et al.* (1989) conceptualized the impact of sexual abuse on children in PTSD terms. They made the important point that children will not tell you about their subjective distress until you ask the right questions. When they did just that, they found that sexual abuse victims did not score above the norms on depression and anxiety, but did so on PTSD items, particularly those involving intrusive thoughts about what had happened to them.

Another difference between disasters and physical/sexual abuse is that disasters are public. Usually the therapists can readily talk about details to the child and usually the child does not feel guilt or shame about being involved. By contrast, abuse happens in secret with the children threatened against revealing the abuse. Thus, while it is useful up to a point to conceptualize the effects of abuse in PTSD terms, these important distinctions need to be borne in mind. Children who experience a single event of abuse differ from those who experience multiple abuse in that the latter present more pervasive disorders (Kiser *et al.*, 1991). Indeed, it was such considerations that led Terr (1991) to differentiate single from repeated traumas, and suggest that greater dissociation was related to repeated trauma.

There are moderate associations between measures of dissociation and trauma in adolescent patients (Sanders & Giolas, 1991). The majority of 19 children given a DSM diagnosis of borderline personality in one study reported significant traumatic experiences, and over a third satisfied criteria for PTSD (Famularo *et al.*, 1991). Taken with the adult literature on the relationship between major stress and dissociation, such findings place real stressors at the centre of the search for significant aetiological factors in many forms of psychopathology in childhood.

SOME METHODOLOGICAL CONSIDERATIONS

By their nature, catastrophes and disasters are usually not anticipated, or at the very best only short warning periods are given. When they strike, people are rightly concerned to restore order and provide help first, with thoughts of studying effects given low priority. Indeed, there may be no relevantly qualified personnel on hand. Thus, many of the existing studies of the effects of disasters have been case studies which, however moving in their descriptions, have often lacked scientific credibility. As Garmezy (1986) noted, such studies have used a wide variety of often non-standard assessment instruments and have rarely included control groups to permit adequate estimation of the effects of the stressors. Sampling bias is common and one is rarely told how representative the small samples reported are of the total population affected.

More importantly, both clinically and for research, it is now well-established that parents and teachers grossly underestimate the distress experienced by child survivors of disasters (Earls *et al.*, 1988). This probably stems from three overlapping factors. Firstly, children and adolescents are very sensitive to parental distress and do not wish to add to it by telling parents of their private difficulties (Yule & Williams, 1990). At other times, adolescents particularly may be scared that they are going mad and do not wish to share this with anyone. Secondly, there is evidence that teachers do not wish to believe that children may be badly affected and so unconsciously underplay the levels of distress they report (McFarlane, 1987; McFarlane *et al.*, 1987). Thirdly, many of the early studies asked parents and teacher to complete general rating scales intended to screen out common problems and never intended to measure subjective distress. In all studies where children have been interviewed directly and asked to complete rating scales on symptoms of subjective distress, the children have consistently reported much higher rates of psychopathology than have either parents or teachers (Galante & Foa, 1986; Handford *et al.*, 1986; McFarlane, 1987; McFarlane *et al.*, 1987; Martini *et al.*, 1990; Belter *et al.*, 1991).

There are now a variety of measures suitable for establishing posttraumatic reactions in children. The Children's Post Traumatic Stress Reaction Index (Frederick & Pynoos, 1988) shows good internal consistency and relates well to clinical judgement of severity of PTSD (Yule *et al.*, 1992). Saigh's (1989) Children's Posttraumatic Stress Disorder Inventory also has good psychometric properties. Horowitz's Impact of Events Scale (Horowitz *et al.*, 1979) has been found useful with children aged 8 and over (Yule & Williams, 1990; Yule & Udwin, 1991), especially in conjunction with a battery that also measures anxiety and depression (Yule & Udwin, 1991). Various semistructured interviews are beginning to appear, but they mainly merely turn DSM criteria into question form and do not enquire about a sufficiently broad range of reactions to be useful for research purposes.

Studies of premorbid adjustment are almost doomed to failure as the chances of any sizeable sample having been properly studied prior to a disaster are slim. Unfortunately (scientifically speaking), when such an opportunity arose, it was in the context of the Three Mile Island nuclear disaster which was, according to Handford *et al.* (1986), a silent disaster with no apparent physical damage to property, and the children were not separated from their parents during the evacuation that some experienced.

Critics have suggested that survivors involved in compensation cases may exaggerate their symptoms. Since many recent studies have involved claimants, this is an important issue. Glaser *et al.* (1981) interviewed a number of survivors who had chosen not to pursue legal redress. No significant differences were found in the levels of reported symptoms between litigants and non-litigants. Given that 14 years after the collapse the estimated rate of PTSD had dropped only from 44% to 28% among adult survivors, the compensation did not seem to have made a dramatic difference to morbidity. To date, no similar study has been undertaken with child survivors involved in litigation.

Disasters will continue to happen and it is increasingly recognized internationally that mental health services need to be ready to deal with the emotional sequelae (Department of Health, 1991; World Health Organization, 1992). Researchers need to agree on both a minimum protocol that can be used to assess children following a disaster and a menu of protocols that can be applied to study different types of disasters and their possible different effects as opportunities arise. Such a strategy has been highly effective in research on adult PTSD (Raphael *et al.*, 1989).

TREATMENT AND PREVENTION

Crisis intervention

Critical incident stress debriefing

Formal psychological debriefing can help adult victims of disaster (Duckworth, 1986; Dyregrov, 1988). Where children have been traumatized in school groups, then school is the natural place to focus help (Yule & Gold, 1993). Ayalon (1988) provides sensible suggestions culled from a variety of theoretical perspectives. Yule and Udwin (1991) described their use of critical incident stress debriefing with girls who survived the sinking of the Jupiter. Self-report data 5 months after the incident suggested that this reduced levels of stress, particularly those manifested in intrusive thoughts (Yule, 1992). Given the few evaluative studies of debriefing and the assumption that people will adapt to trauma at different rates, caution must be exercised before offering debriefing as a panacea to all survivors.

Individual treatment

To date, there is little evidence that drug treatments have a central role; the focus has been mainly on cognitive behavioural treatments that aim both to help survivors make sense of what happened and to master their feelings of anxiety and helplessness. Asking children to draw their experience often assists recall of both the event and the emotions (Newman, 1976; Blom, 1986; Galante & Foa, 1986; Pynoos & Eth, 1986). Drawings were not used as projective techniques, but as ways of assisting talking about the experience.

Most survivors recognize that sooner or later they must face up to the traumatic event. The problem for the therapist is to help the survivor reexperience the event and the emotions that it engenders in such a way that the distress can be mastered rather than magnified. Therapeutic exposure sessions that are too brief may sensitize rather than desensitize (Rachman, 1980), so the therapist may need to use much longer exposure sessions than normal (Saigh, 1986). Fuller suggestions of useful techniques to promote emotional processing are given elsewhere (Rachman, 1980; Richards & Lovell, 1990; Richards & Rose, 1991; Yule, 1991).

Exposure under supportive circumstances seems to deal well with both intrusive thoughts and behavioural avoidance. The other major symptom of child PTSD that requires attention is sleep disorder. A careful analysis will reveal whether the problem is mainly one of getting off to sleep or in waking because of intrusive nightmares related to the disaster. In the former case, implementing relaxing routines before bed and masking thoughts with music may help. In the latter, there are now some promising cognitive behavioural techniques for alleviating nightmares (Marks, 1978, 1987; Halliday, 1987; Seligman & Yellen, 1987; Palace & Johnston, 1989).

Group intervention

Where natural groupings exist in communities and schools, it makes sense to direct some therapeutic support through such groups (Farberow & Gordon, 1981; Galante & Foa, 1986; Ayalon, 1988; Yule & Williams, 1990; Yule & Udwin, 1991). The aims of such therapeutic groups should include the sharing of feelings, boosting children's sense of coping and mastery, and sharing ways of solving common problems.

Family and social support

Family and social support has long been recognized as a key protective factor against the adverse effects of stress on children (Garmezy, 1984). Adult survivors of disaster make better progress where they make use of social support (Joseph *et al.*, 1992). In general, as Flannery's (1990) review attests, social support acts as a buffer against many stressors and so, following a disaster, the formation of supportive networks should not be left to chance.

Stress inoculation

Meichenbaum (1975, 1977; Meichenbaum and Cameron 1983) argued that children should be taught various coping strategies to anticipate and deal with common life stressors. These focused on analysing the problems, monitoring maladaptive thoughts, monitoring behaviours, and practising coping strategies such as problem-solving, relaxation and behavioural rehearsal. Such preventive approaches have been well-utilized in preparing children for the stress of hospital procedures (Melamed, 1977).

Ayalon (1983) suggested the use of such stress-inoculation techniques, among many others, to prepare Israeli children to cope with the effects of terrorist attacks. These ideas seem eminently sensible, but their implementation awaits systematic evaluation.

CONCLUSIONS

It is now well-established that children and adolescents can manifest adult-like PTSD after experiencing an acute and major stressor. However, there is uncertainty on the extent to which ICD and DSM categories accurately reflect the range of symptoms presented by children, the extent to which children fail to show some of the adult symptoms, and on the way symptom presentation varies with developmental age. This means that studies of children following disasters should enquire into a wider range of symptoms than those encapsulated in the 'official' check lists. Indeed, there is still room for naturalistic descriptions of children's reactions.

Children's reactions to major stressors can last for many years and be quite disabling. Treatment studies have only just begun, and although cognitive behavioural approaches offer promise, it is still not clear to what extent these need to be adapted to meet the developmental levels of the children.

As with adults, it appears that where children believe they could have died during the disaster, then they show increased psychopathology later. It is far from clear whether very young children, who cannot fully comprehend the implication of danger, are thereby protected from developing acute stress reactions. This, and other developmental aspects, requires considerably more research.

The study of children's reactions to disasters offers unique opportunities to investigate important themes in developmental psychopathology. As Dollinger *et al.* (1984) and Yule et al. (1990) have shown, basic questions relating to the aetiology of fears can be posed while assessing the need for help. Careful thought about what questions to answer will lead to better studies in the future. Longitudinal studies will establish the natural history of PTSD in children, whether it has a phasic course as expected in adults, and what factors determine continuity and discontinuity into adult life. Better cross-sectional studies can investigate the nature of risk and protective factors within the children themselves and their families, within essentially random samples of the population.

Further disasters will occur. By their nature, they cannot be predicted, but the scientific community could agree a common core methodology that could be applied to studying the effects of disasters on children wherever appropriate, as has been agreed with respect to adult studies (Raphael et al., 1989).

REFERENCES

American Psychiatric Association (1980) *Diagnostic and Statistical Manual of Mental Disorders*, 3rd edn. American Psychiatric Association, Washington, DC.

American Psychiatric Association (1987) *Diagnostic and Statistical Manual of Mental Disorders*, 3rd edn, revised. American Psychiatric Association, Washington, DC.

American Psychiatric Association (1994) *Diagnostic and Statistical Manual of Mental Disorders*, 4th edn, *DSM-IV*. American Psychiatric Association, Washington, DC.

Ayalon O. (1983) Coping with terrorism: the Israeli case. In: Meichenbaum D. & Jaremko M.E. (eds) *Stress Reduction and Prevention*, pp. 293–339. Plenum, New York.

Ayalon O. (1988) *Rescue! Community Oriented Preventive Education for Coping with Stress*. Nord Publications, Haifa.

Belter R.W., Dunn S.E. & Jeney P. (1991) The psychological impact of Hurricane Hugo on children: a needs assessment. *Advances in Behavioural Research Therapy*, **13**, 155–161.

Birleson P. (1981) The validity of depressive disorder in childhood and the development of a self-rating scale: a research report. *Journal of Child Psychology and Psychiatry*, **22**, 73–88.

Birleson P., Hudson I., Buchanan D.G. & Wolff S. (1987) Clinical evaluation of a self-rating scale for depressive disorder in childhood (Depression Self-Rating Scale). *Journal of Child Psychology and Psychiatry*, **28**, 43–60.

Black D. & Kaplan T. (1988) Father kills mother: issues and problems encountered by a child psychiatric team. *British Journal of Psychiatry*, **153**, 624–630.

Black D., Kaplan T. & Harris Henddricks J. (1991) Children who witness parental killing. Paper presented at European Society for Child and Adolescent Psychiatry, London, September 1991.

Bloch D.A., Silber E. & Perry S.E. (1956) Some factors in the emotional reactions of children to disaster. *American Journal of Psychiatry*, **133**, 416–422.

Blom G.E. (1986) A school disaster — intervention and research aspects. *Journal of the American Academy of Child Psychiatry*, **25**, 336–345.

Bradburn I.S. (1991) After the earth shook: children's stress symptoms 6–8 months after a disaster. *Advances in Behavioural Research Therapy*, **13**, 173–179.

Burke J.D., Borus J.F., Burns B.J., Millstein K.H. & Beasley M.C. (1982) Changes in children's behavior after a natural disaster. *American Journal of Psychiatry*, **139**, 1010–1014.

Burke J.D., Moccia P., Borus J.F. & Burns B.J. (1986) Emotional distress in fifth-grade children ten months after a natural disaster.

Journal of the American Academy of Child Psychiatry, **25**, 536–541.

Coddington R.D. (1972a) The significance of life events as etiologic factors in the diseases of children. I: A survey of professional workers. *Journal of Psychosomatic Research*, **16**, 7–18.

Coddington R.D. (1972b) The significance of life events as etiologic factors in the diseases of children. II: A study of a normal population. *Journal of Psychosomatic Research*, **16**, 205–213.

Department of Health (1991) *Disasters: Planning for a Caring Response*. HMSO, London.

Dollinger S.J., O'Donnell J.P. & Staley A.A. (1984) Lightning-strike disaster: effects on children's fears and worries. *Journal of Consultation and Clinical Psychology*, **52**, 1028–1038.

Duckworth D. (1986) Psychological problems arising from disaster work. *Stress Medicine*, **2**, 315–323.

Dyregrov A. (1988) Critical incident stress debriefings. Unpublished manuscript, Research Center for Occupational Health and Safety, University of Bergen, Norway.

Earls F., Smith E., Reich W. & Jung K.G. (1988) Investigating psychopathological consequences of a disaster in children: a pilot study incorporating a structured diagnostic approach. *Journal of the American Academy of Child and Adolescent Psychiatry*, **27**, 90–95.

Famularo R., Kinscherff R. & Fenton T. (1991) Posttraumatic stress disorder among children clinically diagnosed as borderline personality disorder. *Journal of Nervous Mental Disorders*, **179**, 428–431.

Farberow N.L. & Gordon N.S. (1981) *Manual for Child Health Workers in Major Disasters*. DHHS publication no. ADM 81-1070. Washington DC, US Government Printing Office.

Flannery R.B. (1990) Social support and psychological trauma: a methodological review. *Journal of Traumatic Stress*, **3**, 593–611.

Foa E.B., Steketee G. & Olasov-Rothbaum B.O. (1989) Behavioural-cognitive conceptualizations of post-traumatic stress disorder. *Behaviour Research and Therapy*, **20**, 155–176.

Frederick C.J. (1985) Children traumatized by catastrophic situations. In: Eth S. & Pynoos R. (eds) *Post-Traumatic Stress Disorder in Children*, pp. 73–99. American Psychiatric Press, Washington D.C.

Frederick C.J. & Pynoos R. (1988) *The Child Post-Traumatic Stress Disorder (PTSD) Reaction Index*. University of California, Los Angeles.

Galante R. & Foa D. (1986) An epidemiological study of psychic trauma and treatment effectiveness after a natural disaster. *Journal of the American Academy of Child Psychiatry*, **25**, 357–363.

Garmezy N. (1984) Stress resistant children: the search for protective factors. In: Stevenson J.E. (ed) *Recent Research in Developmental Psychopathology*, pp. 213–233. Pergamon, Oxford.

Garmezy N. (1986) Children under severe stress: critique and comments. *Journal of the American Academy of Child Psychiatry*, **25**, 384–392.

Garmezy N. & Masten A. (1990) The adaptation of children to a stressful world: mastery of fear. In: Arnold L.E. (ed) *Childhood Stress*, pp. 459–473. Wiley International, New York.

Garmezy N. & Rutter M. (1985) Acute reactions to stress. In: Rutter M. & Hersov L. (eds) *Child and Adolescent Psychiatry: Modern Approaches*, 2nd edn, pp. 152–176. Blackwell Scientific Publications, Oxford.

Gibbs M.S. (1989) Factors in the victim that mediate between disaster and psychopathology: a review. *Journal of Traumatic Stress*, **2**, 489–514.

Glaser G.G., Green B.L. & Winget C. (1981) *Prolonged Psychosocial Effects of Disaster: A Study of Buffalo Creek*. Academic Press, New York.

Goodwin J. (1988) Post-traumatic symptoms in abused children. *Journal of Traumatic Stress*, **4**, 475–488.

Goodyer I.M. (1990) *Life Experiences, Development and Childhood Psychopathology*. John Wiley, Chichester.

Goodyer I.M., Kolvin I. & Gatzanis S. (1985) Recent undesirable life events and psychiatric disorder in childhood and adolescence. *British Journal of Psychiatry*, **147**, 517–523.

Goodyer I.M., Wright C. & Altham P.M.E. (1988) Maternal adversity and recent stressful life events in anxious and depressed children. *Journal of Child Psychology and Psychiatry*, **29**, 651–667.

Green B.L., Korol M., Grace M.C., Vary M.G., Leonard A.C., Gleser G.C. & Smitson-Cohen S. (1991) Children and disaster: age, gender, and parental effects on PTSD symptoms. *Journal of the American Academy of Child and Adolescent Psychiatry*, **30**, 945–951.

Halliday G. (1987) Direct psychological therapies for nightmares: a review. *Clinical Psychology Review*, **7**, 501–523.

Handford H.A., Mayes S.O., Mattison R.E., Humphrey F.J., Bagnato S., Bixler E.O., & Kales J.D. (1986) Child and parent reaction to the TMI nuclear accident. *Journal of the American Academy of Child Psychiatry*, **25**, 346–355.

Herman J.L. (1992) Complex PTSD: a syndrome in survivors of prolonged and repeated trauma. *Journal of Traumatic Stress*, **5**, 377–391.

Hodgkinson P.E. & Stewart M. (1991) *Coping with Catastrophe: A Handbook of Disaster Management*. Routledge, London.

Horowitz M.J. (1976) *Stress-response syndromes*. Jason Aronson, New York.

Horowitz M.J., Wilner N. & Alvarez W. (1979) Impact of event scale: a measure of subjective stress. *Psychosomatic Medicine*, **41**, 209–218.

Jehu D. (1988) *Beyond Sexual Abuse: Therapy with Women who were Victims in Childhood*. John Wiley, Chichester.

Jones J.C. & Barlow D.H. (1992) A new model for posttraumatic stress disorder: implications for the future. In: Saigh P.A. (ed) *Posttraumatic Stress Disorder: A Behavioral Approach to Assessment and Treatment*, pp. 147–165. Macmillan, New York.

Joseph S.A., Brewin C.R., Yule W. & Williams R. (1991) Causal attributions and psychiatric symptomatology in survivors of the Herald of Free Enterprise disaster. *British Journal of Psychiatry*, **159**, 542–546.

Joseph S., Williams R., Yule W. & Andrews B. (1992) Crisis support and psychiatric symptomatology in adult survivors of the Jupiter cruise ship disaster. *British Journal of Clinical Psychology*, **31**, 63–73.

Joseph S., Brewin C., Yule W. & Williams R. (1993) Causal attributions and post traumatic stress in adolescents. *Journal of Child Psychology and Psychiatry*, **34**, 247–253.

Kinzie J.D., Sack W.H., Angell R.H., Manson S. & Rath B. (1986) The psychiatric effects of massive trauma on Cambodian children: I. The children. *Journal of the American Academy of Child Psychiatry*, **25**, 370–376.

Kiser L.J., Heston J., Millsap P.A. & Pruitt D.B. (1991) Physical and sexual abuse in childhood: relationship with post-traumatic stress disorder. *Journal of the American Academy of Child and Adolescent Psychiatry*, **30**, 776–783.

Kolb L.C. (1988) A critical survey of hypotheses regarding posttraumatic stress disorders in light of recent findings. *Journal of Traumatic Stress*, **1**, 291–304.

Lacey G.N. (1972) Observations on Aberfan. *Journal of Psychosomatic Research*, **16**, 257–260.

Lee I. (1991) Second international conference on wartime medical services. *Medicine and War*, **7**, 120–128.

Lonigan C.J., Shannon M.P., Finch A.J., Daugherty T.K. & Taylor C.M. (1991) Children's reactions to a natural disaster: symptom severity and degree of exposure. *Advances in Behavioural Research Therapy*, **13**, 135–154.

McFarlane A.C. (1987) Family functioning and overprotection following a natural disaster: the longitudinal effects of post-traumatic morbidity. *Australian and New Zealand Journal of Psychiatry*, **21**, 210–218.

McFarlane A.C., Policansky S. & Irwin C.P. (1987) A longitudinal study of the psychological morbidity in children due to a natural disaster. *Psychological Medicine*, **17**, 727–738.

Macsoud M.S. (in press) The war traumas of Lebanese children. *Journal of Traumatic Stress*.

Macsoud M.S., Dyregov A. & Raundalen M. (1992) Traumatic war experiences and their effects on children. In: Wilson J.P. & Raphael B. (eds) *International Handbook of Traumatic Stress Syndromes*. Plenum, New York.

Malmquist C. (1986) Children who witness parental murder: posttraumatic aspects. *Journal of the American Academy of Child Psychiatry*, **25**, 320–325.

Marks I. (1978) Rehearsal relief of a nightmare. *British Journal of Psychiatry*, **133**, 461–465.

Marks I. (1987) Nightmares. *Integrated Psychiatry*, **5**, 71–73.

Martin S. & Little B. (1986) The effects of a natural disaster on academic abilities and social behavior of school children. *British Columbian Journal of Special Education*, **10**, 167–182.

Martini D.R., Ryan C., Nakayama D. & Ramenofsky M. (1990) Psychiatric sequelae after traumatic injury: the Pittsburgh Regatta accident. *Journal of the American Academy of Child and Adolescent Psychiatry*, **29**, 70–75.

Meichenbaum D. (1975) Self instructional methods. In: Kanfer F. & Goldstein A. (eds) *Helping People Change*, pp. 357–391. Pergamon, New York.

Meichenbaum D. (1977) *Cognitive Behavior Modification: An Integrated Approach*. Plenum, New York.

Meichenbaum D. & Cameron R. (1983) Stress inoculation training: toward a general paradigm for training coping skills. In: Meichenbaum D. & Jaremko M.E. (eds) *Stress Reduction and Prevention*, pp. 115–154. Plenum, New York.

Melamed B.G. (1977) Psychological preparation for hospitalization. In: Rachman S. (ed) *Contributions to Medical Psychology*, vol. I, pp. 43–74. Pergamon, London.

Milgram R.M. & Milgram N.A. (1976) The effects of the Yom Kippur war on anxiety level in Israeli children. *Journal of Psychology*, **94**, 107–113.

Milgram N.A., Toubiana Y.H., Klingman A., Raviv A. & Goldstein I. (1988) Situational exposure and personal loss in children's acute and chronic stress reactions to a school bus disaster. *Journal of Traumatic Stress*, **1**, 339–352.

Monaghan J.H., Robinson J.O. & Dodge J.A. (1979) The children's life events inventory. *Journal of Psychosomatic Research*, **23**, 63–68.

Nader K., Pynoos R.S., Fairbanks L. & Frederick C. (1991) Childhood PTSD reactions one year after a sniper attack. *American Journal of Psychiatry*, **147**, 1526–1530.

Newman C.J. (1976) Children of disaster: clinical observation at Buffalo Creek. *American Journal of Psychiatry*, **133**, 306–312.

O'Donohue W. & Eliot A. (1992) The current status of posttraumatic stress disorder as a diagnostic category: problems and proposals. *Journal of Traumatic Stress*, **5**, 421–439.

Ornitz E.M. & Pynoos R.S. (1989) Startle modulation in children with posttraumatic stress disorder. *American Journal of Psychiatry*, **146**, 866–870.

Palace E.M. & Johnston C. (1989) Treatment of recurrent nightmares by the dream reorganization approach. *Journal of Behavior Therapy and Experimental Psychiatry*, **20**, 219–226.

Parry Jones W. (1991) Children of Lockerbie. Paper presented at Guys Hospital meeting.

Paykel E.S. (1974) Life stress and psychiatric disorder. In: Dohrenwend B.S. & Dohrenwend B.P. (eds) *Stressful Life Events: Their Nature and Effects*, pp. 135–149. Wiley, New York.

Pruett K. (1979) Home treatment of two infants who witnessed their mother's murder. *Journal of the American Academy of Child Psychiatry*, **18**, 647–657.

Pynoos R.S. & Eth S. (1986) Witness to violence: the child interview. *Journal of the American Academy of Child Psychiatry*, **25**, 306–319.

Pynoos R.S. & Nader K. (1988) Psychological first aid and treatment approach for children exposed to community violence: research implications. *Journal of Traumatic Stress,* **1**, 243–267.

Pynoos R.S., Frederick C., Nader K., Arroyo W., Steinberg A., Eth S., Nunez F. & Fairbanks L. (1987). Life threat and posttraumatic stress in school-age children. *Archive of General Psychiatry,* **44**, 1057–1063.

Pynoos R.S., Goenjian A., Karakshian M., Tashjian M., Manjikian R., Manoukian G., Steinberg A.M. & Fairbanks L. (in press) Posttraumatic stress reactions in children after the 1988. Armenian earthquake. *British Journal of Psychiatry.*

Rachman S. (1980). Emotional processing. *Behavior Research and Therapy,* **18**, 51–60.

Raphael B. (1986). *When Disaster Strikes: A Handbook for the Caring Professions.* Hutchinson, London.

Raphael B., Lundin T. & Weisaeth L. (1989) A research method for the study of psychological and psychiatric aspects of disaster. *Acta Psychiatrica Scandinavica* **80**, Suppl. 353.

Reynolds C.R. & Richmond B.O. (1978) What I think and feel: a revised measure of children's manifest anxiety. *Journal of Abnormal Child Psychology,* **6**, 271–280.

Richards D. & Lovell K. (1990) Imaginal and *in-vivo* exposure in the treatment of PTSD. Paper read at Second European Conference on Traumatic Stress, Netherlands, September 1990.

Richards D. & Rose J. (1991) Exposure therapy for post-traumatic stress disorder: four case studies. *British Journal of Psychiatry,* **158**, 836–840.

Rubonis A.V. & Bickman L. (1991) Psychological impairment in the wake of disaster: the disaster–psychopathology relationship. *Psychological Bulletin* **109**, 384–399.

Sack W.H. (1990) Paper presented at 98th Annual Convention of the American Psychological Association, Boston, MA.

Saigh P.A. (1986). *In vitro* flooding in the treatment of a 6-yr-old boy's posttraumatic stress disorder. *Behaviour and Research Therapy,* **24**, 685–688.

Saigh P.A. (1989) The development and validation of the Children's Posttraumatic Stress Disorder Inventory. *International Journal of Special Education,* **4**, 75–84.

Saigh P.A. (1991) The development of posttraumatic stress disorder following four different types of traumatization. *Behavioural Research and Therapy,* **29**, 213–216.

Sanders B. & Giolas M.H. (1991) Dissociation and childhood trauma in psychologically disturbed adolescents. *American Journal of Psychiatry,* **148**, 50–54.

Schetky D.H. (1978) Pre-schoolers' response to murder of their mothers by their fathers: a study of four cases. *Bulletin of the American Academy of Psychiatry and the Law,* **6**, 45–47.

Seligman M.E.P. (1971) Phobias and preparedness. *Behavior Therapy,* **2**, 307–320.

Seligman M.E. & Yellen A. (1987) What is a dream? *Behavior Research and Therapy,* **25**, 1–24.

Sullivan M.A., Saylor C.F. & Foster K.Y. (1991) Post-hurricane adjustment of preschoolers and their families. *Advances in Behavioural Research Therapy,* **13**, 163–171.

Suomi S.J. (1991) Early stress and adult emotional; reactivity in rhesus monkeys. In: Bock G.R. & Whelan J. (eds) *The Childhood Environment and Adult Disease.* Ciba Foundation Symposium 156,

pp. 3–16. John Wiley, Chichester.

Terr L.C. (1979) The children of Chowchilla. *Psychoanalytical Study of Children,* **34**, 547–623.

Terr L.C. (1983) Chowchilla revisited: the effects of psychic trauma four years after schoolbus kidnapping. *American Journal of Psychiatry,* **140**, 1543–1550.

Terr L.C. (1988) What happens to early memories of trauma? A study of twenty children under age five at the time of documented traumatic events. *Journal of the American Academy of Child Adolescent Psychiatry,* **27**, 96–104.

Terr L.C. (1991) Childhood traumas — an outline and overview. *American Journal of Psychiatry,* **148**, 10–20.

Tsui E.P. (1990) The 'Jupiter' sinking disaster: effects on teenagers school performance. MSc dissertation, University of London, Institute of Psychiatry.

van der Kolk B., Greenberg M., Boyd H. & Krystal J. (1985) Inescapable shock, neurotransmitters, and addiction to trauma: toward a psychobiology of posttraumatic stress disorder. *Biological Psychiatry,* **20**, 314–325.

Weisaeth L. (1983) The study of a factory fire. Doctoral dissertation, University of Oslo.

Wicks B. (1988) *No Time to Wave Good-bye.* Bloomsbury, London.

Williams R., Joseph S. & Yule W. (1993) Disaster and mental health. In: Bhurga D. & Leff J. (eds) *Principles of Social Psychiatry.* Blackwell Scientific, Oxford.

Wolfe V.V., Gentile C. & Wolfe D.A. (1989) The impact of sexual abuse on children: a PTSD formulation. *Behavior Therapy,* **20**, 215–228.

World Health Organization (1992) *The ICD-10 Classification of Mental and Behavioural Disorders: Clinical descriptions and diagnostic guidelines.* World Health Organization, Geneva.

World Health Organization (1992) *Psychosocial Consequences of Disasters: Prevention and Management.* World Health Organization, Geneva.

Yeaworth R.C., York J., Hussey M.A., Ingle M.E. & Goodwin T. (1980) The development of an adolescent life change event scale. *Adolescence,* **15**, 91–97.

Yule W. (1991) Work with children following disasters. In: Herbert M. (ed) *Clinical Child Psychology: Social Learning, Development and Behaviour,* pp. 349–363. John Wiley, Chichester.

Yule W. (1992) Posttraumatic stress disorder in child survivors of shipping disasters: the sinking of the 'Jupiter'. *Psychotherapy and Psychosomatics,* **57**, 200–205.

Yule W. & Gold A. (1993) *Wise before the Event: Coping with Crises in Schools.* Calouste Gulbenkian Foundation, London.

Yule W. & Udwin O. (1991) Screening child survivors for posttraumatic stress disorders: experiences from the 'Jupiter' sinking. *British Journal of Clinical Psychology,* **30**, 131–138.

Yule W. & Williams R. (1990) Posttraumatic stress reactions in children. *Journal of Traumatic Stress,* **3**, 279–295.

Yule W., Udwin O. & Murdoch K. (1990) The 'Jupiter' sinking: effects on children's fears, depression and anxiety. *Journal of Child Psychology and Psychiatry,* **31**, 1051–1061.

Yule W., Bolton D. & Udwin O. (1992) Objective and subjective predictors of PTSD in adolescents. Paper presented at World Conference of International Society for Traumatic Stress Studies, Trauma and Tragedy, Amsterdam, 21–26 June, 1992.

Chapter 23
Suicide and Attempted Suicide

David Shaffer & John Piacentini

Children and teenagers who complete suicide and those who threaten or unsuccessfully attempt to commit suicide have some features in common — about a third of suicide completers will have made a prior attempt and attempters are the group that is at greatest risk for later suicide — but in many respects they are different. This chapter will deal with both conditions. The first section reviews the epidemiology of completed suicide and describes what is known of child and teen suicide victims. The second section reviews the characteristics, natural history and treatment of suicide attempters. A final section deals with strategies to prevent suicide.

COMPLETED SUICIDE

Incidence

Suicide in childhood and early adolescence (up to age 15) is uncommon in all countries and societies (Shaffer & Fisher, 1981). The incidence increases markedly in the late teens and continues to rise until the early 20s (Fig. 23.1). The toll exerted by suicide among children and teens is remarkably similar in the US and UK. In 1989, the suicide rate for children aged 5–14 years was 0.7 per 100 000 in the US and 0.8 per 100 000 in the UK. This accounted for 0.3% of all deaths occurring in this age group in the US and 0.5% in the UK. Among 15–19-year-olds the rate was 13.2 per 100 000 in the US (13% of all deaths) and 7.6 per 100 000 (14% of all deaths) in the UK. The rate among male teens has increased markedly in recent years, starting in the mid-1960s in the US, but in only the mid-1980s in the UK (Fig. 23.2). Rates among male teens have also increased in many other countries (Kolmos, 1987; Dyck *et al.*, 1988; Skegg & Cox, 1991). In both countries, suicide is less common among females. The suicide rate varies by region and culture and this is unlikely to be due to reporting differences because such variations are apparent even in a single country. Thus, in the US, suicide is strikingly less common among blacks than whites.

Age

These epidemiological data suggest that some factors either increase risk in older adolescents or offer protection to children and younger adolescents. A number of social and cognitive features of childhood could provide children and young adolescents with some form of protection that is lost as they grow older.

Isolation has long been viewed as a determinant of suicide (the creation of hotlines is based on the belief that suicidal intent can be lessened by communication). The child's life in a family and at school provides rich social and emotional support that makes isolation uncommon. However, many neglected children spend a substantial part of their home lives alone, in the New York study (see below) none of the suicides aged less than 15 years had evidence of abuse or neglect, and there is no evidence that suicide in such children is anything but rare. It has been suggested that some of the psychological tasks of adolescence, i.e. individuation and separation, are stressful and that these enhance suicide risk. That may be the case, but an examination of the year-by-year incidence of teenage suicide (Shaffer & Fisher, 1981) shows rates to increase linearly from 13 to reach a peak at age 24 that is then sustained. By that time such adolescent concerns should be less important.

Despair and hopelessness are known to be predictors of suicide in adults (see below). Considered logically, these cognitions require an ability to think into the future and weigh alternative hypotheses, better developed in adolescent formal operational thinking than in middle childhood. However, hopelessness has been reported as a feature of depression in young children (Kovacs & Beck, 1977) and a decision to commit suicide in response to stress could as plausibly be considered a product of failing to appreciate all available options. Other features of adolescent thinking such as a greater awareness of the self as seen by others and a pre-occupation with abstract notions could increase vulnerability to depression and suicide. It has also been suggested that suicide requires access to lethal methods and skills in planning that are better developed in older adolescents. A youngster who intends to hang himself needs to find an appropriate and private site or a degree of technical sophistication. This is not an entirely plausible explanation because a degree of privacy is available to most 12–15-year-olds who, nevertheless, have a strikingly low suicide rate. Further, most suicide threats in young children involve a threat to jump from a height or into traffic: both are potentially effective methods that are readily accessible to most children and can be executed without much planning.

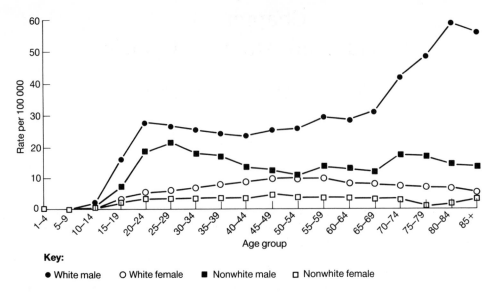

Fig. 23.1 Suicide at different ages (US 1984).

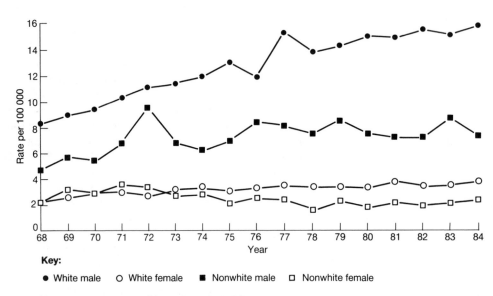

Fig. 23.2 Adolescent suicide rates (15–19-year-olds) (US 1968–1984).

There is a large body of literature suggesting that proneness to suicide is increased by the younger child's concept of the reversibility of death (see Schilder & Wechsler, 1934; Freud & Burlingham, 1944; Nagy, 1965; Koocher, 1973; McIntire & Angle, 1973, for reviews and studies on this topic). A child who believes that death is reversible will be less inhibited about engaging in suicidal behaviour. However, what needs to be explained is not why suicidal behaviour is common, but the reverse. Believing that death is reversible may be common in children, but suicide is uncommon. It cannot, therefore, follow that the one finding explains the other.

On balance, therefore, the notion of early childhood protection is implausible and it seems more likely that the striking age gradient is a function of risk factors that only start to operate in later adolescence. This applies to both affective illness and alcohol abuse, two leading risk factors for suicide in adults and adolescents (Brent *et al.*, 1989; Gould *et al.*, 1990; Shaffer *et al.* in preparation), that are uncommon before the mid-teens (Kashani & Simonds, 1979), but are increasingly prevalent after that.

Gender

In North America and Europe, suicide is more common in males than in females at all ages except the very young. However, in several countries in Latin America and Asia, sex rates are equal and, in some, the majority of suicides are committed by women (Barraclough, 1987).

It is likely that two separate factors contribute to the observed sex differences in well-developed countries: (1) *psychopathology*: aggressive behaviour and substance abuse are potent risk factors for suicide (see below) and both are more common in young males than females; and (2) *method choice*: female suicides are most commonly due to overdose or jumping from a height, compared with hanging or firearms by males (National Center for Health Statistics 1979–1990). In countries with advanced treatment resources and strict regulation of potentially lethal ingestants, ingestions are rarely 'successful'. However, if the rate of female self-poisoning is high, if the type of self-poisoning used is untreatable (e.g. paraquat ingestion in South-East Asia and the South Pacific; Haynes, 1987) or if good medical services are not readily available then the female-to-male ratio should increase and it does.

Ethnicity

Cultural factors are conveniently studied in a multiethnic country such as the US where recording and reporting procedures are uniform across different groups. In the US, suicide is generally more common in whites than in nonwhites in all groups (see Fig. 23.1) and varies greatly among different Native American groups (May, 1987). Some Native American groups have rates more than 20-fold higher than the national average; others approximate that for the nation as a whole.

White–black differences in the US are greatest in areas of long black settlement in the south and southeast and are least in the western states. This is compatible with protection from some feature of black society in areas of long settlement that may have been lost during migration. It is not clear whether this factor is a function of different attitudes towards suicide (e.g. that suicide is less well-justified or is a feature of insanity or cowardice) or whether, in old established areas, blacks have more effective social support systems than whites (Gibbs & Martin, 1964; Bush, 1976; May, 1987). It seems unlikely that ethnic differences are due to confounding socioeconomic status (SES) effects. Black teen suicides have a somewhat higher SES than the black population at large (Gould *et al.*, in preparation).

Explicit cultural sanctions or prohibitions against suicide are not clearly related to ethnic differences. For example, the Japanese sanction suicide under certain circumstances and the Catholic church strongly prohibits suicide, yet the Japanese youth suicide rate is lower than in most of western and eastern Europe (World Health Organization, 1988) and suicide rates show great variability in countries with predominantly Catholic populations.

There are at least two possible explanations for cultural variations in suicide rates. The first is that the almost universal negative perception of suicide protects all but a few individuals who, by virtue of character disorder or psychopathology, are prone to suicide at times of personal stress. However, subtle variations in the strength or nature of these attitudes can influence the suicide rates. An alternative explanation is unrelated to culture. It would be that contagion (see below) is a crucial factor that operates *within* cultural groups independently of attitudinal differences. An individual who had close contact with a suicide of the same cultural group would be more likely to commit suicide him- or herself. If this were true, it could account for the quite stable regional differences that exist within a country. Once a given rate has been established, it should maintain itself over long periods.

Secular changes

In all countries where an increase in youth suicide has been observed, it has been more marked in males and in older teens. This pattern is apparent in suicide mortality data from the US presented in Figure 23.2. Increases have been generally regular and consistent over the past two decades and this, coupled with similar findings from countries that use quite different ascertainment procedures, suggests that the increase is a real one and not a function of any change in reporting practice.

Reviewing North American data in the late 1970s, some authorities interpreted the increase as a cohort effect (Murphy & Wetzel, 1980; Solomon & Heller, 1980), i.e. that the suicide rate was determined by some influence on a whole generation that could be expected to operate throughout its life. However, data that have accumulated since then (National Center for Health Statistics 1979–1990) suggest that the increased incidence is present only through the second and third decades of life. As generations that had a high youth suicide rate reached the fourth decade of life the rate of increase diminished and their suicide rate was comparable to those in earlier generations. Although this could be due to the premature death of suicide-prone individuals at an early age, it is also compatible with the increase being due to some aetiological factor that operates most potently in young males and whose prevalence has increased during this period. Substance and alcohol abuse fit this paradigm well (see below).

Suicide method

In the US, the large majority of teenage boys commit suicide by shooting themselves or by hanging. In the UK, hanging is the most common method. Teenage girls are more likely to die from an overdose or jump from a height.

The method used to commit suicide varies according to the victim's place of residence (Moens *et al.*, 1988; Fisher & Shaffer, 1990; Brent *et al.*, 1991), suggesting that it is, in part, determined by availability. For example, in a demographically varied area surrounding New York City (Fisher *et al.*, in preparation), hanging occurred in all areas, but death by firearms was most prevalent in rural areas, where firearms are commonly kept for hunting. Self-asphyxiation, which usually involves feeding automobile exhaust back into a car parked in a garage, occurred most often in suburban areas and jumping from a height occurred exclusively in urban areas.

A proportion of male hanging victims are found under

circumstances, e.g. being in a state of semiundress or in cross-dress, evidence of recent orgasm, and the presence at the scene of death of fetishistic objects, that suggest that their death is associated with erotic activity (Stearns, 1953; Coe, 1974; Sheehan & Garfinkel, 1988). Sheehan and Garfinkel (1988) suggested that this form of death may account for up to a third of all hangings. However, in the New York study described below, only 3 of 135 male hangings were of this sort and in published accounts of alleged autoerotic deaths, there have been few in which there was independent evidence of habitual semistrangulation; the sex, seasonal and ethnic distribution has resembled that of suicide, and, in those cases where behavioural and psychiatric information has been available, depression and substance abuse were common (Sheehan & Garfinkel, 1988). Taken together, these facts suggest that rather than many autoerotic accidental deaths being misclassified as suicide, the reverse is more likely to be true.

Terminal events

Several studies (Shaffer, 1974; Shaffi *et al.*, 1988) have shown that adolescents most often commit suicide during a disciplinary crisis, e.g. while awaiting a punishment or other consequence of committing a crime or breaking school rules. A typical situation will be that a teenager is discovered truanting or stealing and is told by the school or police that his or her parents will be informed in the near future. The teen commits suicide shortly after and before the family finds out. Other common precipitants include a public humiliation such as being excluded from a party when drunk; the threat of separation from a girl- or boyfriend; or reading about a suicide in a novel or newspaper or seeing a film that includes a suicide (Shaffer, 1974). Other suicides occur in the context of an acute depression with no obvious external precipitant. A proportion of suicides occur on the anniversary of a friend's death. In one study (Shaffer, 1974), just over one-quarter of the children died within 2 weeks of their own birthdays.

About half of all suicides had discussed or threatened suicide within 24 hours of their deaths. Previous attempts had been noted in about 50% of female and 25% of all male teen suicides (Shaffer, 1974).

AETIOLOGICAL MECHANISMS

Family history

A large number of studies (Roy, 1983) have found an excess of psychopathology and of suicidal behaviours in the families of adult suicide victims. In the New York study of adolescents, approximately half of the suicides had a first-degree relative with a history of attempted or completed suicide compared with less than half that proportion in controls. Familiality was greatest in the families of teenagers who had depression or marked depressive features at psychological autopsy. The mechanisms for familiality have been examined in both large twin registry (Roy *et al.*, 1991) and adopted-away samples

(Kety, 1986; Wender *et al.*, 1986) and suggest a genetic element. Concordance in the twin registry study was 12% for monozygous and 2% for dizygous twins, a significant difference. Detailed evaluation of psychiatric status in a small and unrepresentative sample of twins (Roy *et al.*, 1991) suggests that concordance for suicide is associated with concordance for specific forms of psychiatric disorder.

Imitation, identification or contagion may play a role in familial suicide. In short-term prospective studies, Brent *et al.* (In submission) followed up the adolescent siblings of 26 suicides over a 12-month period and found no excess of suicidal behaviour in them, although suicidal ideation was prominent, especially when significant depression was present. In the New York study, a small number of parents did commit suicide during the period of bereavement after their child's death.

Imitation and contagion

There is evidence from several quarters that suicidal behaviour is facilitated by exposure to news or stories about suicide. Direct evidence includes case accounts of individuals who committed suicide shortly after seeing a film or reading a book or news story that featured a suicide (Shaffer, 1974). Other research evidence is 'ecological', that is to say that there is an apparent and statistically robust relationship between the occurrence of the purported stimulus, such as publishing or broadcasting a newspaper or television story about suicide, and a subsequent increase in suicide or suicide attempt rate, but no evidence on whether a given individual suicide was exposed to the purported stimulus. Evidence of this sort is available for increased morbidity following newspaper accounts of suicides in prominent individuals (Phillips, 1974, 1979, 1980, 1984; Bollen & Phillips, 1981, 1982; Wasserman, 1984); televised dramatizations that feature teen suicide (Holding, 1974, 1975; Gould & Shaffer, 1986; Gould *et al.*, 1988) and televised news stories (Schmidtke & Hafner, 1986). The excess of suicides in such circumstances lasts for 1−2 weeks, is proportional to the number of times that the news is repeated and mainly affects young people (Phillips & Carstensen, 1986). Studies of imitation using the same stimulus have not always been consistent (Berman, 1988; Gould *et al.*, 1988) but, given that the context of exposure is subject to large variations in the age and size of the exposed viewership and the context in which the material is seen (e.g. whether or not the programmes were accompanied by material that could direct a disturbed viewer to obtain help, etc.), some variability in the consequences of even a single stimulus is not surprising. Evidence for contagion also comes from the well-documented occurrence of cluster or epidemic suicides that are estimated to account for up to 4% of all teen suicides in the US and to be increasing in incidence (Gould, 1990). In a suicide cluster, an unexpected number of deaths occur in a short period of time in a circumscribed community. There is no evidence that clusters occur as a response to significant changes in the community itself and little is known about the characteristics of the suicides. In a description of one cluster (Davidson *et al.*, 1989) the victims, like sporadic suicides, were predominantly male and several had a history of past suicidal attempts. It does not appear that imitative suicides are necessarily close or knew the initial victim well (Brent *et al.*, In submission).

Biological abnormalities

A number of biological correlates of suicide have been identified in adult suicides and suicide attempters (see Stanley & Mann, 1987, for a review). The most frequently replicated finding, first reported by Asberg *et al.* in 1986, is the presence of significantly lower concentrations of the serotonin metabolite 5-HIAA in the cerebrospinal fluid (CSF) of suicide attempters and completers than in age- and sex-matched nonsuicidal controls. These findings have been elaborated and include autoradiographic studies that show a low density of presynaptic serotonin receptors and high concentrations of postsynaptic receptors. There is some evidence that low serotonin is associated with impulsive, labile and aggressive behaviour and these character traits may be more important correlates than psychiatric diagnosis, for the association has been found in suicides with a variety of psychiatric diagnoses.

Despite the large number of studies that have reported these abnormalities, a number of unanswered questions remain. The specific behavioural correlates of low serotonin states have yet to be documented in large samples; there are conflicting reports about whether 5-HIAA levels are stable or fluctuate with mental state, and it is not known in what proportion of teen or adult suicide victims such abnormalities occur.

In one promising development, Asberg *et al.* (1986) noted a 1-year suicide completion rate of 21% among adult suicide attempters whose CSF 5-HIAA was less than 90 µg/ml compared with only a 2% death rate among attempters with higher levels. If, as has been held, declining or stable low levels of 5-HIAA predict a poor prognosis, then secondary or tertiary prevention could be served by routine CSF monitoring of patients who have made a suicide attempt, with special care being given to those with abnormally low levels.

Perinatal morbidity

Studies in the US (Salk *et al.*, 1985) found an approximately threefold excess of perinatal morbidity in the records of consecutive suicides compared with controls. This was highly significant. The mothers of the suicides also received less prenatal care and were more likely to smoke and take alcohol during pregnancy, suggesting that this relationship could be a function either of some neurological sequel of the obstetric morbidity, or of maternal psychopathology. In Sweden, Jacobson *et al.* (1987) have reported broadly similar findings.

Associated psychiatric disorder

Suicide is rare in groups with no psychopathology (Winokur & Tsuang, 1975). High rates of suicide have been found in both follow-up studies of psychiatric patients (Pokorny, 1964, 1983) and in retrospective psychological autopsy studies of consecutive suicides in adults (Robins *et al.*, 1959; Dorpat & Ripley, 1960; Barraclough *et al.*, 1969; Rich *et al.*, 1988) in adults as well as among children and teenagers. Most of these studies (Dizmang *et al.*, 1974; Sanborn *et al.*, 1974; Shaffer, 1974; Shaffi et al., 1985; Fowler *et al.*, 1986; Rich *et al.*, 1986; Brent *et al.*, 1988) have been small, with 30 or fewer subjects, and have either been uncontrolled or used unusual comparison groups (Shaffi *et al.*, 1985; Brent *et al.*, 1988). However, results are emerging from two much larger studies that have included normal controls in Pittsburg (Brent *et al.*, In submission) and in New York (Shaffer *et al.*, in preparation).

The New York study addressed 170 suicides recorded among children and adolescents aged 19 or under over a 2-year period. Of these suicides, 122 were examined in detail through structured interviews with surviving family members and teenage friends. A similar number of normal controls matched for age, sex, and ethnicity were recruited by random telephone dialing in the same area. Psychiatric disorder was far more prevalent in suicides than in controls and two-thirds of each sex met DSM-III criteria for a psychiatric diagnosis. The remaining third, although not meeting diagnostic criteria, were clearly symptomatic. Most had some psychiatric symptoms and many were experiencing significant dysfunction before their death. Approximately half of all suicides had had previous contact with a mental health professional. After making allowance for differences due to the number of informants, very few of the suicides were found to be free of significant psychiatric symptomatology. Quite marked sex differences were found. Approximately a third of each sex met criteria for an anxiety disorder but, while conduct disorder and alcohol or drug abuse (often occurring together) were common among males, with just under a half having one or other or both of these diagnoses, none of the girls were found to have a significant substance abuse problem and a somewhat smaller proportion had a conduct disorder. Criteria for major depression were met by a third of the girls, but by only half as many boys. Most cases appeared to fall into one of three broad categories: (1) an irritable, impulsive, volatile and erratic group who were over-sensitive to criticism; (2) a group who were excessively anxious about forthcoming events, were afraid of making mistakes, found it difficult to adapt to new circumstances, and who were perfectionistic, and (3) a group, mainly girls, who clearly met criteria for major depressive disorder and were often being treated for this at the time of their death.

The prevalence of alcohol abuse increased markedly with age. Approximately two-thirds of 17–19-year-old *male* teenagers (who constituted over half of the sample) had a significant alcohol abuse problem. This finding of a sex-specific risk factor that is known to have increased in prevalence during recent years suggests that alcohol abuse may have been the determining factor in recent increases in male suicide. The high prevalence of antisocial behaviour in both sexes is in line with the biological findings described above.

Although alcohol abuse and disruptive behaviour disorders were the most prevalent diagnoses, their base rate in the general population is high, and value for prediction is therefore low. Using these findings coupled with age- and sex-specific base rate estimates (Fleiss, 1981), Gould *et al.* (1990) have demonstrated that, at least among psychopathological variables, previous suicide attempts in males and/or depression in either sex are the most specific psychiatric risk factors for suicide. Thus, while in the US the annual incidence of suicide in male adolescents is under 15/100 000, the annual incidence among male attempters approaches 270/100 000, and male depressives would be 100/100 000. Among adolescent females, the general incidence is less than 4/100 000, but among depressed female teens, this is increased 20-fold to 80/100 000. The increase among female attempters is less striking, at 20/100 000.

Family circumstances

In the New York study, approximately half of the suicides who had not already left home were living with two biological parents, compared with two-thirds of the controls. There was no significant excess of either marital discord between parents of suicides compared with controls, or of more hostile parent–child relationships. However, the frequency and intensity of parent–teen communication was less good in suicides than in controls even after taking account of parent and teen psychopathology.

ATTEMPTED SUICIDE

Epidemiology

Prevalence

Estimates of the incidence of suicide attempts in teenagers range widely, no doubt reflecting differences in definitions and samples. Incidence reports from clinics are difficult to interpret because many attempters do not seek medical treatment and they may be misdiagnosed when they do (McIntire & Angle, 1973). Community surveys suggest that suicidal ideation is common in adolescents and that the incidence of suicide attempts, while much lower, nevertheless represents a significant problem. The Centers for Disease Control (CDC; 1991) surveyed over 11 000 high school students (ranging in age from roughly 14 to 17 years) regarding the presence of suicidal behaviour in the past 12 months and found that 27% had thought about suicide during this time period, 16.3% had made a specific plan, 8.3% had made an attempt, and 2% made attempts requiring medical attention. Based on these results, the CDC estimated that almost 300 000 high school students in the US made a serious suicide attempt in 1990.

Data from the first US state (Oregon) to require reporting of all suicide attempters under the age of 18 requiring hospital treatment indicated a 0.2% hospital-treated attempt rate in 1988 (Andrus *et al.*, 1991). Surveys of *lifetime* suicidality have generally found US teens to report somewhat higher lifetime suicide attempt rates than their Canadian and European counterparts. Smith and Crawford (1986) and Harkavy-Friedman *et al.* (1987) reported lifetime attempt rates of 8.4% and 9% respectively for high school students based on anonymous surveys, while Pronovost *et al.* (1990) found a 3.5% lifetime attempt rate in a school-based survey of 2850 French-Canadian 12–18-year-olds from Quebec. Kienhorst *et al.* (1990) found that 2.2% of Dutch secondary education students (aged 14–20 years) reported having made a suicide attempt at some point in their lifetime, while Larsson *et al.* (1991) reported that 4% of a representative school-based sample of 605 Swedish 13–18-year-olds had made a lifetime attempt and 2% had made attempts in the past year. Teen attempts place a significant burden on clinical resources (Lukianowitz, 1986; Leese, 1969; Mattson *et al.*, 1969; Pfeffer *et al.*, 1980, 1984).

Secular change

Changes in the number of teen attempters attending clinics in the UK and Australia suggest a marked growth in referrals in the 1960s and 1970s (Oliver *et al.*, 1971; Kreitman & Schreiber, 1979). Hawton and Goldacre (1982), for example, found a 28% increase in admission rates for self-poisoning among 12–20-year-olds in the Oxford region between 1974 and 1979, with the increase being more pronounced in individuals aged 15 and under. One study in the UK, however, found a significant decline between 1980 and 1985 in overdose with psychotropic-type substances among 16–20-year-old females which they attributed to increased vigilance by physicians in prescribing psychotropic drugs and the subsequent decreased availability of these medications (Sellar *et al.*, 1990). There is no information about changes in the incidence of suicide behaviour that does not lead to hospital care.

Age

Suicide attempts and ideation appear to be less common before puberty and there are inconsistent reports that they increase in frequency through adolescence. Pfeffer *et al.* (1984) reported that 1% of normal schoolchildren age 6–12 years had made a suicide attempt. Garrison *et al.* (1991) reported a 1-year prevalence rate for attempts of around 1.5% in a school-based survey of 12–14-year-olds. Studies in the Mid-West (Dubow *et al.*, 1989) and North East US (Velez & Cohen, 1988) have found no relationship between age and prevalence of attempts, although in the Mid-West study, suicidal ideation peaked in the ninth grade. In a study in France, Choquet and Mencke (1989) reported an increase in the frequency of suicidal ideation through adolescence among girls but not boys.

Gender

Females are more likely than males to attempt suicide, although sex differences are less striking in community than in clinical samples. In their community study of high school students, the CDC (1991) survey found that females outnumbered males by a factor of about 1.6 to 1 for all types of suicidal behaviour. Similar differences have been found in unselected samples of US college students (Meehan *et al.*, 1992), Native Americans (Blum *et al.*, 1992), French-Canadian adolescents (Provonost *et al.*, 1990) and French suburban adolescents (Choquet & Mencke, 1989). In their survey of Swedish adolescents, Larsson *et al.* (1991) found that females were three times more likely than males (6 compared to 2%) to report a lifetime attempt.

In clinic samples, female attempters outnumber males by factors of from 3 : 1 to 7 : 1. Piacentini *et al.* (1991) found 77% of an adolescent sample of 273 consecutive emergency room admissions for suicidal behaviour to be female, with the gender difference being higher for attempters (86%) than ideators (53%). Similar proportions have been found in hospitalized attempters in Hong Kong (74% female; Chung *et al.*, 1987) and the Oxford region of the UK (71%; Sellar *et al.*, 1990). In the last study, sex differences narrowed from 4 : 1 among 12–15-year-olds to 2 : 1 among 16–20-year-olds. Although female attempters are more likely to present for treatment, males are significantly more likely to be hospitalized, perhaps because of an appreciation of the increased risk for male completion (Trautman & Rotheram, 1987; Piacentini *et al.*, 1991).

Ethnicity

The CDC (1991) survey found that high-school-aged Hispanics living in the US had higher attempt rates (12%) than either whites (7.9%) or blacks (6.5%). A reported rate among Native Americans of 17% (Blum *et al.*, 1992) is higher than any of these.

Social class

A community sample of almost 1400 US 7th–12th graders (Dubow *et al.*, 1989), reported subjects of low socioeconomic status to be at increased risk for both suicidal ideation and attempts.

Method and lethality

In the US and UK, among hospital-referred attempts, self-poisoning with analgesics or psychotropics is the most common method (Hawton & Goldacre, 1982; Rotheram-Borus & Trautman, 1988; Spirito *et al.*, 1989). Violent methods, such as jumping, hanging, and shooting, are more likely to be made by males (Otto 1972, Miller *et al.*, 1979; Mehr *et al.*, 1982; Hawton, 1986).

Most attempts have little lethal potential. In studies in the UK (Hawton *et al.*, 1982a) and in New York City (Rotheram-Borus *et al.*, 1990; Piacentini *et al.*, 1991), physicians rated the likely untreated consequences of self-poisoning. Fifty-eight per cent and 70% of attempts were rated as certainly survivable while death was rated as more likely than not in only 8% and 2% in the two countries respectively. Spirito *et al.* (1988b) and Garfinkel *et al.* (1982) reported a similarly restricted range of lethality using a slightly different method of risk classification (the Risk–Rescue Rating Scale; Weissman & Worden, 1972). Adolescent attempters generally overestimate the potential lethality of their behaviour. Piacentini *et al.* (1991) compared attempter and psychiatrist estimates of lethality in a series of emergency room presentations and found that, while 26% of attempts were rated as having a potential to cause death by the adolescents, only 2% were considered lethal by the physicians. A significant relationship between increased medical lethality of suicide attempts in hospitalized adolescents and male gender, the presence of affective disorder (both individual and familial), substance abuse, persistent ideation, the ingestion of psychotropic agents, and the degree of planning of the attempt has been reported by Brent and his colleagues (1987). The availability of a lethal agent appears to be a more important determinant of lethality for impulsive attempters, while suicidal intent and presence of affective disorder and substance abuse were the strongest predictors of lethality for depressed, hopeless individuals engaging in premeditated attempts.

Intent

Because of teenagers' *naïveté* about what constitutes medically lethal behaviour, attempts have been made to gauge intent by asking teenagers directly whether or not they want to die. Although anywhere from 30 to 50% say they do, most take no or at best passive precautions against discovery (Piacentini *et al.*, 1991). Hawton *et al.* (1982a) reported that only 29% of adolescent reports of lethal intent were confirmed by the evaluating psychiatrist. Altogether 34% of attempters reported wanting to die and 42% reported not caring whether they lived or died. Most adolescent attempters deny persistent intent after their attempt and are glad that they recovered. A substantial minority of attempters deny the suicidal implications of their behaviour (Spirito *et al.*, 1989).

Precipitants

Interpersonal (mainly family) conflict is the most commonly reported precipitant of an adolescent suicide attempt. Overall, about three-quarters will identify conflict with a family member or friend (Tishler *et al.*, 1981; Rotheram-Borus & Trautman, 1988; Pronovost *et al.*, 1990), but girls are significantly more likely to do so than boys. Other less common precipitants include school problems, rejection, drug or alcohol problems, an abusive environment and bereavement. Up to one-third of adolescent attempters are unable to identify a clear precipitating event for their attempt (Hawton *et al.*, 1982b). Lack of an obvious precipitant appears to be more characteristic of attempts occurring in the context of a depressive illness.

Clinical features

Depressive disorders

Affective and disruptive disorders and substance abuse place adolescents at increased risk for attempted suicide. Teen suicide attempters have been reported to be anywhere from 3 to 18 times more likely to be depressed than unselected controls (Smith & Crawford, 1986; Velez & Cohen, 1988; Garrison et al., 1991) depending on the diagnostic criteria used and samples studied. Some (Marks & Haller, 1977; Taylor & Stansfeld, 1984a), but not all studies have found more depression than in psychiatric controls (Mattson et al., 1969; Pfeffer et al., 1980; Pfeffer, 1981; Cohen-Sandler et al., 1982; Spirito et al., 1987; Brent et al., 1988). Community surveys have revealed rates of depression of 19–42% (Smith & Crawford, 1986; Velez & Cohen, 1988) with the rate being much higher — 25–82% — in hospitalized youngsters. There is some evidence that a positive relationship exists between severity of depression and the severity of suicidal behaviour (Bettes & Walker, 1986; Pfeffer et al., 1988). Nevertheless, it is clear that while affective disturbance is a potent risk factor for suicidal behaviour, a substantial number of suicidal adolescents are not depressed.

Disruptive disorders

A number of studies have found aggression, anger and other antisocial behaviours to be as or more common than depression in suicidal adolescents (Garfinkel et al., 1982; Bettes & Walker, 1986; Joffe et al., 1988; Velez & Cohen, 1988; Choquet & Mencke, 1989; Trautman et al., 1991). Rates of conduct disorder in suicidal adolescents have ranged from 26% in an inpatient sample (Brent et al., 1988) to 46% of a consecutive series of minority female attempters (Trautman et al., 1991). Gispert and colleagues reported a significant correlation between intensity of anger and both seriousness of the index attempt (Gispert et al., 1985) and an increased likelihood of future attempts (Gispert et al., 1987). Although conduct disorder often co-occurs with childhood depressive illness (McGee et al., 1990), many attempters have conduct problems without any affective symptoms (Pfeffer et al., 1983).

Substance use disorders

Many attempters abuse drugs or alcohol with reported rates ranging from 13 to 42% depending on the sample and definition of abuse (Hawton et al., 1982c; Brent et al., 1988; Spirito et al., 1989). Substance abuse has been found to be more common in attempters than in community controls (Garfinkel et al., 1982; McKenry et al., 1983), but not clinic controls (Spirito et al., 1987; Trautman et al., 1991). The relationship may be stronger in the US than in the UK (Hawton, 1986; Spirito et al., 1989). Only a small minority of attempters (5–11%) report being intoxicated at the time of their attempt (Garfinkel et al., 1982; Piacentini et al., 1991).

Comparison between suicide attempters and completers

Comparisons between adolescent attempters and completers are made difficult by the lack of detailed epidemiological data on adolescent suicide attempters. To date, the few studies examining similarities and differences between these two groups have relied on unrepresentative hospital-based samples of attempters demographically matched to the completer group. Brent et al. (1991) compared a consecutive sample of 47 adolescent completers from Western Pennsylvania with 47 hospitalized attempters matched for age, gender and ethnicity and found completed suicides to be characterized by higher levels of suicidal intent and lower rates of affective, but not substance abuse or conduct, disorders. Brent et al. also found that completers were almost five times as likely as attempters to have guns in their homes. Firearms were used by the majority of completers (69%), and almost all of the completers with guns in their homes, versus none of the attempters. There is some evidence from broader emergency room-based studies that certain subgroups of attempters may be more similar to suicide completers than others. In a chart review study of 131 consecutive adolescent attempters presenting to a hospital emergency room, Brent (1987) identified two subgroups of adolescents: one group of depressed, hopeless youngsters with high suicidal intent who made premeditated lethal attempts and a second group that was characterized by adjustment or behavioural disturbance, a lack of hopelessness, and who made impulsive attempts of varying lethality.

Cognitive factors

A number of cognitive factors such as hopelessness, impaired problem-solving abilities or coping strategies, and an abnormal attributional style have been related to depressive disturbance. There is less evidence linking these types of cognitive dysfunction to suicidality.

Hopelessness

Studies in adults indicate that hopelessness is a better predictor of suicidal intent and behaviour than depression (Dyer & Kreitman, 1984; Beck et al., 1985). The predictive relationship has not been examined among adolescents and there is disagreement about the strength of the relationship at the time of the attempt. Spirito et al. (1988a) and Swedo et al. (1991) found higher levels in hospitalized attempters compared with nonsuicidal psychiatric and normal controls, but two other studies (Asarnow et al., 1987; Rotheram-Borus & Trautman, 1988) failed to find significant correlations, after controlling for depression. Pillay and Wassenaar (1991) found no relationship between the degree of hopelessness and the expectation of rescue.

Problem-solving and coping

Suicidal youngsters have been found to generate fewer alternative solutions to interpersonal problem situations (Levenson, 1974; Asarnow *et al.*, 1987; Orbach *et al.*, 1987; Rotheram-Borus *et al.*, 1990) and to show greater inflexibility in dealing with problem situations (Levenson & Neuringer, 1971) than either psychiatric or normal controls. Rotheram-Borus *et al.* (1990) reported that female adolescent attempters were more 'problem-focused' and more likely to employ wishful thinking when dealing with interpersonal problems than either nonsuicidal psychiatric or normal controls. Young suicidal inpatients have been found to use fewer cognitive mediational strategies for coping with stress (Asarnow *et al.*, 1987) and to predict more negative consequences for their solutions than hospitalized nonsuicidal controls (Schotte & Clum, 1987). Taken together, these studies suggest that attempters are more focused on their problems, generate fewer and less effective solutions for dealing with stressful situations and are more pessimistic about their chances for success.

Attributional style

Dysfunctional attributional style, in which negative events are considered to be one's own fault (internal), long-lasting (stable) and impacting on all aspects of one's life (global), is a common characteristic of depression in both adults and children (Abramson *et al.*, 1978; Beck *et al.*, 1979; Kaslow *et al.*, 1984, 1988). In only one study (Hart *et al.* unpublished data, 1988) was a similar relationship found in hospitalized attempters. Two others (Asarnow *et al.*, 1987; Rotheram-Borus *et al.*, 1990) failed to find a relationship to suicidality after controlling for depression, and Spirito *et al.* (1991) found that adolescent suicide attempters were actually more likely than psychiatric controls to make positive attributions.

Impulsivity

Adolescent suicide attempters are commonly referred to as impulsive and clinic-based studies suggest that the majority of attempts in this age group are not premeditated. Two studies in New York City found that up to 70% of a consecutive series of emergency-room admissions described their attempts as impulsive while only 10–15% reported thinking about their attempt for more than a day (Rotheram-Borus *et al.*, 1990; Piacentini *et al.*, 1991). In spite of this, very few studies have examined the relationship between impulsive style and suicidal behaviour in adolescents due in part, perhaps, to the difficulty in measuring this variable (Spirito *et al.*, 1989). The little evidence from adults and adolescents that does exist, however, suggests that impulsivity is probably not a characteristic of all adolescent suicide attempters but rather may be a

marker for a heterogeneously distinct subgroup who are less likely to be depressed and hopeless and show lower suicidal intent and lethality than their nonimpulsive counterparts (Brent, 1987; Brown *et al.*, 1991).

Family factors

The parents of suicide attempters have been described as having high rates of psychiatric illness and marital and parent–child conflict, although evidence that either of these problems is more prevalent than in the families of other psychiatric patients is limited (Shaffer, 1974; Taylor & Stansfeld, 1984a; Trautman & Shaffer, 1984; Rubenstein *et al.*, 1989; Asarnow, 1992). There are also uncontrolled accounts of hostile, punitive, indifferent and insensitive parenting (Jacobs, 1971; Yusin *et al.*, 1972; McIntire & Angle, 1973). Attempters have been reported to perceive their parents as placing extremely high expectations on them and being over-controlling. The teenagers may view their relationship with their parents as being more dysfunctional than the parents acknowledge (McIntire & Angle, 1973; McKenry *et al.*, 1982) and, in many instances, conflicts arise from unresolved differences about what is or isn't age-appropriate behaviour for a teenager. However, biased perceptions of this sort are common, if not normal, in adolescents and are unlikely to be sufficient explanation for what is essentially an uncommon condition. Adolescent suicide attempters have been shown to experience more family turmoil (e.g. parental separation, change in caretaker or living situation) and total stressful life events than both depressed and normal controls (Jacobs, 1971; Cohen-Sandler *et al.*, 1982; Gispert *et al.*, 1985; De Wilde *et al.*, 1992). They are also more likely than normal, but not depressed, controls to have been sexually and/or physically abused at some time in their lives.

Course

Many adolescent attempters experience continued disturbance after their acute attempt and up to 50% make further attempts (Spirito *et al.*, 1989). Follow-up studies indicate that between 0.1 and 11% will eventually commit suicide (Otto, 1972; Motto, 1984; Goldacre & Hawton, 1985; Shaffer *et al.*, 1988a,b; Spirito *et al.*, 1989). Later suicide has been associated with greater disturbance at the time of initial contact and is many times higher in psychiatrically hospitalized patients than in outpatients. It is also more common in older teens. A high proportion of repeat attempts occur during the first 2 years after the initial attempt. Otto (1972) reported that 70% of the attempters who ultimately completed suicide died by methods similar to their initial attempt, the remainder using a more lethal method. Male attempters are anywhere from three to seven times as likely as female attempters ultimately to commit suicide.

Risk factors for nonfatal repetition are similar to those for completed suicide. They include male gender, poor communication, a history of previous attempts, depressive symptomatology and hopelessness (Stanley & Barter, 1970; McIntire *et al.*, 1977; Goldacre & Hawton, 1985; Gispert *et al.*, 1987; Choquet & Mencke, 1989; Sellar *et al.*, 1990; Pfeffer *et al.*, 1991).

In addition to repetition, suicidal behaviour in childhood and adolescence has been associated with other adverse psychiatric and psychosocial outcomes as well. Otto (1972) found that the suicide attempters at 10−15-year follow-up were much more likely than controls to be unmarried or divorced and to be listed in national registries as having criminal behaviour, alcohol problems or disability pensions.

Treatment and evaluation

Initial evaluation

Many teen attempters will first be seen in the casualty/ emergency room. The initial task, after medical stabilization, is to determine whether or not an inpatient hospitalization is needed. Although the pros and cons of hospitalization have not been studied systematically, knowledge of risk factors derived from studies of both completers (e.g. Shaffer, 1974; Shaffer *et al.*, 1988a,b) and attempters (e.g. Hawton, 1986; Brent, 1987) suggest that admission should be considered for the following groups: those who use a method other than ingestion or superficial cutting; males; teens with persistent ideation or a history of recurrent attempts; those with depressive or psychotic symptoms or alcohol/substance abuse; and teens with no adult guardian or companion who can ensure the safety of the environment (i.e. remove all medications, guns, knives, etc.) and monitor the youngster until the first follow-up appointment. It is common practice to require attempters to contract (either verbally or in writing) with the clinician that they will not make a further attempt before the next clinic visit, or if the urge to harm themselves becomes too great, to return to the clinic or emergency room immediately.

Ensuring that the patient returns

Although this will vary from clinic to clinic, published reports suggest that close to half of all adolescent suicide attempters fail to receive any formal therapeutic intervention following their emergency-room experience (Kienhorst *et al.*, 1987; Spirito *et al.*, 1989), and that many of the remainder fail to complete their recommended course of treatment (Litt *et al.*, 1983; Taylor & Stansfeld, 1984a,b; Trautman & Rotheram, 1988; Swedo, 1989; Trautman *et al.*, 1989; Piacentini *et al.*, 1991). These proportions may be even higher in younger attempters. Factors associated with noncompliance include previous suicidal behaviour, persistent suicidal intent, a large number of psychiatric symptoms, depression, family rigidity, poor communication, vague discharge treatment plans and past dissatisfaction with treatment. Maternal substance abuse, depression and poor physical health may be associated with *improved* compliance (Trautman, 1989; Piacentini *et al.*, 1991).

Outpatient treatment

There have, to date, been no systematic evaluations, controlled or otherwise, of outpatient treatment interventions with child and adolescent suicide attempters, and most treatment studies with adult attempters have used the inherently weak strategy of relying on natural variations in the treatment experience, examining outcome as a function of the amount or type of treatment received. Given these limitations, the adult studies suggest that psychiatric intervention of any type (even that as minimal as intermittent telephone contact) has a positive effect in reducing subsequent suicidal attempts and social adjustment with no one type of treatment being superior to any other (Greer & Bagley, 1971; Chowdhury *et al.*, 1973; Motto, 1976; Welu, 1977; Gibbons *et al.*, 1978; Gibbons, 1980; Motto *et al.*, 1981; Liberman & Eckman, 1981).

Given the acute time interval within which most adolescent suicidal crises erupt and recede and the fact that a majority of patients fail to stay in treatment for more than a few sessions, a brief crisis-oriented treatment approach makes sense for most adolescent attempters (Trautman, 1989). Within this framework, a number of treatment approaches have been proposed for adolescent suicide attempters. Most are based on teaching some form of cognitive problem-solving techniques and involve other family members (Richman, 1981; Trautman & Shaffer, 1984; Hawton, 1986; Trautman & Rotheram, 1988; Trautman, 1989; Gutstein & Rudd, 1990; Lerner & Clum, 1990). The use of a cognitive-behavioural approach is based on the assumption that attempters have poor social problem-solving abilities, use ineffective coping strategies, and have dysfunctional cognitive styles, although evidence for this is by no means convincing (see above). The primary goals of family-based cognitive-behavioural treatment are to: (1) increase the positive affective state of the family; (2) teach the adolescent attempter and other family members how to recognize the situations and events in the child's environment that lead to family conflict, emotional upset, and suicidal behaviour; and (3) teach family members how to generate and test feasible solutions to family problems in order to anticipate and defuse situations that may precipitate suicidal behaviour (Richman, 1979; Trautman, 1989; Miller *et al.*, 1992).

Given the importance of familial conflict in precipitating most attempts, it is certainly reasonable to involve the family. A cognitive behavioural approach that emphasizes positive events and personal strengths will hopefully reduce the high levels of conflict, blame and negativity which are often present shortly after an attempt (Stuart, 1980; Trautman & Shaffer, 1984; Miller *et al.*, 1992).

Two very small controlled studies, one with older adolescents (Lerner & Clum, 1990) and one with adults (Salkovskis *et al.*, 1990), have shown a cognitive-behavioural problem-solving approach to be more effective than unstructured or supportive treatments in reducing depression and hopelessness in suicidal patients at posttreatment and 3−12-month follow-up. In addition, Salkoviskis *et al.* found that adult attempters receiving problem-solving treatment reported less suicidal ideation and made fewer repeat attempts than attempters in the comparison condition.

Other treatment strategies that have been described as useful for suicidal adolescents include family therapy (Richman, 1984), group therapy (Glaser, 1978) and psychopharmacological interventions (Trautman, 1989). However, these approaches have not been systematically evaluated and in the case of group therapy (high degree of contagion of adolescent suicidality) and psychopharmacological treatment (easy availability of lethal medication), the evidence suggests they should be used with great caution, if at all.

SUICIDE PREVENTION

For many years suicide was seen as a logical behaviour that could be enjoined by anyone. It was, therefore, not feasible to consider its prevention. However, as research into the individual characteristics of suicide completers has progressed, the factors that define risk, such as depression and alcohol abuse, have been refined and narrowed and suicide prevention has become a more attainable goal.

Who is at risk?

Armed with better knowledge of the characteristics of suicide, a logical procedure is to identify high-risk cases and provide them with optimal treatment and follow-up. Other prevention strategies that fit this model include crisis management or limiting access to potential methods for committing suicide.

Case-finding

This can be either direct or indirect. *Indirect* case-finding is used in some suicide education programmes to train pupils, teachers, and parents to spot the warning signs of suicide among their friends, pupils or children. Problems with this approach include the fact that many at-risk teens do not show visible symptoms and that behaviours that denote risk, such as depression or alcohol abuse, are prevalent in nonsuicidal teens. Furthermore, it cannot be assumed that assigning teenagers the task of case-finding other teenagers is without social or psychological risk for the teen case-finder, who must either persuade the friend to obtain help or, if that fails, break a confidence and disclose the evaluation to a responsible adult. It also seems that this approach is difficult to implement. Teenagers who have received systematic training in case-finding are no more likely to recommend treatment to their distressed friends than those who do not (Vieland *et al.*, 1991).

Direct case-finding elicits risk status from the teenagers themselves. This is reasonable because older teenagers' self-identification of problems is both highly correlated with a clinician's determination of need for treatment and, in the case of depression and dysthymia, identifies a different group of troubled teens than teacher or parent nominations (Kovacs, 1981; Achenbach & Edelbrock, 1987; Bird *et al.*, 1990). A number of forms have been developed to identify presuicidal

states in teenagers (Smith & Crawford, 1986; Harkavy-Friedman *et al.*, 1987; Office of Disease Prevention and Health Promotion, 1989), but their value in predicting suicide-prone teens has yet to be demonstrated. Regardless of the method used, the value of case-finding will be restricted by the very high base rate of some high-risk conditions (e.g. alcohol abuse, anxiety disorders and aggressive behaviour), sparse treatment resources and limited knowledge on optimal treatment.

Crisis services

The original argument for intervention (Schneidman & Farberow, 1965; Litman *et al.*, 1965) was that suicide intent is often associated with a critical stress event that is usually contemplated with psychological ambivalence and that arises in the context of mental disturbance. If the model of suicide presented in Figure 23.3 is accurate, then crisis services are potentially efficient because they operate at the final common pathway to death.

Crisis services are usually provided by so-called telephone hotlines. Some are staffed by teenagers (Simmons *et al.*, 1986), but most by specially trained adult listeners who give information about how to access appropriate services. Some, especially those that are part of a multiservice agency, carry out more active case management, making appointments with the appropriate clinical service and following up if the appointment is not kept. Relatively few offer direct therapy on the telephone and most will break confidentiality if they judge that it will avert a suicide, calling parental or police help. An exception is the Samaritan organization whose befriending process emphasizes acceptance, warmth, and *confidentiality* (Hirsch, 1981).

The efficacy of crisis intervention has usually been tested by determining whether the establishment of a service results in lower suicide morbidity in a given area. The research is inevitably ecological, i.e. there is no information on whether suicides that occurred had contacted the crisis service to no avail, or the reverse, whether highly suicidal individuals were redirected from their intended plan by the crisis service. Regardless, the balance of evidence is that crisis services have no or at best, very limited effects on the suicide rate (Barraclough *et al.*, 1977; Bridge *et al.*, 1977; Jennings *et al.*, 1978; Miller *et al.*, 1984). Possible explanations for this (see Shaffer *et al.*, 1989, for a review) are the predominance of female callers, who are at relatively low risk for suicide, the indifferent quality of much of the advice given (Bleach & Claiborn, 1974; Apsler & Hodas, 1975; Slaiku *et al.*, 1975; Knowles, 1979; Hirsch, 1981), and the fact that a significant proportion of suicides occur when the victim is preoccupied or disorganized, under the influence of alcohol, or in an otherwise agitated state where he or she may not be able to summon the resources to make or benefit from an appropriate call. Only a small proportion of teens know how to access a hotline (Litman *et al.*, 1965; Greer & Anderson, 1979).

It is probably a mistake to dismiss hotlines as well-inten-

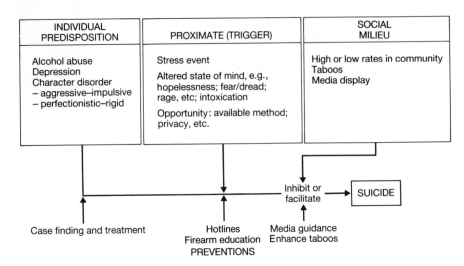

Fig. 23.3 Pathway model of suicide.

tioned, but ineffective. Hotlines are widely available in the US and provide help for a needy and otherwise underserved population. King (1977) showed that only 8% of callers were currently receiving other mental health services. In a survey of high school students who had attended a suicide education programme (Shaffer *et al.*, 1988a), one of the few significant effects was an increase in a declared willingness to use a hotline when experiencing emotional difficulties, there being no increase in willingness to use any other type of service. There is a need to develop a standardized but clinically informed screening procedure coupled with active case management procedures and to broaden interest in hotlines, particularly among troubled boys, with appropriately directed advertising.

Educational programmes

Educational programmes generally aim at one or more of the following goals (Shaffer *et al.*, 1988a,b; Garland *et al.*, 1989):
1 To heighten awareness of the problem, by showing taped vignettes of teenagers who have attempted suicide or by quoting disturbing statistics, e.g. that suicide is the second leading cause of death in teenagers.
2 To promote indirect case-finding (see above).
3 To promote disclosure of suicidal intentions or ruminations. This is done by presenting a model of suicide that is intended to be nonstigmatizing. Thus, the programme may state that suicide is *not* a feature of mental illness but is a response to common adolescent stress such as pressure to succeed, family upsets, residential mobility, changing value systems, use of drugs and alcohol etc. This may be reinforced by showing taped vignettes of attractive youngsters who have made a previous attempt for these reasons.
4 To provide staff and students with information about mental health resources, specifically how they operate and how they can be accessed.

Didactic, school-based suicide prevention programmes can be criticized for following a low-risk strategy. The over-

whelming number of adolescents who are exposed to the programmes carry no risk for suicide. Further, there is no evidence that such programmes modify attitudes about suicide or help-seeking in either normal or high-risk students (Spirito *et al.*, 1988b; Shaffer *et al.*, 1990, 1991; Vieland *et al.*, 1991). The failure of a purely didactic approach is broadly in line with educational strategies to prevent alcohol and drug abuse (Office of Substance Abuse Prevention, 1989) and early sexual activity (Kirby, 1985). There is some suggestion that such programmes do shift students to a model of suicide that is held to be nonstigmatizing by the designers, i.e. one that renders suicide understandable in the context of stress, rather than a psychopathological model (Shaffer *et al.*, 1991). These programmes have not solved the dilemma of how to make suicide less shameful without, at the same time, reducing the prohibitions that may contribute to making suicide a mercifully rare event.

Limiting access to methods

Because youth suicide is often an impulsive act, it is reasonable to expect that limiting access to commonly used methods could prevent its, occurrence in some instances. The so-called British experience is a frequently cited example of how this can happen. The British suicide rate declined *pari passu* with the replacement of poisonous domestic coal gas with carbon monoxide-free natural gas (Hassall & Trethowan, 1972; Kreitman, 1976). Over the period of transition, British suicide rates fell by 26%, with most of the decline being attributed to a decrease in deaths from domestic gas asphyxiation with no compensatory increase in suicidal deaths by other methods. British rates, in contrast to those in most other countries, remained at the new lower level (Farberow, 1985) for many years. Most suicides in the US are committed with legally owned and registered firearms. It would be reasonable to expect that the early British experience could be replicated by effective firearm control in that country, but by extension one would only expect a similar transient effect.

Postvention

Postvention refers to an intervention implemented after a suicide with direct survivors or in the victim's school or community. Postvention could serve several preventive functions, by (1) providing a structure for understanding the death, thus alleviating some of the guilt and isolation experienced by family survivors (Calhoun *et al.*, 1982; Rogers *et al.*, 1982; Henley, 1984); (2) minimizing the scapegoating that can affect parents, teachers, the school, or particular peers; and (3) reducing the likelihood of imitation either within the family or within the community or both.

There have been no controlled studies on postvention and reports of reduction in guilt and sadness in a 2-month volunteer-led survivors support group (Rogers *et al.*, 1982) could have occurred spontaneously.

CONCLUSION: A MODEL FOR SUICIDE

Psychodynamic models explain suicide as a consequence of either intrapsychic dynamics, such as the need to identify with or join a deceased love object, the internalization of anger, or of interpersonal goals, such as manipulations either to gain love or inflict punishment (Abraham, 1927; Zilboorg, 1936; Freud, 1957; Toolan, 1962). However, phenomena such as self-denigratory thought or morbid preoccupations with deceased loved ones can be reversed with antidepressant medication and so are more likely to be a consequence, rather than a cause, of a mood disturbance.

Sociological models hold suicide to be an intended or understandable behaviour given an individual's life situation or position in society. Variations on the model include concepts such as a lack of social integration or anomie, group dynamics such as racial or sexual prejudice, that foster or lessen identification with others and political-economic pressures such as cycles of unemployment or increases in cohort size that increase pressure for educational employment resources. The individual is seen to be responding to social forces beyond his or her control. This model cannot stand alone and it is not suggested that *all* individuals in an anomalous position in society or experiencing a particular stress will seek suicide as a solution. Studies carried out to examine some sociological models are open to the so-called ecological fallacy, i.e. they relate mortality statistics to measurable variables such as total population, unemployment rates, phases in the economic cycle, ethnic mixture in geographic units, immigration patterns, migration, crime and divorce rates, etc. A causal relationship cannot be inferred because when one factor, for example, unemployment rate, varies, others may vary with it, or the variation may occur against a backdrop of more general change. Most of the sociological models listed above are not supported by studies of individual suicides which, in general, fail to find impaired access to educational or employment resources that could not be better explained as a consequence of deviant behaviour or social drift.

The *psychiatric disease model* is supported by psychological studies that posit that suicide occurs as a consequence of the distortions of perception and judgement that characterize a disturbance of mental state brought about by a psychiatric illness such as depression or intoxication. Suicide is not seen as a disease, but rather as a symptom or sign of an underlying disturbance of mental state.

A model that takes account of many of the correlates described above and that is heuristic for prevention is provided in Figure 23.3 (Shaffer *et al.*, 1988b). It assumes that suicide does not occur capriciously, and mainly affects predisposed individuals. Important predispositions include major mood disorder and certain personality types. Very few individuals who are not thus affected will be at risk for suicide. Predisposed individuals will usually make their suicide attempt or commit suicide after some stressful event — often a consequence rather than a cause of their disorder — has induced an extreme emotion, such as fear, unhappiness, hopelessness or rage. This mental state may lead to suicide if judgement is impaired by drugs or alcohol or identification with a glamorously or heroically portrayed suicide model in a movie or on TV. Finally, the means of committing suicide in an acceptable and effective way will need to be at hand.

ACKNOWLEDGEMENTS

This work was made possible by NIMH Research Training Grant MH 38198—11A2 and Research Training Grant MH 16434, NIMH Center Grant MH 43878 AI, the Centers for Disease Control Grant R49 CCR202598, NIMH Project Grants ROI MH 38198, ROI MH416898 and R18MH48059—02 and grants from the American Mental Health Foundation and the Leon Lowenstein Foundation.

REFERENCES

Abraham K. (1927) Notes on the psychoanalytic investigation and treatment of manic-depressive insanity and allied conditions. In: Jones E. (ed) *Selected Papers*, pp. 137—156. Hogarth Press, London.

Abramson L.Y., Seligman M.E.P. & Teasdale J.D. (1978) Learned helplessness in humans: critique and reformulation. *Journal of Abnormal Psychology*, **87**, 49—74.

Achenbach T.M. & Edelbrock C. (1987) *Manual for the Youth Self-Report and Profile*. University of Vermont, Department of Psychiatry, Burlington, VT.

Andrus J.K., Flemming D.W., Heumann M.A., Wassell J.T., Hopkins D.D. & Gordon J. (1991) Surveillance of attempted suicide among adolescents in Oregon, 1988. *American Journal of Public Health*, **81**, 1067—1069.

Apsler R. & Hodas M. (1975) Evaluating hotlines with simulated calls. *Crisis Intervention*, **6**, 14—21.

Asarnow J. (1992) Suicidal ideation and attempts during middle childhood: associations with perceived family stress and depression among child psychiatric inpatients. *Journal of Clinical Child Psychology*, **21**, 35—40.

Asarnow J.R., Carlson G.A. & Guthrie D. (1987) Coping strategies, self-perceptions, hopelessness, and perceived family environments in depressed and suicidal children. *Journal of Consulting and Clinical Psychology*, **55**, 361—366.

Asberg M., Nordstrom P. & Traskman-Bendz L. (1986) Cerebrospinal fluid studies in suicide. In: Mann J.J. & Stanley M. (eds) *Psychobiology of Suicidal Behaviour*, pp. 243–255. New York Academy of Sciences, New York.

Barraclough B.M. (1987) Sex ratio of juvenile suicide. *Journal of the American Academy of Child and Adolescent Psychiatry*, **26**, 434–435.

Barraclough B.M., Bunch J., Nelson B. & Sainsbury P. (1969) The diagnostic classification and psychiatric treatment of 100 suicides. In: *Proceedings of the Fifth International Conference for Suicide Prevention*. London.

Barraclough B.M., Jennings C., Moss J.R., Hawton K., Cole D., O'Grady J. & Osborne M. (1977) Suicide prevention by the Samaritans. *Lancet*, **ii**, 237–238.

Beck A.T., Rush A.J., Shaw B.F. & Emergy G. (1979) *Cognitive Therapy of Depression*. Guilford Press, New York.

Beck A.T., Steer R.A., Kovacs M. & Garrison B. (1985) Hopelessness and eventual suicide: a 10-year prospective study of patients hospitalized with suicidal ideation. *American Journal of Psychiatry*, **142**, 559–563.

Berman A.L. (1988) Fictional depiction of suicide in television films and imitation effects. *American Journal of Psychiatry* **145**, 982–986.

Bettes B.A. & Walker E. (1986) Symptoms associated with suicidal behavior in childhood and adolescence. *Journal of Abnormal Psychology*, **14**, 591–604.

Bird H., Yager T., Staghezza B., Gould M., Canino G. & Rubio-Stipec M. (1990) Impairment in the epidemiological measurement of childhood psychopathology in the community. *Journal of the American Academy of Child and Adolescent Psychiatry*, **29**, 796–803.

Bleach G. & Claiborn W.L. (1974) Initial evaluation of hot-line telephone crisis centers. *Community Mental Health Journal*, **10**, 387–394.

Blum R.W., Harmon B., Harris L., Bergeisen L. & Resnick M.D. (1992) American Indian-Alaska native youth health. *Journal of the American Medical Association*, **267**, 1637–1644.

Bollen K.A. & Phillips D.P. (1981) Suicidal motor vehicle fatalities in Detroit: a replication. *American Journal of Sociology*, **87**, 404–412.

Bollen K.A. & Phillips D.P. (1982) Imitative suicides: a national study of the effects of television news stories. *American Sociological Review*, **47**, 802–809.

Brent D. (1987) Correlates of medical lethality of suicide attempts in children and adolescents. *Journal of the American Academy of Child and Adolescent Psychiatry*, **26**, 87–91.

Brent D., Perper J. & Allman C. (1987) Alcohol, firearms, and suicide among youth: temporal trends in Allegheny County, Pennsylvannia, 1960 to 1983. *Journal of the American Medical Association*, **257**, 3369–3372.

Brent D., Perper J.A., Goldstein C., Kolko D., Allan M., Allman C. & Zelenak J. (1988) Risk factors for adolescent suicide: a comparison of adolescent suicide victims and suicide inpatients. *Archives of General Psychiatry*, **45**, 581–588.

Brent D., Kerr M., Goldstein C., Bozigar J., Wartella M. & Allan M. (1989) An outbreak of suicide and suicidal behavior in a high school. *Journal of the American Academy of Child and Adolescent Psychiatry*, **28**, 918–924.

Brent D., Perper J., Allman C., Moritz G., Wartella M. & Zelenak J. (1991) The presence and accessibility of firearms in the homes of adolescent suicides: a case-control study. *Journal of the American Medical Association*, **266**, 2989–2995.

Brent D., Perper J.A., Moritz G., Liotus L., Schweers J., Roth C., Baylach L. & Allman C. (in submission.) Psychiatric impairment of the loss of an adolescent sibling to suicide.

Bridge T.P., Potkin S.G., Zung W.W. & Soldo B.J. (1977) Suicide prevention centers: ecological study of effectiveness. *Journal of Nervous and Mental Disease*, **164**, 18–24.

Brown L., Overholser J., Spirito A. & Fritz G. (1991) The correlates of planning in adolescent suicide attempts. *Journal of the American Academy of Child and Adolescent Psychiatry*, **30**, 95–99.

Bush J.A. (1976) Suicides and blacks: a conceptual framework. *Suicide and Life-Threatening Behavior*, **6**, 216–222.

Calhoun L.G., Selby J.W. & Selby L.E. (1982) The psychological aftermath of suicide: an analysis of current evidence. *Clinical Psychological Review*, **2**, 409–420.

Centers for Disease Control (1991) Attempted suicide among high school students-United States, 1990. *Morbidity and Mortality Weekly Report*, **40**, 633–635.

Choquet M. & Mencke H. (1989) Suicidal thoughts during early adolescence: prevalence, associated troubles and help-seeking behavior. *Acta Psychiatrica Scandinavica*, **81**, 170–177.

Chowdhury N., Hicks R.C. & Kreitman N. (1973) Evaluation of an aftercare service for parasuicide (attempted suicide) patients. *Social Psychiatry*, **8**, 67–81.

Chung S.Y., Luk S.L. & Lieh Mak F. (1987) Attempted suicide in children and adolescents in Hong Kong. *Social Psychiatry*, **22**, 102–106.

Coe J.I. (1974) Sexual asphyxias. *Suicide and Life-Threatening Behavior*, **4**, 171–175.

Cohen-Sandler R., Berman A.L. & King R.A. (1982) Life stress and symptomatology: determinants of suicidal behavior in children. *Journal of the American Academy of Child Psychiatry*, **21**, 178–186.

Davidson L., Rosenberg M., Mercy J.A., Franklin J. & Simmons J. (1989) An epidemiologic study of risk factors in two teenage suicide clusters. *Journal of the American Medical Association*, **262**, 2687–2692.

De Wilde E.J., Kienhorst C.W.M., Diekstra R.F.W. & Wolters W.H.G. (1992) The relationship between adolescent suicidal behavior and life events in childhood and adolescence. *American Journal of Psychiatry*, **149**, 45–51.

Dizmang M., Watson J., May P. & Bopp J. (1974) Adolescent suicide at an Indian reserve. *American Journal of Orthopsychiatry*, **44**, 43–49.

Dorpat T.L. & Ripley H.S. (1960) A study of suicide in the Seattle area. *Comprehensive Psychiatry*, **1**, 349–359.

Dubow E.F., Kausch D.F., Blum M.C., Reed J. & Bush E. (1989) Correlates of suicidal ideation and attempts in a community sample of junior high and high school students. *Journal of Clinical and Child Psychology*, **18**, 158–166.

Dyck R.J., Newman S.C. & Thompson A.H. (1988) Suicide trends in Canada, 1956–1981. *Acta Psychiatrica Scandinavica*, **77**, 411–419.

Dyer J.A.T. & Kreitman N. (1984) Hopelessness, depression and suicidal intent in parasuicide. *British Journal of Psychiatry*, **144**, 127–133.

Farberow N.R. (1985) *Youth Suicide: An International Problem*. Report of the National Conference on Youth Suicide, pp. 9–34. Youth Suicide National Center, Washington, DC.

Fisher P. & Shaffer D. (1990) Facts about adolescent suicide: a review of national mortality statistics and recent research. In: Rotheram-Borus M.J., Badley J. & Obolensky N. (eds) *Planning to Live: Evaluating and Treating Suicidal Teens in Community Settings*, pp. 3–32. National Resource Center for Youth Services, University of Oklahoma.

Fisher P., Shaffer D., Gould M., Trautman P. & Flory M. (in preparation) An epidemiological study of child and adolescent suicide. IV. The act of suicide.

Fleiss J.L. (1981) *Statistical Methods for Rates and Proportions*, 2nd edn. John Wiley, New York.

Fowler R.C., Rich C.L. & Young D. (1986) San Diego Suicide Study II. Substance abuse in young cases. *Archives of General Psychiatry*, **43**, 962–968.

Freud A. & Burlingham D. (1944) *Infants Without Families*. International Universities Press, New York.

Freud S. (1957) *Mourning and Melancholia* (standard edn.) pp. 237–

260. Hogarth Press, London.

Garfinkel B.D., Froese A. & Hood J. (1982) Suicide attempts in children and adolescents. *American Journal of Psychiatry*, **139**, 1257–1261.

Garland A., Shaffer D. & Whittle B. (1989) A survey of youth suicide prevention programs. *Journal of the American Academy of Child and Adolescent Psychiatry*, **28**, 931–934.

Garrison C.Z., Jackson K.L., Addy C.L., McKeown R.E. & Waller J.L. (1991) Suicidal behavior in young adolescents. *American Journal of Epidemiology*, **133**, 1005–1014.

Gibbons J.S. (1980) Management of self-poisoning: social work intervention, In: Farmer R. & Hirsch S. (eds) *The Suicide Syndrome*. Croom Helm, London.

Gibbons J.S., Butler J., Urwin P. & Gibbons J.L. (1978) Evaluation of a social work service for self-poisoning patients. *British Journal of Psychiatry*, **133**, 111–118.

Gibbs J.P. & Martin W.T. (1964) *Status of Integration and Suicide*. University of Oregon Press, Eugene, OR.

Gispert M., Wheeler K., Marsh L. & Davis M.S. (1985) Suicidal adolescents: factors in evaluation. *Adolescence*, **20**, 753–762.

Gispert M., Davis M.S., Marsh L. & Wheeler K. (1987) Adolescent suicide repeaters: factors in evaluation. *Hospital and Community Psychiatry*, **38**, 390–393.

Glaser K. (1978) The treatment of depressed and suicidal adolescents. *American Journal of Psychotherapy*, **32**, 252–269.

Goldacre M. & Hawton K. (1985) Repetition of self-poisoning and subsequent death in adolescents who take overdoses. *British Journal of Psychiatry*, **146**, 395–398.

Gould M.S. (1990) Suicide clusters and media exposure. In: Blumenthal S.J. & Kupfer D.J. (eds) *Suicide Over the Life Cycle: Risk Factors, Assessment and Treatment of Suicidal Patients*, pp. 517–532. American Psychiatric Press, Washington, DC.

Gould M.S. & Shaffer D. (1986) The impact of suicide in television movies: evidence of imitation. *New England Journal of Medicine*, **315**, 690–694.

Gould M.S., Shaffer D. & Kleinman M. (1988) The impact of suicide in television movies: replication and commentary. *Suicide and Life-Threatening Behavior*, **18**, 90–99.

Gould M.S., Shaffer D. & Davies M. (1990) Truncated pathways from childhood: attrition in follow-up studies due to death. In: Robins L. & Rutter M. (eds) *Straight and Devious Pathways from Childhood to Adulthood*, pp. 3–10. Cambridge University Press, Cambridge.

Gould M.S., Fisher P., Shaffer D. & Flory M. (Submitted for publication.) Environmental and familial characteristics of adolescent suicide completers.

Greer S. & Anderson M. (1979) Samaritan contact among 325 parasuicide patients. *British Journal of Psychiatry*, **135**, 263–268.

Greer S. & Bagley C.R. (1971) Effect of psychiatric intervention in attempted suicide: a controlled study. *British Medical Journal*, **1**, 310–312.

Gutstein S. & Rudd D. (1990) An outpatient treatment alternative for suicidal youth. *Journal of Adolescence*, **13**, 265–277.

Harkavy-Friedman J.M., Asnis G.M. & Boeck M. (1987) Prevalence of specific suicidal behaviors in a high school sample. *American Journal of Psychiatry*, **144**, 1203–1206.

Hassall C. & Trethowan W.H. (1972) Suicide in Birmingham. *British Medical Journal*, **1**, 717–718.

Hawton K. (1986) *Suicide and Attempted Suicide Among Children and Adolescents*. Sage Publications, Beverly Hills, CA.

Hawton K. & Goldacre M. (1982) Hospital admissions for adverse effects of medicinal agents (mainly self-poisoning) among adolescents in the Oxford region. *British Journal of Psychiatry*, **141**, 106–170.

Hawton K., Cole D., O'Grady J. & Osborn M. (1982a) Motivational aspects of deliberate self-poisoning in adolescents. *British Journal of Psychiatry*, **14**, 286–291.

Hawton K., O'Grady J., Osborn M. & Cole D. (1982b) Adolescents who take overdoses: their characteristics, problems and contacts with helping agencies. *British Journal of Psychiatry*, **140**, 118–123.

Hawton K., Osborn M., O'Grady J. & Cole D. (1982c) Classification of adolescents who take overdoses. *British Journal of Psychiatry*, **140**, 124–131.

Haynes R.H. (1987) Suicide and social response in Fiji: a historical survey. *British Journal of Psychiatry*, **151**, 21–26.

Henley S.H.A. (1984) Bereavement following suicide: a review of the literature. *Current Psychological Research and Reviews*, **3**, 53–61.

Hirsch S. (1981) A critique of volunteer-staffed suicide prevention centres. *Canadian Journal of Psychiatry*, **26**, 406–410.

Holding T.A. (1974) The B.B.C. 'Befriender' series and its effect. *British Journal of Psychiatry*, **124**, 470–472.

Holding T.A. (1975) Suicide and 'The Befrienders'. *British Medical Journal*, **3**, 751–753.

Jacobs J. (1971) *Adolescent Suicide*. Wiley Interscience, New York.

Jacobson B., Eklund G., Hamberger L., Linnarsson D., Sedvall G. & Valverius M. (1987) Perinatal origin of adult self-destructive behavior. *Acta Psychiatrica Scandinavica*, **76**, 364–371.

Jennings C., Barraclough B.M. & Moss J.R. (1978) Have the Samaritans lowered the suicide rate? A controlled study. *Psychological Medicine*, **8**, 413–422.

Joffe R.T., Offord D.R. & Boyle M.H. (1988) Ontario child health study: suicidal behavior in youths aged 12–16 years. *American Journal of Psychiatry*, **145**, 1420–1423.

Kashani J. & Simonds J.F. (1979) The incidence of depression in children. *American Journal of Psychiatry*, **136**, 1203–1205.

Kaslow N.J., Rehm L.P. & Siegel A.W. (1984) Social-cognitive and cognitive correlates of depression in children. *Journal of Abnormal Child Psychology*, **12**, 605–620.

Kaslow N.J., Rehm L.P., Pollack S.L. & Siegel A.W. (1988) Attributional style and self-control behavior in depressed and nondepressed children and their parents, *Journal of Abnormal Child Psychology*, **16**, 163–175.

Kety S. (1986) Genetic factors in suicide. In: Roy A. (ed) *Suicide*, pp. 41–45. Baltimore, MD.

Kienhorst C.W.M., Wolters W.H.G., Diekstra R.F.W. & Otte E. (1987) A study of the frequency of suicidal behavior in children aged 5 to 14. *Journal of Child Psychology and Psychiatry*, **28**, 153–165.

Kienhorst C.W.M., De Wilde E.J., Van Den Bout J., Diekstra R.F.W & Wolters W.H.G. (1990) Characteristics of suicide attempters in a population-based sample of Dutch adolescents. *British Journal of Psychiatry*, **156**, 243–248.

King G.D. (1977) An evaluation of the effectiveness of a telephone counselling center. *American Journal of Community Psychology*, **5**, 75–83.

Kirby D. (1985) Sexuality education: a more realistic view of its effects. *Journal of School Health*, **55**, 421–424.

Knowles D. (1979) On the tendency for volunteer helpers to give advice. *Journal of Counseling Psychology*, **26**, 352–354.

Kolmos L. (1987) Suicide in Scandinavia. *Acta Psychiatrica Scandinavica*, **76**, 11–16.

Koocher G.P. (1973) Childhood, death, and cognitive development. *Developmental Psychology*, **9**, 369–375.

Kovacs M. (1981) Rating scales to assess depression in school-aged children. *Acta Paedopsychiatrica*, **46**, 305–315.

Kovacs M. & Beck A.T. (1977) An empirical-clinical approach toward a definition of childhood depression. In: Schulterbrandt J.G. & Raskin A. (eds) *Depression in Childhood: Diagnosis Treatment and Conceptual Models*, pp. 1–26. Raven Press, New York.

Kreitman N. (1976) The coal gas story: United Kingdom suicide rates,

1960−71. *British Journal of Preventive and Social Medicine*, **30**, 86−93.

Kreitman N. & Schreiber M. (1979) Parasuicide in young Edinburgh women, 1968−1975. *Psychological Medicine*, **9**, 469−479.

Larsson B., Melin L., Breitholtz E. & Andersson G. (1991) Short-term stability of depressive symptoms and suicide attempts in Swedish adolescents. *Acta Psychiatrica Scandinavica*, **83**, 385−390.

Leese S.M. (1969) Suicide behaviour in 20 adolescents. *British Journal of Psychiatry*, **115**, 479−480.

Lerner M. & Clum G. (1990) Treatment of suicide ideators: a problem-solving approach. *Behavior Therapy*, **21**, 403−411.

Levenson M. (1974) Cognitive correlates of suicidal risk. In: Neuringer C. (ed) *Psychological Assessment of Suicidal Risk*, pp. 150−163. Charles C. Thomas, Springfield, IL.

Levenson M. & Neuringer C. (1971) Problem-solving behavior in suicidal adolescents. *Journal of Consulting and Clinical Psychology*, **37**, 433−436.

Liberman R.P. & Eckman T. (1981) Behavior therapy vs insight-oriented therapy for repeated suicide attempters. *Archives of General Psychiatry*, **38**, 1126−1130.

Litman R., Farberow N., Shneidman E., Heilig S. & Kramer J. (1965) Suicide prevention telephone service. *Journal of the American Medical Association*, **192**, 107−111.

Litt I.F., Cuskey W.R. & Rudd S. (1983) Emergency room evaluation of the adolescent who attempts suicide: compliance with follow-up. *Journal of Adolescent Health Care*, **4**, 106−108.

Lukianowitz N. (1968) Attempted suicide in children. *Acta Psychiatrica Scandinavica*, **44**, 415−435.

McGee R., Feehan M., Williams S., Partridge F., Silva P. & Kelly J. (1990) DSM-III disorders in a large sample of adolescents. *Journal of the American Academy of Child and Adolescent Psychiatry*, **29**, 611−619.

McIntire M.S. & Angle C.R. (1973) Psych biopsy in self poisoning of children and adolescents. *American Journal of Disturbed Children*, **126**, 42−46.

McIntire M.S., Angle C.R., Wikoff R.L. & Schlict M.L. (1977) Recurrent adolescent suicidal behavior. *Pediatrics*, **60**, 605−608.

McKenry P.C., Tishler C.L. & Kelley C. (1982) Adolescent suicide: a comparison of attempters and nonattempters in an emergency room population. *Clinical Pediatrics*, **21**, 266−270.

McKenry P.C., Tishler C.L. & Kelley C. (1983) The role of drugs in adolescent suicide. *Suicide and Life-Threatening Behavior*, **13**, 166−175.

Marks P.A. & Haller D.L. (1977) Now I lay me down for keeps: a study of adolescent suicide attempts. *Journal of Clinical Psychology*, **33**, 390−400.

Mattson A., Seese L.R. & Hawkins J.W. (1969) Suicidal behavior as a child psychiatric emergency. *Archives of General Psychiatry*, **20**, 100−109.

May P.A. (1987) Suicide and self-destruction among American Indian youths. *American Indian and Alaska Native Mental Health Research*, **1**, 52−69.

Meehan P.J., Lamb J.A., Saltzman L.E. & O'Carroll P.W. (1992) Attempted suicide among young adults. *American Journal of Psychiatry*, **149**, 41−44.

Mehr M., Zeltzer L.K. & Robinson R. (1982) Continued self-destructve behaviors in adolescent suicide attempters: Part II. *Journal of Adolescent Health Care*, **2**, 182−187.

Menninger K. (1938) *Man Against Himself.* Harcourt, Brace & World, New York.

Miller J., Sakinofsky I. & Streiner D.L. (1979) The family and social dynamics of adolescent parasuicide. In: *Proceedings of the 10th International Conference for Suicide Prevention and Crisis Intervention, Ottawa.*

Miller H.L., Coombs D.W., Leeper J.D. & Barton S. (1984) An analysis of the effects of suicide prevention facilities on suicide rates in the United States. *American Journal of Public Health*, **74**, 340−343.

Miller S., Rotheram-Borus M., Piacentini J., Graae F. & Castro-Blanco D. (1992) *Successful Negotiation/Acting Positively (SNAP): A Brief Cognitive-behavioral Therapy Manual for Adolescent Suicide Attempters and their Families.* Unpublished. New York State Psychiatric Institute, New York.

Moens G.F.G., Lycsch M.J.M. & Vand De Voorde H. (1988) The geographical pattern of methods of suicide in Belgium: implications for prevention. *Acta Psychiatrica Scandinavica*, **77**, 320−327.

Motto J.A. (1976) Suicide prevention for high-risk persons who refuse treatment. *Suicide and Life-Threatening Behaviors*, **6**, 223−230.

Motto J.A. (1984) Suicide in male adolescents. In: Segdak H.S., Ford A.B. & Rushforth N.B. (eds) *Suicide in the Young*, pp. 227−244. John Wright PSG, Boston.

Motto J.A., Heilbron D.C., Juster R.P. & Bostrom A. (1981) Communication as a suicide prevention program. *Dépression et Suicide*, 148−154.

Murphy G.E. & Wetzel R.D. (1980) Suicide risk by birth cohort in the United States, 1949−1974. *Archives of General Psychiatry*, **37**, 519−523.

Nagy M.L. (1965) The child's view of death. In: Feifel H. (ed) *The Meaning of Death*, pp. 79−98. McGraw-Hill, New York.

National Center for Health Statistics (1979−90) *Vital Statistics of the United States.* US Department of Health and Human Services, Mortality Statistics Branch (published and unpublished data.); 1990; Inclusive Vol. II: parts A−B.

Office for Substance Abuse Prevention (1989) *Prevention of Mental Disorders, Alcohol and Other Drug Use in Children and Adolescents.* Shaffer D., Phillips I. & Enzer N. (eds) US Department of Health and Human Services, Rockville, MD.

Office of Disease Prevention and Health Promotion (1989) *National Adolescent Health Survey.* Department of Health and Human Services, Washington, DC.

Oliver R.G., Kaminski Z., Tudor K. & Hetzel B.S. (1971) The epidemiology of attempted suicide as seen in the causalty department, Alfred Hospital, Melbourne. *Medical Journal of Australia*, **1**, 833−839.

Orbach I., Rosenheim E. & Hary E. (1987) Some aspects of cognitive functioning in suicidal children. *Journal of the American Academy of Child Psychiatry*, **26**, 181−185.

Otto U. (1972) Suicidal acts by children and adolescents: a follow-up study. *Acta Psychiatrica Scandinavica Supplementum*, **233**, 5−123.

Pfeffer C.R. (1981) The distinctive features of children who threaten and attempt suicide. In: Wells L.F. & Stewart I.R. (eds) *Self Destructive Behavior in Children and Adolescents*, pp. 106−121. Van Nostrand Reinhold, New York.

Pfeffer C.R., Conte H.H., Plutchik R. & Jerrett I. (1980) Suicide behavior in latency-age children: an outpatient population. *Journal of the American Academy of Child Psychiatry*, **19**, 703−710.

Pfeffer C.R., Plutchik R. & Mizruchi M.S. (1983) Suicidal and assaultive behavior in children: classification, measurement, and interrelations. *American Journal of Psychiatry*, **140**, 154−157.

Pfeffer C.R., Zuckerman S., Plutchik R. & Mizruchi M. (1984) Suicidal behavior in normal school children: a comparison with child psychiatric inpatients. *Journal of the American Academy of Child Psychiatry*, **23**, 416−423.

Pfeffer C.R., Newcorn J., Kaplan G., Mizruchi M.S. & Plutchick R. (1988) Suicidal behavior in adolescent psychiatric patients. *Journal of the American Academy of Child and Adolescent Psychiatry*, **27**, 357−361.

Pfeffer C.R., Klerman G.L., Hurt S.W., Lesser M., Peskin J.R. & Siefker C.A. (1991) Suicidal children grow up: demographic and clinical risk factors for adolescent suicide attempts. *Journal of the American Academy of Child and Adolescent Psychiatry*, **30**, 609−616.

Phillips D.P. (1974) The influence of suggestion on suicide: substantive and theoretical implication of the Werther effect. *American Socio-*

logical Review, **39**, 340–354.

Phillips D.P. (1979) Suicide, motor vehicle fatalities, and the mass media: evidence toward a theory of suggestion. *American Journal of Sociology*, **84**, 1150–1174.

Phillips D.P. (1980) Airplane accidents, murder and the mass media: towards a theory of imitation and suggestion. *Social Forces*, **58**, 1001–1004.

Phillips D.P. (1984) Teenage and adult temporal fluctuations in suicide and auto fatalities. In: Sudak H.S., Ford A.B. & Rushforth N.B. (eds) *Suicide in the Young*, pp. 69–80. John Wright-PSG, Littleton, MA.

Phillips D.P. & Carstensen L.L. (1986) Clustering of teenage suicides after television news stories about suicide. *New England Journal of Medicine*, **315**, 685–689.

Piacentini J., Rotheram-Borus M.J., Trautman P. & Graae F. (1991) Psychosocial correlates of treatment compliance in adolescent suicide attempters. Presented at the Association for Advancement of Behavior Therapy Meeting, New York, NY.

Pillay A.L. & Wassenaar D.R. (1991) Rescue expectations and hopelessness in adolescent parasuicides. *Perceptual and Motor Skills*, **72**, 363–366.

Pokorny A.D. (1964) Suicide rates in various psychiatric disorders. *Journal of Nervous and Mental Disorders*, **139**, 499–506.

Pokorny A.D. (1983) Prediction of suicide in psychiatric patients. *Archives of General Psychiatry*, **40**, 249–257.

Pronovost J., Cote L. & Ross C. (1990) Epidemiological study of suicidal behavior among secondary school students. *Canada's Mental Health*, **3**, 9–15.

Rich C.L., Young D. & Fowler R.C. (1986) San Diego suicide study. *Archives of General Psychiatry*, **43**, 577–586.

Rich C.L., Fowler R.C., Fogarty L.A. & Young D. (1988) San Diego suicide study: III. Relationships between diagnosis and stressors. *Archives of General Psychiatry*, **45**, 589–592.

Rich C.L., Young J.G., Fowler R.C., Wagner J. & Black N.A. (1990) Guns and suicide: possible effects of some specific legislation. *American Journal of Psychiatry*, **147**, 342–346.

Richman J. (1979) The family therapy of attempted suicide. *Family Process*, **18**, 131–142.

Richman J. (1981) Family treatment of suicidal children and adolescents. In: Stuart I.R. & Wells C.F. (eds) *Self Destructive Behavior in Children and Adolescents*. Van Nostrand Reinhold, New York.

Richman J. (1984) The family therapy of suicidal adolescents: promises and pitfalls. In: Sudak H.S., Ford A.B. & Rushforth N.B. (eds) *Suicide in the Young*, pp. 393–406. John Wright-PSG, Little, MA.

Robins E., Gassner S., Kayes J., Wilkinson JRR. & Murphy G. (1959) The communication of suicide intent: a study of 134 consecutive cases of successful (completed) suicide. *American Journal of Psychiatry*, **115**, 724–733.

Rogers J., Sheldon A., Barwick C., Leftofsky K. & Lancee W. (1982) Help for families of suicide: survivors support program. *Canadian Journal of Psychiatry*, **27**, 444–448.

Rotheram-Borus M.J. & Trautman P. (1988) Hopelessness, depression, and suicidal intent among adolescent suicide attempters. *Journal of the American Academy of Child and Adolescent Psychiatry*, **27**, 700–704.

Rotheram-Borus M.J., Trautman P.D., Dopkins S.C. & Shrout P.E. (1990) Cognitive style and pleasant activities among female adolescent suicide attempters. *Journal of Consulting and Clinical Psychology*, **58**, 554–561.

Roy A. (1983) Family history of suicide. *Archives of General Psychiatry*, **40**, 971–974.

Roy A., Segal N.L., Centerwall B.S. & Robinette C.D. (1991) Suicide in twins. *Archives of General Psychiatry*, **48**, 29–32.

Rubenstein J., Hellen T., Housman D., Rubin C. & Stechlor G. (1989) Suicidal behavior in normal adolescents: risk factors and protective factors. *American Journal of Orthopsychiatry*, **59**, 59–71.

Salk L., Sturner W., Lipsett L., Reilly B. & Levat R. (1985) Relationship of maternal and perinatal conditions to eventual adolescent suicide. *Lancet*, **1**, 624–627.

Salkovskis P., Atha C. & Storer D. (1990) Cognitive-behavioural problem solving in the treatment of patients who repeatedly attempt suicide. *British Journal of Psychiatry*, **157**, 871–876.

Sanborn D.E., Sanborn C.J. & Cimbolic P. (1974) Two years of suicide: a study of adolescent suicide in New Hampshire. *Child Psychiatry and Human Development*, **3**, 234–242.

Schilder P. & Wechsler D. (1934) The attitudes of children toward death. *Journal of General Psychology*, **45**, 406–451.

Schmidtke A. & Hafner H. (1986) Die vermittlung von selbstmord-motivation und selbstmordhandlung durch fiktivemodelle. *Nervenarzt*, **57**, 502–510.

Schneidman E. & Farberow N. (1965) Statistical comparisons between attempted and committed suicides. In: Farberow N. & Schneidman E. (eds) *The Cry for Help*, pp. 19–47. McGraw-Hill, New York.

Schotte D.E. & Clum G.A. (1987) Problem-solving skills in suicidal psychiatric patients. *Journal of Consulting and Clinical Psychology*, **55**, 49–54.

Sellar C., Hawton K. & Goldacre M.J. (1990) Self-poisoning in adolescents: hospital admissions and deaths in the Oxford region 1980–1985. *British Journal of Psychiatry*, **156**, 866–870.

Shaffer D. (1974) Suicide in childhood and early adolescence. *Journal of Child Psychology and Psychiatry*, **15**, 275–291.

Shaffer D. & Fisher P. (1981) The epidemiology of suicide in children and young adolescents. *Journal of the American Academy of Child Psychiatry*, **20**, 545–565.

Shaffer D., Garland A. & Underwood M. (1988a) *An Evaluation of Three Youth Suicide Prevention Programs in New Jersey*. Unpublished manuscript.

Shaffer D., Garland A., Gould M., Fisher P. & Trautman P. (1988b) Preventing teenage suicide: a critical review. *Journal of the American Academy of Child and Adolescent Psychiatry*, **27**, 675–687.

Shaffer D., Garland A. & Bacon K. (1989) Prevention issues in youth suicide. In: Shaffer D., Philips I. & Enzer N. (eds) *Prevention of Mental Disorders, Alcohol and Drug Abuse in Children and Adolescents*, pp. 373–412. OSAP Prevention Monograph 2. Alcohol, Drug Abuse and Mental Health Administration, Washington DC.

Shaffer D., Vieland V., Garland A., Rojas M., Underwood M. & Busner C. (1990) Adolescent suicide attempters: response to suicide prevention programs. *Journal of the American Medical Association*, **264**, 3151–3155.

Shaffer D., Garland A., Vieland V., Underwood M. & Busner C. (1991) The impact of curriculum-based suicide prevention programs for teenagers. *Journal of the American Academy of Child and Adolescent Psychiatry*, **30**, 588–596.

Shaffer D., Gould M., Fisher P., Trautman P., Kleinman M. & Moroshima A. (in preparation) An epidemiological study of child and adolescent suicide. II. Clinical diagnosis.

Shaffi M., Carrigan S., Whittinghill J.R. & Derrick A. (1985) Psychological autopsy of completed suicide in children and adolescents. *American Journal of Psychiatry*, **142**, 1061–1064.

Shaffi M., Steltz-Lenarsky J., Derrick A.M., Beckner C. & Whittinghill R. (1988) Comorbidity of mental disorders in the post-mortem diagnosis of completed suicide in children and adolescents. *Journal of Affective Disorders*, **14**, 227–233.

Sheehan W. & Garfinkel B.D. (1988) Case study: adolescent autoerotic deaths. *Journal of the American Academy of Child and Adolescent Psychiatry*, **27**, 367–370.

Simmons J.T., Comstock B.S. & Franklin J.L. (1986) *Prevention/Intervention Programs for Suicidal Adolescents*. Prepared for: The Prevention and Intervention Work Group of the Secretary of Health and

Human Services' Task Force on Youth Suicide. Oakland, California, June 6, 1986.

Skegg K. & Cox B. (1991) Suicide in New Zealand 1957–1986: the influence of age, period and birth-cohort. *Australia and New Zealand Journal of Psychiatry*, **25**, 181–190.

Slaiku K.A., Tulkin S.R. & Speer D.C. (1975) Process and outcome in the evaluation of telephone counselling referrals. *Journal of Consulting and Clinical Psychology*, **43**, 700–707.

Smith K. & Crawford S. (1986) Suicidal behaviors among 'normal' high school students. *Suicide and Life-Threatening Behaviors*, **16**, 313–325.

Solomon M.J. & Heller C.O. (1980) Suicide and age in Alberta Canada, 1951–1977. *Archives of General Psychiatry*, **37**, 511–513.

Spirito A., Stark L.J., Fristad M., Hart K. & Owens-Stively J. (1987) Adolescent suicide attempters hospitalized on a general pediatrics floor. *Journal of Pediatric Psychology*, **12**, 171–189.

Spirito A., Williams C.A., Stark L.J. & Hart K.J. (1988a) The Hopelessness Scale for Children: psychometric properties with normal and emotionally disturbed adolescents. *Journal of Abnormal Child Psychology*, **16**, 445–458.

Spirito A., Overholser J., Ashworth S., Morgan J. & Benedict-Drew C. (1988b) Evaluation of a suicide awareness curriculum for high school students. *Journal of the American Academy of Child and Adolescent Psychiatry*, **27**, 705–711.

Spirito A., Brown L., Overholser J. & Fritz G. (1989) Attempted suicide in adolescence: a review and critique of the literature. *Clinical Psychology Review*, **9**, 335–363.

Spirito A., Overholser J. & Hart K. (1991) Cognitive characteristics of adolescent suicide attempters. *Journal of the American Academy of Child and Adolescent Psychiatry*, **30**, 604–608.

Stanley E.J. & Barter J.T. (1970) Adolescent suicidal behavior. *American Journal of Orthopsychiatry*, **40**, 87–96.

Stanley M. & Mann J.J. (1987) *Biological Factors Associated with Suicide*. New York. Supported in part by NIMH grants #MH40048-01 and #MH40210. The Lowenstein Foundation and an Irma T. Hirschi Trust Research Scientist Award.

Stearns A.W. (1953) Cases of probable suicide in young persons without obvious motivation. *Journal of the Maine Medical Association*, **44**, 16–23.

Stuart R. (1980) Helping couples change: a social learning approach to marital therapy. Guilford Press, New York.

Swedo S. (1989) Postdischarge therapy of hospitalized adolescent suicide attempters. *Journal of Adolescent Health Care*, **10**, 541–544.

Swedo S., Rettew D., Kuppenheimer M., Lum D., Dolan S. & Goldberger E. (1991) Can adolescent suicide attempters be distinguished from at-risk adolescents? *Pediatrics*, **88**, 620–629.

Taylor E.A. & Stansfeld S.A. (1984a) Children who poison themselves I. A clinical comparison with psychiatric controls. *British Journal of Psychiatry*, **145**, 127–132.

Taylor E.A. & Stansfeld S.A. (1984b) Children who poison themselves II. Prediction of adherence for treatment. *British Journal of Psychiatry*, **14**, 132–135.

Tishler C.L., McKenry P.C. & Morgan K.C. (1981) Adolescent suicide attempts: some significant factors. *Suicide and Life-Threatening Behavior*, **11**, 86–92.

Toolan J.M. (1962) Suicide and suicide attempts in childhood and adolescence. *American Journal of Orthopsychiatry*, **118**, 719–724.

Trautman P. (1989) *Suicide treatment modalities of adolescent suicide attempters*. Report of the Secretary's Task Force on Youth Suicide. Vol. 3: Prevention and Interventions in Youth Suicide. Alcohol, Drug Abuse, and Mental Health Administration, DHHS Pub No. (ADM) 89–1623, Washington, DC.

Trautman P.D. & Rotheram M.J. (1987) Referral failure among adolescent suicide attempters. Poster presented at the Annual Meeting of the American Academy of Child Psychiatry, Los Angeles, CA.

Trautman P.D. & Rotheram M.J. (1988) Cognitive therapy with children and adolescents. In: Frances A. & Hales R. (eds) *Review of Psychiatry VII*, pp. 584–607. American Psychiatric Press, Washington, DC.

Trautman P.D. & Shaffer D. (1984) Treatment of child and adolescent suicide attempters. In: Sudak H.S., Ford A.B. & Rushforth N.B (eds) *Suicide in the Young*, pp. 307–324. John Wright-PSG, Boston.

Trautman P., Kaplan S., Pelcovitz D., Lewin N., Cortonea R., Magito D. & Kriegel E. (1989) *Home Visits with Treatment Non-compliant Adolescent Suicide Attempters*. American Academy of Child Psychiatry, New York, NY.

Trautman P.D., Rotheram-Borus M.J., Dopkins S. & Lewin N. (1991) Psychiatric diagnoses in minority female adolescent suicide attempters. *Journal of the American Academy of Child and Adolescent Psychiatry*, **4**, 617–622.

Velez C. & Cohen P. (1988) Suicidal behavior and ideation in a community sample of children: maternal and youth reports. *Journal of the American Academy of Child and Adolescent Psychiatry*, **27**, 349–356.

Vieland V., Whittle B., Garland A., Hicks R. & Shaffer D. (1991) The impact of curriculum-based suicide prevention programs for teenagers: an 18-month follow-up. *Journal of the American Academy of Child and Adolescent Psychiatry*, **30**, 811–815.

Wasserman I.M. (1984) Imitation and suicide: a reexamination of the Werther effect. *American Sociological Review*, **49**, 427–436.

Weissman A. & Worden W. (1972) Risk-rescue rating in suicide assessment. *Archives of General Psychiatry*, **26**, 553–560.

Welu T.C. (1977) A follow-up program for suicide attempters. *Suicide and Life-Threatening Behavior*, **7**, 17–30.

Wender P., Kety S., Rosenthal D., Schulsinger F., Ortmann J. & Lunde I. (1986) Psychiatric disorders in the biological and adoptive families of adopted individuals with affective disorders. *Archives of General Psychiatry*, **43**, 923–929.

Winokur G. & Tsuang M. (1975) The Iowa 500: suicide in mania, depression and schizophrenia. *American Journal of Psychiatry*, **132**, 650–651.

World Health Organization (1985–1989) *World Health Statistic Annual*. WHO, Geneva.

Yusin A., Sinay R. & Nihira K. (1972) Adolescents in crisis: evaluation of a questionnaire. *American Journal of Psychiatry*, **129**, 574–577.

Zilboorg G. (1936) Consideration on suicide with particular reference to that of the young. *American Journal of Orthopsychiatry*, **7**, 15–35.

Chapter 24
Anorexia and Bulimia Nervosa

Hans-Christoph Steinhausen

In contrast to early forms of eating disorder originating in childhood, such as rumination, failure to thrive, pica, faddiness and obesity, the age period for the onset of anorexia nervosa and bulimia nervosa is most typically adolescence. Prepubertal onset is rare for anorexia nervosa and the first onset peak is around 14 years. Onset for bulimia nervosa is in most cases at the end of adolescence, peaking initially at around 19 years. Thus, anorexia nervosa is typically connected with the transition from childhood to adolescence and, in most cases, bulimia nervosa reflects the transition from adolescence to young adulthood. The differentiation of these two disorders is not only based on clinical symptoms and the different pattern of age at onset, but also on the findings of a recent twin study that suggests that heritability may be high in anorexia but low in bulimia nervosa (Treasure & Holland, 1990). It is, therefore, justifiable to describe these two disorders separately in this chapter.

ANOREXIA NERVOSA

Clinical features

Anorexia nervosa is characterized by highly specific behavioural and psychopathological symptoms and significant somatic signs. Despite the fact that the majority of cases are female and that the onset of the disorder most frequently occurs during adolescence, there are both cases in which males are afflicted and cases of premenarchal onset.

Behaviour and psychopathology

The core psychopathological feature of anorexia nervosa is the dread of fatness. There are many synonyms for this symptom, e.g. weight phobia, fear of becoming fat, or drive for thinness. In the behavioural sense, it implies that the patient is deeply convinced that her/his body is too large. This pursuit of thinness may, in the classical case, persist even at times when the patient is extremely emaciated. Typically, the following pattern emerges. In the beginning, the patient starts with dieting, just as any teenager might do who is concerned that she/he is overweight, as measured by the standards of her/his (peer) culture. Or perhaps, the patient is indeed slightly overweight and is taunted and teased by family members, schoolmates and peers. This feeling of being overweight may be related to the whole body or to particular parts, such as the thighs or buttocks.

The typical diet starts with a reduction of sweets and high-caloric, carbohydrate-rich foods, and the patient soon becomes an expert with regard to the caloric content of all sorts of food and beverages. Weeks or even months may pass before this behaviour is noticed by others. By this time the patient may have lost control over dieting. Usually at this stage of the disease process the adolescent anorectic has not yet recognized the abnormal nature of her/his behaviour and denies the illness. Indeed, she/he feels better being thin and does not seek any help, despite the perceived concern of family members who feel helpless in the face of the powerful behaviour of the patient.

In many of the patients this distorted drive for thinness is associated with a disturbance in body image. Despite being emaciated, the patient does not perceive herself as being thin or even ugly. This perceptual disorder is an overvalued idea and comes close to having delusional proportions. It pertains not only to body shape, but also to interoceptive disturbances, i.e. the inability accurately to identify internal sensations such as hunger, satiety or affective states. Thus, the patients not only perceive their physical dimensions inaccurately but also, with increasing duration of starvation, they fail to notice sensations of hunger and satiety. In addition, they are rather vague or defensive about their feelings and are susceptible to undue influence by significant others. This in turn reinforces the bodily mistrust and the fear of loss of control. Dieting continues and may be accompanied by further efforts to reduce weight and to control bodily functions. Such efforts can include rigorous exercise, abuse of laxatives or diuretics and vomiting, that are intended not only to promote weight loss but also to regulate bodily functions rigidly. From the purging and vomiting behaviour there is only a small step to binge-eating, in which the patient consumes enormous amounts of food within a very short period of time. This bulimic component is followed by either a restrictive period of fasting for several days or else vomiting, to prevent weight gain. Bulimic features within the spectrum of anorexia nervosa are, however, rather infrequent during adolescence.

Aside from these very specific behavioural features of anorexia nervosa, there are further psychopathological symptoms that are shared with other psychiatric disorders. These include poor self-esteem, rigid dichotomous 'either/or' thinking, a highly restricted realm of interests and cognition that excludes almost everything but the topics of food and weight and the loss of social contacts. Anorectic patients very rarely engage in sexual activity, and when they do, they usually experience it as being unpleasant and joyless. This might apply more to restrictive anorectics than to the bulimic anorectics (Coovert & Kinder, 1989).

Many of these psychopathological features, which also include irritability, mood swings and insomnia, are effects of starvation. This in turn brings up the question of the relation between anorexia nervosa and depression. Clearly, many patients show signs of a depressive syndrome. The overlap that exists between the manifestations of anorexia nervosa and those of depression, including major affective disorder, is considerable (Altshuler & Weiner, 1985; Levy & Dixon, 1985; Laessle *et al.*, 1987a; Strober, 1991). However, in many cases, depressive symptoms are, at least partially, the result of the effects of starvation.

Finally, many patients manifest obsessional behaviour, including compulsive behaviour and obsessional thinking about foods. This pertains not only to the peculiar eating habits — e.g. eating rituals — but also to other areas such as food and nonfood-related hoarding. Premorbid personality traits can be identified in the history. The phenomenological overlap of the two disorders seems to depend mainly on starvation, and there is no evidence that anorexia nervosa is a variant of obsessive-compulsive disorder (Holden, 1990).

Physical characteristics

Anorectic patients are apparently emaciated and show effects of downregulation of the autonomic nervous system, indicated by bradycardia, hypotension and hypothermia. In addition, complications arise as a consequence of the effects of the eating disorder on virtually every organ system and deserve careful consideration (see review by Kaplan, 1990).

A number of medical illnesses might well be considered for differential diagnosis. These include tuberculosis, acquired immune deficiency disease, primary endocrine disturbances such as anterior pituitary insufficiency, Addison's disease, hyperthyroidism, diabetes mellitus, inflammatory bowel disease, hypothalamic tumours and a variety of malignancies. All of these are conditions that manifest significant and prominent weight loss but lack the psychological characteristics of anorexia nervosa, i.e. the deliberate attempt to reduce weight by exercise, purging, vomiting or dieting. There are also a variety of drugs that are associated with weight loss and influence appetite. Binge-eating also occurs in a number of rare medical illnesses and certain chronic illnesses such as premorbid obesity and diabetes, which, in turn, can act as risk factors for the development of eating disorders. Finally, there are also instances in which symptoms in patients with an eating disorder are misdiagnosed as being a medical illness (Kaplan, 1990).

Specific features of premenarchal cases and of anorexia nervosa in males

The manifestation of anorexia nervosa before the age of 14 or before the menarche is rare. However, the clinical features of the prepubertal cases are essentially similar (Gislason, 1988; Gowers *et al.*, 1991). Greater premorbid feeding problems and behavioural problems (Jacobs & Isaacs, 1986) and frequent delay in diagnosis and referral for psychiatric treatment (Fosson *et al.*, 1987) were observed in recent reports. Weight loss in these very young patients arrests the process of puberty. Russell (1985) emphasizes the devastating effect on a girl's physical development in so far as the disease not only causes prolonged delay of puberty with late menarche, but also seriously and permanently interferes with growth in stature and breast development. Thus, early diagnosis and competent treatment are vitally important for the development of the child.

Anorexia nervosa in males is a rare phenomenon, although it is possibly also underdiagnosed (Andersen & Mickalide, 1983). The combination of prepubertal onset and male sex is extremely rare. There are no systematic descriptions of series of boys who develop anorexia nervosa during adolescence. In general there is agreement that, from the clinical point of view, the illness is strikingly similar in the two sexes (Burns & Crisp, 1984; Vandereycken & Vandenbroucke, 1984; Sterling & Segal, 1985; Scott, 1986a; Fichter & Daser, 1987; Oyebode *et al.*, 1988; Steiger, 1989). With regard to the significant features of male patients, various studies report conflicting findings with respect to an earlier onset of the disease, atypical gender role behaviour, more grave symptomatology and poor prognosis.

Clinical assessment

A thorough examination of patients with an eating disorder requires the assessment of the history, development of the symptoms, psychopathology and family functioning. More specifically, the behavioural assessment of the anorectic and bulimic spectrum of symptoms should be focused upon. In addition, structural interviews and rating scales, as well as self-report questionnaires, can augment the assessment process. Techniques for the assessment of disturbances of body image (Ben-Tovim & Walker, 1991), however, serve research purposes more than clinical ones.

The behavioural assessment should start with issues concerning food intake and eating behaviours, including thoughts and attitudes towards eating and weight. This should be followed by a systematic analysis of further significant clinical symptoms and an analysis of events and emotional states preceding food refusal or binge/purge episodes. Furthermore, the patient should be asked to report any attempts to alter eating behaviour. The assessment can be enhanced through the inclusion of one of the structured interviews recently designed for this purpose. This include the Eating Disorder Examination (Cooper & Fairburn, 1987), the Clinical Eating

Disorder Rating Instrument (Palmer *et al.*, 1987) and the Structural Interview for Anorexia and Bulimia Nervosa (Fichter *et al.*, 1990).

Self-administered self-report questionnaires are a further source of assessment data. Examples of such instruments include the Eating Attitude Test (Garner & Garfinkel, 1979; Garner *et al.*, 1982), which was originally designed for epidemiological purposes, and the Eating Disorders Inventory (Garner *et al.*, 1983). Both questionnaires were designed in Canada with primarily adult samples. Transcultural studies have called into question the original cut-off scores for the delineation of clinical cases and the transcultural validity of some of the scales, especially in the adolescent age range (Steinhausen, 1984; Neumärker *et al.*, 1992; Steinhausen *et al.*, 1992).

Finally, the variety of potential medical complications requires a careful physical assessment, including a list of routine laboratory investigations. The latter should include serum electrolytes, liver enzymes, complete blood count, blood urea nitrogen and an electrocardiogram. Significant abuse of laxatives might require endoscopic or roentgenographic examination to assess the extent of bowel damage.

Classification

DSM-IV and ICD-10 share many similarities with regard to defining criteria of anorexia nervosa. These pertain to the criteria of weight loss, body-image distortion, amenorrhoea and the so-called weight phobia. However, the two systems differ somewhat with regard to the definition of these criteria. Both define weight loss in terms of a weight that is 15% below that expected for age and height but ICD-10 helpfully refers to Quatelet's Body Mass Index as one way of defining that expectation. This is important because the clinical significance of a certain weight loss in a person of large stature is not the same as for a person of medium or small stature. Both systems of classification consider the special situation of prepubertal patients who fail to make the expected growth.

There are further advantages of the recent ICD-10 as compared with the DSM-IV. It not only covers the criterion 'self-induced loss of weight' but also provides a clinically useful operational definition of this criterion. Furthermore, ICD-10 links the body-image distortion to the main theme of psychopathology, namely, fear of becoming obese. Thus, ICD-10 deemphasizes the idea that body-image distortion is a specific defining criterion of anorexia nervosa. This view is in accord with a recent paper that criticized the utility of the concept of body-image disturbance, which was seen as having contributed nothing to the understanding of the psychopathology of the eating disorders, and promoted the viability of weight phobia or fear of fatness, which were considered the *sine qua non* of anorexia nervosa (Hsu & Sobkiewicz, 1991). Finally, the widespread endocrine disorder in anorexia nervosa is clearly indicated in the ICD-10 set of criteria, whereas the DSM-IV refers only to amenorrhoea.

Despite the recent progress in the classification of anorexia nervosa, typology of this disorder is not considered by the ICD-10 classification scheme. This is remarkable considering that there is some evidence to justify subtyping anorectic patients into those who exclusively starve—the so-called restricters—those who starve and purge but do not binge—the so-called purgers—and those who binge. These sub-types are considered in the DSM-IV scheme. There are several arguments in favour of this typology: differential medical complications, age and duration of illness and long-term outcome (Steinhausen & Glanville, 1983; Vandereycken & Pierloot, 1983; Halmi, 1985; Steinhausen *et al.*, 1992). There is, however, also evidence that it may be premature to distinguish between restricters and the bulimic variant of anorexia nervosa. This comes from a study by Welch *et al.* (1990), who failed to identify separate clusters for these two groups of patients based on clinical data and various questionnaire scales that relate to the eating disorders and depression. Currently, little is known with regard to the validity of these subtypes, i.e. whether they reflect different entities or only different indices of severity that may alternate over time in individual patients. Nevertheless, clinicians should perhaps be aware of the pragmatic aspects of this typology because bulimic features in anorexia nervosa clearly warrant differential treatment efforts.

In closing this section on classification, it must be stated that both the syndrome and the spectrum character of the eating disorders make it clear that there are atypical cases of anorexia nervosa that do not fulfil the entire sets of criteria listed in the two major systems of classification. Atypical cases, such as those with an absence of amenorrhoea or significant weight loss, or with key symptoms present only to a mild degree, are considered in both the DSM-IV and the ICD-10.

Epidemiology

Most of our current knowledge about the frequencies of the eating disorders stems from incidence and prevalence studies that are based on either psychiatric case registers or medical records of hospitals in circumscribed areas. Obviously, such studies lead to an underestimation of the true incidence and prevalence because not all community cases will be referred to doctors or hospitals.

Incidence rates of eating disorders reported in studies from various European countries and North America range from 0.35 in Monroe County, New York (Jones *et al.*, 1980) to 8.2 in Rochester, Minnesota (Lucas *et al.*, 1991) per 100 000 person-years. There is no evidence that morbidity registration by general practitioners leads to higher figures than psychiatric case registers or the analysis of hospital records or the combination of these sources. Accordingly, an incidence rate of 6.3 per 100 000 population was reported in a recent Dutch study Hoek (1991) based on general practitioners' registration and the use of DSM-III and DSM-III-R criteria.

The even higher incidence reported in the study by Lucas *et al.* (1991) is based on a study period of 50 years, the longest period to date. This study also provides the strongest evidence that there has been an increase in the incidence of anorexia nervosa. The Rochester data show that the incidence rates for 10–19-year-old females have increased by 36% every 5 years for the 35 years from 1950 to 1984. Similar trends of increasing incidence rates were also observed in Monroe County (Jones *et al.*, 1980), North-East Scotland (Kendell *et al.*, 1973; Szmukler *et al.*, 1986), and at least partly up to the 1970s in the Canton of Zurich, Switzerland (Willi *et al.*, 1990). However, using data that were collected between 1972 and 1981 in England and Wales, Williams and King (1987) demonstrated that the increased number of new cases could be accounted for by demographic changes in the general population. Their observation of a relative increase in the number of young women in the general population who have been diagnosed as having an eating disorder has so far not been studied or replicated in other regions.

So far, the majority of studies reporting prevalence figures show that less than 1% of the adolescent population is affected. Older studies reported 0.66% in Sweden (Nylander, 1971) and 0.46% in the UK (Crisp *et al.*, 1976). More recent studies show an even wider range between 0.22 and 0.84% in various European and North American adolescent populations (Cullberg & Engstrom-Lindberg, 1988; Råstam *et al.*, 1989; Whitaker *et al.*, 1990; Lucas *et al.*, 1991). With regard to regional differences, the Dutch study by Hoek (1991) shows that anorexia nervosa — in contrast to bulimia nervosa — is found with almost equal frequency in rural and urbanized areas. However, all epidemiological data support the clinical experience that anorexia nervosa is eight to 11 times more common in females than in males (Råstam *et al.*, 1989; Nielsen, 1990; Lucas *et al.*, 1991).

In contrast to clinical series, little evidence of anorexia nervosa being associated with higher social class has emerged from epidemiological studies. The one register study by Kendell *et al.* (1973) that reports a significant relationship is based on a very small sample of patients. Cultural factors are clearly operative. Whereas anorexia nervosa is rarely observed among blacks in the US, UK and Africa (Pumariega *et al.*, 1984; Andersen & Hay, 1985; Thomas & Szmukler, 1985; Silber, 1986; Dolan, 1991), and is almost absent in the Chinese population, with only a few cases being reported from Hong Kong (Lee & Chiu, 1989), it is quite common in Japan (Suematsu *et al.*, 1985). There is some evidence that outside the western culture, the disease may be restricted to prosperous backgrounds and the upper social strata. Reports of increasing rates of eating disorders that have recently been reported in some cross-cultural studies may be due to either the adoption of western cultural values (Nasser, 1988) or to conceptual errors and problems of translation of diagnostic instruments (Patton & King, 1991).

Finally, a recent epidemiological study on abnormal eating attitudes in London schoolgirls (Patton *et al.*, 1990) showed that dieting in the great majority of girls was found to be a benign practice, without incidence of progression to clinical status. A previous psychiatric history and some association between general psychiatric morbidity and eating disorders in this sample give rise to the assumption that there is an extra set of factors that strengthens excessive dieting. Thus, the view that there is discontinuity from normal dieting is supported by this study.

Aetiology

Considering the diversity and complexity of both anorexia and bulimia nervosa, single-factor aetiology can hardly be considered for these disorders. Current theories emphasize multifactorial origin coupled with multiple determinants and risk factors (Garfinkel & Garner, 1982; Hsu, 1983) and their interaction within a developmental framework. This model is based on the following determinants: individual, familial, sociocultural and biological factors, precipitating events and perpetuating factors.

Individual factors

Developmentalists of differing theoretical backgrounds underscore the patients' intense fear of becoming physically and emotionally mature (Crisp, 1980) and their fundamental ego deficits in autonomy and mastery over one's body — a sense of personal ineffectiveness, according to Bruch (1973). Psychodynamic theory has linked these deficits to the failure of the parents to regard the developing child as an individual in her/his own right by treating the child as something to complement the parents' needs (Selvini-Palazzoli, 1974). However, these rather plausible assumptions have rarely been tested empirically.

From a developmental point of view, eating disorders are most likely to manifest in adolescence because of the convergence of physical changes and psychosocial challenges with which the adolescent must cope. The increase in body fat, which is most dramatic in adolescent girls, is frequently associated with increased concern about weight and efforts to control it. Dieting behaviour emerges as the body develops and as the changes in physical appearance, bodily feelings and reproductive status require reorganization and transformation of the body image (Attie *et al.*, 1990).

Whereas it is not known whether disturbances of self-perception of body size and of internal affective and visceral states — i.e. body image and body satisfaction — are part of the predisposition or sequelae of the illness, there is evidence of an increased rate of premorbid obesity and even higher birth weight in a number of patients suffering from anorexia (Garner *et al.*, 1982). As Crisp (1980) speculated with regard to the natural history of the disorder, the earlier heightened nutritional state in weight pathologies may lead to an earlier prepubertal growth spurt. This and the accompanying sexual development would require an earlier confrontation with the developmental demands of adolescence, for which the individual may be unprepared. In addition, premorbid obesity may expose the adolescent to humiliation and force her/him to use dieting and other weight-reducing measures. Recent epidemiological studies, however, have called the aetiological relevance of premorbid obesity into question because it appeared to be more closely identified with dieting than with eating disorders (Patton *et al.*, 1990).

Careful clinical history-taking often reveals a premorbid personality pattern of compliance, perfectionism and dependence. These children present few if any educational problems prior to the onset of the eating disorder. Early eating and digestive problems in childhood may also be present (Manchi & Cohen, 1990). There is little evidence that psychosexual factors are involved in the causation of eating disorders (Scott, 1987). Whereas a high proportion of adverse sexual experiences in childhood has been reported in anorectic women (Palmer *et al.*, 1990), the pathogenic relevance of these experiences to the subsequent illness is uncertain.

Finally, in recent years there has been discussion as to whether or not anorexia nervosa is a depression equivalent or a depressive spectrum disorder. Arguments in favour of this idea are mainly based on the greater than average frequency of depressive symptoms found among anorectic patients, the response of some of the patients to antidepressants, comparable physiological abnormalities and the elevated incidence of the two disorders reported in family studies. However, each of these lines of evidence is unclear, so that both the equivalence and depressive spectrum disorder hypotheses must be seriously questioned (Altshuler & Weiner, 1985; Strober, 1991).

Familial factors

Empirical tests of family system models, i.e. Minuchin *et al.* (1978), reflected in anorectic patients and their families, revealed less coherent family characterization than proposed by these theories or even opposite types of family interaction (Kog & Vadereycken, 1988) and have lent no support to the notion of a typical anorexia nervosa family (Råstam & Gillberg, 1991). Nevertheless, there is sufficient empirically based evidence that a significant amount of disturbed communication and interaction is present in families with anorectic patients (Kog & Vadereycken, 1985, 1988; Humphrey, 1988, 1989). Beyond the importance of communication and interaction patterns, there are further family risk factors that may play a role in the multifactorial determination of the eating disorders. These include the higher incidence of weight problems in the family and the high incidence of physical illness, affective disorders and alcoholism in the relatives (Kog & Vandereycken, 1985).

Sociocultural factors

Several characteristics of the eating disorders suggest that sociocultural factors are to be found among the pathogenic components. These include the extremely uneven sex distribution, the typical adolescent age of onset, the increasing incidence in recent decades, and the association of anorexia nervosa to western life style and cultural values. Accordingly, the pressure in western societies to achieve, the importance of physical attractiveness and the emphasis on slimness and dieting in women may all help to contribute to increased risk for the development of eating disorders in a considerable number of females, particularly in specific groups such as ballet dancers, athletes and modelling students (Garfinkel & Garner, 1982; Strober, 1991).

Biological factors

There is sufficient evidence that, once malnutrition and starvation have started, significant alterations occur in a broad spectrum of physiological parameters (Wakeling, 1985). These include hypothalamic−pituitary−thyroid mechanisms, catecholamine metabolism and endogenous opioid activity. In a review of the research in these areas, Weiner (1985) stated that once weight loss and starvation occur, the usual mechanisms for the release and inhibition of various regulators of eating behaviour change, and a new set of regulating mechanisms is established. Whereas the increased body of knowledge on these pathophysiological mechanisms has not necessarily contributed to a better understanding of the origins of anorexia nervosa, it is clear that many of the pathophysiological alterations serve to sustain the disorder. These pathophysiological changes represent effects of starvation and cause the syndrome of anorexia nervosa to be self-perpetuating (Garfinkel & Kaplan, 1985). Ploog and Pirke speculated that this process leads to a perversion of the hunger drive and drew parallels to addictive disorders (1987). More specifically, Marrazzi and Luby (1986) introduced the hypothesis of an autoaddiction opioid model of chronic anorexia nervosa.

Twin studies and family studies provide the bulk of evidence supporting the hypothesis of genetic predisposition for anorexia nervosa. A review of twin studies states that 44−50% of monozygotic twins are concordant for anorexia nervosa, whereas, unfortunately, there are no comparable series of anorectic dizygotic twins (Scott, 1986b). A more recent study found 56% of monozygotic twin pairs to be concordant for anorexia nervosa and only 5% concordance among dizygotic twins (Holland *et al.*, 1988). Heritability was found to be high, especially in restricting anorexia nervosa with adolescent onset, whereas it was almost nonexistent among patients with bulimia nervosa (Treasure & Holland, 1990). However, as Strober (1991) correctly pointed out, direct recruitment and voluntary referral in this study may have led to potentially biased conditions of ascertainment. Thus, predisposing elements are best accounted for by genetically transmitted dispositional traits.

Further tentative support is given by other family studies in which it was shown that the frequency of anorexia nervosa in family members and relatives greatly exceeds normal expectations (Scott, 1986b). In addition, family studies have shown a higher than expected prevalence of affective disorders in relatives of anorectic patients, especially in those with coexisting depression. However, these studies revealed that the factors affecting genetic liability for developing anorexia nervosa are different from those that are operant in the transmission of affective disorders (Strober *et al.*, 1990). Of course, these familial findings cannot rule out the possibility of such relatives playing an environmentally causative role. They are, however, compatible with a 'diathesis-stress' model in which a genetic predisposition towards anorexia nervosa and adverse environmental effects are linked (Scott, 1986b).

Precipitating events

As in many other psychiatric disorders, significant events in the individual's life have been reported to have preceded the manifestation of anorexia nervosa. External precipitants have been identified in from 50 to 100% in various studies, whereas the type of precipitant is not specific to the eating disorders. Common initiating factors include separation and loss, disruptions of family homeostasis, new environmental demands, direct threat of loss of self-esteem and, in a small number of patients, physical illness (Garfinkel & Garner, 1982). As a consequence of these threats of the patient's sense of worth and control over the world, preoccupation with the body is increased and weight-reducing measures are initiated.

Perpetuating factors

Anorexia nervosa becomes chronic in a considerable number of patients. Several factors are known to sustain the illness. According to Garfinkel and Garner (1982), these factors begin with the starvation syndrome and end with iatrogenic factors. Starvation intensifies the patient's preoccupation with food and negatively affects self-concepts and mental state. It also produces a reduction of interests and social isolation. In addition, vomiting is another powerful sustaining factor. Delayed gastric emptying and chronic constipation lend the sensation of fullness after meals and serve to prolong dieting. Furthermore, distorted body perceptions may be linked with a feeling of being out of control after small increases in weight.

The chain of detrimental factors is continued by certain cognitive factors such as positive self-reinforcement resulting from weight loss or phobic avoidance of weight gain and/or personality features such as obsessiveness, the generally restricted ability to cope with stress and the level of impulse control. Unresolved predisposing factors from the patient's family or her own biography may also add to chronicity, unless they are addressed in psychotherapy. Secondary gain in terms of receiving considerable attention from the environment is another powerful perpetuating factor, as is the prevailing cultural emphasis on slimness. Finally, there are also iatrogenic factors that are responsible for the perpetuation of the illness. According to Garfinkel and Garner (1982), these include rapid weight gain programmes that neglect both provisions for instituting external controls for the patient and attention to other psychosocial issues, failure to recognize the necessity of weight gain to counteract the effects of starvation, and the infliction of humiliating punishments for failures to achieve treatment goals.

Treatment

Patients who suffer from anorexia nervosa definitely require intensive professional intervention due to the inherent complications and the danger of chronicity which are found in a large proportion of the patients. Although there is a variety of treatment approaches, comparative studies that evaluate the effects of treatment are scarce. Currently, the main psychotherapeutic approaches used with adolescent anorectic patients are individual psychotherapy, behaviour therapy and family therapy. However, before reporting on these treatment approaches and their respective effects, a more general outline of the basic therapeutic requirements will be given.

General principles

As is the case in other psychiatric and medical conditions, the treatment of anorectic patients must be based on a comprehensive and detailed assessment of both the mental and the physical status. After this, the treating physician must decide whether an inpatient or outpatient setting is more appropriate. This decision rests partly on rather nonspecific factors such as the availability of treatment modalities or the 'treatment philosophy' of a given centre or therapist. At many treatment centres in recent years, management shifted increasingly from inpatient to outpatient treatment, with emphasis placed on family therapy and on empowering parents as controllers of the patient's food intake. This shift may be due to the greater awareness of the eating disorders both among physicians and the public, resulting in many patients presenting before they have become severely emaciated. Unfortunately, beyond the evidence that early intervention and hospitalization might be a positive prognostic factor, there is a lack of solid empirical data to form a rationale for the selection of the type and setting of treatment intervention (Steinhausen & Glanville, 1983). Certain clinical criteria, for example severe emaciation (less than 70% of the average weight), are definite indications for hospital treatment. Familial factors, too, might tip the scales in favour of inpatient treatment, for example in cases where conflict within a family precludes or hinders outpatient treatment. Inpatient treatment does have certain specific advantages that should be acknowledged. These include the fostering of what might otherwise be a fragile treatment alliance, greater awareness on the part of the physician of complications and/or responses to intervention and the possibility of using a psychoeducational approach in which the patient's eating behaviour is modified to foster healthy nutritional attitudes and habits and to ensure the maintenance of an acceptable weight. Outpatient treatment might be considered in cases in which purging and vomiting are not part of the clinical picture, the family is very supportive and the patient is highly motivated and cooperative. However, perhaps because anorectic patients characteristically deny that they are ill and in need of treatment, high motivation for treatment is not usual among these patients.

The recent increase in numbers of clinical cases has affected admission rates not only in psychiatric institutions but in paediatric and medical wards as well. Whereas it is evident that severely emaciated patients need intensive medical treatment, the psychological needs of the majority of these patients are better met on psychiatric wards, where it is easier to create a psychotherapeutic milieu and to initiate a treatment alliance. Again, the emergence of special units and centres in many countries in the recent past is mainly due to the increase in admissions. Clearly, these units are attractive in terms of accumulated clinical experience, but there is no definite evidence that they should form the basis for service. Eating-disordered patients can also be adequately treated on adolescent psychiatric wards that treat a variety of different problems and patients.

Independent of treatment selection, weight restoration is the first major goal of treatment. The minimum target weight should be specified at the beginning of the treatment rather than later during the course of therapy. Although there is a lack of conformity in the literature regarding the degree of final weight restoration, many clinicians would agree that the goal should be set to within 10% of the recommended weight appropriate for age and height. Taking into account the patient's fear of loss of control, rather than a rapid weight gain, a *gradual* but steady gain averaging about 0.2 kg/day is aimed for. The patient, therefore, eats smaller portions but more frequent meals per day.

The regular intake of an adequate number of calories per day should start at 1500 and gradually increase to between 2000 and 3000 calories derived from four to six meals per day. With the help of a dietician, the definite number of calories should be determined according to individual needs and whether the programme is one for weight gain or one for weight maintenance. Other schemes for calculating adequate calorie intake emphasize the reliance on the weight at admission plus a 50% increase for activity and 50% increase every fifth day. Besides weight restoration, close monitoring of fluid and electrolyte balance, including the correction of imbalances, is an important part of the ongoing medical management. The provision of information feedback on weight gain and dietary reeducation are further essential components. There are conflicting views concerning the inclusion of tube feeding, intravenous feeding or parenteral hyperalimentation for weight gain. Whereas these measures are often recommended in medical settings, many psychotherapists are concerned about the psychological side-effects, i.e. the disturbance of the fragile staff cooperation and the psychotherapeutic alliance with the patient. However, it is clear that these interventions can be life-saving in the extremely ill patient.

Many clinicians consider a supportive and secure relationship with the treatment team to be the cornerstone of successful inpatient treatment. This especially applies to the nurse who is present during mealtimes and can encourage the patient to eat and to ventilate feelings that are related to eating (Russell, 1981). Regular monitoring of weight with feedback to the patient is another essential treatment component. There is sufficient clinical evidence that improvement of the patient's weight also contributes to an improvement in her/his morbid mental state. Therefore, weight-reducing behaviour such as hyperactivity, purging and vomiting needs to be controlled, and the patient should be confronted about this in psychotherapy.

Here, the therapeutic milieu of the ward contributes significantly to this area of treatment, i.e. reducing the patient's morbid fear of fatness, establishing a sense of self-esteem and confidence and treating concomitant psychiatric disorders such as depression. Supportive and encouraging relationships with the staff can reduce the necessity of using coercive measures like tube feeding or parenteral nutrition, although such measures may none the less remain necessary in a small number of life-endangering situations. The individual emotional problems of the patient form the second major goal of treatment and need to be met through psychotherapeutic methods, regardless of the treatment setting. Despite the variety of theoretical foundations that underlie the different psychotherapeutic approaches, there is a growing trend to combine therapeutic methods in the sense of multimodal approaches.

Individual psychotherapy

As with other psychiatric disorders, certain prerequisites must be fulfilled to institute individual psychotherapy with the anorectic patient. These include sufficient motivation and intact cognitions. These prerequisites may be absent in cases where the patient is emaciated and manifests impaired psychological functioning, when severe depression is present, when the course of the anorexia nervosa is chronic, when severe intellectual limitations are present, when the family sabotages therapeutic efforts, or when the patient is a very young preadolescent.

Most psychotherapeutic experience in the eating disorders seems to come from the treatment of adults and a small number of older adolescents. We can therefore not be certain whether or not most of the recommendations and limitations pertain to the majority of adolescent patients. Accordingly, the shift in emphasis from the traditional psychoanalytic approach to a more fact-finding method, including careful attention to the patient's emotions, sensations, ideas and cognitions (Bruch, 1973; Selvini-Palazzoli, 1974; Crisp, 1980; Garner & Bemis, 1985), has dealt mainly with older patients and has not been documented for adolescent anorectic patients.

However, one may assume that there is considerable agreement among clinicians that supportive psychotherapy is an important component in multidimensional treatment strategies for adults and adolescents alike. If psychotherapy is tailored to the individual level of cognitive development and the emotional needs of the young patient, and if the adolescent can utilize empathetic support, education, problem-solving, cognitive restructuring and insight, then she/he will certainly profit from this measure. Furthermore, the continuation of psychotherapy after discharge from hospital treatment may contribute to the prevention of relapses.

Behaviour therapy, including cognitive methods

In the last two decades, behavioural methods for the treatment of eating disorders have become increasingly popular. The main approaches are operant-conditioning procedures and cognitive methods (Bemis, 1987; Harris & Phelps, 1987). In some instances, social skill training programmes may also be used. Whereas operant-conditioning procedures may be introduced regardless of age, cognitive methods may be more suitable for the older adolescent and the adult. Again, there is no clear evidence coming from systematic research that indicates the earliest age at which cognitive therapies might be introduced or delineating guidelines for modifying cognitive interventions for use with adolescent anorectic patients.

Operant-conditioning measures in general are more frequently employed in the hospital setting where the control of target behaviours, e.g., eating behaviour and/or weight gain, is more easily accomplished. The advantages of choosing one of these target behaviours over the other have been critically reviewed by Bemis (1987). Both negative and positive reinforcement contingencies are operative. The hospital itself can be an implicit negative reinforcer in terms of being experienced as an aversive environment that can be left only through sufficient weight gain. Other negative reinforcers may include bed rest, seclusion and tube feeding. However, many of these rather coercive measures are no longer components of a standard inpatient programme. Rather, most operant programmes claim to be based mainly on positive reinforcers like access to recreational activities, visiting privileges or freedom of movement within or outside the hospital. Critics have objected that these privileges are also negative reinforcers because they imply relief from the prior situation of being deprived from these opportunities. In addition, it has been argued that isolation and deprivation of reinforcers are not required for effective treatment (Garfinkel, 1985). More information on the procedural issues of the choice of reinforcement schedule, the choice of conditions to facilitate weight gain and the choice of criteria for the termination of operant conditioning is provided in the review by Bemis (1987).

The use of a cognitive-behavioural approach in the treatment of anorectic patients has been strongly advocated by Garner and Bemis (1985). Methods emphasize teaching the patient to examine the validity of her/his beliefs on a here-and-now basis. The intervention starts with an analysis of the patient's distorted thinking patterns such as selective abstraction, over-generalization, magnification, dichotomous thinking, personalization and superstitious thinking. Intervention techniques include, among others, articulation of beliefs, decentring, decatastrophizing, challenging beliefs through behavioural exercises, prospective hypothesis testing, reattribution techniques and others. Additional strategies are aimed at improving self-esteem, which is seriously affected in the typical anorectic patient, and providing assistance for overcoming deficits in self-awareness or personal trust.

Family therapy

The conceptualization of the eating disorders as a symptom of family dysfunction has become quite popular among clinicians. In an attempt to expand the structural model, Todd (1985) has both addressed the limitations of the model and discussed the combinations of family therapy with behaviour modification, cognitive-behaviour therapy and individual psychotherapy. Apart from these more pragmatic considerations, family therapy had been advocated as the treatment of choice in anorectic patients for a number of years until more critical comments recently arose.

Accordingly, some authors caution against the exclusive use of family therapy in a condition that is clearly multidetermined (Gilchrist & McFarlane, 1986), whereas others object that the family therapy movement is based on personal beliefs rather than on solid research (Vandereycken, 1987a; Kog & Vandereycken, 1988). Objections pertain, for instance, to the possibility of finding no family dysfunctioning at all, the assumption that a family crisis is necessarily a sign of family pathology, and the uncritical use of family therapy without consideration for indications and contraindications. Currently, there is some converging clinical agreement about the usefulness of family-oriented treatment approaches in fairly young children who still live in intact families. However, the inexperienced family therapist should be warned with regard to chronic patients, those with delayed psychosocial development, single-parent families, broken homes, families in which one or both parents display severe psychopathology, and families in which previous family therapeutic attempts failed (Vandereycken, 1987a).

Other limitations stem from a small number of empirical studies. Hall (1987) illustrated selection factors for family therapy in the treatment of anorexia nervosa. Most of her patients who underwent family therapy were mainly younger, had a recent onset of illness, and lived in an intact nuclear family with cooperative parents. In the only thoroughly controlled trial that compared family therapy with individual supportive therapy in cases of anorexia nervosa and bulimia nervosa (Russell et al., 1987), family therapy was found to be superior to individual therapy in patients whose illness was not chronic and had begun before the age of 19 years. There was a trend for individual supportive therapy to be more effective in older patients.

As with other child and adolescent disorders, clinical practice, especially in a residential treatment programme, certainly profits most from a multifaceted approach that combines diet, behavioural contracts, individual and group psychotherapy, and occupational and art therapy with family-oriented philosophy. This family-oriented approach implies that various interventions from educational guidance to counselling are used and that family therapy should be introduced when there is a clear indication to do so. Further research is clearly needed to substantiate this pragmatic view.

Psychopharmacological treatment

Several medications have been used in the treatment of anorexia nervosa both clinically and in controlled studies. These include, among others, neuroleptics, appetite stimulants and antidepressants. Among the neuroleptics, phenothiazines are still used by many clinicians, perhaps more in the treatment of adults than adolescents. Research evidence of their usefulness in the treatment of anorexia nervosa is very limited. Both pimozide and sulpiride were shown to have limited success in accelerating weight gain in some patients. However, considering that their hazards outweigh their benefits, it has to be concluded that neuroleptics are generally of no clinical value in the treatment of anorexia nervosa (Vandereycken, 1987b).

Among the appetite stimulants, tetrahydrocannabinol (THC) and cyproheptadine (CYP) were tested. While THC was not found useful (Pryor *et al.*, 1990), there is some evidence that there is a differential effect of CYP on the anorectic bulimic subgroup (Halmi *et al.*, 1986). Antidepressants would seem to be indicated in anorectic patients with accompanying depression. Because of the frequent comorbidity of these two entities, several antidepressants were subjected to controlled trials in these patients. Whereas these studies clearly show that some of the antidepressants that were studied (amitriptyline, clomipramine, monoamine oxidase inhibitors, lithium and fluoxetine) may have some effect on weight gain or improve dysphoria and depression (Pryor *et al.*, 1990), the clinical value of these findings is rather limited, especially in adolescent anorectic patients.

Evaluation of treatment

Whereas there is little doubt that anorectic patients benefit from multifaceted treatment programmes, and that these programmes have on the whole been proven to be effective (Steinhausen, 1985; Steinhausen & Seidel, 1992), there has been little work done to evaluate the effects of different components of treatment for different patients. Noticeable exceptions include most studies that report on behavioural methods. These studies demonstrate that operant conditioning has short-term effectiveness in inducing weight gain, whereas nothing is known on the broader spectrum of effects (Bemis, 1987). Cognitive-behavioural interventions have been systematically evaluated in bulimic patients but not in purely anorectic patients (see below).

As shown in the previous section, there is one unique study comparing the effects of family therapy and supportive individual therapy (Russell *et al.*, 1987). Further studies that evaluate the merits of these therapeutic approaches and the differential predictors of outcome are clearly warranted. Finally, as stated above, a wide spectrum of pharmacological agents has been carefully tested so that clinical practice can make use of these studies.

Outcome and prognosis

Over the last four decades, a considerable body of knowledge on the outcome and prognosis of anorexia nervosa has accumulated that has been reviewed by the author and his group (Steinhausen & Glanville, 1983; Steinhausen *et al.*, 1991). Without going too much into methodological details, the following conclusions can be drawn from a total of 68 follow-up studies published in the English and German-speaking literature from the 1950s to the 1980s. Follow-up periods range from 1 to 33 years.

With regard to the most salient features of anorexia nervosa, it may be concluded that, in approximately 60% of the patients, weight is restored, whereas normalization of menstruation occurs in a mean of 55%, and eating behaviour returns to normal in approximately 44% of the patients. However, it must be noted that there is a wide fluctuation across studies, with figures for the first two parameters ranging mostly between 50–70% and 30–70% for eating behaviour.

There are few solid data on psychiatric diagnosis associated with anorexia nervosa and no indication that any disorder may be significantly related to the outcome. Firstly, depression and, secondly, obsessive-compulsive states have been noted more frequently in some follow-up studies, whereas development of psychotic disorders is rare. Psychosocial adaptation in terms of employment, interpersonal relationships, marriage and sexuality is the most diverse and elusive outcome parameter to study. Whereas close to two-thirds or even more of the former patients accomplish employment and normal educational careers, only a minority enters marriage or a stable partnership.

When the common medical classification criteria for recovery, improvement and chronicity were applied, it was found that about half of the anorexia nervosa patients had recovered, 30% had improved over time and 20% suffered from a chronic course of the disorder. Mortality figures have declined in the last decade to less than 5%.

In addition to these central trends in the outcome of anorexia nervosa, evidence is accumulating that a number of prognostic factors are either favourably or unfavourably operant in the disease course. According to a number (frequencies in parentheses) of studies, favourable prognostic factors include: early age at onset (10), hysterical personality (7), conflict-free parent–child relationship (7), a short interval between onset of symptoms and treatment intervention (8), a short duration of inpatient treatment with no readmissions (6), and high social status and level of education (6). It must be noted, however, that the findings of a smaller number of other studies call into question the predictive value of these factors. Hyperactivity and dieting as weight-reduction strategies are prime examples of factors that a long list of studies have found to be of no consequence with regard to outcome. The picture is even clearer for the factors that are prognostically unfavourable: vomiting (7), bulimia (8), great loss of weight (4), chronicity or compulsiveness (8) and premorbid developmental or clinical abnormalities (4) have all been almost unequivocally related to poor outcome.

Finally, there is only little information available as to whether, within the spectrum of eating disorders, there are changes in diagnostic status. In his review, Hsu (1988) concluded from very limited information that twice as many restrictive anorectic patients develop bulimia than do bulimic anorectic patients become restrictive, that most bulimic anorectic patients retain their bulimia, and that bulimia nervosa is the second most common follow-up diagnosis, with anorexia nervosa prevailing as the most frequent follow-up diagnosis. These conclusions are largely based on older patients and are not in agreement with the preliminary findings of a follow-up study of adolescent inpatients in Berlin (Steinhausen & Seidel, 1992). Here, the most common outcome diagnosis of purely anorectic cases was still anorexia nervosa, and the conversion of anorexia nervosa to bulimia was only rarely encountered. Even in a very small subgroup of anorectic patients with bulimic features, the bulimic symptoms tended to remit rather than to persist.

BULIMIA NERVOSA

Clinical features

In a paper that has become a classic in the field, Russell (1979) introduced the term bulimia nervosa to describe an ominous variant of anorexia nervosa. A series of patients were described in this paper who were characterized by two criteria: '(i) an irresistible urge to overeat, followed by self-induced vomiting or purging and (ii) a morbid fear of becoming fat.' The author noted that self-induced vomiting or purging are secondary devices used by the patients to counteract the effects of overeating and to prevent weight gain, and that they are dangerous behaviours in that they tend to be habit-forming and can lead to physical complications. As is characteristic of patients with the usual form of anorexia nervosa, Russell's patients were determined to keep their weight below a self-imposed threshold, but in contrast with true anorexia nervosa, the patients tended to be heavier, more sexually active, and more likely to menstruate regularly and to maintain fertility. Furthermore, Russell observed frequent severe depressive symptoms and a high risk of suicide.

Behaviour and psychopathology

The typical eating pattern of the bulimic patient (Gandour, 1984) is characterized by the rapid consumption of a large amount of food. Estimates of the caloric intake of these eating binges range from 3000 to 20000 calories. These binges are often experienced as an altered state of consciousness in which the patient is out of control of her/his behaviour. The frequency of binges varies among patients considerably — from several times a day to less than once a week or fortnight. Binges can last from minutes to several hours and can be precipitated by feelings of anxiety, tension, boredom and

loneliness. At least in the beginning, the binge itself brings temporary relief from negative mood states. However, the longer the binges continue, the more the patient experiences feelings of guilt, shame and anger.

Among the accompanying or counteracting behaviours, self-induced vomiting is not a necessary symptom for diagnosis. Whereas not all bulimics are vomiters, most vomiters are probably bulimics. Binge-eating usually precedes the vomiting. With increasing duration and severity of the disorder, patients do not require any mechanical device to induce vomiting but, rather, learn to vomit by reflex by contracting their abdominal and thoracic muscles. Purgative abuse of laxatives or other drugs is less often used than vomiting. However, most purgers also display vomiting.

Bulimic patients are not only preoccupied with constant thoughts about weight, body size and food. The most frequently associated mental state is depression. As with anorexia nervosa, this association has led some researchers to hypothesize that bulimia might be a variant of affective disorder. Although there is strong evidence that bulimia is often accompanied by depression or is secondary to the disorder, it would be premature to accept this hypothesis as fact (Hinz & Williamson, 1987). Other personality characteristics include anxiety, emotional lability, strong needs for approval and external control, impulsiveness and compulsiveness (Gandour, 1984).

Physical characteristics

The majority of bulimic patients are of normal weight for their height. Menstrual irregularities occur frequently, although amenorrhoea is not as common among bulimics as it is among anorectics. The list of medical complications associated with bulimia is a long one (Kaplan, 1990). Many of these complications are serious and are often overlooked; however, they may lead to the diagnosis in those patients who do not come into consultation because of bulimia.

Specific features in males

Bulimia is rarely observed in males. Symptomatology and demographic characteristics are similar in both sexes (Andersen, 1990; Fichter & Hoffmann, 1990). However, disturbances of psychosexual development, gender identity and homosexuality have been observed more frequently than in healthy males. In addition, sexual activity is more frequently inhibited in heterosexually oriented bulimic men than in healthy ones (Fichter & Hoffmann, 1990).

Clinical assessment

Because the weight of most bulimic patients is within the normal range, there is, in contrast to anorexia nervosa, no direct clinical sign of the disease. Some patients may be detected by chance through careful routine physical assessment or during consultations that were made for other purposes. Thus, a large proportion of cases remain undetected unless the patients themselves report their symptoms. Diagnostic interviews and questionnaires can then be used to assist diagnosis and assessment. Examples of these measures were given in the respective section on anorexia nervosa. Further questionnaires that are designed more specifically for bulimic patients were reviewed by Fairburn *et al.* (1990). Taking the large number of medical complications into consideration, careful physical assessment is mandatory.

Definition and classification

The ICD-10 defines four major criteria:

1 There is a persistent preoccupation with eating, irresistible craving for food, and the patient succumbs to episodes of overeating in which large amounts of food are consumed in short periods of time.

2 The patient attempts to counteract the fattening effects of food by one or more of the following.

(a) self-induced vomiting;

(b) purgative abuse;

(c) alternating periods of starvation;

(d) the use of such drugs as appetite suppressants, thyroid preparations or diuretics. When bulimia occurs in diabetic patients, they may choose to neglect their insulin treatment.

3 The psychopathology consists of a morbid dread of fatness, and the patient sets her-/himself a sharply defined weight threshold that is well below her premorbid weight and far below what would be clinically designated as optimal or healthy.

4 There is often a history of an earlier episode of anorexia nervosa, the interval ranging from a few months to several years. This episode may have been fully expressed, or may have assumed a minor, cryptic form with a moderate loss of weight and/or a transient phase of amenorrhoea.

DSM-IV criteria are largely comparable with regard to the first two criteria, but do not include the content of ICD-10 criteria (3) and (4). It emphasizes, rather, the feeling of lack of control over eating behaviour during the eating binges, and specifies an average of two binge-eating episodes per week for 3 months. Purging and nonpurging sub-types are specified only in the DSM-IV scheme. Both systems mention the category of atypical bulimia nervosa. It is reserved for cases in which one or more of the key features is absent. Most commonly, this applies to patients with normal or even excessive weight.

Epidemiology

Fairburn and Beglin (1990) have recently critically reviewed the available literature on the epidemiology of bulimia nervosa. They conclude that, as methods have improved, consensus has increased regarding the prevalence rate among adolescents and young adult women, which is about 1%. However, the authors critically add that the studies that cite this figure may all be underestimating the actual rate.

A number of studies report epidemiological data that were obtained in adolescent populations in various countries (Crowther *et al.*, 1985; Gross & Rosen, 1987; Drewnowski *et al.*, 1988; Stein & Brinza, 1989; Striegel-Moore *et al.*, 1989; Timmerman *et al.*, 1990). Prevalence rates in this age range vary considerably — between 0.7 and 7.7%. However, the validity of many of these findings is questionable. With the exception of the study by Stein and Brinza (1989), self-report studies based on questionnaires were performed rather than interview studies. The groups under study were often not representative samples, as in studies of college student populations, and response rates were often unsatisfactory. Finally, varying case definitions and inaccuracy in case detection are the major shortcomings of these and other studies that are exclusively based on questionnaires.

A tentative synopsis of epidemiological studies would most likely report the following conclusions: independently of age, bulimia nervosa is more common than anorexia nervosa in nonclinical populations so that one would expect to find both more adult and more adolescent patients with bulimia nervosa than with anorexia nervosa. The majority of bulimic patients are adults with a peak onset of the disorder around the age of 19 years. Analogous to anorexia nervosa, females by far outnumber males. In contrast to epidemiological data, bulimic patients are underrepresented in clinical samples of eating-disordered adolescent patients (e.g. Steinhausen & Seidel, 1992).

Aetiology

A model of aetiology of bulimia nervosa has to share many aspects of the model of anorexia nervosa outlined above. For the most part, the same determinants are operative in both disorders, namely, individual, familial, sociocultural and biological factors, precipitating events and perpetuating factors. Because these factors were extensively described above, they will not be discussed again. The vicious cycle in bulimic patients is perhaps even more pronounced than in patients with anorexia nervosa. Due to their low self-esteem and affective instability, the bulimic behaviour of these patients serves to secure emotional stability and conformity with external standards for weight and shape. However, the resulting psychological changes — which include fatigue, irritability and depression — and the physical effects in terms of malnutrition lead again to binge-eating behaviour, which in turn induces affective instability.

The virtually inescapable nature of this process has led to the suggestion that bulimia be conceptualized as an addictive disorder. The discussion not only rests on phenomenological issues (e.g. preoccupation with obtaining the substance, loss of control, adverse consequences, poor motivation for treatment, etc.) but also on a higher-than-expected prevalence of substance abuse among the relatives of bulimic patients and a possible involvement of endogenous opioid systems in the pathogenesis of bulimia. Vandereycken (1990) has critically discussed these issues and warned about overemphasis of the attractiveness of the analogy of the two phenomena by addressing the problems of partial similarity. This analogy model certainly has no promising quality for the delineation of specific aetiological factors.

In an attempt to clarify the significance of bulimia in juvenile anorexia nervosa, Strober (1981) found that, in comparison with nonbulimic anorectics, bulimic anorectic patients evidenced higher levels of core anorectic symptomatology and were more likely to show affective disturbance and alcohol use. Furthermore, bulimia was more strongly associated with affective instability and premorbid behavioural abnormalities. The family environment of bulimics was more conflict-ridden, less cohesive and structured, more emotionally distant, and exhibited greater psychiatric and physical morbidity. The author concluded from his findings that the pre-disposition for bulimia is rooted in early disturbances in ego functioning, personality adaptation and other factors that are aetiologically related to maladjustment. In light of the findings coming from a family study of psychiatric disorders in the first-degree relatives of patients with bulimia nervosa (Kassett *et al.*, 1989), the possibility of a common diathesis for bulimia nervosa and major affective disorder has been proposed.

Support for the assumption that biological factors of vulnerability are important in the aetiology of bulimia nervosa comes from recent twin studies. Fichter and Noegelm (1990) and Hsu *et al.* (1990) found higher concordance rates for bulimia nervosa in two series of monozygotic twins as compared with dizygotic twins.

Treatment

A variety of treatment strategies are available to bulimic patients. These include psychological methods — i.e. individual and group psychotherapy, cognitive and behavioural treatment — and biological approaches such as medication and nutritional management. Self-help and support groups have also received considerable attention.

Hospitalization has been recommended by a number of experienced clinicians and experts in the field (Russell, 1979; Garfinkel & Garner, 1982) as a method for breaking through the vicious cycle of starvation, binge-eating and vomiting. However, others have emphasized that the vast majority of patients with bulimia nervosa can be treated on an outpatient basis (Freeman, 1991) and that, initially, inpatient treatment in bulimia nervosa is rarely required. The latter should be reserved in those cases in which there are serious medical problems, serious concurrent psychiatric disturbances that would warrant hospitalization in their own right and unremitting severe symptoms that have not responded to adequate trials of outpatient treatment (Yager, 1988). Individual or group approaches with bulimic patients in both inpatient and outpatient settings depend on the willingness of the patient to cooperate and on the disorder being uncomplicated, i.e. free of laxative abuse, alcohol or drugs, psychosis, suicidal or antisocial behaviour.

Practical treatment advice includes diary-keeping and self-monitoring of eating behaviour and meals, self-induced vomiting and any abuse. In addition, dietary and eating advice must be given and educational material for implementing weight control is helpful (Freeman, 1991). Among the various treatment approaches, three stand out and deserve additional comments: cognitive-behavioural treatment, group therapy and psychopharmacological treatment. As in the whole field of bulimia nervosa, most of the experience comes from the treatment of adult patients.

Cognitive-behavioural treatment

This treatment approach has received the widest attention, at least among all controlled trials of psychotherapy for bulimia nervosa (Mitchell, 1991). With the intent to disrupt the habitual binge-eating, vomiting and laxative abuse, programmes are centring around the monitoring of eating and weight stimulus control and the provision of information, and education and advice regarding the normalization of eating behaviour in early stages of the treatment. Later, during the course of the therapeutic process, dysfunctional thoughts, beliefs and values that perpetuate the eating problem are identified and modified, and finally, a maintenance programme is instituted (Fairburn, 1985). Further characteristics of this approach were described above in the section on the treatment of anorectic patients.

Group therapy

Given the large number of bulimic individuals, group therapy has been recommended at least in centres in which large numbers of eating-disordered patients are seen. The potency of the group treatment of adolescent patients, in addition to other therapeutic elements, was seen in forcing the discussion of a number of important issues such as that of the context of secrecy and isolation in which bulimia takes place, the rigid and irrational ideas of the patients, alternative strategies for coping with stress and conflicts and the confrontation and working through of psychologically painful emotional states (Stuber & Strober, 1987).

Psychopharmacological treatment

A large number of psychopharmacological agents has been tested in bulimia nervosa, including anticonvulsants, antidepressants, lithium and fenfluramine. Scientifically, the antidepressants clearly turned out to be the most promising agents (Mitchell, 1988). According to some studies, they have a short-term effect in terms of reduced frequency of binge-eating. However, the mechanisms underlying the effectiveness of these agents is not understood. Long-term efficacy is jeopardized by high relapse rates upon withdrawal of medication and the frequent changes of drugs required over time. Because it is unlikely that the effectiveness of the antidepressants rests on the treatment of underlying depression, the clinician is left without any sound basis on which to make decisions concerning treatment management (Mitchell, 1988).

Evaluation of treatment

Given the fact that bulimia nervosa has been studied for only little more than a decade, there is a surprisingly high number of studies evaluating the effects of different treatment approaches. Recent reviews indicate that cognitive-behavioural interventions and drug therapy are clearly effective (Garner, 1987; Laessle *et al.*, 1987b; Fairburn, 1988; Mitchell, 1991). However, common methodological problems, including the failure to use a control group, overreliance on self-report outcome measures, small sample sizes and great variation in the inclusion criteria, the duration of treatment and the length of follow-up contribute to the difficulties that arise in interpreting the findings (Cox & Merkel, 1989). Recent comparative studies indicate that cognitive-behavioural approaches are superior to antidepressants (Mitchell, 1991) and interpersonal psychotherapy (Fairburn *et al.*, 1990), whereas intensive group psychotherapy is superior to antidepressant treatment (Mitchell *et al.*, 1990).

Outcome and prognosis

In his first description of the disorder, Russell (1979) emphasized that bulimia nervosa was a tenacious and intractable disorder. This may have been due to the fact that many of the bulimic patients had concurrent anorexia nervosa. Indeed, as described above in the section on outcome of anorexia nervosa, these patients had a poor prognosis. However, the spectrum of bulimic patients is much broader than the overlap with anorexia nervosa, and the last decade produced a small number of first-outcome studies (Swift *et al.*, 1987; Herzog *et al.*, 1988; Mitchell, 1988; Hsu & Sobkiewicz, 1989). Only a few of these outcome studies reported data on weight and menstruation, whereas disturbed eating behaviour was evident in a considerable proportion of the former patients at follow-up. Figures ranged from less than 30% to close to 90% in different studies. Depression was the most common psychiatric symptom, being reported by 15−36% of the subjects. Psychosexual functioning, recovery and relapse rates were scarcely studied at all and, in addition, there is also only very scant information concerning the crossover from bulimia to anorexia nervosa.

So far, no prognostic factor has been found to be consistently predictive of outcome across studies. Poor outcome may be related to a history of alcohol abuse, suicide attempts and increased depression at follow-up. In contrast with anorexia nervosa, which is often chronic and unremitting, bulimia nervosa often takes an episodic course with remissions and relapses.

CONCLUSIONS

The increased frequencies of clinical cases of eating-disordered patients and the awareness of both laypersons and professionals with regard to these disorders has stimulated research and the accumulation of expertise to a great extent in the recent past. In general, we have learned a considerable amount about clinical phenomenology, epidemiology, treatment and outcome of the eating disorders. Unfortunately, much of this knowledge stems from studies of adult patients. This is surprising because disease onset typically occurs during adolescence. Therefore, one of the main hopes for the future is that the eating disorders be studied more intensively during the period of initial manifestation.

Aetiology is one of the most difficult topics of the various areas of research. Currently, as in other fields of psychiatry, rather loosely tailored models try to integrate a large body of diverse factors and assumptions. Hopefully, with the advancement of genetic research tools, the identification of those individuals who are vulnerable to developing eating disorders will be possible. This may also contribute to a revised system of classification in terms of valid subtypes.

With regard to treatment, there is an urgent need to evaluate the various approaches. Given the high costs of medical treatment, regardless of setting and approach, and given the high relapse and chronicity rates, both the patients and society must have an interest in the question of which patients are most apt to profit best from certain well-evaluated treatment approaches. Studies of this kind should be connected with outcome studies that must concentrate on longer follow-up periods.

Finally, it would be most interesting to plan and perform large-scale epidemiological studies in adolescent school populations that aim at preventing the massive abuse of dieting and other weight-reducing practices and at identifying those individuals who are considerably at risk for the development of eating disorders. Studies of this kind would ideally combine effects of primary and secondary prevention.

REFERENCES

Altshuler K.Z. & Weiner M.F. (1985) Anorexia nervosa and depression — a dissenting view. *American Journal of Psychiatry*, **142**, 328−332.

American Psychiatric Association (1993) *Diagnostic and Statistical Manual of Mental Disorders*, Fourth Edition, (in press), Washington, DC.

Andersen A.E. (1990) *Males with Eating Disorders*. Brunner/Mazel, New York.

Andersen E.E. & Hay A. (1985) Racial and socioeconomic influences in anorexia nervosa and bulimia. *International Journal of Eating Disorders*, **4**, 479−488.

Andersen A.E. & Mickalide A.D. (1983) Anorexia nervosa in the male — an underdiagnosed disorder. *Psychosomatics*, **24**, 1066−1075.

Attie I., Brooks-Gunn F. & Petersen A.C. (1990) A developmental perspective on eating disorders and eating problems. In: Lewis M. & Miller S.M. (eds) *Handbook of Developmental Psychopathology*, pp. 409–420. Plenum Press, New York.

Bemis K.M. (1987) The present status of operant conditioning for the treatment of anorexia nervosa. *Behaviour Modification*, **11**, 432–463.

Ben-Tovim D.I. & Walker M.K. (1991) Women's body attitudes — a review of measurement techniques. *International Journal of Eating Disorders*, **10**, 155–168.

Bruch H. (1973) *Eating Disorders*. Basic Books, New York.

Burns T. & Crisp A.H. (1984) Outcome of anorexia nervosa in males. *British Journal of Psychiatry*, **145**, 319–325.

Cooper Z. & Fairburn C. (1987) The eating disorder examination: a semi-structured interview for the assessment of the specific psychopathology of eating disorders. *International Journal of Eating Disorders*, **6**, 1–8.

Coovert D.L. & Kinder B.N. (1989) The psychosexual aspects of anorexia nervosa and bulimia nervosa: a review of the literature. *Clinical Psychology Review*, **9**, 169–180.

Cox G.L. & Merkel W.T. (1989) A qualitative review of psychosocial treatments for bulimia. *Journal of Nervous and Mental Disease*, **177**, 77–84.

Crisp A.H. (1980) *Anorexia Nervosa: Let Me Be*. Academic Press, London.

Crisp H.H., Palmer R.L. & Kalney R.S. (1976) How common is anorexia nervosa? A prevalence study. *British Journal of Psychiatry*, **128**, 549–554.

Crowther J.H., Post G. & Zaynor L. (1985) The prevalence of bulimia and binge eating in adolescent girls. *International Journal of Eating Disorders*, **4**, 29–42.

Cullberg J. & Engstrom-Lindberg M. (1988) Prevalence and incidence of eating disorders in a suburban area. *Acta Psychiatrica Scandinavica*, **78**, 314–319.

Dolan B. (1991) Cross-cultural aspects of anorexia nervosa and bulimia — a review. *International Journal of Eating Disorders*, **10**, 67–80.

Drewnowski A., Yee D.K. & Krahn D.D. (1988) Bulimia in college women — incidence and recovery rates. *American Journal of Psychiatry*, **145**, 733–755.

Fairburn C.G. (1985) Cognitive-behavioural treatment for bulimia. In: Garner D.M. & Garfinkel P.E. (eds) *Handbook of Psychotherapy for Anorexia Nervosa and Bulimia*, pp. 160–192. Guilford Press, New York.

Fairburn C.G. (1988) The current status of the psychological treatments for bulimia nervosa. *Journal of Psychosomatic Research*, **32**, 635–646.

Fairburn C.G. & Beglin S.J. (1990) Studies of the epidemiology of bulimia nervosa. *American Journal of Psychiatry*, **147**, 401–408.

Fairburn C.G., Steere F. & Cooper P.F. (1990) Assessment of the specific psychopathology of bulimia nervosa. In: Fichter M.M. (ed) *Bulimia Nervosa: Basic Research, Diagnosis, and Therapy*, pp. 37–56. John Wiley, Chichester.

Fichter M.M. & Daser C. (1987) Symptomatology, psychosexual development, gender identity in 42 anorexic males. *Psychological Medicine*, **17**, 409–418.

Fichter M.M. & Hoffmann R. (1990) Bulimia nervosa in the male. In: Fichter M.M. (ed) *Bulimia Nervosa: Basic Research, Diagnosis and Therapy*, pp. 99–111. John Wiley, Chichester.

Fichter M.M. & Noegelm R. (1990) Concordance for bulimia nervosa in twins. *International Journal of Eating Disorders*, **9**, 255–264.

Fichter M.M., Elton M., Engel K., Meyer A.-E., Poustka F., Mall H. & von der Heydra S. (1990) The structured interview for anorexia and bulimia nervosa (SIAB): development and characteristics of a (semi-) standardized instrument. In: Fichter M.M. (ed) *Bulimia Nervosa: Basic Research, Diagnosis and Therapy*, pp. 57–70. John Wiley, Chichester.

Fosson A., Knibbs J. & Bryant-Waugh R. (1987) Early onset anorexia nervosa. *Archives of Disease in Childhood*, **62**, 114–118.

Freeman C.P. (1991) A practical guide to the treatment of bulimia

nervosa. *Journal of Psychosomatic Research*, **35**(suppl. 1), 40–49.

Gandour J.J. (1984) Bulimia — clinical description, assessment, aetiology, and treatment. *International Journal of Eating Disorders*, **3**, 3–38.

Garfinkel P.E. (1985) Review: The treatment of anorexia nervosa in Toronto. *Journal of Psychiatric Research*, **19**, 405–412.

Garfinkel P. & Garner D. (1982) *Anorexia Nervosa — A Multidimensional Perspective*. Brunner/Mazel, New York.

Garfinkel P. & Kaplan A.S. (1985) Starvation based perpetuating mechanisms in anorexia nervosa and bulimia. *International Journal of Eating Disorders*, **4**, 651–666.

Garner D.M. (1987) Psychotherapy outcome research with bulimia nervosa. *Psychotherapy and Psychosomatics*, **48**, 129–140.

Garner D.M. & Bemis K.M. (1985) Cognitive therapy for anorexia nervosa. In: Garner D.M. & Garfinkel P.E. (eds) *Handbook of Psychotherapy for Anorexia Nervosa and Bulimia*, 2nd edn, pp. 107–146. Guilford Press, London.

Garner D.M. & Garfinkel P.E. (1979) The eating attitudes test: an index of the symptoms of anorexia nervosa. *Psychological Medicine*, **9**, 273–279.

Garner D.M., Olmstead M.P., Bohr Y. & Garfinkel P.E. (1982) The eating attitude test. Psychometric features and clinical correlates. *Psychological Medicine*, **12**, 871–878.

Garner D.M., Olmstead M.P. & Polivy J. (1983) Development and validation of a multidimensional eating disorder inventory for anorexia nervosa and bulimia. *International Journal of Eating Disorders*, **2**, 15–34.

Gilchrist P.N. & McFarlane C.M. (1986) Family therapy in the treatment of anorexia nervosa. *International Journal of Eating Disorders*, **5**, 659–668.

Gislason I.L. (1988) Eating disorders in childhood (ages 4 through 11 years). In: Blinder B.F., Chaitin B.F. & Goldstein R. (eds) *The Eating Disorders*, pp. 285–293. PMA, New York.

Gowers S.G., Crisp A.H., Joughin N. & Bhat A. (1991) Premenarcheal anorexia nervosa. *Journal of Child Psychology and Psychiatry and Allied Disciplines*, **32**, 515–524.

Gross J. & Rosen J.C. (1987) Bulimia in adolescents: prevalence and psychosocial correlates. *International Journal of Eating Disorders*, **7**, 51–62.

Hall A. (1987) The place of family therapy in the treatment of anorexia nervosa. *Australian and New Zealand Journal of Psychiatry*, **21**, 568–574.

Halmi K.A. (1985) Review: Classification of the eating disorders. *Journal of Psychiatric Research*, **19**, 113–120.

Halmi K.A., Eckert E., Lasu T.F. & Cohen F. (1986) Anorexia nervosa. Treatment efficacy of cyproheptadine and amitriptyline. *Archives of General Psychiatry*, **43**, 177–181.

Harris F.C. & Phelps C.F. (1987) Anorexia and bulimia. In: Hersen M. & Van Hasselt V.B. (eds) *Behaviour Therapy with Children and Adolescents. A Clinical Approach*, pp. 465–484. Wiley-Interscience, New York.

Herzog D.B., Keller M.B. & Lavori P.W. (1988) Outcome in anorexia nervosa and bulimia nervosa. A review of the literature. *Journal of Nervous and Mental Disease*, **176**, 131–142.

Hinz L.D. & Williamson D.A. (1987) Bulimia and depression: a review of the affective variant hypothesis. *Psychological Bulletin*, **102**, 150–158.

Hoek H.W. (1991) The incidence and prevalence of anorexia nervosa and bulimia nervosa in primary care. *Psychological Medicine*, **21**, 455–460.

Holden N.L. (1990) Is anorexia nervosa an obsessive-compulsive disorder? *British Journal of Psychiatry*, **157**, 1–5.

Holland A.J., Sicotte N. & Treasure J. (1988) Anorexia nervosa — evidence for a genetic basis. *Journal of Psychosomatic Research*, **32**, 561–572.

Hsu L.K.G. (1983) The aetiology of anorexia nervosa. *Psychological Medicine*, **13**, 231−238.

Hsu L.K.G. (1988) The outcome of anorexia nervosa: a reappraisal. *Psychological Medicine*, **18**, 807−812.

Hsu L.K.G. & Sobkiewicz T.A. (1989) Bulimia nervosa: a four- to six-year follow-up study. *Psychological Medicine*, **19**, 1035−1038.

Hsu L.K.G. & Sobkiewicz T.A. (1991) Body image disturbance: time to abandon the concept for eating disorders. *International Journal of Eating Disorders*, **10**, 15−30.

Hsu L.K.G., Chesler B.E. & Santhouse R. (1990) Bulimia nervosa in eleven sets of twins: a clinical report. *International Journal of Eating Disorders*, **9**, 275−282.

Humphrey L.L. (1988) Relationships within subtypes of anorexic, bulimic, and normal families. *Journal of the American Academy of Child and Adolescent Psychiatry*, **27**, 544−551.

Humphrey L.L. (1989) Observed family interactions among subtypes of eating disorders using structural analysis of social behaviour. *Journal of Consulting Clinical Psychology*, **57**, 206−214.

Jacobs B.W. & Isaacs S. (1986) Pre-pubertal anorexia nervosa − a retrospective controlled study. *Journal of Child Psychology and Psychiatry and Allied Disciplines*, **27**, 237−250.

Jones D.J., Fox M.M., Babigian H.M. & Hutton H.E. (1980) Epidemiology of anorexia nervosa in Monroe County, New York: 1960−1976. *Psychosomatic Medicine*, **42**, 551−558.

Kaplan A.S. (1990) Biomedical variables in the eating disorders. *Canadian Journal of Psychiatry*, **35**, 745−753.

Kassett J.A., Gershon E.S., Maxwell M.E., Gurolt J.J., Kazuba D.M., Smith A.L., Brandt H.A. & Jimerson D.C. (1989) Psychiatric disorders in the first-degree relatives of probands with bulimia nervosa. *American Journal of Psychiatry*, **146**, 1468−1471.

Kendell R.E., Hale D.J., Hailey A. & Babigian H.M. (1973) The epidemiology of anorexia nervosa. *Psychological Medicine*, **3**, 200−203.

Kog E. & Vandereycken W. (1985) Family characteristics of anorexia nervosa and bulimia: a review of the research literature. *Clinical Psychology Review*, **5**, 159−180.

Kog E. & Vandereycken W. (1988) The facts: a review of research data on eating disorder families. In: Vandereycken W.E.K., Kog E. & Vanderlinden J. (eds) *The Family Approach to Eating Disorders: Assessment and Treatment of Anorexia Nervosa and Bulimia*, pp. 25−67. PMA, New York.

Laessle R.G., Kittl S., Fichter M.M., Wittchen H.U. & Pirke K.M. (1987a) Major affective disorder in anorexia nervosa and bulimia − a descriptive diagnostic study. *British Journal of Psychiatry*, **151**, 785−789.

Laessle R.G., Zoettl C. & Pirke K.-M. (1987b) Metaanalysis of treatment studies for bulimia. *International Journal of Eating Disorders*, **5**, 647−653.

Lee S. & Chiu H.F.K. (1989) Anorexia nervosa in Hong Kong − why not more in Chinese? *British Journal of Psychiatry*, **154**, 683−688.

Levy A.B. & Dixon K.N. (1985) The relationship between anorexia nervosa and depression: a reevaluation. *International Journal of Eating Disorders*, **4**, 389−406.

Lucas A.R., Beard C.M., O'Fallon W.M. & Kurland L.T. (1991) Fifty-year trends in the incidence of anorexia nervosa in Rochester, Minnesota: a population-based study. *American Journal of Psychiatry*, **148**, 917−922.

Manchi M. & Cohen P. (1990) Early childhood eating behaviour and adolescent eating disorders. *Journal of the American Academy of Child and Adolescent Psychiatry*, **29**, 112−117.

Marrazzi M.A. & Luby E.E. (1986) An auto-addiction opioid model of chronic anorexia nervosa. *International Journal of Eating Disorders*, **5**, 191−208.

Minuchin S., Rosman B.L. & Baker L. (1978) *Psychosomatic Families*. Harvard University Press, Cambridge, MA.

Mitchell P.B. (1988) The pharmacological management of bulimia nervosa: a critical review. *International Journal of Eating Disorders*, **7**, 29−41.

Mitchell J.E. (1991) A review of the controlled trials of psychotherapy for bulimia nervosa. *Journal of Psychosomatic Research* **35**(suppl. 1), 23−32.

Mitchell J.E., Pyle R.L., Eckert E., Hatsukami D., Pomeroy C. & Zimmerman R. (1990) A comparison study of antidepressants and structured intensive group psychotherapy in the treatment of bulimia nervosa. *Archives of General Psychiatry*, **47**, 149−160.

Nasser M. (1988) Cultural and weight consciousness. *Journal of Psychosomatic Research*, **32**, 573−578.

Neumärker U., Dudeck U., Vollrath M., Neumärker K.J. & Steinhausen H.-C. (1992) Eating attitudes among adolescent patients and normal school girls in East Berlin and West Berlin. A transcultural comparison. *International Journal of Eating Disorders*, **12**, 281−289.

Nielsen S. (1990) The epidemiology of anorexia nervosa in Denmark from 1973 to 1987: a nationwide register study of psychiatric admission. *Acta Psychiatrica Scandinavica*, **81**, 507−514.

Nylander I. (1971) The feeling of being fat and dieting in a school population. *Acta Sociomedica Scandinavica*, **3**, 17−26.

Oyebode F., Boodhoo J.A. & Schapira K. (1988) Anorexia nervosa in males: clinical features and outcome. *International Journal of Eating Disorders*, **7**, 121−124.

Palmer R., Christie M., Cordle C., Davies D. & Kenrick J. (1987) The clinical eating disorder rating instrument (CEDRI): a preliminary description. *International Journal of Eating Disorders*, **6**, 9−16.

Palmer R.L., Oppenheimer R., Dignon K., Chaloner D.A. & Howells K. (1990) Childhood sexual experiences with adults reported by women with eating disorders − an extended series. *British Journal of Psychiatry*, **156**, 699−703.

Patton G.C. & King M.B. (1991) Editorial: Epidemiological study of eating disorders: time for a change of emphasis. *Psychological Medicine*, **21**, 287−291.

Patton G.C., Johnson-Sabine E., Wood K., Mann A.H. & Wakeling A. (1990) Abnormal eating attitudes in London schoolgirls − a prospective epidemiological study: outcome at twelve-month follow-up. *Psychological Medicine*, **20**, 383−394.

Ploog D.W. & Pirke K.M. (1987) Psychobiology of anorexia nervosa. *Psychological Medicine*, **17**, 843−860.

Pryor T., McGilley B. & Roach N.E. (1990) Psychopharmacology and eating disorders − dawning of a new age. *Psychiatric Annals*, **20**, 711−722.

Pumariega A.J., Edwards P. & Mitchell C.B. (1984) Anorexia nervosa in black adolescents. *Journal of the American Academy of Child and Adolescent Psychiatry*, **23**, 111−114.

Råstam M. & Gillberg C. (1991) The family background in anorexia nervosa: a population based study. *Journal of the American Academy of Child and Adolescent Psychiatry*, **30**, 283−289.

Råstam M., Gillberg C. & Garton M. (1989) Anorexia nervosa in a Swedish urban region. *British Journal of Psychiatry*, **155**, 642−646.

Russell G.F.M. (1979) Bulimia nervosa: an ominous variant of anorexia nervosa. *Psychological Medicine*, **9**, 429−448.

Russell G.F.M. (1981) The current treatment of anorexia nervosa. *British Journal of Psychiatry*, **138**, 164−166.

Russell G.F.M. (1985) Premenarchal anorexia nervosa and its sequelae. *Journal of Psychiatric Research*, **19**, 363−369.

Russell G.F.M., Szmukler G.I., Dare C. & Eisler I. (1987) An evaluation of family therapy in anorexia nervosa and bulimia nervosa. *Archives of General Psychiatry*, **44**, 1047−1056.

Scott D.W. (1986a) Anorexia nervosa in the male: a review of clinical epidemiological and biological findings. *International Journal of Eating Disorders*, **5**, 799−820.

Scott D.W. (1986b) Anorexia nervosa: a review of possible genetic factors. *International Journal of Eating Disorders*, **5**, 1−20.

Scott D.W. (1987) The involvement of psychosexual factors in the causation of eating disorders: time for a reappraisal. *International Journal of Eating Disorders*, **6**, 199–213.

Selvini-Palazzoli M. (1974) *Self-Starvation*. Chaucer, London.

Silber T.J. (1986) Anorexia nervosa in blacks and Hispanics. *International Journal of Eating Disorders*, **5**, 121–128.

Steiger H. (1989) Anorexia nervosa and bulimia in males — lessons from a low-risk population. *Canadian Journal of Psychiatry Revue Canadienne de Psychiatrie*, **34**, 419–424.

Stein D.M. & Brinza S.R. (1989) Bulimia: prevalence estimates in female junior high and high school students. *Journal of Clinical Child Psychology*, **18**, 206–213.

Steinhausen H.-C. (1984) Transcultural comparison of eating attitudes in young females and anorectic patients. *European Archives of Psychiatry and Neurological Sciences*, **234**, 198–201.

Steinhausen H.-C. (1985) Evaluation of inpatient treatment of adolescent anorexic patients. *Journal of Psychiatric Research*, **19**, 371–375.

Steinhausen H.-C. & Glanville K. (1983) Follow-up studies of anorexia nervosa — a review of research findings. *Psychological Medicine*, **3**, 239–249.

Steinhausen H.-C. & Seidel R. (1992) A prospective follow-up study in early-onset eating disorders. In: Herzog W., Deter H.C. & Vandereycken W. (eds) *The Course of Eating Disorders: Long-Term Follow-Up Studies of Anorexia and Bulimia Nervosa Course*. Springer, Berlin.

Steinhausen H.-C., Neumärker K.-J., Vollrath M., Dudeck U. & Neumärker U. (1992) A transcultural comparison of the Eating Disorder Inventory in former East and West Berlin. *International Journal of Eating Disorders*, **12**, 407–416.

Steinhausen H.-C., Rauss-Mason C. & Seidel R. (1991) Follow-up studies of anorexia nervosa: a review of four decades of outcome research. *Psychological Medicine*, **21**, 447–451.

Sterling J.W. & Segal J.D. (1985) Anorexia nervosa in males: a critical review. *International Journal of Eating Disorders*, **4**, 559–572.

Striegel-Moore R.H., Silberstein L.R., French P. & Rodin F. (1989) A prospective study of disordered eating among college students. *International Journal of Eating Disorders*, **8**, 523–532.

Strober M. (1981) The significance of bulimia in juvenile anorexia nervosa — an exploration of possible etiologic factors. *International Journal of Eating Disorders*, **1**, 28–43.

Strober M. (1991) Family-genetic studies of eating disorders. *Journal of Clinical Psychiatry*, **52**(suppl. 10), 9–12.

Strober M., Lampert C., Morrell W., Burroughs J. & Jacobs C. (1990) A controlled family study of anorexia nervosa: evidence of familial aggregation and lack of shared transmission with affective disorders. *International Journal of Eating Disorders*, **9**, 239–253.

Stuber M. & Strober M. (1987) Group therapy in the treatment of adolescents with bulimia: some preliminary observations. *International Journal of Eating Disorders*, **6**, 125–132.

Suematsu H., Kuboki T. & Itoh T. (1985) Statistical studies on the prognosis of anorexia nervosa. *Psychosomatics*, **43**, 104–112.

Swift W.J., Ritholz M., Kalin N.H. & Kaslow N. (1987) A follow-up study of thirty hospitalized bulimics. *Psychosomatic Medicine*, **49**, 45–55.

Szmukler G., McCane C., McCrone L. & Hunter D. (1986) Anorexia nervosa: a psychiatric case register study from Aberdeen. *Psychological Medicine*, **16**, 49–58.

Thomas J.P. & Szmukler G.I. (1985) Anorexia nervosa in patients of Afro-Caribbean extraction. *British Journal of Psychiatry*, **146**, 653–656.

Timmerman M.G., Wells L.A. & Chen S. (1990) Bulimia nervosa and associated alcohol abuse among secondary school students. *Journal of the American Academy of Child and Adolescent Psychiatry*, **29**, 118–222.

Todd T.C. (1985) Anorexia nervosa and bulimia — expanding the structural model. In: Mirkin M.P. (ed) *Handbook of Adolescent and Family Therapy*, pp. 223–244. Gardner Press, New York.

Treasure J. & Holland A. (1990) Genetic vulnerability to eating disorders: evidence from twin and family studies. In: Remschmidt H. & Schmidt M.H. (eds) *Anorexia Nervosa*, pp. 59–68. Hogrefe & Huber, Toronto.

Vandereycken W. (1987a) The constructive family approach to eating disorders: critical remarks on the use of family therapy in anorexia nervosa and bulimia. *International Journal of Eating Disorders*, **6**, 455–468.

Vandereycken W. (1987b) The use of neuroleptics in the treatment of anorexia nervosa patients. In: Garfinkel P.E. & Garner D.M. (eds) *The Role of Drug Treatments for Eating Disorders*, pp. 74–89. Brunner/Mazel, New York.

Vandereycken W. (1990) The addiction model in eating disorders: some critical remarks and a selected bibliography. *International Journal of Eating Disorders*, **9**, 95–102.

Vandereycken W. & Pierloot R. (1983) The significance of subclassification in anorexia nervosa: a comparative study of clinical features in 141 patients. *Psychological Medicine*, **13**, 543–549.

Vandereycken W. & Vandenbroucke S. (1984) Anorexia nervosa in males — a comparative study of 107 cases reported in the literature (1970 to 1980). *Acta Psychiatrica Scandinavica*, **70**, 447–454.

Wakeling A. (1985) Neurobiological aspects of feeding disorders. *Journal of Psychiatric Research*, **19**, 191–201.

Weiner H. (1985) The physiology of eating disorders. *International Journal of Eating Disorders*, **4**, 347–388.

Welch G., Hall A. & Renner R. (1990) Patient subgrouping in anorexia nervosa using psychologically-based classification. *International Journal of Eating Disorders*, **9**, 311–322.

Whitaker A., Johnson J., Shaffer D., Rapoport J.L., Kalikow K., Walsh T., Davies M., Braiman S. & Dolinsky A. (1990) Uncommon troubles in young people. Prevalence estimates of selected psychiatric disorders in a nonreferred population. *Archives of General Psychiatry*, **47**, 487–496.

Willi J., Giacometti G. & Limacher B. (1990) Update on the epidemiology of anorexia nervosa in a defined region of Switzerland. *American Journal of Psychiatry*, **147**, 1514–1518.

Williams P. & King M. (1987) The 'epidemic' of anorexia nervosa: another medical myth? *Lancet* (January), 205–208.

World Health Organization (1991) Tenth Revision of the International Classification of Diseases, Chapter V (F): Mental and Behavioural Disorder (Including Disorder of Psychological Development). *Clinical Descriptions and Diagnostic Guidelines*, WHO, Geneva.

Yager J. (1988) The treating of eating disorders. *Journal of Clinical Psychiatry*, **49**(suppl), 18–25.

Chapter 25
Obsessive-Compulsive Disorder

Judith L. Rapoport, Susan Swedo & Henrietta Leonard

DEFINITION:
THE CONCEPT AND CURRENT ISSUES

Until recently, obsessive-compulsive disorder (OCD) was unfamiliar to most child psychiatrists, even though classic descriptions of the disorder featured cases with childhood presentation (Janet, 1903). The recognition that OCD was more common in adults than previously believed, and the retrospective reports that one-half to one-third of adult subjects had their onset in childhood or adolescence, focused the attention of the child psychiatric community on this chronic and often disabling disorder (Karno *et al.*, 1988).

Until the mid 19th century, obsessive-compulsive phenomena were considered to be a variant of insanity. However, as the disorder was better defined, it came into focus as one of the neuroses. The descriptions of repetitive, unwanted thoughts or rituals often characterized by magical thinking, and usually kept private by the sufferer, were relatively constant observations. In the late 1800s, biological hypotheses flourished. Debate about core deficits and the relative importance of volitional, intellectual and emotional impairments (all of which are in some way abnormal in OCD), have flourished for over 100 years (Berrios, 1989).

Freud (1909, 1913) provided some of the most interesting and creative speculations on the similarity between obsessive-compulsive phenomena, children's games and religious rites. Although psychoanalytic theory has not added usefully to the treatment or understanding of the aetiology of severe OCD, the broad questions raised by Freud about continuity and discontinuity within individual development and OCD, as well as with secular and religious rituals, remain fascinating issues. In addition, the observation of association between certain neurological disorders and OCD has led to the most intriguing aspects of current neurobiological research: the possible localization of brain circuits mediating such behaviour and mechanism for behavioural encoding. Over the past decade, interest in these social and developmental questions, together with increased recognition of paediatric OCD, has generated an astonishing amount of clinical observation, and basic science and clinical treatment research (Rapoport, 1986; Rapoport, 1989a,b,c and d).

EPIDEMIOLOGY

The Epidemiological Catchment Area (ECA) study of over 18 500 adult individuals in five different sites in the US included OCD as a separate category and provided the first large-scale information on the prevalence of this disorder (Robins *et al.*, 1981). Using a structured interview, the Diagnostic Interview Schedule (DIS), designed for lay interviewers, lifetime prevalence rates ranged from 1.9 to 3.3% across the sites. Even when other disorders were excluded, the rates were 1.2—2.4%. These rates were 25—60 times greater than had been estimated on the basis of clinical populations (Karno *et al.*, 1988). The mean age of onset across the sites ranged from 20 to 25 years, with 50% developing symptoms in childhood or adolescence (Karno & Golding, 1990), providing further support for retrospective accounts of the frequent paediatric onset of this disorder (Black, 1974).

The ECA findings have been criticized on the grounds that interviewers were not trained clinicians and on the uncertain validity of the DIS (see discussion in Karno *et al.*, 1988). To address these criticisms, while examining the rate in a younger population, Flament *et al.* (1988) carried out the only epidemiological study of an adolescent population to date that examined the prevalence of OCD. As part of the two-stage study of 5596 adolescents (Whitaker *et al.*, 1990), the Leyton Obsessional Inventory was administered (along with other questionnaires on general mental health, anxiety and eating disorders) to the entire high school population of a county 80 miles from New York City.

The second stage of the study used a semistructured clinical interview carried out by child psychiatrists with extensive clinical experience with OCD. Clinical vignettes were compiled on the basis of these interviews and a high agreement for OCD, compulsive personality and subclinical OCD was obtained (overall kappa of 0.85).

A total of 20 subjects received a lifetime diagnosis of OCD (18 current and 2 with past illness). Fifteen of the 20 had one or more other lifetime psychiatric diagnoses (10 current), with depression, bulimia or overanxious disorder most common. Four had been in psychological treatment at some time (but never for OCD).

The weighted prevalence figure (without exclusion)

obtained was 1.9% in agreement with the ECA estimates for adults.

The symptom presentation and associated disorders for the epidemiological sample resembled that for clinical samples. The clinical significance of a diagnosis of OCD even in a community sample of adolescents was reinforced by a 2-year follow-up of these children (Berg *et al.*, 1989a). The chronicity and the continued impairment of the community sample in Berg's follow-up study, and the availability of effective treatments, make it important that child mental health workers pay serious attention to this disorder.

PHENOMENOLOGY AND CLASSIFICATION

OCD is defined in both ICD-10 and DSM-IV (American Psychiatric Press, in press) as repetitive intrusive thoughts and/or rituals that are unwanted and which interfere significantly with function or cause marked distress. The severity criteria avoid confusion with the many childhood habits which are a part of normal development, and the content and at least relative insight into the unreasonableness of the behaviours differentiate OCD from other disorders.

A major change from DSM-III (American Psychiatric Press, 1980) to DSM-III-R (American Psychiatric Press, 1987), continued in DSM-IV — making it less compatible with ICD-10 — is the omission of exclusionary criteria for a diagnosis of schizophrenia. The change was made because of the broad comorbidity of OCD (Karno *et al.*, 1988), and convincing evidence of coexistence with schizophrenia (see Lewis *et al.*, 1991, for review). DSM-IV, of course, urges multiple diagnosis as appropriate and both Karno *et al.* and our own experience suggest that almost 50% of OCD subjects will also merit another axis I diagnosis, often an anxiety or affective disorder (Swedo *et al.*, 1989c).

Current debates about diagnostic criteria — including whether obsessions are inevitably present, and what degree of insight is required concerning the irrationality of symptoms — are of particular importance for childhood OCD. Both DSM-IV and ICD-10 state that compulsions are designed to neutralize or prevent some dreaded event. This may be in error. About 40% of children with typical compulsive rituals deny associated obsessions (Swedo *et al.*, 1989c), and surprisingly similar figures are also available for adults (Karno *et al.*, 1988), suggesting that neutralization is not relevant at any age. While some children may not be willing or able to verbalize associated thoughts, long-term contact with these subjects indicates that many children steadfastly report only rituals (accompanied by vague discomfort if these rituals are not carried out), without associated thoughts. The degree of insight needed for the diagnosis is also in dispute, as some (young and old) patients, at least some of the time, 'believe' their obsessions. However, generally children do not differ from adults in this respect. While in theory it might seem that young children would be particularly prone to 'believe' their obsessional thoughts, experience to date suggests that the DSM-IV adult criteria are appropriate for the diagnosis in

childhood (Rapoport, 1989a,c; Swedo *et al.*, 1989c). It seems however that for both adults and children, diagnostic criteria must acknowledge that compulsions can and do occur in the absence of obsessions, and that partial 'belief' in the necessity for these thoughts/behaviours is seen, particularly in severe cases.

Because of the range of associated phenomena and comorbidity, and because the boundaries of OCD are still being explored, classification, differential diagnosis, comorbidity and associated features are still conceptually muddled. For this reason, classification and phenomenology are discussed together.

Clinical presentation

Childhood-onset OCD has been documented as early as age 2, and certain general patterns are consistent across the few published sizeable series (Despert, 1955; Adams, 1973). In a National Institute of Mental Health (NIMH) sample of 70 consecutive patients, the mean age at onset was 10.1 ($\pm$ 3.52) years, with 8 of the patients having early onset, that is, obsessive-compulsive symptoms before age 7. Males tend to have an earlier onset of symptoms than females, particularly among patients with onset before age 7 (Swedo *et al.*, 1989c). Early-onset illness may represent a variant of OCD, possibly one more closely related to Tourette's disorder (see below). Although the clinical presentation in young children is similar to that in older children and adolescents, familial OCD appears to be increased among young children, suggesting that genetic factors may be more prominent in this subgroup.

There has only been one published family study for childhood-onset OCD. Lenane *et al.* (1990) conducted in-person structured interviews of first-degree relatives of 46 consecutive paediatric OCD patients; one-quarter (25%) of the patients had a first-degree relative with OCD. Fifteen (17%) of the 90 parents interviewed met diagnostic criteria for OCD, with 9% of mothers and 25% of fathers affected.

The presenting symptoms for 70 paediatric OCD patients seen at the NIMH are shown in Table 25.1. (The series is described in detail in Swedo *et al.*, 1989c.) Rituals were more frequently the presenting complaint than were obsessions. Obsessions dealt primarily with contamination, danger to self or others, symmetry or moral issues. A combination of rituals and obsessions was most common, and 'pure' obsessives were rare compared with the more frequent 'pure' ritualizers.

Washing rituals were by far the most common, occurring at some time during the course of the illness in 85% of patients, but repeating and checking rituals were also frequent. Handwashing was slightly more frequent than showering, and the two activities accounted for virtually all of the washing rituals (no subject took prolonged baths). A number of children used chemicals, such as alcohol or detergents, to clean their hands, provoking eczematoid dermatitis.

In 90% of cases the symptoms had changed over time. Most children began with a single obsession or compulsion at onset, continued with this for months to years, and then gradually

Table 25.1 Presenting symptoms in 70 consecutive children and adolescents with primary OCD (adapted from Goodman *et al.*, 1989)

Reported symptoms at initial interview	*n*	Percentage
Obsessions		
Concerns with dirt, germs or environmetal toxins	28	40
Something terrible happening (e.g. fire, death or illness of self or loved one)	17	24
Symmetry, order or exactness	12	17
Scrupulosity (religious obsessive)	9	13
Concern or disgust with bodily wastes or secretions (urine, stool, saliva)	6	8
Lucky or unlucky numbers	6	8
Forbidden, aggressive or perverse sexual thoughts, images or impulses	3	4
Fear might harm others or self	3	4
Concern with household items	2	3
Intrusive nonsense sounds, words or music	1	1
Compulsions		
Excessive or ritualized hand-washing, showering, bathing, toothbrushing or grooming	60	85
Repeating rituals (e.g. going in or out the door, up or down)	36	51
Checking (e.g. doors, locks, stove, appliances, emergency brake on car, paper route, homework)	32	46
Miscellaneous rituals (e.g. writing, moving, speaking)	18	26
Rituals to remove contact with contaminants	16	23
Touching	14	20
Measures to prevent harm to self or others	11	16
Ordering or arranging	12	17
Counting	13	18
Hoarding/collecting rituals		
Rituals of cleaning household or inanimate objects	4	6

* Obsessions or compulsions are totalled; thus the total exceeds 70.

acquired different thoughts or rituals. In grade school years, counting and symmetry were common; a period of excessive washing was particularly frequent in early and mid-adolescence; sexual thoughts or rituals became increasingly common in later adolescence, usually dissipating by 18 years of age, to be supplanted by more general ruminations and doubts.

When considered, the diagnosis of OCD is straightforward, even with very young subjects. Subjects with an early age at onset (below age 6) had begun their rituals or obsessions in easily recognizable fashion, with only minor allowances for developmental level; in some cases the child had not yet mastered the task performed compulsively by older children

and adults. For example, one 6-year-old boy, who was compelled to draw zeros repetitively, had started at age 3 to circle manhole covers on city streets. His tantrums when this behaviour was interrupted and his subjective distress at having to do this, together with lack of other behavioural abnormalities led to the diagnosis of OCD.

A 7-year-old boy, who checked doors and light switches, had been seen at 3 years of age because he walked only on the edges of floor tiles. Two subjects had started excessive hand-washing at age 4. A 5-year-old boy had suddenly become 'unable' to enter his garden gate without going back and forth three times; by age 9 he was unable to go through doorways at all; when the number of repetitions had reached 500, he was hospitalized.

Approximately one-third of these patients report that certain stimuli trigger their rituals. A 16-year-old girl with elaborate front-door touching and stepping rituals could 'sneak' into her house by a side door, avoiding the sight of the front door, and successfully averting the rituals. Several hoarders would close their eyes to avoid seeing scraps of paper on the street that would set off the collecting urge.

Secrecy is typical, hand-washing may be disguised as more frequent voiding, and rituals are carried out in private, so that children are symptomatic for months before their parents are aware of a problem. Teachers and peers become aware only with much greater severity.

As with Tourette's disorder, children may expend great effort 'controlling' their behaviours in public and 'let go' when at home. This partial voluntary control of symptoms baffles and angers parents.

All but the most severely affected patients find keeping busy, having others structure their time and carrying out physical activity to be helpful in suppressing obsessive-compulsive symptoms, while stress of any sort usually aggravates them.

Course and natural history

There are no prospective studies yet completed on high-risk samples for OCD, such as studies of offspring of adults with this disorder. However, retrospective data from the NIMH sample indicated that almost half of the sample had had 'micro episodes' years before becoming ill, in which excessive rigidity, repetitive rituals (e.g. wearing the same clothes for a month, refusal to take a different path through the house) were the subject of concern, albeit briefly (Leonard *et al.*, 1990).

The clinical course of the disorder indicates some developmental influence on symptoms over time, as discussed earlier. However, these are only generalizations and particular subtypes such as repetitive tunes may persist as the only symptom over the entire course of the illness.

Clinical course may be chronic or episodic, and spontaneous remission even after years of illness occurs in perhaps a third of patients (Karno & Golding, 1990). About 10% of patients have a continuous deteriorating course.

Prospective follow-up studies of childhood OCD are rare. Earlier studies (Berman, 1942; Warren, 1965) found half of cases doing poorly at follow-up, as did Hollingsworth *et al.* (1980) and Zeitlin (1986) in later studies. The problem has not been solved by the availability of drug treatment as the only prospective follow-up of 27 children treated with clomipramine (CMI) also found poor outcome for approximately 50% of the cases. The majority still met criteria for OCD 2–5 years later (Flament *et al.*, 1990). Surprisingly, neither baseline measures nor a positive response to CMI predicted long-term outcome. More recently, Leonard *et al.* (1993) carried out a 2–7-year prospective follow-up of 54 OCD children and adolescents who had more vigorous behavioural and drug treatment. While the group appeared to be functioning slightly better than the earlier group of Flament *et al.*, (1988) only 18 (33%) subjects were symptom-free and 20 still met criteria for OCD. Of the 34 subjects with few or subclinical OC symptoms, 21 (61%) had ongoing drug treatment (H.L. Leonard, unpublished data). Drug treatment is still of some long-term benefit, however, as discontinuation brings further worsening (Leonard *et al.*, 1991a).

Associated disorders

In adults, OCD has a broad range of comorbidity similar to that seen for other major axis I disorders (Karno *et al.*, 1988). Based on clinical experience, and the adolescent epidemiological study, childhood OCD also has a strong association with eating disorders (Whitaker *et al.*, 1990). Because eating disorders were exclusionary in the NIMH paediatric studies, they do not appear in these data. Concurrent psychiatric diagnoses that were seen with childhood-onset OCD in the NIMH study are given in Table 25.2.

With the exception of Tourette's and specific developmental disorders, the pattern of associated disorders follows that reported for adult clinical series (Swedo *et al.*, 1989c). Only about 26% of children have OCD as a single diagnosis, although a secondary diagnosis may be relatively mild.

Table 25.2 Associated psychopathology with severe primary childhood OCD*

Associated disorder
Axis I disorders
Tourette's disorder
Major depression
Anxiety disorders
Alcohol substance abuse
Conduct/oppositional disorder
Attention deficit/hyperactivity disorder
Eating disorder
Axis II disorders
Specific developmental disorders

* Current and lifetime.

Depression, either lifetime or current, and anxiety disorders were most common, and are equally likely to predate or follow the onset of OCD.

Although occurring less frequently than affective and anxiety disorders, disruptive behaviour disorder or substance abuse also appear to be increased (Bolton & Turner, 1984, Swedo *et al.*, 1989c). Increased incidence of neurological 'soft' signs in childhood anxiety disorder has been reported by Shaffer *et al.* (1985). We noted chronic motor tics had been present at baseline in over 30% of the NIMH study patients and, as will be seen from the discussion below, whether this is a distinct subgroup or simply an associated (tic) disorder remains unsettled (Denckla, 1989). The tics were seen more often in younger patients, those with acute illness and in males. In some cases, touching rituals were utilized to disguise an involuntary tic. It is unknown just how the pattern and severity of obsessive-compulsive symptoms differ between patients with Tourette syndrome and those with primary OCD, but preliminary impressions are that compulsions associated with Tourette syndrome may be more likely to involve touching than washing, and may be less severe than in primary OCD.

Choreiform movements are also found in one-third of the children and adolescents with OCD. The absence of these movements on follow-up examination 2–5 years later has been interpreted to mean that they are a marker of a pathological process aetiological to OCD (Denckla, 1989), but may simply reflect the tendency for childhood tic disorders, including Tourette's, to improve with time.

Only 20% of our paediatric sample was judged to have compulsive personality disorder. This seems to be less common than reported for adults (Rasmussen & Tsuang, 1984; Black *et al.*, 1988), although recent findings using more systematic diagnosis of personality disorder indicate that the prevalence of compulsive personality disorder in adult OCD patients may be less than previously believed (Joffe *et al.*, 1988). The limitations of standardized instruments for assessing personality disorders and the lack of paediatric indication for this diagnosis have obscured the issue. It is also possible that, even in preadolescents, compulsive personality disorder can develop as a secondary or adaptive response to very early-onset OCD.

Case illustrations

Case 1

A 14-year-old boy, whose symptoms had begun gradually, recalls at a very early age having to wash his hands repetitively. He was unable to associate an obsessive thought with this ritual, but he felt compelled to perform it. By age 6 years he had developed an obsessive fear of tornadoes. He would repeatedly check the sky for clouds, listen to all weather reports, and query his mother about approaching storms.

The tornado obsession faded over time and was replaced by a generalized fear of harm coming to himself or his family. He responded with extensive protective ritualization to keep his family safe and to protect himself. Particularly at times of separating, such as bedtime or leaving for school, the patient would be compelled to repeat actions perfectly or to check repetitively. When asked how many times he would have to repeat an action, he replied, 'It depends. The number isn't always the same, I just have to do it *right*'. When asked how he knew when it was right, he said, 'I don't know, it just *feels* right'.

As the patient entered puberty, he became obsessed with acquired immunodeficiency syndrome (AIDS) and was convinced that he would acquire it through his mouth. He began spitting in an effort to cleanse his mouth, and would spit every 15–20 seconds. In addition, he began extensive washing rituals. Despite these cleansing and washing compulsions, his personal appearance was slovenly and dirty. He never tied his shoelaces because they had touched the ground and were 'contaminated'; if he tied them, his hands would be 'dirty' and he would have to wash until they were 'clean' again. Remarkably, although his family was aware that 'something has been wrong for a long time', most of the content of his obsessions was kept secret. This case illustrates the quite usual variety of symptoms with change over time; exacerbation of washing rituals is common in puberty.

Case 2

A 16-year-old girl had symptoms that began abruptly, shortly after the onset of menses. She called herself 'a prisoner of my own mind'. Her obsessions centred around fear of harm to her parents. She was plagued by recurrent thoughts of her mother dying in a car accident, her father being killed by an intruder, or both her parents dying of burns received in a house fire. Always a light sleeper, she began to get up during the night to check. She spent hours checking that the doors were locked, that the coffee pot was unplugged, and that the family dog was safely ensconced in the garage. Despite her obsessions about fire, however, she did not check the smoke detector, an excellent example of the irrationality of this superficially rational disorder.

She involved her family in her rituals. Her mother made a checklist that the daughter carried to school, and both parents had to check the 24 items on the list, signing that they had done so. At night, she would wake her father to help her check. The family involvement was so profound that behavioural treatment could only take place after a period of family counselling in which the parents were helped to separate from their daughter's illness.

Differential diagnosis and obsessive-compulsive spectrum concept

The broad comorbidity of OCD and array of associated features makes the diagnosis in theory seem difficult; in practice, however, it is usually quite straightforward to decide if true clinical obsessions and/or compulsions are present rather than symptoms of another disorder such as depressive rumi-

nations or phobic avoidance. For example, when OCD is comorbid with bulimia or anorexia, the content of the obsessions or compulsions must be typical, e.g. washing, arranging, counting, and not fixed overfocused ideas about food, diet, etc. Phobic disorders are similarly distinguished by the content of the preoccupation (more often heights, spiders, the dark, etc.) and by the absence of discomfort when the phobic object is absent. Because of the common comorbidity of OCD and other anxiety disorders, however, simultaneous separation anxiety and even social phobia are seen together with classic OCD even in young children. Depressive ruminations are distinguished by their content, as are psychotic preoccupations.

The differential diagnosis from Tourette's is the most problematic, and the relationship between the two disorders remains obscure. Distinguishing between a compulsion or a tic may be difficult, as patients with Tourette's syndrome often have complex behavioural overlay on their tics. Some 20–80% patients with clear Tourette's have been reported to have obsessive-compulsive symptoms or OCD, and this has been documented in several studies (Frankel *et al.*, 1986; Pauls *et al.*, 1986; Grad *et al.*, 1987). While in theory the two disorders could be closely associated disorders (comparable to the relationship between anxiety and depression, for example), the strong relationship suggests instead a common aetiology, at least for some cases.

A subgroup of OCD (particularly in males with early onset who also have tics) may represent an alternative form of Tourette's. In Tourette's, there is an increased familial rate of OCD independently of the presence of obsessive-compulsive symptoms in the proband. Increased familial rates of Tourette's and tics are seen with OCD probands, particularly for their male relatives (Leonard *et al.*, 1992).

Any Tourette's–OCD formulation, however, is likely to be oversimplified; OCD unrelated to Tourette's syndrome (e.g. without tics or attention deficit disorder (ADD) or in females with later onset) is associated with a variety of other basal ganglia disorders. As discussed below, both Tourette's and OCD may be manifestations of basal ganglia dysfunction secondary to a number of causes, including genetic, toxic, traumatic and infectious agents.

Concept of obsessive-compulsive spectrum

The greater focus on the complex perseverative motor pattern in the early years of the disorder has led to a consideration of a broad group of behaviours in relation to OCD. Firstly, it is clear that the everyday habits or isolated mannerisms so common in normal development seem quite discontinuous from OCD as these had no predictive significance within a community sample (Berg *et al.*, 1989a) and as discussed below (Leonard *et al.*, 1990). At least some other repetitive unwanted behaviours of childhood onset may fall into an obsessive-compulsive spectrum crossing current diagnostic categories. For example, trichotillomania (compulsive hair-pulling) and onychophagia (pathological nail-biting), two disorders (the former is grouped as an impulsive disorder, not otherwise classified; the latter is not mentioned in DSM-III-R), may actually be variants of OCD. The phenomenology, treatment response and associated disorders suggest that these too are 'hard-wired', inappropriately released grooming behaviours (Swedo, 1989; Swedo *et al.*, 1989a; Leonard *et al.*, 1991b). Eating disorders, paraphilias, kleptomania and compulsive gambling have also been suggested as candidates for an obsessive-compulsive spectrum of behaviours responding to serotonin reuptake blocking drugs. Treatment studies are the least informative with respect to classification. However, selective benefit of serotonin reuptake blockers (in comparison to desipramine, an effective antidepressant without serotonergic reuptake properties), which is a treatment profile unique to OCD and *not* seen in depression, has now been demonstrated for both trichotillomania (Swedo *et al.*, 1989a) and severe pathological nail-biting (Leonard *et al.*, 1991b). A more cogent argument for an obsessive-compulsive spectrum would come from evidence of genetic relatedness. Family studies of trichotillomania have found increased rate of OCD (as well as trichotillomania) in first-degree relatives (Lenane *et al.*, 1992). Other putative spectrum disorders have not been studied from this perspective.

OCD's current categorization as an anxiety disorder is not ideal. But the complexity of the new familial, biological and pharmacological links argues against any change until more consistent information becomes available.

THEORIES OF AETIOLOGY AND CURRENT RESEARCH

Psychological factors

Psychological theories of OCD have encompassed psychoanalytic as well as more general nonpsychodynamic aetiological hypotheses. For example, Kanner (1962), favouring a psychological explanation, stated that children with OCD were often reared with an 'overdose of parental perfectionism'. It is ironic that Freud's 1909 case of the Rat Man has been seen for so long as a paradigm of a psychologically determined illness. In that case, the central role of ambivalence, anal sadistic concerns with control, and the salience of defences of reaction formation, intellectualization, isolation and undoing are made clear as well as the critical importance of magical thinking. Freud (1913) went on to formulate a theory of pregenital organization of the libido determined by constitutional rather than experimental factors, and crucial to the obsessional neurosis. The constitutional factors were again stressed by Anna Freud (1965), who claimed no single predisposing feature for obsessive-compulsive children. There has been little support from the psychoanalytic literature for psychogenic aetiology and an impressive array of child psychoanalytic writers have pointed out the spectrum of premorbid personalities that exist in OCD and the extreme difficulty — if not impossibility — in treating severe OCD psychoanalytically (Esman, 1989). Isolated case reports of posttraumatic OCD following rape or incest are intriguing, however, and such phenomena should be studied systematically, before any simple pronouncement on psychological causation is made.

Implicit in most textbook descriptions of OCD has been the analogy to normal developmental phenomena and to superstitions. The magical thinking and ritualistic behaviours of common superstitions, although brief, ego-syntonic and non-interfering, hold obvious features in common with OCD. Superstitious rituals before sports events are particularly similar to obsessive-compulsive rituals. But it is not clear what such analogy really implies for OCD. Leonard *et al.* (1990), for example, found that superstitious beliefs or behaviours of children with OCD were no more severe or numerous than those of normal peers. Moreover, when 'micro episodes' of OCD resembling current presenting obsessive-compulsive symptoms were discounted, normal childhood developmental rituals also were not exaggerated. Thus OCD cannot be viewed as exaggerated behaviours on a continuum with population samples. The 'release' of OCD symptoms appears to be discontinuous from the cultural rituals and beliefs.

Because of the interest in both psychological and biological aspects of OCD, the interplay between cultural setting and presentation of OCD might shed light on the relative importance of these influences. What observations there are testify to the universality of washing rituals, and the similar pattern in sex ratio and age of presentation in childhood OCD in Japan (Honjo *et al.*, 1989) or India (Khanna & Srinath, 1988). Further studies are needed here, as if childhood-onset OCD were truly invariant across cultures that differed widely in their emphasis, for example, on hygiene, it would support a more biologically determined syndrome.

Fragmentary data suggest that in fact rather similar presentations can be found across cultures, such as one ethnopsychiatric study of rural Ghana (Field, 1960) in which cleaning rituals and irrational repugnant ideas about harm were readily recognizable.

The efficacy of behaviour therapy in OCD indicates at least some role for learning in the maintenance of OCD. The efficacy of this treatment does not prove a learning aetiology for OCD, but any theory, biological or psychological, must account for behaviour therapy's (usually partial) effect. To date, no systematic evidence for abnormal past learning experience has been shown for OCD, and within the behaviourist learning framework, the behavioural concept of preparedness has implicit the notion of canalized learning, as do all biological theories of OCD (Seligman, 1971; Marler, 1981).

Biological factors in OCD

Basal ganglia dysfunction

Understanding the aetiological role of the frontal lobe—basal ganglia circuits in OCD is one of the most exciting current challenges of psychiatry. Clues provided by historical reports of association with basal ganglia disease, brain-imaging techniques such as computed tomography (CT) and positron emission tomography (PET) and results of neurotransmitter and hormonal manipulations must be integrated into a neuropathological framework determined by basic scientific research. For reviews, see Wise and Rapoport (1989), Swedo and Rapoport (1990) and Rapoport (1991).

Association with basal ganglia disorders

The striking and selective association between OCD and basal ganglia disease is summarized in Table 25.3. The best description of neurologically based OCD comes from Constantin von Economo's treatise (1931) on postencephalitic Parkinson's disease, which followed an outbreak of encephalitis lethargica in 1916–1917. Von Economo (1931) noted the compulsory nature of the motor tics and ritual-like behaviours that his patients exhibited. His neuropathological examinations revealed primarily basal ganglia destruction. Von Economo's patients, like OCD patients, described 'having to' act, while not 'wanting to' — i.e. they experienced a neurologically based loss of volitional control.

The association between Tourette's disorder, a presumed basal ganglia disorder, and OCD (Frankel *et al.*, 1986; Pauls *et al.*, 1986) has been noted earlier: the increased incidence of motor tics observed in children and adolescents with OCD, as well as choreiform movements, all suggest basal ganglia pathology in association with OCD (Denckla, 1989; Wise & Rapoport, 1989).

Sydenham's chorea (SC) is a basal ganglia disorder characterized by sudden involuntary, purposeless, jerking movements of the extremities. Husby *et al.* (1976) demonstrated antibodies directed against the cytoplasm of the subthalamic and caudate nuclei in patients with SC, to a greater extent than in those patients with rheumatic fever (RF) without chorea. The association between OCD and SC was noted by Chapman *et al.* (1958), who reported obsessive-compulsive symptoms in 4 of 8 children with SC, and by Freeman and colleagues (1965) in their comparison of adults with and without a history of SC during childhood.

A systematic investigation of obsessive-compulsive symptoms in 23 children and adolescents with an episode of SC revealed increased OCD and obsessive-compulsive symptoms as compared to a group of 14 RF controls (Swedo *et al.*, 1989b). SC patients scored significantly higher than did RF patients on the Yes and Interference scales of the Leyton Obsessional Inventory — Child Version. Three of the SC and none of the RF patients had significant obsessional interference and met DSM-III criteria for OCD. It is particularly noteworthy that the increase in compulsive behaviours and obsessive thoughts occurred selectively in the SC patients, as SC differs from RF only in the presence of basal ganglia dysfunction in SC and its absence in RF. Current research with acute SC subjects shows a parallel course between onset and decline of chorea and of obsessive-compulsive symptoms (S. Swedo, unpublished data).

As seen in Table 25.3, a number of basal ganglia disorders are associated with OCD. Several are under current investigation, including those which have their onset in childhood or adolescence. Specific basal ganglia lesions in individuals also have resulted in obsessive-compulsive behaviours (see Laplane *et al.*, 1984; Rapoport, 1991).

Surgical lesions that result in the disconnection of the basal ganglia from the frontal cortex are therapeutic in OCD (Chiocca & Martzuzza, 1990; Mindus, 1991). Currently, the preferred psychosurgeries for OCD are capsulotomy and cingulectomy. In capsulotomy, bilateral basal lesions are made in the anterior limb of the internal capsule in order to interrupt frontal–cingulate projections; however, the surgical target lies within the striatum, near the caudate nuclei. In order to perform a cingulectomy, the surgeon lesions the anterior portion of the cingulate gyrus, interrupting tracks between the cingulate gyrus and the frontal lobes and destroying all of the efferent projections of the anterior cingulate cortex. Both

Table 25.3 Regional effects of basal ganglia disease and association with obsessive-compulsive disorder (OCD)

Disease	Cause	Basal ganglia area most affected	Most prominent signs	Association with OCD
Sydenham's chorea	Autoimmune cross-reaction in streptococcus A/B	Caudate and putamen	Chorea	+++
Huntington's chorea	Genetic	Caudate and putamen	Chorea	+
Wilson's disease	Genetic	Putamen and caudate	Tremor and rigidity	?
Vascular disease	Vascular	Putamen	Dystonia	+
Parkinson's disease				
Idiopathic	Unknown	SNC	Akinetic rigidity	−
Postencephalitic	Infection	SNC	Akinetic rigidity	++
Seqawa's dystonia	Genetic	Unknown	Dystonia	++
Tourette's disorder	Genetic	Unknown	Motor/vocal tics	+++

procedures result in significant reduction of obsessions and compulsions. The success of psychosurgery is, of course, not conclusive evidence of a basal ganglia defect in OCD, as the lesions could be anywhere 'upstream' from the site of treatment, but it does contribute to a biological model and focuses interest on frontal—striatal tracts.

As summarized elsewhere (Rapoport, 1991) several brain-imaging studies implicate frontal lobes and basal ganglia in OCD. A volumetric analysis of noninfusion head CTs from 10 males with childhood-onset OCD and 10 healthy controls found the caudate nuclei significantly smaller in the OCD group (Luxenberg et al., 1988). The lack of radioactive exposure in magnetic resonance imaging will allow for direct examination of children and adolescents, and comparison with a group of normal controls, but to date this CT finding has not been replicated.

Four ^{18}FDG PET studies conducted at the NIMH and University of California at Los Angeles have found regional glucose metabolism in OCD to be elevated in the orbital frontal cortex, cingulate gyri and/or caudate nuclei of the OCD patient groups (Baxter et al., 1985, 1987). In general, the studies have been consistent in these selective increases in these areas. These findings are consistent with the hypothesized basal ganglia—frontal lobe dysfunction of OCD (Swedo et al., 1989d; Wise & Rapoport, 1989). Moreover, the findings are both replicable and the particular pattern appears specific to OCD (Baxter et al., 1987).

Implicit in a basal ganglia model is a neuroethological perspective on OCD (Swedo, 1989) in which OC symptoms are viewed as inappropriately released fixed patterns. The adaptive significance of such innate specification is related to the nonrandom structure of natural environments.

All current models, both biological and psychological, fail to account for the episodic nature of the disease, i.e. its waxing and waning course, and the behavioural specificity of the disorder — washers wash and checkers check. To date, however, the notion of obsessive and compulsive behaviour, as an expression of basal ganglia disorder has been most useful, accounting for a wide variety of observations and predicting others.

H_2-receptors, cholinergic and α-receptors, and has antidopaminergic properties). Its metabolite, desmethylchlomipramine, also effectively blocks serotonin reuptake. Fluoxetine, which also appears effective in childhood OCD, has a highly potent and selective serotonin reuptake-inhibiting effect (Riddle et al., 1989; Leonard et al., 1991c).

The response of childhood OCD to CMI and not to the equally effective antidepressant desipramine (DMI), as discussed elsewhere in this chapter (Leonard et al., 1989a), indicates a remarkable specificity of effect for the serotonin uptake inhibitors for this condition.

No unselected group of depressed patients, for example, would show such a differential response. Thus, the profile of drug response in OCD differs from that seen in depression or anxiety disorders which respond to a broad array of antidepressants and antianxiety agents and which highlight a unique role for serotonin blockers in this disorder.

In a study with children and adolescents (Flament et al., 1985, 1987), response to CMI correlated with pretreatment platelet serotonin concentration. A high pretreatment level of serotonin was a strong predictor of clinical response and within this sample, platelet serotonin concentrations were lower in the more severely ill patients. However, there were no differences in serotonin concentration from age- and sex-matched controls.

Cerebrospinal fluid samples from 43 OCD children and adolescents participating in an ongoing study were analysed for cerebrospinal fluid monoamines in the largest cerebrospinal fluid study in OCD to date and the only one in childhood OCD (Swedo et al., 1992). Cerebrospinal fluid 5-hydroxyindole acetic acid, the major metabolite of serotonin, correlated most strongly with response to CMI; i.e. the most successful responders had the higher levels of 5-hydroxyindole acetic acid in the cerebrospinal fluid.

The serotonergic hypothesis is undoubtedly too simplistic to account for the efficacy of CMI and other serotonin reuptake blockers; the antiobsessional effect may actually result from an alteration in the balance of serotonin and the other monoamines and/or change in receptor functions (Murphy et al., 1989).

Serotonin, other neurotransmitters and hormones

The serotonergic hypothesis of OCD comes from the selective efficacy of drugs that have specific serotonergic activity (Insel et al., 1985), and challenge tests with metacholorophenyl-piperazine (mCPP), a serotonergic agonist (Murphy et al., 1989; Pigott et al., 1991). Challenges with mCPP (Zohar et al., 1987, 1988; Pigott et al., 1991) show that OCD symptoms may be exacerbated by this serotonin agonist. CMI may downregulate serotonergic responsivity and metergoline, a serotonin antagonist, may protect against mCPP's behavioural effect (Pigott et al., 1991).

The most widely studied of the antiobsessional drugs is CMI, which is a *relatively* selective and potent inhibitor of active serotonin uptake in the brain (it also blocks histamine

Other neurotransmitters

Dopaminergic dysfunction in OCD is suggested not only by the obsessive-compulsive symptoms in patients with basal ganglia disorders (see Table 25.3), but also by the increase in obsessive-compulsive symptoms following high-dose stimulant administration (Frye & Arnold, 1981) and occasional amelioration of symptoms following dopamine blocking agents (Goodman et al., 1990; Swedo & Rapoport, 1990). High-dose stimulant administration has been thought to result in simple stereotypies, rather than in more complex compulsive or obsessive behaviour; however, 'compulsive' symptoms following high-dose amphetamines have been observed in children with attention-deficit disorder and hyperactivity (Borcherding et al., 1990), particularly compulsive ritualization with high-dose d-amphetamine (1 mg/kg) and methylphenidate (2 mg/kg) administration. For example, a 7-year-old boy spent several hours each evening vacuuming the carpet in his home, and another played with Lego blocks for 2 days, stopping only to eat and sleep. As in OCD, these children may become overly concerned with details and erase holes in their papers trying to get a single letter perfectly shaped.

However, the obsessive-compulsive behaviours are not ego-dystonic in these stimulant-induced cases. (Borcherding *et al.*, 1990) has speculated that compulsions and obsessions may result from dopaminergic overactivity and that serotonin dysregulation is required for ego-dystonicity. Tourette's disorder and OCD may be at opposite ends of a spectrum of dopamine—serotonin disequilibrium. In Tourette's, dopaminergic overactivity overcomes serotonergic inhibition and results primarily in motor and vocal tics. By contrast, OCD is primarily a serotonergic defect. Here, a primary lack of serotonin results in an inability to inhibit normal dopaminergic activity and fixed action patterns (obsessions and compulsions) are inappropriately released. Ego-dystonicity could then be related to the primary serotonin defect, or secondary to the loss of volitional control (Swedo & Rapoport, 1990).

Neuroendocrine dysfunction

Although most OCD investigations concentrate on hormonal aberrations as secondary rather than primary to the disorder, case reports and anecdotal experience suggest that hormonal dysfunction and OCD may be aetiologically related (Swedo, 1989). OCD symptoms may be worse during early puberty, and female patients often experience an increase in obsessive thoughts and rituals immediately before their menses. A controlled study of the cyclicity of OCD symptoms in relationship to the menstrual cycle is currently under way. Other hints at neuroendocrine factors in OCD include postpartum OCD, and reports of successful antiandrogen therapy (Casas *et al.*, 1986). In the Spanish study, 5 out of 5 patients with OCD experienced a remission in their symptoms following treatment with cyproterone acetate, a potent antiandrogen. At the NIMH, 3 patients (2 boys ages 8 and 15, and 1 girl 14 years old) have been treated with spironolactone, a peripheral antiandrogen, particularly antitesterone agent, and testolactone, a peripheral antioestrogen medication. Both experienced a temporary reduction of obsessions and compulsions, but relapsed within 3—4 months (S. Swedo, unpublished observation).

In the epidemiological study of OCD in high school students cited earlier (Flament *et al.*, 1988), males with OCD were smaller and lighter than the community normal controls and males with other psychiatric illnesses (Hamburger *et al.*, 1989). There were no differences in the size of females with and without OCD. The small size of the OCD males could be due to an effective lack of growth hormone, or to a delay in the pubertal growth spurt, although of course, no causality is demonstrated by the relationship.

Ethology, animal grooming and contamination rituals

The focus on grooming behaviours in childhood-onset OCD, the links to trichotillomania and nail-biting and the neurobiological studies cited above contribute to our ethological perspective on OCD (Swedo, 1989; Winslow, 1989; Wise & Rapoport, 1989). It is beyond the scope of this chapter to review the extensive literature on hormones and animal grooming behaviour (see Swedo, 1989, for review). Because novelty and conflict situations are strong releasers of adrenocorticotrophic hormone (ACTH), resulting in increased grooming behaviour, it was hypothesized that ACTH was involved in animal grooming. Peripheral administration failed to elicit grooming behaviour, but intracerebral and intracranial injections of ACTH elicit a dose-dependent grooming response (see studies of Dunn *et al.*, 1979; Gispen & Isaacson, 1981). ACTH (1 μg) injected into the lateral ventricle of a rat causes it to groom for 90% of the subsequent hour, in a pattern indistinguishable from natural grooming. The ACTH response seems to be mediated by a variety of neurotransmitter systems, as dopaminergic antagonists and opiate antagonists prevent the ACTH grooming response. The similarities between this situationally inappropriate ritual and the repetitive behaviours of OCD are striking and worthy of further investigation.

An ethological bias on OCD still leaves entirely open the question of what sort of innate programmes could serve to focus the developing child's attention on particular aspects of environmental stimulation that forms blocks of behavioural organization, later 'released' as OCD. Adaptive significance of such innate specification is assumed, but runs the danger of teleological argument. The 'release' of obsessive-compulsive routines by certain stimuli does recall animal releasing mechanisms, but how particular stimuli (dirt, excretions) might become so potent remains obscure.

Wise and Rapoport (1989) have proposed a model in which the striatum functions as a feature detector/filter that triggers the release of species-typical behaviours. The ventromedial aspect of the caudate nucleus receives input from the anterior cingulate and orbital frontal cortex, and the other from cortical association areas thought to be involved in the recognition of objects and sounds (superior and inferior temporal areas). The caudate may act as the stimulus detector, and another portion of the striatum as the internal motivation detector. These striatal assemblies converge to inhibit pallidal discharge, resulting in expression of a fixed action pattern or behaviour. While evidence of selective response to certain stimuli has been demonstrated in normal infants (e.g. response to voice tones), no studies have yet been done on trigger stimuli in childhood OCD. Such studies, particularly with high-risk groups, would be of great interest.

TREATMENT

Behavioural treatment

In adults, behavioural treatment is established as a major

therapeutic tool in OCD. Behavioural treatment has not been systematically studied in children and adolescents, but what data there are suggests that the techniques employed with adults will also be appropriate for children (for reviews, see Wolff & Rapoport, 1988; Berg *et al.*, 1989b).

Only 20 publications on the use of behavioural treatment of OCD in children could be found since 1967. All were clinical reports consisting of only 1 or 2 patients, except for the reports by Apter *et al.* (1984) and Bolton *et al.* (1983) of 8 and 15 patients respectively. The use of concurrent treatments, absence of baseline observations or established treatment time course, and the use of mixed objective rating scales for obsessions, anxiety and fear make these papers only suggestive.

Response prevention was the predominant treatment (9 studies) but was usually utilized in addition to other treatment techniques. Bolton *et al.* (1983), in the largest paediatric behavioural report, a retrospective record analysis of children admitted to the hospital over a 4-year period, used response prevention in 11 of 15 obsessive adolescents. Follow-up of this group documented continued gains for over half of the sample. Response prevention with *in vivo* exposure, the most successful approach with adults, has been used successfully (Zikis, 1983; Apter *et al.*, 1984). Thought stopping for obsessive ruminations has also been sucessfully applied (Campbell, 1973; Friedman & Silvers, 1977).

The involvement of family members is an important consideration in behavioural treatment. Family dynamics and psychopathology in relationship to the OCD patient's treatment and recovery have been addressed in adults (Hoover & Insel, 1984) and for children (Hafner *et al.*, 1981). Familial over-involvement, marital stress and family psychopathology can interfere with the success of behaviour modification, so involving the family in a positive way is essential.

As long as the child is motivated and able to understand directions, he or she is suitable for behaviour treatment. Not surprisingly, cooperation of hospitalized adolescents is often a problem, as is the secretiveness of many of these patients.

For the cooperative child or adolescent, however, behavioural treatment usually starts with a careful listing of symptoms, time duration and triggering situations. Together with the therapist, the child works out a plan for gradually increasing exposure to the triggering stimuli (e.g. dirty hands) without carrying out the response (in this example, handwashing). An assistant may be employed to supervise the exercises for reassurance and/or to ensure compliance.

A major void in the literature is in studies comparing drug and behavioural treatments for unselected groups of OCD children. There are few guidelines to suggest which children will respond to which treatment, although 'pure' obsessions are more difficult to treat behaviourally than are rituals. Our clinical experience indicates that at least half of our referrals to local behaviour therapists do not enter into treatment because either the symptoms are not considered amenable to behavioural control (e.g. obsessions predominant) or the child is not able to comply. Referral for behaviour therapy remains a complex clinical balance between the availability of behav-

ioural treatment, cooperation on the part of the child, and the child's symptom pattern.

Pharmacological treatment

In contrast to remarkable resistance to traditional psychotherapeutic interventions, numerous controlled trials in adults have shown the efficacy of drug treatment with the serotonin reuptake blocker CMI for OCD (Zohar *et al.*, 1987), and in two studies (Flament *et al.*, 1985; Leonard *et al.*, 1989b), to paediatric cases. Doses resembled those for adults (up to 3 mg/kg as tolerated).

A mean dose ($\pm$ s.d.) of 140 ($\pm$ 30) mg/day for adolescents produced improvement in symptoms that could usually be seen by 3 weeks, and 75% of child or adolescent patients had some degree of improvement. Drug response could not be predicted from baseline measures of age, intelligence, mode or age of onset, or duration or severity of illness. As with adults, drug-induced improvement was independent of initial depression (although primarily depressed subjects had been excluded; Flament *et al.*, 1985).

CMI was also significantly better than DMI, a selective noradrenergic reuptake blocker, in ameliorating the OCD symptoms by week 5 ($p = 0.001$ on the NIMH OCD Scale), while DMI was no more effective in improving OC symptoms than placebo had been in the Flament *et al.* (1985) study (Leonard *et al.*, 1989b). In fact, when DMI was given as the second active medication, in the crossover, 64% of patients experienced some degree of relapse. Depression ratings also increased during DMI, probably due to the demoralization experienced by the patients as their obsessive-compulsive symptoms returned. CMI was in general well-tolerated, but it has a slightly higher incidence of tremor and 'other' (sweating, flushing, middle insomnia) side-effects than do other tricyclic antidepressants in children (Leonard *et al.*, 1989b).

Fluoxetine, a bicyclic serotonin reuptake blocker, has been reported to be effective for OCD in adults in open studies (Fontaine & Chouinard, 1986; Jenike *et al.*, 1989) and in a single-blind trial (Turner *et al.*, 1985). A multicentre controlled trial is ongoing for adults with OCD. Fluoxetine is currently available by prescription, with an indicated use as an antidepressant for adults. Its safety and efficacy in the paediatric age group have not yet been established, although there are numerous anecdotal reports of efficacy in children. Riddle *et al.* (1989) concluded that fluoxetine appeared to be safe and well-tolerated in dosages of 10–40 mg day in a group of 10 children and adolescents with primary OCD, or Tourette's syndrome and OCD. A group of 15 adolescents who completed the NIMH trial and did not respond to, or could not tolerate CMI's side-effects, have been tried on fluoxetine without untoward side-effects and most showed a clinical response.

Augmentation of CMI with L-tryptophan and/or lithium to maximize a partial response has been reported to be beneficial in adult individuals (Rausmussen & Tsuang, 1984; Jenike *et al.*, 1989). Experience with augmentation in children is limited and remains to be explored.

In summary, the efficacy of CMI has been demonstrated for the treatment of childhood OCD, and is the current psychopharmacological treatment of choice. Fluoxetine may also prove to be safe and effective in the paediatric population, but systematic studies are needed.

An antiobsessional drug treatment may be needed for an indefinite duration. A controlled discontinuation study with a group of children with severe primary OCD who had been maintained on CMI for 4 months to 2 years found that almost all relapsed when DMI was (blindly) substituted (Leonard *et al.*, 1991a), in spite of the fact that drug control of symptoms was not complete. Ideally the combination of behaviour therapy with drug discontinuation may prevent such relapse, but this has yet to be demonstrated. As all of our patients ultimately are referred to behavioural treatment as well as drug treatment, we have no systematic data on the long-term relative benefits of either treatment.

Support groups

An important advance in the treatment of OCD has been the organization of support groups for patients and their families. Patients who previously had been secretive about their disorder showed immediate and warm response to the chance to share their difficulty with other sufferers. Their secrecy is usually secondary to fear of ridicule or, worse, fear that they will be considered 'crazy'.

Because avoidant behaviour is a complication of OCD, the support groups serve a social function for many. But the information-sharing is probably their major function and certainly those most successful groups have education, local referral service and information about research on OCD as their major goals. Groups vary to the extent that they have professional leadership, age separation or families separate from patients. In some sites, adolescent support groups have been particularly strong (Lenane, 1989).

The obvious benefit of these US groups has led to establishment of OCD support groups in Canada, Australia and Sweden, with new groups forming in a number of other countries as this is being written. Information on these groups and sample newsletters may be obtained from the OCD Foundation, PO Box 9573, New Haven, CT 06535, US. In the absence of such groups, clinicians are urged to help adolescent patients make contact with appropriate affected peers.

REFERENCES

Adams P.L. (1973) *Obsessive Children.* Penguin Books, New York.

American Psychiatric Association (1980) *Diagnostic and Statistical Manual of Mental Disorders*, 3rd edn. American Psychiatric Association, Washington DC.

American Psychiatric Association (1987) *Diagnostic and Statistical Manual of Mental Disorders*, 3rd edn, revised. American Psychiatric Association, Washington DC.

American Psychiatric Association (1994) *Diagnostic and Statistical Manual of Mental Disorders — 4th Edition — DSM-IV.* American Psychiatric Association, Washington DC.

Apter A., Berhout E. & Tyano S. (1984) Severe obsessive compulsive disorder in adolescence: a report of eight cases. *Journal of Adolescence*, **7**, 349–358.

Baxter L.R., Phelps M.E., Mazziotta J.C., Schwartz J.M., Gerner R.H., Selin C.E. & Sumida R.M. (1985) Cerebral metabolic rates for glucose in mood disorders: studies with positron emission tomography and fluorodeoxyglucose. *Archives of General Psychiatry*, **42**, 441–447.

Baxter L.R., Phelps M.E., Mazziotta J.E., Guze B.H., Schwartz M.J. & Selin C.E. (1987) Local cerebral glucose metabolic rates in obsessive-compulsive disorder: a comparison with rates in unipolar depression and in normal controls. *Archives of General Psychiatry*, **44**, 211–218.

Berg C.Z., Rapoport J.L., Whitaker A., Davies M., Leonard H., Swedo S.E., Braiman S. & Lenane M. (1989a) Childhood obsessive compulsive disorder: a two-year prospective follow-up of a community sample. *Journal of the American Academy of Child and Adolescent Psychiatry*, **28**, 528–533.

Berg C.Z., Rapoport J.L. & Wolff R.P. (1989b) Behavioral treatment for obsessive-compulsive disorder in children. In: Rapoport J.L. (ed) *Obsessive Compulsive Disorder in Children and Adolescents*, pp. 169–185. American Psychiatric Association, Washington DC.

Berman L. (1942) Obsessive-compulsive neurosis in children. *Journal of Nervous and Mental Disease*, **95**, 26–39.

Berrios G.E. (1989) Obsessive compulsive disorder: its conceptual history in France during the 19th century. *Comprehensive Psychiatry*, **30**, 283–295.

Black A. (1974) The natural history of obsessional neurosis. In: Beech H. (ed) *Obsessional States*, pp. 19–54. Methuen, London.

Black D., Yates W., Noyes R., Pfohl B. & Reich J. (1988) Personality disorder in obsessive compulsives. Presented at 137th Meeting of the American Psychiatric Association, Montreal, May 12, 1988.

Bolton D. & Turner T. (1984) Obsessive compulsive neurosis with conduct disorder: a report of two cases. *Journal of Child Psychology and Psychiatry*, **25**, 133–139.

Bolton D., Collins S. & Steinberg D. (1983) The treatment of obsessive-compulsive disorder in adolescence: a report of 15 cases. *British Journal of Psychiatry*, **142**, 456–464.

Borcherding B., Keysor C., Rapoport J.L., Elia J. & Amass J. (1990) Motor vocal tics and compulsive behaviors on stimulant drugs: is there a common vulnerability? *Psychiatry Research*, **33**, 83–94.

Campbell L. (1973) A variation of thought-stopping in a twelve year old boy: a case report. *Journal of Behavior Therapy and Experimental Psychiatry*, **4**, 69–70.

Casas M.E., Alvarez P., Duro C., Garcia Ribera C., Udina C., Velat A., Abella D., Rodriguez-Espinosa J., Salva P. & Jane F. (1986) Antiandrogenic treatment of obsessive compulsive neurosis. *Acta Psychiatrica Scandinavica*, **73**, 221–222.

Chapman A.H., Pilkey L. & Gibbons M.J. (1958) A psychosomatic study of eight children with Sydenham's chorea. *Pediatrics*, **21**, 582–595.

Chiocca E.A. & Martzuzza R. (1990) Neurosurgical therapy of obsessive compulsive disorder. In: Jenike M., Baer L. & Minichiello W. (eds) *Obsessive Compulsive Disorders: Theory and Management*, pp. 283–294. Year Book, Littleton, MA.

Denckla M.B. (1989) The neurological examination. In: Rapoport J.L. (ed) *Obsessive Compulsive Disorder in Children and Adolescents*, pp. 107–118. American Psychiatric Press, Washington DC.

Despert L. (1955) Differential diagnosis between obsessive-compulsive neurosis and schizophrenia in children. In: Hoch P.H. & Zubin J. (eds) *Psychopathology of Childhood*, pp. 240–253. Grune & Stratton, New York.

Dunn A.J., Green E.J. & Isaacson R.L. (1979) Intracerebral adrenocorticotropic hormone mediates novelty-induced grooming in the rat. *Science*, **203**, 281–283.

Esman A. (1989) Psychoanalysis and general psychiatry: obsessive-compulsive disorder as paradigm. *Journal of the American Psychoanalytic Association*, **37**, 319–336.

Field M. (1960) *An Ethno-psychiatric Study of Rural Ghana*, pp. 399–406. Northwestern University Press, Evanston, IL.

Flament M.F., Rapoport J.L., Berg C.J., Sceery W., Kilts C., Mellstrom B. & Linnoila M. (1985) Clomipramine treatment of childhood compulsive disorder: a double-blind controlled study. *Archives of General Psychiatry*, **42**, 977–983.

Flament M.F., Rapoport J.L., Murphy D.L., Berg C.J. & Lake R. (1987) Biochemical changes during clomipramine treatment of childhood obsessive compulsive disorder. *Archives of General Psychiatry*, **44**, 219–225.

Flament M.F., Whitaker A., Rapoport J., Davis M., Berg C.Z., Kalikow K., Sceery W. & Shaffer D. (1988) Obsessive compulsive disorder in adolescence. *Journal of the American Academy of Child and Adolescent Psychiatry*, **27**, 764–771.

Flament M.F., Koby E., Rapoport J.L., Berg C.J., Zahn T., Cox C., Denckla M. & Lenane M. (1990) Childhood obsessive-compulsive disorder: a prospective follow-up study. *Journal of Child Psychology and Psychiatry*, **31**, 363–380.

Fontaine R. & Chouinard G. (1986) An open clinical trial of fluoxetine in the treatment of obsessive compulsive disorder. *Journal of Clinical Psychopharmacology*, **6**, 98–101.

Frankel M., Cummings J.L., Robertson M.M., Trimble M.R., Hill M.A. & Benson D.F. (1986) Obsessions and compulsions in Gilles de la Tourette's syndrome. *Neurology (NY)*, **36**, 378–382.

Freeman J., Aron A.M., Collard J. & MacKay M.C. (1965) The emotional correlates of Syndenham's chorea. *Pediatrics*, **35**, 42–49.

Freud A. (1965) *Normality and Pathology in Childhood*. International University Press, New York.

Freud S. (1895) Obsessions and phobias: their physical mechanisms and their etiology. In: Strachey J (ed) *The Standard Edition of the Complete Psychological Works of Sigmund Freud*, vol. 1, (1957) pp. 128–137. Hogarth Press, London.

Freud S. (1909) Notes on a case of obsessional neurosis. In Strachey J. (ed) *The Standard Edition of the Complete Psychological Works of Sigmund Freud*, vol. 10 (1957), pp. 153–318. Hogarth Press, London.

Freud S. (1913) The predisposition to obsessional neurosis. In: Strachey J. (ed) *The Standard Edition of the Complete Psychological Works of Sigmund Freud*, vol. 12 (1957), pp. 311–326. Hogarth Press, London.

Friedman C. & Silvers F. (1977) A multimodality approach to inpatient treatment of obsessive compulsive disorder. *American Journal of Psychotherapy*, **31**, 456–465.

Frye P. & Arnold L. (1981) Persistent amphetamine-induced compulsive rituals: response to pyridoxine (B_6). *Biological Psychiatry*, **16**, 583–587.

Gispen W.H. & Isaacson R.L. (1981) ACTH-induced excessive grooming in the rat. *Pharmacology and Therapeutics*, **12**, 209–240.

Goodman W.K., Price L.H., Rasmussen S.A., Mazure C., Fleischmann R.L., Hill C.L., Heninger G.R. & Charney D.S. (1989) The Yale–Brown Obsessive Compulsive Scale. I. Development, use and reliability. *Archives of General Psychiatry*, **46**, 1006–1011.

Goodman W.K., Mcdougle C.J., Price L.H., Riddle M.A., Pauls, D.L. & Leckman J.F. (1990) Beyond the serotonin hypothesis: a role for dopamine in some forms of obsessive compulsive disorder? *Journal of Clinical Psychiatry*, **51** (suppl), 36–43.

Grad L.R., Pelcovitz D., Olson M., Mathews M. & Grad G.J. (1987) Obsessive-compulsive symptomatology in children with Tourette's syndrome. *Journal of the American Academy of Child Psychiatry*, **26**, 69–73.

Hafner R., Gilchrist P. & Bowling J. (1981) The treatment of obsessional neurosis in a family setting. *Australian and New Zealand Journal of Psychiatry*, **15**, 145–151.

Hamburger S.D., Swedo S., Whitaker A., Davies M. & Rapoport J.L. (1989) Growth rate in adolescents with obsessive-compulsive disorder. *American Journal of Psychiatry*, **146**, 652–655.

Hollingsworth C.E., Tanguay P.E., Grossman L. & Pabst P. (1980) Long-term outcome of obsessive-compulsive disorder in childhood. *Journal of the American Academy of Child and Adolescent Psychiatry*, **19**, 134–144.

Honjo S., Hirano C.C., Murase S., Kaneko T., Sugiyama T., Ohtaka K., Aoyama T., Takei Y., Inoko K. & Wakabayashi S. (1989) Obsessive compulsive symptoms in childhood and adolescence. *Acta Psychiatrica Scandinavica*, **80**, 83–91.

Hoover C.F. & Insel T.R. (1984) Families of origin in obsessive compulsive disorder. *Journal of Nervous and Mental Disease*, **172**, 207–215.

Husby G., Van de Rijn I., Zabriskie J.B., Abdin Z.H. & Williams R.C. (1976) Antibodies reacting with cytoplasm of subthalamic and caudate nuclei neurons in chorea and acute rheumatic fever. *Journal of Experimental Medicine*, **144**, 1094–1110.

Insel T.R., Mueller E.A., Alterman I., Linnoila M.M. & Murphy D.L. (1985) Obsessive-compulsive disorder and serotonin: is there a connection? *Biological Psychiatry*, **20**, 1174–1188.

Janet P. (1903) *Les Obsessions et la Psychiatrie*, vol. 1. Felix Alan, Paris.

Jenike M.A., Buttolph L., Baer L., Ricciardi J. & Holland A. (1989) Open trial of fluoxetine in obsessive-compulsive disorder. *American Journal of Psychiatry*, **146**, 909–911.

Joffe R., Swinson R. & Regan J. (1988) Personality features of obsessive compulsive disorder. *American Journal of Psychiatry*, **45**, 1127–1129.

Kanner L. (1962) *Child Psychiatry*, 3rd edn. Charles C. Thomas, Springfield, IL.

Karno M. & Golding J. (1990) Obsessive compulsive disorder. In: Robins L. & Regrer D.A. (eds) *Psychiatric Disorders in America: The Epidemiologic Catchment Area Study*. Free Press, New York.

Karno M., Golding J., Sorenson S. & Burnam A. (1988) The epidemiology of obsessive compulsive disorder in five US communities. *Archives of General Psychiatry*, **45**, 1094–1099.

Khanna S. & Srinath S. (1988) Childhood obsessive compulsive disorder. *Psychopathology*, **21**, 254–258.

Laplane D., Baulac M., Widlocher D. & Dubois B. (1984) Pure psychic akinesia with bilateral lesions of basal ganglia. *Journal of Neurology, Neurosurgery and Psychiatry*, **47**, 377–385.

Lenane M. (1989) Support groups. In: Rapoport J. (ed) *Obsessive Compulsive Disorder in Children and Adolescents*. American Psychiatric Press, Washington DC.

Lenane M.C., Swedo S.E., Leonard H.L., Pauls D.L., Sceery W. & Rapoport J.L. (1990) Psychiatric disorders in first degree relatives of children and adolescents with obsessive compulsive disorder. *Journal of the American Academy of Child and Adolescent Psychiatry*, **29**, 407–412.

Lenane M.C., Swedo S.E., Rapoport J.L., Leonard H., Sceery W. & Guroff J.K. (1992) Rates of obsessive compulsive disorder in first degree relatives of patients with trichotillomania: a research note. *Journal of Child Psychology and Psychiatry*, **33**, 925–933.

Leonard H.L., Swedo S., Rapoport J., Koby E., Lenane M., Cheslow D. & Hamburger S. (1989a) Treatment of childhood obsessive compulsive disorder with clomipramine and desmethylimipramine: a double-blind crossover comparison. *Archives of General Psychiatry*, **46**, 1088–1092.

Leonard H.L., Goldberger E.L., Rapoport J.L., Cheslow D.L. & Swedo S.E. (1990) Childhood rituals: normal development or obsessive compulsive symptoms? *Journal of the American Academy of Child and Adolescent Psychiatry*, **29**, 17–23.

Leonard H.L., Swedo S., Lenane M., Rettew D., Cheslow D., Hamburger S.D. & Rapoport J.L. (1991a) A double-blind desipramine substitution during long-term clomipramine treatment in children and adolescents with obsessive compulsive disorder. *Archives of General Psychiatry*, **48**, 922−926.

Leonard H.L., Lenane M., Swedo S., Rettew D. & Rapoport J. (1991b) A double-blind comparison of clomipramine and desipramine treatment of severe onychophagia (nailbiting). *Archives of General Psychiatry*, **48**, 821−827.

Leonard H.L., Swedo S.E. & Rapoport J.L. (1991c) Diagnosis and treatment of obsessive compulsive disorder in children and adolescents. In: Pato M.T. & Zohar J. (eds) *Current Treatments of Obsessive Compulsive Disorder Clinical Practice #18*, pp. 87−102. American Psychiatric Association Press, Washington DC.

Leonard H.L., Lenane M., Swedo S., Rettew D., Gershon E. & Rapoport J.L. (1992) Tics and Tourette's syndrome: a 2 to 7 year follow-up of 54 obsessive compulsive children. *American Journal of Psychiatry*, **149**, 1244−1251.

Leonard H.L., Swedo S., Lenane M., Rettew D.C., Hamburger M.S., Bartko J.J. & Rapoport L.L. (1993) A two to seven year follow-up study of 54 obsessive compulsive children and adolescents. *Archives of General Psychiatry*, **50**, 429−438.

Lewis S., Chitkara B. & Revely A.M. (1991) Obsessive compulsive disorder and schizophrenia in the three identical twin pairs. *Psychological Medicine*, **21**, 135−141.

Luxenberg J.S., Swedo S.E., Flament M.F., Friedland R.P., Rapoport J.L. & Rapoport S.I. (1988) Neuroanatomic abnormalities in obsessive-compulsive disorder detected with quantitative x-ray computed tomography. *American Journal of Psychiatry*, **145**, 1089−1093.

Marler P. (1981) Innate programs for perceptual development: An ethological view. In: Gollin E.S. (ed) *Developmental plasticity: Behavioral DNA Biological Aspects of Variations in Development*, pp. 135−172. Academic Press, New York.

Mindus P. (1991) *Capsulotomy in Anxiety Disorders: A Multidisciplinary Study*. Karolinska Institute Press, Stockholm.

Murphy D., Zohar J., Pato M., Pigott T. & Insel T. (1989) obsessive compulsive disorder as a 5 HT subsystem behavioral disorder. *British Journal of Psychiatry*, **155** (suppl), 15−24.

Pauls D.L., Towbin K.E., Leckman J.F., Zahner G.E.P. & Cohen D. (1986) Gilles de la Tourette's syndrome and obsessive-compulsive disorder: evidence supporting a genetic relationship. *Archives of General Psychiatry*, **43**, 1180−1182.

Pigott T.A., Zohar J., Hill J.L., Berstein S.E., Grover G.N., Zohar-Kadouch R.C. & Murphy D.L. (1991) *Biological Psychiatry*, **29**, 418−426.

Rapoport J.L. (1986) Annotation: childhood obsessive compulsive disorder. *Journal of Child Psychology and Psychiatry*, **27**, 289−296.

Rapoport J.L. (ed) (1989a) *Obsessive Compulsive Disorder in Children and Adolescents*. American Psychiatric Press, New York.

Rapoport J.L. (1989b) The neurobiology of obsessive compulsive disorder. *Journal of the American Medical Association*, **260**, 2888−2890.

Rapoport J.L. (1989c) The new biology of obsessive compulsive disorder. *Scientific American*, **260**, 82−89.

Rapoport J.L. (1989d) Childhood obsessive compulsive disorder. *Journal of Child Psychology and Psychiatry*, **27**, 289−295.

Rapoport J.L. (1989e) *The Boy Who Couldn't Stop Washing*. E.P. Dutton, New York.

Rapoport J.L. (1991) Recent advances in obsessive compulsive disorder. *Neuropsychopharmacology*, **5**, 1−9.

Rasmussen S.A. & Tsuang M.T. (1984) The epidemiology of obsessive compulsive disorder. *Journal of Clinical Psychiatry*, **45**, 450−457.

Riddle M., Hardin M. & King R. (1989) Fluoxetine treatment of children and adolescents with Tourette's and obsessive compulsive disorders. Paper presented at Annual Meeting of the American Academy of Child and Adolescent Psychiatry. New York, October, 1989.

Robins L., Helzer J., Crougham J. & Ratcliffe K. (1981) The NIMH epidemiologic catchment area study. *Archives of General Psychiatry*, **38**, 381−389.

Seligman M. (1971) Phobias and preparedness. *Behavior Therapy*, **2**, 307−320.

Shaffer D., Schonfeld I., O'Connor P.A., Stockman C., Trautman P., Shafer S. & Ng S. (1985) Neurological soft signs: their relationship to psychiatric disorders and intelligence in childhood and adolescence. *Archives of General Psychiatry*, **44**, 342−351.

Swedo S. (1989) Rituals and releasers: an ethological model of OCD. In: Rapoport J.L. (ed) *Obsessive Compulsive Disorder in Children and Adolescents*, pp. 269−288. American Psychiatric Press, Washington DC.

Swedo S.E. & Rapoport J.L. (1990) Neurochemical and neuroendocrine considerations of obsessive-compulsive disorders in childhood. In: Deutsch S.I., Weizman A. & Weizman R. (eds) *Application of Basic Neurosciences to Child Psychiatry*, pp. 275−284. Plenum Medical Books, New York.

Swedo S.E., Leonard H.L., Rapoport J.L., Lenane M.C., Cheslow D.L. & Goldberger E.L. (1989a) Clomipramine vs. desmethylimipramine treatment of trichotillomania: a double-blind crossover comparison. *New England Journal of Medicine*, **321**, 497−501.

Swedo S.E., Rapoport J.L., Cheslow D.L., Leonard H.L., Ayoub E.M., Hosier D.M. & Wald E.R. (1989b) High prevalence of obsessive-compulsive symptoms in patients with Sydenham's chorea. *American Journal of Psychiatry*, **146**, 246−249.

Swedo S., Rapoport J.L., Leonard H.L., Lenane M. & Cheslow D. (1989c) Obsessive compulsive disorder in children and adolescents: clinical phenomenology of 70 consecutive cases. *Archives of General Psychiatry*, **46**, 335−341.

Swedo S.E., Schapiro M.B., Grady C.L., Cheslow D.L., Leonard H.L., Kumar A., Friedland R., Rapoport S.I. & Rapoport J.L. (1989d) Cerebral glucose metabolism in childhood-onset obsessive compulsive disorder. *Archives of General Psychiatry*, **46**, 518−523.

Swedo S., Leonard H.L., Kruesi M.J.P., Rettew D., Listwak S.J., Berrettini W., Stipetic M., Hamburger S., Gold P.W., Potter W.Z. & Rapoport J.L. (1992) Cerebrospinal fluid neurochemistry of children and adolescents with obsessive compulsive disorder. *Archives of General Psychiatry*, **49**, 29−36.

Turner S., Jacob R. & Beidel D. (1985) Fluoxetine treatment of obsessive compulsive disorder. *Journal of Clinical Psychopharmacology*, **5**, 207−212.

Von Economo C. (1931) *Encephalitis Lethargica: Its Sequelae and Treatment*. Oxford University Press, London.

Warren W. (1965) A study of adolescent psychiatric inpatients and the outcome six or more years later. *Journal of Child Psychology and Psychiatry*, **6**, 141−160.

Whitaker A., Johnson J., Schaffer D., Kalikow K., Walsh T., Davies M., Braimon S. & Dolinsky S. (1990) Uncommon troubles in young people: prevalence estimates of selected psychiatric disorders in a non-referred adolescent population. *Archives of General Psychiatry*, **47**, 487−496.

Winslow J. (1989) Neuroethology of obsessive-compulsive behavior. In: Zohar J., Rasmussen S. & Insel T. (eds) *Psychobiology of Obsessive Compulsive Disorder*, pp. 208−226. Springer Verlag, New York.

Wise S. & Rapoport J.L. (1989) Obsessive-compulsive disorder: is it basal ganglia dysfunction? In: Rapoport J.L. (ed) *Obsessive-Compulsive Disorder in Children and Adolescents*, pp. 327−347. American Psychiatric Press, Washington DC.

Wolff R.A. & Rapoport J.L. (1988) Behavioral treatment of childhood compulsive disorder. *Behavior Modification*, **12**, 252−266.

Zeitlin H. (1986) *The Natural History of Psychiatric Disorder in Children*.

Oxford University Press, New York.

Zikis P. (1983) Treatment of an 11 year old obsessive compulsive ritualizer tiqueur girl with *in vivo* exposure and response prevention. *Behavioural Psychotherapy*, **11**, 75−81.

Zohar J., Mueller E.A., Insel T.R., Zohar-Kadouch R. & Murphy D. (1987) Serotonergic responsitivity in obsessive-compulsive disorder: comparison of patients and healthy controls. *Archives of General Psychiatry*, **44**, 946−951.

Zohar J., Insel T., Zohar-Kadouch R., Zohar-Kadouch R. & Murphy D. (1988) Serotonergic responsivity in obsessive-compulsive disorder: effects of chronic clomipramine treatment. *Archives of General Psychiatry*, **45**, 167−172.

Chapter 26
Tic Disorders

James F. Leckman & Donald J. Cohen

Tic disorders are transient or chronic conditions associated with difficulties in self-esteem, family life, social acceptance or school or job performance that are directly related to the presence of motor and/or phonic tics. Although tic symptoms have been reported since antiquity, systematic study of individuals with tic disorders dates only from the 19th century with the reports of Itard (1825) and Gilles de la Tourette (1885). Gilles de la Tourette, in his classic study of 1885, described 9 cases of tic disorder characterized by motor 'inco-ordinations' or tics, 'inarticulate shouts accompanied by articulated words with echolalia and coprolalia'. In addition to identifying the cardinal features of severe tic disorders, his report noted an association between tic disorders and obsessive-compulsive symptoms as well as the hereditary nature of the syndrome in some families.

In addition to tics, individuals with tic disorders may present with a broad array of behavioural difficulties including disinhibited speech or conduct, impulsivity, distractibility, motoric hyperactivity and obsessive-compulsive symptoms (Leckman & Cohen, 1988). Professional opinion has been divided on how broadly to conceive the spectrum of maladaptive behaviours associated with Tourette's syndrome (Shapiro *et al.*, 1988). This controversy is fuelled in part by the genuine frustration that parents and educators encounter when they attempt to divide an individual child's repertoire of problem behaviours into those that are 'Tourette-related' and those that are not. Population-based epidemiological studies and family-genetic studies have begun to clarify these issues, but much work remains to be done.

In this chapter, a brief discussion of the phenomenology and classification of tic disorders precedes a review of the aetiology, neurobiological substrates, assessment and management of these conditions. The general perspective that will be presented is that Tourette's syndrome and other aetiologically related disorders, including some forms of obsessive-compulsive disorder, are model neurobiological disorders in which it may be possible to understand the genetic and environmental (epigenetic) mechanisms that interact to produce syndromes of varying severity. Advances in understanding the causes and determinants of tic disorders may lead to the development of more rational and effective interventions.

DEFINITIONS AND CLASSIFICATIONS

A tic is a sudden, repetitive movement, gesture or utterance that typically mimics some aspect or fragment of normal behaviour. Usually of brief duration, individual tics rarely last more than a second. Many tics tend to occur in bouts with a brief inter-tic interval. Individual tics can occur singly or together in an orchestrated pattern. They vary in their intensity or forcefulness. Motor tics vary from simple abrupt movements such as eye-blinking, head jerks or shoulder shrugs to more complex, purposive-appearing behaviours such as facial expressions or gestures of the arms or head. In extreme cases, these movements can be obscene (copropraxia) or self-injurious, e.g. hitting or biting. Phonic or vocal tics can range from simple throat-clearing sounds to more complex vocalizations and speech. In severe cases, coprolalia (obscene speech) is present.

By the age of 10 years, most individuals with tics are aware of premonitory urges that may either be experienced as a focal perception in a particular body region where the tic is about to occur (like an itch or a tickling sensation) or as a mental awareness (Leckman *et al.*, 1993). These premonitory phenomena contribute to an individual's sense that tics are a voluntary response to unpleasant stimuli that are momentarily relieved by the performance of tics. Indeed, most adolescent and adult subjects describe their tics as either voluntary or as having both voluntary and involuntary aspects (Lang, 1991). In contrast, many young children are oblivious to their tics and experience them as wholly involuntary movements or sounds. Most tics can also be suppressed for brief periods of time. The warning given by premonitory urges may contribute to this phenomenon.

Current classification of tic disorders in ICD-10 (World Health Organization, 1988) includes transient tic disorder (F95.0), chronic motor or vocal tic disorder (F95.1), combined vocal and multiple tic disorder (Tourette's syndrome; F95.2) and residual categories (F95.8 and F95.9). The ICD-10 diagnostic descriptions are largely based on the diagnostic criteria contained in DSM III-R and DSM-IV (American Psychiatric Association, 1987, 1993).

The ICD-10 descriptions focus on the phenomenology and natural history of the disorder and are readily applied in clinical settings. Objections can be raised to the statement contained in the description of Tourette's syndrome that 'tics disappear during sleep'. Based on several empirical studies, it appears that, although tics are markedly diminished during the sleep of children and adolescents with Tourette's syndrome, they do not disappear completely (Glaze *et al.*, 1983; Jankovic & Rohaidy, 1987). The statement that 'symptoms [tics] frequently worsen during adolescence', although consistent with clinical experience, is not well-supported by empirical data. The ICD-10 description of Tourette's syndrome also overlooks the frequent presence of premonitory urges, the bout-like occurrence of tics, the waxing and waning character of the disorder (with variations in the repertoire of tics occurring over weeks to months), and the usual amelioration of the condition that occurs during mid to late adolescence and early adulthood.

As with many other child psychiatric disorders, both the ICD-10 and DSM-IV groupings suffer from uncertainties on how best to categorize conditions that potentially encompass a broad range of symptoms that wax and wane in severity. The current nosological boundaries are set by convention and clinical usage and may not reflect true aetiological differences.

PREVALENCE

Transient tic behaviours are commonplace among children. Community surveys indicate that 1–13% of boys and 1–11% of girls manifest frequent 'tics, twitches, mannerisms or habit spasms' (Zahner *et al.*, 1988). The instability of these estimates is in part due to the wording of items on symptom inventories, the identity of the informant and the demographic characteristics of the sample studied. Children between the ages of 7 and 11 years appear to have the highest estimated prevalence rates, in the range of 5%. Although boys are more commonly affected with tic behaviours than girls, the male to female ratio in most community surveys is less than 2 : 1. For example, in the Isle of Wight study of 10–11-years-olds, 5.9% of boys and 2.9% of girls were reported by their parents to have 'twitches, mannerisms, tics of face or body' (Rutter *et al.*, 1970). Urban living may be associated with elevated rates (Rutter *et al.*, 1974). Although most reports on tics have come from European, American and Asian sources, race and socioeconomic status have not been shown to influence the point prevalence of tics.

Much less is known concerning the prevalence of tic disorders. Once thought to be rare, current estimates from registers of clinically diagnosed subjects and a single school surveillance study have arrived at relatively high but widely divergent prevalence estimates ranging from 2.9 per 10 000 in Monroe County, New York (Caine *et al.*, 1988) to 59 per 10 000 in a single California school district (Comings *et al.*, 1990). More recently, Apter and colleagues have reported a prevalence rate of 4.5 per 10 000 for full-blown Tourette's syndrome among 16–17-year-olds in Israel (Apter *et al.*, in press). The basis of these discrepancies may be due to methodological differences rather than true differences in prevalence rates. These data do provide evidence that children

are five to 12 times more likely to be identified as having a tic disorder than adults and that males are more commonly affected than females (with male-to-female ratios of 9 : 1 and 3 : 1 for children and adults respectively; Burd *et al.*, 1986a,b). Although other demographic characteristics have not been systematically investigated, some authors have suggested that tic disorders may be more common among Caucasian and oriental racial groups.

CLINICAL DESCRIPTIONS

With the exception of Tourette's syndrome (Bruun, 1988; Shapiro *et al.*, 1988), relatively few cross-sectional or longitudinal studies of tic disorders have been performed, so that most of the information provided below is based on clinical experience and anecdotal reports.

Transient tic disorder

Almost invariably a disorder of childhood, transient tic disorder is usually characterized by one or more simple motor tics that wax and wane in severity over weeks to months. The anatomical distribution of these tics is usually confined to the eyes, face, neck or upper extremities. Transient phonic tics, in the absence of motor tics, can also occur, though more rarely. The age of onset is typically 3–10 years. Boys are at greater risk. The initial presentation may be unnoticed. If medical consultation is sought, family practitioners, paediatricians, allergists and ophthalmologists are typically the first to see the child. Missed diagnoses are common, particularly as the symptoms may have completely disappeared by the time of the consultation. As prescribed by the prevailing diagnostic criteria, the subsequent natural history of this condition is limited to fewer than 12 consecutive months of active symptomatology. As such, this is often a retrospective diagnosis as the clinician is unable to know with certainty which children will show progression of their symptoms and which children will display a self-limiting course.

Chronic motor or vocal tic disorder

This chronic condition can be observed in children and adults. Like other tic disorders, it is characterized by a waxing and waning course and a broad range of severity. Chronic simple and complex motor tics are the most common manifestations. A majority of tics involve the eyes, face, head, neck and upper extremities. Although some children may display other developmental difficulties such as attention deficit hyperactivity disorder, the disorder is not incompatible with an otherwise normal course of childhood. This condition can also appear as a residual state, particularly in adulthood. In such instances, a predictable repertoire of tic symptoms may only be seen during periods of heightened stress or fatigue.

Chronic vocal tic disorder by all accounts is a rare condition. Some authors exclude 'chronic cough of adolescence' from this category (Shapiro *et al.*, 1988).

Tourette's syndrome (combined vocal and multiple motor tic disorder)

The most severe tic disorder is best known by the eponym Gilles de la Tourette's syndrome. Typically the disorder begins in early childhood with transient bouts of simple motor tics such as eye-blinking or head jerks. These tics may initially come and go, but eventually they become persistent and begin to have adverse effects on the child and family. The repertoire of motor tics can be vast, incorporating virtually any voluntary movement by any portion of the body. Although some patients have a rostral–caudal progression of motor tics (head, neck, shoulders, arms, torso), this course is not predictable. As the syndrome develops, complex motor tics may appear. Typically they accompany simple motor tics. Often they have a camouflaged or purposive appearance, e.g. brushing hair away from the face with an arm, and can only be distinguished as tics by their repetitive character. They can involve dystonic movements. In a small fraction of cases (< 5%), complex motor tics have the potential to be self-injurious and further to complicate management. These self-injurious symptoms may be relatively mild, e.g. slapping or tapping, or quite dangerous, e.g. punching one side of the face, biting a wrist or gouging eyes to the point of blindness.

On average, phonic tics begin 1–2 years after the onset of motor symptoms and are usually simple in character, for example, throat-clearing, grunting, squeaks. More complex vocal symptoms such as echolalia, palilalia and coprolalia occur in a minority of cases. Other complex phonic symptoms include dramatic and abrupt changes in rhythm, rate and volume of speech.

Motor and phonic tics tend to occur in bouts. Their frequency ranges from nonstop bursts that are virtually uncountable (> 100 tics per minute) to rare events that occur only a few times a week. Single tics may occur in isolation or there may be orchestrated combinations of motor and phonic tics that involve multiple muscle groups.

The forcefulness of motor tics and the volume of phonic tics can also vary tremendously from behaviours that are not noticeable (a slight shrug or a hushed guttural noise) to strenuous displays (arm thrusts or loud barking) that are frightening and exhausting.

By the age of 10, most children and adolescents have some awareness of the premonitory urges that frequently precede both motor and vocal tics (see above). These urges add to the subjective discomfort associated with having a tic disorder. They may also contribute to an individual's ability to suppress the tics for longer periods of time.

The factors that determine the degree of disability and handicap versus resiliency are largely unknown (see below) but are likely to include the presence of additional developmental, mental and behavioural disorders; the level of support and understanding from parents, peers, and educators; and the presence of special abilities (as in sports) or personal attributes (intelligence, social abilities and personality traits). The behavioural and emotional problems that frequently complicate Tourette's syndrome range from impulsive, dis-

inhibited and immature behaviour to compulsive touching or sniffing. At present, there are no clear dividing lines between these disruptive behaviours and complex tics on the one hand and comorbid conditions of attention deficit hyperactivity disorder and obsessive-compulsive disorder on the other. As described below, some of these conditions may be alternative expressions of the same underlying vulnerability such as obsessive-compulsive disorder; others may be intimately related by virtue of shared pathophysiological mechanisms such as attention deficit hyperactivity disorder; and still others may be the consequence of having a chronic disorder that is socially disfiguring, such as affective and anxiety syndromes. Defining the limits of tic disorders *vis à vis* other forms of psychopathology remains one of the most controversial and difficult areas for families, clinicians and researchers. Some investigators believe that the spectrum of Tourette's syndrome includes attentional deficits, impulsivity, hyperactivity, disruptive behaviour, learning disabilities, pervasive developmental disorders, affective and anxiety disorders, as well as tics and obsessive-compulsive disorder (Comings, 1990). Twin, family and genetic linkage studies in combination with prospective longitudinal studies of at-risk individuals and intensive neurobiological studies, have the potential to clarify these associations (Leckman *et al.*, 1987c).

Although most children with Tourette's syndrome are loving and affectionate, maintaining age-appropriate social skills appears to be a particularly difficult area for many patients with Tourette's syndrome (Dykens *et al.*, 1990; Stokes *et al.*, 1991). It is not uncommon to encounter children who are 2–4 years behind their age-mates in making and maintaining friendships. Whether this is due to the stigmatizing effects of the tics, the patient's own uneasiness, or some more fundamental difficulty linked to the neurobiology of this disorder is unknown.

Consistent with available epidemiological data, tic disorders tend to improve in late adolescence and early adulthood. In many instances, the phonic symptoms become increasingly rare or may disappear altogether, and the motor tics may be reduced in number and frequency. Complete remission of both motor and phonic symptoms has also been reported (Bruun, 1988; Shapiro *et al.*, 1988). In contrast, adulthood is also the period when the most severe and debilitating forms of tic disorder can be seen. The factors that influence the continuity of tic disorders from childhood to adolescence to adulthood are not well-understood but probably involve the interaction of normal maturational processes occurring in the central nervous system with the neurobiological mechanisms responsible for Tourette's syndrome, the exposure to cocaine, other CNS stimulants, androgenic steroids, and the amount of intramorbid emotional trauma and distress experienced by affected individuals during childhood and adolescence. In addition, it should be emphasized that tic disorders may be aetiologically separable, so that some of these factors may influence the pathogenesis and intramorbid course for some tic disorders but not others. Other factors may have a more uniform impact.

In contrast to this usual pattern of diminishing tic symptoms in early adulthood, it is not uncommon for patients to report an increase in their obsessive-compulsive symptoms.

AETIOLOGY AND PATHOGENESIS

During the course of the past decade, Tourette's syndrome and related conditions have emerged as model disorders for researchers interested in the interaction of genetic, neurobiological and environmental (non-genetic) factors which shape clinical outcomes from health to chronic disability over the life span.

Genetic factors

Twin and family studies provide evidence that genetic factors are involved in the vertical transmission within families of a vulnerability to Tourette's syndrome and related disorders (Pauls & Leckman, 1986, 1988). The concordance rate for Tourette's syndrome among monozygotic twin pairs is greater than 50% while the concordance of dizygotic twin pairs is about 10% (Price *et al.*, 1985). If co-twins with chronic motor tic disorder are included, these concordance figures increase to 77% for monozygotic and 30% for dizygotic twin pairs. Differences in the concordance of monozygotic and dizygotic twin pairs indicate that genetic factors play an important role in the aetiology of Tourette's syndrome and related conditions. These figures also suggest that nongenetic factors are critical in determining the nature and severity of the clinical syndrome.

Other studies indicate that first-degree family members of Tourette's syndrome probands are at substantially higher risk for developing Tourette's syndrome, chronic motor tic disorder and obsessive-compulsive disorder (OCD) than unrelated individuals (Pauls *et al.*, 1991). Overall, the risk to male first-degree family members approximates 50% (18% Tourette's syndrome, 31% chronic motor tics and 7% OCD) while the overall risk to females is less (5% Tourette's syndrome, 9% chronic motor tics and 17% OCD). These rates are substantially higher than might be expected by chance in the general population, and greatly exceed the rates for these disorders among the relatives of individuals with other psychiatric disorders except OCD.

The pattern of vertical transmission among family members has led several groups of investigators to test whether or not mathematical models of specific genetic hypotheses could account for these data. While not definitive, the bulk of this work favours models of autosomal dominant transmission (Pauls & Leckman, 1986, 1988). These studies have prompted the identification of large multigenerational families to facilitate genetic linkage studies (Kurlan *et al.*, 1986). Genetic linkage studies are now ongoing and more than 60% of the autosomal genome has been examined thus far; however, these studies have not yet been successful in determining the chromosomal location of the putative Tourette's syndrome gene or genes (Pauls *et al.*, 1990; Pakstis *et al.*, 1991). Questions concerning what constitutes the affected phenotype may have contributed to the lack of success in this effort. Future studies may attempt to reduce possible false-positive cases in the linkage analyses by using more stringent definitions. It is also possible that the assumption of autosomal dominant transmission is erroneous.

Neurobiological substrates

The basal ganglia and related cortical and thalamic structures have been implicated in the pathobiology of Tourette's syndrome and OCD (see Chappell *et al.*, 1990, for review). This evidence includes the ameliorative effects on tic behaviours following neurosurgical lesions to thalamic nuclei and following procedures that isolate regions of the prefrontal cortex.

Preliminary evidence from positron emission tomography (PET) studies suggests that Tourette's syndrome patients have decreased regional metabolic activity in frontal, cingulate and insular cortices (Chase *et al.*, 1986). In contrast, subjects with OCD appear to have increased regional metabolic activity in the caudate nuclei (Baxter *et al.*, 1987, 1988; Benkelfat *et al.*, 1990) and a variety of cortical areas (orbital, prefrontal, cingulate and sensorimotor; Baxter *et al.*, 1987, 1988; Nordahl *et al.*, 1989; Swedo *et al.*, 1989). Magnetic resonance imaging (MRI) studies also have provided preliminary evidence of volume differences within the basal ganglia in Tourette's syndrome subjects (Singer *et al.*, 1993; Peterson *et al.*, 1993).

Functionally, the basal ganglia are composed of pathways that contribute to the multiple parallel corticostriatothalamocortical (CSTC) circuits that concurrently subserve a wide variety of sensorimotor, motor, oculomotor, cognitive and limbic processes (Alexander *et al.*, 1986; Goldman-Rakic & Selemon, 1990). It has been hypothesized that Tourette's syndrome and aetiologically related forms of OCD are associated with a failure to inhibit subsets of the CSTC minicircuits (Leckman *et al.*, 1991a). Based on the functional neuroanatomy of the CSTC circuits, we have suggested that the frequently encountered tics involving the face are associated with a failure of inhibition of those minicircuits that include the ventromedian areas of the caudate and putamen that receive topographical projections from the orofacial regions of the primary motor and premotor cortex. We and others (Laplane *et al.*, 1989) also have hypothesized that obsessions with aggressive and sexual themes would be associated with a failure to inhibit portions of the limbic minicircuits, while the counting obsessions and the obsessive need for symmetry and exactness result from a failure to inhibit prefrontal minicircuits.

Other aspects of the circuitry of the basal ganglia may provide important clues concerning the anatomical distribution of motor tics and the 'choice' of obsessive themes frequently encountered in forms of OCD related to Tourette's syndrome. Specifically, the unidirectional input from the amygdala and the bed nucleus of the stria terminalis to widespread areas of the nucleus accumbens and ventral portions of the caudate and putamen appears to overlap those areas most affected in Tourette's syndrome-related OCD (Nauta, 1982; Russchen *et al.*, 1985). Studies in primates and humans have also shown that stimulation of the amygdala produces motor and vocal activity reminiscent of the symptoms of Tourette's syndrome (McLean & Delgado, 1953; Baldwin *et al.*, 1954).

In addition, reciprocal connections between midbrain sites (periaqueductal grey, substantia nigra and the ventral tegmental area), portions of the hypothalamus and structures in the basal ganglia and amygdala are likely to play a critical role in the genesis and maintenance of the symptoms of Tourette's syndrome. These connections may also contribute to the stress sensitivity (including sensitivity to thermal stress observed in a limited number of subjects) and to the more frequent expression of Tourette's syndrome in males than females (many of these structures contain receptors for gonadal steroids and are responsive to alterations in their hormonal environment).

Although the neurophysiological defect that underlies Tourette's syndrome and aetiologically related conditions remains unknown, a more complete understanding of these disorders will likely illuminate mechanisms that regulate the activity of the multiple parallel CSTC circuits that subserve much of the normal cognitive, behavioural and emotive repertoire.

Neurochemical and neuropharmacological data

Extensive immunohistochemical studies of the basal ganglia have demonstrated the presence of a wide spectrum of differently distributed classic neurotransmitters, neuromodulators and neuropeptides (Parent, 1986; Graybiel, 1990). The functional status of a number of these systems has been evaluated in Tourette's syndrome (see Leckman *et al.*, 1987b, for a review). In particular, mesencephalic monoaminergic (dopaminergic, noradrenergic and serotonergic) projections that modulate the activity of the CSTC circuits have been repeatedly implicated in both Tourette's syndrome and OCD. Other evidence has focused attention on the endogenous opioid projections from the striatum to the pallidum and substantia nigra (Chappell *et al.*, 1990).

Dopaminergic systems

Based largely on parallels between the tics, vocalizations and obsessive-compulsive behaviours seen in some patients with encephalitis lethargica, Devinsky has suggested that Tourette's syndrome is the result of altered dopaminergic function in the midbrain (Devinsky, 1983). Other data implicating central dopaminergic mechanisms include clinical trials in which haloperidol and other neuroleptics which preferentially block dopaminergic D_2-receptors have been found to be effective in the partial suppression of tics in a majority of Tourette's syndrome patients (Shapiro *et al.*, 1989). Tic suppression has also been reported following administration of agents that reduce dopamine synthesis (see Shapiro & Shapiro, 1988, for a review). Alternatively, increased tics have been reported following withdrawal of neuroleptics and following exposure to agents which increase central dopaminergic activity, such as L-dopa and CNS stimulants, including cocaine. Transient increases in tics following thermal stress (in a subset of patients) may also be mediated by increased dopaminergic activity (Lombroso *et al.*, 1992).

Investigators have also reported that Tourette's syndrome patients have lower mean levels of homovanillic acid (HVA), a major metabolite of brain dopamine, in cerebrospinal fluid (Cohen *et al.*, 1978; Butler *et al.*, 1979; Singer *et al.*, 1982) and in certain brain regions (Anderson *et al.*, 1992). Recent preliminary PET studies of brain dopamine D_2-receptors, however, do not support the view that there are increased numbers of these receptors in the few Tourette's syndrome patients that have been studied. Additional imaging studies are needed to address fully the potential abnormalities of receptor number, affinity and distribution across the growing family of dopamine receptors. Indeed, the recent molecular characterization of a large family of dopaminergic receptors holds considerable promise both in terms of potential treatments as well as the development of safe and effective pharmacological probes for neuroimaging studies. For example, allelic variations in the D_2 dopamine receptor gene may be of significance in Tourette's syndrome as they may influence the number of D_2-receptors in the striatum (Noble *et al.*, 1991).

Postmortem brain studies have reported a striking increase in the number of presynaptic dopamine carrier sites in the striatum (Singer *et al.*, 1991). However, given the small number of brains studied ($N = 3$), this study must be considered preliminary.

Noradrenergic systems

Evidence of noradrenergic involvement in the pathophysiology of Tourette's syndrome is based largely on the beneficial effects of clonidine (Cohen *et al.*, 1979). Although the effectiveness of clonidine has not been uniformly supported (Goetz *et al.*, 1987), we have reported a large double-blind placebo-controlled trial that demonstrated a beneficial effect on motor tics and some of the other behavioural symptoms associated with Tourette's syndrome (Leckman *et al.*, 1991b).

The neurobiological basis for these effects has not been established. However a number of reports indicate that brain noradrenergic afferents project to the ventral tegmental area (VTA), a collection of dopamine-containing neurons that innervate mesolimbic areas (nucleus accumbens, olfactory tubercles, amygdala) and mesocortical sites such as the prefrontal cortex, and that these inputs may be of functional significance in regulating the activity of the VTA (Tassin *et al.*, 1979; Herve *et al.*, 1982). As noted above, many of these sites are part of the ventral striopallidal complex and related neural circuits that are involved in the control of motor behaviours that are responsive to emotional stimuli.

At the level of receptor function, clonidine has been viewed traditionally as a selective alpha$_2$-adrenoceptor agonist active at either pre- or postsynaptic sites. Previous reports have speculated that the effectiveness of clonidine in treating Tourette's syndrome may be due to the ability of alpha$_2$-adrenoceptor agonists to reduce the firing rate and the release of noradrenaline from central noradrenergic neurons and to modulate indirectly the firing of dopamine neurons in the ventral tegmental area (Grenhoff & Svensson, 1989). Evidence of heterogeneity among the alpha$_2$ class of adrenoceptors and their distinctive distribution within relevant brain regions adds further complexity and suggests that these subtypes may account for the differential responsiveness of particular behavioural features of this syndrome to clonidine treatment.

Serotonergic systems

Serotonergic mechanisms have been invoked repeatedly as playing a role in the pathophysiology of both Tourette's syndrome and OCD. The most compelling evidence relates to OCD and is based largely on the well-established efficacy of potent serotonin reuptake inhibitors (RUIs) such as clomipramine and fluvoxamine in the treatment of OCD (see Goodman et al., 1990, for a review). Additional evidence has come from pharmacological challenge studies in which serotonergic agonists such as metachlorophenylpiperazine (mCPP) were found to exacerbate obsessive-compulsive symptoms in some patients (Zohar et al., 1987; Charney et al., 1988) or were associated with a blunted plasma prolactin response (Charney et al., 1988; Hollander et al., 1989). This last observation was interpreted as evidence for downregulation of postsynaptic serotonin receptors in some OCD patients.

In addition, recent preliminary postmortem brain studies in Tourette's syndrome have shown that serotonin and the related compounds tryptophan and 5-hydroxyindoleacetic acid may be globally decreased in the basal ganglia and other areas receiving projections from the dorsal raphe (Anderson et al., 1992). Although preliminary, these postmortem findings are consistent with previous observations that Tourette's syndrome subjects exhibit significantly lower levels of 5-hydroxyindoleacetic acid in the cerebrospinal fluid (Cohen et al., 1978; Butler et al., 1979; Singer et al., 1982; Leckman et al., 1988), plasma tryptophan (Leckman et al., 1984; Comings, 1990), and whole-blood serotonin (Comings, 1990) in comparison to normal controls.

Endogenous opioid peptides

Endogenous opioid peptides, localized in structures of the extrapyramidal system (reviewed in Nieuwenhuys, 1985), interact with central dopaminergic and (GABA) ergic neurons (Quirion et al., 1985; Li et al., 1986), and are likely to be importantly involved in the gating of motor functions (Herrera-Marschitz et al., 1986). Two of the three families of opioid peptides, dynorphin and met-encephalin, are highly concentrated and similarly distributed in the basal ganglia and substantia nigra (Nieuwenhuys, 1985). In addition, significant levels of opiate receptor binding have been detected in both primate and human neostriatum and substantia nigra (Kuhar et al., 1973).

Opioid peptides have been implicated directly in the pathophysiology of Tourette's syndrome by Haber and co-workers, who reported decreased levels of dynorphin A(1–17) immunoreactivity in striatal fibres projecting to the globus pallidus in the brain of a patient with severe Tourette's syndrome (Haber et al., 1986). This observation, coupled with the neuroanatomical distribution of dynorphin, its broad range of motor and behavioural effects, and its modulatory interactions with striatal dopaminergic systems, suggests that dynorphin may play a role in the pathobiology of Tourette's syndrome. Additional evidence comes from a cerebrospinal fluid study of dynorphin A(1–8) (Leckman et al., 1988) and from studies of the opiate antagonists (Sandyk et al., 1986; Chappell et al., 1990, 1992) and agonists (Chappell et al., 1990). Data from these studies lend additional support to the hypothesis that opioids exert a modulatory effect on Tourette's syndrome symptoms. However, the results appear to be most consistent with an effect mediated by mu rather than kappa receptors.

Gender-specific endocrine factors

If Tourette's syndrome is transmitted within families as an autosomal dominant trait, then males and females should be at equal risk. However, as previously noted, males are more frequently affected than females (Shapiro et al., 1988). This observation has led us to hypothesize that androgenic steroids act at key developmental periods to influence the natural history of Tourette's syndrome and related disorders (Leckman et al., 1987a). These developmental periods include the prenatal period when the brain is being formed, adrenarche when adrenal androgens first appear at age 5–7 years and puberty. Androgenic steroids may be responsible for these effects or they may act indirectly through oestrogens formed in key brain regions by the aromatization of testosterone.

The importance of gender differences in expression of associated phenotypes is also clear given the observation that women are more likely than men to develop obsessive-compulsive symptoms without concomitant tics (Pauls et al., 1991) and that boys are much more likely than girls to display disruptive behaviours (Comings & Comings, 1987).

Surges in testosterone and other androgenic steroids during critical periods in fetal development are known to be involved in the production of long-term functional augmentation of subsequent hormonal challenges (as in adrenarche and during puberty) and in the formation of structural CNS dimorphisms (Sikich & Todd, 1988). In recent years several sexually dimorphic brain regions have been described, including portions of the amygdala (and related limbic areas) and the hypothalamus (including the medial preoptic area that mediates the body's response to thermal stress; Boulant, 1981). These regions contain high levels of androgen and oestrogen receptors and are known to influence activity in the basal ganglia both directly and indirectly (Fehrbach et al., 1985). It is also of note that some of the neurochemical and neuropeptidergic systems implicated in Tourette's syndrome and related disorders, such as dopamine, serotonin and the opioids, are involved with these regions and appear to be regulated by sex-specific factors.

Further support for a role for androgens comes from pilot study data from open trials of antiandrogens to patients with severe OCD (Casas *et al.*, 1986) in which all the subjects reported a remission in their symptoms while on medication and an exacerbation when the medication was withdrawn. In a pilot study, 2 boys with OCD were treated with spirono-lactone, a peripheral antitestosterone agent, and with testo-lactone, a peripheral antioestrogen agent. Both experienced a temporary reduction of their obsessive-compulsive symptoms which lasted for 3–4 months (Swedo & Rapoport, 1990). Finally, a case report has described 2 athletes with a history of Tourette's syndrome who experienced exacerbations of their tics while using androgenic steroids (Leckman & Scahill, 1990).

Other nonendocrine factors may contribute to these gender differences, but the data are limited and no cogent hypotheses concerning such mechanisms have been advanced.

Perinatal factors

The search for nongenetic factors which mediate the expression of a genetic vulnerability to Tourette's syndrome and related disorders has also focused on the role of adverse perinatal events. This interest dates from the report of Pasamanick and Kawi (1956) who found that mothers of children with tics were 1.5 times more likely to have experienced a complication during pregnancy than the mothers of children without tics. Other investigations have reported that among monozygotic twins discordant for Tourette's syndrome, the index twins with Tourette's syndrome had lower birth weights than their unaffected co-twins (Leckman *et al.*, 1987b; Hyde *et al.*, 1992). Severity of maternal life stress during pregnancy and severe nausea and/or vomiting during the first trimester have also emerged as potential risk factors in the development of tic disorders (Leckman *et al.*, 1990). In contrast, two studies have failed to document any association between adverse perinatal events and manifestations of Tourette's syndrome (Shapiro *et al.*, 1988).

Psychological factors

Tic disorders have long been identified as stress-sensitive conditions (Jagger *et al.*, 1982; Shapiro *et al.*, 1988). Typically, symptom exacerbations follow in the wake of stressful life events. As noted by Shapiro *et al.* (1988), these events need not be adverse in character. Clinical experience suggests that in some unfortunate instances a vicious cycle can be initiated in which tic symptoms are misunderstood by the family and teachers, leading to active attempts to suppress the symptoms by punishment and humiliation. These efforts can lead to a further exacerbation of symptoms and further increase in stress in the child's interpersonal environment. Unchecked, this vicious cycle can lead to the most severe manifestations of Tourette's syndrome and dysthymia as well as maladaptive characterological traits. Although psychological factors are

insufficient to cause Tourette's syndrome, the intimate association of the content and timing of tic behaviours and dynamically important events in the lives of children makes it difficult to overlook their contribution to the intramorbid course of these disorders.

In addition to the intramorbid effects of stress and anxiety that have been well-characterized, premorbid stress may also play an important role as a sensitizing agent in the pathogenesis of Tourette's syndrome among vulnerable individuals (Leckman *et al.*, 1984). Although the mechanisms that mediate this stress response are unclear, it is likely that the immediate family environment, e.g. parental discord, and the coping abilities of family members play some role (Leckman *et al.*, 1990; Carter & Pauls, 1991).

DIFFERENTIAL DIAGNOSIS

The differential diagnosis of simple motor tics includes a variety of hyperkinetic movements: myoclonus, tremors, chorea, athetosis, dystonias, akathitic movements, paroxysmal dyskinesias, ballistic movements and hyperekplexia (Fahn & Erenberg, 1988). These movements may be associated with genetic conditions such as Huntington's chorea or Wilson's disease; structural lesions, as in hemiballismus (associated with lesions to the contralateral subthalamic nucleus); infectious processes as in Sydenham's chorea; idiopathic functional instability of neuronal circuits, as in myoclonic epilepsy; and pharmacological treatments such as acute akathisia and dystonias associated with the use of neuroleptic agents. Differentiation between these conditions and tic disorders is usually accomplished on clinical grounds and is based on the presentation of the disorder and its natural history. For example, although aspects of tics such as their abruptness, their paroxysmal timing or their suppressible nature may be similar to symptoms seen in other conditions, it is rare for all of these features to be combined in the absence of a *bona fide* tic disorder. Occasionally diagnostic tests are needed to exclude alternative diagnoses.

Complex motor tics can be confused with other complex repetitive behaviours such as stereotypies or compulsive rituals. Differentiation among these behaviours may be difficult, particularly among retarded individuals with limited verbal skills. In other settings where these symptoms are closely intertwined, as in individuals with both Tourette's syndrome and OCD, efforts to distinguish between complex motor tics and compulsive behaviours may be futile. In cases of a tic disorder, it is unusual to see complex motor tics in the absence of simple tics. Involuntary vocal utterances are uncommon neurological signs in the absence of a tic disorder. Huntington's disease may be associated with sniffing and brief sounds. Involuntary moaning can be heard in Parkinson's disease, particularly as a result of L-dopa toxicity. Complex phonic tics characterized by articulate speech typically can be distinguished from other conditions including voluntary coprolalia. Because of their rarity in other syndromes, phonic tics can play an important role in differential diagnosis.

Anamnesis, family history, observation and neurological examination are usually sufficient to establish the diagnosis of a tic disorder. There are no confirmatory diagnostic tests. Neuroimaging studies, electroencephalogram-based studies and laboratory tests are usually noncontributory except in atypical cases.

Inventories such as the Tourette's Syndrome Questionnaire (Jagger *et al.*, 1982) completed by the family prior to their initial consultation can be valuable ancillary tools to gain a long-term perspective of the child's developmental course and the natural history of the tic disorder. In addition, several valid and reliable clinical rating instruments have been developed to inventory and quantify recent tic symptoms, including the Yale Global Tic Severity Scale (Leckman *et al.*, 1989) and the Shapiro Tourette Syndrome Severity Scale (Shapiro *et al.*, 1988), and some clinicians make regular use of standardized video tape protocols to assess current tic severity (Tanner *et al.*, 1982; Goetz *et al.*, 1987; Shapiro *et al.*, 1988).

ASSESSMENT

Once the diagnosis has been established, care should be taken to focus on the overall course of an individual's development, not simply on his or her tic symptoms. This may be a particular problem in the case of Tourette's syndrome where the symptoms can be dramatic and there is the temptation to organize all of an individual's behavioural and emotional difficulties under a single all-encompassing rubric.

The principal goal of an initial assessment is to determine the individual's overall level of adaptive functioning and to identify areas of impairment and distress. Close attention to the strengths and weaknesses of the individual and his or her family is crucial. Relevant dimensions include the presence of comorbid mental, behavioural, developmental or physical disorders; family history of psychiatric and/or neurological disease; relationships with family and peers; school and/or occupational performance; and the history of important life events.

Medication history is important, particularly if the disorder is long-standing or if medications have been prescribed for physical disorders. It may be necessary to evaluate the adequacy of the prior trials with pharmacological agents used to treat tic disorders.

TREATMENT

Tic disorders are frequently chronic, if not lifelong, conditions. Continuity of care is desirable and should be considered before embarking on a course of treatment. Major approaches include education and supportive interventions and treatment with neuropsychopharmacological agents. Usual clinical practice focuses initially on the educational and supportive interventions. Pharmacological treatments are typically held in reserve. Given the waxing and waning course of the disorders, it is likely that whatever is done (or not done) will lead in the short term to some improvement. The decision to employ psychoactive medications is usually made after the educational and supportive interventions have been in place for a period of months and it is clear that the tic symptoms are sustained and are themselves a source of impairment in terms of self-esteem, relationships with the family or peers, or the child's ability to perform at school.

Educational and supportive interventions

Although the efficacy of educational and supportive interventions has not been rigorously assessed, they appear clinically to have positive effects by reshaping familial expectations and relationships (Cohen *et al.*, 1988). This is particularly true when the tic behaviours have been misconstrued by the family and others as voluntary and intentionally provocative. Families also find descriptions of the natural history comforting in that the disorders tend not to be relentlessly progressive and usually improve during adulthood. This information often contradicts the impressions gained from the available lay literature on Tourette's syndrome which typically focuses on the most extreme cases.

For children, contact with their teachers can be enormously valuable. By educating the educators, clinicians can make significant progress towards securing for the child a positive and supportive environment in the classroom. If possible, teachers need to respond to outbursts of tics with understanding and positive regard. Repeatedly scolding a child for tics can be counterproductive with serious sequelae: the child may develop a negative attitude to authority figures and may be reluctant to attend school and classmates may feel freer to tease the child. Other useful strategies that teachers may consider include providing short breaks out of the classroom to let the tics out in private; allowing students with severe tics to take tests in private so that a child does not have the pressure to suppress tics during the test period; and being flexible with regard to the scheduling of oral presentations so that the child is not expected to make an oral presentation at a point when the tics are severe (Bronheim, 1991).

Pharmacological treatments

For individuals who are experiencing significant impairment as a result of their tic behaviours, treatment with medications can provide a source of relief. Although virtually every agent in the *vade-mecum psychopharmacologium* has been used in the treatment of Tourette's syndrome, only the relatively selective D_2-receptor antagonists, haloperidol and pimozide, have consistently been shown to be effective in clinical practice as well as during the course of double-blind clinical trials.

Haloperidol and pimozide

Approximately 70% of Tourette's syndrome patients respond favourably to either haloperidol or pimozide (Shapiro *et al.*, 1989). The mean reduction of symptom severity is also in the 70–80% range. In general, it is useful to start treatment with low doses of medication and to make any necessary increases gradually. Typically, treatment is initiated with a low dose (0.25 mg of haloperidol or 1 mg of pimozide) given before sleep. Further increments (0.5 mg of haloperidol or 1 mg of pimozide) may be added at 7–14-day intervals if the tic behaviours remain severe. In most instances, 0.5–6.0 mg/day of haloperidol or 1.0–10.0 mg/day of pimozide administered over a period of 4–8 weeks is sufficient to achieve adequate control of tic symptoms.

Tic symptoms often continue to wax and wane, at a much reduced level, even during periods of neuroleptic treatment. Generally it is not a good idea to 'chase' the tic symptoms with adjustment in medication dosage. Such adjustments generally are not beneficial, and may expose the subjects to additional unwanted physical effects of the medication, many of which appear to be dose-related. In general, prescribing the smallest amount of neuroleptic needed to gain reasonable symptom control is a useful guideline.

The major limiting factor in the use of neuroleptics is the emergence of side-effects, including acute dystonias, akathisia, akinesia, cognitive impairment, weight gain and phobias (Shapiro & Shapiro, 1988). A majority of subjects will experience one or more of these effects, and a significant proportion of these subjects elect to discontinue treatment if the side-effects are not controlled. In addition to these effects, pimozide may have an adverse effect on cardiac conduction in some Tourette's syndrome subjects, particularly at doses above 10–12 mg/day. Tardive dyskinesia has also been reported in Tourette's syndrome patients with chronic exposure to neuroleptics. Given the short-term and long-term hazards of neuroleptic medication, many clinicians elect to use these medications only in severe cases.

Clonidine

Clonidine hydrochloride, a selective alpha$_2$-adrenergic receptor agonist, may be effective for a proportion of Tourette's syndrome subjects (Cohen *et al.*, 1979; Leckman *et al.*, 1991b). Clinical trials indicate that subjects can expect on average a 25–35% reduction in their symptoms over an 8–12-week period. Motor tics may show greater improvement than phonic symptoms. The usual starting dose is 0.05 mg on arising. Further 0.05 mg increments at 3–4-hour intervals are added weekly until a dosage of 5 μg/kg is reached or the total daily dose exceeds 0.25 mg.

Although clonidine is clearly less effective than haloperidol and pimozide, it is considerably safer. The principal side-effect associated with its use is sedation, which occurs in 10–20% of subjects and which usually abates with continued use. Other side-effects include dry mouth, transient hypotension and rare episodes of worsening behaviour. Clonidine should be tapered and not withdrawn abruptly, to reduce the likelihood of symptom or blood pressure rebound.

Treatment of associated behavioural disorders

There is a diversity of opinion concerning the treatment of patients with attention deficit hyperactivity disorder and Tourette's syndrome. While most clinicians endorse the use of educational interventions and other behavioural techniques to manage the symptoms of attention deficit hyperactivity disorder, controversy surrounds the use of CNS stimulant medications such as methylphenidate and d-amphetamine, which may exacerbate tic symptoms in some patients. Many clinicians avoid the use of CNS stimulants, preferring in their stead desipramine or clonidine. Others use the CNS stimulants with caution or combine them with neuroleptics. The recent reports of sudden death associated with the use of desipramine in a small number of child subjects have further restricted the options of some clinicians. Extensive educational and physical evaluations in the context of well-informed parents and a close working relationship with school personnel should optimize the safety and effectiveness of whichever approach is selected.

The treatment of obsessive-compulsive symptoms is less problematic, with many patients responding to selective serotonin RUIs such as clomipramine, fluoxetine and fluvoxamine or the combination of one of these agents and a neuroleptic. The use of behavioural and cognitive approaches to the treatment of OCD in child patients with tic symptoms has not been explored.

Behavioural, cognitive and other psychotherapeutic treatments

The characteristic suppressibility of tic symptoms may have broad implications for treatment. Prior to seeking professional consultation, many families will have experimented with a variety of *ad hoc* behavioural approaches on their own. It is useful to elicit information concerning these efforts and their sequelae.

A variety of cognitive and behavioural approaches have been used with Tourette's syndrome subjects. A battery of habit reversal training techniques encompassing awareness training, self-monitoring, relaxation training, competing response training (where a movement is performed that is opposite to a particular tic), and contingency management has been reported to reduce markedly tic symptoms at home and in a clinic setting (Azrin & Peterson, 1990). Additional studies are needed to confirm the effectiveness of these techniques.

The most frequently used component of this battery is some version of relaxation training which may employ tensing followed by relaxation, imagery or deep breathing. Some of these methods can be temporarily helpful. However, most families report that these techniques lose their effectiveness. Other techniques, such as massed negative practice (where the patient deliberately performs the tic movement as quickly and as forcefully as possible) have been studied, with mixed results (Azrin & Peterson, 1988).

Not surprisingly, tic symptoms can have a powerful impact

on the inner life of individuals with Tourette's syndrome. They can emerge as important determinants of self-esteem and self-definition. Traditional psychotherapeutic approaches can be helpful in helping patients and their families to understand and cope with their illness and to address intrapsychic conflicts that affect or result from tic symptoms. It is unlikely, however, that such interventions will abolish the tic symptoms.

PROGNOSIS

The prognosis for tic disorders is generally good with most individuals experiencing their worst tic symptoms from 9 to 15 years of age. The course in adulthood is variable but most patients have a more or less stable repertoire of tic symptoms that wax and wane over a reduced range of severity (Bruun, 1988).

Poorer prognoses are associated with comorbid developmental and mental disorders, chronic physical illness, unstable and unsupportive family environments, and exposure to psychoactive drugs, such as cocaine. Potential complications include the emergence of OCD, character pathology associated with a chronic stigmatizing disorder, and physical injuries secondary to self-abusive motor tics.

RESEARCH PROSPECTS

As outlined in this chapter, a broad array of research opportunities are now being actively pursued. Based largely on advances in related fields of science, genetic and neurobiological studies show particular promise. Progress in these areas may herald significant advances in early detection and diagnosis as well as advances in treatment.

ACKNOWLEDGEMENTS

Portions of this chapter are based on a chapter in the book, *Child and Adolescent Psychiatry: A Comprehensive Textbook* (1991), ed. M. Lewis (Williams and Wilkins, Baltimore MD). We are grateful for permission to use them here.

REFERENCES

Alexander G.E., Delong M.R. & Strick P.L. (1986) Parallel organization of functionally segregated circuits linking basal ganglia and cortex. *Annual Review of Neuroscience*, **9**, 357–381.

American Psychiatric Association (1987) *Diagnostic and Statistical Manual of Mental Disorders*, 3rd edn, revised. American Psychiatric Association Press, Washington, DC.

American Psychiatric Association (1993) *DSM-IV Draft Criteria*. American Psychiatric Association, Washington, DC.

Anderson G.M., Polack E.S., Chatterjee D., Leckman J.F., Riddle M.A. & Cohen D.J. (1992) Postmortem analysis of subcortical monoamines and aminoacids in Tourette syndrome. In: Chase T.N., Friedhoff A.J. & Cohen D.J. (eds) *Tourette Syndrome: Genetics, Neurobiology, and Treatment*, pp. 253–262. Raven Press, New York.

Apter A., Zohar A., Pauls D.L., Bleich A., Kron S. & Cohen D.J. (in press) A population-based epidemiological study of Gilles de la Tourette's syndrome among adolescents in Israel. *Archives of General Psychiatry*, in press.

Azrin N.H. & Peterson A.L. (1988) Habit reversal for the treatment of Tourette syndrome. *Behaviour Research and Therapy*, **11**, 347–355.

Azrin N.H. & Peterson A.L. (1990) Treatment of Tourette syndrome by habit reversal: a waiting-list control group comparison. *Behaviour Therapy*, **21**, 305–318.

Baldwin M., Frost L.L. & Wodd C.D. (1954) Investigation of primate amygalda. *Neurology*, **4**, 586–598.

Baxter L.R., Phelps M.E., Mazziota J.C., Guze B.E., Schwartz J.M. & Selin C.E. (1987) Local cerebral glucose metabolic rates in obsessive-compulsive disorder. *Archives of General Psychiatry*, **44**, 211.

Baxter L.R., Schwartz J.M., Phelps M.E., Mazziota J.C., Barrio J., Rawson R.A., Engel J., Guze B.H., Selin C. & Sumida R. (1988) Cerebral glucose metabolic rates in obsessive-compulsive disorder. *Archives of General Psychiatry*, **145**, 1560–1563.

Benkelfat C., Nordahl T.E., Semple W.E., King A.C., Murphy D.L. & Cohen R.M. (1990) Local cerebral glucose metabolic rates in obsessive compulsive disorder patients treated with clomipramine. *Archives of General Psychiatry*, **47**, 840–848.

Boulant J.A. (1981) Hypothalamic mechanisms in thermoregulation. *Federal Proceedings*, **40**, 2843–2850.

Bronheim S. (1991) An educator's guide to Tourette syndrome. *Journal of Learning Disabilities*, **24**, 17–22.

Bruun R.D. (1988) The natural history of Tourette's syndrome. In: Cohen D.J., Bruun R.D. & Leckman J.F. (eds) *Tourette's Syndrome and Tic Disorders*. Wiley, New York.

Burd L., Kerbeshian L., Wikenheiser M. & Fisher W. (1986a) Prevalence of Gilles de la Tourette's Syndrome in North Dakota adults. *American Journal of Psychiatry*, **143**, 787.

Burd L., Kerbeshian L., Wikenheiser M. & Fisher W. (1986b) A prevalence study of Gilles de la Tourette syndrome in North Dakota. school-age children. *Journal of the American Academy of Child Psychiatry*, **25**, 552.

Butler I.J., Koslow S.H., Seifert W.E. Jr., Caprioli R.M. & Singer H.S. (1979) Biogenic amine metabolism in Tourette syndrome. *Annuals of Neurology*, **6**, 37.

Caine E.D., Mcbride M.C., Chiverton P., Bamford K.A., Rediess S. & Shiao S. (1988) Tourette syndrome in Monroe County school children. *Neurology*, **38**, 472–475.

Carter A.S. & Pauls D.L. (1991) Preliminary results of a prospective family study of Tourette's syndrome. *Psychiatric Genetics*, **2**, 26–27.

Casas M., Alvarez E., Duro P., Garcia-Ribera C., Udina C., Velat A., Abella D., Rodriguez-Espinosa J., Salvap P. & Jané F. (1986) Antiandrogenic treatment of obsessive-compulsive neurosis. *Acta Psychiatrica Scandinavica*, **73**, 221–222.

Chappell P., Leckman J.F., Pauls D. & Cohen D.J. (1990) Biochemical and genetic studies of Tourette's syndrome: implications for treatment and future research. In: Deutsch S., Weizmar A. & Weizmar R. (eds) *Application of Basic Neuroscience to Child Psychiatry*, pp. 241–260. Plenum, New York.

Chappell P.B., Leckman J.F., Riddle M.A., Anderson G.M., Listwack S.J., Ort S.I., Hardin M.T., Scahill L.D. & Cohen D.J. (1992) Neuroendocrine and behavioral effects of naloxone in Tourette syndrome. In: Chase T.N., Friedhoff A.J. & Cohen D.J. (eds) *Tourette Syndrome: Genetics, Neurobiology, and Treatment*, pp. 253–262. Raven Press, New York.

Charney D.S., Goodman W.K., Price L.H., Woods S.W., Rasmussen S.A. & Heninger G.R. (1988) Serotonin function in obsessive-compulsive disorder. *Archives of General Psychiatry*, **45**, 177–185.

Chase T.N., Geoffrey V., Gillespie M. & Burrows B.H. (1986) Structural and functional studies of Gilles de la Tourette's syndrome. *Revue Neurologique (Paris)*, **142**, 851–855.

Cohen D.J., Shaywitz B.A., Caparulo B., Young J.G. & Bowers M.B.

Jr. (1978) Chronic, multiple tics of Gilles de la Tourette's disease: CSF acid monoamine metabolites after probenecid administration. *Archives of General Psychiatry*, **35**, 245.

Cohen D.J., Young J.G., Nathanson J.A. & Shaywitz B.A. (1979) Clonidine in Tourette's syndrome. *Lancet*, **2**, 551.

Cohen D.J., Ort S.I., Leckman J.F., Riddle M.A. & Hardin M.T. (1988) Family functioning and Tourette's syndrome. In: Cohen D.J., Bruun R.D. & Leckman J.F. (eds) *Tourette's Syndrome and Tic Disorders*, p. 179. Wiley, New York.

Comings D.E. (1990) *Tourette Syndrome and Human Behaviour*, pp. 59–302. Hope Press, Duarte, CA.

Comings D.E. & Comings B.G. (1987) A controlled study of Tourette syndrome. I. Attention-deficit disorder, learning disorders, and school problems. II. Conduct. *American Journal of Human Genetics*, **41**, 701–760.

Comings D.E., Himes J.A. & Comings B.G. (1990) An epidemiological study of Tourette's syndrome in a single school district. *Journal Clinical Psychiatry*, **51**, 463–469.

Devinsky O. (1983) Neuroanatomy of Gilles de la Tourette's syndrome: possible midbrain involvement. *Archives of Neurology*, **40**, 508.

Dykens E., Leckman J.F., Riddle M.A., Hardin M. & Schwartz S. (1990) Intellectual, academic, and adaptive functioning Tourette syndrome with and without attention deficit disorder. *Journal of Abnormal Child Psychology*, **18**, 607–615.

Fahn S. & Erenberg G. (1988) Differential diagnosis of tic phenomena: a neurologic perspective. In: Cohen D.J., Bruun R.D. & Leckman J.F. (eds) *Tourette's Syndrome and Tic Disorders*, p. 41. Wiley, New York.

Fehrbach S.E., Morell J.I. & Pfaff D.W. (1985) Identification of medial preoptic neurons that concentrate estradiol and project to the midbrain in the rat. *Journal of Comparative Neurology*, **247**, 364–382.

Gilles de la Tourette (1885) Etude sur une affection nerveuse caractérisée par de l'incoordination motrice accompagnée d'echolalie et de copralalie. *Archives of Neurology*, **9**, 158.

Glaze D.G., Frost J.D. & Jankovic J. (1983) Sleep in Gilles de la Tourette syndrome: disorder of arousal. *Neurology*, **33**, 586–592.

Goetz C.G., Tanner C.M., Wilson R.S., Carroll V.S., Como P.G. & Shannon K.M. (1987) Clonidine and Gilles de la Tourette syndrome: double-blind study using objective rating method. *Annals of Neurology*, **31**, 307–310.

Goldman-Rakic P.S. & Selemon L.D. (1990) New frontiers in basal ganglia research. *Trends in Neuroscience*, **13**, 244–245.

Goodman W.K., McDougle C.J. & Price L.H. (1990) Beyond the serotonin hypothesis: a role for dopamine in some forms of obsessive compulsive disorder? *Journal of Clinical Psychiatry*, **51**, 36–43.

Graybiel A.M. (1990) Neurotransmitters and neuromodulators in the basal ganglia. *Trends in Neuroscience*, **13**, 244–254.

Grenhoff J. & Svensson T.H. (1989) Clonidine modulates dopamine cell firing in rat ventral tegmental area. *European Journal of Pharmacology*, **165**, 11–18.

Haber S.N., Kowall N.W., Vonsattel J.P., Bird E.D. & Richardson E.P. (1986) Gilles de la Tourette's syndrome: a postmortem neuropathological and immunohistochemical study. *Journal of the Neurological Sciences*, **75**, 225.

Herrera-Marschitz M., Christensson-Nylander I., Sharp T., Staines W., Reid M., Hokfelt T., Terenius L. & Ungerstedt U. (1986) Striato-nigral dynorphin and substance P pathways in the rat. *Experimental Brain Research*, **64**, 193–207.

Herve D., Blanc G., Glowinski J. & Tassin J.P. (1982) Reduction of dopamine utilization in the prefrontal cortex but not the nucleus accumbens after selective destruction of the noradrenergic fibers innervating the ventral tegmental area of the rat. *Brain Research*, **237**, 510–516.

Hollander E., Decarla C., Cooper T. & Liebowitz M.R. (1989) Repeat

M-CPP challenge during fluoxetine treatment in obsessive-compulsive disorder. *Biological Psychiatry*, **25**, 5A–9A.

Hyde T.M., Aaronson B.A., Randolph C., Rickler K.C. & Weinberger D.R. (1992) Relationship of birth weight to the phenotypic expression of Gilles de la Tourette's syndrome in monozygotic twins. *Neurology*, **42**, 652–658.

Itard J.M.G. (1825) Memoire sur quelques fonctions involontaires des appareils de la locomotion de la prehension et de la voix. *Archives of General Medicine*, **8**, 385.

Jagger J., Prusoff B.A., Cohen D.J., Kidd K.K., Carbonari C.M. & John K. (1982) The epidemiology of Tourette's syndrome: a pilot study. *Schizophrenia Bulletin*, **8**, 267.

Janovic J. & Rohaidy H. (1987) Motor, behavioral and pharmacologic findings in Tourette's syndrome. *Canadian Journal of Neurological Science*, **14**, 541–546.

Kuhar M.J., Pert C.B. & Snyder S.H. (1973) Regional distribution of opiate receptor binding in monkey and human brain. *Nature*, **245**, 447–450.

Kurlan R., Behr J., Medved L., Shoulson I., Pauls D.L., Kidd J.R. & Kidd K.K. (1986) Familial Tourette's syndrome: report of a large pedigree and potential for linkage analysis. *Neurology*, **36**, 722.

Lang A. (1991) Patient perception of tics and other movement disorders. *Neurology*, **41**, 223–228.

Laplane D., Levasseur M., Pillon B., Dubois B., Baulac M., Mazoyer B., Tran-Dinh S., Sette G., Danze F. & Baron J.C. (1989) Obsessive-compulsive and other behavioral changes with bilateral basal ganglia lesions. *Brain*, **112**, 699–725.

Leckman J.F. & Cohen D.J. (1988) Descriptive and diagnostic classification of tic disorders. In: Cohen D.J., Bruun R.D. & Leckman J.F. (eds) *Tourette's Syndrome and Tic Disorders*, p. 3. Wiley, New York.

Leckman J.F. & Scahill L. (1990) Possible exacerbation of tics by androgenic steroids. *New England Journal of Medicine*, **322**, 1674.

Leckman J.F. Cohen D.J., Price R.A., Minderaa R.B. & Anderson G.M. & Pauls D.L. (1984) The pathogenesis of Gilles de la Tourette's syndrome. A review of data and hypothesis. In: Shah A.B., Shah N.S. & Donald A.G. (eds) *Movement Disorders*, pp. 257–272. Plenum, New York.

Leckman J.F., Price R.A., Walkup J.T., Ort S.I., Pauls D.L. & Cohen D.J. (1987a) Letter to the editor: nongenetic factors in Gilles de la Tourette's syndrome. *Archives of General Psychiatry*, **44**, 100.

Leckman J.F., Walkup J.T., Riddle M.A., Towbin K.E. & Cohen D.J. (1987b) Tic disorders. In: Meltzer H.Y. (ed) *Psychopharmacology: The Third Generation of Progress*, p. 1239. Raven, New York.

Leckman J.F., Weissman M.M., Pauls P.L. & Kidd K.K. (1987c) Family-genetic studies and the identification of valid diagnostic categories in adult and child psychiatry. *British Journal of Psychiatry*, **151**, 39–44.

Leckman J.F., Riddle M.A., Berrettini W.H., Anderson G.M., Hardin M., Chappell P.B., Bissette G., Nemeroff C.B., Goodman W.K. & Cohen D.J. (1988) Elevated CSF dynorphin A[1–8] in Tourette's syndrome. *Life Science*, **43**, 2015.

Leckman J.F., Riddle M.A., Hardin M.T., Ort S.I., Swartz K.L., Stevenson J. & Cohen D.J. (1989) The Yale Global Tic Severity Scale: initial testing of a clinician-rated scale of tic severity. *Journal of the American Academy of Child and Adolescent Psychiatry*, **28**, 566.

Leckman J.F., Dolnansky E.S., Hardin M.T., Clubb M., Walkup J.T., Stevenson J. & Pauls D.L. (1990) Perinatal factors in the expression of Tourette's syndrome: an exploratory study. *Journal of the American Academy of Child and Adolescent Psychiatry*, **29**, 220–226.

Leckman J.F., Knorr A.M., Rasmusson A.M. & Cohen D.J. (1991a) Basal ganglia research and Tourette's syndrome. *Trends in Neuroscience*, **14**, 94.

Leckman J.F., Hardin M.T., Riddle M.A., Stevenson J., Ort S.I. & Cohen D.J. (1991b) Clonidine treatment of Gilles de la Tourette's syndrome. *Archives of General Psychiatry*, **48**, 324–328.

Leckman J.F., Walker D.E. & Cohen D.J. (1993) Premonitory urges in Tourette's syndrome. *American Journal of Psychiatry*, **150**, 98–102.

Li S., Sivam S.P. & Hong J.S. (1986) Regulation of the concentration of dynorphin A[1–8] in the striatonigral pathway by the dopaminergic system. *Brain Research*, **398**, 390–392.

Lombroso P.J., Mack G., Scahill L., King R.A. & Leckman J.F. (1992) Exacerbation of Tourette's syndrome associated with thermal stress: a family study. *Neurology*, **41**, 1984–1987.

McLean P. & Delgado J. (1953) Electrical and chemical stimulation of frontotemporal portion of limbic system in the waking animal. *EEG Clinics in Neurophysiology*, **5**, 91–100.

Nauta W.J.H. (1982) Limbic innervation of the striatum. In: Friedhoff A.J. & Chase T.N. (eds) *Advances in Neurology, Gilles de la Tourette Syndrome.* Raven, New York.

Nieuwenhuys R. (1985) *Chemoarchitecture of the Brain.* Springer Verlag, New York.

Noble E.P., Blum K., Ritchie T., Montgomery A. & Sheridan P.J. (1991) Allelic association of the D_2 dopamine receptor gene with receptor-binding characteristics in alcoholism. *Archives of General Psychiatry*, **48**, 648–654.

Nordahl T.E., Benkelfat C., Semple W.E., Gross M., King A.C. & Cohen R.M. (1989) Cerebral glucose metabolic rates in obsessive compulsive disorder. *Neuropsychopharmacology*, **2**, 23–28.

Pakstis A.J., Heutinik P., Pauls D.L., Kurlan R., Van de Wetering B.J., Leckman J.F., Sandkuyl L.A., Kidd J.R., Breedveld G.J., Castiglione C.M., Weber J., Sparkes R.S., Cohen D.J., Kidd K.K. & Öostra B.A. (1991) Progress in the search of genetic linkage with Tourette syndrome: an exclusion map covering more than 50% of the autosomal genome. *American Journal of Human Genetics*, **48**, 281–294.

Parent A. (1986) *Comparative Neurobiology of the Basal Ganglia.* Wiley, New York.

Pasamanick B. & Kawi A. (1956) A study of the association of prenatal and paranatal factors in the development of tics in children. *Journal of Pediatrics*, **48**, 596.

Pauls D.L. & Leckman J.F. (1986) The inheritance of Gilles de la Tourette syndrome and associated behaviors: evidence for autosomal dominant transmission. *New England Journal of Medicine*, **315**, 993.

Pauls D.L. & Leckman J.F. (1988) The genetics of Tourette's syndrome. In: Cohen D.J., Bruun R.D. & Leckman J.F. (eds) *Tourette's Syndrome and Tic Disorders*, p. 91. Wiley, New York.

Pauls D.L., Pakstis A.J., Kurlan R., Kidd K.K., Leckman J.F., Cohen D.J., Kidd J.R., Como P.G. & Sparkes R.S. (1990) Segregation and linkage analysis of Gilles de la Tourette's syndrome and related disorders. *Journal of the American Academy of Child and Adolescent Psychiatry*, **29**, 195–203.

Pauls D.L., Raymond C.L., Stevenson J.F. & Leckman J.F. (1991) A family study of Gilles de la Tourette, *American Journal of Human Genetics*, **48**, 154–163.

Peterson B.S., Riddle M.A., Cohen D.J., Katz L.D., Smith J.C., Hardin M.T. & Leckman J.F. (1993) Reduced basal ganglia volumes in Tourette's syndrome using 3-dimensional reconstruction techniques from magnetic resonance images. *Neurology*, **43**, 941–949.

Price A.R., Kidd K.K., Cohen D.J., Pauls D.L. & Leckman J.F. (1985) A twin study of Tourette's syndrome. *Archives of General Psychiatry*, **42**, 815–820.

Quirion R., Gaudreau P., Martel J.C., St-Pierre S. & Zamir N. (1985) Possible interactions between dynorphin and dopaminergic systems in the rat basal ganglia and substantia nigra. *Brain Research*, **331**, 358–362.

Russchen F.T., Bakst I., Amaral D.G. & Price J.L. (1985) The amygdalostriatal projections in the monkey: an anterograde tracing study. *Brain Research*, **329**, 241–257.

Rutter M., Tizard J. & Whitmore K. (eds) (1970) *Education, Health, and Behaviour.* Longman, London.

Rutter M., Yule W., Berger M., Yule B., Morton J. & Bagley C. (1974) Children of West Indian immigrants: I. Rates of behavioural deviance and psychiatric disorder. *Journal of Child Psychology and Psychiatry*, **15**, 241–262.

Sandyk R., Iacono R.P. & Allender J. (1986) Naloxone ameliorates compulsive touching behavior and tics in Tourette's syndrome. *Annals of Neurology*, **20**, 437.

Shapiro A.K. & Shapiro E.S. (1988) Treatment of tic disorders with haloperidol. In: Cohen D.J., Bruun R.D. & Leckman J.F. (eds) *Tourette's Syndrome and Tic Disorders.* Wiley, New York.

Shapiro A.K., Shapiro E.S., Young J.G. & Feinberg T.E. (eds) (1988) *Gilles de la Tourette Syndrome*, 2nd edn. Raven, New York.

Shapiro E.S., Shapiro A.K., Fulop G., Hubbard M., Mandeli J., Nordlie J & Phillips R.A. (1989) Controlled study of haloperidol, pimozide, and placebo for the treatment of Gilles de la Tourette's syndrome. *Archives of General Psychiatry*, **46**, 722.

Sikich L. & Todd R.D. (1988) Are neurodevelopmental effects of gonadal hormones related to sex differences in psychiatric illness? *Psychiatric Development*, **6**, 277–310.

Singer H.S., Tune L.E., Butler I.J., Zaczek R. & Coyle J.T. (1982) Clinical symptomatology, CSF neurotransmitter metabolites, and serum haloperidol levels in Tourette Syndrome. In: Friedhoff A.J. & Chase T.N. (eds) *Advances in Neurology, vol. 35, Gilles de la Tourette Syndrome*, p. 187. Raven, New York.

Singer H.S., Hahn I.-H. & Moran T.H. (1991) Abnormal dopamine uptake sites in postmortem striatum from patients with Tourette's syndrome. *Annals of Neurology*, **30**, 558–562.

Singer H.S., Reiss A.L., Brown J., Aylward E.H., Shih B., Chee E., Harris E.L., Reader M.J., Chase G., Bryan N. & Denckla M.A. (1993), Volumetric MRI changes in basal ganglia of children with Tourette's syndrome. *Neurology*, **43**, 950–956.

Stokes A., Bawden H.N., Camfield P.R., Backman J.E. & Dooley J.M. (1991) Peer problems in Tourette's disorder. *Pediatrics*, **87**, 936–942.

Swedo S.E. & Rapoport J.L. (1990) Neurochemical and neuroendocrine considerations of obsessive compulsive disorders in childhood. In: Deutsch S.I., Weizman A. & Weizman R. (eds) *Application of Basic Neuroscience to Child Psychiatry.* Plenum, New York.

Swedo S.E., Schapiro M.E., Grady C.L., Cheslow D.L., Leonard H.L., Kumar A., Friedland R., Rapoport S.I. & Rapoport J.L. (1989) Cerebral glucose metabolism in childhood-onset obsessive compulsive disorder. *Archives of General Psychiatry*, **46**, 518–523.

Tanner C.M., Goetz C.G. & Klawans H.L. (1982) Cholinergic mechanisms in Tourette's syndrome. *Neurology*, **32**, 1315.

Tassin J.P., Lavielle S., Herve D., Blanc G., Thierry A.M., Alvarez C., Berger B. & Glowinski J. (1979) Collateral sprouting and reduced activity of the rat mesocephalic dopaminergic neurons after selective destruction of ascending noradrenergic bundles. *Brain Research*, **4**, 1569–1582.

World Health Organization (1988) ICD-10 (1988), draft of chapter V, mental, behavioral, and developmental disorders. *Clinical Descriptions and Diagnostic Guidelines.* World Health Organization, Geneva.

Zahner G.E.P. Clubb M.M., Leckman J.F. & Pauls D.L. (1988) The epidemiology of Tourette's syndrome. In: Cohen D.J., Bruun R.D. & Leckman J.F. (eds) *Tourette's Syndrome and Tic Disorders*, p. 79. Wiley, New York.

Zohar J., Mueller A., Insel T.R., Zohar-Kadouch R.C. & Murphy D.L. (1987) Serotonergic responsivity in obsessive-compulsive disorder. *Archives of General Psychiatry*, **44**, 946–951.

Chapter 27
Feeding and Sleeping Disorders

David Skuse

INTRODUCTION

Both feeding and sleeping behaviour in early childhood are examples of developmental tasks that, if they are to be achieved successfully, demand an ability for the self-regulation of behaviour. From their earliest days infants must have the capacity to experience hunger and satiation, so that they can elicit sufficient nurture in order to satisfy the energy costs of growth and activity. Similarly, they should be able to regulate their sleep patterns so that they can obtain sufficient sleep to ensure a state of psychological and physical health. Evidently the two behavioural repertoires have much in common: they are essential and universal developmental tasks; they entail interaction with a caregiver to varying extents, and both are subject to frequent perturbations in otherwise normal children. Feeding and sleeping difficulties are two of the most common problems encountered by parents.

Feeding is an intermittent activity that requires a young infant to have, or to attract, the attention of a caregiver. Both partners normally make an active contribution to that interaction. The cry of the human infant is highly effective in eliciting nurturance and bodily contact (Bernal, 1972) and is known to induce anticipatory milk let-down and increase breast temperature in a lactating mother (Vuorenskoski *et al.*, 1969). Mothers who are attuned to their infants' signals are often able to distinguish a hungry cry from other cry signals (Wasz-Hockert *et al.*, 1985). So that they may ensure the nurturing environment responds adaptively to their needs, infants must be able to signal those demands clearly and unambiguously, a facility that is normally well-developed by 4 months or so (Harris & Booth, 1992). Infants who are neurologically in some way abnormal, suffering for example from cerebral palsy (Rogers, 1988), or who have been born preterm (McGehee & Eckerman, 1983) may emit signals that are difficult for their mothers to interpret. Temperamental variability may also play a part in determining the insistence and clarity with which infants make their needs known; for example, the possession of a 'difficult' temperament may have quite different consequences for children's development according to the environmental circumstances in which they are being raised. On the one hand, in a fascinating study by DeVries (1984), Masai infants stood a better chance of survival in a famine if they were predisposed to be demanding of their

mothers than if they had passive and 'easy' dispositions. Within their culture qualities of assertion are prized and feeding patterns reflect that point. In contrast, a study in inner London (Wolke *et al.*, 1990) found evidence that a substantial proportion of infants who had failed to thrive were temperamentally fussy and difficult to soothe, qualities which seemed to contribute towards a maladaptive style of parent–child interaction in which their needs were not met by irritated and harassed mothers.

FEEDING

Historical trends in infant feeding

Trends in feeding practices between 1910 and the early 1970s in the UK are now being reversed. Over that period the proportion of infants being fed by breast fell from 70% at the time they left hospital to just 24%. By the mid 1970s 80–95% of infants were receiving nonmilk solids by 3 months of age. A dramatic change has taken place within the past two decades. Following substantial publicity emphasizing the benefits of breast-feeding, the proportion of mothers putting babies to the breast has increased to nearly 70%. About 2 out of 3 mothers are still breast-feeding at 6 weeks and approximately 50% at 3 months. However, there is still substantial variation between social classes; in 1985 the incidence of breast-feeding amongst mothers from families with professional qualifications (social class I) was 81% (Registrar General's Classification of Occupations, 1980). It was only 43% among families from unskilled manual workers (social class V; Department of Health and Social Security, 1988).

During the first 6 months of life a child's rate of weight gain is greater than it will ever be again until puberty. The energy cost of that growth is exceptionally high, constituting 30% of normal energy intake at 1–2 months and falling to just 3% by 9–12 months after birth (Bergman & Bergman, 1986). An infant's weight typically doubles in 4–6 months and triples within a year. In order to sustain this remarkable growth rate an adequate supply of calories is needed. Chronic early malnourishment may lead to permanent stunting (Skuse, 1989). Healthy babies who are being breast-fed consume a daily volume of milk at any given age that varies across a two- to threefold range (Whitehead & Paul, 1981). Studies have shown that from 2 to 8 months after birth, normal rates of growth can be achieved by energy intakes that are substantially smaller than the current recommended dietary allowance (Whitehead, 1985). However, towards the end of the first year there is a closer correspondence with the World Health Organization/Food and Agriculture Organization (WHO/FAO) recommendations, possibly because of increased activity levels (FAO/WHO/UNU (United Nations University), 1985). Commenting on these findings, Whitehead (1983) was emboldened to state: 'it is wisest for paediatricians, nutritionists, and health workers to recognise that the mother is probably the best judge of what her baby needs: where there are no economic or social pressures on her, and where her baby is growing well, then she should be advised to follow her instincts and not to be unnecessarily influenced by experts'. Whilst this is undoubtedly true for the majority or normal children, there is recent evidence that a substantial minority of otherwise healthy infants, who are relatively undemanding and easy babies, do not get fed adequately precisely because they do not make life difficult for their mothers (Habbick & Gerrard, 1984). A baby's lack of demand can lead to reduced milk production (Dewey & Lonnerdal, 1986), whereas more frequent nursing can increase it (Drewett et al., 1987b; Illingworth, 1991). Harris and Booth (1992) recently proposed that such relatively undemanding infants fail to feed adequately, hence do not put on weight at a normal rate, because they do not experience the same degree of hunger as the majority.

Failure to thrive at the breast is a well-recognized phenomenon, and is especially likely to occur where there are long intervals between feeds and uninterrupted sleep at night (Evans & Davies, 1977; Keane et al., 1988). Normally the frequency of on-demand feeds rises to 2-hourly in the early days after birth and breast milk production increases to meet the challenge. It is inappropriate to breast-feed according to a strict timetable (Department of Health and Social Security, 1988). Frequent suckling stimulates the mother's secretion of prolactin which in turn contributes to an increased milk supply. If that mother wishes to continue breast-feeding she should not give any other fluid to her child (Goldberg & Adams, 1983). Were she to respond as many mothers do, by providing supplementary formula from a bottle, her supply of breast milk would remain static. Consequently, before long she would seem to have 'insufficient milk'. In fact 'insufficient milk' is the most commonly given but usually spurious reason for premature cessation of lactation. True failure of lactation can occur but is rare (Llewellyn-Jones, 1983). Recent work has suggested that feeding size is largely determined by the infant and is not usually limited by maternal factors (e.g. Dewey & Lonnerdal, 1986; Neville et al., 1988). Unfortunately, we do not yet know which factors influence feeding size and interval, and the extent to which these variables are influenced by learning and experience.

The total fat content of breast milk is low at the beginning of each feed, and caloric intake depends upon the extent to which the breast is emptied. Fat provides much of the energy and all of the associated essential fatty acids needed; it is also the carrier of fat-soluble vitamins A, D, E and K, and of prostaglandins. During the course of any single feed fat content may increase by as much as four times, though the extent is very variable. Therefore brief feeds, for whatever reason, can lead to chronic undernourishment. So can feeds from one breast that terminate relatively early because the baby is put on to the other breast before the fat-rich hind milk has been consumed. Breast-feeding may be adequate as a sole source of food up to 4–6 months of age, but the length of time infants can fulfill their nutritional needs from breast milk alone varies considerably (Ahn & MacLean, 1980; Hitchcock et al., 1981). Exclusively breast-feeding may be associated with a relative decline in weight gain after 8–12 weeks, an eventuality that causes anxiety not only to mothers but also to health visitors and family doctors. Yet less rapid weight gain from the third month onwards is perfectly compatible with good infant health (Whitehead et al., 1989). The weight gain trajectories of infants who are breast-fed through the first year differ substantially from charts of normal growth drawn up in the early 1960s when bottle-feeding was predominant (Tanner et al., 1966a,b).

A variety of problems can be associated with breast-feeding; many mothers give up because of nipple pain, and pain from uterine contractions, both of which are more common in the early days (Drewett et al., 1987a). More frequent nursing does not make nipple pain more likely (Illingworth, 1991). Fretful irritable infants may be more difficult to breast-feed. If the infant is thereby chronically undernourished, such behaviour may become exacerbated, and a vicious cycle established. Maternal worry and tiredness can also adversely affect the production of milk, by interfering with the neurohumoral let-down reflex (Davies, 1979).

Introduction of mixed feeding

During the first years of life infants make a transition from single to multiple food sources; there are increasing opportunities for self-control of food intake and, subsequently, new social contexts for eating involving peers and adult caretakers. At some time, usually in the early to middle part of the first year after birth, infants are introduced to foods that bear some relationship to the adult diet of their culture. Developmental changes in food acceptance patterns accompany this broadening of choice. They include, firstly, alterations in child and mother factors that contribute to the control of food intake such as the desire to self-feed. The second, change is the emergence of neophobia (a preference for familiar over novel foods) and its reduction through repeated exposure. Thirdly, preferences and aversions are acquired, through the associative conditioning of food cues to the social contexts and physiological consequences of eating. Fourthly, conventions are learned about when to eat and when to stop eating (meal initiation and satiety). Finally, so-called cuisine rules are acquired (Birch, 1990b). Cuisine rules involve learning how to distinguish edible from inedible substances, which food and flavour combinations are socially sanctioned, and also social norms about when foods should be eaten; for example, which foods it is appropriate to eat at which mealtimes.

When the introduction of solid foods into an infant's diet is being discussed, the term weaning is often encountered. It has a rather uncertain meaning, and should be avoided. A preferable way of describing the procedure by which an infant's food is changed from predominantly milk or formula to that of a solid diet (Lebenthal, 1985) is to speak of mixed feeding. Mixed feeding refers to the use of any food other than human milk or infant formula, and includes the use of nonproprietary milks (e.g. cow's milk) as well as semisolid foods (Department of Health and Social Security, 1988). The present-day recommendation in the UK is that solid food should be introduced into an infant's diet between the ages of about 4 and 6 months (Department of Health and Social Security, 1988). However, practices vary considerably between different cultures. The introduction of mixed feeding is a stage of transition for the infant in terms of behavioural organization (Lipsitt *et al.*, 1985), and accompanies a change from the reflexive behaviour patterns seen in the young infant (e.g. suckling) to a voluntary response system. During the intermediate period, which occurs at different times for different individuals, but is almost always between 60 and 150 days postterm, the child may become restless and fretful.

During the latter part of the first year there may be a 'sensitive' period for the introduction of solid foods. If children are not exposed to solids that require chewing by about 6–7 months of age they tend to be resistant to accepting these textures in later childhood (Illingworth & Lister, 1964). Feeding problems can then result, with refusal to accept lumpy foods and even vomiting. In their original hypothesis on this matter, Illingworth and Lister provided a few case histories, but theirs was by no means the report of a scientific investigation. Yet their conclusions and advice fit very closely with the experience of feeding young children. Consequently virtually no one has subsequently tried to study the matter systematically, the original paper being for over 25 years taken as the last word on the matter! Cameron (1968) did reexamine the issue with the aid of a small retrospective series of children who had been operated on for tracheooesophageal fistula, but unfortunately the results were inconclusive with respect to this hypothesis. Children who have not had the experience of chewing firm solids by a year or so will have immature and restricted tongue movements, and consequently firm foodstuffs will not be masticated adequately for ease of swallowing. Attempts to swallow will lead to an aversive gag response and subsequent refusal to ingest anything but liquid or puréed material.

Some recent work by Harris *et al.* (1990) has suggested a sensitive period may also exist early in the first year for tastes as well as textures. Normally, solid food is liable to be introduced into the diets of infants from about 4 months, from nutritional necessity (Harris, 1988). New tastes are readily accepted at this time, and tolerance of those tastes persists into later childhood. Outright rejection of new foods (neophobia) does not normally occur until later on in the first year. If food preferences really are conditioned by exposure in the early months, delayed introduction of a wide range of tastes until

after 6 months or so is likely to meet with food refusal, especially by individuals who are temperamentally difficult (Harris & Booth, 1992). Whilst this hypothesis has yet to be tested scientifically, apart from the very limited condition of salt preference (Harris *et al.*, 1990), the observation fits closely with clinical experience.

Feeding disorders

There have been few studies of the prevalence of serious feeding disorders among the infant population in general. Dahl and colleagues (Dahl & Sundelin, 1986; Dahl *et al.*, 1986; Dahl, 1987; Dahl & Kristiansson, 1987) conducted a survey in Uppsala, Sweden, using child health clinic records. Mothers were visited at home in order to interview them, and to observe their children being fed. The proportion of those with significant feeding difficulties between 3 and 7 months of age was about 1.4%, defined rather strictly according to three criteria. Firstly, the mother and health clinic nurse must have agreed that a problem was present. Secondly, it should have persisted without interruption for at least 1 month. Thirdly, simple advice on management provided by the clinic nurse had not been sufficient to eliminate the problem. Of 50 identified cases the sex distribution was equal. The majority presented with refusal to feed, but about 1 in 6 had either persistent colic or vomiting. Overall, only 14% had a physical disorder which was believed to be contributing to the feeding difficulties. Lindberg *et al.* (1991) undertook two questionnaire surveys to determine the prevalence of feeding problems in infants between 6 and 16 months, again among Swedish families. They found about a quarter of families in both samples had had significant difficulties at one time, and about 1 in 10 were still having difficulties. These higher proportions than were found by Dahl no doubt reflect different diagnostic criteria. Typical symptoms included refusing to eat, not showing hunger and being oppositional during mealtimes. A different approach was taken by Forsyth *et al.* (1985a) who studied a sample of 373 singletons born during a 4-month period at a Newhaven, Connecticut, hospital. In the first part of the study mothers were interviewed a few days after birth. They were asked about their expectations of later feeding problems, such as crying, colic and spitting. The researchers then tried to discover what proportion actually had developed difficulties 4 months later. A follow-up telephone survey found about one-third of mothers believed their infant had a moderate or severe problem connected with feeding. The proportions of those with difficulties within the breast- and bottle-feeding populations were broadly similar. On the whole, mothers who had higher social adversity scores were substantially more likely to report difficulties at follow-up.

Colic

There is no widely accepted definition of colic, but the diagnosis is usually based on paroxysms of intense inconsolable crying which commence after feeding, occur during the evening hours, and are associated with other symptoms such as flushing of the skin, flexing of the legs and abdominal distension. Colic usually begins 2—4 weeks after birth and persists for 3—4 months. The cause is unknown, but about 16—30% of infants are said to suffer from it at some time (Hide & Guyer, 1982; Forsyth *et al.*, 1985b). The distress engendered by the condition can drive parents to despair, and leads to decreased confidence in their ability to manage their infant successfully. Because there is no consensus about its aetiology, little can be said about the best way to manage the problem. Over the past 20—30 years there has been a ground-swell of opinion that the condition could be due to some specific allergic reaction to the protein content of milk or, on the other hand, that milk intolerance might be caused by the partial malabsorption of lactose (Lothe *et al.*, 1982; Jakobsson & Lindberg, 1983). Studies that have eliminated cow's milk from the diet of colicky babies have yielded contradictory results, in part because of poor methodological techniques. Even when a recent attempt was made to rectify these deficiencies, findings were equivocal (Forsyth, 1989): whilst there was some evidence that colic improved when artificial feeds based on cow's milk formulas were eliminated and replaced by a casein-hydrolysate formula, the benefits did not persist but diminished over time. The phenomenon of colic is commonly encountered; even without treatment it is usually self-limiting in duration. Food allergy or intolerance is probably the cause of symptoms in only 12—15% of colicky infants. A 2—3-month trial of a hypoallergenic formula may be warranted in selected cases, but parents should not be left with the idea that the infant will have a lifelong food allergy.

Reflux vomiting

Regurgitation of foods because of gastrooesophageal reflux is common in the young infant but in most cases it is little more than an inconvenience. However, in a minority it is an important clinical problem resulting in failure to thrive, haematemesis, iron-deficiency anaemia, oesophagitis, structure formation, apnoea, obstructive airway disease and aspiration pneumonia (Milla, 1990; Orenstein & Orenstein, 1988). Reflux may occur because of a variety of defects of function and structure of the oesophagus; in symptomatic children most reflux episodes are due to transient relaxation of the lower oesophageal sphincter, which is asynchronous with swallowing (Mahony *et al.*, 1988). The prevalence of the condition is difficult to ascertain, as most infants who regurgitate do not come to medical attention. Even in those who do, about two-thirds of symptoms resolve by 9, or at the most 18 months (Carre, 1959). The relevance of this disorder for those concerned with child behaviour is twofold. Firstly, because as many as 90% of instances of reflux occur without associated vomiting (Paton *et al.*, 1988), the condition may present as irritability or posturing of the head and neck that superficially resembles torticollis (Bray *et al.*, 1977). Secondly, frequent reflux of stomach contents and acid into the oesophagus can cause a persistent burning sensation that becomes associated with mealtimes, and an affected child is therefore often reluctant to eat for no obvious reason. If there

is associated vomiting, quite apart from the impact on the child, there may be profound consequences on the caretaker, in whom feelings of demoralization can be induced. Investigation of suspected gastrooesophageal reflux should ideally be undertaken by a paediatric gastroenterologist. The problem can potentially be controlled by a number of interventions including modified positioning, thickening of foods, pharmacological agents and surgery depending on the severity of symptoms.

Rumination

This rather rare condition is defined as 'the repeated voluntary regurgitation of gastric contents, without associated nausea or gastro-intestinal disorder' (American Psychiatric Association, 1987). It is encountered predominantly among children, although it is occasionally also observed in adults and, in both populations, it has a higher prevalence among those with mental retardation. There is usually an associated failure to gain weight or weight loss. It derives importance from the fact that, although not common in the general population of children, the condition is potentially fatal (Sauvage *et al.*, 1985). Incidentally, there is evidently a problem with a defining criterion that states 'without nausea', for this would be difficult to establish in infancy. The onset of rumination is usually within the first year of life. During the earliest phase it may be difficult to distinguish from the regurgitation or possetting seen in normal infants. Recent work has suggested two distinct forms of the condition should be differentiated. Firstly, so-called psychogenic rumination (Mayes *et al.*, 1988), which has its onset during infancy and occurs in children who are otherwise developmentally normal. This form is allegedly associated with a significant disturbance in the mother—child relationship, such as neglect, or failure of adequate attachment experiences (Sauvage *et al.*, 1985). Secondly, self-stimulatory rumination, the form that is closely associated with mental retardation, may have its onset at any time from infancy through adulthood. The role of psychosocial factors is less certain in this latter condition (Mayes *et al.*, 1988). Because rumination is relatively rare, and only scattered case reports are available on its characteristics, there is little certainty about its natural history or prognosis. Medical complications such as gastrooesophageal reflux (Shepherd *et al.*, 1987) are likely to be contributory in infancy and initial treatment should be aimed at the underlying condition, although it may be difficult to establish which disorder preceded the other. However, in many instances there will be associated disturbances in the caregiver—infant relationship, which are bound up with the symptoms in a complex interaction of cause and effect. For the caregiver of a child who persistently ruminates, her failure to feed the child successfully may render the very act of feeding aversive; the noxious odour of vomit pervades the scene and clothes may become saturated with regurgitated material.

Treatment is urgent because of potential medical complications including haematemesis, dehydration and caries. Note that as gastric acid erodes the teeth they can become exquisitely painful, and the scene is set for food refusal, even after the rumination has been successfully treated. Dental intervention in which capping of the affected teeth is undertaken is then indicated. Behavioural management is usually indicated. A variety of aversive techniques including electroshock were used in the past but these have now been superseded by nonaversive approaches (Singh *et al.*, 1982; Whitehead *et al.*, 1985; Glasscock *et al.*, 1986; Mestre *et al.*, 1988).

Oral–motor dysfunction

In order to feed successfully the infant must acquire a range of developmental skills, which include sucking, chewing, biting and swallowing. This repertoire of oral–motor functions gradually evolves to allow the efficient management of foods with an increasing variety of consistencies. Voluntary control is gradually acquired over the process of nutritional acquisition, but at the outset infants are equipped simply with just a few essential reflexes including the rooting response, the suckle–swallow reflex and reflex closure of the vocal chords on swallowing. A basic component of control at this time is rhythmicity, exerted at the subcortical level, through the brainstem and midbrain (Evans-Morris, 1985). Until recently, it has been insufficiently appreciated by non-specialists that relatively minor perturbations in neurological maturation, as well as overt disorders of neurological organization, can have a significant impact on the ability of young children to feed successfully by impairing oral–motor competence. The earliest oral–motor skill to be achieved by breast-fed infants is known as suckling (distinct, it should be noted, from sucking) in which subtle control of the tongue is required to allow a repetitive negative intraoral pressure to be generated, which alternates with compression of the nipple against the upper jaw and hard palate. Poor suckling activity is likely to be found in otherwise normal infants who are premature, but it is then a transient phenomenon. The postconception age required for the establishment of suckle–swallow coordination is 34–37 weeks (Braun & Palmer, 1985). Feeding difficulties with their onset at a very early stage in the first year may be the only finding in subjects with mild cerebral palsy, manifesting as dysrythmias or disregulation of the suckling rhythm (Evans-Morris, 1985). Varying degrees of deficiency in suckle competence may also be found in infants with more obvious manifestations of brain damage (Evans-Morris, 1989). In infants of over 34 weeks' gestation, abnormalities of suckling and swallowing are unlikely to result from immaturity and usually have a pathological basis (Hill & Volpe, 1981).

Disorders of oral–motor development may play a role in the aetiology of some cases of failure to thrive in infancy (Mathisen *et al.*, 1989). As a consequence of such disorders an overt feeding problem can be created, which exacerbates preexisting tensions in the mother–infant relationship. Difficulties with sucking, chewing or swallowing, tongue-thrusting, involuntary tonic biting of the nipple or spoon, excessive drooling and an intolerance of the texture of developmentally appropriate foods may be present. Although it has been postulated that such disorders are likely to be associated with excessively long mealtimes (Lewis, 1982), direct observation of affected infants being fed within their own homes has shown precisely the opposite is often true. Many mothers who are confronted by a child whom it is exceptionally difficult and frustrating to feed simply want the procedure to be over as quickly as possible. This is not only the case where oral–motor dysfunctions are associated with failure to thrive (Mathisen *et al.*, 1989) in which the brief duration of feeding probably contributes towards a deficient energy intake. It is also true in cases of cerebral palsy, where overt brain damage (Reilly & Skuse, 1992) can be associated with profound disorders of oral–motor functioning.

Feeding difficulties in relation to cerebral palsy are due to three main aetiological factors: (1) the child's difficulty with head control, poor mouth closure and persistent tongue thrust; (2) a delayed swallow reflex; and (3) poor pharyngeal peristalsis. The chief consequence of these abnormalities is that it takes far longer than normal for the child to masticate and swallow a mouthful of food. During swallowing there may be an escape of food into the pharynx before laryngeal closure, causing gagging and permitting aspiration of foodstuff into the lungs. Because pharyngeal transit of food is itself disordered, or protracted, aspiration is a serious risk. Perhaps it is not surprising, in view of the associated difficulties, that children with cerebral palsy often fail to achieve an adequate food intake for normal growth. Not only do they have problems dealing with the nutrition that is presented to them but, if they are totally dependent upon being fed by others, those with communication difficulties may not be able to signal hunger or satiety adequately. They may not be able to make their food preferences known. Gastrooesophageal reflux often contributes to their discomfort; up to 75% of children with cerebral palsy are affected, according to some surveys (Rempel *et al.*, 1988). The consequence of such feeding disorders may be serious, influencing not only children's physical development, in the sense of malnutrition, but also their sense of well-being and social relationships. Feeding interactions characterized by numerous episodes of food spillage, coughing, choking, regurgitation and spitting engender intense emotions in parents whose failure to feed adequately their child is likely to lead to feelings of guilt and despair, reflected in high levels of depressive symptoms (Reilly & Skuse, 1992).

A number of approaches to the management of feeding disorders in association with cerebral palsy have been suggested. Firstly, the management of contextual factors such as positioning is important. Many feeding problems will be greatly improved by the provision of adaptive seating arrangements (Hulme *et al.*, 1987; Mulcahy *et al.*, 1988). The provision of oral–motor therapy is said by some to be an effective way of improving oral–motor functioning (Alexander, 1987), although others have taken the view that this is not necessarily of value (Ottenbacher *et al.*, 1983). Some have suggested the consistency of presented food should be modified, so that it resembles paste (Jones, 1989), although again this recommendation is controversial. Less severely affected children can be helped to eat and drink independently by the use of special aids and utensils, such as wide-bore plastic drinking straws and non-slip mats (Jones, 1992).

Some medical conditions

Other significant disorders of feeding in infancy may be associated with structural defects of the oropharynx (Illingworth, 1969). The majority of these will be self-evident, such as cleft palate, macroglossia (as in the Down's syndrome), and the Pierre Robin syndrome which is associated with micrognathia. However, the congenital anomaly of submucous cleft palate will not be detected unless the palate is palpated, as the associated nasal regurgitation and nasal speech often pass unnoticed (Moss et al., 1990).

It is important to bear in mind that relatively subtle disorders of gastric motility can be associated with abnormal patterns of feeding (Milla, 1986). In recent years a variety of new techniques for the investigation of oesophageal and small intestinal motility have become available for use with children (Sondheimer, 1988; Cucchiara et al., 1990). Such disorders may present with food refusal, often engendered by parental or even professional attempts at force-feeding, which is all too often the initial response to a young child who is reluctant to eat. Efforts to break the child's will are doomed to failure. Investigations may reveal delayed gastric emptying or abnormal small bowel motility. In many cases it is possible to produce a dramatic improvement with a simple medical treatment, by prescribing the novel prokinetic drug cisapride which enhances gut motility (Cucchiara et al., 1990). However, this drug is not yet licensed for use with children, and so should only be prescribed after a specialist assessment.

Pica

Pica is a disorder with an onset usually between 12 and 24 months, in which there is persistent eating of substances that have no nutritional value (Bicknell, 1975). Because very young infants normally put a whole variety of objects in their mouths, for exploratory purposes, it would be unwise to make the diagnosis before the age of 2 years unless the behaviour has been so persistent as to appear developmentally inappropriate (Rozin, 1990). In older children the frequency of the behaviour is also usually taken as a defining feature; according to ICD-10 (World Health Organisation, 1992) it has to occur at least twice weekly and persist for a month or more to have clinical relevance. Pica may be associated with psychiatric conditions such as autism (Raiten & Massaro, 1986; Accardo et al., 1988), schizophrenia and the Kleine—Levin syndrome. However, it is more commonly associated with mental retardation, in which case the behaviour may persist from childhood into adulthood. Good epidemiological data on this matter are not available, but estimates of the prevalence of pica among institutionalized mentally retarded persons range from 10 to 25% (Danford & Huber, 1982; McAlpine & Singh, 1986); severely retarded individuals are at greatest risk.

Among children who are not mentally retarded there is an unsurprising association with lack of parental supervision and with neglect, hence the condition is associated with relative environmental deprivation (Madden et al., 1980) and parental psychopathology. The clinical importance of pica is threefold. Firstly, it may be one presenting feature of a developmental disorder such as childhood autism or mental retardation. Secondly, it may be a behavioural indicator of a child who is suffering serious neglect or abuse. Thirdly, the persistent consumption of materials such as cloth, paint, dirt, hair, straw and wood can lead to medical complications which include lead poisoning, intestinal obstruction and infestations with Toxocara or Toxoplasma. The condition is potentially lethal (Barnhard & Mittleman, 1986).

FEEDING AS AN INTERACTIONAL PROCESS

Certain infant feeding disorders are said to reflect a developmental problem of separation and individuation (Chatoor et al., 1988). Food refusal is hypothesized to be the outward manifestation of an underlying conflict between autonomy and dependence. The peak age of onset is between 6 months and 3 years of age. In some cases the degree of selectivity about which foods are accepted is so great that there is associated failure of somatic growth; parents become anxious, frustrated and over-involved, failing to give appropriate contingent responses to the child's needs. Chatoor et al. (1988), drawing on notions about the origins of adolescent anorexia nervosa (Bruch, 1973; Selvini Palazzoni, 1978), have suggested such food refusal may be designated infantile anorexia nervosa. However, Sturm and Stancin (1990) have challenged this hypothesis; it is unwise to draw parallels between food refusal in later childhood and the phenomenon as observed in infancy for the following reasons. Firstly, the criteria used to make a diagnosis of anorexia nervosa, such as distortions of body image, which are necessary in both DSM-IV (American Psychiatric Association, in press) and ICD-10, could not be applied to infants. Secondly, there is no good empirical evidence to support the assertion by Chatoor et al. that temperamental qualities determine whether a child at risk will manifest anorexia nervosa during infancy, or anorexia during adolescence. The argument is not about the description of the condition, which is well-recognized by clinicians who deal with feeding problems in early childhood, but about the extent to which one can infer the infant's motives in refusing to eat. Whether or not we accept Chatoor's formulation of the problem, there is no doubt that infants with persistent food refusal often have 'difficult' temperaments in other respects too, in the sense that they tend to be poorly regulated in other aspects of their behaviour and respond negatively to novel stimuli (Prior, 1992). Their need to control incoming stimuli may derive from a strong need for autonomy. Alternatively, they may have a heightened sensitivity to novelty, so that unfamiliar stimuli are perceived as aversive. Or perhaps they are exquisitely aware of internal signals of satiety.

Eating disorders in the older preschool child

Investigations into the prevalence of feeding problems among preschool children have found a remarkably high proportion are affected. Minde and Minde (1986) reviewed the available epidemiological data; estimates of between 12 and 34% were usual, although one study of parents of preschool children (Eppright *et al.*, 1969) reported 75% had had a problem with their child refusing to eat at mealtimes.

Many toddlers who decline to eat a normal diet in terms of quantity and quality will have been difficult feeders from an early age — fussy, resisting the introduction of any new foods, suffering from frequent colic, and vomiting persistently after, or even during, mealtimes. In general, other things being equal, young children show a preference for familiar over novel foods. There is very little information available on the emergence and developmental course of neophobic responses, but anecdotal evidence suggests they may not exert a major influence until after the first year of life (Birch, 1990a). Neophobia diminishes in severity when repeated samplings of food are not followed by negative consequences; novel foods eventually become an accepted part of the diet. During the transitional period, as children are being introduced to the adult diet of their culture, the adaptive value of a wary response must be weighed against the children's need to experience variety in their diets. Unfortunately, most parents are unaware that this initial rejection of a new food is usually a transitory phenomenon, which can be reduced by means of repeated exposure. Instead they interpret the initial rejection as reflecting the child's immutable dislike of the new food. Rather than presenting it again, parents will then remove the food from the child's diet, thereby eliminating the possibility that the neophobic response will be reduced and consequently failing to broaden the variety of foods their child will accept.

As has already been discussed, recent work suggests that there could be a sensitive period, between about 4 and 6 months of age, during which infants will usually accept virtually any taste, and if they have a number of exposures to that taste a preference may be induced which persists into later childhood (Birch & Marlin, 1982; Harris & Booth, 1992). Consequently, extreme faddiness in preschoolers may be more frequently encountered amongst those whose early feeding experiences were of a very bland and limited diet up until at least 6 months of age. In the 1920s and 1930s Clara Davis conducted several pioneering studies on the selection of diets by infants and young children (Davis, 1928, 1938). The results of her research have been widely interpreted by health professionals to mean that, given a variety of choices, infants will instinctively select and consume a well-balanced diet. Such a broad conclusion was not drawn by Davis, nor can it be concluded from her research or from that of any other investigator (Story & Brown, 1987). Davis's experiment was to offer only a variety of nutritious unsweetened foods. Young infants have a distinct preference for sweeter tastes (Cowart, 1981; Birch, 1990b), although this preference may be modified

by subsequent dietary experiences (Beauchamp & Moran, 1984). So an important question not addressed by her research is what would have been selected given the availability of desserts, ice cream, pastries, sweets and similar items.

Food refusal may develop on the basis of learned aversions to certain foods, perhaps because they have in the past been associated with unpleasant experiences. Rozin and Fallon (1987) point out that the single most common precursor to the dislike of specific foods in adulthood is that the food in question was, in the past, associated with vomiting. Such an aversion typically reflects close temporal contiguity between ingestion and the episode of vomiting; the apparent causal relationship might well have been coincidental but that is irrelevant to this example of a 'one-trial' learning process.

Management

A wide variety of professionals may become involved with children who are refusing to eat, including health visitors, general practitioners, paediatricians, speech therapists and psychologists. Usually the problem does not present to a specialist until a relatively late stage, for the simple reason that most cases are self-limiting and adequate advice is given, along the lines of 'Don't worry, he'll grow out of it'. More severe and protracted instances are referred for specialist investigation. Such referrals may be motivated by the observation that the child is failing to gain weight, or by anxiety about the consequences of nutritional inadequacies such as iron-deficiency anaemia. Because of the range of potentially important aetiological factors, severe and persistent food refusal should be assessed by a multidisciplinary team, comprising at the very least a clinical psychologist, paediatrician, dietitian and speech therapist. The purpose of bringing such a broad range of expertise to bear on the problem is to establish at the outset whether organic factors are playing a significant role in causing or maintaining the feeding problem; these may be subtle, as in the case of submucous cleft or disordered gut motility.

The extent to which medical investigations should be pursued will have to be determined on the basis of an initial assessment, which should comprise not only a comprehensive history of the problem but also direct observations of the child being fed. Ideally observations are undertaken in the home and video-recorded for later discussion by the team. Obviously it would be inappropriate to subject all children with food refusal to a battery of invasive tests; the purpose of a multidisciplinary approach is to formulate a plan that is appropriately tailored to the needs of the individual child (Skuse & Wolke, 1992; Wolke & Skuse, 1992).

There is remarkably little literature on a systematic approach to dealing with children who refuse to eat, most reports being of single case studies. Often these describe children who would not accept oral food after a period of parenteral, naso-gastric or gastrostomy feeding (Blackman & Nelson, 1985; Geertsma *et al.*, 1985). An exception are the recent books by Macht (1990) and Douglas (1989) which do concentrate on the problem as it presents in children who are otherwise perfectly well.

Many children who present with food refusal or extreme faddiness will have been force-fed by their parents at some time. A variety of techniques may have been employed, including holding the child's nose so that the mouth must open to breathe, during which the food is pushed in. Force-feeding almost always leads to an exacerbation of the problem in the longer term. By a simple process of paired associate learning a child comes to fear the feeding situation because of the aversive experience. Soon the very act of food preparation, perceived long before any food has actually been presented, causes distress and tantrums. By the time the caretaker is ready to present the child with a meal there is no alternative but to force-feed yet again.

A further recommended tactic, which goes against the grain with most parents, is that they should discontinue diversionary tactics and games around feeding, in order to encourage the child to accept food. Whilst playing 'aeroplanes' may encourage a normal child to eat up his or her greens, a chronic food refuser will simply use such approaches to his or her own advantage so that mealtimes become impossibly protracted occasions in which games are substituted for food consumption. Mealtimes are for eating and should be time-limited; 20 minutes is a reasonable maximum for preschool children. To begin with, only the foods the child is known to accept should be presented. Small quantities of different foods, each presented separately, are better accepted than large quantities thrown together on one plate. Refusal should be ignored; coaxing is usually self-defeating. Social reinforcement is a crucial element to any treatment programme and works with the great majority of children. Aberrant behaviours are not rewarded, of course; face aversion may be necessary in these circumstances. If success is encountered it may be advantageous to permit frequent closely spaced meals both to increase the overall nutritional intake and to allow frequent exposure to positive reinforcement. Social reinforcement may be enhanced by the family at large, so the child should be encouraged to eat with other family members. In many cases participant observation of normal peer feeding behaviour serves as a powerful motivator for change; seemingly intractable feeding problems often resolve when the self-feeding child has an opportunity to eat at the nursery's communal lunch (Birch, 1980). Peer group modelling is not only effective in encouraging children to eat who are otherwise reluctant to accept anything. It is also a potent way of increasing the range of accepted foods. Note that children who are eating well in the communal situation should be receiving positive social reinforcement for their behaviour. Another technique used to increase the range of accepted foods is to allow a child to take food from another's plate, be it parent, sibling or friend. Children are especially attracted to foods they see others enjoying. This technique will only work with relatively neutral foods for obvious reasons; if the child has a strong aversion to the taste in question it will not be accepted.

Parents often use palatable, preferred foods as rewards for children's performance of desired behaviours. A series of experiments was designed to investigate the effects of these practices on the acquisition of food preferences (Birch, 1990b). The results are clear: repeatedly associating a food with a distinctive social context systematically changes children's preferences, in either a positive or negative direction, depending on the social context employed. If preschool children are offered a food about which they have no strong feelings in order to obtain a (nonfood) reward, this feeding practice produces significant *negative* shifts in their attitude towards that food (Birch *et al.*, 1982, 1984). The reason for this finding is not entirely clear, but one possibility is that the coercive nature of the feeding strategy generates negative emotions which become associated with the food in question. In a fascinating study that was designed to investigate the effects of the use of foods themselves as the reward component of a contingency, it was found that when repeatedly presented with neutral foods as rewards for a desired (noneating) behaviour (whether or not in conjunction with positive adult attention), these erstwhile neutral foods became highly preferred by children (Birch, 1980). An interpretation of these findings is that food cues are becoming associated with the positive or negative affect generated by the social context.

Finally, there is the issue of whether giving a desired foodstuff should be used as a reward, for example, in order to increase consumption of other less desirable foodstuffs. Research conducted with preschool children showed that if there is contingent pairing between the consumption of two foods, then the instrumental food will be cognitively devalued and its consumption on future occasions actually decreases (Birch *et al.*, 1987). For example, in our culture adult caretakers habitually attempt to increase children's consumption of vegetables. It is certainly possible that the reason children do not like to eat vegetables reflects a cultural stereotype. They know their peers will not eat vegetables either. One strategy used to induce children to consume these nutritionally desirable foods is to encourage them to eat the vegetable in order to obtain an extrinsic food reward (e.g. dessert). Such practices can have unintended and negative effects on the quality of a child's diet; preferences for highly palatable (typically high-fat, high-sugar) foods are enhanced, while nutritionally desirable foods can become even more disliked. So, for example, the tactic 'eat up your greens and you can have some ice cream' results in children perceiving greens as even less attractive, and enhances their preference for ice cream. Food can be used as a reward, but encouraging consumption of a preferred food should not be employed as an instrument task. Unfortunately, experience shows that the paradoxical injunction 'eat up your ice cream and you can have some greens' evokes bemusement, rather than consumption.

SLEEP

Sleep is a behavioural state of perceptual disengagement from and unresponsiveness to the environment accompanied by characteristic electroencephalogram (EEG) changes, in which there is potentially a quick reversibility to the wakeful state (Zepelin, 1987). It is now known that the sleep cycle is regulated by a neuronal system situated in the core of the brain, which extends from the medulla through the brainstem and hypothalamus into the forebrain (Jones, 1989). Within sleep two distinct states have been recognized, on the basis of EEG, muscle tone and eye movement data. They are the rapid eye movement state (REM) and the nonrapid eye movement state (NREM). NREM sleep is conventionally divided into four stages: stage 1 and 2 are associated with light sleep whereas stage 3 and 4 are associated with deep sleep and a high threshold for arousal. REM sleep is characterized by EEG activity that is rather like the wakeful state; the arousal threshold is variable. NREM and REM sleep alternate cyclically through the night, the cycle time gradually extending through early life from 50–60 minutes in the neonate to 90 minutes in later childhood and adulthood. Both sleep states are interrupted by brief arousals (Carskadon & Dement, 1987). Normally sleep is entered through NREM activity after a brief period known as the hypnogogic state, which in adults is experienced as fragmented images and disrupted thought patterns. In early sleep the NREM sleep cycles are dominated by stages 3 and 4 but as the night progresses stages 1 and 2 predominate. Early-morning waking is usually from REM sleep.

The function of sleep is still controversial despite over 50 years of research into the matter. Numerous theories abound, seemingly falling into two broad categories: firstly, those that emphasize the need for energy conservation (Snyder, 1966; 1969; Berger & Walker, 1972; Zepelin & Rechtschaffen, 1974), and secondly, those that suggest that there is a need to 'refresh' the neuronal network (Jouvet, 1975). Horne (1988) combined these hypotheses into one, by suggesting that NREM sleep stages 3 and 4 were necessary for cerebral restitution, the rest of sleep being dispensable apart from the marginal energy-conserving role of stage 2 NREM sleep. Dreaming takes place solely during the period of mental activity known as REM sleep, and this is thought to perform a special function in very young infants, being involved in the stimulation of nerve growth. Winson (1990) has proposed that about the age of 2, when the hippocampus becomes functional, REM sleep takes on a further task — it is part of a basic mammalian memory process, the means by which animals form strategies for survival and evaluate current experience in light of those strategies.

Methods of data collection

The most widely used technique of obtaining data about children's sleep is the parental record, which is naturally dependent on the parent in question observing not only the transition to sleep but also being aware of episodes of waking. Several pioneering studies have used this approach (Moore & Ucko, 1957; Parmalee *et al.*, 1964; Bernal, 1973; Jacklin *et al.*, 1980). Other methods include time-lapse infrared video, EEGs,

activity monitors and heart and respiration recordings. All have their advantages and disadvantages. Evidently, the more intrusive the method of sleep recording employed, the more likely one is to collect data that are unrepresentative. For example, Anders and Sostek (1975) criticize polygraph studies conducted in laboratories because 'the first night effect' leads to a reduction in the amount of active REM sleep. In a departure from conventional approaches Thoman and her colleagues (see Thoman & Whitney, 1989) used a pressure-sensitive crib to produce signals of the infant's respiration and body movements. Home-based actigraphic monitoring is also claimed to give information which comes close in accuracy to the laboratory polysomnograph (Sadeh *et al.*, 1991).

Developmental progression of sleep

The fetus is thought not to be truly awake, but to alternate between active sleep and quiet sleep. Movements, including swallowing, kicking and breathing, occur during active sleep (Rigatto, 1989). Neonates born before 30 weeks' gestation spend 90% of their sleep time in REM sleep compared with 50% at term. At term, the neonate spends about 75% of each 24-hour period asleep but this reduces to about 50% by 6 months of age. Longitudinal studies have shown that this relatively small decrease is associated with a considerable change in the organization of sleep. Using parental diaries to obtain a longitudinal record between birth and 22 weeks, Parmalee *et al.* (1964) found the average daily maximal sleep period in the first postnatal week was just 4 hours, but this increased to over 8 hours in the 16th week. The establishment of a diurnal pattern, the longest periods of sleep being overnight, is influenced by environmental as well as maturational factors (Kleitman & Engelmann, 1953). The behavioural organization of sleep–wake cycles was studied by Anders and Keener (1985) by using all-night time-lapse video somnograms of infants at 2, 4, 8, 24, 36 and 52 weeks in their home environments. They found that for full-term infants both the sleep onset latency times and the length of time to their first period of quiet sleep gradually reduced over the first year of life. Brief periods of nightwaking were usual but the infants usually settled themselves and went back to sleep again, although occasionally they cried out. Parents' awareness of their child's waking depends largely on whether he or she sleeps with the parents, how often they check the child is asleep and whether they are disturbed by cries. Anders (1979) found that a sample of 2-month infants spent on average about 9% of the night's sleep time awake, but this had declined to 6% by 9 months. Interestingly, premature infants seem to be better self-soothers than older infants (Hoppenbrouwers *et al.*, 1988). There is some evidence that mental performance at 24 weeks postterm may be predicted by sleep indices in premature infants; those who most rapidly evolve a mature pattern of long quiet periods of sleep early in the night have superior cognitive performance at follow-up. This matter has been investigated by a number of researchers, including Beckwith and Parmalee (1986). As part of a prospective longitudinal study of preterm infants they measured sleep state organization and EEG patterns at 40 postconception weeks. They found poorer performance both at 4 months postterm and at 8 years in children who had had less mature neurophysiological organization at term, but only for those who had been brought up in relatively unstimulating and unresponsive home environments during the intervening years.

Social and family factors

There are relatively few epidemiological data on family factors associated with sleeping arrangements and sleep problems in children. No consistent social class differences in the prevalence of sleep problems have been found, but it has been reported that social stresses such as financial difficulties, illnesses and unsatisfactory housing are more frequent among families whose children are poor sleepers (Richman, 1981; Lozoff et al., 1985).

There is abundant evidence that maternal depression is associated with children's sleeping difficulties. For example, Richman (1981) discovered a higher rate of psychiatric symptoms among the mothers of 1–2-year-old children who were subject to frequent and persistent nightwaking. A subsequent study of toddlers (Richman, 1985) reported a higher risk of maternal depression in a case group than in controls without sleep problems, also an association with family stress and a lack of confiding relationships between the spouses. Father's mental state may also be influenced by a sleepless child (Simonoff & Stores, 1987). The relationship between cause and effect was investigated by Zuckerman et al. (1987); maternal depression at 8 months was associated with sleep problems that persisted from 8 months to 3 years, suggesting that, at least in this sample, the psychological disturbance was *not* simply a consequence of the mother's disrupted sleep. There is nevertheless a danger that children who do sleep poorly and constantly demand parental attention at night may be at greater risk of abuse.

A review of the popular literature on child rearing among western cultures would suggest it is not unusual for parents to share a bed with their child; warnings are issued about the potentially dire consequences of such behaviour. Yet studies of what parents actually do, as opposed to what they are advised to do, have found co-sleeping is really rather common. In a sample of infants aged 1–2 years, identified in a British epidemiological survey, 35% of night wakers were to be found sleeping in their parents' bed, compared to 7% of controls (Richman, 1981). In the study conducted by Klackenberg (1982), about 35% of Swedish youngsters were still sharing their parents' bed for at least part of the night at 5 years of age; there was no evidence for a different pattern of bed sharing according to the family's socioeconomic status. In the US Lozoff et al. (1984) found it occurred at least occasionally in 35% of white and 70% of black families they interviewed. In a study of Hispanic-American families in New York the prevalence of frequent all-night co-sleeping was said to be 21% for children aged between 6 and 48 months, although

the figure in white urban families from middle America is only about 6% (Schachter et al., 1989). Children are more likely to share their parents' bed if they are ill or frightened (Rosenfeld et al., 1982).

Other cultures are far more openly tolerant of co-sleeping. Super and Harness (1982) found that the Kipisgis of Kowet in Kenya routinely allow infants to sleep with their mothers and to suckle if they wake. This pattern of sleep is associated with significantly shorter periods of continuous sleep during the first year than American infants (6.4 versus 9 hours at 16 weeks). Zuckerman et al. (1987) also report differences according to mother's cultural origins; co-sleeping is more prevalent among mothers from West Indian and African families (46%) and from non-Asian countries (29%) than from Asian (17%) and the UK (16%). Although it has been proposed that solitary nocturnal sleep is a deviant activity from an anthropological point of view (McKenna et al., 1990), and may even be a risk factor for the sudden infant death syndrome (SIDS), this opinion has yet to reach wide acceptance.

VARIETIES OF SLEEP DISORDER

At any age four main categories of specific sleep disturbance can be identified (Stores, 1991): (1) disorders of initiating and maintaining sleep (insomnia); (2) disorders of the sleep–wake cycle; (3) episodic types of behaviour made worse by sleep or occurring exclusively during sleep (parasomnia); and (4) disorders of excessive daytime sleepiness (hypersomnia). In children a distinction ought to be made between sleep disorders and sleep behaviour: sleep disorders will present a problem to someone, be it the parent or the child. Sleep behaviours are not necessarily regarded as a problem; some behaviours such as headbanging might be whereas others, such as snoring, are not.

Most studies on sleep disorders in children have concentrated on nightwaking; this is the most frequent cause of concern to parents and a frequent reason for seeking a professional opinion on management. The second most common problem is the child who fails to settle at night, who will not go to sleep within a reasonable period after being set down in bed, and who calls persistently for parental attention. Other sleep disorders are less common but perhaps expert advice is sought about proportionately more of them: these include nightmares, night terrors, sleepwalking (somnambulism), sleep talking and tooth grinding (bruxism). It is not unusual for these problems to co-occur. Stores (1991) has recently drawn attention to the fact that not only are common disorders of sleep often confused with one another but they may even be misdiagnosed as epilepsy. Conversely, nocturnal epileptic attacks may be misdiagnosed as sleep disorders.

Nightwaking

Whether or not nightwaking is regarded as a problem by parents will depend on what they believe to be normal. Few think that infants less than 3–4 months of age can be expected to sleep through the night without interruption. Even after 4 months there is considerable variation in their expectations. Scott and Richards (1990a) recently conducted a survey on this matter. They found that about 1 in 4 infants, at 1 year of age, were waking 5 or more nights a week. Ten per cent of their mothers did not regard that as a problem. However, 37% of those whose babies woke less often did regard their sleep pattern as a problem. These findings have implications for studies that rely solely on parental reports for their identification of children with sleep disorders.

Nightwaking at 14 months was studied by Bernal (1973) using data from the Cambridge Longitudinal Study (Richards & Bernal, 1972). About a third of infants were still waking regularly at 14 months; there was no relationship between sleep problems, gender, birth order or social class. Those who woke most regularly had had persistently shorter periods of continuous sleep from 8 weeks of age. During the preschool years there is good evidence that the proportion of children who manifest nightwaking behaviour which comes to the attention of their parents is reasonably similar between 1 and 5 years of age (Beltramini & Hertzig, 1983). About 57% wake occasionally at 1 year; the figure is 61% at 5 years. There is however a modest decline in the proportion who wake every night from about 1 in 3 at 3 years to 1 in 5 at 5 years. Whilst various factors have been investigated as possible associates of sleep difficulties and nightwaking, inconsistent findings are reported. There is probably no association with broad indicators of socioeconomic status, mother's age or educational history, although specific aspects of environmental disorganization such as overcrowding and poor housing conditions are significant factors (Chavin & Tinson, 1980; Scott & Richards, 1990b).

Breast-fed infants tend to wake more frequently during the night than artificially fed infants; they also have fewer total hours sleep per 24-hour cycle during the first 2 years of life (Wright *et al.*, 1983; Wright, 1987; Keane *et al.*, 1988). When their infants wake during the night parents often conclude that they are hungry, so one of the major tasks for every parent is to discover what feeding regime is most likely to ensure an uninterrupted night's sleep. This is especially true after the child reaches 3–4 months of age when mixed feeding is likely to have been introduced (Tuchman, 1988).

By 2 months of age breast-fed infants have a diurnal pattern of large meals in the early morning and small meals at the end of the day. At 4 months the pattern switches to large meals at the end of the day, which is adaptive, allowing the infant to cope with a prolonged period of night starvation. Mothers of bottle-fed infants often prefer this technique because their ability to control the quantity given in the evenings means fewer overnight feeds. Mothers often also wish to introduce solid foods at an early stage, prior to bedtime, because they believe this will assure them a longer period of uninterrupted sleep. Although there is a substantial folklore on the supposed benefits of giving, say, cereal just before bedtime, until recently there was little empirical evidence on the matter. Macknin *et al.* (1989) studied this

issue and found no statistically significant trends for infants given bedtime cereal to sleep through the night with any greater consistency than controls, whether it was introduced at 5 weeks or at 4 months of age. By 20 weeks nearly 60% of infants from both groups were sleeping for at least 8 consecutive hours. Wright *et al.* (1983) reported that the mean age at which breast-fed children slept through the night was about 13 weeks, whereas the equivalent figure for bottle-fed infants was just under 11 weeks. Dahl (Dahl & Sundelin, 1986; Dahl *et al.*, 1986) conducted a follow-up of infants who had been originally studied at a mean age of 7.3 months (range 3–11.8 months) 3 months after the original assessment, and again 18 months later. The children had had significant feeding problems when first seen. Normal controls were matched to this case group and in all, 42 pairs of subjects were studied. At the 3-month follow-up sleeping problems were far more frequent among those infants in the refusing to eat group (40%) than among the controls (4%), although by the 18-month follow-up the prevalence of sleeping difficulties was rather similar in both groups, about 1 in 3 children being affected. However, the sleeping problems of children with feeding difficulties had had an earlier onset and in general persisted for a longer period of time than those of the controls.

The influence of the child's birth order upon sleeping difficulties is occasionally thought to be important. But the interpretation of data suggesting that first- or second-born children wake more often (Moore & Ucko, 1957; Richman, 1985) may merely reflect reduced parental anxiety with later-born children. Other studies have failed to find any association between age at sleeping through the night and parity (van Tassel, 1985; Zuckerman *et al.*, 1987). If parental expectations do indeed play a role in determining the 'problem' in first-borns, automated recordings of sleep behavioural organization should reveal no differences in nightwaking with parity, and that is indeed the case (Anders *et al.*, 1985; Thoman & Whitney, 1989). Nor does there seem to be any significant association between gender and sleep problems, whether the matter has been studied with the aid of parental report (Jacklin *et al.*, 1980) or by automated recording devices (Anders *et al.*, 1985). A sole exception to this picture is the study of van Tassel (1985) which found males were rather more likely to show sleep disturbance in the first and the second years of life.

In contrast to the generally non-significant influence of demographic characteristics, specific problems during pregnancy, delivery and labour have often been shown to bear some predictive relationship to later sleep difficulties (Blurton-Jones *et al.*, 1978; Richman, 1981). Longitudinal studies by Moore and Ucko (1957) and Bernal (1973) also found poorer Apgar-like ratings at birth were associated with greater (parentally defined) sleep problems in later infancy. The Bernal study is of particular interest because all births were uncomplicated home deliveries. However, despite the consensus that perinatal events can be important influences, there is very little evidence for an association with low birth weight, or prematurity.

Drug treatment

The sustained benefit of drug treatment for sleep problems in early childhood has not been established. Despite this, drugs continue frequently to be prescribed for the condition. Few investigators have examined the matter systematically, using appropriate case-control designs and double-blind prescriptions. An exception is the Richman (1985) study which aimed to determine the effectiveness of trimeprazine tartrate in a sample of children aged 1−2 years with a severe sleep problem, as reported by parents, who had been identified from a community survey. The drug was administered for 2 weeks after a baseline sleep pattern had been established by means of sleep diaries. Despite improvement in the time taken to fall asleep and the frequency of nightwakings, these effects were of little clinical significance. Benefits were not sustained during a 6-month follow-up, suggesting that the habitual sleep pattern of the children had not been altered. Rather similar findings were obtained by Simonoff and Stores (1987) who reported a reduction in the number of nightwakings in a 4-week trial of trimeprazine tartrate with children aged 7−37 months. The benefits were not sustained once treatment had been discontinued.

Behaviour management

The initial step in managing a disorder of sleep is to get the child to bed. Subsequently, one must deal with disturbances during the course of the night. The recommended procedures can be summarized briefly as follows; they derive from the work of Douglas and Richman (1984). Firstly, a behavioural analysis should be made of the sleep problem, including antecedents, behaviour and consequences. Secondly, an analysis of the family relationship should be undertaken, including airing of any major difficulties. An assessment is made of the emotional states of both parents and other family members. Thirdly, a discussion should be undertaken about possible causes of the sleep problem and about scope for change. Fourthly, goals should be set for change and a programme of treatment outlined. Finally, implementation of treatment programmes should occur, including keeping of sleep diaries and regular attendance of both parents for review of progress.

Management tactics to deal effectively with bedtime tantrums have been proposed by Adams and Rickert (1989). The approach that seems to be most acceptable to parents entails what they have termed positive routines. The child's bedtime is changed to coincide with the time when he or she naturally falls asleep, and before going to bed parent and child engage in a series of mutually enjoyable, but not too stimulating activities. Over the course of the treatment period bedtimes are systematically brought forward until eventually the child is put to bed at a reasonable hour.

Most children wake transiently during the night. These waking periods are usually no more than 5% of the total overnight duration of sleep, but if the child is unable to settle and cries they become a problem for the parents. Accordingly, an effective approach to sleep management would be to encourage the child to settle him- or herself (Douglas & Richman, 1984). Persistent parental intervention may reflect intrafamilial factors such as marital disharmony, over-anxiety or a lack of parental confidence rather than any intrinsic abnormality in the child's ability to self-regulate sleeping behaviour. Behavioural approaches to the treatment of night-waking encompass four main techniques: (1) extinction; (2) positive reinforcement, shaping and grading behaviour; (3) antecedent conditions; and (4) discrimination learning. Extinction means removing any reinforcing response to the child's waking behaviour. Usually it entails failing to respond to crying for as long as it takes the child to cease using the technique to gain parental attention. Although fine in theory, in practice this approach is rarely practicable. Quite apart from the stress persistent crying causes to the parents themselves, there may be adverse effects on other family members and neighbours. Furthermore, intermittent reinforcement will serve to make the problem even worse, so parents who are successful in ignoring their child's cries 6 nights out of 7 gain no benefit.

Positive reinforcement is possible with children whose verbal age is greater than 3 years. Evidently the child must be motivated to obtain the reward on offer for the procedure to be successful. Social reinforcement may be sufficient, but star charts and similar techniques are often employed too. The behaviour to be reinforced should be contrued in positive terms, and it may be necessary to approximate the desired goal by shaping and grading procedures. Initially the child would be rewarded for a relatively easily achieved goal, such as settling down on going to bed without making a fuss. The criteria by which success is defined should be unambiguous. Then the reinforcement may be given for a relatively more difficult task, such as going through the entire night without attracting parental attention. This technique is far more acceptable to parents than the extinction procedure, although it is more vulnerable to regression and is susceptible to corruption through inadvertent positive reinforcement for undesirable behaviours.

Prognosis of non-specific sleeping difficulties

There are few detailed studies on the longitudinal course of sleeping disorders in childhood, or on the association between such disorders and other disturbances of behaviour and emotional adjustment. The measures used of disordered sleep in epidemiological investigations are necessarily crude and the meaning of such continuities as are found is difficult to interpret. Zuckerman *et al.* (1987) conducted a longitudinal study of children with sleep problems from 8 months to 3 years of age. Just over 40% of those with sleeping difficulties towards the end of the first year had a sleep problem as measured on the Behavior Screening Questionnaire (Richman & Graham, 1971) at 3 years of age. Few interpersonal or environmental factors seem to account for the continuities seen, with the exception of maternal depression, but associated nonsleep-related behaviour problems such as tantrums, oppositional behavioural and poor attention were more common among those with persistent sleep difficulties.

Garrison and Earls (1985) reported on a sample of 3-year-olds from New England and studied them again at 6 years of age. There was only a modest correlation between sleep problems as measured on the Behavior Screening Questionnaire (Richman & Graham, 1971) at 3 years and the Child Behavior Checklist (Achenbach & Edelbrock, 1983) which was administered at 6 years. Relevant items on the Child Behavior Checklist were nightmares, sleeps more than most children during day/night, sleeps less than most children.

The follow-up phase of a British epidemiological survey (Richman *et al.*, 1982) allowed continuities of sleep problems from the preschool years to middle childhood to be examined. The study found that the majority of children who had night settling difficulties, nightwaking, or who were sleeping in parents' beds at 3 years were not presenting these problems at 8 years of age. Interestingly, when the earlier histories of the 8-year-olds with sleeping difficulties were examined it was found that about half of them had had those behaviours at 3 years, and the continuities were actually stronger than were found in other behaviour disorders. Continuities of sleeping difficulties between 5 and 9 years have also been examined by the Dunedin Longitudinal Study (Clarkson *et al.*, 1986). No association was found between sleep difficulties and the sex, intelligence or educational attainments of children.

Parasomnias

Parasomnias include both sleepwalking (somnambulism) and night terrors, both of which are much more common in children than in adults (Kales *et al.*, 1987). Up to 30% of children are estimated to have had at least one episode of sleepwalking (Klackenberg, 1987), although the behaviour is only habitual in just 2.5%, and it occurs in about the same proportion of the adult population (Handford *et al.*, 1991). Episodes typically last less than 20 minutes, during which movements may appear to be purposeful. Sleepwalking children rarely show any facial expression and behave as though they are unaware of being observed; they are relatively unreactive to their immediate environment. Although they may walk only from room to room, it is not unusual for the somnambulating child to attempt to leave the house. The aetiology of the condition is unknown, but it has been alleged that characteristic EEG patterns may be observed (Jacobson *et al.*, 1969). In a few cases febrile convulsive episodes have been thought to precede the onset of the condition (Kales *et al.*, 1979).

The prognosis is good; the incidence peaks in children aged 5–7 years of age, and is much lower after 9 years. Of 75 children who had had at least one episode between 6 and 16 years of age, only 6 children sleepwalked for as long a period as 10 years, and not one was brought to medical attention for somnambulism (Klackenberg, 1982). Cirigmotta *et al.* (1982)

found, in a very large epidemiological survey of both children and adults, that by the age of 14 years over three-quarters of sleepwalkers had not had an event for at least 2 years and 50% of the sample had had no event after the age of 9. There may be an important genetic contribution to the behaviour; Bakwin (1970) reported that monozygotic twins were concordant for sleepwalking considerably more frequently than dizygotic twins. Guilleminault and Silvestri (1982) discovered 65% of somnambulists had a positive family report of sleepwalking or night terrors.

Night terrors are another example of these so-called arousal disorders (Broughton, 1968) which typically occur within 2–3 hours of the onset of sleep, within a deep NREM part of the cycle. They should be distinguished from nightmares, which are frightening dreams that occur during REM sleep, usually during the latter part of the night. Children may or may not wake during nightmares, but if they do so they can give a vivid account of what they were dreaming about. In contrast, children having night terrors cry out, thus attracting parental attention, but they only appear to be awake. Characteristically, a scene is described in which there is intense agitation, a terrified visage, autonomic overactivity (producing flushing and sweating) and apparently purposeful movements. The dramatic qualities of extreme agitation and an appearance of intense terror or panic cause alarm in parents. The condition is rather unusual, probably occurring in no more than about 3% of otherwise healthy children (Kurth *et al.*, 1965; Jacobson *et al.*, 1969; Klackenberg, 1987).

During a night terror children may rush about the bedroom, although they rarely go far (Kales *et al.*, 1980). Although parasomnias may occasionally be associated with epileptic seizures, this is rare (Pedley & Guilleminault, 1977; Guilleminault, 1987a). Guilleminault advised that nocturnal complex seizures can be distinguished from true night terrors by the fact that the former events comprise a conjunction of violent actions and stereotypical behaviour, and do not usually take place during the first third of the sleep period; brutal headbanging or other violent activity may be the only manifestations of a complex partial seizure during sleep. The differential diagnosis can occasionally be difficult, but if epileptiform activity does account for the symptoms they can usually be controlled completely by anticonvulsant medication such as carbamazepine or diphenylhydantoin.

The prognosis is usually good. DiMario and Emery (1987) found that, in a small series of children whose onset of night terrors was before 7.5 years, 50% had lost their symptoms by 8 years although just over a third persisted into adolescence. It is unusual for the condition to persist beyond adolescence and it has been suggested that those who do suffer from symptoms in adulthood are much more likely to have significant psychopathology (Handford *et al.*, 1991). Management is symptomatic; the child should merely be prevented from injuring him- or herself or from placing him- or herself in a dangerous situation in which injury is likely. Reassurance is all that is necessary; it is not usually appropriate to prescribe hypnotics or other psychotrophic medication (e.g. benzodiazepines) for most children with the disorder, although it can be reserved for especially severe and persistent cases. The child should not be woken; to do so induces confusion and distress. There is typically no memory the following morning for episodes of night terrors or of somnambulism.

Nightmares

Nightmares are frightening dreams that occur during REM sleep, usually in the latter part of the night. Children may or may not awake during nightmares. A survey of 900 children, aged from 6 to 12 years, found that 1 in 5 reported having nightmares (Vela-Bueno *et al.*, 1985), but it is likely that most young children experience them at one time or another (Bauer, 1976). We do not know how often waking in preverbal children is related to nightmares, although Beltramini and Hertzig (1983) reported that 5% of 1-year-olds in their sample had nightmares according to their parents' judgement.

In some cases both nightmares and night terrors occur in association with other manifestations of posttraumatic stress disorder. It has been claimed that, in overanxious and post-traumatic stress disorders, relatively specific features are described (van der Kolk, 1987). Typical characteristics include recurrent nightmares in which the traumatic event is relived. A combination of psychotherapy, behaviour management and the short-term prescription of hypnotic medication may be useful in alleviating the symptoms of this condition (Dollinger, 1986).

Headbanging and rocking

Rocking and headbanging at night are spontaneous movements in which the child rhythmically moves his or her torso or head in a back-and-forth motion, whilst asleep or in a drowsy state (Dollinger, 1985). The behaviour may be ritualistic or performed consciously, whilst the child is awake, as a preparation for sleep. The intensity of the movement varies from relatively slight to vigorous; in the latter instance parents are often alarmed and medical intervention is sought. Kravitz and Boehm found in their survey of 200 normal infants that headbanging had a peak onset at 8–9 months but it probably has an earlier onset in developmentally advanced children, and somewhat later in those whose development is delayed or who are brain-damaged (Kravitz and Boehm, 1971; Thelen, 1979). In a similarly sized sample Klackenberg (1987) found the prevalence was similar in boys and girls, and was maximal up to about 12 months of age (30% of normal infants). The condition occurs in less than 5% of children over 2 years of age (Werry *et al.*, 1983).

Body rocking is a much more common phenomenon, occurring in up to 43% of normal children at 9 months (Klackenberg, 1987). It is usually transient and does not persist beyond 2 years of age in more than 3% or so of subjects. The child is said to be unaware of the behaviour and to be unconcerned about it (Dollinger, 1985). Aetiology is unknown, although numerous hypotheses have been proposed including maternal deprivation, understimulation and erotic gratification, the evidence for each of which consists of case reports (Freiden *et al.*, 1979; Walsh *et al.*, 1981).

Treatment approaches have included a variety of behaviour modification tactics. Extinction has been combined with the removal of reinforcing stimuli (Dougherty & Lane, 1976) or by a regime whereby a reward is earned for not engaging in the behaviour (Balaschak & Mostofsky, 1980). Over-correction has been successful in some instances, in the sense of a required sequence of behaviours being contingent upon the undesired behaviour, this sequence being incompatible with persistence of that behaviour. The technique is alleged to work reasonably well according to the few case reports that are available (Linschied *et al.*, 1981; Strauss *et al.*, 1983).

Hypersomnias

Hypersomnias includes a general tendency to daytime somnolence (which affects about 5% of the general population), the Kleine–Levin syndrome, which is relatively rare, and true narcolepsy, which is also very uncommon.

Daytime sleepiness has its onset in early adolescence, boys being affected rather more frequently than girls (Bixler *et al.*, 1979). The need for sleep does not seem to change significantly as children enter adolescence, although there are relatively few longitudinal studies on this subject. An exception is the work of Carskadon and Dement (1987) in which a longitudinal study was performed at the Stanford University Summer Sleep Laboratory on a sample of adolescents comprising 12 girls and 15 boys over the course of 7 years. These authors concluded that a percentage of 'normal' adolescents have a significant disturbance of waking function as a result of three factors: (1) a normal postpubertal increase in daytime sleepiness; (2) the restriction of nocturnal sleep to meet societal expectations or obligations (e.g. late night movies and discotheques); and (3) the cumulative impact of chronic sleep restriction. They conclude: 'the truly alert adolescent may be exceptional!'.

Narcolepsy

Narcolepsy is a lifelong disorder of unknown cause with a primary complaint of excessive daytime sleepiness. Patients also typically have one or more of these associated symptoms: cataplexy, sleep-onset paralysis and hypnagogic hallucinations (Zarcone, 1973). Reports on the prevalence of narcolepsy in the general population suggest that this is less than 1% (Dement *et al.*, 1973).

Clinically it is important to establish the diagnosis and to evaluate the severity of excessive daytime sleepiness and sleep disturbance. This may be accomplished by polysomnography. The condition is associated with pathological manifestations of REM sleep, including sleep-onset REM periods or a reduction of time between sleep onset and the first REM sleep period. The age of onset of the condition in children is usually around puberty, although the diagnosis may not be confirmed until later adolescence. It is excessively rare before 11 years of age (Guilleminault, 1987b). In the Young *et al.* (1988) study of patients aged 15 years or younger presenting with the condition, the mean age was 11.6 years with a slight excess of boys.

The presenting feature in children is usually uncontrollable attacks of daytime sleepiness. These tend to occur several times a day during monotonous sedentary activities such as watching television, sitting in class or reading. The episodes of sleep last from a matter of seconds to 30 minutes or so; so long as stages 3−4 sleep have not been entered, the subject may awake feeling refreshed. During the onset of the overt sleep episodes there may be repetitive microsleeps associated with periods of extreme drowsiness. Individual microsleeps last from 1 to 10 seconds, increasing in frequency, finally coming in rapid succession and sometimes associated with automatic activity such as gestural, ambulatory or speech automatisms (Guilleminault *et al.*, 1975). During microsleeps the subject's eyes are open but gaze is unresponsive and verbal production may be garbled or out of context.

Hypnagogic hallucinations occur at sleep onset, sometimes during daytime naps but more frequently just prior to the nocturnal onset of sleep. Such hallucinations may be very unpleasant and frightening and their content may be bizarre; they are seen in association with both child-onset and adult-onset narcolepsy (Young *et al.*, 1988). A related symptom, also seen at the onset of sleep, but occasionally on waking as well, is sleep paralysis. Episodes of sleep paralysis are temporary and completely reversible; during these the subject feels unable to move or sleep and often has the feeling of breathing shallowly. This symptom is probably rather less common in children than the other features associated with narcolepsy.

Cataplexy is closely related to sleep paralysis (Guilleminault, 1976). It has been defined as an abrupt and reversible decrease or loss of muscle tone most frequently elicited by emotions such as laughter, anger or surprise. Occasionally, limited to the muscles of the head and neck, it can involve the entire voluntary musculature and in a typical cataleptic attack the jaw sags, the head falls forward, the arms drop to the side and the knees bend. The subject may completely collapse to the floor but consciousness usually remains intact, at least in the initial stage of the attack. Cataplectic episodes may last for only a few seconds to many minutes and in some cases go on to REM sleep; individuals with cataplexy usually enter REM sleep immediately after the onset of normal sleep, rather than after the 70−90 minutes of NREM sleep which is seen in normal individuals. In contrast to the symptoms of the condition seen in adults, the associated symptoms of cataplexy, hypnagogic hallucinations and sleep-onset paralysis began at virtually the same time as the excessive daytime sleepiness in children, all symptoms beginning within a year or so of one another.

Hereditary factors are certainly important in the predisposition to narcolepsy: between 10 and 50% of patients have at least one affected first-degree relative (Kessler *et al.*, 1974). A link has been found between narcolepsy and the DR2

antigen of the human leukocyte antigen system (Langdon *et al.*, 1984; Honda *et al.*, 1985); possibly 100% of Japanese narcoleptics are DR2-positive. Biochemical and pharmacological studies have been reviewed by Guilleminault (1987a) and Garreau *et al.* (1990).

Children suffering from narcolepsy often suffer academically; because of fear of their hypnagogic hallucinations and sleep paralysis older children may well believe they have a serious mental illness. Social embarrassment is likely, especially if cataplexy is a predominant syndrome. The prognosis is not good and medication, whilst offering short-term relief, is not a long-term solution. Approaches to medical treatment included the prescription of stimulants such as pemoline, methylphenidate and amphetamines; also, tricyclic antidepressants, of which chlorimipramine is one of the most frequently used in the UK. Viloxazine hydrochloride is said to produce good control of the symptoms of cataplexy (Guilleminault *et al.*, 1986) but the drug is not recommended for children.

The Kleine−Levin syndrome is very rare and occurs predominantly in boys, usually in the early teenage years towards the end of puberty (Critchley, 1962). Symptoms typically include hypersomnia and hyperphagia, with irritability, aggressiveness and sexual disinhibition (Billiard, 1989). The syndrome manifests with sudden outbreaks, often preceded by a prodromal phase characterized by fever, vomiting, photophobia and irritability. Outbreaks last between 1 and 2 weeks, but onset and recovery phases are acute. Physical examination usually shows no positive signs; there may be some diffuse paroxysmal slowing of the EEG. The aetiology of the Kleine−Levin syndrome is unknown. The prognosis is good and the condition virtually always resolves by late adolescence (Garreau *et al.*, 1990). Treatment has included the prescription of stimulants such as amphetamines and methylphenidate. Lithium carbonate is alleged to be associated with improvement in some cases.

Excessive sleepiness is also seen in association with the Prader−Willi syndrome, a condition characterized by neonatal hypotonia, mental retardation, hyperphagia, obesity, hypogonadism and short stature, which is thought to be due to hypothalamic dysfunction. Somnolence is said to be an almost universal symptom of the condition, especially in severely obese patients who may become cyanotic because of sleep apnoea (Vela Bueno *et al.*, 1984). There is a similarity between this condition and the Pickwickian syndrome (Laurence *et al.*, 1981). It is hypothesized that the sleep-onset REM periods and oxygen desaturation observed in the Prader−Willi syndrome are caused by hypothalamic disturbances (Okawa & Sasaki, 1987).

Sleep apnoea

This condition is defined as intermittent periods of cessation of breathing during sleep (Handford *et al.*, 1991) which last more than a few seconds and are often followed by loud and prolonged snoring sounds. Two broad types of sleep apnoea are described, obstructive and central. In some cases the problem involves a mixture of both types.

Obstructive sleep apnoea is caused by the mechanical obstruction of the child's airway, usually because of hyperplastic tonsils and adenoids (Potsic, 1989). Other less frequent causes include mandibular malformations, micrognathia, acromegaly and a glottal web (Kales *et al.*, 1987). Subjects typically have a history of excessive daytime sleepiness; their attacks of repetitive nocturnal breathing cessation are associated with loud snorting and gasping sounds (Handford *et al.*, 1991). Additional symptoms can include excessive body movements during sleep, sweating, secondary enuresis, cognitive impairment and early-morning headaches. In infants the condition of obstructive sleep apnoea associated with hyperplastic tonsils and adenoids can be associated with severe failure to thrive (Everett *et al.*, 1987; Hodges & Wailoo, 1987); the impaired rate of growth is rapidly rectified following tonsillectomy and adenoidectomy.

Some examples of SIDS are thought to be associated with centrally determined sleep apnoea (Milner, 1987; Oren *et al.*, 1987). Higher risk is believed to attach to sleeping in a prone position, the relative risks having been estimated to lie between 1.9 and 12.5 times the risk for an infant sleeping supine or on his or her side (Dwyer *et al.*, 1991). A number of recent reports have suggested that public education on this matter has led to a significant fall in the incidence of SIDS in the UK (Wigfield *et al.*, 1992), the Netherlands (de Jonge & Engelberts, 1989) and Australia (Beal, 1988).

Another environmental factor believed to attach to the risk of SIDS during sleep is the amount of bedding and overnight temperature (Fleming *et al.*, 1990). There is an inverse association between the incidence of the syndrome and climatic temperature, falls in the latter being linked to an increase in deaths about 6 days later (Murphy & Campbell, 1987; Campbell, 1989). Recent work (Ponsonby *et al.*, 1992) has found evidence for an increase in relative risk of about 1.26 for every excess thermal insulation unit (tog), this risk factor acting independently of that associated with the prone sleeping position.

Sleep disturbances and other conditions

Children with mental retardation may be at a special risk of sleep disturbance, one of the most common complaints of their caregivers being that they are overactive at night, although others may be regarded as hypersomnolent. Clements *et al.* (1986) found sleep difficulties occurred in over 34% of mentally retarded children under the age of 15 years, and in a substantial minority were associated with self-injury, stereotyped movements, destructive or otherwise nonsocially directed aggressive behaviour. Families were thereby put under tremendous stress and the detrimental impact on their social life, including school work of siblings, was significant. In some cases specific physical abnormalities contribute to the clinical picture. For example, macroglossia in children with Down's syndrome has been alleged to cause sleep apnoea in

some circumstances (Silverman, 1988). Among the many reports on sleep and mental retardation, those on sleep abnormalities in association with Down's syndrome are the most numerous (Okawa & Sasaki, 1987) but findings have not been consistent, possibly because the severity of the syndrome and the stage at which sleep abnormalities are studied are so variable (Okawa & Sasaki, 1987).

Autistic syndromes, also known as pervasive developmental disorders, are associated with sleep problems, which often have their onset in infancy (Hosino *et al.*, 1984). Symptoms include restlessness, stereotypied activities and a difficulty getting off to sleep. There may also be noctural or early-morning wakening (Inamura, 1984).

Sleep disturbances are also common in Tourette's syndrome, including insomnia (difficulty getting off to sleep, intermittent waking during the night and early-morning waking) and bruxism (for review, see Robertson, 1989). The increased proportion of stage 3 and 4 sleep is sometimes excessively high and that of REM sleep rather too low, in association with the excessive night wakings (Glaze *et al.*, 1983). Treatment with a dopamine-blocking agent such as haloperidol or pimozide may improve the sleep pattern (Handford *et al.*, 1991).

Perhaps unsurprisingly, a link has been drawn between disorders of attention, hyperactivity and sleep difficulties (Taylor, 1986). Parents of hyperactive children are far more likely to consider them to have sleep problems than the parents of normal children (Kaplan *et al.*, 1987). This may be because they wake excessively frequently at night and cause disruption to the household, but they may not require less sleep. Whether there is truly a physiological explanation that links their sleep disorder with dysfunction of the catecholamine system, as claimed by Mefford and Potter (1989) remains unproven. Evidence has been adduced by Ramos Platon *et al.* (1990) to show in unmedicated subjects that polysomnographic indices can distinguish attention deficit disorder without hyperactivity from attention deficit disorder with hyperactivity, the latter group of subjects showing greater sleep fragmentation and a lesser degree of sleep efficiency.

Sleep abnormalities are also part of the characteristic clinical picture of the Rett syndrome. This is a progressive disorder of unknown aetiology which occurs in females and is characterized by autistic behaviour, dementia, ataxia and loss of purposeful use of hands, together with seizures (Glaze *et al.*, 1987). Studies of the sleep patterns seen in this condition have demonstrated a decreased proportion of REM sleep, which is associated with abnormal respiratory activity.

Sleep disorders are well-known features of depression in adults, and much the same sorts of disorder may be found in association with depression in children and adolescents (Puig-Antich, 1987). Hawkins *et al.* (1985) found depressed adolescents and young adults showed extended sleep periods, up to double those of normal controls. Whether or not depressed children have reduced REM sleep latencies is debatable: some studies suggest that this disorder (characteristic for adult depressives) is seen in prepubertal children (Emslie *et al.*,

1987, 1990). However, other studies have failed to find parellels between the classic REM sleep characteristics associated with the adult depressive syndrome and the sleep patterns of depressed adolescents (Goetz *et al.*, 1987).

Within the past few years another type of sleep disorder, manifesting in bizarre behaviour, has been described in which the affected individual acts out his or her dreams (Mahoward & Schenck, 1989). Although most cases have been reported in middle-aged men, a few descriptions of similar behaviours have been made in children between 2 and 10 years of age (Schenck *et al.*, 1986; Herman *et al.*, 1989). There is an association in these cases with a brainstem lesion which could be responsible by disrupting the control of REM sleep. It has been in the context of seemingly purposeful, often violent sexual acts, committed whilst allegedly asleep that mistaken diagnoses of epilepsy are occasionally made (Stores, 1991). On the other hand, complex partial seizures of frontal origin, which have only recently been described in children, may present with very strange nocturnal behaviours, occasionally being mistakenly taken for evidence of nightmares (Stores *et al.*, 1991). Attacks differ from true sleep disorders because there is no associated dreaming, they occur very frequently and have an abrupt onset and termination.

CONCLUSIONS

Feeding and sleeping behaviours are universal self-regulatory tasks which, in order to develop successfully according to cultural expectations, require the sensitive attention of a caregiver, usually the child's mother. Substantial secular trends have been observed both in feeding practices and expectations about appropriate sleeping behaviour. In western societies such matters are sensitive to the prevailing views of doctors and other 'experts' about what is good for young children. Remarkably little is known as a result of empirical research on the normal development of such basic attributes as appetite, food preferences and aversions, nor is there any consensus view on the function of sleep or the significance of individual differences in sleep patterns during infancy. Consequently, much of the advice given to parents on the management of disorders of feeding and sleeping is based as much upon folklore and personal experience as it is upon any real understanding of the mechanisms involved.

A study of the feeding relationship between a dependent infant and its mother may give the impression that herein lie the origins of social dialogue; certainly when things go wrong in this emotionally charged situation there can be repercussions upon wider aspects of their relationship. In such cases a vicious cycle may be generated in which the child fails to thrive, the mother suffers an increasing burden of guilt, and professional intervention may be less than helpful, especially if the finger of blame is pointed at the 'inadequate' parent. The vulnerability of neurologically impaired children to major feeding difficulties is not at all well-recognized. When a consequence of such a feeding disorder is nutritional compromise, mental development may be put at risk, arising both from impaired energy intake and from micronutrient deficiencies.

Sleeping difficulties are also relatively common, but may be engendered in part by inappropriate societal expectations about what constitutes a normal sleep pattern. Fortunately, there is abundant evidence that the majority of problems concern difficulty getting off to sleep or excessive nightwaking, both of which are readily responsive to simple behaviour management. For some reason abnormalities of sleep have attracted far greater interest from researchers than disorders of feeding, at least during the preschool period. Accordingly, there is a very substantial literature on the classification of sleep disorders and a reasonable understanding of their physiological basis. Despite this encouraging picture, the medical treatment of sleep disorders still seems to be a rather 'hit or miss' affair and few clear recommendations can be made.

REFERENCES

Accardo P., Whitman B., Caul J. & Rolfe U. (1988) Autism and plumbism. A possible association. *Clinical Paediatrics (Philadelphia)*, **27**, 41–44.

Achenbach T.M. & Edelbrock C.S. (1983) *Manual for the Child Behavior Checklist and Revised Child Behavior Profile.* University of Vermont, Department of Psychiatry, Burlington, VT.

Adams L.A. & Rickert V.I. (1989) Reducing bedtime tantrums: comparison between positive routines and graduated extinction. *Pediatrics*, **84**, 756–761.

Ahn C.E. & MacLean W.C. (1980) Growth of the exclusively breast fed infant. *American Journal of Clinical Nutrition*, **33**, 183–192.

Alexander R. (1987) Oral–motor treatment for infants and young children with cerebral palsy. *Seminars in Speech and Language*, **8**, 87–99.

American Psychiatric Association (1994) *Diagnostic and Statistical Manual of Mental Disorders*, 4th edn, DSM-IV. American Psychiatric Association, Washington, DC.

American Psychiatric Association (1987) *Diagnostic and Statistical Manual-III-R*. American Psychiatric Association, Washington DC.

Anders T.F. (1979) Night-waking in infants during the first year of life. *Pediatrics*, **63**, 860–864.

Anders T.F. & Keener M.A. (1985) Developmental course of nighttime sleep-wake patterns in full-term and premature infants during the first year of life. *Sleep*, **8**, 173–192.

Anders T.F. & Sostek A.M. (1975) The use of time lapse video recording of sleep–wake behavior in human infants. *Psychophysiology*, **13**, 155–158.

Anders T.F., Keener M.A. & Kraemer H. (1985) Sleep–wake organization, neonatal assessment and development in premature infants during the first year of life. II. *Sleep*, **8**, 193–206.

Bakwin H. (1970) Sleepwalking in twins. *Lancet*, **ii**, 446–447.

Balaschak B.A. & Mostofsky D.I. (1980) Treatment of nocturnal headbanging by behavioural contracting. *Journal of Behaviour Therapy and Experimental Psychiatry*, **11**, 117–120.

Barnhard J.S. Jr & Mittleman R.E. (1986) Unusual deaths associated with polyphagia. *American Journal of Forensic Medicine*, **7**, 30–34.

Bauer D. (1976) An exploratory study of developmental changes in children's fears. *Journal of Child Psychology and Psychiatry*, **17**, 69–74.

Beal S.M. (1988) Sleeping position and the sudden infant death syndrome. *Medical Journal of Australia*, **149**, 562.

Beauchamp G.K. & Moran M. (1984) Acceptance of sweet and salty tastes in 2 year old children. *Appetite*, **5**, 291–305.

Beckwith L. & Parmalee A.H. (1986) EEG patterns of preterm infants, home environment and later IQ. *Child Development*, **57**, 777–785.

Beltramini A.U. & Hertzig M.E. (1983) Sleep and bedtime behaviour in preschool aged children. *Pediatrics*, **71**, 153–158.

Berger R.J. & Walker J.M. (1972) A polygraphic study of sleep in the tree shrew (*Tupais glis*). *Brain Behaviour Evolution*, **5**, 54–69.

Bergman R.L. & Bergman K.E. (1986) Nutrition and growth in infancy. In: Falkner F. & Tanner J.M. (eds) *Human Growth: A Comprehensive Treatise. Vol. 3: Methodology, Ecological Genetic and Nutritional Effects on Growth*, pp. 389–413. Plenum Press, London.

Bernal J. (1972) Crying during the first 10 days of life, and maternal responses. *Developmental Medicine and Child Neurology*, **14**, 362–372.

Bernal J.F. (1973) Night waking in infants during the first 14 months. *Developmental Medicine and Child Neurology*, **15**, 760–769.

Bicknell D.J. (1975) *Pica: A Childhood Symptom*. Butterworths, London.

Billiard M. (1989) The Kleine–Levin syndrome. In: Roth T. & Dement W.C. (eds) *Principles and Practices of Sleep Medicine*, pp. 377–378. W.B. Saunders, Philadelphia.

Birch L.L. (1980) Effects of peer models' food choices and eating behaviors on preschoolers' food preferences. *Child Development*, **51**, 489–496.

Birch L.L. (1990a) The control of food intake by young children: the role of learning. In: Capaldi E.D. & Powley T.L. (eds) *Taste, Experience, and Feeding*, American Psychiatric Association, pp. 116–138. Washington, DC.

Birch L.L. (1990b) Development of food acceptance patterns. *Developmental Psychology*, **26**, 515–519.

Birch L.L. & Marlin D.W. (1982) I don't like it: I never tried it: effects of exposure on two-year-old children's food preferences. *Appetite*, **3**, 353–360.

Birch L.L., Birch D., Marlin D. & Kramer L. (1982) Effects of instrumental eating on children's food preferences. *Appetite*, **3**, 125–134.

Birch L.L., Marlin D.W. & Rotter J. (1984) Eating as the 'means' activity in a contingency: effects of young children's food preference. *Child Development*, **55**, 431–439.

Birch L.L., McPhee L., Shoba B.C., Steinberg L. & Krehbiel R. (1987) 'Clean up your plate': effects of child feeding practices on the development of intake regulation. *Learning and Motivation*, **18**, 301–317.

Bixler E.O., Kales A., Soldatos C.R., Kales J.D. & Healey S. (1979) Prevalence of sleep disorders in the Los Angeles metropolitan area. *American Journal of Psychiatry*, **136**, 1257–1262.

Blackman J.A. & Nelson C.L.A. (1985) Reinstituting oral feedings in children fed by gastrostomy tube. *Clinical Pediatrics*, **24**, 434–438.

Blurton-Jones N., Ferreira M.C.R., Brown M.F. & MacDonald L. (1978) The association between perinatal factors and later night waking. *Developmental Medicine and Child Neurology*, **20**, 427–434.

Braun M.A. & Palmer M.M. (1985) A pilot study of oral–motor dysfunction in 'at risk' infants. *Physical and Occupational Therapy in Pediatrics*, **5**, 13–25.

Bray P.F., Herbst J.J., Johnson D.G., Book L.S., Ziter F.A. & Condon V.R. (1977) Childhood gastroesophageal reflux: neurologic and psychiatric syndromes mimicked. *Journal of the American Medical Association*, **237**, 1342–1345.

Broughton R.J. (1968) Sleep disorders: disorders of arousal? *Science*, **159**, 1071–1078.

Bruch H. (1973) *Eating Disorders, Obesity and Anorexia Nervosa and the Person Within*. Basic Books, New York.

Cameron H.C. (1968) The 'critical period' hypothesis, and emotional and speech disorders, related to dysphagia in infancy. DPM Thesis, University of Condor.

Campbell M.J. (1989) Sudden infant death syndrome and environmental temperature: further evidence for a time-lagged relationship. *Medical Journal of Australia*, **151**, 365–367.

Carre I.J. (1959) The natural history of the partial thoracic stomach (hiatus hernia) in children. *Archives of Disease in Childhood*, **34**, 344–353.

Carskadon M.A. & Dement W.C. (1987) Sleepiness in the normal adolescent. In: Guilleminault C. (ed) *Sleep and its Disorders in Children*, pp. 53–66. Raven Press, New York.

Chatoor I., Egan J., Getson P., Menvielle E. & O'Donnell R. (1988) Mother–infant interactions in infantile anorexia nervosa. *Journal of the American Academy of Child and Adolescent Psychiatry*, **27**, 535–540.

Chavin W. & Tinson S. (1980) Children with sleep difficulties. *Health Visitor*, **53**, 477–480.

Cirigmotta F., Zucconi M., Bondini S., Lenzi P.L. & Lugaresi E. (1982) Enuresis, sleepwalking and nightmares: an epidemiological survey in the Republic of San Marino. In: Guilleminault C. & Lugaresi E. (eds) *Sleep/Wake Disorders: Natural History, Epidemiology and Long-term Evolution*, pp. 237–241. Raven Press, New York.

Clarkson S., Williams S. & Silva P.A. (1986) Sleep in middle childhood — a longitudinal study of sleep problems in a large sample of Dunedin children aged 5–9 years. *Australian Paediatric Journal*, **22**, 31–35.

Clements J., Wing L. & Dunn G. (1986) Sleep problems in handicapped children: a preliminary study. *Journal of Child Psychology and Psychiatry*, **27**, 399–407.

Cowart B.J. (1981) Development of taste perception in humans: sensitivity and preference throughout the life span. *Psychological Bulletin*, **90**, 43–73.

Critchley M. (1962) Periodic hypersomnia and megaphagia in adolescent males. *Brain*, **85**, 627–656.

Cucchiara S., Staiano A., Boccieri A., DeStefano M., Capozi C., Manzi G. & Camerlingo F. (1990) Effects of cisapride on parameters of oesophageal motility and on the prolonged intra-oesophageal pH test in infants with gastro-oesophageal reflux disease. *Gut*, **31**, 21–25.

Dahl M. (1987) Early feeding problems in an affluent society. iii) follow-up at two years: natural course, health, behaviour and development. *Acta Paediatrica Scandinavica*, **76**, 872–880.

Dahl M. & Kristiansson B. (1987) Early feeding problems in an affluent society. iv) impact on growth up to two years of age. *Acta Paediatrica Scandinavica*, **76**, 881–888.

Dahl M. & Sundelin C. (1986) Early feeding problems in an affluent society: i) categories and clinical signs. *Acta Paediatrica Scandinavica*, **75**, 370–379.

Dahl M., Eklund G. & Sundelin C. (1986) Early feeding problems in an affluent society: ii) determinants. *Acta Paediatrica Scandinavica*, **75**, 380–387.

Danford D.E. & Huber A.M. (1982) Pica among mentally retarded adults. *American Journal of Mental Deficiency*, **87**, 141–146.

Davis D.P. (1979) Is inadequate breast-feeding an important cause of failure to thrive? *Lancet*, **1**, 541–542.

Davis C.M. (1928) Self selection of diet by newly weaned infants: an experimental study. *American Journal of Diseases in Children*, **36**, 651–679.

Davis C.M. (1938) The self selection of diet experiment: its significance for feeding in the house. *Ohio State Medical Journal*, **34**, 862–868.

de Jonge G.A. & Engelberts A.C. (1989) Cot deaths and sleeping position. *Lancet*, **2**, 1149–1150.

Dement W.C., Carskadon M.A. & Ley R. (1973) The prevalence of narcolepsy. II. *Sleep Research*, **2**, 147 (abstract).

Department of Health and Social Security (1988) *Present Day Practice in Infant Feeding*, third report. DHSS Report on Health and Social Subjects no. 32. Her Majesty's Stationery Office, London.

DeVries M.W. (1984) Temperament and infant mortality among the Masai of East Africa. *American Journal of Psychiatry*, **141**, 1189–1194.

Dewey K.G. & Lonnerdal B. (1986) Infant self-regulation of breast milk intake. *Acta Paediatrica Scandinavica*, **75**, 893–898.

DiMario F.J. Jr & Emery E.S. (1987) The natural history of night terrors. *Clinics in Pediatrics (Philadelphia)*, **26**, 505–511.

Dollinger S.J. (1985) Childhood sleep disturbances. *Advances in Clinical Child Psychology*, **9**, 279–332.

Dollinger S.J. (1986) The measurement of children's sleep disturbances and somatic complaints following a disaster. *Child Psychiatry and Human Development*, **16**, 148–153.

Dougherty E.H. & Lane J.R. (1976) Naturalistic alternatives to extinction: an application to self-injurious bedtime behaviour. *Journal of Behaviour Therapy and Experimental Psychiatry*, **7**, 373–375.

Douglas J. (1989) *Behavioural Problems in Young Children: Assessment & Management*, pp. 67–93. Tavistock/Routledge, London.

Douglas J. & Richman N. (1984) *My Child Won't Sleep*. Penguin, Harmondsworth.

Drewett R.F., Kahn H., Parkhurst S. & Whiteley S. (1987a) Pain during breastfeeding: the first three months postpartum. *Journal of Reproductive and Infant Psychology*, **5**, 183–186.

Drewett R., Payman B.C. & Whiteley S. (1987b) Effect of complementary feeds on sucking and milk intake in breastfed babies: an experimental study. *Journal of Reproductive and Infant Psychology*, **5**, 133–143.

Dwyer T., Ponsonby A.-L.B., Newman N.M. & Gibbons L.E. (1991) Prospective cohort study of prone sleeping position and sudden infant death syndrome. *Lancet*, **337**, 1244–1247.

Emslie G., Roffwarg H. & Rush A. (1987) Sleep EEG findings in depressed children and adolescents. *American Journal of Psychiatry*, **144**, 668–670.

Emslie G., Rush A.J. & Weinberg W.A. (1990) Children with major depression show reduced rapid eye movement latencies. *Archives of General Psychiatry*, **47**, 119–124.

Eppright E.S., Fox H.M., Fryer B.S., Lamkin G.H. & Vivian V.M. (1969) Eating behaviour of preschool children. *Journal of Nutrition Education*, **1**, 16–19.

Evans T.J. & Davies D.P. (1977) Failure to thrive at the breast: an old problem revisited. *Archives of Disease in Childhood*, **52**, 974.

Evans-Morris S. (1985) Developmental implications for the management of feeding problems in neurologically impaired infants. *Seminars in Speech and Language*, **6**, 293–315.

Evans-Morris S. (1989) Development of oral–motor skills in the neurologically impaired child receiving non-oral feedings. *Dysphagia*, **3**, 135–154.

Everett A.D., Koch W.C. & Saulsbury F.T. (1987) Failure to thrive due to obstructive sleep apnea. *Clinical Pediatrics (Philadelphia)*, **26**, 90–92.

FAO/WHO/UNU (1985) *Energy and Protein Requirements*. Technical Report Series no. 724. World Health Organization, Geneva.

Fleming P.J., Gilberg R., Azaz Y., Berry J., Rudd P., Stewart A. & Hall E. (1990) Interaction between bedding and sleeping position and the sudden infant death syndrome: a population-control study. *British Medical Journal*, **301**, 85–89.

Forsyth B.W.C. (1989) Colic and the effect of changing formulas: a double-blind, multiple, crossover study. *Journal of Pediatrics*, **115**, 521–526.

Forsyth B.W.C., Leventhal J.M. & McCarthy P.L. (1985b) Mothers' perceptions of problems of feeding and crying behaviors. *American Journal of Diseases of Children*, **139**, 269–272.

Forsyth B.W.C., Leventhal J.M. & McCarthy P.L. (1985b) Problems of early infancy, formula changes, and mothers' beliefs about their infants. *Journal of Pediatrics*, **106**, 1012–1017.

Freiden J.R., Jankowski J.J. & Singer W.D. (1979) Nocturnal head-banging as a sleep disorder: case report. *American Journal of Psychiatry*, **136**, 1469–1470.

Garreau B., Barthélémy C., Bruneau N., Martineau J. & Rothenberger A. (1990) Sleep disturbances in children: from the physiological to the clinical. In: Rothenberger A. (ed) *Brain Behaviour in Child Psychiatry*, pp. 317–342. Springer-Verlag, Berlin.

Garrison W. & Earls F. (1985) Change and continuity in behaviour problems from the preschool period through school entry: an analysis of mothers' reports. In: Stevenson J. (ed) *Recent Research in Developmental Psychopathology*, pp. 51–65. Pergamon, Oxford.

Geertsma M.A., Hyams J.S., Pelletier J.M. & Teiter S. (1985) Feeding resistance after parenteral hyperalimentation. *American Journal of Diseases of Children*, **139**, 255–256.

Glasscock S.G., Friman P.C., O'Brien S. & Christopherson E.R. (1986) Varied citrus treatment of ruminant gagging in a teenager with Batten's disease. *Journal of Behavior Therapy and Experimental Psychiatry*, **17**, 129–133.

Glaze D.G., Frost J.D. & Jankovic J. (1983) Sleep in Gilles de la Tourette's syndrome: disorder of arousal. *Neurology*, **33**, 586–592.

Glaze D.G., Frost J.D., Zoghbi H.Y. & Percy A.K. (1987) Rett's syndrome. Correlations of electroencephalographic characteristics with clinical staging. *Archives of Neurology*, **44**, 1053–1056.

Goetz R.R., Puig-Antich J., Ryan N., Rabinowich H., Ambrosini P.J., Nelson B. & Krawiec V. (1987) Electroencephalographic sleep of adolescents with major depression and normal controls. *Archives of General Psychiatry*, **44**, 61–68.

Goldberg N.M. & Adams E. (1983) Supplementary water for breast fed babies in a hot and dry climate — not really a necessity. *Archives of Disease in Childhood*, **58**, 73–74.

Guilleminault C. (1976) Cataplexy. In: Guilleminault C., Dement W.C. & Passouant P. (eds) *Narcolepsy*, pp. 125–143. Spectrum, New York.

Guilleminault C. (1987a) Disorders of arousal in children: somnambulism and night terrors. In: Guilleminault C. (ed) *Sleep and its Disorders in Children*, pp. 243–252. Raven Press, New York.

Guilleminault C. (1987b) Narcolepsy and its differential diagnosis. In: Guilleminault C. (ed) *Sleep and its Disorders in Children*, pp. 181–194. Raven Press, New York.

Guilleminault C. & Silvestri R. (1982) Disorders of arousal and epilepsy during sleep. In: Sturman M.B., Shouse M. & Passouant P. (eds) *Sleep and Epilepsy*, pp. 513–531. Academic Press, New York.

Guilleminault C., Billiard M., Monplaisir J. & Dement W.C. (1975) Altered states of consciousness in disorders of daytime sleepiness. *Journal of Neurological Science*, **26**, 377–393.

Guilleminault C., Mancuso J., Quera Salva M.A., Hayes B., Mitler M., Poirier G. & Monplaisir J. (1986) Viloxazine hydrochloride in narcolepsy: a preliminary report. *Sleep*, **9**, 275–279.

Habbick B.F. & Gerrard J.W. (1984) Failure to thrive in the contented breast fed baby. *Canadian Medical Association Journal*, **131**, 765–768.

Handford H.A., Mattison R.E. & Kales A. (1991) Sleep disturbances and disorders. In: Lewis M. (ed) *Child and Adolescent Psychiatry*, pp. 715–725. Williams & Wilkins, Boston.

Harris G. (1988) Determinants of the introduction of solid food. *Journal of Reproductive and Infant Psychology*, **6**, 241–249.

Harris G. & Booth I.W. (1992) The nature and management of eating problems in preschool children. In: Cooper P. & Stein A. (eds) *The Nature and Management of Feeding Problems and Eating Disorders in Young People*. Monographs in Clinical Pediatrics. Harwood Academic, New York.

Harris G., Thomas A. & Booth D.A. (1990) Development of salt taste in infancy. *Developmental Psychology*, **26**, 534–538.

Hawkins D.R., Taub J.M. & von der Castel R.L. (1985) Extended sleep (hypersomnia) in young depressed patients. *American Journal of Psychiatry*, **142**, 905–910.

Herman J.H., Blaw M.E. & Steinberg J.M. (1989) REM behaviour disorder in a two year old male with evidence of brainstem pathology. *Sleep Research*, **18**, 242.

Hide D.W. & Guyer B.M. (1982) Prevalence of infant colic. *Archives of Disease in Childhood*, **57**, 559–560.

Hill A. & Volpe J.J. (1981) Disorders of sucking and swallowing in the newborn infant: clinicopathological correlations. *Progress in Perinatal Neurology*, **1**, 157–181.

Hitchcock N.E., Gracey M. & Owles E.N. (1981) Growth of healthy breast-fed infants in the first six months. *Lancet*, **ii**, 64–65.

Hodges S. & Wailoo M.P. (1987) Tonsillar enlargement and failure to thrive. *British Medical Journal*, **295**, 451.

Honda Y., Doi Y., Juyi T. & Satake M. (1985) Positive HLA-DR2 finding as a prerequisite for the development of narcolepsy. *Folia Psychiatrica Neurologica Japonica*, **39**, 203–204.

Hoppenbrouwers T., Hodgman J., Anakawa K., Geidel S.A. & Sterman M.B. (1988) Sleep and waking states in infancy: normative studies. *Sleep*, **11**, 387–401.

Horne J.A. (1988) *Why we Sleep: The Functions of Sleep in Humans and Other Mammals*. Oxford University Press, Oxford.

Hoshino Y., Watanade E., Watanade H., Yashimi Y., Kaneko M. & Kumashiro H. (1984) An investigation on sleep disturbance of autistic children. *Folia Psychiatrica et Neurologica Japonica*, **38**, 45–51.

Hulme J.B., Shaver J., Acher S., Mullette L. & Eggert C. (1987) Effects of adaptive seating on the eating and drinking of children with multiple handicap. *American Journal of Occupational Therapy*, **41**, 81–89.

Illingworth R.S. (1969) Sucking and swallowing difficulties in infancy: diagnostic problem of dysphagia. *Archives of Disease in Childhood*, **44**, 655–665.

Illingworth R.S. (1991) *The Normal Child*. Churchill Livingstone, London.

Illingworth R.S. & Lister J. (1964) The critical or sensitive period, with special reference to certain feeding problems in infants and children. *Journal of Pediatrics*, **65**, 839–849.

Inamura K. (1984) Sleep–wake patterns in autistic children. *Japanese Journal of Child and Adolescent Psychiatry*, **25**, 205–217.

Jacklin C.N., Snow M.E., Gahart M. & Maccoby E.E. (1980) Sleep pattern development from 6 through 33 months. *Journal of Pediatric Psychology*, **5**, 295–303.

Jacobson A., Kales J.D. & Kales A. (1969) Clinical and electrophysiological correlates of sleep disorders in children. In: Kales A. (ed) *Physiology and Pathology: A Symposium*, pp. 109–118. J.B. Lippincott, Philadelphia.

Jakobsson I. & Lindberg T. (1983) Cow's milk proteins cause infantile colic in breastfed infants: a double-blind crossover study. *Pediatrics*, **71**, 268–271.

Jones M. (1992) Enabling independence in daily living. In: McCarthy G.T. (ed) *Physical Disability in Childhood. An Interdisciplinary Approach to Management*, pp. 553–570. Churchill Livingstone, London.

Jones P.M. (1989) Feeding disorders in children with multiple handicaps. *Developmental Medicine and Child Neurology*, **31**, 398–406.

Jouvet M. (1975) The function of dreaming: a neurophysiologists point of view. In: Gazzaniga M.S. & Blakemore C. (eds) *Handbook of Psychobiology*, pp. 499–527. Academic Press, New York.

Kales J.D., Kales A., Soldatos C.R., Chamberlin K. & Martin E.D. (1979) Sleepwalking and night terrors related to febrile illness. *American Journal of Psychiatry*, **136**, 1214–1215.

Kales J.D., Kales A., Soldatos C.R., Caldwell A.B., Charney D.S. & Martin E.D. (1980) Night terrors: clinical characteristics and personality patterns. *Archives of General Psychiatry*, **37**, 1413–1417.

Kales A., Soldatos C.R. & Kales J.D. (1987) Sleep disorders: insomnia, sleepwalking, night terrors, nightmares, and enuresis *Annals of Internal Medicine*, **106**, 582–592.

Kaplan B.J., McNicol J., Conte R.A. & Moghadam H.K. (1987) Sleep disturbance in preschool-aged hyperactive and nonhyperactive children. *Pediatrics*, **80**, 839–845.

Keane V., Charney E., Stratus J. & Roberts K. (1988) Do solids help baby sleep through the night? *American Journal of Diseases of Children*, **142**, 404–405.

Kessler S., Guilleminault C. & Dement W.C. (1974) A family study of 50 REM narcoleptics. *Acta Neurologica Scandinavica*, **50**, 503–512.

Klackenberg G. (1982) Somnambulism in childhood: prevalence, course and behavioural correlation. *Acta Paediatrica Scandinavica*, **71**, 495–499.

Klackenberg G. (1987) Incidence of parasomnias in children in a general population. In: Guilleminault C. (ed) *Sleep and its Disorders in Children*, pp. 99–113. Raven Press, New York.

Kleitman N. & Engelmann T.G. (1953) Sleep characteristics in infants. *Journal of Applied Physiology*, **6**, 269.

Kravitz H. & Boehm J.J. (1971) Rhythmic habit patterns in infancy: their sequence, age of onset and frequency. *Child Development*, **42**, 399–413.

Kurth V.E., Gohler I. & Kanaape H.H. (1965) Untersuchungen uber der Pavor Nocturnus bei Kindern. *Psychiatrie Neurologie und Medizinische Psychologie (Leipzig)*, **17**, 1–7.

Langdon N., VanDam M., Walsh K.I., Vaughan R.W. & Parkes D. (1984) Genetic markers in narcolepsy. *Lancet*, **ii**, 1178–1180.

Laurence B.M., Brito A. & Wilkinson J. (1981) Prader–Willi syndrome after age 15 years. *Archives of Disease in Childhood*, **56**, 181–186.

Lebenthal E. (1985) Impact of digestion and absorption in the weaning period on infant feeding practices. *Pediatrics*, **75**, 207–213.

Lewis J.A. (1982) Oral motor assessment and treatment of feeding difficulties. In: Accardo P. (ed) *Failure to Thrive in Infancy and Early Childhood — A Multidisciplinary Team Approach*, pp. 265–295. University Park Press, Baltimore.

Lindberg L., Bohlin G. & Hagekull B. (1991) Early feeding problems in a normal population. *International Journal of Eating Disorders*, **10**, 395–405.

Linschied T.R., Copeland A.P., Jacobstein D.M. & Smith J.L. (1981) Over-correction treatment for nighttime self-injurious behavior in two normal children. *Journal of Pediatric Psychology*, **6**, 29–35.

Lipsitt L.P., Crook C. & Booth C.A. (1985) The transitional infant: behavioral development and feeding. *American Journal of Clinical Nutrition*, **41**, 485–496.

Llewellyn-Jones D. (1983) *Breastfeeding — How to Succeed*. Faber and Faber. London.

Lothe L., Lindberg T. & Jakobsson I. (1982) Cow's milk formula as a cause of infantile colic: a double-blind study. *Pediatrics*, **70**, 7–10.

Lozoff B., Wolf A.W. & Davis N.S. (1984) Cosleeping in urban families with young children in the United States. *Pediatrics*, **74**, 171–182.

Lozoff B., Wolf A.W. & Davis N.S. (1985) Sleep problems in pediatric practice. *Pediatrics*, **75**, 477–483.

McAlpine C. & Singh N.N. (1986) Pica in institutionalized mentally retarded persons. *Journal of Mental Deficiency Research*, **30**, 171–178.

McGehee L.J. & Eckerman C.O. (1983) The preterm infant as a social partner: responsive but unreadable. *Infant Behaviour and Development*, **6**, 461–470.

McKenna J.J., Mosko S., Dangy C. & McAninch J. (1990) Sleep and arousal patterns of co-sleeping human mother–infant pairs: a preliminary physiological study with implications for the study of sudden infant death syndrome (SIDS). *American Journal of Physical Anthropology*, **83**, 331–347.

Macht J. (1990) *Poor Eaters: Helping Children who Refuse to Eat*. Plenum Press, New York.

Macknin M.L., Medendorp S.V. & Maier M.C. (1989) Infant sleep and bedtime cereal. *American Journal of Diseases of Children*, **143**, 1066–1067.

Madden N.A., Russo D.C. & Cataldo M.F. (1980) Environmental influences on mouthing in children with lead intoxication. *Journal of Pediatric Psychology*, **5**, 207–216.

Mahony M.J., Migliavacca M., Spitz L. & Milla P.J. (1988) Motor disorders of the oesophagus in gastrooesophageal reflux. *Archives of Disease in Childhood*, **63**, 1333−1118.

Mahoward M.W. & Schenck C.H. (1989) REM sleep behaviour disorder. In: Kryger M.H., Roth T. & Dement W.C. (eds) *Principles and Practices of Sleep Medicine*, pp. 389−401. W.B. Saunders, Philadelphia.

Mathisen B., Skuse D., Wolke D. & Reilly S. (1989) Oral−motor dysfunction and failure to thrive amongst inner-city children. *Developmental Medicine and Child Neurology*, **31**, 293−302.

Mayes S.D., Humphrey F.J. 2d, Handford H.A. & Mitchell J.F. (1988) Rumination disorder: differential diagnosis. *Journal of the American Academy of Child and Adolescent Psychiatry*, **27**, 300−302.

Mefford I.N. & Potter W.Z. (1989) A neuroanatomical and biochemical basis for attention deficit disorder with hyperactivity in children: a defect in tonic adrenaline mediated inhibition of locus coeruleus stimulation. *Medical Hypotheses*, **29**, 33−42.

Mestre J.R., Resnick R.J. & Berman W.F. (1988) Behavior modification in the treatment of rumination. *Clinical Pediatrics*, **22**, 488−491.

Milla P.J. (1986) Intestinal motility and its disorders. *Clinics in Gastroenterology*, **15**, 121−136.

Milla P.J. (1990) Reflux vomiting. *Archives of Disease in Childhood*, **65**, 996−999.

Milner A.D. (1987) Recent theories on the cause of cot death. *British Medical Journal*, **295**, 1366−1367.

Minde K. & Minde R. (1986) *Infant Psychiatry: An Introductory Text*. Sage Publications, London.

Moore T. & Ucko L.E. (1957) Night waking in early infancy: Part I. *Archives of Disease in Childhood*, **32**, 333−343.

Moss A.L., Jones K. & Pigott R.W. (1990) Submucous cleft palate in the differential diagnosis of feeding difficulties. *Archives of Disease in Childhood*, **65**, 182−184.

Mulcahy C.M., Poutney T.E., Nelham R.L., Green E.M. & Billington G.D. (1988) Adaptive seating for motor handicap: problems, a solution, assessment and prescription. *Physiotherapy*, **74**, 531−536.

Murphy M.F.G. & Campbell M.J. (1987) Sudden infant death syndrome and environmental temperature: an analysis using vital statistics. *Journal of Epidemiology and Community Health*, **41**, 63−71.

Neville M.C., Keller R., Seacat J., Lutes V., Neifert M., Casey C., Allen J. & Archer P. (1988) Studies in human lactose: milk volumes in lactating women during the onset of lactation and full lactation. *American Journal of Clinical Nutrition*, **48**, 1375−1386.

Okawa M. & Sasaki H. (1987) Sleep disorders in mentally retarded and brain impaired children. In: Guilleminault C. (ed). *Sleep and its Disorders in Children*, pp. 269−290. Raven Press, New York.

Oren J., Kelly D.H. & Shannon D.C. (1987) Familial occurrence of sudden infant death syndrome and apnea of infancy. *Pediatrics*, **80**, 355−357.

Orenstein S.R. & Orenstein D.M. (1988) Gastro-oesophageal reflux and respiratory disease in children. *Journal of Pediatrics*, **112**, 847−858.

Ottenbacher K., Bundy A. & Short M.A. (1983) Development and treatment of oral−motor dysfunction: a review of clinical research. *Physical and Occupational Therapy in Pediatrics*, **3**, 1−13.

Parmalee A.H., Wenner W.H. & Schulz H.R. (1964) Infant sleep patterns: from birth to 16 weeks of age. *Pediatrics*, **65**, 576−582.

Paton J.Y., Nanayakkhara C.S. & Simpson H. (1988) Vomiting and gastro-oesophageal reflux. *Archives of Disease in Childhood*, **63**, 837−856.

Pedley T.A. & Guilleminault C. (1977) Episodic nocturnal wanderings responsive to anticonvulsant drug therapy. *Annals of Neurology*, **2**, 30−35.

Ponsonby B.Y.A.-L., Dwyer T., Gibbons L.E., Cochrane J.A., Jones M.E. & McCall M.J. (1992) Thermal environment and sudden infant death syndrome: case-control study. *British Medical Journal*, **304**, 277−282.

Potsic W.P. (1989) Sleep apnea in children. *Otolaryngologic Clinics of North America*, **22**, 537−544.

Prior M. (1992) Childhood temperament. *Journal of Child Psychology and Psychiatry*, **33**, 249−279.

Puig-Antich J. (1987) Psychobiologic markers of prepubertal major depression. *Journal of Adolescence and Health Care*, **8**, 509−529.

Raiten D.J. & Massaro T. (1986) Perspectives on the nutritional ecology of autistic children. *Journal of Autism and Developmental Disorders*, **16**, 133−143.

Ramos Platon M.J., Vela Bueno A., Espinar Sierra J. & Kales S. (1990) Hypnopolygraphic alterations in attention deficit disorder (ADD) children. *International Journal of Neurosciences*, **53**, 87−101.

Registrar General's Classification of Occupations (1980) London, HMSO.

Reilly S. & Skuse D. (1992) Characteristics and management of feeding problems in young children with cerebral palsy. *Developmental Medicine and Child Neurology*, **34**, 379−388.

Rempel G.R., Colwell S.O. & Nelson R.P. (1988) Growth in children with cerebral palsy fed via gastrostomy. *Pediatrics*, **82**, 857−863.

Richards M.P.M. & Bernal J. (1972) An observational study of mother−infant interaction. In: Blurton-Jones N. (ed) *Ethological Studies of Child Behaviour*. Cambridge University Press, Cambridge.

Richman N. (1981) A community survey of characteristics of one to two year olds with sleep disruptions. *Journal of the American Academy of Child Psychiatry*, **20**, 281−291.

Richman N. (1985) A double-blind drug trial of treatment in young children with waking problems. *Journal of Child Psychology and Psychiatry*, **26**, 591−598.

Richman N. & Graham P. (1971) A behavioural screening questionnaire for use with 3-year-old children. *Journal of Child Psychology and Psychiatry*, **12**, 5−33.

Richman N., Stevenson J. & Graham P.J. (1982) *Pre-school to School: A Behavioural Study*. Academic Press, London.

Rigatto H. (1989) Control of breathing during sleep in the fetus and neonate. In: Kryger H., Rother T. & Dement W.C. (eds) *Principles and Practice of Sleep Medicine*, pp. 237−248. W.B. Saunders, Philadelphia.

Robertson M.M. (1989) The Gilles de la Tourette syndrome: the current status. *British Journal of Psychiatry*, **154**, 147−169.

Rogers S.J. (1988) Characteristics of social interactions between mothers and their disabled infants: a review. *Child: Care, Health and Development*, **14**, 301−317.

Rosenfeld A.A., Wenegrat A.O., Haavik D.K., Wenegrat B.G. & Smith C.R. (1982) Sleeping patterns in upper middle class families when the child awakens ill or frightened. *Archives of General Psychiatry*, **39**, 943−947.

Rozin P. (1990) The importance of social factors in understanding the acquisition of food habits. In: Capaldi E.D. & Powley T.L. (eds) *Taste, Experience, and Feeding*, pp. 255−270. American Psychiatric Association Washington, DC.

Rozin P. & Fallon A.E. (1987) A perspective on disgust. *Psychological Review*, **94**, 23−41.

Sadeh A., Lavie P., Scher A., Tirosh E. & Epstein R. (1991) Actigraphic home-monitoring sleep-disturbed and control infants and young children: a new method for pediatric assessment of sleep-wake patterns. *Pediatrics*, **87**, 494−499.

Sauvage D., Leddet L., Hameur L. & Barthelemy C. (1985) Infantile rumination; diagnosis and follow-up of twenty cases. *Journal of the American Academy of Child Psychiatry*, **24**, 197−203.

Schachter F.F., Fuchs M.L., Bijur P.E. & Stone R.K. (1989) Cosleeping and sleep problems in Hispanic-American urban young children. *Pediatrics*, **84**, 522−529.

Schenck C.H., Bundlie S.R., Patterson A.L. & Mahoward M.W. (1986) Rapid eye movement sleep behavior disorder. A treatable parasomnia affecting older adults. *Journal of the American Medical Association*, **257**, 1786−1789.

Scott G. & Richards M.P.M. (1990a) Night waking in infants: effects of providing advice and support for parents. *Journal of Child Psychology and Psychiatry*, **31**, 551–567.

Scott G. & Richards M.P.M. (1990b) Night waking in 1-year-old children in England. *Child: Care, Health and Development*, **16**, 283–302.

Selvini Palazzoni M. (1978) *Self-starvation*. Jason Aronson, Northvale.

Shepherd R.W., Wren J., Evans S., Lander M. & Ong T.H. (1987) Gastro-oesophageal reflux in children. Clinical profile, course, and outcome with active therapy in 126 cases. *Clinical Pediatrics*, **26**, 55–60.

Silverman M. (1988) Airway obstruction and sleep disruption in Down's sydrome. *British Medical Journal*, **296**, 1618–1619.

Simonoff E. & Stores G. (1987) Controlled trial of trimeprazine tartrate for night waking. *Archives of Disease in Childhood*, **62**, 253–257.

Singh N.N., Manning P.J. & Angell M.J. (1982) Effects of an oral hygiene punishment procedure on chronic rumination and collateral behaviors in monozygous twins. *Journal of Applied and Behavioral Analysis*, **15**, 309–314.

Skuse D. (1989) Emotional abuse and delay in growth. *British Medical Journal*, **299**, 113–115.

Skuse D. & Wolke D. (1992) The nature and consequences of feeding problems in infants. In: Cooper P. & Stein A. (eds) *The Nature and Management of Feeding Problems and Eating Disorders in Young People*, pp. 1–25. Monographs in Clinical Pediatrics. Harwood Academic Publications, New York.

Snyder F. (1966) Towards an evolutionary theory of dreaming. *American Journal of Psychiatry*, **123**, 121–136.

Snyder F. (1969) Sleep and REM as biological engimas. In: Kales A. (ed) *Sleep: Physiology and Pathology*, pp. 266–280. J.B. Lippincott, Philadelphia.

Sondheimer J.M. (1988) Gastro-oesophageal reflux: update on pathogenesis and diagnosis. *Pediatric Clinics of North America*, **35**, 103–116.

Stores G. (1991) Confusions concerning sleep disorders and the epilepsies in children and adolescents. *British Journal of Psychiatry*, **158**, 1–7.

Stores G., Zaiwalla Z. & Bergel N. (1991) Frontal lobe complex partial seizures in children: a form of epilepsy at risk of misdiagnosis. *Developmental Medicine and Child Neurology*, **33**, 998–1009.

Story M. & Brown J.E. (1987) Do young children instinctively know what to eat? *New England Journal of Medicine*, **316**, 103–107.

Strauss C.C., Rubinoff A. & Atkeson B.M. (1983) Elimination of nocturnal headbanging in a normal 7 year old girl using overcorrection plus rewards. *Journal of Behaviour Therapy and Experimental Psychiatry*, **14**, 269–273.

Sturm L. & Stancin T. (1990) Do babies get anorexia? *Journal of the American Academy of Child and Adolescent Psychiatry*, **29**, 316–318.

Super C.M. & Harness S. (1982) The Infant's niche in rural Kenya and Metropolitan America. In: Adler L.C. (ed) *Cross-cultural Research at Issue*, pp. 47–55. Academic Press, New York.

Tanner J.M., Whitehouse R.H. & Takaishi M. (1966a) Standards from birth to maturity for height, weight, height velocity and weight velocity: British children 1965, part I. *Archives of Disease in Childhood*, **41**, 454–471.

Tanner J.M., Whitehouse R.H. & Takaishi M. (1966b) Standards from birth to maturity for height, weight, height velocity and weight velocity: British children 1965, part II. *Archives of Disease in Childhood*, **41**, 613–635.

Taylor E. (1986) *The Overactive Child*. Clinics in Developmental Medicine, no. 97. MacKeith Press/Blackwell, Oxford.

Thelen E. (1979) Rhythmical stereotypies in normal human infants. *Animal Behavior*, **27**, 699–715.

Thoman E.B. & Whitney M.P. (1989) Sleep states of infants monitored in the home: individual differences, developmental trends, and origins of diurnal cyclicity. *Infant Behavior and Development*, **12**, 59–75.

Tuchman D.N. (1988) Dysfunctional swallowing in the pediatric patient: clinical considerations. *Dysphagia*, **2**, 203–208.

van der Kolk B. (1987) The trauma spectrum: the interaction of biological and social events in the genesis of the trauma response. *Journal of Traumatic Stress*, **1**, 273–290.

van Tassel E.B. (1985) The relative influence of child and environmental characteristics on sleep disturbance in the first and second years of life. *Developmental and Behavioral Pediatrics*, **6**, 81–86.

Vela-Bueno A., Kales A., Soldatos C.R., Dobladez Blanco B., Campos-Castell J., Espino-Hurtado P. & Olivian-Palacios J. (1984) Sleep in the Prader–Willi syndrome. *Archives of Neurology*, **41**, 294–296.

Vela-Bueno A., Bixler E.O., Dobladez-Blanco B., Rubo M.E., Marrison R.E., Kales A. (1985) Prevalence of night terrors and nightmares in elementary school children: a pilot study. *Research Communication in Psychology, Psychiatry and Behaviour*, **10**(3), 177–188.

Vuorenskoski V., Wasz-Hockert O., Koivisto E. & Lind J. (1969) The effect of cry stimulus on the temperature of the lactating breast of primiparae: a thermographic study. *Experientia*, **25**, 1286.

Walsh J.K., Kramer M. & Skinner J.E. (1981) A case report of jactatio capitis nocturna. *American Journal of Psychiatry*, **138**, 524–526.

Wasz-Hockert O., Michelsson K. & Lind J. (1985) Twenty-five years of Scandinavian cry research. In: Lester B.M. & Boukydis C.F.Z. (eds) *Infant Crying: Theoretical and Research Perspectives*, pp. 349–354. Plenum, New York.

Werry J.S., Carlielle J. & Fitzpatrick B.A. (1983) Rhythmic motor activities (stereotypies) in children under 5: etiology and prevalence. *Journal of the American Academy of Child Psychiatry*, **22**, 329–336.

Whitehead R.G. (1983) Breast feeding and growth. *Pediatric Association*, **5**, 114–129.

Whitehead R.G. (1985) Infant physiology, nutritional requirements and lactational adequacy. *American Journal of Clinical Nutrition*, **41**, 447–458.

Whitehead R.G. & Paul A.A. (1981) Growth standards for early infancy. *Lancet*, **ii** (letter), 419–420.

Whitehead W.E., Drescher V.M., Merrill-Corbin E. & Cataldo M.F. (1985) Rumination syndrome in childhood treated by increasing holding. *Journal of Pediatric Gastroenterology and Nutrition*, **4**, 550–556.

Whitehead R.G., Paul A.A. & Cole T.J. (1989) Diet and the growth of healthy infants. *Journal of Human Nutrition and Dietetics*, **2**, 73–84.

Wigfield R.E., Fleming P.J., Berry P.J., Rudd P.T. & Golding G. (1992) Can the fall in Avon's sudden infant death rate be explained by changes in sleeping position? *British Medical Journal*, **304**, 282–283.

Winson J. (1990) The meaning of dreams. *Scientific American*, Nov., **263**(8), 42–48.

Wolke D. & Skuse D. (1992) The management of infant feeding problems. In: Cooper P. & Stein A. (eds) *The Nature and Management of Feeding Problems and Eating Disorders in Young People*, pp. 27–59. Monographs in Clinical Pediatrics. Harwood Academic Publications, New York.

Wolke D., Skuse D. & Mathisen B. (1990) Behavioral style in failure to thrive infants: a preliminary communication. *Journal of Pediatric Psychology*, **15**, 237–254.

World Health Organization (1992) *The ICD-10 Classification of Mental and Behavioural Disorders: Clinical Descriptions and Diagnostic Guidelines*. World Health Organization, Geneva.

Wright P. (1987) Mothers' assessment of hunger in relation to meal size in breastfed infants. *Journal of Reproductive and Infant Psychology*, **5**, 173–181.

Wright P., MacLeod H.A. & Cooper M.J. (1983) Waking at night: the effect of early feeding experience. *Child: Care, Health and Development*,

9, 309–319.

Young D., Zorick F., Wittig R., Roehrs T. & Roth T. (1988) Narcolepsy in a pediatric population. *American Journal of Diseases of Children*, **142**, 210–213.

Zarcone V. (1973) Narcolepsy. *New England Journal of Medicine*, **288**, 1156–1166.

Zepelin H. (1987) Mammalian sleep. In: Kryger H., Roth T. & Dement W.C. (eds) *Principles and Practice of Sleep Medicine*, pp. 30–49. W.B. Saunders, Philadelphia.

Zepelin H. & Rechtschaffen A. (1974) Mammalian sleep, longevity and energy metabolism. *Brain Behaviour Evolution*, **10**, 425–470.

Zuckerman B., Stevenson J. & Bailey V. (1987) Sleep problems in early childhood: continuities, predictive factors, and behavioral correlates. *Pediatrics*, **80**, 664–671.

Chapter 28
Attachment Disorders in Infancy and Childhood

Charles H. Zeanah & Robert N. Emde

Attachment disorders occupy a unique position among the disorders of child psychiatry, both in terms of nosology and traditions of research.

In terms of nosology, attachment disorders are unusual in that they necessarily imply a designation of disorder in the individual, but one that has arisen from a disturbance in the individual's caregiving context. Although some have argued that the caregiving relationship context is the appropriate unit for diagnosis in children under 3 years of age (Sameroff & Emde, 1989), existing systems of psychiatric nosology designate disorders *within* rather than *between* individuals. DSM-III-R (American Psychiatry Association, 1987), for example, considers a mental disorder to be 'a clinically significant behavioral or psychological syndrome or pattern that occurs *in a person* [emphasis added] and that is associated with present distress (a painful symptom) or disability (impairment in one or more important areas of functioning) or with a significantly increased risk of suffering death, pain disability, or an important loss of freedom' (p. xxii). From this standpoint, attachment disorders must be discussed as they are experienced by and affect the young child.

In terms of research, there are separate traditions that form a background for the designation of disorder, but there is little research that joins these traditions and virtually no research on the currently designated syndromes themselves. A highly productive research tradition stems from attachment theory and methods in developmental psychology and that assesses secure and insecure patterns of attachment in young children and their caregivers. Such research will be highlighted in this chapter. Other research traditions stem from investigations of child maltreatment (including a variety of adverse caregiving environments) and children raised in institutions without the opportunity to develop selective attachments. Common features of this research include a concern with children under 5 years who have problems with social relatedness, yet there has not been explicit attention given to research on the syndrome designations arrived at in DSM-IV (American Psychiatric Association, 1991), ICD-10 (World Health Organization, 1992) or their predecessors. Consequently, direct information about validity, prevalence, course and treatment of attachment disorders is incomplete.

THE SYNDROMES OF ATTACHMENT DISORDER

Clinicians and researchers have been concerned since mid-century with problems of young children who have difficulties in social relatedness in contexts of less than adequate caregiving (Goldfarb, 1945; Spitz, 1945; Bowlby, 1951; Kempe *et al.*, 1962; Tizard & Tizard, 1971; Rutter, 1972, 1979; Call, 1980). The classification of syndromes of disordered attachment, however, is a relatively recent development.

Classification

Both DSM-IV and ICD-10 now designate two major types of 'reactive attachment disorder of childhood' (although the latter gives this particular label to one type only). Both classification systems refer to a persistent disturbance in the child's social relatedness that begins before age 5 years, that extends across social situations and that is distinguished from autism and pervasive developmental disorders.

One type of disorder is designated as 'inhibited' (DSM-IV), wherein ambivalent, inhibited or hypervigilant responses are centred on one or more adults. The other type is designated as 'disinhibited', wherein there is indiscriminant oversociability with a relative lack of selectivity in the persons from whom comfort is sought, poorly modulated social interactions with unfamiliar persons across a range of social situations and a failure to show selective attachments. DSM-IV (American Psychiatric Association, 1991) considered whether to require that there be evidence of grossly pathogenic care, such as harsh treatment by caregiver, frank neglect, disregard of child's physical needs, or repeated changes in caregivers. ICD-10 does not make this requirement, although the child must have the capacity for social responsiveness, as revealed in interactions with 'non-deviant' adults.

In the ICD-10 system, for example, contradictory or ambivalent social responses are expected to be present across social contexts, although allowances are made for relationship variability. In other words, infants should display unusual social responses in more than one relationship, although these responses may be considerably less evident in some relationships (e.g. with preschool teachers as opposed to parents).

In contrast, DSM-IV is more emphatic that abnormal social behaviour is expected to be apparent in most social contexts.

Differential diagnosis

In young children who present with markedly aberrant social behaviour, a diagnosis of attachment disorder should be considered. Other conditions that are associated with deviant social behaviour in the first few years of life include pervasive developmental disorders, language disorders and mental retardation.

By definition, children who receive a diagnosis of pervasive developmental disorder are excluded from attachment disorder in both the DSM-IV and the ICD-10 systems. Young children who have primary language disorders may have associated cognitive and social delays, although the language delays are significantly greater than the cognitive delays and the deviant social behaviour. Thus, the clinician needs to consider the form as well as the presence of aberrant social behaviour. The characteristic features of autistic social impairment (see Chapter 33) will suggest a diagnosis of pervasive developmental disorder instead.

Children with mental retardation are excluded by definition from both the inhibited and disinhibited DSM-IV types of attachment disorders. Absence of a history of grossly pathogenic care in a young child with significant social delays or deviance, assuming it can be ascertained, excludes a diagnosis of attachment disorder in DSM-IV. In ICD-10, children diagnosed with reactive attachment disorder are required to exhibit the capacity for normal social relatedness when interacting with 'appropriately responsive, non-deviant adults'. This effectively excludes children whose mental retardation renders them so delayed socially that their relatedness is impaired with responsive adults. Children who present with significant cognitive, language and social delays and who have a known or suspected history of extreme neglect or other form of adverse care may present significant diagnostic challenges.

Clinical experience suggests that some children from especially punitive or impoverished environments may appear quite delayed on standardized tests and exhibit aberrant social behaviours, but they may make rapid developmental gains in more favourable caregiving contexts over a period of weeks to months. Thus, these children may demonstrate the capacity for normal social relatedness with appropriately responsive adults, although it may not be clear to the clinician what a particular child's capacity really is at a particular moment in time. For this reason, serial assessments of children following a change in caregiving environments may prove useful.

RESEARCH ON ATTACHMENT: KNOWLEDGE BASE FOR CLINICAL SYNDROMES

Although criteria have been available for diagnosing attachment disorders for over 10 years, little research has examined the validity of these criteria. The criteria appear to have been derived from research on social behaviour in maltreated children and from studies of children raised in institutions. A large body of data from developmental research on attachment in childhood, however, has not yet been integrated into the nosologies. Research on attachment has focused on normal or high-risk populations rather than clinical populations. Nevertheless, this research bears on the questions of qualitative differences in attachment relationships and deals with disturbed parent–child relationships. Since it seems clear that diagnostic criteria must be drawn from research in relevant domains, and that future research is likely to address such an integration, we believe that a review of these disparate bodies of research is useful in order to reexamine the diagnostic criteria of the syndromes presented earlier.

Social behaviour in maltreated children

Research on social behaviour of maltreated children appears to have influenced the descriptions of attachment disorders in DSM-IV and ICD-10. Gaensbauer and Sands (1979) observed a number of unusual affective communications and social behaviours in infants and toddlers who had been maltreated. During interactions with their caregivers, abused/neglected infants exhibited affective withdrawal, anhedonia, inconsistent and unpredictable signals, indiscriminant sociability, ambiguity and ambivalence, and proneness to anger and distress. The authors asserted that these distorted affective communications, which are reminiscent of many of the socially aberrant behaviours of attachment disorders as described in DSM-IV and ICD-10, further compromise social interchanges between maltreated infants and their caregivers.

George and Main (1979) observed 10 children 1–3 years old with a history of physical abuse in daycare settings. In daycare settings where they observed the children, the abused infants exhibited more aggressive behaviours towards their peers and their caregivers than did control children. They were also significantly less likely to approach their caregivers and when they did so it was more likely to be ambivalent: to the side, to the rear or by backstepping. In response to distress in their peers, the abused children demonstrated significantly less concern for and more physical attacks, fear and anger towards the distressed child. In contrast, the control children exhibited more interest, empathy, sadness or concern. The investigators were struck by the co-mingling of caregiving and aggression which seemed to stimulate one another in these children (Main & George, 1985).

Other controlled studies of peer relations of maltreated children have indicated that maltreated children become aggressive more quickly when frustrated, exhibit fewer prosocial behaviours in peer interactions, and exhibit aggressive responses to distress in peers (Herrenkohl & Herrenkohl, 1981; Hoffman-Plotkin & Twentyman, 1984; Howes & Eldridge, 1985). In reviewing this research, Mueller and Silverman (1989) conclude that despite some methodological shortcomings, the studies converge in finding two major patterns of peer relations: a withdrawn, uninvolved pattern and an aggressive, disruptive pattern.

Other socially aberrant behaviours have been observed in hospitalized infants who are failing to thrive. Although failure to thrive is a complexly determined syndrome, there is little question that many of these infants are raised in emotionally deprived environments. Infants who fail to thrive without organic contributors to their growth failure exhibit expressionless faces, abnormal gaze (hyperalert, undirected eyes, avoidance, disinterest), lack of smile and lack of directed vocalization (Powell & Low, 1983). The intensity and frequency of these behaviours have been shown to be greater in infants who are failing to thrive than in a comparison group of hospitalized infants who were growing normally (Powell *et al.*, 1987).

Social withdrawal, out-of-context aggression, odd and ambivalent social approaches and unusual signalling behaviours have all been observed in studies of maltreated children and are also included in the official nosologies' descriptions of attachment disorders.

Children raised in institutions

Influential descriptive studies by Goldfarb (1945) and Spitz (1945, 1946) led Bowlby (1951) to conclude that infants raised in institutions were irreversibly adversely affected by the absence of a close and continuous relationship with a caregiving adult (for a review of Spitz's early hospitalism studies and the subsequent critical commentary surrounding it, see Emde, 1983). Deficits purported to occur included cognitive delays, language impairments, attentional deficits and a lasting inability to form close interpersonal relationships.

Provence and Lipton (1962), for example, studied infants reared in a single institution and pointed out that infants there, compared to home-reared infants, suffered from lack of a specific attachment figure, limited time with an interactive partner, lack of emotional investment of caregiver and caregiving procedures administered on a rigid schedule rather than in response to infant needs. In addition, the institutional environment was physically impoverished, albeit clean and orderly. Infants had significant social, language, motor and cognitive delays by the end of the first year. Compared to home-reared infants, the institution-reared infants also exhibited reduced thumb-sucking, self-exploration and genital manipulation. Deviant social behaviours, such as failure to adapt to holding and rocking, were apparent, as well.

In a now classic study, Skeels (1966) reported on a 30-year follow-up study of 25 children originally raised in an orphanage. A policy shift resulted in an opportunity for planned intervention for a small number of children less than 3 years old. The intervention consisted of transfer of 13 of the more cognitively delayed children from one institution to another. This change was an intervention because the original institution provided less developmental stimulation and less consistent caregiving relationships for the children. Eventually, 11 of the 13 children in the intervention group were adopted. Although the focus of the follow-up was on cognitive development, the long-term results dramatically illustrate divergent patterns of competence in adulthood. All 13 individuals in the intervention group were self-supporting, whereas in the contrast group, 1 of the individuals had died in a state institution and 4 others were still wards of institutions. The intervention group completed a median of 12th grade, whereas the comparison group completed a median of third grade. Further, 11 of 13 individuals in the intervention group were married, but only 2 of the 12 individuals in the contrast group were married. These results dramatically illustrated that some of the most severe consequences of infant institutionalization can be prevented.

Rutter (1972) pointed out that institutional rearing included a variety of adverse conditions beyond the separation that Bowlby had emphasized, including low caregiver-to-child ratios, multiple caregivers from shift work and staff turnover, and poor stimulation. Oftentimes, institutional management openly discouraged workers from developing personal relationships with the children in their care.

A study that disentangled many of the confounds noted above was conducted in London by Tizard and her colleagues (Tizard & Rees, 1974, 1975; Tizard & Hodges, 1978). They conducted a longitudinal investigation of 65 children raised for 2–4 years in British residential nurseries. In these nurseries, children lived in small, mixed-age groups, were provided with books and toys, and staff-to-child ratios were high. These residential nurseries provided great improvements in the physical surroundings and instrumental caregiving environments compared to the institutions studied a generation earlier by Spitz and Goldfarb. Nevertheless, each child was cared for by large numbers of adults and close relationships were officially discouraged. As a result, children were significantly hampered in their attempt to establish meaningful relationships with preferred caregivers. An average of 24 different nurses had worked with each child for at least 1 week during the first 2 years of life, and by age $4\frac{1}{2}$ years, the number had increased to 50.

Children who were adopted, who were restored to their original families and who remained in the institution were compared with one another and with a London working-class comparison group who had never been institutionalized. At age $4\frac{1}{2}$ years, 24 of the children had been adopted, 15 had been restored to their original families and 26 remained in institutions. Although mean IQ scores were within the average range in all three groups, the adopted children had significantly higher scores, were friendlier and more cooperative with examiners, and showed less distractibility and restlessness during the test situation (Tizard & Rees, 1974). Adopted children also had fewer behavioural problems than all others (Tizard & Rees, 1975).

The investigators also examined attachment behaviours in the children. At age 2 years, the London working-class children showed a definite preference for a small number of caregivers (generally parents or grandparents). The institutionalized children, on the other hand, also had preferred caregivers among the nursery staff, but they expressed their preferences differently. Specifically, they protested separations and exhibited proximity-seeking much as the working-class children had done when they were younger. By age $4\frac{1}{2}$ years, the only children described as 'very clingy' were those from the institutions.

Nevertheless, 18 of the 26 children were described by their nurse as exhibiting superficial or little attachment to anyone. Of these, 8 children seemed largely detached from everyone, hardly following the staff around and showing little interest in strangers. The other 10 children were described as not having deep attachments, and they were markedly attention-seeking, clingy and overfriendly with strangers. A minority of adopted and restored institutional children exhibited overfriendly behaviour towards strangers that was a cause of concern for their families.

This research on institution-reared children from the study conducted by Tizard and her colleagues has made it possible to examine the effects of lack of specific and sustained attachments to caregivers independent of physical and emotional deprivation. Their findings provide clear support for indiscriminant sociability associated with excessive clinging as in the ICD-10 category disinhibited attachment disorder of childhood. They also provide some support for the socially withdrawn and deviant behaviours described in the DSM-IV and ICD-10 reactive attachment disorder categories.

Attachment research and insecure attachment

Research on attachment from the developmental perspective began in the 1960s when Mary Ainsworth conducted a longitudinal investigation of 26 middle-class mothers and their infants in Baltimore, Maryland. She was interested in individual differences in the child's use of the attachment figure as a secure base from which to explore the environment (Ainsworth *et al.*, 1978). Mothers and infants were visited in their homes for 4 hours of naturalistic home observation every 3 weeks during the first year of life. The investigators recorded notes on their observations of mothers and infants, and these notes were later coded with a number of rating scales. Following Bowlby's (1969/1982) ethological attachment theory, Ainsworth and her colleagues had hypothesized broadly that individual differences in maternal sensitivity and emotional availability during the first year of life would be related to differences in the infants' security of attachment at 1 year.

In order to assess security of attachment, these investigators developed a brief laboratory paradigm known as the Strange Situation Procedure. This was developed as a moderately stressful procedure designed to examine the balance between the infant's motivational systems of attachment and exploration. In the Strange Situation, an infant's caregiver is instructed to sit in a sparsely furnished playroom with her infant (aged 12–20 months) in front of her on the floor next to a few age-appropriate toys. After 3 minutes, a stranger enters and gradually engages the infant. After 3 more minutes, the caregiver leaves the room for up to 3 minutes (less if the infant becomes too distressed), and then she returns. She spends 3 minutes with the infant and then leaves again. This time the infant is left alone for up to 3 minutes before the stranger returns. The infant spends 3 minutes with the stranger, and in the final episode the caregiver returns for a second reunion.

According to attachment theory, infants should be comfortable in the presence of their caregiver and should be motivated to explore the novel environment of the playroom and the toys. The stress induced by brief separation from the caregiver should activate the infant's attachment system and deactivate the exploratory system. When the caregiver returns, the infant should seek proximity and comfort from the caregiver proportionate to the degree of distress the infant experienced during the separation. Having attained comfort, the infant should return within a short time to exploring the environment, as the effects of the attachment system diminish and the effects of the exploratory system intensify. When infants behave in a manner demonstrating this kind of attachment–exploration balance, they are said to be *securely attached* to that caregiver. In the Ainsworth's (Ainsworth *et al.*, 1978) nonclinical sample, 57% of the infants were classified as secure.

Another group of infants become extremely distressed by the separation, and during the reunion episodes they generally seek proximity to the caregiver. Instead of obtaining comfort, however, they continue to protest angrily even when held by the caregiver. They may behave ambivalently, alternately seeking and rejecting the caregiver's attempts to soothe them. In fact, they seem to resist the caregiver's attempts to soothe them. For this reason, their attachment is classified *resistant* to the caregiver with whom they are assessed. In the Ainsworth *et al.* (1978) sample, 17% of the infants were classified in this manner.

A final group of infants behaved in a manner that Ainsworth and her colleagues had not anticipated. They seemed remarkably undistressed by the separation from their caregivers, often hardly noticing the departure. When the caregiver returned, the infants in this group ignored them, or they made an initial approach but then dramatically turned away and seemed actively to avoid the caregivers. For this reason, they are classified *avoidantly attached* to that caregiver (26% of the Ainsworth *et al.* sample). Despite the outward appearance of calm in this group, they tend to experience extremely high levels of physiological arousal during the reunion episodes of the Strange Situation (Sroufe & Waters, 1977). For this reason in part, the avoidance they display is believed to be defensive and to reflect attempts to suppress their own need for comfort (Main, 1982; Main & Weston, 1982; Cassidy & Kobak, 1988).

Investigations in middle-class American samples other than Ainsworth *et al.* (1978) generally have found similar proportions of secure, avoidant and resistant infants. In high-risk and clinical samples more insecurely attached infants and more infants who are unable to be classified into one of these three initial patterns are apparent.

Disorganized/disoriented attachment

A new pattern of attachment of special interest to clinicians, the disorganized/disoriented type, has been described recently. In a number of investigations of attachment, a small proportion of infants could not be classified into the secure, avoidant or resistant categories. Main and Solomon (1986) reviewed unclassifiable cases from a number of investigations and proposed a fourth type of attachment that seems to be more prevalent in samples of high-risk infants. This type is characterized by disorganized or disoriented attachment behaviour. Additionally, Main and Solomon found that some infants previously classified secure, avoidant or resistant met criteria for the *disorganized/disoriented* group. This realization helped resolve some of the previously puzzling findings in the literature, such as why 40–50% of abused and neglected infants were classified securely attached to their maltreating parent.

The disorganized/disoriented classification is made on the basis of the child's behaviour in the presence of the caregiver during the Strange Situation Procedure. The behaviours used to classify the infant as disorganized indicate disturbances in the functioning of the use of the caregiver as a secure base and a safe haven. The child demonstrates conflict behaviours, fear of the caregiver, confusion, disordered temporal sequences, stereotypies or other anomalous behaviour (Main & Solomon, 1990). Because these behaviours may occur in children whose attachment otherwise could be classified into one of the secure, avoidant or resistant patterns, or in children whose attachment does not fit one of the other three patterns, disorganized attachment may represent a dimension rather than a category. At least some of the anomalous behaviours indicative of disorganized attachment are similar to the aberrant social behaviours in maltreated children and of the symptoms of attachment disorders in DSM-IV and ICD-10.

Main and Hesse (1990) have speculated that disorganized attachment results from extremely unpredictable caregiver interactive behaviour. They reason that unpredictability leads the infant to be afraid for or afraid of the caregiver. Conflict behaviour results because the source of security for the infant is also the source of fear. Empirical support for this formulation comes from demonstrations that parents who have unresolved losses or traumatic experiences (Ainsworth & Eichberg, 1992), parents who have serious affective disorder (Radke-Yarrow *et al.*, 1985; DeMulder & Radke-Yarrow, 1991), parents who are active alcoholics (O'Connor *et al.*, 1987) and parents who are maltreating (Carlson *et al.*, 1989), all have high proportions of infants who are classified as disorganized. One of the problems in evaluating this work is that the proportion of disorganized infants in low-risk middle-class populations is not yet clear, making findings in high-risk samples difficult to interpret. Carlson *et al.* (1989) found 82% disorganized classifications of infants in their maltreating group and only 19% disorganized classifications among their demographically similar control group infants. DeMulder and Radke-Yarrow (1991) also found almost 20% of the middle-class control children in their sample to be classified disorganized. At present, insuf-

ficient work with low-risk samples has been completed to know if 20% disorganized is representative of those samples.

Antecedents and stability of infant attachment classification

In the developmental literature on attachment, Strange Situation classifications are said to be stable and to be related systematically to prior patterns of mother infant interaction. We will discuss briefly each of these claims in light of available evidence.

Stability of the three major classifications between infants aged 12 and 18 months has ranged from 53% (Thompson *et al.*, 1982) to 96% (Waters, 1978), and in most investigations it is around 75% (Lamb *et al.*, 1985). In high-risk, low-income samples stability is lower, and changes from secure to insecure classification have been systematically related to an increase in stressful life events reported by mothers (Vaughn *et al.*, 1979). Changes in attachment classifications in this disadvantaged sample were also related to quality of caregiving in mothers. That is, when mothers who were rated as providing excellent care were compared to mothers rated as providing inadequate care, striking differences emerged in the stability of the child's attachment classification. Mothers in the excellent care group had infants with 81% stability and mothers in the adequate care group had infants with only 48% stability (Egeland & Sroufe, 1981). These findings have implications for intervention in that they suggest that the basic organization of an infant's approach to caregiving relationships is malleable depending upon consistency in the caregiving environment.

The most consistent findings about prior interactive patterns are that mothers who are rated as providing sensitive care to their infants during the first year of life have infants who are more likely to be securely attached in the Strange Situations (Ainsworth *et al.*, 1978; Belsky *et al.*, 1984; Egeland & Farber, 1984; Grossman *et al.*, 1985; Vaughn & Waters, 1990). Although the magnitude of this finding has been questioned (Goldsmith & Alansky, 1987), its consistency across investigations is noteworthy. Still, we have much more to learn about the process by which infants become securely or insecurely attached.

Although differences in the behaviour of mothers of secure and insecure infants have been consistently demonstrated, it has been more difficult to identify differences in the interactive behaviour of mothers that precedes the various patterns of insecure attachments. Ainsworth *et al.* (1978) suggested that mothers of avoidant infants were more rejecting (turning away the infants' bids for contact and comfort) and that mothers of resistant infants were more inconsistent than mothers of infants later classified secure. Findings about these assertions in subsequent investigations generally have been mixed, although methods of assessment and specific hypotheses have also varied.

Using transcripts from the Ainsworth *et al.* (1978) sample, Main and Stadtman (1981) found more aversion to physical contact among the mothers of infants later classified avoidant in the Strange Situation. No specific replications of this finding have been conducted. On the other hand, Belsky *et al.* (1984) failed to demonstrate predicted differences in the amount of physical contact between mothers of securely attached and mothers of avoidantly attached infants. These same investigators did find, as predicted, that mothers of infants later classified resistant in the Strange Situation were the least responsive to them in naturalistic home-based observations. No investigations reporting on interactive precursors of infants classified disorganized are yet available.

Significance of infant attachment classifications

From the outset, attachment researchers have argued that infant attachment classifications are not characteristics of the infant *per se*, but instead reflect qualitative features of the attachment relationship with the caregiver with whom the infant is assessed in the Strange Situation. At least three lines of evidence support this assertion.

The strongest evidence that the Strange Situation classification is a relationship characteristic rather than a characteristic of the infant is that infants' attachment may be classified differently with different caregivers. In a number of studies, there has been no relationship between the infant's Strange Situation classifications with different caregivers. In a recent metaanalysis, however, it was possible to predict to a modest but significant degree an infant's classification with one parent by knowing the infant's classification to the other parent (Fox *et al.*, 1991). Despite this tendency, it is clear that an infant's attachment to one caregiver is not necessarily the same as the infant's attachment to another caregiver. This argues against attachment as an endogenous infant characteristic since it varies with different relationships.

Secondly, along these lines, there is little evidence suggesting attachment classifications are within-the-individual temperamental traits. Although some evidence has accumulated that a temperamental characteristic designated 'proneness to distress' distinguishes infants classified avoidant and resistant with their mothers, there is no evidence that temperament characteristics distinguish secure and insecure infants (Lamb *et al.*, 1985; Sroufe, 1985; Belsky & Rovine, 1987). Thus, temperament seems not to influence attachment security directly, but it may influence how security or insecurity is expressed (Belsky & Nezworski, 1988).

A final line of evidence about attachment classifications and relationship patterns comes from an investigation of attachment to mothers and to fathers in London (Steele *et al.*, 1993). In this sample, prenatally measured maternal characteristics predicted the baby's attachment to the mother but not to the father over a year later, and prenatally measured paternal characteristics predicted the infant's attachment to the father but not to the mother over a year later. These differential antecedents of attachment to mother and to father suggest relationship specificity of Strange Situation classifications. Relationship specificity of the classifications begs the question of whether or not symptoms of attachment disorders also may

vary widely across different relationships between the infant and different attachment figures.

Over time, infants apparently develop a more unified attachment organization. What begins as a dyadic characteristic, or perhaps several distinct dyadic characteristics, is integrated by the infant into an overall predisposition towards attachment relationships (and perhaps other types of relationships) in general. Thus, although 6-year-old children have distinctive attachment classifications with each parent (Main & Cassidy, 1988), by the time of adolescence and adulthood individuals are thought to have integrated their experiences in an overall predisposition towards attachment relationships (Main *et al.*, 1985; Zeanah & Anders, 1987).

Bowlby (1969/1982) hypothesized that the integration of early relationship experiences into an overall organization of attachment occurs through representational or internal working models. These are dynamic internal representations, maintained partially or completely out of awareness, that are hypothesized to structure and organize perception and the interpretation of experience in interaction with others. In particular, these models are believed to organize an individual's perceptions of, feelings about, expectations of and behaviours in attachment relationships (Bowlby, 1980; Bretherton, 1985; Main *et al.*, 1985). Although open to modifications through new experiences, these models are presumed to become more resistant to change with increasing age.

In this context, infants' attachment classifications, as measured by the Strange Situation Procedure (Ainsworth *et al.*, 1978), and adult attachment classifications, as measured by the Adult Attachment Interview (Main & Goldwyn, in press) are asserted to reflect qualitative differences in internal working models or internal representations of attachment (Bretherton, 1985; Main *et al.*, 1985; Sroufe, 1988).

Adult attachment classifications

Main and her colleagues developed the Adult Attachment Interview to assess individual differences in adults' internal representation of attachment relationship experiences (Main *et al.*, 1985; Main & Goldwyn, in press). In this structured interview, adults are asked about childhood relationship experiences, as well as about their current perspectives on these experiences. Verbatim transcripts are audio-taped and then transcribed. The narratives are then coded with specific rating scales as well as with an overall classification. Scoring relies not only on the content of the experiences described but even more on the organization of that content. The degree to which the individual has access to memories and feelings congruent with descriptions of attachment relevant experiences and seems to have integrated those experiences coherently is crucial to scoring. Four patterns in adults, analogous to the infant Strange Situation classifications, have been described: (1) autonomous; (2) dismissing; (3) preoccupied; and (4) unresolved.

Adults classified *autonomous* convey during the interview a valuing of attachment relationships and acknowledge that they have significant and sometimes lasting effects. They describe both positive and negative aspects of their childhood relationship experiences in a balanced and open way. They demonstrate a tolerance for imperfection in themselves and in their caregivers and may be explicitly forgiving of mistreatment without minimizing its harmful effects on them. Throughout the interview, they are able to provide specific examples of global descriptions and to convey a consistent, clear and believable sense of their attachment experiences. The autonomous or secure group in adults corresponds to the infant secure group.

Adults who dismiss the importance or the effects of attachment relationship experiences are classified *dismissing*. During the Adult Attachment Interview, they may be unable to support global descriptors with specific memories or may report painful experiences without having any emotional responses to the events. They tend to idealize their caregivers and to claim to have been unaffected by clearly adverse experiences. During questioning about attachment-relevant experiences, such as separations, they minimize having been affected, although they experience elevated levels of physiological arousal (Dozier, 1991). The dismissing adult group corresponds to the infant avoidant group.

A third group of adults, classified *preoccupied*, present highly incoherent narratives about their childhood relationship experiences. They may seem to be struggling psychologically in the present with their families of origin and to have difficulty in providing a comprehensible overview of their experiences. Although they may recall a large number of vignettes about their childhood, they exhibit either confused and passive thinking or unmodulated anger or fear about their relationships. This group corresponds to the infant resistant group.

The final group of attachment classification in adults, *unresolved*, corresponds to the infant disorganized/disoriented classification. This group may share underlying characteristics with any of the other three classifications but also exhibits narrative characteristics of unresolved mourning after a significant loss or unresolved trauma following extreme abuse or other traumatic experiences. The characteristics exhibited by individuals in this group in their narratives include irrational beliefs, excessive fear or guilt, inability to stay with the topic, or other indications of not having satisfactorily resolved their traumatic experiences.

Dismissing, preoccupied and unresolved classifications are sometimes referred to as insecure. These adult attachment classifications are not interpreted as veridical accounts of an individual's childhood relationship history, but rather to reflect an individual's current perspective on or state of mind with respect to those experiences.

Preliminary studies have found that adult attachment classifications are related to both mother and infant behaviour. Autonomous maternal attachment, as measured by the Adult Attachment Interview, appears to be an important protective factor for infant development. Crowell and Feldman (1988) found that only 10% of the mothers of clinic-referred 2–4-year-olds were classified autonomous but 45% of the mothers of demographically matched comparison children were classified autonomous. In two other clinical samples, Benoit and her colleagues reported similar findings. Only 4% of the mothers of hospitalized infants with failure to thrive were classified autonomous compared to 40% of the mothers of carefully matched hospitalized infants who were growing normally (Benoit *et al.*, 1989). None of 20 mothers whose infants had serious sleep disorders were classified autonomous, whereas over 40% of the control group mothers were classified autonomous (Benoit *et al.*, 1992).

Further, Crowell and Feldman (1988, 1991) found that mothers' attachment classifications predicted mother and child behaviour in a problem-solving paradigm. The effects on infant behaviour were especially powerful because the effect of the mothers' attachment classifications remained even after the mothers' current interactive behaviours were controlled for (statistically removed). These preliminary findings suggest that adult attachment classifications are importantly indicative of adaptive parenting characteristics. Whether they are specific to attachment remains to be demonstrated.

Intergenerational transmission of attachment

Explicit in attachment theory has been the notion that an individual's pattern of attachment depends in large part on experiences with the attachment figure in early childhood. Measures of infant and adult internal representations of attachment have refined this assertion by testing the hypothesis that adults' current perspective on their own childhood relationship history is predictive of their own child's attachment to them.

To date, a number of investigations have examined the concordance between adult and infant attachment using the Adult Attachment Interview and the Strange Situation, where concordance is defined as parents classified autonomous with infants classified secure, parents classified dismissing with infants classified avoidant, parents classified preoccupied with infants classified resistant, and parents classified unresolved and infants classified disorganized. Studies in which the Adult Attachment Interview was administered concurrently or following the Strange Situation have found concordance rates of about 69–75% (Main & Goldwyn, in press; Ainsworth & Eichberg, 1992; Zeanah *et al.*, 1993). Recently, three other investigations have assessed the concordance between prenatally administered Adult Attachment Interviews and Strange Situation Procedures administered at 12 or 15 months. These investigations produced similar findings of concordance ranging from 66 to 74% between parents' attachment classifications in pregnancy and infant attachment classifications assessed over 1 year later (Benoit *et al.*, 1991; Fonagy *et al.*, 1991; Ward *et al.*, 1991). These results suggest either that the direction of effects in early infancy is largely mother to infant, or that some third factor explains attachment in both parents and infants.

Clinical implications of attachment classifications

It is widely asserted that Strange Situation classifications and Adult Attachment classifications are assessments of individuals' internal representations of attachment relationship experiences (Bretherton, 1985, 1987; Main *et al.*, 1985; Cicchetti *et al.*, 1990; Zeanah, in press). Evidence in support of this assertion comes in part from the concordance of adult and infant attachment cited earlier, and in part from evidence that mothers of differing attachment classifications perceive and interpret infant distress differently (Zeanah *et al.*, 1993). This evidence, of course, does not preclude multiple influences on the formation and development of an individual's internal representations of attachment.

For a time, there was confusion in the literature about the relationship between insecure attachment classifications and psychopathology. As categories whose labels are not neutral, attachment classifications tend to become reified and may be confused with diagnoses. It is important for clinicians to remember that classifications are not diagnoses, and in fact, that insecure attachment is not necessarily pathological.

Belsky and Nezworski (1988) and others have described insecure attachment classifications as adaptations, or more properly as maladaptions. That is, the insecure pattern may represent children's adaptations to the particular circumstances of their attachment relationships, although these patterns may not prepare them for successful adaptation in the world outside their families. Sroufe (1988) has pointed out that insecure attachments in infants are risk factors which probabilistically increase the likelihood of later psychiatric disorders in the child, even though only a minority of children will ever develop such disorders.

With regard to adult attachment classifications, the situation is similar. Findings from several investigations assessing adult attachment and child adaptation indicate that autonomous attachment in adults appears to be an important protective factor, although insecure adult attachment is not a particularly meaningful risk factor (Zeanah, in press). That is, in high-risk or clinical samples, mothers classified autonomous are extremely unlikely to have infants with clinical disorders, but even in low-risk samples, nearly half of parents assessed are classified insecurely attached.

It should not be surprising that a categorical scheme that includes only three or four different types would include a broad range of adaptations within each type. Secure attachment may provide some protection against psychopathology generally, but it does not confer absolute protection. Similarly, insecure attachments may increase an individual's risk for psychopathology without being linearly related to subsequent psychiatric disorders (Sroufe, 1988).

COURSE AND PROGNOSIS OF DISORDERS OF ATTACHMENT

To date, there have been no investigations on the course of attachment disorders as defined by standard nomenclature.

Still, data from longitudinal investigations of the consequences of institutional rearing and investigations from developmental research are both relevant to questions of course and prognosis. These data make it possible to evaluate Bowlby's (1951) assertions about the effects of maternal deprivation on intelligence, on behaviour problems and on social relationships.

Consequences of insecure infant attachment in later childhood

Insecure attachment in infancy predicts subsequent behavioural problems, impulse control problems, conflicts and struggles with caregivers and seriously problematic peer relationships (Sroufe, 1983; Lewis *et al.*, 1984; Erickson *et al.*, 1985; Troy & Sroufe, 1987; Easterbrooks & Goldberg, 1990). Insecure attachment has also been related to lower self-esteem in 6-year-old children (Cassidy, 1988). Infants who are insecurely attached at 1 year of age to their mothers are less enthusiastic and less compliant, and exhibit more negative affect and less positive affect sharing towards their mothers at 2 years of age in free play and in a problem-solving paradigm (Matas *et al.*, 1978; Waters *et al.*, 1979). Infants who were classified insecurely attached are also less socially competent with peers and less ego-resilient (flexible, self-reliant, curious, involved) in preschool and kindergarten (Arend *et al.*, 1979). These results are also apparent in slightly older children. For example, in an investigation of families of lower social class, 4−5-year-old children were rated by their teachers in a research nursery school programme on a large number of measures. Children with a history of insecure attachment to their primary caregivers were rated to be less empathic, to have lower self-esteem, to be less socially competent, and to be less ego-resilient than children with a history of secure attachment (Sroufe, 1983).

Investigations examining infant attachment classifications predicting later behaviour problems have produced mixed results when parents rate behaviour problems (Lewis *et al.*, 1984; Bates *et al.*, 1985; Fagot & Kavanagh, 1990) but more consistent results when teachers rate behaviour problems (Erickson *et al.*, 1985; Fagot & Kavanagh, 1990). Generally, infants who were insecurely attached to their mothers at age 1 year are significantly more likely to be rated by their teachers as having symptoms of behaviour disorders in the preschool years. Two recent investigations in high-risk samples have found that disorganized attachment classifications, in particular, strongly predict preschool behaviour problems (Hubbs-Tait *et al.*, 1991; Lyons-Ruth *et al.*, 1993).

With regard to social functioning, insecure attachment in infancy has been associated with less competent social behaviour with unfamiliar adults (Main *et al.*, 1985), more problematic interactions in the home with parents (Solomon *et al.*, 1987), and with seriously disturbed patterns of peer interaction (Troy & Sroufe, 1987).

Consequences of institutional rearing

In general, results from investigations of ex-institutional children converge with findings from developmental research about the sequelae of insecure attachments. We have already reviewed the Skeels (1966) intervention study with its 30-year follow-up of a small number of infants raised in institutions. That study illustrates broadly that many of the consequences of institutional rearing in infancy can be reversed in early childhood by providing enriched environments with consistent caregiving experiences.

The longitudinal investigation of Tizard and her colleagues following ex-institutional children yielded important data about the children's functioning at school age and at mid-adolescence. The advantage of results from their study as opposed to older studies is that many of the deplorable conditions that had existed in previous institutions were improved so that it was possible to examine effects of lack of selective attachment relatively unconfounded by physical deprivation, lack of stimulation and lack of opportunities for social interaction. As early as age 4 years, there was no demonstrable effect of institutionalization on IQ. In later assessments, it became clear that IQ was largely dependent upon characteristics of the children's subsequent placements (Tizard & Hodges, 1978; Hodges & Tizard, 1989a). There was a suggestion that the children placed in adoptive homes following institutionalization before age $4\frac{1}{2}$ years made more substantial gains in IQ than those placed after this age.

With regard to behavioural symptoms, the effects of early institutional rearing were more complicated and more worrisome. When the ex-institutional children were 8 years old, according to ratings by their parents, they did not exhibit more behavioural problems than a comparison group of inner-city children who had lived only with their families. According to their teachers, however, the ex-institutional children showed more externalizing symptoms, such as restlessness, attention-seeking behaviour and disobedience than did comparison children (Tizard & Hodges, 1978). By the time the children were 16 years old, differences in behaviour problems were apparent in parent interviews, in teacher ratings and in interviews with the adolescents themselves. In fact, 35–50% of the ex-institutional adolescents tended to be regarded by their teachers as restless and distractible, as irritable and oppositional and as having quarrelsome peer relationships (Hodges & Tizard, 1989a).

Social and family relationships, the most likely arena in which to detect sequelae of attachment disorders, in fact, showed the most profound effects of early institutional rearing (Hodges & Tizard, 1989b). Emphasis in this research was on attachment from the quantitative rather than the qualitative perspective of developmental attachment research. Adopted ex-institutional children were 'better' attached to their parents than were ex-institutional children who had been restored to their original families. Both adopted and restored ex-institutional children apparently had more difficulties with their siblings than their controls, but the difficulties for the restored group were especially pronounced.

With regard to peer relations, ex-institutional children exhibited more problems. Compared to controls who had never been institutionalized, these adolescents were more adult-oriented, more likely to have difficulties in peer relations, less likely to report a best friend, less likely to turn to a peer for emotional support, and less likely to be selective in choosing a friend.

Research to date is not yet conclusive on the question of at what age it may no longer be possible to reverse the effects of disordered early attachments. Clarke and Clarke (1976) reviewed a number of contributions from the scientific literature regarding early deprivation and its consequences and concluded that granted 'a radical change in circumstances', there is 'virtually no psychosocial adversity' from which children cannot recover. Their review resulted in an appeal for more careful empirical analysis of the needs of individual children and the avoidance of oversimplified notions that could give rise to self-fulfilling prophecies about deleterious consequences. The same could be said about avoiding oversimplified notions about recovering from early adversity. It is often difficult to arrange a radical change in circumstances, and research indicates that individual differences are marked in response to adversity. Moreover, the child who has suffered early deprivation can contribute to problems even with an improved environment and, in fact, may alter that environment through maladaptive behaviours. Still, the overwhelming evidence is that wider and continuing problems need not occur when an early adverse environment is corrected by a later salutary one. Correction can occur to a far greater extent than our theories might have predicted, and we have realized more fully that successful interventions may make use of self-righting tendencies (Waddington, 1940; Emde, 1981).

Taken together, these results suggest several tentative conclusions about the course and prognosis of attachment disorders. Firstly, limited opportunities in the early years to form selective attachments to a relatively small number of individuals is a significant risk factor for subsequent functioning. Secondly, more profound effects are apparent in the area of social adaptation and less profound effects in the cognitive domain, with intermediate effects on symptoms of behaviour problems. Thirdly, the quality of attachment relationships is an important mediator between early experiences and subsequent functioning. The ultimate, far-reaching question about the course of attachment disorders concerns the kinds of parenting provided by individuals whose own attachment histories are disordered. No prospective data are yet available to address this question, although several longitudinal investigations currently underway may provide these data in the future.

ASSESSMENT

Assessment of disorders of attachment should focus on the child's relationships with attachment figures. Young children's use of primary attachment figures as secure bases from which to explore and as safe havens to which to return during stress should be evaluated by history and by observation. Functioning of the goal-corrected partnership between the older pre-school child and the attachment figure may also be assessed by history and by observation. These data provide clinically useful indicators of attachment. Particular attention should be paid to the relationship-specificity of symptomatic behaviour.

Although several structured research methods of assessing attachment exist, they are unlikely to be of diagnostic help to the clinician. The Strange Situation Procedure, for example, is designed to classify infant attachment patterns in a research setting rather than to diagnose attachment disorders in a clinical setting. Strange Situation classification is adequate for studying groups of infants but not sufficiently meaningful to warrant application to any particular infant for a number of reasons. Firstly, because insecure attachments are risk factors rather than disorders, infants classified insecurely attached may have reasonably well-functioning relationships and may never become symptomatic. Secondly, the links between naturalistic behaviour (which is of most interest for the clinician) and Strange Situation classifications in the laboratory are too variable for particular infants. Thirdly, the Strange Situation Procedure places significant constraints on the behaviour of the attachment figure. Ideally, assessment procedures should allow partners to behave sufficiently natural-istically to reflect their usual ways of being together (Crowell & Fleischmann, 1993). Fourthly, there is considerable room for measurement error with the Strange Situation Procedure due to situational factors.

Gaensbauer and Harmon (1981) developed a modified version of the Strange Situation for use with clinical samples, but they cautioned against accepting reunion behaviour alone as the criterion for assessing security. Although generally finding that infant reunion behaviour reflected relationship histories with particular caregivers, they also reported some striking exceptions. Affective behaviours in nonreunion episodes of their procedure were often indicative of disturbed attachment relationships even when reunions alone suggested security.

Aber and Baker (1990) developed procedures for evaluating attachment in a service programme for toddlers. They video-taped a standardized intake interview that included a single brief separation from the parent. They coded the child's explo-ration and reunion behaviour during the interview. They also modified the Waters and Deane (1985) Q-Set to make it appropriate for use by teachers at the centre and included a parent–child problem-solving paradigm. From these three sources, four summary variables were determined for each child: (1) secure communication; (2) flexible attention-deployment strategy; (3) separation insecurity; and (4) reunion rejection. Although they appear clinically useful, these vari-ables have not been assessed in clinical or high-risk samples, nor with children who meet criteria for attachment disorders.

What should be of interest to the clinician is the functioning attachment relationships in the real world rather than the laboratory. The Attachment Q-Set (Waters & Deane, 1985) may serve as a useful guide to the clinician interested in observing secure base behaviours in children between 1 and 5 years old, especially in distinguishing security from behav-iours reflecting sociability and dependence. Still, this measure

will not lead directly to a diagnosis of attachment disorder.

These problems with standardized measures notwithstand-ing, clinicians who assess children for attachment disorders should evaluate a number of areas of functioning. Inquiries and observations should evaluate the child's patterns of comfort-seeking, reliance on caregivers for help when needed, showing affection to caregivers, cooperativeness, exploratory behaviour and controlling behaviour. Children with attach-ment disorders may not seek comfort from significant care-givers when upset, hurt or frightened, or may seek comfort in unusual ways (e.g. a child who cries in distress but approaches the caregiver walking backwards). Children who are unable or unwilling to seek help from caregivers when needed, or conversely, those who rely excessively on caregivers may be manifesting disturbed attachments. Children with attachment disorders may appear comfortable with caregivers, but they are unlikely to interact warmly and affectionately with them. Cooperation is the hallmark of the goal-corrected partnership and should be apparent in the child's negotiations with the caregiver. Inhibited exploratory behaviour in the child in the presence of the attachment figure or excessively disinhibited exploratory behaviour (e.g. the child fails to check back with the caregiver in unfamiliar environments) may reflect dis-ordered attachment. Finally, controlling behaviour in the young child expressed towards the caregiver has been associ-ated in both the clinical and research literatures with role-reversed attachment relationships (Main & Cassidy, 1988; Solomon *et al.*, 1984; Zeanah & Klitzke, 1991).

In all of these areas, more weight should be given to pervasive patterns of interacting than to isolated instances. According to current criteria, the symptoms should extend across a number of relationships, although variability in the disturbances in different relationships may be apparent. Further, clinicians must determine that the disturbances are sufficiently severe to warrant a diagnosis of attachment disorder rather than merely reflect an insecure attachment relationship.

MANAGEMENT

Clinicians are likely to encounter attachment disorders in children who have not had an opportunity to form lasting relationships (e.g. those in multiple foster placements) and in those who have had stable but extremely disturbed relation-ships. Intervention for disorders of attachment may include general and specific approaches.

General parent-centred approaches to attachment disorders in children include interventions that may be applied to a number of psychiatric disorders in young children. Examples include supportive interventions with caregivers and inter-ventions designed to improve caregivers' consistency and effectiveness in limit-setting.

Several recent intervention studies have used supportive interventions with parent–child dyads and have assessed infant attachment, measured by Strange Situation classifi-cations, as an outcome variable. The interventions were designed to ameliorate a variety of risk conditions for infants, including failure to thrive (Drotar *et al.*, 1985), preterm status (Beckwith, 1988), having a mother with limited support (Barnard *et al.*, 1988) and having an adolescent mother (Osofsky *et al.*, 1988). Curiously, none of these interventions found differences in outcome with respect to security of attachment in intervention and control groups. Some investigators have speculated that beneficial effects of the intervention on attachment may be delayed beyond the second year — the period for which the Strange Situation has been validated. Another possibility is that these generally supportive interventions were neither specific nor intense enough to change patterns of attachment relationships.

With regard to limit-setting, Speltz (1990) has developed and described a parent-training approach to treatment of disruptive behaviour disorders in preschoolers that attempts to integrate operant principles and attachment theory. Greenberg and Speltz (1988) provided the rationale for this approach by pointing out that many behaviour-disordered symptoms in preschool children appear to be maladaptive efforts at joint planning and communication that are central to the attachment goal-corrected partnership described by Bowlby (1969/1982).

According to Speltz (1990), the intervention follows a three-session evaluation and involves an additional 10–16 sessions divided into four phases. In the first phase, parents are educated about developmental issues relevant to the child's problems. The effort is to make parents' expectations about the child's capabilities more realistic and to reinterpret some of the child's oppositional behaviour as reflections of the child's developmentally appropriate need for increased control in the relationship. In the second phase, child-directed play sessions allow the child to experience increased actual and perceived control in interacting with the parents. Emphasis in this phase is placed also on reinterpreting parents' beliefs about the child's maladaptive behaviours. The third phase focuses on limit-setting. In the final phase, the therapist provides communication training to enable parent and child to increase their ability to develop and negotiate plans and goals successfully. This intervention places important emphasis on both parent perceptions and behaviours, but formal evaluation of its effectiveness is not yet available.

More specific interventions for disordered attachments are also available. Even when cared for in institutions, infants often develop a preferred caregiver and an attachment to that individual. For infants who have failed to form primary attachments, such as institutionalized infants whose caregiving is so limited or inconsistent that an attachment does not form, the introduction of a reasonably available and consistent caregiving figure will lead to the development of an attachment relationship. Infants are born with an apparently strong biological propensity to form and to maintain attachments, so that the introduction of an emotionally available attachment figure is the initial treatment of choice. For very young infants, this may be sufficient, but for older children with a longer history of disrupted attachments, supplemental treatment may be indicated (Harmon *et al.*, 1983). Clearly, we still

know too little about the limits of adaptability and about how much the absence of an attachment figure in some or all of the early years can be overcome by subsequent relationships.

A specific examination of intervention for insecure infant attachment relationships comes from an investigation of attachment between women of lower socioeconomic status and their infants in San Francisco who had recently immigrated to the US from Mexico and Central America (Lieberman *et al.*, 1991). Intervenors were bicultural, bilingual women with masters degrees in psychology or social work who received special training and ongoing supervision from experienced clinicians in infant–parent psychotherapy (Lieberman & Pawl, 1993; Fraiberg, 1981). Pretreatment assessments with the Strange Situation divided the sample into three groups: (1) insecure intervention ($n = 29$); (2) insecure control ($n = 23$); and (3) secure control ($n = 30$). The focus of the home-based psychotherapy was on the emotional experience of the mothers and infants — both as reported and as observed.

In $1\frac{1}{2}$-hour sessions conducted weekly for 1 year, the therapists attempted to provide the mother with a corrective attachment relationship so that she could change her attachment relationship with her infant. The therapist attempted to help the mothers articulate and integrate their emotional experiences in the important past and current relationships in their lives. Specifically, the therapist addressed the legitimacy of the mother's longing for protection and safety, both when she was a child and currently as an adult, and explored unsettling feelings of anger and ambivalence towards others (including the child and the therapist). When feasible, the therapist also tried to provide concrete elements of protection by helping mothers obtain needed services.

Results indicated significant increases in more desirable maternal and child interactive behaviours, and an enhanced goal-corrected partnership compared to control infants. Unfortunately, the mothers' own attachment classifications were not assessed in this investigation. This would have been useful because the mothers' representation of attachment was an important target of the intervention. The degree to which a parent's own perspective on attachment must change in order for her behaviour with their child to change is an important question for the field. Further, it is not clear how many of the insecurely attached infants in the intervention group would have met criteria for attachment disorders, making it unclear whether the results could be generalized to that subgroup.

SUMMARY AND CONCLUSIONS

We began this chapter by indicating that attachment disorders are unusual in that they imply disorder not only within the individual but also in the individual's caregiving context. Difficulties in child social relatedness in circumstances of problematic caregiving have been a clinical concern since the dawn of child psychiatry. Diagnostic criteria for attachment disorders have been available for just over 10 years. Still, little research has addressed the validity of the criteria that currently exist in either the DSM or ICD systems, and there is not a clear consensus about how best to communicate about problematic behaviours in their relevant contexts. There is no disagreement, however, about the fact that syndromes of problematic attachment are of major clinical importance.

We have reviewed separate research literatures dealing with different aspects of these syndromes, including social behaviour in maltreated children, children raised in institutions, and children who evidence 'insecure' attachment patterns. The latter designation comes from a major body of developmental research stemming from the theories of John Bowlby and Mary Ainsworth that has not yet been sufficiently integrated into our current diagnostic classification systems. Because we consider it likely that children with insecure attachment patterns represent risk conditions for attachment disorders, and because this developmental research literature illustrates important cross-generational patterns of risk with implications for intervention, we have devoted a considerable portion of the chapter to reviewing this domain.

We are aware of no research specifically on the course and prognosis of attachment disorders as currently designated; however, we reviewed research on consequences of institutional rearing and of insecure attachment patterns. These data suggest that insufficient opportunity in the early years to form selective attachments to a relatively small number of caregivers is a significant risk for subsequent problems in social adaptation.

Assessment of attachment disorders relies on direct observations of the child interacting with primary caregivers and with the examiner, as well as on historical information from multiple informants. Particular attention needs to be given to the relationship-specificity of symptomatic behaviour. Management depends upon the syndrome of disorder: for infants who have failed to form attachment relationships, the introduction of a consistent and emotionally available caregiving figure is the treatment of choice; for infants who have formed disordered attachments a variety of treatments aimed at improving the caregiving relationship may be appropriate. Again, research to aid in selecting appropriate treatments is lacking, even though clinical activity and intervention in problems of disturbed parent–child relationships are considerable (Fraiberg, 1981; Provence, 1983; Minde & Minde, 1986; Cicchetti & Carlson, 1989; Greenspan *et al.*, 1987; Lieberman & Pawl, 1988; Aber & Baker, 1990; Speltz, 1990). Considering the discrepancy between the lack of clinical syndrome-based research and clinical intervention activity, as well as the excitement of recently burgeoning developmental knowledge about attachment, we can think of no more fertile area for clinical research in the future.

REFERENCES

Aber J.L. & Baker A. (1990) Security of attachment in toddlerhood: modifying assessment procedures for joint clinical and research purposes. In: Greenburg M.T., Cicchetti D. & Cummings E.M. (eds) *Attachment in the Preschool Years*, pp. 427–462. University of Chicago Press, Chicago.

Ainsworth M.D.S. & Eichberg C. (1992) Effects on infant–mother attachment of mother's unresolved loss of an attachment figure or other traumatic experience. In: Marris P., Stevenson-Hinde J. & Parkes C. (eds) *Attachment Across the Life Cycle*, pp. 160–183. Routledge, New York.

Ainsworth M.D.S., Blehar M., Waters E. & Wall S. (1978) *Patterns of Attachment: A Psychological Study of the Strange Situation*. Lawrence Erlbaum, Hillsdale, NJ.

American Psychiatric Association (1987) *DSM III-R*, American Psychiatric Association, Washington, DC.

American Psychiatric Association (1991) *DSM-IV Options Book*, American Psychiatric Association, Washington, DC.

Arend R., Gove F. & Sroufe L.A. (1979) Continuity of individual adaptation from infancy to kindergarten: a predictive study of ego-resiliency and curiosity in preschoolers. *Child Development*, **50**, 950–959.

Barnard K., Magyary D., Sumner G., Booth C.L., Mitchell S.K. & Spieker S. (1988) Prevention of parenting alterations for women with low social support. *Psychiatry*, **51**, 248–253.

Bates J.E., Maslin C.A. & Frankel K.A. (1985) Attachment security, mother–child interaction, and temperament as predictors of behavior-problem ratings at age three years. In: Bretherton I. & Waters E. (eds) *Growing Points in Attachment Theory and Research*. Monographs of the Society for Research in Child Development 50, serial no. 209, pp. 167–193.

Beckwith L. (1988) Intervention with disadvantaged parents of sick preterm infants. *Psychiatry*, **51**, 242–247.

Belsky J. & Nezworski T. (1988) Clinical implications of attachment. In: Belsky J. & Nezworski T. (eds) *Clinical Implications of Attachment*, pp. 3–17. Lawrence Erlbaum, Hillsdale, NJ.

Belsky J. & Rovine M. (1987) Attachment and temperament: an empirical rapprochement. *Child Development*, **58**, 787–795.

Belsky J., Rovine M. & Taylor D.G. (1984) The Pennsylvannia infant and family development project, 3: the origins of individual differences in infant–mother attachment: maternal and infant contributions. *Child Development*, **55**, 718–728.

Benoit D., Zeanah C. & Barton M. (1989) Maternal attachment disturbances in failure to thrive. *Infant Mental Health Journal*, **10**, 185–202.

Benoit D., Vidovic D. & Roman J. (1991) Transmission of attachment across three generations. Paper presented to the Biennial Meeting of the Society for Research in Child Development, Seattle, WA.

Benoit D., Zeanah C.H., Boucher C. & Minde K.K. (1992) Sleep disorders in early childhood: association with insecure maternal attachment. *Journal of the American Academy of Child and Adolescent Psychiatry*, **31**, 86–93.

Bowlby J. (1951) *Maternal Care and Child Health*. World Health Organization, Geneva.

Bowlby J. (1969/1982) *Attachment and Loss: Attachment*. Basic Books, New York.

Bowlby J. (1980) *Attachment and Loss: Loss*. Basic Books, New York.

Bretherton I. (1985) Attachment theory: retrospect and prospect. In: Bretherton I. & Waters E. (eds) *Growing Points of Attachment Theory and Research*. Monographs of the Society for Research in Child Development 50, serial no. 209, pp. 3–38.

Bretherton I. (1987) New perspectives on attachment relations: security, communication, and internal working models. In: Osofsky J. (ed) *Handbook of Infant Development*, pp. 1061–1100. Wiley-Interscience, New York.

Call J.D. (1980) Attachment disorders in infancy. In: Kaplan H.I. & Freedman A.M. (eds) *Comprehensive Textbook of Psychiatry*, 3rd edn, pp. 2586–2597. Williams & Wilkins, Baltimore, MD.

Carlson V., Cicchetti D., Barnett D. & Braunwald K.G. (1989) Finding order in disorganization: lessons for research from maltreated infants' attachments to their caregivers. In: Cicchetti D. & Carlson V. (eds) *Child Maltreatment: Theory and Research on the Causes and Consequences of Child Abuse and Neglect*, pp. 494–528. Cambridge University Press, Cambridge.

Cassidy J. (1988) Child–mother attachment and the self at age six. *Child Development*, **57**, 331–337.

Cassidy J. & Kobak R. (1988) Avoidance and its relation to other defensive processes. In: Belsky J. & Nezworski T. (eds) *Clinical Implications of Attachment*, pp. 300–326. Lawrence Erlbaum, Hillsdale, NJ.

Cicchetti D. & Carlson V. (1989) Preface. In: Cicchetti D. & Carlson V. (eds) *Child Maltreatment: Theory and Research on the Causes and Consequences of Child Abuse and Neglect*, pp. xiii–xx. Cambridge University Press, Cambridge.

Cicchetti D., Cummings E.M., Greenburg M.T. & Marvin R. (1990) An organizational perspective on attachment beyond infancy: implications for theory, measurement and research. In: Greenburg M.T., Cicchetti D. & Cummings E.M. (eds) *Attachment in the Preschool Years*, pp. 3–50. University of Chicago Press, Chicago, IL.

Clarke A.M. & Clarke A.D.B. (1976) *Early Experience: Myth and Evidence*. Open Books, London.

Crowell J. & Feldman S. (1988) The effects of mothers' internal models of relationships and children's behavioral and developmental status on mother–child interaction. *Child Development*, **59**, 1273–1285.

Crowell J.A. & Feldman S.S. (1991) Mothers' working models of attachment relationships and mother and child behavior during separation and reunion. *Developmental Psychology*, **27**, 597–605.

Crowell J. & Fleischmann M. (1993) Use of structured research instruments in clinical assessments. In: Zeanah C.H. (ed) *Handbook of Infant Mental Health*, pp. 210–222. Guilford Press, New York.

DeMulder E.K. & Radke-Yarrow M. (1991) Attachment with affectively ill and well mothers: concurrent behavioral correlates. *Development and Psychopathology*, **3**, 227–242.

Dozier M. (1991) Psychophysiology in adult attachment interviews: converging evidence for deactivating strategies. Paper presented to the Biennial meeting of the Society for Research in Child Development, Seattle, WA.

Drotar D., Malone C.A., Devost L., Brickell C., Mantz-Clumpner C., Negray J., Wallace M., Woychik J., Wyatt B., Eckerle D., Bush M., Finlon M.A., El-Amin D., Nowak M., Satola J. & Pallotta J. (1985) Early preventive intervention in failure to thrive: methods and early outcome. In: Drotar D. (ed) *New Directions in Failure to Thrive: Implications for Research and Practice*, pp. 119–138. Plenum Press, New York.

Easterbrooks A. & Goldberg W. (1990) Security of toddler–parent attachment: relation to children's sociopersonality functioning during kindergarten. In: Greenburg M.T., Cicchetti D. & Cummings M.T. (eds) *Attachment in the Preschool Years*, pp. 221–244. University of Chicago Press, Chicago, IL.

Egeland B. & Farber E.A. (1984) Infant–mother attachment: factors related to its development and changes over time. *Child Development*, **55**, 753–771.

Egeland B. & Sroufe L.A. (1981) Attachment and early maltreatment. *Child Development*, **52**, 44–52.

Emde R.N. (1981) Changing models of infancy in the nature of early development: remodelling the foundation. *Journal of the American Psychoanalytic Association*, **9**, 179–219.

Emde R.N. (ed) (1983) *Rene A. Spitz: Dialogues from Infancy*. Selected papers, pp. 1–484. International Universities Press, New York.

Erickson M.F., Sroufe L.A. & Egeland B. (1985) The relationship between quality of attachment and behavior problems in preschool in a high-risk sample. In: Bretherton I. & Waters E. (eds) *Growing Points of Attachment Theory and Research*. Monographs of the Society

for Research in Child Development 50, serial no. 209, pp. 147–166.

Fagot B.L. & Kavanagh K. (1990) The prediction of antisocial behavior from avoidant attachment classifications. *Child Development*, **61**, 864–873.

Fonagy P., Steele H. & Steele M. (1991) Maternal representations of attachment during pregnancy predict the organization of infant–mother attachment at one year of age. *Child Development*, **62**, 891–905.

Fox N.A., Kimmerly N.L. & Schafer W.D. (1991) Attachment to mother/attachment to father: a meta-analysis. *Child Development*, **62**, 210–225.

Fraiberg S. (1981) *Clinical Studies in Infant Mental Health: The First Year of Life*. Basic Books, New York.

Gaensbauer T.J. & Harmon R.J. (1981) Clinical assessment in infancy using structured playroom situations. *Journal of the American Academy of Child Psychiatry*, **20**, 264–280.

Gaensbauer T.J. & Harmon R.J. (1982) Attachment in abused/neglected and premature infants. In: Emde R.N. & Harmon R.J. (eds) *The Development of Attachment and Affiliative Systems*, pp. 263–288. Plenum Press, New York.

Gaensbauer T.J. & Sands M. (1979) Distorted affective communications in abused/neglected infants and their potential impact on caregivers. *Journal of the American Academy of Child Psychiatry*, **18**, 236–250.

George C. & Main M. (1979) Social interactions in young abused children: approach, avoidance, and aggression. *Child Development*, **50**, 306–318.

Goldfarb W. (1945) Effects of psychological deprivation in infancy and subsequent stimulation. *American Journal of Psychiatry*, **102**, 18–33.

Goldsmith H.H. & Alansky J.A. (1987) Maternal and infant temperamental predictors of attachment: a meta-analytic review. *Journal of Consulting and Clinical Psychology*, **55**, 805–816.

Greenberg M.T. & Speltz M.L. (1988) Attachment and the ontogeny of conduct problems. In: Belsky J. & Nezworski T. (eds) *Clinical Implications of Attachment*, pp. 177–218. Lawrence Erlbaum, Hillsdale, NJ.

Greenspan S., Wieder S., Lieberman A., Nover R., Robinson M. & Lourie R. (1987) *Infants in Multirisk Families*. International Universities Press, Madison, CT.

Grossman K., Grossman K., Spangler G., Suess G. & Unzner L. (1985) Maternal sensitivity and newborns' orientation responses as related to quality of attachment in northern Germany. In: Bretherton I. & Waters E. (eds) *Growing Points of Attachment Theory and Research*. Monographs of the Society for Research in Child Development 50, serial no. 209, pp. 233–256.

Harmon R., Wagonfield S. & Emde R.N. (1983) Anaclitic depression: a follow-up from infancy to puberty. *Psychoanalytic Study of the Child*, **38**, 67–94.

Herrenkohl R.C. & Herrenkohl E.C. (1981) Some antecedents and developmental consequences of child maltreatment. *New Directions for Child Development*, **II**, 57–76.

Hodges J. & Tizard B. (1989a) IQ and behavioural adjustment of ex-institutional adolescents. *Journal of Child Psychology, Psychiatry, and Allied Disciplines*, **30**, 53–75.

Hodges J. & Tizard B. (1989b) Social and family relationships of ex-institutional adolescents. *Journal of Child Psychology, Psychiatry, and Allied Disciplines*, **30**, 77–97.

Hoffman-Plotkin D. & Twentyman C. (1984) A multimodal assessment of behavioral and cognitive deficits in abused and neglected preschoolers. *Child Development*, **55**, 794–802.

Howes C. & Eldridge R. (1985) Responses of abused, neglected and non-maltreated children to the behaviors of their peers. *Journal of Applied Developmental Psychology*, **6**, 261–270.

Hubbs-Tait L., Eberhart-Wright A., Ware L., Osofsky J., Yockey W. & Fusco J. (1991) Maternal depression and infant attachment: behavior problems at 54 months in children of adolescent mothers. Paper presented to the Biennial Meeting of the Society for Research in Child Development. Seattle, WA.

Kempe C.H., Silverman F.N., Steele B.B., Droegemueller W. & Silver H.K. (1962) The battered child syndrome. *Journal of the American Medical Association*, **181**, 17–24.

Lamb M.E., Thompson R.A., Gardner W. & Charnov E.L. (1985) *Infant–Mother Attachment: The Origins and Developmental Significance of Individual Differences in the Strange Situation.* Lawrence Erlbaum, Hillsdale, NJ.

Lewis M., Feiring C., McGuffog C. & Jaskir J. (1984) Predicting psychopathology in six-year-olds from early social relations. *Child Development*, **55**, 123–136.

Lieberman A.F. & Pawl J.H. (1988) Clinical applications of attachment theory. In: Belsky J. & Nezworski T. (eds) *Clinical Implications of Attachment*, pp. 327–351. Lawrence Erlbaum, Hillsdale, NJ.

Lieberman A.F. & Pawl J.H. (1990) Disorders of attachment and secure base behavior in the second year of life: conceptual issues and clinical intervention. In: Greenburg M.T., Cicchetti D. & Cummings E.M. (eds) *Attachment in the Preschool Years*, pp. 375–398. University of Chicago Press, Chicago, IL.

Lieberman A.F. & Pawl J. (1993) Infant–parent psychotherapy. In: Zeanah C.H. (ed) *The Handbook of Infant Mental Health*, pp. 427–442. Guilford Press, New York.

Lieberman A.F., Weston D. & Pawl J.H. (1991) Preventive intervention and outcome with anxiously attached dyads. *Child Development*, **62**, 199–209.

Lyons-Ruth K., Alpen L. & Repacholi B. (1993) Disorganized infant attachment classification and maternal psychosocial problems as predictors of hostile-aggressive behavior in the preschool classroom. *Child Development*, **64**, 572–585.

Main M. (1982) Avoidance in the service of attachment: a working paper. In: Immelman K., Barlow G.W., Petrinovich I. & Main M. (eds) *Behavioral Development: The Bielfield Interdisciplinary Project*, pp. 651–693. Cambridge University Press, Cambridge.

Main M. & Cassidy J. (1988) Categories of response to reunion with the parent at age 6: predictable from infant attachment classifications and stable over a 1-month period. *Developmental Psychology*, **24**, 415–426.

Main M. & George C. (1985) Responses of abused and disadvantaged toddlers to distress in agemates: a study in the day care setting. *Developmental Psychology*, **21**, 407–412.

Main M. & Goldwyn R. (in press) Interview-based adult attachment classifications: related to infant–mother and infant–father attachment. *Developmental Psychology*.

Main M. & Hesse E. (1990) Parents' unresolved traumatic experiences are related to infant disorganized attachment status: is frightened and/or frightening parental behavior the linking mechanism? In: Greenburg M.T., Cicchetti D. & Cummings E.M. (eds) *Attachment in the Preschool Years*, pp. 161–184. University of Chicago Press, Chicago, IL.

Main M. & Solomon J. (1986) Discovery of an insecure, disorganized/disoriented attachment pattern: procedures, findings and implications for the classification of behavior. In: Yogman M. & Brazelton T.B. (eds) *Affective Development in Infancy*, pp. 95–124. Ablex, Norwood, NJ.

Main M. & Solomon J. (1990) Procedures for identifying infants as disorganized/disoriented during the Ainsworth Strange Situation. In: Greenburg M.T., Cicchetti D. & Cummings E.M. (eds) *Attachment in the Preschool Years*, pp. 121–160. University of Chicago Press, Chicago.

Main M. & Stadtman J. (1981) Infant responses to rejection of physical contact by the mother. *Journal of the American Academy of Child Psychiatry*, **52**, 292–307.

Main M. & Weston D. (1982) Avoidance of the attachment figure in infancy: descriptions and interpretations. In: Parkes C.M. & Stevenson-Hinde J. (eds) *The Place of Attachment in Human Behavior*, pp. 31–59. Basic Books, New York.

Main M., Kaplan N. & Cassidy J. (1985) Security in infancy, childhood and adulthood: a move to the level of representation. In: Bretherton I. & Waters E. (eds) *Growing Points of Attachment Theory and Research*. Monographs of the Society for Research in Child Development 50, serial no. 209, pp. 66–106.

Matas L., Arend R.A. & Sroufe L.A. (1978) Continuity of adaptation in the second year: the relationship between quality of attachment and later competence. *Child Development*, **49**, 547–556.

Minde K.K. & Minde R. (1986) *Infant Psychiatry: An Introductory Textbook*. Sage Publications, London.

Mueller E. & Silverman N. (1989) Peer relations in maltreated children. In: Cicchetti D. & Carlson V. (eds) *Child Maltreatment: Theory and Research on the Causes and Consequences of Child Abuse and Neglect*. Cambridge University Press, Cambridge.

O'Connor M.J., Sigman M. & Brill N. (1987) *Journal of Consulting and Clinical Psychology*, **55**, 831–836.

Osofsky J., Culp A.M. & Ware L.M. (1988) Intervention challenges with adolescent mothers and their infants. *Psychiatry*, **51**, 236–241.

Powell G.F. & Low J.F. (1983) Behavior in nonorganic failure to thrive. *Journal of Developmental and Behavioral Pediatrics*, **8**, 18–24.

Powell G.F., Low J.F. & Speers M.A. (1987) Behavior as a diagnostic aid in failure to thrive. *Journal of Developmental and Behavioral Pediatrics*, **8**, 18–24.

Provence S. (1983) *Psychotherapy for Infants and Families*. International Universities Press, New York.

Provence S. & Lipton R.C. (1962) *Infants Reared in Institutions*. International Universities Press, New York.

Radke-Yarrow M., Cummings E.M., Kuczynski L. & Chapman N. (1985) Patterns of attachment in two- and three-year olds in normal families and families with parental depression. *Child Development*, **56**, 884–893.

Rutter M. (1972) *Maternal Deprivation Reassessed*. Penguin, London.

Rutter M. (1979) Maternal deprivation, 1972–1978: New findings, new concepts, new approaches. *Child Development*, **50**, 283–305.

Sameroff A.J. & Emde R.N. (1989) *Relationship Disturbances in Early Childhood*. Basic Books, New York.

Skeels H.M. (1966) *Adult Status of Children with Contrasting Early Life Experiences*. Monographs of the Society for Research in Child Development 31, serial no. 105.

Solomon J., George C. & Ivins B. (1987) Mother–child interaction in the home and security of attachment at age six. Paper presented to the Biennal Meeting of the Society for Research in Child Development, Baltimore.

Speltz M. (1990) The treatment of preschool conduct problems: an integration of behavioral and attachment concepts. In: Greenburg M.T., Cicchetti D. & Cummings E.M. (eds) *Attachment in the Preschool Years*, pp. 399–426. University of Chicago Press, Chicago, IL.

Spitz R. (1945) Hospitalism: an inquiry into the genesis of psychiatric conditions in early childhood. *Psychoanalytic Study of the Child*, **1**, 53–74.

Spitz R. (1946) Anaclitic depression: an inquiry into the genesis of psychiatric conditions in early childhood. *Psychoanalytic Study of the Child*, **1**, 53–74.

Sroufe L.A. (1983) Infant–caregiver attachment and patterns of adaptation in preschool: the roots of maladaptation and competence. In: Perlmutter M. (ed) *Minnesota Symposium in Child Psychology*, vol. 16, pp. 41–81. Lawrence Erlbaum, Hillsdale, NJ.

Sroufe L.A. (1985) Attachment classification from the perspective of infant–caregiver relationships and infant temperament. *Child Development*, **56**, 1–14.

Sroufe L.A. (1988) The role of infant–caregiver attachment in development. In: Belsky J. & Nezworski T. (eds) *Clinical Implications of Attachment*, pp. 18–40. Lawrence Erlbaum, Hillsdale, NJ.

Sroufe L.A. & Waters E. (1977) Heart-rate as a convergent measure in clinical and developmental research. *Merrill-Palmer Quarterly*, **23**, 3–28.

Steele M., Steele H. & Fongay P. (1993) Associations among attachment classifications of mothers, fathers and their infants: Evidence for a relationship-specific perspective. Paper presented to the Biennial Meeting of the Society for Research in Child Development, New Orleans, LA.

Thompson R.A., Lamb M.E. & Estes D. (1982) Stability of infant–mother attachment and its relation to changing life circumstances in an unselected middle class sample. *Child Development*, **53**, 144–148.

Tizard B. & Hodges J. (1978) The effect of early institutional rearing on the development of eight year old children. *Journal of Child Psychology, Psychiatry, and Allied Disciplines*, **19**, 99–118.

Tizard B. & Rees J. (1974) A comparison of the effects of adoption, restoration to the natural mother, and continued institutionalisation on the cognitive development of four-year-old children. *Journal of Child Psychology, Psychiatry, and Allied Disciplines*, **16**, 61–73.

Tizard B. & Rees J. (1975) The effect of early institutional rearing on the behaviour problems and affectional relationships of four-year-old children. *Journal of Child Psychology, Psychiatry, and Allied Disciplines*, **16**, 61–73.

Tizard J. & Tizard B. (1971) Social development of 2-year-old children in residential nurseries. In: Schaeffer H.R. (ed) *The Origins of Human Social Relations*. Academic Press, London.

Troy M. & Sroufe L.A. (1987) Victimization among preschoolers: role of attachment relationship history. *Journal of the American Academy of Child and Adolescent Psychiatry*, **26**, 166–172.

Vaughn B. & Waters E. (1990) Attachment behavior at home and in the laboratory: Q-sort observations and strange situation classifi-

cations of one-year-olds. *Child Development*, **61**, 1965–1973.

Vaughn B., Egeland B., Sroufe L.A. & Waters E. (1979) Individual differences in infant–mother attachment at twelve and eighteen months: stability and change in families under stress. *Child Development*, **50**, 971–975.

Waddington C.H. (1940) *Organizers and Genes*. Cambridge University Press, Cambridge.

Ward M.J., Botyanski N.C., Plunkett S.W. & Carlson E.A. (1991) The concurrent and predictive validity of the AAI for adolescent mothers. Paper presented to the Biennial meeting of the Society for Research in Child Development, Seattle, WA.

Waters E. (1978) The reliability and stability of individual differences in infant–mother attachment. *Child Development*, **49**, 483–494.

Waters E. & Deane K. (1985) Defining and assessing individual differences in attachment relationships: Q-methodology and the organization of behavior in infancy and early childhood. In: Bretherton I. & Waters E. (eds) *Growing Points of Attachment Theory and Research*. Monographs of the Society for Research in Child Development 50, serial no. 209, pp. 41–65.

Waters E., Wippman J. & Sroufe L.A. (1979) Attachment, positive affect, and competence in peer group: two studies in construct validation. *Child Development*, **50**, 821–829.

World Health Organization (1992) *ICD-10*. World Health Organization, Geneva.

Zeanah C.H. (in press) Subjectivity in parent–infant relationships: contributions from attachment research. *Adolescent Psychiatry*.

Zeanah C.H. & Anders T.F. (1987) Subjectivity in parent–infant relationships: a discussion of internal working models. *Infant Mental Health Journal*, **8**, 237–250.

Zeanah C.H. & Klitzke M. (1991) Role reversal and the self-effacing solution: observations from infant–parent psychotherapy. *Psychiatry*, **54**, 346–357.

Zeanah C.H., Benoit D., Barton M.L., Regan C., Hirshberg L. & Lipsitt L. (1993) Representations of attachment in mothers and their one-year-old infants. *Journal of the American Academy of Child and Adolescent Psychiatry*, **32**, 278–286.

Chapter 29
Enuresis

David Shaffer

Nocturnal enuresis is usually defined as repeated involuntary passage of urine during sleep in the absence of any identified physical abnormality in children aged above 5 years. Although the condition is not psychogenic, it is often associated with psychiatric disorder and enuretic children are frequently referred to psychiatrists for treatment. When an enuretic child is treated successfully, behaviour, mood and social adjustment may change for the better (Moffatt *et al.*, 1987). It is therefore quite proper that child psychiatrists should acquire a knowledge of the prevalence and natural history of the condition and its association with other pathological states, as well as a mastery of the techniques of treatment.

WHEN IS NIGHT WETTING ABNORMAL?

The likelihood that a child will acquire continence spontaneously over a 12-month period is reduced sharply after age 4. In the Baltimore developmental study (Oppel *et al.*, 1968), the prognosis for becoming dry over a following 12-month period fell from over 40% among wet 2-year-olds through 20% of wet 3-year-olds, to only 6% of wet 4-year-olds. This low rate of spontaneous remission persisted through the rest of childhood. Other longitudinal studies (Miller *et al.*, 1960; Kaffman & Elizur, 1977; Verhulst *et al.*, 1985) that have used similar criteria (1–3 nights wet per month) confirm a general trend for rates of incontinence to decline between ages 2 and 4 and thereafter to remain largely stable, although Verhulst *et al.* (1985) show a continuing sharp decline among Dutch girls until age 6. Defining enuresis as persistent incontinence after age 4 is also supported by findings by Kaffman and Elizur (1977) who found that, while incontinent 3-year-olds were no more likely to have associated psychopathology than continent 3-year-olds, at later ages psychopathology was more common in enuretics. Additional support comes from Järvelin *et al.*'s finding (1988) that the offspring of parents who were wet after age 4 were at significant excess risk for enuresis.

PREVALENCE AND NATURAL HISTORY

The prevalence of enuresis shows a small increase between ages 4 and 7 because a proportion of children who were previously dry acquire secondary enuresis. Thereafter, the prevalence declines steadily. The prevalence of enuresis in adults is not known, although Forsythe and Redmond (1974) found that 3% of 1129 enuretics were still wetting after the age of 20 years. Prevalence varies as a function of the frequency taken to define the condition (De Jonge, 1973). Children who wet nightly are those most likely to be referred for treatment (Foxman *et al.*, 1986), but they constitute only a small proportion (15%) of those who have been wet at least once in the previous 3 months. Rutter *et al.* (1973) found that, while 15% of 7-year-old boys were wet less often than once a week, only 7% wet more than once a week.

Bed-wetting is equally common in each sex until age 5 years. Boys then predominate, so that by age 11 years they are twice as likely to be wet as girls (Oppel *et al.*, 1968; Rutter *et al.*, 1973; Essen & Peckham, 1976). This is in part because male enuretics are less likely to remit spontaneously but also because boys are more likely to develop secondary enuresis (see below; Essen & Peckham, 1976). Wetting rarely stops suddenly among children who have remained enuretic into middle childhood. It is preceded by a period of sporadic wetting and finally occurs only when the child is unwell or during cold weather (Miller *et al.*, 1960). At any age the likelihood of becoming dry is greatest for those who wet intermittently, for primary than for secondary enuretics, for girls than for boys (after age 11 years), and for middle-class than for working-class children (Miller *et al.*, 1960; Essen & Peckham, 1976). In the US bed-wetting is more common in blacks than in whites (Oppel *et al.*, 1968; Dodge *et al.*, 1970) and in oriental immigrants to Israel than in immigrants of European descent (Thaustein & Halevi, 1962). These differences may reflect social disadvantage rather than genetic differences.

Primary and secondary enuresis

At all ages the enuretic population comprises a mixture of children who have always been wet and children who started to wet after a period of continence (secondary or 'onset' enuretics). As many as 25% of preschoolers who achieve continence for at least 6 months will start to wet again (Oppel *et al.*, 1968) and over half of 7–12-year-old enuretics have previously been dry for at least 6 months (Miller *et al.*, 1960; Oppel *et al.*, 1968; Fergusson *et al.*, 1986; Foxman *et al.*, 1986). Secondary enuresis has its onset most often between the ages of 5 and 7 years and is uncommon after age 11. The likelihood that a child will start to wet if he or she has stayed dry until age 7 is only about 1% (Miller *et al.*, 1960; Oppel *et al.*, 1968; Miller, 1973; Essen & Peckham, 1976; McGee *et al.*, 1984). Most, but not all, of the prospective longitudinal studies quoted have found secondary enuresis to be more common in boys.

Prospective studies with baseline information on behaviour suggest that children who go on to develop secondary enuresis have more psychiatric symptoms before the onset of the enuresis than children of the same age who never become wet (Rutter *et al.*, 1973; McGee *et al.*, 1984).

Daytime wetting

Between 2 and 4% of 5–7-year-olds wet at least once a week during the day and about 8% are wet at least monthly (De Jonge, 1973). Only 1% of 12-year-olds wet at least 1 day per month (Oppel *et al.*, 1968). Daytime wetting is more common in girls than boys. About half of day-wetters are also enuretic at night. At age 5, about 1 in 6 boy and 1 in 3 girl nocturnal enuretics also wet during the day. These proportions fall by a half by age 7 (Blomfield & Douglas, 1956; Hallgren, 1956; Järvelin *et al.*, 1988). Day-wetting alone or in combination with night-wetting is associated with higher rates of psychiatric disturbance (Rutter *et al.*, 1973) and genitourinary tract anomalies and infection (Hallgren, 1956; Savage *et al.*, 1969) than nocturnal enuresis.

AETIOLOGY

The cause of bed-wetting cannot usually be identified in an individual child, but a number of associations have been noted in group studies.

Biological factors

Family/genetic influences

Enuresis runs in families. Approximately 70% of clinically referred enuretics have a first-degree relative who was enuretic as a child (Bakwin, 1961). Familiality is not an artefact of clinic referral because it is also found in nonreferred samples. In their study of a New Zealand birth cohort ($n = 1265$), Fergusson *et al.* (1986) found that a family history of enuresis was the most important predictor of delayed bladder control and in a Finnish community study Järvelin *et al.* (1988) calculated a relative risk for enuresis of 7.1 among offspring of male and 5.2 among offspring of female enuretics. In a twin study in unreferred subjects that verified zygosity by blood studies, Bakwin (1973) showed that concordance for enuresis was significantly higher in monovular than in binovular twins (68 versus 36%). Although there have been no reared-apart studies, Kaffman (1962) found an excess of enuretics among the relatives of early-wetting children living on a kibbutz (reared in part by adults other than their parents).

The relationship between a positive family history and some of the associated features of enuresis has not been studied in unselected samples. In two small clinical studies familiality was as common in primary as in secondary enuretics (Mikkelsen *et al.*, 1980; Shaffer *et al.*, 1984). In one of these studies (Shaffer *et al.*, 1984) a relationship was found between a positive family history and a higher rate of parental discord and — if the mother had been enuretic — a higher rate of psychiatric symptomatology in the child.

Circadian rhythms

Urine output is normally reduced at night to approximately one-third of the daytime rate. During the first year of life (Hellbrugge, 1960) this rhythm is absent and infants excrete urine at a constant rate. Lewis *et al.* (1970) published two detailed case reports of enuretic children with immature circadian rhythms, and hypothesized that nocturnal polyuria might have contributed to their condition. More recently Nørgaard *et al.* (1985) and Rittig *et al.* (1989) have studied diurnal variation of circulating vasopressin, urinary excretion rate and urinary osmolality in 15 enuretics aged 11–17 years and 11 age-, weight- and sex-matched nonenuretic controls. The enuretics had a significantly less marked change in diurnal rhythm with higher nocturnal urinary excretion rate and lower urine osmolality. Repeated studies are needed to determine whether this is a robust finding and whether it is reversed with behavioural treatment or when spontaneous remission occurs.

Bladder size and function

A number of studies (Starfield, 1967; Esperanca & Gerrard, 1969; Järvelin *et al.*, 1990, 1991) have found lower maximum urinary voided volumes in enuretics than controls, although with considerable overlap between both groups. Using age- and weight-standardized norms, Gardner and Shaffer (1984) and Shaffer *et al.* (1984) found that 55% of a population of self-referred enuretics in a school clinic had a functional bladder volume greater than 1 s.d. below that expected. Low functional bladder volume was significantly related to behavioural disturbance and was more common in children with current language or speech difficulties. It was unrelated to primary or secondary status, positive family history or social disadvantage. The nature of the difference is not clear. Cystometric studies (Troup & Hodoson, 1971; Nørgaard *et al.*, 1989a; Nørgaard, 1991) indicate that the anatomical bladder capacities of enuretics during anaesthesia or sleep do not differ from controls. Nørgaard (1991) measured spontaneous bladder activity of enuretics during sleep and concluded that bladder function is essentially normal, but that urine production was abnormally large (see the section on circadian rhythms, above). It is not clear whether functional bladder volume is causally related to enuresis. Successful treatment with behaviour therapy occurs without an increase in functional bladder volume (FBV; Fielding, 1980; Shaffer *et al.*,

1984; Geffken *et al.*, 1986), bladder capacity overlaps between enuretics and nonenuretics of the same age, and some enuretics with small bladder capacities have dry as well as wet nights. However, FBV could play a role in initiating the condition. Coupled with other developmental delays, it makes it difficult for a toddler to learn bladder control.

Developmental changes in the bladder neck

Hutch (1972) described a series of anatomical changes that take place at the base of the bladder during the first 6 years of life that appear to increase the effectiveness of the internal sphincter. These developments were significantly delayed in a group of enuretics. These findings have not been replicated and are of uncertain significance, given that nocturnal continence is acquired in many children before the changes are complete.

Other developmental delays

Two large prospective birth cohort studies (Essen & Peckham, 1976; Fergusson *et al.*, 1986) and a large retrospective clinical study (Steinhausen & Gobel, 1989) have noted a relationship between enuresis and early delay in motor, language and social milestones. These were not confirmed in a third prospective cohort study that used somewhat more limited measures (McGee *et al.*, 1984). Clinical studies suggest that psychiatric symptoms are more common in enuretics with a history of motor and speech delay (Hallgren, 1957; Mikkelsen *et al.*, 1980; Shaffer *et al.*, 1984). Community studies by Miller (1973) and Essen and Peckham (1976) found that enuretics were shorter than nonenuretics and Douglas (1973) reported an association between bed-wetting in the mid-teens and delayed puberty.

Minor neurological abnormalities

Among referred clinical enuretics, psychiatric disturbance is more prevalent in those with minor neurological signs (Mikkelsen *et al.*, 1980; Shaffer *et al.*, 1984). In a longitudinal study of an unselected birth cohort, enuresis was significantly more common in females in whom abnormal motor signs (poor coordination etc.) had persisted through middle childhood (Lunsing *et al.*, 1991).

Intelligence

In an unselected population, enuretics did not differ from nonenuretics with respect to IQ (McGee *et al.*, 1984). However in a study that oversampled for handicapped and retarded children, enuresis was several times more prevalent in those groups than in the general population (Järvelin *et al.*, 1988).

Sleep abnormalities

In a prospective longitudinal study, Fergusson *et al.* (1986) noted that toddlers aged 1 and 2 who slept more than 15 hours a day were likely to develop bladder control at a later age than those who slept for shorter periods. It is not known whether the pattern of excess sleep quantity continues as the child gets older. Mikkelsen and Rapoport (1980) studied enuresis and sleep architecture and noted that enuretics wet at all stages of sleep on a seemingly random basis, the frequency of events within one sleep stage being proportional to the amount of time spent by the individual in that sleep stage. In unreplicated research, Nørgaard *et al.* (1989b) found that increases in urinary flow do not influence sleep stage and changes in sleep stage do not affect intravesical pressure. However, in a larger study using different recording techniques, Watanabe and Azuma (1989) found that, while normal subjects showed a sleep stage change from 4 to 1 when bladder volume approached capacity, leading to awakening and then conscious voiding, most enuretics showed the sleep stage change, but failed to wake further.

Epilepsy

The rate of enuresis is similar in both epileptic and nonepileptic children (Poussaint *et al.*, 1967; Rutter *et al.*, 1970a).

Neuropharmacology: neuroleptic-induced enuresis

The powerful antienuretic activity of the tricyclic antidepressants (TCAs) has led to speculation about the neuropharmacological basis of enuresis. The rapidity of action and the fact that they work on children with and without associated psychiatric problems make it improbable that it is a function of their antidepressant effect. Although TCAs reduce the amount of rapid eye movement (REM) sleep, enuretics do not have abnormalities of sleep architecture (Mikkelsen *et al.*, 1980) and other drugs such as the amphetamines do the same, yet have no antienuretic effect. Imipramine increases functional bladder volume during waking and in sleep (Shaffer *et al.*, 1979). A degree of bladder relaxation may be brought about by the drug's anticholinergic activity but more potent anticholinergics such as propantheline and methscopalamine are ineffective in enuresis (Wallace & Forsythe, 1969; Rapoport *et al.*, 1980) and TCAs with weaker anticholinergic properties such as n-aminoimipramine (Petersen *et al.*, 1973) and desmethylimipramine (Rapoport *et al.*, 1980) are as effective in reducing enuresis as imipramine. Imipramine has mild antidiuretic and powerful local anaesthetic properties. However, direct recording from the sacral dorsal roots during bladder filling (Shaffer *et al.*, 1979) is unaffected by the presence of imipramine in the urine, which makes it unlikely that it operates through a local anaesthetic or muscle depressant action.

Imipramine inhibits reuptake of noradrenaline at the synaptic junction. Rapoport *et al.* (1980) suggested that the similar potency of imipramine and desipramine in enuresis is compatible with an adrenergic mechanism for the antienuretic effects of TCAs. In animal experiments imipramine potentiates the effect of hypogastric (sympathetic) stimulation on beta-mediated detrusor relaxation and alpha-mediated contraction of the base (Shaffer *et al.*, 1979). However, the alpha-blocking agent indoramin has no action on enuresis (Shaffer *et al.*, 1978), while both amphetamine and methylphenidate, which have potent adrenergic actions, are ineffective in enuresis (Breger, 1962; McConaghy, 1969).

Urinary incontinence during sleep has been reported to occur during administration of the neuroleptics thioridazine (Melleril), thiothixene (Navane) and chlorpromazine among both adults and children with no prior history of enuresis (Van Putten *et al.*, 1972; Nurnberg & Ambrosini, 1979; Shenoy, 1980; Boon, 1981). Wetting ceases when the neuroleptic is discontinued. The mechanism of neuroleptic-induced enuresis is unknown. It has been suggested that the alpha-adrenergic blocking effects of the neuroleptics result in relaxation of the internal sphincter but, in the case reports listed above, there were no other symptoms of alpha blockade such as hypotension, and thiothixene is a relatively weak alpha-blocking drug.

Psychosocial factors

Toilet training

Prospective studies in New Zealand (Fergusson *et al.*, 1986) and Israel (Kaffmann & Elizur, 1977) suggest that enuresis is more likely among children who start toilet training after age 18 months. The rate of enuresis at 6–8 years old among children reared in a kibbutz where training was started before 20 months was 5% compared with nearly 20% among these who started training later. This is unlikely to be because parents who experience difficulty training their infants defer the process, for in the Israeli study the onset of training varied as a function of kibbutz rule rather than the individual characteristics of the child.

Stress experiences

There is conflicting evidence on the relationship between *early* stress events and later enuresis. In an early longitudinal study, Douglas (1973) found that children who had had more stressful life events at 3–4 years of age had a twofold increase in the risk of enuresis. However a prospective study that used multivariate techniques to reduce the problem of confounded predictors (Fergusson *et al.*, 1986) found no relationship between primary enuresis, childhood stressors, psychosocial disadvantage or social class. There seems to be a clearer relationship between stressful events and the onset of secondary enuresis. Stresses found to be associated with late onset of enuresis include birth of a younger sibling (Werry & Cohrssen, 1965), severe head injury (Chadwick, 1985) and natural disaster (Durkin *et al.*, pers. comm.).

ASSOCIATED CONDITIONS

Urinary tract infection

Five per cent of clinically referred enuretics have evidence of a urinary tract infection (UTI; Kunin *et al.*, 1962; Shaffer *et al.*, 1968) — five times the rate found in the general population (Savage *et al.*, 1969). Conversely, the prevalence of enuresis in infected girls is five times greater than that found in the general population (Dodge *et al.*, 1970). Infection is most common in female enuretics, in those who wet frequently and in day-wetters (Kunin *et al.*, 1962; Shaffer *et al.*, 1968; Dodge *et al.*, 1970; Halliday *et al.*, 1987; Järvelin *et al.*, 1990). There is some evidence that enuresis may facilitate ascending infection. Infected enuretic girls who continue to wet are more likely to become reinfected than enuretic girls who become dry (Dodge *et al.*, 1970). Effective antibiotic treatment in infected enuretics cannot be relied upon to cure the enuresis. Jones *et al.* (1972) found that 24% of infected enuretic girls stopped wetting after their infection had been treated, but the study was uncontrolled and similar cure rates have been described with other nonspecific interventions (see below).

Urinary tract abnormalities

Reports of a high prevalence of urinary tract abnormalities in enuretics are usually based on patients seen in urology clinics and so may be subject to referral bias. In one of the few studies on an unselected group of enuretics, Järvelin *et al.* (1990) used ultrasonography and uroflowmetry to investigate 145 day- and/or night-wetters and age-/sex-matched nonenuretic controls identified from a large unreferred population of young schoolchildren. There were no significant differences in the rate of structural abnormality and/or incomplete bladder voiding between night-wetters and controls, but there was a significant excess among day-wetters. The most common abnormalities were residual urine after double micturition and a hypertrophic bladder wall. Day-wetting girls were more likely to have a past history of urinary tract infection and to be constipated. The investigators concluded that urological investigation should be routine in children who wet during the day but is not indicated in those who only wet at night.

The use of surgical procedures to correct minor abnormalities in the absence of gross pathology has been strongly criticized (Smith, 1969). Surgery is sometimes performed on the basis of unreliable measures of outflow obstruction such as apparent detrusor hypertrophy (Cendron & Lepthard, 1972) and seemingly abnormal voiding pressures (for which good standardization data are not available; Gleason & Latimer, 1962; Cooper, 1968; Pompeius, 1971). Signs commonly attributed to ouflow obstruction such as bladder diverticula and trabeculation can occur without anatomical obstruction and may be a feature of uninhibited detrusor contractions in children with an unstable bladder (Johnston *et al.*, 1978). There have been no controlled studies to show that urethral dilatation or bladder neck repair can be an effective treatment of enuresis.

Constipation

Constipation has been reported to be common among enuretics referred to a nephrology department (O'Regan *et al.*, 1986) and in female enuretics with a history of past UTI (Järvelin *et al.*, 1990). It has been suggested that a distended rectum effectively reduces bladder capacity and leads to detrusor irritability and enuresis. O'Regan *et al.* reported remission of enuresis after aggressive treatment of the constipation with Fleet's enema.

Psychiatric disorder

Psychiatric disturbance is present in only a minority of enuretics but it is two to six times more common than in nonenuretics (Table 29.1). The association has been found in community studies and so is not a referral artefact, nor can it be explained by differences in social background. The association is strongest in girls, in children who also wet during the day and in secondary enuretics (Hallgren, 1956; Rutter *et al.*, 1973; Essen & Peckham, 1976; McGee *et al.*, 1984).

Type of disorder

Symptoms that have been thought to be specifically related to enuresis have included tics, temper tantrums, nail-biting, firesetting and cruelty to animals (Felthous & Bernard, 1978; Jacobson, 1985). However systematic studies have failed to show a consistent or specific pattern for associated psychiatric symptoms (Lickorish, 1964; Rutter *et al.*, 1973; Mikkelsen *et al.*, 1980), or a specific association with deviant personality profiles, including passive-aggression, emotional immaturity or passivity (Achenbach & Lewis, 1971).

Nature of the association

There is evidence of a dynamic link between psychiatric disorder and enuresis. Essen and Peckham (1976) found that 7-year-old children who would become dry by age 11 years had an intermediate level of problems compared to children who had never been wet and those who would remain wet. In the Isle of Wight longitudinal study (Rutter *et al.*, 1973), children who were both wet and disturbed at the age of 10 years were more likely to have stopped wetting by age 14 if they were no longer psychiatrically disturbed. Such findings would be compatible with enuresis being either a cause or a consequence of psychiatric disorder.

Enuresis as a symptom of underlying disturbance

Many enuretics who wet frequently at home are dry when they sleep with relatives or on holiday (Molling *et al.*, 1962; Stein *et al.*, 1965). Relatives point to these phenomena as an example of bed-wetting being a purposeful and hostile act. However such children often admit to anxiety about wetting when in an unusual setting and their dryness may be bought at the expense of fitful sleep. Treatment studies offer little support for this model. Psychotherapy is ineffective in reducing enuresis (Werry & Cohrssen, 1965; Deleon & Mandell, 1966). Anxiolytic drugs have no antienuretic effect and the efficacy of the TCAs (see below) is independent of the psychiatric status of the child. Furthermore they operate more rapidly than would be expected if their antienuretic effect was mediated through a mood disorder (Blackwell & Currah, 1973). If wetting was a direct manifestation of psychiatric disorder, one might expect that purely symptomatic therapies such as the night alarm would be less effective in disturbed than in nondisturbed enuretics, but this is not the case (Behrle *et al.*, 1956; Young & Morgan, 1973).

Enuresis as a cause of psychiatric disorder

Bed-wetting is a distressing and, in some cases, stigmatizing condition. A number of studies have shown that enuretics who have been successfully treated with the night alarm become more assertive, independent and happy and that they gain in self-confidence (Behrle *et al.*, 1956; Lovibond, 1964; Baker, 1969; Moffatt *et al.*, 1987). These changes do not seem to be due to a nonspecific effect of treatment intervention as they were less marked when treatment was unsuccessful. However, two studies (Shaffer *et al.*, 1984; Moffatt *et al.*, 1987) found no change in psychiatric symptoms among children

Table 29.1 Association between enuresis and psychiatric disturbance

Age (years)	Boys			Girls		
	Wet % deviant	Dry % deviant	Deviance ratio	Wet % deviant	Dry % deviant	Deviance ratio
5	15.4	8.7	(1.8)	17.9	3.8	(4.7)
7	15.4	17.4	(0.9)	39.3	11.3	(3.5)**
9/10	17.9	10.1	(1.8)*	14.3	5.7	(2.5)**
14	13.8	5.4	(2.6)	25.0	3.9	(6.4)**

* *P* < 0.05; ** *P* < 0.01.

treated successfully with the night alarm. This confirms a general clinical impression that curing a disturbed child's enuresis may make the child happier and relieve one source of stress, but it rarely cures the disturbance.

Enuresis and psychiatric disorder as results of a third factor

Several factors are common to both enuresis and psychiatric disorder. Enuresis is more common in children living in broken or single-parent homes, in families in which there are extremes of poverty, repeated disruptions of maternal care, a reliance on welfare support, inadequate nutrition and clothing, and parental delinquency, in large crowded families and in children who have received institutional care (Miller *et al.*, 1960; Douglas, 1973; Miller, 1973; Rutter *et al.*, 1973; Essen & Peckham, 1976). Umphress *et al.* (1970) found that parents of bed-wetters were less concerned over home-making, wage-earning or the mental and physical health of their children. Oppel *et al.* (1968) found that poor marital adjustment was significantly more common amongst the parents of girl enuretics than amongst either nonenuretics or amongst boy enuretics. Most of these factors are known also to be associated with psychiatric disorder in childhood (Rutter *et al.*, 1970b). It could be that families with these characteristics have child-rearing practices that are conducive to the persistence of wetting, but that other aspects of their lives predispose to psychiatric disturbance.

It is also possible that there is a shared relationship with biological mechanisms. Reference has been made above to the association between enuresis and delayed motor, speech and pubertal development that are all known to be predictors of psychiatric disturbance. In two studies that have compared disturbed and nondisturbed enuretics, disturbance was associated with neurological signs and a history of developmental delay (Rapoport *et al.*, 1980; Shaffer *et al.*, 1984). Hallgren (1957) and Shaffer *et al.* (1984) found that the previously enuretic mothers of enuretic children were more likely to have marital difficulties than nonenuretic mothers. In this case both could share a biological antecedent or there might be biological transmission of the predisposition to bed-wetting and environmental transmission of family disturbance. Regardless of the mechanism of association there is no evidence to support the psychodynamic idea that wetting is either necessary or beneficial to the disturbed child.

INVESTIGATING ENURESIS

Frequently associated conditions such as developmental delay, learning difficulties, UTI, constipation and concurrent psychiatric disturbance should be ruled out. Enquiries should be made about a past history of UTI, dysuria and frequency and daytime incontinence. If behaviour therapy is to be used, it is important to know about sleeping arrangements, associated behaviour problems, the family's and the child's attitude to enuresis (lack of concern may predict poor compliance with a night alarm), previous treatment failures and their cause.

A microscopic and bacteriological examination of urine should be obtained routinely. Further urological investigations should be confined to children with a history of urological symptoms, day-wetting or evidence of UTI on bacteriological examination of urine. Studies that have routinely investigated nocturnal enuretics radiologically have shown very low rates (less than 1%) of intravenous pyelogram or micturating cystography abnormality (Forsythe & Redmond, 1974; McKendry & Stuart, 1974) and, when present, there was nearly always some other reason for suspecting an organic lesion (Redman & Seibert, 1979). Rates in daytime wetters are consistently higher (Halliday *et al.*, 1987; Järvelin *et al.*, 1990). The American Academy of Pediatrics (1980) recommended that all enuretics be investigated by examination and culture of the urine, but that radiological investigation be reserved for children with documented UTI.

TREATMENT OF NIGHT-WETTING

Comparatively few bed-wetters receive treatment. In 1960, Miller *et al.* found that fewer than 30% of 11-year-old enuretics had ever been assessed or treated for their complaint. The Rand survey of low-/moderate-income families in the US taken in the 1970s (Foxman *et al.*, 1986) reported a slightly higher (38%) rate and noted that treatment referral was more common among families headed by a well-educated parent and for female and older enuretics and those who admitted to distress over wetting. Approximately a third of children referred for treatment were not given any, a third were prescribed medication and the remainder a miscellany of interventions. Only 3% were prescribed a night alarm system, the only known curative treatment. These findings are a cause of concern because the same study found that approximately a third of 5–13-year-old enuretics were greatly distressed by their symptom. Why is it that two-thirds of parents don't seek treatment and why do the large majority of physicians provide either no treatment or treatment that will not cure the condition? Clinical experience suggests that many families accept bed-wetting as an unavoidable part of growing up. The reason for the physicians' behaviour is less clear. No doubt many erroneously believe that the child will soon grow out of the condition; many no doubt do not know how to demonstrate the night alarm apparatus or know that it is often taxing for parents; yet others may be concerned about prescribing potentially toxic medication such as the TCAs. It is not known whether the introduction of safer (but more expensive) medication such as desmopressin (see below) has changed this profile.

Record-keeping and reinforcement for dry nights

Maintaining a chart on which dry nights are recorded for at least 2 weeks is good clinical practice. It provides a baseline against which the effects of future treatment can be judged and it has a therapeutic effect in a minority of enuretics. It will result in a marked reduction, and in some cases a cure, in up to 20% of enuretics (Schmitt, 1982; Devlin & O'Cathain, 1990).

Retention control training

In 1948 Smith suggested a method of training enuretics to increase the FBV by deferring micturition by systematic reinforcement during the day — retention control training (RCT). However, subsequent controlled studies have failed to show that RCT increases FBV and indicate that it is consistently less effective than the night alarm (Fielding, 1980) and, when added, does not improve outcome compared to the night alarm alone (Geffken *et al.*, 1986). A variation of RCT (Cardozo *et al.*, 1978a,b) uses intravesical pressure feedback. Although this reduces the amplitude of detrusor contractions, there is no evidence that it affected nighttime enuresis.

Surgery

A variety of surgical treatments have been recommended for enuretics who show evidence of outflow tract obstruction but no other evidence of dysfunction. The methods include urethral dilation, meatotomy or bladder neck repair and cystoplasty to enlarge the bladder or, to modify the neurological control of the bladder, division of the sacral nerves or the detrusor by bladder transection (Janknegt *et al.*, 1979; Torrens & Hald, 1979; Kvarstein & Mathison, 1981). The efficacy of these procedures has never been demonstrated in clinical trials. Hazards include urinary incontinence, recurrent epididimitis and aspermia (Smith, 1969).

Drug treatment

Although the evidence is that pharmacological treatment only occasionally cures enuresis, in the US and probably elsewhere it is overwhelmingly the most common approach used by medical practitioners (Foxman *et al.*, 1986). Four main classes of drugs have been used to treat enuresis: (1) the synthetic antidiuretics; (2) the TCA's; (3) the sympathomimetic stimulants; and (4) anticholinergics.

Synthetic antidiuretics

Random assignment, double-blind, placebo controlled clinical trials (Terho & Kekomaki, 1984; Dimson, 1986; Miller & Klauber, 1990) have demonstrated an antienuretic effect of the synthetic antidiuretic vasopeptide DDAVP (desamino-D-arginine vasopressin). Sukhai *et al.* (1989) found that a combination of desmopressin and the alarm (see below) was more effective than the alarm alone. The synthetic drug exerts an antidiuretic effect for significantly longer than natural vasopressin and also lacks the natural hormone's pressor effect. The hormone is usually administered intranasally with a dose-metred pump. Plasma concentrations reach a peak after 45

minutes and continue to exert an effect from 6 to 12 hours (Ramsden *et al.*, 1982; Richardson & Robinson, 1985). Absorption is reduced when the child has a cold or nasal allergy. Oral preparations have been developed (Westgren *et al.*, 1986) that appear to be as effective as intranasal hormone (Fjellestad-Paulsen *et al.*, 1987). The oral dose is 10 times the usual intranasal dose.

Under trial conditions, using doses of 20−40 µg intranasally at night, just under a half of children cease wetting completely while a further 40% show a marked reduction in wetting frequency. These effects are comparable to those of the TCAs. However, again as with the TCAs, when treatment is discontinued most, but by no means all (Miller *et al.*, 1989), cases will relapse, making the treatment in the long term inferior to the night alarm (Wille, 1986).

A number of studies have suggested that response rate is proportional to the increase in osmolality produced and by extension to the dose provided. Osmolalities above 800 mosmol/kg are more likely to be associated with good results (Fjellestad-Paulsen *et al.*, 1987). In a large multisite study children treated with 40 µg did better than those treated with 20 µg (Miller & Klauber, 1990).

The most common side-effects have been nasal pain and congestion, rhinitis and conjunctivitis. Other unwanted effects include transient headache, nausea and abdominal pain. Urine osmolality increases gradually, but remains within the normal range (Miller & Klauber, 1990); nevertheless children who are being treated with the hormone should refrain from drinking in the evening. A number of studies have reported an increase in body weight but frank water intoxication with hyponatraemia and seizures is rare and has been reported in only a small number of children, including 1 with cystic fibrosis. Endogenous antidiuretic hormone secretion — as measured by a water deprivation test — does not appear to be suppressed even after treatment of over a year (Rew & Rundle, 1989). The most significant limitation of DDVP is that, as with the TCAs (see below), when treatment is stopped, most but not all children revert to their initial wet night frequency. DDVP appears to be as effective as the TCAs but has fewer side-effects and is a generally safer drug. It is therefore reasonable to favour its use over treatment with the TCAs.

The mode of action of DDVP is not known. The reduction in urinary flow may be sufficient to maintain bladder volume below that which will induce micturition contraction. Alternatively, if the studies that suggest a primary vasopressin deficiency in enuresis are confirmed, it may be correcting that natural deficiency.

Tricyclic antidepressants

The effect of the TCA imipramine (IMI) in reducing the frequency of bed-wetting was first reported by MacLean in 1960. Since then many random-assignment, double-blind, placebo-controlled studies have confirmed their effectiveness. Other TCAs such as amitriptyline, nortriptyline and des-methylimipramine (Blackwell & Currah, 1973) and related tetracyclics, such as maprotiline, have a similar effect (Simeon _et al._, 1981). IMI will reduce wetting frequency in about 85% of bed-wetters and will suppress wetting completely in about 30%. Relapse after withdrawal of medication may be immediate or delayed, but within 3 months of stopping treatment, nearly all children treated with IMI will be wetting again at or near their previous wetting frequency (Shaffer _et al._, 1968). The technique of stopping the drug — gradual or abrupt withdrawal — does not seem to influence the relapse rate. The effect of very prolonged treatment has not been studied.

The effect is closely related to the total plasma concentration of IMI and its principal metabolite, desipramine (DMI). Although some children will show a response at a lower level, there appears to be no benefit for exceeding a combined IMI—DMI plasma level above 60 ng/ml (Rapoport _et al._, 1980; De Gatta _et al._, 1984, 1990). This will usually require a maximum nighttime dose of between 1 and 2.5 mg/kg (Jorgensen _et al._, 1980). Under no circumstances should the upper limit exceed 5 mg/kg (Rohner & Sanford, 1975) and elctrocardiogram monitoring is advised if the dose goes above 3.5 mg/kg to detect signs of conduction delay (Saraf _et al._, 1978; Mikkelsen & Rapoport, 1980).

Mikkelsen (1991) suggests that it is reasonable to begin with a dose of 25 mg at night to identify those children who respond to low doses. The dose would then be increased by 25 mg a night every 4—7 days. Providing that dosage is adequate, the effect will nearly always be noted within 1 week of starting or changing treatment. Tolerance develops between 2 and 6 weeks after the start of treatment in many children (Jorgensen _et al._, 1980; Rapoport _et al._, 1980). There is no evidence that children ever show a delayed response.

Unwanted effects are uncommon with a combined IMI—DMI serum level below 50 ng/ml, but are invariably present when it rises above 100 ng/ml. The most frequent of these are dry mouth, dizziness, headache and constipation. Some hyperactive children may show a worsening of their restlessness and distractibility. Goel and Shanks (1974) have reported a number of cases of acute TCA poisoning in children. Manifestations of toxicity include cardiac irregularities, convulsions, hallucinations, retention of urine and ataxia. Death, when it occurs, is usually due to a cardiac arrhythmia.

Other drugs

Sympathomimetic stimulants

Sympathomimetic stimulants have been used to reduce the depth of sleep, but there is no evidence that enuretics sleep more heavily than nonenuretics (see above) and no evidence that this class of medication is effective in enuresis (McConaghy, 1969). There is some evidence that stimulants accelerate response to behaviour therapy (Young & Turner, 1965).

Anticholinergic drugs

Anticholinergic drugs, such as belladonna, propantheline, oxybutynin chloride and terodiline reduce the frequency of detrusor contractions of a neurogenic type, delay the desire to void and increase functional bladder capacity, but double-blind controlled studies show they do _not_ reduce night-wetting, although they may have a role to play in day-wetting (Wallace & Forsythe, 1969; Rapoport _et al._, 1980; Baigrie _et al._, 1988; Elmer _et al._, 1988; Lovering _et al._, 1988). They almost invariably produce unwanted effects that include dry mouth, dysphagia, stomal ulcers, blurred vision, headache, dizziness, drowsiness, constipation and nausea (Baigrie _et al._, 1988).

Treatment involving night-waking

Night lifting and fluid restriction before bed

These common-sense measures are frequently adopted by the parents of younger bed-wetters and the failure of a parent to have tried either or both of these methods may be an indication of a negative or negligent attitude towards the condition or the child. Studies of their efficacy in well-established enuresis (Roberts & Schoellkopf, 1951; Hagglund, 1965; Fournier _et al._, 1987) suggest that, although the procedures may lead to a small initial reduction in wetting frequency, their effect, if any, is short-lived. This is not to say that lifting and restriction may be more effective in bed-wetters who are never referred for specialist treatment. A good response to one of these techniques may be one of the reasons why professional advice is not sought.

The night alarm

Pfaundler (1904) devised an alarm system to alert nursery nurses to when an infant needed changing. He also tried the apparatus on an enuretic child and noted that the enuresis improved. Despite this early report of a successful treatment for enuresis, the method was only applied irregularly (see Forsythe & Butler, 1989, for a historical account) until Mowrer and Mowrer (1938), working from conditioning theory, developed a similar device. The Mowrer apparatus consisted of an auditory alarm linked to two electrodes, separated in one way or another, upon which the child slept. When the child was incontinent the urine established contact between the two electrodes, the alarm sounded and the child woke. This system, with a number of technical refinements, including, most currently, a mini body alarm (Schmitt, 1986) in which a sensor is attached to the child's pyjama pants and the alarm is carried on a wrist band or in a pocket, has continued to be used and constitutes the most effective form of therapy now available. Instruments that apply a mild electric shock after an enuretic event seem to be no more effective than devices with an auditory signal and are understandably less acceptable to the family (Crosby, 1950; Lovibond, 1964; Netley _et al._, 1984).

Cure — most commonly defined as 14 nights of continuous dryness — with the night alarm varies from 50 to 100%, with most studies reporting a success rate approximating 80% (see Forsythe & Butler, 1989, for a review). Studies with the body alarm (Malum *et al.*, 1982; Forsythe & Butler, 1989; Butler *et al.*, 1990a) report similar success rates. Primary and secondary enuretics and those with and without a positive family history seem to do equally well with the night alarm. Children who do less well include those with associated day-wetting (Fielding, 1985), psychiatric disorders, family stress and when the children appear to be unconcerned about the symptom. Although the bell is often not considered suitable for families who live in poor housing conditions, this factor alone does not predict low response rates when other predictive factors are taken into account (Dische *et al.*, 1983; Devlin & O'Cathain, 1990). Significant cure or improvement rates have also been reported among the retarded (Sloop & Kennedy, 1973; Smith, 1981; Hanson *et al.*, 1988) and other institutionalized children, although treatment may need to be continued for longer in such children.

Duration of treatment

One of the inconveniences of the night alarm is that it takes many weeks before cure is obtained. Cure is usually reached during the second month of treatment (Kolvin *et al.*, 1972), but significantly sooner with the body alarm (Butler *et al.*, 1990a). Response may be hastened by increasing the intensity of the auditory stimulus (Finley & Wansley, 1977) or by the simultaneous use of methylamphetamine, a stimulant drug (Young & Turner, 1965) and more recently (Sukhai *et al.*, 1989) the antidiuretic desmopressin. Bollard and Nettelbeck (1982) suggested that the addition of regular scheduled night-waking to an alarm procedure would shorten the period to continence, but this has not been confirmed (Whelan & Houts, 1990). Young and Morgan (1973) and Dische *et al.* (1983) examined the characteristics associated with a delayed response to treatment. Age of the child and initial wetting frequency were unrelated but a failure of the child to waken with the alarm and maternal anxiety and disturbed home background were.

Premature termination of treatment

Although the night alarm offers the only known cure for enuresis, it is a difficult treatment that tends to be unpopular with both clinicians (who are much more likely to prescribe medication) and with families who often abandon treatment prematurely. In some studies premature termination rates run as high as 48% (Turner *et al.*, 1970). Aspects of treatment that may lead to premature termination include failure to understand or to follow the instructions; failure of the apparatus to wake the child; and irritation at false alarms (Turner, 1973). These common problems are addressed in the final section of this chapter.

Early termination is also more likely in families that have made little previous effort to treat their child (including the use of such home-spun techniques as fluid restriction and night-waking), those who are intolerant of enuresis and among children who have other behaviour problems (Geffken *et al.*, 1986; Wagner & Johnson, 1988). These research findings suggest that the initial evaluation should include an assessment of associated behaviour problems (see above), enquiries about the family's attitudes toward the condition and the nature and extent of previous treatment. The family should be warned that the treatment is slow to take effect, and that it will involve their substantial involvement at inconvenient hours of the night. Exacting a commitment to continue with the treatment for at least 12 weeks, coupled with careful monitoring that the treatment is indeed being provided (see below) may also be helpful. The negative aspects of treatment should be set against the probable gains in having clean beds and an expectation that there will be an improvement in the child's self esteem and level of contentment.

Relapse after initial cure

Most children who become dry with the night alarm will have occasional isolated relapses (Deleon & Mandell, 1966). More significant relapse occurs in slightly over a third of children who have become dry for at least 2 weeks, usually within 6 months of completing treatment (Doleys, 1977). Although a number of research projects have attempted to identify the predictors of relapse, perhaps because of differences in the duration of follow-up and the criteria adopted for relapse, no findings have been consistently replicated across studies (Turner, 1973; Young & Morgan, 1973; Doleys, 1977; Fielding, 1985; Butler *et al.*, 1990b). In a naturalistic retrospective study that has not yet been replicated, Houts *et al.* (1984) reported that enuretics who had previously been treated with IMI were more likely to relapse after successful treatment with the night alarm.

Two techniques have been proposed to reduce the relapse rate — intermittent reinforcement and overlearning. Intermittent reinforcement requires special apparatus that wakens the patient after only a proportion of micturitions (Finley *et al.*, 1973). This apparatus is not readily available, although Lovibond (1964) suggested that using ordinary apparatus on only 3 or 4 days in each week should have the same effect. There is however no good evidence that this method is effective. Overlearning involves two procedures: continuing the treatment after criterion for cure (i.e. 2 weeks dryness) has been reached and trying to precipitate further enuretic events by fluid loading. Young and Morgan (1972) and Houts *et al.*, 1984) reported that these procedures significantly reduced the relapse rate. In practice, the fluid-loading procedure usually induces waking rather than triggering the alarm. In view of this, Forsythe and Butler (1989), finding no significant reduction in relapse rates between children who retained the alarm for 2, 3 or 4 weeks of uninterrupted dryness, suggest that the procedure may have marginal value.

Side-effects

The only known side-effect of night alarm treatment is 'buzzer ulcers' that may arise when the child lies in a pool of ionized urine. While this was a problem with high-voltage buzzers, almost all contemporary waking devices are transistorized and sample their sensor only intermittently, thus permitting the use of low-voltage batteries that have a minimal risk of causing acid-burn injury (Malum *et al.*, 1982).

Mode of action

Classical and operant conditioning theories have been advanced to explain the efficacy of the alarm system. In the classical conditioning paradigm, bladder distension or the micturition contraction is assumed to be the indifferent stimulus (IS). Treatment introduces an unconditioned stimulus (US; the auditory signal) in proximity to the IS which then acquires the properties of a conditioned stimulus, leading to a conditioned response (CR; waking). In favour of a classical conditioning model are: (1) when the introduction of the US is delayed, treatment is compromised (Collins, 1973); and (2) extinction of the CR after initial cure can be inhibited by intermittent reinforcement (Finley *et al.*, 1973) and by over-learning (Young & Morgan, 1972; see below).

In favour of avoidance learning or punishment training as a form of operant conditioning is the gadget effect, whereby the child becomes dry when the apparatus is placed on the bed but not switched on (Deleon & Mandell, 1966). The greater effectiveness of the twin-signal apparatus (Lovibond, 1964; Hansen, 1979), which emits a moderate-volume auditory signal when micturition is first detected and a second much louder aversive noise several seconds later, suggested that the apparatus works primarily through punishment training. Turner (1973) makes the point that the night alarm focuses family attention on the wetting habits of the child so that dry nights are more liable to be noted and rewarded by praise, and suggests that social learning is an important component in the bell's efficacy.

Scheduled night-waking and massed practice: the dry bed technique

The dry bed technique (Azrin *et al.*, 1973; Ballard & Wood-roofe, 1977; Azrin & Thienes, 1978) includes high fluid intakes, frequent behavioural rehearsal of proper toileting, RCT (see above), training in rapid awakening (with the use of a night alarm), and rapid reinforcement for correct micturition.

The procedure is burdensome and, without the simultaneous use of a night alarm, the dry bed procedure produces substantially the same results as no treatment at all. (Nettelbeck & Langeluddecke, 1979, Bollard & Nettelbeck, 1981; Butler *et al.*, 1988; Kaplan *et al.*, 1989; Whelan & Houts, 1990). Mattson and Ollendick (1977) have reported such adverse effects as temper tantrums and withdrawn behaviour after using the method.

INVESTIGATION AND TREATMENT OF DAY-WETTING

Day-wetting, whether it occurs alone or in combination with night-wetting, is more likely to be associated with urinary tract abnormalities and with other psychiatric symptoms than simple night-wetting (see above). Investigation should therefore include taking a complete psychiatric history and a history of genitourinary tract symptoms. Urine should always be checked for infection and this should be repeated monthly for at least 3 months. Uroradiological studies or ultrasound should be performed if there is any suspicion of abnormality.

The history should be taken carefully to determine where and when day-wetting is most likely to occur. In some cases, daytime wetting is situation-specific. The patient is a young, timid child who has started to wet only since starting school, and wets only at school and never during weekends or holidays. In these children, school anxiety may be the most important factor, the child being reluctant to use the school lavatories or leave the classroom during lessons. A suggestion to the teacher that she or he tactfully encourage the child to use the toilet at regular intervals may be all that is needed.

Until recently there have been few established treatments available for day-wetters. Close observation of day-wetters (Fielding *et al.*, 1978) indicates that they experience an urge before micturition takes place but that this is either ignored or — in the case of day-wetters with an irritable bladder — occurs so close to the micturition contraction that it cannot be heeded in time. Treatment — habit training — has therefore focused on identifying the time of day when day-wetting is most likely to occur (in most cases between noon and 5 p.m.) and reinforcement is given for anticipatory toileting during that period (Berg *et al.*, 1982). A more intensive behavioural treatment that can be carried out over a few days (Azrin *et al.* 1974; Foxx & Azrin, 1973) involves forcing fluid to increase the number of toileting responses available for reinforcement and applying punishment for 'accidents'.

The development of portable body alarms with a sensor that is worn in underwear and an alarm that is carried in a pocket or on a wrist band offers considerable promise for this condition. Halliday *et al.*, (1987) found that such a device cured two-thirds of a series of day-wetters and that cure was for the most part maintained over the following 2 years. Two versions of the device were tested — one in which the signal occurred only after wetting had taken place; the other was set to sound at predetermined intervals. There were no significant differences in the findings from each alarm and the authors recommend that the noncontingent alarm was preferable. It avoids the inconvenience of a sensor and is more acceptable to children who are often embarrassed when the alarm sounds after wetting in school. Treatment with IMI is ineffective (Meadow & Berg, 1982) but double-blind placebo-controlled studies with the anticholinergics terodiline and oxybutynin (Baigrie *et al.*, 1988; Elmer *et al.*, 1988) show that, while they have no effect on night-wetting, they significantly reduce day-wetting frequency.

CONCLUSIONS

This chapter has reviewed many factors known to be associated with bed-wetting. These include biological associations such as an increased rate of urinary infection, apparent abnormalities in the rate of development of the structures at the base of the bladder, a low threshold of responsiveness of the bladder and a genetic predisposition. There are also a number of associations of a social or environmental nature. Enuretic children are more likely to come from large or broken or impoverished or unhappy families. Their parents may be less caring and are more likely to have allowed or been forced to allow their children to be separated from them during early childhood. Enuresis occurs more often in children living in institutions and it may respond to psychosocial changes and interventions that have in common the effect of increasing the attention that is paid to the child and possibly to the bed-wetting.

A social motivational model would seem to bring together many of these apparently disparate associations. Enuresis can then be viewed as a socially unacceptable response that has persisted either because the social reinforcement or social inhibitory influences have not acted at an optimal level, or because biological deviance renders the force of these influences inadequate. Azrin *et al.* (1973) have pointed out that social reactions to the act of bed-wetting are delayed because the event takes place at night and the child does not wake after the event. In some cases, the effectiveness of even these delayed responses is reduced still further by the unsatisfactory nature of the child's environment. In other cases, the appropriate social response is hindered by abnormal bladder function. The night alarm is effective because it focuses the family's attention on the symptom in a consistent fashion and because it reduces the delay between the act of wetting and the social response. The TCAs and daytime training are presumably effective because they facilitate the child's appropriate inhibitory response.

Irrespective of the cause of bed-wetting, it is important that practitioners appreciate that this common symptom can be treated successfully in nearly all cases, that there are no contraindications to treatment, and that treatment, as well as bringing practical relief to the family, will often benefit the child socially and emotionally.

ACKNOWLEDGEMENT

This work was made possible by Research Training Grant MH 38198–11A2, NIMH Center Grant MH 43878–03AI to The Center to Study Youth Depression, Anxiety and Suicide.

REFERENCES

Achenbach T. & Lewis M. (1971) A proposed model for clinical research and its application to encopresis and enuresis. *Journal of the American Academy of Child Psychiatry*, **10**, 535–554.

American Academy of Pediatrics — Committee on Radiology (1980) Excretory urography for evaluation of enuresis. *Pediatrics*, **65**, 644–645.

Azrin N.H. & Thienes P.M. (1978) Rapid elimination of enuresis by intensive learning without a conditioning apparatus. *Behaviour Research and Therapy*, **9**, 342–354.

Azrin N.H., Sneed T.J. & Foxx R.M. (1974) Dry bed: a rapid method of eliminating bed wetting (enuresis) of the retarded. *Behaviour Research and Therapy*, **11**, 427–434.

Azrin N.H., Sneed T.J. & Foxx R.M. (1974) Dry bed wetting: Rapid elimination of childhood enuresis. *Behaviour Research and Therapy*, **12**, 147–156.

Baigrie R.J., Kelleher J.P., Fawcett D.P. & Pengelly A.W. (1988) Oxybutynin: Is it safe? *British Journal of Urology*, **62**, 319–322.

Baker B.L. (1969) Symptom treatment and symptom substitution in enuresis. *Journal of Abnormal Psychology*, **74**, 42–49.

Bakwin H. (1961) Enuresis in children. *Journal of Pediatrics*, **58**, 806–819.

Bakwin H. (1973) The genetics of bed wetting. In: Kolvin I., MacKeith R. & Meadow R.S. (eds) *Bladder Control and Enuresis*, pp. 73–77. Clinics in Developmental Medicine, nos. 48/49. Heinemann/Spastics International Medical Publications, London.

Ballard R.J. & Woodroofe P. (1977) The effect of parent-administered dry-bed training on nocturnal enuresis in children. *Behaviour Research and Therapy*, **15**, 159–165.

Behrle F.C., Elkin M.T. & Laybourne P.C. (1956) Evaluation of a conditioning device in the treatment of nocturnal enuresis. *Pediatrics*, **17**, 849–855.

Berg I., Forsythe I. & McGuire R. (1982) Response of bedwetting to the enuresis alarm. Influence of psychiatric disturbance and maximum functional bladder capacity. *Archives of Disease in Childhood*, **57**, 394–396.

Blackwell B. & Currah J. (1973) The psychopharmacology of nocturnal enuresis. In: Kolvin I. MacKeith R. & Meadow S.R. (eds) *Bladder Control and Enuresis*, pp. 231–257. Clinics in Developmental Medicine, nos. 48/49. Heinemann/Spastics International Medical Publications, London.

Blomfield J.M. & Douglas J.W.B. (1956) Bedwetting — prevalence among children aged 4–7 years. *Lancet*, **1**, 850–852.

Bollard J. & Nettelbeck T. (1981) A comparison of dry bed training and standard urine — alarm conditioning treatment of childhood bedwetting. *Behaviour Research and Therapy*, **19**, 215–226.

Bollard J. & Nettelbeck T. (1982) A component of analysis of dry-bed training for treatment for bedwetting. *Behaviour Research and Therapy*, **20**, 383.

Boon F. (1981) Nocturnal enuresis and psychotropic drugs. *American Journal of Psychiatry*, **138**, 538.

Breger E. (1962) Hydroxyzine hydrochloride and methylphenidate hydrochloride in the management of enuresis. *Journal of Pediatrics*, **61**, 443–447.

Butler R.J., Brewin C.R. & Forsythe W.I. (1988) A comparison of two approaches to the treatment of nocturnal enuresis and the prediction of effectiveness using pre-treatment variables. *Journal of Child Psychology and Psychiatry*, **29**, 501–509.

Butler R.J., Forsythe W.I. & Robertson J. (1990a) The body-worn alarm in treatment of childhood enuresis. *British Journal of Child Psychiatry*, **44**, 237–241.

Butler R., Brewin C. & Forsythe I. (1990b) Relapse in children treated for nocturnal enuresis: Prediction of response using pre-treatment variables. *Behavioural Psychology*, **18**, 65–72.

Cardozo L.D., Abrams P.D., Stanton S.L. & Feneley R.C. (1978a) Idiopathic bladder instability treated by biofeedback. *British Journal of Urology*, **50**, 521–523.

Cardozo L.D., Stanton S.L., Hefner J. & Allan V. (1978b) Biofeedback in the treatment of detrusor instability. *British Journal of*

Urology, **50**, 250–254.

Cendron J. & Lepthard V. (1972) Maladie du col vesical chez l'enfant. *Urologica Internationalis,* **27**, 355–360.

Chadwick O. (1985) Psychological sequelae of head injury in children. *Developmental Medicine and Child Neurology,* **27**, 69–79.

Collins R. (1973) Importance of the bladder-cue buzzer contingency in the conditioning treatment for enuresis. *Journal of Abnormal Psychology,* **82**, 299–308.

Cooper D.G.W. (1968) Bladder studies in children with neurogenic incontinence with comments on the place of pelvic floor stimulation. *British Journal of Urology,* **40**, 157–174.

Crosby N.D. (1950) Essential enuresis. Treatment based on physiological concepts. *Medical Journal of Australia,* **2**, 533–543.

De Gatta M.M., Garcia M.J., Acosta A., Rey F., Gutierrez J.R. & Dominguez-Gil A. (1984) Monitoring of serum levels of imipramine and desipramine and individualization of dose in enuretic children. *Therapeutic Drug Monitoring,* **6**, 438–443.

De Gatta M.M., Galindo P., Rey F., Gutierrez J., Tamayo M., Garia M. & Dominguez-Gil A. (1990) The influence of clinical and pharmacological factors on enuresis treatment with imipramine. *British Journal of Clinical Pharmacology,* **30**, 693–698.

De Jonge G.A. (1973) A survey of the literature. In: Kolvin I., MacKeith R.C. & Meadow S.R. (eds) *Bladder Control and Enuresis,* pp. 39–46. Clinics in Developmental Medicine, nos. 48/49. Heinemann/Spastics International Medical Publications, London.

Deleon G. & Mandell W. (1966) A comparison of conditioning and psychotherapy in the treatment of enuresis. *Journal of Clinical Psychology,* **22**, 326–330.

Devlin J.B. & O'Cathain C. (1990) Predicting treatment outcome in nocturnal enuresis. *Archives of Disease in Childhood,* **65**, 1158–1161.

Dische S., Yule W., Corbett J. & Hand D. (1983) Childhood nocturnal enuresis: factors associated with outcome of treatment with an enuresis alarm. *Developmental Medicine and Child Neurology,* **25**, 67–81.

Dimson S.B., (1986) DDAVP and urine osmality in refractory enuresis. *Archives of Disease in Childhood,* **61**, 1104–1107.

Dodge W.F., West E.F., Bridgforth M.S. & Travis L.B. (1970) Nocturnal enuresis in 6- to 10-year-old children. *American Journal of Disease in Childhood,* **120**, 32–35.

Doleys D.M. (1977) Behavioral treatments for nocturnal enuresis in children: a review of the recent literature. *Psychological Bulletin,* **84**, 30–54.

Douglas J.W.B. (1973) Early disturbing events and later enuresis. In: Kolvin I., MacKeith R. & Meadow S.R. (eds) *Bladder Control and Enuresis,* pp. 109–117. Clinics in Developmental Medicine, nos. 48/49. Heinemann/Spastics International Medical Publications, London.

Elmer M., Norgaard J.P., Djurhuus J.C. & Adolfsson T. (1988) Terodiline in the treatment of diurnal enuresis in children. *Scandinavian Journal of Primary Health Care,* **6**, 119–124.

Esperanca M. & Gerrard J.W. (1969) Nocturnal enuresis: comparison of the effect of imipramine and dietary restriction on bladder capacity. *Canadian Medical Association Journal,* **101**, 721–724.

Essen J. & Peckham C. (1976) Nocturnal enuresis in childhood. *Developmental Medicine and Child Neurology,* **18**, 577–589.

Felthous A.R. & Bernard H. (1978) Enuresis, firesetting, and cruelty to animals: the significance of two thirds of this triad. *Journal of Forensic Sciences,* **45**, 240–246.

Fergusson D.M., Horwood L.J. & Shannon F.T. (1986) Factors related to the age of attainment of nocturnal bladder control: an 8-year longitudinal study. *Pediatrics,* **78**, 884–890.

Fielding D. (1980) The response of day and night wetting children and children who wet only at night to retention control training and the enuresis alarm. *Behaviour Research and Therapy,* **18**, 305–317.

Fielding D. (1985) Factors associated with drop out, relapse and failure in the conditioning treatment of nocturnal enuresis. *Behavioral Psychotherapy,* **13**, 174–185.

Fielding D., Berg I. & Bell S. (1978) An observational study of posture and limb movements of children who wet by day and at night. *Developmental Medicine and Child Neurology,* **20**, 453–461.

Finley W.W. & Wansley R.A. (1977) Auditory intensity as a variable in the conditioning treatment of enuresis nocturna. *Behaviour Research and Therapy,* **15**, 181–185.

Finley W.W., Besserman R.L., Clapp R.K. & Finley P. (1973) The effect of continuous, intermittent and placebo reinforcement on the effectiveness of the conditioning treatment for enuresis nocturna. *Behaviour Research and Therapy,* **11**, 289–297.

Fjellestad-Paulsen A., Wille S. & Harris A.S. (1987) Comparison of intranasal and oral desmopressin for nocturnal enuresis. *Archives of Disease in Childhood,* **62**, 674–677.

Forsythe W.I. & Butler R.J. (1989) Fifty years of enuretic alarms. *Archives of Disease in Childhood,* **64**, 879–885.

Forsythe W.I. & Redmond A. (1974) Enuresis and spontaneous cure rate. A study of 1129 enuretics. *Archives of Disease in Childhood,* **49**, 259–263.

Fournier J., Garfinkel B., Bond A., Beauchesne H. & Shapiro S. (1987) Pharmacological and behavioral management of enuresis. *Journal of the American Academy of Child and Adolescent Psychiatry,* **26**, 849–853.

Foxman B., Valdez R.B. & Brook R.H. (1986) Childhood enuresis: prevalence, perceived impact, and prescribed treatments. *Pediatrics,* **77**, 482–487.

Foxx R.M. & Azrin N.H. (1973) Dry pants. A rapid method of toilet training children. *Behaviour Research and Therapy,* **11**, 435–442.

Gardner A. & Shaffer D. (1984) Expected values for the Starfield test of functional bladder volume in children. Unpublished manuscript.

Geffken G., Johnson S.B. & Walker D. (1986) Behavioral interventions for childhood nocturnal enuresis: the differential effect of bladder capacity on treatment progress and outcome. *Health Psychology,* **5**, 261–272.

Gleason D.M. & Latimer J.K. (1962) The pressure flow study: a method for measuring bladder neck resistance. *Journal of Urology,* **87**, 844–852.

Goel K.M. & Shanks R.A. (1974) Amitryptyline and imipramine poisoning in children. *British Medical Journal,* **1**, 261–263.

Hagglund T.B. (1965) Enuretic children treated on fluid restriction or forced drinks. A clinical and cystometric study. *Annales Paediatrica Fennica,* **11**, 84–90.

Hallgren B. (1956) Enuresis. A study with reference to certain physical, mental and social factors possibly associated with enuresis. *Acta Psychiatrica Neurologica Scandinavica,* **31**, 405–436.

Hallgren B. (1957) Enuresis: a clinical and genetic study. *Acta Psychiatrica Neurologica Scandinavica* **32**, 1–154, (suppl. 114).

Halliday S., Meadow S.R. & Berg I. (1987) Successful management of daytime enuresis using alarm procedures: a randomly controlled trial. *Archives of Disease in Childhood,* **62**, 132–137.

Hansen G.D. (1979) Enuresis control through fading, escape and avoidance training. *Journal of Applied Behavior Analysis,* **12**, 303–307.

Hanson R.H., Thompson T. & Wieseler N.A. (1988) Methodological considerations in enuresis-treatment research. A three-treatment comparison. *Behavior Modification,* **12**, 335–352.

Hellbrugge T. (1960) The development of circadian rhythm in infants. *Cold Spring Harbour Symposium on Quantitative Biology,* **25**, 311–323.

Houts A.C., Peterson J.K. & Liebert R.M. (1984) The effect of prior imipramine treatment on the results of conditioning therapy in children with enuresis. *Journal of Pediatric Psychology,* **9**, 505–509.

Hutch J.A. (1972) *Anatomy and Physiology of the Bladder, Trigone and Urethra.* Appleton-Century-Crofts, New York.

Jacobson R.R. (1985) The subclassification of child firesetters. *Journal of Child Psychology and Psychiatry*, **26**, 769−775.

Janknegt R.A., Moonen W.A. & Schrienemechars L.M.H. (1979) Transsection of the bladder as a method of treatment in adult enuresis nocturna. *British Journal of Urology*, **51**, 275−277.

Järvelin M.R., Vikevainen-Tervonen L., Moilanen I. & Huttunen N.P. (1988) Enuresis in seven-year-old children. *Acta Paediatrica Scandinavica*, **77**, 148−153.

Järvelin M.R., Huttunen N.P., Seppanen J., Seppanen U. & Moilanen I. (1990) Screening of urinary tract abnormalities among day and nightwetting children. *Scandinavian Journal of Urology and Nephrology*, **24**, 181−189.

Järvelin M.R., Moilanen I., Kangas P., Moring K., Vikevainen-Tervonen L., Huttunen N.P. & Seppanen J. (1991) Aetiological and precipitating factors for childhood enuresis. *Acta Paediatrica Scandinavica*, **80**, 361−369.

Johnston J.H., Koff S.A. & Classberg K.I. (1978) The pseudo-obstructed bladder in enuretic children. *British Journal of Urology*, **550**, 550−510.

Jones B., Gerrard J.W., Shokeir M.K. & Houston C.S. (1972) Recurrent urinary infection in girls: relation to enuresis. *Canadian Medical Association Journal*, **106**, 127−130.

Jorgensen O.S., Lober M., Christiansen J. & Gram L.F. (1980) *Clinical Pharmacokinetics*, **5**, 386−393.

Kaffman M. (1962) Enuresis amongst kibbutz children. *Journal of the Medical Association of Israel*, **63**, 251−253.

Kaffman M. & Elizur E. (1977) Infants who become enuretics. A longitudinal study of 161 kibbutz children. *Monograms of the Society into Research in Child Development*, **42**, 170.

Kaplan S., Breit M., Gauthier B. & Busner J. (1989) A comparison of three nocturnal enuresis treatment methods. *Journal of the American Academy of Child and Adolescent Psychiatry*, **28**, 282−286.

Kolvin I., Taunch J., Currah J., Garside M.F., Nolan J. & Shaw W.B. (1972) Enuresis: a descriptive analysis and a controlled trial. *Developmental Medicine and Child Neurology*, **14**, 715−726.

Kunin C.M., Zacha E. & Paquin A.J. Jr (1962) Urinary tract infections in school children: an epidemiologic, clinical and laboratory study. *New England Journal of Medicine*, **266**, 1287−1296.

Kvarstein B. & Mathison W. (1981) Sigmoidocystoplasty in adults with enuresis. *Surgery, Gynecology and Obstetrics*, **153**, 65−66.

Lewis H.E., Lobban M.C. & Tredre B.E. (1970) Daily rhythms of renal excretion in a child with nocturnal enuresis. *Journal of Physiology*, **201**, 42−43.

Lickorish J.R. (1964) One hundred enuretics. *Journal of Psychosomatic Research*, **7**, 263−267.

Lovering J.S., Tallett S.E. & McKendry J.B.J. (1988) Oxybutynin efficacy in the treatment of primary enuresis. *Pediatrics*, **82**, 104−106.

Lovibond S.H. (1964) *Conditioning and Enuresis*. Pergamon, Oxford.

Lunsing R.J., Hadders-Algra M., Touwen B.C.L. & Huisjes H.J. (1991) Nocturnal enuresis and minor neurological dysfunction at 12 years: a follow-up study. *Developmental Medicine and Child Neurology*, **33**, 439−445.

McConaghy N. (1969) A controlled trial of imipramine, amphetamine, pad and bell, conditioning and random awakening in the treatment of nocturnal enuresis. *Medical Journal of Australia*, **2**, 237−239.

McGee R., Makinson T., Williams S., Simpson A. & Silva P. (1984) A longitudinal study of enuresis from five to nine years. *Australian Paediatric Journal*, **20**, 39−42.

McKendry J.B. & Stuart D.A. (1974) Enuresis. *Pediatric Clinics of North America*, **21**, 1019−1028.

Maclean R.E.G. (1960) Imipramine hydrochloride and enuresis. *American Journal of Psychiatry*, **117**, 551.

Malum H., Knapp M.S. & Hiller E.J. (1982) Electronic bed-wetting alarm and toilet trainer. *British Medical Journal*, **285**, 22.

Mattsson J.L. & Ollendick T.H. (1977) Issues in training normal children. *Behavior Therapy*, **8**, 549−553.

Meadow R. & Berg I. (1982) Controlled trial of imipramine in diurnal enuresis. *Archives of Diseases of Children*, **57**, 714−716.

Mikkelsen E.J. (1991) Modern approaches to enuresis and encopresis. In: Lewis M. (ed) *Child and Adolescent Psychiatry: A Comprehensive Textbook*, pp. 583−591. Williams & Wilkins, Baltimore, MD.

Mikkelsen E.J. & Rapoport J.L. (1980) Enuresis: psychopathology sleep stage and drug response. *Urologic Clinics of North America*, **7**, 361−377.

Mikkelsen E.J., Rapoport J.L., Nee L., Gruenau C., Mendelson W. & Gillin J.C. (1980) Childhood enuresis I. Sleep patterns and psycho-pathology. *Archives of General Psychiatry*, **37**, 1139−1145.

Miller K. & Klauber G.T. (1990) Desmopressin acetate in children with severe primary nocturnal enuresis. *Clinical Therapeutics*, **12**, 357−366.

Miller F.J.W., Court S.D.M., Walton W.S. & Knox E.G. (1960) *Growing Up in Newcastle-upon-Tyne*. Oxford University Press, London.

Miller K., Goldberg S. & Atkin B. (1989) Nocturnal enuresis: experience with long-term use of intranasally administered desmopressin. *Journal of Pediatrics*, **14**, 723−726.

Miller P.M. (1973) An experimental analysis in retention control training in the treatment of nocturnal enuresis in two institutionalized adolescents. *Behavior Therapy*, **4**, 288−294.

Moffatt M.E.K., Kato C. & Pless I.B. (1987) Improvements in self-concept after treatment of nocturnal enuresis: randomized control trial. *Journal of Pediatrics*, **110**, 647−652.

Molling P.A., Lockner A.W., Sauls R.S. & Eisenberg L. (1962) Committed delinquent boys. *Archives of General Psychiatry*, **7**, 70−76.

Mowrer O.H. & Mowrer W.M. (1938) Enuresis: a method for its study and treatment. *American Journal of Orthopsychiatry*, **8**, 436−459.

Netley C., Khanna F., McKendry J. & Lovering J. (1984) Effects of different methods of treatment of primary enuresis on psychologic functioning in children. *Canadian Medical Association Journal*, **131**, 577−579.

Nettelbeck T. & Langeluddecke P. (1979) Dry-bed training without an enuresis machine. *Behaviour Research and Therapy*, **17**, 403−404.

Nørgaard J.P. (1991) Pathophysiology of nocturnal enuresis. *Scandinavian Journal of Urology and Nephrology*, (suppl. 140, 7−31).

Nørgaard J.P., Pedersen E.B. & Djurhuus J.C. (1985) Diurnal anti-diuretic hormone levels in enuretics. *Journal of Urology*, **134**, 1029−1031.

Nørgaard J.P., Hansen J.H., Wildschiotz G., Sorensen S., Rittig S. & Djurhuus J.C. (1989a) Sleep cystometries in children with nocturnal enuresis. *Journal of Urology*, **141**, 1156−1159.

Nørgaard J.P., Rittig S. & Djurhuus J.C. (1989b) Nocturnal enuresis: an approach to treatment based on pathogenesis. *Journal of Pediatrics*, **114**, 705−710.

Nurnberg H.G. & Ambrosini P.J. (1979) Urinary incontinence in patients receiving neuroleptics. *Journal of Clinical Psychiatry*, **40**, 271−274.

Oppel W.C., Harper P.A. & Rider R.V. (1968) Social, psychological and neurological factors associated with enuresis. *Pediatrics*, **42**, 627−641.

O'Regan S., Yazbeck S., Hamberger B. & Schick E. (1986) Constipation: a commonly unrecognized cause of enuresis. *American Journal of Diseases of Children*, **140**, 260−261.

Petersen K.E., Anderson O.O. & Hansen T. (1973) The mode of action of imipramine and related drugs and their value in the treatment of different categories of enuresis nocturna. *Acta Paediatrica Scandinavica*, (suppl. 236), 63−64.

Pfaundler M. (1904) Demonstration eines Apparetes zur selbstatig Signalisieursang stattgehabter Bettnassung. *Verhandlungen der*

Gesellschaft Kinderheilkunde, **21**, 219−220.

Pompeius R. (1971) Cystometry in paediatric enuresis. *Scandinavian Journal of Urology and Nephrology*, **5**, 222−228.

Poussaint A.F., Koegler R.R. & Riehl J.L. (1967) Enuresis, epilepsy and the EEG. *American Journal of Psychiatry*, **123**, 1294−1295.

Ramsden P., Hindmarsh J.R., Price D., Yeates W. & Bowditch J. (1982) DDAVP for adult enuresis: a preliminary report. *British Journal of Urology*, **54**, 256−258.

Rapoport J.L., Mikkelsen E.J., Zavardil A., Nee L., Gruenau C., Mendelson W. & Gillin C. (1980) Childhood enuresis II. Psychopathology, tricylic concentration in plasma, and antienuretic effect. *Archives of General Psychiatry*, **37**, 1146−1152.

Redman J.E. & Seibert J.J. (1979) Urographic evaluation of the enuretic child. *Journal of Urology*, **122**, 699−801.

Rew D.A. & Rundle J.S.H. (1989) Assessment of the safety of regular DDAVP therapy in primary nocturnal enuresis. *British Journal of Urology*, **63**, 352−353.

Richardson D.W. & Robinson A.G. (1985) Desmopressin. *Annals of Internal Medicine*, **103**, 228−239.

Rittig S., Knudsen U., Nørgaard J., Pedersen E. & Djurhuus J. (1989) Abnormal diurnal rhythm of plasma vasopressin and urinary output in patients with enuresis. *American Journal of Physiology*, **256**, 664.

Roberts K.E. & Schoellkopf J.A. (1951) Eating, sleeping and elimination practices in a group of $2\frac{1}{2}$-year-olds. *American Journal of Diseases of Children*, **82**, 144−152.

Rohner T. & Sanford E. (1975) Imipramine toxicity. *Journal of Urology*, **114**, 402−403.

Rutter M.L., Graham P.J. & Yule W. (1970a) *A Neuropsychiatric Study in Childhood*. Clinics in Developmental Medicine, nos. 35/36. Heinemann/Spastics International Medical Publications, London.

Rutter M., Tizard J. & Whitmore K. (eds) (1970b) *Education, Health and Behaviour*. Longmans, London.

Rutter M.L., Yule W. & Graham P.J. (1973) Enuresis and behavioural deviance: some epidemiological considerations. In: Kolvin I., MacKeith R. & Meadow S.R. (eds) *Bladder Control and Enuresis*, pp. 137−147. Clinics in Developmental Medicine, nos. 48/49. Heinemann/Spastics International Medical Publications, London.

Saraf K., Klein D., Gittelman-Klein R., Gootman N. & Greenhill P. (1978) EKG effects of imipramine treatment in children. *Journal of the American Academy of Child Psychiatry*, **17**, 60−69.

Savage D.C.L., Wilson M.I., Ross E.M. & Fee W.M. (1969) Asymptomatic bacteriuria in girl entrants to Dundee primary schools. *British Medical Journal*, **3**, 75−80.

Schmitt B.D. (1982) Nocturnal enuresis: an update on treatment. *Pediatric Clinics of North America*, **29**, 21−31.

Schmitt B.D. (1986) New enuresis alarms: safe, successful and child operable. *Contemporary Pediatrics*, **3**, 1−6.

Shaffer D., Costello A.J. & Hill J.D. (1968) Control of enuresis with imipramine. *Archives of Disease in Childhood*, **43**, 665−671.

Shaffer D., Hedge B. & Stephenson J.D. (1978) Trial of an alpha adrenolytic drug (Indoramin) for noctural enuresis. *Developmental Medicine and Child Neurology*, **20**, 183−188.

Shaffer D., Stephenson J.D. & Thomas D.V. (1979) Some effects of imipramine on micturition and their relevance to their antienuretic activity. *Neuropharmacology*, **18**, 33−37.

Shaffer D., Gardner A. & Hedge B. (1984) Behavior and bladder disturbance in enuretic children: a rational classification of a common disorder. *Developmental Medicine and Child Neurology*, **26**, 781−792.

Shenoy R.S. (1980) Nocturnal enuresis caused by psychotropic drugs. *American Journal of Psychiatry*, **137**, 739−740.

Simeon J., Maguire J. & Lawrence S. (1981) Maprotiline effects in children with enuresis and behavioral disorders. *Progress in Neuropsychopharmacology*, **5**, 495−498.

Sloop E.W. & Kennedy W.A. (1973) Institutionalized retarded nocturnal enuretics treated by a conditioning technique. *American Journal of Mental Deficiency*, **77**, 717−721.

Smith D.R. (1969) Critique of the concept of vesical neck obstruction in children. *Journal of the American Medical Association*, **207**, 1686−1692.

Smith L.J. (1981) Training severely and profoundly mentally handicapped nocturnal enuretics. *Behaviour Research and Therapy*, **19**, 67−74.

Smith S. (1948) *The Psychological Origin and Treatment of Enuresis*. University of Washington Press, Seattle, WA.

Starfield S.B. (1967) Functional bladder capacity in enuretic and non-enuretic children. *Journal of Pediatrics*, **70**, 777−781.

Stein Z.A. & Susser M.W. (1965) Sociomedical study of enuresis among delinquent boys. *British Journal of Preventive and Social Medicine*, **19**, 174−181.

Stein Z.A., Susser M.W. & Wilson A.E. (1965) Families of enuretic children. I: Family type and age. II: Family culture, structure and organisation. *Developmental Medicine and Child Neurology*, **7**, 658−676.

Steinhausen H.C. & Gobel D. (1989) Enuresis in child psychiatric clinic patients. *Journal of the American Academy of Child and Adolescent Psychiatry*, **28**, 279−281.

Sukhai R.N., Mol J. & Harris A.S. (1989) Combined therapy of enuresis alarm and desmopressin in the treatment of nocturnal enuresis. *European Journal of Pediatrics*, **148**, 465−467.

Terho P. & Kekomaki M. (1984) Management of nocturnal enuresis with a vasopresin analogue. *Journal of Urology*, **131**, 952−957.

Thaustein J. & Halevi H.S. (1962) Enuresis among school entrants in the changing population of Israel. *British Journal of Preventive and Social Medicine*, **18**, 40−45.

Torrens M. & Hald T. (1979) Bladder denervation procedures. *Urological Clinics of North America*, **6**, 283−293.

Troup C.W. & Hodoson N.S. (1971) Nocturnal functional bladder capacity in enuretic children. *Journal of Urology*, **105**, 129−130.

Turner R.K. (1973) Conditioning, treatment of nocturnal enuresis: present studies. In: Kolvin I., MacKeith R. & Meadow S.R. (eds) *Bladder Control and Enuresis*, pp. 195−210. Clinics in Developmental Medicine, nos. 48/49. Heinemann/Spastics International Medical Publications, London.

Turner R., Young G. & Rachman S. (1970) Treatment of nocturnal enuresis by conditioning techniques. *Behaviour Research and Therapy*, **8**, 367−381.

Umphress A., Murphy E., Nickols J. & Hammar S. (1970) Adolescent enuresis. A social study of family interaction. *Archives of General Psychiatry*, **22**, 237−244.

Van Putten T., Malkin M.D. & Weiss M.S. (1972) Phenothiazine-induced stress incontinence. *Journal of Urology*, **109**, 625−626.

Verhulst F.C., Van Der Lee J.H., Akkerhuis G.W., Sanders-Woudstra J.A.R., Timmer F.C. & Donkhorst I.D. (1985) The prevalence of nocturnal enuresis: do DSM-III criteria need to be changed? A brief research report. *Journal of Child Psychology*, **26**, 989−993.

Wagner W.G. & Johnson J.T. (1988) Childhood nocturnal enuresis: the prediction of premature withdrawal from behavioral conditioning. *Journal of Abnormal Child Psychology*, **16**, 687−692.

Wallace I.R. & Forsythe W.I. (1969) The treatment of enuresis. A controlled clinical trial of propantheline, propantheline and phenobarbitone, and placebo. *British Journal of Clinical Practice*, **23**, 207−210.

Watanabe H. & Azuma Y. (1989) A proposal for a classification system of enuresis based on overnight simultaneous monitoring of electroencephalography and cystometry. *Sleep*, **12**, 257−264.

Werry J.S. & Cohrssen J. (1965) Enuresis: an etiologic and therapeutic study. *Journal of Pediatrics*, **67**, 423−431.

Westgren U., Wittstrom C. & Harris A.S. (1986) Oral desmopressin in central diabetes insipidus. *Archives of Disease in Children*, **61**, 247–250.

Whelan J.P. & Houts A.C. (1990) Effects of a waking schedule on primary enuretic children treated with full-spectrum home training. *Health Psychology*, **9**, 164–176.

Wille S. (1986) Comparison of desmopressin and enuresis alarm for nocturnal enuresis. *Archives of Disease in Children*, **61**, 30–33.

Young G.C. & Morgan R.T.T. (1972) Overlearning in the conditioning treatment of enuresis. *Behaviour Research and Therapy*, **10**, 147–151.

Young G.C. & Morgan R.T.T. (1973) Rapidity of response to the treatment of enuresis. *Developmental Medicine and Child Neurology*, **15**, 488–496.

Young G.C. & Turner R.K. (1965) CNS stimulant drugs and conditioning treatment of nocturnal enuresis. *Behaviour Research and Therapy*, **3**, 93–101.

Chapter 30
Faecal Soiling

Lionel Hersov

The term faecal soiling is used to describe disorders of bowel function and control excluding constipation without soiling occurring in children over a certain age in the absence of any structural abnormality or disease. It avoids arguments about the use and definition of terms such as encopresis and psychogenic megacolon. The age at which faecal incontinence is considered abnormal varies. In fact, there is much variation in the age at which control is achieved by children in different cultures (Whiting & Child, 1953; Anthony, 1957) and probably within our own culture, depending on parental expectation (Brazelton, 1962). Stein and Susser (1967), studying the development of bladder and bowel control in 671 British preschool children, concluded that seasonal variation, depth of sleep, family size, birth rank, maternal age, occupational class and economic status could not be shown to influence achievement of control. This was achieved by more than half the children in the age group of 18—24 months and almost all of the children aged $2\frac{1}{2}$ years had achieved this both by day and night. At 42—48 months, nearly 100% of the sample had achieved control. Quay and Werry (1972) suggest that these findings and those of Bellman (1966) point to 4 years as a more realistic minimum age for judging abnormality of bowel control.

EPIDEMIOLOGY

Bellman (1966) studied the prevalence of encopresis — the passage of relatively normal stools in inappropriate places including underclothing. She used a parent questionnaire for 8863 7-year-olds in their first year of school. Responses showed that bowel control was firmly established in the majority during the child's fourth year. There was a decreasing frequency of encopresis in the children until 16 years of age, when the numbers were practically zero. Among children between 7 and 8 years of age, the frequency was 1.5%, with boys (2.3%) predominant over girls (0.7%) in a ratio of 3.4 : 1. More recently, Rutter *et al.* (1970) found the presence of at least once-a-month soiling among 10—12-year-olds on the Isle of Wight to be 1.3% for boys and 0.3% for girls. Davie *et al.* (1972), using retrospective reports, found soiling by day after 5 years of age in slightly over 10% of children in their cohort study and this occurred three times more commonly in boys than girls. The higher rate in boys is also a con-

stant finding in clinical studies of soiling children attending paediatric and psychiatric clinics (Anthony, 1957; Davidson *et al.*, 1963; Berg & Jones, 1964; Olatawura, 1973; Levine, 1975). Rutter *et al.* (1970) also found a highly significant association between enuresis and soiling, in keeping with similar findings by Hallgren (1956), Davidson *et al.* (1963), Bellman (1966), Stein and Susser (1967) and Levine (1975).

CLASSIFICATION OF FAECAL INCONTINENCE

There have been many schemes of classification in the literature on soiling (Anthony, 1957; Pinkerton, 1958; Coekin & Gairdner, 1960; Easson, 1960; Davidson *et al.*, 1963; Woodmansey, 1967; Gavanski, 1971; Olatawura, 1973; Levine, 1982, 1983). These have emphasized variables such as constitutional factors in bowel function, psychodynamic factors in the child, factors in the school, deviant parent—child relationships and expectations with regard to bowel training. A classification based on physiological defecation dynamics will no doubt come in the future.

The differences in these clinical studies and the conclusions drawn from them are very likely to be artefacts of the different clinical populations seen by paediatricians and child and adolescent psychiatrists. Paediatricians are more likely to see younger children from socially disadvantaged homes whose soiling is due to faulty training (Berg & Jones, 1964), or short-lived cases of retention with overflow (Jolly, 1976; MacCarthy, 1976). They are less likely to see the older child whose pattern of faecal soiling is more fixed and often associated with gross personal pathology and family problems which make treatment difficult, for these are usually referred to the psychiatrist. The classification put forward here is based on the description of the soiling behaviour which is then used to identify the psychological mechanisms leading to the soiling. From this, a rational treatment plan can be derived which has its basis in a multifactorial formulation. A combined physical and psychological approach is required in most cases, whatever the initial cause might have been.

It is necessary to distinguish between 3 types of faecal soiling; (1) where it is known that there is adequate bowel control in the sense that the child can control the physiological process of defecation but deposits normal faeces in inappropriate places; this is also described as encopresis; (2) cases where there is a true failure to gain bowel control, as shown by the fact that the child is either unaware that he or she is soiling or, while being aware, is unable to control the bowels; and (3) cases in which the soiling is due to excessively fluid faeces which may be the result of diarrhoea due to physical disease or anxiety, or which may arise from constipation leading to retention with overflow. Faecal impaction may be found in three-quarters of such cases (Levine, 1975).

In the first group, where bowel control has been adequately established, stools are normal but control may break down in circumstances of psychological stress, e.g. birth of a sibling, admission to hospital, starting at school or a traumatic separation from parents and sexual abuse (Boon, 1991). Usually, control is regained when the stress is relieved, provided the situation is well-managed and the home environment stable. In other circumstances of psychological stress arising from parental disharmony, family instability and punitive management, there is no loss of control but the child may respond by depositing faeces in unlikely places, often, it appears, to cause maximum irritation to the family; there may also be smearing of faeces and other evidence of psychiatric disorder, including antisocial behaviour. At the same time, the children often show massive denial of soiling and covert aggressiveness in their dealings with other family members.

In the second group with failure to learn bowel control, the stools are normal in consistency and appearance, but deposited randomly in clothes, often both at school and at home. A few children may suffer from severe mental retardation or neurological disorders such as cerebral palsy or spina bifida, which impair their capacity to learn bowel control. Others, who are of normal intelligence and without major physical handicap, are often socially aggressive and come from socially disadvantaged families where parents may be limited in personality and intellect (Anthony, 1957; Easson, 1960; Berg & Jones, 1964; Rutter, 1975). The reasons for failure to gain control may be in faulty or inconsistent training or in stresses interfering with the acquisition of control during the toddler training period.

In the third group, the stools are abnormal in appearance and consistency, sometimes as the result of gastrointestinal disease and ulcerative colitis. Diarrhoea can also occur in states of severe anxiety, under stress, or when a child has to confront a situation which is greatly feared. In other children who pass small amounts of foul, watery stools, examination may reveal faecal masses in a palpable colon, a normal anal reflex but a rectum packed with hard faeces, so that retention with overflow is present (see Levine & Bakow, 1976, for a classification system according to degree of constipation and soiling). There may be a history of an episode of painful defecation possibly due to an anal fissure with holding back of stools, and eventually constipation and impaction. In other cases, there is a history of a constant struggle between parent and child over bowel training and use of the lavatory, associated with reluctance to open bowels and faecal retention in the mother's presence or near a pot or toilet (Garrard &

Richmond, 1952; Anthony, 1957; Pinkerton, 1958; Call *et al.*, 1963; Woodmansey, 1967).

Faecal soiling, unlike enuresis, occurs most commonly during the day, but occasionally the child may pass formed stools in the bedclothes. Soiling at night seems to have a poor prognosis (Levine, 1982). A rarer form of soiling at night is due to anal masturbation where bedclothes are stained but formed stools are only rarely passed (Clark *et al.*, 1990). Children will usually deny the behaviour, but inspection of the fingernails will often show faecal material, so giving a clue to the anal masturbation.

A fourth group display inappropriate toiletting behaviour on the basis of 'fear' of using the toilet. Such children fear sitting on the lavatory or even being near it, and several studies have recorded what might be described as toilet phobias (Gelber & Meyer, 1965; Ashkenazi, 1975; Doleys & Arnold, 1975). Others have described a pot refusal syndrome (Berg & Jones, 1964; Gavanski, 1971).

PHYSIOLOGY AND PSYCHOLOGY OF BOWEL CONTROL

Physiology

Normal faecal continence has been described by Gaston (1948) as the ability to retain faeces until is convenient. This ability results from the interplay of several functions. Firstly, there is the rectal response to distension by faecal material and the acute sensitivity of the upper anal canal to contact (Duthie & Gairns, 1960). Rectal sensation is difficult to define and children are often unable to respond to questions about whether they have a feeling of rectal fullness or can sense the passage of a stool. In normal people, distension of the lower rectum with a balloon produces pelvic floor discomfort and an associated sense of urgency (Parks, 1975).

Secondly, the motor element of the external sphincter and the puborectoanalis sling of the levator ani make up the striated sphincter together with the smooth muscle of the internal sphincter (Nixon, 1973). These two types of muscle serve different functions. The striated sphincter is able to contract strongly to prevent the passage of stool at an inconvenient time when it is forced down by a rectal contraction wave. This sphincter can only function for up to 30 seconds or so, long enough to contain the rectal contraction wave until it passes. The internal sphincter can maintain persistent tonic activity, so preventing leakage of stool between periods of rectal activity by maintaining closure of the resting anal canal. Both sphincter activities complement each other in conditions of normal continence, but clinical experience (Nixon, 1975) suggests that the external sphincter is of much less importance than the puborectoanalis sling and the internal sphincter.

Loening-Baucke and Younoszai (1982), after measuring anal sphincter function using a strain gauge, conclude that the basic problem in chronically constipated children appears to be an abnormal internal anal sphincter which is weak and less responsive to rectal distension than in nonconstipated children. Loening-Baucke and Cruikshank (1986) found that 46% of children with chronic constipation and encopresis were unable to defecate water-filled balloons — a much higher rate than in healthy children. They demonstrated that contraction of the external sphincter during defecation, instead of relaxation, was responsible for the failure to expel balloons. They argue that increased external sphincter activity during the act of bearing down for defecation prevents stool expulsion and could have caused the chronic faecal retention noted in the patients. The children who failed to expel balloons were significantly less likely than other children with soiling to recover after conventional laxative treatment. Wald *et al.* (1986) compared anorectal sensory and motor function, expulsion dynamics and continence mechanisms in encopretic and healthy children. They concluded that a significant number of boys with encopresis have abnormal anorectal expulsion dynamics which may contribute to chronic faecal retention and incontinence.

Anorectal manometry is now regarded as a standard procedure for the investigation of functional disorders of the anorectum, especially in the investigation of children with severe constipation where Hirschsprung's disease needs exclusion (Clayden & Agnarsson, 1991). Varying findings in anal pressures have been reported in children with constipation, probably due to the different types of equipment used. As further studies elucidate expulsion dynamics along the above lines, we can hope for the development of measures to differentiate chronic cases from others, and so lead into more rational treatments of faecal soiling in the future.

However, at present manometry should not be used in mild constipation, but should be considered if faulty anorectal expulsion dynamics are suspected in chronic cases of constipation and soiling. There is little, if any, place for biopsy and anal dilation in the usual case of faecal soiling.

Thirdly, in addition to mechanical support of muscles anchoring the anus which allows the muscles to act at a mechanical advantage, rectal motility to accommodate faeces is important. The resilience of the wall of the anal canal plays some part in maintaining the resting tone of the normal anal canal which is cleverly constructed to allow a weak muscle to resist a strong force. The motility of the anal muscle causes it to pucker into folds, as the canal is narrowed, so plugging the anal canal and exerting a strong obstructive action (Nixon, 1973).

Psychology

Bowel control is a very complex function, including involuntary peristaltic waves of contraction of the colon, the physiological mechanisms of sphincter function described above, and the voluntary initiation and delay of defecation under different conditions and in terms of different social and cultural demands. Voluntary defecation is a total neuromuscular response, not a simple localized reaction, and it involves maturational factors interacting with social learning. The development of patterns of bowel behaviour fluctuates as the child matures, and the acquisition of the new skill of bowel control must be understood in terms of greater maturity and personality differences, rather than just habit formation and learning (Gesell *et al.*, 1974).

By 40 weeks, the infant is able to sit and reacts adaptively to toilet training, but by 1 year, 'successes' are less frequent and resistance again appears. At 15 months, the child can stand upright and the irregularities and resistances lessen, for he or she now likes to go to the toilet, and some children instinctively assume the squat pattern. The developmental task is to achieve a working balance between contraction and relaxation, and at first, each comes under voluntary control separately. By 18 months, speech is developing and the articulate child who is able to say the word for toilet can relate this to the bowel movement, and so increase voluntary control. He or she will remain trained, unlike a second type of child who has the same amount of training but is slow in learning. He or she is not so apt with words and does not seize on the essentials of the toilet situation in terms of process and product. He or she may even smear stools, and does not relate the act of toilet-going to the social situation, or even to his or her mother and may pass a stool when standing in the playpen.

Gesell *et al.* (1974) point out that some 2-year-olds are often trainable if left to their own devices after their pants have been taken off. By the age of 3 years, there is increased ability to withhold and postpone, and the child accepts and even asks for help. Bowel function has become a private affair by the age of 4 years, with insistence on a closed toilet door with curiosity as to how bowel function occurs in others. The child is interested in the size, shape and colour and consistency of stools, outspoken in making comments and pleased with his or her productiveness.

Training, that is, regular sitting on the toilet after meals and praise when a stool is produced, works reasonably well in most children, and by 3 or 4 years of age, can be taken for granted, but some children appear to make no progress towards having bowel movements on the toilet. This can lead to disappointments and emotional tensions in parents, particularly where children engage in frequent stool-smearing as well. Parents may try to deal with this with punitive measures of varying severity, sometimes leading to habitual 'holding back' of stools, chronic constipation, rectal inertia and overflow incontinence (Nixon, 1961). The call to stool is diminished in the presence of an enlarged rectum and the absence of stretch required to produce the sensation of fullness.

Regularity of the bowels was almost the first rule of health in Victorian times, and the first subject asked about by a doctor in cases of illness. The process of bowel training was left to folk wisdom and oral tradition, and the subject was omitted entirely in otherwise comprehensive manuals of child care (Robertson, 1976).

Toilet training is a major topic of interest to modern writers on the subject of child care, and advice to mothers appears frequently in various magazine articles. The pendulum has swung from a rather casual approach in the 1950s to more structured advice, and it is likely that conflicting advice may often be given to a mother by her neighbours, the health visitor or the doctor in the maternity and child welfare clinic. Caldwell (1964), in a survey of the trends in the time of starting toilet training, concluded that this has gradually been postponed over the past 30 years or so. She has also commented that it is a universal training situation, that is, learning not to soil within the immediate living area is expected of infants in every human social group that has been observed. This is not confined to humans, for piglets learn to excrete in a corner of the pen away from the living area, and it appears that those piglets reared without their mothers have a random pattern of elimination and are continually dirty (Laird, 1973).

The use of the term training here does not imply a systematic and deliberate process according to protocol but the regular experience of a parent introducing a child to the use of the toilet followed by praise and encouragement for a successful result. Early coercive training means putting the young infant on the pot, hoping that a reflex response will lead to a result and keeping the child there for long periods until defecation occurs. The situation is very different in older children who are able to understand and use language. Here, associations are built up between a successful result and parents' satisfaction and approval until the child eventually makes the behaviour his or her own.

Studies on the reactions of children to bowel training (Huschka, 1942), using clinical case histories, found an association between training begun before 8 months of age and completed by 18 months and emotional disturbance in the children. Prugh (1954) found a high incidence of constipation and faecal incontinence in boys (and, to a lesser extent, girls) who had been trained early and coercively according to Huschka's (1942) criteria. Both studies are open to criticism on the grounds of unreliability of parents' accounts of past toilet training.

Anthony (1957) set out to investigate the alleged causal relationships between bowel training, bowel functioning and the presence of certain subsequent negative attitudes in the children. The initial focus on the act of soiling and the precipitating effect proved fruitless, as abnormal toilet functioning had by then become an automatic and stereotyped activity. The abnormal training methods of mothers of soiling children then became the main subject for investigation. Anthony (1957) drew attention to the 'potting couple', a situation between mother and child that has a system of stimulus cues for communication. Under normal conditions, the mother responds promptly to the child's physiological cues, and her own communications in return make the child aware of his or her own cues, so that he or she is able to achieve eventual autonomy in bowel function. However, there were some mothers in the study who missed the stimulus cues so that their child's learning became deficient, and others who misinterpreted cues and responded inappropriately without regularly reinforcing the appropriate behaviour.

There are problems in the hypothesis that abnormal training methods lead to bowel dysfunction. Not all children who are coercively trained develop faecal soiling, and not all children who have bowel dysfunction experience abnormal training. Moreover, in primitive societies, children who receive deviant training according to our standards do not appear prone to bowel dysfunction. Anthony (1957) suggested that the degree of coercion is but one factor within the context of the total mother—child situation and may have different effects depending on the mother's motivation and degree of general responsiveness to the child's needs.

Anthony (1957) used an ingenious experimental method to study the connections between methods of toilet training and encopresis (defined here as the regular passage of a formed motion of normal consistency into clothes, bedclothes or any receptacle not intended for the purpose). Seventy-six clinic children aged 4–15 years were studied, and at least three types of soiling were identified: (1) *continuous* — children who do not appear ever to have been continent and whose soiling is part of a general messiness and lack of concern for cleanliness; (2) *discontinuous* — children with faecal soiling in contrast to the orderly tenor and cleanliness of their everyday life. They usually have normal stools with a few showing episodic retention; and (3) *retentive* — children with stubborn constipation later giving way to soiling. Statistically significant associations were found between continuous soiling and neglectful training, and between coercive training and the discontinuous and retentive group. The paper contains a mass of clinical observations and vivid descriptions of parental attitudes, family interactions and children's behaviour. It is often difficult to separate the statistically significant findings from the rest of the detail and therefore to discern the frequency of differentiating factors between the three groups, for the descriptions are composite rather than discrete.

ASSOCIATED FACTORS

Constitutional factors

Coekin and Gairdner (1960) analysed 69 cases of soiling and found 44 in which they maintained soiling could be very simply accounted for on a mechanical basis with primary constipation. A history of constipation in the first 6 months of life was present in 12 (27%) of the cases. They gave case histories to support their contention of a congenital basis for constipation in these children and argue that in the remaining 7% of cases, a congenital factor provided a predisposition to later constipation and soiling. This view of constipation and soiling finds little support, apart from Davidson *et al.* (1963) who write of predisposition to constipation and formed stools, rendering the child more amenable to toilet training and consequent early control over defecation.

Psychogenic factors in the child

Coekin and Gairdner (1960) also judged psychogenic factors to play an important or predominant part in a smaller group of cases and feel the term encopresis is more appropriately applied to these. There was less evidence of constipation and only a few showed faecal masses in the abdomen, so that in the majority, the stool passed was of normal consistency but was studiously deposited in the wrong place. They remarked, too, that nearly all the children showed obvious signs of emotional disorder and many came from 'unsatisfactory' homes. Bemporad (1978) describes an entrenched personality disorder often complicated by organic problems and reinforced by disturbed family relations.

Family pathology

Later papers on supposed family factors (Bemporad *et al.*, 1971; Hoag *et al.*, 1971; Baird, 1974; Bemporad, 1978) have not provided convincing data of any particular pattern of family structure and function that can be clearly differentiated from that found in other types of childhood psychiatric disorder, although Wolters (1974) found a high frequency of family disharmony and marital problems.

Developmental factors in the child

Slow language development and poor coordination have been noted (Bemporad *et al.*, 1971), while Olatawura (1973) recorded low intelligence, neurological impairment and associated neurotic and developmental disorder among his group of discontinuous encopretics. McTaggart and Scott (1959) described enuresis, stubbornness and negativism, immature speech, hyperactivity, temper tantrums, withdrawal, school phobia, feeding problems, transvestism and firesetting as associated factors in 10 out of 12 children with encopresis. It is difficult to decide from the above data whether such behaviour is primary or secondary to the encopresis, although Bellman (1966) inclined to the view that they are probably aetiological rather than secondary to the encopresis.

There is also confusion in the literature over the significance of soiling as an indicator of psychiatric disorder. It can obviously coexist with other psychiatric disorders. Some regard it as evidence of serious general disturbance in psychological function, others as a developmental disorder in itself, with persistent soiling followed by secondary disturbance of affect, interpersonal behaviour and relationships. In younger children, successful treatment of the soiling results in concomitant disappearance of the associated symptoms and improvement in disturbed parent–child relationships. In older children, both the soiling and the associated difficulties have proved more difficult to alter for the better.

MANAGEMENT

Management of the individual case depends on a comprehensive assessment of the type of faecal soiling and the mechanisms responsible for its occurrence (see the section on classification, above), including evaluation of possible organic factors affecting bowel function such as Hirschsprung's disease (Vaughan *et al.*, 1975), a developmental and family history, clinical interviews and physical examination and records of toilet-going behaviour. The latter help define the pattern of soiling — parent and child motivation for treatment and ability to comprehend, follow and carry out instructions. Levine (1982) favours a plain X-ray of the lower abdomen, with appropriate safeguards, for the detection of abundant retained faeces, and regards a barium enema as seldom, if ever, necessary.

It can be argued that a child with a constipated loaded colon is easy to spot and that clinical examination would reveal this. Under these circumstances an X-ray is unnecessary. Demonstration by X-ray of a loaded colon to patient and parents may have some advantages in explaining the clinical picture.

The records of toiletting behaviour provide a baseline for the assessment of treatment effects. This should include frequency, magnitude of each episode, where and when it occurred and whether or not the lavatory was appropriately used. Attention should also be paid to whether or not appropriate toiletting occurred, rather than just a focus on accidents, with special attention paid to the occurrence of 'fear' (Doleys, 1983).

If the pattern of soiling seems mainly that of a younger child who has failed to gain bowel control, some form of bowel training is needed. Attention will also be required to the wider social and psychological problems which are usually found in the families of these children. Various procedures can be used, such as simple star charts recording success in using the toilet regularly, or more complex schemes of material and social reinforcement contingent on normal defecation in the toilet (Neale, 1963; Gelber & Meyer, 1965; Sluckin, 1975; Doleys, 1983; Fielding & Doleys, 1988).

In those cases where soiling is due to secondary overflow of loose motions from partial blockage of the bowel, examination will reveal the reasons for this in the form of palpable faecal masses on abdominal palpation (Bell & Levine, 1954), as well as a packed rectum on digital anal examination, and a characteristic X-ray appearance of the rectum (Barr *et al.*, 1979). This clinical picture can arise in different ways. Young children may experience pain on defecation due to the passage of large hard faeces, or a lesion such as an anal fissure. They come to fear going to the lavatory, hold back their faeces and become constipated. In severe cases, there is a diminution in the normal call to stool (Nixon, 1975) so that the previously existing regular pattern is now disrupted and increasing faecal impaction occurs. A second mechanism leading to retention comes into play when there is a struggle between parents and child over toilet training. A parent using strict coercive methods and punishment may encounter a child striving for autonomy who refuses to open the bowels on demand. This response may increase punitive attempts to make the child conform, leading to negativism and fearfulness in the child, and finally severe constipation, bowel distension and overflow of fluid faeces.

In both instances, the first line of treatment is to clear the blockage of faeces in the bowel, for this will remove pain and fear, especially in the younger child, and prevent gross impaction of faeces in the pelvis which may cause retention of urine

(MacCarthy, 1976). Bowel washouts are considered appropriate in severe cases (Nixon, 1961), but this approach is criticized by Berg and Jones (1964) and Jolly (1976) on the grounds that it merely produces temporary emptying of the bowels without dealing with the basic psychological mechanisms of retention. If the relationship between physiological events and the psychological factors is considered when problems arise, a combined physiological and psychological approach is needed regardless of the initial cause (Clayden & Agnarsson, 1991).

For this reason many clinicians try to tailor the treatment to the individual child. Some clinicians favour enemas initially — either a phosphate enema or the use of a microenema containing sodium alkylsulphoacetate (Micralax). The child is then put on a regular bowel training programme using senna laxatives, usually with a stool softener such as docusate or lactulose to ensure the passage of soft, painless stools. Any painful anal conditions should be treated, but it is often more important to try to alter the struggle between parent and child over toilet training or soiling, along with other faulty patterns of interaction. Sometimes methods of bowel training using systematic reinforcement have been effective without parent participation (Neale, 1963; Young & Goldsmith, 1972), but there are many advantages in the involvement of parents in a retraining programme. Tensions may exist in a family so that the soiling child is liable to be scapegoated for general uncleanliness and negative behaviour, and some form of parental counselling is usually required to ensure that treatment is carried out systematically and not given up if immediate success is not achieved.

Levine (1982) has developed a treatment approach that emphasizes education and demystification of patient and parents. They both need to be reassured that many other children have the same problem, in the hope that this will counter the feeling of isolation that is often felt. Levine (1983) uses drawings and diagrams to show patient and parents the abnormal mechanisms of stretched-out bowels that have lost their 'feelings' and muscle tone. The function of the normal colon is explained and then a plausible explanation of the particular child's problems of retention. Treatment consists of enemas, suppositories, a bowel training programme and follow-up. This can be carried out on an outpatient basis, but Levine (1983) stresses the importance of vigorous catharsis at the outset. In a few cases, hospitalization is required for the initial clearout or when it is detrimental for the parents to be giving enemas to their child. Clayden and Agnarsson (1991) have developed a booklet which is given out routinely to the children attending their clinics. The language is aimed at 10–12-year-olds but can be read by younger children. It aims to demystify the subject and facilitate better cooperation with treatment.

Doleys (1983) and Fielding and Doleys (1988) review behavioural procedures in the treatment of soiling, focusing on the arrangements of environmental consequences to initiate and establish appropriate behaviour. In clear discussions of the various methods used, emphasis is placed on defining the target behaviour for treatment which may differ in individual children, depending on the particular patterns of soiling and its associated factors, such as the retention or nonretention of faeces. The goal of treatment is regular independent use of the toilet, but follow-up should continue for 18–24 months past treatment because of the risk of relapse, which is high and sometimes requires years of treatment (Levine, 1983).

Those children who have apparently achieved bowel control and then begin soiling as part of a more general psychiatric disorder often prove difficult to treat because of abnormal emotional and behavioural traits in the child, and deviant parental and family attitudes towards the developing child's emotional and social needs. Such children may need a combination of different forms of treatment aimed in the first instance at relieving constipation. Many children can reduce or even avoid constipation by increasing their intake of dietary fibre by including fruit and sources of green fibre, as well as proprietary cereals containing bran. Once constipation is relieved, a system of simple rewards for regular toilet use is begun (Neale, 1963). Very often, the child suffers much guilt, shame and anxiety, and the family show obsessional traits and overconcern about cleanliness, requiring some form of family therapy to deal with these attitudes and other problems of family interaction. A bowel training programme may be difficult to carry out while family tensions are high, but can be introduced effectively at a later stage if the soiling is continuing as a habit.

Young and Goldsmith (1972) describe an interesting combination of individual psychotherapy, milieu therapy and behaviour modification in the treatment of a 9-year-old boy attending a day-treatment centre. Encopresis began at age 7 years during a visit to a relative, associated with enuresis, anxiety, uncleanliness, petty stealing and compulsive collecting. Two years of individual psychotherapy, parental casework and environmental manipulation had little effect on the cause of the encopresis, which flared up in stress situations of separation, rejection by peers, fear of teacher and crisis at home. A behaviour modification programme was set up in which the boy chose his own reinforcers and took part in buying them. With improvement in soiling, this meek, submissive and passive boy displayed violent attacks on his peers, disruptive classroom behaviour and aggression in therapy sessions. Similar behaviour was reported by Balson (1973) in an 8-year-old boy in treatment. Both case reports discussed the issue of symptom substitution and concluded that the aggressive behaviour was probably primary, so that successful treatment of the secondary (defensive) soiling led to its reemergence. Young and Goldsmith (1972) also pointed out that the parents did not participate at all in the treatment programme beyond providing clean underwear, but that the change in behaviour did generalize to the child's total living situation, although it was entirely carried out in the day centre.

Olness et al. (1980) used biofeedback in 40 patients aged 4–15 years with histories of chronic constipation and soiling, ranging from 3 to 15 years. All had undergone multiple diagnostic studies and treatment. A balloon inserted in the anus at the level of internal and external sphincter transmitted pressure changes to an oscilloscope visible to the children. They were trained to alter their sphincteric responses voluntarily using anal and buttock muscles. The usual laxatives and enemas were discontinued, and regular toilet-going was emphasized. The authors claim the 24 patients acquired normal bowel habits with complete cessation of soiling, while 14 continued minor soiling. Three out of 6 children with associated nocturnal enuresis became dry in a month. The treatment was not recommended as the initial therapy of choice for very young children and only after a thorough trial of other methods. Other workers have used direct conditioning of the anal sphincter (Kohlenberg, 1973; Engel *et al.*, 1974).

At present, the most important lines of treatment include assessment of the degree of constipation underlying faecal soiling and treatment of this with appropriate enemas, laxatives, stool softeners and high-fibre diet. Coincidentally, a behavioural programme to establish regular and effective toilet use and defecation should be established, allied to demystification of the problem using drawings and diagrams. The parents should be closely involved in the treatment programme from the outset. While many cases can be effectively treated as outpatients, some will need hospital admission for a short period for closer supervision of treatment. In all cases, regular follow-up to maintain the treatment programme is crucial because of the risk of relapse and this may need to be continued for some time.

RESULTS OF TREATMENT

Bellman (1966), in a follow-up of 186 children with encopresis seen at two psychiatric clinics, found a steady decline of the symptoms from age 6 years in boys and 8 years in girls until it disappeared in all by 10 years, except for relapses in 2 cases at 17 and 19 years respectively. There are few controlled trials of treatment, so that the relative effectiveness of different types of treatment is most difficult to judge. Coekin and Gairdner (1960) and Davidson *et al.* (1963) claimed a high success rate (80–90%) in soiling with constipation using laxatives and enemas. Good results with psychotherapy were claimed by McTaggart and Scott (1959), with 10 out of 12 children either cured or improved, while Pinkerton (1958) recorded success in 21 of 30 cases using three techniques of eliciting fantasy, free drawing and expression of aggression. Berg and Jones (1964) claimed freedom from symptoms for a minimum of 6 months in 33 of 38 cases (87%) with severe constipation, using a combination of oral laxatives and simple psychological treatment. The results were also good (8 successful out of 10 cases) in those with training problems without constipation.

Levine and Bakow (1976) treated 127 children (mean age 8 years 2 months; 87% boys, 13% girls) with a mean duration of soiling of 3 years. Half of the sample were free of symptoms (i.e. had gone 6 months without soiling) within 1 year of the start of treatment. Over one-quarter showed marked improvement and a little under one-tenth were essentially unchanged.

The latter included children with a high level of behavioural, developmental and academic problems. Landman *et al.* (1983) set out certain features in the history which define a high-risk group at first presentation. These include soiling accidents at night, hyperactivity and attention deficit disorder and external locus of control, which appears to make internalizing new attitudes on the problem difficult for the child. Such children require a broader interdisciplinary approach from the outset than the closely monitored paediatric approach which led to symptomatic improvement in the majority of cases.

Berg *et al.* (1983) carried out a double-blind randomly controlled trial of laxative (Senokot) in moderate dosage in 40 children with severe and persistent soiling, often with a history of faecal retention, who had all received much prior treatment from family doctors and paediatricians. At least one-third failed to respond, even though significant improvement occurred overall following 3 months' outpatient treatment using a behavioural approach and laxative, placebo or no medication. It appeared that the laxative used as a supplement to behavioural treatment did not help relieve the problem in those children who did not respond to the original trial, and who were continued in treatment for a further 3 months. Those children who do not respond to behavioural management in this form may need to be considered for hospital inpatient treatment where treatment can be more intensive and more control can be exercised.

CONCLUSIONS

The evidence to date suggests a multifactorial aetiology for faecal soiling, and that soiling often occurs in the context of a broader emotional disturbance. Physiological predisposition to a particular pattern of bowel function may play a part, together with the age at which bowel training is begun and the methods of training used. Parent–child relationships, family structure and function and environmental stresses are also influential, possibly more so in those cases of faecal soiling which are associated with a diagnosable psychiatric disorder. It is clear that no single treatment will suffice for the varieties of soiling encountered in clinical practice. A programme embodying several methods of treatment, including counselling, individual and family therapy and behaviour modification in various combinations, as well as the use of enemas, laxatives, softeners and high-fibre diet, should be instituted in terms of the type of faecal soiling and the underlying mechanisms. Newer techniques of anorectal manometry should in time become regular aids to diagnosis. These methods of diagnosis and treatment will be effective in the majority of children treated as outpatients, but in some difficult problems the resources of a day-hospital or an inpatient unit may be required.

REFERENCES

Anthony E.J. (1957) An experimental approach to the psycho-pathology of childhood: encopresis. *British Journal of Medical Psychology*, **30**, 146–175.

Ashkenazi Z. (1975) The treatment of encopresis using a discriminative stimulus and positive reinforcement. *Journal of Behaviour Therapy and Experimental Psychiatry*, **6**, 155−157.

Baird M. (1974) Characteristic interaction patterns in families of encopretic children. *Bulletin of the Menninger Clinic*, **38**, 144−153.

Balson P.M. (1973) Case study: encopresis. A case with symptom substitution. *Behaviour Therapy*, **4**, 134−136.

Barr R.G., Levine M.D. & Wilkinson R.H. (1979) Occult stool retention. A clinical tool for the evaluation in school-aged children. *Clinical Paediatrics*, **18**, 674−686.

Bell A.I. & Levine M.I. (1954) The psychological aspects of paediatric practice. 1 Causes and treatment of chronic constipation. *Paediatrics*, **14**, 259−266.

Bellman M. (1966) Studies on encopresis. *Acta Paediatrica Scandinavica*, (suppl), 170.

Bemporad J.R. (1978) Encopresis. In: Wolman B., Egon J. & Ross A. (eds) *Handbook of Treatment of Mental Disorders in Childhood and Adolescence*. Prentice Hall, New Jersey.

Bemporad J.L., Pfeifer C.M., Gibb L., Cortner R.H. & Bloom W. (1971) Characteristics of encopretic patients and their families. *Journal of the American Academy of Child Psychiatry*, **10**, 272−292.

Berg I. & Jones K.V. (1964) Functional faecal incontinence in children. *Archives of Diseases in Childhood*, **39**, 465−472.

Berg I., Forsythe I., Holt P. & Watts J. (1983) A controlled trial of Senokot in faecal soiling treated by behavioural methods. Journal of Child Psychology and Psychiatry, **23**, 543−549.

Boon F. (1991) Encopresis and sexual assault. *Journal of the American Academy of Child and Adolescent Psychiatry*, **30**, 479−482.

Brazelton T.B. (1962) A child-orientated approach to toilet training. *Paediatrics*, **29**, 121−128.

Caldwell B.M. (1964) The effects of infant care. In: Hoffman M.L. & Hoffman L.W. (eds) *Review of Child Development Research*, vol. 1, pp. 80−87. Russell Sage Foundation, New York.

Call J.D., Christianson M., Penrose F.R. & Backlar M. (1963) Psychogenic megacolon in three pre-school boys. A study of aetiology through collaborative treatment of child and parents. *American Journal of Orthopsychiatry*, **33**, 923−928.

Clark A.F., Taylor P.J. & Bhates S.R. (1990) Nocturnal faecal soiling and anal masturbation. *Archives of Disease in Childhood*, **65**, 1367−1368.

Clayden G. & Agnarsson U. (1991) *Constipation in Childhood*. Oxford University Press, Oxford.

Coekin M. & Gairdner D. (1960) Faecal incontinence in children. *British Medical Journal*, **2**, 1175−1180.

Davidson M., Kugler M. & Bauer C. (1963) Diagnosis and management in children with severe and protracted constipation and obstipation. *Journal of Paediatrics*, **62**, 261−275.

Davie R., Butler N. & Goldstein H. (1972) *From Birth to Seven*. Longman, London.

Doleys D.M. (1983) Enuresis and encopresis. In: Ollendick T.H. & Hersen M. (eds) *Handbook of Child Psychopathology*, pp. 201−226. Plenum Press, New York.

Doleys D.M. & Arnold S. (1975) Treatment of childhood encopresis: full cleanliness training. *Mental Retardation*, **13**, 14−16.

Duthie H.L. & Gairns F.W. (1960) Sensory nerve endings and sensation in the anal region of man. *British Journal of Surgery*, **47**, 585−595.

Easson R.I. (1960) Encopresis-psychogenic soiling. *Canadian Medical Association Journal*, **82**, 624−628.

Engel B.T., Nikoomanesh P. & Schuster M.M. (1974) Operant conditioning of rectosphincteric responses in the treatment of faecal incontinence. *New England Journal of Medicine*, **290**, 646−649.

Fielding D.M. & Doleys D.M. (1988) Elimination problems: enuresis and encopresis. In: Mash E.J. & Terdal L.G. (eds) *Behavioral Assessment of Childhood Disorders*, 2nd edn, pp. 586−623. Guilford Press, New York.

Garrard S.O. & Richmond J.B. (1952) Psychogenic megacolon manifested by faecal soiling. *Paediatrics*, **10**, 474−581.

Gaston E.A. (1948) The physiology of faecal continence. *Surgical Gynecology and Obstetrics*, **87**, 280−290.

Gavanksi M. (1971) The treatment of non-retentive secondary encopresis with imipramine and psychotherapy. *Canadian Medical Association Journal*, **104**, 227−231.

Gelber H. & Meyer V. (1965) Behaviour therapy and encopresis, the complexities involved in treatment. *Behaviour Research and Therapy*, **2**, 227−231.

Gesell A., Ilg F.L. & Ames L.B. (1974) *Infant and Child in the Culture of Today*, revised edn. Harper Row, New York.

Hallgren B. (1956) Enuresis I: a study with references to the morbidity risk and symptomatology. *Acta Psychiatrica Scandinavica*, **31**, 379−403.

Hoag J.M., Norriss N.G., Himeno E.T. & Jacobs J. (1971) The encopretic child and his family. *Journal of the American Academy Child Psychiatry*, **10**, 242−256.

Huschka M. (1942) The child's response to coercive bowel training. *Psychosomatic Medicine*, **4**, 301−308.

Jolly H. (1976) A paediatrician's view on the management of encopresis. *Proceedings of the Royal Society of Medicine*, **69**, 21−22.

Kohlenberg R.J. (1973) Operant conditioning of human anal sphincter pressure. *Journal of Applied Behavior Analysis*, **6**, 201−208.

Laird R. (1973) The excretory habits of piglets. In: Kolvin I., MacKeith R. & Meadow S.R. (eds) *Bladder Control and Enuresis*, p. 22. Clinics in Developmental Medicine nos. 48/49. Spastics International Medical Publications/Heinemann, London.

Landman G.B., Levine M.D. & Rappaport L. (1983) A study of treatment resistance among children referred for encopresis. *Clinical Paediatrics*, **23**, 499−505.

Levine M.D. (1975) Children with encopresis: a descriptive analysis. *Paediatrics*, **56**, 412−416.

Levine M.D. (1982) Encopresis, its potentiation evaluation and alleviation. *Medical Clinics of North America*, **29**, 315−330.

Levine M.D. (1983) Encopresis. In: Levine M.D., Carey W.B., Crocker A.C. & Gross R.T. (eds) *Developmental Behavioral Pediatrics*, pp. 586−595. W.B. Saunders, Philadelphia.

Levine M.D. & Bakow H. (1976) Children with encopresis; a study of treatment outcome. *Paediatrics*, **50**, 845−852.

Loening-Baucke V. & Cruikshank B.M. (1986) Abnormal defecation dynamics in chronically constipated children with encopresis. *Journal of Pediatrics*, **108**, 562−566.

Loening-Baucke V.A. & Younoszai M.K. (1982) Abnormal anal sphincter response in chronically constipated children. *Journal of Pediatrics*, **100**, 213−218.

MacCarthy D. (1976) Encopresis. *Proceedings of the Royal Society of Medicine*, **69**, 19−20.

McTaggart A. & Scott M. (1959) A review of twelve cases of encopresis. *Journal of Pediatrics*, **54**, 762−768.

Neale D.H. (1963) Behavior therapy and encopresis in children. *Behavioural Residential Therapy*, **1**, 139−149.

Nixon H. (1961) Discussion of megacolon and megarectum. *Proceedings of the Royal Society of Medicine*, **54**, 1037.

Nixon H. (1973) Sphincter cripples. *Proceedings of the Royal Society of Medicine*, **66**, 575−578.

Nixon H. (1975) The diagnosis and management of faecal incontinence in children. *Archive Chirugia. Neerlandicum*, **27**, 171−177.

Olatawura M. (1973) Encopresis: a review of thirty-two cases. *Acta Paediatrica Scandinavica*, **62**, 358−364.

Olness K., McParland F.A. & Piper J. (1980) Biofeedback: a new modality in the management of children with faecal soiling. *Journal of Pediatrics*, **96**, 505−509.

Parks A. (1975) Anorectal incontinence. *Proceedings of the Royal Society of Medicine*, **68**, 21–30.

Pinkerton P. (1958) Psychogenic megacolon in children: the implications of bowel negativism. *Archives of Disease in Childhood*, **33**, 371–398.

Prugh D.G. (1954) Childhood experience and colonic disorder. *Annals of the New York Academy of Science*, **58**, 355–376.

Quay H.C. & Werry J.S. (eds) (1972) *Psychopathological Disorders in Childhood*. Wiley, New York.

Robertson P. (1976) Home as a nest: middle class childhood in nineteenth-century Europe. In: de Mause L. (ed) *The History of Childhood*. Souvenir Press, London.

Rutter M. (1975) *Helping Troubled Children*. Penguin, Harmondsworth.

Rutter M., Tizard J. & Whitmore K. (eds) (1970) *Education, Health and Behaviour*. Longman, London.

Sears R.R., Macoby E.E. & Levine H. (1957) *Patterns of Child Rearing*. Row Peterson, Evanston, IL.

Sluckin A. (1975) Encopresis: a behavioral approach described. *Social Work Today*, **5**, 643–646.

Stein Z. & Susser M. (1967) Social factors in the development of sphincter control. *Developmental Medicine and Child Neurology*, **9**, 692–700.

Vaughan V.C., McKay R.J. & Nelson W.E. (1975) *Textbook of Pediatrics*, 10th edn. W.B. Saunders, Philadelphia.

Wald A., Chandra R., Chiponis D. & Gabel S. (1986) Anorectal function and continence mechanisms in childhood encopresis. *Journal of Paediatric Gastroenterology and Nutrition*, **5**, 346–351.

Whiting J.W. & Child I.L. (1953) *Child Training and Personality*. Yale University Press, New Haven, CT.

Wolters W.H.G. (1974) *Kinderin mid Encopresis: een Psychosomatische Benadering*. Elinkivijk, Utrecht.

Woodmansey A.C. (1967) Emotion and the motions: an inquiry into the causes and prevention of functional disorders of defecation. *British Journal of Medical Psychology*, **40**, 207–223.

Young G.I. & Goldsmith A. (1972) Treatment of encopresis in a day treatment program. *Psychotherapy Theory, Research and Practice*, **9**, 231–235.

Chapter 31
Drug and Alcohol Use and Misuse

Michael Farrell & Eric Taylor

INTRODUCTION

Preventing young people from embarking on substance misuse has long been, and remains, a priority for society. Adults and parents now perceive that their children frequently live in environments with high levels of drug availability, both legal and illegal. Young people should be provided with factual information about drugs to help them make responsible decisions that minimize the risk to their health and future well-being. It is a reasonable assumption that the larger the number of young people who experiment with a range of drugs, the larger will be the number who develop problems related to drug use.

Young people may be puzzled by the behaviour of their adult role models, who consume tobacco despite the clear warnings on the health risks associated and may also consume alcohol in a manner that is hazardous to health. Many teenagers of both sexes continue to initiate tobacco smoking (Warburton *et al.*, 1991) and perceive themselves as taking acceptable risks when they consume certain drugs.

To date there is little information to indicate what proportion of drug experimenters will develop problems or who is more likely to do so. Broad prevention strategies in the field of education (Schinke *et al.*, 1991) are therefore the central thrust of social approaches to young people's substance use.

What is a drug problem?

Many descriptive terms are unsatisfactory: words such as addict, junkie, dipsomaniac and alcoholic are not only imprecise but also value-laden. Some progress has been made towards a better terminology. Although the boundaries between drug use and drug misuse are poorly defined, the concepts remain useful.

The Royal College of Psychiatrists (1987), wishing to emphasize potential risks, deliberately adopted a broad definition of drug misuse in terms of the use of substances that threatened harm to the individual or to society. However, their use by any individual does not necessarily bring harm to that person and, in treating patients, it is preferable to adopt the clinical perspective of the *problem drug-taker*, defined as 'Any person who experiences social, psychological, physical or legal problems related to intoxication and/or regular excessive consumption and/or dependence as a consequence of his own use of drugs or other chemical substances' (Advisory Council on the Misuse of Drugs, 1982).

Different aspects of drug and alcohol misuse need to be distinguished, because they do not all appear in the same individuals. The World Health Organization *Document on Nomenclature and Classification* (1981) made a helpful distinction between the following forms of substance-related problem:

1 *Unsanctioned use*: use of a drug that is not approved by society, or by a group within that society.

2 *Hazardous use*: use of a drug that will probably lead to harmful consequences for the user — either dysfunction or harm.

3 *Dysfunctional use*: use of a drug that leads to impaired psychological or social functioning (e.g. loss of job or marital problems).

4 *Harmful use*: use of a drug that is known to have caused tissue damage or mental illness in a particular person. One type of dysfunctional and harmful use is *dependence*. This is a cluster of phenomena related to difficulty in refraining from repeated drug taking. They include a sense of compulsion to take the substances involved, a wish to stop in the face of continued use, the presence of tolerance and withdrawal symptoms and the use of the substances to suppress withdrawal symptoms, and rapid return to using the substances even after a period of voluntary abstinence. They constitute one of the dimensions of substance misuse.

DSM-IV (American Psychiatric Association, in press) and ICD-10 (World Health Organization, 1992) have adopted this kind of broad approach, making a distinction between consumption, dependence symptoms and adverse consequences. In DSM-III-R (American Psychiatric Association, 1987) 'psychoactive substance abuse' was characterized as maladaptive and lasting for a period greater than 1 month and was distinguished from psychoactive substance dependence by lack of withdrawal symptoms. In ICD-10 (World Health Organization, 1992) the type of psychoactive substance used is first classified, followed by its further categorization into hazardous, harmful or dependent patterns of use (or withdrawal, intoxication, psychotic or other organic syndromes resulting from the substance). DSM-IV (American Psychiatric Association, in press) takes a similar line.

These distinctions can be difficult to make for young people, and the borderline between experimental and group use on the one hand and the various patterns of misuse on the other is hard to draw. The decision is perhaps easiest when clear dependence is evident but, at least as judged by self-descriptions, this is less common in adolescents than in adults. Research on drinking has emphasized two main dimensions — intensity of use and use-related problems (White, 1987), both of which may range from mild to severe.

PREVALENCE OF ALCOHOL AND DRUG USE

Drug use and drug availability are very different from three decades ago. Many young people experiment with a range of drugs and only a few will go on to use them on a more regular or problematic basis. There may, of course, be substantial problems arising from experimental use, such as the deaths that can result from first-time solvent inhalation. Nevertheless, it is a weakness of many population studies that they report only the frequency of drugs 'ever used'. Ideally there should be data on the quantity and frequency of all drug use. Some estimation could be then made of the range of populations at risk and the critical thresholds for cumulative risk.

The drugs most widely used by adolescents are those that are most socially acceptable — alcohol, tobacco and marijuana. The greatest morbidity is incurred from the use of alcohol and tobacco. In a survey by the British Office of Population Censuses and Surveys (1986) 79% of 13-year-olds said that they had drunk alcohol and 29% that they usually drank once a week. At this age, the great majority drank at home but by the age of 15 43% said that they drank in public houses. By 17 years of age, 90% have consumed alcohol at least once and 62% drink in public houses. Swadi (1988) reported comparable figures from a self-report study of London schoolchildren. More than 10% of 11–16-year-olds were using alcohol as often as once a week or more.

The figures for illicit drug use are scanty and may not be very reliable; their validity has not been examined against other measures of drug use. Swadi (1988) asked some 3000 London schoolchildren about their use of solvents or illegal drugs; the numbers who had ever tried any of these rose from 13% at the age of 11 to 26% at 16. Regular use rose more sharply, from 2 to 16%. Estimates of the misuse of volatile substances range from 3 to 11% in children at secondary school (Swadi, 1988; Chadwick et al., 1989; Edeh, 1989).

The use of *minor tranquillizers* by adolescents is likely to reflect the availability of these drugs in their homes. Both British and American studies suggest that 5–10% of young people have taken nonprescribed tranquillizers but that very few are involved in their regular consumption (Miller et al., 1983; Johnson et al., 1986, 1988; Coggans & Danes, 1989).

Cannabis had been used by 3–5% of children aged 11–16 in two large-scale surveys in the UK (Health Education Authority, 1992). In older teenagers the rate had risen to 17% in the British Crime Survey (Mott, 1985). This was still lower than the high (but declining) rates in the US. The American

High School Survey data report that in 1980 60% of seniors had tried cannabis but by 1991 this had fallen to 37% ever used, with 14% having used cannabis in the previous month (National Institute for Drug Abuse, 1992).

There have been some school-based surveys of the use of a range of other drugs (Plant et al., 1984; Swadi, 1988; Wright & Pearl, 1990; Health Education Authority, 1992). The use of *heroin* and *cocaine* is low — probably below 1%. There are however some localities of higher-prevalence drug use where heroin and cocaine may each be used by some 2% of secondary schoolchildren (Parker et al., 1986; Swadi, 1988; Wright & Pearl, 1990). The UK has seen a recent dramatic increase in the interest in *hallucinogens* fed by the youth music culture of rave parties (Farrell, 1989; Pearson et al., 1991). Survey data provide figures for estimated population drug use but it is also important to develop a monitoring system to assess the demands on services for problem drug use in the young. At present there are very few such data available. The number of addicts notified to the Home Office (1992) continues to increase but the larger increases have occurred in the older age groups. The number of new addicts age under 21, at 1200, was still fewer than in 1985 and 1986 when this age group accounted for nearly a quarter of all new addicts compared with 15% in 1991. It is estimated that in the UK in 1991 over 200 under-15-year-olds and approximately 1400 15–19-year-olds made contact with services for drug problems.

The overall UK picture appears to be one of high initiation to tobacco and alcohol with high levels of regular consumption and experimentation with solvents, cannabis and, more recently, hallucinogens, but low rates of heroin and cocaine use. The pattern emerging from the US studies is that of a falling prevalence of new initiates to illicit drug use but also local pockets of high-density problem drug use associated with a complex range of social problems.

Drug use and misuse in society are likely to fluctuate in prevalence (Mustò, 1987). A society's experience with one set of drugs may not be useful when a novel drug is introduced. Such waves of drug use are likely to leave a population of long-term users in their wake. Since the drug scene changes quickly, it would be helpful to have regular monitoring of representative national samples of schoolchildren.

AETIOLOGY

Associated social factors

The research of the last two decades has given us knowledge about many associations and possible causes of substance use (see below). These include broad aspects of society, for culture provides the normative expectations of behaviour; aspects of the individual, including inheritance, personality characteristics, response to substances and personal goals; and aspects of the interpersonal environment, including family, peers and neighbourhood.

This knowledge about correlations has not yet led to a clear developmental understanding of substance use and misuse.

Several limitations of the studies therefore need to be noted to appreciate why there should still be so much uncertainty.

There are several types of substance use and their associations may well vary. Some types of use can be thought of as progression: beginning with experimental and occasional use and going on to regular and then heavy use, multiple drug use and other modes of consumption such as injecting. Some people stop using drugs even after very heavy use, or acquire the protective skills of moderate consumption; others persist for long periods. It would, of course, be too simple to think of these types of use as an invariant developmental sequence. Some individuals progress very rapidly to dependence after a brief career of substance use. As dependence develops, the range of drugs used often narrows. The importance of considering different stages is that they may well have different risk factors.

Existing studies typically identify their cases on the basis of amount of substance use. Accordingly, there may be a danger of overemphasizing the factors associated with the initiation of substance use at the expense of those that determine progression to dependence and other forms of harm. Conversely, studies where the subjects are referred patients may well fail to detect the factors that led to the beginning of the pathway of substance misuse. The possibility of different factors at different stages is exemplified by the Danish adoption study reported by Goodwin *et al.* (1973). Alcoholic men (who had been adopted) had an excess number of alcoholics among their biological parents; those who were heavy drinkers (but not alcoholic) had an excess of biological parents who used no alcohol. The finding is not necessarily a contradiction but might indicate an inherited factor specifically for the progression to alcohol dependence.

There are many other ways in which substance misusers form a heterogeneous group, and many of the differences cannot be seen as stages in a career of misuse. For example, some but by no means all young misusers show psychiatric syndromes — most commonly a conduct disorder or antisocial personality disorder. The reasons for this comorbidity are complex (see the section on relation with antisocial disorders, below). The result is that some of the apparent factors in aetiology may be associations of other psychiatric conditions rather than the substance misuse itself. As another example, there are many possible reasons for substance misuse, including individual psychopathology, a constitutionally determined response to drug use in which pleasurable effects predominate over unpleasant, a personal disposition to take risks and pursue momentary pleasure, an alienation from conventional norms of behaviour, and exposure to cultural pressure (especially from other young people) to take drugs. We do not know whether these represent types of misuse or a set of factors that usually coexist; but if most users belong to only one of the types then the aetiological factors of each type are probably obscured by confounding them into a single concept of drug misuse.

Clinicians therefore need to judge the contribution of different aetiological factors on an individual, biographic basis.

There is, as yet, no single set of causes that can be universally invoked. Nevertheless, it is important to know the associations in order to avoid the trap of placing false emphasis on factors that are only coincidentally present.

Using drugs is so common that it cannot plausibly be regarded in itself as an abnormal activity. Alcohol and drug use are vividly portrayed to young people as aspects of the adult world. Curiosity and pleasure-seeking are often reported by young people as motives for initial use. The seeking after autonomy in adolescence frequently involves a wide range of risk-taking behaviour, including experimental drug use (Newcomb & Bentler, 1988). The neighbourhood, and especially the peer group, can have a powerful influence on whether young people start to use drugs. This is largely a matter of attitudes rather than simply of deprivation: the more parents are integrated into their neighbourhood in high-use areas, the greater the likelihood that their children will use illicit drugs (Elliott *et al.*, 1984). Longitudinal studies of African-American adolescents in Harlem have indicated that there has been a large drop in the use of heroin, and the perceived attractiveness of heroin has fallen, but that this is not associated with direct government intervention or with fluctuations in drug price and purity (Messerei & Brunswick, 1987). In short, social attitudes play a stronger part than the availability of drugs or social anomie.

The reasons for using alcohol and other drugs at all may well be different from those for using them heavily. Many factors are known to be associated with high alcohol consumption in community samples, and the same associations characterize those taking large amounts of other drugs (Bucholz, 1990). They include male gender, being white, being a Catholic or a Protestant, having at least one parent who drinks heavily, having friends who drink or take illegal drugs, underperforming at school, being antisocial in other ways and having an unconventional lifestyle that does not follow parental expectations. Some epidemiological investigations find an association with unemployment and social deprivation (Parker *et al.*, 1986; Pearson, 1987). Of course, some of these findings might be the result of using drugs. It is therefore important to note the picture that emerges when one follows young people longitudinally.

Andréasson *et al.* (1992) have reported a very large cohort (some 50 000) who were studied systematically when they were Swedish conscripts in 1969–1970 and who have been followed up to determine their alcohol consumption. High consumption was predicted chiefly by whether they used alcohol when first studied, by their degree of antisocial behaviour and whether they had contacts with police and child care authorities. The negative findings were striking: most social factors were very weak predictors of later alcohol use. Social class of the family of origin, for example, did not predict; and those factors that did predict were hard to interpret, with heavier drinking being predicted by poor 'home well-being' but good 'family economy'. This does not mean that background social factors are of no importance, but it does imply that the important factors are likely to be rather more specific than the presence or absence of adversity. Brook and Brook (1990) have reviewed a number of surveys and concluded that the main environmental variables associated with substance abuse of all kinds are those of neighbourhood crime, poverty and decay; an atmosphere of tolerance of drug use and perception of drug use as relatively safe; a lack of community support structures; and the ready availability of illicit drugs.

GENETIC INFLUENCES

Genetic inheritance is involved in the development of alcoholism, but the findings are complex and to some extent contradictory (Mullan, 1989). The possibility of genetic influences is established by the finding that animals can be selectively bred for high levels of alcohol ingestion (Deitrich & Spuhler, 1984). The most consistent evidence for this mode of transmission in humans comes from cross-fostering analyses of adopted men. They show an excess of alcoholism in the biological rather than the adoptive relatives of problem drinkers (Goodwin *et al.*, 1973; Cloninger *et al.*, 1981). To put the findings another way, the risk of 'alcoholism' in adopted males rises from about 5% in those without a family history to about 20% in those who had an 'alcoholic' biological parent. The definition of 'alcoholism' is not wholly satisfactory for developmental purposes. Case register and self-report measures probably blur together the amount of alcohol used, the development of dependence, involvement with the law and the appearance of physical illness.

The comparison of monozygotic with dizygotic same-sex twins has been used extensively for the insight it gives into heritability. An older generation of studies indicated an elevated risk — approximately doubling — in monozygotic twins by comparison with dizygotic (Kaij, 1960). Some of this may have represented an influence upon the complications of alcoholism rather than alcoholism itself; and indeed a twin study by Hrubec and Omenn (1981) found a similar size of genetic influence upon the biological end-points of hepatic cirrhosis and alcoholic psychosis. Gurling *et al.* (1981) reported a contrasting result, in which concordance rates for monozygotic and dizygotic twins were very similar, at about 20%. This negative result has also had its methodological problems: the identification of probands may have been partly based upon other psychiatric problems besides alcoholism, so that a genetic contribution to alcohol use or dependence could have been obscured by the presence of many other aetiological factors for the individuals concerned.

More recent studies have been able to apply modern methodology and unbiased methods of identifying twin pairs from population registers. They are in agreement that there is at least a modest genetic influence. Kaprio *et al.* (1987), Heath and Martin (1988) and Pickens *et al.* (1991) all estimate a heritability of 40–50%. Heath and Martin (1988) found this to apply to teenage drinking as well as to the adult misuse of alcohol. The modern twin studies also agree that environmental influences play an important part.

It is possible to identify some of the factors involved in determining the degree of heritability. Pickens *et al.* (1991) were able to distinguish between heavy drinking (in which heritability was less than 40% and there was a larger contribution from shared environmental influences) and dependent drinking (for which heritability was about 60% and little of the environmental influence could be ascribed to factors common to both twins). This is in line with the finding from an adoptive study (see above) that genetic influences play a stronger role in dependent than in heavy but non-dependent drinking. Gender and marital status also influence findings, with heritability being higher in females than males, in unmarried females than in wives, and in older than younger women (Heath & Martin, 1988). Presumably heritability is lower in married females because they are subject to non-genetic influences from the husbands.

Genetic factors in other types of drug abuse have received surprisingly little research attention. Cadoret *et al.* (1986) were able to compare the biological and the adoptive relatives of young adopted adults who had abused drugs. They found evidence for genetic influences; and also, even after controlling for those genetic influences, an effect of the adoptive environment (indicated by divorce or psychiatric illness in the adopting family).

The way that genetic and environmental factors interact is crucial, little understood, and worthy of more systematic investigation. What is inherited? It might be a quality of personality such as sensation-seeking (von Knorring *et al.*, 1987; Cloninger *et al.*, 1988) or a chemical reaction to alcohol. This chapter will therefore go on to consider the role of personality variables, especially those linked to antisocial behaviour; the pharmacological determinants of drug effects; and the longitudinal course of substance misuse.

Relation with antisocial disorders

One of the strongest associations of substance abuse is the presence of conduct disorder or delinquency (Kandel, 1980; Johnson *et al.*, 1991). This is not only because drugs lead to crime, because conduct disorder often comes first. Several longitudinal studies have shown that boys who exhibit aggressive and antisocial behaviour have an increased risk of later alcoholism and drug-taking (McCord & McCord, 1960; Robins, 1966; McCord, 1972; Monelly *et al.*, 1983; Vaillant, 1983).

There are several possible reasons for this association. Antisocial boys may have, or be at risk for developing, a complex of attitudes that lead to reckless drug use; or may simply come more into the company of other people who themselves use drugs heavily. Experimental drug use could be viewed as a dimension of experimental delinquent behaviour (Hammersley *et al.*, 1990). Alternatively, the association might stem from intended compensatory effects of drug use. Problem behaviour theory (Jessor & Jessor, 1977) views behaviours such as substance use and premature sexual initiation as functional, serving to offset psychological or social deficits and achieve personal goals. The Jessors hypothesize that adolescents with fewer social skills, lack of effective coping strategies in their repertoire and a general feeling of inadequacy in coping with interpersonal situations are at greater risk of substance misuse. Alternatively again, the association between conduct disorder and substance abuse might come about because the pathogenetic factors for the two disorders overlap.

Longitudinal studies will be needed to determine which of these pathways apply (see Chapter 18). Longitudinal studies have already begun to give support to the notion of overlapping pathogenetic mechanisms, by identifying risk factors that precede the onset of both drug use and delinquency (Farrington & Hawkins, 1991). These risks, however, are not necessarily independent of conduct disorder behaviours or of drug abuse by other family members. They include psychological changes that can be seen as part of aggressive, antisocial behaviour (Elliott *et al.*, 1984), family problems, family substance abuse and physical or sexual abuse (Dembo *et al.*, 1989).

Genetic and longitudinal studies should have a good deal to contribute to clarifying the mechanisms that are involved. Studies of the children of alcoholics make it very clear that they are at risk for disorders of conduct as well as for alcoholism. For example, Drake and Vaillant's (1988) 33-year longitudinal study of children of alcoholics found that, in adolescence, 38% of the sample had poorer adjustment than their peers. By mid-life 25% were diagnosed with at least one personality disorder; these personality problems had strong continuities with adolescent adjustment difficulties, whereas alcoholism itself did not. In another study, antisocial personality disorder not only independently influenced the risk for developing alcoholism but was a stronger predictor of alcoholism than was a positive family history (Stabeneau, 1990). These findings of the predictive power of antisocial personality, together with cross-fostering evidence for the genetic transmission of antisocial personality in drug misusers (Cadoret *et al.*, 1986), have led to suggestions that the genetic risk lies in personality factors, that in turn lead on to heavy substance use or a dependent pattern of use (Tarter *et al.*, 1984). On the other hand, the children of alcoholics have also been found to be characterized by unusual responses to alcohol, with strong positive reactions from an early stage of alcohol use and an early appearance of craving (Schuckit, 1984). This altered response has a basis in the metabolism of alcohol, for the children of alcoholics show altered levels of blood acetaldehyde after a dose of alcohol (Schuckit, 1987). Future work will have to distinguish genetic from environmental influences upon biochemical and personality variables as well as on patterns of substance misuse.

PHARMACOLOGICAL ASPECTS

It is clear that drugs are rewarding, and probable that they interact with reward systems in the brain. Dopamine pathways originating from the ventral tegmental area have attracted a great deal of work: amphetamine, cocaine and morphine derivatives all enhance the rewarding effect of electrical brain stimulation in this area of the brain, are all rewarding when injected into the area, and no longer maintain self-administration so powerfully after dopamine-depleting lesions of the ventral tegmentum (Bozarth, 1987). Other brain areas may do the same; indeed, individual neurons from hippocampal slices may be operantly conditioned by direct cellular application of dopamine or cocaine (Stein & Belluzzi, 1987). Cerebral endorphins have intrinsic rewarding properties and some will increase the rate of self-administration of heroin by rats and the rate of an operant response that delivers electrical stimulation to the ventral tegmentum (van Ree, 1987).

This allows the possibility that inherited or acquired differences in reward systems could underlie individual vulnerability to self-stimulation with drugs, but does not establish it as a known pathogenesis. Evidently, knowledge of brain areas involved in reward does not automatically mean that they explain individual differences.

It is possible to see the motivating effects of drugs as the major determinant of their misuse — in fact this is probably the dominant theory in popular culture. The theory of gateway drugs argues that there is a sequencing from one drug on to another, beginning with alcohol and tobacco and going up a scale of 'hardness'. Some support to the pharmacological explanation comes from the animal work, for it seems that some 80% of the animals tested for intravenous cocaine or heroin self-administration learn to self-administer the drug and take it, if allowed, at very high levels (Deneau *et al.*, 1969; Yokel, 1987). The important implication of this type of study is that it suggests that preexisting conditions, such as psychopathology, are not necessary for the drug to exert its control on behaviour and that continued exposure to the drug is adequate to motivate drug-taking behaviour.

Such a theory is, in general, too simple to explain many of the complexities of human drug use. A classic investigation explaining why came from the follow-up of Vietnamese veterans who returned to the US after exposure to liberally available heroin (Robins *et al.*, 1974; Robins, 1980). Very many of those who had been addicted gave up the drug use when they returned to their homeland and their civilian life. Those who did not were the ones who had had the most troubled social adjustment before their Vietnamese experience, not the ones who had most heavily indulged. Cultural as well as personal factors were important; inner-city blacks were the most likely to use narcotics heavily yet, of those who did use narcotics, rural whites were the most likely to continue dependent drug use when they returned. The exposure to the drug was therefore not the key variable in determining the development of sustained use or of dependence.

There may nevertheless be circumstances in which pharmacological effects are a dominating influence. Cocaine and its derivatives are particularly powerful reinforcers. A very wide variety of animal species learn to self-administer it and produce a very high rate indeed of the responses that obtain the drug — even to the point of exhaustion, despite punishment of those same responses, and with neglect of alternative reinforcers such as food itself (Johanson, 1988). One of the most cited experiments in the field of drug abuse is one in which rhesus monkeys, given unlimited access to cocaine, self-administered it to the point of toxicity and death (Johanson *et al.*, 1976). Even here, however, it should be noted that the scientific story is a good deal more complicated than the dangerous power of the drug. The monkeys who killed themselves only did so under a regime of continuously available cocaine; when access was limited to a few hours each day then there was a very controlled pattern of self-administration which led to a steady, regular intake of a constant amount of drug each hour regardless of the strength of the preparation that was given. It is not certain what leads to the loss of control — perhaps the cocaine produces stereotypic behaviour that includes the drug-obtaining response as a stereotypy. What is clear is that external restraints modify the extent to which even cocaine can dictate behaviour.

LONGITUDINAL COURSE

Initiation and continuation of drug use need to be seen in a developmental context with personal and pharmacological factors (e.g. type of drug, amount and frequency of use) influencing the subsequent use of that drug, the chances of stopping and the likely use of other drugs. There might be different influences at different stages.

Bozarth (1991) suggested that the early phases of drug use are influenced chiefly by psychosocial factors, while repeated use of the drug may result in compulsive use because the substance itself has strong motivational properties and appears to govern much of the individual's behaviour (see pharmacological aspects, above). This would explain why the best predictor of the future use of a drug is the quantity and frequency of previous use of that drug. But, at least for many drugs, it remains equally possible that excessive and sustained use is determined by the same factors that led to initial experimenting, including the peer group, or that there is a biochemical risk in some individuals specifically for developing dependence.

Perhaps no one developmental explanation will suffice. The possibility of heterogeneity, both in alcoholism and in other types of substance use, has been raised from the genetic evidence. Cadoret *et al.* (1986), in the adoptive study already cited, found evidence for at least two routes to substance abuse among their adopted sample. Antisocial behaviour was linked to antisocial behaviour in biological relatives, and so was probably inherited, at least in part (though the possibility of drug effects on the developing fetus could not be dismissed); in this case the antisocial behaviour seemed to be the main link that in its turn led on to the abuse of drugs. In addition, there was a direct link between alcoholism in the biological relatives and alcohol and drug abuse in the subjects. One could therefore suppose that there are genetic influences on both alcohol intake and on behaviour, and that the use of other drugs is secondary to those. If such a conclusion were justified, then it would help to target high-risk groups for

prevention and suggest the kind of intervention that should be tried.

Very early use may constitute a distinct pathway into misuse. The earlier adolescents start drug or alcohol use, the more likely they are to have a persisting problem (Robins & Przybek, 1985). It would be helpful to know more about why this is, so as to know whether delaying initiation is in itself a good preventive strategy. The simplest explanation is probably wrong: that early onset is determined by exactly the same factors that determine whether drugs are used at all. The main evidence here is that the age of initiation has remained constant over periods when the overall prevalence is changing sharply (Messerei & Brunswick, 1987). Perhaps the substances used have a more profound effect upon the immature nervous system, so that young users are more at risk for dependence. Perhaps those individuals who are precocious in using substances before their peers are also those who are unrestrained in their later use and consequently at enhanced risk of dependence. In either event, clinicians should take early substance use seriously and be prepared to intervene at lower levels of substance abuse than for older people.

There have been a few longitudinal studies of the longer-term consequences of substance use in adolescence. Kandel *et al.* (1986) reported on a follow-up of 1004 men and women from the age of 15–25 years, finding strong independent effects of illicit drugs on increased delinquency, unemployment, divorce and abortions. Drug use at any one time was the strongest predictor for further use; drug effects depended on the extent of cumulative use and appeared to be drug-specific. Similarly, Newcomb and Bentler (1988) reported that heavy drug use (but not alcohol use) in adolescence interfered with normal maturational processes prominent during this developmental period, resulting in a variety of negative consequences in early adulthood, including impaired social functioning and physical and psychological disturbance.

ASSESSMENT

One of the first issues in assessment is the extent and pattern of drug use. Adolescents are sometimes referred after relatively minor experience of drugs. On the one hand, one should not give too great a pathological significance to occasional, experimental use. Infrequent episodes are of little clinical significance if they have always been a peer group activity, or instigated by a friend or family member, or prompted by curiosity. On the other hand, the full extent of substance use by young people is often not appreciated.

The rate of detection of substance problems in adult medical and psychiatric services (Farrell & David, 1988) is low. The same applies to the young. Alcohol and other drug misuses have been identified as probably the most commonly missed paediatric diagnoses (MacDonald, 1984). There is a need for a greater index of suspicion and more regular enquiry on substance use. Standardized screening instruments can assist staff in the identification of problems.

Two brief screening instruments are the Adolescent Alcohol

Involvement Scale (AAIS; Mayer & Filstead, 1979) and the Youth Diagnostic Screening Test (Alibrandi, 1978). The Michigan Alcohol Screening Test (Selzer, 1971) and the CAGE (Mayfield *et al.*, 1974) are two instruments regularly used to screen the adult population but neither seems particularly appropriate for a younger population. The Drug Abuse Screening Test (DAST) was developed by Skinner (1982). The 20-item DAST yields a quantitative index of problems related to psychoactive drug use.

Several studies using chemical measures of drug use have confirmed the general reliability of self-report questionnaires in assessing substance use (Stimson & Oppenheimer, 1982; Barnea *et al.*, 1987; Gossop *et al.*, 1987). However, to date there is little to suggest that any of these instruments is preferable to a reasonable index of suspicion and a readiness to enquire in a sensitive nonjudgemental manner about experience of drug and alcohol use.

Standardized assessment instruments have also been elaborated to cover a wide range of substance-related problems. One recent extensive application involved incorporation of different questionnaires to develop a method for the evaluation and treatment of adolescent substance abuse (Tarter, 1990). The package comprises a drug use screening inventory (DUSI) which is followed by the administration of questionnaires, inventories and scales relevant to 10 problem domains: (1) substance use; (2) behaviour patterns; (3) health status; (4) psychiatric status; (5) social competency; (6) family systems; (7) school performance/adjustment; (8) work adjustment; (9) peer relationships; and (10) leisure recreation. The product of this assessment is a needs assessment and diagnostic summary which leads to the development of a treatment plan. Most importantly, the assessment determines whether there are other nonsubstance-related disorders present and whether the alcohol or drug problem is indeed the most severe problem among the 10 domains. This is a 149-item questionnaire that can be completed in 20 minutes and provides a score on absolute problem density and overall problem index score, as well as a relative problem density score. A very similar instrument has been developed by the National Institute for Drug Abuse, entitled the Adolescent Assessment/Referral System (Tarter, 1990; Radhert, 1991). The well-established Addictions Severity Index (ASI; McLellan *et al.*, 1986) has been modified to the Teen-Addiction Severity Index (T-ASI; Kaminer *et al.*, 1991) and assesses seven domains: (1) substance use; (2) school status; (3) employment support status; (4) family relationships; (5) peer and social relationships; (6) legal status; and (7) psychiatric status. All these systems are promising, but do not yet have good reliability or validity data.

Individual assessment

A full personal and developmental history is an essential framework for putting drug use in context in the adolescent and the adult (Glass *et al.*, 1991). Smoking, alcohol and other drug use should be directly enquired about and it may be reasonable and facilitating to assume that people will have had some exposure to or use of drugs. Enquiries should include which drugs (including alcohol) have been used in the previous 24 hours, the previous month and ever used, as three separate categories. The drinking history should clearly outline details of first drinking experience, age when regular weekend drinking began or even regular weekday drinking. Questions should cover personal and social problems incurred due to alcohol consumption.

The distinction between longitudinal drug history and recent drug use provides an opportunity to put recent use in a broader context. As well as enquiring about specific drug use, the route of drug use for each drug should be clarified as oral, nasal, smoked or injected. Enquiry should be made about human immunodeficiency virus (HIV) risk-taking behaviour, such as injecting and sharing injecting equipment. Physical examination should include a check for evidence of injection marks. In a thorough assessment a full physical examination may reveal evidence of fresh injection marks, old scars and other physical sequelae of drug use (Farrell, 1991).

The assessment should determine whether a person is dependent. Dependence is unusual in the teenage population but is probably indicative of highly problematic use. Evidence of dependence includes daily use, withdrawal symptoms and relief of withdrawal symptoms with drug use, increased tolerance, a subjective sense of loss of control, and an exclusive focus of activities around drug use and drug-using peers.

Direct enquiry about criminal involvement and pending court cases is necessary as pending legal cases may frequently be a major reason for a young drug user seeking professional help. A picture of the broader social support network should be obtained — both the networks for drug users and those for nondrug users. A psychosexual history should include unsafe sexual practices. The possibility that the person has been involved with male or female prostitution should be considered.

Detection and confirmation of substance misuse should galvanize the clinician to do a thorough psychiatric assessment with an effort to disentangle which symptoms are antecedent to drug use and which are consequent of it. In practice the distinction is not easily drawn.

The development of standardized assessment and referral procedures supported by urine toxicology tests has helped clarify that a substantial number of young people may be referred for assessment who do not have a regular or serious pattern of alcohol or other drug abuse but require intervention on other aspects of their lives (Babor *et al.*, 1991).

Laboratory investigations

Clinical practice and research should not rely on one measure of drug use and ideally a wide range should be included in order to validate self-reports and findings (Strang *et al.*, 1989). Urine testing may be used to confirm the presence or absence of drugs. Doctors who perform urine drug screening tests should know the limits of the methods and have a sensitivity to the ethical and legal issues involved. They must also ensure that laboratory data are tailored to clinical and historical information. Interpretation of positive screens should involve repeat confirmatory tests and careful clinical consultation with the individual concerned. The commonest and most reliable laboratory method of urine testing uses thin-layer chromatography to detect opiates, amphetamines, cocaine, solvents, barbiturates, benzodiazepines and cannabis (Lancet Editorial, 1987). However urinalysis will not detect hallucinogens such as LSD.

Confirmation of a drug within a particular group requires the use of gas—liquid chromatography or high-pressure liquid chromatography, both of which are more expensive (Lancet Editorial, 1987). Such urine tests provide a snapshot of drug use depending on the half-life of the individual drug. Substances such as cannabis may be present in the urine for up to 3 weeks after consumption. The analysis of the drug content of hair is a new method that provides a longer timeframe of drug exposure. However, hair analysis is still at the research stage, with few data available on test sensitivity and specificity or likelihood of false-positive tests from environmental exposure.

It is recommended that all adolescents presenting with psychiatric symptoms should be screened, as should adolescents presenting with acute-onset behavioural problems, and high-risk adolescents such as runaways and delinquents.

Family assessment

The young drug user needs to be understood both in the context of the individual maturational process and the family life cycle (see Chapter 5). A family history of alcohol or drug-related problems substantially increases the risk of involvement with substance problems (Huberty & Huberty, 1976; Deren, 1986). The assessment should look for evidence of parental criminality and substance abuse — alcohol in particular. There are frequent reports of multigenerational substance abuse families (Huberty & Huberty, 1976; Stanton & Todd, 1982).

TREATMENT

There is a need to tailor the level of treatment to the severity of the problem. All too often the type of treatment provided for a substance problem is most strongly influenced by the package of treatment available at the agency being contacted rather than by individual need (Institute of Medicine, 1990a; Babor *et al.*, 1991).

Good treatment planning is dependent on good initial assessment and careful problem definition. Well-defined treatment goals, along with regular review of the capacity to achieve defined goals, will guide most practitioners in an otherwise complicated field. Most young people will present to a non-specialist agency for help. This is the most appropriate initial source of help. Unfortunately, many professionals may feel unskilled to cope with substance problems and wish to refer to a more specialist agency. The prevalence and range of substance problems make it essential that most generic workers coming into contact with young people seeking help for problems should possess sufficient skills and knowledge to assess and manage an alcohol or drug problem. Both substance and other underlying problems will need to be addressed.

The primary objective of substance misuse treatment services must be to identify, assess and make a treatment plan appropriately tailored to the severity of the presenting problem. It is common for people to misuse drugs for many years before they decide to seek help for such behaviour (Oppenheimer *et al.*, 1988). The importance of the involvement of generic services is that many young people who are misusing alcohol or other drugs may have more severe social or psychiatric problems; if these are the presentation, substance misuse may go unrecognized as an aggravating or precipitating factor in the overall problem. People who are involved in regular and heavy use of a range of substances are likely to incur physical, psychological and social consequences. Interventions may involve some dealings with schools and courts and medical services.

Specific interventions around the substance problem can focus on strategies to help individuals clarify aspects of their behaviour that they wish to change and to provide help in motivating and maintaining behaviour change. Helping people recognize the costs incurred from their alcohol or drug use is frequently a challenging task in treatment interventions with substance misusers; this is particularly the case with young people who may identify drug use as one of the more positive aspects of a difficult life. Prochaska and Di Clemente (1983) in their cycles of change model have categorized stages of change into precontemplators, contemplators and action phase. Thus, young people may be involved in drug use and have no interest in changing their behaviour and thus be in the precontemplator category, as are many people who continue to smoke cigarettes. Motivational interviewing techniques (Miller, 1983) may need to be devised to coax people from precontemplation and to help them grasp the level of problems associated with their drug use. This might involve individuals in looking at both the benefits and drawbacks of their behaviour, in order to enhance cognitive dissonance associated with the substance use. The subtlety and openness of approach required should not be underestimated, because any blanket judgemental approach is likely to meet intense and entrenched resistance from the client.

Social learning theory and cognitive behavioural therapy have been the most influential approach to working with drug users over the past decade. Conditioning and learning theory have dominated recent research and treatment models in the field of alcohol and drug dependence (Wikler, 1965; Bandura, 1977; Marlatt & Gordon, 1985; Childress *et al.*, 1988). Relapse prevention has been most influential in providing a broad conceptual framework for the generalist. It aims to help people recognize the conditions in which they are most likely to involve themselves in patterns of substance use they wish to avoid. Such high-risk situations include negative affective states, interpersonal conflict or social pressure. Having identified individual high-risk situations, alternative coping strategies are then developed to assist in the maintenance of behaviour change.

There may be significant differences between teenagers and adults in the process of relapse. Some studies suggest that social pressures are the major factor in younger people's relapse. Adolescents with substance problems in high-risk situations appear to use behavioural coping strategies more effectively than cognitive ones (Brown *et al.*, 1990).

Cue exposure has been developed in the treatment of alcohol, opiate and cocaine dependence (O'Brien *et al.*, 1974; Blakey & Baker, 1980; Rankin *et al.*, 1983, Childress *et al.*, 1988; Powell *et al.*, 1990). Cue exposure research demonstrates that particular situations such as a pub, the sight of an alcoholic drink or of a preferred drug can stimulate a powerful craving that triggers a train of events resulting in relapse to drug use. In cue exposure treatment, particular cues are identified and the craving response extinguished gradually through graded exposure therapy. This treatment method remains experimental but clarifies the role of relapse prevention in identifying high-risk situations.

Family involvement, when possible, can mobilize support around the young person (see Chapter 55). Systems-based approaches are commonly used in working with families with substance abuse problems but behavioural-based approaches also have an important place in helping the family to redefine boundaries and set goals (Bry, 1988). Families who are looking for new coping strategies might find support with the Minnesota-based family support organizations, such as Families Anonymous.

Young people coming for treatment are likely to be more chaotic and problematic than the population samples of young people misusing drugs who have been studied over the past decade (Kandel *et al.*, 1986; Newcomb & Bentler, 1988). Adult treatment populations generally experience a number of years of problematic substance use before presenting to treatment agencies. Experience with Vietnam veterans made it clear that only a tiny minority of addicted men entered treatment, and that they were a very selected group with poor outcome (Robins *et al.*, 1974). Severe substance misuse will substantially disrupt other aspects of development such as education, peer relationships, family support and criminal involvement, so that what are pretreatment factors in the adult population are important outcome measures in the young. The young misuser is embarking on a career of narrowing options.

Treatment outcome varies according to the population studied and the definition of the outcome. Particular attention has been paid to pretreatment patient variables. Factors such as being younger, married, employed, having less initial symptomatology, psychopathology or dependence are associated with better outcome in terms of abstinence and social functioning. However such predictors of treatment only account for 10−30% of the outcome variance and posttreat-

ment environmental factors are also important. In the younger population careful study will need to be made of social functioning in the family, school, peer and work environment both before and after treatment.

A number of descriptive treatment outcome studies of young people generally report that treatment programmes appear to reduce heroin and cocaine use but have limited impact on alcohol and marijuana use (Rush, 1979; Sells & Simpson, 1979; Hubbard *et al.*, 1983; Friedman & Beschner, 1985). Of course, many young users move away from drug use without entering formal treatment programmes (Biernacki, 1986). It is important to remember that changeability and discontinuity during development are encountered as well as the simple progression of risks. Young people move into or out of a wide range of experimental behaviours as their work, study or living environment changes.

Specialized treatment for young people in the UK is virtually nonexistent. Inpatient treatment is available, although the advisability of admitting young inexperienced drug users into settings with individuals with long drug-using histories is doubtful. There is, accordingly, a hiatus in the availability of treatment services for this group. A few residential treatment facilities exist based on 12-step programmes or Concept House models of treatment (Cook, 1988; Rosenthal, 1989). However, in the US, there are extensive treatment facilities ranging from intensive outpatient to long-term residential treatment. Rosenthal (1989) has argued that many disturbed adolescents would benefit from the containing environment of such a therapeutic community and in the US there are residential schools for adolescent drug users which focus on the acquisition of occupational skills in a highly structured environment. Concern has also been expressed about the use of involuntary treatment in the private residential sector in the US.

Inpatient and residential treatment is expensive and to date there are few empirical data to suggest that they are better than community-based treatment. Friedman and Beschner (1985) and Wheeler and Malmquist (1987) reviewed treatment approaches in the US but found an absence of evaluation of efficacy. One may however hope that some of the difficulties in the way of evaluation can be removed. There has been a substantial improvement in the availability of standardized instruments, and an increasing perception that young people are an important focus for both treatment and prevention. The advent of HIV has also increased the need for early intervention strategies to minimize the long-term harm from experimental adolescent drug use.

Harm minimization involves the provision of information and interventions which reduce the damaging nature of any continued drug use. This requires an ability on the part of the therapist and the patient to work at several levels simultaneously. Thus, there should be strong advice to abstain from any further drug use, but also information on first-aid resuscitation and advice about safer syringe-cleaning technique and where to obtain sterile injecting equipment (Stimson *et al.*, 1988). Such an approach might involve dissuading young people from misusing solvents while at the same time ensuring that they have the information to know which sorts of activities (such as inhalation of butane gas) carry the highest risks (Anderson, 1990). Services will need to have policies on their approach to people under the age of 16 with reference to the supply of injecting equipment and the provision of detoxification and substitute drug treatment.

DRUG MISUSE AND HIV/AIDS

Young people are a key target audience in the promotion of safer sexual and risk-taking behaviour through educational and mass media channels. Their experience and knowledge are limited, and interventions need to be aimed initially at informing teenagers of the range of risks. Intoxication is likely to impair vigilance and result in the abandonment of safer sexual practice (Robertson & Plant, 1988; Leigh, 1990). This has long been an issue in unplanned teenage pregnancies and the advent of HIV has highlighted the need for a more concerted approach to teenage contraceptive and sexual health education. It is estimated that young people possess relatively high levels of knowledge on the basic facts of HIV and acquired immunodeficiency syndrome (AIDS; Bury, 1991) but there is little evidence to suggest that such knowledge has had a major impact on behaviour (Weisman *et al.*, 1991). The newly recruited population of young drug users and drug injectors poses a particular problem for HIV prevention campaigns by having low AIDS awareness and high risk of involvement in sharing activity.

Specific drugs

Particular issues arise with different substances. The rates of use will be influenced by local availability and also the local characteristics of drug misuse. For example, in Scotland and the North of England in the late 1980s and early 1990s, there was a rise in the number of people injecting medically prescribed substances such as buprenorphine and temazepam (Sakol *et al.*, 1989). It is not clear why such patterns should develop in one locality and not elsewhere where there is the potential for similar levels of availability of the substances.

A brief overview of relevant substances is provided, but for more detailed coverage the chapter by Jaffe (1990) is recommended.

Alcohol

Alcohol is a cerebral depressant. It is the most commonly misused drug in society. Many young people experience alcohol-related problems but dependence is unusual until a later age. Young people are most likely to experience problems with alcohol as a result of acute intoxication. The longer-term sequelae will be determined by their eventual adult drinking patterns, and the relationship between teenage drinking and adult drinking is far from being a direct continuity (Fillmore & Midanik, 1984).

Acute intoxication may result in traumatic accidents, drownings or occasionally fatal alcohol poisoning. Young people account for a disproportionate number of alcohol-related road traffic accidents, possibly as a result of their inexperience with both alcohol and driving. However, other factors such as the level of impulsivity and impact of alcohol on risk-taking decision-making may also be involved. Young people may also experience alcohol dependence with withdrawal symptoms and may require appropriate medical management. Such heavy consumption may be associated with benzodiazepine abuse and the combined withdrawal may result in *grand mal* convulsions.

Heavy alcohol consumption is associated with chronic liver, gastrointestinal, neurological and endocrine complications as well as malnutrition. There are few available data on the prevalence of such problems among young people. This may be because many of these problems arise as a result of long-term drinking but it may also be due to lack of clinical suspicion of alcohol as a co-factor in physical morbidity in the young.

Opiates

Only a small number of people report using opiates on a regular basis, but it is this class of drug that figures most prominently in the demands on drug treatment services. Heroin is the most commonly used drug in the illicit market but a wide range of drugs such as codeine, Diconal (dipipanone and cyclazine mixture), dextromoramide (Palfium), and the mixed agonist/antagonist opioid buprenorphine (Temgesic) may be used.

Heroin may be smoked or injected or taken intranasally by snorting. Chasing the dragon is the term for smoking heroin and this is a common mode of initiation into heroin use which may continue as smoking or may progress to heroin injecting (Gossop *et al.*, 1988). The first use may be associated with nausea and vomiting. There are no good data available on the proportion of experimenters who go on to develop regular or dependent use. Regular use will result in a higher tolerance to opiates. Withdrawal when dependent will occur 8–12 hours after the last dose. This can give rise to restlessness, irritability, increased bowel activity with diarrhoea and crampy abdominal pain, yawning, sneezing and coryza, nausea and vomiting. Such withdrawal symptoms will also be associated with intense craving for the drug.

The prescription of oral methadone is the commonest approach to the management of opiate withdrawal. Dosage is calculated on the basis of a conversion factor of a daily use of 1 g of heroin being equivalent to 80 mg of methadone (Department of Health, 1991). Apart from the immediate treatment of withdrawal symptoms with an opiate substitute, methadone treatment is also given as a substitute drug over the short, medium and long term to achieve social rehabilitation of the drug user. The role of methadone has been reevaluated in the era of HIV in the hope that methadone might be effective in reducing injecting drug users' risk-taking behaviour, and thereby reducing the spread of HIV (Cooper, 1989). There is a need for a more detailed analysis of the components of treatment that impact on risk-taking behaviour.

Methadone treatment is one of the more extensively evaluated forms of treatment intervention. A number of large-scale prospective studies and multicentre studies have been conducted (Simpson & Sells, 1982; Hubbard *et al.*, 1989; Ball & Ross, 1991). There have however been only three randomized controlled trials (Dole *et al.*, 1969; Newman & Whitehill, 1979; Gunne & Gronbladh, 1981). Within the limited aims of maintenance treatment this modality has been demonstrated to be moderately effective (Institute of Medicine, 1990b) but overall it must be viewed as a longer-term treatment option for the opiate-dependent individual. Such treatment should be viewed as one of a number of treatment options and not the preferred option for those with a short history of opiate dependence.

Recent advances have included the development of long-acting oral antagonists such as naltrexone which have an affinity for the opiate receptors and block any effect from self-administered opiates. The aim of such medication is to enhance an individual's capacity to maintain a drug-free state after detoxification from opiates. Despite its initial promise, this drug has found only a limited place in the treatment of opiate dependence (Gonzales & Brogden, 1988).

STIMULANTS

Stimulants like cocaine and amphetamines may be taken in powder form, intranasally or by injection. Cocaine with the hydrochloride component removed is known as crack and is smokable in this form as it volatizes. Stimulants generally produce an elevation of mood and a sense of increased energy with reduction in appetite and a marked reduction in sleep. At higher doses some people may become anxious or irritable, talkative, agitated and some may develop a frank psychosis which may be related to the amount of stimulant consumed. People smoking cocaine may shift from irregular to compulsive use over a short period of time. The classic pattern of compulsive consumption is bingeing, lasting from 12 hours to 3 days, which is then followed by a crash with a period of sleepiness, depression and withdrawal with mounting craving for further cocaine (Gawin & Ellinwood, 1988). Both cocaine and amphetamines probably exert their reinforcing effect by increasing synaptic concentrations of dopamine (see above). Binges and longer-term stimulant use also result in depletion of synaptic monoamines and this may be a mechanism for the development of affective disorders with depression, anxiety and suicidal ideation (Gawin & Ellinwood, 1988).

As the number of people using cocaine has increased, so have the reports of the physical complications in toxicity of cocaine (Cregler, 1989). Toxic paranoid psychoses are dose-related and therefore occur particularly in situations where there is high drug tolerance (Post, 1975). The commonest signs are visual hallucinations, pseudohallucinations and tactile hallucinations ('cocaine bugs'). Stereotypical behaviour

may also occur. Unlike the opiates, there is only a small place for substitute prescribing. The tricyclic antidepressant desipramine has been used in the treatment of stimulant-induced affective disorders and has been reported to reduce cocaine consumption in controlled studies (Gawin & Kleber, 1984; Gawin *et al.*, 1989). Other researchers have looked at strategies to antagonize cocaine's effect on dopaminergic systems. Clinical trials of amantadine, bromocriptine (Dakis *et al.*, 1987) and flupenthixol (Gawin & Ellinwood, 1988) have been mounted but have not found clear superiority over placebo; a small effect is possible in view of the relative lack of power in the studies. A controlled trial of cue exposure has reported positive treatment results in severe cocaine dependence (Childress *et al.*, 1988).

Psychedelics (hallucinogens)

MDMA (known as ecstasy or E)

This is a combined stimulant and hallucinogen and also possesses stimulant properties. The current popularity of this drug is a particular source of concern because of the basic animal research that suggests that both MDMA (methylene-dioxy-metho-amphetamine) and MDA (methylene-dioxy-amphetamine) are toxic to serotonergic neurons (Battaglia *et al.*, 1987). Animal studies have not been replicated in humans. This is a drug that does not appear to produce compulsive use but is associated with a rapid development of tolerance. Effects are likely to be mild euphoria, general sense of well-being, increased activity and reduced sleep. At higher doses it may result in a paranoid psychosis. Clinical descriptions of affective complications with depression, anxiety and suicidal ideation are now being reported and there have been a few cases of chronic paranoid psychosis (McGuire & Fahy, 1991). A small number of deaths have been reported.

LSD

Hallucinogenic substances have been known to humanity for many generations, ranging from psilocybin and peyote to mescaline or magic mushrooms (*Psilocybe semilanceata*; 'liberty caps'). These hallucinogens achieved great popularity in the late 1960s and have had a resurgence in popularity in the late 1980s and 1990s in association with the consumption of MDMA. LSD appears to act particularly on the serotonin receptor (Pierce & Peroutka, 1988). Psychological effects appear at extremely low doses of LSD — as little as 20–25 µg. The subjective effect is of visual distortions, disturbance in sense of time and increased sensitivities to colours and sound with a loss of the sense of boundaries between self and the world. Users are particularly sensitive to the environment and the experience of a calm and structured environment may result in a pleasant experience, whereas a threatening or chaotic environment may result in marked anxiety, panic and even paranoia. Such experiences are titled 'bad trips' and are best handled by reassurance in a supportive environment.

Long-term consequences of LSD use are unclear. The most frequently reported adverse effect is that of flashbacks which are recurrences of the subjective effects long after use of the drug. A flashback may be quite similar to a panic attack because it is characterized by distress associated with experiencing the phenomena. Flashbacks may be precipitated by use of marijuana, anxiety, fatigue or movement into a dark environment (Jaffe, 1990). A small number of people may develop long-term psychotic illnesses. It is not clear whether this is a result of LSD use or an indication of premorbid psychopathology.

Cannabis

Marijuana has been the most commonly used illicit drug in the western world since the late 1960s. The active ingredient, delta-9-tetrahydrocannabinol, produces most of the characteristic subjective effects such as relaxation, increased sense of well-being, sleepiness, spontaneous laughter and giggling, distortion in the sense of time and impairment of short-term memory (Hollister, 1986).

An immediate effect is impairment of coordination and psychomotor skills with consequent handicap in driving skills or handling machinery. Because of the slow rate of elimination of marijuana, residual effects may persist for a number of days after consumption if high doses have been consumed. Long-term cannabis smoking is associated with bronchitis and the smoke is even more carcinogenic than tobacco (Wu *et al.*, 1988). Cannabis may induce mild dependence but overall appears to be a weekly reinforcing drug. High doses may result in the development of anxiety and paranoid ideas and at sufficiently high doses delta-9-tetrahydrocannabinol can result in a frank toxic psychosis. Clinical experience seems to indicate that cannabis can be a factor in provoking, aggravating or prolonging psychotic experiences. Indeed, cannabis use predicted the later development of schizophrenia in a large study of Swedish conscripts, even allowing for general social disadvantage (Andréasson *et al.*, 1987). There is however little evidence to support a distinctive clinical syndrome (Johnson, 1991).

Tranquillizers

Barbiturates, benzodiazepines and related compounds

Benzodiazepines are readily available in many homes and are frequently used by young people in association with alcohol. Abuse of benzodiazepines appears to be characterized by binge use or the regular taking of large quantities (up to four times the recommended dose). It is not clear if the different benzodiazepines have varying abuse liability but most clinicians think that the shorter-acting ones are more often abused. In the UK this has centred around temazepam abuse, frequently injected and therefore frequently with physical complications (Sakol *et al.*, 1989). Benzodiazepine dependence is a more unusual problem among young people. Barbiturates are now rarely used in the UK.

Volatile substance abuse

Volatile substance abuse occurs in young people but seldom persists into adulthood. Solvents are cheap and readily available, particularly as household products. Adhesives, typewriter correcting fluids and thinners, butane gas, lighter fuel, fire extinguishers and other aerosols are the most commonly used substances (Flanagan *et al.*, 1990). Compounds such as glue are usually inhaled from a plastic bag, and aerosols may also be sprayed into a plastic bag so that the propellant can be inhaled. Otherwise lighter fuel may be directly sprayed on to the back of the larynx, resulting in pharyngeal and laryngeal oedema and consequent breathing difficulties. There were 145 volatile substance abuse-related deaths in the UK in 1990 (Pottier *et al.*, 1992). Butane gas as lighter fuel is particularly implicated in the recent high death rate from volatile substance abuse in the UK (Anderson, 1990). Suspicion may be aroused by unusual smells on children's clothes or accumulation of large quantities of abusable products.

Inhalation initially gives rise to a pleasurable reaction but higher dosage may result in incoordination, confusion and hallucinations. Deaths sometimes result from accidental falls. It appears that most of the physical complications are reversible on cessation of use but there is still uncertainty about the possibility of long-term neuropsychological deficits (Chadwick *et al.*, 1989).

Arylcyclohexylamines

Phenylcyclidine (PCP, 'angel dust' or 'crystal') had a brief ascendancy in the US but is now in more limited use. This drug has never penetrated the UK or other European markets, despite being relatively easy to synthesize. It has a combination of depressant, hallucinogenic and analgesic actions. Its complications can present major management and containment problems to emergency room staff. They include acute behavioural disturbance, coma and convulsions. Patients with these problems should be managed in a nonstimulating environment. Coma may be preceded or followed by psychotic and bizarrely aggressive behaviour (Jaffe, 1990). The psychosis may be treated with haloperidol.

Anabolic steroids

Originally it was thought that the use of anabolic steroids was confined to the upper echelons of competitive sport. Clinical experience makes it clear that such drugs may also be used by a wider population, although there are as yet no epidemiological studies. The contamination of sport by drug misuse has aroused alarm and governments in the US and Europe are looking for forceful strategies to stamp out such activities (Shapiro, 1991). It is not quite clear what are the exact benefits of anabolic steroids, but athletes report that they enable them to train harder and recover more quickly from their training schedules. There is little evidence to suggest that these drugs are dependence-inducing. The most serious physical complications are in young users where the steroids may result in premature fusion of the epiphyses and inhibit growth. There is also concern that athletes may be at risk of HIV from using communal injecting equipment. Steroid use may be associated with aggression and psychosis (Pope & Katz, 1987). Careful epidemiological work is required to determine the extent of anabolic steroid use in sport and to document the adverse physical effects. It would also be helpful to determine if there is any objective advantage to drug use in sport.

PREVENTION

The profound influence of social and environmental factors on the initiation and maintenance of drug use suggests the possibility of psychosocial prevention. Substantial educational programmes now exist with the specific aim of reducing initiation into drug use. As the age of initiation into drug use declines, some consider that such educational programmes should be extended to the primary schools. Traditional prevention programmes have focused on the provision of information, arousal of fear, appeal to moral sense, effective education and alternative activities such as adventure weekends and similar activities that enhance sense of achievement and may provide a natural high. Evaluations have consistently indicated that the benefit of these approaches is very limited (Dorn & Thompson, 1976; Kinder *et al.*, 1980; Schaps *et al.*, 1982).

The more modern approaches to prevention include components dealing with resistance skills, psychological inoculation and personal and social skills training (Schinke *et al.*, 1991).

Many of these interventions are derived from approaches developed to prevent young people from starting to smoke. Evaluations of such procedures have started to appear and, despite methodological short-comings, indicate that they increase the number of young people avoiding tobacco smoking (Glasgow & McCaul, 1985). Many of these programmes depend on peer-led groups where individuals who are popular among their classmates are trained to deliver the programme. It is not clear how applicable this approach is to other substances. The clear message of abstinence from tobacco may be more acceptable and transmissible than the mixed message about controlled alcohol use or the even more difficult message about marijuana use.

It is difficult to ascertain the role of mass media campaigns other than to highlight issues that need to be dealt with by parents, schools and communities more locally. In a comprehensive review of the English language literature on prevention strategies, Dorn and Murji (1992) chart the evolution of drug prevention through the following stages:

1 Providing information to individual decision-makers, i.e. young people who are about to start smoking, drinking or drug taking.
2 Seeking to remedy supposed deficits of moral values or living skills.
3 Bolstering peer resistance strategies in the context of anti-drug norms.

4 Providing alternatives to drug use through youth and community participation.
5 Reemphasizing enforcement measures against users with a focus on the point of purchase of drugs.

Overall, there is room for limited gains through prevention campaigns if the aims of such campaigns are realistic and modest and appropriately targeted. There is no good evidence that current prevention efforts affect the rate of drug experimentation. There is a need for a greater focus on more regular drug users through advice and helping agencies at a local level and such behaviour seems unlikely to be affected in any significant way by national campaigns. However it may be possible to increase risk perception, harm reduction and AIDS awareness with broad educational campaigns. Whatever the perceived limitations of educational campaigns, there seems little justification for the limited levels of activity in this arena in many schools and countries. There is a need for a clear educational strategy as part of overall health education. All children need to receive clear and concise information from an early age on the risks of drug use. Ideally such information should be provided within both the school and the family setting.

There is likely to be substantial overlap between treatment and prevention approaches and the benefits from each intervention would be a key part of a multidimensional approach aiming at cumulative small gains rather than imaginary masterstrokes.

REFERENCES

Advisory Council on the Misuse of Drugs (1982) *Treatment and Rehabilitation Report*. Department of Health and Social Security, London.

Alibrandi T. (1978) *Young Alcoholics*. Comp Care, Minneapolois, MN.

American Psychiatric Association (1994) *Diagnostic and Statistical Manual of Mental Disorders*, 4th edn (DSM-IV). American Psychiatric Association, Washington DC.

American Psychiatric Association (in press) *Diagnostic and Statistical Manual of Mental Disorders — DSM-IV — 4th edition*. American Psychiatric Association, Washington DC.

Anderson H.R. (1990) Increase in deaths from deliberate inhalation of fuel gases, and pressurised aerosols. *British Medical Journal*, **41**, 301.

Andréasson S., Allbreck P., Engstrom A. & Rydberg U. (1987) Cannabis and schizophrenia: a longitudinal study of Swedish conscripts. *Lancet*, **2**, 1483–1486.

Andréasson S., Allbreck P., Brandt L. & Romelsjö A. (1992) Antecedents and covariates of high alcohol in young men. *Alcoholism: Clinical and Experimental Research*, **16**, 708–713.

Babor T.F., Del Boca F.K., Mc Laney M.A., Jacobi B., Higgins-Biddle J. & Hass W. (1991) Just say Y.E.S. Matching Adolescents to appropriate interventions for alcohol and other drug related problems. *Alcohol World; Health and Research*, **15**, 77–86.

Ball J.C. & Ross A. (1991) *The Effectiveness of Methadone Maintenance Treatment: Patients, Programs, Services, and Outcome*. Springer-Verlag, New York.

Bandura A. (1977) Self-efficacy: toward a unifying theory of behavioural change. *Psychological Review*, **84**, 191–215.

Barnea Z., Rahau G. & Teichman M. (1987) The reliability and consistency of self reports on substance use in a longitudinal study. *British Journal of Addiction*, **82**, 891–898.

Battaglia G., Yeh S.Y., O'Hearn E., Molliver M.E., Kuhar M.J. & de

Souza E.B. (1987) 3−4 methylenedioxymethamphetamine and 3−4 methylenedioxyamphetamine destroy serotonin terminals in rat brain: quantification of neurodegeneration by measurement of [³H] paroxetine labelled serotonin uptake sites. *Journal of Pharmacology and Experimental Therapeutics*, **242**, 911−916.

Biernacki P. (1986) *Pathways from Heroin Addiction: Recovery Without Treatment*. Temple University Press, Philadelphia PA.

Blakey R. & Baker R. (1980) An exposure approach to alcohol abuse. *Behaviour Research and Therapy*, **18**, 319−325.

Bozarth M. (1987) Ventral tegmental reward system. In: Engel J., Oreland L., Ingvar D.H., Pernow B., Rössner S. & Pellborn L.A. (eds) *Brain Reward Systems and Abuse*, pp. 1−17. Raven Press, New York.

Bozarth M. (1991) Drug addiction as a psychobiological process. In: Warburton D.M. (ed) *Addictions, Controversies*, pp. 112−134. Harwood Academic Publishers, Chur, Switzerland.

Brook D. & Brook J. (1990) The etiology and consequences of adolescent drug use. In: Watson R. (ed) *Drug and Alcohol Abuse Prevention*, pp. 339−362. Humana Press, Clifton, NJ.

Brown S.A., Mott M.A. & Myers M. (1990) Adolescent alcohol and drug treatment outcome. In: Watson R. (ed) *Drug and Alcohol Abuse Prevention*, pp. 373−404. Humana Press, Clifton, NJ.

Bry B.H. (1988) Family-based approaches to reducing adolescent substance use: theories, techniques and findings. In: Rahdbert E.R. & Grabowski J. (eds) *National Institute of Drug Abuse Research Monograph 77. Adolescent Drug Abuse: Analyses of Treatment Research*. National Institute on Drug Abuse, Rockville, MD.

Bucholz K.K. (1990) A review of correlates of alcohol use and alcohol problems in adolescence. In: Galonte M. (ed) *Recent Developments in Alcoholism*, vol. 8, pp. 111−124. Plenum, New York.

Bury J. (1991) Teenage sexual behaviour and the impact of AIDS. *Health Education Journal*, **50**, 43−48.

Cadoret R.J., Troughton E., O'Gorman T.W. & Heywood M.A. (1986) An adoption study of genetic and environmental factors in drug abuse. *Archives of General Psychiatry*, **43**, 1131−1136.

Chadwick O., Anderson R., Bland J. & Ramsey J. (1989) Neuropsychological consequences of volatile substance abuse: a population based study of secondary school pupils. *British Medical Journal*, **298**, 1679−1684.

Childress A.R., Ehrman R., McLellan A.T. & O'Brien C. (1988) Conditioned craving and arousal in cocaine addiction. In: Harris L.S. (ed) *Problems of Drug Dependence*, National Institute on Drug Abuse Research Monograph, pp. 74−80. National Institute on Drug Abuse, Rockville, MD.

Cloninger C.R., Bohman M. & Sigvardsson S. (1981) Inheritance of alcohol abuse: cross-fostering analysis of adopted men. *Archives of General Psychiatry*, **38**, 861−868:

Cloninger C.R., Sigvardsson S. & Bohman M. (1988) Childhood personality predicts alcohol abuse in young adults. *Alcoholism*, **12**, 494−503.

Coggans S. & Davies J. (1989) *National Evaluation of Drug Education in Scotland: Final Report*. University of Strathclyde, Strathclyde.

Cook C.C.H. (1988) The Minesota Model in the management of drug and alcohol dependency: miracle, method or myth? *British Journal of Addiction*, **83**, 625−634.

Cooper J. (1989) Methadone treatment and AIDS. *Journal of the American Medical Association*, **62**, 1664−1681.

Cregler L.L. (1989) Adverse consequences of cocaine abuse. *Journal of the National Medical Association*, **81**, 27−38.

Dakis C., Gold A.S., Sweeney D., Byron J.P. & Climko R. (1987) Single dose bromocriptine reverses cocaine craving. *Psychiatric Research*, **20**, 261−264.

Deitrich R.A. & Spuhler K. (1984) Genetics of alcoholism and alcohol actions. In: Smart R.G., Cappell H.D., Glaser F.B., Israel Y., Kalant

H., Popham R.E., Schmidt W. & Sellers E.M. (eds) *Research Advances in Alcohol and Drug Problems*, vol. 8, pp. 47−98. Plenum, New York.

Dembo R., Williams L., La Voie L., Berry E., Getreeu A., Wish E.D., Schmeidler J. & Washburn M. (1989) Physical abuse, sexual victimization and illicit drug use: replication of a structural analysis among a new sample of high risk youths. *Violence and Victims*, **4**, 121−138.

Deneau G., Yanagita T. & Seevers M.H. (1969) Self-administration of psychoactive substances by the monkey: a measure of psychological dependence. *Psychopharmacologica*, **16**, 30−48.

Department of Health (1991) *Drug Misuse and Drug Dependence: Guidelines on Clinical Management*. Report of a medical working group. Her Majesty's Stationery Office, London.

Deren S. (1986) Children of substance abusers: a review of the literature. *Journal of Substance Abuse Treatment*, **3**, 77−94.

Dole V.P., Robinson J.W., Orraca J., Towns E., Searcy P. & Caine E. (1969) Methadone treatment of randomly selected criminal addicts. *New England Journal of Medicine*, **280**, 1372−1375.

Dorn N. & Murji K. (1992) *Drug Prevention: A Review of the English Language Literature*. Institute for the Study of Drug Dependence, London.

Dorn N. & Thompson A. (1976) Evaluation of drug education in the longer term is not an optional extra. *Community Health*, **7**, 154−161.

Drake R.E. & Vaillant G.E. (1988) Predicting alcoholism and personality disorder in a 33 year longitudinal study of children of alcoholics. *British Journal of Addiction*, **83**, 799−807.

Edeh J. (1989) Volatile substance abuse in relation to alcohol and illicit drugs: psychosocial perspectives. *Human Toxicology*, **8**, 313−317.

Elliott D.S., Huizinga D. & Ageton S.S. (1984) *Explaining Delinquency and Drug Use*. Sage, Beverly Hills.

Farrell M. (1989) Ecstasy and the oxygen of publicity. *British Journal of Addiction*, **84**, 943.

Farrell M. (1991) Physical complications of drug abuse. In: Glass I.B. (ed) *The International Handbook of Addiction Behaviour*, pp. 120−125. Routledge, London.

Farrell M.P. & David A.S. (1988) Do psychiatric registrars take a proper drinking history? *British Medical Journal*, **296**, 395−396.

Farrington D.P. & Hawkins J.D. (1991) Predicting participation, early onset and later persistence in officially recorded offending. *Criminal Behaviour and Mental Health*, **1**, 1−33.

Fillmore K. & Midanik L. (1984) Chronicity of drinking problems among men: a longitudinal study. *Journal of Studies on Alcohol*, **45**, 228−236.

Flanagan R.J., Ruprah M., Meredith T.J. & Ramsey J. (1990) An introduction to the clinical toxicology of volatile substances *Drug Safety*, **5**, 359−383.

Friedman A.S. & Beschner G.M. (1985) *Treatment Services for Adolescent Substance Abusers*. National Institute for drug abuse research monograph. National Institute for Drug Abuse, Rockville, MD.

Gawin F. & Ellinwood E.H. (1988) Cocaine and other stimulant: actions, abuse and treatment. *New England Journal of Medicine*, **318**, 1173−1182.

Gawin F. & Kleber H. (1984) Cocaine abuse treatment: open pilot trial with desipramine and lithium carbonate. *Archives of General Psychiatry*, **41**, 903−909.

Gawin F., Kleber H., Byck R., Rounsville B.J., Kosten T.R., Jarlow P.I. & Morgan C. (1989) Desipramine facilitation of initial cocaine abstinence. *Archives of General Psychiatry*, **46**, 117−121.

Glasgow R.E. & McCaul K.D. (1985) Life skills training programs for smoking prevention: critique and directions for future research. In: Bell C. & Battjes R. (eds) *Prevention Research: Deterring Drug Abuse Among Children and Adolescents*. Government Printing Office, Washington DC.

Glass I.B., Farrell M. & Hajek P. (1991) Tell me about the client: history taking and formulating the case. In: Glass I.B. (ed) *The International Handbook of Addiction Behaviour*, pp. 191–206. Routledge, London.

Gonzalez J.P. & Brogden R.N. (1988) Naltrexone: a review. *Drugs*, **35**, 192–213.

Goodwin D.W., Schulsinger F., Hermansen L., Guze S.B. & Winokur G. (1973) Alcohol problems in adoptees raised apart from alcoholic biological parents. *Archives of General Psychiatry*, **28**, 238–243.

Gossop M., Green L., Phillips G. & Bradley B. (1987) What happens to opiate addicts immediately after treatment: a prospective follow up study. *British Medical Journal*, **294**, 1377–1380.

Gossop M., Griffiths P. & Strang J. (1988) Chasing the dragon: characteristics of heroin chasers. *British Journal of Addiction*, **83**, 1159–1162.

Gunne L.M. & Gronbladh L. (1981) The Swedish methadone maintenance program: a controlled study. *Drug and Alcohol Dependence*, **7**, 249–256.

Gurling H.M.D., Clifford L.A. & Murray R.M. (1981) Genetic contribution to alcohol dependence and its effects in brain function. In: Gedda L., Pinsi P. & Nance W.A. (eds) *Twin Research* pp. 77–87. Alan R. Liss, New York.

Hammersley R., Forsyth A. & Lavelle T. (1990) The criminality of new drug users in Glasgow. *British Journal of Addiction*, **85**, 1583–1594.

Health Education Authority (1992) *Tomorrow's Young Adults. 9–15 Year Olds Look at Alcohol, Drugs, Exercise and Smoking*. Health Education Authority, London.

Heath A.C. & Martin N.G. (1988) Teenage alcohol use in the Australian twin register: genetic and social determinants of starting to drink. *Alcoholism: Clinical and Experimental Research*, **12**, 736–741.

Hollister L. (1986) Health aspects of cannabis. *Pharmacological Review*, **38**, 1–20.

Home Office (1992) *Statistics of the Misuse of Drugs: Addicts Notified, United Kingdom 1991*. Home Office Statistical Bulletin, London.

Hrubec Z. & Omenn G.S. (1981) Evidence of genetic predisposition to alcoholic cirrhosis and psychosis: twin concordances for alcoholism and its biological end points by zygosity among male veterans. *Alcoholism*, **5**, 207–215.

Hubbard R., Cavanaugh S., Graddock S. & Rachel J. (1983) *Characteristics, Behaviours and Outcomes for Youth in TOPS Study: Report submitted to National Institute for Drug Abuse*. Research Triangle Institute, Research Triangle Park, NC.

Hubbard R.L., Marsden J.V., Rachal H.J., Harwood E.R., Cavanaugh, E.R. & Ginzberg H.M. (1989) *Drug Abuse Treatment: A National Study of Effectiveness*. The University of North Carolina Press, Chapel Hill, NC.

Huberty C.E. & Huberty D.J. (1976) Treating the parents of adolescent drug abusers. *Contemporary Drug Problems*, **4**, 573–592.

Institute of Medicine (1990a) Broadening the base of treatment for alcohol problems: a report of a study by a committee of the Institute of Medicine, Division of Mental Health and Behavioural Medicine. National Academy of Sciences, Washington DC.

Institute of Medicine (1990b) Treating drug problems: a study by a committee of the Institute of Medicine, Division of Mental Health and Behavioural Medicine. National Academy of Sciences.

Jaffe J. (1990) Drug addiction and drug abuse. In: Goodman L.S. & Gilman A. (eds) *The Pharmacological Basis of Therapeutics*. Macmillan, New York.

Jessor R. & Jessor S.L. (1977) *Problem Behaviour and Psychosocial Development: A Longitudinal Study of Youth*. Academic Press, New York.

Johanson C.E. (1988) Behavioral studies of the reinforcing properties of cocaine. In: Clouet D., Asghar K. & Brown R. (eds) *Mechanisms of Cocaine Abuse and Toxicity*, pp. 107–124. National Institute on Drug Abuse Research Monograph 88. National Institute on Drug Abuse, Rockville, MD.

Johanson C.E., Baister R.L. & Bonese K. (1976) Self-administration of psychomotor stimulant drugs: the effects of unlimited access. *Pharmacology and Biochemistry of Behaviour*, **4**, 45–51.

Johnson B.A. (1991) Cannabis. In: Glass I.B. (ed) *The International Handbook of Addiction Behaviour*, pp. 69–76. Routledge, London.

Johnson L.D., O'Malley P.M. & Bachman J.G. (1986) *Drug Use Among American High School Students, College Students and Other Young Adults: National Trends Through 1985*. National Institute on Drug Abuse Research Monograph. National Institute on Drug Abuse, Rockville, MD.

Johnson L.D., O'Malley P.M. & O'Malley P. (1988) *Illicit Drug Use, Smoking and Drinking by America's High School Students and Young Adults: 1975–1985*. National Institute on Drug Abuse Research Monograph. National Institute on Drug Abuse, Rockville, MD.

Johnson B.D., Wish E.D., Schmeidler J. & Huizinga D. (1991) The concentration of delinquent offending: serious drug involvement and high delinquency rates. *Journal of Drug Issues*, **21**, 205–229.

Kaij L. (1960) *Alcoholism in Twins: Studies on the Etiology and Sequelae of Abuse of Alcohol*. Almqvist & Wiksell, Stockholm.

Kaminer Y., Bukstein O. & Tarter R.E. (1991) The teen-addiction severity index: rational and reliability. *International Journal of Addictions*, **26**, 219–226.

Kandel D.B. (1980) Drug and drinking behaviour among youth. *Annual Review of Sociology*, **6**, 235–285.

Kandel D., Davies M., Karus D. & Yamaguchi K. (1986) The consequences in young adulthood of adolescent drug involvement. *Archives of General Psychiatry*, **43**, 746–754.

Kaprio J., Koskenvuo M., Langinvainio H., Romanov K., Sarna S. & Rose R.J. (1987) Genetic influences in use and abuse of alcohol: a study of 5638 adult Finnish twin brothers. *Alcoholism: Clinical and Experimental Research*, **11**, 349–356.

Kinder B., Pape N. & Walfish S. (1980) Drug and alcohol education programs: a review of outcome studies. *International Journal of Addictions*, **15**, 1035–1054.

Lancet Editorial (1987) Screening for drugs of abuse. *Lancet*, **i**, 365–366.

Leigh B.C. (1990) Alcohol and unsafe sex: an overview of the research literature. In: Seminara D., Ross Watson R. & Palowski A. (eds) *Alcohol Immunomodulation and AIDS*. Alan R. Liss, New York.

McCord J. (1972) Aetiological factors in alcoholism. *Quarterly Journal for the Study of Alcohol*, **33**, 1020–1027.

McCord W. & McCord J. (1960) *Origins of Alcoholism*. Stanford University Press, Stanford, CA.

MacDonald D. (1984) *Drugs, Drinking and Adolescents*. Year Book, Chicago, IL.

McGuire & Fahy T. (1991) Chronic paranoid psychosis after misuse of MDMA. *British Medical Journal*, **302**, 697.

McLellan A.T., Childress A.R., Ehrman R., O'Brien C.P. & Pashko S. (1986) An improved diagnostic evaluation instrument for substance abuse patients: the Addiction Severity Index. *Journal of Nervous and Mental Diseases*, **168**, 26–33.

Marlatt G.A. & Gordon J.R. (1985) *Relapse Prevention: Maintenance Strategies in Addictive Behaviour Change*. Guilford Press, New York.

Mayer J. & Filstead W.J. (1979) The adolescent alcohol involvement scale: an instrument for measuring adolescent use and misuse of alcohol. *Journal of Studies of Alcohol*, **40**, 291–300.

Mayfield D., McLeod G. & Hall P. (1974) The CAGE questionnaire: validation of a new alcoholism screening instrument. *American Journal of Psychiatry*, **131**, 1121–1123.

Messerei P. & Brunswick A.F. (1987) Heroin availability and aggregate levels of use: secular trends in an urban black cohort. *American Journal of Drug and Alcohol Abuse*, **13**, 109–133.

Miller J.D., Cisin I.H., Gardenere-Keaton H., Harrell A.V., Wirtz P.W.,

Abelson H.I. & Fishburne P.M. (1983) *National Survey On Drug Abuse: Main Findings 1982*. National Institute on Drug Abuse Research Monograph. National Institute on Drug Abuse, Rockville, MD.

Miller W. (1983) Motivational interviewing with problem drinkers. *Behavioural Psychotherapy*, **11**, 147–172.

Monelly E.P., Hartl E.M. & Elderkin R. (1983) Constitutional factors predictive of alcoholism in a follow up of delinquent boys. *Journal of Studies of Alcohol*, **44**, 530–537.

Mott J. (1985) Self-reported cannabis use in Great Britain in 1981. *British Journal of Addiction*, **80**, 37–43.

Mullan M. (1989) Alcoholism and the 'new genetics'. *British Journal of Addictions*, **84**, 1433–1440.

Musto D. (1987) *The American Disease. The Origins of Narcotic Control*. Oxford University Press, Oxford.

National Institute for Drug Abuse (1992) *Report on American High School Survey*. National Institute on Drug Abuse, Rockville, MD.

Newcomb M.D. & Bentler P.M. (1988) *Consequences of Adolescent Drug Use*. Sage, Beverly Hills, CA.

Newman R.G. & Whitehill W.B. (1979) Double blind comparison of methadone and placebo maintenance treatments of narcotic addicts in Hong Kong. *Lancet*, **ii**, 485–488.

O'Brien C.P., Chaddock B., Woody G.E. & Greenstein R. (1974) Systematic extinction of addiction-associated rituals using narcotic antagonists. *Psychosomatic Medicine*, **36**, 458.

Office of Population Censuses and Surveys (1986) *Adolescent Drinking*. Her Majesty's Stationery Office, London.

Oppenheimer E., Sheehan M. & Taylor C. (1988) Letting the client speak: drug misusers and the process of help seeking. *British Journal of Addiction*, **83**, 635–648.

Parker H., Bakx K. & Newcombe R. (1986) *Drug Use in Wirral: The First Report of the Wirral Misuse of Drugs Project*. Subdepartment of Social Work Studies, University of Liverpool, Liverpool.

Pearson G. (1987) *The New Heroin Users*. Basil Blackwell, Oxford.

Pearson G., Ditton J., Newcombe R. & Gilman M. (1991) *Drug Misuse in Britain: National Audit of Drug Misuse Statistics*. ISDD, London.

Pickens R.W., Svikis D.S., McGue M., Lykken D.T., Heston L.L. & Clayton P.J. (1991) Heterogeneity in the inheritance of alcoholism: a study of male and female twins. *Archives of General Psychiatry*, **48**, 19–28.

Pierce P.A. & Peroutka S.J. (1988) Antagonism of 5-hydroxytryptamine 2 receptor-mediated phosphatidyl-inositol turnover by d-lysergic acid diethylamide. *Journal of Pharmacology and Experimental Therapeutics*, **247**, 918–925.

Plant M., Peck D. & Samuel E. (1984) *Alcohol, Drugs and School-leavers*. Tavistock, London.

Pope H.G. & Katz D.L. (1987) Body builders psychosis. *Lancet*, **1**, 863.

Post R.M. (1975) Cocaine psychoses: a continuum model. *American Journal of Psychiatry*, **132**, 225–231.

Pottier A.C.W., Taylor J.C., Norman C.L. *et al.* (1992) *Trends in Deaths Associated With Abuse of Volatile Substance 1971–1990*. St Georges Hospital Medical School, London, report no. 5.

Powell J., Gray J., Bradley B., Kasvikis Y., Strang J., Barrett L. & Marks I. (1990) The effects of exposure to drug-related cues in detoxified opiate addicts: a theoretical review and some new data. *Addictive Behaviours*, **15**, 339–354.

Prochaska J.O. & DiClemente C.C. (1983) Stages and processes of self-change of smoking: towards a more integrative model of change. *Journal of Consulting and Clinical Psychology*, **51**, 390–395.

Radhert E.R. (1991) (ed) *The Adolescent Assessment/Referral System Manual*. Department of Health and Human Services, Public Health Service; Alcohol, Drug Abuse and Mental Health Administration, Rockville, MD.

Rankin H., Hodgson R. & Stockwell T. (1983) Cue exposure and response prevention with alcoholics: a controlled trial. *Behaviour Research and Therapy*, **21**, 435–446.

Robertson J.A. & Plant M.A. (1988) Alcohol, sex and the risks of HIV infection. *Drug and Alcohol Dependence*, **22**, 75–78.

Robins L.N. (1966) *Deviant Children Grown Up*. Williams & Wilkins, Baltimore, MD.

Robins L. (1980) Epidemiological findings in drug abuse. In: Purcell E. (ed) *Psychopathology of Childhood and Youth: A Cross Cultural Perspective*. Josiah Macy Jr Foundation, Packamack Lake, NJ.

Robins L.N. & Przybeck T.R. (1985) Age of onset of drug use as a factor in drug and other disorders. In: La Rue Jones C., Battjes R.J. (eds) *Etiology of Drug Abuse, Implications for Prevention*. National Institute on Drug Abuse Research Monograph 56. National Institute on Drug Abuse, Rockville, MD.

Robins L.N., Helzer J.E. & Goodwin D.W. (1974) Drug users in Vietnam: a follow up on return to USA. *American Journal of Epidemiology*, **99**, 235–249.

Rosenthal M. (1989) The therapeutic community exploring the boundaries. *British Journal of Addiction*, **84**, 141–150.

Royal College of Psychiatrists (1987) *Drugs Scenes*. A report on drugs and drug dependence. Royal College of Psychiatrists, London.

Rush T. (1979) Predicting treatment outcome. In: Beschner G. & Friedman A. (eds) *The Pennsylvania Substance-Abuse System in Youth Drug Abuse: Problems, Issues and Treatment*. Lexington Books, Lexington, MA.

Sakol M., Stark C. & Sykes R. (1989) Buprenorphine and temazepam abuse by drug takers in Glasgow — an increase. *British Journal of Addiction*, **84**, 434–441.

Schaps E., Moskowitz J., Condon J. & Malvin J. (1982) Process and outcome evaluation of a drug education course. *Journal of Drug Education*, **12**, 253–364.

Schinke S.P., Botvin G.J. & Orlandi M.A. (1991) *Substance Abuse in Children and Adolescents. Evaluation and Intervention*. Developmental Clinical Psychology; 22. Sage, Beverly Hills, CA.

Schuckit M.A. (1984) Subjective responses to alcohol in sons of alcoholics and control subjects. *Archives of General Psychiatry*, **41**, 879–884.

Schuckit M. (1985) Studies of populations at high risk for alcoholism. *Journal of Psychiatric Development*, **3**, 31–65.

Schuckit M.A. (1987) Biological vulnerability to alcoholism. *Journal of Consulting and Clinical Psychology*, **55**, 301–309.

Sells S. & Simpson D. (1979) Evaluation of treatment outcome for youths in the drug abuse reporting program (DARP): a follow up study. In: Beschner G. & Friedman A.S. (eds) *Youth Drug Abuse: Problems, Issues and Treatment*. Lexington Books, Lexington, MA.

Selzer M.L. (1971) The Michigan alcoholism screening test: the quest for a new diagnostic instrument. *American Journal of Psychiatry*, **127**, 1653–1658.

Shapiro H. (1991) Running scared: the use of drugs in sport. *British Journal of Addiction*, **86**, 5–8.

Simpson D.D. & Sells S.B. (1982) Effectiveness of treatment for drug abuse: an overview of the DARP research program. *Advances in Alcohol and Substance Abuse*, **2**, 7–29.

Skinner H.A. (1982) The drug abuse screening test. *Addictive Behaviour*, **7**, 363–371.

Stabeneau J. (1990) Additive independent risk factors that predict risk for alcoholism. *Journal of Study of Alcohol*, **51**, 164–174.

Stanton D. & Todd T.C. (1982) *The Family Therapy of Drug Abuse and Addiction*. Guilford, New York.

Stein L. & Belluzzi J.D. (1987) Reward transmitters and drugs of abuse. In: Engel J., Oreland L., Ingvar D.H., Pernow B., Rössner S. & Pellborn L.A. (eds) *Brain Reward Systems and Abuse*, pp. 19–34. Raven Press, New York.

Stimson G.V. & Oppenheimer E. (1982) *Heroin Addiction Treatment and*

Control. Tavistock, London.

Stimson G.V., Alldritt L., Dolan K. & Donoghue M. (1988) Syringe exchange schemes for drug users in England and Scotland. *British Medical Journal*, **296**, 1717–1719.

Strang J., Bradley B. & Stockwell T. (1989) Assessment of drug and alcohol use. In: Thompson C. (ed) *The Instruments of Psychiatric Research*, pp. 211–236. John Wiley, Chichester.

Swadi H. (1988) Drug and substance use among 3333 London adolescents. *British Journal of Addiction*, **83**, 935–942.

Tarter R.E. (1990) Evaluation and treatment of adolescent substance abuse: a decision tree method. *American Journal of Drug and Alcohol Abuse*, **16**, 1–46.

Tarter R.E., McBride H., Buonpane N., Dorothea R.N. & Schneider N. (1977) Differentiation of alcoholics: childhood history and drinking pattern. *Archives of General Psychiatry*, **34**, 761–768.

Tarter R.E., Hegedus A.M., Goldstein G., Shelly C. & Alterman A.I. (1984) Adolescent sons of alcoholics: neuropsychological and personality characteristics. *Alcoholism: Clinical and Experimental Research*, **8**, 216–222.

Vaillant G.E. (1983) *The Natural History of Alcoholism: Causes, Patterns and Paths to Recovery.* Harvard University Press, Cambridge, MA.

van Ree J.M. (1987) Reward and abuse: opiates and neuropeptides. In: Engel J., Orland L., Ingvar D.H., Pernow B., Rössner S. & Pellborn L.A. (eds) *Brain Reward Systems and Abuse*, pp. 75–88. Raven Press, New York.

von Knorring L., Oreland L. & von Knorring A.L. (1987) Personality traits and platelet MAO activity in alcohol and drug abusing teenage boys. *Acta Psychiatrica Scandinavica*, **75**, 307–314.

Warburton D., Revell A.D. & Thompson D.H. (1991) Smokers of the future. *British Journal of Addiction*, **86**, 621–625.

Weisman C.S., Plichta S., Nathanson C.A., Ensminger M. & Robinson J.C. (1991) Consistency of condom use for disease prevention among adolescent users of oral contraceptives. *Family Planning Perspective*, **23**, 71.

Wheeler K. & Malmquist J. (1987) Treatment approaches in adolescent chemical dependency. *Pediatric Clinic of North America*, **34**, 437–447.

White H.R. (1987) Longitudinal stability and dimensional structure of problem drinking in adolescents. *Journal of Studies on Alcohol*, **48**, 541–550.

Wikler A. (1965) Conditioning factors in opiate addiction and relapse. In: Willner D.I. & Kassenbaum G.G. (eds) *Narcotics*, pp. 85–100. McGraw Hill, New York.

World Health Organization (1981) *Documents on Nomenclature and Classification.* WHO, Geneva.

World Health Organization (1992) *The ICD-10 Classification of Mental and Behavioural Disorders: Clinical Descriptions and Diagnostic Guidelines.* World Health Organization, Geneva.

Wright J.D. & Pearl L. (1990) Knowledge and experience of young people regarding drug abuse, 1969–1989. *British Medical Journal*, **300**, 99–103.

Wu T.C., Tashkin D.P., Djahed D. & Rose J.E. (1988) Pulmonary hazards of smoking marijuana as compared with tobacco. *New England Journal of Medicine*, **318**, 347–351.

Yokel R.A. (1987) Intravenous self-administration: response rates, the effects of pharmacological challenges and drug preference. In: Bozarth M.A. (ed) *Methods of Assessing the Reinforcing Properties of Abused Drugs*, pp. 1–35. Springer-Verlag, New York.

Chapter 32
Developmental Disorders of Speech and Language

D.V.M. Bishop

A 5-year-old marches up to his mother with a glass in hand and demands: 'wan doo' ('want juice'). A toddler shows no understanding of spoken language, but the audiologist declares she has normal hearing. A teenager responds to the question: 'Can you draw the curtains?' by finding paper and pencil and drawing a picture. In each case, the child's language departs from what is normal at that age, but the manifestations of language disorder are remarkably varied. This chapter aims to help those without a background in psycholinguistics to recognize when language is abnormal, and to understand the causes, assessment, diagnosis and management of these diverse disorders.

THE CONCEPT OF SPECIFIC SPEECH AND LANGUAGE DISORDER

In order to learn to speak, the child must be exposed to language and have the necessary biological equipment to decode and produce speech: adequate sensory apparatus to perceive language input, a brain that can detect and learn the underlying structure of language and an articulatory apparatus which can be programmed to produce speech sounds. Language disorders can result if children have inadequate exposure to language or if they suffer from medical conditions that compromise the biological bases for language learning. However, in the majority of children who present with speech and language difficulties there is no obvious cause. Hearing is normal, nonverbal intelligence is adequate, there is no physical or emotional disorder that can account for the language problems and the home language environment seems unremarkable. This chapter will be mainly concerned with considering the definition and diagnosis of these mysterious disorders and documenting what we know about their nature and cause.

Terminology: developmental dysphasia and specific speech and language disorder

Developmental language disorders of unknown origin were first described around the turn of the century by neurologists who noticed similarities between the symptoms observed in children and those seen in aphasic adults after focal brain lesions. The term developmental dysphasia was coined to describe cases where the language difficulties appeared to be selective, and were not explicable in terms of hearing loss or mental handicap. Terms such as developmental dysphasia and congenital aphasia remain popular in continental Europe, but in the UK and North America they have been largely superseded by expressions such as specific speech and language disorder or developmental language disorder. There are several reasons for this. One is that neurological labels can be misleading in implying that there is independent evidence of a neurological basis for the condition. Parents may react with great relief on being told that their child is dysphasic, saying that at last someone has given them an explanation for their child's difficulties. They fail to appreciate that the diagnosis is no explanation at all, only a shorthand description of the problem. A further reason for rejecting a label such as developmental dysphasia is that it suggests we are dealing with a single condition, whereas children with unexplained speech and language difficulties may have widely different problems.

Contemporary specifications of diagnostic criteria: DSM-IV and ICD-10

In DSM-IV (American Psychiatric Association, in press) specific developmental speech and language disorders are classified as one of the group of disorders usually diagnosed in infancy, childhood or adolescence. Diagnostic criteria are shown in Figure 32.1.

ICD-10 (World Health Organization, 1992) also includes a category of specific developmental disorders of speech and language (code F80) and draws a similar threefold distinction between specific speech articulation disorder (F80.0); expressive language disorder (F80.1); and receptive language disorder (F80.2). It also includes under this broad heading acquired aphasia with epilepsy (Landau–Kleffner syndrome; F80.3) and additional categories of other disorder (F80.8) and unspecified disorder (F80.9). These last two subcategories will not be considered further here: category F80.8 (other) covers lisping, which is seldom of clinical significance, and category F80.9 (unspecified) is a default category to be used only when other subcategories do not apply.

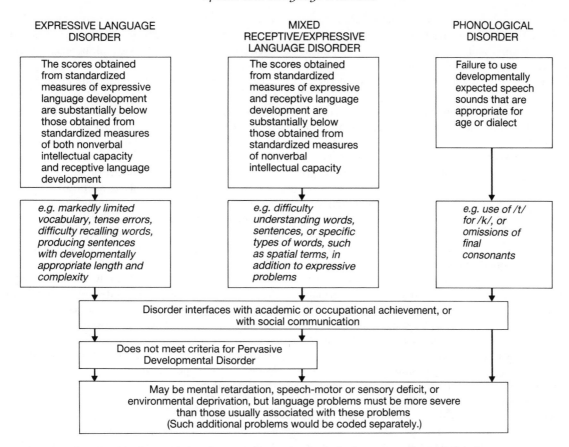

Fig. 32.1 DSM-IV (American Psychiatric Association, in press) diagnostic criteria for language and speech disorders.

Subtypes of specific speech and language disorders

Subtypes within DSM-IV and ICD-10

Both DSM-IV and ICD-10 distinguish between disorders affecting only expressive language and those where receptive language is impaired. Although this subgrouping is reasonably straightforward to apply, it is undoubtedly an oversimplification. For example, receptive problems include difficulties in decoding speech sounds (e.g. failure to distinguish between 'gate' and 'date'), limited knowledge of word meaning (e.g. treating 'gate' and 'fence' as synonyms), problems in interpreting complex grammatical constructions (e.g. uncertainty about the sequence when told 'shut the gate after you cross the field'), and a tendency to be over-literal (e.g. the child who replies 'yes' without moving when asked 'can you shut the gate'). Likewise, the category of expressive language disorder groups together children with diverse difficulties.

Although both systems include a category for children with specific problems of speech sound production, DSM-IV has abandoned the earlier term 'developmental articulation disorder' for 'phonological disorder'. This reflects increasing recognition that for many children such difficulties are linguistic rather than motor in origin. The child is usually physically capable of producing correct sounds, but has problems in learning how to classify speech sounds. For instance, the child may not realize that 'see' and 'soup' begin with the same phoneme (Bird & Bishop, 1992).

Classifications based on neurolinguistic criteria

An alternative approach to classification has been adopted by Rapin and Allen (1983) who proposed a nosology based on clinical observation of linguistic characteristics of language impairment. Unlike other systems, this classification is not restricted to children with specific language disorders, but is intended to be applied to all children with language difficulties, irrespective of whether other disorders, such as autism, are present.

The commonest type of disorder that they recognize is *phonologic–syntactic syndrome*, where the child has problems in learning the speech sound system (phonology) and has limited mastery of grammatical structures (syntax) in expressive language. Most children who would be classified as cases of expressive language disorder in DSM-IV would fit this category. Rapin and Allen distinguish phonologic–syntactic syndrome from *phonologic programming deficit syndrome*, in which the expressive difficulties are so severe as to render the child largely unintelligible, but normal comprehension is preserved.

A very different type of expressive disorder is *lexical–syntactic deficit syndrome*, where the child speaks clearly, but has problems with word-finding and sentence formulation. Because the child's speech does not sound obviously abnormal, this type of problem may be overlooked unless standardized assessments are used.

A rare type of receptive language disorder described by Rapin and Allen is *verbal auditory agnosia*, which is diagnosed when a child with severe comprehension problems appears to be having difficulty interpreting speech sounds. Many children with acquired aphasia with epilepsy would receive this diagnosis, although the diagnosis would also be applied to other children with severe comprehension problems occurring as a developmental disorder.

Comprehension problems of a different kind are seen in children with *semantic–pragmatic syndrome*. Semantics is the branch of linguistics concerned with meaning, and pragmatics deal with how language is used in different contexts. The diagnostic label specifies that for these children the abnormalities are in language content and use, rather than with aspects of language form (i.e. grammar and phonology). Rapin (1982) summarized the clinical characteristics of such children as including fluent, clearly articulated speech that may be echolalic, word-finding problems and impaired comprehension of discourse. The children are talkative and may be described as 'hyperverbal'. Those who fit this clinical picture produce language that seems odd and inappropriate, rather than just poor for their age.

Although the nosology proposed by Rapin and Allen appears to be a step forward in refining our classification of developmental language disorders, anyone attempting to apply this framework in a clinical setting will find that the diagnostic boundaries remain imprecisely specified, and some children defy attempts at classification within this system. Several studies have found that the profile of language impairment can change as children mature (Bishop & Edmundson, 1987a; Scarborough & Dobrich, 1990; Whitehurst *et al.*, 1991a), and it is possible that some of the subgroups that have been described correspond to different points in development rather than to distinct clinical entities. A multicentre longitudinal study is currently under way in the US to evaluate Rapin and Allen's nosological framework (Rapin, 1987).

ASSESSMENT OF THE CHILD WITH SPEECH AND LANGUAGE PROBLEMS

Parental interview

General guidelines for interviewing parents are given in Chapter 3. Here, attention will be restricted to points that commonly arise when interviewing parents of children with speech and language disorders.

An interview can not only provide important information about the child's characteristics, but will also give an indication of the level of parental anxiety and their attitude to the child and to professional agencies. It is not uncommon for parents of first-born children to be unaware that their child's progress is slow until the child starts at nursery school when the discrepancy with verbal skills of other children becomes obvious.

Parents should be asked for specific instances of language behaviour, rather than for general statements. Norms for milestones, described by Neligan and Prudham (1969; see Table 32.1), can give a preliminary indication of the severity of language delay in relation to other attainments, but it should be borne in mind that parental recall after several years is likely to be unreliable. However, a parental report of regression of language skills is an unusual and potentially important observation, and should be taken seriously. Many children with delayed language development also have other behaviour disorders, but these may be ignored unless the parent is carefully questioned, because the parent finds it easier to seek help for language difficulties.

The perinatal, medical and family history may provide some clues as to the aetiology of disorder, although it is not uncommon to find an uneventful history in children with developmental speech and language disorders. Few such children have any clear indications of neurological disease, and it can be difficult to estimate the importance of common perinatal hazards such as prematurity or toxaemia in the aetiology of these disorders.

Physical examination

The physical examination of children in general is covered in Chapter 6. For the child with speech and language problems, a careful examination of the structural and functional integrity of the speech apparatus is especially important. One needs to be alert to the possibility of physical anomalies such as submucous cleft palate which may interfere with speech production. Detailed guidelines for the examination of neurological mechanisms concerned with control of the speech apparatus are provided by Brown (1985). Involuntary grimacing, drooling, abnormalities of the gag reflex and impairment of sucking and swallowing are important upper motor neuron signs. Most children with a speech disorder caused by

Table 32.1 Age (in months) for passing language milestones (based on Neligan & Prudham, 1969)

Percentile	Single words*		Sentences†	
	Boys	Girls	Boys	Girls
3rd	8.7	8.6	17.5	16.2
10th	10.0	9.8	19.1	18.4
25th	11.6	11.5	21.4	20.4
50th	12.4	12.3	23.8	22.9
75th	15.0	14.6	26.8	25.0
90th	18.0	17.3	32.5	30.8
97th	21.9	20.1	36.0+	36.0

* Three or four different words for people or objects, correctly used.
† Three or more words, strung together to make some sort of sense.

neurological disease will have delayed motor milestones, with abnormalities of muscle tone, persistent primitive reflexes and/or involuntary movements.

Medical investigations

There are relatively few cases of speech and language disorder in children where management will be significantly influenced by the outcome of laboratory tests or neurophysiological investigations. One exception is where language skills have regressed after a period of normal development. This history is suggestive of acquired epileptic aphasia (see below) and should prompt a full electroencephalographic (EEG) investigation, including a sleep recording.

Although there may be no direct implications for management, biological investigations may be of value, either in providing parents with an explanation for their child's disorder or in ruling out unwarranted fears. Bishop (1987) noted that chromosome analysis seldom gives positive findings, and is most likely to reveal anomalies in children with severe expressive speech and language problems, where speech is described as dyspraxic, and where there is associated clumsiness. Procedures such as computed tomography (CT) and magnetic resonance imaging (MRI) are unlikely to demonstrate any underlying brain lesion, except in cases where there are severe comprehension problems with associated behavioural problems (see review by Bishop, 1987).

Assessment of hearing and auditory perception

Failure to detect hearing loss is one of the most serious diagnostic errors that is made in this field, leading some authors to recommend that *all* children referred for speech and language assessment should have a full audiological evaluation (Coplan, 1987). However, in many countries such a policy would place an intolerable burden on audiological services. It is dangerous to rely on informal observations of the child's responsiveness to sound (Coplan, 1987; McCormick, 1988a), but there are reliable screening tests suitable for administration in the community health setting (McCormick, 1988b).

Where a child does not give clear and unambiguous evidence of normal hearing on a screening test, then full assessment by an audiologist is required. There are well-established behavioural procedures for assessing hearing using pure tone audiometry in children over 3 years of age, but these are unsuitable for younger children whose concentration and cooperation are less good. Over the past two decades, a range of electrophysiological procedures has been devised to provide accurate threshold estimation in such cases. The most popular method is brainstem evoked response audiometry, a non-invasive technique in which repetitive clicks or tones are presented, and the electrical response in the brain is recorded and averaged across many stimuli. There is good agreement between threshold estimation based on electrophysiology and that obtained with behavioural audiometry (Parving & Elberling, 1982).

Tympanometry is a quick and simple procedure for assessing middle ear function (Brooks, 1987), but is not recommended in isolation from other methods because of the relatively high proportion of cases that give abnormal recordings that merely reflect transient changes in the absence of any clear pathology or educationally significant hearing impairment.

Some children with receptive language disorder show a marked discrepancy between audiological test results and reactions to auditory stimuli outside the test situation. Such children may show poor discrimination between auditory stimuli or variable reactivity to sound from one occasion to another, and yet if hearing is found to be adequate on the basis of procedures such as electrocochleography or brainstem evoked response, then the verdict 'normal hearing' is all too often returned, and the ball placed firmly back in the court of other specialists. Where such an inconsistent picture is observed, three possibilities must be considered.

The first is that the audiological assessment was inaccurate or incomplete. False negatives (i.e. a diagnosis of normal hearing when there is hearing loss) should not occur when behavioural audiometry is performed by a qualified specialist, because the procedure is designed to prevent use of non-auditory cues or lucky guesses. However, McCormick (1988a) found that where screening tests were administered by individuals who have only brief training in their use (e.g. as in the hearing checks administered by health visitors in the UK), there may be a high rate of error. He found this could be dramatically improved by better training. Electrophysiological methods are generally regarded as highly accurate, but they are insensitive to hearing loss below 1000 Hz. A false-negative diagnosis is most likely when reliance is placed on a single measure of peripheral hearing, such as acoustic reflex or tympanometry (Berlin, 1978).

The second possibility to consider is that the child has a progressive hearing loss. It is worth insisting on repeated audiological testing a few months after the first assessment if the child's behaviour continues to suggest poor hearing.

If neither of these two explanations applies, then this suggests the child has a central auditory impairment. Speech processing involves discrimination between transient stimuli with complex spectra, and there is evidence from animal studies that cortical lesions can impair such discriminations, yet conventional audiometric techniques do not evaluate this ability; they merely require the child to detect that a sound has occurred. Unfortunately, there are no nonverbal tests standardized on children that test higher auditory functions. The diagnosis of central auditory impairment is sometimes made on the basis of abnormal auditory responses which, in adults, are known to be indicative of lesions of auditory cortex. These include problems in understanding distorted or filtered speech and difficulties in integrating auditory signals from the two ears (Jerger, 1964). There are, however, dangers in using tests that involve speech stimuli to diagnose central auditory impairment in a child with poor language.

Assessment of nonverbal communication, social development and play

In normal children, the emergence of language is closely tied to development of other aspects of symbolic and communicative behaviour. Thus, before the first words are produced, the infant uses gestures and gaze patterns to perform communicative functions such as requesting or showing. The normal infant is highly sociable, aware of and interested in others, seeking to gain the caregiver's attention and responsive to communicative overtures. Most children who have difficulty in using verbal communication will compensate for this by using nonverbal methods of communication, such as gestures — failure to do so is suggestive of autistic disorder. Most language assessments for toddlers include some items concerned with the use of nonverbal communication (see the section on measuring speech and language function, below), and the Symbolic Play Test (Lowe & Costello, 1976) provides a useful index of developmental level of play.

Assessment of nonverbal intelligence

Delayed language development is often the first warning sign of unexplained general delays in development. Montgomery (1988) found that speech delay was the commonest presenting symptom in children aged between 2 and 6 years who had no identifiable syndrome but had IQs below 70. It is therefore important to assess intelligence in any young child presenting with delayed language development. Procedures for assessing intelligence are reviewed in Chapter 7, and this chapter will simply mention features of special relevance to language-impaired children, where one needs a measure of intellectual level that is as free as possible from the effects of language disorder. The Stanford–Binet Intelligence Scale (Terman & Merrill, 1960) is not suitable for this purpose, because it includes many items involving expressive and receptive language. The performance subtests of the Wechsler scales (Wechsler, 1974, 1990) are more appropriate and are well-standardized. Other tests that are widely used in this context are the Columbia Mental Maturity Scale (Burgemeister *et al.*, 1972), and Raven's Matrices (Raven, 1963). Although these tests use verbal instructions, there is seldom any problem in conveying to the child what is required. However, in young children with severe comprehension problems, there may be reason to prefer a test that involves no verbal instructions at all. The Leiter International Performance Scale (Leiter, 1969) was designed for use with deaf children, and makes ample use of demonstration without verbal instructions. Interpretation of results, however, is hindered by the lack of up-to-date standardization data.

One may encounter reluctance among psychologists to use intelligence tests with language-impaired children. Stark and Tallal (1981) reported that 50 out of 132 children referred to them as cases of specific speech and language disorders had non-verbal IQs below 85, with at least 10 of these scoring below 60. There was a widespread belief by those referring the children that genuine abilities were masked by language problems. However, these children showed no evidence of latent abilities when tested using instruments standardized on deaf populations. Overall, it does seem that nonverbal IQ provides useful diagnostic and prognostic information, provided that those interpreting test results appreciate the error of measurement associated with test scores.

Measuring speech and language function

Below 3 years of age

Many children below the age of 3 years are reluctant to speak in the presence of strangers and have limited ability to cooperate in formal comprehension tests. Traditionally, paediatricians have relied on parental estimates of a few critical milestones, but in recent years there has been dissatisfaction with such gross indices, and a recognition that retrospective parental report is often inaccurate. This has led to a move towards more detailed assessment schedules, where parents describe current features of communicative behaviour. One widely used scale is the Early Language Milestone (ELM) Scale, designed by Coplan *et al.* (1982), which provides developmental norms for a range of visual as well as verbal communication skills in children aged from 0 to 36 months. A sample chart is shown in Figure 32.2.

More recently, a comprehensive assessment of early language, the MacArthur Communicative Development Inventories, has been developed and standardized on children learning a range of different languages (Dale, 1991; Fenson *et al.*, 1991). Parents check words that their child produces and understands, indicate the types of gestures and communicative actions used, and provide an indication of complexity of language by selecting from pairs of alternatives the utterance that is most like the language produced by their child.

Coplan and Gleason (1988) noted that few physicians are knowledgeable about speech sound production, and many have difficulty recognizing delayed or deviant articulation in young children. They conducted a study in which parents were simply asked: 'How clear is your child's speech? That is, how much of your child's speech can a stranger understand: (1) less than half; (2) about half; (3) three-quarters; (4) all or almost all?' They found a gradual increase in intelligibility: with virtually complete intelligibility being reported for 25% of 2-year-olds, rising to 90% of $4\frac{1}{2}$-year-olds. They recommend that children who score below the 10th centile for their age should be referred for detailed evaluation by a speech and language therapist. In practice, this criterion would select any child who was less than 50% intelligible at 22 months, less than 75% intelligible at 37 months, or less than fully intelligible by 47 months.

Although it is frequently stated that parents are the best people to evaluate the language competence of young children, some caution is required. Many parents overestimate verbal comprehension abilities, because the child makes good use of context and nonverbal communicative cues to interpret what

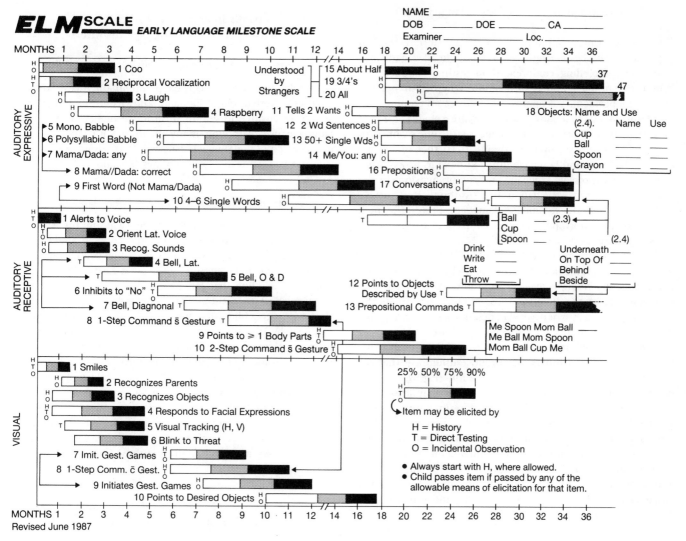

Fig. 32.2 Sample chart from the Early Language Milestone Scale. (From Coplan *et al.*, 1982.)

is said. Furthermore, parental characteristics that are associated with high risk of language disorder in offspring are precisely those that are likely to make parents unreliable informants. Mothers who themselves are inarticulate or illiterate may be daunted by the language used in questionnaires, particularly if written responses are required, and those who suffer from depression or other psychiatric disorders may have difficulty in providing accurate information about their children. Where possible, one should supplement parental report with direct observation of the child's communicative functioning with a familiar adult in a natural setting. This not only provides confirmation of the adult's account; it also can indicate how the child *uses* language communicatively, and how the adult responds to communicative attempts. Simply observing the child with a parent in a waiting area can provide relevant information. Home videos can also be useful.

3–6 years of age

When children are old enough for more formal testing, it is best to ask a speech and language therapist for a detailed language assessment, but there are some quick and simple procedures that can be used by those with little specialist linguistic knowledge to get an idea of how the child's performance relates to that of others of the same age. Two tests suitable for British children are the Action Picture Test (Renfrew, 1988), which uses single pictures to elicit responses containing particular grammatical structures from the child, and the Bus Story Test (Renfrew, 1969), which requires the child to listen to a story accompanied by cartoon pictures and then retell it to an adult. Normative data on British children are available to indicate whether expressive language content and form are broadly within normal limits, and the tests have been found to have good predictive validity in identifying children who are at risk for persistent language difficulties (Bishop & Edmundson, 1987a).

Whenever there is indication of delay or deviance in expressive speech or language, a more detailed language assessment, including comprehension testing, is called for. Where the primary aim is to diagnose whether or not the child has a problem, it is appropriate to place an emphasis on standardized tests that allow one to compare a child's performance with that of others of the same age. If one's aim is to make a diagnosis based on DSM-IV or ICD-10, then only three aspects of speech and language function need to be assessed: articulation, expressive language and comprehension. In the UK, the Edinburgh Articulation Test (Anthony *et al.*, 1977) and the Reynell Developmental Language Scales (Reynell, 1977) are the most popular standardized instruments for assessing these functions.

Global tests of expressive and receptive language function do not give a very detailed picture of a child's abilities. For instance, some children may obtain a low score on a test of expressive language because they produce grammatically simplified sentences when asked to describe a picture (e.g. 'big dog go woof'); others may use general terms rather than specific vocabulary items (e.g. 'that one there, it's big, it's doing that'), and yet others may produce utterances that are only tangentially relevant to the situation (e.g. 'I've got a rabbit at home'). A comprehension disorder may arise for a number of reasons, e.g. difficulty in discriminating speech sounds, lack of knowledge of word meaning, poor memory for long sentences, difficulty in understanding grammatically complex utterances, or problems in drawing inferences about what is not directly stated. Useful accounts of standardized and informal assessment procedures for a more fine-grained language assessment can be found in Wiig and Semel (1984) and Lahey (1988).

7 years and above

There is a dearth of standardized language tests suitable for school-aged children. One reason for this is that normal children reach ceiling levels on many tests by 5 or 6 years of age. However, more complex aspects of grammar and vocabulary remain to be mastered, as well as appreciation of discourse and written language. The Test for Reception of Grammar (Bishop, 1989a) is a standardized comprehension test suitable for school-aged children which tests understanding of a range of late-acquired structures, such as 'neither . . . nor' and 'not only . . . but also' constructions, as well as sentences with various types of subordinate clause. The Test of Adolescent Language (Hammill *et al.*, 1980) is designed to assess high-level language in adolescents, e.g. requiring the testee to extract meaning from longer passages of language, and to answer questions that involve drawing inferences.

Pitfalls in assessment of children with speech and language disorders

Reliance on IQ testing to establish language ability

Verbal IQ tests are concerned predominantly with testing children's verbal reasoning and knowledge, and they are largely insensitive to grammatical impairments or abnormal language use. Although many children with language disorders do have a relatively low verbal IQ, this is not necessarily the case (Cohen *et al.*, 1989; Haynes & Naidoo, 1991).

Assuming that children mean what they say

Some young children use language that, on the surface, sounds extremely sophisticated, incorporating vocabulary and phrases (e.g. 'you see', 'well, actually') that are usually only found in the conversation of adults. It is easy to fall into the trap of concluding that language is not a problem for such children, and to assume that they mean what they say. However, the child may have learnt the surface form of language by imitation, with little grasp of the content, and so produce utterances with little understanding of their meaning. Comprehension testing will then reveal significant impairments. For example, the author observed a child who produced utterances such as 'We went on a bus because Lee was sick out of the window'. This type of language suggested a diagnosis of thought disorder, but further testing indicated that the child simply did not understand the meaning of connectives such as 'because', 'but' and 'and', and used these interchangeably to join utterances together.

Relying solely on clinical observation and ignoring standardized tests

Even those experts who regularly see children with language disorders find it difficult to estimate a child's language level relative to a peer group just on the basis of informal observation. Clinicians seldom see normally developing children, and so internal standards of what it is reasonable to expect at a given age can drift downwards. Reliance on clinical observation is likely to lead to overestimation of a child's language abilities.

Relying solely on standardized tests and ignoring clinical observation

Some language-impaired children, especially older children with the clinical features of 'semantic–pragmatic syndrome' (see above) may perform very well in a formal assessment, but reveal difficulties in communication in more open-ended situations such as when one attempts to converse with the child. Standardized tests are important, but they must be supplemented with other information about how the child uses language in everyday interactions.

In many languages, no standardized tests exist to assess children's verbal competence and it is tempting to use translated versions of tests with British or American norms. However, this is a dangerous procedure. Differences between languages are such that it is not safe to assume that translated items will be of equivalent difficulty. Restandardization on the native population is essential. It is preferable to have no quantitative index of comprehension than to give a spurious impression of accuracy by misuse of norms from another language.

Inadequate assessment of speech, language and hearing in children with low IQ and/or a clinical syndrome

There is a tendency by some clinicians to lose all interest in a child's language abilities once an explanation for the disorder has been found and the diagnosis of specific language impairment has been ruled out. However, those whose language problems occur in the context of other disorders merit just as much concern as those with more selective difficulties.

Hecox (1982) noted that when a chromosomal anomaly results in dysmorphic features, there is a tendency to assume that the child is mentally retarded and to treat this as an adequate explanation for delayed language. However, many such children, including those with Down's syndrome as well as those with rarer short and long arm deletions, are at particularly high risk for peripheral hearing loss. Furthermore children with cleft palate typically have unremitting middle ear disease which can affect their articulatory proficiency (Hubbard *et al.*, 1985). Craniofacial anomalies should therefore alert the clinician to the need for audiological investigation. Similar considerations apply to neurological conditions that cause dysarthria: in children with Möbius syndrome, for instance, there may be involvement of the auditory nerve as well as cranial nerves VI and VII. High-frequency hearing loss is associated with athetoid cerebral palsy. The message is simple: where a child already has a major handicapping condition, audiological investigation is crucial.

Presence of a physical basis for a speech disorder does not exclude the possibility of additional language difficulties — on the contrary, the two types of disorder frequently co-occur. It is important therefore to assess language skills using comprehension tests that do not involve speech in any child who presents with a speech difficulty. Cerebral palsied children with severe physical handicaps can pose a major diagnostic challenge. In a young child with limited motor control and little or no speech, it can be difficult to establish how far the problem is purely one of anarthria or dysarthria, with intact underlying language skills, and how far there are more general difficulties with language comprehension. There are sufficient documented cases of underestimation of cognitive and linguistic potential of severely handicapped individuals to make one very wary of relying on initial impressions to assess comprehension. Multiple choice methods of assessment can be used provided one can find a response that the individual can reliably use to select between alternatives (whether this be by eyepointing, blinking or operating a computer keyboard).

DIFFERENTIAL DIAGNOSIS OF SPECIFIC SPEECH AND LANGUAGE DISORDERS

Identifying language impairment in practice

The first problem for those wishing to apply the diagnostic criteria specified in DSM-IV or ICD-10 is how to quantify speech and language in relation to the child's age. A 3-year-old who said 'tat' for 'cat', 'fower' for 'flower' or 'him jump' rather than 'he jumped' would not be regarded as having a disorder, whereas a 6-year-old who persisted in such usage would give cause for concern. These examples are clear enough, but what about the child who is still saying 't' for 'k', reducing consonant clusters or speaking in two-word utterances at the age of 4 years? In English-speaking countries one can at least turn to a substantial research database for guidance. However, other languages contain different sounds and grammatical constructions and in many cases little is known about normal patterns of acquisition. In countries where no suitable standardized tests exist, one must rely on the examples of language behaviour given in DSM-IV and ICD-10 to identify cases where children are falling below expected age levels. For instance, ICD-10 specifies that the absence of single words (or word approximations) by 2 years and the failure to generate simple two-word phrases by the age of 3 years are significant signs of delay.

Where standardized tests are available, these provide a basis for quantifying the abnormality of a given language level relative to the child's age. It is common practice to convert results into language-age-equivalent scores, which are arrived at by finding the age at which the obtained score is the average (Stark & Tallal, 1981). There are, however, major problems with this approach (McCauley & Swisher, 1984; Bishop, 1989c). The statistical abnormality of a lag in language age relative to chronological age will vary from test to test. A 2-year gap between language age and chronological age sounds like a severe problem, but for many language tests in common use, such a discrepancy is not at all unusual in the normal population.

One way of avoiding this problem is to use standardized language tests to identify children whose scores are statistically abnormal, e.g. more than 2 s.d. below the mean. However, if we rely on a statistical definition of disorder, we create a new dilemma, because then the prevalence of disorder will remain constant across different ages and different cultures. One may, for instance, be alarmed to hear that some surveys find as many as 16% of children to have a speech and language impairment. However, if the presence of disorder is defined in terms of the child scoring at least 1 s.d. below the population mean, then this is exactly the prevalence figure one will obtain — and it would remain the same even if the language level of the whole population increased dramatically. In ICD-10 it is noted that older children do show progressive improvement and it is implied that the diagnosis of specific speech and language impairment may be appropriate in children whose test scores are in the normal range, but who previously had particularly severe difficulties with an abnormal pattern of language functioning. It is evident that, although recommendations such as these are probably the best that can realistically be proposed in our current state of knowledge, they do leave an uncomfortably large amount of room for subjective variation in making a diagnosis.

Distinguishing specific from more general delays

It is easy enough to identify cases of severe mental handicap where language and nonverbal abilities are both well behind age level, but there is far greater difficulty in making a diagnosis when a child with language difficulties has nonverbal intelligence that is below age level but not in the mentally handicapped range. This is a very common situation. Several longitudinal studies have found that low scores on tests of nonverbal IQ are two to three times as common in children with poor language attainments (Silva, 1987). For example, in a survey of 7-year-olds (Silva *et al.*, 1984), 57 out of 827 children failed an articulation screening test. Ten per cent were mentally handicapped (IQ less than 70) and 33% had IQs between 76 and 89.

Whether these children are included as cases of specific developmental language disorder depends on the definition we adopt. Some authorities use a cut-off approach, where the child must achieve some minimal level of nonverbal ability (e.g. an IQ of 70) in order to meet diagnostic criteria. However, this leads to two problems. If the cut-off is set relatively low, there is a danger of including children who do not appear to have a substantial discrepancy between verbal and nonverbal functioning; to take an extreme case, we could end up including a child with a nonverbal IQ of 71 and a verbal score of 69. However, if a higher cut-off is set, then we will exclude cases where a child with a low nonverbal IQ has a language problem far more severe than is compatible with overall functioning, e.g. an 8-year-old child with a nonverbal IQ of 75 who is totally mute.

Current diagnostic criteria specified in DSM-IV and ICD-10 avoid such problems by diagnosing specific language disorder in terms of the mismatch between verbal and nonverbal abilities, irrespective of the level of nonverbal skills. However, in neither diagnostic scheme is any precise statement made as to how the mismatch between verbal and nonverbal abilities is to be quantified, leaving the interpretation of this part of the definition open to individual judgement.

It is possible to use the correlation between verbal and nonverbal tests to estimate the size of discrepancy between two scores that is statistically abnormal (Payne & Jones, 1957). Using unpublished data reported by Silva (1987), we can compute that around 6% of children would be expected

to have a score on the Reynell Developmental Language Scales that was 1 s.d. below IQ assessed using the Wechsler Scales for Children IQ. In our current state of knowledge, a useful rule of thumb for deciding when there is a significant language impairment discrepant with IQ would be that the child should obtain a score on a language test that is at least 2 s.d. below the mean, with an IQ score that is at least 1 s.d. above the language level.

It should be noted that, although the traditional approach of differentiating specific speech and language disorders from more global developmental delays has been described here, the validity of this distinction has been called into question (Leonard, 1983). In many countries the bulk of special educational resources is directed at those children who demonstrate normal nonverbal abilities, when other children with similar levels of language impairment may receive little specialist help, because they do poorly on nonverbal measures. This difference in provision might be justified if children with specific language impairments proved to be qualitatively different from those with more global difficulties, either in terms of types of language difficulty or in response to intervention. However, this remains to be demonstrated.

When can language disorder be attributed to hearing loss?

To learn spoken language, one must be able to hear it. Children with profound congenital hearing loss (in excess of 90 dB) have tremendous difficulty learning spoken language, even when (exceptionally) there is early identification with provision of hearing aids and auditory training (see Mogford, 1988, for a review). Lipreading cannot provide the same information as listening, because many sounds (such as m, p and b) are indistinguishable visually. One cannot simply bypass the hearing impairment by teaching the child to read if the child does not have adequate language skills to appreciate what the written form maps on to. The milder the degree of hearing loss, the greater the probability that the child will produce intelligible speech, succeed at lip-reading, show evidence of using internal speech and acquire functional reading skills (Quigley, 1978; Conrad, 1979).

Lack of precise knowledge about the relationships between less severe hearing loss and language impairment means that there will necessarily be a degree of subjectivity in deciding whether an observed language disorder can be attributed to sensory impairment. Most children designated as partially hearing have verbal deficits (Fundudis *et al.*, 1979) and many people would argue that even mild losses can play a part in causing language difficulties. In general, however, it is not reasonable to attribute language difficulties to conductive hearing loss associated with otitis media, except where the condition is chronic and unremitting (see the section on aetiology of specific speech and language disorders, below). Age at which hearing is lost is important. Even a few years of normal hearing early in life can make a tremendous difference to the child's language development.

Distinguishing specific language impairment and autistic disorder

ICD-10 specifies that children with specific language disorder show normal social reciprocity, normal make-believe play, normal use of parents for comfort, near-normal use of gestures and only mild impairments in nonverbal communication. In contrast, language difficulties in autistic children are part of a broader social impairment affecting nonverbal as well as verbal means of communication (see Chapter 33). From an early age, autistic children do not use gestures and patterns of gaze to establish joint attention with others (Loveland & Landry, 1986; Mundy *et al.*, 1986, 1990; Landry & Loveland, 1988). There are also a number of characteristics of the language itself that distinguish the two types of disorder, as demonstrated by Bartak *et al.* (1975) in a study that explicitly compared language of receptive aphasic and autistic children (Fig. 32.3). Language features identified by formal assessments (e.g. age at passing language milestones and articulation status) did not clearly distinguish the two groups. However, abnormal use of language and lack of nonverbal communication and symbolic behaviour were more common in the children with autism.

Although there are clear differences between well-defined groups of autistic and receptive aphasic children, this does not mean that the diagnostic boundaries are clear. Bartak *et al.* (1977) found that some children in their comparative study could not be classified as either autistic or dysphasic, because their behaviour and language fell between these two categories. Bishop (1989b) suggested that autistic disorder and semantic–pragmatic disorder may be on a continuum. In both disorders there is abnormality of language content and use, but autistic children have communicative impairments that are both more severe and more extensive.

Acquired epileptic aphasia (Landau–Kleffner syndrome)

In 1957, Landau and Kleffner described a rare form of receptive language disorder in which there was deterioration of previously acquired language skills associated with EEG abnormalities, and, in some cases, seizures. Typically, there are profound comprehension problems and the child may initially be thought to be deaf. Onset is usually between the ages of 3 and 6 years, and may be gradual or precipitous. An EEG may reveal spike waves in the temporal lobes, especially during sleep. In some cases, there are fluctuations in the severity of the language impairment, usually associated with underlying seizure activity.

In terms of classification, this disorder sits uneasily between acquired and developmental disorders. ICD-10 includes acquired epileptic aphasia among developmental language disorders, but the natural history suggests this is an acquired disorder. However a specific causal agent has yet to be identified and the prognosis is unlike that of other acquired language disorders in childhood, in that the younger the child at onset, the least recovery is seen (Bishop, 1985). Many children who have onset below 5 years of age have severe comprehension problems persisting into adulthood and may understand only a small vocabulary spoken by a familiar person, despite years of therapeutic effort. Although there are exceptional cases of dramatic recovery, it is common to find that anticonvulsant medication succeeds in normalizing the EEG without any corresponding improvement in language functions (Deonna, 1991).

There may be difficulties in distinguishing acquired epileptic aphasia from other disorders where there is a history of regression, especially cases of late-onset autism. However, in classical cases of acquired epileptic aphasia the desire to

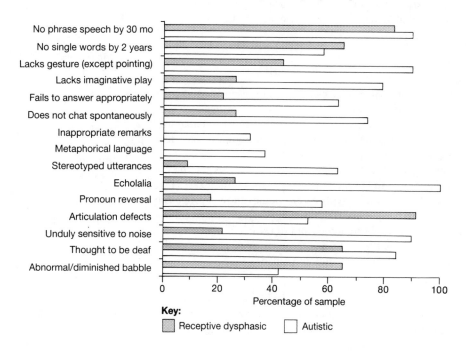

Fig. 32.3 Summary of findings from the study by Bartak *et al.* (1975) comparing 19 autistic children with 23 children with developmental receptive dysphasia. Most characteristics were scored positive if the child had ever shown that behaviour, regardless of whether it was still present at the time of assessment.

communicate is retained and the child is socially responsive with preserved nonverbal abilities.

Disorders of speech production

In common parlance, the terms *speech* and *language* are often treated as synonyms, but more precise usage restricts the meaning of speech to the activity of articulating speech sounds, whereas language refers to the communication of thoughts by the use of meaningful units combined in a systematic way. Problems with the physical production of speech include structural or functional disorders affecting the tongue, lips and palate, voice disorders caused by disease or stress of the vocal cords, and disruption of the smooth sequencing of speech output, i.e. disorders of fluency.

Structural and neurological abnormalities of the speech apparatus

A question of clinical interest is how far speech difficulties in apparently normal young children may be caused by minor structural abnormalities of the articulators. In the past, it was common for children to be operated on for tongue-tie, i.e. an abnormally short frenum. The effectiveness of this procedure has never been adequately evaluated, but it has largely fallen into disfavour, as there has been growing awareness that physical proportions of the articulators are a poor predictor of speech characteristics, even in children with major disproportion of the articulatory apparatus (Peterson-Falzone, 1982).

Strictly speaking, the term *dysarthria* covers speech impairments arising from both anatomical and neurological causes, but in practice its use is often restricted to speech difficulties caused by neurological impairment. Brown (1985) provides a comprehensive review of neurological conditions that can cause dysarthria in children, indicating how the level of the lesion will determine the scope and nature of the motor impairment that is seen.

Voice disorders

A harsh or hoarse voice can be an indication of an underlying disease process, but can also arise as the consequence of vocal abuse, i.e. excessive screaming, shouting or coughing. In extreme cases, benign growths (vocal nodules) may develop on the margins of the vocal folds. Although they are not life-threatening, they have adverse consequences for the child's functioning and surgical removal may be necessary. Parents report that children with vocal nodules show a propensity to argue, to become hysterical when things do not go their way, to disobey until threatened and to complain of others' unfairness (Green, 1989). They often have poor peer relations and tend to be distractible and immature.

Disorders of fluency

Stuttering is diagnosed when there is a disturbance of the rhythm of speech, with hesitations, prolongations and rep-etitions of sounds within words. For many years stuttering was thought to reflect antagonistic emotional impulses (Meyer, 1945). According to one school of thought, long-term stuttering can be caused by inappropriate handing of developmental dysfluency, where adults draw attention to and try to correct the child's speech. Some contemporary treatment programmes attempt to treat stuttering indirectly by modifying the attitude of the child and family towards the disorder. However, genetic studies have demonstrated high heritability for stuttering, suggesting that, although the family environment may play some part in determining the course of the disorder, constitutional factors play a significant role in aetiology (Kidd, 1980).

Selective (elective) mutism

Occasionally children are referred because they have ceased speaking (mutism), having previously produced normal or near-normal speech. Broadly speaking, two quite different alternatives have to be considered: (1) the ability to speak has been lost as the result of organic brain pathology (acquired aphasia); and (2) the ability to speak has not changed but its *use* has been impaired as a result of socioemotional disturbance. The latter has been termed selective or elective mutism and refers to a psychiatric condition in which the child can talk, but does so only in the presence of a handful of intimates (Kratochwill, 1981; Rutter & Lord, 1987; Tancer, 1992). Both types of disorder arise during the preschool years and require quite different forms of treatment; accordingly, their differential diagnosis is important.

It may be thought that the differential diagnosis from aphasia should be easily made, because brain pathology severe enough to cause language disturbance should also result in clear evidence of neurological impairment. However, this is not always so, especially in the case of acquired epileptic aphasia, where an organic basis can be difficult to demonstrate. Differential diagnosis is made on the basis of two key features that separate selective mutism from aphasia. Firstly, in aphasia, the loss of speech is evident in all situations. By contrast, in selective mutism, the failure to use speech is situation-specific, being unimpaired in certain social circumstances with particular characteristics. Typically, children with selective mutism speak when on their own with their friends, and sometimes with their parents, but do not do so at school, in public situations or with strangers. However, other patterns occur occasionally. Secondly, in aphasia, problems typically extend beyond the use of spoken language; in most cases language comprehension is impaired, and older children may show loss of literacy skills. By contrast, children with selective mutism will show competence in spoken language in certain situations (this may be confirmed by getting the family to tape-record conversations in situations where the child does talk, or by observations through a one-way mirror) and will show no deterioration of comprehension, reading or writing. If careful attention is paid to these two key features, there is usually no difficulty in making the distinction.

An initial reluctance to speak when children first start school is not uncommon; Brown and Lloyd (1975) reported a rate of 7.2 per 1000. This phenomenon was particularly common among recent immigrants learning a new language. However, this initial reluctance nearly always remits without the need for any intervention. Persistent selective mutism (lasting at least 6 months) is much rarer — with a rate of only about 0.7 per 1000 (Brown & Lloyd, 1975; Kolvin & Fundudis, 1981). Accordingly, it is an uncommon cause for referral at both speech clinics (Cantwell *et al.*, 1981) and psychiatric facilities (Wilkins, 1985). The syndrome occurs somewhat more frequently in girls than in boys.

Although selectivity in use of language is a required diagnostic feature, speech/language impairment, developmental immaturity and cognitive impairment constitute important risk factors, and it is important that an accompanying developmental language disorder is not overlooked. Not surprisingly, children who lack proficiency in language are likely to become anxious about speaking in public situations. In addition, it is common for children with selective mutism to exhibit temperamental or behavioural features such as negativism, shyness, controlling or oppositional tendencies, poor peer relations and social isolation. Often the families show no unusual features, but maternal overprotection does seem to be relatively common.

The reports on course and outcome are rather contradictory. Prognosis is excellent for the more frequent syndrome of reluctance to speak on starting school, but long-established cases of selective mutism can be quite difficult to treat. The 2–10-year follow-up by Sluckin *et al.* (1991) suggested that individual behavioural approaches using techniques such as graded change or reinforcement were most effective, but their study did not constitute a controlled trial and the conclusion must be tentative. Some children continued to show a degree of selective mutism that continued over some years; this occurred most often when there was marked family psychopathology.

Language impairment in Duchenne muscular dystrophy

A gap between language ability and nonverbal intelligence is well-documented in Duchenne muscular dystrophy, although the mechanism is not fully understood (Marsh & Munsat, 1974; Karagan *et al.*, 1980). It is important to be aware of this association, because language delay, associated with motor clumsiness, may be the first presenting symptom (Kaplan *et al.*, 1986) and failure to make a correct diagnosis will leave parents uninformed of risks to other offspring.

PREVALENCE OF SPECIFIC LANGUAGE IMPAIRMENT

The topic of prevalence goes hand in hand with the issue of diagnosis. This may be illustrated by considering the longitudinal study conducted by Fundudis *et al.* (1979). These authors followed up a group of children who had originally been seen at the age of 3 years as part of the Newcastle Child Development Study (Neligan & Prudham, 1969). In the original study, normative data on language milestones were collected and 3% of children were reported by their parents as not stringing words together at the age of 36 months. Fundudis *et al.* followed up children who had not achieved this milestone and compared their progress with that of a control group. The sample was subdivided into those whose language delay was secondary to other major impairments, and those with no other abnormality. Their data are summarized in Table 32.2. The overall prevalence of speech and language delay was by definition 3%, because the criterion for disorder was language development at or below the third centile. However, only one child in the entire sample was deemed to have a problem serious enough to merit the diagnosis of severe developmental dysphasia. No details of his language difficulties are provided. If we accept that this child is the only one in the sample who would merit a clinical diagnosis, then this gives a prevalence estimate of 1 per 3000 (which is, however, a highly unreliable estimate, being based on a single case!). There were, however, many more children who fell below the third centile for language development at 3 years of age, in the absence of any other known disorder (residual speech retardation), who started to walk at the normal age. If we regard these children as cases of developmental language disorder, we obtain a prevalence estimate of around 2%.

As well as illustrating how prevalence rates depend on

Table 32.2 Classification of 100 children who scored below the third centile on a language screen at 36 months — data from Fundudis *et al.* (1979)

	n	Estimated population prevalence per 1000
Cerebral palsy	5	1.67
Autism	2	0.67
Elective mutism	2	0.67
Cleft palate/dysarthria	2	0.67
Profound deafness	2	0.67
Marked intellectual handicap (IQ less than 65) in absence of other conditions	7	2.33
Severe dysphasia	1	0.33
Residual speech retardation Not walking at 15 months (mean PIQ at age 7 years = 88.6)	23	7.67
Walked before 16 months (mean PIQ at age 7 years = 98.3)	59	19.67

* The total is 103 because these categories are not mutually exclusive: presumably three children were doubly coded. PIQ, Performance IQ.

definition, this study demonstrated the dangers of equating statistical abnormality with clinical significance. Only 11 children with residual speech retardation had received any speech therapy. Although it is possible that the lack of intervention arose partly because of inadequate speech therapy provision, it seems likely that in many cases these children were not regarded as giving cause for concern. Some might argue that because the early language development of these children was well below average in statistical terms, they should have been treated. However, this is dangerous logic, as it means that we will end up advocating treatment for a constant proportion of children, regardless of whether their verbal difficulties are severe enough to interfere with daily life and/or academic attainments (cf. DSM-IV). We need better ways of identifying those children whose language impairments are truly handicapping. It is not possible to give prevalence estimates for such disorders, but it seems clear that figures would be well below the 15–25% reported by some contemporary surveys (e.g. Beitchman *et al.*, 1986a).

PROGNOSIS OF SPECIFIC LANGUAGE IMPAIRMENT

Language delay or language disorder?

We know that in the normal population there is considerable variability in the ages of passing developmental milestones, and there can be quite substantial mismatches between different aspects of maturation. For instance, some children who are otherwise developing normally may be very late in passing through puberty. It seems reasonable to suppose that there will be some children who show a similar lag in language development, not because of any underlying disorder but simply because they constitute the tail end of a normal distribution of language development. One would expect that after a slow start they would develop normally, and they should not therefore be a focus for therapeutic concern. This distinction between late developers and those with true disorders is sometimes referred to as a contrast between language *delay* (corresponding to the tail of the normal distribution) and language *disorder**. This distinction is fairly straightforward to make conceptually, but the problem for the clinician is how to distinguish these subgroups in practice. In ICD-10 it is suggested that four criteria may be used to provide an indication of a clinically significant disorder, namely severity, course, pattern and presence of associated problems. In terms of pattern of problems, it is often suggested that the child with delay will resemble a younger normal child, whereas the child with disorder will have language that does not correspond to any normal stage of development. Furthermore, the child with language delay is expected to follow a normal course, whereas the child with disorder might show early plateaux in development (Stark *et al.*, 1983).

Empirical validation of these ideas has only recently been attempted. Thal *et al.* (1991) investigated outcome in 10 children who scored below the 10th centile for language production when aged 18–32 months. Six of these children scored within the normal range for their age when seen 12 months later. The main factor distinguishing those with transient and persistent problems was level of comprehension: the 'late bloomers' had all had normal levels of language comprehension when first assessed. Other researchers have focused on children whose language deficits are restricted to expressive language. Fischel *et al.* (1989) studied a group of 2-year-olds who had a substantial delay in expressive language, but normal comprehension and nonverbal ability. Five months after initial diagnosis, all children were reassessed on an expressive vocabulary scale, and it was found that one-third scored in the normal range, one-third were still markedly impaired and the remainder were intermediate. These authors concluded that children with expressive vocabularies of 8 words or less at 2 years of age are unlikely to show spontaneous improvement, whereas those with larger vocabularies usually do improve.

A recent study by the same group (Whitehurst *et al.*, 1991a) confirmed the generally good prognosis for specific expressive language delay. A group of 27 children who had been diagnosed as cases of specific expressive language delay at 2 or 3 years of age were followed up and given a battery of language tests. Irrespective of whether the children had been enrolled into a treatment programme, progressive improvement was seen with age and the vast majority of children were problem-free by 5 years of age. This optimistic picture contrasts with recent work by Rescorla and Schwartz (1990), who studied a sample of 2-year-olds with normal comprehension and intelligence who were behind age level on an expressive language measure when first seen. When followed up at 3–4 years of age, more than half of them still had major expressive problems, with scores on language structure measures that were at least 1.5 s.d. below age level. Most of these children had expressive vocabularies well above Fischel *et al.*'s cut-off of 8 words when first seen. Rescorla and Schwartz argued that persisting expressive deficits in language-delayed children may have been missed in other studies because language structure was not adequately measured. However, the more recent study by Whitehurst *et al.* did measure a range of language functions, but no deficits were reported. More longitudinal research is required to reconcile these findings.

The longitudinal study by Bishop and Edmundson (1987a) showed that nearly half of a sample of 4-year-olds with specific language impairment went on to catch up with their peer group, maintaining this good outcome at 8 years of age (Bishop & Adams, 1990). No qualitative differences in language deficits emerged between those children whose problems resolved and those whose problems persisted, although the initial impairments of the latter group were more severe and more likely to include significant comprehension problems.

A small amount of research has been carried out relevant to the question of whether delay and disorder are aetiologically distinct. Bishop and Edmundson (1987b) found no difference

---

* However, language delay is often used in a less specific sense to refer to any child whose language development lags behind the normal level for a child of that age.

in frequency of potential aetiological factors between children who had persistent language difficulties and those who improved. However, Whitehurst *et al.* (1991b) obtained some circumstantial evidence supporting a distinction between early language delay and disorder. In contrast to studies of older language-impaired children, they found no indication of a raised family history of language problems in families of 2-and 3-year-olds with specific expressive delays. This is, of course, the same type of child for whom they reported a good spontaneous recovery.

What implications do these studies have for clinical practice? It does seem reasonable to give an optimistic prognosis for the 2-year-old with expressive language delay but normal intelligence and comprehension. The longitudinal studies and family history data of Whitehurst and colleagues suggest this type of language delay is distinct from more persistent disorder. In children aged under 27 months, language difficulties should not give cause for concern except where there are comprehension problems or where expressive vocabulary is severely delayed (around 8 words or less). However, all children whose expressive vocabularies consist of less than 50 words at the age of 24 months should be monitored carefully. If a child is still well below normal limits by the age of 30 months, then the data of Rescorla and Schwartz suggest that spontaneous catch-up is less likely, and it may be appropriate to initiate some kind of intervention.

Data from Bishop and Edmundson (1987a) provide some preliminary guidelines for distinguishing 4-year-olds who will grow out of their difficulties from those who are likely to have persisting problems. In general, children who are able to retell the gist of a simple story they had heard, albeit using simple language, are likely to have a good outcome, whereas those who fail to give a consecutive account of events have a poorer prognosis. Isolated phonological problems usually resolve by 5 years of age, but those occurring in association with other language difficulties have a poorer outcome (Bishop & Adams, 1990).

Long-term outcome of severe speech and language disorders

Residential schools for children with specific speech and language disorders are in a unique position to provide data on the outcome of children with severe language problems. An early study by Griffiths (1969) followed up 49 children who had attended John Horniman School. Nearly three-quarters of these children had speech and language levels within normal limits when followed up at the age of 7−16 years, but many had educational difficulties. The best outcome was found for those who had difficulties predominantly affecting speech, and the poorest for those who had abnormal auditory function and comprehension problems.

A recent study of school-leavers from another English residential school, Dawn House School, provides a wealth of data about outcome from children with a range of different speech and language disorders (Haynes & Naidoo, 1991). Standardized language tests were administered to children leaving school at 13 years of age, and results were combined to divide children into those whose understanding and speech would be adequate for everyday interactions with others, and those who had persisting problems that would interfere with communication. Around two-thirds of the children were functioning within normal limits for language comprehension and speech when they left school, and just over half were judged to be functioning adequately in terms of language production. Of 118 school-leavers, 62 were able to rejoin their normal peers, understand class instructions, express themselves coherently and generally participate gainfully in normal education. However, 40% of children still had noticeable and disabling language problems when they moved on from their special school, usually after several years of intensive therapy and education. Language tests given at school entry were found to be good predictors of outcome. A further follow-up was conducted with 34 ex-pupils who had reached the age of 18 years. Information was obtained in most cases by telephone interview with the ex-pupil or a parent. In only 3 cases was it reported that there were no residual problems with spoken or written language. Difficulties that were reported included problems in pronouncing long words, difficulty in filling in forms and in using the telephone, self-consciousness about odd-sounding speech, and difficulty in following films. Despite these remaining problems, the majority of these young people were employed or in full-time further education, with only 3 having had no real experience of stable employment.

A poor long-term prognosis for *receptive* language disorders was found by Rutter *et al.* (1992) and Rutter and Mawhood (1991), who followed up a sample previously studied by Cantwell *et al.* (1989) when they were in their 20s. Only half of these men had normal conversational skills. Half had abnormal use of prosody (i.e. pitch and tone of speech), although these problems were much less marked than those seen in a comparison group of individuals with autism. Interestingly, there appeared to be a progressive drop in *nonverbal* IQ in the language-disordered group, with the mean score falling from 108 when first assessed to 96 in middle childhood, to 78 in adulthood. Only one-third of these men were living independently away from parents when seen in their mid 20s, and one-third had been in continuous paid employment. The psychiatric status of this group will be considered more fully in the next section.

COMORBIDITY

Emotional and behaviour disorders

Associations between language problems and behaviour problems have been extensively documented. Stevenson and Richman (1978) reported a prevalence of behaviour problems of 58% in children with delayed language development compared with 14% in a random sample of 705 3-year-olds. In an epidemiological study of 5-year-old Canadian children, Beitchman *et al.* (1986b) identified 142 cases of speech and language disorders, who were compared with a normally developing control group. The estimated frequency of psychiatric disorder (using DSM-III criteria) was 49% for those with speech and language disorder, compared with 12% for controls. Attention deficit disorder was diagnosed in 30% of this sample. However, neither of these studies distinguished between *specific* speech and language disorders and other types of problem, so one cannot tell whether the associations with psychiatric disturbance represented specific correlates of language impairment, or whether they were a function of generally delayed development. The only studies that concentrate on children whose language difficulties are not attributable to low IQ are clinic-based, and so susceptible to referral bias (parents may be more likely to seek help if a language-impaired child also manifests behaviour difficulties). Nevertheless, although such studies may overestimate the population prevalence of psychiatric disorders among language-impaired children, they do provide useful information for those who see children in clinical settings, because they indicate that a high rate of psychiatric disorder is found in such cases. Baker and Cantwell (1982) studied 300 children attending a community speech and hearing clinic and found prevalence rates for psychiatric disorder of 29% in children with speech disorders (mostly articulation disorders, but also some cases of stuttering and other disorders), 45% in those with speech and language disorders and 95% in those with pure language disorders. Cohen *et al.* (1989) approached the question from the opposite direction, by assessing speech and language functions in 37 children attending an outpatient mental health clinic. Of the children referred solely for a psychiatric problem, 28% had a moderate or severe language disorder that had not been previously suspected or diagnosed. They suggested that language disorders tended to be overlooked in children with disruptive behaviour, and recommended that there should be routine screening of language in child psychiatric populations. This conclusion is endorsed by an unpublished survey described by Baltaxe and Simmons (1990) who studied 362 consecutive admissions to an inpatient department of child and adolescent neuropsychiatry. They found that 63% of children diagnosed as having emotional disorders had communication handicaps.

There are many candidate explanations for the association between language difficulties and psychiatric problems. One possibility is that the language disorder causes behaviour problems to develop. Various mechanisms could be involved. A common view is that the frustration experienced by the child who cannot communicate leads to acting-out behaviour. Prizant and Wetherby (1990) suggested that, even if the child does not experience a high rate of frustrating experiences, limited language skills may affect responses to everyday events. Language provides a framework for thinking about the self in relation to past and future events, which may be used to regulate arousal and emotional states. The child who lacks this framework may find it difficult to show self-control and to defer gratification. Yet another possibility is that the child's communicative difficulties lead to social rejection and/or educational failure, and these negative experiences lead to low self-esteem and associated emotional and behaviour problems.

Of course, these routes from language impairment to behaviour disorder are not mutually exclusive. A second class of explanation proposes that the association between language difficulties and psychopathology reflects a causal link *from* emotional disturbances in infancy *to* language disturbances. This could arise if caregivers avoid an irritable and/or unresponsive child, so reducing the amount of reciprocal communicative interaction. A third type of explanation views the association between language and behavioural problems as symptoms of a common underlying cause, such as neurological immaturity. Finally, it is known that mothers of language-impaired children report high levels of stress (Fundudis *et al.*, 1979; Beitchman *et al.*, 1986b), and it may be that psychosocial stressors that coexist with language impairment also lead to psychiatric disorders.

Prizant and Wetherby (1990) suggested that it may be oversimplistic to adopt a unidirectional view of relationships between early language and socioemotional development and they suggest that the transactional model of Sameroff and Chandler (1975) provides a more satisfactory framework for explaining relationships between language and socioemotional development. According to this theory, developmental outcomes are the result of dynamic interrelationships between child behaviour, caregiver responses to behaviour and environmental factors that influence both child and caregiver.

Some clues as to mechanism can be obtained by considering the frequency and nature of behavioural and emotional problems in relation to the type of language disorder. The first point to note is that associations between language delay and behaviour problems have been reported for preschool children who have not experienced educational failure and whose experiences of social rejection are likely to have been mild (e.g. Stevenson & Richman, 1978). Associations with behaviour disorders vary according to the *nature* of the language disorder. Although children with pure expressive language disorders do exhibit more difficult behaviour than control children (Caulfield *et al.*, 1989), in general the highest rates of disorder are reported for children with comprehension problems (Cantwell *et al.*, 1981).

Cantwell *et al.* (1989) followed the progress of a group of 14 boys who were identified as cases of developmental receptive dysphasia at the age of 4–9 years. When followed up 2–3 years later, most children had made significant gains in language skills, yet a substantial proportion had poor peer relations, with several apparently showing a deterioration in this aspect of functioning. According to their parents, one-third lacked friends and one-half did not participate in social groups. The authors noted that the difficulties in making friends at a time when language was improving goes against the notion that the socioemotional problems are just a secondary consequence of language impairment. Although the dysphasic children did not meet criteria for autistic disorder, some of them demonstrated repetitive stereotyped behaviour and an apparent lack of interest in social relationships, with lack of sympathy being remarked upon in a third of children at follow-up. A further follow-up into adulthood revealed that in their mid 20s many of these men were socially isolated; out of a total group of 17, 4 were married and 2 had a close heterosexual relationship. One-third had never had either a close friendship or a love relationship, and a further third had had only a close friendship but no love relationship (Rutter *et al.*, 1992). These observations suggest that in a subset of children with receptive language disorders, there may be a primary social impairment that persists even though the more obvious language difficulties resolve. Another possible reason for deterioration of peer relationships is increased sensitivity to and intolerance of abnormality by normal children as they grow older. Thus a mild language disorder at 10 years of age could be more damaging to peer relationships than a severe disorder at 6 years, simply because other children are better able to detect the abnormality and are more likely to reject the child who is perceived as different.

One further intriguing finding from this follow-up study was that 3 out of 25 males with a history of severe receptive language disorder developed a florid paranoid psychosis in late adolescence (Rutter & Mawhood, 1991). It is possible that language delay and psychosis are different manifestations of an underlying constitutional liability to disorder. Alternatively, the stress of social isolation and comprehension difficulties may play a role in precipitating psychosis.

It is important that peer relationships are taken into consideration when deciding on educational placement for a language-impaired child. Current trends are for children with special needs to be educated in regular classrooms, but such integration into the mainstream is merely nominal if children remain socially isolated. It would be interesting to use sociometric methods to evaluate how far language-impaired children become socially integrated with other children in normal classrooms.

Literacy problems

Several longitudinal studies of language-impaired children have found poor acquisition of literacy skills as children grow older, but on the whole these have not focused on children with *specific* language delay, but have rather grouped together all children who are slow to speak, irrespective of general ability. Thus in studies such as those by Richman *et al.* (1982), Silva *et al.* (1987) and Fundudis *et al.* (1979), it is possible that the strong link between early language delay and later literacy problems arose because language delay was the earliest indication of borderline intelligence. Bishop and Adams (1990) found that with a group of children with a history of *specific* speech and language disorders there was considerable variation in outcome, and many children did score in the normal range on language and literacy tests when followed up at 8 years of age. Most children with poor reading attainments had comprehension problems that affected understanding of both written and oral language. Overall, this study confirmed that early language delay is a risk factor for later literacy problems, but only in those children where there is persistence of oral language difficulties. This conclusion contrasts with the conventional wisdom that problems usually persist beneath the surface in children with delayed language development and interfere with acquisition of literacy.

Motor impairment

Although few children with specific speech and language disorders have any 'hard' neurological signs, clumsiness is frequently noted. Robinson (1987) reported that 90% of pupils attending a residential school for children with speech and language disorders scored in the impaired range on the Test of Motor Impairment (Stott *et al.*, 1984) and several experimental studies have confirmed an association between specific language disorder and motor deficits (Johnston *et al.*, 1981; Bishop & Edmundson, 1987b; Noterdaeme *et al.*, 1988). There is debate as to whether this is a sign of neuromotor immaturity or indicative of neurological damage or dysfunction.

RISK FACTORS

Gender

In almost every series of children reported with specific speech and language disorders, an excess of males has been found. Robinson (1987) averaged findings from 10 studies to give a male : female ratio of 2.82 : 1.

Family background

Although specific speech and language disorders can be seen in all kinds of social circumstances, children with delayed language development are more likely than other children to come from large families, to live in poor housing, and to have parents who have unsatisfactory work patterns and more contact with social agencies and higher levels of marital tension, stress and psychiatric problems (Fundudis *et al.*, 1979; Beitchman *et al.*, 1986b). Several studies have found an abnormally high concentration of affected individuals in the immediate families of children with developmental language disorders (Neils & Aram, 1986; Bishop & Edmundson, 1987b; Tallal *et al.*, 1989; Tomblin, 1989).

Multiple birth

Language development is delayed in twins relative to singletons, even when nonverbal ability has been controlled for (Mittler, 1970; Hay *et al.*, 1987). Although the language delay seen in twins is of considerable theoretical interest, it is unclear whether the prevalence of clinically important language disorders is any higher in twins than in singletons. In fact, awareness of the association between language delay and twinning may lead clinicians to dismiss the importance of serious language problems when they occur in twins, on the grounds that 'twins are usually slow in language'. Where a child aged 3 years or above meets criteria for language disorder, then this should be taken seriously, regardless of whether the child is a twin.

AETIOLOGY OF SPECIFIC SPEECH AND LANGUAGE DISORDERS

The aetiology of specific speech and language disorders is not known, but most experts would agree that such conditions are likely to have an organic basis, and are not the result of inadequate verbal stimulation by parents. One line of evidence comes from studies of hearing children whose parents are profoundly and congenitally deaf. These children seldom develop significant language problems, although the spoken language they hear is limited in quantity and quality (Schiff-Myers, 1988). Language development also shows great resilience in the face of obvious inadequacies of standards of care: children of depressed mothers seldom have significant language difficulties, despite disruption of normal patterns of mother−child interaction (Cox *et al.*, 1987; Murray, 1992) and, although language delays are seen in children of abusive mothers, the effects seem to be small and not specific to language (Allen & Wasserman, 1985). This is not to say that environmental factors are unimportant. The nature of a child's home background may influence the severity and course of a disorder, and treatment programmes aimed at creating an optimal communicative environment in the home are to be welcomed, provided parents are not made to feel guilty and responsible for causing their child's difficulties.

Recurrent otitis media

The past two decades have seen an explosion of research into the linguistic sequelae of secretory otitis media. The advent of tympanometry has made it easy to identify middle ear disease, and epidemiological surveys have found that at a given point in time, between 20 and 50% of children below the age of 4 years have fluid in the middle ear. In most cases, the disease resolves spontaneously, but some children have repeated bouts of otitis media, and in others a chronic condition develops, and the fluid in the middle ear may become suppurative and eventually burst the eardrum.

Secretory otitis media leads to a conductive hearing loss usually ranging from 15 to 40 dB. For many years it was thought that this was too slight to have any significance for development. However, in 1969, Holm and Kunze reported significant deficits on language tests for 16 children with a history of chronic otitis media, compared with a group of matched controls. The literature on this topic has since burgeoned, and many feel that there is now good evidence that there are long-term detrimental effects on language development after recurrent episodes of otitis media, even when hearing has returned to normal (e.g. Feagans, 1986).

However, many of the studies that report associations between otitis media and language impairment are methodologically inadequate because they rely on clinic-referred samples of children with otitis media. As Bishop and Edmundson (1986) pointed out, the presence of language delay influences whether otitis media will be diagnosed, and whether it will be treated aggressively if detected. Epidemiological surveys, which avoid such sources of bias, typically find much smaller effects of otitis media on language development, especially if attention is restricted to children who have normal hearing at the time of language testing. Bishop and Edmundson concluded that otitis media is unlikely to be a major factor in the aetiology of specific speech and language disorders, but it may interact with other factors so that occurrence of otitis media in a child already vulnerable for language disorder would assume importance. Despite uncertainty about the causal link between otitis media and language impairments, most clinicians feel it is appropriate to adopt an aggressive approach to treatment of otitis media when this is found in a child with significant language difficulties.

Brain damage

We know from studies of adults that lesions of circumscribed areas of the left cerebral hemisphere typically cause aphasia, whereas damage to the homologous areas of the right hemisphere or to other areas of the left hemisphere leaves language unaffected (see Chapter 11). One might therefore reasonably assume that integrity of these areas of the left hemisphere was critical for normal language development. However, it is a remarkable fact that a brain lesion that would, in an adult, result in severe and persistent aphasia can be incurred by an infant or young child with little evidence of any adverse effect on subsequent language development. The limiting case is that of left hemidecortication, which is sometimes carried out for the treatment of infantile hemiplegia with intractable seizures. Although children undergoing this surgery are usually mildly or moderately mentally retarded, there is little evidence of any negative consequences for language development, provided the lesion is acquired very early in life. Basser (1962) explained such results by arguing that good recovery is possible in the child because the right hemisphere is able to mediate language functions if the left hemisphere is damaged early in life. However, as the child grows older, the right hemisphere becomes increasingly committed to other cognitive functions and correspondingly less able to process verbal information. Bilateral lesions, on the other hand, will have a poor prognosis, because the possibility of right hemisphere compensation is reduced.

A left hemisphere lesion acquired after the child has started to speak will often cause aphasic symptoms. For many years it was thought that left hemisphere lesions acquired in early and middle childhood had a good prognosis, provided the right hemisphere was intact enough to act in a compensatory role. However, recent studies, using standardized tests rather than relying on clinical impression, paint a bleaker picture, especially for children aged over 6 years (Woods & Carey, 1979). Most recovery usually takes place in the first 3 months after injury, with relatively slow progress after this period

(Lees & Neville, 1990). Many children have persisting difficulties and make slow academic progress, with written language being particularly poor (Alajouanine & Lhermitte, 1965). A recent study following the progress of 3 Japanese child-onset aphasics into adulthood (Watamori *et al.*, 1990) found that, despite superficial recovery of functional communication ability, all continued to have difficulties in adult life that limited their employment prospects. Problems included slowness in comprehending written and oral language, difficulty in engaging in conversation with colleagues and limited ability to draw inferences.

Limited quantity of speech is the symptom most frequently noted after left hemisphere damage in children (Hecaen, 1976) and this may explain why children's language difficulties may go unremarked: it is easier to detect language errors in a talkative child than in one who appears shy and monosyllabic. The clinical lesson to be learned from research conducted over the past decade is that cognitive outcome must be monitored as scrupulously as physical outcome after brain injury in a child. Regular follow-up assessment of language abilities using age-appropriate materials is essential to identify areas in need of remediation and to aid prognosis.

Although focal brain damage undoubtedly can lead to aphasia in children, it does not seem to provide a reasonable explanation for most children with developmental language disorders, where typically there is no hard evidence of neurological damage. However, techniques such as ultrasound show that minor damage to the brain can occur in children who do not appear grossly neurologically abnormal, especially premature babies of low birth weight. This raises the question of whether specific language disorder could be explained in terms of Pasamanick's (1952) concept of the continuum of reproductive casualty, which maintains that developmental disorders can result from a perinatal brain lesion that is not sufficient to produce physical handicap. In recent years there have been numerous follow-up studies of low birth weight infants who are high risk of intraventricular haemorrhage, and some of these do describe language deficits relative to full birth weight controls (e.g. Dunn, 1986; Largo *et al.*, 1986; Vohr *et al.*, 1989). However, where other aspects of development are measured it is usually found that any effects of such early brain damage are general rather than specific, with nonverbal abilities being consistent with language level. Perinatal brain damage does not reliably increase the risk of *specific* language impairment.

Prenatal influences on brain development

The development of high-resolution brain imaging techniques has allowed us to examine the structure of the brain *in vivo* in far greater detail than was hitherto possible. Although studies on children with developmental disorders are understandably rare, those that have been conducted emphasize that a brain may be neurologically abnormal, despite the fact that there are no areas of destruction of tissue of the kind that would be identified on CT. A study by Jernigan *et al.* (1991) used blind,

quantitative analysis of MRI scans to contrast brain structures in children with developmental language disorders with those of normal control children and a group of children with mental handicap. There was no evidence of major structural lesions in the language-impaired children, but the quantitative analysis revealed departures from the usual pattern of cerebral asymmetries, plus a significant decrease bilaterally in the size of an area corresponding to superior temporoparietal cortex. This study, then, provides support for the notion that the biological basis of developmental language disorder may be an abnormality of early neurological development, rather than damage to a normally developing system. The next question to consider is what type of factor might disrupt early development.

Genetic factors

Although there are certain chromosomal anomalies that are associated with specific speech and language disorders, especially those where there is an extra X chromosome (Haka-Ikse *et al.*, 1978; Bender *et al.*, 1983; see also Chapter 10), the majority of language-impaired children have a normal karyotype (Mutton & Lea, 1980; Friedrich *et al.*, 1982). However, the familial aggregation of speech and language disorders suggests that genotype does play a role in the aetiology of specific speech and language disorders. It seems unlikely that this reflects imitation of inadequate language models from parents or siblings, because unaffected and affected children often coexist in the same family. Few family pedigrees are as clear-cut as that recently described in a three-generation family with a dominant pattern of inheritance for specific language disorder (Hurst *et al.*, 1990). However, it seems likely that genetic constitution will prove to be a risk factor for language disorder that may become manifest under certain environmental conditions. Future progress in understanding genetic factors will be closely linked to advances in subclassifying disorders: it is likely that at present we are grouping together subgroups of children with diverse aetiologies.

Nongenetic prenatal influences

There are numerous factors that can influence the development of the fetus, e.g. drugs and hormones in the maternal blood stream, exposure to ionizing radiations and infections. One factor that has been postulated as playing an important role in development of language areas of the brain is the level of testosterone in the fetal circulation. Geschwind and Galaburda (1987) proposed a complex theory that included the postulate that high levels of testosterone retard development of the left cerebral hemisphere, leading to later speech and language disorders (stuttering, dyslexia and developmental language disorders) and left-handedness. One observation motivating this postulate was the sex difference in the incidence of speech and language disorders. However, there is little independent evidence for a selective influence of testosterone on left hemisphere development, and Pennington *et al.*

(1987) have pointed out that individuals with adrenogenital syndrome, who have abnormally high levels of prenatal testosterone, do not show elevated rates of language disorders. Furthermore, although it is widely believed that left- or mixed-handedness is a risk factor for developmental speech and language disorders, few studies have found this association (Bishop, 1990).

INTERVENTION AND EDUCATION

When to intervene

A common answer to the question: 'At what age should intervention start?' is 'the sooner the better'. The obvious advantage of early intervention is that one has the opportunity to act before the disorder becomes too entrenched, and may also avoid the negative consequences that arise when children become aware of failure (Cantwell & Baker, 1987). However, there are drawbacks to early intervention. Many children with early language delay do grow out of their difficulties, so the younger the child is when identified, the higher is the probability that one has picked up a child whose disorder would resolve if left untreated. This message is emphasized by two controlled studies of home-based intervention for 2–3-year-old children with early language delay, both of which found that *all* children made substantial gains, regardless of whether they were treated (Stevenson *et al.*, 1982; Whitehurst *et al.*, 1991). Some would reply that this does not matter and that it is better to treat a child who may not need it than to deny treatment to those who do. However, treatment may engender worry in parents and self-consciousness in children. Furthermore, in times of scarce resources it is important to ensure that it is directed only at those who really are in need.

Although one might question the wisdom of direct intervention with very young children, parents will need advice and guidance, even when the prognosis is good. This should focus on: (1) alleviating inappropriate guilt or anxiety by emphasizing that major language difficulties in children are unlikely to be caused by factors in the home environment; (2) discouraging parents from using coercion to 'teach' language to their child. Strategies such as withholding a sweet until the child repeats a word are likely to be counterproductive; (3) encouraging acceptance of the child's communicative efforts, be these verbal or non verbal. Verbal and articulate families may need to be made aware of the need to slow down the pace of conversation, to give the language-impaired child time to formulate utterances, and to use simple, straightforward language to a child who has comprehension problems.

Structured versus naturalistic language therapy

In the past, most forms of speech therapy involved teaching language skills directly by imitation and modelling. The therapist identifies which aspects of the child's language system are impaired and focuses on these in drills that provide opportunities to work selectively on areas of difficulty. The area where this approach is still commonly used is in treating phonological problems. The aim is to identify the pattern of errors that the child makes, and then to give extensive practice in producing contrastive sounds. More recently, the development of electropalatography has made it possible to give children visual feedback showing how the tongue makes contact with the palate, which can then be compared with a model (Hardcastle *et al.*, 1987). In general, the evidence for efficacy of highly structured therapy is strongest for treatment directed towards phonological problems (see e.g. Tyler *et al.*, 1987).

In recent years there has been a move away from structured programmes, especially when teaching grammatical competence and appropriate language use. One reason was that therapists became disillusioned when they found that children who could produce acceptable language in therapy sessions persisted in using impaired language in more natural situations. Webster and McConnell (1987) suggested that structured language training may actually hinder language development because it alters the linguistic and social environment: children are not encouraged to use language to communicate their needs, but merely to give correct responses to adult initiations.

The swing of the pendulum away from structured approaches to language training led some to advocate a policy of general language stimulation, especially in cases where the home background is thought to be disadvantaged. In practice, language stimulation is often interpreted to mean attendance at a nursery, where there is plenty of opportunity to mix with other children. Tizard (1983) questioned this rationale. She found that working-class mothers used much more complex language to their children than did nursery teachers, and children used language for complex purposes more often at home than at school. Thus, although a great deal of language is produced in the nursery setting, individual children experience relatively few communicative exchanges with adults. Nurseries can provide plentiful and stimulating opportunities for play and social interaction with peers, but they are noisy places, where the language-impaired child has to compete for adult attention with other small children with more sophisticated language skills.

In recent years, attempts have been made to strike a balance between structured didactic training approaches and more naturalistic techniques. In *milieu* teaching the aim is to use a range of methods to teach specific target skills in a natural setting. Warren and Bambara (1989) demonstrated that this approach could be effective in teaching specific syntactic–semantic forms to mentally retarded children, with good generalization of skills to other settings.

Alternative and augmentative means of communication

An alternative or supplementary form of communication, such as signed language, is sometimes considered if the child has severe auditory comprehension difficulties. In such cases there is often concern that the child will no longer attend to sound, and so will never recover oral comprehension skills. However, there is no evidence that mastery of a signed language interferes with learning spoken language. On the contrary, it seems that the signed language can provide the child with a conceptual framework that will facilitate oral language learning, by showing what the lip patterns and associated sounds refer to. Although there have been no systematic comparisons of different educational approaches for children with severe receptive language disorders, most experts agree that some form of signed language, as a supplement rather than an alternative to speech, is beneficial in providing the child with a route into language learning.

Signing may also play a part in the education of children with very severe speech disorders. This would include those with dysarthria or anarthria, and some cases of dyspraxia. Other methods of visual communication, such as computerized communication aids, may also be used, although it must be appreciated that many of these children have poor literacy skills. Communication boards using symbols such as Blissymbolics (Archer, 1977) may provide a communication channel for young children who cannot use written language. As in the case of children with comprehension problems, clinical observations suggest that oral language is facilitated rather than inhibited by providing the child with a communication aid (Shane, 1987).

THE ROLE OF THE CHILD PSYCHIATRIST

A multidisciplinary perspective is particularly important in the assessment and management of developmental language disorders. Speech and language therapists, psychologists, audiologists, teachers, neurologists and paediatricians all have a role to play in helping understand and treat these complex conditions, but the importance of the child psychiatrist should not be overlooked. We now know that there is a very high rate of communication difficulties among children referred to psychiatric services, and that in many cases these go undiagnosed. We also know that language disorder is a risk factor for later development of a range of emotional and behavioural problems. Greater involvement of psychiatrists in diagnosis, prevention and treatment of these disorders is to be encouraged.

REFERENCES

Alajouanine T. & Lhermitte F. (1965) Acquired aphasia in children. *Brain*, **88**, 653–662.
Allen R. & Wasserman G.A. (1985) Origins of language delay in abused infants. *Child Abuse and Neglect*, **9**, 335–340.
American Psychiatric Association (1994) *Diagnostic and Statistical Manual of Mental Disorders*, 4th edn., *DSM IV*. American Psychiatric Association, Washington DC.
Anthony A., Bogle D., Ingram T.T.S. & McIsaac M.W. (1971) *The Edinburgh Articulation Test*. Churchill Livingstone, Edinburgh.
Archer L.A. (1977) Blissymbolics: a nonverbal communication system.
Journal of Speech and Hearing Disorders, **42**, 568–579.
Baker L. & Cantwell D.P. (1982) Psychiatric disorder in children with different types of communication disorder. *Journal of Communication Disorders*, **15**, 113–126.
Baltaxe C.A.M. & Simmons J.Q. (1990) The differential diagnosis of communication disorders in child and adolescent psychopathology. *Topics in Language Disorders*, **10**, 17–31.
Bartak L., Rutter M. & Cox A. (1975) A comparative study of infantile autism and specific developmental receptive language disorder. I. The children. *British Journal of Psychiatry*, **126**, 127–145.
Bartak L., Rutter M. & Cox A. (1977) A comparative study of infantile autism and specific developmental receptive language disorder. III. Discriminant function analysis. *Journal of Autism and Childhood Schizophrenia*, **7**, 383–396.
Basser L.S. (1962) Hemiplegia of early onset and the faculty of speech with special reference to the effects of hemispherectomy. *Brain*, **85**, 427–460.
Beitchman J.H., Nair R., Clegg M. & Patel P.G. (1986a) Prevalence of speech and language disorders in 5-year-old children in the Ottawa-Carleton region. *Journal of Speech and Hearing Disorders*, **51**, 98–110.
Beitchman J.H., Nair R., Clegg M., Ferguson B. & Patel P.G. (1986b) Prevalence of psychiatric disorders in children with speech and language disorders. *Journal of the American Academy of Child and Adolescent Psychiatry*, **25**, 528–535.
Bender B., Fry E., Pennington B., Puck M., Salbenblatt J. & Robinson A. (1983) Speech and language development in 41 children with sex chromosome abnormalities. *Pediatrics*, **71**, 262–267.
Berlin C.I. (1978) Electrophysiological indices of auditory function. In: Martin F.N. (ed) *Pediatric Audiology*, pp. 113–173. Prentice-Hall, Englewood Cliffs, NJ.
Bird J. & Bishop D. (1992) Perception and awareness of phonemes in phonologically impaired children. *European Journal of Disorders of Communication*, **27**, 289–311.
Bishop D.V.M. (1985) Age of onset and outcome in 'acquired aphasia with convulsive disorder' (Landau–Kleffner syndrome). *Developmental Medicine and Child Neurology*, **27**, 705–712.
Bishop D.V.M. (1987) The causes of specific developmental language disorder ('developmental dysphasia'). *Journal of Child Psychology and Psychiatry*, **28**, 1–8.
Bishop D.V.M. (1989a) *Test for Reception of Grammar*, 2nd edn. Department of Psychology, University of Manchester.
Bishop D.V.M. (1989b) Autism, Asperger's syndrome and semantic–pragmatic disorder: where are the boundaries? *British Journal of Disorders of Communication*, **24**, 107–121.
Bishop D.V.M. (1989c) Quantitative aspects of specific developmental disorders. In: Munsat T. (ed) *Quantification of Neurologic Deficit*, pp. 327–344. Butterworths, Boston.
Bishop D.V.M. (1990) *Handedness and Developmental Disorder*. Clinics in Developmental Medicine 110. Blackwell Scientific, Oxford.
Bishop D.V.M. & Adams C. (1990) A prospective study of the relationship between specific language impairment, phonological disorders and reading retardation. *Journal of Child Psychology and Psychiatry*, **31**, 1027–1050.
Bishop D.V.M. & Edmundson A. (1986) Is otitis media a major cause of specific developmental language disorders? *British Journal of Disorders of Communication*, **21**, 321–338.
Bishop D.V.M. & Edmundson A. (1987a) Language-impaired four-year-olds: distinguishing transient from persistent impairment. *Journal of Speech and Hearing Disorders*, **52**, 156–173.
Bishop D.V.M. & Edmundson A. (1987b) Specific language impairment as a maturational lag: evidence from longitudinal data on language and motor development. *Developmental Medicine and Child Neurology*, **29**, 442–459.
Brooks D. (1987) Assessment of hearing in children. In: Yule W. &

Rutter M. (eds) *Language Development and Disorders*, pp. 337–349. Clinics in Developmental Medicine nos. 101–102. Blackwell Scientific, Oxford.

Brown J.K. (1985) Dysarthria in children – neurologic perspective. In: Darby J.K. (ed) *Speech and Language Evaluation in Neurology: Childhood Disorders*, pp. 133–184. Grune & Stratton, Orlando, FL.

Brown J. & Lloyd H. (1975) A controlled study of children not speaking at school. *Journal of the Association of Workers for Maladjusted Children*, **3**, 49–63.

Burgemeister B., Blum L. & Lorge I. (1972) *Columbia Mental Maturity Scale*. Harcourt Brace Jovanovich, Orlando, FL.

Cantwell D.P. & Baker L. (1987) *Developmental Speech and Language Disorders*. Guilford Press, New York.

Cantwell D.P., Baker L. & Mattison R. (1981) Prevalence, type, and correlates of psychiatric diagnoses in 200 children with communication disorder. *Developmental and Behavioral Pediatrics*, **2**, 131–136.

Cantwell D.P., Baker L., Rutter M. & Mawhood L. (1989) Infantile autism and developmental receptive dysphasia: a comparative follow-up into middle childhood. *Journal of Autism and Developmental Disorders*, **19**, 19–31.

Caulfield M.B., Fischel J.E., DeBaryshe B. & Whitehurst G.J. (1989) Behavioral correlates of developmental expressive language disorder. *Journal of Abnormal Child Psychology*, **17**, 187–201.

Cohen N.J., Davine M. & Meloche-Kelly M. (1989) Prevalence of unsuspected language disorders in a child psychiatric population. *Journal of the American Academy of Child and Adolescent Psychiatry*, **28**, 107–111.

Conrad R. (1979) *The Deaf Schoolchild*. Harper & Row, London.

Coplan J. (1987) Deafness: ever heard of it? Delayed recognition of permanent hearing loss. *Pediatrics*, **79**, 206–213.

Coplan J. & Gleason J.R. (1988) Unclear speech: recognition and significance of unintelligible speech in preschool children. *Pediatrics*, **82**, 447–452.

Coplan J., Gleason J.R., Ryan R., Burke M.G. & Williams M.L. (1982) Validation of an early language milestone scale in a high-risk population. *Pediatrics*, **70**, 677–683.

Cox A.D., Puckering C., Pound A. & Mills M. (1987) The impact of maternal depression in young children. *Journal of Child Psychology and Psychiatry*, **28**, 917–928.

Dale P.S. (1991) The validity of a parent report measure of vocabulary and syntax at 24 months. *Journal of Speech and Hearing Research*, **34**, 565–571.

Deonna T.W. (1991) Acquired epileptiform aphasia in children (Landau–Kleffner syndrome). *Journal of Clinical Neurophysiology*, **8**, 288–298.

Dunn H.G. (ed) (1986) *Sequelae of Low Birthweight: The Vancouver Study*. Clinics in Developmental Medicine. nos. 95–96. MacKeith Press, London.

Feagans L. (1986) Otitis media: a model for long term effects with implications for intervention. In: Kavanagh J.F. (ed) *Otitis Media and Child Development*, pp. 192–208. York Press, Parkton, MD.

Fenson L., Dale P.S., Reznic S., Bates E., Thal D., Hartung J. & Reilly J. (1991) *Technical Manual for the MacArthur Communicative Development Inventories*. Developmental Psychology Laboratory, San Diego State University, San Diego, CA.

Fischel J., Whitehurst G., Caulfield M. & Debaryshe B. (1989) Language growth in children with expressive language delay. *Pediatrics*, **82**, 218–227.

Friedrich U., Dalby M., Staehelin-Jensen T. & Bruun-Petersen G. (1982) Chromosomal studies of children with developmental language retardation. *Developmental Medicine and Child Neurology*, **24**, 645–652.

Fundudis T., Kolvin I. & Garside R.F. (1979) *Speech Retarded and Deaf Children: Their Psychological Development*. Academic Press, London.

Geschwind N. & Galaburda A. (1987) *Cerebral Lateralization: Biological Mechanisms, Associations and Pathology*. MIT Press, Cambridge, MA.

Green G. (1989) Psycho-behavioral characteristics of children with vocal nodules: WPBIC ratings. *Journal of Speech and Hearing Disorders*, **54**, 306–312.

Griffiths C.P.S. (1969) A follow-up of children with disorders of speech. *British Journal of Disorders of Communication*, **4**, 46–56.

Haka-Ikse K., Stewart D.A. & Cripps M.H. (1978) Early development of children with sex chromosome aberrations. *Pediatrics*, **62**, 761–766.

Hammill D., Brown B.S., Larsen S.C. & Wiederholt J. (1980) *Test of Adolescent Language*. Pro-Ed, Austin, TX.

Hardcastle W.J., Morgan Barry R. & Clark C.J. (1987) An instrumental phonetic study of lingual activity in articulation-disordered children. *Journal of Speech and Hearing Research*, **30**, 171–184.

Hay D.A., Prior M., Collett S. & Williams M. (1987) Speech and language development in preschool twins. *Acta Geneticae Medicae et Gemellologiae*, **36**, 213–223.

Haynes C. & Naidoo S. (1991) *Children with Specific Speech and Language Impairment*. Clinics in Developmental Medicine, 119. Blackwell Scientific, Oxford.

Hecaen H. (1976) Acquired aphasia in children and the ontogenesis of hemispheric functional specialization. *Brain and Language*, **3**, 114–134.

Hecox K. (1982) Pediatric applications of the brainstem auditory evoked response. In: Chiarenza G.A. & Papkostopoulos D. (eds) *Clinical Applications of Cerebral Evoked Potentials in Pediatric Medicine*, pp. 397–414. Excerpta Medica, Amsterdam.

Holm V. & Kunze L. (1969) Effect of chronic otitis media on language and speech development. *Pediatrics*, **43**, 833–839.

Hubbard T.W., Paradise J.L., McWilliams B.J., Elster B.A. & Taylor F.H. (1985) Consequences of unremitting middle-ear disease in early life: otologic, audiologic, and development findings in children with cleft palate. *New England Journal of Medicine*, **312**, 1529–1534.

Hurst J.A., Baraitser M., Auger E., Graham F. & Norell S. (1990) An extended family with a dominantly inherited speech disorder. *Developmental Medicine and Child Neurology*, **32**, 352–355.

Jerger J. (1964) Auditory tests for disorders of the central auditory mechanism. In: Fields W.S. & Alford B.R. (eds) *Neurological Aspects of Auditory and Vestibular Disorders*, pp. 77–93. C.C. Thomas, Springfield, IL.

Jernigan T., Hesselink J.R., Sowell E. & Tallal P. (1991) Cerebral structure on magnetic resonance imaging in language- and learning-impaired children. *Archives of Neurology*, **48**, 539–545.

Johnston R.B., Stark R.E., Mellits E.D. & Tallal P. (1981) Neurological status of language-impaired and normal children. *Annals of Neurology*, **10**, 159–163.

Kaplan L.C., Osborne P. & Elias E.R. (1986) The diagnosis of muscular dystrophy in patients referred for language delay. *Journal of Child Psychology and Psychiatry*, **27**, 545–549.

Karagan N.J., Richman L.C. & Sorensen J.P. (1980) Analysis of verbal disability in Duchenne muscular dystrophy. *Journal of Nervous and Mental Diseases*, **168**, 419–423.

Kidd K.K. (1980) Genetic models of stuttering. *Journal of Fluency Disorders*, **5**, 187–201.

Kratochwill T.R. (1981) *Selective Mutism: Implications for Research and Treatment*. Erlbaum, Hillsdale, NJ.

Kolvin I. & Fundudis T. (1981) Elective mute children: psychological development and background factors. *Journal of Child Psychology and Psychiatry*, **22**, 219–232.

Lahey M. (1988) *Language Disorders and Language Development* MacMillan, New York.

Landau W.M. & Kleffner F.R. (1957) Syndrome of acquired aphasia with convulsive disorder in children. *Neurology*, **7**, 523–530.

Landry S. & Loveland K. (1988) Communication behaviors in autism and developmental language delay. *Journal of Child Psychology and Psychiatry*, **29**, 621–634.

Largo R.H., Molinari L., Pinto L.C., Weber M. & Duc G. (1986) Language development of term and preterm children during the first five years of life. *Developmental Medicine and Child Neurology*, **28**, 333–350.

Lees J.A. & Neville B.G.R. (1990) Acquired aphasia in childhood: case studies of five children. *Aphasiology*, **4**, 463–478.

Leiter R. (1969) *Leiter International Performance Scale*. C.H. Stoelting, Chicago.

Leonard L.B. (1983) Discussion: Part II: Defining the boundaries of language disorders in children. In: Miller J., Yoder D. & Schiefelbusch R. (eds) *Contemporary Issues in Language Intervention*. ASHA Reports no. 12. American Speech-Language-Hearing Association, Rockville, MD.

Loveland K. & Landry S. (1986) Joint attention in language in autism and developmental language delay. *Journal of Autism and Developmental Disorders*, **16**, 335–349.

Lowe M. & Costello A. (1976) *Symbolic Play Test — Experimental Edition*. NFER-Nelson, Windsor.

McCauley R.J. & Swisher L. (1984) Use and misuse of norm-referenced tests in clinical assessment: a hypothetical case. *Journal of Speech and Hearing Disorders*, **49**, 338–348.

McCormick B. (1988a) *Screening for Hearing-Impairment in Young Children*. Croom Helm, London.

McCormick B. (1988b) Behavioural hearing tests 6 months to 5 years. In: McCormick B. (ed) *Paediatric Audiology: 0 to 5 years*, pp. 97–115. Taylor & Francis, London.

Marsh G.G. & Munsat T.L. (1974) Evidence for early impairment of verbal intelligence in Duchenne muscular dystrophy. *Archives of Disease in Childhood*, **49**, 118–122.

Meyer B.C. (1945) Psychosomatic aspects of stuttering. *Journal of Nervous and Mental Diseases*, **101**, 127–157.

Mittler P. (1970) Biological and social aspects of language development in twins. *Developmental Medicine and Child Neurology*, **12**, 741–757.

Mogford K. (1988) Oral language acquisition in the prelinguistically deaf. In: Bishop D. & Mogford K. (eds) *Language Development in Exceptional Circumstances*, pp. 110–131. Churchill Livingstone, Edinburgh.

Montgomery T.R. (1988) Clinical aspects of mental retardation: the chief complaint. *Clinical Pediatrics*, **27**, 529–531.

Mundy P., Sigman M., Ungerer J. & Sherman T. (1986) Defining the social deficits of autism: the contribution of nonverbal communication measures. *Journal of Child Psychology and Psychiatry*, **27**, 657–669.

Mundy P., Sigman M. & Kasari C. (1990) A longitudinal study of joint attention and language development in autistic children. *Journal of Autism and Developmental Disorders*, **20**, 115–128.

Murray L. (1992) The impact of postnatal depression on infant development. *Journal of Child Psychology and Psychiatry*, **33**, 543–561.

Mutton D.E. & Lea J. (1980) Chromosome studies of children with specific speech and language delay. *Developmental Medicine and Child Neurology*, **22**, 588–594.

Neils J. & Aram D.M. (1986) Family history of children with developmental language disorder. *Perceptual and Motor Skills*, **63**, 655–658.

Neligan G.A. & Prudham D. (1969) Norms for four standard developmental milestones by sex, social class and place in family. *Developmental Medicine and Child Neurology*, **11**, 413–422.

Noterdaeme H., Amorosa H., Ploog M. & Scheimann G. (1988) Quantitative and qualitative aspects of associated movements in children with specific developmental speech and language disorders and in normal pre-school children. *Journal of Human Movement Studies*, **15**, 151–169.

Parving A. & Elberling C. (1982) Clinical application of electrocochleography (ECoG) in children. In: Chiarenze G.A. & Papakostopoulos D. (eds) *Clinical Applications of Cerebral Evoked Potentials in Pediatric Medicine*, pp. 345–361. Excerpta Medica, Amsterdam.

Pasamanick B. (1952) Patterns of research in mental hygiene. *Psychiatric Quarterly*, **26**, 577–589.

Payne R.W. & Jones H.G. (1957) Statistics for the investigation of individual cases. *Journal of Clinical Psychology*, **13**, 115–121.

Pennington B.F., Smith S.D., Kimberling W.J., Green P.A. & Haith M.M. (1987) Left-handedness and immune disorders in familial dyslexics. *Archives of Neurology*, **44**, 634–639.

Peterson-Falzone S. (1982) Articulation disorders in orofacial anomalies. In: Lass N.J., McReynolds L., Northern J. & Yoder D.E. (eds) *Speech, Language and Hearing. Vol II: Pathologies of Speech and Language*, pp. 611–637. W.B. Saunders, Philadelphia.

Prizant B.M. & Wetherby A.M. (1990) Toward an integrated view of early language and communication development and socio-emotional development. *Topics in Language Disorders*, **10**, 1–16.

Quigley S.P. (1978) Effects of early hearing impairment on normal language development. In: Martin F.N. (ed) *Pediatric Audiology*, pp. 35–63. Prentice-Hall, Englewood Cliffs, NJ.

Rapin I. (1982) *Children with Brain Dysfunction*. Raven Press, New York.

Rapin I. (1987) Developmental dysphasia and autism in pre-school children: characteristics and subtypes. In: *Proceedings of the First International Symposium on Specific Speech and Language Disorders in Children*, pp. 20–35. AFASIC, London.

Rapin I. & Allen D. (1983) Developmental language disorders: nosologic considerations. In: Kirk U. (ed) *Neuropsychology of Language, Reading and Spelling*, pp. 155–184. Academic Press, New York.

Raven J. (1963) *Raven's Progressive Matrices*. NFER-Nelson, Windsor.

Renfrew C.E. (1969) *The Bus Story: A Test of Continuous Speech*. C.E. Renfrew, North Place, Headington.

Renfrew C.E. (1988) *Action Picture Test, 2nd edn*. C.E. Renfrew, North Place, Headington.

Rescorla L. & Schwartz E. (1990) Outcome of toddlers with specific expressive language delay. *Applied Psycholinguistics*, **11**, 393–407.

Reynell J. (1977) *Reynell Developmental Language Scales* (revised). NFER-Nelson, Windsor.

Richman N., Stevenson J. & Graham P. (1982) *Preschool to School: A Behavioural Study*. Academic Press, London.

Robinson R.J. (1987) Introduction and overview. In: *Proceedings of the First International Symposium on Specific Speech and Language Disorders in Children*, pp. 1–19. AFASIC, London.

Rutter M. & Lord C. (1987) Language disorders associated with psychiatric disturbance. In: Yule W. & Rutter M. (eds) *Language Development and Disorders*. Clinics in Developmental Medicine, nos. 101–102, pp. 206–233. Blackwell Scientific, Oxford.

Rutter M. & Mawhood L. (1991) The long-term psychosocial sequelae of specific developmental disorders of speech and language. In: Rutter M. & Casaer P. (eds) *Biological Risk Factors for Psychosocial Disorders*, pp. 233–259. Cambridge University Press, Cambridge.

Rutter M., Mawhood L. & Howlin P. (1992) Language delay and social development. In: Fletcher P. & Hall D. (eds) *Specific Speech and Language Disorders in Children*, pp. 63–78. Whurr, London.

Sameroff A.J. & Chandler M.J. (1975) Reproductive risk and the continuum of caretaking casualty. In: Horowitz F.D. (ed) *Review of Child Development Research*, vol. 4, pp. 187–244. University of Chicago Press, Chicago.

Scarborough H.S. & Dobrich W. (1990) Development of children with early language delay. *Journal of Speech and Hearing Research*, **33**, 70–83.

Schiff-Myers N. (1988) Hearing children of deaf parents. In: Bishop D. & Mogford K. (eds) *Language Development in Exceptional Circumstances*, pp. 47—61. Churchill Livingstone, Edinburgh.

Shane H. (1987) Trends in communication aid technology for the severely speech-impaired. In: Yule W. & Rutter M. (eds) *Language Development and Disorders*, pp. 408—421. Clinics in Developmental Medicine, nos. 101—102. Mac Keith Press, London/Blackwell Scientific Publications, Oxford.

Silva P. (1987) Epidemiology, longitudinal course and some associated factors: an update. In: Yule W. & Rutter M. (eds) *Language Development and Disorders*. Clinics in Developmental Medicine, nos. 101—102, pp. 1—15. Mac Keith Press, London.

Silva P., Justin C., McGee R. & Williams S.M. (1984) Some developmental and behavioural characteristics of seven-year-old children with delayed speech development. *British Journal of Disorders of Communication*, **19**, 147—154.

Silva P.A., Williams S.M. & McGee R. (1987) A longitudinal study of children with developmental language delay at age three: later intelligence, reading and behaviour problems. *Developmental Medicine and Child Neurology*, **29**, 630—640.

Sluckin A., Foreman N. & Herbert M. (1991) Behavioural treatment programmes and selectivity of speaking at follow-up in a sample of 25 selective mutes. *Australian Psychologist*, **26**, 132—137.

Stark R.E. & Tallal P. (1981) Selection of children with specific language deficits. *Journal of Speech and Hearing Disorders*, **46**, 114—122.

Stark R.E., Mellits E.D. & Tallal P. (1983) Behavioral attributes of speech and language disorders. In: Ludlow C.L. & Cooper J.A. (eds) *Genetic Aspects of Speech and Language Disorders*, pp. 37—52. Academic Press, New York.

Stevenson J. & Richman N. (1978) Behaviour, language and development in three-year-old children. *Journal of Autism and Childhood Schizophrenia*, **8**, 299—313.

Stevenson P., Bax M. & Stevenson J. (1982) The evaluation of home based speech therapy for language delayed pre-school children in an inner city area. *British Journal of Disorders of Communication*, **17**, 141—148.

Stott D.H., Moyes F.A & Henderson S.E. (1984) *Test of Motor Impairment*. Psychological Corporation, New York.

Tallal P., Ross R. & Curtiss S. (1989) Familial aggregation in specific language impairment. *Journal of Speech and Hearing Disorders*, **54**, 164—173.

Tancer N.K. (1992) Elective mutism: a review of the literature. In: Lahey B.B. & Kazdin A.E. (eds) *Advances in Clinical Child Psychology*, vol. 14, pp. 265—288. Plenum, New York.

Terman L.M. & Merrill M.A. (1960) *Stanford-Binet Intelligence Scale*. Houghton Mifflin, Boston, MA.

Thal D., Tobias S. & Morrison D. (1991) Language and gesture in late talkers: a 1-year follow-up. *Journal of Speech and Hearing Research*, **34**, 604—612.

Tizard B. (1983) Language and social class: is verbal deprivation a myth? *Journal of Child Psychology and Psychiatry*, **24**, 533—542.

Tomblin J.B. (1989) Familial concentration of developmental language impairment. *Journal of Speech and Hearing Disorders*, **54**, 287—295.

Tyler A.A., Edwards M.L. & Saxman J.H. (1987) Clinical application of two phonologically based treatment procedures. *Journal of Speech and Hearing Disorders*, **52**, 393—409.

Vohr B.R., Garcia-Coll C. & Oh W. (1989) Language and neurodevelopmental outcome of low-birthweight infants at three years. *Developmental Medicine and Child Neurology*, **31**, 582—590.

Warren S.F. & Bambara L.M. (1989) An experimental analysis of milieu language intervention: teaching the action-object form. *Journal of Speech and Hearing Disorders*, **54**, 448—461.

Watamori T.S., Sasanuma S. & Ueda S. (1990) Recovery and plasticity in child-onset aphasics: ultimate outcome at adulthood. *Aphasiology*, **4**, 9—30.

Webster A. & McConnell C. (1987) *Children with Speech and Language Difficulties*. Cassell, London.

Wechsler D. (1974) *Wechsler Intelligence Scale for Children — Revised*. Psychological Corporation, New York.

Wechsler D. (1990) *Wechsler Preschool and Primary Scale of Intelligence — Revised*. Psychological Corporation, New York.

Whitehurst G.J., Fischel J.E., Lonigan C.J., Valdez-Manchaca M.C., Arnold D.S & Smith M. (1991a) Treatment of early expressive language delay: if, when, and how. *Topics in Language Disorders*, **11**, 55—68.

Whitehurst G.J., Arnold D.S., Smith M., Fischel J.E., Lonigan C.J. & Valdez-Manchaca M.C. (1991b) Family history in developmental expressive language delay. *Journal of Speech and Language Disorders*, **34**, 1150—1157.

Wiig E. & Semel E. (1984) *Language Assessment and Intervention for the Learning Disabled*. C.C. Merrill, Columbus, OH.

Wilkins R. (1985) A comparison of elective mutism and emotional disorders in children. *British Journal of Psychiatry*. **146**, 198—203.

Woods B. & Carey S. (1979) Language defects after apparent clinical recovery from childhood aphasia. *Annals of Neurology*, **6**, 405—409.

World Health Organization (1992) *The ICD-10 Classification of Mental and Behavioral Disorders: Clinical Descriptions and Diagnostic Guidelines*. World Health Organisation, Geneva.

Chapter 33
Autism and Pervasive Developmental Disorders

Catherine Lord & Michael Rutter

The story of autism represents a prototype of the interplay between clinical and scientific progress in the field of child psychiatry in the 20th century. Questions of classification, the nature of brain–behaviour relationships, implications of psychological theory for treatment and the pragmatics of helping individuals and families cope with a debilitating life-long disorder all lie in the short history of the syndrome of autism. Autism is not only a unique disorder, but a window into the linkages among neurobiology, human behaviour and effective treatment in child psychiatry.

HISTORY OF AUTISM

Kanner's syndrome: autistic disturbances of affective contact

In the early 19th century, there were accounts of children whose behaviour now sounds hauntingly familiar (Vaillant, 1962). However, it was nearly 150 years later before the process of identifying what was specific about these children began with the careful observations of a clinician who brought the commonalities and special qualities of these behaviours to public attention. Kanner's original paper described 11 children seen over the course of 5 years who struck him as sharing 'fascinating peculiarities' (Kanner, 1943), including delayed echolalia, pronoun reversal, failure to use speech to communicate, an anxious desire to preserve sameness, repetitive behaviours, failure to anticipate being lifted, a general lack of awareness of other people's existence or feelings and a lack of ability to play imaginatively with other children. Kanner was particularly impressed by the existence of these behaviours in children who functioned at a retarded level in many respects but who gave the impression of normal intelligence, and seemed to have an inborn inability to relate to people and situations.

Kanner's description of autism continues to be one of the most vivid representations of the behaviour of autistic children, though his assumptions about normal intelligence have not been supported. At about the same time, Asperger independently described a group of children who were similar in many ways to Kanner's first 11 patients (Frith, 1991). In the ensuing years, there were other accounts of children who had some of the characteristics of autism, but who were regarded as showing schizophrenia or psychosis (Bender, 1941; Mahler, 1952). In part, this confusion may have been perpetuated by the term autism, with its connotations of an active withdrawal into a rich fantasy life (Bosch, 1970); this is ironic, because the relative absence of creativity and fantasy constitutes one of the cardinal symptoms of the syndrome of autism.

Kanner's early papers illustrate the important contribution of detailed clinical observations in serving to highlight a hitherto unrecognized pattern and forcing a change in concept. He described how the children were similar to each other and yet different from other children with mental handicap or emotional disorder and he gave their disorder a name, autism. This description made it possible for systematic study to begin.

The first studies took three forms: descriptions of the incidence and course of autism, empirical studies designed to identify the cognitive deficits underlying autism, and studies emphasizing the development of a behavioural technology and its implications for our understanding and treatment of autism. The first two developments are considered below; the third development, the impact of behavioural methods and theory, is discussed in relation to treatment at the end of the chapter.

Clinical and epidemiological studies of autism

In the 1960s and early 1970s, studies on both sides of the Atlantic confirmed that children with behaviours similar to those described by Kanner could reliably be discriminated from children with mental handicaps or with other psychiatric disorders (Rutter & Lockyer, 1967; Treffert, 1970; DeMyer et al., 1972). The importance of a distinctive pattern of deficits in social relatedness, communication and unusual interests and repetitive behaviours was supported. Autism was found to differ from mental handicap in the ratio of males to females (about 3 : 1 in autism; Lord & Schopler, 1985), in patterns of cognitive dysfunction (Hermelin & O'Connor, 1970; Lockyer & Rutter, 1970; Rumsey, 1992) and in an unusual onset of seizures in adolescence (Rutter, 1970). Autism was found to be different from schizophrenia in its onset during infancy or early preschool years, more frequent indications of overt organic impairment, specific patterns of cognitive deficit and association with mental handicap (Rutter, 1972). The prevalence of autism is now estimated at 2–5 per 10 000, with numbers expanding to 10—20 per 10 000 if broader definitions are used (Wing & Gould, 1979; Bryson *et al.*, 1988).

Two outcomes of these original descriptive studies, supported by later follow-up studies and other epidemiological research, were critical to the understanding of autism. Firstly, there were the links between autism and seizures, signs of neurological impairment and mental retardation; these provided evidence that autism is a developmental disorder with a neurobiological, rather than psychogenic, basis (Minshew, 1991). Secondly, findings that intelligence is as meaningful, stable and measurable a construct for autistic children as for any other children have been particularly important because of the implication that any consideration of the specific deficits of autism needs to take into account a child's developmental level (Rutter, 1979, 1983). Fewer than one-third of autistic children were found to have general cognitive abilities in the normal range of intelligence, even when language handicaps were taken into account (Lockyer & Rutter, 1970; Kolvin, 1971; Asarnow *et al.*, 1987). Autistic children range in intelligence from severe mental handicap to above-normal test performance. Because normal children's social and communicative behaviour varies with mental age, and because autism is characterized by *deviance* and not just impairment in these functions, the clinical assessment of autistic children must include evaluation of their cognitive level in order to determine if social and communicative behaviour is out of keeping with the child's developmental level (Rutter, 1985a).

Empirical studies of cognition and autism

At about the same time as the epidemiological studies, two developmental psychologists began a programme of experimental research on autism (Hermelin & O'Connor, 1970), studying how autistic children took in information through vision, touch or hearing, and how they used this information in simple memory and motor tasks. Their studies showed, among other things, that autistic children looked for shorter periods of time at social and nonsocial visual patterns and tended to persist in making the same motor responses for longer periods of time than nonautistic mentally handicapped children. They concluded that autism involved a specific cognitive deficit, different from (though often associated with) mental retardation, that had to do with difficulties in perceiving order or meaning in events. Their work showed that it was possible to study, in a controlled, scientific manner, the thinking of children who were for the most part nonverbal and often not particularly cooperative.

Like the early descriptions of Kanner, many of the early theoretical constructs of Hermelin and O'Connor underlie the current thinking on autism. Thus, notions of autism-specific over selectivity (Schreibman & Lovaas, 1973), impairments in drive for coherence (Frith, 1989) and deficits in organization and attention that may differentially affect modalities (Ozonoff *et al.*, 1991a; Courchesne *et al.*, in press) can be related back to these original studies, although some interpretations have changed.

Empirical studies of cognition and social relations

The documentation of autistic children's difficulties in recalling visual sequences was a first step in beginning to account for the particular pattern of social and communicative deficits characteristic of autism. Hobson (1984, 1987) took a next step, also using experimental methods from developmental psychology, to look specifically at autistic children's recognition of socially significant information, such as gestures, facial expressions and vocal expressions of affect. Hobson, following the lead of Hermelin and O'Connor, used a methodology of employing control tasks, as well as control groups, to assess the extent to which autistic children were differentially handicapped in their responses to social or affect-related information (for example, recordings of angry or happy tones of voice) compared to nonsocial input (e.g. sounds of train whistles or lawn mowers).

As with Hermelin and O'Connor's findings regarding processing in different modalities, the search for nonsocial tasks that are identical in information-processing demands (such as speed of processing required, complexity of elements) to the demands of social situations is still continuing (Hobson, 1991). Questions that arose from the earlier work of Hermelin and O'Connor also remain relevant. For example, one study showed that autistic children *could* sort photographs of faces by age and sex of the model, but often chose first to sort by type of hat, suggesting that interest and attention, as well as ability, may be involved (Weeks & Hobson, 1987). In addition, when autistic children were matched with mentally handicapped children on vocabulary rather than on nonverbal tests, group differences were weaker, indicating that, to a substantial extent, the autistic children's difficulties in socio-emotional discrimination may be accounted for by exceptionally poor language comprehension compared with other skills (Prior *et al.*, 1990; Ozonoff *et al.*, 1991a). Hobson's work has been very important in focusing attention on social cognitive deficits, even though his hypothesis that a deficit in emotional appreciation, specific to autism, underlies the behavioural and cognitive abnormalities has not been fully supported to date (Rutter & Bailey, 1993).

A second programme of research that occurred coincidentally with Hobson's work also used methods taken directly from experimental psychology to explore the idea that autistic individuals have a specific cognitive deficit in mentalizing — a lack of 'theory of mind' (Leslie, 1987; Baron-Cohen, 1989a). This approach opened up new concepts in its attempts to account for the broad social, linguistic and behavioural deficits of autism by positing a very specific cognitive deficit in understanding knowledge and thinking. It is based on experimental tasks that have shown that autistic children have difficulty understanding from the social context what other people are likely to be thinking. For example, normal and nonautistic mentally handicapped individuals readily appreciate that, if someone is out of a room while an object is moved from one place to another, on her return, she will look for it in its original location and not where it actually is. This is because most individuals realize that the person has no access to the information that the object has been moved. Autistic individuals are much less likely to show this appreciation. Theoretical accounts of these results have emphasized social-cognitive deficits in metarepresentation (Leslie & Happé, 1989; Baron-Cohen *et al.*, 1993) and 'automated' modules of imagination (Harris, 1989), as well as more general deficits in organization and 'executive functioning' (Ozonoff *et al.*, 1991a). However, all variants unite in the importance of the difference between autistic children and nonautistic children in the ease with which they can understand other people's thinking. An example of this is seen in the extent to which we take for granted a normally developing toddler's understanding of a simple act of pretence, such as pretending that a doll is crying.

When children of similar age and ability have been studied, research findings have been remarkably robust (Fein *et al.*, 1987; Prior *et al.*, 1990; Ozonoff *et al.*, 1991a), although few studies have directly contrasted the different theories, and questions of interpretation remain. It now seems well-established that autism involves deficits in the understanding of goals and attention, together with deficits in mentalizing, in appreciating what other people are likely to be thinking, and in a range of executive planning functions (Rutter & Bailey, in press). Moreover, it seems reasonable to suppose that these might underlie many of the social abnormalities in autism, and possibly some of the language abnormalities. What is much less clear is whether these deficits represent just one modular cognitive function or several separate functions; how the deficits evident at early ages relate to those found later; and how cognitive deficits might explain the stereotyped, repetitive behaviours also characteristic of autism (see below; Rutter & Bailey, 1993).

Structured observations of social-cognitive behaviours

Research from structured observations has also made important contributions to our understanding of autism-specific cognitive deficits. Working with preschool and early-school-age youngsters, Mundy and colleagues (1986) identified specific deficits in joint attention; that is, a child's tendency to look at or direct attention to an object that is being attended to by another person. Thus, young autistic children are as likely to reach for toys and to respond to being tickled as mental-age-matched nonautistic peers, but less likely to show something or to follow a point to an object of interest (Loveland & Landry, 1986; Mundy *et al.*, 1986). More cognitively advanced autistic children are able to point in order to request objects and understand the idea of doing so, but typically do not point to draw someone's attention to something they are interested in (Baron-Cohen, 1989b).

Specific deficits in the socially directed expression of affect and the coordination of vocalizations of speech with nonverbal behaviours have also been identified (Mundy *et al.*, 1986; Hertzig *et al.*, 1989). Autistic children are less likely to smile spontaneously at people or back to people (rather than to themselves); they are less likely to look at someone, gesture

and vocalize than other children matched in language or other cognitive skills (Dawson & Adams, 1984; Kasari *et al.*, 1990). In particular, they are less likely to look at people when faced with an ambiguous action, such as someone putting a hand on that of the child as if to stop him or her doing something (Phillips *et al.*, 1992). Deficits in these behaviours are important theoretically because they occur much earlier in normal development than the acquisition of metarepresentation or theory of mind, and so suggest that specific explanations of autism positing difficulties only in higher-order cognitive processes may not be sufficient (Klin *et al.*, 1992).

DIAGNOSIS

Diagnostic frameworks

At present, the two most commonly used diagnostic frameworks are ICD-10 (World Health Organization, 1992) and DSM-III-R (American Psychiatric Association, 1987), with DSM-IV (American Psychiatric Association, in press) about to appear. The systems both identify three areas of deficit required for a diagnosis of autism: communication, social development and restricted and repetitive behaviours and interests. Both require the recognition of some type of abnormality prior to age 36 months. Yet each child and adult is different in how autism is manifested. Symptoms change over time, as do expectations for normal behaviour. Even with its indefinite borders, autism probably remains one of the most reliably diagnosed psychiatric disorders in children (Cantwell *et al.*, 1979). Currently, autism is classified as a pervasive developmental disorder, a term that is intended to cover children and adults who have severe lifelong difficulties in social and communicative skills beyond those accounted for by general delay (Rutter & Schopler, 1992). This term has recently come under some criticism, but no appropriate alternative has yet been suggested. Clinical characteristics of autism are described briefly below.

Clinical characteristics

Social deficits

While autism is defined by a triad of deficits, there is a growing consensus that it is the distinctive aberrations in social development that are most specific and perhaps most handicapping across the range of individuals with the disorder (Volkmar, 1987). The most characteristic aspects of the social deviance of autism have to do with difficulties in reciprocal social interaction and the ability to form relationships (Siegel *et al.*, 1989). As infants, some autistic youngsters do not like to be held and do not hold their arms up to be lifted or adjust their bodies when being held, while others are very clingy or indiscriminately cuddly (Le Couteur *et al.*, 1989). What these behaviours have in common is a difficulty with the give-and-take of social behaviour, even at an infant level, that is manifested in a nonautistic child by being able both to catch someone's eye and respond to another's attempt to direct his or her attention to a toy or a family member. A lack of spontaneous imitation of others' behaviour and a paucity of interactions such as showing, giving and vocalizing that seem to have no other purpose than to communicate interest in another person and the world are also characteristic of autism (Rogers & Pennington, 1991).

In the preschool years, autistic children can be differentiated from mentally handicapped children or children with language impairments or other delays by a lack of interest in other children, a limited range of facial expression and unusual eye contact (Lord, 1993). By the time they are 4 or 5 years old, many autistic children are distressed by separation from their parents (Rogers *et al.*, 1991), but they are less likely to use their parents as a secure base in new situations, or to offer comfort to others in a simple way (such as bringing a baby brother his blanket). They often do not greet their parents in clear and positive ways upon reunion or follow them about, getting under foot and wanting to be part of the family. Other abnormalities include a lack of seeking to share their own enjoyment, such as getting their parents to come when they have built something interesting or when a favourite television character appears (Le Couteur *et al.*, 1989). However, it is important to note that most autistic children do not show deficits in all of these areas; many children have one or more behaviours for brief periods of time or in particular situations that seem surprisingly social.

Communication

If the full IQ range is included, about half of autistic children fail to develop functional speech; however, most of those who remain without speech are also severely mentally retarded (Rutter, 1978). Although autism is characterized by delayed language acquisition, it is the deviant quality of communication that is most specific to autistic individuals. Deficits in understanding of language in autistic children with severe mental handicaps and those with more normal nonverbal intelligence are important, both in differentiating autistic children from children with other disorders and in the ways in which they affect children's lives (Lord, 1985). Many young autistic children respond to noises in such unusual ways that they appear deaf, though usually there are some sounds (e.g. a favourite television commercial or a sweet wrapper) to which they respond consistently. Reports of whether autistic children babble less than or differently from other children with language delays have been inconclusive, but what seems to be missing in autism is the social back-and-forth of vocalizations seen even in very young normally developing infants (Le Couteur *et al.*, 1989). Use of gesture is delayed, particularly referential gestures (Baron-Cohen, 1989b) and emotional gestures, such as expressions of astonishment or sympathy (Attwood *et al.*, 1988).

When speech develops, the most characteristic aspect in autism is its lack of, or unusual, social quality (Tager-Flusberg & Anderson, 1991). Autistic children do not carry on to-and-fro conversations, even at the level of toddlers just putting words together. Although as their language develops some autistic children ask questions, these questions tend to be about the children's preoccupations (e.g. 'How tall were you when you were 2?') or they reflect concerns about upcoming events (e.g. 'When is lunchtime?'); they are rarely directed at inquiring about someone else's state of mind or interests (Tager-Flusberg, 1992). Some autistic children are talkative, but generally this speech is repetitive or more of a monologue than socially directed communication. Some autistic children, although they are able to speak, do so only infrequently, and primarily to ask for things (Stone & Caro-Martinez, 1990).

Other special characteristics of the language of autistic children include reversing pronouns (e.g. referring to themselves as 'you' or 'he'), delayed echolalia or stereotypical speech borrowed from other people or the media (e.g. repeating commercials or phrases from their teacher out of context, although sometimes with meaning), abnormalities of pitch, stress, rhythm and intonation (e.g. talking in a monotone or with sing-song intonation) and neologisms or making up words (such as 'sharda' for a ranger's hat; Fay & Schuler, 1980; Prizant & Wetherby, 1985; Volden & Lord, 1991). Immediate echolalia, or repeating what someone has just said, is common in young autistic children, but is found in other populations with language comprehension problems as well.

Restricted and repetitive interests and behaviours

Stereotyped behaviours and interests constitute the third set of criteria for autism. There is a tendency not to use toys in the intended functional fashion (except for simple movement or noise-maker play things); however, many behaviours in this category are difficult to differentiate from general delays in very young children (Lord, 1993). Usually, stereotyped patterns become more noticeable in older preschool autistic children when they become preoccupied by a specific part of a toy, such as spinning the wheels on a toy car or opening and closing the door of a toy house. Dressing up or spontaneous, flexible, imaginative play with dolls or teddy bears, is rare in autistic children, though many autistic children can carry out simple actions such as feeding a doll or pretending to talk on the phone (Ungerer & Sigman, 1981; Lewis & Boucher, 1988; Jarrold *et al.*, 1993). Some older, less retarded children develop complex routines with objects or dolls that they act out over and over again (Le Couteur *et al.*, 1989). Unusual reactions to sounds or sights, such as extreme agitation when someone sings or at the sight of a man with a beard, also occur in some autistic individuals.

Many autistic children and adults are interested in the sensory properties of objects. They smell or taste or feel objects that have no obvious interest to others. Peering at objects or visual patterns, often using peripheral vision, is common in autism. Stereotyped, repetitive movements, particularly of the hands and fingers within the visual field, are also common (Le Couteur *et al.*, 1989). Some autistic children injure themselves deliberately, for instance by biting their wrists, banging their heads or slapping themselves. These behaviours occur in other disorders besides autism, including severe mental handicap and sensory impairments. In autism, they are more likely to occur in very retarded children, but are found in autistic persons without severe retardation as well (Rumsey *et al.*, 1985). Some autistic children become attached to an unusual object such as a vacuum cleaner nozzle or a bottle cap and want to carry it with them wherever they go. As they grow older, many autistic children develop specific interests or preoccupations, often with repetitive topics, such as maps or birthdates or shoe sizes (Le Couteur *et al.*, 1989). Younger children may show similar behaviours by drawing elevator buttons or crossing sticks to form the shape of a Y. As they mature, autistic children may become upset if daily routines are not followed to minute detail (e.g. sandwiches not cut on the diagonal, bath water not up to a certain level) or if trivial aspects of the environment are changed, such as moving the furniture in the dining room. Many adults continue to need structure and routine, though the very strong reactions to minor changes often diminish.

Autism and mental retardation

Views on the relationship between autism and mental retardation have swung to and fro over the years. Kanner's (1943) initial view that the low IQ often found in autistic individuals was in some way not 'real' held sway for many years, but it can be firmly rejected in the light of the consistent evidence that their IQ scores have the same properties found in other groups (Rutter, 1979). Wing (1981), in reviewing the findings of her epidemiological study, noted that the triad of social, play and language impairment (a broader concept than autism) was strongly associated with IQ (a rate of 1.8% in the 50−69 range, extending to 82% in the 0−19 range). Some investigators have interpreted this association as meaning that there is an invariant relationship between low IQ and autism. However, the evidence firmly indicates that this is not the case. Thus, autism rarely occurs in Down's syndrome individuals in spite of their severe mental retardation (Wing & Gould, 1979). Moreover, the familial loading associated with autism (see the section on genetic studies below) mainly applies to language and social abnormalities in individuals of normal intelligence; there is no loading for mental retardation as such. Accordingly, the view that autism is simply a concomitant of mental handicap can also be firmly rejected.

Most theory of mind researchers (see the section on empirical studies of cognition and social relations, above), by contrast, have tended to set aside the occurrence of mental retardation in their attempts to explain autism, on the grounds that their task is only to account for that which is specific to autism (see Baron-Cohen *et al.*, 1993). However, that ignores the close association between autism and mental retardation. Not only do some three-quarters of autistic individuals have an IQ below 70, but also IQ is the single most powerful predictor of outcome in autism (Venter *et al.*, 1992). In addition, familial loading in autism is significantly associated with verbal IQ

(Rutter *et al.*, 1993). Verbal cognitive impairment must be considered as an intrinsic (albeit not quite invariant) part of autism. Autism tends to be associated with a distinctive cognitive pattern, with visuospatial skills greatest and verbal abstraction and conceptualization skills weakest (Venter *et al.*, 1992). Also, it is important to note that a significant minority of autistic individuals have unusual cognitive skills as well as deficits; *idiot savant* talents seem to be particularly common in autism, (Frith, 1989) and these, too, require explanation.

NEUROBIOLOGY OF AUTISM

Having validated autism as a distinctive syndrome characterized by a specific cognitive, social and behavioural pattern, researchers have sought to identify the pathophysiology of these deficits (Bailey, 1993). This has not been an easy task. Even the most apparently straightforward findings have been difficult to replicate across samples and laboratories. Links between findings and models have often been tenuous at best. However, improvements in technology offer the hope of much clearer understanding and treatment of the neurobiological bases of autism in the not too distant future.

Neuroanatomy

Autopsy studies

Attempts (based on a variety of research strategies) have been made to localize autism in the medial temporal lobe, thalamic nuclei, basal ganglia, vestibular system, pons and neocerebellum. Autopsy studies have shown that autistic individuals do not have gross lesions, obvious gliosis or abnormal gyral configurations or myelinization (Bauman, 1991). What has been shown is increased cell-packing density and reduced nerve cell size bilaterally in the limbic system, variable loss of Purkinje cells and, to a lesser extent, granule cells in the neocerebellar cortex (Bauman, 1991). To date, these findings have not been found to be associated with seizures or use of medication. However, they have also not been found to be associated with severity of clinical symptoms. Because this research is based on small numbers of subjects, most though not all of whom have been mentally handicapped as well as autistic, interpretations must be cautious. To date, the autopsy studies have lacked mental retardation controls and the degree to which any finding is specific to autism remains unknown (Bailey, 1993).

Retrograde cell loss and atrophy that would be expected following perinatal or postnatal damage have not been found in autism. These findings, together with the absence of gross lesions, have led some investigators to begin to suggest that the timing of any developmental aberration in autism should be narrowed to the second trimester or up to 30−32 weeks' gestation (Ciaranello *et al.*, 1982; Bauman, 1991); on the other hand, the association with congenital anomalies suggests the first trimester (see below).

Imaging studies

While initially promising, findings from computed tomography (CT) scans have been inconsistent, but suggest that there may be enlargement of central nervous system (CNS) fluid spaces in some autistic individuals (Courchesne, 1991). Courchesne's (1989, 1991) magnetic resonance imaging (MRI) studies indicated reductions in the size of neocerebellar regions of vermal lobes VI and VII. These findings have been partially replicated by some investigators and not at all by others (Courchesne, 1991; Minshew, 1991; Kleiman *et al.*, 1992; Piven *et al.*, 1992). Like the autopsy findings, they have not been found to be related to clinical symptoms. Cerebellar dysfunction in early development in otherwise normally developing children is generally associated with neuromotor rather than cognitive difficulties, a finding that does not fit easily with attempts to account for autism by cerebellar abnormalities (Bailey, 1993).

Only a very small number of functional imaging studies have been undertaken in autistic individuals and the findings so far are inconclusive and somewhat contradictory (Minshew, 1991). However, all have been performed under resting conditions and activation studies are likely to be more informative.

One finding from basic research in neurobiology may be relevant for autism. Primate research has generated interest in the ideas of shifts in the functional equivalence of behaviours; that is, the idea that similar behaviours may be reliant on different CNS systems at different points in development. For example, monkeys with dorsolateral frontal lobe lesions at 1 year of age are able to carry out delayed-response tasks, whereas the same monkeys at 3 years of age cannot (Goldman-Rakic *et al.*, 1983). These findings are interesting because of their similarity to descriptions of deterioration (or at least failure to progress) in autistic children's communicative and social skills during their second and third years of life. The implication of the primate research is that such changes may not be caused by new abnormalities but, rather, may be due to shifts in the functional organization of brain–behaviour relationships.

Our understanding of neural bases of different behaviours has been directly related to the ease with which deficits can be detected and quantified (Goldman-Rakic *et al.*, 1983). Brain–behaviour links are much better understood for sensory and motor systems than for affective and social behaviour. The accurate measurement of the unique pattern of deficits in autism across the areas of communication, social skills and repetitive interests and behaviours provides a challenge to scientists interested in identifying these links.

Neurophysiology

EEG/epilepsy studies

Findings of the increased incidence of epilepsy and abnormal electroencephalograms (EEGs) in autistic children, compared with other psychiatric populations, were one of the first pieces of evidence that autism is an organic, rather than psychogenic, disorder (Ornitz, 1978). The particular pattern of epilepsy, with one peak of incidence during early childhood and a second, unusual peak during adolescence, suggests that electrophysiological abnormalities are an integral part of the clinical manifestation of autism, not just the co-occurrence of two different disorders. Some autistic children have seizures in the preschool period (the proportion may be higher in the profoundly retarded), but the incidence rises to some 25–40% by early adulthood (Rutter, 1970; Deykin & MacMahon, 1979; Olsson *et al.*, 1988; Volkmar & Nelson, 1990). Major motor seizures are most common, though complex partial seizures may be more frequent than estimated earlier. There is a clear association between epilepsy in autism and mental handicap (Bartak & Rutter, 1976; Olsson *et al.*, 1988). The onset of seizures in adolescence is sometimes, but not usually, associated with marked behavioural changes and regression (Rutter, 1970; Kobayashi *et al.*, 1992).

Estimates of EEG abnormalities have ranged from 10 to 83%, with one recent study showing 32–43% of autistic subjects exhibiting abnormalities with one EEG and 58% with repeat EEGs. As with other neurobiological research, measurement error and interpretation are significant considerations. Diffuse or focal spikes, slow waves and paroxysmal spike-and-wave activity with mixed discharge are the most common abnormalities (Minshew, 1991). Most abnormalities are bilateral, and even unilateral findings have tended not to be clearly localized.

Evoked potentials

Neurophysiological research has provided some interesting findings, but has been plagued by fundamental difficulties in replication. Earlier work did not control for intelligence and so comparisons of mentally handicapped autistic children with normal children may have primarily indicated the effect of mental handicap on measures. Some of the first neurophysiological studies of autism suggested moderate to severe delays in wave I (auditory) and prolonged brainstem transmission (Tanguay, 1976), but recent studies have generally not shown simple differences in transmission time (Courchesne, 1991).

Recently there has been an interest in event-related potentials — measures that reflect the transmission of sensory information through the brainstem and its processing by the brain. Attenuation of auditory P300 has been found in autistic subjects of normal intelligence compared with controls (Courchesne & Lincoln, 1985). Visual potentials were reduced, but less obviously so, and negative components, potentials originating from the frontal cortex that also cross modalities, were found to be absent in the same individuals.

These results have been interpreted to suggest that autism is associated with less efficient strategies for cortical information-processing (Courchesne & Lincoln, 1985). Autistic individuals may have a reduced capacity to attach appropriate levels of importance, particularly to auditory information, and may not increase attention when they detect new auditory or visual information. These hypotheses are intriguing and reminiscent of the ideas of Hermelin and O'Connor in the early cognitive studies, but clear links, either to neuroanatomy or to behaviour, have not yet been identified. Alternative explanations for these findings and specific effects of stimulus changes and other methodological factors require careful consideration. At this stage, simple replication of findings across samples and laboratories is a necessary step before results can be taken seriously (Young *et al.*, 1982).

Neurochemistry

Neurochemical studies of autism are potentially informative on the neurobiology of autism, but so far the findings have been inconclusive (Elliot & Ciaranello, 1987; Cook, 1990; Bailey, 1993). Because few studies have included more than one measure, contradictory findings are difficult to interpret.

CNS neurotransmitters in autism have been studied in spinal fluid, blood and urine, as well as assays of platelets containing enzymes that help regulate the level of neurochemicals by metabolizing other chemicals to inactive states. Increased blood levels of serotonin have been found in about one-third of mentally handicapped autistic children and about one-half of nonautistic severely retarded children; there is some evidence that hyperserotonaemia runs in families. Decreased levels of 5-hydroxyindoleacetic acid (5-HIAA), the primary metabolite of serotonin, have been found in autistic children, with no differences in cerebrospinal fluid-based 5-HIAA reported in other studies. Other neurochemical studies have been unable to find a significant relationship between cerebrospinal fluid levels of homovanillic acid, the principal metabolite of dopamine, and autistic symptoms, though one study found a relationship with motor disturbance (Young *et al.*, 1982). Blood levels of noradrenaline have been elevated in autistic children compared with normal controls, but studies of urinary excretion have yielded mixed results (Young *et al.*, 1982). Other investigators have suggested associations between autism and autoimmune disorders, inborn errors of purine metabolism and lactate acidosis (Stubbs, 1977). Opioids, including reduced blood levels of endorphins and overactivity of endogenous opioids, have also been suggested as possible factors, but interpretation of studies has been hindered by methodological constraints (Elliot & Cianarello, 1987; Cook, 1990). Except for the nonspecific finding of hyperserotonaemia in about a third of autistic mentally handicapped youngsters, other results await replication before serious attempts to interpret them are worthwhile.

Neuropsychological models

Neuropsychological models of autism have arisen in three ways: by general analogy with other disorders with known sites of localization, by specific analogy on the basis of experimental data, and from neuroanatomical evidence. On the basis of results of classic experimental tasks, earlier theories suggested autism-specific delays in lateralization. These theories have received less attention as the process of lateralization has become viewed as more complex and as the effects of developmental delay on task performance have been better understood. The temporal lobes were also of interest because of analogies between the communication handicaps that define autism and the language deficits seen in adults with temporal lobe lesions. However, the lack of replicable neuroanatomical findings and an awareness that the findings from the study of acquired lesions in adults cannot necessarily be extrapolated to developmental disorders arising in early life have reduced the enthusiasm for this area as the site of autism (Fein *et al.*, 1984).

An analogous model of autism as a frontal lobe disturbance, because of its association with flat affect, poor motivation and motor stereotypies (Damasio & Maurer, 1978), has recently attracted attention because of experimental findings that performance on tasks that require high levels of 'executive functioning', an ability hampered by frontal lesions, is specifically impaired in high-functioning autistic adolescents and adults (Ozonoff *et al.*, 1991a; Rumsey, 1992; Ozonoff, in press). Imaging studies have not yet supported these findings. The nature of the proposed deficit in functioning, manifestations of which have varied from study to study, needs to be better understood, but this is currently a promising area for future research.

Analogous models of limbic system dysfunction, including motivational deficits, stereotypies and differences in orientation and arousal, have also been proposed (Dawson & Lewy, 1989). While cognitive deficits in autism do not fit easily into these models, the neuroanatomical evidence of increased cell density and decreased cell size does provide some support for abnormalities in this area (Bauman, 1991).

Origins of neurobiology

Because most autistic children are described by their parents as showing some abnormal development from infancy, the search for the cause of autism has focused mainly on two areas: genetics and obstetric factors. However, some autistic children seem to have a period of regression during the preschool years. There is no evidence in the great majority of cases that this regression is associated with infection or trauma. The notion of functional equivalence, that is, that different parts of the brain may be required for similar behaviours at different stages of development, may help explain the unusual course of the disorder.

Genetic studies

Chromosomal and single gene disorders

Over the years, autism has been reported to be associated with phenylketonuria (PKU), tuberous sclerosis and neurofibromatosis, all of which are single-gene disorders (Reiss *et al.*, 1986;

Folstein & Rutter, 1988; Smalley *et al.*, 1988; Smalley, 1991). The link with PKU is based on nonsystematic studies and the association is now perhaps in some doubt. In any case, with neonatal screening, untreated PKU is now rare and therefore is of negligible current importance as a cause of autism. The connection with neurofibromatosis is based only on a few isolated case reports, the disease is rare, and it is likely that it, too, is an infrequent cause of autism (Mouridsen *et al.*, 1992). The association with tuberous sclerosis is the best documented (Smalley *et al.*, 1991, 1992; Hunt & Shepherd, 1993) and there is no doubt that some autistic individuals have this condition. The above studies of people with tuberous sclerosis have found that autism rarely occurs in those of normal intelligence; the association may be with the degree of handicap and not with the medical condition *per se*.

Following the development of cytogenetic methods of detecting the fragile X anomaly, there was an enthusiastic claim that at least 47% of autistic individuals had chromosome anomalies, about half of whom showed the fragile X (Gillberg & Wahlström, 1985). Other studies have shown that this estimate is too high and the rate of fragile X in autism is probably about 2.5% (Bailey *et al.*, 1993), with only the occasional cases being associated with other chromosomal anomalies. Clearly, part of the reason for the misleadingly high early estimates derived from loose laboratory criteria: very low (1−3%) rates of fragile X expression probably had quite a different implication (Bolton *et al.*, 1992). However, it is likely that varying diagnostic criteria for autism were also responsible. Recent studies have emphasized the rather different quality of the social deficit (marked social anxiety and averted gaze combined with friendliness) in most fragile X individuals (Cohen *et al.*, 1989; Wolff *et al.*, 1989). It is now clear that although there is a low-level association between autism and the fragile X anomaly (in both males and females — Bolton & Rutter, 1990; Bailey *et al.*, 1993), most fragile X individuals show a rather different behavioural pattern and the anomaly accounts for only a tiny proportion of cases of autism. Nevertheless, in view of its importance with respect to genetic counselling, screening for the fragile X anomaly and other chromosome anomalies is indicated (see Chapters 6 and 10).

Twin and family studies

Because the rate of autism in siblings was so low (an estimate of 2% on the data available in the 1960s/1970s), there was a general reluctance to consider a genetic aetiology in cases without a known medical condition, even though it had become accepted that autism arose on the basis of some form of organic brain dysfunction. A realization that this rate, although low in absolute terms, represented a 50−100-fold increase over the general population incidence led to the first systematic population-based twin study of autism (Folstein & Rutter, 1977a,b). The results showed a 37% concordance for autism in 11 monozygotic (MZ) pairs versus 0% in 10 dizygotic (DZ) pairs — a difference that pointed to a strong genetic component. The findings also showed that most of the MZ pairs, but only 1 in 10 of the DZ, were concordant for some type of cognitive deficit, usually involving language delay. A recent follow-up showed that these cognitive deficits were also associated with social impairment (Rutter, 1991; Rutter *et al.*, in press). The original study was important because of the implication that it might not be autism as such that is inherited, but rather some broader type of cognitive/social deficit that included, but was not confined to, autism (Rutter *et al.*, 1993).

A further UK population-based twin study using standardized interview and observation methods with cytogenetic investigations to detect the fragile X more than doubled the sample size (Rutter *et al.*, 1993). Pooling the two studies produced an MZ concordance for autism of 60 versus 0% in the DZ pairs. As in the Folstein and Rutter study, autism was associated also with social and/or cognitive deficits (92% MZ concordance versus 10% DZ concordance). The Scandinavian twin study by Steffenburg and her colleagues (1989) produced autism concordance figures of 91 versus 0% but did not show the broader phenotype evident in both the UK studies (Rutter *et al.*, 1993).

All three twin studies found that obstetric complications differentiated twins with autism from their co-twins without autism. At first, this was interpreted as indicating the possible role of environmentally induced brain damage. However, Rutter *et al.* (1993) went on to show that obstetric complications were very strongly associated with minor congenital anomalies. As most of the latter derive from abnormal development in the early part of pregnancy, the implication is that the obstetric complications probably stem from a genetically abnormal fetus and do not represent an environmental effect at all (see Chapter 10).

The most extensive systematic standardized family genetic study was undertaken by Bolton and colleagues (submitted), who compared the families of autistic individuals with those of Down's syndrome individuals (Rutter *et al.*, 1993). In keeping with previous studies (Folstein & Rutter, 1988; Smalley *et al.*, 1988), it was found that the rate of autism in siblings was 3%. However, a further 2% had a somewhat atypical syndrome of autism and a further 4% a combination of cognitive and social abnormalities (in each case versus 0% in the siblings of Down's syndrome individuals). When isolated cognitive and social abnormalities were included, the rate of disorder in the sibs was just over 14%. Piven *et al.*'s (1992) findings were broadly comparable. An epidemiological study of autism in Utah produced the somewhat higher figure of 4.5% for sibling recurrence risk of autism (Jorde *et al.*, 1991).

The family data take the twin findings beyond the general support of a strong genetic component in three key respects. Firstly, Bolton *et al.* (in press) found that the more severe the autism (as judged by a symptom count from the Autism Diagnostic Interview; Le Couteur *et al.*, 1989), or the lower the verbal IQ, the greater the familial loading (Rutter *et al.*, 1993). This suggests that multiple genes are involved, and not just one major gene (Rutter *et al.*, 1993). If this were so, the familial loading would also be expected to be higher for autistic females than males. There is an inconsistent tendency for this to be so (August *et al.*, 1981; Tsai *et al.*, 1981; Tsai & Beisler, 1983; Jorde *et al.*, 1991; Lord *et al.*, 1991; Bolton *et al.*, in press), but the statistical power to detect a sex difference was low in all studies, so the matter remains in some doubt. Secondly, the very marked fall-off in rate going from MZ co-twins to DZ co-twins or sibs (Folstein & Rutter, 1977a,b; Steffenburg *et al.*, 1989; Bailey *et al.*, submitted) and the further marked fall-off from first-degree to second-degree relatives (Jorde *et al.*, 1991) also points to the operation of multiple genes (Risch, 1990).

The third contribution of the family data is the confirmation that the phenotype extends beyond the traditional diagnostic boundaries to include a mixture of cognitive (mainly language-related) and social deficits in individuals of normal intelligence (Wolff *et al.*, 1988; Piven *et al.*, 1990; Landa *et al.*, 1991, 1992, Rutter *et al.*, in press). Despite earlier suggestions to the contrary (Baird & August, 1985), the phenotype does not appear to include mental retardation when it is associated with autism in the same individual. It seems that, although autism is likely to be genetically heterogeneous (see below), the genetic contribution is probably autism-specific and not part of undifferentiated mental retardation (Rutter, 1991).

Comings and Comings (1991) have suggested that the main phenotype also includes Tourette's syndrome, and Gillberg (1992) has argued that anorexia nervosa also ought to be added; however, the evidence to date supporting both suggestions seems unconvincing. Two studies (DeLong & Dwyer, 1988; Piven *et al.*, 1992) reported an apparently increased familial loading for affective disorder, but it is not yet clear whether this is genetically mediated.

The association, albeit weak, between autism and various single-gene conditions shows that to some extent autism must be genetically heterogeneous. The history of medical genetics suggests that further heterogeneity is to be expected. The rather different twin and family findings in cases of autism associated with profound mental retardation raise the possibility that it might include genetically distinct subvarieties (Rutter, 1991).

The only linkage study published to date (Spence *et al.*, 1985) produced inconclusive findings; a recent molecular genetic study focusing on the long arm of the X chromosome (Melmer *et al.*, submitted) could neither demonstrate nor rule out a genetic locus in the region of the fragile X site.

Genetic counselling

It is important to inform families with an autistic child who are considering having further children that there is a genetic risk of about 3% that a subsequent child will show autism, and a somewhat greater risk that he or she will have some type of broader social-cognitive disorder of a less seriously handicapping variety. This risk is greater if further offspring are male. Unfortunately, in the absence of knowledge on the mode of inheritance, it is not possible to give more precise risks of an individualized kind. The risk of an unaffected sibling having an autistic child is very low (although the available data do not provide precise figures for this risk).

Obstetric factors in autism

A generally higher incidence of prenatal problems has been found in autistic children compared with their siblings, or with normative data (Tsai, 1987; Nelson, 1991). Factors found to differentiate autistic from other children in two or more studies include advanced maternal age, birth order (either first- or fourth-born or later), use of medication, meconium staining, prematurity, postmaturity and early or midtrimester bleeding (Tsai, 1987). Autism has generally not been associated with perinatal factors, including birth asphyxia, except those that are often related to prenatal conditions (Goodman, 1990; Nelson, 1991). Delayed cry, apnoea, difficulties in resuscitation, low Apgar scores and respiratory distress have inconsistently been related to autism, but the evidence indicates that they are more likely to be manifestations of intrinsic disorders of the fetus than birth factors whose effects are environmentally mediated (Goodman, 1990; Rutter *et al.*, 1993). Presumably, obstetric complications can occasionally serve as causes of autism but the evidence suggests that this accounts for few cases.

Other environmental causes

Despite claims to the contrary (Gillberg, 1992), the twin findings (see above) indicate that environmental causes are unlikely to play more than a minor aetiological role in autism (Rutter, 1991; Rutter *et al.*, 1993). The best established association is with congenital rubella (Chess, 1971), but these cases have been found to show a markedly atypical course, involving frequent recovery from the autism (Chess, 1977). With modern immunization programmes, rubella is not likely to account for more than the occasional rare case. There are isolated case reports of autism associated with a few other environmental causes (such as congenital cytomegalovirus; Stubbs *et al.*, 1984), but all seem to be quite rare. There is no consistent evidence of any psychosocial environmental causal factor.

Autism and known medical conditions

Gillberg (1990, 1992) has argued, on the basis of his findings, that some two-fifths (37%) of autistic children have a diagnosable medical condition. Other studies have produced much lower estimates — in the region of 10% (Ritvo *et al.*, 1990; Smalley, 1991; Rutter *et al.*, in press). Three main explanations for the disparity in estimates need to be considered: regional differences in aetiology (as suggested by Gillberg, 1992), differences in the stringency of diagnostic criteria for the medical conditions, and the possibility that the medical conditions are mainly associated with atypical autism or autism accompanied by severe retardation rather than autism as such. The issue is an important one because of its implications. Although regional variations in patterns of causal influences are possible, the suggestion lacks supporting evidence. Clearly, differences in stringency of medical diagnostic criteria may play some part, as shown by the marked drop over time in the rate of fragile X reported in autism, and the uncertain meaning of some of the other laboratory findings. However, the third possibility that the association is mainly with atypical autism or autism accompanied by severe retardation may well constitute the main explanation (see review by Rutter *et al.*, in press). The implication is that the diagnostic distinctions within the broad grouping of pervasive developmental disorders, including that between autism and atypical autism, may well be medically important (Rutter & Schopler, 1992). It also seems that the need for systematic medical investigations may be especially great when autism is associated with profound retardation and/or when the clinical picture is atypical or unusual in some way (see Chapter 6).

COURSE OF AUTISM

Age of onset and early regressions

Most autistic children are identified by their parents as showing some abnormalities or delays in the second year of life, and many parents suspect problems long before this. Age of onset was originally important in discriminating autism from schizophrenia. Children with the symptoms of autism show abnormalities by 30 or 36 months, in contrast to schizophrenia-related disorders that generally develop in the early or late teens (Kolvin, 1971). Otherwise, discriminations among autistic children on the basis of age of onset have not been particularly useful. Education and having had a previous child are both factors that affect parents' ability to recognize early developmental abnormalities typical of autism (Volkmar *et al.*, 1985), so that age of onset may often be more age of recognition than the actual onset of symptoms. The abnormalities identified by parents of autistic children when they are still toddlers are often not specific to autism (such as language delay and difficulties in settling, eating and sleeping) and so it is not surprising that they are not recognized by parents earlier (Dahlgren & Gillberg, 1989), even though it may be possible for experienced clinicians to identify autism in some children at early ages (Gillberg *et al.*, 1990; Lord, 1991).

About one-quarter to one-third of parents of autistic children report a loss of speech in the first years of life (Rogers & DiLalla, 1990), often accompanied by changes in social behaviour. These regressions usually consist of the loss of most or all of the child's few communicative meaningful words. One study found that most children who lost words had been using them for less than 6 months (Kurita, 1985). Few children regained speech within a year, though many did so eventually. Some studies have shown worse prognoses for children who experience early language regressions (Kurita, 1985) and others no differences (Rogers & DiLalla, 1990), but none have suggested it is a positive sign.

Few longitudinal studies are available that allow us to follow the development of individual children but, as they enter their early teens, many autistic children are described by their parents as more flexible and more socially directed, within the constraints of autism (Cantwell *et al.*, 1989). However, a minority of autistic youngsters show marked regressions in behaviour and occasionally in cognitive skills (Rutter, 1970; Gillberg & Steffenburg, 1987), and rather more show increases in aggression and difficult behaviour. It has been claimed that such deterioration is more likely when there are associated epileptic seizures, but this is not a regular occurrence.

Autism during adulthood

Adulthood can seem very slow in coming for autistic young people, perhaps because of their lack of independence, but clinical experience suggests that at least some autistic adults experience real behavioural and social improvements in their late 20s and early 30s (Mesibov, 1984). On the other hand, autism is a lifelong disorder and the prognosis for complete independence is limited. Autistic individuals with severe mental handicap require supervised living and working situations throughout their lives; opportunities for such situations within communities, rather than in institutions, have increased within the last decade. Apart from a few notable exceptions (Grandin & Scariano, 1986), almost all autistic adults, even those with normal intelligence, require some help in finding and keeping jobs and coping with responsibilities and social demands (Rutter *et al.*, 1992). How independent an autistic adult with mild or no mental handicap will be often depends as much on community resources and the effort and luck of family members seeking vocational and residential placements as on the individual's own characteristics. There are only limited data on the development of new problems in adult life. A large-scale, long-term follow-up study has shown that some autistic adults develop depressive disorders, and clear-cut obsessional disorders sometimes occur (S. Goode, personal communication). There were no cases of schizophrenia, although these did arise in a comparison group with developmental disorders of receptive language (Rutter & Mawhood, 1991; Rutter *et al.*, 1992). Contrary to a report from Burd *et al.* (1987) the development of Tourette's syndrome was rare.

ASSESSMENT AND INTERVENTION

Assessment of children or adults referred because of concerns about possible autism is a multifaceted, multidisciplinary process. Information about the child's history, current behaviour and cognitive skills is necessary and best obtained from a combination of parental and teacher report, observation and standardized assessment. Though the diagnosis of autism may often seem apparent simply from observation, there are many cases, particularly of young children or adolescents, where it is not clear whether such a diagnosis is appropriate, and other cases where such a decision would have been wrong because of a lack of pertinent information. The process of diagnosis is one of eliminating alternative explanations for the child's behaviour (e.g. undiagnosed severe hearing impairment, gross neglect or deprivation), establishing a baseline of the child's ordinary cognitive functioning and behaviour and then selecting among differential diagnoses. This process can be carried out in several hours for most children, if good information from other sources is organized beforehand and if experienced clinicians work together to build on each other's knowledge.

Because autism is a developmental disorder, it is often helpful to begin detailed questioning with a chronological account, starting not with pregnancy, but by getting the parents to describe when and why they were first suspicious that something was not quite right with their child's development. Once the timing and nature of these concerns have been established, it is then easier to go back and enquire about the pregnancy, delivery and neonatal period, working forward from there. Information is then needed about the areas of development that are most associated with autism: communication, socialization, play and specific behaviours. Some clinicians choose to ask specifically about each of these areas as they occurred in early development and then move on to current behaviours. Another approach is to begin more focused questioning about current behaviours in each of the areas and, when it is appropriate within specific questions, refer back to the child's behaviour at earlier ages. Because autism is most clearly diagnosed in the later preschool years (4–5 years), if the child is older, it is important to get information about this period. It is also necessary to enquire about other aspects of behaviour and emotional development, such as fears and worries and aggression to self, objects or others.

The Autism Diagnostic Interview — Revised is a semistructured standardized interview for caregivers of autistic children and adults that has recently become available (Le Couteur *et al.*, 1989; Lord *et al.*, submitted). The full interview takes about 90 minutes and requires some training. It results in a diagnostic algorithm for ICD-10 or DSM-IV draft criteria and provides a structure for questioning and interpreting responses. Other ways of organizing information may also be effective, but it is important for the clinician to have a framework into which he or she can put the information gathered from the interview.

Information about adaptive behaviour, using well-standardized instruments, such as the Vineland Adaptive Behaviour Scales (Sparrow & Cicchetti, 1985), can also be helpful, not just in structuring information about everyday skills such as eating and dressing and independent travel, but also in providing data that compare to established norms in these areas. Scores for autistic children and adults follow distinctive patterns with very low scores in socialization, low scores in communication and closer to normal scores in daily living (Volkmar *et al.*, 1987).

Observation/interview of the child

The goal of a clinical observation is to witness behaviours across the areas described in the interview. Several protocols for semistructured observations of autistic children and adults are available. These include the Psychoeducational Profile (Schopler *et al.*, 1990), an educationally oriented instrument that is administered in about an hour and is appropriate for children with mental ages of between about 2 and 5 years. Various checklists are also available (Sevin *et al.*, 1991) that do not structure the clinician's behaviour, but do provide a framework for rating or characterizing behaviours associated with autism. These include the Autism Behavior Checklist (Krug *et al.*, 1980), the Childhood Autism Rating Scale (Schopler *et al.*, 1986) and the Behavioral Rating Instrument for Autistic and other Atypical Children (Ruttenberg *et al.*, 1974).

The Autism Diagnostic Observation Schedule (Lord *et al.*, 1989) attempts both to structure the clinician's behaviour by providing activities in which to observe children and adolescents and to structure the behaviours to be observed by specifying features to rate in the context of a 20-minute observation/interview. It is appropriate for children with expressive verbal skills at least at the 3-year-old level. Through providing a range of social 'presses', such as to ask for help, demonstrate how to do something, tell a story or play with miniatures, or carry on a conversation, the clinician, with training, moves up and down within a hierarchy of structure. This allows observation of the child's social behaviour across a variety of contexts from no demand whatsoever (in which case, many autistic children do nothing at all), to general demands to interact by offering toys or engaging in a simple conversation (difficult for most autistic children) to more specific demands to interact within structured activities (such as taking turns building something, a task that is easier socially for most autistic youngsters). Language demands are also deliberately manipulated. A similar instrument for lower-functioning and younger children has also been developed (DiLavore *et al.*, in preparation).

What is difficult about observing social behaviour, particularly in a setting that is unfamiliar to the child and when there are time constraints, is that most autistic children look their best under conditions of high structure. However, it is not possible to evaluate a child's spontaneous social behaviour if the clinician is, by his or her own actions, structuring the situation so well that all the child has to do is respond. On the other hand, when autistic children are left in a completely unstructured environment, they often do not do much at all, and little information is gained. Thus, the clinician must walk a fine line between providing clear social expectations and tasks and stepping back to observe the quality of the child's affect and social interactions.

With younger and more mentally handicapped children, direct observation may also provide information about behaviours such as unusual sensory interests, hand and finger mannerisms, simple rituals (such as tapping puzzle pieces before placing them) and repetitive actions. It may be useful to have available objects that frequently elicit such behaviours, such as a toy with a pull-string, cars with wheels and small objects such as blocks. With older and/or higher-functioning children and adolescents, it may be difficult to elicit these behaviours during a short observation in an unfamiliar setting, even though they do occur in other environments, so this information may need to be gleaned from the parent or teacher reports (Lord *et al.*, 1989).

Cognitive assessment

There are numerous standardized intelligence tests for which information concerning reliability and validity with autistic children and adolescents is available (Parks, 1988). In general, it is most useful to employ a test that separates verbal from performance skills (such as the Wechsler (1974) scales or the Differential Abilities Scales; Elliott, 1990) or to compare scores on nonverbal tests (such as Raven's Matrices; Raven, 1956) with those from language or verbal scales, although in this case care must be taken that standardization is comparable. In deciding on which nonverbal test to use, a crucial feature is the likelihood that it will gain the child's cooperation. On that criterion, the Merrill—Palmer Scale (Stutsman, 1931) has much to commend it in spite of its outdated standardization; the board form of Raven's (1956) Coloured Progressive Matrices, and the Leiter International Performance Scale (Arthur, 1952; Shah & Holmes, 1985) are useful. For tests of language see Chapter 32. For very young or low-functioning children, the Bayley Scales of Infant Development (Bayley, 1969), the Mullen Scales of Early Learning (Mullen, 1989), or the Cattell (1960) may be necessary. For lower-functioning adults and adolescents, the Adolescent and Adult Psychoeducational Profile provides useful information for educational and vocational planning (Mesibov *et al.*, 1989).

Communication and language assessment should be carried out by a clinician familiar with autism and should consist of evaluation of articulation; comprehension, including both single words and more complex language; and expressive language complexity and form. If the child speaks or signs, a brief language sample taken during the psychological or communication assessment can be very useful to evaluate pragmatics. If the child is nonverbal, it is often helpful to coordinate the communication assessment either with the psychological testing or the social observation or both.

For older higher-functioning children and adolescents, achievement testing may be appropriate. In this regard, it is important to use tests that differentiate reading comprehension from decoding, because autistic children may have much better rote decoding skills than understanding of what they read (Frith & Snowling, 1983; Venter *et al.*, 1992). Similarly, straightforward computational ability should be compared to solving practical arithmetic problems.

Medical examination and investigations

The purpose of the medical examination is to provide a general assessment of the child's neurodevelopmental status, identify questionable findings that require further study, and ensure that medical or dental problems, such as dental caries or drug toxicity, are not contributing to a child's difficulties. Systematic audiological testing for all children with speech delay and measurement of visual acuity, if vision is in doubt, are standard prerequisites to an adequate examination. A history of pregnancy, illnesses with a possible neurological component and any possibility of seizures should be taken, as well as a family history of developmental delay, learning or language problems, neurological disease and psychiatric disorder. A standard neurological assessment, including an examination of the skin for evidence of tuberous sclerosis, should be undertaken. When there is any doubt in any of these areas, referral to a specialist experienced with young handicapped children should be made (see Chapter 6 for a discussion of medical tests and investigations).

Differential diagnosis of autism and other pervasive developmental disorders

Because autism is a heterogeneous developmental disorder diagnosed on the basis of a pattern of deficits, diagnosis must be a step-by-step process of determining which behaviours can be accounted for by alternative explanations, such as profound mental handicap or deafness or severe neglect, and then whether the remaining features of the child's behaviour fit best with autism or another disorder (Rutter, 1985a). Multiaxial frameworks such as ICD-10 and DSM-IV are well-suited to this purpose, with their explicit recognition of the need to consider intellectual level, specific developmental delays, other psychiatric disorder and psychosocial factors in each decision.

In order to assess the meaning of the child's behaviour, the first step is to determine the child's current intellectual level and an estimated mental age, based on nonverbal skills (Table 33.1). A second step is evaluation of the child's receptive and expressive language abilities. A third step is consideration

Table 33.1 Diagnosis of autism

---

1 Determine child's cognitive level (nonverbal and verbal).
2 Determine child's language abilities.
3 Consider whether child's behaviour is appropriate for his or her:
   (a) Age
   (b) Mental age
   (c) Language age.
4 If not, consider special problems in
   (a) Social skills
   (b) Play
   (c) Communication
   (d) Other behaviours.
5 Identify any medical conditions.
6 Consider other relevant psychosocial factors.

---

of whether the child's behaviour is appropriate for his or her chronological, mental and language development. Behaviours that are in keeping with a very low developmental level, even if they involve severe social and communicative impairment, are not diagnostic of autism. A diagnosis of autism is not indicated because of repetitive behaviours and visual fascination if the child's highest level of functioning in any area except gross motor skills is, for example, 3 or 4 months. Similarly, a child with a severe expressive and receptive language disorder may fail to carry on conversations because of very limited language ability, not because of autism.

Most autistic children have some behaviours, or lack of behaviours, that are not appropriate at any developmental level beyond very early infancy. If behaviours or deficits in behaviours are identified that cannot be accounted for by general developmental or specific language delay, then the fourth step is to consider the differential diagnosis of psychiatric conditions responsible for the deviant patterns of development. The fifth and sixth steps then, respectively, address the possibility of contributory medical conditions and psychosocial factors.

Differential diagnosis consists of discriminating autism from other psychiatric and developmental conditions that lead to abnormalities in language, play and social development. Often it is helpful to begin chronologically and to consider if there was ever a period of normal development. If there was a period of clearly normal development extending beyond 2 years, the possibilities of elective mutism, disintegrative disorder and schizophrenia in children must be considered.

Particular care is needed in the diagnosis of autism in preschool children, especially if they are also severely retarded. It is quite difficult to determine if the pattern of social relationships, communication and behaviour is deviant if the level of development is very low. The few available follow-up data on toddlers who meet criteria for autism suggest that quite a few do not appear autistic when older (Knobloch & Pasamanick, 1975; Gillberg *et al.*, 1990; Lord, 1991).

Elective mutism

Electively mute children may, like autistic children, be socially withdrawn and unresponsive, but they generally do not show the specific abnormalities of language associated with autism, except for delay and articulation problems in some cases (Kolvin & Fundudis, 1981). They have spontaneous, creative play, carry on conversations and have appropriate attachments and normal verbal social interactions with family members, and show social reciprocity with some people (see Chapter 32).

Rett's syndrome

Rett's syndrome is a behaviourally defined syndrome (see also Chapter 11) that is quite different from autism in course and in being found exclusively (or almost exclusively) in girls. Although its manifestations differ from autism in most stages of development, it can produce autistic-like behaviours in toddlers and preschool children (Hagberg *et al.*, 1983; Rett Syndrome Diagnostic Criteria Working Group, 1988). Development appears normal in the first year, but then head growth begins to decelerate and over the next 2 years there is a loss of purposive hand skills and verbal communication (if it was already established). There is social impairment and stereotypical hand-wringing or hand-clapping midline movements (often these movements are accompanied by wetting of the hands with saliva); hyperventilation is also quite common. Gait and truncal ataxia usually appears between 1 and 4 years. As the child with Rett's syndrome grows older, motor and mental handicaps increase, although social interest may seem to increase within the limits of the profound mental handicap. Thus, although some toddlers and preschool children with Rett's syndrome may show some autistic features, there are many behavioural differences between autism and Rett's syndrome. The differential diagnosis is not usually difficult after the age of 4 or 5 years (Olsson & Rett, 1987, 1990).

Disintegrative disorder

Disintegrative disorder (or Heller's disease) occurs when normally developing children suddenly or over a period of several months show marked behaviour changes and developmental regression after age 2, often in association with some loss of coordination and bowel or bladder function (Corbett *et al.*, 1977; Volkmar & Cohen, 1989; Kurita *et al.*, 1992). Behavioural changes include social withdrawal, reduced response to sounds, complete loss of communication, unusual sensory behaviours and development of simple rituals and hand and finger stereotypies, much like those of autistic children. However, disintegrative disorder differs from autism in the loss of motor and self-help skills and usually, too, in the lack of more complex stereotyped behavioural patterns (although simple motor stereotypies may occur). This rare disorder can sometimes be linked to measles encephalitis, cerebral lipoidoses, leukodystrophies or other neurological conditions but in most cases no clear cause is ever identified. Even in cases where progressive neurological disorder is eventually identified, initial medical tests are often negative and sometimes diagnoses of hysterical reactions are considered. Thus, it is important to repeat medical investigations if a child's condition does not improve.

Two different courses are typical of children with regressions occurring after the first few years. Most common are regressions that extend over several months and then plateau, resulting in a developmental and behavioural pattern that looks much like autism with severe mental handicap (Hill & Rosenbloom, 1986). In some cases, deterioration continues, with increased motor dysfunction, development of seizures and localized neurological signs (Corbett *et al.*, 1977).

Another disorder that overlaps in symptomatology but that does not have quite so poor a prognosis is Landau–Kleffner syndrome of acquired aphasia with epilepsy (Miller *et al.*, 1984). Children with this disorder lose receptive and expressive language usually over a period of months, typically in conjunction with the development of seizures or transient EEG abnormalities (see Chapter 32). Some social withdrawal and unusual behaviours may occur, but usually relatively normal social relationships are maintained with parents and others known to the child. Nonverbal cognitive functioning remains intact. In most cases, the outlook for these children is better than for children with disintegrative psychoses or autism, and sometimes language is eventually regained.

Schizophrenia developing in childhood or adolescence

Generally, it is not difficult to distinguish schizophrenia from autism, except in rare cases of high-functioning autistic adolescents whose unusual thought processes may sometimes sound as if they are delusional (Dykens *et al.*, 1991). Children with schizophrenia do not show the language abnormalities or difficulties in language comprehension of autistic children (Asarnow *et al.*, 1987). Cantor and colleagues (1982) described a particular pattern of early onset of schizophrenia in children with hypotonia, good eye contact, presence of thought disorder, delusions and hallucinations (in some cases, though, these may be difficult to recognize) and often a family history of schizophrenia. The nosological validity of this group is not certain, but there is no doubt that there are serious, ill-understood nonautistic disorders that may manifest in childhood.

Receptive-expressive language disorders

As discussed earlier, when language delay is the presenting complaint, autism can usually be ruled out when there is reciprocal social behaviour and an absence of autism-specific language and nonverbal communication patterns. There is a rare group of children with severe receptive language disorders who may have some immediate echolalia, some social impairment and sometimes limited imaginative play (Morehead & Morehead, 1976). In most cases, these children do have reciprocal social interactions, relationships with friends and family members and a wider variety of interests than most autistic children. They seldom have the unusual preoccupations and rituals seen in autism. On the other hand, many of these children also have long-term social difficulties (Cantwell *et al.*, 1989; Rutter *et al.*, 1992) and semantic−pragmatic language deficits clearly overlap with the communication problems associated with autism (Bishop, 1989).

Severe psychosocial deprivation

If the child's development has been unusual from early on, effects of severe early deprivation must be considered. There is no evidence that minor 'lack of experience' such as not attending a preschool or having a rather unstimulating baby-sitter contributes to autism. However, children who have experienced severe neglect do show language delay, abnormal social behaviour and sometimes unusual habits and motor stereotypies (Hoffman-Plotkin & Twentyman, 1984; Skuse, 1984; see Chapters 13 and 28). These children generally do not have marked language comprehension difficulties, the broader communication abnormalities associated with autism, or failure to make social communicative use of the language they have. They show normal social reciprocity when relationships are established.

Wing's triad of abnormality in social skills, communication and play

Two different distinctions represent the most difficult differential diagnoses for autism. First is the question of how to classify the many severely to profoundly retarded children who, like autistic children, show specific, additional delays in language comprehension, social interaction and play, but display more social reciprocity and spontaneous socially directed communication than do most autistic children (Wing & Gould, 1979). For children who are profoundly retarded, it can be difficult to determine if their skills in particular areas are deviant or just very severely delayed. Many moderately retarded children with additional language delays benefit from the same educational and treatment strategies as children with autism, so there is some press to broaden the diagnostic category to include them (Wing & Gould, 1979). On the other hand, as we have discussed earlier, neurobiological research will be greatly hampered if subject populations are not well-defined. For the purposes of communication among professionals, it seems best for now to restrict the term autism to children and adults who meet the full criteria, and use other variants such as atypical autism to describe those who do not (Rutter & Schopler, 1992).

Asperger's syndrome

Second are the questions of whether autism can occur in persons of normal intelligence without language delay and whether it is worth creating a separate diagnostic category for high-functioning individuals with patterns of deficit similar to autism, with or without language delay (Tantam, 1988; Szatmari *et al.*, 1990; Frith, 1991). Undoubtedly there are children who show autistic-like difficulties in early social development and behaviour, but who do not have easily demonstrable language or cognitive delays in the preschool years. One proposal has been to use the term Asperger's syndrome (Tantam, 1988), to refer to individuals without cognitive delay who have severely impaired social understanding and reciprocity, pragmatic difficulties and unusual, circumscribed interests (World Health Organization, 1992). Currently, there is controversy over the exact nature of Asperger's syndrome, how it compares to autism without mental retardation and whether it can occur at all in mentally handicapped individuals (Szatmari *et al.*, 1989; Ozonoff *et al.*, 1991b). It is also not clear exactly how Asperger's syndrome fits with concepts of schizoid personality (Wolff, 1991; see Chapter 38). However, it is important to recognize that there are individuals with severe social impairments and behaviours (much like those seen in autism) who are not mentally handicapped or even language-delayed in a way that is easy to measure. These individuals tend to have milder symptoms of all sorts, to have less restricted interests and fewer bizarre behaviours than classically autistic subjects. They may be identified somewhat later, require fewer specialized educational services, and have somewhat better outcome than most autistic children (Szatmari *et al.*, 1990). Whether or not the differences between autism and Asperger's syndrome are qualitative or quantitative has yet to be determined. However, there have been few comparative studies; research has been plagued from the start by a lack of clear definition of the syndrome. It is difficult to draw firm conclusions from the evidence available to date, and systematic investigations of well-defined groups are greatly needed.

TREATMENT AND INTERVENTION

At about the same time as major changes occurred in the conceptualization of autism as a disorder that could be understood through careful study of cognitive functioning (Hermelin & O'Connor, 1970; Rutter, 1983), a different sort of reconceptualization of autism was also developing in North America. Earlier treatment models had been based on psychoanalytic interpretations of autism (Rank, 1949; Goldfarb *et al.*, 1966). Positive results of such treatment had been difficult to document and many clinicians began wondering, given increasing evidence of neurobiological abnormalities associated with autism, if unusual aspects of the parent–child relationship might be more likely to be due to factors intrinsic to the child than to the environment provided by the parents.

In the late 1960s behavioural treatment methods for autism were formally introduced by researchers interested, not so much in autism, but in applying their newly developed techniques to the challenge of teaching the basics of social behaviour and communication. Ironically, this experiment offered a wellspring of hope for the treatment of autism. The techniques were based on the belief that all behaviour is learned and so, if the correct technology could be developed, anyone using appropriate methods should be able to teach autistic children the skills they lack. While the outcome has not been as simple or positive as hoped, the systematic use of behavioural methods with autistic children has had a real impact on management of difficult behaviours, acquisition of self-help skills and educational treatment (Carr, 1985).

Initial expectations for behavioural treatment were limitless, with the hope that all autistic children could learn all missing skills. However, it became apparent that this was not the case, and that developmental factors, including level of mental handicap, also had very significant effects (Schopler, 1976). Behaviour programmes became increasingly individualized and, to a greater extent, limits of outcome began to be recognized, although each year sees new treatments, offered as yet-to-be-documented cures. It is now well-known that a variety of different treatments and educational practices result in far greater gains for autistic children who are not severely mentally handicapped than those who are severely mentally retarded (Bartak & Rutter, 1973; Lovaas, 1987). Even though absolute developmental hierarchies are not necessary (e.g. children do not always have to crawl before they walk), treatment goals must be linked to developmental level. For example, teaching a child with no language comprehension and a mental age of under a year to give his mother's keys to her when he wants to go outside is much more likely to be useful than speech treatment trying to evoke imitation of speech sounds as a step towards speech.

Other limits to behavioural techniques that were recognized early on were difficulties in maintenance and generalization of a change (Lovaas *et al.*, 1973). The fact that an autistic child has learned a new skill, particularly if the learning has occurred in an environment that is unusually intense and different from everyday situations, does not mean that the child will use that skill in another environment (Lord, 1984). Many programmes now include deliberate plans for 'sloppy teaching', recognizing that acquisition of a skill in a highly contrived situation may be more rapid, but that slower learning in a more natural environment may eventually allow a child greater independence in his or her own setting (Carr, 1985; Mesibov, 1986; see Chapter 60). 'Natural' language teaching programmes, incidental learning protocols, building successful experiences into learning and providing supervised access to normal environments and normal experiences with which we hope autistic children will be able to cope as adults (e.g. restaurants, interactions with noisy peers) are all strategies that have evolved as a result of these findings (Koegel *et al.*, 1988; Watson *et al.*, 1988).

Organization of treatment services

Because autistic children and adolescents require many different sorts of treatment and support and because these services generally change over time, the most important role of the primary clinician is often that of a coordinator of services who remains stable across the child's development. The complexity of treatment options and the individual differences among autistic children mean that forming a relationship with parents, often by seeing a child and family frequently for an initial series of visits, is necessary for the clinician to judge what is most appropriate for the individual child and his or her caregivers. Knowledge and experience with autism do not fall handily into professional divisions, so it is important to make use of the skills of well-trained clinicians across disciplines in the community. In one community, a skilled speech and language clinician from a children's hospital may run an excellent group for mothers of young autistic children, while in another community a similar group for adolescents and their siblings may be run by a psychologist or social worker employed by the Autism Society.

To date, although there have been claims to the contrary, there is no recognized cure for autism, so appropriate treatment must address both immediate and long-term needs of

Table 33.2 Overall treatment programme

Appropriate medical care
Treatment of medical conditions (when present)
Correction of hearing/vision defects
Dental care
Genetic counselling
Discussion with parents of diagnosis, prognosis and treatment

Special educational provision
Suitable class, unit or school
Extra services as required
Vocational support and training

Family support
Use of behavioural/developmental methods
Counselling
Practical help
Respite
Support
Books

Direct treatment
Medication
Social skills groups
Speech and language treatment
Psychotherapy
Other therapies
Independent treatment

the autistic child and his or her family (Rutter, 1985b). As shown in Table 33.2, this is typically a multidisciplinary process including psychiatry and paediatrics, special education, psychology and communication disorders specialists, as well as social work and other therapists. Different models for services are available, from those emphasizing 'generalists', who are individuals from any discipline who are intensively trained to provide a range of treatment and consultation services (Schopler & Olley, 1982), to multidisciplinary clinics in which each professional takes responsibility for the child's needs in a particular area. Regardless of the model, effectiveness seems likely to depend on the skill, experience and knowledge of the individuals *about autism* and their ability to work together with each other and the family.

Goals of treatment

In determining goals, four basic aims (Rutter, 1985b) should be borne in mind:
1 Fostering social and communicative development.
2 Enhancing learning and problem-solving.
3 Decreasing behaviours that interfere with learning and access to opportunities for normal experiences.
4 Helping families cope with autism.
Because these goals are large, it is important to break them down into specific immediate and long-term needs and solutions. For example, the overall aim of promoting an autistic

child's language development may be broken into specific goals of helping her to participate in structured conversations, increasing the frequency of her spontaneous communication and extending her oral vocabulary. The aim of decreasing an adolescent boy's aggression toward his mother may be operationalized by helping the teenager entertain himself with a scrapbook, setting up a behaviour programme for the mother and son with well-defined warnings, consequences and alternative behaviours to hitting, recommending a community respite programme and prescribing medication. Each of these goals may require its own plan and strategy. Often, solutions involve not just deliberately trying to change the child's behaviour, but modifying the physical environment and others' behaviours, and revising the expectations placed on the child.

Methods of treatment

Education

Education has been by far the most powerful source of improvement for autistic children and adolescents in the last 50 years. With access to appropriate educational services, far fewer children are placed in long-stay institutions (Schopler & Olley, 1982). Earlier studies suggested that, for higher-functioning children, there was a direct relationship between time spent in a classroom working on an academic subject, such as reading, and improvements in that subject (Bartak & Rutter, 1973). A recent study found that high-functioning autistic adolescents, compared to a similar sample from 20 years ago, had better reading, maths and spelling and that their academic attainment was significantly correlated with verbal intelligence (when this was not the case in the earlier sample). These findings were interpreted as suggesting that, with appropriate education, more autistic children are using the intellectual skills that they possess to acquire functional academics (Venter *et al.*, 1992). On the other hand, few children, even in this relatively high-functioning sample, attained academic skills at mental-age level, particularly in reading comprehension. On the whole, effects specific to different educational methods have not been found for autistic children with severe or profound mental handicap.

One question concerns integration or mainstreaming and the extent to which autistic youngsters should be placed in self-contained classrooms specifically for autistic children, self-contained classrooms for more broadly defined groups (e.g. learning disabilities, mental handicap) or be supported in regular programmes with various resources (see Chapter 63). There are few interpretable data comparing the outcome of children who have received various levels of integration. Few autistic children are able to survive behaviourally if placed completely in the mainstream with no extra support, and of those who do, it is not clear that they are benefiting academically from this exposure. On the other hand, there are cognitive benefits to being exposed to the broader curricula typically available in standard educational programmes and social benefits to being surrounded by nonhandicapped agemates, or in the case of autistic children who are mildly to moderately mentally handicapped, by nonautistic children of equivalent intellectual level. Much seems to depend on whether the programme is well-structured, positive in attitude and prepared to cope with the individual needs of the children (Strain, 1983; Harris *et al.*, 1990). In general, the policy of seeking the least restrictive environment as defined individually for each child is reasonable, but finding this environment is often easier said than done.

Family support

Family support can come in many forms, from local or national societies, such as the National Society for Autistic Children in the UK, the Association for Retarded Citizens and the Autism Society of America, curriculum-oriented parent training programmes (Koegel *et al.*, 1982; Harris, 1984), parent-as-co-therapist models (Schopler & Olley, 1982) and support groups for parents or siblings of handicapped individuals (see Chapter 53). It is important to recognize that families vary in the kinds of support and information that they need and want and that, even within a family, roles and concerns of the two parents may be quite different (Bristol, 1987). Helping parents know what they should do (e.g. control a child's tantrums) is often not nearly as helpful as showing them ways they might do it. In order to do this, familiarity with the child and the family is essential. Helping parents accept the disappointment and fear that they feel, know that ambivalent feelings are acceptable, and that they are not alone in these feelings, is part of treatment. Practical help with finding respite services and dealing with social services may often be as important as emotional support or teaching management techniques. For this reason, familiarity with community resources and the willingness to work with the agencies involved in direct service are essential for any professional or clinic serving individuals with autism.

There are several intensive specialized treatment methods for which strong claims have been made for their efficacy. These include the Higashi Daily Life Therapy (Quill *et al.*, 1989); the Option Method (Kaufman, 1976); and Holding Therapy (Richer & Zappella, 1989; Wimpory & Cochrane, 1991). These treatments differ substantially in their rationale; systematic evaluations have yet to be undertaken and their value remains quite uncertain.

Specific therapies

There are many individual therapies available to families, especially with young autistic children, including speech and language treatment, occupational therapy, physical therapy, psychotherapy for older, verbal adolescents and adults and various new specific treatment regimes, such as facilitated communication and auditory training, that have tended to come and go over the years. Most autistic children can benefit from focused programming in communication. It is possible to

work on communication with children who are functioning even at an infant level, if appropriate strategies and goals are employed. Individual communication treatment can be beneficial, but may be less important in the long run than helping parents and teachers understand how to modify their communications and their expectations. For example, parents may be helped to respond positively to any communicative attempts by children who have very little speech (Howlin & Rutter, 1987).

Other therapies may be appropriate depending on the child's specific deficits in areas such as gross and fine motor skills. Brief psychotherapy, in which specific problems and solutions are identified, may be helpful with adolescents and young adults who are sufficiently verbal to be able to discuss their social difficulties and/or who may have co-occurring depression or anxiety. Social skills training and social groups may also be beneficial, particularly for higher-functioning adolescents and adults, in offering an opportunity to practise social behaviours that are taken for granted in other populations, and in providing a positive social experience to young people who may be extremely isolated from peers (Mesibov, 1984; Williams, 1989).

Behaviour management

Formal principles of classical and operant conditioning have now become second nature to teachers and clinicians working with autistic children, including simple strategies such as providing clear warnings that a context is going to change (i.e. making a picture schedule that can be pointed to in order to warn a boy that he will be returning to his desk after free time), taking care not to reward unknowingly behaviours that are undesirable, and teaching alternative, reinforceable behaviours to a child in order to eliminate an undesirable behaviour (e.g. teaching a child to shake hands upon greeting rather than to smell people's wrists). Along with positive principles of learning, a better understanding of structure and ways to organize the environment to make it more meaningful and predictable to autistic individuals often reduces the need for intense behaviour programmes aimed at negative behaviours (Schopler, 1976). Providing regular *vigorous* exercise and setting up a schedule, such as allowing an autistic adolescent to engage in 'silly talk' for 15 minutes at the end of the day if he or she has earned credits for not hitting, may reduce the need to develop programmes to deal with aggression (Kern *et al.*, 1984). Sophisticated behavioural techniques are also available for severe self-injury and aggression when needed (Carr, 1977; Gaylord-Ross, 1980). Lovaas (1987; McEachin *et al.*, 1993) reported that unusually intensive behavioural treatment beginning at a very young age led to major gains for most children. This finding has provided an impetus for further investigations of intensive early interventions, but its results have yet to be replicated and uncertainties exist about selection of groups, the diagnosis of these very young autistic children and the completeness of the recovery (Schopler *et al.*, 1989).

Vocational training and support

Real gains have been made in the last 10 years in placing and keeping autistic adults in paid employment and in community work settings, although unfortunately these opportunities vary greatly across communities (Van Bourgondien & Schopler, 1990). School programmes that emphasize general vocational behaviours, such as task completion, dealing with delayed contingencies and self-management as well as specific skills (such as cooking or gardening), have been one factor in this improved outlook (Mesibov, 1986; Dunlap *et al.*, 1987). Another factor is on-the-job coaching and continued regular support as well as work placement and training (Van Bourgondien & Schopler, 1990). Original hopes that many autistic individuals would be able to function completely independently in jobs after initial periods of support have not been met, but ways of providing appropriate cost-effective back-up for placements are being developed. Unfortunately, probably the most important factor determining where an autistic adult spends his or her days is the persistence and determination of parents or community advocates to find a niche for him or her. Many more community services for adults are needed, particularly those funded with the recognition that autism is a lifelong disorder and so individualized long-term support is required.

Pharmacological treatment

By adolescence, a large proportion of autistic individuals, at least in the US, are prescribed medication to help control their behaviour (Rumsey *et al.*, 1985). Drugs may sometimes be helpful in bringing about modest improvements in behaviour but, despite optimistic claims by enthusiasts, there is so far no evidence that any drug produces major benefits or affects the basic deficits of autism (Campbell *et al.*, 1987; Sloman, 1991).

Earlier research mainly focused on use of the major neuroleptics (see Chapter 51). It was found that haloperidol reduced stereotypies, aggression and tempers, and probably it is the most effective drug for treating very severe behavioural disturbance that cannot be managed by other means. However, it causes a very high risk of dyskinesia and dystonias (probably in the region of 1 in 4 cases, even with a conservative dose). These are particularly likely to occur following drug withdrawal and most are reversible; nevertheless, irreversible dystonias can arise. The frequency of extremely unpleasant side-effects rules out haloperidol for anything other than use after other treatments have been tried and failed. Chlorpromazine has generally not been particularly effective and its marked sedative action constitutes a major disadvantage. Studies of the less sedative drug, thioridazine, in developmentally disabled children (Aman & Singh, 1991) suggest that it may constitute a better alternative for the treatment of agitation (perhaps especially in adolescents and adults), although there is a paucity of evidence regarding its benefits in autistic individuals.

Stimulants may occasionally be helpful, perhaps especially with autistic children who are not severely retarded, but tend not to be particularly effective in mentally handicapped children. There has been some concern that they can produce severe dysphoria and also aggravate stereotypies and tics in some children (Aman, 1982), so their general use is not recommended (Sloman, 1991). Tricyclic antidepressants, lithium, and serotonin-uptake inhibitors (such as clomipramine and fluoxetine) have all been said to help some autistic children but systematic data on their general efficacy are lacking. The limited available evidence suggests that further studies of the last group of drugs (which have been used to treat both depression and obsessional disorders in nonautistic individuals) may be worthwhile (perhaps especially if depressive symptoms and ritualistic behaviours are prominent), but they have side-effects (Riddle *et al.*, 1991) and their benefits in the treatment of autism remain uncertain. Beta-blockers have been used in autistic individuals to control aggression and self-injurious behaviour, but little is known about their efficacy and their use remains at the experimental stage (Arnold & Aman, 1991).

In recent years, there have been several claims regarding drugs that supposedly are specifically useful in autism. The use of very high doses of vitamin B_6 in conjunction with magnesium is longest established and has strong advocates (Rimland, 1987); nevertheless the supporting evidence remains meagre and the routine use of megavitamins is not justified (Sloman, 1991). Because it was known that a third of autistic children show hyperserotonaemia, there was initial excitement over the claim (rather prematurely made on the basis of an uncontrolled study of just 3 children) that fenfluramine produced intellectual and behavioural gains in autistic children (Geller *et al.*, 1982). However, subsequent controlled studies have shown only inconsistent evidence of minor improvements; fenfluramine does indeed lower serotonin levels but such minor benefits as occur following its use are not related to this effect (Campbell, 1988; Aman & Kern, 1989).

In 1979, Panksepp suggested that autistic symptoms might stem from abnormalities in the endogenous opiate system. It seemed to follow that opiate antagonists might be useful in treatment, perhaps especially for self-injurious behaviour (Panksepp & Sahley, 1987). A small number of trials point to modest positive effects but, again, usage is at the experimental stage (Campbell *et al.*, 1990; Leboyer *et al.*, 1992). Because the fragile X anomaly is detected cytogenetically through the growth of chromosomes in low-folate culture media, it has been suggested that folic acid may be useful in the treatment of children with this anomaly; however, the benefits are rather unconvincing (Aman & Kern, 1991).

Finally, anticonvulsants are, of course, indicated for the control of seizures in autistic individuals, just as they are in any other group. Sometimes the use of anticonvulsants may be associated with behavioural benefits.

In summary, there is no evidence to date that pharmacological treatments in autism provide the dramatic benefit that may be seen in some other psychiatric conditions, such as schizophrenia. Accordingly, there is no indication for their routine use, particularly as most active drugs involve a significant risk of side-effects (Gadow, 1992). Nevertheless, the judicious use of medication in some individuals has a place as part of a broad-based therapeutic strategy that includes psychoeducational treatment, family support and behavioural management. Careful monitoring is essential, particularly given the limited evidence on the cost—benefits of pharmacotherapy in autism.

PROGNOSIS AND OUTCOME IN AUTISM

Autism is most easily recognized in the later preschool years, around 4 to 6 years of age. As autistic children enter school, many show substantial improvements in social behaviour and communication at a simple level (Harris *et al.*, 1990). As discussed earlier, adolescence can be difficult because of increased aggression and irritability. These problems usually subside, but not always. The strongest predictors of long-term outcome with respect to overall social functioning, as well as academic attainment, are the child's cognitive level and degree of language impairment, together with level of adaptive functioning (the last being particularly important in very young nonverbal children; Rutter, 1970; Lotter, 1978; Howlin & Rutter 1987; Lord & Schopler, 1989; Rutter *et al.*, 1992; Venter *et al.*, 1992). The great majority of children with a performance IQ below 50 or 60 will remain severely handicapped and dependent on others for help in meeting their day-to-day needs throughout life. Those with a performance IQ in the mildly retarded range, but who at age 5 years still have very limited language, may make a fair social adjustment but a good outcome is unlikely. By contrast, if the child has a normal nonverbal intelligence and useful communicative language by age 5 with no more than mild receptive language impairment, there is about a 50—50 chance of a good level of social adjustment in adult life. Scarcely any adults with autism achieve complete normality. That is, they may well show considerable autonomy (taking independent holidays, for example), but most will require a degree of shelter in their work and support in their living arrangements.

Within subgroups of autistic individuals who have a normal nonverbal intelligence, verbal skills show quite a strong association with outcome. In addition to IQ and language, the overall level of behavioural disturbance (particularly with respect to aggression and pervasively intrusive repetitive behaviours) is of some prognostic importance (Venter *et al.*, 1992). Good services (with respect to education, family support and behavioural interventions) make a real, albeit modest, difference in social outcome but they do not remove the basic handicaps (Howlin & Rutter, 1987).

CONCLUSIONS

Autism represents a disorder worthy of study in its own right and also as a model of enquiry in the fields of child psychiatry, psychology and special education. As with the mixture of disease and symptoms represented by the variety of fevers, our understanding of autism is dependent on the careful description of the features specific to it and recognition of

deficits that are associated with but not central to the disorder. The past decade has yielded significant knowledge about the prevalence and course of autism, improvements in methods of assessment and education, documentation of cognitive and social deficits, and awareness of ongoing issues of classification and genetic patterns. There has been little change, however, in our understanding of the underlying neuropathophysiology or in the ability to prevent or treat basic aspects of the disorder. The challenge for the next decade will be to forge these links between behaviour, neurobiology, treatment and prevention.

REFERENCES

Aman M.G. (1982) Stimulant drug effects in developmental disorders and hyperactivity: toward a resolution of disparate findings. *Journal of Autism and Developmental Disorders*, **12**, 385—398.

Aman M. & Kern R. (1989) Review of fenfluramine in the treatment of the developmental disabilities. *Journal of the American Academy of Child and Adolescent Psychiatry*, **28**, 249—565.

Aman M.G. & Kern R.A. (1991) Mental retardation: the efficacy of folic acid in fragile X syndrome and other developmental disabilities. *Journal of Child and Adolescent Psychopharmacology*, **1**, 285—299.

Aman M.G. & Singh N.N. (1991) Pharmacological intervention. In: Matson J.L. & Mulick J.A. (eds) *Handbook of Mental Retardation*, pp. 347—372. Pergamon Press, New York.

American Psychiatric Association (1987) *Diagnostic and Statistical Manual of Mental Disorders (DSM III-R)*, 3rd edn, revised. American Psychiatric Association, Washington, DC.

American Psychiatric Association (1994) *Diagnostic and Statistical Manual of Mental Disorders*, 4th edn — DSM-IV. American Psychiatric Association, Washington, DC.

Arnold L.E. & Aman M.G. (1991) Beta blockers in mental retardation and developmental disorders. *Journal of Child and Adolescent Psychopharmacology*, **1**, 361—373.

Arthur G. (1952) *The Arthur Adaptation of the Leiter International Performance Scale*. The Psychological Service Center Press, Chicago, IL.

Asarnow R.F., Tanguay P.E., Bott L. & Freeman B.J. (1987) Patterns of intellectual functioning in non-retarded autistic and schizophrenic children. *Journal of Child Psychology and Psychiatry*, **28**, 273—280.

Attwood A., Frith J. & Hermelin B. (1988) The understanding and use of interpersonal gestures by autistic and Down syndrome children. *Journal of Autism and Developmenal Disorders*, **18**, 241—258.

August G.J., Stewart M.A. & Tsai L. (1981) The incidence of cognitive disabilities in the siblings of autistic children. *British Journal of Psychiatry*, **138**, 416—422.

Bailey A.J. (1993) The biology of autism. *Psychological Medicine*, **23**, 7—11.

Bailey A.J., Bolton P., Butler L., Le Couteur A., Murphy M., Scott S., Webb T. & Rutter M. (1993) Prevalence of the fragile X anomaly amongst autistic twins and singletons. *Journal of Child Psychology and Psychiatry*, **34**, 673—688.

Bailey A.J., Le Couteur A., Gottesman I.I., Bolton P., Simonoff E. & Rutter M. (submitted) Autism as a strongly genetic disorder: evidence from a British twin study.

Baird T.D. & August G.J. (1985) Familial heterogeneity in infantile autism. *Journal of Autism and Developmental Disorders*, **15**, 315—321.

Baron-Cohen S. (1989a) The autistic child's theory of mind: a case of specific developmental delay. *Journal of Child Psychology and Psychiatry*, **30**, 285—298.

Baron-Cohen S. (1989b) Perceptual role-taking and proto-declarative pointing in autism. *British Journal of Developmental Psychology*, **7**, 113–127.

Baron-Cohen S., Tager-Flusberg H. & Cohen D. (1993) *Understanding Other Minds: Perspectives from Autism*. Oxford University Press, Oxford.

Bartak L. & Rutter M. (1973) Special educational treatment of autistic children: a comparative study: I. Design of study and characteristics of units. *Journal of Child Psychology and Psychiatry*, **14**, 161–179.

Bartak L. & Rutter M. (1976) Differences between mentally retarded and normally intelligent autistic children. *Journal of Autism and Childhood Schizophrenia*, **6**, 109–120.

Bauman M. (1991) Microscopic neuroanatomic abnormalities in autism. *Pediatrics*, **31**, 791–796.

Bayley N. (1969) *Manual for the Bayley Scales of Infant Development*. Psychological Corporation, New York.

Bender L. (1941) Childhood schizophrenia. *The Nervous Child*, **1**, 138–140.

Bishop D.V.M. (1989) Autism, Asperger's syndrome and semantic-pragmatic disorder: where are the boundaries? *British Journal of Disorders of Communication*, **24**, 107–121.

Bolton P., & Rutter M. (1990) Genetic influences in autism. *International Review of Psychiatry*, **2**, 65–78.

Bolton P., Pickles A., Butler L., Summers S., Webb T., Lord C., LeCouteur A., Bailey A. & Rutter M. (1992) Fragile X in families multiplex for autism and related phenotypes: prevalence and criteria for cytogenetic diagnosis. *Psychiatric Genetics*, **2**, 277–300.

Bolton P., Macdonald H., Pickles A., Rios P., Goode S., Crowson M., Bailey A. & Rutter M. (1994) A case-control family history study of autism. *Journal of Child Psychology and Psychiatry*, **35**, 877–900.

Bosch G. (1970) *Infantile Autism* (translated by Jordan D. & Jordan I.). Springer-Verlag, New York.

Bristol M. (1987) Mothers of children with autism or communication disorders: successful adaptation and the ABCX model. *Journal of Autism and Developmental Disorders*, **17**, 469–486.

Bryson S.E., Clark B.S. & Smith T.M. (1988) First report of a Canadian epidemiological study of autistic syndromes. *Journal of Child Psychology and Psychiatry*, **29**, 433–445.

Burd L., Fisher W.W., Kerbeshian J. & Arnold M.E. (1987) Is development of Tourette disorder a marker for improvement in patients with autism and other pervasive developmental disorders? *Journal of the American Academy of Child Psychiatry*, **26**, 162–165.

Campbell M. (1988) Fenfluramine treatment of autism. *Journal of Child Psychology and Psychiatry*, **29**, 1–10.

Campbell M., Perry R., Small A. & Green W. (1987) Overview of drug treatment in autism. In: Schopler E. & Mesibov G.B. (eds) *Neurobiological Issues in Autism*, pp. 341–352. Plenum Press, New York.

Campbell M., Anderson L.T., Small A.M., Locascio J.J., Lynch N.S. & Choroco M.C. (1990) Naltrexone in autistic children: a double-blind and placebo-controlled study. *Psychopharmacology Bulletin*, **26**, 130–135.

Cantor S., Evans J., Pearce J. & Pezzot-Pearch T. (1982) Childhood schizophrenia: present but not accounted for. *American Journal of Psychiatry*, **139**, 758–762.

Cantwell D.P., Russell A.T., Mattison R. & Will L. (1979) A comparison of DSM-II and DSM-III in the diagnosis of childhood psychiatric disorders. I. Agreement with expected diagnosis. *Archives of General Psychiatry*, **36**, 1208–1213.

Cantwell D.P., Baker L., Rutter M. & Mawhood L. (1989) Infantile autism and developmental receptive dysphasia: a comparative follow-up into middle childhood. *Journal of Autism and Developmental Disorders*, **19**, 19–32.

Carr E.G. (1977) The motivation of self-injurious behavior: a review of some hypotheses. *Psychological Bulletin*, **84**, 800–816.

Carr E.G. (1985) Behavioral approaches to language and communication. In: Schopler E. & Mesibov G.B. (eds) *Communication Problems in Autism*, pp. 38–54. Plenum Press, New York.

Cattell P. (1960) *The Measurement of Intelligence of Infants and Young Children*. Psychological Corporation, New York.

Chess S. (1971) Autism in children with congenital rubella. *Journal of Autism and Childhood Schizophrenia*, **1**, 33–47.

Chess S. (1977) Follow-up report on autism in congenital rubella. *Journal of Autism and Childhood Schizophrenia*, **7**, 69–81.

Ciaranello R., Vandenberg S. & Anders T. (1982) Intrinsic and extrinsic determinants of neural development: relation to infantile autism. *Journal of Autism and Developmental Disorders*, **12**, 115–145.

Cohen I.L., Vietze P.M., Sudhalter V., Jenkins E.C. & Brown W.T. (1989) Parent–child dyadic gaze patterns in fragile X males and non-fragile X males with autistic disorder. *Journal of Child Psychology and Psychiatry*, **30**, 845–856.

Comings D.E. & Comings B.G. (1991) Clinical and genetic relationships between autism-pervasive developmental disorder and Tourette syndrome: a study of 19 cases. *American Journal of Medical Genetics*, **39**, 180–191.

Cook E.H. (1990) Autism: review of neurochemical investigation. *Synapse*, **6**, 292–308.

Corbett J., Harris R., Taylor E. & Trimble M. (1977) Progressive disintegrative psychosis of childhood. *Journal of Child Psychology and Psychiatry*, **18**, 211–219.

Courchesne E. (1989) Neuroanatomical systems involved in infantile autism: the implications of cerebellar abnormalities. In: Dawson G. (ed) *Autism: Nature, Diagnosis, and Treatment*, pp. 119–143. Guilford Press, New York.

Courchesne E. (1991) Neuroanatomic imaging in autism. *Pediatrics*, **31**, 781–799.

Courchesne E. & Lincoln A. (1985) Event-related brain potential correlates of the processing of novel visual and auditory information in autism. *Journal of Autism and Developmental Disorders*, **15**, 55–76.

Courchesne E., Akshoomoff N., Townsend J., Yeung-Courchesne R., Lincoln A., James H., Haas R., Schriebman L. & Lau L. (1993) Impairment in shifting attention in autistic and cerebellar patients. In: Broman S.H. & Grafman J.K. (eds) *Atypical Cognitive Deficits in Developmental Disorders: Implications for Brain Function*. Lawrence Erlbaum, Hillsdale, NJ.

Dahlgren S.O. & Gillberg C. (1989) Symptoms in the first two years of life: a preliminary population study of infantile autism. *European Archives of Psychiatric and Neurological Science*, **283**, 169–174.

Damasio A.R. & Maurer R.G. (1978) A neurological model for childhood autism. *Archives of Neurology*, **35**, 777–786.

Dawson G. & Adams A. (1984) Imitation and social responsiveness in autistic children. *Journal of Abnormal Child Psychology*, **12**, 209–226.

Dawson G. & Lewy A. (1989) Arousal, attention, and the socio-emotional impairments of individuals with autism. In: Dawson G. (ed) *Autism: Nature, Diagnosis, and Treatment*, pp. 49–74. Guilford Press, New York.

DeLong G. & Dwyer J. (1988) Correlation of family history with specific autistic subgroups: Asperger's syndrome and bipolar affective disease. *Journal of Autism and Developmental Disorders*, **18**, 593–600.

DeMyer M.K., Alpern G.D., DeMyer W.E., Churchill D.W., Hingtgen J.N., Bryson C.Q., Pontius W. & Kimberlin C. (1972) Imitation in autistic, early schizophrenic, and nonpsychotic abnormal children. *Journal of Autism and Childhood Schizophrenia*, **2**, 264–287.

Deykin E.Y. & MacMahon B. (1979) The incidence of seizures among children with autistic symptoms. *American Journal of Psychiatry*, **136**, 1310–1312.

DiLavore P., Lord C., Rutter M. (in press) Pre-linguistic autism diagnostic observation schedule. *Journal of Autism and Developmental Disorders*.

Dunlap G., Koegel R., Johnson J. & O'Neill R. (1987) Maintaining performance of autistic clients in community settings with delayed contingencies. *Journal of Applied Behavior Analysis*, **20**, 185−191.

Dykens E., Volkmar F. & Glick M. (1991) Thought disorder in high-functioning autistic adults. *Journal of Autism and Developmental Disorders*, **21**, 291−302.

Elliot G. & Ciaranello R. (1987) Neurochemical hypotheses of childhood psychoses. In: Schopler E. & Mesibov G.B. (eds) *Neurobiological Issues in Autism*, pp. 245−262. Plenum Press, New York.

Elliott C.D. (1990) *Differential Abilities Scales*. Psychological Corporation, Orlando, FL.

Fay W. & Schuler A.L. (1980) *Emerging Language in Autistic Children*. University Park Press, Baltimore, MD.

Fein D., Humes M., Kaplan E., Lucci D. & Waterhouse L. (1984) The question of left hemisphere dysfunction in infantile autism. *Psychological Bulletin*, **95**, 258−281.

Fein D., Pennington B. & Waterhouse L. (1987) Implications of social deficits in autism for neurological dysfunction. In: Schopler E. & Mesibov G.B. (eds) *Neurobiological Issues in Autism*, pp. 127−144. Plenum Press, New York.

Folstein S. & Rutter M. (1977a) Genetic influences and infantile autism. *Nature*, **265**, 726−728.

Folstein S. & Rutter M. (1977b) Infantile autism: a genetic study of 21 twin pairs. *Journal of Child Psychology and Psychiatry*, **18**, 297−321.

Folstein S. & Rutter M. (1988) Autism: familial aggregation and genetic implications. *Journal of Autism and Developmental Disorders*, **18**, 3−30.

Frith U. (1989) *Autism: Explaining the Enigma*. Blackwell, New York.

Frith U. (1991) *Autism and Asperger Syndrome*. Cambridge University Press, Cambridge.

Frith U. & Snowling M. (1983) Reading for meaning and reading for sound in autistic and dyslexic children. *British Journal of Developmental Psychology*, **1**, 329−342.

Gadow K.D. (1992) Pediatric psychopharmacotherapy: a review of recent research. *Journal of Child Psychology and Psychiatry*, **33**, 153−197.

Gaylord-Ross R. (1980) A decision model for the treatment of aberrant behavior in applied settings. In: Sailor W., Wilcox B. & Brown L. (eds) *Methods of Instruction for Severely Handicapped Students*, pp. 135−158. Paul H. Brooks, Baltimore, MD.

Geller E., Ritvo E., Freeman B. & Yuwiler A. (1982) Preliminary observations on the effect of fenfluramine on blood serotonin and symptoms in three autistic boys. *New England Journal of Medicine*, **307**, 165−169.

Gillberg C. (1990) Autism and pervasive developmental disorders. *Journal of Child Psychology and Psychiatry*, **31**, 99−119.

Gillberg C.L. (1992) The Emanuel Miller memorial lecture 1991: Autism and autistic-like conditions: subclasses among disorders of empathy. *Journal of Child Psychology and Psychiatry*, **33**, 813−842.

Gillberg C. & Steffenburg S. (1987) Outcome and prognostic factors in autism and similar conditions: a population-based study of 46 cases followed through puberty. *Journal of Autism and Developmental Disorders*, **17**, 273−287.

Gillberg C. & Wahlström J. (1985) Chromosome abnormalities in infantile autism and other childhood psychoses: a population study of 66 cases. *Developmental Medicine and Child Neurology*, **27**, 293−304.

Gillberg C., Ehlers S., Schaumann H., Jakobsson G., Dahlgren S., Lindblom R., Gabenholm A., Tjuus R. & Blidner E. (1990) Autism under age 3 years: a clinical study of 28 cases referred for autistic symptoms in infancy. *Journal of Child Psychology and Psychiatry*, **31**, 921−934.

Goldfarb W., Goldfarb N. & Pollack R. (1966) A three year comparison of day and residential treatment of schizophrenic children. *Archives of General Psychiatry*, **14**, 110−128.

Goldman-Rakic P.S., Isseroff A., Schwartz M.L. & Bugbee N.M. (1983) The neurobiology of cognitive development. In: Haith M.M. & Campos J.J. (eds) *Infancy and Developmental Psychobiology, Vol. 2., Mussen's Handbook of Child Psychology*, (4th edn) pp. 281−344. Wiley, New York.

Goodman R. (1990) Technical note: are perinatal complications causes or consequences of autism? *Journal of Child Psychology and Psychiatry*, **31**, 809−812.

Grandin T. & Scariano M. (1986) *Emergence: Labeled Autistic*. Arena Press, Navanto, CA.

Hagberg B., Aicardi J., Dias K. & Ramos O. (1983) A progressive syndrome of autism, dementia, ataxia and loss of purposeful hand use in girls: Rett's syndrome: report of 35 cases. *Annals of Neurology*, **14**, 471−479.

Harris P.L. (1989) The autistic child's impaired conception of mental states. *Development and Psychopathology*, **1**, 191−196.

Harris S. (1984) Intervention planning for the family of the autistic child: a multilevel assessment of the family system. *Journal of Marital and Family Therapy*, **10**, 157−166.

Harris S.L., Handleman J.S., Kristoff B., Bass L. & Gordon R. (1990) Changes in language development among autistic and peer children in segregated and integrated preschool settings. *Journal of Autism and Developmental Disorders*, **20**, 23−31.

Hermelin B. & O'Connor N. (1970) *Psychological Experiments with Autistic Children*. Pergamon Press, New York.

Hertzig M., Snow M. & Sherman M. (1989) Affect and cognition in autism. *Journal of the American Academy of Child and Adolescent Psychiatry*, **28**, 194−199.

Hill A. & Rosenbloom L. (1986) Disintegrative psychosis of childhood: teenage follow-up. *Developmental Medicine and Child Neurology*, **28**, 34−40.

Hobson R.P. (1984) The autistic child's recognition of age-related features of people, animals and things. *British Journal of Developmental Psychology*, **1**, 343−352.

Hobson R.P. (1987) The autistic child's recognition of age- and sex-related characteristics of people: an experimental investigation. *Journal of Autism and Developmental Disorders*, **17**, 63−80.

Hobson R.P. (1991) Methodological issues for experiments on autistic individuals' perception and understanding of emotion. *Journal of Child Psychology and Psychiatry*, **32**, 1135−1158.

Hoffman-Plotkin D. & Twentyman C.T. (1984) A multimodal assessment of behavioral and cognitive deficits in abused and neglected preschoolers. *Child Development*, **55**, 794−802.

Howlin P. & Rutter M. (1987) *Treatment of Autistic Children*. John Wiley, Chichester.

Hunt A. & Shepherd C. (1993) A prevalence study of autism in tuberous sclerosis. *Journal of Autism and Developmental Disorders*, **23**, 329−339.

Jarrold C., Boucher J. & Smith P. (1993) Symbolic play in autism —a review. *Journal of Autism and Developmental Disorders*, **23**, 281−307.

Jorde L.B., Hasstedt S.J., Ritvo E.R., Mason-Brothers A., Freeman B.J., Pingree C., McMahon W.M., Peterson B., Jenson W.R. & Moll A. (1991) Complex segregation analysis of autism. *American Journal of Human Genetics*, **49**, 932−938.

Kanner L. (1943) Autistic disturbances of affective contact. *Nervous Child*, **2**, 217−250.

Kasari C., Sigman M., Mundy P. & Yirmiya N. (1990) Affective sharing in the context of joint attention interactions of normal, autistic, and mentally retarded children. *Journal of Autism and Developmental Disorders*, **20**, 87−100.

Kaufman B.N. (1976) *Son Rise*. Warren Books, New York.

Kern L., Koegel R. & Dunlap G. (1984) The influence of vigorous versus mild exercise on autistic stereotyped behaviors. *Journal of Autism and Developmental Disorders*, **12**, 399−419.

Kleiman M.D., Neff S. & Rosman N.P. (1992) The brain in infantile autism: are posterior fossa structures abnormal? *Neurology*, **42**, 753–760.

Klin A., Volkmar F.R. & Sparrow S.S. (1992) Autistic social dysfunction: some limitations of the theory of mind hypothesis. *Journal of Child Psychology and Psychiatry*, **33**, 861–876.

Knobloch H. & Pasamanick B. (1975) Some etiologic and prognostic factors in early infantile autism and psychosis. *Pediatrics*, **55**, 182–191.

Kobayashi R., Murata T. & Yoshinaga K. (1992) A follow up study of 201 children with autism in Kyushu and Yamaguchi areas, Japan. *Journal of Autism and Developmental Disorders*, **22**, 395–411.

Koegel R.L., Schreibman L., Britten K.R., Burke J.C. & O'Neill R.E. (1982) A comparison of parent training to direct clinic treatment. In: Koegel R.L., Rincover A. & Egel A.L. (eds) *Educating and Understanding Autistic Children*, pp. 260–279. College Hill Press, San Diego, CA.

Koegel R., O'Dell M. & Dunlap G. (1988) Producing speech use in nonverbal autistic children by reinforcing attempts. *Journal of Autism and Developmental Disorders*, **18**, 525–538.

Kolvin I. (1971) Psychosis in childhood — a comparative study. In: Rutter M. (ed) *Infantile Autism: Concepts, Characteristics, and Treatment*, pp. 7–26. Churchill Livingstone, Edinburgh.

Kolvin I. & Fundudis T. (1981) Elective mute children: psychological development and background factors. *Journal of Child Psychology and Psychiatry*, **22**, 219–232.

Krug D.A., Arick J. & Almond P. (1980) Behavior checklist for identifying severely handicapped individuals with high levels of autistic behavior. *Journal of Child Psychology and Psychiatry*, **21**, 221–229.

Kurita H. (1985) Infantile autism with speech loss before the age of 30 months. *Journal of the American Academy of Child Psychiatry*, **24**, 191–196.

Kurita H., Kita M. & Miyake Y. (1992) A comparative study of development and symptoms among disintegrative psychosis and infantile autism with and without speech loss. *Journal of Autism and Developmental Disorders*, **22**, 175–188.

Landa R., Wzorek M., Piven J., Folstein S. & Isaacs C. (1991) Spontaneous narrative discourse characteristics of parents of autistic individuals. *Journal of Speech and Hearing Research*, **34**, 1339–1345.

Landa R., Piven J., Wzorek M., Gayle J.O., Chase G.A. & Folstein S.E. (1992) Social language use in parents of autistic individuals. *Psychological Medicine*, **22**, 245–254.

Leboyer M., Bouvard M.P., Launay J., Tabuteau F., Waller D., Dugas M., Kerdelhue B., Lensing P. & Panksepp J. (1992) Brief report: a double-blind study of naltrexone in infantile autism. *Journal of Autism and Developmental Disorders*, **22**, 309–328.

Le Couteur A., Rutter M., Lord C., Rios P., Robertson S., Holdgrafer M. & McLennan J.D. (1989) Autism Diagnostic Interview: a semi-structured interview for parents and caregivers of autistic persons. *Journal of Autism and Developmental Disorders*, **19**, 363–387.

Leslie A.M. (1987) Pretense and representation: the origins of 'theory of mind.' *Psychological Review*, **94**, 412–426.

Leslie A.M. & Happé F. (1989) Autism and ostensive communication: the relevance of metarepresentation. *Development and Psychopathology*, **1**, 205–212.

Lewis V. & Boucher J. (1988) Spontaneous, instructed and elicited play in relatively able autistic children. *British Journal of Developmental Psychology*, **6**, 325–329.

Lockyer L. & Rutter M. (1970) A five to fifteen-year follow-up study of infantile psychosis: IV. Patterns of cognitive ability. *British Journal of Social and Clinical Psychology*, **9**, 152–163.

Lord C. (1984) The development of peer relations in children with autism. In: Morrison F.J., Lord C. & Keating D.P. (eds) *Applied Developmental Psychology*, vol. 1, pp. 165–229. Academic Press, New York.

Lord C. (1985) Autism and the comprehension of language. In: Schopler E. & Mesibov G.B. (eds) *Communication Problems in Autism*, pp. 257–281. Plenum, New York.

Lord C. (1991) Follow-up of two year-olds referred for possible autism. Paper presented at the biennial meeting of the Society for Research in Child development, Seattle, April 1991.

Lord C. (1993) Complexity of social behavior in autism. In: Baron-Cohen S., Tager-Flusberg H. & Cohen D. (eds) *Understanding Other Minds: Perspectives from Autism*, pp. 292–316. Oxford University Press, Oxford.

Lord C. & Schopler E. (1985) Differences in sex ratios in autism as a function of measured intelligence. *Journal of Autism and Developmental Disorders*, **15**, 185–193.

Lord C. & Schopler E. (1989) The role of age at assessment, developmental level, and test in the stability of intelligence scores in young autistic children. *Journal of Autism and Developmental Disorders*, **19**, 483–499.

Lord C., Rutter M., Goode S., Heemsbergen J., Jordan H. & Mawhood L. (1989) Autism Diagnostic Observation Schedule: a standardized observation of communicative and social behavior. *Journal of Autism and Developmental Disorders*, **19**, 185–212.

Lord C., DiLavore P. & Schopler E. (1991) Sex differences in autism. Paper given at the Annual meeting of the American Psychiatric Association, New Orleans, May 1991.

Lord C., Rutter M. & Le Couteur A. (in press) Autism Diagnostic Interview – Revised: A revised version of a diagnostic interview for caregivers of individuals with possible pervasive developmental disorders. *Journal of Autism and Developmental Disorders*.

Lotter V. (1978) Follow-up studies. In: Rutter M. & Schopler E. (eds) *Autism: A Reappraisal of Concepts and Treatment*, pp. 475–495. Plenum Press, New York.

Lovaas O.I. (1987) Behavioral treatment and normal educational and intellectual functioning in young autistic children. *Journal of Consulting and Clinical Psychology*, **55**, 3–9.

Lovaas O.I., Koegel R., Simmons J.Q. & Long J.S. (1973) Some generalization and follow-up measures on autistic children in behavior therapy. *Journal of Applied Behavior Analysis*, **6**, 131–166.

Loveland K. & Landry S. (1986) Joint attention and language in autism and developmental language delay. *Journal of Autism and Developmental Disorders*, **16**, 335–349.

McEachin J.J., Smith T. & Lovaas O.I. (1993) Long-term outcome for children with autism who received early intensive behavioral treatment. *American Journal on Mental Retardation*, **97**, 359–372.

Mahler M.S. (1952) On childhood psychosis and schizophrenia: autistic and symbiotic psychoses. *Psychoanalytic Study of the Child*, **7**, 286–305.

Melmer G., Bolton P., Hodgkinson S., Holmes D., Lord C., Rutter M. & Gurling H.M.D. (submitted) Genetic linkage analysis of the fragile X region in autism.

Mesibov G.B. (1984) Social skills training with verbal autistic adolescents and adults: a program model. *Journal of Autism and Developmental Disorders*, **14**, 395–404.

Mesibov G.B. (1986) A cognitive program for teaching social behaviors to verbal autistic adolescents and adults. In: Schopler E. & Mesibov G.B. (eds) *Social Behavior in Autism*, pp. 265–280. Plenum Press, New York.

Mesibov G.B., Schopler E. & Caison W. (1989) The Adolescent and Adult Psychoeducational Profile: assessment of adolescents and adults with severe developmental handicaps. *Journal of Autism and Developmental Disorders*, **19**, 33–40.

Miller J.F., Campbell T.F., Chapman R.S. & Weismer S.E. (1984) Language behaviour in acquired childhood aphasia. In: Holland A.

(ed) *Language Disorders in Children*, pp. 57–99. College-Hill Press, San Diego, CA.

Minshew N. (1991) Indices of neural function in autism: clinical and biological implications. *Pediatrics*, **31**, 774–780.

Morehead D.M. & Morehead A.E. (eds) (1976) *Normal and Deficient Child Language*. University Park Press, Baltimore, MD.

Mouridsen S.E., Bachmann Anderson L., Sörensen S.A., Rich B. & Isager T. (1992) Neurofibromatosis in infantile autism and other types of childhood psychoses. *Acta Paedopsychiatrica*, **55**, 15–19.

Mullen E. (1989) *Mullen Scales of Early Learning*. T.O.T.A.L. Child, Cranston, RI.

Mundy P., Sigman M., Ungerer J. & Sherman T. (1986) Defining the social deficits of autism: the contribution of nonverbal communication measures. *Journal of Child Psychology and Psychiatry*, **27**, 657–669.

Nelson K. (1991) Prenatal and perinatal factors in the etiology of autism. *Pediatrics*, **87**, 761–766.

Olsson B. & Rett A. (1987) Autism and Rett syndrome: behavioural investigations and differential diagnosis. *Developmental Medicine and Child Neurology*, **29**, 429–441.

Olsson B. & Rett A. (1990) A review of the Rett syndrome with a theory of autism. *Brain and Development*, **12**, 11–15.

Olsson I., Steffenburg S. & Gillberg C. (1988) Epilepsy in autism and autistic-like conditions: a population-based study. *Archives of Neurology*, **45**, 666–668.

Ornitz E.M. (1978) Biological homogeneity or heterogeneity. In: Rutter M. & Schopler E. (eds) *Autism: A Reappraisal of Concepts and Treatment*, pp. 243–250. Plenum Press, New York.

Ozonoff S. (in press) Executive functions in autism. In: Schopler E. & Mesibov G.B. (eds) *Learning and Cognition in Autism*. Plenum Press, New York.

Ozonoff S., Pennington B.F. & Rogers S.J. (1991a) Executive function deficits in high functioning children with autism: relationship to theory of mind. *Journal of Child Psychology and Psychiatry*, **32**, 1081–1106.

Ozonoff S., Rogers S.J. & Pennington B.F. (1991b) Asperger's syndrome: evidence of an empirical distinction from high-functioning autism. *Journal of Child Psychology and Psychiatry*, **32**, 1107–1122.

Panksepp J. (1979) A neurochemical theory of autism. *Trends in Neuroscience*, **2**, 174–177.

Panksepp J. & Sahley T. (1987) Possible brain opioid involvement in disrupted social intent and language development of autism. In: Schopler E. & Mesibov G.B. (eds) *Neurobiological Issues in Autism*, pp. 357–367. Plenum Press, New York.

Parks S.L. (1988) Psychometric instruments available for the assessment of autistic children. In: Schopler E. & Mesibov G.B. (eds) *Diagnosis and Assessment in Autism*, pp. 123–136. Plenum Press, New York.

Phillips W., Baron-Cohen S. & Rutter M. (1992) The role of eye-contact in goal-detection: evidence from normal toddlers and children with autism or mental handicap. *Development and Psychopathology*, **4**, 375–383.

Piven J., Gayle J., Chase J., Fink B., Landa R., Wzorek M. & Folstein S. (1990) A family history study of neuropsychiatric disorders in the adult siblings of autistic individuals. *Journal of the American Academy of Child and Adolescent Psychiatry*, **29**, 177–183.

Piven J., Nehme E., Simon J., Barta P., Pearlson G. & Folstein S.E. (1992) Magnetic resonance imaging in autism: measurement of the cerebellum, pons and fourth ventricle. *Biological Psychiatry*, **31**, 491–504.

Prior M., Dahlstrom B. & Squires T.L. (1990) Autistic children's knowledge of thinking and feeling states in other people. *Journal of Child Psychology and Psychiatry*, **31**, 587–602.

Prizant B.M. & Wetherby A.M. (1985) Intentional communicative behavior of children with autism: theoretical and practical issues. *Australian Journal of Human Communication Disorders*, **13**, 21–59.

Quill K., Gurry S. & Larkin A. (1989) Daily life therapy: a Japanese model for educating children with autism. *Journal of Autism and Developmental Disorders*, **19**, 625–635.

Rank B. (1949) Adaptation of the psychoanalytic technique for the treatment of young children with atypical development. *American Journal of Orthopsychiatry*, **19**, 130–139.

Raven J.C. (1956) *Guide to Using the Coloured Progressive Matrices*. H.K. Lewis, London.

Reiss A.L., Feinstein C. & Rosenblum K.N. (1986) Autism and genetic disorders. *Schizophrenia Bulletin*, **12**, 724–728.

Rett Syndrome Diagnostic Criteria Working Group (1988) Diagnostic criteria for Rett syndrome. *Annals of Neurology*, **23**, 425–428.

Richer J. & Zappella M. (1989) Changing social behaviour: the plus of holding. *Communications*, **23**, 35–39.

Riddle M.A., King R.A., Hardin M.T., Scahill L., Ort S.I., Chappell P., Rasmusson A. & Leckman J. (1991) Behavioral side-effects of fluoxetine in children and adolescents. *Journal of Child and Adolescent Psychopharmacology*, **1**, 193–198.

Rimland B. (1987) Megavitamin B_6 and magnesium in the treatment of autistic children and adults. In: Schopler E. & Mesibov G.B. (eds) *Neurobiological Issues in Autism*, pp. 389–405. Plenum, New York.

Risch N. (1990) Linkage strategies for genetically complex traits. Parts I–III. *American Journal of Human Genetics*, **46**, 222–253.

Ritvo E.R., Mason-Brothers A., Freeman B.J., Pingree C., Jenson W.R., McMahon W.M., Petersen P.B., Jorde L.B., Mo A. & Ritvo A. (1990) The UCLA–University of Utah epidemiologic survey of autism: the etiologic role of rare diseases. *American Journal of Psychiatry*, **147**, 1614–1621.

Rogers S. & DiLalla D. (1990) Age of symptom onset in young children with pervasive developmental disorders. *Journal of the American Academy of Child and Adolescent Psychiatry*, **29**, 863–872.

Rogers S. & Pennington B. (1991) A theoretical approach to the deficits in infantile autism. *Development and Psychopathology*, **3**, 137–162.

Rogers S., Ozonoff S. & Maslin-Cole C. (1991) A comparative study of attachment behavior in young children with autism or other psychiatric disorders. *Journal of the American Academy of Child and Adolescent Psychiatry*, **30**, 483–488.

Rumsey J.M. (1992) Neuropsychological studies of high level autism. In: Schopler E. & Mesibov G.B. (eds) *High-Functioning Individuals With Autism*, pp. 44–64. Plenum Press, New York.

Rumsey J.M., Rapoport M.D. & Sceery W.R. (1985) Autistic children as adults: psychiatric, social, and behavioral outcomes. *Journal of the American Academy of Child Psychiatry*, **24**, 465–473.

Ruttenberg B.A., Kalish B.I., Wenar C. & Wolf E.G. (1974) *Behavioral Rating Instrument for Autistic and Other Atypical Children*. Developmental Center for Autistic Children, Philadelphia, PA.

Rutter M. (1970) Autistic children: infancy to adulthood. *Seminars in Psychiatry*, **2**, 435–450.

Rutter M. (1972) Childhood schizophrenia reconsidered. *Journal of Autism and Childhood Schizophrenia*, **2**, 315–337.

Rutter M. (1978) Language disorder and infantile autism. In: Rutter M. & Schopler E. (eds) *Autism: A Reappraisal of Concepts & Treatment*, pp. 85–104. Plenum Press, New York.

Rutter M. (1979) Language, cognition and autism. In: Katzman R. (ed) *Congenital and Acquired Cognitive Disorders*, pp. 247–264. Raven Press, New York.

Rutter M. (1983) Cognitive deficits in the pathogenesis of autism. *Journal of Child Psychology and Psychiatry*, **24**, 513–532.

Rutter M. (1985a) The treatment of autistic children. *Journal of Child Psychology and Psychiatry*, **26**, 193–214.

Rutter M. (1985b) Infantile autism. In: Shaffer D., Erhardt A. & Greenhill L. (eds) *A Clinician's Guide to Child Psychiatry*, pp. 48–78. Free Press, New York.

Rutter M. (1991) Autism as a genetic disorder. In: McGuffin P. & Murray R. (eds) *The New Genetics of Mental Illness*, pp. 225–244. Heinemann Medical, Oxford.

Rutter M. & Bailey A. (1993) Thinking and relationships: mind and brain — some reflections on 'theory of mind' and autism. In: Baron-Cohen S., Tager-Flusberg H. & Cohen D. (eds) *Understanding Other Minds: Perspectives from Autism*, pp. 481–504. Oxford University Press, Oxford.

Rutter M. Lockyer L. (1967) A five to fifteen year follow-up study of infantile psychosis. I: Description of sample. *British Journal of Psychiatry*, **113**, 1169–1182.

Rutter M. & Mawhood L. (1991) The long-term psychosocial sequelae of specific developmental disorders of speech and language. In: Rutter M. & Casaer P. (eds) *Biological Risk Factors for Psychosocial Disorders*, pp. 233–259. Cambridge University Press, Cambridge.

Rutter M. & Schopler E. (1992) Classification of pervasive developmental disorders: some concepts and practical considerations. *Journal of Autism and Developmental Disorders*, **22**, 459–482.

Rutter M., Mawhood L. & Howlin P. (1992) Language delay and social development. In: Fletcher P. & Hale D. (eds) *Specific Speech and Language Disorders in Children*. pp. 63–78. Whurr Publishers, London.

Rutter M., Bailey A., Bolton P. & Le Couteur, A. (1993) Autism: Syndrome definition and possible genetic mechanisms. In: Plomin R. & MaClearn G.E. (eds) *Nature, Nurture, and Psychology*, pp. 269–284. APA Books, Washington DC.

Rutter M., Bailey A., Bolton P. & Le Couteur A. (1994) Autism and known medical conditions: Myth and substance. *Journal of Child Psychology and Psychiatry*, **35**, 311–322.

Schopler E. (1976) Towards reducing behavior problems in autistic children. In: Wing L. (ed) *Early Childhood Autism*, pp. 221–246. Pergamon Press, London.

Schopler E. & Olley G. (1982) Comprehensive educational services for autistic children: the TEACCH model. In: Reynolds C.R. & Gutkin T.R. (eds) *The Handbook of School Psychology*, pp. 629–643. Wiley, New York.

Schopler E., Reichler R.J. & Renner B.R. (1986) *The Childhood Autism Rating Scale (CARS) For Diagnostic Screening and Classification of Autism*. Irvington Publishers, New York.

Schopler E., Short A. & Mesibov G. (1989) Relation of behavioral treatment to 'normal functioning': comment on Lovaas. *Journal of Consulting and Clinical Psychology*, **57**, 162–164.

Schopler E., Reichler R.J., Bashford A., Lansing M.D. & Marcus L.M. (1990) *Psychoeducational Profile Revised*. Pro-Ed, Austin, TX.

Schreibman L. & Lovaas O.I. (1973) Overselective response to social stimuli by autistic children. *Journal of Abnormal Child Psychology*, **1**, 152–168.

Sevin J.A., Matson J.L., Coe D.A., Fee V.C. & Sevin B.M. (1991) A comparison and evaluation of three commonly used autism scales. *Journal of Autism and Developmental Disorders*, **21**, 551–556.

Shah A. & Holmes N. (1985) The use of the Leiter International Performance Scale with autistic children. *Journal of Autism and Developmental Disorders*, **15**, 195–204.

Siegel B., Vukicevic J., Elliot G. & Kramer H. (1989) The use of signal detection theory to assess DSM-III-R criteria for autistic disorder. *American Academy of Child and Adolescent Psychiatry*, **28**, 542–548.

Skuse D. (1984) Extreme deprivation in early childhood — I. Diverse outcomes for three siblings from an extraordinary family. *Journal of Child Psychology and Psychiatry*, **25**, 523–541.

Sloman L. (1991) Use of medication in pervasive developmental disorders. *Psychiatric Clinics of North America*, **14**, 165–182.

Smalley S. (1991) Genetic influences in autism. *Psychiatric Clinics of North America*, **14**, 125–139.

Smalley S., Asarnow R. & Spence M. (1988) Autism and genetics: a decade of research. *Archives of General Psychiatry*, **45**, 958–961.

Smalley S., Smith M. & Tanguay P. (1991) Autism and psychiatric disorders in tuberous sclerosis. *Annals of New York Academy of Science*, **615**, 382–383.

Smalley S.L., Tanguay P.E., Smith M. & Gutierrez G. (1992) Autism and tuberous sclerosis. *Journal of Autism and Developmental Disorders*, **22**, 339–355.

Sparrow S.S. & Cicchetti D.V. (1985) Diagnostic uses of the Vineland Adaptive Behavior Scales. *Journal of Pediatric Psychology*, **10**, 215–225.

Spence M., Ritvo E., Marazita M., Funderburk S., Sparkes S. & Freeman B. (1985) Gene mapping studies with the syndrome of autism. *Behavior Genetics*, **15**, 1–13.

Steffenburg S., Gillberg C., Helgren L., Anderson L., Gillberg I., Jakobsson G. & Bohman M. (1989) A twin study of autism in Denmark, Finland, Iceland, Norway, and Sweden. *Journal of Child Psychology and Psychiatry*, **30**, 405–416.

Stone W. & Caro-Martinez L. (1990) Naturalistic observations of spontaneous communication in autistic children. *Journal of Autism and Developmental Disorders*, **20**, 437–454.

Strain P.S. (1983) *The Utilization of Classroom Peers as Behavior Change Agents*. Plenum Press, New York.

Stubbs E. (1977) Autistic children exhibit undetectable hemagglutination-inhibition antibody titers despite previous rubella vaccination. *Journal of Autism and Childhood Schizophrenia*, **6**, 269–274.

Stubbs E.G., Ash E. & Williams C.P.S. (1984) Autism and congenital cytomegalovirus. *Journal of Autism and Developmental Disorders*, **14**, 183–189.

Stutsman R. (1931) Guide for administering the Merrill-Palmer Scale of Mental Tests. In: Terman L.M. (ed) *Mental Measurement of Preschool Children*, pp. 139–262. Harcourt, Brace & World, New York.

Szatmari P., Bremner R. & Nagy J. (1989) Asperger's syndrome: a review of clinical features. *Canadian Journal of Psychiatry*, **34**, 554–560.

Szatmari P., Tuff L., Finlayson M.A. & Bartolucci G. (1990) Asperger's syndrome and autism: neurocognitive aspects. *Journal of the American Academy of Child Psychiatry*, **29**, 130–136.

Tager-Flusberg H. (1992) Autistic children's talk about psychological states: deficits in the early acquisition of a theory of mind. *Child Development*, **63**, 161–172.

Tager-Flusberg H. & Anderson M. (1991) The development of contingent discourse ability in autistic children. *Journal of Child Psychology and Psychiatry*, **32**, 1123–1134.

Tanguay P. (1976) Clinical and electrophysiological research. In: Ritvo E.R. (ed) *Autism: Diagnosis, Current Research and Management*, pp. 75–84. Spectrum, New York.

Tantam D. (1988) Asperger's syndrome. *Journal of Child Psychology and Psychiatry*, **29**, 245–253.

Treffert D.A. (1970) Epidemiology of infantile autism. *Archives of General Psychiatry*, **22**, 431–438.

Tsai L. (1987) Pre-, peri-, and neonatal factors in autism. In: Schopler E. & Mesibov G.B. (eds) *Neurobiological Issues in Autism*, pp. 179–189. Plenum Press, New York.

Tsai L. & Beisler J.M. (1983) The development of sex differences in infantile autism. *British Journal of Psychiatry*, **142**, 373–378.

Tsai L., Stewart M.A. & August G. (1981) Implications of sex differences in the familial transmission of infantile autism. *Journal of Autism and Developmental Disorders*, **23**, 700–703.

Ungerer J.A. & Sigman M. (1981) Symbolic play and language comprehension in autistic children. *Journal of the American Academy of Child Psychiatry*, **20**, 318–337.

Vaillant G. (1962) John Haslam on early infantile autism. *American Journal of Psychiatry*, **119**, 376.

Van Bourgondien M. & Schopler E. (1990) Critical issues in the residential care of people with autism. *Journal of Autism and Developmental Disorders*, **20**, 391−400.

Venter A., Lord C. & Schopler E. (1992) A follow-up study of high-functioning autistic children. *Journal of Child Psychology and Psychiatry*, **33**, 489−507.

Volden J. & Lord C. (1991) Neologisms and abnormal functional usage of language in autistic speakers. *Journal of Autism and Developmental Disorders*, **21**, 1−22.

Volkmar F. (1987) Social development. In: Cohen D. & Donnellan A. (eds) *Handbook of Autism and Pervasive Developmental Disorders*, pp. 41−61. John Wiley, New York.

Volkmar F.R. & Cohen D.J. (1989) Disintegrative disorder or 'late onset' autism. *Journal of Child Psychology and Psychiatry*, **30**, 717−724.

Volkmar F. & Nelson I. (1990) Seizure disorders in autism. *Journal of the American Academy of Child and Adolescent Psychiatry*, **29**, 127−129.

Volkmar F.R., Stier D.M. & Cohen D.J. (1985) Age of recognition of pervasive developmental disorder. *American Journal of Psychiatry*, **142**, 1450−1452.

Volkmar F.R., Sparrow S.S., Goudreau D., Cicchetti D.V., Paul R. & Cohen D.J. (1987) Social deficits in autism: An operational approach using the Vineland Adaptive Behavior Scales. *Journal of the American Academy of Child and Adolescent Psychiatry*, **26**, 156−161.

Watson L., Lord C., Schaffer B. & Schopler E. (1988) *Teaching Spontaneous Communication to Autistic and Developmentally Handicapped Children*. Irvington Press, New York.

Wechsler D. (1974) *Manual for the Wechsler Child Intelligence Scale-Revised*. Psychological Corporation, San Antonio, TX.

Weeks S. & Hobson R. (1987) The salience of facial expression for autistic children. *Journal of Child Psychology and Psychiatry*, **28**, 137−152.

Williams T. (1989) A social skills group for autistic children. *Journal of Autism and Developmental Disorders*, **19**, 143−156.

Wimpory D. & Cochrane V. (1991) Criteria for evaluative research — with special reference to holding therapy. *Communications*, **25**, 15−17.

Wing L. (1981) Language, social, and cognitive impairments in autism and severe mental retardation. *Journal of Autism and Developmental Disorders*, **11**, 31−44.

Wing L. & Gould J. (1979) Severe impairments of social interaction and associated abnormalities in children: epidemiology and classification. *Journal of Autism and Developmental Disorders*, **9**, 11−29.

Wolff S. (1991) 'Schizoid' personality in childhood and adult life. *British Journal of Psychiatry*, **159**, 615−635.

Wolff S., Narayan S. & Moyes B. (1988) Personality characteristics of parents of autistic children. *Journal of Child Psychology and Psychiatry*, **29**, 143−154.

Wolff P., Gardner J., Paccia J. & Lappen J. (1989) The greeting behavior of fragile X males. *American Journal of Mental Retardation*, **93**, 406−411.

World Health Organization (1992) *The ICD-10 Classification of Mental and Behavioural Disorders: Clinical Descriptions and Diagnostic Guidelines*. World Health Organization, Geneva.

Young J., Kavanagh M., Anderson G., Shaywitz B. & Cohen D. (1982) Clinical neurochemistry of autism and associated disorders. *Journal of Autism and Developmental Disorders*, **12**, 147−165.

Chapter 34
Schizophrenic and Allied Disorders

John Scott Werry & Eric Taylor

INTRODUCTION

Overview

Schizophrenia is a serious mental illness characterized primarily by particular abnormalities of thinking, perception and emotion (World Health Organization, 1991). It is responsible for a major part of the cost of publicly funded psychiatric services in most countries (Sharfstein & Clark, 1978).

Schizophrenia is usually first diagnosed in late adolescence or young adulthood, between the ages of 15 and 35 (Zigler & Levine, 1981). Nevertheless, it has been recognized since the writing of Kraepelin that the onset can be in childhood (Eisenberg, 1957). Modern approaches to understanding schizophrenia in children needed to clear away two notions: a psychodynamic view that considered psychosis as a manifestation of extreme severity of psychopathology and psychosocial stress, rather than as a group of qualitatively different disorders; and a muddling together of autism and childhood schizophrenia (Rutter, 1972; Kydd & Werry, 1981; Russell, 1992).

Child schizophrenia has also been affected by a perennial argument in child psychopathology on whether or not child forms are discontinuous with, and should be classified separately from, adult forms. The same issue applies to depression and anxiety disorders. Most reviews (e.g. Eisenberg, 1957; Rutter, 1972; Beitchman, 1985; Werry, 1992) have concluded that differences are mostly developmental and quantitative rather than of kind. The distinctiveness of the different childhood psychoses and the assumption of similarity of child and adult schizophrenia were made official in 1978 in ICD-9 (World Health Organization, 1978) and in 1980 in DSM-III (American Psychiatric Association, 1980). Both these diagnostic schemes abolished the separate category of childhood schizophrenia and ICD-10 (World Health Organization, 1991) and DSM-IV (American Psychiatric Association, in press) follow the same line.

There are some useful reviews of child and adolescent schizophrenia (Rutter, 1972; Beitchman, 1985; Prior & Werry, 1986; Asarnow *et al.*, 1989; Berney, 1990; Werry 1992) but data are sparse, especially for adolescent schizophrenia. Clinicians will for some time be dependent on extrapolations from adults to children (McClellan & Werry, in press). This chapter will therefore summarize core knowledge derived in adults with greater attention given to topics particularly germane to children and adolescents.

TERMINOLOGY IN CHILD AND ADOLESCENT SCHIZOPHRENIA

Schizophrenia, beginning before age 13, is usually referred to as prepubertal schizophrenia. Since puberty is a biological developmental stage encompassing a wide age range, this term is misleading and should be avoided. Werry (1992) has suggested that schizophrenia beginning before age 17—18 should be called early-onset schizophrenia (EOS) and that before age 13, very-early-onset schizophrenia (VEOS). These terms will be used here.

Definition

Schizophrenia is summarized in ICD-10 (World Health Organization, 1992) as a group of disorders 'characterized in general by fundamental and characteristic distortions of thinking, and perception and affects that are inappropriate or blunted. Clear consciousness and intellectual capacity are usually maintained '... The disturbance involves the most basic functions which give the normal person a feeling of individuality, uniqueness and self-direction' (World Health Organization, 1992).

On the whole, modern psychiatry agrees that schizophrenia is a group of diseases best understood and researched by the methods of medical science (Carpenter, 1987). However, while Kraepelin brought order out of nosological chaos, there never has been and still is not a single, universally accepted definition of schizophrenia. Variations in diagnosis produce different patient populations with different clinical pictures and differing outcomes (Andreasen, 1987; Bland & Kaloda, 1988; Westermeyer & Harrow, 1988). Most of the dispute has centred less on the disabling core disorder with its marked change in function accompanied by distinctively bizarre symptoms than where the borders should be drawn. The major split is between a narrow Kraepelinian view, reborn in DSM-III and its successors (American Psychiatric Association 1980, 1987, in press), which emphasizes both a core of first-ranked (or Schneiderian) symptoms and chronicity (minimum

6 months' duration); and Eugen Bleuler's view, which challenged the inexorability of poor prognosis and expanded symptomatology to include reaction to symptoms (Angst, 1988; Bland & Kaloda, 1988) in rather the same way that Hughlings Jackson, the great neurologist, did with his 'release symptoms' in neurology. ICD lies between these two poles.

The problem of definition is particularly germane in children. Firstly, acute and florid schizophrenic symptoms are rare but there is a numerically significant group of very odd, dysfunctional individuals called schizoid, schizotypal, borderline or schizophrenia spectrum (Volkmar *et al.*, 1988; Asarnow *et al.*, 1989; Petti & Vela, 1990; Russell, 1992). Secondly, the problem of how to understand concurrent affective states is difficult, because affective symptoms are common in VEOS (Asarnow & Ben-Meir, 1988). Thirdly, some symptoms are modified and may be atypical because of cognitive immaturity (see the section on developmental effects on core symptomatology below).

No clinician or researcher can operate without some diagnostic standard such as DSM-IV (American Psychiatric Association, in press) or ICD-10 (World Health Organization, 1992). The two schemes, though developed in close cooperation, are not exactly similar. DSM-IV tends to be more legalistic, setting out in minute detail just what and how many symptoms are needed, while ICD-10 (in its clinical diagnostic guidelines) concentrates more on the conceptual core and symptom array and leaves more to clinical judgement (Rutter, 1989). The result is that the US definition of schizophrenia has moved from one of the loosest to the narrowest in the world with substantial improvement of reliability and specificity of diagnosis (Bland & Kaloda, 1988) — but with considerable sacrifices in sensitivity, and exclusion of some of the more atypical cases that are more common in children and adolescents. Despite their popularity and legitimacy, neither DSM nor ICD is entirely satisfactory, nor have they set to rest competing views on just how schizophrenia should be defined (Angst, 1988). As in so many areas of psychiatry, reviewers have had to assume that researchers in different traditions are dealing with the same underlying concepts — or there would have been no reviews (Beitchman, 1985; Kolvin & Berney, 1990; Russell, 1992; Werry, 1992).

All current definitions rely on clinical symptoms and features considerably 'downstream' from whatever the causative brain disorders may be, and hence are derivative, lacking absolute sensitivity and specificity. The clinician must choose some definition that is clinically practicable and tied to a usable systematic body of knowledge about epidemiology, symptomatology, correlates, outcome and treatment. On the whole, ICD and DSM will fit this need and have the advantage of universality, though using DSM will result in a narrower and more ominous disorder (Angst, 1988; Bland & Kaloda, 1988). No attempt will be made here to specify exactly what these ICD and DSM criteria are because not only is this repetitious, but it leads to the false and dangerous belief that diagnosis can be carried out from memory without reference to the diagnostic manual. There is already evidence, elsewhere in child psychiatry, that an important source of error in diagnosis is failure to follow diagnostic rules (Prendergast *et al.*, 1988). In an appendix, DSM offers useful, but probably underused, diagnostic decision trees, each beginning with a broad symptom area (e.g. psychotic symptoms). Increasingly, such decision trees are becoming part of structured history-taking and interviews (Gutterman *et al.*, 1987; Reich, 1990) and in desktop computerized systems within the range of every clinician (DTREE; Firth, 1990). Since the diagnosis of schizophrenia in children and adolescents is such a serious one socially and prognostically, and errors may dog a patient for years, their use is to be encouraged.

Subcategories of schizophrenia

Subcategorizing schizophrenia by the predominant pattern of symptomatology is widely accepted: *paranoid* where self-referent delusions predominate; *catatonic* with conspicuous psychomotor symptoms; *disorganized or hebephrenic* with marked thought disorder and silly affect; *undifferentiated* where many poorly formulated symptoms are seen; *simple* where the onset and progress are insidious but relentless and flagrant psychotic symptoms absent or inconspicuous; and *residual* with disability and active symptoms. A new ICD-10 subtype, *postschizophrenic depression*, is self-explanatory, except that the depression is noted as seldom severe enough to meet the criteria for a major depression, though carrying an increased risk of suicide.

While most of these subtypes are well-established, there is recurring doubt about their reliability and constancy throughout the course of the disorder (Angst, 1988). In children and adolescents (EOS), there has not been much study of these subcategories but the preponderant subtype varies so much from centre to centre (Werry, 1992) that there must be considerable doubt about their reliability. There are insufficient long-term studies to comment on their stability in EOS.

Reliability of diagnosis

Under research conditions, where interview techniques and diagnostic criteria are explicated and diagnosers are trained in such techniques, good interrater reliability of both symptoms (Kay, 1990) and diagnosis can be achieved in adults (Bland & Kaloda, 1988). While there has been little formal study of this in EOS, indications are that reliability is equally attainable (Volkmar *et al.*, 1988; Caplan *et al.*, 1989, 1990; Russell *et al.*, 1989; Werry *et al.*, 1991), although systemized methods of assessment and formal calculations of reliability have been used only occasionally (Caplan *et al.*, 1989; Russell *et al.*, 1989). A more searching question is what happens in ordinary clinical practice (Quay, 1986). Numbers of EOS in DSM field trials were very small and kappas were lower than 0.81 in adults (Quay, 1986); what really obtains in clinical practice remains unknown.

SYMPTOMATOLOGY

Core symptoms

Most definitions, including DSM-IV and ICD-10, rely on symptoms described by the Germanic school of Kraepelin, Bleuler and Schneider. A more recent and widely used regrouping of these symptoms, reflected in DSM-IV, is *positive* (or active) and *negative* (or deficit) (Andreasen, 1987; Kay, 1990). Positive symptoms include delusions, hallucinations, thought disorder, excitement and suspiciousness; negative symptoms are usually considered to comprise flattening of affect, alogia, apathy, anhedonia and asociality (see below). This distinction is reliable, has different correlates and prognostic implications and probably represents two fundamental dimensions of the psychopathology of schizophrenia rather than groups of truly independent symptoms (Kay, 1990; Dollfus *et al.*, 1991). There is probably a third dimension — disorganization (Dollfus *et al.*, 1991). Disorganization may be particularly relevant for EOS because it could capture the devastating functional effect that schizophrenia has on development.

Delusions

These are fixed, false beliefs inappropriate to the person's culture, peer group or developmental level, that do not respond to reasonable explanations to the contrary. Delusions are not unique to schizophrenia but in it, delusions are often bizarre and unbelievable. They may, especially in children, be fleeting or half-formed (especially if accompanied by hallucinations). Delusions are found in children in most studies though the frequency varies greatly (Garralda, 1985; Spencer *et al.*, 1991; Werry, 1992). As to type, most have been paranoid (persecutory, reference etc.) or ill-formed with few classical Schneiderian delusions (of thought echo, insertion, withdrawal or broadcasting; Garralda, 1985; Russell *et al.*, 1989; Spencer *et al.*, 1991).

Hallucinations

These are perceptions occurring in the absence of any or sufficient sensory stimulus and, as a consequence, not observed by anyone else present at the same time. Hallucinations are found outside schizophrenia and also occur in nonpsychotic states in children (Rothstein, 1981; Garralda, 1984a; Burke *et al.*, 1985) but are uncommon, the frequency in psychiatric outpatients being 1% or less (Rothstein, 1981; Garralda, 1984a). Care is needed in defining hallucinations in children, because they may have difficulty accurately describing them. Hallucinations may be confused with eidetic imagery, fantasy and sleep-related illusions. Among psychiatric diagnoses, they occur most commonly in schizophrenia and depression but are seen also in organic, conduct, anxiety and other disorders (Garralda, 1984a; Burke *et al.*, 1985; Russell, 1992). A history of relatives with major psychiatric disorders

may increase the risk in children who do not have schizophrenia or depression (Burke *et al.*, 1985).

Hallucinations do not necessarily portend later development of psychosis (Garralda, 1984b). Nevertheless, hallucinations are the most consistently reported symptoms in EOS (Russell, 1992; Werry, 1992). One study found few qualitative differences in the phenomenology of hallucinations between EOS and nonpsychotic children with hallucinations (Garralda, 1984a), though the psychotic children had far more *additional* indicators of schizophrenia, emphasizing the fact that schizophrenia cannot be diagnosed on hallucinations alone. Hallucinations are usually auditory (Garralda, 1985; Spencer *et al.*, 1991; Werry, 1992) but may be visual, tactile, olfactory or somatic (Andreasen, 1987).

Formal thought disorder (incoherence, illogicality and loosening of associations)

This is a disorder of the logic of thinking and talking that makes for difficulty in understanding particular comments or the overall thread of conversation. This is a feature of EOS, though the reported frequency varies from 40 to 80% (Arboleda & Holzman, 1985; Garralda, 1985; Werry, 1992). When dissected and measured systematically, important differences between children and adults emerge (Caplan *et al.*, 1990). Because of the lack of discursive speech in children, Caplan and co-workers used a story-telling method. Loosening of association and illogical thinking were highly specific to schizophrenic children in comparison with normals, but were also found, though less severely, in schizotypal children, suggesting that these may be either a predisposing trait (Asarnow *et al.*, 1989) or that schizophrenia and schizotypal disorder are part of the same spectrum separated only by severity (Caplan *et al.*, 1989, 1990; Russell, 1992). In contrast to adults, incoherence and poverty of content of thinking were found to be infrequent in children, though they have been reported by others using less exact, developmentally appropriate methods than the story-telling technique (Garralda, 1985; Werry, 1992). Another study (Arboleda & Holzman, 1985) found an increased frequency of formal thought disorder in hospitalized children with schizophrenia and also in the children of schizophrenic mothers. In children, care must be taken not to confuse formal thought disorder with developmental language disorders (Cantwell & Baker, 1987).

Affective changes (flattening or inappropriateness)

These are alterations in the transitory changes in emotional inflexion that accompany and facilitate both transmitted and received communication. Their absence (or flattening) is what makes computer-synthesized voices on electronic equipment sound so inhuman and is responsible for the characteristic 'glass wall' effect that makes some schizophrenic patients seem remote and unknowable.

Flattened affect is a negative symptom representing a deficit of normal function. Both flattened and inappropriate affect are common in EOS (Garralda, 1985; Spencer *et al.*, 1991; Werry, 1992). Depressive symptoms are also frequent in EOS (Asarnow & Ben-Meir, 1988; Asarnow *et al.*, 1991) but differ qualitatively from the characteristic inappropriate/flat affective changes of schizophrenia.

Catatonic behaviour

These are mostly motor: muteness, frozen immobility, bizarre posturing, waxy flexibility and motor negativism. This type of symptom appears uncommon in EOS (Spencer *et al.*, 1991; Werry, 1992) and is also less common in developed countries (World Health Organization, 1991). They are not specific to schizophrenia, and are also encountered in organic encephalopathies and in affective disorders.

Other negative symptoms

These are deficits of function. They do not only arise later in the disorder but are also characteristic of the acute phases (Kay, 1990). The Positive and Negative Symptom Scale gives an explicit measure, in which the main negative symptoms are blunted affect, emotional withdrawal, poor rapport, passive/apathetic social withdrawal, difficulty in abstract thinking, lack of spontaneity and stereotyped thinking (Kay *et al.*, 1987). They have received little study in EOS (Remschmidt *et al.*, 1991; Russell, 1992), which is regrettable given their importance in continuing management. In acute schizophrenia, negative symptoms are associated with a benign family history and predict a better eventual outcome, but a chronic negative syndrome reflects an intractable deficit disorder (Kay, 1990). These are the symptoms of schizophrenia most closely related to cognitive impairment, but their developmental significance clearly varies with the stage of the disorder or the age of the patient.

Other diagnostic features

Definitions vary in the extent to which they require a clear, adverse change in adaptive function and in the duration of symptoms. Unlike ICD-10 (World Health Organization, 1992), which has a time requirement only for the active phase (1 month), DSM requires a 6-month duration which may include prodrome, active and recovery phases (see below). The prognosis for schizophrenia is likely to be worse if the definition eliminates anyone who recovers quickly (Westermeyer & Harrow, 1988). In a study of child (VEOS) schizophrenia, diagnosed by both DSM-III-R (American Psychiatric Association, 1987) and ICD-10 criteria, Spencer *et al.* (1991) found that the duration of the disorder in all cases exceeded 6 months, as have others (Werry, 1992) but this is not so true in adolescence where a number of cases with brief initial episodes were found at long-term follow-up to be schizophrenic (Werry *et al.*, in press). This suggests that the diagnosis cannot be made accurately in all cases during the first episode, and that all such young patients should be followed carefully for some time.

Schizophrenia is uncommon until late adolescence, so that ICD or DSM should be consulted carefully before making the diagnosis and the diagnosis should not be made unless the symptoms are multiple, pervasive and persistent and the effect on adaptive function substantial.

Developmental effects on core symptomatology

While symptoms of schizophrenia are qualitatively similar in children and adolescents to those in adults, there are developmental variations (Garralda, 1985; Caplan *et al.*, 1989, 1990; Russell *et al.*, 1989; Spencer *et al.*, 1991; Werry, 1992). As noted, some of the classical core symptoms like passivity phenomena, poverty of thinking and incoherence may be infrequent in children. As would be expected given their less well-organized cognition (Caplan *et al.*, 1989, 1990), delusions in children are less frequent and complex than in adults, and less often have sexual or other adult themes (Russell *et al.*, 1989; Russell, 1992).

Other symptoms such as disorganized thinking and other aspects of thought disorder (Arboleda & Holzman, 1985; Caplan *et al.*, 1989, 1990), hallucinations (Rothstein, 1981; Garralda, 1984a; Burke *et al.*, 1985) may be present in other childhood diagnoses (such as developmental language disorder; Cantwell & Baker, 1987) or even in normal children, creating special hazards in diagnosis not found in adults. Many of these developmental differences have not been well-studied and in no cases have there been actual direct comparisons with adults. Even so, it does seem reasonable to conclude that, in the adolescent group, differences from adult symptoms will be less conspicuous but that, as with development in general, immaturity will produce greater variation.

The best studied developmental effect is in cognition (Arboleda & Holzman, 1985; Caplan *et al.*, 1989, 1990) where the severity of illogical thinking and loose associations (formal thought disorder) are correlated with age. This is because thought disorder represents a deficit in sensitivity to the listener's needs to be able to follow the flow of ideas and this skill is developmentally acquired. An important implication is that the onset of a disorder of this fundamental social skill before it is well-established should have a much greater impact than later, leading to greater disability.

A big controversy, still unresolved, is whether schizophrenia is wrongly excluded in non- or preverbal children because language is integral to much of the defining symptomatology (Cantor *et al.*, 1982; Russell *et al.*, 1989). This may be less of a problem developmentally, since schizophrenia has yet to be demonstrated even at the lower limits of well-established language, that is, earlier than about 5 years of age (Werry, 1992). However, it is a problem when development is abnormal and language is delayed or does not develop. For example, in a review of schizophrenia in mentally retarded persons, Reid (1983) declared it could not be detected in those without language. Nevertheless, where there is a marked change in behaviour accompanied by behaviour suggestive of hallucinations, catatonia and/or accompanied by inappropriate affect, schizophrenia could still be reasonably inferred, especially if there is a good response to antipsychotic medication.

Cultural effects on symptomatology

There can be little argument that the content of positive symptoms like hallucinations and delusions will be culture-bound. The importance of this cultural effect lies in diagnosis, since patients from minority cultures may be misdiagnosed as schizophrenic when they have beliefs (such as the spirit of a dead relative entering the body of a Polynesian child) which are not regarded as unusual in their own culture. In these cases, it is always necessary to get both evidence of deterioration in function and validation of abnormality of ideation from members of the same culture.

PHASES OF THE DISORDER

Schizophrenia is ordinarily a phasic disorder and this must be clearly understood both for recognizing the disorder in its various manifestations and for treating each phase appropriately (Kane, 1987). Nevertheless, not all patients will follow the characteristic phasic course outlined below (Carpenter & Kirkpatrick, 1988) and DSM which, unlike ICD, put so much emphasis on the different phases has now admitted that their separation often presents great difficulty (American Psychiatric Association, 1991). In children (VEOS), where premorbid abnormality is often substantial and the course chronic, this is a particular problem.

The prodrome

This is a variable period from hours or days to months (Werry, 1992), during which there is a clear change in adaptive function, often accompanied by premonitory but insufficient signs of developing psychosis. This differs from premorbid schizotypal or schizoid personality mainly by the clear change in function. This distinction may be difficult when the deterioration is insidious over many years or, in VEOS, lifelong (see Cantor *et al.*, 1982; Volkmar *et al.*, 1988). In one study the prodrome lasted as long as 5 years (Spencer *et al.*, 1991), which raises doubts about its validity as a concept distinct from premorbid personality abnormality in some cases.

The active phase

In this, the patient is clearly psychotic and the characteristic, mostly positive, symptoms of schizophrenia are present. In EOS this phase ordinarily lasts about 1−6 months, though it may be over 1 year (Spencer *et al.*, 1991; Werry *et al.*, 1991; Werry, 1992). Antipsychotic drug treatment can mitigate and sometimes shorten this phase (Spencer *et al.*, in press). It is failure to recognize the slow pace of this phase that leads to unacceptable practices such as frequent changes in treatment, polypharmacy and excessive dosage.

The recuperative/recovery phase

Symptoms abate or mitigate during this period, which may last for several months, but while signs of psychosis may disappear, some degree of impairment is usually discernible by those who know the patient well (like parents or teachers) — especially negative symptoms like anergia or inattention (Werry *et al.*, 1991). ICD-10 (World Health Organization, 1992) describes a postschizophrenic depression which is a recuperative phase characterized by flattening of affect with complaints of depression. Knowledge of this phase will prevent unreasonable pressure being brought to bear on the child.

The residual phase

Unfortunately, particularly after the second and subsequent episodes, recovery is incomplete in about 80% of cases (Westermeyer & Harrow, 1988; Werry *et al.*, 1991; Werry, 1992), leaving a residuum of social impairment, negative symptoms and isolated or minor positive symptoms, all of which result in a varying degree of handicap.

Chronically ill patients

There is a small group of patients who never recover from the first or second episodes, despite good treatment (Brenner *et al.*, 1990) and remains more or less actively ill, though with fluctuations, for many years (Eggers, 1978). These patients are among the most disabled and difficult to manage (Brenner *et al.*, 1990). Failure to recognize this outcome can lead to gross overtreatment with medication, discomfort and even psychosis through side-effects and to the neglect of more rehabilitation-oriented measures (Kane, 1987; McClellan & Werry, 1992).

EXAMINATION AND ASSESSMENT

One of the attractions (and weaknesses) of psychiatry is that it is still very much 'bedside' medicine. Diagnosis is dependent on good history-taking and examination and schizophrenia is no different in this respect from the rest of child and adolescent psychiatry. Yet, child and adolescent psychiatry has still to agree on a universally acceptable method of history-taking and examination of demonstrated reliability and validity. Although there have been many attempts to modify techniques to suit the needs of adolescents, there are few such measures for children (Russell, 1992) — most recently, for example, the Interview for Childhood Disorders and Schizophrenia (Russell *et al.*, 1989), the Kiddie Formal Thought Disorder Rating Scale (Caplan *et al.*, 1989), the Kiddie Positive and Negative Symptom Scales for children and adolescents (K-PANSS; Fields *et al.*, 1991), and the psychosis subscale of the Pictorial Instrument for Children (Ernst *et al.*, 1991). There are structured diagnostic interviews for children and adolescents, most centred on DSM-III-R (American Psychiatric Association, 1987), which also cover psychotic symptoms

(Gutterman *et al.*, 1987; Edelbrook & Costello, 1988), such as the Diagnostic Interview Schedule for Children (DISC, Edelbrook & Costello, 1988), Kiddie-Schedule for Affective Disorders and Schizophrenia (K-SADS) and Diagnostic Interview for Children and Adolescents (DICA; Russell *et al.*, 1989). They tend to be cumbersome and time-consuming and so far have not won wide acceptance in clinical work. What may change this situation is the development of both shorter forms and user-friendly computer-driven interviews.

In any case, the diagnosis cannot be made validly unless an adequate survey for the signs and symptoms of schizophrenia and of its differential diagnoses is carried out by whatever means (Russell, 1992). As noted above, no diagnosis should be made without reference to the proper criteria, preferably through the use of a decision tree. Psychiatry lacks the audit of the pathological laboratory, but it can compensate for this by making sure that the serious diagnoses like schizophrenia are made with strict adherence to accepted criteria. Medical methods — physical, laboratory, neurological and neuro-imaging examinations — assume rather more importance in the differential diagnosis of schizophrenia than in much of the rest of child and adolescent psychiatry because of the similarity of some of the psychotic symptoms to those seen in organic disorders such as delirium, dementia or disintegrative disorder.

In order to evaluate progress of the disorder with treatment, it is important to define what the problems and symptoms are, so that changes may be noted and documented, not left to such vagaries as 'better' or 'improved', although such measures as the Clinical Gobal Impressions (Lipman *et al.*, 1965) do have a place in estimating overall progress. The widely known Brief Psychiatric Rating Scale (Overall & Gorham, 1962) and Scales for Positive and Negative Symptoms (Andreasen, 1987; Kay, 1990) are useful for specific symptoms, even though they were developed for adults. The ways of measuring thought disorder in children developed by Caplan *et al.* (1989, 1990) may also have some value clinically.

Assessment of the child and the family, as opposed to the illness of schizophrenia, requires no special comment since such assessment is integral to and well-accepted in the practice of child and adolescent psychiatry. It is not qualitatively different in schizophrenia from any other disorder apart, perhaps, from more interest in family history of major psychiatric disorder and in certain family dynamics like expressed emotion (see below, and Goldstein, 1987). Even so, there are some formal methods of assessing social and family function developed for use in schizophrenic adults (Goldstein, 1987; Liberman, 1988; Brenner *et al.*, 1990) which may be of particular help in EOS, especially in adolescents.

AETIOLOGY

Schizophrenia is complexly caused and influenced (Carpenter, 1987; Meltzer, 1987). Biological factors are primary, but the disorder is shaped and influenced by psychosocial factors.

Genetic inheritance

Many types of research have given evidence that there is a substantial genetic component. Family studies leave little doubt that schizophrenia manifests as a familial disorder (Tsuang *et al.*, 1991). The risk is about 8% if one has a sibling with the disorder, 12% if a parent is affected, 40% if both parents, and 55% if an identical twin has schizophrenia. The risk rates in EOS are probably higher, though there is little good research (Hanson & Gottesman, 1976; Werry, 1992). Recent work generally confirms that, in males at least, onset before the age of 17 is associated with an increased risk for other relatives (Pulver *et al.*, 1990). The elevated risk applies chiefly to schizophrenic and schizotypal disorders. It has been suggested that the traditional, strict genetic separation from affective disorder needs to be qualified, since bipolar affective disorder is twice as common among the relatives of people with schizophrenia as is found in a control group (Kendler *et al.*, 1985; McGuffin *et al.*, 1987). This led Crow (1986) to argue for a genetic continuum of the psychoses — though the lack of an elevated risk for schizophrenia in those with affective disorder has restrained most psychiatrists from following suit. It is perhaps more probable that an inherited affective disorder can sometimes manifest with symptoms close enough to schizophrenia to meet the criteria for the latter diagnosis. In keeping with this view is the better prognosis for people with schizophrenia who have a family history of affective disorder (Kendler & Tsuang, 1988).

Adoption studies have gone further, to give convincing evidence that the biological, rather than the adoptive, relationship is responsible for familial transmission, estimating genetic heritability at between 0.6 and 0.7 and environmental familial factors as accounting for less than 20% of the variance in liability (Kendler, 1988). Two particularly important groups should be noted. The first is the biological paternal half-siblings of schizophrenic adoptees, who are at greater risk than those of control adoptees even though they do not share a common pre- or perinatal background. The second group to note is the biological offspring of normal parents, adopted by people who developed schizophrenia. They are not at risk for schizophrenia — so vertical cultural transmission of disorder is not a likely mechanism (Wender *et al.*, 1977). Adoptive designs are not always well-chosen for revealing aspects of the environment: gene−environment interactions are not well-tested for and the adoptive environment may bring its own stresses. Nevertheless, they can be indicative, as in the report by Tienari *et al.* (1990) that an adverse environment in the adopting family is associated with the development of schizophrenia spectrum disorders in the biological offspring of mothers with schizophrenia.

Twin studies also very strongly support a genetic component, through the difference between concordance rates for monozygotic twins (about 55%) and same-sex dizygotic twins (about 12%; Gottesman & Shields, 1982). They have also made it clear that there is a range of genetic expression: the nonschizophrenic monozygotic twins of people with schizophrenia are at increased risk of schizotypal and schizoid personality, and of other forms of personality disorder, and they are just as likely as their schizophrenic twins to have a child who develops schizophrenia (Fischer, 1971; Gottesman & Bertelson, 1989). It is therefore quite possible to carry the genetic liability without showing the disorder.

Quantitative modelling studies have not yet given clear knowledge about the mode of inheritance (Gottesman *et al.*, 1987).

A fully penetrant dominant gene is excluded because the risk for the offspring of a schizophrenic parent falls far short of 0.5 (see above); similarly, a penetrant recessive gene is not the cause because the risk for a child of two schizophrenic parents is much less than 1.0 (the actual value is about 0.4). Single-gene models have therefore been complicated by supposing reduced penetrance, an environmental cause for some affected individuals, and an interaction between genetic and environmental influences leading to a continuum of liability with a threshold for showing the disorder. Even so, these models have not fared well against statistical testing: they do not predict the pattern of affected relatives well enough (Tsuang *et al.*, 1991).

Models that suppose multiple genes to be involved have fared better in statistical analysis and deserve serious consideration. Multifactorial polygenic models cope well with the findings that the risk for schizophrenia rises with the number of affected relatives and that schizophrenia is found in varying severity, with increasing severity raising the risk of a relative being affected (McGue *et al.*, 1983). It is also quite possible that multiple polygenic influences could coexist with a single gene of large effect.

The complexity of findings might arise from a heterogeneity of disorders, each of which has a simple pattern of inheritance, or from a simply inherited genotype that is expressed in complex ways. Latent structure analysis applied to two samples has proposed that a supposed underlying trait of brain dysfunction may have at least two independent phenotypic manifestations — one being schizophrenia, the other dysfunctions of smooth pursuit eye movements (Matthysse *et al.*, 1986). The latent trait, but not schizophrenia, conforms to an autosomal dominant mode of transmission. Large samples of carefully ascertained cases are needed for these forms of analysis and much research is still required.

Molecular genetics has so far contributed chiefly by attempts to localize the genes involved: DNA is cut by enzymes into segments varying greatly from person to person, and these segments are widespread genetic markers for linkage analysis. The method has not yet yielded localization of involved genes. The claim that schizophrenia genes were sited on chromosome 5 (Sherrington *et al.*, 1988) has been refuted by subsequent studies (Kennedy *et al.*, 1988; St Clair *et al.*, 1989; Crowe *et al.*, 1991).

Environmental factors

Early brain damage

The genetic studies considered above have also indicated that some environmental contribution to the disorder is to be expected. They do leave open the question of how the environment operates — does it, for instance, interact with genetic constitution or are there some environmental causes that are sufficient? Temporal lobe epilepsy can give rise to a psychiatric syndrome resembling schizophrenia, and drug intoxication (especially with amphetamine) can do the same: it seems likely that those causes do not require a genetic predisposition.

Several sources of evidence relate to the possibility that early damage to the brain can contribute to the risk of schizophrenia. Neuropathological findings might reveal the nature of any brain alteration: birth injury might be the cause, viral infection is a possibility, and the effects of season of birth and immigration are relevant to environmental causes. They will be considered separately.

Neuropathological findings

Postmortem studies in the last decade have found that some structural brain abnormalities are more common in schizophrenia. Schizophrenic brains are, as a group, a little lighter than those of normal controls, and have smaller temporal lobe structures, but they do not usually show the gliosis that might be expected in a degenerative disorder (Bogerts *et al.*, 1985; Brown *et al.*, 1986; Bruton *et al.*, 1990). Jakob and Beckman (1986) found that schizophrenic brains are more likely to show heterotopic pre-alpha cells in the entorhinal cortex, suggesting an abnormality of neuronal migration (which would be expected to date from the first years of life).

In vivo studies by neuroimaging obviously give less pathological detail, but are consistent in finding an increased rate of abnormalities in schizophrenia, and allow for clinicopathological correlations. Cerebral ventricular enlargement has been found repeatedly in subgroups of people with schizophrenia; it is present very early in the evolution of the disoder (Nyback *et al.*, 1982; Weinberger *et al.*, 1982) and it is not related to the extent of treatment with neuroleptics (Williams *et al.*, 1985). Indeed, the study by Williams *et al.* (1985) suggested that larger ventricles were more probable in those with a poor social adjustment before the illness started.

Both histological and neuroimaging data are therefore suggestive — but not definitely confirmatory — of an early-onset and nonprogressive abnormality of the brain in some cases of schizophrenia. The findings come from group studies, and neuroimaging should not yet be a routine investigation for schizophrenia since the precision of findings is not yet good enough for individual diagnosis.

The aetiology of these findings is not yet known. They could be determined genetically, or they could result from damage to the developing brain. It has been claimed that they bear witness to an aetiology in brain damage, on the grounds that they may be more common in sporadic than in familial schizophrenia. The best evidence here is a replicated finding from neuroimaging studies of monozygotic twins who are discordant for schizophrenia. The affected twin is more likely to have enlarged ventricles and a decreased volume of the temporal lobe (Reveley *et al.*, 1982; Murray *et al.*, 1985; Suddath *et al.*, 1989). However, further thought should make it evident that these twin findings do not establish an environmental aetiology. Discordance in monozygotic twin pairs does not imply an environmental cause: as already described above, an unaffected co-twin is still likely to transmit the disorder, so there must be a genetic contribution even when a twin is unaffected. The cerebral changes in the affected twin therefore do *not* imply that they were environmentally caused; they are more likely to come about because of an effect of brain abnormalities upon the expression of an inherited tendency, or an effect of whatever factors lead to expression of the genotype upon cerebral structure.

Obstetric complications

There is little doubt that people with schizophrenia are more likely than the general population to have an abnormal birth history (Lewis & Murray, 1987). This association has been taken to imply that damage at birth may be sufficient to predispose an individual to schizophrenia. However, the meaning of the association is still in doubt and it would be premature to regard it as causal. There are uncertainties over the specificity of the finding, whether it can be attributed to confounding factors, the direction of causality, and the extent to which it characterizes an identifiable subgroup of those with schizophrenia.

Obstetric complications (OCS) are specific to schizophrenia in the sense that they are more common than in a mixed group of other adult psychiatric patients (Lewis & Murray, 1987). However, OCS are also more common in childhood developmental disorders such as hyperkinesis and intellectual retardation, and do not seem to be causative (see Chapter 6). It is possible therefore that the association is not with schizophrenia as such, but with the developmental impairment that may accompany it. Correlational studies within groups of patients suffering from schizophrenia suggest that the presence of OCS is linked to early onset of disorder (Lewis *et al.*, 1989), chronicity of disorder (McNeil & Kaij, 1978) and radiological abnormalities of the cerebral ventricles (Owen *et al.*, 1988). All these associations seem to be between OCS and neurodevelopmental impairment rather than with the syndrome of schizophrenia.

It is also important to appreciate that OCS are markers for other forms of disadvantage. Since poverty and low social class can characterize both schizophrenia and people encountering OCS, they will need to be allowed for before attributing causality to the OCS in either the group or the individual case. Indeed, the direction of causality may be from brain disorder to OCS rather than the other way round. A fetus with an abnormal brain is likely to encounter a more difficult birth experience (Goodman, 1988).

Even if damage at birth or in pregnancy were to be accepted as causal factors for schizophrenia — and, as we have seen, this is far from being the case in present knowledge — the question would still arise of whether they are sufficient causes in a subgroup, or contributing in interaction with other factors. One would expect, if OCS cause a predisposition in themselves, that they would be more common in schizophrenics who did not show evidence of other causes such as a genetic diathesis. The evidence here is conflicting: some studies do, and some do not, indicate that OCS are more common in schizophrenics without a family history of schizophrenia than in those from families with more than one affected member (reviewed by Lewis, 1990). No conclusion seems possible yet. Clinicians need to be very cautious before interpreting the pathogenic significance of OCS in a diagnostic formulation. They should certainly not be raising the possibility of schizophrenia merely because the pregnancy or birth was complicated.

Seasonality and virus infection

There appear to be season-of-birth effects in schizophrenia. More than 40 articles (reviewed by Bradbury & Miller, 1985), taken together, yield a strong case for an increased rate of winter births among schizophrenic patients who are known to therapeutic services. The effect varies with geographical location: for example, it is stronger in the northern than in the southern states of the US. The reasons are not known with any certainty; they are often taken to point to a seasonally varying pathogen such as an infective agent, but are not known to be accounted for by any such agent.

Mednick *et al.* (1987) were able to relate the clinical diagnosis of schizophrenia to birth information in a cohort of young adults in Copenhagen. An A2 influenza epidemic occurred in 1957 and could be timed from records of hospital admissions. The later development of schizophrenia was more common in those who had been in the second trimester of gestation during the epidemic. Accordingly, efforts have been made to link the dates of birth of people with known schizophrenia to historical records of influenza rates. Maternal infection with influenza during the second trimester of gestation has been associated epidemiologically with the later development of schizophrenia in some studies, but not others (Eaton, 1991). Sham *et al.* (1992) reported national data from England and Wales in 1938–1960 and estimated that between 1 and 2% of schizophrenic births could be explained by the number of influenza deaths in the previous months. This is obviously circumstantial evidence; though persuasive, it does not amount to a known pathogenesis. One of the research problems is the unsatisfactory nature of the nationally and routinely gathered data about schizophrenia admissions.

Immigration

It has been apparent for 20 years, from routinely gathered admission data, that first-admission rates for schizophrenia among first-generation Afro-Carribean migrants to the UK are raised two- or threefold (Glover, 1989). This increase is not found in other migrant groups, such as those from Asia. The reasons for this have attracted much controversy. Littlewood and Lipsedge (1981), for example, administered a standardized psychiatric interview to a series of patients admitted with religious delusions, found a different pattern of symptomatology in West Indian migrants, and suggested that very many were showing acute reactive disturbances, for which 'schizophrenia' was a misdiagnosis. Racism in the mental health services was therefore suggested as a contribution to the apparently high rates of diagnosis, and received some support from the further finding of disproportionately high rates of compulsory detention and police involvement (Harrison *et al.*, 1984). On the other hand, a case vignette study by Lewis *et al.* (1990) examined the diagnostic practices of British psychiatrists directly, and concluded that any stereotyping worked the other way round, i.e. the psychiatrists involved underdiagnosed schizophrenia in patients identified as West Indian by comparison with white patients.

A prospective study, based on an epidemiological catchment area in Nottingham using standardized case-finding techniques and extensive contextual histories of symptom exclusion, was therefore of considerable significance (Harrison *et al.*, 1988). The findings were contrary to the expectations of the investigators: the annual incidence rates for the 16–29 age group were 29 per 10 000 in the Afro-Caribbeans and 2 in the non-Caribbean general population. Allowing for errors in measurement, the rate for Afro-Caribbeans was at least six times higher than in the general population. This rate was based on a rigorous and operational definition of schizophrenia that should have excluded reactive psychoses.

This very large difference was not attributable to elective migration. The vast majority of cases were second-generation — they had either been born in the UK or had been brought in as children. The difference is so great that it seems to point to an environmental cause; but it does not by itself favour any one of the major aetiological theories. The difference is present both for males and females, and both for those migrants born in the West Indies and those born in the UK. Routinely gathered statistics suggest that the risk may be greater for those from Jamaica than those from Trinidad (Glover, 1989). Certainly further research will need to take account of the detailed operation of specific causes. The epidemic cannot be attributed solely to the experience of immigration as it is affecting selectively those from the Caribbean.

Obstetric damage has been suggested, especially as Afro-Caribbean infants are not only more likely than Europeans to be of low birth weight (which would apply equally to Asian babies), but also (unlike Asians) are more likely to survive low birth weight (Griffiths *et al.*, 1989). However, as indicated above, complications are not an established cause of schizophrenia. Exposure to unfamiliar viruses is also a possible explanation, as considered above, but cannot yet be regarded as anything more than one possibility among many.

Psychogenic factors

While popular in art (e.g. Ophelia or Lucia di Lammermoor), with the lay public and with some professionals, the notion of psychological factors as a primary cause of schizophrenia has lost credence, mostly for lack of evidence despite decades of research (Goldstein, 1987). Emphasis therefore has shifted to the stress-diathesis model (Goldstein, 1987), in which psychosocial factors are seen interacting with biological, especially in affecting the course of the disorder once established. The power of psychosocial procedures has been repeatedly rediscovered, for example, in the 'moral treatment of the insane' of the late 18th century, Bleuler's work ethos for patients, the 'open door policy' of the 1950s, and the community care of the present era, with its carefully focused social skills training (Liberman *et al.*, 1986; Brenner *et al.*, 1990; Wing, 1990). Research has focused on chronic adversity, the effects of defined life events and the influence of close personal (especially family) relationships.

Psychiatric epidemiology has consistently found a disproportionate number of schizophrenics in inner-city areas with high levels of social adversity. The classic study by Faris and Dunham (1939) in Chicago suggested that social drift was responsible. The issue was studied further by British investigators who distinguished the social class of people with schizophrenia from that of their families of origin. Goldberg and Morrison (1963) found that hospital patients were in lower status occupations than their fathers: the parental generation did not show an excess of adverse social conditions. The conclusion seems clear: that the chronic adversity under which so many schizophrenics live is the result rather than the initiating cause of their condition.

Most studies of EOS have not shown this lower social class bias but this is probably an artefact of referral patterns in centres doing most of the studies (Werry, 1992). Schizophrenia is common in the homeless (Lamb, 1990), and a study of homeless adolescents in the US revealed that 29% had four or more 'psychotic' symptoms (Mundy *et al.*, 1990). Though the study was not designed to yield psychiatric diagnoses, it suggests that EOS is similar to later-onset schizophrenia in contributing to vagrancy.

Acute stresses have been studied as precipitants of schizophrenic illness. The best known work is still that of Brown and Birley (1968) who recorded the occurrence of life events in the 3 months prior to an acute hospital admission, and found a significant excess in the 3 weeks before onset by comparison with nonschizophrenic controls. The effect extended even to independent events that could scarcely be the result of illness; they had the effect of bringing forward the time of onset of symptoms rather than of being a sufficient cause (Brown *et al.*, 1972).

The best established psychosocial influence is that of

stressors on the patient arising within the family, especially from parents (Goldstein, 1987). While many theories have come and gone, the most sustained, most reliably measurable and best validated arise from the systematic work of the Maudsley group of Brown, Leff, Rutter and others (see Hirsch & Leff, 1975). Having first noted that patients discharged to parental care did worse than those who went to other relatives or lodgings, they were then able to define the specific stressors as negative affective ambience or expressed emotion, as it is now more commonly known. A number of studies have shown expressed emotion to the patients to be implicated in the production of relapses (Goldstein, 1987; Kane, 1987), and when this emotion is specifically addressed and improved, the rate is reduced (Leff *et al.*, 1982; Goldstein, 1987), suggesting some causal connection.

However, recent studies in child and adolescent psychiatry (Hibbs *et al.*, 1991; Sanchez-Lachay *et al.*, 1991; Stubbe *et al.*, 1991) have shown that the changes described in families of adults with schizophrenia are not specific to that disorder, occurring in most families with an adolescent suicide attempter, or with a child with a disruptive behaviour disorder, and in nearly a quarter of families seen in a community child psychiatric clinic. Critical comments were associated particularly with disruptive behaviour disorders, and emotional over-involvement with anxiety disorders. This does not, of course, diminish the power of the hypothesis or role of treatment in schizophrenia, only its specificity.

Pathogenesis

Whether the causes are genetic or environmental, it will be important to identify the neurological and psychological changes through which the disorder is brought about.

At a *neurochemical* level, the main contender is the dopamine hypothesis which is derived from the observation that most of the effective antipsychotic drugs are dopamine blockers. This theory posits overactivity in the mesolimbic dopaminergic system which has important regulatory functions in cognition, motivation and emotion. Apart from psychopharmacological support, there are some not unanimous receptor studies that suggest overactivity or supersensitivity of D_2-receptors (Meltzer, 1987). However, other biogenic substances like noradrenaline (Brier *et al.*, 1990), neuropeptides and serotonin (Meltzer, 1987) have also been implicated. Positron and single photon emission tomography make it possible to assay neurotransmitter receptors in different regions of the brain. This has confirmed that most current neuroleptic drugs probably work through blockade of dopamine (D_2) receptors; but that clozapine has a different mechanism — probably serotonin or D_4 receptors are involved (Pilowsky *et al.*, 1992).

Neurodevelopmental abnormalities have been described in subgroups of people with schizophrenia. They include speech and language delays, 'soft' signs, lowered intelligence, decreased span of attention and hypofrontality (Aylward *et al.*, 1984; Asarnow *et al.*, 1989; Walker & Lewine, 1990). All these phenomena are more common in EOS, especially VEOS, than

in adults, and they often predate the onset of psychosis (Asarnow *et al.*, 1989).

The relationship between these different sorts of abnormality is still not fully worked out. Crow (1985) proposed two types of schizophrenia: one inherited and marked by acute symptomatology and neurochemical changes (type 1) and the other marked by chronic deficit symptoms and neuropathological changes (type 2). The distinction was elaborated by Murray and Lewis (1987) and Weinberger (1987), with the extension of the type 2 into a neurodevelopmental disorder, based on early brain damage, with premorbid impairment and a chronic course. The idea has several implications that need drawing out separately.

Firstly, there is no doubt that schizophrenia can have an insidious onset and can be preceded by years of poor social adjustment. Zeitlin (1986) provided a case-note study of individuals who had been patients at a psychiatric hospital both as adults and as children. The resulting group, while highly selected, was well-chosen for examining continuities of disorder. Individuals with a diagnosis of schizophrenia in adult life were often characterized as children by a combination of developmental delays and personality abnormalities. Retrospective studies of adult schizophrenics have emphasized that those with early onset of illness are especially likely to have shown poor childhood adjustment (Foerster *et al.*, 1991).

Secondly, the premorbid abnormalities are not simply the nonspecific presence of psychiatric disturbance. Neurological and cognitive changes are disproportionately common (Zeitlin, 1986). It remains to be seen whether there is anything specific about these developmental changes or whether they would show the same range of abnormalities as in children with developmental delays who do not develop schizophrenia. Longitudinal studies of children at high risk are relevant here: a few investigations have followed the offspring of schizophrenics from childhood to early adult life. Erlenmeyer-Kimling and Cornblatt (1987) found that high-risk children, who suffered psychiatric hospitalization as young adults, were characterized as children by impaired scores on a range of tests of their attention (continuous performance test, span of apprehension and digit span). This does not yet prove that the premorbid changes are a specific result of brain disorder, for they might have been part of a generalized cognitive impairment. Nevertheless, the similarity to the attentional impairment that is frequently found in schizophrenia adds some evidence to the possibility of a developmental track that leads through impaired attention to schizophrenia.

Thirdly, the neuropathological changes reviewed above are comparable with a very early onset, and their association with cognitive impairment allows for the possibility that they might be causal. However, the evidence for their resulting from brain damage is scanty, and the argument for a distinct syndrome of neurological impairment is correspondingly flawed. Nevertheless, even if this 'strong' form of the neurodevelopmental hypothesis were to fail, the hypothesis that early neurodevelopmental changes are precursors of some forms of schizophrenia commands a good deal of support.

The premorbid changes are not yet distinctive enough to make a confident diagnosis of incipient schizophrenia in childhood. They may however reasonably be taken to contribute to the clinical questions of giving a prognosis for children who are the offspring of schizophrenic parents and of whether a disturbance in such a child is likely to be the beginning of schizophrenia.

EPIDEMIOLOGY

Schizophrenia has a whole-life prevalence of a little less than 1%, and an incidence of about 0.1% per year, though rates are greatly influenced by the criteria used and the group studied (Torrey, 1987). Comparisons between different areas are hazardous because of varying diagnostic practices. Nationally collected statistics of first contacts with psychiatric services have been collated for Scotland by Eagles et al. (1988) and for England by Der et al. (1990): both suggest that the incidence may have fallen through the 1970s and 1980s. The conclusion is weak, however, because of the possibility of shifts in diagnostic practice over this time. The frequency of EOS is unknown, though VEOS is clearly rare. There is a rapid increase in adolescence, with peak incidences reached in males between the ages of 15 and 25 and in females about 25–35 (Zigler & Levine, 1981), after which there is a rapid decline.

Earlier studies generally describe an approximately equal number of men and women in series of people with schizophrenia; more recently, a slight male preponderance has been described (Lewin, 1988). It is not clear whether the change is due to a secular trend or the adoption of more stringent diagnostic criteria.

It is much clearer that there are substantial differences between males and females with a diagnosis of schizophrenia. Schizophrenic males have long been known to show an earlier age of onset, worse premorbid adjustment, more cognitive impairment and a less favourable response to neuroleptic drugs (reviewed by Goldstein & Tsuang, 1990). This pattern of differences raises the possibility that the gender differences arise because of bias in the diagnosis: perhaps many women with affective disorders are misclassified as schizophrenic. It is therefore important to note that the same pattern of gender differences is found when standardized interview techniques are used to make the diagnosis (Goldstein & Link, 1988).

Comparisons between males and females with diagnosed schizophrenia have shown other differences. Affected females are more likely than males to have relatives with a diagnosis of schizophrenia (Bellodi et al., 1986); by the same token, female monozygotic twins have higher concordance rates than males (Kringlen, 1987). In spite of this genetic loading, the outcome is better for females (Salokangas & Stengard, 1990). This better outlook is less surprising in that some female characteristics (more affective symptoms, better premorbid adjustment) are also good prognostic signs.

These findings have led to the suggestion that the gender differences come about because a lower proportion of female than male patients suffer from the 'neurodevelopmental' type of schizophrenia (Castle & Murray, in press). Direct evidence for this is lacking, but some support comes from a latent class analytic approach applied by Goldstein et al. (1990) to two cohort family studies from Iowa. The analysis tested whether there was a subgroup of schizophrenic men who showed low familial risk, deficit symptoms, poor premorbid adjustment and winter birth. They found that men were, as expected, more likely to meet these criteria — but some women also met them. The conclusion was that both males and females had similar subtypes of schizophrenia, but the prevalence was different.

COURSE AND OUTCOME

The course of schizophrenia is variable (Eggers, 1978; Carpenter & Kirkpatrick, 1988). Some of this is due to differences in definition (Westermeyer & Harrow, 1988) but there is also variation across individuals and at different times within individuals (Eggers, 1978). Nevertheless, the disorder is usually fluctuating, with each episode often marked by prodrome, active and recuperative phases, followed by recovery/quiescent/residual periods (Kane, 1987), as outlined above. While on average episodes last about 1 year and probably longer in VEOS (Asarnow et al., 1991; Spencer et al., 1991), these figures are rough guidelines only, but do emphasize the need for patience in dealing with this disorder. The number of episodes in a life-time in EOS can vary from 1 to very many (Eggers, 1978). In adults the disorder tends to reach a plateau after about 5–10 years (McGlashan, 1988a; Westermeyer & Harrow, 1988) and/or about 4 active episodes (Angst, 1988).

In adults, the reported recovery rate is 25–40% (Westermeyer & Harrow, 1988). Studies of outcome in EOS are infrequent (Asarnow et al., 1991; Werry et al., 1991; Werry, 1992). While it is widely held that outcome is worse than the adult figure of 25% recovery, the difference in fact is small. One study found that older onset augured a slightly worse prognosis, though there were few cases of VEOS (Werry & McClellan, 1992). What seems clear, though, is that only a very small minority will recover without further episodes.

Another issue is that of continued decline. Here the data in EOS are scant but, as in the adult disorder, some continued deterioration seems to be common (Asarnow et al., 1991; Werry et al., 1991), though the degree is variable (Eggers, 1978).

Predictive factors have been considered above: in adults, they include female sex, good premorbid personality and function, an acute onset, precipitating events, confusional states and a family history of mood disorder. The World Health Organization international study of schizophrenia (Sartorius et al., 1986) has suggested that the prognosis may be better in developing countries — perhaps because of a higher rate of acute forms of illness, perhaps because of better social supports (Sartorius et al., 1986). In one of the few formal studies of predictors of longer-term outcome in EOS

(Werry & McClellan, 1992), it was found that practically all the variance was explained by premorbid function and personality, and degree of recovery from the first episode.

From the clinical perspective then, EOS has to be regarded as a serious, episodic but ultimately usually chronic progressive disorder producing considerable disability and requiring continued psychiatric supervision. One hopeful note is that when the disorder finally becomes quiescent, there may be a very slow but limited improvement over many years (Angst, 1988).

COMPLICATIONS

Suicide is the commonest cause of premature death for people with schizophrenia: the life-time risk is about 15%, with most of the suicides occurring within 10 years of the onset of the disorder (Caldwell & Gottesman, 1990; Cohen *et al.*, 1990). This mortality rate is clinically significant — much higher than in a similar age cohort and as high as in affective disorders where the risk is better recognized (Caldwell & Gottesman, 1990). Whether the risk is higher in EOS cannot yet be answered since data are few and samples small (Asarnow *et al.*, 1991; Werry, 1992).

Several studies have compared schizophrenics who have killed themselves with control groups of schizophrenics who have not. Statistical associations of suicide in this group have been found, but the level of predictiveness for individuals is too low to allow really effective prevention. Some of the associations of suicide would characterize any group of people killing themselves: male gender; depressive symptoms and, especially, hopelessness (Drake & Cotton, 1986; Roy *et al.*, 1986); social isolation; and a history of previous suicide attempts (Nyman & Jonsson, 1986; Allebeck *et al.*, 1987). Other factors are more specific to schizophrenia: young men with high levels of premorbid functioning and high expectations are particularly at risk (Dingman & McGlashan, 1986; Caldwell & Gottesman, 1990). The period after discharge is a particularly dangerous time (Barner-Rasmussen, 1986).

The services for young people with schizophrenia need to be very aware of this high risk, and to place an emphasis upon supporting self-esteem and helping to sustain patients through their downward revision of personal expectations.

Deteriorating academic performance and failure to acquire vocational skills, social drift and incompetence with its attendant risk of self-neglect and victimization, loss to follow-up and noncompliance with treatment are probably the most important complications clinically. Caplan *et al.* (1990) also posited that in VEOS there may be a serious disruption of the normal development of listener-sensitive skills vital to communication. As noted above, schizophrenia in young persons is an important contribution to homelessness (Mundy *et al.*, 1990), though this affects only a small minority of patients.

While the public greatly fears schizophrenic patients and often wishes them put out of sight, there is much more of a risk of social embarrassment and unacceptable nonconformity than of frank aggression. When crimes of violence are committed by psychiatric patients, they attract a notoriety which makes them seem more frequent than they really are.

Recent pushes towards deinstitutionalization in the US show that incarceration is a complication of the disorder, less because of crimes than of public nuisance and the absence of systems of community care (Lamb, 1990). Nevertheless, threats to public safety and to prominent figures do occur occasionally — the M'Naughten Rules resulted from the assassination of Prime Minister Peel's secretary in the UK and the White House security staff in the US deal each year with a surprisingly large number of deluded patients who threaten the President (Shore *et al.*, 1989).

DIFFERENTIAL DIAGNOSIS

Autism

This is distiguished by the absence, transitoriness, insignificance or insufficiency of the key schizophrenic symptoms (especially hallucinations and delusions), and the pervasiveness and predominance of the characteristic language patterns, unrelatedness, and other key symptoms of autism (Kolvin, 1971; Green *et al.*, 1984; Green & Padron-Gayol, 1986; Volkmar *et al.*, 1988). The very early onset that is usual for autism should also help in differential diagnosis. Though some schizophrenic children have been abnormal since infancy (Watkins *et al.*, 1988; Asarnow *et al.*, 1989; Werry, 1992), this premorbid abnormality is less developmentally catastrophic than in autism.

There may be special difficulties in nonverbal children such as the mentally retarded, but marked behavioural change with externally observable signs of schizophrenia can be suggestive. A trial of antipsychotic medication may help to clarify the diagnosis. Whether or not children with autism can subsequently become schizophrenic, either independently or by having a greater vulnerability, is a different issue. There is no reason *a priori* that the two should not coexist by chance (Watkins *et al.*, 1988). If early brain damage facilitates the onset of both disorders, the risk could well be raised. DSM has a special differential diagnostic criterion for schizophrenia that, if autism has been diagnosed previously, hallucinations or delusions must now be prominent.

There are now a few reports of both disorders coexisting (Petty *et al.*, 1984; Watkins *et al.*, 1988; Volkmar & Cohen, 1991) with, as expected, the onset of schizophrenia much later than that of autism (ordinarily after age 5). However, this comorbidity appears rare and the risk is not increased — Volkmar and Cohen (1991) found only 1 such case in a sample of 163 well-documented cases of autism, though not all had yet attained the age of maximum incidence for schizophrenia.

Schizotypal and schizoid disorders

Schizoid disorder is characterized primarily by egocentricity and aloofness from human relationships and schizotypal disorder by eccentricity and oddness of ideation short of frank thought disorder or delusions (see Chapter 38). Ordinarily, differential diagnosis from schizophrenia should not be a problem if DSM-IV (American Psychiatric Association, in press) or ICD-10 (World Health Organization, 1992) criteria are followed, since both schizotypal and schizoid disorders are characterized by a life-style that is usually neither totally incapacitating nor characterized by inexorably deteriorating function, there is no active psychotic phase and schizophrenic-positive-type symptoms are mild, localized and/or inconspicuous in schizotypal disorder and absent in schizoid disorder. However, schizoid and especially schizotypal disorder may present considerable diagnostic difficulty when function is marginal, and/or where there is continuing deterioration with no clear point of onset and/or presence but insufficiency of positive symptoms (Cantor *et al.*, 1982; Asarnow & Ben-Meir, 1988; Volkmar *et al.*, 1988; Caplan *et al.*, 1990; Russell, 1992).

There is a belief, anchored by some data, that schizotypal disorder is linked to schizophrenia by familial distribution, as a risk factor and symptomatologically as merely a milder version (Asarnow *et al.*, 1989; Andrews, 1990). Thus, some of this effort to separate them may be spurious. In ICD-10 this spectrum concept is recognized in that schizotypal disorder is placed in the group which includes schizophrenia rather than among the personality disorders; but DSM-IV does not follow suit. There are some data to support this spectrum view in children (Caplan *et al.*, 1990; Russell, 1992). It has therefore become common to find studies in children combining schizotypal and schizophrenic children, no doubt, at least partly, to increase sample sizes (Volkmar *et al.*, 1988; Caplan *et al.*, 1990; Asarnow *et al.*, 1991; Butler *et al.*, 1991; Russell, 1992).

It may be asked whether it is important clinically to separate schizotypal disorder and schizophrenia. In doubtful cases, it seems sensible to carry out a trial of antipsychotic medication, remembering that schizotypal disorder may also respond to medication, in much lower dosage (Andrews, 1990). On the other hand, it seems premature simply to state that the substantial literature on schizophrenia applies equally to schizotypal disorder. Before leaving schizotypal and schizoid disorder, as Russell (1992) points out, it is worth noting that there are two main types of strange children — one whose symptomatology is more like autism, where the most prominent feature is lack of interest in social interaction with rigid patterns of behaviour, and the other characterized more by eccentricity of behaviour and ideation, which is more like schizophrenia. In DSM terms these would be schizoid and schizotypal personality disorders but in children, whose cognition is immature, it may be more difficult to separate them than Russell implies (Petti & Vela, 1990). A further complication is that Petti and Vela include Asperger's disorder in this group as well.

Mood disorders

There is good evidence that, when the presentation of major depression or mania in adolescence or childhood is accompanied by hallucinations, delusions or thought disorder, the differential diagnosis from schizophrenia may be very difficult (Joyce, 1984; Bashir *et al.*, 1987; McGlashan, 1988b; Strober *et al.*, 1989; Carlson, 1990; Werry *et al.*, 1991). There is a large overlap between schizophrenic and affective symptomatology (Apter *et al.*, 1987; Bashir *et al.*, 1987; McGlashan, 1988b; Russell *et al.*, 1989; Carlson, 1990). The error has operated largely to misclassify psychotic mood disorder as schizophrenia (Joyce, 1984; Carlson, 1990; Werry *et al.*, 1991), though some of the cases may be schizoaffective (McGlashan, 1988b; Eggers, 1989). Rules for differential diagnosis are given in DSM-IV (positive symptoms occurring for more than 2 weeks in the absence of manic or depressed mood), but difficulty is admitted. Strober *et al.* (1989) emphasize premorbid social withdrawal/anxiety, insidiousness of onset, mood-incongruent delusions/hallucinations and protractedness as more characteristic of schizophrenia, though none is absolute. Homotypic family history may also be helpful in alerting to the possibility of bipolar disorder (Werry *et al.*, 1991). Nevertheless, the picture in children and adolescents may become clear only with time and calls for punctilious follow-up of all cases of EOS (Werry *et al.*, 1991).

Schizoaffective disorder

This term has a variety of meanings to describe patients who have both mood and schizophrenic symptoms. ICD-10 merely requires the coexistence of prominent mood and schizophrenic symptoms such that a clear diagnosis of either disorder cannot be made. In DSM, three criteria are required: overlap in time between mood and schizophrenic symptoms, the occurrence at some point of schizophrenic symptoms in the absence of mood symptoms, and mood symptoms being a prominent and sustained part of the clinical picture. There are two main subtypes, schizomanic and schizodepressive (Samson *et al.*, 1988). Some children and adolescents first diagnosed as schizophrenic will incur a diagnosis of schizoaffective disorder at longer-term follow-up (Eggers, 1989; Werry *et al.*, in press).

The importance of making this differential diagnosis is tied to the validity of schizoaffective disorder as a category. Patients with the combination of schizophrenic and affective symptoms resemble those with affective disorders in neurodevelopmental status: they show less cognitive impairment than those with schizophrenia (Lindenmeyer *et al.*, 1989), and they less often have a history of obstetric complications (Foerster *et al.*, 1991). Their outcome is considerably better then than that of schizophrenic people with no affective symptoms, but worse than for affective disorders (Kendler & Tsuang, 1988). They show raised frequencies of both schizophrenic and mood disorders in relatives (Samson *et al.*, 1988) and, most importantly, addition of mood-adjusting drugs may increase benefits over use of antipsychotic medication alone. Scientific uncertainty over the status of the category remains; it is wise to include it in clinical formulations because of prognostic and therapeutic implications.

Organic disorders

Obviously, these are best diagnosed by finding a clear-cut physical cause, but this is not always possible. Dementias in childhood are rare and usually characterized by marked intellectual decline and neurological signs, rather than positive schizophrenic symptoms (Gudex & Werry, 1990). Delirium is more likely to be confused with schizophrenia since hallucinations and ill-formed delusions may be present, and not all children with delirium are obviously physically ill. However, with careful examination, including neuropsychological testing where necessary, it will be found that disorientation is not present in schizophrenia and intellectual function is better preserved, though not unaffected (Aylward *et al.*, 1984; Caplan *et al.*, 1990). Drug-induced delirium is always a possibility in children and adolescents, and requires careful review for both medical and illicit substances which might be causal. On the whole though, psychiatric aspects of delirium and dementia have been little studied in children (Gudex & Werry, 1990) so their phenomenology is rather unclear.

Other psychoses

This is a heterogeneous group of relatively unresearched disorders that are of particular interest in children and adolescents. They may differ from schizophrenia in several respects. Firstly, there are disorders that show rapidity of recovery, or insufficient duration for schizophrenia (acute schizophrenia-like psychotic disorder). Many of these will prove to be schizophrenia after continued observation or upon recurrence (Werry *et al.*, 1991; Werry *et al.*, in press). Secondly, symptomatology may be insufficient or changing too rapidly to meet the diagnosis of schizophrenia (delusional disorder, acute psychotic disorder or atypical psychosis). Thirdly, the presence of clear and unusual stressors may suggest the brief reactive form of acute psychosis. Great care is needed in making this controversial diagnosis (Torrey, 1987; Angst, 1988) since there is a close similarity with the criteria for schizophrenia that is not helped by the substitution of an *internal* state common in acute schizophrenia (emotional turmoil) for its *external* consequences (social dysfunction), allowing the admission of stressors (which may result from, rather than cause, the onset of schizophrenia), and a short duration which can occur in the first episode or prodrome of what turns out subsequently to be schizophrenia (Werry *et al.*, in press). Such reactive psychoses are said to be more common in developing countries or immigrants from them (Torrey, 1987). Some of these cases will prove to be malingering or dissociative states. Inconsistent and outlandish symptomatology and/or rapid fluctuations between psychotic and normal states should raise suspicion.

Borderline (personality) disorder

This disorder has not been well-studied in children and adolescents, even though the term, derived from psychoanalysis, has been around for many years and has been used in a variety of ways in children, adding to the confusion (Petti & Vela, 1990). The characteristic symptoms are intense, demanding interpersonal relationships, emotional instability, impulsiveness, self-harm and hallucinations (see Chapter 38).

Alcohol and drug abuse

These can present difficulty, especially where the symptomatology is characterized by hallucinosis rather than full delirium. A high index of suspicion, careful enquiry and appropriate toxicological tests are needed. Short-lived episodes of a few hours are highly suggestive of drug-induced states. However, the position may be quite complicated when there is a history of abuse of alcohol and/or drugs like cannabis (as is frequently the case; Dixon *et al.*, 1991) but the psychosis endures. Not surprisingly, the risk of such concurrence is increased by a family history of abuse and adolescent adjustment problems (Dixon *et al.*, 1991). While there is some connection between abuse and the onset or relapse of schizophrenia, the nature of this relationship is unclear — it may be causal/precipitant or it may represent self-medication of symptoms of schizophrenia. Drug abuse does not necessarily augur a worse prognosis, possibly since to get and use drugs requires some degree of personality integration (Dixon *et al.*, 1991).

TREATMENT

Children and adolescents with schizophrenia present a challenge to the clinician since they are seriously and repeatedly ill, and even during periods of quiescence their educational and social development often continues to be disrupted. Further, their position of dependence within a family or similar social network broadens the context of treatment. As noted, in order to treat schizophrenic persons, it is essential to have a good grasp of the *course* of schizophrenia and the *limitations of treatment* — while therapies can lessen the frequency and severity of psychotic episodes and reduce disability, none can, as yet, cure the disorder (McGlashan, 1988a). Without this knowledge, overtreatment, frequent and premature changes of treatment or therapists, overoptimism and misinformation to caretakers will result. It is equally important to understand the symptomatology and particular disabilities which schizophrenia produces. On the whole, positive symptoms call for a different approach from negative ones. By their high social visibility, the former attract more attention and opprobrium; but by blunting affect, impoverishing thinking and eroding zest, negative symptoms are particularly distressing to relatives and to patients, because they are the ones most destructive of remembered premorbid levels of personal and social functions. Both positive and negative symptoms make compliance with treatment programmes difficult by eliding insight, producing immobility, social unacceptability and inertia (Amador *et al.*, 1991). This means that an unusual degree of energy, persistence and active outreach is needed in treatment.

In case management, two major themes may be defined, though this separation is artificial and neither can operate without the other: (1) *nonspecific* management, which is person-, patient- and family-oriented, largely pragmatic and mostly derived from general therapeutic principles, clinical wisdom and humanism; (2) *specific* treatment — for schizophrenia. The knowledge for this comes largely from the scientific study of schizophrenia, is disorder-oriented and transcends any particular patient in broad principles.

Nonspecific management

Here the emphasis is on a severely ill or handicapped child or adolescent and on accurate assessment of distress, abilities and disabilities and how best to relieve suffering and adjust the child to the world and the world to the child. This calls for all the usual skills of the multidisciplinary child mental health team well-anchored in a knowledge of community resources. These general measures, despite the probably neurobiological aetiology of schizophrenia, play a major part in the management of schizophrenic children and adolescents (Liberman *et al.*, 1986; Goldstein, 1987; Brenner *et al.*, 1990; Amador *et al.*, 1991). The only special features in patients with schizophrenia — and then only a matter of frequency and degree — stem from proneness to severe disabilities like inertia, eccentricity, poor social judgement, lack of insight and noncompliance (Amador *et al.*, 1991).

An argument can be made not to refer patients on to adult services prematurely. While adult services may be very skilled in the management of schizophrenia, few have good understanding of the special needs of children and adolescents, especially of their need for supervision, protection and education and of the necessity for dealing with the whole family. It is therefore important that, wherever, possible, regional child and adolescent psychiatric services have the full range of services needed to take care of young schizophrenic patients and their families — inpatient, daypatient, paediatric, educational, activity, respite, community, rehabilitative and welfare.

Specific treatment

Unfortunately, there is very little research on treatment in EOS and therefore it is necessary to work from the assumption that EOS and adult schizophrenia are the same disorder or group of disorders (McClellan & Werry, 1992).

Pharmacotherapy

Drugs used in the treatment of schizophrenia are considered in Chapter 51, and clinical issues are emphasized here. *This short summary should not be taken as sufficient to practise pharmacotherapy in schizophrenia and fuller discussions should be consulted* (e.g. Bassuck *et al.*, 1983; Kane, 1987; Dollfuss & Petit, 1988; McClellan & Werry, 1992; Werry & Aman, 1993).

Antipsychotic (neuroleptic) medication is the cornerstone of treatment and there is now massive evidence to show that, though there are many unanswered questions, these drugs are very helpful in schizophrenia in adults (Kane, 1987). There is no evidence to support the widely held view that pharmacotherapy is ineffective in EOS — in fact, the very few studies suggest the contrary (Dollfus & Petit, 1988, pp. 14–15; McClellan & Werry, 1992; Spencer *et al.*, 1992). Despite many claims of superiority upon introduction, with the exception of clozapine, no active neuroleptic has been shown to be any more effective than any other against the disorder, particular subtypes or symptoms or individuals (Kane, 1987). Although antipsychotic efficacy is similar, side-effects do differ in number and type (primarily preponderance of atropinic or extrapyramidal) and individual drugs may be preferred on this account. It is generally recommended that the clinician should be thoroughly familiar with two or three drugs with different side-effect profiles rather than the whole spectrum (McClellan & Werry, 1992).

Depot preparations, in which a single injection will last as long as 1 month, have a place when compliance by patient or family is poor. In some countries these preparations have not been approved for use in children. Most take several weeks to achieve a pharmacodynamic equilibrium and it is customary to stabilize the patient first on oral medication to establish dosage levels, efficacy and side-effects. While neuroleptics do not cure the disorder (McGlashan, 1988a), they can mitigate acute psychotic symptoms and prevent relapses in a majority. There are some patients who respond poorly and a few do just as well (or rather, badly) without medication (Kane, 1987; Brenner *et al.*, 1990).

Therapeutic failure can result from incorrect dosage or failure to persist; the International Group for the Study of Refractory Schizophrenia requires a period of 2 years of continuous symptoms despite 'reasonable and customary' pharmacological and psychosocial treatment before a diagnosis of *refractory* may be made (Brenner *et al.*, 1990). It is important to note, too, in this definition that since psychosocial treatment can have an enhancing effect on medication (Goldstein, 1987), apparent refractoriness to drugs may be due to failure to combine it with psychosocial treatment.

The side-effects of antipsychotic medication are common, so proper advance warning must be given, and patients must be examined regularly so as to minimize their effects through reducing dosage if possible, changing from one class of antipsychotic to another or using antidotal substances.

Other drugs are also in use. Lithium, carbamazepine and other antimanic drugs have been tried in schizophrenia and are said to be helpful when there is a history of manic-like episodes. Similarly, antidepressants may occasionally be helpful, particularly in the postpsychotic (recuperative) phase which may take depressive features. None of these is yet properly established (McClellan & Werry, 1992) and they bring all the risks that come with polypharmacy. In individual cases, however, it may be worth trying these drugs with careful monitoring of effects and, wherever possible, within a baseline/treatment/baseline paradigm.

The value of electroconvulsive therapy in schizophrenia is controversial, but it may have some value in severely catatonic patients whose lives are in danger because of insufficient fluid and electrolyte intake (Andrews, 1984).

Psychosocial interventions

In contrast to the clear-cut role of medication, the role of psychosocial treatments specific for schizophrenia is vexatious because, with a few exceptions, research in this area has generally been of poor quality (Goldstein, 1987; Kane, 1987). There is a strong need for investigations using blind raters, standardized measures and adequately long follow-up. Whereas the emphasis 20 years ago was on trying to cure the disorder, there has been a marked shift towards mitigating the disability and preventing relapse and away from specific to nonspecific psychosocial interventions (see above). The potential for psychosocial interventions is clear. The predictive power of psychosocial variables on the course of disorder and the transcultural differences in outcome suggest that it should be possible to modify the course.

A handful of studies has shown that interventions specifically aimed at family-expressed emotion can improve outcome. This treatment is targeted on behaviour emitted by parents (expressed emotion) and relies heavily on educational methods (Goldstein, 1987; Liberman, 1988). It is time-consuming and requires training. It is important to remember that the patient's 'family' is whatever group the patient is living in — including hospital. A promising line of investigation suggests that there may be some interaction between pharmacotherapy and this type of family intervention, in that there may be patients who respond better to one than the other, and/or patients whose maintenance dose may be lowered if concomitant family intervention is made.

Another proven area is behavioural intervention. Social skills training is valuable in adults with schizophrenia (Liberman *et al.*, 1986; Goldstein, 1987; Liberman, 1988). It draws on assumptions and techniques used in other disorders, that should be readily transferable to schizophrenia by any competent behaviour therapist. Special 'packages' for schizophrenia are available (Liberman, 1988). Cognitive-behavioural therapy aims to teach self-control of symptoms, and can achieve clinical remission, even in some drug-resistant cases (Tarrier *et al.*, in press). There is no evidence that insight-oriented psychotherapy is helpful in schizophrenia and indeed it may be harmful (Goldstein, 1987; Kane, 1987).

Other lines of management should also be made available, though good controlled evidence of their efficiency is still lacking and will need more research. They include efforts to develop a satisfactory social network around a patient, given that many young patients become very isolated within their families. Early and crisis intervention strategies need an adequately organized and responsive team that has a sufficiently trusting relationship with patient and family that relapses can be detected early and treated vigorously. Education and training for employment may require sheltered residential settings, especially for the most impaired young

people where adverse family interactions cannot be modified. Chronic illness can be helped by strategies emphasizing coping with illness and giving to individuals and their families enough knowledge and practical strategies to help them adjust — such as skills in controlling delusional thinking (Chadwick & Lowe, 1990).

Pilot work has suggested that intensive intervention at the onset of schizophrenia may make full recovery more probable (Falloon, 1992). This, if confirmed scientifically, would be of particular relevance to the treatment of young patients, especially those in their first episode of illness.

Many communities have lay support groups, such as MIND, the Richmond or Schizophrenia Fellowships, which can be comforting and informative to patients and helpful to professionals in developing and lobbying for resources and in support of research. While these may not rank as true psychosocial 'treatments', they may be able to achieve a great deal in a practical way.

In summary, while there are one or two promising leads as to the value of specific psychosocial interventions in schizophrenia, the prudent clinician will favour pragmatic and nonspecific approaches rooted in the care of handicapped children and adolescents in general and directed to the individual needs of each child and towards family and community resources.

Hospitalization and asylum

This is one of the most contentious issues in the current management of schizophrenia (Wing, 1990). In this debate, one must distinguish justifiable short-term (less than 4 weeks) admission during the first episode for a thorough diagnostic work-up or, subsequently, for adjustment of medication regimens, or for respite care, from the policies of the past in which hospitalization was used as the principal means of care of patients or automatically for the management of relapses or for any kind of socially unacceptable behaviour. There is now abundant evidence from controlled studies that community care does as well as and probably better than hospital care and that patients and families prefer it (Stein & Test, 1980; Muijen *et al.*, 1991). However, effective and humane community care is little cheaper, if at all (though this may not be true after the establishment phase), requires retraining of staff and puts added strain on both community and professionals which must be dealt with prophylactically (Muijen *et al.*, 1991).

Many patients will continue to have severe and growing disability, and there is a need for a range of facilities, including those that can care for the most seriously disabled and rejected by society (Lamb, 1990; Wing, 1990). The word asylum for such persons has reemerged, in the original sense in which it was used by the humanitarian reformers at the turn of the 18th century — one of refuge and humane protection rather than its debased sense of large, custodial hospital care (Wing, 1990). In the US there is great concern that ideologically driven antipathy to hospital care has allowed governments to conceal parsimony as humane care and to discharge patients without provision of adequate community facilities, thus contributing to the growing problem of homelessness there (Lamb, 1990). Children and adolescents are less vulnerable to these problems because of societal expectations of and mechanisms for their protection and care and because child and adolescent psychiatrists are more used to providing comprehensive community care routinely. Nevertheless, in most affluent countries there are growing bands of homeless youths whose ranks contain some psychotic patients. Further, child and adolescent psychiatrists should not stand aside from the debate on what facilities their community should have for the psychiatrically disabled adult, since most of their schizophrenic patients will ultimately require such services.

PREVENTION AND HIGH-RISK RESEARCH

Successful primary prevention is most likely to stem from a good understanding of aetiology and a clear definition of predictive or risk factors. In the current absence of the former, the search for the latter has to be largely empirical. Not surprisingly therefore, most of the research in this area has begun with those at *genetic* risk. Signs of neurointegrative and social dysfuntion (see the section on pathogenesis, above) appear in infancy but become clearer and more pronounced in middle childhood and adolescence. None so far can be said to have achieved the status of high-risk indicators of robust sensitivity or specificity for schizophrenia as a whole. Most children with such findings will *not* go on to develop schizophrenia, making them of little practical clinical value.

The possible role of brain damage early in life (Goldstein, 1987; Harrison, 1990) would call for good prenatal and perinatal care in general but especially in mothers with a family history of schizophrenia. This is a good goal in itself, but it is not yet clear that it would have specific effects on later schizophrenia. The genetic theories call for vigorous research to identify the aberrant gene or genes and their neurobiochemical derivatives. The stress-diathesis theory would call for a focus in research on stress reduction in those at risk of schizophrenia. Such studies are difficult, and must be prolonged. Preventive intervention is not yet justified.

SUMMARY AND CONCLUSIONS

Schizophrenia is rare in children but increases rapidly in frequency throughout adolescence. All the evidence suggests that EOS is a variant of the adult form and is best treated as such, though there may be some minor differences from adults in such areas as outcome, familial risk, frequency of premorbid personality and neurodevelopmental anomalies, response to medication and symptomatology. In most instances, schizophrenia is a serious disorder which has a devastating effect on academic and social development. The presence of genetic influences is clear, but the detailed aetiology of schizophrenia remains unknown and treatment must therefore be pragmatic. Neuroleptic or antipsychotic medication is the cornerstone of treatment, though its value in EOS is unproven. While it may be useful for mitigating symptoms

and minimizing relapses, it does not cure the disorder. Psychosocial treatment, including social skills training and family education, can enhance the effect of medication, prevent relapse and soften disability.

While a small number of cases may remit, in the majority the disorder is marked by recurring phases of psychosis and recuperation with variable residual disability increasing as life proceeds. Social drift and lack of insight make compliance a problem. It is especially difficult to differentiate schizophrenia from bipolar mood disorder with psychosis in children and adolescents, so that careful follow-up of every patient with a diagnosis of EOS is necessary.

In its totality, EOS presents child and adolescent psychiatry with a challenge that can only be met by a multidisciplinary team which, in addition to knowing about schizophrenia, is skilled in dealing with chronically handicapped children and their families and with the community in which the child lives. Adolescent schizophrenia should not be left by default to adult psychiatry.

While it would be foolish to try to duplicate in children or adolescents much of the massive search for the cause of schizophrenia, there is a need to see the extent to which some aspects of adult research, especially treatment, are valid for children and adolescents. In addition, because EOS occurs early in life before other experiential factors can greatly complicate the biopsychosocial picture or make obtaining accurate neurodevelopmental history impossible, and because EOS probably has special characteristics such as higher genetic loadings and more premorbid neurodevelopmental anomalies, it offers some unique advantages for research into this serious disorder.

ACKNOWLEDGEMENT

Portions of this are adapted from Werry J.S. (1992) Child and adolescent schizophrenia: a review in the light of DSM-III-R. *Journal of Autism and Developmental Disorders*, reproduced with permission of the publisher.

REFERENCES

Allebeck P., Varla A., Kristjansson E. & Wiztedt B. (1987) Risk factors for suicide among patients with schizophrenia. *Acta Psychiatrica Scandinavica*, **76**, 414–419.

Amador X.F., Strauss D.H., Yale S.A. & Gorman J.M. (1991) Awareness of illness in schizophrenia. *Schizophrenia Bulletin*, **17**, 113–132.

American Psychiatric Association (1980) *Diagnostic and Statistical Manual of Mental Disorders – 3rd edition – DSM-III*. American Psychiatric Association, Washington DC.

American Psychiatric Association (1987) *Diagnostic and Statistical Manual of Mental Disorders – 3rd edition revised – DSM-III-R*. American Psychiatric Association, Washington DC.

American Psychiatric Association (1994) *Diagnostic and Statistical Manual of Mental Disorders*, 4th edn (DSM-IV). American Psychiatric Association, Washington DC.

Andreasen N.C. (1987) The diagnosis of schizophrenia. *Schizophrenia Bulletin*, **13**, 25–34.

Andrews G. (1984) Treatment outlines for the management of schizophrenia. *Australia and New Zealand Journal of Psychiatry*, **18**, 19–38.

Andrews G. (1990) Treatment outlines for paranoid, schizotypal, and schizoid personality disorders: the quality assurance project. *Australia and New Zealand Journal of Psychiatry*, **24**, 339–350.

Angst J. (1988) European long-term follow-up studies of schizophrenia. *Schizophrenia Bulletin*, **14**, 501–513.

Apter A., Bleich A. & Tyano S. (1987) Affective and psychotic psychopathology in hospitalized adolescents. *Journal of the American Academy of Child and Adolescent Psychiatry*, **27**, 116–120.

Arboleda C. & Holzman P.S. (1985) Thought disorder in children at risk for psychosis. *Archives of General Psychiatry*, **42**, 1000–1013.

Asarnow J.R. & Ben-Meir S. (1988) Children with schizophrenia spectrum and depressive disorders: a comparative study of premorbid adjustment, onset pattern, and severity of impairment. *Journal of Child Psychology and Psychiatry*, **29**, 477–488.

Asarnow J.R., Bates S., Tompson M., Goldstein M.J. & Hornstein N. (1991) Depressive and schizophrenia spectrum disorders in childhood: a followup study. Paper presented to the annual meeting of the American Academy of Child and Adolescent Psychiatry, San Francisco.

Asarnow R.F., Asarnow J.R. & Strandburg R. (1989) Schizophrenia: a developmental perspective. In: Cicchetti D. (ed) *Rochester Symposium on Developmental Psychology*, pp. 189–220. Cambridge University, New York.

Aylward E., Walker E. & Bettes B. (1984) Intelligence in schizophrenia: meta-analysis of the research. *Schizophrenia Bulletin*, **10**, 430–459.

Barner-Rasmussen P. (1986) Suicide in psychiatric patients in Denmark 1971–1981. *Acta Psychiatrica Scandinavica*, **73**, 449–455.

Bashir M., Russell J. & Johnson G. (1987) Bipolar affective disorder in adolescence: a 10 year study. *Australia and New Zealand Journal of Psychiatry*, **21**, 36–43.

Bassuck E.L., Schoonover S.C. & Gelenberg A.J. (1983) *The Practitioner's Guide to Psychoactive Drugs*, 2nd edn. Plenum, New York.

Beitchman J.H. (1985) Childhood schizophrenia: a review and comparison with adult-onset schizophrenia. *Psychiatric Clinics of North America*, **8**, 793–814.

Bellodi L., Bussoleni C., Scorza-Smeraldi R., Grassi G., Zacchetti L. & Smeraldi E. (1986) Family study of Schizophrenia. *Schizophrenia Bulletin*, **12**, 120–128.

Bland R.C. & Kaloda J. (1988) *Diagnosis*. In: Tsuang M.L. & Simpson J.S. (eds) *Handbook of Schizophrenia* (vol. 3) pp. 1–25. *Nosology, Epidemiology and Genetics*. Elsevier, Amsterdam.

Bogerts B., Meerts E. & Schonfeldt-Bausch R. (1985) Basal ganglia and limbic system pathology in schizophrenia. *Archives of General Psychiatry*, **42**, 784–791.

Bradbury T.N. & Miller G.A. (1985) Season of birth in schizophrenia: a review of evidence, methodology and etiology. *Psychological Bulletin*, **98**, 569–594.

Brenner H.D., Dencker S.J. & Goldstein M.J. (1990) Defining treatment refractoriness in schizophrenia. *Schizophrenia Bulletin*, **4**, 551–565.

Brier A., Wolkowitz O.M., Roy A., Potter W.Z. & Pickar D. (1990) Plasma norepinephrine in chronic schizophrenia. *American Journal of Psychiatry*, **147**, 1467–1470.

Brown G.W. & Birley J.L.T. (1968) Crises and life changes and the onset of schizophrenia. *Journal of Health and Social Behaviour*, **9**, 203–214.

Brown G.W., Birley J.L.T. & Wing J.K. (1972) Influence of family life on the course of schizophrenic disorders: a replication. *British Journal of Psychiatry*, **121**, 241–258.

Brown R., Colter N., Corsellis J.A.N., Crow T.J., Firth C.D., Jagoe R., Johnstone E.C. & Marsh L. (1986) Postmortem evidence of structural brain changes in schizophrenia: differences in brain weight, temporal horn area and parahippocampal gyrus compared with affective disorder. *Archives of General Psychiatry*, **43**, 36–42.

Bruton C.J., Crow T.J., Firth C.D., Johnstone E.C., Owens D.C. & Roberts G.W. (1990) Schizophrenia and the brain. *Psychological Medicine*, **20**, 285–304.

Burke P., Del Becarro M., McCauley E. & Clark C. (1985) Hallucinations in children. *Journal of the American Academy of Child and Adolescent Psychiatry*, **24**, 71–75.

Butler P., Whitaker A., Setterberg S., Rao U., Ramirez P., Jaffer M. & Upstill C. (1991) Executive function deficits in early onset schizophrenia. Paper presented to the annual meeting of the American Academy of Child and Adolescent Psychiatry, San Francisco.

Caldwell C.B. & Gottesman I.I. (1990) Schizophrenics kill themselves too: a review of risk factors for suicide. *Schizophrenia Bulletin*, **16**, 571–589.

Cantor S., Evans J., Pearce J. & Pezott-Pearce T. (1982) Childhood schizophrenia: present but not accounted for. *American Journal of Psychiatry*, **139**, 758–762.

Cantwell D.P. & Baker L. (1987) *Developmental Speech and Language Disorders in Children*. Guilford, New York.

Caplan R., Guthrie D., Fish B., Tanguay P.E. & David-Lando G. (1989) The Kiddie Formal Thought Disorder Rating Scales: clinical assessment, reliability and validity. *Journal of the American Academy of Child and Adolescent Psychiatry*, **28**, 408–416.

Caplan R., Perdue S., Tanguay P.E. & Fish B. (1990) Formal thought disorder in childhood onset schizophrenia and schizotypal personality disorder. *Journal of Child Psychology and Psychiatry*, **31**, 1103–1114.

Carlson G.A. (1990) Child and adolescent mania: diagnostic considerations. *Journal of Child Psychology and Psychiatry*, **31**, 331–342.

Carpenter W.T. (1987) Approaches to knowledge and understanding of schizophrenia. *Schizophrenia Bulletin*, **13**, 17–24.

Carpenter W.R. & Kirkpatrick B. (1988) The heterogeneity of the long-term course of schizophrenia. *Schizophrenia Bulletin*, **14**, 645–652.

Castle D.H. & Murray R.M. (1991) The neurodevelopmental basis of six differences in schizophrenia. *Psychological Medicine*, 21, 565–575.

Chadwick P. & Lowe F. (1990) The measurement and modification of delusional beliefs. *Journal of Consulting and Clinical Psychology*, **58**, 225–232.

Cohen L.J., Test M.A. & Brown R.L. (1990) Suicide and schizophrenia: data from a prospect of community treatment study. *American Journal of Psychiatry*, **147**, 602–607.

Crow T.J. (1985) The two syndrome concept: origins and current status. *Schizophrenia Bulletin*, **9**, 471–486.

Crow T.J. (1986) The continuum of psychosis and its implication for the structure of the gene. *British Journal of Psychiatry*, **149**, 419–429.

Crowe R.R., Black D.W., Wesner R., Andreasen N.C., Cookman A. & Roby J. (1991) Lack of linkage to chromosome Sq11-q13 markers in six schizophrenia pedigrees. *Archives of General Psychiatry*, **48**, 357–361.

Der G., Gupta S. & Murray R. (1990) Is schizophrenia disappearing? *Lancet*, **335**, 513–516.

Dingman C. & McGlashan T. (1986) Discriminating characteristics of suicides. *Acta Psychiatrica Scandinavica*, **74**, 91–97.

Dixon L., Haas G., Weiden P.J., Sweeney J. & Frances A.J. (1991) Drug abuse in schizophrenic patients: clinical correlates and reason for use. *American Journal of Psychiatry*, **148**, 224–230.

Dollfus S. & Petit M. (1988) *Efficacite et tolerance des psychotropes chez l'enfant*. Expansion Scientific Française, Paris.

Dollfus S., Petit M., Lesieur P. & Menard J.F. (1991) Principal component analysis of PANSS and SANS-SAPS global ratings in schizophrenic patients. *European Psychiatry*, **6**, 251–259.

Drake R.E. & Cotton P.G. (1986) Depression, hopelessness and suicide in chronic schizophrenia. *British Journal of Psychiatry*, **148**, 554–559.

Eagles J.M., Hunter D. & McCance C. (1988) Decline in the diagnosis of schizophrenia among first contacts with psychiatric services in North East Scotland 1969–1984. *British Journal of Psychiatry*, **152**, 793–798.

Eaton W.W. (1991) Update on the epidemiology of schizophrenia. *Epidemiological Review*, **13**, 302–328.

Edelbrock C. & Costello A.J. (1988) Structured psychiatric interviews for children. In: Rutter M., Tuma A.H. & Lam I. (eds) *Assessment and Diagnosis in Child Psychopathology*, pp. 87–112. David Fulton, London.

Eggers C. (1978) Course and prognosis in childhood schizophrenia. *Journal of Autism and Childhood Schizophrenia*, **8**, 21–36.

Eggers C. (1989) Schizoaffective disorders in childhood: a followup study. *Journal of Autism and Developmental Disorders*, **19**, 327–342.

Eisenberg L. (1957) The course of childhood schizophrenia. *Archives of Neurology and Psychiatry*, **78**, 69–83.

Erlenmeyer-Kimling L. & Cornblatt B. (1987) The New York High-Risk Project: a follow-up report. *Schizophrenia Bulletin*, **13**, 451–461.

Ernst M., Pouget E., Silva R.R., Godfrey K. & Welkowitz J. (1991) Pictorial Instrument for Children: psychosis and conduct disorder subscales. Paper presented to the annual meeting of the American Academy of Child and Adolescent Psychiatry, San Francisco.

Falloon I.R.H. (1992) Early intervention for first episodes of schizophrenia. *Psychiatry*, **55**, 1–12.

Faris R.B.L. & Dunham H.W. (1939) *Mental Disorders in Urban Areas*. University of Chicago Press, Chicago, IL.

Fields J., Kay S., Grochowski S., Grosz D., Hyman R.B. & Lindemayer J.P. (1991) Assessing positive and negative symptoms in children and adolescents. Paper presented to the Annual Meeting of the American Academy of Child and Adolescent Psychiatry, San Francisco.

Firth M. (1990) *DTREE*. Multihealth Systems, Toronto.

Fischer M. (1971) Psychoses in the offspring of schizophrenic monzygotic twins and their normal co-twins. *British Journal of Psychiatry*, **118**, 43–52.

Foerster A., Lewis S., Owen M. & Murray R. (1991) Pre-morbid adjustment and personality in psychosis: effects of sex and diagnosis. *British Journal of Psychiatry*, **158**, 171–176.

Garralda M.E. (1984a) Hallucinations in children with conduct and emotional disorders: I. The clinical phenomena. *Psychological Medicine*, **14**, 589–596.

Garralda M.E. (1984b) Hallucinations in children with conduct and emotional disorders: II. The follow up study. *Psychological Medicine*, **14**, 597–604.

Garralda M.E. (1985) Characteristics of the psychoses of late onset in children and adolescence (a comparative study of hallucinating children). *Journal of Adolescence*, **8**, 195–207.

Glover E.R. (1989) Differences in psychiatric admission patterns between Caribbeans from different blends. *Social Psychiatry and Psychiatric Epidemiology*, **24**, 209–211.

Goldberg E.M. & Morrison S.L. (1963) Schizophrenia and social class. *British Journal of Psychiatry*, **109**, 785–802.

Goldstein M.J. (1987) Psychosocial issues. *Schizophrenia Bulletin*, **13**, 157–171.

Goldstein J.M. & Link B.G. (1988) Gender differences in the clinical expression of schizophrenia. *Journal of Psychiatric Research*, **22**, 141–155.

Goldstein J.M. & Tsuang M.T. (1990) Gender and schizophrenia: an introduction and synthesis of the findings. *Schizophrenia Bulletin*, **16**, 179–183.

Goldstein J.M., Santangelo S.L., Simpson J.C. & Tsuang M.T. (1990) The role of gender in identifying subtypes of schizophrenia: a latent class analytic approach. *Schizophrenia Bulletin*, **16**, 263–276.

Goodman R. (1988) Are complications of pregnancy and birth causes of schizophrenia? *Developmental Medicine and Child Neurology*, **30**, 391–395.

Gottesman I. & Bertelson A. (1989) Confirming unexpressed genotypes for schizophrenia. *Archives of General Psychiatry*, **46**, 867–872.

Gottesman I.I. & Shields J. (1982) *Schizophrenia: The Epigenetic Puzzle*. Cambridge University Press, Cambridge.

Gottesman I.I., McGuffin P. & Farmer A.E. (1987) Clinical genetics as clues to the 'real' genetics of schizophrenia: a decade of modest gains while playing for time. *Schizophrenia Bulletin*, **13**, 39–64.

Green W.H. & Padron-Gayol M. (1986) Schizophrenic disorder in childhood: its relationship to DSM-III criteria. In: Shagass C. (ed) *Biological Psychiatry 1985*, pp. 1484–1486. Elsevier Science, Amsterdam.

Green W.H., Campbell M., Hardesty, A.S., Grega D.M., Padron-Gayal M., Shell J. & Erdenmeyer-Kimling L. (1984) A comparison of schizophrenic and autistic children. *Journal of the American Academy of Child Psychiatry*, **23**, 399–409.

Griffiths R., White M. & Stonehouse M. (1989) Ethnic differences in birth statistics from Central Birmingham. *British Medical Journal*, **298**, 94–95.

Gudex M. & Werry J.S. (1990) Organic and substance use disorders. In: Tonge B., Burrows G.D. & Werry J.S. (eds) *Handbook of Studies in Child Psychiatry*, pp. 107–122. Elsevier, Amsterdam.

Gutterman E.M., O'Brien J.D. & Young J.G. (1987) Structured diagnostic interviews for children and adolescents: current status and future directions. *Journal of American Academy of Child and Adolescent Psychiatry*, **26**, 621–630.

Hanson D.R. & Gottesman I.I. (1976) The genetics, if any, of infantile autism and childhood schizophrenia. *Journal of Autism and Childhood Schizophrenia*, **6**, 209–234.

Harrison G. (1990) Searching for the causes of schizophrenia: the role of migrant studies. *Schizophrenia Bulletin*, **16**, 663–671.

Harrison G., Ineichen B., Smith J. & Morgan H.E. (1984) Psychiatric hospital admissions in Bristol: II Social and clinical aspects of compulsory admission. *British Journal of Psychiatry*, **145**, 605–611.

Harrison G., Owens D., Holton T., Neilson D. & Boot D.A. (1988) A prespective study of severe mental disorder in Afro-Caribbean patients. *Psychological Medicine*, **18**, 643–657.

Hibbs E.E., Hamburger S.D., Lenane M., Rapoport J.L., Kruest M.J.P., Keysor C.S. & Goldstein M.J. (1991) Determinants of expressed emotion in families of disturbed and normal children. *Journal of Child Psychology and Psychiatry*, **32**, 757–770.

Hirsch S.R. & Leff J.P. (1975) *Abnormalities in Parents of Schizophrenics*. Oxford University Press, London.

Jakob H. & Beckmann H. (1986) Prenatal development disturbances in the limbic allocortex in schizophrenics. *Journal of Neural Transmission*, **65**, 303–326.

Joyce P.R. (1984) Age of onset in bipolar affective disorder and misdiagnosis of schizophrenia. *Psychological Medicine*, **14**, 145–149.

Kane J.M. (1987) Treatment of schizophrenia. *Schizophrenia Bulletin*, **13**, 171–186.

Kay S.R. (1990) Significance of the positive negative distinction in schizophrenia. *Schizophrenia Bulletin*, **16**, 635–652.

Kay O.R., Fiszbein A. & Opler L.A. (1987) The positive and negative syndrome seale (PANSS) for schizophrenia. *Schizophrenia Bulletin*, **13**, 261–276.

Kendler K.S. (1988) The genetics of schizophrenenia: an overview. In: Tsuang M.T. & Simpson J.C. (eds) *Handbook of Schizophrenneia*, vol. 3, pp. 437–462. Elsevier, New York.

Kendler K.S. & Tsuang M.T. (1988) Outcome and familial psychopathology in schizophrenia. *Archives of General Psychiatry*, **45**, 338–346.

Kendler K.S., Gruenberg A.M. & Tsuang M.T. (1985) Psychiatric illness in first degree relatives of schizophrenic and surgical control patients. *Archives of General Psychiatry*, **42**, 770–779.

Kennedy J.L., Giuffra L.A., Moises H.W., Cavalli-Sforze L.L., Pakstiz A.J., Kidd J.R., Castiglione C.M., Sjogren B., Wetterberg L. & Kidd K.K. (1988) Evidence against linkage of schizo to markers on chromosome S in a Northern Swedish pedigree. *Nature*, **336**, 167–170.

Kolvin I. (1971) Studies in the childhood psychoses. *British Journal of Psychiatry*, **118**, 381–419.

Kolvin I. & Berney T.P. (1990) Childhood schizophrenia. In: Tonge B., Burrows G.D. & Werry J.S. (eds) *Handbook of Studies in Child Psychiatry*, pp. 123–136. Elsevier, Amsterdam.

Kringlen E. (1987) Contributions of genetic studies on schizophrenia. In: Hafner H., Gattas W.F. & Janzarik W. (eds) *Search for the Causes of Schizophrenia*, pp. 123–142. Springer-Verlag, Berlin.

Kydd R.R. & Werry J.S. (1981) Schizophrenia in children under 16 years. *Journal of Autism and Developmental Disorders*, **12**, 343–357.

Lamb H.R. (1990) Will we save the homeless mentally ill? *American Journal of Psychiatry*, **147**, 649–657.

Leff J., Kuipers L., Berkowitz R., Eberlein-Vries R. & Sturgeon D. (1982) A controlled trial of social intervention in the families of schizophrenic patients. *British Journal of Psychiatry*, **141**, 121–134.

Lewin R.R. (1988) Gender and schizophrenia. In: Tsuang M.T. & Simpson J.C. (eds) *Handbook of Schizophrenia: Neurology, Epidemiology and Genetics of Schizophrenia*, pp. 379–397. Elsevier Press, Amsterdam.

Lewis G., Croft-Jeffreys C. & David A. (1990) Are British psychiatrists racist? *British Journal of Psychiatry*, **157**, 410–415.

Lewis S.W. (1990) Computerized tomography in schizophrenia 15 years on. *British Journal of Psychiatry*, **157**(suppl. 9), 16–24.

Lewis S.W. & Murray R.M. (1987) Obstetric complications, neurodevelopmental deviance and risk of schizophrenia. *Journal of Psychiatric Research*, **21**, 413–421.

Lewis S.W., Murray R.M. & Owen M.J. (1989) Obstetric complications in schizophrenia: methodology and mechanisms. In: Schultz S.C. & Tamminga C.A. (eds) *Schizophrenia: Scientific Progress*. Oxford University Press, New York.

Liberman R.P. (1988) *Psychiatric Rehabilitation of Chronic Mental Patients*. American Psychiatric Association Press, Washington DC.

Liberman R.P., Mueser T.J. & Wallace C.J. (1986) Social skills training for schizophrenic individuals at risk for relapse. *American Journal of Psychiatry*, **143**, 523–526.

Lindenmeyer J.P., Kay S.R. & Van Praag H.M. (1989) Schizoaffective disorder: a distinct diagnostic entity. In: *Proceedings of the Annual Meeting of the American Psychiatric Association*, p. 305. American Psychiatric Association, Washington DC.

Lipman R., Cole J.O., Pank L. & Rickels K. (1965) Sensitivity of symptom and non symptom-focused criteria of outpatient drug therapy. *American Journal of Psychiatry*, **122**, 24–27.

Littlewood R. & Lipsedge M. (1981) Some social and phenomenological characteristics of psychotic immigrants. *Psychological Medicine*, **11**, 289–302.

McClellan J.M. & Werry J.S. (1992) Schizophrenia. *Psychiatric Clinic of North America*, **15**, 113–148.

McGlashan T.H. (1988a) A selective review of recent North American long-term followup studies of schizophrenia. *Schizophrenia Bulletin*, **14**, 515–542.

McGlashan T.H. (1988b) Adolescent versus adult onset mania. *American Journal of Psychiatry*, **145**, 221–223.

McGue M., Gotlesman I.I. & Rao D.C. (1983) The transmission of schizophrenia under a multifactorial threshold model. *American Journal of Human Genetics*, **35**, 1161–1178.

McGuffin P., Murray R.M. & Reveley A.M. (1987) Genetic influence on the psychoses. *British Medical Bulletin*, **43**, 531–556.

McNeil T.F. & Kaij L. (1978) Obstetric factors in the development of schizophrenia. In: Wynne L.C., Cromwell R.L. & Matthysse S. (eds) *The Nature of Schizophrenia*, pp. 401–429. John Wiley, New York.

Makita K. (1966) The age of onset of childhood schizophrenia. *Folia Psychiatrica Neurologica Japonica*, **20**, 111–121.

Matthysse S., Halzman P.S. & Lange K. (1986) The genetic transmission of schizophrenia: application of mendelian latent structure analysis to eye tracking dysfunctions in schizophrenia and affective disorder. *Journal of Psychiatric Research*, **20**, 57–76.

Mednick S.A., Parnos J. & Schulsinger F. (1987) The Copenhagen High Risk Project 1962–1986. *Schizophrenia Bulletin*, **13**, 485–495.

Meltzer H.Y. (1987) Biological studies in schizophrenia. *Schizophrenia Bulletin*, **13**, 93–128.

Muijen M., Marks I.M. & Connolly J. (1991) The Daily Living Programme: a controlled study for the care of the severely mentally ill in Camberwell. In: Hall P. & Brockington I.F. (eds) *The Closure of the Mental Hospital*, pp. 121–123. Gaskell, London.

Mundy P., Robertson M., Robertson J. & Greenblatt M. (1990) The prevalence of psychotic symptoms in homeless adolescents. *Journal of the American Academy of Child and Adolescent Psychiatry*, **29**, 724–731.

Murray R.M. & Lewis S.W. (1987) Is schizophrenia a neurodevelopmental disorder? *British Medical Journal*, **295**, 681–682.

Murray R.M., Reveley A.M., Reveley M.A., Shur E. & Lewis S.W. (1985) Genes and environment in schizophrenia. In: Sakai T. & Tsuboi T. (eds) *Genetic Aspects of Human Behaviour*, pp. 63–74. Igakushoin, Tokyo and New York.

Nyback H., Weisel R.A., Berggren B.K. & Hindmarsh T. (1982) Computed tomography of the brain in patients with acute psychosis and healthy volunteers. *Acta Psychiatrica Scandinavica*, **65**, 403–414.

Nyman A. & Jonsson H. (1986) Patterns of self-destructive behaviour in schizophrenia. *Acta Psychiatrica Scandinavica*, **73**, 252–262.

Overall J.E. & Gorham D.R. (1962) The brief psychiatric rating scale. *Psychological Report*, **10**, 799–812.

Owen M.J., Lewis S.W. & Murray R.M. (1988) Obstetric complications and schizophrenia: a computed tomographic study. *Psychological Medicine*, **18**, 331–339.

Petti T.A. & Vela R.M. (1990) Borderline disorders of childhood: an overview. *Journal of the American Academy of Child and Adolescent Psychiatry*, **29**, 327–337.

Petty L.K., Ornitz E.M., Michelman J.D. & Zimmerman E.G. (1984) Autistic children who become schizophrenic. *Archives of General Psychiatry*, **41**, 129–135.

Pilowsky L.S., Costa D.C., Ell P.J., Murray R.M., Verhoeff N.P.L.E. & Kerwin R.W. (1992) Clozapine, single photon emission tomography, and the D_2 dopamine receptor blockade hypothesis of schizophrenia. *Lancet*, **340**, 199–202.

Prendergast M., Taylor E., Rapoport J.L., Bartko J., Donnelly M., Zametkin A., Ahearn M.B., Dunn G. & Weiselberg H.M. (1988). The diagnosis of hyperactivity: a US–UK cross national study of DSM-III and ICD9. *Journal of Child Psychology and Psychiatry*, **29**, 289–301.

Prior M. & Werry J.S. (1986) Autism, schizophrenia and allied disorders. In: Quay H.C. & Werry J.S. (eds) *Psychopathological Disorders of Childhood*, 3rd edn, pp. 156–210. Wiley, New York.

Pulver A.E., Brown C.H., Wolyntec P., McGrath J., Tam D., Adler L., Carpenter T. & Childs B. (1990) Schizophrenia: age at onset, gender and familial risk. *Acta Psychiatrica Scandinavica*, **82**, 344–351.

Quay H.S. (1986) Classification. In: Quay H.C. & Werry J.S. (eds) *Psychopathological Disorders of Childhood*, 3rd edn, pp. 1–34. Wiley, New York.

Reich W. (1990) *The Diagnostic Interview for Children (DICA)*. Multihealth Systems, Toronto.

Reid A.H. (1983) Psychiatry of mental handicap. *Journal of the Royal Society of Medicine*, **76**, 587–592.

Remschmidt H., Martin M., Schulz E., Guttenbrunner C. & Fleischhaker C. (1991) The concept of positive and negative symptoms in schizophrenia. In: Maneros A., Andreasen N.C. & Tsuang M.T. (eds) *Negative Versus Positive Symptoms*, pp. 219–242. Springer, Berlin.

Reveley A.M., Reveley M.A., Clifford C. & Murray R.M. (1982) Cerebral ventricular size in twins discordant for schizophrenia. *Lancet*, **1**, 540–541.

Rothstein A. (1981) Hallucinatory phenomena in children. *Journal of the American Academy of Child Psychiatry*, **20**, 623–635.

Roy A., Schreiber J., Mazonson A. & Pickar D. (1986) Suicidal behaviour in chronic schizophrenia: a follow-up study. *Canadian Journal of Psychiatry*, **31**, 737–740.

Russell A.T. (1992) Schizophrenia. In: Hooper S.R., Hynd G.W. & Mattison R.E. (eds) *Assessment and Diagnosis of Child and Adolescent Psychiatric Disorders: Current Issues and Procedures*, pp. 23–63. Lawrence Ehrlbaum, Hillsdale, NJ.

Russell A.T., Bott L. & Sammons C. (1989) The phenomenology of schizophrenia occurring in childhood. *Journal of the American Academy of Child and Adolescent Psychiatry*, **29**, 399–407.

Rutter M. (1972) Childhood schizophrenia reconsidered. *Journal of Autism and Childhood Schizophrenia*, **2**, 315–337.

Rutter M. (1989) Child psychiatric disorders in ICD-10. *Journal of Child Psychiatry and Psychology*, **30**, 499–514.

St Clair D., Blackwood D., Muir W., Baillie D., Hubbard A., Wright A. & Evans H.J. (1989) No linkage of chromosome 5q11–q13 markers to schizophrenia in Scottish families. *Nature*, **339**, 305–309.

Salokangas R.K.R. & Stengard E. (1990) Gender and short-term outcome in schizophrenia. *Schizophrenia Research*, **3**, 333–345.

Samson J.A., Simpson J.C. & Tsuang M.T. (1988) Outcome studies of schizoaffective disorder. *Schizophrenia Bulletin*, **14**, 543–549.

Sanchez-Lachay A., Trautaman P.D. & Lewin N. (1991) Expressed emotion and cognitive family therapy of suicide attempters. Paper presented to the annual meeting of the American Academy of Child and Adolescent Psychiatry, San Francisco.

Sartorius N., Jablensky A., Korten A., Ernberg G., Anker M., Cooper J.E. & Day R. (1986) Early and first-contact incidence of schizophrenia in different cultures: a preliminary report of the initial evaluation phase of the WHO study of determinants of outcome in severe mental disorder. *Psychological Medicine*, **16**, 909–928.

Sham P.C., O'Callaghan E., Takei N., Murray E.K., Hare E.H. & Murray R.M. (1992) Schizophrenia following prenatal exposure to influenza epidemics between 1939 and 1960. *British Journal of Psychiatry*, **160**, 461–466.

Sharfstein S.S. & Clark H.W. (1978) Economics and the chronic mental patient. *Schizophrenia Bulletin*, **4**, 399–414.

Sherrington R., Brynjolfsson J., Petursson H., Potter M., Dudleston K., Barraclough B., Wasmuth J., Dobbs M. & Gurling H. (1988) Localization of a susceptibility locus for schizophrenia on chromosomes. *Nature*, **336**, 164–167.

Shore D., Filson C.R., Johnson W.E., Rae D.S., Muchrer P., Kelley D.J., Davis T.S., Waldman I.N. & Wyatt R.J. (1989) Murder and assault arrests of White House cases: clinical and demographic correlates of violence subsequent to civil commitment. *American Journal of Psychiatry*, **146**, 645–651.

Spencer E.K., Meeker W., Kafantaris V., Padron-Gayol M. & Campbell M. (1991) Symptom duration in schizophrenic children: DSM-III-R compared with ICD-10 criteria. Presented at the Annual Meeting of the American Academy of Child and Adolescent Psychiatry, San Francisco.

Spencer E.K., Kafantaris V., Padron-Gayol M., Rosenberg C.M. & Campbell M. (1992) Haloperidol in schizophrenic children. *Psychopharmacology Bulletin*, **28**, 183–186.

Spivak B., Radwan M., Brandon J., Molcho A., Chring R., Tyano S. & Weizman A. (1991) Cold agglutinin autoantibodies in psychiatric patients: their relation to diagnosis and pharmacological

treatment. *American Journal of Psychiatry*, **143**, 244: **247**.

Stein L. & Test M. (1980) Alternative to mental hospital treatment: conceptual model, treatment and evaluation. *Archives of General Psychiatry*, **37**, 392–397.

Strober M., Hanna G. & McCracken J. (1989) Bipolar disorder. In: Last C.G. & Hersen M. (eds) *Handbook of Child Psychiatric Diagnosis*. pp. 299–316. Wiley, New York.

Stubbe D., Zahner G.R., Goldstein M.J. & Leckman J.F. (1991) Diagnostic specificity of a brief measure of expressed emotion. Paper presented to the annual meeting of the American Academy of Child and Adolescent Psychiatry, San Francisco.

Suddath R.L., Casanova M.D., Goldberg T.E., Daniel D.G., Kelsoe J.R. & Weinberger D.R. (1989) Temporal lobe pathology in schizophrenia: a quantitative magnetic resonance imaging study. *American Journal of Psychiatry*, **146**, 464–472.

Tarrier N., Beckett R., Harwood S., Baker A., Yusupoff L. & Ugarteburu I. (1993) A trial of two cognitive behavioural methods of treating drug-resistant residual psychotic symptoms in schizophrenic patients: I. Outcome. *British Journal of Psychiatry*, **162**, 524–532.

Tienari P., Labiti I., Sorri A., Naarala M., Morning J., Kaleva M., Wahlberg K.E. & Wynne L.C. (1990) Adopted-away offspring of schizophrenics and controls: the Finnish adoptive family. Study of schizophrenia. In: Robins L. & Rutter M. (eds) *Straight and Devious Pathways from Childhood to Adulthood*, pp. 365–379. Cambridge University Press, Cambridge.

Torrey E.F. (1987) Prevalence studies in schizophrenia. *British Journal of Psychiatry*, **150**, 598–608.

Tsuang M.T., Gilbertson M.W. & Faraone S.V. (1991) The genetics of schizophrenia: current knowledge and future directions. *Schizophrenia Research*, **4**, 157–171.

Volkmar F.R. & Cohen L.J. (1991) Comorbid association of autism and schizophrenia. *American Journal of Psychiatry*, **148**, 1705–1707.

Volkmar F.R., Cohen D.J., Hoshino Y., Rende R.D. & Rhea P. (1988) Phenomenology and classification of the childhood psychoses. *Psychological Medicine*, **18**, 191–201.

Walker E. & Lewine R.J. (1990) Prediction of adult-onset schizophrenia from childhood home movies of the patient. *American Journal of Psychiatry*, **147**, 1052–1056.

Watkins J.M., Asarnow R.F. & Tanguay P. (1988) Symptom development in childhood onset schizophrenia. *Journal of Child Psychology and Psychiatry*, **29**, 865–878.

Weinberger D.R. (1987) Implications of normal brain development for the pathogenesis of schizophrenia. *Archives of General Psychiatry*, **44**, 660–669.

Weinberger D.R., Delisi L.E., Perman G.P., Targum S. & Wyatt R.J. (1982) Computed tomography in schizophreniform disorder and other acute psychiatric disorders. *Archives of General Psychiatry*, **39**, 778–783.

Wender P.H., Rosenthal D., Rainer J.D., Greenhill L. & Sarlin M.B. (1977) Schizophrenic's adopting parents: psychiatric status. *Archives of General Psychiatry*, **34**, 777–784.

Werry J.S. (1992) Child and adolescent (early-onset) schizophrenia: a review in the light of DSM-III-R. *Journal of Autism and Developmental Disorders*, **22**, 601–624.

Werry J.S. & Aman M.G. (1993) *A Practitioner's Guide to Psychoactive Drugs in Children and Adolescents*. Plenum, New York.

Werry J.S. & McClellan J.M. (1992) Predicting outcome in child and adolescent schizophrenia and bipolar disorder. *Journal of the American Academy of Child and Adolescent Psychiatry*, **31**, 147–150.

Werry J.S., McClellan J.M. & Chard L. (1991) Childhood and adolescent schizophrenia, bipolar and schizoaffective disorders: a clinical and outcome study. *Journal of the American Academy of Child and Adolescent Psychiatry*, **30**, 457–465.

Werry J.S., McClellan J.M. Andrews L.K. & Ham M. (in press) Some studies of child and adolescent schizophrenia. *Schizophrenia Bulletin.*

Westermeyer J.F. & Harrow M. (1988) Course and outcome in schizophrenia. In: Tsuang M.T. & Simpson J.S. (eds) *Handbook of Schizophrenia*, vol. 3. *Nosology, Epidemiology and Genetics.* Elsevier, Amsterdam.

Williams A.O., Reveley M.A., Kolakowska T., Ardern M. & Mandelbrote B.K. (1985) Schizophrenia with good and poor outcome: II. Cerebral ventricular size and its clinical significance. *British Journal of Psychiatry*, **146**, 239−246.

Wing J.K. (1990) The functions of asylum. *British Journal of Psychiatry*, **157**, 822−827.

World Health Organization (1978) *International Classification of Diseases (9th edition).* World Health Organization, Geneva.

World Health Organization (1992) *The ICD-10 Classification of Mental and Behavioural Disorders: Clinical Descriptions and Diagnostic Guidelines.* World Health Organization, Geneva.

Zeitlin H. (1986) *The Natural History of Psychiatric Disorder in Children.* Maudsley Monograph no. 29. Oxford University Press, Oxford.

Zigler E. & Levine J. (1981) Age on first hospitalization of schizophrenia. *Journal of Abnormal Psychology*, **90**, 458−467.

Chapter 35
Mental Retardation

Stephen Scott

INTRODUCTION

In recent years considerable advances have been made in the understanding and management of children and adolescents with mental retardation (MR). Medical discoveries have led, for example, to the recognition of the fragile X syndrome as the commonest identifiable inherited cause of MR after Down's syndrome, the discovery of the precise location of the genetic defect responsible, and the delineation of the behavioural characteristics of affected individuals. Psychological investigations of children with MR have led to a better understanding of how their cognitive and emotional processes develop, both in general and in specific conditions such as autism. Psychiatric studies have elucidated more clearly which factors predispose to disturbed behaviour, and which treatments are effective. In society in general the drive towards better integration of people with MR into the community has led more children with MR to be educated in mainstream schools. Large institutions have been closed down and community care facilities have been developed. None the less, there is still far to go in implementing the main goals of 'normalization' (Nirje, 1969), namely the promotion of as ordinary a life as possible in the community, and general acceptance that people with MR should have a valued social role (Wolfensberger, 1983).

This chapter begins by examining the general definition and causes of MR, then proceeds to focus specifically on psychiatric and behavioural disorders and their management. In the conclusion, opportunities for preventing organic causes of MR are considered. Educational aspects are discussed separately in Chapter 63, while the provision of special services is covered in Chapter 60.

DEFINITION

Many authorities define intelligence as a theoretical cognitive capacity (e.g. Guilford, 1979). However, others suggest it is the practical ability to 'solve real-life tasks' (Kimble *et al.*, 1984), a quality which confers adaptability, particularly to new situations. In this vein Sternberg's *Handbook of Human Intelligence* defines intelligence as 'goal-directed adaptive behaviour' (Sternberg & Salter, 1982). Likewise, each of these criteria can contribute to the definition of MR: either intel-lectual capacity or adaptation to the real world can be used, or they can be combined.

If *intellectual capacity* is used as the only criterion, the advantage is that there is no prejudgement of adaptability. Impairment can be judged independently, and can arise for different reasons, such as physical disability, behaviour problems, educational difficulties or lack of day-to-day living skills. There may be no impairment, although naturally at more severe levels this is increasingly unlikely. Another advantage is that the psychometric properties of IQ measures have been well worked-out, with explicit strengths and weaknesses in this context:

1 They are objectively standardized, reliable measures which remain relatively stable over the developmental span as the individual grows up; moreover, low scores have greater stability over time than average or high ones (Silverstein, 1982).
2 Although the reliability is high, there will inevitably be some measurement error. The American Psychiatric Association (APA) recognizes this in its definition by allowing 5 IQ points of leeway in its chosen levels.
3 A cut-off point has to be selected. The tests are designed to have a normal (Gaussian) distribution with a mean of 100 and a standard deviation of 15, so that a score of less than 85 (−1 s.d.), as used in the 1961 American Association for Mental Retardation (AAMR) definition, included 16% of the population. A score of 70 (−2 s.d.) includes 2.28% and was adopted in the 1973 AAMR definition, which thus arbitrarily cut the number of Americans with MR by over 20 million at a stroke.
4 Wherever the cut-off is taken, there will be few differences between those just above it, say with a score of 71, and those just below it, say with a score of 69.
5 IQ test scores are more often low in those from disadvantaged backgrounds. Using IQ as the only criterion will therefore include many more people of low socioeconomic status. This is discussed later in the chapter.

If an IQ under 70 is used as the sole criterion, it will include a large proportion of people who have no social impairment and are able to cope with life without any special services. Many would argue that if any term is necessary, low IQ is more accurate and acceptable than MR. Some would go further, and say that to use the label MR for those who failed a test known to give lower scores to those from ethnic minorities and disadvantaged backgrounds is an act of gross discrimination, and highly pejorative. Indeed, in a famous ruling in California (*Larry P.* v. *Riles*, 1974), educators were forbidden to use IQ tests in determining special class placements.

Using *social adaptation* as the only criterion fails to distinguish those of normal intelligence who have a psychiatric disorder, a specific learning disability, or who are socially impaired for some other reason. It harks back to the days when many such people were placed in institutions for the retarded.

Using both *intellectual capacity* and *social adaptation* as criteria means that the condition is only considered to be present if it is associated with impairment. This is in line with the principles for diagnosing any disorder in the World Health Organization (WHO; ICD-10; 1992) and APA (DSM-IV; American Psychiatric Association, 1993) classificatory systems. It avoids labelling the group with low IQ but no impairment mentioned above. It gives an indication of what an individual can and cannot do, which is essential for the administration of special help and services.

The major authoritative bodies in the field now use both intellectual level and social adaptation as criteria. The WHO in ICD-10 takes a flexible approach to what evidence may be used:

> Mental retardation is a condition of arrested or incomplete development of the mind, which is especially characterized by impairment of skills manifested during the developmental period, which contribute to the overall level of intelligence, i.e. cognitive, language, motor, and social abilities ... Adaptive behaviour is always impaired ... The assessment of intellectual level should be based on whatever information is available, including clinical findings, adaptive behaviour and psychometric performance (WHO, 1992).

The latest definition from the AAMR puts further emphasis on current adaptation, and now specifies the areas:

> Mental retardation refers to substantial limitations in present functioning. It is manifested as significantly subaverage intellectual functioning, existing concurrently with related disabilities in two or more of the following applicable adaptive skill areas: communication, self-care, home living, social skills, community use, self-direction, health and safety, functional academics, and work.

Mental retardation begins before age 18 (AAMR, 1992). 'Significantly subaverage intellectual functioning' is defined as 'an IQ score approximately 70–75 or less'. The APA in DSM-IV (1993) takes a similar approach but adaptive functioning is defined in more general terms.

Social adaptation is not a fixed quantity — it is a varying state of functioning rather than a set trait. It depends on how well the child's personal characteristics match the situation he or she is in. For example, the child may have low mobility, a medical problem such as epilepsy, disturbed behaviour, educational difficulties or trouble with self-care. Whether or not this affects the child's independence will vary according to the demands made and the facilities available. A change in educational or occupational status, type of residence or in the

availability of support can alter the child's ability to cope. Therefore a consequence of including adaptation in the definition of retardation is that it varies over time and place. This can be an advantage from the point of view of not giving a child a label for life. However, because the criteria used are so variable, it can make comparison between groups or over time difficult. Further local factors will influence whether or not children are judged to require additional services and so be registered as having MR by agencies in the area. These include the measures used to assess impairment, the availability of resources, administrative convenience, the prevailing ideology, and so on.

In recent years there has been considerable progress in overcoming some of these difficulties by developing more objective measures of adaptive behaviour. Two scales are widely used, the revised Vineland (Sparrow *et al.*, 1984) and the revised Adaptive Behaviour Scale (ABS) of the AAMR (Nihira *et al.*, 1974). To take the latter as an example, Part I is concerned with personal independence, which includes 10 domains, such as self-direction, responsibility, and socialization. Part II measures 14 areas of maladaptive behaviour, including inappropriate interpersonal manners, hyperactive behaviours and sexually aberrant activities. Norms have been developed based on many thousands of people with MR; reliability for Part I is good but is less so for Part II (Bean & Roszkowski, 1982). As people vary considerably across domains, reporting of subscales gives a more useful picture of functioning than a single overall figure. These scales of adaptive behaviour are increasingly being used for assessment and prognostic purposes (Futterman & Arndt, 1983; Perry & Factor, 1989), and the circumstances when scores on these differ from intelligence tests are being characterized (Atkinson, 1990).

There are also global scales of social functioning, as used in general child and adolescent psychiatry. These include the Children's Global Assessment Scale (Shaffer *et al.*, 1983), and Axis 6 in ICD-10 (WHO, 1992). They are unidimensional impressionistic assessments of impairment whose criteria are not detailed, being based on statements such as 'moderately impaired in two or more domains'. While they may give an overall idea of how impaired a child with MR is in comparison to one with a psychiatric disorder, their lack of detail makes their usefulness in decision-making limited.

From an administrative and clinical standpoint, it is useful to restrict the definition of mental retardation to those who fulfil both criteria. However, from the scientific and research viewpoint it is important to know about all people with low intellectual function, whatever term is used. In this way the extent of social impairment and associated clinical problems can be examined independently, as correlates, rather than as the defining characteristic. Therefore this chapter will use intellectual function alone as the basic criterion. Naturally, many children at lower levels will also be impaired, but here it will not automatically be presumed to be the case. Readers used to including impairment in the definition may prefer to think in terms of low IQ when they come across the term MR in this chapter.

TERMINOLOGY

Many terms have been used this century, reflecting changes in understanding and attitudes. For example, the English legal system in 1913 distinguished between idiocy, imbecility and feeble-mindedness. A typical attitude in that era, from a man who was relatively progressive in his outlook, is that of the American, Walter Fernald:

> The feebleminded are a parasitic, predatory class, never capable of self-support or managing their own affairs . . . Feebleminded women are almost invariably immoral and if at large usually become carriers of venereal disease . . . Every feebleminded person is a potential criminal . . . (1912, quoted in Davies & Ecob, 1959).

Subsequent dissatisfaction with the negative connotations of these terms was one of the influences leading the legal terminology to change in England and Wales to mental subnormality in 1959 and then to mental handicap in 1983. When involuntary detention is involved under the Mental Health Act (1983), the term mental impairment is used.

Different terms have evolved in the context of education. In the UK the terms severe and moderate learning difficulties were officially introduced following the Warnock Report in 1978. Many professionals currently favour the term learning disability. There is continuing debate among interested groups about the most appropriate terms to use and how best to dispel prejudice, which seems to taint every new term as time goes by. This chapter uses the term mental retardation for the time being, since it is widely used throughout the English-speaking world by medical and other disciplines, and does not necessarily imply impairment, whereas mental handicap does. Whatever term is used, there is a need to emphasize the value of the individual as a person with exactly the same rights and entitlements as anyone else in society. This can be reflected in terminology by speaking of a *person with retardation* rather than a retarded person or retardate.

The effect of a label will depend on what ensues. If the label leads to a better appreciation of the child's needs and the provision of an environment where tasks are achievable and rewarded with encouragement, then a sense of competence and self-esteem can be fostered and considerable benefit may accrue. If, however, it leads to underexpectation and under-stimulation, prejudice, and exclusion from social and work opportunities, then much harm may be done. Equally, the same negative outcome can arise in those *not* labelled or recognized as having special needs, if they do not get understanding help and then fail and are blamed. The study by Granat and Granat (1978) of 19-year-olds with MR which had not been recognized in the school years by the authorities revealed that they none the less experienced considerable anguish and social failure. Thus it is not simply the presence or absence of an official label that is important, but the nature of the actual experience the individual has as a consequence.

One way of reducing the negative impact of a label on an individual is to acknowledge the contribution of the social context in causing any difficulty. The WHO (1980) has put forward a model linking four different levels of process:

$$disease \rightarrow impairment \rightarrow disability \rightarrow handicap$$

This distinguishes four stages: disease process, organ system failure, difficulties in the performance of personal functions, and inability to carry out a normal social role. For example, a *disease* of the eighth cranial nerve can lead to *impairment* of hearing, *disability* in receiving verbal communication, and *handicap* the opportunity for social activities. Although the terms are used in a more restricted sense than is usual, the model serves to show that over-emphasis on an individual's disease or deficits can lead to unnecessary pessimism by focusing on what cannot be changed. Including the social context highlights the opportunities and responsibilities others have to improve the quality of life of people with MR, by giving appropriate support and training, and by making the surroundings and environment more facilitating.

LEVEL OF MENTAL RETARDATION

The WHO distinguishes four different degrees of MR according to intellectual level: mild: IQ 50−70; moderate: IQ 35−49; severe: IQ 20−34; and profound: IQ <20. The American terminology is the same, although at each of the IQ levels a range of 5 points is allowed (i.e. 20−25, 35−40, 50−55, 70−75). The proportion of people in each category is very different. The vast majority, typically 80% or so, have mild MR. Around 12% have moderate MR, 7% severe MR, while profound MR is uncommon, occurring in less than 1%.

In the remainder of this chapter the three lower categories will be coalesced, so the convention will be that mild retardation = IQ 50−70 and severe retardation = IQ under 50. The distinction between people with mild and severe retardation is based on phenomenology and is very important since it flags differences in many characteristics, as set out in Table 35.1. This distinction will recur at several points in the chapter.

PREVALENCE

A summary of selected studies is given in Table 35.2. The majority of studies based on total populations give overall rates for people with IQ under 70 of around 2−3%, as shown in part (a) of Table 35.2. This is hardly surprising since the tests are designed on theoretical grounds to have 2.28% below this cut-off, as discussed above. However, the overall figure disguises some interesting differences in each subgroup. In people with *mild* MR all the surveys agree there are wide variations according to socioeconomic status (SES). For example, in the extensive study by Broman *et al.* (1987), mild MR was found in 7.8% of black children in the low SES group but in only 1.2% of the high; comparable figures for white children were 3.3 and 0.3% respectively. Thus there is a striking paucity, relatively speaking, of mild MR in families with advantaged SES. In contrast, the rate is high in disadvantaged families. This, together with the racial mix, accounts for

Table 35.1 Characteristics of children with severe and mild mental retardation (MR)

	Severe retardation	Mild retardation
Definition	IQ under 50	IQ 50–70
Social functioning	Invariably marked impairment	Many have minor or no impairment
Cause	Organic pathology in majority	Organic pathology in minority
Family history	Parents and siblings usually of normal intelligence	Parents and siblings often at lower levels of intelligence
Background	Fairly equal distribution across SES levels	Much commoner at lower SES levels
	Neglect at home unlikely	Neglect at home more likely
Appearance	Dysmorphic features often evident	Normal appearance
Medical complications	Physical handicap common (e.g. cerebral palsy)	Physical handicap uncommon
	Major health problems frequent Life expectancy shortened Fertility low	Health in normal range Life expectancy normal Fertility usually normal
Psychiatric complications	Severe and pervasive disorders such as hyperactivity, autism and self-injury especially common Presentation of disorders often altered, mental state may be difficult to determine	Disorders similar in type to those found in children without MR, but occur more frequently Form of disorders and mental state examination similar to children without retardation

SES, Socioeconomic status.

the higher than usual overall rate (7.4%) also found in the Lemkau and Imre (1969) study, which was conducted in a poor rural part of the USA. The causes underlying these differences are discussed below.

The rate of *severe* MR is much less influenced by SES and typically is between 0.3 and 0.5% (reviewed by Richardson & Koller, 1985). This is 10 times the theoretically expected rate of 0.048%. It is mainly due to organic causes, as discussed below.

When the overall prevalence rate is based on the dual criteria of IQ <70 plus impairment as judged by being on a local retardation register, it is usually under 1%, as shown in part (b) of Table 35.2. This lower rate occurs because more than half those with mild MR are judged not to require special services. The *total* administrative rates of retardation, as reflected by local registers, are often about a third higher, since they usually include a substantial proportion of people with IQs a little over 70 who are none the less impaired (Birch *et al.*, 1970; Rutter *et al.*, 1970a).

SOCIAL FUNCTIONING OVER THE LIFE SPAN

The relationship between intellectual and social functioning is clear for those with severe MR: effectively all require special support as children, and this need continues into adulthood. Where there is an identified organic cause, it often has critical consequences for the degree of handicap as they grow older. For example, severe cerebral palsy limits mobility when the children become too heavy to lift, and predisposes to potentially fatal pneumonia; adults with Down's syndrome are at high risk of presenile dementia of the Alzheimer type.

In children with mild MR, more than half are usually judged not to require significant special support. This raises the question whether these 'unimpaired' children, who would not be classed as having MR using dual criteria, are in fact any different from average-intelligence controls. The Isle of Wight survey (Rutter *et al.*, 1970a) of 10- and 11-year-olds found that 20 of the 48 children with IQ under 70 were in special schools, and 28 were in normal schools; almost all of these children had an IQ of 55 or above. Compared with controls, those in normal schools were none the less handicapped in a number of ways. Educationally, half were more than 30 months behind in their reading accuracy. Neurologically, a quarter were abnormal on clinical examination — twice the control rate. Psychiatrically, over a third were deviant on parent and teacher report scales — four times the control rate. Therefore children with IQ under 70 who are not classified as handicapped may none the less often be significantly impaired. The adult outcome of such individuals was considered in a large Swedish follow-back study by Granat and Granat (1978). A group of 19-year-old men with an IQ less than 84 (mean 76) who had never been registered as having MR were interviewed after random selection. Half had significant social

Table 35.2 Prevalence of mental retardation (MR): selected studies

Author and site	Ascertainment	Measures	Prevalence
(a) Studies based on total populations. Criterion is IQ under 70			
Rutter *et al.* (1970a) (Isle of Wight, England)	Total cohort of 9 and 10-year-olds; $n = 2334$; screened by group IQ tests plus multiple criteria	WISC restandardized for sample	2.53%
Birch *et al.* (1970) (Aberdeen, Scotland)	All 8–10-year-olds in regular and special schools (>95% of total population); $n = 8274$	Moray House intelligence test	2.42%
Granat and Granat (1973) (Sweden)	Random sample of male 19-year-olds; $n = 5605$	Ullerkas Sjukhus IQ test and Stanford-Binet	2.21%
Mercer (1973a,b) (Riverside, CA)	'Disproportionate random sampling' with weighting; $n = 644$	Stanford–Binet LM and Kuhlman–Binet	2.14%
Reschly & Jipson (1976) (Pima County, AZ)	Stratified random sample of first-to seventh-grade children in regular and special schools; $n = 950$	WISC-R	3.53%
Lemkau and Imre (1969) (Rose County, US)	All households with 1–19-year-olds visited; $n = 7383$	Stanford–Binet	7.44%
Broman *et al.* (1987) (various states in US)	All eligible births in 12 obstetric hospitals followed up until age 7; $n = 17\,432$ white children and $n = 19\,412$ black children	WISC-R	1.68% White children 5.27% Black children
(b) Studies based on regional service registers. Criteria are IQ under 70, plus impairment as judged by service providers			
Rutter *et al.* (1970a) (Isle of Wight, England)	All 9- and 10-year-olds receiving MR services or in special school; population base 2334	WISC restandardized for sample	1.33%
Birch *et al.* (1970) (Aberdeen, Scotland)	8–10-year-olds on regional MR register, plus multiple agency search; population base 8274	Moray House intelligence test	0.92%
Hagberg *et al.* (1981a) (Gothenburg, Sweden)	8–12-year-old local children on national MR register, plus suspicion of all school nurses and psychologists; population base 24498	Swedish WISC or Terman–Merrill	0.67%
Gillberg *et al.* (1983) (Gothenburg, Sweden)	10-year-old local children on national MR register; population base 3448	Swedish WISC	0.91%
Baird and Sadovnick (1985) (British Columbia, Canada)	All 14–28-year-olds on health surveillance register; population base 739785	WISC and others	0.56%
Gostason (1985) (Kopparberg County, Sweden)	Stratified sample of 20–60-year-olds on local MR register, plus multiagency search; population base 14915	Swedish SP IQ test	0.59%

WISC, Wechsler Intelligence Scale for Children; WISC-R, WISC — Revised.

adjustment difficulties. Cluster analysis revealed 50% with personal problems, 25% with work problems and 25% who had committed repeated criminal acts. Taken together with the Isle of Wight findings, this suggests that there is considerable impairment in unregistered people with mild MR across different ages, which by definition cannot be attributed to the process of official labelling.

Although up to half of people with mild MR are administratively registered as needing special services in childhood, this proportion reduces to well under a quarter in adulthood.

The question arises whether those who received services in childhood but do not as adults really are no longer impaired. Possibly once they leave school their capacity to cope increases, since the demands are different and more flexibly met. Indeed, Kushlick and Blunden (1974) concluded: 'Mild subnormality appears to be a temporary incapacity characterized mainly by educational difficulties experienced at school' (p. 42); others have called mild MR '6-hour retardation', since they presume it is purely a function of being in the school context (MacMillan, 1982). Richardson and Koller (1992) followed up at age 22 the Aberdeen cohort of 9–11-year-olds originally determined by Birch *et al.* (1970) to have an IQ under 70 and be registered impaired. Of those with mild MR who received special services as children, 80% did not as adults. Adjustment was measured in this group using four relatively objective measures of functioning: (1) amount of social interaction of any kind; (2) frequency of socializing with peers; (3) behaviour disturbance; and (4) job history. Some 27% functioned adequately on all four measures, so can reasonably be considered as resilient since leaving school. At the other end of the scale, 15% functioned adequately on none or only one of the measures, and must clearly be considered as remaining vulnerable in the postschool years. In a regression analysis to find which factors predicted a better outcome, family stability, brain disorder and IQ level came out top in that order, but together only accounted for 13% of the variance. However, personality, motivation and behaviour disorders were not included in the analysis, and studies are needed to see if they are more predictive of later social functioning.

Edgerton (1984) followed up adults in their mid 30s who were chosen for discharge from an institution for the mentally subnormal in the US. They had been there for an average of 20 years and had a mean IQ of 65, and had passed a vocational training programme. Over the next two decades following their discharge, unstructured interviews were carried out to get an 'anthropological' view. Their lives were remarkably varied and had a fair degree of complexity. Two particular themes were emphasized: firstly, the great importance of unofficial benefactors, ordinary persons in the community who helped them with their problems, typically a spouse, relative, professional person or employer; and secondly, the lengths they went to hide all traces of their past and to pass as normal, an activity in which the benefactors participated as part of a benevolent conspiracy. Some improvement in competence was noted at the follow-ups, but this was very variable, and competence seemed less important than confidence, with independence less vital than a sense of well-being. There was an overall feeling of vulnerability and Edgerton concluded, 'they themselves feel limited, often painfully so' (1984).

Overall adjustment in adulthood according to IQ has also been studied. Ross *et al.* (1985) determined the proportion of people who had achieved self-sufficiency and found none in the group with an IQ less than 40, 20% with 40–49, 42% with 50–59, 71% with 60–69 and 84% with 70–79. Weaver (1946) studied over 8000 recruits inducted into the US army, most of whom had an IQ of less than 75, and 54% of the men and 62% of the women were judged to have made a satisfactory adaptation to military life. The difference in IQ between the successful and unsuccessful groups was small: they had mean scores of 72 and 68 respectively. In summary, longitudinal studies of outcome in adulthood for people with mild MR are fairly unanimous in showing close to half significantly impaired. Put the other way round, the majority make more or less adequate adjustments to society, usually without official special help. More studies are needed to elucidate

which characteristics make the difference in coping ability, and how they may be developed.

CAUSES OF MENTAL RETARDATION

Three main influences give rise to MR: organic, polygenic and sociocultural. Each has a role to play in shaping the intelligence of a given individual, although their relative importance will vary from person to person. Historically, writers have divided people with MR into two groups according to aetiology, as if the causes were mutually exclusive. In 1933 Lewis distinguished between pathological retardation caused by trauma, central nervous system malformation, mongolism and other syndromes, and subcultural retardation with no identifiable cause, due to the lower end of normal genetic variation. In 1963 Penrose modified this two-group approach to retardation by playing down the significance of trauma in the pathological group, and proposed that the subcultural group was caused by social influences as well as genetic variation. The two-group approach still has its adherents, for example, Zigler and colleagues (Zigler & Hodapp, 1986; Burack, 1990). While it is a useful starting point, it has serious limitations.

It is useful because it highlights that overt organic causes underlie many of the characteristics of the severe group. Firstly, children with a demonstrable organic cause usually have lower mean IQ, typically 30–40 in most studies. In the extensive investigation by Broman *et al.* (1987), 72% of white children with severe MR had an organic cause identified, compared to only 14% with mild MR. Secondly, the unexpectedly high overall prevalence of severe retardation — 10 times greater than that predicted by normal variation — is largely explained by organic causes. The observed rate fits a model in which there is a normal curve based on the general population, plus a second distribution, representing the organic group, with a mean IQ of 30 and a tail skewed to the right extending into the normal range (Dingman & Tarjan, 1960). Thirdly, some (but by no means all) of the associated medical complications are due to particular organic causes rather than a severe level of retardation in itself. Finally, in children with an *overt* organic cause, the other two main influences do not appear to exert much effect — polygenic influences are slight, as judged by the IQ levels of their parents and siblings which are normal, and SES seems not to contribute, in so far as the overtly organically affected children come equally from high and low SES families (Birch *et al.*, 1970; Rutter *et al.*, 1970a; Broman *et al.*, 1987). Before considering the limitations to the two-group approach, recent advances in the understanding of how each of the three main causes operate will be reviewed.

Organic influences

For an organic cause to be attributed, clear evidence of a condition associated with impaired brain function must be demonstrated. This may be direct, as in cerebral palsy, epilepsy, hydrocephalus, or indirect, as in congenital syndromes with dysmorphic features usually accompanied by MR. A list of some causes according to the time they operate is given in Table 35.3.

A number of points need to be made to amplify the tabulated causes:

1 Typically, the proportion of children with *severe* retardation found to have an organic cause is 55—75% (Gustavson *et al.*, 1977; Laxova *et al.*, 1977; Fryers & MacKay, 1979; Elwood & Darragh, 1981; Einfeld, 1984; Broman *et al.*, 1987). Prenatal causes predominate, with the first three causes contributing around 10—15% each: idiopathic cerebral palsy, Down's syndrome and fragile X syndrome. The next three causes contribute around 5—10% each: other chromosomal anomalies, single gene disorders and dysmorphic syndromes, and idiopathic epilepsy. All the remaining prenatal causes are uncommon. Perinatal causes and postnatal causes each account for only about 5% of the total, in most series.

2 A far smaller proportion of children with *mild* retardation is found to have an organic cause, typically 10—25% (Hagberg *et al.*, 1981b; Einfeld, 1984; Broman *et al.*, 1987; Lamont & Dennis, 1988). The proportion is greater in high SES families where, although there are just as many organically affected children, there are far fewer due to nonorganic (sociocultural/polygenic) causes. The mix of organic causes in mild MR is different, with fewer instances of Down's syndrome, less quadriplegic cerebral palsy but more hemiplegic and diplegic, more idiopathic epilepsy and different dysmorphic syndromes. There will also be many cases where subtle organic influences have impaired intelligence but have gone undetected since overt signs are absent (see below).

3 Recent advances in genetics have led to the recognition of the fragile X syndrome (Lubs, 1969) and appreciation of its prevalence — 1 in 1000 boys in the careful study of Webb *et al.* (1986) The precise location of the genetic defect in a number of syndromes has recently been ascertained, as on chromosome 22 at q11 for the DiGeorge syndrome (Schinzel, 1988), and on chromosome 15 at q11—13 for the Prader—Willi syndrome (Butler, 1990). It has become clear that there is no automatic correspondence between a genetic defect and disease: thus an apparently identical genetic abnormality can lead to full-blown phenylketonuria or a clinically insignificant rise in phenylalanine; the fragile X anomaly may lead to dysmorphic features and severe MR, or normal appearance and average intelligence. This has important implications when it comes to attributing an organic cause, as discussed below.

4 Research on noxious environmental influences shows that levels of exposure well below those which produce clinically obvious damage may still have harmful effects. Consuming large amounts of alcohol during pregnancy can give rise to the characteristic dysmorphic features and associated MR of the fetal alcohol syndrome, where the effect on brain embryology has been shown in over 1000 animal studies (West, 1986). Exposure to lower amounts was investigated by Streissguth *et al.* (1989), who found that the group of mothers who took 4 drinks a day or more (40 g alcohol, or 1.5 oz — 3 US drinks) had children whose average IQ was 5 points lower when tested at 4 years of age.

Clear-cut symptoms of lead poisoning can occur after chronic exposure to high levels, but this is rare. Rutter's (1980) review of the risk of lower levels concluded there was good evidence that when blood lead was raised above 60 µg/dl, IQ was likely to be reduced by 3—4 points, even in asymptomatic children. Whether lower levels than this also impair intellect is harder to disentangle from the many covariables, and is still unclear despite several more recent surveys (Taylor, 1991).

The effect of malnutrition has also proved hard to separate out from a myriad of coexisting factors. Whilst Dobbing (1968) showed that the main growth spurt of the brain was from the last trimester of pregnancy until 2 years of age, unequivocal evidence that this period is one of particular vulnerability has been hard to find. Evidence from studies in a number of developing countries suggests that for growth-retarded children, both nutritional supplementation and psychosocial stimulation need to be given to get the best gains in mental development, rather than either alone (Grantham-McGregor *et al.*, 1991). In industrialized countries, many believe that the level of infant nutrition is more than adequate for optimal brain development. However, the study by Lucas *et al.* (1992) on premature infants found that those fed breast milk, rather than formula, had IQs 8 points higher at 7 years of age — a finding which needs to be replicated.

5 Perinatal factors contribute rather little independently in most cases. The high frequency cited in older studies was partly due to a failure to take into account their common occurrence in control groups, and partly due to the single-factor analysis of results. Multivariate analyses show that, while adverse perinatal events are indeed associated, they are usually *markers* of retardation which reflect a preexisting cause (Nelson & Ellenberg, 1986; Broman *et al.*, 1987). For example, many genetic disorders are associated with an increased incidence of difficult births, and although improved conditions and perinatal care have led to a dramatic decrease in perinatal mortality in recent decades, there has been relatively little reduction in the incidence of cerebral palsy in infants born at term (Stanley & Alberman, 1984). However, severe birth asphyxia does still occur in modern centres. The rate is around 5 per 1000 deliveries, and 20% of these babies suffer moderate to severe postasphyxial encephalopathy, best predicted by fits in the neonatal period (Scott, 1976; Levene *et al.*, 1985). As development proceeds, the later manifestations are cerebral palsy with MR; birth asphyxia does not lead to mental retardation in the absence of neurological signs (National Institutes of Health, 1985). Thus, for this minority of infants the perinatal period is crucial. However, the asphyxia has to be severe, and many babies are resilient: only 10% of newborns with an Apgar score of 0—3 for 15 minutes are at increased risk of later cerebral palsy (Nelson & Ellenberg, 1981). In conclusion, the majority of children who experience perinatal adversity do not develop retardation or neurological

Table 35.3 Some organic causes of mental retardation

Nature of cause	Example
PRENATAL: GENETIC	
Chromosomal anomalies	
Autosomes	Trisomy 21 (Down's syndrome)
Sex chromosomes	47,XXX (triple X syndrome)
	5p- (*cri-du-chat* syndrome)
Genetic errors	
Inborn errors of metabolism	
Carbohydrate	Galactosaemia (AR)
Amino acid	Phenylketonuria (AR)
Fat	Lipofuscinosis (Batten's disease (AR))
Mucopolysaccharide	Hunter's syndrome (X)
Dysmorphic syndromes	
Genetic locus known	Fragile X syndrome (X)
	Prader—Willi syndrome
	Angelman syndrome
Genetic locus unknown	de Lange syndrome
	Rubinstein—Taybi syndrome
	Many others
Nervous system diseases	Tuberous sclerosis (AD)
PRENATAL: ENVIRONMENTAL	
Infection	Rubella
	Toxoplasmosis
	Cytomegalovirus
	Human immunodeficiency virus
Toxin	Fetal alcohol syndrome
Serious systemic maternal disease	Diabetes
	Septicaemia
PRENATAL: MULTIFACTORIAL	
Defects of brain development	Cerebral palsy
	Epilepsy
	Hydrocephalus
Dysmorphic syndromes	Many
PERINATAL	
Maternal cardiovascular shock	Preeclampsia
Fetal distress and hypoxia/acidosis	Birth complication or other cause
Complications of prematurity	Intraventricular haemorrhage
	Respiratory distress syndrome
POSTNATAL	
Trauma	Road traffic accident
Infection	Meningitis
	Encephalitis
Endocrine	Hypothyroidism
Neoplasm	Brain tumour
Iatrogenic	Cranial irradiation
Toxin	Lead poisoning

AR, Autosomal recessive; X, X-linked; AD, autosomal dominant.

dysfunction, and conversely the majority of children with retardation do not experience perinatal adversity.

Concerns that the advent of sophisticated neonatal intensive care would lead to a great increase in MR amongst the survivors have not been borne out in practice (Williams *et al.*, 1987; Largo *et al.*, 1989; Stewart *et al.*, 1989). A metaanalysis of follow-up studies of low birth weight babies found overall mean IQ scores of 97.8 compared to 104.8 in controls (Aylward *et al.*, 1989). However, the very low birth weight group (less than 1500 g) do have an increased rate of cerebral palsy, leading to a rise in the total population rate, estimated at 0.1 per 1000 newborn by Hagberg *et al.* (1989).

6 Evidence from direct investigation of brain pathology have shown anatomical abnormalities in some 75–90% of people with severe retardation who lived in institutions (Crome & Stern, 1972; Jellinger, 1972; Shaw, 1987). The abnormalities varied from grossly obvious malformations to subtle developmental and postinflammatory changes. In Shaw's study a quarter had brains which appeared normal, so it would be wrong to conclude yet that nearly all severe retardation is due to pathological processes. So far there have not been any neuropathological investigations of people with mild retardation.

Newer techniques such as electron microscopy and neurotransmitter assays have added little as yet, although quantitative light microscopy is promising. Using this method, Huttenlocher (1991) has suggested that MR may be related to less dendritic branching and fewer synaptic connections of neurons, and has shown these changes in the brains of animals with experimentally engineered phenylketonuria. The high incidence of Alzheimer-type brain changes in older people with Down's syndrome have lead to vigorous investigation of the neuropathology in trisomy 21, with the prospect of discovering the precise gene responsible (see Chapter 10).

7 Organic influences do not necessarily operate directly through either genetic or environmental mechanisms — more complex interrelationships can occur. For example, genetically determined maternal hyperphenylalaninaemia in untreated phenylketonuric mothers constitutes an environmental risk to the fetus (Levy & Waisbren, 1983), and environmental ionizing radiation prior to conception produces gene mutations that result in mental and physical defects in the offspring (Thomson & Thomson, 1986).

Polygenic influences

There have been many studies estimating the genetic influence on IQ in the normal range. Most of this influence is found to be additive and attributable to polygenic mechanisms, with rather little influence attributable to all-or-none dominant/recessive mechanisms. Reviews of family (Bouchard & McGue, 1981), twin (Loehlin & Nichols, 1976; Wilson, 1983; Sundet *et al.*, 1988) and adoption studies (Plomin *et al.*, 1990) offer fairly good agreement that about 50% (±20%) of the variability of IQ in a given population is genetically transmitted. Although a large number of genes may be involved, Gottesman

(1968) has shown that a five-gene model can predict the observed distribution of intelligence well.

In contrast, there have been far fewer studies looking at the genetic transmission of MR. Earlier studies suggested a marked difference between mild and severe MR, and this has been borne out by subsequent research. In *severe* MR there seems to be little polygenic influence. Thus, in the large study by Broman *et al.* (1987), the mean IQ of siblings of white children with severe MR was 103, suggesting the severe MR was due to one-off nonadditive genetic mechanisms (such as new chromosomal abnormalities or single-gene errors) or environmental influences not shared by other members of the family. The comparable figure for IQ of siblings of children with *mild* MR was 85, suggesting a strong familial influence. The main empirical family study of MR to date is that by Reed and Reed (1965). They found that if one parent had MR (of any degree), the risk to the offspring was 14%, rising to 40% if both parents were affected. Further analysis of this data set (Johnson *et al.*, 1976) confirmed that mild retardation was strongly familial, but severe was not.

The question then arises how much the familial transmission of mild MR shown in family studies is due to polygenic and how much to environmental influences. That polygenic influences play a significant part is suggested by the regression towards the mean of IQ scores of the offspring of parents with mild MR, despite being brought up in unfavourable environments; and by the higher IQ of half-siblings raised in the same family whose other parent is of normal IQ. To answer the question more definitively requires studies of people with mild MR using twin and adoption strategies, but none has been published to date, although a twin study is under way (Detterman, 1987).

In the absence of such studies, any attempt to hazard a guess at the likely importance of polygenic influences on an individual child with MR is fraught with difficulties. Polygenic influences should lead a child's IQ to fall within the range of natural variation around the mean of the parents' IQ, assuming the effect of the rearing environment and any organic causes can be precisely accounted for in both generations. In practice these assumptions and the range of the natural variation preclude an accurate estimate. However, it is true to say that the further the child's intelligence is below that of its parents, the higher the probability there is an organic or environmental cause at work, and so investigations should be pursued accordingly.

Whether those whose MR is due principally to polygenic influences have special characteristics as a group has been little studied. Zigler and Hodapp (1986) suggest that such a group comprise a third of people with MR and described them as polygenic isolates. Clarke (1985) has also identified such a group, whom she calls 'normal variants without psychosocial adversity'.

Psychosocial and cultural influences

Cultural influences affect the ability to do any task: the

opportunity to learn how to do it is necessary in addition to the capacity. Children from socially disadvantaged backgrounds perform less well on intelligence tests and, as might be expected, verbal subtest scores are more affected than those reflecting performance tasks. Attempts have been made to develop relatively culture-free or at least culture-fair tests, and the possibility of unfairness has led to intelligence testing being abandoned by some professionals. This raises the question whether children from disadvantaged backgrounds who score in the mildly retarded range only do poorly on tests of academic ability, but are otherwise competent in terms of everyday adaptation and coping. It is important to be aware of these reservations when interpreting IQ tests, which are discussed further in Chapter 7 and in the book by Loehlin *et al.* (1975). Despite these caveats, intelligence tests play a very important role in research and clinical practice. Their usefulness and validity are shown by their good correlation overall with social adaptation and psychiatric disorder, and in prompting closer examination where this is not the case.

The extent to which intelligence may be affected by different environments has been conceptualized in terms of a reaction range for a given genotype, calculated by Cronbach (1975) to be around 12 points. Empirical studies show a size of effect of at least this order during childhood. Dumaret (1985) compared children adopted away early to advantaged homes with their full or half-siblings who remained with their mothers in a disadvantaged environment. The adopted-away group had IQ gains on average of 10 points or more and a considerable reduction of scholastic failure, although they did not do as well as SES-matched classmates. Capron and Duyme (1989) compared children adopted into the upper end of the SES spectrum with those adopted into the lower end and found a 12-point difference in IQ, and moreover this effect was just as big whether the children's biological parents came from an advantaged or disadvantaged background. Since the adoption strategy does not cover prenatal influences such as nutrition, smoking and alcohol, the overall effect of environmental influences is likely to be greater. As children grow older, there is good evidence that the environmental contribution to differing intelligence levels comes less and less from common family background variables, and increasingly from unique influences not shared by other members of the young person's family (McCartney *et al.*, 1990).

A number of early intervention programmes such as the Abedecarian project (Ramey *et al.*, 1984), the Milwaukee project (Garber, 1988) and the Yale project (Provence & Naylor, 1983) have targeted infants of mothers with MR in socially deprived districts. A variety of child- and mother-oriented intervention methods were used, and typical findings were that preschool IQs and attainment test scores were boosted considerably, often by 10–20 points or more. However, after a few years of schooling, when the programmes had stopped, these tended to fade out, although some gains in attainment and social adjustment persisted. Whether the impressive early gains would have been maintained if the programmes had continued to a later age remains unresolved.

The evidence therefore suggests that for psychosocial changes to have a large and permanent effect on IQ, they need to be prolonged. There does not seem to be any brief critical period during which either deprivation or enrichment is crucial (Skuse, 1984); rather, the development of intelligence is the product of ongoing transactions with the environment (Sameroff, 1975).

The extent to which SES might affect the number of children with MR can be approached both theoretically and empirically. Theoretically, a reduction of 10 points in the average IQ of a population where it is normally distributed will lead to a rise in the proportion with MR from 2.28 to 10%. Empirically, epidemiological surveys do show such large differences. In the UK the Isle of Wight study (Rutter *et al.*, 1970a) found an almost fivefold difference between the rate of MR in higher and lower social classes. In the US comparable differences were found in the Broman *et al.* (1987) study, cited above.

In order to see which psychosocial aspects of low SES lead to poor cognitive development, both the Kauai studies (Werner & Smith, 1982) and the Rochester Longitudinal Study (Sameroff *et al.*, 1987) have followed up children from birth to adolescence. The latter study measured 10 correlates of social class such as maternal mental disorder and education level, parental attitudes and positive interactions with the child, family support levels and stressful life events. Those children with no risk factors had an IQ more than 30 points higher than those with 8 or 9. No single factor was the main predictor; rather it was the total number of factors present that was relevant. When present, these factors exerted as strong an effect at higher SES levels as at lower. Interestingly, one-fifth of the children in the high-risk group nevertheless were 'resilient' and did better than expected in tests of cognitive ability. The main distinguishing characteristic was that their parents took a restrictive attitude with clear rules and emotional warmth, described by the authors as 'making it safe in chaos'.

Causation as a multifactorial process

From the evidence cited above, it is clear that to classify an individual with MR as affected exclusively either by an organic cause or by familial–cultural aetiology is too simple. In the so-called familial–cultural group, organic causes may be operating undetected. Both genetic and environmental organic factors may give rise to impaired cognitive function without evident signs or positive test results. For example, the variability of expression of a single-gene disorder may lead to subtle brain impairment rather than the full-blown condition; undernutrition, maternal infection or alcohol intake may have similar consequences and also go undetected. Many of these organic environmental influences operate more frequently in deprived groups so their effects may erroneously be attributed to purely psychosocial mechanisms. Equally, where an organic condition has been identified, this does not mean that polygenic or social influences are no longer relevant in determining cognitive ability. Because of this overlap, to pigeonhole a person into one of two groups is misleading. It is more accurate to take three-factor approach and assess the extent to which polygenic, psychosocial and organic influences each affect a given individual.

PSYCHIATRIC AND BEHAVIOURAL DISORDERS

Psychiatric and behavioural disorders are particularly important for children and adolescents with MR since, in addition to the subjective distress they cause the individual, they restrict opportunities to engage in many normal activities. Holmes (1988) found that people with mental handicap who had behaviour problems had reduced freedom of movement, less training in domestic, social and self-help skills, fewer leisure activities at home and fewer friends than those without such problems. Psychiatric and behavioural disorders are a major source of stress for the family, as discussed later in the chapter. Their prevalence in people with MR has been the subject of a number of studies, which are shown in Table 35.4. For simplicity, the term psychiatric disorder will be used here to include behavioural disorders which in either case are marked enough to lead to significant distress and impairment.

A number of conclusions can be drawn from these studies:
1 Psychiatric disorders are three to four times commoner in children and adults with MR than in the general population. The only study to examine this epidemiologically on the basis of IQ alone was that of Rutter *et al.* (1970a).
2 The range of disorders found is similar to that found in children in general. Conduct and emotional disorders are both increased by about the same proportion. Some disorders occur much more frequently, notably hyperactivity, pervasive developmental disorders and stereotypies and self-injurious behaviour.
3 In children with *mild* MR the rate of disorder is high, typically being around three times commoner than in children in general. This goes against a commonly held view that children with mild MR are not at significantly increased risk.
4 In those with *severe* MR, most surveys which use standardized instruments find about half have significant psychiatric difficulties; the rate of disorder is higher in the more profoundly affected.
5 There is an overall relationship between intellectual level and the presence of disorder. As well as rates increasing with more severe degrees of retardation, this holds true within the normal IQ range, where those of higher ability have lower rates of disorder, emotional problems excepted.
6 There is no significant decline in the proportion with psychosocial problems from childhood to adulthood. The idea that most behavioural difficulties of people identified as having retardation while at school evaporate when they grow up is false.

Specific disorders

In children and adolescents with mild MR, the presentation of disorders is generally similar to those without retardation. However in severe MR where speech and communication are limited, the presentation often does not fit into an easily recognizable pattern. There may be considerable difficulty in finding out how individuals are feeling, and in eliciting what is distressing them. Deciding whether delusions or hallucinations are present can be problematic since they may be poorly formed, and in children with profound retardation it may be hard to make any diagnosis at all. Some of the specific difficulties of particular relevance in more severe retardation are as follows.

Aggression

Aggressive and destructive behaviour is termed by some challenging behaviour to emphasize that the problem and responsibility for managing it lie with the system of care as a whole as well as the individual (Emerson *et al.*, 1988). Other than the overall level of retardation, aggressive behaviour is the most important consideration leading to institutional placement (Bruininks *et al.*, 1988), and in the breakdown of community placements (Borthwick-Duffy *et al.*, 1987). It increases the likelihood of being sacked from employment (Salzberg *et al.*, 1988), of physical abuse from institutional staff (Rusch *et al.*, 1986) and is the commonest reason to be put on tranquillizers and to be referred to psychiatric services. The prevalence increases with severity of intellectual impairment (Jacobson, 1982a) and follow-up studies indicate that it is highly persistent (Koller *et al.*, 1983; Matson *et al.*, 1991).

Affective and emotional disorders

Until recently, professionals have often been reticent at recognizing the existence of depression in people with MR (Sovner & Hurley, 1983). In the last decade this has changed and there are several accounts of the modification of self-report measures to make them suitable for screening people with mild MR (Beck *et al.*, 1987; Reynolds & Baker, 1988). However, they do not include the objective criteria a clinician would use, and their correlation with a standardized clinical interview such as the modified Hamilton is often very low: 0.24 in the study by Kazdin *et al.* (1983). There is therefore no substitute for a proper clinical evaluation. This is particularly difficult in people with severe and profound MR who cannot usually express their mood, and in whom slowness, lack of interest in surroundings, social withdrawal and disturbed sleeping and eating may be intrinsic features of their severe MR. Depression may therefore have to be judged on *changes* in these characteristics. These difficulties help explain the relatively low rates found in many surveys of severe MR using standardized instruments, e.g. 2% in children under 15 (Corbett, 1985), 0.2% in young persons under 21 (Jacobson, 1982a) and 0.6% using modified DSM-III-R criteria in adults (Matson *et al.*, 1991). If the true rate is equal to or higher than that of the general population, a lot of depression is going unrecognized and untreated.

Table 35.4 Prevalence of psychiatric disorders in people with retardation: selected studies

Author and site	Sample and IQ instrument	Psychiatric measure	Rate of psychiatric disorder			
			Children with mental retardation			Controls
(a) Studies based on total populations of children with IQ under 70						
Rutter et al. (1970a) (Isle of Wight, England)	All 9- and 10-year-olds screened by group IQ test, plus multiple ascertainment. Then individual WISC. Retarded n = 59	Standardized parent and teacher rating scales plus child psychiatric interview. Multiaxial criteria, including impairment categories		Parent questionnaire	30%	8%***
				Teacher questionnaire	42%	10%***
				Child interview only	24%	1.4%
(b) Studies based on regional service registers including children with IQ under 70 and impairment as judged by service providers						
Birch et al. (1970) (Aberdeen, Scotland)	All 8–10-year-olds given group IQ test, plus multiple ascertainment. Retarded n = 78	Standardized parent and teacher questionnaires plus psychiatric interview		Mild	34%	None
				Severe	45%	None
Koller et al. (1982, 1983) (Aberdeen, Scotland)	Birch et al.'s (1970) sample plus 7- and 11-year-olds followed up at age 22	Retrospective account of behaviour problems until age 16, and from 16; disturbance classified into one emotional and three conduct categories	Until 16 years	Mild	35%	6%*
				Severe	46%	6%**
			Ages 16–22	Mild	41%	14%*
				Severe	48%	14%*
Corbett (1977) Wing (1977) (Camberwell, London)	All those on local MR register; n = 140 children, 402 adults. WISC on children	Standardized interviews and instruments as used by Rutter et al. (1970a)	Children	Severe	47%	None
			Adults	Severe	46%	None
Jacobson (1982a,b) (New York State)	All those of any age receiving MR services in New York State: n = 8784 under 21; n = 21 643 over 21	Survey of problem behaviour frequency data	Under 21	Mild	48%	None
				Severe	54%	None
			Adults	Mild	49%	None
				Severe	66%	None
Gillberg et al. (1986) (Gothenburg, Sweden)	All 13–17-year-olds in the 5-year cohort studied by Hagberg et al. (1981a) on MR services register, plus multiple ascertainment; then given Swedish WISC or Terman–Merrill. Retarded n = 164	Parent semistructured interview, child psychiatric interview; own criteria, influenced by ICD-9 and DSM-III		Mild	57%	None
				Severe	64%	None
Gath and Gumley (1986) (Health region, England)	All 6–17-year-olds with Down's syndrome known to school health service in region: n = 193; Controls with MR at same school matched for verbal and motor handicap: n = 154: controls without MR sibling next in age: n = 101 (no IQ test)	Parent semistructured interview; parent- and teacher-completed Rutter scales. Adaptive Behaviour Scale of AAMR. ICD-9 diagnosis		Down's	30%	11%**
				MR controls	36%	12%***

continued on p. 628

Table 35.4 (continued)

(c) Studies based on regional service registers of adults with IQ under 70 and impairment as judged by service providers

Author and site	Sample and IQ instrument	Psychiatric measure	Children with mental retardation	Rate of psychiatric disorder	Controls
Gostason (1985) (Kopparberg County, Sweden)	Random stratified sample of those aged 20–60 on national MR register living in county: $n = 112$; control: $n = 112$. Swedish intelligence test	Pyschopathology rating scale psychiatric interview→DSM-III diagnosis	Mild Severe	17% 55%	8% NS 8%***
Lund (1985) (Aarhus County: Denmark)	Cluster sample of those over 20 on national MR register living in county: $n = 302$ (no IQ test)	MRC Handicap, Behaviour and Skills schedule, including Vineland; psychiatric interview→DSM-III diagnosis		27%	None
Iverson & Fox (1989) (Midwest County, US)	Random stratified sample of those over 20 in county on local MR register: $n = 165$	Psychopathology rating scale; (PIMRA)→DSM-III diagnosis	Mild Severe	55% 29%	None

* P, <0.05; ** P, <0.01; *** P, <0.001; NS, not significant.
WISC, Wechsler Intelligence Scale for Children; MR, mental retardation; AAMR, American Association for Mental Retardation; MRC, Medical Research Council.

Swings in mood and emotional lability occur more commonly, but often do not fit the pattern of a particular disorder. Mania may have to be diagnosed mainly on over-activity and behavioural signs such as excitement, irritability and nervousness; in their series of 5 adolescent cases, McCracken and Diamond (1988) caution against over-reliance on psychotic symptoms. Anxiety is frequently evident among children and adolescents with less severe retardation, especially when they face a change in daily routine. The picture may be mixed and include obviously psychosomatic symptoms.

Stereotypies and self-injurious behaviour

Stereotyped or repetitive and apparently purposeless activities such as mannerisms, rocking, hand-flapping and pica are common in those with severe retardation, occurring in about 40% of children and 20% of adults (Corbett, 1979). They need to be differentiated from recognizable patterns of neurological involuntary movement disorders including chorea, athetosis and dyskinesias, as well as the side-effects of neuroleptic medication. Differentiation from obsessions may not be possible where the subjective mental state cannot be determined (Baron-Cohen, 1989). Repeated self-injurious behaviour occurs in about 10% of children and adults in a mild form; less common are more destructive acts such as headbanging, gouging of skin, biting of limbs and eye-poking.

Stereotypies and self-injurious behaviour have been viewed as a form of functional communication in individuals who have few alternative ways to express their needs and little control over their environment. The evidence for this includes the fact that they are especially common in retarded children with severe social and communication disorders, the blind and deaf, and in those who have restricted mobility (Oliver *et al.*, 1987), and that teaching a means of communication can reduce self-injury (Bird *et al.*, 1989). In some children they may arise in an unstimulating, barren environment when self-stimulation may be a motive, whereas others may show a high rate in an environment that is overstimulating, leading to overarousal. Sorting out which circumstances lead to a high frequency of self-injury calls for a careful functional analysis, as described below.

A high incidence of self-injurious behaviour has been confirmed in individuals with the Lesch—Nyhan syndrome (Christie *et al.*, 1982), but not in the largest published series of those with the Cornelia de Lange syndrome (Beck, 1987). Organic theories of underlying mechanisms have tended to arise from the effectiveness of medication. The opiate antagonists naloxone and naltrexone were found to be effective in one study (Barrett *et al.*, 1989) and the theory that endorphins mediate the behaviour is supported by reports of raised levels in self-cutting behaviour (Coid *et al.*, 1983; Sandman *et al.*, 1990). Dopaminergic receptor supersensitivity has also been proposed as a mechanism.

Pervasive developmental disorders

The classical syndrome of autism is rare, being found in 2—4 per 10 000 children overall. Two-thirds have an IQ of less than 70, so they constitute around 1% of all children with retardation and 2 or 3% of the severely affected. Onset must be before 3 years of age and strict criteria have to be met in the three domains of lack of reciprocal social interaction, limited and abnormal speech and communication, and repetitive stereotyped behaviour. However, if less strict criteria are applied, autistic-like syndromes are found much more commonly in children with severe MR. Wing and Gould (1979) defined a triad of slightly less severe impairments in the same three domains as classical autism (except that in the third domain restricted imaginative play and interests are emphasized, rather than repetitive stereotyped behaviour; in practice there is usually a high degree of overlap). In their survey of mobile children with severe MR, they found that fully half had clear abnormalities in all three domains. Thus pervasive developmental disorders are very common in severe MR. Their recognition is important since appropriate management can reduce the level of difficulty but calls for special expertise, as described in Chapter 33.

Hyperactivity

A number of children with severe MR are persistently over-active, impulsive, and distractible with a short attention span. Usually the picture has been present from early childhood, and is particularly common where there is overt evidence of brain injury such as epilepsy or cerebral palsy, or if marked language disorder is present. Before making a diagnosis, allowance must be made for the normal activity level and attention span of an individual of the same mental age. Hyperactivity may be the dominant problem, or be part of a wider picture of aggression, stereotypy and self-injury.

Maltreatment and abuse

Many children with retardation and their families have characteristics that in the general population are recognized as high-risk factors for maltreatment. In the children these include irritating sleep and crying problems when young, hard-to-manage behaviour problems, and an inability to defend themselves. In the parents, negative feelings towards the child and stress due to increased care requirements occur commonly. Once maltreatment has taken place, the children are often less able to report what has happened. Despite many assertions that abuse does occur more frequently in this group, there have been almost no systematic studies to back this up. Studies of children with retardation in institutions (Ammerman *et al.*, 1989) do clearly indicate high rates of abuse of all kinds, but this is also found in some institutions looking after children without MR. Over-dependence on adults and compliance with their wishes make sexual abuse a particular risk, although again few systematic investigations have been carried out (Tharinger *et al.*, 1990).

Sexual problems

The sexual needs and sexual education of adolescents with retardation are increasingly recognized in the literature, although carers are still often reluctant to acknowledge them (Craft, 1987). Inappropriate sexual overtures and public masturbation may be embarrassing, but there is no evidence to support the claim that males with retardation are over-represented in the statistics of sexual offences (Stevens *et al.*, 1988).

Sleep problems

These are particularly common in children with severe retardation, with waking problems occurring in two-thirds in the survey by Quine (1991), and settling problems in half.

Schizophrenia and psychoses

These are rare until later adolescence. Poverty of thinking is especially characteristic, but delusions are often less elaborate and hallucinations may be simple and repetitive. Motor manifestations may be indistinguishable from the mannerisms sometimes seen in people with more severe retardation (Reid, 1989). Diagnosis of schizophrenia according to positive symptoms may not be possible, but may be suspected due to the emergence of new odd or bizarre behaviour, together with worsening social and intellectual functioning, once an organic cause has been ruled out. A trial of antipsychotic drugs is a last resort.

Loss of skills and regression

This picture must be taken seriously since it raises the possibility of a neurodegenerative disorder and warrants investigation by a paediatric neurologist. The diagnosis of disintegrative disorder or psychosis is not a very specific one and encompasses a number of underlying conditions (Corbett, 1987). Regression is discussed more fully in Chapter 11.

REASONS FOR THE HIGHER INCIDENCE OF PSYCHIATRIC DISORDERS IN CHILDREN WITH RETARDATION

The evidence cited earlier shows that lower levels of intellectual functioning are associated with higher levels of psychiatric disorder. A number of mechanisms could underlie this relationship. Firstly, the increased rate of disorders could arise directly in association with the particular medical cause of the child's retardation, either a specific diagnosis as in Down's syndrome, or a more general condition such as a brain disorder. Secondly, a neglected, inconsistent environment may lead to both stunted intellectual development and to disordered behaviour. Thirdly, the raised level of problems could be a consequence of having MR irrespective of the cause. For example, having restricted abilities may lead the

person to fail to cope with situations, and fail to get their needs fulfilled, resulting in frustration and aggression. Low self-esteem may arise from inside, by individuals comparing themselves with others, and from outside, through prejudice and labelling. Fourthly, the direction of effect could be the other way around, with the psychiatric problems leading to impaired intellectual performance. In practice this seldom operates since developmental delay and low intelligence usually antedate the onset of disorder, and the IQ stays in the same range when the disorder has remitted. This is not to deny the clinical experience that the resolution of emotional and behavioural disturbances can lead to great improvement in academic functioning, but there is seldom a significant rise in measured intelligence.

Specific medical conditions

Certain organic causes of retardation are associated with particular disorders and behaviour patterns. At its most direct the link may be mediated through demonstrably abnormal brain structure, as with early-onset Alzheimer's disease in Down's syndrome. More often the link is between the medical condition and observed behaviour, with no mechanism yet shown. For example, children with Lesch—Nyhan syndrome frequently mutilate themselves (Christie *et al.*, 1982), those with Williams syndrome have a particular language disorder, sometimes called cocktail party speech (Udwin & Yule, 1990), and those with Prader—Willi syndrome tend to binge on food and become obese (Zipf *et al.*, 1990). The association between certain medical syndromes and particular patterns of behaviour is discussed more fully in Chapter 37. Here the focus is on how this may link with particular disorders. For example, children with the fragile X syndrome sometimes have an unusual profile of cognitive abilities and litany-like speech, and are often socially anxious and have a particular manner of turning away and avoiding gaze on greeting (Wolff *et al.*, 1989). The extent to which this may predispose to autism is debated. Earlier reports that up to a quarter of people with autism had the fragile X syndrome (Gillberg & Wahlström, 1985) have not been supported by more recent studies. For example, the investigation by Bailey et al. (1993) used carefully applied research criteria and found a rate of under 5%. Closer study reveals qualitative differences in behavioural characteristics from those seen in classical autism (Turk, 1992a).

A corollary of this notion is that a medical condition might *protect* from certain psychiatric disorders. Children with Down's syndrome have long been recognized as particularly sociable and outgoing, so one might imagine they would be immune from pervasive developmental disorders. Certainly in the study by Wing and Gould (1979) referred to earlier, only 1 of the 28 people with Down's syndrome had the triad of impairments, compared to the majority of those with retardation due to other causes. Two other studies found a less dramatic reduction, to about half the rate. Gillberg *et al.* (1986) found 17% of adolescents with Down's had autism or the triad of impairments compared to 43% of controls, while Gath and Gumley

(1986) found that 10% of children with Down's had ICD-9 autism or childhood-specific psychosis compared to 18% of controls.

Brain disorders

Before considering whether brain disorders predispose to psychiatric problems, the term needs to be clarified. In so far as intellectual level is accepted as an indirect measure of brain function, then mental retardation can be said to reflect *lack of function*. This is different from positive evidence of brain *malfunction* or disorder, as seen in conditions where there is structural change, such as cerebral palsy, or electrical disturbance, as in epilepsy. Brain disorder is not synonymous with organically determined retardation, since on the one hand children may have a brain disorder but an IQ in the average range, and on the other, many children with organic conditions such as Down's syndrome show no evidence of a brain disorder.

We need to see whether having controlled for lack of function, brain malfunction adds a further risk. Once matched for IQ, do the children with brain disorders have more problems? The Isle of Wight general study of 10- and 11-year-olds (Rutter *et al.*, 1970a) looked at those who had an IQ of less than 70 and were attending school. At interview, those with signs of a brain disorder had a higher rate of psychiatric problems than those without, but on parent and teacher questionnaires they had the same rate — an equivocal result. In the companion neuropsychiatric study of 5–15-year-olds (Rutter *et al.*, 1970b) psychiatric disturbance was found to be four times commoner in children with epilepsy than in those without; both groups had similar IQs in the normal range. In the children with structural brain disorder, rates of psychiatric disturbance were also very high but comparison with controls matched for IQ less than 70 was not made. None the less, it seems highly likely that brain disorder does exert an independent effect in this range. There is no unique pattern of psychiatric disturbance where there is brain disorder, but hyperactivity and autism occur far more frequently.

Just how important brain malfunction can be is seen in children with intractable status epilepticus arising from widespread disorder in the temporal lobe. After the whole diseased cerebral hemisphere is removed, their intellectual function improves dramatically, although they have lost up to half their cerebrum (Hopkins & Klug, 1991). This shows the harmful effect the malfunctioning part exerted. More detail of the relationship between psychiatric disturbance and brain disorder is given in Chapter 11.

Adverse environment

Low SES is associated with mild retardation and with some behaviour disorders, notably conduct disorder. Therefore the same environmental influences could give rise to both. Indeed, many of the factors found to be associated with poor intellectual development in the Rochester Longitudinal Study (Sameroff *et al.*, 1987) are similar to those known to be associated with conduct disorder (Kazdin, 1987), for example large family size, maternal mental illness, few positive interactions with the child and ineffectual child-rearing practices. However, this is not the whole explanation, since some of the low SES factors which impair intellectual development such as poor nutrition or linguistic stimulation are not known to foster conduct disorder. In contrast, family discord or disrupted attachments of the 'broken' home variety have not been closely linked to impeded intellectual development. Thus, although a general programme to improve living conditions might be expected to improve both conduct disorder and MR, the mechanisms through which it would work would differ.

Being reared in adverse conditions does not explain the increased incidence of those disorders which have not been shown to be strongly related to any specific environmental influence, for example most emotional disorders. Nor will it affect disorders which are principally genetically determined, such as autism.

Capacity to cope

Children with retardation often have a reduced ability to respond to the problems of everyday life. This is likely to lead to anxiety when the child cannot understand or control an important situation. Where inability to communicate or change a situation results in significant needs going unmet, frustration and aggression may follow. Indirect evidence for this mechanism is the strong association between communication disorders and psychiatric disorders both in children with retardation (Rutter *et al.*, 1970a; Wing & Gould, 1979; Jacobson, 1982b) and in children of average intelligence (Silva, 1987). Moreover some disorders improve when means of communication are taught (Bird *et al.*, 1989).

If failure to cope is an important mechanism, then if children with MR are in an environment where their needs are rapidly met and catered for, disorder levels should be low. In clinical practice it is not uncommon to see a marked decrease in the level of disturbance when children are transferred from insensitive and poorly trained carers to understanding and responsive ones, although there are few formal studies documenting this. Equally, if the capacity to cope is important, one would expect that the use of adaptability scales would add power to the use of IQ alone to predict disorder. This has been shown to be the case for autism (Rodrigue *et al.*, 1991) but has not been studied for other disorders. One would also expect that personality disorder, when properly diagnosed on the basis of long-standing inability to negotiate relationships and cope with everyday situations, would be especially common. Reid and Ballinger's (1987) study found this to be so.

Low self-worth as judged by self and others

A poor view of their worth can arise from the children's own judgement of their performance, or from comments and reactions by others. Experiencing repeated failure can lead to low self-esteem with feelings of helplessness and hopelessness, even in the absence of external criticism. Studies show that people with MR have less ambitious idealized selves than controls (Weisz, 1990), but whether this is healthy realism or a sign of debased self-worth which might predispose to depression is not clear. Fear of being stigmatized by others was shown to be a major theme for people with mild MR discharged from an institution in the follow-up study by Edgerton (1984). Having a behaviour disturbance in addition to learning difficulties often greatly increases peer rejection. In the Isle of Wight neuropsychiatric study (Rutter *et al.*, 1970b), children with cerebral palsy (half of whom had an IQ less than 70) *and* a psychiatric disorder were far more often rated as being disliked by their peers than children with cerebral palsy alone.

Interaction of factors

In terms of the development of psychiatric disorders, are children with MR more or less vulnerable to environmental influences than other children? The question is more than academic since if their condition has rendered them relatively immune to psychosocial influences, then a management approach based on altering these cannot be expected to bring about much improvement. If on the other hand they are far more sensitive than most children to their environment, improving it may reduce disturbance levels right down to those of the general population. The evidence would seem to suggest that, in general, children with retardation are certainly not less vulnerable to psychosocial influences than those of average intelligence. Rutter *et al.* (1970b) found that for those with a structural brain disorder, half of whom had an IQ of less than 70, maternal malaise and a 'broken' home were highly associated with psychiatric disorder. Gath's (1990) review of longitudinal studies of children with Down's syndrome found poor marital relationships and parental psychiatric disorder were both highly predictive of subsequent disorder in the children.

Breslau (1990) failed to find an interaction between family environment and psychiatric symptoms in children with brain disorders whose IQ was in the normal range, but conclusions must be guarded since the brain-disordered group had rates of symptoms little higher than the controls. Bender *et al.* (1987) found no increase in psychosocial impairment in children with sex chromosome abnormalities compared to controls where there was no family dysfunction, but where this was present, the impairment rate increased many times, demonstrating a powerful interaction; no such interaction was seen for language disorders.

In conclusion, the evidence so far suggests that for several psychiatric disturbances, children with MR are at least as responsive to changes in psychosocial environment as children of average intelligence, if not more so. How low the rates of disturbance might go in optimal conditions requires detailed studies. To increase their accuracy, these will need to include the child's particular experience of the aspect under study rather than only a general measure of its level in the family,

because children with MR are often treated differently from their siblings.

Resilience and recovery

In addition to considering the mechanisms discussed above which may give rise to psychiatric disorders, it is equally important to look for the positive characteristics that seem to protect children from developing disturbance. What is it that makes some children with MR resilient? It may be the same factors as for all children, such as a close confiding relationship with one parent or carer, other social support, and a source of self-esteem (Rutter, 1983). Alternatively some characteristics may be especially important for children with MR, such as having the confidence to take the initiative and not become over-dependent on others (Weisz, 1990).

Another useful approach would be to examine the continuity of psychiatric disorders over time, which has so far been little studied in people with MR. Whether the form of disorder remains similar (homotypic continuity) or changes (heterotypic continuity) needs to be studied, as do the individual and environmental characteristics of those who recover from disorder, and those who develop it anew later in life. Armed with such information about the nature of disorder and the mechanisms underlying it, intervention could be planned more effectively and successfully.

PSYCHOLOGICAL IMPACT ON THE FAMILY

Early effects

For many families, hearing that they have a child with MR is reported as one of the biggest shocks of their lives (Raech, 1966). How they are told is of particular importance. Where a condition is evident at birth, as for example in Down's syndrome, parents express a strong preference to be told as soon as possible, with dissatisfaction rising with delay (Carr, 1970; Nursey *et al.*, 1991). Fortunately an increasing proportion of parents are being told within the first week (Quine & Pahl, 1987). After hearing the news many writers observe that there are stages of adjustment which parents go through, akin to those of grieving. Clinical studies of parents (reviewed by Blacher, 1984) describe an initial response characterized by shock, bewilderment, emotional numbness and disbelief. Parents may deny the reality of the retardation and therefore believe a 'cure' or some kind of therapy will relieve the problem, and may make repeated visits to different professionals — 'doctor-shopping' (Anderson, 1971).

As time goes on there may then be a stage of emotional disorganization, with crying and disappointment, mixed in with self-blame and guilt. The parents may grieve for the child they would have had, and feel anger. This may be expressed towards themselves, the baby, hospital staff, or others (Drotar *et al.*, 1975). The attachment of the mother to the infant may diminish and this may be reflected in the amount of caring behaviour exhibited towards the child (Emde & Brown, 1978).

The third stage is characterized by adjustment and acceptance. This enables the parents to refocus their attention from themselves to the needs of both the affected child and the other family members (Wright, 1976). Some go further and become involved in advocacy and voluntary organizations to help other handicapped children. There is considerable variation in the time taken to reach this stage and there may never be an absolute state of acceptance; indeed Wikler *et al.* (1981) found the parents of children with MR experienced chronic sorrow rather than time-bound grief. However, it would be inaccurate only to focus on negative outcomes; some families describe being strengthened and brought together. In Saenger's (1962) study, with the exception of a few cases of severe rejection, parents of young children with retardation were devoted and affectionate.

The stages provide a useful framework for understanding rather than a fixed sequence; for example, while going through them parents may at times return to earlier sets of feelings. Being aware of the stages can help the clinician in the timing and nature of interventions with parents.

Burden of care

The practical demands of looking after a child with MR can be considerable. In Aarhus, Denmark, where services are highly developed, Dupont (1980) found that families who had a child between 6 and 14 years old with severe retardation living at home devoted 7 hours a day, 7 days a week to the care of the child. Some 80% had disturbed sleep; only one-quarter of the children could be left alone for as long as half an hour; 77% had reduced their contacts with friends and 59% had stopped going on holidays. In a study of comparable children in Salford, UK, Wilkin (1979) found that in the great majority of families it was the mother who took nearly all the responsibility for caring for the child and for household tasks; a similar picture was found by Carr (1975). Wilkin remarks that a more appropriate term for community care is maternal care.

Family factors moderating stress

Over 30 years ago Tizard and Grad (1961) concluded it was not possible to show that having a child with MR necessarily had an adverse effect on family life, but rather that the better-adjusted families seemed more able to cope with the problems of an abnormal child. Since then, studies on the effect of severity of disability have continued to show the variability of response. Some find increased parental stress irrespective of the level of handicap (Ferguson & Watt, 1980; Wallander *et al.*, 1990), while others find it increases further with more severe disabilities (Beckman, 1991; Orr *et al.*, 1991). Recently there has been increasing interest in applying stress and coping models in this context. Frey *et al.* (1989) found that each of the five variables in the Lazarus and Folkman (1984) model contributed to parent outcome: (1) social networks;

(2) problem-solving skills; (3) general and specific beliefs; (4) utilitarian resources; and (5) health/energy/morale. Several studies indicate that family climate and informal networks are more important in supporting parents than formal service provision. Siblings seem to be affected far less than parents, and maintain a normal range of activities (Stoneman *et al.*, 1991), despite having a high level of day-to-day involvement and a strong feeling of responsibility for the affected child's welfare (Wilson *et al.*, 1989).

Impact of child psychiatric disturbance

From the point of view of the family, the presence of psychiatric disturbance in a child is often more difficult to cope with than the demands arising from a severe level of retardation. Quine and Pahl (1985) studied the parents of severely retarded children and found that while continence, lack of mobility, low self-help skills and communication ability were not related to maternal malaise scores, behaviour problems were very significantly associated. When all variables were entered into a regression analysis, they emerged as the most important stress-inducing factor, followed by nighttime disturbance and maternal social isolation. The Manchester Down's Syndrome Cohort study (Byrne *et al.*, 1988; Sloper *et al.*, 1991) distinguished between the parents' malaise, which was significantly associated with child behaviour problems, and their positive satisfaction with life, which was associated with a high degree of self-sufficiency in the children, but not the mere absence of behaviour problems. Eventually some families seek respite, and in the study by Tausig (1985), behaviour problems were the most important factor determining requests for institutional care of children and adolescents, outweighing level of retardation.

Family life cycle

The impact on families changes as the child grows up. While parents usually expect to look after children until the teenage years, they may have expected to have less responsibility after this. They may find it harder to cater for and control their child, at a time when they themselves are becoming less strong and other siblings who have helped out have left home. Often fewer services are on offer for adults with retardation compared with children, which along with the other considerations has been shown to influence requests for institutional care (Tausig, 1985; Selzer & Krauss, 1989).

ASSESSMENT

A good assessment requires both general psychiatric skills and specific knowledge of mental retardation. From the outset it is helpful to bear in mind that, as well as getting a clear description of events, one is looking to assess both the causes and effects of the MR, and the causes and effects of the behaviour problem. Wherever possible, family practitioners and other agencies should be contacted to fill in the picture.

Family history

It is helpful to draw out an extended family tree and hear something about the character and occupation of each member, to give an idea of ability level and any personality difficulties. A useful way to elicit learning difficulties in relatives is to ask about any special or extra education they may have had, and reading or spelling problems. Psychiatric disorders should be specifically enquired about, as well as unusual withdrawn personalities suggestive of the autistic spectrum. A rough estimate of the intellectual level of the parents and the siblings can be made from their school and work performance.

Pregnancy and birth

Infertility treatment, miscarriages and stillbirths should be enquired about directly since they may indicate an organic cause and may not be mentioned spontaneously (see Chapter 6). Each partner's attitude to the pregnancy, and their lifestyle at the time need to be explored with some delicacy to get a realistic estimate of exposure to risk factors about which they may be sensitive, such as alcohol, drugs and human immuno-deficiency virus (HIV). Cross-checking with other informants is valuable. Brief flu-like illnesses may indicate teratogenic infections such as rubella, cytomegalovirus or herpes, especially if accompanied by a rash, while chronic maternal illnesses such as epilepsy, hypothyroidism and hypertension may compromise fetal well-being. Vaginal bleeding may indicate placental malfunction. If the pregnancy or birth were complicated in any way, details should be sought from the obstetric hospital, with parental permission. Ultrasound scans may have shown anomalies or intrauterine growth retardation — infants who are very small for their gestational age are at higher risk of MR. Fetal heart and blood pH tests may have indicated fetal asphyxia. As noted earlier, most children with quite poor Apgar scores develop normally, but if the score remains low after 15 minutes the risk of developmental delay increases significantly; asphyxia with seizures is a particularly bad prognostic sign.

Development and education

The pattern of development should be established. Parents often find it easier to pinpoint dates if they are encouraged to recall personal events at the time. When they first suspected something was wrong, what they were told, and how they coped will all shape their current concerns. There may have been general delay in all milestones, often with some sparing of gross motor skills. Assessment of the development of social and communication skills is paramount, where two particular questions need to be answered. Firstly, is there a deficit over and above that expected from the general level of development? Communication disorders (see Chapter 32) are disproportionately common in children with MR and have important implications for diagnosis and treatment. For

example, sometimes finding a better way to communicate with the child can reveal a higher than expected level of nonverbal functioning to the parents, and reduce behaviour disturbance (Howlin & Rutter, 1987). Secondly, has the development of social and communication skills been *deviant* in quality rather than just *delayed* in level? To determine this requires detailed descriptions of situations such as greetings, the offering and seeking of comfort, the to-and-fro character of conversations, pointing to share meaning rather than just to indicate wants, and so on. The findings may point to a pervasive developmental disorder, for example the reversal of pronouns, abnormal gaze, lack of turn-taking and other features characteristic of autism.

Reports of school performance should include details of abilities and any tests taken, and not just bland statements. Differences in the frequency and nature of problem behaviour at school compared with at home may illuminate precipitants and suggest management strategies. Friendships with peers and capacity to join in turn-taking games should be assessed, along with exposure to ridicule. A school visit is often helpful, and for example might reveal that behaviour described as naughty is in fact hyperactive.

Medical history

Physical disorders must be enquired about since they are very common in children with severe MR. They can be divided into those which arise from damage to the nervous system and general health concerns. Central nervous system involvement may be manifest by motor, sensory or epileptic disturbances. Motor disabilities such as cerebral palsy usually impair mobility; they include spasticity, ataxia and athetosis. Sensory impairments of hearing or vision add an additional obstacle to effective cognitive functioning and affect about a quarter of children with severe retardation. Epileptic seizures occur at some stage in about a third of people with severe MR (Corbett *et al.*, 1975). They are particularly common when there is other evidence of cerebral damage, and uncommon when the retardation is due to chromosomal abnormalities such as Down's syndrome. The range of types is the same as for children in general, although some are strongly associated with MR, for example infantile spasms (Jeavons *et al.*, 1970). The age of onset varies according to the diagnosis, so that fits in severe quadriplegia often begin within the first few days of life, infantile spasms usually start between 7 and 12 months, *grand mal* onset peaks in middle childhood and the seizures associated with autism typically start in the teenage years. Epilepsy is discussed further in Chapter 11.

Current behaviour

In addition to a detailed description of the present difficulty and the circumstances in which it occurs, more general recent changes in the life of the child should be elicited. An account of a typical day may be very revealing. Parental reaction to and coping with problem behaviour should be assessed, including the effects on their mental state and their own relationship, the impact on the siblings, and the need for support or respite. If there is sexually inappropriate behaviour, consideration will need to be given as to whether this seems to be understandable in terms of developmental stage, or whether sexual abuse seems probable.

Social circumstances

Who has looked after the child during his or her life needs to be documented and potential exposure to physical and environmental deprivation assessed. Financial and housing difficulties may add considerably to the stress of looking after a handicapped child. Whether or not the parents have had contact with social services should be asked directly, since an affirmative answer may indicate previous parenting difficulty and possible abuse. Through the painstaking gathering of information from social services and other agencies, Oliver (1988) found 11 cases of violence-induced mental handicap in a district with a population of 200 000.

Mental state examination

As mentioned previously, in children with mild MR this can be done in more or less the usual way, whereas in those who are severely affected with poor verbal skills a precise assessment of mental state may be impossible. None the less, it is always important to try to speak to children and try various overtures, in order to see their reaction and where possible find out their views. If little is elicited, then observation becomes the mainstay, and should be attempted in as many settings as possible, e.g. parting and reuniting with parents, activity when left alone with favourite objects, when given new toys, while feeding, etc. The amount and quality of any communication should be observed and compared with that reported in the history. If there is a discrepancy, parents should be asked whether the behaviour observed is typical.

Physical examination

This should focus on three areas: dysmorphic features, neurological abnormalities and signs of general health problems (see Chapter 6). The search for dysmorphic features characteristic of syndromes should if possible be guided by the psychiatric condition. Where no particular syndrome is suspected, the head and hands are especially worth examining in detail for congenital malformations. If an anomaly is found, an atlas of malformations should be consulted, e.g. the update of Smith's classic (Jones, 1988).

General health problems in children with severe and profound retardation may become quite marked before they are detected if the child cannot articulate the symptoms. Therefore it is important to look for common conditions such as middle ear infection, constipation and dental decay that can lead to considerable pain and a marked deterioration in behaviour while unrelieved. More ominous conditions that may occur include pneumonia, which is the commonest final cause of death in children with MR who have restricted mobility. Where the cause of the MR is identified, the specific medical problems known to be associated should be sought. For example, contractures and hip dislocation occur frequently in cerebral palsy, while cataracts, hypothyroidism, congenital heart disease and leukaemia occur more commonly in Down's syndrome. Searching for these is a part of good practice and may lead to reduction of behaviour problems — Gunsett *et al.* (1989) found 10 of 56 referred clients had previously undetected medical problems whose treatment reduced the need for behavioural programmes. Possible abuse should be borne in mind, especially in institutions, and suspicious marks and bruises should be recorded and photographed.

Medical investigation

Where the history and examination suggest specific diagnostic possibilities, including HIV, then confirmatory tests are indicated, as described in Chapter 6. However, in the majority of cases no particular symptoms and signs are present and a general screen is needed. This should have three components: chromosomal examination, tests for other causes, and general health investigations. The chromosomal examination should include the fragile X anomaly, in which the physical appearance is often normal. The screen for other causes should include a urinary amino acid screen, tests of thyroid function, blood lead and blood creatine phosphokinase since muscular dystrophy in boys may first present with cognitive and language difficulties. A recent survey at the Maudsley Hospital in London found that more extensive routine testing had too low a hit rate to be worthwhile. Tests for syphilis, plasma amino acids, plasma electrolytes and numerous tests for individual rare neurodegenerative conditions revealed no unexpected findings in more than 500 children with MR and a psychiatric disorder (S. Scott, unpublished data). However, this is not to say that these tests should be permanently banished if there seems to be an indication — for example, there has been a recent dramatic increase in syphilis in poor urban areas of the US, particularly in neighbourhoods where drug abuse and prostitution are widespread (Dorfman & Glaser, 1990). Equally, the diagnostic yield from an electroencephalogram or computed tomography scan is likely to be negligible if there is no specific indication (Green, 1987; Brett, 1991).

The general health screening tests are more often helpful. A full blood count may reveal anaemia or an eosinophilia suggestive of parasitic infestation; urine microbiology and hepatitis B serology are worth doing since both conditions are more common in children with MR; and liver function tests may be abnormal due to medication. Tests of hearing and vision should always be arranged as they often reveal impairment.

Psychometric assessment

Investigation of cognitive abilities and attainments including reading should preferably be carried out by an experienced psychologist, and evaluation of strengths and weaknesses on an adaptive behaviour scale is desirable. If psychometric testing is not carried out on children who are failing at school and are suspected of having MR, there is a danger of missing specific reading retardation. In the Isle of Wight survey, 7% of the children were backward in reading (28 months or more behind their chronological age), but only a quarter of these were intellectually retarded (Rutter *et al.*, 1970a). Since the nature of the problem, the management and the prognosis are very different for the two conditions, it is essential they are differentiated.

Putting it together

Diagnosis using a multiaxial framework such as ICD-10 or DSM-IV is helpful since as well as focusing on the psychiatric problem, it leads to systematic consideration of specific developmental delays, possible medical causes, the family environment and psychosocial functioning. The completed assessment should go further than this and formulate as far as possible the relative contribution of organic, genetic and environmental influences on the aetiology of the retardation, and the predisposing, precipitating and maintaining factors in the psychiatric problem. It should consider the impact of the difficulties, and identify personal and family strengths which may be used as a basis for planning change.

MANAGEMENT OF PSYCHIATRIC AND BEHAVIOURAL DISORDERS

The overall plan of management deriving from the assessment should aim not just to get rid of undesirable behaviour, but also to promote desirable behaviour and build worthwhile experiences. To do this, special education must be considered (see Chapter 63), as well as the contribution available from special services for the handicapped (see Chapter 60). As in all clinical work with children, before starting an individual treatment programme family issues need to be addressed. Where they are judged to have had a role in the cause or maintenance of a problem, they may require intervention. In any case, acknowledging the effect of the problem on the family helps to promote their engagement and willingness to implement a treatment programme. Some specific approaches to the management of psychiatric disorders are discussed below.

Psychological treatment

Behaviour modification

This has proved a powerful method for both increasing desirable behaviours and decreasing undesirable behaviours.

It can be particularly helpful for people with more severe MR since it does not require the use of language or conscious motivation. Specific daily activities can be worked on, such as self-help skills, toilet-training, and the use of communication and language. The technique is less successful with overall social skills, as it is hard to get the newly learned behaviours to generalize widely (Robertson *et al.*, 1984). In the approach to a problem behaviour, an individual functional analysis should be formulated after careful direct observation of the antecedents of the behaviour, its frequency and duration and the consequences (for details of behavioural techniques, see Chapter 50). In children with MR the target of treatment must be realistically achievable, objectively measurable and if possible should include promotion of positive behaviours which already are seen, rather than only elimination of negative ones. Thus for a hyperactive boy, rather than aiming only to reduce running around, it would be preferable to aim to increase his sitting down to say a minute at a time. Having set a target, a number of options are available.

Firstly, changing the antecedents alone may be sufficient to avoid triggering the behaviour (stimulus control). While the need for social attention is often a prime stimulus setting off difficult behaviour in children without MR, in those with MR a range of possibilities needs to be considered. Iwata and colleagues (1982) have developed a method of systematically varying environmental stimuli to see which are relevant. Using this method, Murphy and Oliver (1987) give examples of some children who stop self-injuring when they are given adult attention, but others who are the opposite and stop when they are free from it, and a third group who stop when they are provided with stimulating toys.

Secondly, it may be possible to diminish the undesirable behaviour by replacing it with new behaviours. A suitable reinforcer has to be identified. Where social attention does not work, it is worth trying a variety of primary reinforcers including food, drinks, music, flashing lights, toys, etc. to see which is most often selected. If still no preference is evident, the Premack principle (Premack, 1959) can be applied by seeing what the child does when left alone, and using that as a reinforcer. Whichever reinforcer is chosen, the desired behaviour may need to be built up using shaping and prompting techniques, followed by gradual fading out of the schedule when the new pattern is established. De Kock *et al.* (1984) give an example of how disruptive mealtime behaviour was eliminated by differential reinforcement of appropriate behaviour.

Thirdly, specific techniques for decreasing undesirable behaviour can be applied. The usual first line is to try extinction by removing contingent rewards. For example, if functional analysis showed that attention seemed to be the reward, ignoring the behaviour would be tried; or if, say, it showed that the reward was that the child was allowed to stop a task each time she screamed, getting her to continue the task would be tried. However, sometimes nonaversive punishment techniques are required. The indications include: (1) where the consequence of the behaviour is too harmful to countenance the temporary rise in frequency which occurs using extinction, for example with severe self-injury; (2) where a quick result is essential; (3) where control of the rewarding consequence is impossible, as with the attention of other residents in an institution; and (4) where other methods have failed.

Nonaversive punishment techniques include time out and response cost. The former refers to time out from positive reinforcement, for example by removal from a socially stimulating environment to a quiet room. It can be very effective for children with MR, but the time-out period should be short, certainly under 15 minutes, and other more desired behaviours must be rewarded (Murphy & Oliver, 1987). The latter refers to the removal of reward systems such as tokens or stars, thereby setting up a response cost of the behaviour. The problem here is that the reward system has to be in place to start with, and then to change it by taking away the rewards often leads to considerable protest from the children.

The use of aversive punishment techniques such as unpleasant tastes and smells, restraint, covering the head, water spray and even electric shocks (e.g. Foxx *et al.*, 1986) is questionable ethically, and can lead to abuse. Such abuse is more likely where there is a lack of skilled support for alternative psychological management, and carers are stretched and feel angry because of repeated acts of challenging behaviour. In both the UK and the US there have been enquiries following abuse of aversive punitive techniques in institutions; in some states, such as Massachusetts and Michigan, their use is banned and alternatives must be used (Nolley *et al.*, 1982). However the literature suggests they can be very helpful for individuals when properly used (Lennox *et al.*, 1988), which has led to calls for proper regulation rather than banning aversive techniques altogether (Matson & Taras, 1989).

Fourthly, any of these techniques may be combined into more complex treatment protocols. With more able children they may be used with self-instruction, which can increase generalization. Because all of these techniques are time-consuming, there has been increasing interest in the effectiveness of teaching parents and carers how to use them (Carr, 1990; Baker *et al.*, 1991) either individually or in groups (Callias, 1987). The application of these methods for people with mental handicap is succinctly described in the text by Yule and Carr (1987).

Individual psychotherapy

When working with children with retardation there is a danger in overlooking their own thoughts and feelings, and consequently ignoring the opportunity to effect change through them. For example, cognitive techniques have been shown to be effective in reducing anxiety in children with mild MR (Lindsay *et al.*, 1989). The techniques and benefits of psychodynamic psychotherapy have been persuasively described by Sinason (1992) for individual children with severe and profound handicap, but bigger-scale systematic studies are lacking (Hurley, 1989).

Family therapy

Family systems thinking has been helpful in highlighting how having a child with retardation may affect the development of different stages in the family life cycle. Sloman and Konstantereas (1990) offer a management approach taking these issues into account from birth onwards. Black (1987) describes the management of families which have developed particular problems around a child with retardation, and gives examples using structural family therapy, genograms and discussion of belief systems.

Drug treatment

General principles

Firstly, medication should *not* be the first or only treatment for difficult-to-manage behaviour. A careful assessment of all likely contributing factors should have been carried out, including physical health and recent alterations in everyday routine, and appropriate psychological and environmental changes made before drugs are considered.

Secondly, all the usual features of good general prescribing practice should be maintained, such as baseline electrocardiogram and blood tests where appropriate, explanation of side-effects to the child and carers, agreement before starting of clear criteria for assessment of improvement, regular review to consider stopping, etc. (see Chapter 51).

Thirdly, the practitioner should be experienced in prescribing for this group; nonspecialists prescribe people with MR more drugs, and for longer (Raft *et al.*, 1975).

Fourthly, consent needs to be obtained. In England and Wales the Children Act (1989) widened the definition of who holds parental responsibility and so who can give consent. With the increasing emphasis on individual rights, the extent to which the child's views should be taken into consideration has grown. For young people over 16 with MR, the grounds on which they may refuse treatment if they have the capacity to make their own decisions have changed in recent case law to include well-being as well as strict physical health. They may now be entitled in some circumstances to refuse unpleasant treatment even if it is life-prolonging, for example in terminal cancer (Gunn, 1990). Bicknell (1989a,b) has drawn up guidelines for getting consent from children and adults with mental handicap who are not legally competent.

Prevalence

Use of psychotropic drugs to control behaviour remains too common (Aman & Singh, 1988) and can be reduced with benefit (see Chapter 51). Consideration is given here to studies in people with MR for drugs commonly used for aggression and hyperactivity.

Neuroleptics

Thioridazine, chlorpromazine and haloperidol are the most frequently prescribed to control behaviour, in addition to their use for psychoses. While high doses certainly have a role as sedatives in the management of acute outbursts of violence, whether long-term usage of lower, less sedative doses is of benefit is less clear. The difficulty is that doses which control disruptive behaviour often also suppress constructive behaviour, as well as the alertness necessary to learn — a high price in children where learning is already difficult. Once clearly sedative doses of neuroleptics are used, impairment can be demonstrated in formal tests of learning and laboratory tests of attention. At lower levels however, some studies indicate that cognitive ability is improved, partly due to the reduction of behaviour difficulties.

In 1971 Sprague and Werry listed minimum design requirements for drug research in developmental disabilities, but very few studies have met them. An early placebo-controlled study of haloperidol found hyperactivity, assaultiveness and self-injury improved in children and young adults with MR (Burk & Menolascino, 1968). However Aman *et al.* (1989) found haloperidol produced minimal changes in adults with MR on any measures, even in moderately high dosage (0.05 mg/kg per day, equivalent to 2.5 mg/kg per day chlorpromazine), though a subgroup with marked stereotypy did improve. In a study of haloperidol with autistic children, Campbell *et al.* (1978) found that it reduced stereotypies and withdrawal behaviour in older but not younger children, and had complex interactions with teaching programmes, often helping learning in lower doses; higher doses were clearly sedative.

Studies on thioridazine also report mixed results. In adolescents with severe retardation, Singh and Aman (1981) found that, compared to placebo, it reduced hyperactivity, bizarre behaviour and stereotypies just as effectively whether given at 2.5 or 5.2 mg/kg per day (chlorpromazine-equivalent dose the same), and did not impair performance on instruction-following or attention tests. Two studies in young adults with retardation found that withdrawing thioridazine led to small but significant increases in inappropriate behaviours overall. However, there was a wide range of individual responses; some people's behaviour improved on withdrawal while others deteriorated seriously (Heistad *et al.*, 1982; Schroeder & Gualtieri, 1985).

All the recognized side-effects of neuroleptics also occur in people with retardation. One of the most troublesome in the long term is tardive dyskinesia. The typical prevalence rate in people with retardation exposed to neuroleptics is approximately 30% (Kalachnik, 1984). Although increased age operates as a risk factor independently of total accumulated dose, children and adolescents are by no means exempt, and Paulson *et al.* (1975) found it in 20% of 11–16-year-olds with MR. There does not appear to be an increased risk for people with MR, organic brain injury (Golden, 1988) or any specific diagnosis, possibly excepting phenylketonuria (Richardson *et al.*, 1986). However, as in the general population, female

sex confers an increased risk, as does total lifetime dose (Kane, 1991).

Lithium

Following accounts of the effectiveness of lithium in controlling aggressive behaviour in general adult psychiatry, trials of lithium in adults with retardation behaving aggressively have been reported (Tyrer *et al.*, 1984; Craft *et al.*, 1987; Spreat *et al.*, 1989). Useful responses occurred in about two-thirds of patients. Blood levels needed to be at the higher end of the therapeutic range (0.7–1.0 mmol/l), and treatment had to be for 6–8 weeks before all responses were evident. Controlled trials in children with MR have not been carried out. Trials in aggressive children without MR have shown modest results. Two found statistically significant improvements (Campbell *et al.*, 1984; Carlson *et al.*, 1992) but these were often not judged clinically worthwhile enough to continue the drug, and Greenhill *et al.* (1973) found only 2 of 9 children with hyperactivity and aggression improved.

Stimulants

Stimulants such as methylphenidate do not seem to be helpful for hyperactivity in children with severe and profound retardation (Aman, 1982; Gadow, 1992). However, recent studies provide firmer evidence that stimulants can be safe and effective for some hyperactive children with mild to moderate MR (Payton *et al.*, 1989; Handen *et al.*, 1990; Aman *et al.*, 1991a,b; Gadow, 1992), although responses and side-effects may be more idiosyncratic (Handen *et al.*, 1991).

PREVENTION AND AMELIORATION OF MENTAL RETARDATION RESULTING FROM ORGANIC CAUSES

Prevention of MR calls for an understanding of its multifactorial causation, as discussed above. Psychosocial interventions were briefly reviewed in the section on causes, above, and more extensive review is beyond the scope of this chapter. Here the focus will be on organic causes, which are responsible for the majority of cases of severe MR and contribute significantly to mild MR. Since cure of established MR (i.e. restoration to complete normality) is virtually non-existent in the present state of knowledge, prevention is of primary importance.

Genetic aspects of prevention

In a very few conditions, children with established genetic disorders can be prevented from developing MR. Current interventions are at the later two points in the process whereby a gene leads to a gene product (such as an enzyme), which in turn works on a chemical substrate in the body. For example, in phenylketonuria and galactosaemia, treatment is by restricting dietary intake of the substrate which accumulates at toxic levels in the disorders — phenylalanine and galactose respectively. If started early, subsequent intellectual development of the children is usually within the normal range (Hayes *et al.*, 1988; Fishler *et al.*, 1989). In the case of congenital hypothyroidism, the missing gene product, the hormone thyroxine, can be produced artificially and so replaced each day, again with a good outcome (New England Congenital Hypothyroidism Collaborative, 1990). In most conditions however the missing gene product cannot be produced artificially and delivered to the right part of the body. Attempts are therefore being made to engraft donor tissue to make the lacking product within the body. For example, the enzymes lacking in leukodystrophies are present in the white blood cells of unaffected people, and this has recently led to successful treatment through bone marrow transplant (Menkes, 1990). Neural transplants from fetuses have begun to be performed to try to prevent the movement difficulties and dementia in adults with Parkinson's disease (Sladek & Gash, 1988), and may in the future be applicable for some conditions causing MR in children, for example those known to be due to the lack of particular enzymes necessary for nerve cell development. The ultimate step would be to be able to intervene at the level of the genes themselves. This is not currently feasible, but the necessary knowledge and techniques are being developed extremely rapidly. For example, genetic material has been successfully inserted into mouse gametes, leading what would have been a female to develop as a normal male. Practical gene therapy for genetic disorders may not be far off (Weatherall, 1991).

Genetic counselling and prenatal diagnosis remain the mainstay of genetic prevention, since treatment of the type discussed above is only possible for very few conditions at present. Most genetic counselling is prompted when someone in the family is already affected, often a child or sibling. To be able to provide an accurate prediction of the recurrence risk as precise a diagnosis as possible is necessary. Then for disorders with known Mendelian patterns of transmission, recurrence risk percentages can be exact, for example 25% for an autosomal recessive disorder in a sibling of an affected individual, 50% for an autosomal dominant disorder transmitted through a parental carrier. The recurrence risks for chromosomal disorders are usually based on empirical data since most arise *de novo*, for example they are around 1% for standard nondisjunction trisomy 21. This is not always so: some cases of Down's syndrome are due to a translocation inherited from one parent, as in the 21/21 form, where the recurrence risk is 100%. Other syndromes of unknown aetiology thought to have a significant genetic component can also be forecast on empirical grounds; for example neural tube defects such as spina bifida with hydrocephalus have a recurrence risk in first-degree relatives of about 4% (Berg, 1992).

Sometimes genetic counselling is sought before any affected children are born, if the risk is thought to be high. Consanguinity raises the risk of autosomal recessive conditions, advanced maternal age the risk of chromosomal nondisjunctions such as standard Down's syndrome, and membership of certain ethnic groups may confer heightened risk, as with Tay—Sachs disease in Ashkenazi Jews or thalassaemia in those of Mediterranean origin. Preconceptual screening is sometimes possible where there is a test for carrier states, as with thalassaemia. Couples then have to decide what to do, bearing in mind the risk, the seriousness of the condition and their personal values. Options to prevent the risk or make it extremely small include the avoidance of future pregnancies, or the use of donor sperm or *in vitro* fertilization of a donor ovum. These options raise considerable emotional and ethical issues, but some may find them less arduous than to proceed with their own pregnancy and face the higher risk of a child with MR, or pregnancy termination following prenatal diagnosis.

Prenatal diagnosis is becoming available for a rapidly increasing number of conditions (Weaver, 1989). Techniques include high-resolution ultrasonography to look for morphological anomalies such as spina bifida, and the more invasive amniocentesis and chorionic villous sampling, both of which lead to fetal death in around 0.5% of procedures. Unfortunately at present the scope for prenatal treatment is limited though occasionally possible (Schulman, 1990), and the main option is for termination of pregnancy if an uncurable anomaly is detected, many of which are associated with MR. The ethical issues raised are sensitive, and widely varying outlooks on the moral legitimacy of abortion continue to be debated passionately around the world. The stress on couples is considerable and calls for sensitive handling by the professional (Black, 1990).

Environmental aspects of prevention

Many opportunities arise for prevention in light of the recent advances in knowledge of organic environmental causes, reviewed earlier. Prenatally, these include avoidance of alcohol during pregnancy, changing from anticonvulsants such as phenytoin to less teratogenic alternatives, reducing relevant infections early in pregnancy and preventing undernutrition of mothers before and during pregnancy. The services required for prevention are considered further in Chapter 60. Prevention also calls for general political initiatives that cannot be effected by health departments alone.

Postnatally, both nutritional supplementation and enhanced stimulation produce better gains in intellectual development than either alone (Grantham-MacGregor *et al.*, 1991). Folic acid supplements around conception and early in pregnancy are now officially recommended in both the UK and the US because it is highly likely that they reduce the incidence of neural tube defects (MRC Vitamin Study Group, 1991), even though not all studies show an effect (Mills *et al.*, 1989). Perinatal improvements in obstetric care and neonatal intensive care continue to improve the outlook for those experiencing perinatal adversity (Stewart *et al.*, 1989). Prevention of intraventricular haemorrhages amongst the very premature remains a major challenge.

Postnatally, advances have also been made. *Haemophilus influenzae* type b is the commonest cause of meningitis in children under 4 years old and each year in the UK around 65 die and 150 are left with permanent brain damage and MR (Department of Health, 1992a). A vaccine has now been made which produces immunity in over 95% of cases, and it was introduced throughout the UK in 1992. In Finland it led to a reduction in cases from 203 in 1986 to 12 in 1991. Accidents are the commonest cause of death for children over 1 year of age in the UK and also lead to a significant number of head injuries with MR, particularly from road traffic accidents. The government has recently targeted a 33% reduction in fatal accidents in children by the year 2005 (Department of Health, 1992b) which, if achieved, should be accompanied by a reduction in MR due to head injury.

Amelioration

Once MR is established, amelioration generally becomes the predominant focus of attention, in which educational and general service provision play a leading role. Medication can seldom ameliorate the primary deficit in intellectual functioning in any general way, despite unsubstantiated claims to the contrary (Black *et al.*, 1966). Because the causes are so diverse, a more rational approach is to target specific conditions where there is reason to believe intervention might work. For example, in Klinefelter syndrome (47,XXY) there is a lack of testosterone, and replacement led to improvement in behaviour and adaptation in the majority of cases in the study of Nielsen *et al.* (1988). Since lack of folic acid led to the appearance of chromosomal breaks in the fragile X syndrome, some researchers tried giving it to improve the functioning of affected individuals. Results have been equivocal in terms of both intellectual level and behaviour (Turk, 1992b). The role of psychotropic medication in improving behavioural and psychiatric disturbances has been reviewed above; the drug treatment of epilepsy can improve intellectual functioning considerably in some instances.

Surgery also has a role to play. Operations to insert shunts to prevent build-up of cerebrospinal fluid in hydrocephalus usually improve intellectual prognosis considerably, and have been attempted on fetuses *in utero* before significant fluid accumulates, but with less success (Manning *et al.*, 1986). The benefit of partial temporal lobectomy in intractable epilepsy originating at that site was mentioned previously. There is a wide range of general surgical procedures which have particular relevance to groups of children with MR. These include orthopaedic surgery to improve spinal deformities and release tendon contractures in cerebral palsy, resulting in greatly improved mobility (Fixsen, 1992), cardiac surgery for the congenital heart defects common in Down's syndrome and, more controversially, plastic surgery to 'improve' appearances in Down's syndrome and so increase acceptance in the community (see Chapter 60).

CONCLUSION

In recent years there have been considerable advances in the understanding of MR and associated difficulties. The recognition of organic causes has been given a strong impetus by the discoveries of the new genetics, which also promises new opportunities for prevention in the future. The nature of social impairment has been more clearly defined and good measuring instruments developed. There is better understanding of how families cope and what they find most difficult, with psychiatric disorders figuring prominently. The extent and types of psychopathology in some specific groups have been mapped out. There is now a need for follow-up studies on epidemiologically defined samples in which intellectual level and impairment are assessed independently. In this way, individual, family and environmental factors associated with recovery, persistence or development of new disorders can be investigated. Such information will be invaluable for planning interventions. Currently there are too few systematic studies of treatment of psychiatric disorders in children with MR, although they are so prevalent. The demonstration that behaviour modification is effective for some behaviours is extremely useful, and there is now a need to evaluate a wider range of psychotherapies, such as family work and parent management training, for a wider range of conditions, including depression, hyperactivity and pervasive developmental disorders. While most professionals deplore simple sedation as a means of reducing antisocial behaviour, in some circumstances medication can relieve disorder and promote the opportunity for learning. The conditions where this applies need to be much more systematically evaluated.

All these advances in understanding will be of little benefit to children with MR if they are not made available to them. The skills of many disciplines are required, so over-emphasis on one approach is detrimental. Traditionally this area has often been characterized by a lack of services, reflecting a feeling that little can be done. In fact the advances reviewed in this chapter show that there are now many opportunities to develop services and apply our knowledge, offering the prospect for the children and their carers to lead more rewarding lives.

REFERENCES

Aman M.G. (1982) Psychoactive drug effects in developmental disorders and hyperactivity: toward a resolution of disparate findings. *Journal of Autism and Developmental Disabilities*, **12**, 385–398.

Aman M.G. & Singh N.N. (1988) Patterns of drug use, methodological considerations, measurement techniques, and future trends. In: Aman M.G. & Singh N.N. (eds) *Psychopharmacology and the Developmental Disabilities*. Springer Verlag, New York.

Aman M.G., Teehan C.J., White A.J., Turnott S.H. & Vaithianathan C. (1989) Haloperidol treatment with chronically medicated residents: dose effects on clinical behavior and reinforcement contingencies. *American Journal on Mental Retardation*, **93**, 452–460.

Aman M.G., Marks R.E., Turbott S.H., Wilsher C.P. & Merry S.N. (1991a) Clinical effects of methylphenidate and thioridazine in intellectually subaverage children. *Journal of the American Academy of Child and Adolescent Psychiatry*, **30**, 246−256.

Aman M.G., Marks R.E., Turbott S.H., Wilsher C.P. & Merry S.N. (1991b) Methyl-phenidate and thioridazine in the treatment of intellectually subaverage children: effects on cognitive-motor performance. *Journal of the American Academy of Child and Adolescent Psychiatry*, **30**, 816−824.

American Association for Mental Retardation (1992) *Definition and Classification in Mental Retardation*, 9th edn. American Association for Mental Retardation, Washington, DC.

American Psychiatric Association (1994) *Diagnostic and Statistical Manual of Mental Disorders*, 4th edn (DSM-IV). Washington American Psychiatric Association, Washington, DC.

Ammerman R.T., Van Hasselt V.B., Hersen M., McGonigle K.K. & Lubetsky M.J. (1989) Abuse and neglect in psychiatrically hospitalized multihandicapped children. *Child Abuse and Neglect*, **13**, 335−343.

Anderson K.A. (1971) The shopping behavior of parents of mentally retarded children: the professional person's role. *Mental Retardation*, **9**, 3−5.

Atkinson L. (1990) Intellectual and adaptive functioning: some tables for interpreting the Vineland in combination with intelligence tests. *American Journal of Mental Retardation*, **95**, 198−203.

Aylward G.P., Pfeiffer S.I., Wright A. & Verhulst S.J. (1989) Outcome studies of low birth weight infants published in the last decade: a meta-analysis. *Journal of Pediatrics*, **115**, 515−520.

Bailey A., Bolton P., Butler L., Le Couteur A., Murphy M., Scott S., Webb T. & Rutter M. (1993) Prevalence of the Fragile X anomaly amongst autistic twins and singletons. *Journal of Child Psychology and Psychiatry*, **34**, 673–688.

Baird P.A. & Sadovnick A.D. (1985) Mental retardation in over half a million consecutive livebirths − an epidemiological study. *American Journal of Mental Deficiency*, **89**, 323−330.

Baker B.L., Landen S.J. & Kashima K.J. (1991) Effects of parent training on families of children with mental retardation: increased burden or generalized benefit? *American Journal on Mental Retardation*, **96**, 127−136.

Baron-Cohen S. (1989) Do autistic children have obsessions and compulsions? *British Journal of Clinical Psychology*, **28**, 193−200.

Barrett R.P., Feinstein C. & Hole W.T. (1989) Effects of naloxone and naltrexone on self-injury: a double-blind, placebo-controlled analysis. *American Journal on Mental Retardation*, **93**, 644−651.

Bean A.G. & Roszkowski M.J. (1982) Item-domain relationships in the Adaptive Behavior Scale (ABS). *Applied Research in Mental Retardation*, **3**, 359−367.

Beck B. (1987) Psycho-social assessment of 36 de Lange patients. *Journal of Mental Deficiency Research*, **31**, 251−258.

Beck D.C., Carlson G.A., Russell A.T. & Brownfield F.E. (1987) Use of depression rating instruments in developmentally and educationally delayed adolescents. *Journal of the American Academy of Child and Adolescent Psychiatry*, **26**, 97−100.

Beckman P.J. (1991) Comparison of mothers' and fathers' perception of the effect of young children with and without disabilities. *American Journal of Mental Retardation*, **95**, 585−595.

Bender B.G., Linden M.G. & Robinson A. (1987) Environment and developmental risk in children with sex chromosome abnormalities. *American Academy of Child and Adolescent Psychiatry*, **26**, 499−503.

Berg J.M. (1992) Reducing mental and related handicaps: a biomedical perspective. In: Tizard B. & Varma V. (eds) *Vulnerability and Resilience in Human Development*, pp. 126−136. Jessica Kingsley, London.

Bicknell J. (1989a) Consent for children and adolescents who have an intellectual handicap. *Archives of Disease in Childhood*, **64**, 1529−1532.

Bicknell J. (1989b) Consent and people with mental handicap. *British Medical Journal*, **299**, 1176−1177.

Birch H.G., Richardson S.A., Baird D., Horobin G. & Ilsley R. (1970) *Mental Subnormality in the Community: A Clinical and Epidemiological Study*. Williams & Wilkins, Baltimore.

Bird F., Dores P.A., Moniz D. & Robinson J. (1989) Reducing severe aggressive and self-injurious behaviors with functional communication training. *American Journal of Mental Retardation*, **94**, 37−48.

Blacher J. (1984) Sequential stages of parental adjustment to the birth of a child with handicaps: fact or artifact? *Mental Retardation*, **22**, 55−68.

Black D. (1987) Handicap and family therapy. In: Bentovim A. Gorell Barnes G. & Cooklin A. (eds) *Family Therapy: Complementary Frameworks of Theory and Practice*. Academic Press, London.

Black D.B., Kato J.G. & Walker G.W.R. (1966) A study of improvement in mentally retarded children accruing from siccacell therapy. *American Journal of Mental Deficiency*, **70**, 499−508.

Black R.B. (1990) Prenatal diagnosis and fetal loss: psychosocial consequences and professional responsibilities. *American Journal of Medical Genetics*, **35**, 586−587.

Borthwick-Duffy S.A., Eyman R.K. & White J.F. (1987) Client characteristics and residential placement patterns. *American Journal of Mental Deficiency*, **92**, 24−30.

Bouchard T.J. Jr & McGue M. (1981) Familial studies of intelligence: a review. *Science*, **212**, 1055−1059.

Breslau N. (1990) Does brain dysfunction increase children's vulnerability to environmental stress? *Archives of General Psychiatry*, **47**, 15−20.

Brett E. (1991) *Paediatric Neurology*, 2nd edn. Churchill Livingstone, Edinburgh.

Broman S., Nichols P.L., Shaughnessy P. & Kennedy W. (1987) *Retardation in Young Children: A Developmental Study of Cognitive Deficit*. Lawrence Erlbaum, Hillsdale, NJ.

Bruininks R.H., Hill B.K. & Morreau L.E. (1988) Prevalence and implications of maladaptive behaviors and dual diagnosis in residential and other services. In: Stark J.A., Menolascino F.J., Albarelli M.H. & Gray V.C. (eds) *Mental Retardation and Mental Health: Classification, Diagnosis, Treatment, Services*, pp. 3−29. Springer Verlag, New York.

Burack J.A. (1990) Differentiating mental retardation: the two-group approach and beyond. In: Hodapp R.M., Burack J.A. & Zigler E. (eds) *Issues in the Developmental Approach to Mental Retardation*, pp. 27−48. Cambridge University Press, Cambridge.

Burk H.W. & Menolascino F.J. (1968) Haloperidol in emotionally disturbed mentally retarded individuals. *American Journal of Psychiatry*, **124**, 1589−1591.

Butler M.G. (1990) Prader−Willi syndrome: current understanding of cause and diagnosis. *American Journal of Medical Genetics*, **35**, 319−332.

Byrne E.A., Cunningham C.C. & Sloper P. (1988) *Families and their Children with Down's Syndrome. One Feature in Common*. Routledge, London.

Callias M. (1987) Teaching parents, teachers and nurses. In: Yule W. & Carr J. (eds) *Behaviour Modification for People with Mental Handicaps*, 2nd edn., pp. 211−244. Croom Helm, New York.

Campbell M., Anderson L.T., Meier M., Cohen I.L., Small A.M., Samit C. & Sachar E.J. (1978) A comparison of haloperidol and behavior therapy and their interaction in autistic children. *Journal of the American Academy of Child Psychiatry*, **17**, 640−655.

Campbell M., Small A.M., Green W.H., Jennings S.J., Perry R., Bennett W.G. & Anderson L. (1984) Behavioral efficacy of haloperidol and lithium carbonate − a comparison in hospitalized aggressive children with conduct disorder. *Archives of General Psychiatry*, **41**, 650−656.

Capron C. & Duyme M. (1989) Assessment of effects of socio-economic status on IQ in a full cross-fostering study. *Nature*, **340**, 552–554.

Carlson G.A., Rapport M.D., Pataki C.S. & Kelly K.L. (1992) Lithium in hospitalized children at 4 and 8 weeks: mood, behavior and cognitive effects. *Journal of Child Psychology and Psychiatry*, **33**, 411–425.

Carr J. (1970) Mongolism: telling the parents. *Developmental Medicine and Child Neurology*, **12**, 213–221.

Carr J. (1975) *Young Children with Down's Syndrome*. Butterworth, London.

Carr J. (1990) Supporting the families of people with behavioural/psychiatric difficulties. *International Review of Psychiatry*, **2**, 33–42.

Christie R., Bay C., Kaufman I.A., Bakay B., Borden M. & Nyhan W.L. (1982) Lesch–Nyhan disease: clinical experience with nineteen patients. *Developmental Medicine and Child Neurology*, **24**, 293–306.

Clarke A.M. (1985) Polygenic and environmental interactions. In: Clarke A.M., Clarke A.D.B. & Berg J.M. (eds) *Mental Deficiency: The Changing Outlook*, 4th edn., pp. 267–291. Methuen, London.

Coid J., Allolio B. & Rees L.H. (1983) Raised plasma metenkephalin in patients who habitually-mutilate themselves. *Lancet*, **2**, 545–546.

Corbett J.A. (1977) Population studies in mental retardation. In: Graham P. (ed) *Epidemiological Approaches in Child Psychiatry*, pp. 305–322. Academic Press, London.

Corbett J.A. (1979) Psychiatric morbidity and mental retardation. In: James F.E. & Smith R.P. (eds) *Psychiatric Illness and Mental Handicap*, pp. 11–25. Gaskell, London.

Corbett J.A. (1985) Mental retardation: psychiatric aspects. In: Rutter M. & Hersov L. (eds) *Child and Adolescent Psychiatry*, pp. 661–678. Blackwell Scientific Publications, Oxford.

Corbett J. (1987) Development, disintegration and dementia. *Journal of Mental Deficiency Research*, **31**, 349–356.

Corbett J.A., Harris E. & Robinson R. (1975) Epilepsy. In: Wortis J. (ed) *Mental Retardation and Developmental Disabilities*, vol. VII, pp. 79–111. Brunner/Mazel, New York.

Craft A. (1987) *Mental Handicap and Sexuality: Issues and Perspectives*. Costello, Tunbridge Wells.

Craft M., Ismail I.A., Krishnamurti D., Mathews J., Regan A., Seth R.V. & North P.M. (1987) Lithium in the treatment of aggression in mentally handicapped patients: a double-blind trial. *British Journal of Psychiatry*, **150**, 685–689.

Crome L. & Stern J. (1972) *Pathology of Mental Retardation*, 2nd edn. Churchill Livingstone, Edinburgh.

Cronbach L.J. (1975) Five decades of controversy over mental testing. *American Psychologist*, **30**, 1–14.

Davies S.P. & Ecob K.C. (1959) The challenge to the schools. In: Davies S.P. (ed) *The Mentally Retarded in Society*. Columbia University Press, New York.

de Kock U., Mansell J., Felce D. & Jenkins J. (1984) Establishing appropriate alternative behaviour of a severely disruptive mentally handicapped woman. *Behavioral Psychotherapy*, **12**, 163–174.

Department of Health (1992a) *Immunisation against Infectious Disease*. HMSO, London.

Department of Health (1992b) *The Health of the Nation*. HMSO, London.

Detterman D. (1987) Mental retardation, cognition, and achievement in twins. Research grant awarded by the National Institute of Child Health and Human Development, Washington, DC.

Dingman H.F. & Tarjan G. (1960) Mental retardation and the normal distribution curve. *American Journal of Mental Deficiency*, **64**, 991–994.

Dobbing J. (1968) Vulnerable periods in developing brain. In: Davison A.N. & Dobbing J. (eds) *Applied Neurochemistry*. Blackwell Scientific Publications, Oxford.

Dorfman D.H. & Glaser J.H. (1990) Congenital syphilis presenting in infants after the newborn period. *New England Journal of Medicine*, **323**, 1299–1302.

Drotar D., Baskiewicz A., Irvin N., Kennell J.H. & Klaus M.H. (1975) The adaptation of parents to the birth of an infant with a congenital malformation: a hypothetical model. *Pediatrics*, **56**, 710–717.

Dumaret A. (1985) IQ, scholastic performance and behaviour of sibs raised in contrasting environments. *Journal of Child Psychology and Psychiatry*, **26**, 553–580.

Dupont A. (1980) A study concerning the time-related and other burdens when severely handicapped children are reared at home. *Acta Psychiatrica Scandinavica*, **62** (suppl. 285), 249–257.

Edgerton R.B. (1984) (ed) *Lives in Process: Mildly Retarded Adults in a Large City*. AAMD, Washington, DC.

Einfeld S.L. (1984) Clinical assessment of 4500 developmentally delayed individuals. *Journal of Mental Deficiency Research*, **28**, 129–142.

Elwood J.H. & Darragh P.M. (1981) Severe mental handicap in Northern Ireland. *Journal of Mental Deficiency Research*, **25**, 147–155.

Emde R.N. & Brown C. (1978) Adaptation to the birth of a Down's syndrome infant. *Journal of the American Academy of Child Psychiatry*, **17**, 299–323.

Emerson E., Cummings R., Barrett S., Hughes H., McCool C. & Toogood A. (1988) Challenging behaviour and community services: 2. Who are the people who challenge services? *Mental Handicap*, **16**, 16–19.

Ferguson N. & Watt J. (1980) The mothers of children with special educational needs. *Scottish Educational Review*, **12**, 21–31.

Fishler K., Azen C.G., Friedman E.G. & Koch R. (1989) School achievement in treated PKU children. *Journal of Mental Deficiency Research*, **33**, 493–498.

Fixsen J.A. (1992) Orthopaedic surgery for cerebral palsy. *Hospital Update*, **18**, 803–805.

Foxx R.M., McMorrow M.J., Bittle R.G. & Bechtel D.R. (1986) The successful treatment of a dually diagnosed deaf man's aggression with a programme that included contingent electric shock. *Behavior Therapy*, **17**, 170–186.

Frey K.S., Greenberg M.T., Fewell R.R. (1989) Stress and coping among parents of handicapped children: a multidimensional approach. *American Journal of Mental Retardation*, **94**, 240–249.

Fryers T. & MacKay R.I. (1979) The epidemiology of severe mental handicap. *Early Human Development*, **3**, 277–294.

Futterman A.D. & Arndt S. (1983) The construct and predictive validity of adaptive behavior. *American Journal of Mental Deficiency*, **87**, 546–550.

Gadow K.D. (1992) Pediatric psychopharmacotherapy: a review of recent research. *Journal of Child Psychology and Psychiatry*, **33**, 153–195.

Garber H.L. (1988) *The Milwaukee Project: Preventing Mental Retardation in Children at Risk*. American Association on Mental Retardation, Washington, DC.

Gath A. (1990) Down syndrome children and their families. American Journal of Medical Genetics Supplement, **7**, 314–316.

Gath A. & Gumley D. (1986) Behaviour problems in retarded children with special reference to Down's syndrome. *British Journal of Psychiatry*, **149**, 156–161.

Gillberg C. & Wahlström J. (1985) Chromosome abnormalities in infantile autism and other childhood psychosis: a population study of 66 cases. *Developmental Medicine and Child Neurology*, **27**, 293–304.

Gillberg C., Persson E., Grufman M. & Themner U. (1986) Psychiatric disorders in mildly and severely mentally retarded urban children and adolescents: epidemiological aspects. *British Journal of Psychiatry*, **149**, 68–74.

Gillberg C., Svenson B., Carlström G., Waldenström E. & Rasmussen

P. (1983) Mental retardation in Swedish urban children: some epidemiological considerations. *Applied Research in Mental Retardation*, **4**, 207−218.

Golden G.S. (1988) Tardive dyskinesia and developmental disabilities. In: Aman M.G. & Singh N.N. (eds) *Psychopharmacology of the Developmental Disabilities*, pp. 197−216. Springer-Verlag, New York.

Gostason R. (1985) Psychiatric illness among the mentally retarded: a Swedish population study. *Acta Psychiatrica Scandinavica*, **71** (suppl. 318), 1−117.

Gottesman I.I. (1968) Biogenetics of race and class. In: Deutch M., Katz I. & Jensen A.R. (eds) *Social Class, Race and Psychological Development*. Holt, Rinehart & Winston, New York.

Granat K. & Granat S. (1973) Below-average intelligence and mental retardation. *American Journal of Mental Deficiency*, **78**, 27−32.

Granat K. & Granat S. (1978) Adjustment of intellectually below-average men not identified as mentally retarded. *Scandinavian Journal of Psychology*, **19**, 41−51.

Grantham-McGregor S.M., Powell C.A., Walker S.P. & Hines J.H. (1991) Nutritional supplementation, psychosocial stimulation, and mental development of stunted children: The Jamaican study. *Lancet*, **338**, 1−5.

Green S.H. (1987) Who needs a brain scan? *Archives of Disease in Childhood*, **62**, 1094−1096.

Greenhill L.L., Reider R.O., Wender P.H., Buchsbaum M. & Zahn P. (1973) Lithium carbonate in the treatment of hyperactive children. *Archives of General Psychiatry*, **28**, 636−640.

Guilford J.P. (1979) *Cognitive Psychology with a Frame of Reference*. Edits, San Diego.

Gunn M.J. (1990) The law and learning disability. *International Review of Psychiatry*, **2**, 13−22.

Gunsett R.P., Mulick J.A., Fernald W.B. & Martin J.L. (1989) Indications for medical screening prior to behavioral programming for severely and profoundly mentally retarded clients. *Journal of Autism and Developmental Disorders*, **19**, 167−172.

Gustavson K.H., Holmgren G., Jonsell R. & Son Blomquist H.K. (1977) Severe mental retardation in children in a northern Swedish county. *Journal of Mental Deficiency Research*, **21**, 161−181.

Hagberg B., Hagberg G., Lewerth A. & Lindberg U. (1981a) Mild mental retardation in Swedish school children — I. Prevalence. *Acta Paediatrica Scandinavica*, **70**, 441−444.

Hagberg B., Hagberg G., Lewerth A. & Lindberg U. (1981b) Mild mental retardation in Swedish school children — II. Etiologic and pathogenetic aspects. *Acta Paediatrica Scandinavica*, **70**, 445−452.

Hagberg B., Hagberg G., Olow I. & von Wendt L. (1989) The changing panorama of cerebral palsy in Sweden. *Acta Paediatrica Scandinavica*, **78**, 1−8.

Hagerman R.J. (1989) Genes and chromosomes in autism. In: Gillberg C. (ed) *Diagnosis and Treatment of Autism*. Plenum, New York.

Handen B.L., Breaux A.M., Gosling A., Ploof D.L. & Feldman D. (1990) Efficacy of methylphenidate among mentally retarded children with attention deficit hyperactivity disorder. *Pediatrics*, **86**, 922−930.

Handen B.L., Feldman H., Gosling A., Breaux A.M. & McAuliffe S. (1991) Adverse side effect of methylphenidate among mentally retarded children with ADHD. *Journal of the American Academy of Child and Adolescent Psychiatry*, **30**, 241−245.

Hayes A., Bowling F.G., Fraser D., Krimmer H.L., Marrinan A. & Clague A.E. (1988) Neonatal screening and an intensive management programme for galactosaemia: early evidence of benefits. *Medical Journal of Australia*, **149**, 21−25.

Heistad G.T., Zimmerman R.L. & Doebler M.I. (1982) Long-term usefulness of thioridazine for institutionalized mentally retarded patients. *American Journal of Mental Deficiency*, **87**, 243−254.

Holmes N. (1988) *The Quality of Life of Mentally Handicapped Adults and their Parents*. Unpublished PhD thesis, University of London.

Hopkins I.J. & Klug G.L. (1991) Temporal lobectomy for the treatment of intractable complex partial seizures of temporal lobe origin in early childhood. *Developmental Medicine and Child Neurology*, **33**, 26−31.

Howlin P. & Rutter M. (1987) *Treatment of Autistic Children*. Wiley, Chichester.

Hurley A.D. (1989) Individual psychotherapy with mentally retarded individuals, a review and call for research. *Research in Developmental Disabilities*, **10**, 261−275.

Huttenlocher P.R. (1991) Dendritic and synaptic pathology in mental retardation. *Pediatric Neurology*, **7**, 79−85.

Iverson J.C. & Fox R.A. (1989) Prevalence of psychopathology among mentally retarded adults. *Research in Developmental Disabilities*, **10**, 77−83.

Iwata D.A., Dorsey M.F., Slifer K.J., Bauman K.E. & Richman G.S. (1982) Toward a functional analysis of self-injury. *Analysis and Intervention in Developmental Disabilities*, **2**, 3−20.

Jacobson J.W. (1982a) Problem behavior and psychiatric impairment within a developmentally disabled population I: Behavior and frequency. *Applied Research in Mental Retardation*, **3**, 121−139.

Jacobson J.W. (1982b) Problem behavior and psychiatric impairment within a developmentally disabled population II: Behavior severity. *Applied Research in Mental Retardation*, **3**, 369−381.

Jeavons P.M., Harper J.R. & Bower B.D. (1970) Long-term prognosis in infantile: a follow-up report on 112 cases. *Developmental Medicine and Child Neurology*, **12**, 413−421.

Jellinger K. (1972) Neuropathological features of unclassified mental retardation. In: Cavanagh J.B. (ed) *The Brain in Unclassified Mental Retardation*, pp. 293−306. Churchill Livingstone, London.

Johnson C.A., Ahern F.M. & Johnson R.C. (1976) Level of functioning of siblings and parents of probands of varying degrees of retardation. *Behavior Genetics*, **6**, 473−477.

Jones K.L. (1988) *Smith's Recognizable Patterns of Human Malformation*, 4th edn. W.B. Saunders, Philadelphia.

Kalachnik J.E. (1984) Tardive dyskinesia and the mentally retarded: a review. In: Breuning S.E., Matson J.L. & Barrett R. (eds) *Mental Retardation and Developmental Disabilities*, vol. 2, pp. 329−356. JAI Press, Greenwich, CT.

Kane J.M. (1991) *Tardive Dyskinesia: A Task Force Report of the American Psychiatric Association*. American Psychiatric Press, Washington, DC.

Kazdin A. (1987) *Conduct Disorders in Childhood and Adolescence*. Sage, London.

Kazdin A.E., Matson J.L. & Senatore V. (1983) Assessment of depression in mentally retarded adults. *American Journal of Psychiatry*, **140**, 8.

Kimble G., Garmezy N. & Zigler E. (1984) *Principles of General Psychology*, 5th edn. Wiley, New York.

Koller H., Richardson S.A., Katz M. & McLaren J. (1982) Behavior disturbance in childhood and the early adult years in populations who were and were not mentally retarded. *Journal of Preventive Psychiatry*, **1**, 453−468.

Koller H., Richardson S.A. & Katz M. (1983) Behavior disturbance since childhood among a 5-year birth cohort of all mentally retarded young adults in a city. *American Journal of Mental Deficiency*, **87**, 386−395.

Kushlick A. & Blunden R. (1974) The epidemiology of mental subnormality. In: Clarke A.M. & Clarke A.D.B. (eds) *Mental Deficiency: The Changing Outlook*, 3rd edn. Methuen, London.

Lamont M.A. & Dennis N.R. (1988) Aetiology of mild mental retardation. *Archives of Disease in Childhood*, **63**, 1032−1038.

Largo R.H., Pfister D., Molinari L., Kundu S., Lipp A. & Duc G. (1989) Significance of prenatal, perinatal and postnatal factors in the development of aga preterm infants at five to seven years.

Developmental Medicine and Child Neurology, **31**, 440–456.

Larry P. v. *Riles*, 343 F. Suppl. 1306, aff'd 502 F 2d 963 (9th Cir., 1974).

Laxova R., Ridler M.A.C. & Bowen-Bravery M. (1977) An etiological survey of the severely retarded Hertfordshire children who were born between January 1, 1965 and December 31, 1967. *American Journal of Medical Genetics*, **1**, 75–86.

Lazarus R.S. & Folkman S. (1984) *Stress, Appraisal and Coping*, Springer, New York.

Lemkau P.V. & Imre P.D. (1969) Results of a field epidemiologic study. *American Journal of Mental Deficiency*, **73**, 858–863.

Lennox D.B., Miltenberger R.G., Spengler P. & Erfanian N. (1988) Decelerative treatment practices with persons who have mental retardation: a review of five years of the literature. *American Journal on Mental Retardation*, **92**, 492–501.

Levene M.I., Kornberg J. & Williams H.C. (1985) The incidence and severity of post asphyxial encephalopathy in full term infants. *Early Human Development*, **11**, 21–28.

Levy H.L. & Waisbren S.E. (1983) Effects of untreated maternal phenylketonuria and hyperphenylalaninemia on the fetus. *New England Journal of Medicine*, **309**, 1269–1274.

Lewis E. (1933) Types of mental deficiency and their social significance. *Journal of Mental Science*, **79**, 298–304.

Lindsay W.R., Baty F.J. & Michie A.M. (1989) A comparison of anxiety treatments with adults who have moderate and severe mental retardation. *Research in Developmental Disabilities*, **10**, 129–140.

Loehlin J.C. & Nichols R.C. (1976) *Heredity, Environment and Personality*. University of Texas Press, Austin, TX.

Loehlin J.C., Lindzey G. & Spuhler J.N. (1975) *Race Differences in Intelligence*. W.H. Freeman, San Francisco.

Lubs H.A. (1969) A marker X chromosome. American Journal of Human Genetics, **21**, 231–244.

Lucas A., Morley R., Cole T.J., Lister G. & Leeson-Payne C. (1992) Breast milk and subsequent intelligence quotient in children born preterm. *Lancet*, **339**, 261–264.

Lund J. (1985) The prevalence of psychiatric morbidity in mentally retarded adults. *Acta Psychiatrica Scandinavica*, **72**, 563–570.

McCartney F., Harris M.J. & Bernieri F. (1990) Growing up and apart. *Psychological Bulletin*, **107**, 226–237.

McCracken J.T. & Diamond R.P. (1988) Bipolar disorder in mentally retarded adolescents. *Journal of the American Academy of Child and Adolescent Psychiatry*, **27**, 494–499.

MacMillan D.L. (1982) *Mental Retardation in School and Society*, 2nd edn. Little, Brown, Boston.

Manning F.A., Harrison M.R. & Rodeck C.H. (1986) Catheter shunts for fetal hydrone-phrosis and hydrocephalus. Report of the International Fetal Surgery Registry. *New England Journal of Medicine*, **315**, 336–340.

Matson J.L. & Taras M.E. (1989) A 20 year review of punishment and alternative methods to treat problem behaviors in developmentally delayed persons. *Research in Developmental Disabilities*, **10**, 85–104.

Matson J.L., Gardner W.I., Coe D.A. & Sovner R. (1991) A scale for evaluating emotional disorders in severely and profoundly mentally retarded persons: development of the diagnostic assessment for the severely handicapped (DASH) scale. *British Journal of Psychiatry*, **159**, 404–409.

Menkes J. (1990) Leucodystrophies. *New England Journal of Medicine*, **322**, 54–55.

Mercer J. (1973a) *Labelling the Mentally Retarded*. University of California Press, Berkeley, CA.

Mercer J. (1973b) The myth of three percent prevalence. In: Meyers C.E. (ed) *Socio-Behavioral Studies in Mental Retardation. Monographs of the American Association for Mental Deficiency*, No. 1. Washington, DC.

Mills J.L., Rhoads G.G., Simpson J.L., Cunningham G.C., Conley M.R., Lassman M.R., Walden M.E., Depp O.R., Hoffman H.J. & the National Institute of Child Health and Human Development Neural Tube Defects Study Group (1989) The absence of a relation between the periconceptional use of vitamins and neural-tube tube defects: *New England Journal of Medicine*, **321**, 430–435.

MRC Vitamin Study Group (1991) Prevention of neural defects results of the MRC vitamin study. *Lancet*, **238**, 131–137.

Murphy G. & Oliver C. (1987) Decreasing undesirable behaviours. In: Yule W. & Carr J. (eds) *Behaviour Modification for People with Mental Handicaps*, 2nd edn., pp. 143–161. Croom Helm, New York.

National Institutes of Health (1985) Report on causes of mental retardation and cerebral palsy from the task force on joint assessment of prenatal and perinatal factors associated with brain disorders. *Pediatrics*, **76**, 457–458.

Nelson K.B. & Ellenberg J.H. (1981) Apgar scores as predictors of chronic neurological disability. *Pediatrics*, **68**, 36–44.

Nelson K.B. & Ellenberg J.H. (1986) Antecedents of cerebral palsy: multivariate analysis of risk. *New England Journal of Medicine*, **315**, 81–86.

New England Congenital Hypothyroidism Collaborative (1990) Elementary school performance of children with congenital hypothyroidism. *Journal of Pediatrics*, **116**, 27–32.

Nielsen J., Pelsen B. & Srensen K. (1988) Follow-up of 30 Klinefelter males treated with testosterone. *Clinical Genetics*, **33**, 262–269.

Nihira K., Foster R., Shellhaas M. & Leland H. (1974) *AAMD Adaptive Behavior Scale*. American Association of Mental Deficiency, Washington, DC.

Nirje B. (1969) The normalization principle and its human management implications. In: Kugel R. & Wolfensberger W. (eds) *Changing Patterns in Residential Services for the Mentally Retarded*. Government Printing Office, Washington, DC.

Nolley D., Butterfield B., Fleming A. & Muller P. (1982) Non-aversive treatment of severe self-injurious behaviour: multiple replications with DRO and DRI. In: Hollis J.H. & Meyers C.E. (eds) *Life-Threatening Behaviour*. American Association on Mental Deficiency, Washington, DC.

Nursey A.D., Rohde J.R. & Farmer R.D.T. (1991) Ways of telling new parents about their child and his or her mental handicap: a comparison of doctors' and parents' views. *Journal of Mental Deficiency Research*, **35**, 48–57.

Oliver J.E. (1988) Successive generations of child maltreatment: the children. *British Journal Psychiatry*, **153**, 543–553.

Oliver C., Murphy G.H. & Corbett J.A. (1987) Self-injurious behaviour in people with mental handicap: a total population study. *Journal of Mental Deficiency Research*, **31**, 147–162.

Orr R.R., Cameron S.J. & Day D.M. (1991) Coping with stress in families with children who have mental retardation: an evaluation of the double ABCX Model. *American Journal of Mental Retardation*, **95**, 444–450.

Paulson G.W., Rizvi C.A. & Crane G.E. (1975) Tardive dyskinesia as a possible sequel of long-term therapy with phenothiazines. *Clinical Pediatrics*, **14**, 953–955.

Payton J.B., Burkhart J.E., Hersen M. & Helsel W.J. (1989) Treatment of ADDH in mentally retarded children: a preliminary study. *Journal of the American Academy of Child and Adolescent Psychiatry*, **28**, 761–767.

Penrose L.S. (1963) *The Biology of Mental Defect*. Sidgwick & Jackson, London.

Perry S. & Factor D.C. (1989) Psychometric validity and clinical usefulness of the Vineland Adaptive Behavior Scales and the AAMD Adaptive Behavior Scale for an autistic sample. *Journal of Autism and Developmental Disorders*, **19**, 41–56.

Plomin R., DeFries J.C. & McClearn G.E. (1990) *Behavioral Genetics: A*

Primer, 2nd edn. W.H. Freeman, New York.

Premack D. (1959) Towards empirical behaviour laws. 1. Positive reinforcement. *Psychological Review*, **66**, 219–233.

Provence S. & Naylor A. (1983) *Working with Disadvantaged Parents and Children: Scientific Issues and Practice*. Yale University Press, New Haven, CT.

Quine L. (1991) Sleep problems in children with mental handicap. *Journal of Mental Deficiency Research*, **35**, 269–290.

Quine L. & Pahl J. (1985) Examining the causes of stress in families with severely mentally handicapped children. *British Journal of Social Work*, **15**, 501–517.

Quine L. & Pahl J. (1987) First diagnosis of severe handicap: a study of parental reactions. *Developmental Medicine and Child Neurology*, **29**, 232–242.

Raech H. (1966) A parent discusses initial counselling. *Mental Retardation*, **2**, 25–26.

Raft D., Davidson J., Toomey T.C., Spencer R.F. & Lewis B.F. (1975) Inpatient and outpatient patterns of psychotropic drug responding by non-psychiatrist physicians. *American Journal of Psychiatry*, **132**, 1309–1312.

Ramey C., Campbell F. & Finkelstein N. (1984) Course and structure of intellectual development in children at high risk for developmental retardation. In: Brooks P., Sperber R. & McCauley C. (eds) *Learning and Cognition in the Mentally Retarded*. Erlbaum, Hillsdale, NJ.

Reed E.W. & Reed S.C. (1965) *Mental Retardation: A Family Study*. Saunders, Philadelphia.

Reid A.H. (1989) Schizophrenia in mental retardation: clinical features. *Research in Developmental Disabilities*, **10**, 241–249.

Reid A.H. & Ballinger B.R. (1987) Personality disorder in mental handicap. *Psychological Medicine*, **17**, 983–987.

Reschly D. & Jipson F. (1976) Ethnicity, geographic locale, age, sex, and urban rural residence as variables in the prevalence of mild retardation. *American Journal of Mental Deficiency*, **81**, 154–161.

Reynolds W.M. & Baker J.A. (1988) Assessment of depression in persons with mental retardation. *American Journal on Mental Retardation*, **93**, 93–103.

Richardson S. & Koller H. (1985) Epidemiology. In: Clarke A.M., Clarke A.D.B. & Berg J.M. (eds) *Mental Deficiency: The Changing Outlook*, 4th edn. Methuen, London.

Richardson S. & Koller H. (1992) Vulnerability and resilience in adults who were classified as mildly mentally handicapped in childhood. In: Tizard B. & Varma V. (eds) *Vulnerability and Resilience in Human Development*, pp. 102–123. JKP, London.

Richardson M.A., Haugland G., Pass R. & Craig T.J. (1986) The prevalence of tardive dyskinesia in a mentally retarded population. *Psychopharmacology Bulletin*, **22**, 243–249.

Robertson I., Richardson A.M. & Youngson S.C. (1984) Social skills training with mentally handicapped people: a review. *British Journal of Clinical Psychology*, **23**, 241–264.

Rodrigue J.R., Morgan S.B. & Geffken G.R. (1991) A comparative evaluation of adaptive behavior in children and adolescents with autism, Down syndrome, and normal development. *Journal of Autism and Developmental Disorders*, **21**, 187–196.

Ross T.T., Begab M.J., Dondis E.H., Giampiccolo J.S. & Meyers C.E. (1985) *Lives of the Mentally Retarded: A Forty-Year Follow-Up Study*. Stanford University Press, Stanford, CA.

Rusch R.G., Hall J.C. & Griffin H.C. (1986) Abuse-provoking characteristics of institutionalized mentally retarded individuals. *American Journal of Mental Deficiency*, **90**, 618–624.

Rutter M. (1980) Raised lead levels and impaired cognitive/behavioral functioning. *Developmental Medicine and Child Neurology*, **42** (suppl.), 1–26.

Rutter M. (1983) Stress, coping and development: some issues and some questions. In Garmezy N. & Rutter M. (eds) *Stress, Coping and Development in Children*. McGraw-Hill, New York.

Rutter M., Tizard J. & Whitmore K. (eds) (1970a) *Education, Health and Behaviour*, Longman, London.

Rutter M., Graham P. & Yule W. (1970b) *A Neuropsychiatric Study in Childhood*. Spastics International Medical Publications Heinemann, London.

Saenger G. (1962) Social factors in the institutionalization of retarded individuals. In: Richards B.W. (ed) *Proceedings of the London Conference on the Scientific Study of Mental Deficiency (1960)*, pp. 642–649. May & Baker, Dagenham.

Salzberg C.L., Lignugaris-Kraft B. & McCuller G.L. (1988) Reasons for job loss: a review of employment termination studies of mentally retarded workers. *Research in Development Disabilities*, **9**, 153–170.

Sameroff A. (1975) Early influences on development: fact or fancy? *Merill Palmer Quarterly*, **21**, 267–294.

Sameroff A., Seifer R., Barocas R., Zax M. & Greenspan S. (1987) IQ scores of 4-year-old children: social-environmental risk factors. *Pediatrics*, **79**, 343–350.

Sandman C.A., Barron J., Chicz-de Met A. & De Met E.M. (1990) Plasma and endorphin levels in patients with self-injurious behaviour. *American Journal of Mental Retardation*, **95**, 84–92.

Schinzel A. (1988) Microdeletion syndromes, balanced translocations, and gene mapping. *Journal of Medical Genetics*, **25**, 454–462.

Schroeder S.R. & Gualtieri C.T. (1985) Behavioral interactions induced by chronic neuroleptic therapy with persons with mental retardation. *Psychopharmacology Bulletin*, **21**, 323–326.

Schulman J.D. (1990) Treatment of the embryo and the fetus in the first trimester: current status and future prospects. *American Journal of Medical Genetics*, **35**, 197–200.

Scott H. (1976) Outcome of very severe birth asphyxia. *Archives of Disease in Childhood*, **51**, 712.

Selzer M.M. & Krauss M.W. (1989) Aging parents with mentally retarded children: family risk factors and sources of support. *American Journal of Mental Retardation*, **94**, 303–312.

Shaffer D., Gould M.S., Brasic J., Ambrosini P., Fisher P., Bird H. & Aluwahlia S. (1983) A children's global assessment scale (C-GAS). *Archives of General Psychiatry*, **40**, 1228–1231.

Shaw C.-M. (1987) Correlates of mental retardation and structural changes of the brain. *Brain and Development*, **9**, 1–8.

Silva P.A. (1987) Epidemiology, longitudinal course and some associated factors: an update. In: Yule W. & Rutter M. (eds) *Language Development and Disorders*. Clinics in Developmental Medicine, nos. 101/102, pp. 1–15.

Silverstein A.B. (1982) Note on the constancy of IQ. *American Journal of Mental Deficiency*, **77**, 380–382.

Sinason V. (1992) *Mental Handicap and the Human Condition: New Approaches from the Tavistock*. Free Association Books, London.

Singh N.N. & Aman M.G. (1981) Effects of thioridazine dosage on the behavior of severely retarded persons. *American Journal of Mental Deficiency*, **85**, 580–587.

Skuse D. (1984) Extreme deprivation in early childhood: II. Theoretical issues and a comparative review. *Journal of Child Psychology and Psychiatry*, **25**, 543–572.

Sladek J.R. & Gash D.M. (1988) Nerve-cell grafting in Parkinson's disease. *Journal of Neurosurgery*, **68**, 337–351.

Sloman L. & Konstantereas M. (1990) Why families with biological deficits require a systems approach. *Family Process*, **29**, 417–429.

Sloper P., Knussen C., Turner S. & Cunningham C. (1991) Factors related to stress and satisfaction with life in families of children with Down's syndrome. *Journal of Child Psychology and Psychiatry*, **32**, 655–676.

Sovner R. & Hurley A.D. (1983) Do the mentally retarded suffer from affective illness? *Archives of General Psychiatry*, **40**, 61–67.

Sparrow S., Balla D. & Cicchetti D. (1984) *Vineland Adaptive Behavior Scales*. American Guidance Service, Circle Pines, MN.

Sprague R.L. & Werry J.S. (1971) Methodology of psychopharmacological studies with the retarded. In: Ellis N.R. (ed) *International Review of Research in Mental Retardation* vol. 5, pp. 147–210. Academic Press, New York.

Spreat S., Behar D., Reneski B. & Miazzo P. (1989) Lithium carbonate for aggression in mentally retarded persons. *Comprehensive Psychiatry*, **30**, 505–511.

Stanley F. & Alberman E. (1984) *The Epidemiology of the Cerebral Palsies*. Clinics in Developmental Medicine, no. 87. SIMP Blackwell, London.

Sternberg R.J. & Salter W. (1982) Conceptions of intelligence. In: Sternberg R. (ed) *Handbook of Human Intelligence*, pp. 3–28. Cambridge University Press, Cambridge.

Stevens S., Evered C., O'Brien R. & Wallace E. (1988) Sex education: who needs it? *Mental Handicap*, **16**, 166–170.

Stewart A.L., Costello A.M., Hamilton P.A., Baudin.J., Townsend J., Bradford B.C. & Reynolds E.O.R. (1989) Relationship between neurodevelopmental status of very preterm infants at one and four years. *Developmental Medicine and Child Neurology*, **31**, 756–765.

Stoneman Z., Browdy G.H., Davis C.H., Crapps J.M. & Malone D.M. (1991) Ascribed role relations between children with mental retardation and their younger siblings. *American Journal of Mental Retardation*, **95**, 537–550.

Streissguth A.P., Barr H.M., Sampson P.D., Darby B.L. & Martin D.C. (1989) IQ at age 4 in relation to maternal alcohol use and smoking during pregnancy. *Developmental Psychology*, **25**, 3–11.

Sundet J.M., Tambs K., Magnus P. & Berg K. (1988) On the question of secular trends in the heritability of intelligence test scores: a study of Norwegian twins. *Intelligence*, **12**, 47–60.

Tausig M. (1985) Factors in family decision making about placement for developmentally disabled individuals. *American Journal of Mental Deficiency*, **89**, 352–361.

Taylor E. (1991) Toxins and allergens. In: Rutter M. & Casaer P. (eds) *Biological Risk Factors for Psychosocial Disorders*. Cambridge University Press, Cambridge.

Tharinger D., Horton C.B. & Millea S. (1990) Sexual abuse and exploitation of children and adults with mental retardation and other handicaps. *Child Abuse and Neglect*, **14**, 301–312.

Thomson J.S. & Thomson M.W. (1986) *Genetics in Medicine*, 4th edn, p. 263. W.B. Saunders, Philadelphia.

Tizard J. & Grad J.C. (1961) *The Mentally Handicapped and their Families*. Oxford University Press, London.

Turk J. (1992a) The fragile-X syndrome: on the way to a behavioural phenotype. *British Journal of Psychiatry*, **160**, 24–35.

Turk J. (1992b) Fragile X and folic acid. In: Hagerman R.J. & McKenzie P. (eds) *Proceedings of the 3rd International Fragile X Conference*. Spectra Publishing, Dillon, CO.

Tyrer S.P., Walsh A., Edwards D.E., Berney T.P. & Stephens D.A. (1984) Factors associated with a good response to lithium in aggressive mentally handicapped subjects. *Progress in Neuro-Psychopharmacology and Biological Psychiatry*, **8**, 751–755.

Udwin O. & Yule W. (1990) Expressive language of children with Williams syndrome. *American Journal of Medical Genetics*, (suppl. 6), 108–114.

Wallander J.L., Pitt L.C. & Mellins C.A. (1990) Child functional independence and maternal psychosocial stress as risk factors threatening adaptation in mothers of physically or sensorially handicapped children. *Journal of Consulting and Clinical Psychology*, **58**, 818–824.

Weatherall D.J. (1991) Gene therapy in perspective. *Nature*, **349**, 275–276.

Weaver T.R. (1946) The incident of maladjustment among mental defectives in military environments. *American Journal of Mental Deficiency*, **51**, 238–246.

Weaver D.D. (1989) *Catalog of Prenatally Diagnosed Conditions*. Johns Hopkins University Press, Baltimore, MD.

Webb T., Bundey S., Thake A. & Todd J. (1986) The frequency of the fragile X chromosome among school children in Coventry. *Journal of Medical Genetics*, **23**, 396–399.

Weisz J.R. (1990) Cultural–familial mental retardation: a developmental perspective on cognitive performance and 'helpless' behavior. In: Hodapp R.M., Burack J.A. & Zigler E. (eds) *Issues in the Developmental Approach to Mental Retardation*, pp. 137–168. Cambridge University Press, Cambridge.

Werner E.E. & Smith R.S. (1982) *Vulnerable but Invincible: A Longitudinal Study of Resilient Children and Youth*. McGraw-Hill, New York.

West J.R. (1986) *Alcohol and Brain Development*. Oxford University Press, London.

Wikler L., Wasow M. & Hatfield E. (1981) Chronic sorrow revisited: parent versus professional depiction of the adjustment of parents of mentally retarded children. *American Journal of Orthopsychiatry*, **51**, 63–70.

Wilkin D. (1979) *Caring for the Mentally Handicapped Child*. Croom Helm, London.

Williams M.L., Lewandowski L.J., Coplan J. & Deugenio D.B. (1987) Neurodevelopmental outcome of preschool children born preterm with and without intracranial hemorrhage. *Developmental Medicine and Child Neurology*, **29**, 243–249.

Wilson J., Blacher J. & Baker B.L. (1989) Siblings of children with severe handicaps. *Mental Retardation*, **27**, 167–173.

Wilson R.S. (1983) The Louisville twin study: developmental synchronies in behavior. *Child Development*, **54**, 298–316.

Wing L. (1977) The use of case registers in child psychiatry and mental retardation. In: Graham P. (ed) *Epidemiological Approaches in Child Psychiatry*, pp. 00–00. Academic Press, London.

Wing L. & Gould J. (1979) Severe impairments of social interaction and associated abnormalities in children: epidemiology and classification. *Journal of Autism and Developmental Disorders*, **9**, 11–29.

Wolfensberger W. (1983) Social role valorisation: a proposed new term for the principle of normalisation. *Mental Retardation*, **21**, 234–239.

Wolff P.H., Gardner J., Paccia J. & Lappen J. (1989) The greeting behaviour of fragile X males. *American Journal of Mental Retardation*, **93**, 406–411.

World Health Organization (1980) *International Classification of Impairments, Disabilities and Handicaps*. WHO, Geneva.

World Health Organization (1992) *The ICD-10 Classification of Mental and Behavioural Disorders: Clinical Descriptions and Diagnostic Guidelines*. WHO, Geneva.

Wright L.S. (1976) Chronic grief: the anguish of being an exceptional parent. *The Exceptional Child*, **23**, 160–169.

Yule W. & Carr J. (1987) *Behaviour Modification for People with Mental Handicaps*, 2nd edn. Croom Helm, New York.

Zigler E. & Hodapp R.M. (1986) *Understanding Mental Retardation*. Cambridge University Press, Cambridge.

Zipf W.B., O'Dorisio T.B. & Berntson G.G. (1990) Short-term infusion of pancreatic polypeptide: effect on children with Prader–Willi syndrome. *American Journal of Clinical Nutrition*, **51**, 162–166.

Chapter 36
Reading and
Other Learning Disabilities

Barbara Maughan & William Yule

INTRODUCTION

For most children, learning to read, spell and do arithmetic presents some challenges; for some, mastering these basic academic skills creates inordinate difficulties. Severe, specific learning problems affect a substantial minority of children, and show a strong tendency to persist. In childhood, they are also frequently associated with psychiatric disorder (Rourke & Fuerst, 1991; Hinshaw, 1992). Professionals in child psychiatry will meet many learning-disabled children, and may be consulted on a range of questions: what causes unexpected learning problems? do they run in families? will children's skills improve as they get older? and what sorts of remedial help, at what stages, are likely to be most beneficial? It is these questions that we focus on here.

Disorders of reading, spelling, writing and arithmetic are all recognized in DSM-IV (American Psychiatric Association, in press) and ICD-10 (World Health Organization, 1992). They share many features in common (and indeed many children face problems in each area), but different types of learning disability also have important distinguishing features. To date, we know a great deal more about the development of reading, and reading disabilities, than we do about spelling or arithmetic problems. Because of that, we focus primarily on reading, and take up specific issues in relation to other difficulties more briefly at the end of the chapter. There has been a massive expansion of research on reading in recent years, most notably in cognitive psychology, and in promising advances in genetic methodologies. We highlight some of the central issues here; fuller discussions of these and other topics are provided by Bryant and Bradley (1985), Goswami and Bryant (1990), Pennington (1990), Snowling (1991) and Snowling and Thomson (1991).

READING SKILLS
AND THEIR ACQUISITION

Like speech and language, reading and writing are uniquely human achievements, of extraordinary complexity and power. They enable us to record knowledge, thoughts and feelings in symbolic forms, and communicate them to others across time and space. Although writing systems have been in existence for thousands of years, literacy was quite restricted, even in western societies, until the relatively recent past. Only a few generations ago, most of our ancestors were unable to sign their names. Little wonder that our understanding of these complex skills is still in its infancy.

Problems in learning to read are best seen in the context of what we know about fluent reading and its acquisition. Frith (1985) and Marsh *et al.* (1981) proposed stage models of reading acquisition, in which different skills are added at different points. When they first begin to read, children recognize words as whole units, almost certainly on the basis of visual cues. At this *logographic* stage they have no strategies for deciphering unfamiliar words. To do this, they need to master the alphabetic principles of letter–sound correspondences, breaking words down into smaller units. This constitutes the second, *alphabetic* or *sequential decoding* stage. Finally, in what Frith called the *orthographic* stage, children move towards the automaticity typical of later fluent reading, recognizing strings or sequences of letters without phonological conversion.

These models provide a useful way of organizing much developmental data, though they have not gone unchallenged (Stuart & Coltheart, 1988; Goswami & Bryant, 1990; Temple, 1990). Following from the stage approach, however, some models of reading difficulties view poor readers as delayed at an early stage of reading development (Snowling, 1991). Others argue that it may be more helpful to analyse the skills involved in fluent reading, and track poor readers' deficits from there. For the fluent reader, extracting meaning from print is a rapid and largely automatic process. We recognize and understand familiar words directly, as whole units, without any awareness of intervening processes. When we meet new words we approach them with quite specific strategies: breaking them down into smaller units, perhaps sounding them out, or guessing at their meaning from contextual cues. Much research on reading in the 1970s and 1980s was directed at understanding the processes involved in these two routes to word recognition, the one apparently direct and immediate, the other more indirect, and drawing on phonological skills (Coltheart, 1978; Patterson, 1981). More recently, more complex models have been proposed (Seidenberg & McClelland, 1989; Van Orden *et al.*, 1990). Even so, understanding the skills involved in reading both familiar and unfamiliar words remains a fundamental concern.

Educationalists often stress a 'top down' approach, beginning with comprehension and moving to the specifics of word recognition. Here, the reader is seen as actively searching for meaning, guessing at new words from contextual cues, and testing out predictions against the text in a 'psycholinguistic guessing game' (Goodman, 1976). Others (e.g. Perfetti, 1985) stress 'bottom-up' processes, beginning with simple perceptual skills and ending with comprehension. Somewhere between these two, Stanovich (1980) proposed an interactive-compensatory model, in which reliance on context varies as a function of reading skill.

Whichever model is favoured, a task analysis of reading highlights the complex range of cognitive skills involved. The reader must make fine visual discriminations, including closure (as between o and c), line to curve transformations (as between u and v), and rotational transformations (e.g. b and d, or m and w). The ability to make these transformations follows a regular developmental course (Gibson, 1965). In written English, left-to-right sequencing, both of letters within words and words within sentences, is also crucial for accurate reading: 'god' is not the same as 'dog', nor 'dog bit man' the same as 'man bit dog'.

Phonological skills are also important. In languages with alphabetic writing systems, the letters and letter strings of written words represent particular sound segments of spoken words — individual phonemes, syllables, and between these, elements often referred to as subsyllabic units. Sensitivity to the sound patterns of spoken words, and the ability to segment them into smaller units, have been shown to be crucial to reading (Bradley & Bryant, 1983). The reader must store both phonological and visual codes in memory, and match between these two modalities. Most important of all, reading is a linguistic skill, aimed at comprehension. The child who can read mechanically, but does not understand what he or she has read, has not yet mastered what reading is all about.

Reading shows strong links with general as well as specific cognitive skills. Reading attainment correlates about +0.6 with measures of IQ (Yule *et al.*, 1974, 1981), and, like other forms of learning, depends on motivation and task involvement, and on the learning opportunities open to the child. Reading achievement varies markedly with socioeconomic background, birth order and parental interest (Davie *et al.*, 1972; Hewison & Tizard, 1980; McManus & Mascie-Taylor, 1983). Once these factors have been taken into account, reading progress then often differs according to the school a child attends (Mortimore *et al.*, 1988). There are clearly important environmental influences on reading achievement; as we discuss in later sections, there is also persuasive evidence for genetic effects.

Difficulties in any of these areas might plausibly contribute to problems in learning to read. They have been strongly linked to speech and language problems (Stevenson, 1989) and to temperamental attributes such as poor concentration (Rutter *et al.*, 1970). A number of handicapping conditions (including epilepsy and cerebral palsy) are associated with higher than expected rates of underachievement in reading, and children with localized head injuries, especially of the left cerebral hemisphere, have also been found to have difficulties in reading (Chadwick *et al.*, 1981).

The first clinical reports of dyslexia — then viewed as word-blindness — appeared almost a century ago (Hinshelwood, 1895). Since then, many different approaches to classifying and conceptualizing reading problems have emerged. They have been viewed as specific deficits or more general developmental delays; as contingent on, or independent of, general intelligence; and as discrete disorders or the extremes of the normal range. Debates on many of these issues continue in the literature today. Consensus has, however, emerged on one important issue. In the past, reading failure was assumed to be a unitary phenomenon. This view is no longer regarded as tenable. Reading-disabled children show many different patterns of difficulties, and different types of learning problems can be identified. We thus begin by considering questions of classification.

CLASSIFICATION OF LEARNING DISABILITIES

Three basic distinctions have to be made in the differential diagnosis of low scholastic achievement (Rutter, 1974). Firstly, there must be a differentiation according to the type of skill involved (reading, spelling, mathematics). Secondly, failure to acquire educational skills must be differentiated from a later loss of those skills. And thirdly, it is important to distinguish between generally *low* achievement, poor for the child's age, and more specific disabilities, that involve *under*achievement in relation to age and IQ (Rutter & Yule, 1975). The first two points are widely accepted, but the third remains controversial. Here, we begin by examining the controversy regarding identification, then look at the value of classifying types of reading disability by psychological functions.

General reading backwardness and specific reading retardation

Implicitly or explicitly, most clinical and research studies have distinguished between children with specific difficulties in reading, discrepant from their general abilities, and those for whom poor reading performance forms part of a wider pattern of intellectual difficulties. Underachievement in reading has been operationalized in widely differing ways, and we come on to discuss questions of measurement below. In general, however, children have been taken to show specific underachievement in reading if their performance is discrepant from expectations based on both age or grade and IQ. This concept of specific underachievement is central to most definitions of learning disabilities, and to both ICD (World Health Organization, 1992) and DSM (American Psychiatric Association, in press) diagnostic criteria for reading and other academic skills disorders.

Underachievement in reading has been reported in all countries where it has been studied (Aaron & Malatesha Joshi, 1987). Prevalence rates depend, of course, on the definitions taken: most estimates of severe underachievement fall in the range from 3 to 10%. In the Isle of Wight epidemiological studies (Rutter *et al.*, 1970), specific reading retardation (SRR), defined as achievement more than 2 standard errors of prediction below expectation in relation to age and IQ, was found to affect just under 4% of 10-year-olds. General reading backwardness (GRB), reflecting similarly severe difficulties assessed in relation to age alone, affected 8%. In the Inner London comparative study the respective rates were almost double, at 10% SRR and 19% GRB (Berger *et al.*, 1975). Specific reading problems may be somewhat less common in languages such as Italian, which have much more regular orthographies than English (Lindgren *et al.*, 1985), but rates broadly within the 4–10% range have been found in countries with widely differing writing systems, including nonalphabetic scripts (Stevenson *et al.*, 1982).

Recently, distinctions between low achievers and underachievers have come under scrutiny from a number of quarters (Stanovich, 1991). Some commentators have questioned the appropriateness of using IQ as a benchmark for assessing reading problems, objecting to what is seen as a 'capacity' notion of IQ (Siegel, 1988, 1989). This is not, of course, a necessary implication of the use of IQ tests in predicting reading; many children read above the level predicted from their IQ (Yule *et al.*, 1974; Rodgers, 1983), and lower-ability children can maintain the same levels of progress in reading as their more able peers (Share *et al.*, 1989). The use of a test of general intelligence to predict reading is a convenient way of predicting the specific skill from the general, and involves no claims that IQ causes or constrains reading ability. The procedure is purely empirical, and stands or falls by its utility. The central question is whether underachievers form a distinct — and possibly qualitatively different — group from other poor readers.

The first systematic comparisons came from the Isle of Wight and London studies (Rutter *et al.*, 1970; Berger *et al.*, 1975; Rutter & Yule, 1975), which highlighted a series of differences between SRR and GRB groups that have subsequently been tested in other samples. The first major finding of the Isle of Wight and London studies was distributional: SRR occurred more often in these populations than would be expected if poor readers simply formed the bottom of the normal curve on reading skills (Rutter & Yule, 1975). On statistical grounds alone, there are bound to be some children with extreme degrees of underachievement in reading. SRR might thus represent simply the lower end of a normal continuum, with nothing else remarkable about the children. In the Isle of Wight and London studies, however, children with SRR formed a 'hump' at the bottom of the normal curve. Van der Wissel and Zegers (1985) have argued that some of the excess of SRRs could have been due to floor and ceiling effects on group tests. Some other population studies have also reported bimodality in the distribution of underachievement in reading (Stevenson, 1988; Dobbins & Tafa, 1992), while others have not (Rodgers, 1983; Shaywitz *et al.*, 1992).

Distributional differences could, of course, arise for a number of reasons. If children with specific reading problems form a qualitatively distinct group, other tests are perhaps more important. In particular, we might expect differentiable subgroups to show different patterns of correlates; differences in prognosis and response to treatment; and possibly also differences in functional impairments in reading and related cognitive skills. Genetic studies might also show different patterns of heritability.

Beginning with the question of correlates, the Rutter and Yule (1975) studies highlighted a series of differences between backward and retarded readers: (1) children with SRR were much more likely to be boys (a ratio of 3 or 4 to 1) whereas the sex distribution for GRB was nearly equal; (2) overt neurological disorders were much more frequent in the GRB group; (3) children with GRB tended to have a wide range of developmental difficulties including motor and praxic abnormalities, whereas SRR was strongly associated only with speech and language impairment; and (4) more of the GRB children came from socially disadvantaged homes.

These differences were largely replicated by Silva *et al.* (1985) in their general population study of 9-year-old New Zealand boys, though their SRR group showed less extensive language problems. Ingram *et al.* (1970) found that children with SRR were less likely to have neurological or electroencephalogram abnormalities, but more likely to show primitive spelling errors of audiophonic origin. Few other studies have been able to assess this range of correlates. The question of sex ratios has, however, attracted widespread attention. Clinic studies of reading disability almost invariably follow the Isle of Wight and London findings in showing a marked excess of boys. More recent studies (Shaywitz *et al.*, 1990; Wadsworth *et al.*, 1992) have replicated the excess of boys in referred groups but found more balanced sex ratios among research-defined poor readers. Once again, comparisons are complicated by definitional differences, especially in terms of severity: the excess of boys among underachievers may be focused at the extremes of the distribution of underachievement. Cases at this level of severity will often be found in clinic samples, but need large general population studies to identify to any significant degree.

Differences in the pattern of children's reading-related skills might also help identify different subgroups of poor readers. Here, current evidence is inconsistent. Elliott (1989), for example, found that GRB and SRR children showed very different patterns of subscores on the British Ability Scales. Jorm *et al.* (1986a) reported that SRR was associated with deficits in phonological processing, while Ellis and Large (1987) found relatively normal phonological skills but disabilities in visual processing. Fredman and Stevenson (1988) found significant differences between GRB and SRR in phonological, whole-word reading skills on both regular and irregular words, but these were not maintained when reading age and IQ were controlled. Aaron (1989), however, found that a non-specific poor reading group did not differ from younger normal readers, while a dyslexic group was poorer in decoding and spelling, and showed heavier dependence on context.

Follow-up and treatment studies, examining the educational outlook for different groups, provide yet further tests. We know of no systematic evaluations of response to treatment among SRR and GRB children as yet. It is clear that the outcome of both GRB and SRR is poor (Yule, 1985), but this does not imply that there may not be important differences between these subtypes. A follow-up of the Isle of Wight samples (Yule, 1973) found that, despite their higher general intelligence, children with SRR made significantly less progress in reading and spelling between the ages of 10 and 14 than children with GRB, but more progress in mathematics. A follow-up of the more socially disadvantaged Inner London groups, however, found few backward-retarded differences in progress during schooling (Maughan *et al.*, in press). The meaning of the disorder may thus be somewhat different in different social and cultural contexts.

Finally, there is the question of differences in the pattern of genetic influences. We discuss more general aspects of the genetic evidence on reading disabilities in a later section. Here, we focus on findings from one of the most interesting new techniques in this area, designed to test how far extreme scores on a distribution reflect discrete disorders or the extremes of the normal range (Plomin & Rende, 1991). To date, these approaches have only been applied in a very few studies of reading disabilities, and results are not yet conclusive (DeFries *et al.*, 1987). The findings thus far are, however, consistent with the existence of a distinct group of severe underachievers, but require extension and replication before we can be certain of this picture.

At present, then, the evidence from these various comparisons is mixed. There are a number of indicators that severely underachieving readers form a distinct group, differing in important ways from generally backward readers, but not all the evidence is consistent. As in most aspects of reading research, definitional and methodological differences may well play a part in these variations in findings. We must await further clarification to resolve these important debates.

Dyslexia and other subtypes

From a somewhat different perspective, others have argued for a subcategory of dyslexia within the severely reading disabled population. Dyslexia is often assumed to involve 'pure' difficulties of constitutional origin that show a common need for a specific form of treatment. The World Federation of Neurology produced a much quoted definition of developmental dyslexia: 'A disorder manifested by difficulty in learning to read despite conventional instruction, adequate intelligence, and socio-cultural opportunity. It is dependent upon fundamental cognitive disabilities which are frequently of constitutional origin' (Critchley, 1970).

It is now widely accepted that this is not a scientifically or clinically useful definition, partly because there is no consensus on how to operationalize it, but largely because it is a negative rather than a positive definition (Reid, 1969; Boder, 1971). Other attempts at defining dyslexia have also left a

great deal to be desired (see Rutter, 1969; Rutter & Yule, 1975; Rourke & Strang, 1983) and most efforts to separate out a dyslexic core from within a broader group of children with specific reading retardation have largely failed. One of the earliest distinctions was to differentiate between auditory and visual dyslexia on the basis of children's pattern of results on a battery of tests. Myklebust (1965) claimed that having identified a child's cognitive weakness, the child should then be taught through his or her strengths. Unfortunately, attractive as this idea is, there is little evidence that this sort of diagnostic-prescriptive teaching has been successful (Yule, 1976).

Feagans and McKinney (1991) have recently reviewed approaches to subtyping in the learning disabilities field more generally. Among clinical/inferential approaches, Boder's (1973) early studies of reading and spelling errors had considerable influence. Based on clinical impressions, Boder distinguished three main groups of dyslexics: (1) a *dysphonetic* subgroup, making up almost two-thirds of her sample, whose difficulties centred on the use of phonological strategies; (2) a *dyseidetic* subgroup, whose problems seemed primarily visual; and (3) an *alexic* or mixed group, showing both types of difficulty. Although her results have proved difficult to replicate in detail, a not dissimilar pattern has emerged from a number of other subtyping studies.

More recently, multivariate statistical procedures have been used to identify subtypes. Some studies (Lyon & Watson, 1981) have identified differentiable groupings, but others have found less consistent results. Vogler *et al.* (1989), for example, found little support for distinct subtypes, and argued that subgroupings derived from statistical clustering procedures require careful validation. A number of writers have recently proposed a model of heterogeneity without clustering, where individuals' score profiles on reading-related cognitive skills are best seen as continuously distributed on a number of different dimensions (Fletcher & Satz, 1985; Stanovich, 1988).

Very different approaches to subgrouping have emerged from developmental models of the reading process, and from cognitive neuropsychological studies of acquired dyslexia. The developmental approach (Snowling, 1991) assumes that different subgroups of poor readers may have become delayed at different stages of reading development. Cognitive neuropsychological studies have examined possible analogues between developmental and acquired reading problems. Psycholinguistic analyses of the reading errors of brain-injured patients (Patterson, 1981) have identified three main types of acquired reading problem: (1) *phonological dyslexia*, in which patients show essentially normal word recognition, but have particular difficulties with non-words; (2) *surface dyslexia*, in which phonological skills are not impaired, but there are difficulties in recognizing irregular words; and (3) *deep dyslexia*, where patients seem able to extract meaning from words they are unable to read out loud, and make semantic errors (such as reading 'canary' for 'parrot').

To date, few if any cases of developmental reading problems have been found to parallel deep dyslexia (Ellis, 1991), but there have been individual case studies of children argued to be examples of both developmental phonological dyslexia (Temple & Marshall, 1983) and developmental surface dyslexia (Coltheart *et al.*, 1983). Other studies, however, have shown that some younger normal readers make errors of the kind taken as 'symptoms' of developmental dyslexia (Bryant & Impey, 1986; Baddeley *et al.*, 1988). This might argue for a delay (or possibly arrest) rather than a deficit model.

At this stage, then, there is little evidence in favour of clear subtypes among disabled readers, nor of a pure dyslexic subgroup. The features that are said to characterize dyslexia are closely similar to those that empirical findings show to be associated with specific reading retardation. In both cases, the reading difficulties are severe, specific and persistent, and in both there is a strong association with serious and often bizarre spelling errors that frequently involve audiophonic decoding and which tend to persist into adult life (Critchley, 1970; Boder, 1971; Rutter & Yule, 1973). There is a strong connection with developmental impairment of various specific cognitive functions, especially those involving speech and language, and good evidence for an important biological component that includes genetic factors. There are two important respects in which the concept of dyslexia seems to be mistaken: firstly, the supposition that it is a distinct unitary condition; and secondly, that the presence of a biological condition means that environmental influences are unimportant. Quite the converse is true. Children with a biological impairment may be *more* vulnerable to environmental adversities, and reading difficulties are best seen as the outcome of an interaction between constitutional deficits and environmental hazards.

Measuring underachievement

To identify any sort of learning disability we need some means of assessing underachievement, to determine whether children are performing less well than expected. Underachievement is a matter of degree, and we need to ask what should be the expected level of attainment for any child, and what constitutes achievement significantly below that level.

From the beginning of educational attainment measurement, people have considered the difference between tested reading age and actual chronological age or grade level. This difference (sometimes expressed as a ratio of RA : CA, which is mathematically equivalent) examines degrees of general backwardness in reading. But where is the cut-off point to be placed to identify a severely underfunctioning group? Clearly being 1 year (or grade) behind at age 7 years is much more serious than being 1 year behind at age 14 years (Otto & Fredricks, 1963; Lyle & Goyen, 1969; Applebee, 1971), so arbitrary sliding scales were introduced.

Accomplishment quotients — the ratio of attainment age to expectancy age (or mental age) — were fashionable and, despite serious criticisms on statistical grounds (Crane, 1959; Thorndike, 1963; Yule *et al.*, 1974; Yule, 1979), reappear in recent literature (Erickson, 1975; Finucci *et al.*, 1982). Inevi-

tably, as IQ and reading do not run exactly in parallel, children who are well above average on one measure will be less superior on the second, and vice versa, assuming that the correlation is linear. Thus, indices such as achievement ratios or learning quotients will overestimate the number of highly intelligent children with specific reading retardation.

The most appropriate procedure is the use of some kind of regression equation in which achievement is predicted on the basis of the observed correlations between educational attainment, age and IQ in the general population (Thorndike, 1963; Angoff, 1971). This approach has been widely applied in reading research (Rutter *et al.*, 1970; Berger *et al.*, 1975; Yule *et al.*, 1981, 1982; Share & Silva, 1986; Shaywitz *et al.*, 1992). It enables both the calculation of the degree of the child's underachievement in reading and an estimate of the expected frequency of different degrees of underachievement. The decision on what cut-off point to use for a clinically significant degree of specific reading retardation is necessarily somewhat arbitrary, and any difference or dicrepancy score is inherently unreliable. Only by taking extreme differences will the resulting index be reasonably stable. Follow-up studies show that children whose achievement in reading is more than 2 standard errors of prediction below expectation tend to have a very persistent disability that constitutes a real handicap (Yule, 1973; Rutter *et al.*, 1976; Maughan *et al.*, 1985). As we have seen, this extreme cut-off point picks up between 3 and 10% of the general school population.

These differing approaches to assessment are not merely theoretical niceties. They have very real practical implications, because different definitions identify different children. Thus, many of the apparent disagreements in the research literature stem from researchers studying different types of reading difficulty. Much more worrying is that different children will be given or denied access to specialist remedial help depending on which definitions are employed.

CAUSES AND CORRELATES

A wide variety of factors seem likely to contribute to reading problems. We focus here on three central issues: cognitive skills, neuropsychological deficits and the role of genetic influences.

Cognitive skills

Cognitive skills are clearly central to successful reading, and cognitive deficits of many kinds have been proposed as correlates and possible causes of reading problems. In practice, there are often considerable methodological difficulties in testing these suggestions. As Bryant and his co-workers have argued, one of the most frequently used approaches — comparing good and poor readers on the skills of interest — raises tricky methodological issues, and results are often difficult to interpret (Bryant & Impey, 1986; Bryant & Goswami, 1990). Because a great deal of work in the field has adopted some variant of this approach, it is worth setting out the problems in some detail.

Many early studies used an age match, comparing poor and competent readers of the same chronological age. Any deficits poor readers show in this type of study may well give pointers to the roots of their problems, but the findings are almost always open to other interpretations too. The difficulty stems from the reciprocities between reading and other cognitive skills: almost all skills that contribute to reading have also been shown to be improved by it. Poor vocabulary, for example, undoubtedly plays a part in the development of early reading problems, but from the age of about 8, reading in its turn contributes a good deal to the growth of vocabulary. Stanovich (1986) has argued that 'Matthew effects' of this kind (the rich getting richer, and the poor poorer), occur in a wide range of areas. If poor readers are worse at skill *x* than age-matched peers, that deficit could be an effect, just as much as a cause, of their reading problems.

An alternative approach, the reading age match, overcomes these difficulties by comparing poor readers with younger children of the same reading age. Here, differences cannot reflect variations in reading skill, as the groups are matched for this. But because the poor readers are older, they will have better developed general cognitive skills than controls, and also longer experience of failure and frustration with reading. If they achieve similarly to younger normal readers, they may be compensating for real deficits by bringing other skills into play. If they perform less well on particular tasks, anxiety or frustration may be inhibiting their performance.

As Bryant and Goswami (1990) point out, these problems cast doubt on the interpretation of many cross-sectional studies. To be more confident about causal factors, longitudinal and training studies are also needed. But one pattern of cross-sectional findings can be important, to rule out potential causal factors. If good and poor readers of the same chronological age do *not* differ on a particular skill, that skill cannot be contributing to the poor readers' difficulties. Bryden (1972) used this approach to demonstrate that poor readers do not show cross-modal deficits, and similar designs have been used to demonstrate that problems of visual perception and memory are not the causes of most children's difficulties in reading.

These findings are especially important given the widespread assumption, supported by many pioneers in the field (Hinshelwood, 1895; Orton, 1937) that reading difficulties reflected generalized weaknesses in perceiving and remembering visual patterns. In general, more recent evidence has failed to support this view. In the Isle of Wight predictive studies, verbal intelligence was found to be a better predictor of reading attainment than results on a battery of visual–motor tests both at age 7 (Butler, 1971; Maxwell, 1972) and at the end of compulsory schooling (Yule & Gold, 1980). On the basis of extensive experimental investigations, Vellutino (1979), Jorm (1983) and others concluded that problems of visual perception and memory do not lie at the heart of most children's difficulties in reading. Visuospatial defects may be important causes of reading impairment in young children

(Rutter & Yule, 1973), and there has been renewed interest in specific visual problems in the context of studies of hemispheric and ocular dominance (Stein & Fowler, 1985; Stein, 1989). To date, however, methodological problems have complicated the interpretation of these findings (Bishop, 1989), as well as those on the use of tinted lenses to correct visual problems in poor readers (Wilsher & Taylor, 1988). At this stage, it seems most appropriate to conclude that specific visual problems may contribute to some children's difficulties in reading, but that they affect only a small proportion of the reading-disabled population.

Difficulties in phonological processing, by contrast, seem likely to be of much more general importance. There has been an immense research effort in this field in recent years, beginning with cross-sectional comparisons, but also including longitudinal and training studies. Wagner and Torgeson (1987), Snowling (1987), Goswami and Bryant (1990) and Rack *et al.* (1992) provide recent reviews of this important work.

Phonological skills are important contributors to reading for all children. It is now clear, for example, that awareness of rhyme and alliteration assessed before children start school is a strong predictor of later reading (Bryant & Bradley, 1985; Bryant *et al.*, 1990). We also know that phonological skills show specific links with reading and spelling, that hold after controls for IQ (MacLean *et al.*, 1987), and that alerting children to the sound structures of words helps their reading progress (Olson *et al.*, 1990).

Many poor readers have particular difficulties in phonological processing. They have striking problems reading nonsense words such as 'dake' or 'molsmit', which must in one way or another involve the use of phonological skills (Baddeley *et al.*, 1982; Frith & Snowling, 1983; Olson *et al.*, 1990). Their difficulties seem to centre especially on segmenting the sounds of words, and in relating sounds to letters (Snowling, 1980; Olson *et al.*, 1985). They have also been found to show deficits in nonword repetition (Snowling *et al.*, 1986), object naming (Snowling *et al.*, 1988), and in using phonological codes in short-term memory. Follow-up studies (Temple, 1990; Hulme & Snowling, 1992) show that these difficulties are often highly resistant to change. And finally, genetic evidence (see below) suggests that heritable influences act on the phonological aspects of word recognition.

We know less as yet about the mechanisms underlying these links. Phonological skills may be important to reading at a number of levels (Hulme *et al.*, 1991): in understanding grapheme–phoneme correspondences; in learning the relationships between larger units of letter strings and their spoken counterparts; and, via a rather different route, by alerting children that analogies between the sounds of words (such as 'beak' and 'peak') might also be found in their written forms. The major research efforts currently underway in these areas hold out the promise of greatly increasing our understanding of the difficulties that beset many children as they learn to read.

Neuropsychological accounts of specific reading retardation

One of the most enduring conceptual themes in the field of reading disabilities (Orton, 1937) has been the supposed link between hemispheric specialization and SRR. Bakker (1983) noted that there are two sets of theories that stress the importance of functioning of the left cerebral hemisphere.

The first type of theory is associated with Satz and his colleagues (Satz & Sparrow, 1970; Satz & Friel, 1973; Satz *et al.*, 1976). Satz developed the concept of maturational lag and attached it to the concept of differential maturation of the left cerebral hemisphere. If poor readers have a left cerebral hemisphere that is developing at a slower rate than their right, then the problems they display at any one age should be quantitatively, rather than qualitatively, different from their normal peers. In particular, the types of errors they make on any task should be similar to those seen in testing younger, normal readers. Various specific predictions follow from this formulation, for example, younger poor readers will show more visuomotor problems than will older poor readers; older poor readers will show greater deficits on conceptual integration and language tasks. Thus, by focusing on the lateralization of function in the differential development of the two cerebral hemispheres, Satz built an elegant model that took account of many previously disparate findings in the appreciation that the peripheral indices of cerebral nervous system lateralization of function alter with age. But not all the evidence supports this formulation. Satz's theory seems to predict, for example, that early measures of language should be poor predictors of later reading difficulty, but this is not the case (Butler, 1971; Maxwell, 1972; Yule & Gold, 1980). Likewise, Bryant and Bradley's (1985) demonstration that phonetic analysis capacity predicts later reading disability argues against part, at least, of Satz's model.

The second type of lateralization theory is that proposed by Masland (1975). He argued that dyslexics have more difficulty than normal children with interhemispheric transfer, and that this is especially true of boys in whom superior spatial functioning in the right hemisphere impedes transfer across hemispheres, such transfer of information being essential to link visual matter with temporally presented linguistic matter. Considerable interest remains in the relationship between dichotic dominance tasks and reading (Bakker *et al.*, 1980; Bakker, 1983) and similar concerns underlie the recent theorizing on the relationship between handedness, right–left shift and reading ability (Annett & Manning, 1990).

Although raised incidences of left- and mixed-handers have been reported among poor readers in clinic samples (Critchley, 1970; Naidoo, 1972; Annett & Kilshaw, 1984), these have not been replicated in epidemiological studies (Clark, 1970; Rutter *et al.*, 1970; Satz & Fletcher, 1987). In a recent report on a general population sample, Annett and Manning (1990) found that poor readers included both strongly sinistral and strongly dextral cases, consistent with a genetic model suggesting that laterality and ability might be related through a balanced polymorphism with heterozygote advantage. In addition, however, backward readers tended to have poor right-hand skills, while retarded readers were the only group with good left-hand skills and a high proportion of nonright-handers. The findings applied to both sexes, but were stronger in boys.

There is general agreement from neuropsychological studies employing large batteries of tests that SRR is not a homogeneous condition (Knights & Bakker, 1976; Benton & Pearl, 1978; Dalby, 1979; Rourke & Strang, 1983). Dalby (1979) discussed the alternatives of a delay in maturation or a qualitatively different deficit. The implication of the delay hypothesis is that poor readers should eventually 'catch up'. However, most remain handicapped in spelling and many fail to gain adequate reading skills. On the other hand, the lack of catch-up could stem from an interference with earlier learning. Dalby noted that hemispheric specialization occurs much earlier in life than hitherto realized — a finding in favour of the concept of SRR as a qualitatively distinct condition.

Magnetic resonance imaging (MRI) studies, both of neuro-anatomical structure and of *in vivo* functioning, open the way to examining neurological differences between reading-disabled and normal children directly. Initial studies, reviewed by Pennington (1991), pointed to differences in the size and symmetry of the planum temporale. This area is known to be implicated in phonological processing. It is recognized that planum symmetry cannot account for all aspects of reading disability, but may well account for part of the disorders noted. As work with this new technology expands, MRI studies promise to clarify many of the unsolved neuropsychological questions related to reading difficulties.

Genetic influences

From the time of the very earliest reports of dyslexia (Hinshelwood, 1917), reading problems were noted as strongly familial. Studies of representative samples of poor readers have confirmed this picture, with estimates of familial risk of 35–45% in the parents of affected boys, and somewhat under 20% in the families of girls (Vogler *et al.*, 1985). Well-designed twin studies have in the main suggested important heritable factors. Using a new multiple regression technique, LaBuda and colleagues (LaBuda *et al.*, 1986; LaBuda & DeFries, 1990) have estimated about 30% heritability for the cognitive phenotype in reading disability, controlling for the effects of IQ, and quite similar estimates have emerged from other studies. The main exception to this pattern comes from a study of London 13-year-old twins (Stevenson *et al.*, 1987), where heritabilities for reading problems were low, although significant genetic influences were found for spelling skills and disabilities. The authors suggested that their findings might reflect declining genetic effects on reading with age. As yet, age variations in heritabilities have not been found in other studies (Olson *et al.*, 1991), so the reasons for these somewhat differing conclusions remain to be clarified.

Family studies have examined possible modes of genetic transmission. Segregation analyses (Finucci *et al.*, 1976;

Lewitter *et al.*, 1980) have suggested that there is probably genetic heterogeneity, with polygenic inheritance in some families, but the possibility of single gene effects in others. The consistent finding of lower gender ratios in affected relatives than in index cases (Finucci & Childs, 1981; Vogler *et al.*, 1985) is compatible with a gender-influenced polygenic threshold model (DeFries, 1989). Linkage studies (Smith *et al.*, 1990) have also supported the hypothesis of heterogeneity, but found evidence of an autosomal dominant form of reading disability, with linkage to chromosome 15, in some 15–20% of the families studied. As all of the families in this sample had histories consistent with autosomal dominant transmission, other possible linkages also seem likely to be involved (Smith *et al.*, 1990). Further studies are clearly needed to elucidate this picture.

Genetic strategies are also being used to tackle some of the central debates in the reading disabilities field. The first of these concerns the disorder/dimension question: do reading disabilities constitute a separate disorder, or simply the extremes of a the normal range? Plomin and Rende (1991) discussed an important advance in genetic modelling, first applied in the area of reading problems (DeFries *et al.*, 1987). The technique incorporates quantitative measures of dimensions in the analysis of qualitative disorders (DeFries & Fulker, 1985, 1988), and provides estimates of a new genetic parameter: group heritability, reflecting the extent to which average differences between probands and individuals in unselected populations are due to genetic effects. This measure can be compared to the more usual estimates of individual heritability to assess how far severely affected cases represent the extremes of the normal distribution.

Drawing on evidence from a number of different fields, Plomin (1991) has proposed that mild, common disorders may represent the extremes of normal continua, but that severe, rare problems may be aetiologically distinct. These differential patterns might reflect either greater or lesser genetic influences on severe conditions: in schizophrenia, for example, more severe forms indicate greater genetic involvement, while severe mental retardation appears less heritable than variation in the normal IQ range.

In the case of reading problems, group heritabilities are only about half the magnitude of individual heritabilities (DeFries *et al.*, 1987). This pattern is consistent with a model of reading disability as aetiologically distinct from the continuous dimension of reading ability, and, while still showing important genetic influences, less strongly heritable than variations in reading skills in the normal range. This in turn highlights the role of environmental factors. Scarborough (1991) suggested that it may be specific, nonshared environmental influences that are most important within families with reading-disabled children, and that these may in part be driven by the child. In her study, poor-readers-to-be were less interested in literacy experiences at any early age. The person–environment correlations recently emerging in many behaviour genetic studies may thus also prove important in relation to reading disabilities.

Finally, genetic studies have also begun to examine which components of the reading process are most likely to be subject to genetic influence. Recent investigations (Olson *et al.*, 1989, 1991; Stevenson, 1991) have assessed both phonological and orthographic skills, and found markedly different patterns of heritability in these two areas. In a large sample of twins, around half of the probands' deficits in word recognition were estimated as reflecting genetic influences. The relationship between phonological coding and word recognition appeared to be strongly genetically determined, with a genetic correlation of 0.62 (± 0.12). By contrast, associations with orthographic coding were not significant (0.22 ± 0.17); the effects of orthographic skills on word recognition thus seemed primarily attributable to environmental influences.

Taken together with the extensive work on phonological deficits in the cognitive literature, these findings are likely to be of major importance. Set in the context of work on links with IQ, they suggest yet other possibilities. Stevenson (1991), for example, has argued for the possibility of different genetic mechanisms, each contributing to different aspects of reading. One, reflecting general genetic effects shared with IQ, may contribute to orthographic skills, while a second, more modular and specific pathway, may provide links with phonological processing. These and other studies promise exciting new advances in our understanding of reading problems in the next few years.

ASSOCIATIONS BETWEEN READING DIFFICULTIES AND BEHAVIOURAL AND PSYCHIATRIC PROBLEMS

There is ample (and perhaps not surprising) evidence that many learning-disabled children show behaviour problems in the classroom (McKinney, 1989). But rates of more pervasive behavioural and psychiatric disorders are also elevated in reading-disabled groups. Backward readers may be vulnerable to emotional as well as conduct problems (Richman *et al.*, 1982; Kellam *et al.*, 1983; Jorm *et al.*, 1986b) but specific, IQ-discrepant reading difficulties have been particularly linked with disruptive behaviours. Early evidence suggested strong associations with conduct disorder: in the Isle of Wight studies of 10-year-olds, a quarter of specifically retarded readers showed antisocial behaviour in middle childhood, and a third of those with conduct problems were also reading-retarded (Rutter *et al.*, 1970). This overlap is much higher than would be expected by chance. More recent work has explored reasons for this particular pattern of comorbidity, and pointed to possible developmental changes in the nature of the association over time.

Rutter *et al.* (1970) set out three broad hypotheses that might account for reading–behaviour problem links. Firstly, the behaviour problems might be primary, and give rise to reading difficulties by interfering with a child's learning. Secondly, reading problems might be primary, and lead, perhaps through lowered self-esteem or frustration, to the expression of behaviour disorder. Or thirdly, both difficulties might share common roots in organic, temperamental or environmental adversities. Some combination of these models, including reciprocal as well as unidirectional influences, may prove the most likely picture in practice.

Longitudinal evidence has been central in testing out these various possibilities. Studies beginning early in childhood have shown that both sets of problems, or precursors to them, are often evident by the time children start school, well before they have been exposed to a formal curriculum (McMichael, 1979; McGee *et al*, 1988). This argues for a shared risk factor model, and a range of possible contenders has been put forward: low social class (Offord & Poushinsky, 1981); maternal depression and anxiety (Richman *et al.*, 1982); adverse temperamental features in the child; cognitive deficits (August & Garfinkel, 1990); speech and language problems (Silva, 1987); and neurodevelopmental immaturity (Beitchman, 1985). Each, either singly or in interaction with others, may be important for some groups of children.

If shared risk factors account for at least some of the links in early childhood, reciprocal effects may also be important at later stages. Poor readers show increases in behaviour problems across the primary school years (McGee *et al.*, 1988), and although fewer studies have examined the effects of behaviour problems on reading progress, they seem very likely to occur. Fergusson and Horwood (1992), for example, found modest effects of inattentiveness and overactivity on reading progress between the ages of 10 and 12, and Rowe and Rowe (1992) argued for similar processes across a wider age range, though only on the basic of cross-sectional measures. For some children, the pattern of conjoint reading and behaviour problems can have cumulating effects over time.

Longitudinal studies have also been important in highlighting changes in the nature of the behaviour problems characteristic of poor readers at different ages. Although the broad picture of links with externalizing behaviours remains, recent findings have placed greater emphasis on associations with inattentive, overactive behaviours in young children, and the emergence of conduct symptoms at a rather later point. Hinshaw (1992) provided a valuable review of evidence in this area. For some children, associations between reading and conduct problems might largely reflect comorbidity with attention deficit disorder with hyperactivity (Frick *et al.*, 1991); we need further evidence to clarify this picture. What is already clear, however, is that poor readers may well show changing patterns of behaviour problems across childhood, and that clinical assessments need to take these developmental progressions into account.

Fewer studies have traced links between reading and psychiatric problems in adolescence. Two separate questions arise here: firstly, do reading difficulties make it more likely that earlier behaviour problems will persist, and secondly, do they increase vulnerabilities to new disorders, arising for the first time in the teens? On the first point, the evidence seems clear. The Isle of Wight, inner London and Dunedin follow-ups all found that reading problems play little if any role in the persistence of psychiatric disorder after middle childhood

(Rutter *et al.*, 1976; Maughan *et al.*, 1985; McGee *et al.*, 1992). On the second issue — links with new adolescent disorders — findings are more mixed. The Isle of Wight studies suggested that adolescent disorders showed few links with educational difficulties of any kind. Bruck (1985), however, found rather higher rates of late adolescent adjustment problems among reading-disabled girls in a clinic sample, and the Dunedin study (McGee *et al.*, 1992) has shown a small but significant effect of reading problems on new disorders at age 15, this time specifically in boys.

At present, then, the picture is rather mixed on disorder in the teens. In the delinquency field, however, there is a long tradition of research positing links between school failure and juvenile offending. Reviews of this extensive literature (Hirschi & Hindelag, 1977; Rutter & Giller, 1983; Brier, 1989; Hawkins & Lishner, 1987) suggest a range of possible causal mechanisms: shared risk factors, continuities from earlier behaviour problems, or experiences of failure at school that alienate young people from mainstream societal values, and so encourage them to seek status and satisfaction elsewhere.

Much of this literature has focused on general underachievement at school, rather than reading difficulties *per se*. Wadsworth (1979) found that links between early reading scores and delinquency up to age 21 could largely be accounted for by social class and birth order effects. The first follow-up of the Inner London sample (Maughan *et al.*, 1985) found a trend towards higher rates of juvenile offending in both behaviourally deviant and nondeviant poor readers, suggesting some increased risk associated with uncomplicated reading problems. The few studies reporting on offending in adulthood have not found elevated rates of criminality among poor readers (Bruck, 1985; Spreen, 1988; Maughan *et al.*, 1993). These scattered findings clearly need to be replicated. They begin to suggest, however, that any increases in poor readers' delinquency in the teens may reflect relatively time-limited reactions or vulnerabilities, rather than ongoing deviant tendencies.

The limited evidence of psychosocial adjustment in early adulthood suggests a generally more positive picture. Bruck (1985) found no excess of severe adjustment problems in the young adult members of her clinic sample, and the same was true in the Inner London adult follow-up (Hagell & Maughan, 1993). The only differences between the groups here emerged on measures of independent living. Over a third of poor reading men (by comparison with only 1 in 8 controls) were still living at home, with their families of origin, in their late 20s. More had also delayed expected transitions into early adult roles. Social context may thus be especially important for poor readers' adjustment. Many of the problems evident in the school years may be avoidable in adult environments that are supportive, or present a known (and perhaps somewhat restricted) range of challenges, and where reading skills are of limited salience.

These findings are clearly encouraging, but are based on a very small number of studies. A recent large-scale follow-up of more broadly defined group of high school underachievers in the US (McCall *et al.*, 1992) found that they lacked persistence in both their working and personal lives. Follow-up studies also suggest that the subjective experience of continued reading difficulties in adulthood is not without its effects. Naylor *et al.* (1990), in a report specifically excluding subjects with major psychopathology, nevertheless noted that 'many subjects reported strong feelings of inferiority, insecurity and frustration' (p. 227). The Inner London study examined both global self-esteem and the more specific issue of poor readers' attributions for success and failure (Hagell, 1991). Although global measures of self-esteem did not differ between the reading groups, poor readers showed a strong tendency to attribute their difficulties to internal causes, and to hold negative, self-blaming assumptions about their literacy problems. From middle childhood onwards, academic self-esteem is clearly sensitive to underachievement at school, and perhaps especially to difficulties in reading (Chapman *et al.*, 1990). McCall *et al.* (1992) found consistently poorer self-concepts among underachievers, associated not only with lower current evaluations of their capabilities, but also lower educational and occupational aspirations for the future. The implications of reading problems for views of self, quite as much as for disorder, need to be borne in mind in clinical assessment and formulating treatment plans.

PROGNOSIS

What is the outlook for children with reading disabilities? To date, some 40 follow-up studies have explored different facets of this question — how far reading problems persist, their implications for educational attainment, and the longer-term issues of poor readers' occupational and social adjustment over time. A number of reviews have summarized these findings (Watson *et al.*, 1982; Finucci, 1986; Spreen, 1988).

The follow-up picture is clearest on the persistence of reading problems *per se*. Almost without exception, well-designed studies of both clinic-referred and community-based samples have reported high levels of continuing reading difficulties. In the Isle of Wight follow-ups (Rutter *et al.*, 1976), over half the children identified as reading-retarded at age 10 were still reading more than 2 s.d. below the mean some 4 years later. A similar pattern emerged from follow-ups of the Inner London sample (Maughan *et al.*, 1985, 1992). Spreen's (1988) review of longer-term follow-ups, mainly of clinic samples, confirmed the persistence of quite severe reading and spelling problems in adulthood in the great majority of studies. Many poor readers appear to fall further behind their peers as time goes on (Badian, 1988; Maughan *et al.*, in press; but see also Decker, 1989), although small groups do achieve functionally adequate comprehension skills. Initial severity and general intellectual skills seem important here. There are few differences in prognosis for boys and girls (Trites & Fiedorowicz, 1976; LaBuda & DeFries, 1989; Maughan *et al.*, in press), and the effects of parental socioeconomic status reading progress are at most weak. The Isle of Wight studies (Rutter *et al.*, 1976) showed that retarded readers made poorer progress in reading

and spelling in the early teens than their backward-reading counterparts; absolute reading scores were also lower for retarded readers in the inner London follow-ups, but analyses of progress showed no differences between the groups.

Longitudinal assessments of cognitive deficits suggest that these are highly persistent, even for the small groups of poor readers who make relatively good progress in reading comprehension. Bruck (1990) studied 20 ex-clinic attenders, all in college at the time of the follow-up. Despite quite good comprehension skills, they were inaccurate and slow at word recognition, relied heavily on spelling—sound information and context, and showed general patterns of performance similar to those of beginning normal readers and dyslexic children. Individual case studies (Temple, 1990; Hulme & Snowling, 1992) have reported similar findings: phonological difficulties remain, despite considerable progress in oral reading and comprehension. Rather than mastering alphabetic reading skills, many poor readers may thus depend on compensatory skills, such as acquiring an extensive sight vocabulary, if they are to make good progress in reading.

Educational attainment seems to be strongly influenced by social background (O'Connor & Spreen, 1988). Finucci *et al.* (1985), Bruck (1985) and Naylor *et al.* (1990) all reported positive educational outcomes for children from mainly middle-class samples. With adequate supports, disabled readers clearly can make good educational progress, though often more slowly than their nondisabled peers. Less favourable findings have been reported for less socially advantaged groups, where early drop-out from formal schooling seems a particularly characteristic feature. Spreen (1987), found that approaching two-thirds of attenders at a neurological clinic dropped out before completing high school, and only 12% entered college. The first Inner London follow-up (Maughan *et al.*, 1985) also found high rates of early leaving among poor-reading boys, especially those with associated behaviour problems. The second follow-up confirmed this pattern (Maughan *et al.*, 1993). Some poor readers went on to gain vocational qualifications, but contrasts with the comparison group were still marked in the 20s: half the poor readers remained without any academic or vocational qualifications, and only 1 of the 110 with relevant follow-up information had achieved a degree.

Occupational attainments generally mirror educational outcomes. Studies of middle-class groups report subjects in management or the professions, though not in the most reading-intensive areas. Even here, however, the socio-economic status of disabled readers in adulthood is often rather lower than that of their parents. The Inner London sample, by contrast, showed a predictably less positive picture. The great majority of the poor readers were in manual occupations in their late 20s, many in semi- or unskilled work. They showed little downward mobility by comparison with their parents' occupations, but they had also failed to achieve the improvememts in occupational status made by many members of the comparison group.

Adjustment and performance at work have been relatively

little studied. Some reports (White, 1985) have suggested lower employment satisfaction among LD (learning disabled) groups, while others (Bruck, 1985) have found few differences. In the London follow-up, measures of social functioning at work showed no differences between good and poor readers, though men in the retarded reading group had experienced more unemployment since leaving school. Across a range of studies, there are suggestions that poor readers take considerable care in selecting occupational settings, and that, provided the literacy demands of the workplace are manageable, they perform well there. Such niche-picking is clearly an adaptive approach to coping with continuing reading deficits.

The limited information available on other aspects of adult adjustment has been touched on in earlier sections. In general, most disabled readers appear to function well in early adulthood provided they select or remain in manageable and supportive environments. This requirement may, of course, bring disadvantages. Restrictions on horizons, aspirations and more directly on living standards may well result in the longer term. The implications of learning difficulties are likely to vary with age and individuals' social situations. Perhaps inevitably, school life can present major problems. In adulthood, environments can more readily be chosen, so that many of the more pressing effects of basic skills deficits can be circumscribed or circumvented. We must await further follow-ups to clarify the balance of personal costs and benefits that this involves at different stages of the life course.

REMEDIAL INTERVENTION

Almost any remedial intervention can produce short-term gains in reading, but these disappear, in comparison with untreated controls, over the following months or years (Silberberg *et al.*, 1973; Tobin & Pumfrey, 1976; Yule, 1976; Spache, 1981; Hewison, 1982). Even the 'differential diagnosis — prescriptive teaching' approach that attempts to tailor remedial approaches to supposed underlying deficits does not work (Bateman, 1969; Hammill & Wiederholt, 1973; Arter & Jenkins, 1974), presumably because the supposed deficits are correlates rather than causes of the reading difficulties.

Most would agree that screening by 7–9 years should enable help to be given before a sense of failure sets in (Department of Education and Science, 1975). Some argue that the sense of failure should be treated by counselling or psychotherapy, but the evidence for such indirect approaches to reading is scanty and contradictory (Lawrence, 1971, 1973; Elliott & Pumfrey, 1972). Feelings of failure can be tackled simultaneously with teaching reading skills and more direct ways of motivating poor readers have been well-tested by Staats and his colleagues using social learning techniques (Staats *et al.*, 1967, 1970; Staats, 1968).

Clay (1985) is the latest to combine individual instruction that emphasizes reward with an emphasis on teaching basic phonic and other skills. Her Reading Recovery approach has been widely adopted in New Zealand, the US and now in the UK, and preliminary results indicate that the concentrated daily programme early in children's school careers brings significant and lasting results for many poor readers in 3 or 4 months. Hatcher *et al.* (in press) review the value of phonological awareness training and incorporated that in their longitudinal study of remedial teaching of 7-year-old poor readers. Phonological training alone was found to be less successful than phonological training plus reading, a strategy modelled on the work of Clay (1985). They concluded that spending an equivalent time on either component (reading or phonology) in isolation was less effective than the combination.

There is little evidence that psychotropic drugs can directly improve reading attainment (Aman, 1980), although treating overactivity with methylphenidate may have indirect benefits through making the child more accessible to instruction (Gittelman, 1983). Studies of the effects of nootropic drugs — in particular piracetam — seem potentially more promising (Wilsher 1991). Although the neuropsychological effects of piracetam have not been adequately studied, it appears to improve left hemisphere functioning. A large multicentre trial (Wilsher *et al.*, 1987) showed consistent effects on reading comprehension, though findings on single-word reading were more mixed. Longer-term follow-ups are needed to assess how far these effects were maintained.

Increasingly there is evidence that the role of parents may be as great as that of teachers in supporting children's reading (Tizard *et al.*, 1982). Parents in inner-city areas were asked to listen daily to their children reading from books taken home from school. This minimal intervention significantly reduced the number of poor readers and the effect lasted over 3 years (Hewison, 1988). Indeed, this study provides the strongest evidence to date for the effects of any remedial intervention, although the mechanisms of change are not understood. Parents have been involved as co-therapists in other successful schemes (Morgan & Lyon, 1979). Hopefully, educators will experiment with the most judicious mix of parental involvement, motivational techniques, attention to rhyming and phonological skills, and other appropriate curriculum teaching based on empirical findings.

SPELLING AND WRITING DIFFICULTIES

Too often it has been assumed that once children have learned to read, spelling will develop without further tuition. Fortunately, most children do seem to learn to spell reasonably well, despite the vicissitudes of English spelling. However, while young children can read more words than they can spell, two-thirds of children tested by Bradley and Bryant (1979) could spell at least one word that they could not read. This suggests that the two skills may be relatively independent. Indeed, ICD-10 (World Health Organization, 1992) recognizes that, although spelling disorders are frequent concomitants of reading problems, they can also occasionally occur in their absence. However, little is known of the prevalence, antecedents, course, correlates or outcome of specific spelling disorders isolated from reading problems.

Children who could spell words they could not read were found more frequently among poor readers than normal readers. Bradley and Bryant (1979) examined the types of spelling errors and concluded that young children and backward readers primarily depend on phonological cues when they spell, although not when they read.

Frith (1978) has argued that there can be no simple one-to-one sound—symbol correspondence since not only do sounds have no natural segments, but also pronunciations are constantly changing. Since English has borrowed words from many sources and since words get changed over the years, an understanding of context and meaning is often as important as any knowledge of sound—symbol correspondence in deciding on spelling.

More recently, Goswami (1991) has drawn attention to a different way of conceptualizing sound analysis within words and thereby illuminated some early spelling practices of young children. Literate adults may think they spell words using letters, and if forced they may say that they use different combinations of letters to represent different sounds or phonemes. But children new to spelling do not know all these things and have to discover or learn or be taught them. The task is to get a word they are thinking of down on to paper.

For a while, people assumed that this was done by analysing the separate phonemes that make up a word and then representing them correctly (according to some spelling convention). But many short words are instead analysed into two component parts, the *onset* and the *rime*. A word such as 'top' consists of 't' (onset) and 'op' (rime). In as far as there is a natural segmentation of words, this seems to be it.

Young children try to spell words in this way. For example, the words 'car', 'bell' and 'hen' are often spelled 'cr', 'bl', and 'hn' because the rime sounds the same as individual letters that children can already write down (Treiman, 1985). Goswami (1991) also argued that there may be ways of cueing children to use the appropriate endings or rimes. Teaching them to spell 'beak' assisted them to spell related words such as 'peak' and 'weak' but not words such as 'bask', even though the latter has as many phonemes in common with the cue word as do the other analogue words (Goswami, 1988). Studies such as this not only give new insights into the development of spelling and of reading, but they also suggest new strategies for teaching spelling to children with difficulties. The major implication is that in teaching implicit or explicit rules of spelling, then one should be careful which exemplars to use to maximize learning and transfer of learning. Once again, a phonic-based approach to introductory and remedial teaching is coming to the fore, as it did many years ago (Gillingham & Stillman, 1956; Hornsby & Shear, 1975).

There are two major aspects of writing difficulties that must be considered separately. Firstly, there is the physical aspect of writing, where difficulties may be related to various apraxias or other aspects of clumsiness. Secondly, there is the ability to express ideas coherently in written form, involving such literary skills as spelling, punctuation and good paragraph formation. The literature on expressive writing problems is very slight (Lynch & Jones, 1989; Newcomer & Barenbaum, 1991), and reliable assessments are hampered by the lack of well-standardized tests. In DSM-IV (American Psychiatric Association, 1993) problems in spelling, handwriting and grammatical expression are all classified together as features of disorders of written expression. In ICD-10 (World Health Organization, 1992), difficulties in expressive writing do not appear in the main classifications of academic skills disorders, but can be recorded among other disorders of scholastic skills. In most instances, problems of this kind will occur alongside one of the other academic skill disorders, or in the context of disruptive behaviour problems. Little if anything is known at this stage about the prevalence or course of expressive writing problems that present as isolated learning disabilities.

Specific developmental disorders of motor function (developmental coordination disorders) may manifest in fine motor skills associated with writing, or may be part of a gross motor clumsiness. Clumsy children do not form a homogeneous group (Henderson, 1987). Although opinion is divided, it would appear from the few follow-up studies that most children with developmental motor clumsiness still have difficulties with coordination in their teens, and that they share the poor self-concept and other school problems typical of other learning-disabled groups at this stage (Losse *et al.*, 1991).

ARITHMETICAL DIFFICULTIES

Problems with number have been less, and less systematically, studied than problems in language (O'Hare *et al.*, 1991). In a society that is increasingly numerate and computer-literate, numerical difficulties are increasingly important. There is no agreement on whether it is preferable to assess children's attainments in mathematics in term of basic operations (addition, subtraction, multiplication and division), or in terms of higher-order concepts as applied to particular problems (as in algebra, geometry, trigonometry or calculus). Indeed, these may be very different processes mediated by different brain mechanisms. Thus, mathematics in primary or elementary schools is predominantly about learning basic arithmetic, whereas in secondary schools higher-order mathematics comes to the fore. It is not unknown for some children to excel at basic arithmetic, but to fail badly in higher-order mathematics.

The recognition of difficulties with number and their association with psychiatric disorders has been hampered by the major shifts in fashions within the teaching of mathematics in schools. Traditional mathematics had emphasized rote learning of tables and the like, probably placing a great load on verbal memory. Modern mathematics, claiming to be related to Piagetian theorizing about number, placed more emphasis on direct experience of weighing and measuring. In the UK, it is only in the 1990s that the National Curriculum is trying to combine the best of the two approaches and, when working, children will be more readily judged against standard attainment tasks. Then there will be more awareness of difficulties in arithmetic and mathematics.

It was long believed that most difficulties in mathematics were related to wider language difficulties (Cohn, 1961, 1971). The studies of selected clinic cases of severe mathematical difficulties, or dyscalculia, suggested these had much more in common with difficulties in visuospatial functions subserved by the parietal lobes (Slade & Russell, 1971; Money, 1973).

Rourke and his colleagues have pursued a different way of studying arithmetical difficulties (Rourke & Finlayson, 1978; Rourke & Strang, 1983; Rourke & Fuerst, 1991). Studying children attending a neuropsychology clinic, they contrasted two groups of children poor in arithmetic: (1) those whose arithmetic was better than their reading and spelling; and (2) those whose reading and spelling were normal, but whose arithmetic was weak. The former perfomed well on visuospatial tasks but appeared to have a general language disorder; the latter had intact verbal skills but poor visuospatial skills and did badly on complex psychomotor tasks.

Share *et al.* (1988) partly replicated these findings in the Dunedin longitudinal study. However, they examined the cross-over effect separately in boys and girls, and found it only occurred in boys. Moreover, they were unable to confirm the deficits in complex motor skills. Thus, there is some confirmation that specific arithmetic difficulties may be related to right hemisphere functioning, at least in boys.

Although difficulties in arithmetic and mathematics are recognized in both DSM and ICD, there are as yet no good data on prevalence rates. The Isle of Wight follow-up study (Yule, 1973) reported that children with severe and specific reading retardation also had problems in mathematics, but that they made relatively more progress in maths during their secondary school years. This suggested that, although related, the underlying processes in reading, spelling and mathematics were somewhat independent.

It has long been noted that difficulties in arithmetic and mathematics are associated with anxiety (Lansdown, 1978). The question is whether arithmetic difficulties are more strongly related to anxiety or other neurotic disorders than are reading difficulties, which tend to be related to conduct problems. This has recently been examined in a series of studies by Rourke and Fuerst (1991). They concluded that children with good reading and spelling relative to their scores on arithmetic showed much more clinically significant psychopathology than did those who show poor reading and spelling relative to their arithmetic. In particular, the former group (in a sense those with specific deficits in arithmetic) showed much more anxiety or internalized psychopathology.

Thus, studies of specific deficits in arithmetic and/or mathematics are slowly beginning to examine the question of the nature and extent of links with child psychopathology. As yet, there is a less sophisticated typology of arithmetical difficulties, and given the complex nature of mathematical processing (Bryant, 1991), these early studies are necessarily crude. However, there is evidence that boys and girls must be considered separately; that there is an increased rate of psychopathology in children with specific arithmetical difficulties; and that this psychopathology is predominantly anxiety.

CLINICAL PRESENTATION AND MANAGEMENT

We conclude with some brief comments on the clinical assessment and management of children with learning disabilities. As we have seen, because of the high rates of comorbidity between learning and psychiatric disorders, learning difficulties may well be present in many children referred primarily for behavioural or emotional reasons, and psychiatric problems are frequent concomitants of learning difficulties. The first need, then, is for comprehensive psychological and psychiatric investigations of all children where this joint pattern is likely to be present.

When a child presents at the clinic for investigations of reading difficulties, a full psychometric assessment must be undertaken. At the very least, this should include assessment of general intelligence on a well-standardized, individually administered test together with standardized assessments of reading and spelling. It is important to assess the child's abilities to decode from print, and also the level of comprehension from a prose text. If the child scores very poorly, then knowledge of the alphabet, phonic values for letters and letter combinations and other similar early reading skills should be assessed. More experimental investigations of phonology may also be undertaken. Snowling and Thomson (1991) include some useful suggestions on methods of assessing mathematical skills and difficulties.

In addition, visual acuity, hearing and handedness should all be ascertained. During the spelling test, observations should be made on the child's pen grip, paper positioning and hand-writing, as messy hand-writing is often dismissed (Alston & Taylor, 1984). Children who are left-handed will require instruction on appropriate pen holds to avoid tiring 'hooked' writing and will need practice in placing the paper to the left of midline so that they can get visual feedback of what they write (Clark, 1957). The history from the parents should pay particular attention to early language development as well as current language and speech problems. Parents should also be asked if any first-degree relative has had any major difficulty with reading and with spelling (the latter being particularly important as adults often manage to conceal reading problems but are less successful in hiding spelling difficulties).

If learning difficulties are identified, clinicians should notify the appropriate educational authorities, and ensure that children receive suitable remedial help and other supports. Remedial tuition will be most important at younger ages, but for older children additional time or other aids in sitting examinations may also be crucial. Technical aids, such as word-processors with spell-checkers, can be a boon at many points.

As we have seen, children's views of themselves as learners are likely to be especially vulnerable, and may well compound academic problems over time. Remedial help cannot be relied on to improve self-esteem alone, and direct attention will often need to be given to the child's understanding of the nature of his or her difficulties. It is important that learning-disabled children, their parents and their teachers should be helped to come to a realistic perspective on their problems. They are not the result of laziness or stupidity, but they can constitute very real handicaps, especially during schooling, and these need to be taken seriously. A balanced view will avoid self-blame, but will also involve recognition and acceptance of the child's problem. Minimizing the effects of learning disabilities calls for informed support from parents and teachers, and a considerable degree of persistence on the part of children themselves. If these can be harnessed, the outlook for many children with learning disabilities can be much improved.

REFERENCES

Aaron P.G. (1989) Qualitative and quantitative differences among dyslexic, normal and non dyslexic poor readers. *Reading and Writing*, **1**, 291–309.

Aaron P. & Malatesha Joshi R. (1987) *Reading and Writing Disorders in Different Othographic Systems*. Kluwer, Dordrecht.

Alston J. & Taylor J. (1984) *The Handwriting File*. LDA, Wisbech, Cambridgeshire.

Aman M.G. (1980) Psychotropic drugs and learning problems – a selective review. *Journal of Learning Disabilities*, **13**, 87–97.

American Psychiatric Association (1994) *Diagnostic and Statistical Manual of Mental Disorders*, 4th edn (DSM-IV). American Psychiatric Association, Washington, DC.

Angoff W.H. (1971) Scales, norms and equivalent scores. In: Thorndike R.L. (ed) *Educational Measurement*, 2nd edn. American Council on Education, Washington, DC.

Annett M. & Kilshaw D. (1984) Lateral preference and skill in dyslexics: implications of the right shift theory. *Journal of Child Psychology and Psychiatry*, **25**, 357–377.

Annett M. & Manning M. (1990) Reading and a balanced polymorphism for laterality and ability. *Journal of Child Psychology and Psychiatry*, **31**, 511–529.

Applebee A.N. (1971) Research in reading retardation: two critical problems. *Journal of Child Psychology and Psychiatry*, **12**, 91–113.

Arter J.A. & Jenkins J.R. (1974) Differential diagnosis – prescriptive teaching: a critical appraisal. *Review of Educational Research*, **49**, 517–555.

August G.J. & Garfinkel B.D. (1990) Comorbidity of ADHD and reading disability among clinic-referred children. *Journal of Abnormal Child Psychology*, **18**, 29–45.

Baddeley A.D., Ellis N., Miles T.R. & Lewis V.J. (1982) Developmental and acquired dyslexia: a comparison. *Cognition*, **11**, 185–199.

Baddeley A.D., Logie R. & Ellis N. (1988) Characteristics of developmental dyslexia. *Cognition*, **29**, 197–228.

Badian N.A. (1988) The prediction of good and poor reading before kindergarten entry: a nine-year follow-up. *Journal of Learning Disabilities*, **21**, 98–123.

Bakker D.J. (1983) Hemispheric specialization and specific reading retardation. In: Rutter M. (ed) *Developmental Neuropsychiatry*, pp. 498–506. Guilford Press, New York.

Bakker D.J., Light R., Kok A. & Bouma A. (1980) Cortical responses to word reading by right-and-left-eared normal and reading-disturbed children. *Journal of Clinical Neuropsychology*, **2**, 1–2.

Bateman B. (1969) Reading, a controversial view: research and rationale. In: Tarnopol L. (ed) *Learning Disabilities: An Introduction to Educational and Medical Management*, pp. 289–304. Charles C. Thomas, Springfield, IL.

Beitchman J.H. (1985) Speech and language impairment and psychia-

tric risk: toward a model of neurodevelopmental immaturity. *Psychiatric Clinics of North America*, **8**, 721–735.

Benton A.L. & Pearl D. (eds) (1978) *Dyslexia: An Appraisal of Current Knowledge*. Oxford University Press, New York.

Berger M., Yule W. & Rutter M. (1975) Attainment and adjustment in two geographical areas II: the prevalence of specific reading retardation. *British Journal of Psychiatry*, **126**, 510–519.

Bishop D.V.M. (1989) Unstable vergence control and dyslexia — a critique. *British Journal of Ophthalmology*, **73**, 223–235.

Boder E. (1971) Developmental dyslexia: prevailing diagnostic concepts and a new diagnostic approach. In: Myklebust H.R. (ed) *Progress in Learning Disabilities*, vol. 2, pp. 293–321. Grune & Stratton, New York.

Boder E. (1973) Developmental dyslexia: a diagnostic approach based on three atypical reading-spelling patterns. *Developmental Medicine and Child Neurology*, **15**, 663–687.

Bradley L. & Bryant P. (1979) Independence of reading and spelling in backward and normal readers. *Developmental Medicine and Child Neurology*, **21**, 504–514.

Bradley L. & Bryant P.E. (1983) Categorizing sounds and learning to read — a causal connection. *Nature*, **301**, 419–421.

Brier N. (1989) The relationship between learning disability and delinquency: a review and reappraisal. *Journal of Learning Disabilities*, **22**, 546–553.

Bruck M. (1985) The adult functioning of children with specific learning disability: a follow-up study. In: Siegel I. (ed) *Advances in Applied Developmental Psychology*, pp. 91–129. Ablex, Norwood, NJ.

Bruck M. (1990) Word recognition skills of adults with childhood diagnoses of dyslexia. *Developmental Psychology*, **26**, 439–454.

Bryant P.E. (1991) Mathematical difficulties. Paper delivered to the Conference of the British Dyslexia Association, Oxford.

Bryant P.E. & Bradley L. (1985) *Children's Reading Problems*. Blackwell, Oxford.

Bryant P.E. & Goswami U. (1990) Comparisons between backward and normal readers — a risky business. *British Psychological Society Education Review*, **14**, 3–29.

Bryant P.E. & Impey L. (1986) The similarities between normal readers and developmental acquired dyslexics. *Cognition*, **24**, 121–137.

Bryant P.E., MacLean M., Bradley L.L. & Crossland J. (1990) Rhyme and alliteration, phoneme detection, and learning to read. *Developmental Psychology*, **26**, 429–438.

Bryden M.P. (1972) Auditory-visual and sequential-spatial matching in relation to reading reliability. *Child Development*, **43**, 824–832.

Butler S. (1971) *Predicting Reading Failure in the Infant School*. Unpublished PhD Thesis, University of London.

Chadwick O., Rutter M., Thompson J. & Shaffer D. (1981) Intellectual performance and reading skills after localized head injury in childhood. *Journal of Child Psychology and Psychiatry*, **22**, 117–139.

Chapman J.W., Lambourne R. & Silva P.A. (1990) Some antecedents of academic self-concept: a longitudinal study. *British Journal of Educational Psychology*, **60**, 142–152.

Clark M.M. (1957) *Left-Handedness and Writing Problems*. University of London Press, London.

Clark M.M. (1970) *Young Fluent Readers*. Heinemann, London.

Clay M. (1985) *The Early Detection of Reading Difficulties*, 3rd edn. Heinemann, Tadworth, Surrey.

Cohn R. (1961) Dyscalculia. *Archives of Neurology*, **4**, 301–307.

Cohn R. (1971) Arithmetic and learning disabilities. In: Myklebust H.R. (ed) *Progress in Learning Disabilities*, vol. 2, pp. 322–389. Grune & Stratton, New York.

Coltheart M. (1978) Lexical access in simple reading tasks. In: Underwood G. (ed) *Strategies in Information Processing*, pp. 151–216. Academic Press, London.

Coltheart M., Masterson J., Byng S., Prior M. & Riddoch J. (1983) Surface dyslexia. *Quarterly Journal of Experimental Psychology*, **35A**, 469–496.

Crane A.R. (1959) An historical and critical account of the accomplishment quotient idea. *British Journal of Educational Psychology*, **29**, 252–259.

Critchley M. (1970) *The Dyslexic Child*. Charles C. Thomas, Springfield, IL.

Dalby J.T. (1979) Deficit or delay: neuropsychological models of developmental dyslexia. *Journal of Special Education*, **13**, 239–264.

Davie R., Butler N. & Goldstein H. (1972) *From Birth to Seven: A Report of the National Child Development Study*. Longman, London.

Decker S.N. (1989) Cognitive processing rates among disabled and normal reading adults: a nine-year follow-up study. *Reading and Writing: An Interdisciplinary Journal*, **2**, 123–134.

DeFries J.C. (1989) Gender ratios in reading-disabled children and their affected relatives: a commentary. *Journal of Learning Disabilities*, **22**, 544–545.

DeFries J.C. & Fulker D.W. (1985) Multiple regression analysis of twin data. *Behaviour Genetics*, **15**, 467–473.

DeFries J.C. & Fulker D.W. (1988) Multiple regression analysis of twin data: etiology of deviant scores versus individual differences. *Acta Geneticae Medicae et Gemellologiae: Twin Research*, **37**, 205–216.

DeFries J.C., Fulker D.W. & LaBuda M.C. (1987) Evidence for a genetic aetiology in reading disability of twins. *Nature*, **329**, 537–539.

Department of Education and Science (1975) *A Language for Life* (The Bullock Report). HMSO, London.

Dobbins D.A. & Tafa E. (1992) The 'stability' of identification of underachieving readers over different measures of intelligence and reading. *British Journal of Educational Psychology*, **61**, 155–163.

Elliott C.D. (1989) Cognitive profiles of learning disabled children. *British Journal of Developmental Psychology*, **7**, 171–178.

Elliott C.D. & Pumfrey P.D. (1972) The effects of non-directive play in some maladjusted boys. *Educational Research*, **14**, 157–161.

Ellis A.W. (1991) *Reading, Writing and Dyslexia: A Cognitive Analysis*. Lawrence Erlbaum, London.

Ellis N.C. & Large B. (1987) The development of reading: as you seek so shall you find. *British Journal of Psychology*, **78**, 1–28.

Erickson M.T. (1975) The Z-score discrepancy method for identifying reading-disabled children. *Journal of Learning Disabilities*, **8**, 308–312.

Feagans L.V. & McKinney J.D. (1991) Subtypes of learning disability: a review. In: Feagans L.V., Short E.V. & Meltzer L.J. (eds) *Subtypes of Learning Disabilities*, pp. 3–31. Lawrence Erlbaum, Hillsdale, NJ.

Fergusson D.M. & Horwood L.J. (1992) Attention deficit and reading achievement. *Journal of Child Psychology and Psychiatry*, **33**, 375–385.

Finucci J.M. (1986) Follow-up studies of developmental dyslexia and other learning disabilities. In: Smith S.D. (ed) *Genetics and Learning Disabilities*, pp. 97–121. Taylor and Francis, Philadelphia, PA.

Finucci J.M. & Childs B. (1981) Are there really more dyslexic boys than girls? In: Ansara A., Geschwind N., Galaburda A., Albert M. & Gartrell N. (eds) *Sex Differences in Dyslexia*, pp. 11–19. Orton Dyslexia Society, Townson, MD.

Finucci J.M., Guthrie J.T., Childs A.C., Abbey H. & Childs B. (1976) The genetics of specific reading disability. *Annals of Human Genetics*, **40**, 1–23.

Finucci J.M., Isaacs S.D., Whitehouse C.C. & Childs B. (1982) A quantitative index of reading disability for use in family studies. *Developmental Medicine and Child Neurology*, **24**, 733–744.

Finucci J.M., Gottfredson L.S. & Childs B. (1985) A follow-up study of dyslexic boys. *Annals of Dyslexia*, **35**, 117–136.

Fletcher J.M. & Satz P. (1985) Cluster analysis and the search for learning disability subtypes. In: Rourke B. (ed) *Neuropsychology of Learning Disabilities*. Guilford Press, New York.

Fredman G. & Stevenson J. (1988) Reading processes in specific reading retarded and reading backward 13 year olds. *British Journal of Developmental Psychology*, **6**, 67–108.

Frick P.J., Kampaus R.W., Lahey B.B., Loeber R., Christ M.A.G., Hart E.L. & Tannenbaum L.E. (1991) Academic underachievement and the disruptive behavior disorders. *Journal of Consulting and Clinical Psychology*, **59**, 289–294.

Frith U. (1978) Spelling difficulties. *Journal of Child Psychology and Psychiatry*, **19**, 279–285.

Frith U. (1985) Beneath the surface of developmental dyslexia. In: Patterson K.E., Marshall J.C. & Coltheart M. (eds) *Surface Dyslexia*, pp. 301–330. Routledge & Kegan-Paul, London.

Frith U. & Snowling M. (1983) Reading for meaning and reading for sound in autistic and dyslexic children. *British Journal of Developmental Psychology*, **1**, 329–342.

Gibson E.J. (1965) Learning to read. *Science*, **148**, 1066–1072.

Gillingham A. & Stillman B.W. (1956) *Remedial Training for Children with Specific Disability in Reading, Spelling and Penmanship*. Educational Publishing Services, Cambridge, MA.

Gittelman R. (1983) Treament of reading disorders. In: Rutter M. (ed) *Developmental Neuropsychiatry*, pp. 530–541. Guilford Press, New York.

Goodman K.S. (1976) Reading: a psycholinguistic guessing game. In: Singer H. & Ruddell R.B. (eds) *Theoretical Models and Processes of Reading*, 2nd edn, pp. 497–508. International Reading Association, Newark, DE.

Goswami U. (1988) Children's use of analogy in learning to spell. *British Journal of Developmental Psychology*, **6**, 21–33.

Goswami U. (1991) Recent work on reading and spelling development. In: Snowling M. & Thomson M. (eds) *Dyslexia: Integrating Theory and Practice*, pp. 108–121. Whurr Publishers, London.

Goswami U. & Bryant P. (1990) *Phonological Skills and Learning to Read*. Lawrence Erlbaum, London.

Hagell A. (1991) The social psychology of illiteracy: An Attributional Perspective. Unpublished PhD Thesis, University of London.

Hagell A. & Maughan B. (1993) Poor readers in adulthood: psychosocial outcomes. Unpublished manuscript, MRC Child Psychiatry Unit, Institute of Psychiatry, London.

Hammill D.D. & Wiederholt J.L. (1973) Review of the Frostig Visual Perception Test and the related training program. In: Mann L. & Sabatino D. (eds) *The First Review of Special Education*, pp. 33–48. Buttonwood Farms, Philadelphia, PA.

Hatcher P., Hulme C. & Ellis A. (in press) Ameliorating early reading failure by integrating the teaching of reading and phonological skills: the phonological linkage hypothesis.

Hawkins J.D. & Lishner D.M. (1987) Schooling and delinquency. In: Johnson E.H. (ed) *Handbook on Crime and Delinquency Prevention Child Development*, pp. 179–221. Greenwood Press, New York.

Henderson S.E. (1987) The assessment of 'clumsy' children: old and new approaches. *Journal of Child Psychology and Psychiatry*, **28**, 511–527.

Hewison J. (1982) The current status of remedial intervention for children with reading problems. *Developmental Medicine and Child Neurology*, **24**, 183–186.

Hewison J. (1988) The long term effectiveness of parental involvement in reading: a follow-up to the Haringey Reading Project. *British Journal of Education Psychology*, **58**, 184–190.

Hewison J. & Tizard J. (1980) Parental involvement and reading attainment. *British Journal of Educational Psychology*, **50**, 209–215.

Hinshaw S.P. (1992) Externalizing behavior problems and academic underachievement in childhood and adolescence: causal relationships and underlying mechanisms. *Psychological Bulletin*, **111**, 127–155.

Hinshelwood J. (1895) Word-blindness and visual memory. *Lancet*, **2**, 1564–1570.

Hinshelwood J. (1917) *Congenital Word-blindness*. Lewis, London.

Hirschi T. & Hindelag M.J. (1977) Intelligence and delinquency: a revisionist review. *American Sociological Review*, **42**, 571–587.

Hornsby B. & Shear F. (1975) *Alpha to Omega: The A–Z of Teaching Reading, Writing and Spelling*. Heinemann, London.

Hulme C. & Snowling M. (1992) Deficits in output phonology: an explanation of reading failure? *Cognitive Neuropsychology*, **9**, 47–72.

Hulme C., Snowling M. & Quinlan P. (1991) Connectionism and learning to read: steps towards a psychologically plausible model. *Reading and Writing: An Interdisciplinary Journal*, **3**, 159–168.

Ingram T.T.S., Mason A.W. & Blackburn I. (1970) A retrospective study of 82 children with reading disability. *Developmental Medicine and Child Neurology*, **12**, 271–281.

Jorm A. (1983) Specific reading retardation and working memory: a review. *British Journal of Psychology*, **74**, 311–342.

Jorm A., Share D., Maclean R. & Matthews R. (1986a) Cognitive factors at school entry predictive of specific reading retardation and general reading backwardness: a research note. *Journal of Child Psychology and Psychiatry*, **27**, 45–54.

Jorm A.F., Share D.L., Matthews R. & Maclean R. (1986b) Behaviour problems in specific reading retarded and general reading backward children: a longitudinal study. *Journal of Child Psychology and Psychiatry*, **27**, 33–43.

Kellam S.G., Brown C.H., Rubin B.R. & Ensminger M.E. (1983) Paths leading to teenage psychiatric symptoms and substance use: developmental epidemiological studies in Woodlawn. In: Guze S.B., Earls F.J. & Barratt J.E. (eds) *Childhood Psychopathology and Development*, pp. 17–51. Raven Press, New York.

Knights R.M. & Bakker D.J. (eds) (1976) *The Neuropsychology of Learning Disorders: Theoretical Approaches*. University Park Press, Baltimore, M.D.

LaBuda M. & DeFries J.C. (1989) Differential prognosis of reading-disabled children as a function of gender, socioeconomic status, IQ and severity: a longitudinal study. *Reading and Writing: An Interdisciplinary Journal*, **1**, 25–36.

LaBuda M.C. & DeFries J.C. (1990) Genetic etiology of reading disability: evidence from a twin study. In: Pavlidis G. (ed) *Dyslexia*, pp. 47–76. Wiley, New York.

LaBuda M.C., DeFries J.C. & Fulker D.W. (1986) Multiple regression analysis of twin data obtained from selected samples. *Genetic Epidemiology*, **3**, 425–433.

Lansdown R. (1978) Retardation in mathematics: a consideration of multifactorial determination. *Journal of Child Psychology and Psychiatry*, **19**, 181–185.

Lawrence D. (1971) The effects of counselling on retarded readers. *Educational Research*, **13**, 119–124.

Lawrence D. (1973) *Improved Reading Through Counselling*. Ward Lock Educational, London.

Lewitter F.I., DeFries J.C. & Elston R.C. (1980) Genetic models of reading disability. *Behavioral Genetics*, **10**, 9–30.

Lindgren S.D., De Renzi E. & Richman L.C. (1985) Cross-national comparisons of developmental dyslexia in Italy and the United States. *Child Development*, **56**, 1404–1417.

Losse A., Henderson S.E., Elliman D., Hall D., Knight E. & Jongmans M. (1991) Clumsiness in children — do they grow out of it? A 10-year follow up study. *Developmental Medicine and Child Neurology*, **33**, 55–68.

Lyle J.C. & Goyen J. (1969) Performance of retarded readers on the WISC and educational tests. *Journal of Abnormal Psychology*, **74**, 105–112.

Lynch E.M. & Jones S.D. (1989) Process and product: a review of the research on LD children's writing skills. *Learning Disability Quarterly*, **12**, 74–96.

Lyon R. & Watson B. (1981) Empirically derived subgroups of learning disabled readers: diagnostic characteristics. *Journal of Learning Disabilities*, **14**, 256–261.

McCall R.B., Evahn C. & Kratzer L. (1992) *High School Underachievers: What do they Achieve as Adults?* Sage, Newbury Park.

McGee R., Share D., Moffitt T.E., Williams S. & Silva P.A. (1988) Reading disability, behaviour problems and juvenile delinquency. In: Saklofske D.H. & Eysenck S.B.G. (eds) *Individual Differences in Children and Adolescents: International perspectiveness*, pp. 150–172. Hodder and Stoughton, London.

McGee R., Feehan M., Williams S. & Anderson J. (1992) DSM-III disorders from age 11 to age 15 years. *Journal of the American Academy of Child and Adolescent Psychiatry*, **31**, 50–59.

McKinney J.D. (1989) Longitudinal research on the behavioural characteristics of children with learning disabilities. *Journal of Learning Disabilities*, **22**, 141–150.

MacLean M., Bryant P.E. & Bradley L. (1987) Rhymes, nursery rhymes and reading in early childhood. *Merrill-Palmer Quarterly*, **33**, 255–282.

McManus I.C. & Mascie-Taylor C.G.N. (1983) Biosocial correlates of cognitive abilities. *Journal of Biosocial Science*, **15**, 289–306.

McMichael P. (1979) The hen or the egg? Which came first — antisocial emotional disorder or reading disability? *British Journal of Educational Psychology*, **49**, 226–235.

Marsh G., Friedman M., Welch V. & Desberg P. (1981) A cognitive-developmental theory of reading acquisition. In: MacKinnon G.E. & Waller T.G. (eds) *Reading Research: Advances in Theory and Practice*, vol. 3, pp. 199–221. Academic Press, New York.

Masland R.L. (1975) Neurological bases of correlates of language disabilities: diagnostic implications. *Acta Symbolica*, **6**, 1–34.

Maughan B., Gray G. & Rutter M. (1985) Reading retardation and antisocial behaviour: a follow-up into employment. *Journal of Child Psychology and Psychiatry*, **26**, 741–758.

Maughan B., Hagell A., Rutter M. & Yule W. (in press) Poor readers in secondary school. *Reading and Writing: An Interdisciplinary Journal*.

Maughan B., Hagell A. & Rutter M. (1993) Reading problems and antisocial behaviour: the picture in adulthood. Unpublished manuscript, MRC Child Psychiatry Unit, Institute of Psychiatry, London.

Maxwell A.E. (1972) The WPPSI: a marked discrepancy in the correlations of the subtests for good and poor readers. *British Journal of Mathematical and Statistical Psychology*, **25**, 283–291.

Money J. (1973) Turner's syndrome and parietal lobe functions. *Cortex*, **9**, 387–393.

Morgan R. & Lyon E. (1979) 'Paired reading' — a preliminary report on a technique for parental tuition of reading-retarded children. *Journal of Child Psychology and Psychiatry*, **20**, 151–160.

Mortimore P., Sammons P., Stoll L., Lewis D. & Ecob R. (1988) *School Matters*. Open Books, London.

Myklebust H.R. (1965) *Development and Disorders of Written Language: Picture Story Language Test*. Grune & Stratton, New York.

Naidoo S. (1972) *Specific Dyslexia*. Pitman, London.

Naylor C.E., Felton R.H. & Wood F.B. (1990) Adult outcome in developmental dyslexia. In: Pavlidis G.Th. (ed) *Perspectives on Dyslexia*, vol. 2, pp. 215–229. Wiley, London.

Newcomer P.L. & Barenbaum E.M. (1991) The written composing ability of children with learning disabilities: a review of the literature from 1980 to 1990. *Journal of Learning Disabilities*, **24**, 578–593.

O'Connor S. & Spreen O. (1988) The relationship between parents' socioeconomic status and education level and adult occupational and educational achievement of children with learning disabilities. *Journal of Learning Disabilities*, **21**, 148–153.

Offord D.R. & Poushinsky M.F. (1981) School performance IQ and female delinquency. *International Journal of Social Psychiatry*, **21**, 267–283.

O'Hare A.E., Brown J.K. & Aitken K. (1991) Dyscalculia in children. *Developmental Medicine and Child Neurology*, **33**, 356–361.

Olson R., Kliegel R., Davidson B. & Foltz G. (1985) Individual and developmental differences in reading disability. In: Waller T. (ed) *Reading Research: Advances in Theory and Practice*, vol. 4, pp. 1–64. Academic Press, London.

Olson R.K., Wise B.W., Conners F., Rack J. & Fulker D. (1989) Specific deficits in component reading and language skills: genetic and environmental influences. *Journal of Learning Disabilities*, **22**, 339–349.

Olson R.K., Wise B.W., Conners F. & Rack J. (1990) Organization, heritability, and remediation of component word recognition and language skills in disabled readers. In: Carr T.H. & Levy B.A. (eds) *Reading and its Development: Component Skills Approaches*, pp. 261–322. Academic Press, New York.

Olson R.K., Rack J.P., Conners F.A., DeFries J.C. & Fulker D.W. (1991) Genetic etiology of individual differences in reading disability. In: Feagans L.V., Short E.J. & Meltzer L.J. (eds) *Subtypes of Learning Disabilities*, pp. 113–135. Lawrence Erlbaum, Hillsdale, NJ.

Orton S.T. (1937) *Reading, Writing and Speech Problems in Children*. Norton, New York.

Otto W. & Fredricks R.C. (1963) Relationships of reactive inhibition to reading skill attainment. *Journal of Educational Psychology*, **54**, 227–230.

Patterson K.E. (1981) Neuropsychological approaches to the study of reading. *British Journal of Psychology*, **72**, 151–174.

Pennington B.F. (1990) The genetics of dyslexia. *Journal of Child Psychology and Psychiatry*, **31**, 193–201.

Pennington B.F. (1991) Overview: introduction to special edition on genetics, neurology and neuropsychology of reading disabilities. *Reading and Writing: An Interdisciplinary Journal*, **3**, 191–201.

Perfetti C.A. (1985) *Reading Ability*. Oxford University Press, New York.

Plomin R. (1991) A behavioral genetic approach to learning disabilities and their subtypes. In: Feagans L.V., Short E.J. & Meltzer L.J. (eds) *Subtypes of Learning Disabilities*, pp. 83–111. Lawrence Erlbaum, Hillsdale, NJ.

Plomin R. & Rende R. (1991) Human behavioral genetics. *Annual Review of Psychology*, **42**, 161–190.

Rack J.P., Snowling M. & Olson R.K. (1992) The nonword reading deficit in developmental dyslexia: a review. *Reading Research Quarterly*, **27**, 29–53.

Reid J.F. (1969) Dyslexia: a problem in communication. *Educational Research*, **10**, 126–133.

Richman N., Stevenson J. & Graham P.J. (1982) *Pre-school to School: A Behavioural Study*. Academic Press, London.

Rodgers B. (1983) The identification and prevalence of specific reading retardation. *British Journal of Educational Psychology*, **53**, 369–373.

Rourke B.P. & Finlayson M.A.J. (1978) Neurophysiological significance of variations in patterns of academic performance: verbal and visual-spatial abilities. *Journal of Abnormal Child Psychology*, **6**, 121–133.

Rourke B.P. & Fuerst D.R. (1991) *Learning Disabilities and Psychosocial Functioning: A Neuropsychological Perspective*. Guilford Press, New York.

Rourke B.P. & Strang J.D. (1983) Subtypes of reading and arithmetic disabilities: a neuropsychological analysis. In: Rutter M. (ed) *Developmental Neuropsychiatry*, pp. 473–488. Guilford Press, New York.

Rowe K.J. & Rowe K.S. (1992) The relationship between inattentiveness in the classroom and reading achievement (part B): an exploratory study. *Journal of the American Academy of Child and Adolescent Psychiatry*, **31**, 357–368.

Rutter M. (1969) The concept of 'dyslexia'. In: Wolff P. & McKeith R.C. (eds) *Planning for Better Learning*, pp. 129–139. Clinics in Developmental Medicine no. 33. Heinemann/Spastics International Medical Publications, London.

Rutter M. (1974) Emotional disorder and educational underachievement. *Archives of Disease in Childhood*, **49**, 249–256.

Rutter M. & Giller H. (1983) *Juvenile Delinquency: Trends and Perspectives*. Penguin, London.

Rutter M. & Yule W. (1973) Specific reading retardation. In: Mann L. & Sabatino D. (eds) *The First Review of Special Education*, pp. 1–50. Buttonwood Farms, Philadelphia, PA.

Rutter M. & Yule W. (1975) The concept of specific reading retardation. *Journal of Child Psychology and Psychiatry*, **125**, 181–197.

Rutter M., Tizard J. & Whitmore K. (eds) (1970) *Education, Health and Behaviour*. Longman, London.

Rutter M., Tizard J., Yule W., Graham P. & Whitmore K. (1976) Isle of Wight studies 1964–1974. *Psychological Medicine*, **6**, 313–332.

Satz P. & Fletcher J.M. (1987) Left-handedness and dyslexia: an old myth revisited. *Journal of Pediatric Psychology*, **12**, 291–298.

Satz P. & Friel J. (1973) Some predictive antecedents of specific learning disability: a preliminary one year follow-up. In: Satz P. & Ross J.J. (eds) *The Disabled Learner: Early Detection and Intervention*, pp. 79–98. Rotterdam University Press, Rotterdam.

Satz P. & Sparrow S. (1970) Specific developmental dyslexia: a theoretical formulation. In: Baker D.J. & Satz P. (eds) *Specific Reading Disability: Theory and Method*. Rotterdam University Press, Rotterdam.

Satz P., Friel J. & Rudegeair F. (1976) Some predictive antecedents of specific reading disability: a two, three and four year follow up. In: Guthrie J.T. (ed) *Aspects of Reading Acquisition*, pp. 111–140. Johns Hopkins Press, Baltimore, MD.

Scarborough H. (1991) Antecedents to reading disability: preschool language development and literacy experiences of children from dyslexic families. *Reading and Writing: An Interdisciplinary Journal*, **3**, 219–233.

Seidenberg M. & McClelland J. (1989) A distributed, developmental model of word recognition. *Psychological Review*, **94**, 523–568.

Share D.L. & Silva P.A. (1986) The stability and classification of specific reading retardation: a longitudinal study from age 7 to 11. *British Journal of Educational Psychology*, **56**, 32–39.

Share D.L., Moffitt T.E. & Silva P.A. (1988) Factors associated with arithmetic-and-reading disability and specific arithmetic disability. *Journal of Learning Disabilities*, **21**, 313–320.

Share D.L., McGee R. & Silva P.A. (1989) IQ and reading progress: a test of the capacity notion of IQ. *Journal of the American Academy of Child and Adolescent Psychiatry*, **28**, 97–100.

Shaywitz S.E., Shaywitz B.A., Fletcher J.M. & Escobar M.D. (1990) Prevalence of reading disability in boys and girls: results of the Connecticut Longitudinal Study. *Journal of the American Medical Association*, **264**, 998–1002.

Shaywitz S.E., Escobar M.D., Shaywitz B.A., Fletcher J.M. & Makuch R. (1992) Evidence that dyslexia may represent the lower tail of a normal distribution of reading ability. *New England Journal of Medicine*, **326**, 145–150.

Siegel L.S. (1988) Evidence that IQ scores are irrelevant to the definition and analysis of reading disability. *Canadian Journal of Psychology*, **42**, 201–215.

Siegel L.S. (1989) IQ is irrelevant to the definition of learning disabilities. *Journal of Learning Disabilities*, **22**, 469–478.

Silberberg N.E., Iversen I.A. & Goins J.T. (1973) Which remedial method works best? *Journal of Learning Disabilities*, **6**, 547–557.

Silva P.A. (1987) Epidemiology, longitudinal course, and some associated factors: an update. In: Yule W. & Rutter M. (eds)

Language Development and Disorders, pp. 1–15. Mac Keith London/Blackwell Scientific Publications, Oxford.

Silva P.A., McGee R. & Williams S. (1985) Some characteristics of 9-year-old boys with general reading backwardness or specific reading retardation. *Journal of Child Psychology and Psychiatry*, **26**, 407–421.

Slade P.D. & Russell G.F.M. (1971) Developmental dyscalculia: a brief report on four cases. *Psychological Medicine*, **1**, 292–298.

Smith S.D., Pennington B.F., Kimberling W.J. & Ing P.S. (1990) Familial dyslexia: use of genetic linkage data to define subtypes. *Journal of the American Academy of Child and Adolescent Psychiatry*, **29**, 204–213.

Snowling M.J. (1980) The development of grapheme-phoneme correspondence in normal and dyslexic readers. *Journal of Experimental Child Psychology*, **29**, 294–305.

Snowling M. (1987) *Dyslexia*. Blackwell Scientific Publications, Oxford.

Snowling M.J. (1991) Developmental reading disorders. *Journal of Child Psychology and Psychiatry*, **32**, 49–77.

Snowling M. & Thomson M. (1991) *Dyslexia: Integrating Theory and Practice*. Whurr, London.

Snowling M., Stackhouse J. & Rack J.P. (1986) Phonological dyslexia and dysgraphia: a developmental analysis. *Cognitive Neuropsychology*, **3**, 309–339.

Snowling M., Van Wagtendonk B. & Stafford C. (1988) Object naming deficits in developmental dyslexia. *Journal of Research in Reading*, **11**, 67–85.

Spache G.D. (1981) *Diagnosing and Correcting Reading Disabilities*, 2nd edn. Allyn and Bacon, Boston.

Spreen O. (1987) *Learning Disabled Children Growing Up: A Follow-up into Adulthood*. Swets & Zeitlinger, Lisse, Netherlands.

Spreen O. (1988) Prognosis of learning disability. *Journal of Consulting and Clinical Psychology*, **56**, 836–842.

Staats A.W. (1968) *Learning, Language and Cognition*. Holt, Rinehart & Winston, New York.

Staats A.W., Minke K.A., Goodwin W. & Landeen J. (1967) Cognitive behavior modification: 'motivated learning' reading treatment with subprofessional therapist-technicians. *Behaviour Research and Therapy*, **5**, 283–299.

Staats A.W., Minke K.A. & Butts P. (1970) A token reinforcement remedial reading programme administered by block therapy-technicians to black problem children. *Behaviour Therapy*, **1**, 331–353.

Stanovich K.E. (1980) Toward an interactive-compensatory model of individual differences in the development of reading fluency. *Reading Research Quarterly*, **16**, 32–71.

Stanovich K.E. (1986) Matthew effects in reading: some consequences of individual differences in the acquisition of literacy. *Reading Research Quarterly*, **21**, 360–407.

Stanovich K.E. (1988) Explaining the differences between the dyslexic and the garden variety poor reader: the phonological-core variable-difference hypothesis. *Journal of Learning Disabilities*, **21**, 590–612.

Stanovich K.E. (1991) The theoretical and practical consequences of discrepancy definitions of dyslexia. In: Snowling M. & Thomson M. (eds) *Dyslexia: Integrating Theory and Practice*, pp. 125–143. Whurr, London.

Stein J.F. (1989) Visuospatial perception and reading problems. *Irish Journal of Psychology*, **22**, 487–492.

Stein J.F. & Fowler M.S. (1985) Effect of monocular occlusion on visuomotor perception and reading in dyslexic children. *Lancet*, **ii**, July, 69–73.

Stevenson J. (1988) Which aspects of reading ability show a 'hump' in their distribution? *Applied Cognitive Psychology* **2**, 77–85.

Stevenson J. (1989) Language development and delays and the prediction of later reading failure. In: Brambring M., Losel F. &

Skowroneck H. (eds) *Children at Risk: Assessment and Longitudinal Research*. de Gruyter, Berlin.

Stevenson J. (1991) Which aspects of processing text mediate genetic effects? *Reading and Writing: An Interdisciplinary Journal*, **3**, 249–269.

Stevenson H.W., Stigler J.W., Lucker G.W., Lee S.Y., Hsu C.-C. & Kitamura S. (1982) Reading disabilities: the case of Chinese, Japanese, and English. *Child Development*, **33**, 1164–1181.

Stevenson J., Graham P., Fredman G. & McLoughlin V. (1987) A twin study of genetic influences on reading and spelling ability and disability. *Journal of Child Psychology and Psychiatry*, **28**, 229–247.

Stuart M. & Coltheart M. (1988) Does reading develop in a sequence of stages? *Cognition*, **30**, 139–181.

Temple C. (1990) Foop is still Floop: a six year follow-up of phonological dyslexia and dysgraphia. *Reading and Writing: An Interdisciplinary Journal*, **2**, 209–221.

Temple C.M. & Marshall J.C. (1983) A case study of developmental phonological dyslexia. *British Journal of Psychology*, **74**, 517–533.

Thorndike R.L. (1963) *The Concepts of Over- and Under-Achievement*. Teachers College, Columbia University, New York.

Tizard J., Schofield W.N. & Hewison J. (1982) Collaboration between teachers and parents in assisting children's reading. *British Journal of Educational Psychology*, **52**, 1–15.

Tobin D. & Pumfrey P.D. (1976) Some long term effects of the remedial teaching of reading. *Educational Review*, **29**, 1–12.

Treiman R. (1985) Onsets and rimes as units of spoken syllables: evidence from children. *Journal of Experimental Child Psychology*, **39**, 161–181.

Trites R.L. & Fiedorowicz C. (1976) Follow-up study of children with specific (or primary) reading disability. In: Knights R.M. & Bakker D.J. (eds) *The Neuropsychology of Learning Disorders: Theoretical Approaches*, pp. 41–50. University Park Press, Baltimore, MD.

Van der Wissel A. & Zegers F.E. (1985) Reading retardation revisited. *British Journal of Developmental Psychology*, **3**, 3–19.

Van Orden G.C., Pennington B.F. & Stone G.O. (1990) Word identification in reading and the promise of subsymbolic psycholinguistics. *Psychological Review*, **97**, 488–522.

Vellutino F. (1979) *Dyslexia: Theory and Research*. MIT Press, Cambridge, MA.

Vogler G.P., DeFries J.C. & Decker S.N. (1985) Family history as an indicator of risk for reading disability. *Journal of Learning Disabilities*, **18**, 419–421.

Vogler G., Baker L.A., Decker S.N., DeFries J.C. & Huizinga D. (1989) Cluster analytic classification of reading disability subtypes. *Reading and Writing: An Interdisciplinary Journal*, **1**, 163–167.

Wadsworth M. (1979) *Roots of Delinquency: Infancy, Adolescence and Crime*. Martin Robertson, Oxford.

Wadsworth S.J., DeFries J.C., Stevenson J., Gilger J.W. & Pennington B.F. (1992) Gender ratios among reading-disabled children and their siblings as a function of parental impairment. *Journal of Child Psychology and Psychiatry*, **33**, 1229–1239.

Wagner R.K. & Torgeson J.K. (1987) The nature of phonological processing and its causal role in the acquisition of reading skills. *Psychological Bulletin*, **101**, 192–212.

Watson B.U., Watson C.S. & Fredd R. (1982) Follow-up studies of specific reading disability. *Journal of the American Academy of Child Psychiatry*, **21**, 376–382.

White W.J. (1985) Perspectives on the education and training of learning disabled adults. *Learning Disabilities Quarterly*, **8**, 231–236.

Wilsher C.R. (1991) Is medicinal treatment of dyslexia advisable? In: Snowling M. & Thomson M. (eds) *Dyslexia: Integrating Theory and Practice*, pp. 204–212. Whurr, London.

Wilsher C.R. & Taylor J.A. (1988) Commentary: tinted glasses and dyslexia. *Journal of Research in Reading*, **11**, 50–52.

Wilsher C.R., Bennett D., Chase C.H., Conners C.K., Dhanni M. & Feagans L. (1987) Piracetam and dyslexia: effects on reading tests. *Journal of Clinical Psychopharmacology*, **7**, 230−237.

World Health Organization (1992) *The ICD-10 Classification of Mental and Behavioural Disorders. Clinical Descriptions and Diagnostic Guidelines.* World Health Organization, Geneva.

Yule W. (1973) Differential prognosis of reading backwardness and specific reading retardation. *British Journal of Educational Psychology*, **43**, 244−248.

Yule W. (1976) Issues and problems in remedial education. *Developmental Medicine and Child Neurology*, **18**, 675−682.

Yule W. (1979) Correlates of reading retardation among junior school children: An Epidemiological Study. Unpublished PhD thesis, University of London.

Yule W. (1985) Comments on Van der Wissel and Zegers: reading retardation revisited. *British Journal of Developmental Psychology*, **3**, 11−13.

Yule W. & Gold R.D. (1980) *Isle of Wight Prediction Study: 1967−1979. Final Report to SSRC and Nuffield Foundation.* Obtainable from authors, Institute of Psychiatry, London.

Yule W., Rutter M., Berger M. & Thompson J. (1974) Over- and underachievement in reading: distribution in the general population. *British Journal of Educational Psychology*, **44**, 1−12.

Yule W., Gold R.D. & Busch C. (1981) WISC-R correlates of academic attainment at 16½ years. *British Journal of Educational Psychology*, **51**, 237−240.

Yule W., Lansdown R. & Urbanowicz M. (1982) Predicting educational attainment from WISC-R in a primary school sample. *British Journal of Clinical Psychology*, **21**, 43−46.

Chapter 37
Behavioural Phenotypes

Jonathan Flint & William Yule

Although it is well-established that rates of psychiatric disorder are increased in mentally retarded children and adults, the idea that there could be significant behavioural differences between the biological disorders causing mental retardation has not been so readily accepted. Instead, mental retardation due to any cause is often considered to result in a largely undifferentiated pattern of motor, cognitive, linguistic and behavioural abnormalities or, in short, a uniform behavioural phenotype (Ellis, 1969; MacMillan, 1982). Indeed, categorizing behaviour by aetiology is sometimes discouraged, because it is said to imply incurability, with detrimental social consequences for sufferers (Goodman, 1990).

Three lines of research have led to a reassessment of the relationship between behavioural phenotypes and biological causes of mental retardation. Firstly, self-help groups have challenged the view that parents are to blame for many of the behaviours that previously led to institutionalization. Closer cooperation between professionals and the families of retarded children has drawn attention to the existence of similar problem behaviours in children with the same syndrome, and this has renewed interest in the psychological assessment of behavioural phenotypes. Counter to the predictions of the undifferentiated hypothesis of mental retardation, specific impairments have been detected in different syndromes.

Secondly, proponents of the developmental approach to mental retardation have begun to look at the development of different types of organically retarded children and claim to have found important differences (Zigler & Hodapp, 1991). For instance, it is said that the cognitive development of Down's syndrome children gradually decelerates with increasing age (Hodapp & Zigler, 1990) while IQ scores of boys with fragile X are fairly steady until puberty when IQ declines (Dykens & Leckman, 1990). Pursuing this line of enquiry further has led these investigators to compare behavioural profiles (mainly cognitive) of the different groups and argue that there are 'aetiology-specific strengths and weaknesses' (Hodapp & Dykens, 1991).

Thirdly, molecular genetic techniques are now able to define the biological basis and characterize the genes responsible for some forms of mental retardation, as is happening in the case of fragile X (Pieretti et al., 1991; Verkerk et al., 1991). This information has already provided new ways of classifying disorders (such as by the amount of DNA deleted, the type of mutation responsible or the parental origin of the abnormality) so that more aetiologically homogeneus groups emerge. Moreover, molecular genetic techniques have begun to characterize genes that are involved in learning and memory processes in other species (Chen et al., 1986; Hardin et al., 1990; Grant et al., 1992; Levin et al., 1992; Silva et al., 1992a,b); it is suspected that homologous genes will be important in equivalent human activities. Interest in the belief that there may be specific 'behavioural genes' has therefore reawakened.

All these approaches indicate that there may be a closer connection than previously suspected between the organic basis of mental retardation and its behavioural consequences. This has important implications for management: we have already mentioned the change in the attribution of parental blame. Thus it is a characteristic of Cornelia de Lange syndrome children that they reject physical contact; it is not a failure of parenting. Additionally, the recognition of specific deficits (for instance, poor visuospatial abilities in Turner's syndrome) may allow early intervention, and possibly prevention of secondary handicaps (Marfo, 1991).

Moreover, if there are relatively discrete pathways linking biology with behaviour (and the evidence that this is so is presented below) then these conditions present us with a unique opportunity. They are primarily disorders of single genes or chromosomal anomalies which are now vulnerable to dissection with new molecular genetic techniques. It may therefore be possible to isolate the genetic basis of some forms of pathological behaviour, and by doing so there is every reason to expect that we will learn about the biological basis of normal behaviour.

CHARACTERIZATION OF BEHAVIOURAL PHENOTYPES

What is a behavioural phenotype? As we shall see later it is not at all clear what should be included within the definition, but we shall begin with two requirements. Firstly, a behavioural phenotype should consist of a distinctive behaviour that occurs in almost every case of a genetic or chromosomal disorder, and rarely (if at all) in other conditions. Secondly, we should be able to say that this behaviour has a direct and specific relationship to the genetic or chromosomal anomaly that gives rise to the physical manifestations of the syndrome.

A problem with these requirements is that, when they are strictly applied, only three syndromes can be said to have a behavioural phenotype. A severe form of self-mutilating behaviour is found in all cases of the Lesch–Nyhan syndrome; overeating and abnormal food-seeking behaviour characterize children (but not infants) with the Prader–Willi syndrome (PWS); there is a pathognomonic loss of purposeful hand movements in Rett's syndrome and the emergence of midline hand-wringing stereotypies. In these syndromes the diagnosis would be questioned in the absence of the behaviour: indeed, could not even be advanced in the case of Rett's syndrome.

However, behavioural phenotypes are also recognized that consist of a collection of behavioural abnormalities that, individually, are not usually thought to have any psychiatric significance. Such behavioural phenotypes are less consistently associated with a syndrome than is the case for self-injurious behaviour in Lesch–Nyhan syndrome; also, in addition to purely behavioural features, they often include cognitive, linguistic and social processes as part of the behavioural phenotype. To take two examples: in a survey of 16 children with Sotos syndrome, 5 displayed precocious sexual behaviour, and 11 had sleep problems (Rutter & Cole, 1991); in Williams syndrome evidence has accumulated that a large minority (perhaps 40%) have 'cocktail party speech', characterized by an excessive use of clichés, fluency, perseverations and a habit of introducing irrelevant personal experiences into conversations (Udwin & Yule, 1990). Such observations are intriguing, but there are formidable methodological problems to be overcome before accepting that there is any specific and direct relationship between the biological disorder underlying the syndrome and the putative behavioural phenotype.

To find a behavioural phenotype in these cases, the most crucial point to establish is that an association between the syndrome and a behaviour, cognitive abnormality or psychiatric disorder holds in the presence of appropriate controls. Comparing the frequency of a behaviour in a syndrome with estimates of population rates can be misleading because of sampling bias and diagnostic differences. Good examples of the dangers that emerge if adequate care is not taken can be found in the investigation of the phenotypes of fragile X and XYY syndromes (Witkin *et al.*, 1976; Einfeld & Hall, 1992; Fisch, 1992). Moreover it is often not at all clear what the appropriate controls are. Thus in seeking to decide whether the 'approaching' temperamental trait of Williams syndrome is a component of the behavioural phenotype, it may be necessary to control for effects of the facial appearance and 'smiling behaviour' on parents. Dilts *et al.* (1990) argue that the engaging smile and appearance 'facilitate attachment through promoting and positively reinforcing social interaction'. Without at least considering such possibilities we may be misled into seeing a particular temperament as a direct result of the biology of the condition.

But there are also problems which can obscure the detection of a behavioural phenotype. Firstly, it is not clear what to include as part of a behavioural phenotype. Standard assessment procedures may not detect distinctive behavioural abnor-

malities. There is something to be learnt here from older literature which, although producing observations of questionable validity, at least had the advantage of being free of the homogenizing effect of questionnaires and diagnostic criteria. It is difficult to see how observations made in the first part of this century about the musicality, imitative abilities and sexual behaviour of Down's syndrome children could have emerged had investigators relied upon the Bayley Scales of infant behaviour, the Wechsler Intelligence Scale for Children (WISC) and the Vineland Adaptive Behaviour Scale (Belmont, 1971). The use of more structured protocols may help here (O'Brien, 1991) but at present we often cannot be certain that a syndrome has been adequately examined for the presence of a behavioural phenotype. The discovery of such features as hyperacusis in Williams syndrome, skin-picking in PWS and social gaze avoidance in fragile X syndrome has not emerged from a rigorous inquisition into all possible behavioural anomalies. There is still a fair element of chance determining what comes to investigators' notice.

Secondly, there are problems in relying on physical findings (rather than the rarely available genotype analysis) to define homogeneous clinical syndromes. Identical physical phenotypes can arise from mutations in different genes (or from mutations in the same gene) and in chromosomal disorders there is no straightforward relationship between the size or type of chromosomal aberration and the phenotype. While different genotypes may result in a homogeneous physical syndrome, this may not be true for the behavioural phenotype. Consequently, studies which use physical stigmata for syndrome diagnosis may find variation in the behavioural abnormalities which could be due to variation in the genotype. In such instances a behavioural phenotype would be missed. The problem is most likely to occur in studies of chromosomal disorders, where a large number of genetic loci are involved in the phenotype. Deletions of different sizes could affect genes determining the behavioural phenotype but not the physical condition, or somatic mosaicism could be present in central nervous system but not other cell lineages, thus dissociating behavioural from physical manifestations. Until recently such problems could be considered largely theoretical, but there is now evidence that genes in Down's syndrome affecting mental development are indeed separate from those affecting the physical phenotype (Epstein, 1986, 1991; McCormick *et al.*, 1989; Korenberg *et al.*, 1991).

So there are difficulties in deciding what to include in a behavioural phenotype, whether aetiological heterogeneity can produce a single physical but multiple behavioural phenotypes, and how to determine whether a behaviour is characteristic of a syndrome. These difficulties should caution any over-hasty acceptance of the existence of a behavioural phenotype. We touch again on these points in the discussion of individual syndromes.

In the rest of the chapter we discuss the relatively well-established examples of behavioural phenotypes, and then consider the more difficult problem posed by syndromes where distinctive patterns of behaviour have been observed, but studies have not demonstrated such a close and invariant relationship with a behavioural abnormality. We then ask what information we can expect to gain from molecular analysis of syndromes with behavioural phenotypes, and what light this may cast on the biology of normal behaviour. Finally, we deal with the implications of the existence of behavioural phenotypes for the management of children with these syndromes.

SYNDROMES WITH A DISTINCTIVE AND SPECIFIC BEHAVIOURAL PHENOTYPE

Lesch–Nyhan syndrome

Lesch–Nyhan syndrome is due to complete deficiency of the enzyme hypoxanthine phosphoribosyltransferase. The gene is located on the X chromosome so the disorder is only manifest in males (though there are rare exceptions; Yukawa, 1992). Heterozygotes (that is, females) have a partial enzyme deficiency which produces hyperuricaemia and causes a form of gouty arthritis and renal stones in early adulthood.

Lesch–Nyhan syndrome has a particularly striking behavioural phenotype: almost as soon as they have teeth, children with the disorder will bite themselves and others. The biting is so severe that they can sever their fingers, and lose portions of their lips and tongues. In the largest reported series, all 19 had extensive loss of lip tissue (Christie *et al.*, 1982). In 12 cases the diagnosis of Lesch–Nyhan syndrome was not made until after the onset of self-mutilation, emphasizing the diagnostic value of the behavioural phenotype.

Self-injurious behaviour is common in the mentally retarded population, but two features of the behaviour in Lesch–Nyhan syndrome indicate that it is a specific abnormality. Firstly, self-injurious behaviour in Lesch–Nyhan disease is unusually severe and resistant to behavioural intervention (Anderson *et al.*, 1977). Although differential reinforcement of incompatible behaviour and punishment has been effective in some cases, no consistent benefit has been reported. Indeed sometimes intervention has worsened the behaviour (Anderson *et al.*, 1977). This suggests that the behaviour is less environmentally determined than is commonly the case. Moreover, although patients are clearly aware of their disability, they often appear to have surprisingly little control over it. Christie *et al.* (1982) quote one boy who spoke to his hand when it was freed from its restraints, saying, 'Be good, right hand'. Nyhan describes how 'when protective coverings or restraints are removed, the patient's personality undergoes a dramatic change. He appears terrified. He screams, I think, for help, to protect him from himself' (Nyhan, 1976).

Secondly, Lesch–Nyhan individuals also harm others, and can be as verbally aggressive as they are physically. Fourteen of the patients reported by Christie *et al.* (1982) tried to hit others, and 11 to bite those around them. Nyhan (1976) described 1 patient who, immediately after appearing overjoyed at the sight of his mother, threw a toy at her and lacerated her leg. The fact that these children self-harm more

often than they attack those around them may be due to lack of opportunity: most patients are incapacitated by spasticity and postural tremors (choreoathetosis and opisthotonus are found in almost every case; 7 of the patients in Christie *et al.*'s series (1982) had dislocated hips, possibly as a result of spasticity). Generalized aggression, physical and verbal, to self and others, characterizes the behavioural phenotype.

Both these features suggest that self-injurious behaviour in Lesch–Nyhan syndrome is qualitatively different from self-injurious behaviour in most other mental retardation syndromes. It has an involuntary character and appears to be part of a more general disturbance.

Prader–Willi syndrome

PWS provides an informative contrast with Lesch–Nyhan syndrome. Here again a behavioural abnormality (overeating) is said to be a hallmark of the condition, but closer examination has failed to reveal any attributes which clearly distinguish overeating in PWS from overeating in other forms of obesity. Consequently we have to be careful in drawing the conclusion that the behaviour is a direct consequence of the genetic abnormality.

PWS is characterized by small stature, hypogonadism, infantile hypotonia and mental retardation. It is due to a chromosomal abnormality affecting part of the long arm of chromosome 15. The degree of mental retardation is variable (IQ 20–90), with as many as 50% of individuals with scores above the retarded range (Sulzbacher *et al.*, 1981; Greenswag, 1987; Curfs *et al.*, 1991). Despite the fact that in the first few years of life PWS children characteristically fail to thrive, from about 2 years of age (range 1–6 years) they begin foraging for food. If food is withheld they are said to steal, even consuming 'inedible' material, such as frozen food (Zellweger & Schneider 1968; Holm & Pipes, 1976; Taylor & Caldwell, 1985). Extreme obesity results: one-third of cases weigh more than 200% of ideal body weight (Schoeller *et al.*, 1988) and death from the complications is not unknown.

This description suggests that the eating behaviour has some unusual, perhaps unique qualities, that would make us believe it had an organic determinant. In fact there is nothing to support such an assertion (but then little research has addressed the issue). Investigation into the food-seeking behaviour shows that PWS individuals, like the rest of us, have food preferences; they do not consume food indiscriminately, but consistently choose sweet over salty or sour foods, and will consume less of their preferred food rather than more of a less desirable morsel. Moreover the higher the IQ, the more marked this preference is (Taylor & Caldwell, 1985; Caldwell *et al.*, 1986).

It has not been possible to explain this behaviour as the consequence of a metabolic dysfunction, but this is not to say that impaired central satiety mechanisms must be to blame. PWS patients have low resting metabolic rates which are not due to a reduced fat-free mass, and one-fifth of cases have reduced glucose tolerance (Holm, 1981; Cassidy, 1984; Butler,

1990). Foraging behaviour may be secondary to a metabolic derangement still to be discovered, but the available evidence points to a central mechanism.

The difficulty with accepting overeating as a unique aspect of the syndrome is that, as Taylor (1988) emphasizes, it is possible that the behaviour is partly learned. Because it is believed that dietary therapy is unworkable, PWS individuals are frequently put in a position where they have no access to any food. Consequently they may learn to overeat whenever food does become available. Taylor goes on to point out that food-related behaviours may be a function of cognitive level, and that those with marked food preferences, deprived of their desired food, are likely to gorge themselves whenever they can eat what they want. This is not to say that all eating behaviour in PWS is learned. The point is that, in contrast to Lesch—Nyhan syndrome, behavioural analysis provides no good reason to rule out a significant environmental determinant.

Overeating is the best established component of the PWS behavioural phenotype, but it is probably not the only one. Cognitive testing has suggested that PWS subjects have strengths in puzzle-solving and visual organization skills (Holm, 1981; Curfs *et al.*, 1991), although comparing PWS and obese IQ-matched individuals, Taylor (1988) argued that the cognitive characteristics were not unique to the syndrome, as they occurred in the controls as well.

There have not been any similarly controlled studies of other behavioural features. It is clear that PWS children and adults have a wide variety of psychiatric disorders; it is not clear why this should be. Over half of the 35 adolescents surveyed by Whitman and Accardo (1987) received a DSM-III diagnosis, with a high preponderance of neurotic disorders (compulsive and anxious types). However they included no matched controls in their survey. Over 90% of PWS adolescents exhibit some degree of daytime sleepiness, but this could be due to sleep apnoea secondary to obesity, rather than being more directly related to the chromosomal lesion.

A better case can be made for the presence of a typical temperamental profile. Hall and Smith (1972) noted that 71% of the 32 individuals they assessed had violent outbursts; Cassidy (1984) concluded that PWS children were affectionate and compliant, but prone to outbursts of rage. Greenswag (1987), who surveyed 232 PWS individuals, found that PWS children were described as good-natured, but often belligerent (not always over food); similar conclusions were reached by Hanson (1981). Unfortunately, as we do not know whether this pattern of behaviour has any special relationship to the psychosocial pressures of being obese, to carers' responses to food-seeking behaviour or to other physical features of the syndrome (such as the lack of secondary sexual characteristics), we cannot say to what extent the behaviour is a result of the primary genetic lesion.

One other behaviour may turn out to be organically determined; that is the unusual picking and scratching that PWS individuals indulge in (Hanson, 1981; Clarke *et al.*, 1989). Comparison with weight- and IQ-matched controls indicates that the behaviour is specific to PWS; moreover, the stereotyped nature of the behaviour (almost tic-like), with no obvious environmental determinant, suggests an organic cause.

Rett's syndrome

Rett's syndrome is a rare condition (its prevalence was estimated at 1 in 15 000 girls in Hagberg's (1985) Swedish study) which has attracted attention because of its remarkable behavioural phenotype. It is an example of a syndrome where a behaviour is pathognomonic: there is loss of purposeful hand movements and their replacement by midline hand-wringing stereotypies.

Rett's syndrome has only been described in females. Although the inheritance has not been unequivocally established, there is now an increasing body of evidence that it is due to an abnormal gene on the X chromosome, behaving in a dominant fashion (Killian, 1986; Riccardi, 1986; Journel *et al.*, 1990; Zoghbi *et al.*, 1990). Children with Rett's syndrome are apparently normal until 6–12 months when motor and cognitive skills begin to deteriorate. From 12 to 18 months there is a regression in language skill, deceleration of head circumference, the appearance of seizures (in 80% of cases) and the emergence of the behavioural profile (Naidu *et al.*, 1986).

From as early as 12 months, abnormal hand movements appear, such as twirling of the hands at the sides, tapping the chest, pulling hair or ears. Gradually the movements become more stereotyped, less purposeful, and occur increasingly in the midline, sometimes being performed behind the child's back, but always in the midline (Naidu *et al.*, 1986). By 5 years characteristic hand-wringing, licking, sucking and biting occur in virtually all children. The biting is never as disfiguring as in Lesch—Nyhan syndrome, but other problems emerge due to the persistence of the movements. They interfere significantly with motor performance, and may produce skin abrasions (Hagberg *et al.*, 1985; Olsson & Rett, 1985).

There seems little doubt that these movements are a direct outcome of the biological basis of Rett's syndrome. A similar developmental pattern of movements has not been observed in other conditions and the use of operant methods has demonstrated that the stereotypies are unlikely to have been shaped by the environment (Iwata *et al.*, 1986). Furthermore the gradual development of the movements suggests they emerge as a function of central nervous system maturation. It is interesting in this regard that Nomura *et al.* (1984) report that almost all Rett's syndrome children under 7 who grasp objects are left-handed, yet examination of children over 7 years old showed right-hand preference (Olsson & Rett, 1986). Furthermore the hand stereotypies are part of a more general neurodevelopmental abnormality: language never progresses beyond the possession of 2 or 3 phrases or words and there are often signs of poor motor development; gait apraxia may develop, some children being unwilling to walk at all, and hyperreflexia with sustained ankle clonus can be found.

A number of other behaviours have been considered part of the behavioural phenotype: hyperventilation, breath-holding, bruxism and tremulousness are all common (Naidu *et al.*, 1986), but not specific to Rett's syndrome. As autism is the commonest wrong diagnosis of Rett's syndrome, there have been some attempts to argue that autistic features comprise part of the behavioural phenotype. The most careful study to date (Olsson & Rett, 1987) compared the behaviour of 27 children with Rett's syndrome with 18 autistic children and 18 with severe brain damage and autistic traits. A few features occurred sufficiently frequently in Rett's syndrome and infrequently in autistic children to qualify as characteristic: episodic hyperventilation, broad-based stance and apraxic gait, lack of proper thumb opposition and some abnormalities of social interaction. Although most children smiled at people's faces, they did so with equal frequency to familiar and unfamiliar adults and failed to accommodate, appearing to look through the person. However Olsson and Rett concluded that the social interaction of Rett's syndrome children corresponded to the mental age of their behaviour in general. They found that once additional factors such as severe mental retardation and brain insults are taken into account, the abnormal social interaction, suggestive of autism, occurs no more frequently than in other organic brain disorders.

SYNDROMES WHERE BEHAVIOURAL PHENOTYPES ARE FOUND IN MOST INDIVIDUALS

There are a number of conditions where no single behavioural abnormality is present in all cases, but where distinctive deficits occur sufficiently often to arouse suspicion that they are a direct result of the biological disorder. The fragile X and Williams syndromes have attracted most attention, and are discussed next. The basis for believing in the existence of characteristic behavioural phenotypes in these syndromes is that a pattern of behaviour is found in a number of individuals, who differ in personality variables, cultural background and socioeconomic status. It is then likely that the collection of abnormalities is due to what these individuals have in common, namely the syndrome. However this still does not rule out the possibility that the behaviour is a secondary consequence of other features of the syndrome (for example, the physical); as yet there is no unambiguous evidence that the phenotype bears a direct relationship to the organic determinant.

Williams syndrome

Williams syndrome (or idiopathic infantile hypercalcaemia) is diagnosed on the basis of the presence of a characteristic face (wide mouth, long philtrum, thick lips, turned-up nose; often called elfin facies) and heart defect (supravalvular aortic stenosis, peripheral pulmonary artery stenosis; Burn, 1986; Morris *et al.*, 1988). It is a rare disorder (1 in 50 000 live births; Martin *et al.*, 1984) of unknown cause, although disturbance

of calcium homeostasis is implicated (Friedman & Mills, 1969; Westgren *et al.*, 1988; Jones, 1990). It is unclear whether it is aetiologically heterogeneous.

The case for a behavioural phenotype in Williams syndrome is made on the basis of a constellation of behavioural features, including abnormalities of cognitive, linguistic and social skills.

Initial investigations of cognitive skills using general intelligence tests suggested that Williams syndrome children had better verbal than visuospatial skills (von Arnim & Engel, 1964; Bennett *et al.*, 1978). Considerable interindividual variation and scores at the lower limit of the WISC made it difficult to confirm this finding (Martin *et al.*, 1984; Arnold *et al.*, 1985), but Udwin *et al.*'s (1987) assessment of 44 Williams syndrome children showed significantly lower performance than verbal IQ scores. A controlled study by Crisco *et al.* (1988) of 22 Williams syndrome children looked specifically at auditory and visual information-processing skills. They confirmed that affected children have a cognitive profile unlike that of children with other developmental delays, and that it is characterized by diminished visuoperceptual functions. However, not all children show this pattern, and more detailed investigation suggests that the deficit may only affect specific visuospatial abilities. Bellugi *et al.* (1990), in a study of 6 Williams syndrome adolescents, were able to show that despite poor drawing, block design and spatial transformation abilities, Williams syndrome children could discriminate between unfamiliar human faces under differing conditions.

A similarly complex picture emerges from studies of Williams syndrome linguistic abilities. Anecdotal reports of an unusual use of language (von Arnim & Engel, 1964; Meyerson & Frank, 1987) are supported by parents' and teachers' reports that about half Williams syndrome children chatter incessantly, using stereotyped and formal speech patterns (Udwin *et al.*, 1987). In the most carefully controlled study to date of Williams syndrome speech characteristics, Udwin and Yule examined 43 children and found no differences in the range and frequency of utterances between Williams syndrome and controls, but did find that Williams syndrome children produce more idioms and social phrases (Udwin & Yule, 1990). Within the Williams syndrome group they identified a group with 'cocktail party speech' (fluent articulate speech with an excess of clichés, social phrases, irrelevancies and false starts). Cocktail party speech occurs in 35–40% of the sample, so cannot be regarded as characteristic. Bellugi and co-workers (1990) in their smaller sample found that when Williams syndrome children were asked to name animals, they offered 'unicorn, pterandon, brontosaurus', in contrast to Down's syndrome children whose choices were more expected. In summary, the Williams syndrome behavioural phenotype includes a tendency to use more adult vocabulary and social phrases.

Early descriptions of Williams syndrome children as 'polite, open and gentle', (von Arnim & Engel, 1964) or 'affectionate and lovable' (Williamson, 1964) are belied by the high rates of behavioural disturbance more recent investigators have found (Udwin *et al.*, 1987; Tomc *et al.*, 1990). But, as Tomc *et al.* (1990) observe, Williams syndrome children differ from other 'difficult' children in that temperamentally they are more approaching than withdrawing.

Finally there are a number of other unrelated abnormalities of behaviour, including eating and sleeping difficulties, fascination with particular objects and hyperacusis. Perhaps only the latter can be said to have any close relation with the syndrome because it occurs so frequently — over three-quarters of cases in three surveys (Martin *et al.*, 1984; Arnold *et al.*, 1985; Dilts *et al.*, 1990). There has been no systematic investigation into the nature of this association.

So, although there have been few controlled studies of the behavioural phenotype in Williams syndrome, there is evidence that a specific cognitive and linguistic profile and hyperacusis constitute a behavioural phenotype. It is hard to explain the emergence of this pattern in Williams syndrome individuals from different backgrounds, exposed to different environments, except by appealing to some effect of the biological disorder that they all share.

However, the extent to which we can explain the pattern as a direct outcome of the biological disorder in Williams syndrome is in doubt. We are hampered by our ignorance of the fundamental genetic or chromosomal lesion and we cannot rule out the possibility that some behaviours develop as adaptations to the physical abnormalities, or that there may be a hierarchy of behaviours, with those that are direct consequences of biology predisposing the individual to develop other compensatory or adaptive behaviours. Dilts *et al.*'s (1990) suggestion about the aetiology of the 'approaching' temperament has already been mentioned; they also propose that for the distractible Williams syndrome child with poor manual skills there may be an incentive and advantages in developing conversation skills. Only carefully controlled investigations of the Williams syndrome phenotype will decide how far biology is determining behaviour.

Fragile X syndrome

Fragile X syndrome is the commonest cause of inherited mental retardation. On the basis of population surveys in Sweden and England the prevalence of affected males has been estimated at about 1 in 1250 (Gustavson *et al.*, 1986; Webb *et al.*, 1986). The physical features are an untrustworthy guide to diagnosis (mild facial dysmorphology, macroorchidism, epilepsy and a generalized disorder of connective tissue presenting as joint hyperextensibility and mitral valve prolapse). The genetic basis of the condition is complex, though recent advances in molecular genetics have begun to explain it (see Chapter 10).

Because of the unreliability of physical stigmata, and the difficulties in cytogenetic diagnosis, there has been considerable interest in establishing whether cognitive and behavioural features can distinguish fragile X individuals from other groups of the mentally retarded. Unfortunately, variability within the syndrome and the unusual mode of inheritance (Sherman *et al.*, 1985; Fu *et al.*, 1991; Yu *et al.*, 1991) make the usual problems of confirming an association with a behavioural

phenotype particularly taxing. Genotypes differ between individuals even within the same family (Rousseau *et al.*, 1991) and it is probable that reliable association studies can only be done with subjects categorized using molecular analysis, as some workers have now begun to do (Hinton *et al.*, 1992).

Psychological functioning in three areas has been scrutinized: cognitive abilities, speech and social interaction. On available evidence, only abnormalities in the latter can reasonably be said to contribute to a behavioural phenotype but, as the psychological descriptions are imprecise and many of the studies insufficiently controlled, future work may reveal additional characteristic features.

The search for a distinctive cognitive profile has to take into consideration the variation in intellectual ability in fragile X males. Between 80 and 90% of males have IQs less than 50, and about a third are profoundly retarded (Prouty *et al.*, 1988; Hagerman & Sobesky, 1989). Cognitive assessments agree that IQ falls with age (Hagerman *et al.*, 1986; Prouty *et al.*, 1988) but not all males are so affected, prompting Fisch *et al.* (1992) to argue that fragile X males are a 'heterogeneous composition of 2 types of affected individuals'.

Despite these complications, Kemper *et al.* (1988), in a controlled study, found a characteristic cognitive profile in 15 of 20 fragile X children (a profile found in only 1 control), indicating specific deficits in sequential processing. These authors draw upon their assessments of fragile X females (Kemper *et al.*, 1986) to argue that there is a relative deficit in arithmetical abilities and a relative strength in some linguistic abilities, and that this may be part of a focal (parietal) central nervous system lesion (which they call a developmental Gerstmann syndrome). Unfortunately there are still too many inconsistent findings for their claim to be substantiated. Dykens *et al.* (1988) compared fragile X males, autistic and retarded individuals of unknown cause and found no evidence of a characteristic cognitive profile.

Many authors have commented on the presence of a distinctive speech abnormality in fragile X males (Howard-Peebles *et al.*, 1979; Jacobs *et al.*, 1980; Newell *et al.*, 1983; Paul *et al.*, 1984; Hanson *et al.*, 1986). Jacobs *et al.* (1980, 1983) claim to have identified a characteristic 'jocular' form of speech and Rhoads (1982) enthusiastically diagnosed fragile X on the basis of a telephone conversation with an adult. Hanson *et al.* (1986) in a study of 10 mildly intellectually impaired fragile X men (IQ >70) described the presence of 'cluttering', which they define as 'fast and fluctuating rate of speech and repetitions of sounds, words or phrases'. Sudhalter *et al.* (1990, 1992), again working with a small sample of moderately impaired men, found an excess of repetitive language compared to Down's syndrome and autistic controls.

The speech disturbance appears to be restricted to a subgroup of fragile X — the adult and mildly impaired population. Prouty *et al.* (1988) found only 3 cases of repetitive speech in their sample of 100 mostly preadolescent males. Even if the speech disorder is characteristic, there is little to suggest it has any close connection to the biological cause of fragile X. As

Sudhalter *et al.* (1990) observe, the speech pattern could be a consequence of social anxiety. There is evidence (discussed below) that fragile X males are unusually sensitive to social gaze, and may therefore be responding with deviant language.

Considerable dispute has resulted from claims that there are pathogenetic links between fragile X and autism (Brown *et al.*, 1986; Hagerman *et al.*, 1986). Cohen *et al.* (1991) argued that the number of reported associations in the literature exceeded that predicted by the hypothesis that the two were independent, but they did not establish whether the prevalence of autism among fragile X subjects was significantly higher than in mentally retarded controls. Fisch (1992) reviewed 19 studies of autistic males and 21 studies of mentally retarded males: 5.5% of the mentally retarded males and fragile X chromosomes and 5.4% of autistic males. He concluded that there is no attributable risk of autism from fragile X.

Nevertheless the interest in this issue has produced the most consistent finding yet of a behavioural abnormality. A series of studies by different investigators has shown that fragile X men maintain eye contact poorly (Levitas *et al.*, 1983; Borghraef *et al.*, 1987, Bregman *et al.*, 1988; Cohen *et al.*, 1988, 1989; Einfeld *et al.*, 1989, Reiss & Freund, 1992). The proportion showing this behaviour varies from study to study (half of Bregman *et al.*'s sample, 86% of the 23 cases seen by Levitas *et al.* (1983)). Cohen *et al.*'s (1988) controlled study showed social avoidance in 20% of fragile X (compared to 10% in Down's syndrome and 5% of nonretarded controls). Their more detailed analysis of social behaviour showed that social avoidance in 24 fragile X boys could be distinguished from similar behaviour in autistic children. The fragile X sample discriminated strangers from parents and had a greater sensitivity to their parents' initiation of social gaze.

So it seems that a proportion of fragile X males (perhaps one-half) have characteristic abnormal social behaviour (distinct from autistic), though it is not at all clear what the relationship is between this abnormality and the genetic lesion (Cohen *et al.*, 1991). Evidence for a distinctive linguistic or cognitive profile is still flimsy.

SYNDROMES WITH A CLAIM TO A BEHAVIOURAL PHENOTYPE

There remains a large group of syndromes where there is some evidence for a behavioural phenotype. It can be heuristically divided into two. The first category includes those cases where a few case reports or initial surveys have hinted that there is a behavioural phenotype, but adequately controlled investigations have yet to be carried out. In the second category are aneuploidies (in particular, trisomy 21 and the sex chromosome anomalies; see Chapter 10). Associations between aneuploidies and behaviour are bedevilled by the problem of the size of the genotype. Even though chromosome 21, the possession of an extra copy of which confers Down's syndrome, is the smallest human chromosome, it consists of some 50 000 000 bp of DNA (Chumakov *et al.*, 1992) and therefore hundreds, probably thousands, of genes. Even if we

do establish the presence of a phenotype, how are we to know which genes are involved? With so many genes there are numerous possible interactions, and variation can occur at many of these loci.

The problem of attributing behavioural phenotypes to aneuploidies is similar to that posed by the existence of the best known putative behavioural phenotype of all, the behavioural differences that result from having either an XX or XY karyotype. The combination of sociocultural influences, a variety of physiological differences and a corresponding complexity at the genetic level makes it extremely difficult to determine how a genetic abnormality could be directly affecting behaviour.

Should we even use the term behavioural phenotype at all unless there is evidence of a more discrete biological determinant? In the case of Down's and Turner's syndrome, very small regions of the relevant chromosomes can produce most, if not all features (see Chapter 10); though it is not known whether this is true of the other aneuploidies. For this reason we have included aneuploidies in our discussion. However no one has tried to categorize behavioural phenotypes according to the extent or type of chromosomal lesion (Epstein *et al.*, 1991) so we cannot be certain that any direct associations exist between a single or small number of genes and the behavioural abnormalities.

Preliminary data supporting a behavioural phenotype

Phenylketonuria

Phenylketonuria is due to a deficiency in the liver enzyme phenylalanine hydroxylase or, more rarely, to defects in the biosynthesis of its co-factor tetrahydrobiopterin. It is an autosomal recessive condition (the phenylalanine hydroxylase gene is located on chromosome 12; Lidsky *et al.*, 1985) which, if untreated, leads to mental retardation with IQs below 50 in 95% of cases (Wright & Tarjan, 1957).

Phenylketonuria might seem an ideal syndrome to have a behavioural phenotype; not only is it a single-gene disorder producing intellectual retardation, but the biochemical disturbance (excess phenylalanine) affects metabolic pathways implicated in many behavioural disorders, of which the best known is the dopaminergic. Mild elevations in the concentration of plasma phenylalanine can lead to central dopaminergic depletion (as well as affecting other amines) and to widespread alterations in transmitter metabolism (Scriver *et al.*, 1989). Surely this must have significant behavioural consequences, even for early-treated children?

Yet the evidence for a specific behavioural or cognitive profile is meagre. Treated phenylketonuria children do have an increased rate of mannerisms, hyperactivity, unresponsiveness and solitariness as compared to controls, but this does not go so far as to constitute a characteristic behavioural phenotype (Stevenson *et al.*, 1979; Smith *et al.*, 1988).

A slightly better case can be made for specific effects on

intellectual function. The discovery of neuropsychological deficits in treated patients with average IQ (Williamson *et al.*, 1981; Koch *et al.*, 1982), together with loss of intellectual function and electroencephalogram changes after relaxation of dietary treatment (Lou *et al.*, 1985; Seashore *et al.*, 1985; Holtzman *et al.*, 1986; Matthews *et al.*, 1986), indicate that biochemical disturbances in phenylketonuria do have a direct effect on cognitive abilities, but only one study has identified a characteristic deficit. Welsh *et al.* (1990) looked for evidence of poor abilities on tasks of frontal lobe processes (planning, maintenance and organized search), on the grounds that alteration in dopamine metabolism might affect these functions. Comparison of 11 treated preschool children with age- and IQ-matched controls showed that phenylketonuria children did have prefrontal dysfunction. The sample studied was small, but the results highlight the value of careful neuropsychological assessment. Similar studies may be useful in the recognition of cognitive phenotypes in other syndromes.

Brachmann–Cornelia de Lange syndrome

The de Lange syndrome (Cornelia de Lange or Brachmann–de Lange syndrome) is another instance where the case for a behavioural phenotype rests on the discovery of a pattern of abnormalities. The syndrome is clinically diagnosed, primarily by recognition of facial and hand features, which include confluent eyebrows, long philtrum, posteriorly rotated ears, short, low-set or absent thumbs and abnormal digit patterns (Preus & Rex, 1983). Other features include hirsutism, talipes and contracted elbows; the phenotype is extremely variable (Hawley *et al.*, 1985; Opitz, 1985; de Die-Smulders *et al.*, 1992). There have been some reports of de Lange syndrome occurring in association with abnormalities of chromosome 3 and it may turn out to be a contiguous gene syndrome (see Chapter 10).

An early study by Johnson *et al.* (1976) best delineates the behavioural phenotype in de Lange syndrome. What makes their work remarkable is its freedom from standard protocols of cognitive and linguistic function. They make their case for a behavioural phenotype on observations of what most people would accept as behaviour, namely, what the children actually do in certain situations. They video-taped 9 patients in eight standardized conditions and then measured four types of behaviour. The subjects were found to lack facial expression, show a paucity of social responses, arch their backs and turn away from adults (including parents) who tried to comfort them and to perform repetitive, sometimes self-mutilatory acts without any obvious provocation (as if self-programmed).

Velocardio facial syndrome

This is probably the commonest syndrome of clefting. It is an autosomal dominant condition and is diagnosed on the basis of the following clinical features: cleft palate, congenital heart disease, facial dysmorphology (including minor ear abnor-malities, malar flatness and prominent nose; Arvystas & Shprintzen, 1984).

Its claim to a behavioural phenotype depends on the cognitive profile, which Shprintzen and Goldberg (1986) include as a diagnostic feature. In an uncontrolled study of 26 patients, Golding-Kushner *et al.* (1985) reported consistent deficiencies in mathematical ability, reading comprehension and tests of auditory and visual association. The same authors noted a characteristic personality profile marked by bland affect, impulsive behaviour and poor social interaction. Without more controlled data we cannot decide how distinctive these features are.

Infantile hydrocephalus

Over 30 years ago Taylor (1961) described a behavioural phenotype in children with spina bifida complicated by hydro-cephalus. She maintained that the verbal abilities of the pre-school child gave an inappropriately good impression of intellectual ability; psychological assessment revealed specific deficits in perception and reasoning. However as the child grew older, the discrepancy between observed verbal ability and cognitive function became less apparent. Such children were said to have cocktail party syndrome (Hadenius *et al.*, 1962), meaning that 'they love to chatter, but think illogically'. In a survey of 120 cases of spina bifida, Spain (1974) claimed that 27.5% had the syndrome. However, other investigators failed to find differences between hydrocephalics and matched controls (Fleming, 1968; Parsons, 1969).

Tew (1979) surveyed 59 unselected cases of spina bifida and found 41% had evidence of the cocktail party syndrome. Children with the syndrome had lower IQs and poorer social skills, suggesting that these variables may be more important in the genesis of the behavioural phenotype than hydro-cephalus. There have been no controlled studies to examine this point. In a more recent study of behavioural problems, Fernell *et al.* (1991) concluded that the excess of inattentive-ness and hyperactivity was due to mental retardation rather than being a specific association with hydrocephalus.

Sotos syndrome

Sotos syndrome consists of large body size, acromegaloid features, advanced bone age, developmental delay and a nonprogressive neurological disorder (Cole & Hughes, 1990). The cause is unknown. Case reports have suggested that there are specific delays in language and motor development, and attention deficits (Sotos & Cutler, 1977; Bloom *et al.*, 1983; Sotos *et al.*, 1984). Rutter and Cole (1991) investigated 16 children and found wide variation in cognitive abilites, but some consistency in behavioural patterns. Thirteen of the children had tantrums, 11 had sleep problems and 10 had object phobias (of eggs, insects, dogs, washing machines and the colour green). Eight children were socially isolated: they had no close friends and showed a preference for solitary activity.

Tuberous sclerosis

Tuberous sclerosis is an autosomal dominant condition with a prevalence of about 1 in 10 000 (Hunt & Lindenbaum, 1984) which is characterized by a skin condition (adenoma seba-ceum), epilepsy and mental retardation. Equally characteristic is the wide variation in clinical presentation. Some affected individuals have nothing to show except a few mild skin changes; others are severely mentally retarded, afflicted by treatment-resistant epilepsy. With the exception of skeletal muscle and peripheral nerves, all tissues may be affected by hamartomas, areas of abnormal cell proliferation (Gomez, 1988). The genetics is also not straightforward: about 60% of cases are probably new mutations (Gomez, 1988) and the disorder is now known to be genetically heterogeneous with disease loci on chromosomes 9, 11 and 12 (Fryer et al., 1987; Smith et al., 1990; Fahsold et al., 1991).

Two studies have tried to establish an association between tuberous sclerosis and autism. Hunt and Dennis (1987) com-pared data on 69 children with both tuberous sclerosis and infantile spasms (therefore a relatively homogeneous group) with similar data on a larger group of children with infantile spasms of mixed aetiology (Riikonen & Amnell, 1981). They argued that behavioural differences between the two groups would therefore not be attributable to the epilepsy. About half of the tuberous sclerosis group had both autism and hyper-kinetic behaviour, as compared to 8% in the controls. The majority of their sample was severely mentally retarded, and all the autistic individuals fell into this category. Smalley et al. (1991) evaluated 24 children with tuberous sclerosis and found 4 with autism. They also were all mentally retarded and had had seizures since infancy. It remains to be determined therefore whether the association is mediated by mental retardation.

Angelman's syndrome

Angelman's syndrome is very rare, and arises from chromo-somal abnormalities affecting chromosome 15q11–13. This is the same region implicated in the aetiology of PWS, but the loci responsible for the two conditions are distinct (Wagstaff et al., 1992).

Children with Angelman's syndrome have wide mouths, pointed chins, prominent jaws, a jerky ataxia affecting all limbs, seizures and a characteristic electroencephalogram (Dooley et al., 1981; Robb et al., 1989). Their retardation is extreme. In a review of 36 children, Robb et al. (1989) reported that only 7 had any language and the largest vocabu-lary was three words. There is some indication that there is more speech delay than expected from other measures of intellectual development. More specific features of a behav-ioural phenotype were first noted in 1981 (Hersh et al., 1981). In a review of 28 children attentional and social abnormalities were documented. For prolonged periods children with Angelman's syndrome failed to establish eye contact, and were noted to have short attention spans. There was no correlation between seizure activity and these behavioural abnormalities. The problem with this study is again that no controls were included. Poor social relationships and short attention spans are certainly not the preserve of children with Angelman's syndrome.

Aneuploidies

Down's syndrome

Down's syndrome (trisomy 21) is the commonest genetic form of mental retardation with a prevalence of between 1 and 1.5 per 1000 live births. This, and the relative ease of diagnosis from physical features and cytogenetic analysis, has meant that Down's syndrome has received a good deal of attention from psychologists, keen to identify the psychologi-cal correlates of an extra chromosome (Gibson, 1978). Much of this research was carried out at a time when it was more generally accepted that stereotypes of behaviour and person-ality existed in association with medical conditions, and Belmont (1971) gives a synopsis of 54 behavioural studies of Down's syndrome. However the vast majority of these (and later) studies have compared Down's syndrome children with normal controls so we often do not have adequate information on the specificity of behavioural abnormalities. Three main areas dominate the literature: cognitive abilities, temperament and psychiatric disorders. However, in all three areas the variation is great and there is no really convincing evidence for a discrete behavioural phenotype.

The search for a characteristic psychometric pattern in Down's syndrome has been going on for as long as psycho-metric tests have existed. Overall, trisomy 21 individuals do worse than mentally retarded controls on verbal subtests of cognitive ability and do better on visuospatial subtests (Lyle, 1959; Nakamura, 1965; Gibson, 1978; Silverstein et al., 1982; Snart et al., 1982), but there is wide variation in achievement and no distinctive abilities or deficits emerge. Moreover we know from Carr's studies (1988) how important environ-mental effects are on verbal and academic abilities.

A different approach to cognitive assessment has been taken by psychologists assessing attention, perception and memory. On the one hand there have been attempts to define a specific cognitive abnormality by inference from measures of infor-mation processing. Thus Zekulin-Hartley (1981) reported that Down's syndrome children have a left ear advantage, which, together with other indications of unusual information processing (Pipe, 1983), led to the suggestion that there might be a disorder of cerebral lateralization underlying a general cognitive deficit. However at present there are contradictory results (Kerr & Blais, 1985, 1987; Elliot et al., 1987) and no controlled studies comparing Down's syndrome individuals with other aetiological groups.

On the other hand some investigators have taken a more naturalistic approach. In one of the best studies Krakow and Kopp (1983) compared normal, mentally retarded and Down's syndrome children in a video-taped free-play situation. Subtle but characteristic differences between Down's syndrome children and the two control groups emerged in the style of play. Down's syndrome children did not glance around at their environment as much, focusing all their attention on the toys. The Down's group was more like the normal controls in that they spent more time playing than in doing nothing, which was more characteristic of the behaviour of other retarded children. There is therefore some evidence of a distinctive attentional difference.

A long-established stereotype of temperament in Down's syndrome is that the child is affectionate, placid and easy to manage. There is little to support this view, as was evident to Belmont over 20 years ago (Belmont, 1971). Recent surveys show that between 10 and 20% of Down's syndrome children have a difficult temperament (Gunn *et al.*, 1981; Bridges & Cicchetti, 1982; Gunn & Berry, 1985). Comparison with developmentally delayed controls indicates some differences in activity, approach and distractibility, but no distinctive profile emerges (Marcovitch *et al.*, 1986).

Sadly, there have been no recent attempts to characterize a temperamental feature much commented on in earlier literature: that Down's syndrome children are as responsive to music and rhythm as much as (if not more than) normal children. Belmont's (1971) review concludes that 'institutional samples of mongoloids' have 'almost no musical inclinations of any kind', but the issue has been scantily investigated.

Finally, three groups have investigated the association between Down's syndrome and psychiatric disorder (Menolascino, 1965, 1967; Gath & Gumley, 1986; Myers & Pueschel, 1991). The overall rate of psychiatric disorder is probably no higher than in children mentally retarded for other reasons. Gath and Gumley (1986) compared 193 Down's syndrome children with an age-, sex- and handicap-matched control group. They reported a significant behavioural disorder in 38% of the Down's syndrome children and 49% of the controls. No single diagnostic category is characteristic; indeed most psychiatric disorders have been described in association with Down's syndrome. Some have suggested that schizophrenia is frequently found in adults, but the data are sparse (Heaton-Ward, 1977; Lund, 1988).

Do some diagnoses occur less than expected? There have been very few cases of mania (Sovner *et al.*, 1985; Cook & Leventhal, 1987; McLaughlin, 1987), and, given the degree of mental impairment, some authors have suggested that autism is rare (Wakabayashi, 1979; Bregman & Volkmar, 1988). However the surveys of Down's syndrome children cannot confirm this. Gath and Gumley (1986) diagnosed autism in 2 Down's syndrome children and 3 controls (a rate of 2.6%). In Myers and Pueschel's (1991) study only 3 of the 261 Down's syndrome individuals under 20 years of age received a diagnosis of autism (0.6% of the total), but without a control group it is not possible to generalize this finding. Lund (1988) found 5 cases in his survey of 44 adults (11%). The association with autism is weak, but there is no evidence that it is peculiarly weak. There is also no evidence that as a group, Down's syndrome have an excess of attention deficit

disorder, although one report suggests a subgroup may be so diagnosed (36% of the sample studies by Green *et al.*, 1989).

However the association of Down's syndrome with dementia of the Alzheimer's type is now well-established (Oliver & Holland, 1986) and was an important clue in localizing a predisposing locus for Alzheimer's disease to chromosome 21 (Goate *et al.*, 1991). Nevertheless, while it is true that almost all Down's people have the neuropathological changes typical of Alzheimer's dementia (Whalley, 1982), clinically the disease is not so universally present. In a study of 63 Down's syndrome adults, Fenner *et al.* (1987) found intellectual deterioration in only one-third of those over 35 years old, and Gibson *et al.* (1988) found no evidence of intellectual decline when they tested a group of Down's syndrome subjects in their 30s compared to matched controls. The difficulty with such studies is that no one knows how Alzheimer's disease manifests itself in a trisomy 21 background. How much of the behaviour is due to the aneuploidy, how much to Alzheimer's and how much to an interaction between the two?

Dysarthria, apraxias, agnosias and other evidence of impairment of cortical function found in Alzheimer's disease in the general population are hard to detect in the presence of intellectual impairment, and are rarely mentioned in the literature. Most tests of cognitive, memory and social functioning are not standardized for the Down's syndrome population, and in some studies subjects perform below the floor of the instruments used (Fenner *et al.*, 1987). It is difficult to know what the behavioural manifestations of Alzheimer's disease are in Down's syndrome individuals, and how reliable are the estimates of its prevalence.

Dalton and co-workers have attempted to overcome these difficulties by developing tests specifically for persons with Down's syndrome (Dalton & Crapper, 1984; Dalton & Crapper-McLachlan, 1986; Dalton & Wisniewski, 1990). They argue that it *is* possible to detect a clinical picture similar in some ways to that found in individuals with normal karyotypes and Alzheimer's disease: there is memory loss in the early stages, a decrease in spontaneous communication and movement, and disorientation in space and time. Later the Down's syndrome adult loses the ability to make sense of perceptions, to communicate and to move voluntarily. The final stages of the disorder are indistinguishable from those found in the general population. Nevertheless there have been no attempts to correlate the clinical features of dementia with postmortem neuropathology and the existence of Down's syndrome individuals in their 60s and 70s with no clinical manifestations of dementia underlines the difficulty of arguing for a direct relationship between the trisomy and the occurrence of Alzheimer's disease.

In summary, despite many attempts, there have been few successes in describing any characteristic behavioural abnormalities in Down's syndrome. A distinctive attentional behaviour is perhaps the closest we can get to defining the behavioural phenotype. However, with closer scrutiny of the molecular lesion it may become possible to look at genotypically defined subgroups, and hence arrive at more uniform phenotypes. Certainly that should help determine if there is a specific genotype–behaviour correlation.

Sex chromosome aneuploidies

There have been many claims for the distinctive psychological characteristics of individuals with sex chromosome abnormalities. On one hand there are those who see evidence that there are genes on one or both sex chromosomes that predispose to psychiatric disorder (for example, it has been said that schizophrenia is found more commonly in those with an extra X chromosome; reviewed in Polani, 1969, and Crow, 1988). On the other hand attempts have been made to delineate behavioural phenotypes for particular syndromes. Only the latter need concern us here. Ongoing longitudinal studies from 6 centres have provided a large amount of information about the cognitive and behavioural profiles associated with all sex chromosome aneuploidies (Evans *et al.*, 1991; Kemper *et al.*, 1991; Nielsen & Wohlert, 1991; Ratcliffe *et al.*, 1991; Robinson *et al.*, 1991a,b; Stewart *et al.*, 1991), yet only Turner's syndrome can be said to have a behavioural phenotype (because of a distinctive cognitive profile).

Klinefelter's syndrome (XXY)

Early work described a special personality type in Klinefelter's syndrome (Pasqualini *et al.*, 1957; Forssman & Hambert, 1963): antisocial, prone to outbursts of temper and lacking in enterprise. More recent work has continued to describe the XXY boy as quiet, unassertive, passive and with a tendency to withdraw from group activities. Most of these reports are comparisons with XYY children, whose temperament is different on all these traits. Theilgaard (1984) found that Klinefelter's men had fewer sexual partners, reported less sexual desire and had masturbated less than XYY men. Klinefelter's men were also more dependent, and had more problems with male identity. Money *et al.* (1974) came to similar conclusions. Schiavi *et al.* (1988) also found delayed sexual development, lower sexual drive and activity in XXY compared to XYY. Like their predecessors, they could find no convincing correlation between behavioural abnormalities and plasma hormone levels.

While these findings may eventually cast some light on the biological basis of sexual behaviour, they cannot be said to establish a behavioural phenotype for Klinefelter's, or XYY. No one has established a distinctive behavioural pattern that occurs specifically in either syndrome. The karyotype has some role in determining deviations from a norm in terms of sexual identity and behaviour but this does not amount to a behavioural phenotype.

Buccal smear examination of males with schizophrenia has indicated an increased prevalence of XXY among schizophrenics (Anders *et al.*, 1968; MacLean *et al.*, 1968; Dasgupta *et al.*, 1973), but, as most of these studies were done without operationalized diagnoses of schizophrenia, this finding may be another manifestation of an unusual (but not necessarily characteristic) personality.

There is a normal IQ range in Klinefelter's men, with all studies showing an excess of language-related disabilities (Ratcliffe *et al.*, 1991; Robinson *et al.*, 1991b; Stewart *et al.*, 1991). There is disagreement as to whether this is an expressive (Graham *et al.*, 1988; Walzer *et al.*, 1991) or receptive deficit (Netley & Rovet, 1982a). In a blind study with normal controls, Bender *et al.* (1983) found both receptive and expressive language disorder. The same group argued that dyslexia is the commonest psychological disorder in Klinefelter's (Bender *et al.*, 1986), but their sample is small (14) and they find the same disability in XYY men. Netley and Rovet (1984, 1987) argued that, prior to adolescence, left hemisphere language functions were specifically impaired in XXY men, but their more recent studies, on an older age group, show no difference from controls (Stewart *et al.*, 1991). Klinefelter's men have a continuum of psychological disabilities, mostly centred on problems with language, but no specific deficit can be reliably identified.

XYY syndrome

Cognitive assessment of XYY subjects shows that half have language and reading difficulties, similar to the problems afflicting Klinefelter's individuals (Bender *et al.*, 1986; Ratcliffe *et al.*, 1991). Ratcliffe *et al.* (1991) found a greater susceptibility to psychiatric illness in XYY children (half of their sample was referred to a child psychiatrist, in contrast to 9% of controls) but this could be attributed to higher rates of family problems (maternal psychiatric illness, marital breakdown) and to other predisposing factors (for example, temperament and birth abnormalities).

The personality characteristics of XYY men have been mentioned in the discussion of Klinefelter's syndrome.

Most interest in the behaviour of XYY has concentrated on the finding of Jacobs and co-workers that this karyotype occurred at a disproportionately high frequency among inmates of a maximum security hospital in Scotland (Jacobs *et al.*, 1965, 1971). The best study of this issue confirmed that those with an XYY karyotype were more often criminal, mostly because of property offences (Witkin *et al.*, 1976). The authors went on to establish why this might be. They found that educational achievement, parental socioeconomic status and IQ scores were associated with criminal behaviour in both XY and XYY men, each contributing independently to the chance of acquiring a criminal record. As XYY men were of lower intelligence and had achieved less well at school than XY men, it could be that criminality was correlated with these variables and not with any more specific factor. In fact it seems that intellectual and educational variables were enough to increase criminal prevalence from the population value of 9.3 to 17.2%, whereas the observed figure among the XYY population was just over 40%. So the extra Y exerts its effects partly through lowered intelligence; it is not clear how the remaining increased risk can be explained, but it cannot be assumed to be a direct result of the chromosomal aneuploidy.

Turner's syndrome (45,XO)

Two areas have attracted attention in behavioural research on Turner's sydrome: psychopathology and cognitive abilities.

There have been a few reports of an association between anorexia nervosa and Turner's syndrome, but it has not been established whether the prevalence is above that in a control population (Liston & Shershow, 1973; Darby *et al.*, 1981; Larocca, 1985). In general no increase of psychiatric disorder has been reported in adults. However, they are more likely than their peers and siblings to be socially isolated, unmarried and living with their parents (Nielsen *et al.*, 1977; McCauley *et al.*, 1986; Downey *et al.*, 1989). Is this part of a behavioural phenotype?

Almost certainly not, because these difficulties can be related to the physical abnormalities of Turner's syndrome. Short stature and lack of secondary sexual characteristics increase the risk of behavioural problems. Money and Mittenthal (1970) compared the outcome of two groups of Turner's syndrome adolescents, one treated with oestrogens and one not. The latter group were more socially isolated and withdrawn. The effect of short stature on psychological development has been assessed in studies on children with growth hormone deficiency. Untreated children were found to be more socially immature.

Cognitive abnormalities are more securely established as part of a behavioural phenotype: women with Turner's syndrome have a specific deficit in nonverbal ability or spatial functioning (Shaffer, 1962; Money, 1963; Alexander *et al.*, 1964; Garron, 1977; Rovet & Netley 1980, 1982; Ratcliffe *et al.*, 1991; Robinson *et al.*, 1991b). There has been disagreement as to whether there is also generally reduced intelligence. The fact that performance measures on IQ testing are low means that the full-scale IQs will be lower than normal, and some have argued this accounts for the reported low intelligence (Buckley, 1971; Garron, 1977). Measures of verbal IQ have been found to be normal (as compared to controls) in some studies (Netley, 1986), low (Bender *et al.*, 1984; Robinson *et al.*, 1991b) or even above average (Nielsen *et al.*, 1977) in others.

Two explanations can be proffered for the low performance IQ. It could be part of a general neurological dysfunction, or it could be a more specific abnormality of cortical function (Netley & Rovet, 1982b). In favour of the first view is the observation that attention disorders and hyperactivity occur in Turner's syndrome at increased frequency (Bender *et al.*, 1984). These disorders lower scores on performance testing and would therefore account for the low perfomance IQ. However no neurological abnormalities have been detected on clinical testing, electroencephalogram or computed tomography scans (Buchsbaum *et al.*, 1974; Nielsen *et al.*, 1977). Evidence for the alternative view comes from neuropsychological studies. Netley & Rovet (1982b) compared 35 Turner's syndrome individuals with IQ-matched controls and showed that the Turner's subjects were less likely to have a right ear advantage on dichotic listening tests, and that this advantage was associated with the greatest performance IQ

deficits. Pennington *et al.* (1985) compared Turner's syndrome individuals with brain-damaged women. They found the neuropsychological measures of the Turner's group best matched a group with diffuse brain damage, rather than those with focal left or right hemisphere lesions. The variability in lesion site, size and effect on abilities makes it difficult to interpret such findings unambiguously, but they are consistent with Netley and Rovet's view that there is an abnormality of neurodevelopment in Turner's syndrome (possibly producing abnormal lateralization), a conclusion also reached by Waber (1979).

THE RELATIONSHIP BETWEEN GENETIC LESIONS AND BEHAVIOURAL ABNORMALITIES

Most people would agree that genes do not determine human behaviour directly, but instead control developmental and metabolic processes in the central nervous system. Our knowledge of these processes is still so rudimentary and the investigations into behavioural phenotypes so preliminary that any discussion of mechanisms involved in the path from abnormal gene to disturbed behaviour will inevitably be speculative. It would be premature to draw any conclusions from the available data on the syndromes discussed above and we do not intend to do so.

However there is one very pertinent question that should be addressed: is the genetic dissection of behavioural phenotypes, now possible with molecular techniques, likely to be a useful way of unravelling the relationship between gene and behaviour? We have so far assumed that it is, but there is evidence to suggest the opposite. The molecular basis of two conditions described above (Lesch−Nyhan syndrome and phenylketonuria) has been well-known for some years, without this adding a great deal to our knowledge of the genetic basis of behaviour. The study of these two syndromes is something of a cautionary tale for those hoping to find a 'gene for overeating' in PWS or a 'gene for language' in Williams syndrome. As we will see later, results emerging about the genetic basis of behaviour in species other than humans paint a more hopeful picture, but we start with a consideration of the relationship between behaviour and genes in Lesch−Nyhan syndrome and phenylketonuria.

Molecular basis of behaviour in Lesch−Nyhan syndrome and phenylketonuria

The function of the abnormal enzyme (hypoxanthine phosphoribosyltransferase) in Lesch−Nyhan syndrome is well-understood, its biochemical characteristics and the DNA sequence of the gene known, but none of this information has clarified how a defect in a protein found in all cell types could produce such a specific behavioural phenotype (Stout & Caskey, 1988; Oliver & Head, 1990; Winchel & Stanley, 1991). Researchers have gone so far as to introduce a mutation into the hypoxanthine phosphoribosyltransferase gene of the mouse, in the hope presumably of producing self-injurious mice (Hooper *et al.*, 1987; Kuehn *et al.*, 1987). The mice grew up to be placid animals, not even venting hostility against their less than beneficient creators (Finger *et al.*, 1988).

More conventional studies have suggested that abnormalities in dopaminergic and serotoninergic systems exist. There is a 10—30% decrease in the function of dopamine-containing neurons (Lloyd *et al.*, 1981), and rats made supersensitive to dopamine by injection of 6-hydroxydopamine into the nigrostriatal area in the neonatal period will bite their forelimbs incessantly when given a dopamine agonist. There is also some evidence that dopamine blockade alters self-mutilation in Lesch—Nyhan patients (Goldstein *et al.*, 1985).

Seven studies have looked at the effect of 5-hydroxytryptophan on self-injurious behaviour in Lesch—Nyhan syndrome, and two found the treatment effective (Winchel & Stanley, 1991). However the effect is not reliable. How a deficiency in purine metabolism in early life disrupts serotonergic transmission or dopamine function in the basal ganglia is unclear, but it may lead to impaired arborization of nigrostriatial neurons (Stout & Caskey, 1988); the hypothesis remains untested.

Even less is known about the relationship between mutations in phenylalanine hydroxylase and the behavioural phenotype of phenylketonuria. The effects of raised plasma phenylalanine concentrations are so diverse that it has been impossible to use our knowledge of the biochemical deficit to gain any clear understanding of how behaviour is disturbed. Plasma concentrations above 1.2 mmol/l depress dopamine excretion, and lead to widespread alterations in transmitter metabolism (Scriver *et al.*, 1989). Prolonged exposure to high phenylalanine levels affects myelination and dendritic arborization (Bauman & Kemper, 1982; Lacey & Terplan, 1987), and it is argued that brain structures and functions are differentially sensitive to these changes, but as yet we have no idea where to look for these differences.

Behavioural genes in flies and mice

The examples of Lesch—Nyhan syndrome and phenylketonuria force us to ask whether the molecular excavation of genes involved in behavioural phenotypes is likely to be a useful way of understanding the relationship between gene and behaviour. Until recently the only species in which behavioural genes had been identified by working backwards from phenotype to genotype was the fruitfly. This might not seem a very hopeful place to start unearthing the genetic basis of social interaction, but the work on *Drosophila* does have some lessons for the study of behavioural phenotypes in humans. It tells us what we may expect to learn from molecular characterization of behavioural genes.

Following the demonstration in 1974 that *Drosophila* could learn to distinguish between two tubes with different odours, one of which was paired with an electric shock, mutants were isolated that lacked this ability (Quinn & Greenspan, 1984). The genes affected in two cases (*dunce* and *rutabaga*) have now been isolated. Interestingly, the same physiological sys-

tem is affected in both mutants: the genes are involved in the regulation of intracellular cyclic adenosine monophosphate, an ubiquitous second messenger molecule. The finding presents a paradox: the proteins encoded by these genes are present in all body tissues, and probably all stages of development (Shotwell, 1983; Levin *et al.*, 1992), yet mutations have circumscribed effects.

The *Drosophila* workers can provide other examples of this paradox: other behavioural genes have broad tissue distributions, the best example being the *period* gene, necessary for the functioning of the biological clock underlying circadian rhythms. Despite the gene's widespread distribution, mutants are defective in song rhythm regulation (Kyriacou, 1990).

Two features of these behavioural genes suggest a possible resolution of the paradox. Firstly, flies devoid of these genes are viable. This goes against the idea that behavioural genes are part of essential cellular processes. Secondly, there *is* evidence that other behaviours can be affected by these genes. *Dunce* is involved in sexual behaviour (females without the gene are sexually hyperactive; Bellen & Kiger, 1987) and *period* alters locomotor activity.

How can it be that mutations in genes affecting basic cell metabolic processes result not in death, but in multiple, discrete behavioural abnormalities? We have an answer to this conundrum from the recent investigations into genes involved in tissue-specific and developmental regulation.

One of the major ways in which cells establish and maintain a differentiated state (as neurons, lymphocytes or fibroblasts) is by combining protein subunits to interact with DNA and other proteins. Dozens of proteins may be able to bind to the DNA in front of and around a gene, each combination providing a different effect on the level of gene transcription and its sensitivity to other cellular signals (such as cyclic adenosine monophosphate concentrations). The combinatorial potential allows for redundancy (many proteins appear to have similar binding sites and can swap with one another) and hence provides a robust system which can manage if one or two proteins go astray. It also provides a way of producing immense diversity out of relatively few proteins (McGinnis & Krumlauf, 1992). We should not be surprised if the same sorts of genes (or even the same gene) have effects on apparently unrelated systems. For instance, neurogenic genes in *Drosophila* are crucial for oogenesis (Ruohola *et al.*, 1991) and for mesoderm formation (Corbin *et al.*, 1991). Both these features (redundancy and multiple effects, or pleiotropy) are found in behavioural genes.

Thus we can say that behavioural genes in *Drosophila* have general roles in cell function and development. The specific effects found in mutants come about because of disturbances in balanced systems that involve the cooperation of numerous different regulatory factors. The behavioural genes are hence pleiotropic and display a degree of redundancy.

The rather general nature of this conclusion suggests that it will turn out to be applicable in other species, a view supported by recent results from work in mice. No one has as yet started from a behavioural mutant and isolated a gene (as has happened in *Drosophila* and is the proposed method of identifying behavioural genes in the syndromes described in this chapter), but in animals an alternative approach is available. Where an experimenter has a candidate behavioural gene it is possible to create animals lacking the gene, and observe how the deficiency affects the animal's behaviour. In mice, genes involved in a neurophysiological function (long-term potentiation) affecting visuospatial learning have been investigated using this technique.

For over two decades the phenomenon of long-term potentiation (LTP) in the hippocampus has been implicated in memory functions. Pharmacological agents that block one class of hippocampal glutamate receptors (*N*-methyl-D-aspartate (NMDA) receptors) prevent LTP, and also disturb spatial learning, but it has not been clear whether this is a specific effect or due to a more general disturbance of hippocampal neuronal circuitry. Researchers have made mice lacking genes for enzymes that transduce signals downstream of NMDA receptor activation. We can think of these genes as controlling second messenger functions (analogous to the genes involved in cyclic adenosine monophosphate level regulation in *Drosophila*). LTP was affected by altering these genes and spatial learning was specifically diminished (Grant *et al.*, 1992; Silva *et al.*, 1992a,b).

There are two features that relate these mice to the *Drosophila* mutants discussed above, and which have important implications for behavioural phenotypes in humans. The first is that, as Silva *et al.* (1992a) comment, 'the most remarkable feature of the mutant mice is the apparent lack of widespread abnormality'. A specific effect has resulted from disruption of an enzyme widespread in the brain. The second is that the same conclusion was reached when a *different* gene was disrupted (this gene too had been implicated in LTP; Grant *et al.*, 1992). In both mutants, although LTP was reduced, it was not eliminated entirely. The conclusion is that a number of proteins contribute to the production of LTP, and that there is some redundancy in the function of each.

So, although it does look as if behavioural genes can be found, this does not necessarily mean we will understand the *pathway* from gene to behaviour. We should expect to find genes involved in networks of interacting regulatory mechanisms. The mechanisms themselves can be fairly general (the control of second messenger traffic, or the developmental regulation of cell specificity, for example), causing specific effects to result from an imbalance in the network.

Implications for syndromes with behavioural phenotypes

The behavioural phenotypes of many of the syndromes discussed above are characterized by a pattern of abnormalities in cognitive, linguistic, social and behavioural fields (perhaps best exemplified by Williams syndrome). We might take this as evidence that the gene—behaviour relationship is even more indirect and diffuse than we first thought.

Yet we can recognize here one of the features associated with behavioural genes in other species, namely pleiotropy. If the findings in other species are confirmed our own, then the genes responsible for human behavioural phenotypes may also code for tissue-ubiquitous proteins. Multiple effects would then be the result of different cellular, metabolic and developmental systems using the same genes for different purposes.

The second feature we stressed, redundancy of function, will only emerge when the genetic basis of more syndromes has been characterized. We would predict that syndromes with similar behavioural abnormalities (for instance, self-injurious behaviour) could well have mutations in different genes.

We can summarize this by saying that work on other species has two implications for the study of human behavioural phenotypes. Firstly, it confirms the generally accepted view that specific behaviours are unlikely to be associated with specific genes. Secondly, it shows that specific behaviours can result from alterations in a system (developmental, structural, metabolic or otherwise) which is fairly robust and involves numerous interacting factors.

This means, for example, that we will probably not find a gene for language. Certainly there are families where language disorder segregates as an autosomal dominant mutation (Hurst *et al.*, 1990) and neuropsychologists have characterized the affected members as possessing specific grammatical disabilities (a failure to appreciate the 'deep structure' of language, to use Chomsky's term; Chomsky, 1988; Gopnik, 1990). But, on the evidence quoted above, we should not be surprised to discover that the mutation lies within a mundane cellular process, such as axonal sprouting. Perhaps dyslexia will turn out to be due to a mutation in a gene that carries out the same cellular function in humans and yeast. The specific effects will then only be understood within the broader framework of gene regulation and interaction, in the ways now being elucidated in developmental genetics (McGinnis & Krumlauf, 1992).

Does work on the molecular genetics of human behavioural phenotypes bear this out? The difficulty here is that in only a very few cases have genes been isolated for syndromes with behavioural phenotypes. A gene for fragile X has been cloned, but we have very little idea about what it does. Fortunately, more is known about a candidate gene for Turner's syndrome.

Dissection of the molecular lesions that can give rise to the Turner phenotype has led to the isolation of a gene that codes for a ribosomal protein (Fisher *et al.*, 1990). There are few more basic elements of cellular machinery than the ribosome, which is responsible for the translation of messenger RNA into protein. All cells express the candidate Turner gene, so we face the same problem posed by the *Drosophila* mutants: how can interfering with a basic cellular mechanism have specific effects?

The ribosome is a massive structure of RNA and over 80 protein subunits. One reason why it has so many components is that it allows cells many ways to control its function. The ribosome is an obvious major control site, affecting as it does cellular protein synthesis. It is quite conceivable that variations in the rate of protein synthesis could be altered in different cell types by the absence of a single ribosomal subunit. The consequence would be a cell-type-specific effect from changes in a protein apparently involved in a general cellular function.

There are obvious parallels here with the mutations in other species discussed above.

Finally, consider the example of Kallmann syndrome. The physical stigmata of Kallmann syndrome are hypogonadatrophic hypogonadism and anosmia. The reported behavioural components of Kallmann syndrome are mild mental retardation and slow mirror movements of the hands and feet; unfortunately there has been no work to establish the behavioural phenotype more precisely. What type of gene is responsible?

The gene has sequence similarity to neural cell adhesion molecules that guide neuronal migration (Franco et al., 1991; Legouis et al., 1991). Cell migration and axon growth are not preprogrammed activities, but involve discrete navigational steps mediated by cellular interactions, which in turn require cell surface molecules. Errors in this process are implicated in a number of psychiatric disorders. Disturbances of cortical cytoarchitecture have been implicated in dyslexia (Galaburda et al., 1985) and schizophrenia (Roberts, 1990) and in the rat mossy fibre connections in the hippocampus correlate with performance in shuttle-box learning (Schwegler et al., 1981; Schwegler & Lipp, 1983). So the discovery of a gene with a phenotype that includes a learning disability is intriguing. We may soon have a clearer idea of the relationship between a single-gene disorder, aberrant cytoarchitecture and behavioural phenotype.

Within the next few years a large number of the genes responsible for behavioural phenotypes will come into the hands of molecular biologists. There are reasons to expect that we will then learn much more about the relationship between genes and behaviour; however, we should not be surprised if this relationship turns out to be not quite as we expect.

IMPLICATIONS FOR MANAGEMENT

One of the driving forces in the discovery of behavioural phenotypes has been the endeavours of parents to make professionals aware that more than parenting is to blame for their children's behaviour. For those who take the view that mental retardation is a uniform phenotype, parental failure is an obvious explanation for the appearance of psychiatric disorder in a child with mental retardation. We have argued in this chapter that there are close connections between behaviour and genetic lesion, but it would be wrong to make parents feel guilty if their child did not fit the stereotype suggested by the behavioural phenotype; after all, not every Williams syndrome child has a sociable temperament.

On one hand, with the exceptions of the Rett's and Lesch-Nyhan syndromes, there is considerable variation in behavioural phenotypes. There should be no rigid expectations about how a child will behave. On the other hand, genetic determinants often affect behaviour by their ability to evoke certain environmental responses, rather than by directly altering behaviour. Thus in Williams syndrome it has been proposed that the child's characteristic engaging smile will facilitate attachment, hence improving social interactions

(Dilts et al., 1990). Scarr and McCartney's (1983) concept of genotype–environment correlation may be the most appropriate model to apply here. Social immaturity in Turner's women can be explained on similar lines as the outcome of short stature and failure to develop secondary sexual characteristics.

There are no specific management measures that follow from a knowledge of a behaviour phenotype, but there are two general issues. The first is the management of parents' expectations; parents should know about potentially negative characteristics, and be relieved of the burden of blaming themselves for a difficult child who should be 'easy'. This applies to almost all the syndromes described here. The second is that, as we learn more about the pathway from gene to behaviour, we see ways in which we can alter the development of maladaptive behaviours (Marfo, 1991). Our knowledge here is still at a rudimentary stage but it would be appropriate for any clinician dealing with a child with a syndrome to consider how the physical and behavioural features are interrelated. In the case of Turner's syndrome, hormonally induced puberty can be justified on the difference it will make to later psychosocial adjustment. Carr (1988), noting how academic performance in Down's syndrome children can be raised above the levels indicated by their IQ, raises the possibility of building up their self-esteem by improving their academic performance. Where the behaviours are more closely determined by the organic lesion, then different interventions will be necessary.

REFERENCES

Alexander D., Walker H.T. & Money J. (1964) studies in direction sense: I. Turner's syndrome. *Archives of General Psychiatry*, **10**, 337–339.

Anders J., Jagliello G., Polani P., Gianelli F., Hammerton J. & Lieberman D. (1968) Chromosome findings in chronic psychotic patients. *British Journal of Psychiatry*, **114**, 1167–1174.

Anderson L., Dancis J., Alpert M. & Herrmann L. (1977) Punishment learning and self-mutilation in Lesch–Nyhan disease. *Nature*, **265**, 461–463.

Arnold R., Yule W. & Martin N. (1985) The psychological characteristics of infantile hypercalcaemia: a preliminary investigation. *Developmental Medicine and Child Neurology*, **27**, 49–59.

Arvystas M. & Shprintzen R.J. (1984) Craniofacial morphology in the velocardio facial syndrome. *Journal of Craniofacial Genetics and Developmental Biology*, **4**, 39–45.

Bauman M.L. & Kemper T.L. (1982) Morphologic and histoanatomic observations of the brain in untreated human phenylketonuria. *Acta Neuropathologica*, **58**, 55–63.

Bellen H.J. & Kiger J.A. (1987) Sexual hyperactivity and reduced longevity of *dunce* females of *Drosophila melanogaster*. *Genetics*, **115**, 153–160.

Bellugi U., Bihrle A., Jernigan T., Trauner D. & Doherty S. (1990) Neuropsychological, neurological, and neuroanatomical profile of Williams syndrome. *American Journal of Medical Genetics*, (suppl. 6), 115–125.

Belmont J.M. (1971) Medical behavioural research: retardation. In: Fellis N.R. (ed) *International Review of Research in Mental Retardation*, pp. 1–81. Academic Press, New York.

Bender B., Fry E., Pennington B., Puck M., Salbenblatt J. & Robinson A. (1983) Speech and language development in 41 children with sex chromosome anomalies. *Pediatrics*, **71**, 262–267.

Bender B., Puck M., Salbenblatt J. & Robinson A. (1984) Cognitive development of unselected girls with complete and partial X monosomy. *Pediatrics*, **73**, 175–182.

Bender B.G., Puck M.H., Salbenblatt J.A. & Robinson A. (1986) Cognitive development of children with sex chromosome abnormalities. In: Smith S. (ed) *Genetics and Learning Disabilities*, pp. 175–201. Taylor and Francis, London.

Bennett F., LaVeck B. & Sells C. (1978) The Williams elfin facies syndrome: the psychological profile as an aid in syndrome identification. *Pediatrics*, **61**, 303–306.

Bloom A.S., Reese A., Hersh J.H., Podruch P.E., Weisskopf B. & Dinno N. (1983) Cognition in cerebral gigantism: are estimates of mental retardation too high? *Journal of Developmental and Behavioural Pediatrics*, **4**, 250–252.

Borghgraef M., Fryns J., Dickens A. & van den Berghe H. (1987) Fragile X syndrome: a study of the psychological profile in 23 prepubertal patients. *Clinical Genetics*, **32**, 179–186.

Bregman J.D. & Volkmar F.R. (1988) Autistic social dysfunction and Down syndrome. *Journal of the American Academy of Child and Adolescent Psychiatry*, **27**, 440–441.

Bregman J.D., Leckman J.F. & Ort S.I. (1988) Fragile X syndrome: genetic predisposition to psychopathology. *Journal of Autism and Developmental Disorders*, **18**, 343–354.

Bridges F.A. & Cicchetti D. (1982) Mothers' ratings of the temperament characteristics of Down syndrome infants. *Developmental Psychology*, **18**, 238–244.

Brown W.T., Jenkins E.C., Cohen I.L., Gisch G.S., Wolf-Schein E.G., Gross A., Waterhouse L., Fein D., Mason-Brothers A., Ritvo E., Ruttenberg B.A., Bentley W. & Castells S. (1986) Fragile X and autism: a multicenter survey. *American Journal of Medical Genetics*, **23**, 341–352.

Buchsbaum M., Henkin R.L. & Christiansen R.L. (1974) Age and sex differences in averaged evoked responses in a normal population with observations on patients with gonadal dysgenesis. *Electroencephalography and Clinical Neurophysiology*, **37**, 137–144.

Buckley F. (1971) Preliminary report on intelligence quotient scores of patients with Turner's syndrome: a replication study. *British Journal of Psychiatry*, **119**, 513–514.

Burn J. (1986) Williams syndrome. *Journal of Medical Genetics*, **23**, 389–395.

Butler M.G. (1990) Prader–Willi syndrome: current understanding of cause and diagnosis. *American Journal of Medical Genetics*, **35**, 319–332.

Caldwell M.L., Taylor R. & Bloom S. (1986) An investigation of the use of preferred and nonpreferred food as a reinforcer to increase activity of individuals with Prader–Willi syndrome. *Journal of Mental Deficiency Research*, **30**, 347–354.

Carr J. (1988) Six weeks to twenty one years old: a longitudinal study of children with Down's syndrome. *Journal of Child Psychology and Psychiatry*, **29**, 407–431.

Cassidy S.B. (1984) Prader–Willi syndrome. *Current Problems in Pediatrics*, **14**, 1–55.

Chen C.N., Denome S. & Davis R.L. (1986) Molecular analysis of cDNA clones and the corresponding genetic coding sequences of the *Drosophila dunce*+ gene, the structural gene for cAMP phosphodiesterase. *Proceedings of the National Academy of Sciences, USA*, **83**, 9313–9319.

Chomsky N. (1988) *Language and Problems of Knowledge*. MIT Press, Cambridge, MA.

Christie R., Bay C., Kaufman I.A., Bakay B., Borden M. & Nyhan W.L. (1982) Lesch–Nyhan disease: clinical experience with nineteen patients. *Developmental Medicine and Child Neurology*, **24**, 293–306.

Chumakov I., Rigault P., Guillou S., Ougen P., Billaut A., Guasconi G., Gervy P., LeGall I., Soularue P., Grinas L., Bougueleret L., Bellanne-Chantelot C., Lacroix B., Barillot E., Gesnouin P., Pook S., Vaysseix G., Frelat G., Schmitz A., Sambucy J.-L., Bosch A., Estivill X., Weissenbach J., Vignal A., Riethman H., Cox D., Patterson D., Gardiner K., Hattori M., Sakaki Y., Ichikawa H., Ohki M., Le Paslier D., Heilig R., Antonarakis S. & Cohen D. (1992) Continuum of overlapping clones spanning the entire human chromosome 21q. *Nature*, **359**, 380–387.

Clarke D.J., Waters J. & Corbett J.A. (1989) Adults with Prader–Willi syndrome: abnormalities of sleep and behaviour. *Journal of the Royal Society of Medicine*, **82**, 21–24.

Cohen I.L., Gisch G.S., Sudhalter V., Wolf-Schein E.G., Hanson D., Hagerman R., Jenkins E.C. & Brown W.T. (1988) Social gaze, social avoidance and repetitive behavior in fragile X males: a controlled study. *American Journal of Mental Retardation*, **92**, 436–446.

Cohen I.L., Vietze P.M., Sudhalter V., Jenkins E.C. & Brown W.T. (1989) Parent–child dyadic gaze patterns in fragile X males and in non-fragile X males with autistic disorder. *Journal of Child Psychology and Psychiatry*, **30**, 845–856.

Cohen R.L., Sudhalter V., Pfadt A., Jenkins E.C., Brown W.T. & Vietze P.M. (1991) Why are autism and the fragile-X syndrome associated? Conceptual and methodological issues. *American Journal of Human Genetics*, **48**, 195–202.

Cole T.R.P. & Hughes H.E. (1990) Sotos syndrome. *Journal of Medical Genetics*, **27**, 571–576.

Cook E.H. & Leventhal B.L. (1987) Down's syndrome with mania. *British Journal of Psychiatry*, **150**, 249–250.

Corbin V., Michelson A.M., Abmayr S.M., Neel V., Alcamo E., Maniatis T. & Young M.W. (1991) A role for the *Drosophila* neurogenic genes in mesoderm differentiation. *Cell*, **67**, 311–323.

Crisco J.J., Dobbs J.M. & Mulhern R.K. (1988) Cognitive processing of children with Williams syndrome. *Developmental Medicine and Child Neurology*, **30**, 650–656.

Crow T.J. (1988) Sex chromosomes and psychosis. *British Journal of Psychiatry*, **153**, 675–683.

Curfs L.M.G., Wiegers A.M., Sommers J.R.M., Borghgraef M. & Fryns J.P. (1991) Strengths and weaknesses in the cognitive profile of youngsters with Prader–Willi syndrome. *Clinical Genetics*, **40**, 430–434.

Dalton A.J. & Crapper D.R. (1984) Incidence of memory deterioration in aging persons with Down's syndrome. In: Berg J.M. (ed) *Perspectives and Progress in Mental Retardation, Vol. II: Biomedical Aspects*, pp. 55–62. University Park Press, Baltimore, MD.

Dalton A.J. & Crapper-McLachlan D.R. (1986) Clinical expression of Alzheimer's disease in Down's syndrome. *Psychiatric Clinics of North America*, **9**, 659–670.

Dalton J. & Wisniewski H. (1990) Down's syndrome and the dementia of Alzheimer disease. *International Review of Psychiatry*, **2**, 43–52.

Darby P.L., Garfinkel P.E., Vale J.M., Kirwan P.J. & Brown G.M. (1981) Anorexia nervosa and 'Turner syndrome': cause or coincidence? *Psychology and Medicine*, **11**, 141–145.

Dasgupta J., Dasgupta D. & Balasubrahmanyan M. (1973) XXY syndrome, XY/XO mosaicism and acentric chromosomal fragments in male schizophrenics. *Indian Journal of Medical Research*, **61**, 62–70.

de Die-Smulders C., Theunissen P., Schrander-Stumpel C. & Frijns J.P. (1992) On the variable expression of the Brachmann-de Lange syndrome. *Clinical Genetics*, **41**, 42–45.

Dilts C.V., Morris C.A. & Leonard C.O. (1990) Hypothesis for development of a behavioural phenotype in Williams syndrome. *American Journal of Medical Genetics*, Suppl. 6, 126–131.

Dooley J.M., Berg J.M., Pakula Z. & MacGregor D.L. (1981) The puppet-like syndrome of Angelman. *American Journal of Diseases of Children*, **135**, 621–624.

Downey J., Ehrhart A.A., Grueu R., Bell J.J. & Morishima G. (1989)

Psychopathology and social functioning in women with Turner syndrome. *Journal of Nervous and Mental Disease*, **177**, 191–201.

Dykens E. & Leckman J. (1990) Developmental issues in fragile X syndrome. In: Hodapp R.M., Burack J.A. & Zigler E. (eds) *Issues in the Developmental Approach to Mental Retardation*, pp. 226–245. Cambridge University Press, New York.

Dykens E., Leckman J., Paul R. & Watson M. (1988) Cognitive, behavioral and adaptive functioning in fragile X and non-fragile X retarded men. *Journal of Autism and Developmental Disorders*, **18**, 41–52.

Einfeld S. & Hall W. (1992) Behavior phenotype of the fragile X syndrome. *American Journal of Medical Genetics*, **43**, 56–60.

Einfeld S., Molony H. & Hall W. (1989) Autism is not associated with the fragile X syndrome. *American Journal of Medical Genetics*, **34**, 187–193.

Elliot D., Weeks D.J. & Elliot C.L. (1987) Cerebral specialization in individuals with Down syndrome. *American Journal of Mental Deficiency*, **92**, 263–271.

Ellis N. (1969) A behavioral research strategy in mental retardation: defense and critique. *Journal of Mental Deficiency*, **73**, 557–566.

Epstein C.J. (1986) *The Consequences of Chromosome Imbalance: Principles, Mechanisms, Models*. Cambridge University Press, New York.

Epstein C.J., Korenberg J.R., Anneren G., Antonarakis S.E., Ayme S., Courchesne E., Epstein L.B., Fowler A., Groner Y., Huret J.L., Kemper T.L., Lott I.T., Lubin B.H., Magenis E., Opitz J.M., Patterson D., Priest J.H., Pueschel S.M., Rapoport S.I., Sinet P.-M., Tanzi R.E. & de la Cruz F. (1991) Protocols to establish genotype–phenotype correlations in Down syndrome. *American Journal of Human Genetics*, **49**, 207–235.

Evans J., de von Flindt R., Greenberg C. & Hamerton J. (1991) Physical and psychological findings in adolescents with sex chromosome abnormalities ascertained in the Winnipeg cytogenetic study of newborns: 1970–1973. *Birth Defects (Original Article Series)*, **26**, 189–200.

Fahsold R., Rott H.-D. & Lorenz P. (1991) A third gene locus for tuberous sclerosis is closely linked to the phenylalanine hydroxylase gene locus. *Human Genetics*, **88**, 85–90.

Fenner M.E., Hewitt K.E. & Torpy D.M. (1987) Down's syndrome: intellectual and behavioural functioning during adulthood. *Journal of Mental Deficiency Research*, **31**, 241–249.

Fernell E., Gillberg C. & von Wendt L. (1991) Behavioural problems in children with infantile hydrocephalus. *Developmental Medicine and Child Neurology*, **33**, 388–395.

Finger S., Heavens R.P., Sirinathsinhji D.R., Kuehn M.R. & Dunnett S.B. (1988) Behavioral and neurochemical evaluation of a transgenic mouse model of Lesch–Nyhan syndrome. *Journal of Neurological Science*, **86**, 203–213.

Fisch G.S. (1992) Is autism associated with the fragile X syndrome? *American Journal of Medical Genetics*, **43**, 47–55.

Fisch G.S., Shapiro L.R., Simensen R., Schwartz C.E., Fryns J.P., Borghgraef M., Curfs L.M., Howard-Peebles P.N., Arinami T. & Mavrou A. (1992) Longitudinal changes in IQ among fragile X males: clinical evidence of more than one mutation? *American Journal of Medical Genetics*, **43**, 28–34.

Fisher E.M., Bee-Romero P., Brown L.G., Ridley A., McNeil J.A., Lawrence J.B., Willard H.G., Bleber F.R. & Page D.C. (1990) Homologous ribosomal protein genes on the human X and Y chromosomes: escape from X inactivation and possible implications for Turner syndrome. *Cell*, **63**, 1205–1218.

Fleming C.P. (1968) The verbal behaviour of hdyrocephalic children. *Developmental Medicine and Child Neurology*, **15**, 74–82.

Forssman H. & Hambert G. (1963) Incidence of Klinefelters syndrome among mental patients. *Lancet*, **i**, 1327.

Franco B., Guioli S., Pragliola A., Incerti B., Bardoni B., Tonlorenzi R.,

Carrozo R., Maestrini E., Pieretti M., Taillon-Miller P., Brown C., Willard H., Lawrence C., Persico M., Camerino G. & Ballabio A. (1991) A gene deleted in Kallmann's syndrome shares homology with neural cell adhesion and axonal path-finding molecules. *Nature*, **353**, 529–536.

Friedman W. & Mills L. (1969) The relationship between vitamin D and the craniofacial and dental anomalies of the supravalvular aortic stenosis syndrome. *Pediatrics*, **43**, 12–18.

Fryer A.E., Chalmers A., Connor J.M., Fraser I., Povey S., Yates A.D., Yates J.R.W. & Osborne J.P. (1987) Evidence that the gene for tuberous sclerosis is on chromosome 9. *Lancet*, **i**, 659–661.

Fu Y.-H., Kuhl D.P.A., Pizzuti A., Pieretti M., Sutcliffe J.S., Richards S., Verkerk A.J.M.H., Holden J.J.A., Fenwick R.G. Jr, Warren S.T., Oostra B.A., Nelson D.L. & Caskey C.T. (1991) Variation of the CGG repeat at the fragile X site results in genetic instability: resolution of the Sherman paradox. *Cell*, **67**, 1047–1058.

Galaburda A.M., Sherman G.F., Rosen G.D., Aboitz F. & Geschwind N. (1985) Developmental dyslexia: four consecutive patients with cortical anomalies. *Annals of Neurology*, **18**, 222–233.

Garron D.C. (1977) Intelligence among persons with Turner's syndrome. *Behavior Genetics*, **7**, 105–127.

Gath A. & Gumley D. (1986) Behaviour problems in retarded children with special reference to Down's syndrome. *British Journal of Psychiatry*, **149**, 156–161.

Gibson D. (1978) *Down's Syndrome: The Psychology of Mongolism*. Cambridge University Press, Cambridge.

Gibson D., Groeneweg G., Jerry P. & Harris A. (1988) Age and pattern of intellectual decline among Down syndrome and other mentally retarded adults. *International Journal of Rehabilitation Research*, **11**, 47–55.

Goate A., Chartier-Harlin M.-C., Mullan M., Brown J., Crawford F., Fidani L., Giuffra L., Haynes A., Irving N., James L., Mant R., Newton P., Rooke K., Roques P., Talbot C., Pericak-Vance M., Owen M. & Hardy J. (1991) Segregation of a misense mutation in the amyloid precursor protein gene with familial Alzheimer's disease. *Nature*, **349**, 704–706.

Golding-Kushner K., Weller G. & Shprintzen R. (1985) Velocardio facial syndrome: language and psychological profiles. *Journal of Craniofacial Genetics and Developmental Biology*, **5**, 259–266.

Goldstein M., Anderson L.T. & Reuben R. (1985) Self mutilation in Lesch–Nyhan disease is caused by dopaminergic denervation. *Lancet*, **i**, 338–339.

Gomez M.R. (1988) *Tuberous Sclerosis*. Raven Press, New York.

Goodman J.F. (1990) Technical note: problems in etiological classifications of mental retardation. *Journal of Child Psychology and Psychiatry*, **31**, 465–469.

Gopnik M. (1990) Feature blind grammar and dysphasia. *Nature*, **344**, 615.

Graham J.M., Bashir A.S., Stark R.E., Silbert A. & Walzer S. (1988) Oral and written language abilities of XXY boys: implications for anticipatory guidance. *Pediatrics*, **81**, 795–806.

Grant G.N., O'Dell T.J., Karl K.A., Stein P.L., Soriano P. & Kandel E.R. (1992) Impaired long-term potentiation, spatial learning and hippocampal developmental in *fyn* mutant mice. *Science*, **258**, 1903–1910.

Green J.M., Dennis J. & Bennets L.A. (1989) Attention disorder in a group of young Down's syndrome children. *Journal of Mental Deficiency Research*, **33**, 105–122.

Greenswag L.R. (1987) Adults with Prader–Willi syndrome: a survey of 232 cases. *Developmental Medicine and Child Neurology*, **29**, 145–152.

Gunn P. & Berry P. (1985) The temperament of Down's syndrome toddlers and their siblings. *Journal of Child Psychology and Psychiatry*, **26**, 973–979.

Gunn P., Berry P. & Andrews R.J. (1981) The temperament of Down's syndrome infants: a research note. *Journal of Child Psychology and Psychiatry*, **22**, 189–194.

Gustavson K.-H., Blomquist H. & Holmgren G. (1986) Prevalence of fragile-X syndrome in mentally retarded boys in a Swedish county. *American Journal of Medical Genetics*, **23**, 581–588.

Hadenius A., Hagberg B., Hyffnes-Bensch K. & Sjogren I. (1962) The natural prognosis of infantile hydrocephalus. *Acta Pediatrica Scandinavica*, **51**, 117–124.

Hagberg B. (1985) Retts syndrome: prevalence and impact on progressive severe mental retardation in girls. *Acta Paediatrica Scandinavica*, **74**, 405–408.

Hagberg B., Goutieres F., Hanefeld F., Rett A. & Wilson J. (1985) Rett syndrome: criteria for inclusion and exclusion. *Brain and Development*, **3**, 372–373.

Hagerman R. & Sobesky W. (1989) Psychopathology in the fragile X syndrome. *American Journal of Orthopsychiatry*, **59**, 142–152.

Hagerman R.J., Jackson A.W., Levitas A., Rimland B. & Braden M. (1986) An analysis of autism in fifty males with fragile X syndrome. *American Journal of Medical Genetics*, **23**, 359–374.

Hall B.D. & Smith D.W. (1972) Prader–Willi syndrome: a résumé of 32 cases including an instance of affected first cousins, one of whom is of normal stature and intelligence. *Pediatrics*, **81**, 286–293.

Hanson J.W. (1981) A view of the etiology and pathogenesis of Prader–Willi syndrome. In: Holm V.A., Sulzbacher S.J. & Pipes P.L. (eds) *The Prader–Willi Syndrome*, pp. 23–32. University Park, Baltimore, MD.

Hanson D.M., Jackson A.W. & Hagerman R.J. (1986) Speech disturbances (cluttering) in mildly impaired males with the Martin-Bell/fragile X syndrome. *American Journal of Medical Genetics*, **23**, 195–206.

Hardin P., Hall J. & Rosbash M. (1990) Feedback of the *Drosophila* period gene product on circadian cycling of its messenger RNA levels. *Nature*, **343**, 536–540.

Hawley P.P., Jackson L.G. & Kurnit D.M. (1985) Sixty-four patients with Brachmann-de Lange syndrome: a survey. *American Journal of Medical Genetics*, **20**, 453–459.

Heaton-Ward A. (1977) Psychosis in mental handicap. *British Journal of Psychiatry*, **130**, 525–533.

Hersh J.H., Bloom A.S., Zimmerman A.W., Dinno N.D., Greenstein R.M., Weisskopf B. & Reese A.H. (1981) Behavioral correlates in the happy puppet syndrome: a characteristic profile? *Developmental Medicine and Child Neurology*, **23**, 792–800.

Hinton V.J., Dobkin C.S., Halperin J.M., Jenkins E.C., Brown W.T., Ding X.H., Cohen I.L., Rousseau F. & Miezejeski C.M. (1992) Mode of inheritance influences, behavioral expression and molecular control of cognitive deficits in female carriers of the fragile X syndrome. *American Journal of Medical Genetics*, **43**, 87–95.

Hodapp R.M. & Dykens F.M. (1991) Towards an etiology specific strategy of early intervention with handicapped children. In: Marfo K. (ed) *Early Intervention in Transition*, pp. 41–60. Praeger, New York.

Hodapp R. & Zigler E. (1990) Applying the developmental perspective to individuals with Down syndrome. In: Cicchett D. & Bceghly M. (eds) *Down syndrome: The Developmental Perspective*, pp. 1–28. Cambridge University Press, New York.

Holm V. (1981) The diagnosis of Prader–Willi syndrome. In: Holm V.A., Sulzbacher S.J. & Pipes P. (eds) *Prader Willi Syndrome*, pp. 27–44. University Park Press, Baltimore, MD.

Holm V.A. & Pipes P.L. (1976) Food and children with Prader–Willi syndrome. *American Journal of Diseases of Children*, **130**, 1063–1067.

Holtzman N.A., Kronmal R.A., van Doorninck W., Azen C. & Koch R. (1986) Effect of age at loss of dietary control on intellectual performance and behavior of children with phenylketonuria. *New England Journal of Medicine*, **314**, 593–598.

Hooper M.L., Hardy K., Handyside A., Hunter S. & Monk M. (1987) HPRT-deficient (Lesch–Nyhan) mouse embryos derived from germ-line colonization by cultured cells. *Nature*, **326**, 292–295.

Howard-Peebles P.N., Stoddard, G.R. & Mims M.G. (1979) Familial X linked mental retardation, verbal disability and marker X chromosome. *American Journal of Human Genetics*, **31**, 214–222.

Hunt A. & Dennis J. (1987) Psychiatric disorder among children with tuberous sclerosis. *Developmental Medicine and Child Neurology*, **29**, 190–198.

Hunt A. & Lindenbaum R.H. (1984) Tuberous sclerosis: a new estimate of prevalence within the Oxford region. *Journal of Medical Genetics*, **21**, 272–277.

Hurst J.A., Baraitser M., Auger E., Graham F. & Norell S. (1990) An extended family with a dominantly inherited speech disorder. *Developmental Medicine and Child Neurology*, **32**, 347–355.

Iwata B.A., Pace G.M., Willis K.D., Gamache T.B. & Hyman S.L. (1986) Operant studies of self-injurious hand biting in the Rett syndrome. *American Journal of Medical Genetics*, **24**, 157–166.

Jacobs P.A., Brunton M., Melville M.M., Brittain R.P. & McClemont W.F. (1965) Aggressive behaviour, mental subnormality and the XYY male. *Nature*, **208**, 1351–1352.

Jacobs P.A., Price W.H., Richmond S. & Ratcliff R.A.W. (1971) Chromosome surveys in penal institutions and approved schools. *Journal of Medical Genetics*, **8**, 49–58.

Jacobs P., Glover T. & Myer M. (1980) X-linked mental retardation: a study of seven families. *American Journal of Medical Genetics*, **7**, 471–489.

Jacobs P.A., Mayer M., Matsuura J., Rhoads F. & Yee S. (1983) A cytogenetic study of a population of mentally retarded males with special reference to the marker X syndrome. *Human Genetics*, **63**, 139–148.

Johnson H.G., Ekman P. & Friesen W. (1976) A behavioural phenotype in the de Lange syndrome. *Pediatric Research*, **10**, 843–850.

Jones K.L. (1990) Williams syndrome: an historical perspective of its evolution, natural history and etiology. *American Journal of Medical Genetics*, (suppl. 6), 89–96.

Journel H., Melki J., Turleau C., Munnick A. & de Grouchy J. (1990) Rett phenotype with X/autosome translocation: possible mapping to the short arm of chromosome X. *American Journal of Medical Genetics*, **35**, 142–147.

Kemper M.B., Hagerman R.J., Ahmad R.S. & Mariner R. (1986) Cognitive profiles and the spectrum of clinical manifestations in heterozygous fra(X) females. *American Journal of Medical Genetics*, **23**, 139–156.

Kemper M.B., Hagerman R.J. & Altshul-Stark D. (1988) Cognitive profiles of boys with the fragile X syndrome. *American Journal of Medical Genetics*, **30**, 191–200.

Kemper T.L., Lott I.T., Lubin B.H., Magenis E.I., Opitz J.M., Patterson D., Priest J.H., Pueschces S.M., Rapoport S.I., Sinet P.-M., Tanzi R.E., de la Cruz F., Evans J.A., de von Flindt R., Greenberg C.R. & Hamerton J.L. (1991) Physical and psychological findings in adolescents with sex chromosome abnormalities ascertained in the Winnipeg cytogenetic study of newborns: 1970–1973. *Birth Defects: Original Articles Series*, **26**(4), 189–199.

Kerr R. & Blais C. (1985) Motor skill acquisition by individuals with Down syndrome. *American Journal of Mental Deficiency*, **90**, 313–318.

Kerr R. & Blais C. (1987) Down syndrome and the extended practice of a complex motor task. *American Journal of Mental Deficiency*, **91**, 591–597.

Killian W. (1986) On the genetics of Rett syndrome: analysis of family and pedigree data. *American Journal of Medical Genetics*, (suppl. 1), 369–376.

Koch R., Azen C.G., Friedman E.G. & Williamson M.L. (1982) Preliminary report on the effects of diet discontinuation in PKU. *Journal of Pediatrics*, **100**, 870–875.

Korenberg J.R., Kalousek D.K., Anneren G., Pulst S.-M., Hall J.G., Epstein C.J. & Cox D.R. (1991) Deletion of chromosome 21 and normal intelligence: molecular definition of the lesion. *Human Genetics*, **87**, 112–118.

Krakow J.B. & Kopp C. (1983) The effects of developmental delay on sustained attention in young children. *Child Development*, **54**, 1143–1155.

Kuehn M.R., Bradley A., Robertson E.J. & Evans M.J. (1987) A potential animal model for Lesch–Nyhan syndrome through introduction of HPRT mutations into mice. *Nature*, **326**, 295–298.

Kyriacou C. (1990) The molecular ethology of the *period* gene in *Drosophila*. *Behavior Genetics*, **20**, 191–211.

Lacey D.J. & Terplan K. (1987) Abnormal cerebral cortical neurons in a child with maternal PKU syndrome. *Journal of Child Neurology*, **2**, 201–204.

Larocca F.E.F. (1985) Concurrence of Turner's syndrome, anorexia nervosa, and mood disorders: case report. *Journal of Clinical Psychiatry*, **46**, 296–297.

Legouis R., Hardelin J.-P., Levilliers J., Claverie J.-M., Compain S., Wunderle V., Millasseau P., Le Paslier D., Cohen D., Caterina D., Bougueleret L., Delemarre-Van de Waal H., Lutfalla G., Weissenbach J. & Petit C. (1991) The candidate gene for the X-linked Kallmann syndrome encodes a protein related to adhesion molecules. *Cell*, **67**, 423–435.

Levin L.R., Han P.-L., Hwang P.M., Feinstein P.G., Davis R.L. & Reed R.R. (1992) The *Drosophila* learning and memory gene *rutabaga* encodes a Ca^{2+}/calmodulin-responsive adenylyl cyclase. *Cell*, **68**, 479–489.

Levitas A., McBogg P. & Hagerman R. (1983) Behavioral dysfunction in the fragile X syndrome. In: Hagerman R.J. & McBogg P. (eds) *The Fragile X Syndrome: Diagnosis, Biochemistry and Intervention*, pp. 153–173. Spectra, CO.

Lidsky A.S., Law M.L., Morse H.G., Kao T., Robin M., Ruddle F.H. & Woo S.L.C. (1985) Regional mapping of the phenylalanine hydroxylase gene and the phenylketonuria locus in the human genome. *Proceedings of the National Academy of Sciences, USA*, **82**, 6221–6225.

Liston E.H. & Shershow L.W. (1973) Concurrence of anorexia nervosa and gonadal dysgenesis: a critical review with practical considerations. *Archives of General Psychiatry*, **29**, 834–836.

Lloyd K.G., Hornykiewicz O. & Davison L. (1981) Biochemical evidence of dysfunction of brain neurotransmitter in the Lesch–Nyhan syndrome. *New England Journal of Medicine*, **305**, 1106–1111.

Lou H.C., Guttler F., Lykkelund C., Bruhn P. & Niederwieser A. (1985) Decreased vigilance and neurotransmitter synthesis after discontinuation of dietary treatment for phenylketonuria in adolescents. *European Journal of Pediatrics*, **144**, 17–20.

Lund J. (1988) Psychiatric aspects of Down's syndrome. *Acta Psychiatrica Scandinavica*, **78**, 369–374.

Lyle J. (1959) The effect of an institution environment upon the verbal development of imbecile children. 1. Verbal intelligence. *Journal of Mental Deficiency Research*, **3**, 122–128.

McCauley E., Ito J. & Kay T. (1986) Psychosocial functioning in girls with Turner's syndrome and short stature: social skills, behavior problems, and self-concept. *Journal of the American Academy of Child Psychiatry*, **25**, 105–112.

McCormick M.K., Schinzel A., Petersen M.S., Stetton G., Driscoll D.J., Cantu E.S. & Tranebjaerg I. (1989) Molecular characterization of the 'Down syndrome' region of chromosome 21. *Genomics*, **5**, 325–331.

McGinnis W. & Krumlauf R. (1992) Homeobox genes and axial patterning. *Cell*, **68**, 283–302.

McLaughlin M. (1987) Bipolar affective disorder in Down's syndrome. *British Journal of Psychiatry*, **151**, 116–117.

MacLean N., Court-Brown W., Jacobs P., Mantle D. & Strong J. (1968) A survey of sex chromatin abnormalities in mental hospitals. *Journal of Medical Genetics*, **5**, 165–172.

MacMillan D. (1982) *Mental Retardation in School and Society*. Little, Brown, Boston.

Marcovitch S., Goldberg S., MacGregor D. & Lojkasek M. (1986) Patterns of temperament variation in three groups of developmentally delayed preschool children: mother and father ratings. *Developmental and Behavioural Pediatrics*, **7**, 247–252.

Marfo K. (1991) *Early Intervention in Transition*. Praeger, New York.

Martin N.D.T., Snodgrass G.J.A. & Cohen R.D. (1984) Idiopathic infantile hypercalcaemia — a continuing enigma. *Archives of Disease in Childhood*, **59**, 605–613.

Matthews W.S., Barabas G., Cusack E. & Ferrari M. (1986) Social quotients of children with phenylketonuria before and after discontinuation of dietary treatment. *American Journal of Mental Deficiency*, **91**, 92–94.

Menolascino F.J. (1965) Psychiatric aspects of mongolism. *American Journal of Mental Deficiency*, **69**, 653–660.

Menolascino F.J. (1967) Psychiatric findings in a sample of institutionalized mongoloids. In: *Journal of Mental Subnormality*, **13**, 67–74.

Meyerson M.D. & Frank R.A. (1987) Language, speech and hearing in Williams syndrome: intervention approaches and research needs. *Developmental Medicine and Child Neurology*, **29**, 258–270.

Money J. (1963) Two cytogenetic syndromes: psychologic comparisons 1. Intelligence and specific-factor quotients. *Journal of Psychiatric Research*, **2**, 223–231.

Money J. & Mittenthal S. (1970) Lack of personality pathology in Turner's syndrome: relation to cytogenetics, hormones, and physique. *Behavior Genetics*, **1**, 43–56.

Money J., Annecillo C., Van Orman B. & Borgaonkar D.S. (1974) Cytogenetics, hormones and behaviour disability: comparison of XYY and XXY syndromes. *Clinical Genetics*, **6**, 370–382.

Morris C., Demsey S., Leonard C., Dilts C. & Blackburn B. (1988) Natural history of Williams syndrome: physical characteristics. *Journal of Pediatrics*, **113**, 318–326.

Myers B.A. & Pueschel S.M. (1991) Psychiatric disorders in persons with Down syndrome. *Journal of Nervous and Mental Disease*, **179**, 609–613.

Naidu S., Murphy M., Moser H.W. & Rett A. (1986) Rett syndrome — natural history in 70 cases. *American Journal of Medical Genetics*, **24**, 61–72.

Nakamura H. (1965) An enquiry into systematic differences in the abilities of institutionalized adult mongoloids. *American Journal of Mental Deficiency*, **69**, 661–665.

Netley C. (1986) Summary overview of behavioural development in individuals with neonatally identified X and Y aneuploidy. *Birth Defects (Original Article Series)*, **22**, 293–306.

Netley C. & Rovet J. (1982a) Verbal defects in children with 47 XXY and 47 XXX Karyotypes: a descriptive and experimental study. *Brain and Language*, **17**, 58–73.

Netley C. & Rovet J. (1982b) Atypical hemispheric lateralization in Turner syndrome subjects. *Cortex*, **18**, 377–384.

Netley C. & Rovet J. (1984) Hemispheric lateralization in 47 XXY Klinefelters syndrome boys. *Brain and Cognition*, **3**, 10–18.

Netley C. & Rovet J. (1987) Relations between a dermatoglyphic measure, hemispheric specialization and intellectual abilities in 47 XXY males. *Brain and Cognition*, **6**, 153–160.

Newell K., Samborn B. & Hagerman R. (1983) Speech and language dysfunction in the fragile X syndrome. In: Hagerman R.J. & McBogg P.M. (eds) *The Fragile X Syndrome — Diagnosis, Biochemistry and Inter-*

vention, pp. 175–200. Spectra, CO.

Nielsen J. & Wohlert M. (1991) Sex chromosome abnormalities found among 34 910 newborn children: results from a 13 year incidence study in Arhus, Denmark. *Birth Defects: Original Articles Series*, **26**, 209–224.

Nielsen J., Nyborg H. & Dahl G. (1977) Turner's syndrome. A psychiatric–psychological study of 45 women with Turner's syndrome, compared with their sisters and women with normal karyotypes, growth retardation and primary amenorrhoea. *Acta Jutlandica*, **XLV**, Medicine Series 21, Århus.

Nomura Y., Segawa M. & Hasegawa M. (1984) Rett syndrome — clinical studies and pathophysiological consideration. *Brain and Development*, **6**, 475–486.

Nyhan W.L. (1976) Behavior in the Lesch–Nyhan syndrome. *Journal of Autism and Childhood Schizophrenia*, **6**, 235–252.

O'Brien G. (1991) *Behavioural Measurement in Mental Handicap*. SSBP, Oxford.

Oliver C. & Head D. (1990) Self-injurious behaviour in people with learning disabilities: determinants and interventions. *International Review of Psychiatry*, **2**, 101–116.

Oliver C. & Holland A.J. (1986) Down's syndrome and Alzheimer's disease: a review. *Psychological Medicine*, **16**, 307–322.

Olsson B. & Rett A. (1985) Behavioural observations concerning differential diagnosis between Rett syndrome and autism. *Brain and Development*, **7**, 281–289.

Olsson B. & Rett A. (1986) Shift to righthandedness in Rett syndrome around age 7. *American Journal of Medical Genetics*, **24**, 133–141.

Olsson B. & Rett A. (1987) Autism and Rett syndrome: behavioural investigations and differential diagnosis. *Developmental Medicine and Child Neurology*, **29**, 429–441.

Opitz J. (1985) The Brachmann-de Lange syndrome: editorial comment. *American Journal of Medical Genetics*, **22**, 89–102.

Parsons J.G. (1969) Short term verbal memory in hydrocephalic children. *Developmental Medicine and Child Neurology*, **20**, 75–79.

Pasqualini R.Q., Vidal G. & Bur G.E. (1957) Psychopathology of Klinefelter's syndrome. *Lancet*, **ii**, 164–167.

Paul R., Cohen D.J., Breg W.R., Watson M. & Herman S. (1984) Fragile X syndrome: its relation to speech and language disorders. *Journal of Speech and Hearing Disorders*, **49**, 328–332.

Pennington B.F., Heaton R.K., Karzmark P., Pendleton M.G., Lehman R. & Shucard D.W. (1985) The neuropsychological phenotype in Turner syndrome. *Cortex*, **21**, 391–404.

Pieretti M., Zhang F., Fu Y.-H., Warren S.T., Oostra B.A., Caskey C.T. & Nelson D.L. (1991) Absence of expression of the *FMR-1* gene in fragile X syndrome. *Cell*, **66**, 817–822.

Pipe M.E. (1983) Dichotic listening performance following auditory discrimination training in Down syndrome and developmentally retarded children. *Cortex*, **19**, 481–491.

Polani P.E. (1969) Abnormal sex chromosomes and mental disorder. *Nature*, **223**, 680–686.

Preus M. & Rex A.P. (1983) Definition and diagnosis of the Brachmann-De Lange syndrome. *American Journal of Medical Genetics*, **16**, 301–312.

Prouty L.A., Rogers R.C., Stevenson R.E., Dean J.H., Palmer K.K., Simensen R.J., Coston G.N. & Schwartz C.E. (1988) Fragile X syndrome: growth, development, and intellectual function. *American Journal of Medical Genetics*, **30**, 123–142.

Quinn W.G. & Greenspan R.J. (1984) Learning and courtship in *Drosophila*: two stories with mutants. *Annual Review of Neurosciences*, **7**, 67–93.

Ratcliffe S.G., Butler G.E. & Jones M. (1991) Edinburgh study of growth and development of children with sex chromosome abnormalities. IV. *Birth Defects: Original Articles Series*, **26**, 1–44.

Reiss A.L. & Freund L. (1992) Behavioral phenotype of fragile X

syndrome: DSM-III-R autistic behavior in male children. *American Journal of Medical Genetics*, **43**, 35–46.

Rhoads F. (1982) X linked mental retardation and fragile X or marker-X syndrome. *Pediatrics*, **69**, 668–669.

Riccardi V.M. (1986) The Rett syndrome: genetics and the future. *American Journal of Medical Genetics*, (suppl. 1), 389–402.

Riikonen R. & Amnell G. (1981) Psychiatric disorders in children with earlier infantile spasms. *Developmental Medicine and Child Neurology*, **23**, 747–760.

Robb S.A., Pohl K.R.E., Baraitser M., Wilson J. & Brett E.M. (1989) The 'happy puppet' syndrome of Angelman: review of the clinical features. *Archives of Disease in Childhood*, **64**, 83–86.

Roberts G.W. (1990) Schizophrenia: the cellular biology of a functional psychosis. *Trends in Neurological Science*, **13**, 207–211.

Robinson A., Bender B.G. & Linden M.G. (1991a) Summary of clinical findings in children and young adults with sex chromosome anomalies. *Birth Defects: Original Articles Series*, **26**, 225–228.

Robinson A., Bender B.G., Linden M.G. & Salbenblatt J.A. (1991b) Sex chromosome aneuploidy: the Denver prospective study. *Birth Defects: Original Articles Series*, **26**, 59–115.

Rousseau F., Heitz D., Biancalana V., Blumenfeld S., Kretz C., Boue J., Tommerup N., van der Hagen C., DeLozier-Blanchet C., Croquette M.-F., Gilgenkrantz S., Jalbert P., Voelckel M.A., Oberle I. & Mandel J.-L. (1991) Direct diagnosis by DNA analysis of the fragile X syndrome of mental retardation. *New England Journal of Medicine*, **325**, 1673–1681.

Rovet J. & Netley C. (1980) The mental rotation task performance of Turner syndrome subjects. *Behavior Genetics*, **10**, 437–443.

Rovet J. & Netley C. (1982) Processing deficits in Turner's syndrome. *Developmental Psychology*, **18**, 77–94.

Ruohola H., Bremer K.A., Baker D., Swedlow J.R., Jan L.Y. & Jan Y.N. (1991) Role of neurogenic genes in establishment of follicle cell fate and oocyte polarity during oogenesis in *Drosophila*. *Cell*, **66**, 433–449.

Rutter S.C. & Cole T.R.P. (1991) Psychological characteristics of Sotos syndrome. *Developmental Medicine and Child Neurology*, **33**, 898–902.

Scarr S. & MacCartney K. (1983) How people make their own environments: a theory of genotype–environment effects. *Child Development*, **54**, 424–435.

Schiavi R.C., Theilgaard A., Owen D.R. & White D. (1988) Sex chromosome anomalies, hormones, and sexuality. *Archives of General Psychiatry*, **45**, 19–24.

Schoeller D.A., Levitsky L.L., Bandini L.G., Dietz W.W. & Walczak A. (1988) Energy expenditure and body composition in Prader–Willi syndrome. *Metabolism*, **37**, 115–120.

Schwegler H. & Lipp H.-P., (1983) Hereditary covariations of neuronal circuitry and behaviour: correlations between the proportions of hippocampal synaptic fields in the region inferior and two-way avoidance in mice and rats. *Behaviour and Brain Research*, **7**, 1–39.

Schwegler H., Lipp H.-P., van der Loos H. & Buselmaier W. (1981) Individual hippocampal mossy fibre distribution in mice correlates with two-way avoidance performance. *Science*, **214**, 817–819.

Scriver C.R., Kaufman S. & Woo S.L.C. (1989) The hyperphenylalaninemias. In: Scriver C.R., Beaudet A.L., Sly W.S. & Valle D. (eds) *The metabolic basis of inherited disease*, 6th edn, pp. 495–546. McGraw-Hill, New York.

Seashore M.R., Friedman E., Novelly R.A. & Bapat V. (1985) Loss of intellectual function in children with phenylketonuria after relaxation of dietary phenylalanine restriction. *Pediatrics*, **75**, 226–232.

Shaffer J.W. (1962) A specific cognitive deficit in gonadal aplasia (Turner's syndrome). *Journal of Psychology*, **18**, 403–406.

Sherman S.L., Jacobs P.A., Morton N.E., Froster-Iskenius U., Howard-Peebles P.N., Nielsen K.B., Partington M.W., Sutherland G.R., Turner G. & Watson M. (1985) Further segregation analysis of the fragile X syndrome with special reference to transmitting males. *Human Genetics*, **69**, 289–299.

Shotwell S.L. (1983) Cyclic adenosine 3':5'-monophosphate phosphodiesterase and its role in learning in *Drosophila*. *Journal of Neurosciences*, **3**, 739–747.

Shprintzen R.J. & Goldberg R.B. (1986) Multiple anomaly syndromes and learning disabilities. In: Smith S. (ed) *Genetics and Learning Disabilities*, pp. 153–173. Taylor and Francis, London.

Silva A.J., Stevens C.F., Tonegawa S. & Wang Y. (1992a) Deficient hippocampal long-term potentiation in α-calcium-calmodulin kinase II mutant mice. *Science*, **257**, 201–206.

Silva A.J., Paylor R., Wehner J.M. & Tonegawa S. (1992b) Impaired spatial learning in α-calcium-calmodulin kinase II mutant mice. *Science*, **257**, 206–211.

Silverstein A.B., Legutki G., Friedman S.L. & Takayama D.L. (1982) Performance of Down syndrome individuals on the Stanford-Binet Intelligence Scale. *American Journal of Mental Deficiency*, **86**, 548–551.

Smalley S., Smith M. & Tanguay P. (1991) Autism and psychiatric disorders in tuberous sclerosis. *Annals of the New York Academy of Sciences*, **615**, 382–383.

Smith I., Beasley M.G., Wolff O.H. & Ades A.E. (1988) Behavior disturbance in 8-year-old children with early treated phenylketonuria. *Journal of Pediatrics*, **112**, 403–408.

Smith M., Smalley S., Cantor P., Pandolo M. & Gomez M.I. (1990) Mapping of a gene determining tuberous sclerosis to human chromosome 11q14–11q23. *Genomics*, **6**, 105–114.

Snart F., O'Grady M. & Das J.P. (1982) Cognitive processing by subgroups of moderately mentally retarded children. *American Journal of Mental Deficiency*, **86**, 465–472.

Sotos J.F. & Cutler E. (1977) Cerebral gigantism. *American Journal of Diseases of Children*, **131**, 625–627.

Sotos J.F., Dodge P.R., Muirhead D., Crawford J.D. & Talbot N.B. (1984) Cerebral gigantism in childhood. *New England Journal of Medicine*, **271**, 109–116.

Sovner R., Hurley A.N. & Labrie R. (1985) Is mania incompatible with Down's syndrome? *British Journal of Psychiatry*, **146**, 319–320.

Spain B. (1974) Verbal and performance ability in pre-school children with spina bifida. *Developmental Medicine and Child Neurology*, **16**, 773–781.

Stevenson J.E., Hawcroft J., Lobascher M., Smith I., Wolff O.H. & Graham P.J. (1979) Behavioral deviance in children with early treated phenylketonuria. *Archives of Disease in Childhood*, **54**, 14–18.

Stewart D.A., Bailey J.D., Netley C.T. & Park E. (1991) Growth, development, and behavioral outcome from mid-adolescence to adulthood in subjects with chromosome aneuploidy: the Toronto study. *Birth Defects: Original Articles Series*, **26**, 131–188.

Stout J.T. & Caskey C.T. (1988) The Lesch–Nyhan syndrome: clinical, molecular and genetic aspects. *Trends in Genetics*, **4**, 175–178.

Sudhalter V., Cohen I.L., Silverman W. & Wolf-Schein E.G. (1990) Conversational analyses of males with fragile X, Down syndrome and autism: a comparison of the emergence of deviant language. *American Journal of Mental Retardation*, **94**, 431–441.

Sudhalter V., Maranion M. & Brooks P. (1992) Expressive semantic deficit in the productive language of males with fragile X syndrome. *American Journal of Medical Genetics*, **43**, 65–71.

Sulzbacher S., Crnic K.A. & Snow J. (1981) Behavioural and cognitive disabilities in Prader Willi syndrome. In: Holm V.A., Sulzbacher S.J. & Pipes P.L. (eds) *The Prader–Willi Syndrome*, pp. 147–159. University Park Press, Baltimore, MD.

Taylor E. (1961) *Psychological Appraisal of Children with Cerebral Defects*. Harvard University Press, Cambridge, MA.

Taylor R.L. (1988) Cognitive and behavioral characteristics. In: Caldwell M.L. & Taylor R.L. (eds) *Prader–Willi Syndrome: Selected Research and Management Issues*, pp. 29–42. Springer-Verlag, New York.

Taylor R. & Caldwell M.L. (1985) Type and magnitude of food preferences of individuals with Prader–Willi syndrome. *Journal of Mental Deficiency Research*, **29**, 109–112.

Tew B. (1979) The cocktail party syndrome in children with hydrocephalus and spina bifida. *British Journal of Disorders of Communication*, **14**, 89–101.

Theilgaard A. (1984) A psychological study of the personalities of XYY and XXY men. *Acta Psychiatrica Scandinavica*, **315**, 1–133.

Tomc S.A., Williamson N.K. & Pauli R.M. (1990) Temperament in Williams syndrome. *American Journal of Medical Genetics*, **36**, 345–352.

Udwin O. & Yule W. (1990) Expressive language of children with Williams syndrome. *American Journal of Medical Genetics*, Suppl. 6, 108–114.

Udwin O., Yule W. & Martin N. (1987) Cognitive abilities and behavioural characteristics of children with idiopathic infantile hypercalcaemia. *Journal of Child Psychology and Psychiatry*, **28**, 297–309.

Verkerk A.J.M.H., Pieretti M., Sutcliffe J.S., Fu Y.-H., Kuhl D.P.A., Pizzuti A., Reiner O., Richards S., Victoria M.F., Zhang F., Eussen B.E., van Ommen G.-J.B., Blonden L.A.J., Riggins G.J., Chastain J.L., Kunst C.B., Galjaard H., Caskey C.T., Nelson J.D.L., Oostra B.A. & Warren S.T. (1991) Identification of a gene (*FMR-1*) containing a CGG repeat coincident with a breakpoint cluster region exhibiting length variation in fragile X syndrome. *Cell*, **65**, 905–914.

von Arnim G. & Engel P. (1964) Mental retardation related to hypercalcaemia. *Developmental Medicine and Child Neurology*, **6**, 366–377.

Waber D.P. (1979) Neuropsychological aspects of Turner's syndrome. *Developmental Medicine and Child Neurology*, **21**, 58–70.

Wagstaff J., Knoll J.H.M., Glatt K.A., Shugart Y.Y., Sommer A. & Lalande M. (1992) Maternal but not paternal transmission of 15q11–13-linked nondeletion Angelman syndrome leads to phenotypic expression. *Nature Genetics*, **1**, 291–294.

Wakabayashi S. (1979) A case of infantile atuism associated with Down's syndrome. *Journal of Autism and Developmental Disorders*, **9**, 31–36.

Walzer S., Bashir A.S. & Silbert A.R. (1991) Cognitive and behavioral factors in the learning disabilities of 47,XXY and 47,XYY boys. *Birth Defects: Original Articles Series*, **26**, 45–58.

Webb T.P., Bundey S.E., Thake A. & Todd J. (1986) Population incidence and segregation ratios in the Martin-Bell syndrome. *American Journal of Medical Genetics*, **23**, 573–580.

Welsh M.C., Pennington B.F., Ozonoff S., Rouse B. & McCabe E.R. (1990) Neuropsychology of early-treated phenylketonuria: specific executive function deficits. *Child Development*, **61**, 1697–1713.

Westgren M., Eastham W.N., Ghandourah S. & Woodhouse N. (1988) Intrauterine hypercalcaemia and non-immune hydrops fetalis — relationship to Williams syndrome. *Prenatal Diagnosis*, **8**, 333–337.

Whalley L.J. (1982) The dementia of Down's syndrome and its relevance to aetiological studies of Alzheimer's disease. *Annals of the New York Academy of Sciences*, **396**, 39–53.

Whitman B.Y. & Accardo P. (1987) Emotional symptoms in Prader–Willi syndrome adolescents. *American Journal of Medical Genetics*, **28**, 897–905.

Williamson D.A.J. (1964) Supravalvular aortic stenosis associated with mental retardation and characteristic facies. *Proceedings of the Royal Society of Medicine*, **57**, 118–119.

Williamson M.L., Koch R., Azen C. & Chang C. (1981) Correlates of intelligence test results in treated phenylketonuric children. *Pediatrics*, **68**, 161–167.

Winchel R.M. & Stanley M. (1991) Self injurious behaviour: a review of the behaviour and biology of self mutilation. *American Journal of Psychiatry*, **148**, 306–317.

Witkin H.A., Mednick S.A., Schulsinger F., Bakkestrom E., Christiansen K.O., Goodenough D.R., Hirschhorn K., Lundsteen C., Owen D.R., Philip J., Rubin D.B. & Stocking M. (1976) XYY and XXY men: criminality and aggression. *Science*, **193**, 547–555.

Wright S.W. & Tarjan G. (1957) Phenylketonuria. *American Journal of Diseases of Children*, **93**, 405–419.

Yu S., Pritchard M., Kremer E., Lynch M., Nancarrow J., Baker E., Holman K., Mulley J.C., Warren S.T., Schlessinger D., Sutherland G.R. & Richards R.I. (1991) Fragile X genotype characterized by an unstable region of DNA. *Science*, **252**, 1179–1181.

Yukawa T. (1992) A female patient with Lesch–Nyhan syndrome. *Developmental Medicine and Child Neurology*, **34**, 534–546.

Zekulin-Hartley X.Y. (1981) Hemispherical asymmetry in Down's syndrome children. *Canadian Journal of Behavioural Science*, **13**, 210–217.

Zellweger H. & Schneider H. (1968) Syndrome of hypotonia, hypomentia, hypogonadism-obesity (HHMO) or Prader–Willi syndrome. *American Journal of Diseases of Children*, **115**, 588–598.

Zigler E. & Hodapp R.M. (1991) Behavioral functioning in individuals with mental retardation. *Annual Review of Psychology*, **42**, 29–50.

Zoghbi H.Y., Ledbetter D.H., Schultz R., Percy A.K. & Glaze D.G. (1990) A *de novo* X; 3 translocation in Rett syndrome. *American Journal of Medical Genetics*, **35**, 148–151.

Chapter 38
Personality Disorders

Jonathan Hill & Michael Rutter

Traditionally, most child psychiatrists have been reluctant to use the diagnostic category of personality disorder because it seemed to imply a fixity of outcome that was inconsistent with their view of the fluidity of personality development in early life. Accordingly, until very recently, most child psychiatry textbooks have not included a chapter on the topic. However, one of the key diagnostic features for many concepts of personality disorder is that its onset should have occurred in childhood or, at least, no later than late adolescence. Indeed, the American Psychiatric Association scheme in its various editions (e.g. 1987) *requires* the presence of conduct disorder before the age of 15 years for the diagnosis of antisocial personality disorder. Accordingly, it seems crucial to consider what is known about personality disorders, with special reference to the two key questions for child psychiatrists of the extent to which there is continuity in personality disturbance between childhood and adult life, and whether it is useful to apply the diagnosis in childhood and adolescence.

CONCEPTS OF PERSONALITY DISORDER

Attempts to classify personality types and dimensions go back to antiquity but concepts of personality disorder are of much more recent origin (Frances & Widiger, 1986; Rutter, 1987; Tyrer *et al.*, 1991). Although there are numerous variations on the specifics, the unifying notion is the idea that there are pervasive and persistent abnormalities of overall personality functioning that cause social impairment and/or subjective distress, but that are not due to episodic disorders of mental state, and that are not the result of qualitatively disordered thought processes (as exemplified by psychiatric phenomena). The basic assumption is that, in some way, personality disorders are different from other psychotic conditions such as schizophrenia, depression or anxiety states. The extent to which empirical evidence supports this basic dichotomy is considered below but, first, it is necessary to note the rather different routes by which particular personality disorders have come to be recognized.

Firstly, there are those that derive from the clinical observation that there are individuals who show enduring patterns of inflexible and seriously maladaptive behaviour that seem to fall outside the traditional criteria for mental illnesses or psychiatric syndromes. The need to have a term to describe these patterns of abnormal behaviour led to the concepts of psychopathy put forward by writers such as Hare (1970), Henderson (1939) and Cleckley (1941).

Secondly, there are the categories of personality disorder that derive from concepts of the impairments associated with extremes of personality dimensions, and of the personalities most prone to suffer from episodic mental disorders. Schneider's (1923, 1950) notion of psychopathic personalities (defined quite differently from the psychopathy formulations of Hare, of Henderson and of Cleckley) provides the main historic origin of this approach. In more recent times, Tyrer (1988) has done most to develop these ideas and to investigate their application. Many of the ICD-10 specific personality disorder categories (e.g. paranoid, anankastic and anxious) represent this tradition (World Health Organization, 1992).

Thirdly, some categories have their origins in empirical observations of the continuities between psychopathological disorders in childhood and pervasive social malfunction in adult life. The DSM-IV (American Psychiatric Association, in press) diagnosis of antisocial personality disorder is the most obvious example of this type, with its starting point in the findings of the long-term longitudinal studies pioneered by Robins (1966, 1978) and replicated by others (see Chapter 18). However, Wolff's concept of schizoid personality has somewhat similar roots (Wolff, 1991a,b; Wolff *et al.*, 1991).

Fourthly, some categories stem fairly directly from theoretical, especially psychoanalytic, notions. The DSM-IV diagnosis of borderline personality disorder constitutes the prototype here (Kernberg, 1967, 1975). However, it should be noted that, although originally conceptualized in psychodynamic terms, it has come to be defined behaviourally following the work of Gunderson (e.g. Gunderson & Singer, 1975; Gunderson *et al.*, 1981), Loranger (Loranger *et al.*, 1987, 1991), Spitzer (Spitzer *et al.*, 1979) and others.

Finally, a few categories have come, at least in part, from genetic findings. Meehl (1962) coined the term schizotypy to describe the postulated characteristics of schizophrenia-prone individuals, and the Danish adoption studies showed that the biological families of adopted schizophrenic probands included a raised rate of personality disorders that seemed to exhibit some features reminiscent of schizophrenia (Kety *et al.*, 1971). Spitzer *et al.* (1979) developed more explicit criteria for this type of personality syndrome which has come to be termed schizotypal personality disorder.

It will be appreciated that these approaches represent rather different concepts of what is meant by personality disorder and hence imply different sets of validating criteria. The situation is complicated by the fact that sometimes the same terms have been used to mean quite different things, and by the fact that sometimes the different approaches have landed up at much the same finishing point. Thus, for example, Wolff (1991a) argued that her concept of schizoid personality disorders largely overlaps with other people's diagnosis of schizotypal personality disorder but also overlaps with Asperger's syndrome (Frith, 1991), which most people have viewed as related to autism (see Chapter 33). It is scarcely surprising, therefore, that there is a good deal of uncertainty in the findings on validation (Docherty *et al.*, 1986; Siever & Klar, 1986; Tarnopolsky & Berelowitz, 1987; Siever & Davis, 1991). Accordingly, it may be more helpful to tackle the issue of validation according to a series of different concepts, rather than as a single issue.

VALIDATION

Separation from episodic disorders

Because all the concepts postulate a separation between personality disorders and episodic psychiatric conditions, it is appropriate to start with this issue. The distinction was called in question by the finding from several different studies that the scores of psychiatric patients on various personality questionnaires became more normal when their episodic conditions remitted (Ingham, 1966; Kerr *et al.*, 1970; Reich *et al.*, 1987). However, that finding is not necessarily relevant if personality disorders are viewed as something more than (or different from) deviant scores on a personality scale. Loranger *et al.* (1991) undertook one of the few pertinent tests in their test—retest study of changes in the diagnosis of personality disorder (on a standardized interview) in a series of 84 psychiatric patients. The investigation is limited by the fact that the interval between assessments was only 1 week to 6 months, but there were major changes in mental state during this period. The key finding was that there was no effect of change in mental state on the diagnosis of personality disorder, supporting the personality disorder—episodic disorder distinction. Nevertheless, remission was associated with some fall in personality disorder symptoms and the diagnosis of personality disorder showed only moderate temporal stability (κ = 0.55).

Rutter, 1977; Rutter and Quinton, 1984 tackled the issue over a longer time span by testing whether personality disorder predicted the course of handicapping symptoms in patients over a 4-year period. The results showed that personality disorder was a strong predictor of course (59% marked persistence versus 18% in those without personality disorder), whereas duration of symptoms was *un*related to outcome in the absence of personality disorder. More recently, Quinton *et al.* (in preparation) examined the course of disorder in the same group of patients over a 15—20-year period. Persistent social role impairment was much more frequent in those diagnosed as showing personality disorder initially (61% versus 17%); moreover this difference was not accounted for by either the length or clinical severity of the initial associated episodic condition. On the other hand, nearly a fifth of the subjects with an initial diagnosis of personality disorder showed no social role impairment at follow-up.

It may be concluded that the empirical findings indicate that the diagnosis of personality disorder is *not* simply synonymous with long-standing or severe episodic disorders. However, that conclusion fails to deal with two other key issues concerning the distinctiveness of personality disorders: the comorbidity with episodic disorders and the distinction between personality disorders and chronic psychiatric conditions.

All clinical studies have shown very high rates of personality disorder in patients with episodic conditions — nearly half in inpatient samples and 20—40% in outpatient groups (Docherty *et al.*, 1986; Tyrer *et al.*, 1991). These figures are much higher than the rates of 6—13% that are typical of general population samples (Casey & Tyrer, 1986; Merikangas & Weissman, 1986). However, even in the latter, comorbidity with episodic disorders is very common (Casey & Tyrer, 1986; Robins & Regier, 1991). The comorbidity cannot be just an artefact of some sort of halo effect in diagnosis at the time of acute mental disturbance because longitudinal studies of patients with personality disorders have shown them to have an increased liability to affective disorders (Docherty *et al.*, 1986).

The implications of this consistent finding for the conceptual separation of personality disorders and episodic conditions will necessarily vary according to the mediating mechanisms involved (Docherty *et al.*, 1986), and these remain quite uncertain (as is the case with most instances of psychiatric comorbidity — see Achenbach, 1990/1991; Caron & Rutter, 1991). Thus, for example, the association could mean that personality disorder constitutes a risk factor for episodic conditions, perhaps because it involved less adequate coping skills or because it created increased psychosocial stressors. If so, the two classes of disorder could be quite distinct in spite of their association. Alternatively, both the personality disorder and the episodic condition could reflect different manifestations of the same underlying liability, in which case the distinction would be a misleading one. Because the mechanisms are not likely to be the same for all varieties of personality disorder, the issues are discussed further below in relation to different personality disorder categories.

What is clear, however, is that the association with episodic conditions is clinically important. The evidence is reasonably consistent that personality disorders are associated with a worse immediate response to treatment and a worse overall outcome for episodic mental disturbances (Docherty *et al.*, 1986; Shea *et al.*, 1990; Reich & Green, 1991). This seems to apply to a range of affective disorders and to panic disorders, and possibly also to obsessional disorders. However, so far as the last is concerned, Baer *et al.* (1992) found that a worse outcome was associated only with schizotypal, borderline and avoidant personality disorders, and with the co-occurrence of several different forms of personality disorder. As with comorbidity, there is a need to elucidate the underlying mechanism. Is it, for example, a question of poor treatment compliance, or does the effect reflect a difference in the meaning of the episodic disorders, or is it just that the presence of personality disorder reflects a greater number or severity of psychosocial stressors and adversities that serve to maintain the episodic condition?

The suggestion that the episodic conditions that accompany personality disorders are in some crucial respects different from those that do not constitutes a real possibility. Thus, for example, several studies have found a lower rate of abnormal responses to the Dexamethasone Suppression Test in patients whose affective disorders were associated with a borderline personality disorder than in those with 'pure' major depressive disorders (Docherty *et al.*, 1986). Also, Rutter *et al.* (in press) found that antisocial disorders and pervasive social malfunction were *not* associated with an increased risk for bipolar affective disorders or for the more severe varieties of unipolar major affective disorder. The meaning of both the comorbidity between personality disorders and episodic conditions and the effect of the former on the course of the latter is an important research issue that has yet to be tackled.

Separation from chronic disorders

The conceptual distinction between personality disorders and chronic psychiatric conditions raises other difficult questions. Usually it has been assumed that the latter are more episodic in their course, do not reflect a basic characterological defect, are more amenable to change, and are ego-dystonic in the sense that they represent a difference from the person's ordinary functioning that is a source of distress to the individual and which the person wishes to change. However, as Hirschfeld (1986) pointed out, none of these assumptions is fully borne out by the empirical evidence, although there may be something to the suggestions. Certainly, it is clear that the treatment of personality disorders poses many problems and that there is a strong tendency to persistence (Liebowitz *et al.*, 1986). However, there is some indication that both drugs (Stein, 1992) and psychological treatments (Higgitt & Fonagy, 1992) may bring limited benefits with adults.

The postulate that personality disorders are in some sense more fundamentally part of a person's basic character than is the case with other psychiatric 'syndromes is a particularly difficult notion to tackle because it is not at all clear what it means. Thus, for example, in what sense is autism (see Chapter 33) or mental retardation (see Chapter 35) or even schizophrenia (see Chapter 34) not part of a person's basic make-up? If the postulate is based on the expectation that the genetic contribution to personality disorders would be greater, that is clearly wrong. As McGuffin and Thapar's (1992) review brings out, there is evidence of genetic influences on several sorts of personality disorder, but these do not stand out as any stronger than those involved in many other psychiatric con-

ditions. Another way of interpreting the postulate would be to suggest that the genetic contribution for personality disorders is the same as that in the related personality dimensions. Such evidence is lacking and, in any case, there is considerable uncertainty on just what is the link between personality dimensions and personality disorders (Rutter, 1987). Broadly comparable issues arise with respect to biological features. There is evidence of biological abnormalities associated with personality disorders (Siever & Davis, 1991), and these do seem to have some parallels with those accompanying extremes of personality dimensions (McBurnett, 1992). However, they overlap to an equal extent with those found with conduct disorders (see Chapter 18) and with hyperkinetic/attention deficit disorders (see Chapter 17).

The problem of this approach is highlighted by the fact that conduct disorders in childhood are treated in the same way as other psychiatric conditions but yet, very frequently, they lead on to syndromes in adult life that are regarded as personality disorders (Robins, 1991; also see Chapter 18). If there is a fundamental distinction between personality disorders and other psychiatric conditions, what does this continuity mean? This difficult question is discussed below in relation to the findings on antisocial personality disorder. However, it is evident that there is no clear-cut separation between personality disorders and other chronic psychiatric conditions.

Differentiations among personality disorders

The World Health Organization (1992) classification, ICD-10, makes a basic differentiation between organic personality disorders (meaning those resulting from a severe head injury, encephalitis and other forms of overt brain disease or damage); enduring personality changes deriving from some catastrophic experience, personality abnormalities that reflect the residue of some mental illness (e.g. residual schizophrenia); and what they term specific personality disorders. The American Psychiatric Association (1987, in press) scheme DSM makes broadly comparable distinctions. This chapter is concerned only with this last group of specific personality disorders, because the others have only an extremely limited application in childhood and adolescence.

However, even this group includes 11 different categories in DSM-IV and nine in ICD-10. The repeated finding (e.g. Pfohl *et al.*, 1986; Morey, 1988; Oldham *et al.*, 1992) that individuals who meet the criteria for one of these personality disorders usually do meet the criteria for one or more others raises serious questions about discriminant validity among the different supposedly specific personality disorders. The issue has been tackled in several different ways. Blashfield (1990) asked a large group of clinicians to assign individual criteria to the existing categories in DSM-III-R and ICD-10. Three main findings stand out: firstly, schizoid and schizotypal personality disorders appeared phenomenologically rather separate from the remainder; secondly, there were many criteria that were placed in different categories by different clinicians (suggesting substantial overlap in meaning among categories); and thirdly, there was poor correspondence between some DSM-III-R and ICD-10 categories with the same name.

Livesley and Schroeder (1990) used factor analysis to examine the constructs associated with personality disorders. Their results suggested that three main dimensions (paranoid behaviour, social avoidance and perceptual-cognitive distortion) might constitute a better basis for classification than the DSM categories. Kass *et al.* (1985) had used a similar approach earlier, with findings that seemed to support the DSM-III-R broad subdivision into the three clusters of odd/eccentric, dramatic/emotional/erratic, and anxious/fearful, and Widiger and Rogers (1989) argued that these might constitute the fundamental distinctions.

Oldham *et al.* (1992) examined the particular patterns of overlap between pairs of personality disorder categories and noted that several appeared counterintuitive — for example, the co-occurrence of borderline and obsessional personality disorders. However, their main recommendation was that, in view of the extensive co-occurrence of supposedly different personality disorder categories, there was a need for a category of extensive personality disorder. Their suggestion is in keeping with Hill *et al.*'s (1989) suggestion that pervasive social role impairment seemed to be the unifying feature across many forms of personality disorder.

Alternative approaches are provided by the pattern of comorbidity with different psychiatric conditions (Docherty *et al.*, 1986; Reich & Thompson, 1987), by family clustering, and by genetic data (Siever & Klar, 1986; McGuffin & Thapar, 1992). On the whole, the patterns of comorbidity with episodic disorders have not been particularly helpful. The anxious/fearful group of personality disorders (including the obsessional type) has been mainly associated with anxiety and obsessional disorders (McKeon *et al.*, 1984; Nestadt *et al.*, 1991), although not in a type-specific fashion. Also, borderline personality disorders have been mainly associated with affective disorders (Docherty *et al.*, 1986). However, in both cases, the specificity of the association is in some doubt because most studies have not been comparative.

The most clear-cut finding from family studies is the association between schizophrenia and a loading of schizotypal personality disorders in the biological relatives (Kendler *et al.*, 1981, 1984). However, a significant (but weaker and less specific) association has been found with paranoid personality disorders (Kendler & Gruenberg, 1982; Kendler *et al.*, 1985). The findings with respect to schizoid personality disorders are contradictory (Kety *et al.*, 1975; Kendler *et al.*, 1984). It may be concluded that the odd/eccentric cluster of personality disorders seems to differ from others in their familial (probably genetic) association with schizophrenia. However, three caveats are necessary. Firstly, it should follow that there is also a familial loading for schizophrenia in the relatives of individuals with a schizotypal personality disorder but this has not been found so far — possibly because of lack of power in the studies (McGuffin & Thapar, 1992). Secondly, the evidence is much stronger in the case of schizotypal personality disorders than with either paranoid or schizoid types. It is probably for

this reason that, in ICD-10, schizotypal disorders are grouped with schizophrenia whereas the other two are not. Thirdly, there is some continuing uncertainty on the key diagnostic features of schizotypal personality disorder and, in particular, on how much weight should be attached to unusual perceptual experiences and odd thinking patterns (in addition to the socioemotional impairment, paranoid features and eccentric behaviour).

The family and genetic data on other personality disorders are distinctly sparse (Merikangas & Weissman, 1986; McGuffin & Thapar, 1992). There is some evidence that borderline personality disorders cluster in families and also are associated with affective disorders in other family members but it remains quite uncertain whether the familial loading has a genetic basis. There seems to be a genetic component to antisocial personality disorder but it may not be very strong. Also little is known about genetic factors in anxious personality disorders. There is evidence from twin studies of a modest genetic component to both specific phobias (Kendler *et al.*, 1992a) and generalized anxiety disorder (Kendler *et al.*, 1992b), but in the latter case it does not seem to be separate from that for depression (Kendler *et al.*, 1992c), and in the former case there seems to be both a general vulnerability to phobias and specific vulnerabilities to particular types of phobia (Kendler *et al.*, 1992a). It is clear that, from a genetic perspective, there must be very considerable uncertainty about the constituents of an anxious personality disorder (Barlow, 1988). However, such evidence as there is there seems to indicate that none of these other personality disorders shows the specific familial association with schizophrenia found with schizotypal personality disorders.

In summary, it may be concluded that there is the best evidence for the distinctiveness of schizotypal personality disorders, although considerable doubts remain on the boundaries with paranoid and schizoid personality disorders. There is some support for the grouping of antisocial, borderline, histrionic and narcissistic categories — the so-called dramatic/emotional erratic cluster, but little validating evidence on the distinctions between them. Least is known about the various anxious/fearful/dependent personality disorders.

SPECIFIC PERSONALITY DISORDERS

In view of the lack of good discriminant validity among the many specific personality disorders (between them, ICD-10 and DSM-IV list 14), only a few of the key categories that may be particularly relevant in childhood and adolescence will be discussed.

Antisocial personality disorders

Although the adjective antisocial might seem to imply that the personality disorder necessarily involves criminal behaviour, it is apparent from DSM-IV (American Psychiatric Association, in press) that this is not so. The diagnostic criteria include an inability to sustain consistent work behaviour, antisocial acts, aggression, failure to honour financial obligation, failure to plan ahead, disregard for the truth, recklessness, irresponsible parenting, failure to sustain a monogamous relationship and a lack of remorse (of which symptoms the individual has to exhibit four or more).

The evidence on the strong links between conduct disorder in childhood and antisocial personality disorder in adult life is reviewed in Chapter 18 and will not be rediscussed here. However, three issues in relation to these findings need some consideration with respect to personality disorders: (1) whether the continuity is only with antisocial personality disorders or whether it extends to other forms of psychopathology; (2) the mediating mechanisms that may underlie this continuity; and (3) whether disturbance of conduct in childhood should be reconceptualized as a personality disorder.

Most early follow-up studies were confined to males and focused almost exclusively on antisocial personality disorder as an outcome so that the first issue could not be addressed adequately. Retrospective data from the American Epidemiological Catchment Area studies were therefore important in their indication that the adult psychopathology associated with conduct disorders in childhood extended substantially more widely, especially in females (Robins, 1986). Findings from childhood to adulthood longitudinal studies in the UK have shown the same (Zoccolillo et al., 1992; Rutter et al., in press). The adult outcome usually seems to involve some form of pervasive social malfunction (and hence presumably some form of personality disorder) but it also includes an increased risk of depressive or dysthymic disorders. In keeping with earlier findings, it is very common, especially in males, for the pervasive social malfunction in adult life to take the form of antisocial personality disorder but it need not do so. These more recent studies also indicate that, at least in groups from a seriously disturbed family background, the adult outcome is worse than the earlier investigations had suggested; the majority of children with conduct disorder showed extensive social difficulties in adult life.

However, this caveat is important in view of the uncertainty on the mechanisms mediating the continuities between childhood and adult life. It is clear that persistence into adult life is more likely with conduct disorders of early onset associated with hyperactivity and poor peer relationships (Loeber & Dishion, 1983; Farrington et al., 1990; Magnusson & Bergman, 1990; Robins, 1991; see Chapter 18). However, it is also apparent that persistence is more likely when there is a parental personality disorder and associated family discord and disorganization (Rutter & Quinton, 1984; Loeber & Stouthamer-Loeber, 1986; Quinton et al., 1990; Sampson & Laub, 1993). There has been a tendency to assume that, because the persistence of conduct disorders is very high, this must imply that it is due to some intrinsic factor in the child. This need not be so. The limited evidence to date suggests only a modest to moderate genetic component (DiLalla & Gottesman, 1989; McGuffin & Thapar, 1992) and there are numerous ways in which strong continuities over time may come about (Rutter, 1989; Rutter & Rutter, 1993), as well as many different ways in which individual characteristics may

play a role in influencing person–environment interactions (Caprara & Rutter, in press; Engfer et al., in press). Thus, there is evidence for effects that come about through the influence of reputations, of acting in ways that bring about further psychosocial stresses and adversities or which fail to promote social ties and supports, and of behaviours that provide negative interpersonal interactions. In their reanalysis of Glueck's follow-up data on delinquent youths, Sampson and Laub (1993) argue persuasively that the key mediator may be the presence or absence of social bonds and controls. Conduct disorder in childhood leads to criminal behaviour in adult life not so much because this is inevitable (although there are important individual influences) but rather because antisocial behaviour in childhood is likely to predispose to weak social commitments in work, friendship and marriage and that these, in turn, make crime in adult life more likely. By the same token, however, if there are sufficiently powerful salient life events and socialization experiences of the right kind in adult life, this strong indirect chain can be broken. Both these results and those of others (Quinton & Rutter, 1988; Quinton et al., 1990) point to the importance of a harmonious marriage in that connection.

These considerations are relevant to the third issue of whether disturbances of conduct should be reconceptualized as personality disorders. The question certainly needs to be addressed in view of the strength of the continuities between the two. However, there are several reasons why that step would seem to carry more disadvantages than advantages. Firstly, by no means all children with conduct disorder go on to exhibit a personality disorder in adult life; even in high-risk groups about a quarter do not. Although there are good pointers to features likely to predispose to a worse adult outcome, prediction at the individual level would still be a rather uncertain matter. Secondly, the risk of personality disorder in adult life may be substantially lower for children with conduct disorder from less disturbed family backgrounds: the possibility certainly needs study. Thirdly, if the continuities are, at least in part, indirectly mediated, it cannot be assumed that the basis for the adult disorder is isomorphic with that for the childhood condition, although it could turn out to be so. Finally, if there is no clear-cut distinction between personality disorders and other psychiatric conditions (see above), it is not obvious what would be gained from this step.

Borderline personality disorder

The overall concept of borderline personality disorder is of a pervasive pattern of instability of interpersonal relationships, self-image, affects and control over impulses. The operationalization of this concept has varied somewhat over the years but the criteria have usually included a pattern of unstable and intense interpersonal relationships with alternating over-idealization and devaluation, frantic efforts to avoid real or imagined abandonment, an unstable or distorted self-image, impulsiveness, recurrent suicidal behaviour, affective instability with intense episodic dysphoria, chronic feelings of emptiness, and a lack of control over anger (American Psychiatric Association, in press). Not surprisingly, in that it is included in the criteria, the diagnosis has been made particularly often in suicidal patients in both adolescence (Martuunen *et al.*, 1991) and adult life. However, the association seems to be not entirely tautological in that, even when that diagnostic criterion was omitted in the Friedman *et al.* (1983) study, patients with both depression and borderline personality disorders, still had an elevated risk of suicidal attempts compared with those depressed patients without borderline personality disorder.

There are several standardized interviews for the diagnosis of borderline personality disorder in adults (Gunderson *et al.*, 1981; Stangl *et al.*, 1985; Loranger *et al.*, 1987), but so far there are none applicable in childhood. Nevertheless, there have been several attempts to apply the adult criteria to children and adolescents (Greenman *et al.*, 1986; Ludolph *et al.*, 1990; Meijer & Treffers, 1991). From the limited available evidence there is more difficulty in doing so in younger age groups than in older teenagers. Ludolph *et al.*'s (1990) comparison of adolescent girls with borderline personality disorder and girls in the same inpatient unit with other psychiatric diagnoses showed that the background factors that most clearly separated the groups were grossly inappropriate parental behaviour, expulsion or removal from the home and sexual abuse. These findings parallel those in adults (Herman *et al.*, 1989; Ogata *et al.*, 1990; Patrick *et al.*, in press). Patrick *et al.* (in press) compared borderline personality disorder and dysthymic patients, finding that the former experienced worse parental care (as assessed on the Parental Bonding Instrument) and more unresolved/disorganized attachment relationships (as assessed on the Adult Attachment Interview). They argued that adults' modes of representing adverse early experiences may be intimately related to styles of interpersonal functioning and that borderline personality disorder may be associated with a particular kind of representational thought. The notion warrants further exploration, and follow-up studies of children exposed to sexual abuse (see Chapter 14) and those experiencing grossly disrupted attachment experiences (see Chapter 28) would be particularly informative. Probably these would be more useful than attempts to devise a set of criteria that could be applied as such to younger age groups. However, borderline personality disorder is a diagnosis that needs to be considered in adolescents and the adult criteria appear reasonably applicable, at least during the later teenage years.

Schizotypal personality disorder

The general concept of schizotypal personality disorder is that of a pervasive pattern of social and interpersonal deficits marked by acute discomfort with, and reduced capacity for, close relationships as well as by cognitive or perceptual distortions and eccentricities of behaviour, beginning by early adulthood (American Psychiatric Association, in press). There has been only a small number of attempts to apply the criteria

in childhood but one study suggested an overlap with pervasive developmental disorders, although not autism as such (Nagy & Szatmari, 1986); another suggested a course similar to that of schizophrenia arising in childhood (Asarnow & Ben-Meir, 1988); and a third suggested that there was a pattern of communication deficits similar to, but milder than, those found in schizophrenia (Caplin & Guthrie, 1992). There is every reason to suppose that the concept of a spectrum of schizophrenic disorders, including schizotypal personality disorder, applies in the preadult years as well as later. However, whether the diagnosis can be made reliably and validly in childhood is another matter, and that has still to be determined.

Schizoid personality disorder

The usual concept of schizoid personality disorder is of a pervasive pattern of detachment from social relationships and a restricted range of expression of emotions in interpersonal settings (American Psychiatric Association, in press). Thus, ICD-10 criteria (World Health Organization, 1992) include a lack of pleasure in activities, emotional coldness, apparent indifference to praise or criticism, a limited capacity to express either positive or negative emotions, and lack of close friends, a preference for solitary activities, a marked insensitivity to prevailing social norms and an excessive preoccupation with fantasy and introspection. The literature on the syndrome is almost confined to adults. However, since the 1970s (Wolff & Barlow, 1979), Wolff has pressed the case for the application of the diagnosis in childhood. Unfortunately for comparative purposes, her criteria differ in several key respects from those generally applied with adults. Thus, she has specified *increased* sensitivity and paranoid ideas, whereas ICD-10 and DSM-IV indicate marked *insensitivity*, and she has included an unusual or odd style of communicating which would ordinarily be part of schizotypal, not schizoid, personality disorders (Wolff & Chick, 1980; Wolff, 1991a,b). The initial findings in childhood suggested some similarities with autism (Wolff & Barlow, 1979) and the follow-up showed substantial continuity with schizotypal personality disorder in adult life (Wolff *et al.*, 1991). She put the case that her concept is similar to that of Asperger (see Chapter 33) and used her findings to argue for a continuum between autism and schizophrenia. The genetic data make that implausible but certainly it is the case that both conditions are associated with developmental and social abnormalities in childhood (see Chapter 34).

It cannot be claimed that anyone's concepts of the different varieties of personality disorder are well-validated and it is all too evident that there is an undesirable overlap between the criteria for schizoid and schizotypal personality disorders, and between both of these and Asperger's syndrome. Wolff's follow-up data are convincing in their demonstration that her criteria were successful in picking out a group of children with disorders that would show a high degree of persistence into adult life. On the other hand, as she has suggested (Wolff, 1989), it may well turn out that her concept covers a heterogeneous group of conditions.

UTILITY OF PERSONALITY DISORDER DIAGNOSES IN CHILDHOOD

In concluding the chapter, it is necessary to return to the question with which it began — whether it is useful to apply personality disorder diagnoses in childhood. The answer is implicit in both the ideas and findings that have been reviewed. Unquestionably, it has been informative to study continuities in psychopathology between childhood and adult life. Indeed, that appears to be a particularly valuable research strategy provided that it seeks to identify mechanisms as well as quantify statistical connections. Thus, the adult outcome findings for conduct disorder in childhood have done much both to validate the diagnosis and to raise important questions about heterogeneity and about mediating mechanisms. Similarly, the childhood antecedents of borderline personality disorder may turn out to be very useful in delineating the aetiological pathways involved in this form of adult psychopathology. The neurodevelopmental factors involved in schizophrenia (see Chapter 34) have been helpful in opening up a new approach to the pathogenesis of that disorder and studies of schizoid and schizotypal phenomena may ultimately also be informative in the same connection.

It is likely that a study of developmental processes in relation to a wide range of psychopathology will prove informative on some of the mechanisms involved in continuity (Rutter & Rutter, 1993; Rutter, in press). That should include psychobiological approaches to personality variables that seem to create a psychiatric risk (McBurnett, 1992). However, the lack of a clear demarcation between personality disorders and other psychiatric conditions indicates that there are no particular theoretical implications of whether or not personality disorders are diagnosed in early life. The evidence suggests that practical considerations will mean that some extrapolations downwards will be easier than others and there does not seem much to be gained by forcing childhood disorders into adult criteria. On the other hand, equally, child psychiatrists need to pay close attention to the findings on adult disorders in order to consider which have implications for child and adolescent psychiatry. Also, it is apparent that at least some of the personality disorder concepts are applicable during adolescence and need to be considered clinically (as well as investigated further) in this age period.

CONCLUSIONS

It is easy to cast scorn on concepts of personality disorder, arguing that they are mythical entities (Blackburn, 1988), and it is all too obvious that many basic questions about their conceptualization and meaning remain, as almost all reviews cited in this chapter have concluded. Nevertheless, as the same reviews have shown, the concepts have come into being because there are important clinical phenomena that have to be accounted for. Substantial progress has been made delineating the key issues, and research over the years to come should serve to determine which diagnostic distinctions are useful and which are not.

REFERENCES

Achenbach T.M. (1990/1991) 'Comorbidity' in child and adolescent psychiatry: categorical and quantitative perspectives. *Journal of Child and Adolescent Psychopharmacology*, **1**, 271−278.

American Psychiatric Association (1987) *Diagnostic and Statistical Manual of Mental Disorders*, 3rd edn. − revised; DSM-III-R. American Psychiatric Association, Washington, DC.

American Psychiatric Association (1994) *Diagnostic and Statistical Manual of Mental Disorders*, 4th edn (DSM-IV). American Psychiatric Association, Washington, DC.

Asarnow J.R. & Ben-Meir S. (1988) Children with schizophrenia spectrum and depressive disorders: a comparative study of premorbid adjustment, onset pattern and severity of impairment. *Journal of Child Psychology and Psychiatry*, **29**, 477−488.

Baer L., Jenike M., Black D.W., Treece C., Rosenfeld R. & Greist J. (1992) Effect of axis II diagnoses on treatment outcome with clomipramine in 55 patients with obsessive-compulsive disorder. *Archives of General Psychiatry*, **49**, 862−866.

Barlow D.H. (1988) *Anxiety and its Disorders: The Nature and Treatment of Anxiety and Panic*. Guilford Press, New York.

Blackburn R. (1988) On moral judgements and personality disorders: the myth of psychopathic personality revisited. *British Journal of Psychiatry*, **153**, 505−512.

Blashfield R.K. (1990) An American view of the ICD-10 personality disorders. *Acta Psychiatrica Scandinavica*, **82**, 250−256.

Caplin R. & Guthrie D. (1992) Communication deficits in childhood schizotypal personality disorder. *Journal of the American Academy of Child and Adolescent Psychiatry*, **31**, 961−967.

Caprara G.V. & Rutter M. (in press) Individual development and social change: Some concepts and issues. In Rutter M. & Smith D. (eds) *Psychosocial Disorders in Young People: Time Trends and Their Origins*. Wiley, Chichester.

Caron C. & Rutter M. (1991) Comorbidity in child psychopathology: concepts, issues and research strategies. *Journal of Child Psychology and Psychiatry*, **32**, 1063−1080.

Casey P.R. & Tyrer P.J. (1986) Personality, functioning and symptomatology. *Journal of Psychiatric Research*, **20**, 363−374.

Cleckley H. (1941) *The Mask of Sanity*. Henry Kimpton, London.

DiLalla L.F. & Gottesman I.I. (1989) Heterogeneity of causes for delinquency and criminality: lifespan perspective. *Development and Psychopathology*, **1**, 339−349.

Docherty J.P., Fiester S.J. & Shea T. (1986) Syndrome diagnosis and personality disorder. In: Frances A.J. & Hales R.E. (eds) *American Psychiatric Association Annual Review*, vol. 5, pp. 315−355. American Psychiatric Press, Washington, DC.

Engfer A., Walper S. & Rutter M. (1994) Individual characteristics as a force in development. In: Rutter M. & Hay D.F. (eds) *Development through Life: A Handbook for Clinicians*, pp. 79−111. Blackwell Scientific Publications, Oxford.

Farrington D.P., Loeber R. & Van Kannen W.B. (1990) Long-term criminal outcomes of hyperactivity-impulsivity-attention deficit and conduct problems in childhood. In: Robins L. & Rutter M. (eds) *Straight and Devious Pathways from Childhood to Adulthood*, pp. 62−81. Cambridge University Press, Cambridge.

Frances A.J. & Widiger T. (1986) The classification of personality disorders: an overview of problems and solutions. In: Frances A.J. & Hales R.E. (eds) *American Psychiatric Association Annual Review*, vol. 5, pp. 240−258. American Psychiatric Press, Washington, DC.

Friedman R.C., Arnoff M.P., Clarkin J.F., Corn R. & Hurt S.W. (1983) History of suicidal behavior in depressed borderline patients. *American Journal of Psychiatry*, **140**, 1023−1026.

Frith U. (1991) *Autism and Asperger Syndrome*. Cambridge University Press, Cambridge.

Greenman D.A., Gunderson J.G., Cane M. & Saltzman P.R. (1986)

An examination of the borderline diagnosis in children. *American Journal of Psychiatry*, **143**, 998−1003.

Gunderson J.G. & Singer M.T. (1975) Defining borderline patients: an overview. *American Journal of Psychiatry*, **132**, 1−10.

Gunderson J.G., Kolb J.E. & Austin V. (1981) The diagnostic interview for borderline patients. *American Journal of Psychiatry*, **138**, 896−903.

Hare R.D. (1970) *Psychopathy: Theory and Research*. John Wiley, New York.

Henderson D.K. (1939) *Psychopathic States*. Norton, New York.

Herman J.L., Perry J.C. & van de Kolk B.A. (1989) Childhood trauma in borderline personality disorder. *American Journal of Psychiatry*, **146**, 490−495.

Higgitt A. & Fonagy P. (1992) Psychotherapy in borderline and narcissistic personality disorder. *British Journal of Psychiatry*, **161**, 23−43.

Hill J., Harrington R., Fudge H., Rutter M. & Pickles A. (1989) The adult personality functioning assessment: development and reliability. *British Journal of Psychiatry*, **155**, 24−35.

Hirschfeld R.M.A. (1986) Forward to section III − personality disorders. In: Frances A.J. & Hales R.E. (eds) *American Psychiatric Association Annual Review*, vol. 5, pp. 233−239. American Psychiatric Press, Washington, DC.

Ingham J.G. (1966) Changes in MPI scores in neurotic patients; a three year follow-up. *British Journal of Psychiatry*, **112**, 931−939.

Kass F., Skodal A.E., Charles E., Spitzer R.L. & Williams J.B.W. (1985) Scaled ratings of DSM-II personality disorders. *American Journal of Psychiatry*, **142**, 627−630.

Kendler K.S. & Gruenberg A.M. (1982) Genetic relationship between paranoid personality disorder and the 'schizophrenic spectrum' disorders. *American Journal of Psychiatry*, **139**, 1185−1186.

Kendler K.S., Gruenberg A.M. & Strauss J.S. (1981) An independent analysis of the Copenhagen sample of the Danish adoption study of schizophrenia. II. The relationship between schizotypal personality disorders and schizophrenia. *Archives of General Psychiatry*, **38**, 982−984.

Kendler K.S., Masterson C.C., Ungaro R. & Davis K.L. (1984) A family history study of schizophrenic related personality disorders. *American Journal of Psychiatry*, **141**, 424−427.

Kendler K.S., Masterson C.C. & Davis K.L. (1985) Psychiatric illness in first-degree relatives of patients with paranoid psychosis, schizophrenia and medical illness. *British Journal of Psychiatry*, **147**, 524−532.

Kendler K.S., Neale M.C., Kessler R.C., Heath A.C. & Eaves L.J. (1992a) The genetic epidemiology of phobias in women: the interrelationship of agoraphobia, social phobia, situational phobia and simple phobia. *Archives of General Psychiatry*, **49**, 273−281.

Kendler K.S., Neale M.C., Kessler R.C., Heath A.C. & Eaves L.J. (1992b) Generalized anxiety disorder in women: a population-based twin study. *Archives of General Psychiatry*, **49**, 267−272.

Kendler K.S., Neale M.C., Kessler R.C., Heath A.C. & Eaves L.J. (1992c) Major depression and generalized anxiety disorder: same genes, (partly) different environments? *Archives of General Psychiatry*, **49**, 716−722.

Kernberg O.F. (1967) Borderline personality organization. *Journal of the American Psychoanalytic Association (New York)*, **15**, 641−685.

Kernberg O.F. (1975) *Borderline Conditions and Pathological Narcissism*. Jason Aronson, New York.

Kerr T.A., Schapira D., Roth M. & Garside R.F. (1970) The relationship between the Maudsley Personality Inventory and the course of affective disorders. *British Journal of Psychiatry*, **116**, 11−19.

Kety S.S., Rosenthal D. & Wender P.H. (1971) Mental illness in the biological and adoptive families of adopted schizophrenics. *American Journal of Psychiatry*, **128**, 302−306.

Kety S.S., Rosenthal D., Wender P., Schulsinger F. & Jacobsen B.

(1975) Mental illness in the biological adoptive families who have become schizophrenic: a preliminary report based on psychiatric interviews. In: Fieve R., Rosenthal D. & Brill H. (eds) *Genetic Research in Psychiatry*, pp. 147−166. Johns Hopkins University Press, Baltimore, MD.

Liebowitz M.R., Stone M.H. & Turkat D. (1986) Treatment of personality disorders. In: Frances A.J. & Hales R.E. (eds) *American Psychiatric Association*, vol. 5, pp. 356−393. American Psychiatric Press, Washington, DC.

Livesley W.J. & Schroeder M.L. (1990) Dimensions of personality disorder. The DSM-III-R cluster A diagnoses. *Journal of Nervous and Mental Disease*, **178**, 627−635.

Loeber R. & Dishion T.J. (1983) The predictors of male delinquency: a review. *Psychological Bulletin*, **94**, 68−99.

Loeber R. & Stouthamer-Loeber M. (1986) Family factors as correlates and predictors of juvenile conduct problems and delinquency. In: Tonry M. & Morris N. (eds) *Crime and Justice*, vol. 7, pp. 29−149. Chicago University Press, Chicago, IL.

Loranger A.W., Susman V.L., Oldham J.M. & Russakoff L.M. (1987) The personality disorder examination: a preliminary report. *Journal of Personality Disorders*, **1**, 1−13.

Loranger A.W., Lenzenweger M.F., Gartner A.F., Susman V.L., Herzig J., Zammit G.K., Gartner J.D., Abrams R.C. & Young R.C. (1991) Trait−state artifacts and the diagnosis of personality disorders. *Archives of General Psychiatry*, **48**, 720−728.

Ludolph P.S., Westen D., Misle B., Jackson A., Wixom M.A. & Wiss C. (1990) The borderline diagnosis in adolescents: symptoms and developmental history. *Archives of General Psychiatry*, **147**, 470−476.

McBurnett K. (1992) Psychobiological approaches to personality and their applications to child psychopathology. In: Lahey B.B. & Kazdin A.E. (eds) *Advances in Clinical Child Psychology*, vol. 14, pp. 107−164. Plenum, New York.

McGuffin P. & Thapar A. (1992) The genetics of personality disorder. *British Journal of Psychiatry*, **160**, 12−23.

McKeon J., Roa B. & Mann A. (1984) Life events and personality traits in obsessive-compulsive neurosis. *British Journal of Psychiatry*, **144**, 185−189.

Magnusson D. & Bergman L.R. (1990) A pattern approach to the study of pathways from childhood to adulthood. In: Robins L. & Rutter M. (eds) *Straight and Devious Pathways from Childhood to Adulthood*, pp. 101−115. Cambridge University Press, Cambridge.

Martuunen M.J., Aro H.M., Henriksson M.M. & Lönnquist J.K. (1991) Mental disorders in adolescent suicide: DSM-III-R axes I and II diagnoses among 13−19-year-olds in Finland. *Archives of General Psychiatry*, **48**, 834−839.

Meehl P.E. (1962) Schizotaxia, schizotypy, schizophrenia. *American Psychologist*, **17**, 827−838.

Meijer M. & Treffers P.D.A. (1991) Borderline and schizotypal disorders in children and adolescents. *British Journal of Psychiatry*, **158**, 205−212.

Merikangas K.R. & Weissman M.M. (1986) Epidemiology of DSM-III axis II personality disorders. In: Frances A.J. & Hales R.E. (eds) *American Psychiatric Association Annual Review*, vol. 5, pp. 258−278. American Psychiatric Press, Washington, DC.

Morey L.C. (1988) Personality disorders in DSM-III and DSM-III-R: convergence, coverage and internal consistency. *American Journal of Psychiatry*, **145**, 573−577.

Nagy J. & Szatmari P. (1986) A chart review of schizotypal personality disorders in children. *Journal of Autism and Developmental Disorders*, **16**, 351−367.

Nestadt G., Romanoski A.E., Brown C.H., Chahal R., Merchant A., Folstein M.F., Gruenberg E.M. & McHugh R.R. (1991) DSM-III compulsive personality disorder: an epidemiological survey. *Psychological Medicine*, **21**, 461−471.

Ogata S.N., Silk K.R., Goodrich S., Lohr N.E., Westen D. & Hill E.M.

(1990) Childhood sexual and physical abuse in adult patients with borderline personality disorder. *American Journal of Psychiatry*, **147**, 1008–1013.

Oldham J.M., Skodol A.E., Kellman H.D., Hyler S.E., Rosnick L. & Davies M. (1992) Diagnosis of DSM-III-R personality disorders by two structured interviews: patterns of comorbidity. *American Journal of Psychiatry*, **149**, 213–220.

Patrick M., Hobson R.P., Castle D., Howard R. & Maughan B. (in press) Personality Disorder and the Mental Representation of Early Social Experience. *Development and Psychopathology*.

Pfohl B., Coryell W., Zimmerman M. & Stangl D.A. (1986) DSM-III personality disorders: diagnostic overlap and internal consistency of individual DSM-III criteria. *Comprehensive Psychiatry*, **27**, 21–34.

Quinton D. & Rutter M. (1988) *Parenting Breakdown: The Making and Breakdown of Intergenerational Links*, Averbury, Aldershot, Hampshire.

Quinton D., Rutter M. & Gulliver L. (1990) Continuities in psychiatric disorders from childhood to adulthood in the children of psychiatric patients. In: Robins L. & Rutter M. (eds) *Straight and Devious Pathways from Childhood to Adulthood*, pp. 259–278. Cambridge University Press, Cambridge.

Quinton D., Gulliver L. & Rutter M. (in press) A fifteen to twenty year follow-up of adult psychiatric patients. I: Psychiatric disorder and social functioning. *British Journal of Psychiatry*.

Reich J.H. & Green A. (1991) Effect of personality disorders on outcome of treatment. *Journal of Nervous and Mental Disease*, **179**, 74–82.

Reich J. & Thompson W. (1987) DSM-III Personality disorder clusters in three populations. *British Journal of Psychiatry*, **150**, 471–475.

Reich J., Noyes R., Hirschfeld R., Coryell W. & O'Gorman T. (1987) State effects on personality measures in depressed and panic patients. *American Journal of Psychiatry*, **144**, 181–187.

Robins L.N. (1966) *Deviant Children Grown Up*. Williams & Wilkins, Co. Baltimore, MD.

Robins L.N. (1978) Sturdy childhood predictors of adult antisocial behavior: replications from longitudinal studies. *Psychological Medicine*, **8**, 611–622.

Robins L.N. (1986) The consequences of conduct disorder in girls. In: Olweus D., Block J. & Radke-Yarrow M. (eds) *Development of Antisocial and Prosocial Behaviour: Research, Theories and Issues*, pp. 385–414. Academic Press, Orlando, FL.

Robins L.N. (1991) Conduct disorder. *Journal of Child Psychology and Psychiatry*, **32**, 193–212.

Robins L.N. & Regier D.A. (eds) (1991) *Psychiatric Disorders in America: The Epidemiologic Catchment Area Study*. The Free Press, New York.

Rutter M. (1977) Prospective studies to investigate behavioral change. In: Strauss J.S., Babigian H.M. & Rolff M. (eds) *The Origins and Course of Psychopathology*, pp. 223–247. Plenum, New York.

Rutter M. (1987) Temperament, personality and personality disorder. *British Journal of Psychiatry*, **150**, 433–458.

Rutter M. (1989) Pathways from childhood to adult life. *Journal of Child Psychology and Psychiatry*, **30**, 23–51.

Rutter M. (1993) Developmental psychopathology as a research perspective. In: Magnusson D. & Casaer P. (eds) *Longitudinal Research on Individual Development: Present Status and Future Perspectives*, pp. 127–152. Cambridge University Press, Cambridge.

Rutter M. & Quinton D. (1984) Parental psychiatric disorder: effects on children. *Psychological Medicine*, **14**, 853–880.

Rutter M. & Rutter M. (1993) *Developing Minds: Challenge and Continuity Across the Lifespan*. Penguin, Harmondsworth, Middlesex/Basic Books, New York.

Rutter M., Harrington R., Quinton D. & Pickles A. (1994) Adult

outcome of conduct disorder in childhood: Implications for concepts and definitions of patterns of psychopathology. In: Ketterlinus R.D. & Lamb M.E. (eds) *Adolescent Problem Behaviors: Issues and research*, pp. 52–80. Lawrence Erlbaum Associates, Hillsdale, NJ.

Sampson R.J. & Laub J.H. (1993) Crime and deviance in the life course. *Annual Review of Sociology*, **18**, 63–84.

Schneider K. (1923) *Die Psychopathischen Personlichkeiten*. Springer, Berlin.

Schneider K. (1950) *Psychopathic Personalities*, 9th edn. (English translation, 1958.) Cassell, London.

Shea M.Y., Pilkonis P.A., Beckham E., Collins J.F., Elkin I., Sotsky S.M. & Docherty J.P. (1990) Personality disorders and treatment outcome in the NIMH treatment of depression collaborative research program. *American Journal of Psychiatry*, **147**, 711–718.

Siever L.J. & Davis K. (1991) A psychobiological perspective on the personality disorders. *American Journal of Psychiatry*, **148**, 1647–1658.

Siever L.J. & Klar H. (1986) A review of DSM-III criteria for the personality disorders. In: Frances A.J. & Hales R.E. (eds) *American Psychiatric Association Annual Review*, vol. 5, pp. 279–314. American Psychiatric Press, Washington, DC.

Spitzer R.L., Endicott J. & Gibbon A.M. (1979) Crossing the border into borderline personality and borderline schizophrenia: the development of criteria. *Archives of General Psychiatry*, **36**, 17–24.

Stangl D., Pfohl B., Zimmermann M., Bowers W. & Corenthal C. (1985) A structured interview for the DSM-III personality disorders. *Archives of General Psychiatry*, **42**, 591–596.

Stein G. (1992) Drug treatment of the personality disorders. *British Journal of Psychiatry*, **161**, 167–184.

Tarnopolsky A. & Berelowitz M. (1987) Borderline personality: a review of recent research. *British Journal of Psychiatry*, **151**, 724–734.

Tyrer P. (ed) (1988) *Personality Disorders: Diagnosis, Management and Course*. Wright, London.

Tyrer P., Casey P. & Ferguson B. (1991) Personality disorder in perspective. *British Journal of Psychiatry*, **159**, 463–472.

Widiger T.A. & Rogers J.H. (1989) Prevalence and comorbidity of personality disorders. *Psychiatric Annals*, **19**, 132–136.

Wolff S. (1989) Schizoid disorders of childhood and adolescence. In: Last C.G. & Hersen M. (eds) *Handbook of Child Psychiatric Diagnosis*, pp. 209–232. John Wiley, New York.

Wolff S. (1991a) 'Schizoid' personality in childhood and adult life. I: The vagaries of diagnostic labelling. *British Journal of Psychiatry*, **159**, 615–619.

Wolff S. (1991b) 'Schizoid' personality in childhood and adult life. III: The childhood picture. *British Journal of Psychiatry*, **159**, 629–635.

Wolff S. & Barlow A. (1979) Schizoid personality in childhood: a comparative study of schizoid, autistic and normal children. *Journal of Child Psychology and Psychiatry*, **20**, 29–46.

Wolff S. & Chick J. (1980) Schizoid personality in childhood: a controlled follow-up study. *Psychological Medicine*, **10**, 85–100.

Wolff S., Townshend R., McGuire R.J. & Weeks D.J. (1991) 'Schizoid' personality in childhood and adult life. II. Adult adjustment and the continuity with schizotypal personality disorder. *British Journal of Psychiatry*, **159**, 620–628.

World Health Organization (1992) *ICD-10: The ICD-10 Classification of Mental and Behavioural Disorders. Clinical Descriptions and Diagnostic Guidelines*. World Health Organization, Geneva.

Zoccolillo M., Pickles A., Quinton D. & Rutter M. (1992) The outcome of childhood conduct disorder: implications for defining adult personality disorder and conduct disorder. *Psychological Medicine*, **22**, 971–986.

Chapter 39
Psychiatric Aspects of
Somatic Disease and Disorders

David A. Mrazek

The impact of chronic paediatric illnesses on child development has been well-recognized (Pless & Roghmann, 1971; Cadman *et al.*, 1987; Gortmaker *et al.*, 1990). These reports indicate that the risk for psychological problems is approximately twice the rate of disturbance found in children without chronic illness. However, the majority of children with chronic medical illnesses do not have a psychiatric illness. In those children who have developed a psychiatric disturbance, the thesis has been developed that their severe paediatric illness may have contributed as a risk factor to the development of their psychopathology. While a high degree of individual variability exists, elevated rates of affective disorder and anxiety disorders have been noted in some clinical samples of children with physical illnesses. However, there is little evidence to suggest a strong association between chronic medical disability and the onset of either schizophrenia or autism, with the exception of associations, such as temporal lobe epilepsy and encephalitis, which most plausibly reflects a possible common organic aetiology.

A systematic approach to understanding the range of negative outcomes associated with serious paediatric illnesses can be facilitated by taking the perspective that the adaptation of children is in large part the product of the relevant risk and protective factors that shape their experiences and ultimately impact the expression of their genes. An emotionally well-adjusted child with a supportive family who has experienced a series of early successes can be expected to cope well with the early onset of a serious physical illness. This is not to suggest that the physical symptoms and emotional disruptions associated with the disease do not provide a challenge for both the child and the family, but ráther that the child will eventually succeed in meeting the challenge. In contrast, an infant with a difficult temperament who early in life is hard to soothe is likely to experience less appropriate and sensitive early parental stimulation and is subsequently more likely to develop insecure attachment relationships. For a child with few early successes and some biological limitations, the onset of a severe physical illness may prove to be overwhelming. When the onset of severe physical disease occurs simultaneously with other disruptions in the emotional homeostasis of the child, the risk for a negative outcome is enhanced. The evidence that such negative reciprocal interactions are central to problems in emotional development is primarily clinical, although additive models highlighting the impact of multiple hospitalizations have empirical support (Quinton & Rutter, 1976).

While there is little evidence to suggest that early severe chronic paediatric disease is a primary risk factor for psychotic illnesses, the onset of frightening physical symptoms can precipitate an initial psychotic episode. More generally, if the emotional burdens required to manage the child's physical disease are sufficiently great, these life stressors may precipitate the initial expression of other psychiatric disturbances. The precise mechanisms by which such psychiatric vulnerabilities are unmasked are still poorly understood, but through the study of children at high genetic risk for both a psychiatric and medical disorder, physiological and environmental factors that affect gene expression will become clearly elucidated.

Two strategies exist for the investigation of these important interactions. The first is to quantify a wide range of potential stressors for the target disease and carefully monitor the initial expression and subsequent exacerbations of illness in vulnerable children. An alternative is to examine carefully the recent past experience of children who have had a recent onset of a significant disease. This second strategy is subject to the serious methodological weakness of retrospective justification. However, given the current state of our understanding of these interactions, new data derived from retrospective studies are still needed in order to design what should ultimately be more informative prospective assessments.

Another major research strategy is to identify illness-specific factors. This has the attractive feature of being more precise. While it is possible to speculate that a particular physiological mechanism may link the symptoms of a physical illness and a set of psychiatric symptoms, there are surprisingly few models. An exception is the clinically observed association that depression is common in children with severe asthma. Three competitive neurobiological hypotheses exists. The first is that an underlying disturbance in autonomic regulation such as a shift in the sensitivity of cholinergic receptors to parasympathetic stimulation (Cockcroft *et al.*, 1977) may place a child at greater risk for environmentally triggered bronchial constriction while at the same time influencing the central nervous system in such a way as to result in increased dysphoric mood (Charney *et al.*, 1981; Miller, 1987; Mrazek & Klinnert, 1991). A second potential mechanism could be that the contents of mast cells or basophils are released as a consequence of an immunologically mediated immunoglobulin E (IgE) reaction. These cells contain a wide range of substances that include both bronchial constrictors and neuropeptides (Leff, 1988) and some of these neurohumoral proteins have been shown to be involved in central neuroregulation of dysphoric states (Snyder, 1980, 1982). A third potential mechanism could be primarily genetic, based on the possibility that a major gene involved in the regulation of respiratory control and a major gene involved in the regulation of central neurotransmitters are located in close proximity to each other on the same chromosome. Yet another hypothesis is that psychophysiological changes are secondary to the negative subjective experiences of the asthmatic child and this explanation is based on the observation that severe episodes of respiratory insufficiency are often described as extremely frustrating and result in considerable social restrictions. The chronic experience of severe attacks subsequently becomes linked to repeated episodes of unhappiness, discouragement and depressed mood (see Chapter 42). Only through systematic investigations will the most salient mechanism or combination of mechanisms responsible for this phenomenon become more clearly understood. Unfortunately, such investigations are difficult to conduct as a consequence of current methodological limitations. To continue the previous illustration, the study of depression in physically ill children is often confounded by the use of instruments designed to assess mood disturbance that equate physical symptoms with signs of affective disease. Clearly, there has been considerable progress in this area (Heiligenstein & Jacobsen, 1988). More definitive studies will be possible once biological markers for affective disturbance have been clearly established.

ILLNESS-SPECIFIC RISK FACTORS

A quantitative and analytical approach to the examination of the relationship of paediatric illness to early emotional development can be facilitated by conceptualizing the occurrence of a physical illness as a complex set of emotional stressors that have specific component characteristics. Such a frame of reference increases the precision with which variability in psychological outcome can be examined. This strategy also provides a bridge between those clinical investigators interested in studying the effects of chronic illness as a generic condition and other researchers who have been interested in evaluating components of one of several specificity hypotheses that suggest that particular medical conditions are associated with more distinctive behavioural outcomes. If two diseases share similar illness-specific risk factors, it is logical to expect that their impact on emotional development should be similar. In contrast, if two illnesses share only a single characteristic such as persistent chronicity, but have different causes, courses and outcomes, it would *not* be reasonable to expect that such contrasting conditions would have a similar impact on the emotional adjustment of a child.

Age of child at time of illness onset

To appreciate the impact of specific risk factors on development, it is necessary to place the onset of the illness into a developmental context. Clearly, stressors that are particularly disruptive for toddlers are quite different from those stressors that are disorganizing for adolescents. Furthermore, the concept of illness for children evolves in parallel with their cognitive development (Burbach & Peterson, 1986; Perrin & Gerrity, 1981; Millstein *et al.*, 1981).

Early studies of hospitalization suggest that the separation phenomenon was particularly difficult for children in their second to fourth years of life (Prugh *et al.*, 1953). In examining the very early experiences of severely asthmatic children with multiple hospitalizations in the first 3 years of life, a sensitive period between 6 months and 2 years also seemed to be associated with later behavioural difficulties (Mrazek, 1993). Given that disruptions in formation of primary attachment relationships during the first 2 years of life have been shown to have persistent effects on later relationships, those illnesses that result in unplanned and prolonged early separations from primary attachment figures would be predicted to have a more disruptive effect on subsequent emotional development.

During the school years, illnesses that interfere with the participation of children in normal family and school events are conceptualized to be particularly potent stressors. During this period, sex differences also begin to play a role. Boys appear to be more sensitive to illnesses that interfere with their ability to participate in athletics, while girls may be more sensitive to problems that result in their not being able to participate fully in the support provided by their school-age peer group.

In adolescence, diseases that interfere with the process of establishing greater independence are particularly problematic (Orr *et al.*, 1984). Acceptance by a peer group and development of an intimate sexual relationship become critical. Medical problems with sexual stigma such as venereal disease or that involve physical deformity such as facial burns or injury can have a more dramatic emotional impact than more debilitating illnesses that are essentially invisible (Love *et al.*, 1987).

Given that developmental capacities and issues shape how children perceive their illnesses, it is surprising how little empirical research has been directed towards examining the impact of age of onset of illness on children with specific paediatric diagnoses. One factor that complicates such investigations is the limitations in current methods of assessing the efficacy of familial protective factors that clearly affect the outcome of the child. In this regard, a family that may be particularly good at providing a secure environment for a young child may find it difficult to facilitate the independence of a teenager who suffers from an illness that requires careful management. More attention to the developmental implications of both the course of paediatric illness and the appropriate family responses is needed in order to clarify how significant these developmental factors are in the ultimate expression of psychological disturbance.

Parental responsibility related to the paediatric illness

A powerful factor related to the adaptation of a child to serious paediatric illness is the response of the family. While problematic parenting should be considered a major risk factor, exceptionally sensitive and effective parenting could well be conceptualized as a potent protective factor. Chronic paediatric illness has been conceptualized as a stressor on the parent's marriage that can further interfere with parenting (Sabbeth & Leventhal, 1984). Given that siblings of children with chronic illness have also been reported to have more behaviour problems (Tritt & Esses, 1988) there is some evidence of considerable system dysfunction that may be mediated through some breakdown in parenting effectiveness. While deriving a definition of adequate parenting is surprisingly difficult, this methodological step forward is necessary in order to categorize more protective families reliably. Negative parenting has been more frequently described.

Unfortunately, in some circumstances parents actually play a role in the onset of a paediatric illness through negligence, poor judgement, or frank abuse. In the most extreme example, Münchausen's syndrome by proxy, a parent intentionally creates illness. A wide range of physical illnesses have been simulated by disturbed parents (Meadow, 1982, 1985). What is critical to consider is that parents may not share the commitment of the medical teams to cure the illness of the child. If this is the case, the disturbed behaviour of the parent is likely to be far more problematic for the ultimate psychological adaptation of the child than any discomfort or disruption associated with the illness.

Another circumstance that can influence the ability of the family to support the medical plan is when an accidental injury occurs as the result of an action by the parent. An illustration would be the case of a father who is responsible for a vehicle collision in which he is uninjured, but his daughter sustains multiple fractures. The capacity of the father to be able to focus on his daughter's recovery as a primary goal despite his own emotional reactions and guilt can have a very positive impact on her recovery as well as his ultimate working-through of the feelings associated with the accident.

In other circumstances, it is even more difficult to attribute responsibility. For example, when a child develops a severe infectious illness during a period of intense family stress, an appropriate question to raise is whether any actions taken by the parents could have prevented the illness if they had not been overwhelmed in their attempts to cope with other life events. Specifically, caretaking questions such as whether the child should have been left in a strange child-care centre or exposed to a sick child are quite concrete and may provide a proximal link between parental action and the onset of the illness. Subsequently, the issue of whether the child received prompt treatment for the infection is legitimate to raise and may well have affected the course. The temptation is to provide reassurance to the parents by minimizing the links between their actions and the course of the physical illness.

Such a strategy is often supported by the belief that any guilt that the parents sustain as a result of their mismanagement of the illness will ultimately have a negative impact on the child and is irrelevant to the subsequent management of the infection. However, this perspective must be counterbalanced with the knowledge that potential future exposure to other risk factors for physical illness may be enhanced by minimizing the importance of parental behaviour and responsibility. Clearly, the risks are markedly different if the child has an upper respiratory infection or meningitis.

A special circumstance exists related to genetic or familial illnesses. Once parents decide to have a child, the transmission of a particular genetic trait becomes an estimated probability. Parents cannot influence whether they will actually pass on an affected gene or not. However, both parents should be made aware of any increased risk for physical illnesses that their children may have as a consequence of the genetic characteristics of the parents. When the genetic risk for illness in the child is remote, this gamble is generally viewed as well-justified. In these cases, the occurrence of an unlikely outcome tends to result in a relatively limited negative impact on the subsequent adaptation of the family. However, when the genetic risk is clearly known to be high, as in the case of parents who have previously had a child with cystic fibrosis, the decision to have another child is taken with full knowledge that there is a 25% likelihood that the next child will have the illness, as well as a 50% chance that he or she will be a carrier of the autosomal recessive condition. In this case, the 'blame' is shared equally by both parents as they are by definition both heterozygotes or carriers for cystic fibrosis. However, in most circumstances when a genetic illness is evident, and only one parental pedigree is implicated, the situation is further complicated by the potential of one parent blaming the other for the responsibility of passing on the undesirable gene.

In some ways, it is easier for the family to respond to the onset of physical illness if the aetiology of the disease does not imply any parental responsibility. However, as more is understood about environmental risk factors and genetic vulnerability, such circumstances are likely to become less common.

Accuracy and timeliness of the establishment of the diagnosis

The process by which the diagnosis is established can play a significant role in the ability of the child and parent to adapt to the illness. A number of factors play a role. The first is the duration of time required to come to closure on the nature of the problem. The second is the certainty with which the diagnosis can be made. A third is the sensitivity with which the diagnosis and its implications are transmitted to the child and the family.

The diagnostic skill of the physician is important as it often establishes the affective nature of the physician–patient relationship which can ultimately affect the long-term treatment for the child. A rapid and accurate diagnosis can facilitate this relationship while a misdiagnosis can lead to an acutely adversarial relationship.

Prompt determination of the diagnosis is clearly the standard of care. Furthermore, even if arrival at the diagnosis is delayed through unavoidable postponements in diagnostic testing, sensitive communication to the family regarding diagnostic progress can mitigate the negative effects of a prolonged period of uncertainty. Some illnesses are simply more easily recognized. A child who develops the classic sign of insatiable thirst coupled with an abnormal fasting serum glucose is not likely to be missed as being diabetic. In contrast, a number of illnesses can mimic asthma. These include vocal cord dysfunction that can be impossible to differentiate from asthma in the doctor's office and requires bronchoscopy for a definitive identification (Christopher *et al.*, 1983). Given that there is a strong association between vocal cord dysfunction and emotional disturbance, this differential diagnostic possibility should be considered carefully by a psychiatric consultant when asked to consider the role of emotional factors in children with treatment-resistant asthma.

Illnesses such as some of the leukaemias can be definitively diagnosed upon inspection of the blood cells, but may have prodromal symptoms that are quite vague and do not trigger the appropriate diagnostic evaluation. Unfortunately, in cases where malignancies are discovered in relatively advanced stages, the question of why the appropriate early investigations were not pursued is difficult to avoid and will often negatively affect subsequent treatment.

An issue that is difficult to resolve is how to communicate the implications of a grave or terminal diagnosis to a child and family. While the standard of care is to provide complete disclosure, the implications of sharing devastating information with a family in crisis are often difficult to ascertain. The entire situation can be further complicated if the physician is ambivalent about the need to share the grave implications of a serious disease with a relatively young child. The intensity of the conflict is illustrated by the care with which some physicians organize their practices to avoid these unhappy interactions. In these cases, a child psychiatrist can be particularly helpful by providing the paediatrician with some perspective on the emotional needs of the patient and the family of the child to ensure that they have the opportunity to explore implications of the disease on the future of the family. Such a strategy is facilitated by the use of a multidisciplinary team approach to comprehensive care (Bingley *et al.*, 1980).

One method that physicians use to cope with their paediatric patients with terminal illnesses is to begin to focus on the treatment of the disease and avoid talking about how the child is coping with the symptoms and prognosis. Increasingly, psychoneuroimmunological evidence suggests very similar illnesses can evoke a wide range of host responses. An important aspect of paediatric clinical care is to be able to help the family sustain hope for an optimal outcome while providing a realistic perspective on the medical risks that the child is facing.

Interference with function

Disability associated with chronic illness varies enormously. However, this variability in disability is rarely considered as an independent variable in the analysis of risk factors associated with specific illnesses, despite the clear link with long-term adaptation (Cadman *et al.*, 1987; Mattsson, 1972). Another factor that is rarely assessed is the substantive differences that the same disability will have at different periods of development. While interferences with intellectual processing play a negative role at all stages of development, it becomes a more serious problem with a wider range of implications when the child reaches the age in school when cognitive processing is critical for advancement. Similarly, the inability to drive a car has little negative impact prior to the age when it is legally permitted, but can have very strong negative social connotations for older adolescents.

Disability is strongly related to the severity of the illness. An asthmatic child with easily controlled asthma may have virtually no functional disability whereas a severely asthmatic child may find it impossible to attend school consistently. While both children may have some difficulty adapting to their illness, the probability of the occurrence of emotional difficulty is associated with more severe illness (McNichol *et al.*, 1973). A similar relationship between severity of renal disease and emotional adaptation has been noted (Garralda *et al.*, 1988).

Impact on physical appearance

One of the most common concerns of chronically ill children is their anxiety about being physically different. This concern has often been seen to be a central aspect of a diminished sense of self-esteem (Burns & Zweig, 1980). Given the importance of a positive physical appearance to the formation of a sense of self-worth, it is not surprising that disfiguring illnesses are associated with increased emotional vulnerability (Breslau & Marshall, 1985).

Many illnesses result in no negative impact on physical appearance. Most asthmatic children appear to be physically normal until late in the course of their illness after long periods of respiratory compromise or as a result of physical changes secondary to treatment with chronic corticosteroids. Other illnesses such as atopic dermatitis can result in extensive unattractive skin lesions that are not associated with long-term physical handicap or any concern for problems in athletic or cognitive achievement.

Again there is a rarely appreciated association between age of illness and impact of problems in appearance. Specifically, very young children may have relatively little negative feedback regarding physical deformity from those adults who care for them. However, as the peer group of a child assumes greater importance, emotional rejection based on negative response from other children can precipitate depressed mood. The classic period of peak sensitivity is adolescence when children with severe problems of physical appearance most often show disturbances in emotional adaptation. Interestingly, little empirical evidence is available to demonstrate this frequent clinical observation.

Persistence of symptoms

Diseases vary in their pattern of symptom expression. Illnesses such as asthma and epilepsy frequently have long periods of remission in which children may have extended opportunities to interact with peers and attend school in the absence of physical reminders of their disease. Other illnesses are either unremitting or result in a gradual worsening of physical discomfort and disability.

Illnesses with more persistent or unremitting symptoms would be expected to have a more negative impact on emotional adaptation. However, there is little evidence to suggest chronicity as a primary factor. A possible alternative explanation is that some children with persistent disturbance learn to come to grips with their problems in a more effective manner than children with episodic symptoms. In any case, variability regarding this characteristic requires further investigation.

Hope for recovery

A brief encounter with a serious illness that results in a complete recovery is unlikely to have any negative impact on emotional development. However, children with a more uncertain prognosis have been described as having a Damocles syndrome (Koocher & O'Malley, 1981). These children must come to live with considerable uncertainty about their long-term survival.

A primary concern in the treatment of children with a terminal prognosis is that they do not prematurely give up and subsequently become clinically depressed. Some children are able to maintain a strong optimistic sense about their eventual recovery with little support and in the face of quite grave odds. Even children with a terminal prognosis are sometimes able to come to some peace with their impending death.

PSYCHIATRIC CONSIDERATION OF SPECIFIC PHYSICAL ILLNESSES

Asthma

Asthma is the most prevalent chronic illness of childhood. In the US and UK, estimates of prevalence vary from approximately 3% using questionnaires that focus on having previously been diagnosed as having asthma to 12% based on having reported episodes of wheezing in the past year. The highest rates are reported in isolated populations, particularly among Pacific Islanders, where reported prevalence varies between 20 and 30%. The lowest prevalence rates have been reported in Scandinavia, Switzerland, Israel and Japan, where less than 2% of children have been identified (Cookson,

1987). Three primary factors have been put forward to explain these differences. The first is that differences in genetic vulnerabilities exist in different racial and ethnic populations. This has been particularly suggested as an explanation for why small populations with a high frequency of consanguineous matings have high prevalence rates. A second factor is variability in the methodology of ascertainment of 'caseness'. Clearly studies that accept a history of episodic wheezing as the equivalent of the diagnosis will have elevated rates. A more recent suggestion has been that variability in the physical environment may explain increased prevalence. However, this explanation does not address the paradoxical finding that the lowest rates were found in some of the most developed industrial countries.

Asthma is defined as a reversible reactive airway disease triggered by a variety of immunological, infectious, physiological and emotional triggers. There is increasing evidence that asthma has a genetic component, and its expression probably involves multiple gene loci. There is strong evidence that (IgE) plays a central role in the mechanism of symptom expression in allergic asthma and that the regulation of IgE antibody level is under genetic control.

Asthma is probably best conceptualized as a syndrome with multiple aetiological origins. In this regard, it illustrates interactions that occur between physiological and psychological processes. Some children appear to have a simple form of asthma that is limited to attacks that are allergically triggered. Conversely, some asthmatic children appear to have no allergic symptoms, but their illness is triggered by a wide variety of physical and psychological factors. The majority of children present a more complex clinical picture that involves an interaction of triggers that ultimately result in bronchial constriction.

In this regard, it is interesting to note that both an immunological risk factor in the form of elevated serum IgE and a psychological risk factor measured by early difficulties in parenting are predictive of the onset of asthma in children at increased genetic risk for developing the disease (Mrazek *et al.*, 1991).

There is little evidence to suggest that mild asthma, defined as wheezing episodes easily controlled by inhaled bronchodilators, is associated with increased early psychopathology. However, quite severely asthmatic children, who have persistent functional disability and require multiple medications, including corticosteroids, to control their symptoms, have been shown to be at increased risk for emotional disturbance. Epidemiological studies have focused on the issue of severity of illness as a predictor of psychopathology (McNichol *et al.*, 1973). Subsequent studies have highlighted the importance of understanding the development of emotional symptoms within the context of other risk factors for psychopathology (Steinhausen *et al.*, 1983). Even preschool samples composed of very seriously asthmatic children have had rates of psychopathology in excess of 50% (Mrazek *et al.*, 1984). These high levels of disturbance can be contrasted with the relatively positive adaptation of very young asthmatics who have suffered from milder forms of the disease (Gauthier *et al.*, 1977, 1978). In severely asthmatic older children, affective disorder is common and has serious implications for survival (Miller, 1987). Both the presence of affective symptoms and disturbance in family functioning were independently associated with a higher probability of fatal episodes in very severely asthmatic children. Physiological variables associated with asthma death in this cohort were the occurrence of hypoxic seizures, a previous respiratory arrest and rapid decrement in steroid dose (Strunk *et al.*, 1985).

Given the complex immunological factors associated with the onset of asthma, it is not surprising that families often develop a variety of idiosyncratic beliefs about the illness. Awareness that there are genetic aspects associated with the development of asthma places it in the class of illnesses that can challenge parental attitudes about their level of personal responsibility. Parents who carry genes associated with known illnesses must make a decision regarding their plans to have children. Parents who had mild asthma virtually never consider their illness a cause for worry, but many severely asthmatic adults seriously weigh the potential risk for their offspring. The decision of a severely asthmatic woman to have a child is often complicated by the realization that her own disease may become more difficult to control over the course of the pregnancy. Approximately one-third of asthmatic women do experience some increase in their asthmatic symptoms during a pregnancy. Furthermore, it is increasingly clear that how well the physical and emotional environment of the child is managed is likely to have an influence on the ultimate evolution of the child's symptoms. This realization places the non-affected parent in a position of shared responsibility regarding the child's outcome. Given this increased awareness, it is more difficult for parents to ascribe the onset of the illness in a child to simply being bad luck. Conversely, the avoidance of the development of symptoms in a child at increased genetic risk is increasingly viewed as a consequence of good caretaking and parenting.

The establishment of the diagnosis of asthma can actually be quite difficult. Controversy exists over what symptoms are sufficient to establish the diagnosis. More strict criteria have been suggested and, if utilized, would result in lower prevalence estimates. Yet another consideration is that recurring wheezing in infancy associated with respiratory infections can resemble an asthmatic attack. However, the prognostic implications of infectious wheezing or wheezing bronchitis are very different than the diagnosis of asthmatic episodes in the absence of infection. Clearly, the perception and response of the family will be quite different if the first wheezing attack is perceived as simply an isolated symptom associated with one of the inevitable respiratory illnesses of early childhood, rather than the beginning of a chronic illness. Increasingly, evidence exists to suggest that early asthmatic attacks should be treated intensively and that such treatment will minimize the likelihood of the development of chronic asthma. A reasonable perspective is to consider the first attack of wheezing in a vulnerable child as a symptom providing evidence of the existence of genetic underlying vulnerability to asthma. Such a position should be accompanied by considering strategies to minimize additional symptoms through management of the child's exposure to allergens, infections and intense emotional distress.

In very mild asthmatics, there is virtually no disability. The illness can be controlled quite effectively through the use of inhaled bronchodilators. In more progressive forms of the illness, chronic corticosteroids are required, and limitations on physical activity occur as a consequence of respiratory symptoms, as well as a variety of corticosteroid side-effects that can affect vision, learning and physical development.

Mild asthmatics have a completely normal physical appearance. In contrast, severe debilitating disease that requires corticosteroid treatment often results in Cushingoid stigmata, growth retardation and scoliosis and carries the most risk for having problems adapting to the developmental challenges of adolescence.

Asthma tends to be an episodic illness which allows children to have intervals without symptoms during which they can function normally. These remissions provide reasonable hope that the illness will eventually be controlled. However, for very severely asthmatic children, the future is less positive. There is considerable evidence that fatal asthmatic episodes are increasing (Sly, 1988) and that the risk of a fatal episode is elevated if the child has an emotional disturbance or there is family dysfunction (Strunk *et al.*, 1985). While these risks are most acute for severely asthmatic children who require corticosteroids to control their symptoms, rare examples of children with milder disease who have died from asthma have been reported.

In summary, asthma presents a prototype of how multiple factors interact to influence the development of the chronically ill child. It is necessary to understand both the aetiology of the disease and approaches to its management in order for psychiatric interventions to have the largest impact. While asthmatic children as a group appear to be at increased risk for psychopathology, these difficulties are most relevant for children with severe illness in the context of families who are having difficulties adapting to the illness and providing the child with appropriate support and structure.

Atopic dermatitis

Atopic dermatitis or eczema is an allergic skin condition that almost always begins during the first years of life and is mediated by IgE sensitization, usually resulting in quite localized areas of skin involvement. In a minority of children with atopic dermatitis, severe lesions develop that are very distressing. The diagnosis is based on the presence of an intense pruritic rash that usually begins on the face and extensor aspects of the extremities. Serum IgE levels are often very elevated. Eczema usually resolves during childhood, but the condition can persist throughout life. Occasionally atopic dermatitis develops in adulthood.

The incidence of atopic dermatitis in childhood is probably

less than 5% (Halpern *et al.*, 1973). Only a small number of these children suffer from the more pervasive or debilitating forms of the illness. Evidence of a genetic aetiology is supported by family studies (Ferguson *et al.*, 1983), and the underlying hypersensitive IgE response is hypothesized to have a genetic basis.

Studies of adults have suggested an increased prevalence of depression and other emotional disorders in patients with atopic dermatitis (Preston, 1969). Small clinical studies have reported that exacerbations of skin lesions were associated with life stressors (Ullman *et al.*, 1977). The paediatric clinical literature includes reports of individual children who have responded well to psychological interventions (Mirvish, 1978), although systematic analyses of interventions have not been available. There is some suggestion that early avoidance of antigenic foods and prolonged breast-feeding may decrease the likelihood of illness in at-risk samples (Matthew *et al.*, 1977; Zeiger *et al.*, 1986).

Atopic dermatitis is predominantly a disease of early childhood that illustrates the clinical objective of supporting children in acute distress before they have the cognitive ability to cope with their discomfort. Parents must find a means of preventing their infants from aggravating the illness by scratching the lesions. Given that these infants are often upset and uncomfortable for prolonged periods, it is surprising that there have been no systematic studies examining the association between the early onset of severe eczema and later emotional difficulties. Furthermore, the illness often resolves in the first 2 years of life so that many children are completely amnesic for the experience. This unusual set of disease characteristics would allow an examination of the hypothesis that early disruption of the caretaking relationship due to frustrations involved in controlling the child to prevent excoriation of pruritic lesions may be associated with later interpersonal difficulties.

Atopic dermatitis is a familial illness, but one with relatively few long-term implications. Therefore, parents are less concerned about their children inheriting the disease. However, the primary treatment of the illness involves medicating the lesions, preventing scratching and identifying potential allergens in order to eliminate these substances from the environment of the child. Parents must therefore be alert to their child's behaviour and be prepared to make difficult life changes. A common conflict is making the decision to give up a family pet after it is recognized that contact with the animal appears to be a primary precipitant for the skin lesions.

Differential diagnosis is not usually a problem. Seborrhoeic dermatitis may be confused with eczema, but the psychological consequences of a delay in arriving at the accurate diagnosis are minimal as seborrhoeic dermatitis is a self-limited rash that is usually confined to the scalp and flexural areas of the extremities.

One implication of making the diagnosis of atopic dermatitis is the recognition that the child is at risk for other allergic problems such as hayfever and IgE-mediated asthma. If the child has a family history for asthmatic illness, the diagnosis of eczema can be conceptualized as an indicator of elevated risk for the later onset of allergically mediated asthma.

In older children with persistent and severe eczema, issues of disability and physical appearance become relevant. While it is rare that any permanent disability is created, wrapping the arm of the child to control acute episodes makes it difficult to participate in sports and engage in other physical activities.

When eczema spreads to the arms and face, it can be quite unattractive. The skin can become encrusted and weepy if the child is allowed to scratch the skin and the excoriated lesions become secondarily infected. Supportive families are usually able to tolerate the changes in the appearance of their child with minimal difficulty. However, there are some parents who place a high value on physical appearance which they may psychologically equate as an equivalent of their own attractiveness. The sudden development of unattractive secondary lesions can lead to an overt rejection of a previously highly valued child. Early sensitization of the parents to the negative implications of this rejection is often effective. Although eczema has the appearance of an infectious disease, it is not contagious. The irrational fear of contracting the disease from the child should be directly addressed while emphasizing the need to provide continued emotional support which includes physical contact.

When the lesions of the skin persist, they often have a more serious impact on the child's sense of self-esteem. In these cases, more aggressive psychiatric treatment is indicated to help the child cope with his or her appearance. Throughout the process, the ultimate favourable prognosis can be stressed. This strategy is particularly effective if severe rashes have been typical for the family. Involving previously affected family members whose skin has healed is a good strategy to use with younger children who have a problem with abstract projections into the future regarding the course of their illness.

Cystic fibrosis

Cystic fibrosis is one of the most prevalent autosomal recessive genetic illnesses of childhood. In Caucasian populations, approximately 5% of adults are carriers of the gene and approximately 0.05% of children are affected. While the pattern of inheritance has been recognized for years, a number of recent discoveries have been made regarding its pathophysiology. Specifically, it has been determined that the illness is caused by a mutation in a single gene that encodes for cystic fibrosis transmembrane conductance regulator (Riordan *et al.*, 1989). A central aspect of the mechanism appears to be a defect in the chloride channels that affect chloride permeability. A range of mutations at this gene site exist and their differences may explain variability in the clinical presentation of the illness. For example, one mutation may primarily affect chloride channel function in the sweat glands and pancreatic ducts while another may affect airway epithelia. While the range of physical symptoms is broad, classic features include chronic bronchial airway obstruction that often leads to respiratory infections and maldigestion that results from defects in the production of pancreatic enzymes. Other organs that may be affected include the liver, intestines and genitals, usually through a mechanism that involves an increase in the viscosity of secretions.

There has been a significant increase in the life span of children with cystic fibrosis. Currently, the mean age of survival is approximately 30 years of age. However, sexual development is usually delayed and 98% of the males are sterile (Taussig *et al.*, 1976). Pregnancy in females with cystic fibrosis is a high-risk medical condition because of the likelihood of deterioration of the respiratory function of pregnant patients. Problems in adjustment to the limitations of the illness have been specifically reported during adolescence (Bywater, 1981).

Cystic fibrosis is almost always diagnosed during infancy or in early childhood. The diagnosis is always suspected in families in which there is a pedigree with a high incidence of affected relatives. Even in the less frequent circumstance of the marriage of two carriers with no first- or second-degree affected relatives, a preliminary diagnosis is usually established once multiple symptoms emerge.

It is now technically possible to identify affected individuals through prenatal screening. However, there has been considerable controversy regarding the pursuit of this policy. Perinatal screening has been questioned as a potentially harmful practice based on the perspective that early intervention is relatively limited for these children. This position is based on the view that the stigma related to making the diagnosis is harmful, despite the reality that it is typical that the disease will become expressed in the first years of a child's life. The manner in which the medical community resolves what are acceptable practices regarding cystic fibrosis will provide an early indicator of how other illnesses will soon be handled in an era of increased genetic awareness.

There is wide variability regarding what is an appropriate familial response given genetic counselling. At one end of the spectrum, genetic counsellors have advised against two carriers of an autosomal recessive gene having children, based on the 25% probability of having an affected child. This has traditionally been the advice given to families after having had a child with cystic fibrosis. However, some parents are quite willing to take this level of risk in the hope of having additional children, independent of whether their offspring will be normal or have the disease. At the very least, given the very substantial burden of caring for a child with cystic fibrosis, it is critical to provide comprehensive information regarding the commitment necessary to deliver the pulmonary care and physical therapy that these children require, as well as being frank about expected complications and life expectancy.

Strong family support appears to be an important protective factor for the emotional development of children with cystic fibrosis (Venters, 1981). However, Steinhausen *et al.* (1983) conducted a multivariate study that identified severity of cystic fibrosis as the primary predictor of psychiatric disturbance in their small sample. In the group with severe illness, approximately one-third of the children developed serious emotional disturbance and another 22% had less severe prob-

lems. The development of eating disorders has been specifically cited as being more common in children with cystic fibrosis (Pumariega *et al.*, 1986). While a broad range of concerns have been reported to be associated with cystic fibrosis (Steinhausen & Schindler, 1981), the most frequently identified issues have been related to concerns about the illness itself. These have included anxiety about the treatment of the disease. While the probability of a shortened life span was rated to be the most difficult disease-related emotional issue by children with cystic fibrosis, this problem was rarely discussed until late in the course of the illness (Petzel *et al.*, 1984).

Previous therapeutic approaches have included medical and emotional supportive strategies for children with cystic fibrosis (Mrazek, 1985). A focus on achieving medical compliance has been advocated (Czajkowski & Koocher, 1986). However, with the discovery of the cystic fibrosis gene, there is now optimism that innovative treatment can be developed at the molecular level. Ultimately, the evolution of gene therapy may dramatically alter the entire experience of the illness.

Juvenile-onset insulin-dependent diabetes mellitus

Juvenile-onset insulin-dependent diabetes mellitus (IDDM) is an uncommon paediatric illness in young children, affecting very few preschoolers, and only about 0.2% of school-age children and adolescents. It is a disease of the islet cells of the pancreas and has classically been characterized as a deficiency in the production of insulin.

IDDM does not affect the early parent–child relationship because of its later onset. Therefore, there have been speculations that the psychological sequelae associated with the illness are less pervasive. Hypotheses for the better adjustment of diabetic children have included the following: (1) that the early emotional development of these children is essentially normal; (2) that when the onset of the diabetes does occur, prompt diagnosis and specific treatment are available; and (3) that there is minimal evidence of central nervous system involvement.

There is an increased familial risk for the development of diabetes (Riley *et al.*, 1990) and diabetic complications (Seaquist *et al.*, 1989). Although the specific pattern of inheritance has not been established, progress in the identification of children at increased risk is being made through molecular genetic techniques (Baisch *et al.*, 1990). While it has been hypothesized that emotional stressors could play a role in the initial onset of the illness, Kovacs *et al.* (1985) did not report such an association in their cohort. However, there does appear to be a relationship between stressor scores and both low serum glucose levels and triglyceride concentrations in diabetic adolescents (Chase & Jackson, 1981). An association between disturbances in family interaction and overall diabetic control of adolescents, as measured by elevated glycosylated haemoglobin, has also been demonstrated at the 5-year follow-up assessment after initial diagnosis (Gustafsson *et al.*, 1987).

Characteristics of mothers' interactions with even preschool children have been shown to distinguish children who had difficulty in maintaining adequate glycaemic control from those who were easily controlled (Garrison *et al.*, 1990). While diabetic patients are at slightly increased risk for emotional disturbance, generally more modest rates have been reported (Wilkinson, 1987). In his study of adult diabetics, 18% were diagnosed with a psychiatric disorder and these were predominantly some form of depressive or anxiety disturbances. More severe chronic diabetic samples have been shown to be at greater risk with 51% having been identified as having a psychiatric diagnosis in a sample evaluated for pancreatic transplantation (Popkin *et al.*, 1988). A special risk in depressed diabetics is attempted suicide by the method of insulin overdose (Kaminer & Robbins, 1988). Problems in adjustment to the diagnosis of diabetes in children have also been reported (Ahnsjo *et al.*, 1981).

Fortunately, few physical deformities are associated with IDDM. However, Moran (1984) has reported relatively high levels of anxiety in children related to their fears of hypoglycaemic and hyperglycaemic coma as well as later vascular complications. During adolescence, it is common for teenagers to have difficulty adhering to the relatively strict dietary protocols and restrictions in their activity. The link between environmental stressors and diabetic control in children has also been studied (White *et al.*, 1984). In these studies ketoacidosis was linked to either dietary indiscretion or insulin mismanagement in only a minority of the cases (5–10%). However, in a majority of cases family difficulties were felt to be associated with less adequate control.

A major concern for many children with IDDM is the uncertainty that is associated with the future course of their illness. This includes both fear of severe ketoacidotic episodes and diabetic sequelae. More cognitive difficulties have been demonstrated in diabetic children with more persistent illness (Gath *et al.*, 1980). Poor diabetic control was correlated with: (1) the presence of psychiatric disorder; (2) difficulties in reading; and (3) adverse psychosocial risk factors. Cognitive difficulties in the abstract visual reasoning subscale of the Stanford–Binet Intelligence Scale have even been noted in children with relatively mild hyperglycaemia if the onset of their illness occurred before 5 years of age (Golden *et al.*, 1989).

Kovacs *et al.* (1985) described variability in the coping of diabetic children. Approximately 64% of the children in this cohort reported some social withdrawal and sadness but did not merit a diagnosis, while 36% could be diagnosed with a psychiatric disturbance. Affective disorders were the most frequent diagnoses. Fortunately, 93% of the children with these disturbances recovered over the course of the first year of their diabetic illness.

The interaction of psychiatric disturbance and the control of diabetic symptoms continues to be an area of investigation. Severe psychiatric disturbance in either the child or parent has been shown to account for approximately 44% of the variance in blood glucose level. It has also been shown to predict low

glycosylated haemoglobin concentration in the children (Fonagy *et al.*, 1987). In this study, nearly one-third of the children had an emotional or behavioural difficulty and these children were determined to be less responsible in caring for their illness.

Leukaemia

The most common paediatric malignancy is leukaemia. It has a prevalence of less than 0.05% during childhood. The introduction of chemotherapy and irradiation therapy has dramatically altered the clinical course of the illness. Currently, the 5-year life expectancy of children with this diagnosis exceeds 50%. While these odds are a dramatic improvement over the recent past, many children still succumb to the disease. The term the Damocles syndrome has been appropriately coined to describe the chronic state of uncertainty that characterizes the lives of these children (Koocher & O'Malley, 1981).

The genetic basis of leukaemia is not well-understood. There are certain subtypes of the disease that appear to be familial, but the majority of children with leukaemia do not have a positive pedigree for the disease. Leukaemia represents a disease where there is little evidence that life stressors affect the onset. Furthermore, there is little to suggest that any defined parental disturbance or behaviour is associated with its occurrence. The reaction of the family to the initial diagnosis is usually disbelief and anger.

Complications can arise in the establishment of the diagnosis of leukaemia. A primary problem is that many of the early signs of the illness are nonspecific, such as increased infections, lethargy and weakness. Once the illness is suspected, the diagnosis can be made definitively through laboratory examination. However, as it is now universally agreed that prompt and aggressive treatment is highly beneficial for the long-term survival of these patients, unnecessary delays in establishment of the diagnosis can lead to both guilt and the attribution of blame.

During the early phases of the illness, there is little physical deformity. Later, weight loss and prominent bruising can be a problem. However, the severe prognosis that is associated with the later stages of the illness usually overshadows the changes that occur in physical appearance.

There have been relatively few studies documenting elevated levels of emotional disturbance in children with leukaemia (Kupst *et al.*, 1984; Greenberg *et al.*, 1989). However, Sawyer *et al.* (1986) did demonstrate elevated levels of behavioural and emotional disturbance when children with leukaemia were compared to their siblings. While these children gradually seemed to adjust to their illness over the 4-year follow-up period, they were still found to have more difficulties in school, as documented by both parent and teacher reports (Sawyer *et al.*, 1989).

The care and treatment of leukaemia are inevitably a burden for both the child and parent. The necessity for repeated painful bone marrow biopsies as well as other invasive procedures can make hospitalizations frightening experiences for these children. Furthermore, the use of cranial irradiation has been shown to have a variety of negative sequelae. These include specific neuropsychological deficits, particularly if the treatment is administered before the child is 8 years of age (Moehle & Berg, 1985). If both cranial radiation and intrathecal methotrexate treatment are employed, a larger number of psychological sequelae are noted, as well as associated abnormal computed tomography (CT) scans (Pavlovsky *et al.*, 1983). Brouwers *et al.* (1984) also demonstrated abnormalities on CT scans as well as more frequent neuropsychological deficits and attentional disturbances in patients with documented evidence of atrophy. Very few patients showed calcifications, but these children did demonstrate the greatest neuropsychological dysfunction. These findings are similar to results from studies that examine cognitive function in children with primary brain tumours receiving whole-brain radiotherapy (Packer *et al.*, 1989).

Physical symptoms without physical disease

Several patterns of somatic dysfunction commonly present in the absence of known organic disease. In the past they have often been classified on the basis of supposedly different forms of psychic aetiology (psychosomatic, hysterical, dissociative, conversion, etc.). These terms, however, have largely fallen out of use because of the unreliability involved in the description of psychological mechanisms. The World Health Organization (1992) classification of diseases has substituted a simpler classification based upon the nature of the bodily functions that are impaired. Some of these have received a great deal of clinical and research attention in children, for example, disorders of micturition (see Chapter 29), defecation (see Chapter 30), feeding and sleeping (see Chapter 27). It is clear from the study of these disorders that they reflect a complex interaction between physical and psychological factors, the details of which vary between disorders.

The same complexity is likely to apply to the less well-researched types of dysfunction. What they have in common is that they present as a physical disorder, but no such illness can be found that can explain the symptoms. They comprise complete and partial paralyses or incoordination (dissociative movement disorders), convulsions of the limbs (pseudoseizures; see Chapter 11), anaesthetic areas of the skin, loss of visual acuity or accommodation or parts of the visual field (dissociative sensory loss), pains and other unpleasant sensations (persistent pain disorder), diarrhoea, palpitations, hyperventilation, sweating, flushing and tremor (somatoform autonomic dysfunction), fatigue (neurasthenia), preoccupation with the possibility of an underlying disease (hypochondriacal disorder) and multiple somatic symptoms that are very persistent and may come from any or all of the above types (somatization disorder).

The concept of disorders defined chiefly by the absence of a physical explanation is necessary but troublingly negative and gives rise to a number of difficulties. Firstly, an affected child may have an underlying physical disease that has not yet become apparent. This is shown by two kinds of evidence: some children with a diagnosis of psychogenic physical disorder prove on follow-up to have relevant organic pathology (Caplan, 1970); and some children with organic brain disease have been previously diagnosed as showing hysteria (Rivinus *et al.*, 1975). Some particularly common diagnostic traps are the postural abnormalities of dystonia musculorum deformans, the amblyopia seen in cerebral and retinal degenerations, the pseudoseizures that are produced by some people who really have epilepsy as well, and the episodic abdominal pain that may result from a variety of causes, including parasitic infestations and volvulus of the intestine.

A second, related difficulty is the uncertainty about how far to go in the investigation of possible physical causes. Intensive investigation is often thought to carry a risk of increasing the certainty with which a child and family may espouse a physical theory of cause, though empirical evidence is lacking. Sometimes the form of the symptom is in itself enough to argue strongly against a physical cause: for example, diplopia appearing when one eye is covered hints strongly at a nonphysical explanation. (Even here, however, conditions such as dislocation of the lens can produce monocular diplopia and confound the unwary diagnostician.) Similarly, if a symptom is clearly related in time to an external stressor (e.g. if pain is confined to the period before going to school) then history and examination may well be sufficient grounds on which to base diagnosis (see Chapter 6). On the other hand, physical illness can arise even in children with psychologically determined disorders, and necessary investigations may be overlooked because of a psychiatric label. Good communication between paediatrician and psychiatrist is crucial (see Chapter 52) and physical reappraisal of disorders believed to be psychogenic should be undertaken if they do not improve when a stress believed to be responsible has been ameliorated.

A third difficulty in the concept of nonorganic physical presentations is the limitation of scientific knowledge of organic causes. Many illnesses have in the past been regarded as purely psychogenic that are now known to have organic contributions: Crohn's disease, narcolepsy and asthma have all been regarded as direct manifestations of specific intrapsychic conflicts. No doubt there are some causes of diffuse abdominal pain that are at present unsuspected; some cases of pain should therefore be regarded as crypto- rather than psychogenic.

Fourthly, one of the common presentations is a psychogenic exaggeration of the incapacity imposed by an organic illness (Goodyer & Taylor, 1985). Children with epilepsy may present pseudoseizures too; an infective illness may be followed by a prolonged adoption of the sick role (Dubowitz & Hersov, 1976). The disentangling of these strands may need prolonged assessment and subtlety of judgement.

Such problems of definition make it impossible to obtain satisfactory estimates of prevalence. The commonest of the somatic symptoms attributed to psychological causes is diffuse pain, often in the head or abdomen. Abdominal pain affected 32% of young adolescents with a frequency of at least once a month; headache, 67%, in a survey of two Swedish cities by Larsson (1991). However, in this as in other surveys there is no means of determining which cases could be confidently attributed to psychological disturbance. There is an association between somatic symptoms and self-reports of high levels of emotional distress in psychiatrically referred children (Ryan *et al.*, 1987), children with chronic illness (Wallander *et al.*, 1988) and epidemiological surveys (Kashani *et al.*, 1989; Larsson, 1991), but the direction of causality is not addressed by the research. There is a need for studies that will apply more detailed measures to categorize children with unexplained somatic symptoms into those with clear evidence of relation to psychological stressors, those with other evidence of psychiatric disorder, and those where only the somatic symptom itself is testimony to the possibility of a psychological cause.

Somatization disorder is very seldom diagnosed in children. However, adults with the condition very often give a history of having been affected from childhood. The condition gives rise to issues similar to those presented by the personality disorders, and its childhood antecedents should repay investigation.

Particular care needs to be taken over the assessment of somatic symptoms when the patient and the professional come from different cultures. Cultures vary in the words used to describe illness, and in their readiness to seek help: for instance, Thai parents rate children's problems as less serious and more likely to improve than do American parents (Weisz *et al.*, 1991). A skilled translator can help to reduce linguistic barriers to understanding the complaints, but there may be more profound differences. The conceptualization of personal distress varies between cultures, in line with societies' theories about the causes of suffering. Kleinman (1986) examined the Chinese concept of neurasthenia, which is defined solely in terms of somatic symptoms, and found many similarities between those affected and those falling into the western category of depression. For example, the vast majority of those with neurasthenia responded to antidepressant medication. The somatic terminology in China followed a political and social insistence that the roots of any personal malaise should be sought in physical illness. Of course, this did not mean that the somatic complaints were unreal, or that the Chinese patients really had depression rather than neurasthenia. The implication is that the meaning of a somatic complaint needs to be interpreted in the light of knowledge about the culture's understanding of illness.

In the treatment of somatic symptoms, most authorities advocate an attempt to help the child and family understand why abnormal illness behaviour has developed so as to achieve a more adaptive solution to problems (Goodyer & Taylor, 1985). Suggestion and encouragement towards a gradual resumption of normal function are often useful (Dubowitz & Hersov, 1976). However, trials of therapy are lacking and there is not even much systematic description of the treated or untreated natural history. What there is does not wholly support conventional clinical practices. Recurrent abdominal pain, for example, is regarded as having a very good outlook by most paediatricians (Graham, 1986); but follow-up studies of children seen by paediatric services for this condition indicate that nearly half continue to suffer the same symptoms in adult life (Apley & Hale, 1973; Christensen & Mortensen, 1975). These studies of outcome do of course concentrate on a most atypical group simply by virtue of being based upon groups that have been referred to hospital paediatrics. The vast majority of cases are managed by primary care clinicians who are likely to operate an efficient filter. Much can be done by primary care professionals, especially in consultation with mental health specialists, to ensure the kind of family understanding that may prevent the escalation of anxiety and somatic symptomatology (see Chapter 62).

GENERAL THERAPEUTIC CONSIDERATIONS

The role of the psychiatrist in the management of paediatric patients with serious illnesses is in transition. Traditionally, the primary therapeutic role has been to help children cope with their circumstances. Treatment has been expanded to include active interventions that involve parents and the family members as well as psychopharmacological management.

A recent development has been the increased awareness of the interactions of multiple risk factors that are frequently associated with the initial onset of many physical illnesses. Emotional stressors have been recently demonstrated to be linked to the onset of asthmatic symptoms (Mrazek *et al.*, 1991), and it is hypothesized that a wide range of highly complex illnesses may involve similar mechanisms. As new knowledge about the genetic basis of specific physical illnesses is established, the challenge of developing protective early interventions will become more clinically imperative. For these interventions to be appropriately employed, new techniques involving multiple specialists will need to be developed, and intervention trials designed and conducted to identify appropriate treatments and validate their efficacy.

In the past, chronically ill children who exhibited depressive symptoms were not always recognized (Costello *et al.*, 1988) and when recognized were often not always treated psychiatrically. In part this was due to an expectation that children with severe physical limitation would understandably begin to show social withdrawal and signs of discouragement. With the use of multimodal forms of treatment that include not only medication, but also family support and individual counselling, it is now the expectation that psychiatric symptoms should be directly addressed. Rehabilitation efforts for chronically ill children are also now more clearly known to have multiple benefits. While it may not be possible completely to resolve either the underlying physical illness or the psychiatric and behavioural symptoms of some patients, achieving a better overall level of emotional adaptation is an appropriate objective. For example, the respiratory status of severely asthmatic children has been shown to improve when they participate in an active exercise training (Strunk *et al.*, 1989). Furthermore, overall decrease in the medical utilization of severely asthmatic children was demonstrated after their participation in a comprehensive rehabilitation programme with active psychiatric involvement (Strunk *et al.*, 1989). Similar results may be possible for a wide range of chronic problems and should be the focus of active investigations.

REFERENCES

Ahnsjo S., Humble K., Larsson Y., Settergren-Carlsson G. & Sterky G. (1981) Personality changes and social adjustment during the first three years of diabetes in children. *Acta Paediatrica Scandinavica*, **70**, 321–327.

Apley J. & Hale B. (1973) Children with recurrent abdominal pain: how do they grow up? *British Medical Journal*, **3**, 7–9.

Baisch J.M., Weeks T., Giles R., Hoover M., Stastny P. & Capra J.D. (1990) Analysis of HLA-DQ genotypes and susceptibility in insulin-dependent diabetes mellitus. *New England Journal of Medicine*, **322**, 1836–1841.

Bingley L., Leonard J., Hensman S., Lask B. & Wolff O. (1980) Comprehensive management of children on a paediatric ward: a family approach. *Archives of Disease in Childhood*, **55**, 555–561.

Breslau N. & Marshall I.A. (1985) Psychological disturbance in children with physical disabilities: continuity and change in a 5-year follow-up. *Journal of Abnormal Child Psychology*, **13**, 199–216.

Brouwers P., Riccardi R., Poplack D. & Fedio P. (1984) Attentional deficits in long-term survivors of childhood acute lymphoblastic leukemia (ALL). *Journal of Clinical Neuropsychology*, **6**, 325–330.

Burbach D.J. & Peterson L. (1986) Children's concepts of physical illness: a review and critique of cognitive-developmental literature. *Health Psychology*, **5**, 307–325.

Burns W.J. & Zweig A.R. (1980) Self-concepts of chronically ill children. *Journal of Genetic Psychology*, **137**, 179–190.

Bywater E.M. (1981) Adolescents with cystic fibrosis: psychosocial adjustment. *Archives of Disease in Childhood*, **56**, 538–543.

Cadman D., Boyle M., Szatmari P. & Offord D.R. (1987) Chronic illness disability, and mental and social well-being. *Pediatrics*, **79**, 805–813.

Caplan H. (1970) Hysterical 'conversion' symptoms in childhood. M.Phil dissertation, University of London.

Charney D., Mendes D. & Heninger G. (1981) Receptor sensitivity and the mechanism of action of antidepressant treatment. *Archives of General Psychiatry*, **38**, 1160.

Chase H.P. & Jackson G.G. (1981) Stress and sugar control in children with insulin-dependent diabetes mellitus. *Journal of Pediatrics*, **98**, 1011–1013.

Christensen M.F. & Mortensen O. (1975) Long-term prognosis in children with recurrent abdominal pain. *Archives of Disease in Childhood*, **50**, 110–114.

Christopher K.L., Wood R.P. II, Eckert R.C., Blager F.B., Raney R.A. & Souhrada J.F. (1983) Vocal-cord dysfunction presenting as asthma. *New England Journal of Medicine*, **308**, 1566–1570.

Cockcroft D.W., Ruffin R.E., Dolovich J. & Hargreave F.E. (1977) Allergen-induced increase in non-allergic bronchial reactivity. *Clinical Allergy*, **7**, 503–513.

Cookson J.B. (1987) *Prevalence Rates of Asthma in Developing Countries and their Comparison with those in Europe and North America*. Glenfield General Hospital, Leicester, England.

Costello E.J., Edelbrock C., Costello A.J., Dulcan M.K., Burns B.J. & Brent D. (1988) Psychopathology in pediatric primary care: the new hidden morbidity. *Pediatrics*, **82**, 415–424.

Czajkowski D.R. & Koocher G.P. (1986) Predicting medical compliance among adolescents with cystic fibrosis. *Health Psychology*, **5**, 297–305.

Dubowitz V. & Hersov L. (1976) Management of children with non-organic (hysterical) disorders of motor function. *Developmental Medicine and Child Neurology*, **25**, 67–80.

Ferguson E.M., Horwood L.J. & Shannon W.T. (1983) Parental asthma, parental eczema and asthma and eczema in childhood. *Journal of Chronic Disease*, **36**, 517–524.

Fonagy P., Moran G.S., Lindsay M.K.M., Kurtz A.B. & Brown R. (1987) Psychological adjustment and diabetic control. *Archives of Diseases of Children*, **55**, 371–375.

Garralda M.E., Jameson R.A., Reynolds J.M. & Postlethwaite R.J. (1988) Psychiatric adjustment in children with chronic renal failure. *Journal of Child Psychologist and Psychiatrist*, **29**, 79–90.

Garrison W.T., Biggs D. & Williams K. (1990) Temperament characteristics and clinical outcomes in young children with diabetes mellitus. *Journal of Child Psychology and Psychiatry*, **31**, 1079–1088.

Gath A., Smith M.A. & Baum D.J. (1980) Emotional, behavioural, and educational disorders in diabetic children. *Archives of Disabilities in Children*, **55**, 371–375.

Gauthier Y., Fortin C., Drapeau P., Breton J.J., Quintal L., Weisnagel J., Tetreault L. & Pinard G. (1977) The mother–child relationship and the development of autonomy and self-assertion in young (14–30 months) asthmatic children. *Journal of the American Academy of Child Psychiatry*, **16**, 109.

Gauthier Y., Fortin C., Drapeau P., Breton J.J., Gosselin J., Quintal L., Weisnagel J. & Lamarre A. (1978) Follow-up study of 35 asthmatic preschool children. *Journal of the American Academy of Child Psychiatry*, **17**, 69.

Golden M.P., Ingersoll G.M., Brack C.J., Russell B.A., Wright J.C., Huberty T.J. (1989) Longitudinal relationship of asymptomatic hypoglycemia to cognitive function in IDDM. *Diabetes Care*, **12**, 89–93.

Goodyer I. & Taylor D.C. (1985) Hysteria. *Archives of Disease in Childhood*, **60**, 680–681.

Gortmaker S.L., Walker D.K., Weitzman M. & Sobol A.M. (1990) Chronic conditions, socioeconomic risks, and behavioral problems in children and adolescents. *Pediatrics*, **85**, 267–276.

Graham P. (1985) Psychology and the health of children. *Journal of Child Psychology and Psychiatry*, **26**, 333–347.

Graham P. (1986) *Child Psychiatry: A Developmental Approach*, p. 328. Oxford Medical Publications, Oxford.

Greenberg H.S., Kazak A.E. & Meadows A.T. (1989) Psychologic functioning in 8 to 16 year old cancer survivors and their parents. *Journal of Pediatrics*, **114**, 488–493.

Gustafsson P.A., Cederblad M., Ludvigsson J. *et al.* (1987) Family interaction and metabolic balance in juvenile diabetes mellitus. A prospective study. *Diabetes Research and Clinical Practice*, **4**, 7–14.

Halpern S.R., Sellars W.A. & Johnson R.B. (1973) Development of childhood allergy in infants fed breast, soy or cow's milk. *Journal of Allergy Clinical Immunology*, **51**, 139.

Heiligenstein E. & Jacobsen P.B. (1988) Differentiating depression in medically ill children and adolescents. *American Academy of Child and Adolescent Psychiatry*, **27**, 716–719.

Kaminer Y. & Robbins D. (1988) Attempted suicide by insulin overdose in insulin-dependent diabetic adolescents. *Pediatrics*, **81**, 526–528.

Kashani J.H., Rosenberg T.K. & Reid J.C. (1989) Developmental perspective in child and adolescent depressive symptoms in a community sample. *American Journal of Psychiatry*, **146**, 871–875.

Kleinman A. (1986) *Social Origins of Distress and Disease: Depression Neurasthenia and Pain in Modern China*. Yale University Press, New Haven, CT.

Koocher G.P. & O'Malley J.E. (1981) *The Damocles Syndrome*. McGraw Hill, New York.

Kovacs M., Feinberg T.L., Paulauskas S., Finkelstein R., Pollock M. & Crouse-Novak M. (1985) Initial coping responses and psychosocial characteristics of children with insulin dependent diabetes mellitus. *Journal of Pediatrics*, **106**, 827–834.

Kupst M.J., Schulman J.L., Maurer H., Honig G., Morgan E. & Fochtman D. (1984) Coping with pediatric leukemia: a two-year follow-up. *Journal of Pediatric Psychology*, **9**, 149–163.

Larsson B.S. (1991) Somatic complaints and their relationship to depressive symptoms in Swedish adolescents. *Journal of Child Psychology and Psychiatry*, **32**, 821–832.

Leff A.R. (1988) Neurohumoral regulation of airway contractile responses. *Chest*, **93**, 1285–1287.

Love B., Byrne C., Roberts J., Browne G. & Brown B. (1987) Adult psychosocial adjustment following childhood injury: the effect of disfigurement. *Journal of Burn Case and Rehabilitation*, **8**, 280–285.

McFadyen A., Broster G. & Black D. (1991) The impact of a child psychiatry liaison service on patterns of referral. *British Journal of Psychiatry*, **158**, 93–96.

McNichol K., Williams H., Allan H. & McAndrew I. (1973) Spectrum of asthma in children. III. Psychological and social components. *British Medical Journal*, **4**, 16.

Matthew D.J., Taylor B., Norman A.P., Turner M.W. & Soothill J.F. (1977) Prevention of eczema. *Lancet*, **1**, 321–324.

Mattsson A. (1972) Long-term physical illness in childhood: a challenge to psychosocial adaptation. *Pediatrics*, **50**, 801–811.

Meadow R. (1982) Munchausen syndrome by proxy. *Archives of Disease in Childhood*, **57**, 92–98.

Meadow R. (1985) Management of Munchausen syndrome of proxy. *Archives of Disease in Childhood*, **60**, 385–393.

Miller B.D. (1987) Depression and asthma: a potentially lethal mixture. *Journal of Allergy and Clinical Immunology*, **80**, 48.

Millstein S.G., Adler N.E. & Irwin C.E. (1981) Conceptions of illness in young adolescents. *Pediatrics*, **68**, 834–839.

Minuchin S. & Fishman H. (1979) The psychosomatic family in child psychiatry. *American Academy of Child Psychiatry*, **18**, 76–90.

Mirvish I. (1978) Hypnotherapy for the child with chronic eczema. *South African Medical Journal*, **54**, 410–411.

Moehle K.A. & Berg R.A. (1985) Academic achievement and intelligence test performance in children with center at diagnosis and one year later. *Developmental Behavior in Pediatrics*, **6**, 62–64.

Moran G.S. (1984) Psychoanalytic treatment of diabetic children. In: Solnit A.J., Eissler R.S. & Neubauer P.B. (eds) *The Psychoanalytic Study of the Child*, pp. 407–447. Yale University Press, New Haven, CT.

Mrazek D.A. (1985) Cystic fibrosis: a systems analysis of psychiatric consequences. *Advances in Psychosomatic Medicine*, **14**, 119–135.

Mrazek D.A. (1993) Disturbed emotional development in severely asthmatic children. In: West A. & Christie M.J. (eds) *Quality of Life in Childhood Asthma*, pp. 67–76. Carden, Chichester.

Mrazek D.A. & Klinnert M. (1991) Asthma: Psychoneuroimmunological considerations. In: Ader R., Felten D.L. & Cohein N. (eds) *Psychoneuroimmunology II*, pp. 1013–1035. Academic Press, Orlando.

Mrazek D., Anderson I. & Strunk R. (1984) Disturbed emotional development of severely asthmatic preschool children. In: Stevenson J. (ed) *Recent Research in Developmental Psychopathology*, pp. 81–94. Pergamon Press, Oxford.

Mrazek D.A., Klinnert M., Mrazek P. & Macey T. (1991) Early asthma onset: consideration of parenting issues. *Journal of the American Academy of Child and Adolescent Psychiatry*, **30**, 277–282.

Orr D.P., Weller S.C., Satterwhite B. & Pless I.B. (1984) Psychosocial implications of chronic illness in adolescence. *Journal of Pediatrics*, **104**, 152–157.

Packer R.J., Sutton L.N., Atkins T.E., Radcliffe J., Bunin G.R., D'Angio G., Siegel K.R. & Schut L. (1989) A prospective study of cognitive function in children receiving whole-brain radiotherapy and chemotherapy: 2-year results. *Journal of Neurosurgery*, **70**, 707–713.

Pavlovsky S., Castano J., Leiguarda R., Fisman N., Chamoles N., Moreno R. & Arizaga R. (1983) Neuropsychological study in patients with ALL. *American Journal of Pediatric Hematology*, **5**, 79–86.

Perrin E.C. & Gerrity P.S. (1981) There's a demon in your belly: children's understanding of illness. *Pediatrics*, **67**, 841–849.

Perrin J.M., MacLean W.E. & Perrin E.C. (1989) Parental perceptions of health status and psychologic adjustment of children with asthma. *Pediatrics*, **83**, 1.

Petzel S.V., Bugge I., Warwick W.J. & Budd J.R. (1984) Long term adaptation of children and adolescents with cystic fibrosis: identification of common problems and risk factors. In: Blum R.W. (ed) *Chronic Illness and Disabilities in Childhood and Adolescence*, pp. 413–427. Grune & Stratton, New York.

Pless I.B. & Roghmann K.J. (1971) Chronic illness and its consequences: observations based on three epidemiologic surveys. *Journal of Pediatrics*, **79**, 351–359.

Popkin M.K., Callies A.L., Lentz R.D., Colon E.A. & Sutherland D.E. (1988) Prevalence of major depression, simple phobia, and other psychiatric disorders in patients with long-standing type I diabetes mellitus. *Archives of General Psychiatry*, **45**, 64–68.

Preston K. (1969) Depression and skin diseases. *The Medical Journal of Australia*, **5**, 326–329.

Prugh D.G., Straub E.M., Sands H.H., Kirschbaum R.M. & Lenihan E.A. (1953) A study of the emotional reactions of children and families to hospitalization and illness. *American Journal of Orthopsychiatry*, **23**, 70–106.

Pumariega A.J., Pursell J., Spock A. & Jones J.D. (1986) Eating disorders in adolescents with cystic fibrosis. *Journal of the American Academy of Child Psychiatry*, **25**, 269–275.

Quinton D. & Rutter M. (1976) Early hospitalization and later disturbances of behavior: an attempted replication of Douglas' findings. *Developmental Medicine and Child Neurology*, **18**, 447–459.

Riley W.J., MacLaren N.K., Krischer J., Spillar R.P., Silverstein J.H., Schatz D.A., Schwarts S., Malone J., Shah S., Vadheim C. & Rotter J.I. (1990) A prospective study of the development of diabetes in relatives of patients with insulin-dependent diabetes. *New England Journal of Medicine*, **323**, 1167–1172.

Riordan J.R., Rommens J.M., Kerem B., Alon N., Rozmahel R., Grzelczak A., Zielenski J., Lok S., Plavsic N., Chou J.L., Drumm M., Iannuzzi M.C., Collins F.S. & Tsui L.C. (1989) Identification of the cystic fibrosis gene: cloning and characterization of complemetary DNA. *Science*, **245**, 1066–1073.

Rivinus T.M., Jamison D.L. & Graham P.J. (1975) Childhood organic neurological disease presenting as psychiatric disorder. *Archives of Disease in Childhood*, **50**, 115–119.

Ryan N.D., Puig-Antich J., Ambrosini P., Rabinovich H., Robinson D., Nelson B., Iyengar S. & Twomey J. (1987) The clinical picture of major depression in children and adolescents. *Archives of General Psychiatry*, **44**, 854–861.

Sabbeth B.F. & Leventhal J.M. (1984) Marital adjustment to chronic childhood illness: a critique of the literature. *Pediatrics*, **73**, 762–768.

Sawyer M., Crettenden A. & Toogood I. (1986) Psychological adjustment of families of children and adolescents treated for leukemia. *American Journal of Peadiatric Hematology Oncology*, **8**, 200–207.

Sawyer M.G., Toogood I., Rise M., Haskell C. & Baghurst P. (1989) School performance and psychological adjustment of children treated for leukemia. *American Journal of Pediatric Hematology and Oncology*, **11**, 146–152.

Seaquist E.R., Goetz F.C., Rich S. & Barbosa J. (1989) Familial clustering of diabetic kidney disease. *New England Journal of Medicine*, **320**, 1161–1165.

Sly M. (1988) Co-morbidity from asthma in children 1979–1984. *Annuals of Allergy*, **60**, 433–443.

Snyder S.H. (1980) Brain peptides as neurotransmitters. *Science*, **209**, 976.

Snyder S.H. (1982) Neurotransmitters and CNS disease: schizophrenia. *Lancet*, **2**, 970.

Steinhausen H. (1982) Locus of control among psychosomatically and chronically ill children and adolescents. *Journal of Abnormal Child Psychology*, **10**, 609–616.

Steinhausen H. & Schindler H. (1981) Psychosocial adaptation in children and adolescents with cystic fibrosis. *Developmental and Behavioral Pediatrics*, **2**, 3.

Steinhausen H., Schindler H. & Stephan H. (1983) Correlates of psychopathology in sick children. An empirical model. *Journal of the American Academy of Child Psychiatry*, **22**, 559.

Strunk R.C., Mrazek D.A., Wolfson G.S. & LaBrecque J.F. (1985) Physiological and psychological characteristics associated with deaths from asthma in childhood: a case-controlled study. *Journal of the American Medical Association*, **254**, 1193–1198.

Strunk R.C., Mrazek D.A., Fukuhara J.T., Masterson J., Ludwick S.K. & LaBrecque J.F. (1989) Cardiovascular fitness in children with asthma correlates with psychologic functioning of the child. *Pediatrics*, **84**, 460–464.

Taussig L., Cohen M. & Sieber O. Jr (1976) Psychosexual and psychosocial aspects of cystic fibrosis. *Medical Aspects of Human Sexuality*, **10**, 101–102.

Tritt S.G. & Esses L.M. (1988) Psychosocial adaptation of siblings of children with chronic medical illnesses. *American Journal of Orthopsychiatry*, **58**, 211–220.

Ullman K.C., Moore R.W. & Reidy M. (1977) Atopic eczema: a clinical psychiatric study. *Journal of Asthma Research*, **14**, 91–99.

Venters M. (1981) Familial coping with chronic and severe childhood illness: the case of cystic fibrosis. *Social Science Medicine*, **15A**, 289–297.

Wallander J.L., Varni J.W., Babani L., Banis H.T. & Wilcox K.T. (1988) Children with chronic physical disorders: maternal reports of their psychological adjustment. *Journal of Pediatric Psychology*, **13**, 197–212.

Weisz J.R., Suwanlert S., Chaiyasit W., Weiss B. & Jackson E.W. (1991) Adult attitudes toward over- and under-controlled child problems: urban and rural parents and teachers from Thailand and the United States. *Journal of Child Psychology and Psychiatry*, **32**, 645–654.

White K., Kolman M.L. Wexler P., Polin G. & Winter R.J. (1984) Unstable diabetes and unstable families: a psychosocial evaluation of diabetic children with recurrent ketoacidosis. *Pediatrics*, **73**, 749–755.

Wilkinson G. (1987) The influence of psychiatric, psychological and social factors on the control of insulin-dependent diabetes mellitus. *Journal of Psychosomatic Research*, **31**, 277–286.

World Health Organization (1992) *The ICD-10 Classification of Mental and Behavioural Disorders: Clinical Descriptions and Diagnostic Guidelines*, World Health Organization, Geneva.

Zeiger R.S., Heller S., Mellon M., O'Connor R. & Hamburger R.N. (1986) Effectiveness of dietary manipulation in the prevention of food allergy in infants. *Journal of Allergy and Clinical Immunology*, **78**, 224–238.

Chapter 40
Psychiatric Aspects of Human Immunodeficiency Virus in Childhood and Adolescence

Chris Thompson, Pamela Westwell & Deborah Viney

The first reports of an apparently new disease began to appear in the late 1970s among homosexuals, haemophiliacs, Haitians and intravenous drug users in the US. It was at first difficult to recognize the disorder because of its wide range of manifestations; infections with normally nonpathogenic organisms and rare tumours were prominent. The occurrence first among stigmatized groups has tended to determine and heighten the ethical debate, but as time has gone by, and with the discovery of the causative virus and its natural history, the disease has fallen into place among the retroviral conditions. However the fact that it is a fatal, sexually transmitted or blood-borne disease continues to guarantee a certain level of prurient interest from the general population, and a genuine ethical debate.

Readers of this chapter must be aware of the difference between human immunodeficiency virus (HIV) infection, which may be asymptomatic, and acquired immunodeficiency syndrome (AIDS), which is a clinical syndrome. There are also differences in the epidemic between the US, Europe, and the less developed nations. While much of our knowledge is drawn from adults, only a part of it is applicable to children. We have indicated where direct knowledge is available for children and where it has been necessary to extrapolate from work with adults.

THE VIRUS

HIV is a member of the retrovirus family which also includes human lymphotrophic viruses I and II, which cause types of adult leukaemia, and HIV-II which is closely related to HIV-I but is endemic only in West Africa. In the cylindrical core of HIV is the RNA genome and the reverse transcriptase by which the virus replicates. This is surrounded by a glycoprotein envelope that has receptors for specific host cells, especially the CD4 subset of the T-cell population, to which it attaches prior to invasion. By a process of syncytia formation and cell death the CD4 population of cells is reduced, leading to severely impaired cell-mediated immunity and a host of secondary opportunistic infections and malignancies, often by organisms which are not usually pathogenic. In addition the virus attaches to, invades and destroys macrophages in the central nervous system, which become pathological multinucleated giant cells before disintegrating. It is likely that the destruction of the giant cells produces neuronal damage by an 'innocent bystander' effect since direct invasion of neurons by the virus has not been seen. These two related pathological effects of the virus produce the two major clinical syndromes of HIV infection, AIDS and HIV encephalopathy, sometimes known as AIDS dementia (Bryant & Ratner, 1991). In fact the relationship between these two clinical syndromes is still under investigation and it may be more appropriate to state that HIV encephalopathy is one of the syndromes that can occur in the course of AIDS.

EPIDEMIOLOGY

The first report of AIDS in children came from the US in 1982. By 1987 AIDS was the ninth largest cause of death in 1—4-year-olds and the seventh in 15—24-year-olds in the US. However, the populations most at risk, poor, black and Hispanic communities, show a much higher prevalence, AIDS being the third most frequent killer of 1—4-year-olds. By 1990 there had been 2000 reports of children with AIDS in the US (2% of all AIDS cases; Koop, 1991). UK figures showed 44 reports to the same date in children under 14 (AIDS/HIV quarterly surveillance tables: PHLS AIDS centre and Communicable diseases (Scotland) Unit, June 1990). Even allowing for the fourfold difference in total population between these two countries, the excess morbidity in the US is obvious, and correspondingly AIDS is very low-ranking as a cause of death in children in the UK.

It is now known that there has been for some time a very large epidemic in Africa with cases being retrospectively diagnosed, as long ago as 1976. There and in other developing countries, paediatric AIDS constitutes 15—25% of all cases, higher than in the US because of the greater prevalence of a heterosexual source of infection and therefore the greater chance of vertical transmission from mother to child. Some 5—10% of young adults in urban areas of Zaire, Zambia, Kenya and Rwanda were shown to be infected in a study by Biggar (1986). There are associations with city life, higher socioeconomic status and high levels of heterosexual activity (Pinching, 1986). As the proportion of adult heterosexual infection increases in the developed world, so the proportion of paediatric AIDS cases will increase in parallel. The World Health Organization estimates that more than 1 million children were affected by the end of 1992, half of whom had AIDS (Mok, 1991).

SOURCES OF INFECTION IN CHILDREN

There are four major sources of infection in children and adolescents, of which three are also found in adults: (1) vertical transmission; (2) infection by blood products; (3) sexually transmitted disease; and (4) intravenous drug use.

Vertical transmission

The only source of infection not currently found in the adult population is vertical transmission. Females account for 9–13% of all AIDS cases and an infected mother may pass the virus transplacentally to the fetus (Oxtoby, 1991). The presentation therefore occurs mostly during infancy (Wittenberg & Lazenby, 1989). Only about 50–65% of all babies born to infected mothers are infected with the virus. However, it takes up to 15 months for the passively transferred maternal HIV antibodies to clear from the infant's blood, allowing a negative diagnosis to be made in a proportion of those with antibodies at birth.

The precise mode of transmission of the virus is still unknown, but in most cases is presumed to be transplacental. At the time of writing, the frequency of transmission in breast milk is unclear. In a 17-month follow-up study of 212 mother–infant pairs who were negative at birth, 16 mothers converted during the postnatal period and 9 of their infants became seropositive (Van de Perre *et al.*, 1991). However, taking into account the timing of the seroconversion, only the 4 children (25% of those at risk) who had late (4–21 months) seroconversion can be said to have definitely acquired it through breast milk or colostrum (Pizzo & Butler, 1991). Therefore the risk of infection through this route appears to lie between 25 and 50%. However the danger of infections of other kinds when bottle-feeding in the Third World needs to be weighed against the risk of HIV infection in breast milk (Read, 1986; Gibb, 1991).

There was a 38% increase in vertical transmission in the US between 1988 and 1989. The usual mode of infection by which the mother acquired the virus was sharing of needles in illicit drug use (70% of all infected women) and intercourse with an infected man (about 30%), who usually himself acquired it from infected needles.

This form of infection accounts for 70–80% of all paediatric cases and is increasing. In capital cities of East Africa, e.g. Kampala, the HIV-positive rate among pregnant women is 20–30%, although this figure is lower in rural areas. Similar figures are seen in some areas of South-East Asia and in Latin America, and the recent trends have been upwards.

Some 25% of children infected at birth will develop AIDS in the first year of life (17% die) and 80% will have AIDS by the end of the fourth year (Mok, 1991).

Infection by blood products

The majority of these cases are patients with haemophilia who received nonheat-treated clotting factor concentrates prior to 1983. This source of infection is now less common due to screening and heat treatment of blood products. Prior to this precaution the risk of receiving the infection depended upon the severity of haemophilia. In the severe group about 75% were infected, 45% in the moderate group and 25% in the mild group (Eyster, 1991). Individuals with other illnesses who have been transfused with infected whole blood have also been at risk, e.g. neonatal blood transfusions (Church, 1984).

Compared with other children with AIDS, haemophiliac children tend to be older but they have a case : fatality ratio which is the same as in children with AIDS from other causes (Jason *et al.*, 1988). In a study of 57 haemophiliac boys with HIV infection the most accurate prognostic indicator was shown to be a persistently falling CD4 count, indicating the imminent development of clinical symptoms (Williams *et al.*, 1988). Darby *et al.* (1990) and Lee *et al.* (1989) have shown that the length of the asymptomatic interval decreases with increasing age at seroconversion. Seven years later 6% of those aged under 25 at seroconversion, 20% aged 25–44, and 34% aged 45 and over had developed AIDS.

Sexually transmitted disease

Adolescents are frequently sexually active and are therefore at risk of developing AIDS if they have unprotected sex. Among adolescents with HIV infection those who are older, male (80%) or from the ethnic minorities (in the US) predominate (Gayle & D'Angelo, 1991). Those with a homosexual preference are particularly at risk in this age group (Belfer *et al.*, 1988). Many of these teenagers also have troubles at school, with substance abuse and with authority as well as histories of emotional difficulties and sexually transmitted diseases.

Intravenous drug use

Figures are usually given for intravenous drug use combined with sexual contact in a 'behaviour-related' category, since in many cases both risk behaviours are present. Older adolescents are again at highest risk. Sexual and intravenous drug use combined account for 10% of US cases of AIDS aged 13–14, 20% aged 15–16, and 70% aged 17–19. The critical age for education about AIDS therefore appears to be around 12–14 (Overby *et al.*, 1989).

CLINICAL FEATURES OF HIV INFECTION AND AIDS IN CHILDHOOD AND ADOLESCENCE

Broadly speaking the effects of the virus in childhood and adolescence are the same as in adults, causing immune deficiency with secondary diseases on the one hand and central nervous system (CNS) involvement on the other (which itself is secondary to viral attack upon CNS immune system). However in the young the prevalence of the various complications varies from age to age and the pattern also differs from adults.

When attempts were made to stage the disease in a similar way to adults it was found that many symptomatic children did not reach Centers for Disease Control (CDC) criteria for AIDS. Therefore a new paediatric system of staging was developed, as described below (US Department of Health and Human Services, 1987).

During the early stages the patient is asymptomatic (stage P-1). In this stage there may be normal immune function (stage P-1A) or the immune function may start to deteriorate (stage P-1B). This may occur for some time before clinical signs and symptoms appear. The evidence can be found in an absolute lymphopenia and reduced CD4 count, a reducing CD4 : CD8 ratio and raised immunoglobulin levels.

As symptoms develop the patient enters class P-2 in which a number of diseases can occur. There may be nonspecific findings, such as failure to thrive (P-2A). Progressive neurological disease (P-2B) includes loss of developmental milestones, acquired microcephaly or cerebral atrophy, and progressive symmetrical motor deficits (see below).

Apart from these direct effects on the CNS leading to neurological and psychiatric syndromes, other secondary diseases may also have an influence on mental state. For example, confusional states or neoplasms with cerebral secondaries can occur. These other diseases include lymphoid interstitial pneumonitis (P-2C), secondary infectious diseases (P-2D) or secondary cancers (P-2E).

The diagnosis of HIV infection is made by observation of the presence of one of the index diseases and/or by laboratory testing. This may include HIV antibody or antigen testing as well as the laboratory tests referred to above. In very young infants up to 15 months of age the presence of HIV antibody is unreliable as an indicator of disease since it may have been passively transferred from the mother without viral passage.

In infancy there is often a failure to thrive, developmental delay and regression, focal neurological deficit, pyramidal tract signs, seizures, progressive dementia due to encephalopathy, somnolence and coma, microcephaly, and opportunistic infections and malignancies (Wittenberg & Lazenby, 1989; Brouwers *et al.*, 1991).

Differential diagnosis

Psychological symptoms in a child whose mother is known to be HIV-positive can have several causes. In infancy, there is the possibility of emotional deprivation secondary to maternal loss, since the mothers are, almost by definition, unwell with a terminal illness. In addition the infant may be suffering from withdrawal symptoms of the mother's drug use and in rare cases a congenital abnormality may be present.

Where the onset of, for example, refusal to eat and mutism coincides with the death of the mother they may well be part of the psychological response to the death rather than due to the development of the disease. Similarly, mothers with AIDS may be deprived themselves and unable to care adequately for their babies, leading to malnutrition, and physical or emotional neglect.

It is rare that the mother who is a drug user (or is otherwise at risk) is of unknown HIV status, but under these circumstances the HIV status of the infant should be suspected to be positive if there is failure to thrive for no apparent reason, or if it is out of proportion to that which would be expected in the social circumstances of the family with drug abuse.

In older children and adolescents the results of antibody testing are more reliable. However it is necessary before testing to ensure that there is consent from an adult, and when it seems appropriate from the adolescent as well. The decision to carry out a test should never be taken lightly and a full assessment of the likely benefits and risks of the test to the patient should be made with the multidisciplinary child health team.

NEUROLOGICAL MANIFESTATIONS OF AIDS IN CHILDREN AND ADOLESCENTS

In adult patients, there are a number of neurological features of active HIV infection, including progressive dementia, spinal cord degeneration, myoclonus and epilepsy. Together these are often referred to as AIDS dementia complex or HIV encephalopathy.

A similar syndrome has been found to occur in older children as well as in infants. Epstein *et al.* (1985) reported 4 children (age 9 months to 11 years) with AIDS who had loss of developmental milestones, and weakness with pyramidal tract signs. Two were ataxic; 1 was cortically blind and had myoclonus in the later stages. Two had isolated seizures during the course of the illness. Two had secondary microcephaly and all 4 had cortical atrophy on computerized scanning. At postmortem there was gross cortical atrophy, microglial nodules and intranuclear inclusions similar to those found in adults.

In a further report (Epstein *et al.*, 1986) the results of 36 children with HIV were described in detail. A progressive encephalopathy developed in 1 out of 3 otherwise asymptomatic children, 3 out of 12 with symptoms falling short of AIDS and 16 out of 21 with AIDS. The neurological disease appeared to run in parallel with the immunodeficiency, as is the case in the adult disease. It was a sign of a poor prognosis: indeed it had an almost invariably fatal outcome (Epstein *et al.*, 1988). The incubation period from the initial infection to encephalopathy varied greatly from 2 months to 5 years. Active brain infection with HIV was clearly demonstrated in 8 of the 14 children in whom it was examined, correlating reasonably well but not fully with the presence of clinical symptoms.

Ultmann *et al.* (1985) also reported a cohort of 16 children aged 6 months to 6 years with AIDS or symptomatic HIV infection who showed delayed milestones, especially motor milestones. This was most pronounced in the AIDS group in which there was a loss of previously achieved milestones, and more severe cognitive abnormalities on testing. However, on follow-up after 14 months a very variable picture emerged (Ultmann *et al.*, 1987). Five had died and neurological deterioration was seen in a further 9. These 9 had encephalopathy, acquired microcephaly, and pyramidal tract signs. Computed tomography (CT) scan showed varying atrophy with ventricular dilatation and calcification, particularly in the basal ganglia. At neuropathology there was calcification in the blood vessels of the basal ganglia (Belman *et al.*, 1986), corticospinal tract degeneration and nonspecific white matter changes (Belman *et al.*, 1985). On formal cognitive testing 2 showed regression in function, 6 were progressing as expected for age and 2 were performing better than expected. Developmental progression was in some cases compatible with deteriorating clinical/ neurological course. Treatment and rehabilitation therefore needed to be tailored to individual requirements.

In a group of 68 children with symptomatic HIV infection, 61 had CNS dysfunction (Belman *et al.*, 1988), while only 10 children had opportunistic CNS pathogens or malignancy. The course was steadily progressive in 11, indolent in 31, and static in 17 with cognitive abnormality alone (7) or cognitive plus neurological abnormality (10). Those children with a static course showed normal or mildly atrophic CT scans but poor brain growth (Brouwers *et al.*, 1991).

In a less pessimistic report from the European Collaborative Study only 31% of children with already established AIDS had significant CNS symptoms. Even HIV-negative children had minor neurological symptoms due to drug withdrawal — an important differential diagnosis (Newell, 1990). This may account for the failure to find the virus in the brains of all the children with apparent encephalopathy who come to postmortem. For example, the virus was identified in the brains of only 2 out of 4 children with HIV encephalopathy by Shaw *et al.* (1985), and by more sophisticated techniques in only 3 out of 7 children with the disease by Vazeux *et al.* (1991).

Clinicians need to remember that there are many causes of dementia (see Chapter 11) that can mimic AIDS, and differential diagnosis is needed. There are sometimes pronounced neurological symptoms and signs in children with AIDS. These appear particularly to affect rapidly developing brain areas such as cortex and basal ganglia. However there are many other causes of neurological and intellectual decline in such children and there is great variability in the course of the illness. It is therefore important not to place too much prognostic significance upon a single abnormal test result but to wait until there is objective evidence of declining neurological and cognitive function before diagnosing HIV infection of the CNS.

NEUROPSYCHOLOGICAL FINDINGS

Few studies have described the cognitive symptoms in perinatally infected children surviving to an age when they can be tested. During infancy the delayed acquisition of milestones —

especially motor — referred to in the previous section are prominent signs. There is also a delay in the development of expressive language functions. This syndrome is probably analogous to the HIV encephalopathy in adults.

In adults, the course of the encephalopathy in relation to the immune deficiency is generally parallel. Those who have symptomatic infection are more at risk of compromised cognitive function. However there remains some controversy surrounding claims that there are subtle early manifestations of direct viral action within the CNS during the asymptomatic stage. Grant (1990) has recommended that these early signs be classified as 'neurobehavioural disorders associated with HIV' to distinguish them from the AIDS dementia, where symptoms must reach criteria for global dementia. However a consensus statement from the World Health Organization (1988) does not lend support to the concept of early cognitive changes in asymptomatic patients. Often when such supposedly asymptomatic patients are reassessed retrospectively they are found to have been suffering from very early symptoms not yet recognized or to have had a falling CD4 count. Goethe *et al.* (1989) found no excess of abnormal cognitive tests in asymptomatic adults compared with HIV-negative controls, a finding confirmed by the very large multicentre AIDS Cohort Study (McArthur *et al.*, 1989). Lunn *et al.* (1991) found that the severity of cognitive abnormalities correlated with the grade of the disease.

In children the initial results from the European Collaborative Study (Cogo *et al.*, 1990) of children born to HIV-infected mothers confirm reports that systemic disease almost always precedes neurological disease. The rate of encephalopathy was put at 8–13% for serious signs and a further 6% for minor signs. This compares with rates of 1.2 and 3% respectively in the HIV-negative group, attributed to drug withdrawal states. These rates are lower than reports from other smaller studies, a finding which emphasizes the variability of such findings, probably because of differing thresholds for diagnosis and variations in the general levels of health care in the study groups.

In formalizing the cognitive testing in children, most investigators have chosen age-appropriate tests such as the Bayley Scales of infant development, the Stanford–Binet intelligence tests, the Kauffman assessment battery for children and the Wechsler Intelligence Scale for Children. Brouwers *et al.* (1990) have discussed the specificity of the cognitive findings for HIV patients. However, the two main findings of high inter- and intratest score scatter and some apparently nonprogressive deficits cannot be said to identify a specific profile. The abilities which are more susceptible to selective deficits are those associated with expressive behaviour, and expressive language function may be deficient despite intact receptive verbal function. Detailed results will of course depend upon the age of the child and the severity and speed of progression of the disease.

Three types of progression have been identified: (1) subacute progressive encephalopathy; (2) plateau course; and (3) static encephalopathy.

Subacute progressive encephalopathy

Infants and young children will show a deterioration of play, loss of previously acquired language and socially adaptive skills, progressive motor dysfunction and various neurological signs. They become increasingly apathetic and lose interest in their environment. There is a decrease in gesture and vocalization, an alert and wide-eyed expression, but with a lack of spontaneous facial movement. In the final stage the child is mute, dull-eyed and quadriparetic. Older children show loss of interest in school and gradually slow down. Attention deficit disorders may develop or worsen, and emotional lability can occur.

Plateau course

In this type the evidence becomes gradually more obvious that the rate of normal cognitive development is slowing. This becomes clear both from the norms for the age and from the child's own prior rate of achievement. No initial loss of previously acquired developmental milestones occurs but the mental development age remains the same for months. Further progression after this stage varies but the progressive course described above may eventually supervene. Infrequently a child may appear to improve after the plateau stage but the rate of acquisition of new skills remains slow. The cognitive performance gradually falls into the range of the learning-disabled (e.g. IQ 50–70).

Static encephalopathy

About 25% of symptomatic children show nonprogressive cognitive and motor deficits. Such children continue to acquire new developmental skills and their IQs remain stable for their age. Hyperactivity is common. Brain growth is normal in rate (Epstein *et al.*, 1988).

The study of the effects of HIV infection acquired at different ages in childhood may provide more general information about the developing brain and its vulnerabilities. The observation, for example, that the most rapidly developing areas are most affected seems to be borne out in the observations to date. However, the amount and the nature of the information which is so far available would not allow of any useful generalizations.

Progressive intellectual decline in children who were not previously known to be infected but who were at risk, requires full investigation. There are, however, many other causes of such a decline, including other brain diseases and psychiatric disorders, which should also be borne in mind. When intellectual decline appears as a symptom in isolation from immunological complications of AIDS then further complications are seldom a long time developing. Usually in these cases the CD4 count is already falling and immunological deficiencies are beginning, although still subclinical.

PSYCHOLOGICAL ASPECTS

Empirical data on the psychological and family correlates of HIV infection are sparse and to date most of the evidence is drawn from the experience of workers in the field or from comparisons with other chronic childhood diseases.

HIV infection almost always coexists with preceding social adversity. At any time the condition can become symptomatic. It affects not only the individual but also the lives and continuity of the whole family. The families have their future expectations affected and may experience a wide range of negative emotions such as fear of loss, guilt, anxiety and anger. They have to cope with a powerful stigma and the consequent isolation.

The reaction of an adult to a diagnosis of HIV infection in his or her child is often denial. This can recur throughout the course of the disease. Often it is a normal response but it may sometimes interfere with the care of the child (Spiegal & Mayers, 1991).

Feelings of guilt are common in all parents, irrespective of the mode of transmission. Where vertical transmission is concerned the reality of the mother's drug use often adds to the burden of guilt which is felt even by the parents of children infected via blood or blood products. For example, where a mother has treated her haemophiliac son at home, the thought that she made the tranfusion can cause great feelings of guilt. Such feelings are exacerbated during periods of active illness, causing problems in the family and sometimes between the family and medical staff. Expressions of anger towards the hospital, especially in iatrogenic infection, or towards other at-risk groups such as intravenous drug users or homosexuals are not uncommon. It is often useful for the professionals involved to facilitate the expression of this anger.

In general, families choose to tell only a small number of close relatives about the diagnosis, often continuing to hedge or lie about it even after the child's death. Sometimes a grandparent is kept out of the secret, for fear of old-fashioned attitudes. As a result of the close guarding of the secret, health professionals are often the only source of support (Mok, 1989), placing a greater than usual burden on them.

A major source of distress is the uncertainty of the prognosis. The child's slow deterioration is often devastating to the parents and the neurological and cognitive signs are often the most difficult to accept. (Weiner & Septimus, 1991). In vertical transmission the extra source of uncertainty imposed by the 15-month wait to see if antibodies disappear is particularly hard. In addition the parent and the child are often ill at the same time. The ill mother will have greater problems in providing the health care and emotional needs of the child (Spiegal & Mayers, 1991). In the Third World there are additional problems of poverty and its hygiene and nutritional consequences. In developed countries the families are often unstable and prostitution, intravenous drug use and unemployment are major factors to be taken into account in clinical decision-making about the future of the child.

Children infected via blood products have to cope with the

diagnosis, treatment and uncertain future of two diseases (Waters *et al.*, 1988). However such children have already been challenged by their preexisting disease to develop coping skills and professional and lay support networks, and this may be an important factor in their apparent resilience in dealing with their HIV status. For example, Logan *et al.* (1990) found no excess psychiatric morbidity in HIV-positive compared to HIV-negative haemophiliacs.

The siblings of children with any chronic disease tend to be a neglected group (Eiser, 1990). Parents focus so much attention on the sick child that they have little time for the needs of the healthy sibling. This places the healthy siblings at increased risk for emotional and conduct disorders. In HIV infection the siblings are often not told the diagnosis, even though they may guess or be suspicious. If they are told the diagnosis they may be drawn closer to the family, at the expense of becoming more aware of the stigma attached to them (Weiner & Septimus, 1991). Studies identifying a high incidence of behavioural disturbance in the siblings of HIV-infected children must however be treated with caution, because of the large number of associated variables such as parental drug use (Harris, 1990).

Normal children born to HIV-infected mothers are also victims of the epidemic. Between 30 and 50% of children born to HIV-infected mothers will not themselves be infected. The reason for this is unclear but it parallels the situation in transfusion-acquired HIV where 10% of those exposed to the virus fail to develop infection. Some children will have been born to mothers or fathers who contract HIV infection after the birth. The World Health Organization estimates that there will be over 1 million such children during the 1990s (Mok, 1991). They will clearly not suffer from AIDS but will suffer the traumas of maternal (and sometimes paternal) illness and death, often at a very young age and, especially in the Third World, they are likely to suffer the consequences of an inadequate system of care for orphans and one-parent families. Grandparents may be called upon to become directly involved with the child's care before or after the death of the parent while they are themselves struggling with the loss of their own child.

Adoption may need to be considered at some point, leading to a great many questions about the prognosis for the child, the cause of the HIV infection in the parents, etc. Under these circumstances doctors need to act in concert with adoption agencies to the highest ethical standards, especially where they concern the right to confidentiality. The health, social and financial implications of this epidemic of orphans have not yet been properly assessed.

When assessing families with HIV infection of one or more members it is important to keep in mind the physical and cognitive limitations placed upon the ill members by the disease, which may limit their ability to work in psychotherapeutic approaches in some cases. Nevertheless the psychosocial implications of the disease are vast for the family and their social environment and some attention should always be paid to the psychological and social welfare of all members of the family, including those who do not have the illness.

MANAGEMENT OF HIV INFECTION IN CHILDREN

Aims of treatment

Treatment must have three objectives, of which the first and overriding priority is the aggressive treatment of the diseases arising from the immune deficiency. It is not within the scope of this chapter to discuss all the available treatments for all of the complications of HIV infection.

Appropriate antiretroviral therapy (e.g. zidovudine) should be given at an appropriate stage in the disease process. Knowledge on this point is in a stage of evolution. Zidovudine can improve the prognosis in adults for those with established AIDS (Fischl *et al.*, 1987).

In children, Blanche *et al.* (1988) found that 100 mg intravenously every 6 hours for 14 days followed by the same dose orally for 6 months was associated with marked improvement in 2 out of 8 children with AIDS and a transient improvement in another 3. One child with encephalopathy was among the improvers. CD4 counts increased transiently in 4 children.

Pizzo *et al.* (1988) carried out an open multiple-dose comparison study of between 0.5 and 1.8 mg/kg per hour of continuous-infusion zidovudine in 21 children aged 14 months to 2 years, all of whom were symptomatic and 13 of whom had neurodevelopmental abnormalities. The optimum dose for efficacy and side-effect limitation appeared to be 0.9–1.4 mg/kg per hour. There appeared to be an improvement in the developmental abnormalities in all 13 children with encephalopathy. The IQ scores of these 13 rose over the course of the 6-month follow-up by a mean 15 points. CT and positron emission tomography scan findings also improved in some patients. The improvement persisted for 12 months. In general there were also improvements in immunological parameters but these appeared to be independent of the improvements in neurological function.

A study to examine more specifically the effect of zidovudine on neuropsychological function was carried out by Brouwers *et al.* (1990). Eight of 13 children were classified as having encephalopathy before treatment. After 6 months of continuous infusion there was a 15.5-point increase in general IQ. The group of 10 who survived to 1 year retained these gains. The authors concluded strongly and rather illadvisedly that 'neuropsychological functioning was significantly improved with continuous infusion AZT'. The studies of zidovudine in children to date have been open studies but they suggest at least the possibility that disease progression, including CNS disease, can be modified to some degree.

Increasingly there is clinical evidence that zidovudine can slow the rate of progression to AIDS in early symptomatic HIV-positive individuals. Therefore the trend is to treat earlier than before, in spite of the sometimes high toxicity of the drug. Since the toxic effects appear to be greater in more advanced disease there is a logic in early treatment. Thus if a child appears to have borderline abnormalities on psychological testing in the absence of other obvious symptoms of the disease, and there is evidence of deterioration of function without other likely cause, then the decision to prescribe zidovudine should be considered.

HIV appears to be compatible with prolonged survival in some cases so the disease process must be prevented from interfering with the development of the child as much as possible. This can bring with it clinical, psychological and social problems, often with profound ethical dilemmas. Is a child with HIV to be schooled with other children? Are staff and parents prepared for the problems this will bring to the child, and for the antagonism of inadequately educated parents of other children (Mok, 1991)? It is necessary to provide information to the parents of the infected child about the treatment of the condition, and they must be assisted in understanding and managing the illness and its symptoms.

At a certain stage in development the children themselves will, of course, also need help and advice to manage their own health. At what stage the diagnosis is made clear to the child will depend primarily upon the degree of intellectual and emotional development, but also upon the degree of physical development. It would clearly be inappropriate, for example, to withhold the diagnosis from a teenager who was about to become or who might already be sexually active.

It is important that the child is integrated into as normal a life for as long as possible. Children should be encouraged to go to school, college or clubs and to participate in extramural activities. In the UK there is no obligation to inform teachers of the HIV status of the child as normal playground and schoolroom first aid should be sufficient to stop the spread of infection even from spilled blood. Parents may choose to inform teachers of their child's illness so the child can be protected from contact with potentially lethal infections in others, but the need for absolute confidentiality must be stressed.

Attempts should be made to prevent the illness and its consequences from disrupting family life. Confidentiality is essential in this regard since there have been many reports of exclusion from school and bullying by other children and the Press. Families should be made aware of their rights and helped to find their way round the complex network of the health care system.

Finally, there is a need to prevent the spread of HIV infection especially among the vulnerable groups at the beginning of their sexual experiences. One report has found that HIV-positive haemophiliac adolescents had excellent knowledge of the cause, natural history and transmission of AIDS but were nevertheless failing to practise safe sex. Nine out of 26 respondents were sexually active but only 1 was using a condom (Overby *et al.*, 1989). There is thus a need to ensure that health education messages are not only simple and understandable but that they take into account as far as possible the social skills level, the peer group pressures and other situational factors affecting the target groups.

The health education of those primarily at risk from intravenous drug usage will be more complex and demanding. It will involve giving information on harm reduction in drug-taking behaviour and safe sex, to a group whose cognitive function and impulse control may frequently be impaired by the drugs themselves, by uncontrollable urges for a fix, and sometimes by the early effects of AIDS encephalopathy. All of these factors are multiplied by the reluctance of this group to come forward to formal health care services and by their high levels of social disadvantage and dislocation.

Psychiatric and psychological interventions

Some individuals and families will require more detailed assessment and treatment from the child and adolescent teams either in clinics or in liaison with paediatricians (Krener & Miller, 1989). This might involve some or all of the following: (1) cognitive testing; (2) medical treatment; (3) family psychotherapy; and (4) social and institutional issues.

Cognitive testing

Cognitive testing is useful. Recommendations for antiviral therapy may sometimes be based on evidence of failure to achieve milestones in infants and children or decline in intellectual abilities in older adolescents. While this undoubtedly does occur, the clinical utility of the cognitive findings is usually marginal since there is usually much firmer evidence of disease progression to be found in the results of the immunological testing (see above). Nevertheless, cognitive testing can sometimes contribute to the decision to commence or withhold antiretroviral treatment.

Medical treatment

The medical treatment of the children may involve periods of hospitalization, painful medical procedures and long-term prophylaxis. In other chronic diseases the preparation of the child for hospitalization has been found to be important (Eiser, 1990). Anxiety management and stress reduction can markedly improve the child's quality of life.

Counselling should occur both before and after HIV testing if possible. After disclosure of the positive test result, individual psychotherapy may be appropriate for the older child or adolescent. Frequent themes will be the fear among gay youth, of disclosure of homosexuality, the problems of addiction and personality disorder in some, denial of infection or of the need for safe sex in promiscuous adolescents and anger against doctors in those who have received infected blood products. The aim may not be to 'cure' the patients of such conflicts but at least to maintain a channel of communication with professionals for early intervention, to support the patient, to allow ventilation of feelings and to encourage harm-minimization procedures in the drug takers. Other agencies which have a role in the process will be youth groups, schools, drug treatment programmes and voluntary bodies, e.g. Haemophilia Society, Body Positive, and Terence Higgins Trust.

Family psychotherapy

It is important to provide family support to those who, for example, have a child with perinatal infection. The parents themselves may be unwell and/or suffering from the guilt of causing their infant's disease. The developmental delay frequent in such children will have to be explained to the parents and day care or foster care may be considered at an appropriate time. Similar issues are frequently encountered in the families of transfusion recipients, with the exception that there is more rage at the medical attendants for allowing the infected transfusion than guilt about being the cause, although the latter is also often encountered in this group as well ('I should have known'). This anger may make the families difficult to work with at first, especially if there is ongoing litigation against the physician.

Social and institutional issues

The advent of the HIV epidemic has had a broad impact upon the sex and health education of children, sparking renewed debate about the ethics of sex education and complaints that it should either not be carried out at all or, conversely, that sex is now too much portrayed as dangerous (Belfer *et al.*, 1988).

Staff burnout on AIDS wards is high, as it is in other settings where the care is for those who are terminally ill, especially where the majority of patients are young. Staff support groups can serve a useful function if sensitively and expertly carried out. Ethical dilemmas abound in the care of this group and staff frequently need the time to discuss their feelings about what they might see as a bad decision by more senior physicians, or about the results of treatment being less than satisfactory (Wittenberg & Lazenby, 1989).

Fostering and adoption are sometimes necessary because of parental illness and death or because of social problems in the family resulting from the risk activities. In such cases the merits and disadvantages of any placement must be very carefully weighed. Foster parents should be fully informed about the very low risks in looking after an HIV-positive child. The dangers to the immunocompromised child are considerably higher than those to the parent from the child. High standards of hygiene are therefore essential. On the attitudinal side, a tolerant attitude towards the parental risk behaviour and a nonjudgemental attitude towards the child are absolutely essential (Mok, 1989).

REFERENCES

Belfer M.L., Krener P.K. & Miller F.B. (1988) AIDS in children and adolescents. *Journal of the American Academy of Child and Adolescent Psychiatry*, **27**, 147–151.

Belman A.L., Ultmann M.H., Horoupian D., Novick B., Spiro A.J., Rubinstein A., Kurtzberg D. & Cone-Wesson B. (1985) Neurological complication in children with acquired immune deficiency syndrome. *Annals of Neurology*, **18**, 560–566.

Belman A.L., Lantos G., Horoupian D., Novick B.E., Ultmann M.H., Dickson D.W. & Rubinstein A. (1986) AIDS: Calcification of the basal ganglia in infants and children. *Neurology*, **36**, 1192–1199.

Belman A.L., Diamond G., Dickson D., Horoupian D., Llena J., Lantos G. & Rubinstein A. (1988) Pediatric acquired immunodeficiency syndrome, neurologic syndromes. *American Journal of Diseases of Children*, **142**, 29–35.

Biggar R.J. (1986) The clinical features of HIV infection in Africa. *British Medical Journal*, **293**, 1453–1454.

Blanche S., Caniglia M., Fischer A., Rouzioux C., Burgard M., Tardieu M., Duhamel G. & Griscelli C. (1988) Zidovudine therapy in children with acquired immunodeficiency syndrome. *American Journal of Medicine*, **85**, 203–207.

Brouwers P., Moss H., Wolters P., Eddy J., Balis F., Poplack D.G. & Pizzo P.A. (1990) Effect of continuous infusion zidovudine therapy on neuropsychologic functioning in children with symptomatic human immunodeficiency virus infection. *Journal of Pediatrics*, **117**, 980–985.

Brouwers P., Belman A.L. & Epstein L.G. (1991) Central nervous system involvement: manifestations and evaluation. In: Pizzo P.A. & Wilfert C.M. (eds) *Pediatric AIDS; The Challenge of HIV Infection in Infants, Children and Adolescents*, pp. 318–335. Williams & Wilkins, Baltimore, MD.

Bryant M.L. & Ratner L. (1991) Biology and molecular biology of HIV. In: Pizzo P.A. & Wilfert C.M. (eds) *Pediatric AIDS; The Challenge of HIV Infection in Infants, Children and Adolescents*, pp. 53–74. Williams & Wilkins, Baltimore, MD.

Church J.A. (1984) Transfusion-associated acquired immune deficiency syndrome in infants *Journal of Pediatrics*, **105**, 731–737.

Cogo P., Laverda A.M., Ades A.E., Newell M.L. & Peckham C.S. (1990) Neurologic signs in young children with human immunodeficiency virus infection. *Paediatric Infectious Diseases Journal*, **9**, 402–406.

Darby S.C., Doll R., Thakrar B., Rizza C.R. & Cox D.R. (1990) Time from infection with HIV to onset of AIDS in patients with haemophilia in the UK. *Statistics in Medicine*, **9**, 681–689.

Eiser C. (1990) *Chronic Childhood Diseases*. Cambridge University Press, Cambridge.

Epstein L.G., Sharer L.R., Joshi V.V., Fojas M.M., Koenigsberger M.R. & Oleske J.M. (1985) Progressive encephalopathy in children with acquired immune deficiency syndrome. *Annals of Neurology*, **17**, 488–496.

Epstein L.G., Sharer L.R., Oleske J.M., Connor E.M., Goudsmit J., Bagdon L., Robert-Guroff M. & Koenigsberger M.R. (1986) Neurologic manifestations of human immunodeficiency virus infection in children. *Pediatrics*, **78**, 678–687.

Epstein L.G., Sharer L.R. & Goudsmit J. (1988) Neurological and neuropathological features of human immunodeficiency virus infection in children. *Annals of Neurology*, **23**, S19–S23.

Eyster M.E. (1991) Transfusion and coagulation factor acquired disease. In: Pizzo P.A. & Wilfert C.M. (eds) *Pediatric AIDS; The Challenge of HIV Infection in Infants, Children and Adolescents*, pp. 22–37. Williams & Wilkins, Baltimore, MD.

Fischl M.A., Richman M.D., Grieco M.H., Gottlieb M.S., Volberding P.A., Laskin O.L., Leedom J.M., Groopman J.E., Mildvan D., Schooley R.T., Jackson G.G., Durack D.T., King D. & the AZT collaborative working group. (1987) The efficacy of azidothymide (AZT) in the treatment of patients with AIDS and AIDS-related complex. *New England Journal of Medicine*, **317**, 185–191.

Gayle H.D. & D'Angelo L.J. (1991) Epidemiology of AIDS and HIV infection in adolescents. In: Pizzo P.A. & Wilfert C.M. (eds) *Pediatric AIDS; The Challenge of HIV Infection in Infants, Children and Adolescents*, pp. 38–50. Williams & Wilkins, Baltimore, MD.

Gibb D.M. (1991) HIV infection in children. *Hospital Update*, 267–281.

Goethe K.E., Mitchell J.E., Marshall D.W., Brey R., Cahill W., Leger G.D., Hoy L. & Boswell N. (1989) Neuropsychological and neurological function of HIV seropositive asymptomatic individuals. *Archives of Neurology*, **46**, 129−133.

Grant I. (1990) The neuropsychiatry of human immunodeficiency virus. *Seminars in Neurology*, **10**, 267−275.

Harris (1990) Paper presented at the VIth International Conference on AIDS, San Francisco THD123.

Jason J.M., Stehr-Green J., Holman R.C. & Evatt B.L. (1988) Human immunodeficiency virus in hemophilic children. *Pediatrics*, **82**, 565−570.

Koop C.E. (1991) Foreward. In: Pizzo P.A. & Wilfert C.M. (eds) *Pediatric AIDS; The Challenge of HIV Infection in Infants, Children and Adolescents*, Williams & Wilkins, Baltimore, MD.

Krener P. & Miller F.B. (1989) Psychiatric response to HIV spectrum disease in children and adolescents. *Journal of the American Academy of Child and Adolescent Psychiatry*, **28**, 596−605.

Lee C.A., Phillips A., Elford J., Miller E.J., Bofii M., Griffiths P.D. & Peter B.A. (1989) The natural history of human immunodeficiency virus infection in a haemophiliac cohort. *British Journal of Haematology*, **73**, 228−234.

Logan F.A., Maclean A., Howie C.A., Gibson B. & Parry-Jones W.L. (1990) Psychological disturbance in children with haemophilia. *British Medical Journal*, **301**, 1235−1236.

Lunn S., Skydsbjerg M., Schulsinger H., Parnas J., Pedersen C. & Mathiesen L. (1991) A preliminary report on the neuropsychologic sequelae of human immunodeficiency virus. *Archives of General Psychiatry*, **48**, 139−142.

McArthur J.C., Cohen B.A. & Seher O.A. (1989) Low prevalence of neuropsychological abnormalities in otherwise healthy HIV-infected individuals: Results from the multi-centre AIDS cohort study. *Annals of Neurology*, **26**, 601−611.

Mok J. (1989) Paediatric HIV infection. In: Green J. & McCreamer A. (eds) *Counselling in HIV Infection and AIDS*, pp. 157−166. Blackwell Scientific Publications, Oxford.

Mok J. (1991) HIV infection in children. *British Medical Journal*, **302**, 921−922.

Newell M.L. (1990) The European collaborative study on children born to HIV positive women. *MRC News*, **48**, 11−12.

Overby K.J., Lo B. & Litt I.F. (1989) Knowledge and concerns about acquired immune deficiency syndrome and their relationship to behaviour among adolescents with haemophilia. *Pediatrics*, **83**, 204−210.

Oxtoby M.J. (1991) Perinatally acquired HIV infection. In: Pizzo P.A. & Wilfert C.M. (eds) *Pediatric AIDS; The Challenge of HIV Infection in Infants, Children and Adolescents*, pp. 3−21. Williams & Wilkins, Baltimore, MD.

Pinching A.J. (1986) AIDS and Africa: lessons for us all. *Journal of the Royal Society of Medicine*, **79**, 501−503.

Pizzo P.A. & Butler K.M. (1991) In the vertical transmission of HIV timing may be everything. *New England Journal of Medicine*, **325**, 652−654.

Pizzo P.A., Eddy J., Falloon J., Balis F.M., Murphy R.F., Moss H.,

Wolters P., Brouwers P., Jarosinski P., Rubin M., Broder S., Yarchoan R., Brunetti A., Maha M., Nusinoff-Lehrman S. & Poplack D. (1988) Effect of continuous intravenous infusion of zidovudine (AZT) in children with symptomatic HIV infection. *New England Journal of Medicine*, **319**, 889−896.

Read S.E. (1986) AIDS a new sexually transmitted disease. *Pediatrics Medicine*, **1**, 137−141.

Shaw G.M., Harper M.E., Hahn B.H., Epstein L.G., Gajdusek D.C., Price R.W., Navia B.A., Petito C.K., O'Hara C.J., Groopman J.E., Cho E.-S., Oleske J.M., Wong-Staal F. & Gallo R.C. (1985) HTLV III infection in brains of children and adults with AIDS encephalopathy. *Science*, **227**, 177−182.

Spiegal L. & Mayers A. (1991) Psychosocial effects of AIDS in children and adolescents. *Paediatric Clinics of North America*, **38**, 153−168.

Ultmann M.H., Belman A.L., Ruff H.A., Novick B.E., Cone-Wesson B., Cohen H.J. & Rubinstein A. (1985) Developmental abnormalities in infants and children with acquired immune deficiency syndrome (AIDS) and AIDS-related complex. *Developmental Medicine and Child Neurology*, **27**, 563−571.

Ultmann M.H., Diamond G.W., Ruff H.A., Belman A.L., Novick B.E., Rubinstein A. & Cohen H.J. (1987) Developmental abnormalities in children with acquired immunodeficiency syndrome(AIDS) a follow up study. *International Journal of Neuroscience*, **32**, 661−667.

US Department of Health and Human Services (1987) *Morbidity and Mortality Weekly Report*, **36**, 15. 225−235.

Van de Perre P., Simonon A., Msellati P., Hitimana D.-G., Vaira D., Bazubagira A., Van Goethem C., Stevens A.M., Karita E., Sondag-Thull D., Dabis F. & Lepage P. (1991) Postnatal transmission of human immunodeficiency virus type I from mother to infant. *New England Journal of Medicine*, **325**, 593−598.

Vazeux R., Henin D., Ciaudo C., Tardieu M. & Montagnier L. (1991) Pathogenesis and biological markers of HIV-1 associated dementia. *Biological Psychiatry*, **29**, 176S.

Waters B.G.H., Ziegler J.B., Hampson R. & McPherson A.H. (1988) The psychosocial consequences of childhood infection with human immunodeficiency virus. *Medical Journal of Australia*, **149**, 198−202.

Weiner S. & Septimus A. (1991) Psychosocial considerations and support for the child family. In: Pizzo P.A. & Wifert C.M. (eds) *Paediatric AIDS; The Challenge of HIV Infection in Infants, Children and Adolescents*, pp. 577−594. Williams & Wilkins, Baltimore, MD.

Williams M.D., Al-Rubei K. & Hill F.G.H. (1988) A prospective study of HIV infected haemophiliac boys and the prognostic significance of immune and haematological abnormalities. *Thrombosis and Haemostasis*, **60**, 97−101.

Wittenberg J. & Lazenby A. (1989) AIDS in Infancy: diagnostic, therapeutic and ethical problems. *Canadian Journal of Psychiatry*, **34**, 576−580.

World Health Organization (1988) *Report of the Consultation on the Neuropsychiatric Aspects of the HIV Infection*, WHO, Geneva.

Chapter 41
Psychiatric Aspects of Specific Sensory Impairments

Peter Hindley & Rachel M.A. Brown

INTRODUCTION

Sensory impairments (SIs) can have profound effects on children's development. The more profound the impairment and the earlier the onset (see Table 41.1), the greater the effect. Although deaf, blind and multisensory impaired (MSI) children represent the minority of children with SIs, in these children the effects of SI can be seen most clearly and they and their families are faced with the greatest challenges in adapting to their impairment. This chapter concerns itself primarily with this group but makes reference to children with less severe impairments.

At birth, the perceptual systems of infants without SI are predisposed to enable the infant to interact with the social environment. The perceptual systems do not function independently: rather perception is intermodal, the infant initially perceiving the world in unified percepts (Butterworth, 1989). Amongst the multiple stimuli in the world of infants, they seem particularly attuned to human voices, faces and smells. Equally the infant's parents and caregivers are sensitive to the infant's facial expressions, vocalizations and movements. Each partner is primed to enter into a sequence of rapidly developing, reciprocal and mutually responsive social interactions

which are highly dependent on the infant's intact perceptual systems and the caregivers' ability to share their infant's experience.

Deaf, blind and MSI infants and their parents are faced with considerable difficulties. The infants' capacity for intermodal perception is reduced, they receive less sensory information and attend to different sensory aspects of the world. Most parents of SI children do not have SIs. Some 5–10% of deaf children have deaf parents (Rawlings & Jensema, 1977) and probably less than 1% of blind children have blind parents (C. Rowbury, personal communication). For most parents, the birth of a child with SI will be their first direct experience of SI. They are faced with at least two tasks: surviving the news that their child has SI; and beginning to understand the different world that their infant inhabits. Many SI children manage to adapt successfully, some less so. However, before examining the developmental and psychiatric aspects of SI, it is important to consider some additional medical features of SI and some of the cultural aspects of deafness.

Epidemiology of sensory impairment

Hearing impairment (HI)

Approximately 1 in 1000 children will have moderate to profound congenital and bilateral early onset HI (Martin, 1982), rising to 4 in 1000 if acquired losses are included (Bamford & Saunders, 1991). Mild, transient hearing losses are far commoner — the annual incidence of acute otitis media reaches a peak of approximately 50% of children in their second year of life, falling to below 10% by the ninth year (Haggard & Hughes, 1991). These children are unlikely to experience a hearing loss but some 20% of children aged 2–5 will have otitis media with effusion, of whom a minority will experience persistent, unilateral or bilateral losses in the mild to moderate range.

The aetiology of childhood hearing impairment, in the developed world, is changing rapidly. The incidence of early onset and acquired hearing impairment as a consequence of infectious diseases is falling, whilst the proportion of inherited, congenital and early onset hearing impairment is rising (Newton, 1985; Bamford & Saunders, 1991). At the same time, although the number of children born with congenital

Table 41.1 Definitions of sensory impairment

Hearing impairment		Visual impairment
Physical descriptor of degree of impairment		
Mild	20–40 dB	PS: 3 in 60–6 in 60
Moderate	41–70 dB	Snellen
Severe	71–95 dB	Blind: less than 3 in 60 or visual
Profound	96+ dB	field defect, less than 20 degrees at maximum diameter
Terms used to describe children and adults with SI		
Hard of hearing: moderate to profound acquired HI		PS: partially sighted, sufficient vision for pattern recognition and visually directed reach, can read with special visual aids
Deaf: severe to profound congenital or early onset HI		
Deaf: culturally deaf, use sign language and member of deaf community		Blind: cannot use materials involving sight

Degree of hearing loss is measured in the better ear at 0.25, 0.5, 1, 2 and 4 KHz. Conversational speech is roughly 50–70 dB.

rubella syndrome is falling as a consequence of immunization programmes, very low-birth-weight babies account for an increasing proportion of congenital hearing impairment (Davis, 1990). These children are at greater risk of additional impairments, such as brain abnormalities.

The prevalence of brain abnormalities in a total population of deaf children has been estimated at 16% (Freeman *et al.*, 1975). In the main, children with inherited deafness are less likely to show evidence of brain abnormalities than deafness as a result of intrauterine or postnatal infections. The important exception is Usher's syndrome. The syndrome consists of congenital deafness in association with retinitis pigmentosa leading to acquired visual impairment and it is the single largest inherited cause of deaf–blindness. It is also associated with mental retardation (Das, 1989). Congenital rubella syndrome is manifest in a large number of organ systems. In addition to a strong association with mental retardation (Sidle, 1985) and blindness, there is good evidence for both a congenital and a delayed onset encephalitis (Sever *et al.*, 1985). Both very low-birth-weight children and children with early onset and acquired deafness as a consequence of infections such as meningitis, are at greater risk of brain abnormalities.

Visual impairment (VI)

In the UK, Peckham and Pearson (1976) recorded 0.3 in 1000 blind and partially sighted children at 6 years and 0.6 in 1000 at 11, in the 1958 National Child Development study. Most of the children were placed in special schools and units for VI children or in Learning Difficulty Schools. Hereditary retinopathies account for 25–50% of VI children (Hill *et al.*, 1986; Jan *et al.*, 1977). Cortical blindness, congenital anomalies and congenital cataracts are other important causes. Congenital rubella and other infective conditions account for about 10%. More effective neonatal care has lead to a drop in retinopathy of prematurity but it is still an important cause in Very Low-Birth-Weight (VLBW) babies (Dunn, 1986). Hereditary retinopathies, tumours, accidents and poisoning account for most cases of acquired VI (Jan *et al.*, 1977).

Additional impairments often compound the difficulties of VI children. In a clinic based study of a mixed population of blind and partially sighted children, 51% had intellectual impairments and 40% other additional impairments (Hill *et al.*, 1986). The most common additional impairments were cerebral palsy (15%), epilepsy (11%) and HI (9%). Similarly, Jan *et al.* (1977) found that 24% of their total population of VI children and young people had 'hard' signs of CNS disorder. Developmental delay is common but less so amongst children with hereditary VI (Hill *et al.*, 1986). Amongst children with severe intellectual impairments VI appears to be underestimated (Colbourne-Brown & Tobin, 1982).

Multisensory impairment (MSI)

Hearing impairments combined with visual impairments do not combine additively. If one sense is impaired the others can compensate or help to ensure the most effective use of the residual senses. When two senses are impaired these compensatory mechanisms are lost, leading to what McInnes and Treffry (1982) have termed multiple sensory impairment. Variations in the type and severity of each specific impairment and a strong association with additional mental and physical impairments result in a population of children about whom it is extremely difficult to generalize.

Reliable estimates of the prevalence of MSI are difficult to obtain and many of the published figures are unreliable because of difficulties in ascertaining cases. The estimated prevalence rate is 0.01 in 1000 (Best, 1983) in children. However, estimated prevalence rates for MSI vary considerably (Trybus, 1985) and it is likely that Best's figure is an underestimate. Similarly, findings concerning the aetiology of MSI vary from survey to survey, mainly as a result of different methods of ascertainment. At the time of Trybus' review (1985) congenital rubella syndrome remained the single largest cause of MSI, but estimates of the prevalence of MSI as a result of congenital rubella varied from 34 to 56%. In his review, Trybus suggests that hereditary conditions are the next largest cause and it is likely that the proportion of children with hereditary MSI will have risen since the early 1980s.

Additional impairments are also common amongst MSI children with rates of mental handicap ranging from 34 to 55% and rates of brain abnormalities ranging from 12 to 28% (Trybus, 1985).

Cultural and linguistic aspects of deafness

The factors outlined above, create an extremely heterogeneous group of deaf children. Yet most children with congenital or early onset, severe and profound hearing impairment (the vast majority being sensorineural) will grow into adults who join the deaf community (Kyle & Allsop, 1982). The deaf community is a group of people joined together by a shared language — signed language — and shared experiences — primarily residential deaf schools and deaf clubs (Brien, 1991; Padden & Marcowicz, 1976) and consists of both deaf and hearing people. In the past most deaf adults would have attended deaf schools but changes in educational policy in the UK and the US mean that increasing numbers of children are being educated in units attached to mainstream schools or integrated fully into the classroom. This has considerable implications for the deaf community of the future.

Signed languages

Signed languages are naturally occurring languages, which have developed amongst the various different deaf communities of the world: in the US, American Sign Language (ASL); in Britain, British Sign Language (BSL); and in France, French Sign Language (FSL). Kyle and Woll (1985) provide a useful introduction to BSL and Klima and Bellugi (1979) to

ASL. Signed languages are all visuospatial languages which use spatial relationships created by face, hands and body to express syntactic and semantic forms (Bellugi *et al.*, 1988). The national signed languages are both grammatically and lexically distinct from the spoken languages of the native community and from each other. However, certain syntactic features, such as the use of topic–comment sentence structure and aspectual rather than verb-tense modification, occur in many signed languages but differ in the ways they are expressed. The differences between national sign languages are of a similar order to the differences between English and French.

Signed languages and spoken languages coexist and a degree of linguistic interference inevitably occurs. English features become more prominent in formal addresses, whilst BSL predominates in informal conversation and story-telling (Cicourel, 1978). Educationalists have artificially adapted signed languages, to allow for simultaneous communication in spoken and signed language. Thus BSL signs are altered and used in English-word order to allow English grammar to be visually presented, in combination with spoken English, in Signs Supporting English. American Sign Language has been similarly altered to produce a variety of different educational forms (Maxwell, 1990).

A vigorous political, educational and linguistic debate about the best method of communication with deaf children is occurring in two main areas. The first of these is the use of spoken language against signed languages (Freeman, 1976). For over one hundred years some educationalists, the oralists, have argued that the use of gestures and signed language inhibits the child's ability to acquire spoken language, which, they say, with special audiological and educational methods can develop in all deaf children (Clark, 1989; Van Uden, 1977). This is in the face of evidence that deaf children acquire language more readily if it is presented in sign (Brasel & Quigley, 1977) and the many deaf children who leave school without useful spoken language (Conrad, 1979). Secondly, a debate has developed over the last twenty years about the effects of combining signed and spoken languages (Maxwell, 1990). At a linguistic level, presenting signed and spoken languages simultaneously leads to linguistic interference. Educationally it has been argued that a bilingual approach, using ASL as a first language and then teaching English as a second language will be more effective than using simul-taneous communication (Strong, 1988). A bilingual pro-gramme has recently been started in the UK, using BSL and English but, as yet, has not been fully evaluated (Daunt, 1991). Politically, some members of the American and Brtish deaf communities argue that tinkering with ASL or BSL is akin to cultural vandalism.

The study of signed languages has provided the opportunity to examine the influence of the medium of communication on language. Structurally signed languages are true languages, using a constrained set of elements to generate infinite meanings (Klima & Bellugi, 1979). Both the process of devel-opment and the milestones of development parallel those of spoken languages (Caselli & Volterra, 1989; Meadow, 1980). Neuropsychological studies show that signed languages are processed in the left temporal lobe (for right-handers), despite their visuospatial nature (Bellugi *et al.*, 1988).

DEVELOPMENTAL ASPECTS OF SENSORY IMPAIRMENT

The developmental fit (Super & Harkness, 1986) between SI infants and their sighted and hearing parents may sometimes be poor (see below). However, it seems likely that SI children born to SI parents will enter an environment more attuned to the child's developmental needs. What are the features of relationships in such families?

Sensory impaired children of sensory impaired adults

Our knowledge of this group of children is almost exclusively confined to deaf people. There is limited research concerning deaf children of oral-deaf parents (Galenson *et al.*, 1979) and the research concerning blind children of blind parents appears to be limited to one study (Rowbury, 1991). All of the studies relating to early development, entailed detailed observations of small numbers of children (1–6 children) but there are some consistent themes in the results.

Some 5–10% of deaf children are born to deaf parents (see above). For most deaf parents, the birth of a deaf child does not come as a shock and is often a relief, tempered by knowledge of the difficulties that that child will face (Erting, 1987). Studies using the Still Face paradigm (Cohn & Tronick, 1983) show that within the first 6 months of life deaf infants rely on visual information more than hearing controls and that deaf mothers use more positive facial expression than hearing mothers of deaf infants (Meadow-Orlans *et al.*, 1987). In addition, deaf mothers ensure that their hands, faces and eyegaze are within the infant's visual field (Erting *et al.*, 1989).

Using simultaneous videotaping of deaf mothers and their deaf infants, Erting *et al.*, (1989) have shown that the mothers slow and enlarge their signing and use repetition, changes which the authors compare to spoken 'Motherese'. These adaptations of signs seem intended to enable shared attention and joint referencing to occur. They point to a fundamental difficulty that both blind and deaf children share in establishing language, that is how to ensure that linguistic symbol and referent object can, as far as possible, be within the same visual or auditory field and so salient to and contingent upon each other. Unimpaired children can divide their attention *between* visual and auditory fields. Sensory impaired children must either divide their attention *within* the visual or auditory field or between touch and either hearing or vision. Sensory impaired parents use a variety of methods to manage the field of shared attention. Deaf parents use both touch and adap-tations of sign language to overcome divided attention (Harris *et al.*, 1988). These adaptations include moving signs within the signing space and signing on the child's body. In a study comparing a blind mother of a blind child and a sighted mother of a blind child, the blind mother relied more on touch and less on speech to maintain shared attention (Rowbury, 1991). The blind mother also seemed to use speech to maintain communication and help her child acquire information whilst the sighted mother seemed to use speech to elicit communication and action from her child. By 1 year deaf mothers are more able than their hearing counterparts to establish and sustain meaningful interactions with their children (Gregory & Barlow, 1986).

It may be that for deaf children of deaf parents the establishment of shared attention and joint referencing, and the mutuality that these infer, form the basis for the relatively normal pattern of development that follows. Thus the development of attachments (Meadow *et al.*, 1981; Meadow *et al.*, 1983), symbolic play (Spencer *et al.*, 1990) and sign language (Caselli & Volterra, 1989) in deaf children of deaf parents parallel those of hearing children of hearing parents. The exception to these findings is a study of attachment formation in deaf children of oral-deaf parents, in which delayed and deviant patterns of attachment predominated (Galenson *et al.*, 1979).

As deaf children of deaf parents pass through the school system their levels of attainment in all areas are on average superior to those of their deaf counterparts, when groups matched for nonverbal IQ are compared (Balow & Brill, 1972; Meadow, 1968b). In adult life deaf people with deaf parents are often community leaders.

SI children of hearing and sighted parents

Family responses

The diagnosis of a sensory impairment is a distressing experience for most parents. It seems likely that early onset, profound impairments will be the most distressing. Studies of parental responses show a mixed picture.

Deaf children

Many parents of deaf children suspect that their infants are deaf before the diagnosis is made (Hall, 1989). In the past these suspicions have often been denied by professionals (Freeman *et al.*, 1975; Meadow, 1968a) and the parents labelled as neurotic, contributing to delays in diagnosis. However, the delay between suspicion and diagnosis means that for some parents the confirmation of their fears yields an initial sense of relief. For others the manner in which the news is broken leaves a long-lasting sense of distress and anger. It has been suggested that the intensity of emotion surrounding diagnosis is akin to grief (Schlesinger & Meadow, 1971) and that if these feelings remain unresolved they can lead to a persistent sense of powerlessness in the parents (Schlesinger, 1988). However, in a total population survey of deaf children (ages 5–16) in the Greater Vancouver area, most parents were thought to have accepted that their child

was deaf and adjusted well to their needs (Freeman *et al.*, 1975). In adjusting to their deaf child, hearing parents often talk of the need to re-examine the past and rediscover their child and themselves anew.

VI children

The diagnosis of blindness tends to be made within the first few months of life but diagnosis can be delayed for some infants because they use their residual vision (Freeman, 1977; Jan *et al.*, 1977). Again, in the past, the way in which the news has been broken has often provoked distress (Jan *et al.*, 1977). Freeman *et al.* (1989) have suggested that the diagnosis of blindness is 'one of the greatest shocks that parents ever undergo'. For some mothers this may provoke a depressive response and there is anecdotal evidence to suggest that blind babies may be particularly vulnerable to this experience (Burlingham, 1961; Wills, 1970). Adaptation to VI is possible, if difficult, but in a total population study Jan *et al.* (1977) found that one-third of mothers had recent major psychiatric problems, one-third of marriages had major difficulties and one-quarter of siblings had behavioural problems. However, similar rates were found amongst control families.

MSI children

There has been no systematic study of parental responses to the diagnosis of MSI. However, Peggy Freeman (1975) has described her experience as the mother of a child with MSI. She describes her distress and need to compensate for her child's impairments. Retrospectively she feels she should have viewed things differently '. . . but to see such a child (as any other) who has certain abilities — our task and that of all who along life's road will in turn share with us this task, is to see that our child makes the best possible use of these abilities, never mind about the things he doesn't possess, use those he has.' (Freeman, 1975 p. viii).

Early interaction

The lack of either vision or hearing, or both vision and hearing poses a variety of difficulties for the SI infant and his sighted or hearing parents. Although some blind infants are reported to smile selectively at 1 month (Fraiberg, 1977) and deaf infants use vocalizations which are very similar to hearing babies during their first year, the absence or distortion of visual or auditory feedback is reflected in their interactions with their parents. Blind babies are deprived of important visual cues and their smiles and facial expressions appear to be weaker and less sustained than sighted children (Fraiberg, 1977; Warren, 1984). Shared visual activities are important sources of communication between parents and infants but a blind infant cannot show interest with eyegaze. Indeed, the response to an interesting sound may be to quieten and still, which parents may interpret as a rebuff.

In contrast deaf infants make greater use of visual cues.

Using the Still Face paradigm (Cohn & Tronick, 1983), Meadow-Orlans *et al.* (1987) showed that at 6 months deaf infants showed greater reliance on visual information and used visual scanning when distressed. However, their hearing mothers had greater difficulty in comforting their infants than both the deaf mothers of deaf infants and hearing mothers of hearing infants. In addition deaf infants appear to use more self-comforting during the Still Face, in comparison with hearing infants (Koester & Trim, 1991).

In hearing infants, these early interactions develop into the prelinguistic games from which language develops. How does this process occur in SI children? Both deaf and blind infants use manual gestures in this prelinguistic phase (Fraiberg, 1977; Koester & Trim, 1991). However, this process is somewhat delayed in blind infants because their sense of object constancy is often delayed (Fraiberg, 1977). In addition the delay in self-initiated motor activity, often seen in blind children (Adelson & Fraiberg, 1974) may limit infants' experience of and interest in exploring their world.

Sighted and hearing parents are faced with the task of establishing joint referencing and shared attention in a mutually responsive way. There are a number of studies of blind infants suggesting successful and unsuccessful paths. For deaf infants the literature is almost exclusively concerned with unsuccessful adaptation.

Blind infants do give subtle social cues — both by manual gesture and vocalization. Mothers who are able to pay close attention to these subtle signals (Urwin, 1983) and ensure that they give their infant a continuing sense of their presence by voice and by touch (Preisler & Palmer, 1986), seem able to establish non-visual prelinguistic games. It seems that a lack of sensitivity and responsiveness to these cues can inhibit the development of such interactions (Rowland, 1983); for one of Rowland's mothers this lack of sensitivity seemed to manifest itself in a need to be constantly touching her baby.

For deaf infants, mothers appear to make greater use of facial expression, both by using more smiling and exaggerating their expressions (Koester & Trim, 1991). However, Gregory and Barlow (1986) found that mothers of 1-year old deaf children had great difficulty in establishing and maintaining shared attention. One of the consequences of these difficulties is the emergence of an over-controlling, intrusive style of parenting (Meadow, 1987; Spencer & Gutfreund, 1990), which has also been noted in sighted mothers of blind children (Kekelis & Andersen, 1984).

Language, imaginative play and emotional attachments

There is evidence that deaf infants in hearing families and in the absence of formal signed language, develop visuospatial systems of communication which are initially purely gestural but become referential (Feldman *et al.*, 1978; Mohay, 1982, 1989). Moreover, some of these systems share some of the syntactic features of ASL (Goldin-Meadow & Mylander, 1984).

Brasel and Quigley's study (1977) suggests that the use of sign language with deaf children enhances both signed and spoken language but our evidence as to what factors promote sign language development in deaf children of hearing mothers is confined to one study. Mather (1990) suggests that making use of eyegaze, adaptations of sign to take advantage of direction in ASL and using miniature signs all assist in the establishment of dialogue with deaf preschoolers. In a finding that is echoed in the work on spoken language Mather also suggests that non-native signers use more closed questions and fewer wh- (i.e. what, where, when etc.) questions, both of which inhibit the development of discourse.

Spoken language in deaf children is both delayed and different in comparison to hearing children. Gregory and Mogford (1981) in a longitudinal study of 8 deaf children found that on average first words emerged at 16 months and 10 words at 23 months. The two children in the study with the most profound hearing losses reached the ten-word stage at 4 years. Whilst the hearing children took a month, on average, to go from the 50-word stage to 100 words, the deaf children took 6 months. In addition the deaf children's vocabulary was primarily of social and affective words, whilst the hearing children knew more object and event-related words. White and White (1984) have suggested that these delays may be partly explained by hearing parents' over-controlling interaction and lack of responsiveness to their deaf children's changing language. However, Wood *et al.* (1986) suggest that although this pattern occurs between teachers of the deaf and their pupils it is possible to overcome it. They found that when teachers listened to their pupils talking, they tended to correct their mistakes rather than following the children and encouraging them to talk about the subject by asking open wh- questions. When these findings were pointed out to teachers, using videotapes of teacher–pupil interactions, teachers were able to change their behaviour, leading to an increase in the children's spoken language.

Otitis media with effusion (OME) is now thought to have a significant but not major effect on language development (Haggard & Hughes, 1991), since it primarily affects expressive language whereas moderate to profound losses affect both receptive and expressive language.

Some blind children show delays in both expressive and receptive language (Reynell, 1978, 1979). Blind children are more likely to use echolalia, standardized formulaic statements and pronoun reversal (Freeman & Blockberger, 1987; Urwin, 1983) but there is doubt about the significance and function of these types of speech. It has been suggested that blind children's echolalic and formulaic statements may be attempts to maintain communication (Urwin, 1981, 1983) much as sighted children do by manual and vocal gestures. Equally Lewis (1987) has suggested that a blind child's pronoun reversal simply reflects the effect of lack of vision on the child's understanding of deixis, rather than the fundamental confusion over the boundaries between one person and another that Fraiberg suggests (1977).

In some respects the emergence of symbolic play and social attachments demonstrates an opposite trend to that described above. Deaf children begin to display symbolic play at around the same age as that seen in hearing children. However, it is less well-elaborated and appears to contain extraneous elements (Gregory & Mogford, 1982). In contrast blind children demonstrate less symbolic play (Fraiberg, 1977) and it is possible that instead they use spoken fantasy play (Urwin, 1981).

There are similarities in the development of social attachments. As long as hearing mothers use some form of gesture, attachment formation in deaf children, as measured by the 'Strange Situation' (Ainsworth *et al.*, 1978), does not appear delayed (Greenberg & Marvin, 1979). Although the 'Strange Situation' has not been used with blind children, Fraiberg (1977) suggests that the emergence of stranger anxiety and separation protest are both delayed.

Social development

For many SI children their first contacts outside the home will be with sighted and hearing children and adults. Hearing adults appear to have difficulties initiating and maintaining interactions with deaf preschoolers (Lederberg, 1984). Deaf preschoolers appear to be less socially skilled than their hard of hearing and hearing peers (Levy-Schiff & Hoffman, 1985) but it is not clear if the diminished social interaction seen between HI and hearing children is a consequence of self-selection or peer rejection (Arnold & Tremblay, 1979; Levy-Schiff & Hoffman, 1985). This picture is even more extreme for blind preschoolers who appear isolated from (Jan *et al.*, 1977), and at times reject their peers and either turn to adults for social interaction or to self-stimulation (Preisler & Palmer, 1989).

The relative social isolation of VI children continues into middle and late childhood (Jan *et al.*, 1977) with a considerable proportion (15%) reported as having no friends. However, we do not have a good understanding of peer relationships in VI children and adolescents.

Freeman's *et al.* (1975) study of deaf children, showed similar degrees of peer isolation to that observed by Jan *et al.* (1977) but we have a somewhat better understanding of the changing pattern of peer relationships amongst HI children.

Kennedy's prospective sociometric study of deaf and hard of hearing children in integrated settings suggests that they are popular in their early school careers (Kennedy & Bruininks, 1974). However, as they progress their popularity wanes (Kennedy *et al.*, 1976), so that in their third year of school they are significantly less likely to be selected as friends. In adolescence deaf and hard of hearing children make use of both hearing and deaf peer groups at school (Ladd *et al.*, 1984; Markides, 1989). This does not extend to friendships and activities out of school (Ladd *et al.*, 1984). Markides' findings suggests that hearing children are extremely unlikely to choose a deaf peer as a friend.

Schools for the deaf provide children with a larger peer group but there are no studies to tell us what use children make of it. Informally, deaf adults often refer to their peers at school as their real brothers and sisters and deaf authors cite the residential school as the arena in which children join deaf society and culture (Higgins, 1987).

Personality development of SI children

Much of the earlier developmental work with SI children concerned personality development. Ammerman *et al.* (1986) provide a review of this literature for blind children and Meadow (1980) for deaf children. These authors refute the notion of a blind or deaf personality but list some of the common findings. Deaf children are described as egocentric, impulsive and immature, whilst blind children are said to show greater dependency, are more introverted and have more emotional adjustment problems than their sighted peers. However both Ammerman *et al.* (1986) and Meadow (1980) cast doubt on the methodology of much of the work on which these findings are based. For instance many of the studies of deaf children were carried out using pencil and paper tests whilst none of the studies of blind children included children under 13 and many included young adults.

Cognitive development, reading and intellectual assessment

Cognitive development

Sensory impairment can affect cognitive development in a number of ways. Lowenfeld (1948) suggested that VI could have three main effects: (1) directly reducing the range and variety of experience; (2) indirectly, by reducing opportunities because of limitations of mobility; and (3) by reducing the child's control over the environment. Furth (1973) has suggested that the main effect of deafness would be through reduced opportunities for experience and training because of linguistic deprivation. O'Connor and Hermelin (1970) suggest that deaf children have difficulties in processing temporally arranged information and that blind children have difficulty in processing spatially arranged information.

Investigators using Piagetian models have suggested that blind children are delayed in their development of classification and conversation skills (Warren, 1984) and that deaf children are delayed in their development of conservation skills (Meadow, 1980; Lewis, 1987). However, criticisms have been levelled at both sets of studies because of uncertainty about the relevance of the tasks to deaf and blind children's everyday experience. In addition for deaf children there are the inevitable doubts about the children's ability to understand the task. At the level of formal operational thinking Furth (1973) reported that half of his deaf adolescents were able to reason abstractly.

Reading and writing

Conrad (1979) in his study of all British deaf school leavers, reported that half of the group were reading at 9 years or less and that only 2.5% of the group were reading at chronological age. Reading ages correlated with level of hearing loss and IQ score. Wood *et al.* (1986) in their analysis of reading errors suggest that deaf children do not make the same sorts of errors as hearing children and that they seem to be using non-syntactically based strategies when reading. The writing of deaf children contains more nouns and verbs than hearing children and they make errors which hearing children rarely make such as omitting 'is'. It has been suggested that for signing children their writing reflects the grammar of their native sign language (Kyle & Woll, 1985). In their review of the effects of OME on reading, Haggard and Hughes (1991) suggest that persistent, mild HI can lead to small but significant delays in reading.

Braille reading for blind children appears to be a more demanding task than reading for sighted children. Many blind children continue to make mistakes over the identification of Braille letters into their early teens (Lorimer, 1981) and average Braille reading speeds for blind teenagers are about half those of sighted teenagers (Williams, 1971).

Intellectual assessment

The use of standardized tests poses many problems for SI children. The verbal scales of such tests are not appropriate for deaf children, equally the performance scales cannot be used with blind children and many verbal items are visually loaded. One response has been to use the performance scales for deaf children and the verbal scales, excluding the visual items for blind children. This solution begs the question as to whether or not part-scales accurately reflect children's intellectual functioning (Ammerman *et al.*, 1986; Blennerhassett, 1990). Graham and Shapiro's (1953) study of the relative effectiveness of pantomimed and spoken IQ tests with deaf and hearing children, suggest that presenting tests to deaf children in pantomime may lead to an underestimation of their abilities.

Two strategies have been developed to overcome these objections. The first is the use of performance scales specifically for deaf children such as the Hiskey—Nebraska and Leiter and the adaptation of scales specifically for blind children, e.g. the Perkins—Binet. The psychometric properties of both sets are well-established but there is some doubt as to the validity of the Perkins—Binet (Ammerman *et al.*, 1986). The second strategy has been to translate the verbal scale of the Wechster Intelligence Scales for Children (WISC-R) into ASL and re-assess its psychometric properties (Blenner-hassett, 1990). Scores on the verbal subscale presented in ASL correlate with reading and writing achievement tests for deaf children of both deaf and hearing parents.

PSYCHIATRIC ASPECTS OF SI

Hearing impairment

Assessment

Psychiatric assessments of deaf children must be adapted to suit the individuals involved, that is both patient and clinician. In deciding how to carry out the assessment a number of variables need to be considered: language usage; communicative competence; school placement; hearing status of parents; and the family response to deafness.

Language usage is the single factor most likely to determine whether or not referral to specialist services for deaf children is needed. A general child psychiatrist undertaking an assessment of a deaf child, is strongly advised to work with an interpreter. Both clinician and interpreter will have to adapt: the clinician finding that the interpreter becomes her ears and eyes, especially in assessing nonverbal communication and interaction (Hoyt *et al.*, 1981; Hindley, 1993); the interpreter will need to consult with the clinician prior to and after the assessment, which may conflict with his professional and ethical position as a neutral facilitator of communication (Stansfield & Veltri, 1987). If the clinician has a limited knowledge of sign but undertakes the assessment alone he or she should do so with caution. The clinician's well intentioned attempts to engage the child, may well colour the interaction. This can lead to the clinician missing important nonverbal cues and prevent the child from disclosing painful feelings and experiences (Hindley, 1993). Oral/aural children may well manage without an interpreter but some benefit from a speechreader/communicator. Many younger children and multihandicapped children may not have sufficient language to take part in an interview and direct observations at home and in school will then be essential.

Residential schools are often where the foundations of Deaf cultural identity are laid. For children attending residential schools close liaison with teaching and care-staff can yield important information. However, many parents find it understandably disturbing to send their children away from home. Envious and jealous feelings can develop between parents and school which for some parents are compounded by the ease with which children and staff communicate. Equally staff members can see themselves as more competent and caring than parents. The nature of these relationships adds to the importance of involving parents in any psychiatric consultation, except in exceptional circumstances. For deaf parents consideration needs to be given to their earlier experience of hearing professionals. Deaf parents may see such people as interfering and intrusive, attempting to dominate and control by providing counselling rather than information (Erting, 1987). A deaf mental-health-worker can provide vital insights in all these areas.

Two aspects of mental-state assessment can be particularly difficult with deaf children. Inexperienced clinicians may find it difficult to distinguish written sign language from thought disordered writing (Evans & Elliott, 1981; Kitson & Fry, 1990). Even the experienced can find it difficult to distinguish idiosyncratic sign from thought disordered sign. Again a deaf colleague is essential. Assessment of mood and affect can also pose problems. How can one distinguish between narrative related changes of affect and true affect? Developmental studies suggest that the shape of the mood contour can help to make the distinction (Snitzer Reilly *et al.*, 1989). Abrupt changes in affect are associated with narrative related mood, whilst true mood changes more smoothly (N. Kitson, personal communication).

In addition, assessment of psychological functioning can be difficult. Poor expertise in sign language and inexperience in working with deaf children can lead to unreliable assessments, particularly in the case of children with additional impairments, such as mental retardation and visual impairment (Bond, 1986). Whilst a number of nonverbal assessment instruments exist, it is only recently that attempts have been made to translate verbal subscales into ASL (Blennerhassett, 1990). Elliott *et al.* (1987) provide a useful guide to both psychiatric and psychological assessments of deaf children and adults.

Finally what do the child, siblings and parents make of the child's deafness? The presence of a deaf child can have a profound influence on the family but this will change as the family develops (Harvey, 1989). For the child, parental and societal attitudes will affect his or her self-image. They may see their deafness as unimportant, or they may see themselves as proud members of the deaf community or as impaired individuals whose deafness is a source of shame (Hindley, 1993).

Epidemiology

There have been a number of studies of psychiatric disorder in deaf and hard of hearing children and adolescents (see Table 41.2). The studies which included control groups (Rutter *et al.*, 1970; Fundudis *et al.*, 1979) or comparison groups (Schlesinger & Meadow, 1972) suggested that the prevalence of disorder in the HI groups was 2.5–3 times that seen in the control groups. The rates of disorder ranged from 15.4% to 60.9%. The exception to these findings is a small, uncontrolled study suggesting the rate of disorder amongst HI children was the same or less than that seen in hearing children (MacLean & Becker, 1979).

Two sets of mechanisms are likely to contribute to the differing findings. Firstly there were differences in the methods of ascertainment and sizes of the populations studied. Secondly different rating instruments were used (see Table 41.3) and prevalence rates were calculated in different ways.

Two of the studies were whole population studies (Rutter *et al.*, 1970; Freeman *et al.*, 1975), whilst the others were studies of whole school populations. In comparison with the other studies (see Table 41.2), Rutter *et al.* (1970) studied a small number of patients and so their prevalence figure is likely to be unreliable. Some of the studies concentrated on either children (Fundudis *et al.*, 1979) or adolescents (Hindley, 1993) whilst others studied children and adolescents (Rutter *et al.*, 1970; Freeman *et al.*, 1975; Aplin, 1985, 1987). Freeman *et al.* (1975) suggest that younger children are likely to show higher rates of disorder but Aplin's findings (1985, 1987) do not confirm this. Similarly there were differences in the range of hearing losses amongst the children studied (see Table 41.2). Although level of hearing loss alone does not appear to be a significant factor in the aetiology of psychiatric disorder

Table 41.2 Prevalence of psychiatric disorders in hearing impaired (HI) children and adolescents and hearing controls

Study	Number of HI children	Range of HI	Prevalence of disorder	
			HI group (%)	Control (%)
Rutter, Graham and Yule (1970)	13	moderate–profound	15.4	6.6
Schlesinger and Meadow (1972)	512	severe–profound	31.2	9.7
Freeman, Malkin and Hastings (1975)	120	severe–profound	22.0	—
Fundudis, Kolvin and Garside (1979)	54	moderate–profound	deaf: 54 H/H: 28	18
Aplin (1985)	61	profound	36.1	—
Aplin (1987)	42	mild–profound	16.6	—
Hindley (1993)	81	moderate–profound	deaf: 42.4 H/H: 60.9	—

Deaf: severe to profound, early onset hearing impairment.
H/H (hard of hearing): moderate to profound acquired hearing impairment.

Table 41.3 Psychiatric rating scales in prevalence studies

Study	Teacher scale	Parent scale	Parent i/view	Child i/view
Aplin (1985, 1987)	*			
Schlesinger and Meadow (1972)	*			
Fundudis *et al.* (1979)	*	*		
Freeman *et al.** (1975)	*	*	*	
Hindley (1993)	*	*	*	*

* Freeman *et al.* (1975) included an observation of the child but did not interview the child.

(Williams, 1970; Aplin, 1985; Hindley, 1993) it appears that factors associated with level of loss are, e.g. type of schooling (see below). Finally, although some of the studies do not report rates of additional impairments (Fundudis *et al.* (1979); Aplin (1987); Schlesinger & Meadow (1972)) such rates do vary between different schools and so affect the prevalence rates of psychiatric disorder.

A variety of rating instruments were used. All bar one used scales developed in hearing populations and suitably adapted. However, speech related items in some scales made them unreliable (Fundudis *et al.*, 1979; Prior *et al.*, 1988). Hindley (1993) developed teacher and parent scales to screen for psychiatric disorder in deaf children but psychiatric ratings were based on interviews with parents and children, using a BSL interpreter with the deaf children. Studies using teacher or parent questionnaires found a preponderance of conduct disorders (Fundudis *et al.*, 1979; Aplin, 1985) but when children were interviewed there was a preponderance of anxiety disorders. However, although Hindley (1993) interviewed all children who had screened positive for psychiatric disorder, he only interviewed a proportion of children screened negative and an adjusted prevalence rate was calculated using a pre-established false negative rate. In contrast, Freeman *et al.* (1975) interviewed all parents and so were able to calculate a true prevalence rate.

Mental retardation

The prevalence of hearing impairment in mentally retarded school children has been estimated to be of the order of 17% (Jitts & Keyes, 1983). This figure is likely to be an underestimate (Kropka & Williams, 1986). Schein (1975) suggested that the rate of mental retardation, amongst children enrolled in hearing impaired programmes in the US, lay in the range 17–19%. However, given the difficulties outlined above, the accuracy of these figures may be doubted.

Aetiology

Degree of deafness alone does not appear to be an important aetiological factor in psychiatric disorder in HI children. However, there has been considerable interest in the role of impaired communication in the genesis of psychiatric disorders. Some authors have asserted that lack of communication accounts for much of the disorder seen in deaf children (Lesser & Easer, 1972; Schlesinger & Meadow, 1972; Stokoe & Battison, 1975). This can be understood in relation to distortions of parent–child interaction and deprivation of social experiences (Feinstein, 1983). Rainer (1976) suggested that the absence of the anxiety reducing effects of the mother's voice may also account for increased personality difficulties in deaf adolescents and adults.

Attempts to study the effects of different school settings are difficult to interpret because school placement is dictated by a number of factors, some of which are, of themselves, likely to affect rates of psychiatric disorder (Fundudis *et al.*, 1979). It is not surprising that to date findings are inconsistent. In contrast to Hindley's (1993) findings, both Fundudis *et al.* (1979) and Aplin (1985, 1987) found increased rates of disorder amongst children attending deaf schools against those attending hearing impaired units or in integrated settings. However, neither of these studies involved interviews with the children. The hard of hearing children in Hindley's (1993) study reported more unsatisfactory school experiences, had fewer friends and had poorer self-images. All these factors were significantly related to psychiatric disorder. Anecdotally, the hard of hearing children reported much higher rates of stigmatization and victimization. Just as in studies of hearing children, in deaf children IQ score is inversely related to risk of psychiatric disorder (Williams, 1970; Schlesinger & Meadow, 1972; Aplin, 1985). In a similar vein, certain aetiological groups seem to be at risk. The most extensively studied group are children with congenital rubella syndrome (Vernon, 1967; Chess *et al.*,

1971; Chess & Fernandez, 1980; Desmond *et al.*, 1978). In addition to increased rates of impulsivity and attention difficulties, the rate of autism seems to be higher, particularly amongst the deaf–blind group (Chess *et al.*, 1971). Vernon (1967) suggests that there are increased rates of central language disorder in children with congenital rubella. However, there are no standardized instruments to assess sign language development, moreover the widely varying linguistic environments of deaf children make the assessment of language disorder extremely difficult.

In one study (Silva *et al.*, 1982) children with OME were found to be at greater risk of both emotional and behavioural problems, as measured by Rutter A and B scales. Amongst these there is a significant preponderance of children with short attention span and restlessness.

There is now increasing evidence that HI children are at greater risk of both physical and sexual abuse (Kennedy, 1990). This may be particularly so in residential schools (Brookhouser, 1987). It is unclear if this is a risk factor associated with residential schools in general or that deaf children in residential schools are more vulnerable because of communication difficulties.

Intervention

Although there are a number of psychiatric units for deaf children in the US, they are few and far between. A specialist outpatient service exists in the UK and The Netherlands but many countries have no such facilities. In the early 1960s Rainer and Altshuler (1966) described the then revolutionary service for deaf adults in New York State and more recently Sleebloom-van Raaij (1991) has offered her experience in setting up a similar unit in The Netherlands. These authors emphasize the importance of close consultation with the deaf community, when planning and running a service. However, whilst deaf adults are able to congregate in urban areas, deaf children are more diffusely spread across the country. Treating deaf children in hearing inpatient units poses considerable problems in communication and socialization for both staff and children (McCune, 1988). Although an inpatient unit for deaf children may be of help for severe disturbance, there will be a continuing need for community based treatments. Whilst specialist services may not be able to treat all children, consultation to residential deaf schools may be one effective way of reaching the children.

Feinstein (1983) and Feinstein and Lytle (1987) give moving accounts of work with early and late teenagers, using a residential school as a treatment setting. The early paper shows how group psychotherapy can enhance mutual understanding and diminish behavioural problems. Using a questionnaire designed to assess social–emotional adjustment in deaf children (Meadow *et al.*, 1980), they have also shown how stressful transfer to residential school can be for hard of hearing children (Lytle *et al.*, 1987). Evans (1987) provides a comprehensive review of treatment methods, whilst Lou (1989) describes a social-cognitive approach to improving social functioning. Greenberg & Kusché (1993) have developed a preventative mental programme specifically for deaf children.

Much of the psychoanalytical literature considers the relationship between language and personality formation. The therapeutic relationship is seen as offering the possibility of giving the young, deaf, child the experience of a reciprocally responsive relationship (Zalewska, 1989). On the other hand, parental concern with the acquisition of spoken language is seen as making communication a source of intense anxiety and conflict (Rainer, 1976). Psychotherapy using an interpreter inevitably leads to transference relationships that include the interpreter (Hoyt *et al.*, 1981).

Some families will adjust easily to the presence of a child with HI, others will find it more difficult. Amongst these families, as with other families with disabled family members, patterns of over-protection, idealization and rejection often emerge. For families with a deaf child, difficulties of communication will compound these patterns of interaction (Harvey, 1989) and deaf adolescents may find themselves torn between their hearing families and the deaf community with whom they wish to identify (Shapiro & Harris, 1976).

Adult outcome

A community survey of deaf adults (Checinski, 1993) has suggested that the rate of psychiatric disorder is increased, with a substantial proportion of deaf people, estimated at 30%, experiencing an episode of depression. Depressed deaf people have been referred to a community psychiatric service for deaf people (Elliott *et al.*, 1987) but this does not seem to be so for inpatient services. Amongst these populations, very few depressed deaf people are seen, the prevalence of schizophrenia appears to be equivalent to that in hearing populations and there is a preponderance of people with behavioural disorders (Rainer & Altshuler, 1966; Denmark, 1985).

Visual impairment

Assessment

The developmental path of VI children can differ considerably from sighted children. On these grounds Jan *et al.* (1977) suggest that clinicians who are inexperienced in working with these children should be cautious in making diagnoses.

The realization that a family has a visually impaired infant has a considerable impact in emotional and practical terms and both need to be borne in mind whilst assessing family functioning. When assessing the individual child, reduced facial expression (Fraiberg, 1977) may lead to difficulties in assessing affect and responsiveness, whilst uncertainties over the significance of language features such as echolalia (Urwin, 1983) and pronoun reversal (Lewis, 1987) may lead to difficulties in diagnosing pervasive developmental disorders.

Although a variety of IQ tests have been used with VI

children, Ammerman *et al.* (1986) suggest that there are three areas of difficulty in doing so. Firstly, it is not clear if the verbal subscales of tests such as the WISC-R measure the same abilities in blind children as in sighted children. Secondly, many of the tests, developed specifically for VI children, have not been fully validated. Thirdly, many of these tests do not distinguish between the different populations of VI, i.e. PS versus blind.

Epidemiology

Although there is no study which provides a comparable control group, rates of psychiatric disorder appear to be raised amongst VI children. Jan *et al.* (1977) studied a total population of legally blind children and young people aged between 0 and 20 years old. They assessed 92 out of 115 subjects and also recruited a neighbourhood control group matched for age and sex. Assessments were carried out using modified Rutter A and B scales, parental interviews, psychiatric interviews with the subjects and home observations. However, the content and structure of the interviews are not given. Psychiatric diagnoses were made by a child psychiatrist and the severity of dysfunction was assessed on a 4 point scale. Unfortunately, diagnostic criteria were not given and some of the terms used lacked specificity, e.g. behaviour disturbance and developmental disorder.

Fourteen of the children were totally blind, 13 had light perception and the remaining 65 were partially sighted. Over half of the population had additional impairments (49) and 29% had hard signs of CNS disorder. Forty-five per cent of the population were rated as having moderate or severe psychiatric disorders, of which mental handicap (18.6%), developmental disorder (15.1%) and adjustment reaction (10.5%) were the most common. Unfortunately, similar information was not provided for the control group.

One other study has used a control group (Van Hasselt *et al.*, 1986), using Achenbach's Child Behaviour Checklist (CBCL, teacher and parents versions) and Youth Self Report Form (YSRF) (Achenbach & Edelbrock, 1983). The data are reported as mean total scores, so that prevalence rates cannot be compared. However, differences in symptomatology between VI and sighted adolescents do emerge. Their subjects were VI male adolescents aged 13–19. Eighteen attended residential school, 17 publicly funded day-schools and there were 17 sighted controls. None of the subjects had additional handicaps and the subjects and controls were matched for age, IQ and a teacher's rating of their physical attractiveness. The VI adolescents attending residential school were more disturbed than the two other groups on all three questionnaires. The VI adolescents attending publicly funded school were also more disturbed than the controls on all three. The CBCL-P revealed that residential students scored higher on uncommunicative, obsessive–compulsive and hostile-withdrawn subscales. In addition VI adolescents in the publicly funded schools rated higher on school adjustment problems and were more anxious, according to the CBCL-T.

Patterns of symptomatology appear to change, according to the group of children studied. Kitzinger and Hunt (1985) used Richman's Sleep and behaviour questionnaires (1977), in a study of pre-school children with severe VI and mental handicap. Whilst temper tantrums, control problems and overactivity were relatively uncommon, a third of the group demonstrated social withdrawal, lack of relationship to other children, self-injurious behaviour and poor compliance at bedtime. In addition feeding problems also appear to be more common (Jan *et al.*, 1977). Ollendick *et al.* (1985) found a pattern of fears amongst VI adolescents that seemed to reflect the dangers that VI individuals face in the everyday world. Schnittjer and Hirshoren (1981) used Quay and Peterson's (1989) Behaviour Problem Checklist (BPC) to survey the pattern of problems displayed by a group of children and young people aged 6–21 attending a residential school. Their factor analysis revealed 3 dimensions — conduct disorder, personality problem and inadequacy–immaturity — that corresponded to factors found in sighted populations of children, using the BPC.

Aetiology

Jan *et al.*'s (1977) study is the most important source of information regarding the aetiology of psychiatric disorder in VI children. In line with studies of sighted children, they found that CNS disorder, multiple impairments, maternal mental illness and marital breakdown were all important aetiological factors. As with deafness, rates of additional impairments varied according to the aetiology of VI and so in turn affected rates of psychiatric morbidity. Severity of VI was also related to psychiatric disorder with blind children being more likely to show psychopathology than partially sighted children. Visually impaired children attending residential schools demonstrate higher rates of disturbance (Van Hasselt *et al.*, 1986) but it is unclear whether this is a result of referral bias or whether factors within the school foster the development of psychiatric disorder.

Although it seems likely that VI children will be victims of emotional, physical or sexual abuse only the latter is described in the literature (Elonen & Zwarensteyn, 1975). Using a limited number of case studies they suggest that sexual abuse has a severely deleterious effect on most blind children.

VI and autism

In 1958, Keeler described 5 children, who were blind as a result of retrolental fibroplasia, and whom he diagnosed as autistic. In addition he described 35 other children, with retrolental fibroplasia, and partial features of autism. This was in sharp contrast to two groups of children, one blinded at birth and the other later in childhood, amongst whom he found only one child with partial features of autism. Keeler (1958) suggested that three factors — brain damage, blindness *per se* and emotional deprivation — most probably interacting with each other, accounted for this picture.

Keeler's findings have been partially replicated by Chase (1972). She found an excess of children with autistic features, associated with signs of neurological damage, amongst children with retrolental fibroplasia. These findings have not been replicated amongst children with congenital rubella. Although Chess *et al.* (1971) found an excess of children with both a complete and partial autistic syndrome, there was a particular association with signs of brain damage and MSI but not blindness alone. Goodman and Ashby (1990) have described three children with delayed visual maturation and autism, who appeared to have improved considerably after limited follow-up. Rogers and Newhart-Larson (1989) have described 5 children with Leber's amaurosis and autism.

A number of possible mechanisms for the apparent association between autism and VI have been proposed. Goodman (1990) suggests that, for the children he studied, delayed neuronal maturation may account for both changes in visual functioning and autistic symptoms. Chase (1972) suggests that neurological abnormalities are most likely to account for the increase in autism. In contrast, Fraiberg (1977) suggests that many nonautistic blind children pass through a period of development, akin to autism, but which is a temporary handicap and reflects, in part, difficulties in the infant–mother relationship that stem from the effects of blindness on early interpersonal relations. Minter *et al.*'s (1991) findings support Fraiberg's view but also suggest that the prevalence of autism is increased amongst blind children.

Hobson (1991) suggests that greater understanding of the 'autistic-like' features of congenitally blind children may cast light on those aspects of autism which are a consequence of distortions in the infant–mother relationship and so subject to amelioration through psychological intervention. However, as Hobson (1991) implies, it may not be appropriate to consider many of the abnormalities of social behaviour and language development that nonautistic blind children demonstrate as 'autistic-like'. Many of the behaviours demonstrated by autistic children can be understood as attempts to communicate and cope with a social world which they do not understand. Behaviours which are superficially similar in blind children, may in fact reflect blind children's attempts to communicate with a world that they have difficulty in knowing.

Intervention

Reports by Jan *et al.* (1977), that almost 30% of their study population had received tranquillizers or sedatives may reflect how difficult it is to treat psychiatric disturbance in VI children. However, a wide range of psychological interventions for psychiatric disorders in VI children have been described. In single case studies, psychodynamic approaches are said to have produced striking improvements (Adelson, 1983; Fraiberg, 1977; Warren, 1984). Specially adapted social skills programmes have been described by Van Hasselt (1983) and his colleagues (Van Hasselt *et al.*, 1985a, 1985b). For VI children with additional intellectual impairments a variety of behavioural interventions have been used, such as: contingent stimulation (Williams, 1978); substitute activity (Raver &

Dwyer, 1986); positive reinforcement, punishment and peer feedback (Blasch, 1978); and modification of mealtime behaviour (Sisson & Dixon, 1986). Finally, the parenting of a VI child, with or without additional impairments can be extremely stressful and programmes to reduce parental stress have been developed (Kirkham *et al.*, 1986; Webb, 1990).

Developmental and psychiatric aspects of MSI

The combination of the effects of MSI and the brain abnormalities associated with its various causes, yields a highly complex developmental picture. The combination of HI and VI results in major distortions in the child's relationship with his environment. Not only are many perceptions absent but those that remain are often distorted. The interaction of perception and action is disrupted and the fundamental psychological processes that lead to adaptive development — motivation, anticipation and communication — are severely impaired (McInnes & Treffry, 1982). The child encounters difficulties in perceiving the environment and in managing the stimulation that the environment affords. In fact, the environment can be experienced as intrusive and threatening. In addition, those abilities that the child does have are often underestimated or interpreted by carers as maladaptive.

As a consequence the development of MSI children can take a number of paths. For the rare children like Helen Keller, whose sensory impairments were acquired rather than congenital, development is relatively complete; but for most it will be severely curtailed in all domains without specialist intervention. Motor development often takes one of two paths. Those children who have been understimulated are passive and disinterested whilst those who have been over-stimulated are overactive. Self-stimulating, self-destructive and aggressive behaviours are common. Language and communication are often severely limited or absent, as are self-help and more abstract cognitive skills. It is perhaps not surprising that the child often withdraws from social interaction.

Multisensory impaired children can be extremely taxing on parental resources. They call for enormous effort and considerable change in parents (Freeman, 1975, 1985). Similar flexibility and resourcefulness is called for in the professionals who set out to help them (Walton, 1989). McInnes and Treffry (1982) describe an effective programme of intervention whereby an adult, the intervener, becomes the child's eyes and ears and so allows communication between the child and the environment to begin. The child is initially extremely dependent on the intervener, but, as the child's ability to perceive and communicate with the world develops, the intervener encourages increasing independence and slowly withdraws.

CONCLUSIONS

In the course of this chapter we have considered the extent to which the behaviour and development of SI children is differ-ent or deviant. This question is most clearly stated in the case of deaf children. Here are a group of children with a language that differs from spoken languages in both its medium and many of its syntactic features. They are a group of children who grow to join a community of people who are connected but separate from the hearing community. Yet it is amongst hearing people working with deaf people that the notion of a 'psychology of deafness' has been most fiercely resisted. Lane (1987) has argued that such theories are, by definition, paternalistic representing a hearing person's ill-informed and prejudiced view of a cultural minority. In contrast, with blind children there has been a recognition that the study of their development reveals a diversity in their developmental paths (Urwin, 1983) which is of importance in its own right. Indeed it may be possible to reverse Lane's argument and suggest that the study of deaf children of deaf parents, in one sense the psychology of deafness, will lead to a better informed study of deaf children of hearing parents and the reversal of paternalism.

For both deaf and blind children a number of areas of research present themselves. For deaf children of hearing parents, there is a need for greater understanding as to how such parents can foster the development of sign language. In contrast with blind children, our knowledge of blind children of blind parents is rudimentary but what we know suggests (Rowbury, 1991) that this is potentially a rich vein. Equally our knowledge of the development of peer and sibling relationships in blind children is at a basic level. Although we have a better understanding of the peer relationships of HI children, this is true for children in mainstream programmes and not in residential or day schools for deaf children.

Given the increasing emphasis on mainstreaming of SI children, our understanding of peer relationships should play an important part in determining the strengths and weaknesses of mainstream and separate educational programmes. Unfortunately, the non-curricular aspects of education seem to pass many SI children by. Finally, despite the decades of debate between oralists and manualists in deaf education, there is, as yet, no reliable way of identifying which children most benefit from which system, except by seeing who fails. This sentences many HI children to repeated failure both academically and linguistically.

Although there have been a number of well-thought through prevalence studies, none as yet has used a fully developed methodology, particularly interviews with the children, and a fully assessed control group. For HI children it would allow an assessment of the effects of different educational approaches on mental health. For VI children this would allow investigators to assess the relative influences and interactions of VI, brain abnormalities, mental retardation and parental responses on psychopathology. These are particularly important in trying to resolve the possible association between VI and autism. Even less is known about the psychopathology of MSI children.

Our knowledge of the effectiveness of psychological and physical interventions in SI children is minimal. There would seem strong grounds for actively fostering the involvement of deaf people in the development and provision of children's mental health services for deaf children. Are there similar grounds for involving blind people with blind children? In turn we may ask how such services should be organized. For such comparatively small groups of children there is a good argument for developing specialist services. There are such services for deaf children but not for blind children. However, there is a danger of professional isolation and there are logistical and practical difficulties in trying to deliver services to a widely dispersed population. Perhaps the onus of responsibility lies with the professionals working in these fields to inform their colleagues of the intellectual and emotional challenges and excitements entailed in working with these children and their families.

REFERENCES

Achenbach T.M. & Edelbrock C.S. (1983) *Manual for the Child Behaviour Checklist and Revised Behaviour Profile.* University Associates in Psychiatry, Burlington, VT.

Adelson E. (1983) The role of vision in early development. In: Mills A.E. (ed) *Language Acquisition in the Blind Child: Normal and Deficient.* pp. 1–12. Croom Helm, London.

Adelson E. & Fraiberg S. (1974) Gross motor development in infants blind from birth. *Child Development,* **45**, 114–126.

Ainsworth M.D.S., Blehar M.C., Waters E. & Wall S. (1978) *Patterns of attachment: A psychological study of the Strange Situation.* Erlbaum, Hillsdale, NJ.

Ammerman R.T., Van Hasselt V.B. & Hersen M. (1986) Psychological Adjustment of visually handicapped children and youth. *Clinical Psychology Review,* **6**, 67–85.

Aplin D.Y. (1985) Social and emotional adjustments of hearing-impaired children in special schools. *Journal of the British Association of Teachers of the Deaf,* **9**, 84–94.

Aplin D.Y. (1987) Social and emotional adjustment of hearing-impaired children in ordinary and special schools. *Educational Research Volume 29,* 56–64.

Arnold D. & Tremblay A. (1979) Interaction of deaf and hearing preschool children. *Journal of Communication Disorders,* **12**, 245–251.

Balow I.H. & Brill R.G. (1972) An evaluation study of reading and academic achievement levels of sixteen graduating classes of the California School for the Deaf, Riverside, CA.

Bamford J. & Saunders E. (1991) *Hearing impairment, auditory perception and language disability* (2nd edn.), Whurr, London.

Bellugi U., Klima E.S. & Poizner H. (1988) Sign Language and the Brain. In: Plum F. (ed) *Language, Communication and the Brain.* Association for Research in Nervous and Mental Disease, 66, Raven Press, New York.

Best C. (1983) The 'new' deaf-blind? Results of a national survey of deaf-blind children in ESN (S) and hospital schools. *British Journal of Visual Impairment,* **1**, 11–13.

Blasch B.B. (1978) Blindisms: treatment by punishment and reward in laboratory and natural settings. *Journal of Visual Impairment and Blindness,* **72**, 215–230.

Blennerhassett L. (1990) Intellectual Assessment. In: Moores D.F. & Meadow-Orlans K.P. (eds) *Educational and Developmental Aspects of Deafness.* Gallaudet University Press, Washington DC.

Bond D.E. (1986) Psychological Assessment of the Hearing Impaired, Additionally Impaired and Multi-handicapped Deaf. In: Ellis D. (ed) *Sensory Impairments in Mentally Handicapped People.* Croom Helm, London.

Brasel K.E. & Quigley S.P. (1977) Influence of certain language and communication environments in early childhood on the development of language in deaf individuals. *Journal of Speech and Hearing Research,* **20**, 81–94.

Brien D. (1983) Is there a Deaf Culture? In: Gregory S. & Hartley G.M. (eds) *Constructing Deafness.* Pinter Publishers, London, in association with the Open University.

Brookhouser P.E. (1987) Ensuring the safety of deaf children in residential schools. *Otolaryngology Head and Neck Surgery,* **97**, 361–368.

Burlingham D. (1961) Some notes on the development of the blind. *Psychoanalytic Study of the Child,* **16**, 121–145.

Butterworth G. (1989) Events and encounters in infant perception. In: Slater A. & Bremner G. (eds) *Infant Development.* Lawrence Earlbaum Associates: London, Hove and Hillsdale.

Caselli M.C. & Volterra V. (1989) From communication to language in hearing and deaf children. In: Volterra V. & Erting C.J. (eds) *From Gesture to Language in Hearing and Deaf Children.* Springer-Verlag, Berlin.

Chase J.B. (1972) *Retrolental Fibroplasia and Autistic Symptomatology.* New York American Foundation for the Blind, New York.

Checinski K. (1993) 'An estimate of the point prevalence of psychiatric disorder in prelingually deaf adults living in the community'. M.D. thesis submitted Cambridge University 1993.

Chess S. & Fernandez P. (1980) Do Deaf Children have a Typical Personality? *Journal of American Academy of Child Psychiatry,* **19**, 654–664.

Chess S., Korn S.J. & Fernandez P.B. (1971) *Psychiatric Disorders of Children with Congenital Rubella.* Brunner and Mazel, New York.

Cicourel A.V. (1978) Sociolinguistic aspects of the use of Sign Language. In: Schlesinger I.M. & Namir L. (eds) *Sign Language of the Deaf: psychological, linguistic and sociological perspectives.* Academic Press, London.

Clark M. (1989) *Language Through Living for Hearing Impaired Children.* Hodder and Stoughton, London.

Cohn J. & Tronick E.Z. (1983) Three month old infants' reaction to simulated maternal depression. *Child Development,* **54**, 185–193.

Colbourne-Brown M. & Tobin M. (1982) Integration of the educationally blind. *New Beacon,* **66**, 781, Royal National Institute for the Blind.

Conrad R. (1979) *The Deaf School Child: Language and Cognitive Function.* Harper Row, London.

Das V. (1989) Heterogeneity in Usher's syndrome. In: Best A.B. (ed) *Papers on the Education of the Deaf-Blind, Proceedings of Warwick August '89.* International Association for the Education of the Deaf-Blind, London.

Davis A. (1990) Neonatal hearing screening: part of an integrated advance in audiological health services for the 1990s. *British Association of Audiological Scientists Newsletter,* **17**.

Daunt, W. (1991) *Bilingual Education for Deaf Children: From Policy to Practice. Proceedings of a Conference held at Nottingham, Nov. 1990.* LASER, Kimpton, Herts. UK.

Denmark J.C. (1985) A study of 250 patients referred to a department of psychiatry for the deaf. *British Journal of Psychiatry,* **146**, 282–286.

Desmond M.M., Fisher E.S., Vorderman A.L., Schaffer H.G., Andrew L.P., Zion T.E. & Catlin F.I. (1978) The longitudinal course of congenital rubella encephalitis in non-retarded children. *Journal of Pediatrics,* **93**, 584–591.

Dunn H.G. (1986) Neurological, psychological and opthalmological sequelae of low birthweight. In: Dunn H.G. (ed) *Sequelae of Low Birthweight: The Vancouver Study.* Mackeith Press, Oxford and Philadelphia.

Elliott H., Glass L. & Evans J.W. (1987) *Mental Health Assessment of Deaf*

Clients: a practical manual. College-Hill Press, Boston.

Elonen A.S. & Zwarensteyn S.B. (1975) Sexual trauma in Young Blind Children. *New Outlook for the Blind*, **69**, 440–442.

Erting C.J. (1987) Cultural conflict in a school for deaf children. In: Higgins P.C. & Nash J.E. (eds) *Understanding Deafness Socially.* Charles Thomas, Springfield, Illinois.

Erting C.J., Prezioso C. & O'Grady Hynes M. (1989) The interactional context of deaf mother-infant communication. In: Volterra V. & Erting C.J. (eds) *From Gesture to Language in Hearing and Deaf Children.* Springer-Verlag, Berlin.

Evans J.W. (1987) Mental Health treatment for Hearing Impaired Adolescents and Adults. In: Heller B.W., Flohr L.M. & Zegans L.S. (eds) *Psychosocial Interventions with Sensorially Disabled Persons.* Grune Stratton, Orlando.

Evans J.W. & Elliott H. (1981) Screening criteria for the diagnosis of schizophrenia in deaf patients. *Archives of General Psychiatry*, **36**, 787–790.

Feinstein C.B. (1983) Early adolescent deaf boys: a biopsychosocial approach. *Adolescent Psychiatry*, **11**, 147–162.

Feinstein C.B. & Lytle R. (1987) Observations from clinical work with high school aged deaf adolescents attending a residential school. *Adolescent Psychiatry: Developmental and Clinical Studies*, **14**, 461–477.

Feldman H., Goldin-Meadow S. & Gleitman L. (1978) Beyond Herodotus: the creation of language by linguistically deprived children. In: Lock A. (ed) *Action, Gesture and Symbol: The Emergence of Language.* Academic Press, London.

Fraiberg S. (1977) *Insights from the Blind: Comparative Studies of Blind and Sighted Infants.* Basic Books, New York/Souvenir Press, London.

Freeman P. (1975) *Understanding the deaf-blind child.* Heineman, London.

Freeman P. (1985) *The deaf/blind infant: a programme for care.* William Heineman, London.

Freeman R.D. (1976) The deaf child: controversy over teaching methods. *Journal of Child Psychology and Psychiatry*, **17**, 229–232.

Freeman R.D. (1977) Psychiatric aspects of sensory disorders and intervention. In: Graham P. (ed) *Epidemiological Approaches in Child Psychiatry*, 275–304. Academic Press, London.

Freeman R.D. & Blockberger S. (1987) Language development and sensory disorder: visual and hearing impairments. In: Rutter M. & Yule M. (eds) *Language Development and Disorder*, 234–247. Blackwell Scientific, Oxford.

Freeman R.D., Malkin S.F. & Hastings J.O. (1975) Psychosocial Problems of Deaf Children and their Families: a Comparative Study. *American Annals of the Deaf*, **120**, 275–304.

Freeman R.D., Goetz E., Richards D.P., Groenveld M., Blockberger S., Jan J.E. & Sykanda A.M. (1989) Blind children's early emotional development: do we know enough to help? *Child Care, Health and Development*, **15**, 3–28.

Fundudis T., Kolvin I. & Garside R. (1979) *Speech Retarded and Deaf Children: their psychological development.* Academic Press, London.

Furth H.G. (1973) *Deafness and Learning. A Psychological Approach.* Belmont CA, Wadsworth.

Galenson E.M., Miller R., Kaplan E. & Rothstein A. (1979) Assessment of development in the deaf child. *Journal of the American Academy of Child Psychiatry*, **18**, 128–142.

Goldin-Meadow S. & Mylander C. (1984) Gestural Communication in Deaf Children: the Effects and Non-effects of Parental Input on Early Language Development. *Monographs of the Society for Research in Child Development Serial No. 207, vol. 49, nos. 3–4.*

Goodman R. (1990) Making sense of links between blindness and autism: pitfalls and possibilities. *Proceedings of the Behavioural Phenotypes Study Group Symposium, November 1990*, Welshpool, UK.

Goodman R. & Ashby L. (1990) Delayed visual maturation and autism. *Developmental Medicine and Child Neurology*, **32**, 814–819.

Graham E.E. & Shapiro E. (1953) Use of the Performance Scale of the W.I.S.C. with the deaf child. *Journal of Consulting Psychology*, **17**, 396–398.

Greenberg M.T. & Marvin R.S. (1979) Patterns of attachment in profoundly deaf pre-school children. *Merrill-Palmer Quarterly*, **25**, 263–679.

Greenberg M.T. and Kusché C.A. (1993) *Promoting Social and Emotional Development in Deaf Children: The PATHS Project.* University of Washington Press, Washington, DC.

Gregory S. & Barlow S. (1986) *Interaction between deaf babies and their deaf and hearing mothers.* Paper presented to the Language Development and Sign Language Workshop, Bristol.

Gregory S. & Mogford K. (1981) Early language development in deaf children. In: Woll B., Kyle J.G. & Deuchar M. (eds) *Perspectives on BSL and Deafness.* Croom Helm, London.

Gregory S. & Mogford K. (1982) The development of symbolic play in young deaf children. In: Rogers I.D.R. & Sloboda J. (eds) *The Acquisition of Symbolic Skills.* Plenum Press, London.

Haggard M. & Hughes E. (1991) *Screening children's hearing.* HMSO, London.

Hall D.M.B. (1989) *Health for all children: a programme for child health surveillance; the report of the Joint Working Party on Child Health Surveillance.* Oxford University Press, Oxford.

Harris M., Clibbens J., Chasin J. & Tibbits R. (1988) The third chicken is a duck: linguistic experience and early sign language development. In: Collins G. (ed) *Proceedings of the Child Language Seminar*, University of Warwick.

Harvey M.A. (1989) *Psychotherapy with deaf and hard-of-hearing persons: A Systemic Model.* Lawrence Erlbaum, Hillsdale NJ.

Higgins P.C. (1987) In: Higgins P.C. & Nash J.E. (eds) *Understanding Deafness Socially.* Charles Thomas, Springfield, IL.

Hill A.E., McKendrick P., Poole J.J., Pugh R.E., Rosenbloom L. & Turnbull R. (1986) The Liverpool Visual Assessment Team: 10 Years Experience. *Child: Care, Health and Development*, **12**, 37–51.

Hindley P.A. (1993) *Signs of Feeling: A prevalence study of psychiatric disorder in deaf and partially hearing children and adolescents.* Royal National Institute for the Deaf, Research Report, London.

Hobson R.P. (1991) What is autism? *Pervasive Developmental Disorders*, **14**, 1–17.

Hoyt M.F., Siegelman E.Y. & Schlesinger H.S. (1981) Special Issues Regarding Psychotherapy with the Deaf. *American Journal of Psychiatry*, **138**(6), 807–811.

Jan J.E., Freeman R.D. & Scott E.P. (1977) *Visual Impairment in Children and Adolescents.* Grune and Stratton, New York.

Jitts S. & Keyes C. (1983) Incidence of hearing loss in a population of school-aged, intellectually handicapped children. *Australian Journal of Audiology*, **5**, 71–75.

Keeler W.R. (1958) Autistic patterns and defective communication in blind children with retrolental fibroplasia. In: Hoch P.H. & Zubin J. (eds) *Psychopathology of Communication.* 64–83. Grune and Stratton, New York.

Kekelis L.S. & Andersen E.S. (1984) Family communication styles and language development. *Journal of Visual Impairment and Blindness*, **78**, 54–65.

Kennedy M. (1990) No more secrets — please. *Deafness*, **6**, 10–12.

Kennedy P. & Bruininks R.H. (1974) Social status of hearing impaired children in regular classrooms. *Exceptional Children*, **40**, 336–343.

Kennedy P., Northcott W., McCauley R. & Williams S.M. (1976) Longitudinal sociometric and cross-sectional data on mainstreaming hearing-impaired students: implications for pre-school programming. *The Volta Review*, **78**, 71–81.

Kirkham M.A., Schilling R.R., Norelius K. & Schinke S.P. (1986) Developing coping styles and social support networks: an intervention outcome study with mothers of handicapped children. *Child:*

Care, Health and Development, **12**(5), 313—323.

Kitson N. & Fry R. (1990) Prelingual deafness and psychiatry. *British Journal of Hospital Medicine*, **44**, 353—356.

Kitzinger M. & Hunt H. (1985) The effect of residential setting on sleep and behaviour patterns of young visually-handicapped children. In: Stevenson J.E. (ed) *Recent Research in Developmental Psychopathology*. Pergamon Press, Oxford.

Klima E.S. & Bellugi U. (1979) *The Signs of Language*. Harvard University Press, Cambridge, MA.

Koester L.S. & Trim M.V. (1991) *Face-to-face Interactions with Deaf and Hearing Infants: Do Maternal or Infant Behaviours Differ?* Biennial Meeting of the Society for Research in Child Development, Seattle.

Kropka B.I. & Williams C. (1986) The Epidemiology of Hearing Impairment in People with a Mental Handicap. In: Ellis D. (ed) *Sensory Impairments in Mentally Handicapped People*. Croom Helm, London.

Kyle J.G. & Allsop L. (1982) *Deaf people and the community: final report to the Nuffield Foundation*. School of Education, Bristol University, Bristol.

Kyle J. & Woll B. (1985) *Sign Language: the study of deaf people and their language*. Cambridge University Press, London.

Ladd G.W., Munson H.L. & Miller J.K. (1984) Social integration of deaf adolescents in secondary-level mainstream programs. *Exceptional Children*, **50**, 420—423.

Lane H. (1987) *Paternalism and the Deaf: An Open Letter to Mme. Umuyevi*. Paper presented at the Congress of the World Federation of the Deaf, Helsinki.

Lederberg A.R. (1984) Interaction between Deaf Preschoolers and Unfamiliar Hearing Adults. *Child Development*, **55**, 598—606.

Lesser S.R. & Easer B.R. (1972) Personality differences in the perceptually handicapped. *Journal of the American Academy of Child Psychiatry*, **11**, 458—466.

Levy-Shiff R. & Hoffman M.A. (1985) Social behaviour of hearing-impaired and normally hearing children. *British Journal of Educational Psychology*, **55**, 111—118.

Lewis V. (1987) *Development and Handicap*. Basil Blackwell, Oxford.

Lorimer J. (1981) The limitations of Braille as a medium for communication and the possibility of improving reading standards. *The British Psychological Society Division of Educational and Child Psychology Occasional Papers*, **5**, 62—72.

Lou M.W. (1989) A social-cognitive approach to improving the social functioning of deaf adolescents and young adults. In: Watson D., Long G., Taff-Watson M. & Harvey M. (eds) *Two Decades of Excellence: A Foundation for the Future*. Monograph **14**, 69—77. ADARA, Little Rock, Ar.

Lowenfeld B. (1948) Effects of blindness on the cognitive functions of children. *Nervous Child*, **7**, 45—54.

Lytle R.R., Feinstein C. & Jonas B. (1987) Social and Emotional Adjustment in Deaf Adolescents after Transfer to a Residential School for the Deaf. *Journal of the American Academy of Child and Adolescent Psychiatry*, **26**, 237—241.

McCune N. (1988) Deaf in a hearing unit: coping of staff and adolescents. *Journal of Adolescence*, **11**, 21—23.

McInnes J.M. & Treffry J.A. (1982) *Deaf-Blind Infants and Children: a developmental guide*. Open University Press, Milton Keynes.

MacLean G. & Becker S. (1979) Studies of the psychosocial adjustment of the hearing impaired. *Canadian Journal of Psychiatry*, **24**, 744—748.

Markides A. (1989) Integration: the speech intelligibility, friendships and associations of hearing impaired children in secondary schools. *Journal of the British Association of Teachers of the Deaf*, **13**, 63—72.

Martin J.A.M. (1982) Aetiological factors relating to childhood deafness in the European Community. *Audiology*, **21**, 149—158.

Mather S.M. (1990) Home and classroom communication. In: Moores

D.F. & Meadow-Orlans K.P. (eds) *Educational and Developmental Aspects of Deafness*. Gallaudet University Press, Washington, DC.

Maxwell M.M. (1990) *Simultaneous communication: the state of the art and proposals for change*. Sign Language Studies, **69**, 333—390.

Meadow K.P. (1968a) Parental responses to the medical ambiguities of deafness. *Journal of Health and Social Behaviour*, **9**, 299—309.

Meadow K.P. (1968b) Early manual communication in relation to the deaf child's intellectual, social and communicative functioning. *American Annals of the Deaf*, **113**, 29—41.

Meadow K.P. (1980) *Deafness and Child Development*. Edward Arnold, London.

Meadow K.P. (1987) Understanding Deafness: Socialization of Children and Youth. In: Higgins P.C. & Nash J.E. (eds) *Understanding Deafness Socially*. Charles Thomas, Springfield, Illinois.

Meadow K.P., Greenberg M.T. & Erting C. (1983) Attachment behaviour of deaf children with deaf parents. *Journal of the American Academy of Child Psychiatry*, **22**, 23—28.

Meadow K.P., Greenberg M.T., Erting C. & Carmichael H. (1981) Interactions of deaf mothers and deaf preschool children: comparisons with three other groups of deaf and hearing dyads. *American Annals of the Deaf*, **126**, 454—468.

Meadow K.P., Karchmer M., Petersen L. & Rudner L. (1980) *Manual for Meadow/Kendall Social-Emotional Assessment Inventory for Deaf Students*. Gallaudet College, Washington, DC.

Meadow-Orlans K.P., Erting E., Day P.S., MacTurk R., Prezioso C. & Gianino A. (1987) *Deaf and Hearing Mothers of Deaf and Hearing Infants: Interaction in the First Year of Life*. Paper presented at the 10th World Congress of the World Federation of the Deaf, Helsinki.

Minter M., Brown R. & Hobson P. (1991) *Congenital blindness and autism: exploring possible links*. British Psychological Society, Developmental Psychology Section Annual Conference, Cambridge University.

Mohay H. (1982) A preliminary description of the communication systems evolved by the deaf children in the absence of a sign language model. *Sign Language Studies*, **34**, 73—90.

Mohay H. (1989) The interaction of Posture and Speech in the Language Development of The Profoundly Deaf Child. In: Volterra Y.J. & Erting C.J. (eds) *From Gesture to Language in Hearing and Deaf Children*, Springer-Verlag, Berlin.

Newton V.E. (1985) Aetiology of bilateral sensorineural hearing loss in young children. *Journal of Laryngology and Otology*, Suppl 10, pp. 41—44.

O'Connor N. & Hermelin B. (1978) *Seeing and Hearing and Space and Time*. Academic Press, London.

Ollendick T.H., Matson J.L. & Helsel W.J. (1985) Fears in visually-impaired and normally-sighted youths. *Behavior Research and Therapy*, **23**, 375—378.

Padden C. & Marcowicz H. (1976) *Cultural Conflicts between Hearing and Deaf Communities, in Proceedings of the Seventh World Congress of the World Federation of the Deaf*. National Association of the Deaf, Washington, DC.

Peckham C. & Pearson R. (1976) The Prevalence and Nature of Ascertained Handicap in the National Child Development Study. *Public Health Reports*, **90**, 111—121.

Preisler G. & Palmer C. (1986) The function of vocalization in early parent-blind child interaction. In: Lindblom B. & Zetterstrom R. (eds) *Precursors of Early Speech*. Wenner-Gren International Symposium Series 44. Macmillan Press, Basingstoke.

Preisler G. & Palmer C. (1989) Thoughts from Sweden: the blind child at nursery school with sighted children. *Child: Care, Health and Development*, **15**, 45—52.

Prior M.R., Glazner J., Sanson A. & Debelle G. (1988) Research Note: Temperament and behavioural adjustment in hearing impaired children. *Journal of Child Psychology and Psychiatry*, **29**, 209—216.

Quay H.C. & Peterson D.R. (1979) *Manual for the Behavior Problem Checklist.* (Available from D.R. Peterson, 39 North Fifth, Highland Park, New Jersey 08904.)

Rainer J.D. (1976) Some observations on affect induction and ego development in the deaf. *International Review of Psychoanalysis*, **3**, 121–123.

Rainer J.D. & Altshuler K.Z. (1966) *Comprehensive Mental Health Services for the Deaf.* Department of Medical Genetics, New York State Psychiatric Institute.

Raver S. & Dwyer R.C. (1986) Using a substitute activity to eliminate eye poking in a 3-year-old visually-impaired child in the classroom. *The Exceptional Child*, **33**, 65–72.

Rawlings B.W. & Jensema C.J. (1977) *Two studies of the families of hearing impaired children.* Office of Demographic Studies, Gallaudet University, Washington DC.

Reynell J. (1978) Developmental patterns of visually-handicapped children. *Child: Care, Health and Development*, **4**, 291–303.

Reynell J. (1979) *Manual for the Reynell-Zinkin Developmental Scales for Young Visually-Handicapped Children. Part 1.* NFER, Windsor.

Richman N. (1977) Is a behaviour checklist for preschool children useful? In: Graham P.J. (ed) *Epidemiological Approaches in Child Psychiatry.* Academic Press, London.

Rogers S.J. & Newhart-Larson S. (1989) Characteristics of infantile autism in five children with Leber's congenital amaurosis. *Developmental Medicine and Child Neurology*, **31**(5), 598–608.

Rowbury C. (1991) *Referential Communication between a Blind mother and a Blind child.* Paper presented at the British Psychological Society developmental Section Annual Conference, September 1991, Cambridge.

Rowland C. (1983) Patterns of interaction between three blind infants and their mothers. In: Mills A.E. (ed) *Language Acquisition in the Blind Child.* Croom Helm, Beckenham.

Rutter M., Graham P. & Yule W. (1970) A neuropsychiatric study in childhood. *Clinics in Developmental Medicine Nos. 35/36.* Spastics International Medical Publications, London.

Schein J.D. (1975) Deaf students with other disabilities. *American Annals of the Deaf*, **120**, 92–99.

Schlesinger H. (1988) Questions and answers in the development of deaf children. In: Strong M. (ed) *Language, Learning and Deafness.* Cambridge University Press, Cambridge.

Schlesinger H. & Meadow K.P. (1972) *Sound and Sign.* University of California Press, Berkeley.

Schnittjer C.J. & Hirshoren A. (1981) Factors of problem behavior in visually-impaired children. *Journal of Abnormal Child Psychology*, **9**, 517–522.

Sever J.L., South M.A. & Shaver K.A. (1985) Delayed manifestations of congenital rubella. *Reviews of Infectious Diseases*, **7**, Suppl 1, pp. 164–169.

Shapiro R.J. & Harris R. (1976) Family Therapy in Treatment of the Deaf: A Case Report. *Family Process*, **15**, 83–97.

Sidle N. (1985) *Rubella in Pregnancy: a Review of Rubella as an Infection in Pregnancy, its Consequences and Prevention.* SENSE, London.

Silva P.A., Kirkland C., Simpson A., Stewart I.A. & Williams S.M. (1982) Some developmental and behavioural problems associated with bilateral otitis media with effusion. *Journal of Learning Disorders*, **15**, 417–421.

Sisson L.A. & Dixon M.J. (1986) Improving mealtime behaviors of a multihandicapped child using behavior therapy techniques. *Journal of Visual Impairment and Blindness*, **80**, 855–858.

Sleeboom I. (1992) Issues of importance to be considered in setting up new mental health services for the deaf. In: *Proceedings of the Second International Congress of the European Society for Mental Health and Deafness, Namur, May 1991.* La Bastole, Namur.

Snitzer Reilly J., McIntyre M.L. & Bellugi U. (1989) Faces: The Relationship between Language and Affect. In: Volterra V. & Erting C.J. (eds) *From Gesture to Language in Hearing and Deaf Children.* Springer-Verlag, Berlin.

Spencer P.E. & Gutfreund M.K. (1990) Directiveness in Mother–Infant Interactions. In: Moores D.F. & Meadow-Orlans K.P. (eds) *Educational and Developmental Aspects of Deafness.* Gallaudet University Press, Washington DC.

Spencer P.E., Deyo D. & Grindstaff N. (1990) Symbolic play development of deaf and hearing toddlers. In: Moores D.F. & Meadow-Orlans K.P. (eds) *Educational and Developmental Aspects of Deafness.* Gallaudet University Press, Washington DC.

Stansfield M. & Veltri D. (1987) Assessment from the Perspective of the Sign Language Interpreter. In: Elliot H., Glass L. & Evans J.W. (eds) *Mental Health Assessment of Deaf Clients: a practical manual.* College-Hill Press, Boston.

Stokoe W.C. & Battison R. (1975) 'Sign language, mental health and satisfactory interaction'. Unpublished paper. Linguistics Research Laboratory, Gallaudet College, Washington DC.

Strong M. (1988) A bilingual approach to the education of young deaf children: ASL and English. In: Strong M. (ed) *Language, Learning and Deafness.* Cambridge University Press, Cambridge.

Super C.M. & Harkness S. (1986) The developmental niche: a conceptualization at the interface of child and culture. *International Journal of Behavioural Development*, **9**, 545–569.

Trybus R.J. (1985) Demographics and population character research in deaf-blindness. In: Stahlecker J.E., Glass L.E. & Machalow S. (eds) *State of the Art: Research Priorities in Deaf-Blindness.* Center on Deafness, UCSF, California.

Urwin C. (1981) Early language development in blind children. *The British Psychological Society Division of Educational and Child Psychology Occasional Papers*, **5**, 78–93.

Urwin C. (1983) Dialogue and cognitive functioning in the early language of three blind children. In: Mills A.E. (ed) *Language Acquisition in the Blind Child.* Croom Helm, Beckenham.

Van Hasselt V.B. (1983) Social adaptation in the blind. *Clinical Psychology Review*, **3**, 87–102.

Van Hasselt V.B., Hersen M. & Kazdin A.E. (1985a) Assessment of social skills in visually handicapped adolescents. *Behaviour Research and Therapy*, **23**, 53–63.

Van Hasselt V.B., Kazdin A.E., Hersen M., Simon J. & Mastantuono A.M. (1985b) A behavioral-analytic model for assessing social skills in blind adolescents. *Behavior Research and Therapy*, **23**, 395–405.

Van Hasselt V.B., Kazdin A.E. & Hersen M. (1986) Assessment of Problem Behaviour in Visually Handicapped Adolescents. *Journal of Clinical Child Psychology*, **15**, 135–141.

Van Uden A.M.J. (1977) *A world of language for deaf children. Part 1: Basic principles.* Swets and Zeitlinger, Amsterdam and Lisse.

Vernon M. (1967) Characteristics associated with post-rubella children: psychological, educational and physical. *Volta Review*, **69**, 176–185.

Walton L. (1989) Working with parents. In: Best A.B. (ed) *Papers on the education of the deaf-blind, vol. 2. Proceedings of Warwick August '89, A European Conference of the International Association of Educators of the Deaf Blind.*

Warren D. (1984) *Blindness and Early Childhood Development.* 2nd edn. American Foundation for the Blind, New York.

Webb B. (1990) Mutual support for families of children with eye cancer. *Child: Care, Health and Development*, **16**, 319–329.

White S.J. & White R.E.C. (1984) The deaf imperative: characteristics of maternal input to hearing-impaired children. *Topics in Language Disorders*, **4**, 38–49.

Williams C. (1978) Strategies of intervention with the profoundly retarded visually-handicapped child: a brief report of a study of stereotype. *Occasional Papers, Volume II, Number II*, 68–72. British

Psychological Society, Leicester.

Williams C.E. (1970) Some psychiatric observations on a group of maladjusted deaf children. *Journal of Child Psychology and Psychiatry*, **11**, 1–18.

Williams M. (1971) Braille reading. *The Teacher of the Blind*, **59**, 103–116.

Wills D.M. (1970) Vulnerable periods in the early development of blind children. *Psychoanalytic Study of the Child*, **25**, 461–479.

Wood D., Wood H., Griffiths A. & Howarth I. (1986) *Teaching and Talking with Deaf Children*. John Wiley, Chichester.

Zalewska M. (1989) Non-verbal psychotherapy of deaf children with disorders in personality development. *Journal of the Rehabilitation of the Deaf*, **22**, 55–71.

Chapter 42
Psychological Aspects of Chronic Physical Sickness

David C. Taylor & D. Mary Eminson

INTRODUCTION

. . . for there is much pain that is quite noiseless; and vibrations that make human agonies are often a mere whisper in the roar of human existence (George Eliot, *Felix Holt, The Radical*)

The intuitive assumption is that suffering a chronic sickness would be burdensome to a child, and a source of sorrow to its family. But the intuition requires of us that we should have some ideas about how the burden and the sorrow would be expressed in the feelings and behaviour of the people involved. Or, if they are not obviously expressed, whether that reveals a failure of research design, is a measure of the quality of coping of those involved, or suggests that our intuition about burden and sorrow was erroneous. Initially we must consider what is meant by the terms in the intuitive statement, and the relationships assumed between them. We must also consider how the burden and sorrow can be alleviated.

Chronic sickness

Under scrutiny chronic sickness is seen as one of medicine's clumsy portmanteau terms; extensible to include about 30% of children in some surveys (Pless & Roghman, 1971), frequently measured at around 15% (Gortmaker & Sappenfield, 1984; Cadman *et al.*, 1987), but which, constrained by the adjective severe, can be reduced to 2–4% of children. Perrin and MacLean (1988) described this latter group of children as having 'severe health conditions that affect their daily activities on a regular basis'. They form a small proportion of children who see physicians but they deserve particular consideration since the scale and duration of medical involvement with them are considerable.

Relationships between chronic sickness and suffering

It would also seem intuitively likely that the degree of psychological impact should generally parallel the severity of the physical sickness. As the term chronic has been loosely applied in research and used to cover variably large proportions of children, little correspondence might be found in some studies that include a large proportion of low-impact conditions. Also,

it could happen that the ways in which the burden and sorrow are expressed might not conform with readily identifiable categories in psychiatric nosology. Studies that rely upon fixed schedules of diagnostic criteria, therefore, may fail to record what is intuitively being experienced. Some research has been regarded as falling short by failing to give proper consideration to the developmental variable (Cerreto & Travis, 1984; Eiser, 1991). Quite different yardsticks will be necessary, for example, to examine the effect of an illness on a child's social functioning as between 2 and 18 years of age. No single measure could cover this. The expectations of normal family activities also alter through that period, as does how siblings expect to share in these activities. The mode of expression of any sickness changes with time (Jessop & Stein, 1988). The chronic sick population is made up of different proportions of various diseases at different ages (Kohler & Jakobsson, 1987). Thus congenital abnormalities, childhood epilepsy, cystic fibrosis, diabetes and cancers have their onset at various ages, altering the constitution of the chronic sick as a group.

Research might also fail to confirm the intuition by seeking too precise a correspondence between specific sickness and psychological states. Some have even argued the case for behavioural phenotypes, suggesting thereby the closest correspondence between disease and behaviour (Udwin *et al.*, 1987; see Chapter 37). Should such close correspondence fail to be secured, then a general sense of weakening of the effects of chronic sickness on behaviour might be created.

Research approaches

The most numerous studies are those that have looked at the psychological and psychiatric aspects of specific disease groups, probably because clinical services tend to be organized around particular conditions (see Chapter 39). This research has, for the reasons outlined above, often failed to yield clear answers about the effect of the chronic sickness. More recently, a non-categorical approach to chronic sickness has been preferred (Jessop & Stein, 1988; Wallander *et al.*, 1988), bearing in mind that, although there are differences in the biomedical aspects, the broader issues of being sick are held in common across many disease categories and that most of the associations between chronic sickness and psychological distress are taken up by quite general associations about being ill. The non-categorical approach encourages consideration of those aspects of children's and families' emotional, social and cognitive development where *any* chronic illness might have an impact. This view underlies the structure of this chapter, which explores the common effects of sickness by reference to various diseases and illnesses.

Extremes of the noncategorical view, however, lead to a perspective in which the role of disease is underregarded. Perrin and MacLean (1988), for example, favoured the view that there was nothing really different about children with chronic sickness and that they were best understood as normal children in an abnormal situation. Such views underestimate the variety of potentially discoverable interrelationships between brain and specific bodily diseases and do not stipulate the part played by different experiences of pain, limitation, self-perceived stigma, or malaise in the various disease processes. Cadman *et al.* (1987) and Breslau (1985) provide examples of research designs which do reveal those interactions.

Terminology

The language which is used to discuss these different components of sickness is potentially very confusing. It was clarified by Taylor (1979) and his definitions will be employed here. The word disease is reserved for the biomedical, structural aspect of sickness; that part which claims the special expertise of physicians. Illness relates more to the personal experience of being sick, both its inner experiential aspects and its description to others, including its role-play component. Predicament describes that special and particular place in psychosocial space which each individual uniquely occupies and which is susceptible of profound modification, among many other things, by being ill with a disease. The problem for psychological research is to capture the essence of what appears to be perceived intuitively by ordinary people, by affected families, by health practitioners, and by specialists working with people with chronic sickness. The problem for practitioners is to have a framework for understanding the basis on which a wide variety of associations between physical sickness and psychological disorder present clinically.

MODES OF PRESENTATION OF CHRONICALLY SICK CHILDREN TO PSYCHIATRISTS AND PSYCHOLOGISTS

The presentation of a child with chronic sickness or a family with a sick member to a mental health professional is almost invariably at the request of a member of the team treating the child's medical disorder. In a well-provided liaison practice, the psychologist or psychiatrist may have the luxury of meeting most of the patients and making his or her own judgement about who best to help, but this is unusual.

Adherence to treatment

There is an implied contract between parents, patients and the medical team which involves the assumption that by attending at all, the family agrees to accept and comply with the interventions proposed. A breach of that contract at any point provokes anxiety. A common reason for presentation to psychiatrists and psychologists is having failed to comply, in various of the possible ways, with the wishes of the medical team treating the physical illness. This may include screaming, struggling, panicking, and vomiting — behaviours not ordinarily thought of in studies of compliance. Compliance with any treatment regime is a constraint upon autonomy. The most casual personal acquaintance with trying to complete a course of antibiotics reveals this. The constraints created by compliance with a scheme of treatment of chronic sickness can be prodigious in scale and lifelong in duration; consider diabetes, renal disease, leukaemia. In the treatment of children the constraints tax not only the child but its entire family (Blum, 1984). Compliance by parents relates to their understanding of the seriousness of the disease in their child, the complexity of the regimen, the convenience of therapy, their attitude to the physician and the conventions of their culture. Health-beliefs play a significant part: for example, parents whose children actually have a particular disease tend to rate that disease as less serious than other parents do (Marteau & Johnston, 1986).

The advent of powerfully intrusive, expensive treatments requiring precise treatment adherence and some risk (for example, renal and heart transplants, limb lengthening) has stimulated requests from some medical teams for assessment of *future* adherence. Such invitations are probably best used as opportunities for information-sharing with all parties, ensuring that everyone concerned is made precisely aware of the future progress of the disease without proper treatment and the limits that must be set on further interventions unless adherence is secured. In the process, opportunities will arise for a good deal of psychological work to be done.

As the word compliance of itself suggests a coercive constraint, whereas adherence retains an element, at least, of autonomy and since the locus of control is best vested in the patient (Shagena *et al.*, 1988), perhaps that attitude to treatment by professionals symbolized in the concept of adherence deserves to triumph (Blackwell, 1976). It suggests a more mutual approach by patient and physician towards treating the sickness.

Psychological mechanisms underlying nonadherence

Denial as a defence is commonly enacted through treatment nonadherence but at times the negative feelings of parents may be expressed through over-rigorous attention to the fine detail of the treatment schedule; this is to the eventual disadvantage of the child who finally reacts negatively towards it. Rejection of treatments that are painful, nauseating, stigmatizing or physically constraining provides a self-apparent explanation for the more outspoken nonadherent responses. Drugs that obviously alter the mental state of children, for example anticonvulsants, are often unilaterally rejected by parents. More problematic are adherence failures in less obviously undesirable treatments. In these situations the treatment lapses are more readily understood as an aspect of acting out through manipulation of the sickness. This is a powerful option for certain sick children. However unlooked for, the sickness becomes a potentially lethal weapon in the child's hands, especially when the consequences are predictable and follow swiftly upon a lapse in treatment. In such circumstances, for example in diabetes, haemophilia or asthma, children can become inappropriately powerful; Nocon (1991) speaks of 'tyranny' by the asthmatic child. On occasion, the most successful treatment adherence may be shown to be associated with a poorer psychological outcome (Close *et al.*, 1986). The mechanism merits elucidation but it may be another cost of being over-precise in treatment.

Rebelliousness under cover of the sick role is not confined to treatment nonadherence but can reflect the uncertainty that parents feel about the appropriateness of their ordinary discipline for their sick child, their apprehension of guilt and responsibility for the sickness, and their fear that their reactions might precipitate a relapse of sickness. These issues are likely to be particularly potent in adolescence. Parental guilt may be reality-based where the sickness is the result of deliberate abuse, or a prior want of care such as failure to immunize. It may be experienced as more or less real, for example genetic guilt, or less specifically as somehow having been a poor provider *in utero*.

Problems arising at school: absenteeism, disciplinary issues and performance

Problems arising at school are another source of referrals. Drotar *et al.* (1981) and others (Bywater, 1981), who have not found chronically sick children to suffer increased risk of psychological disorder through parental enquiries, have not found problems in school either. Some suggest (Perrin & MacLean, 1988) that school absenteeism is a suitable measurement of adjustment but in an interesting study of a wide variety of chronic diseases, Fowler *et al.* (1985) were able to distinguish absenteeism from relative school failure. In that study of 270 participating families, school achievement was poorest for epilepsy, sickle cell disease and spina bifida, whereas absenteeism was highest for the cystic fibrosis group. The causes of absenteeism are diverse but mainly mediated by nonmedical issues (Klerman, 1988). In the Ontario Child Health Study (Cadman *et al.*, 1987) the odds ratio for 'not doing well at school' was 4.7 for the chronic illness group with disability but not significantly increased for chronic illness alone. These findings do not entirely support the non-categorical case and suggest that there are effects which are severity-related or are brain-related effects of illness or treatment.

Disciplinary issues in school are partly a feature of the reduction in expectation. This can disadvantage the chronic sick (Hartlage & Green, 1972). School problems also arise from disorders or treatments which affect cerebral functioning. The loss of routine, stability and predictability of school attendance lead to educational disadvantage, lowered academic expectations and further behavioural and attendance problems (Richards, 1986).

Psychiatric disorders

Children presenting with frank, major psychiatric disorder directly attributable to the physical sickness or its treatment are rare but the most deserving of the medical aspect of the psychiatrist's skills. Specific psychoses, both schizophrenic (Taylor, 1975) and manic (Taylor, 1989a), have been reported in children with cerebral lesions. Organic psychoses with features of confusion and disorientation occur in non-convulsive status epilepticus (Stores, 1986), in cerebral infection and acute trauma. Organically based deterioration of cerebral functioning is a feature of drug intoxication, especially with anticonvulsants, but is also a feature of encephalitic and postencephalitic states. Confusional psychoses can be seen following renal transplantation. The behavioural features of infantile autism are an aspect of cerebral dysfunction in reaction to certain cerebral diseases, such as tuberous sclerosis (Hunt & Dennis, 1987), and in reaction to those encephalopathies of unknown origin associated with infantile spasms (Kolvin *et al.*, 1971).

Depressive illness is among the most frequent associations with chronic illness and can be severe enough to include suicidal ideation. Our impression is that depressive ideation is normally noticed in research studies rather more often than in referral practice in busy paediatric hospitals. Phobias, anxiety and acting out in various distressing ways have a more immediate impact upon paediatricians. Sorrow and sadness they perhaps regard as self-evident consequences of being so sick. Impulsiveness and hyperactivity, with their behavioural consequences, may be the cause of referral in children whose disease and its treatment are affecting cerebral functioning (Williams *et al.*, 1989).

DEVELOPMENTAL CONSIDERATIONS

One major problem in understanding the psychological effects of chronic sickness in children is that the impact is clearly influenced by the degree of developmental maturation which has been achieved by the age of onset of the disease. In addition, available developmental schedules are imprecise, so the correlation between the stage of development and any psychological effect is uncertain (Eiser, 1991). The stage of development not only affects the way (and the degree) in which the disease has its impact on the individual and his or her understanding of it, but also influences the way in which a family perceives its impact, the extent to which siblings will be affected and the degree to which the child will be able even to approach the challenges of later periods of development.

The child's own understanding of sickness was previously thought to be limited largely by cognitive developmental considerations. Recently other explanations have been advanced (Eiser, 1991). It is evident that young children may have considerably greater knowledge than previously thought (Kendrick *et al.*, 1986), whereas hospitalization may also bring about deviation in emotional development (Harris, 1989).

The point in the developmental schedule where a family learns of a chronic sickness is not necessarily the same as the time the disease occurred, but provides the opportunity for a variety of explanations and responses. For example, an infantile hemiplegia identified at birth can be blamed on events in pregnancy, or on the obstetrician, or on either parent as an inherited 'fault'. If recognized later, the responsibility may be attributed not only to these, but also to neonatal paediatricians, immunization, or even to a conspiracy of silence among professionals. The period before the recognition of the sickness may acquire, in retrospect, a special 'pre-lapsarian' quality. Clinically these issues are important in each family's adjustment, as is the extent to which the couple have successfully reared other children and demonstrated themselves as adequate parents. The interaction of disease, family predicament and developmental stage makes for considerable diversity (Shapiro, 1983; Reiss *et al.*, 1986).

Acquiring or recognizing a chronic illness at later stages of a child's development exposes both child and family to much wider public and peer evaluation, as expectations increase outside a strictly private family arena. A chronically sick child may previously have been only dimly aware of its deviation and now has deficiencies and stigmata exposed and brought into consciousness. Whilst expectations of physical and academic achievements increase, peer group interactions become more crucial and have greater potential to cause distress. Conversely, contact with children with a similar sickness can prove more supportive at this stage.

Puberty arises from within, having profound biological effects upon physical systems previously stable, but it has intense significance as a social signal as well. Adolescents see before them issues of the management of their sexuality, the chances of their being married and having children, whether or not they will be able to enter the world of work. They may feel the proximity of death (Harper, 1983). These issues arise at the time when rates of neurosis, depression and suicide are also on the increase among other adolescents. The majority of adolescents who are suffering severe health conditions are substantially precluded from these crucial psychosocial achievements and they represent significant losses unless the adolescents themselves are equipped with adequate coping skills, or are sufficiently defended, or are individually unchallenged because they are developmentally not capable of experiencing the crisis.

PHYSICAL EFFECTS ON THE CHILD

Complete separation of the physical from the psychological effects of chronic illness is impossible but enumeration of the variety of ways in which function is altered may assist our understanding. Results of some of the studies of specific conditions are considered here, with their effects on psychological functioning.

Increased mortality

Reliable and important cohort studies reveal increased mortality among the chronically sick. The study by Pless *et al.* (1989) was based upon a definition that led to 106 per 1000 of a whole population sample followed to the age of 15 being regarded as chronically sick. By the age of 34 years 10 months, over 95% of males and females from nonmanual-class homes who had not been chronically sick were alive, as were over 92% of those from manual-class homes. The highest death rate was among females with chronic sickness from manual-class-homes, of whom only 85% survived. In all the remaining categories about 10−11% had died. The impact of child mortality figures generally as evidence of the peril of disease is reduced by the fact that about 40% of child mortality derives from accidents. Nevertheless these figures summarize the reality of the peril and are the sources of sorrow at loss in the chronic sick.

Some diseases reduce life expectancy through gradual deterioration, whereas others increase the risk of sudden death. Duchenne muscular dystrophy, among other such disorders, is associated with gradual and inexorable deterioration of function, though this may soon change because of new treatments. Studies reveal that there is an increase in depression among these youths (Leibowitz & Dubowitz, 1981). Children with renal failure and their families (Garralda *et al.*, 1988; Reynolds *et al.*, 1988; Soskolne & Kaplan De-Nour, 1989) reveal extensive but varied and complex effects on psychological and social functioning. Under the stress, especially of in-hospital renal dialysis, family life is disrupted and parents report increased rates of mental health problems. The children show increased rates of psychiatric disorder, tending to increase with the severity of their renal disease. In a study of a very severe congenital heart disease (transposition of the great vessels), O'Dougherty *et al.* (1983) showed that both biological and psychosocial factors contributed to the quality of later competence after surgery. Children of over-stressed parents who were socioeconomically less well-placed did less well than others.

Some 1400 new diagnoses of cancer per year are made in the UK (Van Dongen-Melman & Sanders-Woudstra, 1986; Morris-Jones, 1987; Lansdown & Goldman, 1988) and, as prognosis improves, the prevalence of children with cancer, or who have formerly suffered from cancer, increases. Should there be sequelae of successful treatment, they will become more evident as children and adolescents with psychological disturbance.

The threat of sudden death

Taylor (1969) described the epileptic seizure as 'a brief excursion through madness into death'. The core of the negative stereotype of epilepsy is dyscontrol and death. Fifty per cent of mothers who watched their child have a febrile convulsion (among the most benign of all seizure manifestations) feared that the child was dying (Baumer *et al.*, 1981). The reality of death was revealed in the cohort study by Britten *et al.* (1986) from the study by Pless *et al.* (1986). A total of 467 children were identified as suffering a chronic illness, of whom 55 suffered epilepsy. Britten *et al.* showed that 37 of these were uncomplicated and 18 cases were complicated, i.e. they apparently manifested other obvious signs of cerebral disease. One-third of the complicated group (6 of 18) had died and 6 of the 37 so-called uncomplicated group had also died by the 36-year follow-up. The death rate in both groups was therefore very substantially increased. All the deaths were among children whose epilepsy had started before they were 15 years of age. Similarly, 10% of the children with epilepsy had died by the time of the 25-year follow-up by Harrison and Taylor (1976) of Ounsted's population study of epilepsy in Oxfordshire. The lesser mortality reflected the fact that febrile convulsions were included in Ounsted's definition of epilepsy. Rapid or sudden deaths 'out of the blue' occur frequently in populations of people with epilepsy. Deaths also occur by accident, in baths or fires in particular. Deaths also occur in sleep, probably because abnormal electrocerebral activity interferes with the vital centres. Status epilepticus accounts for only about 25% of the deaths.

Diabetes, asthma and haemophilia are disorders in which quite rapid deaths can occur — diabetics in hypoglycaemic or hyperglycaemic coma, asthmatics in respiratory or cardiac failure, haemophiliacs by dramatic exsanguination. A recent small-scale study assessed a group of 43 children with clotting disorders, 46 diabetic children, and 42 normal controls. Diabetic children who were aged 3–5 revealed an increased rate of behavioural difficulties. Rates of psychological disorder among older children with either diabetes or haemophilia were not different from controls (Logan *et al.*, 1990). There is little recent research and there is a conflict of views among older studies so that it is not easy to understand these counter-intuitive results. Perhaps the stress is not directly upon the lives of these relatively young persons but comes, when it comes, by reflection from their families. Those who are unsupported and have relatively poor medical help or who are treated in a manner in which their psychological needs are unmet, as might well have been the case 20 years ago, may reflect back their distress through their children. More recently, better psychological support to carers may have been reflected in reduced rates. It is worth remembering that there are a few, late, unexpected deaths (Molander, 1982) from a variety of causes. These sudden unexpected deaths of young people can lead to considerable distress in families.

The threat of recurrence

Especially in the management of childhood cancers and leukaemias but also in epilepsy there is a peculiar tension about episodes of freedom from illness. The disease appears to have retreated. But it leaves the intensely painful predicament of being well but under threat. Is this renewal of health a recovery or just an interval? The question heightens the sense of future doom should recurrence arise. In the heterogeneous group of children who received bone marrow transplantation studied by Pot-Mees (1989), the transition from having been sick to becoming normal was a further crisis event leading to behavioural deviation. Fear of recurrence was a common stressor.

Impairment of brain function

There is now almost universal agreement across all research that it is those disorders that affect cerebral functioning directly that impose the greatest risk of behavioural disorders. Epilepsy appears to heighten the chances even further (Rutter *et al.*, 1970; Hoare, 1984; Hoare & Kerley, 1991). Organic cerebral dysfunction also occurs in cancer and its treatment, giving rise to rates of organic mental disorder of 14% in one study (Rait *et al.*, 1988). Severe learning difficulties, cerebral palsy and hydrocephalus are all associated with high rates of both epilepsy and behavioural problems. A few studies conclude otherwise (Wallander & Hubert, 1987).

Deterioration of function

There are disorders, examples of which can be given for most of the body systems, in which deterioration of function is progressive and relentless. Affected individuals are both living with their disease and dying of it. While many of these conditions are inborn, they, and other conditions, will exert their impact at various times in early childhood and hence allow more or less of the developmental schedule to have been unfolded normally. Congenital metabolic disorders such as the mucopolysaccharidoses come to attention with failing performance or dementia. The metabolic diseases are not all treatable and lead to gradual self-intoxication, deterioration and death. Certain epilepsies are associated with specific (for example, Batten's disease, subacute sclerosing panencephalitis) or nonspecific, relentless deterioration. All these syndromes are associated with cerebral dysfunction and in their various phases can produce any of the whole range of psychiatric disorders as a result of the increased distortion of normal development and progressive deterioration. The rate of progress of the disease and the particular predicament of the child provide further variety in outcomes.

Living and dying with muscular dystrophy would seem to be a very different experience from living and dying with cystic fibrosis. Yet research suggests no specific behavioural portrait for either condition but merely some increase, mainly of depression (Leibowitz & Dubowitz, 1981; Steinhausen *et al.*, 1983) and, more rarely, dementia in muscle disease (Gordon, 1988). Indeed, clinical experience and the paucity of psychological research in these fields lead to the suggestion that, in the absence of brain dysfunction or acting out, the psychological impact of these disorders is less evident to clinicians than intuition would suggest. Specific chronic diseases are rarely powerful enough, in effect, to place their individual stamp on biography and behaviour, though they might stamp it firmly on morphology. Relatively little referral to psychiatrists is made of more severe and progressive heart disease, although the outcome of surgical intervention of otherwise fatal cardiac disorders is modified by neurological and psychosocial variables (O'Dougherty *et al.*, 1983). Certain highly influential papers (Drotar *et al.*, 1981, for example) drew attention to the finding that psychological disorder was not *necessarily* related to experiencing chronic physical sickness — in that particular case, cystic fibrosis. These authors are often quoted subsequently as supporting that counterintuitive case, rather than supporting the case that such behavioural abnormalities that arise in children always arise within the wider context of family life and that there is simply no *necessary* connection between the disease and psychological disorder.

Limitation of sensory inputs

Sensory inputs are limited by deficits in the special senses, most obviously by blindness and deafness (see Chapter 41). Consideration should also be given to those features of chronic sickness that limit exploration. These pervasively reduce the facility with which the chronic sick can explore and control their environment. The import of these limitations is acknowledged through the provision of special equipment, mobility allowances and legislation to enable access to public places by people with mobility problems. Legislation to enable more chronically sick children to participate in ordinary schools and nurseries and for them to live in the community has, as basic premises, not only a humanitarian view but also a belief that by promoting a rich variety of experiences through ordinary exploration the handicaps of the chronically sick will be minimized.

Personality alteration

The question of personality alteration as an effect of the constraints on cerebral functioning determined by certain genetic disorders is intriguing to psychiatrists. The paradigm would be the supposed similarity of disposition of Down's syndrome children (see Chapter 37). These genetic constraints could be pervasive through the organism and across ontogeny but they might be the outcome of a once-for-all effect exerted *in utero*. The personality of people with epilepsy was also, it was argued, so constrained as a consequence of suffering that illness. Tizard (1962) disposed of such arguments. They reemerged in other disguises (Bear & Fedio, 1977). Taylor (1971, 1989b) attempted to interweave the developmental schedule with the various forms of infantile epilepsy which were age-dependent to explicate the different psychological outcomes, but the endeavour requires much more research. The very size of the vocabulary of epithets required to describe the personality of epileptics bears witness to the extent to which, even when constrained by severe and brain-related

sickness, human personality struggles towards variety. Cerreto and Travis (1984) attempting a similar task in diabetes also concluded that more investigations with more consistent groups of children of similar developmental age and socio-economic background were needed. The variety of outcomes should not be surprising, given the genetic uniqueness of people and huge predicamentary differences which they experience.

Unwanted medical and surgical treatment effects

All treatment is a balance of advantage over disadvantage. The greater the peril, the more noxious the disease, the more its morbidity, the greater the relative harm that can be borne in its treatment. In extreme circumstances the danger of treatments becoming grotesque is ever present (Taylor, 1990). Some sorts of harm are self-evident in the treatment schedule, for example amputation treatments or callosal section, whilst medications carry unwanted effects: cyclophosphamide, phenytoin, steroids. Other harm is a severe risk, at what all parties to the treatment regard as acceptable odds, for catastrophes such as the death of a transplant donor, or later malignancy as a result of previous treatment by irradiation. Limb-lengthening may involve months of distant hospitalization and being wheelchair-bound in adolescence; the result can be a young adult who is still short-statured and whose body proportions may remain abnormal. The harm is clear but may need to be denied by those involved in meeting their various needs.

But the passage of acquired immunodeficiency syndrome (AIDS) through blood products, or Creutzfeldt—Jacob disease through implants, or the loss of IQ in the treatment of leukaemia by cranial irradiation were unsuspected sources of harm, as was the blindness caused by high levels of oxygen given to newborns, the precipitation of diabetes in renal transplant patients, and other medical disasters of that kind. The existence of such risks constitutes part of the peril of sickness. Being sick exposes children to additional risks. If the effects are nonspecific, as they so often prove to be in research studies, we can conclude that being severely imperilled is a noxious event in itself. Work on posttraumatic stress syndromes and life events research may contribute to our understanding of the mechanisms involved.

PSYCHOLOGICAL EFFECTS ON THE CHILD

The social construction of sickness

The sick are a minority group negatively valued within society. Brief occupation of the category 'sick' is sanctioned but 'get well soon' cards are an admonition as well as a gesture of sympathy. Chronic is a word which has a pejorative, prejudicial element within its meanings. Prejudice implies prejudgement made on the basis of inadequate evidence. It now includes ascribing to an individual attributes said to characterize the group to which they belong, which are of such overwhelming importance that they override that individual's own characteristics (Taylor, 1987). One problem of minority group membership is that prejudices accrue. These may be no more noxious than that certain assumptions are made about the limitations which the sick person might experience, but the consequence of these putative limitations would be loss of esteem and hence of self-esteem.

Even the special allowances that are made for the sick, such as special educational facilities, or increased financial provision, or a parking permit, can carry a negative connotation and unwontedly betray minority group membership. Of course these allowances also represent, in a positive manner, society's recognition of the burdens of the disabled. The extent of the allowances made to the chronic sick — financial, situational, occupational, educational — also represent society's control over its deviant members. The scale of available help relative to the gross national product represents the real level of concern within society.

Stigma

Minority group membership is declared by the exhibition of signs or symbols which Goffman (1963) called stigmata. Some of the stigmata of the group dying of cancer, for example, are cachexia, alopecia and weakness. Strenuous efforts are made to correct the obvious signs, to the extent that parents may have the facial appearance of their dysmorphic child made more 'normally' Caucasian. But stigmata can also be behavioural; tics, funny walks, inappropriate social signalling, physical limitations and metabolic signs, including odours, also constitute stigmata. Among the symbols that stand in for physical deficits are such paraphernalia as Zimmer frames, crutches, wheelchairs, eye patches, helmets, hearing aids, leg braces and modified clothing. Membership of sufferers' groups provides an antidote to the prejudice created by stigma. Over-enthusiastic membership brings other potential threats, however; such group membership combines normalization with stigmatization. These elements are among those that make up the social construction of disability (Resnick, 1984).

Diseases also vary in the speed and manner which they betray their stigma; in epilepsy and diabetes the declaration may be sudden and cataclysmic; in muscle diseases their appearance may be both insidious and unrelenting.

The science called dysmorphology, which is dependent upon codifying children into groups by their striking and unusual facial and somatic characteristics, relies upon stigmata. The stigmata also provide material for negative peer evaluations. 'Mong' is currently popular, and not necessarily limited to those with Down's syndrome. Cerebral palsy and muscular dystrophy are among the so-called crippling diseases, the negative social image of which has allowed the word cripple to become a negative epithet. Dwarfism provides the over-riding characteristic for children with coeliac disease, pituitary insufficiency or achondroplasia. Cancers can lead directly or indirectly to disfigurement. To be stereotyped by one's physical characteristics, especially by negative characteristics, is to lose autonomy, esteem, and self-identity (for example, the 'Elephant Man').

Effect on body image

The most poignant evocation of distress to the body image in sick children is probably that of Stevie Smith in her lines beginning, 'I am not God's little lamb, I am God's sick Tiger...'. Many of the constraints of sickness lead towards dependence and the anger and resentment resulting from that. This is most evidently possible in the bedfast or the wheelchair-bound, or those confined within orthopaedic appliances such as the Milwaukee brace. But, together with limitations upon exploratory activity and a diminished world view, the sick child is more psychologically dependent both as a direct consequence of the sickness and also as a consequence of changes in the perspective adults have of such a child. For children with epilepsy, for example, the availability of rectally administered diazepam also allows the possibility of inappropriate intimate intrusion by anxious parents. The precariousness of diabetic children permits of a degree of invigilation of their habits and ingestions such that locus of control remains external to the growing child and self-esteem can suffer in consequence. This may be the mechanism which explains the excess of depression in those whose diabetes is well-controlled. Sitting down in a wheelchair symbolizes a sort of dependence which allows the sitter to be belittled and patronized. There are few data however. Offer *et al.* (1984), using the Offer Self Image Questionnaire, reported that children with asthma or cancer retained surprisingly normal self-image, though the body image of males with cancer was decreased. Males and females with cystic fibrosis, however, showed marked impairment of their body image.

Personal identity is a crucial, core concept in psychiatry. It is supposed as an ideal construct, an achievement which, though unique to each individual, comes within an implied norm (Charmaz, 1983). While it may not seem a very robust structure, it is actually better defined by the more evident deviations from it and failures to achieve it which are attributed to genetic factors or experiential factors, and chronic sickness may mediate its effects by either of these.

Effects of unusual facial appearance

Certain genetic disorders impose common facial characteristics and, presumably, other common constraints upon development. Concern about the constraint imposed in social interactions by certain facial stigmata is evidenced in the popular appeal of cosmetic plastic surgery (see Chapter 60). Defects which are medically inconsequential and socially trivial may be construed as alien to the personality within. More serious surgery, facial reconstruction, aims to obviate congenital stigmata with a view to normalizing the individual's potential. Such a view tends to be derived from perceived stigma based upon the prejudices of others. But the drive may come from the family's need to see in their child something more congruent with their hopes, or from the individual with ambitions to have a form more appropriate to his or her self-image. These considerations apply across the whole range of chronic sicknesses and concern the management of all stigmata.

Effects of size

Certain disorders are characterized by atypical stature for age. Increased growth for age is, psychologically, generally an advantage to boys but a disadvantage to girls (Jones, 1957; Mussen & Jones, 1957; Jones & Mussen, 1958; Brooks-Gunn et al., 1985). Small stature tends to imply delayed puberty and leads to being regarded by others as being younger than chronological age (Brooks-Gunn & Warren, 1985). Thus developmental age can be seen as a potential source of deviation and hence of handicap, in the World Health Organization sense of handicap as 'a disadvantage for a given individual, resulting from an impairment, that limits the fulfilment of a role that is normal for that individual depending on age, sex, and social, and cultural, factors' (World Health Organization, 1980). In the growth clinics of children's hospitals there gather many parents concerned about the achievement of ideal stature because of the presumed disadvantages of more extreme physical size. Obesity is similarly regarded in contemporary society; what is currently a negative social stereotype is now sanctioned by medical research indicating increased health risks (Brownell & Stunkard, 1983).

Genitalia

Ambiguity of sex role is sometimes associated with ambiguous genitalia. Ambiguous genitalia increase the confusion of parents too and so sex reallocations or sex-confirming allocations towards the genitalia of one or other sex are regarded as appropriate. These early surgical interventions and subsequent hormonal manipulations are usually successful. Psychiatrists become involved with the failures and the failure, though it may seem to come from across the range of potential physiological sources of error, is commonly located in attitudinal and behavioural components of parenting. There remains much to be learned about the hormonal mechanisms underlying sexual identity.

Effects of psyche on soma

Finally, one potential effect of chronic illness upon psychological functioning could be expressed through the illness itself. It is known that the psychological set in which cancer treatment is received by adults is one of the determining factors in outcome. There is no reason to suppose it is different for children. Psychological mechanisms have been imputed as a basis for some organ transplant failures (Levy, 1986). Evidence about personality disposing towards certain illness in childhood is generally lacking.

IMPACT ON PARENTS AND FAMILIES: BURDENS OF CARE

Psychological burdens

When children are diagnosed as having a sickness that will be severe and chronic, much of the emotional trauma and turmoil of the parents are taken as self-evident, necessary consequences of the perceived threat implied in the diagnosis. The threat is not only to the child — indeed the child may experience no evident threat. The threat to parents is the threat of loss and the threat of the burden of care. These feelings are compounded with guilt. Threat of loss allows rather better adjustment to eventual loss but also extends the period of grief premonitory to the loss. The chronic threat was called the Damocles syndrome (Koocher & O'Malley, 1981). Loss includes loss of perfection, loss of potential, loss of opportunity (Taylor, 1992). Sorrow is perhaps the most appropriate expression for these well-founded, coherent, negative affects.

The threat of loss promotes defences in parents so that psychiatrists and others are at times referred patients because of the disturbing nature of the defences in parents (Taylor, 1992). Denial is common but particularly tempting in conditions such as mental handicap (severe learning difficulty) that demand no special treatment. Anger is liable to be projected on to physicians. Some referrals can be seen as a mechanism to deflect this anger from the team treating the physical illness.

The effects upon the partnership of parents may also be profound, although simple patterns are not discernible (Sabbeth & Leventhal, 1984). Planning for future pregnancies becomes burdened by fear of genetic effects and concern about available energy and time. There are broad differences of view about the effects of chronic illness in a child upon its siblings (Lobato et al., 1988). Clearly family structures vary widely in age and sex composition, in intimacy, in the amount of accommodation available, and in well-being before the impact of the illness. Precise effects are therefore unlikely to be widely generalizable. In any given family, the repercussions upon siblings and upon family life deserve close enquiry (Sargent, 1983). There are likely to be differences of view about the problems of siblings, depending upon who it is in the family that is asked to express a view, and the stage reached in each family's life cycle.

Practical burdens

Labour

The experience of chronic sickness as a burden is common across most diseases. The burden is in part created by the extra labour involved in the process of living. Respiratory or muscular or cardiac disadvantage increases the work cost of activities. Working under the disadvantage of sedative drugs, in unwished for locations, in unwanted occupations, decreases the reward of engagement in life. While young children may appear to cope, it is often because the burden of care is carried by their parents. The actual increase of physical labour of parents was well-identified, for example by Edebol-Tysk (1989) in her series of studies of very heavily handicapped tetraplegic young people in Sweden. Feeding, lifting, turning, attending to toileting were immensely consuming of time, occupying nearly 25 hours per week. Even so, one-third of the group lived at home.

Cost

The burden of care has been estimated in financial terms too (Jacobs & McDermott, 1989) as being one way of measuring its total impact. There is a loss of earning by the patient but also by the carers, increased costs of diets and special foods, hospital outpatient visits and inpatient visiting and the increased burden on certain clothing. Accommodation may need to be restructured or changed; special forms of transport may be needed. Special equipment and drugs also add to expense and the burden of care.

Access

Even given proper transport, access to buildings and recreational activities can still be difficult.

IMPLICATIONS FOR TREATMENT BY CLINICIANS

An appreciation by the psychiatrist of the significant physical effects of the disease and its treatment on the patient is crucial. In addition, an appraisal of the child and family's predicament must be undertaken by setting the present sickness into the context of the development of the family and of the particular child. Lask (1988) provided a useful model of interaction of social and environmental factors with the stability, adaptability, understanding, and the coping skills in the child and family.

Another device for coping in most chronic sickness is to enable the carers by providing them with knowledge and resource to assist with their coping. These trends may be reducing the frequency of associated psychiatric disorder. Psychiatrists have the necessary skills in their ordinary armamentarium. Given that they can sustain a credible knowledge of the disease under treatment, many of those skills can help:

1 A variety of techniques is now available for dealing with short-term, acute distresses: relaxation and hypnosis are amongst them.

2 Any of the therapeutic techniques in the psychiatrist's armamentarium may be useful for psychiatric and psychological disturbance. Each psychiatrist will naturally incline to use his or her best skills in this endeavour.

3 Discussions with parents and whole families may help to ease discomforts and remedy unhelpful reactions.

4 Support to the team treating the physical illness may be a potent way of ensuring that psychological issues are considered.

FURTHER RESEARCH

The issues facing the chronic sick are more than those constituted in managing the disease itself, or its treatments, or its varying physical ramifications. Being sick is a social and psychological construct in itself, to be understood both from the perspective of the sufferer and from the perspective of those who care about that person, as well as by everyone who has concerns about the sick in society. Currently, AIDS looms to confront every imaginable aspect of the association of chronic sickness and psychological reaction, threatening children and adolescents in ways more serious and more frequent than ever syphilis did. Ibsen, himself a physician, foresaw that predicament in *Ghosts*. 'The disease I have as my birthright [he points to his forehead and adds very softly] is seated here . . . it's seated here waiting. And it may break out at any day — at any moment.' The predicament of the AIDS children and adolescents will be even more painful by being even more acute (see Chapter 40).

There are now some sound major studies of epidemiology of chronic sickness producing a basis for understanding the problems of the chronically sick (Gortmaker & Sappenfield, 1984; Cadman *et al.*, 1987; Kohler & Jakobsson, 1987; Pless *et al.*, 1989). The studies that derive from birthday cohorts provide unequivocal evidence of the peril to life implicit in the term chronic sick. The reduction of mortality and the elimination of certain diseases are in the hands of the microbiologists. The reduction of morbidity, of the broader dimensions of sickness, will require better doctoring, through facilitation of coping by offering appropriate strategies to those people who are under perceivable threat (Eiser, 1990). The management of severe psychological distress requires a clinical approach which is sensitive to the recognition of distress as well as able to provide assistance with its treatment.

Much of the depressive illness in the community at large is a transient reaction to an episodic stress. What is the appropriate treatment for a depressive response to the imminence of inevitable death? To what extent and up to what time is it appropriate to intervene? What are the indices of having made the best of a chronically sick life, and what the index of having coped well with a death? Knowledge of these issues is necessary to our management in such cases.

Epidemiological work stands beside the cohort studies to amplify our grasp on the level of provision of services that might be needed. These require local replication. In particular, the painstaking work of Edebol-Tysk (1989) needs to be replicated among other disease groups, since there are likely to be considerable differences in effort cost in the management of different disease states. The managers of medicine now require more studies of the precise burden of financial costs and the labour costs of the burden of care. In the audit of intervention these indices could be crucial in showing the benefit, or the cost, of certain interventions. Is it worth preventing siblings becoming disturbed; or mother becoming depressed; or father taking to becoming chronically sick himself? These are measurable in financial as well as humanitarian terms. Negative prejudice accrues to certain diseases and adequate research is needed to keep cost–benefit in the minds of medicine's managers.

Distress of mind is the most difficult to study but perhaps techniques of relating experiences and of the personal consequences of having had chronically sick children can be subsumed into a scientifically valid research endeavour (Goldberg & Simmons, 1988). More of the sensitive child-oriented but essentially scientific work, such as that of Wilkinson (1988), could help us to depict realistically from the child's perspective what we feel empathically about the plight of the sick child.

CONCLUSIONS

Much of what health care workers experience from the distress of those who are chronically ill and of their friends and relatives comes empathically or can be foreseen intuitively. The distress has been memorably portrayed in painting, in poetry and in the novel. Yet it remains hard to portray meaningfully through the vehicle of acceptable scientific research. Our intuition about distress, for example, leads us to suppose that it would be universal across a group of parents, or a group of adolescents, who received notice of a poor-prognosis sickness. Yet it appears that the measures being used in research reveal only increased *rates* of disorder rather than generally elevated *levels* of distress and dysfunction. Further, the measures are the measure of the resultant of two effects, the crisis and the coping. It also seems to us that, when parents and teachers participate in research studies, there is a closing of ranks to avoid vilifying chronically sick children by portraying their behaviour negatively. Equally, sensible relatives may diminish their own suffering when considering it against what their loved one is losing. It is probably not the appropriate strategy for research to persist with trying to depict the occurrence of the various psychological illnesses of predetermined categorization and intended for more general purposes. Research had better adopt a more inquisitive position, to try to determine in what ways distress is experienced and what coping is successful. To help the chronically sick child we have first to achieve a meaningful account of what they suffer.

The current of opinion prefers to regard as important those components of sickness which are likely to be held in common between various sicknesses rather than depict the consequences of each disease. Medicine, however, is likely to retain its disease-related boundaries and to presume that the expertise of its treatment teams depends upon more specific skills and less on the appreciation of the general principles of the reactions of the chronic sick and their families. It could be mental health workers who therefore provide the basis of necessary expertise in coping with the more general psycho-

logical and social issues and meeting those needs in a variety of chronic illness clinics. The needs to be met, and our effectiveness in meeting them, deserve further research. The results could speak not only to further our knowledge of mental disorders but will deepen our knowledge of what constitutes good medicine.

REFERENCES

Baumer J.H., David T.J., Valentine S., Roberts J. & Hughes B. (1981) Many parents think their child is dying when having a first febrile convulsion. *Developmental Medicine and Child Neurology*, **23**, 462–464.

Bear D.M. & Fedio P. (1977) Quantitative analysis of interictal behaviour in temporal lobe epilepsy. *Archives of Neurology*, **34**, 454–467.

Blackwell B. (1976) Treatment adherence. *British Journal of Psychiatry*, **129**, 513–531.

Blum R.W. (1984) Compliance with therapeutic regimens among children and youths. In: Blum R.W. (ed) *Chronic Illness and Disabilities in Childhood and Adolescence*, pp. 143–158. Grune & Stratton, Orlando, FL.

Breslau N. (1985) Psychiatric disorder in children with physical disabilities. *Journal of the American Academy of Child Psychiatry*, **24**(1), 87–94.

Britten N., Morgan K., Fenwick P.B.C. & Britten H. (1986) Epilepsy and handicap from birth to age 36. *Developmental Medicine and Child Neurology*, **28**, 719–728.

Brooks-Gunn J. & Warren M.P. (1985) The effects of delayed menarche in different contexts: dance and non-dance students. *Journal of Youth and Adolescence*, **14**, 285–299.

Brooks-Gunn J., Petersen A.C. & Leichorn D. (1985) The study of maturational timing effects in adolescence. *Journal of Youth and Adolescence*, **14**, 149–161.

Brownell K. & Stunkard A. (1983) Behavioural treatment for obese children and adolescents. In: McGrath P. & Firestone P. (eds) *Pediatric And Adolescent Behavioural Medicine: Issues In Treatment*, pp. 277–283. Springer, New York.

Bywater E.M. (1981) Adolescents with cystic fibrosis: psychological adjustment. *Archives of Disease in Childhood*, **56**, 538–543.

Cadman D., Boyle M., Szatmari P. & Offord D.R. (1987) Chronic illness, disability, and mental and social well-being: findings of the Ontario Child Health Study. *Pediatrics*, **79**(5), 805–813.

Cerreto M.C. & Travis L.B. (1984) Implications of psychological and family factors in the treatment of diabetes. *Pediatric Clinics of North America*, **31**(3), 689–710.

Charmaz K. (1983) Loss of self: a fundamental form of suffering in the chronically ill. *Journal of the Sociology of Health and Illness*, **5**, 168–195.

Close H., Davies A.G., Price D.A. & Goodyer I. (1986) Emotional differences in diabetes mellitus. *Archives of Disease in Childhood*, **61**, 337–340.

Drotar D., Doershuk C.F., Stern R.C., Boat T.F., Boyer W. & Matthews L. (1981) Psychosocial functioning of children with cystic fibrosis. *Pediatrics*, **67**(3), 338–343.

Edebol-Tysk K. (1989) Spastic tetraplegic cerebral palsy epidemiology and care load. Thesis. University of Gothenburg, Sweden.

Eiser C. (1990) *Chronic Childhood Disease: An Introduction To Psychological Theory And Research*. Cambridge University Press, Cambridge.

Eiser C. (1991) Cognitive deficits in children treated for leukaemia. *Archives of Disease in Childhood*, **66**(1), 164–168.

Fowler M., Johnston M. & Atkinson S. (1985) School achievement and absence in children with chronic health conditions. *Journal of*

Pediatrics, **106**, 683−687.

Garralda M.E., Jameson R.A., Reynolds J.M. & Postlethwaite R.P. (1988) Psychiatric adjustment in children with chronic renal failure. *Journal of Child Psychology and Psychiatry*, **29**(1), 79−90.

Goffman E. (1963) *Stigma: Notes On The Management Of Spoiled Identity*. Prentice Hall, New York.

Goldberg S. & Simmons R.J. (1988) Chronic illness and early development. *Pediatrician*, **15**, 13−20.

Gordon N. (1988) Muscle and brain disease. *Developmental Medicine and Child Neurology*, **30**, 536−549.

Gortmaker S.L. & Sappenfield W. (1984) Chronic childhood disorders: prevalence and impact. *Pediatric Clinics of North America*, **31**, 3−18.

Harper D.C. (1983) Personality correlates and degree of impairment in male adolescents with progressive and nonprogressive physical disorders. *Journal of Clinical Psychology*, **39**(6), 859−867.

Harris P.L. (1989) The experience of emotion. In: Harris P.L. (ed) *Children and Emotion: The Development of Psychological Understanding*, pp. 173−192. Blackwell Scientific Publications, Oxford.

Harrison R.M. & Taylor D.C. (1976) Childhood seizures: a 25 year follow up. *Lancet*, **i**, 948−951.

Hartlage L.C. & Green J.B. (1972) The relation of parental attitudes to academic and social achievement in epileptic children, *Epilepsia*, **13**, 21−24.

Hoare P. (1984) The development of psychiatric disorder among school children with epilepsy. *Developmental Medicine and Child Neurology*, **26**, 3−13.

Hoare P. & Kerley S. (1991) Psychosocial adjustment of children with chronic epilepsy and their families. *Developmental Medicine and Child Neurology*, **33**, 201−215.

Hunt A. & Dennis J. (1987) Psychiatric disorder among children with tuberous sclerosis. *Developmental Medicine and Child Neurology*, **29**, 190−198.

Jacobs P. & McDermott S. (1989) Family caregiver costs of chronically ill and handicapped children: method and literature review. *Public Health Reports*, **104**(2), 158−163.

Jessop D.J. & Stein R.E.K. (1988) Essential concepts in the care of children with chronic illness. *Pediatrics*, **15**, 5−12.

Jones M.C. (1957) The later careers of boys who were early or late maturing. *Child Development*, **28**, 113−128.

Jones M.C. & Mussen P.H. (1958) Self conceptions, motivations and interpersonal attitudes of early- and late-maturing girls. *Child Development*, **29**, 491−501.

Kendrick C., Culling J., Oakhill T. & Mott M. (1986) Children's understanding of their illness and its treatment within a Paediatric Oncology Unit. *Newsletter of the Association of Child Psychology and Psychiatry*, **8**(2), 16−20.

Klerman L.V. (1988) School absence − a health perspective. *Pediatric Clinics of North America*, **35**(6), 1253−1269.

Kohler L. & Jakobsson G. (1987) *Children's Health And Well-Being In The Nordic Countries*. Clinics in Developmental Medicine no. 98. MacKeith Press, Oxford.

Kolvin I., Ounsted C. & Roth M. (1971) Studies in the childhood psychoses. V: Cerebral dysfunction and childhood psychoses. *British Journal of Psychiatry*, **118**, 407−414.

Koocher G.E. & O'Malley J.E. (1981) *The Damocles Syndrome: Psychosocial Consequences of Surviving Childhood Cancer*. McGraw-Hill, New York.

Lask B. (1988) Psychosocial factors in childhood diabetes and seizure disorders: the family approach. *Pediatrician*, **15**, 95−101.

Lansdown R. & Goldman A. (1988) Annotation: the psychological care of children with malignant disease. *Journal of Child Psychology and Psychiatry*, **29**(5), 555−567.

Leibowitz B. & Dubowitz V. (1981) Intellect and behaviour in Duchenne muscular dystrophy. *Developmental Medicine and Child Neurology*, **23**(5), 577−590.

Levy N.B. (1986) Renal transplantation and the new medical era. *Advances in Psychosomatic Medicine*, **15**, 167−179.

Lobato D., Faust D. & Spirito A. (1988) Examining the effects of chronic disease and disability on children's sibling relationships. *Journal of Pediatric Psychology*, **13**(3), 389−407.

Logan F.A., Maclean A., Howie C.A., Gibson B., Hann I.M. & Parry-Jones W.L. (1990) Psychological disturbance in children with haemophilia. *British Medical Journal*, **301**, 1253−1256.

Marteau T.M. & Johnston M. (1986) Determinants of beliefs about illness: a study of parents of children with diabetes, asthma, epilepsy and no chronic illness. *Journal of Psychosomatic Research*, **30**(6), 673−683.

Molander N. (1982) Sudden natural death in later childhood and adolescence. *Archives of Disease in Childhood*, **57**, 572−576.

Morris-Jones P.H. (1987) Advances in managing childhood cancer. *British Medical Journal*, **245**, 4−6.

Mussen P.H. & Jones M.C. (1957) Self-conception, motivations and interpersonal attitudes of late- and early maturing boys. *Child Development*, **20**, 243−256.

Nocon A. (1991) The social impact of childhood asthma. *Archives of Disease in Childhood*, **66**(4), 458−460.

O'Dougherty M., Wright F.S., Garmezy N., Loewenson R.B. & Torres F. (1983) Later competence and adaptation in infants who survive severe heart defects. *Child Development*, **54**, 1129−1142.

Offer D., Ostrove E. & Howard K. (1984) Body image, self perception and chronic illness in adolescence. In: Blum R.W. (ed) *Chronic Illness and Disabilities in Childhood and Adolescence*, pp. 59−74. Grune & Stratton, Orlando, FL.

Perrin J.M. & MacLean E.W. (1988) Children with chronic illness: the prevention of dysfunction. *Pediatric Clinics of North America*, **35**, 1325−1337.

Pless I.B. & Roghman J. (1971) Chronic illness and its consequences. *Journal of Pediatrics*, **79**, 351−359.

Pless I.B., Cripps H.A., Davies J.M.C. & Wadsworth M.E.J. (1989) Chronic physical illness in childhood: psychological and social effects in adolescence and adult life. *Developmental Medicine and Child Neurology*, **31**, 746−755.

Pot-Mees C. (1989) *The Psychosocial Effects of Bone Marrow Transplantation in Children*. Eburon, Holland.

Rait D.S., Jacobsen P.B., Lederberg M.S. & Holland J.C. (1988) Characteristics of psychiatric consultations in a pediatric cancer center. *American Journal of Psychiatry*, **145**(3), 363−364.

Reiss D., Gonzalez S. & Kramer N. (1986) Family process, chronic illness, and death. *Archives of General Psychiatry*, **43**, 795−804.

Resnick M. (1984) The social construction of disability and handicap in America. In: Blum R.W. (ed) *Chronic Illness and Disabilities in Childhood and Adolescence*, pp. 29−46. Grune & Stratton, Orlando, FL.

Reynolds J.M., Garralda M.E., Jameson R.A. & Postlethwaite R.J. (1988) How parents and families cope with chronic renal failure. *Archives of Disease in Childhood*, **63**, 821−826.

Richards W. (1986) Allergy, asthma, and school problems. *Journal of School Health*, **56**, 151−152.

Rutter M., Graham P. & Yule W. (1970) *A Neuropsychiatric Study in Childhood*. Clinics in Developmental Medicine no. 35/36. Lavenham Press/Spastics International Medical Publications, London.

Sabbeth B.F. & Leventhal J.M. (1984) Marital adjustment to chronic childhood illness: a critique of the literature. *Pediatrics*, **73**(6), 762−767.

Sargent A.J. (1983) The sick child and the family. *Journal of Pediatrics*, **102**(6), 982−987.

Shagena M.M., Sandler H.K. & Perrin E.C. (1988) Concepts of illness and perception of control in healthy children and in children with chronic illness. *Developmental Behavior and Pediatrics*, **9**(5), 252−256.

Shapiro J. (1983) Family reactions and coping strategies in response to the physically ill or handicapped child: a review. *Social Science and Medicine*, **17**(14), 913−931.

Soskolne V. & Kaplan De-Nour A. (1989) The psychosocial adjustment of patients and spouses to dialysis treatment. *Social Science and Medicine*, **29**(4), 497−502.

Steinhausen H.-C., Schindler H.-P. & Stephan P. (1983) Correlates of psychopathology in sick children: an empirical model. *Journal of the American Academy of Child Psychiatry*, **22**(6), 559−564.

Stores G. (1986) Non convulsive status epilepticus in children. In: Pedley T.A. & Meldrum B.S. (eds) *Recent Advances in Epilepsy (3)*, pp. 53−64. Churchill Livingstone, Edinburgh.

Taylor D.C. (1969) Some psychiatric aspects of epilepsy. In: Herrington R.N. (ed) *Current Problems in Neuropsychiatry*, pp. 106−69. Headley Brothers, Ashford.

Taylor D.C. (1971) Psychiatry and sociology in the understanding of epilepsy. In: Gelder M.G. & Mandlebrote B.M. (eds) *Psychiatric Aspects of Medical Practice*, pp. 161−187. Staples, London.

Taylor D.C. (1975) Factors influencing the occurrence of schizophrenia-like psychosis in patients with temporal lobe epilepsy. *Psychiatric Medicine*, **5**, 249.

Taylor D.C. (1979) The components of sickness: diseases, illnesses and predicaments. *Lancet*, **ii**, 1008−1010.

Taylor D.C. (1987) Epilepsy and prejudice. *Archives of Disease in Childhood*, **62**, 209−211.

Taylor D.C. (1989a) Affective disorder in epilepsies: a neuropsychiatric review. *Behavioral Neurology*, **2**, 49−68.

Taylor D.C. (1989b) Psychosocial components of childhood epilepsy. In: Hermann B. & Seidenberg M. (eds) *Childhood Epilepsies: Neuropsychological Psychosocial and Intervention Aspects*, pp. 119−142. John Wiley, Chichester.

Taylor D.C. (1990) Annotation: callosal section for epilepsy and the avoidance of doing everything possible. *Developmental Medicine and Child Neurology*, **32**(3), 267−270.

Taylor D.C. (1992) Mechanisms of coping with handicap. In: McCarthy G. (ed) *The Physically Handicapped Child*, 2nd edn. pp. 53−64. Churchill Livingstone, Edinburgh.

Tizard B. (1962) The personality of epileptics. *Psychological Bulletin*, **59**, 196−210.

Udwin O., Yule W. & Martin N. (1987) Cognitive abilities and behavioural characteristics of children with infantile idiopathic hypercalcaemia. *Journal of Child Psychology and Psychiatry*, **28**, 297−309.

Van Dongen-Melman J.E.W.M. & Sanders-Woudstra J.A.R. (1986) Psychosocial aspects of childhood cancer: a review of the literature. *Journal of Child Psychology and Psychiatry*, **27**(2), 145−180.

Wallander J.L. & Hubert N.C. (1987) Social dysfunction in children with developmental disabilities: empirical basis and a conceptual model. *Clinical Psychological Review*, **7**, 205−221.

Wallander J.L., Varni J.W., Babani L., Banis H.T. & Wilcox K.T. (1988) Children with chronic physical disorders: maternal reports of their psychological adjustment. *Journal of Pediatric Psychology*, **13**(2), 197−212.

Wilkinson S.R. (1988) *The Child's World of Illness: The Development of Health and Illness Behaviour*. Cambridge University Press, Cambridge.

Williams P., Stores G. & Styles E. (1989) A controlled study of the cognitive effects of carbamazepine and sodium valproate as single treatments in children with epilepsy. In: Manelis J., Bental E., Loeber J. & Dreifuss F. (eds) *Advances in Epileptology*, vol. 17, pp. 150−152. Raven Press, New York.

World Health Organization (1980) *International Classification of Impairments, Disabilities and Handicaps*. World Health Organization, Geneva.

Chapter 43
Atypical Psychosexual Development

Richard Green

TYPICAL PSYCHOSEXUAL DEVELOPMENT

Psychosexual development describes what has been termed sexual identity or gender identity development. It encompasses three components. The first is the earliest awareness by the child of belonging to one of two categories of human beings: like mummy or like daddy, like me or not like me, male or female. Determining the age at which this basic feature evolves is difficult, in part due to the limited capacity of very young children for verbal expression. By age 3 most children may be able to select a doll figure of the gender consistent with their own and by 4 they may be able to select correctly the sex-typed adult doll into which they expect to grow (Rabban, 1950). Four out of 5 2-year-olds correctly answered the question, 'Are you a boy or a girl?' and at 3, about 80% also correctly answered, 'Are you like this doll [a boy] or this doll [a girl]?' Also, at about 3, 80% correctly answered, 'Are you going to be a mummy or a daddy?' (Levin *et al.*, 1972). This first component of sexual or gender identity may be called core morphological identity, or anatomical identity (Green, 1987).

The second component may be called sex-typed behaviour, gender-role behaviour and, popularly, masculinity and femininity. It comprises activities that discriminate males and females at various ages in a given culture. With young children, it manifests itself primarily in toy and activity preferences. The age at which this component emerges is also imprecisely known. Sex differences in play styles have been documented late in the second year and more frequently at ages 3 and 4 years (Gessell, 1940; Rabban, 1950; Hartup & Zook, 1960). Research suggests, however, that even 1-year-old children show gender-typed toy preferences. One-year-old girls may prefer soft toys and dolls, whereas boys may prefer transportation toys (Fagot, 1974) and robots (Jacklin *et al.*, 1973). At 2–3 years, when observed in a free-play setting, boys are more aggressive towards peers (Pedersen & Bell, 1970) and show more rough-and-tumble play (Smith & Connolly, 1972). These observations have been confirmed in other cultures, including the Philippines, India, Okinawa, Mexico and Kenya (Whiting & Whiting, 1975).

The third component of sexual or gender identity, the direction of erotic and romantic interests, may be called sexual orientation. It is even more problematic with respect to age of onset. Whereas it typically manifests itself during early adolescence in erotic fantasies, some preadolescents report erotic interests and the research described below shows a high correlation between the first two components of sexual identity in young children and later sexual orientation. The latter observation suggests the presence of sexual orientation in a nascent form well before puberty.

THE STUDY OF PSYCHOSEXUAL DEVELOPMENT

Strategies utilized in studying psychosexual development include research with anatomically intersexed children, anatomically normal children, children with typical and atypical patterns of behaviour, and the retrospectively recalled childhoods of sexually atypical and typical adults.

Major advances in understanding psychosexual development derived from the study of anatomically intersexed children (Money *et al.*, 1957). With these pseudohermaphroditic infants inconsistencies existed between the several anatomical and physiological criteria of sex, including chromosomal sex, gonadal sex, hormonal sex, internal reproductive structures and external genital morphology. The most significant finding was that an additional variable, psychological sex, could be inconsistent with any or most of these body variables and would usually develop in concert with the sex to which the infant was assigned at birth. Thus sex-typed socialization experiences during the first years appeared to predominate over the anatomical or physiological criteria of sex. The time-frame during which the first component of sexual identity, the awareness of being male or female, evolved in the child was in the first 2–3 years. This basic identity element appeared to be irreversible after that period. Attempts to reassign intersexed children to their 'correct' sex (based on anatomical criteria) after more sophisticated medical diagnosis were unsuccessful after about age 2½ years.

Generalizing from findings with the anatomically intersexed to the anatomically normal child is debatable, however. Critics argue that, in consequence of their anatomically intersexed state, these children were exposed to intersex phenomena during prenatal development which rendered them more amenable to environmental influences on sexual identity (Diamond, 1965; Zuger, 1970). Supporting this argument are a few reports of persons considered to be either male or female at birth, and raised accordingly, but who harboured the idea that they belonged to the other sex, and with puberty developed cross-sex body changes (Baker & Stoller, 1968). Further, a report putting the earlier work to test has been the study of a pair of monozygotic male twins where one underwent traumatic amputation of his penis neonatally in a circumcision accident. Here was a male child whose prenatal contributions to maleness were not compromised by any intersex state and who could be compared with a genetically comparable sibling. The twin whose penis was amputated was reassigned as female within the time period posited by the hermaphrodite research to permit successful socialization as a female. Early reports suggested that the child's sexual identity had emerged as female and that the child was living as the relatively normal sister of the male twin (Money & Ehrhardt, 1972). However, a follow-up report during adolescence and a subsequent report in young adulthood indicated that identity as female has not been confirmed and that the person is currently living as a man (Diamond, 1982, 1991).

Other intersex states have also suggested the importance of the prenatal endocrine composition on later sexual identity, in particular the syndrome in which the enzyme, 5-alpha-reductase, is deficient (the enzyme that transforms testosterone to dihydrotestosterone). Persons with this inherited defect appear to be female at birth although their genitals are not entirely normal. Presumably in the earliest generations, however, they were considered to be normal girls and were socialized accordingly. With puberty, they virilize with considerable phallus growth and a male chest pattern and muscular development. Then, during a 2–4-year period, they evolve a male identity and an erotic orientation towards females. The endocrinological interpretation for this transition is that whereas dihydrotestosterone (absent) is required for prenatal genital differentiation, but not for pubertal genital differentiation, testosterone (present prenatally and postnatally) organized the fetal brain to mediate a later male sexual identity (Imperato-McGinley *et al.*, 1979). By contrast, the socialization argument sees the society in which these individuals live as being so harsh towards homosexuality that the easier social course for them is to live as heterosexual men after their body virilizes. Subsequent generations of these children are identified neonatally and are now known to be those who will undergo pubertal body masculinization. Consequently, understanding the relative contributions of endocrine and socialization influence is confounded.

HORMONAL INFLUENCES ON SEX DIFFERENCES AND BEHAVIOURS

The clearest data showing an association between prenatal sex steroid levels and postnatal sex-typed behaviours are in the syndrome of congenital virilizing adrenal hyperplasia (CAH), formerly called the adrenogenital syndrome. Here there is excessive androgen production by the adrenal gland, beginning prenatally. CAH girls in childhood, compared to their hormone-normal sisters, have been reported by parents

to be more likely to engage in rough-and-tumble play and sports, and less likely to engage in doll play and infant care (Ehrhardt & Baker, 1974). More recent research also documents, with direct observation, a male-type toy preference by girls with CAH (Berenbaum & Hines, 1992). These findings are in parallel to those with the nonhuman primate: pregnant rhesus monkeys, when injected with androgen, bear female offspring who also engage in behaviours that are considered male-like (Young *et al.*, 1964). As for later psychosexual development, women with CAH — even those treated shortly after birth with cortisol, which suppresses excessive adrenal androgen — show higher rates of bisexuality and homosexuality (Money *et al.*, 1984).

The finding of a relationship between prenatal diethylstilboestrol (DES) exposure in females and later sexual orientation is another source of interest regarding a prenatal chemical influence on psychosexual development. DES is a synthetic oestrogen formerly given to women who were habitual aborters. When females whose mothers received DES during pregnancy were compared with non-DES-exposed sisters and nonrelated controls, more DES women were homosexual or bisexual (Ehrhardt *et al.*, 1985).

Studies of males exposed to 'female' pregnancy-maintaining drugs *in utero*, however, have not yielded consistent findings for sex-typed behaviours. Our early study suggested that prepubertal males whose mothers received oestrogens during pregnancy were less aggressive and less athletic (Yalom *et al.*, 1973). In a subsequent study we looked at young adult males exposed prenatally to DES, or DES with progestational agents, or progestin alone. Men exposed to progesterone tended to recall boyhood behaviours that departed from the conventional male mode towards femininity, whereas the DES men tended to recall more conventionally masculine boyhoods. No examples of clinically significant cross-gender childhood behaviours, nor elevated rates of bisexual or homosexual behaviour were found (Kester *et al.*, 1980).

Prenatal sex hormone levels have implications for early socialization experiences and the influence of such experiences on psychosexual development. Of particular relevance is the suggested impact of hormones on rough-and-tumble and doll play. Boys and girls with substantially different levels of these behaviours, compared to their same-sex peers, will have a different socialization experience with other children and a different family experience with their mother and father. These disparate patterns may influence emerging sexual identity.

CROSS-CULTURAL ASPECTS

Cross-culturally, among typical boys and girls, common sex-typed behavioural characteristics are observed. Rough-and-tumble play is more commonly found among boys and doll play or interest in newborns among girls (Whiting & Whiting, 1975). But many societies have contained subgroups of young males and females with substantial cross-gender behaviour. These behaviours typically began during the earliest years and remained lifelong (Green, 1968). A noted example is the Berdache among the Native American Indians. Among the Mohave, boys who would become Shamans would 'pull back their penis between their legs and then display themselves to women, saying, "I too am a woman"'. These boys refused to play with boys' toys or dress in boys' attire. Similarly, there were girls who rejected dolls and girls' attire, and would refuse feminine chores (Devereux, 1937). What is lacking in these phenomenological accounts is their developmental aetiology.

MALE AND FEMALE CHILDHOOD CROSS-GENDER BEHAVIOUR

Retrospective reports by nearly all transsexuals of their childhood behaviours attest to the enduring significance of a cross-gender identity in both boys and girls. Recalled childhood behaviours by adult homosexuals also describe significantly higher rates of cross-gendered interests and activities during childhood (Saghir & Robins, 1973; Bell *et al.*, 1981; Grellert *et al.*, 1982; Harry, 1982). Gender nonconformity during childhood was the best predictor of later male or female homosexuality with several hundred nonpatient subjects (Bell *et al.*, 1981). Gender nonconformity meant that fewer homosexuals recalled enjoying gender-typical activities and more enjoyed atypical activities.

Cross-culturally, cross-sex behaviours during childhood have been linked with adult homosexuality. Male homosexuals are more likely than heterosexuals in Brazil, Guatemala, the Philippines and the US to recall doll-play, cross-dressing and the play and activities of girls (Whitam & Mathy, 1986). Conversely, female homosexuals in Brazil, Peru, the Philippines, and the US more often recall playing with boys' toys, less often with girls' toys, more often dressing up in mens' clothes, and more frequently being considered a tomboy (Whitman & Mathy, 1991b).

Beginning in the late 1960s, I began evaluating, in prospective research, boys whose behaviours were similar to the retrospectively recalled boyhoods of adult male transsexuals. As the study evolved, and others' research demonstrated substantial overlap in the recalled boyhood behaviours of homosexual and transsexual males, it became likely that what we were evaluating was a precursor of homosexuality (because of the much higher prevalence of homosexuality than transsexualism; Green, 1974).

Sixty-six families with boys whose behaviours, for the most part, would today be diagnosed as the gender identity disorder of childhood were studied. Fifty-six of the families were demographically matched with a family where the boys were unselected for sex-typed characteristics. Both groups were interviewed with a semistructured protocol that was audio-tape-recorded. Children were observed systematically and given psychological tests. Provisions were made for periodic follow-up.

At initial evaluation approximately four-fifths of the boys stated their preference for being girls. Nearly all were extensively involved in cross-dressing, with the dressing beginning by the sixth birthday. To the question, 'How often does your son cross-dress?' the mother's reply was, 'As often as you let him'. Playmate preference was for girls. When playing house or mother−father games, mother or another female was the usual role taken. When media characters were imitated, they were heroines. A favourite toy was Barbie or another female-type dress-up doll. Pictures drawn were typically of females. These boys had a marked aversion to rough-and-tumble play and sports.

Vignettes: onset of atypical behaviour

Mother A: It started out as he liked to play with high heels . . . He always wanted my high heels (at about 2, 2½).
Mother B: At 2 years . . . he liked to put things on his hair, towels, anything that looked like hair . . . As far as his feminine actions and everything, he has been like this since he was a very small child.

Doll play

Doctor: What are his favourite toys?
Father: Barbie . . . anything feminine. He's got two GI Joes, and he doesn't play with them.

Pictures drawn

Mother: [He draws] girls. Only girls. Practically refuses to draw pictures of boys . . .

Peer group teasing

Mother: I told him, 'Go out and play with the boys' . . . and when he tries . . . they tease him and make fun of him and they don't want to play with him.

Reason for wanting to be a girl

Boy (age 5): Because you dress up and make up, because you dress in girl's clothes which I like the best . . . I wish I was a girl.

The age at which psychosexually atypical children were evaluated affected the presenting picture. Younger children are more likely to express directly their wish to be the other sex. Older children have learned that it is not possible to change sex and/or that these statements meet with disapproval. Older children's desire to be the other sex may be inferred from their cross-gender activity preference, particularly roles taken in fantasy games.

The cross-gendered toy preferences of these children were documented in an experimental playroom. When given the opportunity to play with boy-type or girl-type toys, and observed via a one-way mirror, cross-gendered boys and age-matched girls made similar selections that differed from age-matched boys. Toys that best discriminated between the groups were a dress-up doll and a truck (Green *et al.*, 1972b).

Cross-gendered mannerisms were also documented. Cross-gendered boys, ages 4–10, and age-matched boys and girls were similarly attired so as to conceal gender, and video-taped walking, running, throwing a ball and narrating a story (picture only). Raters clearly distinguished the age-matched boys and girls, but were uncertain as to the gender of the atypical boys (Green *et al.*, 1983).

Girls whose behaviours were 'tomboyish' have also been studied in our research programme, although most would not be diagnosed with the gender identity disorder of childhood. In contrast to a demographically matched control group, they were more likely to engage in sports and rough-and-tumble play, have a male peer group, play less often with dolls, play more with trucks, and state their wish to grow up to be like their father rather than like their mother (Green *et al.*, 1982).

'Tomboys' do not experience stigma comparable to 'sissies'. None of the 'tomboys' in our study were seen by parents as rejected by peers (compared to 18% for 'sissies'), 44% were seen as good mixers (compared to 28%), and 32% were seen as leaders (compared to 15%; Green *et al.*, 1980).

More recently, I have also evaluated and treated girls with gender identity disorder.

Vignette

Mother C: She doesn't want to be a girl. When she was 2, she said, 'Go to the store and buy me a penis'. She thinks it fell off when she was inside me. When she was 4, she said, 'I am a boy'.

Because there is more latitude culturally in sex-typed behaviours by girls, identifying clinically significant behaviour is more difficult. However, there is a different quality to gender identity disorder girls and 'garden-variety tomboys'. Their insistence on wanting to be a boy and their adamant refusal to wear girl's clothes are qualitatively and quantitatively distinctive.

PSYCHOLOGICAL TESTING

Two tests, the It-Scale for Children, and the Draw-a-Person, were administered to the boys. The It-Scale presents the child with a card depicting a neuter stick-figure ('It'). 'It' then selects, from a series of cards, masculine or feminine toys, articles, activities and playmates (Brown, 1956). The Draw-a-Person test, as used in this research, required the child to draw a person, with no clue given as to whether a male or female should be drawn. On the It-Scale, the cross-gendered boys scored similarly to same-age girls but differently from same-age boys. On the Draw-a-Person test, cross-gendered boys were more likely to draw a female first, whereas the contrast boys were more likely to draw a male first (the typical response; Green *et al.*, 1972a). 'Tomboys' were more likely to draw a male first.

AETIOLOGY

The aetiology of atypical psychosexual development in children remains controversial. There is evidence supporting a variety of psychodynamic and social learning theories as well as growing evidence of a physiological or inherited contribution.

Much of the developmental psychology research on the acquisition of sex roles has been adapted to explaining atypical development. Thus, positive reinforcement of atypical sex-typed behaviours in children by significant adults is seen as contributing to a greater degree of expression of such behaviours. The role of the father has gained increasing currency in developmental literature from two research sources. One is the less conventionally masculine behaviours of boys from father-absent homes (Hetherington, 1966) and the other is the observation that fathers appear to be stricter enforcers, at least for boys, of conventional sex-typed behaviour (Biller, 1981). Less research has been done on the acquisition of atypical sex-typed behaviours by girls.

In our 15-year prospective study, a positive correlation was found between mothers' attitude towards cross-gender behaviour in the boys and the extent to which the sons displayed such behaviour. Thus, when mothers were neutral to supportive, at least initially, of a son's cross-gender behaviours, the boys had higher ratings of such behaviours at initial evaluation (Green, 1987). Similarly, the extent of the boys' cross-gender behaviour was positively related to whether the father had wanted a daughter during this pregnancy (Roberts *et al.*, 1987). However, the popular theory that parents, particularly a mother, may 'treat a son like a girl', or perhaps a father may 'treat a daughter like a son', was found in only a few families with gender-atypical children.

However, over-interpretation of parental positive reinforcement of cross-gender behaviour in clinical samples is possible due to insufficient research on families' responses to cross-gender behaviour in conventional children. In my experience, nearly 20% of families of boys with gender identity disorder had family album photographs of their young sons cross-dressed, indicating apparently positive attention. None of the families of any demographically matched gender-typical boys had such photographs. But, was this because cross-dressing never occurred, occurred too infrequently to be memorialized, or because the parents ignored or discouraged it? From non-clinical studies, a recent metaanalysis of parental gender socialization reported that 'encouragement of sex-typed activities and perceptions of sex-stereotyped characteristics is helpful'. It found mean effect scores of 0.34, 0.49 and 0.43 for mothers, fathers, and both parents combined (Lytton & Romney, 1991). Future studies of children with gender identity disorder need to assess not only reactions to cross-gender behaviour but to isogender behaviour. Discouragement of boyish behaviour may be at least as significant developmentally.

The father–son relationship in our research emerged as a prominent variable in association not only with initial cross-gender behaviours, but also with later sexual orientation.

Accounts given by both parents of the extent of father—son shared time in the boy's first 4 years revealed substantially less between fathers and cross-gendered sons compared to fathers in the contrast families. Additionally, within the cross-gendered boy families, when there were two male children, less father—son shared time was reported for the cross-gendered son. Finally, at follow-up, when sexual orientation of the sons was assessed as young men, higher rates of homosexual fantasy and behaviour were associated with less father—son shared time in those early years within the cross-gendered boy group (Green, 1987).

Psychodynamic approaches to atypical development look to the more specific role of the mother in the separation individuation phase of development for the male. Stoller's early work found excessive mother—son skin-to-skin contact during the boy's earliest years which inhibited the psychological separation of son from mother (Stoller, 1968). Other research found separation anxiety to be prominent (Coates & Person, 1985).

Physical attractiveness of the male child may also influence gender identity. Stoller reported that maternal descriptions of the appearance of precross-gender identified sons was remarkably feminine. 'We have noticed that they often have pretty faces, with fine hair, lovely complexions, lovely movements, and especially big, piercing, liquid eyes' (Stoller, 1975). Our more systematic research constructed interviews and a rating scale of parental responses to questions regarding the recalled appearance of the infant son's face. Two raters, blind to whether the tape-recorded interview responses emanated from a cross-gendered or contrast family, rated transcripts on a 6-point scale. Descriptions given by the parents of cross-gendered boys were rated as more beautiful and feminine (Green, 1987). Thus, Stoller's anecdotal observation was extended to a quasi-experimental design, but again with the possibility of distortions in parental recall and reporting. Recently, a more experimentally designed study has yielded consistent findings. Raters judged a facial and upper torso photograph taken at the time of the clinical evaluation of cross-gendered boys at about age 8 years and compared them with a matched clinical control group (Zucker *et al.*, 1993). Cross-gendered boys were rated as more attractive, beautiful, cute and pretty. Possibly the physically attractive feature of the child triggers response patterns in parents and others which is reinforcing of feminine behaviour.

Less research has been conducted on female children with atypical gender patterns. Extensive cross-sex identity in females was seen by Stoller (1975) as resulting in part from an extremely distant mother—daughter relationship and compensatory identification with the father. There might also be substantial reinforcement of 'tomboyish' behaviours by father. A female transsexual monozygotic co-twin of a feminine sister was reported by both twins to have been encouraged and expected to do household chores such as helping father roof the house or do concrete and stone work, whereas the feminine twin was given feminine jobs or excused from these chores. One twin received toys typically given to boys, the other a gift useful in quiet play. On their eighth or ninth birthday, one received a pet bird, the other a boy's bicycle (Green & Stoller, 1971).

CHILDREN OF THE SEXUALLY ATYPICAL

The direct influence of parental sexual identity on children's sexual identity is not obvious. What characterizes the parents of psychosexually atypical children is their typicality. It was the rare parent in my series of families with a gender identity disorder boy who was bisexual. None was transsexual or transvestite. Conversely, my studies of parents with atypical sexual identity found their children to be sexually typical.

I evaluated 16 children raised by 7 male-to-female and 9 female-to-male transsexuals. The children were 3—20 years old (mean 4.9) and lived in the atypical households for 1—16 years (mean 4.9). None of the older children was homosexual, bisexual, transsexual or transvestite. None of the younger children had a gender identity disorder (Green, 1978).

Our research with lesbian mothers and their children evaluated 56 children of 50 lesbian-identified women and 48 children of 40 demographically matched heterosexual women. The average age of the children was 8 and they had lived in the single-parent (mother) homes for an average of 4 years. No evidence of gender identity disorder was found in any of the children (Green *et al.*, 1986).

PHYSIOLOGICAL CONTRIBUTIONS

Posited physiological contributions to early sex-typed behaviours derive from research in genetics and with prenatal endocrine variations. Genetic implications for atypical psychosexual development derive indirectly from genetic studies of homosexual orientation. The extent to which cross-gender behaviour in childhood is the early manifestation of a later homosexual orientation, deriving from a common physiological basis, suggests a genetic aetiology of atypical early behaviours. The classic Kallman (1952) study of (presumably) male monozygotic twins found 100% concordance for homosexuality in 37 pairs. Although the study has been questioned methodologically, and smaller studies have shown twin pairs discordant for sexual orientation, newer research has demonstrated the substantial contribution of genetics. A 52% concordance rate for homosexual orientation was found in male monozygotic twins who were reared together (Bailey & Pillard, 1991). These rates are higher than among dizygotic twins (22%) or non-twin male siblings (9%). Similarly, another report finds a 48% concordance rate for female monozygotic twins reared together, also higher than among dizygotic twins (16%), or non-twin siblings (14%) (Bailey *et al.*, 1993).

Because of the confound of a common environment on monozygotic pairs, twins separated at birth provide a more powerful model of the relative contributions of nature versus nurture. Unfortunately for research purposes, few twins are separated at birth and in far fewer cases would at least one be expected to emerge as homosexual. A report of two such male pairs is of interest. In one, the twins discovered each other in their 20s and both were homosexual. In the second, whereas one twin was homosexual, the second was married and a father but in his adolescence had engaged in a 3-year same-sex relationship. The data for reared-apart female twins are much less compelling for a genetic basis, with none of four pairs being concordant for lesbianism (Eckert *et al.*, 1986).

In my prospective research I evaluated one set of mono-zygotic twins in which only one showed the gender identity disorder of childhood (Green, 1974, 1987). Both emerged as bisexual, but the previously cross-gendered twin was con-siderably more homosexual. Perhaps their common genetics worked as a constraint on the degree to which their sexual orientation diverged, notwithstanding their considerably disparate early gender-typed behaviour.

Other family studies of nontwin siblings also provide support for a genetic basis of sexual orientation. Higher rates of homosexual brothers have been found for homosexual men (Pillard & Weinrich, 1986) and higher rates of homosexual sisters for homosexual women (Pillard *et al.*, 1982). These family studies, however, have a substantial confound from environmental influences.

The best, but not yet final genetic study is the recent suggestion that DNA markers on the X chromosome are linked to male homosexuality. The markers were found in two-thirds of 40 pairs of homosexual brothers. The presence of the markers on the X chromosome (passed by the mother) is consistent with the finding that in these families male homosexuality was also found in maternal uncles and male cousins but not in fathers or paternal relatives (Hamer *et al.*, 1993).

The prenatal stress theory of sexual orientation derives from the finding that stress to the pregnant rodent results in less male behaviour by male offspring. One explanatory theory is that stress androgens from the adrenal compete with more powerful testicular androgens and lead to less masculinization. The other is that stress alters fetal testicular enzyme activity (Ward, 1972).

Two studies supporting this theory in the human emanate from a research laboratory in Germany. A model of extreme prenatal stress was taken as the 1941–1946 years in Germany, the years that included World War II. When men were assessed at a venereal disease clinic, rates of homosexuality were higher for those born during those war years than during the few years before or after (Dorner *et al.*, 1983). However, this finding is confounded by the fact that these war years were the same years in which there was generalized father absence from the home, a popular environmental theory of homo-sexuality. The second study had homosexual, bisexual and heterosexual men report stressful events during their gestation as told to them by their mothers. Mothers of homosexual men reportedly recalled more stress. This finding, however, was not confirmed in two other German studies (Wille *et al.*, 1987). Research in the US has been suggestive, at best. Mothers of more homosexually oriented men recalled slightly

more severe stress 9–12 months before the pregnancy and during the second trimester. No relationships were found for female children (Ellis *et al.*, 1988). However, another American study found that recalled maternal stress during each trimester did not correlate with ratings of sexual orientation or with reports of childhood cross-gender behaviour in males.

Another celebrated test of a prenatal endocrine difference in homosexual versus heterosexual males utilized the sex-typed pattern of luteinizing hormone (LH) response to rising levels of blood oestradiol (the hormonal basis of ovulation). The theory here is that the LH response is a marker for the extent of prenatal androgenization of the central nervous system. There is evidence, however, that the LH response may also be related to current testicular function. Initial reports found an attenuated, but female-type, LH response pattern in homosexual men (Dorner *et al.*, 1975). Our research found that over one-half of a sample of homosexual men showed a response similar to heterosexual females and different from heterosexual males (Gladue *et al.*, 1984). Another study, however, using a somewhat different approach to ascertain the LH response, did not find a significant difference between homosexual and heterosexual men (Gooren, 1986), nor did another following the original protocol (Hendricks *et al.*, 1989).

The recent finding of an anatomical difference in the brain of homosexual men is provocative. At autopsy, homosexual men were found to have a smaller INAH-3 nucleus in the anterior hypothalamus compared to presumably heterosexual men, and similar in size to presumably heterosexual women (no sex histories were available for the latter two groups; (LeVay, 1991)). Although there was nucleus size overlap between groups, mean differences were significant. No data are available for this nucleus size in female homosexuals to ascertain whether it is comparable to heterosexual males. The source of this difference, if it is genuine, remains obscure, but could be related to androgen levels during prenatal or neonatal development.

TREATMENT

Several treatment goals present for children with atypical psychosexual development. Short-term goals are directed at the child's discontent over being the sex to which it was born, and social conflicts the child is experiencing, particularly with the peer group, in consequence of atypical behaviours. Parents often have a longer-range goal of preventing the development of atypical patterns of sexuality. However, they should be aware at the outset that there is no controlled psychotherapy outcome research demonstrating that intervention of any type during childhood for atypical psychosexual expression affects later sexual orientation. Although some reports describe behavioural changes in such children, notably boys, with lessening of discontent with being male and a reduction of stigmatizing feminine behaviours, there is no firm evidence that such change effects later sexuality. In fact, in my long-term research study, approximately one-quarter of the boys entered one of a variety of treatments during childhood, but the rates of bisexual and homosexual orientation in the treated group did not differ from that of the untreated group. Thus, parents' goals should be directed at the immediate conflict the child is experiencing, with assurance that addressing short-term goals should have a positive effect on their child's later self-image and social adjustment, irrespective of sexual orientation.

One long-term treatment goal with more prospect of success is preventing transsexualism. More optimism can be expressed here based on two factors. The first is the relatively low incidence of transsexualism compared to homosexuality. The second is that intervention addressed specifically at discontent with being the sex to which the child was born would appear to have more prospect of success, with its rather clearly identified focus, than attempting to intervene with a 5-year-old in a manner that affects later patterns of sexual arousal.

Another goal with at least theoretical optimism for success is the prevention of fetishistic cross-dressing (transvestism). Because an obvious symptom of gender identity disorder is cross-dressing, parents and therapists work to reduce and eliminate this behaviour. Cross-dressing in the male usually does not become sexually arousing until puberty. Thus, interrupting the behaviour before its reinforcement conditioned by genital arousal and orgasm may abort the development of fetishistic cross-dressing.

A variety of strategies have been utilized in the treatment of cross-gendered children, notably boys. They have included psychodynamically oriented therapy, behaviour therapy, family therapy and eclectic approaches.

The most systematic attack on cross-gender behaviours in boys has been by the behaviour therapists (e.g. Rekers, 1982). Specific behaviours have been positively and negatively reinforced, sometimes through a token economy system, othertimes through selective attention and regard by significant adults. These interventions result in substantial decreases in cross-gender behaviours. At follow-up, 2 boys treated in that programme were interviewed by me and found to be bisexual (Green, 1987). No other long-term sexual orientation data have been published on the larger series of cross-gendered boys treated by Rekers and co-workers (1990).

In the psychodynamic literature an emphasis is placed on early object relations and general ego functioning with a focus on understanding the mother–child and father–child relationship, plus the parental dynamics that affect their support of cross-gender behaviour in the child (for reviews, see Zucker, 1985, 1990; Zucker & Green, 1991a,b). Reports of treatment of cross-gendered girls are few (see review by Zucker & Green, 1992).

A factor stressed in many case reports is the parental attitude toward masculine and feminine behaviours in children, and subtle parental reinforcement of cross-gender behaviour. Treatment attempts to interrupt these influences. An additional therapy component has been to engage the father more actively in the life of his son. To some extent this is through a reeducation process whereby the father becomes more comfortable in engaging in activities that are mutually enjoyable, rather than expecting the boy to conform to a more aggressive, masculine stereotype.

Parents may be seen concurrently or sequentially with the child. Parents typically have vacillated in their approach to the child's gender behaviour. There may be parental disagreement over its significance. Parents must be in concert in their attitudes towards the child's exaggerated cross-gender behaviour and should become comfortable in setting limits. The penalty the child is paying *vis-à-vis* the peer group can be an important stimulus here where parents are ambivalent about conformity to conventional sex roles — a not invalid ideal, but one which is causing their child social distress.

The relative deficit in the father–son shared experience in our research in association with atypical psychosexual development argues for addressing this deficiency. Whether the child's behaviours discourage father participation, or the father's disinterest diverts the boy to female companions and caregivers, enhancing the father–son relationship should be a positive experience for both. To the extent that, for some homosexual men, the emotional gratification from same-sex relationships derives from boyhood alienation from the male parent and male peers (male affect starvation), this intervention may affect later relationships. Even if the direction of erotic interest derives exclusively from the INAH-3 nucleus of the hypothalamus, a more positive father–son relationship benefits both partners.

Modifying peer group composition is another goal. With cross-gendered boys, other male children are seen as too rough. The boy gravitates towards a female peer group, resulting in stigmatization and adoption of feminine gestures and mannerisms, which, in turn, enhance stigma. Parents need to find other boys whose interests are not exaggeratedly rough-and-tumble, but rather are more sedentary, to provide a comfortable milieu for their son that includes same-sex peers. Young children see the world in black and white, including the world of gender. Thus, if they do not conform to what they see as the requirements of their given sex, they conclude that they must be the opposite sex. A world of greys must be painted in. Boys need to appreciate that not all boys are rough-and-tumble, athletic and aggressive, and girls need to appreciate that many girls are athletic and do not enjoy doll play.

Markedly cross-gendered mannerisms set the child apart from same-sex age-mates and result in teasing. Often, these gestures and vocal patterns are not conscious. Parents can alert their children to such mannerisms so as to bring them under volitional control.

Parents must hear that the aims of therapy are not to transform their child into a stereotypically masculine boy or feminine girl, but to impart gender balance into a developmental schema that has gone awry. While some may object to a societal insistence that children conform to sex-role expectations, the social distress experienced by severely atypical children needs to be emphasized with its consequent problems in self-image and perhaps in later social adjustment.

THE OUTCOME OF ATYPICAL PSYCHOSEXUAL DEVELOPMENT IN CHILDREN

My 15-year prospective study revealed that, of the two-thirds of previously cross-gendered boys who were reevaluated, three-quarters were bisexually or homosexually oriented in adolescence or young adulthood. By contrast, none of the previously conventionally sex-typed boys were homosexual and the only one who was bisexual was the monozygotic twin of a substantially cross-gendered boy (Green, 1987).

Other prospective research, although less systematic, also demonstrates the association between early cross-gender behaviour in boys and subsequent homosexual orientation. A follow-up on 55 males seen for early feminine behaviours, 39 of whom were preadolescent when evaluated, was reported by Zuger (1984). About two-thirds of the full sample were reported to be homosexual, although it is not clear how many were in the group seen prior to teenage, and the number who were bisexual is not reported. In another study, 16 boys described in medical records made during childhood as showing feminine behaviour were interviewed during adulthood. Two had become homosexual, 3 transsexual, and 1 a transvestite (Lebovitz, 1972). My study with John Money of 'feminine boys' in the late 1950s and early 1960s (Green & Money, 1960) found in an early follow-up that 3 of 5 were exclusively homosexual and 2 were bisexual (Green, 1974). Three of the original 5 were reported in a later follow-up of 9 previously 'feminine boys' where at least 8 were predominantly homosexual (Money & Russo, 1979).

Because transsexualism and transvestism are mental disorders and homosexuality and bisexuality are not, it would be helpful to clinicians who see children with atypical psychosexual development if specific childhood behaviours predictive of these outcomes could be distinguished.

DISCUSSION

As with most behaviours, there is a continuum for psychosexual development. At one end are traditionally (stereotypically to some) sex-typed children, at the other are children with the complete picture of gender identity disorder. Just where on the spectrum a child's development is sufficiently atypical to warrant concern, if not diagnosis, is problematic. From the perspective of potential future transsexualism, perhaps it is where children want to be the other sex. From the perspective of current distress, perhaps it is where their behaviours result in substantial teasing.

Psychosexual development in children bears more than research significance. Although there was much talk a decade ago about a unisex movement that would sweep away traditional expectations of boy versus girl behaviours, little change has appeared. Boys and girls who radically differ from cultural expectations continue to experience social distress. To the extent that the stigma attached to deviant sex role behaviour is ultimately reduced, children with atypical psychosexual development may elicit less attention and concern from peers and parents. To date this has not happened.

Politics has captured much of the controversy over the extent to which sex-typed behaviours are innate or the influence of culture. Not only in the lay press, but also among professionals, the same research is seen as buttressing opposing viewpoints. Selective data reporting resembles the polemics of the lawyer's brief, not the balanced perspective of the scientist. Further, the increased vitality of the association between sex-typed behaviours in boys and girls and later sexual orientation invokes the cultural and political passions surrounding homosexuality.

The extent to which sexual orientation is determined before birth, or acquired postnatally, and the extent to which it is modifiable, has religious and legal ramifications. Religious conservatives claim that homosexuals choose to be sexually deviant and can change their 'sinful' behaviour. American law provides special protection for stigmatized groups where the trait for which they are discriminated against is 'immutable'.

The clinician responsible for the child with a gender identity disorder is confronted with all facets of this complex. Parents want to know whether their child's atypical development is inborn or acquired. Children cannot understand (as if there were a rational answer) why girls can wear trousers, but boys can't wear dresses. Parents remain fearful that their child will become homosexual (if not transsexual), and do not care that psychiatry no longer considers homosexuality to be a mental disorder.

Striking a professional balance that contributes to the child's interest in reducing short-term stigma and enhancing long-term self-image, while integrating the parents into an effective intervention strategy, is no small task. It requires sympathizing with views supporting an increased flexibility of sex roles, at all ages, while empathizing with the pain of the teased atypical child. It includes enhancing emotional ties between child and parents so that, irrespective of the child's later sexuality, the family bond will be strong.

Finally, away from our offices and institutions, we can invoke our professional and community standing to effect social and legal change that is therapeutic to all those with atypical psychosexual development, whether or not they become patients.

REFERENCES

Bailey J. & Pillard R. (1991) A genetic study of male sexual orientation. *Archives of General Psychiatry*, **48**, 1089–1096.

Bailey J., Willerman L. & Parks C. (1991) A test of the maternal stress theory of human male homosexuality. *Archives of Sexual Behavior*, **20**, 277–293.

Bailey M., Pillard R., Neale M. & Agyei Y. (1993) *Heritable factors influence sexual orientation in women. Archives of General Psychiatry*, **50**, 217–223.

Baker H. & Stoller R. (1968) Can a biological force contribute to gender identity? *American Journal of Psychiatry*, **124**, 1653–1658.

Bell A., Weinberg J. & Hammersmith S. (1981) *Sexual Preference.* Indiana University Press, Bloomington, IN.

Berenbaum S. & Hines M. (1992) Early androgens are related to childhood sex-typed toy preferences. *Psychological Science*, **3**, 203–206.

Biller H. (1981) The father and sex-role development. In: Lamb M. (ed) *The Role of the Father in Childhood Development*, 2nd edn. John Wiley, New York.

Brown D. (1956) Sex role preference in young children. *Psychological Monographs*, **70**(421).

Coates S. & Person E. (1985) Extreme boyhood femininity. Isolated behavior or pervasive disorder? *Journal of American Academy of Child Psychiatry*, **24**, 702–709.

Devereux G. (1937) Institutionalized homosexuality of the Mohave Indians. *Human Biology*, **9**, 508–527.

Diamond M. (1965) A critical evaluation of the ontogeny of human sexual behavior. *Quarterly Review of Biology*, **40**, 147–175.

Diamond M. (1982) Sexual identity, monozygotic twins reared in discordant sex roles and a BBC follow-up. *Archives of Sexual Behavior*, **11**, 181–186.

Diamond M. (1991) Personal communication. University of Hawaii, Department of Anatomy, Hawaii, USA.

Dorner G., Rohde W. & Stahl F. (1975) A neuroendocrine predisposition for homosexuality in men. *Archives of Sexual Behavior*, **4**, 1–8.

Dorner G., Schenk B., Schmiedel B. & Ahrens L. (1983) Stressful events in prenatal life of bi- and homosexual men. *Experimental and Clinical Endocrinology*, **81**, 83–87.

Eckert E., Bouchard T. & Bohler J. (1986) Homosexuality in monozygotic twins reared apart. *British Journal of Psychiatry*, **148**, 421–426.

Ehrhardt A. & Baker S. (1974) Fetal androgens, human central nervous system differentiation, and behavioral sex differences. In: Friedman R., Richart R. & Vande Wiele R. (eds) *Sex Differences in Behavior*, pp. 35–51. John Wiley, New York.

Ehrhardt A., Meyer-Bahlburg H., Rosen L., Feldman J., Veridiano N., Zimmerman I. & McEwen B. (1985) Sexual orientation after prenatal exposure to exogenous estrogen. *Archives of Sexual Behavior*, **14**, 57–75.

Ellis L., Ames M., Peckham W. & Burke D. (1988) Sexual orientation of human offspring may be altered by severe maternal stress during pregnancy. *Journal of Sex Research*, **25**, 152–157.

Fagot B. (1974) Sex differences in toddlers' behavior and parental reaction. *Developmental Psychology*, **10**, 554–558.

Gessell A. (1940) *The First Five Years of Life.* Methuen, London.

Gladue B., Green R. & Hellman R. (1984) Neuroendocrine response to estrogen and sexual orientation. *Science*, **225**, 1496–1499.

Gooren L. (1986) The neuroendocrine response of luteinizing hormone to estrogen administration in heterosexual, homosexual and transsexual subjects. *Journal of Clinical Endocrinology and Metabolism*, **63**, 583–588.

Green R. (1968) Transsexualism. Mythological, historical and cross-cultural aspects. In: Benjamin H. (ed) *The Transsexual Phenomenon.* Julian Press, New York.

Green R. (1974) *Sexual Identity Conflict in Children and Adults.* Basic Books, New York; Gerald Duckworth, London.

Green R. (1978) Sexual identity of 37 children raised by homosexual or transsexual parents. *American Journal of Psychiatry*, **135**, 692–697.

Green R. (1987) *The 'Sissy Boy Syndrome' and the Development of Homosexuality.* Yale University Press, New Haven.

Green R. & Money J. (1960) Incongruous gender role: nongenital manifestations in prepubertal boys. *Journal of Nervous and Mental Disease*, **131**, 160–168.

Green R. & Stoller R. (1971) Two monozygotic (identical) twin pairs discordant for gender identity. *Archives of Sexual Behavior*, **1**, 321–327.

Green R., Fuller M. & Rutley B. (1972a) It-scale for children and draw-a-person test: 30 feminine versus 25 masculine boys. *Journal of Personality Assessment*, **36**, 349–352.

Green R., Fuller M., Rutley B. & Hendler J. (1972b) Playroom toy preferences of 15 masculine and 15 feminine boys. *Behavior Therapy*, **3**, 425–429.

Green R., Williams K. & Harper J. (1980) Cross-sex identity: peer group integration and the double standard of childhood sex typing. In: Samson J. (ed) *Enfance et Sexualité/Childhood and Sexuality.* Les Editions Etudes Vivantes, Montreal.

Green R., Williams K. & Goodman M. (1982) Ninety-nine 'tomboys' and 'non-tomboys': behavioral contrasts and demographic similarities. *Archives of Sexual Behavior*, **11**, 247–266.

Green R., Neuberg D. & Finch S. (1983) Sex-typed motor behaviors of 'feminine' boys, conventionally masculine boys and conventionally feminine girls. *Sex Roles*, **9**, 571–579.

Green R., Mandel J., Hotvedt M., Gray J. & Smith L. (1986) Lesbian mothers and their children. *Archives of Sexual Behavior*, **15**, 167–184.

Grellert E., Newcomb M. & Bentler P. (1982) Childhood play activities of male and female homosexuals. *Archives of Sexual Behavior*, **11**, 451–478.

Hamer D.H., Hu S., Magnuson V.L., Hu N. & Pattatucci A.M.L. (1993) A linkage between DNA markers on the X-chromosome and male sexual orientation. *Science*, **261**, 321–327.

Harry J. (1982) *Gay Children Grown Up.* Praeger, New York.

Hartup W. & Zook E. (1960) Sex-role preferences in 3 and 4 year old children. *Journal of Consulting and Clinical Psychology*, **24**, 420–426.

Hendricks S., Graber B. & Rodriguez-Sierra J. (1989) Neuroendocrine responses to exogenous estrogen. *Psychoneuroendocrinology*, **14**, 177–185.

Hetherington E. (1966) Effects of paternal absence on sex-typed behavior in Negro and white preadolescent males. *Journal of Personality and Social Psychology*, **4**, 87–91.

Imperato-McGinley J., Peterson R., Gautier T. & Sturia E. (1979) Androgen and the evolution of male-gender identity among male pseudohermaphrodites. *New England Journal of Medicine*, **300**, 1233–1237.

Jacklin C., Maccoby E. & Dick A. (1973) Barrier behavior and toy preference. *Child Development*, **44**, 196–200.

Kallman E. (1952) Comparative twin study on the genetic aspects of male homosexuality. *Journal of Nervous and Mental Disease*, **115**, 283–298.

Kester P., Green R., Finch S. & Williams K. (1980) Prenatal female hormone administration and psychosexual development in human males. *Psychoneuroendocrinology*, **5**, 269–285.

Lebovitz P. (1972) Feminine behavior in boys. *American Journal of Psychiatry*, **128**, 1283–1289.

LeVay S. (1991) A difference in hypothalamic structure between heterosexual and homosexual men. *Science*, **253**, 1034–1037.

Levin S., Balistrier J. & Schukit M. (1972) The development of sexual discrimination in children. *Journal of Child Psychology and Psychiatry*, **13**, 47–53.

Lytton H. & Romney D. (1991) Parents' differential socialization of boys and girls: a meta-analysis. *Psychological Bulletin*, **109**, 267–296.

Money J. & Ehrhardt A. (1972) *Man and Woman, Boy and Girl.* Johns Hopkins Press, Baltimore, MD.

Money J. & Russo A. (1979) Homosexual outcome of discordant gender identity/role. *Journal of Pediatric Psychology*, **4**, 29–41.

Money J., Hampson J. & Hampson J. (1957) Imprinting and the establishment of gender role. *Archives of Neurology and Psychiatry*, **77**,

333–336.

Money J., Schwartz M. & Lewis V. (1984) Adult heterosexual status and fetal hormonal masculinization and demasculinization. *Psychoneuroendocrinology*, **9**, 405–414.

Pedersen F. & Bell R. (1970) Sex differences in preschool children without histories of complications of pregnancy and delivery. *Developmental Psychology*, **3**, 10–15.

Pillard R. & Weinrich J. (1986) Evidence of familial nature of male homosexuality. *Archives of General Psychiatry*, **43**, 808–812.

Pillard R., Poumadere J. & Carretta R. (1982) A family study of sexual orientation. *Archives of Sexual Behavior*, **11**, 511–520.

Rabban M. (1950) Sex-role identification in young children in two diverse social groups. *Geriatric Psychology Monographs*, **42**, 81–158.

Rekers G. (1982) *Shaping Your Child's Sexual Identity*. Baker Book House, Grand Rapids, MI.

Rekers G., Kilgus M. & Rosen A. (1990) Long-term effects of treatment for gender identity disorder of childhood. *Journal of Psychology and Human Sexuality*, **3**, 121–153.

Roberts C., Green R., Williams K. & Goodman M. (1987) Boyhood gender identity development: a statistical contrast of two family groups. *Developmental Psychology*, **23**, 544–557.

Saghir M. & Robins M. (1973) *Male and Female Homosexuality*. Williams & Wilkins, Baltimore, MD.

Schmidt G. & Clement V. (1990) Does peace prevent homosexuality? *Archives of Sexual Behavior*, **19**, 183–187.

Smith P. & Connolly K. (1972) Patterns of play and social interaction in preschool children. In: Jones N. (ed) *Ethological Studies of Child Behaviour*. Cambridge University Press, Cambridge.

Stoller R. (1968) *Sex and Gender*. Science House, New York.

Stoller R. (1975) *Sex and Gender, Vol. 2: The Transsexual Experiment*, p. 43. Jason Aronson, New York.

Ward I. (1972) Prenatal stress feminizes and demasculinizes the behavior of males. *Science*, **175**, 82–84.

Whitam F. & Mathy R. (1991a) *Male Homosexuality in Four Societies*. Praeger, New York.

Whitam F. & Mathy R. (1991b) Child cross-gender behavior of homosexual females in Brazil, Peru, the Philippines, and the United States. *Archives of Sexual Behavior*, **20**, 151–170.

Whiting B. & Whiting J. (1975) *Children of Six Cultures*. Harvard University Press, Cambridge, MA.

Wille R., Borchers D. & Schultz W. (1987) *Prenatal Distress*. International Academy of Sex Research, Tutzing, Germany.

Yalom I., Green R. & Fisk N. (1973) Prenatal exposure to female hormones: effect on psychosexual development in boys. *Archives of General Psychiatry*, **28**, 554–561.

Young W., Goy R. & Phoenix C. (1964) Hormones and sexual behavior. *Science*, **142**, 212–218.

Zucker K. (1985) Cross-gender identified children. In: Steiner B. (ed) *Gender Dysphoria*. Plenum, New York.

Zucker K. (1990) Treatment of gender identity disorders in children. In: Blanchard R. & Steiner B. (eds) *Clinical Management of Gender-Identity Disorders in Children and Adults*. American Psychiatric Press, Washington, DC.

Zucker K., Green R. (1991a) Gender identity disorders in children and adolescents. In: Lewis M. (ed) *Child and Adolescent Psychiatry*. Williams & Wilkins, Baltimore, MD.

Zucker K. & Green R. (1991b) Gender identity and psychosexual disorders. In: Wiener J. (ed) *Textbook of Child and Adolescent Psychiatry*. American Psychiatric Association Press, Washington, DC.

Zucker K. & Green R. (1992) Psychosexual disorders in children and adolescents. *Journal of Child Psychology, Psychiatry and Allied Disciplines*, **33**, 107–151.

Zucker K., Wild J. & Bradley S. (1993) Physical attractiveness in boys with gender identity disorder. *Archives of Sexual Behavior*, **22**, 23–36.

Zuger B. (1970) Gender role determination: a critical review of the evidence from hermaphroditism. *Psychosomatic Medicine*, **32**, 449–463.

Zuger B. (1984) Early effeminate behavior in boys. *Journal of Nervous and Mental Disease*, **172**, 90–97.

Chapter 44
Implications for the Infant of
Maternal Puerperal Psychiatric Disorders

R. Channi Kumar & Alison E. Hipwell

INTRODUCTION

The young infant is entirely dependent upon others for its survival; for most babies the mother is the primary source of nurturance, physical as well as psychological. This chapter examines how the presence of maternal mental illness may have a detrimental effect on the developing infant, and how some of such ill-effects may be prevented or mitigated. It is, of course, an over-simplification to seek to draw direct links between maternal mental illness and adverse effects in the child because of the multiple, complex and interacting influences that impinge upon the developmental process. Genes, environmental toxins (including psychotropic drugs), nutritional deficits, social customs, accidents (including well-meaning interventions such as operative procedures) may all take their toll on the fetus or the neonate, and the part played by maternal psychiatric disorder is inevitably enmeshed in a web of interconnecting influences. The effects on the child of observable maternal psychopathology may be both amplified and distorted by many of the causal mechanisms behind the mother's illness as well by some of its associations and consequences.

Rutter and Cox (1985) and Rutter (1989) have signposted some of the most important channels through which adverse effects of parental psychiatric disorders may be transmitted to children and these are listed below with some examples which refer particularly to consequences for infants of maternal disorders. Mental illness in fathers as a risk factor is an important subject in its own right and research is needed into similarities and differences in outcome for the infant when either mothers or fathers or when both parents are affected. In this chapter we shall focus primarily on illness in mothers and refer to possible increased risks to infants when the mother's illness also then affects her partner. The main pathways leading to adverse effects in infants are as follows:

1 Direct effects of maternal psychopathology that impact on the child in various ways; the most extreme consequences of maternal mental illness are cases of infanticide (D'Orban, 1979; Kumar & Marks, 1992), injury, failure to thrive and other forms of abuse and harm (Bentovim, 1991). It should be borne in mind, however, that not all mothers or parents who act in this way meet objective and agreed criteria for psychiatric disorder.

2 Indirect effects through the additional increased risk of disorder in the marital partner. Recent studies (Harvey & McGrath, 1988; Lovestone & Kumar, 1993) have shown that 40–50% of men whose spouses were admitted to psychiatric mother-and-baby units were themselves unwell, mainly with recent-onset depressive disorders following the mothers' illnesses.

3 Marital disharmony, which very often precedes or is exacerbated by maternal conditions such as postnatal depression, has been shown, for example, to contribute significantly to the adverse effects of maternal depression on the child's cognitive development (Cogill et al., 1986). Secure parental relationships and healthy fathers provide an important element of protection in the milieu of the developing child. Brown and colleagues have shown in several studies (Brown & Harris, 1978; Brown, 1988) how lack of intimacy or undependability in the husband adds to the risk of maternal depression.

4 Impairment of maternal functioning and of interaction with the child. An early pointer was provided by Weissman et al. (1972) who described observing 'immobilization in the maternal role' in women who were severely depressed after childbirth.

5 Temporary or permanent separations of the infant from its mother and sometimes from the family as a consequence of the mother's illness in the context of disturbed family relationships. The pros and cons of joint admission of mothers and their infants into psychiatric mother-and-baby units, and the assessment of risk to the infant through impulse or neglect, are major relevant problems needing further research (Kumar, 1992).

6 Genetic factors could be involved (see review by Rutter et al., 1990). As understanding grows of the genetic mechanisms of the transmission of diseases, a new era is in sight in which prevention of many disorders may become a practical possibility. This subject is, however, outside the scope of this chapter.

7 Psychotropic drugs in pregnancy — the possibility of teratogenicity became an awful reality following the thalidomide tragedy, and expectant mothers are advised to avoid potential toxins, prescribed and unprescribed. Sometimes however, the severity of a mother's illness requires drug therapy, for example, with drugs such as tricyclic antidepressants or phenothiazines or butyrophenones, which are not thought to cause malformations. However, hardly anything is known in humans about behavioural or developmental teratogenicity (see, for example, Hawkins, 1983).

A typical clinical history illustrates some of the ways in which a mother's illness puts the infant at risk.

A young woman with a family history of schizophrenia and who is of below average intelligence is herself schizophrenic. She is maintained on neuroleptic medication which, despite reducing her fertility, does not prevent her from becoming pregnant. Paternity is uncertain. The father of the baby is suspected to be a schizophrenic or he may be another sexual partner who has a personality disorder and is also alcoholic. Either way, and perhaps most importantly, neither man is going to play any significant part in the child's future. The expectant mother does not regularly attend antenatal care and is unable to stop smoking, occasional drinking and recreational use of other, unspecified drugs. She lives for some of the time with friends and for some of the time with her parents, but she has been discouraged in the past from staying in the parental home because, for several years, she was sexually abused by her father. He has recently returned home after serving a short prison sentence for assault and burglary. Her mother is devoted and caring but is preoccupied by debts, by inadequate housing and by the needs of 3 other younger children, 1 of whom is already on probation because of drug-related offences. She herself has been taking benzodiazepines for several years and cannot see herself as being of much practical help after the grandchild is born.

It is late in the pregnancy and the expectant mother and her future baby are the subject of an increasingly worried case conference at which her social worker reports that when he last saw her, she was obviously in a psychotic state and was adamant that she was going to keep and bring up her baby. She had accepted an offer of temporary accommodation, but had not liked a hostel for mothers and babies which was run by the local authority. She had also been refusing to attend her psychiatric outpatient appointments and had not wanted to see her community nurse because all he did was to offer injections which made her sleepy and stiff. She was certainly not going to have any injections after the birth because she was planning to breast-feed. Apart from this conviction she had no other clear plans for looking after the baby and had not yet made any anticipatory purchases such as a pram, or a cot, or clothes and nappies. She would get these after the delivery when she had some extra money.

The participants of the case conference engage in a sometimes heated discussion about potential risks to the baby but eventually agree that they are powerless at this stage, without factual evidence, to take legal steps to protect the baby's future health and safety, and they also agree that this mother and baby will need the maximum available supervision and support. There is the usual wistful wish that if only there were a foster mother who could take in both the mother and the baby then all would be well. Anxiety mounts when no one can think of any suitable surrogate mother-cum-grandmother,

and it reaches a crescendo when someone asks what criteria of observable neglect or significant harm to the baby (Lynch, 1991) will be used in deciding whether or not to remove the infant from the mother. It is agreed that the meeting will recommend the placing of the infant's name on the 'at-risk' register, if only because this will ensure regular review of the case.

There is a sense of relief when someone suggests a voluntary placement in a psychiatric mother-and-baby unit because expert assessment is needed of this woman's competence and motivation as a mother. She may also accept treatment for herself as part of the package. The psychiatrist present argues that the staff of the unit in question are reluctant to take such patients because all the warning signs are there that the child will eventually be fostered and that the proposed admission is a way of deferring a painful decision. What is needed is a realistic assessment in which the mother might be required to sort out her own needs in the community, and to have supervised and regular access to the baby at a foster-parent's home to show her level of motivation and competence. It is nevertheless resolved that admission to the mother-and-baby unit is the only viable option, that the mother will be informed of this and that her social worker will negotiate the admission. Someone enquires how one manages in places where there are no mother-and-baby units and asks what will happen if the proposed admission proves not to be possible. Everyone agrees that there is a lack of research findings to aid decision-making in such difficult cases.

This lengthy vignette is not fabricated; it lists a series of hazards, some actual and some potential, to the baby's health and development. It is intended to make the point that the mother's psychopathology is best regarded as a kind of compass-bearing to help navigation through poorly chartered waters. It also emphasizes the fact that mothers with pre-partum mental illnesses are, in their way, as important a group as those who develop postpartum psychoses and postnatal depressions. Finally, the case history shows up an important gap in the way that clinical services attempt to meet the needs of mentally ill mothers and their babies. Much, or even most of the concern that is expressed focuses on the baby in terms of the risks to its safety, health and welfare. But there is usually no one present at case conferences such as the one described, or indeed in ward meetings in mother-and-baby units, who has first-hand knowledge and expertise in the field of child development. Child psychiatrists by and large work with older children, and adult general psychiatrists who are responsible for the care of mentally ill mothers do not normally have any special knowledge of infant development.

Although the infant of the schizophrenic mother in the vignette might begin its life already loaded with disadvantages, this is not necessarily the case for many others whose mothers develop psychoses or nonpsychotic depressions after the delivery. In these latter cases, therefore, there is a great opportunity for primary prevention; that is, to identify and to treat those features of maternal illness that may provoke later problems in otherwise healthy infants. There is also a major opportunity for secondary prevention; that is, to identify early signs of later problems in vulnerable infants, and to target therapeutic measures at them to prevent, overcome and compensate for such effects. Firstly, however, it is necessary to study the natural history of infant development in the context of maternal illness. Although there is an extensive psychiatric literature on the ways in which parental pathology has an impact on the developing infant's psyche, and thus lays the foundations for adult disorder (Rutter, 1966, 1981; Weissman & Paykel, 1974; Weissman *et al.*, 1984; Rutter & Cox, 1985), there has been comparatively little direct observation and longitudinal study of infants exposed to different kinds of maternal psychopathology (see reviews in Rutter, 1988).

Recent research has shown that normal infants of just 6 weeks of age respond in highly specific ways to the interactional style and emotional tone of their primary caregiver (Cohn & Tronick, 1987; Murray, 1988). In experimental settings where the mother is asked suddenly to adopt a blank facial expression to her infant or where the timing of the mother's speech and behaviour is arranged to be out of phase with her baby's behaviour, infants initially show signs of protest which develop into distress and avoidance (Brazelton *et al.*, 1975; Murray, 1980; Murray & Trevarthen, 1985; Cohn & Tronick, 1987). Some theorists argue that positive expression and responsive caregiving are particularly crucial during infancy such that maternal psychopathology at this time will have a long-term influence on later language, peer interaction (e.g. Bakeman & Brown, 1980), social responsiveness (Tronick *et al.*, 1982), performance on developmental assessments (Field *et al.*, 1983) and even the reaction of others to the child (Field *et al.*, 1988).

An examination of the possible effects of maternal psychopathology on the developing infant must divide the material in two ways — firstly, in terms of the different psychiatric syndromes, and secondly in terms of the timing of their onset or occurrence in relation to pregnancy and childbirth. This is both logical and convenient because the maternal conditions fall into two main groups: (1) those illnesses that antedate pregnancy and in a sense are complicated by childbearing; and (2) those illnesses that begin after childbirth and thus are complications of childbearing. Psychiatric illnesses do not on the whole arise during pregnancy (Kendell *et al.*, 1987).

IMPLICATIONS FOR THE CHILD OF DISORDERS THAT PRE-DATE PREGNANCY

There may be a tendency to assume that infants of women with chronic mental illness are more at risk than those whose mothers have suffered an onset of illness after the delivery. This may, in fact, not be the case because chronically ill women, their partners and families, as well as health professionals, may have made many personal and social adaptations to the presence of chronic illness. Such adaptations may serve a protective function after the baby is born. A variety of resources, ranging from day nurseries to help from

relatives, may have been brought into readiness because some of the implications of the mother's illness are already recognized by others and also by the mother herself. In contrast, a mother who becomes ill for the first time after childbirth is in unknown territory and the responses of herself and her family to her illness and to the infant's part in it may be coloured by the belief that, directly or indirectly, the baby is somehow to blame.

Schizophrenic disorders account for many of the cases in which clinicians are asked to provide opinions for case conferences or for court hearings where there are concerns about a mother's wish to retain the sole or the primary responsibility for the care of her infant. The basic issues are the same, however, in relation to other conditions such as chronic manic-depressive illness, severe mental impairment, personality disorder, etc. Such concerns do not typically arise when mothers experience first episodes of psychosis after childbirth because the normal pattern among women with previously stable personalities and social backgrounds is that of substantial recovery (Brockington *et al.*, 1982).

Child psychiatrists may, therefore, be invited to assess a mentally ill mother who is contesting actions by social services under child protection procedures. There is an inherent conflict of interests between the mother's wishes and the child's needs. What is in balance is a judgement of the prognosis, which in turn is based upon a detailed assessment of the psychiatric diagnosis and the history of the mother's mental illness, her medical and social history, her current and likely future social circumstances, the degree of impairment in daily living skills and the supports and treatments that are available to her. Against this background, the psychiatrist must attempt to evaluate her expressed motivation as a parent, her insight into the problems facing her, and her competence, consistency and sensitivity in her interactions with her infant. A single session of observation in an unfamiliar setting is unlikely to do justice to the mother. In such circumstances it is also difficult to be confident about the reliability of any conclusions concerning the extent, nature and severity of possible risk now and in the future to the infant's safety and welfare. The present procedures for dealing with such difficult problems are best described as *ad hoc*, and careful thought is needed about how such assessments should be conducted.

The cliché of the good-enough mother does not easily incorporate a woman such as the one described in the case vignette earlier in the chapter. Furthermore, what may be good enough for a 3-month-old infant in the setting of a semisupervised hostel in the community may be damaging for a 3-year-old in a disorganized home. There is therefore a serious and urgent need for a collection of clinical case histories where definite concerns have been expressed about the abilities of mentally ill women to care for their young infants. A review of the procedures that were used, the information that was required and the decisions that were reached in this setting would provide a helpful basis for attempting a more systematic approach to the evaluation of maternal safety and competence. Finally, a follow-up is needed to ascertain what happens when mothers lose care and control of their infants and also when they do not. What is the outcome for mother and child?

Personal experience indicates that women who are most likely to be statutorily separated from their infants in the first few months are those with chronic schizophrenic illnesses, with substantial cognitive and social impairment and a lack of family and marital support. But what are the important and relevant prognostic factors for women who have less severe illnesses, episodic paranoid hallucinatory psychoses, schizo-affective disorders, bipolar illnesses or nonpsychotic disorders such as chronic depressions allied with personality problems, drug or alcohol abuse, or crippling phobias and obsessions?

The brief overview of the major syndromes which follows focuses on the ways in which disturbances of maternal behaviour may mediate problems in infants. It is assumed that the reader will bear in mind the points made earlier about the illnesses being only one part of all the adverse influences that may be brought into play.

Schizophrenia

One might expect that a mother with a chronic schizophrenic disorder in a severe paranoid hallucinatory or defect state would be unable to provide an optimal nurturing and responsive environment for her infant. The child may be exposed to the mother's blunted emotions, poverty or distortion of speech, avolition, or anhedonia on the one hand, or excesses such as hallucinations, delusions and bizarre behaviour on the other. The heterogeneous nature of the illness and its extensive influence on day-to-day functioning suggest that studies should focus on the effects of manifestations of particular constellations of problems. Studies, however, have generally failed to do so and this heterogeneity is reflected in research findings.

Schizophrenic mothers, for example, have been described as touching and playing less with their 4-month-old infants than a control sample of women (Garmezy, 1974), although separation from their infants during the acute phase of their illnesses may have contributed to the patterns of behaviour that were subsequently observed. Psychotic hospitalized mothers, particularly schizophrenics, have also been described as being more likely to perceive their infants as passive creatures and to interpret their cues, such as smiles, as 'accidental grimaces' compared with mothers in a control group (Cohler et al., 1970). By contrast, Schachter et al. (1977) observed schizophrenic mothers to be *more* responsive and affectionate, and to play more with their 14-month-old infants than did controls. All the participants in this study, however, were informed of the study's hypothesis, which may have differentially increased anxiety and motivation among the schizophrenic mothers to perform well.

McNeil et al. (1983) have carried out a major longitudinal study of infants of mothers with histories of various kinds of psychotic illnesses. They found consistently less social contact between schizophrenic mothers and their infants in com-parison with healthy mothers up to 6 months. Subsequently, at 1 year on a modified version of the Strange Situation Test (Ainsworth & Wittig, 1969; Näslund et al., 1984), these children were more likely to show anxious attachment and were less likely to be afraid of strangers. At 12 months, their mothers also displayed greater tension, and a higher frequency of vocal discrepancy (positive intonation combined with nega-tive content) in a feeding and play situation. By contrast, Sameroff et al. (1982) reported no difference in attachment security between infants of schizophrenic mothers and either those of mothers with nonpsychotic depression or personality disorder or those of healthy controls.

In addition to reports of the impact of maternal psycho-pathology on the child, McNeil and Kaij (1984) have suggested that the infants of mothers with schizophrenia may contribute to nonoptimal maternal behaviour as a result of being tem-peramentally more difficult and more reactive to stimulation. This suggestion is supported by the observation of Gamer et al. (1976), who reported that these infants were more inhibited. Similarly, Ragins et al. (1975) described infant characteristics such as less spontaneity and a lesser tendency to imitate, less responsivity to verbal stimulation and heightened distress to separation from the mother than healthy control infants. These studies, however, cannot disentangle the bidirectional effects of disturbed mother–infant interactions.

In a study which examined both cognitive and emotional development, Gamer et al. (1976) investigated outcome in 15 women who had been hospitalized in the puerperium. These investigators found that infants of mothers with schizophrenia tended to perform worst on tests of object constancy at age 1. They were also less likely to approach their mothers and interact positively with them after a brief separation, which, it could be argued, is suggestive of anxious attachment to the mother. These infants were, however, also more likely to have had multiple caretakers during the mother's illness. A similar study by Sobel (1961) reported that children who were fostered later manifested fewer behavioural and develop-mental problems than those who were reared at home, thus highlighting the significance of environmental factors in the transmission of psychopathology from parent to child.

A personal, unpublished investigation of 20 schizophrenic mothers admitted with their infants into a psychiatric unit (Kumar et al., 1993) has shown that 50% were separated from their infants at the point of discharge and some additional separations occurred later. Poor prognostic factors were the severity and duration of the illness prior to the pregnancy, the lack of supportive relationships (in particular from a stable partner or other family members) and the extent of maternal cognitive impairment. Thus, the results of studies of the mother–infant relationship in the context of schizophrenia must be interpreted with great caution because of the selection bias that may have operated, i.e. only a proportion of less severely disabled mothers who were able to sustain a maternal care-taking role may have been studied.

Manic-depressive disorder

There have been few investigations of the effects of bipolar illnesses on interactions between mothers and infants. As with schizophrenia, research methodology has had to contend with the heterogeneity of mothers' symptoms both within a group of individuals with the same diagnosis and within a specific clinical episode for any one person. The infant may be alternately or almost simultaneously exposed to an elated, hyperactive, overstimulating and/or distractible caregiver, or one who is inactive, apathetic, tearful and/or expressionless. The effects of this variability should again be borne in mind in an attempt to understand differences in research findings.

Gaensbauer *et al.* (1984) reported a study of 7 male infants and their mothers where 1 parent (4 mothers and 3 fathers) was known to have been suffering from a bipolar disorder. Davenport *et al.* (1984) described some additional important details about the parents; their illnesses were recurrent and severe. On average each of the parents had been hospitalized at least 4 times and the duration of the illnesses prior to the study ranged between 2 and 23 years. Five of the spouses of these patients had received a diagnosis of unipolar depression and 1 of substance abuse. Tests of mothers and infants were conducted in a laboratory setting at 12, 15 and 18 months of age and controls, who were matched for age, race and socio-economic status, were also studied. Free-play, structured interactions and a modified Strange Situation test were observed. The case infants were indistinguishable from the controls in their attachment behaviour at 12 months. However, at 15 and 18 months, they showed more avoidance of their mothers in the same procedure and tended to display more negative responses to their mothers during play. An association between parental bipolar illness and disturbance in the child's expression of emotion was also described by Zahn-Waxler *et al.* (1984). Using the same sample of 7, by now 2-year-old boys (see Gaensbauer *et al.*, 1984), these investigators described the children as being more likely to display aggression towards an unfamiliar adult and towards a playmate when the mother was absent, and were more likely to have difficulty engaging in friendly, sharing play with peers. These children were preoccupied with distress during others' conflicts and had little capacity for pleasure when the source of conflict had been removed.

In their slightly older sample of 2–3-year-olds of mothers with major affective illness, Radke-Yarrow *et al.* (1985) reported that insecure attachments were relatively frequent, particularly among children of mothers with bipolar disorder. The risk of insecure infant–mother attachment was not raised in families where the father was also depressed.

In contrast, similar measures of Swedish mothers (McNeil, 1988) with histories of affective psychosis (unipolar and bipolar combined) did not show any such differences from controls up to a year. Longer-term follow-up (McNeil, 1988) confirmed these findings; one reason for the different results may be that the Swedish mothers were less severely and less chronically ill than their American counterparts, with corre-spondingly less associated dysfunction in their family and social lives.

When clinical outcome was examined in our unpublished series (Kumar *et al.*, 1993) of 56 women with affective psychotic illnesses who were admitted following delivery into a psychiatric mother-and-baby unit, 20% of the infants were initially discharged into the care of someone other than the mother. All but 2 infants were eventually reunited with their mothers and for only 4 of the babies was it necessary for social services to go through formal procedures to protect the infants (at-risk registers, fostering, adoption or wardship proceedings). The relatively benign outcome of postpartum affective psychosis may be contrasted with the poor prognosis of maternal schizophrenia, which illness, in practically every case, was evident before conception and pregnancy.

Chronic depressive disorders

The only investigators to have separately examined and compared the impact of chronic versus 'pure' postnatal depression are Murray and her colleagues. Their findings will be discussed in the context of research into postnatal depression, below.

Obsessive-compulsive disorder and phobic anxiety states

Phobic symptoms are very common and disabling phobias are found in about 2% of adults (Agras *et al.*, 1969). Obsessive-compulsive disorder shows a similar pattern and is not as rare as was originally thought; prevalence rates between 0.1 and 2% have been reported following community surveys (Rasmussen & Eisen, 1990) and estimates vary depending on the methods for ascertaining cases and the periods under study (Marks, 1987). Rutter *et al.* (1970) found no cases of obsessive-compulsive disorder in their survey of 10–11-year-olds in the Isle of Wight. Yet rituals and superstitions are very common in children's play and day-to-day life (Gesell *et al.*, 1974). Is there any link between parental phobic or obsessional behaviour and child disorder? There do not seem to have been any systematic observational studies of mother–infant interaction and subsequent follow-up of such children in the context of obsessive-compulsive disorder, and clinical anecdotes give conflicting impressions. Marks (1987) commented that parents who suffer from severe obsessive-compulsive disorder may cease to look after their children and increase their emotional deprivation by bizarre physical restrictions. He cites an example of a 2-year-old boy who was cooped up in a play-pen all day lest he crawl into 'infected' areas. Despite this, Marks (1987) concluded that 'it is a tribute to their resilience that most children of obsessive compulsives who grow up in such abnormal environments have no obvious problems themselves'. On *a priori* grounds it would seem that the acquisition of obsessional symptoms would be facilitated by growing up in the presence of an obsessional parent. Yet it seems that when disturbing or disabling obsessional symptoms are seen in children they are usually part of some other condition such as autism.

Exactly how phobias are acquired is also obscure. Children's fears and phobias reflect maternal psychopathology, suggesting some degree of imitative learning (Windheuser, 1977). On the other hand, the repertoire of stimuli that is typically associated with phobic avoidance and obsessional rituals seems to reflect preparedness, that is, there is an element of biological advantage in avoiding crowds, heights, contamination etc. (de Silva *et al.*, 1977). Thus, interpretations of similarities between symptoms in parents and child in terms of imitative learning may be spurious. It may be worth looking for more general links: are phobic and obsessional symptoms more prevalent in the parents of children who are school refusers? Are there observable group differences in the way that mothers with obsessional and phobic disorders interact with and rear their infants?

Anorexia nervosa and bulimia nervosa

Apart from a number of case reports, the literature on the impact of maternal eating disorders on the fetus and infant is sparse. Evidence is mixed whether maternal symptoms diminish (Lacey & Smith, 1987) or worsen (Steward *et al.*, 1987) during pregnancy, but there is some suggestion that the infants may be at increased risk of intrauterine malnutrition and congenital abnormalities. It is not known, however, whether these infants are at risk in the long-term for impaired growth and its neurodevelopmental sequelae. A study reported by Lacey and Smith (1987) has raised concern that bulimic mothers may try to slim their infants down during the first year of life, despite their weights being in the normal range. This phenomenon, however, was observed in only 3 of the 20 mothers included in their study. Similarly, Woodside and Shekter-Wolfson (1990), in their sample of 12 mothers or fathers with anorexia or bulimia nervosa, described many examples of highly distorted parent–child relationships. Two of the parents had abandoned their children altogether as a result of their eating disorder, while in other families the children had become extremely involved in their parent's illness by cooking for them or dieting in response to parental weight loss. In some families the parent was wearing the children's clothes. Brinch *et al.* (1988) reported that 17% of a group of 50 mothers with a history of anorexia nervosa described their children as failing to thrive during the first year postpartum. However, the mothers were interviewed between 4 and 22 years after their children were born and these retrospective findings must be interpreted with caution, but other reports by van Wezel-Meijler and Wit (1989) and by Stein and Fairburn (1989) also raise concerns about inadequate child nutrition and care within their samples of eating-disordered mothers.

A controlled study using observational methods is currently being completed on the effects of maternal eating disorder psychopathology on the development of 1-year-old infants (Stein *et al.*, 1991b). Preliminary findings indicate that the index mothers expressed more negative emotion towards their infants during meals but not during play when compared with controls; however, there were no differences comparing cases and controls during either feed or play on measures of positive expressed emotion. The index mothers were more intrusive towards their infants during both meals and play when compared with controls. In addition, the infants of index mothers were lighter than those of controls; infant weight was related to the degree of conflict between mother and infant that was observed during meals and to the extent of the mother's concern about her shape. These findings are suggestive of some specificity in transmission of disturbance but further comparative research is needed, including groups with other parental psychiatric disturbance.

Substance abuse

Maternal substance abuse is associated with increased rates of complications during pregnancy, labour and delivery and is believed to have a wide range of effects on the fetus and infant which are dependent on the dose, timing and conditions of exposure (West, 1986). After delivery, these mothers have also been described as being at high risk for difficulties in parenting, including child neglect and abuse (Lawson & Wilson, 1979). However, it is still not possible to draw out the separate implications for the child of maternal abuse of, for example alcohol, during or after pregnancy due to the likely associations between alcohol consumption and maternal personality characteristics, physical and mental health, intelligence, social circumstances, multigenerational and/or multiple substance abuse, and the impact of being reared in a drug- or alcohol-seeking environment. It is clear that many kinds of psychological stressors are associated with the environments of children whose parents abuse drugs or alcohol, and it is particularly difficult to tease out the effects on the fetus from those occurring postnatally on the infant. A comprehensive and comparative review of adverse effects of different kinds of substance abuse is beyond the scope of this chapter and some of the main problems are illustrated by reference to selected studies of alcohol, opioid and cocaine abuse.

A longitudinal prospective study carried out in Sweden by Aronson *et al.* (1985) sheds some light on the risks involved for the fetus. The offspring of alcoholic mothers who had been reared by foster parents showed hyperactivity, inattention and poor motor skills, and were also found to have lower IQ scores than their controls despite showing no signs of fetal alcohol syndrome (Jones & Smith, 1973). Streissguth *et al.* (1984) reported that the 4-year-old children born to heavy drinkers displayed attention and reaction time abnormalities compared with children born to light and infrequent drinkers. Similar findings have been reported in several studies, although there is some discussion as to the existence of a threshold of safe exposure, or whether abnormalities of balance in particular are observed among 'social drinking' mothers (Streissguth *et al.*, 1984; Barr *et al.*, 1990). One of the few studies to have investigated the association between maternal alcohol abuse and the early infant—mother relationship is that carried out by O'Connor *et al.* (1987). In their sample of primiparous, middle-class mothers, an increase in attachment insecurity was observed among infants of moderate-to-heavy drinkers compared with the offspring of abstinent or light drinkers. Furthermore, no association was revealed between attachment classification and infant characteristics at birth or 1 year.

It is known that many infants who are prenatally exposed to opioids undergo some degree of withdrawal after delivery which may last up to 6 months and is manifested as irritability, high-pitched crying, tenseness of muscles, tremulousness, regurgitation (e.g. Kron *et al.*, 1975) and also rejection of their mothers' attempts to console them (Strauss *et al.*, 1975). Chasnoff and Griffith (1991) have also reported that cocaine-exposed neonates have low thresholds for overstimulation and significant difficulty with self-regulation when these thresholds are exceeded, which is likely to have far-reaching effects in a range of contexts if this difficulty continues over several years (Howard *et al.*, 1989). In the early postnatal period, therefore, such infant behaviours are likely to be primarily associated with problems in infant—caregiver interaction patterns. However, Jeremy and Bernstein (1984) reported no differences in patterns of mother—infant interaction between the 4-month-olds of mothers maintained on methadone during pregnancy compared with infants of control mothers. The mothers who abused drugs showed worse interaction and communication with their infants but this was related more to lack of current maternal resources than to drug use *per se*.

Studies concerned with the effects of drug abuse are beset by numerous methodological difficulties such as the confounding effects of nutritional deficits, concurrent infections, multiple drug use, differential effects of motivation and sample attrition, chaotic lifestyle of substance-abusing mothers and other mental health problems such as clinical depression and anxiety, or personality characteristics such as low tolerance to frustration and neediness for immediate gratification. It is therefore not possible to predict the developmental outcomes for these high-risk children until more is known about the additive and interactive effects of the multiple risk factors to which they are exposed.

IMPLICATIONS FOR THE INFANT OF PSYCHIATRIC DISORDERS THAT FOLLOW CHILDBIRTH

Postpartum psychosis

Acute psychotic breakdowns consistently occur after about 1 in 1000 births (Kendell *et al.*, 1987). These illnesses are predominantly affective in their symptomatology (Dean & Kendell, 1981; Brockington *et al.*, 1982; Meltzer & Kumar, 1985) and almost always necessitate admission of the mother to psychiatric hospital, which in the UK usually means joint admission with the baby (see the section on clinical management of mothers with psychosis, below). The illness is commonest in first-time mothers and it usually develops within 1—2 weeks of childbirth. Most mothers are able to leave hospital after stays of 1—3 months, and the prognosis in the medium term is excellent, with full recovery being the norm (Platz & Kendell, 1988). These disorders therefore offer an opportunity to study the impact of a severe perturbation of mother—infant interaction, limited to the early months of the child's life, albeit with the associated complications of admission to an institution. Comparisons may be possible with other settings such as in the US or Scandinavia where infants remain at home or are fostered while the mother is an in-patient. The results of such comparisons may have a major influence on the ways in which services for mentally ill mothers are organized and provided, because the incidence of postpartum psychosis appears to be broadly the same in whichever cultural and racial context the condition has been studied (Kumar, 1993).

Other issues relevant to the impact of postpartum psychoses on the infant and on the mother—infant relationship that can be investigated include the comparison of dyads and of infant development in which some mothers given selected psychotropic drugs continue to breast-feed and others are advised to bottle-feed. There is no clear rationale based on pharmacokinetics and on existing anecdotal knowledge of toxicological observations in infants, to make informed recommendations about whether or not it is safe to breast-feed while taking most psychotropic drugs (Buist *et al.*, 1990).

Brew and Seidenberg (1950), Margison (1982) and Tetlow (1955), among others, have observed the interactions of psychotic mothers with their infants, concluding that they are rejecting, inconsistent and hostile. Such reports would suggest that serious maternal mental disorder in the postpartum period is likely to raise the risk of the development of insecure infant—mother attachment as the conditions fostering healthy development are absent. Having said this, only two studies are known to have systematically investigated attachment security in the infants of mothers with postpartum psychosis: the Swedish longitudinal study (which used a modified Strange Situation procedure; Näslund *et al.*, 1984; McNeil *et al.*, 1988) and in the UK, the study by Hipwell (1992).

Näslund *et al.* (1984) showed that serious maternal mental disturbance during the infants' first year of life was not related to insecure infant—mother attachment. Indeed, among the group of mothers who were known to have been psychotic and clearly disturbed at this time, there was a tendency for the infants to be *more* likely to be classified as securely attached. However, it is likely that the modifications made to the procedure resulted in an unusually low proportion of insecure attachment classifications (D'Angelo, 1986). McNeil *et al.* (1988) reported no negative effects of maternal post-partum psychosis on infant emotional, social, cognitive or physical development compared with normal controls. Fewer infants of mothers with postpartum psychosis were reported by their mothers to have developmental problems at 6 months and at 6 years. In addition, fewer of these children had mental disorders, social difficulties or developmental delay than the offspring of mothers with a history of psychotic illness but no relapse during the first 12 months postpartum. The authors suggested that the physical separation of mother and child occurring as a result of the postpartum illness had a more positive effect on the child than being cared for by a mother with a history of psychotic illness but with no current symptoms in the postpartum period.

In a follow-up study of 27 mother–infant dyads who had been jointly admitted to a British mother-and-baby unit, Hipwell (1992) found that the type of attachment at 12 months was dependent on the nature of the mother's affective psychotic illness. Infants whose mothers had experienced a manic episode of illness were disproportionately represented by secure attachment classifications whereas infants whose mothers had been psychotically or nonpsychotically depressed (i.e. without any manic episodes) were more likely to have developed insecure attachment relationships with their mothers. The former group of mothers were observed to be more sensitive and appropriate in their interactions with their children at 1 year and were more positive in their attitudes towards their infants throughout the period of study than the depressed-only group of mothers. Although at 12 months postpartum, only one woman was assigned a psychiatric diagnosis of minor depression (Spitzer *et al.*, 1978), it is nevertheless possible that there were some underlying residual ideas of superiority and euphoria among the mothers who had had a manic episode of illness, which continued to influence their behaviour with, and attitudes towards, the child.

Postnatal depression

Postnatal depression (non-psychotic depression) is 100 times more common than postpartum psychosis. Many longitudinal studies, especially in primiparae, suggest that about 10% of such mothers become depressed in the first few weeks and months after delivery, who were not depressed before (Pitt, 1968; Kumar, 1982; O'Hara & Zekoski, 1988). There is currently a debate about whether many such women would have become depressed anyway, given the high annual period prevalence of depressive disorder in women of child-bearing age (Brown & Harris, 1978). Current opinion (Cooper *et al.*, 1988; J.L. Cox *et al.*, 1993) is that there is a rise in the rate of depression in the 3 months which follow delivery and that some at least of these depressions would not have occurred but for the destabilizing effects of childbirth. Of course the opposite may hold for some women, i.e. they are protected from depression because of having a child (Miller, 1989) — this kind of suggestion is supported by studies of suicide rates (Appleby, 1991) that indicate a lower rate in the year immediately after childbirth. Overall, however, increased rates of female depressive disorder generally, in comparison with men, can be ascribed mainly to child-bearing (Gater *et al.*, 1989; Bebbington *et al.*, 1991).

The importance for the infant of maternal depression was originally highlighted by Weissman *et al.* (1972) who pointed out that the cardinal symptoms of misery, apathy, irritability, agitation or retardation, social isolation and a failure to cope, when coloured by guilt about inadequacy as a mother, could all have a major bearing on the mother's relationship with her child. Indeed, there is now a substantial body of evidence to suggest that the interactions of depressed mothers with their infants compared with normal controls are less active, playful, decisive and responsive, with lower levels of warm acceptance of the child (Livingood *et al.*, 1983; Field, 1984; Field *et al.*, 1985; Persson-Blennow, 1986; Heptinstall *et al.*, 1987; Murray, 1988; see also a review by Downey & Coyne, 1990). However, Cohn *et al.* (1986) argued that depressed mothers could be divided into several quite distinct groups in terms of their interactions with their infants: (1) a pattern characterized by disengagement and apathy; (2) mothers who attempted to engage their babies but who were also highly intrusive and angry; and (3) mothers who related positively to their infants. Their results suggested that maternal disengagement was more distressing for the infant than the rough handling and intrusive behaviour of the second group. It is therefore clearly essential to take into account the way in which maternal depression is manifested and is thus experienced by the infant. The infants have been variously reported to be more drowsy, passive, less content, more distressed and fussy (Field *et al.*, 1985), to look at their mothers less and to engage in more self-directed activity than controls (Murray & Trevarthen, 1985). In a later study, Field *et al.* (1988) also suggested that not only did the infants' 'depressed' style of interacting generalize to their interactions with nondepressed strangers, but it also seemed to elicit depressedlike behaviour in the nondepressed adult.

Depressed mothers have also been found to describe their 3-month-old infants more often in critical and negative terms (Kumar & Robson, 1984) and several studies have now been reported in which mothers who are depressed describe difficulties themselves in relating with their children (Uddenberg & Nilsson, 1975) or that their children are more difficult (Wrate *et al.*, 1985; Caplan *et al.*, 1989). Finally, there are findings of cognitive impairment in such children (Cogill *et al.*, 1986; Hay & Kumar, submitted), aspects of which may be evident early on in measures of object constancy (Murray, 1992) and it is possible that the timing of the mother's depression may result in differences in the ways that the children are affected. One of the problems of longitudinal studies of the potential impact of postnatal depression is that such disorders are episodic and that it may be difficult to separate out the possible consequences of postnatal depression *per se* from effects of intervening or concurrent depression in the mother at the time of the follow-up assessment. Furthermore, depression is not 'all or nothing' and it is necessary to investigate associations with categorical diagnoses as well as with subclinical episodes of depressive symptoms (Wrate *et al.*, 1985).

In relation to this, Murray (1988) has suggested that the timing of the episode of depression was influential in the mother's behaviour: mothers who experienced depression before the birth of their first child were less deviant than those who experienced their first depression in the context of motherhood. In this study, the postnatally depressed mothers were more preoccupied with their own condition than their infant's, and used fewer interrogatives in interaction with their 3-month-old infants than either controls or previously depressed mothers. They were less likely to expand or extend the child's vocalizations in a child-centred way and were the only group who were controlling and overtly critical of their babies. The infants, in turn, were less alert, spent less time looking at their mothers and demonstrated more self-directed activity, even at this early stage.

LONG-TERM EFFECTS ON THE CHILD

Infants' coping responses to maternal depression may become persistent and continue after the mother has recovered and may extend to other people too. In this way, what was an effective pattern of adaptation to an environmental deficit becomes over-generalized or fixed. However, both maternal depression and child problems may be caused by preexisting conditions such as marital or family stress, and broad interpersonal processes in the lives of depressed mothers must be considered (Rutter, 1981). For example, the mother's own inadequate care as a child may have contributed to her current depression and, in fact, may have a greater influence on her own parenting abilities than her depressive illness *per se*. Studies have rarely accounted for comorbidity, and the influences of alcoholism, drug dependence and personality disorder in association with depression are often ignored. In fact, Rutter and Quinton (1984) suggested that family discord may be a greater risk factor than parental depression or personality disorder for emotional and behavioural disturbance in school-aged children.

Recent studies (Cogill *et al.*, 1986; A. Cox *et al.*, 1987; Stein *et al.*, 1991a; Hay & Kumar, submitted) have provided support for the hypothesis that early problems in patterns of mother–infant interaction may set in train a course of events which is not easily amenable to change. A. Cox *et al.* (1987) have shown that, even when the mother's depression remitted, the quality of the mother–child interaction and the child's behaviour problems did not improve over a 6-month follow-up. Stein *et al.* (1991a) have also reported that differences in the interactions with their children of 49 women with previous postpartum depression and 49 individually matched nondepressed controls could still be detected at 19 months postpartum. The mothers who had been depressed were observed to interact less, and facilitate the child's play less. In turn, their children were less likely to smile, talk and/or share toys during play, were less sociable towards strangers and were more likely to show marked distress during a brief separation from their mothers.

A longitudinal study of the impact of postnatal depression on infant cognitive, social and behavioural development assessed over the first 18 months postpartum has been carried out by Murray (1988, 1992). The children of mothers who had never been depressed before but who had become depressed after the birth ('pure' postnatal depression as opposed to women with histories of intermittent or chronic depression) were found to be slower to develop object constancy at both 9 and 18 months. This cognitive delay was found to be significantly related to the quality of the mother–infant relationship in the early postpartum weeks. General cognitive and language development did not appear to be affected but, in boys, postnatal depression was associated with a greater vulnerability to adverse effects of lower social class. This study also examined the quality of attachment between the mother and her 18-month-old child using the Strange Situation procedure (Ainsworth & Wittig, 1969). The infants of postnatally depressed women were found to be more insecurely attached to their mothers than were infants of healthy control mothers and those whose depressive episode had only been before childbirth.

Longitudinal studies that have followed mothers from pregnancy or parturition until the children are 3 or 4 years old have provided useful but often conflicting evidence relating to the mechanisms of developmental disorder (Uddenberg & Englesson, 1978; Sameroff *et al.*, 1982; Ghodsian *et al.*, 1984). In most instances, behavioural disturbance in the child has been most strongly associated with concurrent depression. Wrate *et al.* (1985) found that 3-year-old children whose mothers had had a brief and mild depressive episode postpartum showed more behavioural disturbance than did controls. Perhaps more importantly, these mothers were also characterized as having been more anxious about their children.

A study by Kumar and colleagues (Cogill *et al.*, 1986) followed up a cohort of mothers previously investigated by Kumar and Robson (1984) and showed that maternal depression at some time in the first year after delivery was associated with poorer performance on the McCarthy Scale of Children's Abilities when the children were 4 years old, whereas concurrent depression had no effect. Lower scores were independently linked to marital conflict, socioeconomic disadvantage and a history of paternal psychiatric problems. These findings suggest that these adverse family factors may have direct effects on the child as well as indirectly via their effects on the mother's mental health. Behavioural disturbance in the children at age 4 was also associated with lower scores on the McCarthy Scales (Caplan *et al.*, 1989). Preliminary results from a recent follow-up study (Pawlby *et al.*, 1992; Sharp *et al.*, 1992) provide a partial replication of these findings and, in addition, indicate that boys more than girls are likely to show cognitive and behavioural disturbances. Four-year-old girls of mothers who were postnatally depressed showed patterns of submissive interaction but no cognitive impairment.

INFANTICIDE

The literature on mothers who kill their babies has been reviewed by Margison (1982) and by Kumar and Marks

(1992). In English law (Bluglass, 1978, 1990) infanticide is treated as manslaughter provided that the act occurs within the first year after delivery and that it can be shown that the balance of the mother's mind was disturbed by reason of her not having fully recovered from the effect of giving birth to the child, or by reason of the effect of lactation consequent upon the birth of the child. A number of surveys (see reviews by Margison, 1982; Kumar & Marks, 1992) point to the presence of psychiatric disorder in a proportion of such mothers, most commonly depression with associated suicidal ideation (D'Orban, 1979; West, 1965), and, more rarely, schizophrenia (Gregger & Hoffmeyer, 1969; DaSilva & Johnstone, 1981). Women with manic illnesses may also place their children at extreme risk, for example through the belief that they have supernatural powers (Margison, 1982). Some women may be tortured by obsessional impulses to harm their infants (Chapman, 1959) but in keeping with this condition they rarely act on their impulses. There are no clear guidelines for assessing risk, and Margison advocates paying particular attention to mothers with a previous history of violent behaviour. Other empirically important warning signs are the presence of delusions that are nihilistic or that the child is possessed or has unusual and supernatural powers. However, many mothers with such beliefs do not harm their infants and it is not yet possible to pick out in advance the tragic few who do.

The important study by D'Orban (1979) showed that less than a third of women who were charged with killing their infants were definitely mentally ill at the time. Minor psychiatric symptoms such as depression, irritability, exhaustion and apathy were present in about 50% of women categorized as 'batterers' or those who had killed the child either as retaliation against the spouse or because it was unwanted. The great majority of women who had committed neonaticide, i.e. killed the child in the first day, were free of any such symptoms.

A survey of infant homicides in England and Wales in the years 1982–1988 (Marks & Kumar, 1993) has shown that the first year of life is the time when one is most at risk of being murdered; this risk is four times greater than the risk for the population as a whole and the perpetrator is almost always a parent. The first day is the time of maximum risk, when about 20% of all infant homicides occur and virtually all are at the hands of the mother. Aside from observations such as those of D'Orban (1979), there has been very little systematic research into parental psychopathology and different kinds of infant homicide, such as battering, retaliatory, altruistic, mentally ill, neonaticide (D'Orban, 1979), or indeed into the validity of such categorizations, or others based on motive (Resnick, 1969) or source of impulse (Scott, 1973). Very little is known about the possible mechanisms underlying neonaticide. Is it related to concealment and denial of the pregnancy? Is it a consequence of a severe disorder of mother–infant attachment? Is it planned or impulsive? Does it recur after subsequent pregnancies? What is the underlying maternal personality like?

The Infanticide Act in England, passed in 1938, is a very special form of humanitarian legislation, originally designed to protect women from the death penalty for murder on the grounds of diminished responsibility arising out of the (physiological) upheavals of childbirth. Most infant homicides do not occur in the context of severe mental illness and fathers are as likely as mothers to murder babies older than a day. Even when similarly violent or wounding offences are compared, most men are sentenced to prison and most women are placed on probation. This is the picture in England and Wales (Marks & Kumar, 1993) and probably in the UK and in some Commonwealth countries. There do not seem to have been any reports of investigations that have compared homicidal mothers with fathers who have killed infants, to try to identify similarities or differences in factors which associate with risk to infants. Women who kill their infants are treated differently in different countries and much may be learned by comparing rates of infant homicides if reliable statistics are available (Cristoffel, 1990; Daly & Wilson, 1988). In the US there is no comparable legislation to the Infanticide Act and there are variations between states in the ways in which women who kill their infants are prosecuted and sentenced. It is not uncommon for women to be serving prison sentences of 8–10 years for offences they are unlikely ever to commit again. However, we know very little about recidivism or about long-term sequelae for such women or for the rest of their families.

CLINICAL MANAGEMENT OF MOTHERS WITH PSYCHOSIS: JOINT ADMISSION OF MOTHERS AND BABIES

Admission of a mother to a psychiatric hospital may mean separation from her infant at a time when their relationship is starting to develop. Prolonged separation of mothers and children is believed to be detrimental to the psychological development of the child as well as to the ongoing process of attachment (Bowlby, 1977). With this rationale, the practice of joint mother-and-infant admissions has become more widespread (Buist et al., 1990; Margison, 1990), especially in the UK since it was first proposed by Main (1948). A number of studies carried out over the last 30 years have provided support for the feasibility of specialized mother-and-baby units in as much as the burden on nursing staff is manageable, there is no clearly increased risk of physical injury to the child and there appears to be no adverse effect on the mental health of the mother.

Baker et al. (1961) reported that joint admission of mothers and babies resulted in shorter hospital stays, lower relapse rates and a greater likelihood of the mother adequately caring for her child. However, these findings have not always been supported by other studies (Glaser, 1962; Bardon et al., 1968; Stewart, 1989). Nevertheless, it is generally accepted that the mother's recovery is hastened by the practice of joint admission, either as a result of the continued contact with her infant and the associated confidence in her role as a mother or the particularly supportive and structured environment which is created by grouping women together with similar illnesses. The mother may learn by direct observation of other adult–infant interactions how to care for and play with her baby. Destructive, ambivalent and guilty feelings, obsessional thoughts and misinterpretations can be detected by staff and dealt with promptly. Joint admission may also facilitate attachment by allowing breast-feeding for infants whose mothers are taking certain psychotropic drugs. Mothers who become ill as a result of environmental difficulties but with no obvious problem in their feelings for their baby will also benefit from joint admission by the very fact that separation from the child and the ensuing effects on their relationship will only add to the crises that brought them into hospital.

However, assessing the positive value of joint admission is complicated by variations in admission criteria between units. Systematic studies have yet to test the validity of claims about the benefits for the mother or, even more surprisingly, for the developing child. In the latter case, another methodological puzzle presents itself. In an attempt to ascertain the potential advantages and disadvantages for the infant of joint admission with a psychotic mother, how can one separate out the effects of the mother's illness from the fact that the pair have been placed in an institution with the influences of multiple caretakers or risks from other patients in addition to the child's own mother?

A feature of mother-and-baby units, like that of neonatal intensive care units, is that care-taking is carried out by a large number of different people not all of whom are able to learn individual characteristics of a particular baby; their interventions, therefore, may not always be sensitive to the infant's current mood or activity and may interfere with the normal development of infant self-regulation (Minde & Benoit, 1991). Grunebaum *et al.* (1975) described a study which compared 7 infants of mentally ill mothers who were jointly admitted to hospital, 7 babies of mentally ill mothers not treated in hospital, and 14 babies of normal mothers. It was revealed that while the social development of the children in the former two groups was judged to be impaired at 18 months compared with controls, the 'joint admission' children attained markedly higher developmental quotients than the other groups, mainly as a result of higher scores on active language development. The authors suggested that the infant's experience of multiple caretakers and heightened and varied environmental stimulation in the hospital proved to be beneficial to cognitive development at this time. On the other hand, a number of studies do suggest that there are adverse effects of multiple care-giving on interpersonal development. For example, Provence and Lipton (1962) noted the impaired social responsiveness of institutionally reared babies. Even in an institution with quite good levels of social stimulation, A. Stevens (unpublished data) reported that the dispersion of care among a large number of caretakers seemed to delay the development of important attachment relationships.

A number of factors may further heighten the risk of maladaptation of infants whose mothers become psychotic in the puerperium. These include the mother's own difficulties in establishing patterns of mutually responsive interaction with her infant due to heavy sedation from antipsychotic drugs; discontinuation of breast-feeding; and some degree of limited access to the baby as a result of staff concerns about safety and competence of care. Another important consideration which will indirectly affect the mother and infant's long-term outcome is the impact of their joint admission on the quality of the marital or familial relationship (Harvey & McGrath, 1988; Lovestone & Kumar, 1993), the concerns felt by the family about the baby's safety and the difficulty that the partner/father may experience in getting to know the newborn.

Assessment of risk for the infant must be the most important consideration in the provision of joint care. In community-based samples, researchers have repeatedly tried to identify factors arising before and after childbirth that could indicate mothers who are at high risk for child abuse or neglect. In one of the few prospective studies carried out, Gray *et al.* (1979) identified a very large range of maternal characteristics and social problems potentially associated with risk for the child. Systematic measures of current and future risk among inpatient populations of mentally ill mothers and their infants, however, remain to be defined. A detailed psychiatric history would go some way to raising awareness about the functioning of particular patients who have shown violent or impulsive behaviour in the past or who have experienced command hallucinations or persecutory delusions. A measure that could formally assess characteristics such as maternal motivation and competence to care safely for the infant both during psychiatric illness and after remission of symptoms in an acute episode would clearly be invaluable from a clinical point of view. Preliminary analyses suggest that the Bethlem Mother–infant Interaction Scale devised on a specialized mother-and-baby unit may be useful in predicting care-giving difficulties from observations in the early weeks of joint admission (Kumar, 1986; Hipwell *et al.*, 1990). Simmonds (1991) emphasizes, however, that measures intended to assess risk should only be a part of the decision-making process of experts and that their routine use could clearly have serious consequences where false negatives or positives occur.

Joint care thus poses a number of specific problems such as assessment of risk, regulation of access and support in developing an appropriate mother–infant relationship. The practice of domiciliary care of carefully selected severely depressed or manic mothers has recently been shown to be a viable alternative to admission to a mother-and-baby unit (Oates, 1988). In this study, the women were managed at home if they were free from active suicidal or infanticidal ideas, lived within reach of the base hospital in case of emergency, and were not living alone and had the support of family and friends. The minimal disruption to the family, the individuality of care provided by the community nurse, encouraging maternal self-confidence and autonomy in her own home, were described as particular benefits of this type of management. No major difference in the clinical recoveries of 17 patients who had been admitted previously with an episode of puerperal psychosis was reported, although these women felt their recovery had been faster when managed at home.

Clinical management of mothers with nonpsychotic disorders

The vast majority of child-bearing women with mental disorders do not come to the attention of psychiatric services. Epidemiological and case register studies (Nott, 1982; Oates, 1989) have demonstrated contact rates between 4 and 15 per 1000 deliveries, of which about 2 per 1000 represent admissions (Meltzer & Kumar, 1985; Kendell *et al.*, 1987). The prevalence of depression after childbirth is at least 10% and therefore, about 90% of depressed mothers remain exclusively under the care of their family doctors. To this number may be added cases of other preexisting nonpsychotic disorders such as phobias and obsessive-compulsive disorders, many of which may also not have been referred for specialist assessment and treatment. The majority of postnatal depressions are self-limiting and resolve within 6 months but, for about a quarter of those affected, childbirth marks the beginning of chronic and persistent depression (Pitt, 1968; Watson *et al.*, 1984), and for a similar proportion, the start of recurrent, remitting and relapsing depressive disorder (Kumar & Robson, 1984). Studies of child-bearing women in the community have shown that about half of those meeting operational clinical criteria for 'caseness' remain undetected by family doctors (Kumar & Robson, 1984; Sharp, 1992) or by health visitors (Briscoe, 1986).

The first priority therefore is to improve the detection of women with nonpsychotic postnatal psychiatric disturbances and a very significant step in this direction has been made by the development of screening questionnaires such as the Edinburgh Postnatal Depression Scale (J.L. Cox *et al.*, 1987). Such methods, allied with the introduction of systematic psychiatric liaison for obstetrics (Appleby *et al.*, 1988; J.L. Cox *et al.*, 1992), may greatly improve detection rates. However, an essential next step is to develop indices that will help in picking out women most in need of interventions such as counselling (Holden *et al.*, 1989), pharmacotherapy (Henderson *et al.*, 1991) or measures specifically targeted at improving the quality of interaction between mother and infant (Murray, 1992).

The childbirth experience in the present context is best summarized as reflecting *discontinuities* of care. As the mother passes from family doctor to student midwife or to junior obstetricians for subsequent antenatal visits, then meets new faces in the delivery suite and subsequently in the postnatal ward where she must undergo checks from obstetricians and paediatricians before leaving hospital to go back into the care of the community midwives, health visitors and her family doctor, it is not surprising that changes in her mental state are missed. Even when vigorous attempts are made to detect women at risk, or those already suffering with psychiatric

problems in antenatal clinics and postnatal wards (Appleby *et al.*, 1988), a significant proportion — nearly 30% — fail to keep clinic appointments. It is possible that many such non-attenders are also the most needy; they may be overwhelmed by the problems of coping with other small children without support from their partners or others and cannot contemplate travelling to a hospital clinic while feeling depressed and run down with an infant and toddlers in tow. There is a need for a coordinated policy of care based upon links between hospital and community primary health care services, social services and voluntary agencies. Such resources, to be effective, must also be capable of being delivered at home and the contribution of child psychiatrists to the development and shaping of these services seems indispensable.

From a practical, clinical perspective the prevention of possible harm to the child begins in pregnancy and depends upon effective liaison. The checklist of questions that follows in Table 44.1, is intended as an *aide-mémoire* — it is neither comprehensive, nor are all the items relevant to every patient. It has been prepared in the hope that going through such a list and acting upon the information available or lack of it may obviate some of the crises that occur on postnatal wards or at home after discharge from the obstetric unit.

CONCLUSIONS

A review of the current literature on maternal psychiatric illness and child adjustment and development is complicated by the diversity of questions asked and methods used. The merits and drawbacks of a variety of procedures to assess mother–infant interaction are discussed by Melhuish *et al.* (1988), who conclude that an integration of methods is essential for future research and clinical practice. Ideally, highly detailed observations of short duration which describe the interactive roles and behaviours of mother and infant should be combined with longer observations in naturalistic settings that provide a more typical, though global, account. Such systematic assessments in the early postpartum months may then be placed in the context of long-term, longitudinal investigations of developmental outcome for the child and its network of relationships.

Despite the very considerable advantages of longitudinal research designs (see reviews in Rutter, 1988), it is surprising how little research has been carried out along the lines described by Melhuish *et al.* (1988). Much of the recent effort has been directed at investigations of putative consequences of maternal depressive disorders and the results have already been fruitful in generating strategies for early detection of maternal psychopathology (J.L. Cox *et al.*, 1987) and, eventually, prevention of adverse effects in infants (Murray, 1992). Similar investigations of phobic and obsessional parents and their children remain to be carried out and systematic longitudinal studies are underway into eating disorders. There is a dearth of longitudinal studies of children of psychotic parents and it is therefore difficult at this stage to do more than speculate about the potential risk to the infant

Table 44.1 Some questions to ask when a woman with a history of mental illness becomes pregnant and decides to keep the baby

Pregnancy

Antenatal clinic	Has she booked in?
	Do obstetricians and midwives know of her psychiatric history?
Family doctor, health visitor, and psychiatrist	Do they know she is pregnant?
	Have they seen her recently?
Social services	Is a planning meeting necessary to discuss possible concerns about child protection?
	Does she need counselling and practical help, e.g. about housing?
	Does she need an allocated social worker?
Medication	Has it been reviewed since her pregnancy became known?

Labour, delivery and early puerperium

Admission	Will she see staff she has met before?
	Is there a contact number for the liaison psychiatrist?
	Have arrangements been made, if needed, to call upon a psychiatric nurse to 'special' her, after delivery?
	Do the obstetric and paediatric teams know what medication she is taking?
Postnatal management	Is the baby staying with her or in a nursery?
	How long is the planned stay on the postnatal ward and where is she going from there?
	Has an assessment by a psychiatrist been organized?
	Are social services convening a child protection conference, and have they got all the relevant clinical data?
Discharge separately from baby	If she is being separated from the baby, has she been prepared for this and does she know her rights?
	What part are her partner and her family playing?
	Where is she going, and do receiving staff know about her needs?
	Who will organize access to the baby?
Discharge with baby	What level of supervision, if any, is needed?
	Have social services assessed her need for facilities such as day nursery, home help, etc.?
	Who will organize reviews of the child's welfare and what information is required for such reviews?
	Who is responsible for the mother's clinical management?

from a disturbed mother through impulse or neglect within the context of a given illness, the mother's personal characteristics and her previous and current social background. In fact, across all types of maternal psychiatric disorders, some knowledge of the sorts of parent—infant interactions that carry the most serious risks for the child is urgently needed. Decisions about care and custody of infants may become easier to make if there is eventually a well-documented set of narrative and semisystematic observations of series of infants and their families. One way of selecting families for investigation might be if either parent of an infant aged less than a year was in contact with psychiatric or with social services during the first postnatal year or previously during the pregnancy. Such a database might also greatly facilitate the setting up of more focused longitudinal research into the detection and prevention of different sources and forms of risk to the developing infant and child.

REFERENCES

Agras W.S., Sylvester D. & Oliveau D. (1969) The epidemiology of common fears and phobias. *Comprehensive Psychiatry*, **10**, 151—156.

Ainsworth M.D.S. & Wittig B.A. (1969) Attachment and exploratory behaviour of 1-year-olds in a strange situation. In: Foss B.M. (ed) *Determinants of Infant Behaviour*, Vol. 4. Methuen, London.

Appleby L. (1991) Suicide during pregnancy and the first postnatal year. *British Medical Journal*, **302**, 137—140.

Appleby L., Fox H., Shaw M. & Kumar R. (1988) The psychiatrist in the obstetric unit: establishing a liaison service. *British Journal of Psychiatry*, **154**, 510—515.

Aronson M., Kyllerman M., Sabel K.G., Sandin B. & Olegard R. (1985) Children of alcoholic mothers: developmental, perceptual, and behavioural characteristics as compared to matched controls. *Acta Paediatrica Scandinavica*, **74**, 27—35.

Bakeman R. & Brown J.V. (1980) Early interaction: consequences for social and mental development at 3 years. *Child Development*, **51**, 437—447.

Baker A.A., Morison M., Game J.A. & Thorpe J.G. (1961) Admitting schizophrenic mothers with their babies. *Lancet*, **2**, 237—239.

Bardon D., Glaser Y., Protheroe D. & Weston D.H. (1968) Mother and baby unit. Psychiatric survey of 115 cases. *British Medical Journal*, **ii**, 755—758.

Barr H.M., Streissguth A.P., Darby B.L. & Simpson P.D. (1990) Prenatal exposure to alcohol, caffeine, tobacco, and aspirin: effects on fine and gross motor performance in 4-year-old children. *Developmental Psychology*, **26**, 339—348.

Bebbington P.E., Tennant C. & Harry J. (1991) Gender, parity and the prevalence of minor affective disorder. *British Journal of Psychiatry*, **158**, 40—45.

Bentovim A. (1991) Significant harm in context. In: Adcock M., White R. & Hollows A. (eds) *Significant Harm: Its Management and Outcome*, pp. 125—135. Significant Publications, Croydon.

Bluglass R. (1978) Infanticide. *Bulletin of the Royal College of Psychiatrists*, **2**, 130—141.

Bluglass R. (1990) Infanticide and filicide. In: Bluglass R. & Bowden P. (eds) *Principles and Practice of Forensic Psychiatry*, pp. 523—528. Churchill Livingstone, Edinburgh.

Bowlby J. (1977) The making and breaking of affectional bonds: I, Aetiology and psychopathology in the light of attachment theory. *British Journal of Psychiatry*, **130**, 201—210.

Brazelton T.B., Tronick E.Z., Adamson L., Als H. & Wise S. (1975) Early mother−infant interaction. In: Hofer M. (ed) *Parent−Infant Interaction*, pp. 137−154. Elsevier, Amsterdam.

Brew M.F. & Seidenberg R. (1950) Psychotic reactions associated with pregnancy and childbirth. *Journal of Nervous and Mental Diseases*, **111**, 408−423.

Brinch M., Isager T. & Tolstrup K. (1988) Anorexia nervosa and motherhood: reproduction pattern and mothering behaviour of 50 women. *Acta Psychiatrica Scandinavica*, **77**, 611−617.

Briscoe M. (1986) Identification of emotional problems in postpartum women by health visitors. *British Journal of Psychiatry*, **292**, 1245−1247.

Brockington I.F., Winokur G. & Dean C. (1982) Puerperal psychosis. In: Brockington I.F. & Kumar R. (eds) *Motherhood and Mental Illness*, pp. 37−69. Butterworth, Cambridge.

Brown G.W. (1988) Causal paths, chains and strands. In: Rutter M. (ed) *Studies of Psychosocial Risk: The Power of Longitudinal Data*, pp. 285−314. Cambridge University Press, Cambridge.

Brown G.W. & Harris T. (1978) *Social Origins of Depression*. Free Press, New York.

Buist A.E., Norman T.R. & Dennerstein L. (1990a) Breastfeeding and the use of psychotropic medication: a review. *Journal of Affective Disorders*, **19**, 197−206.

Buist A.E., Dennerstein L. & Burrows G.D. (1990b) Review of a mother−baby unit in a psychiatric hospital. *Australian and New Zealand Journal of Psychiatry*, **24**, 103−108.

Butler Committee (1975) *Report of the Committee on Mentally Abnormal Offenders*. (Chairman: Lord Butler of Saffron Malden.) Cmnd 6244. Her Majesty's Stationery Office, London.

Caplan H.L., Cogill S.R., Alexandra H., Robson K.M., Katz R. & Kumar R. (1989) Maternal depression and the emotional development of the child. *British Journal of Psychiatry*, **154**, 818−822.

Chapman A.H. (1959) Obsessions of infanticide. *Archives of General Psychiatry*, **1**, 28−31.

Chasnoff I.J. & Griffith D.R. (1991) Maternal cocaine use: neonatal outcome. In: Fitzgerald H. & Lester B. (eds) *Theory and Research in Behavioral Pediatrics*, vol. 5, pp. 1−17. Plenum Press, New York.

Cogill S.R., Caplan H.L., Alexandra H., Robson K.M. & Kumar R. (1986) Impact of maternal postnatal depression on cognitive development of young children. *British Medical Journal*, **292**, 1165−1167.

Cohler B.J., Weiss J. & Grunebaum H. (1970) Child-care attitudes and emotional disturbances in mothers of young children. *Genetic Psychological Monographs*, **82**, 3−47.

Cohn J.F. & Tronick E.Z. (1987) Mother−infant interaction: the sequence of dyadic states at 3, 6, and 9 months. *Child Development*, **54**, 185−193.

Cohn J.F., Matias R., Tronick E.Z., Connell D. & Lyons-Ruth K. (1986) Face-to-face interactions of depressed mothers and their infants. In: Tronick E.Z. & Field T. (eds) *Maternal Depression and Infant Disturbance*. New Directions for Child Development, no. 34, pp. 31−45. Jossey-Bass, San Francisco, CA.

Cooper P.J., Campbell E.A., Day A., Kennerly H. & Bond A. (1988) Non-psychotic psychiatric disorder after childbirth: a prospective study of prevalence, incidence, course and nature. *British Journal of Psychiatry*, **152**, 799−806.

Cox A., Puckering C., Pound A. & Mills M. (1987) The impact of maternal depression in young children. *Journal of Child Psychology and Psychiatry*, **28**, 917−928.

Cox J.L., Holden J.M. & Sagovsky R. (1987) Detection of Postnatal depression: development of the Edinburgh Postnatal Depression Scale. *British Journal of Psychiatry*, **150**, 782−786.

Cox J.L., Kumar R., Oates M., Foreman D. & Anderson H. (1992) Report of the General Psychiatry Section working party in postnatal mental illness. *Psychiatric Bulletin of the Royal College of Psychiatrists*, **16**, 519−522.

Cox J.L., Murray D. & Chapman G. (1993) A controlled study of the onset, duration and prevalence of postnatal depression. *British Journal of Psychiatry*, **163**, 27−31.

Cristoffel K.K. (1990) Violent death and injury in US children and adolescents. *American Journal of Diseases of Children*, **144**, 697−706.

Daly M. & Wilson W. (1988) *Homicide*. Aldine de Gruyter, New York.

D'Angelo E.J. (1986) Security of attachment in infants with schizophrenic, depressed and unaffected mothers. *Journal of Genetic Psychology*, **147**, 421−422.

DaSilva L. & Johnstone E.C. (1981) A follow-up study of severe puerperal psychiatric illness. *British Journal of Psychiatry*, **139**, 346−354.

Davenport Y.B., Zahn-Waxler C., Adland M. & Mayfield A. (1984) Early child-rearing practices in families with a manic-depressive parent. *American Journal of Psychiatry*, **141**, 230−235.

Dean C. & Kendell R.E. (1981) The symptomatology of puerperal illnesses. *British Journal of Psychiatry*, **139**, 128−133.

de Silva P., Rachman S. & Seligman M.E.P. (1977) Prepared phobias and obsessions: therapeutic outcome. *Behaviour Research and Therapy*, **15**, 65−77.

D'Orban P.T. (1979) Women who kill their children. *British Journal of Psychiatry*, **134**, 560−571.

Downey G. & Coyne J.C. (1990) Children of depressed parents: an integrative review. *Psychological Bulletin*, **108**(1), 50−76.

Field T.M. (1984) Early interactions between infants and their postpartum depressed mothers. *Infant Behaviour and Development*, **7**, 517−522.

Field T.M., Dempsey J. & Shuman H.H. (1983) Five-year follow-up of preterm respiratory distress syndrome and postterm postmaturity syndrome infants. In: Field T. & Sostek A. (eds) *Infants Born at Risk: Physiological, Perceptual, and Cognitive Processes*. Grune & Stratton, New York.

Field T., Sandberg D., Garcia R., Veg-Lahr N., Goldstein S. & Guy L. (1985) Pregnancy problems, postpartum depression, and early mother−infant interactions. *Developmental Psychology*, **21**, 1152−1156.

Field T.M., Heal B., Goldstein S., Perry S., Schanberg S., Zimmerman E. & Kuhn C. (1988) Infants of depressed mothers show 'depressed' behavior even with nondepressed adults. *Child Development*, **59**, 1569−1579.

Gaensbauer T.J., Harmon R.J., Cytryn L. & McKnew D.H. (1984) Social and affective development in infants with a manic-depressive parent. *American Journal of Psychiatry*, **141**, 223−229.

Gamer E., Gallant D. & Grunebaum H.U. (1976) Children of psychotic mothers. *Archives of General Psychiatry*, **33**, 311−317.

Garmezy N. (1974) Children at risk: the search for the antecedents of schizophrenia. Part II: Ongoing research programmes and intervention. *Schizophrenia Bulletin*, **9**, 55−125.

Gater R.A., Dean C. & Morris J. (1989) The contribution of childbearing to the sex difference in the first admission rates for affective psychosis. *Psychological Medicine*, **19**, 719−724.

Gesell A., Ile F.L. & Ames L.B. (1974) *Infant and Child in the Culture of Today*. Harper & Row, New York.

Ghodsian M., Zajicek E. & Wolkind S. (1984) A longitudinal study of maternal depression and child behaviour problems. *Journal of Child Psychology and Psychiatry*, **23**(1), 91−109.

Glaser Y.I.M. (1962) A unit for mothers and babies in a psychiatric hospital. *Journal of Child Psychology and Psychiatry*, **3**, 53−60.

Gray J.D., Cutler C., Dean J. & Kempe C.H. (1979) Prediction and prevention of child abuse. *Seminars in Perinatology*, **3**, 85−90.

Gregger J. & Hoffmeyer O. (1969) Murder of several children by schizophrenic mothers. *Psychiatrica Clinica*, **2**, 14−24.

Grunebaum H.U., Weiss J.L., Cohler B.J., Hartman C.R. & Gallant D.H. (1975) *Mentally Ill Mothers and their Children*. University of Chicago, Chicago, IL.

Harvey I. & McGrath G. (1988) Psychiatric morbidity in spouses of women admitted to a mother and baby unit. *British Journal of Psychiatry*, **152**, 506–510.

Hawkins D.F. (1983) *Drugs and Pregnancy — Human Teratogenesis and Related Problems*. Churchill Livingstone, Edinburgh.

Hay D. & Kumar R. (1993) Developmental specificity of the impact of maternal depression on intellectual development: a reanalysis and test of competing hypotheses. (Submitted.)

Henderson A.F., Gregoire A.J.P., Kumar R. & Studd J.W.W. (1991) Treatment of severe postnatal depression with oestradiol skin patches. *Lancet*, **338**, 816–817.

Heptinstall E., Puckering C., Skuse D., Start K., Dowdney L. & Zurszpiro S. (1987) Nutrition and mealtime behaviour in families of growth retarded children. *Human Nutrition: Applied Nutrition*, **41**, 390–402.

Hipwell A.E. (1992) Postpartum maternal mental illness and the psychological development of the infant. PhD thesis, University of London.

Hipwell A.E., Kumar R. & Melhuish E. (1990) Mental illness and mother–infant interaction. Paper presented at 5th International Conference of Marcé Society, York, England.

Holden J., Sagovsky R. & Cox J.L. (1989) Counselling in a general practice setting: controlled study of health visitor intervention in treatment of postnatal depression. *British Medical Journal*, **298**, 223–226.

Howard J., Beckwith L., Rodning C. & Kropenske V. (1989) The development of young children of substance-abusing parents: insights from 7 years of intervention and research. *Zero to Three*, **9**, 8–12.

Jeremy R.J. & Bernstein V.J. (1984) Dyads at risk: methadone-maintained women and their 4-month-old infants. *Child Development*, **55**, 1141–1154.

Jones K.L. & Smith D.W. (1973) Recognition of the fetal alcohol syndrome in early infancy. *Lancet*, **2**, 999–1001.

Kendell R.E., Chalmers J.C. & Platz C. (1987) Epidemiology of puerperal psychoses. *British Journal of Psychiatry*, **150**, 662–673.

Kron R.E., Kaplan S.L., Finnegan L.P., Litt M. & Phoenix M.D. (1975) An assessment of the behavioural change in infants undergoing narcotic withdrawal: comparative data from clinical and objective methods. *Addictive Diseases*, **2**, 257–275.

Kumar R. (1982) Neurotic disorders in childbearing women. In: Brockington I.F. & Kumar R. (eds) *Motherhood and Mental Illness*. Academic Press, London.

Kumar R. (1986) Postpartum mental illness: a method for assessment of mother–infant interaction. In Cox J.L., Kumar R., Margison F.R. & Downey L.J. (eds) *Puerperal Mental Illness*, pp. 44–56, Duphar, Southampton.

Kumar R. (1992) Mentally ill mothers and their babies: what are the benefits and risks of joint hospital admission? In: Cowen P.J. & Hawton K. (eds) *Practical Problems in Psychiatry: Some Clinical Guidelines*, pp. 184–197. Oxford University Press, Oxford.

Kumar R. (1993) Postnatal mental illness: a transcultural perspective (submitted).

Kumar R. & Marks M. (1992) Infanticide and the law in England and Wales. In: Hamilton J.A. & Harberger P.N. (eds) *Postpartum Psychiatric Illness: A Picture Puzzle*, pp. 256–273. University of Pennsylvania Press, Philadelphia, PA.

Kumar R. & Robson K.M. (1984) A prospective study of emotional disorders in childbearing women. *British Journal of Psychiatry*, **144**, 35–47.

Kumar R., Platz C. & Yoshida K. (1993) Clinical audit of 100 consecutive admissions to a psychiatric mother and baby unit. (submitted).

Lacey H.J. & Smith G. (1987) Bulimia nervosa: the impact of pregnancy on mother and baby. *British Journal of Psychiatry*, **150**, 777–781.

Lawson M.S. & Wilson G.S. (1979) Addiction and pregnancy: two lives in crisis. *Social Work in Health Care*, **4**, 445–457.

Livingood A.B., Dean P. & Smith B.D. (1983) The depressed mother as a source of stimulation for her infant. *Journal of Clinical Psychology*, **39**(3), 369–375.

Lovestone S. & Kumar R. (1992) Postnatal psychiatric illness: impact on spouses (submitted).

Lynch M. (1991) Significant harm: the paediatric contribution. In: Adcock M., White R. & Hollows A. (eds) *Significant Harm: Its Management and Outcome*, pp. 125–135. Significant Publications, Croydon.

McNeil T.F. (1988) Women with nonorganic psychosis: psychiatric and demographic characteristics of cases with versus without postpartum psychotic episodes. *Acta Psychiatrica Scandinavica*, **78**, 603–609.

McNeil T.F. & Kaij L. (1984) Offspring of women with nonorganic psychoses: progress report. In: Watt N., Anthony E.J., Wynne L. & Rolf J. (eds) *Children at Risk for Schizophrenia: A Longitudinal Perspective*. Cambridge University Press, New York.

McNeil T.F., Kaij L., Malmquist-Larsson A., Näslund B., Persson-Blennow I., McNeil N. & Blennow G. (1983) Offspring of women with nonorganic psychosis: development of a longitudinal study of children at high risk. *Acta Psychiatrica Scandinavica*, **68**, 234–250.

McNeil T.F., Persson-Blennow I., Binett B., Harty B. & Karyd U.-B. (1988) A prospective study of postpartum psychoses in a high-risk group. 7. Relationship to later offspring characteristics. *Acta Psychiatrica Scandinavica*, **78**, 613–617.

Main T.F. (1948) Mothers with children in a psychiatric hospital. *Lancet*, **ii**, 845–847.

Margison F.R. (1982) The pathology of the mother–child relationship. In: Brockington I.F. & Kumar R. (eds) *Motherhood and Mental Illness*, pp. 191–222. Academic Press, London.

Margison F.R. (1990) Infants of mentally ill mothers: the risk of injury and its control. *Journal of Reproductive and Infant Psychology*, **8**(2), 137–146.

Marks I. (1987) *Fears, Phobias and Rituals*. Oxford University Press, Oxford.

Marks M. & Kumar R. (1993) Infanticide in England and Wales. *Medicine, Science and the Law*, (in press).

Melhuish E.C., Gambles C. & Kumar R. (1988) Maternal mental illness and the mother–infant relationship. In: Kumar R. & Brockington I.F. (eds) *Motherhood and Mental Illness 2*, pp. 191–211. Wright, London.

Meltzer E.S. & Kumar R. (1985) Puerperal mental illness, clinical features and classification: a study of 142 mother-and-baby admissions. *British Journal of Psychiatry*, **147**, 647–654.

Miller P. (1989) Life events technology: is it adequate for the task? In: Cox J.L., Paykel E.S. & Page M.L. (eds) *Childbirth as a Life Event*. Duphar Laboratories, Dorset.

Minde K. & Benoit D. (1991) Infant psychiatry: its relevance for the general psychiatrist. *British Journal of Psychiatry*, **150**, 173–184.

Murray L. (1980) The sensitivities and expressive capacities of young infants in communication with their mothers. Ph.D. thesis, University of Edinburgh.

Murray L. (1988) Effects of postnatal depression on infant development: direct studies of early mother–infant interactions. In: Kumar R. & Brockington I.F. (eds) *Motherhood and Mental Illness 2*, pp. 159–190. Wright, London.

Murray L. (1992) The impact of postnatal depression on infant development. *Journal of Child Psychology and Psychiatry*, **33**, 543–561.

Murray L. & Trevarthen C. (1985) Emotional regulation of interactions between 2 month olds and their mothers. In: Field T.M. & Fox N.A. (eds) *Social Perception in Infants*. Ablex, Norwood, NJ.

Näslund B., Persson-Blennow I., McNeil T., Kaij L. & Malmquist-Larsson A. (1984) Offspring of women with nonorganic psychosis:

infant attachment to the mother at 1 year of age. *Acta Psychiatrica Scandinavica*, **69**, 231–241.

Nott P. (1982) Psychiatric illness following childbirth in Southampton: a case register study. *Psychological Medicine*, **12**, 557–561.

Oates M.R. (1988) The development of an integrated community-orientated service for severe postnatal mental illness. In: Kumar R. & Brockington I.F. (eds) *Motherhood and Mental Illness 2*, pp. 133–158. Wright, London.

Oates M.R. (1989) Normal emotional changes in pregnancy and the puerperium. *Baillière's Clinical Obstetrics and Gynaecology*, **3**, 791–804.

O'Connor M.J., Sigman M. & Brill N. (1987) Disorganization of attachment in relation to maternal alcohol consumption. *Journal of Consulting and Clinical Psychology*, **6**, 831–836.

O'Hara M. & Zekoski E.M. (1988) Postpartum depression: a comprehensive review. In: Kumar R. & Brockington I.F. (eds) *Motherhood and Mental Illness 2*, pp. 17–77. Wright, London.

Pawlby S.J., Schmücker G.A., Allen H.A., Kumar R., Sharp D.J. & Hay D.F. (1992) Links between a mother's interactive style and her child's development, with special reference to maternal depression. Paper presented at British Psychological Society Conference, Developmental Psychology Section, Edinburgh.

Persson-Blennow I. (1986) Current research in Sweden. In: Cox J.L., Kumar R., Margison F.R. & Downey L.J. (eds) *Puerperal Mental Illness*, pp. 34–39. Duphar, Southampton.

Pitt B. (1968) 'Atypical' depression following childbirth. *British Journal of Psychiatry*, **114**, 1325–1335.

Platz C. & Kendell R.E. (1988) A matched-control follow-up and family study of 'puerperal psychoses'. *British Journal of Psychiatry*, **153**, 90–94.

Provence S. & Lipton R.C. (1962) *Infants in Institutions: A Comparison of their Development with Family-reared Infants During the First Year of Life*. International Universities Press, New York.

Radke-Yarrow M., Cummings E.M., Kuczynski L. & Chapman M. (1985) Patterns of attachment in 2- and 3-year-olds in normal families and families with parental depression. *Child Development*, **56**, 884–893.

Ragins N., Schachter J., Elmer E., Preisman R., Bowes A. & Harway V. (1975) Infants and children at risk for schizophrenia. *Journal of Child Psychiatry*, **14**, 150–177.

Rasmussen S.A. & Eisen J.L. (1990) Epidemiology of obsessive-compulsive disorder. *Journal of Clinical Psychiatry*, **51**(2), 10–13.

Resnick P.J. (1969) Child murder by parents: a psychiatric review of filicide. *American Journal of Psychiatry*, **126**, 325–333.

Rutter M. (1966) *Children of Sick Parents: An Environmental and Psychiatric Study*. Institute of Psychiatry, Maudsley Monographs no. 16. Oxford University Press, Oxford.

Rutter M. (1981) *Maternal Deprivation Reassessed*, 2nd edn. Penguin Books, Harmondsworth, Middlesex.

Rutter M. (1988) *Studies of Psychosocial Risk: The Power of Longitudinal Data*. Cambridge University Press, Cambridge.

Rutter M. (1989) Psychiatric disorder in parents as a risk factor for children. In: Schaffer D., Phillips I. & Enzer N.B. (eds) *Prevention of Mental Disorders, Alcohol and Other Drug Use in Children and Adolescents*, pp. 157–189. OSAP Prevention Monograph 2. Office of Substance Abuse Prevention, US Department of Health and Human Services, Rockville, MD.

Rutter M. & Cox A. (1985) Other family influences. In: Rutter M. & Hersov L. (eds) *Child and Adolescent Psychiatry: Modern Approaches*, 2nd ed. pp. 58–81. Blackwell Scientific Publications, Oxford.

Rutter M. & Quinton D. (1984) Parental psychiatric disorder: effects on children. *Psychological Medicine*, **14**, 853–880.

Rutter M., Tizard J. & Whitmore K. (eds) (1970) *Education, Health and Behaviour*, Longman, London.

Rutter M., MacDonald H., LeCouter A., Harrington R., Bolton P. & Bailey A. (1990) Genetic factors in child psychiatric disorders. II. Empirical findings. *Journal of Child Psychology and Psychiatry*, **31**, 39–83.

Sameroff A.J., Seifer R. & Zax M. (1982) Early development of children at risk for emotional disorder. *Monographs of the Society for Research in Child Development*, **47**(7), 1–82.

Schachter J., Elmer E., Ragins N. & Wimberley F. (1977) Assessment of mother–infant interaction: schizophrenic and non-schizophrenic mothers. *Merrill-Palmer Quarterly*, **23**(3), 193–205.

Scott P.D. (1973) Parents who kill their children. *Medicine, Science and the Law*, **13**, 120–126.

Seager C.P. (1960) A controlled study of postpartum illness, *Journal of Mental Science*, **106**, 214–230.

Sharp D. (1992) Childbirth related emotional disorders: a prospective longitudinal study in primary care. Ph.D. Thesis, University of London.

Sharp D.J., Pawlby S.J., Schmücker G.A., Kumar R., Hay D.F. & Allen H.A. (1992) Maternal depression and child development. Paper presented at 6th International Conference of the Marcé Society, Edinburgh.

Simmonds J. (1991) Making professional judgements of significant harm. In: Adcock M., White R. & Hollows A. (eds) *Significant Harm: Its Management and Outcome*. Significant Publications, Croydon.

Sobel D. (1961) Children of schizophrenic patients: preliminary observations on early development. *American Journal of Psychiatry*, **118**, 512–517.

Spitzer R.L., Endicott J. & Robins E. (1978) Research Diagnostic Criteria: Rationale and Reliability. *Archives of General Psychiatry*, **36**, 773–782.

Stein A. & Fairburn C. (1989) Children of mothers with bulimia nervosa. *British Medical Journal*, **299**, 777–778.

Stein A., Gath D.H., Bucher J., Bond A., Day A. & Cooper P.J. (1991a) The relationship between post-natal depression and mother–child interaction. *British Journal of Psychiatry*, **158**, 46–52.

Stein A., Woolley H. & Fairburn C.G. (1991b) The infants of mothers with an eating disorder. Paper presented at the conference of the European congress of Child and Adolescent Psychiatry, London.

Stewart D.E. (1989) Psychiatric admission of mentally ill mothers with their infants. *Canadian Journal of Psychiatry*, **34**, 34–37.

Stewart D.E., Raskin J., Garfunkel P.E., McDonald O. & Robinson G.E. (1987) Anorexia nervosa, bulimia and pregnancy. *American Journal of Obstetrics and Gynecology*, **157**, 1194–1198.

Strauss M.E., Lessen-Firestone J.K., Starr R.H. & Ostrea E.M. (1975) Behaviour of narcotics-addicted newborns. *Child Development*, **46**, 887–893.

Streissguth A.P., Martin D.C., Barr H.M. & Sandman B.M. (1984) Intrauterine alcohol and nicotine exposure: attention and reaction time in 4-year-old children. *Developmental Psychology*, **20**, 533–541.

Tetlow C. (1955) Psychoses of childbearing. *Journal of Mental Science*, **101**, 629–639.

Tronick E.Z., Ricks M. & Cohn J.F. (1982) Maternal and infant affective exchange: patterns of adaptation. In: Field T. & Fogel A. (eds) *Emotion and Early Interaction*. Lawrence Erlbaum, Hillsdale, NJ.

Uddenberg N. & Englesson I. (1978) Prognosis of postpartum mental disturbance. A prospective study of primiparous women and their 4-year-old children. *Acta Psychiatrica Scandinavica*, **58**, 201–212.

Uddenberg N. & Nilsson L. (1975) The longitudinal course of paranatal emotional disturbance. *Acta Psychiatrica Scandinavica*, **52**, 160–169.

van Wezel-Meijler G. & Wit J.M. (1989) The offspring of mothers with anorexia nervosa: a high risk group for undernutrition and stunting? *European Journal of Paediatrics*, **149**, 130–135.

Watson J.P., Elliott S.A., Rugg A.J. & Brough D.I. (1984) Psychiatric disorder in pregnancy and the first postnatal year. *British Journal of Psychiatry*, **144**, 453−462.

Weissman M.M. & Paykel E.S. (1974) *The Depressed Woman: A Study of Social Relationships*. University of Chicago Press, Chicago, IL.

Weissman M.M., Paykel E.S. & Klerman G.L. (1972) The depressed woman as a mother. *Social Psychiatry*, **7**, 98−108.

Weissman M.M., Prusoff B.A. Gammon G.D., Merikangas K.R., Leckman J.F. & Kidd K.K. (1984) Psychopathology in the children (ages 6−18) of depressed and normal parents. *Journal of American Academy of Child Psychiatry*, **23**, 78−84.

West D.J. (1965) *Murder Followed by Suicide*. Heinemann, London.

West J.R. (1986) *Alcohol and Brain Development*. Oxford University Press, London.

Windheuser H.J. (1977) Anxious mothers as models for coping with anxiety. *Behaviour Analysis Model*, **2**, 39−58.

Woodside D.B. & Shekter-Wolfson L.F. (1990) Parenting by parents with anorexia nervosa and bulimia nervosa. *International Journal of Eating Disorders*, **9**, 303−309.

Wrate R.M., Rooney A.C., Thomas P.F. & Cox J.L. (1985) Postnatal Depression and Child Development: a three-year follow-up study. *British Journal of Psychiatry*, **146**, 622−627.

Zahn-Waxler C., Cummings E.M., McKnew D.H. & Radke-Yarrow M. (1984) Altruism, aggression, and social interactions in young children with a manic-depressive parent. *Child Development*, **55**, 112−122.

Chapter 45
Psychological Reactions to Life-Threatening and Terminal Illnesses and Bereavement

Dora Black

INTRODUCTION

This chapter considers the psychological effects on children of different ages and stages of development of having a life-threatening or terminal illness, the effects on children of having a parent who dies or has a life-threatening or terminal illness, and the consequences for families of the death of a child. Other chapters in this volume deal with aspects of loss of a parent (Chapter 12), chronic nonfatal illness (Chapter 42), the psychiatric consequences of specific illnesses (Chapter 39) and acquired immunodeficiency syndrome (AIDS; Chapter 40). This chapter will describe especially the clinical aspects of prevention, treatment and long-term outcome.

LIFE-THREATENING ILLNESS IN CHILDREN

Until the advent of immunization, vaccination and antibiotics, death in childhood, mainly from infectious diseases, was common in the developed world as it still is in many parts of the world where, in addition, death from starvation, war, neglect, exploitation, accidents and disaster result in high death rates in infants, children and adolescents.

The main causes of death in childhood in England and Wales today are shown in Table 45.1. Apart from road traffic accidents, malignancy, especially leukaemia, congenital conditions, muscular dystrophy, end-stage renal failure, sudden infant death syndrome and AIDS are the main killers in children, with suicide becoming important as a cause of death in adolescents.

Many of the killing diseases of 20 years ago are less likely to kill today. Acute lymphocytic leukaemia, for example, the commonest malignant disease in childhood, was almost invariably fatal within 2 years, but now has a 47% 5-year survival rate and in many cases is cured (Birch *et al.*, 1988). Chronic renal failure was invariably fatal until the advent of haemodialysis and renal transplant. In both these conditions, deaths still occur from the disease and from the complications of treatment.

For most families now the task is having to find a way of living in the shadow of death and having to find a way of living until death, however far or near death may be. This has

Table 45.1 Deaths in childhood (from Office of Population Censuses and Surveys, 1985)

Cause	Number	%
Infections	212	2
Neoplasms	420	5
Endocrine	210	2
Neurological	396	5
Respiratory	588	7
Congenital abnormalities	1990	23
Perinatal	2291	26
Sudden deaths (cause unknown)	1226	14
All accidents and poisoning	983	11
Other	359	4
Total deaths	8675	100

been described as turning an acute catastrophe into a chronic catastrophe with families being in a 'physical and psychosocial limbo' (Cohen & Wellisch, 1978). The advent of therapies which produce this effect is relatively recent. When leukaemia killed within 2 years, child and family distress was high and hope was low so that at diagnosis, processes of anticipatory mourning were initiated and in a way, the certainty of death enabled doctors and nurses to find effective ways of offering comfort and support because they could predict the future. Today there is a realization that we have to find a way of helping patients and families to live with the uncertain outcome and the handicapping effects of treatment, such as stunted growth and delayed puberty, prolonged dependence, disfigurement and sterility. This has led to the greater involvement of mental health professionals in liaison work (see Chapter 58) so that in some centres in developed countries all children with life-threatening diseases and their families are seen and assessed by a member of the child psychiatric team. Whether this is a cost-effective use of a scarce resource awaits proper evaluation. It has been argued that since these are normal children and families undergoing abnormal experiences, the use of psychiatric professionals is unjustified and adds the burden of psychiatric stigma to families already facing the pain of their child's serious illness (Chesler & Barbarin, 1987). On the other hand, the high levels of anxiety and depression found in adults with cancer (Maguire *et al.*,

1978) have led to the argument that routine assessment is justified if it leads to treatment improving mental health and if it has an effect on survival and the quality of life until death. The debate for adults is reviewed by Watson (1983).

LIFE-THREATENING ILLNESS AND SUDDEN DEATH IN PARENTS

Cancer and heart disease are the two great premature killing diseases in parents in the developed world. Other conditions that may kill prematurely include road traffic and other accidents, multiple sclerosis, renal and liver failure and mental illness leading to suicide.

The incidence of childhood bereavement in the west because of the death of a parent is approximately 1.6% (Black, 1978).

The child's developing understanding of illness

In children and adolescents, the reactions to illness will depend on their understanding of what is happening to them. We therefore turn first to the studies on children's understanding of illness and death.

Eiser (1985), reviewing studies of the changes in understanding of illness as the child grows, has suggested that at least three stages exist in the development of the child's knowledge of the body. In the first stage (up to 7 years) children confuse internal and external aspects of the body; their knowledge of the existence and position of different organs is rudimentary, and their knowledge of function seems to lag behind knowledge of position. Between 7 and 11 there is some development of knowledge but the child does not relate the various parts of the body until adolescence. The child's understanding of the causes of illness similarly develops in three stages (Bibace & Walsh, 1980, 1981). Between 4 and 7 years children may attribute the cause of illness to magic or believe it is a punishment. Between 7 and 10, the child sees illness as contagious and it is not until adolescence that more complex causations are usually understood.

The stage theory of development has its critics. For example, one study (Millstein *et al.*, 1981) found that there was some evidence of a developmental process underlying concepts of illness, but that healthy adolescents used adult-like concepts within a framework more commonly used by children. Others have questioned the concept of stages, since development is conceptualized as more of a continuum (Mandler, 1983).

Eiser, in reviewing these criticisms, points out that children show more sophisticated concepts when playing than when questioned and that experience determines understanding to a considerable extent (Eiser, 1989). Thus sick young children display considerably more mature understanding than healthy children (Bluebond-Langner, 1978; Kendrick *et al.*, 1986). She concludes that the stage theory is valid and that we need to study what children know within a framework of developmental changes that occur in other areas of cognition, particularly memory, learning and information processing. Young children need concrete structures to demonstrate their

knowledge of events. A small study of 20 children who suffered psychic trauma before the age of 5 confirmed this conclusion. Terr found that children traumatized before the age of 36 months could not describe the event in words but the behavioural memories remained quite accurate (Terr, 1988). These findings have importance for the treatment of young children in particular. Painful and frightening treatments may not appear to have been remembered because the child cannot verbalize the experience but their behaviour, if attended to, can tell us clearly that they have remembered, as illustrated by the following case:

> Jeannie, aged 4, was treated at 15 months for a medulloblastoma that involved hospital admission, venepunctures and neurosurgery. She made a full recovery and seemed to have forgotten her traumatic experiences until she was readmitted with a fractured femur. Her extreme reaction to the attempt to draw a blood sample indicated that the previous experiences had been remembered although they could not be verbalized.

Medical procedures are sometimes misunderstood by young children who may see them as punishments and perceive doctors and nurses as wanting to hurt them (Brewster, 1982). One of the difficulties that results from the tendency to involve parents more in administering treatment (e.g. in continuous ambulatory peritoneal dialysis for end-stage renal failure) is that they too come to be seen by the child as behaving punitively. Long term benefits of treatment are not appreciated until adolescence.

The development of the concept of death in children

Reactions in children are likely to depend upon their age and stage of development. Here we are concerned with reactions to life-threatening illness. The child would have to appreciate the threat to life to react to it. At what age do children understand about death? Early studies suggested that it was not until the onset of puberty that children understood that death was different from life in a number of respects: that it was universal, irreversible and that there was a causal agent (Anthony, 1971). More recent studies have demonstrated that children as young as 5 years have quite well-developed concepts of death. Lansdown and Benjamin (1985), for example, found that by 5 years 60–80% of children understood the above ideas so that it is likely that some 4 and even a few 3-year-olds will be able to grasp that they have an illness that might kill them. By 9 years the majority of children had well-developed concepts of death. Others (Bluebond-Langner, 1978; Reilly *et al.*, 1983) have found that age was less important than experiencing a relapse in the disease in the knowledge that a fellow patient had died of the same condition. From these studies we can conclude that experience and stage of understanding interact so that from the age of 5, and possibly earlier, experience of someone dying, especially with the same disease, is likely to increase knowledge and may arouse death anxiety in children.

A small study of death conceptualization in children with

leukaemia, aged 4–9 years (Clunies-Ross & Lansdown, 1988) found that whilst there was little difference in the overall concepts between sick and healthy children, there were differences in content (Table 45.2).

There was some suggestion that healthy children aged 7 and under showed a greater understanding of the causes of death and the appearance of a dead body than did leukaemic children. The leukaemic children showed a greater understanding of the irrevocability of death and the cessation of bodily function. A study of the drawings of the leukaemic children indicated that they felt a degree of psychological isolation, even when they had ample company; this is confirmed in clinical work (Emanuel *et al.*, 1990). Such a play construction is illustrated in Figure 45.1.

PSYCHOLOGICAL REACTIONS TO SERIOUS ILLNESS

One of the components of life-threatening illness is the experience of all the consequences of any chronic and serious illness (see Chapter 42). Illnesses may impose limitations in mobility, cause pain, lead to frequent hospitalizations, require frequent venepunctures and injections or involve unpleasant or painful investigations and treatments. These may include operations and unpleasant-tasting or toxic medications, resulting in nausea and vomiting. They may lead to changes in appearance, for example, radiotherapy and chemotherapy causing alopecia or steroid therapy causing a Cushingoid appearance, or may in some cases lead to cognitive defects. The treatment or the disease may stunt growth and interfere with sexual functioning by delaying puberty or causing sterility. Bone marrow transplants, if mismatched, may lead to graft-versus-host

Table 45.2 Understanding of the different components of the concept of death by age and health status: percentage of children showing complete understanding (from Clunies-Ross & Lansdown, 1988)

| | Age (years) | | | | | | | |
| | 5 | | 6 | | 7 | | 8 | |
	H	L	H	L	H	L	H	L
Separation	82	80	100	100	100	100	100	50
Universality	76	60	82	100	57	88	100	100
Causality	82	40	82	0	67	55	100	100
Irrevocability	71	100	73	100	100	100	96	100
Appearance	35	0	32	0	19	11	65	50
Insensitivity	88	0	82	100	95	89	96	50
Cessation of bodily function	71	100	86	100	95	89	96	100

H, healthy children; L, leukaemic children.

disease, a disfiguring and often fatal condition. Cognition may be impaired by irradiation of the brain.

Schooling may be interrupted repeatedly, and friendships disrupted. The preoccupations of the patient compared with those of his or her healthy siblings and friends may differ so markedly that no *rapprochement* seems possible. In adolescence, the development of interest in the opposite sex, in careers and planning for the future may not be seen as high priorities in a still prepubertal child facing death or life-threatening illness.

Epidemiological studies of the prevalence of psychiatric disorder make it clear that rates are raised in children with

Fig. 45.1 A 5-year-old boy with leukaemia, in his play with his psychotherapist, indicates that he is afraid that death will come through the defences of his castle. The boy in the next room had just died from the same illness; his parents wished to keep this news from him.

serious illness (Rutter *et al.*, 1970; Pless & Roghmann, 1971; Eisen *et al.*, 1980; Walker *et al.*, 1981; Cadman *et al.*, 1987). The picture in clinically referred populations is not so clear. Several studies of adults with cancer have found that there is a high incidence of anxiety and depression (Greer, 1985). In children, the evidence for emotional disorders is less definite. The problems that develop will depend to some extent on the developmental stage reached by the child. Major psychiatric disorders, rare in childhood, do not seem appreciably more common in children with serious illness (Kellerman *et al.*, 1980; Greenberg *et al.*, 1989) and may even be less frequent than in the healthy population (Kaplan *et al.*, 1987; Worchel *et al.*, 1988). Considering the massive interruption to normal life that serious diseases and their treatments impose on child and family, such results require some explanation.

The studies mentioned above used standardized and validated questionnaires. Studies that use standardized clinical interviews find more morbidity (Burns & Zweig, 1980; Koocher *et al.*, 1980; Slavin, 1981), and it may be that questionnaires are too insensitive and seriously underestimate the psychiatric morbidity in sick children (Graham & Rutter, 1973). There is also a secular trend towards a reduction in morbidity and this may reflect the improvement in psychosocial preventive interventions (Greenberg *et al.*, 1989). Recent studies have moved away from the concept of psychiatric disorder and have looked instead at behaviour, self-concept, competence, self-esteem and locus of control (Burns & Zweig, 1980; Kellerman *et al.*, 1980; Zeltzer *et al.*, 1980; Chesler & Barbarin, 1987; Eiser, 1990a). Studies of adolescents' self-esteem have not found major differences between chronically ill and healthy subjects, although the former tend to be more dependent on family and less sexually developed (Kellerman *et al.*, 1980; Zeltzer *et al.*, 1980; Offer *et al.*, 1984; McAnarney, 1985).

One has to ask why the findings from children's studies are different from adults? Are children developmentally less able to express depressive affects, do they use denial mechanisms to a greater extent than adults, or is their affective response predicated on the emotional tone of their family and clinicians? Is it possible that adults are unable or unwilling to recognize the distress of children or are children adept at hiding their feelings to protect their parents? Recent work on childhood depression has shown that the prevalence is higher than was previously thought (Kolvin *et al.*, 1991) and it is underdiagnosed. Families can protect or stress their children and there is a high correlation between parental and patient functioning. Probably all these factors and others, as yet unidentified, play a part in the differences in the rate of psychiatric disorder in children and adults suffering from the same diseases.

There are few studies of the effects on infants of serious illness. Neonates undergoing surgery for life-threatening congenital abnormalities were examined at 3 years in one study. There was an increased incidence of behaviour problems and difficulties in the mother–child relationship compared with controls and this was enhanced when there were repeat admissions and other adversities (Ludman *et al.*, 1992).

EFFECTS ON FAMILY MEMBERS OF LIFE-THREATENING ILLNESS IN CHILDREN

Siblings

Do siblings of children with life-threatening illness show an increased rate of disturbance? The question is difficult to answer. Many studies do not distinguish the degree of severity or life-threat of the diseases. Others do not analyze the sibling group by age or gender or by relationship with the sick child. There was a twofold increase in the incidence of emotional disorders including depression and anxiety in the siblings of chronically sick children in the Ontario Child Health population study and a slightly increased incidence of poor peer relationships, but no increase in conduct or school problems (Cadman *et al.*, 1988). Smaller studies using questionnaires and semistructured interviews have found a higher level of disturbance in the siblings at all ages (Tolley, 1987; Cairns *et al.*, 1979; Iles, 1979; Lavigne & Ryan, 1979; Spinetta, 1981; Cohen, 1985; Perez-Ortega, 1986) but the symptoms described are wide-ranging and rarely amount to a definite psychiatric disorder. In some cases, when compared to the sick patient, the healthy sibling exhibited more distress in relation to social isolation, fear of confronting family members with negative feelings and concern with failure (Cairns *et al.*, 1979). Poor communication and disturbed relationships within the family, as well as poor social support, predicted behavioural problems in the siblings (Cohen, 1985; Richmond, 1985). The one study with negative findings in the siblings of children with cystic fibrosis (Gayton *et al.*, 1977) failed to control for the age of the sick child so that the perception of life-threat in the small group must have been variable.

Siblings' understanding of the illness appears to be age-related, with some delays in understanding concepts, compared with other children, that may be caused by avoidance of discussion of illness in families with sick children (Caradang *et al.*, 1979; O'Brien, 1987). Siblings appear to be at increased risk (approximately double) for developing psychological disturbance that appears related to demographic characteristics of the family, level of family functioning and disease characteristics. Illness-related knowledge is different in siblings of ill children compared with siblings of healthy controls.

The majority of siblings of sick children appear to be well-adjusted and do not have a psychiatric disorder. Most of the studies however have been cross-sectional and have not looked at long-term effects.

Parents

When children are seriously ill, mothers are usually more involved in nursing and caring for them and in accompanying them to hospital than fathers and have therefore been most extensively studied. Mothers have been found to suffer in excess from depression (Daniels *et al.*, 1987; Jessop *et al.*, 1988). Maguire (1983) found that 28% of mothers of children with leukaemia had morbid anxiety or depression at 12–18 months after diagnosis compared with 8% of controls, a finding confirmed by a more recent study in which one-third of parents of children with cancer had continuing moderate to severe anxiety (Hughes & Lieberman, 1990). There may be gender-related differences in the reactions of mothers and fathers. In one study 145 parents of children who died from neoplasms were asked about functioning during the child's last illness using a semistructured interview. Mothers reported a greater degree of difficulty with the problems of helplessness, loss of confidence in the ability to be a good parent, financial difficulties, being avoided by others, growing apart from their spouse and fear of being unable to cope if the child should die, than fathers who reported significantly greater difficulty with two problems — feeling left out of the ill child's life and being worried that their spouse was too preoccupied with the ill child (Cook, 1984). Another study failed to find significant gender differences in a group of middle-class white parents attending a support group, although the parents of the children who died did worse than those of the children who survived (Morrow *et al.*, 1981).

EFFECTS ON MARRIAGE

Marriages are stressed by the demands of treatment for serious illness. Often the treating specialist hospital is at a distance and parents are separated as one accompanies the child and the other tries to keep the rest of the family going and earn a living. It is surprising therefore that most studies have not found an increase in divorce or separation (see Sabbeth & Leventhal, 1984, for review), although marital distress is increased and this becomes worse as the disease worsens (Jessop *et al.*, 1988). It seems that the stress of a serious and prolonged illness in a child is likely to make a poor marriage worse but may strengthen the relationship in an already close marriage, so that the result is that the studies show no increase in marital breakdown resulting from the stress of illness in the child.

FAMILY STUDIES

Spinetta *et al.* (1988) report a study of long-term adjustment in families of children with cancer, in which they compared 38 families of a child who survived with 13 families of one who died, after 5 years. They constituted 69% of an original treated sample. The families of children who died scored at less adaptive levels of functioning on items measuring return to normal activities, zest for living, making plans for the future, recognizing and accepting the family members' needs, admitting the need for emotional support from friends or family and having placed the cancer in a more reasonable and less overwhelming perspective.

Barbarin and Chesler, (1986) looked at the coping strategies of 74 parents of children with cancer and found that they were not related to income or gender. Those parents who had a good relationship with the medical staff tended to use coping

strategies such as denial, acceptance or relying on religion. More highly educated parents tended to use information-seeking more than the others.

The interaction of family members as the disease progresses and as the children grow is very complex and difficult to study. Most studies are cross-sectional rather than longitudinal and models for describing these complex interactions are not yet satisfactory. The way that parents, under stress themselves because of the demands of their child's illness, react to their sick child, the siblings and each other must depend on their own personality strengths, the degree of family and social support, finances, work demands and satisfactions, and the perceived and actual support of the hospital staff (Wallander *et al.*, 1989). There is a need for research that focuses upon the family, not just on individual functioning; that approaches the situation from a more positive stance of asking how people cope with the stresses upon them; and that takes account of the perceptions of those involved in the situation (Wallander *et al.*, 1989).

FACTORS ASSOCIATED WITH ADAPTATION OF CHILD AND FAMILY

Disease variables

The threat of death itself is important. Howarth (1972), for example, found that 40% of children with life-threatening illness had psychiatric disorders, compared with 8% of those with nonlife-threatening ones. Wallander *et al.* (1988) found no differences in the incidence of psychological problems in children with a variety of diseases, few of which were life-threatening.

Psychosocial variables

Psychosocial variables predicting better family functioning and better psychological outcome for the sick child include openness of communication, possession of religious beliefs and a positive approach to the illness, as well as good emotional support, a good marital relationship and family cohesiveness (Rolland, 1984; Chesler & Barbarin, 1987; Eiser, 1990a). Family income appears more important in the American studies than in the UK, where there are no direct charges for treatment (Eiser, 1990b).

Open communication involves talking with children about their illness in an age-appropriate manner, involving them in decisions about their treatment as far as possible, not taking away hope, protecting them from despair but enabling them to feel that they can trust their parents and medical carers to talk to them truthfully. The evidence that we have is that refusing to talk about issues of death and dying with children who have life-threatening diseases impedes their coping (Spinetta & Deasey-Spinetta, 1981; Slavin *et al.*, 1982). Children often know more than they let on to their parents, especially when they realize that it would pain their parents to be made aware of the child's knowledge and distress. This tendency to protect parents is commonly found and needs addressing in therapeutic work (Spinetta *et al.*, 1973; Spinetta & Deasey-Spinetta, 1981). How well the child functions seems very dependent on the good mental health of the mother (Jessop *et al.*, 1988).

Individual variables

Age affects compliance with treatment, understanding, ability to tolerate unpleasant sensations and affects, separation anxiety, loneliness, sense of control and self-esteem and many other variables. In general, the younger the child is at the onset of a disease, the more difficult is the adaptation. An exception to this is in the area of compliance with treatment where adolescents are less compliant than younger children (Blum, 1984).

Personality variables are difficult to examine in children with long-standing serious illness, as their personality development may have been constricted by pain, disability, lack of opportunity to develop friendships, the demands of treatment regimes and parental factors. The child's cognitive style, use of denial and perception of locus of control are probably all relevant but have been less studied than in adults.

Treatment setting

Children can be treated in a hospital ward, a hospice for children or at home. Mulhern and colleagues found that parents were more anxious, depressed and defensive after death in hospital than at home and when children died at home the long-term outcome was better for the parents (Mulhern *et al.*, 1983; Lauer *et al.*, 1989), although the reactions of siblings have not been similarly studied.

Although children's hospices have only been in existence for a short time, the evidence is that they do have a specific role and can be helpful where dying at home is not an option because of the complex medical and nursing needs of the child, or because of factors such as the needs of siblings or others (Corr & Corr, 1985; Stein *et al.*, 1989; Stein & Woolley, 1990). More specialist units are developing home care teams so that children can receive more care at home and preliminary studies are encouraging (Edwardson, 1983; Koocher, 1984; Martinson *et al.*, 1985; Martinson, 1986; Chambers *et al.*, 1989).

Professional support and behaviour

When physicians advocate protection of the child from knowledge of the diagnosis, the mental health of the child on follow-up is worse than when open communication is practised (Slavin *et al.*, 1982). Parents also appreciate staff openness and remember the method of imparting the bad news vividly many years later. Accurate information, delivered with skill and sympathy and updated regularly, lessens the parents' sense of helplessness and isolation and sets up a therapeutic alliance (Woolley *et al.*, 1989).

It is only recently that the high cost of parenting a seriously ill child has been recognized by primary carers. Family doctors rarely enquire about family functioning when a child is ill (Rosser & Maguire, 1982).

Parents who feel supported by the community and family, as well as by professionals, are more likely to adapt, particularly if they are older. The young parent whose child dies and who has poor social supports is at risk of psychiatric illness (Morrow *et al.*, 1981).

Involvement of children in treatment decisions

This is an area where there is little research but many opinions. The advent of the Children Act in the UK in 1989 has forced physicians to consider the need for consent for treatment from the child if he or she is thought to be able to understand the issues involved. One centre that has studied involving children in consent found that children were less likely to choose the treatment that was experimental than their parents and would opt for palliative care only. Severe depression and behavioural problems occurred rarely and communication was better within the family (Nitschke *et al.*, 1982; Kamps *et al.*, 1987). It is not surprising that children do not choose the more distressing and uncertain experimental treatments if they are given a choice, but it raises ethical questions about the desirability of giving children a choice when they cannot be properly informed. Conversely, can there be trials of hazardous treatments in children, given the difficulty of obtaining informed consent? These issues are discussed by the Working Party on Research on Children (1991). Children as young as 9 years can participate successfully in health care decision-making (Weithorn & Campbell, 1982). A controlled study of adolescents who refused treatment for cancer found that they were more likely than the consenting adolescents to be prone to anxiety and coped with distress by believing that their lives were determined by fate or God. Treating the anxiety enabled many of them to accept treatment which in some cases restored their health (Blotcky *et al.*, 1985). This subject clearly requires more study.

TREATMENT AND MANAGEMENT OF PSYCHOLOGICAL PROBLEMS IN CHILDREN WITH LIFE-THREATENING ILLNESS AND THEIR FAMILIES

Many of the problems in patients and families discussed above are related to the attempt of the individual to adapt to an abnormal situation. For that reason it is important that the medical team and the psychiatric team are seen to be working together from the beginning to enhance psychological functioning and to prevent avoidable psychological distress (Black *et al.*, 1990). The psychiatric team should be able to offer a wide range of psychiatric and psychological therapies and to advise the medical team on the psychological needs of patient, family and staff. Most approaches today are eclectic in orientation and clinicians take the view that the interaction of child, family and professional systems must be addressed when treatment plans are made. This is best done by the two teams scheduling regular meetings to discuss each patient and family (see Chapter 58).

Specific symptoms can be controlled by a careful assessment and an application of the appropriate techniques. *Needle phobia* should be preventable by preparing children and taking time to help them to relax, if necessary using relaxation or hypnosis and an anaesthetic cream (Manne *et al.*, 1990). An important part of the psychiatrist's or psychologist's input to medical teams is that of educating junior medical and nursing staff on these preventive measures. If treatment is necessary, it involves behavioural desensitization techniques (see Chapter 50).

Physical techniques of *pain control* can be supplemented with hypnotic and autohypnotic techniques (Hilgard & LeBaron, 1982, 1984; Olness & Gardner, 1988).

Patients receiving chemotherapy can develop an antici-patory *nausea* so that they begin to vomit at the smell of the medication or the approach of the nurse, or even when entering the hospital. The way the parents manage their children is associated with the development of the syndrome: those children receiving threats of punishment fare worse (Dolgin & Katz, 1988). Hypnosis and relaxation (Zeltzer *et al.*, 1983), as well as desensitization, may help, but the symptoms are resistant to psychological and pharmacological treatments and may need a combination of treatments (Sokel *et al.*, 1990), as illustrated by the following case:

> Angela, aged 10, developed reflex vomiting when she was given courses of chemotherapy for a malignant tumour of her eye. She vomited every 5 minutes for 24 hours following treatment. Antiemetic drugs gave only limited relief. She responded to a combination of desensitization using a hierarchy and a psychotherapeutic relationship with her psychiatrist.

Anxiety will respond to psychotherapeutic methods, medi-cation, cognitive approaches, hypnosis and relaxation (LeBaron & Zeltzer, 1984; Spirito *et al.*, 1984; Cozzi *et al.*, 1987; Pfefferbaum *et al.*, 1987; Redd *et al.*, 1987; Wall & Womack, 1989; Kuttner *et al.*, 1988; Emanuel *et al.*, 1990; Noeker & Petermann, 1990) but there are few controlled trials comparing treatments. Jay and her colleagues (1987) studied 56 children undergoing bone marrow transplant comparing a cognitive-behavioural approach, diazepam and a no-treatment control group. The cognitive approach produced significantly lower behavioural distress, lower pain ratings and pulse rates, but in general there is no clear indication that one treatment is superior to others and the choice is likely to be determined by the availability of expertise. Addressing parental anxiety using counselling techniques is an important part of the treatment of the child, and family therapy (Black, 1989) may be helpful here, but the only controlled trial of family therapy is for asthma (Lask & Matthew, 1979).

Death anxiety (Spinetta & Maloney, 1975) in child and family is best tackled with a family therapy approach that aims at improving communication and helps the family to use relaxation techniques to help the child and themselves. Hypnosis and relaxation can play a large part in making the terminally ill child comfortable and easing distress for the family; nurses working with such children have found it worthwhile learning the techniques. Teaching the child how to use self-hypnosis may also be helpful. Most of the studies are of small groups and are uncontrolled and we await further studies (Kellerman *et al.*, 1983; Olness & Gardner, 1988).

Depression

Where depressive symptoms are present, the need for pharmacotherapy should be assessed by a child and adolescent psychiatrist. Depression, especially in adolescents, may inter-fere with compliance with the treatment regime and com-pliance may improve with treatment of the depression. Depression and withdrawal can be a consequence of the child or adolescent's perception of the need to protect the parent and may respond to family therapy where the promotion of open communication takes place.

Compliance

Compliance difficulties also may respond to family therapy. Such families are often enmeshed and give subtly contradictory messages to the children. For example, a parent may be overtly encouraging compliance, but may unconsciously or covertly be giving a simultaneous message that leads the child to reject treatment (Altschuler *et al.*, 1991). This may happen particularly when there is conflict between the parents:

> Colin, aged 10, suffered from end-stage renal failure. After a kidney transplant, he failed to take his immunosuppressants and risked rejecting his transplant. At a family interview it became clear that the parents were in severe conflict and that the father, who had been away from home at the time that Colin was undergoing surgery, was subtly encouraging him to rebel against his mother's authority. Although the father was not overtly wishing Colin to become ill again, the effect of his denigration of the mother's authority was to put Colin in a double-bind. If he obeyed his mother he was disappointing his father. If he did not, he risked losing his transplant and would have to return to a greater dependence on his mother who would have to dialyse him 4 times a day. A family therapy approach using strategic interventions enabled the parents to form an effective co-parenting coalition so that Colin was released from the pathological triangulation.

Support for parents, therapy for siblings and support for staff are the other pillars of a liaison psychiatric team's inter-vention strategy.

Many of the psychotherapeutic approaches that have been developed have not been adequately evaluated — the evalu-ation of cognitive behavioural and psychopharmacological approaches in adults is further advanced. Nevertheless, parents and older adolescents often wish to explore and question existential aspects of their serious life-threatening illness and need a counsellor or psychotherapist who will voyage with them on this quest. Comaroff and Maguire (1981) studied 60 families of children with leukaemia and found that the experience of uncertainty and the search for meaning were the characteristic features of the impact of the disease upon sufferers and their families. Judd's (1989) account of her psychotherapeutic work with a boy dying of leukaemia is a good example of a sensitive therapist travelling with a child and his family whilst they explore existential issues.

Attendance at a summer camp with other children with the same disease has been advocated as helping to educate the children about their disease and treatment, and to enable them to explore issues with which they may not wish their parents to be troubled (Smith *et al.*, 1987; Bluebond-Langner *et al.*, 1990).

Given the findings related to locus of control, outlined above, some authors have emphasized the importance of helping the child to gain autonomy and mastery within the limitations imposed by the disease, the treatment and the developmental status of the child (Blotcky *et al.*, 1985; Black, 1989). The use of play therapy as a way of introducing knowledge about illness and helping the child to model control and gain mastery seems attractive but there has been little attempt at evaluation (Adams, 1976).

If there is a child psychiatric liaison team available that can offer a wide range of interventions, choosing which one or more of those available should be used must depend on the coping style of the child, the availability of professional time and skill and the cost-effectiveness of the procedure (Smith *et al.*, 1989). Most centres however will only be able to call on the services of one or two psychiatric professionals: a psychiatrist, social worker, psychologist or psychotherapist. It may then be most economical for that person to be used for staff support and education, so that the nurses or paediatricians carry out the bulk of the interventions (Graham & Jenkins, 1985). In a well-staffed unit, different techniques may be necessary for different symptoms at different times in the illness:

> Jandy, a 5-year-old girl, developed leukaemia. She lived with her uncle and aunt after her parents had been killed when she was 3½ years old in a country torn by civil war. Her carers had 3 other young children, were struggling to establish themselves in a new country and had little understanding of Jandy's need for a parent to be with her in the hospital, believing she was well cared for. Jandy developed a severe behavioural disorder as an inpatient, with which the nurses found it difficult to cope. She would reject their help, scream loudly for long periods and demand to be put to bed most of the day. The interventions devised by the psychiatric team included the use of a behavioural programme to encourage age-appropriate behaviour (attending school, staying up during the day, deferring gratification), support and explanation for the nurses and physicians, the provision of psychotherapy aimed at helping Jandy to mourn the

loss of her parents and separation from her new family, domestic help for her carers, social work help to them to enable them to visit more frequently, and the provision of a 'ward granny', a volunteer who was free of family commitments and who could provide a consistent mother-figure during Jandy's admission.

In our present state of knowledge, the best approach is an eclectic one utilizing ideas from many sources: learning and systems theories, psychodynamic theory, psychiatry, philosophy and anthropology (Comaroff & Maguire, 1981).

TERMINAL ILLNESS AND DEATH

Although parents and child may know that the child has a life-threatening illness, day-to-day living continues without that awareness being constantly present. Life may continue for many years and thoughts of dying, if they were present, may be pushed to the backs of their minds. At some stage, however, there is a change that brings the terminal phase of illness. This may be a worsening of the illness, a lack of response to treatments which have hitherto been effective or the failure of an operation or other procedure. This is often coupled with the knowledge of the death of a fellow patient with the same condition. The terminal phase of a life-threatening illness may be defined as one where curative treatments are not applicable but palliation is given. Some physicians and surgeons refuse to acknowledge this stage and children may then die without there having been an opportunity for them and their families to round off their relationships. Some situations deteriorate so rapidly that it is not possible to delineate a terminal phase.

There is evidence that children, even young ones, are aware that they are dying. They may pick up these cues from parents and hospital staff, who in one study gave significantly less time and attention to children who were terminally ill than to others (Waechter, 1971). They may not let anyone know what they know.

The handling of the period leading up to death is crucial to the functioning of the family during the time after death. A study of the way that bad news was broken and the reaction of professionals (Finlay & Dallimore, 1991) indicated the importance of sensitive handling, allowing enough time, viewing the body, requesting organ donation and follow-up and support from hospital staff. The following case shows how this may happen:

> Alison, aged 10 years, was transferred to a regional neurosurgical unit after respiratory arrest following status asthmaticus. She was brain-dead, and the parents requested help in deciding how to tell the other children. They were seen by the child psychiatrist and child psychiatric nurse, who arranged for the other children to come to the hospital and see their sister, helped the parents to talk with them about what had happened and supported the family in their grief. There was a particular concern for the older brother who also had stress-induced asthma and arrangements were made for him to have

relaxation exercises and to be taught autohypnosis. Bereavement counselling was arranged nearer home but the nurse on the intensive care unit and the child psychiatric nurse remained available by phone. The parents were grateful to be asked to donate Alison's organs, feeling that something of her would go on living and benefit others.

Family doctors rarely enquire about family functioning during the illness of a child or parent, so that one of the main supports to families coping with serious illness in our society is often unavailable (Rosser & Maguire, 1982).

BEREAVEMENT

Parental bereavement

In a normal grief reaction in adults (Parkes, 1986) the acute pangs of grief last few weeks or months at most, the depressive phase can go on for a few months and by the first or at most the second anniversary there is considerable improvement. However, many parents feel that they never really recover from the loss of a child. They may adjust to it, they may be able to resume their everyday activities and may even derive some pleasure from life, but they feel they remain vulnerable, and they are not the same people they were before (Osterweis *et al.*, 1984). For some parents, the new identity is a stronger one — they feel they have been 'through the fire' and that nothing can affect them so profoundly again. The cost may be a reduction in their sensitivity to their other children or their partner, which may threaten the marriage or even disrupt it.

Parents who lose a child experience a fundamental change in their beliefs about their family's future security. Their grief reaction is more likely to take a pathological course. For example, a retrospective study of parents losing an infant in the neonatal period (Dyregrov, 1990) found high levels of anxiety, especially in the mothers, and in those who perceived themselves as lacking in support from others. Grief may be absent, delayed, prolonged or distorted. These pathological bereavement reactions occur more commonly when the loss is sudden, unexpected, untimely or horrific; when there have been deaths preceding or following and where social supports are lacking (Parkes, 1985).

Factors affecting parental grief

Relationship with the dead child

There appear to be gender differences in the expression and response to grief following the loss of an infant (Dyregrov & Matthiesen, 1987; Bohannon, 1991). Mothers tend to grieve more intensely and for longer and they are more at risk for pathological grief reactions. This probably reflects their different roles with the sick child, mothers often being closer to their dying child and fathers being excluded by virtue of their need to earn a living and to care for the remaining children (Cook, 1984). However Rando found few differences between the sexes in their grieving behaviour when a child died from cancer (Rando, 1983). The gender differences in grieving seem to be related to the age at the death of a child. Fathers may take longer than mothers to become attached to their child and if the death is in infancy, may not be as affected as the mothers. A recent study confirms this supposition. There appear to be no gender differences in parental functioning if the child was more than 1 year old at death (Sumner & Dinwiddie, 1991).

Biological factors

The discovery that the mitotic response of leukocytes is depressed in the recently bereaved (Bartrop *et al.*, 1977) has led to the search for immune factors in bereavement (Schleifer *et al.*, 1983). This seems to be related to the severity of the depressive phase of the grief reaction (Schleifer *et al.*, 1984).

Psychosocial factors

The effect of multiple events and traumas on the adaptation of children and parents to bereavement is cumulative rather than inoculating. Thus two or more family deaths following one another swiftly will lower resistance to psychiatric disorder in adults (Parkes, 1985, 1986). Parents who have experienced bereavement in childhood are more vulnerable to loss in adult life (Brown *et al.*, 1971). One psychosocial variable that has been shown to affect outcome is the provision of support by family, friends and professional staff. (Chesler & Barbarin, 1987).

Length of illness and place of death

There is some evidence that the place of death has an influence on the course of mourning. Parents were more anxious and depressed after a death in hospital, and home deaths resulted in a better long-term outcome for the parents (Mulhern *et al.*, 1983; Lauer *et al.*, 1989). High rates of morbidity after a child's death are more likely when there has been prebereavement psychological ill health and this correlates with the length of illness prior to death (Rando, 1983).

One of the problems in evaluating the research on bereaved parents is that it often fails to control for the length of the preceding illness. Since life-threatening illness in children may affect family functioning adversely, it is likely that the parents and siblings will be entering a period of mourning in an already disturbed or distressed state of mind.

Bereavement in children

The effects of bereavement on development are considered in Chapter 12 — this section describes the clinical aspects.

Classification of childhood bereavement reactions in ICD-9 (1977) and ICD-10 (1992) relies on accurately assessing the presence of discrete symptoms and syndromes such as conduct disorder, emotional disorder or separation anxiety disorder. In

DSM-III-R and DSM-IV (American Psychiatric Association, 1987, in press) there is a category of uncomplicated bereavement which, it has been argued by Vida and Grizenko (1989), does not satisfy the observations made about childhood bereavement. At least it acknowledges the need for recognition of the trigger to the development of symptoms.

Most studies of bereaved children focus on their reactions to the death of a parent and there is much less known about reactions to the loss of other attachment figures such as siblings, grandparents, friends and animals. There are few studies that have used control groups of nonbereaved individuals studied at the same time and most have not used standardized measures and have relied on parent interviews rather than interviewing the children themselves. Most studies have not obtained unselected, systematically gathered samples of bereaved children and relevant independent variables are not identified or controlled for. Many studies are limited by small sample size and differences fail to reach significance (Vida & Grizenko, 1989).

The loss of a parent by death has interested theoreticians for many years. Freud (1917) noted the effect of loss on his adult patients, and Bowlby (1969, 1972, 1980) developed the theory of attachment as a biological organizer of human behaviour, with the inevitable converse phenomenon of loss.

Parkes (1986) was one of the first to study widows systematically and to identify the high morbidity that occurs after the loss of a spouse. He identified factors that predicted which individuals would be at risk for pathological grief reactions. Bowlby and others, mainly working clinically with children in psychoanalytic therapy, suggested that children might be at high risk of developing pathological grief reactions after the death of a parent (Bowlby, 1963; Miller, 1971; Furman, 1974). A series of studies have showed that adults bereaved as children are more likely to develop psychiatric disorders, especially depression (reviewed by Black, 1978) and, more recently, bereaved children have been shown to have a high level of distress (Kaffman & Elizur, 1979, 1983; Raphael, 1982; Elizur & Kaffman, 1982, 1983; Black & Urbanowicz, 1985). Other studies (Van Eerdewegh *et al.*, 1982, 1985), using parent interview, identified levels of morbidity that were raised but significantly lower than those obtained by studying children directly.

Children are more likely than adults to have difficulties with the comprehension of death and the processes of grief and mourning. They are more likely to develop pathological mourning reactions because of limitations in their understanding, lack of information and changes in their lives (Bowlby & Parkes, 1970; Goodyer, 1990a).

Symptoms in bereaved children are often delayed and may be due to the consequences of the loss rather than the loss itself. Children who lose their mothers suffer also a reduction in the quantity as well as quality of care (Weller *et al.*, 1991). The finding that adult psychopathology following childhood loss of a parent is correlated with the adequacy of care following the death (Harris *et al.*, 1986) has implications for preventive intervention.

Children's grief reactions

Children who have reached school age are as capable as adults of comprehending death, of expressing grief and experiencing mourning. The reactions may appear different because they often take an immature form. The influences on the expression of grief and the ability to mourn in children are related to cognitive, emotional and physical development (Raphael, 1983).

Cognitive development

The child's ability to comprehend the various components of the concept of death have been well-studied and the consensus is that, by 5 years, most children can understand that death is irreversible, universal, has a cause, involves permanent separation and that dead people differ from live people in a number of respects. They are immobile, unfeeling, cannot hear, see, smell or speak. All their bodily functions cease and they do not require to drink or eat. The concept of corporeal deterioration is more difficult for young children to comprehend and this concept is not fully formed until nearer puberty (Kane, 1979; Reilly *et al.*, 1983; Lansdown & Benjamin, 1985).

Other cognitive difficulties involve immaturities in searching for the dead parent, an important component of the process of mourning, and anticipating both the death and the prospect of missing the dead parent. There is a developmental progression in the ability to envisage how one might feel on future occasions. For example, it would be difficult for young children to imagine that they might miss their mother when they next go on holiday. Anticipatory mourning for all the small and large events and situations at which the mother will no longer be present is therefore more difficult and, when the event comes, the child is unprepared for the emotional experience of renewed loss.

Cognition plays a part in reunion fantasies, which are concrete in early childhood:

> Harry, aged 3 when his father died, said when he visited his grandmother in the same hospital, 1 year later: 'Good, now we can see Daddy again'. His mother had believed that he accepted his father's death and was surprised that he had held on to the hope of reunion for so long. It clearly was revived by the visit to the last place he had seen his father alive.

Children are rarely prepared for the death of a parent or a sibling and yet we know from adults that mourning is aided by anticipation of the inevitability and proximity of death (Parkes, 1986). If children are informed, they have lower levels of anxiety than those who are not, even within the same family (Rosenheim & Reicher, 1985).

Cognitive limitations also affect the child's ability to recall memories, especially in the absence of contextual cues (Johnson & Foley, 1984). These are often denied them by protective adults who do not wish to remind them of their loss. The places they visited with their parent are avoided, so mourning for the lost parent is inhibited. Whereas adults can take themselves to the places in reality and in fantasy, it is more difficult for children to do so.

The loss of a parent is associated with difficulties in learning and failure to maintain progress at school (Van Eerdewegh *et al.*, 1982).

Emotional development

Children's capacity to sustain sad affects increases gradually with age and maturity. Not only may they avoid the experience of the pain of grief but young children do not sustain affects for long periods and their apparent lack of sadness may deceive their caretakers into believing that they are unaffected by the loss.

One way in which children obtain understanding of events is through repetitive play, which may be distressing to adults because it lacks appropriate affective expression. Children need to be able to understand the reality of death in order to mourn and yet they are given less opportunity to see for themselves the physical deterioration, and then the immobility and unresponsiveness of the dead parent. They may be prevented from going to the funeral and protected from the grief of the adults.

Children may be protected from reminders of the dead parent and this handicaps them in the normal process of grieving and resolving grief. Their concrete thinking and egocentric view of the world make it more likely that young children will feel guilty and responsible for the parent's disappearance. Longings for death and even suicidal ideas are common as part of reunion fantasies but are rarely acted upon (Weller *et al.*, 1991).

Another aspect of emotional development is the continuing need for caretakers. Children who have lost one parent feel anxious lest other one will also die or disappear. This leads them to monitor their surviving parent and parental expressions of grief may be misinterpreted as illness. Children may hide their own grief in order to protect their parent, and avoid upsetting them. Adolescents in the process of separating from parents may either take a step back in the process and become more involved with the family, particularly if they are the eldest or of the same sex as the deceased parent (Birtchnell, 1971), or they may react by rejecting the family and developing new and possibly premature procreative partnerships.

Children may not understand the source of the emotions of grief and suffer alone without seeking elucidation from carers or other adults. The misconstruing of emotions may lead to hypochondriasis or other psychosomatic symptoms. The ability to attribute anxiety, depression and other dysphoric emotions accurately develops with maturation. They may feel ashamed of their reactions, believing themselves to be experiencing unique emotions. Education about emotional reactions should be a part of the curriculum in schools but rarely is (Ward *et al.*, 1989), as shown by the following case:

> Carla was 4 years old when her mother died after a few weeks' illness. At 6, she was seen by a child psychiatrist because of disturbed sleep and hypochondriasis. She was

cared for by her father and a devoted child-minder and assessment revealed that she interpreted every delay in her father's return as evidence that he too had died. Her various symptoms served to keep him at home where she could keep an eye on him.

Physical development

Preverbal children react to loss with bodily responses. Previously continent children may become enuretic or soil, lose their appetites, fail to settle to sleep or become restless. Mobility may be temporarily lost. Previously secure children may cling to the remaining parent and refuse to separate. Infections and other illnesses are commoner in young children following loss of a parent (Raphael *et al.*, 1980).

EFFECTS OF PARENTAL DEATH

Infants and young children

Children younger than 4 probably have little concept of death and their reactions to the disappearance of a parent from whatever cause are similar. Thus a parent away for a few hours, and one absent for longer, evoke the same separation anxiety in children older than a few weeks or months (Bowlby, 1969). The longer the absence, the greater the distress; until protest gives way to despair and depression, and that in turn to detachment. Although early authors believed that the intensity of the reaction was related to dependence needs and that there would be no grief reaction if an infant's need for care was met (Wolfenstein, 1966), later authors have emphasized the ability of even very young children to mourn (Furman, 1974; Bowlby, 1980). Their reactions tend to be bodily ones and sad affects are not easily sustained. Depressive reactions have been described however in very young children (see Chapter 19).

Young schoolchildren

Children from 5 to 11 years are more likely to be able to comprehend the physical changes death brings and are helped by being able to perceive these changes for themselves. Adults find this difficult to contemplate and so children are cut off from using their cognitions to comprehend death. Their characteristic response to the death of a parent is activity and conduct disorders tend to predominate. Suicidal thoughts are common in bereaved children and adolescents (Balk, 1983, Weller *et al.*, 1991) but rarely lead to suicide attempts. Young children may believe that if they were to die they would be reunited with their dead parent.

Adolescents

The capacity to sustain sad affects becomes commoner around puberty and so does the ability to express grief directly rather than through bodily symptoms or behavioural disturbances.

The adolescent's biological and psychological drive towards greater autonomy conflicts with the tendency to become more dependent when bereaved and this may give rise to a seeming indifference or lack of feeling that can alarm and puzzle the adults in his or her world. The finding that the oldest child in the family of the same sex as the dead parent is more at risk for psychological problems (Birtchnell, 1971) may reflect this.

Psychiatric symptoms in bereaved children

Many of the studies that look at childhood bereavement rely on parental report alone and it has been suggested that psychopathology is underestimated (Raphael, 1982). One of the few studies to interview, using standard measures, a large nonclinical sample of bereaved children themselves, as opposed to their surviving parents, in the early months, found that most school-aged children were able to express their grief and were functioning well. Overall, only 17% of children showed significant problem behaviour in the early months following bereavement. The loss of the mother caused the greatest discontinuity in the lives of the children, and boys found more difficulty than girls in expressing their feelings of loss. The study was uncontrolled, and only 51% of a population sample consented to be interviewed (Silverman & Worden, 1992). Obviously, when referred children only are interviewed, much higher levels of distress are identified (Raphael, 1982).

Studies that look at children about 1 year after the death of a parent have found higher levels of morbidity than those that examine the children in the immediate aftermath. Approximately 40% of children were found to have dysfunctional symptoms in one study (Black & Urbanowicz, 1985) and other studies have found an even higher incidence of symptoms (Kaffman & Elizur, 1979, 1983; Elizur & Kaffman, 1982). Using adult definitions of depression, one study found that bereaved children have an increased incidence of depression (11%) compared with a control group (4%); (Van Eerdewegh *et al.*, 1982). Follow-up studies indicate a substantial improvement but with a residual higher level of dysfunction compared with the general population (Black & Urbanowicz, 1987).

Studies of children attending psychiatric clinics (Rutter, 1966) show a marked excess of parental deaths in the clinic group compared with the general population.

Long-term effects of bereavement in children

Adults bereaved as children have an approximately double risk of developing depression, especially if they experience a subsequent loss (Birtchnell, 1970; Brown *et al.*, 1971). Factors that modify the outcome are reviewed by Black (1978) and include age (younger is worse), sex (girls seem more vulnerable), mode of death (sudden deaths and violent ones such as suicide or murder are associated with a worse outcome) and subsequent experiences (good care lessens the risks). It was concluded that bereaved children are more likely to develop psychiatric disorders both in childhood and in adult life, although the risk is small. Children most at risk are those bereaved young and those whose surviving parent has a prolonged grief reaction.

Life events

The effects of the illness and death of a member of a family on the other family members have been looked at in the life events research that was systematized by Brown and his colleagues who, amongst other variables, examined the sequelae for women of losing their mother in childhood and found correlations with psychiatric disorders, particularly depressive disorder in adult life (Brown *et al.*, 1971). Goodyer has shown similar findings for bereaved children (Goodyer, 1990c–d). The state of the surviving parent's health influences the well-being of the child following bereavement (Black & Urbanowicz, 1985; Goodyer & Altham, 1991; Silverman & Worden, 1992).

EFFECTS OF THE DEATH OF A SIBLING

Children who lose a sibling have been less studied than those bereaved of a parent. One study (Pettle, Michael & Lansdown, 1986) of 28 children found that 2 or 3 years after the death, a high proportion of the children were emotionally or behaviourally disturbed and had a low self-esteem. The dead sibling was idealized and school work was suffering. If the child had been prepared for the sibling's death, had participated in the patient's care and had been able to take leave of him or her and joined in the community rituals, the outcome appeared to be better. Interestingly, there was no correlation between parental and child adaptation.

Although the majority of children cope with the death of their sibling without developing symptoms, for a few the cost of being the survivor and having to carry all the parental expectations may be great.

EFFECTS ON OTHERS

Grandparents are often involved as carers for the other children and supports for the parents. They are rarely included in any support provided by the hospital and no studies have been done of their reactions. Because they usually have to learn about the illness and prognosis at second hand, they may be bewildered and can be obstructive. They may encourage fruitless and expensive searches for alternative treatments. Other relatives may be similarly in the dark, while carrying a burden of support and care. Their grief reactions need acknowledgement.

Friends of the child are often denied recognition of their loss. They are given even less information than adults and because of their immaturity are not able to comprehend what is being discussed over their head. Rituals such as that described by Arngrimmson (1984) conducted at school or by a club can be therapeutic.

Those doctors, nurses, teachers and other professionals caring for a child who dies are themselves bereaved. They may have known him or her for many years and have come to love him or her. It is important that the senior members of the team acknowledge this and support their staff through their own grief. The dangers of neglecting this are that the individuals may develop maladaptive psychological defences or they give so much of themselves that they burn out (Raphael, 1982). The rewards of caring for dying children are immense but the stresses too have to be recognized (Dominica, 1987) and those in charge must ensure rest periods and an opportunity to work through the grief of the staff through group meetings with a leader who has skill and knowledge in bereavement counselling. Many wards find it helpful to have a meeting following a death and use it to review their contact with the dead child and the joys and sorrows of their relationship. It is important for those less closely associated with the child and family to express condolences to the staff nearest the child. In this way it is acknowledged that feelings matter and a ward ethos develops which gives due regard to their importance.

INTERVENTION WITH BEREAVED CHILDREN AND PARENTS

Before and immediately after death

There is now good evidence that many of the pathological grief reactions outlined above can be prevented or modified by intervention either before the death when possible or during the period following death. Parkes (1980), in a review of controlled studies of the efficacy of bereavement counselling for adults, concluded that it was helpful in preventing the onset of symptoms after loss, and Black and Urbanowicz's (1985) controlled trial of family therapy with children bereaved of a parent suggested that the postbereavement morbidity of 40% at 1 year could be reduced to 20% by 6 sessions of family meetings that focused on promoting shared grief and mourning within the family and encouraging communication about the dead parent. Furman and her colleagues' sensitive work with individual children, whilst not controlled, gives pointers to the problems that bereavement poses for children and how they can be helped (Furman, 1974). Others have set up programmes offering group meetings for bereaved children on the premiss that it is helpful for children to know that others are similarly affected by bereavement (Fleming & Balmer, 1991), but the intervention has not been evaluated.

When children are referred immediately after bereavement, mental health practitioners can be instrumental in ensuring that the care the child is receiving is optimal. This may involve periods of relief from the company of a grief-stricken widowed parent, advice about how to cope with other children's questions and adults' expressions of condolence, factual information about the cause of death and the processes of death, burial and cremation and advice to the carers about viewing the body, attending the funeral, returning to school, and

promoting healthy mourning (Cathcart, 1988; Weller *et al.*, 1988). The following case shows how this may happen:

> Stuart, aged 7, was referred by the nurses on the intensive care unit where his father was recovering from a massive overdose of antidepressants, prescribed by his general practitioner for a depressive illness which ensued after his wife left him. Two days later, whilst Stuart was walking his dog, his mother died suddenly from a cerebral haemorrhage and Stuart could not get back into the house. His neighbour took him to his aunt, who requested help in breaking the news to Stuart of his mother's death. During the psychiatric interview with Stuart he revealed that he had seen his mother 'asleep', although his aunt believed that he had not entered the house after his mother's death. Asked about his worries, Stuart confided that he was scared his mother had died and that no one would tell him. His father and aunt were told of this worry and were helped to talk to Stuart about it. Stuart burst into tears but was able to accept comfort from his aunt and later accompanied his uncle to see his mother's body. In his sessions with the therapist he was able to explore the beliefs of his religion and to grieve for his mother. The therapist, whilst respecting the family belief system, was able to help the family to give explanations consistent with healthy mental functioning and appropriate to the child's stage of development and understanding.

Controlled trials of counselling for bereaved parents have shown that the high incidence of prolonged grief reactions can be reduced where there has been a perinatal death by the provision of brief interventions that allow for the ventilation of sad feelings and promote communication about the dead child (Forrest *et al.*, 1982; Woodward *et al.*, 1985).

Pathological grief reactions in child or parent

There is no specific syndrome that results from a prolonged or deviant grief reaction in a child and the treatment is that of the presenting disorder. As in all psychiatric disorders, a careful history will have been taken, and any bereavements evaluated as possible precipitating or predisposing factors. In adults the technique of forced or operational mourning has been shown to be effective, if the patient has depressive symptoms and has been bereaved (Mawson *et al.*, 1981), but this has not been evaluated in children. In principle, there seems no reason why it should not be equally effective and it has been shown that forcing mourning is not harmful in early bereavement (Black & Urbanowicz, 1987).

THE INTERACTION OF TRAUMA AND GRIEF

This chapter has been largely concerned with the effects on children of life-threatening and terminal illness and bereavement. It has been suggested that children who experience traumatic events that result in bereavement may be inhibited in the expression and resolution of grief by the presence of posttraumatic stress disorder, resulting particularly from witnessing parental death or mutilation (Eth & Pynoos, 1985). Clinical experience supports such a hypothesis but there is no research evidence yet to support or refute it.

CONCLUSION

Although there are raised levels of morbidity in children facing life-threatening and terminal illness and bereavement, and in their parents and siblings, the great majority do not come to psychiatric attention and appear to negotiate their developmental tasks without needing treatment. Nevertheless, there is evidence that some of the morbidity can be prevented and, whilst there appears to be less morbidity in seriously ill children than in adults, there will be a need for therapeutic services for bereaved children who are more prone to develop psychological problems than adults. Psychiatric and psychological therapies can be of help with children who develop reactions to physical treatments. It is clear that the resilience of children is associated in some degree with the well-being of the surviving parent in childhood bereavement.

Much of the morbidity associated with serious life-threatening illness and bereavement should be preventable. Child and adolescent psychiatrists and other members of the team working together with paediatricians, nurses, general practitioners, teachers and others may make a significant contribution to the mental health of children and their parents, and be in a position to intervene early when dysfunction begins, to prevent secondary and tertiary disability. There is a paucity of good evaluation studies of psychological therapies in this area (as in others) which should be remedied.

Many of the studies in this field are marred by poor or absent controls, small numbers and selection biases (Stroebe & Stroebe, 1989). Conclusions therefore have to be tentative but at least one researcher on the effect of life experiences on the development of childhood psychopathology (Goodyer, 1990c) has concluded that we should be considering the implications of our present knowledge for the development of public policy in relation to the care of bereaved children and the prevention of distress through stress inoculation programmes and preventive interventions.

REFERENCES

Adams M.A. (1976) A hospital play programme: helping children with serious illness. *American Journal of Orthopsychiatry*, **46**, 416–424.

Altschuler J., Black D., Trompeter R., Fitzpatrick M. & Peto H. (1991) Adolescents in end-stage renal failure — a pilot study of family factors in compliance, and treatment considerations. *Family Systems Medicine*, **9**(3), 229–247.

American Psychiatric Association (1987) *Diagnostic and Statistical Manual of Mental Disorders-DSM-III-R*. APA, Washington DC.

American Psychiatric Association (1994) *Diagnostic and Statistical Manual of Mental Disorders*, 4th edn (DSM-IV). American Psychiatric Association, Washington, DC.

Anthony S. (1971) *The Discovery of Death in Childhood and After*. Allen Lane, The Penguin Press, London.

Arngrimmson B. (1984) A community crisis resolved by a mourning ritual. *Bereavement Care*, **3**(2), 18–19.

Balk D. (1983) Adolescents' grief reactions and self-concept perceptions following sibling death: a study of 33 teenagers. *Journal of Youth and Adolescence*, **12**, 137–161.

Barbarin O.A. & Chesler M. (1986) The medical context of parental coping with childhood cancer. *American Journal of Community Psychology*, **44**, 221–235.

Bartrop R.W., Lazarus L., Luckhurst E., Kiloh L.G. & Penny R. (1977) Depressed lymphocyte function after bereavement. *Lancet*, **1**, 834–836.

Bibace R. & Walsh M.E. (1980) Development of children's concepts of illness. *Pediatrics*, **66**, 912–917.

Bibace R. & Walsh M.E. (1981) Children's conceptions of illness. In: Bibace R. & Walsh M.E. (eds) *New Directions for Child Development*, vol. 14. Jossey-Bass. San Francisco.

Birch J.M., Marsden H.B., Morris Jones P.H., Pearson D. & Blair V. (1988) Improvements in survival from childhood cancer: results of a population based survey over 30 years. *British Medical Journal*, **296**, 1372–1376.

Birtchnell J. (1970) Early parent death and mental illness. *British Journal of Psychiatry*, **116**, 281–288.

Birtchnell J. (1971) Early parent death in relation to size and constitution of sibship. *Acta Psychiatrica Scandinavica*, **47**, 250–270.

Black D. (1978) Annotation: The bereaved child. *Journal of Child Psychology and Psychiatry*, **19**, 287–292.

Black D. (1989) Life-threatening illness, children and family therapy. *Journal of Family Therapy*, **11**, 81–101.

Black D. & Urbanowicz M.A. (1985) Bereaved children — family intervention. In: Stevenson J.E. (ed) *Recent Research in Developmental Psychopathology*, pp. 179–187. Pergamon, Oxford.

Black D. & Urbanowicz M.A. (1987) Family intervention with bereaved children. *Journal of Child Psychology and Psychiatry*, **28**, 467–476.

Black D., McFadyen A. & Broster G. (1990) Development of a psychiatric liaison service. *Archives of Disease in Childhood*, **65**, 1373–1375.

Blotcky A.D., Cohen D.G., Conatser E. & Klopovich P. (1985) Psychosocial characteristics of adolescents who refuse cancer treatment. *Journal of Consulting and Clinical Psychology*, **53**, 729–731.

Bluebond-Langner M. (1978) *The Private Worlds of Dying Children*. Princeton University Press, Princeton, NJ.

Bluebond-Langner M., Perkel D., Goertzel T., Nelson K. & McGeary J. (1990) Children's knowledge of cancer and its treatment: impact of an oncology camp experience [see comments]. *Journal of Pediatrics*, **116**, 207–213.

Blum R. (1984) Compliance with therapeutic regimens among children and youth. In: Blum R. (ed) *Chronic Illness and Disabilities in Childhood and Adolescence*. Grune & Stratton, New York.

Bohannon J.R. (1991) Grief responses of spouses following the death of a child — a longitudinal study. *Omega — Journal of Death and Dying*, **22**, 109–121.

Bowlby J. (1963) Pathological mourning and childhood mourning. *Journal of the American Psychoanalytic Association*, **11**, 500–541.

Bowlby J. (1969) *Attachment and Loss* vol. 1. Hogarth Press, London.

Bowlby J. (1972) *Attachment and Loss*, vol. 2. Hogarth Press, London.

Bowlby J. (1980) *Attachment and Loss*, vol. 3. Hogarth Press, London.

Bowlby J. & Parkes C.M. (1970) Separation and loss within the family. In: Anthony E.J. & Koupernile C. (eds) *The Child in his Family*. John Wiley, New York.

Brewster A.B. (1982) Chronically ill hospitalized children's concepts of their illness. *Pediatrics*, **69**(3), 355–362.

Brown G.W., Harris T. & Copeland J.R. (1971) Depression and loss. *British Journal of Psychiatry*, **130**, 1–18.

Burns W.J. & Zweig A.R. (1980) Self-concepts of chronically ill children. *Journal of Genetic Psychology*, **137**, 179–190.

Cadman D., Boyle M., Szatmari P. & Offord D.R. (1987) Chronic illness, disability, and mental and social well-being: findings of the Ontario Child Health Study. *Pediatrics*, **79**(5), 805–813.

Cadman D., Boyle M.H. & Offord D.R. (1988) The Ontario Child Health Study: social adjustment and mental health of siblings of children with chronic health problems. *Journal of Developmental and Behavioral Pediatrics*, **9**, 117–121.

Cairns N.U., Clark G.M., Smith S.D. & Lanksy S.B. (1979) Adaptation of siblings to childhood malignancy. *Journal of Pediatrics*, **95**(3), 484–487.

Caradang M.L.A., Folkins C.H., Hines P.A. & Steward M.S. (1979) The role of cognitive level and sibling illness in children's conceptualizations of illness. *American Journal of Orthopsychiatry*, **49**, 474–481.

Cathcart F. (1988) Seeing the body after death. *British Medical Journal*, **297**, 997–998.

Chambers E.J., Oakhill A., Cornish J.M. & Curnick S. (1989) Terminal care at home for children with cancer. *British Medical Journal*, **298**, 937–940.

Chesler M. & Barbarin O. (1987) *Childhood Cancer and the Family: Meeting the Challenge of Stress and Support*. Brunner/Mazel, New York.

Clunies-Ross C. & Lansdown R. (1988) Concepts of death, illness and isolation found in children with leukaemia. *Child: Care, Health and Development*, **14**, 373–386.

Cohen D.S. (1985) Pediatric cancer: predicting sibling adjustment. *Dissertation Abstracts International*, **46**(2-B), 637.

Cohen M.M. & Wellisch D.K. (1978) Living in limbo. Psychosocial intervention in families with a cancer patient. *American Journal of Psychotherapy*, **32**, 561–571.

Comaroff J. & Maguire P. (1981) Ambiguity and the search for meaning: childhood leukaemia in the modern clinical context. *Journal of Social Science in Medicine*, **15B**, 115–123.

Cook J.A. (1984) Influence of gender on the problems of parents of fatally ill children. *Journal of Psychosocial Oncology*, **2**, 71–91.

Corr C.A. & Corr D.M. (1985) Pediatric hospice care. *Pediatrics*, **76**, 774–780.

Cozzi L., Tryon W.W. & Sedlacek K. (1987) The effectiveness of biofeedback-assisted relaxation in modifying sickle cell crises. *Biofeedback and Self Regulation*, **12**, 51–61.

Daniels D., Miller J.J., Billings A.G. & Moos R.H. (1987) Psychosocial risk and resistance factors among children with chronic illness, healthy siblings, and healthy controls. *Journal of Abnormal Child Psychology*, **15**, 295–308.

Dolgin M.J. & Katz E.R. (1988) Conditioned aversions in pediatric cancer patients receiving chemotherapy. *Journal of Developmental and Behavioral Pediatrics*, **9**, 82–85.

Dominica F. (1987) Reflections on death in childhood. *British Medical Journal*, **294**, 108–110.

Dyregrov A. (1990) Parental reactions to the loss of an infant child — a review. *Scandinavian Journal of Psychology*, **31**, 266–280.

Dyregrov A. & Matthiesen S.B. (1987) Similarities and differences in mothers' and fathers' grief following the death of an infant. *Scandinavian Journal of Psychology*, **28**, 1–15.

Edwardson S.R. (1983) The choice between hospital and home care for terminally ill children. *Nursing Research*, **32**, 29–34.

Eisen M., Donald C., Ware J.E. (1980) *Conceptualization and Measurement of Health for Children in the Health Insurance Study*. Rand, Santa Monica, CA.

Eiser C. (1985) Changes in understanding of illness as the child grows. *Archives of Disease in Childhood*, **60**, 489–492.

Eiser C. (1989) 'Let's play doctors and nurses': a script analysis of children's play. *Early Child Development and Care*, **49**, 17–25.

Eiser C. (1990a) Psychological effects of chronic disease. *Journal of Child Psychology and Psychiatry*, **31**, 85–98.

Eiser C. (1990b) *Chronic Childhood Illness*. Cambridge University Press, Cambridge.

Elizur E. & Kaffman M. (1982) Children's bereavement reactions following death of the father: II. *Journal of the American Academy of Child Psychiatry*, **21**(5), 474–480.

Elizur E. & Kaffman M. (1983) Factors influencing the severity of childhood bereavement reactions. *American Journal of Orthopsychiatry*, **55**(4), 668–676.

Emanuel R., Colloms A., Mendelsohn A., Muller H. & Testa R. (1990) Psychotherapy with hospitalized children with leukaemia: is it possible? *Journal of Child Psychotherapy*, **16**(2), 21–38.

Eth S. & Pynoos R.S. (1985) Interaction of trauma and grief in childhood. In: Eth S. & Pynoos R.S. (eds) *Post Traumatic Stress Disorder in Children*, pp. 169–183. American Psychiatric Association, Washington, DC.

Finlay I. & Dallimore D. (1991) Your child is dead. *British Medical Journal*, **302**, 1524–1525.

Fleming S. & Balmer L. (1991) Group intervention with bereaved children. In: Papadatou D. & Papadatos C. (eds) *Children and Death*. Hemisphere, Washington, DC.

Forrest G.C., Standish E. & Baum J.D. (1982) Support after perinatal death: a study of support and counselling after perinatal bereavement. *British Medical Journal*, **285**, 1475–1479.

Freud S. (1917) *Mourning and Melancholia*. Hogarth Press, London.

Furman E. (1974) *A Child's Parent Dies*. Yale University Press, New Haven, CT.

Gayton W.F., Friedman S.B., Tavormina J.F. & Tucker F. (1977) Children with cystic fibrosis: 1. Psychological test findings of patients, siblings and parents. *Pediatrics*, **59**(6), 888–894.

Goodyer I.M. (1990a) *Life Experiences, Development and Childhood Psychopathology*. John Wiley, Chichester.

Goodyer I.M. (1990b) Family relationships, life events and childhood psychopathology [published erratum appears in *Journal of Child Psychology and Psychiatry*, (1990) **31**(3), 491]. *Journal of Child Psychology and Psychiatry*, **31**, 161–192.

Goodyer I.M. (1990c) Recent life events and psychiatric disorder in school age children. *Journal of Child Psychology and Psychiatry*, **31**(6), 839–848.

Goodyer E.M. & Altham P.M.E. (1991) Lifetime exit events and recent social and family adversities in anxious and depressed school-age children and adolescents — I. *Journal of Affective Disorders*, **21**, 219–228.

Graham P. & Jenkins S. (1985) Training of paediatricians for psychosocial aspects of their work. *Archives of Disease in Childhood*, **60**, 777–780.

Graham P. & Rutter M. (1973) Psychiatric disorder in the young adolescent: a follow-up study. *Proceedings of the Royal Society of Medicine*, **66**, 1226–1229.

Greenberg H.S., Kazak A.E. & Meadows A.T. (1989) Psychologic functioning in 8- to 16-year-old cancer survivors and their parents. *Journal of Pediatrics*, **114**, 488–493.

Greer S. (1985) Cancer: psychiatric aspects. In: Granville-Grossman K. (ed) *Clinical Psychiatry*, pp. 87–104. Churchill Livingstone, Oxford.

Harris T., Brown G.W. & Bifulco A. (1986) Loss of parent in childhood and adult psychiatric disorder: the role of lack of adequate parental care. *Psychological Medicine*, **16**, 641–659.

Hilgard J.R. & Lebaron S. (1982) Relief of anxiety and pain in children and adolescents with cancer: quantitative measures and clinical observations. *International Journal of Clinical and Experimental Hypnosis*, **30**, 417–442.

Hilgard J.R. & LeBaron S. (1984) *Hypnotherapy of Pain in Children with*

Cancer. Kaufman, Los Angeles, CA.

Howarth R.V. (1972) The psychiatry of terminal illness in children. *Proceedings of the Royal Society of Medicine*, **65**, 1039−1040.

Hughes P.M. & Lieberman S. (1990) Troubled parents: vulnerability and stress in childhood cancer. *British Journal of Medical Psychology*, **63**, 53−64.

ICD-9 (1977) *Manual of the International Statistical Classification of Diseases, Injuries and Causes of Death*. World Health Organization, Geneva.

ICD-10 (1992) *Classification of Mental and Behavioural Disorders*. World Health Organization, Geneva.

Iles J.P. (1979) Children with cancer: healthy siblings' perceptions during the illness experience. *Cancer Nursing*, **2**, 371−377.

Jay S.M., Elliott C.H., Katz E. & Siegel S.E. (1987) Cognitive-behavioral and pharmacologic interventions for childrens' distress during painful medical procedures. *Journal of Consulting and Clinical Psychology*, **55**, 860−865.

Jessop D.J., Riessman C.K. & Stein R.E.K. (1988) Chronic childhood illness and maternal mental health. *Journal of Developmental and Behavioral Pediatrics*, **9**, 147−156.

Johnson M.K. & Foley M.A. (1984) Differentiating fact from fantasy: the reliability of children's memory. *Journal of Social Issues*, **40**, 33−50.

Judd D. (1989) *Give Sorrow Words — Working with a Dying Child*. Free Association Press, London.

Kaffman M. & Elizur E. (1979) Children's bereavement reactions following death of the father. *International Journal of Family Therapy*, **1**, 203−229.

Kaffman M. & Elizur E. (1983) Bereavement responses of kibbutz and non-kibbutz children following death of father. *Journal of Child Psychology and Psychiatry*, **24**, 435−442.

Kamps W.A., Akkerboom J., Nitschke R., Kingma A., Holmes H.B. & Humphrey G.B. (1987) Altruism and informed consent in chemotherapy trials of childhood cancer. Special issue: Psychosocial aspects of chemotherapy in cancer care: the patient, family, and staff. *Loss, Grief and Care*, **1**, 93−110.

Kane B. (1979) Children's concepts of death. *Journal of Genetic Psychology*, **134**, 141−153.

Kaplan S.L., Busner J., Weinhold C. & Lenon P. (1987) Depressive symptoms in children and adolescents with cancer: a longitudinal study. *Journal of the American Academy of Child and Adolescent Psychiatry*, **26**, 782−287.

Kellerman J., Zeltzer L., Ellenberg L., Dash J. & Rigler D. (1980) Psychological effects of illness in adolescence. I. Anxiety, self-esteem, and perception of control. *Journal of Pediatrics*, **97**, 126−131.

Kellerman J., Zeltzer L., Ellenberg L. & Dash J. (1983) Adolescents with cancer: hypnosis for the reduction of the acute pain and anxiety associated with medical procedures. *Journal of Adolescent Health Care*, **4**, 85−90.

Kendrick C., Culling J., Oakhill T. & Mott M. (1986) Children's understanding of their illness and its treatment within a paediatric oncology unit. *Newsletter of the Association for Child Psychology and Psychiatry*, **8**, 16−20.

Kolvin I., Barrett M.L., Bhate S.R., Berney T.P., Famuyiwa O.O., Fundudis T. & Tyrer S. (1991) The Newcastle Child Depression Project diagnosis and classification of depression. *British Journal of Psychiatry*, **159**, 9−21, Suppl. 11.

Koocher G.P. (1984) Terminal care and survivorship in pediatric chronic illness. *Clinical Psychology Review*, **4**, 571−583.

Koocher G.P., O'Malley J.E., Gogan J.L. & Foster D.J. (1980) Psychological adjustment among pediatric cancer survivors. *Journal of Child Psychology and Psychiatry*, **21**, 163−173.

Kuttner L., Bowman M. & Teasdale M. (1988) Psychological treatment of distress, pain, and anxiety for young children with cancer. *Journal of Developmental and Behavioral Pediatrics*, **9**, 374−381.

Lansdown R. & Benjamin G. (1985) The development of the concept of death in children aged 5−9 years. *Child: Care, Health and Development*, **11**, 13−20.

Lask B. & Matthew D. (1979) Childhood asthma — a controlled trial of family psychotherapy. *Archives of Disease in Childhood*, **54**(2), 116−119.

Lauer M.E., Mulhern R.K., Schell M.J. & Camitta B.M. (1989) Long-term follow-up of parental adjustment following a child's death at home or hospital. *Cancer*, **63**, 988−994.

Lavigne J.V. & Ryan M. (1979) Psychologic adjustment of siblings of children with chronic illness. *Pediatrics*, **63**, 616−627.

LeBaron S. & Zeltzer L.K. (1984) The role of psychotherapy in the treatment of children with cancer. *Psychotherapy in Private Practice*, **2**, 45−49.

Ludman L., Lansdown R. & Spitz L. (1992) Effects of early hospitalization and surgery on the emotional development of 3 year olds: an exploratory study. *European Child and Adolescent Psychiatry*, **1**, 186−195.

McAnarney E.R. (1985) Social maturation: a challenge for handicapped and chronically ill adolescents. *Journal of Adolescent Health Care*, **6**, 90−101.

Maguire G.P. (1983) The psychological sequelae of childhood leukaemia. *Recent Results in Cancer Research*, **88**, 47−56.

Maguire G.P., Lee E.G., Bevington D.J., Kucheman C.S., Crabtree R.J. & Cornell C.F. (1978) Psychiatric problems in the first year after mastectomy. *British Medical Journal*, **1**, 963−965.

Mandler J. (1983) Representation. In: Flavell J.H. & Markman E.M. (eds) *Handbook of Child Psychology, vol. III: Cognitive Development*. Wiley, New York.

Manne S., Redd W., Jacobsen P., Gorfinkel K., Schorr O. & Rapkin B. (1990) Behavioral intervention to reduce child and parent distress during venipuncture. *Journal of Consulting and Clinical Psychology*, **58**, 562−572.

Martinson I.M. (1986) Home care for the dying child with cancer: feasibility and desirability. *Loss, Grief and Care*, **1**, 97−114.

Martinson I.M., Nesbit M.E. & Kersey J.H. (1985) Physician's role in home care for children with cancer. *Death Studies*, **9**, 283−293.

Mawson D., Marks I.M., Ramm L. & Stern R.S. (1981) Guided mourning for morbid grief: a controlled study. *British Journal of Psychiatry*, **138**, 185−193.

Miller J.B.M. (1971) Children's reactions to the death of a parent: a review of the psychoanalytic literature. *Journal of the American Psychoanalytic Association*, **19**, 697−719.

Millstein S.G., Adler N.E. & Irwin C.E. (1981) Conceptions of illness in young adolescents. *Pediatrics*, **68**(6), 834−839.

Morrow G., Hoagland A. & Carnrike C. (1981) Social support and parental adjustment to pediatric cancer. *Journal of Consulting and Clinical Psychology*, **49**, 763−765.

Mulhern R.K., Lauer M.E. & Hoffman R.G. (1983) Death of a child at home or in the hospital: subsequent psychological adjustment of the family. *Pediatrics*, **71**, 743−747.

Nitschke R., Humphrey G.B., Sexauer C.L., Catron B., Wunder S. & Jay S. (1982) Therapeutic choices made by patients with end-stage cancer. *Journal of Pediatrics*, **101**, 471−476.

Noeker M. & Petermann F. (1990) Treatment-related anxieties in children and adolescents with cancer. *Anxiety Research*, **3**, 101−111.

O'Brien E.L. (1987) Living with chronically ill siblings: a developmental study. *Dissertation Abstracts International*, **47**(12-B), 15075.

Offer D., Ostrov E. & Howard K.I. (1984) Body image, self-perception and chronic illness in adolescence. In: Blum R. (ed) *Chronic Illness and Disabilities in Childhood*. Grune & Stratton, New York.

Office of Population Censuses and Surveys (1985) *Mortality Statistics*

(Childhood). Series DH3 no. 19. Table 16, p. 34. OPCS, London.

Olness K. & Gardner G.G. (1988) *Hypnosis and Hypnotherapy with Children*. Grune & Stratton, Philadelphia, PA.

Osterweis M., Solomon F. & Green M. (1984) *Bereavement: Reactions, Consequences and Care*. National Academy Press, Washington, DC.

Parkes C.M. (1980) Bereavement counselling: does it work? *British Medical Journal*, **281**, 3–6.

Parkes C.M. (1985) Bereavement. *British Journal of Psychiatry*, **146**, 11–17.

Parkes C.M. (1986) *Bereavement: Studies of Grief in Adult Life*, 2nd edn. Penguin, Harmondsworth, Middlesex.

Perez-Ortega P. (1986) The psychological adjustment of school-age siblings of paediatric cancer patients: a pilot study. *Dissertation-Abstracts International*, **47**(4-B), 1736.

Pettle Michael S.A. & Lansdown R.G. (1986) Adjustment to the death of a sibling. *Archives of Disease in Childhood*, **61**, 278–283.

Pfefferbaum B., Overall J.E., Boren H.A., Frankel L.S., Sullivan M.P. & Johnson K. (1987) Alprazolam in the treatment of anticipatory and acute situational anxiety in children with cancer. *Journal of the American Academy of Child and Adolescent Psychiatry*, **26**, 532–535.

Pless I.B. & Roghmann K.J. (1971) Chronic illness and its consequences: observations based on three epidemiologic surveys. *Journal of Pediatrics*, **79**, 351–359.

Pless I.B. & Satterwhite B. (1975) Chronic illness. In: Haggerty R.J., Roghmann K.J. & Pless I.B. (eds) *Child Health and the Community*. John Wiley, New York.

Rando T.A. (1983) An investigation of grief and adaptation in parents whose children have died from cancer. *Journal of Pediatric Psychology*, **8**, 3–20.

Raphael B. (1982) The young child and the death of a parent. In: Parkes C.M. & Stevenson-Hinde I. (eds) *The Place of Attachment in Human Behaviour*. Tavistock, London.

Raphael B. (1983) *Anatomy of Bereavement*. Basic Books, New York.

Raphael B., Field J. & Kvelde H. (1980) Childhood bereavement: a prospective study as a possible prelude to future preventive intervention. In: Anthony E.J. & Chiland C. (eds) *Preventive Psychiatry in an Age of Transition*. John Wiley, New York.

Redd W.H., Jacobsen P.B., Die-Trill M., Dermatis H., McEvoy H. & Holland J.C. (1987) Cognitive/attentional distraction in the control of conditioned nausea in pediatric cancer patients receiving chemotherapy. *Journal of Consulting and Clinical Psychology*, **55**, 391–395.

Reilly T.P., Hasazi J.E. & Bond L.A. (1983) Children's conceptions of death and personal mortality. *Journal of Pediatric Psychology*, **8**(1), 21–31.

Richmond S.L. (1985) Factors influencing sibling reaction to childhood cancer. *Dissertation-Abstracts International*, **46**(6-B), 2051.

Rolland J.S. (1984) Toward a psychosocial typology of chronic and life-threatening illness. *Family Systems Medicine*, **2**, 245–262.

Rosenheim E. & Reicher R. (1985) Informing children about a parent's terminal illness. *Journal of Child Psychology and Psychiatry*, **26**, 995–998.

Rosser J.E. & Maguire P. (1982) Dilemmas in general practice: the care of the cancer patient. *Social Science in Medicine*, **16**, 315–322.

Rutter M. (1966) *Children of Sick Parents*. Oxford University Press, Oxford.

Rutter M., Tizard J. & Whitmore K. (eds) (1970) *Education, Health and Behaviour*. Longman Press, London.

Sabbeth B. & Leventhal J. (1984) Marital adjustment to chronic childhood illness: a critique of the literature. *Pediatrics*, **73**, 762–767.

Schleifer S.J., Keller S.E., Camerino M., Thornton J.C. & Stein M. (1983) Suppression of lymphocyte stimulation following bereavement. *Journal of the American Medical Association*, **250**, 374–377.

Schleifer S.J., Keller S.E., Meyerson A.T., Raskin M.J., Davis K.L. &

Stein M. (1984) Lymphocyte function in major depressive disorder. *Archives of General Psychiatry*, **41**, 484–486.

Silverman P.R. & Worden J.W. (1992) Children's reactions in the early months after the death of a parent. *American Journal of Orthopsychiatry*, **62**, 93–104.

Slavin L. (1981) Evolving psychosocial issues in the treatment of childhood cancer: a review. In: Koocher G. & O'Malley J. (eds) *The Damocles Syndrome*. McGraw-Hill, New York.

Slavin L., O'Malley J., Koocher G. & Foster D. (1982) Communication of the cancer diagnosis to pediatric patients: impact on long-term adjustment. *American Journal of Psychiatry*, **139**, 179–183.

Smith K.E., Gotlieb S., Gurwitch R.H. & Blotchy A.D. (1987) Impact of a summer camp experience on daily activity and family interactions among children with cancer. *Journal of Pediatric Psychology*, **12**, 533–542.

Smith K.E., Ackerson J.D. & Blotcky A.D. (1989) Reducing stress during invasive medical procedures: relating behavioral interventions to preferred coping style in pediatric cancer patients. Special issue: Pediatric pain, distress, and intervention. *Journal of Pediatric Psychology*, **14**, 405–419.

Sokel B.S., Devane S.P., Bentovim A. & Milla P.J. (1990) Self hypnotherapeutic treatment of habitual vomiting. *Archives of Disease in Childhood*, **65**, 626–627.

Spinetta J.J. (1981) The sibling of the child with cancer. In: Spinetta J.J. & Deasy-Spinetta P. (eds) *Living with Childhood Cancer*. C.V. Mosby, St Louis, MO.

Spinetta J.J. & Deasey-Spinetta P. (1981) Talking with children who have life-threatening diseases. In: Spinetta J.J. & Deasy-Spinetta P. (eds) *Living with Childhood Cancer*. C.V. Mosby, St Louis, MO.

Spinetta J. & Maloney J. (1975) Death anxiety in the outpatient leukemic child. *Pediatrics*, **56**, 1035–1037.

Spinetta J.J., Rigler D. & Karon M. (1973) Anxiety in the dying child. *Pediatrics*, **52**, 841–845.

Spinetta J.J., Murphy J.L., Vik P.J., Day J. (1988) Long-term adjustment in families of children with cancer. Special issue: Clinical research issues in psychosocial oncology. *Journal of Psychosocial Oncology*, **6**, 179–191.

Spirito A., Russo D.C. & Masek B.J. (1984) Behavioral interventions and stress management training for hospitalized adolescents and young adults with cystic fibrosis. *General Hospital Psychiatry*, **6**, 211–218.

Stein A. & Woolley H. (1990) An evaluation of hospice care for children. In: Baum J.D., Dominica F. & Woodward R.N. (eds) *Listen, My Child Has a Lot of Living to Do*, pp. 66–90. Oxford University Press, Oxford.

Stein A., Forrest G.C., Woolley H. & Baum J.D. (1989) Life threatening illness and hospice care. *Archives of Disease in Childhood*, **64**, 697–702.

Stroebe M.S. & Stroebe W. (1989) Who participates in bereavement research? a review and empirical study. *Omega*, **20**(1), 1–29.

Sumner M. & Dinwiddie R. (1991) Loss on a paediatric intensive care unit: parents' perceptions. *Care of the Critically Ill*, **7**, 64–66.

Terr L. (1988) What happens to early memories of trauma? A study of 20 children under age 5 at the time of documented traumatic events. *Journal of the American Academy of Child and Adolescent Psychiatry*, **27**(1), 96–104.

Tolley E.S. (1987) Factors affecting the behavioural adaptation of children following the diagnosis of cancer in a brother or sister: an examination of child and sibling access characteristics. *Dissertation-Abstracts-International*, **48**(6-A), 1543.

Van Eerdewegh M.M., Bieri M.D., Parrilla R.H. & Clayton P.J. (1982) The bereaved child. *British Journal of Psychiatry*, **140**, 23–29.

Van Eerdewegh M.M., Clayton P.J. & Van Eerdewegh P. (1985) The bereaved child: variables influencing early psychopathology. *British*

Journal of Psychiatry, **147**, 188−194.

Vida S. & Grizenko N. (1989) DSM-III-R and the phenomenology of childhood bereavement: a review. *Canadian Journal of Psychiatry*, **34**, 148−155.

Waechter E.H. (1971) Children's awareness of fatal illness. *American Journal of Nursing*, **7(6)**, 1168−1172.

Walker D., Gortmaker S. & Weitzman M. (1981) *Chronic Illness and Psychosocial Problems Among Children in Genesee County*. Harvard School of Public Health Publications, Boston.

Wall V.J. & Womack W. (1989) Hypnotic versus active cognitive strategies for alleviation of procedural distress in pediatric oncology patients. *American Journal of Clinical Hypnosis*, **31**, 181−191.

Wallander J.L., Varni J.W., Babani L., Banis H.T. & Wilcox K.T. (1988) Children with chronic physical disorders: maternal reports of their psychological adjustment. *Journal of Pediatric Psychology*, **13**, 197−212.

Wallander J.L., Varni J.W., Babani L., Banis H.T. & Wilcox K.T. (1989) Family resources as resistance factors for psychological maladjustment in chronically ill and handicapped children. *Journal of Pediatric Psychology*, **14**, 157−173.

Ward B. (1992) *Good Grief!*, 2nd edn. Ward 19, Bawtree Road, Uxbridge, Middx, UBE 1TT.

Watson M. (1983) Psychosocial intervention with cancer patients: a selected review. *Psychological Medicine*, **13**, 839−846.

Weithorn L. & Campbell S. (1982) The competency of children and adolescents to make informed treatment decisions. *Child Development*, **53**, 1589−1598.

Weller E.B., Weller R.A., Fristad M.A., Cain S.E. & Bowes J.M. (1988) Should children attend their parent's funeral? *Journal of the American Academy of Child and Adolescent Psychiatry*, **27**, 559−562.

Weller R.A., Weller E.B., Fristad M.A. & Bowes J.M. (1991) Depression in recently bereaved prepubertal children. *American Journal of Psychiatry*, **148**, 1536−1540.

Wolfenstein M. (1966) How is mourning possible? *Psychoanalytic Study of the Child*, **21**, 93−123.

Woodward S., Pope A., Robson W.J. & Hagan O. (1985) Bereavement counselling after sudden infant death. *British Medical Journal*, **290**, 363−365.

Woolley H., Stein A., Forrest G. & Baum J. (1989) Imparting the diagnosis of life threatening illness in children. *British Medical Journal*, **298**, 1623−1626.

Worchel F.F., Nolan B.F., Willson V.L., Purser J.S., Copeland D.R. & Pfefferbaum B. (1988) Assessment of depression in children with cancer. *Journal of Pediatric Psychology*, **13**(1), 101−112.

Working party on research on children (1991) *The Ethical Conduct of Research on Children*. Medical Research Council, London.

Zeltzer L., Kellerman J., Ellenberg L., Dash J. & Rigler D. (1980) Psychologic effects of illness in adolescence. II. Impact of illness in adolescents — crucial issues and coping styles. *Journal of Pediatrics*, **97**(1), 132−138.

Zeltzer L., Kellerman J., Ellenberg L. & Dash J. (1983) Hypnosis for reduction of vomiting associated with chemotherapy and disease in adolescents with cancer. *Journal of Adolescent Health Care*, **4**, 77−84.

Chapter 46
History of Child and Adolescent Psychiatry

William Ll. Parry-Jones

INTRODUCTION

The principal justification for this chapter lies in the potential benefits to be derived from the application of historical understanding to psychiatry. In most branches of medicine, theoretical and technical advances have been so rapid and substantial that historical aspects have only limited current application. This is not the case, however, in child and adolescent psychiatry, where for most of its history, scientific progress has been slow and discontinuous and there are a number of practical and conceptual dilemmas. Many questions bear on the future of the subspecialty, concerning its scope, its place in psychiatry and medicine, and issues about staff roles and organization. Despite the dangers of exaggerating the pragmatic value of history, particularly as a guide to the future (Warren, 1971), historical analysis can contribute positively to the clarification and resolution of some current issues (Parry-Jones, 1989). It can, for example, illuminate the development of aetiological theories, the past management of enduring clinical and social problems and the vagaries of service evolution.

The central theme of this chapter runs from the 16th to the mid 20th century, with the aim of addressing issues not dealt with previously. The main objective is to juxtapose the available evidence, however fragmentary, concerning the emergence of the psychiatry of childhood and youth as a medical discipline. The focus is on British developments and English-language sources, with reference to significant influences and pertinent literature from continental Europe and the US. The roots of modern child and adolescent psychiatry, which cannot be divorced from the evolution of psychiatry as a whole, have to be sought in a complex, dispersed but interacting network of facts and disciplines. Interpretational difficulties arise, for example, from changing connotations of the terms infancy, childhood and adolescence over the centuries. Kett (1977) observed that, in the early 19th century, not only was childhood dependence within the home much shorter, but adolescence scarcely existed. In the course of this chapter, the age of 20 years is taken as the upper limit, since this was used relatively consistently in literature on lunacy, particularly in 19th-century asylum statistics.

HISTORIOGRAPHY OF CHILDHOOD INSANITY

The way medical history is written, its authenticity, coverage and orientation, needs to be subjected to comparable analytic and evaluative scrutiny as would be operative with scientific research methodology. Recent years have seen the extensive reexamination of 18th- and 19th-century lunacy institutions and practice, with greater use of primary sources and revisionist interpretations (Bynum *et al.*, 1985/1988; Porter, 1987; Scull, 1989). Child and adolescent psychiatry, however, has received very limited research. Brief historical introductions in textbooks usually repeat conventional — sometimes erroneous — ideas with little advancement of historical knowledge, involving simplistic, past—present comparisons and excessive reliance on secondary sources and historical reviews (Kauffman, 1976). Modern writers have often failed to acknowledge the theoretical and practical advances of previous centuries and to have taken the view that 'prior to the 1920s there was no body of knowledge or clinical practice integrated enough to merit being set aside as an organized specialty' (Kanner, 1959). Rosenblatt (1971) even concluded that before the Freudian era 'the history of the treatment of children is in some respects hardly worth writing'. The social position of mentally disordered children over the centuries, the significance of child psychopathology and the emergence of discrete mental disorders have received minimal research attention. Definition of the enduring aspects of some forms of insanity, in face of the ever-widening range of problems brought under the aegis of psychiatry, has particular relevance. Despite methodological and practical difficulties, there is a pressing need for historical research, especially evaluation of the classical and medieval heritage (Parry-Jones, 1992). There are, however, a number of useful reviews addressing principally the more modern aspects of the history of the medical specialty (Witmer, 1940; Crutcher, 1943; Lowrey, 1944; Kanner, 1948, 1959; Rubinstein, 1948; Cameron, 1956; Walk, 1964; Duché, 1990; Stone, 1973; Nissen, 1974, 1991; Howells & Osborn, 1981; Brandon, 1986; Von Gontard, 1988; Wardle, 1991a,b).

HISTORY OF CHILDHOOD, ADOLESCENCE AND THE FAMILY

Familiarity with child development and nurture, integral to modern child psychiatry, needs to be associated with an awareness of continuities and discontinuities with previous beliefs and practices. Patterns of childhood experience, child-rearing, parent—child relations and family evolution have become popular historical research themes (Ariès, 1962; Bremner *et al.*, 1970/1971; Laslett & Wall, 1972; de Mause, 1976; Rabb & Rotberg, 1976; Pollock, 1983; Wilson, 1980; Walvin, 1984). The expanding historiography of the family creates a background against which the apparently widening range of social, emotional, behavioural and educational problems of juveniles and parents, and the consequent burgeoning of caring services, become more comprehensible.

The influence of social, cultural, economic and demographic changes in defining the limits of childhood is fundamental in historical studies of child welfare. From the late 18th century, for example, the British population grew rapidly, especially in industrialized areas. Traditionally, lower-class children had an early introduction to adult responsibilities, in the family and the workplace, with little child-to-adult transition time, while upper-class children underwent a lengthened educational dependence. Despite changes in the prevailing view of children from the 17th century onwards, this pattern persisted in western culture until children's status changed following the humanitarian reform movement. From 1833, child labour was restricted by successive Factory Acts; compulsory elementary education was introduced in 1870, with growing awareness of the psychological components of childhood, individual differences and the deterministic significance of early life experiences. Such changes, reflected in literature and art, where the child became a focus of romantic interest, contrasted with the harsh realities of child prostitution, incest and rape in 19th-century cities. In 1871, when the age of consent was raised from 12 to a mere 13 years, infant rape was already featuring as a medicolegal issue (Adams, 1843; Wilde, 1859), formalizing even earlier concern about infant violation.

Interest in the developmental stages of infancy, childhood and adolescence has not been confined to modern times. They had attracted attention from antiquity, with continuing currency of the terms *puer, puella, adolescens* and *pueritia* during the Middle Ages (Demaitre, 1977; Gordon, 1986). As early as the 13th century, *De Proprietatibus Rerum* (de Glanville, 1535) incorporated perceptive descriptions of bodily and behavioural maturational changes. Some historians, however, contend that the modern concept of adolescence emerged as a socially created stage only during the late 19th and early 20th centuries, reflecting demographic and industrial changes, with puberty as the biological determinant (Demos & Demos, 1969). Although this interpretation requires revision (Fox, 1977; Kett, 1977), it is clear that Hall's seminal work (1904) made adolescence a new focus for study. Innovative accounts of female adolescence were published (Anonymous, 1921).

Age-related problems were generated by lengthening formal education and dependence on parents.

The changing role and status of children were associated with alterations in child-rearing practices and sustained high infant mortality rates. De Mause (1976) identified six modes of parent—child relations, as parents became more tuned in to the needs of their offspring, culminating in the permissive, mid 20th-century helping mode. This contrasted with the conformist 19th-century socialization mode, and the 18th-century intrusive mode, subordinating the child's will. Western family life and structure have changed radically over the last two centuries, with decreasing family size, increasing state dependence, incursion of specialist agencies, female emancipation, greater health expertise, parental role-sharing and declining authority, self-fulfilment concerns and emphasis on the status and rights of children. However, this evolutionary process has been erratic and Stone (1979) identified 'the only steady linear change' over 400 years as 'growing concern for children', with treatment oscillating 'cyclically between the permissive and the repressive'. Demands on parents necessitated increased counselling, reflected in expanding literature, on parenthood, child-training and childhood sexuality (Combe, 1841; Jackson, 1882; Crichton-Miller, 1923). Such parent-guidance literature was supported by numerous popular manuals on family health (M'Gregor-Robertson, 1907) and birth control (Stopes, 1920).

WELFARE, PROTECTION AND CORRECTION

The welfare of destitute, deprived and delinquent juveniles has always encroached upon the physician's role. Its history is covered in other works (Craig, 1946; Heywood, 1959). This chapter reviews chiefly the 19th-century developments, when the boundaries of child psychiatry were being delineated.

The effectiveness of the Elizabethan Poor Law Act (1601) in protecting helpless children was variable and the time-hallowed abandonment of unwanted offspring, including the mentally and physically defective, continued (Boswell, 1988). The first institution for destitute children, the Foundling Hospital, London, opened in 1747 (McClure, 1981). Despite its admirable objectives, there was opposition to additional foundations on the grounds of encouraging abandonment, the deprivation of proper parenting and high institutional infant mortality. By the early 19th century, there were many orphans and foundlings in overcrowded, unsalubrious work-houses (Crowther, 1981). Child labour in coalmines and factories and compulsory apprenticeship burgeoned. Gradually, educational provisions were made in workhouse and district schools and boarding-out in families developed, but parochial supervision remained inefficient. The year 1872 saw the first legislation for infant life protection; adoption was legalized in 1926 and a distinction drawn between adoption and fostering (Trasler, 1960; Schor, 1982). The Children Act (1948) laid the modern foundations for the care of children deprived of normal home life.

Philanthropic concern for needy children was pioneered by 19th-century rescue societies, notably the Destitute Children's Dinner Society (1864), the National Children's Home and Orphanage (1869) and Dr Barnardo's Homes (1870). Following American precedents, societies for the prevention of cruelty to children emerged, culminating in the National Society for the Prevention of Cruelty to Children (1889). The conspicuous social problems of vagrant children in the late 18th and early 19th centuries initiated the Ragged School Movement. The Marine Society (1756) established a school for convicts' children, usually regarded as the earliest agency for delinquent youth. However, these organizations, and short-lived institutions like the County of Warwick Juvenile Criminal Asylum, made little impact on early 19th-century juvenile crime, when any child over 7 was considered as capable of committing felony (Beach, 1900). Convicted juveniles were sent to prisons and houses of correction, amid growing dissatisfaction about their numbers and recidivism. Encouraged by Carpenter's work in Bristol (1851) and concern about harsh conditions at Parkhurst Prison for Boys, industrial and reformatory schools (later, approved schools) were established, for training, detention and social rehabilitation (Carlebach, 1970; Ribton-Turner, 1887). Borstal institutions were established, from 1908, to train young offenders needing higher security than the approved schools (MacKellar, 1913; Barman, 1934). Probation was introduced in 1907 and the Children Act (1908) led to the foundation of the British juvenile court system. Early child guidance focused on delinquents. Outside the approved school system, the early 20th century saw innovative, progressive residential schools and therapeutic communities for delinquent and disturbed children. In the US, the first White House Conference on Care of Dependent and Neglected Children, in 1909, introduced the principles of the child welfare movement. The child mental health movement, therefore, developed in a social context distinct from hospital-based adult psychiatry.

CHILD MENTAL DEVELOPMENT

The background to modern developmental psychology is relevant to the child psychiatrist because of the long-standing interrelationship between developmental theories and the interpretation of insanity. Its history from the 19th century onwards falls into three stages (White, 1979): (1) child study, in the 19th and early 20th centuries; (2) child development, in the 1920s and 1930s, emphasizing scientific research; and (3) developmental psychology from the 1950s, within mainstream psychology (Sears, 1975). Recently, the concept of developmental psychopathology has emerged (see below). Gradually, during the 19th century, psychology evolved from a philosophical to a scientific discipline. Concepts of child development still reflected the 17th-century theories of Locke, who believed that from birth children were susceptible to moulding into productive citizens (Locke, 1690). His emphasis on more liberal education contrasted with Rousseau's views, stressing spontaneity, direct sensory experience and learning

by active involvement. Rousseau's understanding of the developing mind and emphasis on feelings gave impetus to child study and education (Rousseau, 1762). In the late 18th and early 19th centuries, Pestalozzi (Green, 1912) and Froebel (1893) developed educational theories and practices that influenced the emergence of 'educational therapy'.

Darwin's theory of evolution raised challenging problems concerning development and variation. He described the development of one of his own children (Darwin, 1877), highlighting similarities between the mental processes of humans and animals, particularly in terms of emotional expression (Darwin, 1872), in ways that were significant for alienists, notably H. Maudsley (1835–1918). Although Darwinism remained influential, some support persisted for Lamarckian views concerning the inheritance of acquired characteristics, and for the evolutionary theories of Spencer. Galton (1869), founder of eugenics, explored the extent to which heredity or environment determined individual differences in personality, mental capacity and psychopathology. The nature/nurture debate and questions about immutability or plasticity of childhood continued into the 20th century (Gesell, 1925; Watson, 1925). By the close of the 19th century, interest in child study was developing rapidly in Europe and the US, with further biographical accounts of infant development (Champneys, 1881; Shinn, 1893) and an advanced description of reflex development, growth and behaviour patterns (Preyer, 1894). These complemented observational child behaviour studies that had been accumulating over the preceding century, following work in Germany by Tiedemann (Dennis, 1949). In the US, Hall's *Pedagogical Seminary* (1891) covered both normal and exceptional children (Bohannon, 1896). Sully, founder of the British Association for Child Study, published his own recapitulationary theories (1895), and the century closed with a flurry of developmental works. Adolescent development was not overlooked and Clouston (1891) focused on developmental disorders of this period, clearly distinguishing adolescence (18–25 years) from puberty (Clouston, 1880). A recurrent post-Darwinian theme was ancestral recapitulation: passage through developmental stages characterized those of the race. In practical terms, the doctrine 'ontogeny recapitulates phylogeny' was transferred from embryological to mental development and recast as 'infant psychology recapitulates race psychology'. These ideas were expanded by Baldwin (1894), and Hall (1904) described such concepts as psychic evolution and archeopsychisms. Child study and 'paidology' in Europe and the US was documented by Claparède (1911). Twentieth-century developmental theories were influenced predominantly by the Freuds and subsequent child psychoanalysts; by Claparède's 'functionalist' approach; Piaget's cognitive-developmental studies (1926); Kohlberg's moral development theories (1964); Vygotsky's sociocultural views (1962); Werner's organic approach (1948) and Erikson's psychosocial perspective of the life cycle (1959).

Developmental psychology tended to concentrate on normal processes and to describe the typical course of development rather than individual differences. The modern discipline of developmental psychopathology examines factors leading to variations in lines of development, continuities and discontinuities between normal and morbid development, and the convergence of genetic and environmental factors in determining deviant types of development. The course of disorder is seen less as the evolution of a disease and more as the outcome of multiple complex interactions. While building on earlier concepts, elaborated by the early study of mental development, it reflects increasing awareness of the range of factors affecting development and the active contribution that children make in determining their environment.

RECOGNITION OF PSYCHOLOGICAL INFLUENCES AND MENTAL DISEASES WITHIN CHILDREN'S MEDICINE

Current issues in the relationship between child and adolescent psychiatry and paediatrics become more comprehensible with historical perspective. The first references to psychological disturbance are incorporated in early works on children's medicine. Although Savonarola (who died in 1462) discussed child welfare in his work on maternal care (Demaitre, 1977), the earliest printed treatise on children's diseases was published in Italy by Bagellardus (1472). The first book on children's diseases (translated into English in 1540) was Roesslin's German treatise (Still, 1931), followed by the first English paediatric text (Phaer, 1545). Both discussed epilepsy and night terrors and Phaer added 'Pissing in the Bedde'. Works on childhood disorders continued to appear, increasing in the late 18th century. Harris (1742), however, stated that the management of sick children, usually in the hands of nurses and old women, remained 'a sort of guesswork'. His work was superseded by Underwood (1789), whose section on 'the passions of the mind' represented 'an early essay in infant psychology' (Abt & Garrison, 1965). Although dispensaries catered for sick children from the late 18th century, some early hospitals excluded them and the inadequacy and inappropriateness of general hospitals for children were recognized. Foundations such as the Hospital for Sick Children, Great Ormond Street, London, provided the framework for the new discipline of paediatrics (Franklin, 1964), but made no provision for mentally ill children.

Although there appear to be no specific references to insanity in early English-Language paediatric texts, various psychological and social factors were recognized. Exposure of children to sudden or continual fear, producing vomiting and possibly epilepsy, for example, was described by Von Rosenstein (1776) and there were frequent references to convulsions induced in breast-fed infants by maternal dietary indiscretions or mental 'passions' (Underwood, 1789). Armstrong (1808) stressed the dangers of 'precocious employment of the mental faculties', which contributed to 'the great increase of nervous complaints', held to have doubled over the preceding century. Parkinson's guides (1800, 1801, 1807), for parents and families, revealed remarkable insight into child management. It is significant that interest in childhood insanity was slow to enter paediatric literature, except for topics such as convulsions (Clarke, 1815), sleep disturbance and bed-wetting (Glicklich, 1951). West (1848), founder of Great Ormond Street Hospital, discussed night terrors and, later (1854), reflecting wider trends, included 'disorders of the mind' and idiocy. He mentioned hypochondriasis and malingering, but stressed the importance of moral insanity, affirming that 'mental disorder in childhood seems ... almost invariably to assume this character'. His later writings (1860, 1871) featured substantial sections on mental disorders. Although the classical theory concerning maternal psychological impressions on the fetus (Paré, 1649; Turner, 1732; Talbot, 1898) was discussed in an early American paediatric textbook (Dewees, 1826), Adams (1897) noted that the topic of insanity was not mentioned in American paediatric literature from 1789 to 1896.

Notable early 20th-century paediatric authors (Rachford, 1905; Cameron, 1918) focused on functional nervous diseases, reflecting growing recognition of the effects of emotion on health, the problems of neurotic children and their consequences in adulthood. Guthrie (1909), for example, discussed neurotic fears, fretting, home-sickness and educational overstrain. In the early 1930s, a closer alliance developed between child psychiatry and paediatrics, despite mutual suspicion and uncertainty about their respective boundaries (White House Conference on Child Health and Protection, 1932). In the borderland between psychiatry and paediatrics, the work of Kanner (1959) and Winnicott (1931, 1958) was outstanding. However, some paediatricians were critical of psychiatry (Brenneman, 1931), cautioning about its overuse. Paterson (1941) warned against the tendency 'when 'Child Psychology' is so much in vogue, to attribute all the faults of behaviour to faulty management and environment', stressing that organic disease remained 'the probable cause of many behaviour problems'. Generally, mental problems 'remained a sideline, without great originality in paediatric writings' (Von Gontard, 1988), thereby facilitating the emergence of child psychiatry as a separate discipline.

MENTAL RETARDATION

Mental retardation and its management are integral to the history of psychiatry as a whole and of specific relevance in child and adolescent psychiatry (Kanner, 1964; Jones, 1967; Rosen *et al.*, 1971; Scheerenberger, 1983). From medieval times, lunatics were distinguished from idiots, but systematic improvement of the condition of mentally retarded children started only in the 19th century. Some impetus was given by Itard's experimental education and socialization of the wild boy of Aveyron (Itard, 1801), the best known of the documented feral children (Anonymous, 1768; Ireland, 1875a; Malson, 1972). His principles had long-term implications for idiots, imbeciles and 'functionally' retarded children, by encouraging remedial education. During the early 19th century, behaviourally disturbed, retarded juveniles, who were not kept at home, were confined in madhouses, asylums and workhouses. By the second half of the century, separate institutions for their education, rehabilitation or custody began to be established, with gradual differentiation of the causes of mental defect, e.g. Mongolian idiocy (Down, 1867) and the Idiots Act (1886), first provided separately for defectives. Classification remained unrefined, perceived causation included organic disease, degeneracy, intermarriage and intemperance, and anthropological explanations and ethnographic categorization continued to be influential (Bogdan, 1988).

Schools for 'fatuous patients' opened in France in the early 19th century, notably at the Bicêtre, Paris, where outstanding contributions were made by Ferrus, Voisin and Séguin in 1846 (Duché, 1990). The much-visited institution for cretins at Abendberg, Switzerland, was influential briefly (Guggenbuhl, 1845). Some British idiot establishments functioned from the late 1840s but, even by the 1880s, few institutionalized idiots were in specialized accommodation. Child provisions began with a small private institution at Bath in 1847 and, in 1849, the Idiot Asylum, Park House, London, opened. Others soon followed, including the Earlswood Idiot Asylum, Surrey, and the Darenth Schools at Dartford, Kent (1878) for 1000 imbecile children. Similar developments occurred throughout Europe and the US (Brady, 1865; Beach, 1900; Barr, 1904). By 1882, there were 11 American institutions for the feeble-minded, their aim being employment, establishing good habits and moral standards.

Where specialist institutional provisions were inadequate, concern mounted about the admission of mentally retarded children to lunatic asylums. Children as young as 4 were in confinement, most were idiots and many were epileptic (Ireland, 1886). Wise (1865) illustrated the inadequate specialized provision by referring to the plight of a 12-year-old Irish imbecile girl who, predictably, would need admission to the poorhouse or the lunatic asylum in late adolescence, when already 'less hope can be held out for a complete cure'.

In view of the grossly inadequate capacity of idiot asylums, some county asylums built annexes for imbecile children. The earliest idiot asylum superintendents advocated the benefits of institutional training in a 'family home' setting. At Barre, Massachusetts, for example, the superintendent recommended segregation because the normal child might thoughtlessly reject the weaker one, 'who, thus repulsed will perhaps not put forth a second effort but shrinks back into still duller apathy' (Brown, 1853). This view was endorsed by a former superintendent of the Darenth Schools (Beach, 1895). In a plea for greater separation according to degree of handicap, the Boston institution trustees emphasized, moralistically, the inadvisability of placing children with capacity for improvement 'in frequent contact with revolting objects, of whom it would be blasphemy to say that they were made in the image and after the likeness of God' (Greene, 1882).

Pessimism about curability of inherited disease, and fears, fostered by eugenic ideology, of the proliferation of retardation encouraged institutionalization. Segregation of idiots and imbeciles in colonies, particularly delinquents and fertile, feeble-minded females, persisted into the 1950s, However, a

degree of optimism continued in educational, industrial and moral training, involving collaboration between physicians and teachers (Shuttleworth & Potts, 1910).

The possibility of intercurrent insanity, such as melancholia, was always acknowledged. Down (1887), for example, described 'children intermediate between the idiot and lunatic, children of neurotic parents who breakdown under any vital strain' and Ireland (1898) discussed 'mad idiots', 'imbecile lunatics' and 'moral imbecility', a variant of moral insanity applied to criminal children (Sullivan, 1915).

For feeble-minded children, who were neither certifiable imbeciles nor in need of confinement, belated educational provisions were made in the UK, under the Elementary Education (Defective and Epileptic Children) Act (1899) which created special classes and schools (Shuttleworth, 1888; Kelynack, 1915). Identification and classification were refined by the application of the assessment tests of Binet and Simon (1914). It was not until the Education Act (1944) that the integration of some retarded children into ordinary schools was initiated.

Although the study and management of mental retardation in the 20th century deviated from child psychiatry, these fields remained closely allied. Valuable common ground was experienced in the management of disordered behaviour, and idiot asylums and colonies 'served as a model for the organization of large groups of in-patient children with educational and behavioural problems' (Von Gontard, 1988).

CHRONOLOGY OF THE EMERGING SPECIALTY

Classical and medieval influences

Despite the remoteness of classical and medieval writings, the evident concern for the physical and psychological well-being of infants and children means that these periods cannot be dismissed as irrelevant to the history of child psychiatry. Among pertinent contributions of Hippocrates, (460−370 BC), for example, were the concepts of the seven ages of man and the assignment of nonsupernatural causes to childhood convulsions. Aristotle (384−323 BC) works discussed parent−offspring resemblances and the significance of remoter ancestral links, but rejected the maternal impressions theory, which recurred intermittently until the 19th century, in explanation of childhood physical anomalies and behavioural disturbances. Celsus (25 BC−50 AD) advised that 'children should not be treated as adults', noted that epilepsy and insanity occurred in youth, and that puberty was a critical stage (Abt & Garrison, 1965). Soranus (93−138 AD) concluded detailed child-care discussion with practical advice on weaning. Play should be used to distract the gluttonous child from dietary restrictions, while the fastidious infant's appetite should be 'whetted by variety' (Still, 1931). The infant-care treatise of Galen (130−200 AD) emphasized the normal child's innate goodness and the need to prevent its corruption and excessive disturbance. Paul of Aegina, in the 7th century, discussed hydrocephalus, epilepsy and enuresis, and the Arabian physician, Rhazes (c. 860–932 AD), referred to night terrors, sleeplessness and convulsions. In the 10th century, Avicenna advised on child training and character formation. Excesses of anger, low spirits and over-enforced learning were prejudicial, but exercise was beneficial.

During the Middle Ages, the complex strands of Graeco-Roman and Arabic medicine intermingled with traditional medieval folk medicine and medical explanations synthesized classical, pagan and Christian elements. The 13th-century work of de Glanville (1535) is representative of the neglected period of 'scholastic medicine' (Demaitre, 1977). It influenced subsequent child-care literature and was avant-garde in explaining mental illness by natural causes, rather than demonology. In medieval times, religious experience, demonic possession and psychologically abnormal experiences were not clearly differentiated and 'A wide spectrum of behavior that would be considered extremely pathological today was accepted as normal' (Kroll, 1973). The late Middle Ages witnessed extraordinary hysterical mass phenomena, such as the Children's Pilgrimage and the Dancing Mania. These were interpreted as religious zeal, physical illness, mental disturbance or supernatural visitations, and mental disorders continued to be attributed to such influences for centuries. Physical nurture and moral training were not overlooked during the Middle Ages (Shahar, 1990) and Kroll and Bachrach (1986) found little evidence of child abuse and neglect in their study of early medieval Europe. Mental disorder and child care were studied by Clarke (1975) and Gordon (1986), using records of miraculous cures at medieval shrines. Identified juvenile abnormalities included madness, hysterical and suicidal behaviour, food refusal associated with demonic possession and infantile failure to thrive. The latter, like congenital deformity and hydrocephalus, was interpreted, for centuries, as supernatural replacement of normal infants by defective changelings.

Sixteenth and 17th centuries

During this period, references to childhood insanity remain elusive and general texts on madness appear to contribute no information on children. Alexis of Piemont's herbal remedy (1562) for children suffering from 'the Lunatike disease' is unique, attributing disorder to a worm entering the heart, causing 'suche a passion that often tymes it kylleth them'. Such connections between worms and childhood 'fatuity' persisted (Anonymous, 1832). It was recognized that children could be problematic and disappointing to their parents and also that the parental role required a preventive dimension. Elyot's popular health guide (1541) recommended moderate food and drink, exercise and 'quietnesse in livinge' during 'adolescency' and admitted there were many children 'whose lyves either for incorrigible vices, or infortunate chances, have ben . . . grevous unto theyr parentes'. His view that juvenile education (Elyot, 1557) should avoid coercion was shared by Mercurialis (1584) and Burton (1621). The latter regarded

education as a possible source of melancholy, reprimanding parents who were 'too sterne, always threatning, chiding, brawling, whipping or striking' and also the doting and over-indulgent. The significance of hereditary influences on physique and temperament was already acknowledged by writers including Burton (1621) and Charleton (1674).

The Poor Law Act (1601) made no separate provision for the confinement of lunatics and idiots and those not causing social disturbance remained at liberty. Later, public tolerance changed, marking the beginning, throughout Europe, of increasing incarceration of lunatics and the origins of the private madhouse system (Parry-Jones, 1972). However, little information is extant about the practical effects of these changes on disturbed juveniles. Seventeenth-century perceptions of madness, demonic possession and witchcraft were intertwined, as illustrated in Baddeley's account (1622) of the boy of Bilson. This 13-year-old displayed features of possession, with fits, when 'hee appeared both deafe and blinde, writhing his mouth . . . groning and panting', unresponsive to physical stimuli. Fraudulence was demonstrated when it was discovered that he coloured his urine with black ink. Other cases attracting supernatural explanations and allegations of imposture included a Cornish maidservant, fed by 'Fairies' (Pitt, 1696) and Margaret Rule of Boston, Massachusetts, visited by spectres (Fowler, 1861). Despite progressive secularization and medicalization of madness, allegations of demonic possession in juveniles continued (Heaton, 1822; Griesinger, 1867). Similarly, pathological food abstinence was interpreted as due to miraculous or satanic influences, natural causes or imposture. Notable 'fasting girls' included Margaret of Spire, Apollonia Schreier of Bern (Lentulus, 1604) and Miss Duke of St Mary Axe (Morton, 1689). Counterfeit fasters were exposed, including 10-year-old Barbara Kramers, demonstrated to be a malingerer, not a miracle (Wier, 1660). Medical texts of this period also contain frequent references to pubescent girls with pica (Parry-Jones & Parry-Jones, 1992), involving irrational consumption of bizarre substances (Peirce, 1697).

Eighteenth century

Although institutional care expanded rapidly in madhouses, lunatic hospitals and public subscription asylums, the number and condition of pauper lunatics in prisons, workhouses and madhouses caused alarm, culminating in progressive construction of asylums under the County Asylums Act (1808). Information is sparse about juvenile admission to workhouses and houses of correction, but scattered numerical data are retrievable for asylums and madhouses. For example, at Bethlem from 1772 to 1787, 4.7% of the 2829 admissions were under 20 years, with only 1 under 10 and most between 15 and 20 (Black, 1788, 1810). Haslam (1798) reported figures for 1784–1794, when 6.8% of admissions were aged from 10 to 20 years. In comparison, from 1784 to 1792, at the Bicêtre, Paris, between 4 and 12 maniacs aged 15–20 were admitted annually (Pinel, 1806).

Childhood disorders featured sporadically in 18th-century lunacy texts. Arnold's account of nosology and aetiology, for example, did not deal with juvenile psychopathology, apart from vulnerability to 'nostalgic insanity' or homesickness (Arnold, 1782/1786). Published cases reflected developing awareness of psychosomatic correlations and juvenile insanity. Disorders included premenstrual nightmares (Bond, 1753); 'nervous atrophy' (a condition later likened to anorexia nervosa; Whytt, 1765) and fatal bulimia emetica in a 10-year-old boy (Martyn, 1745; Parry-Jones & Parry-Jones, 1991). Juvenile convulsions were well-documented (e.g. Cheyne, 1733) and de Mandeville (1715) discussed 'epileptick' and 'hysterick' fits in children, and believed their psychological and reproductive immaturity rendered them less disposed to 'hysterick passion' than adult women. Accounts of hysterical disorders always included a high proportion of teenage girls (Pomme, 1777).

In the mid-century, insightful observations were made about infantile jealousy and sibling rivalry. Baker (1755) discussed the effects of envy, suggesting that 'even . . . in the very cradle, unmistakable signs of jealousy may be seen . . . . It is possible to see an infant . . . languish . . . from this emotion as if from some wasting disease', curable only by the removal, or less attentive treatment, of 'the rival infant'. Crichton (1798) referred to the effects of education and hereditary taint, repeating Greding's case of a boy born 'raving mad' in 1763. Perfect (1778) described 2 19-year-old girls with 'hysteric' fits, and of 61 cases that he published in 1787, 4 were adolescents. In 1791 he described the home treatment of a boy aged 11, who displayed depression, alternating with confusion and acutely disturbed, 'obstreporous' states.

Nineteenth century

Developments during the 19th century were far-reaching and the volume of evidence is so substantial that the emergent themes require considerable selectivity.

Growing interest in childhood insanity

During the first half of the century, the increasing publication of unusual cases and references to young lunatics indicated mounting medical interest. As asylums burgeoned, juveniles featured in general lunacy practice and writings; the description and treatment of their disorders fell naturally within the scope of physicians dealing predominantly with adults. Haslam (1809), apothecary to Bethlem, for example, reported 3 children under 10, including a boy aged 7, whose features have been interpreted as suggesting infantile autism (Vaillant, 1962). Cox (1804) described 2 teenage cases, including a depressed 18-year-old girl, and Burrows (1828) referred to a 12-year-old boy with 'demency or fatuity', choreiform movements and speech impairment, who died unimproved aged 18. Among 51 cases described by A. Morison (1828), 6 were under 20, including a 14-year-old boy with prepubertal mania and, later (1848) his youngest case, a girl aged 6. Prichard

(1835) recorded a colleague's observations on a girl of 7, whose behaviour disorder, with rudeness, defiance, cruelty and stealing, aptly fitted his new category of moral insanity. Epilepsy continued to be reported widely and, of 38 cases mentioned by Andree (1846), 18 were juveniles, including a 13-year-old girl with 'Hysteric fits from fright'. Mania in a girl of 6, admitted to Bethlem in 1842, was regarded as sufficiently unusual to warrant publication (T.C. Morison, 1848).

In the US, Rush (1812) reported 4 children, including a pair of 2-year-olds, suffering from 'cholera infantum' and 'internal dropsy of the brain', who displayed 'the countenance of madness', biting 'first their mothers, and afterwards their own flesh'. Although Rubinstein (1948) discovered few other references to childhood insanity in American literature before the end of the century, some cases had been recorded by the mid-century (Macdonald, 1846). Subsequently, articles appeared in the *American Journal of Insanity*, with other substantial publications from the 1880s (Spitzka, 1883). There were comparable developments in Europe. In France, Esquirol (1845) discussed the influence of age on presentation of insanity and, in Germany, Nissen (1974) highlighted the work of Schule, differentiating child from adult disorders, and of Georgens and Deinhardt, pioneer educational therapists.

From the 1850s, childhood madness featured regularly in general psychiatric works and publications proliferated. Crichton-Browne (1860) reviewed childhood psychopathology comprehensively and Conolly (1862) published clinically perceptive papers on juvenile insanity. Griesinger (1867) discussed childhood insanity in relation to the impact of age; although infrequent before puberty, almost all forms were thought to occur, including mania and melancholia. The work of Brierre de Boismont (1855) gave impetus to wider studies of childhood hallucinations (Wilkins, 1987). Maudsley's textbook (1867) included a chapter 'On the Insanity of Early Life', a topic extended in 1879, culminating in separate chapters on the insanities of children and adolescents in 1895. Most British and American psychiatric textbooks began incorporating sections on children, gradually differentiating juvenile insanity from idiocy, epilepsy and neurological disorders. Towards the end of the century, monographs on childhood insanity appeared, including works by Emminghaus (1887) in Germany (described by Harms (1960) as 'a blueprint for the future development of the field') and Moreau de Tours (1888) and Manheimer (1899) in France. Ireland's influential work (1898) on childhood mental deficiency incorporated a chapter on insanity. Child cases appeared frequently in medical and psychiatric journals, with growing interest in statistical aspects. Wilmarth's study (1894) of 1000 cases, for example, attributed one-third to organic factors.

Specifically adolescent disorders became a new focus of interest, with references, in the first half-century, to the effects of puberty and associated increased vulnerability to insanity, particularly in females (Parkman, 1817). Puberty became accepted as a physiological cause of mental disturbance and 'developmental', 'pubescent' or adolescent' insanity was described frequently (Keay, 1888; Clouston, 1891, 1892, 1898; Maudsley, 1895), although sometimes contested conceptually. Pubescent insanities included emotional and conduct abnormalities, with impaired self-control, waywardness, irritability and irresponsibility. As in modern presentations, obtrusive, mischievous behaviour was characteristic and even 'genuine' insanity was 'frequently accompanied by noisy and violent action' (Blandford, 1877). Adolescence was perceived as important for the emergence of 'ancestral influences' and atavisms (Lewis, 1899) and for its predisposition to dementia praecox and manic-depressive insanity (Kraepelin, 1919, 1921; Bleuler, 1950).

Prevalence of juvenile insanity

Apparently increasing incidence of insanity generated alarm and controversy (Powell, 1813; Jarvis, 1852). Available data preclude accurate estimation, in the general population, of juveniles identified as lunatics or idiots and, in the US, Fletcher (1895) claimed that no statistics were available. Various attempts were made to obtain figures; statistics for a German district in the 1870s indicated that, excluding congenital cases, 'one in 70 584 children [under 15] annually became insane' (Spitzka, 1890).

Some indications are obtainable from returns of British pauper lunatics to the Commissioners in Lunacy. In 1843, for example, 5.7% of 16 704 pauper lunatics in England and Wales were under 20, and, in 1859 and 1889, the proportions of pauper lunatics or idiots under 16 were 0.2 and 0.55% respectively (Commissioners in Lunacy, 1889). Asylum admission statistics (see below) were used as a measure of prevalence and, using Scottish asylum and demographic data, Clouston (1898) estimated that insanity requiring admission occurred in 1 in 21 900 juveniles under 20.

Range and presentation of disorders

Prevailing 19th-century views confirmed that all forms of insanity occurred in juveniles, although comparative rarity created descriptive and classificatory problems, making it difficult to generalize about characteristic symptoms and presenting forms (Ireland, 1898). The lack of a well-defined nosology of childhood insanity fostered idiosyncratic systems and it was not until the 1960s that classification achieved a wider concensus. West (1860), for example, interpreted most early disorders as moral rather than intellectual. Although hallucinations, fixed ideas and adult forms of insanity rarely presented, he conceded that children could lapse into uncontrollable or chronic disorder. Maudsley's neurological and developmental classification (1867) comprised monomania, choreic delirium, cataleptoid insanity, epileptic insanity, mania, melancholia and affective insanity.

Various forms of monomania were described (A. Morison, 1828, 1848; Emminghaus, 1887) and categorized according to content, e.g. demonomania and kleptomania, and childhood erotomania, satyriasis and nymphomania were discussed (Beach, 1898). Melancholic states attracted considerable atten-

tion and Maudsley (1895) proposed a developmental sequence, explaining changes in presentation according to age. In infants, melancholic expression comprised a 'primitive language of cries, grunts, exclamations, tones of sounds, gestures and features'. Older children might have 'fits of moaning melancholy and apprehensive fears' and, later, typical melancholic symptoms. Mania, with loquacity, exaltation, excitement and overactivity, was described, including 'folie circulaire' (Ireland, 1875b). States of extreme excitability, hypersensitiveness and 'mental explosiveness' were reported in young children (Clouston, 1899).

In the late 19th century, incidence of child suicide was thought to be escalating (Beach, 1898) and attempts were made to collect statistical information, for example, in England and Wales, from 1861 to 1888, 148 boys and 113 girls under 15 committed suicide (Strahan, 1893). In an exceptional study, Durand-Fardel (1855) emphasized the importance of a child's emotional life and possible adverse effects by parents and teachers. Precipitants included 'correction for a trifling fault' (Winslow, 1840) and educational pressure. Westcott (1885) noted 'cases of children killing themselves because unable to perform school tasks', although abolition of corporal punishment 'has removed one fertile cause of suicide in childhood'.

Juvenile crime similarly aroused concern (Day, 1858), particularly thieving by young boys. Despite punitive confinement in houses of correction, reoffending was high and one preferred solution was provision of day refuges for unemployed boys (Buchanan, 1846). Juvenile delinquency did not impinge directly on the asylum doctor's work, since management was chiefly in reformatories. Some physicians developed interest in delinquency, especially its hereditary aspects (Winslow, 1895) and, in the early 20th century, it constituted a central theme of the mental hygiene movement, following the establishment of juvenile courts (Anderson, 1924). Moral insanity, applied frequently to juveniles (Millar, 1863; Tuke, 1885), referred not simply to antisocial behaviour, but to affective disturbances without delusions and hallucinations and Savage (1881) believed that many 'so-called spoiled children' were 'morally of unsound mind', blaming poor heredity as much as faulty education. Conversely, moral imbecility (Spitzka, 1890) covered most features of current conduct disorder. Late 19th-century authors referred to homicide by children, which was generally regarded as 'an unreflective act', influenced by imitation (Alexander, 1893).

There was a growing literature on childhood hysteria (Conolly, 1862; Mills, 1890), which covered convulsive and nonconvulsive presentations and a spectacular range of disorders, especially in females, e.g. trance, anaesthesia, aphonia, paralyses and feigned illnesses. Savage (1885), for example, reported a bereaved 11-year-old boy, whose hysterical symptoms included gait disturbance. Anorexia nervosa was described and named by Lasègue (1873) and Gull (1874), although self-inflicted fasting in young females had extensive antecedents (Parry-Jones & Parry-Jones in preparation). During the late 19th century, adolescent cases were reported increasingly (Marshall, 1890). Despite Gull's emphasis on 'a morbid mental state', surprisingly little psychiatric interest focused on the condition, which was managed chiefly at home or in general infirmaries (Parry-Jones, 1985), although some clinicians maintained that the asylum was the appropriate location for refeeding 'fasting girls' (Spitzka, 1890).

There was increasing emphasis on connections between insanity and masturbation, sometimes occurring at an early age (Spitzka, 1883; Neuman, 1975). Before 1700, references were sparse, the practice being castigated on religious rather than medical grounds. During the 18th century, cases of onanism began to be published, e.g. a 17-year-old youth, reduced to 'a mere skeleton' by 'self-pollution' (de Valangin, 1768). Coote (1867) observed that 'disturbance of the erotic passion ... tacitly recognised, but not openly expressed', filled asylums with young people and Maudsley (1868) viewed it as 'a most hopeless form of disease'. In an age of repressive sexual attitudes, masturbation was a vice, believed to cause insanity and generating fearful warnings about 'self-abuse' (Woodward, 1838). Drastic treatments included chastity belts, pinning of the prepuce, circumcision and clitoridectomy (Brown, 1866; Yellowlees, 1892). According to Jalland and Hooper (1986), however, 'Morality rather than medical science was the real issue in the spread of masturbation mania'.

Profile of asylum inmates

The clearest profile of presenting clinical problems is derivable from asylum records, complemented by published cases. From the mid-century, asylum case books standardized admission and discharge data, giving variable amounts of information on clinical conditions and management. Medical labelling and precise diagnostic statements were rare, permitting only speculative retrospective diagnoses.

A study of juveniles admitted to Oxfordshire asylums (Parry-Jones, 1990) provides an illustration of presenting disorders. In a series of 46 patients aged up to 16, for example, admitted to Oxfordshire County Asylum from 1846 to 1866, the sexes were about equal and the youngest were aged 5. Twenty-five epileptics presented major management problems and many early fatalities. Nineteen patients were diagnosed as idiotic — a category fraught with terminological imprecision. Acutely disturbed, noisy and destructive behaviour was characteristic in this study and in contemporaneous case reports (T.C. Morison, 1848). Only 2 children were hallucinated (see Wilkins, 1987) and, of 4 with delusional ideas, 2 were paranoid. No patients were termed melancholic, but depressive features are recognizable and a boy of 15 showed manic-depressive phenomena. Several were suicidal, including a 15-year-old, who cut his throat and threatened to kill his brothers. Some excited states suggest mania and 1 girl aged 16 was restless, talked incessantly and unconnectedly and uttered profanities. It is significant that the fee-paying Warneford Asylum, Oxford, specifically excluded idiots and the range of disorders was much wider, with less violent behaviour.

Causation

By this period, a wide range of possible causes, both psychological and organic, were recognized, comprising almost any experiential circumstances, sometimes distinguishing predisposing from exciting causes. Physical causes, perceived as acting mainly on the brain and nervous system, included menstruation, masturbation, intoxication by alcohol or drugs, epilepsy, meningitis, fevers and trauma, particularly head injury and sunstroke. The main psychological causes were shocks, anxiety, disappointments, bereavements, jealousy, excessive study, religious excitement and parental maltreatment. Some manifestations were considered to be imitative (Beach, 1898). Although such assigned causes appear simplistic out of their historical context, serious attempts were made to establish pathogenesis in relation to hereditary factors, the effects of early experience and developmental stage.

The importance of heredity was an enduring theme (Crichton, 1798; Hallaran, 1818). Connate disorders were distinguished from hereditary susceptibilities, which generated either disposition to disorder, with poor preventive prospects, or predisposition, triggered by external causes and carrying better prognosis (Adams, 1814). Offspring 'tainted' by ancestral insanity were thought to require special care from infancy (Ellis, 1838). Clouston (1892) linked poor heredity with liability to developmental neuroses, and certain kinds of mental retardation and criminality were perceived popularly as atavistic regression to primitive states or races (Laycock, 1861; Dagonet, 1876).

Adverse early nurturing experiences and defective education generated increasing comment (Culverwell, 1837) and preventive steps were advocated, additional to the early identification of 'incubating' insanity. Phrenological theories, for example, were recommended 'to counteract by education in infancy the original defects of organisation' (Forster, 1815). The value of early training and moral education was upheld to prevent the formation of 'injurious habits ... often fatal to the health of the mind' (Abercrombie, 1837) and Parkinson (1801, 1807) warned parents against the adverse, potentially lifelong, psychological effects of 'excessive indulgence' and inconsistency. Educational methods, over-emphasis on scholastic attainment and excessive 'mental exertion' attracted frequent criticism (Combe, 1835), particularly the premature schooling of young children, except for their moral education (Brigham, 1832; Ellis, 1838). Belief in the value of preventive and corrective measures in the 19th century anticipated the early 20th-century concept of mental hygiene (Clouston, 1906).

Influence of age and developmental stage

The influence of age on the onset, symptoms and outcome of insanity was acknowledged and age on first attack and on admission was recorded in asylum documentation. While some published series incorporated infants and children (e.g. German cases cited by Arlidge, 1864), the prevailing view, particularly early in the century, was that insanity did not occur or was very rare before puberty. This was usually attributed to the fact that children's minds and brain functions were too undeveloped for mental impressions to have any lasting effect (Rush, 1812). Broussais (1833) added that 'the intensity of impressions may be a substitute for their durability', alluding to the vulnerability to mental alienation of children with 'premature development of the encephalon'. Children could become insane, according to Brigham (1832), 'from strong mental excitement, and injurious development of the moral faculties'. Spurzheim (1836) specifically attributed the rarity of childhood insanity to delicate 'cerebral organization', incapable of bearing 'strong morbid affection without entirely losing its fitness for the mind and endangering life'. Until the brain developed, its disturbance precipitated organic diseases, not insanity. The stage of mental development, therefore, determined the form of disorder and the brain's susceptibility to disease.

The concept and process of child development were discussed increasingly and, by the 1860s, the clinical importance of its understanding was recognized. Enlightened physicians needed 'to take every stage of existence into consideration, and to weigh well every influence to which the being is liable', (Crichton-Browne, 1860). Various developmental sequences of disorders were proposed. Esquirol (1845), for example, claimed: 'Mental alienations might ... be divided ... into imbecility for childhood, mania and monomania for youth, lypemania or melancholy for consistent age, and into dementia for advanced life'. Allbutt (1889) contributed a rare description of infant insanity, which 'betrayed itself ... in its own muscular groups, in its one place of contact with external things. The insane baby bites, and biting was the range of its symptoms, the external measure of its madness'. Adopting a strong developmental approach, Maudsley (1895) maintained that a child could not 'go mad ... before it has got some mind to go wrong, and then only in proportion to the quantity and quality of mind which it has'. His sequence of disorders was influenced by the concept of phylogenetic recapitulation. In infants, the simple reflex state of functioning meant that disorder presented with symptoms of deranged sensorimotor function and quasiconvulsive actions, like instinctive acts of animals. He likened mental derangement in 'ill-born infants' to 'attacks of blind and dangerous frenzy [in an elephant] in which it runs amuck ... trumpeting shrilly, and doing furious destruction ... Were the insane child as strong as the elephant, it would be just as destructive.' In older children, the indistinguishability of real and unreal worlds could result in hallucinations, delirious dramatization, night terrors and somnambulism. Mania had the character of delirium since 'the imagination of children cannot rise above the inferior grade of fancy' (Maudsley, 1895).

Griesinger (1867) had attributed the rarity of monomania to the absence of a 'persistent ego' and the fact that 'the mobility of this age does not allow single insane ideas to become persistent and systematised, as at a late period'. The developmental sequence proposed by Hurd (1895) ranged from congenital epilepsy or idiocy, childhood night terrors and transitory mania to adolescent melancholia, hysteria and paranoia, with comparative immunity between the ages of 7 and 10. Confronting such a plethora of developmental ideas, Ireland (1898) concluded, insightfully, that accurate portrayal of childhood insanity 'would need a series of shifting views of the most frequent symptoms for every six months'. Generally, disorders in children over 12 were thought to differ little from adult forms and adolescent disorders were considered, increasingly, in relation to physiological and psychological maturation. On a surprisingly modern note, Clouston (1892) concluded that: 'The physiology of adolescence, its psychology, its neurology and its psychiatry, must all hang together, being explained and unified by the facts of the development of the capacity and desire to propagate the species, then going on'.

Management

Sparse information is available about the numbers or methods of treatment of mentally disordered juveniles, either as dispensary and infirmary outpatients or by local practitioners. Many physicians conducted 'chamber-practice', of which no known records remain, other than published cases or those reported to medical societies. Accounts of care in asylums are, therefore, the principal sources.

Before the establishment of county asylums, workhouses provided short- and long-term care of pauper lunatics and idiots unfit for life in the community. They were expected to contain disturbed juveniles, especially idiots, and only dangerous, acute or curable cases were transferred, often belatedly, to asylums. Occasionally, separate lunatic and infant wards were established, but overcrowding and inadequate care predominated. Little is known about the welfare of juvenile lunatics and idiots in British workhouses or American poorhouses (Bremner *et al.*, 1970/1971).

Asylum admission statistics

Throughout the 19th century, there is conclusive evidence that children were admitted alongside adult patients to madhouses, county, borough and public subscription asylums, but information is variable and difficult to locate, particularly for younger children and especially for the early period. Farr (1838) showed that admissions under the age of 20 to Bethlem from 1830 to 1834; Charenton, France from 1826 to 1833; and Lincoln from 1820 to 1835 were 6.2, 8.0 and 5.9% respectively. Earle's statistics of European and American asylums (1841) revealed proportions of 7.2% for 10–20-year-old admissions to English and French asylums, and 4.7% for American asylums. A decennial report, 1846–1855, of Bethlem recorded over 6.5% of admissions under 20 (Hood, 1856). Utilizing data relating to 20 asylums and over 21 000 admissions, Thurnam (1845) showed that 0.4% were under 10 and 5.4% between 10 and 20 years.

In England and Wales, reports of the Commissioners in Lunacy from 1843 supply useful data. From 1855–1858, for example, the proportion of juvenile admissions (up to 19 years) to public subscription asylums (12.0%) was twice that to county asylums (6.4%) (Commissioners in Lunacy, 1861). Such data allow the tentative conclusion that 1 or 2 children up to 14 years could be expected to be admitted annually to county asylums, with up to 3 into fee-paying asylums. Modern studies of the records of the York Retreat (Digby, 1984), Bethlem (Wilkins, 1987) and private and public asylums in Oxfordshire (Parry-Jones, 1972, 1990) corroborate the previous 19th-century statistics.

Asylum treatment

Nineteenth-century physicians generally favoured removal from home to establish control unhindered by parental and family interference. A madhouse proprietor, S.G. Bakewell (1836), for example, maintained: 'No patient has a fair chance of recovery unless he be separated from family ... influence ... and under non-irritating control'. West (1854) favoured residential family care by 'some person competent to enter into their pursuits and to share their pleasures', although postpubertal deterioration might necessitate asylum admission. Similarly, Allbutt (1889) insisted that insane children, unless seriously disturbed, could be managed at home, thereby avoiding 'the systematic watchfulness' of asylum doctors. Sometimes the need for asylum care was disputed, e.g. the peremptory discharge of an unmanageable 7-year-old boy with moral insanity which was contested by the family's physician (Millar, 1863). Despite public sensitivity concerning asylum confinement, no scandalous accounts of juvenile maltreatment have emerged and children received no special or separate consideration in the Reports of the Commissioners in Lunacy.

Archival sources confirm the admission of children to adult wards, little or delicate ones living on the female side and boys usually being transferred to male wards when about 7, and there are no known accounts of special provisions made by attendants. At the Oxfordshire County Asylum, children played on the wards, becoming the pets of chronic female patients and often behaving disruptively with their peers and annoying elderly patients. The management of idiots and containment of aggressive and overactive children in adult wards were perennial problems (Parry-Jones, 1990). Treatment of small numbers of juveniles, as part of the normal routine in 19th-century asylums, was facilitated somewhat by the prevailing tendency to interpret lunatics' behaviour as childlike, responding as if they were dependent children (Beard, 1881; Porter, 1989).

As was the case with adults, medication was used extensively. Purgatives, opium, hyoscyamine and belladonna were popular and bathing and a range of dietaries were used. Children benefited from the advantages implicit in moral management, particularly the minimal restraint, grouping according to clinical state, provision of amusements, exercise, employment, educational activities and religious services. Selective use of seclusion, strait waistcoats or ticking dresses, however, continued in acute disturbance.

Length-of-stay figures showed considerable variation, ranging from brief, sometimes repeated admissions, to long-term confinement. In the Oxfordshire study (Parry-Jones, 1990), length of stay of county asylum pauper patients was consistently longer than for paying patients at the Warneford Asylum, where there was more active treatment, a different range of disorders and the constraint of fees. Composite evidence regarding outcome is more readily available from printed sources, including asylum annual reports (Thurnum, 1845; Hood, 1856). In a modern study of Bethlem admissions from 1830 to 1899, juvenile cure rates were 63% (males) and 68% (females), the high percentage probably reflecting the selective admission criteria (Wilkins, 1987). At the Royal Edinburgh Asylum, 1874–1879, where 10% of admissions were aged 14–21, 93 juveniles were discharged recovered, 40 relieved, 26 became incurable and 3 died, supporting the conclusion that adolescent insanity was 'very curable' (Clouston, 1898). However, the degree of recovery is always difficult to evaluate, owing to variable statistical presentation and ambiguous terminology, which was acknowledged at the time (Earle, 1877). Generally, restoration was gauged by symptom removal or return to socially acceptable behaviour.

TWENTIETH CENTURY: INTO MODERN TIMES

The most significant advances in the understanding and care of disturbed children and adolescents have occurred since the Second World War, with progressive expansion of clinical services, research, teaching, training and professional activities. Documentation and secondary sources for this period are freely available and developments have been reviewed by Eisenberg (1969), Hersov (1986), Clarke and Clarke (1986), Chess (1988), Parry-Jones (1989), Duché (1990) and Wardle (1991a). Other chapters deal with the growth of scientific knowledge about disorders.

Child study and welfare

Early 20th-century child study was shaped by scientific advances in neuropathology, neurophysiology and psychology (Keir, 1952; Zenderland, 1988). Intelligence testing, introduced by Binet and Simon (1905), directed attention on the individual child's needs. Infant assessment techniques were pioneered by Gesell (1925), and Piaget's work (1926), on intellectual development, was influential. The well-established eugenics movement advocated harsh measures, including compulsory sterilization of the socially incompetent and 'permanent sequestration in state colonies of all epileptics, insane and feeble-minded' (Wallin, 1914).

The educational needs of retarded, handicapped and 'difficult' children were identified, promoting the emergence of educational psychology and remedial education. The British Child Study Association introduced psychological, sociological and anthropometric examination methods and the school medical services developed in 1907. Witmer's pioneering psychoeducationally focused child clinic at the University of Pennsylvania, in 1896, was replicated in universities, normal colleges, medical schools, asylums, reformatories and in relation to juvenile courts (Wallin, 1914).

Mental hygiene, child guidance and child psychiatry

The Mental Hygiene Movement, which developed in the US, was a driving force in promoting prevention and treatment agencies (Bassett, 1934; Deutsch, 1945). Commencing with the Connecticut Mental Hygiene Society (Beers, 1908) — later the National Committee for Mental Hygiene — it attracted prominent figures, including Healy and Meyer. Meyer's psychobiological approach influenced clinical work with children, redirecting thinking from hereditary degeneracy and fatalistic asylum care towards prevention (Witmer, 1940). In 1909, Healy founded the Chicago Juvenile Psychopathic Institute, combining psychiatric, psychological and social techniques, in delinquency treatment (Levy, 1968). From 1922, demonstration child guidance clinics opened, supported by the Commonwealth Fund's programme for delinquency prevention (Anderson, 1924; Stevenson & Smith, 1934). This focus soon changed to unacceptable behaviour, habit and personality problems, school difficulties and effects of crises, generally excluding problems of mental defectives, epileptics and the neurologically handicapped (Healy, 1917; Burt, 1925). By the 1930s, the therapeutic stance became less directive and moralistic, emphasizing social case work and environmental change (Horn, 1984). The major shift from individual to family therapy occurred only in the late 1940s and 1950s (Parry-Jones, 1991).

Development of the child guidance method in the UK was encouraged by training of personnel in the US (Burke & Miller, 1929; Stevenson & Smith, 1934; Keir, 1952; Sampson, 1980). In 1927, the Jewish Health Organization of Great Britain set up the East London Child Guidance Clinic (Renton, 1978); the Child Guidance Council was founded in 1928, followed closely by the London Child Guidance Clinic, which pioneered the first training programme for psychiatric social workers. By 1944, there were 95 clinics, mainly organized by local education authorities (Howells, 1965), focusing particularly on the controversial handicap category of maladjustment (Bridgeland, 1971). An entirely new model of interdisciplinary collaboration by psychologists, psychiatric social workers and psychiatrists was created which shaped child psychiatrists' working relationships and service delivery patterns for half a century. It has been suggested that this phase inaugurated child psychiatry (Kanner, 1960; Earls, 1979). From the outset, distinction was drawn between the physician's traditional role with cases of aberration from normal, and deviations within the normal range, which constituted the majority of cases and became the concern of the new psychological specialists. Child guidance 'conceived its task to be primarily that of adjusting the growing individual to his own immediate environment . . . rather than . . . curing a mental illness or treating a psychiatric patient' (Keir, 1952).

Juvenile outpatient services were being developed also by mental hospitals (Feversham Committee, 1939) and by paediatric services. In London, two children's departments opened, at the Tavistock Clinic (1926) and the Maudsley Hospital (1930). The Boston Psychopathic Hospital accepted child outpatients from 1912 — a rare facility at American state hospitals before 1920 (Witmer, 1940). In 1930, a children's psychiatric service opened at Johns Hopkins Hospital, Baltimore, Maryland. Although inpatient units were established in the 1920s in the US (Klopp, 1932; Barker, 1974), the children's inpatient unit at the Maudsley Hospital was not opened until 1947 (Cameron, 1949). In Heidelberg, a comprehensive child psychiatric outpatient clinic was established by Homburger (1926) in 1917 (Kanner, 1959; Nissen, 1974).

Psychoanalytic theory had a significant and increasing influence on child study and on early attempts at understanding and treating emotional disorder (see Chapter 54). It became a dominant approach during the 1950s and 1960s (Chess, 1988) and the fact that neurotic disorders formed the central paradigm for clinical work tended to exclude children with disorders, such as the psychoses, who needed other treatment approaches. Subsequently, an increasing eclecticism has guided practice in most countries. Behaviourism also emerged in the early 20th century: its main protagonist, Watson (1919) envisaged a new approach to psychology, discarding concepts of introspection and consciousness. Innovative behavioural treatments followed, such as for enuresis (Mowrer & Mowrer, 1938).

Scope of the new specialty

The unifying term child psychiatry emerged in the 1930s, and Kanner (1960) attributed its origin to Tramer, at a Swiss Psychiatric Society meeting, in 1933. The term *psychiatrie infantile* was utilized at a Paris child psychiatry congress in 1934. The scope of the new specialty was defined progressively. Kanner's paediatric liaison at Johns Hopkins University was highly respected (Senn, 1948), and his textbook (1935) gave the specialty organization and enhanced scientific standing. Influenced by the new medical psychology, child psychiatrists directed attention away from the disease model, organ pathology, heredity, syndromal description and physical treatment, towards psychosocial and psychodynamic theories. The new child-oriented specialty, therefore, diverged from asylum psychiatry and became distanced from the most severely disturbed, particularly adolescents. Separate services for adolescents were not established in the UK until after World War II, later than in the US (Curran, 1939), and proliferating in the late 1960s (Slaff, 1981; Parry-Jones, 1984).

During the early 20th century, there had been ambiguity concerning the constituents of 'adolescent insanity' and its distinction from other emotional and behavioural disorders and defects of 'moral sense'. The outlook was held to be poor for adolescents with either manic-depressive insanity (Kraepelin, 1921) or dementia praecox (Norman, 1928). Regarding the latter, Younger (1914) advised that 'These patients should never be allowed to be at large, in spite of the grief caused to the parents by the removal of their child . . . prognosis is usually . . . gloomy . . . and treatment is of little avail'. Such views highlighted the dichotomy between asylum-based management of major morbidity and more optimistic treatments in outpatient and child guidance clinics.

Clinical innovation and research increased slowly through the early part of the century (Gordon, 1939). Examples include the introduction of follow-up programmes and outcome studies (Glueck & Glueck, 1930; Kanner, 1937); Penrose's identification (1938) of the genetic basis of Down's syndrome; and the description and labelling of early infantile autism by Kanner (1943), highlighting the scientific importance of careful clinical observation. The more recent scientific history is described in the chapters of this volume dealing with individual disorders and modes of treatment.

CONCLUSIONS

The history of the identification and treatment of mentally disordered children and youth emerges as a continuum, extending over centuries, with periods of accelerated change. It is misguided, therefore, to seek origins simply in terms of recognizable modern specialization, and rarely justifiable to claim primacy of theories, interventions or publications. Inevitably, the 18th and 19th centuries have featured prominently, as mentally defective and severely disturbed juveniles were managed, more identifiably, within medicine and, ultimately, within psychiatry. The major 19th-century developments, however, cannot be isolated from their formative antecedents. Although there was no distinctive specialization, the observation and description of abnormal children and attempts to understand and differentiate between child and adult psychopathology by using contemporaneous child development theories inaugurated the compilation of a body of specialist theoretical and practical knowledge. Modern reviewers of the history of child psychiatry have tended to underestimate the level of pre-20th-century awareness of child development and of the aetiological significance accorded to early life experiences and influences, such as changing parent–child relationships. Such neglect and devaluation of earlier contributions have been determined by factors such as the primacy attached to psychoanalytic interpretation of intrapsychic and interpersonal processes, especially in the US, with consequent disregard of earlier approaches which failed to address the child's 'inner life'. These attitudes have been perpetuated and compounded by bias, and by historiographic inadequacies, especially over-generalization and the failure to set historical facts in the context of the ethos and value systems of their contemporary culture.

The multidisciplinary specialty which took shape in the 1920s was a confluence of theories and expertise from paediatrics, asylum medicine, training and custodial care of the mentally retarded, psychoanalysis, psychology, psychiatric social work, remedial education and criminology. As its compass and service boundaries broadened rapidly, child psychiatrists followed and augmented these trends, regardless of whether they called for conventional medical or psychiatric expertise. This has contributed to current ambiguity in defining the province of work, distinctive knowledge and clinical skills of child and adolescent psychiatrists. Scientific progress in the differentiation, classification, understanding and treatment of serious mental disorders in children and adolescents has been slow and discontinuous, with few specifically psychiatric advances. The main source of progress has been careful clinical observation and description, sometimes of chance occurrences such as the unpredicted effects of medication, leading to the construction of theoretical models which shaped clinical practice. In turn, the findings of applied therapeutic techniques have furthered scientific knowledge. In addition, many theoretical and practical developments, which have enhanced the quality of care of disturbed juveniles, have stemmed from changes in social policy affecting the status of children, and from improved educational methods, together with advances in paediatrics and the biological and behavioural sciences. The impression that this suggests continuous progress in the medical specialty of child psychiatry is misleading and requires qualification. Empirical research and evaluation, for example, are only a feature of the relatively recent past, and the emphasis within the specialty has remained technique-oriented, related to treatment modes, continuously coming into and passing out of favour, with insufficient evaluation.

An integral theme of this chapter has been consideration of the role of physicians engaged in clinical work with mentally abnormal juveniles and with the emergence of fundamental theoretical and practical contributions. Notwithstanding limitations in knowledge and differences of emphasis, continuities between previous centuries and the present are perceptible. These include fundamental issues of societal humanitarian concern for the health and welfare of children and youth, and acceptance that alleviation of a wide range of mental and behavioural disorders falls, specifically, within the physician's province. There has been lasting recognition of the causative importance of physical and psychological factors, singly or interactively, and awareness of the influence of heredity, early life experiences, nurturing and educational practices. Continuities may be seen also in attempts to correlate patterns of mental disorder with underlying processes of normal physical and mental development, and in the prevention of morbidity by early intervention, based on a long-standing belief in childhood antecedents of adult disorder.

A multiplicity of innovative aetiological hypotheses and therapeutic practices have been promulgated over the centuries. Nevertheless, the history of the interpretation and treatment of child and adolescent psychopathology illustrates how readily — even dangerously — ideas can be transformed into certainties, and causation and treatment enveloped in all-embracing credos, both biological and psychodynamic. Among examples of such transformations, one of the most far-reaching in its implications was the predominant reliance on psychoanalytic theories, during the middle quarters of the 20th century, which served to distance the growing specialty from the influence of other scientific disciplines, especially the basic biological sciences. It is in such a context that the historical approach fulfils one of its most effective roles, by providing a longitudinal perspective, a wider compass and an appropriate corrective.

REFERENCES

Abercrombie J. (1837) *The Culture and Discipline of the Mind. Addressed to the Young*, 4th edn. W. Whyte, Edinburgh.

Abt A.F. & Garrison F.H. (1965) *History of Pediatrics*. W.B. Saunders, Philadelphia.

Adams J. (1814) *A Treatise on the Supposed Hereditary Properties of Diseases*. J. Callow, London.

Adams J. (1843) What acts are essential to constitute rape? *Lancet*, **i**, 933.

Adams S.S. (1897) Evolution of pediatric literature in the United States. *Archives of Pediatrics*, **14**, 401–429.

Alexander H.C.B. (1893) Insanity in children. *Journal of the American Medical Association*, **21**, 511–519.

Alexis of Piemont (1562) *The Secretes of the Reverende Maister Alexis of Piemount Contayning Excellent Remedies Agaynst Divers Dyseases*. N. England, London.

Allbutt T.C. (1889) Insanity of children. *Journal of Mental Science*, **35**, 130–133.

Anderson V.V. (1924) The demonstration clinics conducted by the Division of the Prevention of Delinquency of the National Committee for Mental Hygiene. The first year's experience. *American Journal of Psychiatry*, **III**, 779–790.

Andree J. (1846) *Cases of the Epilepsy, Hysteric Fits, and St Vitus Dance, with the Process of Cure*. W. Meadows & J. Clarke, London.

Anonymous (1768) *An Account of a Savage Girl, Caught Wild in the Woods of Champagne*. A. Kincaird & J. Bell, Edinburgh.

Anonymous (1832) Fatuity from an accumulation of ascarides *Boston Medical and Surgical Journal*, **V**, 76.

Anonymous (1921) *A Young Girl's Diary. Prefaced with a Letter by Sigmund Freud* (translated by E. & C. Paul). George Allen & Unwin, London.

Ariès P. (1962) *Centuries of Childhood: A Social History of Family Life*. Jonathan Cape, London.

Arlidge J.T. (1864) Foreign psychological literature. *Journal of Mental Science*, **9**, 238–239.

Armstrong G. (1808) *An Account of the Diseases most Incident to Children*. T. Cadell & W. Davies, London.

Arnold T. (1782/1786) *Observations on the Nature, Kinds, Causes, and Prevention of Insanity, Lunacy or Madness. Vol. I. Containing Observations on the Nature, and Various Kinds of Insanity. Vol. II. Containing Observations on the Causes and Prevention of Insanity*. G. Robinson, Leicester.

Baddeley R. (1622) *The Boy of Bilson: or a True Discovery of the late Notorious Impostures of Certaine Romish Priests in their Pretended Exorcisme, or Expulsion of the Devill out of a Young Boy*. F.K. for W. Barret, London.

Bagellardus P. (1472) *De Infantium Aegritudinibus et Remediis*. Bartholomaeus de Valdezoccho & Martinus de Septem Arboribus, Padua.

Baker G. (1755) *De Affectibus Animi et Morbis inde Oriundis*. Thurbourn, Cambridge.

Bakewell S.G. (1836) *An Essay on Insanity*, 2nd edn. E. Cox, London.

Baldwin J.M. (1894) *Mental Development in the Child and the Race: Methods and Processes*. Macmillan, London.

Barker P. (1974) History. In: Barker P. (ed) *The Residential Psychiatric Treatment of Children*, pp. 1–26. Crosby Lockwood Staples, London.

Barman S. (1934) *The English Borstal System. A Study of the Treatment of Young Offenders*. P.S. King, London.

Barr M.W. (1904) *Mental Defectives their History, Treatment and Training*. P. Blackiston's, Philadelphia, PA.

Bassett C. (1934) *Mental Hygiene in the Community*. Macmillan, New York.

Beach F. (1895) *The Treatment and Education of Mentally Feeble Children*. J. & A. Churchill, London.

Beach F. (1898) Insanity in children. *Journal of Mental Science*, **44**, 459–474.

Beach F. (1900) Presidential address. *Journal of Mental Science*, **46**, 623–653.

Beard G.M. (1881) *The Asylums of Europe*, p. 7. G.M. Beard, Cambridge.

Beers C. (1908) *A Mind that Found Itself*. Longmans Green, New York.

Binet A. & Simon T. (1905) Application des méthodes nouvelles au diagnostic du niveau intellectuel chez les enfants normaux et anormaux d'hospice et d'école primaire. *L'Année Psychologique*, **XI**, 245–366.

Binet A. & Simon T. (1914) *Mentally Defective Children* (translated by W.B. Drummond). E. Arnold, London.

Black W. (1788) *A Comparative View of the Mortality of the Human Species, at All Ages ... Illustrated with Charts and Tables*. C. Dilly, London.

Black W. (1810) *A Dissertation on Insanity; Illustrated with Tables, and Extracted from between two and three thousand Cases in Bedlam*. G. Smeeton, London.

Blandford G.F. (1877) *Insanity and its Treatment: Lectures on the Treatment, Medical and Legal, of Insane Patients*. Oliver & Boyd, Edinburgh.

Bleuler E. (1950) *Dementia Praecox or the Group of Schizophrenias* (translated by J. Zinkin). International Universities Press, New York.

Bogdan R. (1988) *Freak Show: Presenting Human Oddities for Amusement and Profit*. University of Chicago Press, Chicago.

Bohannon E.W. (1896) A study of peculiar and exceptional children. *Pedagogical Seminary*, **IV**, 3–60.

Bond J. (1753) *An Essay on the Incubus, or Night-mare*. D. Wilson & T. Durham, London.

Boswell J. (1988) *The Kindness of Strangers. The Abandonment of Children in Western Europe from Late Antiquity to the Renaissance*. Vintage Books, New York.

Brady C. (1865) *The Training of Idiotic and Feeble-minded Children*, 2nd edn. Hodges, Smith, Dublin.

Brandon S. (1986) The early history of psychiatric care of children. In: Turner T. & Cule J. (eds) *Child Care Through the Centuries*, pp. 61–78. STS Publishing, Cardiff.

Bremner R.H., Barnard J., Hareven T.K. & Mennel R.M. (eds) (1970/1971) *Children and Youth in America. Vol. 1 1600–1865; Vol. 11 1866–1932*. Harvard University Press, Cambridge, MA.

Brenneman J. (1931) The menace of psychiatry. *American Journal of Diseases of Childhood*, **42**, 376–402.

Bridgeland M. (1971) *Pioneer Work with Maladjusted Children. A Study of the Development of Therapeutic Education*. Staples Press, London.

Brigham A. (1832) *Remarks on the Influence of Mental Cultivation upon Health*. F.J. Huntington, Hartford, CT.

Brierre de Boismont A. (1855) *A History of Dreams, Visions, Apparitions, Ecstasy, Magnetism, and Somnambulism*. Lindsay & Blakiston, Philadelphia, PA.

Broussais F.J.V. (1833) *On Irritation and Insanity*. (translated by T. Cooper). R. Hunter, London.

Brown G. (1853) *Report of the Private Institution for the Education of Idiots, Imbeciles, Backward and Eccentric Children: Barre, Mass*. J. Henry Goddard, Barre, MA.

Brown I.B. (1866) *On the Curability of Certain Forms of Insanity, Epilepsy, Catalepsy, and Hysteria in Females*. Robert Hardwicke, London.

Buchanan W. (1846) *Juvenile Offenders. Remarks on the Causes and State of Juvenile Crime in the Metropolis*. W. Buchanan, London.

Burke N.H.M. & Miller E. (1929) Child mental hygiene — its history, methods and problems. I. The history of the movements towards child mental hygiene. *British Journal of Medical Psychology*, **9**, 218–242.

Burrows G.M. (1828) *Commentaries on the Causes, Forms, Symptoms, and Treatment, Moral and Medical of Insanity*. Underwood, London.

Burt C. (1925) *The Young Delinquent*. University of London Press, London.

Burton R. (1621) *The Anatomy of Melancholy, What It Is. With all the Kinds, Causes, Symptomes, Prognostickes, and Severall Cures of it ... by Democritus Junior*. Cripps, Oxford.

Bynum W.F., Porter R. & Shepherd M. (1985/1988) *The Anatomy of Madness*, vols. I–III. Routledge, London.

Cameron H. (1918) *The Nervous Child*. Oxford University Press, London.

Cameron K.L. (1949) A psychiatric inpatient department for children. *Journal of Mental Science*, **95**, 560–566.

Cameron K. (1956) Past and present trends in child psychiatry. *Journal of Mental Science*, **102**, 599–603.

Carlebach J. (1970) *Caring for Children in Trouble*. Routledge & Kegan Paul, London.

Carpenter M. (1851) *Reformatory Schools for the Children of the Perishing and Dangerous Classes, and for Juvenile Offenders*. C. Gilpin, London.

Champneys F.H. (1881) Notes on an infant. *Mind*, **6**, 104–107.

Charleton W. (1674) *A Natural History of the Passions*. Printed by T.N. for J. Magnes, in the Savoy [London].

Chess S. (1988) Child and adolescent psychiatry come of age: a 50 year perspective. *Journal of the American Academy of Child and Adolescent Psychiatry*, **27**, 1–7.

Cheyne G. (1733) *The English Malady: or, a Treatise of Nervous Diseases of All Kinds*, pp. 220–222. G. Strachan & J. Leake, London.

Claparède E. (1911) *Experimental Pedagogy and The Psychology of the Child* (translated by M. Louch & H. Holman). E. Arnold, London.

Clarke A.M. & Clarke A.D.B. (1986) Thirty years of child psychology: a selective review. *Journal of Child Psychology and Psychiatry*, **27**, 719–759.

Clarke B. (1975) *Mental Disorder in Earlier Britain. Exploratory Studies*. University of Wales Press, Cardiff.

Clarke J. (1815) *Commentaries on Some of the Most Important Diseases of Children*, pp. 78–112. Longman, Hurst, Rees, Orme, & Brown, London.

Clouston T.S. (1880) *Puberty and Adolescence Medico-Psychologically Considered*. Oliver & Boyd, Edinburgh.

Clouston T.S. (1891) *The Neuroses of Development, Being the Morison Lectures for 1890*. Oliver & Boyd, Edinburgh.

Clouston T.S. (1892) Development insanities and psychoses. In: Tuke D.H. (ed) *A Dictionary of Psychological Medicine*, vol. 1, pp. 357–371. Churchill, London.

Clouston T.S. (1898) *Clinical Lectures on Mental Disorders*, 5th edn. J. & A. Churchill, London.

Clouston T.S. (1899) States of over-excitability, hypersensitiveness, and mental explosiveness in children, and their treatment by bromides. *Scottish Medical and Surgical Journal*, **IV**, 481–490.

Clouston T.S. (1906) *The Hygiene of Mind*. Methuen, London.

Combe A. (1835) *The Principles of Physiology Applied to the Preservation of Health, and to the Improvement of Physical and Mental Education*, 3rd edn. Maclachlan & Stewart, Edinburgh.

Combe A. (1841) *A Treatise on the Physiological and Moral Management of Infancy*, 2nd edn. Maclachlan & Stewart, Edinburgh.

Commissioners in Lunacy (1861) *Fifteenth Report*. Parliamentary Papers, London.

Commissioners in Lunacy (1889) *Forty-third Report*. Parliamentary Papers, London.

Conolly J. (1862) Recollections of the varieties of insanity, Part II,

Cases and consultations. Nos. I–V Juvenile insanity. *Medical Times and Gazette*, **i**, 27–29, 130–132, 234–236, 372–374; **ii**, 2–4.

Coote H. (1867) On lunacy in the young. *British Medical Journal*, **2**, 52.

Cox J.M. (1804) *Practical Observations on Insanity*. C. & R. Baldwin, London.

Craig W.S. (1946) *Child and Adolescent Life in Health and Disease. A Study in Social Paediatrics*. E. & S. Livingstone, Edinburgh.

Crichton A. (1798) *An Inquiry into the Nature and Origin of Mental Derangement*. 2 Vols. T. Cadell & W. Davies, London.

Crichton-Browne J. (1860) Psychical diseases of early life. *Journal of Mental Science*, **6**, 284–320.

Crichton-Miller H. (1923) *The New Psychology and the Parent*. Jarrolds, London.

Crowther M.A. (1981) *The Workhouse System 1834–1929. The History of an English Social Institution*. University of Georgia Press, Athens, GA.

Crutcher R. (1943) Child psychiatry. A history of its development. *Psychiatry*, **6**, 191–201.

Culverwell R.J. (1837) *Hints to the Nervous and Dyspeptic on the Causes and Cure of Nervousness, Indigestion, Haemorrhoids, and Constipation ...* R.J. Culverwell, London.

Curran F.J. (1939) Organisation of a ward for adolescents in Bellevue Psychiatric Hospital. *American Journal of Psychiatry*, **95**, 1365–1388.

Dagonet H. (1876) *Nouveau Traité Élémentaire et Pratique des Maladies Mentales*, pp. 474–483. Librairie J.B. Baillière, Paris.

Darwin C. (1872) *The Expression of the Emotions in Man and Animals*. Murray, London.

Darwin C. (1877) A biographical sketch of an infant. *Mind*, **II**, 285–294.

Day S.P. (1858) *Juvenile Crime; its Causes, Character, and Cure*. J.F. Hope, London.

de Glanville B. (1535) *De Proprietatibus Rerum* (translated by J. Trevisa). T. Berthelet, London.

Demaitre L. (1977) The idea of childhood and childcare in medical writings of the Middle Ages. *Journal of Psychohistory*, **4**, 461–490.

de Mandeville B. (1715) *A Treatise of the Hypochondriack and Hysterick Passions ...*, 2nd edn, pp. 177–179. Dryden Leach, London.

de Mause Ll. (ed) (1976) *The History of Childhood. The Evolution of Parent–child Relationships as a Factor in History*. Souvenir Press, London.

Demos J. & Demos V. (1969) Adolescence in historical perspective. *Journal of Marriage and the Family*, **31**, 632–638.

Dennis W. (1949) Historical beginnings of child psychology. *Psychological Bulletin*, **46**, 224–235.

Deutsch A. (1945) The history of mental hygiene. In: *One Hundred Years of American Psychiatry*, pp. 325–365. American Psychiatric Association, New York.

de Valangin F. (1768) *A Treatise on Diet, or the Management of Human Life*. F. De Valangin, London.

Dewees W.P. (1826) *A Treatise on the Physical and Medical Treatment of Children*. J. Miller, London.

Digby A. (1984) The changing profile of a 19th-century asylum: the York Retreat. *Psychological Medicine*, **14**, 739–748.

Down J.L. (1867) Observation on an ethnic classification of idiots. *Journal of Mental Science*, **13**, 121–123.

Down J.L. (1887) *On Some of the Mental Affections of Childhood and Youth, being the Lettsomian Lectures delivered to the Medical Society of London in 1887 ...* J. & A. Churchill, London.

Duché D.-J. (1990) *Histoire de la Psychiatrie*. Presses Universitaires de France, Paris.

Durand-Fardel M. (1855) Étude sur le suicide chez les enfants. *Annales Médico-Psychologiques*, **1**, 61–79.

Earle P. (1841) *A Visit to Thirteen Asylums for the Insane in Europe; to which are added a Brief Notice of Similar Institutions in Transatlantic Countries and in the United States ... With Copious Statistics*. J. Dobson,

Philadelphia, PA.

Earle P. (1877) *The Curability of Insanity*. E.H. Roberts, Utica, NY.

Earls F. (1979) Epidemiology and child psychiatry: historical and conceptual development. *Comprehensive Psychiatry*, **20**, 256–269.

Eisenberg L. (1969) Child psychiatry: the past quarter century. *American Journal of Orthopsychiatry*, **39**, 389–401.

Ellis W.C. (1838) *A Treatise on the Nature, Symptoms, Causes, and Treatment of Insanity, with Practical Observations on Lunatic Asylums . . .*, pp. 42–45. S. Holdsworth, London.

Elyot T. (1541) *The Castel of Helthe*. Berthelet, London.

Elyot T. (1557) *The Boke named the Gouvernor*. London.

Emminghaus H. (1887) *Die Psychischen Störungen des Kindesalters*. Laupp, Tubingen.

Erikson E. (1959) *Identity and the Life Cycle*. W.W. Norton, New York.

Esquirol E. (1845) *Mental Maladies. A Treatise on Insanity* (translated by E.K. Hunt). Lea & Blanchard, Philadelphia, PA.

Farr W. (1838) *On the Statistics of English Lunatic Asylums and the Reform of Their Public Management*. Sherwood, Gilbert & Piper, London.

Feversham Committee (1939) *The Voluntary Mental Health Services. The Report of the Feversham Committee*. Feversham Committee, London.

Fletcher W.B. (1895) Mental development and insanity of children. *International Clinics*, **1**, 138–147.

Forster T. (1815) Sketch of the New Anatomy and Physiology of the Brain and Nervous System of Drs. Gall and Spurzheim Considered as Comprehending a Complete System of Phrenology. *The Pamphleteer: Respectfully Dedicated to Both Houses of Parliament*, **V**, 220–244.

Fowler S.R. (1861) *Salem Witchcraft; Comprising more Wonders of the Invisible World. Collected by Robert Calef; and Wonders of the Invisible World, by Cotton Mather*. H.P. Ives & A.A. Smith, Salem, MA.

Fox V.C. (1977) Is adolescence a phenomenon of modern times? *Journal of Psychohistory*, **5**, 271–290.

Franklin A.W. (1964) Children's hospitals. In: Poynter F.N.L. (ed) *The Evolution of Hospitals in Britain*, pp. 103–121. Pitman Medical, London.

Froebel F.W.A. (1893) *The Education of Man*. D. Appleton, New York.

Galton F. (1869) *Hereditary Genius, its Laws and Consequences*. Macmillan, London.

Gesell A. (1925) *Mental Growth in the Preschool Child*. Macmillan, New York.

Glicklich L.B. (1951) An historical account of enuresis. *Pediatrics*, **8**, 859–876.

Glueck S. & Glueck E.T. (1930) *500 Criminal Careers*. Knopf, New York.

Gordon E.C. (1986) Child health in the Middle Ages as seen in the miracles of five English saints, AD 1150–1220. *Bulletin of the History of Medicine*, **60**, 502–522.

Gordon R.G. (1939) (ed) *A Survey of Child Psychiatry. Contributed by Contemporary British Authorities*. Oxford University Press, London.

Green J.A. (1912) *Pestalozzi's Educational Writings*. E. Arnold, London.

Greene H.M. (1882) *A Few Facts in regard to the Kansas State Asylum for Idiotic and Imbecile Youth, Lawrence, Kansas. With References to the Work of Kindred Institutions*. Kansas, Topeka, KS.

Griesinger W. (1867) *Mental Pathology and Therapeutics*. New Sydenham Society, London.

Guggenbuhl J.J. (1845) *Extracts from the First Report of the Institution on the Abendberg, near Interlachen, Switzerland; for the Cure of Cretins* (translated by W. Twining). Harrison, London.

Gull W.W. (1874) Anorexia nervosa (apepsia hysterica, anorexia hysterica). *Transactions of the Clinical Society of London*, **7**, 22–28.

Guthrie L.G. (1909) *Functional Nervous Disorders in Childhood*. Henry Frowde/Hodder & Stoughton, London.

Hall G.S. (1904) *Adolescence: Its Psychology and its Relations to Physiology, Anthropology, Sociology, Sex, Crime, Religion and Education*, 2 vols. D. Appleton, New York.

Hallaran W.S. (1818) *Practical Observations on the Causes and Cure of Insanity*. Edwards & Savage, Cork.

Harms E. (1960) At the cradle of child psychiatry. Hermann Emminghaus' Psychische Stoerungen des Kindesalters (1887) *American Journal of Orthopsychiatry*, **30**, 186–190.

Harris W. (1742) *A Full View of All the Diseases Incident to Children*. A. Millar, London.

Haslam J. (1798) *Observations on Insanity: With Practical Remarks on the Disease*. F. & C. Rivington, London.

Haslam J. (1809) *Observations on Madness and Melancholy including Practical Remarks on these Diseases together with Cases*, J. Callow, London.

Healy W. (1917) *The Individual Delinquent*. Little, Brown, Boston.

Heaton J. (1822) *The Extraordinary Affliction and Gracious Relief of a Little Boy; Supposed to be the Effects of Spiritual Agency*, 2nd edn. J. Heaton, Plymouth.

Hersov L. (1986) Child psychiatry in Britain — the last 30 years. *Journal of Child Psychology and Psychiatry*, **27**, 781–801.

Heywood J.S. (1959) *Children in Care. The Development of the Service for the Deprived Child*. Routledge & Kegan Paul, London.

Homburger A. (1926) *Psychopathologie des Kindesalters*. Springer, Berlin.

Hood W.C. (1856) *Statistics of Insanity; Being a Decennial Report of Bethlem Hospital, from 1846 to 1855 inclusive*. D. Batten, London.

Horn M. (1984) The moral message of child guidance 1925–1945. *Journal of Social History*, **18**, 25–36.

Howells J.G. (1965) Organization of child psychiatric services. In: Howells J.G. (ed) *Modern Perspectives in Child Psychiatry*, pp. 251–284. Oliver & Boyd, Edinburgh.

Howells, J.G. & Osborn M.L. (1981) The history of child psychiatry in the United Kingdom. *Acta Paedopsychiatrica (Basel)*, **46**, 193–202.

Hurd H.M. (1895) *Some Mental Disorders of Childhood and Youth*. Friedenwald, Baltimore, MD.

Ireland W.W. (1875a) An inquiry into some accounts of children being fostered by wild beasts. *Journal of Mental Science*, **20**, 185–200.

Ireland W.W. (1875b) German retrospect. *Journal of Mental Science*, **20**, 615–631.

Ireland W.W. (1886) On the admission of idiotic and imbecile children into lunatic asylums. *Journal of Mental Science*, **32**, 182–193.

Ireland W.W. (1898) *The Mental Affections of Children, Idiocy, Imbecility and Insanity*. J. & A. Churchill, London.

Itard J.M.G. (1801) *De l'Éducation d'un Homme Sauvage, ou, des Premiers Développemens Physiques et Moraux du Jeune Sauvage de L'Aveyron*. Goujon Fils, Paris.

Jackson H.H. (1882) *The Training of Children*. N.Y. & Brooklyn, New York.

Jalland P. & Hooper J. (1986) *Women from Birth to Death. The Female Life Cycle in Britain 1830–1914*. Humanities Press International, Atlantic Highlands, NJ.

Jarvis E. (1852) On the supposed increase of insanity. *American Journal of Insanity*, **8**, 333–364.

Jones K. (1967) *Mental Health and Social Policy 1845–1959*, pp. 41–90. Routledge & Kegan Paul, London.

Kanner L. (1935) *Child Psychiatry*. Charles C. Thomas, Springfield, IL.

Kanner L. (1937) Problem children growing up. *American Journal of Psychiatry*, **94**, 691–699.

Kanner L. (1943) Autistic disturbances of affective contact. *Nervous Child*, **2**, 217–250.

Kanner L. (1948) Outline of the history of child psychiatry. In: Kagan S.R. (ed) *Victor Robinson Memorial Volume, Essays on History of Medicine*. Froben Press, New York.

Kanner L. (1959) The thirty-third Maudsley Lecture: trends in child psychiatry. *Journal of Mental Science*, **105**, 581–593.

Kanner L. (1960) Child psychiatry: retrospect and prospect. *American Journal of Psychiatry*, **117**, 15–22.

Kanner L. (1964) *A History of the Care and Study of the Mentally Retarded.* C. Thomas, Springfield, IL.

Kauffman J.M. (1976) Nineteenth century views of children's behavior disorders: historical contributions and continuing issues. *Journal of Special Education,* **10**, 335–349.

Keay J. (1888) A case of insanity of adolescence. *Journal of Mental Science,* **34**, 69–72.

Keir G. (1952) Symposium on psychologists and psychiatrists in the child guidance service. III. A history of child guidance. *British Journal of Educational Psychology,* **22**, 5–29.

Kelynack T.N. (ed) (1915) *Defective Children.* J. Bale & Danielsson, London.

Kett J.F. (1977) *Rites of Passage: Adolescence in America, 1790 to the Present.* Basic Books, New York.

Klopp H.I. (1932) The children's institute of the Allentown state hospital. *American Journal of Psychiatry,* **88**, 1108–1118.

Kohlberg L. (1964) Development of moral character. In: Hoffman M.L. & Hoffman L.W. (eds) *Review of Child Development Research,* vol. 1. Russell Sage Foundation, New York.

Kraepelin E. (1919) *Dementia Praecox and Paraphrenia* (translated by R.M. Barclay). E. & S. Livingstone, Edinburgh.

Kraepelin E. (1921) *Manic-Depressive Insanity and Paranoia* (translated by R.M. Barclay). E. & S. Livingstone, Edinburgh.

Kroll J. (1973) A reappraisal of psychiatry in the Middle Ages. *Archives of General Psychiatry,* **29**, 276–283.

Kroll J. & Bachrach B. (1986) Child care and child abuse in early medieval Europe. *Journal of the American Academy of Child Psychiatry,* **25**, 562–568.

Lasègue E.C. (1873) On hysterical anorexia. *Medical Times and Gazette,* **2**, 265–266, 367–369.

Laslett P. & Wall R. (eds) (1972) *Household and Family in Past Time.* Cambridge University Press, Cambridge.

Laycock T. (1861) *The Scientific Place and Principles of Medical Psychology: An Introductory Address.* Murray & Gibb, Edinburgh.

Lentulus P. (1604) *Historia Admiranda de Prodigiosa Appolloniae Schreierae virginis in agro Bernensi Inedia.* Bern.

Levy D. (1968) Beginnings of the child guidance movement. *American Journal of Orthopsychiatry,* **38**, 799–804.

Lewis W.B. (1899) *A Text-Book of Mental Diseases: With Special Reference to the Pathological Aspects of Insanity.* C. Griffin, London.

Locke J. (1690) *An Essay Concerning Humane Understanding.* E. Holt for T. Basset, London.

Lowrey L.G. (1944) Psychiatry for children. A brief history of developments. *American Journal of Psychiatry,* **101**, 375–388.

McClure R. (1981) *Coram's Children. The London Foundling Hospital in the Eighteenth Century.* Yale University Press, New Haven, CT.

MacDonald J. (1846) Insanity. *New York Journal of Medicine,* **VI**, 8–9.

MacKellar C.K. (1913) *The Treatment of Neglected and Delinquent Children in Great Britain, Europe, and America, with Recommendations as to Amendment of Administration and Law in New South Wales.* W.A. Gullick, Sydney.

Malson L. (1972) *Wolf Children* (translated by E. Fawcett *et al.*) NLB, London.

Manheimer M. (1899) *Les Troubles Mentaux de l'Enfance: Précis de Psychiatrie Infantile.* Société d'Éditions Scientifiques, Paris.

Marshall C.F. (1890) A fatal case of anorexia nervosa. *Lancet,* **1**, 149–150.

Martyn J. (1745) Communication of a letter from J. Cookson, M.D. concerning the boy who has an extraordinary boulimia, or craving appetite. *Philosophical Transactions of the Royal Society,* **XLIII**, 380–381.

Maudsley H. (1867) *The Physiology and Pathology of the Mind,* pp. 259–293. Macmillan, London.

Maudsley H. (1868) Illustrations of a variety of insanity. *British Medical Journal,* **1**, 387–388.

Maudsley H. (1879) *The Pathology of Mind,* pp. 256–295. Macmillan, London.

Maudsley H. (1895) *The Pathology of Mind. A Study of its Distempers, Deformities, and Disorders,* pp. 364–414. Macmillan, London.

Mercurialis H. (1584) *De Morbis Puerorum.* Basle.

M'Gregor-Robertson J. (1907) *The Household Physician,* 2 Vols. Gresham, London.

Millar J. (1863) On a case of moral insanity in a child. *Lancet,* **1**, 576–577.

Mills C.K. (1890) Hysteria. In: Keating J.M. (ed) *Cyclopaedia of the Diseases of Children, Medical and Surgical,* vol. IV, pp. 958–1007. Young J. Pentland, Edinburgh.

Moreau de Tours P. (1888) *La Folie chez les Enfants.* Baillière, Paris.

Morison A. (1828) *Cases of Mental Disease, with Practical Observations on the Medical Treatment. For the Use of Students.* Longman/S. Highley, London.

Morison A. (1848) *Outlines of Lectures on the Nature, Causes and Treatment of Insanity,* 4th edn. Longman, Brown, Green, & Longmans, London.

Morison T.C. (1848) Case of mania occurring in a child 6 years old. *Journal of Psychological Medicine and Mental Pathology,* **1**, 317–318.

Morton R. (1689) *Phthisiologia seu exercitationes de Phthisi.* S. Smith, London.

Mowrer O.H. & Mowrer W.M. (1938) Enuresis: a method for its study and treatment. *American Journal of Orthopsychiatry,* **8**, 436–459.

Neuman R.P. (1975) Masturbation, madness, and the modern concepts of childhood and adolescence. *Journal of Social History,* **8**, 1–27.

Nissen G. (1974) History of child psychiatry in Germany. *Medical Bulletin of the US Army, Europe,* **31**, 228–234.

Nissen G. (1991) The history of child and adolescent psychiatry. In: Seva A. (ed) *The European Handbook of Psychiatry and Mental Health,* vol. II, pp. 1459–1467. Editorial Anthropos, Barcelona.

Norman H.J. (1928) *Mental Disorders. A Handbook for Students and Practitioners.* E. & S. Livingstone, Edinburgh.

Paré A. (1649) *The Workers of that Famous Chirurgion Ambrose Parey Translated out of Latine and Compared with the French by Thomas Johnson.* R. Cotes & W. Dugard, London.

Parkinson J. (1800) *Dangerous Sports: A Tale Addressed to Children.* H.D. Symonds, London.

Parkinson J. (1801) *Medical Admonitions to Families, Respecting the Preservation of Health, and the Treatment of the Sick,* 4th edn. H.D. Symonds, London.

Parkinson J. (1807) *Observations on the Excessive Indulgence of Children, Particularly Intended to Show its Injurious Effects on their Health, and the Difficulties it Occasions in their Treatment during Sickness.* H.D. Symonds, London.

Parkman G. (1817) *Management of Lunatics, with Illustrations of Insanity.* J. Eliot, Boston.

Parry-Jones B. & Parry-Jones W.Ll. (1991) Bulimia: an archival review of its history in psychosomatic medicine. *International Journal of Eating Disorders,* **10**, 129–143.

Parry-Jones B. & Parry-Jones W.Ll. (1992) Pica: symptom or eating disorder? A historical analysis. *British Journal of Psychiatry,* **160**, 341–354.

Parry-Jones B. & Parry-Jones W.Ll. (in preparation) *Fashions in Fasting: A Historical View of Self-Inflicted Starvation.* Blackwell Publishers, Oxford.

Parry-Jones W.Ll. (1972) *The Trade in Lunacy. A Study of Private Madhouses in England in the Eighteenth and Nineteenth Centuries.* Routledge & Kegan Paul, London.

Parry-Jones W.Ll. (1984) Adolescent psychiatry in Britain: a personal view of its development and present position. *Bulletin of the Royal College of Psychiatry,* **8**, 230–233.

Parry-Jones W.Ll. (1985) Archival exploration of anorexia nervosa.

Journal of Psychiatric Research, **19**, 95−100.

Parry-Jones W.Ll. (1989) The history of child and adolescent psychiatry: its present day relevance. *Journal of Child Psychology and Psychiatry*, **30**, 3−11.

Parry-Jones W.Ll. (1990) Juveniles in 19th century Oxfordshire asylums. *British Journal of Clinical and Social Psychiatry*, **7**, 51−58.

Parry-Jones W.Ll. (1991) The development of the psychotherapies: a brief historical overview. In: Weller M. & Eysenck M. (eds) *The Scientific Basis of Psychiatry*, 2nd edn., pp. 417−429. Saunders, London.

Parry-Jones W.Ll. (1992) Historical research in child and adolescent psychiatry: scope, methods and application. *Journal of Child Psychology and Psychiatry*, **33**, 803−811.

Paterson D. (1941) *Sick Children: Diagnosis and Treatment*, 4th edn., p. 372. Cassell, London.

Peirce R. (1697) *Bath Memoirs: or, Observations in Three and Forty Years Practice at the Bath*. H. Hammond, Bristol.

Penrose L.S. (1938) A clinical and genetic study of 1280 cases of mental defect. *Special Report Series. Medical Research Council*, No. 229. His Majesty's Stationery Office, London.

Perfect W. (1778) *Methods of Cure, in Some Particular Cases of Insanity: The Epilepsy, Hypochondriacal Affection, Hysteric Passion, and Nervous Disorders*. W. Perfect, Rochester, Great Britain.

Perfect W. (1787) *Select Cases in the Different Species of Insanity, Lunacy or Madness, with the Modes of Practice as adopted in the Treatment of Each*. Gillman, Rochester, Great Britain.

Perfect W. (1791) *A Remarkable Case of Madness, with the Diet and Medicines Used in the Cure*. W. Perfect, Rochester, Great Britain.

Phaer T. (1545) *The Regiment of Life whereunto is added a Treatyse of the Pestilence with The Boke of Chyldren*. E. Whitchurche, London.

Piaget J. (1926) *The Language and Thought of the Child* (translated by M. Gabain). Routledge & Kegan Paul, London.

Pinel P. (1806) *A Treatise on Insanity, in which are Contained the Principles of a New and More Practical Nosology of Maniacal Disorders than has yet been Offered to the Public* (translated by D.D. Davis), p. 112. Cadell & Davies, Sheffield.

Pitt M. (1696) *An Account of one Ann Jefferies, now living in the County of Cornwall, who was fed for Six Months by a Small Sort of Airy People call'd Fairies*. R. Cumberland, London.

Pollock L.A. (1983) *Forgotten Children. Parent−Child Relationships 1500−1900*. Cambridge University Press, Cambridge.

Pomme P. (1777) *A Treatise on Hysterical and Hypochondriacal Diseases, in which A New and Rational Theory is Proposed*. P. Elmsly, London.

Porter R. (1987) *Mind-Forg'd Manacles. A History of Madness in England from the Restoration to the Regency*. Athlone Press, London.

Porter R. (1989) *A Social History of Madness. Stories of the Insane*, pp. 182−183. Weidenfeld & Nicolson, London.

Powell R. (1813) Observations upon the comparative prevalence of insanity, at different periods. *Medical Transactions*, **4**, 131−160.

Preyer W. (1894) *Mental Development in the Child* (translated by H.W. Brown). E. Arnold, London.

Prichard J.C. (1835) *A Treatise on Insanity and Other Disorders Affecting the Mind*. Sherwood, Gilbert & Piper, London.

Rabb T.K. & Rotberg R.I. (eds) (1976) *The Family in History. Interdisciplinary Essays*. Octagon Books, New York.

Rachford B.K. (1905) *The Neurotic Disorders of Childhood*. E.B. Treat, New York.

Renton G. (1978) The East London Child Guidance Clinic. *Journal of Child Psychology and Psychiatry*, **19**, 309−312.

Ribton-Turner C.J. (1887) *A History of Vagrants and Vagrancy and Beggars and Begging*. Chapman & Hall, London.

Rosen M., Clark G.R. & Kivitz M.S. (1971) *The History of Mental Retardation. Collected Papers*, 2 vols. University Park Press, Baltimore, MD.

Rosenblatt B. (1971) Historical perspectives of treatment modes. In:

Rie H.E. (ed) *Perspectives in Child Psychopathology*, pp. 51−84. Aldine Atherton, Chicago, IL.

Rousseau J.J. (1762) *Émile, ou, de l'Éducation*. J. Néaulme, Amsterdam.

Rubinstein E.A. (1948) Childhood mental disease in America. A review of literature before 1900. *American Journal of Orthopsychiatry*, **18**, 314−321.

Rush B. (1812) *Medical Inquiries and Observations Upon Diseases of the Mind*. Grigg, Philadelphia, PA.

Sampson O.C. (1980) *Child Guidance. Its History, Provenance and Future*. Occasional Paper Vol. 3 No. 3. British Psychological Society, Leicester.

Savage G.H. (1881) Moral insanity. *Journal of Mental Science*, **27**, 147−155.

Savage G.H. (1885) Case of marked hysteria in a boy of eleven years. *Journal of Mental Science*, **31**, 201−202.

Scheerenberger R.C. (1983) *A History of Mental Retardation*. P.H. Brooks, Baltimore, MD.

Schor E.L. (1982) The foster care system and health status of foster children. *Pediatrics*, **69**, 521−528.

Scull A. (1989) *Social Order/Mental Disorder*. Routledge, London.

Sears R.R. (1975) Your ancients revisited. A history of child development. In: Hetherington M. (ed) *Review of Research in Child Development*, vol. 5. University of Chicago Press, Chicago, IL.

Séguin E. (1846) *Traitement Moral, Hygiène et Éducation, des Idiots et des Autres Enfants Arriérés*. Baillière, Paris.

Senn M.J.E. (1948) Pediatrics in orthopsychiatry. In: Lowrey L.G. (ed) *Orthopsychiatry, 1923−1948. Retrospect and Prospect*, pp. 300−309. American Orthopsychiatric Association, New York.

Shahar S. (1990) *Childhood in the Middle Ages*. Routledge, London.

Shinn M.W. (1893) *Notes on the Development of a Child*. University of California Press, Berkeley, CA.

Shuttleworth G.E. (1888) The education of children of abnormally weak mental capacity. *Journal of Mental Science*, **34**, 80−84.

Shuttleworth G.E. & Potts W.A. (1910) *Mentally Deficient Children. Their Treatment and Training*, 3rd edn. H.K. Lewis, London.

Slaff B. (1981) The history of adolescent psychiatry. In: Feinstein S.C., Looney J.G., Schwartzberg A.Z. & Sorosky A.D. (eds) *Adolescent Psychiatry*, vol. IX, pp. 7−21. University of Chicago Press, Chicago, IL.

Spitzka E.C. (1883) *Insanity. Its Classification, Diagnosis and Treatment. A Manual for Students and Practitioners of Medicine*, pp. 378−380. Bermingham, New York.

Spitzka E.C. (1890) Insanity. In: Keating J.M. (ed) *Cyclopaedia of the Diseases of Children, Medical and Surgical*, vol. 4, pp. 1038−1053. Young J. Pentland, Edinburgh.

Spurzheim J.G. (1836) *Observations on the Deranged Manifestations of the Mind; or Insanity*. Marsh, Cape & Lyon, Boston, MA.

Stevenson G.S. & Smith G. (1934) *Child Guidance Clinics: A Quarter Century of Development*. The Commonwealth Fund, New York.

Still G.F. (1931) *The History of Paediatrics. The Progress of the Study of Diseases of Children up to the End of the XVIIIth Century*. Oxford University Press, London.

Stone L. (1979) *The Family, Sex and Marriage. In England 1500−1800*. Penguin Books, Harmondsworth.

Stone M.H. (1973) Child psychiatry before the 20th century. *International Journal of Child Psychotherapy*, **2**, 264−308.

Stopes M.C. (1920) *Radiant Motherhood. A Book for Those Who are Creating the Future*. G.P. Putnam's Sons, London.

Strahan S.A.K. (1893) *Suicide and Insanity. A Physiological and Sociological Study*. Swan Sonnenschein, London.

Sullivan W.C. (1915) Criminal Children. In: Kelynack T.N. (ed) *Defective Children*, pp. 81−97. J. Bale & Danielsson, London.

Sully J. (1895) *Studies of Childhood*. Longmans, Green, London.

Talbot E.S. (1898) *Degeneracy: Its Causes, Signs, and Results*. W. Scott, London.

Thurnam J. (1845) *Observations and Essays on the Statistics of Insanity, and on Establishments for the Insane; to which are added the Statistics of the Retreat, near York*. Gilpin, London.

Trasler G. (1960) *In Place of Parents*. Routledge & Kegan Paul, London.

Tuke D.H. (1885) Moral or educational insanity. *Journal of Mental Science*, **31**, 174–190.

Turner D. (1732) *The Force of the Mother's Imagination upon her Foetus in utero . . . .* London.

Underwood M. (1789) *A Treatise on the Diseases of Children, with General Directions for the Management of Infants from the Birth*. J. Mathews, London.

Vaillant G.E. (1962) John Haslam on early infantile autism. *American Journal of Psychiatry*, **119**, 376.

Von Gontard A. (1988) The development of child psychiatry in 19th century Britain. *Journal of Child Psychology and Psychiatry*, **29**, 569–588.

Von Rosenstein N.R. (1776) *The Diseases of Children and their Remedies* (translated by A. Sparrman), pp. 180–183. T. Cadell, London.

Vygotsky L.S. (1962) *Thought and Language*. Wiley/MIT Press, New York.

Walk A. (1964) The pre-history of child psychiatry. *British Journal of Psychiatry*, **110**, 754–767.

Wallin J.E.W. (1914) *The Mental Health of the School Child. The Psycho-educational Clinic in relation to Child Welfare. Contributions to a New Science of Orthophrenics and Orthosomatics*. Yale University Press, New Haven, CT.

Walvin J. (1984) *A Child's World. A Social History of English Childhood 1800–1914*. Penguin, Harmondsworth.

Wardle C.J. (1991a) Twentieth-century influences on the development in Britain of services for child and adolescent psychiatry. *British Journal of Psychiatry*, **159**, 53–68.

Wardle C.J. (1991b) Historical influences on services for children and adolescents before 1900. In: Berrios G.E. & Freeman H. (eds) *150 Years of British Psychiatry 1841–1991*, pp. 279–293. Gaskell, London.

Warren W. (1971) You can never plan the future by the past. *Journal of Child Psychology and Psychiatry*, **11**, 241–257.

Watson J.B. (1919) *Psychology from the Standpoint of a Behaviorist*. Lippincott, Philadelphia, PA.

Watson J.B. (1925) *Behaviorism*. Kegan Paul, Trench, Trubner, London.

Werner H. (1948) *Comparative Psychology of Mental Development*. Harper & Row, New York.

West C. (1848) *Lectures on the Diseases of Infancy and Childhood*, 1st edn., pp. 128–131. Longman, Brown, Green, & Longmans, London.

West C. (1854) *Lectures on the Diseases of Infancy and Childhood*, 3rd edn, pp. 185–206. Longman, Brown, Green, & Longmans, London.

West C. (1860) On the mental peculiarities and mental disorders of childhood. *Medical Times and Gazette*, **1**, 133–137.

West C. (1871) *On Some Disorders of the Nervous System in Childhood;* being the Lumleian Lectures delivered . . . in March 1871. Longmans, Green, London.

Westcott W.W. (1885) *Suicide; its History, Literature, Jurisprudence, Causation and Prevention*. H.K. Lewis, London.

White S.H. (1979) Children in perspective. *American Psychologist*, **34**, 812–820.

White House Conference on Child Health and Protection (1932) *Psychology and Psychiatry in Pediatrics: The Problem. Report of the Sub-Committee on Psychology and Psychiatry*. Century, New York.

Whytt R. (1765) *Observations on the Nature, Causes, and Cure of those Disorders which have been Commonly called Nervous Hypochondriac or Hysteric*, pp. 303–305. T. Becket & P. Du Hondt, London, & J. Balfour, Edinburgh.

Wier J. (1660) *Opera Omnia*. Amsterdam.

Wilde W.R. (1859) Evidence of rape on infants. *Medical Times and Gazette*, **2**, 21–22.

Wilkins R. (1987) Hallucinations in children and teenagers admitted to Bethlem Royal Hospital in the 19th century and the possible relevance to the incidence of schizophrenia. *Journal of Child Psychology and Psychiatry*, **28**, 569–580.

Wilmarth A.W. (1894) Causation and early treatment of mental disease in children. *Journal of the American Medical Association*, **23**, 271–274.

Wilson A. (1980) The infancy of the history of childhood: an appraisal of Philippe Ariès. In: Nadel G.H. (ed) *History and Theory. Studies in the Philosophy of History*, vol. XIX, pp. 132–153. Wesleyan University Press, Middletown, CT.

Winnicott D.W. (1931) *Clinical Notes on Disorders of Childhood*. Heinemann, London.

Winnicott D.W. (1958) *Collected Papers: Through Paediatrics to Psychoanalysis*. Tavistock Publications, London.

Winslow F. (1840) *The Anatomy of Suicide*. H. Renshaw, London.

Winslow L.S.F. (1895) *Youthful Eccentricity: a Precursor of Crime*. Funk & Wagnalls, New York.

Wise T.A. (1865) *Observations on the Claims of Infirm and Imbecile Children on Public Attention*. J.J. Bradford, Cork.

Witmer H.L. (1940) *Psychiatric Clinics for Children, with Special Reference to State Programs*. Commonwealth Fund, New York.

Woodward S.B. (1838) *Hints for the Young, on a Subject Relating to the Health of Body and Mind*. Weeks, Jordan, Boston, MA.

Yellowlees D. (1892) Masturbation. In: Tuke D.H. (ed) *A Dictionary of Psychological Medicine*, vol. II, pp. 784–786. J. & A. Churchill, London.

Younger E.G. (1914) *Insanity in Every-day Practice*. Baillière, Tindall & Cox, London.

Zenderland L. (1988) Education, evangelism, and the origins of clinical psychology: the child-study legacy. *Journal of the History of the Behavioral Sciences*, **24**, 152–165.

PART 4
APPROACHES TO TREATMENT

Chapter 47
Prevention

Philip Graham

While resources are so clearly inadequate to meet the needs of the numbers of children with mental health problems, the notion that such problems might be prevented from occurring in the first place is obviously attractive (Offord, 1987). In this chapter, knowledge relevant to preventive activity will be summarized. Attention is also drawn to a number of more comprehensive recent multiauthored books on this subject (US Department of Health and Human Services, 1989; Goldston *et al.*, 1990; Pueschel & Mulick, 1990).

DEFINITION

By convention, three types of preventive activity are recognized (Henderson, 1988). Primary prevention involves intervention that reduces the incidence of disorder. Secondary prevention comprises treatment that reduces the duration of the disorder, and tertiary prevention covers rehabilitative activity that reduces the disability arising from an established disorder. Secondary and tertiary forms of prevention are covered in other chapters, and will not be dealt with here. It is worth pointing out however that this classification into primary and tertiary preventive activity is imperfect. Much treatment is at least of potentially preventive significance. Children with anxiety states treated successfully with cognitive-behaviour therapy (see Chapter 49) are at least in theory less likely to develop further anxiety states in the future because they have been given the techniques to avoid them. A suicide prevention programme might fail to prevent adolescents from attempting suicide, but might alert parents and peers to seek early help and treatment when such an attempt occurred, thus avoiding a preventable death. Nevertheless, this threeway classification is helpful in creating broadly useful categories.

In considering primary prevention, the concepts of risk, protective factors and vulnerability are crucial. A *risk factor* is a variable, the presence of which increases the liability of an individual to suffer from a particular disorder. The identification of a risk factor does not necessarily mean that it is causally related to the disorder in question. Thus, for example, coming from a single-parent family might be a risk factor for antisocial behaviour, yet results of studies might suggest that children from single-parent families are at risk because they are financially disadvantaged, and that once they are compared with children from two-parent families living at a similar economic level, their extra risk for antisocial disorder disappears. Obviously in planning preventive activity, a knowledge not only of risk factors but also of their causal significance and of the processes involved (Rutter, 1990) is vital.

It is also important to know the level of risk associated with a particular factor. The fact that a variable is significantly highly correlated with a disorder does not mean that individuals showing the variable are at high risk. In large-scale studies, highly significant correlations may be found even when the risk is quite low. A more helpful concept is that of *relative risk* (the ratio of the incidence rate of the disorder in those possessing a risk factor to the incidence rate in those not possessing the risk factor). A closely related statistic is the *odds ratio* — the product of cases with the risk factor and noncases without the risk factor (true positives and true negatives), divided by the product of cases without the risk factor and noncases with the risk factor (false positives and false negatives). *Attributable risk* is an even more helpful statistic from the point of view of anyone planning preventive activity. This describes the difference in the incidence of a disorder between those with and without a risk factor, and gives an estimate of the degree to which the incidence of a disorder could be reduced if the risk factor were completely eliminated. It is rarely possible to identify attributable risk accurately in multifactorially determined child psychiatric disorders, but in some developmental disorders it is possible to provide such an estimate. It is possible, for example, to calculate attributable risk for Down's syndrome in women over the age of 38 years, i.e. the level of reduction in the incidence of Down's syndrome if all women of this age had amniocentesis and therapeutic terminations if found to be carrying an affected fetus.

Protective factors are those that, if present, reduce an individual's likelihood of suffering from a particular disorder. The individual concerned may be at high, low or average risk, and the protective factor may operate differently depending on whether risk factors are present or not. In some cases, for example, a protective factor may operate specifically when a risk is present, but not when the risk is absent. In these circumstances there is an interactive process between the risk and the protective factor (Rutter, 1987). In other situations a protective factor may act additively, reducing the rate of the disorder whether or not the stress is present — in these circumstances it is uncertain whether it is appropriate to refer to the factor as protective or merely as denoting reduction of risk (Jenkins & Smith, 1990).

Finally, the terms vulnerability and invulnerability must be mentioned. These are usually taken to refer to the state of children who, when exposed to a particular level of risk, are, for one reason or another, particularly likely or unlikely to develop disorder. Typically, vulnerable children are considered to be those who, although in low-risk situations, perhaps because of their temperamental characteristics, have an increased tendency to develop disorders, and invulnerable children are those who, although in high-risk situations, perhaps for the same reasons or because they have been 'steeled' by previous adverse experiences, do not develop disorders.

In the child psychiatric field, information that is most relevant to preventive interventions usually comes from longitudinal research studies that have identified the aetiological significance of risk factors and examined their modifiability (American Academy of Child and Adolescent Psychiatry, 1990). Logically such information should be used in the design of preventive interventions aimed at reducing the presence of these risk factors. Controlled trials can then be mounted to determine to what degree, if any, the risk factors have been altered and, if there has been an alteration, what effect this has had on the disorder in question. Although it is difficult to point to an example in the field of child psychiatric disorders in which this approach has been convincingly successful, many elements have been present in preventive programmes described later in this chapter in relation, for example, to preterm infants, hospitalized children and children exposed to other stressful circumstances.

There are however a variety of reasons why preventive interventions fail, even when based on this approach. Firstly, it may be impossible at this stage of knowledge to identify risk factors that are amenable to preventive activity. Such a situation currently exists in relation to childhood autism and various other psychiatric disorders. Secondly, studies apparently identifying risk factors may be faulty, either because of the use of unreliable methods or because of unsatisfactory interpretation of results. Thirdly, risk factors may turn out to be only risk indicators, and not involved in causal mechanisms. For example, as mentioned above, low socioeconomic status, as assessed by parental occupation, may be a risk indicator for delinquency, but changing parental occupation is unlikely to alter the rate of delinquency. It is more likely that causal mechanisms involve indicators linked to low socioeconomic status, such as poverty and unemployment. The distinction between risk indicators that are or are not involved in causal mechanisms is often difficult, but Rutter (1988) discussed helpful pointers. He particularly highlighted the usefulness of identifying a dose effect. If the length, frequency or severity of a particular risk factor is associated with the likelihood of the presence of an outcome variable, it is more likely that a causal mechanism is involved. Fourthly, interventions designed to achieve change in the prevalence of risk factors may fail to do so. Unless a serious attempt is made to

evaluate the effectiveness of interventions using a controlled approach, valuable resources may be wasted on measures that appear sensible but, in fact, have little or no impact.

In planning preventive programmes for child psychiatric disorders, it is sensible to base activities on existing information, especially if this is derived from longitudinal studies in which a causal mechanism has been identified, or from cross-sectional studies in which attributable risk has been shown to be high. For example, if the staff of a child psychiatric department were considering putting aside time to undertake preventive activity, they might wish to choose between the prevention of disorders in children who were bereaved of a parent, or in children whose parents were separated or divorcing. In these circumstances, it is relevant to know that the relative risk of disturbance in children of divorcing or separating parents is much higher than in those who have lost a parent by death (see Chapter 12). It would also be relevant that attributable risk is higher in divorced and separating parents because the rate of separation and divorce is so much higher than bereavement. Of course, relative and attributable risk are not the only factors that might sway the decision of the staff of a clinic — the motivation of potential clients, the effectiveness of available intervention and the clinical interest and skill of the staff in question would also be relevant — but clearly existing knowledge concerning risk and protective factors should be one major influence determining the choice.

TYPES OF PREVENTIVE ACTIVITY

Preventive activities and programmes can be classified according to their aims and focus. Measures may be directed: (1) towards the improvement of living conditions of a population on the assumption, to be examined below, that the quality of living conditions indirectly affects the rate of child mental health problems; (2) towards a total population of children of specific ages and/or their parents, with the focused aim of preventing mental disorders generally; or (3) towards individuals known or thought to be at risk for specific mental health problems with the aim of preventing their occurrence. In each of these three types of preventive activity it is relevant to consider the evidence that the variable it is intended to change indeed reflects a risk mechanism for child psychiatric disorder as well as evidence that preventive programmes exist that are effective or show promise of being effective.

In the discussion that follows, most attention is given to measures aimed to reduce psychiatric disorders. Influences on development, intelligence and learning disorders are, however, discussed where these were targeted or influenced in addition. Preventive activities in relation to learning disorders are discussed more fully by Silver and Hagin (1989).

Prevention by improvement in the quality of living conditions

It may seem common sense that children eating well-balanced diets, living in economically secure circumstances in spacious homes, with at least one parent in employment, and with good prospects of employment themselves, will show fewer mental health problems than those living in less advantaged conditions. Cross-cultural studies do not, in fact, lend support to this commonsensical notion. For example, using the same behavioural questionnaires for measurement, roughly similar rates of deviance are found in countries with very different levels of economic development throughout the world (Graham, 1979). There are probably several reasons for this somewhat surprising state of affairs.

1 It is important to draw a distinction between absolute and relative deprivation (Runciman, 1972). Children whose diet falls below a particular calorific level or who are deficient in an essential dietary constituent may well suffer psychological problems, while those above this level may well not differ from others with a much more varied diet. Children living in crowded but settled circumstances may not differ in rates of mental health problems from those living in much more spacious circumstances, while those living in homeless families' accommodation might be seriously affected. This type of threshold effect may be of major significance.

2 Related to the distinction between absolute and relative deprivation are the perceptions of parents concerning the quality of living conditions they have a right to expect. Unemployed parents and teenagers with expectations of economic conditions of full employment may well be more depressed and frustrated than those brought up in areas where unemployment is the norm.

3 Although there is evidence (see below) that the quality of living conditions is important in determining the level of mental health problems, especially if absolute deprivation is considered, it is clear that whatever the standard of living, the quality of family relationships plays an overriding part in determining the risk of disturbance in a child. There is an interaction between the quality of family relationships and the standard of living — but the association is not a strong one, and the quality of family relationships has an important effect that is independent of living conditions. Affluent parents are only slightly less likely to reject their children, to quarrel, separate and divorce than are parents living in impoverished circumstances.

Housing

The links between quality of housing and child mental health problems have been reviewed by Quinton (1988). Population density appears of little importance. On the other hand, living in the upper floors of high-rise accommodation, where supervision of the child's play is inevitably more difficult, is associated with depression in the mothers of young children (Richman, 1974). Such high-rise accommodation is also not infrequently associated with high rates of vandalism and delinquency in teenagers, probably partly because of the increased opportunities for theft, and partly because of the fact that problem families tend to get housed in less desirable circumstances.

The deleterious effects of homelessness in families with children have been reviewed by Alperstein and Arnstein (1988). Uncontrolled studies (Fox *et al.*, 1990) of children living in homeless families' accommodation (hotels, hostels etc.) have revealed very high rates of developmental delay as well as emotional and behavioural problems. Parents have high rates of depression.

The implications of these studies for preventive activity are considerable. It is inappropriate for families with young children to be housed in circumstances where there is no opportunity for the children to play safely. By attention to environmental management and design of housing estates, there are ways of making delinquent acts more difficult to commit (Clarke, 1985). These include the appointment of caretakers in flats, improved lighting, 'defensible space' architecture, as well as the promotion of community neighbourhood activity. The scandal of homeless families in the major cities of North America and the UK, resulting in children being brought up in a series of unsuitable environments, requires improved housing policies with priority given to the maintenance of family stability.

Employment

The importance of opportunities of full employment in the mental health of teenage boys is confirmed by the work of Banks and Jackson (1982) who showed that in the years after leaving school, older teenagers who had failed to find a job showed more psychiatric symptoms than those in employment. These results held up after the behaviour of the boys while at school had been taken into account. It has also been shown in longitudinal studies that teenagers who are in and out of employment are more likely to offend when unemployed. The specific risk in crimes involving material gain among the unemployed suggests that the relative poverty associated with unemployment is an important mediating factor (Farrington *et al.*, 1986). There are also strong suggestions of links between unemployment and mental ill health in adults (Smith, 1985). Some mothers of young children find significant social support in their place of work and, if they do, this may reduce their rate of minor psychiatric disorder, especially depression and anxiety states (Bebbington *et al.*, 1984). Taken together, these findings suggest that government policies achieving full employment are likely to result in lower rates of psychiatric disorder in children and adolescents.

Nutrition

The period of maximum brain growth occurs between early fetal life and 12 months of age (Morgan, 1990). It is likely therefore that the effects of malnutrition will be greatest when experienced in the first year of life, and that prevention of malnutrition will be most effective when focused on this age period. Although a policy of encouraging breast-feeding will reduce rates of malnutrition in Third World countries, there is no evidence that this is the case in economically developed countries, even though there are other advantages (reduced rates of gastroenteritis etc.) to breast-feeding. The deleterious effects of early malnutrition on later intellectual development in children in Third World countries has been clearly documented. Although it is very difficult to disentangle the effects of malnutrition from other forms of social disadvantage with which it is so often associated (Richardson, 1984), controlled studies have been carried out demonstrating long-lasting beneficial effects on psychosocial interventions in malnourished children (Grantham-McGregor *et al.*, 1987).

In developed countries, poor growth velocity resulting in nonorganic failure to thrive (NOFT) in the first year of life is associated with later developmental delay and learning difficulties as well as a high rate of behavioural and emotional disorders (Skuse, 1989). However in the developed world, NOFT is usually unrelated to lack of available food. Much more commonly it is linked to the interaction between faulty feeding practices and factors within the child such as oral–motor dysfunction (Mathisen *et al.*, 1989). Drotar (1990) suggested the following principles of preventive management in children at risk for NOFT:

1 Early diagnosis, by surveillance of the infant population.
2 Assessment of the child's physical and psychological status, the parent–child relationship and family context.
3 Stabilization or reversal of the child's acute physical symptoms by physical and nutritional intervention.
4 Addressing specific problems in the parent–child or family system that are maintaining NOFT and contributing to risk for emotional disorders.

Whereas the importance for later intellectual development of an adequate nutritious diet is well-established, there is controversy over claims that specific vitamins or mineral supplementation promote brain development or intelligence (Benton & Buts, 1990; Schoenthaler *et al.*, 1991). It is possible that vitamin and mineral supplements do specifically enhance the nonverbal ability of children on poor diets, and therefore that such supplementation could be desirable for children on inadequate diets that cannot otherwise be improved. The matter requires further investigation.

Economic status

There is a view that mental health problems are largely, if not wholly, the result of financial inequalities, and that if such inequalities can be eradicated, such problems would no longer occur. If this is the case, this would have very considerable implications for preventive activity.

Although there is rather little clear-cut direct information on this subject, it is nevertheless possible to draw reasonably definite conclusions from indirect evidence. Most information about financial inequalities is derived from studies of links between social status and mental health problems. Social status is usually measured by the occupation of the main breadwinner, and is reasonably closely related to income. In general, child psychiatric disorders, with a few exceptions (see Chapters 18, 24 and 56) are only weakly related to socioeconomic status. In contrast, intellectual development and educational achievement are much more strongly related (Rutter & Madge, 1976). Further indirect evidence pointing to

the same conclusions comes from comparisons of social class differences in intelligence and educational attainment between countries with different income differentials. It is notable that in Sweden, where the differential between the highest and the lowest incomes is relatively small, the differences between the social classes in IQ and academic achievement appear considerably reduced (Hagberg *et al.*, 1981). In contrast, the evidence suggests that the rate of psychiatric disorders in children and adolescence is no different in Sweden and other Scandinavian countries than in other developed nations.

The evidence cited above cannot be taken to relate only to economic factors, for low income is related to poor housing, inadequate diet, risk of unemployment, size of family, physical ill health, parental mental ill health and a number of other adverse influences. Nevertheless, the evidence does point to a major influence of social adversity on intelligence and a relatively minor influence on psychiatric disorder. Again, from the point of view of the development of government policy, this suggests that the removal or reduction of economic inequalities and the alleviation of serious poverty might be expected to have a significant influence on the intellectual development of the population, but much less effect on the rates of child psychiatric disorder.

Preventive activities directed towards children at different developmental levels

Routine pre- and perinatal care

Preventive possibilities in the field of child mental health begin well before conception. Indeed, in the sense that the best foundation for parenthood lies in the secure child-centred early life of parents themselves, prevention can be said to begin as early as the parents' own infancy. From the point of view of professional intervention, classes in preparation for parenthood held in secondary (high) schools that are practically oriented (concentrating, for example, not just on normal development but on how to deal with common early feeding and sleeping problems) represent an early opportunity for prevention. There is however no satisfactory evidence for or against the suggestion that exposure to such information results in better parenting subsequently.

Further, although classes along similar lines for pregnant women and their partners probably do result in greater knowledgeability concerning normal child development and its deviations, given the amount of effort going into such educational activity, it is perhaps surprising that there is little evidence for effectiveness in changing parental behaviour and child outcome in the general population. Such evidence is largely linked to similar interventions for high-risk groups (see below).

There are however many ways in which obstetricians, midwives and public health nurses can promote healthy child development in their routine antenatal and postnatal care (Newton, 1988). Such measures include the delivery of regular antenatal monitoring by the same staff (so that continuity of care is achieved), sympathetic handling of anxiety, behavioural help to mothers who smoke or drink more than a moderate amount of alcohol, and identification and rapid treatment of depressive states. In the period immediately after birth, there should be encouragement of early mother–baby contact, taking account of the mother's need to rest and recuperate after a physically and emotionally exhausting experience. Early reports (Klaus & Kennell, 1976) of the importance of early contact for satisfactory bonding were exaggerated (Sluckin *et al.*, 1983), but there is every reason why mothers should have ready access to their babies immediately after birth.

Pre- and perinatal care of the 'high-risk' mother and infant

In contrast to the relative lack of scientific studies on the effects of psychosocial interventions in routine pre- and perinatal care, there is a good deal of encouraging information on the effects of intervention in the 'high-risk' mother and baby.

1 Successful interventions have been described in the *prenatal* period. Olds *et al.* (1986a) carried out a randomized trial involving four levels of intervention with pregnant women identified as at high risk because of their young age, single-parent status, low socioeconomic status or a combination of these disadvantages. The interventions involved routine care, routine care with free transport to and from clinic appointments, and routine care, free transport and regular home visiting by a trained nurse. (The additional effects of a postnatal visiting programme on rates of child abuse are described below). Home visiting made a significant difference in that those who had this intervention, if aged less than 17 years, had heavier babies and fewer preterm deliveries. They made more use of nutritional supplementation advice. Osofsky *et al.* (1988) came to similar conclusions as a result of a study of the effects of home visitation, but here the results were less clear-cut. It seemed that the benefits were only obtained by the pregnant teenagers who accepted home visiting, and these were a less disadvantaged group in the first place than those who did not 'take' to home visiting.

2 *Postnatal intervention* in groups at high risk, either because of the social disadvantage of the family or the prematurity of the baby, has also shown positive results. Programmes have been devised that focus on preterm babies and these have been successful in enhancing developmental level, improving mother–child interaction and reducing the number of later behaviour problems (Gutelius *et al.*, 1977; Barrera *et al.*, 1986; Beckwith, 1990; Infant Health and Development Program, 1990). The results are not necessarily short-lived. Thus Seitz *et al.* (1985) found that, although there were no beneficial effects on intelligence, a programme involving home visiting, day care and paediatric care from early pregnancy through to 30 months postpartum had a demonstrable effect on the mother's capacity to support herself and the child's school attendance when the child was 10 years old.

Attention to mother–baby contact and to the quality of the environment in units for sick or premature neonates is likely to result in improved outcome (Wolke, 1987). Mothers of premature babies interact less with their infants 3 months after discharge than mothers of full-term babies (Minde *et al.*, 1983). There is evidence that, after exclusion of the obviously handicapped, very low birth weight babies show high rates of behaviour problems as well as motor clumsiness at 6 years (Marlow *et al.*, 1989). Some of these deviations may be preventable with early intervention. For example, using a home visitor intervention programme (Beckwith, 1990), it was possible to show that mother–child interaction and maternal sensitivity could be significantly increased, and Rauh *et al.* (1988) obtained similar results with an 11-session intervention programme with additional benefits on developmental quotients.

Components necessary to the success of these programmes seem to involve home intervention by trained workers, usually public health nurses, who visit regularly, build up trusting relationships with the mothers, and provide both emotional support and practical guidance based on developmental concepts. Further, the longer the intervention is maintained, the better the results (Horacek *et al.*, 1987). Similarly successful results have been obtained with groups of disadvantaged 'at-risk' mothers and babies who were not born preterm (e.g. Horacek *et al.*, 1987; Lally *et al.*, 1988). Horacek *et al.* (1987) found that intervention along the lines described above from the time the baby was 3 months old reduced rates of retention in grade once the children reached elementary school. These positive results are not necessarily generalizable to low-risk groups. Belsky (1985), for example, found no effects on developmental level as a result of administering the Brazelton Neonatal Behavioural Assessment with accompanying active guidance to a group of largely middle-class mothers.

Preschool intervention

A high proportion of children who present in primary school with behaviour problems and learning difficulties have been showing signs of disturbance before they entered mainstream schooling. Consequently, it is rational to consider whether interventions aimed at the preschool child might result in a reduction in the rate of school-based problems.

Preschool educational programmes

Although there have been other studies with interesting results (Johnson & Walker, 1987), most information concerning the effectiveness of intervention in preventing mental retardation and behavioural and emotional disorders through preschool educational programmes arises from studies based on the massive Head Start programme initiated by President Johnson in the US in the mid 1960s. Apart from the fact that the programmes were focused on young children living in disadvantaged circumstances, they were very varied in nature. In some, the intervention was limited to a small number of additional sessions of child care of unspecified quality, whereas in others the intervention was much more intensive, regular and long-lasting. In some, mothers were heavily involved but in others, apart from agreeing to cooperate, they were not involved at all.

Controlled evaluation was built into a relatively small number of the programmes, and initial results, reported shortly after the children had entered mainstream schooling, were, on the whole, rather disappointing and showed few, if any, effects on intelligence and educational attainment that lasted more than a year after the children entered mainstream schooling.

However in the 1980s, the results of a number of long-term longitudinal studies were published, demonstrating at least limited effectiveness of some of the more intensive and well-documented controlled interventions. In particular, Lazar and Darlington (1982) synthesized the results of 12 studies in which children exposed to programmes of varying types and degrees of intensity were followed up to the ages of 9–19 years. Some of these children had had year-round experience 5 days a week for as long as 2 years, whereas others only had a session a week delivered at home by a paraprofessional. All the studies were controlled, but with a varying degree of randomization. There were major problems of attrition or drop-out in some of the studies, but in others very satisfactory levels of contact were maintained. The findings strongly suggested that, compared to controls, those children who attended the programmes were less likely to be referred to special classes or to repeat grades. Their mothers were more likely to be satisfied with their educational attainment.

The long-term results of some of the studies were striking, and some have been separately reported. For example, Berrueta-Clement *et al.* (1984), reported the long-term results of an intensive intervention in which the disadvantaged children, then aged 3–4 years, attended a special class 5 mornings a week for 7 months of the year. Their parents were visited at home once a week by a teacher. This experimental group did better than controls in a wide range of measures. They achieved better academic results from the time they entered school until they left high school. At the age of 19 years they were more often employed, more often self-supporting, and were less dependent on welfare. There were fewer pregnancies among the girls. A further report (Berrueta-Clement *et al.*, 1987) provides more detail on the outcomes in relation to delinquency. Interestingly, although the programme children had quite markedly fewer police-documented arrests, there were few differences between the two groups in self-reported offences, leaving the possibility open that in many areas of antisocial activity the programme children grew up no less antisocial, but better at avoiding police contact.

The requirements for successful preschool educational intervention programmes have been stated to include a developmentally appropriate curriculum, groups of fewer than 20 3–5-year-olds with 2 adults to each group, trained staff, supervisory support and in-service training, sensitivity to the child's noneducational needs, and developmentally appropriate evaluation procedures (Rae-Grant, 1991). Added to these must be included high-quality caregiver–child verbal interactions, and an experienced programme director (Phillips *et al.*, 1987). It should be emphasized that mere attendance at a preschool programme confers no benefit in itself in terms of educational or social outcome (Stevenson & Ellis, 1975). Benefits are likely to accrue only if the child attends a facility that provides a better-quality experience than the child would receive at home. Of course, in many circumstances, mainly for economic reasons, women do send their children to facilities that provide a poorer quality of experience than they themselves would be able to provide. This is unavoidable in the social circumstances that pertain, and the indirect benefits to the child in terms of improved material conditions may be considerable, but it cannot be accepted that this is a desirable state of affairs or in any way preventive of future educational or social difficulties. Nor can the effects of intensive preschool interventions to high-risk children be generalized to justify preschool or kindergarten experience in relatively large classes for children who are not socially or biologically disadvantaged. Such experience may be desirable, but there is little firm evidence to confirm its value.

Other approaches

Some workers have targeted specific childhood symptomatology in an attempt to prevent its occurrence. Thus Brazelton (1962) counselled parents systematically to follow a child-centred approach to toilet training. The study was not controlled, but the results are strikingly positive. Cullen (1976) also regularly counselled parents of infants and young children using a child-centred approach and, in a controlled follow-up study, was able to demonstrate positive effects on rates of habit problems and fearfulness, although not aggressive behaviour. Finally, there have been attempts to reduce rates of child abuse, particularly by focusing on groups at risk. Preventive possibilities and programmes have been reviewed by Leventhal (1988) and Dubowitz (1989). Unfortunately, the specificity and sensitivity of predictive screening measures are not sufficiently high to allow the accurate early identification of many abused children. A number of studies have however found at least short-term effects on rates of abuse, of which one of the most striking is that reported by Olds *et al.* (1986b). In this study, the prenatal component of which has already been described above, a postnatal visiting programme was found to reduce rates of child abuse when the experimental group was compared to controls.

Middle childhood programmes

There are distinctly fewer studies published reporting primary preventive programmes in middle childhood (school entry to early teenage) than for the preschool or adolescent age group. Nevertheless, there are significant opportunities for prevention in this age group when, for the first time, the legal obligation to attend a school means that there is access to the total child population. Different approaches have been reviewed by

Durlak (1985). Some, such as social cognitive problem-solving (see Chapter 48) are discussed elsewhere in this book and will not be considered here.

On the basis of information gathered from around 1000 6–12-year-olds in the Ontario Child Health Study, Boyle and Offord (1990) suggested that, at least in programmes directed towards the primary prevention of conduct disorders, for reasons of cost-effectiveness there should be a focus on high-risk groups, and indeed this has been the approach most commonly pursued.

The Yale New Haven Primary Prevention Study focused on a small number of elementary schools attended mainly by black, disadvantaged children. At the onset of the study, the schools in which the intervention occurred were the least successful in the educational achievement of their pupils and in school attendance rates (Comer, 1985). The programme devised had four elements: (1) a representative governance and management group; (2) a focus on parent participation both in management and in volunteer help in the classroom; (3) a mental health team providing both therapy and consultation; and (4) an academic programme. It is unclear what additional staff resources were involved. Over a period of 7 years, the schools involved obtained the best attendance records in the area, and the children reached grade levels in their educational attainments. A follow-up in middle school 3 years after the children had left their elementary schools suggested that the children were achieving significantly better than controls who had attended different elementary schools (Cauce *et al.*, 1987).

Parent participation alone was the main focus in a study in a deprived area in London, UK, in which parents were encouraged to listen to their children reading each evening at a level indicated by their teachers. This simple intervention that necessitated regular parent–teacher communication was compared with the addition of extra classroom tuition in reading and to no intervention. The parent-involvement group of children reached significantly better reading levels than the other two groups (which did not differ from each other) over a period of a year, and these gains over the other groups were maintained over a period of 3 years follow-up (Hewison, 1988).

The reduction of educational retardation achieved by such preventive methods is highly likely to result in a similar reduction in antisocial behaviour, because evidence suggests that a significant proportion of conduct disorders arises as a result of the feelings of failure accompanying learning difficulties (Rutter *et al.*, 1970a). A more direct approach to the prevention of conduct disorders has been taken by Hawkins *et al.* (1991) who focused on about 450 second-grade children. The parents of these children had parenting skill training sessions, and their teachers received tutorials in classroom management and social skills training using a cognitive-behavioural approach (see Chapter 49). Over the following year there were significant reductions in aggressive behaviour in white boys and self-destructive behaviour in white girls. No effects were reported in black chil-

dren, nor have further follow-up data been reported.

The rather slender volume of research reported in preventive programmes in middle childhood needs supplementation, for this is a time when children might be expected to be open to behaviour change, and when there is a real opportunity for individual teachers who spend much more time with the same children than is the case in secondary school to have a positive impact on children at risk.

Adolescent programmes

In that about half the psychiatric disorders occurring in adolescent boys and a much higher proportion in adolescent girls are of relatively recent onset (Rutter *et al.*, 1976), the possibilities for prevention in this age group may be considerable. Programmes described in other sections of this chapter are of considerable relevance to the adolescent group. For example, much of the work on the impact of different types of school organization (see below) has been carried out in secondary or junior high schools.

However there are particular components of school organization that are relevant to adolescents, especially the transition from primary or elementary to secondary, junior high or middle school. The relatively immature child moving from a school setting in which much of the day has been spent in one classroom with a familiar teacher may become disturbed as a result of the complexity of secondary school life. Felner and Adan (1988) have demonstrated that a secondary school intake programme designed to provide the incomer with a home base and opportunities for counselling can result in a lower subsequent drop-out rate and lower rates of delinquency and substance abuse when comparisons are made with an untreated control group. This study is possibly unique in attempting to evaluate the effectiveness of school counselling, but it is not possible to establish from the findings whether the counselling had an independent beneficial effect. There is however considerable anecdotal evidence that the availability of school counselling along the lines described by Jones (1984) can provide teenagers with an opportunity to discuss life problems either individually or in groups in a way that reduces the likelihood of the subsequent development of stress-related disorders. More evaluative work is greatly needed in this area.

In addition to measures directed generally towards the prevention of adolescent disturbance, a number of workers have established or reviewed programmes directed towards specific mental health problems occurring in adolescence. These include the following:

1 *Suicide and suicidal attempts.* Shaffer and his colleagues (1988) have written extensively on both school-based programmes and 'hot-lines' (emergency telephone counselling), established over recent decades, especially in the US, to prevent suicidal behaviour. Although there is a large number of school-based programmes in the US, in fact they cover only a small proportion of the adolescent population at risk, and are of doubtful value. Garland *et al.* (1989) are critical of professionals who

put emphasis on a stress-based explanatory model of suicidal behaviour rather than a mental illness model, and believe that such programmes could be more cost-effective if directed towards high-risk groups.

'Hot-lines' run from suicide crisis centres are rather little used by adolescents, although they have the advantages of anonymity, the sense of control they give the caller, and the possibility of linkage with care services (Shaffer et al., 1990). 'Hot-line' services might be more attractive to teenagers if they were more clearly aiming to service high-risk groups and gave more attention to the personality and training of telephone counsellors. In the meantime, possibly the most effective method of reducing suicidal behaviour in teenagers might be to discourage television companies from putting on programmes in which glamorous youngsters make suicidal attempts as a response to stress. There is evidence that when such programmes are broadcast they are followed by a definite increase in adolescent suicidal behaviour (Shaffer et al., 1990).

2 *Antisocial behaviour and delinquency.* Improvements in school organization along the lines described below might be expected to result in a reduction in antisocial behaviour generally, but two more focused approaches have recently been described that seem to offer considerable promise. These programmes are not specifically geared to adolescence, but they are particularly relevant to this age group.

Olweus (1989), at the request of the Norwegian Education Department, undertook a study of the prevalence of bully—victim offences in Norwegian schools and found that 9% of children in grades 1—9 were regularly bullied and 7—8% self-reported bullying other children. With the cooperation of government officials, teachers, parents and parent organizations, he then systematically introduced an intervention programme that he was able to show by controlled studies reduced bullying events by as much as 50%. The programme involved the introduction of an authoritative adult—child model of interaction; positive active involvement of parents and teachers; and the consistent use of nonhostile, noncorporal punishment sanctions on rule violations. Specifically the programme included an information booklet on the subject for all teachers and school managers, a folder carrying information to inform parents of both bullies and victims, a 25-minute video-cassette giving typical case histories of bully—victim events with suggestions on how to handle them, and a short inventory for completion by children on the degree to which bullying went on in their schools and the attitudes of their teachers to its occurrence. This successful programme has been described in some detail because the multiple levels of the intervention and quality of the evaluation seem to provide a model for other preventive research.

A very different approach to the prevention of antisocial behaviour outside the school has been described by Jones and Offord (1989). They introduced a nonacademic skills programme to children aged 5—15 living in a disadvantaged inner-city area, comparing outcome in officially reported antisocial behaviour in this area and another area in which there was no specific intervention. The nonacademic skills involved a range of sporting activities, scouting, orienteering, etc. The results are a little difficult to evaluate because the prestudy rate of antisocial behaviour, as assessed by security breach reports, police charges and fire calls, was very considerably higher at the outset in the experimental than in the control area. However there was certainly a very marked reduction in neighbourhood antisocial behaviour in the experimental area that would be difficult to explain purely on the basis of statistical artefact. Interestingly, there was no significant change in the behaviour of children in the experimental area at home or in school — the changes that occurred were specifically linked to neighbourhood behaviour. The results of the study are also encouraging, especially in relation to possibilities for prevention with disadvantaged children who find few rewards in academic school activities.

Some more individualized, and therefore more expensive preventive programmes have been reported. Thus, in a controlled trial, Klein et al. (1977) found a short-term behaviourally oriented family system treatment of families with a delinquent child to be successful in preventing similar problems in the siblings of the index child. A range of other preventive programmes targeted at rates of delinquency are discussed by Rutter and Giller (1983) and by Offord (1987).

3 *School organization.* Preventive programmes in schools directed towards children and adolescents of different ages have been discussed above. However, in view of evidence collected over the last 10—15 years, especially in the UK and US, there is also a need to consider the way in which characteristics of schools themselves affect rates of behaviour and emotional disorder, and the preventive opportunities that might arise as a result of altering these characteristics.

The evidence in this connection is summarized by Maughan (1988). Firstly, there are major differences between schools in rates of behavioural and emotional problems in children attending them. These differences are only to some degree accounted for by neighbourhood variables and by the characteristics of the children on school entry. The differences are persistent over time — an individual school has a relatively stable record in producing high or low rates of children with psychiatric disorder (Rutter et al., 1979).

More effective schools are characterized, according to Maughan (1988) by purposeful leadership, involvement of staff in decision-making, consistency and consensus among staff concerning the aims of the school, and parental involvement. For pupils at classroom level, the need is for a pleasant, work-oriented environment, effective classroom management, stimulating teaching and opportunities for children to be involved in and take responsibility for aspects of their lives at school.

Although the findings concerning the importance of these characteristics are reasonably clear-cut, it has been much more difficult to ascertain whether attempts at altering schools and classrooms do result in change and, more importantly, if changes are achieved, whether this has an impact on rates of psychiatric disorder. Anecdotal evidence certainly suggests that the quality of leadership provided by a headteacher is crucial and recently, in the UK, much more attention has been given in selection to the leadership qualities of potential headteachers and to their training in management skills. There is also more emphasis in teacher training on classroom management. The skills required of a teacher of a class of 30—35 pupils in dealing with 1 or 2 disruptive children without negating the education of the whole class are vital, but it has not been easy to delineate these precisely or to develop methods to train teachers to exercise them effectively.

Preventive approaches to children in high-risk situations

Children with acute and chronic illness

Hospitalization

Hospitalization is a common experience for children of all ages, but particularly for those in the preschool age group. In the UK, and the figures are similar in most developed countries, about 1 in 20 children under the age of 16 is admitted to hospital each year, and by the age of 16, about 1 in 4 children will have experienced a hospital admission.

In the 1950s and 1960s, repeated hospitalizations were associated with high rates of later behavioural and emotional problems (Douglas, 1975; Quinton & Rutter, 1976). It was unclear whether repeated hospitalizations caused such problems or whether children at risk for psychiatric disorder for other reasons were hospitalized more frequently. More recent evidence (Shannon *et al.*, 1984) suggests that changes in procedures in children's hospitals and paediatric wards in general hospitals may have resulted in a reduction in subsequent behavioural and emotional problems for hospitalized children. If this is the case, then such procedures can be seen to have preventive possibilities and will be briefly summarized here (see also Chapter 58).

They include the following (Byrne & Cadman, 1987; Graham, 1991):

1 Adequate preparation, for example (in planned admissions) by the use of preadmission visits to the paediatric unit, and the use of relevant story books appropriate to the child's age.

2 Rooming-in facilities, especially for children under 5 and seriously ill or vulnerable older children.

3 Round-the-clock visiting hours for parents and siblings, with a welcoming attitude from staff.

4 Adequate preparation geared to the child's level of understanding for all painful or unpleasant procedures and for the aftermath of surgical operations.

5 Training of medical and nursing staff working with children in the alleviation of distress.

6 The presence of trained teachers for children admitted for longer than brief periods and who are well enough to benefit from continuing education.

7 A child-centred ward atmosphere with waking times, mealtimes, etc. geared to children's needs rather than staff needs.

8 Adequate social work, psychological and psychiatric back-up services with regular opportunities for discussion of psychosocial aspects of ward policies as well as individual children and their families.

9 Allocation of nursing staff to individual children, so that children and families become familiar with a small group of nurses who themselves will be better able to meet the needs of the individual child.

10 Opportunities for medical and nursing staff (especially those working under unusually stressful conditions with care of very sick babies) to express their feelings about their work and receive support both from each other and, where appropriate, from mental health professionals less directly involved in care.

The general principle underlying virtually all these measures is an awareness that the smaller the discrepancy between the child's environment in hospital and that at home, the less will be the child's distress (Brown, 1979). The evidence for the effectiveness of the measures described above is largely anecdotal, but the results of a limited number of studies (e.g. Melamed & Siegel, 1975; Fergusson, 1979; Wolfer & Visintainer, 1979; Schwartz *et al.*, 1983) support their value as far as the effectiveness of adequate preparation is concerned.

Children with chronic illness

Children with chronic physical disorders have twice the expected rate of psychiatric disorder, and rates of psychiatric disorder are higher still in children with physical disorders affecting the brain, including especially cerebral palsy and epilepsy (Rutter *et al.*, 1970b). Measures such as immunization and genetic counselling that reduce rates of cerebral disorders may therefore be seen to be preventive of psychiatric as well as neurological conditions.

Because of the high rates of psychiatric disorder in the children they see, it is important that child health professionals should be sensitive to the psychosocial needs of their patients and families (American Academy of Child and Adolescent Psychiatry, 1990). Unfortunately, methodologically sound studies of social work counselling in children with chronic disorders have not been able to demonstrate positive effects on behaviour, though many parents perceive such counselling as helpful (Nolan *et al.*, 1987).

Children of mentally ill parents

The impact on the child of psychiatric disorder in a parent is discussed in Chapter 12. It is clear that parental mental illness is a factor putting a child at high risk of disorder, but that the risk is not related to the type of disorder. More relevant is the associated presence of marital discord, the lack of stability in child care the illness may produce, the exposure of the child to morbid symptomatology and the ability of one or both parents to maintain adequate parenting capacity (Rutter & Quinton,

1984; Quinton et al., 1990). It is not usually possible in an individual child to determine the degree to which a disorder is genetically or environmentally linked to an illness in a parent, but the results of investigations suggest that preventive approaches to this high-risk group may well be effective.

Unfortunately there does not appear to be any evaluated intervention programme for children of parents with psychiatric disorders, although the sections in this chapter reporting evaluated programmes for children whose parents have marital problems and substitute child care are relevant (see below). Nevertheless, the evidence does suggest certain preventive procedures may be helpful; many of these have been considered by Silverman (1989).

A first requirement, sometimes sadly lacking, is that professionals dealing with adults with psychiatric disorders should be aware of the fact that such people often have children who may be adversely affected. Such awareness should, in itself, lead to various simple measures. The well parent should be encouraged to discuss the problems of the ill parent with any children at an age-appropriate level, so that communication is facilitated. Family sessions with a mental health professional present may be helpful in this respect and, of course, such family sessions may illuminate the patient's psychopathology and reveal it to be part of wider dysfunction within the family. The presence of marital discord will suggest the need for counselling, and such counselling should involve discussion of ways in which the impact of such discord on the children might be reduced.

If the parent needs to be hospitalized or the parental capacity of the ill parent, usually the mother, is significantly reduced, mental health professionals will need to work closely with other family members and, if these are unable to cope, with child welfare services, to ensure that child care is maintained at a satisfactory level. The need for continuity of care and, except in unusual circumstances, for continuing contact between parent and child should be borne in mind by both mental health and child welfare agencies. Children of mentally ill parents may have an increased need for developing affectionate relationships with members of the extended family and for out-of-home activities.

Children of parents with disharmonious or broken marriages

Although many children survive the experience of growing up in a family where parents are in chronic conflict, separated or divorced, without developing a psychiatric disorder, the presence of marital disharmony puts a child at high risk for the development of emotional and behaviour problems (see Chapter 12). Factors that predict childhood disturbance in this situation are the sex of the child (boys show more overt disturbance than girls), inability of the parents to cooperate over child-care issues, impaired parenting (especially in terms of lack of consistency) and a critical attitude of one or both parents to the child.

These findings carry implications for possible preventive approaches. Some measures that have already been discussed are relevant. In particular, curriculum material used in secondary schools in preparation for parenthood needs to contain material that is relevant to situations in which marital conflict prejudices child care. Some of the content of antenatal and postnatal discussion groups can similarly be focused on this issue, especially as the advent of a child inevitably brings a need for adjustments in the marital relationship. Unfortunately, emotionally deprived parents most in need of discussion of this nature are those least likely to attend such groups. However there is some possibility that nurse home-visiting programmes for deprived young mothers (Olds et al., 1986b), may achieve their positive effect in child behaviour, at least partly by their effects on women's capacity to relate to their partners.

In most developed countries, agencies exist to assist couples who are having marital difficulties. Such agencies may have the general aim of assisting all aspects of marital relationships or, as in the case of conciliation agencies, they may aim specifically to assist couples who have decided to separate to achieve this end through cooperative discussion rather than in litigious conflict. Although only a small number of programmes of this type — of which the best known is that described by Wallerstein (1990) — are specifically aimed to provide counselling for children involved in marital separation and divorce, most professionals working in such agencies would regard it as part of their task to ensure that children's needs are considered by parents in coming to decisions about the future. Although anecdotally, programmes such as those described by Wallerstein (1990) are helpful in preventing the development of childhood behaviour and emotional disorders, there is little satisfactory evidence from controlled studies that this is indeed the case. However, interestingly, Stolberg and Garrison (1985) found that a cognitive problem-solving programme aimed directly at either separated mothers or their 7–13-year-old children was only effective on the individuals who received the treatment. The children did not improve if only their mothers received treatment, and the converse was also true.

The great majority of parents with disharmonious marriages do not attend such agencies. They are however frequently in touch with health professionals, particularly family doctors, but also social workers and general psychiatrists, presenting with other problems that turn out to arise from their marital difficulties. The family doctor may be consulted about headache, gastrointestinal or other physical symptoms, the social worker about financial problems and the psychiatrist about depression or anxious mood. A variety of health professionals are therefore in touch with parents whose child-rearing capacities may be impaired by marital conflict. One of the responsibilities of these professionals is to bear in mind the needs of children when counselling such parents. The powerful emotions experienced by couples in conflict in relation to each other often obscure their capacities to be sensitive to their children's needs, and such professionals can be helpful in redressing the balance.

Finally, the preventive potential of appropriate legislation relating to separation and divorce needs consideration. Such legislation needs to be drafted to protect children's interests. A review of divorce legislation in different countries is beyond the scope of this chapter, but the UK 1989 Children Act encourages parents engaged in divorce proceedings to make a joint statement of the arrangements they propose for their children. These statements are then considered by the Court to decide whether they are satisfactory, or whether there is a need for one or more specific orders to be made. Such orders may specify the arrangements concerning with whom the child is to live (residence order), and with whom the child is to be allowed social contact (contact order). Professionals asked to provide advice to the Court where there is conflict about these matters will naturally regard the children's interests as paramount. Such legislation and professional advice must be seen as having considerable potential for prevention of childhood psychiatric disorders.

Children exposed to acute stress

Acute stress reactions are discussed in Chapters 21 and 22. From the point of view of preventive approaches, the acute stresses children face can be classified as: (1) life-threatening situations, such as severe illness and natural disasters; (2) major psychosocial stresses such as moving house away from the district, family breakdown, severe illness or death in a close family member; and (3) minor psychosocial stress, e.g. starting or changing schools, school examinations, or the move of a close friend away from the district. Obviously what may be a minor stress for one child may, for a variety of reasons, be a major stress for another. In any event, the experience of an acute stress puts the child at risk for the development of a psychiatric disorder. In this section, attention will be paid to general principles that may govern preventive interventions. Other chapters discuss more specific preventive issues (e.g. in relation to the death of a parent — see Chapter 45, and in relation to posttraumatic stress disorder — see Chapter 22).

In considering preventive approaches in acute stress circumstances, it is useful to consider the coping skills a child may naturally use. These are summarized by Hamburg *et al.* (1982) as: (1) containing distress within tolerable limits; (2) maintaining self-esteem; (3) preserving interpersonal relationships; and (4) meeting the conditions of the new situation. The principles involved in achieving these aims are likely to be the same regardless of the stress. They have been comprehensively discussed in preventive terms by Pynoos and Nader (1990) in relation to children exposed, or at risk of exposure, to natural disasters.

Preventive activity before the stress occurs involves the development of confident preparedness. For example, children at high risk of natural disaster should understand the nature of the event that might occur, and the physical measures they will need to protect themselves. Children about to enter hospital (see above) need to know what to expect in the way of environment, visits, investigations and operations. Children about to start or change schools benefit from a visit to the new school beforehand. Such preparation for anticipated stress has been elaborated to apply to a range of potentially upsetting events with the development of the concept of stress inoculation (Meichenbaum, 1985).

During the stressful situation itself, individual coping strategies are of major importance and have been well-summarized by Hamburg *et al.* (1982). They include the cognitive regulation of increasing awareness of the threat, the handling of multiple, concurrent stresses by processing these sequentially one at a time and the construction of cognitive buffers against disappointment with the development of contingency plans if the desired outcome does not occur. Obviously these strategies will be more suitable for older children, but they are also relevant for the parents, whose reactions will be of major importance in mediating the reactions of younger children.

Eth and Pynoos (1985) summarized poststress preventive goals as the amelioration of traumatic stress and facilitation of grief work, prevention of interference with child development and promotion of competence in dealing with the new situation. Although these principles were formulated in relation to natural disasters, they are also relevant to the child's experience of other acute life stresses. Children changing schools do indeed often experience grief in relation to the previous school they have lost.

The achievement of these goals after the experience of the acute stress is likely to be best achieved through the family. The availability of close family members to support the child and interpret new experiences in a positive way will be vital in this connection. Professionals involved in helping children following acutely stressful situations should therefore ensure that family integrity is maintained and that parents, in particular, are helped to communicate with their children about the experiences they have suffered. When an acute stress has occurred in school or has occurred out of school but with a high proportion of children in a particular school or classroom affected, school-based mental health interventions may be helpful. Ensuring that children are well-informed about what has actually happened and thus suppressing inaccurate rumours, facilitating group discussions and providing other opportunities for children to express their feelings have all been found, on an anecdotal basis, to reduce the development of psychiatric disorder. Providing individual counselling and treatment for children disturbed by acute stress is classed as secondary prevention, and is outside the scope of this chapter, but is discussed in Chapter 22.

Children where parental care has broken down

Children whose biological parents are unable to provide adequate care for them are at particular risk for the development of emotional and behaviour disorders. The provision of adequate substitute care is of particular importance in infancy and early childhood where the pattern may be set for the whole of the child's development. Issues such as the need for a 'care plan' so that young children do not drift from one placement to another, the desirability of very early adoption when it is clear that a child's family is going to find it too difficult to provide continuing care, the superiority of long-term over short-term fostering when, for one reason or another, adoption is not feasible, are discussed in Chapters 15 and 16. Here it is only necessary to point out that effective professional intervention in these circumstances has a strong preventive effect (Schaefer *et al.*, 1981; Steinhauer, 1988). Regrettably, too often the alternative to an unstable family situation is an unstable and inadequate pattern of substitute care. Apart from the social and individual outcome, the economic consequences of a lack of resources for good early substitute care often entail much greater expenditure on institutional care later in the child's life.

CONCLUSION

Increased knowledge deriving from studies carried out over the past two decades has made effective prevention in the field of child psychiatry a real possibility. Numerous preventive activities have indeed been undertaken. Until recently, knowledge has lagged behind innovation in this field, and there has been a lack of information on how to intervene in order to achieve the desired result (Rutter, 1982). There are now signs that the situation is changing, and that preventive activities will soon be able to move forward with a sounder knowledge base.

REFERENCES

Alperstein G. & Arnstein E. (1988) Homeless children — a challenge for pediatricians. *Pediatric Clinics of North America*, **35**, 1413–1425.
American Academy of Child and Adolescent Psychiatry (1990) *Prevention in Child and Adolescent Psychiatry: The Reduction of Risk for Mental Disorders*. American Academy for Child and Adolescent Psychiatry, Washington, DC.
Banks M. & Jackson P. (1982) Unemployment and risk of minor psychiatric disorder in young people: cross-sectional and longitudinal evidence. *Psychological Medicine*, **12**, 786–798.
Barrera M., Rosenbaum P. & Cunningham S. (1986) Early home intervention with low birth-weight infants and their parents. *Child Development*, **51**, 20–33.
Bebbington P., Sturt E., Tennant C. & Hurry J. (1984) Misfortune and resilience: a community study of women. *Psychological Medicine*, **14**, 346–364.
Beckwith L. (1990) Preventive interventions with parents of premature infants. In: Goldston S.E., Yager J., Heinicke C.M. & Pynoos R. (eds) *Preventing Mental Health Disturbances in Childhood*, pp. 41–54. American Psychiatric Press, Washington, DC.
Belsky J. (1985) Experimenting with the family in the newborn period. *Child Development*, **56**, 407–414.
Benton D. & Buts J.-P. (1990) Vitamin/mineral supplementation and intelligence. *Lancet*, **335**, 1158–1160.
Berrueta-Clement J.R., Schweinhart L.J., Barnett W.S., Epstein A.S. & Weikart D.P. (1984) *Changed Lives: The Effects of the Perry Pre-school Program on Youth through Age 19*. High Scope Press, Ypsilanti, MI.
Berrueta-Clement J.R., Schweinhart L.J., Barnett W.S. & Weikart D.P. (1987) The effects of early educational intervention on crime

and delinquency in adolescence and early adulthood. In: Burchard J.D. & Burchard S.N. (eds) *Prevention of Delinquent Behaviour*, pp. 220–238. Sage, London.
Boyle M.H. & Offord D.R. (1990) Primary prevention of conduct disorder. *Journal of the American Academy of Child and Adolescent Psychiatry*, **29**, 227–233.
Brazelton T.B. (1962) A child-oriented approach to toilet-training. *Pediatrics*, **29**, 121–128.
Brown B. (1979) Beyond separation: some new evidence on the impact of brief hospitalization in young children. In: Hall D. & Stacey M. (eds) *Medicine, Illness and Society. Beyond Separation: Further Studies of Children in Hospital*. Routledge & Kegan Paul, London.
Byrne C.M. & Cadman D. (1987) Prevention of the adverse effects of hospitalization in children. *Journal of Preventive Psychiatry*, **3**, 167–190.
Cauce A.M., Comer J.P. & Schwartz D. (1987) Long-term effects of a systems-oriented school prevention program. *American Journal of Orthopsychiatry*, **57**, 127–131.
Clarke R.V.G. (1985) Delinquency, environment, and intervention. *Journal of Child Psychology and Psychiatry*, **26**, 505–523.
Comer J.P. (1985) The Yale-New Haven Primary Prevention Project: a follow-up study. *Journal of the American Academy of Child Psychiatry*, **24**, 154–160.
Cullen K.J. (1976) A 6 year controlled trial of prevention of children's behavior disorders. *Journal of Pediatrics*, **88**, 662–666.
Douglas J.W.B. (1975) Early hospital admission and later disturbances of behaviour and learning. *Developmental Medicine and Child Neurology*, **17**, 456–480.
Drotar D. (1990) Prevention of emotional disorders in children with non-organic failure to thrive. In: Goldston S.E., Yager J., Heinicke C.M. & Pynoos R.S. (eds) *Preventing Mental Health Disturbances in Childhood*, pp. 85–105. American Psychiatric Press, Washington, DC.
Dubowitz H. (1989) Prevention of child maltreatment: what is known. *Pediatrics*, **83**, 570–577.
Durlak J. (1985) Primary prevention of school maladjustment. *Journal of Consulting and Clinical Psychology*, **53**, 623–630.
Eth S.R. & Pynoos R.S. (1985) *Post-traumatic Stress Disorder in Children*. American Psychiatric Association, Washington, DC.
Farrington D.P., Gallagher B., Morley L., Ledger R.J. & West D.J. (1986) Unemployment, school leaving and crime. *British Journal of Criminology*, **26**, 335–356.
Felner R.D. & Adan A.A. (1988) The school transitional environmental project: an ecological intervention and evaluation. In: Price R.H., Cowen E.L., Lorion R.P. *et al.* (eds) *Fourteen Ounces of Prevention*, pp. 111–122. American Psychological Association, Washington, DC.
Fergusson B.F. (1979) Preparing young children for hospitalization: a comparison of two methods. *Pediatrics*, **64**, 656–664.
Fox S.J., Barrnett J., Davies M. & Bird H.R. (1990) Psychopathology and developmental delay in homeless children. *Journal of the American Academy of Child and Adolescent Psychiatry*, **29**, 732–735.
Garland A., Shaffer D. & Whittle B. (1989) A national survey of school based, adolescent suicide prevention programs. *Journal of the American Academy of Child and Adolescent Psychiatry*, **28**, 931–934.
Goldston S.C., Yager J., Heinicke C.M. & Pynoos R.S. (1990) (eds) *Preventing Mental Health Disturbances in Childhood*. American Psychiatric Press, Washington, DC.
Graham P. (1979) Epidemiological approaches to child mental health in developing countries. In: Purcell E.F. (ed) *Psychopathology of Youth: A Cross-Cultural Perspective*, pp. 28–45. Josiah Macy Junior Foundation, New York.
Graham P. (1991) *Child Psychiatry: A Developmental Approach*, 2nd edn. Oxford University Press, Oxford.

Grantham-McGregor S., Schofield W. & Powell C. (1987) Development of severely malnourished children who received psychosocial stimulation: a 6 year follow-up. *Pediatrics*, **79**, 247–254.

Gutelius M.F., Kirsch A.D., MacDonald S., Brooks M.R. & McErlean T. (1977) Controlled study of child health supervision: behavioral results. *Pediatrics*, **60**, 294–304.

Hagberg B., Hagberg G., Lewerth A. & Linberg U. (1981) Mild mental retardation in Swedish schoolchildren. II. Etiologies and pathogenetic aspects. *Acta Paediatrica Scandinavica*, **70**, 445–452.

Hamburg D.A., Elliott G.R. & Parron D.L. (1982) (eds) *Health and Behavior*, pp. 63–90. National Academy Press, Washington, DC.

Hawkins J.D., von Cleve E. & Catalano R.F. (1991) Reducing early childhood aggression: results of a primary prevention program. *Journal of the American Academy of Child and Adolescent Psychiatry*, **30**, 208–217.

Henderson A.S. (1988) *An Introduction to Social Psychiatry*, p. 155. Oxford Medical Publications, Oxford.

Hewison J. (1988) The long-term effectiveness of parent involvement in reading: a follow-up to the Haringey Reading Project. *British Journal of Educational Psychology*, **58**, 184–190.

Horacek H.J., Ramey C.T., Campbell F.A., Hoffmanuk K.P. & Fletcher R.H. (1987) Predicting school failure and assessing early intervention with high-risk children. *Journal of the American Academy of Child and Adolescent Psychiatry*, **26**, 758–763.

Infant Health and Development Program (1990) Enhancing the outcomes of low birth-weight, premature infants: a multisite randomized trial. *Journal of the American Medical Association*, **263**, 3035–3042.

Jenkins J.M. & Smith M.A. (1990) Factors protecting children in disharmonious homes. *Journal of the American Academy of Child and Adolescent Psychiatry*, **29**, 60–69.

Johnson D.L. & Walker T. (1987) The primary prevention of behavior problems in Mexican-American children. *American Journal of Community Psychology*, **15**, 375–385.

Jones A. (1984) *Counselling Adolescents: School and After*, 2nd edn. Kogan Page, London.

Jones M.B. & Offord D.R. (1989) Reduction of antisocial behaviour in poor children by non-school skill development. *Journal of Child Psychology and Psychiatry*, **30**, 737–750.

Klaus M. & Kennell J. (1976) *Maternal–infant bonding. The Impact of Early Separation or Loss on Family Development*. CV Mosby, St Louis, MO.

Klein N.C., Alexander J.F. & Parsons B.V. (1977) Impact of family systems intervention on recidivism and sibling delinquency: a model of primary prevention and program evaluation. *Journal of Consulting and Clinical Psychology*, **45**, 469–474.

Lally J.R., Mangione P.L. & Honig A.S. (1988) The Syracuse University Family Development Research Program: long-range impact as an early intervention with low-income children and their family. In: Powell D.R. (ed) *Parent Education as Early Childhood Intervention: Emerging Directions in Theory, Research and Practice*, pp. 79–104. Annual Advances in Applied Developmental Psychology, vol. 3. Ablex, Norwood, NJ.

Lazar I. & Darlington R. (1982) Lasting effects of early education: a report for the Consortium for Longitudinal Studies. *Monographs of Society for Research in Child Development*, **47**, 1–151.

Leventhal J.M. (1988) Can child maltreatment be predicted during the peri-natal period? Evidence from longitudinal cohort studies. *Journal of Reproductive Infant Psychology*, **6**, 139–161.

Marlow N., Roberts B.L. & Cooke R.W.I. (1989) Motor skills in extremely low birthweight children at the age of 6 years. *Archives of Disease in Childhood*, **64**, 839–847.

Mathisen B., Skuse D., Wolke D. & Reilly S. (1989) Oral–motor dysfunction and failure to thrive in inner city infants. *Developmental Medicine and Child Neurology*, **31**, 293–302.

Maughan B. (1988) School experiences as risk/protective factors. In: Rutter M. (ed) *Studies of Psychosocial Risk*, pp. 200–220. Cambridge University Press, Cambridge.

Meichenbaum D. (1985) *Stress Inoculation Training*. Pergamon Press, New York.

Melamed B.G. & Siegel L.J. (1975) Reduction of anxiety in children facing hospitalization and surgery by use of filmed modelling. *Journal of Consulting and Clinical Psychology*, **43**, 511–521.

Minde K., Whitelaw A., Brown J. & Fitzhardinge P. (1983) Effect of neonatal complications in premature infants on early parent–infant interventions. *Developmental Medicine and Child Neurology*, **25**, 763–777.

Morgan R.L.G. (1990) Nutrition and brain development. In: Pueschel S.M. & Mulick J.A. (eds) *Prevention of Developmental Disabilities*, pp. 261–286. Paul H. Brookes, Baltimore, MD.

Newton R.W. (1988) Psychosocial aspects of pregnancy: the scope for intervention. *Journal of Reproductive and Infant Psychology*, **6**, 23–39.

Nolan T., Vagulis I. & Pless I.B. (1987) Controlled trial of social work in childhood chronic illness. *Lancet*, **2**, 411–415.

Offord D.R. (1987) Prevention of behavioural and emotional disorders in children. *Journal of Child Psychology and Psychiatry*, **28**, 9–20.

Olds D., Henderson C.R., Tatelbaum R. & Chamberlin R. (1986a) Improving the delivery of pre-natal care and outcomes of pregnancy: a randomized trial of nurse home visitation. *Pediatrics*, **77**, 16–28.

Olds D.L., Henderson C.R., Chamberlin R. & Tatelbaum R. (1986b) Preventing child abuse and neglect: a randomised trial of nurse home visitation. *Pediatrics*, **78**, 65–78.

Olweus D. (1989) Bully/victim problems among schoolchildren: basic facts and effects of a school based intervention program. In: Rubin K. & Pepler D. (eds) *The Development and Treatment of Childhood Aggression*. Erlbaum, Hillsdale, NJ.

Osofsky J.D., Culp A.M. & Ware L.M. (1988) Intervention challenges with adolescent mothers and their infants. *Psychiatry*, **51**, 236–241.

Phillips D., McCartney K. & Scarr S. (1987) Child-care quality and children's social development. *Developmental Psychology*, **23**, 537–543.

Pueschel S.M. & Mulick J.A. (1990) *Prevention of Developmental Disabilities*. Paul H. Brooker, Baltimore, MD.

Pynoos R.S. & Nader K. (1990) Mental health disturbance in children exposed to disaster; preventive interventive strategies. In: Goldston S.E., Yager J., Heinicke C.M. & Pynoos R.S. (eds) *Preventing Mental Health Disturbances in Childhood*, pp. 211–234. American Psychiatric Press, Washington, DC.

Quinton D. (1988) Urbanism and child mental health. *Journal of Child Psychology and Psychiatry*, **29**, 11–20.

Quinton D. & Rutter M. (1976) Early hospital admission and later disturbances of behaviour: an attempted replication of Douglas' findings. *Developmental Medicine and Child Neurology*, **18**, 447–459.

Quinton D., Rutter M. & Gulliver L. (1990) Continuities in psychiatric disorders from childhood to adulthood in the children of psychiatric patients. In: Robins L. & Rutter M. (eds) *Straight and Devious Pathways from Childhood to Adulthood*, pp. 259–278. Cambridge University Press, Cambridge.

Rae-Grant N. (1991) Primary prevention. In: Lewis M. (ed) *Child and Adolescent Psychiatry: A Comprehensive Textbook*, pp. 918–929. Williams & Wilkins, Baltimore, MD.

Rauh V.A., Achenbach T.M., Nurcombe B., Howell C.T. & Teti D.M. (1988) Minimizing adverse effects of low birthweight: 4 year results of an early intervention program. *Child Development*, **59**, 544–553.

Richardson S.A. (1984) Consequences of malnutrition for intellectual development. In: Dobbing J. (ed) *Scientific Studies in Mental Retardation*, pp. 233–250. Macmillan Press, London.

Richman N. (1974) The effects of housing on pre-school children and their mothers. *Developmental Medicine and Child Neurology*, **16**, 53–58.

Runciman W.G. (1972) *Relative Deprivation and Social Justice*. Penguin, Harmondsworth.

Rutter M. (1982) Prevention of children's psychosocial disorders: myth and substance. *Pediatrics*, **70**, 883–894.

Rutter M. (1987) Psychosocial resilience and protective mechanisms. *American Journal of Orthopsychiatry*, **57**, 316–331.

Rutter M. (1988) Longitudinal data in the study of causal processes: some uses and some pitfalls. In: Rutter M. (ed) *Studies of Psychosocial Risk: The Power of Longitudinal Data*, pp. 1–28. Cambridge University Press, Cambridge.

Rutter M. (1990) Psychosocial resilience and protective factors. In: Rolf J., Masten A.S., Cicchetti D., Neuchterlein K.H. & Weintraub S. (eds) *Risk and Protective Factors in the Development of Psychopathology*, pp. 181–214. Cambridge University Press, Cambridge.

Rutter M. & Giller H. (1983) *Juvenile Delinquency: Trends and Perspectives*, pp. 323–336. Penguin Books, Harmondsworth.

Rutter M. & Madge N. (1976) *Cycles of Disadvantage*, pp. 110–117. Heinemann, London.

Rutter M. & Quinton D. (1984) Parental psychiatric disorder: effects on children. *Psychological Medicine*, **14**, 853–880.

Rutter M., Tizard J. & Whitmore K. (1970a) *Education, Health and Behaviour*. Longmans, London.

Rutter M., Graham P. & Yule W. (1970b) *A Neuropsychiatric Study in Childhood*. Clinics in Developmental Medicine 35/36. Heinemann Medical Books, London.

Rutter M., Graham P., Chadwick O. & Yule W. (1976) Adolescent turmoil: fact or fiction. *Journal of Child Psychology and Psychiatry*, **17**, 35–56.

Rutter M., Maughan B., Mortimore P. & Ouston J. (1979) *Fifteen Thousand Hours*. Open Books, London.

Schaefer M.H., Kliman G., Friedman M.J. & Pasquariella M.A. (1981) Children in foster care: a preventive service and research program for a high risk population. *Journal of Preventive Psychiatry*, **1**, 47–56.

Schoenthaler S.J., Amos S.P., Eysenck H.J., Peritze E. & Yudkin J. (1991) Controlled trial of vitamin-mineral supplementation: effects on intelligence and performance. *Personality and Individual Differences*, **12**, 351–362.

Schwartz H.B., Albino J.E. & Tedesco L.A. (1983) Effects of psychological preparation on children hospitalized for dental operations. *Journal of Pediatrics*, **102**, 634–638.

Seitz V., Rosenbaum L.K. & Apfel N.H. (1985) Effects of family support intervention: a 10 year follow-up. *Child Development*, **56**, 376–391.

Shaffer D., Garland A., Gould M., Fisher P. & Trautman P. (1988) Preventing teenage suicide: a critical review. *Journal of the American Academy of Child and Adolescent Psychiatry*, **27**, 675–687.

Shaffer D., Garland A., Fisher P., Bacon K. & Vieland V. (1990) Suicide Crisis Centres: a critical reappraisal with special reference to the prevention of youth suicide. In: Goldston S.E., Yager J., Heinicke C.M. & Pynoos R. (eds) *Preventing Mental Health Disturbances in Childhood*, pp. 135–165. American Psychiatric Press, Washington, DC.

Shannon F.T., Fergusson D.M. & Dimond M.E. (1984) Early hospital admissions and subsequent behaviour in 6 year olds. *Archives of Diseases in Childhood*, **59**, 815–819.

Silver A. & Hagin R. (1989) Prevention of learning disorders. In: *Prevention of Mental Disorders, Alcohol and Other Drug Use in Children and Adolescents*. US Department of Health and Human Services OSAP Prevention Monographs 2. US Department of Health and Human Services, Rockville, MD.

Silverman M.M. (1989) Children of psychiatrically ill parents: a preventive perspective. *Hospital and Community Psychiatry*, **40**, 1257–1265.

Skuse D. (1989) Psychosocial adversity and impaired growth: in search of causal mechanisms. In: Wilkinson G. (ed) *The Scope of Epidemiological Psychiatry: Essays in Honour of Michael Shepherd*, pp. 240–263. Routledge, London.

Sluckin W., Herbert M. & Sluckin A. (1983) *Maternal Bonding*. Blackwells, London.

Smith R. (1985) 'What's the point. I'm no use to anybody.' The psychological consequences of unemployment. *British Medical Journal*, **291**, 1338–1341.

Steinhauer P.D. (1988) The preventive utilization of foster care. *Canadian Journal of Psychiatry*, **33**, 459–467.

Stevenson J. & Ellis C. (1975) Which 3 year olds attend pre-school facilities? *Child: Care, Health and Development*, **1**, 397–411.

Stolberg A.L. & Garrison K.M. (1985) Evaluating a primary prevention programme for children of divorce. *American Journal of Community Psychology*, **13**, 111–124.

US Department of Health and Human Services (1989) *Prevention of Mental Disorders, Alcohol and Drug Use in Children and Adolescents*. OSAP Prevention Monograph 2. Office for Substance Abuse and Prevention, Rockville, MD.

Wallerstein J.S. (1990) Preventive interventions with divorcing families: a reconceptualization. In: Goldston S.E., Yager J., Heinicke C.M. & Pynoos R.S. (eds) *Preventing Mental Health Disturbances in Childhood*, pp. 167–185. American Psychiatric Press, Washington, DC.

Wolfer J.A. & Visintainer M.A. (1979) Pre-hospital psychological preparation for tonsillectomy patients: effects on children's and parents' adjustment. *Pediatrics*, **64**, 646–655.

Wolke D. (1987) Environmental neonatology. *Archives of Disease in Childhood*, **62**, 987–988.

Chapter 48
Training in Interpersonal Cognitive Problem-Solving

David S. Pellegrini

Acquiring the requisite skills for interacting successfully with peers constitutes one of the most important accomplishments of childhood. In addition to providing a source of social support and pleasure (Monck, 1991), peers fulfil a host of other developmental functions. For example, as agents of socialization they communicate and reinforce standards of behaviour (Hartup, 1980). In addition, peers provide instruction in a variety of social, cognitive, linguistic and motor skills (Parker & Asher, 1987). Their role in shaping sexual and aggressive behaviour may be especially critical (Suomi, 1980).

Poor peer relations are characteristic of children demonstrating a wide variety of behavioural and emotional difficulties. Indeed, relational problems are often the primary reason why children are referred for therapy. Given the critical role that peers appear to play in development, it is not surprising that peer relationship difficulties in childhood have been linked with maladjustment later in life, as well. For example, in a well-known study Cowen *et al.* (1973) found that negative peer evaluations in third grade were superior to a variety of other adjustment indices in predicting mental health problems 11 years later. Roff *et al.* (1972) found that young children who were disliked by their peers were more likely to engage in juvenile delinquency. Correlational findings of this kind cannot conclusively establish that poor peer relations *cause* current or later maladjustment. However, while the predictive power of social withdrawal has yet to be examined adequately, the strength and consistency of findings across a wide range of studies provide strong support for considering peer rejection and social aggression to be clear indices of risk for difficulties later in life, most notably school failure, juvenile delinquency and adult criminality (see Parker & Asher, 1987, for a review). Moreover, they highlight the importance of treating peer relationship difficulties directly.

A number of different strategies have been devised for remedying peer relationship difficulties. Most assume that these difficulties arise from critical response deficits in the individual's repertoire (McFall, 1976). A shy and inhibited child, for example, might lack conversational, assertive or other social skills essential for effective social interaction. This is not to say that response excesses (e.g. social anxiety, aggression) are unimportant. Rather, it is frequently assumed that as the child acquires essential social skills through training, whatever excesses exist will automatically disappear.

More recently, however, it has become apparent that excessive negative behaviours require direct remedial efforts in conjunction with efforts to remediate response deficits (Bierman *et al.*, 1987).

Three social skill training (SST) approaches have been adopted most frequently with children experiencing peer relationship difficulties (Asher, 1978; Gresham, 1985). Various *operant techniques* (e.g. response–cost contingencies, selective attention, praise) have been employed to foster prosocial behaviours (participation, cooperation, communication) while discouraging undesirable behaviours (aggression, withdrawal). In contrast, *modelling* strategies teach appropriate social behaviours by requiring children to observe adult or child models (sometimes live, often filmed) demonstrating competent performance in particular social situations. *Coaching* strategies, on the other hand, describe and teach general principles of competent social performance, although behavioural examples or models are also usually provided. Typically, elements of all three SST approaches are intermingled in a comprehensive training effort. Modelling and coaching programmes also generally provide participating children with opportunities to rehearse targeted skills in the context of supervised peer interaction (Ladd & Mize, 1983).

Both operant and modelling approaches to SST teach inductively; that is, it is up to the observer to infer principles of effective social interaction from a number of reinforced or depicted (modelled) behaviours (Marlatt, 1972). Coaching strategies teach inductively; the learner is expected to use the general principles provided to generate appropriate social behaviours in a variety of future situations. On the other hand, both modelling and coaching approaches have been described as cognitive-behavioural in orientation, since they rely less prominently upon environmental contingencies and more prominently on cognitive changes for the maintenance of newly acquired social behaviours outside the therapeutic setting (Kendall & Braswell, 1982).

Wasserman (1983) suggested that the demand characteristics of cognitive-behavioural techniques may at times exceed the information-processing capabilities of children at a particular age or developmental level. Such basic incongruities may account for the occasional failure of such techniques to produce desired changes in social behaviour or the failure of such changes to generalize across situations and time. In this context it is worth noting, therefore, that operant tech-niques — which have been successfully employed with a wide variety of clinical populations — have proven to be effective with mentally retarded, autistic and otherwise seriously disabled youngsters (Gresham, 1981). Such techniques may be particularly useful with children whose information-processing capabilities are limited. On the other hand, while operant techniques offer powerful tools for shaping social behaviour, such training efforts typically fail to demonstrate generalization and maintenance of effects when the applied contingencies are withdrawn (Gresham, 1981, 1985).

Early efforts to apply operant techniques to remedy social skill deficits tended to focus on very discrete responses, such as the amount and timing of eye contact with peers. Results were somewhat disappointing in that newly acquired behav-iours often did not lead to greater social acceptance. Sub-sequent training efforts focused on broader response classes, with more positive results (Oden & Asher, 1977). Modelling and coaching approaches, in particular, seem promising for teaching complex social behaviours.

One troublesome aspect of modelling approaches, however, derives from the influence of model—observer similarity on training results. Gresham (1985) has suggested that targeted children must perceive close similarity between themselves and the model in order to attend to, retain and/or perform modelled behaviours. Such specificity of effects diminishes the applicability of modelling approaches with heterogeneous groups.

Nevertheless, a wide variety of studies have suggested that various combinations of treatment procedures (modelling, coaching, praise, response—cost contingencies, etc.) are effec-tive in increasing adaptive social behaviour and decreas-ing negative social behaviour in children (Gresham, 1985). Although specific consequences (such as time out) for pro-hibited negative behaviours, like hitting, have frequently not been included in cognitively oriented SST programmes (Ladd, 1981; Coie & Krehbiel, 1984), the inclusion of operant tech-niques appears to facilitate further skill training. Unfor-tunately, however, few direct comparisons of treatment approaches have been conducted to date (see Gresham & Nagle, 1980, for an exception). Thus, it is not possible at this point to identify and evaluate the specific SST components that are responsible for behaviour change.

Despite the promise and utility of traditional SST approaches, however, positive training effects frequently fail to generalize across behaviours, settings and time (Sarason, 1981; Gresham, 1985). Moreover, while it is often assumed that cognitive-behavioural procedures *per se* should produce greater general-ization effects than strictly behavioural approaches (Kendall & Finch, 1979; Kendall & Braswell, 1982), there is little evidence to support the notion that modelling or coaching interventions lead to greater generalization than operant strategies. Finally, the failure of these SST programmes to increase peer accept-ance, despite observed increases in skilful behaviour and decreases in negative behaviour, is a recurrent problem (Bierman & Furman, 1984; Bierman *et al.*, 1987).

Recently a great deal of enthusiasm has been generated for

a fourth SST approach, also cognitive-behavioural in orien-tation, that focuses on rectifying interpersonal cognitive problem-solving (ICPS) deficits in maladjusted children. Like coaching, ICPS training assumes that cognitions mediate social behaviour. However, whereas coaching strategies have gener-ally focused on cognitive content or what a child knows about effective social interaction, ICPS programmes place explicit theoretical emphasis on training covert thinking *processes* (identifying problems, generating alternative solutions, etc.). The promise of such a programme is that by training at the level of processes that theoretically mediate competence across a broad range of situations, generalization will be built in as an integral part of treatment (Urbain & Kendall, 1980). Through ICPS training it may also be possible to teach generally well-functioning children a set of coping skills that they could then apply independently to deal with diverse problem situations arising in everyday life (Meichenbaum *et al.*, 1981).

This chapter reviews current knowledge regarding the nature and development of interpersonal problem-solving ability. Training programmes designed to foster the *cognitive* components of problem-solving in children will be described, and evidence regarding the efficacy of such programmes will be evaluated.

THE NATURE AND DEVELOPMENT OF INTERPERSONAL PROBLEM-SOLVING

Research into human problem-solving has a long and exten-sive history in psychology, going back at least as far as Dewey's landmark treatise in 1933 (see reviews by Duncan, 1959; Davis, 1966; Gagne, 1970). Early on, Jahoda (1958) emphasized the theoretical link between effective inter-personal problem-solving and both social and emotional adjustment. She noted that the individual who can recognize and admit a problem, reflect on possible solutions and take action was less likely to suffer frustration due to chronically unresolved interpersonal needs.

Despite the persuasiveness of Jahoda's reasoning, however, empirical investigation has until recently focused almost exclusively on problem-solving applied to nonsocial tasks, such as puzzles, mazes and anagrams. Consequently, we know relatively little about the nature of interpersonal problem-solving skills and the process by which they are applied in social interaction. What little theory is available for application to treatment efforts has been adopted from exper-imental work with nonsocial stimuli. It is very unlikely, however, that models of nonsocial problem-solving are completely applicable to the social world.

The inappropriateness of this theoretical transposition can be attributed largely to fundamental differences in the nature of social and nonsocial objects. Piaget (1966) argued that physical objects become known to children in two com-plementary ways. Through figurative knowing children come to recognize an object's configuration or perceptual features. Through operative knowing children understand how the object came to be. Following Piaget, Youniss (1975) suggested that the behaviours exhibited by people are analogous to the physical features of nonsocial objects, so that children acquire figurative knowledge of another person just as they do of any object. Similarly, interpersonal interaction and the process of mentally constructing the nature of interpersonal relationships provide the basis for operative knowledge of persons akin to the operative knowledge of objects.

However, whereas physical objects present fairly regular and relatively accessible stimulus features for abstraction, people exhibit surface features that reflect multiple underlying thoughts and feelings. These thoughts and feelings interact and change in complicated and frequently subtle ways. Complex inferences are required to understand such covert processes (Damon, 1977). Moreover, children come to understand other people largely through coming to understand themselves (Selman & Byrne, 1974). Self-reflection does not pertain to the understanding of physical objects, and thereby provides a unique source of operative knowledge with respect to the social world.

Consider also the nature of the problems that have provided most of the data for model-building efforts. In the broadest sense, any situation for which no effective response alternative is immediately evident can be considered a problem. Researchers concerned with nonsocial problem-solving have focused almost exclusively on uncommon situations or situations never before encountered by most individuals (such as how to build four equal and equilateral triangles with six matchsticks). Because of this unfamiliarity, one's traditional behaviours or previously learned paradigms are not applicable and may even be an impediment to the discovery of an effective solution. Problem-solving is instead dependent upon uncommon or creative responses that were previously very low in one's response hierarchy (Duncan, 1959). As a result, nonsocial problem-solving has come to be characterized generally as the sudden achievement of insight regarding the 'one correct solution' to the problem at hand.

In the interpersonal problem-solving literature there has also been a concern with situations — in this case, social situations — in which traditional or initial responses are not adaptive. However, these researchers and the training programmes that they have developed have focused almost exclusively on common-place situations that arise repeatedly in everyday life (for example, what to do when another child refuses to share a toy). This focus seems appropriate, since most interpersonal situations probably are problematic not because they are unfamiliar, but because they are shaped by multiple, conflicting (or at least noncomplementary) goals both within and across interactants. In such situations there are typically a number of workable solutions, with each alternative involving different costs and benefits. The paramount importance of interpersonal communication, considering another's feelings and point of view, and compromise are clearly unique to the interpersonal problem-solving process. Consequently, successful problem-solving in the social arena is perhaps better described as reaching resolution and compromise than as discovering a solution.

Moreover, unlike most nonsocial problems, social situations are generally transactional in nature. A behavioural response from one individual tends to provoke an overt or covert response from the other individual(s) involved, which may provoke yet another response from the first respondent, and so on (see Dodge, 1986, for a discussion of how such negative behavioural cycles may operate among aggressive children and their peers). Thus, a problematic interpersonal situation is not static; its conditions are continually changing as it evolves towards resolution. Successful interpersonal problem-solving activity, then, is likely to be characterized by give-and-take and by the flexible application of generally common-place behavioural responses. Affect management and impulse control probably play more prominent roles in social than in nonsocial problem-solving, as well (Dodge, 1991).

What, then, can be said about the nature of the interpersonal problem-solving process? Firstly, it is clear that the process is multifaceted, with both cognitive and enactive (i.e. behavioural) components. Considered from such a broad perspective, interpersonal problem-solving reflects or subsumes many different dimensions or components already attributed to global constructs like social competence and social cognition. However, the interpersonal problem-solving domain is usefully distinguished both by its problem focus and its greater concern with underlying processes than with cognitive content or behavioural skills.

Secondly, these components appear to operate relatively independently, in that social thought and social action are not always closely related (Shantz, 1983; Rubin & Krasnor, 1986). This phenomenon is clearly evident among extremely withdrawn children, whose social deficits appear to be related to an inability to translate their otherwise adequate cognitive repertoire of problem-solving strategies into effective behavioural exchanges (Rubin & Rose-Krasnor, 1992), perhaps because affective arousal impedes their performance. Behavioural problem-solving competence commonly lags behind cognitive problem-solving competence among children who have difficulty inhibiting responses, as well.

Thirdly, it is clear that effective problem-solving in the social arena is typically a multistep or multistage process. Among the first to recognize this aspect of problem-solving, Dewey's (1933) model distinguished among the following five stages: (1) sensing a difficulty; (2) locating or defining the difficulty; (3) suggesting possible solutions; (4) considering consequences; and (5) accepting a solution. Similar stages have been proposed by Wallas (1926), Johnson (1955) and Jahoda (1958), among others. Merrifield *et al.* (1962) were among the first to recognize that unsuccessful problem-solving may return the individual to a previous point in the process. They added a reapplication stage to their model. D'Zurilla and Goldfried (1971) subsequently appended a final stage of outcome verification, which provides a firmer basis for any reapplication that might occur. Recent attempts to delineate the problem-solving process have retained this recyclical quality (Rubin & Rose-Krasnor, 1992).

While commonalities among such theoretical models are striking, there are some notable differences as well. These theoretical differences are reflected in divergent approaches to problem-solving training. For example, some theorists seek to identify the sequence of stages in the problem-solving process and the discrete problem-solving activities (e.g. the generation of alternatives, decision-making) that occur at each stage (D'Zurilla & Goldfried, 1971). However, Newell and Simon (1972), among others, have raised serious objections to all such stage models. For example, steps may overlap in time or be unstable in the sequence in which they occur. Moreover, not every problem-solving thought or action can be unequivocally delegated to a single step or stage. Even the process of successful problem-solving may be characterized by multiple embedded interruptions and detours, and vague, difficult-to-model ideas (Flavell, 1976). This complex recycling and the simultaneous occurrence of most real-life problem-solving events renders the problem-solving process less accessible to training than might be initially apparent. Consequently, a number of researchers (Osborn, 1963; Spivack *et al.*, 1976) have focused on identifying and training the generic skills that cut across the problem-solving process.

Although research pertaining to the emergence and growth of interpersonal problem-solving skills is still in its infancy, it is becoming increasingly clear that each and every component of the problem-solving process undergoes important developmental change (Rubin & Rose-Krasnor, 1992). However, relatively few researchers have taken such changes fully into account when designing (or evaluating) ICPS training programmes (Kendall, 1984). Developmental change is evident, first and foremost, with respect to the interpersonal goals that define and drive children's problem-solving efforts. For example, only with the growth of self-awareness that occurs around age 2 do social exchanges begin to reflect concern with self-presentation (Kagan, 1989). The enhancement of one's social status relative to peers becomes a common social goal when social comparison begins to determine self-esteem in middle childhood (Ruble *et al.*, 1980). Finally, prosocial goals are more likely to shape interpersonal exchanges as children develop the ability to understand the perspectives of others (Selman & Schultz, 1990).

Similar changes tied to general cognitive development are evident with respect to processing of the social environment. With the emergence of operational thinking skills that occurs around age 7 (Piaget, 1966), children are newly able to go beyond the surface features of a social situation. Their capacity to decentre (consider more than one aspect of a given person or situation) and to evaluate psychological (not just physical) aspects of their peers results in more complex and useful encoding of information relevant to problem-solving. The growing sophistication of such information-processing enhances children's capacity to understand the nature of the problems confronting them (problem identification), as well as their capacity to evaluate how well their selected strategies are working with respect to achieving their goals (outcome verification).

A final illustration of developmental change pertains to the generation of alternative problem-solving strategies and the selection and coordination of strategies into a coherent problem-solving plan. Whereas the number of strategies that children can generate appears to level off by the time of school entry (Rubin & Krasnor, 1983; Guerra & Slaby, 1989), considerable evolution continues to occur in the types of strategies that children generate. With increasing age, children begin to show a preference for verbal strategies over physical ones. In addition, problem-solving strategies come to reflect increasing cognitive complexity and children's growing ability to understand and consider their peers' needs, thoughts and feelings (Rubin & Rose-Krasnor, 1992).

From the preceding discussion it is clear that changes in interpersonal problem-solving follow developmental changes in cognitive functioning more generally (Flavell, 1985). Moreover, the quality or success of interpersonal problem-solving depends upon the cognitive processes available to the individual at any point in time. However, developmental (and non-developmental) influences beyond cognitive structures also affect cognitive processing and, therefore, interpersonal problem-solving.

For example, Gal'perin (1969) described the developmental process through which cognitive processing becomes automatic: from initial familiarization with a task, through its material representation, leading to performance acts related to external speech, and culminating in the completion of the task guided by internal speech alone (see Kendall, 1984, for a discussion of the therapeutic implications of this theoretical model). Developmental changes in affect regulation constitute yet another probable source of influence on the emergence and refinement of problem-solving (Clark & Isen, 1981; Holmbeck & Kendall, 1991; Dodge, 1991).

Among the host of other factors that are likely to play a role in the emergence of individual differences in interpersonal problem-solving skills, socialization experiences appear to be particularly important. For example, Shure and Spivack (1978) found that the capacity to generate multiple alternative solutions to interpersonal dilemmas was greatest for girls whose mothers employed inductive techniques (calling attention to the consequences of alternative solutions) for handling conflict situations. Similarly, Jones *et al.* (1980) reported that authoritarian, restrictive mothers were most likely to have children who preferred evasive strategies for resolving interpersonal dilemmas (see also Rubin *et al.*, 1989). The quality of the parent–child relationship may, indirectly, also shape interpersonal problem-solving (Rubin & Rose-Krasnor, 1992). For example, Goldberg *et al.* (1989) reported that preschoolers who were insecurely attached as infants were less likely to demonstrate flexibility in resolving interpersonal problems and emphasized aggressive strategies for solving problems.

Peer socialization experiences must also be considered. For example, the firmly established preference for agonistic strategies demonstrated by aggressive children (Dodge, 1986) undoubtedly stems, in part, from the fact that such strategies, while socially unacceptable, are frequently successful in attaining short-term goals. That is, the experience of aggressive children tends to reinforce and maintain the deficiencies in their interpersonal problem-solving repertoire (Rubin & Rose-Krasnor, 1992).

ICPS TRAINING METHODS

Problem solvers draw on, and appear to be limited by, their repertoire of social-cognitive and social-behavioural competencies (e.g. role-taking and assertiveness skills), as well as by their store of social knowledge (familiarity with social rules and conventions) in generating, evaluating and applying potential solutions to social dilemmas that confront them (Spivack *et al.*, 1976; Marsh *et al.*, 1980). Consequently, efforts to enhance interpersonal problem-solving often incorporate training in such related social competencies as part of a broad-based remedial effort.

Perhaps the most systematic, comprehensive and influential approach to problem-solving training has been developed by Myrna Shure, George Spivack and their colleagues at Hahnemann University in Philadelphia. The Hahnemann group concentrates on developing three *cognitive* skills that they consider to be central to effective problem-solving:

1 *Alternative thinking*: the ability to generate multiple alternative solutions to an interpersonal problem situation.

2 *Consequential thinking*: the ability to foresee the immediate as well as the long-range consequences of a particular alternative, and to use this information in the decision-making process.

3 *Means—ends thinking*: the ability to elaborate or plan a series of specific actions to attain a given goal, to recognize and devise ways around potential obstacles, and to use a realistic time framework in constructing a means to the goal.

While a wide variety of ICPS skills have been described by various other investigators (Feldhusen *et al.*, 1972), these three have consistently differentiated youngsters who display varying degrees of behavioural maladaptation from those who do not, although means—ends thinking appears to be a higher-order skill that does not emerge until sometime in middle childhood (Spivack *et al.*, 1976).

To foster ICPS skills and a problem-solving orientation to social interaction, Shure and Spivack (1971) developed a sequential series of lessons incorporating games, discussion and group interaction techniques. Originally devised for use by teachers with their preschool classes, the programme content was subsequently adapted for kindergarten (Shure & Spivack, 1974) and elementary schoolchildren (Shure, 1982), as well as for more flexible application by parents with a single preschool child at home (Shure & Spivack, 1978). Quite recently, all of the original Hahnemann programmes were completely revised for use in ongoing research and training efforts (M.B. Shure, personal communication).

Training scripts designed for use with preschoolers begin with simple word concepts that will form the foundation for subsequent problem-solving thought and instruction. For example, the words 'or' and 'different' are taught to help children think later on about alternative ways to solve a problem ('I can hit him *or* I can tell him that I'm mad . . .

hitting is *different* from telling'). In addition to building linguistic competence, the Hahnemann programme fosters a variety of other concepts and skills deemed to be prerequisites for effective problem-solving as follows:

1 *Emotional awareness.* Sensitivity to the feelings and preferences of oneself and others undoubtedly increases the likelihood that one's problem-solving efforts will be successful. Beginning with generally familiar emotional concepts (happy, sad, angry) and building to more complex ones (disappointed, frustrated, relieved), children are taught that the same person can feel different ways at different times ('I can ask her later when she's feeling better'), and that not everyone feels the same way about the same things ('Bobby likes it when I act silly; Jim doesn't'). Games focus upon the reasons why people feel and act as they do, and on ways to influence how another person feels and acts in an interpersonal situation.

2 *Information-gathering.* To help children develop a sensitivity to cues regarding how others feel, exercises are included for building information-gathering skills. In these games, children use clues to guess of whom the leader is and is not thinking; listen to messages whispered quickly; and respond to incongruous conversations (e.g. A says: 'My knee is bleeding' and B responds: 'Tomorrow is my brother's birthday'). Discussions focus on the consequences of jumping to quick and often faulty conclusions ('Did Jeanne not wave because she's mad at me, or did she just not see me? If I don't talk to her next, she might really get mad'), and on how one can discover another's feelings by listening, observing and asking.

3 *Understanding motives.* As a precursor to consequential thinking, children are taught to consider not just the feelings of other people, but what they might be thinking in an interpersonal situation ('Why did Frank do that? Would Paul still be mad if he found out what Frank was really thinking?'). To help children understand multiple viewpoints, they are asked to describe what is going on in pictures and in scripted pantomimes.

Following these preliminary lessons, the Hahnemann programmes shift the focus of training to skills that theoretically are central to the problem-solving process itself. Again, a variety of scripted games and group exercises are employed to encourage the emergence of problem-solving thought. Interpersonal problems introduced by teachers or children serve as a basis for group discussion focused on the generation of alternative solutions, consideration of consequences and the planning of a careful, step-by-step route to a given interpersonal goal. Formal lessons are supplemented by a problem-solving approach to behavioural management whenever real-life problems arise. Programme implementers (parents or teachers) are taught to adopt a style of dialogue whereby children are encouraged to think through the problem at hand.

In their most recent versions for teachers, the Hahnemann training programmes attempt to integrate ICPS concepts more fully into the entire school curriculum. For example, a mathematics teacher might reinforce the notion of alternative thinking by calling attention to the multiple ways of arriving at 8 (a pair of 4s, 8 1s, etc.). Similarly, teachers are encouraged to engage children in problem-solving dialogues throughout the day, not just in the heat of problem situations (e.g. 'How else might we line up for recess?').

Unlike other cognitive-behavioural treatment strategies (such as coaching), the emphasis throughout is on teaching children *how* to think about interpersonal situations and problems, not on *what* to think. The goal is not to generate a particular belief system in the child, but rather a way to reason and to use one's own beliefs and values in decision-making relative to problems that arise. The assumption underlying this approach is that, while the success with which a problem is solved on any given occasion may be determined by what one thinks, in the long run one is more likely to come up with adaptive solutions to a wide variety of complex situations once ICPS processes have been mastered. Because of the transactional nature of interpersonal interaction, it is simply not possible to provide a list of behavioural strategies that will invariably resolve particular interpersonal dilemmas. A child with well-developed ICPS skills should react with less frustration and greater flexibility when a particular strategy does not work, and should be better able to think of other ways to handle the problem than a child with ICPS deficiencies.

This emphasis on the training of cognitive processes does not imply lack of interest in what children actually think or do. Theoretically, good cognitive problem solvers may choose to act in socially unacceptable ways. Indeed, Spivack *et al.* (1976) noted that well-adjusted children can conceptualize solutions that may have a negative impact on others (e.g. hit a peer to obtain a toy) just as poorly adjusted children can. However, the former appear to be better able to generate socially appropriate solutions as well, and to identify the likely short-term and long-term consequences of the alternatives at hand. Thus, an emphasis on the process of problem-solving should lead children naturally to adopt socially appropriate, effective and maximally satisfying solutions as their own.

The following dialogues (from Shure, 1981) illustrate two contrasting approaches to SST with children, as reflected in different approaches to conflict mediation in the classroom. In the first example, a teacher tries unsuccessfully to coach a child in a socially appropriate way to get a peer to share a toy:

Teacher (*T*): Daniel, why did you grab that shovel from Jamie?
Child (*C*): He never shares.
T: You can't grab toys. Jamie doesn't like that. You should ask.
C: It's not fair. He won't give it to me.
T: If you grab like that, he won't play with you anymore.
C: I don't care.
T: Daniel, I told you to ask him for it.
(Daniel asks, is refused, and either in frustration or by decision, hits Jamie.)

In the second example, a teacher attempts to remain neutral regarding specific strategies, while asking questions that stimulate problem-solving thought.

Teacher (*T*): Shelly, what happened when you grabbed that doll from Tasha?
Child (*C*): She snatched it back.

T: What else happened?
C: She hit me.
(Teacher guides child to consider consequences.)
T: How did that make you feel?
C: Mad.
T: How do you think Tasha feels?
C: Mad.
(Teacher guides child to think of own and other's feelings.)
T: You're mad and Tasha's mad. Can you think of a *different* way to get Tasha to let you have that doll?
C: But she said no. And I want it!
T: If you try really hard, I bet you can think of an idea.
(Teacher encourages child not to give up.)
C: (to Tasha) Let's have a puppet show. We can take turns holding it [the doll].
(Tasha agrees, if she can go first.)

Clearly, the role of the help-giver differs in these two approaches. For the ICPS therapist the goal is not to teach or supply ready-made solutions to problems (the end-product of problem-solving thought), but to act as a catalyst and guide through the process itself.

The Hahnemann approach has served as a prototype for, or is representative of, a variety of other ICPS training efforts with children. For example, a number of other investigators (Weissberg, 1985, 1989; Elias *et al.*, 1986; Battistich *et al.*, 1989) have developed similar programmes (or revised earlier ones) that attempt to enhance ICPS skills and other social competencies by integrating an ICPS approach throughout the total school environment. Indeed, the growing awareness that social skills deficits are implicated in both academic failure and health-compromising behaviour has led to a proliferation of state and local mandates in the US for school programmes of this kind to promote social competence in the formative years (Weissberg, 1990).

However, not every programme purporting to teach cognitive problem-solving has retained such an exclusive focus on process rather than content. Most published accounts appear to represent an amalgam of both elements (Ollendick & Hersen, 1979; Battistich *et al.*, 1989). Moreover, many other ICPS programmes place additional emphasis on translating cognitive problem-solving into behavioural terms (Goldfried & Goldfried, 1975; McClure *et al.*, 1978). Strategies employed for fostering ICPS skills also differ from programme to programme. While all rely on direct verbal instruction in problem-solving principles, a variety of other techniques are at times applied, including modelling of effective problem-solving thought and behaviour; environmental and self-reinforcement; role-play and rehearsal; self-instruction training; feedback; and group discussion. Finally, the aspects of social functioning targeted for change also vary widely, ranging from impulse control, to prosocial behaviour, to actual peer acceptance. Given the complex and multifaceted nature of most ICPS training — especially those 'omnibus' training programmes that attempt to enhance problem-solving and adjustment through longterm changes in the school environment — it has become extremely difficult to determine just what the differential impact and 'active ingredients' of such programmes might be.

OUTCOME STUDIES

A number of attempts have been made to demonstrate the impact and relevance of ICPS training with children and adolescents in group settings. The most persuasive findings to date have been presented by the Hahnemann researchers. In their initial effort, (Spivack and Shure 1974; Shure & Spivack, 1980) enlisted schoolteachers to train 113 lower-class black children attending inner-city nursery schools. Prior to treatment, 44 of these children were identified as impulsive and aggressive with peers, 28 as inhibited, and 41 as well-adjusted, on the basis of teacher ratings of classroom behaviour. Training occurred daily for 3 months and included 46 20−30-minute scripted lessons, games and dialogues. Teachers also applied problem-solving techniques of communication whenever interpersonal problems arose in the classroom.

Posttesting indicated that children trained in this fashion improved relative to a matched no-treatment control group on measures of alternative and consequential thinking. Behavioural ratings favoured the experimental group at posttesting, as well. Of the youngsters displaying impulsive behaviours at pretest, 50% were judged to be well-adjusted following ICPS training compared to only 21% of the controls ($P<0.01$). Among initially inhibited youngsters, 75% of the trained group moved into the adjusted category compared with only 35% of controls ($P<0.05$). Since teachers served as both programme implementers and evaluators, the possibility of rating bias could not be ruled out. However, new ratings made the following year by kindergarten teachers unfamiliar with the children's previous training or social behaviour suggested that adjustment gains were real and had been maintained. Moreover, the impulsive and inhibited children who showed the greatest gains in cognitive skills also made the greatest gains in behaviour − strong evidence that ICPS skill acquisition *mediated* the observed changes.

Unfortunately, the investigators failed to control for adult attention and other nonspecific treatment factors (e.g. special group membership, expectancy for change) in their study design. It is possible that such unexplored factors were partially responsible for the behavioural gains associated with ICPS training. However, the gains did not appear to be a function of IQ. Of the 69 initially maladjusted children tested, the mean Stanford−Binet IQ of the 41 whose behaviour improved was 104 (s.d. 10.33, range 73−126), not significantly different from a mean of 102 (s.d. 10.80, range 70−117) among the 28 whose aberrant behaviour persisted.

Similar methods and remedial impact were reported by Shure and Spivack (1979) with 74 black children attending inner-city kindergartens. Prior to treatment, teachers rated 16 of these youngsters as impulsive, 4 as inhibited, and 54 as well-adjusted. Thirty-nine of the experimental children had previously participated in the nursery school training programme. The concepts taught were essentially the same in both years, although the content was more sophisticated for the older children. Posttesting indicated that children trained for the first time during kindergarten improved relative to a matched no-treatment control group on measures of alternative and consequential thinking. Moreover, 2 years of training generally resulted in significantly greater cognitive gains than 1 year of training occurring in either nursery school or kindergarten. Related gains in teacher-rated adjustment were once again apparent. After training, 70% of initially maladapted children were judged to be adjusted compared with only 6% of maladapted controls ($P<0.01$). However, 2 years of cognitive training did not appear to yield additional gains in adjustment relative to 1 year of training at either point in time. Again, no attention-control group or independent evaluation of behavioural impact was undertaken.

A variety of other SST programmes incorporating ICPS components have produced beneficial results with older maladjusted children and adolescents, as well. For example, Sarason (1968) and Sarason and Ganzer (1969, 1973) taught a variety of skills to 128 institutionalized delinquents. Training centred around social, educational and vocational situations commonly faced by adolescents, such as learning how to interview for a job. Counsellors placed considerable emphasis on alternative and consequential thinking processes, although they also highlighted desirable and undesirable ways of coping. Training resulted in improved self-descriptions, a more internal locus of control and better behavioural ratings from the counsellors themselves, relative to a no-treatment control condition. Moreover, a significant decrease in recidivism was apparent a full 2−3 years afterwards.

Such results are impressive, since delinquents as a group have been particularly unyielding to treatment (Little & Kendall, 1979). Unfortunately, however, the investigators failed to assess ICPS ability before and after training. Thus, one cannot be sure: (1) that the adolescents targeted for training in fact had preexisting cognitive deficits underlying their obvious behavioural deficits in the interpersonal problem-solving arena; (2) that they acquired the relevant skills in the course of training; and (3) that observed changes in adjustment were mediated by such cognitive skill acquisition.

The same methodological shortcoming limits the conclusions that can be drawn about adjustment gains following ICPS-oriented training in a number of other studies, as well: Ollendick and Hersen (1979) with incarcerated delinquents; Giebink et al. (1968) and Elias (1979) with emotionally disturbed boys in residential treatment centres; Pitkanen (1974), Schneider (1974) and Robin et al. (1976) with maladjusted, aggressive children; and Meijers (cited in Meichenbaum, 1977) with socially anxious schoolchildren.

Less encouraging have been a variety of other studies (Rickel et al., 1983) in which the acquisition of ICPS skills failed to produce observable improvement in social adjustment. One such noteworthy failure was reported by Sharp (1981), who attempted to replicate the findings of Spivack and Shure (1974) while eliminating and/or controlling for earlier methodological problems. For example, nursery school teachers were not used as trainers. Instead, they were told only that participants would be meeting daily with project staff as part of a special programme designed to enrich language, number and thinking skills. An attention-control group was also included rather than a simple no-treatment control. This condition also served to keep teachers 'blind' as to which children actually received the training. Finally, teachers' ratings of classroom behaviour were supplemented by 'blind' observers' ratings of social behaviour during play periods. Fifty-four black, low-income nursery school children were randomly assigned to one of three experimental conditions: (1) the original 46-session ICPS training programme designed by Spivack and Shure (1974); (2) a modified training programme that substituted games, songs and story-telling exercises for the first 12 lessons otherwise concerned with language concepts; and (3) a cognitive enrichment programme stressing language skills and number concepts.

Posttesting suggested that initially maladjusted children who received the complete training programme made the greatest gains in alternative thinking, although no training effects on consequential thinking were apparent. Otherwise, results differed sharply from those reported by Spivack and Shure (1974). In the training group, 5 out of 15 children who were rated aberrant at pretest were rated adjusted at posttest. However, 8 out of 20 children who were rated adjusted at pretest were rated aberrant after training. The number of trained children who improved behaviourally did not differ significantly from the number who deteriorated over the same period. Similarly, observational findings suggested that general activity levels, as well as aggression and dominance, increased from pretest to posttest for both adjusted and aberrant children across all three conditions.

This discrepancy in results may be accounted for by several factors. For example, Spivack and Shure (1974) may have been misled by their failure to supplement teacher reports of behaviour with observational or other unbiased sources of data. On the other hand, as Sharp herself observed (1981), the lack of behavioural improvement in the present study may be attributed to the failure to provide children with *in vivo* experience and reinforcement of problem-solving strategies (a central component of the original programme).

Urbain (1980) was also relatively unsuccessful in his attempts to intervene with second- and third-graders identified by teachers as impulsive and aggressive with peers. This study compared a behavioural intervention programme (contingency management) with two different cognitive approaches (self-instructional plus either ICPS or social perspective-taking training). Training in self-instruction was based on prior research (Camp, 1977; Camp *et al.*, 1977) suggesting that young aggressive boys fail to employ private speech successfully in self-regulation on a variety of cognitive and motor tasks, despite adequate verbal intelligence. To remediate such verbal-mediational deficits, critical self-statements are first modelled for children (e.g. 'What is my problem? What are all the things that I can do?'). Gradually, children are encouraged to verbalize their own statements, and then to fade vocalizations into covert self-instructions. Training was carried out

by the investigator himself in small group settings outside the classroom. Like Sharp (1981), no provision was made for *in vivo* training, and posttesting indicated little specificity of outcome. All three training conditions led to improvement on social-cognitive measures, whereas none produced significant overall improvement in teacher-rated behaviour. Nevertheless, a moderate relationship was observed between behavioural improvement and improvement in social-cognitive functioning.

Whereas most ICPS training efforts have focused on maladjusted and generally lower-class children, attempts to teach ICPS skills to nonclinical and to middle- and upper-middle-class groups have been proliferating of late, as interest in the potential of such training for prevention has grown. With few exceptions, these studies have been very consistent in producing gains in ICPS skills. However, immediate associated changes in social behaviour or peer acceptance have been particularly elusive in such studies. Moreover, data addressing the long-term impact of such intervention efforts are sparse.

In one such prevention effort, Gesten *et al.* (1979) devised a 17-lesson ICPS treatment programme for use by teachers with suburban, middle-class second- and third-grade children. The programme emphasized role-playing, video-tape modelling and class discussion of interpersonal problems. Results indicated that the full training programme resulted in greater cognitive gains than did an abridged version or a no-treatment control condition. Moreover, children receiving the full programme showed the greatest problem-solving persistence on a posttreatment simulated problem situation. However, parallel gains in teacher-rated adjustment or peer acceptance were not evident. Similar findings were reported by Allen *et al.* (1976).

In an attempt to strengthen Gesten *et al.*'s (1979) programme, Weissberg *et al.* (1981) increased the number of classroom lessons to 52 and devised 6 parent training sessions to support children's use of newly acquired ICPS skills. Teachers were once again employed to implement the programme. This time, however, participants included a group of black, inner-city, lower-class third-graders, as well as a group of white, suburban, middle-class youngsters, to test directly the differential effectiveness of such training with the two groups. Results indicated that both groups improved with training on a variety of ICPS measures. In addition, trained children tried more solutions and persisted longer than controls in a simulated problem situation.

Adjustment findings were more complex and disconcerting. In the suburban sample, trained children improved more than controls on teacher ratings of behavioural problems (e.g. reduced acting out) and competencies (e.g. enhanced assertiveness), although adjustment and ICPS gains were not significantly correlated. By contrast, teacher-rated data suggested that the same training programme may have had a negative impact on urban children, among whom experimentals declined significantly on 5 out of 9 rating dimensions. These findings were unexpected in that the urban group also acquired key ICPS skills, and prior ICPS interventions with inner-city preschoolers had yielded significant gains in teacher-rated adjustment (Spivack & Shure, 1974).

Teacher reactions to the training programme itself help to clarify the adjustment findings. Weissberg *et al.* (1981) reported that experimental teachers in the suburban schools felt that brainstorming alternative solutions helped children to express ideas more creatively. Urban experimental teachers, on the other hand, found that the same process produced mostly aggressive solutions and, in so doing, negatively affected class discipline. One such teacher expressed her discomfort with the programme at the outset and implemented it reluctantly. Such expectations (positive and negative) undoubtedly introduced bias into teacher-based outcome measures. Such detrimental effects were not reflected in measures of self-esteem, trait anxiety or sociometric status, in which no experimental–control group differences were apparent.

A more successful prevention effort was reported by Ridley and Vaughn (1982), who randomly assigned 40 preschoolers to an experimental or control group. Experimental subjects were trained in ICPS skills 4 days a week for 10 weeks. The experimental group showed a significant increase, compared to controls, in both cognitive and behavioural problem-solving skills. These gains were maintained at follow-up 3 months later. Moreover, gains in problem-solving skills were associated with improved social behaviour based on classroom observation (Vaughn & Ridley, 1983). Similar results were reported by Feis and Simons (1985) with preschoolers, as well as by Elardo and Caldwell (1979) in their multifaceted training programme designed for middle-class fourth- and fifth-graders.

Provocative evidence for the preventive impact of ICPS training is most apparent when long-term follow-up data are examined. For example, in the year following the completion of Gesten *et al.*'s (1979) ICPS training study, former control children in the suburban, middle-class sample deteriorated relative to former experimental children on measures of teacher- and peer-rated adjustment. Indeed, at 1-year follow-up, experimentals exceeded controls on 7 out of 10 social competence and pathology factors as rated by new teachers who were unaware of the previous training. In addition, sociometric findings indicated that experimental children liked their peers more and were more popular in return than children who were not trained.

Similarly, Shure and Spivack (1979) have noted that, after only 1 year of exposure to the Hahnemann programme in nursery school, 25 out of 27 youngsters (93%) who were initially judged to be adjusted continued to be so in kindergarten, while 5 out of 6 (83%) maintained this status to the end of first grade. With 2 years of training, 11 out of 14 initially adjusted youngsters (78%) continued to be judged so to the end of first grade. By contrast, 19 out of 27 initially adjusted control children (67%) were adjusted in kindergarten, but only 1 out of 6 (17%) were at the end of first grade. It appears, then, that ICPS training may insulate young children from developing social adjustment problems over time.

Finally, a number of successful attempts have been made to reduce social adjustment problems in children through ICPS training in a family context (Pfiffner *et al.*, 1990). The family

unit is the setting in which many significant and possibly prototypical interpersonal problems arise. To test the effectiveness of parent-based ICPS training, Shure and Spivack (1978) instructed black, inner-city, lower-class mothers in the use of problem-solving methods with their nursery school children. Forty mother–child pairs were matched as closely as possible on the problem-solving abilities of both members of the dyad, as well as on the child's school adjustment, age and sex. Twenty pairs were then randomly selected for intervention, while their counterparts served as no-treatment controls. Prior to treatment, 7 of the experimental children and 16 of the controls were judged by their teachers to be inhibited or impulsive and aggressive with peers. Mothers in the experimental condition were taught to administer the sequence of structured lessons, games and dialogues at home with their children. Exercises for parents were interspersed throughout the programme script, designed to parallel skills that they would be transmitting to their children. The programme continued on a daily basis over a 3-month period.

Posttesting indicated that trained mothers improved in their problem-solving thinking about mother–child and child–child problems, but not in their thinking about adult problems (the latter not being the focus of training efforts). Moreover, trained mothers reported shifts toward a more problem-solving approach to child-rearing. Mother-trained children also made substantial increases in alternative and consequential thinking relative to control children, although no group differences were apparent on a measure of interpersonal problem sensitivity. Most importantly, ICPS increases in children were associated with significant improvements in classroom behaviour, as judged by teachers who were blind to the treatment conditions. Of the initially aberrant children, 71% were rated as well-adjusted in the classroom following home treatment, in comparison to only 31% of controls. Youngsters whose behaviour improved also increased their alternative thinking skills significantly more than did those whose behaviour stayed the same.

Alexander and Parsons (1973) also incorporated ICPS components into a primarily behavioural, short-term family therapy programme for juvenile status offenders. Posttesting indicated significant improvement on a number of family interaction measures (for example, verbal reciprocity) relative to a short-term client-centred therapy approach, a psychodynamic family programme and a no-treatment control group. In a second study, Parsons and Alexander (1973) similarly noted the superiority of their ICPS-oriented programme relative to no-treatment and discussion-oriented control groups. A subsequent follow-up of both training programmes $2\frac{1}{2}-3\frac{1}{2}$ years later indicated that the problem-solving intervention resulted in sibling court involvement one-third to one-half below that of the comparison groups and a significantly lower recidivism rate (Klein *et al.*, 1977). It is not clear, however, to what extent ICPS skill acquisition actually mediated these adjustment gains.

Not every ICPS intervention effort with families has had beneficial results, however. Both Robin *et al.* (1977) and Blechman *et al.* (1976a,b) produced significant gains in problem-solving thought and behaviour in the therapeutic context, but these new skills failed to transfer to the home environment. Foster (1978) attempted to facilitate generalization of training by having therapists assign and discuss homework tasks of graded difficulty each week and discuss specific ways in which problem-solving and communication skills could be used at home. While several beneficial effects did occur, there was little evidence for increased effectiveness of generalization training methods over skill training alone. Moreover, with the exception of Shure and Spivack (1978), no studies have considered the extent to which family-based treatment effects generalize to the peer context.

DISCUSSION

Available findings suggest that a wide variety of approaches are effective for teaching ICPS skills to children. Beginning as early as nursery school (Sharp, 1981) and extending at least into fifth grade (Elardo & Caldwell, 1979), children have consistently demonstrated the capacity to improve their performance significantly on measures of ICPS. Moreover, both normal (Winer et al., 1982) and behaviourally maladjusted children across a wide IQ range (Shure & Spivack, 1980) have been able to learn such skills.

Taken as a whole, findings to date also suggest that ICPS training has beneficial effects going beyond improved cognitive test performance, although such effects are less reliably observed. Positive changes in social behaviour have been achieved with numerous groups, ranging from preschoolers demonstrating early signs of behavioural maladjustment (Spivack & Shure, 1974), to disturbed schoolchildren in residential treatment (Elias, 1979), to generally recalcitrant juvenile delinquents (Ollendick & Hersen, 1979). Moreover, while long-term follow-up data are sparse, initial findings suggest substantial holding power for treatment effects, at least in the early years following training (Shure & Spivack, 1979).

However, a metaanalysis of ICPS training studies, undertaken by Denham and Almeida (1987), suggests that the magnitude of training effects, on both ratings of adjustment and on observed behaviour, are somewhat greater for vulnerable or 'at-risk' children (e.g. children showing early signs of maladjustment, lower-class children) than for severely maladjusted or normal children. Training also appears to have stronger effects on younger children. Moreover, while classroom teachers (Allen et al., 1976), parents originally deficient in problem-solving skills (Shure & Spivack, 1978; Pfiffner et al., 1990) and clinicians (Spivack & Shure, 1974) have all been successful at fostering both ICPS skill acquisition and adjustment gains, experienced investigators appear to be most successful. Finally, where beneficial effects on adjustment have been noted, ICPS skill acquisition appeared to *mediate* those effects.

While ICPS training appears to offer a useful focus for remedial and prevention efforts with children and adolescents, it is clear that newly acquired cognitive skills do not translate automatically into more adaptive social behaviour (Sharp,

1981). Indeed, training efforts lasting at least 40 sessions appear to be more effective than shorter training programmes (Denham & Almeida, 1987). Explicit, guided practice in the problem-solving process in the child's real-life environment may be particularly critical for the generalization of training effects.

However, ICPS gains, even when accompanied by improved social behaviour, may not guarantee greater peer acceptance for previously rejected or neglected children. As noted earlier, this is neither surprising nor unique to ICPS training, but is common to other SST approaches as well (Bierman et al., 1987). Widespread assumptions that newly acquired social competencies of any kind will, of their own accord, translate into improved social status and peer acceptance over time appear to be unfounded.

Peer expectations and friendship networks may be relatively rigid, and a prior history of negative or egocentric social behaviour may alienate peers. As a result, treated children may have few opportunities to engage peers in positive interactions that would foster the generalization and maintenance of treatment effects. Thus, not only do children with social difficulties require specific skill training, but peers' behaviour towards, and perceptions of, target children may also require direct intervention and modification (Strain & Fox, 1981).

While the utility of ICPS training continues to garner empirical support, investigators would do well to incorporate a number of methodological improvements in future training studies. For example, the use of more optimal control groups is essential to demonstrate that the cognitive aspects of any problem-solving training approach are truly effective. Component contrast or alternative treatment groups may be required for longer-term treatment programmes, in which a strict attention-control may not be feasible (O'Leary & Borkovec, 1978). Direct comparison with other commonly employed SST approaches (such as coaching and modelling) would also be particularly informative regarding the relative therapeutic effectiveness of ICPS training for different types of children. Finally, the systematic inclusion of therapy manipulation checks would be advantageous in future studies. Such checks allow one to determine whether theoretical distinctions between contrasted treatment approaches are, in fact, being applied in ongoing treatment efforts (Kendall & Wilcox, 1980).

Whenever cognitive components of an intervention are said to be important in producing behavioural change, confirmation requires pre- and postassessment of the relevant cognitive variables (Kendall et al., 1981). However, the choice of an appropriate method for assessing problem-solving skills is a difficult one. Current approaches are quite diverse and each one has its own set of advantages and limitations (Krasnor & Rubin, 1981; Gresham, 1985). Observational strategies represent a particularly promising new approach, despite being time-consuming, costly and variable in their rate of data acquisition. While probably not suitable for prevention studies — where it is generally necessary to assess large numbers of children in as efficient a way as possible — observational methods may be ideal for the periodic evaluation of randomly selected individuals in the course of training. In this way, it may be possible to determine whether newly taught cognitive skills are being effectively implemented in unstructured social interaction, while avoiding training-to-task problems.

Unfortunately, no problem-solving assessment device has been adequately validated to date (Gresham, 1985). The inadvertent use of an invalid measure may distort our view of the problems at hand (e.g. What is the most effective way to teach problem-solving?) and may lead us to seek solutions in the wrong places (Ford, 1979). In the absence of properly validated measures of any kind, investigators concerned with cognitive training effects are well advised to consider multiple-method assessment for establishing both problem-solving deficits and improvements.

Future studies would also benefit from the use of 'blind' raters for evaluating the impact of training on adjustment (Sharp, 1981; Rickel *et al.*, 1983). Since ICPS interventions are frequently embedded within the school environment (Elardo & Caldwell, 1979; Weissberg, 1985; Battistich *et al.*, 1989), with teachers themselves serving as the programme implementers, special attention must be paid to obtaining unbiased evaluations of training effectiveness (e.g. in follow-up evaluations from teachers blind to the treatment condition).

The use of multiple sources of assessment (self-report, teacher and peer ratings, behavioural observations, etc.) would also be advantageous for assessing a broad range of social and behavioural outcomes. Researchers are advised to consider not only whether ICPS training produces significant effects, but also whether it returns deviant or 'at-risk' children back to within normal limits on various outcome measures (Kendall & Wilcox, 1980). Finally, more long-term assessment of treatment outcome is essential. This is particularly true with regard to primary prevention efforts where immediate effects may not be readily observable and where the true test of clinical utility is the test of time.

It should be clear at this point that a host of problems, questions and issues pertinent to ICPS training have yet to be properly addressed. For example, it is not clear whether particular ICPS skills are more critical than others in terms of mediating adjustment at any particular point in time. A careful and comprehensive task analysis of various problematic social situations should shed some light on this issue. Future studies designed to train single problem-solving components in isolation or in limited, rationally derived combinations would be informative. The systematic process research undertaken by Nezu and D'Zurilla (1981; D'Zurilla & Nezu, 1980) with normal adults provides a useful model for such treatment research with children.

The developmental unfolding of interpersonal problem-solving ability also requires further description and explication. Most developmental studies of problem-solving to date have restricted their focus to examination of particular components (social goal formation, strategy selection, response flexibility, etc.) in a static framework (Rubin & Rose-Krasnor, 1992). Additional research is required to understand how the individual components of problem-solving come to be coordinated in an adaptive, smoothly flowing process.

Every ICPS training programme appears to attach a central role to instruction in and practice of alternative thinking or brainstorming techniques. However, Langer (1978) has argued that, for the most part, social behaviour is unthinking in nature and proceeds according to overlearned social scripts. Social situations that call for more reflective cognitive processing (situations that are novel or where any action might have important consequences) may be relatively uncommon (Krasnor & Rubin, 1981). Indeed, the majority of young children may not spontaneously consider alternative solutions to most hypothetical social dilemmas.

The ICPS process may actually vary in different populations of children (normal versus disturbed; middle class versus lower class), or at different ages or developmental stages within the same population. On the other hand, the process itself may be constant, while having different implications and repercussions for different kinds of children. For example, while most children may not brainstorm spontaneously in most social situations, the failure to do so may generally have little significance for the well-adjusted child whose natural recourse is to a relatively mature and effective problem-solving strategy. The same failure in an aggressive child may lead to peer conflict or goal frustration due to the type of problem solution typically relied upon. If so, then the aggressive child may require initial training in brainstorming primarily to establish more mature scripts, as well as impulse-control training to encourage more reflective problem-solving. The normal child, on the other hand, may benefit more from instruction regarding when brainstorming is desirable (i.e. metacognitive training) than from instruction regarding how to do it. Thus, the nature of a truly effective and efficient training programme may differ markedly depending upon whether its purpose is prevention or rectification, as well as upon the kinds of central or concomitant problems which are cause for concern in a given sample of children.

A related issue concerns the need to sort out the more effective from less effective training elements in the diverse programmes currently in vogue. Because such programs are multifaceted and often long-lasting (e.g. Battistich *et al.*, 1989), it is difficult to determine what their 'active ingredients' might be. The disappointing results of Urbain (1980) and Sharp (1981), as well as the metaanalysis of Denham and Almeida (1987), support the widespread suggestion that 'dialoguing' may be one such ingredient (e.g. Elardo & Caldwell, 1979; Rickel *et al.*, 1983; Weissberg, 1985). Dialoguing with teachers (or parents) during the course of actual interpersonal problems provides children with both practice in ICPS skill use, as well as reinforcement for their efforts (Denham & Almeida, 1987). Kendall (1977) argued that the application of systematically applied behavioural contingencies is another ingredient necessary to ensure the effectiveness of any cognitive training programme.

A final issue concerns the most advantageous setting for fostering ICPS ability. A number of researchers (Weissberg,

1985; Battistich *et al.*, 1989) have argued convincingly that ICPS training works best when it is firmly embedded in the child's natural environment, such as the school. ICPS training curricula can be readily incorporated into the classroom to beneficial effect.

Since children undoubtedly learn a great deal about interpersonal behaviour within their families, the family context provides another logical focus for therapeutic intervention, and ICPS training in parent–child dyads appears promising. However, Youniss (1980) has argued that fundamental differences exist in the structure of parent–child and child–child relationships and in the rules or conventions that govern them. In the former dyad, conflicts are resolved unilaterally, with decisions emanating primarily from parents. In the latter dyad, conflicts tend to be resolved reciprocally, at least by middle childhood, when friendships blossom. Principles of problem-solving among family members may not transfer readily to the peer group. Thus, a recent innovation designed by Selman and Schultz (1990) for fostering interpersonal problem-solving skills in the context of dyadic peer interaction is of particular interest. A direct comparison of the therapeutic effectiveness of ICPS training approaches in different contexts (school, family and peer dyads) would be enlightening.

CONCLUSIONS

While ICPS training is sensible and appealing as an SST approach, outcome data indicate that it is not simplistic. A programme's content and mode of presentation may differentially affect its impact depending upon the age and sociodemographic attributes of target populations (Weissberg *et al.*, 1981). For example, the nonevaluative approach to ICPS training may be initially (if not chronically) disruptive in an inner-city school setting, where a greater premium is placed on behavioural control than on self-expression. Family-based ICPS training may be most effective in early childhood, but less effective than peer-based training in middle childhood and adolescence, when the changing nature of peer relations demands greater reciprocity. Such parameters must be better understood if the promise of this approach to rectification and prevention is to be realized.

In the meantime, however, practitioners might profitably incorporate elements of ICPS training in their therapeutic efforts with socially maladjusted youngsters. Instruction in alternative and consequential thinking seems especially warranted for nonreflective children who act impulsively and aggressively with peers, as well as for children whose limited social repertoires are matched by a poverty of ideas regarding effective social interaction. Elements of the problem-solving approach appear to have a useful part to play in the treatment of other clinical conditions, as well. For example, guided practice in brainstorming and the role-playing of effective problem-solving might increase feelings of personal efficacy in children suffering from depression and low self-esteem. Parents might also benefit from instruction in the problem-solving approach for managing disruptive or unco-operative behaviour at home. Finally, the ICPS emphasis on teaching youngsters how to think about their problems, and not just what to think, seems applicable to a wide range of therapeutic approaches.

REFERENCES

Alexander J.F. & Parsons B.V. (1973) Short-term behavioral intervention with delinquent families. *Journal of Abnormal Psychology*, **81**, 219–225.

Allen G.J., Chinsky J.M., Larcen S.W., Lochman J.E. & Selinger H.V. (1976) *Community Psychology and the Schools: A Behaviorally Oriented Multilevel Preventive Approach*. Lawrence J. Erlbaum, Hillsdale, NJ.

Asher S.R. (1978) Children's peer relations. In: Lamb M.E. (ed) *Social and Personality Development*, pp. 91–113, Holt, Rinehart, & Winston, New York.

Battistich V., Solomon D., Watson M., Solomon J. & Schaps E. (1989) Effects of an elementary school program to enhance prosocial behavior on children's cognitive-social problem-solving skills and strategies. *Journal of Applied Developmental Psychology*, **10**, 147–169.

Bierman, K.L. & Furman W. (1984) The effects of social skills training and peer involvement on the social adjustment of preadolescents. *Child Development*, **55**, 151–162,

Bierman K.L., Miller C.L. & Stabb S.D. (1987) Improving the social behavior and peer acceptance of rejected boys: effects of social skill training with instructions and prohibitions. *Journal of Consulting and Clinical Psychology*, **55**, 194–200.

Blechman E., Olson D. & Hellman I. (1976a) Stimulus control over family problem-solving behavior: the family contract game. *Behavioral Therapy*, **7**, 686–692.

Blechman E., Olson D., Schornagel C., Halsdorf M. & Turner A. (1976b) The family contract game: technique and case study. *Journal of Consulting and Clinical Psychology*, **44**, 449–455.

Camp B.W. (1977) Verbal mediation in young aggressive boys. *Journal of Abnormal Psychology*, **86**, 145–153.

Camp B., Blom G., Herbert F. & Van Doornick W. (1977) 'Think aloud': a program for developing self-control in young aggressive boys. *Journal of Abnormal Child Psychology*, **5**, 157–168.

Clark M.S. & Isen A.M. (1981) Toward understanding the relationship between feeling states and social behavior. In: Hastorf A.H. & Isen A.M. (eds) *Cognitive Social Psychology*, pp. 73–108. Elsevier, New York.

Coie J. & Krehbiel G. (1984) Effects of academic tutoring on the social status of low achieving, socially rejected children. *Child Development*, **55**, 1465–1478.

Cowen E.L., Pederson A., Babigian H., Izzo L.D. & Trost M.A. (1973) Long-term follow-up of early detected vulnerable children. *Journal of Consulting and Clinical Psychology*, **41**, 438–446.

Damon W. (1977) *The Social World of the Child*. Jossey-Bass, San Francisco, CA.

Davis G. (1966) Current status of research and theory in human problem-solving. *Psychological Bulletin*, **66**, 36–54.

Denham S. & Almeida M. (1987) Children's social problem-solving skills, behavioral adjustment, and interventions: a meta-analysis evaluating theory and practice. *Journal of Applied Developmental Psychology*, **8**, 391–409.

Dewey J. (1933) *How We Think*. Heath, New York.

Dodge K.A. (1986) A social information processing model of social competence in children. In: Perlmutter M. (ed) *Cognitive Perspectives on Children's Social and Behavioral Development. The Minnesota Symposia on Child Psychology* (vol. 18), pp. 77–126. Erlbaum, Hillsdale, NJ.

Dodge K.A. (1991) Emotion and social information processing. In: Garber J. & Dodge K.A. (eds) *The Development of Emotion Regulation and Dysregulation*, pp. 159–181. Cambridge University Press, New York.

Duncan C.P. (1959) Recent research on human problem-solving. *Psychological Bulletin*, **56**, 397–429.

D'Zurilla T.J. & Goldfried M.R. (1971) Problem-solving and behavior modification. *Journal of Abnormal Psychology*, **78**, 107–126.

D'Zurilla T.J. & Nezu A. (1980) A study of the generation-of-alternatives process in social problem-solving. *Cognitive Therapy and Research*, **4**, 67–72.

Elardo P.T. & Caldwell B.M. (1979) The effects of an experimental social development program on children in the middle childhood period. *Psychology in the Schools*, **16**, 93–100.

Elias M.J. (1979) Helping emotionally disturbed children through prosocial television. *Exceptional Children*, **46**, 217–218.

Elias M.J., Gara M., Ubriaco M., Rothman P.A., Clabby J.F. & Schuyler T. (1986) Impact of a preventive social problem-solving intervention on children's coping with middle-school stressors. *American Journal of Community Psychology* **14**, 259–275.

Feis C.L. & Simons C. (1985) Training preschool children in interpersonal cognitive problem solving skills. *Prevention in Human Services*, **4**, 59–70.

Feldhusen J.F., Houtz J.C. & Ringenbach S. (1972) The Purdue Elementary Problem-Solving Inventory. *Psychological Reports*, **31**, 891–901.

Flavell J.H. (1976) Metacognitive aspects of problem-solving. In: Resnick L.B. (ed) *The Nature of Intelligence*, pp. 231–235. Lawrence J. Erlbaum, Hillsdale, NJ.

Flavell J.H. (1985) *Cognitive Development*, 2nd edn. Prentice-Hall, Englewood Cliffs, NJ.

Ford M.E. (1979) The construct validity of egocentrism. *Psychological Bulletin*, **86**, 1169–1188.

Foster S. (1978) Reducing family conflict: the impact of skill-training and generalization programming. Paper presented at the American Psychological Association Convention, Toronto.

Gagne R.M. (1970) *The Conditions of Learning*. Holt, Rinehart and Winston, New York.

Gal'perin P.Y. (1969) Stages in the development of mental acts. In: Cole M. & Maltzman I. (eds) *A Handbook of Soviet Psychology*. Basic Books, New York.

Gesten E.L., Flores De Apodaca R.F., Rains M., Weissberg R.P. & Cowen E.L. (1979) Promoting peer-related social competence in school. In: Kent M.W. & Rolf J.E. (eds) *The Primary Prevention of Psychopathology, III: Social Competence in Children*, pp. 220–247. University Press of New England, Hanover, NH.

Giebink J.W., Stover D. & Fahl M. (1968) Teaching adaptive responses to frustration to emotionally disturbed boys. *Journal of Consulting and Clinical Psychology*, **32**, 366–368.

Goldberg S., Lojkasek M., Gartner G. & Corter C. (1989) Maternal responsiveness and social development in preterm infants. In: Bornstein M.H. (ed) *Maternal Responsiveness: Characteristics and Consequences*, pp. 89–103. Jossey-Bass, San Francisco, CA.

Goldfried M.R. & Goldfried A.P. (1975) Cognitive change methods. In: Kanfer F.H. & Goldstein A.P. (eds) *Helping People Change*, pp. 89–116. Pergamon Press, New York.

Gresham F.M. (1981) Social skills training with handicapped children: a review. *Review of Educational Research*, **51**, 139–176.

Gresham F.M. (1985) Utility of cognitive-behavioral procedures for social skills training with children: a critical review. *Journal of Abnormal Child Psychology*, **13**, 411–423.

Gresham F.M. & Nagle R.J. (1980) Social skills training with children: responsiveness to modeling and coaching as a function of peer orientation. *Journal of Consulting and Clinical Psychology*, **48**, 718–729.

Guerra N.G. & Slaby R.G. (1989) Evaluative factors in social problem solving by aggressive boys. *Journal of Abnormal Child Psychology*, **17**, 277–289.

Hartup W. (1980) Peer relations and family relations. Two social worlds. In: Rutter M. (ed) *Scientific Foundations of Developmental Psychiatry*, pp. 280–292. Heinemann Medical, London.

Holmbeck G.N. & Kendall P.C. (1991) Clinical-childhood-developmental interface: implications for treatment. In: Martin P.R. (ed) *Handbook of Behavior Therapy and Psychological Science: An Integrative Approach*. Pergamon, New York.

Jahoda M. (1958) *Current Concepts of Positive Mental Health*. Basic Books, New York.

Johnson D.M. (1955) *The Psychology of Thought and Judgment*. Harper, New York.

Jones D.C., Rickel A.V. & Smith R.L. (1980) Maternal child-rearing practices and social problem-solving strategies among pre-schoolers. *Developmental Psychology*, **16**, 241–242.

Kagan J. (1989) *Unstable Ideas: Temperament, Cognition, and Self.* Harvard University Press, Cambridge, MA.

Kendall P.C. (1977) On the efficacious use of verbal self-instructional procedures with children. *Cognitive Therapy and Research*, **1**, 331–341.

Kendall P.C. (1984) Social cognition and problem solving: a developmental and child–clinical interface. In: Gholson B. & Rosenthal T.L. (eds) *Applications of Cognitive-Developmental Theory*, pp. 115–148. Academic, New York.

Kendall P.C. & Braswell L. (1982) Cognitive-behavioral self-control therapy for children: a component analysis. *Journal of Consulting and Clinical Psychology*, **50**, 672–689.

Kendall P.L. & Finch A.J. (1979) Developing nonimpulsive behavior in children: cognitive-behavioral strategies for self control. In: Kendall P.C. & Hollon S.D. (eds) *Cognitive-behavioral interventions: Theory, Research and Procedures*, pp. 37–80. Academic Press, New York.

Kendall P.C., Pellegrini D.S. & Urbain E. (1981) Approaches to assessment for cognitive-behavioral interventions with children. In: Kendall P.C. & Hollon S.D. (eds) *Assessment Strategies for Cognitive-Behavioral Interventions*, pp. 227–285. Academic Press, New York.

Kendall P.C. & Wilcox L.E. (1980) A cognitive-behavioral treatment for impulsivity: concrete versus conceptual training in non-self-controlled problem children. *Journal of Consulting and Clinical Psychology*, **48**, 80–91.

Klein N.C., Alexander J.F. & Parsons B.V. (1977) Impact of family systems intervention on recidivism and sibling delinquency: a model of primary prevention and program evaluation. *Journal of Consulting and Clinical Psychology*, **45**, 469–474.

Krasnor L.R. & Rubin K.H. (1981) The assessment of social problem-solving skills in young children. In: Merluzzi T., Glass C. & Genest M. (eds) *Cognitive Assessment*, pp. 452–476. Guilford Press, New York.

Langer E. (1978) Rethinking the role of thought in social interactions. In: Harvey J., Ickes W. & Kidd R. (eds) *New Directions in Attribution Research*, vol. 2, pp. 35–58. Lawrence J. Erlbaum, Hillsdale, NJ.

Ladd G.W. (1981) Effectiveness of social learning method for enhancing children's social interaction and peer acceptance. *Child Development*, **52**, 171–178.

Ladd G.W. & Mize J. (1983) A cognitive-social learning model of social skill training. *Psychological Review*, **90**, 127–157.

Little V.L. & Kendall P.C. (1979) Cognitive-behavioral intervention with delinquents: problem-solving, role-taking and self-control. In: Kendall P.C. & Hollon S.D. (eds) *Cognitive-Behavioral Intervention: Theory, Research, and Procedures*, pp. 81–115. Academic Press, New York.

McClure L.F., Chinsky J.H. & Larcen S.W. (1978) Enhancing social problem-solving performance in an elementary school setting.

Journal of Educational Psychology, **70**, 504—513.

McFall R.M. (1976) Behavioral training: a skill-acquisition approach to clinical problems. In: Spence J.T., Carson R.C. & Thibaut J.W. (eds) *Behavioral Approaches to Therapy,* pp. 227—259. General Learning Press, Morristown, NJ.

Marlatt G.A. (1972) Task structure and the experimental modification of verbal behavior. *Psychological Bulletin,* **78**, 335—350.

Marsh D.T., Serafica F.C. & Barenboim C. (1980) Effect of perspective-taking training on interpersonal problem-solving. *Child Development,* **51**, 140—145.

Meichenbaum D. (1977) *Cognitive-Behavior Modification: An Integrative Approach.* Plenum Press, New York.

Meichenbaum D., Henshaw D. & Himal N. (1981) Coping with stress as a problem-solving process. In: Krone W. & Laux L. (eds) *Achievement Stress and Anxiety,* pp. 127—142. Hemisphere Press, Washington, DC.

Merrifield P.R., Guilford J.P., Christensen P.R. & Frick J.W. (1962) *Psychology Monograph,* **76**, 10 pp.

Monck E. (1991) Patterns of confiding relationships among adolescent girls. *Journal of Child Psychology and Psychiatry,* **32**, 333—345.

Newell H. & Simon H. (1972) *Human Problem-Solving.* Prentice-Hall, Englewood Cliffs, NJ.

Nezu A. & D'Zurilla T.J. (1981) Effects of problem definition and formulation on decision-making in the social problem-solving process. *Behavioral Therapy,* **12**, 100—106.

Oden S. & Asher S. (1977) Coaching children in social skills for friendship-making. *Child Development,* **48**, 496—506.

O'Leary K.D. & Borkovec T.D. (1978) Conceptual, methodological, and ethical problems of placebo groups in psychotherapy research. *American Psychology,* **33**, 821—830.

Ollendick T.H. & Hersen M. (1979) Social skills training for juvenile delinquents. *Behavioral Research and Therapy,* **17**, 547—554.

Osborn A.F. (1963) *Applied Imagination: Principles and Procedures of Creative Problem-Solving,* 3rd edn. Charles Scribner's Sons, New York.

Parker J.G. & Asher S.R. (1987) Peer relations and later personal adjustment: Are low-accepted children at risk? *Psychological Bulletin,* **102**, 357—389.

Parsons B.V. & Alexander J.F. (1973) Short-term family intervention: a therapy outcome study. *Journal of Consulting and Clinical Psychology,* **41**, 195—201.

Pfiffner L.J., Jouriles E.N., Brown M.M. & Etscheidt M.A. (1990) Effects of problem solving therapy on outcomes of parent training for single-parent families. *Child and Family Behavior Therapy,* **12**, 1—11.

Piaget J. (1966) *The Psychology of Intelligence.* Littlefield, Adams, Totowa, NJ.

Pitkannen L. (1974) The effect of simulation exercises on the control of aggressive behavior in children. *Scandinavian Journal of Psychology,* **15**, 169—177.

Rickel A.U., Eshelman A.K. & Loigman G.A. (1983) Social problem solving training: a follow-up study of cognitive and behavioral effects. *Journal of Abnormal Child Psychology,* **11**, 15—28.

Ridley C.A. & Vaughn S.R. (1982) Interpersonal problem solving: an intervention program for preschool children. *Journal of Applied Developmental Psychology,* **3**, 177—190.

Robin A., Schneider M. & Dolnick M. (1976) The turtle technique: an extended case study of self-control in the classroom. *Psychology in the Schools,* **13**, 449—453.

Robin A.L., Kent R., O'Leary D., Foster S. & Prinz R. (1977) An approach to teaching parents and adolescents problem-solving communication skills: a preliminary report. *Behavioral Therapy,* **8**, 639—643.

Roff M., Sells S.S. & Golden M.M. (1972) *Social Adjustment and Personality Development in Children.* University of Minnesota Press, Minneapolis, MN.

Rubin K.H. & Krasnor L.R. (1983) Age and gender differences in the development of a representative social problem solving skill. *Journal of Applied Developmental Psychology,* **4**, 463—475.

Rubin K.H. & Krasnor L.R. (1986) Social-cognitive and social behavioral perspectives on problem solving. In: Perlmutter M. (ed) *Cognitive Perspectives on Children's Social and Behavioral Development. The Minnesota Symposia on Child Psychology,* vol. 18, pp. 1—68. Erlbaum, Hillsdale, NJ.

Rubin K.H. & Rose-Krasnor L.R. (1992) Interpersonal problem-solving and social competence in children. In: Van Hasselt V.B. & Hersen M. (eds) *Handbook of Social Development: A Lifespan Perspective,* pp. 283—323. Plenum, New York.

Rubin K.H., Mills R.S.L. & Krasnor L.R. (1989) Parental beliefs and children's social competence. In: Schneider B., Atilli G., Nadel J. & Weissberg R. (eds) *Social Competence in Developmental Perspective,* pp. 313—331. Kluwer International Publishers, Dordrecht, Netherlands.

Ruble D.N., Boggiano A.K., Feldman N.S. & Loebel J.H. (1980) Developmental analyses of the role of social comparison in self-evaluation. *Developmental Psychology,* **16**, 105—115.

Sarason B.R. (1981) The dimensions of social competence: contributions from a variety of research areas. In: Wine J.D. & Smye M.D. (eds) *Social Competence,* pp. 100—122. Guilford Press, New York.

Sarason I.G. (1968) Verbal learning, modeling and juvenile delinquency. *American Psychology,* **23**, 254—266.

Sarason I.G. & Ganzer V.J. (1969) Developing appropriate social behaviors of juvenile delinquents. In: Krumholtz J. & Thorenson C. (eds) *Behavior Counseling Cases and Techniques,* pp. 178—193. Holt, Rinehart and Winston, New York.

Sarason I.G. & Ganzer V.J. (1973) Modeling and group discussion in the rehabilitation of juvenile delinquents. *Journal of Consulting Psychology,* **20**, 442—449.

Schneider M. (1974) Turtle technique in the classroom. *Teaching Exceptional Children,* **8**, 22—24.

Selman R.L. & Byrne D.F. (1974) A structural-developmental analysis of levels of role-taking in middle childhood. *Child Development,* **45**, 803—806.

Selman R.L. & Schultz L.H. (1990) *Making a Friend in Youth: Developmental Theory and Pair Therapy.* University of Chicago Press, Chicago, IL.

Shantz C. (1983) Social cognition. In: Flavell J. & Markham E. (eds) *Cognitive Development,* vol. 4, pp. 495—555; Mussen P. (ed) *Manual of Child Psychology.* Wiley, New York.

Sharp K.C. (1981) Impact of interpersonal problem-solving training on pre-schoolers' social competency. *Journal of Applied Developmental Psychology,* **2**, 129—143.

Shure M.B. (1981) Social competence as a problem-solving skill. In: Wine J.D. & Smye M.D. (eds) *Social Competence,* pp. 158—185. Guilford Press, New York.

Shure M.B. (1982) *Interpersonal Cognitive Problem-Solving for Fifth-Grade Children: Training Program Script.* Department of Mental Health Sciences, Hahnemann Medical College, Philadelphia, PA.

Shure M.B. & Spivack G. (1971) *Solving Interpersonal Problems: A Program for 4-Year-Old Nursery School Children: Training Script.* Department of Mental Health Sciences, Hahnemann Medical College, Philadelphia, PA.

Shure M.B. & Spivack G. (1974) *A Mental Health Program for Kindergarten Children.* Department of Mental Health Sciences, Hahnemann Medical College, Philadelphia, PA.

Shure M.B. & Spivack G. (1978) *Problem-Solving Techniques in Child Rearing.* Jossey-Bass, San Francisco, CA.

Shure M.B. & Spivack G. (1979) Interpersonal cognitive problem-solving and primary prevention: programming for pre-school and kindergarten children. *Journal of Clinical Child Psychology*, **2**, 89–94.

Shure M.B. & Spivack G. (1980) Interpersonal problem-solving as a mediator of behavioral adjustment in pre-school and kindergarten children. *Journal of Applied Developmental Psychology*, **1**, 29–44.

Spivack G., Platt J. & Shure M.B. (1976) *The Problem-Solving Approach to Adjustment*. Jossey-Bass, San Francisco, CA.

Spivack G. & Shure M.B. (1974) *Social Adjustment of Young Children: A Cognitive Approach to Solving Real-life Problems*. Jossey-Bass, San Francisco, CA.

Strain P.S. & Fox J.J. (1981) Peer social initiations and the modification of social withdrawal: a review and future perspective. *Journal of Pediatric Psychology*, **6**, 417–433.

Suomi S.J. (1980) Peers, play, and primary prevention in primates. In: Kent M.W. & Rolf J.E. (eds) *Primary Prevention of Psychopathology, III: Social Competence in Children*, pp. 127–149. University Press of New England, Hanover, NH.

Urbain E.S. (1980) Interpersonal problem-solving training and social perspective-taking training with impulsive children via modeling, role-play, and self-instruction. Doctoral dissertation, University of Minnesota, MN.

Urbain E.S. & Kendall P.C. (1980) Review of social-cognitive problem-solving interventions with children. *Psychological Bulletin*, **88**, 109–143.

Vaughn S.R. & Ridley C.A. (1983) A preschool interpersonal problem solving program: does it affect behavior in the classroom? *Child Study Journal*, **13**, 1–12.

Wallas G. (1926) *The Art of Thought*. Watts, London.

Wasserman T.H. (1983) The effects of cognitive development on the use of cognitive behavioral techniques with children. *Child Family Therapy*, **5**, 37–50.

Weissberg R.P. (1985) Designing effective social problem solving for the classroom. In: Schneider B., Rubin K. & Ledingham J. (eds) *Children's Peer Relations: Issues in Assessment and Intervention*, pp. 225–242. Springer-Verlag, New York.

Weissberg R.P. (1989) Challenges inherent in translating theory and basic research into effective social competence promotion programs. In: Schneider B., Atilli G., Nadel J. & Weissberg R. (eds) *Social Competence in Developmental Perspective*, pp. 313–331. Kluwer International Publishers, Dordrecht, Netherlands.

Weissberg R.P. (1990) Support for school-based social competence promotion. *American Psychology*, **xx**, 986–988.

Weissberg R.P., Gesten E.L., Rapkin B.D., Cowen E.L., Davidson E., Flores De Apodaca R. & McKim B. (1981) Evaluation of a social problem-solving training program for suburban and inner-city third-grade children. *Journal of Consulting and Clinical Psychology*, **49**, 251–261.

Winer J.I., Hilpert P.L., Gesten E.L., Cowen E.L. & Shubin W.E. (1982) The evaluation of a kindergarten social problem-solving program. *Journal of Primary Prevention*, **2**, 205–216.

Youniss J. (1975) Another perspective on social cognition. In: Pick A.D. (ed) *Minnesota Symposia on Child Psychology*, vol. 9, pp. 173–193. University of Minnesota Press, Minneapolis, MN.

Youniss J. (1980) *Parents and Peers in Social Development*. University of Chicago Press, Chicago, IL.

Chapter 49
Cognitive-Behavioural Therapies

Philip C. Kendall & John Lochman

Cognitive-behavioural approaches can be described as a rational amalgam: a purposeful attempt to preserve the demonstrated positive effects of behavioural therapy within a less doctrinaire context and to incorporate the cognitive activities of the client into the efforts to produce therapeutic change (Kendall & Hollon, 1979). Accordingly, cognitive-behavioural strategies with children and adolescents include behavioural performance-based procedures as well as cognitive interventions to produce changes in thinking, feeling and behaviour (Kendall, 1991a). The cognitive-behavioural analyses of child and adolescent disorders and adjustment problems, as well as related analyses of treatment-produced gains, include considerations of the child's internal and external environment and represent an effort to integrate behaviourism with cognitive therapy (Meichenbaum, 1977). The model places greatest emphasis on the learning process and the influence of the contingencies and models in the environment while recognizing the importance of the individual's cognitive style in the development and remedying of psychological distress. Cognitive-behavioural therapies do not insult the role of affect and the social context. Rather, they integrate cognitive, behavioural, affective, social and contextual strategies for change. The cognitive-behavioural model includes the relationships of cognition and behaviour to the affective state of the organism and the functioning of the organism in the larger social context.

THE THERAPEUTIC ATTITUDE

We can describe the attitude (or mental posture) of the cognitive-behavioural therapist working with children and adolescents using the terms consultant, diagnostician and educator.

As consultant, the therapist is a person who does *not* have all the answers, but one who has some ideas worthy of trying out and some ways to examine whether or not the ideas have value for the individual client. Telling a child and/or adolescent exactly what to do is not the idea; giving the client an opportunity to try something and helping him or her to make sense of the experience is the idea. The therapist as consultant strives to develop skills in the client that include thinking on his or her own and moving towards independent, mature problem-solving. The youngster and therapist interact in a collaborative problem-solving manner. When the client asks: 'Well, what am I supposed to do?' the therapist might reply: 'Let's see, what do you want to accomplish here?' and then 'What are our options?' or 'What's another way we could look at this problem?' The exchange is geared towards facilitating the process of problem-solving.

The mental attitude associated with diagnostician is one of going beyond the verbal report and/or behaviour of the client and his or her significant others. The diagnostician integrates data and, judging against a background of knowledge of psychopathology, normal development and psychologically healthy environments, makes meaningful decisions. Mental health professionals cannot let others tell us what is wrong and what needs to be fixed when we are working with children and adolescents with psychological problems. That a parent or teacher says that a child is hyperactive is not sufficient to initiate a medication regime and/or a cognitive-behavioural therapy. The fact that a parent or teacher suspects hyperactivity is one piece of useful information, but there are alternative hypotheses that must be considered. For example, the child's behaviour may be within normal limits but appearing as troubled when judged against inappropriate parental (or teacher) expectations about child behaviour. There is also the possibility of alternative disorders; hyperactivity may be the term used by the referring adults, but aggressive noncompliance may be a better description in terms of mental health professionals' concepts. A dysfunctional family interaction pattern may need the greatest attention, not the child *per se*. In a nutshell, the cognitive-behavioural therapist, as is true of competent clinicians of several theoretical orientations, serves as a diagnostician by taking into account the various sources of information and, judging against a background of knowledge, determines the nature of the problem and the optimal strategy for its treatment.

Lastly, the therapeutic attitude of cognitive-behaviour therapists is as an educator: the term educator communicates that we are talking about interventions for learning behaviour control, cognitive skills, and emotional development, and we are talking about optimal ways to communicate to help someone to learn. A good educator stimulates the students to think — to think for themselves. An active and involved educator is a good therapist. Importantly, a good educator observes the student and helps to maximize strengths while reducing hindrances. Individualized attention means that individuals can and should do things differently. A good educator pays attention to what the learner is saying to himself or herself, as this internal dialogue can be interfering with performance. An effective therapist, just as an effective teacher, is involved in the process.

The mental attitude of the cognitive-behavioural therapist working with children and adolescents is one that has a collaborative quality (therapist as consultant), integrates and decodes information (therapist as diagnostician) and teaches through experiences with involvement (therapist as educator). A high-quality intervention is one that alters how the client makes sense of experiences and the way the client will behave in the future.

Building a 'coping' template

Cognitive-behavioural theorists have promoted the notion that individuals perceive and make sense of the world through their cognitive structures, also referred to as schema. Such a template has an influence on what is perceived and how it is processed and understood. Children and adolescents are in the process of developing ways to view their world, so cognitive-behavioural therapists use shared experiences to help youth reconceptualize problems into situations requiring coping. That is, the treatment goal is for the child to develop a new cognitive structure, or a modified existing structure — a schema for coping — through which he or she can now look at formerly distressing situations. Therapy helps to reduce the support for dysfunctional schemas and construct a new schema, through which the child can identify and solve problems. An effective intervention capitalizes on creating behavioural experiences with emotional involvement, while paying attention to the cognitive activities of the participant. The therapist guides both the youngster's attributions about prior behaviour and his or her expectations for future behaviour. Thus, the youngster can acquire a cognitive structure for future events that include the adaptive skills and appropriate cognition associated with adaptive functioning. The child's acquisition and use of a coping template is a major goal of the treatment — a goal that requires combining many skills taught to the child and the therapist's use of several treatment strategies.

Areas of application

Cognitive-behavioural approaches to interventions for children and adolescents have been applied in a variety of areas (Kendall, 1991a). The present coverage will provide a selective review of applications and their outcomes across four areas: (1) anger and aggression; (2) attention deficit disorder with hyperactivity (ADDH); (3) anxiety; and (4) depression. In each of these areas our review will describe the nature of the disorder, including the cognitive and behavioural features of the disorder, components of the intervention and illustrative outcomes.

Anger and aggression

While aggressive and oppositional behaviours are relatively common in mild forms during early childhood, aggressive behaviours become clinically significant if they occur with high frequency or intensity, or if the behaviour occurs in multiple settings (e.g. home and school; see Loeber & Dishion, 1983; also Chapter 18). Clinically significant aggressive behaviour occurs in 5–10% of children, with boys outnumbering girls by about 3:1 (Quay, 1986; Kazdin, 1987; see also Pepler & Rubin, 1991). Physical and verbal aggression are important symptoms of the disruptive behaviour disorders (especially oppositional defiant disorder and conduct disorder) but they are present in children and adolescents with a variety of disorders (e.g. ADDH, dysthymic disorder). Clinical concern has focused on children with aggressive behaviour because of the substantial stability of aggressive behaviour over time (Olweus, 1979; Huesmann *et al.*, 1984), and because childhood aggressive behaviour has emerged as a significant risk marker for subsequent substance abuse, delinquency and school failure (Lochman *et al.*, 1990; Coie *et al.*, 1991).

Research in the last decade has documented a range of *social-cognitive* distortions and deficiencies (Kendall, 1985, 1991b) which are present in aggressive children. Consistent with Dodge's (1985, 1986) information-processing model, aggressive children have been found to recall high rates of hostile cues present in social stimuli (Milich & Dodge, 1984; Dodge *et al.*, 1986), to attend to few cues when interpreting the meaning of others' behaviour (Dodge & Newman, 1981), to attribute others' behaviour in ambiguous situations to their hostile intentions (Dodge *et al.*, 1986, 1990), to under-perceive their own level of aggressiveness and their responsibility for early stages of dyadic conflict (Lochman, 1987), and to generate fewer verbal assertion solutions and more action-oriented and aggressive solutions to social problems (Richard & Dodge, 1982; Asarnow & Callan, 1985; Lochman & Lampron, 1986). These results suggest that aggressive children are hypervigilant in scanning their social environment for hostile cues, and that their tendencies to perceive hostile intentions in others' behaviour leads them to respond in a nonverbal, action-oriented manner. This set of social-cognitive dysfunctions has been found to be more evident in reactive-aggressive children than in proactive-aggressive children (Dodge & Coie, 1987).

Other cognitive operations, schemas and appraisal processes that have been conceptualized as influencing moment-to-moment information-processing in aggressive children have been investigated. Aggressive children have an unusual pattern of affect-labelling (Garrison & Stolberg, 1983), as they anticipate that they will have fewer feelings of fear or sadness in difficult social situations. When they suddenly experience these vulnerable internal states, aggressive children are likely to be ill-prepared to cope in a competent manner, and they are apt to label the generalized arousal as anger. Provocation-induced arousal has been found to produce progressively more action-oriented responses in aggressive children (Gordon *et al.*, 1986). Aggressive children's type of cognitive operations has also been found to influence their problem-solving. When aggressive children respond to social conflicts in a deliberate rather than automatic manner they generate higher rates of competent, assertive solutions (Lochman *et al.*, 1989; Rabiner *et al.*, 1990). This indicates that the tendency for preadolescent aggressive children to think of nonverbal action-oriented solutions is due in part to their retrieval of highly salient solutions from memory when they used quick, automatic processing of social events rather than using deliberate memory retrieval strategies.

Cognitive schemas such as outcome expectations and social goals are another source of influence on attributions and problem-solving. Aggressive children expect that an aggressive solution will reduce aversive reactions from others and allow them to acquire tangible positive outcomes (Perry *et al.*, 1986), and an aggressive adolescent believes that aggressive behaviour will enhance self-esteem, avoid a negative image and would not cause victims to suffer (Slaby & Guerra, 1988). In a study of outcome values, Boldizar *et al.* (1989) found that aggressive children placed more value on controlling the victim, and less value on victims suffering, victim retaliation, peer rejection and negative self-evaluation. Similarly, Lochman *et al.* (1991a) have found that aggressive boys value social goals of dominance and revenge more, and a social goal of affiliation less, than do nonaggressive boys. While the aggressive and nonaggressive adolescents in this study did not have differences in the content of their problem-solving in general, aggressive boys' problem solutions were more aggressive and involved less bargaining when their solutions to achieve their main social goal were examined.

Collectively, these findings provide an empirical focus for cognitive-behavioural interventions with aggressive children. In addition to addressing children's attributional processes and problem solutions, cognitive-behavioural programmes should assess and intervene with children's affect-labelling, and their pervasive cognitive schemas for social goals and outcome expectations, and should reinforce the salience of more competent solutions which are quickly retrieved from their 'memory bins' when the children respond quickly and automatically. To address these distortions and deficiencies cognitive-behavioural intervention programmes use a combination of treatment components, including self-monitoring, self-instruction, perspective-taking, social problem-solving, affect-labelling and relaxation (Lochman *et al.*, 1991a).

Self-monitoring and self-instruction components assist children in accurately monitoring their arousal state, labelling the arousal as coexisting with an appropriate emotional state, recognizing situations that typically provoke intense feelings of anger and frustration, and using inhibitory self-instructions (e.g. 'Stop! Think! What can I do?') to slow down the automaticity of their response, permitting more deliberate memory retrieval processes to occur. Social perspective-taking components focus on helping children to be more aware of nonhostile cues in social situations, and to become aware of the variety of intentions that peers and adults might have in ambiguous social situations (e.g. when peers are 'scolding'

with you; when somebody bumps you or cuts in front of you; when a peer does not respond to your questions). Social problem-solving training (see Chapter 48) is a core element in most cognitive-behavioural interventions and involves assisting children in thinking of a wider array of possible solutions to perceived social provocations, with particular emphasis on verbal assertion, bargaining and compromise solutions and on competent enactment of selected solutions.

Research on immediate posttreatment and follow-up effects has indicated that cognitive-behavioural therapy is a promising form of treatment and secondary prevention of conduct and oppositional disorders (Kazdin, 1987). Using a 20-session problem-solving skills training programme (PSST: a combination of the Spivack & Shure, 1974 and Kendall & Braswell, 1985, programmes) with psychiatric inpatient children, Kazdin *et al.* (1987b) found that PSST produced a significant reduction in parents' and teachers' ratings of aggressive behaviour at posttesting and at a 1-year follow-up. These results have been replicated in a study combining PSST with parent behavioural management training with inpatient children (Kazdin *et al.*, 1987a), and in a study with antisocial children treated in outpatient and inpatient settings (Kazdin *et al.*, 1989). Positive treatment effects for cognitive-behavioural therapy have also been found with day-hospital conduct disorder children (Kendall *et al.*, 1990a, 1991) and with hospitalized aggressive adolescents (Feindler *et al.*, 1986). Treatment and client characteristics predictive of outcome have been examined in a series of studies with a 12–18-session school-based anger coping programme. Reductions in independently observed disruptive classroom behaviour and in parents' ratings of aggressive behaviour and improvements in self-esteem were enhanced when the cognitive-behavioural anger coping programme was augmented with a behavioural goal setting component (Lochman *et al.*, 1984) and when the programme was lengthened to include 18 weekly group sessions (Lochman, 1985). Teacher consultation (Lochman *et al.*, 1989) and nonsocial self-instructional training (Lochman & Curry, 1986) have not augmented the significant intervention effects. Aggressive boys who initially had the poorest problem-solving skills have been found to have the greatest behavioural improvement after the anger coping programme (Lochman *et al.*, 1985). In a 3-year follow-up study, aggressive boys treated in the anger coping programme maintained significant improvements in self-esteem and social problem-solving skills, and had a markedly lower substance use rate (Lochman, 1991) in comparison to untreated aggressive boys. In summary, these studies have documented positive intervention effects across home and school settings posttreatment, and at least partial maintenance of treatment gains at 1–3-year follow-ups.

Attention deficit disorder with hyperactivity

Currently, the diagnostic category of ADDH reflects a conceptualization in which motor and cognitive components coexist (see Chapter 17). ADDH involves heightened motor activity, impulsivity, deficits in attention and deficits in rule-governed behaviour (Barkley, 1990). In addition to the cognitive and behavioural components, ADDH may involve an association with conduct problems and aggression (Prinz *et al.*, 1981; Hinshaw, 1987).

The multifaceted nature of ADDH has implications for determining the type of treatment to follow. For instance, treatment that produces positive effects in one symptom area may not impact on functioning in another area. The most widely used treatment approach in the US is stimulant medication. This has been shown to reduce motor activity, aggression and noncompliance, as well as produce improvements in relationships with mothers, peers and teachers (Humphries *et al.*, 1978; Barkley & Cunningham, 1979, 1980; Whalen *et al.*, 1980, 1981; Barkley *et al.*, 1984; Whalen *et al.*, 1987). The appeal of stimulant medication lies in the relatively rapid behaviour improvements that it produces.

Despite the apparent effectiveness of medication in addressing facets of ADDH, this treatment approach remains controversial. Opponents question the ethics of giving children drugs, arguing that medication is being relied upon to control children's behaviour. The long-term efficacy of the treatment is in question: children often return to their pretreatment levels of functioning when medication is removed, suggesting that they have failed to learn skills related to enduring patterns of improved behaviour. Also, medication is not considered to be effective before the age of 4.

Reacting to the negative factors associated with medication, researchers and clinicians have sought alternative treatments (e.g. behaviour modification, cognitive-behavioural treatment and parent training). Broadly speaking, research on alternative treatments has involved both examining their efficacy independently of medication and in combination with medication.

Next to stimulant medication, behaviour modification has emerged as the most effective alternative or adjunctive treatment for ADDH. The appeal is several-fold. Firstly, unlike the criticism of stimulant medication that it fails to teach new ways of behaving, new behaviour is the target of behaviour modification. Also, some children simply do not respond to medication and some have parents who do not want to have their children on medication. Parents may also face the problem of disruptive behaviour in the home because the medication may not be administered in the evening hours due to its negative effects on sleep. When parents are involved in behaviour modification, they gain skills in coping with their child's behaviour.

Numerous studies have examined the effectiveness of behavioural modification in treating hyperactive children and several reviews of the research are available (Barkley, 1990). Studies include the examination of behaviour modification with and without the administration of stimulant drugs and thus address both the individual and additive effects of the different treatments. Opinion varies as to which is the primary treatment and which is a satisfactory adjunct or alternative. One suggestion has been that a combined use of medication and behaviour modification may provide the opportunity for the child's disruptive behaviour to be reduced initially and his or her attention enhanced via medication so that learning may occur from the behaviour modification; however, Gittelman *et al.* (1980) found that combined treatment and drug treatment alone did not differ significantly from one another; both treatment behaviour conditions markedly reduced impulsive, disruptive and inattentive classroom behaviours.

Although parents are often involved in the behaviour modification programmes for their children, parent management programmes offer a form of behaviour modification that specifically helps parents to gain parenting skills; as Weiss and Hechtman (1986) note, these broad-based programmes have the added benefit of enhancing the family atmosphere as siblings come to benefit from the improved parenting skills, parents gain a sense of self-esteem in being able to manage their children's behaviour more effectively, and marital tensions stemming from the frustrations of the child's disruptive behaviour drop.

With its attention to cognitive processes (e.g. problem-solving, anticipation of the consequences of actions), as well as observable behaviour, cognitive-behaviour therapy (CBT) appeared particularly well-suited to the problems of the ADDH child, many of which have been linked to deficits in cognitive processing. However, the data suggest that while cognitive-behavioural training can reduce impulsivity, it has not been uniformly found to rectify all features of ADDH. Kendall and Braswell's (1985) programme for treating impulsivity (see training tasks in the *Stop and Think Workbook*: Kendall, 1992) provides an illustration of an integrated cognitive-behavioural approach. Included in the programme are reward and response−cost contingencies, self-instructional training, coping modelling and role-plays under conditions of emotional arousal. Self-instruction training (Meichenbaum & Goodman, 1971) can be said to address the cognitive deficits associated with poor problem-solving (both social and nonsocial) in ADDH children. The goal of treatment is to help the child internalize the steps involved in problem-solving — recognizing the problem, reflecting on solutions, making a decision and taking action.

Despite the promising results with impulsive children and the apparent theoretical match of CBT with symptoms of ADDH, the effectiveness of CBT as a treatment of ADDH has remained relatively inconsistent. Although some studies have shown promising results (Douglas *et al.*, 1976; Cameron & Robinson, 1980), others have failed to show the positive impact of CBT (Brown *et al.*, 1985; Whalen *et al.*, 1985; Hinshaw & Erhardt, 1991; see Abikoff, 1987, for a review).

Research has also considered the effectiveness of certain versions of cognitive-behavioural treatment in combination with medication. Results of several studies, however (Abikoff & Gittelman, 1985; Brown *et al.*, 1985; Abikoff *et al.*, 1988) did not show CBT to be as effective as medication or providing an enhancing effect over medication when the two treatments were combined. These results suggest that the authors' cognitive-behavioural programme produced limited effects.

However, in considering these results it may be important to recognize that the form of CBT treatment used varies substantially across studies. For instance, Kendall and Reber (1987) noted that the CBT used by Abikoff and Gittleman (1985) did not include the full behavioural component of contingent reinforcement/response—cost for learning the problem-solving skills. Related to this situation, suggestions for the refinement in both the assessment of children's functioning and treatment approaches have emerged. More specifically, Abikoff (1987) argued that effective CBT will require understanding the specific nature of the child's problems, accompanied by a more tailored application of the various components of CBT to the particular child's needs. In a similar vein, Whalen *et al.* (1985) noted that different situations (e.g. academic versus social) may require different cognitive strategies, with the former creating a situation where the task demands are much more clear-cut than the latter, which may involve such variables as inconsistent or ambiguous feedback about the child's behaviour.

In concluding their review, Hinshaw and Erhardt (1991) noted that increasing the effectiveness of CBT may involve more thoroughly balancing cognitive and behavioural components. Due to the variety of components included in CBT packages, treatment may overemphasize the self-instructional aspect without including behavioural elements such as response—cost and other contingency management components. This external structure may be essential for effectively working with ADDH children. Also, it should be noted that contemporary applications of CBT place a greater emphasis on the role of the family in programme implementation (Braswell, 1991; Braswell & Bloomquist, 1991).

Anxiety disorders

Anxiety itself can be a normal and adaptive response to a variety of situations. The ability to recognize and avoid harm and threat is a necessary component of a child's repertoire. Most childhood fears are transitory, emerge in the course of encounters with new challenges and are resolved through facing these demands. In contrast to normal anxious reactions, fears/anxieties that are excessive, that occur beyond the developmental timetable and/or disrupt the child's life are considered maladaptive (see Chapter 20). Although fear is a discrete response to a circumscribed threat, and phobias are severe fears involving persistent behavioural avoidance (Miller *et al.*, 1974; Morris & Kratochwill, 1983; Barrios & Hartmann, 1988), anxiety is more diffuse both in stimulus and response and is more long-standing and disruptive than an isolated fear or phobia (Morris & Kratochwill, 1983; Kendall *et al.*, 1992).

Separation anxiety provides a clear illustration of the contrast between normal and pathological forms of anxiety. Anxiety about separation involves a child being distressed when apart from caregivers: school and social activities are often avoided in order to maintain contact with caregivers (see also Campbell, 1986). Separation anxiety appears naturally and recedes in early childhood and is characterized by the child's protests at times of separation or in anticipation of separation. In contrast, when separation anxiety occurs in a 9- or 10-year-old, this signals a maladaptive anxiety past the developmental timetable, and though it may spring from a child's somewhat realistic concerns about a parent (e.g. in cases of parent conflict), this signals the need for intervention in the child's world to rectify the anxiety provocation.

Clinicians and researchers view childhood anxiety as a multidimensional construct manifested at physiological, behavioural and cognitive levels. Common motor components of anxiety responses include, most prominently, avoidance, as well as shaky voice, rigid posture, crying, nail-biting and thumb-sucking (Barrios & Hartmann, 1988). Physiological reactions include an increase in automatic nervous activity, perspiration, diffuse abdominal pain ('butterflies in the stomach'), flushed face, urgent need to urinate, trembling and gastrointestinal distress (see also Barrios & Hartmann, 1988). The physiological assessment of anxiety in adults has received wide attention (see Himaldi *et al.*, 1985), yet few empirical data on these indicators in children exist (Barrios & Hartmann, 1988; Beidel, 1988), even though these are considered a promising area of research (Barrios *et al.*, 1981; Miller, 1983). An exception is a study by Beidel (1988) where significant differences in autonomic activity were found in anxious children compared with nonanxious controls during a test-taking task. Overall, test-anxious children had significantly higher heart rates than nonanxious controls; however, no differences were found in systolic or diastolic blood pressure. Such results confirm cautions by some (Haynes, 1978) who advocate monitoring more than one physiological indicator, because concurrent indicators may not correlate.

A variety of anxious children's thoughts have been described; these include thoughts of being scared or hurt, self-critical thoughts or thoughts of danger (Barrios & Hartmann, 1988). However, until recently, little empirical work has examined cognitions in clinically anxious children. Francis (1988), in her review of cognitions of anxious children, concluded that: 'no definitive statements about the cognitions of anxious children can be made' (p. 276). Studies using nonclinical samples on circumscribed fears, such as test anxiety (Prins, 1985), have found that high anxiety is associated with negative self-referent cognitions. Examples include: 'I'm going to mess up' and 'I'm going to get hurt again'.

In terms of information-processing, anxious children evidence a distortion or bias: the individual attends to social or environmental cues, but does so in a distorted and dysfunctional manner. Anxious children, for example, seem preoccupied with concerns about evaluations by self and others and the likelihood of severe negative consequences. They seem to misperceive characteristically the demands of the environment and routinely add stress to a variety of situations.

Although the treatment of adult anxiety disorders has received much research attention (Michelson & Ascher, 1987; Barlow, 1988; Kendall & Watson, 1989), the literature on treating child anxiety disorders has been negligible. The cognitive-behavioural treatment of adult panic disorder, for example, has generated empirical support and widespread application (Clark, 1986; Barlow, 1988). As with many treatment efforts, strategies that have proven useful for adults serve as the building blocks in child interventions; with the addition of age-specific intervention materials such as the *Coping Cat Workbook* (Kendall, 1990). In this section we present a brief selection of the treatment components employed in the treatment of anxiety disorders with children. The techniques are presented separately for clarity; however, there is increasing recognition that a combination of strategies is most efficacious (King & Ollendick, 1989; Kendall *et al.*, 1992). Combining strategies is consistent with the multicomponent conceptualization of anxiety: cognitive, behavioural and physiological response pathways. Successful treatment of anxiety addresses each pathway and works towards intercomponent awareness, communication and control. For example, a child who gets stomachaches when anxious would be helped to tune in to his or her stomach as a 'first alert'. Next, the child would need to translate this physiological sensation into a cognitive message: 'My stomach hurts, I must be getting nervous'. At this point, the child would want to control or attenuate the anxiety by problem-solving strategies such as: 'I need to take deep breaths and relax' or; 'I'd better ask what to do because I'm confused'.

Physiological arousal accompanies anxious cognition, thus methods that help identify children's physiological symptoms and teach them methods to reduce the arousal are often employed. Relaxation training is useful in this regard, with scripts available to the child's developmental level (Koeppen, 1974; Ollendick & Cerny, 1981). Often the combination of progressive muscle relaxation, deep breathing and cognitive imagery is used. There are several examples of use of relaxation training with circumscribed anxiety such as test anxiety (Richter, 1984). It remains unclear whether relaxation alone is helpful for anxiety-disordered children. Major concerns include overall age-appropriateness and the question of how well relaxation strategies generalize.

Relaxation training, as well as establishing a fear hierarchy and pairing relaxation with fearful situations, comprises systematic desensitization. The underlying principle in systematic desensitization is the pairing of two incompatible emotional states — fear and relaxation (see Chapter 50). A critical element of desensitization is the hierarchical presentation of feared situations. Beginning with the least threatening situation and building on success experiences allows the child to progress to more frightening situations. Although there is a substantial literature supporting the efficacy of systematic desensitization with children, most studies used nonclinical subjects with circumscribed fears such as speech anxiety, test-anxiety or dog phobia (Deffenbacher & Kemper, 1974): efficacy with more generalized, pervasive fears is not known.

Morris and Kratochwill (1991) suggested that some children may be unable to grasp the idea of an anxiety hierarchy and the clinician may need to accommodate this possibility. They suggested that systematic desensitization may not be the optimal treatment for children under age 9 as they may have difficulty using visual imagery, following instructions and constructing a hierarchy. Nevertheless, systematic desensitization remains one of the often used methods to remedy children's fears.

Modelling involves the demonstration of the desired coping behaviours in a feared or stressful situation such that they can be subsequently imitated by the child. Feedback and reinforcement can be used to maintain the desired behaviours (Ollendick & Francis, 1988). Modelling can be accomplished by having a child observe live or symbolic (video-taped) models, or participating with a live model. Ollendick (1979) suggested that not all modelling experiences are equally powerful: he noted that the more involved the modelling, the more effective the outcome. Using opportunities for the therapist to serve as a coping model for the child has been found to be an effective and powerful therapeutic tool when working with anxiety-disordered children (Kendall *et al.*, 1992). As a coping model, the therapist self-discloses feared situations that are pertinent to the child's difficulties, describes his or her feelings with one situation, shares whether he or she would feel the same or different in the same situation, and models a strategy for coping with one unwanted arousal. A second and perhaps more compelling instance of coping modelling is the shared experience that actually occurs during a session. For example, a therapist locks him- or herself out of his or her office and shows anxiety as a result. Anxious children are surprised that competent adults get nervous. Then, the therapist verbalizes his or her self-talk during these moments such that the child can see how one moves from anxiety to problem-solving to resolutions.

Because practice is essential to most learning, role-plays provide excellent opportunities to try out a variety of coping strategies. The therapist can be active in setting the scene, providing the appropriate amount of concrete detail to engage the child and assisting in creating the scene as authentically as possible. Particularly with younger children who may be less able to identify the precipitating events in their anxious reactions, role-plays can be used to help the therapist notice when the child begins to become distressed.

Cognitive models of psychopathology highlight the impact of maladaptive thinking (e.g. distortions) on maladaptive behaviour, and stress interventions that address the faulty cognitive processing. Self-talk, what we say to ourselves as we make sense of our experience, has been implicated in anxiety (Kendall & Hollon, 1989). For example, an anxious child's self-talk prior to an evaluation may include; 'Oh my gosh, I'm going to run out of time, I'm going to fail and my parents will kill me'. The goal of cognitive interventions is to build a new (or elaborate on an existing) coping template. Building a coping template involves disputing or correcting the characteristic misinterpretation and looking at the events through the alternative template (based on coping).

Problem-solving (Spivack & Shure, 1974; D'Zurilla, 1986; Kendall & Siqueland, 1989), has applications for many different child disorders. Features of problem-solving interventions include problem identification and successive stages of problem definition and formulation, generation of alternative solutions, choice of desired strategy, implementation and evaluation (see Kendall & Siqueland, 1989 for elaboration with youthful clients; see also Chapter 48). Problem-solving skills provide the underlying model for utilizing available coping actions.

In a controlled comparative study, Kanfer et al. (1975) taught children with nighttime fears either positive self-talk, such as: 'I am a brave child. I can take care of myself in the dark, or stimulus-oriented self-talk, e.g. 'There are many good things in the dark. The dark is a fun place to be'. A third group repeated a nursery rhyme as a control. In terms of the amount of time a child could stay in a dark room, the results suggested both active treatments significantly increased the duration of staying alone as compared with the control-group children. Altering self-talk had a positive impact on anxiety.

A second area where cognitive and behavioural interventions have been applied pertains to children facing medical or dental procedures. Although a child facing a bone marrow transplant, chemotherapy or painful dental procedures has a reality-based distress, efforts to increase the coping armamentarium of these children have been successful. Also, they provide guidelines as to what interventions are most helpful to children in other stressful situations. Peterson and her colleagues (Siegel & Peterson, 1980; Peterson & Shigetomi, 1981) demonstrated that children equipped with coping strategies, as compared with either educational information or no preparation, were less anxious, more cooperative and had lower pulse rates (Siegel & Peterson, 1980). Children who received a combination of coping and modelling were even better able to cope with their medical procedure — tonsillectomy (Peterson & Shigetomi, 1981).

In one of the few investigations of an integrated cognitive-behavioural treatment for children with diagnosed anxiety disorders, Kane and Kendall (1989) reported meaningful improvements. Specifically, using a multiple-baseline design with 4 subjects diagnosed as overanxious disorder, reductions in anxiety, as reported by child, parents and an independent diagnostician, were found. These changes showed significant improvements from pretreatment assessment, and returned the child to scores within the normal range as expected from normative data (see Kendall & Grove, 1988, for a discussion of the method of normative comparisons).

In a randomized clinical trial conducted at Temple University, anxiety-disordered young people were assigned to either a treatment or a wait-list condition. Children receiving therapy were taught a variety of strategies, including relaxation, imagery, problem-solving and modification of self-talk. These strategies enabled the child to change the fearful, threat template into one that sees anxiety-provoking situations as situations that can be managed (Kendall, 1989). The active treatment integrates cognitive strategies, such as modifying anxious self-talk and problem-solving, with behavioural strategies of relaxation, exposure, evaluation and reward. These strategies were put into practice in graduated imagined and in vivo exposure opportunities. At posttreatment assessment,

self-report measures (e.g. Revised Children's Manifest Anxiety Scale (RCMAS), State—Trait Anxiety Inventory for Children (STAIC-T), and Children's Depression Inventory (CDI)) for treated subjects evidenced significant reductions in pathological responses and were often within normative ranges. Children's self-rated coping (Coping Questionnaire) was also found to be significantly higher. Parents' reports on the Child Behavior Checklist (CBCL) and on a modified version of the STAIC (completed by the parent) also evidenced significant reductions in reports of anxiety in their children. Diagnoses based on a structured interview were compared from pretreatment to posttreatment: using the parents' diagnostic interview data, 60% of the treated cases had no diagnosis at posttreatment, while only 7% of the wait-list condition showed such a change (Kendall et al., 1992). These findings support the use of cognitive-behavioural treatment for anxiety disorders in young people. After treatment, disordered children were not distinguishable on many dimensions from a nondisturbed reference group — a convincing demonstration of this approach's therapeutic efficacy.

Depression

An emerging area of cognitive-behavioural specialization has been with depressed children and adolescents. Depression is a relatively common mood state, with 40% of 14- and 15-year-olds in the Isle of Wight study reporting feelings of misery and depression (Rutter et al., 1970). As with many areas of developmental psychopathology, some controversy exists about when the classification of affective disorders such as dysthymia and major depressive disorder begin on this continuously distributed set of symptoms (Kendall et al., 1989; see also Chapter 19). Consistent age and gender effects have been noted on depressive symptomatology (Kazdin, 1989), with no sex differences evident in childhood, but with females having a higher rate of adolescent depression than males, and with increases in the ratio of depressive disorders going from childhood to adolescence. Depressive disorders may be combined with anxiety (Brady & Kendall, 1992) and conduct disorders (Kazdin, 1989), and it is important to determine if the depressive symptoms preceded the conduct disorder symptoms, or if the depression followed from the consequences of the conduct disorder problems. Although major depressive disorder includes a more severe set of symptoms, it is not as stable over time as dysthymic disorder. The mean duration of major depressive disorder has been found to be only 32 weeks, with a 92% recovery rate for children 1½ years later (Kovacs et al., 1984). Children who had an earlier onset of their depressive symptoms had a more stable, chronic course for their depressive disorder.

Research on the cognitive characteristics of depressed children and adolescents has found distortions in attributions, self-evaluation and perceptions of past and present events (Rehm & Carter, 1990). In a study of preadolescent children, Kaslow et al. (1988) found that depressed clinic children had more depressogenic attributions than nondepressed clinic children and nonclinic children, since their causal attributions for positive and negative events were similar. Depressed children have a more external locus of control (Mullins *et al.*, 1985), indicating that they feel less capable of obtaining valued consequences through their own behaviour. While these studies did not report attributions separately for positive and negative events, Curry and Craighead (1990) did so with an adolescent inpatient sample. Adolescents with greater depression attributed the cause of positive events to external, unstable and specific causes, consistent with previous findings that adolescents experience more anhedonia. Attributions for positive events were more closely associated with depression than were attributions for negative events. The relationship between attributions and depression has been found only for currently depressed inpatient children and not for children with resolved depression (McCauley *et al.*, 1986).

Depressed children have low levels of self-esteem and low perceived academic competence and social competence (Kaslow *et al.*, 1984; Asarnow *et al.*, 1987). Kaslow *et al.* (1984) examined the nature of these self-evaluation difficulties on a design-copying task, and found depressed children gave more self-punishment and set more stringent scores for poor scores. These depressed children were particularly concerned about not doing well on the task. The low self-evaluations of depressed children also seem to produce distorted perceptions of past and present events (Haley *et al.*, 1985; Rehm & Carter, 1990). Depressed children in the fifth to eighth grades displayed a variety of cognitive errors, including over-generalizing their predictions of negative outcomes, catastrophizing the consequences of negative events, incorrectly taking personal responsibility for negative outcomes and selectively attending to negative features of an event (Leitenberg *et al.*, 1986; Kendall *et al.*, 1990b). In addition to these biased appraisal processes, depressed children have also displayed problem-solving deficits in some studies, with low rates of impersonal problem-solving (Mullins *et al.*, 1985) and a high rate of depressogenic strategies (Asarnow *et al.*, 1987).

Cognitive-behavioural treatment programmes have been developed to address the cognitive distortions seen in depressed children. The treatment components contained in these interventions include: (1) self-control skills involving self-consequation (reinforcing themselves more, punishing themselves less), self-monitoring (paying attention to positive things they do), self-evaluation (setting less perfectionistic standards for their performance) and assertiveness training; (2) social skills, including methods of initiating interactions, maintaining interactions, handling conflict and using relaxation and imagery; and (3) cognitive restructuring, involving confronting children about the lack of evidence for their distorted perceptions (Stark *et al.*, 1991).

Although little research has yet to be reported on the posttreatment effects of cognitive-behavioural therapy with depressed children, a few reports have provided some indication of the potential efficacy of select procedures (Kazdin, 1989; Stark *et al.*, 1991). For example, Reynolds and Coats (1986) compared a cognitive-behavioural intervention and a relaxation intervention to a wait-list control condition. Thirty moderately depressed adolescents were randomly assigned to the three conditions. The two interventions were applied twice weekly for 5 weeks. Both the cognitive-behavioural and the relaxation training interventions produced significant reductions in depression symptoms according to self-reports and clinical ratings in comparison to the wait-list control children. These treatment effects were maintained at a 5-week follow-up, along with reductions in anxiety and improvements in academic self-concept.

In another study Stark *et al.* (1987) assigned 29 moderately to severely depressed children (aged 9–12 years) to self-control, behavioural problem-solving or waiting-list conditions. At posttreatment and at an 8-week follow-up, the self-control and behavioural problem-solving conditions produced significant reductions in depression using self-report and clinical interviews, in comparison to the wait-list subjects. However, between-group treatment effects were not evident on mother's behavioural checklist ratings. This study provided evidence for some generalization of the treatment effects of a home setting (Stark *et al.*, 1991).

The clearest evidence for the specific effects of cognitive-behavioural treatment emerged in the study reported by Stark *et al.* (1991) of 24 depressed children (grades 4–7) assigned to cognitive-behavioural therapy or to traditional counselling. Both interventions lasted 24–26 sessions over 3½ months, and were conducted in small groups. The cognitive-behavioural treatment was a broader intervention than in previous studies, and included self-control, social skills and cognitive restructuring components (Stark, 1990; Stark *et al.*, 1991). At posttreatment, cognitive-behavioural therapy produced greater improvements in depression and reductions in depressive cognition in contrast to the traditional counselling. However, since these treatment gains were not maintained at the 7-month follow-up, the long-term effects of cognitive-behavioural therapy with depressed children have yet to be documented.

PREVAILING CONTROVERSIES

Generalization of behaviour change

Although significant pre–post changes have often been found after cognitive-behavioural interventions, the lack of generalization of treatment effects was an early concern for this mode of treatment (Hobbs *et al.*, 1980; Urbain & Kendall, 1980). Three types of generalization are important here: (1) generalization of behaviour change across settings; (2) generalization across domains of functioning (behaviour, self-esteem, cognition); and (3) generalization of behavioural improvements over time (maintenance). As noted in our summaries of outcome research, all three types of generalization have now been documented with some cognitive-behavioural therapies, although mixed findings across research studies still exist. Thus, it appears to be naive to assume that the outcome of structured cognitive-behavioural interventions will automatically generalize. Instead, procedures designed to have the client *manage* his or her persistent psychopathology (Kendall, 1989) and enhance the generalization process should be built in the intervention from the outset. Five such procedures are suggested below.

Firstly, goal-setting and operant techniques can be used to reinforce the overt behaviour change that begins to emerge as the children start to alter their maladaptive thinking (Lochman et al., 1984; Kazdin et al., 1989). Collaborative goal-setting allows the child and therapist to set delimited attainable targets for behaviour change rather than assuming that the child will begin making broad-scale changes in multiple behaviour across multiple settings. The latter assumption often leads to quick treatment failure. Programmed, contingent use of social reinforcement, activity reinforcements and tangible reinforcements following the monitoring of children's goal attainment are important for maintaining behavioural improvements over time and for extending the improvements to new situations.

Secondly, more intensive interventions provided over longer periods of time are necessary to produce a clinically significant improvement in children who have chronic behavioural difficulties such as frequent and serious aggressive behaviour and ADDH (Kazdin, 1987). The length of time in therapeutic contact with the child appears to be potentially more important than the number of intervention sessions (Lochman, 1990). Cognitive-behavioural interventions that are effective in producing generalized change generally work with the child for a 6-month period or longer.

Thirdly, through role-playing and discussion, a direct focus can be placed on the specific situations in which problems arise for the child. Thus, some children should focus on problems involving perceived unfairness of teachers, others on perceived provocations or rebuffs from peers, and others on conflicts with parents. By identifying the specific antecedents that lead up to the perceived problem in each of these situations, and the environmental obstacles, and facilitating resources (e.g. presence of a patient, understanding uncle who can intervene during family conflicts) that affect the child's response, the child is likely to consider more adaptive solutions.

Fourthly, in the course of the role-plays about these situational problems, the child can focus on refining his or her enactment of the behaviours used to resolve the problem. Whereas a child may readily recognize that a verbally assertive strategy could be important in responding to a certain social problem, he or she may not continue to try to enact the solution because he or she lacks the necessary social skills (e.g. tone of voice and nonverbal expression may convey either hostility or submissiveness).

Fifthly, generalized behaviour change is more likely to occur when self-instruction training provides the child with a problem-solving process that can be easily used across a number of situations, and when the self-instructions are generated through a Socratic directed discovery procedure rather than through didactic training (Kendall & Wilcox, 1980; Schlesseer et al., 1983; Kendall, 1991a). The latter

procedure allows the child to use personally relevant language in his or her self-direction, increasing the child's sense of ownership and control over the cognitive procedures.

Mechanisms of therapeutic change

Cognitive-behavioural therapies are based on the assumption that, through practice and reward, changes in key areas of children's cognitive processing will result in behavioural changes. However, when behavioural changes are found, can we be sure that the changes are due to changes in cognition? Tests of the causal connection between cognitions and behaviour require more stringent research designs (Lochman et al., 1991b). The least stringent level of intervention research would merely document behavioural change that was presumably due to the intervention's focus on cognitive moderator variables. At the second level of stringency, the outcome study documents that there were changes both in behaviour and in cognitive processes. However, at this level, the parallel changes in these two sets of variables are not necessarily causally related. At the third level of stringency, the outcome study should test whether behavioural changes are predicted by the changes in cognitive processes, using analyses such as multiple regression analyses. Although only the third design can provide a strong causal inference about the relationship between cognitive and behavioural change, most cognitive-behavioural intervention research is conducted using the first two types of designs. Future research needs stringently to document whether the causal relationship exists between cognition and behaviour.

The issue of motivation for change has yet to be fully addressed in most cognitive-behavioural interventions. Presumably, cognitive processes and changes are motivated by the positive consequences that are attained and the negative consequences that are avoided. The inclusion of social learning theory constructs such as outcome expectations and outcome values (Boldizar et al., 1989) in cognitive-behavioural models begins to address this gap, as we assess children's expectations that certain behaviours will lead to valued goals and outcomes.

Nonspecific factors that affect treatment outcome have rarely been examined (Reynolds & Coats, 1986). One important nonspecific factor involves the therapeutic relationship between the therapist and the child (Kendall & Morris, 1991). The social reinforcement provided by the therapist can be a major source of motivation for children. The therapeutic relationship assumes particular importance since many behaviourally and emotionally disordered children have weak relationships with parents and teachers, and thus have been minimally motivated by adults' reinforcement. If a positive therapeutic relationship develops, children can become more accepting of therapists' perceptions of events and can be more open to reframing their own interpretations of events (Lochman et al., 1987). Another nonspecific factor that affects treatment outcome involves the reactions and consequences provided after contact with the therapist by significant others in the children's lives. If peers, teachers and parents provide positive feedback for a child's efforts to be somewhat more verbally assertive, and if they are able readily to change their perceptions of and attributions about the child, then the child's behavioural change is likely to be maintained. However, if these interpersonal systems are not readily accepting of the child's recent behaviour changes, then the child's behaviour and cognitions can easily revert to earlier maladaptive levels. Thus, cognitive-behavioural therapy should actively intervene with key individuals in the child's social environment (parents, teacher, possibly even peers) to maintain therapeutic change (Braswell, 1991; Kendall & Morris, 1991).

Relationship to pharmacotherapy

Because of evidence that stimulants (e.g. methylphenidate) have significant effects on children's ADHD (Barkley, 1989), the role of medication in cognitive-behavioural therapy needs additional attention. Several authors have argued for the necessity of multimodal treatment that includes the use of medication (Hinshaw & Erhardt, 1991). It appears that medication and cognitive-behavioural therapy produce different types of effects on children's behaviour, with cognitive-behavioural therapies influencing specific coping strategies and medication influencing overall arousal and activity levels (Barkley, 1989). Future cognitive-behavioural research will need to examine the separate and combined effects of the treatments (Kendall & Lipman, 1991).

Cognitive-behavioural therapies with children and adolescents: strengths and weaknesses

Many of the strengths and weaknesses of the various cognitive-behavioural treatment strategies have been noted briefly throughout this chapter. It is our intent here to be illustrative rather than exhaustive in mentioning a few key strong points and frailties.

Interventions with children and adolescents are perhaps at their best when they mesh effectively with the normal developmental trajectory. In the years of development that are our target, the move towards autonomy and independence is a central developmental challenge. It is a decided strength of the cognitive-behavioural strategy that it works in a collaborative fashion with the young people and, correspondingly, fosters independent development as well as prosocial behaviour change. Relatedly, the beneficial gains that are produced from interventions with youth may persist posttreatment to prevent later psychological distress. The literature on the treatment of adult disorders suggests that cognitive-behavioural therapy may be of possible value in reducing relapse in recurring disorders and, although relatively unstudied in youth, relapse prevention (Marlatt & Gordon, 1985) may be a significant treatment outcome and deserves investigation.

Secondly, and importantly, the cognitive-behavioural therapies are neither monolithic nor narrow-minded. Quite the opposite is true: there are no rules carved in stone, and the emphasis on cognitive information-processing within a context that uses social reward and behavioural procedures to modify maladaptive methods of adjusting is intentionally flexible. True, there is structure and there are goals, but the paths to the goals, if not the goals themselves, remain fluid.

Contemporary cognitive-behavioural therapy has moved beyond the sole focus on the child client and has incorporated strategies that involve the parents, peers and school personnel. The research literature clearly supports the movement to include interpersonal and social contexts and parents as collaborators and/or co-clients, but the treatment evaluation studies have not kept pace with these expanded clinical applications. The direction and movement are strengths (Kendall & Morris, 1991): the need for additional evaluation is a potential weakness.

In addition to the evaluation needs noted above, the basic applications of cognitive-behavioural therapy need added research in terms of assessing whether or not one can achieve the highly sought-after long-term gains — altering the 'high-risk' profile of troubled youth. Comparisons are also needed in terms of the relative efficacy of the treatment as compared to alternate forms of psychological intervention, e.g. parent training or parent therapy, family therapy, for conduct problems (Kendall & Morris, 1991), as well as forms of pharmacotherapy (Kendall & Lipman, 1991) for anxiety and/or depression. Lastly, in part as a result of the nonmonolithic quality of cognitive-behavioural therapies, interventions include many different treatment strategies. Research is needed to untangle the complexity of strategies that are employed, as well as further to delineate those strategies that are best for specific types of childhood problem.

A possible frailty of the cognitive-behaviour therapies is their need for involved, unruffled therapists. Initial efforts at being a cognitive-behavioural problem-solving therapist, even by experienced therapists, are not as potent as later efforts. What are needed are more studies of experienced cognitive-behavioural therapists. That is, therapists improve with the approach as they have more opportunity to use and enjoy it. The fact that the treatments require the therapist to adopt a particular style of interaction may be viewed as a hindrance in certain contexts. Yet, when one does adopt and receive supervised training in the approach, there are data from a variety of research studies to document that the procedures can have beneficial effects for the participating young people.

ACKNOWLEDGEMENTS

Preparation of this manuscript was facilitated by a National Institute of Mental Health grant (44 042) awarded to the first author. The authors wish to thank Tamar Chansky and Elizabeth Kortlander for their contributions.

REFERENCES

Abikoff H. (1987) An evaluation of cognitive behavior therapy for hyperactive children. In: Lahey B.B. & Kazdin A.E. (eds) *Advances in Clinical Child Psychology*, vol. 10, pp. 171–216. Plenum Press, New York.

Abikoff H., Ganeles D., Reiter G., Blum C., Foley C., & Klein R.G.

(1988) Cognitive training in academically deficient ADHD boys receiving stimulant medication. *Journal of Abnormal Child Psychology*, **16**, 411−432.

Abikoff H. & Gittelman R. (1985) Hyperactive children treated with stimulants: is cognitive training a useful adjunct? *Archives of General Psychiatry*, **42**, 953−961.

Asarnow J.R. & Callan J.W. (1985) Boys with peer adjustment problems: social cognitive processes. *Journal of Consulting and Clinical Psychology*, **53**, 80−87.

Asarnow J.R., Carlson G.A. & Guthrie D. (1987) Coping strategies, self-perceptions, hopelessness, and perceived family environments in depressed and suicidal children. *Journal of Consulting and Clinical Psychology*, **55**, 361−366.

Barkley R.A. (1989) Attention deficit-hyperactivity disorder. In: Mash E.J. & Barkley R.A. (eds) *Treatment of Childhood Disorders*, pp. 39−72. Guilford Press, New York.

Barkley R.A. (1990) *Hyperactive Children: A Handbook for Diagnosis and Treatment*, 2nd edn. Guilford Press, New York.

Barkley R.A. & Cunningham C.E. (1979) The effects of methylphenidate on the mother−child interactions of hyperactive children. *Archives of General Psychiatry*, **36**, 201−208.

Barkley R.A. & Cunningham C.E. (1980) The parent−child interactions of hyperactive children and their modification by stimulant drugs. In: Knights R. & Bakker D. (eds) *Treatment of Hyperactive and Learning Disabled Children*, pp. 219−236. University Park Press, Baltimore.

Barkley R.A., Karlson J., Strzelecki E. & Murphy J. (1984) Effects of age and Ritalin dosage on the mother−child interactions of hyperactive children. *Journal of Consulting and Clinical Psychology*, **52**, 750−758.

Barlow D. (1988) *Anxiety and its Disorders: The Nature and Treatment of Anxiety and Panic*. Guilford Press, New York.

Barrios B.A. & Hartmann D.B. (1988) Fears and anxieties. In: Mash E.J. & Terdal L.G. (eds) *Behavioral Assessment of Childhood Disorders*, 2nd edn., pp. 196−264. Guilford Press, New York.

Barrios B.A., Hartmann D. & Shigetomi C. (1981) Fears and anxieties in children. In: Mash E. & Terdal L. (eds) *Behavioral Assessment of Childhood Disorders*, pp. 259−304. Guilford Press, New York.

Barrios B.A. & O'Dell S.L. (1989) Fears and anxieties. In: Mash E.J. & Barkley R.A. (eds) *Treatment of Childhood Disorders*, pp. 167−221. Guilford Press, New York.

Beidel D.C. (1988) Psychophysiological assessment of anxious emotional states in children. *Journal of Abnormal Psychology*, **97**, 80−82.

Boldizar J.P., Perry D.G. & Perry L.C. (1989) Outcome values and aggression. *Child Development*, **60**, 571−579.

Braswell L. (1991) Involving parents in cognitive-behavioral therapy with children and adolescents. In: Kendall P.C. (ed) *Child and Adolescent Therapy: Cognitive-behavioral Procedures*, pp. 316−352. Guilford Press, New York.

Brady E. & Kendall P.C. (1992) Comorbidity of anxiety and depression in children and adolescents. *Psychological Bulletin*, **111**, 244−255.

Braswell L. & Bloomquist M. (1991) *Cognitive-behavioral Therapy with ADDH Children: Child, Family, and School Intervention*. Guilford Press, New York.

Brown R.T., Wynne M.E. & Medenis R. (1985) Methylphenidate and cognitive therapy: a comparison of treatment approaches with hyperactive boys. *Journal of Abnormal Child Psychology*, **13**, 69−88.

Cameron M.I. & Robinson V.M.J. (1980) Effects of cognitive training on academic and on-task behavior of hyperactive children. *Journal of Abnormal Child Psychology*, **8**, 405−419.

Campbell S.B. (1986) Developmental issues. In: Gittelman R. (ed) *Anxiety Disorders of Childhood*, pp. 24−57. Guilford Press, New York.

Clark D.M. (1986) A cognitive approach to panic. *Behavior Research and Therapy*, **24**, 461−470.

Coie J.D., Lochman J.E., Terry R. & Hyman C. (1991) Predicting adolescent disorder from childhood aggression and peer rejection'. Unpublished manuscript, Duke University.

Curry J.F. & Craighead W.E. (1990) Attributional style in clinically depressed and conduct disordered adolescents. *Journal of Clinical and Consulting Psychology*, **58**, 109−116.

Deffenbacher J.L. & Kemper C.C. (1974) Systematic desensitization of test anxiety in junior high students. *School Counselor*, **22**, 216−222.

Dodge K.A. (1985) Attributional bias in aggressive children. In: Kendall P.C. (ed) *Advances in Cognitive-behavioral Research and Therapy*, pp. 72−110. Academic Press, San Diego, CA.

Dodge K.A. (1986) A social information processing model of social competence in children. In: Perlmutter M. (ed) *Minnesota Symposium on Child Psychology*, vol. 18. Lawrence Erlbaum, Hillsdale, NJ.

Dodge K.A. & Newman J.P. (1981) Biased decision making processes in aggressive boys. *Journal of Abnormal Psychology*, **90**, 375−379.

Dodge K.A. & Coie J.D. (1987) Social information processing factors in reactive and proactive aggression in children's peer groups. *Journal of Personality and Social Psychology*, **53**, 1146−1158.

Dodge K.A., Coie J.D. & Brakke N.P. (1982) Behavior patterns of socially rejected and neglected preadolescents: the roles of social approach and aggression. *Journal of Abnormal Child Psychology*, **10**, 389−409.

Dodge K.A., Pettit G.S., McClaskey C.L. & Brown M.M. (1986) Social competence in children. *Monographs of the Society for Research in Child Development*, **51**, (2, Serial No. 213).

Dodge K.A., Price J.M., Bachorowski J. & Newman J.P. (1990) Hostile attributional biases in severely aggressive adolescents. *Journal of Abnormal Psychology*, **99**, 385−392.

Douglas V.I., Parry P., Marton P. & Garson C. (1976) Assessment of a cognitive training program for hyperactive children. *Journal of Abnormal Child Psychology*, **4**, 389−410.

D'Zurilla T. (1986) *Problem-solving Approaches to Therapy*. Springer, New York.

Feindler E.L., Ecton R.B., Kingsley D. & Dubey, D.R. (1986) Group anger-control training for institutionalized psychiatric male adolescents. *Behavior Therapy*, **17**, 109−123.

Francis G. (1988) Assessing cognitions in anxious children. *Behavior Modification*, **12**, 167−281.

Garrison S.T. & Stolberg A.L. (1983) Modification of anger in children by affective imagery training. *Journal of Abnormal Child Psychology*, **11**, 115−130.

Gittelman R., Abikoff H., Pollack E., Klein D.F., Katz S. & Mattes J.A. (1980) A controlled trial of behavior modification and methylphenidate in hyperactive children. In: Whalen C.K. & Henker B. (eds) *Hyperactive Children: The Social Ecology of Identification and Treatment*, pp. 221−243. Academic Press, New York.

Gordon S.E., Lochman J.E. & Ribordy S.C. (1986) A comparative study of cognitive impulsivity, attribution, and problem-solving in aggressive and nonaggressive latency-aged boys'. Unpublished manuscript, Georgetown University.

Haley G., Fine S., Marriage K., Moretti M. & Freeman R. (1985) Cognitive bias and depression in psychiatrically disturbed children and adolescents. *Journal of Consulting and Clinical Psychology*, **53**, 535−537.

Haynes S.N. (1978) *Principles of Behavioral Assessment*. Gardner Press, New York.

Himaldi W.G., Boice R. & Barlow D. (1985) Assessment of agoraphobia: triples response measurement. *Behaviour Research and Therapy*, **23**, 311−323.

Hinshaw S.P. (1987) On the distinction between attentional deficits/hyperactivity and conduct problems/aggression in child psychopathology. *Psychological Bulletin*, **101**, 443−463.

Hinshaw S.P. & Erhardt D. (1991) Attention-deficit hyperactivity disorder. In: Kendall P.C. (ed) *Child and Adolescent Therapy: Cognitive-behavioral Procedures*, pp. 98–130. Guilford Press, New York.

Hobbs Ş.A., Moguin L.E., Tyroler M. & Lahey, B.D. (1980) Cognitive behavior therapy with children: has clinical utility been demonstrated? *Psychological Bulletin*, **87**, 147–165.

Huesmann L.R., Eron L.D., Lefkowitz M.M. & Walker L.O. (1984) Stability of aggression over time and generations. *Developmental Psychology*, **20**, 1120–1134.

Humphries T., Kinsbourne M. & Swanson J. (1978) Stimulant effects on cooperation and social interaction between hyperactive children and their mothers. *Journal of Child Psychology and Psychiatry*, **19**, 13–22.

Kane M.T. & Kendall P.C. (1989) Anxiety disorders in children: a multiple-baseline evaluation of a cognitive-behavioral treatment. *Behavior Therapy*, **20**, 499–508.

Kanfer F., Karoly P. & Newman A. (1975) Reductions of children's fear of the dark by competence-related and situational threat-related verbal cues. *Journal of Consulting and Clinical Psychology*, **43**, 251–258.

Kaslow N.J., Rehm L.P., Pollack S.L. & Siegel A.W. (1988) Attributional style and self-control behavior in depressed and nondepressed children and their parents. *Journal of Abnormal Child Psychology*, **16**, 163–175.

Kaslow N.J., Rehm L.P. & Siegel A.W. (1984) Social and cognitive correlates of depression children: a developmental perspective. *Journal of Abnormal Child Psychology*, **12**, 605–620.

Kazdin A.E. (1987) *Conduct Disorders in Childhood and Adolescence. Developmental Clinical Psychology and Psychiatry*, vol. 9. Saga Publications, Newbury Park, CA.

Kazdin A.E. (1989) Developmental differences in depression. In: Lahey B.B. & Kazdin A.E. (eds) *Advances in Clinical Child Psychology*, vol. 12, pp. 193–220. Plenum Press, New York.

Kazdin A.E., Esveldt-Dawson K., French N.H. & Unis A.S. (1987a) Effects of parent management training and problem-solving skills training combined in the treatment of antisocial child behavior. *Journal of the American Academy of Child and Adolescent Psychiatry*, **26**, 416–424.

Kazdin A.E., Esveldt-Dawson K., French N.H. & Unis A.S. (1987b) Problem-solving skills training and relationship therapy in the treatment of antisocial child behavior. *Journal of Consulting and Clinical Psychology*, **55**, 76–85.

Kazdin A.E., Bass D., Siegel T. & Thomas C. (1989) Cognitive-behavioral therapy and relationship therapy in the treatment of children referred for antisocial behavior. *Journal of Consulting and Clinical Psychology*, **57**, 522–535.

Kendall P.C. (1985) Toward a cognitive-behavioral model of child psychopathology and a critique of related interventions. *Journal of Abnormal Child Psychology*, **13**, 357–372.

Kendall P.C. (1989) The generalization and maintenance of behavior change: comments, considerations, and the 'no-cure' criticism. *Behavior Therapy*, **20**, 357–364.

Kendall P.C. (1990) *The Coping Cat Workbook*. Available from the author, 238 Meeting House Lane, Merion Station, PA 19066, US.

Kendall P.C. (ed) (1991a) *Child and Adolescent Therapy: Cognitive-behavioral Procedures*. Guilford Press, New York.

Kendall P.C. (1991b) Guiding theory for therapy with children and adolescents. In: Kendall P.C. (ed) *Child and Adolescent Therapy: Cognitive-behavioral Procedures*, pp. 3–22. Guilford Press, New York.

Kendall P.C. (1992) *Stop and Think Workbook*, 2nd edn. Available from the author, 238 Meeting House Lane, Merion Station, PA 19066, US.

Kendall P.C. & Braswell L. (1985) *Cognitive-behavioral Therapy for Impulsive Children*. Guilford Press, New York.

Kendall P.C., Cantwell D.P. & Kazdin A.E. (1989) Depression in children and adolescents: assessment issues and recommendations.

Cognitive Therapy and Research, **13**, 109–146.

Kendall P.C. & Grove W. (1988) Normative comparisons in therapy outcome. *Behavioral Assessment*, **10**, 147–158.

Kendall P.C. & Hollon S.D. (1989) Anxious self-talk: development of the Anxious Self-Statements questionnaire. *Cognitive Therapy and Research*, **13**, 81–93.

Kendall P.C. & Hollon S.D. (eds) (1979) *Cognitive-behavioral interventions: theory, research, and procedures*. Academic Press, New York.

Kendall P.C. & Lipman A.J. (1991) Psychological and pharmacological therapy: Methods and modes for comparative outcome research. *Journal of Consulting and Clinical Psychology*, **59(1)**, 78–87.

Kendall P.C. & Morris R.J., (1991) Child therapy: issues and recommendations. *Journal of Consulting and Clinical Psychology*, **59(6)**, 777–784.

Kendall P.C. & Reber M. (1987) Reply to Abikoff and Gittelman's evaluation of cognitive training with medicated hyperactive children. *Archives of General Psychiatry*, **8**, 77–79.

Kendall P.C. & Siqueland L. (1989) Child and adolescent therapy. In: Nezu A.M. & Nezu C.M. (eds) *Clinical Decision Making in Behavior Therapy: A Problem-solving Perspective*. Research Press, Champaign, IL.

Kendall P.C. & Watson D. (eds) (1989) *Anxiety and Depression: Distinctive and Overlapping Features*. Academic Press, New York.

Kendall P.C. & Wilcox L. (1980) A cognitive-behavioral treatment for impulsivity: concrete versus conceptual training in non-self-controlled problem children. *Journal of Consulting and Clinical Psychology*, **48**, 80–91.

Kendall P.C., Reber M., McLeer S., Epps J. & Ronan K.R. (1990a) Cognitive-behavioral treatment of conduct-disordered children. *Cognitive Therapy and Research*, **14**, 279–297.

Kendall P.C., Ronan K.R. & Epps J. (1991) Aggression in children/adolescents: cognitive-behavioral treatment perspective. In: Pepler D.J. & Rubin K.H. (eds) *The Development and Treatment of Childhood Aggression*, pp. 341–360. Lawrence Erlbaum, Hillsdale, NJ.

Kendall P.C., Stark K.D. & Adam T. (1990b) Cognitive deficit or cognitive distortion in childhood depression? *Journal of Abnormal Child Psychology*, **18**, 255–270.

Kendall P.C., Chansky T.E., Kane M., Kim R., Kortlander E., Ronan K.R., Sessa F. & Siqueland L. (1992) *Anxiety Disorders in Youth: Cognitive-behavioral Interventions*. Allyn and Bacon, Needham, MA.

King N.J. & Ollendick T.H. (1989) Children's anxiety and phobic disorders in school settings: classification, assessment, and intervention issues. *Review of Educational Research*, **59(4)**, 431–470.

Koeppen A.S. (1974) Relaxation training for children. *Elementary School Guidance and Counseling*, **9**, 14–21.

Kovacs M., Feinberg T.L., Crouse-Novak M., Paulashas S.L. & Finkelstein R. (1984) Depressive disorders in childhood. A longitudinal prospective study of characteristics and recovery. *Archives of General Psychiatry*, **41**, 229–237.

Leitenberg H., Yost L.W. & Carroll-Wilson M. (1986) Negative cognitive errors in children: questionnaire development, normative data, and comparisons between children with and without self-reported symptoms of depression, low self-esteem, and evaluation anxiety. *Journal of Consulting and Clinical Psychology*, **54**, 528–536.

Lochman J.E. (1985) Effects of different treatment lengths in cognitive behavior interventions with aggressive boys. *Child Psychiatry and Human Development*, **16**, 45–56.

Lochman J.E. (1987) Self and peer perceptions and attributional biases of aggressive and nonaggressive boys in dyadic interactions. *Journal of Consulting and Clinical Psychology*, **55**, 404–410.

Lochman J.E. (1990) Modification of childhood aggression. In: Hersen M., Eisler R. & Miller P.M. (eds) *Progress in Behavior Modification*, vol. XXV, pp. 47–85. Sage, Newbury Park, CA.

Lochman J.E. (1991) 'Cognitive-behavioral intervention with aggressive boys: three year follow-up and preventive effects.' Unpublished manuscript, Duke University.

Lochman J.E., Burch P.P., Curry J.F. & Lampron L.B. (1984) Treatment and generalization effects of cognitive-behavioral and goal-setting interventions with aggressive boys. *Journal of Consulting and Clinical Psychology*, **52**, 915–916.

Lochman J.E. & Curry J.F. (1986) Effects of social problem-solving training and self-instruction training with aggressive boys. *Journal of Clinical Child Psychology*, **15**, 159–164.

Lochman J.E. & Lampron L.B. (1986) Situational social problem-solving skills and self-esteem of aggressive and nonaggressive boys. *Journal of Abnormal Child Psychology*, **14**, 605–617.

Lochman J.E., Lampron L.B., Burch P.R. & Curry J.E. (1985) Client characteristics associated with behavior change for treated and untreated boys. *Journal of Abnormal Child Psychology*, **13**, 527–538.

Lochman J.E., Lampron L.B. & Rabiner D. (1989) Format and salience effects in the social problem-solving of aggressive and nonaggressive boys. *Journal of Clinical Child Psychology*, **18**, 230–236.

Lochman J.E., Lampron L.B., Gemmer T.C., Harris R. & Wyckoff, G.M. (1989) Teacher consultation and cognitive-behavioral interventions with aggressive boys. *Psychology in the Schools*, **26**, 179–188.

Lochman J.E., Meyer B.L., Rabiner D.L. & White J.J. (1991a) Parameters influencing social problem-solving of aggressive children. In: Prinz R. (ed) *Advances in Behavioral Assessment of Children and Families*, vol. 5, pp. 31–63. Jessica Kingsley Publishers, London.

Lochman J.E., Wayland K.K. & Cohen C. (1990, August) *Predication of adolescent behavior problems for subtypes of aggressive boys*. Paper presented at the Annual Convention of the American Psychological Association, Boston, MA.

Lochman J.E., White K.J. & Wayland K.K. (1991a) Cognitive-behavioral assessment and treatment with aggressive children. In: Kendall P.C. (ed) *Child and Adolescent Therapy: Cognitive-behavioral Procedures*, pp. 25–65. Guilford Press, New York.

Loeber R. & Dishion T.J. (1983) Early predictors of male delinquency: a review. *Psychological Bulletin*, **94**, 68–99.

McCauley E., Burke P., Mitchell J. & Moss S. (1986, August) *Cognitive attributes of depression in children and adolescents*. Paper presented at the annual convention of the American Psychological Association, Washington, DC.

Marlatt A. & Gordon J. (eds) (1985) *Relapse Prevention*. Guilford Press, New York.

Meichenbaum D. (1977) *Cognitive Behavior Modification: An Integrative Approach*. Plenum, New York.

Meichenbaum D. & Goodman J. (1971) Training impulsive children to talk to themselves: a means of developing self-control. *Journal of Abnormal Psychology*, **77**, 115–126.

Michelson L. & Ascher L.M. (eds) (1987) *Anxiety and Stress Disorders: Cognitive-behavioral Assessment and Treatment*. Guilford Press, New York.

Milich R. & Dodge K.A. (1984) Social information processing in child psychiatric populations. *Journal of Abnormal Child Psychology*, **12**, 471–490.

Miller L.C. (1983) Fears and anxiety in children. In: C.E. Walker & M.C. Roberts (eds), *Handbook of Clinical Child Psychology*, pp. 337–380. Wiley, New York.

Miller L.C., Barrett C.L. & Hampe E. (1974) Phobias of childhood in a prescientific era. In: Davids A. (ed) *Child Personality and Psychotherapy: Current Topics*. Wiley, New York.

Morris R.J. & Kratochwill T.R. (1983) *Treating Children's Fears and Phobias: A Behavioral Approach*. Wiley, New York.

Morris R.J. & Kratochwill T.R. (1991) Childhood fears and phobias. In: Kratochwill T.R. & Morris R.J. (eds) *The Practice of Child Therapy*, 2nd edn., pp. 76–114. Pergamon Press, New York.

Mullins L.L., Siegel L.J. & Hodges K. (1985) Cognitive problem-solving and life event correlates of depressive symptoms in children. *Journal of Abnormal Child Psychology*, **13**, 305–314.

Ollendick T.H. (1979) Behavioral treatment of anorexia nervosa: a five year study. *Behavior Modification*, **3**, 124–135.

Ollendick T.H. & Cerny J.A. (1981) *Clinical Behavior Therapy with Children*. Plenum Press, New York.

Ollendick T.H. & Francis G. (1988) Behavioral assessment and treatment of childhood phobias. *Behavior Modification*, **12**, 165–204.

Olweus D. (1979) Stability of aggressive behavior patterns in males: a review. *Psychological Bulletin*, **86**, 852–875.

Pepler D.J. & Rubin K.H. (eds) (1991) *The Development and Treatment of Childhood Aggression*. Lawrence Erlbaum, Hillsdale, NJ.

Perry D.G., Perry L.C. & Rasmussen P. (1986). Cognitive social learning mediators of aggression. *Child Development*, **57**, 700–711.

Peterson L., & Shigetomi C. (1981). The use of coping techniques in minimizing anxiety in hospitalized children. *Behavior Therapy*, **12**, 1–14.

Prins P.J.M. (1985). Self-speech and self-regulation of high- and low-anxious children in the dental situation: an interview study. *Behaviour Research and Therapy*, **23**, 641–650.

Prinz R.J., Connor P.A. & Wilson C.C. (1981) Hyperactive and aggressive behaviors in childhood: intertwined dimensions. *Journal of Abnormal Child Psychology*, **9**, 191–202.

Quay H.C. (1986) Conduct disorders. In: Quay H.C. & Werry J.S. (eds), *Psychopathological Disorders of Childhood*, Third Edition, (pp. 35–72). Wiley, New York.

Rabiner D., Lenhart L. & Lochman J.E. (1990) Automatic versus reflective social problem solving in relation to children's sociometric status. *Developmental Psychology*, **26**, 1010–1016.

Rehm L.P. & Carter A.S. (1990) Cognitive components of depression. In: Lewis M. & Miller S.M. (eds) *Handbook of Developmental Psychopathology*, pp. 341–351. Plenum Press, New York.

Reynolds W.M. & Coats K.I. (1986) A comparison of cognitive-behavioral therapy and relaxation training for the treatment of depression in adolescents. *Journal of Consulting and Clinical Psychology*, **54**, 653–660.

Richard B.A. & Dodge K.A. (1982) Social maladjustment and problem solving in school aged children. *Journal of Consulting and Clinical Psychology*, **50**, 226–233.

Richter N.C. (1984) The efficacy of relaxation training with children. *Journal of Abnormal Child Psychology*, **12**, 319–344.

Rutter M.R., Tizard J. & Whitmore K. (eds) (1970) *Education, health, and behavior*. Longman, London.

Schlesser R., Meyers A.W., Cohen R. & Thackwray, D. (1983) Self-instruction interventions with non-self-controlled children: effects of discovery versus faded rehearsal. *Journal of Consulting and Clinical Psychology*, **51**, 954–955.

Slaby R.G. & Guerra N.G. (1988) Cognitive mediators of aggression in adolescent offenders: I. Assessment. *Developmental Psychology*, **24**, 580–588.

Siegel L. & Peterson L. (1980) Stress reduction in young dental patients through coping skills and sensory information. *Journal of Consulting and Clinical Psychology*, **48**, 785–787.

Spivack G. & Shure M.B. (1974) *Social Adjustment of Young Children: A Cognitive Approach to Solving Real-life Problems*. Jossey-Bass, San Francisco, CA.

Stark K. (1990) *Childhood Depression: School-based Intervention*. Guilford Press, New York.

Stark K.D., Reynolds W.M. & Kaslow N.J. (1987) A comparison of the relative efficacy of self-control therapy and a behavioral problem-solving therapy for depression in children. *Journal of Abnormal Child Psychology*, **15**, 91–113.

Stark K., Rouse L. & Livingston R. (1991) Treatment of depression during childhood and adolescence: cognitive-behavioral procedures for the individual and family. In: Kendall P.C. (ed) *Child and Adolescent Therapy: Cognitive-behavioral Procedures*, pp. 165—208. Guilford Press, New York.

Urbain E.S. & Kendall P.C. (1980) Review of social-cognitive problem-solving interventions with children. *Psychological Bulletin*, **88**, 109—143.

Weiss G. & Hechtman L.T. (1986) *Hyperactive Children Grown up*. Guilford Press, New York.

Whalen C.K., Henker B. & Dotemmoto S. (1980) Methylphenidate and hyperactivity: effects on teacher behaviors. *Science*, **208**, 1280—1282.

Whalen C.K., Henker B. & Dotemmoto S. (1981) Teacher response to the methylphenidate (Ritalin) versus placebo status of hyperactive boys in the classroom. *Child Development*, **52**, 1005—1014.

Whalen C.K., Henker B. & Hinshaw S.P. (1985) Cognitive-behavioral therapies for hyperactive children: premises, problems, and prospects. *Journal of Abnormal Child Psychology*, **13**, 319—410.

Whalen C.K., Henker B., Swanson J.M., Granger D., Kliewer W. & Spencer J. (1987) Natural social behaviors in hyperactive children: dose effects of methylphenidate. *Journal of Consulting and Clinical Psychology*, **55**, 187—193.

Chapter 50
Behavioural Methods

Martin Herbert

There can be few therapeutic terms that have suffered so much unwitting misunderstanding (and wilful misrepresentation) as behavioural methods, a generic concept covering behaviour therapy, behaviour modification and cognitive-behavioural interventions. The source of much genuine confusion about the nature, purpose and parameters of behavioural work can be traced to theoretical uncertainties and conceptual ambiguities; a further difficulty could be attributed to the failure to distinguish between strategic and tactical aspects of the approach.

THEORETICAL BACKGROUND

When it comes to theory, at one extreme there is the restricted nondevelopmental, noncognitivist view (unkind critics would say 'tunnel vision') of some behaviourists which manifests itself in a narrow version of *applied behaviour analysis*. The more fundamentalist exegeses, with their insistence on the letter (as opposed to the spirit) of scientific method as applied to human problems, limit the range, and thus the usefulness of behaviourism. This is especially so when it comes to the multilevel, multifactorial 'untidiness' of problems with which so many disturbed children (and their families) challenge the ingenuity of clinicians. In fairness, Cullen (1991) argued that the philosophy of radical behaviourism does not ignore — as many critics claim — people's thoughts and feelings.

At the other end of the theoretical spectrum is the unashamed cognitive elaboration of the behavioural approach. As long ago as 1978, Kazdin made the point, in his history of behaviour therapy, that the discipline had diversified out of all recognition since its formal beginnings in the late 1950s and could no longer be accommodated theoretically by an all-sustaining behaviouristic umbilical cord. Indeed, behaviour therapy had become so variegated in its conceptualizations of behaviour, research methods and techniques, that no unifying schema or set of assumptions could incorporate all extant techniques. Even more so today, it can be said that, although behaviour therapy emphasizes the principles of classical and operant conditioning, it is not restricted to them. It draws upon principles, not only from learning theory, but also from other branches of experimental psychology such as social and developmental psychology and cognitive science. The import-ance of private events and the cognitive mediation of behaviour is recognized, and a major role is attributed to vicarious and symbolic learning processes such as imitation.

Estes (1971) — a learning theorist — noted that only for a very restricted range of immature or profoundly intellectually impaired human beings is their behaviour, from moment to moment, to a large extent describable and predictable in terms of responses to particular stimuli and the rewarding or punishing outcomes of previous stimulus–response sequences. In more mature beings, much instrumental behaviour and more especially a great part of verbal behaviour is organized into higher-order routines and is, in many instances, better understood in terms of the operation of rules, principles, strategies and the like. Parke (1978) commented scathingly that some work with caregivers would seem to imply that mothers' cognitive complexity is scarcely more sophisticated than that of their infants. Contemporary behaviour therapists are more willing to acknowledge that parents have expertise, theories (attributions) about behaviour, and ideologies about child-rearing; also that they make plans for their children that influence their behaviour by placing them in particular niches (e.g. schools) within society (Whiting, 1963; Rutter *et al.*, 1979). These are matters that are important in assessment, and ones that therapists are likely to discuss with caregivers.

One of the outward and visible signs of the infiltration of cognitive science into behavioural work was the publication of the journal *Behavioural Psychotherapy* in 1981. A decade on, in a special anniversary edition, Power (1991) argued that it is essential that behaviour therapy develops a sounder philosophical base that can genuinely represent the constructs with which skilled behaviour therapists work (p. 23). He suggested that the tacit philosophies which inform behaviour therapists at present are somewhat contradictory in nature. (For a critical analysis of the philosophical and scientific basis of learning theory, and its conceptual relationship to behavioural methods, see Erwin, 1979; Mackintosh, 1983; Dickinson, 1987.)

The drift of behaviour therapy to a cognitive mode is paralleled in cognitive therapy by a noticeable, if small, leaning towards psychodynamic thinking (Power, 1989). There have been several rather unconvincing attempts to find common cause (even a theoretical *rapprochement*) between learning theory and psychoanalysis (Dollard & Miller, 1950; Alexander,

1963). Behaviour therapy, historically speaking, began as a reaction against the subjectivism of psychoanalysis. But it is precisely here, the content or 'what' of behaviour and reinforcement (particularly the latter, given its preoccupation with motivation), that psychoanalysis, according to Wachtel (1977), has most to offer an essentially uninformative behaviourism. It has, he claims, much that is useful to say about the kinds of problems children develop.

Yates (1983) stated that the attempts to coordinate and integrate behaviour therapy and psychodynamic therapy in the clinical situation arose from the observation that the clinical practice of behaviour therapists had many important features in common with the clinical practices of psychodynamic psychotherapists (Klein *et al.*, 1969; Wilson & Evans, 1983). Marmor (1971), one of those who believed there are compelling reasons for a *rapprochement*, pointed out that part of the confusion that surrounds any discussion of these basic approaches to therapy is due to the temptation to see them as monolithic, and therefore distinct, entities. The reality is that both approaches cover a wide range of theories and methods. Marmor contended that 'at one end of each spectrum the theories of behavioural and dynamic psychotherapists tend to converge, while at the other end their divergence is very great' (p. 22).

It is generally recognized that *insight*, arising from psychodynamic analysis and interpretation, does not necessarily lead to a change in behaviour; nor does behaviour change inevitably lead to increased awareness, a subjective sense of improvement or, in psychodynamic terms, a change in psychic structures. Perhaps, it is suggested (by Birk & Brinkley-Birk, 1974), more powerful or significant therapeutic change might be achieved by the complementary use of both methods. It should be noted that such arguments for an interface between the psychodynamic and behavioural therapies are adamantly repudiated by many theorists (Levis, 1970; Rachman, 1970).

In the author's opinion, psychoanalysis has most to contribute to the desideratum of an integrative perspective in psychotherapy, as a *semantic* theory about meanings, rather than as a scientific model of practice for childhood psychiatric problems (Rycroft, 1970). Rycroft stated that:

> What Freud did... was not to explain the patient's choice causally but to understand it and give it meaning, and the procedure he engaged in was not the scientific one of elucidating causes but the semantic one of making sense of it. It can indeed be argued that much of Freud's work was really semantic and that he made a revolutionary discovery in semantics, namely that neurotic symptoms are meaningful disguised communications, but that owing to his scientific training and allegiance, he formulated his findings in the conceptual framework of the physical sciences. (p. 328)

In behavioural work, the functional analysis can operate at two levels: at its simplest, behaviour is a function of certain contingent stimuli, originating in the person's internal and external environment. Here the question is: What payoff does the child get for behaving in this way? At a more interpretive

level the child's behaviour has the function of solving (or attempting to solve) a developmental or life problem. To make sense of it one might ask (*inter alia*): What short-term 'solutions' (even if self-defeating in the longer term) do the child's actions provide? Also, what purpose does the child's behaviour serve in terms of his or her family life and its psychological and social dynamics?

At its broadest, all treatments share the objective of producing change, and change implies learning. Indeed, Goldstein *et al.* (1966) proposed that, whatever else it is, psychotherapy must be considered a learning enterprise involving specific behaviours, attitudes or even, possibly, a whole new outlook on life.

The abuse of behavioural methods

There is, finally, another use of the term behavioural methods which has nothing to do with theory, but represents a dangerous extension, indeed hijacking, of its meaning and legitimacy, for applications (e.g. the extreme and punitive use of isolation in secure institutions) which have everything to do with social control and/or the convenience of staff, but nothing to do with therapeutic goals or (too often) professional ethics. This issue is discussed further below.

STRATEGIC AND TACTICAL CONSIDERATIONS

This brings us to the difference between strategic and tactical aspects of behavioural approaches, a distinction that should help to mitigate some of the confusion that surrounds this kind of work.

At the strategic level, behavioural work represents a *theory* (indeed a philosophy) of treatment and behaviour change, rather than a technology or cookbook of *ad hoc* techniques. It is based upon a broad and empirically based theory of normal and abnormal behaviour (Ollendick, 1986; Herbert, 1991). This is not to claim that all behaviours are learned and can therefore (relatively simply) be unlearned. In conditions such as the Lesch–Nyhan syndrome or epilepsy and, indeed, various other organic disorders, learning processes do not constitute a sufficient explanation of abnormal behaviour. Fortunately, this does not mean that a behavioural approach is valueless in such conditions. The fact is that it can work without being tied to a theory about the origins of the behaviour. Indeed, it is one of the strengths of behavioural work that treatment does not depend necessarily (as we shall see) upon the discovery and understanding of the historical causes of the problem. Nevertheless, the identification of the current problem and its contemporary antecedents and consequences may be assisted by information about the patient's past (e.g. attachments, health, reinforcement history, attitudes, life events).

The information is gathered primarily as a source of clues to contemporary conditions which influence the elicitation and maintenance of problematic behaviour rather than as specific treatment objectives in themselves. The behaviour therapist places most emphasis on providing the patient with new learning experiences. If past experiences did contribute significantly to the manner in which (say) an individual's delinquent behaviour has evolved, in practice they are seldom still functional — they no longer directly maintain current deviant behaviour.

At another level, the link between behavioural theory (e.g. how dysfunctional behaviour results from failures or distortions of learning) and the treatment methods of choice can be somewhat tenuous (Erwin, 1979). Psychologists are still uncertain, for example, about why the enuresis alarm (a treatment discussed in more detail later on) is so successful. It could be said, like the use of aspirin, to be an *empirical* rather than *rational* treatment. Aspirins tend to alleviate headaches of various origins; it is not necessary to ascribe their success to a deficit in sodium salicylate!

At the tactical level of behavioural methods as techniques, we have a veritable Pandora's box of potential misunderstandings. I have referred to the confusing (sometimes deliberate obfuscation) of methods of social control with behaviour modification techniques. It must be admitted that there may be room for genuine ambiguity, as behavioural methods are used to help parents manage difficult children. This might well be called social control. Indeed it gives rise to heated philosophical debates about ethical relativism and the desirability of working within the framework of societal values and norms. It is the implementation of an *appropriate* assessment and formulation, and the negotiation of therapeutic goals that are ethically acceptable, that constitutes the authenticating hallmark of behaviour *therapy*. (A Royal College of Psychiatrists working party (to which the author contributed) has produced a paper, *Guidelines to Good Practice in the Use of Behavioural Treatments* (Royal College of Psychiatrists, 1989), to which I will refer later in the chapter.)

Face validity of behavioural theory

In a very real, if informal sense, parents use behavioural methods every one of their child-rearing days, in order to teach, influence and change the children in their care. This is something parents call discipline and psychologists call socialization. Among these methods are material and psychological rewards, praise and encouragement, giving or withholding approval, and other psychological punishments such as reproof or disapproval. As caregivers they give direct instructions, set an example and provide explanations of rules (i.e. inductive methods). Of course they do not always use them systematically and certainly not on the basis of a theoretical knowledge-base or a planned assessment. Although parents are unfamiliar with the 'small print' and terminology of learning theory, behavioural methods, when explained carefully, do tend to have face validity for them. For those who believe in the advantages of a partnership model in work with families, this demystification of the therapeutic process is a definite plus factor (Herbert, 1993).

The central theoretical assumption of behavioural work is that much abnormal behaviour and cognition in children is on a continuum with normal (nonproblematic) behaviour and thought. These phenomena do not differ, by and large, from their normal counterparts in their development, their persistence and the way in which they can be modified. The laws of learning that apply to the acquisition and changing of normal, functional (e.g. socially approved) behaviour and attitudes are assumed to be relevant to the understanding of dysfunctional actions and cognitions. Unfortunately — and it is the case with all forms of learning — the very processes that help the child adapt to life can, under certain circumstances, contribute to maladaptation. An immature child who learns by imitating an adult does not necessarily comprehend when it is undesirable (deviant) behaviour or distorted thinking that is being modelled. The youngster who learns adaptively on the basis of classical and instrumental conditioning processes to avoid or escape from dangerous situations can also learn in the same way (maladaptively) to avoid school or social gatherings. A caregiver may unwittingly reinforce antisocial coercive behaviour by attending, or giving in, to it.

Of course there is much more to learning — and learning to behave dysfunctionally — than is conveyed by these examples. For example, there may be a learned behavioural, cognitive or affective overlay to problems which have (say) an organic basis, and which are therefore accessible to some alleviation by behavioural methods.

Levels of intervention

Behavioural work starts from a clear objective of producing planned, goal-directed change. At least four levels of intervention need to be implemented in concert in order to fulfil long-term goals (Evans, 1989): (1) altering the immediate consequences of the undesirable behaviour and/or belief; (2) reducing the probability of the behaviour or belief by rearranging the environment; (3) facilitating (teaching, reinforcing, shaping) the emergence of alternative skills and attitudes; and (4) designing long-term prevention through imparting new patterns of behaviour and/or attitudes.

At its simplest level (point 1, above) there are certain basic learning tasks that are commonly encountered in child therapy: (1) the acquisition (learning) of a desired response in which the individual is deficient (e.g. compliance, self-esteem, self-control, bladder and bowel control, fluent speech, social or academic skills); and (2) the reduction or elimination (unlearning) of an unwanted response in the child's repertoire (e.g. self-deprecatory self-talk, aggression, temper tantrums, stealing, facial tics, phobic anxiety, compulsive eating) or the exchange of one response for another (e.g. self-assertion in place of tearful withdrawal).

Models of learning

Each of these tasks (and potential ameliorative methods) may be served by one or a combination of the four major types of learning. The categories represent essentially different processes of learning. Childhood phobias exemplify rather well the translation of different principles of learning into methods of treatment. They also illustrate the fact that different procedures (which sometimes appear to be contradictory) can work with the same problem.

Classical conditioning

Stimulus-contingent reinforcement, a model of learning developed by Pavlov (1927), is well-known, and is referred to as classical conditioning. A stimulus (the unconditioned stimulus) is presented to the organism and reflexly elicits a response. A previously neutral stimulus is repeatedly paired with the first and gradually acquires its response-eliciting properties. The response of the organism has been conditioned to the second stimulus (the conditioned stimulus). Emotional reactions of phobic intensity can be evoked directly by classically conditioned aversive stimuli. In turn, fears and phobias can be unlearned by means of specific counterconditioning procedures.

The most often-quoted account of counterconditioning is that of Jones's early treatment of Peter (Jones, 1924). She successfully treated Peter's fear of rabbits by exposing him to the actual feared rabbit in a systematic but gradual manner and in the presence of food (a stimulus that produced an incompatible positive response). More recently, systematic desensitization (as it is now referred to) has relied primarily on relaxation as the competing, and therefore, inhibiting response (Wolpe, 1958).

Although studies have questioned the active therapeutic mechanisms and the necessary ingredients of systematic desensitization, it remains an effective and frequently used procedure with, children and adolescents (Hatzenbuehler & Schroeder, 1978; King *et al.*, 1988).

Operant conditioning

Response-contingent reinforcement is termed instrumental or operant conditioning. Responses are increased or strengthened (and thus shaped) by having consequences that are rewarding (positive reinforcement), or that lead to the avoidance of, or escape from, punishment (negative reinforcement); they are reduced or eliminated by sanctions (fines, penalties, etc.) as outcomes. This model of learning leads to procedures that bring about the systematic manipulation of the behaviour's consequences so as to modify subsequent behaviours of the same type. This may involve the removal of payoffs (positive reinforcers) that customarily follow a maladaptive response and/or the provision of positive reinforcers or penalties following the display of desirable or undesirable actions, respectively. This model requires a thorough assessment of the positive and negative reinforcing stimuli that produce or maintain fearful, antisocial or other unwanted behaviours.

An illustration is provided in a case report by Ayllon *et al.* (1970), who treated a school phobic 8-year-old girl through a home- and school-based operant approach. A shaping procedure was implemented following collection of baseline data in the home and school. The girl was taken to school towards the end of the school day by an assistant who remained with her until school was dismissed. Each successive day, she was taken to school a little earlier. By the seventh day of this procedure, she was able to remain in school all day. The young girl was reinforced (contingent on each step) by the assistant and her mother.

Operant procedures have also been used in the treatment of socially avoidant children (e.g. Clement & Milne, 1967) and children who display a variety of fears, such as fear of the dark, dogs, riding on school buses and sitting on the toilet (Obler & Terwilliger, 1970; Leitenberg & Callahan, 1973; Luiselli, 1978).

Observational learning

Much complex and novel behaviour in childhood is acquired by observing the behaviour of exemplary models: the people children watch in everyday life or symbolic models that they read about or see on television (Bandura, 1977). A method derived from observational learning theory is referred to as modelling. This involves the systematic demonstration in actuality (or symbolically, on film) of a model displaying the required behaviour: a skill, an appropriate prosocial action, or a coping strategy.

Modelling treatments are based upon vicarious conditioning principles: the therapeutic intervention may be directed towards the relationship between the antecedent conditions and the problematic behaviour and/or between the problem behaviour and its consequences. The child is encouraged to imitate the behaviour being demonstrated and is provided with feedback and reinforcement for performance that matches that of the model. Thus operant principles are used to maintain the desired behaviours once they are acquired through the modelling process. Ollendick (1979) concluded, on the basis of available studies, that filmed modelling is effective in about 25–50% of cases, live modelling in about 50–67%, and participant modelling in 80–92%.

Participant modelling consists of live modelling plus contact with a therapist (or fearless peer) who physically guides the child through the fearful situation. Ross *et al.* (1971) provided an illustration of this method. They used modelling (together with social reinforcement) to treat a 6-year-old boy whose fear and avoidance of interactions with age-mates were so extreme that he actively avoided peers and refused even to watch filmed presentations featuring young children. Treatment consisted of establishing generalized imitation, participant modelling and social reinforcement. Following treatment, the child was observed to interact positively with his peers and to display few avoidant behaviours. On follow-up, 2 months after termination of treatment, he was observed to 'join ongoing play groups, initiate verbal contacts, and sustain effective social interactions, all with children who were complete strangers to him' (Ross *et al.*, 1971, p. 277).

Cognitive learning

Cognitive-behavioural work is based upon the assumption that cognitive processes are critical in childhood learning (Bruner, 1975); thus therapists accept as primary data the phenomenology of problems. These might include the child's descriptions of his or her fears or perceptions about temptations to transgress rules. Zatz and Chassin (1983) reported the cognitions of test-anxious children. They not only endorse more self-denigrating statements (e.g. 'I'm doing poorly; I don't do well on tests like this; everyone usually does better than me'), they also make use of fewer facilitative, coping statements (e.g. 'I am bright enough to do this; I am doing the best that I can; I do well on tests like this'). Stefanek *et al.* (1987) have documented a similar pattern of self-statements in fearful, socially withdrawn children.

There is a wide range of cognitive-behavioural procedures (see Chapter 49) but they share a common assumption: that children can be taught to eliminate some of their maladaptive behaviours by challenging their irrational beliefs and faulty logic, by getting them to instruct themselves in certain ways or to associate wanted behaviour with positive self-statements, and unwanted ones with negative self-statements (Graziano & Mooney, 1980, 1982; Weisz & Weiss, 1989). This method is referred to as verbal self-instruction training. The child can also be taught to rearrange contingencies that influence behaviour in such a way that he or she experiences rewarding rather than aversive consequences.

There is another aspect to the issue of cognitive processes — what are called mutual cognitions. Maccoby and Martin (1983) observed that if we are to study the effect of ideas on parenting and on parent–child interactions, we shall need to ask about the causes and consequences of a lack of match in the parent's and children's ideas and expectations that arise from differences in conceptual level. Smooth interactions require that both parent and child must act from the same 'script' (Maccoby, 1984). Mismatches are thought to promote conflict (Damon, 1989).

Social learning theory: a systemic perspective

Many practitioners are of the opinion that social learning theory as developed by (*inter alia*) Bandura (1969, 1986) and Patterson (1982) is sufficiently comprehensive and theoretically coherent to encompass the complex problems and the elaborate ideas and assumptions which are a feature of contemporary cognitive-behavioural casework.

Learning occurs within a social nexus; rewards, punishments and other events are mediated by human agents and within attachment and social systems, and are not simply the impersonal consequences of behaviour. Children do not simply respond to stimuli; they interpret them. They are relating to, interacting with and learning from people who have meaning and value for them. They feel antipathetic to some, attached by respect and/or affection to others, and thus may perceive (say) an encouraging word from the latter as rewarding (i.e. positively reinforcing), but from the former as valueless,

perhaps even aversive. As Bandura (1977) put it, stimuli influence the likelihood of particular behaviours through their predictive function, not because they are automatically linked to responses by occurring together; contingent experiences create expectations rather than stimulus–response connections.

Not surprisingly, behavioural work is increasingly systemic, dealing with caregivers and nominated child 'patients' in their own right as individuals, analysing their relationships to each other (as dyadic attachment subsystems) and their communications, interactions, boundaries and perceptions of one another within a holistic and dynamic family system (Herbert, 1993).

Transition and change: a developmental perspective

Learning, for children, is all about change, as is growth and development. Their parents (and indeed their family) are, like themselves, locked into a developmental life cycle with its stage-related life-tasks. The nature, sources and consequences of parents' ideas about development (Goodnow & Collins, 1990) and the ramifications of transition and change in family life are vitally important in the child therapist's assessment of children and their problems (Herbert, 1991).

Settings

There are three main settings in which behavioural work with children takes place. Behaviour therapy based on the one-to-one (dyadic) or behavioural family therapy (systemic) model tends to take place in the clinic. Behavioural training based on the triadic or behavioural consultation model (using significant caregivers or teachers as mediators of change) generally takes place in the home, or is geared to the home. It may be located in the school or, when it involves group work, in a community centre. Although the distinction between treatment and training is, at times, indistinct, the treatment model is most appropriate to the emotional disorders of childhood (e.g. fears and phobias), the training model to the longer-term problems (e.g. antisocial behaviour and pervasive developmental disorders).

For the author, the behavioural approach is at its best as a fairly eclectic (informed rather than ragbag variety) *problem-solving strategy*. As Yule (1977) put it:

> The applied psychologist looks at a problem and then relates his observations to his knowledge of general psychology and, in the present instance, of child development. He attempts to apply this knowledge so as both to understand the problem better and to effect some change for the better...The difference between this approach and other therapeutic approaches lies in the crucial emphasis placed on evaluating changes in the individual patient and in demonstrating that these changes were the direct result of the intervention procedures (p. 923).

The behavioural problem-solving strategy involves four distinct steps (Herbert, 1987a): (1) specifying the problem(s) clearly and explicitly; (2) formulating explanatory hypotheses to account for the assessment observations; (3) testing these hypotheses; and (4) evaluating the outcome.

ASSESSMENT

A careful assessment is the hallmark of work with individuals. There is no one way of carrying out the task.

Individual behaviour therapy

A conceptual framework for gathering data for assessment and a clinical formulation (in part referred to as a *functional analysis*) is provided in Figure 50.1.

Proximal (current) influences are direct in their effects and close in time to the actions they influence. They are functionally related to behaviour and can thus, as hypotheses about causation, be tested in therapy using single case experimental designs (Morley, 1989). The formulation is directed towards the precise identification of the antecedent, consequent and symbolic conditions which control the problem behaviour. Problem behaviour is assessed in terms of its frequency or intensity; its coexistence with other problems; its duration since onset; and the sense or meaning it has in terms of individual and family psychodynamics.

Behaviour theorists often refer to their assessment in ABC terms, as a simple mnemonic for patients.

A stands for antecedent events.

B stands for *behaviour(s)* — the target behaviour(s) or interactions (also for *belief*: the patient's (perhaps parent's) perception or interpretation of what is happening).

C stands for the consequences that flow from these behaviours/interactions/beliefs.

This linear analysis is elaborated into a recursive sequence such that Cs become As, which generate new Cs, and thus

ramify to affect the actions of others in the vicinity of the main protagonists (say, mother and child).

Target behaviours and/or interactions are chosen for analysis because of their hypothesized significance as problems in the child's (possibly the parent's) repertoire, or in their relationship. Wilson and Evans (1983) studied the reliability of target behaviour selection in behavioural assessment by asking 118 members of the American Association for Advancement of Behavior Therapy to assess three written case descriptions of (1) fearfulness; (2) conduct disorders; and (3) social withdrawal in children. Granted that the means of assessment was somewhat artificial, there was nevertheless a surprisingly low agreement (38%) between clinicians in selecting a first-priority behaviour for treatment. There was considerable variability in selecting behaviours for intervention and, perhaps surprisingly, a substantial (22%) tendency to introduce psychodynamic and intrapsychic terminology, such as 'internalized hostility', 'poor self-concept' and 'insecure child'.

POTENTIAL INTERVENTION METHODS

A simplified list of common therapeutic tasks was given earlier. Table 50.1 provides definitions of some of the available methods and some of the specific clinical applications which have been reported in the literature.

Systemic behaviour therapy

Some versions of family therapy have explicit roots in the application of social learning principles to the resolution of family problems (Patterson, 1982). Treacher and Carpenter (1984, p. 172) draw attention to the striking similarity between aspects of what is often referred to as behavioural family therapy (Herbert, 1985, 1993) and the structural family therapy of Minuchin (1974; see also Chapter 55).

Both approaches focus attention (*inter alia*) on the developmental tasks faced by the family and its members, at various

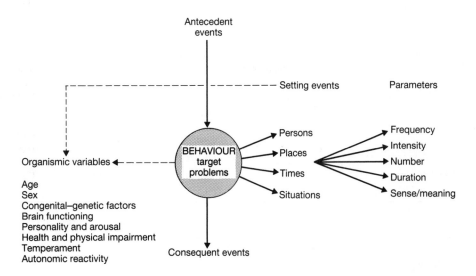

Fig. 50.1 A conceptual framework for an assessment of behaviour problems (adapted from Herbert, 1987a).

Table 50.1 Guide to the application of procedures

Procedure	Method	Some problems dealt with
Positive reinforcement	Present a positive stimulus (a rewarding event or object) following the desired behaviour	Fears and avoidance behaviours Isolated behaviour
Negative reinforcement	Remove a mildly aversive stimulus following the desired behaviour (The above are often combined advantageously in a programme)	Language deficits Hyperactivity Bizarre behaviour Interpersonal conflict Non-compliance/negativism School phobia/truancy Various habit disorders (including toileting deficits: enuresis, encopresis, eating problems etc.) Attentional deficits Academic skills/performance deficits Conduct disorders Delinquency Learning disabilities

Positive reinforcement
  Reinforcing incompatible behaviour (RIB)
 	
  Differential reinforcement of other behaviours (DRO)
	Reinforce behaviour that is incompatible with the unwanted one
	
	Reinforce behaviour other than the undesired one on a regular schedule
		Inappropriate gender behaviour
		Disruptive behaviour
		Agression
		Self-injurious behaviour
		Hyperactivity
		Norm-violating behaviour

Differential reinforcement (including discrimination training and method of successive approximations)	Reinforce desirable behaviours in the presence of the appropriate stimulus; leave them unreinforced in the setting of inappropriate circumstances	Skill/behavioural deficits
Extinction	Withhold reinforcement following inappropriate behaviour	Inappropriate classroom behaviour Temper tantrums Attention-seeking disruptive behaviour Screaming Aggression Excessive crying
Overcorrection	Client makes restitution plus something extra	Disruptiveness
Time out from positive reinforcement (TO)	Withdraw reinforcement for *x* minutes following inappropriate behaviour	Non-attending classroom behaviour Assaultive behaviour Disruptiveness Tantrums Aggression
Response—cost (RC)	Withdraw *x* quantity of reinforcers following inappropriate behaviour (This is a system of fining, i.e. attaching a penalty for unwanted actions)	Stealing Aggression Out-of-seat behaviour in classroom Pestering Delinquency Intractable behaviour Disruptiveness Fire-setting
Avoidance (e.g. covert sensitization)	Present (*in vivo* or in imagination) object to be avoided with aversive stimulus	Unwanted habits, actions

Table 50.1 (*continued*)

Procedure	Method	Some problems dealt with
Skill training Interpersonal skill training (e.g. behaviour rehearsal, assertion training, social skills training)	Self-care/vocational/academic and other skill training Guided rehearsal	Social skill deficits Interpersonal conflict Inappropriate gender behaviour Norm-violating behaviour Delinquency Learning disabilities Toileting skills deficits
Modelling	Get someone suitable to model the desired behaviour, i.e. demonstrate behaviour for child to imitate	Fears and avoidance behaviours Isolated behaviour Social skills deficits Conduct problems Learning disorders Preventive work: preparing children for dental and medical treatment
Stimulus change	Change discriminative stimuli — remove or change controlling antecedent stimuli, i.e. stimuli that are incompatible (interfere) with the desired behaviour	Inappropriate behaviour of various kinds Overeating Non-compliance Attentional deficits
Role-playing, role reversal	Script a role so that the child can rehearse a behaviour and/or situation	Social skills deficits Confrontations, conflict between adolescents and parents
Exposure training (gradual exposure to aversive stimuli, e.g. *in vivo* desensitization)	Expose the child gradually to feared situation while he or she is secure and relaxed	Fears and phobias
Cognitive change methods (e.g. problem-solving skill training)	Teach alternative ways of perceiving, controlling, solving problems	Crisis interventions — problematic situations, including separation, death and other upheavals
Cognitive control	Cognitive restructuring, including problem-solving	Addictive behaviours Conflict situations Interpersonal functioning (conflict) Inhibitions Fears General coping situations Aggression
Self-control/self-management, self-instruction	Various approaches	Interpersonal conflict Impulsivity Fear Academic performance deficits Hyperactivity
Self-confrontation	Video feedback	Obesity Interpersonal conflict Inappropriate parental behaviour
Agreements and contracts	Negotiating goals, discussing rules, achieving compromises in (say) family groups	Disruptive behaviour Stealing Interpersonal conflict School refusal

stages of its (and their) life-span. Day-to-day nuances and patterns of relationship — communication and interaction — between members are inferred from highly charged or repetitive sequences observed and analysed. There is somewhat less emphasis in behavioural family therapy compared with individual treatment on the contingency management of specific target behaviours, and more on broad principles of child management, the setting of limits (boundaries), the interpersonal interactions of members of the family, the marital relationships (which are often poor in the parents of problematic children) and the perceived self-efficacy of caregivers. It lends itself particularly to cases of child abuse where disciplinary, child management, communication and attachment (bonding) difficulties abound (Iwaniec *et al.*, 1985). The approach is multimodal, there being at least three levels (Table 50.2) at which interventions might be focused.

PLANNING A BEHAVIOURAL INTERVENTION

The overall principles governing the choice of treatment should be those of alleviating distress, enhancing personal and social performance and, with it, quality of life. This requires that a treatment should always carry some primary benefit for the individual patient; such benefits should endure beyond the immediacies of the treatment process; and treatment should always be used within an overall planned programme of management. There are also several ethical imperatives to be taken into account when using behavioural treatments in childhood. The Royal College of Psychiatrists working party (1989), referred to earlier, addressed these issues — some of which I summarize and paraphrase below:

1 Children may be limited in their understanding of a treatment or its implications and consequently unable to give full consent. It may, nevertheless, still be necessary to use a behavioural treatment; if so, it is essential that they are applied in such a way as to take the special needs of children into account, particularly those arising from their dependence, immaturity, difficulties in understanding and problems in communicating.

2 In evaluating the acceptability of a behavioural method or goal, the current social and professional consensus, taken in conjunction with the legitimately held values and beliefs of the patient, should be considered in relation to the seriousness of the disturbance and its repercussions to the patient and to society. The majority of behavioural treatments and procedures are ethically unexceptionable but some may give rise to problems and anxieties.

3 If the only effective method available involves distress or risk, the decision to apply it must reflect the importance of the goal to the patient and to others. Such treatments, for example aversion treatments (Lovaas, 1977), should be discussed with a clinical ethical committee.

4 It is essential, speaking about goals, to consider the presenting problems as objectively as possible. Parents sometimes ask for treatment to make their child conform with family values that may be at odds with those of society as a whole. Similar requests are sometimes made when a child fails to fit in with a

Table 50.2 Potential interventions

Systemic level	Dyadic level (Interactions/relationships)	Individual level
Family group discussion/therapy	Enhancing positive interactions	*Parent/Caregiver*
Written contracts	Operant programmes	Training in more effective child-care practice (e.g. use of appropriate sanctions; setting limits; praising)
Negotiation training	Positive reinforcement — 'catching the child out in good behaviour'	
Settling differences		Developmental counselling to enhance knowledge/decrease faulty perceptions/attributions
Contingency contracting (exchange theory)	Decreasing threats, criticism	
Communication enhancement	Encouraging play with children (including demonstrations/modelling)	Cognitive restructuring (reframing)
Clarification of roles and rules		
Improvement of physical/environment resources (e.g. child-minding/day care)	Increasing consistency	Reducing inappropriate anxiety/anger/cynicism
	Negotiating fair/few/clear rules	Relaxation
Cognitive restructuring (reframing)	Marital work	Self-talk
		Self-control training
		Child
		Improving life skills
		Play therapy
		Systematic desensitization
		Skills training

regime at a children's home or school. A judgement must be made about the reasonableness of such a request.

5 The proposed method of treatment should be explained in detail and it is helpful and sensible to offer written explanatory information.

CLINICAL APPLICATIONS

It is an indication of the versatility of modern behaviour therapy that it is possible here to mention only a small sample of the psychiatric, psychiatry/health-related (liaison) and educational problems to which behavioural methods have been applied with some success (Ollendick & Cerny, 1981; O'Leary & Carr, 1982; Blakely & Davidson, 1984; Bornstein & Kazdin, 1985; Herbert, 1991). Their diversity calls for planning on a case-by-case basis, treatment being decided on the basis of a broad-spectrum functional analysis and a knowledge of child development and, of course, the research literature on the effectiveness of particular problems.

The effectiveness of behaviour therapy

Before reviewing some applications of behaviour therapy to particular problems, it is necessary to examine the term effectiveness. It is generally accepted that the claim of psychotherapeutic efficacy requires the demonstration of long-term effects following termination of treatment. How long is a moot point when we are dealing with something as changeable as behaviour in childhood. In any event, the ideal follow-up studies that evaluate and compare treatment methods (controlling the many potentially confounding variables by means of large-scale, randomized experimental designs) are extremely expensive and difficult to implement (Herbert, 1990). Not surprisingly, they are rare in the area of childhood psychotherapy.

The word effectiveness itself is elusive. Conclusions about the relative effectiveness of different therapies may vary, depending: (1) on *whether* one examines interview ratings of symptoms as opposed to direct observations; (2) on *what* signifies a significant clinical change; (3) *where* — i.e. the setting in which — the evaluation is made; and (4) *by whom* — patient or therapist (Kazdin, 1988). To compound the confusion one must ask oneself what constitutes a cure or improvement? How much of an improvement will suffice? Should the therapist be satisfied only with the complete eradication of a problem, or with a more modest reduction in the intensity of (say) anxiety or frequency of some deviant action? There is no simple answer; it depends on the nature of the problem, its implications (e.g. the risk it poses), the context in which it occurs, and so on.

And it is here, precisely, that developmental considerations are important in discussing the efficacy of child treatment. I began this section by mentioning the criterion of stability of change as a measure of effectiveness. But there is a need for caution in applying this to children's behaviour. Depending on the age of the child, and what it is learning, parents have to go on and on repeating themselves, reminding endlessly in the attempt to socialize their children: rewarding them, instructing them, sanctioning antisocial actions and rehearsing prosocial behaviours. Parents do not expect to teach their children in short 'programmatic' bursts of activity, even if they wished it were possible. Teaching goes on until the child has certain crucial social behaviours or the control of antisocial tendencies as habitual (internalized) parts of their repertoire. Time-scales vary, depending on the age and maturity of the child and the nature of the learning task. This is why the author has recommended the systematic scheduling of booster sessions in work with conduct disorder — a problem of childhood where failures of socialization are an important element (Herbert, 1987b).

These difficulties do not release us from the obligation to attempt to validate all therapies and this is a Herculean task if we are to make comparisons; there are over 250 treatments for children and adolescents according to Kazdin (1988). Reviews of different techniques bearing the superordinate title 'psychological therapy' suggest that psychotherapy is better than no treatment for a large number of childhood problems, including anxiety, hyperactivity, social withdrawal and aggression (Kazdin, 1988; Tuma, 1989). But two decades on, we still cannot answer precisely Paul's often-quoted question: '*What* treatment, by *whom*, is more effective for *this* individual with *that* specific problem, under *which* set of circumstances?' (Paul, 1967). We can indicate where behavioural psychotherapy has a promising track record. But it is difficult to provide chapter and verse from rigorous comparison studies, except in a few examples such as the incontinence problems (Smith & Smith, 1987), conduct disorders (Kazdin, 1985, 1987; Herbert, 1987b), and possibly phobic disorders (see King *et al.*, 1988, for the superiority of behavioural approaches over other methods).

Because the frontiers of behaviour therapy are still expanding it is also difficult to answer the question: Which problems are not amenable to this approach? The range of problems has been broadened by the widening concept of behavioural psychotherapy which encompasses 'conversational' therapy, counselling, cognitive and (some would say) psychodynamic thinking. In a word, behavioural work has become, for many practitioners, eclectic (see Johnson *et al.*, 1986, for an account of what they call 'purposive eclecticism' in child treatment).

It has to be acknowledged that there is a great deal of unpredictability in the effects of behavioural interventions. The therapist soon learns that techniques that usually yield the most impressive results are not always effective with certain children. Furthermore, a given technique may, on one day, produce complete control in the case of a particular child, but on the next have no apparent effect at all. Numerous studies have demonstrated that, while behavioural procedures can be applied successfully in such varied settings as clinics, psychiatric hospitals, schools, homes and residential facilities for delinquent or handicapped populations, only rarely is there an automatic transfer of improvement from one situation to another (situational, like temporal, generalization must be worked at).

Nonspecific 'core conditions'

Relationship and other therapeutic process variables cannot be minimized in behaviour therapy any more than in other forms of psychotherapy. They are necessary but not sufficient conditions of change (Frank, 1973). Positive expectations about the outcome of treatment and attitude towards the therapist have been shown to be important elements in determining the success or failure of programmes (Sloane *et al.*, 1975). According to Bandura (1977), a powerful therapeutic ingredient in psychological methods resides in their ability to alter the patient's self-efficacy expectations. These derive primarily from four sources of information: notably, performance accomplishments, but also vicarious experience, verbal persuasion and physiological states. The more reliable the sources, the greater are the changes in perceived self-efficacy, which (in turn) affect both *initiation* (the willingness to get involved in otherwise daunting situations) and *persistence* of coping behaviour in the face of aversive experiences.

BEHAVIOURAL TREATMENT OF PARTICULAR PROBLEMS

Emotional disorders

Depression

Depressive reactions in children are frequently treated as concomitants of school refusal, truancy, failure to thrive, substance abuse and delinquency. But depression has only recently achieved the status of a problem of childhood in its own right. The need for a broad-based intervention with depressive problems seems to be the conclusion of recent studies (e.g. Puig-Antich *et al.*, 1985a,b). Tricyclic medication, behaviour therapy, counselling, psychotherapy and cognitive therapy appear to be the main options, singly or in combination.

Depression in older children (and adolescents) would, on the face of it, seem to lend itself to a cognitive-behavioural approach as depressed patients tend to manifest a high rate of intrusive negative thoughts, including selective ruminations about past events that were unhappy, thoughts about the hopelessness of the future and their helplessness in the face of their perceived dilemma (Seligman, 1975). These cognitive-behavioural methods look promising (Kaslow & Rehm, 1983; Reynolds, 1984; Campbell *et al.*, 1989). Given the tendency of depressed children and adolescents to externalize the location of control in their lives, it would seem sensible to combine psychological methods (which enhance their self-esteem and self-empowerment), with drugs (where indicated) which might well be efficacious, but could also reinforce a sense of passivity and of helplessness.

However, caution is required in making confident claims, as

yet, for a behavioural approach. One of the findings that has emerged strikingly from the drug studies of depression is that, even for disorders of a high degree of severity and of some chronicity, there is a marked placebo response. This has an implication for the use of a waiting-list control condition. Such studies are few and far between in the case of cognitive-behaviour therapy with children and adolescents. An example of what is required is a study by Reynolds and Coats (1986). They randomly assigned 30 moderately depressed adolescents to one of three conditions: (1) cognitive-behavioural therapy; (2) relaxation training; or (3) waiting-list control. In addition to the initial screening, subjects were tested on three occasions: (1) pretreatment assessment; (2) posttreatment assessment; and (3) at a 5-week follow-up assessment. Both cognitive-behaviour therapy and relaxation training were found to be effective in the treatment of the depressed adolescents. When compared with the waiting-list control condition, both treatments demonstrated a significant reduction in depressive symptomatology. Further, these improvements were maintained at the 5-week follow-up assessment. Of interest were the findings in relation to measures of anxiety. On this criterion, the greatest changes occurred for the relaxation training subjects, especially from posttreatment to follow-up assessment. In relation to general self-concept, there were no significant differences between the groups at posttest and follow-up. Both treatment groups, however, reported higher levels of academic self-concept at posttreatment relative to the control group. Yet at follow-up, only the cognitive-behavioural group showed a significantly greater level of academic self-concept compared to the waiting-list control group. Given that this study (and this is still the general pattern in the literature) provides follow-up data on a brief time-scale, it is impossible to draw conclusions about the value of this (or any other) psychological treatment in preventing relapse.

Social skills training has been successfully applied to depressed children who often exhibit poor social skills (Frame *et al.*, 1982).

Anxiety

A wide range of methods based on modelling procedures, operant methods and variations on the theme of systematic desensitization have proved beneficial in the treatment of anxious and fearful children (see Ollendick & King, 1991). This finding was referred to earlier in the chapter; but why should it be so? Part of the answer lies in the fact that problems of a person suffering from phobic fears are not unidimensional. With regard to the particular components of a child's anxiety disorder, they are likely to consist of verbal reports of distress, cognitive, autonomic and motor phenomena which display a degree of specificity with regard to persons, places, times and situations/circumstances, and indeed, with regard to each other (see Fig. 50.1). The specificity of a phobic disorder must be carefully assessed in order to plan an effective programme of treatment; if, for example, the major components of the problem are autonomic and cognitive, then the treatment might focus on modifying the autonomic reactions and cognitions directly.

Systematic desensitization has typically involved imaginal representation of the fear-producing stimuli and has employed muscular relaxation as the competing, inhibiting response. These procedures appear to work quite well with adolescents and older children (Ollendick, 1979); however, younger children appear to have difficulty in acquiring muscular relaxation and in being able to image clearly the fear-producing stimuli (Rosenstiel & Scott, 1977). As a result, *in vivo* desensitization and emotive imagery have become increasingly popular, especially with younger children (Hatzenbuehler & Schroeder, 1978).

Lazarus and Abramovitz (1962) recommend the use of the categories of imagery which arouse feelings of self-assertion, pride, affection, mirth and similar anxiety-inhibiting responses. Methods used in work with children manifesting night-time fears include the use of engaging stories and images of heroic characters to build up a positive affect into which fear-eliciting stimuli are gradually interwoven (King *et al.*, 1989).

An illustration of the emotive imagery approach is provided by Jackson and King (1981) in the treatment of a 5-year-old child with extreme fears of the dark, noises and shadows. Having determined that the child was fond of the comic character Batman (the boy reportedly wore his Batman cape and mask around the house, watched reruns of the Batman series on television, and possessed several toys associated with Batman, including puzzles and a Batmobile), the therapists created a fear hierarchy and then asked the child to imagine that 'he and Batman had joined forces and that he was appointed as a special agent'. Next he was asked to close his eyes and to imagine the fear-producing stimuli in a graduated fashion, while accompanied by Batman. Altogether, there were four sessions of emotive imagery. Treatment, albeit uncontrolled, was successful. In this case study, muscular relaxation has been attempted and was unsuccessful.

Other uncontrolled and controlled case studies have illustrated the potential efficacy of systematic desensitization and its variants in the treatment of a variety of childhood fears such as dogs, the dark, dentists, water, school, bees and loud noises (Blagg & Yule, 1984; Ollendick & King, 1991). Support for the value of operant-based procedures in the treatment of anxious and withdrawn behaviours in children and adolescents is reasonably firm (King *et al.*, 1988). However, as with systematic desensitization, this conclusion is based mainly on comparisons with no-treatment or waiting-list control conditions. Considerably more comparative evaluations with other behavioural procedures, as well as more traditional psychotherapeutic approaches, are necessary for a more precise specification of their efficacy. The same applies to modelling.

Behavioural cognitive methods have been demonstrated to be successful in a series of studies by Graziano and his colleagues. They included 40 clinically phobic children aged 6—13 (Graziano *et al.*, 1979; Graziano & Mooney, 1980).

There was a 2—3-year follow-up (Graziano & Mooney, 1982). The children were severely fearful at night, displaying panic behaviours (e.g. frequent crying and frightened calling out to the parents) that had disrupted family life nearly every night for a mean of 5 years. Improvements were reported for 39 of the 40 children. Maintenance of improvement was reported for 31 of the 34 children studied at follow-up.

Probably the most frequently used cognitive approach with anxious children is verbal self-instruction training. Kanfer *et al.* (1975) treated 5—6-year-old children who were afraid of the dark. Three groups of children were formed. The first group rehearsed active control or competence-mediating statements (e.g. 'I am a brave child and I can handle the dark'); the second group rehearsed statements aimed at reducing the aversive quality of the stimulus situation itself (e.g. 'The dark is not such a bad place to be'); and the third group rehearsed neutral statements (e.g. 'Mary had a little lamb'). When later exposed to a darkness tolerance test, both the competence and stimulus groups surpassed the neutral instruction group in duration. The competence and stimulus groups did not differ significantly from each other, suggesting that adaptive statements were acquired under both conditions.

To summarize, the new and innovative cognitive-based procedures show considerable promise in the treatment of anxious and fearful children. Although initial findings suggest that effects produced in such programmes may be long-term and generalizable, a clear and well-controlled demonstration of such effects is not yet available (Van Hasselt *et al.*, 1979; Kendall, 1984; Kendall *et al.*, 1988).

Conduct disorders

Conduct-disordered children, with their aggressive antisocial behaviour, are capable of wreaking havoc in their own and others' lives, and are also frequently rejected by their peers (Coie, 1990) and/or abused by their parents (Reid *et al.*, 1981). The prevalence of the disorder (4—10% of children in the UK and the US) is probably on the increase, creating a need for a therapeutic service that outstrips, by a long way, the resources available. Prevention becomes a vital issue as these children (particularly 'early starters') are at risk of developing problems later in life such as dropping out of school, alcoholism, drug abuse, juvenile delinquency, adult crime, antisocial personality, marital disruption, interpersonal problems and poor physical health (Kazdin, 1985; Patterson *et al.*, 1989).

Interventions

Structural causes (i.e. socioeconomic factors such as poor housing, inner-city deprivation and alienation) are important in the development of conduct disorders and cannot be ignored, although there may be little the clinician can do directly about them. There are different levels at which therapeutic change of four different types is required: (1) ecological;

(2) operant methods; (3) medication; and (4) behavioural parent training.

Ecological

One function of ecological manipulation is to create productive environments that not only reduce the antecedents for undesirable behaviour but also maximize the opportunities for new learning to occur. The model also includes tactics that physically deter undesirable behaviour from occurring (e.g. making opportunistic thieving physically more difficult).

Operant methods

Behavioural approaches using reinforcement of desired behaviour in the classroom and home have been repeatedly demonstrated to lead to beneficial changes — albeit usually short-term and situation-specific — in disruptive behaviour, aggression, poor cooperation with peers and poor school attendance (Patterson, 1982). Academic performance also responds to classroom reinforcement programmes (O'Leary & O'Leary, 1977).

Medication

Pharmacological agents — notably psychostimulants — have been used since the 1930s to control hyperactivity (Barkley, 1982; Campbell *et al.*, 1989; see also Chapters 17 and 51) for reviews of what are complex and emotive issues). Their use has been a matter of considerable public debate in the US (Schrag & Divoky, 1975).

All these compounds carry their risks of side-effects. One of the greatest risks, paradoxically, is to clinicians — the fact that drugs are so easy to prescribe in the context of a busy general, psychiatric or paediatric practice. Their availability may short-circuit the necessary detailed analysis of the child's motor, attentional and behavioural problems. In the absence of such care, drug therapy can degenerate into a facile and unethical method of social control in the home and the classroom. A behavioural approach can make the use of drugs unnecessary or may, in combination with medication, reduce the time for which they need to be prescribed (Barkley, 1982).

Behavioural parent training

Parent training has provided a promising therapeutic response to the difficult challenge of the conduct disorders. To meet the shortfall in professional resources, agencies have looked increasingly to training parents in group settings. The programmes emphasize methods designed to reduce confrontations, and antagonistic interactions among the family members, to increase the effectiveness of positive interactions and moderate the intensity of parental punishment. The rationale comes from research indicating that parents of aggressive, antisocial children often lack certain basic parenting skills. They frequently indulge in coercive commands and criticisms and high rates of threats, anger, nagging and negative consequences (Snyder & Brown, 1983).

In these groups, parents learn (it is argued) not only a new model of behaviour — a construct system which emphasizes the significance of behavioural consequences and environmental causality — but they assimilate new methods of understanding behaviour. They learn a new language — verbal and nonverbal — for communicating with their children and a more precise way of specifying, defining, observing and thinking about behaviour—environment relationships. There is a belief that the parent's ongoing contact with the child and possession of new skills might facilitate generalization of treatment effects across time.

The seminal influence on parent-training theory (e.g. the coercion hypothesis) and practice, is the work of Patterson, Reid and their colleagues at the Oregon Social Learning Center (OSLC) where they have treated over 200 families with extremely aggressive antisocial children, over a period of some two decades. Five family management practices form the core components of the OSLC programme:

1 Parents are taught how to pinpoint the problematic activities of concern and to track them at home (e.g. compliance versus noncompliance).

2 They are taught reinforcement techniques (e.g. praise, point systems) and disciplinary methods.

3 When parents see their children behaving inappropriately, they learn to apply a mild consequence such as time out or a short-term deprivation of privileges (response—cost).

4 They are taught to monitor (i.e. to supervise) their children even when they are away from home. This involves parents knowing where their children are at all times, what they are doing and when they will be returning home.

5 Finally they are taught problem-solving and negotiation strategies and become increasingly responsible for designing their own programmes. (Twenty hours of direct contact with individual families is the typical pattern in the OSLC treatment package.)

The therapist must be skilled in coping with the resistance to change that characterizes the majority of the families referred for treatment. Ordinarily, this level of clinical skill requires several years of supervised clinical experience (see Hollin *et al.*, 1987, on training in Applied Social Learning Theory).

Another successful parent-training programme for young conduct-disordered children (aged 3—8) has been developed by Webster-Stratton (1981, 1982). It includes components of other fruitful treatment packages (E. Hanf & J. King, unpublished data; Forehand & McMahon, 1981; also Patterson, 1982), as outlined above. There are elements of problem-solving and communication skills (Spivack *et al.*, 1976; D'Zurilla & Nezsu, 1982). The Group Discussion Videotape Modeling programme is notable for its imaginative and systematic use of video-tape modelling methods. The series of 10 video-tapes shows models of differing sexes, ages, cultures, socioeconomic backgrounds and temperaments, so that parents will perceive the models as similar to themselves and their children. In addition, the video-tapes show parent models in natural situations (unrehearsed) with their children 'doing it right' and 'doing it wrong'. The parenting skills (250 vignettes, each of which lasts approximately 1−2 minutes) are shown by a therapist to groups of parents (8−12 parents per group). After each vignette, the therapist leads a group discussion of the relevant interactions and encourages parents' ideas and problem-solving as well as role-playing and rehearsal. The programme has also been given to over 80 parents of conduct-disordered children as a completely self-administered intervention.

A video-tape programme (ENHANCE) based on six video-tape programmes has also been developed to focus on family issues other than parent skills, such as anger management, coping with depression, marital communication skills, problem-solving strategies, and how to teach children to problem-solve and manage their anger more effectively.

An example of a British effort is the Scott programme which was developed for, and validated on, the typical social service clientele of single-parent, low-income or state benefit families (Scott & Stradling, 1987). The programme can be administered by social workers or assistants familiar with the Programme Manual. The programme consists of six 90-minute sessions run at weekly intervals during which a variety of behavioural techniques (e.g. planned ignoring, social reinforcement, time out, response−cost, teaching new skills) are taught, largely through role-play, with a follow-up session a month later. The groups are made up of 5−8 mothers.

Evaluation of behavioural parent training. All the above programmes have received high ratings from parents on acceptability and consumer satisfaction (Cross Calvert & McMahon, 1987; Webster-Stratton, 1989). Significant changes in parents' and children's actions and in parental perceptions of child adjustment have indicated encouraging short-term success (Patterson *et al.* 1973; McMahon & Forehand, 1983; Scott & Stradling, 1987; Webster-Stratton *et al.*, 1988). Observations in the home setting have suggested that parents are successful in reducing children's level of aggression by 20−60% (Patterson, 1982; Webster-Stratton, 1985).

All of the programmes report generalization of behaviour improvements from the clinic setting to the home (Peed *et al.*, 1977; Patterson & Fleischman, 1979; Webster-Stratton, 1984; Scott & Stradling, 1987) over follow-up periods ranging from 6 months to 4 years; also, generalization to untreated child behaviours (Arnold *et al.*, 1975; Fleischman, 1981; Webster-Stratton, 1982, 1990; Forehand & Long, 1986). The Forehand and McMahon (1981) programme did not show generalization from the clinic to the school (Breiner & Forehand, 1981).

Results from the Forehand and McMahon (1981) programme have been shown to be more effective than a family systems therapy (Wells & Egan, 1988). A group version of the programme proved to be more effective than a parent discussion group based on the Systematic Training for Effective Parenting programme (Dinkmeyer & McKay, 1976; Baum

et al., 1986). Webster-Stratton's programme has been replicated with several different populations and has been shown to be superior to a waiting-list control condition (Webster-Stratton, 1981, 1982, 1984). Changes arising from Patterson's programme are superior to family-based psychotherapy, attention-placebo (discussion) and no-treatment conditions (Patterson *et al.*, 1982).

Training formats. Efforts have been made to 'tease out' the specific treatment components and patient attributes that contribute to a successful (or unsuccessful) outcome (Forehand & Atkeson, 1977; Christensen *et al.*, 1980). Component analyses of the Group Discussion Videotape Modeling parent training methods (Webster-Stratton *et al.*, 1988, 1989) seem to suggest that the group approach represents a cost-effective alternative to the conventional parent-training format of individual therapy with a single family. Also, parent-training methods based on video-tape modelling plus parent group discussion and support will produce more sustained and long-term effects than programmes which do not use video-tape modelling or group discussion methods.

As with all new therapeutic approaches subjected to rigorous evaluation (and sadly many are not validated), there is no evidence that behavioural parent training is a panacea. There are many unresolved problems: among these are high drop-out rates, the difficulty of maintaining improvements and the intractability of specific delinquencies such as stealing. Studies cast doubt on whether all families with childhood conduct disorders are equally able to benefit from purely behavioural treatment packages. The issue of what family characteristics affect successful parent-training outcome (and this is a matter of relevance to all therapeutic methods) is very much of current concern.

Ollendick and Cerny (1981) suggest that the failure of some parent-training programmes is due to marital problems between parents or other conflicts within the family. Children from low socioeconomic families generally display more anti-social behaviour and poorer school adjustment, which require longer treatment periods (Herbert, 1987b). Reviews (O'Dell, 1974; Cobb & Medway, 1978) suggest that parental drop-out from training programmes may be linked to factors such as income level and educational background.

Negative findings may reflect an erroneous clinical formulation, or perhaps a lack of ability or training on the part of the therapist; they may reflect an inability of the parents to conceptualize learning principles or a resistance to perceiving improvement in their children's behaviour.

Failure is sometimes a reflection of unremitting stress undermining parents' resolve to set limits, to be consistent, etc. because of their exhaustion and despair. The disappointing results may relate to the parents' own previous experiences of parenting and to ideologies of child care and discipline (in particular, punishment) that are at odds with the assumptions of parent trainers. The somewhat poor outcome reported for parents of lower socioeconomic status, for parents with strong ideologies, or single parents (e.g. Webster-Stratton, 1985) could be due to a lack of perceived relevance in the applied social learning approach. Perhaps parents who have tried for many years to manage an intractable child are looking for 'better' ways of punishing their wayward child (most physical abuse incidents occur in response to what parents perceive as disciplinary encounters) rather than drawn-out programmes that emphasize the positive side of their offspring — a feature of many programmes. In other words, there is an ideological mismatch.

Oppositional/noncompliance problems

We have seen that parents of children with conduct problems give more negative commands than parents of 'normal' youngsters. Parents with reasonably obedient children give more so-called alpha commands. Alpha commands are characterized by being specific and direct, being given one at a time and being followed by a wait of 5 seconds. Parents can be taught to use these, rather than beta commands — chain commands, vague commands, question commands, 'let's' commands, and commands followed by a rational, or verbalization (Peed *et al.*, 1977; Forehand & McMahon, 1981).

Individual or group behavioural programmes attending to both antecedent (e.g. commands) and consequence (e.g. reinforcement) sides of the ABC equation illustrated in Figure 50.1 produce better generalization of effects; each side provides the parent with constructive skills (Forehand & McMahon, 1981).

Eating and mealtime difficulties

Typical mealtime activities that cause concern are refusing food, fiddling with it, leaving the table, having a tantrum, crying and complaining. The effectiveness of a range of behavioural treatment procedures has been demonstrated for reducing disruptive activity and the duration of meals, while increasing food intake (Ireton & Guthrie, 1972). McMahon and Forehand (1978) found that improvements in the inappropriate mealtime behaviours of 3 preschool children and their mothers were associated with the provision of a brochure to parents. The brochure described a way in which behaviour management procedures could be applied to children's disruptive actions during meals.

The provision of written information alone is often sufficient to produce behaviour change for problems which are not severe, long-standing or present across a range of stimulus conditions (Clark *et al.*, 1976).

Bedtime and sleeping difficulties

Behavioural management techniques applied to settling and waking difficulties have been found to be successful in 90% of children between 1 and 5 years old (Richman *et al.*, 1985). Douglas and Richman (1984) produced a manual which has been successfully used by health visitors and in community clinics.

Developmental disorders

Enuresis

Mowrer and Mowrer (1938) provided the necessary impetus for the systematic treatment of enuresis by devising a special training pad which was placed under the child when in bed. The pad, when moistened (with urine) during the night, closed a circuit and rang a bell. It was arranged that when this happened, someone would wake the child, take him or her to the toilet, and change the bed and night clothes. This conditioning technique was very effective.

The evidence for the superiority of the alarm method (with rates of remission between 80 and 90%) over no-treatment and other-treatment control procedures is well-documented for nocturnal enuresis (see Doleys's (1977) review of data based on over 600 subjects). This survey revealed an average relapse rate of 40%; but nearly 60% of these returned to continence after booster sessions.

It has been suggested that the apparatus is based on classical conditioning principles. The idea is that the noise of the buzzer (unconditioned stimulus) causes the child to wake up and attend to the cue of a distended bladder. In this way the child is conditioned to wake up and empty his or her bladder in the night. But what usually happens, contrary to the theory, is that when children using the enuresis alarm become dry, they do not wake up and empty their bladders at night: they sleep through quite dry until morning (White, 1971). Other theorists suggest that operant principles are at work (Lovibond, 1963). In operant terms, the buzzer is an aversive stimulus and the responses of waking and contracting the sphincter are conditioned avoidance responses. Children learn to associate nocturnal voiding with unpleasant consequences; to avoid this, they learn to strengthen their bladder muscles so they can sleep through the night.

Despite the potential of these methods, it is common, in my experience, to meet professionals who are disillusioned because behavioural methods have not worked in their cases. Sometimes uncharitably, one suspects a lack of special skill or experience in the complainants, or a tendency to underrate the painstaking requirements of both the assessment and treatment stages. Many things can go wrong: problems of a technical nature (sweat may trigger the alarm; batteries go flat; the child's clothing and bedding are not prepared properly); inconsistency on the part of the exhausted parents; insufficient expert monitoring of the programme; premature withdrawal of therapy and so on (see Morgan, 1984).

Encopresis

Paediatric assistance is invaluable in the physical aspects of an intervention. The approach tends to involve the use of enemas, laxatives, stool softeners, together with dietary advice — all of importance in the case of retentive encopresis.

Doleys (1978), in his review of treatment studies, found that 93% of cases were successfully treated by the use of behavioural methods. Operant conditioning techniques, in particular a combination of positive and negative reinforcement, have been used to modify the encopresis and smearing (Herbert & Iwaniec, 1981). Sluckin (1975, 1981) has successfully treated cases of encopresis attending an outpatient child guidance clinic. Mothers of the children were instructed to reward them for passing a motion in the toilet. Laxatives were prescribed in order to ensure regular and painless bowel movements. The pain of going to the toilet (for a constipated child) may be sufficiently intense and enduring to set up a conditioned and generalized aversive reaction to the entire process of toileting.

Social deficit problems

Social skills

Social skills programmes have been conducted on behaviourally disordered, developmentally delayed and intellectually impaired children. Most of the studies have concentrated on aspects of their behavioural problems such as unassertiveness, excessive aggression and social withdrawal (Allen *et al.*, 1964; Hart *et al.*, 1968; Michelson & Wood, 1980). The results are encouraging (Beck & Forehand, 1984). There have been a few promising studies of developmentally delayed children (Whitman *et al.*, 1970; Apolloni *et al.*, 1977) who have been helped by this approach.

There is something of a 'hit and miss' feeling to many of these studies, a lack of precise rationale as an underpinning to the training programmes chosen (Ladd, 1984). There is no agreement in the literature on what children should be taught during social skills training. It may be that an emphasis on facilitating active social problem-solving processes, rather than teaching static social skills, will produce the longer-term gains that have so far evaded most interventions (Furman, 1980).

Problem-solving skills

These are discussed in Chapter 48.

Problems of communication

Selective mutism

The child who elects to remain silent in the presence of others or, more accurately, selects to whom he or she will talk, has been treated, in the past, by psychodynamic approaches that stressed infant and childhood experiences that had interfered with the mother—child relationship. Little effort was made to remove the symptom of restricted speech itself. Reed (1963) was among the first to suggest that a child's differential pattern of communication might be subjected to a functional analysis — the frequency of talking in certain situations and/or to certain individuals. Using a behavioural analysis, Cunningham *et al.* (1983) found that the most fruitful treatment strategies were shaping, by rewarding an approximation to the goal in situations where a minimum of speech was

present, by situation fading and individual fading. In situation fading, the child and the person to whom he or she is willing to talk are moved, step by step, from one place where speech is present, to another where speech is not as yet present. In individual fading, new individuals are gradually introduced into situations familiar to the child. A combination of fading and judicious reinforcement procedures leads to the child's being able to talk to an increasing number of people in a variety of situations (see also Labbe & Williamson).

The scarcity of follow-up data on treatment has been addressed (although not in an ideal prospective form) in a retrospective study by Sluckin *et al.* (1991). Twenty-five children, who had at one time been selective mutes, were followed by means of questionnaires administered via their schools, 2—10 years after referral. Eleven had been given individual therapy programmes with a behavioural content and home and school involvement. The remainder received remedial help from special needs teachers in the school setting, with routine Schools Psychological Service support and minimal home contact. Stepwise multiple regression revealed the importance of a history of some form of mental illness in the family as a major determinant of nontalking at follow-up. Those children receiving individual behavioural programmes had made significantly greater improvements than those who had had nonintensive, school-based programmes.

Stuttering

Behaviour therapists view stammering as learned behaviour and, where there is no definite physical defect, as a behaviour pattern that may be directly and successfully retrained by a variety of behaviour-oriented techniques. These include contingency management (Burns & Brady, 1980); distraction (Cherry & Sayers, 1956); the correction of negative habits or poorly developed speech patterns (Dalali & Sheehan, 1974); and systematic desensitization of anxiety about speaking (Boucheau & Jeffry, 1973).

Language delays

The most appropriate treatment for children with language delays has not yet been established. Howlin (1984) has reviewed a number of schemes for parental involvement in the treatment of children with language delays. These range from those centred on children with delays associated with intellectual impairment and autism through to those involving expressive language delays primarily as the result of inadequate or inappropriate stimulation at home. She found that, although few of these approaches to treatment had been adequately evaluated, those that involved the parents in home-based activities as part of a *structured learning programme* of remedial help for the children, were likely to show significant improvements. The same general principle applies to the treatment of autistic children, where behavioural methods have been shown to bring worthwhile long-term benefits (Howlin & Rutter, 1987; see also Chapter 33).

Clark and Rutter (1981) found that, as the demands for social response from autistic children are increased, the children are more likely to produce a social response. This kind of observation has encouraged psychologists and teachers to use behavioural methods to shape up social behaviour, skills and speech (De Myer *et al.*, 1981). Harris and Handleman (1987) make the point that, although treatment focuses primarily on the creative application of traditional operant procedures, interventions with parents and siblings extend to the full range of cognitive-behavioural methods.

A plethora of aversive procedures (water mist, nasty-tasting substances, etc.) have been used to suppress the unwanted and dangerous behaviours (e.g. aggression, self-injury, self-stimulation) characteristic of some autistic children. Recent years have witnessed a welcome search for nonaversive alternatives, such as physical exercise (jogging) and incompatible distractions of a stimulating, pleasant nature.

Psychophysiological (psychosomatic) disorders

Bronchial asthma

What makes asthma so interesting from the aspect of learned behaviour is the fact that breathing, while largely an involuntary activity, is also subject to voluntary control. This means that specific attacks of asthma might be conceptualized in classical conditioning and/or operant learning terms. Creer *et al.* (1982) described a successful five-component treatment package which contains elements of monitoring breathing, relaxation and appropriate use of medication.

A careful assessment may uncover the presence of positive or negative reinforcement from various sources, such as avoidance of social activities which are feared or unpleasant school activities. Unacceptable behaviours (e.g. temper tantrums) may become reinforced by parents who are afraid of provoking an asthmatic episode.

Diabetes mellitus

Rates of nonadherence to vital treatment regimes are very high in childhood diabetes. Behavioural methods have been put to work to increase compliance to treatment plans, and to good effect (see review by Fonagy *et al.*, 1989). Ioannou (1991) sets out some of the principles and practical strategies for helping parents and children to cope with fear and pain surrounding injections and other physical treatments.

Glucose levels are influenced by environmental variables, including psychological stress, which gives scope for behavioural stress management packages (Rose *et al.*, 1983).

Anorexia nervosa

The operant paradigm generally applied to this serious disorder, includes (*inter alia*) restricting the anorexic patient to her or his room and making activities and privileges contingent on weight gain. Those who advocate these methods for the treatment of anorexia nervosa claim that they produce faster and larger weight gains during hospitalization than do other medically or psychiatrically oriented techniques. Swann Van Buskirk (1989), in her review of therapeutic approaches in anorexia nervosa, states that it is sometimes difficult to evaluate these claims because the empirical results have often been complicated by the inclusion of various other forms of psychotherapy.

DISCUSSION

Many psychiatrists (as well as clinical psychologists and social workers) have been antipathetic to behaviour therapy in the past, and remain unimpressed to this day. Yet as long ago as 1973, the American Psychiatric Association issued a Task Force Report on behaviour therapy and concluded as follows:

> The work of the Task Force has reaffirmed our belief that behavior therapy and behavioral principles employed in the analysis of clinical phenomena have reached a stage of development where they now unquestionably have much to offer informed clinicians in the service of modern clinical and social psychiatry (p. 64).

More recently, Kazdin, in his review of the psychotherapies for childhood and their effectiveness, presented evidence — albeit still somewhat tentative — that differences in treatment effects, over a wide range of disorders, favour behavioural rather than nonbehavioural approaches (Kazdin, 1988). Yet, compared with family therapy — still a largely unvalidated collection of treatment methods — behavioural work remains relatively marginal in child psychiatry.

For some critics of behavioural work the belief in the causal role of the family *qua* family in childhood problems has led to a neglect, in my view, of factors intrinsic to the child (e.g. temperament) in the genesis of psychiatric disorder. And behaviour therapy is still viewed as very much a method of treatment aimed at the individual child, and therefore out of key with systemic thinking. For other critics a commitment to ethical relativism — the conviction that there are no objective ethical standards for judging the rightness or wrongness of an act — is the main objection. The one supreme value is to refrain from judging or influencing the values of others. This value position can lead to suspicions that the statement of treatment goals by the behaviour therapist implies an undue influence on the client towards received societal values.

In its most extreme form, one's own personal truth is the only truth one needs to be concerned with. If, for example, psychotherapy method *x* feels right for me, it doesn't matter if I don't have data to substantiate my claims for its value. If I feel uncomfortable about behaviour therapy I can comfortably overlook its claims to be taken seriously. Among these values is sometimes a deep distrust of science and its findings. A scientific approach to treatment is often rejected as impersonal, manipulative (i.e. political) and mechanistic (i.e. simplistic). It is therefore not surprising that a presentation of encouraging behavioural research findings may be met with indifference. Certainly, a healthy scepticism of science is appropriate, but to reject it out of hand would seem to represent a worrying retreat into superstition and irresponsibility. (The *Journal of Consulting and Clinical Psychology*, 1980; **48**, contains several papers on behaviour therapy and ethical relativism.)

It is of interest that, despite behaviour therapists' predilection for explicit and objective methods, Sloane *et al.* (1975) still found that their patients rated them at least as highly on interpersonal factors such as warmth and empathy as nonbehavioural therapists. One might also suggest that the emphasis of behaviour therapy on explicit objectives and self-direction as therapeutic goals, in addition to giving clients access to a self-empowering knowledge base of behavioural principles, makes for a liberating therapeutic philosophy. Indeed, Bandura (1969) has argued that, far from being inconsistent with a humanistic philosophy, behaviour therapy is probably among the most effective means of promoting personal freedom and emotional growth because of its efficacy in enhancing freedom of choice.

CONCLUSIONS

This chapter has described the what, why and how of contemporary behavioural work, bringing it up to date (with its contemporary developmental and cognitive elaborations) from its early behaviouristic origins. Examples are provided of the wide range of methods and the diversity of child and family problems to which they are applied. The systemic nature of much behavioural work is illustrated. It also involves counselling about child development and other issues, in other words — as a partnership with family members — much discussion and debate. The inner life and subjective experiences of caregivers and children (beliefs, attributions, attitudes) are acknowledged to be important phenomena in the assessment and treatment of problems. There is a brief exposition on the ethical and philosophical considerations which still create professional resistances to the behavioural, approach, despite its successful track record with many childhood difficulties.

The point is made that this perspective provides no panacea; as with other therapeutic methods it is a case of 'horses for courses'. The trouble is that we are still not certain which horses are best for which courses — a continuing research task for the future.

What can be asserted confidently is that family-oriented behavioural work is a useful 'craft', and one that is essentially a blend of applied science and art. There is a creditable amount of science — empirical data — available. There is also the art of teaching children and adult caregivers; the art of finding and using imaginative materials to capture the interest of children and adults; the art of explaining abstract principles to, and unravelling complex problems with, patients. There is also the all-important art of increasing patients' perceived self-efficacy by means of a shared therapeutic collaboration. This is a reminder to us of the vital role of therapist–person variables ('core conditions') in treatment. These can no more be neglected in behavioural work than in any other therapy.

REFERENCES

Alexander F. (1963) The dynamics of psychotherapy in the light of learning theory. *American Journal of Psychiatry*, **120**, 440–448.

Allen K.E., Hart B.M., Buell J.S., Harris F.R. & Wolf M.M. (1964) Effects of social reinforcement on isolate behavior of a nursery school child. *Child Development*, **35**, 511–518.

American Psychiatric Association Task Force Report (1973) *Behaviour Therapy in Psychiatry*. American Psychiatric Association, Washington, DC.

Apolloni T., Cooke S.A. & Cooke T.P. (1977) Establishing a normal peer as a behavioral model for developmentally delayed toddlers. *Perceptual and Motor Skills*, **44**, 231–241.

Arnold J.E., Levine A.G. & Patterson G.R. (1975) Changes in sibling behavior following family intervention. *Journal of Consulting and Clinical Psychology*, **43**, 683–688.

Ayllon T., Smith D. & Rogers M. (1970) Behavioural management of school phobia. *Journal of Behavior Therapy and Experimental Psychiatry*, **1**, 125–138.

Bandura A. (1969) *Principles of Behavior Modification*. Holt, Rinehart & Winston, New York.

Bandura A. (1977) *Social Learning Theory*. Prentice-Hall, Englewood Cliffs, NJ.

Bandura A. (1986) Social Foundations of Thought and Action: A Social Cognitive Theory. Prentice-Hall, Englewood Cliffs, NJ.

Barkley R.A. (1982) *Hyperactive Children: A Handbook for Diagnosis and Assessment*. Chichester, Wiley.

Baum C.G., Reyna McGlone C.L. & Ollendick T.H. (1986) The efficacy of behavioral parent training: behavioral parent training plus clinical self-control training, and a modified STEP program for children referred with noncompliance. Paper presented at the meeting of the Association for Advancement of Behavior Therapy, Chicago, IL.

Beck S. & Forehand R. (1984) Social skills training for children: a methodological and clinical review of behaviour modification studies. *Behavioural Psychotherapy*, **12**, 17–45.

Birk L. & Brinkley-Birk A.W. (1974) Psychoanalysis and behaviour therapy. *American Journal of Psychiatry*, **131**, 499–510.

Blagg N.R. & Yule W. (1984) The behavioural treatment of school phobia: a comparative study. *Behaviour Research and Therapy*, **22**, 119–127.

Blakely C.H. & Davidson W.S. (1984) Behavioral approaches to delinquency: a review. In: Karoly P. & Steffen J.J. (eds) *Adolescent Behavior Disorders: Foundations and Contemporary Concerns*. Lexington Books, Lexington, MA.

Bornstein P.H. & Kazdin A.E. (eds) (1985) *Handbook of Clinical Behavior Therapy with Children*. Dorsey Press, Homewood, IL.

Boucheau L.D. & Jeffry C.D. (1973) Stuttering treated by desensitization. *Journal of Behavior Therapy and Experimental Psychiatry*, **4**, 209–212.

Breiner J.L. & Forehand R. (1981) An assessment of the effects of parent training on clinic-referred children's school behavior. *Behavioral Assessment*, **3**, 31–42.

Bruner J.S. (1975) *Beyond the Information Given*. Allen & Unwin, London.

Burns D. & Brady J.P. (1980) The treatment of stuttering. In: Goldstein A. & Foa E.B. (eds) *Handbook of Behavioral Interventions*. Wiley, New York.

Campbell M., Cohen I.L., Perry R. & Small M. (1989) Psychopharmacological treatment. In: Ollendick T.H. & Hersen M. (eds) *Handbook of Child Psychopathology*. Plenum, New York.

Cherry C. & Sayers B.Mc.A. (1956) Experiments upon the total inhibition of stammering by external control and some clinical results. *Journal of Psychosomatic Research*, **1**, 233–246.

Christensen A., Johnson S.M., Phillips S. & Glasgow R.E. (1980) Cost effectiveness in parent consultation. *Behaviour Therapy*, **11**, 208—226.

Clark P. & Rutter M. (1981) Autistic children's responses to structure and to interpersonal demands. *Journal of Autism and Developmental Disorders*, **11**, 201—217.

Clark H.B., Risley T.R. & Cataldo M.F. (1976) Behavioral technology for the normal middle-class family. In: Mash E.J., Hamerlynck L.A. & Handy L.C. (eds) *Behavior Modification and Families*. Brunner/Mazel, New York.

Clement P.W. & Milne D.C. (1967) Group play therapy and tangible reinforcers used to modify the behaviour of 8-year-old boys. *Behaviour Research and Therapy*, **5**, 301—312.

Cobb D.E. & Medway F.J. (1978) Determinants of effectiveness in parent consultation. *Journal of Community Psychology*, **6**, 229—240.

Coie J.D. (1990) Adapting intervention to the problems of aggressive and disruptive rejected children. In: Asher S.R. & Coie J.D. (eds) *Peer Rejection in Childhood*. Cambridge University Press, Cambridge.

Creer T.L., Renne C.M. & Chai H. (1982) The application of behavioural techniques to childhood asthma. In: Russo D.C. & Varni J.W. (eds) *Behavioural Pediatrics: Research and Practice*. Plenum Press, New York.

Cross Calvert S. & McMahon R.J. (1987) The treatment acceptability of a behavioral parent training program and its components. *Behavior Therapy*, **18**, 165—179.

Cullen C. (1991) Radical behaviourism and its influence on clinical therapies. *Behavioural Psychotherapy*, **19**, 47—58.

Cunningham C.E., Cataldo M.F., Mallion C. & Keyes J.B. (1983) A review and controlled single case evaluation of behavioral approaches to the management of elective mutism. *Child and Family Behavior Therapy*, **5**, 25—49.

Dalali I.D. & Sheehan J.G. (1974) Stuttering and assertion training. *Journal of Communication Disorders*, **7**, 97—111.

Damon W. (1989) *The Social World of the Child*. Jossey-Bass, San Francisco, CA.

De Myer K.K., Kingten J.N. & Jackson R.K. (1981) Infantile autism reviewed. A decade of research. *Schizophrenia Bulletin*, **7**, 338—351.

Dickinson A. (1987) Animal conditioning and learning theory. In: Eysenck H.J. & Martin I. (eds) *Theoretical Foundations of Behaviour Therapy*. Plenum Press, New York.

Dinkmeyer D. & McKay G.D. (1976) *Systematic Training for Effective Parenting*. American Guidance Service, Circle Pines, MN.

Doleys D.M. (1977) Behavioral treatments for nocturnal enuresis in children: a review of the recent literature. *Psychological Bulletin*, **8**, 30—54.

Doleys D.M. (1978) Assessment and treatment of enuresis and encopresis in children. In: Hersen M., Eisler R.M. & Miller P.M. (eds) *Progress in Behavior Modification*, vol. 6, pp. 85—121. Academic Press, New York.

Dollard J. & Miller N.E. (1950) *Personality and Psychotherapy*. McGraw-Hill, New York.

Douglas J. & Richman N. (1984) *My Child Won't Sleep*. Penguin, Harmondsworth.

D'Zurilla T.J. & Nezsu A. (1982) Social problem-solving in adults. In: Kendall P.C. (ed) *Advances in Cognitive Behavioral Research and Therapy*, vol. 1. Academic Press, New York.

Erwin E. (1979) *Behaviour Therapy: Scientific, Philosophical and Moral Foundations*. Cambridge University Press, Cambridge.

Estes W.K. (1971) Reward in human learning: theoretical issues and strategic choice points. In: Glaser R. (ed) *The Nature of Reinforcement*. Academic Press, New York.

Evans I.M. (1989) A multi-dimensional model for conceptualizing the design of child behavior therapy. *Behavioural Psychotherapy*, **17**, 237—251.

Fleischman M.J. (1981) A replication of Patterson's 'Intervention for boys with conduct problems'. *Journal of Consulting and Clinical Psychology*, **49**, 342—351.

Fonagy P., Moran G.S. & Higgitt A.C. (1989) Insulin dependent diabetes mellitus in children and adolescents. In: Pearce S. & Wardle J. (eds) *The Practice of Behavioural Medicine*. British Psychological Society/Oxford University Press, Leicester.

Forehand R. & Atkeson B.M. (1977) Generality of treatment effects with parents as therapists: a review of assessment and implementation procedures. *Behavior Therapy*, **8**, 575—593.

Forehand R. & Long N. (1986) A long-term follow-up of parent training participants. Paper presented at the meeting of the Association for the Advancement of Behavior Therapy, Chicago, IL.

Forehand R.L. & McMahon R.J. (1981) *Helping the Noncompliant Child: A Clinician's Guide to Parent Training*. Guilford Press, New York.

Frame C., Matson J.L., Sonis W.A., Fialkov M.J. & Kazdin A.E. (1982) Behavioral treatment of depression in a prepubertal child. *Journal of Behavior Therapy and Experimental Psychiatry*, **3**, 239—243.

Frank J. (1973) *Persuasion and Healing*. John Hopkins University Press, Baltimore, MD.

Furman W. (1980) Promoting appropriate social behavior. In: Lahey, B. & Kazdin A. (eds) *Advances in Clinical Child Psychology*, vol. 3. Plenum, New York.

Goldstein A.P., Heller H. & Sechrest L.B. (1966) *Psychotherapy and the Psychology of Behavior Change*. John Wiley, New York.

Goodnow J.J. & Collins W.A. (1990) *Development According to Parents: The Nature, Sources and Consequences of Parents' Ideas*. Lawrence Erlbaum, Hillsdale, NJ.

Graziano A.M. & Mooney K.C. (1980) Family self-control instruction for children's night-time fear reduction. *Journal of Consulting and Clinical Psychology*, **48**, 206—213.

Graziano A.M. & Mooney K.C. (1982) Behavioral treatment of 'night-fears' in children: maintenance of improvement at 2- to 3-year follow-up. *Journal of Consulting and Clinical Psychology*, **50**, 598—599.

Graziano A.M., Mooney K.C., Huber C. & Ignaziak D. (1979) Self-control instruction for children's fear reductions. *Journal of Behavior Therapy and Experimental Psychiatry*, **10**, 221—227.

Harris S.L. & Handleman J.S. (1987) Autism. In: Hersen M. & Van Hasselt V.B. (eds) *Behavior Therapy with Children and Adolescents*. John Wiley, Chichester.

Hart B.M., Reynolds N.J., Baer D., Brauley E.R. & Harris F.R. (1968) Effects of contingent and noncontingent social reinforcement on the cooperative play of pre-school children. *Journal of Applied Behavior Analysis*, **1**, 73—78.

Hatzenbuehler L.C. & Schroeder H.E. (1978) Desensitization procedures in the treatment of childhood disorders. *Psychological Bulletin*, **85**, 831—844.

Herbert M. (1985) Triadic work with children. In: Watts F. (ed) *Recent Developments in Clinical Psychology*. John Wiley, Chichester.

Herbert M. (1987a) *Behavioural Treatment of Children with Problems: A Practice Manual*, revised edn. Academic Press, London.

Herbert M. (1987b) *Conduct Disorders of Childhood and Adolescence: A Social-learning Perspective*, revised edn. John Wiley, Chichester.

Herbert M. (1990) *Planning a Research Programme: A Guide for Trainees and the Helping Professions*. Cassell, London.

Herbert M. (1991) *Clinical Child Psychology: Social Learning, Development and Behaviour*. Wiley, Chichester.

Herbert M. (1993) *Working with Children and the Children Act*. British Psychological Society, Leicester.

Herbert M. & Iwaniec D. (1981) Behavioural psychotherapy in natural home-settings: an empirical study applied to conduct disordered and incontinent children. *Behavioural Psychotherapy*, **9**, 55—76.

Hollin C., Wilkie J. & Herbert M. (1987) Behavioural social work: training and application. *Practice*, **1**, 297—304.

Howlin P. (1984) Parents as therapists: a critical review. In: Muller D.

(ed) *Remediating Children's Languange: Behavioural and Naturalist Approaches*. Croom Helm, London.

Howlin P. & Rutter M. (1987) *Treatment of Autistic Children*. Wiley, Chichester.

Ioannou C. (1991) Acute pain in childhood. In: Herbert M. *Clinical Child Psychology: Social Learning Development and Behaviour*. John Wiley, Chichester.

Ireton C.L. & Guthrie H.A. (1972) Modification of vegetable eating behavior in preschool children. *Journal of Nutrition Education*, **4**, 100–103.

Iwaniec D., Herbert M. & McNeish S. (1985) Social work with failure-to-thrive children and their families. Part I: Psychosocial factors. Part II: Behavioural casework. *British Journal of Social Work*, **15**, Nos 3 and 4.

Jackson H.J.E. & King N. (1981) The emotive imagery treatment of a child's trauma-induced phobia. *Journal of Behavior Therapy and Experimental Psychiatry*, **12**, 325–328.

Johnson J.H., Rasbury W.C. & Siegel L.J. (1986) *Approaches to Child Treatment*. Pergamon Press, Oxford.

Jones M.C. (1924) The elimination of children's fears. *Journal of Experimental Psychology*, **7**, 382–390.

Kanfer F.H., Karoly P. & Newman A. (1975) Reduction of children's fear of the dark by competence-related and situational threat-related verbal cues. *Journal of Consulting and Clinical Psychology*, **43**, 251–258.

Kaslow N.J. & Rehm L.P. (1983) Childhood depression. In: Morris R.J. & Kratochwill T.R. (eds) *The Practice of Child Therapy*, pp. 27–51. Pergamon Press, New York.

Kazdin A.E. (1978) *History of Behavior Modification: Experimental Foundations of Contemporary Research*. University Park Press, Baltimore, MD.

Kazdin A.E. (1985) *Treatment of Antisocial Behavior in Children and Adolescents*. Dorsey Press, Homewood, IL.

Kazdin A.E. (1987) *Conduct Disorders in Childhood and Adolescence*. Sage, Newbury Park, CA.

Kazdin A.E. (1988) *Child Psychotherapy: Developing and Identifying Effective Treatments*. Pergamon, Oxford.

Kendall P.C. (1984) Cognitive-behavioural self-control therapy for children. *Journal of Child Psychology and Psychiatry*, **25**, 173–179.

Kendall P.C., Howard B.L. & Epps J. (1988) The anxious child: cognitive-behavioural treatment strategies. *Behaviour Modification*, **12**, 281–310.

King N.J., Hamilton D.I. & Ollendick T.H. (1988) *Children's Phobias: A Behavioural Perspective*. Academic Press, London.

King N.J., Cranstoun F. & Josephs A. (1989) Emotive imagery and children's night-time fears: a multiple baseline design evaluation. *Journal of Behavior Therapy and Experimental Psychiatry*, **20**, 125–135.

Klein M.H., Dittman A.T., Parloff M.M. & Gill M.M. (1969) Behaviour therapy: observations and reflections. *Journal of Consulting and Clinical Psychology*, **33**, 259–266.

Labbe E.E. & Williamson D.A. (1984) Behavioral treatment of elective mutism: a review of the literature. *Clinical Psychology Review*, **4**, 273–292.

Ladd G.W. (1984) Social skills training with children: issues in research and practice. *Clinical Psychology Review*, **4**, 317–337.

Lazarus A.A. & Abramovitz A. (1962) The use of 'emotive imagery' in the treatment of children's phobias. *Journal of Mental Science*, **108**, 191–195.

Leitenberg H. & Callahan E.J. (1973) Reinforced practice and reduction of different kinds of fears in adults and children. *Behaviour Research and Therapy*, **11**, 19–30.

Levis D. (1970) Integration of behaviour therapy and dynamic psychiatry techniques: a marriage with a high probability of ending in divorce. *Behavior Therapy*, **1**, 531–537.

Lovibond S.H. (1963) The mechanism of conditioning treatment of enuresis. *Behaviour Research and Therapy*, **1**, 17–21.

Lovaas O.I. (1977) *The Autistic Child: Language Development through Behaviour Modification*. Wiley, New York.

Luiselli J.K. (1978) Treatment of an autistic child's fears of riding a school bus through exposure and reinforcement. *Journal of Behavior Therapy and Experimental Psychiatry*, **9**, 169–172.

McMahon R.J. & Forehand R. (1978) Non-prescriptive behavior therapy: effectiveness of a brochure in teaching mothers to correct their children's inappropriate mealtime behaviors. *Behavior Therapy*, **9**, 814–820.

McMahon R.J. & Forehand R. (1983) Parent training for the non-compliant child: treatment outcome, generalization, and adjunctive therapy procedures. In: Dangel R.F. & Polster R.A. (eds) *Behavioral Parent Training: Issues In Research and Practice*. Guilford, New York.

Maccoby E.E. (1984) Socialization and developmental change. *Child Development*, **55**, 317–328.

Maccoby E.E. & Martin J.P. (1983) Socialization in the context of the family: parent–child interaction. In: Mussen P. (ed) *Handbook of Child Psychology*, vol. 4. Wiley, New York.

Mackintosh N.J. (1983) *Conditioning and Associative Learning*. Oxford University Press, Oxford.

Marmor J. (1971) Dynamic psychotherapy and behaviour therapy: are they irreconcilable? *Archives of General Psychiatry*, **24**, 22–28.

Michelson L. & Wood R. (1980) Behavioral assessment and training of children's social skills. In: Hersen M., Eisler R. & Miller P.M. (eds) *Progress in Behavior Modification*, vol. 9. Academic Press, New York.

Minuchin S. (1974) *Family and Family Therapy*. Harvard University Press, Cambridge, MA.

Morgan R.T.T. (1984) *Behavioural Treatments with Children*. Heinemann Medical, London.

Morley S.V. (1989) Single case methodology in behaviour therapy. In: Lindsay S.J.E. & Powell G.W. (eds) *An Introduction to Clinical Child Psychology*. Aldershot, Gower.

Mowrer O.H. & Mowrer W. (1938) Enuresis: a method for its study and treatment. *American Journal of Orthopsychiatry*, **8**, 436–447.

Obler M. & Terwilliger R.F. (1970) Pilot study on the effectiveness of systematic desensitization with neurologically impaired children with phobic disorders. *Journal of Consulting and Clinical Psychology*, **34**, 314–318.

O'Dell S. (1974) Training parents in behaviour modification: a review. *Psychological Bulletin*, **81**, 418–443.

O'Leary K.D. & Carr E.G. (1982) Childhood disorders. In: Wilson G.T. & Franks C. (eds) *Contemporary Behavior Therapy*. Guilford Press, New York.

O'Leary K.D. & O'Leary S.G. (1977) *Classroom Management: The Use of Behavior Modification*. Pergamon, Oxford.

Ollendick T.H. (1979) Fear reduction techniques with children. In: Hersen M., Eisler R.M. & Miller P.M. (eds) *Progress In Behaviour Modification*. Academic Press, New York.

Ollendick T.H. (1986) Behavior therapy with children and adolescents. In: Garfield S.L. & Bergen A.E. (eds) *Handbook of Psychotherapy and Behavior Change*, 3rd edn. John Wiley, New York.

Ollendick T.H. & Cerny J.A. (1981) *Clinical Behavior Therapy with Children*. Plenum Press, New York.

Ollendick T.H. & King N.J. (1991) Fears and phobias of childhood. In: Herbert M. *Clinical Child Psychology: Social Learning, Development and Behaviour*. John Wiley, Chichester.

Parke R.D. (1978) Parent–infant interaction: progress, paradigms and problems. In: Sackett G.P. (ed) *Observing Behaviour, vol. I: Theory and Applications in Mental Retardation*. University Park Press, Baltimore, MD.

Patterson G.R. (1982) *Coercive Family Process*. Castalia, Eugene, OR.

Patterson G.R. & Fleischman M.J. (1979) Maintenance of treatment effects: some considerations concerning family systems; and follow-up data. *Behavior Therapy*, **10**, 168–185.

Patterson G.R., Cobb J.A. & Ray R.S. (1973) A social engineering technology for retraining the families of aggressive boys. In: Adams H.E. & Unikel I.P. (eds) *Issues and Trends in Behavior Therapy*. Charles C. Thomas, Springfield, IL.

Patterson G.R., Chamberlain P. & Reid J.B. (1982) A comparative evaluation of a parent training program. *Behavior Therapy*, **13**, 638–650.

Patterson G.R., DeBaryshe B.D. & Ramsey E. (1989) A developmental perspective on antisocial behavior. *American Psychologist*, **44**, 329–335.

Paul G.L. (1967) Outcome research in psychotherapy. *Journal of Consulting Psychology*, **31**, 109–118.

Pavlov I.P. (1927) *Conditioned Reflexes* (translated by G.V. Anrep). Clarendon Press, Oxford.

Peed S., Roberts M. & Forehand R. (1977) Evaluation of the effectiveness of a standardised parent training program in altering the interactions of mothers and their noncompliant children. *Behaviour Modification*, **1**, 323–350.

Power M.J. (1989) Cognitive therapy: an outline of theory, practice and problems. *British Journal of Psychotherapy*, **5**, 544–556.

Power M.J. (1991) Cognitive science and behavioural psychotherapy: where behaviour was, there shall cognition be? *Behavioural Psychotherapy*, **19**, 20–41.

Puig-Antich J., Luckens E., Davies M., Goetz D., Brennan-Quattrock J. & Todak T. (1985a) Psychosocial functioning in prepubertal major depressive disorders. I. Interpersonal relationships during the depressive episode. *Archives of General Psychiatry*, **42**, 500–507.

Puig-Antich J., Luckens E., Davies M., Goetz D., Brennan-Quattrock J. & Todak T. (1985b) II. Interpersonal relationships after sustained recovery from affective episode. *Archives of General Psychiatry*, **42**, 511–517.

Rachman S. (1970) Behaviour therapy and psychodynamics. *Behavior Therapy*, **1**, 527–530.

Reed G.F. (1963) Elective mutism in children: a reappraisal. *Journal of Child Psychology and Psychiatry*, **4**, 99–107.

Reid J., Taplin P. & Loeber R. (1981) A social interactional approach to the treatment of abusive families. In: Stewart R. (ed) *Violent Behavior: Social Learning Approaches to Prediction, Management and Treatment*. Brunner/Mazel, New York.

Reynolds W.M. (1984) Depression in children and adolescents: phenomenology, evaluation and treatment. *School Psychology Review*, **13**, 171–182.

Reynolds W.M. & Coats K.I. (1986) A comparison of cognitive-behavioral therapy and relaxation training for the treatment of depression in adolescents. *Journal of Consulting and Clinical Psychology*, **54**, 653–660.

Richman N., Douglas J., Hunt H., Lansdown R. & Levere R. (1985) Behavioural methods in the treatment of sleep disorders — a pilot study. *Journal of Child Psychology and Psychiatry*, **26**, 581–590.

Rose M.I., Firestone P., Heick H.M.C. & Fraught A.K. (1983) The effects of anxiety on the control of juvenile diabetes mellitus. *Journal of Behavioural Medicine*, **6**, 382–395.

Rosenstiel S.K. & Scott D.S. (1977) Four considerations in imagery techniques with children. *Journal of Behavior Therapy and Experimental Psychiatry*, **8**, 287–290.

Ross D., Ross S. & Evans T.A. (1971) The modification of extreme social withdrawal by modification with guided practice. *Journal of Behavior Therapy and Experimental Psychiatry*, **2**, 273–279.

Royal College of Psychiatrists (1989) Report of the Working Party to produce *Guidelines to Good Practice in the Use of Behavioural Treatments*. Approved by Council, October, London.

Rutter M., Maughan B., Mortimore P., Ouston J. & Smith A. (1979) *Fifteen Thousand Hours: Secondary Schools and their Effects on Children*. Open Books, London.

Rycroft C. (1970) Causes and meaning. In: Lee S.G. & Herbert M. (eds) *Freud and Psychology*. Penguin, Harmondsworth.

Schrag P. & Divoky D. (1975) *The Myth of the Hyperactive Child*. Pantheon, New York.

Scott M.J. & Stradling S.G. (1987) Evaluation of a group programme for parents of problem children. *Behavioural Psychotherapy*, **15**, 224–239.

Seligman M.E.P (1975) *Helplessness*. Freeman, San Francisco, CA.

Sloane R.B., Staples F.R., Cristol A.H., Yorkston N.J. & Whipple K. (1975) *Psychotherapy versus Behavior Therapy*. Harvard University Press, Cambridge, MA.

Sluckin A. (1975) Encopresis: a behavioural approach described. *Social Work Today*, **5**, 21, January.

Sluckin A. (1981) Behavioral social work treatment with encopretic children, their families and the school. *Child Care, Health and Development*, **7**, 67–80.

Sluckin A., Foreman N. & Herbert M. (1991) Behavioural treatment programmes and selectivity of speaking at follow-up in a sample of 25 selective mutes. *Australian Psychologist*, **26**(2), 132–137.

Smith P.S. & Smith E.J. (1987) *Continence and Incontinence: Psychological Approaches to Development and Treatment*. Croom Helm, London.

Snyder J. & Brown K. (1983) Oppositional behaviour and noncompliance in pre-school children. Environmental correlates and skill deficits. *Behavioural Assessment*, **5**, 333–348.

Spivack G., Platt J.J. & Shure M.B. (1976) *The Problem-solving Approach to Adjustment*. Jossey-Bass, San Francisco, CA.

Stefanek M.E., Ollendick T.H., Baldock W.P., Francis G. & Yaeger N.J. (1987) Self-statements in aggressive, withdrawn, and popular children. *Cognitive Behaviour Therapy and Research*, **2**, 229–239.

Swann van Buskirk S. (1989) Two-phase perspective on the treatment of anorexia nervosa. *Psychological Bulletin*, **84**, 529–538.

Treacher A. & Carpenter J. (1984) (eds) *Using Family Therapy*. Basil Blackwell, Oxford.

Tuma J.M. (1989) Traditional therapies with children. In: Ollendick T.H. & Hersen M. (eds) *Handbook of Child Psychopathology*, 2nd edn. Plenum, New York.

Van Hasselt V.B., Hersen M., Bellak A.S., Rosenbloom A.S. & Lampacski D. (1979) Tripartite assessment of the effects of systematic desensitization in a multiphobic child: an experimental analysis. *Journal of Behavior Therapy and Experimental Psychiatry*, **10**, 57–66.

Wachtel P.L (1977) *Psychoanalysis and Behavior Therapy*: Toward an Integration. Basic Books, New York.

Webster-Stratton C. (1981) Videotape modeling: a method of parent education. *Journal of Clinical Child Psychology*, **10**, 93–98.

Webster-Stratton C. (1982) The long term effects of a videotape modeling parent education program: comparison of immediate and 1 year followup results. *Behavior Therapy*, **13**, 702–714.

Webster-Stratton C. (1984) A randomized trial of two parent training programs for families with conduct disordered children. *Journal of Consulting and Clinical Psychology*, **52**, 666–678.

Webster-Stratton C. (1985) Predictors of treatment outcome in parent training for conduct disordered children. *Behavior Therapy*, **16**, 223–243.

Webster-Stratton C. (1989) Systematic comparison of consumer satisfaction of three cost-effective parent training programs for conduct problem children. *Behavior Therapy*, **20**, 103–115.

Webster-Stratton C. (1990) Long-term follow-up of families with young conduct problem children: from preschool to grade school. *Journal of Clinical Child Psychology*, **19**, 144–149.

Webster-Stratton C., Kolpacoff M. & Hollinsworth T. (1988) Self-administered videotape therapy for families with conduct disordered children: comparison to two other treatments and a control group. *Journal of Consulting and Clinical Psychology*, **56**, 558–566.

Webster-Stratton C., Kolpacoff M. & Hollinsworth T. (1989) The long-term effectiveness and clinical significance of three cost-effective training programs for families with conduct problem children. *Journal of Consulting and Clinical Psychology*, **57**, 550–553.

Weisz J.R. & Weiss B. (1989) Cognitive mediators of the outcome of psychotherapy with children. In: Lahey B.B. & Kazdin A.E. (eds) *Advances in Clinical Child Psychology*, vol. 12. Plenum Press, New York.

Wells K.C. & Egan J. (1988) Social learning and systems family therapy for childhood oppositional disorder: comparative treatment outcome. *Comprehensive Psychiatry*, **29**, 138–146.

White M. (1971) A thousand consecutive cases of enuresis: results of treatment. *Child and Family*, **10**, 198–209.

Whiting B. (1963) *Six Cultures: Studies of Child Rearing*. John Wiley, New York.

Whitman T.L., Mercurio J.R. & Caponigri V. (1970) Development of social responses in two severely retarded children. *Journal of Applied Behavior Analysis*, **3**, 133–138.

Wilson F.E. & Evans I.M. (1983) The reliability of target-behaviour selection in behavioral assessment. *Behavioral Assessment*, **5**, 15–23.

Wolpe J. (1958) *Psychotherapy by Reciprocal Inhibition*. Stanford University Press, Stanford, CA.

Yates A.J. (1983) Behaviour therapy and psychodynamic psychotherapy: basic conflict or reconciliation and integration? *British Journal of Clinical Psychology*, **22**, 107–125.

Yule W. (1977) Behavioural approaches. In: Rutter M. & Hersov L. (eds) *Child Psychiatry: Modern Approaches*. Blackwell Scientific Publications, Oxford.

Zatz S. & Chassin L. (1983) Cognitions in test-anxious children. *Journal of Consulting and Clinical Psychology*, **51**, 526–534.

Chapter 51
Physical Treatments

Eric Taylor

INTRODUCTION

Physical methods of treatment include some of the most powerful ways of altering the behaviour and mental state of children. They also include some interventions that are ineffective or hazardous yet still widely used. Properly given, they are important aspect of child psychiatric treatment and the expertise should be available in all child mental health services.

The treatments have been controversial, partly because they carry the potential for ill effects, partly because they raise questions of social control, and partly because ideology leads some to oppose all such forms of therapy. In these circumstances it is particularly important that the child psychiatrist is expert in the theoretical and practical aspects of their use. Unfortunately, some turn their backs on the treatment during their training (Schachar, 1985). The result is bound to be a lessened quality of the service that they can give.

In paediatric as in adult psychopharmacology, it is unhelpful to think of drugs as magic bullets. They are not usually specific treatments for specific illnesses. Rather, each drug carries a complex package of actions upon behaviour, chemistry and cognition. Indeed, each drug typically has several actions which may have different dose—response relationships and different time courses.

In any individual case a different balance of actions may be sought. Accordingly the prescriber needs many sources of information. The typical controlled trial yields the knowledge that the treatment is more effective than a control therapy in a group of children with a specific diagnosis. But this is not enough to guide the complex decisions needed. Prescribers also need to set a target for the individual child, which requires knowledge about the range of psychological processes that are affected by the medication; they need to be clear whether an individual child is likely to respond, which requires knowledge from predictive trials of responsiveness; they need to judge the balance of benefits against risks, which requires both knowledge from clinical trials that have used a range of outcome measures and also the results of long-term hazard monitoring; and the understanding of how to prescribe, which requires information about the basic pharmacology of each drug.

Introduction and regulation of drugs

The history of physical treatments includes a variety of ways in which new therapies have been introduced. Unpremeditated clinical observation has played the largest part. For example, Bradley's introduction of the amphetamines was based upon an unexpected discovery (Bradley, 1937). He was using amphetamine as a method of treating the headache that followed lumbar puncture, and noticed that the children were often less hyperactive, less defiant and less 'neurotic' while under the influence of the drug. This type of clinical observation has also played a major role in the discovery of psychoactive drugs for adult psychiatry (Ayd & Blackwell, 1970). Once the observation was made, then the stage was set for the more formal methods of scientific investigation. Controlled trials, the assessment of the effects in animal models and of the neurochemical effects, and the experimental analysis of the nature of the action upon psychological process all played a part.

Other treatments have been introduced directly from adult psychopharmacology. As research into childhood depression indicated the existence of major depressive disorder in young people, trials of antidepressants were a natural step forward. The discovery and application of neuroleptic treatments in adult psychiatry led quickly to attempts to apply them to children's conditions. Such treatments need to be given with caution until evidence for efficacy in children is forthcoming. Children are not just immature adults and the effect of drugs is not necessarily the same at different points in the life span.

Other treatments again have been introduced on the basis of research into the possible neurochemical basis of children's disorders. For example, findings of abnormalities in serotonin metabolism in autism led to the introduction of fenfluramine as a serotonin agonist. The findings are not secure (see Chapter 33), and in any case such a pedigree is no guarantee of the efficacy of the treatment. As will be seen, there are many reservations over the use of fenfluramine in autism. It is likely, however, that increasing knowledge of the basis of disorder will bring more therapies with a rational basis. So far, the introduction of new drugs has usually come from the clinician, not the laboratory.

The next stage after the introduction of a new drug is its assessment in standardized trials. Standardized rating scales (usually completed by parents and school teachers) have been the main outcome measures, together with the use of psychological laboratory tests about the performance of children on different forms of task. The technology is well-established (Psychopharmacology Bulletin, 1973). The sensitivity of measures such as these to the effect of the drug treatment has been so great that they are useful both in group assessments and in the detailed consideration of the response of an individual child. More recently, however, it has been necessary to introduce a wider range of evaluations to give a fuller understanding of the range of actions of drugs. Finer discriminations about the effects on different types of behaviour have needed to be made. Detailed interview techniques with parents, direct observational methods of children, and the self-report of children about their emotional state have all been used increasingly.

The regulation of drugs has often been confused by the existence of established indications for adults, that has allowed drugs to be prescribed routinely for children even before trial evidence has been obtained. On the other hand, manufacturers' data sheets will often include a disclaimer that they are not recommended for use in children, even though they are often used in this way. Much therefore rests on the judgement of the individual physician. Perhaps it is not surprising that practice varies greatly between different centres.

The history of the practical application of drugs has emphasized that scientific considerations are not the only determinants of when treatment is given. The 1960s and 1970s saw a rapid increase in the number of children who were treated with stimulants in the US and other countries influenced by that tradition of psychiatry. It reached a point where of the order of 1% of children were receiving stimulant drugs for hyperactivity (Bosco & Robin, 1980). In the UK and France, by contrast, this increase in the prevalence of using stimulant medication never took place. In both countries stimulant drug treatment is a rarity. Indeed, the best of the stimulant drugs (methylphenidate) is not on the market in the UK. The organization of paediatric care and the dominance of nonbiological theories of disorder have probably been responsible.

EPIDEMIOLOGY

While it is plain that there are major differences between nations and regions in the use of psychotropic drugs, there is relatively little documentation of the true extent of such differences or of the determinants for them. This lack is likely to be rectified with the rise of systems of audit and routinely applied monitoring of drug treatments within systems of health care delivery. The monitoring of adverse events carried out by drug firms in postmarketing surveillance could also be collated to give a full picture of the extent of drug use in a region. At present, however, the information available is rather scanty. Where surveys have been reported, they use a variety of different indices of drug exposure that do not lend themselves to comparison between centres.

The World Health Organization attempted to collate the figures from a variety of nations (World Health Organization, 1985). This comparison involved the use of published data and information obtained for the occasion from case registers. The index used was the prescribing rate, i.e. the number of prescriptions for psychotropic drugs that were issued per year per 1000 children in the whole population. This is an imperfect index, but gives a rough guide to the total use that is made of psychopharmacological agents and can be compared across regions even in current knowledge.

The results of the survey indicated considerable differences. The highest figures came from a survey in Scotland (Bain, 1981), with a rate of 118 prescriptions per 1000 children. Data from the Federal Republic of Germany gave a rate of 102 (for sedatives, neuroleptics, barbiturates and tranquillizers). In Tampere, Finland the figure was 38; in Twente, The Netherlands, 27 (excluding the 'hidden' use of psychotropic drugs in combination with other medicines); in a Swedish study, 8, and in Norway less than 1. The comparable figure in an American survey was 76 for children under the age of 10 years in Tennessee's Medicaid Program (101 for the 10−17-year-olds). This last figure of about 76 per year per 1000 children translated into about 3% of all children for whom psychotropic agents were prescribed (World Health Organization, 1985). The figure was somewhat lower in a group health cooperative programme that served a nearby but more advantaged population.

This shows there are great disparities between different parts of the world but does not, of course, say what pattern of prescribing is correct. For example, in the survey in Twente, a low overall rate of prescription was obtained; but it represented a very large proportion of all the children who were identified by the health services as having a psychological disorder. It could therefore be that high rates of prescription are associated with high rates of detection of disorder. It is also possible that high rates of prescription reflect inappropriate professional practice or the unavailability of psychological means of treatment. It is striking that in all the surveys the great majority of prescriptions issued were for minor tranquillizers and hypnotics. As will be seen later in the chapter, there should be great caution in the use of such medications. The drugs that should perhaps be used most upon the available scientific evidence are the stimulants, yet these were very uncommonly given in all the surveys. There is probably still a lot to do in the dissemination of good psychological therapies into primary care.

DEVELOPMENTAL PHARMACOKINETICS

The indications for drug use in children are often different from those in adults. Furthermore, the fate of an administered drug is not identical in children and adults. A scaled-down adult dose on the basis of body weight is therefore not necessarily a satisfactory guide to the amount of medication to be used in children. Children are not simply more or less sensitive to psychotropic drug effects: many factors determine their sensitivity, which will be different for different drugs. Some of these factors will be summarized briefly: a good account is given by Boreus (1982).

Compliance refers to the important step of getting medicine into the child. The difference from adults is that several people are involved at this step, and any one of them can in effect have a veto. Children themselves may feel hostile to the idea of taking medicine, especially if they feel that it will stigmatize them among other children or if it is presented as a punishment or a result of bad behaviour. Parental attitudes will determine the extent of any placebo effect as well as the likelihood of the child ingesting the prescribed medication. Teachers will have a good deal of influence, both over parents and children; if they use that influence to present medication as hazardous or undesirable then compliance becomes difficult. The particular requirement that is imposed by this consideration is therefore to seek means of ensuring that children do take medicines as prescribed. This would include explanations that are both full and tailored to the understanding of the person, simple written instructions about dosage schedules, dosage schedules that are as simple as can be arranged, and responsiveness to all the concerns that can legitimately be felt by any of the parties involved.

The next major step in determining absorption is the acidity of the stomach. The stomach contents of children tend to be less acidic than those of adults. A weakly acidic drug is therefore likely to be more ionized in a child than in an adult. Since it is the un-ionized fraction that is taken up at this point, then weakly acidic drugs tend to be absorbed more slowly in childhood than in adult life. This could in theory be an effect upon anticonvulsants, amphetamines and antidepressants.

At least in theory, the next factor determining absorption from the gut could be the intestinal microflora. Young children usually have fewer, and fewer types of microorganisms; but the difference is probably not big enough to have much effect upon the absorption of psychotropic drugs. Some drugs such as phenothiazines are metabolized in the gut wall: while the significance of this factor is not known in children, it may perhaps contribute to resistance to phenothiazine medication or to the need for either a surprisingly large oral dose or for parenteral medication.

Once absorbed through the gut, there is a 'first pass' through the liver before the drug is distributed around the body. In general, young children have particularly active livers. They are proportionately large to their body, and very efficient at conjugating and metabolizing many drugs, including antidepressants and phenothiazines. Since the hepatic clearance of drugs takes place rapidly, this factor tends to reduce the bioavailability of an orally administered drug, and does so with particular force during childhood.

Most psychotropic drugs are then distributed in the extracellular fluid of the body. The relative volume of extracellular water is high in young children. During development it tends to fall while fat content rises. The most rapid changes during development are in the first year of life and after puberty in girls. Accordingly, young children may have a dose of drug

distributed in a larger volume than will apply in adult life. This factor also tends to reduce bioavailability during childhood. The dose implications of this factor can be well assessed from surface area tables, since the surface area is closely correlated with the extracellular fluid volume. However, the use of surface area tables introduces possibilities for error, and does not allow for many of the factors determining response, so it is not usually recommended.

The blood–brain barrier tends to be more permeable in children than in adults. In theory this factor will increase the bioavailability of drugs in children. It will to some extent be counteracted, however, by greater amounts of protein entering the cerebrospinal fluid — which will reduce the bioavailability of any drug that binds to protein, such as anticonvulsants.

Pharmacodynamics describes the interaction of drugs with their receptors. The density of receptors in the brain may change over development. For example, dopamine receptors tend to increase for some time after birth and reach their full extent only when the organism is mature. A more precise understanding of this process is likely to be very useful in the future of childhood psychopharmacology. At present it is not possible to predict clearly what is likely to happen in the response of a child at a particular developmental level to a particular medication. Accordingly, the prescriber must be vigilant for the possibility of a quantitatively different action of drug — which may amount to a qualitative difference if, for example, the balance of alpha- and beta-adrenergic activities is altered.

The complexity of pharmacokinetic and pharmacodynamic factors means that recommendations about psychotropic drug doses have to be considered as starting points only. In nearly every case it is necessary to titrate the dose against the desired clinical response. Blood levels are very useful in the monitoring of some drugs, including lithium, the antidepressants, the anticonvulsants and the phenothiazines. They are not useful for the amphetamine-type drugs because of very rapidly fluctuating blood levels and the lack of correlation between blood levels and clinical response. Even for those drugs where blood monitoring is appropriate, it should not be given overwhelming weight. The crossing of the blood–brain barrier and the interaction with central nervous system receptors all happen after the level of distribution of which drug level is an index. Blood levels are a useful aid, but clinical response is the basis for judgement.

STIMULANTS

Amphetamine is chemically similar to the naturally occurring catecholamines in the brain. Other stimulant drugs, such as methylphenidate, are structurally related. Their clinical actions include central stimulation, the reduction of appetite, the production of stereotyped repetitive behaviours, and peripheral sympathomimetic activity. They are little used in adult psychopharmacology, though they are sometimes still valuable in the management of anticonvulsant-induced drowsiness and lethargy. Their action in humans and animals has been very extensively researched, with scores of controlled clinical trials and hundreds of animal experiments. A good deal is therefore known about the bases of their action, but not, it seems, enough to prevent the existence of a sharp controversy about their use and considerable differences in clinical practice between different countries and different services within countries.

Efficacy of drugs in controlled trials

The extensive literature on clinical trials has received several reviews. A quantitative metaanalysis is provided by Ottenbacher and Cooper (1983). More narrative accounts are provided by Taylor (1986) and Gadow (1992). The different types of action need to be considered separately.

Hyperactive behaviour

There can be no argument about the effect of stimulant medication in reducing the level of hyperactive behaviour. This is the commonest target for which the drugs are used. The effect is large, amounting to more than 1 s.d. in effect size (Ottenbacher & Cooper, 1983). This is large enough to make a substantial clinical difference; but not enough to make behaviour normal, for the average child diagnosed and treated is some 2–3 s.d. above the population mean (see Chapter 17).

The effect is not dependent upon the way in which the behaviour is measured: rating scales, standardized psychiatric interviews with parents, interviews with children and direct observations of the child during standardized situations all show that stimulant drugs produce a greater effect than does placebo (Taylor, 1986). Even direct mechanical recording of activity shows that stimulants reduce the amount of movements made (Porrino *et al.*, 1983). However, the effect is not confined to a reduction in movements, which might also be achieved by sedative medication. There is also a qualitative change in that children are rated as more attentive, less disorganized, and engaging for longer in constructive activities (Taylor *et al.*, 1987).

There are still a number of outstanding scientific questions about the nature of the antihyperkinetic effect. For example, it would be important to know whether the effect is to reduce activity in every circumstance. If activity is being reduced through a different action, such as the improvement of attention and self-organization, then activity should rise during situations where high levels of activity are required. By contrast, if the effect is primarily upon motor systems then activity might reduce even in situations, such as the gymnasium, where high levels of activity are expected and valued. On this important point the evidence is conflicting: studies can be cited either way (Rapoport *et al.*, 1980; Porrino *et al.*, 1983). The question needs resolving — but in most practical situations both the improvement of attending behaviour and the reduction of off-task irrelevant activity will be seen during treatment.

One hypothesis of stimulant action is that the effects on

movement are rate-dependent, i.e. the drug produces a reduction in the frequency of high-frequency behaviours and an increase in the frequency of low-frequency behaviours (Robbins & Sahakian, 1979). However, the claim has been refuted statistically (Swanson, 1988), and there is no evidence that low-frequency problem behaviours such as temper tantrums ever become more frequent during treatment with a stimulant drug. The full theory of rate dependence has therefore not been sustained. A weaker version of it, however, is probably true. Those children who show the greatest response to methylphenidate are also those whose hyperactivity was most severe before treatment began (Taylor *et al.*, 1987). The treatment should most pressingly be considered when the problem is itself most severe.

Antisocial behaviour

The many trials upon children with hyperactive behaviour make it clear that defiant, aggressive and otherwise antisocial behaviours are also reduced. The strongest evidence comes from blind placebo-controlled trials using direct observation of aggressive behaviour (Abikoff & Gittelman, 1985; Pelham & Hoza, 1987; Hinshaw *et al.*, 1989; Gadow *et al.*, 1990). However, it is not clear that stimulants are of any benefit for non-hyperactive aggressive children (Campbell *et al.*, 1982). To the contrary, a predictive trial of methylphenidate crossed over with placebo found that the reduction of conduct disorder in disruptive children was predicted by their degree of hyperactivity (Taylor *et al.*, 1987). This implies that a child with conduct disorder who showed no hyperactivity at all would be unlikely to have a useful response to stimulant medication. It would be worth testing this point directly, in a controlled trial that was confined to nonhyperactive but conduct-disordered children. However, such children are uncommon and it has not yet proved possible to amass a series for a trial that can sharply address this question. In the meantime, conduct disorder without hyperactivity should not be seen as an established target for this form of treatment.

Emotional disorder

Adults who use and abuse amphetamines are often seeking the euphoric effect. This effect requires relatively high doses of the drug, especially as tolerance soon appears. Indeed, the most frequent abusing pattern is the rapid escalation of dose to sustain euphoric effects, resulting after a fairly short time in the appearance of unpleasant psychotic symptoms.

The effect of euphoria is not described by children to whom the medication is given. It does not figure as a side-effect when systematic checklists including euphoria as a symptom are given (Conners & Taylor, 1980) and hyperactive children taking medication do not appear to abuse it for euphoria — or at least not before puberty (Goyer *et al.*, 1979). Normal children taking amphetamine do not describe euphoria, in contradistinction to adults (Rapoport *et al.*, 1978). Indeed, misery and agitation are recognized as unwanted effects in the treatment of hyperactive children with stimulants — especially in those with brain damage.

The lack of a euphoric effect may be related to a different reaction by the immature brain. It may also be determined by the set which is created when a drug is prescribed rather than being abused. It has been known for a long time that people given amphetamine may show an enhanced emotional response to different situations, but the nature of the emotion shown and experienced is determined by the context and the subject's knowledge of whether he or she has been given medication, much more than by the drug itself.

There are reasons to suppose that the knowledge that one is taking a drug might have an important influence upon one's self-esteem. One might expect that children may come to attribute their successes to the drug rather than to themselves, and to see their failures as outside their own abilities to correct. The reactions of adults to a child whom they know to be 'on pills' might also be negative and accelerate a process in which children form a lower self-esteem because of their treatment. It must be said that this possibility has not been demonstrated. In the short term, neither methylphenidate nor imipramine showed any greater effects than placebo on a questionnaire measure of self-image (Werry et al., 1980), and a trial seeking effects of methylphenidate, on personal attributions of responsibility, did not find any (Horn et al., 1991).

Methylphenidate produced more self-criticism than placebo in a laboratory game with another child, but this could have reflected effective self-appraisal rather than a pessimistic valuation of one's own worth (Whalen et al., 1979). In the longer term Hechtman et al. (1984) described a trend for self-esteem to be higher in those children who had received methylphenidate during their childhood.

The longer-term effects of stimulants upon mood are still unclear. What is clear is that the immediate effects upon behaviour are not mediated through the induction of euphoria. It would be worrying indeed if this were the case, for it would raise the possibility of dependence upon medication. However, processes of appraising oneself in the world may partly determine the response to treatment. In a comparative trial of behaviour therapy and medication, those children with an external pattern of attributions tended to do less well during therapy based on learning self-control, but were helped by medication or a social reinforcement approach (Bugental et al., 1977).

Cognitive effects

Stimulant drugs have beneficial short-term actions upon laboratory tests of attention. Medication is associated with lower error rates on continuous performance tests of sustained attention (both auditory and visual), more rapid reaction times, more planning and foresight on the Porteus Mazes test, better scores on performance subtests of the Wechsler Intelligence Scales and improved performance in paired-associate learning (Douglas, 1988). There have been attempts to contrast tests on which methylphenidate does show an effect with those upon which it does not. Such attempts do, however, have many pitfalls. For example, in any one study, the absence of evidence for an effect of methylphenidate is not necessarily to be taken as evidence for the absence of effect. It would be necessary to show replication of noneffect upon specific cognitive tests over several studies, and this has on the whole eluded investigators and reviewers.

Attempts have been made to attribute the entire effect of medication to the effects upon a specific psychological process such as that of attention or short-term memory. Solanto (1984) has argued for the constricting effect of the dopaminergic stimulants as underlying the pattern of changes seen. While several such speculations are possible, none of them is established. The difficulty is in the exact definition of the profile of tests that change and the inconstancy of test results between investigations. In present knowledge it would equally be possible to assert the converse, i.e. that the main effect of medication is upon behaviour, that the increased persistence on task activity that is produced will itself enhance performance upon laboratory tests of cognition, and that no more fundamental effect upon attention has been shown.

There has in the past been some concern that the changes in laboratory scores are not paralleled by comparable changes in the real world. Measures of academic attainment have not on the whole been drug-sensitive (Rie et al., 1976). However, methodological problems have also been present here: the absence of an effect of stimulants upon educational performance might be because a longer time than that of the typical trial was required to translate improved capacity into actual performance. More recent research has suggested that stimulant medication, by comparison with placebo, has a beneficial effect upon academic productivity and performance on standardized tests of educational attainment (Douglas et al., 1986). There is no suggestion that such an effect would be obtained in nonhyperactive children. Indeed, there is evidence to the contrary: nonhyperactive children with learning disabilities do not accelerate their learning as a function of stimulant medication (Gittelman-Klein & Klein, 1976).

The recent evidence upon educational performance also suggests that there is a linear relationship between the dose of medication and the effect on school achievement (Douglas et al., 1986). This is, on the face of it, in contradiction to an earlier literature that suggested that there is a curvilinear relationship between dose and cognitive response. Low doses (of the order of 10 mg of methylphenidate per day) were optimal for cognitive test performance in earlier work by Werry and Sprague (1974). This evidence has made most psychiatrists confine their prescriptions to small doses. While this may well be good practice for other reasons (see the section on hazards of treatment, below), it is unlikely that moderate doses (of the order of 20 mg of methylphenidate) will interfere with learning.

Interpersonal effects

Relationships with other children can be influenced, at least in the laboratory, by stimulant drug treatment. Cunningham *et al.* (1985), Pelham *et al.* (1985) and Whalen *et al.* (1989) have provided evidence for improved interpersonal timing and greater acceptability to other children in the hours after taking a dose of methylphenidate. Treated children may even be better at baseball (Pelham *et al.*, 1990).

Laboratory measures of mother–child interaction have been somewhat more equivocal. There is on the whole evidence for more effective interaction in settings where mothers and children are cooperating on a test or mothers are teaching children how to perform a particular activity (Humphries *et al.*, 1978). This effect could, of course, reflect the improved performance of children upon the task rather than any difference in the relationship. In the same way Barkley and Cunningham (1979) described reduced interaction between mothers and children during a free-play setting. Again this could have resulted from the children requiring less input from their parents in order to keep them under control.

A more naturalistic and predictive measure of interaction was applied by Schachar *et al.* (1987), who found that children who showed a behavioural response to methylphenidate were also the recipients of less negative expressed emotion when on methylphenidate than when they were on placebo. This suggested that much of the negative reaction by parents to children was determined by the behaviour of the child. Caution is appropriate: the trial only lasted for 3 weeks, and does not imply that medication is a sufficient means of improving parent–child interactions in the longer term.

Efficacy

The short-term effect of stimulants in trials is not in doubt. There is, however, some persisting doubt about the long-term impact of medication upon development. Long-term trials are very difficult to mount because of the practical and ethical difficulties of withholding a drug that is known to be a powerful agent of change. Ordinarily speaking, the combination of evidence that hyperactive behaviour is a long-term risk factor (see Chapter 17) and that medication reduces the levels of hyperactivity might well be taken as a sufficient justification for therapy. However, doubt arises because of the generally rather poor outcome of treated hyperactive children. Adolescents who as children had been treated at research clinics were still characterized by high levels of antisocial behaviour, delinquency and persisting hyperactivity (Satterfield *et al.*, 1987; Barkley *et al.*, 1990). There seems to be some contradiction between the existence of a powerful treatment and the unsatisfactory nature of the final outcome. This does not discredit medication. Other things may account for the poor outcome: research clinics may well get referrals of particularly intractable cases. It is also possible that the outcome, though poor, is substantially better than it would have been if the medication had been withheld.

Until longer-term studies can be devised, or series of children can be followed in whom the withholding of medication is due to factors other than qualities of the treated child, clinicians have to reckon with the possibility that stimulants may have limited efficacy in the promotion of social adjustment. This might, for example, happen because the effect of stimulants wanes as the months and years pass. In other circumstances tolerance certainly develops, as witness the escalating doses typically used by adult abusers (Connell, 1968). Thus, Charles and Schain (1981) described some children given stimulants who were no longer deriving benefit from it in their adolescence. It is not clear, however, that they had habituated to the effect: perhaps they had grown out of the hyperactivity that was the original target of medication. Sleator *et al.* (1974) studied 42 medicated children to discover whether they had developed tolerance: 25 of the 42 were found to be unaffected by the switch to placebo; but on the other hand the other 17 children became worse with the inactive tablets. For some children, at least, symptomatic benefit is still obtained from stimulants even after years of taking them. It should be possible to determine whether such children will show a poorer social adjustment as well as an increase in symptomatology when switched to placebo.

It is also possible that the efficacy of stimulants in promoting social adjustment is limited by their failure to have an impact upon the factors that are most powerful in promoting outcome. If the major prognostic factors are aspects of family and peer relationships (see Chapter 17) then the reduction of hyperactivity may not be sufficient to improve the outcome of children with hyperactivity. It would then become important to add other treatments as well as or instead of medication.

The place of medication needs to be established by comparison with other therapies. The effect of stimulants is large by comparison with an exclusion diet (Williams *et al.*, 1978). Some studies have compared drugs with behaviour therapy. In single case studies it is clear that the withdrawal of medication may produce deterioration in behaviour, and that behaviour modification can be successful in reducing hyperactive behaviour and increasing on-task activity during lessons (Ayllon *et al.*, 1975; Stableford *et al.*, 1976; Pelham, 1977). Group studies making direct comparison of drug and behaviour therapy have found methylphenidate to be more effective than behaviour therapy alone on symptoms of hyperactivity (Gittelman-Klein *et al.*, 1980); the two forms of treatment seem to be additive (Horn *et al.*, 1991). However, it is possible that the behaviour therapy treatments might have an impact upon other aspects of the symptomatology of an affected child — effects that could be important upon later social adjustment. For example, Loney *et al.* (1979) used behavioural treatment in 12 outpatients, 4 of whom were on methylphenidate. Both treatments increased the amount of time that the affected children spent on task, but in addition the behavioural treatments led to an improvement in other children in the same classroom, presumably because of the way that the teacher changed. Wolraich *et al.* (1978) gave behavioural management, in a reversal design, to 20 hyperactive children, of whom half were receiving methylphenidate and half placebo. Behavioural management did not have much effect upon the hyperactivity as measured by the Conners Scales but did improve academic output. Methylphenidate reduced fidgeting and off-task activity but had little effect upon academic behaviour. In both studies the suggestion was that different forms of treatment may affect different types of problem. The longer-term effect of both the separate treatments and their interaction when combined together should become a focus for study.

Modes of action

There are many actions of stimulants upon the central nervous system and it is not clear which ones are responsible for the clinical effects. Stimulants act on the central nervous system to facilitate transmission across synapses, enhance excitatory activity, increase blood flow and reverse the effects of depressant drugs on the reticular formation. They promote the release of catecholamines, they inhibit the release of the same neurotransmitters through presynaptic receptors, they may directly stimulate dopaminergic and noradrenergic receptors, and they alter the turnover of other neurotransmitters, including serotonin and phenylethylamine.

A chemically dissimilar class of stimulants, the xanthines (such as caffeine) have their effect upon brain by altering concentrations of cyclic adenosine monophosphate in brain tissue and the concentration of intracellular calcium. Together with this they can release catecholamines and potentiate the effects of catecholamines. Their effect on hyperactive children is complex; in normal children they improve attention yet increase activity (Elkins *et al.*, 1981).

Zametkin and Rapoport (1987) described a programme of studies designed to indicate which of the neurochemical actions correlates with clinical response. The clearest correlation came with metabolites of noradrenaline. MHPG (3-methoxy-4-hydroxy-phenyl ethlene glycol) was decreased during amphetamine treatment (Shekim *et al.*, 1979; Shen & Wang, 1984) and the reduction in MHPG and, especially, phenylethylamine correlated with change in hyperactivity (Zametkin *et al.*, 1984). However, the noradrenergic story is obscured again by the lesser effect of methylphenidate on noradrenaline turnover in the face of a strong therapeutic action.

Study of the differential effectiveness of different drugs does not clearly favour any single hypothesis of action. The most effective drugs, such as methylphenidate, dexamphetamine and the monoamine oxidase inhibitors, all have mixed catecholaminergic actions. In general, selectively dopaminergic drugs such as L-dopa, piribidil and nomifensine are not good therapeutic agents (Brown *et al.*, 1979; Langer *et al.*, 1982). Imipramine, which has little dopaminergic action, effectively reduces hyperactivity. More selectively noradrenergic drugs are not studied so much, but clonidine given as a noradrenergic antagonist was found to reduce hyperactive behaviour (Hunt *et al.*, 1985). Its effects in clinical practice are often disappointing. A few drugs, such as pemoline, are considered to be selectively dopaminergic in their properties yet are as effective as amphetamine in the treatment of hyperactivity (Conners & Taylor, 1980). It may be that they work through a different mechanism — and indeed the time course of action seems to be rather different from the other stimulants with the full effect only apparent after some 6 weeks of therapy.

Attempts to block the effect of amphetamines with dopamine or noradrenaline antagonists could help in understanding the mechanism of action, but at present give rather confusing results. Gittelman-Klein *et al.* (1976) found that thioridazine did not antagonize the effects of methylphenidate. Levy and Hobbes (1988) claimed that pretreatment with haloperidol blocked the effect of amphetamine — though on some of their measures the figures made it clear that the difference between placebo and amphetamine was just as great following haloperidol pretreatment as following pretreatment with placebo.

It is clear that we know little about which of the many physiological changes are responsible for the psychological effects. Practically, it is important to appreciate the diversity of actions of effective drugs; if children are refractory to one medication then it may be useful to substitute another of a different chemical class.

Hazards of treatment

Amphetamines and related drugs can all cause transient dose-related side-effects including sleeplessness, headache and abdominal pain. These can usually be managed by reductions of dosage or by redistribution of the dose over the course of the day.

Loss of appetite is often a striking symptom of amphetamine treatment and tolerance to this effect often does not appear in children. Appetite suppression may therefore continue even after months or years of treatment. This and possible neuroendocrine effects have raised concern about the effects of medication on growth. Roche *et al.* (1979) concluded that amphetamine produces at most a small retardation in weight and height. Most children are not affected. If there is slowing of growth, it can still be discerned after 2 years of continuous therapy, but probably not thereafter, and the drugs do not seem to affect adult stature or weight (Klein & Mannuzza, 1988). All treated children should have height and weight monitored and plotted on growth charts. If their rate of growth declines, then a holiday from medication of about 6 weeks will allow catch-up growth to take place (Klein *et al.*, 1988).

Heart rate and blood pressure can be increased: this is not usually of any clinical importance but can be significant in black patients (Brown & Sexson, 1988). Tics can be made worse, even to the point of precipitating Gilles de la Tourette's syndrome (Denckla *et al.*, 1976). The stereotyped and repetitive movements of some children with pervasive developmental disorders can also be aggravated (Campbell, 1975). Dyskinesias may be more common when pemoline is used (Sallee *et al.*, 1989). Psychosis has been reported (Ney, 1967) but published reports are rare. Dependence upon prescribed stimulants seems to be very rare before puberty (see above).

Liver disorder is not common, but may be a hazard with pemoline. Jaffe (1989) described 2 children who died: 1 had liver disease before pemoline was given, and the other suffered a lethal hepatitis after overdose. Baseline and repeated liver function tests are therefore recommended for children given this drug.

Tics, stereotypies and cardiovascular disease are relative contraindications to treatment, but do not forbid the therapy entirely: the balance of risks and benefits should be individually assessed. Methylphenidate was superior to placebo in treating behaviour problems in children with tic disorders (Konkol *et al.*, 1990). Caution in prescription should be taken when an elder relative is at risk for drug abuse and may intercept and sell the medication, or in the treatment of older children. In these circumstances pemoline may be preferred.

Indications and dosage

The main target problem is chaotic, restless, inattentive overactivity that is severe enough to constitute a handicap to the child's development. The clearest indication is the hyperkinetic disorder as defined by severity and pervasiveness of hyperactivity, the absence of affective disorder and the presence of attention deficits (Taylor *et al.*, 1987). Lesser degrees of hyperactivity can also be an indication, depending upon the assessment of the developmental significance of the hyperactive behaviour.

If the chief difficulty is aggressive or unruly behaviour then behaviour modification techniques are likely to be more appropriate. Remedial education and individual counselling may well be more important if learning problems are the main difficulty. For children whose overactivity is a part of emotional disorder and agitation, then psychological treatments should be considered. Behaviour problems in preschool children and the severely intellectually subnormal are not usually an indication for medication.

The first choice of stimulant is usually methylphenidate in a dosage regime of 0.2–0.5 mg/kg daily in divided doses. It is usually preferable to dexamphetamine because of the relative rarity of central nervous system side-effects. However, dexamphetamine (0.1–0.4 mg/kg daily) is also effective and may be preferred in some circumstances, especially epilepsy (because it raises the convulsive threshold) and when methylphenidate is not available (as in the UK,* India and certain other countries). A higher dose of stimulants (methylphenidate 0.5–1.5 mg/kg) can be considered in children failing to respond to lower doses. However, this level of medication is considerably more likely to be associated with adverse effects such as tics and growth retardation; these adverse effects should therefore be considered carefully before embarking on the higher dosage range.

Pemoline (60–100 mg daily) is also a useful drug but is considerably slower to work. It has the corresponding advantage of a single daily dosage and less marked on–off effects. It is not usually a first choice of stimulant because of the relatively high frequency of central effects such as anorexia and because of concerns about hepatotoxicity. However, it has the great advantage that it does not maintain self-administration in animals or a black market among humans, and it is not a controlled drug. It is therefore useful in the treatment of adolescents.

Dosage should not be the slave of body weight. Obese children may well need less and there are marked individual differences in drug metabolism. The dose should be titrated against the response of the target symptom for each individual. Parent and teacher questionnaires such as the abbreviated Conners Questionnaire (Conners, 1973) are clear and useful ways of monitoring effect.

A single-case placebo-controlled design is a powerful way of determining whether an individual child is truly responding to pharmacological rather than placebo properties of the treatment. Usually this is not essential, for the group-based clinical trials make it clear that most of the observed change can be attributed to pharmacological actions. Sometimes, however, there is doubt in an individual; and, if so, a crossover with placebo can be proposed. This can interfere with the business of introducing psychological methods to support a drug-induced improvement, so is not to be embarked on lightly; but the frequent need for medication to be prolonged for years means that a clear decision about whether the drug is efficacious is worth the effort of a comparison with placebo.

If a child is resistant to the effects of stimulants, then the reasons for this should be reviewed. It may be that other problems besides hyperactivity are present and should have precedence in a further treatment plan. Review may also indicate some specific reasons for the failure of stimulants. The coexistence of overt symptoms of emotional disorder predicts a poor response (Taylor *et al.*, 1987; Pliszka, 1989). This combination might well suggest that a different line in medication should be taken, such as imipramine or clonidine (see below). Symptoms of pervasive developmental disorder may also be present: under these circumstances it is likely that amphetamine and related stimulants will be of little effect, and that any beneficial effects upon attention would be outweighed by the worsening of stereotypies and/or the production of a withdrawn and 'frozen' state (Campbell *et al.*, 1972). Low-dosage haloperidol is likely to be preferable in this situation.

TRICYCLIC ANTIDEPRESSANTS

Tricyclic antidepressants are widely used in child psychiatry, chiefly for the indications of enuresis and hyperactivity. Practice varies widely in the use of antidepressants for depressive disorders.

---

* Obtainable on a named-patient basis from The Marketing Director, Ciba-Geigy Pharmaceuticals, Horsham, West Sussex, RH12 4AB.

Effects

Depression

A few studies have now been reported that meet the criteria of selecting subjects with standardized criteria for major depressive disorder, and employing double-blind random allocation designs and standardized outcome measures. They have not established that tricyclics are effective in this age group.

Imipramine was not superior to placebo in the treatment of groups of prepubertal children with carefully diagnosed depression (Petti & Law, 1982; Kashani *et al.*, 1984; Puig-Antich *et al.*, 1987). Puig-Antich *et al.* (1987) suggested that their trial was in fact positive, on the basis of a linear relationship between the plasma level of drug and clinical response. However, this would have implied that a worsening of depression at low plasma levels had as much support as an improvement at high levels; and in any case the correlation could be seen only as an association of unknown significance.

Other studies have not found that response depended upon a high level in the blood. Ryan *et al.* (1986) described a comparison of imipramine and placebo in a group of adolescents: again there was no response, but in this instance plasma level was not a determinant. Geller *et al.* (1989) reported a trial of nortriptyline against placebo in depressed children. This set out to achieve high plasma levels, and was largely successful in doing so. Even so, the proportion of children responding was not significantly higher in the group treated with antidepressants. Kramer and Feiguine (1981) and Geller *et al.* (1990) also failed to find a superiority of antidepressants over placebo in adolescence.

Such results are on the face of it rather disappointing. They do not prove that tricyclics are useless: in several trials (e.g. that of Geller *et al.*, 1989) there was a nonsignificant trend in favour of the drug; but the studies were of low power because of small numbers of children. The effect of antidepressants is so well-established in major depressive disorder in adults that there is still a case for using tricyclic antidepressants in children who show the same presentation as adults.

The reasons for the apparent failure of antidepressant medication in childhood deserve further investigation. The presence of a high placebo response has been noted in several of the trials, and has been invoked as an explanation of the relative lack of antidepressant effectiveness. This does not seem like a full explanation, for even if placebo rates were as high as 50% it would still be possible to detect a drug effect in a reasonably sized group. It is possible that depression is neurochemically different in children, but there is at present little other evidence for such a proposition (see Chapter 19), and the response to other antidepressants is not yet very encouraging. It is possible too that the adult definition of depressive disorder is not really suitable for children, and that a group formally defined as meeting research criteria is not in fact the same as the groups that have been the targets of investigation in later life. Such a suggestion is supported by a rather different pattern of symptomatology in young depressed people (Kovacs, 1986; Mitchell

et al., 1988). Sleep and appetite, for example, are more often increased in early-onset depression than in adults. Other features of depression in young people include responsiveness to environmental change, a high rate of response to placebo and frequent overlap with other types of psychiatric disorder. Indeed, response was worst when children had coexistent conduct disorder (Hughes *et al.*, 1990) or separation anxiety (Ryan *et al.*, 1986). All these would be considered in adult psychiatry as factors likely to work against a large response to antidepressants. Accordingly, the poor response in a broadly defined and heterogeneous group of children with depressive mood should not necessarily be an argument against the use of antidepressants in a less common and more rigorously defined type of depression with endogenous features.

Phobias

Antidepressants in children with phobias have had little research attention. Gittelman-Klein and Klein (1971) found imipramine in a dose of 100−200 mg/day to be superior to placebo in children and adolescents with school phobia. On the other hand, Berney *et al.* (1981) found no superiority for clomipramine (40−75 mg/day) in school phobia, perhaps because the dose was too low. Furthermore, imipramine, in doses similar to those employed by Gittelman-Klein and Klein, was not superior to placebo in the treatment of school refusal in children with symptoms of anxiety and depression (Gittelman & Koplewicz, 1986; Bernstein *et al.*, 1990). Design limitations weaken all these conclusions. The existence of powerful and safe psychological therapies implies that they should be the first line of treatment; antidepressants and other drugs are a second line for those who do not respond.

Obsessive-compulsive disorder

In children, as in adults, there is a place for antidepressants in the control of obsessive-compulsive symptoms (see Chapter 25). A controlled comparison of clomipramine with placebo showed a significant benefit to be obtained with the active drug in doses of 100−200 mg/day (Flament *et al.*, 1985). Motor compulsions responded better than obsessive thoughts. Furthermore, a controlled comparison between clomipramine and desipramine favoured clomipramine: there was a high rate of relapse when children and adolescents switched from it to desipramine (Leonard *et al.*, 1989). This is of great theoretical interest in helping to support the involvement of neural systems using serotonin in the expression of obsessive-compulsive disorder. The clinical effect of drugs such as clomipramine is therefore significant and specific, but it is usually not large. Even the children classed as drug responders in the Flament *et al.* (1985) trial did not recover fully, and relapse on discontinuing the drug was the rule.

Comparisons between drug and psychological therapy have not yet been reported. A chart review study by Bolton *et al.* (1983) suggested that psychological approaches, including response prevention, played a larger part than antidepressant medication, but in the absence of systematic comparison and standardized assessment of outcome it would be unwise to be dogmatic about the relative merits of the treatments. The possibility of longer-lasting effects with therapies based on response prevention argues that they should be given a trial whenever this is feasible. Further, the need for clarity — in understanding the effect of treatments in the long-term management of individual cases — argues that one therapy at a time should be given initially. These considerations will often lead to an initial trial of psychological management, followed by drug treatment for those whose symptoms remain uncontrolled. Sometimes, however, the need for immediate symptom relief will lead to a trial of medication as the first choice, followed by psychological treatment being added to a steady dose of medication.

Hyperactive behaviour

Imipramine is an effective antihyperactivity drug with a good effect upon the full range of symptoms that are influenced by stimulant medication (Werry *et al.*, 1980). Task-relevant behaviour increases and ratings of distractible and disruptive behaviour diminish. The effect is probably different from that of any antidepressant action for it is present in low doses and has a rapid onset.

Recent trials have confirmed the value of desipramine (Donnelly *et al.*, 1986; Biederman *et al.*, 1989) and imipramine (Gualtieri & Evans, 1988). Their hazards (see below) and unpleasant subjective effects mean that they are not the drugs of first choice for hyperactivity. They can be useful in several circumstances, such as the coexistent presence of emotional disorder in a hyperactive child, failure to respond to stimulants (Biederman *et al.*, 1989) and the coexistent presence of hyperactivity with tics (Riddle *et al.*, 1988).

Enuresis

Imipramine, in a dose of 25–50 mg/day, reduces the frequency of bed-wetting in approximately 40% of the children to whom it is given (see Chapter 29). This is not a curative effect, for it relapses when the drug is stopped. The availability of very good psychological treatments for bed-wetting means that imipramine should seldom be used in this situation. It can be helpful for temporary suppression of symptoms, for instance to allow a child with a refractory problem to go on school outings. However, intranasal antidiuretic hormone (desmopressin, 20–40 µg at bedtime) is probably more effective and does not carry the same risk of overdose (Klauber, 1989).

Hazards of treatment

Cardiotoxic side-effects are of particular importance. The myocardium of children is vulnerable to tricyclics, and effects such as tachycardia and elevation of blood pressure have been known for a long time (Kupfer & Detre, 1978; Geller *et al.*,

1985). More recently, particular concern has been raised by the sudden death of 3 prepubertal children receiving desipramine (Riddle *et al.*, 1991). The cases add weight to a previous report of sudden death in a 6-year-old receiving imipramine (Saraf *et al.*, 1974, 1978). Even more worryingly, there is little on which to base a rational preventive strategy. One of the children, at least, had preexisting heart disease which obviously should lead to particular caution. Nevertheless, a normal electrocardiogram is no guarantee against the appearance of cardiotoxic effects. In the low doses typically used for hyperactivity and enuresis (below about 50 mg/day), then such side-effects are not to be anticipated and electrocardiogram monitoring is not essential. Doses above this level, however, should only be given after the baseline electrocardiogram reading has been taken and in the presence of continued monitoring. On the basis of adult experience, newer antidepressants such as fluoxetine and fluvoxamine should be less toxic to the heart, but it is not yet known whether children are more vulnerable than adults to the newer drugs.

The signs of toxicity are a reduction of the P-R interval to less than 200 ms, or of the duration of the QRS complex to less than 120 ms. Blood should also be taken for estimation of drug levels: the serum level must be kept below 300 ng/ml. Careful clinical monitoring, including pulse rate and blood pressure records, is also required.

The familiar unwanted effects of antidepressants — dry mouth, headaches, sedation, malaise — are likely to be as common in children as in adults. The physician should systematically monitor all these, which may not be spontaneously described. Migraine headaches may be provoked by tricyclics. All these unpleasant effects may lead to premature cessation of therapy.

OTHER ANTIDEPRESSANTS

Monoamine oxidase inhibitors

Monoamine oxidase inhibitors are used for depressed children who are refractory to tricyclic antidepressants. A chart review study has suggested that they may be effective in these circumstances (Ryan *et al.*, 1988). Monoamine oxidase inhibitors are superior to placebo in the treatment of hyperactivity (Zametkin *et al.*, 1985).

Controlled trials are clearly called for. Monoamine oxidase inhibitors are rather little used in children because the danger of interactions with foods can be very hard to guard against. However, new monoamine oxidase inhibitors with much less risk are being introduced. Some of them have a more selective effect upon the different types of monoamine oxidase, and therefore a more specific profile of action on cerebral neurotransmitters; some have a reversible effect upon the oxidase enzymes and are safer as a result. They should be good candidates for controlled trials to establish their place in childhood therapeutics.

Serotonergic antidepressants

Efficacy

Several newer antidepressants have their actions largely through serotonin release or by stimulating serotonin receptors. Such drugs, e.g. fluoxetine, have been advocated for the treatment of depression. However, there is as yet no trial evidence for their efficacy in children, and clinical experience has not been very favourable. Therefore, in spite of their great theoretical advantage of lesser cardiotoxicity, they are not recommended for the treatment of depressive disorder.

By contrast, obsessive-compulsive disorder in young people has been shown to be responsive to medication (see above). The superiority of clomipramine to other tricyclics, noted already, supports the use of drugs such as fluoxetine that also act selectively on neural systems using serotonin. An open trial gave further support by suggesting that fluoxetine was indeed effective for obsessive-compulsive disorder in children and adolescents in doses between 10 mg and 40 mg/day (Riddle et al., 1990). It is possible to give fluoxetine and clomipramine at the same time (Simeon et al., 1990).

Hazards

Restlessness and gastrointestinal disturbances were reported in a series treated with fluoxetine (Riddle et al., 1990) but were not particularly hazardous. A very well-publicized campaign has alleged that antidepressants such as these cause severe aggression and self-harm. King et al. (1991) described the emergence of such symptoms in treated adolescents. The interpretation is difficult, for such symptoms are of course very common in untreated depression and may indeed emerge during successful treatment. With any physical treatment, the early stages of recovery from depressive disorder are a time of high risk for suicide. Present evidence does not contraindicate the drugs on these grounds.

Tryptophan

Tryptophan is a precursor of serotonin, and was often given in combination with clomipramine or a monoamine oxidase inhibitor in the treatment of depression. However, an epidemic of eosinophilia with myalgia in 1989 was traced to L-tryptophan consumption. Epidemiological data found most cases in association with the product of one Japanese company (Showa Denko). A dimer of tryptophan (1-1'-ethylidenebis-tryptophan) has been implicated as the responsible compound: it can appear as a byproduct of the manufacture of L-tryptophan anywhere. Until the manufacturing risk has been eliminated, tryptophan is not a recommended treatment. However, it can be prescribed, with caution, in exceptional circumstances — especially where an individual who responded to tryptophan is not helped by alternative therapies. One should suspect eosinophilia with myalgia in any individual receiving the drug who shows severe myalgia, or eosinophilia that is not otherwise explained. Complications include scleroderma, neuropathy and pulmonary hypertension; there have been some 30 deaths.

Electroconvulsive therapy

Electroconvulsive therapy has rarely been given to children, and scientific guidance is not available. It can be considered in the therapy of severe depression and catatonia when drug treatment has had a thorough but unavailing trial.

LITHIUM

Effects

Affective disorders

Lithium has been established clinically for some time in the treatment of children and adolescents with affective psychosis (Youngerman & Canino, 1978). De Long and Aldershof (1987) reported that two-thirds of young people with bipolar affective disorders, aged from 3 to 20 years, responded successfully. This is not a satisfactory report, however, and a full-scale trial meeting current standards of scientific adequacy still has to be completed in children. Strober et al. (1990) described some encouraging results. On the other hand, Carlson et al. (1992) provided careful clinical descriptions of the outcome of children whose clinical features led to the high probability of a lithium-responsive disorder being present. These included the existence of a lithium-responsive first-degree relative or a clearly bipolar course. The children treated were not clearly benefited by it. On the other hand, this negative report is focused essentially upon treatment, and does not necessarily mean that prophylaxis would be a vain endeavour.

The clinical use of lithium in children, therefore, has to proceed by analogy with adult treatment and without clear scientific guidelines. Considerable caution should be exercised. Prescribers should achieve plasma levels between 0.8 and 1.4 mmol/l.

Aggression

The effect of lithium on aggressive behaviour is somewhat better documented. Trials by De Long (1978), Lena (1979) and Campbell et al. (1982) have shown superiority over placebo in aggressive children, and especially in children with a pattern of explosive outbursts of aggression in response to minimum provocation. This should be seen as a reasonable indication for lithium therapy — the indication is severely aggressive behaviour that has persisted in spite of psychological attempts to manage it. The presence or absence of depressive symptomatology or mania is not a consideration in the decision about whether to prescribe for this indication.

Hazards of treatment

The risks of lithium therapy are similar in children and adults (Birch, 1988). Electron microscopy reveals reversible renal changes in people taking lithium. However, this is a mild and transient effect and routine monitoring of renal function is not required. Thyroid function may be reduced and baseline estimation of thyroid function before treatment is recommended. The directly toxic effects of lithium can be lethal — the early signs are often motor central nervous system effects, including tremor and mild confusion. Since these early signs may not appear in mentally retarded children, lithium treatment in this group carries particular hazards of inducing encephalopathy, and it should always be carefully monitored, paying particular attention both to clinical changes and to the plasma levels achieved. Nausea, vomiting, altered taste, thirst and diarrhoea are all possible risks.

NEUROLEPTICS

This group of drugs includes several chemical classes — the phenothiazines (e.g. chlorpromazine), the butyrophenones (e.g. haloperidol) and the thioxanthenes (e.g. flupenthixol). They are grouped together because of their value in the control of psychotic symptoms in adults. They all have multiple actions on brain chemistry, including the blocking of the neurotransmitter actions of dopamine, noradrenaline, serotonin, acetylcholine and octopamine: the balance of actions varies.

Schizophrenia

The treatment of schizophrenia follows the principles established for treatment in adults. Neuroleptics are indicated for treatment of acute episodes, acceleration of recovery and prophylaxis against further illness. However, there is very little controlled trial evidence in children or younger adolescents. Haloperidol and loxapine were both superior to placebo in a study of schizophrenia in adolescence (Pool *et al.*, 1976). Nevertheless, clinical experience suggests that those with a very early onset of schizophrenia all too often show an unsatisfactory response to treatment (Realmulto *et al.*, 1984).

The antipsychotic potency of neuroleptic drugs is in proportion to their efficacy in antagonizing dopamine action in the brain (Creese *et al.*, 1976). (The exception is clozapine, which probably acts in a different way.) The most potent are in some ways the most toxic (see below). Less potent drugs, however, may be more sedative, by virtue of blocking the effects of noradrenaline, and may carry higher risks of less common complications such as bone marrow suppression. The choice of drug for an individual with schizophrenia is therefore quite complex.

In normal circumstances, treatment will be initiated with chlorpromazine or an equivalent drug, progressing if necessary to higher-potency and less sedative phenothiazines such as trifluoperazine or to butyrophenones such as haloperidol. Considerable time is often needed for a full neuroleptic response — of the order of 30 days or even longer. Premature changes of medication should therefore be avoided. Dosage levels will often need to rise to the equivalent of 250 mg chlorpromazine daily, and higher doses are needed to control agitation in some individuals. If response is small after a reasonable trial, then the whole case should be reviewed. An organic cause may then be suspected, or the presence of major psychosocial stress. Mania may have given rise to the clinical picture and, if so, large doses may be needed in the acute stage. Heroically high doses of neuroleptics are sometimes resorted to; trial evidence now appearing suggests that big doses are not more helpful than ordinary ones in the long term (Wing, 1990).

Occasionally an apparently poor response comes because the dosage of neuroleptics has been too high. Delirium and akathisia (a syndrome of restlessness and agitation) can both be induced and masquerade as a relapse of the original symptoms. More often, a poor response can be attributed to insufficient dosage, poor compliance or a rapid metabolism of drug in the intestine. A trial of parenteral neuroleptics can be given when schizophrenia is not controlled by oral medication. Depot preparations are available; but since their onset of action is slow, they are more suitable for longer-term maintenance therapy than for treatment of the acute stage.

Young people with schizophrenia may remain refractory to phenothiazines and allied drugs, even after all the above steps have been taken, psychosocial treatments have also been given, and time for recovery has been allowed. Clozapine can then be considered. An open trial in adolescents with treatment-resistant schizophrenia showed a marked improvement in more than half of those treated (Siefen & Remschmidt, 1986). There is a substantial risk of agranulocytosis, which affected 17 out of 3000 recipients when it was first introduced. This is a much greater risk than applies to other antipsychotics. A further disadvantage of the drug is its very high cost. It must be set against the severity of uncontrolled illness.

Pervasive developmental disorders

Children with autism and related disorders can be given neuroleptics for several reasons. The best established is the control of repetitive, stereotyped behaviours. Such behaviours are reduced by thioridazine more than they are by placebo (Davis *et al.*, 1969). The mechanism is not clear: it could be through a direct action of dopamine blockade on movement control or it could be a more indirect result of reducing agitation. The trial evidence that supports this use is based on low doses: up to the equivalent of 100 mg of chlorpromazine a day. There is no scientific evidence that higher doses are more helpful.

Neuroleptics can also have an influence on broader aspects of behaviour. A review by Winsberg and Yepes (1978) concluded that the effect should be described as a rather general one: it made children more manageable, less agitated and easier to live with, but did not reflect any improvement in the disorder itself.

The drug attracting most research has been haloperidol. In doses of 0.5−1.0 mg/kg, it has been superior to placebo in decreasing withdrawal, hyperactivity and emotional lability (Faretra *et al.*, 1970; Cohen *et al.*, 1980; Anderson *et al.*, 1984) and has remained effective even after years of continuous administration (Campbell *et al.*, 1983). However, doses as large as these are enough to put children at considerable risk of the toxic effects considered below. The balance of benefit and hazard needs more research. Meanwhile, cautious practice will reserve potentially toxic medication for the most severe disturbances of behaviour in which behavioural and other psychological therapies have had a full but unsuccessful trial.

Other drugs have been advocated in the treatment of autism, but none is established. Fenfluramine was introduced, as a serotonergic stimulant, on the basis of open and uncontrolled single-case trials. Great clinical and public interest led rapidly to a series of trials, reviewed by Campbell (1988). Early trials claimed striking results, but technical problems made conclusions hard to draw. More recent trials have been less encouraging (Kahler *et al.*, 1987; Stern *et al.*, 1990) but suggest some beneficial effect on hyperactive behaviour in daily doses of between 1 and 2 mg/kg. To set against this, neurotoxicity is possible and the main effects on neurotransmitter metabolites suggest that it may be acting as another antagonist of dopamine (Barthelemy *et al.*, 1989). The specific research issue was that the benefits of fenfluramine should be seen only in children with altered serotonin levels, and should be a function of returning serotonin levels to normal; this has not proved to be the case.

Naltrexone, an opiate agonist, has been used in doses of 0.5−2.0 mg/kg per day; and it offers to control self-injuring behaviour (Walters *et al.*, 1990). A controlled trial by Campbell *et al.* (1990) showed significantly greater effects than placebo in reducing stereotypies and withdrawal. Though its place in therapy is not yet clear, it has considerable promise and deserves consideration now in the management of repetitive self-injury.

Movement disorders

The treatment of tic disorders and Gilles de la Tourette's syndrome is based chiefly on trials on, and experience with, adults and older adolescents. Even in adults, controlled trials are scanty. Shapiro *et al.* (1989) reported both haloperidol and pimozide to be superior to placebo. In children with tics, Connell *et al.* (1967) found haloperidol to be better than placebo in reducing ratings of tic severity. In practice, there is no doubt that neuroleptics — especially pimozide — are useful therapies. Problems in decision-making come from uncertainty about the comparison with other therapies and about what level of severity in the continuum of tics will call for drug therapy at all.

Clonidine, which predominantly affects noradrenaline receptors, has been shown to be superior to placebo in blind trial (Shapiro & Shapiro, 1982). Doubts about its clinical efficacy remain. It is sedative and so, if used, its effects on concentration and learning need to be assessed. Risks of dystonic reactions are greatly reduced with this medication, so further trials are needed.

Behavioural treatments can sometimes reduce tic frequency (see Chapter 26). They have the great advantage of carrying no hazard to physical health. Their disadvantages are that they require prolonged effort by the patient, and may therefore be abandoned, and that they often fail. Clinical experience suggests that they are more likely to fail when the tics are very frequent, as is often the case in Tourette's syndrome. Failure can be disheartening for patients and families, who may then lose confidence in their advisers or themselves.

A logical treatment strategy is therefore to consider behavioural treatments as the first line of treatment for chronic motor tics of mild to moderate degree. They may on occasions be used as a first line of treatment even for more severely affected people, including those with Tourette's syndrome, providing they are motivated and understand the availability of more potent treatments. When psychological treatments are ineffective or unlikely to help by themselves, and when the degree of handicap imposed by symptoms justifies the risk of the unwanted effects of medication, then a neuroleptic such as pimozide is the next choice. The goal of medication is seldom the complete abolition of tics; this can often be achieved only by hazardously high doses. Rather, the goal is to reduce the social and personal handicap resulting from the tics.

When an initial drug trial is successful, then maintenance treatment may be needed for years. The total dose given should therefore be kept as low as is compatible with satisfactory control. Tourette's syndrome is typically a fluctuating condition, and medication needs correspondingly vary from time to time. A partnership between patient and physician should be developed, with both playing an active part in the regulation of dose levels. The doses required are usually smaller than for schizophrenia — often of the order of 1−5 mg of pimozide — but the range is wide and individual judgement is needed for each case.

Aggression

Aggressive behaviour is the commonest reason for neuroleptics to be given (Aman *et al.*, 1985), yet it is also the worst. In the short term, drugs including chlorpromazine and thioridazine are superior to placebo in reducing assaultive and aggressive behaviour in intellectually impaired children, and haloperidol is superior to either (Campbell *et al.*, 1982). In the short term their use is therefore supported by trial evidence (e.g. in emergency, intramuscular haloperidol 0.1−0.2 mg/kg can be given as a single dose). However, this is not the usual way they are given: long-term, high-dose therapy is all too common. No evidence supports this practice; indeed, when the medication is withdrawn the commonest course is a transient worsening, followed by a return to the levels of aggression that were seen on the drug (Gualtieri *et al.*, 1982). It seems probable that drugs are often given and increased for their transient value, and wrongly maintained in the longer term for people whose aggression would be no worse without them.

Hazards

The neuroleptic malignant syndrome has now been described in children as well as in adults (Diamond & Hayes, 1986; Merry *et al.*, 1986). It is a life-threatening medical emergency and prompt recognition is essential. The cardinal features are pyrexia, muscular rigidity, autonomic dysfunction (such as skin pallor, shivering or sweating) and mental changes (most frequently a mild confusional state). The full syndrome requires all four features to be present (Adityanjee *et al.*, 1988). It is fairly uncommon, with an incidence in the region of 1 in 200 of those at risk (Lazarus, 1986). However, milder variants with only a few of the major characteristics are more common, and seem to merge with other acute extrapyramidal syndromes (Addonizio *et al.*, 1986). Because of the severity of the full syndrome, and the speed with which it evolves, it is wise to suspect the development of neuroleptic malignant syndrome as soon as any of the symptoms appear. For example, unexplained fever in a child receiving neuroleptics should be a signal for urgent assessment and close observation — if necessary, as an inpatient. The clinical syndrome is often accompanied by elevated blood levels of creatinine phosphokinase and a leukocytosis. These are not pathognomonic but can give useful support to the diagnosis when the clinical picture is incomplete; normal levels do not exclude the diagnosis. Neuroleptics should be withdrawn as soon as suspicion becomes high.

The early symptoms proceed rapidly (usually in less than 48 hours) to hyperpyrexia with rigidity and circulatory collapse; hepatic and renal failure can ensue. Intensive care will be needed for a diagnosed case, and supportive measures should include muscular relaxants such as dantrolene. Withdrawal of the neuroleptic should of course be done immediately, if not already carried out; a central dopamine stimulant such as bromocriptine should also be given.

Movement disorders

Similar types of movement disorder appear in children as in adults. Acute dystonic reactions are very common; they appeared in one-third of the children given low-dose haloperidol for hyperactivity by Werry *et al.* (1976). This is so common that children and parents should be warned of the possibility, and it will sometimes be justified to prescribe an antiparkinsonian medication as well, to cover the first few weeks of therapy when the risk is especially high (e.g. procyclidine 2–5 mg/day: same amount for treatment). In the longer term, however, antiparkinsonian drugs should not be

given as they can themselves produce confusion and may increase the risk of dyskinesias. Parkinsonism is less common in children than older patients. Akithisia can appear at any time. Withdrawal dyskinesias appear within 6 weeks of withdrawal of drug and disappear within 4 months; they are common in young people (Gualtieri *et al.*, 1982) and should be taken as a warning of the likely appearance of a tardive dyskinesia. Tardive dyskinesias may be irreversible and handicapping; they are more probable the more medication has been given and no neuroleptic is immune. Sulpiride, however, probably carries a lower rate of movement disorders and should be considered if treatment is likely to be prolonged.

Other hazards

All the many risks of neuroleptics can appear in children: photosensitivity, hypotension, increased appetite, obesity, retinopathy (with thioridazine), corneal opacities (with chlorpromazine), bone marrow suppression (with high doses of low-potency drugs), jaundice, sedation and impaired learning have all been reported. Cognitive effects could be of particular importance to young people, but we still lack acceptable scientific evidence about the effects on children's learning. In acute studies on adults the drugs can slow cognitive performance, but in chronic schizophrenia they may improve as well as worsen performance (Cassens *et al.*, 1990).

MINOR TRANQUILLIZERS AND ANTICONVULSANTS

Anxiolytic and hypnotic drugs can be considered together, for drugs having one effect commonly show the other. Benzodiazepines and antihistamines are the most commonly used. Anticonvulsant drugs have a variety of psychotropic actions, including sedation, besides the main effect of controlling seizures.

Effects

Sleep

In controlled trials, medication such as trimeprazine is capable of improving the rated quality of sleep during the duration of treatment (Simonoff & Stores, 1987). However, the effects are entirely reversible. This implies that there is no logic in the practice of giving a short course of hypnotics in order to reestablish a sleep rhythm. Drugs will not do this by themselves. They might, however, make it more practicable to tackle the self-perpetuating elements in sleep disturbance such as daytime over-tiredness and an excessive reaction from adults. Psychological treatments are available and should be used in preference to medication because they are safer.

Benzodiazepines such as diazepam reduce the time spent in deep (stage 4) sleep and correspondingly reduce parasomnias, such as night terrors. The effect can be dramatic, but is seldom needed since reassurance is usually sufficient in itself.

Anxiety reduction

There is a remarkable dearth of clinical trials for this indication, considering the frequency with which benzodiazepines are prescribed. Clinical experience suggests that benzodiazepines may have an effect in reducing anxiety, at least in the short term. However, even this is not supported well by trial evidence: the best-reported trial shows no superiority over placebo (Lucas & Pasley, 1969).

Attention to the limitations of evidence about the efficacy of drugs would probably reduce the prescription of drugs to children markedly. There are few indications. Short-term treatment may be useful when anxiety prevents progress in psychological treatment such as desensitization, or in reducing acute situational anxiety in the face of essential medical procedures (Pfefferbaum *et al.*, 1987).

Anticonvulsant effects

Anticonvulsants often have a beneficial effect upon the behaviour disturbances of epileptic children if they reduce the frequency of seizures. To set against this, they may exert a harmful effect by a direct action, producing sedation, irritability and hyperactive behaviour, especially when anticonvulsant levels in the blood are high and folate levels are depressed. The balance of these actions requires careful monitoring.

Some authorities have advocated the use of anticonvulsants in children who do not have epilepsy. Several possible indications can be distinguished. Firstly, a trial of anticonvulsants is reasonable when children's behaviour or learning is upset by subconvulsive seizures causing transient cognitive impairment. Transient impairment can be detected by simultaneous behavioural and electroencephalogram assessment (see Chapter 8). It is therefore a form of epilepsy. A second possible indication comes when behaviour disorder is associated with an episodically abnormal electroencephalogram. This does not constitute a diagnosis of epilepsy. No trial has yet focused on exactly this circumstance; clinical experience suggests that anticonvulsants are unhelpful. Thirdly, anticonvulsants have been proposed as general-purpose psychotropics in children with no evidence at all of epilepsy. However, they are not suitable for this purpose (Stores, 1978). The only exception is the use of carbamazepine in rapidly cycling bipolar disorder. Trials of carbamazepine in nonepileptic children with behaviour disorders indicate that the changes produced are essentially those of sedation, carrying the risks of irritability and other adverse behavioural changes (Esser *et al.*, 1984).

Hazards

The benzodiazepines produce a dependence syndrome quite rapidly (Marks, 1978). This is so severe a hazard that only clear and pressing indications would outweigh it. As noted, such indications are very few.

NOOTROPIC DRUGS

A relatively new class of drugs is known as nootropic, because of their claimed ability to improve higher cognitive function. Piracetam, the first of these, is marketed in many countries (though not the UK or US); it is chemically related to the inhibitory neurotransmitter gamma-aminobutyric acid. It has been shown to have a statistically significant superiority over placebo in improving the reading performance of children with specific reading retardation (Di Ianni *et al.*, 1985). Interestingly, it also affects neurophysiological measures of information processing over the left hemisphere (Conners *et al.*, 1984). The effects are relatively small, but no hazards have yet been reported, other than a possible increase in emotional disturbance — for which prescribers should be vigilant. Such drugs are likely to become increasingly important in the future.

DIETARY TREATMENTS

The Feingold or Kaiser-Permanente elimination diet is still widely used for the treatment of hyperactivity. This involves the exclusion of synthetic dyes such as tartrazine, salicylates (including those naturally occurring in fruits) and certain preservatives, including butylated hydroxyanisole. This diet has been largely discredited by controlled trials (Taylor, 1991). It should not be prescribed.

Other types of elimination diet do have some support. A radical elimination diet was suggested by Egger *et al.* (1985) and was promising in a double-blind placebo-controlled trial. In this approach, children are stabilized on a diet containing very few foods to determine whether their behaviour will improve or not. If it does improve then foods are added one at a time to determine the effect of each upon the child. The result is a profile for each child of the particular foods which may upset his or her behaviour. These foods are not by any means confined to artificial additives but include wheatflour, cow's milk, citrus fruits, eggs and chocolate as common targets. When the profile has been found for an individual child, then a blind challenge with that particular food can often be achieved with ingenuity.

CONCLUSIONS

Clinical research has established methods of drug treatments, and a vigorous and expanding literature of clinical trials gives guidance to prescribers in some subjects, especially the control of hyperactivity. Systematic knowledge is still very patchy, and some subject areas such as the therapy of the emotional disorders have received very little scientific study. Much therefore remains to be done.

The psychopharmacological advances of the last decade have for the most part been contributions to understanding the actions and indications of established drugs rather than the introduction of new classes of therapy. We can reasonably expect that future research will continue the process of documenting the nature of drug actions on an increasing range of psychological functions. It should also be possible to understand much more about the developmental impact of drug-induced changes in mental life. Long-term comparison of stimulants against placebo in hyperactive children would be likely to resolve the controversy over their use; such trials could be mounted most acceptably in a country where stimulant medication is not normal practice. The cognitive effects of neuroleptic and other drugs in childhood should become known in enough detail to influence prescribing practice. Comparative trials of medication and psychological therapies in the emotional disorders (especially obsessional disorders, anxiety-based conditions and depression) will show whether there is a place for physical therapies in these conditions, and what the indications should be. Indeed, advances in psychological therapies may restrict some of the current uses of drugs.

More fundamental advances in psychopharmacology are by their nature difficult to foresee. Nevertheless, we shall probably know a great deal more about the relationship between neurochemistry and behaviour, and it will be strange if this does not bring new classes of psychoactive drug and new indications for treatment. Drugs that interact selectively with subpopulations of receptors are steadily appearing and will bring new opportunities for benefit — perhaps even for conditions that are at present unresponsive, such as autism. New hazards may also appear. A greater range of drugs will create the need, and computerized databases of prescribing events will bring the means, for much improved safety monitoring. New ethical problems and professional challenges are also likely. For example, drugs that effectively enhance aspects of school learning can be expected (see the section on nootropic drugs, above). How should they be used? If they are not to undermine educational efforts, or to widen inequality in society, then the relation between education and medicine will need thorough reconsideration and renegotiation.

The financial cost of treatments has not been described in this chapter. Superficial considerations can often make drug therapy seem cheap by comparison with psychological treatments, but this omits the true costs. Since all physical treatments carry physical risks, they are never cheap. They should always be thought of as adjuncts to psychological managements, and adequate monitoring is an essential part of treatment. The importance of drug therapies is that they can in some circumstances produce therapeutic benefits that are greater than those obtained in any other way.

REFERENCES

Abikoff H. & Gittelman R. (1985) The normalizing effects of methylphenidate on the classroom behavior of ADDH children. *Journal of Abnormal Child Psychology*, **13**, 33–34.

Addonizio G., Susman V.C. & Roth S.D. (1986) Symptoms of neuroleptic malignant syndrome in 82 consecutive inpatients. *American Journal of Psychiatry*, **143**, 1587–1590.

Adityanjee M.D., Singh S., Singh G. & Ong S. (1988) Spectrum concept of neuroleptic malignant syndrome. *British Journal of Psychiatry*, **153**, 107–111.

Aman M.G., Field C.J. & Bridgman G.D. (1985) Citywide survey of drug patterns among non-institutionalised retarded persons. *Applied Research in Mental Retardation*, **5**, 159–171.

Anderson L.T., Campbell M., Grega D.M., Perry R., Small A.M. & Green W.H. (1984) Haloperidol in the treatment of infantile autism: effects on learning and behavioral symptoms. *American Journal of Psychiatry*, **141**, 1195–1202.

Ayd F.J. & Blackwell B. (eds) (1970) *Discoveries in Biological Psychiatry*. J.B. Lippincott, Philadelphia, PA.

Ayllon T., Layman D. & Kandel H.J. (1975) A behavioural educational alternative to drug control of hyperactive children. *Journal of Applied Behaviour Analysis*, **8**, 137–146.

Bain D.J.G. (1981) Monitoring and prescribing of psychotropic drugs. In: Murray R.M. (ed) *The Misuse of Psychotropic Drugs*, pp. 70–92. Royal College of Physicians, London.

Barkley R. & Cunningham C. (1979) The effect of methylphenidate on the mother–child interaction and hyperactive children. *Archives of General Psychiatry*, **36**, 201–208.

Barkley R.A., Fischer M., Edelbrock C.S. & Smallish L. (1990) The adolescent outcome of hyperactive children diagnosed by research criteria: I. An 8-year prospective follow-up study. *Journal of the American Academy of Child and Adolescent Psychiatry*, **29**, 546–557.

Barthelemy C., Bruneau N., Jouve J., Martineau J., Muh J.P. & Lelord G. (1989) Urinary dopamine metabolites as indicators of the responsiveness to fenfluramine treatment in children with autistic disorder. *Journal of Autism and Developmental Disorders*, **19**, 241–254.

Berney T., Kolvin I., Bhate S.R., Garside R.F., Jeens J., Kay B. & Scarth L. (1981) School phobia: a therapeutic trial with clomipramine and short-term outcome. *British Journal of Psychiatry*, **138**, 110–118.

Bernstein G.A., Garfinkel B.D. & Borchhardt C.M. (1990) Comparative studies of pharmacotherapy for school refusal. *Journal of the American Academy of Child and Adolescent Psychiatry*, **29**, 773–781.

Biederman J., Baldessarini R.J., Wright V., Knee D. & Harmatz J.S. (1989) A double-blind placebo controlled study of desipramine in the treatment of ADD. I. Efficacy. *Journal of the American Academy of Child and Adolescent Psychiatry*, **28**, 777–784.

Birch N.J. (1988) (ed) *Lithium: Inorganic Pharmacology and Psychiatric Use*. IRL Press, Oxford.

Bolton D., Collins S. & Steinberg D. (1983) The treatment of obsessive-compulsive disorder in adolescence: a report of 15 cases. *British Journal of Psychiatry*, **142**, 456–464.

Boreus L.O. (1982) *Principles of Pediatric Pharmacology*. Churchill Livingstone, New York.

Bosco J.J. & Robin S.S. (1980) Hyperkinesis: prevalence and treatment. In: Whalen C.K. & Henker B. (eds) *Hyperactive Children: The Social Ecology of Identification and Treatment*, pp. 173–190. Academic Press, New York.

Bradley C. (1937) The behavior of children receiving benzedrine. *American Journal of Psychiatry*, **94**, 577–585.

Brown R.T. & Sexson S.B. (1988) A controlled trial of methylphenidate in Black adolescents: attentional, behavioral, and physiological effects. *Clinical Pediatrics*, **27**, 74–81.

Brown G., Hunt R., Ebert M., Bunney W.E. Jr & Kopin I.J. (1979) Plasma levels of d-amphetamine in hyperactive children: serial behavior and motor response. *Psychopharmacology*, **62**, 133–140.

Bugental D.S., Whalen C.K. & Henker B. (1977) Causal attributions of hyperactive children and motivational assumptions of two behavior change approaches: evidence for an interactionist position. *Child Development*, **48**, 874–884.

Campbell M. (1975) Pharmacotherapy in early infantile autism. *Biological Psychiatry*, **10**, 399–423.

Campbell M. (1988) Fenfluramine treatment of autism. *Journal of Child Psychology and Psychiatry*, **29**, 1–10.

Campbell M., Fish B., Shapiro T., Collins P. & Koh C. (1972) Response to triiodothyronine and dextroamphetamine: a study of preschool schizophrenic children. *Journal of Autism and Childhood Schizophrenia,* **2,** 343–358.

Campbell M., Cohen I.L. & Small A.M. (1982) Drugs in aggressive behavior. *Journal of the American Academy of Child Psychiatry,* **21,** 107–117.

Campbell M., Perry R., Bennett W.G., Small A.M., Green W.H., Grega D., Schwartz V. & Anderson L. (1983) Long-term therapeutic efficacy and drug-related abnormal movements: a prospective study of haloperidol in autistic children. *Psychopharmacology Bulletin,* **19,** 80–83.

Campbell M., Anderson L.T., Small A.M., Locascio J.J., Lynch N.S. & Choroco M.C. (1990) Naltrexone in autistic children: a double-blind and placebo-controlled study. *Psychopharmacology Bulletin,* **26,** 130–135.

Carlson G.A., Rapport M.D., Pataki C.S. & Kelly K.L. (1992) Lithium in hospitalised children at 4 and 8 weeks: mood, behavior and cognitive effects. *Journal of Child Psychology and Psychiatry,* **33,** 411–426.

Cassens G., Inglis A.K., Applebaum P.S. & Gutheil T.G. (1990) Neuroleptics: effects on neuropsychological function in chronic schizophrenic patients. *Schizophrenia Bulletin,* **26,** 477–499.

Charles L. & Schain R. (1981) A 4-year follow-up study of the effects of methylphenidate on the behavior and academic achievement of hyperactive children. *Journal of Abnormal Child Psychology,* **9,** 495–505.

Cohen I.L., Campbell M., Posner D., Small A.M., Triebel D. & Anderson L.T. (1980) Behavioural effects of haloperidol in young autistic children: an objective analysis using a within subjects reversal design. *Journal of the American Academy of Child Psychiatry,* **19,** 665–677.

Connell P.H. (1968) The use and abuse of amphetamines. *Practitioner,* **200,** 234–243.

Connell P.H., Corbett J.A., Horne D.J. & Mathews A.M. (1967) Drug treatment of adolescent ticqueurs: a double-blind study of diazepam and haloperidol. *British Journal of Psychiatry,* **113,** 375–381.

Conners C.K. (1973) Rating scales for use in drug studies with children. *Psychopharmacology Bulletin Special Issue: Pharmacotherapy of Children,* **9,** 24–84.

Conners C.K. & Taylor E.A. (1980) Pemoline, methylphenidate and placebo in children with minimal brain dysfunction. *Archives of General Psychiatry,* **37,** 922–930.

Conners C.K., Blouin A.G., Winglee M., Lange L., O'Donnell D. & Smith A. (1984) Piracetam and event-related potentials in dyslexic children. *Psychopharmacology Bulletin,* **20,** 667–673.

Creese I., Burt D.R. & Snyder S.H. (1976) Dopamine receptor binding predicts clinical and pharmacological potencies of antischizophrenic drugs. *Science,* **192,** 481–483.

Cunningham C.E., Siegel L.S. & Offord D.R. (1985) A developmental dose–response analysis of the effects of methylphenidate on the peer interactions of attention deficit disordered boys. *Journal of Child Psychology and Psychiatry,* **26,** 955–972.

Davis K., Sprague R. & Werry J. (1969) Stereotyped behavior and activity level in severe retardates: the effect of drugs. *American Journal of Mental Deficiency,* **73,** 721–727.

De Long G.B. (1978) Lithium carbonate treatment of select behavior disorders in children suggesting manic-depressive illness. *Journal of Pediatrics,* **93,** 689–694.

De Long G.R. & Aldershof A.L. (1987) Long-term experience with lithium treatment in childhood: correlation with clinical diagnosis. *Journal of the American Academy of Child and Adolescent Psychiatry,* **26,** 389–394.

Denckla M.B., Bemporad J.R. & MacKay M.D. (1976) Tics following methylphenidate administration. *Journal of the American Medical Association,* **235,** 1349–1351.

Diamond J.M. & Hayes D.D. (1986) A case of neuroleptic malignant syndrome in a mentally retarded adolescent. *Journal of Adolescent Health Care,* **7,** 419–422.

Di Ianni M., Wilsher C.R., Blank M.S., Conners C.K., Chase C.H., Funkenstein H.H., Helfgott E., Holmes J.M., Lougee L., Maletta G.J., Milewski J., Pirozzolo F.J., Rudel R.G. & Tallal P. (1985) The effects of piracetam in children with dyslexia. *Journal of Clinical Psychopharmacology,* **5,** 272–278.

Donnelly M., Zametkin A.J., Rapoport J.L., Ismond D.R., Weingartner H., Lane E., Oliver J., Linnoila M. & Potter W.Z. (1986) Treatment of childhood hyperactivity with desipramine: plasma drug concentration, cardiovascular effects, plasma and urinary catecholamine levels, and clinical response. *Clinical Pharmacology and Therapeutics,* **39,** 72–81.

Douglas V.I. (1988) Cognitive deficits in children with attention deficit disorder with hyperactivity. In: Bloomingdale L.M. & Sergeant J. (eds) *Attention Deficit Disorder — Criteria, Cognition, Intervention,* pp. 65–81. Pergamon, New York.

Douglas V.I., Barr R.G., O'Neill M.E. & Britton B.G. (1986) Short term effects of methylphenidate on the cognitive, learning and academic performance of children with attention deficit disorder in the laboratory and the classroom. *Journal of Child Psychology and Psychiatry,* **27,** 191–212.

Egger J., Carter C.M., Graham P.J., Gumley D. & Soothill J.F. (1985) Controlled trial of oligoantigenic treatment in the hyperkinetic syndrome. *Lancet,* **i,** 540–545.

Elkins R., Rapoport J., Zahn T.P., Buchsbaum M.S., Weingartner H., Kopin I.J., Langer D. & Johnson C. (1981) Acute effects of caffeine in normal prepubertal boys. *American Journal of Psychiatry,* **138,** 178–183.

Esser G., Schmidt M.H. & Witkop H.J. (1984) Zur Wirksamkeit von Carbamazepin bei hyperkinetischen Kindern. *Zeitschrift fur Kinder und Jugendpsychiatrie,* **12,** 275–283.

Flament M.F., Rapoport J.L., Berg C.J., Sceery W., Kilts L., Mellstrom B. & Linnoila M. (1985) Clomipramine treatment of childhood obsessive-compulsive disorders. *Archives of General Psychiatry,* **42,** 977–983.

Faretra G., Dooher L. & Dowling J. (1970) Comparison of haloperidol and fluphenazine in disturbed children. *American Journal of Psychiatry,* **126,** 1670–1673.

Gadow K.D. (1992) Pediatric psychopharmacotherapy: a review of recent research. *Journal of Child Psychology and Psychiatry,* **33,** 153–196.

Gadow K.D., Nolan E.E., Sverd J., Sprafkin J. & Paolicelli L. (1990) Methylphenidate in aggressive-hyperactive boys. I. Effects on peer aggression in public school settings. *Journal of the American Academy of Child and Adolescent Psychiatry,* **29,** 710–718.

Geller B., Farooki S.Q., Cooper T.B., Chestnut E.C. & Abel A.S. (1985) Serial ECG measurements at controlled plasma levels of nortriptyline in depressed children. *American Journal of Psychiatry,* **142,** 1095–1097.

Geller G., Cooper T.B., McCombs H.G., Graham D. & Wells J. (1989) Double-blind placebo-controlled study of nortriptyline in depressed children using a 'fixed plasma level' design. *Psychopharmacology Bulletin,* **25,** 101–108.

Geller B., Cooper T.B., Graham D.L., Marsteller F.A. & Bryant D.M. (1990) Double-blind placebo-controlled study of nortriptyline in depressed adolescents using a 'fixed plasma level' design. *Psychopharmacology Bulletin,* **25,** 85–90.

Gittelman R. & Koplewicz H.S. (1986) Pharmacotherapy of childhood anxiety disorders. In: Gittelman R. (ed) *Anxiety Disorders of Childhood,* pp. 188–203. Guilford, New York.

Gittelman-Klein R. & Klein D.F. (1971) Controlled imipramine treatment of school phobia. *Archives of General Psychiatry*, **25**, 204–207.

Gittelman-Klein R. & Klein D.F. (1976) Methylphenidate effects in learning disabilities. Psychometric changes. *Archives of General Psychiatry*, **33**, 655–664.

Gittelman-Klein R., Klein D., Katz S., Saraf K. & Pollack E. (1976) Comparative effects of methylphenidate and thioridazine in hyperkinetic children. I. Clinical results. *Archives of General Psychiatry*, **33**, 1217–1231.

Gittelman R., Abikoff H., Pollack E., Klein D.F., Katz S. & Mattes J. (1980) A controlled trial of behaviour modification and methylphenidate in hyperactive children. In: Whalen C.K. & Henker B. (eds) *Hyperactive Children: The Social Ecology of Identification and Treatment*, pp. 221–246. Academic Press, New York.

Goyer P.F., Davis G.C. & Rapoport J.L. (1979) Abuse of prescribed stimulant medication by a 13 year old hyperactive boy. *Journal of the American Academy of Child Psychiatry*, **48**, 170–175.

Gualtieri C.T. & Evans R.W. (1988) Motor performance in hyperactive children treated with stimulants. *Perceptual and Motor Skills*, **66**, 763–769.

Gualtieri C.T., Breuning S.E., Schroeder S.R. & Quade D. (1982) Tardive dyskinesia in mentally retarded children, adolescents and young adults: North Carolina and Michigan studies. *Psychopharmacology Bulletin*, **18**, 62–65.

Hechtman L., Weiss G. & Perlman T. (1984) Young adult outcome of hyperactive children who received long-term stimulant treatment. *Journal of the American Academy of Child Psychiatry*, **23**, 261–269.

Hinshaw S.P., Henker B., Whalen C.K., Erhardt D. & Dunnington R.E. (1989) Aggressive, prosocial, and nonsocial behaviour in hyperactive boys: dose effects of methylphenidate in naturalistic settings. *Journal of Consulting and Clinical Psychology*, **57**, 636–643.

Horn W.F., Ialongo N.S., Pascoe J.M., Greenberg G., Packard T., Lopez M., Wagner A. & Puttler L. (1991) Additive effects of psychostimulants, parent training, and self-control therapy with ADHD children. *Journal of the American Academy of Child and Adolescent Psychiatry*, **30**, 233–240.

Hughes C.W., Preskorn S.H., Weller E., Weller R., Hassanein R. & Tucker S. (1990) The effect of concomitant disorders in childhood depression on predicting treatment response. *Psychopharmacology Bulletin*, **26**, 235–238.

Humphries T., Kinsbourne M. & Swanson J. (1978) Stimulant effects on cooperation and social interaction between hyperactive children and their mothers. *Journal of Child Psychology and Psychiatry*, **19**, 13–22.

Hunt R.D., Minderaa R.B. & Cohen D.J. (1985) Clonidine benefits children with attention deficit disorder and hyperactivity: report of a double-blind placebo-crossover therapeutic trial. *Journal of the American Academy of Child Psychiatry*, **24**, 617–629.

Jaffe S.L. (1989) Pemoline and liver function. *Journal of the American Academy of Child and Adolescent Psychiatry*, **28**, 457–458.

Kahler J.A., Shortland G. & Rolles C.J. (1987) Effect of fenfluramine on autistic symptoms. *British Medical Journal*, **295**, 885.

Kashani J.H., Shekin W.O. & Reid J.C. (1984) Amitriptyline in children with major depressive disorder: a double-blind crossover pilot study. *Journal of the American Academy of Child Psychiatry*, **23**, 348–351.

King R.A., Riddle M.A., Chappell P.B., Hardin M.T., Anderson G.M., Lombroso P. & Scahill L. (1991) Emergence of self-destructive phenomena in children and adolescents during fluoxetine treatment. *Journal of the American Academy of Child and Adolescent Psychiatry*, **30**, 179–186.

Klauber G.T. (1989) Clinical efficacy and safety of desmopressin in the treatment of nocturnal enuresis. *Journal of Pediatrics*, **114**, 719–722.

Klein R.G. & Mannuzza S. (1988) Hyperactive boys almost grown up: III. Methylphenidate effects on ultimate height. *Archives of General Psychiatry*, **45**, 1131–1134.

Klein R.G., Landa B., Mattes J.A. & Klein D.F. (1988) Methylphenidate and growth in hyperactive children: a controlled withdrawal study. *Archives of General Psychiatry*, **45**, 1127–1130.

Konkol R.J., Fischer M. & Newby R.F. (1990) Double-blind, placebo-controlled stimulant trial in children with Tourette's syndrome and attention-deficit hyperactivity disorder. *Annals of Neurology*, **28**, 424.

Kovacs M. (1986) A developmental perspective on methods and measures in the assessment of depressive disorders: the clinical interview. In: Rutter M., Izard C.E. & Read P.D. (eds) *Depression in Young People: Developmental and Clinical Perspectives*, pp. 435–468. Guilford Press, New York.

Kramer A.D. & Feiguine R.J. (1981) Clinical effects of amitriptyline in adolescent depression: a pilot study. *Journal of the American Academy of Child Psychiatry*, **20**, 636–644.

Kupfer D.J. & Detre T.P. (1978) Tricyclic and mono-amine-oxidase-inhibitor antidepressants: clinical use. In: Iversen L.L., Iversen S.D. & Snyder S.H. (eds) *Handbook of Psychopharmacology*, vol. 14, pp. 199–232. Plenum Press, New York.

Langer D.H., Rapoport J.L., Brown G.L., Ebert M.H. & Bunney W.E. (1982) Behavioral effects of carbidopa/levodopa in hyperactive boys. *Journal of the American Academy of Child Psychiatry*, **21**, 10–18.

Lazarus A. (1986) The neuroleptic malignant syndrome: a review. *Canadian Journal of Psychiatry*, **31**, 670–674.

Lena B. (1979) Lithium in child and adolescent psychiatry. *Archives of General Psychiatry*, **36**, 854–855.

Leonard H.L., Swedo S.E., Rapoport J.L., Koby E.V., Lenane M.C., Cheslow D.L. & Hamburger S.D. (1989) Treatment of obsessive-compulsive disorder with clomipramine and desipramine in children and adolescents. *Archives of General Psychiatry*, **46**, 1088–1092.

Levy F. & Hobbes G. (1988) The action of stimulant medication in attention deficit disorder with hyperactivity: dopaminergic, noradrenergic or both? *Journal of the American Academy of Child and Adolescent Psychiatry*, **27**, 802–805.

Loney J., Weissenburger F., Woolson R. & Lichty E. (1979) Comparing psychological and pharmacological treatments for hyperkinetic boys and their classmates. *Journal of Abnormal Child Psychology*, **7**, 133–143.

Lucas A.R. & Pasley F.C. (1969) Psychoactive drugs in the treatment of emotionally disturbed children: haloperidol and diazepam. *Comprehensive Psychiatry*, **10**, 376–386.

Marks J. (1978) *The Benzodiazepines: Use, Overuse, Misuse, Abuse*. MTP Press, Lancaster.

Merry S.N., Werry J.S., Merry A.F. & Birchall N. (1986) The neuroleptic malignant syndrome in an adolescent. *Journal of the American Academy of Child Psychiatry*, **25**, 284–286.

Mitchell J., McCauley E., Burke P.M. & Moss S.J. (1988) Phenomenology of depression in children and adolescents. *Journal of the American Academy of Child and Adolescent Psychiatry*, **27**, 12–20.

Ney P.J. (1967) Psychosis in a child, associated with amphetamine administration. *Canadian Medical Association Journal*, **97**, 1026–1029.

Ottenbacher K.J. & Cooper H.M. (1983) Drug treatment of hyperactivity in children. *Developmental Medicine and Child Neurology*, **25**, 358–366.

Pelham W.E. (1977) Withdrawal of a stimulant drug and concurrent behavioral intervention in the treatment of a hyperactive child. *Behavior Therapy*, **8**, 473–479.

Pelham W.E. & Hoza J. (1987) Behavioral assessment of psychostimulant effects on ADD children in a summer day treatment program. In: Prinz R. (ed) *Advances in Behavioral Assessment of Children and Families*, vol. 3, pp. 3–34. JAI Press, Greenwich, CT.

Pelham W.E., Bender M.E., Caddell J., Booth S. & Moorer S.H. (1985) Methylphenidate and children with attention deficit disorder: dose effects on classroom academic and social behavior. *Archives of General Psychiatry*, **42**, 948−952.

Pelham W.E., McBurnett K., Harper G.W., Murphy D.A., Milich R., Clinton J. & Thiele C. (1990) Methylphenidate and baseball playing in ADHD children: who's on first? *Journal of Consulting and Clinical Psychology*, **58**, 130−133.

Petti T.A. & Law W. (1982) Imipramine treatment of depressed children: a double-blind pilot study. *Journal of Clinical Psychopharmacology*, **2**, 107−110.

Pfefferbaum B., Overall J.E., Boren H.A., Frankel L.S., Sullivan M.P. & Johnson K. (1987) Alprazolam in the treatment of anticipatory and acute situational anxiety in children with cancer. *Journal of the American Academy of Child and Adolescent Psychiatry*, **26**, 532−535.

Pliszka S.R. (1989) Effect of anxiety on cognition, behavior and stimulant response in ADHD. *Journal of the American Academy of Child and Adolescent Psychiatry*, **28**, 882−887.

Pool D., Bloom W., Mielke D.H., Roniger J.J. & Gallant D.M. (1976) A controlled evaluation of loxitane in 75 adolescent schizophrenic patients. *Current Therapeutic Research*, **19**, 99−104.

Porrino L.J., Rapoport J.L., Behar D., Ismond D.R. & Bunney W.E. (1983) A naturalistic assessment of the motor activity of hyperactive boys. II. Stimulant drug effects. *Archives of General Psychiatry*, **40**, 688−693.

Psychopharmacology Bulletin, **9** (suppl.) 1−178. Special issue on pharmacotherapy of children (1973).

Puig-Antich J., Perel J.M., Lupatkin W., Chambers W.J., Tabrizi M.A., King J., Goetz R., Davies M. & Stiller R.L. (1987) Imipramine in prepubertal major depressive disorders. *Archives of General Psychiatry*, **44**, 81−89.

Rapoport J.L., Buchsbaum M., Weingartner H., Zahn T., Ludlow C. & Mikkelsen M. (1978) Dextroamphetamine: behavioral and cognitive effects in normal prepubertal boys. *Science*, **199**, 560−563.

Rapoport J.L., Tepsic P.N., Grice J., Johnson C. & Langer D. (1980) Decreased motor activity of hyperactive children on dextroamphetamine during active gym program. *Psychiatry Research*, **2**, 225−229.

Realmulto G.M., Erickson W.D., Yellin A.M., Hopwood J.H. & Greenberg L.M. (1984) Clinical comparison of thiothixene and thioridazine in schizophrenic adolescents. *American Journal of Psychiatry*, **141**, 440−442.

Riddle M.A., Hardin M.T., Cho S.C., Woolston J.L. & Lechman J.F. (1988) Desipramine treatment of boys with attention-deficit hyperactivity disorder and tics: preliminary clinical experience. *Journal of the American Academy of Child and Adolescent Psychiatry*, **27**, 811−814.

Riddle M.A., Hardin M.T., King R., Scahille L. & Woolston J.L. (1990) Fluoxetine treatment of children and adolescents with Tourette's and obsessive compulsive disorders: preliminary clinical experience. *Journal of the American Academy of Child and Adolescent Psychiatry*, **29**, 45−48.

Riddle M.A., Nelson J.C., Kleinman C.S., Rasmusson A., Leckman J.F., King R.A. & Cohen D.J. (1991) Sudden death in children receiving Norpramin: a review of three reported cases and commentary. *Journal of the American Academy of Child and Adolescent Psychiatry*, **30**, 104−108.

Rie H.E., Rie E.D. & Stewart S. (1976) Effects of methylphenidate on underachieving children. *Journal of Consulting and Clinical Psychology*, **44**, 250−260.

Robbins T.W. & Sahakian B.J. (1979) 'Paradoxical' effects of psychomotor stimulant drugs in hyperactive children from the standpoint of behavioural pharmacology. *Neuropharmacology*, **18**, 931−950.

Roche A., Lipman R., Overall J. & Hung W. (1979) The effects of stimulant medication on the growth of hyperkinetic children. *Pediatrics*, **63**, 847−850.

Ryan N.D., Puig-Antich J., Cooper T.B., Rabinovich H., Ambrosini P., Davies M., King J., Torres D. & Fried J. (1986) Imipramine in

adolescent major depression: plasma level and clinical response. *Acta Psychiatrica Scandinavica*, **73**, 275−288.

Ryan N.D., Puig-Antich J., Rabinovich H., Fried J., Ambrosini P., Meyer V., Torres D., Dachille S. & Mazzie D. (1988) MAOIs in adolescent major depression unresponsive to tricyclic antidepressants. *Journal of the American Academy of Child and Adolescent Psychiatry*, **27**, 755−758.

Sallee F.R., Stiller R.L., Perel J.M. & Everett G. (1989) Pemoline-induced abnormal involuntary movements. *Journal of Clinical Psychopharmacolgy*, **9**, 125−129.

Saraf K.R., Klein D.F., Gittelman-Klein R. & Groff S. (1974) Imipramine side effects in children. *Psychopharmacologia*, **37**, 265−274.

Saraf K.R., Klein D.F., Gittelman-Klein R., Gootman N. & Greenhill P. (1978) EKG effects of imipramine treatment in children. *Journal of the American Academy of Child Psychiatry*, **17**, 60−69.

Satterfield J.H., Satterfield B.T. & Schell A.M. (1987) Therapeutic interventions to prevent delinquency in hyperactive boys. *Journal of the American Academy of Child and Adolescent Psychiatry*, **26**, 56−64.

Schachar R.J. (1985) Evaluating attitudes of child psychiatry residents to psychotropic medication: implications for training. *Canadian Journal of Psychiatry*, **30**, 348−352.

Schachar R., Taylor E., Wieselberg M., Thorley G. & Rutter M. (1987) Changes in family function and relationships in children who respond to methylphenidate. *Journal of the American Academy of Child and Adolescent Psychiatry*, **26**, 728−732.

Shapiro A.K. & Shapiro E. (1982) Clinical efficacy of haloperidol, pimozide, penfluridol and clonidine in the treatment of Tourette syndrome. *Advances in Neurology*, **35**, 383−386.

Shapiro E., Shapiro A.K., Fulop G., Hubbard M., Mandeli J., Nordlie J. & Phillips R.A. (1989) Controlled study of haloperidol, pimozide, and placebo for the treatment of Gilles de la Tourette's syndrome. *Archives of General Psychiatry*, **46**, 722−730.

Shekim W.O., Dekirmenjian H. & Chapel J.L. (1979) Urinary MHPG excretion in minimal brain dysfunction and its modification by d-amphetamine. *American Journal of Psychiatry*, **136**, 667−671.

Shen Y. & Wang Y. (1984) Urinary 3-methoxy-4-hydroxphenylglycol sulfate excretion in 73 school children with minimal brain dysfunction syndrome. *Biological Psychiatry*, **19**, 861−877.

Siefen G. & Remschmidt H. (1986) Results of treatment with clozapine in schizophrenic adolescents. *Zeitschrift fur Kinder und Jugendpsychiatrie*, **14**, 245−257.

Simeon J.G., Thatte S. & Wiggins D. (1990) Treatment of adolescent obsessive-compulsive disorder with a clomipramine-fluoxetine combination. *Psychopharmacology Bulletin*, **26**, 285−290.

Simonoff E.A. & Stores G. (1987) Controlled trial of trimeprazine tartrate for night waking. *Archives of Disease in Childhood*, **62**, 253−257.

Sleator E., Neumann H. & Sprague R. (1974) Hyperactive children: a continuous long term placebo controlled follow-up. *Journal of the American Medical Association*, **229**, 316−317.

Solanto M.V. (1984) Neuropharmacological basis of stimulant drug action in attention deficit disorder with hyperactivity: a review and synthesis. *Psychological Bulletin*, **95**, 387−409.

Stableford W, Butz R., Hasazi J., Leitenberg H. & Peyser J. (1976) Sequential withdrawal of stimulant drugs and use of behavior therapy with two hyperactive boys. *American Journal of Orthopsychiatry*, **46**, 302−312.

Stern L.M., Walker M.K., Sawyer M.G., Oades R.D., Badcock N.R. & Spence J.G. (1990) A controlled crossover trial of fenfluramine in autism. *Journal of Child Psychology and Psychiatry*, **31**, 569−585.

Stores G. (1978) Antiepileptics (anticonvulsants). In: Werry J.S. (ed) *Pediatric Psychopharmacology*, pp. 274−315. Brunner/Mazel, New York.

Strober M., Morrell W., Lampert C. & Burroughs J. (1990) Relapse following discontinuation of lithium maintenance therapy in adolescents with bipolar I illness: a naturalistic study. *American Journal of Psychiatry*, **147**, 457–461.

Swanson J.M. (1988) What do psychopharmacological studies tell us about information processing deficits in ADDH? In: Bloomingdale L.M. & Sergeant J.A. (eds) *Attention Deficit Disorder: Criteria, Cognition, Intervention*, pp. 97–116. Pergamon Press, Oxford.

Taylor E. (1986) Childhood hyperactivity. *British Journal of Psychiatry*, **149**, 562–573.

Taylor E. (1991) Toxins and allergens. In: Rutter M. & Casaer P. (eds) *Biological Risk Factors for Psychosocial Disorders*, pp. 199–232. Cambridge University Press, Cambridge.

Taylor E., Schachar R., Thorley G., Wieselberg H.M., Everitt B. & Rutter M. (1987) Which boys respond to stimulant medication? A controlled trial of methylphenidate in boys with disruptive behaviour. *Psychological Medicine*, **17**, 121–143.

Walters A.S., Barrett R.P., Feinstein C., Mercurio A. & Hole W.T. (1990) A case report of naltrexone treatment of self-injury and social withdrawal in autism. *Journal of Autism and Developmental Disorders*, **20**, 169–176.

Werry J. & Sprague R. (1974) Methylphenidate in children: effect of dosage. *Australian and New Zealand Journal of Psychiatry*, **8**, 9–19.

Werry J., Aman M. & Lampen E. (1976) Haloperidol and methylphenidate in hyperactive children. *Acta Paedopsychiatrica*, **42**, 26–40.

Werry J., Weiss G. & Diamond E. (1980) Impramine and methylphenidate in hyperactive children. *Journal of Child Psychology and Psychiatry*, **21**, 27–35.

Whalen C.K., Henker B., Collins B.E., McAuliffe S. & Vaux A. (1979) Peer interaction in a structured communication task: comparison of normal and hyperactive boys and of methylphenidate (Ritalin) and placebo effects. *Child Development*, **50**, 388–401.

Whalen C.K., Henker B., Buhrmester D., Hinshaw S.P., Huber A. & Laski K. (1989) Does stimulant medication improve the peer status of hyperactive children? *Journal of Consulting and Clinical Psychology*, **57**, 545–549.

Williams J.I., Oram D.M., Tausig F.T. & Webster E. (1978) Relative effects of drugs and diet on hyperactive behavior: an experimental study. *Pediatrics*, **61**, 811–817.

Wing J.K. (1990) The functions of asylum. *British Journal of Psychiatry*, **157**, 822–827.

Winsberg B.G. & Yepes L.E. (1978) Antipsychotics (major tranquillizers, neuroleptics). In: Werry J.S. (ed) *Pediatric Psychopharmacology*, pp. 234–273. Brunner/Mazel, New York.

Wolraich M., Drummond T., Salomon M., O'Brien M. & Sivage C. (1978) Effects of methylphenidate alone and in combination with behavior modification procedures on the behavior and academic performance of hyperactive children. *Journal of Abnormal Child Psychology*, **6**, 149–161.

World Health Organization (1985) *The Prescribing of Psychoactive Drugs for Children*. World Health Organization, Copenhagen.

Youngerman J. & Canino A. (1978) Lithium carbonate use in children and adolescents. *Archives of General Psychiatry*, **35**, 216–224.

Zametkin A.J. & Rapoport J.L. (1987) Noradrenergic hypothesis of attention deficit disorder with hyperactivity: a critical review. In: Meltzer H.Y. (ed) *Psychopharmacology: The Third Generation of Progress*, pp. 837–842. Raven, New York.

Zametkin A.J., Karoum F., Rapoport J.L. *et al.* (1984) Phenylethylamine excretion in attention deficit disorder. *Journal of the American Academy of Child Psychiatry*, **23**, 310–314.

Zametkin A.J., Rapoport J.L., Murphy D.L. *et al.* (1985) Treatment of hyperactive children with monoamine oxidase inhibitors. II. Plasma and urinary monoamine findings after treatment. *Archives of General Psychiatry*, **42**, 969–973.

Chapter 52
Social Work in Child Psychiatry Settings

Judith Lask

This chapter is the only one concerned with the contribution of a particular profession to the field of child psychiatry. This is perhaps a reflection of the important role that social work has played since the beginning of child psychiatry as a separate discipline, and the value placed on the multidisciplinary team approach (Wardle, 1991). In contrast to psychology and psychiatry there has been little social-work-led research and there is a danger that a volume such as this might fail to reflect the social work dimension in service provision. The aim of the chapter is to outline the major issues and developments in social work as they relate to child psychiatry and to provide an overview of the social work contribution to the multidisciplinary team. Hopefully, members of other professions will also take the trouble to read it because most of the issues have direct relevance for everyone working with children and families, both in specialized and more general settings, and whether or not they work directly with social work colleagues.

It is the continued concern for the interplay of individual, family and community factors that has signified the special contribution of social work to child psychiatry and, despite shifts in emphasis due to factors such as changes in social philosophy, political context, legislative framework, and developments in research and practice, this concern has been maintained (Cooper, 1989). An examination of the social work contribution and an assessment of its value are of particular relevance at a time when public services are increasingly called upon to justify their expenditure and, in the UK, there is a trend to withdraw social workers from clinic and hospital settings. In countries that are developing social work and child psychiatry services there is debate about how those services can best be constructed (Desai, 1991).

THE CHANGING ROLE OF SOCIAL WORK IN CHILD PSYCHIATRY

Over time, the social worker's role in the multidisciplinary team has changed in response to developments both in child psychiatry and their own profession. The roots of social work lie in the efforts of individuals and voluntary organizations to meet the needs of the poor, deviant and disadvantaged (Goldstein, 1975) both on an individual basis and as part of wider movements to improve social conditions (Jordan & Parton, 1983). From the beginning of the century social

workers, especially those based in hospitals, developed an interest in psychiatric and psychological issues and sought more knowledge in these areas (Yelloly, 1980). The term psychiatric social worker was coined by Adolf Meyer in 1906 when, through his influence, the first social worker was appointed to the Manhattan State Hospital (Meyer, 1909). The establishment of the first child guidance clinic in Chicago in 1909 was heavily influenced by the work of Healey and Bronner who highlighted the interplay between social disadvantage and personal problems in the development of delinquency (Crutcher, 1943). This clinic employed a multidisciplinary team (including social work) and this model has remained over the years (Meyer, 1909; Kanner, 1955; Wardle, 1991). Initially the role of the social worker was limited to the collection of data, liaison between home and clinic and carrying the clinic's recommendations to schools, social agencies and courts (Wardle, 1991). The first training course was set up at Smith College in 1918 (Timms, 1964) and in 1928, as part of a general trend to follow developments in North America, a group of British social workers went to train at the New York School of Social Work and in the following year the first British mental health course for social workers was established at the London School of Economics and Political Science. There was a growing awareness of the importance of interpersonal relationships in the development of psychiatric disorder (Younghusband, 1978) and it became clear that advice alone did not always achieve changes in the child's environment. In consequence, training in therapeutic skills was introduced into mental health courses (Kanner, 1955).

Although North America and Europe led developments in the field, other parts of the world, especially those colonized by the west, were also developing social work services in a similar fashion. For instance, the first social worker was appointed to the Beijing hospital in 1920 (Chamberlain, 1991) and in 1948 India set up its first specialized training in medical and psychiatric social work. The International Association of Schools of Social Work was established in 1931 and there has been sustained criticism that the North American and European model of training has been inappropriately promoted in Third World countries where community development rather than individual change is seen as the most relevant goal (Resnick, 1980; Midgley, 1981).

This debate about the best focus for social work has also

been important in the UK and highlighted in child psychiatry where the task of belonging to a clinic-based therapeutic team whilst also dealing with wider community issues has proved difficult. During the 1950s there were debates about whether psychiatric social workers were therapists or social workers (Irvine, 1978) and a pull to move in one direction or another rather than hold the two together (Ashdown & Brown, 1953). The criticism that British child guidance clinics underwent in the 1950s and 1960s for not concentrating on the family, relying on long-term treatments and failing to provide a service for working-class deprived clients (Younghusband, 1978) had particular implications for social workers who were seen to have a special role in maintaining community links. In the wake of these criticisms there were calls for the break-up of child guidance teams (Rehin, 1969) but it was reassuring to those committed to a multidisciplinary child guidance service that in 1974 a joint circular (Department of Education and Science, 1974) supported the role of child guidance clinics and the attachment of full-time social workers.

Apart from North America where private, individually oriented social work is well-developed, most social workers are employed by the state or by voluntary agencies that have close links with the state. This has created a further tension for social workers who are concerned with the individual but also operate within the values of the state. For instance, in South Africa, where social workers have had to operate within a context of apartheid, this has raised intense conflicts (Bernstein & Gray, 1991) and some argue that the rise of conservatism and religious fundamentalism throughout the world will place many social workers in a difficult position (Midgley & Sanzenbach, 1989). In communist countries where state has been given precedence over individual needs, social work has often been deemed unnecessary and welfare provision seen as purely an administrative task (Chamberlain, 1991).

In the UK a reorganization of the personal social services in 1971 led to hospital social workers being employed by social services departments rather than health authorities. This meant that they had to carry the same statutory responsibilities as their community-based colleagues and there was no longer a specialized training in psychiatric social work. Inevitably this highlighted the potential conflict between therapy and social control but also provided an opportunity further to strengthen the social work role within the multidisciplinary team, to facilitate more effective interagency liaison and consultation, to place a firmer emphasis on social context and to make a renewed commitment to making the service appropriate for and accessible to the whole community. However, being part of two organizations, often with different priorities, sometimes placed social workers in a difficult position. Pressures on social workers to meet increasing demands in the area of child protection, together with criticism of medically based models (Sheldon, 1984), led to a continuing trend to withdraw social workers from child psychiatry settings (Pietroni, 1991).

Alongside developments in other professions there has been a move away from the long-term individual casework methods which for a time had formed the core of direct work with clients and an inclusion of behavioural, cognitive and family therapy methods in their work. Together with colleagues from other disciplines, social workers are increasingly involved in consultation and liaison with other professionals and assessments both for court work and decision-making by agencies concerned with child protection. Social workers in child psychiatry settings with their particular orientation by viewing emotional, behavioural and psychiatric problems within a community context, together with their knowledge of community resources, have particular skills to contribute to such work.

MAJOR THEORETICAL INFLUENCES

Along with other disciplines working in child psychiatry, social work is not based on one theoretical model but has been moulded by many influences. Concern for wider social issues has been a continuing strand in social work practice (Lees, 1972; Medhat, 1991) and ideas from sociology, psychology, social anthropology, social administration, social policy and organization theory have been incorporated into social work policy and practice (Hardiker & Barker, 1981).

During the 1970s there was a renewed sensitivity to the effect of social and structural factors in creating and maintaining problems. This coincided with the rapid development of the discipline of sociology and a period of interchange between the two disciplines. The development of the sociology of deviance provoked a questioning of the balance of power between different groups in society and the way in which behaviour was labelled as deviant by the group in power (Jordan & Parton, 1983). This concern with differentials of power has led to a criticism of the medical model and its potential consequences for civil liberty (Sheldon, 1984).

Contributions from sociology, social work and child psychiatry have helped our understanding of the effects of poverty on children and their carers. There is a growing body of research relating to poverty and health (Blackburn, 1991) and several authors have suggested that low income combined with disruptive demographic factors and poor external support generate the stress and life crises that put children at risk, and may precipitate child abuse (Richman *et al.*, 1982; Madge, 1983; Blackburn, 1991). We must distinguish between absolute and relative poverty; even in countries where families with children generally have access to sufficient resources to maintain life, many children are living in disadvantageous circumstances with poor housing, diet and amenities that do not live up to the expectations of society in general (Townsend, 1979). Little research attention has been given to the effect on individuals and families of being the 'poor' and the consequent reduction in their capacity to control their own lives. Studies in the UK have shown that the gaps between the wealthy and the poor are not narrowing and differences in health between classes 1 and 5 are widening (Davy Smith *et al.*, 1990). There is also strong evidence that black people and those from ethnic minorities are more at risk of high unemployment low pay and poor social security rights; the particular vulnerability of women to poverty because of their commitment to child care, low pay and poor child-care facilities has been widely noted (Amin & Leech, 1988).

Our particular concern is the direct and indirect effect of these stressors in the development and maintenance of emotional, behavioural and psychiatric problems of children. It is important also to consider physical health and disability because of their wider impact on the child and family. Social workers will have an added interest in the implications of findings for social policy and the development of community resources. There are of course considerable methodological difficulties in isolating the effects of individual factors such as low income, unemployment and poor housing as they often cluster together; but studies show some important associations.

A number of studies show a relationship between poor housing and health problems in children and their parents. Brown and Harris (1978) found an association between over-crowding and levels of depression in women, and Platt *et al.* (1989) found that children living in damp and mouldy housing were more likely to have a number of respiratory symptoms, headaches, fever and irritability than children living in similar dry housing. A survey carried out by the Department of the Environment (1981) found that children who live in flats have a greater incidence of respiratory infections than the general population and a higher level of emotional disturbance than families living in houses. Another study that points to this not simply being an association with housing type is one by Byrne *et al.* (1986), in which they found that in every age group except the over-65s individuals who lived in 'difficult-to-let' areas experienced more psychological distress than people living in more desirable areas, regardless of housing type. Of particular concern in the UK is the growing number of families housed in homeless family accommodation or in bed and breakfast establishments. Their children are at major risk for health and behaviour problems (Bassuk & Rosenberg, 1990). Conditions are usually cramped with poor cooking facilities and frequent moves leading to poor diet, disrupted schooling and poor access to health care (Conway, 1988).

Another area of concern is the effect of poverty on the incidence of child abuse and neglect and on the number of children received into care. Unfortunately government statistics do not record when poverty and associated factors such as poor housing and unemployment are factors in the decision for a child being received into care or placed on a child protection register. In a survey of cases seen by the child protection team at the University of Colorado Hospital over a 15-year period, a positive connection was found between local levels of unemployment and number of cases seen (Irvine, 1985). In the UK, studies of populations of children taken into care show that in Strathclyde 70% of children came from homes where the head of household was unemployed and in Newcastle 80% of children taken into care over a 6-year period came from homes with an income at or below the supplementary benefit level (Oppenheim, 1990).

A study of 2500 children admitted to care in 13 authorities (Bebbington & Miles, 1989) found that before admission only a quarter were living with both parents; almost three-quarters of the families were receiving income support; only 1 in 5 lived in owner-occupied housing; and over half were living in poor neighbourhoods.

There are limitations in studying social service department populations as more affluent families may not use these services and may be in a better position to maintain their privacy (Becker & MacPhereson, 1988). Social workers may also act in a different way towards more affluent and educated clients who are more like themselves (O'Toole *et al.*, 1983), either not recognizing that their children are at risk or offering alternative services such as counselling.

Although studies have shown high levels of stress which do not always come to the notice of professional agencies (Brown & Harris, 1978; Richman *et al.*, 1982), not all families suffering unemployment and poverty have emotional difficulties, abuse their children or have them received into care, nor do all women in adverse circumstances become depressed. We must assume that the effects of poverty and related stresses are mediated by other protective and vulnerability factors. Garmezy (1984) has reviewed the studies that shed light on the nature of protective factors in children and concludes that there are three recurring factors present in a number of the studies. These are personality dispositions in the child, a supportive family milieu and an external support system that encourages and reinforces a child's coping efforts and strengthens these by reinforcing positive values. Studies have highlighted a number of vulnerability factors, including temperament (Graham *et al.*, 1973), parental disharmony (Quinton & Rutter, 1985), loss (Brown *et al.*, 1985), separation (Wolkind & Rutter, 1973) and divorce, especially when accompanied by other stressors (Hetherington *et al.*, 1982).

These findings have important implications for social work policy and practice. Not only will the failure to address poverty be likely to create situations and experiences that will make children vulnerable and less able to cope with later adversities, but it is also necessary to address issues of personal relationships that can protect children and families against that adversity. At the level of social policy the findings indicate the value of more effort being made to support the income of families, to provide better housing and to reduce unemployment. Housing policies that rehouse already vulnerable families on 'difficult-to-let' estates need to be questioned, as do the implications for the emotional, physical and educational development of children living in homeless family accommodation. New children's legislation in the UK encourages the use of resources to avoid children being received into care because of poverty and allows for the support of networks in providing assistance and alternative care for children. Information from research supports these moves but they will require an expansion in public spending.

At the level of organization of service, research points to attention being given to encouraging the take-up of welfare benefits and the targeting of help to vulnerable groups such as those in poor housing, ethnic minorities and unsupported mothers. Those of us who are practitioners in child psychiatry settings must be interested in these wider policies that have an important impact on our clients; but there is also a clear role for us in identifying vulnerable families, putting them in touch with resources and developing the best ways of encouraging harmonious and supportive relationships within families and wider networks. The complex interplay of developmental, emotional, physical and resource issues points to the need for good interdisciplinary cooperation on all levels.

Social support seems to be one important protective factor for children and families and, with a greater emphasis on care in the community (Griffiths, 1988), social work has looked to sociology for helpful ideas about the nature of community and the measurement of social networks and their effectiveness (Sharkey, 1990). The terms network and community support are frequently used in a vague fashion but a more detailed analysis is essential when considering service provision in order that existing community resources can be enhanced and supplemented in the most effective way. This is especially important in countries that do not have the resources for individually targeted services.

Our particular concerns in child psychiatry are the aspects of networks that help to promote the developmental and emotional well-being of children and support their families and carers. Because of the complexity and interrelatedness of factors such as emotional support, poverty, health, employment, emotional disorder and parenting and the lack of large-scale controlled studies, it is generally only possible to draw out associations between well-being and particular kinds of support and impossible entirely to disentangle the effects of emotional support from practical help. The work of Brown and Harris (1978) points strongly to the importance of supportive relationships in protecting vulnerable women from depression. The emotional component of these relationships seems important but the study also points to the importance of practical help in cushioning some of the effects of adverse life events that in turn serve as precipitators of depression. Placing these findings side by side with other evidence of the adverse effect on children of parental depression (Rutter & Quinton, 1984) and the findings of Mills *et al.* (1984) that depressed mothers are likely to be less responsive to the needs of the child, less able to provide consistent discipline and less likely to initiate interaction, the importance of identifying and compensating for network gaps is clear. An extensive review of the work on social networks and health (Specht, 1986) shows a consistent association between weak social networks, lack of social support and poor physical and emotional health.

If social, emotional and practical support are important, how do we identify the situations where there are gaps? Much of the early work of sociologists and anthropologists was concerned with the 'mapping' of networks in fairly stable communities (Bott, 1957), indicating the high level of emotional and practical support that could be provided. These studies are of limited value when considering the more unstable and less geographically based communities that exist in urban areas and could lead to an unrealistic idealization of what communities are able to provide. However, with these limitations, the concepts of network size and density are of value in assessing the support available to individual families and within communities and take us a step further from generalized statements that may not reflect particular cases. Although high network density (i.e. a close-knit community) may be important at times of crisis and at life stages such as infancy and early childhood, evidence from work with the elderly suggests that looser-knit networks may more easily have within them the links and contacts to mobilize the support and help of outside agencies when those networks break down (Granovetter, 1973). In turn, a large network may not be able to provide essential child care if it is geographically widespread. Key issues to be considered are how much a network can cope with before it breaks down and the ability of the network to meet certain specific needs.

The size and effectiveness of social networks seem to be related to levels of affluence (Willmot, 1987) and are enhanced by cars, money, telephones and child care that in turn help unsupported parents to maintain employment. McKee (1987), in looking at the effects of unemployment, points out that there is often a more positive network response to crisis than to long-term need. In addition, low-income families are less likely than high-income families to have the resources to offer services and exchanges of help. These trends are important and point to the need for welfare, child care and health services to target resources in areas of long-term need.

If the strengths and weaknesses of community supports can be identified then provision can be made to support existing arrangements so that they can continue and to provide services to fill gaps. There is a need for research to identify patterns of support in different ethnic groups in order to provide more appropriate services.

Another area of joint concern for social workers and social scientists is the changing nature of the family (Bernades, 1985). This is helpful in understanding the stress of changes such as separation and remarriage on individual children and families (Hetherington, 1988; Wallerstein *et al.*, 1988) and to indicate the kinds of supports that will be most helpful (Tallmen, 1986).

There has been interest in the relevance of an interactionist perspective to social work practice (Day, 1985). The underlying assumption of this perspective is that there is no such thing as a social reality and, as a consequence of this, attention is paid to how meanings are attributed and actions are interpreted. Thus, when assessing the importance of life events it is necessary to consider their meaning for the individual. Similar ideas have come through the route of family therapy (Hoffman, 1988) and have clear implications for the use of the interview both to understand difficulties and to promote change.

The commonly held belief that psychoanalysis has had a profound influence on social work in the UK and the rest of Europe has been challenged (Yelloly, 1980) but in child psychiatry this influence has been strong, especially on the development of casework theory. Criticism for putting too much emphasis on the individual contributed to a move away from psychoanalytic ideas, and concern for a more democratic relationship between worker and client led to an interest in more person-centred (Mearns & Thorne, 1988) and cognitive approaches (Beck, 1976).

Learning theory has had a limited influence on social work practice, although its application has been developed more fully by particular groups (Jehu *et al.*, 1972; Sheldon, 1982). Assumptions that behaviour therapy is manipulative and impersonal have led to its rejection by some, even though it has much to offer, especially when combined within a counselling or family therapy approach.

Over the years, practice has been influenced by studies designed to elicit client perceptions of social work practice and service provision. Unfortunately, studies are generally small, often retrospective and the methodology does not allow any firm conclusions to be drawn. One theme that has been picked up in a number of studies is that clients are more likely to be satisfied if they feel that the social worker has listened to and understood their point of view and concentrated on what they see as their problem (Mayer & Timms, 1970; Fisher *et al.*, 1986; Simpson *et al.*, 1990). There is a strong tendency for clients to prefer a practical, problem-solving approach but one which has a 'human face' (Packman, 1989). Clearly the client's experience is very important but it does not answer the question about the relative effectiveness of different approaches. Recent legislation promotes the ethos of partnership and it is not unreasonable to assume that satisfied clients will be more likely to work closely with social workers. The importance of beginning from a client's view of the problem is widely stated within family therapy (Howe, 1989) and there is a need for more evaluation of issues of engagement and styles of interventions in order to ensure that a wide range of clients have access to a service that they find both acceptable and effective.

In addition to the understanding of child development, attachment (Bretherton & Waters, 1985) and individual and family processes, child psychiatry and psychology have provided a wealth of information with direct relevance to the practice of social work. Earlier I discussed how research has added to our understanding of the effects of poverty and deprivation on children's lives, underlined the importance of environment and pointed to protective and risk factors (Brown & Harris, 1978; Quinton & Rutter, 1984; Rutter, 1987). A range of work addressing the effects of family disruption and alternative forms of care have, together with placement outcome studies, given a helpful basis for decision-making (see Chapter 15 and Wolkind, 1984; Rutter, 1989; Black, 1990).

The provision of day care, its helpfulness to parents and its effects on children have been continued concerns for social work. A review by Belsky (1988) discusses the current information available on the effects on children and isolates those children who experience more than 20 hours a week of nonmaternal care during their first year of life as being particularly at risk of insecurity, aggression and noncompliance that can persist (though the effect decreases) until the age of 8 or 9.

Early anxiety about the detrimental effect of day care on attachment was not borne out by research that concentrated on stranger wariness and separation distress — indeed the value of these as measures was called into question when no evidence was forthcoming for the developmental implications of such behaviour. Studies have moved away from looking at behaviour at separation or confidence in approaching adults to looking at behaviour on reunion with mother. Studies by Waters (1978) convincingly demonstrated that the behaviour of secure infants is characterized by their tendency to greet mothers positively following separation, and to approach and be comforted by her. In each of two investigations to consider attachment to the father, it was discovered that sons with more than 35 hours a week of nonmaternal care were more likely to be classified as insecure in their attachment to their father and as a consequence have two insecure infant–parent relationships (Chase-Lansdale & Owen, 1987; Belsky & Rovine, 1988).

Although these findings do not demonstrate that extensive nonparent care initiated in the first year of life causes insecurity, there is evidence of its association with heightened risk. Initial work suggests that risk may be intensified when the mother's care-giving skills are low and there is marital discord (Belsky & Rovine, 1988). A review by Belsky (1988) concludes that, although studies show that there is a link between more than 20 hours a week of nonparent care in the first year and elevated rates of insecurity, aggression and noncompliance in children, this could also be a function of the quality of care available and/or the experience of growing up in a family that uses nonparental care in the first year. Clearly this is an important area of research and points to the need for day-care workers to identify children at risk and offer extra help to avoid long-term sequelae. When considering the value of day care to a particular family, account must be taken of the effect on the family as a whole in terms of employment opportunities and levels of stress as well as the particular risks to the child. Further research should help us to identify risk factors and how these may be ameliorated.

Casework theory is one example of the struggle to find a theoretical framework in which to place the many strands which make up social work practice but has attracted criticism for theoretical confusion and a reliance on the individual rather than community (Wootton, 1959). Another attempt that gained some support is the unitary model put forward by Pincus and Minahan (1973). This model denoted the various levels of system (such as family and community) that affect an individual and suggests that all should be considered as targets for intervention. This served to bridge the division that had arisen between community work and casework but only had limited influence, perhaps because systems theory has provided a more developed framework and one that gives clearer guidelines for practice. The influence of systems theory (Bateson, 1972) is already strong throughout social work but especially in the field of child psychiatry, where social workers have been at the forefront of its development and application.

VALUES IN SOCIAL WORK

Much has been written about the values underlying social work (Biestek, 1957; Bartlett, 1970). It has been pointed out that a value denotes what is good or desirable, and is a moral imperative which is not empirically verifiable (Halmos, 1965; Bartlett, 1970; Wilkes, 1981). We all hold values, both personal and professional, and these inevitably affect every aspect of our work (Von Glaserfeld, 1988). The question arises whether a discussion of values is useful to social work and in the context of this chapter adds anything to the work of the multidisciplinary team.

Although some would argue that care for the client, much as in medicine, is the core task of social work (Harris, 1990), social workers at times act as agents of social control and work within a politically determined legislative framework. In this way the orientation of social work will vary from country to country; for instance, vital issues for child psychiatry such as the rights of children will be considered differently in different cultures (Hegar, 1990). Authors have commented on the importance of values as a balance to the political pressures on social work (Spicker, 1990). They have also been seen to curb the potential abuse of power and act as a balance to the pervasive managerial style of social work agencies (Wilkes, 1981).

The debate concerning the nature of social work values has been lively and concepts such as self-determination have received much criticism for not taking into account the restraining and authoritative aspects of social work (Whittington, 1971; Webb & McBeath, 1989). Because of concern for the community as well as the individual, a value such as freedom or self-determination cannot be wholly applicable in all circumstances. However, whilst freedom, for instance, must sometimes be limited, the reasons should be explicit and the limitations kept to a minimum. For the reasons stated above, it is important to keep the discussion about values alive within social work and with colleagues from other professions, in the hope that it will prevent the abuses that have taken place in the name of social work and medicine (Butler-Sloss, 1988; *Social Work Today*, 1991).

INTERVENTIONS

This section does not aim to give an overview of each type of intervention as these will be found in other chapters. Rather I will focus on their particular applications by social workers. More attention will be given to casework and counselling as these are not fully covered elsewhere.

Casework and counselling

There have been many attempts to define the terms casework and counselling and to differentiate them both from each other and from psychotherapy (Kraemer, 1987). The similarities and differences depend on the choice of definitions (Walrond-Skinner, 1986) and the terms are often used interchangeably, although the term casework is usually only applied to social work. Perhaps because of earlier criticisms that social workers in child psychiatry were overly reliant on individual approaches to clients' problems, the term counselling is often the preferred term for this work, whilst casework is often used to describe the day-to-day management of a case, often including a variety of interventions.

Although the process of counselling or casework will vary and be dependent on theoretical preference, client and counsellor attributes and agency context, it is possible to draw out some common threads. Underlying any counselling is an acknowledgement of the importance of individual processes in mediating the effects of social relationships, poverty, deprivation and environmental stresses (Holder & Wardle, 1981; Garmezy, 1984). The relationship between client and social worker is the medium through which work is carried out and the nature of this relationship will be an important influence on all aspects of the counselling process. This relationship will in turn be influenced by current knowledge, theoretical preference and professional values. In social work these values determine that counselling is usually client-centred. Rather than offer solutions, social workers will provide a relationship that can help the client look at personal difficulties, identify and use his or her own resources and move towards change. Although there is an element of authority in all therapy, where social workers have the power of legal intervention this authority becomes crucial (Furlong, 1989). It is essential that limits of power and authority are made explicit from the beginning and issues of confidentiality fully discussed.

One of the social worker's roles in the counselling process is to provide a secure and facilitating atmosphere which involves considerations such as punctuality, consistency and privacy. Social workers will always give consideration to the realities of the clients' lives and the way in which they will be affected by the wider systems in which they live. In consequence, where possible assistance will be given to overcome any difficulties such as accessibility, language, child care, low income or problems with timing that might make it difficult for a client to engage in counselling. Attention should be paid to racial, cultural or religious factors that might influence the timing and content of the counselling or the sex of the counsellor (d'Ardenne & Mahtani, 1989; Holland, 1990).

Truax and Carkhuff (1967) showed the importance of communicating warmth, empathy and understanding to the client, and casework theory stresses the importance of acceptance which has more to do with respect than approval (Wilkes, 1981). It also important to allow ventilation of feelings but this alone is not usually enough to create change (Rachman & Wilson, 1980): some systems-based counsellors suggest it should be avoided and discussion should focus on solutions rather than problems (De Shazer, 1986). More traditionally, help is given to clients to explore their problems and identify their own resources and ways of mobilizing them (British Association for Counselling, 1977).

For many clients, counselling is a new experience and if it proves unpleasant or upsetting, especially in the early stages, they may be deterred from seeking help in the future. Clients who are less used to talking about their feelings or have lower educational attainments may experience particular difficulties and the counsellor must take client attributes and expectations into account. The initial period of engagement with the client is crucial in creating a safe-enough context for change to take place.

Studies have shown that casework and counselling have had little effect on the large problems of poverty, deprivation and delinquency (Fischer, 1973) and for this reason relationship work has been denigrated by some segments of social work (Butrym, 1974). Others stress the importance of providing a social work service for everyone and not only the most socially disadvantaged (Huntington, 1981). It may indeed be more relevant in many countries to target resources towards macrodevelopmental needs (Resnick, 1980), but this does not negate the value of counselling for the individual client. Ejaz (1991) describes the situation in India where social workers in rural areas are concerned with community development, whilst among the more affluent urban populations they involve themselves in counselling and family therapy to help with the emotional and relationship difficulties that become visible when basic physical needs are met.

Working with parents

The notion of working with parents is based on a recognition of their importance in the genesis, maintenance and improvement of childhood problems as well as acknowledging that in most circumstances parents have legal responsibility for their children (see Chapter 53). This work might constitute the main intervention, or be used in conjunction with psychotherapy (Kraemer, 1987) or other methods of help, including the provision of appropriate community resources. It may involve one or more sessions, for instance to clarify the nature of a parent's concerns; or gather information on development, current functioning, important relationships and community resources; or may be a longer piece of work with the aim of helping make positive changes for both child and parent. Counselling is often put forward as a general panacea for all ills but it is important always to consider whether or not other forms of intervention such as family therapy or statutory intervention would be more appropriate. It is also essential to ensure that the client wants this kind of help and that it is possible to find a mutually acceptable focus for work. Sometimes it is the referrer who is most concerned about the problem, whilst parents do not see the need for change. Clearly counselling in this situation would not be viable unless the agreed focus was about how to make the referrer less worried.

Many clients, especially those with long dealings with helping agencies, have come to see themselves as failures as parents and sometimes as people. Sometimes just treating a client with respect, focusing on positive aspects of care and highlighting the successful attempts that parents have made to solve their child's difficulties, can change parents' self-perception and promote them to become more active in effecting change. Sometimes it is necessary for counselling to take a longer route that involves exploration of a parent's own previous experiences to highlight the dilemmas and difficulties that make change difficult.

The provision of information and advice on causation, prognosis, available resources and management can be an important part of counselling, especially when a child has a particular problem, such as physical illness, autism (Howlin & Rutter, 1987; Konstantareos, 1990) or mental handicap (Olshankey, 1962), or at times of crisis, such as the loss of a partner or child (Worden, 1983). To distinguish the counselling process from a purely educational intervention, the advice should be given in such a way that there is no expectation to follow it; decisions remain firmly with the client; and there is room to discuss the impact of the information on the individual (Lask & Lask, 1981; Silver, 1991).

Length of contact does not correlate with effectiveness and studies have shown that short-term active interventions using focused techniques to promote behavioural change are generally more effective than long-term, unfocused, open-ended and more passive therapy (Reid & Shyne, 1969; Reid & Hanrahan, 1981).

Although occasionally it is appropriate to meet with one parent or caretaker alone, work can be more effective if any parent actively involved with the child is incorporated in the work. It is necessary to take into account the various forms of family organization, including separated and step-families, and in some cultures it would be appropriate to involve the extended family from the outset.

Working with children and adolescents

Until fairly recently the psychiatrist, psychologist or psychotherapist was the person who carried out direct work with children. However these divisions are breaking down and where individual help is indicated counselling might be the most appropriate kind of intervention. Many children seen in child psychiatry settings live with a great deal of uncertainty about their future, and techniques that start with children's functioning in the real world rather than their inner world are often more appropriate (Winnicott, 1986). Social workers, with their particular knowledge of the community, available resources and legal processes, can be ideally suited to this work, especially when children have needed the protection of statutory intervention. This knowledge will however need to be combined with that of child development and skills in communicating with children (Berry, 1972). Life story work, in which a social worker helps children who have been through many changes discover and recreate the story of their past through research, discussion, visual and written evidence and personal enquiry, is an example of combining social work skills to help children develop a stronger identity. Most child guidance and child psychiatry clinics are called upon to provide a service for children and adolescents who have been sexually abused and counselling will be one of the interventions offered (see Chapter 14).

In England and Wales the implementation of the Children Act (1989), with its firm acknowledgement of the child's right to be part of decision-making, will increase the need for counselling children to think about their own needs and wishes. This will require a combination of counselling skills and knowledge of community and legal frameworks.

As with adults, a range of styles of counselling can be used (Steinberg, 1987) but, whether the emphasis is on psychodynamic, systemic or cognitive approaches, attention must be paid to the power differential between the therapist and child and to issues of confidentiality. In the best interests of the child, confidentiality will have limits and these must be clearly explained. The child will undoubtedly experience the counsellor as an authority figure and care must be taken to avoid behaviour, questioning and comments that could be experienced as abusive. Many children will be unused to adults listening to them and may fear repercussions for themselves or their parents if they divulge information (Berry, 1972). It is important to be honest with children about likely consequences.

Apart from school-based counselling (Rose & Marshall, 1974), there has been no useful research to assess the value of counselling for children and adolescents, although clinical experience indicates that it can be useful (Bentovim *et al.*, 1988). One must look at the range of options for intervention and avoid using counselling as a substitute for more appropriate courses of action such as secure placement, environmental change, family or group work (Dare *et al.*, 1990). In addition, care must be taken to decide on the best person or agency to undertake the work. An association with psychiatry can be unhelpful and other settings such as school or alternative community resources might be more appropriate. On the other hand, the specialist resources of child psychiatry settings might be crucial in work with some children and adolescents. It is also important to be aware of the risk that when someone from outside the child's usual care network does this kind of work, others, such as parents or foster parents, can feel undermined or deskilled. This is an important consideration and if it is possible to help others carry out some or all of the work, this is usually preferable. In making decisions of this kind it is essential to take full account of race, religion, language, culture and disability.

Family therapy, behaviour therapy and group work

Throughout the world social workers have been central to the development of family therapy. It is not surprising that systems theory, with its emphasis on relationships context and the mobilization of networks, provided a welcome framework for understanding the complex problems facing social workers. Family therapy partly developed from work among disadvantaged client groups (Minuchin *et al.*, 1967) and offered to many a more hopeful solution to difficulties than individual approaches. In addition, the ideas proved helpful in understanding and working with the wider professional networks inhabited by families and social workers alike. Systems ideas have been applied to various social work settings (Little & Conn, 1985; Bowman & Jeffcoat, 1990) and family therapy is an established method in child psychiatry (see Chapters 5 and 55).

Many social workers bristle at the mention of behaviour therapy and, apart from a few notable exceptions (Jehu *et al.*, 1972; Sheldon, 1982; Herbert, 1987), it does not feature strongly in social work training and literature. There are of course dangers, as with any other therapy, that it can be used in a manipulative way and Herbert (1987) points out that, because behaviour modification is a directive and often powerful intervention, special attention needs to be paid to ethical issues.

It seems regrettable that techniques that have been shown to be effective are given such little attention in social work practice. The growth of parent training in behaviour therapy techniques (Patterson, 1982; Herbert, 1987; Howlin & Rutter, 1987) fits well with social work where the task is often to help parents develop more confidence and competence in relation to their children and may be used to alleviate problems such as enuresis, behaviour and feeding difficulties that can interfere with a child's development and in some cases contribute towards abuse. Social workers in child psychiatry, because of greater opportunities to learn from colleagues, have been more likely to use behavioural techniques and could probably do more to assist their community-based colleagues to develop and implement these skills (see Chapter 50).

Within social work there is a surprising amount of group work experience. In one review of groups in a London social services department (London Borough of Lambeth, 1984) 31 different groups were running. Intermediate treatment is generally built on group experiences (Jones & Kerslake, 1979) and groups are run for children leaving care, single parents, young parents — particular black and ethnic minority groups — the parents of children with handicap and disability and groups for children, adolescents and adults who have been sexually abused. Most remain unevaluated but can be an important resource for clients. Groups run by social workers usually have a strong emphasis on self-help and will often be based on activities as well as mutual sharing of experience. Hildebrand (1988) describes a range of groups for children and adolescents who have been sexually abused and these are based on a model familiar to social work. The aims are to help the child feel more 'normal', to encourage communication about the abuse whilst also providing education in sexual matters, developing strategies for self-protection and underlining the adult's responsibility for the abuse. Activities and games as well as talking are the media through which this work is done (see Chapter 54).

THE PROVISION OF FINANCIAL AND COMMUNITY RESOURCES

The provision of appropriate financial help and community resources can have an important impact on the physical and psychological health of the family (Blackburn, 1991) and some of the rationale for this was discussed earlier in the chapter. Although child psychiatry agencies will in the main be concerned with the provision of therapeutic services, their assessment should be comprehensive and pay attention to all aspects of family functioning and relationships with wider systems. The social worker has a crucial role to play in this part of the assessment. Although ideally the task should be to help parents to obtain help and advice for themselves, they may need assistance to find the most relevant form of help. In situations where state resources are low, families may need the support of professionals to access important sources of help.

A number of families who come to child psychiatry are reliant on state benefits because of unemployment, the demands of child care, illness or disability. Many are not claiming their full entitlement to benefit and the child psychiatry social worker should have a good knowledge of available resources. These can sometimes be supplemented by applications for charitable help. A washing machine or driving lessons for the parent of a mentally handicapped child can reduce the level of stress considerably. Sometimes educational provision in such areas as parentcraft and literacy might be indicated.

The physical health and behaviour of children and levels of parental stress can be affected by overcrowding and unsatisfactory housing (Brown & Harris, 1978; Gabe & Williams, 1986) and an approach to housing departments can sometimes effect change. Even if this is not possible, an appreciation of the environmental stresses on a family can help engagement and thus the helping process.

When families encounter new and stressful life events such as illness, disability or bereavement, they are often helped by being put in touch with relevant voluntary organizations and self-help groups. Here they will receive specialist information, advice and support, and meet others who have survived their experience.

Research and clinical experience point to high levels of stress and depression in mothers with young children (Brown & Harris, 1978; Richman *et al.*, 1982; Graham, 1986). Community services such as day care, child-minding, playgroups, nurseries or special clubs and leisure activities can help provide important support, much-needed breaks for parents, and social and developmental opportunities for children (Tallmen, 1986). Several studies have shown that where children have disabilities these kinds of services, together with respite care, are particularly important in relieving stress on parents (Chetwynd, 1985; Quine & Pahl, 1985). Although there is wide agreement about the value of such services, a word of caution must be raised about the effect on infants of day care, especially if the quality is poor.

In the UK the relatively low level of take-up of some services by members of black and ethnic minority groups has given cause for concern and there is a trend to set up specialist resources. Social workers should be aware of these resources, as well as of specialist advice and translation services, and make this knowledge available to colleagues.

When there are major concerns for the well-being of a child it will be necessary to involve the relevant statutory agencies and this can usually be done through the team social worker. In the UK local authorities have a responsibility to provide a range of services for children in need, with the aim of protecting them from further harm and preventing their reception

into the care of the local authority. Apart from the services already mentioned, this can include financial help, after-school care, holidays and the provision of tempory accommodation away from the family. Lack of resources often means that important services are not available but it is important for professionals to push hard for those resources to be provided and be explicit about their probable value to a particular child and family. Sometimes children will need longer-term placements and applications for court orders will need to be made. Social workers will be aware of the range of options and have access to information about available resources, including those for children who have particular difficulties.

CONSULTATION AND LIAISON

Many different agencies and professional groups have a part to play in meeting the needs of children and the effectiveness of child psychiatry interventions will often depend on the contributions of other agencies and the quality of professional relationships. Consultation and liaison involve direct contacts between professionals rather than professional and client and form an important part of the work of child psychiatry departments.

Although social workers have a part to play in bringing their own particular perspective to contacts with a wide range of professional groups (see Chapter 61), this section will concentrate on their liaison and consultative roles with other social workers.

Liaison

Good professional relationships developed over time are a very important basis for effective work but tensions in interdisciplinary relationships are often magnified in relations between different agencies (Davis, 1984). In England and Wales, departments of health and social services have a joint responsibility to provide services for children in need and liaison will be carried out at many levels of the organization. However, a significant contribution can be made at the practitioner level. Sometimes firmly held prejudices will hamper effective communication and child psychiatry social workers, with their understanding of the values and potential prejudices of both agencies, are in a good position to identify them and facilitate debate over important issues. These tensions can be enhanced by professional, hierarchical, gender and racial differences.

The referral process can give rise to particular difficulties, with community social workers often feeling that child psychiatry agencies are unhelpful and unwilling to offer help to the multiproblem families with whom they work (Crowther *et al.*, 1990), and on the other hand child psychiatrists feeling frustrated by the deluge of what they consider to be inappropriate referrals and impossible requests (Dare *et al.*, 1990). Neither may understand the reality of the other's work and it is the difficult task of liaison to find a position that is satisfying to both sides and remains helpful to the client.

Regular face-to-face contact between professionals in order

to discuss potential referrals as well as more general issues can facilitate more helpful communication and develop the necessary understanding and respect for each other's skills. There are advantages to this being done, at least on some occasions, in the community social services office. This not only shows a willingness to step down from the 'ivory tower' but also increases the mental health professionals' understanding of the particular pressures of community social work, recent developments in policy and resources. It also enhances familiarity with a particular geographical area and its strengths and needs. When conflicts occur, child psychiatry social workers can feel caught between two sides but if they can avoid feeling totally hopeless, they are in a good position to help develop more effective relationships. In child psychiatry teams with no social worker the task of liaising with other community services remains an important one but will be more difficult because of differences in training, language and ethos.

Consultation

The specialist expertise developed within child psychiatry has direct relevance for the work of social workers in other agencies and most child psychiatry departments will offer them a consultation service (Caplan, 1970; Steinberg, 1989; Dare *et al.*, 1990). This may be on a one-off basis concerning a particular case or may be a series of meetings offered to individuals or groups (Steinberg & Hughes, 1987). In all cases consultation differs from supervision in that the relationship is one of equal collaboration, and responsibility for the case remains with the consultee (Caplan, 1970). In practice this can be problematic, with the consultee looking for supervision (Dare *et al.*, 1990) or feeling that it is necessary to obey the expert (Todd, 1986). The consultee will usually have specialist knowledge and this should not be denied to the consultee but offered in such a way that it is not a prescription for a particular action but is designed to help the consultee's own decision-making. The hope is that the consultation process will help the consultee become generally more confident and effective and in this sense is a good use of resources. Consultation should also not be confused with other kinds of meeting such as referral meetings, case discussions or case-planning meetings, as the roles and responsibilities are very different. The style of consultation may be psychodynamic, behavioural or systemic but in all cases should take account of the professional/client system (Britton, 1981; Dare *et al.*, 1990).

The importance of this is highlighted by the complex cases often brought by social workers. There may be a myriad of professionals involved with the case, each with a different interest and line of responsibility. Frequently there is also some form of statutory involvement so that legal departments and courts also have to be taken into account. In these cases a systems-based consultation is often most helpful (Campbell, 1985; Wynne *et al.*, 1986). An identification of dysfunctional relationships within the professional system (Dare *et al.*, 1990) or even the clarifying of lines of responsibility and the focus for consultation can often free those involved to help the

client more effectively (Bruggen *et al.*, 1973). It is usually helpful for the consultation to include all those directly involved in decision-making and should certainly include a social worker's immediate line manager (Imber-Coppersmith, 1985). This serves to give a better view of the professional system and helps to avoid unhelpful conflicts between the opinion of the manager and the consultant.

Child psychiatry social workers bring a great deal to consultations of this kind. At the time of planning the consultation they will be able to advise on legal issues, ensure that colleagues are aware of the realities of social work in the community, suggest possible involvements from other agencies and outline the available resources and options. Their knowledge of child psychiatry and social work puts them in a good position to understand the issues that will be brought to the consultation and their presence can create a more facilitating atmosphere for the consultees, who will probably view the social worker as more understanding of their situation (Dare *et al.*, 1990).

SOCIAL WORK AND THE LEGAL FRAMEWORK

The legal framework for child psychiatry is fully discussed in Chapter 64 so this section will serve only to highlight the main aspects of the social worker's role. Each country will have a specific legal framework, and here I will refer to the situation in England and Wales, but many points will have general applicability.

Social workers should have a good knowledge of the relevant legislation relating to children and community care and the range of options available. They can act as consultants on particular cases, as well as taking part in planning the department's responses to legislation. Social workers are often involved both directly and indirectly as consultants, with a variety of assessments, both for the Court and to help local authorities with their own-decision making (Crowther *et al.*, 1990).

Social workers also have a particular responsibility for ensuring that the legal rights of children and families are respected. They monitor the practice of the department to ensure that it complies with the law in such areas as consent to treatment, child protection and secure accommodation. In England and Wales children have a right to be consulted about decisions related to them and, depending on their level of understanding, will be given the right to refuse to comply. The weaving of these rights into clinical practice can be a difficult task and certainly demands that full and clear explanations are given.

From time to time child psychiatry social workers who are also employed by the local authority will be required to exercise their legal responsibilities in the course of their work. This could be to identify particular children and young people who may be at risk and to take appropriate action. One example would be an adolescent who had taken an overdose. A social worker might think that the young person could be at risk and undertake a fuller assessment to evaluate the need for further local authority involvement. This could involve the calling of a case conference, provision of community resources to enhance the clinical input from the child psychiatry department, a more active involvement with the family to make necessary changes to avoid statutory action, the calling of a child protection case conference or planning meeting, making arrangements for the young person to be accommodated away from home for a while, or in extreme situations to make applications to the Court for an order to ensure the young person's safety and future development. In these cases the Court will only make an order if it is better than making no order at all. Where social workers are approved under the Mental Health Act (1983) they may — usually when working with adolescents — be required to be involved in applications for compulsory admission. Where possible, statutory action should be taken under children's legislation as this provides the best framework for thinking of the young person's broad needs and avoids the stigma of compulsory mental health admission. In carrying out their statutory duties, social workers will take full account of developmental, language and cultural factors (Mental Health Act, 1983; Children Act, 1989) and work in partnership with those who have parental responsibility for the child.

Some would argue that it is impossible to combine therapy and social control (Haley, 1980), but social workers have a continued struggle to find a way of combining their statutory responsibilities with therapeutic interventions. Therapeutic work is possible within a statutory framework and the family's need to satisfy the demands of a statutory agency can in itself provide a useful impetus for change and clarify what has to be achieved (Crowther *et al.*, 1990). Where the statutory responsibility is held by the social worker on the child psychiatry team, roles will need to be worked out carefully and lines of communication clarified.

WORKING IN A MULTIDISCIPLINARY TEAM

Although the multidisciplinary approach has been criticized by some for being too expensive (Keir, 1952; Tizard, 1983), it is generally promoted as good working practice (Graham, 1986; Steinberg, 1987; Department of Health and Social Security, 1988b). It is an acknowledgement that childhood problems have multiple causation and of the need for a range of people with different trainings and perspectives to address these needs, whilst also retaining the capacity to make a coordinated plan which can be jointly reviewed. In the UK the concept of multidisciplinary teamwork is embodied in new legislation (Children Act, 1989) and its breakdown has been a source of criticism (Butler-Sloss, 1988). It has been suggested that teamwork is difficult to achieve (Pincus & Minahan, 1973) but important for the client (Hudson, 1982).

Interdisciplinary cooperation is essential in order to tackle the wide variety of factors contributing to emotional, behavioural, developmental and psychiatric problems in childhood and to provide the best methods of community care and child protection. A crucial question is how this is best achieved. Hey (1979) draws a helpful distinction between an established team with a common base and a network, such as a case conference, which meets infrequently, with changing constitution to work on a common task (Muir, 1984). At a time of economic crisis when social service and education departments are reassessing the value of the full-time placement of social workers within hospitals, clinics and special schools (Bennathan & Smith, 1991), and when there is increasing reliance on the network level of collaboration, it is important to be clear about any special advantages to a teamwork approach and to ask if the social work perspective can be accessed through a looser form of contact. In countries where welfare, medical and psychiatric services are being developed it will be important to set up the most effective structures. Some advantages suggested for multidisciplinary working have been improved collaboration, development of skills not dictated by one's training, the development of a holistic approach to the client, better service planning and more satisfying work experience for those on the team. Difficulties that have been put forward include increased time spent in meetings, which may result in more rather than less client contact time because of improved communication, the difficulty of being accountable to peers from other professions, the possible isolation from the promotion ladder (this especially applies to social workers) and the increased risk of conflicts and the time needed to resolve these (Huxley, 1985; McGrath, 1991).

Unfortunately, research has contributed very little that is helpful and no direct comparison has been made between different forms of collaboration and models of practice. Some attention has been given to multidisciplinary primary health care but the literature is mainly anecdotal and does not assist in understanding the best models for effective teamwork. Briscoe *et al.* (1983) reported good teamwork relationships between general practitioners and attached social workers in the three group practices they studied, together with a reduction of general practitioner contact with long-term clients. Huntington (1981), from the perspective of occupational sociology, studied the role of the social worker in an Australian general medical practice. She also surveyed the literature and reported collaborative experience from seven countries, concluding that the cultural and structural differences between the professions of medicine and social work presented a real obstacle to teamwork but that intraoccupational situations offered the best opportunity for shared meanings to develop. In her survey of multidisciplinary Mental Handicap Teams in Wales, McGrath (1991) found high levels of worker satisfaction and noted that overtime work tended to be organized on a project basis rather than along traditional lines.

There has been concern among social work employers that because of differentials of status and value within a multidisciplinary team their own policies will not be given sufficient consideration. Freidson (1970) has suggested that the idea of teamwork is a myth in the health field because of the dominant position of the doctors, and Rowbottom and Hey (1978) warn that there is a danger that teams become so cohesive that they are unidisciplinary and the special contribution of each profession is lost. Added to personal and professional issues are the special effects on team relationships of working with disturbed children and their families (Reder & Kraemer, 1980). Overlap of roles and responsibilities, lack of clear lines of communication, unresolved leadership issues and inability to deal with disagreement and conflict can all present problems (Steinberg, 1983; Parry-Jones, 1986). These difficulties can usually be overcome with commitment and respect, but inter-disciplinary teaching, together with training in the special skills required for the various levels of interdisciplinary work, seem crucial (Kane, 1976; Hey *et al.*, 1991).

SOCIAL WORK CONTRIBUTION TO THE MULTIDISCIPLINARY TEAM

There has been little attempt to examine the specific value of social work intervention to treatment but Bateson *et al.* (1989), in a small study, found that when a social worker was involved in cases of deliberate self-harm, the client benefited in terms of satisfaction, the amount of help offered, social circumstances and general health, although not in the level of risk of further self-harm.

Wardle (1991) comments that social workers have often constituted the largest staff group and in many clinics have maintained the continuity and integration of the clinical work. They have tended to concentrate on developing clinical rather than research skills and often undertake further training in particular methods of therapy. Over the years they have developed a specific expertise in working with parents, but more recently their range of skills has widened.

In the past the term social diagnosis has been used to describe the particular kind of assessment that a social worker might undertake (Richmond, 1917; Sainsbury, 1970; Collins & Collins, 1981). The style of assessment will of course depend on the agency (Sainsbury, 1970) and on the particular theor-etical orientation of the social worker, but it will in all cases include information on individual, family and social factors and the relationships between them (Lask & Lask, 1981). Various frameworks for social work assessment have been developed, but not sufficiently to be easily applied in practice and used as a basis for evaluation (Pincus & Minahan, 1973; Goldstein, 1975; Sheldon, 1984; Department of Health and Social Security, 1988a). Such an assessment will inevitably place a greater emphasis on family and social factors than in the traditional child psychiatric classifications (World Health Organization, 1978; American Psychiatric Association, 1980) and provides a helpful dimension to the multidisciplinary assessment.

Social workers also have an important role in bringing their particular perspective into the teaching and training functions of child psychiatry settings. Without their involvement there is a real danger that other disciplines may place too little emphasis on the importance of the relationship with wider systems and be less able to consider the best use of community resources, including statutory intervention to influence the life of a referred child positively.

Apart from bringing a particular perspective to roles which overlap with those of other disciplines, there are tasks and responsibilities specific to social work (Hey *et al.*, 1991). Some of these derive from links with the community and involve not only providing information about community stresses and resources but also keeping colleagues abreast of new policy developments in the welfare services. For many social workers they also include statutory responsibilities, which for them must override all other considerations (see above). Sometimes there may be conflict in the team between the social worker's responsibility to take measures to protect a child and the medical ethic of confidentiality (Crowther *et al.*, 1990). Such debates, arising from different training, values and percep-tions, although at times irksome, can lead to well-thought-out decision-making.

One of the values of a team comprising professionals with different trainings and orientation is that a broader range of issues is kept alive. In addition to some of the issues already raised, there are some other areas of interest for social work. Mentioning them will give another dimension to understand-ing their contribution to the working and development of the child psychiatry team. These issues are of course not the sole concern of social workers but tend to be raised most strongly by them.

One such issue is that of professional style. This is closely related to values and professional orientation. The trend within social work is towards a more reflective professional style (Schon, 1987). This style emphasizes connection rather than distance, client participation rather than expert statements and the importance of context and ascribed meanings in formulating interventions. It is closely related to the idea of partnership and contrasts with the expert professional stance associated with the medical model (Illich, 1976; Schon, 1987). It has been suggested that a partnership model is less likely to create dependence in clients (Popple, 1985) and a common concern for social workers is that interventions, rather than empowering clients, might do the opposite. A continuing struggle for social workers, because of their statutory powers, is the task of weaving together the use of authority with strategies aimed at maximizing the clients' own use of com-munity resources.

Social workers' involvement with socially disadvantaged groups has led them to be aware of the need to ensure that services are widely accessible. In the past child psychiatry has been criticized for only providing a service for a limited range of clients, but an increase in the kinds of interventions and closer links with social services department have led to a widening of the clientele. In many instances black and ethnic minority children are poorly represented among the clientele of child guidance clinics and yet they are more likely to be taken into care or compulsorily admitted to a psychiatric hospital. Although this is a complex issue, it could indicate that these groups are missing out on the opportunity to tackle problems at an early stage in a way that could keep the young child in the family. Social workers, with their close connections with the community, are in a good position to suggest ways of making the service more responsive to these groups and their training sensitizes them to issues of personal and institutional racism (Ahmed, 1986; Dominelli, 1988).

Social workers have also been concerned that interventions themselves should be culturally sensitive (Ahmed, 1986). This concern has also been taken up by other professional groups (Lau, 1984; Ahmed, 1986; Hodes, 1989; Holland, 1990) but social workers' close ties with the community have made it a particular issue for them. O'Brien (1990) stresses the importance of understanding culture in the context of racism and avoiding a 'colour-blind' approach. Ahmed (1986) discusses the setting-up of unhelpful cultural stereotypes and over-dependence on simplistic cultural explanations that neglect the underlying emotional and psychological aspects. In direct work with families attention should be given to stereotyped assumptions about family structures (Deschesney, 1986), problems concerning the use of language, the importance of therapist and worker attributes and the kind and content of interventions (Hodes, 1989). The need to make social work practice sensitive to culture is widely acknowledged (e.g. Desai, 1991) and this is embodied for the first time in British legislation (Children Act, 1989). However, this does not imply that specific cultural practice should be a reason for not complying with the law of the country. Unfortunately there has been no reliable research to substantiate the wealth of clinical impression.

The topic of gender and especially discrimination against women has given rise to a lively debate (Dominelli & McCleod, 1989; Perelberg & Miller, 1990). Interventions such as structural family therapy have been criticized for promoting patterns of male domination (Urry, 1990) and in the field of child sexual abuse there have been concerns that when power differentials between men and women are not taken into account, this can lead to unhelpful blaming of mothers (Dominelli, 1989). Clinical accounts indicate that by making gender assumptions explicit, both men and women can become aware of more choices and possibilities for change. It is clear from the wider community that pay differentials, poor child care, uneven responsibility for child care and male physical violence all contribute to the stresses on women and in consequence affect the quality of experience for children.

RESEARCH AND EVALUATION

During the early 1970s there were three summative reviews of studies of social work practice which showed that it had little impact on the personal and social problems of clients (Mullen & Dumpson, 1972; Segal, 1972; Fischer, 1973). There was growing recognition that 'is social work effective?' was too broad a question, especially when applied to clients with complex problems influenced by many factors and often involved with many helping agencies. More recently, clearer aims and tighter experimental design have led to more encouraging results (Reid & Hanrahan, 1982; Rubin, 1985; Sheldon,

1986). A study by Iwaniec *et al.* (1985) into the effectiveness of behavioural social work interventions for 17 children with failure to thrive and their families is an example of a small study employing a single case study design with weight gain as an independent measure. The results showed an improvement in feeding in over three-quarters of the cases and an impressive reduction in hospital admissions. The study, however, highlights the difficulty of teasing out the effective parts of the social work intervention and the limitations of the absence of an adequate control group.

This kind of study, looking at particular interventions for specific problems in defined client groups, has proved more helpful than large-scale studies of diverse populations. Although there is wide recognition of the need for more social work research and training in research skills (Council on Social Work Education, 1982), evaluation has continued to have a relatively low profile. One factor has been the unwillingness of social work agencies to carry out their own research or give support to individual practitioners. Often agencies are struggling under tight financial constraints and decisions are finance-led rather than based on the results of empirical research. Training in research skills has not been easily available and, although in child psychiatry social workers have often fulfilled the role of therapist in outcome studies, they will continue to need the support of disciplines more sophisticated in research skills.

Among some social workers there is a level of suspicion about the broad value of quantitative research, with accusations that it can be sexist (Davis, 1986), used by academics to criticize social work practitioners unfairly and based on a dubious assumption that it is possible to be objective (Raynor, 1984). Others, however, have stressed the importance of using empirical techniques and not relying on qualitative studies (Thyer, 1989).

The trend towards audit and quality assurance provides an impetus for social work as well as other professions to examine service efficiency, client satisfaction and outcome and to develop methods that can be integrated with practice whilst still fulfilling basic criteria for evaluation and research (Lask, 1980; Sheldon, 1983; Thyer, 1989). However, the tendency to concentrate on studies relating to service delivery to broad groups may fail to identify important factors for individuals and subgroups (Hogarty, 1991). Without resources and training to carry out large-scale controlled studies, social workers will often need to rely on single-case evaluation methods to assess the effectiveness of their work. More training in these methods would afford social workers more opportunity to learn from their own successes and failures.

Social workers have been criticized for not taking enough account of available research evidence in their decision-making (Department of Health and Social Security, 1985; Black, 1990). This is partly due to a lack of training in interpreting and evaluating research evidence but in addition research findings do not always translate easily into policy and practice, and reliance on particular findings can lead to policies that in retrospect have seemed misguided. Ideas about attachment (Bowlby, 1969) were used to argue that children who had undergone many disruptions were not suitable for adoption or long-term fostering. However, recent evidence shows that, although breakdown rates are higher, permanent placement can work for a large number of children who have had disadvantageous beginnings (see Chapter 15).

Social workers are involved in shaping policies that profoundly affect the lives of children and their families. The policies themselves can sometimes prove harmful; however, there is the possibility not only of reducing the risk of harm but also of providing resources that will help children overcome previous harm and in so doing create a protection for the next generation. The sharing of information between child psychiatry and social work is essential in order to decide the best ways forward.

THE FUTURE

The future role of social workers in child psychiatry is uncertain. In the US there is a tendency for many social workers to become therapists and lose their links with the community; in the UK many local authorities have withdrawn social workers from hospital settings in order to cover less specialized work in the community. The demands of new legislation, training initiatives at basic and postqualifying levels, economic climate and greater movement of social workers between European countries will all have their effect. In other parts of the world community development seems to be the most relevant form of social work activity and provides another meeting point for health and welfare services.

This chapter has stressed the unique position of child psychiatry social workers as they bridge the gap between health and social services the individual and the community, and attention must be given to the implications for service if child psychiatry social workers are no longer part of the multidisciplinary team. The challenge for the social workers themselves is to make their role even more effective, both within child psychiatry and in their relationships with social work colleagues in other settings. Through their clinical practice, teaching and research they must continue to promote the importance of wider systems and the necessity of giving attention to the way in which their effects are mediated through families and individuals.

REFERENCES

Ahmed S. (1986) Cultural racism in work with Asian women and girls. In: Ahmed S., Cheetham J. & Small J. (eds) *Social Work with Black Children and Their Parents*. Batsford, London.

American Psychiatric Association (1980) *Diagnostic and Statistical Manual of Mental Disorders — DMS III* (3rd edn). American Psychiatric Association, Washington, DC.

Amin K. & Leech K. (1988) *A New Underclass: Race and Poverty in the Inner City*. Poverty 70 Child Poverty Action Group, London.

Ashdown M. & Brown S. (1953) *Social Services and Mental Health*. Routledge & Kegan Paul, London.

Bartlett H. (1970) *The Common Base of Social Work Practice*. National Association of Social Workers, New York.

Bassuk E. & Rosenberg L. (1990) Psychosocial characteristics of homeless children and children with homes. *Pediatrics*, **85**, 257–261.

Bateson G. (1972) *Steps to an Ecology of Mind*. Ballantine, New York.

Bateson M., Oliver J. & Goldberg D. (1989) Management of cases of deliberate self harm. *British Journal of Social Work*, **19**, 461–478.

Bebbington A. & Miles J. (1989) The background of children who enter local authority care. *British Journal of Social Work*, **19**(5), 349–368.

Beck A. (1976) *Cognitive Therapy and the Emotional Disorders*. Meridian, New York.

Becker S. & MacPherson S. (1986) *Poor Clients: The Extent and Nature of Financial Poverty Among Consumers of Social Work Services*. Nottingham University Benefits Research Unit, Nottingham.

Becker B. & McPhereson S. (1988) *Public Issues Private Pain: Social Work and Social Policy*. Insight Books, London.

Belsky J. (1988) Infant day care and socioemotional development: the United States. *Journal of Child Psychology and Psychiatry*, **29**, 397–406.

Belsky J. & Rovine M. (1988) Non-maternal care in the first year of life and security of infant parent attachment. *Child Development*, **59**, 157–167.

Bennathan M. & Smith H. (1991) The state of services for children in London. *Young Minds Newsletter*, **8**, 10–12.

Bentovim A., Elton A., Hildebrand J., Tranter M. & Vizard E. (eds) (1988) *Child Sexual Abuse within the Family*. Butterworth, London.

Bernades J. (1985) Do we really know what the family is? In: Close P. & Collins R. (eds) *Family and Economy*, pp. 58–72. MacMillan, London.

Bernstein A. & Gray M. (1991) Introducing the South African student to the social work profession. *International Social Work*, **34**(3), 251–264.

Berry J. (1972) *Working with Children*. Routledge & Kegan Paul, London.

Biestek F. (1957) *The Casework Relationship*. Unwin University Books, London.

Black D. (1990) What do children need from parents? *Early Child Development and Care*, **60**, 11–22.

Blackburn C. (1991) *Poverty and Health: Working With Families*. Open University Press, London.

Bowlby J. (1969) *Attachment and Loss, vol 1 Attachment*. Hogarth, London.

Bowman G. & Jeffcoat P. (1990) The application of systems ideas in a social services fieldwork team. *Journal of Family Therapy*, **12**, 243–254.

Bott E. (1957) *Family and Social Network*. Tavistock, London.

Bretherton I. & Waters E. (eds) (1985) *Growing Points of Attachment — Theory and Research*. University of Chicago Press, Chicago, IL.

Briscoe M., Winny J., Chandler V., Mulgrew K., Williment S. & Rushton A. (1983) Long term social work in a primary health care setting. *British Journal of Social Work*, **13**, 559–578.

British Association for Counselling (1977) *Invitation to Membership*, BAC, Rugby, Warwickshire.

Britton R. (1981) Re-enactment as an unwitting professional response to family dynamics. In: Box S. (ed) *Psychotherapy with Families: An Analytic Approach*, Routledge & Kegan Paul, London.

Brown G. & Harris T. (1978) *Social Origins of Depression: A Study of Psychiatric Disorder in Women*. Tavistock, London.

Brown G., Harris T. & Bifulco A. (1985) Long term effects of early loss of parents. In: Rutter M., Izeard C. & Read P. (eds) *Depression in Young People: Developmental and Clinical Aspects*. Guilford Press, London.

Bruggen P., Byng Hall J. & Pitt Aitkens T. (1973) The reason for admission as a focus for work in an adolescent unit. *British Journal of Psychiatry*, **122**, 319–329.

Butler-Sloss E. (1988) *Report of the Inquiry into Child Abuse in Cleveland*. Her Majesty's Stationery Office, London.

Butrym Z. (1974) Ethical standards in counselling. *Social Work Today*, **5**(13), 406–407.

Byrne D., Harrison S. & Keithley J. (1986) *Housing and Health: The Relationship between Housing Conditions and the Health of Council Tenants*. Gower, Aldershot.

Campbell D. (1985) The consultation interview. In: Campbell D. & Draper R. (eds) *Applications of Systemic Therapy: The Milan Approach*, pp. 193–203. Grune & Stratton, London.

Caplan G. (1970) *The Theory and Practice of Mental Health Consultations*. Tavistock, London.

Chamberlain E. (1991) The Beijing seminar: social work education in Asia and the Pacific. *International Social Work*, **34**, 27–35.

Chase-Lansdale P. & Owen M. (1987) Maternal employment in a family context: effects on infant–mother and infant–father attachments. *Child Development*, **58**, 1505–1512.

Chetwynd J. (1985) Factors contributing to stress on mothers caring for an intellectually handicapped child. *British Journal of Social Work*, **15**, 295–304.

Collins J. & Collins M. (1981) *Achieving Change in Social Work*. Heinemann Educational, London.

Conway J. (1988) *Prescription for Poor Health: The Crisis for Homeless Families*. London Food Commission/Maternity Alliance/SHAC/Shelter, London.

Cooper J. (1989) From casework to community care: the end is where we start from. *British Journal of Social Work*, **19**, 177–188.

Council on Social Work Education (1982) Curriculum policy statement for the Master's degree and Baccalaureate degree programs in social work education. *Social Work Education Reporter*, **30**, 10–11.

Crowther C., Dare C. & Wilson J. (1990) 'Why should we talk to you? You'll only tell the court?': On being an informer and a family therapist. *Journal of Family Therapy*, **12**, 105–123.

Crutcher R. (1943) Child psychiatry: the history of its development. *Psychiatry*, **6**, 191–201.

d'Ardenne P. & Mahtani A. (1989) *Transcultural Counselling in Action*. Sage Publications, London.

Dare J., Goldberg D. & Walinets R. (1990) What is the question you need to answer? How consultation can prevent professional systems immobilising families. *Journal of Family Therapy*, **12**, 355–369.

Davis A. (1984) Contemporary social policy towards the mentally disordered. In: Olsen M.R. (ed) *Social Work and Mental Health: A Guide for the Approved Social Worker*, pp. 3–12. Tavistock, London.

Davis L.V. (1986) A feminist approach to social work research. *Affilia*, **1**, 32–37.

Davy Smith G., Bartly M. & Blane D. (1990) The Black report on socioeconomic inequalities in health: 10 years on. *British Medical Journal*, **30**, 18–25.

Day P. (1985) An interview: constructing reality. *British Journal of Social Work*, **15**, 487–501.

Department of Education and Science, Department of Health and Social Security, Welsh Office (1974) *Child Guidance Circular 3/74*. Department of Education and Science, London.

Department of the Environment (1981) *Families in Flats*. Her Majesty's Stationery Office, London.

Department of Health and Social Security (1985) *Social Work Decisions in Child Care*. Her Majesty's Stationery Office, London.

Department of Health and Social Security (1988a) *Protecting Children: A Guide for Social Workers Undertaking a Comprehensive Assessment*. Her Majesty's Stationery Office, London.

Department of Health and Social Security (1988b) *Working Together in Child Abuse: A Guide to Inter-agency Cooperation for the Protection of Children*. Her Majesty's Stationery Office, London.

Desai M. (1991) Issues concerning the setting up of social work specialisations in India. *International Social Work*, **34**, 27–35.

De Shazer S. (1986) Brief therapy: focused solution development. *Family Process*, **25**, 205–222.

Deschesney M. (1986) Jamaican family structure: the paradox of normalcy. *Family Process*, **25**, 293–300.

Dominelli L. (1988) *Anti-Racist Social Work*. Macmillan Educational, London.

Dominelli L. (1989) Betrayal of trust: a feminist analysis of power relationships in incest abuse. *British Journal of Social Work*, **19**, 291–307.

Dominelli L. & McCleod E. (1989) *Feminist Social Work*, Macmillan, London.

Ejaz F. (1991) Social work education in India: perceptions of social workers in Bombay. *International Social Work*, **34**, 253–262.

Fischer J. (1973) Is casework effective? A review. *USA, Social Work*, **1**, 5–20.

Fisher J., Marsh P., Phillips D. & Sainsbury E. (1986) *In and Out of Care: The Experiences of Children, Parents and Social Workers*. Batsford, London.

Friedson E. (1970) *Professional Dominance*. Atherton Press, New York.

Furlong M. (1989) Can a family therapist do statutory work? *Australian and New Zealand Journal of Family Therapy*, **10**, 211–218.

Gabe J. & Williams P. (1986) Is space bad for your health? The relationship between crowding in the home and emotional distress in women. *Sociology of Health and Illness*, **84**, 351–371.

Garmezy N. (1984) Stress resistant children: the search for protective factors. In: Stevenson J. (ed) *Research Into Developmental Psychopathology. Journal of Child Psychiatry and Psychology*, **25**, (suppl 4).

Goldstein J. (1975) A unitary approach: its rationale and structure. In: Ainsworth F. & Hunter J. (eds) *A Unitary Approach to Social Work Practice — Implications for Education and Organisation*. University of Dundee School of Administration, Dundee.

Graham H. (1986) *Caring for the Family*. Health Education Council, London.

Graham P., Rutter M. & George S. (1973) Temperamental characteristics as predictors of behaviour disorder: a year prospective study. *American Journal of Orthopsychiatry*, **43**, 328–339.

Granovetter M. (1973) The strength of weak ties. *American Journal of Sociology*, **78**, 1360–1380.

Griffiths R. (1988) *Community Care: Agenda for Action*. Her Majesty's Stationery Office, London.

Haley J. (1980) *Leaving Home*. McGraw Hill, New York.

Halmos P. (1965) *The Faith of the Counsellors*. Constable, London.

Hardiker P. & Barker M. (1981) (eds) *Theories of Practice in Social Work*. Academic Press, London.

Harris R. (1990) Beyond rhetoric: a challenge for international social work. *International Social Work*, **33**, 203–212.

Hegar R. (1990) The rights and status of children: international concerns for social work. *International Social Work*, **33**, 220–231.

Herbert M. (1987) *Behavioural Treatment of Children with Problems: A Practice Manual*. Academic Press, London.

Hetherington E.M. (1988) Parents, children and siblings 6 years after divorce. In: Hinde R. & Stevenson-Hinde J. (eds) *Relationships within Families*. Cambridge University Press, Cambridge.

Hetherington E., Cox M. & Cox R. (1982) Effects of divorce on parents and children. In: Lamb M. (ed) *Non Traditional Families*, pp. 223–288. Lawrence Erlbaum, Hillsdale, NJ.

Hey A. (1979) Organising teams: alternative patterns. In: Marshall M., Preston-Shoot S. & Wincott E. (eds) *Teamwork — For and Against*. BASW, Birmingham.

Hey A., Minty B. & Trowell J. (1991) Inter-professional and interagency work: theory, practice and training for the nineties. In:

Pietroni M. (ed) *Right or Privilege*, pp. 104–130. CCETSW, London.

Hildebrand J. (1988) The use of groupwork in treating child sexual abuse. In: Bentovim A., Elton A., Hildebrand J., Tranter M. & Vizzard E. (eds) *Child Sexual Abuse in the Family*, pp. 205–237. Wright, London.

Hodes M. (1989) Annotation: culture and family therapy. *Journal of Family Therapy*, **11**, 117–128.

Hoffman L. (1988) A constructivist position for family therapy. *Irish Journal of Psychology*, **9**, 110–129.

Hogarty G. (1991) Social work practice research on severe mental illness: charting a future, research on social work. *Practice*, **1**, 5–31.

Holder D. & Wardle W. (1981) *Teamwork and the Development of a Unitary Approach*. Routledge & Kegan Paul, London.

Holland S. (1990) Psychotherapy, oppression and social action: gender, race and class in black women's depression. In: Perelberg R. & Miller A. (eds) *Gender and Power in Families*, pp. 256–269. Routledge, London.

Howe D. (1989) *The Consumer's View of Family Therapy*. Aldershot, Gower.

Howlin P. & Rutter M. (1987) *Treatment of Autistic Children*. John Wiley, Chichester.

Hudson B. (1982) *Social Work with Psychiatric Patients*. Macmillan, London.

Huntington J. (1981) *Social Work and General Medical Practice: Collaboration or Conflict*. George Allen & Unwin, London.

Huxley P. (1985) *Social Work Practice in Mental Health*. Gower, Aldershot.

Illich I. (1976) *Disabling Professions*. Marion Boyars, London

Imber-Coppersmith V. (1985) Families and multiple helpers: a systemic perspective. In: Campbell D. & Draper R. (eds) *Applications of Systemic Family Therapy*, pp. 203–212. Grune & Stratton, London.

Irvine E. (1978) Psychiatric social work: training for psychiatric social work. In: Younghusband E. (ed) *Social Work in Britain 1950–1975: A Follow Up Study*, vols 1 and 2. George Allen & Unwin, London.

Irvine I. (1985) Child abuse and poverty. In: Becker S. & MacPhereson S. (eds) *Public Issues, Private Pain, Social Work and Social Policy*. Social Services Insight Books, London.

Iwaniec D., Herbert M. & McNeish A. (1985) Social Work with failure to thrive children and their families. *British Journal of Social Work*, **15**(3), 243–260.

Jehu D., Hardiker P., Yelloly M. & Shaw M. (1972) *Behaviour Modification and Social Work*. John Wiley, London.

Jones R. & Kerslake A. (1979) *Intermediate Treatment and Social Work*. Heinemann, London.

Jordan B. & Parton N. (1983) *The Political Dimension of Social Work*. Blackwell, Oxford.

Kane R. (1976) *Interprofessional Teamwork*. Syracuse University School of Social Work, New York.

Kanner L. (1955) *Child Psychiatry*, 3rd edn. Thomas, Springfield, IL.

Keir G. (1952) The history of child guidance. *British Journal of Educational Psychology*, **22**, 5–29.

Konstantareos M. (1990) A psychoeducational model for working with families of autistic children. *Journal of Marital and Family Therapy*, **16**, 59–70.

Kraemer S. (1987) Annotation: working with parents: casework or psychotherapy? *Journal of Child Psychology and Psychiatry*, **28**, 207–213.

Lask B. (1980) Evaluation — why and how? (A guide for clinicians.) *Journal of Family Therapy*, **2**, 199–210.

Lask J. & Lask B. (1981) *Child Psychiatry and Social Work*. Tavistock, London.

Lau A. (1984) Transcultural issues in family therapy. *Journal of Family Therapy*, **6**, 91–112.

Lees R. (1972) *Politics and Social Work*. Routledge & Kegan Paul, London.

Little M. & Conn J. (1985) The application of systemic ideas and techniques to a child care system: always arriving. . .never having arrived. In: Campbell D. & Draper R. (eds) *Applications of Systemic Therapy: The Milan Approach*, pp. 173–180. Grune & Stratton, London.

London Borough of Lambeth (1984) *A Survey of Groupwork*. London Borough of Lambeth, London.

McGrath M. (1991) *Multidisciplinary Teamwork*. Avebury Studies of Care in the Community. Avebury, Gower.

McKee L. (1987) Households during employment: the resourcefulness of the unemployed. In: Brannen J. & Wilson P. (eds) *Give and Take in Families*. Allen & Unwin, London.

Madge N. (1983) (ed) *Families at Risk*. Heinemann Educational, London.

Mayer J. & Timms N. (1970) *The Client Speaks: Working Class Impressions of Casework*. Routledge & Kegan Paul, London.

Mearns D. & Thorne B. (1988) *Person Centered Counselling in Action*. Sage Publications, London.

Medhat M. (1991) Social work practice and local politics in Egypt. *International Journal of Social Work*, **34**, 7–26.

Meyer A. (1909) The problems of the state in the care of the insane. *American Journal of Psychiatry*, **108**, 481–490.

Midgley J. (1981) *Professional Imperialism: Social Work Values in the Third World*, Studies in Social Policy and Welfare vol. xvi. Heinemann Educational, London.

Midgley J. & Sanzenbach P. (1989) Social work, religion and the challenge of fundamentalism. *International Social Work*, **3**, 273–287.

Mills M., Puckering C., Pound A. & Cox A. (1984) What is it about depressed mothers that influences their children's functioning? In: Stevenson J. (ed) *Recent Research in Developmental Psychopathology*, pp. 11–17. Pergamon, Oxford.

Minuchin S., Montalvo B., Guerney B.G., Rossman S.L. & Schurmer F. (1967) *Families of the Slums*. Basic Books, New York.

Muir L. (1984) Teamwork. In: Olsen M.R. (ed) *Social Work and Mental Health: A Guide for the Approved Social Worker*, pp. 189–197. Tavistock, London.

Mullen E.J. & Dumpson J.R. (1972) (eds) *Evaluation of Social Intervention*. Jossey Bass, San Francisco, CA.

O'Brien C. (1990) Family therapy with black families. *Journal of Family Therapy*, **12**, 3–16.

Olshankey S. (1962) Chronic sorrow: a response to having a mentally defective child. *Social Casework*, **43**, 190–193.

Oppenheim G. (1990) *Poverty: The Facts*. Child Poverty Action Group, London.

O'Toole R., Turbett P. & Nalhepa C. (1983) Professional knowledge and diagnosis of child abuse. In: Finkelhorn D., Geddes R., Hetalung G. & Strauss M. (eds) *The Dark Side of Families: Current Family Violence*. Sage, Newbury Park, CA.

Packman J. (1989) Decisions in child care. In: Kahan B. (ed) *Child Care Research Policy and Practice*. Hodder and Stoughton, London.

Parry-Jones W.L. (1986) Multidisciplinary teamwork: help or hindrance? In: Steinberg D. (ed) *The Adolescent Unit*, John Wiley, Chichester.

Patterson G.R. (1982) *Coercive Family Process*. Castalia, Eugene. OR.

Perelberg R. & Miller A. (1990) (eds) *Gender and Power in Families*. Tavistock, London.

Pietroni M. (1991) Historical background. In: Pietroni M. (ed) *Right or Privilege: Post Qualifying Training With Reference to Child Care*, pp. 21–32. CCETSW, London.

Pincus A. & Minahan A. (1973) *Social Work Practice: Model and Method*. FE Peacock, Itasca, IL.

Platt S., Martin C., Hunt M. & Lewis W. (1989) Mould growth and symptomatic health status. *British Medical Journal*, **298**, 1673–1678.

Popple P.R. (1985) The social work profession: a reconceptualisation. *Social Services Review*, **59**, 560–578.

Quine L. & Pahl J. (1985) Examining the causes of stress in families with severely mentally handicapped children. *British Journal of Social Work*, **15**, 501–518.

Quinton D. & Rutter M. (1984) Parents with children in care: 1. Current circumstances and parents: 2. Intergenerational continuities. *Journal of Child Psychology and Psychiatry*, **25**, 211–231.

Quinton D. & Rutter M. (1985) Family pathology and child psychiatric disorder: a 4 year prospective study. In: Nicol A. (ed) *Longitudinal Studies in Child Psychology and Psychiatry: Practical Lessons From Research Experience*, pp. 91–134. Wiley, Chichester.

Rachman S. & Wilson G. (1980) *The Effects of Psychological Therapy*. Pergamon, Oxford.

Raynor P. (1984) Evaluation with one eye closed: the empiricist agenda in social work research. *British Journal of Social Work*, **14**, 1–10.

Reder R. & Kraemer S. (1980) Dynamic aspects of professional collaboration in child guidance. *Journal of Adolescence*, **3**, 165–173.

Rehin G.F. (1969) The practice of psychiatric social work and the future of child guidance clinics. *Case Conference*, **16**, 42–48.

Reid W.J. & Hanrahan P. (1981) The effectiveness of social work: recent evidence. In: Goldberg E.M. & Connelly N. eds) *Evaluative Research in Social Care*, pp. 9–22. Heinemann Educational, London.

Reid W.J. & Hanrahan P. (1982) Recent evaluation of social work: grounds for optimism. *Social Work*, **27**, 328–340.

Reid W.J. & Shyne A.W. (1969) *Brief and Extended Casework*. Columbia University Press, New York.

Resnick R. (1980) Social work education in Latin American and United States: a look to the future. *Journal of Education for Social Work*, **16**, 104–111.

Richman N., Stevenson J. & Graham P. (1982) *Pre School to School: A Behavioural Study*. Academic Press, London.

Richmond M. (1917) *Social Diagnosis*, Free Press, New York.

Rose G. & Marshall T. (1974) *Counselling and School Social Work*. John Wiley, London.

Rowbottom R. & Hey A. (1978) *Organisation of Services for the Mentally Ill: A Working Paper*. BIOSS, Brunel University Uxbridge.

Rubin A. (1985) Practice effectiveness: more grounds for optimism. *Social Work*, **30**, 469–476.

Rutter M. (1987) Psychosocial resilience and protective mechanisms. In: Rolf S., Master A., Cicchetti K., Muechterlein K. & Weintraub S. (eds) *Risk and Protective Factors in the Development of Psychopathology*, Cambridge University Press, New York.

Rutter M. (1989) Pathways from childhood to adult life. *Journal of Child Psychology and Psychiatry*, **30**, 23–51.

Rutter M. & Quinton D. (1984) Parental psychiatric disorder: effects on children. *Psychological Medicine*, **14**, 835–880.

Sainsbury E. (1970) *Social Diagnosis in Casework*. Routledge & Kegan Paul, London.

Schon D. (1987) *Educating the Reflective Practitioner*. Jossey Bass, London.

Segal S.P. (1972) Research on the outcome of social work therapeutic interventions: a review of the literature. *Journal of Health and Social Behaviour*, **13**, 3–17.

Sharkey P. (1990) Social networks and social service workers. *British Journal of Social Work*, **19**, 387–405.

Sheldon B. (1982) *Behaviour Modification: Theory, Practice and Philosophy*. Tavistock, London.

Sheldon B. (1983) The use of single case experimental designs in the evaluation of social work practice. *British Journal of Social Work*, **13**, 477–500.

Sheldon B. (1984) A critical appraisal of the medical model in psychiatry. In: Olsen M.R. (ed) *Social Work and Mental Health: A Guide for Approved Social Workers*, pp. 84–100. Tavistock, London.

Sheldon B. (1986) Social work effectiveness experiments: review and implications. *British Journal of Social Work*, **17**, 573–586.

Silver E. (1991) Should I give advice? A systemic view. *Journal of Family Therapy*, **13**, 295–310.

Simpson B., Corlyon J., McCarthy P. & Walker J. (1990) Client responses to family conciliation: achieving clarity in the midst of confusion. *British Journal of Social Work*, **20**, 557–575.

Social Work Today (1991) Pin down: special report. *Social Work Today*, **22**, 4–9.

Specht H. (1986) Social support, social networks, social exchange and social work practice. *Social Service Review*, **60**, 218–240.

Spicker P. (1990) Social work and self determination. *British Journal of Social Work*, **20**, 221–237.

Steinberg D. (1983) *The Clinical Psychiatry of Adolescence: Clinical Work From a Social and Developmental Perspective*. John Wiley, London.

Steinberg D. (1987) *Basic Adolescent Psychiatry*. Blackwell, London.

Steinberg D. (1989) *Interprofessional Consultation*. Blackwell Scientific Publications, London.

Steinberg D. & Hughes L. (1987) The emergence of work centered issues in consultative work: an observation. *Journal of Adolescence*, **10**, 309–316.

Tallmen M. (1986) Single parents. *Family Relations*. **35**, 215–225.

Thyer B. (1989) First principles of practice research. *British Journal of Social Work*, **19**, 309–324.

Timms N. (1964) Psychiatric social work in Great Britain (1939–62). Routledge & Kegan Paul, London.

Tizard J. (1983) Maladjusted children in the child guidance service. In: Clarke A. & Tizard B. (eds) *The Life and Work of Jack Tizard*, pp. 144–157. British Psychological Society, Leicester.

Todd T.C. (1986) Family systems consultation with mental health professionals. In: Wynne L., McDaniel S. & Weber T. (eds) *Systems Consultation: A New Perspective for Family Therapy*, pp. 53–79. Guilford Press, New York.

Townsend P. (1979) *Poverty in the UK*. Penguin, London.

Truax C.D. & Carkhuff R.R. (1967) *Towards Effective Counselling and Psychotherapy*. Aldine, Chicago, IL.

Urry A. (1990) The struggle towards a feminist practice in family therapy. In: Perelberg R. & Miller A. (eds) *Gender and Power in Families*, pp. 104–117. Routledge, London.

Von Glaserfeld E. (1988) The reluctance to change a way of thinking. *Irish Journal of Psychology*, **9**, 83–90.

Wallerstein J., Corbin B. & Lewis J.M. (1988) Children of divorce: a 10 year study. In: Hetherington E. & Arasteh J. (eds) *Impact of Divorce, Single Parenting and Step-Parenting on Children*. Erlbaum, Hillsdale, NJ.

Walrond-Skinner S. (1986) *Dictionary of Psychotherapy*. Routledge, London.

Wardle C. (1991) Twentieth century influences on the development in Britain of services for child and adolescent psychiatry. *British Journal of Psychiatry*, **159**, 53–68.

Waters E. (1978) The reliability and stability of individual differences in infant mother attachment. *Child Development*, **49**, 483–494.

Webb S. & McBeath G. (1989) Political critique of Kantian ethics. *British Journal of Social Work*, **19**, 491–507.

Whittington C. (1971) Self determination re-examined. *British Journal of Social Work*, **1**, 293–305.

Wilkes R. (1981) *Social Work with Undervalued Groups*. Tavistock, London.

Willmot P. (1987) Friendship networks and social support. London Policy Studies Institute, London

Winnicott C. (1986) *Working with Children*. Routledge & Kegan Paul, London.

Wolkind S. (1984) The child psychiatrist in court: using the contributions of developmental psychology. In: *Taking a Stand*. BAAF, London.

Wolkind S. & Rutter M. (1973) Children who have been 'In care' — an epidemiological study. *Journal of Child Psychology and Psychiatry,* **14**, 97–105.

Wootton B. (1959) *Social Science and Social Pathology.* Allen & Unwin, London.

Worden J. (1983) *Grief Counselling and Grief Therapy.* Springer, New York.

World Health Organization (1978) *International Classification of Diseases,* (9th revision). World Health Organization, Geneva.

Wynne L., McDaniel S. & Weber T. (eds) (1986) *Systems Consultation: A New Perspective for Family Therapy.* Guilford Press, New York.

Yelloly M. (1980) *Social Work Theory and Psychoanalysis.* Van Nostrand Rheinhold, New York.

Younghusband E. (1978) *Social Work in Britain 1950–1975: A Follow Up Study,* vols 1 and 2. George Allen & Unwin, London.

Chapter 53
Parent Training

Maria Callias

There is no single right way to raise children satisfactorily. Parents successfully carry out this complex task using a variety of methods in very diverse family, cultural and social circumstances. Until recently, parents have been regarded as somehow being naturally equipped for this important task. Yet, throughout the ages advice has always been forthcoming, usually from relatives and friends drawing on personal and sociocultural experience and expectations, on the right way of bringing up children. As one spin-off of this century's scientific interest in child development, professionals have joined the ranks of advisers, especially for families experiencing difficulties in rearing their children.

Professional advice is rooted in a wide spectrum of theoretical approaches and research findings (Henry, 1981; Pugh & De'Ath, 1984; Dembo *et al.*, 1985; Herbert, 1988; Brooks, 1991). No single approach is all-encompassing. Approaches overlap, complement each other or may even be contradictory. They differ in their emphasis on particular aspects of parent–child interaction and relationships, on the aspects of family life and difficulties they focus on, the age of the child they apply to and also on which aspects of parenting they remain silent. It is worth noting from the outset that professional advice is rarely based exclusively on well-founded research evidence but tends to be an amalgam of research findings and prevailing societal views (Young, 1990).

Parent training began with the clear aim of meeting the needs of children, especially those presenting with serious problems of conduct or emotion, developmental and intellectual impairments, or who seemed at risk for developing such problems. In addition parent training has begun to focus more directly on adults in their role as parents by providing firstly, education in parenting skills generally; secondly, preparation for parenthood; and thirdly, intervention for parents who are blatantly failing in their task of raising their children. Although practice and research in each of these areas originate in different theoretical and professional traditions, there has been some cross-fertilization over the years as well as parallel independent developments.

The main aim of this chapter is to present an evaluative overview of interventions for parents experiencing difficulties with their children or those regarded as being at risk. As most of the research has been done within a broadly behavioural perspective, the main focus will be on the findings and issues raised by this perspective. To put this in context, the broader spectrum of approaches and their application will be surveyed.

WHAT IS PARENT TRAINING?

The term parent training has come to mean educative interventions with parents that aim to help them cope better with the problems they experience with their children. The term usually applies to approaches within the behavioural/social learning tradition and implies that parents need special teaching in order to be effective. Although there are other theoretical approaches to parent training or counselling (Henry, 1981), behaviourally oriented parent training has been more systematically developed, researched and evaluated than other approaches.

There were several rather different reasons for the major shift from the dyadic model of therapeutic intervention where the therapist works directly with the child to a triadic model in which the therapist works with the parent in order to effect therapeutic or behavioural change in the child (Berkowitz & Graziano, 1972; O'Dell, 1974; Yule, 1975). Firstly, it held promise for overcoming the thorny therapeutic problem of generalizing and maintaining treatment successes achieved in special clinic settings to everyday home and school settings. Secondly, it enabled limited resources to be used to meet the needs of more families than was possible through the conventional dyadic model of intervention. It was also hoped that trained parents would be able to apply their new skills to prevent potential future problems. Finally, in the case of mentally handicapped children, as societal attitudes to their needs and care changed, their parents began pressing for more practical guidance with the task of raising their children.

APPROACHES AND APPLICATIONS

Behavioural parent training

Over the years, behavioural parent training has been used with a wider range of problems (O'Dell, 1974, 1985; Tavormina, 1974; Yule, 1975; Dangel & Polster, 1984; Helm & Kosloff, 1986; Schaefer & Briesmeister, 1989), though most research has been with families with noncompliant children,

918

mentally handicapped children or abused and neglected children (Wiese & Kramer, 1988).

Initially behavioural parent training focused on teaching specific techniques to ameliorate specific child problems. Paralleling developments in cognitive-behavioural treatment, parent training has become more diverse and complex. There is greater emphasis on carrying out a functional analysis of problems, as more flexible problem-solving approaches and on parents' feelings, understanding and reactions to their children's difficulties. Methods of training have also diversified and become more sophisticated. Greater attention is being paid to issues such as the characteristics of children, parents and families in relation to outcome as well as the place of parent training in meeting the needs of families and the nature of the role relationship between parent and professional.

Behavioural parent training was first used with parents of children with externalizing behavioural problems of conduct, including oppositional behaviour and disobedience (McAuley, 1982; Patterson, 1982; Kazdin, 1987; Webster-Stratton, 1991) and with parents of children with mental handicap (Clements, 1985; Cunningham, 1985; Baker, 1986; Helm & Kosloff, 1986; Callias, 1987; Baker *et al.*, 1989). In addition behavioural training has been used with parents of children with other widespread developmental and psychiatric problems such as autism (Howlin *et al.*, 1987; Lovaas, 1987; Marcus & Schopler, 1989) and hyperactivity (Anastopoulos & Barkley, 1989; Whalen & Henker, 1991), as well as with more circumscribed problems such as sleeping difficulties and night-time waking (Graziano & Mooney, 1980, 1982; Richman *et al.*, 1985; Douglas, 1989; Seymour *et al.*, 1989; Scott & Richards, 1990), enuresis (Houts & Mellon, 1989) and school refusal (Yule, 1989).

Although in most cases the problem is identified as the child's problem, the training focuses on the nature of the interaction between the parent and the child — either in the specific context of a circumscribed problem or more generally. Some training is more explicitly directed to altering facets of parent–child relationships or interactions, such as conflict resolution (Robin & Koepke, 1990) or parent–child play interaction (Forehand & McMahon, 1981).

Behavioural parent training has been used to help parents whose parenting skills are more obviously and pervasively inadequate — such as parents who are abusing their children (Isaacs, 1982; Smith, 1984; Wolfe, 1985; Nicol *et al.*, 1988; Wolfe *et al.*, 1988; Azar, 1989; Azar & Siegel, 1990) or who are themselves mildly retarded and experiencing parenting problems (Fantuzza *et al.*, 1986; Feldman *et al.*, 1989). The children of such parents often themselves display behavioural and emotional problems.

Behavioural parent training has focused mainly on parents of younger children (3 years to preadolescence), although some work has been done with adolescents, including delinquents (Bank *et al.*, 1991).

Early intervention

There are several different but overlapping strands to early intervention and prevention of difficulties with parents of infants and preschool children. Early work aiming to prevent high-risk children raised in poverty from failing at school involved early education interventions directed at improving cognitive and scholastic skills. Some of these programmes included some parent training and involvement and others focused mainly on improving parenting skills (Lazar & Darlington, 1982; Seitz, 1990).

In addition, early intervention has focused on preventing problems in the emotional-behavioural domain (sometimes in conjunction with cognitive development) in high-risk young children and families (Offord, 1987; McGuire & Earls, 1991; Wolke, 1991).

One strand of this work concentrates on very small, premature infants. On the basis of assessments of the infant's state on the Brazelton Scales, parents of vulnerable, immature infants receive guidance on how to handle their infants responsively and sensitively (Rauh *et al.*, 1988; Affleck *et al.*, 1989; Wolke, 1991). Other interventions with very low birth weight infants have been based on theories of sensory deprivation or sensory overload of the infant or on attachment theory, or stress the importance of alleviating the parents' own emotional distress over the premature delivery in order to facilitate satisfactory parenting (Wolke, 1991).

There has also been early intervention for families of young children identified as having definitely handicapping conditions such as Down's syndrome or other conditions (Cunningham, 1985; Marfo & Kysela, 1985). One focus of such early intervention is on counselling and guidance for parents' own distress and feelings for their handicapped child. A second focus is on training parents to foster their child's development. Specially trained workers visit the home regularly to offer broadly based counselling that incorporates advice on how to respond sensitively to the infant and how to structure a situation for teaching skills within a developmental framework. The Portage Project (Shearer & Shearer, 1972; Shearer & Loftin, 1984) is one example of an attractive and widely used intervention. It has clear materials and a well-organized, structured system of service delivery which involves trained professionals visiting the home weekly to advise families on the use of materials for assessing and teaching new skills to their child (Daly *et al.*, 1985).

Although most work with parents of infants and toddlers is viewed as preventive, in many cases problems are serious and cause great distress to families. In some settings professionals such as health visitors are being trained to offer practical behavioural advice on managing such difficulties (Stevenson, 1990).

Preparation for parenthood

Prospective parents can be prepared and trained for their parenthood (Michaels & Goldberg, 1988). Programmes are directed either to young adults who are contemplating a family or to adolescents at high risk for embarking on unplanned early child-bearing in an attempt to help them make more informed decisions (Kagan & Seitz, 1988; Osofsky et al., 1988). There are also programmes for prospective parents preparing them to adjust better to the inevitable changes that will occur in their relationship as they make the transition from couple to family (Duncan & Markham, 1988). These programmes differ from the established programmes on preparation for childbirth itself in that the focus is more specifically on the psychological changes that come with parenthood. The work is theoretically rooted in systemic family therapy and other general educative nonbehavioural traditions. The focus is on the couple's relationship and the emotions that accompany the birth of a first child rather than on parenting skills.

Parent training courses

Group training courses for parents of problem children are rooted in three main theoretical traditions: behavioural and social learning theory, Adlerian and Rogerian theories (Henry, 1981; Dembo et al., 1985).

In such courses, groups of parents meet for 8–10 weekly or fortnightly sessions and are taught a systematic curriculum using a variety of materials and teaching methods by specially trained instructors.

Systematic training for effective parenting (STEP; Dinkmeyer & McKay, 1976) is based on Adlerian concepts as developed by Dreikers and Soltz (1972). Parents are taught to interpret their child' misbehaviour in motivational terms as a misguided attempt to feel part of the family. In addition to increasing their understanding of the child's behaviour, parents are also taught how to establish a more cooperative family climate, strategies for reflective listening and problem-solving.

Parent effectiveness training (PET) also focuses on interpersonal relationships within the family but derives from the Rogerian reflective counselling model (Gordon & Sand, 1976). The focus is on teaching improved communication and on the use of negotiation to resolve conflict.

Self-help and support groups

Parents' self-help groups have developed as part of the growing social movement of self-help organisations (Levy, 1976; Pilisuk & Parks, 1980; Lieberman, 1983). Self-help organizations serve many functions which include provision of information, support, practical and psychological help and lobbying for better services. They meet these needs in a variety of ways, including walk-in services, telephone help-lines, volunteer home visiting, meetings and self-help groups. Peers provide the main source of help through members' own efforts, skills, knowledge and concern and if professionals participate their role is usually an ancillary one. Self-help groups differ from professionally run ones in having a pragmatic rather than

theory-driven focus and in the greater mutual reliance of members on one another.

Descriptions of self-help groups for parents tend to be about those with some professional input, however minimal. Some self-help groups have been established within child guidance settings for parents who have been in long-term individual or group therapy and are seen to be in need of continued support and peer help (Dube et al., 1980). Other self-help parent groups have been established in local neighbourhoods, often as part of mother and toddler groups, with the general aim of improving the parenting of socially disadvantaged, isolated or depressed mothers or those at high risk for child abuse or neglect (Peterman, 1981; Munro, 1982; Palfreeman, 1982; Pound & Mills, 1985). Although most self-help groups are run by volunteers, some groups with the explicit aim of improving parenting are run by local organizations offering a telephone crisis service, befriending and home visiting, drop-in centres and baby-sitting (Meacher, 1982). Projects such as Newpin aim to prevent the development of child behaviour problems by explicitly supporting and befriending struggling and possibly depressed mothers, on the assumption that improving maternal mental health and social support are likely to prevent the development of child behaviour problems later (Pound & Mills, 1985).

Parent-training manuals and other materials

Parent-training literature has been pouring on to the market in recent years (Bernal & North, 1978; Clarke-Stewart, 1978; Glasgow & Rosen, 1978; McMahon & Forehand, 1980; Boggs, 1981). In addition to magazines (Young, 1990), there are many books addressing themselves to a wide range of parenting issues. Sometimes several theoretical approaches are presented in one book (Schaefer, 1978; Brooks, 1991). Most books are more focused, either drawing on specific but different theoretical models or addressing discrete child problems. Behaviourally oriented books sometimes provide guides for coping with essentially normal children, but more usually offer advice on coping with aggressive, noncompliant or handicapped children. Some behavioural guides are broadbased in their coverage of general principles for child-rearing or managing child behaviour problems (Patterson, 1975, 1976; Carr, 1980; Herbert, 1985). More focused manuals advise on how to deal with highly circumscribed problems, such as sleeping difficulties (Douglas & Richman, 1984). Many manuals and, more recently, video-tape vignettes (Webster-Stratton, 1981) have been developed for use as an integral part of parent-training programmes. Nearly all these books are available commercially as self-administered treatments or guides to parenting.

In addition, books have been written as guidance to parents in dealing with highly significant but rarely occurring events (Kitzinger & Kitzinger, 1989) or particular circumstances such as step-parenting (Maddox, 1980; Hodder, 1985). Sometimes, vital information is distributed widely in simple leaflets to parents in an attempt to prevent serious accidental maltreatment; for example, a leaflet on coping with persistent crying in infants (Showers, 1992).

Common themes

Common themes run through these very diverse and different ways of helping parents who are already experiencing difficulties with their children, or who are regarded as vulnerable. The first theme is that of training parents directly in aspects of managing child problem behaviour. As noted, cognitive-behavioural and problem-solving approaches have played a major part here but the influence of other theoretical frameworks is evident. The second theme also focuses on child needs but the issues relate far more to fostering appropriate development, play and positive parent–child interactions than to problems with the children. Early interventions emphasize this aspect, but it is also a prominent part of most parent training. The third theme is the focus on the parents themselves as in need of support or help in understanding their own emotional reactions to their child or other personal problems. The underlying assumption is that helping parents in this way will minimize or prevent problems in their children. Many interventions are very clearly rooted within one or other of these models. However, there are blurs and sometimes approaches combine these foci. Developments within cognitive-behavioural parent training will be considered in more detail.

A CLOSER LOOK AT BEHAVIOURAL PARENT TRAINING

Behavioural parent training takes place in a wide range of settings, including clinics, homes and research centres. Training is carried out with individual families or in groups of parents. The child may not be involved in treatment after initial assessment or may be seen regularly with parents. In clinical practice most parent training is done in individual consultation with one set of parents (or the mother only) in the clinic or home setting. Older children and adolescents are usually involved and share in the process of negotiating goals, problem-solving and contracting. When parents and children are seen together, the divide between parent training and behavioural family counselling/therapy is blurred.

The common thread running through all behavioural parent training is the main aim of altering the overt behaviour of the child by teaching the parents relevant principles and skills so that they can alter their child management methods and styles of interacting with the child. A wide variety of methods is used to teach parents and these often include the use of modern technology such as one-way screen observation and video feedback, use of reading material and video vignettes. Parents are usually taught how to define the problem that they are experiencing with their child in more precise behavioural terms, to observe accurately, to keep simple records as a baseline and for monitoring progress, to carry out a functional analysis, and to apply the range of techniques and principles

that are relevant to effecting change (see Chapter 50). Recent extensions include teaching problem-solving strategies, modifying cognitions and anger control.

In individual clinical consultation this process is usually carried out under the guidance of the therapist in a problem-solving manner where programmes are individually designed and tailored to the needs of each family (Callias, 1987; Herbert, 1988). Examples of this flexible but systematic clinical approach in both clinic and home settings include work with families of mentally handicapped children with multiple problems (Callias & Carr, 1975), autistic children (Howlin *et al.*, 1987), school refusal (Blagg & Yule, 1984), conduct disorder and enuresis (Herbert & Iwaniec, 1981) and families abusing their children (Smith, 1984).

Some individual parent training has been based on a more standard training format. The seminal work of the Oregon Social Learning Centre on conduct-disordered, aggressive and delinquent children (Patterson, 1982) provides the starting point for most subsequent developments. Parents are seen individually or in groups and undergo a systematic training programme comprising several sequential steps. After reading a programmed teaching text on social learning principles and being tested on the contents, parents are systematically taught: (1) skills for observing and recording the problems they face with their child; (2) to use reinforcement and effective disciplinary methods; (3) to supervise and monitor their child's out-of-home activities more effectively; and (4) problem-solving and negotiating strategies.

Another influential early model is that of Forehand and McMahon (1981) for families of young oppositional children. In this 10-session programme based on social learning principles and C. Hanf and J. Kling's (unpublished data) two-stage model of child-led and parent-led interactions, the therapist observes the parent — usually the mother — interacting with her child during a game-playing session in a clinic playroom from behind a one-way screen. Using a 'bug-in-the-ear' device, the therapist instructs the parent on how to respond appropriately to her child. During the first 5 sessions (the child's game), play is initiated by the child and the parent is taught to respond sensitively, to give reflective positive feedback and praise but to remain nondirective. The focus then changes to child compliance so that in the later 5 sessions parents are taught effective means of instructing and disciplining the child.

Group parent training is sometimes part of clinical services but more commonly has been carried out in the context of special projects or research programmes. Programmes vary in manner of recruitment, group composition, content covered and teaching methods used. Nevertheless there are some commonalities. Very often families have been recruited through advertisements but families facing more severe clinical problems have also been referred. Group training has been carried out mainly with parents of oppositional and conduct-disordered children (Webster-Stratton, 1991) and mentally handicapped children (Clements, 1985; Callias, 1987). Group training usually comprises a time-limited course with a curriculum that includes both techniques for developing positive interactions or skills and for dealing with problem behaviour. Methods of instruction vary but there are usually didactic components as well as skills teaching by role play or modelling — either live or by video-taped vignettes. A part of each meeting is usually devoted to discussing how parents themselves are applying the principles and techniques to the specific problems of their children. Written materials or manuals are sometimes used. The content of courses varies according to the problems of the children. Programmes for parents of mentally handicapped children emphasize basic self-care skills, language development and play in addition to reducing problem behaviour (Callias, 1987). With conduct-disordered and oppositional children, the focus tends to be on developing positive interactional play between parent and child and techniques of reducing problem behaviour.

An important and promising group-training programme has been developed in the past decade for parents of young conduct-disordered children (Webster-Stratton, 1981, 1984, 1991). The content of this 10-session programme draws from the work of Hanf and Kling (unpublished data), Forehand and McMahon (1981) and Patterson (1982), as well as communication and problem-solving skills (Spivack *et al.*, 1976; D'Zurilla & Nezu, 1982) and uses modelling by video-tape vignettes as the main teaching method. A total of 250 1–2-minute vignettes — of both good and problematic interactions modelled by parents and children of both sexes, diverse ages, socioeconomic and cultural background — provide the basis for discussion and training in group meetings. Parents also carry out homework assignments. The tapes have also been used as self-administered training (Webster-Stratton *et al.*, 1988).

Some parent-training projects combine group treatment with individual training. Group meetings are used to teach parent management principles and sometimes basic child development. In parallel, during home visits, parents are taught to apply management techniques to their own particular problems. Combined group and individual training has been used with families of aggressive antisocial children (Patterson & Reid, 1973; Patterson *et al.*, 1973; Patterson, 1974), abused children (Wolfe *et al.*, 1981; Azar, 1989) and preschool handicapped children (Freeman & Thompson, 1973). Occasionally group treatment has been supplemented by subsequent individual parent training for the few families who have not benefited sufficiently from the group (Brightman *et al.*, 1980).

Parent training is sometimes used in conjunction with other treatments for children: for example, separate parallel groups for parents and for their seriously conduct-disordered children in inpatient treatment (Kazdin *et al.*, 1987), nighttime problems (Graziano *et al.*, 1979; Graziano & Mooney, 1980, 1982) and for treating obesity in childhood (Brownell *et al.*, 1983). Children in these groups have usually been taught a range of cognitive-behavioural strategies for overcoming their problems.

Finally, parent training has also been incorporated as one aspect — albeit a very important one — of a more comprehensive integrated programme for children with serious difficulties such as developmental disorders or autism (Lovaas, 1987; Marcus & Schopler, 1989), for preschool children with serious language delays (Drash & Tudor, 1990) and in inpatient settings (see Chapter 57). An issue with such programmes is that the contribution of parental involvement is difficult to disentangle. However, with complex problems having a poor prognosis and where existing approaches are known to have a minimal effect, it may be more important to demonstrate that maximum-impact strategies work than to tease out the relative contribution of different components.

Summary

Behavioural parent training with individual families and in groups is becoming widely used on its own or as part of a broader treatment approach including the child in outpatient or inpatient treatment. The content of what is taught and methods of teaching vary greatly from project to project. Earlier work concentrated on contingency management of problems. This approach is still commonly used, e.g. with hyperactive children (Whalen & Henker, 1991), and is often sufficient and effective with many circumscribed childrens' problems. Several developments have occurred over recent years. Firstly, there has been a major shift towards considering more seriously the antecedents or settings in which child behaviour problems occur. This has led to an emphasis on teaching mothers to notice and monitor the situations that give rise to problems (including their own perceptions and behaviour) and thus to avoid their recurrence (Wahler & Dumas, 1984). In addition, training programmes have become more complex. Developments occurring within the cognitive-behavioural approaches and problem-solving treatments generally are being incorporated into parent training. Sometimes this is done by including these aspects as new topics and at other times by the manner in which treatments are implemented (Kazdin, 1987; Webster-Stratton, 1991). The main focus still remains on parents' own immediate interactions with their child, aiming either to foster new skills and enjoyable interactions or to deal with behavioural problems and conflicts more effectively. Only a few parent-training programmes address other aspects of parenting, such as monitoring and supervising activities outside the direct surveillance and involvement of the parent (Patterson, 1982; Bank *et al.*, 1991). The clinician embarking on parent training needs to make decisions about how to work with the family, what techniques will be most effective in teaching parents, what to teach them and when parent training is appropriate and with which problems, children and families. Some of these issues will now be considered.

Parent—professional relationships

Parent—professional collaboration and role relationships take many forms today. Over the years there has been a shift towards greater participation and empowerment of parents in the decision-making and care of their children, especially those children with lifelong handicaps (Mittler & Mittler, 1983; Cunningham & Davis, 1985; Marcus & Schopler, 1989). Cunningham and Davis (1985) identified three forms of relationships: expert, transplant and consumer. In the *expert* role relationship, the professional is in charge of both decisions and treatment so parents are not expected to contribute actively. In the *transplant* model, professionals view themselves as the expert resource but parents are co-opted and trained to use special skills with their children under the general supervision and direction of experts, who usually retain decision-making power. Finally, in the *consumer* model, parents decide and choose what they believe is appropriate for their child. As in the transplant model, the professional acts as consultant and instructor but the decision-making is a more equally shared process of negotiation with the aim of reaching mutually accepted decisions. Notions of more equal collaboration and partnership between parents and professionals recognize that each has a different role in relation to the child as well as different knowledge and expertise which needs to be shared in a mutual problem-solving fashion (Mittler & Mittler, 1983; Cunningham & Davis, 1985).

Most parent training occurs within the transplant and collaborative partnership models. There has been a shift over time in the manner and extent of parental involvement. Today skills teaching remains central to most parent training but this is more likely to occur in a climate of joint problem-solving and decision-making.

Individual or group training

There is very little explicit guidance on the issue of whether to prefer individual to group training for particular families. Choices are determined largely by the context of training, with individually based approaches being more common in clinical practice.

The major strength of an individual approach is that it allows for greater flexibility in tailoring the degree of therapists' involvement and amount, nature and place of training to the specific needs of families. Clinic-based work allows for the use of special monitoring and feedback devices, such as bug-in-the-ear and video-tape; with the availability of modern technology, video can often be used at home too. Home-based work has the advantage of allowing the therapist to plan feasible interventions for the setting in which parent–child problems occur; this increases the likelihood of change being maintained. However, home-based work is time-consuming and some homes may offer too many distractions. Individual family work seems preferable for: (1) circumscribed problems that do not require a broad-based approach; (2) rare problems; and (3) multiple and complex difficulties where parenting issues are but one of many problems that need a coordinated but complex intervention.

The impetus for group training came largely from the practical need to maximize the use of limited resources. By their nature, groups introduce other advantages: group methods permit, and to some extent require, a more orderly and systematic coverage of theoretical principles as well as techniques than is usual in individual approaches; the responsibility for helping the child remains clearly in the parents' hands; vicarious learning may occur through hearing how other parents tackle problems and may encourage parents to tackle difficulties that they had previously regarded as immutable; and because groups are usually time-limited, the extent of commitment and aims are more clearly defined and agreed upon than they are in some individually based work.

Group processes have long been regarded as important in adult group therapy (Hartman, 1979; Bloch *et al.*, 1981); they operate in behavioural groups too. Contact with fellow parents can itself be important in reducing feelings of isolation, hopelessness and helplessness. The group provides an opportunity for sharing experiences of both problems and potential solutions, and for mutual peer support and encouragement.

There are, however, problems in running groups. It can be time-consuming to organize, arrange and prepare materials for meetings and to select and prepare participants, especially in settings geared to working with individual families. It may be difficult to arrange for a sufficient number of clients with similar needs to be available at the same time. Some parents and children may not like the exposure of a group and others may not benefit sufficiently from group-based work.

The relative merits of group and individual training have been examined in relation to cost and efficacy. When content of training, child problem and family characteristics are the same, group and individual approaches are equally effective on a range of outcome measures of efficacy, drop-out rates and parental satisfaction, but group approaches are almost always more cost-effective (Kovitz, 1976; Christensen *et al.*, 1980; Brightman *et al.*, 1982; Pevsner, 1982; Webster-Stratton *et al.*, 1988, 1989) unless the individual training involves no therapist contact (Webster-Stratton *et al.*, 1988, Webster-Stratton, 1990).

When group training is compared with a different form of individual training — direct training of mother-child dyads — results of different studies are inconsistent, showing either that individually trained parents improve more and are more satisfied with their treatment than those in group training (Eyberg & Matarazzo, 1980) or no significant differences (Webster-Stratton *et al.*, 1988). A combination of group and individual training is not necessarily more effective than group training alone (Heifetz, 1977; Worland *et al.*, 1980). Nevertheless, parents who do not benefit sufficiently from group training can benefit from subsequent individual attention (Brightman *et al.*, 1980).

Furthermore, although there are no noticeable benefits in the short term with serious problems such as child abuse, the combination of group and individual training seems to yield greater long-term benefits than group training alone with attention-control home visits (Azar, 1989).

In summary, the choice between individual and group treatment will depend on the nature of the problems, the extensiveness of training required and the severity of parenting difficulties. Group treatments, especially those using well-developed materials, may have advantages in settings where many parents share common difficulties and resources are limited. A combination of individual and group training may not show short-term benefits over group training on its own, but may be more effective with serious parenting difficulties in the long term.

Methods of training

Didactic teaching, modelling (live or by video-tape), role-play, discussion and written notes have all been used to train parents. Analogue studies show all teaching methods including manuals to be superior to no training; all are equally effective in imparting principles but, for teaching practical skills, methods requiring active participation or observation (e.g. modelling by film or video-tape, active rehearsal with discussion) are more effective than didactic methods alone (Nay, 1975; Flanagan et al., 1979; O'Dell, 1985).

In whole programmes for parents, group discussion based on video-tape vignettes was as effective as highly individualized bug-in-the-ear direct training of parent–child dyads and more cost-effective (Webster-Stratton et al., 1988, 1989). When this video programme was combined with group discussion and therapist feedback and compared with two other less complex training conditions (group discussion alone and individually self-administered video-tapes), the effect was similar in the short term, but the comprehensive approach appealed more to parents and produced longer-lasting effects than the comparison formats. Although mothers report similar reductions in child behaviour problems after using the self-administered video programme with or without therapist consultation, home observations show significantly less child deviance for parents receiving therapist consultation than those working independently (Webster-Stratton, 1990).

Similarly, video-tape teaching and therapist-directed live teaching are both effective for the development of childrens' self-help skills in mentally retarded children, but live teaching is slightly better (Kashima et al., 1988).

Carefully developed manuals are useful teaching tools. Used independently, they have been shown to be effective for teaching parents to develop new skills and to cope with behaviour problems, but their efficacy for enabling parents to cope with complex or diffuse problems remains uncertain (Bernal & North, 1978; McMahon & Forehand, 1980).

Thus, all teaching methods, including well-designed self-administered material, lead to improvements, but active participation and therapist contact are slightly superior — especially for teaching practical skills — and liked best by parents.

Content of training

Less attention has been paid to the issue of *what* to teach: that is, on content rather than teaching methods. Important issues relate to: the scope of the curriculum; whether parents need to know theory in addition to practical skills; and apparent contradictions in what is taught.

What is taught under the umbrella of cognitive-behavioural training varies considerably according to the perceived needs of participants. The curriculum of skills may cover a wide or narrow range of principles and techniques as they apply to one or several skills or problems that range from specific tantrums or self-care skills to broader interpersonal problems or communication skills. Coverage is usually most comprehensive in programmes for families with widespread parenting problems, as in child abuse (Wolfe et al., 1981; Azar, 1989), neglect (Lutzker, 1990) and conduct disorder (Webster-Stratton, 1991), and most focused when treating specific problems such as sleeping difficulties (Douglas, 1989). Intuitively, this seems sensible. However, even seemingly straightforward problems may require a complex combination of skills if they are to be treated successfully.

In recognition of the limitations of early forms of parent training with their greater emphasis on contingency management for problem behaviour, content expanded to include skills relevant to modifying antecedent conditions, including the contribution of parents' own role and their interpretation of child behaviour (Wahler & Dumas, 1984), as well as other areas of difficulty such as personal adjustment and relationships (Griest et al., 1982), and resulted in better outcomes than more limited training. Current developments include expansions of standard parent-training programmes to incorporate family issues other than parenting skills, such as anger management, coping with depression, marital communication, problem-solving skills and how to teach such problem-solving skills to children (Webster-Stratton, 1991).

Evidence on the issue of whether knowledge of theory enhances parenting skills suggests that teaching principles in addition to practical skills does not improve the acquisition of such skills but it does enhance longer-term effectiveness of training (Glogower & Sloop, 1976; McMahon et al., 1981; O'Dell, 1985). It seems likely that teaching a combination of principles and practical applications will be more effective than either alone. The introduction of problem-solving skills may also facilitate parents' application of their skills to new problems. As yet the specific additional contribution of these elements has not been examined. At least intuitively, problem-solving seems to keep the responsibility for some of the decision-making in the hands of the parents and to provide strategies for tackling new problems.

The issue of apparently contradictory advice is most evident and pertinent in relation to how far parents should actively initiate teaching of appropriate child behaviour and how far they should rely much more on following the child's leads. Most behavioural programmes emphasize a directive parental style, whereas some programmes stress following child cues, for example, early intervention (Marfo & Kysela, 1985) and the 'child game' (Forehand & McMahon, 1981). Teaching parents to respond appropriately to their child's positive spontaneous behaviour and to avoid non-contingent excessive stimulation leads to less fussing in infants (Seifer et al., 1991).

Nevertheless, the validity of advocating this approach in a blanket fashion is being questioned, especially for mentally handicapped children (Cunningham, 1985; Marfo, 1990). Clearly both sensitive responsiveness and clear initiations are necessary. The issue that needs clarification is *when* each of these styles is appropriate.

Summary

Within cognitive-behavioural approaches, what is taught and how it is taught affect the skills and confidence that parents acquire. Any training is generally better than none but the most effective techniques for teaching practical skills involve clearly modelled examples or active role-play. Teaching parents knowledge of principles may not improve their practical skills in the short term but may facilitate generalization and maintenance of change. Parents can be taught either individually or in groups successfully. Group training for parents with similar problems may be more cost-effective and provide additional benefits such as peer support and modelling. Self-administered training by means of manuals or clear video-tape vignettes are effective ways of teaching specific skills. Nevertheless, parents tend to prefer some contact with therapists and this contact seems to improve their confidence as well as skills.

In deciding on the appropriate scope of training, it is necessary to consider the needs of particular families by taking account of their specific problems and also by assessing more carefully their present style of parenting and where their difficulties lie. This issue of matching what it taught, and perhaps also the style of teaching, to parents' individual needs has not received serious attention.

EFFICACY OF PARENT TRAINING

Evaluation and outcome

Methodological problems and issues in the design of studies and evaluation of parent training are similar to those in the field of child interventions and therapy generally (Kazdin, 1988, 1990, 1991; Callias, 1992). Reports of treatments vary enormously from clinical descriptions to sophisticated comparative studies with clearly defined problems, populations, methods of intervention and assessment of change on multiple outcome measures. All studies, even the most sophisticated ones, suffer from some, albeit different, limitations. Moreover, not all approaches have been evaluated (Henry, 1981; Dembo *et al.*, 1985). Thus, conclusions and generalizations can only be tentative and await more compelling demonstration.

The bulk of reports on parent training are descriptions of projects and reports of single case studies or small series of families. There have also been some larger-scale studies involving group comparisons, sometimes with random allocation of families to different conditions. The efficacy of behavioural parent training has been studied in comparisons with waiting-list controls, or with other approaches, including existing

clinical community treatment services or interventions based on different theoretical approaches. Outcome measures have centred on the child (using parental checklists of child behaviour, or standard measures of cognitive or linguistic development in early intervention programmes) but also commonly include parental consumer satisfaction and assessments of parent–child interaction. Changes at the level of parental skills have seldom been studied directly independently of parent–child interaction. Although changing the interaction between parent and child is the ultimate goal of intervention, assessing the impact of intervention only at this level does not allow for disentangling the contributions of parent and child influences on the interaction which is, of course, determined by both participants, the context and other factors that may impinge on them (Hinde & Stevenson-Hinde, 1987). It is necessary to discriminate between parents who lack skills and those who already have adequate parenting skills or have acquired them in training programmes but are unable to implement them for other reasons (Dumas & Albin, 1986). Bearing these caveats in mind, the following findings emerge.

In comparison with *waiting-list* controls, almost all parent-training studies show immediate posttreatment gains on some outcome measures of parent and/or child behaviour despite the wide variety of problems and programmes (O'Dell, 1974, 1985; Tavormina, 1974, 1975; Webster-Stratton, 1984, 1991; Richman *et al.*, 1985; Helm & Kosloff, 1986; Azar, 1989).

Studies comparing behavioural parent training with *existing clinical services* and approaches to the same problems usually show that the behavioural approach is more effective on at least some measures; for example, in the treatment of school refusal (Blagg & Yule, 1984), problems of autistic children (Howlin *et al.*, 1987; Lovaas, 1987) and child abuse (Lutzker & Rice, 1984). Sometimes the advantage of behavioural parent training is to accelerate change; group differences are evident immediately posttreatment but not at subsequent follow-up assessment, usually because other groups catch up rather than because behavioural treatment gains are lost. Examples of such effects are, firstly, the gains made by treated autistic children's earlier functional use of their linguistic skills (Howlin *et al.*, 1987); and secondly, a swifter reduction in re-offending rates by chronic offending delinquent youth treated by parent training than those receiving traditional services (Bank *et al.*, 1991). Sometimes the effect of parent training is not to eliminate difficulties but to reduce the severity and frequency of difficulties such as child abuse (Lutzker & Rice, 1984).

There have been some comparisons of behavioural parent training *with alternative theoretical approaches*. Early work comparing behavioural with reflective counselling for parents of mentally handicapped children showed that both approaches were more effective than no intervention with families experiencing milder problems but not necessarily with more serious problems (O'Dell, 1974; Tavormina, 1974; Graziano, 1977). Sometimes behavioural and reflective counselling changed different domains (Tavormina, 1974, 1975; Hampson & Tavormina, 1980; Rickel *et al.*, 1980; Goldberg *et al.*, 1981).

As might be expected, behavioural methods led to improvements in children's behaviour whereas reflective counselling led to more favourable parental attitudes. Perhaps more surprisingly, however, behavioural methods sometimes resulted in improvements in attitudes as well as behaviour. In the longer term, however, outcomes were usually similar. Some evidence suggests that general parental support on its own is not enough to change child problems. For example, highly anxious primiparous women offered professional or non-professional support for the first 12 months were less anxious both 1 and 5 years later (with parents receiving professional support doing better than those receiving support from non-professional but experienced mothers); but there were no group differences for their children (Barnett & Parker, 1985; Barnett *et al.*, 1991). The children's problems at 5 years of age were best predicted by maternal psychosocial variables, including anxiety and to a lesser extent by their own temperament in infancy. This would suggest that helping parents with only their own problems does not necessarily improve their parenting skills. In contrast, for families experiencing marital discord, parent training with adjunctive therapy focusing on partner support and problem-solving resulted in better maintenance of treatment gains 6 months later than parent training alone (Dadds *et al.*, 1987).

With conduct-disordered children, behavioural parent-training programmes have been shown to be more effective than family-based psychotherapy, discussion (attention placebo) and no treatment, family systems therapy and parent discussion based on Dinkmeyer and McKay's (1976) systematic training for effective parenting (STEP) programme (Webster-Stratton, 1991).

With abusing parents, three interventions — (1) cognitive-behavioural group treatment combined with weekly home visiting to facilitate generalization; (2) the same group treatment and weekly home visits for supportive listening only; and (3) insight-oriented group treatment with supportive home visits — were all more effective than no treatment in the short term, although in the longer term the more intensive treatment yielded better results (Azar, 1989).

Similarly, clinic-based group parent training and multisystemic therapy with individual families conducted at home or in the clinic were equally effective in reducing parental psychiatric symptomatology, overall stress and child problems in abusing and neglecting families, but yielded some treatment-specific effects too (Brunk *et al.*, 1987). Multisystemic therapy was more effective in restructuring parent–child relations whereas parent training was more effective in reducing social problems such as isolation. It should be noted that multisystemic therapy with its wider aetiological perspective encompassed parent training (88% of families received informal parental education) in addition to addressing other problems directly.

Sometimes, parent training is a component *added to existing interventions*, as in the case of two rather different early intervention programmes (Wolfe *et al.*, 1988; Wasik *et al.*, 1990). Young parents of children identified as at risk for child mal-

treatment all attended an informal information and support group while their children attended day-care centres; half the mothers received additional behavioural training (Wolfe *et al.*, 1988). Although both groups showed improvements, the group receiving additional parent training showed better longer-term gains and were regarded as less likely to maltreat their children. In a contrasting study for families with children at risk for cognitive difficulties because of the disadvantaged educational or social circumstances of their parents, children were randomly assigned at birth to: (1) an intensive intervention combining family education with centre-based educational day care for the child; (2) a less intensive intervention of family-based education only; or (3) a no-intervention control group (Wasik *et al.*, 1990). In regular assessments up to the age of $4\frac{1}{2}$ years, children in the educational day care plus family support groups did better than those in the other two groups and no significant effects on cognitive abilities were noted for the family education only group. These two studies suggest that some form of combined or more complex intervention is more effective than a single component intervention (although in each case only one of the components was tested separately).

In general, the results of early intervention studies for high-risk young children have been mixed; overall, programmes including some parent training, usually in addition to direct child education, have yielded the most robust gains (Seitz, 1990; McGuire & Earls, 1991).

The few studies comparing parent training or counselling with *direct therapeutic work with the child* yield contradictory results, perhaps because the interventions derive from different theoretical orientations. Therapy conducted with children at school (either in nondirective playgroups for 7-year-olds or behavioural training by teachers for 11–12-year-olds) more effectively reduced emotional and behavioural problems than individual general counselling for parents and teachers (Kolvin *et al.*, 1981). In contrast, behavioural casework with abusing parents reduced problems more effectively than play therapy with the children (Nicol *et al.*, 1988). A small-scale study with autistic children suggests that outpatient or home-based parent training is more effective than inpatient work with the children (Sherman *et al.*, 1988).

Although individual parent training may involve the child, group training has not usually involved the child directly. In a few studies using parallel groups for parents and children or groups that include both parents and children for treating problems such as night fears, obesity and conduct disorder, treatment gains were greater and more robust when both parents and children were involved in treatment (Tavormina, 1974; Graziano *et al.*, 1979; Graziano & Mooney, 1980, 1982; Brownell *et al.*, 1983; Kazdin *et al.*, 1987).

Most studies have demonstrated statistically significant treatment effects. However, this is not the same as *clinically significant effects* (Kazdin, 1977; Jacobson, 1988). More recently, studies have included such measures in the form of recidivism rates for delinquency (Bank *et al.*, 1991), recurrence of child abuse (Azar, 1989) and reduction of institutionalization for autistic children (Marcus & Schopler, 1989). One problem with these clinically important outcome measures is that they are unlikely to be determined solely by the training that parents receive. Other factors such as availability of adequate community services, social support and detection rates are likely to be relevant too. Such measures also only tap the most serious breakdowns in family coping rather than more common problems.

Increasingly, a reduction of problems to within the normative range for the child's age and sex on behaviour rating scales such as the Child Behavior Inventory (Achenbach & Edelbrock, 1981) is being used as an index of clinically significantly change (Kazdin *et al.*, 1987). These are important measures but again are unlikely to be affected by parent training alone.

In summary, interventions aimed at providing either training in child management or support and understanding to parents will have some effect in the short term, though longer-term effects are more variable. Usually the effects of training parents in child management will have better longer-term outcomes for problems that require improved parenting skills. There is some indication that sometimes working with children as well as parents will be more beneficial than working entirely at the level of parent training. Moreover, what is done with parents does seem to matter: with parents experiencing difficulties in their management of children, some explicit focus on parenting skills seems necessary to effect change in child problems and parenting skills. Addressing additional family problems directly in therapy seems to enhance long-term efficacy.

Not everyone benefits equally from the same parent training. The characteristics of children and families in relation to outcome have received some attention, although several issues remain unresolved.

Child characteristics

In more recent studies the characteristics of children are more clearly defined in terms of the nature of their problems, usually according to DSM (American Psychiatric Association, 1987) or ICD (World Health Organization, 1992) criteria. This is clearly an advance. Nevertheless, the role of considerable individual variation in the severity of these problems as well as other characteristics such as intellectual ability, age and sex in relation to outcome remains unresolved. Such child characteristics are relevant to the nature of intervention, the extent of change and outcome.

Child characteristics are especially pertinent to the evaluation of early curriculum programmes for young developmentally handicapped children who, because of the heterogeneity of their problems and degree of intellectual handicap, might be expected to respond differently (Marfo & Kysela, 1985). Degree of intellectual disability is highly predictive of long-term outcome in children with pervasive developmental handicaps, such as autism (Lockyer & Rutter, 1970). Similarly, although children's problems may fall within the same classifi-

cation, e.g. conduct disorder, their problems may differ considerably in intensity, pervasiveness and severity.

The process of selecting target problems for intervention with children is generally rather an intuitive and fallible process largely dependent on the judgements of parents and therapists based on the scope of the initial assessment. The issues are just beginning to be addressed, with suggestions for minimizing clinician's biases (Weist *et al.*, 1991).

The fact that parental definitions of problems are usually accepted at face value poses problems in circumstances when parental beliefs, attitudes and expectations of children (Sigel, 1985; Goodnow, 1988) may themselves be problematic. Both parental attitudes and child behaviour may be extreme relative to societal norms as, for example, when parents of children who show extreme acting-out behaviour perceive this as less troublesome than parents whose children do not act out (Patterson, 1982). Alternatively, parents may construe fairly normal behaviour as unacceptable by their standards.

More specific descriptions of the characteristics of children and their problems will enhance treatment and its evaluation.

Characteristics of parents and families

As noted from early on, parents who face multiple problems of socioeconomic disadvantage, depression or other psychological distress, single parenthood or who are in discordant marriages or socially isolated find it harder to benefit from parent training than those without such problems (O'Dell, 1974; Patterson & Fleischman, 1979; Wahler, 1980). Nevertheless, such difficulties, for example marital disharmony, do not automatically preclude families from benefiting from behavioural help for their children's problems (Oltmanns *et al.*, 1977).

Understanding how these problems impinge on parenting spurs developments in parent training. Thus, understanding the role of isolation or inharmonious interactions with other people of isolated single parents has led to a greater focus on the role of precipitants of children's behaviour problems (Wahler & Dumas, 1984). It is noteworthy that the same features that led to parents experiencing difficulty with their children (Patterson, 1982; Belsky, 1984) are associated with less favourable outcomes of parent training. Parent training is being expanded to address such problems more directly, usually by adding components to the core child management training (Wahler & Dumas, 1984; Webster-Stratton, 1991) with beneficial effects for families with multiple problems or marital discord (Brunk *et al.*, 1987; Dadds *et al.*, 1987).

A clearer understanding of how parenting and other problems are interwoven (Forehand, 1987) will help to clarify whether interventions are more effective if problems are addressed simultaneously or in succession.

Parent training now usually involves fathers too. However, much less is known about the effects of training on them, on the similarity and differences between fathers' and mothers' parenting styles, the nature and extent of involvement with the child and how far similarities and differences influence outcome of training (Coplin & Houts, 1991). Fathers and mothers benefit equally when trained separately but longer-term gains are slightly better when both parents are involved (Firestone *et al.*, 1980; Adeso & Lipson, 1981; Webster-Stratton, 1985).

Whilst these broader family and personal problems pose issues for parent training and require systematic attention, many parents with such problems do benefit from parent training and there is no good evidence for withholding child management training on *a priori* grounds, provided that parents are motivated to accept treatment and that they can cope with the training requirements.

Drop-out

Parent training or early intervention is demanding and many parents either choose not to take part or drop out before completing the training. Although drop-out rates range from 0 to 50% for both individual and group training (Firestone & Witt, 1982), very few studies examine the reasons for drop-out. The nature and severity of problems, parental motivation and personality, as well as expectations of the intervention seem to play a part. For example, families at high risk for parenting difficulties whose children showed milder problems did not take up the offer of early intervention (Wolfe *et al.*, 1988). In comparison with parents who complete training, parents who drop out tend to have younger and less able children, seek help for girls rather than boys, and are themselves less educated, financially poorer and have more disturbed personalities, but do not differ on family size, marital status and marital satisfaction (Firestone & Witt, 1982).

Organizational and treatment factors also affect drop-outs. Method of recruitment (by advertisement, through schools or clinical referral), the settings and facilities available, such as convenient locations, child-care arrangements and practical timetabling, can lead to effective engagement and involvement of less advantaged families (Rickel *et al.*, 1980; Wolfe *et al.*, 1981). Descriptions of self-help groups suggest that engagement of needy families (who usually drop out of more formal projects) is better in groups run in everyday community settings, such as mother and toddler groups, that rely mostly on informal interchange between parents supplemented with some formal input where necessary (Peterman, 1981; Palfreeman, 1982).

Parental consumer feedback

If parents are to benefit from parent training, they need to find what is taught acceptable. Attitudinal and practical obstacles to implementing behavioural approaches were noted early on (Tharp & Wetzel, 1969). Discussion of these concerns usually enables parents to understand the rationale of principles and to apply appropriate techniques effectively (Tharp & Wetzel, 1969; Callias, 1987). The acceptability of both specific techniques and whole training courses has been investigated empirically. Analogue studies using vignette examples

of particular management techniques show that students (rather than parents experiencing difficulties) favour positive approaches to discipline over more punitive ones (Gullone & King, 1989).

Feedback from parent-training projects shows parents to be enthusiastic and satisfied about the training (Tavormina *et al.*, 1976; Forehand & McMahon, 1981; Holmes *et al.*, 1982; Callias, 1987; Webster-Stratton, 1989). Finer-grain analyses showed preferences for particular training methods and techniques: mothers found group treatment (with or without the use of video vignettes) more helpful than self-directed video training, though fathers were less influenced by treatment modality than mothers; the specific techniques of reward and time out were perceived as most useful, whereas ignore was regarded as most difficult to use and least useful (Webster-Stratton, 1989).

The issue of whether parental satisfaction with their training is related to change in their parenting or in their children's problems is one that is not studied very much. It is noteworthy that parents report feeling very satisfied and supported by training programmes even when more objective outcome measures on child problems show very little change relative to control groups and such problems remain above the level of nonproblem children. This is evident, for example, in some treatment studies of sleep problems of young children (Scott & Richards, 1990) and for autistic children who made few gains in linguistic development (a major aim of the intervention), although they did improve on behaviour problems (Holmes *et al.*, 1982; Howlin *et al.*, 1987). Such discrepancies between small changes in child behaviour on objective measures and warm parental appreciation for the intervention raise several questions about the goals and achievements of parent training. Firstly, parents and therapists may not have the same goals; secondly, small changes in a child's behaviour and progress may greatly improve the quality of family life; thirdly, group data may obscure individul differences in both success and satisfaction; and fourthly, parental satisfaction may not be directly associated with amelioration of problems but may reflect a sense of feeling supported and of achieving some self-efficacy and understanding of the child which is independent of actual changes in the child.

Clearly, outcome measures at the level of child change, parental behaviour and cognitive change, and parental satisfaction are not equivalent. A sharper understanding is needed of both how they are interrelated and how they may be affected by different facets of an intervention.

Therapists' characteristics and integrity of training

In contrast to the extensive research on therapist characteristics in adult therapy (Beutler *et al.*, 1986), the role of the therapists' characteristics, skill and experience in conducting individual and group training has, until recently, been largely ignored in parent training. Yet there are hints that skills and interpersonal relationship skills are relevant. The therapist's style varies considerably depending on theoretical orientation, partly because interventions differ in how far the therapist's behaviour is explicitly specified. Slight evidence suggests that there may be less room for personal style and skill to influence outcome in behavioural parent groups, where the therapist's role is explicitly specified, than in less structured reflective counselling groups (Tavormina, 1975). This does not mean that the therapist's sensitivity and skill are irrelevant in behavioural approaches. Early work in behavioural family intervention showed that a therapist's relationship and structuring skills were especially influential in determining engagement in the initial stages of therapy and made an important contribution to outcome (Alexander *et al.*, 1976). Moreover, although parents do benefit from using training materials independently, contact with a therapist usually increases efficacy (if only marginally) and parents prefer having some therapist contact (Seymour *et al.*, 1989; Scott & Richards, 1990; Webster-Stratton, 1991).

More recently, the role of the therapist is being viewed from a bidirectional, interactive perspective. That is, progress in therapy is viewed as jointly determined by what the client brings into treatment and by the behaviour of the therapist (Alexander *et al.*, 1988; Herbert, 1988).

Overall, there is a need to identify the particular interpersonal skills and attitudinal approaches that foster greater engagement and cooperation. Therapists' interpersonal skills are relevant to three key tasks: (1) engaging families in treatment; (2) ensuring that parents understand and apply new skills appropriately; and (3) supporting and encouraging parents as they implement their new skills. Furthermore, in order to facilitate generalization and maintenance of new parenting styles, therapists may need to consider parenting issues and family problems beyond the teaching of child management techniques. In carrying out these roles, the therapist draws on a much broader base of knowledge and skills than is generally acknowledged. These include consideration of the developmental appropriateness of the particular child management techniques, appropriate expectations of the child and of training tasks, as well as the broader understanding of family functioning and social context.

Research design and methodology

Parent-training studies have become more sophisticated and now often include random allocation to different conditions, longer follow-up of treatment and assessment on a range of measures. Nevertheless, problems remain in relation to research design, the nature of assessment measures, methods of measuring change, the quality and integrity of intervention and adequate control for development (Kazdin, 1988, 1991; Callias, 1992).

Research methodology for evaluating parent training will also need to evolve to meet new challenges. Firstly, there is a need for appropriate research designs for evaluating interventions for such serious problems that ethical and practical considerations preclude the use of traditional randomized group designs (Smith *et al.*, 1984). Secondly, methods are needed for teasing out the therapeutic and other processes influencing long-term outcomes. Finally, there is the challenge of evaluating flexible but systematic interventions tailored to the specific needs of individual families as well as standardized treatments.

CONCEPTUAL FRONTIERS IN PARENT TRAINING

Current parent training addresses important but restricted facets of parenting. Very little attention has been paid to how it relates to other aspects of parenting or the family and sociocultural context in which child-rearing is embedded. Developmental and other child characteristics also receive scant attention.

Parenting comprises more than disciplining children and fostering the development of a child's skills and play. Parents also provide basic physical and emotional care and protection, organize and monitor their children's lives outside the home, liaise with professionals and others in order to gain resources for the child, and recognize and deal appropriately with crises such as children's illnesses. Some of these tasks are beginning to be recognized as teachable skills; for example, monitoring children's out-of-home activities (Patterson, 1982; Bank *et al.*, 1991), recognizing signs of illness and acting upon them (Delgrado & Lutzker, 1988) and helping children avoid injury within the home (Mathews *et al.*, 1987). Parents of children suffering from serious or chronic illness such as cancer or diabetes can be helped to enable their children endure painful medical procedures with less anxiety (Campbell *et al.*, 1986; Manne *et al.*, 1990). Some parent training is addressing the level of emotional and affectionate bonds by helping parents to show affection and responsivity in positive interactions (Affleck *et al.*, 1982; Feldman *et al.*, 1989) and to improve attachment relationships (Jernberg, 1989). The special needs of adoptive and foster parents also require consideration (Rushton, 1989).

The tasks of parenting vary with the age and developmental status of child (Herbert, 1991). Parent training implicitly takes account of developmental issues in working with parents of children of different ages, but an explicit longitudinal, developmental perspective is lacking. Some knowledge of the changing needs of children and the implications for a changing style of parenting may be needed, especially by parents experiencing profound difficulties.

Parent training and counselling of different theoretical persuasions place different value on the behavioural, cognitive or emotional aspects of parenting. Yet these facets of any action or interaction are intimately interlinked. A better understanding of the interrelationships between behaviour, cognition and emotion in parenting (Dix, 1991) has implications for developments in both the content and methods of parent training. Parent training has largely ignored how parental responsibility is shared between parents, styles of parenting and different patterns of family relationships. Such structural and systemic issues are usually addressed by family therapy. Cognitive-behavioural intervention strategies are beginning to be integrated with these approaches (Brunk *et al.*, 1987; Peters & McMahon, 1988).

Individual and cultural variations in child-rearing have received little attention in the treatment of children (Tharp, 1991), including parent training. There is a need to explore the issue of how to make appropriate parent training available in a way that is sensitive to different cultural traditions of child-rearing and family circumstances (Lieh-Mak *et al.*, 1984).

Finally, another important task for future work is to discriminate more explicitly between acceptable individual and cultural differences in parenting practices and those which are failing. Whilst the distinctions between seriously problematic parenting and competent parenting are quite easy to discern, deciding what is 'good-enough' parenting is more problematic.

FROM RESEARCH TO CLINICAL PRACTICE

Despite the issues that remain in understanding parenting and anchoring parent training on firmer empirical foundations, developments over the past 20 years have established parent training as an important form of clinical intervention and as having a role in preventive intervention.

Individual parent training is most common in clinical practice and fits in most easily with the organization of most clinical services. The individual approach clearly allows for a detailed assessment of parenting problems, leading to precise but flexible intervention drawing on research (Herbert, 1987, 1988). This approach is most economical for focused specific problems and is essential for treating more complex and difficult problems.

Groups could be used more often in clinical settings, especially when several families share similar problems.

Behavioural approaches are useful to professionals in other settings who offer advice to parents on a range of topics including behaviour problems. The development of materials and programmes for dealing effectively with common problems, such as sleep difficulties, enables primary care professionals to help families with specific problems more effectively. The provision of training for dealing with more complex or serious problems is necessary too but may require more extensive training or ongoing collaborative work or consultation. The issues involved in making effective parent training available more widely require attention.

This enthusiastic advocacy of parent training and support does not mean that parent training is a panacea. One of the most important tasks of clinicians is to assess the problems and needs of a child and family properly with a view to advising on appropriate interventions. Parent training is one such intervention. A careful assessment of the parenting difficulties can pinpoint the particular needs of the parents, and thus the focus of training. In parallel, the child will usually need to be actively involved in treatment either separately or jointly with parents, depending on the nature of the problems. Parent training is also not a substitute for appropriate education or

for the other treatment and community services required to meet the child's needs.

CONCLUSIONS

Parent training has continued to flourish over the past few years and to be applied to a wide range of parenting and child problems. Most systematic developments have been within the cognitive-behavioural tradition. Overall, cognitive-behavioural interventions have been shown to be more effective than less intensive training in helping parents cope with the particular problems presented by their children.

Further developments in conceptualizing and assessing parenting problems in a manner that draws together behavioural, cognitive and emotional facets coherently will lead to refinements in the content and nature of intervention. Greater attention to individual and sociocultural variations in parenting as well as how tasks are shared within the family will need to play a greater role in parent training. There is likely to be a further expansion of parent training to families facing a wider range of problems, including crisis with their children, chronic ill health and handicaps, as well as parenting in different circumstances such as divorced parents, single parents and foster and adoptive parents. The needs of many of these groups may differ from those of parents of difficult or handicapped children, with whom most of the research has been conducted, and may necessitate different emphasis and issues. For example, with children with chronic serious medical conditions, key issues for parents are those of helping their children cope with regular, painful, medical procedures as well as helping them to lead as normal lives as possible.

Finally, many conceptual and methodological issues require further systematic study. There is a need to develop better methods for assessing the nature of parenting difficulties and to develop better strategies for matching interventions to the specific nature of the difficulties. Whilst much has been achieved and can be used effectively today, further research is essential for developing effective interventions for families whose needs are not well met currently.

REFERENCES

Achenbach T.M. & Edelbrock C.S. (1981) Behavioral problems and competencies reported by parents of normal and disturbed children aged four through sixteen. *Monographs of the Society for Research in Child Development*, Serial No. 188, Vol. 46, No. 1.

Adesso V.J. & Lipson J.W. (1981) Group training of parents as therapists for their children. *Behavior Therapy*, **12**, 625–633.

Affleck G., McGrade B.T., McQueeney M. & Allen D. (1982) Relationship-focused early intervention in developmental disabilities. *Exceptional Children*, **49**, 259–261.

Affleck G., Tennen H., Rowe J., Roscher B. & Walker L. (1989) Effects of formal support on mothers' adaptation to the hospital-to-home transition of high-risk infants: the benefits and costs of helping. *Child Development*, **60**, 488–501.

Alexander J.F., Barton C., Schiavo R.S. & Parsons B.V. (1976) Systems-behavioral intervention with families of delinquents: therapist characteristics, family behavior and outcome. *Journal of*

Consulting and Clinical Psychology, **44**, 656–664.

Alexander J.F., Mas C.H. & Waldron H. (1988) Behavioral and systems family therapies or Auld Lang Syne: shall old perspectives be forgot? In: Peters R. De V. & McMahon R.J. (eds) *Social Learning and Systems Approaches to Marriage and the Family*, pp. 287–314. Brunner/Mazel, New York.

American Psychiatric Association (1987) *DSM-III-R Diagnostic and Statistical Manual of Mental Disorders* (3rd edn, revised). American Psychiatric Association, Washington DC.

Anastopoulos A.D. & Barkley R.A. (1989) A training program for parents of children with attention deficit-hyperactivity disorder. In: Schaefer C.E. & Briesmeister J.M. (eds) *Handbook of Parent Training: Parents as Co-therapists for Children's Behavior Problems*, pp. 83–104. John Wiley, New York.

Azar S.T. (1989) Training parents of abused children. In: Schaefer C.E. & Briesmeister J.M. (eds) *Handbook of Parent Training: Parents as Co-therapists for Children's Behavior Problems*, pp. 414–441. John Wiley, New York.

Azar S.T. & Siegel B.R. (1990) Behavioral treatment of child abuse: a developmental perspective. *Behavior Modification*, **14**, 279–300.

Baker B.L. (1986) Parents as teachers: a programme of applied research. In: Milne D. (ed) *Training Behavior Therapists: Methods, Evaluation and Implementation with Parents, Nurses and Teachers*, pp. 92–117. Croom Helm, London.

Baker B.L., Ambrose S.A. & Anderson S.R. (1989) *Parent Training and Developmental Disabilities*. Monographs of the American Association for Mental Retardation, vol. 13, pp. 1–259. American Association on Mental Retardation, Washington, DC.

Bank L., Marlowe J.H., Reid J.B., Patterson G.R. & Weinrott M.R. (1991) A comparative evaluation of parent training interventions for families of chronic delinquents. *Journal of Abnormal Child Psychology*, **19**, 15–33.

Barnett B. & Parker G. (1985) Professional and non-professional intervention for highly anxious primiparous mothers. *British Journal of Psychiatry*, **146**, 287–293.

Barnett B., Schaafsma M.F., Guzman A.M. & Parker G.B. (1991) Maternal anxiety: a 5-year review of an intervention study. *Journal of Child Psychology and Psychiatry*, **32**, 423–438.

Belsky J. (1984) The determinants of parenting: a process model. *Child Development*, **55**, 83–96.

Berkowitz B.P. & Graziano A.M. (1972) Training parents as behavior therapists: a review. *Behavioral Research and Therapy*, **10**, 297–317.

Bernal M.E. & North J.A. (1978) A survey of parent training manuals. *Journal of Applied Behavior Analysis*, **11**, 533–544.

Beutler L.E., Crago M. & Arizmendi T.G. (1986) Therapist variables in psychotherapy process and outcome. In: Garfield S. & Bergin A. (eds) *Handbook of Psychotherapy and Behavior Change*, 3rd edn, pp. 257–310. John Wiley, New York.

Blagg N.R. & Yule W. (1984) The bahavioural treatment of school refusal — a comparative study. *Behaviour Research and Therapy*, **22**, 119–127.

Bloch S., Crouch E. & Reibstein J. (1981) Therapeutic factors in group psychotherapy: a review. *Archives of General Psychiatry*, **38**, 519–526.

Boggs C.J. (1981) Train up a parent: a review of the research in child rearing literature. *Child Study Journal*, **10**(4), 261–284.

Brightman R.P., Ambrose S.A. & Baker B.L. (1980) Parent training: a school-based model for enhancing teaching performance. *Child Behavior Therapy*, **2**(3), 35–47.

Brightman R.P., Baker B.L., Clark D.B. & Ambrose S.A. (1982) Effectiveness of alternative parent training formats. *Journal of Behavior Therapy and Experimental Psychiatry*, **13**, 113–117.

Brooks J.B. (1991) *The Process of Parenting*, 3rd edn. Mayfield, Mountain View, CA.

Brownell K.D., Kelman J.H. & Stunkard A.J. (1983) Treatment of obese children with and without their mothers: changes in weight and blood pressure. *Pediatrics*, **71**, 515–523.

Brunk M., Henggeler S.W. & Whelan J.P. (1987) Comparison of multisystemic therapy and parent training in the brief treatment of child abuse and neglect. *Journal of Consulting and Clinical Psychology*, **55**, 171–178.

Callias M. (1987) Teaching parents, teachers and nurses. In: Yule W. & Carr J. (eds) *Behavior Modification for People with Mental Handicaps*, 2nd edn, pp. 211–244. Croom Helm, London.

Callias M. (1992) Evaluation of interventions with children and adolescents. In: Lane D. & Miller A. (eds) *Child and Adolescent Therapy: A Handbook*, pp. 39–64. Open University Press, Milton Keynes.

Callias M. & Carr J. (1975) Behaviour modification programmes in a community setting. In: Kiernan C.C. & Woodford F.P. (eds) *Behaviour Modification with the Severely Retarded*, pp. 147–171. Associated Scientific Publishers, Elsevier, North Holland.

Campbell L., Clark M. & Kirkpatrick S.E. (1986) Stress management training for parents and their children undergoing cardiac catheterization. *American Journal of Orthopsychiatry*, **56**, 234–243.

Carr J. (1980) *Helping your Handicapped Child: A Step-by-step Guide to Everyday Problems*. Penguin Books, Harmondsworth.

Christensen A., Johnson S.M., Phillips S. & Glasgow R.E. (1980) Cost effectiveness in behavioral family therapy. *Behavior Therapy*, **11**, 208–226.

Clarke-Stewart K.A. (1978) Popular primers for parents. *American Psychologist*, **33**, 359–369.

Clements J. (1985) Update — training parents of mentally handicapped children. *Newsletter of Association for Child Psychology and Psychiatry*, **7**(4), 2–9.

Coplin J.W. & Houts A.C. (1991) Father involvement in parent training for oppositional child behavior: progress or stagnation? *Child and Family Behavior Therapy*, **13**(2), 29–51.

Cunningham C. (1985) Training and education approaches for parents of children with special needs. *British Journal of Medical Psychology*, **58**, 285–305.

Cunningham C.C. & Davis H. (1985) *Working with Parents: Frameworks for Collaboration*. Open University Press, Milton Keynes.

Dadds M.R., Schwartz S. & Sanders M.R. (1987) Marital discord and treatment outcome in behavioral treatment of child conduct disorders. *Journal of Consulting and Clinical Psychology*, **55**, 396–403.

Daly B., Addington J., Kerfoot S. & Sigston A. (1985) (eds) *Portage: The Importance of Parents*. NFER-Nelson, Windsor, Berkshire.

Dangel R.F. & Polster R.A. (1984) (eds) *Parent Training: Foundations of Research and Practice*. Guilford, New York.

Delgrado L.E. & Lutzker J.R. (1988) Training young parents to identify and report their children's illnesses. *Journal of Applied Behaviour Analysis*, **21**, 311–319.

Dembo M.H., Sweitzer M. & Lauritzen P. (1985) An evaluation of group parent training: behavioural, PET, and Adlerian programs. *Review of Educational Research*, **55**, 155–200.

Dinkmeyer D. & McKay G. (1976) *Systematic Training for Effective Parenting*. American Guidance Service, Circle Pines, MN.

Dix T. (1991) The affective organization of parenting: adaptive and maladaptive processes. *Psychological Bulletin*, **110**, 3–25.

Douglas J. (1989) Training parents to manage their child's sleep problem. In: Schaefer C.E. & Briesmeister J.M. (eds) *Handbook of Parent Training: Parents as Co-therapists for Children's Behavior Problems*, pp. 13–37. John Wiley, New York.

Douglas J. & Richman N. (1984) *My Child won't Sleep*. Penguin, Harmondsworth.

Drash P.W. & Tudor R.M. (1990) Language and cognitive development: a systematic behavioral program and technology for increasing the language and cognitive skills of developmentally disabled and at-risk preschool children. In: Hersen M., Eisler R.M. & Miller P.M. (eds) *Progress in Behavior Modification*, vol. 26, pp. 173–200. Sage Publications, Newbury Park, CA.

Dreikers R. & Soltz V. (1972) (eds) *Happy Children: A Challenge to Parents*. Collins/Fontana, London.

Dube B.D., Mitchell C.A. & Bergman L.A. (1980) Uses of the self-run group in a child guidance setting. *International Journal of Group Psychotherapy*, **30**, 461–479.

Dumas J.E. & Albin J.B. (1986) Parent training outcome: does active parental involvement matter? *Behaviour Research and Therapy*, **24**, 227–230.

Duncan S.W. & Markham H.J. (1988) Intervention programs for the transition to parenthood: current status from a prevention perspective. In: Michaels G.Y. & Goldberg W.A. (eds) *The Transition to Parenthood: Current Theory and Research*, pp. 270–310. Cambridge University Press, Cambridge.

D'Zurilla T.J. & Nezu A. (1982) Social problem-solving in adults. In: Kendall P.C. (ed) *Advances in Cognitive Behavioral Research and Therapy*, vol. 1. Academic Press, New York.

Eyberg S.M. & Matarazzo R.G. (1980) Training parents as therapists: a comparison between individual parent–child interaction training and parent group didactic training. *Journal of Clinical Psychology*, **36**, 492–499.

Fantuzzo J.W., Wray L., Hall R., Goins C. & Azar S. (1986) Parent and social-skills training for mentally retarded mothers identified as child maltreaters. *American Journal of Mental Deficiency*, **91**, 135–140.

Feldman M.A., Case L., Rincover A., Towns F. & Betel J. (1989) Parent education project III: increasing affection and responsibility in developmentally handicapped mothers: component analysis, generalization and effects on child language. *Journal of Applied Behavior Analysis*, **22**, 211–222.

Firestone P. & Witt J.E. (1982) Characteristics of families completing and prematurely discontinuing a behavioral parent-training program. *Journal of Pediatric Psychology*, **7**, 209–222.

Firestone P., Kelly M.J. & Fike S. (1980) Are fathers necessary in parent training groups? *Journal of Clinical Child Psychology*, **9**, 44–47.

Flanagan S., Adams H.E. & Forehand R. (1979) A comparison of four instructional techniques for teaching parents to use time-out. *Behavior Therapy*, **10**, 94–102.

Forehand R. (1987) Parental roles in childhood psychopathology. In: Frame C.L. & Matson J.L. (eds) *Handbook of Assessment in Childhood Psychopathology. Applied Issues in Differential Diagnosis and Treatment Evaluation*, pp. 489–507. Plenum Press, New York.

Forehand R. & McMahon R.J. (1981) *Helping the Noncompliant Child: A Clinician's Guide to Effective Parent Training*. Guilford Press, New York.

Freeman S.W. & Thompson C.L. (1973) Parent–child training for the mentally retarded. *Mental Retardation*, **11(4)**, 8–10.

Glasgow R.E. & Rosen G.M. (1978) Behavioral bibliotherapy: a review of self-help behavior therapy manuals. *Psychological Bulletin*, **85**, 1–23.

Glogower F. & Sloop E.W. (1976) Two strategies of group training of parents as effective behavior modifiers. *Behavior Therapy*, **7**, 177–184.

Goldberg J., Merbaum M., Even T., Getz P. & Safir M.P. (1981) Training mothers in contingency management of school-related behavior. *Journal of General Psychology*, **104(1)**, 3–12.

Goodnow J.J. (1988) Parents' ideas, actions and feelings: models and methods from developmental and social psychology. *Child Development*, **59**, 286–320.

Gordon T. & Sands J. (1976) *PET in Action: Inside PET Families: New Problems, Insights and Solutions in Parent Effectiveness Training*. Wyden Books, New York.

Graziano A.M. (1977) Parents as behavior therapists. In: Hersen M., Eisler R.M. & Miller P.M. (eds) *Progress in Behavior Modification*, vol. 4, pp. 251–298. Academic Press, New York.

Graziano A.M. & Mooney K.C. (1980) Family self-control instruction for children's nightime fear reduction. *Journal of Consulting and Clinical Psychology*, **48**, 206–213.

Graziano A.M. & Mooney K.C. (1982) Behavioral treatment of 'night-fears' in children: maintenance of improvement at $2\frac{1}{2}$ to 3 year follow-up. *Journal of Consulting and Clinical Psychology*, **50**, 398–399.

Graziano A.M., Mooney K.C., Huber C. & Ignasiak D. (1979) Self control instruction for children's fear reduction. *Journal of Behavior Therapy and Experimental Psychiatry*, **10**, 221–227.

Griest D.L., Forehand R., Rogers T., Breiner J., Furey W. & Williams C.A. (1982) Effects of parent enhancement therapy on the treatment outcome and generalization of a parent training program. *Behaviour Research and Therapy*, **20**, 429–436.

Gullone E. & King N.J. (1989) Acceptability of behavioral interventions: child and caregiver perceptions. In: Hersen M., Eisler R.M. & Miller P.M. (eds) *Progress in Behavior Modification*, vol. 24, pp. 132–151. Sage Publications, Newbury Park, CA.

Hampson R.B. & Tavormina J.B. (1980) Relative effectiveness of behavioral and reflective group training with foster mothers. *Journal of Consulting and Clinical Psychology*, **48**, 294–295.

Hartman J.J. (1979) Small group methods of personal change. *Annual Review of Psychology*, **30**, 453–476.

Heifetz L.J. (1977) Behavioral training for parents of retarded children: alternative formats based on instructional manuals. *American Journal of Mental Deficiency*, **82**, 194–203.

Helm D.T. & Kosloff M.A. (1986) Research on parent training: shortcomings and remedies. *Journal of Autism and Developmental Disorders*, **16**, 1–22.

Henry S.A. (1981) Current dimensions of parent training. *School Psychology Review*, **10**, 4–14.

Herbert M. (1985) *Caring for your Children: A Practical Guide*. Basil Blackwell, Oxford.

Herbert M. (1987) *Behavioural Treatment of Children with Problems: A Practice Manual*, 2nd edn. Academic Press, London.

Herbert M. (1988) *Working with Children and their Families*. British Psychological Society, Leicester and Routledge, London.

Herbert M. (1991) *Clinical Child Psychology: Social Learning, Development and Behaviour*. John Wiley, Chichester.

Herbert M. & Iwaniec D. (1981) Behavioural psychotherapy in natural homesettings: an empirical study applied to conduct disordered and incontinent children. *Behavioural Psychotherapy*, **9**, 55–76.

Hinde R.A. & Stevenson-Hinde J. (1987) Interpersonal relationships and child development. *Developmental Review*, **7**, 1–21.

Hodder E. (1985) *The Step-Parent's Handbook*. Sphere Books, London.

Holmes N., Hemsley R., Rickett J. & Likierman H. (1982) Parents as co-therapists: their perceptions of a home-based behavioral treatment for autistic children. *Journal of Autism and Developmental Disorders*, **12**, 331–342.

Houts A.C. & Mellon M.W. (1989) Home-based treatment for primary enuresis. In: Schaefer C.E. & Briesmeister J.M. (eds) *Handbook of Parent Training: Parents as Co-therapists for Children's Behavior Problems*, pp. 60–79. John Wiley, New York.

Howlin P., Rutter M., Berger M., Hemsley R., Hersov L. & Yule W. (1987) *Treatment of Autistic Children*. John Wiley, Chichester.

Isaacs C.D. (1982) Treatment of child abuse: a review of the behavioral interventions. *Journal of Applied Behavior Analysis*, **15**, 273–294.

Jacobson N.S. (1988) (ed) Defining clinically significant change. *Behavioral Assessment*, **10(2)** (special issue).

Jernberg A.M. (1989) Training parents of failure-to-attach children. In: Schaefer C.E. & Briesmeister J.M. (eds) *Hand-*

book of Parent Training: Parents as Co-therapists for their Children's Behavior Problems, pp. 392–413. John Wiley, New York.

Kagan S.L. & Seitz V. (1988) Family support programs for new parents. In: Michaels G.Y. & Goldberg W.A. (eds) *The Transition to Parenthood: Current Theory and Research*, pp. 311–341. Cambridge University Press, Cambridge.

Kashima K.J., Baker B.L. & Landen S.J. (1988) Media-based versus professionally led training for parents of mentally retarded children. *American Journal of Mental Retardation*, **93**, 209–217.

Kazdin A.E. (1977) Assessing the clinical or applied significance of behavior change through social validation. *Behavior Modification*, **1**, 427–452.

Kazdin A.E. (1987) Treatment of antisocial behavior in children: current status and future directions. *Psychological Bulletin*, **102**, 187–203.

Kazdin A.E. (1988) *Child Psychotherapy: Developing and Identifying Effective Treatments*. Pergamon Press, Oxford.

Kazdin A.E. (1990) Psychotherapy for children and adolescents. *Annual Review of Psychology*, **41**, 21–54.

Kazdin A.E. (1991) Effectiveness of psychotherapy with children and adolescents. *Journal of Consulting and Clinical Psychology*, **59**, 785–798.

Kazdin A.E., Esveldt-Dawson K., French N.H. & Unis A.S. (1987) Effects of parent management training and problem-solving skills training combined in the treatment of antisocial child behavior. *Journal of American Academy of Child and Adolescent Psychiatry*, **26**, 416–424.

Kitzinger S. & Kitzinger C. (1989) *Talking with Children about Things that Matter*. Pandora, London.

Kolvin I., Garside R.F., Nicol A.R., Macmillan A., Wolstenholme F. & Leitch I.M. (1981) *Help Starts Here: The Maladjusted Child in the Ordinary School*. Tavistock, London.

Kovitz K.E. (1976) Comparing group and individual methods for training parents in child management techniques. In: Mash E.J., Handy L.C. & Hamerlynck L.A. (eds) *Behavior Modification Approaches to Parenting*, pp. 124–138. Bruner/Mazel, New York.

Lazar I. & Darlington R. (1982) Lasting effects of early education: a report from the consortium for longitudinal studies. *Monographs of the Society for Research in Child Development*, Serial No. 195, Vol. 47, Nos. 2–3.

Levy L.H. (1976) Self help groups: types and psychological processes. *Journal of Applied Behavioral Science*, **12**, 310–322.

Lieberman M.A. (1983) Comparative analyses of change mechanisms in groups. In: Blumberg H.H., Hare A.P., Kent V. & Davies M. (eds) *Small Groups and Social Interaction*, vol. 2, pp. 239–252. John Wiley, Chichester.

Lieh-Mak F., Lee P.W.H. & Luk S.L. (1984) Problems encountered in teaching Chinese parents to be behavior therapists. *Psychologia*, **27**, 56–64.

Lockyer L. & Rutter M. (1970) A 5 to 15 year follow-up study of infantile psychosis. IV Patterns of cognitive ability. *British Journal of Social and Clinical Psychology*, **9**, 152–163.

Lovaas O.I. (1987) Behavioral treatment and normal education/intellectual functioning in young autistic children. *Journal of Consulting and Clinical Psychology*, **55**, 3–9.

Lutzker J.R. (1990) Behavioral treatment of child neglect. *Behavior Modification*, **14**, 301–315.

Lutzker J. & Rice J.M. (1984) Project 12-ways. Measuring outcome of a large in-home service for treatment and prevention of child abuse and neglect. *Child Abuse and Neglect*, **8**, 519–524.

McAuley R. (1982) Training parents to modify conduct problems in their children. *Journal of Child Psychology and Psychiatry*, **23**, 335–342.

McGuire J. & Earls F. (1991) Prevention of psychiatric disorders in early childhood. *Journal of Child Psychology and Psychiatry*, **32**, 129–154.

McMahon R.J. & Forehand R. (1980) Self help behavior therapies in parent training. In: Lahey B.B. & Kazdin A.E. (eds) *Advances in Clinical Child Psychology*, vol. 3, pp. 149–176. Plennum Press, New York.

McMahon R.J., Forehand R. & Griest D.L. (1981) Effects of knowledge of social learning principles on enhancing treatment outcome and generalization in a parent training program. *Journal of Consulting and Clinical Psychology*, **49**, 526–532.

Maddox B. (1980) *Step-parenting*. Unwin Paperbacks, London.

Manne S.L., Redd W.H., Jacobsen P.B., Gorfinkle K., Schorr O. & Rapkin B. (1990) Behavioral intervention to reduce child and parent distress during venipuncture. *Journal of Consulting and Clinical Psychology*, **58**, 565–572.

Marcus L.M. & Schopler E. (1989) Parents as co-therapists with autistic children. In: Schaefer C.E. & Briesmeister J.M. (eds) *Handbook of Parent Training: Parents as Co-therapists for Children's Behaviour Problems*. John Wiley, New York.

Marfo K. (1990) Maternal directiveness in interactions with mentally handicapped children: an analytical commentary. *Journal of Child Psychology and Psychiatry*, **31**, 531–549.

Marfo K. & Kysela G.M. (1985) Early intervention with mentally handicapped children: a critical appraisal of applied research. *Journal of Pediatric Psychology*, **10**, 305–324.

Mathews J.R., Friman P.C., Barone V.T., Ross L.V. & Christophersen E.R. (1987) Decreasing dangerous infant behaviors through parent instruction. *Journal of Applied Behavior Analysis*, **20**, 165–169.

Meacher M. (1982) *Self-help Groups for Parents under Stress: A Contribution to Prevention?* Mental Health Foundation, London.

Michaels G.Y. & Goldberg W.A. (1988) (eds) *The Transition to Parenthood: Current Theory and Research*. Cambridge University Press, Cambridge.

Mittler P. & Mittler H. (1983) Partnership with parents: an overview. In: Mittler P. & McConachie H. (eds) *Parent, Professional and Mentally Handicapped People: Approaches to Partnership*, pp. 8–46. Croom Helm, Beckenham.

Munro H. (1982) Supporting parents in the community — the role of adult education. In: De'Ath E. (ed) *Parenting Papers*, vol. 6, pp. 19–26. National Childrens Bureau, London.

Nay W.R. (1975) A systematic comparison of instructional techniques for parents. *Behavior Therapy*, **6**, 14–21.

Nicol A.R., Smith J., Kay B., Hall D., Barlow J. & Williams B. (1988) A focused casework approach to the treatment of child abuse: a controlled comparison. *Journal of Child Psychology and Psychiatry*, **29**, 703–711.

O'Dell S. (1974) Training parents in behavior modification: a review. *Psychology Bulletin*, **81**, 418–433.

O'Dell S.L. (1985) Progress in parent training. In: Hersen M., Eisler R.M. & Miller P.M. (eds) *Progress in Behavior Modification*, vol. 19, pp. 57–108. Academic Press, London.

Offord D.R. (1987) Prevention of behavioral and emotional disorders in children. *Journal of Child Psychology and Psychiatry*, **28**, 9–19.

Oltmanns T.F., Broderick J.E. & O'Leary K.D. (1977) Marital adjustment and the efficacy of behavior therapy with children. *Journal of Consulting and Clinical Psychology*, **45**, 724–729.

Osofsky J.D., Osofsky H.J. & Diamond M.O. (1988) The transition to parenthood: special tasks and risk factors for adolescent parents. In: Michaels G.Y. & Goldberg W.A. (eds) *The Transition to Parenthood: Current Theory and Research*, pp. 209–232. Cambridge University Press, Cambridge.

Palfreeman S. (1982) Valuing community resources: linking parents and professionals. In: Pugh G. (ed) *Parenting Papers*, vol. 5, pp. 15–22. National Children's Bureau, London.

Patterson G.R. (1974) Intervention for boys with conduct problems: multiple settings, treatments and criteria. *Journal of Consulting and Clinical Psychology*, **42**, 471–481.

Patterson G.R. (1975) *Families: Applications of Social Learning to Family Life* (revised edition). Research Press, Champaign, IL.

Patterson G.R. (1976) *Living with Children* (revised edition). Research Press, Champaign, IL.

Patterson G.R. (1982) *Coercive Family Process*. Castalia Publications, Eugene, OR.

Patterson G.R. & Fleischman M.J. (1979) Maintenance of treatment effects: some considerations concerning family systems and follow-up data. *Behavior Therapy*, **10**, 168–185.

Patterson G.R. & Reid J.B. (1973) Intervention for families of aggressive boys: a replication study. *Behavior Research and Therapy*, **11**, 383–394.

Patterson G.R., Cobb J.A. & Ray R.S. (1973) A social engineering technology for re-training the families of aggressive boys. In: Adams H.E. & Unikel I.P. (eds) *Issues and Trends in Behavior Therapy*. Charles C. Thomas, Springfield, IL.

Peterman P.J. (1981) Parenting and environmental considerations. *American Journal of Orthopsychiatry*, **51**, 351–355.

Peters R. De V. & McMahon R.J. (1988) (eds) *Social Learning and Systems Approaches to Marriage and the Family*. Brunner/Mazel, New York.

Pevsner R. (1982) Group parent training versus individual family therapy: an outcome study. *Journal of Behavior Therapy and Experimental Psychiatry*, **13**, 119–122.

Pilisuk M. & Parks S.H. (1980) Structural dimensions of social support groups. *Journal of Psychology*, **106**(2), 157–177.

Pound A. & Mills M. (1985) A pilot evaluation of NEWPIN — home-visiting and befriending scheme in South London. *Newsletter of Association of Child Psychology and Psychiatry*, **7**(4), 13–15.

Pugh G. & De'Ath E. (1984) *The Needs of Parents: Practice and Policy in Parent Education*. Macmillan Education, Basingstoke, Hampshire.

Rauh V.A., Achenbach T.M., Nurcombe B., Howell C.T. & Teti D.M. (1988) Minimizing adverse effects of low birthweight: four-year results of an early interventions program. *Child Development*, **59**, 544–553.

Richman N., Douglas J., Hunt H., Lansdown R. & Levere R. (1985) Behavioural methods in the treatment of sleep disorders — a pilot study. *Journal of Child Psychology and Psychiatry*, **26**, 581–590.

Rickel A.U., Dudley G. & Berman S. (1980) An evaluation of parent-training. *Evaluation Review*, **4**(3), 389–403.

Robin A.L. & Koepke T. (1990) Behavioral assessment and treatment of parent–adolescent conflict. In: Hersen M., Eisler R.M. & Miller P.M. (eds) *Progress in Behavior Modification*, vol. 25, pp. 178–215. Sage Publications, Newbury Park, CA.

Rushton A. (1989) Post-placement services for foster and adoptive parents — support, counselling or therapy? *Journal of Child Psychology and Psychiatry*, **30**, 197–204.

Schaefer C. (1978) *How to Influence Children: A Handbook of Practical Parenting Skills*. Van Nostrand Reinhold, New York.

Schaefer C.E. & Briesmeister J.M. (1989) (eds) *Handbook of Parent Training: Parents as Co-therapists for Children's Behavior Problems*. John Wiley, New York.

Scott G. & Richards M.P.M. (1990) Night waking in infants: effects of providing advice and support for parents. *Journal of Child Psychology and Psychiatry*, **31**, 551–567.

Seifer R., Clark G.N. & Sameroff A.J. (1991) Positive effects of inter-action coaching on infants with developmental disabilities and their mothers. *American Journal of Mental Retardation*, **96**, 1–11.

Seitz V. (1990) Intervention programs for impoverished children: a comparison of educational and family support models. In: Vasta R. (ed) *Annals of Child Development*, vol. 7, pp. 73–103. Jessica Kingsley, London.

Seymour F.W., Brock P., During M. & Poole G. (1989) Reducing sleep disruptions in young children: evaluation of therapist-guided and written information approaches: a brief report. *Journal of Child Psychology and Psychiatry*, **30**, 913–918.

Shearer D.E. & Loftin C.R. (1984) The Portage Project: teaching parents to teach their preschool children in the home. In: Dangel R.F. & Polster R.A. (eds) *Parent Training: Foundations of Research and Practice*, pp. 93–106. Guilford Press, New York.

Shearer M. & Shearer D. (1972) The Portage Project: a model for early childhood education. *Exceptional Children*, **36**, 172–178.

Sherman J., Barker P., Lorimer P., Swinson R. & Factor D.C. (1988) Treatment of autistic children: relative effectiveness of residential, out-patient and home-based interventions. *Child Psychiatry and Human Development*, **19**(2), 109–125.

Showers J. (1992) 'Don't shake the baby': the effectiveness of a prevention program. *Child Abuse and Neglect*, **16**, 11–18.

Sigel I.E. (1985) (ed) *Parental Belief Systems: The Psychological Consequences for Children*. Lawrence Erlbaum Associates, Hillsdale, NJ.

Smith J.E. (1984) Non-accidental injury to children. A review of behavioural interventions. *Behaviour Research and Therapy*, **22**, 331–347.

Smith J.E., Rachman S.J. & Yule B. (1984) Non-accidental injury to children. III Methodological problems of evaluative treatment research. *Behaviour Research and Therapy*, **22**, 367–383.

Spivack G., Platt J.J. & Shure M.B. (1976) *The Problem-solving Approach to Adjustment*. Jossey Bass, San Francisco, CA.

Stevenson J. (1990) (ed) *Health Visitor Based Services for Pre-school Children with Behaviour Problems*. Occasional Papers no. 2. Association for Child Psychology and Psychiatry, London.

Tavormina J.B. (1974) Basic models of parent counselling: a critical review. *Psychological Bulletin*, **81**, 827–835.

Tavormina J.B. (1975) Relative effectiveness of behavioral and reflective group counselling with parents of mentally retarded children. *Journal of Consulting and Clinical Psychology*, **43**, 22–31.

Tavormina J.B., Hampson R.B. & Luscomb R.L. (1976) Participant evaluations of the effectiveness of their parent counselling groups. *Mental Retardation*, **14**, 8–9.

Tharp R.G. (1991) Cultural diversity and treatment of children. *Journal of Consulting and Clinical Psychology*, **59**, 799–812.

Tharp R.G. & Wetzel R.J. (1969) (eds) *Behavior Modification in the Natural Environment*. Academic Press, New York.

Wahler R.G. (1980) The insular mother: her problems in parent–child treatment. *Journal of Applied Behaviour Analysis*, **13**, 207–219.

Wahler R.G. & Dumas J.E. (1984) Changing the observational coding styles of insular and non-insular mothers. In: Dangel R.F. & Polster R.A. (eds) *Foundations of Research and Practice*, pp. 379–416. Guilford, New York.

Wasik B.H., Ramey C.T., Bryant D.M. & Sparling J.J. (1990) A longitudinal study of two early intervention strategies: project CARE. *Child Development*, **61**, 1682–1696.

Webster-Stratton C. (1981) Modification of mother's behaviors and attitudes through a videotape modelling group discussion program. *Behavior Therapy*, **12**, 634–642.

Webster-Stratton C. (1984) Randomized trial of two parent-training programs for families with conduct disordered children. *Journal of Consulting and Clinical Psychology*, **52**, 666–678.

Webster-Stratton C. (1985) The effects of father involvement in parent training for conduct problem children. *Journal of Child Psychology and Psychiatry*, **26**, 801–810.

Webster-Stratton C. (1989) Systematic comparison of consumer satisfaction of three cost-effective parent training programs for conduct problem children. *Behavior Therapy*, **20**, 103–115.

Webster-Stratton C. (1990) Enhancing the effectiveness of self-administered videotape parent training for families with conduct-problem children. *Journal of Abnormal Child Psychology*, **18**, 479−492.

Webster-Stratton C. (1991) Annotation: strategies for helping families with conduct disordered children. *Journal of Child Psychology and Psychiatry*, **32**, 1047−1062.

Webster-Stratton C., Hollinsworth T. & Kolpacoff M. (1989) The long term effectiveness of three cost-effective parent training programs for families with conduct-problem children. *Journal of Consulting and Clinical Psychology*, **57**, 550−553.

Webster-Stratton C., Kolpacoff M. & Hollinsworth T. (1988) Self-administered videotape therapy for families with conduct disordered children: comparisons to two other treatments and a control group. *Journal of Consulting and Clinical Psychology*, **56**, 558−566.

Weist M.D., Ollendick T.H. & Finney J.W. (1991) Toward the empirical validation of treatment targets in children. *Clinical Psychology Review*, **11**, 515−538.

Whalen G.K. & Henker B. (1991) Therapies for hyperactive children: comparisons, combinations and compromises. *Journal of Consulting and Clinical Psychology*, **59**, 126−137.

Wiese M.R.R. & Kramer J.J. (1988) Parent training research: an analysis of the empirical literature 1975−1985. *Psychology in the Schools*, **25**, 325−330.

Wolfe D.A. (1985) Child-abusive parents: an empirical review and analysis. *Psychological Bulletin*, **97**, 462−482.

Wolfe D.A., Sandler J. & Kaufman K. (1981) A competency-based parent training program for child abusers. *Journal of Consulting and Clinical Psychology*, **49**, 633−640.

Wolfe D.A., Edwards B., Manion I. & Koverola C. (1988) Early intervention for parents at risk of child abuse and neglect: a preliminary investigation. *Journal of Consulting and Clinical Psychology*, **56**, 40−47.

Wolke D. (1991) Supporting the development of low birthweight infants. *Journal of Child Psychology and Psychiatry*, **32**, 723−741.

Worland J., Carney R., Milich R. & Grame C. (1980) Does in-home training add to the effectiveness of operant group parent training? A 2 year evaluation. *Child Behavior Therapy*, **2(1)**, 11−24.

World Health Organization (1992) *The ICD-10 Classification of Mental and Behavioral Disorders: Clinical Descriptions and Diagnostic Guidelines*. World Health Organization, Geneva.

Young K.T. (1990) American conceptions of infant development from 1955 to 1984: what the experts are telling parents. *Child Development*, **61**, 17−28.

Yule W. (1975) Teaching psychological principles to non-psychologists: training parents in child management. *Journal of Association of Educational Psychology*, **10**, 5−16.

Yule W. (1989) Parent involvement in the treatment of the school phobic child. In: Schaefer C.E. & Briesmeister J.M. (eds) *Handbook of Parent Training: Parents as Co-therapists for Children's Behavior Problems*, pp. 223−244. John Wiley, New York.

Chapter 54
Individual and Group Psychotherapy

Judith Trowell

HISTORICAL CONTEXT

Individual child psychotherapy probably began with Freud's (1909) report of Little Hans. Von Hug-Hellmuth (1921) observed children's play and was aware that the play was a means of expression; this led to a specific technique for gaining understanding of children through the medium of play. It was developed by Anna Freud (1926–1927, 1946) and Melanie Klein (1932) and developed in a more specific structural fashion by David Levy (1939) and Virginia Axline (1947, 1964) into play therapy.

Psychodynamic psychotherapy and play therapy flourished in the child guidance clinics in the UK and North America in the 1930s and 1940s. The first clinic opened in Boston, US, in 1921, and in 1927 the East London Child Guidance Clinic was established by Emanuel Miller. The climate was probably made suitable by the founding in 1893 of the British Child Study Association, whose interest centred on normal growth and development by observation of the individual child. This work was being carried out all over Europe and the US (Trowell, 1982; McDermott & Char, 1984).

Since the 1950s there has been a plethora of therapeutic interventions: group therapy, behaviour therapy, family therapy, cognitive-behaviour therapy, environmental manipulation and therapy, and many more (Garfield, 1980; Walrond Skinner, 1986). In 1976 Frank considered some of the features that were common to a variety of the psychological therapies, or 'talking treatments'. These were:

> an intense emotionally charged confiding relationship, a specific therapeutic setting, and a rationale or theoretical framework which prescribes the nature of the intervention. These rationales strengthen the therapeutic relationship providing a basis for hope of improvement. They provide opportunities for cognitive and experiential learning often through a highly emotionally charged relationship. This can lead to an increased sense of mastery and encourage patients to work through/ practise what they have learned.

This outline acknowledges the importance of learning — learning knowledge and learning from experience — which in varying degrees seem to be the core of all psychological therapies. The importance of the role of the therapist and the patient's involvement with, and attachment to, the therapist,

is omitted, as is any consideration of the aptitude and skills of the therapist. Tseng and McDermott (1975, 1979) suggested a more detailed formulation of the common elements in therapy. Rutter (1986) emphasized the need to foster autonomy and self-reliance; to develop steps likely to lead to persistence of therapeutic gains; the need for the development of specific therapeutic techniques; the need for an emphasis on focused short-term interventions; the need to consider therapist qualities; and the importance of family and school interventions.

Psychotherapy services for adults and children had been established for about 30 years by the time separate services for adolescents differentiating them from children and adults emerged in the 1970s. At around this time it was recognized that some adolescents had special needs for treatment and regional units were developed alongside outpatient services (Parry Jones, 1984).

Hersov (1986) reviewed the development of the discipline of child psychiatry and the range of therapies available to the child psychiatrist in the second half of the 20th century. Rutter (1986) looked to the future of 'the next thirty years' and debated the issues for the psychological therapies in child and adolescent psychiatry, suggesting they would continue to be important, given the concept of people as social beings as well as collections of brain cells.

Kazdin (1990) acknowledged the problem of precise definition of psychotherapy, and suggested that:

> Psychotherapy includes interventions designed to decrease distress, psychological symptoms and maladaptive behavior, or to improve adaptive and personal functioning through the use of interpersonal interaction, counselling or activities following a specific treatment plan...Treatment focuses on some facet of how clients feel (affect), think (cognition) and act (behavior).

PSYCHODYNAMIC PSYCHOTHERAPY

Psychodynamic psychotherapy is strongly influenced by Freudian psychoanalysis, modified in the UK by object relations theorists (Winnicott, 1958; Bion, 1967; Klein, 1975a,b) and by attachment theory (Bowlby, 1971, 1975), and modified in the US by ego psychology and self-psychology (Freud, 1936; Erikson, 1956; Kohut, 1971; Kernberg, 1975). The therapy is based on working with the patient on the here-

and-now relationship in the light of past history and external relationships. Use is made of unconscious process, defence mechanisms and transference (the mechanism whereby patients transfer on to their therapist, and repeat, previous disturbed or maladaptive relationships).

Individual child psychotherapy refers to one-to-one psycho-dynamic psychotherapy using verbal or play technique; *group psychotherapy* alludes to psychodynamic techniques applied in a group of children or young people, whether related or unrelated.

INTERPERSONAL PSYCHOTHERAPY

Interpersonal psychotherapy (IPT) was articulated as a theory in the field of interpersonal relations by Harry Stack Sullivan (1953). It now focuses on the patient's current life situations (Klerman *et al.*, 1984). It is time-limited, attends to current symptoms and to the interpersonal context associated with depression, and includes a systematic review of relations with current significant others. It has been developed for the treatment of a single disorder — depression — and is influenced by attachment theory and social support systems. The treatment has been modified for use with adolescents (IPT-A) and this is currently being evaluated (Moreau *et al.*, 1991). The therapy has been adapted to address developmental issues common to adolescents, such as separation from parents, exploration of authority in relation to parents, development of dyadic interpersonal relationships with members of the opposite sex, initial experience with the death of a relative or friend, and peer pressures.

GESTALT THERAPY

Largely founded by Perls (1893–1970), a German psycho-analyst, gestalt therapy is part of the humanistic psychologies. It is largely a training in awareness, in improving the individual's contact with him- or herself and the environment. It also emphasizes personal responsibility and gives equal consideration to mind and body. It uses strategies such as shuttling, when the subject moves attention between figure and ground and so focuses around an issue, and unfinished business, when in the here and now the patient repeats a behaviour until the meaning is known. Working with 'splits' involves using an empty chair with which the patient then has a dialogue. Problems are dealt with in the present tense and externalized for increased access by the client/patient (Perls, 1969).

CREATIVE ARTS THERAPIES

The creative arts therapies have developed since the 1970s. Originally designed for patients in hospitals, they rapidly spread to be used for individuals and groups in outpatient and community settings.

Patients are encouraged to express and explore their con-flicts and difficulties using the specified mode. It can be a very powerful experience and emotionally releasing, because of the very direct use of nonverbal material.

Art therapy

Art therapy can be based on behavioural, humanistic, gestalt or psychoanalytic theory, and done individually or in groups. The aim is to reconcile emotional conflicts, foster self-awareness and personal growth and enable the client to find a more comfortable relationship between his or her inner and outer worlds (Kramer, 1972; Dally *et al.*, 1987; Simon, 1992).

Music therapy

Music can serve as a channel of communication. It is a stimulus for verbalization of emotion; it can be a vehicle for the encouragement of interaction in a group; and it can be used with individuals or groups (Nordoff & Robbins, 1977). Music therapy has several goals: (1) to aid in diagnosis and treatment planning; (2) to establish and cultivate socialization; (3) to promote self-confidence; (4) to control hyperactivity; (5) to foster the development of skills; (6) to assist in the correction of speech impairment; and (7) to facilitate the transition from non-verbal to verbal codification systems.

Drama therapy

Drama provides a structured environment through specifying the roles of the therapist and group members and designating physical and material arrangements. The attempts at recon-struction focus on the sensorimotor, the symbolic and the reflective stages from developmental theory. Characters are chosen for parts in the designed drama; acting out of feelings and attitudes is encouraged via a set script or improvization and role-play. The therapist actively participates, attempting to resolve any impasse and restrain free expression where there is a danger of loss of control (Johnson, 1982).

TRANSACTIONAL ANALYSIS

Influenced by psychoanalytic theory, transactional analysis sees personality as comprising three ego states — parent, child and adult. Through role-play the individual ego states are identified and they are used in personal transactions. The patient is guided through sequential learning experiences to replace maladaptive strategies with more productive ways of relating (Berne, 1964).

Phases of treatment

Reisman's (1973) seven principles still stand:
1 A careful assessment of the nature of the child's psycho-logical difficulties is an essential precondition to psycho-therapy. The therapist must discover the actual psychological mechanisms which underline each child's problems rather

than assuming some mechanism on the basis of theoretical considerations.

2 The therapist listens to the child and allows him or her ample opportunity to express feelings and beliefs. This implies both that therapists do not impose their own views and that the therapeutic situation is so structured as to facilitate communication.

3 The therapist communicates an understanding of the child and the wish to be of help.

4 The therapist and the child should define the purpose and goal of their meeting. These are not necessarily the reasons why the child was referred but it is important that the child appreciates that therapy has a point and a focus.

5 The therapist must make clear what is ineffective or inappropriate in the child's behaviour.

6 When dealing with behaviour that is dependent on social interaction, the therapist may modify it by focusing directly on the interaction.

7 Therapists should plan the ending of the treatment when the advantages of ending outweigh the advantages of continuing.

The way that these principles are understood and used varies with the theoretical and conceptual framework of the therapists. It would be appropriate to add to them the need to consider the child or young person's chronological age, developmental status, gender, race and culture through the phases of the intervention and the child or young person's family interest, social context and network.

In the psychodynamic psychotherapies particular emphasis is given to a developmental history, key relationships, transitions such as starting school — primary and secondary — the move into adolescence, separations and losses, and a careful consideration of the psychological mechanisms used and personality organization. (See Boston, 1989: Appendix A for assessment and Appendix B for progress and termination.)

Developing a working therapeutic alliance is an essential step in the therapy and the rate at which this can be achieved with very damaged children who have had very difficult and distressing experiences is what in part determines the length of the intervention. The length may be described as brief — 4 to 6 sessions; contract — usually 10 sessions to 1 year; or openended — subject to review.

TRAININGS

All the psychotherapies require the development of a trusting and confiding relationship, and the release of powerful, intense feelings. Training in each therapeutic modality can be seen in two parts. Firstly, there is the training in the particular form of intervention. This will consist of theoretical input and then supervised experience. Secondly, there is preparation of the therapists themselves. Many therapy trainings have learnt from experience that it is all too easy for therapists to lose their capacity to retain their objectivity when in close human relationships. Therapists can very easily, at times of personal

stress in their own lives, or when the patient's past difficulties resonate closely with their own past, become overly involved and react inappropriately. There is also a considerable risk of inappropriate sexual behaviour and this needs particular awareness on the part of therapists so that they prevent themselves becoming sexually involved. The psychodynamic, transactional, gestalt, art, music and drama therapies require some personal sessions for their trainees to work on their own conflicts and difficulties in order not to inflict them on their patients and to enable them to work freely and effectively.

One suggestion is that the frequency of sessions, with which therapists can work safely, is linked to the frequency of sessions they received themselves during training. To carry out psychoanalytic psychotherapy with children and adolescents, trainees are expected to spend 4 years in 3–5-times weekly personal therapy sessions in order to prepare them to deal objectively, sensitively and empathically with their patients' emotional distress. In some of the other therapeutic modalities, where the frequency of patient sessions is once or twice weekly, once- or twice-weekly personal sessions are required.

The need, or indeed the value, of this personal preparation of the therapist has not been empirically tested. However, individuals become therapists for a wide range of reasons, one of which is a wish to make sense of some aspect of a traumatic event in their own lives. Adversity is part of normal human development and we all mature and grow through these experiences; but, if aspects of the experience fail to be fully integrated into self-awareness, therapists can be influenced by their past experiences without recognizing this. Some form of personal sessions during training would seem to be valuable to guard against this risk to patients.

CLINICAL PRACTICE OF INDIVIDUAL PSYCHODYNAMIC PSYCHOTHERAPY

Psychodynamic psychotherapy can be intensive (3–5 times weekly), non-intensive (usually once weekly), or brief (short-term) focused therapy.

Children and most young people do not bring themselves for therapy and they may or may not agree they want therapy. They are usually aware that they are worried, upset or angry, and that there are problems at nursery school, at school, at home or outside in the community, or a combination of these.

The child or young person may be brought to the therapy or in some cases the therapist goes to the child, such as to the school. The adults responsible for the child need to be involved in the work, partly to ensure their support and commitment, and partly because they have considerable control over and influence on the child, and their way of relating to and expectations of the child will need to change if the child is to be able to change.

Intensive and nonintensive open-ended individual psychoanalytic psychotherapy used to be offered to depressed, angry, unhappy children, and children with phobias, enuresis, encopresis, learning and behaviour problems in mainstream schools. During the 1980s the range of children and young people who could use and benefit from individual psycho-analytic psychotherapy changed. Intensive and lengthy help is now being sought for children and young people who were previously thought to be unlikely to respond. This has required considerable changes in techniques, with much more emphasis on the here-and-now relationships in the therapy room and in the external world and only some linking back to the past. Language has had to change and much greater use is made of nonverbal communication. The outcome has been that many children and young people with a wide range of disturbance — physical, mental, psychological and emotional — now seek help as families and professionals learn that other similar children have benefited (Trowell, 1985).

Children in fostering and adoption settings were the first of these more severely deprived groups to be offered help. These children, whose placements were breaking down after a previous history of other broken placements, were offered therapy to try to help them make sense of their experiences. The children had to struggle to see how they could and did influence events, and to face events where they could not. Experience with such severely deprived children led on to the therapy being offered to even more damaged children as therapists gained increasing confidence. Children who were physically or mentally handicapped were often unable to use the potential they possessed because of their distress, confusion and rage. These children could grow as people even if their minds or bodies were damaged, and could then benefit from their increased capacity to establish relationships (Boston & Szur, 1983).

The 1980s also saw an explosion in recognized cases of child sexual abuse and the rates of diagnosis of severe physical abuse and neglect also increased. Children who had experi-enced severe physical abuse or neglect or sexual abuse, or combinations of these, became an increasing focus of this work. Many of these children are very troubled and may well also be involved in other therapeutic interventions such as family or group work. Some of them are so troubled, confused and damaged that they are unable to think, learn or own their own feelings and have no sense of themselves as individual human beings. Helping them make sense of their experiences is very painful, difficult work.

The challenge of developmental delay and the place of psychoanalytic psychotherapy is also being tackled. This work is also very demanding and difficult and requires new ways of communicating with children who may be shut off in their own world. Evaluation is in progress (Szur & Miller, 1991).

As an example of psychoanalytic therapy I will describe Lucy, aged four and a half years, who had been anally abused for about 2 years by her father. She came to notice because of her very disturbed behaviour when she started nursery class. She was reported to wet and soil and masturbate excessively. She sat under a table and seemed 'cut off'. She did not join in any activities with the other children but did try to draw or do jigsaws. She talked, but often the adults and children could not follow or make sense of what she said. She didn't talk *to* anyone, or listen.

Lucy lived with her mother; her father was out of the household. She came once weekly to the clinic. She was difficult to contain and ran around the clinic and the room, often very frightened and at times very controlling and dicta-torial. She spent long periods in the laboratory and her play was of monsters who attacked her, or of being a powerful, destructive figure, hitting, spitting and kicking. After about 6 months we had the following conversation.

She had stood up and said: 'I can fly'. She flapped her arms. I said that it seemed as though she wished she could fly and she was trying, but it was pretending and in fact she couldn't. She took some paper to draw and said she had drawn lots of poos coming out of a bottom. I wondered if she had thought like flying when things happened to her bottom. She flushed and said: 'How did you know I played with my bottom?' I said that well, boys and girls do play with their bottoms, but she had also had a daddy who had done things to her bottom. I wondered if, when her bottom was touched, she found herself thinking she could disappear — fly. She took the paper and drew a circle and said: 'This is a poo-hole'; and then she drew lots of poos coming out. I said that was perhaps how she had felt: that she was nothing but a poo-hole, with things going in and out, no good, useless, rubbish. She nodded and said: 'Yes, I'm bad, a poo'.

And slowly over the next months she became able to cry, to talk to people, and to listen, and then to learn.

THE METHODS OF THE PSYCHOANALYTIC CHILD PSYCHOTHERAPIST

Although play is an important part of the therapy and toys are provided, play is only one of many ways in which children convey their feelings and thoughts. Communication is what is important rather than play. The therapy needs to occur in a safe place where the child can communicate intense feelings and anxieties. Part of this safety is provided by offering a session at the same time, on the same day, regularly and with the same toys. The therapist seeks to maintain a neutral non-directive attitude to encourage free expression of feelings, both positive and negative. Within this setting the patient's behaviour is closely observed and an active attempt is made to understand the verbal and nonverbal communications. Tiny details may reveal nonverbalized feelings, fantasies and unconscious conflicts, because children often cannot or choose not to reveal in words what is felt but do so in their actions.

An important aspect of the setting is the provision of con-tainment, so that the fears and terrors can be experienced and survived by child and therapist and then discussed. Interpret-ations are the putting into words of the therapist's understand-ing of what the communications in the room have been about. This aims to help patients gain insight into their feelings and behaviour as they arise; and to enable unconscious fantasies, which may have been distorting perception, to become conscious. For change to occur it is recognized that an experience at an emotional level is required. This occurs in the transference where the patient can reexperience earlier crucial interactions, or the lack of them, and then explore what has been happening (Daws & Boston, 1988).

Brief, short-term, dynamic psychotherapy has been particularly explored by Malan (1963) and Sifneos (1987, 1990), and is particularly suited to patients with psychosocial problems, with difficulties in interpersonal relations and with issues of separation and loss. Selection criteria include the ability to circumscribe the presenting complaint, identification of at least one meaningful (give-and-take) relationship, a response to a tentative interpretation, flexible interactions and some psychological mindedness; but above all a wish to change. This method has been used well by particular age groups. Young parents with small children, where there is a problem in feeding or sleeping or toilet training or temper tantrums, can make good use of 4–6 sessions spaced over time. This can be simply organized as an Under-Fives Counselling Service that does not involve the full consequences of becoming psychiatric patients. Similarly, young people of 16–22 years can make good use of a small number of sessions in a Young People's Counselling Service to help them with normal adolescent turmoil and clarify more serious difficulties.

Similar techniques can be used in a number of settings. Children and young people in hospital can be helped to stabilize their diabetes, or to withstand serious surgery such as renal transplant, heart surgery and bone marrow transplants. The aim is to help these children and young people with their emotional distress, so that by understanding the conflicts, their rage and sadness, they can feel less powerless and respond more appropriately.

Crisis work can also draw on these skills but particular skills are needed in addition, such as immediate debriefing and the importance of linking with other survivors of similar disasters (Pynoos & Nader, 1989/1990).

Counselling has grown considerably as a therapeutic intervention. It draws on a range of theoretical frameworks, particularly psychodynamic and cognitive-behavioural. Counselling may be brief or long-term and may be general and supportive or focused on a topic. Counsellors are frequently in schools, in universities or higher-education settings. Where there are personal or family problems, many children and young people find the stress of academic demands more than they can manage and seek support from an objective, empathic outsider to reflect on the issues and problems they face. Many can then make their own decisions and move forward; others need to move on to more specific therapy.

Topic-focused counselling can cover issues like bereavement, rape, diagnosis of a life-threatening illness and family breakdown. The child or young person can talk over the issues with someone familiar with the particular complexities of their problem.

Client-centred counselling is a particular style based on the ideas of Rogers (1951). Therapist attitudes of genuineness, unconditional positive regard and empathic understanding are used to enable individuals to reorganize their subjective world so as to integrate and actualize the self. The key process is to facilitate the experience of becoming a more spontaneous, autonomous, confident person.

CLINICAL MODIFICATION OF PSYCHODYNAMIC PSYCHOTHERAPY

Psychodynamic treatments have been modified in several ways. Some have been described above (see sections on interpersonal psychotherapy, creative arts therapy and transactional analysis). Developments in using play as the medium of communication, and groups as the setting of therapy, are of particular importance for children.

Play itself is not a therapy, but many children use their play to repeat previous experiences or to try out anticipated experiences. This can involve the use of toys in *creative play* — paints, drawings, plasticine, etc.; *expressive play* — cars, houses, dolls; *fantasy play* — wars, goodies and baddies of all kinds; and *educational play*. Play can also involve large pieces of apparatus like climbing frames, trees, etc. *Play therapy* provides a limited range of toys in a safe setting and the therapist will comment on the play, clarifying the activity. The aim is to put into words what is being enacted, and thus enable children to comment on, question and explore the clarification, and in this way begin to think over their experiences and make sense of them. The range of toys may be greater than in psychodynamic child psychotherapy, e.g. sand and water play and board games for older children, since the aim is to encourage the development of a confiding relationship and the verbalization of personal problems.

EDUCATIONAL THERAPY

Educational therapy uses psychodynamic and cognitive-behavioural theories. Children and young people whose problems are particularly focused upon educational difficulties can respond to this form of help. Educational tasks are tackled and successful accomplishment leads to enhanced self-esteem and self-confidence. Some of the material used — such as interesting stories, literature or poems or particular mathematical difficulties — can reveal areas of anxiety and conflict and can then be sensitively approached and discussed by the therapist. In this way, blocks to learning and emotional growth and understanding can be resolved.

Case management

Case management is another supplement to psychotherapy which is of particular value in childhood. Over a prolonged period of active involvement in therapy it becomes apparent that working as the child's therapist may not leave the professional in the most clear-minded and objective position to undertake the case management. Therapy with a child may be only one part of therapeutic intervention: other children or parents may also be in treatment. There may be issues of education or further investigations that need attention during therapy. Sadly and increasingly often, problems of child protection or family breakdown lead to issues of placement while a child is in therapy, and therefore to a need for case management and possibly legal intervention. Therapy can be preserved, even if confidentiality needs to be broken over child protection issues, if the therapist can ask a case manager to undertake the work required in managing the child, family and network issues. It is very difficult for one person to carry the roles of both individual therapist and case manager.

GROUP THERAPY

Group psychotherapies are important for children. There are two main types: experiential and educative groups.

Group therapy is based on the work of Foulkes (1964) and the Institute of Group Analysis, who insist on the total group interactions being used in the therapy. They emphasize that the group should become group-centred, not leader-centred. The emphasis moves from talking to acting and doing, from content-centred to behaviour in action in a spontaneous rather than controlled manner. The focus is on the present, not the past.

A basic law of group dynamics is that collectively they constitute the very norm from which individuals then deviate. Foulkes (1964) believed that problems arose always within a network of relationships and never within the individual in isolation. The group leader must use the tendency for progressive integration of the group to allow aggressive energies to be set free in order to serve constructive ends. Foulkes (1964) used a sociobiological model and paid great attention to foreground and background, and suggested concepts such as group-specific factors, socialization mirror phenomena, condenser phenomena and exchange, group therapeutic factors and the group as support and communication. The helpful concept of a group matrix is suggested, and the fact that the group matrix preexists the group and dynamically evolves during the life of the group as the group matures.

Experiential groups

Experiential groups are based on the work of Bion (1961). They use the psychoanalytic phenomena of projection and transference as the basis of the therapeutic intervention. The leader comments on what is thought to be going on in the group in the here and now. The concept used is that of basic assumptions: these are patterns of behaviour that grip the group, dependence, pairing, and fight or flight. They make reality interventions difficult, and so to work and learn is a constant struggle for the leader and the group.

The group is either closed, consisting of 6–10 participants who meet regularly for a specific number of sessions, or it may be open, meeting regularly, and members join and leave as is appropriate for them. The group may have one leader or two.

Usually groups consist of participants with a range of problems, and of mixed gender.

Educative groups

Educative groups use a cognitive-behavioural approach and may also use a psychodynamic approach. Examples include social skills groups and groups focusing on a specific problem, such as child sexual abuse groups for survivors of sexual abuse, disaster groups for survivors, groups for children whose parents have divorced, children whose parents are alcoholic, children with cystic fibrosis, diabetes and sickle cell anaemia. The possibilities are endless.

Psychodrama

Psychodrama is another form of group therapy based on the work of Moreno (1964), who believed difficulties arose because of individuals' need to maintain social roles. In the group the principal actor dramatizes his or her conflict and problems by setting the scene and then involving other group members in playing the key roles in a personal drama. Role reversal is when another member plays the identified individual and the principal actor plays other roles. The experience is emotionally very powerful and needs careful exploration of feelings and perceptions with adequate time to ensure the conclusion is beneficial.

Group composition

The composition of groups for children and adolescents needs skilled and careful planning. Participants with a mixture of difficulties can enrich the experience and differences can be worked on. Groups with similar problems feel less isolated and sharing their experiences with others in a similar position can be helpful. Self-esteem and self-confidence can be enhanced in either setting and depend primarily on the skill of the leader or leaders.

With adolescent groups it can be particularly helpful to have two leaders, one male and one female, although some young people are very vocal about their preferences and they may need to be respected. Groups for children and young people with a broad age span can be problematic. Groups tend to work better if banded by age, with 3–4 and 5–6 as the youngest and probably 4–6 children per group. Primary schoolchildren can be grouped together in groups of 6–10. Children passing through puberty (10–14 years of age) may be better in single-gender groups. Groups for young people over 14 years may be single-sex or mixed, partly depending on the reason for setting up the group. Play tends to be the means of communication for young children.

Indications for group therapy

Most difficulties experienced by children and young people can be worked on in group psychotherapy. Not all children and young people are suitable for group psychotherapy. Some require some individual sessions with the leader prior to being able to join the group. Markedly aggressive or disruptive behaviour or florid psychoses may be reasons for not suggesting group therapy. Withdrawn isolated individuals, if they can be encouraged, can do well in group therapy. It is sensible to keep participants at a roughly similar level of intelligence: groups for mentally handicapped individuals can be very useful, but too wide a discrepancy in the group membership limits the work that can be done.

In parallel with the groups for children, it is often extremely helpful to run carers' groups. This maximizes the possibility of change and increases the commitment of the carers to bring the child to the group.

In some instances, such as death of a parent, murder of one parent by another or child abuse affecting all the siblings, it can be very effective to work with the siblings as a group. This may be a focused piece of work, after which the siblings can be considered as individuals with their own needs.

OUTCOME

The question once was: does psychotherapy work? This has given way to the more appropriate questions: which psychotherapy works, with which sorts of patients, with which sort of problems, as practised by what sort of therapist?

In adult psychotherapy there has been considerable psychotherapy outcome research and the lessons learnt have begun to bear fruit in the field of child and adolescent psychotherapy. The rather nihilistic view that no therapy could effect change has begun to be moderated. Heinicke and Strassman (1975) stressed the need to assess specific variables that affect process and outcome in therapy. They delineated key methodological issues in psychotherapy evaluation research. These include: inclusion and exclusion criteria; careful baseline assessment; the need to control for a variety of variables such as age, sex and IQ; the need for homogeneity among treatment groups that are age-appropriate to the initial questions asked; the nature of the therapist and how therapists are assigned to children; and the need to have follow-up assessments made longitudinally after treatment to evaluate 'sleeper' effects.

These issues have been taken seriously. Kolvin *et al.* (1981) studied different interventions for maladjusted children. They studied neurotic and conduct disorders at two different age levels: children of 7—8 (the juniors), and children of 11—12 (the seniors).

Children were identified by screening the population and then the subjects and controls were given a battery of measures for assessment and follow-up. Children were allocated randomly to one of four conditions — (1) control; (2) parent/teacher consultations with a social worker; (3) group therapy (as play for juniors or discussion for seniors); (4) nurture work and behaviour modification for juniors and behaviour modification for seniors. The outcome in general was that there were significantly greater changes in the juniors and seniors in the

group therapy and behaviour modification groups than in the parent/teacher consultations or the controls.

Kolvin *et al.* (1988) go on to argue that previous studies where waiting-list groups or drop-out groups have been used as controls have been unhelpful since many waiting-list patients seek alternative sources of help and drop-out cases were almost certainly not similar to cases that sustain treatment.

Shaffer (1984) reviews the research issues. He notes the number of psychotherapy outcome studies that have emerged in adult psychotherapy research and comments on how the same and different considerations need to be considered in child psychotherapy outcome research. The use of controls presents many problems, including the ethical dilemma, the problem of ascribing meaning if drop-outs are used as controls and the implications of random allocation. Selection of subjects is another difficult area and the solution offered is to match subjects by diagnoses. The impact of parental and family involvement alongside the psychotherapy being evaluated is another important variable to be considered; as are therapist characteristics and the intensity and duration of the therapy. Shaffer goes on to discuss how and when outcome should be measured, and to draw attention to the need for clarity about the theoretical model and method of application being used in the therapeutic intervention under evaluation, with the need for a manual and checks over time.

Casey and Berman (1985) reviewed 75 studies published between 1952 and 1983. They used effect size to compare studies. A positive effect size indicates that the treated group achieved better outcomes and a negative effect size indicates that the control group had a more favourable outcome. They reported that the average outcome of children receiving therapy was more than two-thirds of a standard deviation better than that of untreated children. They also showed that behavioural therapies appeared to have substantially larger effects than nonbehavioural, but this may have been due to difference in outcome measures. Behavioural therapies were more likely to be evaluated by outcome measures that were very similar to activities during treatment. Measures from observers, therapists, parents and subject performance produced effects significantly larger than those from teachers' ratings and children's self-report. The forms of therapy used and evaluated were behavioural in more than half the studies and the other therapies were client-centred therapy, dynamic therapy and mixed techniques. There was a small number of therapies that were too unusual or unclear to include. Individual and group therapy was used and there were no significant differences between them.

Dulcan (1984) considers brief psychotherapy with children and their families. Brief means a range of lengths from 1 to 20 sessions, and those considered use either psychodynamic or educational theoretical frameworks. Methodological problems made assessing outcome difficult. Predictions of good outcome seemed to be high motivation, absence of severe psychopathology and recent onset of symptoms. Therapists need to be experienced and motivated to work in a focused manner. Optimum duration remains unclear, as does the question of whether it should be a fixed contract or renegotiable.

Heinicke and Ramsey Klee (1986) considered the effects of frequency of sessions in psychodynamic psychotherapy with children. The children were in three groups. Two of the groups came from a previous study where the results were that, 2 years after the end of treatment, children seen 4 times weekly showed a greater rate of improvement in reading than those seen once weekly. The third group consisted of children, matched for age and IQ with the previous samples, who received a year of once-weekly and then a year of four-times-weekly treatment. The follow-up was a year after treatment ended, and a range of assessments were used at the beginning and end of treatment. When seen once a week, children showed a significant improvement in reading rate; however, the children who in the second year were seen four times weekly showed a significantly greater improvement in reading over the year after the end of treatment. Overall, the study showed that in the longer term the frequency of psychodynamic psychotherapy sessions did affect the flexibility of adaption and the capacity for relationships as well as the rate of reading improvement. Educational facilities were not different between groups.

Kazdin (1990) reviews the effectiveness of child and adolescent psychotherapy. He points out that mental health problems in children and adolescents are extensive and purchasers of health care are pressing for clarification of effectiveness and the choice of which therapy for which problem for individual clients. He explores the meaning of 'effective': is it reduction of symptoms, improvement in adjustment at home or in the community, an increase in self-reported positive mood, or evaluations by relatives or friends? He urges the need for a high level of specificity in research to look at specific interventions for specified problems, bearing in mind the age and cognitive development of the patients.

A metaanalysis by Weiss *et al.* (1987) examined 100 controlled studies in children aged 4–18 years. It emerged that trained therapists were equally effective with children and adolescents, while students and others were more effective with younger children. Adolescents presented students with more difficulties and the therapy was less effective.

The issue of comorbidity is an interesting one. Specific research into therapy can focus on homogeneous groups of patients but many children meet criteria for more than one disorder. The implications for selection, administration and evaluation of treatment need consideration. The evaluation of combined treatment modalities is needed.

An important review article is that by Barrnett *et al.* (1991) which considers outcome and effectiveness of individual child psychotherapy over the years 1963–1989. It is based on treatments using verbal or play mode, not behavioural or cognitive-behavioural interventions. In their view, psychotherapy research requires: (1) an acceptable level of competence in the skill of the therapist; (2) equivalent skill across all therapists; (3) consistency in applying the skills throughout the treatment trial; and (4) fully described procedures similarly applied by all therapists.

The authors looked at studies where there were a group of children or adolescents receiving individual psychotherapy, where there was at least one comparison group and the study did not focus entirely on cognitive-behavioural, family, group or psychopharmacological methods. They considered 43 studies and these could be grouped into five categories: (1) psychotherapy versus no treatment or drop-out; (2) psychotherapy versus other treatment; (3) therapy variables; (4) patient variables; and (5) therapist variables.

In the first group, conclusions were difficult because of methodological flaws. In the second group individual psychotherapy was found to be equivalent to other forms of therapy in more than half; in about one-third other forms of treatment were superior. In the third group, individual was compared with group psychotherapy, but methodological flaws made conclusions impossible. Studies looking at therapy, patient and therapist variables yielded the same ambiguity because of lack of adherence to basic methodological standards.

Barrnett and colleagues highlight the problems overall as: (1) poor inclusion or exclusion criteria; (2) lack of specification of the characteristics of the therapy and the therapist; (3) poor control groups and poor matching or lack of comparison between control and treatment groups; and (4) errors in the measurement process, unreliable or invalid measures, non-standardized measures or raters not blind.

They concluded that many questions regarding child and adolescent psychotherapy, including efficiency, remain untested, in contrast to the field of adult psychotherapy.

CONCLUSIONS

Outcome research in the field of child and adolescent psychotherapy has much to learn from the adult work, but in addition there are considerable differences that create added problems. Single case studies continue to be the most frequent published accounts of psychodynamic psychotherapy, whether this be individual or group therapy. Attempts are being made to evaluate psychodynamic psychotherapy for children and adolescents but there are still real problems over random allocation, no-treatment control groups, standardized therapeutic interventions and measurement of therapist characteristics that result in very slow progress towards outcome research in the sphere of psychodynamic psychotherapy for children and adolescents.

There is, in addition, a problem that has not yet been resolved in adult psychotherapy research. Difficulties continue in clarifying which aspect of psychotherapy with adults leads to its effectiveness in alleviating distress and disability. Frank (1973) suggests that much of the effectiveness of psychotherapy depends on attributes possessed by all schools. They all combat the patient's demoralization by alleviating specific symptoms of subjective distress and disordered behaviour and employ measures to restore self-confidence and help patients find more effective ways of mastering problems. Frank states that the achievement of these aims requires a conceptual framework and certain activities linked to it. But, he adds, the specific content of these may be largely irrelevant.

To some extent this is confirmed by Wallerstein (1986). The

Menninger Foundation project looked at adults treated with full psychoanalysis or psychoanalytic psychotherapy, and the benefit to the patients did not depend on the application of a theoretical model. Many patients benefited considerably despite incomplete treatment; more of the patients changed on the basis of designedly supportive interventions and mechanisms than had been expected or predicted; the treatments carried more supportive elements than originally intended; and these supportive elements accounted for more of the changes achieved than had been anticipated.

Both Frank and Wallerstein seem to conclude that the important therapeutic agents of change are aspects of the relationship between patients and therapists.

Fonagy and Higgitt (1989) have made a useful contribution to the debate in the adult field and they set out an action plan. They propose a large observational study across many centres, using pre- and posttherapy measures, looking at psychological functioning, objective functioning, client satisfaction, relative satisfaction, as well as therapeutic detail and the patient–therapist relationship. Perhaps a similar model can be developed in the child and adolescent field.

The enormous energy and creativity that have gone into adapting psychodynamic psychotherapy for an increasing range of children and adolescents now need to be channelled into outcome research. Clinical work with very distressed and troubled children, adolescents and their families is an area of great interest. It is now recognized that interventions in childhood and adolescence can bring short- and long-term benefits. Psychodynamic individual and group therapy should join in the kind of outcome studies currently being conducted in other therapies such as family therapy and cognitive-behavioural therapy.

REFERENCES

Axline V.M. (1947) *Play Therapy: The Inner Dynamics of Childhood.* Houghton Miffin, New York.

Axline V.M. (1964) *Dibs: In Search of Self.* Gollancz, London.

Barrnett R.J., Docherty J.P. & Frommelt S.M. (1991) Special article: a review of child psychotherapy research since 1963. *Journal of the American Academy of Child and Adolescent Psychiatry,* **30**, 1–14.

Berne E. (1964) *Games People Play: The Psychology of Human Relationships.* Grove Press, New York.

Bion W.R. (1961) *Experiences in Groups.* Tavistock Publications, London.

Bion W.R. (1967) *Second Thoughts.* Aronson, New York.

Boston M. (1989) In search of a methodology for evaluating psychoanalytic psychotherapy with children. *Journal of Child Psychotherapy,* **15**, 19–50.

Boston M. & Szur R. (1983) *Psychotherapy with Severely Deprived Children.* Routledge & Kegan Paul, London.

Bowlby J. (1971) *Attachment and Loss: vol. 1. Attachment.* Penguin Books, Harmondsworth, Middlesex.

Bowlby J. (1975) *Attachment and Loss: vol. 2. Separation.* Penguin Books, Harmondsworth, Middlesex.

Casey R. & Berman J. (1985) The outcome of psychotherapy with children. *Psychological Bulletin,* **98**, 388–400.

Dally T., Case C., Schaverien J., Weir F., Halliday P., Nowell Hill P. & Waller D. (1987) *Images of Art Therapy: New Developments in Theory and Practice.* Tavistock Publications, London.

Daws D. & Boston M. (1988) *The Child Psychotherapist.* Karnac Books. (Maresfield Library), London.

Dulcan M. (1984) Brief psychotherapy with children and their families: the state of the art. *Journal of American Academy of Child Psychiatry,* **23**, 544–551.

Erikson E.M. (1956) The problem of ego identity. *Journal of the American Psychoanalytical Association,* **4**, 56–121.

Fonagy P. & Higgitt A. (1989) Evaluating the performance of departures of psychotherapy. *Psychoanalytic Psychotherapy,* **4**(2), 121–153.

Foulkes S.S. (1964) *Therapeutic Group Analysis.* George Allen & Unwin, London.

Frank J. (1973) *Persuasion and Healing: A Comparable Study of Psychotherapy.* John Hopkins University Press, London.

Frank J. (1976) Recognition of morale and behaviour change. In: Burton A. (ed) *What Makes Behaviour Change Possible?* Brunner/Mazel, New York.

Freud A. (1926–1927) Introduction to the technique of child analysis. Reprinted in: *The Psychoanalytic Treatment of Children.* Imago, London, 1946.

Freud A. (1936) *The Ego and the Mechanisms of Defense.* International Universities Press, New York.

Freud A. (1946) *The Psychoanalytic Treatment of Children.* International Universities Press, New York.

Freud S. (1909) *Analysis of a phobia in a 5-year-old child.* Standard edition 10. Hogarth Press, London.

Garfield S.C. (1980) *Psychotherapy: An Eclectic Approach.* Wiley, New York.

Heinicke C. & Ramsey Kee D. (1986) Outcome of child psychotherapy as a function of frequency of sessions. *Journal of the American Academy of Child Psychiatry,* **25**, 247–253.

Heinicke C.M. & Strassman L.H. (1975) Towards more effective research on child psychotherapy. *Journal of the American Academy of Child Psychiatry,* **14**, 561–588.

Hersov L. (1986) Child psychiatry in Britain: the last 30 years. *Journal of Child Psychology and Psychiatry,* **27**, 781–802.

Hug-Hellmuth H. von (1921) Zur Technik der Kinderanalyse. *International Zeitschriff für Psychoanalyse,* **7**, 179–197.

Johnson E. (1982) Principles and techniques in drama therapy. *International Journal of Arts and Psychotherapy,* **9**, 83–90.

Kazdin A. (1990) Psychotherapy for child and adolescent. *Annual Review of Psychology,* **41**, 21–51.

Kernberg O. (1975) *Borderline Conditions and Pathological Narcissism.* Aronson, New York.

Klein M. (1932) *The Psychoanalysis of Children.* Hogarth Press, London.

Klein M. (1975a) *Love, Guilt and Reparation and Other Works, 1921–1945.* Hogarth Press, London.

Klein M. (1975b) *Envy and Gratitude and Other Works, 1946–1963.* Hogarth Press, London.

Klerman G., Weissman M., Rounsaville B. & Chevron E. (1984) *Interpersonal Psychotherapy of Depression.* Basic Books, New York.

Kohut H. (1971) *The Analysis of the Self.* International Universities Press, New York.

Kolvin I., Garside R.F., Nicol A.R., Macmillan A., Wolsrenholme E. & Leitch S.M. (1981) *Help Starts Here: The Maladjusted Child in the Ordinary School.* Tavistock Publications, London.

Kolvin I., Garside R.F., Nicol A.R., Macmillan A., Wolsrenholme E. & Leitch S.M. (1988) Psychotherapy is effective. *Journal of the Royal Society of Medicine,* **81**, 261–266.

Kramer E. (1972) *Art as Therapy with Children.* Schocken, New York.

Levy D. (1939) Release therapy. *American Journal of Orthopsychiatry,* **9**, 731–736.

McDermott J. & Char W. (1984) Stage related models of psychotherapy with children. *Journal of the American Academy of Child Psychiatry,* **23**, 537–543.

Malan D.H. (1963) *A Study of Brief Psychotherapy.* Tavistock Publications, London.

Moreau D., Mufson L., Weissman M. & Klerman G. (1991) Interpersonal psychotherapy for adolescent depression: description of modification and preliminary application. *Journal of the American Academy of Child and Adolescent Psychiatry,* **30**(4), 642−651.

Moreno J.L. (1964) *Introduction to Psychodrama,* vol. 1 (3rd edn.). Beacon House, Beacon, New York.

Nordoff P. & Robbins C. (1977) *Creative Music Therapy.* John Day, New York.

Parry Jones W. (1984) Adolescent psychiatry in Britain: a personal view of its development and present position. *Bulletin of the Royal College of Psychiatrists,* **8**, 230−233.

Perls F.S. (1969) *Gestalt Therapy Verbatim.* Real People Press, Moab, UT.

Pynoos R. & Nader K. (1989/1990) *Mental Health Disturbances in Children Exposed to Disaster. Prevention Intervention Strategies.* Expanded version of a paper commissioned by the American Academy of Child and Adolescent Psychiatry Prevention Project.

Reisman J.M. (1973) *Principles of Psychotherapy with Children.* Wiley, New York.

Rogers C. (1951) *Client Centred Therapy in Current Practice: Implications and Theory.* Houghton Mifflin, New York.

Rutter M. (1986) Child psychiatry: looking ahead 30 years. *Journal of Child Psychology and Psychiatry,* **27**, 803−840.

Shaffer D. (1984) Notes on psychotherapy research amongst children and adolescents. *Journal of the American Academy of Child Psychiatry,* **23**, 552−561.

Sifneos P.E. (1987) *Short Term Dynamic Psychotherapy Evaluation and Technique* (2nd edn.). Plenum Medical, New York.

Sifneos P.E. (1990) Short term dynamic psychotherapy in Boston, MA (USA), 1954−1989. *World Psychiatric Association Bulletin,* **1**, 34−38.

Simon M.R. (1992) *The Symbolism of Style: Art as Therapy.* Tavistock/ Routledge, London.

Sullivan H.S. (1953) *The Interpersonal Theory of Psychiatry.* Norton, New York.

Szur R. & Miller S. (eds) (1991) *Extending Horizons: Psychoanalytic Psychotherapy with Children, Adolescents and Families.* Karnac Books, London.

Trowell J. (1982) Over 50 years: child and adolescent psychiatrists in the community. *British Journal of Clinical and Social Psychiatry,* **1**, 67−71.

Trowell J. (1985) The relevance of current clinical practice in child psychotherapy to child psychiatry. *Psychodynamic Psychotherapy,* **1**, 1−12.

Tseng W. & McDermott J. (1975) Psychotherapy, historical roots, universal elements and cultural variations. *American Journal of Psychiatry,* **132**, 378−384.

Tseng W. & McDermott J. (1979) Functional family classification: a proposal. *Journal of the American Academy of Child Psychiatry,* **18**, 22−43.

Wallerstein R. (1986) *Forty two Lives in Treatment: A Study of Psychoanalysis and Psychotherapy.* Guilford Press, New York.

Walrond Skinner S. (1986) *Dictionary of Psychotherapy.* Routledge & Kegan Paul, London.

Weiss J.R., Weiss R., Alicke M.D. & Kloty M. (1987) Effectiveness of psychotherapy with children and adolescents, metaanalytic findings for clinicians. *Journal of Consulting and Clinical Psychology,* **55**, 542−549.

Winnicott D.W. (1958) *Collected Papers: Through Paediatrics to Psychoanalysis.* Tavistock Publications, London.

Chapter 55
Family Therapy

Gill Gorell Barnes

WHAT IS FAMILY THERAPY?

The term family therapy encompasses three things: an observational philosophy, an approach to treating problems in families and a number of methods of treatment. It considers problems in the context both of intimate relationships and of the wider social network of which the family is a part. The aim of treatment is to bring about a change in interactions between dysfunctionally connected parts of a social system. The size of the system and its composition will differ depending on the therapist's definition of the context of the problem, the model of therapy being used or the stage the therapy has reached.

The identified problem may be defined within the context of a number of overlapping social systems: the family household; the extended family; and institutions with whom household members have daily contact such as schools or doctors, health services and other professional services that may be concerned about the family. In recognition of the attention paid to these wider systems reference is often made not to family therapy but to systemic therapy or the systemic approach.

THE SYSTEMIC APPROACH

The principles of the systemic approach underlie all models of therapy used within the broad heading of family therapy and may be summarized as follows:

1 People in families are intimately connected, and focusing on those connections may be a more valid way to understand and promote change in problem-related behaviour than focusing on the perspective of any one individual.

2 People living in close proximity over time set up patterns of interaction made up of relatively stable sequences of interaction.

3 The patterns of interaction, belief and behaviour that therapists observe and address can be understood both as cause and effect of the problem — the 'fit' between the problem and the family.

4 Problems within patterns of family life are related to inappropriate adaptation to some environmental influence or change, either realized or anticipated (Cooklin & Gorell Barnes, 1992).

Change is always conceptualized at two levels — that of the presenting problem and that of the relationship pattern with which it is connected.

Widely differing definitions of the activity of treatment exist (Dare, 1985). A definition that has found agreement among clinicians who are in addition researchers attempting to assess the clinical treatment process runs as follows.

> Family therapy is: any psychotherapeutic endeavour that explicitly focuses on altering the interactions between or among family members and seeks to improve the functioning of the family as a unit, or its subsystems and/or the functioning of individual members of the family. This is the goal regardless of whether or not an individual is identified as 'the patient'. Family therapy typically involves face to face work with more than one family member ... although it may involve only a single member for the entire course of treatment (Gurman *et al.*, 1986, pp. 565–566).

In child psychiatry the unit of treatment will rarely be less than two people, although in exceptional circumstances, such as when a child's parents have died or when a child is moving from one family to another, systemic work with the child alone, exploring his or her beliefs and feelings in relation to the changing contexts of which he or she is a part, may take place for a short period (Jenkins & Asen, 1992). Adolescents can also find this approach welcome.

ENVIRONMENTAL INFLUENCE AND FAMILY LIFE

In the last decade much research into family life and the onset of different forms of psychological illness has explored the impact of stressful life events in terms of the *meanings* that these events are given by individuals, and the impact of these meanings on subsequent choices of relationship (Brown, 1990, 1991). Patterns of childhood deprivation and the attribution of negative meaning to subsequent life events may predispose to continuity of negative experience within a lifetime of an individual or between the generations. However, these and other studies (Quinton & Rutter, 1984; Rutter, 1987a,b) have also looked at how former patterns of deprivation can be changed by subsequent intimate relationships. Such studies provide evidence on a broader scale for the clinical hypothesis that what people believe on the basis of their former life experience is intimately connected to their current overall well-being, to the choices they make and to their capacity to respond with resilience or helplessness in the face of fresh life stress.

Long-term effects of family experience

The long-term effect of family patterns, whether positive or negative, is obviously a question of great importance to all professionals who work with families and have the aim of intervening in systems contributing to problems in children. Maccoby (1980) argued that the main effect of family experience on social development is not the learning of specific behaviours for children growing up, but instead the lasting influences that come from the establishment of modes of interaction with other people; patterns of feeling, thinking and behaving; and from the acquisition of particular patterns of adaptation to changing life circumstances. She suggested that children learn patterns or principles of relating, rather than specific behaviours. These patterns have effects on self-concept, on processes of identification, and on the development of a sustained pattern of social interaction. In particular, dysfunction develops in relation to aggression, quarrelling and the inability to set up mechanisms within the family for problem-solving (Rutter, 1984).

Family therapists look not only at what has brought about behaviour that is considered a problem but by whom it is considered a problem (see Chapter 5). Why is it a problem at this time? In relation to what other events in the lives of members of the family is the problem located? Each problem is likely to have a historical as well as a current dimension in terms of the families' perception of life events. Assessment therefore involves joint appraisal by family and therapist of how these areas were handled in the past; why former solutions do not work in the current context; what new dimensions of family pattern the current problem is challenging; and where the family see that their own resources are inadequate to meet the changes required. This provides a map of family resources and constraints on thinking or action which helps the clinician plan intervention realistically.

FAMILY SYSTEMS AND SOCIAL CHANGE

Early family therapy training was based on a theory of the family as a stable two-parent social system that remained together over time. However, this has changed in the last decade. The many major life transitions experienced through economic pressure, particularly drastic changes in employment patterns and lifestyle following migration, has challenged this notion of a family in a regulated society — functionally organized at different complementary levels. Within the UK, attention now additionally needs to be paid to families formed by fostering and late adoption (see Chapter 16), and to the multiple serial transitions experienced by many children following divorce (see Chapter 12). Lone parenthood, serial

cohabitation and step-families are three forms of family life involving many transitional experiences which are receiving further attention within a systemic framework. The wider changes in patterns of cohabitation, child-bearing and marriage have also led to new thinking about what constitutes a family. The diversity of race and culture within UK society has led to wider recognition of many functional structures for bringing up children, and greater respect for what is unfamiliar among professionals treating families.

Family therapy teaching and research, therefore, have moved towards considering diversity of process in family life, and away from ideas of family normality and pathology. Assumptions based on the stability of family life and the internal coherence of systems patterned over time (which developed in the 1960s) have to be reconsidered in the light of the transitions and disruptions experienced by many families seen in clinical settings in the 1990s. The question of transfer of behaviour, ideas and beliefs from one set of family patterns into others, such as step-families and foster and adoptive families, is now raising interest from researchers in widely differing fields (Reiss, 1988; Sroufe & Fleeson, 1988; Wynne, 1988). However, these transfers have not yet received systematic attention.

Dimensions of family life

Whereas in 1980 a number of studies on the dimensions of family life addressed by therapists showed a common focus on affect, communication, alliances, boundaries and discipline (Gurman & Kniskern, 1981), this may well be different for child psychiatrists in the 1990s. Child psychiatrists are likely to be presented with acute problems of family life, often requiring decisions about whether families can stay together at all, or how a new semblance of family structure can be created for a child. Studies cited here therefore refer to aspects of family interaction that correlate with family health in two-parent intact families studied in Eurocentric contexts (Lewis *et al.*, 1976; Loader *et al.*, 1981; Kinston & Loader, 1984, 1988; Kinston *et al.*, 1987a,b). Few studies relating health to families with different structures due to ethnicity, migration or other transitions appear to have been published (but see Tomlinson, 1983, and Nettles & Pleck, in press, for reviews of findings and issues).

Why see the family at all? An empirical basis for family therapy

In reviewing 20 years of outcome studies, Gurman & Kniskern (1981) concluded that: 'existing evidence from controlled studies of nonbehavioural marital and family therapies suggests that such treatments are often effective beyond chance' (p. 745). Assessment of outcome suggested an overall improvement rate of over 70% in families treated by the methods generally described below. A positive effect on patients was revealed, whether measured either by family interaction or by the behaviour of identified patients. Recent metaanalyses of 19 studies comparing family therapy with other treatment approaches found that patients treated using a family approach did better than patients receiving alternative treatment, minimal treatment or no treatment (Markus *et al.*, 1990). While such data do not cite the structure of families treated, and do not discuss the effective components of treatment, they none the less establish a crude empirical base for working this way.

The following brief history of the development of family therapy in the UK in the context of systems theory takes recent changes in the family and its impact on therapy into account.

FAMILY THERAPY AS AN APPROACH, 1945-1978

Systems thinking and the development of a holistic perspective

The concepts that underlie the collective title of general systems theory were originally developed by Von Bertalanffy (1950) in response to dilemmas arising in the biological sciences during the 1920s. His dissatisfaction lay with the reductionistic mechanistic traditions of science in which events were perceived and explained as linear series of cause-and-effect chains, each intended to unearth a causative antecedent event. His alternative proposition was that scientists should attend to the more general principles that may be used to explain aspects of biological processes leading to increasing complexity of organization in systems. He suggested studying the logical structure, pattern and form of systems organization as the unifying principle of science, which would provide a framework of general theory, allowing one specialist to understand relevant communications from another.

The Macey conferences held during the 1940s in which representatives from anthropology, psychobiology, psychiatry, neurology, anatomy, medicine and electronics attempted to find a common scientific framework for thinking across their disciplines (Von Bertalanffy, 1962) were subsequently influential in developing a philosophy that the whole is qualitatively different from a group of parts. The properties of the whole derive from the properties of the relationships between the parts — interacting with the properties of the parts mutually to define each other. Further history of the development of these ideas of different fields is outlined in Benkovim *et al.*, 1982 and in Gorell Barnes (1985).

Systems thinking, family pattern and family coherence

Systems thinking in family therapy derives principally from the concept of mutual causality or mutual influence, the interrelationship of events within a given framework and from the familiar notion that the whole is greater than the sum of its parts. A system can be defined as an organized arrangement of elements consisting of a network of inter-dependent and coordinated parts that functions as a unit. This arrangement is often referred to as the coherence of the family. Family coherence contains the idea of core family characteristics (Dunn, 1988) that are held in balance in relation to one another; that may be taken in by children as whole patterns — mental representations of sets of relationships (Main *et al.*, 1985); and may be carried forward in life into subsequent social contexts (Sroufe & Fleeson, 1988).

Pattern as a concept in family studies

Models of the systemic properties of pattern in families have been built up theoretically from the properties of a two-person relationship (Hinde, 1979). From the interaction between any two people, properties will emerge that are specific to the interaction itself, and others that are specific to the relationship over time. Some will be observable (the behavioural properties of the relationship); others will be less readily classifiable (the emotional and affective properties of relationship). In the late 1970s different researchers began to show how these two-person interactions may be influenced by the presence of a third person (Clarke-Stewart, 1978; Parke *et al.*, 1979; Pedersen *et al.*, 1979, 1980; Kendrick, 1982; Patterson & Dishion, 1982). These studies looked at and measured the behaviour of families, whereas other studies (Mossige *et al.*, 1979; Reiss, 1981) assessed the less tangible aspects of mutual influence, such as changes in perception and expressed opinion. While the impact of systemic family pattern on the freedom of any individual remains at the level of hypothesis, to be examined in relation to each presenting child, it may be assumed with some confidence that, because of the repetition of daily sequences in family life, and through the attitudes, beliefs and principles expressed in these, family pattern carries a powerful influence on aspects of development (Hinde, 1979, 1981).

Family patterns, researcher observations and the implications for family therapy intervention

Mutual influence and systemic patterning are now well-established concepts in child development research (Hinde & Stevenson-Hinde, 1988). Because they suggest possible self-regulating mechanisms, they underpin the elusive notion of family coherence which family therapy tries to address. An additional concept borrowed from Trevarthen (1979) is that of intersubjectivity. He studied the way in which infants' and mothers' patterns of communication, both verbal and non-verbal, rely on a fine tuning based on former experience of one another over time. The pattern of finely tuned anticipations and responses known to members of the family is the thing that has to be scanned as widely and as sensitively as possible in a therapeutic interview. It is also what needs attention from professionals in the context of working with potential family breakdown as well as with actual break-up, with children going into foster care or with late adoptions. The question of which aspects of family pattern are protective and which may need to be maintained on behalf of children following family break-up is always important to consider.

The carry-forward of pattern

Of additional interest to family therapists is the question of what contributes to the carry-forward of pattern; and conversely, where the pattern is adverse, what acts as protective factors which, in buffering against stress, may allow sufficient flexibility for new patterns to develop (Rutter, 1988, 1989; Radke Yarrow *et al.*, 1989). Two studies that give evidence for the idea of family system characteristics carried forward through the generations are those of Belsky and Pensky (1988) and Caspi and Elder (1988). Belsky and Pensky considered the evidence relating to child maltreatment, spouse abuse and marital instability, and look at the acquisition processes by which young children relate to positive and negative adult interactions. They used the concept of *internal working models* (Bowlby, 1980; Bretherton, 1985; Main *et al.*, 1985; Parkes *et al.*, 1991; Sroufe & Fleeson, 1986, 1988). Internal working models are defined as affectively laden mental representations of the self, other, and of the relationship derived from interactional experiences. These models function outside conscious awareness to direct attention and organize memory in ways that guide interpersonal behaviour and interpretation of social experience. The active role of the individual in interpreting the experienced world and the inclination to assimilate information into preexisting models mean that interpersonal development is likely to be conservative. The individual is likely to disregard inconsistent information or to reinterpret it. In family therapy, the reworking of such models as part of the conscious experience of the session is an important attempt to prevent such powerful mechanisms continuing to operate over time (Byng-Hall, 1986).

Sroufe and Fleeson (1988), also using the concept of internal working models, have suggested that it is the pattern as a whole, the representation of relationships, that is learnt by the child. Represented relationships are carried forward. In studying children who have been abused as they move into subsequent relationship contexts, they observed that children can replay the position of the abused or the abuser relationship. They asserted that relationship systems as wholes have continuity and coherence; that the whole system is reflected in each subrelationship; and that entire representational systems are carried forward. As an assertion, this has powerful implications for family patterns that change within a child's lifetime and bears out clinical experience of the reproduction or reenactment of former family pattern in families that have separated and then remarried.

Family therapists and pattern

Family therapists focus on pattern at different levels: some work primarily at the level of behaviour on the principle that changes in behaviour will be followed by changes in belief about behaviour; others address patterns of belief on the principle that, unless beliefs change, what is permitted in the way of behavioural change will remain unchanged. These different approaches will be discussed further below.

KEY CONCEPTS IN SYSTEMS THINKING

Boundaries, subsystems and information

The boundary of a system is like a notional screen across which information has to be translated from the modality of one system to another. Subsystems in families can be seen to have their own integrity, defined metaphorically by the boundaries between them (Minuchin, 1988). Interactions across subsystems are governed by implicit family rules. The nature of subsystem relationships is therefore of central concern for child psychiatrists in their work with families — who listens to whom; who ignores whom; and who changes as a result of information from another. The boundary between the family and the wider system of which it is a part will also be of importance to child psychiatrists. The way that advice or ideas is delivered from professional to family and the way it is listened to will relate to the professional's ability to join appropriately with the construction of a problem that the family itself brings and effect a change with his or her own contributions.

Circularity and feedback

Living systems have been characterized as on a continuum from chaos (entropy) through rigidity towards greater complexity of patterning, with the further evolution of coherent structure (negentropy; Speer, 1970). Healthy and dysfunctional families have been notionally placed along this continuum in terms of their capacity to develop adaptive and flexible structures in response to feedback, from the environment or from their members (Lewis *et al.*, 1976; Beavers & Hampson, 1990). Feedback may therefore be defined as the system's response to the adaptational change required. It is characterized by negative or deviation-countering operations that maintain homeostasis — i.e. keep things as they are — or as positive deviation-amplifying operations through which change, growth or creativity may occur, sometimes depicted as positive feedback loops and negative feedback loops which increase, change or reestablish balance (Hoffman, 1971; Selvini-Palazzoli *et al.*, 1978; Reiss, 1981; Byng-Hall, 1982).

Homeostasis

In systems theory, as in development, periods of stability and change are considered to be part of the same process, one which characterizes open systems moving through time. Development triggers exploration and a period of reorganization and does not usually progress in an orderly fashion. Much family distress brought to professionals involves an organizational adjustment to a developmental change in one individual. In western industrial society, where much emphasis is put on individual self-expression rather than family harmony, these disruptions are often assumed to be a good or necessary part of development for a young person growing up. The family may, however, experience such disruption as a major stress. Other stressful life events may also create the need for reorganization. In some families the number of accumulated stresses and required reorganizations may be greater than the coherence of the system as a whole can maintain, and fragmentation can ensue. Repeated unexpected life events may undermine the normal capacity to adapt and change.

The concept of homeostasis is of value in two ways. Firstly, in offering clinicians a way of thinking about key characteristics of families that may be interrelated with the presenting problem, their centrality to the family's own definition of itself and the amenability of these characteristics to change have to be considered in relation to any proposed intervention in family pattern. Secondly, where change is induced by nonclinical life events such as divorce or migration, it is useful to consider to what degree aspects of family life have changed and which aspects of former family pattern may need to be maintained, both as aspects of the child's self and of the changing parameters of subsequent family organization.

THE DEVELOPMENT OF FAMILY SYSTEMS THEORY IN THE UK UP TO THE 1970s

In the UK, family therapy developed within the context of a nationwide health service and social service framework — both part of a welfare state that had a strong commitment to families with young children. Contemporary influences therefore included a wide range of treatment approaches, both psychodynamic and behavioural, and a philosophy that connected the well-being of individuals to the wider functioning of a healthy society. This philosophy was expressed both in treatment approaches developed during and after the Second World War, such as group work, therapeutic community work and community work based in civilian populations (Skynner, 1976), and in the importance placed on epidemiological research (Rutter *et al.*, 1975a,b, 1979; Rutter & Madge, 1976; Rutter & Quinton, 1977; Rutter, 1978, 1979, 1981).

FAMILY THERAPY INFLUENCES FROM THE US, 1970–1980

The practice of family therapy with children in the UK began in a number of different child-oriented settings using different models of treatment, e.g. the Tavistock Clinic, London (Bowlby, 1949, 1971; Bell, 1961; Byng-Hall, 1991), Woodberry Down Child Guidance Clinic, London (Skynner, 1969, 1968), the Young People's Unit, Edinburgh, and the Family Institute, Cardiff (Walrond Skinner, 1976).

British practitioners working with families had a number of features in common that distinguished them from colleagues who were not attempting to work as family therapists:

1 They attempted to see the whole nuclear family living in the household of the referred child, at least for the first interview, in the room together.
2 They observed what went on between the family members during the interview and attempted to understand how what went on related to the presenting problem.
3 They commented on their observations and their understanding in different ways, which they hoped would be useful to the family. These comments were sometimes made to each other as co-therapists in front of the family, sometimes were addressed to individual members and sometimes to the family as a group.

Controversy between family therapy practitioners was around how to interview families, and how best to elicit clear pictures of family pattern and its relationship with the problem in a manner that informed both family and therapist. These controversies remain 20 years later. Common dissatisfaction with formal interviews that failed to involve some family members led to the development of a number of new techniques, influenced by colleagues from different schools of family therapy in the US (see Chapter 5).

The three main groups of influence came from the Ackerman Institute, New York, the Philadelphia Child Guidance Clinic and the Mental Research Institute at Palo Alto, California. The first major input came from the Ackerman Institute in 1975 (Ackerman, 1958a,b). Therapists introduced a series of techniques that could be used with families, as well as techniques that could be used in training therapists to look at the relevance of their own family context in the work that they did. Two powerful techniques were known as sculpting and genograms. Sculpting was a dramatic technique that mapped family relationships diagrammatically, using the members of the family themselves to make the sculpt or map. Genograms also mapped family relationship but through the medium of drawing family trees mapped not only historical relationships — lineage — but also current relationships. Each medium allows patterns of relationship to be examined within and between generations. The use of these techniques also freed therapists with families to move from the modality of words to incorporate movement, visual aids and play in the context of family sessions. This was particularly valuable in bringing children more into the activity of the therapy.

HOW DID THESE TECHNIQUES OPERATE?

In a milieu that is highly reliant on verbal skills like child psychiatry, the introduction of techniques that allow both family and therapist to join in a common, nonverbal endeavour to understand family pattern and its impact on the presenting problem, like a sculpt or a family map, operates in an equalizing way. This allows the family to worry less about the expertise of the psychiatrist, and to bring their own resources more to bear on the task in hand. Family and therapist join in reflecting about a third thing, the sculpt or genogram — the depiction of the pattern in which the problem is embedded. Since this depicts the family territory, the family will be more knowledgeable than the professional. This allows the therapist to move to the position of the respectful but curious outsider, the person who can ask the questions that the family have not asked in relation to the problem area they are bringing. The relationship between the therapist's own family map and similarities of pattern to any family with which he or she might be working was also used to explore areas of difficulty experienced by the therapist (Carter & Orfanidis, 1967; Stierlin *et al.*, 1982).

These techniques were never researched in terms of outcome efficacy. They reflected a process of movement within family therapy towards making information about what seemed to be going on in a family equally available to family and therapist. This was part of a growing philosophy characterizing the field that believed the idiosyncratic strengths and resources of any family might be a more important source for developing health and change in relation to problem-solving than any particular body of theory held by a professional.

THE PHILADELPHIA CHILD GUIDANCE CLINIC: STRUCTURAL FAMILY THERAPY

Structural family therapy originally addressed change in families from a different perspective, that of sociological analysis of the impact of social context on poor families. Salvador Minuchin began family therapy as a staff psychiatrist in Wiltwyck School for delinquent boys, where a major project on the dynamics of poor families was undertaken. The observation that the mental health problems of many Puerto Rican families in the study was more a product of their displaced immigrant status than of pathological origin led to major changes of emphasis in technique from a therapy that had formerly been based on a psychodynamic interpretive model. Families were given more information about their milieu, encouraged to develop supportive networks and given opportunity in the therapy sessions to develop their communication and social skills (Minuchin, *et al.*, 1967; Minuchin & Montalvo, 1977). Therapy included action techniques — the enactment of conflict or emotional entanglement — and attempted new resolutions in the room. Therapy was direct and intrusive, and supervision immediate and directed towards intensifying learning for family and therapist simultaneously (Minuchin, 1967; Montalvo, 1973; Aponte, 1976).

In subsequent work at Philadelphia Child Guidance Clinic the concept of the over-organized family was explored in relation to psychosomatic conditions such as diabetes, asthma and anorexia nervosa (Minuchin *et al.*, 1973, 1975; Minuchin & Fishman, 1979). A correlation between certain family traits (enmeshment, over-protectiveness, rigidity, absence of conflict resolution) and the special vulnerability of diabetic patients (Baker *et al.*, 1975) and asthma patients (Liebman *et al.*, 1974a,b, 1976, 1977) was established. In treating anorexia nervosa, the technique of the family meal eaten in the session with the anorectic patient and her family rapidly became world-famous (Rosman *et al.*, 1975, 1976, 1977a,b). Family therapy focused on the destructuring of rigid family

patterns and restructuring according to more functional parameters with clearer boundaries, increased flexibility in transactions and conflict negotiation and detriangulation of the identified patient (Coyne & Anderson, 1988, 1989; Colapinto, 1991). Minuchin subsequently developed a theory of functional family pattern with a related set of therapeutic techniques to help families move from one stage to another when a developmental process had become stuck (Minuchin, 1974).

Techniques and supervision

The techniques that underpin this way of working have been most fully detailed by Minuchin and Fishman (1981). Since the premise of the approach is the inextricable association of family and individual, with the family having the power to organize the data and maintain definitions of self and others, many techniques focus on creating new patterns and boundaries in the family transactions so that individuals can have a new experience of themselves. Because the work was directed to the immediate eliciting of new experience and skills within the session, supervision was direct and focused on learning techniques step by step. Supervisor and team observed the session from behind a one-way mirror. The supervisor was responsible for teaching skills and would often move from behind the screen to join the therapist in the room in increasing the speed or direction of change (Malcolm, 1978; Colapinto, 1983, 1988).

How does structural family therapy work?

Structural family therapy addresses family life through the ground rules that carry the details of everyday transactions in families. These ground rules carry the coding for more abstract family rules, metarules, which govern classes of behaviour. Many transactions obeying the same metarule such as 'help mother' will therefore be equivalent to one another (isomorphic). Working with one transaction, such as a child persistently interrupting a parent, is therefore not an isolated event because it will carry reverberations in other transactions within the family system. Clarification of the principle 'do not interrupt your mother' will in time lead to clarification of the metarule 'your mother is to be listened to when she is speaking and is to be obeyed'.

Structural family therapy works with very small detail in family interaction in the session, closely following verbal and nonverbal communication, disrupting dysfunctional interactions, suggesting alternative transactions, encouraging rehearsal of these in the session; reframing meanings in a positive direction. The benign intentions underlying apparently negative behaviours are often positively connoted. In emphasizing certain aspects of family structure such as intergenerational boundaries, subsystem demarcation and hierarchically organized power and responsibility, it is the most actively interventionalist of the schools of family therapy (Stanton & Todd, 1982; Umbarger, 1983; Karrer &

Schwartzman, 1985; Cooklin, 1986; Reay, 1988). It was also effective. The treatment studies outlined above all show effectiveness of outcome. (A summary of outcome and process studies can be found in Gurman & Kniskern, 1981, pp. 341–358. Comparison of the structural approach with other approaches in recent research studies is discussed in the section on key questions on therapeutic efficacy, below.)

THE PROBLEM IN CONTEXT: STRATEGIC MODELS OF FAMILY THERAPY

The Mental Research Institute (MRI) saw the earliest development of systems theory as it related to a theory of communication in families (Bateson *et al.*, 1956; Jackson, 1957, 1965). Acting as a centre for training, research and therapy, the MRI developed a model of short-term therapy that focused on treating the problem in its social context. A client's complaint was treated as the problem, not as a symptom of something else. A symptom was conceptualized as the result of repetitive dysfunctional interactions produced in response to a perceived deviation or attempted change of rule within an intimate or proximal social group, often itself defined as the solution to another problem (Watzlawick *et al.*, 1967, 1974; Watzlawick, 1978).

Within the group of therapies collectively known as strategic, practitioners subsequently differed in their view of whether the symptom was simply the product of a failed solution to another problem, or whether it carried an important meaning for some other aspect of the systemic functioning of the family. Therapists who follow the brief therapy model, as developed at the MRI, took as their premise the essential resilience of people, which is likely to be depleted at time of critical life transitions or stressful life events. At such times options for solving small problems may diminish and a particular problem may become of greater significance. As energy becomes increasingly directed into trying to solve this problem, so the attempted (failed) solution becomes the problem. Time in therapy is therefore spent understanding how the individuals concerned understand the problem, and the social context in which it occurs. It is assumed that people will have attempted many solutions, and that some of these may have a glimmer of success. The exception to the rule of failure, however small, is therefore sought and amplified. In addition, further unsuccessful attempts may be blocked. A subsequent school of solution-focused therapy in which only the exceptions to the normal pattern are studied by the therapist has subsequently developed (De Shazer *et al.*, 1986). Since people usually apply what seems to them to be common-sense solutions, uncommon solutions may be proposed, thus interrupting the usual pattern of behaviour.

Brief therapy is seen by its practitioners as a simple-to-follow model of therapy. A set of tasks are designed: (1) identifying which family members are motivated for treatment and arranging for them to come to the initial interview; (2) clear and specific data are collected as regards the problem and its attempted solutions; (3) specific goals are set; (4) a plan is formulated to promote benevolent change; (5) interventions to interrupt attempted solutions are implemented; (6) the efficacy of treatment is assessed; and (7) treatment is terminated (Weakland *et al.*, 1974; George *et al.*, 1990; Segal, 1991).

A group of strategic therapists at the Ackerman Institute chose to see the symptom as being part of the mechanism by which the family regulate themselves (Papp, 1984; Keeney & Ross, 1985). To lose the symptom would be to face a dramatic change in the overall organization of the family and a change in the beliefs by which the family hold their collective identity. In redefining the problem, the therapist therefore links the symptom to the system in a number of ways. Rather than challenging the family directly, as in structural family therapy, the therapist acknowledges the importance and power of the symptom, the useful part it plays in stabilizing family life, and expresses curiosity and interest about how the family will manage in the future if the problem goes away. The goal of this work is to create a perceptual redefinition of the problem as having a useful function in the overall current patterning of the family. A shift is thus created in which members think about why this might be and how the family may be regulated or organized in a different way without losing its collective identity.

Further influential forms of strategic therapy in the UK come from the work of Haley (1963, 1967a, 1973, 1976) and Madanes (1981, 1984, 1991). Haley, originally a communications theorist, worked with Minuchin at the Philadelphia Child Guidance Clinic but was also a pupil of Milton Erickson, a hypnotherapist, whose work he chronicled over time (Haley, 1967b, 1968, 1973, 1985). He combined approaches learned from Erickson with the structural directive techniques of Minuchin, and linked these to a life-cycle framework devising interventions for particular problems of childhood, adolescence and young adulthood.

Madanes described similar work in a number of texts, which bring her own distinctive flair for creative tasks that incorporate play and drama into work with families. The common thread in these approaches is: (1) to define a presenting problem in such a way that it can be solved; (2) to create directives, which are to strategic theory what interpretation is to psychoanalysis; and (3) for the therapist to take responsibility for creating strategies that will solve a problem. Strategies are not universal; they are individually created for each problem and each family.

Madanes's thinking is of particular relevance for those working with children. It is distinguished by her use of metaphor. Differences from either a straightforward behavioural approach to family problem-solving or from a brief therapy approach are clearly shown. A child's refusal to go to school, for example, can be seen by the therapist *either* as a straightforward problem of disobedience *or* as a metaphor for other problems in the family such as a parent's depression or need for companionship. In taking this second perspective, consideration of solving the problem will relate not only to its impact on other sequences in the life of the family but to future anticipated consequences of change. If the child is not going to school out of protective or benevolent motives, this is an important aspect to bring into the open and to consider in what ways the behaviour is helpful and in what ways mistaken. Since such mistaken helpfulness also creates a false power for the child over the parents, which may hinder his or her development in other ways, by creating family stability organized around the problem, Madanes described the common purpose of a strategic approach as arranging a new sequence of interactions in which the same end can be achieved without the symptom being required. Madanes, as well as other women therapists cited above (Papp, 1984; Keeney & Ross, 1985) related particularly explicitly to the capacity of children to plan behaviour, whether at conscious or less aware levels.

White, an influential Australian strategic therapist, has incorporated aspects of brief solution focused therapy into his work, which also draws heavily on metaphor and playful tasks. His approach includes a focus on issues of power and the relationship of individual families to the wider socio-political context. His earliest work in the 1980s drew on cybernetics, using the idea of feedback loops and the way problems were caused by deviance amplifying feedback. He developed from Bateson the ideas of double descriptions (contrasting the problem lifestyle with a possible radical new lifestyle) and restraints: what was stopping change occurring, as opposed to what was causing the problem. He also developed the practice of externalizing the problem (White, 1984) by encouraging the family to project the problem into a character or object. They were then encouraged to think of new ways of handling this object. Most recently, his work has moved to look at unique outcomes — the way in which behaviour, which has come to have a dominant definition as problematic, may none the less contain definitions of the identified problem-bearer that contradict the dominant story. By elaborating these exceptions to the rule, people can be encouraged to develop new meanings about themselves which become the dominant story, rather than the stories that others have told about them (White, 1984, 1986; White & Epston, 1989).

Training and supervision

Models of training and supervision as these relate to work with children have been described by Papp (1980, 1984), Madanes (1984), Gorell Barnes and Campbell (1982), Burck & Daniel (1990), Hoffman (1981) and Stanton (1981).

Outcome and strategic therapy

Strategic therapists have published extensively both as theorists and as clinicians. There is a very large case-based descriptive literature of how individual practitioners understand their own methods and techniques to be effective in work with children and adults. Empirical research on work with children is rare. It is further discussed in the section on key questions on therapeutic efficacy, below.

THE MILAN APPROACH

In 1980 a team of psychoanalysts in Milan introduced their model of working as a team, developed over 7 years, to a wider audience. Their original work with anorectic and schizophrenic patients made a theoretical bridge between psychoanalytic and systemic thinking, linking the understanding of unconscious process-controlling family relationships over time with a systemic approach to changing the hidden rules in the families' interactional patterns of communication. Since their work was rooted in three-generational Italian family life they addressed the way family identity became organized around meanings handed down, often without reexamination. All behaviours were seen as serving a function within the overall organization of the family, working to preserve the stability and coherence of the system as it had become organized over time (Selvini Palazzoli *et al.*, 1978).

Working always with an observing team who sat behind a one-way mirror, their highly organized style of work consisted of five formal parts. These have now been incorporated into what is known in the UK as the Milan approach (Selvini-Palazzoli *et al.*, 1980b; Campbell *et al.*, 1991): (1) a presession discussion with the team, during which the therapist gathered information; (2) a session with the family that consisted of questions and which could be interrupted by the observing team with further questions; (3) the discussion of the session with the team in which the therapists met apart from the family to discuss ways in which to conclude the session; (4) the conclusion of the session during which the therapists rejoined the family and presented their comments or prescription; and (5) a discussion of the family's reaction which took place after the family had left.

In the Milan approach the observing team was used as an active alternative to the therapist in taking positions in relation to the family's struggle against one another. The therapist commended the symptomatic behaviour and the part it played in the preservation of family life but questioned the meaning attributed both to this and to all other relationship and belief systems in the family. In their early work, these questions posed during the session were seen primarily as a way of informing the therapist about family functioning, enabling him or her to find the crux of the family meaning system and address this with an end-of-session intervention. However, the impact of questions on the family was rapidly noted as an intrinsic part of the therapeutic process and the provocation of curiosity invoked by listening to the questions of the therapist about relationships in the family and the answers other members gave became seen as the main vehicle inducing change of thinking and belief (Tomm, 1984). The formal method this approach offered to professionals for teamwork with colleagues and for systematic thinking about clinical dilemmas; the consistent use of a hypothesis that guided therapist questioning; the recognition of circularity and mutual influence in the therapeutic process as well as in the family process; and the idea of neutrality in relation to the therapists' stance towards family members characterize the Milan approach and have been further developed throughout the field of family therapy (Tomm, 1987, 1988).

The move from family to context

The Milan approach also highlights how the context within which a *request for therapy or consultation* occurs has to be attended to (Selvini-Palazzoli *et al.*, 1980a; Cecchin, 1987) and the need to construct hypotheses about meanings and premises that organize the agencies' response to the families' action and relationships. This is of particular relevance to child psychiatrists who are frequently used as consultants to wider systems of professionals and family. In attending to the eco-system surrounding the family, more formal ideas about systems consultation were developed (Tomm, 1984; Campbell & Draper, 1985; Imber-Black, 1986, 1987; Wynne *et al.*, 1986, 1987; Andersen, 1987; Anderson & Goolishian, 1987; Jones, 1988, 1992; Campbell *et al.*, 1991). The study of communication in professional systems evolving from this approach has been extended to analyse the multiple and conflicting levels of meaning systems in families and between families and therapists (Cronen *et al.*, 1982; Cronen & Pearce, 1985).

Treatment applicability and research

Although the Milan approach was originally developed as a method of treating families with anorectic and psychotic members, practitioners in the UK have developed its applicability to much wider treatment systems. Campbell and Draper (1985) edited a collection of papers that testified to the variety of applications for this approach, developed in Europe. Their own definition (Campbell *et al.*, 1991) usefully distinguishes the value of this approach from techniques which are directly interventive:

> We would apply our approach to any family in which the alternative solution to the problem has over time become entwined with the families' meaning system so that the alternative solutions are constrained by belief and relationships at one remove from the problem behaviour. Conversely this approach would not be necessary for cases in which feedback from the problem had not created a second order meaning system. We assume that some feedback will create conflict about people's beliefs and relationships. When this happens an individual becomes preoccupied with the context of the message and the relationship to the giver of the message and the content of the message is lost. The result of this loss is that the conflict is incorporated into the family's meaning system. But with some problems, such as a child's sleeping problem, the attempts to solve the problem may *not* have created a comparison between the attempted solution and the relationship between the people involved in the solution and therefore ideas and suggestions from a therapist which are given directly can be accepted because they are not seen as a threat to any relationships or beliefs (Campbell *et al.*, 1991, p. 354).

Outcome

The effectiveness of a Milan approach was reviewed by Bennun (1986); Mashal *et al.*, 1989, Carr (1991) and Simpson (1991). This is discussed further in the section on key questions on therapeutic efficacy, below.

Second-order cybernetics

The study of what has come to be known as second-order cybernetics, in which the role of the therapist and the therapist's meaning system is considered as part of the field of therapeutic interaction, has preoccupied family therapy theorists in the 1980s. The puzzle of 'objectivity' and 'approximation' in relation to the assessment and measurement of reality has long been known to physicists (Capra, 1983) and was part of early family systems theory, as developed by Bateson and the MRI group (Bateson, 1973; Watzlawick, 1978). The famous dictum of Korzybski (1958), 'the map is not the territory' is part of all systems training. However, a reaction to the idea of objective descriptions of family pattern, to the idea of neutrality in the therapist's relationship with the task and to the question of intervention as a one-way process of influence brought the field back to a preoccupation formerly familiar to psychodynamic family therapists under other terminology such as transference, countertransference, projection and projective identification (Dicks, 1963, 1967; Bentovim & Kinston, 1978, 1991; Box, 1981), and to psychologists under the heading of constructivism (Kenny, 1988). The many conversations that have taken place around these topics have considered how a therapist, in construing a problem, by implication becomes part of the problem-determined system in which he or she is creating or constructing the definition of the problem with a family. Von Foerster (1981), in work on neural sets, held that we actively compute our version of the world — the act of observation determines the interpretation of that which is observed. Objective reality is not therefore possible and, in seeking for such a definition, we can only look for 'fit' rather than 'match' (Von Glaserfield, 1984). How a therapist conducts therapy from within a co-constructed therapeutic system has produced much debate. Further theoretical debate arose from the work of Maturana (1978; Maturana & Varela, 1980), whose experiments on the colour vision of frogs convinced him that the nervous system is 'informationally closed'. This was transferred into a theory about human systems through his close work with the Chilean family therapists, Mendez, and her colleagues (Mendez *et al.*, 1988). Family systems were construed as being incapable of instructive interaction: the direct transfer of information. Therapy then could only proceed through construction rather than instruction. Maturana's work and its relevance to family therapy has been discussed by Dell (1985) and usefully criticized by Birch (1991). The constructivist paradigm has been widely critiqued for failing to take account of the structural imbalances of power in society, which control how such problems are thought about and discussed at both visible and invisible levels. Major critiques have come from women therapists (MacKinnon & Miller, 1987; Speed, 1991), from different ethnic perspectives, from the wider development of experience of working with power and abuse in sexually abusing families and from researchers (Shields, 1986).

THE CONTRIBUTION OF WOMEN'S THINKING

During the 1970s women therapists began to develop a *collective* voice which they identified as having features distinct from the preoccupations of men working alongside them. These centred around unacknowledged inequalities in the field itself, both in what was addressed in theory and what was ignored in practice (Boss & Weiner, 1988). Walters (1990) summarized the early feminist approach as including four major components: (1) the conscious inclusion of the different experience of women in their professional, social and family roles in a culture largely organized by male experience; (2) a critique of therapy practices that devalued women and their roles; (3) the integration of feminist theory and women's studies into family therapy thinking; and (4) the use of female modes and models in practice and teaching. In addition, the feminist approach argued for an altered consciousness about the realities of power and control in families, especially those aspects of physical and economic control that oppressed and isolated women and children (Hare-Mustin, 1978, 1987; Goldner, 1985, 1988; Walters *et al.*, 1988; McGoldrick *et al.*, 1989; Perelberg & Miller, 1990).

HOW IS SUCH THINKING RELEVANT TO FAMILY THERAPY IN THE UK?

Recent figures on poverty in the UK reveal the imbalance of economic power both inside marriage and without (Henwood *et al.*, 1981; Glendinning & Millar, 1987). Women are significantly poorer than men throughout Europe (Boh *et al.*, 1989). Women maintain care-giving systems for children, and for elderly and dependent members of the family. The value of such economically unrewarded work is often discounted by men, women and therapists. Awareness of the changing marriage patterning and the effect on family life through the growth of lone, female-headed families in the UK has drawn attention to wider issues of the feminization of poverty. While 16% of all UK families are lone-parent-headed, this figure rises as high as 32% in some inner-city areas (Kiernan & Wicks, 1990). It has now been shown how lone parents are unlikely to rise from the poverty trap (Cook & Watt, 1987). Structural inequalities of this kind therefore need to form an important part of the awareness of all child psychiatrists attempting work with families who may have developed particular forms of adaptation and resilience in response to the survival skills that poverty requires.

BLACK AND MULTIETHNIC PERSPECTIVES ON A FAMILY APPROACH

As different patterns of migration changed the composition of populations in urban areas of the UK, much work with families took place with different cultures and different races from the therapist's own (Brown, 1984; Champion, 1989). While this has long been a part of family therapy thinking in the US (McGoldrick, 1982; Cox, 1986; Ho, 1987; Boyd Franklin, 1989), the difference in the understanding of life experience that this requires from professionals has more recently begun to be addressed in the UK (Campion, 1982; Lau, 1984, 1986, 1988; Cox, 1986; Bott & Hodes, 1989; Goldberg & Hodes, 1992; Messent, 1992; Weiselberg, 1992). There has been a reluctance to document patterns of survival and patterns of breakdown in families from different racial groups in case this could be construed as racial prejudice. Recently, black professionals themselves have become more vocal about the need for white professionals to recognize racial differences and to take a structural pluralist view of society — one that acknowledges there are many perspectives of reality of equal validity. These may be in conflict (Fernando, 1991). The attempt to construct a *homogeneous* view of reality in therapy may disqualify the experience of black families, especially when the inequalities of structure and power built into mental health treatment systems are taken into account (Wynne, 1991).

IMPLICATIONS FOR THE CLINICIAN

To understand the experience of a family from a culture with significant differences to one's own requires having a mind open to new constructions of the patterns of family life, both external and internal, in terms of custom and expectation. Lau (1984, 1986), has argued that in order to be able to mobilize strengths and competency in families with different cultural patterning to the therapist's own, he or she has to be aware of what these strengths may be. Basic assumptions may differentiate western from eastern views of self in relation to others and can overturn primary child development or family therapy texts on healthy family functioning. Respected kinship and authority structures within the frames of Asian and African extended families differ from western families. To understand this requires a change within the discipline of child psychiatry at the level of understanding religion, culture and its impact on family life, as do the different developmental tasks required at the same age period for the child in different cultures (Cooklin, 1993).

O'Brian (1990) also drew attention to the importance of assessing the *referral process* in terms of any potential racist and discriminatory elements. The additional dimension of institutionalized power that a white worker carries when meeting a black family needs to be at the forefront of his or her consciousness. Black authors have asserted that it will certainly be in the families' consciousness (Boyd-Franklin, 1989; O'Brian, 1990) as part of the history they bring to a consultation. Racial awareness therefore needs to be part of the therapeutic pattern developing between therapist and family and alluded to as a part of what takes place between them (Cooklin *et al.*, 1993).

VIOLENCE POWER AND ABUSE

The survivors' contribution to the development of theory of family

Work with families where physical and sexual abuse has been a component part of the ongoing patterning and balance of the family has thrown open questions about the privacy of family boundaries and the maintenance of inequality and power within them. The assumption by parents of 'rights', now replaced in the Children Act (1991) by 'parental responsibility', is under public scrutiny in a wider way than ever before. There is now more public question about what legitimately constitutes a viable family for a child and what constitutes adequate parenting. The degree to which abusive childhood experiences may carry forward into poor adult experience and should be allowed to continue in families is also hotly and repeatedly debated. The relationship of this debate to a practice of work with families based on family systems theory, (respect for family coherence versus the cost for weaker individuals, such as women and children, of maintaining balance in the family at the sacrifice of their own rights and autonomy) is an ongoing dilemma. The position that family therapists need to take in order to work with families where parents abuse their children has been discussed from different perspectives (see Chapters 13 & 14; also Bentovim & Gilmour, 1981; Reid *et al.*, 1981; Dale *et al.*, 1986; Bentovim *et al.*, 1988; Bentovim, 1990).

Work with adult survivors of child sexual abuse highlights the importance of not allowing systems of secrecy within which abusive relationships can continue to be maintained (Jones, 1991). The degree of powerlessness experienced by women and children in abusive situations, the terror this engenders and the ongoing trauma created in the lives of individuals need to be addressed as serious manifestations of the abuse of power within families. Questions relating to power and control in systemic therapy have been addressed by Dell (1989), Hoffman (1985) and Goldner *et al.* (1990), and specific techniques for working with abusing families are addressed in Chapter 14.

THE CONCEPT OF FAMILY COHERENCE: QUESTIONS RAISED BY TRANSITIONS IN FAMILY LIFE

The transitions of divorce and postdivorce living

Divorce now affects 1 in 4 children before the age of 16 (Kiernan & Wicks, 1990). Recent analyses of cohort data (Elliott & Richards, 1991) have shown how the disruptive effect of parental quarrelling and unhappiness can be seen to affect children's performance in school and their emotional well-being some years before a divorce takes place (Jenkins *et al.*, 1988). Research on the impact of divorce therefore cannot answer the question about how these children would have fared had their parents stayed together.

Gorell Barnes (1991a) reviewed some of the divorce literature that shows the multiple pathways followed by children and families after divorce and the differences in family pattern that need to be attended to by professionals. These include: (1) the health of the family in the early stage of reorganization, being aware that mothers will be experiencing higher stress and reduced income (Guidobaldi & Cleminshaw, 1985); (2) the reduction of quarrelling between parents in the postdivorce access situation as an important factor in the maintenance of the child's self-esteem (Lund, 1987; Wallerstein *et al.*, 1988); (3) the importance of supportive networks for lone parents (Bishop & Ingersol, 1989, Johnson, 1988); and (4) clarifying communication with the child about processes in the family and relationships with absent parents (Mitchell, 1985; Gorell Barnes, 1991b).

Isaacs *et al.* (1987) distinguished between marked but transient symptomatic behaviour in children following the decision to divorce and longer-term difficulties. Hetherington (1989a) pointed out the diversity of children's responses. Many children show remarkable resilience and develop enhanced coping mechanisms. Others sustain developmental delay or show delayed effects. There are also some gender differences in children's responses to both divorce and remarriage (Zazlow, 1988a,b; Hetherington, 1989a). The degree to which the coherence of a former family pattern, now dissolved by divorce, may be carried forward into new family situations is not one that is established on a research basis. Concepts from child development studies such as the carrying forward of patterns of relationship or internal working models (Main *et al.*, 1985; Sroufe & Fleeson, 1986, 1988) are valuable in understanding why families who have formed new structures may appear to repeat aspects of patterns that were performed in and had their meaning in former family life.

Lone-parent and extended family structures

Lone-parent families consist of two major groups: the never-married mother and the postcohabitation or postdivorce lone-parent family (Kiernan & Wicks, 1990). The second group forms the largest group in the UK. Never-married mothers form a small percentage of households, most of which are of short duration. Nearly 30% of first births are to unmarried women. The family patterns that these women subsequently develop are various. The meaning of lone parenthood will differ depending on the cultural background of the woman who bears children without a partner. However, certain key factors will affect all lone parents, such as the lack of financial security, the difficulty of earning an adequate income as well as also rearing children (Tuzlack & Hillock, 1986) and the ways in which definitions of relationship between men who form a transient or semipermanent part of the household and the children who rely on a long-term stable relationship with the mother are maintained. In working with lone-parent families it is important to consider wider supportive networks of which they may be a part and to consider kinship as well as friendship systems that may provide important intimate networks for women. Where these are lacking the creation of support systems through such projects as Newpin (Mills *et al.*, 1984) may be an important part of work with the family. The stress that a small family system can manage may be improved by better connections with wider social systems (Johnson, 1988; Klee *et al.*, 1989).

Step-families

Step-families can be formed in a wide variety of ways (Gorell Barnes, 1991a, 1992; Robinson, 1991). Research indicates that the different ways have different sequelae and different outcomes. There is always a danger in extrapolating from trends in postdivorce and step-family literature to any single family.

In considering step-families, four areas of difference from biological families may be useful to note:

1 The formation of an intimate bond between adults in remarriage does not necessarily correlate with the establishment of intimate bonds between parents and step-children. New partners may be seen more by children as rivals for affection than as potential resources for themselves (Clingempeel *et al.*, 1984; Anderson & White, 1986; Amato, 1986; Brand & Clingempeel, 1987; Brand *et al.*, 1988; Hetherington, 1989b).

2 The relationship with former marriage partners and the way access arrangements fit with current relationships in the family need to be considered (Ambert, 1986). The way in which a former partner, now a visiting parent, views a current step-parent will also have an impact on the way the child views a step-parent.

3 General distinctions have been made in the research literature between biological parenting and social parenting (Furstenberg *et al.*, 1985; Furstenberg, 1988). The concept of step-fathers becoming social parents to their step-children and moving away from their own biological children has been much discussed. The impact of such withdrawal of fathers from biological children and the effect of this on the children has not yet been documented.

How do systemic concepts help in working with families after divorce?

When formulating the salient features of the family system to be worked with, it is important to assess: (1) who constitutes the children's current care-giving network; (2) who maintains the regularity of pattern of their daily lives; (3) the nature of the access relationship, whether it is managed reliably and whether there is ongoing acrimony between separated parents to which the child is exposed; and (4) whether the child is given an opportunity to make sense of the changing family context with an adult with whom he or she has a close

relationship — either a relative such as a grandmother, aunt, uncle, etc. or an adult friend. In addition, it is valuable to assess whether there is continuity of home and neighbourhood school and therefore of peer group. All these form aspects of the child's social system, in addition to extended family kin (Visher & Visher, 1988).

The Children Act (1991) emphasizes *collaborative parenthood*. In considering the kinds of family that may develop under the Act it is important to know that children are capable of flexibility in their constructions of how a family may be seen. Whether professionals yet have similar flexibility is less certain. The Act offers many possibilities for developing constructions of partnership between parent and professional and devising networks of responsibility for good-enough child-rearing that widely extend the definitions offered by biological family life.

Efficacy, outcome and treatment applicability: strengths and weaknesses in family therapy

Family therapy in the UK has been widely developed in settings relating to children and adolescents both within their biological families and in situations where family care has been shared with agency care (Treacher & Carpenter, 1984; Street & Dryden, 1988).

What evidence do we have of its usefulness in problems relating to children? Hazelrigg *et al.* (1987) compared family therapy with no treatment and, using behaviour ratings as the treatment measure, found significant effectiveness in all the studies cited concerning children (Garrigan & Bambrick, 1975; Martin, 1977). In comparing family therapy with other treatment methods, all studies cited reported results in the direction favouring family therapy. Using measures of family interaction to assess change, the comparative treatment approaches were education in problem-solving skills (Foster *et al.*, 1983) and individual therapy (Parsons & Alexander, 1973; Johnson & Malone, 1977). Using behaviour ratings to assess change, the comparative treatment approaches were bibliotherapy and group therapy (Stuart *et al.*, 1976) or using nonrecidivism measures at follow-up and education in problem-solving skills are the comparison (Foster *et al.*, 1983) or individual therapy (Klein *et al.*, 1977).

Many of these studies were carried out in the 1970s and therefore may not reflect the changes in the patterns of families presenting for treatment as discussed in this chapter. More recent studies, cited below (Bennun, 1986; Carr, 1991; Simpson, 1991), are likely to reflect these changes.

Within these general findings no conclusions could be drawn about the differential effects of different techniques or methods of intervention. Within the studies analysed, a variety of interventions were used and there was a lack of complete information about types of intervention and sequence of intervention used.

In turning to within-model studies of intervention we can find marked effectiveness for family therapy with children in both the structural approach and the Milan approach, with some evidence for the effectiveness of a brief problem-solving

Chapter 55

approach. The structural approach shows recorded effectiveness for behaviour disorders (Minuchin, 1970; Minuchin & Montalvo, 1977), for diabetic children (Baker *et al.*, 1975), for asthmatic children (Liebman *et al.*, 1974a,b, 1976, 1977), and for anorexia nervosa (Rosman *et al.*, 1975, 1976, 1977b). These studies are of mixed-race populations with a variety of family structures.

Studies of the Milan approach used in child psychiatric settings have shown that it is more effective than other treatment methods in changing wider aspects of family functioning associated with the presenting problem. Bennun (1986) analysed a number of small-scale comparisons of the Milan approach and a brief problem-solving approach and found that, while both methods showed effectiveness, the Milan approach in addition created beneficial change in other aspects of family functioning. Simpson (1991), in a sample of 87 children in a psychiatric setting (4 of whom were treated by the Milan approach as opposed to other treatments), found that all the methods used were effective in treating the children's symptoms. However the Milan approach created associated family change in 97% of cases compared to 44% of the other treatment groups. Carr (1991) reviewed these investigations of the Milan model in which four of the studies relate to children in addition to those reviewed above. Bennun (1986) and Simpson (1991) found that all families treated this way showed sustained improvement at 18-month follow-up. If this finding is replicated on a wider scale it would contrast with the view of Markus *et al.* (1990), whose review did not include these studies of the Milan approach and whose analysis reported that family therapy, like all other therapies, showed a diminished treatment outcome at 18 months.

The efficacy of family therapy with children can also be found in a cluster of studies that related to different stressful life events (Asen *et al.*, 1991), to death (Black & Urbanowicz, 1987) and to illness (Lask & Mathew, 1979; Gustafson, 1983; Kinston *et al.*, 1988). Anorexia has been widely studied in a project described by Dare *et al.* (1990) in which the treatment approach drawing on different aspects of family therapy technique is clearly spelt out. This study is of particular interest in that it linked effective work with children in family therapy to a large group of studies of effective work with families containing an adult patient (Leff *et al.*, 1982, 1985, 1988, 1990; Szmukler *et al.*, 1985; Lam, 1991; Le Grange *et al.*, 1992). The exploration of effectiveness is specifically linked to the study of change in communication patterns and the reduction of critical comments in the family.

If child psychiatrists take as the focus of their work with families dimensions of family life that have an adverse effect on children in different life circumstances, they may well proceed with greater freedom than by attempting to find the right technique or the correct intervention for specific problems. Research in a number of fields has now shown clusters of interaction that have an adverse effect on children and protective factors in families that do make a difference (see Chapter 12). Taking these as starting points and finding ways in which these factors, both negative and positive, are located within different family and cultural contexts provides a way of connecting systemic thinking about families and their interactions to a developmental focus for children.

KEY QUESTIONS ON THERAPEUTIC EFFICACY

During the 1960s and 1970s there were repeated claims that there was no evidence that psychological therapies had any useful level of efficacy. As more recent commentators have indicated (Rutter, 1982, Heinicke, 1989), this negative conclusion is no longer tenable. We do not have to rely on rather dubious metaanalyses of heterogeneous studies of poorly specified treatments. Instead, there are several (but unfortunately not very many) well-concluded investigations that provide a convincing demonstration of efficacy. As noted above, that is so for family therapies as well as other forms of psychological intervention.

Nevertheless, most of the key questions on therapeutic efficacy remain unanswered. Hoch (1964) highlighted three main issues:

1 How do the various treatments compare with one another in their efficacy for particular types of problem?
2 What guidelines are there to decide which patient is likely to respond better to one form of therapy than another?
3 What are the psychological mechanisms by which the various therapies produce beneficial results?

There is no denying the importance of these questions; without satisfactory answers to them, the clinician is in a weak position when deciding how to select a method of treatment. Also, it is clear that the questions are potentially answerable. Yet, as the authors of other chapters on treatment also note (see, for example, Chapter 50), there is a remarkable paucity of relevant evidence. There is reasonable support for the efficacy of each of the main therapeutic modalities, but very little good evidence on their comparative advantages and disadvantages in particular circumstances. Without any doubt, that constitutes one of the most important therapeutic research challenges and it is one that must be met.

Of course, there are successful examples of such research already, such as the Dare and Russell comparison of individual and family therapy for anorexia nervosa, with the finding that the latter was more effective with young people under 18, but less effective with adults (Russell *et al.*, 1987; Dare *et al.*, 1990). Nevertheless, even here, comparable claims have been made for other therapeutic approaches (Crisp *et al.*, 1991), so that the matter cannot be said to be settled. However, the Dare and Russell findings seem to place the onus of proof on those who advocate nonfamily approaches to treatment for adolescents with anorexia nervosa.

Although in this instance, the comparison favoured family therapy, there are examples where the reverse has been the case. Thus, Wells and Egan (1988) undertook a random assignment comparison of social learning-based parent training (SPLT) and systemic family therapy (SFT) for the treatment of oppositional disorder. Many of the outcome measures did not differentiate between the treatments, but children treated with SFT showed more compliance to parent commands after treatment than did those treated with SFT. On this basis, it was claimed that SPLT was a superior treatment (see Chapter 50), where Herbert cites this claim). However, the outcome measure was restricted to behaviour as observed in the clinic (there were no measures of children's behaviour at home or at school) and moreover, the behaviour was one that was a specific focus in SPLT but not SFT. The aims of the study were laudable but the findings fail to provide any valid basis for choice between the treatments.

Other difficulties may be highlighted by reference to two high-quality, ambitious and generally well-planned comparative studies — those by Kolvin *et al.* (1981) and by Nicol *et al.* (in press). Kolvin *et al.* found that parent counselling (which included short-term case work with families at home) was less effective than either group therapy or behaviour modification. The finding is important but, as the authors noted, it is helpful in deciding on the value of family therapy because the approach so rarely involved the whole family and was in any case so weak (usually some 4–6 sessions over a year). Nicol *et al.* compared family therapy, special health visiting, a mother and toddler group and no intervention for the treatment of psychological problems in preschool children. On the whole, there were rather few differences in outcome between these four groups. In terms of children's behaviour, family therapy showed intermediate effectiveness, but it fared worst with respect to developmental progress and consumer satisfaction. As the prime aim of treatment was improvement in children's behaviour, the findings might seem to be moderately favourable for family therapy, in spite of the other more discouraging findings. However, the sample had not sought treatment (it derived from a community screening), the children's problems were heterogeneous, and the pattern of findings varied according to the severity of family adversities and the initial level of the children's behavioural disturbance. Unfortunately, therefore, the findings do not give rise to any straightforward conclusions on which treatment is most suitable for which problems in which circumstances. Other, less satisfactory studies are similarly inconclusive.

As Rutter (1982) noted, in many ways the most convincing demonstration of therapeutic efficacy comes from evidence that, *within* a treated group, the psychopathological benefits are directly proportional to changes in the postulated mediating mechanisms. Such evidence is also vital for improving treatment methods in the future. Thus, for example, with respect to family therapy, it is necessary to ask whether the intended changes in family functioning show a consistent relationship to changes in the child's maladaptive behaviour. Probably the nearest approach is provided by the replicated finding that the relapse rate in schizophrenia is systematically related to reduction in the family's negative expressed emotion, although even here the inferences are not totally unambiguous (Leff & Vaughan, 1985; Goldstein, 1990; Kavanagh, 1992). However, there are regrettably few examples of this kind.

Inevitably, we are left with uncertainty on the mechanisms by which successful treatment brings its benefits. Of course, it should not be supposed that all benefits necessarily stem from specific mechanisms related to the theoretical rationale of the interventions. The relatively high spontaneous remission and placebo response rates argue against that, as does the consistent research finding that widely divergent treatment methods for apparently similar problems seem to have roughly comparable efficacy. As Frank (1967; Frank *et al.*, 1978) argued many years ago (with respect to psychotherapy with adults), much of the benefit from psychological treatments probably derives from a facilitation of natural recuperative processes. Doubtless that is so to some extent, but there is too much evidence pointing to specific therapeutic mechanisms (albeit a diverse range of them) for that to be more than a very partial explanation (Rutter, 1982).

What, then, might be the key elements in the psychological processes associated with successful treatment? Perhaps the crucial point in that connection is that most psychiatric disorders tend to be recurrent or chronic (see, for example, Chapters 18, 19 and 20). Accordingly, a reduction in the risk of recurrence or persistence must constitute an important therapeutic goal (although, of course, amelioration of the immediate psychopathological problem constitutes a proximal target). It may be argued that a reduction in recurrence is likely to require either alteration in the environmental risk factors or strengthening of coping or adaptation processes (Rutter & Giller, 1983). With respect to family therapy, the former constitutes a main focus in view of the evidence that family dysfunction plays a major role in the processes involved in both causation and course (Hines, 1987; Gorell Barnes, 1990a; Rutter, 1991) and the latter, too, are a central concern in relation to attempts to foster more effective family styles of social problem-solving (see Chapters 48 and 49) to note how these goals overlap with those of more individual-oriented psychological treatments). Much further research is needed to test such assumptions but focused investigation to examine therapeutic mechanisms in the context of comparative treatment trials is a priority. Part of that endeavour will have to be an evaluation of family change.

Assessment of change in families: establishmentally viable models

Reiss (1988) linked the slow process of development of commonly held usable theories of family change to three factors. Firstly, there is the abstract nature of systems theory itself, and the influence of other abstractions (Liddle, 1982), such as some of the newer theoretical approaches discussed in this chapter. These are inadequate for generating specific testable hypotheses and for data gathering. Secondly, there is too much preoccupation with the activities of the therapist and not enough focus on the entities of families and their different structures and functional adaptation. Thirdly, there is the fact that therapists do not know enough about the behaviour of families in their own settings and the mechanisms for natural change and self-healing. As discussed in this chapter, the adaptation of theory to the many different forms of family life has not taken place in a way that has led to systematic research.

Olson *et al.* (1983; Olson, 1988) proposed a useful model for establishing baselines and outcome variables at five levels of the family system. These include: (1) the individual; (2) the marriage; (3) the parent−child dyads; (4) the family as a whole and in relation to the community; and (5) the symptoms, presenting problems, treatment goals and outcomes to be specified in each case. Change is to be noted both at the level of symptom change and relationship pattern change.

Gurman (1988) discussed the amenability of different techniques to empirical study, concluding that, while the more behaviourally oriented models lent themselves most clearly to research (Patterson, 1982, 1988; Alexander, 1988; Patterson & Dishion, 1988), the systemic therapies can equally continue to undertake research as long as the results are framed 'within a differential philosophy that recognizes that a research outcome is only one punctuation in a recursive series of events at one point in time' (Gurman, 1988, p. 129). He identified common ingredients in all models of family therapy which may be studied as the coherence of all family therapies:

1 induction in the family of a set of perceptions (beliefs, attributions) about their presenting problem which differs from that which they initially showed;

2 transformation of the family's view of their problem (where clinically appropriate) from individualistic to interactional or systemic (Patterson, 1982; Patterson & Dishion, 1982, 1988; Patterson & Chamberlain, 1988);

3 modification of the permeability of channels available for the exchange of information (communication);

4 creation of alternative modes of problem-solving, whether through direct or indirect intervention;

5 modification of symptom-related affective arousal;

6 modification of generational boundaries and other forms of hierarchical incongruities; and

7 modification of rates of and relative proportion of social and aversive interpersonal behaviour.

Wynne (1988) specified a minimal research description in family systems therapy as including who the participants are (family members, network members, treatment team members and researchers); the family members' expectations, the treatment goals as seen by the therapist and the researchers' concepts and methods. In response to the many different approaches to therapy, the detail of therapeutic method would need to be spelt out in each study. In addition, it would be necessary to specify whether change in the family system or change in the presenting problem should constitute the change criteria. Debate about this include those specifying change in the *symptom* and those who emphasize change in the wider family pattern. Other baseline variables include the treatment setting, the referral process, the therapist's gender and age (Alexander, 1988) and the question of the therapist's previous experience. Problematic aspects of carrying through multi-faceted research projects in the UK have been discussed by

Gale (1979), Hazelrigg *et al.* (1987) and Asen *et al.* (1991).

Family functioning to date has been assessed using a variety of methods: self-report instruments (Moos & Moos, 1981; Olson *et al.*, 1983; Hahlweg *et al.*, 1984); family rating scales such as those reviewed by Grotevant and Carlson (1987) or developed by Kinston and Loader (1984; Kinston *et al.*, 1987a,b, 1988) and coding of standardized samples of family interaction (Benjamin *et al.*, 1986; Grotevant & Carlson, 1987). The problems of model and method — within-model rather than between-model studies — were discussed by Kazdin (1982). Jacobsen (1985, 1988) provided further guidelines on empirical study of the family therapies; Gurman *et al.* (1978, 1986), Frude (1980), Gurman and Kniskern (1981), Gurman (1988), Eisler (1990), Markus *et al.* (1990) and Asen *et al.* (1991) discussed the complexities of evaluating the effects of family therapy.

CONCLUSIONS

Child psychiatrists are well-placed to take forward the integration that is required in the field of family therapy with children. If they take as the focus of their work with families the dimensions of family life that are known to have an adverse effect on children in different life circumstances and connect these to protective factors in families and wider social contexts which are known to make a difference to the impact of stressful experience, they could begin to develop a theory of therapy that relates to many different contexts for children.

The concept of family in the UK has many differing forms. Some of these forms are related to different races, cultures and belief systems and some are the product of wide social changes that create multiple transitions in family life. A theory of family life and what can go wrong within it therefore has to be flexible enough to account for the differences in child-rearing patterns and practices and also allow for the individual assessment of what may be good and bad for a developing child. A family systems approach focuses both on daily interactions and on the beliefs that inform them — the ongoing patterning of the child's milieu which breaks the lasting influences that come from the establishment of modes of interaction with other people. Within this patterning, children learn principles of relating which will be carried forward into other dimensions of their lives. The child psychiatrist as family therapist can mediate future negative effects by addressing the current pattern at the levels both of the presenting problem in the child and its fit with the coherence of the family, as well as addressing wider positive and negative aspects of the family interaction as a whole and the family beliefs about these. Research tentatively suggests that intervention focused at both these levels will have a more enduring effect than focused on the problem alone.

REFERENCES

Ackerman N.W. (1958a) *The Psychodynamics of Family Life: Diagnosis and Treatment of Family Relationships*. Basic Books, New York.

Ackerman N.W. (1958b) The emergence of family diagnosis and treatment: a personal view. *Psychotherapy*, **4**, 125–129.

Alexander J.F. (1988) Phases of family processes research: a framework for clinicians and researchers. In: Wynne L.C. (ed) *The State of the Art in Family Therapy Research: Controversies and Recommendations.* Family Process Press, New York.

Amato P.R. (1986) Family processes in one parent, step-parent and intact families: the child's point of view. *Journal of Marriage and the Family*, **48**, 327–337.

Ambert A.M. (1986) Being a step-parent: live-in and visiting children. *Journal of Marriage and the Family*, **48**, 795–804.

Andersen T. (1987) The reflecting team: dialogue and meta-dialogue in clinical work. *Family Process*, **26**, 415–428.

Anderson H. & Goolishian H. (1987) Systems consultation with agencies dealing with domestic violence. In: Wynne L., McDaniel S. & Weber T. (eds) *Systems Consultation*, pp. 284–299. Guilford Press, New York.

Anderson J.Z. & White G.D. (1986) An empirical investigation of interaction relationship patterns in functional and dysfunctional nuclear families and stepfamilies. *Family Process*, **25**, 407–422.

Aponte H.J. (1976) Under-organisation and the poor family. In: Guerin P. (ed) *Family Therapy: Theory and Practice*, pp. 432–448. New York: Gardner Press.

Asen K., Berkowitz R., Cooklin A., Leff J., Loader P., Piper R. & Rein L. (1991) Family therapy outcome research: a trial for families, therapists and researchers. *Family Process*, **30**, 3–20.

Baker L., Minuchin S., Milman L., Liebman R. & Todd T. (1975) Psychosomatic aspects of juvenile diabetes mellitus. A progress report. In: *Modern Problems in Paediatricts*, vol. 12. Karger, White Plains, NY.

Bateson G. (1973) *Steps to an Ecology of the Mind*. Paladin, St Albans.

Bateson G., Jackson D.D., Haley J. & Weakland J.H. (1956) Towards a theory of schizophrenia. *Behavioural Science*, **1**, 251–265.

Beavers W.R. & Hampson R.B. (1990) *Successful Families: Assessment and Intervention*. W.W. Norton, New York.

Bell J. (1961) *Family Group Therapy*. Public Health Monograph no. 64. US Dept of Health Education and Welfare, US Government Printing Office, Washington, DC.

Belsky J. & Pensky E. (1988) Developmental history, personality and family relationships: toward an emergent family system. In: Hinde R.A. & Stevenson-Hinde J. (eds) *Relationships with Families: Mutual Influences*. Oxford Scientific Publications, Oxford.

Benjamin L.S., Foster S.W., Roberto L.G. & Estroff S.E. (1986) Breaking the family code: analysis of videotapes of family interactions by structural analysis of social behaviour (SASB). In: Greenberg L. & Pinsof W. (eds) *The Psychotherapeutic Process. A Research Handbook*, pp. 391–458. Guilford Press, New York.

Bennun I. (1986) Evaluating family therapy: a comparison of the Milan and problem solving approaches. *Journal of Family Therapy*, **8**, 225–242.

Bentovim A. (1990) Physical violence in the family. In: Bluegass R. & Bowden P. (eds) *Forensic Psychiatry*, pp. 543–561. Livingstone, London.

Bentovim A. & Gilmour L.A. (1981) A family therapy interactional approach to decision making in child care, access and custody cases. *Journal of Family Therapy*, **3**, 65–78.

Bentovim A. & Kinston W. (1978) Brief focal family therapy where the child is the referred patient. *Clinical Journal of Child Psychology, Psychiatry and Allied Disciplines*, **19**, 1–12.

Bentovim A. & Kinston W. (1991) Joining systems theory with psychodynamic understanding. In: Gurman A. & Kniskern D. (eds) *Handbook of Family Therapy*, vol. 2, pp. 284–324. Brunner/Mazel, New York.

Bentovim A., Gorell Barnes G. & Cooklin A. (1982) *Family Therapy: Complementary Frameworks of Theory and Practice*. Academic Press, London.

Bentovim A., Elton A., Hildebrand J., Tranter M. & Vizard E. (1988) *Sexual Abuse Within the Family*. John Wright, Bristol.

Birch J. (1991) Reinventing the already punctured wheel; reflections on a seminar with Humberto Maturana. *Journal of Family Therapy*, **13**, 349–375.

Bishop S.M. & Ingersoll G.M. (1989) Effects of marital conflict and family structure on the self concepts of pre- and early adolescence. *Journal of Youth and Adolescence*, **18**, 25–37.

Black D. & Urbanowicz M. (1987) Family intervention with bereaved families. *Journal of Child Psychology and Psychiatry*, **28**, 467–476.

Boh K., Bak M., Clason C., Pankratova M., Quortup J., Squitt G. & Waervers K. (1989) (eds) *Changing Patterns of European Family Life: A Comparative Analysis of 14 European Countries*. Routledge, London.

Boss P. & Weiner P. (1988) Rethinking assumptions about women's development and family therapy. In: Falicov C.J. (ed) *Family Transitions: Continuity and Change Over the Life Cycle*, pp. 235–254. Guilford Press, New York.

Bott D. & Hodes M. (1989) Structural therapy for a West African family. *Journal of Family Therapy*, **11**, 169–179.

Bowlby J. (1949) The study and reduction of group tension in the family. *Human Relations*, **2**, 123–128.

Bowlby J. (1980) *Attachment and Loss, Vol. 3: Loss, Sadness and Depression*. Penguin Books, Harmondsworth, Middlesex.

Box S. (1981) *Psychotherapy with Families: An Analytic Approach*. Routledge & Kegan Paul, London.

Boyd Franklyn N. (1989) *Black Families in Therapy: A Multi System Approach*. Guilford Press, New York.

Brand E. & Clingempeel W.G. (1987) Interdependencies of marital and step-parent, stepchild relationships and children's psychological adjustment: research findings and clinical implications. *Family Relation*, **36**, 140–145.

Brand E., Clingempeel W.G. & Bowen-Woodward K. (1988) Family relationships and children's psychological adjustment in stepmother and stepfather families: findings and conclusions from the Philadelphia Stepfamily Research Project. In: Hetherington E.M. & Arasteh J.D. (eds) *Impact of Divorce, Single Parenting and Step-parenting on Children*, pp. 249–324. Erlbaum, Hillsdale, NJ.

Bretherton I. (1985) Attachment theory: retrospect and prospect. In: Bretherton I. & Waters E. (eds) Growing Points of Attachment Theory and Research. *Monographs of the Society for Research in Child Development*, 50, 1–2 Serial No. 209, pp. 3–38.

Brown C. (1984) *Black and White Britain. The Third PSI Survey*. Heinemann Educational Books, London.

Brown G. (1990) Some public health aspects of depression. In: Goldberg D. & Tantam D. (eds) *The Public Health Impact of Mental Disorder*, pp. 59–72. Hogrefe and Huber, Toronto.

Brown G. (1991) Life events and clinical depression. In: *Practical Reviews in Psychiatry*, **2**, 5–7.

Burck C. & Daniel G. (1990) Feminism and strategic therapy: contradiction or complementarity. In: Perelberg R.J. & Miller A.C. (eds) *Gender and Power in Families*. Routledge, London.

Byng-Hall J. (1982) Family legends: their significance for the family therapist. In: Bentovim A., Gorell Barnes G. & Cooklin A. (eds) *Family Therapy: Complementary Frameworks of Theory and Practice*, pp. 213–228. Academic Press, London.

Byng-Hall J. (1986) Family scripts: a concept which can bridge child psychotherapy and family therapy thinking. *Journal of Child Psychotherapy*, **12**, 3–13.

Byng-Hall J. (1991) The application of attachment theory to understanding and treatment in family therapy. In: Parkes C.M., Stevenson-Hinde J. & Marrh P. (eds) *Attachment Across the Life Cycle*, pp. 159–215. Routledge, London.

Campbell D. & Draper R. (1985) *Applications of Systemic Family Therapy: The Milan Approach.* Grune & Stratton, London.

Campbell D., Draper R. & Crutchley E. (1991) The Milan systemic approach to family therapy. In: Gurman A.S. & Kniskern D.P. (eds) *Handbook of Family Therapy*, vol. 2, pp. 325–362. Brunner/Mazel, New York.

Campion J. (1982) Young Asian children with learning and behaviour problems: a family therapy approach. *Journal of Family Therapy*, **4**, 153–163.

Capra F. (1983) *The Tao of Physics.* Flamingo, Fontana.

Carr A. (1991) Milan systemic family therapy: a review of 10 empirical investigations. *Journal of Family Therapy*, **13**, 237–265.

Carter E. & Orfanidis M. (1967) Family therapy with one person and the family therapist's own family. In: Guerin P.J. (ed) *Family Therapy*, pp. 193–219. Gardner Press, New York.

Caspi A. & Elder G.H. (1988) Emergent family patterns: the intergenerational construction of problem behaviour and relationships. In: Hinde R.A. & Stevenson-Hinde J. (eds) *Relationships Within Families: Mutual Influences*, pp. 218–240. Oxford Scientific Publications, Oxford.

Cecchin G. (1987) Hypothesizing, circularity and neutrality revisited: an invitation to curiosity. *Family Process*, **26**, 405–513.

Champion T. (1989) Internal migration and spatial population distribution. In: Joshi H. (ed) *The Changing Population of Britain*, pp. 110–132. Blackwell, Oxford.

Clarke-Stewart K. (1978) And Daddy makes three: the father's impact on mother and young child. *Child Development*, **49**, 466–478.

Clingempeel W.G., Ievoli R. & Brand E. (1984) Structural complexity and the quality of stepfather, stepchild relationships. *Family Process*, **23**, 547–560.

Colapinto J. (1983) Beyond technique: teaching how to think structurally. *Journal of Strategic and Systemic Therapies*, **2**, 12–21.

Colapinto J. (1988) The structural way. In: Liddle H.A., Breunlin D.C. & Schwartz R.C. (eds) *Handbook of Family Therapy Training and Supervision.* Guilford Press, New York.

Colapinto J. (1991) Structural family therapy. In: Gurman A.S. & Kniskern D.P. (eds) *Handbook of Family Therapy*, vol. 2. Brunner Mazel, New York.

Cook J. & Watt S. (1987) Racism, women and poverty. In: Glendinning C. & Millar J. (eds) *Women and Poverty in Britain.* Wheatsheaf Books, Harvester Press, Brighton, Sussex.

Cooklin A. (1986) The family day unit: regenerating the elements of family life. In: Fishman H. & Rosman B.L. (eds) *Evolving Models for Family Change*, pp. 122–143. Guilford Press, New York.

Cooklin A. (1993) Psychological changes of adolescence. In: Brooke (ed.) *The Practice of Medicine in Adolescence*, pp. 8–24. Edward Arnold, London.

Cooklin A. & Gorell Barnes G. (1991) Taboos and social order: new encounters for family and therapist. In: Imber Black E. (ed) *Secrets in Families and Family Therapy*, pp. 292–330. W.W. Norton, New York.

Cooklin A., McHugh B. & Dawson N. (1993) *Family Therapy Basics: Video and Computer Distance Learning Pack.* Marlborough Family Service, London.

Cox J. (1986) *Transcultural Psychiatry.* Croom Helm, London.

Coyne J. & Anderson B. (1988) The 'psychosomatic family' revisited, reconsidered. *Journal of Marital and Family Therapy*, **14**, 113–123.

Coyne J. & Anderson B. (1989) The 'psychosomatic family' reconsidered II. Recalling a defective model and looking ahead. *Journal of Marital and Family Therapy*, **15**, 139–148.

Crisp A.H., Norton K., Gowers S., Halek C., Bowyer C., Yeldhan D., Levett G. & Batt A. (1991) A controlled study of the effects of therapies aimed at adolescent and family psychopathology in anorexia nervosa. *British Journal of Psychiatry*, **159**, 325–333.

Cronen V. & Pearce W. (1985) Toward an explanation of how the Milan method works: an invitation to a systemic epistemology and the evolution of family systems. In: Campbell D. & Draper R. (eds) *Applications of Systemic Family Therapy: The Milan Approach*, pp. 69–86. Grune & Stratton, London.

Cronen V., Johnson K. & Lannemann J. (1982) Paradoxes, double binds and reflexive loops: an alternative theoretical perspective. *Family Process*, **20**, 91–112.

Dale P., Davies M., Morrison T. & Waters J. (1986) *Dangerous Families: Assessment and Treatment of Child Abuse.* Routledge, London.

Dare C. (1985) Family therapy. In: Rutter M. & Hersov L. (eds) *Child and Adolescent Psychiatry*, 2nd edn., pp. 204–215. Blackwell Scientific Publications, Oxford.

Dare C., Eisler I., Russell G. & Szmukler G. (1990) The clinical and theoretical impact of a controlled trial of family therapy in anorexia nervosa. *Journal of Marital and Family Therapy*, **16(1)**, 39–57.

Dell P.F. (1985) Understanding Bateson and Maturana; towards a biological foundation for the social sciences. *Journal of Marital and Family Therapy*, **11**, 1–20.

Dell P. (1989) Violence and the systemic view. *Family Process*, **28**, 1–14.

De Shazer S., Berg I.K., Lipchik E., Nunnally E., Molnar A., Gingerich W. & Weiner Davis M. (1986) Brief therapy: focussed solution development. *Family Process*, **25**, 207–222.

Dicks H.V. (1963) Object relations theory and marital studies. *British Journal of Medical Psychology*, **36**, 125–129.

Dicks H.V. (1967) *Marital Tensions: Clinical Studies Towards a Psychological Theory of Interaction.* Routledge & Kegan Paul, London.

Dunn J. (1988) Connections between relationships: implications of research on mothers and siblings. In: Hinde R.A. & Stevenson-Hinde J. (eds) *Relationships Within Families: Mutual Influences*, pp. 168–180. Oxford Scientific Publications, Oxford.

Dunn J. & Kendrick C. (1982) *Siblings: Love, Envy and Understanding.* Harvard University Press, Cambridge, MA.

Eisler I. (1990) Meta-analysis: magic wand or exploratory tool. *Journal of Family Therapy*, **12**, 223–228.

Elliott J. & Richards M. (1991) *Educational Performance and Behaviour, Before and After Parental Separation.* Child Care and Development Group, Free School Love, Cambridge, CB2 3RF.

Fernando S. (1991) *Mental Health, Race and Culture.* Mind Publications Macmillan, Basingstoke.

Foster S., Prinz R. & O'Leary K. (1983) Impact of problem solving communication training and generalization procedures on family conflict. *Child and Behaviour Therapy*, **5**, 1–23.

Frank J.D. (1967) *Persuasion and Healing*, John Hopkins Press, Baltimore, MD.

Frank J.D., Huehn-Sarik R., Imber S.D., Liberman B.L. & Stone A.R. (1978) *Effective Ingredients of Successful Psychotherapy.* Brunner/Mazel, New York.

Frude N. (1980) Methodological problems in the evaluation of family therapy. *Journal of Family Therapy*, **2**, 29–44.

Furstenberg F.F. (1988) Child care after divorce and remarriage. In: Hetherington E.M. & Arasteh J.D. (eds) *Impact of Divorce, Single Parenting and Step-parenting on Children.* Erlbaum, Hillsdale, NJ.

Furstenberg F.F., Winquist-Mord C. & Mead C. (1985) Parenting apart: patterns of childrearing after marital disruption. *Journal of Marriage and the Family*, 893–905.

Gale A. (1979) Problems of outcome research in family therapy. In: Walrond-Skinner S. (ed) *Family and Marital Psychotherapy*, pp. 225–244. Routledge & Kegan Paul, London.

Garrigan J. & Bambrick A. (1975) Short term family therapy with emotionally disturbed children. *Journal of Marriage and Family Counselling*, **1**, 329–343.

George E., Iveson C. & Ratner H. (1990) *Problem to Solution: Brief Therapy with Individuals and Families.* BT Press, London.

Glendinning C. & Millar J. (1987) (eds) *Women and Poverty in Britain*. Wheatsheaf Books, Brighton, Sussex.

Goldberg D. & Hodes M. (1992) The poison of racism and the self poisoning of adolescents. *Journal of Family Therapy*, **17**(1), 51–67.

Goldner V. (1985) Feminism and family therapy. *Family Process*, **24**, 31–47.

Goldner V. (1988) Generation and gender: normative and correct hierarchies. *Family Process*, **27**, 17–31.

Goldner V., Penn P., Sheinberg M. & Walker G. (1990) Love and violence: gender paradoxes in volatile attachments. *Family Process*, **29**, 343–364.

Goldstein M.J. (1990) Factors in the development of schizophrenia and other severe psychopathology in late adolescence and childhood. In: Rolf J., Masten A.S., Cicchetti D., Nuechterlein K.H. & Weintraub S. (eds) *Risk and Protective Factors in the Development of Psychopathology*, pp. 408–423. Cambridge University Press, New York.

Gorell Barnes G. (1985) Systems theory and family theory. In: Rutter M. & Hersov L. (eds) *Child and Adolescent Psychiatry: Modern Approaches*, 2nd edn., pp. 216–232. Blackwell Scientific Publications, Oxford.

Gorell Barnes G. (1990a) Making family therapy work: the application of research to practice. *Journal of Family Therapy*, **12**, 17–29.

Gorell Barnes G. (1991a) Stepfamilies in context: the post divorce process. *Association for Child Psychology and Psychiatry Newsletter*, vol. 13, No. 5, pp. 3–11.

Gorell Barnes G. (1991b) Ambiguities in post divorce relationships. *Journal of Social Work Practice*, **5**, 143–150.

Gorell Barnes G. (1992) *Getting it right the second time round*. Plenary address: Divorce and Remarriage Conference, Jerusalem, May 1992. (National Child Development Cohort 1958: Growing up in stepfamilies' study, with Thompson P., Daniel G. & Burchard N. (in preparation).

Gorell Barnes G. & Campbell D. (1982) The impact of structural and strategic approaches on the supervision process: a supervisor is supervised. Or how to progress from frog to prince. Two theories of change (1978–1980). In: Whiffen R. & Byng Hall J. (eds) *Family Therapy Supervision*, pp. 137–152. Academic Press, London.

Gorell Barnes G., Thompson P., Daniel G. & Burchhandt N. (1992) (in preparation). *Growing up in Step-families: Life Story Interviews*. NCDS Cohort 1958. University of Essex, Department of Sociology and Institute of Family Therapy, London.

Grotevant H.D. & Carlson C.I. (1987) Family interaction coding systems: a descriptive review. *Family Process*, **26**, 49–74.

Guidobaldi S. & Cleminshaw H. (1985) Divorce, family health and child adjustment. *Family Relations*, **34**, 35–51.

Gurman A.S. (1988) Issues in the specification of family therapy interventions. In: Wynne L.C. (ed) *The State of the Art in Family Therapy Research: Controversies and Recommendations*. Family Process Press, New York.

Gurman A.S. & Kniskern D.P. (1981) Family therapy outcome research: knowns and unknowns. In: Gurman A.S. & Kniskern D.P. (eds) *Handbook of Family Therapy*. Brunner/Mazel, New York.

Gurman A.S. & Kniskern D.P. (1991) *Handbook of Family Therapy*, vol. 2. Brunner/Mazel, New York.

Gurman A.S., Kniskern D.P. & Pinsof W. (1978) Research on marital and family therapy. In: Garfield S. & Bergin A. (eds) *Handbook of Psychotherapy and Behaviour Change*, 2nd edn. John Wiley, New York.

Gurman A.S., Kniskern D.P. & Pinsof W.M. (1986) Research on the process and outcome of marital and family therapy. In: Garfield S.L. & Bergin A.E. (eds) *Handbook of Psychotherapy and Behaviour Change: An Empirical Analysis*, 3rd edn. John Wiley, New York.

Gustafson N. (1983) Family therapy for asthmatic children. *Journal of Psychosomatic Research*, **30**, 369–374.

Hahlweg K., Schindler L., Revenstone D. & Brengelmann J. (1984) The Munich therapy study. In: Hahlweg K. & Jacobsen N.S. (eds) *Marital Interaction Analysis and Modification*. Guilford Press, New York.

Haley J. (1963) *Strategies of Psychotherapy*. Grune & Stratton, New York.

Haley J. (1967a) Toward a theory of pathological systems. In: Zuk G.H. & Boszormenyi I. (eds) *Family Therapy and Disturbed Families*. Science and Behavior Books, Palo Alto, CA.

Haley J. (1967b) *Conversations with Milton H. Erickson, vol. 1. Changing Individuals*. Fraigle Press, New York.

Haley J. (1968) *Conversations with Milton H. Erickson, vol. 2. Changing Couples*. Fraigle Press, New York.

Haley J. (1973) *Uncommon Therapy: The Psychiatric Techniques of Milton H. Erickson*. Norton, New York.

Haley J. (1976) *Problem Solving Therapy*. Harper Colophon Books, New York.

Haley J. (1985) *Conversations with Milton H. Erickson, vol. 3. Changing Families*. Fraigle Press, New York.

Hare-Mustin R.T. (1978) A feminist approach to family therapy. *Family Process*, **17**, 181–194.

Hare-Mustin R.T. (1987) The problem of gender in family therapy theory. *Family Process*, **26**, 15–27.

Hazelrigg M., Cooper H. & Borduin C. (1987) Evaluating the effectiveness of family therapy: an integrative review and analysis. *Psychological Bulletin*, **101**, 428–442.

Heinicke C.M. (1989) Psychodynamics psychotherapy with children: current status and guidelines for future research. In: Lahey B.B. & Kazdin A.E. (eds) *Advances in Clinical Child Psychology*, vol. 12, pp. 1–26. Plenum, New York.

Henwood M., Rimmer L. & Wicks M. (1981) *Inside the Family: Changing Roles of Men and Women*. Occasional Paper 6. Family Policy Studies Centre, London.

Hetherington E.M. (1989a) Coping with family transitions: winners, losers and survivors. *Child Development*, **60**, 1–4.

Hetherington E.M. (1989b) Marital transitions: a child's perspective. *American Psychologist*, **44**, 303–312.

Hinde R.A. (1979) *Towards Understanding Relationships*. Academic Press, London.

Hinde R.A. (1981) Family influences. In: Rutter M. (ed) *Scientific Foundations of Developmental Psychiatry*. Heinemann Medical, London.

Hinde R.A. & Stevenson-Hinde J. (1988) (eds) *Relationships Within Families: Mutual Influences*. Oxford Scientific Publications, Oxford.

Hines J.O. (1987) Influences of the home and family environment on childhood dysfunction. In: Lahey B.B. & Kazdin A.E. (eds) *Advances in Clinical Child Psychology*, vol. 10, pp. 1–54. Plenum, New York.

Ho M.K. (1987) *Family Therapy and Ethnic Minorities*. Sage, New York.

Hoch P.H. (1964) Discussion. In: Hoch P.H. & Zubin J. (eds) *The Evaluation of Psychiatric Treatment*, pp. 52–58. Grune & Stratton, New York.

Hoffman L. (1971) Deviation amplifying processes in normal groups. In: Haley J. (ed) *Changing Families*. Grune & Stratton, New York.

Hoffman L. (1981) *Foundations of Family Therapy*. Basic Books, New York.

Hoffman L. (1985) Beyond power and control: toward a 'second order' family systems therapy. *Family Systems Medicine*, **3**, 381–395.

Imber-Black E. (1986) Women, families and larger systems. In: Ault-Riche M. (ed) *Women and Family Therapy*. Aspen Systems, Rockville, MD.

Imber-Black E. (1987) Families, larger systems and the wider social context. *Journal of Strategic and Systemic Therapies*, **5**, 20–35.

Isaacs M.B., Leon G. & Donaghue A.M. (1987) Who are the 'normal' children of divorce? On the need to specify a population. *Journal of*

Divorce, **13**, 107–119.

Jackson D.D. (1957) The question of family homeostasis. *Psychiatric Quarterly Supplement,* **31**, 79–90.

Jackson D.D. (1965) The study of the family. *Family Process,* **4**, 1–20.

Jacobsen N.S. (1985) Toward a non sectarian blueprint for the empirical study of family therapies. *Journal of Marital and Family Therapy,* **11**, 163–165.

Jacobsen N.S. (1988) Guidelines for the design of family therapy outcome research. In: Wynne L.C. (ed) *The State of the Art in Family Therapy Research: Controversies and Recommendations,* pp. 139–158. Family Process Press, New York.

Jenkins H. & Asen K. (1992) Family therapy without the family: a framework for systemic practice. *Journal of Family Therapy,* **14(1)**, 1–14.

Jenkins J., Smith M. & Graham P. (1988) Coping with parental quarrels. *Journal of the American Academy of Child and Adolescent Psychiatry,* **28**, 182–189.

Johnson C.L. (1988) Post-divorce: the organization of relationships between divorcing children and their parents. *Journal of Marriage and the Family,* **50**, 221–231.

Johnson T. & Malone H. (1977) Effects of short term family therapy on patterns of verbal interchange in disturbed families. *Family Therapy,* **4**, 207–213.

Jones E. (1988) The Milan method — quo vadis? *Journal of Family Therapy,* **10**, 325–338.

Jones E. (1991) *Working with Adult Survivors of Childhood Abuse.* Karnal Books, London.

Jones E. (1993) *Family Systems Therapy: Developments in the Milan Systemic Therapies.* John Wiley, Chichester.

Karrer B.M. & Schwartzman J. (1985) The stages of structural family therapy. In: Breunlin D. (ed) *Stages: Patterns of Change over Time.* Aspen, Rockville, MD.

Kavanagh D.J. (1992) Recent developments in expressed emotion and schizophrenia. *British Journal of Psychiatry,* **160**, 601–620.

Kazdin A.E. (1982) Single case experimental designs. In: Kendall P.C. & Butcher J.M. (eds) *Handbook of Research Methods in Clinical Psychology.* John Wiley, New York.

Keeney B. & Ross J.M. (1985) A case study of Olga Silverstein. In: Keeney B. & Ross J.M. (eds) *Mind in Therapy: Constructing Systemic Family Therapies,* pp. 11–85. Basic Books, New York.

Kenny V. (ed) (1988) Radical constructivism, autoprocess and psychotherapy. *Irish Journal of Psychology,* **9**(1), 1988.

Kiernan K. & Wicks M. (1990) *Family Change and Future Policy.* Family Policy Studies Centre, 231 Baker Street, London NW1 6XE.

Kinston W. & Loader P. (1984) Eliciting whole family interaction with a standardized clinical interview. *Journal of Family Therapy,* **6**, 347–363.

Kinston W. & Loader P. (1988) The family task interview: a tool for clinical research in family interaction. *Journal of Marital and Family Therapy,* **13**, 67–88.

Kinston W., Loader P. & Miller L. (1987a) Quantifying the clinical assessment of family health. *Journal of Marital and Family Therapy,* **13**, 49–63.

Kinston W., Loader P. & Miller L. (1987b) Emotional health of families and their members where a child is obese. *Journal of Psychosomatic Research,* **31**, 583–599.

Kinston W., Loader P., Miller L. & Rein L. (1988) Interaction in families with obese children. *Journal of Psychosomatic Research,* **32**, 513–532.

Klee L., Schmidt C. & Johnson C. (1989) Children's definitions of family following divorce of their parents. *Journal of Divorce,* **13(1)**, 109–127.

Klein M., Alexander J. & Parsons B. (1977) Impact of family systems intervention on recidivism and sibling delinquency: a model of

primary prevention and program evaluation. *Journal of Consulting and Clinical Psychology,* **45**, 469–474.

Kolvin I., Garside R.F., Nicol A.R., Macmillan A., Wolstenholme F. & Leitch I.M. (1981) *Help Starts Here: The Maladjusted Child in the Ordinary School.* Tavistock, London.

Korzybski A. (1941) *Science and Sanity.* Science Press, New York.

Lam D.H. (1991) Psychosocial family intervention in schizophrenia: a review of empirical studies. *Psychological Medicine,* **21**, 423–441.

Lask B. & Matthew D. (1979) Family therapy for poorly controlled childhood asthma: a follow-up study. *Archives of Diseases in Childhood,* **54**, 116–117.

Lau A. (1984) Transcultural issues in family therapy. *Journal of Family Therapy,* **6**, 91–112.

Lau A. (1986) Family therapy across cultures. In: Cox J.L. (ed) *Transcultural Psychiatry,* pp. 234–252. Croom Helm, Beckenham, Kent.

Lau A. (1988) Family therapy and ethnic minorities. In: Street E. & Dryden W. (eds) *Family Therapy in Britain,* pp. 270–290. Open University Press, Milton Keynes.

Leff J. & Vaughan C. (1985) *Experienced Emotion in Families.* Guilford, New York.

Leff J.P., Kuipers I., Berkowitz R., Liberlein-Fries R. & Sturgeon D. (1982) A controlled trial of social intervention in schizophrenia families. *British Journal of Psychiatry,* **141**, 121–134.

Leff J.P., Kuipers L., Berkowitz R. & Sturgeon D. (1985) A controlled trial of social intervention in the families of schizophrenia patients; two-year follow up. *British Journal of Psychiatry,* **146**, 594–600.

Leff J.P., Berkowitz R., Shavit N., Strachan A., Glass I. & Vaugn C. (1988) A trial of family therapy v. a relatives' group for schizophrenia. *British Journal of Psychiatry,* **153**, 58–66.

Leff J.P., Berkowitz R., Shavit N., Strachan A., Glass I. & Vaugn C. (1990) A trial of family therapy v. a relatives' group for schizophrenia. Two-year follow-up. *British Journal of Psychiatry,* **150**, 571–577.

Le Grange D., Eisler I., Dare C. & Hodes M. (1992) Family criticism and self-starvation: a study of expressed emotion. *Journal of Family Therapy,* **14(2)**, 177–193.

Lewis J.M., Beavers R., Gossett J.T. & Phillips V.A. (1976) *No Single Thread: Psychological Health in Family Systems.* Brunner/Mazel, New York.

Liddle H.A. (1982) On the problem of eclecticism. A call for epistemological clarification and human scale theories. *Family Process,* **21**, 243–250.

Liebman R., Minuchin S. & Baker L. (1974a) The role of the family in the treatment of anorexia nervosa. *Journal of the American Academy of Child Psychiatry,* **13**, 264–272.

Liebman R., Minuchin S. & Baker L. (1974b) The use of structural family therapy in the treatment of intractable asthma. *American Journal of Psychiatry,* **131**, 535–540.

Liebman R., Minuchin S., Baker L. & Mosman B. (1976) The role of the family in the treatment of chronic asthma. In: Guerin P. (ed) *Family Therapy: Theory and Practice.* Gardner Press, New York.

Liebman R., Minuchin S., Baker L. & Mosman B. (1977) Chronic asthma: a new approach in treatment. In: McMillan M.F. & Henao S. (eds) *Child Psychiatry: Treatment and Research.* Gardner Press, New York.

Loader P., Burck C.C., Kinston W. & Bentovim A. (1981) Method for organising the clinical description of family interaction. *Australian Journal of Family Therapy,* **2**, 131–141.

Lund M. (1987) The non-custodial father: common challenges in parenting after divorce. In: O'Brien M. (ed) *Reassessing Fatherhood: New Observations on Fathers of the Modern Family,* pp. 212–224. Sage Publications, London.

McGoldrick M. (1982) Ethnicity and family therapy: an overview. In:

McGoldrick M., Pearce J. & Giordano J. (eds) *Ethnicity and Family Therapy*. Guilford, New York.

McGoldrick M., Anderson C.M. & Walsh F. (1989) *Women in Families: A Framework for Family Therapy*. W.W. Norton, New York.

MacKinnon L. & Miller D. (1987) The new epistemology and the Milan approach: feminist and sociopolitical considerations. *Journal of Marital and Family Therapy*, **13**, 139−155.

Maccoby E.E. (1980) *Social Development, Psychological Growth and the Parent Child Relationship*. Harcourt Brace Jovanovich, New York.

Madanes C. (1981) *Strategic Family Therapy*. Jossey Bass, San Francisco, CA.

Madanes C. (1984) *Behind the One-Way Mirror: Advances in the Practice of Strategic Therapy*. Jossey Bass, San Francisco, CA.

Madanes C. (1991) Strategic family therapy. In: Gurman A.S. & Kinstern D.P. (eds) *Handbook of Family Therapy*, vol. II. Brunner/Mazel, New York.

Main M. (1992) Metacognitive knowledge, meta cognitive monitoring and singular (coherent) vs. multiple (incoherent) model of attachment. Findings and directions for further research. In: Murray Parkes C. M., Stevenson Hinde J. & Marris P. (eds) *Attachment Across the Life Cycle*. Routledge, London.

Main M., Kaman N. & Cassidy J. (1985) Security in infancy, childhood and adulthood: a move to the level of representation. In: Bretherton I. & Waters E. (eds) Growing Points in Attachment Theory and Research. *Monographs of the Society for Research in Child Development*, vol. 50, pp. 1−2, 66−104, serial no. 209.

Malcolm J. (1978) A reporter at large: the one-way mirror. *New Yorker*, 15 May, pp. 39−114.

Markus E., Lange A. & Pettigrew T. (1990) Effectiveness of family therapy: a meta-analysis. *Journal of Family Therapy*, **12**, 205−221.

Martin B. (1977) Brief family intervention: effectiveness and the importance of including the father. *Journal of Consulting and Clinical Psychology*, **45**, 1002−1010.

Mashal M., Feldman R. & Sigal J. (1989) The unravelling of a treatment paradigm: a follow-up study of the Milan approach. *Family Process*, **28**, 457−470.

Maturana H. (1978) Biology of language: the epistemology of reality. In: Miller G.A. & Lennenberg E. (eds) *Psychology and Biology of Language and Thought*. Academic Press, New York.

Maturana H. & Varela F. (1980) *Autopoiesis and Cognition: The Realization of the Living*. Reidel, Holland.

Mendez C.L., Coddou F. & Maturana H.R. (1988) The bringing forth of pathology. *Irish Journal of Psychology*, **9**, 144−172.

Messent P. (1992) Working with Bangladeshi families in the East End of London. *Journal of Family Therapy*, **14**, 287−304.

Mills M., Puckering C., Pound A. & Cox A. (1984) What is it about depressed mothers that influences their children's functioning? In: Stephenson J.E. (ed) *Recent Research in Developmental Psychopathology. Journal of Child Psychology & Psychiatry*, supplement, No. 4.

Minuchin P. (1988) Relationships within the family: a systems perspective on development. In: Hinde R.A. & Stevenson-Hinde J. (eds) *Relationships within Families: Mutual Influences*, pp. 7−26. Oxford Scientific Publications, Oxford.

Minuchin S. (1967) *Families of the Slums*. Basic Books, New York.

Minuchin S., Montalvo B., Guenney B.G., Rosman B.C. & Schumer F. (1967) *Families of the Slump*. Basic Books, New York.

Minuchin S. (1974) *Families and Family Therapy*. Tavistock, London.

Minuchin S. & Fishman C. (1979) The psychosomatic family in child psychiatry. *Journal of the American Academy of Child Psychiatry*, **18**(1), 76−90.

Minuchin S. & Fishman C. (1981) *Family Therapy Techniques*. Harvard University Press, Cambridge, MA.

Minuchin S. & Montalvo B. (1966) An approach for diagnosis of the low socioeconomic family. *American Psychiatric Research Report*, 20.

Minuchin S. & Montalvo B. (1977) Techniques for working with disorganized low socio economic families. *American Journal of Orthopsychiatry*, **37**, 380−387.

Minuchin S., Baker L., Liebman R., Milman L., Rosman B. & Todd T. (1973) Anorexia nervosa: successful application of a family approach. *Pediatric Research*, **7**, 294.

Minuchin S., Baker L., Liebman R., Milman L., Rosman B. & Todd T. (1975) A conceptual model of psychosomatic illness in children. *Archives of General Psychiatry*, **32**, 1031−1038.

Minuchin S., Rosman B. & Baker L. (1978) *Psychosomatic Families*. Harvard University Press, Cambridge, MA.

Mitchell A. (1985) *Children in the Middle: Living Through Divorce*. Tavistock, London.

Montalvo B. (1973) Aspects of live supervision. *Family Process*, **12**, 343−259.

Moos R.H. & Moos B.S. (1981) *Manual for the Family Environment Scale*. Consulting Psychologist Press, Palo Alto, CA.

Mossige S., Petterson R.B. & Blakar R.M. (1979) Egocentrism and inefficiency in the communication of families containing a schizophrenic member. *Family Process*, **18**, 405−425.

Nettles S. & Pleck J. (in press) Risk resistence and developments: the multiple ecologies of black adolescents in the United States. In: Haggarty R.J., Garmezy N., Rutter M. & Sherrod L.R. (eds) *Stress, Risk, and Resilience in Children and Adolescents: Processes, Mechanisms and Interventions*. Cambridge University Press, New York.

Nicol A.R., Stretch D. & Fundudis T. (in press) *Preschool Children in Troubled Families: Approaches to Intervention and Support*. Wiley, Chichester.

O'Brian C. (1990) Family therapy with black families. *Journal of Family Therapy*, **12**, 3−16.

Olson D.H. (1988) Capturing family change: multi-system level assessment. In: Wynne L.C. (ed) *The State of the Art in Family Therapy Research*. Family Process Press, New York.

Olson D.H., Russell C.S. & Sprenkle D.H. (1983) Circumplex model of marital and family systems: VI. Theoretical update. *Family Process*, **22**, 69−83.

Papp P. (1980) The Greek chorus and other techniques of family therapy. *Family Process*, **19**, 45−58.

Papp P. (1984) *The Process of Change*. Guilford Press, New York.

Parke R.D., Power T.G. & Gottman J.M. (1979) Conceptualizing and quantifying influence patterns in the family triad. In: Lamb M.E., Suomi S.J. & Stephenson G.R. (eds) *Social Interaction Analysis Methodological Issues*, pp. 231−252. University of Wisconsin Press, Madison, WI.

Parkes C.M., Stevenson-Hinde & Marris P. (1991) *Attachment Across the Life Cycle*. Tavistock, Routledge, London.

Parsons P. & Alexander J. (1973) Short term family intervention. A therapy outcome study. *Journal of Consulting and Clinical Psychology*, **48**, 195−201.

Patterson G.R. (1982) *Coercive Family Process*. Castalia Publishing, Eugene, OR.

Patterson G. & Chamberlain P. (1988) Treatment process: a problem at three levels. In: Wynne L.C. (ed) *The State of the Art in Family Therapy Research: Controversies and Recommendations*, pp. 189−226. Family Process Press, New York.

Patterson G.R. & Dishion T.J. (1988) Multilevel family process models: traits, interactions and relationships. In: Hinde R.A. & Stevenson-Hinde J. (eds) *Relationships Within Families: Mutual Influences*, pp. 283−310. Oxford Scientific Publications, Oxford.

Pederson F.A., Rubinstein J. & Yarrow L.J. (1979) Infant development in father-absent families. *Journal of Genetic Psychology*, **135**, 51−61.

Perelberg R.J., Miller A.C. (1990) *Gender and Power in Families*. Routledge, Tavistock, London.

Pinsof W.M. (1988) Strategies for the study of family therapy process.

In: Wynne L.C. (ed) *The State of the Art in Family Therapy Research*, pp. 159–174. Family Process Press, New York.

Quinton D. & Rutter M. (1984) Parents with children in care: 1. current circumstances and parents; 2. intergenerational continuities. *Journal of Child Psychology and Psychiatry*, **25**, 211–231.

Radke Yarrow M., Richards J. & Wilson W.E. (1989) Child development in a network of relationships. In: Hinde R.A. & Stevenson-Hinde J. (eds) *Relationships Within Families: Mutual Influences*, pp. 48–67. Oxford Scientific Publications, Oxford.

Reay R. (1988) Structural family therapy. In: Street E. & Dryden W. (eds) *Family Therapy in Britain*. Open University Press, Milton Keynes.

Reid J.B., Taplin P.S. & Lorber R. (1981) A social interactional approach to the treatment of abusive families. In: Stuart R. (ed) *Violent Behaviour: Social Learning Approaches to Prediction, Management and Treatment*. Brunner/Mazel, New York.

Reiss D. (1981) *The Family's Construction of Reality*. Harvard University Press, Cambridge, MA.

Reiss D. (1988) Theoretical versus tactical inferences, or 'How to do family therapy research without dying of boredom'. In: Wynne L.C. (ed) *The State of the Art in Family Therapy Research: Controversies and Recommendations*. Family Process Press, New York.

Robinson M. (1991) *Family Transformation Through Divorce and Remarriage: A Systemic Approach*. Tavistock/Routledge, London.

Rosman B.L., Minuchin S. & Liebman R. (1975) Family lunch session. An introduction to family therapy in anorexia nervosa. *American Journal of Orthopsychiatry*, **45**, 846–853.

Rosman B.L., Minuchin S., Liebman R. & Baker L. (1976) Input and output of family therapy in anorexia nervosa. In: Claghorn J.C. (ed) *Successful Psychotherapy*. Brunner/Mazel, New York.

Rosman B.L., Minuchin S. & Liebman R. (1977a) Treating anorexia by the family lunch session. In: Scaefer C.E. & Milman H.L. (eds) *Therapies for Children: A Handbook of Effective Treatments for Problem Behaviour*. Jossey Bass, San Francisco, CA.

Rosman B.L., Minuchin S., Liebman R. & Baker L. (1977b) A family approach to anorexia nervosa: study, treatment, outcome. In: Vigersky R.A. (ed) *Anorexia Nervosa*. Raven, New York.

Russell G., Szmukler G., Dare C. & Eisler I. (1987) An evaluation of family therapy in anorexia nervosa and bulimia nervosa. *Archives of General Psychiatry*, **44**, 1047–1057.

Rutter M. (1978) Early sources of security and competence. In: Bruner J.S. & Garton A. (eds) *Human Growth and Development*, pp. 33–61. Oxford University Press, London.

Rutter M. (1979) Protective factors in children's responses to stress and disadvantage. In: Kent M.W. & Rolf J.E. (eds) *Primary Prevention of Psychopathology, vol. 13, Social Competence in Children*, pp. 49–74. University Press of New England, Hanover, NH.

Rutter M. (1981) Stress, coping and development: some issues and some questions. *Journal of Child Psychology and Psychiatry*, **22**, 323–356.

Rutter M. (1982) Psychological therapies in child psychiatry: issues and prospects. *Psychological Medicine*, **12**, 723–740.

Rutter M. (1984) Psychopathology and development II. Childhood experiences and personality development. *Australian and New Zealand Journal of Psychiatry*, **18**, 314–327.

Rutter M. (1987a) Psychosocial resilience and protective mechanisms. In: Rolf S., Master A., Cicchetti D., Muerchterlein K. & Weintraub S. (eds) *Risk and Protective Factors in the Development of Psychopathology*. Cambridge University Press, New York.

Rutter M. (1987b) Psychosocial resilience and protective mechanisms. *American Journal of Orthopsychiatry*, **57**, 316–331.

Rutter M. (1988) Functions and consequences of relationships: some psychopathological considerations. In: Hinde R.A. & Stevenson-Hinde J. (eds) *Relationships with Families: Mutual Influences*,

pp. 332–352. Oxford Scientific Publications, Oxford.

Rutter M. (1989) Intergenerational continuities and discontinuities in serious parenting difficulties. In: Cicchetti D. & Carlson V. (eds) *Child Maltreatment: Theory and Research on the Causes and Consequences of Child Abuse and Neglect*, pp. 317–348. Cambridge University Press, Cambridge.

Rutter M. (1991) A fresh look at 'maternal deprivation'. In: Bateson P. (ed) *The Development of Integration of Behaviour*, pp. 331–374. Cambridge University Press, Cambridge.

Rutter M. & Giller H. (1983) *Juvenile Delinquency: Trends and Perspectives*. Penguin Books, Harmondsworth, Middlesex.

Rutter M. & Madge N. (1976) *Cycles of Disadvantage: A Review of Research*. Heinemann, London.

Rutter M. & Quinton D. (1977) Psychiatric disorder — ecological factors and concepts of causation. In: McGurk H. (ed) *Ecological Factors in Human Development*, pp. 173–187. North Holland, Amsterdam.

Rutter M., Cox A., Tupling C., Berger M. & Yule W. (1975a) Attainment and adjustment in two geographical areas, I. *British Journal of Psychiatry*, **126**, 493–509.

Rutter M., Yule B., Quinton D., Rowlands O., Yule W. & Berger M. (1975b) Attainment and adjustment in two geographical areas: III. Some factors accounting for area differences. *British Journal of Psychiatry*, **126**, 520–533.

Rutter M., Maughan B., Mortimore P., Ouston J. & Smith A. (1979) *Fifteen Thousand Hours: Secondary Schools and Their Effects on Children*. Open Books, London.

Segal L. (1991) Brief therapy: the MRI approach. In: Gurman A.S. & Kniskern D.P. (eds) *Handbook of Family Therapy*, vol. II. Brunner/Mazel, New York.

Selvini Palazzoli M., Boscolo L., Cecchin G. & Prata G. (1978) *Paradox and Counterparadox*. Aronson, New York.

Selvini Palazzoli M., Boscolo L., Cecchin G. & Prata G. (1980a) The problem of the referring person. *Journal of Marital and Family Therapy*, **6**, 3–9.

Selvini Palazzoli M., Boscolo L., Cecchin G. & Prata G. (1980b) Hypothesizing — circularity — neutrality: three guidelines for the conductor of the session. *Family Process*, **19**, 3–12.

Shields C.G. (1986) Critiquing the new epistemologies: toward minimum requirements for a scientific theory of family therapy. *Journal of Marital and Family Therapy*, **12**, 359–372.

Simpson L. (1991) The comparative efficacy of Milan family therapy for disturbed children and their families. *Journal of Family Therapy*, **13**, 267–284.

Skynner A.C.R. (1969) Indications and contraindications for conjoint family therapy. *International Journal of Social Psychiatry*, **15**.

Skynner A.C.R. (1968) Conjoint family therapy. *Journal of Child Psychology and Psychiatry*, **10**, 81–106.

Skynner R. (1976) *One Flesh: Separate Persons: Principles of Family and Marital Psychotherapy*. Constable, London.

Speed B. (1991) Reality exists ok? An argument against constructivism and social constructionism. *Journal of Family Therapy*, **13**, 395–411.

Speer D.C. (1970) Family systems: morphostasis and morphogenesis, or is homeostasis enough? *Family Process*, **9**, 259–278.

Sroufe L.A. & Fleeson J. (1986) Attachment and the construction of relationships. In: Hartup W. & Rubin Z. Erlbaum, Hillsdale, NJ.

Sroufe L.A. & Fleeson J. (1988) The coherence of family relationships. In: Hinde R.A. & Stevenson-Hinde J. (eds) *Relationships Within Families: Mutual Influence*, pp. 27–42. Oxford Scientific Publications, Oxford.

Stanton M.D. (1981) Strategic approaches to family therapy. In: Gurman A.S. & Kniskern D.P. (eds) *Handbook of Family Therapy*, pp. 361–402. Brunner/Mazel, New York.

Stanton M.D. & Todd T.C. (eds) (1982) *The Family Therapy of Drug*

Abuse and Addiction. Guilford Press, New York.

Stierlin H., Wirsching M. & Weber G. (1982) How to translate different dynamic perspectives into an illustrative and experiential learning process: role play, genogram and live supervision. In: Whiffen R. & Byng Hall J. (eds) *Family Therapy Supervision. Recent Developments in Practice*, pp. 93–108. Academic Press.

Street E. & Dryden W. (eds) (1988) *Family Therapy in Britain*. Open University Press, Milton Keynes.

Stuart R., Jayaratne S. & Tripodi T. (1976) Changing adolescent deviant behaviour through re-programming the behaviour of parents and teachers. *Canadian Journal of Behavioural Science*, **8**, 132–144.

Szmukler G., Eisler I., Russell G. & Dare C. (1985) Anorexia nervosa: parental 'expressed emotion' and dropping out of treatment. *British Journal of Psychiatry*, **147**, 265–271.

Tomm K. (1984) One perspective on the Milan systemic approach. *Journal of Marital and Family Therapy*, **10**, 113–125, 253–271.

Tomm K. (1987) Interventive interviewing: parts I and II. *Family Process*, **26**, 3–13, 167–183.

Tomm K. (1988) Interventive interviewing: part III. Intending to ask lineal, circular, strategic or reflexive questions. *Family Process*, **27**, 1–15.

Treacher A. & Carpenter J. (1984) *Using Family Therapy*. Basil Blackwell, Oxford.

Trevarthen C. (1979) Communication and co-operation in early infancy. A description of primary intersubjectivity. In: Bulow A. (ed) *Before Speech: The Beginning of Human Communication*. Cambridge University Press, London.

Tuzlack A. & Hillock D.W. (1986) Single mothers and their children after divorce: a study of those 'who make it'. *Conciliation Courts Review*, **24**, 79–89.

Umbarger C.C. (1983) *Structural Family Therapy*. Grune & Stratton, New York.

Visher E.B. & Visher J.S. (1988) *Old Loyalties, New Ties: Therapeutic Strategies with Stepfamilies*. Brunner/Mazel, New York.

Von Bertalanffy L. (1950) The theory of open systems in physics and biology. *Science*, **3**, 25–29.

Von Bertalanffy L. (1962) General system theory: a critical review. *General Systems*, **7**, 1–20.

Von Foerster H. (1981) *Observing Systems*. Lukesystems, Seaside, CA.

Von Glaserfield E. (1984) An introduction to medical constructivism. In: Watzlawick P. (ed) *The Invented Reality*. W.W. Norton, New York.

Wallerstein J., Corbin S.B. & Lewis J.M. (1988) Children of divorce: a 10 year study. In: Hetherington E.M. & Arasteh J. (eds) *Impact of Divorce, Single Parenting and Step-parenting on Children*. Erlbaum, Hillsdale, NJ.

Walrond Skinner S. (1976) *Family Therapy: The Treatment of Natural Systems*. Routledge & Kegan Paul, London.

Walters M. (1990) A feminist perspective in family therapy. In: Perelberg R.J. & Miller A.C. (eds) *Gender and Power in Families*. Routledge, Tavistock, London.

Walters M., Carter B., Papp P. & Silverstein O. (1988) *The Invisible Web: Gender Patterns in Family Relationships*, pp. 13–33. Guilford Press, New York.

Watzlawick P. (1978) *The Language of Change: Elements of Therapeutic Communication*. Basic Books, New York.

Watzlawick P., Beavin J. & Jackson D. (1967) *Pragmatics of Human Communications: A Study of Interactional Patterns, Pathologies and Paradoxes*. W.W. Norton, New York.

Watzlawick P., Weakland J. & Fisch R. (1974) *Change: Principles of Problem Formation and Problem Resolution*. W.W. Norton, New York.

Weakland J., Fisch R., Watzlawick P. & Bodin A. (1974) Brief therapy: focussed problem resolution. *Family Process*, **13**, 141–168.

Weiselberg H. (1992) Family therapy and ultra orthodox Jewish families: a structural approach. *Journal of Family Therapy*, **14(9)**, 305–330.

Wells K. & Egan J. (1988) Social learning and systems family therapy for childhood oppositional disorder: comparative treatment outcome. *Comprehensive Psychiatry*, **29**, 138–146.

White M. (1984) Pseudo encopresis: from avalanche to victory, from vicious to virtuous cycles. *Family Systems Medicine*, **2**, 150–160.

White M. (1986) Negative explanation, restraint and double description. A template for family therapy. *Family Process*, **25(2)**, 169–184.

White M. & Epston D. (1989) *Narrative Means to Therapeutic Ends*. W.W. Norton, New York.

Wynne L.C. (1987) Professional politics and the concepts of family therapy. Family consultation and systems consultation. *Family Process*, **26**, 153–166.

Wynne L.C. (1988) The 'presenting problem' and theory based family variables. In: Wynne L.C. (ed) *The State of the Art in Family Therapy Research: Controversies and Recommendations*. Family Process Press, New York.

Wynne L.C. (1991) A preliminary proposal for strengthening the multiracial approach of DSM III: possible family oriented sessions. In: Tischler G.L. (ed) *Diagnosis and Classification in Psychiatry. A Critical Appraisal of DSM III*. Cambridge University Press, New York.

Wynne L.C., McDaniel S.H. & Weber T.T. (1986) (eds) *Systems Consultation: A New Perspective for Family Therapy*. Guilford Press, New York.

Zazlow M. (1988a) Sex differences in children's response to parental divorce: research methodology and post divorce family focus. *American Journal of Orthopsychiatry*, **58**, 355–377.

Zazlow M. (1988b) Sex differences in children's response to parental divorce: samples, variables, ages and sources. *American Journal of Orthopsychiatry*, **59**, 117–141.

Chapter 56
Treatment of Delinquents

Carol Sheldrick

INTRODUCTION

Delinquency is very frequent among young people, yet the majority of offenders do not become recidivists. Although some offending behaviour occurs in the context of psychiatric disorder, the mechanisms underlying this association are not known precisely. This means that it is difficult to know how to plan psychiatric interventions. In fact, research suggests that many young offenders do not require specific intervention. Having made these points, this chapter looks first at the judicial response to delinquency. Firstly, the advantages of deterrence and punishment are considered, then the advantages of diversion from the Courts, intervention in the community and finally removal from the community into the prison or child-care system. The disadvantages of these approaches are then discussed, before moving on to consider the medical role in facilitating the judicial process and, finally, in providing more specialized treatment programmes.

Definition

Conduct disorder is a psychiatric category but delinquency is a sociolegal one (West, 1985). The definition of a juvenile delinquent is a young person who has been prosecuted and found guilty of an offence that would be classified as a crime if committed by an adult. In most countries, juvenile delinquency becomes possible only above an age when young people are thought to have acquired criminal responsibility. In the UK this age is currently set at 10 years. However, this age varies a good deal from country to country, with a range extending from 7 to 18 years. There is also an upper limit for juvenile delinquency determined by the age when young people are deemed to have become adult and therefore eligible to be dealt with under the rather different rules of the criminal justice system for adults. Currently in the UK, that age is set at 17 years but in other countries it is as high as 21. As West (1985) pointed out, the numbers of young people classified as delinquent depend on other factors too, such as the standards that the enforcing agencies try to uphold, the readiness of teachers, parents and members of the public to report incidents to the police, the resources allocated to detection and collecting evidence, as well as policy regarding the choice between prosecution or cautioning for juveniles.

THE SIZE OF THE PROBLEM

Antisocial behaviour

Research findings are consistent in showing that the majority of young people (particularly boys) have committed delinquent acts (usually minor ones) at some time. In a sample of London boys, West and Farrington (1973) found that approximately 90% admitted to having gone to X-rated films under age and to travelling without a ticket on public transport; 82% to having played truant and to breaking windows of empty houses; and 65% to having bought cheaply or accepting something known to be, or suspected of being, stolen. Belson (1968) found that 70% of boys had stolen from shops and 35% from family and relatives. Not all boys appear in court, but self-reports pick out most of those with official records; and the higher the score on a schedule of self-reported offences, the greater the likelihood of the young person having an official conviction record (Belson, 1975; Hardt & Hardt, 1977). Similar results have been obtained elsewhere; for example, Short and Nye (1958) in the US, and Christie *et al.* (1965) in Norway.

Conviction rates

Farrington (1990), using data from his longitudinal study of some 400 boys living in inner London and selected randomly from six primary schools (West, 1969, 1982; West & Farrington, 1973, 1977) showed that up to the age of 32, over one-third (37.2%) were convicted of criminal offences. The peak age for the number of offenders and the number of offences was 17, but approximately equal numbers of offences were committed by males as juveniles (age 10–16), as young adults (age 17–20) and as adults (age 21–32). The men who were first convicted at the earliest ages tended to become the most persistent offenders, in committing large numbers of offences at high rates over long time periods. Similar results have been obtained elsewhere; for example, by Lie (1981) in Sweden. Even higher levels were found by Christensen (1967) and Wolfgang *et al.* (1972) in North America. Much less research has been carried out on females but figures quoted by Farrington (1981) suggest that the ratio of males to females acquiring a criminal record is approximaely 4:1.

West (1982) noted that statistics show that officially recorded delinquency careers of young males, followed to the age of 25 years, may be classified into four rather similar-sized groups:

1 Juvenile, one-time offenders who differ only slightly in background and behaviour from their unconvicted peers.

2 Late-comers to crime (also often one-time offenders) who tend to come from unremarkable backgrounds, but who have been rather more troublesome than average as schoolboys.

3 Temporary recidivists, who have multiple convictions in youth, but no more after passing the age of 18 years. They tend to come from relatively deprived backgrounds and to have been troublesome as schoolboys.

4 Persistent delinquents, who tend to start their conviction careers at a particularly early age, to sustain frequent convictions as juveniles and to continue to acquire convictions in their 20s. They generally are from the most deprived family backgrounds and stand out as the most deviant group, both during school years and in early adult life.

Continuity of problem behaviours

The kinds of behaviour that commonly result in a juvenile criminal record in the UK are theft, burglary, taking vehicles without the owner's consent and vandalism, or criminal damage. Crimes of personal violence, drug offences and sex offences constitute a much smaller proportion of juvenile offence records than is commonly supposed, or portrayed in the press. Much juvenile offending is opportunistic and committed impulsively without prior planning.

Up to the age of 18, most offenders show versatile deviant behaviour. They not only commit property offences but also engage in violence or vandalism, and carry weapons and use weapons in fights; they are more likely to express aggressive and antiestablishment attitudes. They tend to engage in heavy gambling, drug use, excessive drinking, smoking, reckless driving and sexual promiscuity, without the use of contraceptives. In addition they are likely to have a low-status job record, punctuated by periods of unemployment, and to be living away from home and to have a poor relationship with their parents. Compared with controls, more are likely to be tattooed and more have a slow pulse rate. West and Farrington (1977) developed a measure of antisocial tendency at the age of 18 based on these components.

If still offending in his 30s, the offender is likely to be separated or divorced from his wife or cohabitee and separated from his children. He tends to be unemployed or to have a low-paid job, to move house frequently, and to live in rented rather than owner-occupied accommodation. His life is still characterized by more evenings out, more heavy drinking and drunk-driving, more drug-taking and more violence than his nonoffending contemporaries. He is more likely to steal from work and to commit other types of property offences (Farrington, 1989). Farrington *et al.* (1988a) developed a measure of general social failure at the age of 32 based on these components.

Overlap with other characteristics/disorders

Although delinquents have many features in common, it has often been noted that some patterns of delinquency overlap with aggression, emotional disturbance, poor peer relationships, hyperactivity and attentional deficits. There is no agreement on the extent to which delinquency is homogeneous or heterogeneous, and no consensus on subdivision. However, it seems that there is an important difference between delinquency of early onset associated with hyperactivity/inattention and poor peer relationships and that which begins in adolescence and is unassociated with these features (Farrington *et al.*, 1990; Magnusson & Bergman, 1990). Whether this difference is quantitative or qualitative remains uncertain.

Causes of offending

Numerous studies have shown that delinquency tends to be much more frequent in adolescents coming from families characterized by large size; poverty; parental criminality; marital conflict; poor parental supervision; cruel, passive or neglecting attitudes; and erratic or harsh discipline (West & Farrington, 1973; McCord, 1979; Wadsworth, 1979). Farrington (1990) has shown that the childhood predictors of conviction up to the age of 32 can be grouped into six major conceptual categories: (1) socioeconomic deprivation (low family income, large family size, poor housing, low socioeconomic status according to the prestige of the family breadwinner); (2) poor parental child-rearing (harsh or erratic discipline, parental disharmony, poor supervision or monitoring, separation of the child from his parents for reasons other than death or hospitalization); (3) family deviance (convicted parents, siblings delinquent or with behaviour problems); (4) low intelligence and attainments and high delinquency rates of the school; (5) hyperactivity−impulsivity−attention deficit, shown by high daring, poor concentration, restlessness and high psychomotor impulsivity; and (6) antisocial child behaviour such as troublesomeness, dishonesty and laziness.

Observational studies of sequences of family interaction in the home have attempted to go further in delineating the processes of maladaptive interaction associated with disturbances of conduct (Patterson, 1981, 1982). Careful empirical observation has shown that parents of aggressive and conduct-disordered children are more punitive, issue more commands, and are more likely to provide attention and positive consequences following deviant behaviour, to lack effective problem-solving techniques and fail to follow through disciplinary threats. There is a lack of clear household rules, of adequate monitoring of the child's behaviour and activities, a lack of encouragement and warm interest in the child and prolonged, coercive, negative interchanges based on irritation and anger.

Farrington (1990) suggested that the link between antisocial child behaviour and offending probably reflects an underlying construct of an antisocial tendency. He went on to suggest that the other five constructs (noted above) are possible causes of this offending. His later work (Farrington, in press) emphasized the need to differentiate between the origins of this individual predisposition and the factors involved in the translation into actual delinquent behaviour. Situational factors play a greater role in the latter (Clarke, 1985).

Sampson and Laub (1993) have drawn attention to another very important distinction: namely, that between individual differences in antisocial tendency and changes over time in *levels* of delinquent behaviour. Thus, even though there is a quite strong tendency for those individuals who are most delinquent in childhood to be still more criminal than average in adult life, there is nevertheless a marked fall in criminal activities in the 20s and 30s age period. Moreover, there is considerable heterogeneity at all ages so that, despite appreciable consistency over time, some people do change markedly in their behaviour. Sampson and Laub's reanalyses of the Gluecks's classical longitudinal study of delinquent and non-delinquent youths clearly point to the beneficial effects of both job stability and marital support in early adult life in reducing criminality.

Putting together the findings from the major longitudinal studies, it is possible to arrive at a tentative model of causal influences. In childhood, individual characteristics such as hyperactivity and cognitive difficulties are associated with an increased risk for markedly troublesome behaviour, which in turn predisposes to delinquent behaviour (Loeber, 1987; Magnusson & Bergman, 1990; Moffitt, 1990). These individual characteristics are first evident as early as the preschool years and certainly are very apparent in the first few years of schooling (White *et al.*, 1990). However, even when prior individual characteristics have been taken into account, it is clear that family disorganization, disruption and deviance (as reflected in poor supervision, erratic discipline, weak relationships and antisocial behaviour) have a strong effect on delinquency — albeit mostly through effects on children's troublesome behaviour. Poverty and poor living conditions are associated with an increased risk of delinquency but probably only because they predispose to family difficulties or make good schooling less likely (Conger *et al.*, 1992; Sampson & Laub, 1993). Having many delinquent friends also seems to foster delinquent activities. Of course, young people choose their own friends but, even so, the values and behaviour of those friends have effects on the young people's own behaviour. It seems that, to an important extent, the predisposition to delinquency is increased by weak bonds with society and hence by a weakening of informal social controls. This process remains important in early adult life and, probably, it is for this reason that job instability and marital disharmony/disruption both increase the likelihood that crime will continue (Sampson & Laub, 1993). Of course, a person's own behaviour plays an important role in predisposing to both job difficulties and marital problems but, however caused, the latter then have an effect on antisocial behaviour. It is necessary to view the mechanisms in step-like terms with a two-way interplay between people and their environment.

Finally, it is necessary to consider a further set of factors

that are involved in a person with an antisocial predisposition actually committing criminal acts. As directly noted, situational and opportunity factors play an important part in that process (Clarke, 1985). A person's own behaviour may influence these — for example, as is seen with the effects of both truancy and unemployment. In addition, it is necessary to add that heavy drinking also predisposes to the commission of criminal acts (Sampson & Laub, 1993).

Implications for management

Although the evidence on the risk factors for delinquency is reasonably consistent, the precise mode of operation of the risk mechanism and of the interplay between risk factors remains uncertain (Rutter & Giller, 1983). It is also unclear whether the factors initiating delinquency are the same as those responsible for maintaining it and those that promote desistance. Farrington (1991) found that the mix of variables was somewhat different for these three features, although there was overlap. In planning effective interventions, it is necessary to consider when there is an opportunity to intervene and when interventions are likely to make a difference, as well as which factors to try to change (Rutter & Giller, 1983). Also, it is still not known whether breaking the chain of behaviours before the full syndrome appears might prevent the development of disorders of either conduct or personality disorder, and how long an interruption in antisocial behaviour is required before one can be reasonably sure that a risk of progression is over.

Farrington (1985) strongly advocated that, because the causes of delinquency are to be found within the individual and the family, intervention should be targeted on them rather than on organizations or on society. Nevertheless, he recognized that actions to reduce the opportunities for crime could be useful (Farrington, 1990) and others have suggested that these are the most practical of preventive policies (Clarke, 1985). On the basis of 20 years of Home Office research, Clarke (1985) argued for a rational choice model of crime and suggested that measures that reduce opportunities for crime are likely to prove more effective than attempts to treat delinquents themselves.

What is clear from the research is that a certain amount of minor law-breaking is the norm, particularly for males, and does not necessarily imply any significant degree of personal maladjustment. Many youths only appear in court once and only a small proportion show a persistent pattern of delinquency. The general trend is towards improvement with age, although the outlook for the worst behaved and most disadvantaged boys is very poor. Specialist resources available within the multidisciplinary teams are based in departments of child psychiatry and in child guidance clinics. These resources are best directed towards identifying and treating those delinquents who persist in their offending, who show the most disturbed and dangerous patterns of offending, and who show the most disturbed past and family backgrounds.

ADVANTAGES OF THE JUDICIAL APPROACH

Punishment and deterrence

In the US the development of child psychiatry as a discipline was tied in with the mental hygiene movement, out of which evolved a therapeutic and humane response to juvenile delinquency. Since the early 1970s, however, attitudes have changed again on both sides of the Atlantic and there is now considerable debate and doubt as to whether this strongly therapeutic orientation is helpful. It has been argued that costly treatment programmes appear to be ineffective and that the only rational alternative is punishment; it also led to the widespread acceptance, in the US at least, of a doctrine that 'nothing works' (Martinson, 1974). There are also those who argue that individuals have a right to punishment, not to benign paternalism in the name of treatment (Taylor *et al.*, 1979; Morris *et al.*, 1980). There is much ongoing discussion about the advantages and disadvantages of a tariff system and the use of mandatory sentences for certain offence categories. A study by McCord (1985), reporting on the criminal histories of 231 boys who committed crimes between the ages of 7 and 17, showed that those juveniles who were processed through the Courts were less likely to be convicted subsequently for serious crimes.

DIVERSION FROM THE COURTS

General considerations

Built into all child-care legislation is an assumption that, even if children appear before the Court, removal of a young person from home should be a last resort; furthermore, that if removed he or she should be placed as near home as possible. Legislation, particularly the Children and Young Persons Act (1969) in the UK, aimed at blurring the distinction between children in need of care and those committing offences (the so-called deprived and depraved), and it sought to prevent increasing numbers of children coming to Court as well as making the treatment of young offenders more flexible than hitherto. This legislation sought to prevent children coming before the Courts for criminal proceedings by introducing cautioning, which was given statutory sanction for the first time.

The Children and Young Person's Act of 1969 demanded, and indeed resulted in, much closer liaison between those working in the community, that is, police, schools and local authority social services departments. The police were involved in setting up juvenile bureaux in police stations so that cautioning could be introduced. Although it is aimed at preventing young people coming before the Courts, it is a formal procedure, with data being collected by the Home Office.

Cautioning

Prior to 1971, the year when the 1969 Act was implemented, children could be given a warning if apprehended whilst committing an offence. This was an informal procedure, conducted at the discretion of the police officer and not recorded officially. Juvenile bureaux, used for cautioning, are comprised of volunteers with an understanding of juvenile problems. Once it has been established that a child has committed an offence, the bureau staff collect information about the child from their own records, from social services, from the school and other relevant agencies. Often they visit the home. On the basis of this information, the chief inspector in the bureau decides on the most appropriate course of action: to take no further action, to caution, or to prosecute. The caution is usually administered, with the consent of the child, parents and victim, in a formal way to emphasize the gravity of the situation. Sometimes the police undertake follow-up supervision and guidance, or they may refer the child to the social service department on a voluntary basis.

Recently the police have introduced a range of informal cautions. Information on the number of such cautions is not currently recorded by the Home Office, although some police forces collect such information (Wilkinson & Evans, 1990).

Trends in the use of diversion from the Courts

The police dealt with nearly twice as many juveniles guilty of serious offences by means of a caution in 1979 compared with 1970 (Home Office, 1979), during which time the number brought before the Courts and sentenced was not diminished. Work by Farrington and Bennett (1981) led them to believe that cautioning had produced a widening of the net, so that official cautions had tended to replace informal, unrecorded warnings, rather than being used in place of Court appearances. The situation since then appears to have changed for the better, however. Richardson and Tutt (1991), using data from the Home Office (1989), pointed out that there has been a 23.2% decrease in the number of 10–16-year-olds in the population in England and Wales over the 10 years from 1979 to 1988. Over 55% fewer juveniles entered the formal court system during 1988 than did in 1979. The number of young people receiving formal cautions has remained virtually constant (82 000 in 1979 and 82 900 in 1988), which means that there has been a considerable increase in their use, for the purpose of diverting young people from the Courts (47% of all male juveniles processed by the police in 1979 and 67% in 1988). As stated above, a range of informal cautions have also been introduced and the extent to which these have added to the numbers being cautioned remains uncertain. Richardson and Tutt (1991) pointed out that these developments in diverting children from Court were further enhanced by the setting up of the Crown Prosecution Service in 1986. The prosecutor's role has been to review police decisions in order to increase the possibility of diversion, though the full impact of this relatively new service has yet to be assessed. Richardson and Tutt (1991) argued, however, that the key to developing the policy of diversion lies with this service.

In 1980 Morris *et al.* had questioned whether the police, whose training and traditions lie in the direction of bringing as many guilty persons as possible before the Courts, were the best persons to decide when to warn, when to refer to a social agency, and when to pass on to magistrates. They suggested the setting-up of an independent legal check to ensure that formal prosecutions by the police really warranted this serious step. In Scotland such a system of this kind exists in the form of the Reporter, an official who sifts complaints from the police and others, and who decides which cases can be dealt with informally with the consent and cooperation of the child, parents, school, local social agencies and perhaps the victim(s), and which cases need to be passed on for a formal tribunal hearing. Children's hearings are made up of three panel members drawn from a list of lay volunteers selected and trained to make decisions about children under 16 years of age. Unlike the Courts, the hearings have no power to impose fines or make committals to penal institutions. Only on instructions of the Lord Advocate are a small number of children prosecuted in the Sheriff Court or in the High Court. These prosecutions are usually reserved for serious cases involving offences against the person (e.g. assault, grievous bodily harm, attempted murder).

INTERVENTIONS DEALING WITH SOCIAL ISSUES

It has been argued that, in the treatment of delinquency, possible interventions include giving more economic resources to poor families, providing juveniles with socially approved opportunities for excitement and risk-taking, deterring offending through an increased probability and level of penalty (although this also has dangers), increasing the physical security or surveillance of potential targets, and encouraging resistance to antisocial peer pressures (Farrington, 1990). Whilst these aims appear to be worthwhile, there is an absence of research proving their efficacy. In practice much intervention in the community is provided by departments of social services and is court-directed.

THE USE OF COURTS FOR CARE PROCEEDINGS AND INTERVENTION IN THE COMMUNITY

In England and Wales, Courts have basically two types of case to hear: care proceedings and criminal proceedings. Under the age of 10 years a child cannot be found guilty of a crime (except homicide) and between 10 and 14 years should not be prosecuted for a crime. This means that all those under the age of 14 years should come before the courts for care proceedings only. An additional safeguard is that the 1969 Act, replaced by the 1989 Act, sets out criteria for taking out care proceedings. Cases heard in juvenile courts have a specially selected panel of magistrates composed of three, occasionally two, lay members, one of whom must be a man and one a woman. Under the terms of the Children Act (1989), a care order may no longer be imposed as a sentence in criminal proceedings. However the fact that a child has committed an offence may indicate that he or she is suffering, or likely to suffer, significant harm, so that the local authority may apply for a care order in respect of that child.

For the majority of young people coming before the Courts for criminal proceedings, the Criminal Justice Act (1991) renames the Juvenile Court as the Youth Court and brings 17-year-olds within its jurisdiction. This change will produce a more logical age limit in line with the age of majority (18 years) and will bring England and Wales into line with most other west European nations. Those charged with very serious offences and/or adults will still come before higher courts as before.

THE USE OF SUPERVISION ORDERS

Supervision orders may still be made in criminal proceedings, the primary consideration being to safeguard and promote the welfare of the child, and not to protect the public. The differences between criminal and civil supervision orders increase under the Children Act (1989). Firstly, supervision orders under the Act may impose requirements on those with parental responsibility for the child and other people with whom the child is living. Secondly, the Act introduces a further requirement which may be imposed under a criminal supervision order, in the case of serious offences only: that the young person will live in accommodation provided by, or on behalf of, the local authority for up to 6 months. It can also stipulate that a young person will not live with a named person during that period. The statutory responsibility lies with the local social services to 'advise, assist and befriend', but the supervisor has powers to return the young person to court if the terms of the order are breached.

Supervision orders with a supervised activity requirement

The supervised activity requirement can be made by magistrates and social services departments have to accept it. Placements are usually drawn from the scheme of intermediate treatment (IT).

IT has been adopted since the White Paper *Children in Trouble* was published in 1968 (Home Office, 1968). The aim is to fill the gap between simple supervision and removal from home. It is designed to allow children to remain at home, but bring them into contact with a different environment, interests and experiences that may be beneficial to them and to enable them to share these interests with other children who have not been before the courts. Although IT is usually community-based, it can be provided in a residential facility for up to 90 days. The concept tends to be vague and wide, as illustrated by the Department of Health and Social Security (1977) listing of objectives: (1) supervision by involvement of children in the centre's recreational and work programme; (2) support in relation to home stresses; (3) the aiding of personal and emotional development; (4) opportunities to develop satisfactory social relationships; (5) rehabilitation to enable the child to transfer learning within the programme to his or her wider environment; (6) education; and (7) social work with the family. As the national survey by Bottoms and his colleagues (1990) indicated, there is considerable variation in how these broad aims are interpreted. However, most programmes include some mix of group activities and individual counselling or life skills training.

REMOVAL FROM THE COMMUNITY

Prison system

Much residential treatment offered to adolescents, in the UK at least, is provided within a secure setting. Rutherford (1980) showed that in 1960, 800 boys aged 14–16 years, representing 4% of all boys of that age group found guilty, were given custodial sentences. By 1978 the figure had risen to 7279 or 12% of those found guilty. After the introduction of the Criminal Justice Act (1982) in May 1983, magistrates had the power to give shorter detention centre orders but, for the first time, were able to sentence adolescents to up to 6 months' youth custody (formerly Borstal training) without recourse to a higher court. In comparing the figures for 6-month periods before and after the introduction of the Act (Home Office, 1984) it was found that the number of 14–16-year-old boys received into custody was the same (3230). However, the number receiving the short detention centre orders (3 weeks up to 4 months) fell by 15% and the number of boys receiving the longer youth custody sentences increased by 69%. Detention centre orders are not available for girls but the small numbers receiving youth custody sentences increased by 77% (45 compared with 22 Borstal sentences in the same period in 1982). The Criminal Justice Act (1988) renamed these two sentences as 'detention in a young offender institution', without changing the sex and age criteria for sentencing. As has already been noted, there has been a very large increase in the numbers of young people diverted from the Courts in the UK from 1979 to 1988. The same trend has been mirrored, even more impressively, by the numbers of young people receiving custodial sentences – 7097 in 1979 and 2176 in 1988, a decrease of 69% (Home Office, 1989). In The Netherlands similar changes occurred in the 1950s and in Germany in the 1980s.

Child-care system

Likewise, there has been extensive use made of secure provision within the child-care system, although, as Cawson (1986) pointed out, the national picture has pursued an almost complete circle. Until the early 1950s there was none available, save for a few detention rooms in some senior approved schools, intended for short-term use. During the 1960s three long-term units for boys were developed within the approved school system but by 1971 there were still only 74 long-term secure places. During the 1970s two youth treatment centres were built for boys and girls and other secure units were built by local authorities, with a number of secure back-up suites built in open establishments. By 1980 there were approximately 300 such places in the country. As a result of experience, staffing and building difficulties and changes in legislation, the provision started to decline in the 1980s.

Since the introduction of the Criminal Justice Act (1982), a young person can be placed in secure accommodation for periods in excess of 72 hours only if application is made to a court. It is of interest that, in contrast to mental health legislation (Mental Health Act, 1983), there is no requirement to make the case for the treatability of the young person. The work of Millham *et al.* (1978) and Cawson and Martell (1979) has shown that referrals to secure units cannot be fully explained in terms of the behavioural characteristics of the young people themselves; referrals also reflect the failure of open establishments to cope with persistent, delinquent absconders.

DISADVANTAGES OF THE JUDICIAL APPROACH

Punishment and deterrence

As discussed above, there is a debate about the use of punishment, a tariff system and the use of mandatory sentences for certain offence categories. Regrettably these arguments tend not to be based on empirical evidence and tend to overlook any personal and social factors that might be amenable to change in individual cases (West, 1982). Others have argued that a judicial approach could be damaging because of the deleterious effects of labelling and stigmatization. Farrington *et al.* (1978) showed that the first appearance in court tends to be followed by an increase in delinquent activities, as well as by increases in hostile attitudes towards the police, aggressive attitudes and behaviour. There was a suggestion that this increase was most likely to follow discharges, rather than more serious judicial responses. However, this process did not seem to be intensified by further convictions and it is unclear whether the initial increase is a result of labelling *per se* (Rutter & Giller, 1983).

THE USE OF THE COURTS FOR CARE PROCEEDINGS AND INTERVENTIONS IN THE COMMUNITY

Despite the expressed intentions of the legislation in the 1970s and 1980s, English and Welsh courts continued to function very much as before. Following the introduction of the 1969 Act, care proceedings for young offenders were encouraged. Nevertheless, between 1971 and 1978 the number actually decreased; likewise, probation and supervision orders also decreased over this period (Home Office, 1979). Even when care orders were made, they were not always used to implement the policy of community care intended in the Act. The role of the social worker was greatly enlarged under the 1969 Act and, as well as providing detailed reports to the Court, social workers became much more involved in the later stages of the court proceedings and in the subsequent management of the adolescent and family.

Many magistrates came to regret the loss of power that was a consequence of the 1969 Act and a failure on the part of social workers to implement community-based court recommendations undoubtedly led to a hardening of opinion and a tendency towards more punitive recommendations. The Criminal Justice Act (1982) further emphasized the role of social workers with respect to the preparation of social inquiry reports, specifying community-based options, with an obligation to see that these were offered to the young person.

SUPERVISION ORDERS WITH A SUPERVISED ACTIVITY REQUIREMENT

In a North American, community-based, nonpunitive programme comparable to IT, a study by O'Donnell *et al.* (1979) showed that nondelinquents had a worse outcome than controls, possibly because of delinquent peer group contamination. The philosophy of IT remains a personal intervention model that is community-based but not community-directed (Rutter & Giller, 1983) and often there is little attention to difficulties in the child's usual environment. There have, nevertheless, been high hopes that it would constitute an effective alternative to custodial care for severe delinquency and to supervision for mild delinquency. In the event, the one prospective large-scale systematic evaluation has shown no substantial differences in outcome between IT and its alternatives, although IT has other benefits (Bottoms, 1993).

Experience has shown that there has been an improvement in the implementation of supervision orders and supervised activity requirement (IT) since the introduction of the Criminal Justice Act (1982). The end of the 1970s saw two major developments in practice: intensive IT, to provide a real alternative to removal from home, and the introduction of new methods for working with groups (Cawson, 1985). Nevertheless there is still substantial disagreement within social work as to the desirability of alternative-to-custody programmes, and many IT programmes are still focused on non-offenders, or even exclude serious delinquents.

COMMUNITY-BASED PROGRAMMES

It seems that social factors such as living in an inner city, having a delinquent peer group and opportunities for crime are also important in maintaining delinquent behaviour. In the UK, Osborn (1980) showed that delinquents move home more frequently than nondelinquents and that those who are already delinquent showed a lower incidence of subsequent convictions on moving out of an inner city. For example, at age 14 years only 5.4% of those living outside London had been convicted since intake, compared with 11.7% of those remaining in London; at 21 years the differential was as great — 15.7% versus 33.1%. The differences did not appear to be secondary to variations in police procedures or detection rates but to a reduction in delinquent behaviour; in addition the move from London was not associated with other changes in lifestyle (e.g. unstable employment record, aggressive attitudes, excessive drinking, smoking and sexual activities). Somewhat similar results had been obtained earlier in The Netherlands by Buikhuisen and Hoekstra (1974). They looked at a group of young male offenders released from prison and found that the reconviction rate was significantly lower in those who moved from their former address than in those who returned to it (60 versus 76%). The benefits were greatest for those who moved away from an unstable family and/or asocial environment.

An important study by McCord (1978) looked at the long-term effects of a treatment programme for boys and their families drawn from densely populated, factory-dominated areas of eastern Massachusetts. The study was based on a 30-year follow-up of over 500 men, one-half of whom had been randomly assigned to a treatment programme at the age of 5–13 years, for an average of 5 years. Treatment consisted of counselling for the boy and his family, introduction to community programmes and summer camps, provision of medical and psychiatric assistance as well as tutoring in academic subjects. Subjective evaluations of the programme suggested that the intervention had been helpful; follow-up data showed otherwise. The treated group actually fared worse than the control group on such measures as criminal behaviour, death at a young age, stress-related disease, alcoholism, serious mental illness, occupational status and job satisfaction.

Berg *et al.* (1978) looked at the effectiveness in dealing with truancy by means of adjournment versus social work intervention following an appearance in court. Ninety-six children brought before Juvenile Courts in Leeds because of failure to attend school were randomly allocated to adjournment and regular recall to Court or to supervision by a social worker or probation officer. In a 6-month follow-up period, the children dealt with by adjournment and recall to Court had not only truanted less but also committed fewer offences leading to conviction or caution than those placed on supervision.

REMOVAL FROM THE COMMUNITY

Prison system

In the UK we have a reputation for locking up a higher proportion of our population than most other western European countries. At one time it was hoped that institutional treatments would be therapeutic and reformative in their effects. Unfortunately, this has not proved to be so and some studies from the US (Empey & Erickson, 1972; Wright & Dixon, 1977) show that noncustodial approaches do better than institutional ones. McCord (1985), in the study referred to above, showed that, contrary to a deterrence theory prediction that more serious punishments would prevent crime, recidivism rates among previously incarcerated boys were not lower than rates among those who received more lenient sentences. In the UK there is no evidence that the Borstal (now renamed the young offender) system is effective in influencing long-term recidivism. Of trainees released in 1972, 64% were reconvicted within 2 years; the figure for boys under the age of 17 years was even higher — 79% (Home Office, 1976).

Child-care system

Despite the intentions of the 1969 Act, everyday practice has not mirrored the intentions of child-care legislation. There is evidence that during the 1960s and 1970s there has been a steadily increasing readiness to remove children from home at an earlier stage. Giller and Morris (1981) found that 40% of their sample of offenders in inner London were committed to care at their first court appearance; furthermore, the social worker described this as a very unusual thing to happen. Cawson (1978) and Thorpe (1977) observed that informal community support measures were often not tried, and that residential placements were made before alternatives had been explored. Cawson (1982) found that many of the young people in residential schools for delinquents jumped quickly through several stages of the tariff and quickly found themselves in care or custody for minor or few offences, and that these individuals were not always those who had committed very serious offences or who had multiple and difficult social problems. Later research by Cawson (1984) showed that half the adolescent offenders committed to care had three or more placements in the 9 months following the care order, and that 1 in 10 had five or more placements in that period. This is all the more depressing since May (1978) and Millham *et al.* (1975) showed that frequent moves in care are predictive of further offending and eventual custody.

Clarke and Cornish (1978) showed similar reconviction rates to those of the prison system (i.e. 69%) from the three houses of an approved school (these being known as community homes with education on the premises, or CH(E)s, since 1969) when they were undertaking research for the Home Office.

It seems unlikely that institutional treatment, retraining or punishment is effective in decreasing delinquency. It is even possible that there is a harmful effect because of the alienation, stigmatization and 'contamination' suffered by those who are incarcerated together with other offenders. Even where treatment gains are observed, it appears that they are lost on return to the community.

THE MEDICAL ROLE IN THE MANAGEMENT OF DELINQUENCY

Assisting the judicial process

The medical role in the assessment and treatment of delin-

quency is a limited one yet psychiatrists are often asked to prepare reports on young offenders for the Court.

For those young people coming before the Courts for criminal proceedings, and where a custodial sentence is being considered, certain reports must be prepared prior to sentencing. The Criminal Justice Act (1991) renames social enquiry reports as presentence reports, which should indicate a range of options, not definite recommendations to the Court. The new Act also states that the Court shall obtain and consider a medical report before passing a custodial sentence if the offender appears to be mentally disordered. Approval under Section 12(2) of the Mental Health Act is a necessary qualification in order to undertake this work.

Psychiatrists may be asked to prepare reports by the Court itself, usually through a social worker or, less often, a probation officer; by a solicitor; or by a Guardian-ad-Litem if care proceedings are involved or if it is anticipated that a secure accommodation order may be made. In all cases it is important to bear in mind that any report is prepared in order to assist the magistrates or judge in coming to a decision, and that it is unhelpful if the report is weighed too heavily in favour of one party versus another.

There are a number of different issues on which psychiatrists may be asked to advise. The first, and most obvious, is to comment on the presence (or absence) of mental illness and the risk of suicide. Indications that might suggest these are reports of self-damage, extreme changes of mood and recent changes in personality. A history of solvent or drug abuse may also give cause for concern. Aspects of the background history, in the absence of any obvious symptoms, such as a previous history of mental illness in the family, may sometimes lead to the request for a psychiatric opinion. A psychiatrist may also be involved in the assessment and management of some developmental delays, physical conditions and illnesses, especially if there is an emotional component. The investigations for speech disorder, enuresis and epilepsy provide examples: the hyperkinetic syndrome of childhood deserves special investigation and treatment. A request may be made for an adolescent to be seen alone, or with his or her family, and in this context it may be possible for a psychiatrist to express a view on the personality and emotional development of the young person, other members of the family or on the functioning of the family as a whole.

Other indications for assessment are unusual or bizarre behaviour either reported in the past, possibly at the time of an offence, or even witnessed in court during a hearing. Inexplicable, repetitive offending, sexual deviancy and dangerous behaviour, such as fire-setting and serious assault against another person, may lead to a psychiatric referral.

As with adults, a specific request for assessment of dangerousness, fitness to plead, diminished responsibility and treatability within the resources of the health service may be requested of psychiatrists.

Dangerousness is particularly difficult to predict, essentially because of the low frequency of such acts. It is well-accepted that past behaviour is the best predictor of future behaviour and factors to be taken into account in the past history suggestive of future dangerousness include an early onset of extreme behaviours such as fire-setting and cruelty to animals or children and an early and extensive history of known offending, particularly if this includes acts of violence. Consideration of the young person's upbringing is important too: harsh, erratic and abusive parenting is often associated with later aggressive and even violent behaviour.

It is not appropriate for a psychiatrist (or psychologist) to become involved in issues concerning the punishment tariff, especially if this entails removing the young person from the community and placing him or her in the prison system. These professionals may support a recommendation for the making of a supervision or care order with intervention in the community, whether or not this includes the offer of out-patient treatment from a department of child psychiatry or child guidance clinic. They may recommend the removal of a young person for treatment within the child-care system or, less often, within psychiatric hospital. Because the notion of alternatives to custody disappears under the Criminal Justice Act (1991), phrases such as 'a direct alternative to custody' should not be used.

Psychiatrists and psychologists often play an important role in consulting to establishments within the child-care system.

TREATMENT INTERVENTIONS

General issues

Study design and evaluation of programmes

It is difficult to assess the value of specific treatment programmes because of the poor quality of many studies (West, 1982; Rutter & Giller, 1983). Some form of comparison is an essential component of evaluation: the most satisfactory way of ensuring this is the use of random allocation of delinquents to treatment programmes versus conditions of no intervention. For practical, ethical and emotional reasons this rarely occurs and, at best, systematic comparisons are made between different kinds of treatment, to which offenders have been allocated in a nonrandom fashion. Many studies are based on small samples, with short follow-up periods and large losses of subjects, which could hardly be expected to yield statistically significant results unless the reduction in convictions were exceptionally pronounced. Traditionally, outcome is measured by reconviction rates, which provide a very insensitive tool. Rates alone do not take account of the possibility that interventions may lead to less serious, possibly less violent offending, nor do they take account of other aspects of social functioning, for example unemployment, social isolation, mental disorder, alcohol and drug abuse. If interventions improved psychological functioning without affecting reconviction rates, a worthwhile aim would have been achieved. It often remains uncertain what procedure is being introduced and evaluated, particularly when global terms such as supervision or counselling are used; interventions, particularly

when poorly defined, are not always introduced and carried through as intensively as originally intended; often the same treatment is given to everyone, regardless of individual need or suitability, with the result that benefits to some may be offset or diluted by nil effects or damage to others; finally, the causal connections between the goals to be remedied and the reduction of delinquent behaviour is left unclear.

Characteristics of the delinquent

Where patterns of delinquency overlap with other problems they may well require treatment in their own right; often this can best be provided by a multidisciplinary team based in a child psychiatry department. These teams are usually headed by a medically qualified practitioner but the medical role in the treatment of delinquency is probably a limited one. Overt neurological disorder or severe psychiatric abnormality is met with only occasionally in adolescent offenders. Those with hyperactivity and attentional deficits may benefit from medication and behavioural psychotherapy, those with emotional disturbance from individual or family psychotherapy. However the numbers that can be helped in these ways are few. It is perhaps important to note that in the inner London study undertaken by Farrington *et al.* (1988a,b) males who were from criminogenic backgrounds who were not convicted nevertheless had other indicators, such as a high score on the General Health Questionnaire, that suggested that they might benefit from some kind of input.

Very few studies have concerned themselves with the possibility that differential treatment effects might be related to differing characteristics of the young person. This was looked at by Adams (1962) in the Pilot Intensive Counselling Organization project. This study, which used experimental and control groups, showed that treated 'amenables' (i.e. those who were bright, verbal, anxious, insightful with awareness of problems, a desire to change and acceptance of treatment) did better than untreated groups with respect to recidivism; also that treated nonamenables tended to do worse.

A different approach comes from the I-level theory of personality development, which proposes that individuals can be described in terms of seven successive levels of interpersonal maturity (Sullivan *et al.*, 1957; Warren, 1966). The California Treatment Project undertaken by Palmer (1973, 1974) and Warren (1969, 1977) used this diagnostic typology. Power-oriented youths did worse with experimental treatment whilst the neurotic group fared significantly better. The neurotic youths were characterized by feelings of inadequacy or rejection or by symptoms of emotional disturbance. Unfortunately, despite the use of control groups, accounts of this study are not clear, yet it remains an important attempt to look at differing needs of offenders and requires further replication.

The amenable/nonamenable and I-level classifications are difficult to translate into behavioural terms and everyday practice for those not conversant with them. However, it does seem that intensive counselling is only likely to be of value with rather anxious, introverted youths who are aware of their personal problems and who want help for them. Different approaches are required for other types of adolescents.

Characteristics of the programme

Although there is a paucity of empirical evidence, it appears that short-term, focused therapies, with explicit aims and definite targets, are generally more effective than traditional, long-term, open-ended psychotherapeutic approaches (Reid & Shyne, 1969).

A problem-oriented approach, based on social learning principles, promises to be the most effective and has been described by Stumphauzer (1986). It lends itself to the use of behavioural methods of intervention using operant principles, modelling, social skills training and problem-solving techniques. They have the added advantage that they have been used in various settings such as the family, the community and within institutions, and can be aimed at improving family functioning, educational and social skills, possibly from a preschool age.

Characteristics of the therapist

As early as 1967, Truax and Carkhuff's work, with adults being treated with Rogerian counselling, emphasized that effective counsellors were characterized by genuineness, empathy and nonpossessive warmth. Subsequent work has shown a great deal of inconsistency in the effects of therapist variables (Mitchell *et al.*, 1977) and other studies have suggested that different qualities are important. Alexander *et al.* (1976) examined therapist variables in relation to interventions with families of delinquents. They found that 60% of the outcome in treated cases was accounted for by structuring and relationship skills (these latter being composed of several behaviourally defined categories, including affection, warmth and humour). Kolvin *et al.* (1981) found substantial differences between therapists in their effectiveness in treating children, but that the important qualities were extroversion, assertiveness and openness. Clearly research indicates that therapist qualities are important, but further studies are required in order to establish which are the most important ones and whether or not they can be taught.

Nonresidential approach to treatment

The individual

Seidman *et al.* (1980) described a community programme in which 11–17-year-old delinquent youths were randomly allocated to a treatment programme or to a control group. The strategies used included behavioural contracting, relationship skills and child advocacy. The number of contacts with police, the seriousness of offences and numbers of referrals to court were all significantly less for the treated group, although no significant changes in the social attitudes of the treated group were discernible.

A later study separated the cognitive-behavioural and relationship components for children with antisocial behaviour, the former being more effective than the latter. Kazdin *et al.* (1989) evaluated the outcomes of 112 children randomly assigned to one of three treatments: (1) problem-solving skills training; (2) problem-solving skills training with *in vivo* practice; or (3) client-centred relationship therapy. The first two groups showed significantly greater reductions in antisocial behaviour and overall behavioural problems, and greater increase in prosocial behaviours. The results were evident immediately after treatment and at 1-year follow-up, and were evident both at home and at school. Despite these encouraging results, comparisons with normal controls showed that the majority of the clinic population remained outside the normal range of behaviour.

The individual and the school

As Farrington (1990) stated, if low intelligence and school problems are causes of offending, then any programme that leads to an increase in school success should lead to a decrease in offending. He quoted the Perry preschool project carried out in Michigan by Schweinhart and Weikart (1980). This compensatory education programme randomly allocated more than 240 disadvantaged black children to experimental and control groups. The daily preschool programme lasted 2 years and aimed to provide intellectual stimulation, an increase of cognitive abilities and increases in later school achievement. The initial gains were short-lived. However the treatment group was found to be significantly better in elementary school motivation, school achievement at 14, teacher ratings or classroom behaviour at 6–9, self-reports of classroom behaviour at 15, and self-reports of offending at 15. A later follow-up study of this group by Berrueta-Clement *et al.* (1984) showed that, at age 19, the experimental group were more likely to be employed, more likely to have graduated from high school, more likely to have received college or vocational training, and less likely to have been arrested (31% as opposed to 51% of the controls). Clearly this study suggests great promise but requires replication.

The family

There are several studies suggesting that family harmony is important in fostering the amelioration of conduct disorders in children. For example, Rutter (1971) studied children who had experienced severe early stresses and who were separated from their parents as a result of family discord and problems. Those who were still in homes characterized by discord and disharmony were compared with those subsequently living in harmonious, happy homes. A change for the better in family circumstances was associated with a marked reduction in the risk of conduct disorder. The work suggested that a good relationship with one parent protected children from developing conduct disorders when brought up in an otherwise discordant, unhappy home. However a prospective study of children's behaviour during the 2 years following parental divorce has indicated that the relationship must be both particularly good and with the parent currently living with the child if there is to be a significant effect (Hetherington *et al.*, 1979a,b).

It is not known how relevant these studies are in relation to delinquency, but behavioural approaches to the modification of family interactions are thought to be promising.

Alexander and Parsons (1973) placed their emphasis on improving family communication and organization, with contingency contracting on specific areas of dispute within the family. Results suggested that intervention is beneficial, though there are doubts because of methodological imperfections.

The most extensive series of behavioural family intervention studies are those undertaken by Patterson and his colleagues at the Oregon Social Learning Center (Patterson *et al.*, 1973; Patterson, 1974, 1979). Both aggressive children and delinquents have been treated using a behaviourally oriented parent-training programme. Parents are helped to use positive, noncoercive methods of control; to interact more positively as a family; to monitor their children's activities better and to deal more decisively with deviant behaviour; to negotiate behavioural contracts with their children; and to develop improved social problem-solving skills. Detailed quantified observational techniques are used to assess parent–child interactions, parental and child behaviours. The findings have shown that both aggression and stealing can be markedly reduced by this approach, but that the benefits are much shorter-lived with the latter group. A subsequent study by Bank *et al.* (1991) has shown the efficacy of this approach in comparison with a control group. Parents exerted quicker control over the official delinquency rates of their sons, who were less likely to become institutionalized. This is all the more impressive since the control group had considerable therapeutic input. The authors concluded, however, that it is unlikely that the approach could be used on a widespread basis because of the emotional cost to the therapists.

Kazdin *et al.* (1987) has shown the superior effects of combined parent management training and cognitive-behavioural problem-solving skills over parent and child contact meetings to discuss treatment and activities. In a later study, Kazdin (1990) looked at the differences between children and families who completed treatment versus those who terminated prematurely. The results indicated that, among cases who terminated treatment prematurely, children showed more severe conduct disorder symptoms and more delinquent behaviours; mothers reported greater stress from their relations with the child, their own role-functioning and life events; and the families were at greater socioeconomic disadvantage than those who remained in treatment. This might suggest that those families most in need of help are those who terminate treatment early but, as Kazdin pointed out, it is possible that these families would not benefit from the treatment offered or may profit better from an alternative service.

REMOVAL FROM HOME

Residential approaches in the community

In general there is little evidence that residential establishments remote from the community are able to help many young offenders and their families and there is a particular problem with respect to the generalization of skills acquired. One of the most important developments was the establishment of residential group homes, closely integrated with the community and run on behavioural lines.

In the UK Reid *et al.* (1980) developed a three-phase programme called SHAPE. Offenders aged 16–23 are placed in a group home with a relatively high level of control, reinforcement and shaping of social skills. In phase 2 these youths move into two-person housing with increased self-management. Finally, independent living and employment are shaped. This was a descriptive account and no results of evaluation are available.

Extensive developments came from the Achievement Place studies in North America (Phillips, 1968; Phillips *et al.*, 1971, 1973; Fixsen *et al.*, 1973; Hoefler & Bornstein, 1975). The model provides a community-based, family-style, group home-treatment programme for 6–8 youths aged 12–15 years who would otherwise be institutionalized. The programme is administered by a couple referred to as teaching parents, who have had a year's professional training. Reinforcement, modelling and instruction are used to establish the necessary skills needed in the social, self-care, academic and prevocational areas that the youths have not already acquired. A motivation (token economy) system, a merit system (without the use of tokens), a self-government system and a comprehensive behavioural skill-training curriculum are all used. The boys attend local schools, have the same friends and visit their parents; the teaching parents are responsible for establishing good working relationships with various community agencies as well as transferring skills to the boy's parents. In the short term, significant changes have been observed in most target areas, such as school attendance, police and Court contacts and subsequent institutionalization. Kirigen *et al.* (1982), however, found no advantages at 1-year follow-up.

Residential approaches removed from the community

It is clear that few adolescents will require residential treatment, particularly in a secure setting, though those that do present a great challenge. It has been noted that some patterns of delinquency overlap with symptoms of psychiatric disturbance, though the numbers are small. Very few adolescents under the age of 17 require detention under the Mental Health Act. None of them are now detained within the special hospital system, and those who are detained are admitted either to the only National Health Service medium-secure unit in the country in Manchester, or to one of the hospitals providing specialists services within the private hospital sector.

Adolescents 17 years or older requiring detention under the Mental Health Act may be admitted to either the private sector or special hospital. The majority of adolescent offenders thought to need a treatment approach in a secure setting are detained using child-care legislation. Some young people are admitted to the National Health Service medium-secure unit referred to above, whilst others are admitted to units in the child-care system, including the two specialized youth treatment centres which are managed by the Department of Health. These establishments have psychiatric and psychological input and, like other therapeutic institutions, provide a variety of treatment approaches ranging from an emphasis on an insight-oriented therapeutic living group experience (Rose, 1990) to behaviourally oriented taken economies (Hoghughi, 1979).

As Bullock *et al.* (1990) stated, the young people in secure child-care units present with a wide variety of problems, which makes it difficult for centres to fashion a clear treatment approach. They argued that the psychiatric and psychological diagnoses, which could help in this respect, tend to emphasize the absence of formal mental illness rather than specify needs and proven remedies. Hoghughi (1992) has attempted to overcome this difficulty by developing a problem profile approach in the assessment of young people.

The relative merits of the different approaches referred to above for different sorts of young people has yet to be determined. However, two different studies have looked at the efficacy of psychotherapy and behavioural methods in institutional settings.

Persons (1966, 1967) studied the effects of group and individual psychotherapy for boys aged 15−19 years, who were matched with a control group. The experimental group showed better institutional adjustment and interpersonal relationships and at 1-year follow-up showed a lower recidivism rate and a better employment record.

In the UK Reid (1982) reported on the ongoing development of a behavioural programme in a secure youth treatment centre, which started as a highly structured token economy system but which has evolved to a more flexible one.

In North America the Cascadia project (Sarason & Ganzer, 1973; Sarason, 1978) provides a good example of the efficacy of individually applied behavioural methods which has been evaluated. Modelling, role-playing and discussion were used to teach social skills in applying for a job, in resisting peer group pressure to engage in antisocial acts, in dealing with social problems, and in planning ahead. Behavioural ratings whilst within the institution and recidivism rates showed that the experimental groups did considerably better than the controls at 33 months and at 5 years. Other studies have been described by Stumphauzer (1986).

Different studies have shown other factors to be important, however. Cross-institutional designs have been used to look at the large differences that exist between institutions in the behaviour shown by similar types of residents whilst in their care. The first Home Office cross-institutional study was designed and carried out by Sinclair (1971, 1975). It was found that the proportion of boys leaving prematurely (as a result of absconding or reoffending) varied between 14 and 78%. Sinclair found that much of the variation was related to characteristics of staff, particularly the wardens. Absconding was less frequent from hostels with a strict discipline, where wardens expressed warmth towards the boys and were in agreement with their wives about how the hostel should be run.

Clarke and Martin (1971), Sinclair and Clarke (1973) and Tutt (1976) have also shown wide variations of 10−75% in absconding and 15−66% in drop-out rates, respectively from CH(E)s. Again, studies by Millham *et al.* (1975) and Sinclair and Clarke (1982) have shown that successful schools are dependent on qualities of staff and combine a harmonious atmosphere, good staff−pupil relationships, kindness, consistency and firmness with high expectations, a high level of activities and vocational training. Dunlop's (1974) more detailed study of eight CH(E)s, catering for boys aged 12−15 on admission, showed that schools which appeared to lay emphasis on trade training and on mature, responsible behaviour had lower rates of absconding and other forms of misbehaviour during admission as well as having marginally, though significantly, better reconviction rates.

Somewhat similar results have been shown in studies of ordinary schools. For example, in their comparison of 12 inner London secondary schools, Rutter *et al.* (1979) showed that delinquency rates were probably affected by school factors such as appropriately high expectations, good group management, effective feedback to the children with ample use of praise, the setting of good models of behaviour by teachers, pleasant working conditions, and giving pupils positions of trust and responsibility.

In summary, it appears that a problem-oriented approach using behavioural methods of intervention is more effective than counselling and psychotherapy. In addition, warmth, consistency, firmness and high but appropriate expectations are essential.

SUMMARY

Delinquency is a large problem, at least in inner cities, yet only about one-quarter of adolescent offenders go on to become recidivists. There is conflicting evidence as to whether treatment aims should be directed towards the individual, the family, the institution or society. Whilst it may seem appropriate to intervene as early as possible in the lives of potential delinquents, there are many practical and ethical issues raised by this. Since 75% of delinquents do not become persistent recidivists, research suggests that they should be dealt with by cautions or community-based programmes. Fortunately it appears that, in the UK at least, there is now an increasing trend away from the court process and incarceration in prison establishments. If treatment is to be offered, there seems to be a consensus of opinion that short-term, focused therapies aimed at improving family functioning, educational, vocational and social skills, possibly from a preschool age, are the most effective. Any treatment gains achieved whilst in residential care appear to be short-lived, particularly if the young person returns to an unstable family or an asocial environment. It therefore seems that residential care should be reserved for those individuals who commit repeated, violent crimes and for those from very damaging family backgrounds who repeatedly abscond or absent themselves from community-based programmes. Whatever setting or professional is used, it seems that warmth, consistency, firmness, high, but appropriate, expectations and clearly defined objectives are essential.

ACKNOWLEDGEMENT

Parts of this chapter, particularly that on the preparation of court reports, are based on an article Treatment of Delinquents, published in *Archives of Disease in Childhood* 1992; **67**, 1392−1397. The author is grateful to the editors for allowing this material to be reproduced.

REFERENCES

Adams S. (1962) The PICO project. In: Johnston N., Savitz L. & Wolfgang M.E. (eds) *The Sociology of Punishment and Correction*, pp. 213−224. Wiley, New York.

Alexander J.F. & Parsons B.V. (1973) Short-term behavioural intervention with delinquent families: impact on family process and recidivism. *Journal of Abnormal Psychology*, **81**, 219−225.

Alexander J.F., Barton C., Schiavo R.S. & Parsons B.V. (1976) Systems-behavioural intervention with families of delinquents: therapist characteristics, family behaviour and outcome. *Journal of Consulting and Clinical Psychology*, **44**, 656−664.

Bank L., Marlowe J.H., Reid J.B., Patterson G.R. & Weinrott M.R. (1991) A comparative evaluation of parent-training interventions for families of chronic delinquents. *Journal of Abnormal Child Psychology*, **19**, 15−33.

Belson W.A. (1968) The extent of stealing by London boys and some of its origins. *Advancement of Science (British Association)*, **25**, 171−184.

Belson W.A. (1975) *Juvenile Theft: The Causal Factors*. Harper & Row, London.

Berg I., Consteridine M., Hullin R., McGuire R. & Tyrer S. (1978) The effect of two randomly allocated court procedures on truancy. *British Journal of Criminology*, **18**, 232−244.

Berrueta-Clement J.R., Schweinhart L.J., Barnett W.S., Epstein A.S. & Weikart D.P. (1984) *Changed Lives*. High/Scope, Ypsilanti, MI.

Bottoms A. (1993) *Evaluation of Intermediate Treatment*. Final Report to the Department of Health, London.

Bottoms A., Brown P., McWilliams B., McWilliams W., Nellis M. & Pratt J. (1990) *Intermediate Treatment and Juvenile Justice*. HMSO, London.

Buikhuisen W. & Hoekstra H.A. (1974) Factors leading to recidivism. *British Journal of Criminology*, **14**, 63−69.

Bullock R., Hosie K., Little M. & Millham S. (1990) The characteristics of young people in youth treatment centres: a study based on leavers from St Charles and Glenthorne between 1982 and 1985. *Journal of Forensic Psychiatry*, **1**, 329−350.

Cawson P. (1978) *Community Homes: A Study of Residential Staff*. DHSS Research Report no. 2. HMSO, London.

Cawson P. (1982) *Young Offenders in Care*. DHSS, London.

Cawson P. (1984) Learning from experience: research and the place-

ments of adolescents in care. *Orchard Lodge Studies of Deviancy*, **4**, 99−114.

Cawson P. (1985) Annotation: intermediate treatment. *Journal of Child Psychology and Psychiatry*, **26**, 675−681.

Cawson P. (1986) *Long Term Secure Accommodation: A Review of Evidence and Discussion of London's Needs*. London Borough's Children's Regional Planning Committee, London.

Cawson P. & Martell M. (1979) *Children Referred To Closed Units*. DHSS Research Report no. 5. Her Majesty's Stationery Office, London.

Christensen R. (1967) *Projected Percentage of US Population with Criminal Arrest and Conviction Records*. President's Commission on Law Enforcement and the Administration of Criminal Justice. Taskforce Report: Science and Technology, US Government Printing Office, Washington, DC.

Christie N., Andenaes J. & Skirbekk S. (1965) A study of self reported crime. In: Christiansen K.O. (ed) *Scandinavian Studies in Criminology*, Vol. 1, pp. 86−116. Tavistock, London.

Clarke R.V.G. (1985) Delinquency, environment and intervention. *Journal of Child Psychology and Psychiatry*, **26**, 505−523.

Clarke R..G. & Cornish D.B. (1978) The effectiveness of residential treatment for delinquents. In: Hersov L.A., Berger M. & Schaffer D. (eds) *Aggression and Anti-Social Behaviour in Childhood and Adolescence*, pp. 143−159. Pergamon Press, Oxford.

Clarke R.V.G. & Martin D.N. (1971) *Absconding From Approved Schools*. Home Office Research Study no. 12. Her Majesty's Stationery Office, London.

Conger R.D., Conger K.J., Elder G.H., Lovenz F.O., Simons R.C. & Whitbeck L.B. (1992) A family process model of economic hardship and adjustment of early adolescent boys. *Child Development*, **63**, 526−541.

Department of Health and Social Security Social Work Service Group (1977) *Intermediate Treatment Planning for Action*. Report of Two Study Groups. DHSS, London.

Dunlop A.B. (1974) *The Approved School Experience*. Home Office Research Study no. 25. Her Majesty Stationery Office, London.

Empey L.T. & Erickson M.L. (1972) *The Provo Experiment: Evaluating Community Control of Delinquency*. D.C. Heath, Lexington, MA.

Farrington D.P. (1981) The prevalence of convictions. *British Journal of Criminology*, **21**, 173−175.

Farrington D.P. (1985) Delinquency prevention in the 1980s. *Journal of Adolescence*, **8**, 3−16.

Farrington D.P. (1989) Later adult life outcomes of offenders and non-offenders. In: Brambring M., Losel F. & Skowronek H. (eds) *Children at Risk: Assessment, Longitudinal Research and Intervention*, pp. 220−244. De Gruyter, Berlin.

Farrington D.P. (1990) Implications of criminal career research for the prevention of offending. *Journal of Adolescence*, **13**, 93−113.

Farrington D.P. (1991) Predicting participation, early onset and later persistence in officially recorded offending. *Criminal Behaviour and Mental Health*, **1**, 1−33.

Farrington D.P. (in press) The challenge of teenage antisocial behaviour. In: Rutter M. (ed) *Psychosocial Disturbances in Young People: Challenges for Prevention*. Cambridge University Press, Cambridge.

Farrington D.P. & Bennett T. (1981) Police cautioning of juveniles in London. *British Journal of Criminology*, **18**, 277−284.

Farrington D.P., Osborn S.G. & West D.J. (1978) The persistence of labelling effects. *British Journal of Criminology*, **21**, 277−284.

Farrington D.P., Gallagher B., Morley L., St Ledger R.J. & West D.J. (1988a) A 24 year follow-up of men from vulnerable backgrounds. In: Jenkins R.L. & Brown W.K. (eds) *The Abandonment of Delinquent Behaviour: Promoting the Turnaround*, pp. 155−173. Praeger, New York.

Farrington D.P., Gallagher B., Morley L., St Ledger R.J. & West D.J. (1988b) Are there any successful men from criminogenic backgrounds? *Psychiatry*, **51**, 116–130.

Farrington D.P., Loeber R. & Van Kammen W.B. (1990) Long-term criminal outcomes of hyperactivity-impulsivity-attention deficit and conduct problems in childhood. In: Robins L. & Rutter M. (eds) *Straight and Devious Pathways from Childhood to Adulthood*, pp. 62–82. Cambridge University Press, Cambridge.

Fixsen D.L., Phillips E.L. & Wolf M.M. (1973) Achievement place: experiments in self government with predelinquents. *Journal of Applied Behavior Analysis*, **6**, 31–49.

Giller H. & Morris A. (1981) *Care and Discretion*. Burnett Books, London.

Hardt R.H. & Hardt S.P. (1977) On determining the quality of the delinquency self-report method. *Journal of Research in Crime Delinquency*, **14**, 247–261.

Hetherington E.M., Cox M. & Cox R. (1979a) Play and social interaction in children following divorce. *Journal of Social Issues*, **35**, 26–49.

Hetherington E.M., Cox M. & Cox R. (1979b) Family interaction and the social, emotional and cognitive development of children following divorce. In: Vaughan V. & Brazelton T. (eds) *The Family: Setting Priorities*, pp. 89–128. Science and Medicine, New York.

Hoefler S.A. & Bornstein P.H. (1975) Achievement place: an evaluative review. *Criminal Justice and Behaviour*, **2**, 146–168.

Hoghughi M. (1979) The Aycliffe token economy. *British Journal of Criminology*, **19**, 384–399.

Hoghughi M. (1992) *Assessing Child and Adolescent Disorders: A Practice Manual*. Sage, London.

Home Office (1968) *Children in Trouble*. Cmnd 3601. Her Majesty's Stationery Office, London.

Home Office (1976) *Report on the Work of the Prison Department*. Cmnd 6542. Her Majesty's Stationery Office, London.

Home Office (1979) *Criminal Statistics England and Wales, 1978*. Her Majesty's Stationery Office, London.

Home Office (1984) *Criminal Justice Act 1982: Reception Into Prison Department Establishments of Young Offenders*. Her Majesty's Stationery Office, London.

Home Office (1989) *Criminal Statistics England and Wales, 1988*. Her Majesty's Stationery Office, London.

Kazdin A.E. (1990) Premature termination from treatment among children referred for antisocial behaviour. *Journal of Child Psychology and Psychiatry*, **31**, 415–425.

Kazdin A.E., Esveldt-Dawson K., French N.H. & Unis A.S. (1987) Effects of parent management training and problem-solving skills training in the treatment of antisocial child behaviour. *Journal of the American Academy of Child and Adolescent Psychiatry*, **26**, 416–424.

Kazdin A.E., Bass D., Siegel T. & Thomas C. (1989) Cognitive-behavioural therapy and relationship therapy in the treatment of children referred for antisocial behaviour. *Journal of Consulting and Clinical Psychology*, **57**, 522–535.

Kirigen K.A., Braukmann C.J., Atwater J.D. & Wolf M.M. (1982) An evaluation of teaching family (achievement place) group homes for juvenile offenders. *Journal of Applied Behavior Analysis*, **15**, 1–16.

Kolvin I., Garside R.F., Nicol A.R., MacMillan A., Wolstenholme F. & Leitch I.M. (1981) *Help Starts Here: The Maladjusted Child in the Ordinary School*. Tavistock, London.

Lie N. (1981) Young lawbreakers: a prospective longitudinal study. *Acta Paediatrica Scandinavica*, Suppl. 288, pp. 5–58.

Loeber R. (1987) Behavioural precursors and accelerators of delinquency. In: Buikhuisen W. & Mednick S.A. (eds) *Explaining Criminal Behaviour*, pp. 51–67. Brill, Leiden, Netherlands.

McCord J. (1978) A 30 year follow-up of treatment effects. *American Psychologist*, **33**, 284–289.

McCord J. (1979) Some child-rearing antecedents of criminal behaviour in adult men. *Journal of Personality and Social Psychology*, **37**, 1477–1486.

McCord J. (1985) Deterrence and the light touch of the law. In: Farrington D.P. & Gunn J. (eds) *Reactions to Crime: The Police, Courts, and Prisons*, pp. 73–85. John Wiley, Chichester.

Magnusson D. & Bergman L.R. (1990) A pattern approach to the study of pathways from childhood to adulthood. In: Robins L. & Rutter M. (eds) *Straight and Devious Pathway from Childhood to Adulthood*, pp. 101–115. Cambridge University Press, Cambridge.

Martinson R. (1974) What works? Questions and answers about prison reform. *Public Interest*, **35**, 22–54.

May J. (1978) *Youngsters in Court: Phase Two*. Warwickshire Social Services Department, Coventry.

Millham S., Bullock R. & Cherret P. (1975) *After Grace — Teeth: A Comparative Study of the Residential Experience of Boys in Approved Schools*. Human Context Books, London.

Millham S., Bullock R. & Hosie K. (1978) *Locking Up Children: Secure Provision Within the Child-Care System*. Saxon House, Farnborough, Hampshire.

Mitchell K.M., Bozarth J.D. & Krauft C.C. (1977) A reappraisal of the therapeutic effectiveness of accurate empathy, non-possessive warmth and genuineness. In: Gurman A.S. & Razin A.M. (eds) *Effective Psychotherapy: A Handbook of Research*, pp. 482–502. Pergamon Press, New York.

Moffitt T.E. (1990) The neuropsychology of juvenile delinquency: a critical review. In: Tonry M. & Morris N. (eds) *Crime and Justice*, vol. 12, pp. 99–169. University of Chicago Press, Chicago, IL.

Morris A., Giller H., Szwed E. & Geach H. (1980) *Justice For Children*. Macmillan, London.

O'Donnell C.R., Lydgate T. & Fo W.S.O. (1979) The buddy system: review and follow-up. *Child Behaviour Therapy*, **1**, 161–169.

Osborn S.G. (1980) Moving home, leaving London and delinquent trends. *British Journal of Criminology*, **20**, 54–61.

Palmer T.B. (1973) Matching worker and client in corrections. *Social Work*, **18**, 95–103.

Palmer T.B. (1974) The Youth Authority's community treatment project. *Federal Probation*, **38**, 3–14.

Patterson G.R. (1974) Interventions for boys with conduct problems: multiple settings, treatments and criteria. *Journal of Consulting and Clinical Psychology*, **43**, 471–481.

Patterson G.R. (1979) Treatment for children with conduct problems: a review of outcome studies. In: Feshbach S. & Fraczek A. (eds) *Aggression and Behaviour Change: Biological and Social Processes*, pp. 83–138. Praeger, New York.

Patterson G.R. (1981) Mothers: the unacknowledged victims. *Monographs of the Society for Research in Child Development*, **46**(5), 1–63.

Patterson G.R. (1982) *Coercive Family Process*. Castalia, Eugene, OR.

Patterson G.R., Cobb J.A. & Ray R.S. (1973) A social engineering technology for retraining the families of aggressive boys. In: Adams H.E. & Unikel I.P. (eds) *Issues and Trends in Behaviour Therapy*, pp. 139–210. Charles C. Thomas, Springfield, IL.

Persons R.W. (1966) Psychological and behavioural change in delinquents following psychotherapy. *Journal of Clinical Psychology*, **22**, 337–340.

Persons R.W. (1967) Relationship between psychotherapy with institutionalized boys and subsequent community adjustment. *Journal of Consulting Psychology*, **31**, 137–141.

Phillips E.L. (1968) Achievement place: token reinforcement procedures in a home-style rehabilitation setting for predelinquent boys. *Journal of Applied Behavior Analysis*, **1**, 213–223.

Phillips E.L., Phillips E.A., Fixsen D.L. & Wolf M.M. (1971) Achievement place: modification of the behaviours of predelinquent boys within a token economy. *Journal of Applied Behavior Analysis*, **4**, 45–59.

Phillips E.L., Phillips E.A., Fixsen D.L. & Wolf M.M. (1973) Achievement place: behaviour shaping works for delinquents. *Psychology*

Today, June, 75–79.

Reid I.D. (1982) A behavioural regime in a secure youth treatment centre. In: Feldman M.P. (ed) *Developments in the Study of Criminal Behaviour, vol. 1. The Prevention and Control of Offending,* pp. 79–106. Wiley, Chichester.

Reid W.J. & Shyne W. (1969) *Brief and Extended Casework.* Columbia University Press, New York.

Reid I.D., Feldman M.P. & Ostapiuk E. (1980) The shape project for young offenders: introduction and overview. *Journal of Offender Counselling, Services and Rehabilitation,* **4**, 233–246.

Richardson N. & Tutt N. (1991) Delinquency and social policy 1979–1989. *Association of Child Psychology and Psychiatry Newsletter,* **13**, 4–9.

Rose M. (1990) *Healing Hurt Minds: The Peper Harow Experience.* Tavistock/Routledge, London.

Rutherford A. (1980) Why should courts make non-custodial orders? In: *Juvenile Offenders: Care, Control or Custody.* Howard League Day Conference Report, London.

Rutter M. (1971) Parent–child separation: psychological effects on the children. *Journal of Child Psychology and Psychiatry,* **12**, 233–260.

Rutter M. & Giller H. (1983) *Juvenile Delinquency: Trends and Perspectives.* Penguin Books, Harmondsworth, Middlesex.

Rutter M., Maughan B., Mortimore P., Ousten J. & Smith A. (1979) *Fifteen Thousand Hours: Secondary Schools and their Effects on Children.* Open Books, London.

Sampson R.J. & Laub J.H. (1993) *Crime in the Making: Pathways and Turning Points Through Life.* Harvard University Press, Cambridge, MA.

Sarason I.G. (1978) A cognitive social learning approach to juvenile delinquency. In: Hare R. & Schalling D. (eds) *Psychopathic Behaviour: Approaches to Research,* pp. 299–317. Wiley, New York.

Sarason I.G. & Ganzer V.J. (1973) Modelling and group discussion in the rehabilitation of juvenile delinquents. *Journal of Counseling Psychology,* **20**, 442–449.

Schweinhart L.J. & Weikart D.P. (1980) *Young Children Grow Up.* High/Scope, Ypsilanti, MI.

Seidman E., Rappaport J. & Davidson W.S. (1980) Adolescents in legal jeopardy: initial success and replication of an alternative to the criminal justice system. In: Ross R.R. & Gendreau P. (eds) *Effective Correctional Treatment,* pp. 103–123. Butterworths, Toronto.

Short J.F. & Nye F.I. (1958) The extent of unrecorded juvenile delinquency: tentative conclusions. *Journal of Criminal Law and Criminology and Police Science,* **49**, 296–302.

Sinclair I.A.C. (1971) *Hostel for Probationers.* Home Office Research Study no. 6. Her Majesty's Stationery Office, London.

Sinclair I.A.C. (1975) The influence of wardens and matrons on probation hostels: a study of quasi-family institution. In: Tizard J., Sinclair I.A.C. & Clarke R.V.G. (eds) *Varieties of Residential Experience,* pp. 122–140. Routledge & Kegan Paul, London.

Sinclair I.A.C. & Clarke R.V.G. (1973) Acting out behaviour and its significance for the residential treatment of delinquents. *Journal of Child Psychology and Psychiatry,* **14**, 283–291.

Sinclair I.A.C. & Clarke R.V.G. (1982) Predicting, treating and explain-ing delinquency: the lessons from research on institutions. In: Feldman P. (ed) *Developments in the Study of Criminal Behaviour, vol. 1. The Prevention and Control of Offending,* pp. 51–78. Wiley, Chichester.

Smith D. (in press) Youth crime and conduct disorders: sociocultural patterns and time trends. In: Rutter M. & Smith D. (eds) *Psychosocial Disorders in Young People: Time Trends and their Origins.* Wiley, Chichester.

Stumphauzer J.S. (1986) *Helping Delinquents Change: A Treatment Manual of Social Learning Approaches.* Haworth Press, New York.

Sullivan C., Grant M.Q. & Grant J.D. (1957) The development of interpersonal maturity: applications to delinquency. *Psychiatry,* **20**, 373–385.

Taylor L., Lacey R. & Bracken D. (1979) *In Whose Best Interests?* The Cobden Trust and MIND (National Association for Mental Health), London.

Thorpe D. (1977) *Services to Juvenile Offenders.* Unpublished paper, University of Lancaster.

Truax C.B. & Carkhuff R.R. (1967) *Towards Effective Counselling and Psychotherapy: Training and Practice.* Aldin, Chicago, IL.

Tutt N. (1976) Recommitals of juvenile offenders. *British Journal of Criminology,* **16**, 385–388.

Wadsworth M. (1979) *Roots of Delinquency: Infancy, Adolescence and Crime.* Martin Robertson, Oxford.

Warren M.Q. (1966) *Interpersonal Maturity Level Classification: Juvenile.* Mimeographed. California Youth Authority, Sacramento, CA.

Warren M.Q. (1969) The case for differential treatment of delinquents. *Annals of the American Academy of Political Science (Philadelphia),* **381**, 47–59.

Warren M.Q. (1977) Correctional treatment and coercion: the differ-ential effectiveness perspective. *Criminal Justice and Behaviour,* **4**, 355–376.

West D.J. (1969) *Present Conduct and Future Delinquency.* Heinemann Educational Books, London.

West D.J. (1982) *Delinquency: Its Roots, Careers and Prospects.* Heinemann Educational Books, London.

West D.J. (1985) Delinquency. In: Rutter M. & Hersov L. (eds) *Child Psychiatry: Modern Approaches,* pp. 414–423. Blackwell Scientific Publications, Oxford.

West D.J. & Farrington D.P. (1973) *Who Becomes Delinquent?* Hei-nemann Educational Books, London.

West D.J. & Farrington D.P. (1977) *The Delinquent Way of Life.* Heinemann Educational Books, London.

White J.L., Moffit T.E., Earls F., Robins L.N. & Silva P.A. (1990) How early can we tell? Predictors of child conduct disorder and ado-lescent delinquency. *Criminology,* **28**, 507–533.

Wilkinson C. & Evans R. (1990) Police cautioning of juveniles: the impact of Home Office circular 14/1985. *Criminal Law Review,* pp. 165–180.

Wolfgang M.E., Figlio R.M. & Sellin T. (1972) *Delinquency in a Birth Cohort.* University of Chicago Press, Chicago, IL.

Wright W.E. & Dixon M.C. (1977) Community prevention and treat-ment of juvenile delinquency: a review of evaluation studies. *Journal of Research Crime and Delinquency,* **14**, 35–67.

Chapter 57
Inpatient and Day-Hospital Units

Lionel Hersov

INTRODUCTION

Inpatient psychiatric units for children were first set up in the US in New York and Philadelphia to care for the large numbers of children with behaviour disorders following the epidemic of encephalitis at the close of World War I (Chess, 1969). The aim was to contain children's behaviour problems by care and management. As other units were opened, they came to provide for children with all types of emotional disturbance who could not be treated as outpatients. There was a change from mainly custodial function to the use of the inpatient setting as a therapeutic agent in itself.

The treatment procedures in these newer units were naturally derived from the outpatient practice of the time, that is, the clinical team approach of psychiatrist, psychologist and psychiatric social worker using mainly psychotherapy and casework. They included the additional features of an individual treatment programme for each child, the constructive use of group interaction and the integrated help of other professional disciplines. Modern inpatient units usually include the disciplines of psychiatry, nursing, psychology, social work, paediatrics, occupational therapy, sometimes child psychotherapy and may include activity therapy, recreational therapy and expressive arts therapy. More specialized units may employ child-care workers and speech and language therapists, depending on the age of the children and the range of disorders that require assessment and treatment (Schulman & Irwin, 1982).

The newer ideas of inpatient placement for assessment and treatment rather than merely containment required dimensions of knowledge over and above that of the child's individual psychopathology (Sonis, 1967). In order to use the environment to bring about therapeutic changes, many issues must be carefully considered. These include the attitudes of staff towards parents (Christ & Wagoner, 1966); the parent's and family's role in treatment; maintaining the child as a viable family member (Palmer *et al.*, 1983); the structure and content of each child's daily treatment programme; and expectations and opportunities provided by a group living situation. In addition, the place and objectives of individual psychotherapy, behavioural psychotherapy, family therapy, parent-training programmes and pharmacotherapy must be taken into account.

Psychiatric treatment methods and systems have changed a great deal in the last decade. Escalating medical costs and financial pressure in the US from third-party payers have brought into being different models of treatment, most often to provide short-term psychiatric care focusing on assessment and recommendation, crisis resolution and the treatment of acute symptoms of disorder.

Acute psychiatric units, especially for adolescents, have grown in numbers, particularly among private facilities, and the pressure still continues to reduce further the duration of hospital treatment, especially with the introduction of methods of managed care. There is also increased interest in partial hospitalization or day-hospital care because of diminished costs and the fact that care is less restrictive than admission to hospital.

INPATIENT TREATMENT

Aims

Earlier views of inpatient treatment as a benign neutral setting to offset the adverse family influences that get in the way of psychotherapy have rightly been superseded by a broader approach (Berlin, 1978; Schulman & Irwin, 1982). This includes both treatment skills developed from clinical experience and practice in managing deviant children of all types in groups, together with individual treatment based on psychodynamic understanding and the principles of learning. The bedrock of inpatient hospital treatment is to provide physical care, meet children's personal and social needs and give the opportunity for satisfying interpersonal experiences along with appropriate education. The reliance on time as the healing agent has been outlawed by the pressures towards shorter hospital stay. There has to be a definite therapeutic attitude and plan to make use of the many opportunities that all disciplines have to help the child and family overcome personal and social problems. The primary aim of an inpatient assessment and treatment is to provide something that cannot be achieved on an outpatient basis (see below). The goal is to return the child to school and community unless the disability requires permanent residential care (Palmer *et al.*, 1983). In the majority of cases today, admission to hospital is one phase in the overall treatment plan which will often have included outpatient treatment before admission, and will usually include further work with the child, family, school and community services after discharge, either in a day unit or as an outpatient. It may also include foster or long-term residential care.

The modern approach favours the linking of general hospital and community services with hospital units that accept responsibility for meeting the psychiatric needs of a community, including children and adolescents and their families. In this framework, the inpatient psychiatric unit for children is in a functional working relationship with the outpatient services and other facilities and community agencies concerned with children in need (Blinder *et al.*, 1978; Shafi *et al.*, 1979). The aim is to provide help for children with a variety of psychiatric disorders by providing the *appropriate* treatment for each problem and not the *same* treatment for all problems. In this sense, the hospital inpatient unit provides a specialized assessment and short-term treatment programme within a range of services. In countries which are developing services, outpatient facilities may take priority over inpatient services where resources are scarce.

Characteristics of inpatient units

How do hospital inpatient units differ from other residential treatment units? Nonhospital educational units for disturbed children have existed in the UK for many years, providing an appropriate environment for social and emotional development (Laslett, 1975). Robinson (1957) defined an inpatient unit as a psychiatric treatment service in a medical institution or unit. Its function is the assessment, diagnosis and treatment in residence of children and adolescents with psychiatric disorders. It provides a 24-hour service and, in many instances, a 7-day-a-week service for children whose family situation and/or severity of disturbance make such a service the treatment of choice, in contrast to outpatient or other forms of treatment. In such units, the decisions about admission, plan of treatment, discharge and disposition based on the diagnostic and therapeutic findings are made ultimately by the psychiatric staff, in discussion and consultation with other professional disciplines in the unit. Increasingly, patients and their families are involved in the process of deciding what is the best plan for patients after they leave hospital, as well as the various agencies in the community. However, while the child is in hospital, the psychiatrist, whether as a consultant or director, carries the final medical and, correspondingly, legal responsibility for the diagnosis and management of patients in his or her care, regardless of the way in which aspects of the daily work are delegated to others.

Uses and abuses of inpatient treatment

An inpatient unit can solve only some, not all, of the problems of a psychiatrically ill child and his or her family when the child has not responded to other efforts at treatment and presents a dilemma in diagnosis and management. Much

effort, dedication and resourcefulness must go into comprehensive treatment planning for a child and his or her family but this may not be enough to overcome the handicaps of a parental personality disorder and the distorting effects of severe deprivation and abuse on the child's development. Too often, parents form an unrealistic picture of what to expect from inpatient admission. Pressure from insurance companies in the US may influence decisions as to whether a hospital inpatient admission becomes a common choice for treatment. Experience shows that it is much better to spell out the objectives and limitations of any treatment plan at a pre-admission meeting, and to let the parents and child look over the unit before admission. They will then have a better picture of the layout, facilities, routine, visiting arrangements and home passes, but above all, what is required of the parents in the treatment plan.

In general, inpatient admission is the treatment of choice in children when:

1 thought, behaviour and affective display are so severely irrational and bizarre that outpatient treatment is impossible, or where the child may do damage to him- or herself or others. There must also be the realistic likelihood that inpatient treatment can offer effective help;

2 socially unacceptable behaviour arises from a degree of psychiatric disorder that is unaffected by ordinary social measures or removal from home and outpatient treatment;

3 a complex psychiatric problem requires skilled observation integrated with specialized assessment, testing and management, including continuous and prolonged observation and of an intensity not possible on an outpatient basis, such as in low-frequency unprovoked rages;

4 the family interaction is so distorted that life at home leads to continuing or progressive interference with the child's development and progress. In this situation, the child may need a controlled therapeutic environment to provide healthier life experiences and relationships. Financial and other pressures to reduce the duration of in-hospital care may mean that such problems can no longer be treated in the long term. However, a goal-directed treatment plan may be set in motion to continue after discharge with the aid of community resources;

5 there is a life-threatening illness such as anorexia nervosa with severe weight loss, intractable asthma or suicidal depressive disorders;

6 there is a need to relate behaviour change to electroencephalogram events in diagnostic problems, as in seizure and pseudo-seizure disorders; and

7 it is necessary to determine if cognitive impairment is due to neglect.

Experience has shown that inpatient treatment has dangers where the disturbed child has become the family scapegoat or target of parental hostility. When the child is admitted, often as a result of great pressure from referral agents or the parents themselves, he or she may become permanently extruded from the family unless powerful efforts are made to keep the child and family in psychological touch. Admission under these circumstances can easily create strong feelings of rejection and consequent anger in the child, and a sense of failure in the parents; this may be very difficult to overcome later (Mandelbaum, 1977).

In the last decade in the US, the numbers of older children and adolescents admitted to inpatient hospital facilities has markedly increased, representing a trend to admit to hospital over other kinds of care. This has been attributed to many reasons, including family turmoil, divorce, remarriage and change of home, but also financial reasons, mainly the profitability of psychiatric facilities in the private hospital industry. In some cases, youngsters who have been placed in hospitals do not require that level of care and may be confined against their will, at the request of their parents or other agencies, without first considering the appropriateness of less restrictive treatment resources. This has rightly been condemned by professional organizations in the US.

It is utterly inappropriate to use an inpatient unit merely as a prelude to boarding school placement unless the time is used to deal with particular difficulties, such as learning disabilities or problems with peer group relationships, as well as other psychiatric problems. At times, however, careful appraisal of the child's and family's responses to hospital admission (Gair & Salomon, 1962) and the child's own needs for help in developing emotional and social independence lead to the decision that admission to a special boarding school would continue the improvement gained in hospital.

THERAPEUTIC MILIEU AND ORGANIZATION

In the treatment of adults, the terms therapeutic community and therapeutic milieu are sometimes used interchangeably. There are differences of opinion over the practical usefulness of a self-governing community of disturbed children and adolescents, although with adolescents, there are usually regular community meetings. In practice, the staff of most inpatient units shape and control the setting for the group of children as a whole, while attempting to meet the treatment needs of the individual child.

By therapeutic milieu is usually meant those aspects of inpatient ward structure, organization and setting that can help to reduce the emotional and behavioural disorders of children. It is assumed that deviant behaviour is largely due to faulty or maladaptive social learning that interferes with a child's capacity to relate to other children and adults, to apply him- or herself in a school setting, to control impulsive and aggressive feelings and behaviour and to conform to the standards of a social group. Deviant behaviour is also the overt accompaniment of internal conflict, experiences of loss, rejection and abuse, distorted family relationships and psychiatric illness. A therapeutic milieu is a structured environment that provides a variety of human relationships, satisfactory emotional interactions, opportunities for new learning and experiences, mastering of new situations and the development of personal and social competence. It should aim to meet the

child's needs for respect, appreciation, approval and praise, to reduce anxiety, guilt and psychological conflict, to strengthen existing competencies and develop new coping skills where possible (Berlin *et al.*, 1984).

In the US, Jemerin and Philips (1988) have discussed the changes in inpatient treatment over the last decade. During this time, there has been a diagnostic shift towards conduct disorders and to children who are impulsive and aggressive, frequently involved with multiple agencies and with a history of neglect and physical and sexual abuse. Different techniques of patient management have developed as hospital stays have become briefer, and loss of control by children has become the major problem of management. This requires the acquisition and use of management and behaviour skills and techniques with less emphasis on understanding the child and his or her motivations. Training is now required in physical management of children, including physical restraint and the use of unlocked seclusion rooms. Nonpunitive restraint and seclusion must be used with great care according to an agreed protocol with all the necessary safeguards, but can help children gain control of destructive or disruptive impulses (Gair *et al.*, 1984). There is less time for verbal problem-solving because the decision to use physical restraint has to be made quickly to avoid complete loss of self-control. At present, the use of seclusion is largely unevaluated and easily abused and needs further research.

Moss and Boren (1971) have set out criteria for the successful conclusion of adult psychiatric treatment which can be equally applied to children and adolescents. They are: (1) description of the problem behaviour; (2) specification of the treatment goals; (3) description of the patient's current effective repertoire of skills and attainments; (4) specification of the therapeutic methods to be used to achieve treatment goals; and (5) a system of objective measurement over time to assess the direction and magnitude of change in response to treatment. Moss and Levine (1980) have embodied these criteria in a behaviourally oriented treatment programme which includes, amongst other approaches, developmental assessment, social skills training, remedial education, a token economy programme to modify behaviour, parent education and training programmes and psychotropic medication.

It has been found at the Maudsley Hospital that a preadmission home visit is most helpful for members of the treatment team to meet the child and family in their own setting. This reduces the psychological distance between home and hospital, and allows the team to appraise the child and his or her whole family. The nurse in the team makes contact with the child on home ground through favourite toys and pets and gradually introduces the notion of hospital admission and life in hospital. The same clinical team welcomes the family to hospital and the same nurse supports the child during the introductory phase on the basis of trust and confidence established during the home visit. A similar method has been adopted in other countries (Arajärvi & Oranen, 1983).

Specific aspects of inpatient treatment

Once the child enters hospital, the specific goals and objectives of treatment must be defined for all those working with child and family. This task should be completed early on, and can sometimes be done on the basis of the initial assessment. More often, a week or 10 days is needed to assess the child and family's response to admission, to amplify the history and observe how the child functions, so establishing a baseline of observations for later comparison. Some units use semi-structured or structured diagnostic interviews to gather data, as well as rating scales of the child's behaviour. While in hospital, attention is paid to children's peer group relation-ships, their communication and interaction with different adults, their handicaps and areas of competence, the factors which reinforce or modify their behaviour and how they talk about their problems, fears, worries and concerns about them-selves and their family, and their hopes for the future.

Treatment planning is a crucial part of the treatment process in hospital. Several decades ago, the pace of planning was leisurely and it was hard to decide when assessment became treatment. Today, with the pressure towards shorter periods in hospital and the estimate of cost-effectiveness in treatment, a systematic form of treatment planning has come into being. Nurcombe (1989) has proposed a goal-directed planning scheme for use during brief periods in hospital lasting 4—6 weeks. This embodies some aspects of problem-oriented clini-cal data collection, leading to the use of diagnostic categories for which treatment is prescribed. Emphasis is placed on the concept of stabilization to enable treatment at a less restrictive level of care than hospital treatment. After a rapid multi-disciplinary diagnostic evaluation, the aim is to stabilize the problems which led to admission and prevented the patient from being safely treated outside hospital. Central problems and potential are rephrased as stabilization goals with the selection of therapy or therapies appropriate to each goal, a designation of a target date for discharge, the stipulation of specific objectives and methods of evaluation. A discharge plan is designed which is negotiated with the family and outpatient and community resources leading to termination of treatment when goals and objectives have been attained. Obviously, there is room for revision of the plan if progress is not maintained, if complications set in, or if deterioration occurs. Integral points of the plan include a diagnostic formu-lation, the definition of pivotal problems and potentials, goals, therapy, objectives of treatment, evaluation, discharge plan-ning and termination. This approach has the weakness that treatment is prescribed for diagnostic categories and not for children.

The arguments against the use of this and other forms of treatment planning (Harper, 1989) include the amount of paper-work engendered, which leads to a mechanical listing of problems and goals for treatment, and the difficulty of deciding on psychodynamic and family objectives. Nurcombe (1989) stated that physical, educational and behavioural objec-tives are much easier to outline and, indeed, some inpatient

units operate very much on these lines, in a rather arid fashion. The overriding question is whether the efficacy of hospital admission and treatment is improved by these methods. Brief hospitalization certainly has a place for a number of short-lived, acute psychiatric problems, but depends very much on the existence of adequate outpatient facilities and community resources to carry on and support ongoing management. Far too often, these are not readily available. Instead of languishing in hospital awaiting a suitable place-ment, children wait at home in distracted families while adequate community services are painfully assembled. Shorter admissions require more planning and definition of treatment objectives but may leave crucial work with child and family undone. Longer admissions run the risk of everything slowing to a halt while awaiting deployment of community resources.

While in hospital, an educational assessment can be carried out, and is often urgently necessary, so that a remedial teaching programme can be set up. A patient may be taken off all drugs to establish a baseline, and response to drugs can be monitored by daily observation and behaviour rating scales, until the appropriate level of medication is arrived at. One-way viewing screens and video-tape recordings are helpful in observing parent—child or family interaction. Objective measures of behaviour help in the evaluation of treatment programmes and involve nursing staff more actively in man-agement (Wilkinson, 1979).

In certain disorders, particularly where young children are affected, an objective of treatment may be to modify parent—child interaction when appropriate, or where inconsistent handling appears to be producing and maintaining behav-ioural disturbance. Family interaction can be observed by the clinical team, or parents can observe the child and therapist together. Parents can watch video-tape recordings of their own interaction with their children and discuss this with the therapists. Treatment planning can then aim to modify faulty interaction and improve behaviour, using techniques of shaping and modelling as well as helping parents develop methods of dealing with any new behaviour problems (Holbrook, 1978). It may be necessary to help parents with mixed or hostile feeling towards their child and the behaviour. Expectations may be unreal, as in the case of brain-damaged children, and interviews focused on these issues can help parents toward a more tolerant understanding of the many difficulties these children have. Parenting skills can be taught to immature young mothers in cases of actual or suspected drug abuse.

The social group on the ward can greatly assist children who have difficulties with social relationships, or one lacking in social skills because of handicaps, such as developmental dysphasia. Others may have withdrawn from social relation-ships as part of a depressive disorder or have missed social experiences because of long-standing school absence (Hersov, 1974). Social skills training programmes (see Chapter 48) can be established for children with severe social incompetence, whereas others will gain confidence and skills by taking part in planned group activities that focus on gaining mastery in a particular skill or game previously feared or avoided (such as swimming, model-making or acting).

The daily programme for an individual child can be structured to overcome a particular difficulty. For example, a graded programme of activities in occupational therapy may be used to overcome poor muscular coordination in a brain-damaged child, or training in the use of gesture or sign language may be used with children with severe language disorders. Very short periods of time out from pleasurable activities can be used as needed throughout the day to help children with impulsive disruptiveness or temper tantrums to gain control (see Chapter 50). This will usually be in conjunction with a parent–training programme to provide continuity and ensure generalization of improved behaviour to situations at home, as well as in hospital. Behaviour contracts may sometimes be set up with parents and children using principles of social learning (Patterson, 1971).

An effective system of communication is needed for any treatment planning, so that all professional disciplines are clear about the goals, objectives, the methods of realizing these within the ward milieu, the family's place in treatment and any changes of plan that are required (Hersov, 1974). The nature of work on inpatient units makes demands on the professional staff's self-understanding, personal stability, resourcefulness, patience and tolerance, as well as requiring a high degree of trained skills in nursing care, and the various forms of social and behavioural treatment. Brown *et al.* (1974) and Wilkinson (1983) have discussed these issues in detail in relation to training programmes for child psychiatric nurses engaged in the hospital care of psychiatrically disordered children.

ROLE OF INDIVIDUAL TREATMENT

The place of individual psychotherapy in the treatment of psychiatrically disturbed children in hospital has altered, in keeping with the changes in the structure and function of therapeutic environments (Noshpitz, 1962; Shaw & Lucas, 1970). The goals may not necessarily be the resolution of unconscious conflicts and the modification of basic character structure. Instead, the objective may be to help the child tolerate emotional distress and develop stronger and more effective defences against anxiety, without attempting to deal with the unconscious causes of conflict. There needs to be a focus on the here-and-now conflicts in real life in order for the child to reach effective solutions and mastery of the situation. The emphasis is on the child's behaviour on the ward, and on his or her expressed concerns in relation to adults and other children. The Life Space Interview (Redl, 1959) is an example of how to deal with immediate crisis situations. In both the ward and individual treatment setting, the patient is offered a chance of a new kind of human relationship, rather than the distorted and anxiety-ridden one he or she may have with his or her parents. In this sense, psychotherapy is reeducative and supportive rather than uncovering. 'No insight, no emotional discharge, no recollec-

tion can be as reassuring as accomplishment in the actual life situation in which the individual has failed' (Alexander & French, 1946, p. 40).

The use of medication in children's inpatient units is really only one aspect of the total treatment plan and behaviour modification techniques are now well-established as useful methods of treatment in a variety of psychiatric problems. Drug treatments are given to help the child become more amenable to other forms of treatment, mentioned earlier. Side-effects of drug treatment should be carefully considered, so that they do not interfere with other treatments and activities. An example would be of the sedative effects of neuroleptic medication on children which interferes with their participation in many activities, as well as interfering with learning. Medication should seldom be given to a child or adolescent only to reduce or extinguish maladaptive social behaviour, although medication may be needed for stabilization or for calming effects with dangerous, assaultative, aggressive and agitated older children and adolescents (Small & Perry, 1989). When medications are used, it is valuable to use standardized rating scales for comparison of effects with and without medication (Kolsko, 1988). (For a detailed account of the use of medication, see Chapter 51.)

THE FAMILY APPROACH TO INPATIENT TREATMENT

In the past, residential treatment programmes for children and adolescents have concentrated on the child or youngster who was placed, with little attention to the family's ability to help in treatment, and after discharge, when the child returns home and is reintegrated into the school and community. As the ultimate aim of hospital treatment is to return the child home to his or her family and back to normal life in school as soon as possible, the work with families is particularly important. A strong case can be made for close contact with a family prior to admission, on the grounds that an understanding of family relationships, parental health or pathology and parenting skills and resources is essential for formulating treatment goals and objectives. Hospital admission tests the resources of child and family to cope with issues of separation and control (La Barbera *et al.*, 1982). A family meeting, as part of the assessment prior to admission, can lead to a clearer understanding of the contextual links between behaviour, affective state and the quality of family relationships. Significant alliances and interactions may be observed which will influence treatment plans. Parental methods of control by bargaining, coercion and differential reinforcement of behaviour can be evaluated. Expectations, sibling relationships and the child's role in the family often emerge clearly. The family meeting can define the need for inpatient treatment, can jointly determine the aims and goals of treatment, allow siblings to view the unit and meet staff, deal with fears and myths about psychiatric disorder and hospitals, and assist the child and family to cope with separation problems.

Hildebrand *et al.* (1981) described the introduction of a full family orientation in a child psychiatric inpatient unit. They mention resistances to this model of treatment among staff, the need for a firm commitment to the approach by the physician in charge, as well as the increased need for staff supervision and training. Jenkins and Loader (1984) highlighted other areas of potential difficulty, namely maintaining a family focus and coping with staff disagreement over case management. They suggested that the child's presenting problem should be assessed from several different perspectives, not only in terms of the child and the immediate family system, but also including the extended family, school and other supporting agencies in the community. As the child becomes integrated into the unit, the child and family initially create a particular pattern of relationships within the ward community which becomes part of the assessment and therapeutic process. This may require a particular way of intervening to maintain therapeutic momentum (Bruggen & Davies, 1977) and the introduction of paradoxical prescriptions of problem behaviour or rituals to provoke change in inpatient settings has been described (Dessee & L'Abate, 1980).

Problems can arise in the integration of individual therapy and family therapy, as well as in blending the different conceptual frameworks of several disciplines in a multidisciplinary team. There is, however, some evidence that family approaches add to successful outcome in that, compared with those treated individually, family-treated patients are able to return to school or work in a shorter time and are readmitted to hospital less frequently (Ro-Trock et al., 1977; Madanes, 1982).

DAY-HOSPITAL UNITS AND TREATMENT

As management in hospital inpatient units became more sophisticated, the gap between the range of treatments available in this setting and that provided in the outpatient or clinic service increased. To bridge the gap, Connell (1961) in the UK developed a day-hospital unit for children. In the US, day-treatment for children with psychiatric disorders dates back to 1943 (Zimet & Farley, 1985) and the numbers of day-treatment programmes have steadily increased over the years (Directory for Exceptional Children, 1980–1981).

Through partial hospitalization, the severely disturbed child could benefit from being in a carefully planned, therapeutic environment on a daily basis, and yet remain with the family for some of the time. This has proved over the years to be a helpful flexible model of intervention with widespread applications.

Aims and objectives

If inpatient treatment aims to reunite the disturbed child and his or her family, with the goal of returning him or her to a normal life in school and community, day-treatment has the goal of maintaining him or her in the family unit. The difference is that the day-unit shares the physical care and nurturance of the child and provides a variable amount of time away from the family during the day (for between 1 and 5 days a week).

There has been a rapid development of day-services of all kinds for children in the community. We need to distinguish between centres that have a specific psychiatric function, and are managed by psychiatric staff, whether called day-hospitals or centres, and those day-centres that may have many overlapping functions with psychiatric settings, but are managed by other agencies and professionals.

In the UK, the day-school for disturbed or 'maladjusted' children is basically an educational provision for children with established psychiatric problems. Although such schools have similar services and facilities to the psychiatric day-centre, the essential difference is that psychiatric staff offer guidance and consultation to schools, but also supervise and take responsibility for treatment of children and families in the psychiatric day-centre (Laufer et al., 1974).

The objectives of day-treatment are to relieve anxiety, promote the development of adaptive skills, improve interpersonal relationships, improve motivation to learn academic skills, develop self-control and raise self-esteem (Zimet & Farley, 1985).

Differences in approach

With no responsibility for 24-hour care, the variation in day-centre settings and configuration can be even wider than in inpatient care. They can be an integral part of an inpatient unit or a separate entity; function in a converted house or purpose-built premises; cater for between 4 and 40 children, with or without parents and siblings; confine their services to specific diagnostic social or age groups; or provide for the whole age and diagnostic range. Children and families can attend daily or for varying numbers of days a week, for months or several years. Centres can be part of a child psychiatric, paediatric or adult psychiatric day-hospital servicing a wide catchment area, or be within walking distance.

Without the need for total care, staff in continuous contact with children can come from a wide range of disciplines. Registered or enrolled nurses can form the core but others can be drawn from among nursery nurses, teachers, social workers, group workers, occupational therapists, recreational therapists, child-care workers and play specialists, in various combinations. In the US, day-programmes generally take a systems approach to treatment, appreciating the interplay within families and the families' environment (Zimet & Farley, 1985). The family system is engaged in the therapy, but specifically designed behaviour management programmes are aimed at children needing this help. Individual and/or group psychotherapy occurs at least once a week in most settings. Communication between staff, and staff and parents is an important feature.

Uses and abuses

Originally, day-treatment was aimed at children requiring more than outpatient treatment, but less than the restrictive setting of an inpatient unit. The argument was advanced that not only can problems of lesser intensity be dealt with, but that it may also be the optimal treatment for all such conditions, even the severe. Complete separation from family does not occur, lessening the danger of mutual rejection and scapegoating. It would appear that children who are in danger of physical harm (whether from abuse or from their own impulses, suicidal or anorexic) require inpatient management. Atkins (1962) claimed equal success with more severely disturbed children using either inpatient or day-hospital treatment. Linnihan (1977) drew attention to the way that adolescent day-treatment can be a satisfactory alternative to institutionalization of emotionally disturbed adolescents.

Where day-centres or inpatient units coexist, flexibility of case management is possible for more severely disturbed children. The day-centre can be used to determine whether a particular child requires a controlled therapeutic environment, whether residential or day special school. It can also be particularly useful in the reuniting-with-family phase of treatment for the child who has been an inpatient and who needs further help before rejoining his or her family and reentering life in the community (Marshall & Stewart, 1969).

Thus, day-hospitals and centres are specifically helpful in the following situations:

1 In those severe and complex problems of thinking, behaviour and family relationships where, because of the age of the child, or the specific patterns of disturbance, separation to a residential unit would not be appropriate. The use of a day-centre in the management of a wide variety of severe disorders has been described (Bentovim & Boston, 1973; Bentovim, 1974).

2 In the management of specific disorders, such as child abuse and parenting breakdown, a day-hospital can provide additional supervision and therapeutic work for reunion of a child who has been separated, for his or her own protection, from his or her family (Bentovim 1977a,b; Asen *et al.*, 1982; Cooklin & Reeves, 1982).

3 Specialized day-centres for psychotic or autistic children have been developed with the possibility of introducing techniques not usually possible in straightforward education settings (e.g. Fenichel *et al.*, 1960; Schopler & Reichler, 1971; Lansing & Schopler, 1978).

4 To provide a therapeutic setting for those children whose psychiatric disorders are of such a degree that family, school and community cannot, for the moment, contain them. At the same time, residential placement may be avoided or postponed to test whether change can be achieved with the child at home.

Therapeutic milieu and organization

The therapeutic milieu and the methods used in many day-hospitals are similar to that created in inpatient units. The organization has to provide for a variety of family relationships, satisfactory interactions and emotional experiences; attempt to meet the emotional needs of all who attend; and improve psychological functioning. The administrative structure is designed to further communication among staff, children and families by regular review of progress by the whole team.

The intake of child and family is particularly important. Some preliminary meetings for explanation, assessment and exploration with the family help to reduce the concern over day-care attendance, especially when regular attendance is expected of child and parents. For parents to label their children and themselves as in need of help requires attention to their resistance and denial at the outset. An individual in the team should be assigned to help with the anxiety engendered in crossing the boundary and remaining 'within the circle'. Further individual family work may be necessary to reinforce attendance (cf. the 'second day packing' phenomenon described by Ounsted *et al.*, 1974).

Relationships with parents are particularly important to create the partnership necessary for regular attendance of the child or of the parents themselves. Work to establish the parents' role in the child's disturbance is needed, either through individual or family work, and to assess the best way of modifying dysfunctional interaction in regular family meetings.

When the focus is on joint work with a parent or a preschool child, these issues are vital. The parent is not an inpatient, yet needs to be responsive to the therapeutic milieu if family relationships are to be modified (Bentovim, 1973). Parent groups are helpful in discussing shared problems or coping with disturbed children. A therapeutic attitude of sharing responsibility and decision-making for the day-unit and its organization with parents may also help them find a role and status which do not foster unhelpful regression.

The amount of time attended depends on the aims and objectives of treatment. If families are severely deprived and disorganized, then intensive attendance, over several days, may be needed (Asen *et al.*, 1982). With less severe problems, a single day or 2 days a week may help. If specific programmes are needed for speech, language or intensive behavioural work, then the child may need to attend far more often than the parents. In children of school age showing severe school refusal, school attendance, as part of the treatment plan, is needed. The flexibility of the day-unit is one of its strengths. A number of intervention methods have been described, depending on whether the groups are treated separately (Frommer, 1967) or conjointly (Bentovim & Boston, 1973; Asen *et al.*, 1982). A variety of individual groups, marital and family interventions can be fitted into the daily programme in predictable fashion.

There are two basic methods of providing treatment for the older child. One uses a school model separate from the inpatient unit, and may rely on specially trained teachers and nurse therapists to maintain the setting and provide regular school work and remedial help, which form the cornerstone of the day. Parents are usually at the margin as older children do not expect parents to be present except for specific events. Activity groups (with painting, drama or music) are generally small to encourage socialization, and the daily programme (Godwin *et al.*, 1966) is arranged in collaboration with the psychiatric team, including remedial teaching and social recreational activities, to encourage competence as well as specific individual and family work with appropriate group meetings and social skills training.

The other common model is that in which the day-patient has an integral place in a joint day- and inpatient unit. This provides considerable flexibility of treatment but can present problems for staff members in their approach to a child who is in their care for 24 hours a day, compared with a child in their charge for a more limited period. In such settings, a child is likely to meet a wider variety of staff and to have separate schooling. Unless there is a reasonable number of day-patients, their needs can often be swamped by the insistent demand of inpatients.

Regular meeting and considerable attention to training (Cooklin & Reeves, 1982) are necessary to maintain a therapeutic milieu, as well as attending to the ongoing needs of specific patients and their families. Projections on to the staff by specific patients and their families need watching. Failure to observe such group phenomena in the staff can create opposition to attempts to carry out treatment. All staff need to provide mutual support and be involved and share in decision-making about intakes. Changes in treatment planning and how to achieve a therapeutic milieu involve the staff in many different treatments such as family therapy, increasing their confidence and sense of shared responsibility.

Specific aspects of milieu therapy

A specific programme for each child must soon be planned, whether he or she attends alone or with parents and siblings. After initial observation and assessment, specific solutions and strategies for particular problems must be devised and fitted into the daily plan. A preschool child with a separation problem requires a relationship with a particular worker or nurse, fostered through shared activities, so that he or she can find adequate comfort to tolerate a parent's brief absence. The worker should have a sufficiently good relationship with the parents so that they can leave with a feeling of trust. Once initial separation is achieved, then the child should be involved in group activities so as to gain confidence in social relationships. Concurrently, individual or group work with parents should aim to uncover the precipitating and maintaining factors leading to the separation problem.

An excessively shy or fearful child also needs a small group which, rather than overwhelm him or her, will draw him or her into shared games, play, music and movement. A regular predictable timetable is required with structured and unstructured periods of play, to develop creativity and control individual and group activities; this will help a child with particular anxieties and help in socialization. Stories and music aid language skills. Regular snacks and mealtimes aid children with feeding problems. Orderly predictable attendance of staff and other children and families provides a stable expectable environment. Holidays and breaks by all are talked about and feelings managed. All these features provide a holding and adaptive framework which encourages confidence and intellectual and social growth.

Aggressive, overactive children need a firm predictable setting and a milieu prepared to use time out from reinforcement techniques or periods of work aimed at lengthening attention and concentration. To increase frustration tolerance and reduce violent responses, the gains from impulsivity have to be reduced, and attention and a social reward given for increased self-control. These methods must be generalized to the child's home by parent training in management of the disturbed behaviour. Families need help to acquire methods which replace punitiveness by firmness. If parents are taken into shared activities with their children, they can learn and then persist in attempts to interact and play with an unresponsive, self-stimulating, handicapped or autistic child, or continue at home with a behavioural or speech programme initiated by a clinical psychologist or speech therapist.

The help of other older children in the unit can be enlisted for a child who feels forced to perpetuate a battle with authority. At times, social pressure from peers can be more powerful than the staff's in helping a child to attend to a teacher with whom he or she has had an earlier conflict. The peer culture can also work against the therapeutic programme. A reasonable degree of identification between worker, parents and children is essential to create a satisfactory therapeutic milieu. Detachment and lack of involvement do not help, and can be experienced as rejection. The balance between reasonable concern and caring on the one hand and over-involvement without understanding is not easy to achieve, but essential for the unit to function well. Consultation and supervision can help the staff group think about interactions, and can be an important element in preserving the therapeutic milieu.

Specific aspects of individual treatments

Individual treatment for a particular child or family needs to be carefully integrated into the therapeutic milieu as a whole. A chaotic or disorganized family will experience the regular sequence of changing activities and regular treatment sessions as threatening, or the opposite, supportive, and their responses can be observed and modified where necessary. The regular family sessions or parent sessions can often be video-taped or the one-way screen used to increase the range of solutions the family learns to employ to deal with the problems arising from disorganization. Experienced workers or therapists can help staff deal with the mass of observations available when a child and family attend for a day, and to sort out the relevant material for monitoring and improving the treatment plan.

A programme of social skills development, speech and language stimulation and behavioural programmes can be designed for a particular child, with or without parental participation. Individual psychotherapy for a child in a day hospital can often appear helpful, yet may confuse the child because of all the other activities going on.

The day-unit can have an important training function, exposing many different professionals to contact with disturbed children and families. The provision of theoretical seminars on child development and behaviour, family interaction and different treatment methods, as well as the teaching of basic skills, helps the staff maintain a therapeutic role without being drawn into roles and behaviour which go against successful treatment. Focused treatment (Kinston & Bentovim, 1981) which puts the presenting problems and family interaction into historical context can help professionals decide what changes they are aiming to achieve, and to evaluate progress in relation to specific targets.

PROBLEMS ASSOCIATED WITH DAY-CENTRES AND HOSPITALS

There are many advantages to flexible day-patient treatment with a variety of treatment strategies available, and the therapeutic power of the group to create a favourable milieu (Gold & Reisman, 1970). This approach has been adopted in many countries in western Europe (see *International Journal of Partial Hospitalization* 1988; **5**, nos 1, 2, for an account). However, problems can arise in the parent–child preschool setting. Frommer (1967) pointed out the high incidence of psychiatric disorders in parents of children attending day-centres. This means that their needs can dominate the centre's resources, to the detriment of the children's needs. There is a definite difference between day-units designed for children and day-hospitals for adults catering for parents. Confusion and inappropriate admissions may arise if the functions of two different types of unit are not kept in mind.

By the same token, the composition of a children's group in a day-unit needs careful consideration. Groups seem to function best with a good mixture of children and of problems. Too many aggressive children or children with severe language problems can distort the group and mitigate against successful treatment, unless units are particularly organized for these problems.

There are also problems for staff working in day-units, centres or hospital inpatient units. Staff in continuous contact with highly disturbed children experience feelings of despair, inadequacy, terror and rage at times. They need a setting to share these feelings without criticism, but with understanding. Problems such as closeness to and identification with certain children, and feelings of rivalry and tension with parents, need to be aired. A sequence of messianic hope, despair and final realistic appraisal of what can be achieved with children and families needs to be gone through (Stroh, 1968) by all workers who start work in such settings.

When workers from such different fields as nursing, teaching, social work and occupational therapy come together, they can pool their resources and teach each other different skills. However, constant contact with problem behaviour and the need to modify their way of working may make staff feel deprived of their professional skills, with blurred roles and fear of losing their professional base. Senior staff of all disciplines need to work together to reduce these anxieties, feelings of loss of self and abilities, so realizing the aim of providing a therapeutic milieu without too much wear and tear on those involved. Helping the staff achieve some personal and professional growth, in turn, helps the children and families.

OUTCOME OF TREATMENT IN INPATIENT AND DAY-HOSPITAL UNITS

There are real problems involved in the study of the effects of treatment, which have been well-discussed by Robins and O'Neal (1969) and Barker (1974). A control group matched for complaints, symptoms and diagnosis, but left untreated or treated in some other way, is needed in order to measure the specific effects of the treatment being studied. The selection of a particular treatment is influenced by many factors, such as the beliefs and convictions of the clinicians involved, and the ways in which the child and family receive and respond to the offer of treatment (Schuham *et al.*, 1964). In a therapeutic milieu, there are many potentially helpful influences acting on the child and family, and it is difficult to tease out the relative effectiveness of each. As a result, the effects of inpatient treatment are little understood because the follow-up studies needed are time-consuming, expensive, methodologically complex and few and far between. In 1984, there were approximately 15 000 children in residential psychiatric treatment in the US (Blotcky *et al.*, 1984). The cost of treatment to families, hospitals and the country in general has come under increasing scrutiny by those responsible, and the effectiveness of treatment is repeatedly questioned, sometimes with decreased financial support.

There are relatively few studies of the outcome of inpatient treatment, affecting the difficulties involved in carrying these out, and none in which there has been a controlled comparison between a treated and untreated group, as it is usually the more severely ill children who are offered inpatient treatment, and there are also problems in obtaining a suitably matched comparison group. The published results of follow-up studies cannot be easily compared as they refer to different clinical populations in different hospital settings, using different methods of assessment such as interviews, questionnaires, telephone conversations and the like.

Winsberg *et al.* (1980) compared community and hospital care of 49 children with severe conduct disorder coming from indigent families with much social disadvantage, emotional distress and father absence. Four-fifths were black or Hispanic families and in two-thirds the father was absent. They were randomly assigned to hospital treatment, described as typical of most municipal teaching hospitals in New York, with no details given, and to community treatment which emphasized social services and pharmacotherapy. A variety of pretreatment measures included psychological assessments, behaviour rating scales. a psychiatric status schedule and a family function checklist. The study is flawed by lack of reliability of behaviour ratings, poor interrater reliability and the fact that one-quarter of hospital cases did not complete their treatment. The conclusions that hospital care offers no advantages over community care are hard to justify, but it appears that children with severe conduct disorders in adverse social circumstances can be dealt with as effectively by community services.

In general, it appears that children with emotional disorder do better in hospital than those with psychotic or organic disorders (Warren, 1965; Levy, 1969; Treffert, 1969; Barker, 1974). However, all studies tend to show that the goal of reuniting a child with his or her family without the need for further treatment is reached in only a small proportion of cases, usually with emotionally disordered children. The majority still require further special help in other hospital units or residential or day-schools for maladjusted children (Capes *et al.*, 1971). In Barker's (1974) words, 'Inpatient treatment was thus often a passport to further help rather than a complete treatment in itself' (p. 307). Lewis *et al.* (1980), in a study of 51 children, found that the majority who had received approximately 2 years of residential treatment fared poorly at follow-up using objective measures of outcome, and their adjustment was often marred by serious psychiatric and antisocial problems. There was a discrepancy between clinical ratings of apparent improvement in function, and actual function objectively assessed. It appeared that neurologically impaired children, or those with psychiatrically ill parents, required lengthier treatment.

Blotcky *et al.* (1984) reviewed 24 child inpatient follow-up studies involving children under the age of 12 and found, on average, children with emotional disorders do well through adolescence and young adulthood: those with more profound personality disorders, psychiatric disorders, clear signs of neurological dysfunction or below-average intelligence do less well. The clinical impression was supported that if the children return to a reasonably well-functioning family, the long-term outcome is improved because effective aftercare can be carried out.

Problems arise on the evaluation of inpatient treatment and many published studies can be criticized on different grounds. Patient groups are usually heterogeneous and descriptions of the specific characteristics of children are poor. Standard diagnostic classifications have been seldom used on the grounds of unreliability and lack of validity. Some studies rely on behavioural descriptions and the use of behaviour rating scales, but these and measures of outcome can be criticized because of the lack of demonstrated reliability. In general, there is still a need for systematic evaluation of treatment programmes in inpatient care (Pfeifer & Strzelecki, 1990), in particular the elements that go into the treatment plan.

The evaluation of day-hospital treatment is beset by similar problems. Children referred are among the most difficult to treat so that comparable control groups or random allocation of treatment modalities is difficult to put into operation. Devlin (1962) reported on children who, although regarded as suitable for inpatient treatment, where randomly assigned to a day-hospital. He noted that, although all children made

gains, parental attitudes were more important in relation to the day-hospital children who were withdrawn from treatment or subsequently admitted to the inpatient unit.

Woolacott *et al.* (1978) carried out a study of the effectiveness of a psychiatric day-centre for preschool children by matching a sample of children referred to the centre with children assessed in an epidemiological survey, and then following both up over a similar period of time. A variety of reliable and valid measures of children's and parents' behaviour were used, including a standardized behaviour questionnaire (Richman & Graham, 1971). There were no significant differences between the groups in outcome, although there were more severely disturbed children in the day-centre group than in the control population, despite attempts being made to match the groups on behavioural ratings, mother's mental health and language disorders. In addition, the day-centre group itself had a preponderance of children with physical illness.

A further 5-year follow-up (Richman *et al.*, 1983) included a second control group matched for the language difficulties, which were a significant reason for reference to a specialist centre. The outcome measures showed a significant improvement in all groups on measures of behaviour and educational progress, but again, no significant between-group differences. The mothers of the day-centre group reported that they themselves had definitely gained help from attendance, largely through discussion with workers and sharing problems with other parents. About one-half thought that attendance had been useful for the child and one-third felt that the child had been helped by school placement. It was of interest to note that the parents did not feel that they had been helped as a family, although attempts had been made to work with all family members. It appears that, where the child has a defined problem, it may be difficult to work effectively on the marriage or the family as a whole.

There are always problems in the evaluation of effectiveness of treatment programmes which are difficult to resolve, particularly when there are many different components to the treatment, and when comparable control groups are difficult to find. In order not to lose within-group differences or specific responses to treatment, Richman and her colleagues (1983) stressed the importance of studying the short-term effectiveness of focused treatments for specific target behaviours or interaction, rather than using broad measures of treatment and outcome. However, the two studies described above showed that control-group comparisons are possible, given the complex setting of a day-centre or hospital. Further research on outcome is clearly necessary.

Zimet *et al.* (1980) carried out a prospective study at a psychoeducational day-treatment programme where children were between 8 and 10 years old. Diagnoses included reactive disorders, childhood psychosis, developmental deviations, psychoneurotic and personality disorders. The average length of stay was 2 years 2 months. A variety of measures were used to assess the children at entry to treatment, termination of treatment 3−6 months later and 15−18 months later. Since an untreated control group was not acquired, a one-group pretest—posttest design was used. They found positive changes in school behaviour, academic performance, IQ, home behaviour and self-concept during the time the children were in the day-centre and at the two follow-up points after treatment was completed.

The outcome data on day treatment so far published permit few conclusions and much additional work is needed. The general impression is that many children benefit, especially the younger children, but the gains are modest and hardly noticeable in certain studies (Woolacott *et al.*, 1978; Richman *et al.*, 1983). Some studies mention the importance of involving the family in treatment when the children seem to do better but again, this is not an invariable finding. Gabel and Finn (1986) reported the consistent impression from outcome studies that they seem effective in reducing or forestalling admission to hospital or placement in a residential school. It also helps some children to return to a less restrictive school placement.

CONCLUSIONS

Hospital treatment of psychiatric disorders in children has steadily evolved since its beginnings where the objectives were containment, to its present, more sophisticated use of milieu therapy embodying psychotherapeutic and behavioural techniques, as well as pharmacotherapy. Current trends in psychiatric treatment are towards less costly short-term treatment in hospital, leading to increasing interest in day-hospitals, family units and mother-and-child treatment services, which include a variety of interventions, including direct work with children in their families. Increasing costs and doubts about the effectiveness of the treatment will put both inpatient and day-units under increasing scrutiny to justify their existence for all but a smallish group of very psychiatrically ill children and adolescents.

REFERENCES

Alexander F. & French T. (1946) *Psychoanalytic Therapy*. Norton, New York.

Arajärvi T. & Oranem A.M. (1983) First contacts with a family whose child is to be admitted to the child psychiatric day ward. *Acta Paedopsychiatrica*, **49**, 119–120.

Asen K., Stein R., Stevens A., McHugh B., Greenwood J. & Cooklin A. (1982) A day unit for families. *Journal of Family Therapy*, **4**, 345–358.

Atkins T. (1962) *Criteria for the Differential Use of Treatment Settings for Children with Emotional Disorders*. Child Welfare League of America, New York.

Barker P. (1974) The results of in-patient care. In: Barker P. (ed) *The Residential Psychiatric Treatment of Children*, pp. 294–309. Crosby Lockwood Staples, London.

Bentovim A. (1973) Group processes in the pre-school centre for children and their parents. *Group Analysis*, **1**, 50–53.

Bentovim A. (1974) Disturbed and under 5. *Special Education*, **62**, 31–36.

Bentovim A. (1977a) Therapeutic systems and settings in the treatment of child abuse. In: Franklin A.W. (ed) *The Challenge of Child Abuse*, pp. 249–259. Academic Press, London.

Bentovim A. (1977b) A psychiatric family day-centre meeting the needs of abused or at-risk pre-school children and their parents. *Child Abuse Register*, **1**, 479–485.

Bentovim A. & Boston M. (1973) A day-centre for disturbed young children and their parents. *Journal of Child Psychotherapy*, **3**, 46–60.

Berlin I. (1978) Developmental issues in the psychiatric hospitalization of children. *American Journal of Psychiatry*, **135**, 1044–1048.

Berlin I., Critchley D.L. & Rassman P.G. (1984) Current concepts in milieu treatment of severely disturbed children and adolescents. *Psychotherapy*, **21**, 118–131.

Blinder B.J., Young W.M., Fineman K.R. & Miller S.J. (1978) The children's psychiatric hospital in the community 1. Concept and development. *American Journal of Psychiatry*, **135**, 848–851.

Blotcky M.J., Dimperio T.J. & Gossett J.T. (1984) Follow-up of children treated in psychiatric hospitals: a review of studies. *American Journal of Psychiatry*, **141**, 1499–1507.

Brown S., Kolvin I., Scott D.McL. & Tweddle E.G. (1974) The child psychiatric nurse: training for residential care. In: Barker P. (ed) *The Residential Psychiatric Treatment of Children*, pp. 273–293. Crosby Lockwood Staples, London.

Bruggen P. & Davies E. (1977) Family therapy in adolescent psychiatry. *British Journal of Psychiatry*, **131**, 433–447.

Capes M., Gould E. & Townsend M. (1971) *Stress in Youth*. Oxford University Press, London.

Chess S. (1969) *An Introduction to Child Psychiatry*, 2nd edn. Grune & Stratton, New York.

Christ A.E. & Wagoner N.N. (1966) Iatrogenic factors in child residential treatment. In: Massenmor J.H. (ed) *Current Psychiatric Therapies*, pp. 46–54. Grune & Stratton, New York.

Connell P.H. (1961) The day-hospital approach in child psychiatry. *Journal of Mental Science*, **107**, 969–977.

Cooklin A. & Reeves D. (1982) Family therapy in a living context: training experiences in a family day unit. In: Whiffen R. & Byng-Hall J. (eds) *Family Therapy Supervision: Recent Developments in Practice*, pp. 243–260. Academic Press, London.

Dessee E. & L'Abate L. (1980) The use of paradox with children in an in-patient setting. *Family Process*, **19**, 59–64.

Devlin M. (1962) Criteria for day treatment type of setting. In: *Criteria for the Differential Use of Treatment Setting for Children with Emotional Disorders*. Child Welfare League of America, New York.

Dingman P.R. (1969) Day programs for children: a note on terminology. *Mental Hygiene*, **53**, 646–647.

Directory For Exceptional Children 1980–1981 (1981) Carter-Sargent, Boston.

Fenichel C., Freedman A.M. & Klapper Z. (1960) A day school for schizophrenic children. *American Journal of Orthopsychiatry*, **30**, 130–143.

Frommer E. (1967) A day hospital for children under 5. *Lancet*, **i**, 377–379.

Gabel S. & Finn M. (1986) Outcome in children's day-treatment programme: review of the literature and recommendations for future research. *International Journal of Partial Hospitalization*, **3**, 261–271.

Gair D.S. & Salomon A.D. (1962) Diagnostic aspects of psychiatric hospitalization of children. *American Journal of Orthopsychiatry*, **32**, 445–460.

Gair D.S., Bullard D.M. & Corwin J.M. (1984) Guidelines for children and adolescents. In: Tardiff K. (ed) *The Psychiatric Uses of Seclusion and Restraint*, pp. 69–85. American Psychiatric Press, Washington, DC.

Godwin M.P., Conor M.E., Atkins S. & Muldoon J.F. (1966) The role of the educational programme in a psychiatric day care center for children and teenagers. *American Journal of Orthopsychiatry*, **36**, 345–346.

Gold J. & Reisman J. (1970) An outcome study of a day-treatment unit school in a community mental health centre. *American Journal of Orthopsychiatry*, **40**, 286–287.

Harper G. (1989) Focal in-patient treatment planning. *Journal of the American Academy of Child and Adolescent Psychiatry*, **28**, 31–37.

Hersov L.A. (1974) Neurotic disorders with special reference to school refusal. In: Barker P. (ed) *The Residential Psychiatric Treatment of Children*, pp. 105–141. Crosby Lockwood Staples, London.

Hildebrand J., Jenkins J., Carter D. & Lask B. (1981) The introduction of a full family orientation in a child psychiatric in-patient unit. *Journal of Family Therapy*, **3**, 139–152.

Holbrook D. (1978) A combined approach to parental coping. *British Journal of Social Work*, **8**, 439–451.

Jemerin J.M. & Philips I. (1988) Changes in in-patient child psychiatry: consequences and recommendations. *Journal of the American Academy of Child and Adolescent Psychiatry*, **27**, 397–403.

Jenkins J. & Loader P. (1984) Family therapy on an in-patient unit: whose problem is it anyway? In: Anthony A.J. (ed) *Yearbook of Child Psychiatry*. Wiley, Chichester.

Kinston W. & Bentovim A. (1981) Creating a focus for brief monital or family therapy. In: Busman S.H. (ed) *Forms of Brief Therapy*, pp. 361–385. Guilford Press, New York.

Kolko D.J. (1988) Daily ratings on a child psychiatric unit: psychometric evaluation of the Child Behaviour Rating Form. *Journal of the American Academy of Child and Adolescent Psychiatry*, **27**, 126–132.

La Barbera J.D., Martin J.E. & Dozier J.E. (1982) Residential treatment of males: the influential role of parental attitudes. *Journal of the American Academy of Child Psychiatry*, **21**, 286–290.

Lansing M.D. & Schopler E. (1978) Individualized education. A public school model. In: Rutter M. & Schopler E. (eds) *Autism: A Reappraisal of Concepts and Treatment*, pp. 439–452. Plenum, New York.

Laslett R. (1975) Aspects of change in the education of maladjusted children. *Journal of the Association of Workers with Maladjusted Children*, **3**, 13–19.

Laufer M.W., Laffey J.J. & Davidson R.E. (1974) Residential treatment for children and its derivatives. In: Caplan G. (ed) *American Handbook of Psychiatry*, vol. 11, 2nd edn., pp. 193–205. Basic Books, New York.

Levy E.Z. (1969) Long-term follow-up of former in-patients at the Children's Hospital of the Menninger Clinic. *American Journal of Psychiatry*, **125**, 1633–1639.

Lewis M., Lewis D.O., Shanok S.S., Klatskin E. & Osborne J.R. (1980) The undoing of residential treatment: a follow-up study of 51 adolescents. *Journal of the American Academy of Child Psychiatry*, **19**, 160–171.

Linnihan D.C. (1977) Adolescent day treatment: a community alternative to institutionalization of the emotionally disturbed adolescent. *American Journal of Orthopsychiatry*, **47**, 679–688.

Lynch M., Steinberg D. & Ounsted C. (1975) Family unit in a children's psychiatric hospital. *British Medical Journal*, **ii**, 127–129.

Madames C. (1982) Strategic family therapy in the prevention of hospitalization. In: Horbin H. (ed) *The Psychiatric Hospital and the Family*. MTP Press, Lancaster.

Mandelbaum A. (1977) A family-centred approach to residential treatment. *Bulletin of the Menninger Clinic*, **41**, 27–39.

Marshall K. & Stewart M.F. (1969) Day treatment as a complementary adjunct to residential treatment. *Child Welfare*, **48**, 40–44.

Moss G.R. & Boren J.J. (1971) Specifying criteria for completion of psychiatric treatment: a behavioristic approach. *Archives of General Psychiatry*, **24**, 441–447.

Moss G.R. & Levine M.J. (1980) A developmental educational and behavioral approach to hospital treatment for children. *Psychiatric International Clinics of North America*, **3**, 501–511.

Noshpitz J.D. (1962) Notes on the theory of residential treatment. *Journal of the American Academy of Child Psychiatry*, **1**, 284–296.

Nurcombe B. (1989) Goal-directed planning and the principles of brief hospitalization. *Journal of the American Academy of Child and Adolescent Psychiatry*, **28**, 26–30.

Ounsted C., Oppenheimer R. & Lindsay J. (1974) Aspects of bonding failure: the psychopathology and psychotherapeutic treatment of families of battered children. *Developmental Medicine and Child Neurology*, **16**, 447–450.

Palmer A., Harper G. & Rivinus T.M. (1983) The 'adaptive process' in the in-patient treatment of children and adolescents. *Journal of the American Academy of Child Psychiatry*, **22**, 286–293.

Patterson G.R. (1971) *Families: Applications of Social Learning to Family Life*. Research Press, Champaign, IL.

Pfeifer S.I. & Strzelecki S.C. (1990) Inpatient psychiatric treatment of children and adolescents: a review of outcome studies. *Journal of the American Academy of Child and Adolescent Psychiatry*, **29**, 847–853.

Redl F. (1959) The life space interview 1. Strategy and techniques of the life space interview. *American Journal of Orthopsychiatry*, **29**, 1–18.

Richman N. & Graham P. (1971) A behavioral screening questionnaire for use with 3 year old children: preliminary findings. *Journal of Child Psychology and Psychiatry*, **12**, 5–33.

Richman N., Graham P. & Stevenson J. (1983) Long-term effects of treatment in a pre-school day centre. *British Journal of Psychiatry*, **142**, 71–77.

Robins L.M. & O'Neal P.L. (1969) The strategy of follow-up studies with special reference to children. In: Harvells J.G. (ed) *Modern Perspectives in International Child Psychiatry*, pp. 785–804. Oliver and Boyd, Edinburgh.

Robinson J.F. (ed) (1957) *Psychiatric In-patient Treatment of Children*. American Psychiatric Association, Washington, DC.

Ro-Trock G.H., Welisch D.K. & Schoolar J.C. (1989) A family therapy outcome study in an in-patient setting. *American Journal of Orthopsychiatry*, **47**, 514–522.

Schopler E. & Reichler R.J. (1971) Parents as cotherapists in treatment of psychiatric children. *Journal of Autism and Childhood Schizophrenia*, **1**, 87–102.

Schuham A.I., Coer M. & Rae-Grant N.I. (1964) Some social-psychological variables influencing parental acceptance of residential treatment for their emotionally disturbed children. *Journal of Child Psychology and Psychiatry*, **5**, 251–261.

Schulman J.L. & Irwin M. (eds) (1982) *Psychiatric Hospitalization of Children*. Charles C. Thomas, Springfield, IL.

Shafi M., McCue A., Ice J.F. & Schwab J.J. (1979) The development of an acute short-term in-patient child psychiatric setting: a paedopsychiatric model. *American Journal of Psychiatry*, **136**, 427–429.

Shaw R. & Lucas A.R. (1970) *The Psychiatric Disorder of Childhood*, 2nd edn. Appleton-Century Crofts, New York.

Small A.M. & Perry R. (1989) Pharmacotherapy. In: Lyman R.D., Prentice-Dunn S. & Gabel S. (eds) *Residential and Inpatient Treatment of Children and Adolescents*, pp. 163–189. Plenum, New York.

Sonis M. (1967) Residential treatment. In: Freedman A.M. & Kaplan H.L. (eds) *Comprehensive Textbook of Psychiatry*. Williams & Wilkins, Baltimore, MD.

Stroh G. (1968) The function of in-service training in the management of disturbed children. *Journal of Child Psychology and Psychiatry*, **9**, 189–207.

Treffert D.D. (1969) Child-adolescent unit in a psychiatric hospital. *Archives of General Psychiatry*, **21**, 745–752.

Warren W. (1965) A study of adolescent psychiatric in-patients and the outcome 6 or more years later. II The follow-up study. *Journal of*

Child Psychology and Psychiatry, **6**, 141−160.

Wilkinson T.R. (1979) The problems and values of objective nursing observations in psychiatric care. *Journal of Advanced Nursing*, **4**, 151−159.

Wilkinson T.R. (1983) *Child and Adolescent Psychiatric Nursing*. Blackwell Scientific Publications, Oxford.

Winsberg B.G., Bialer I., Kupietz S., Botti E. & Balka E. (1980) Home versus hospital care of children with behavior disorders. *Archives of General Psychiatry*, **37**, 413−418.

Woolacott S., Graham P. & Stevenson J. (1978) A controlled evaluation of the therapeutic effectiveness of a psychiatric day-centre for pre-school children. *British Journal of Psychiatry*, **132**, 349−355.

Zimet S.G. & Farley G.K. (1985) Day treatment for children in the United States. *Journal of the American Academy of Child Psychiatry*, **24**, 732−738.

Zimet S.G., Farley G.K., Silver J., Herbert F.B., Robb E.D., Ekanger C. & Smith D. (1980) Behavior and personality changes in emotionally disturbed children enrolled in a psychoeducational day treatment centre. *Journal of the American Academy of Child and Adolescent Psychiatry*, **19**, 240−250.

Chapter 58
Paediatric Liaison Work

Bryan Lask

Child Psychiatry and Paediatrics have enjoyed a long flirtation. It is high time they were married if only for the sake of the children (Apley, 1984, p. 156).

THE NEED FOR PAEDIATRIC LIAISON

Sixty years ago an article was published in the *American Journal of Diseases of Children* welcoming the promise of psychiatry (Plant, 1932). Apley, quoted above, clearly considered that the promise had been fulfilled and consummation was due. What now is the situation? In an era of increasingly sophisticated and highly technological medicine and surgery, it is all too easy to forget the emotional needs of the child and family. Studies have consistently noted high rates of psychopathology in children admitted to hospital. For example, Stocking *et al.* (1972) reported that almost two-thirds of children admitted to a paediatric ward would have benefited from a child psychiatric consultation. Awad and Poznanski (1975) also confirmed a high rate of psychopathology in hospitalized children, and noted that referral to child psychiatry was more likely to be made when the symptoms were of unknown aetiology, depression was suspected or behaviour problems arose on the ward.

Similar findings apply to children seen in outpatient clinics. Apley (1982) and Smithells (1982) noted that in general paediatric clinics about half of the children seen had disorders in which psychological factors play a major aetiological role, and many of the remainder had significant emotional sequelae to their organic disease. Other studies have reported a prevalence for these findings of between 28 and 36% (Fitzgerald, 1985; Cundall, 1987; Garralda & Bailey, 1989).

Paediatricians are quite likely to miss psychiatric disorders. For example, Dulcan *et al.* (1990) reported that 83% of 52 children who received a psychiatric diagnosis using relatively conservative criteria were not identified by the paediatrician as having a psychiatric disorder. They also noted that paediatricians have been found to diagnose psychopathology in 4–7% of patients they see, compared to a prevalence of 17–20% estimated from community samples. Emotional disorders are particularly likely to be overlooked in the presence of an acute treatable medical condition, especially in younger children (Stocking *et al.*, 1972).

Another area of frequently unrecognized pathology is within the families of children with acute or chronic illness. A wide variety of psychosocial problems have been identified, including marital conflict or separation, parental distress or illnesses, ill health in other family members and family dysfunction (Garralda & Bailey, 1989; Dulcan *et al.*, 1990). Kasper and Nyamathi (1988) investigated the needs of parents of children in paediatric intensive care, categorizing these as physical, psychological or social. The majority of parental needs were psychological and failure to fulfil them impairs parental role performance and parent–staff relationships, and increases parental stress. Phipps *et al.* (1989) studied the mothers of 30 infants who had experienced an apnoeic episode and had been placed on an apnoeic monitor. Transient but high levels of mood disturbance were noted. It was possible to predict persistent mood disturbance by monitoring levels of family resources and health locus of control beliefs. Families at risk of maladaptive responses were identified and offered intensive psychosocial support.

Jedlicka-Kohler and Gotz (1988) in their study of 65 children with cystic fibrosis noted that parents frequently over-estimate disease severity. Such differences between subjective and medical evaluation reflect psychiatric complications and point the way to a focus for treatment. Family influences have been shown to be relevant in a wide range of other chronic or recurrent illness, including asthma (Lask & Matthew, 1979), diabetes (Minuchin *et al.*, 1978, pp. 23–51), epilepsy (Rutter *et al.*, 1970; Hoare, 1984), and malignant diseases (Greenberg *et al.*, 1989; Mulhern *et al.*, 1989; Morris & Craft, 1990). Similar observations have been made with regard to chronic disability (Palfrey *et al.*, 1989).

Notwithstanding these areas where psychopathology can be missed, paediatricians are increasingly recognizing the need for help in diagnosing and treating psychiatric problems in sick children and their families, and making use of the available resources (Rothenberg, 1979; Bingley *et al.*, 1980; Dungar *et al.*, 1986; McFadyen *et al.*, 1991).

WHAT IS PAEDIATRIC LIAISON WORK?

Much has been written about consultation in liaison psychiatry, and various definitions exist for both consultation and liaison. For example, Wellish and Pasnau (1979) defined consultation as referring largely to the services performed for physically ill patients and families, often at the bedside in a general hospital, upon referral of the attending physician or other health professional. Liaison refers to the services provided for the physician and staff, tying together the treatment of the patient and family, using educational conferences, psychosocial teaching rounds and holistic treatment plans.

Steinberg and Yule (1986) have argued that consultation is one of many forms of interprofessional activity, and that it differs from liaison work in that the latter usually involves collaboration between two teams who differ in their main focus of interests and methods of working, as is the case between paediatrics and child psychiatry. They see consultation *per se* as having a number of special characteristics. The emphasis is on helping consultees make the most effective use of their experience, skills and resources. The consultant does not take over the responsibility for the child and the consultee remains autonomous in what action to take. Steinberg and Yule add that the consultant–consultee relationship is one of mutual and equal collaboration. However, it can be argued that liaison is also characterized by a mutual and equal collaboration.

No definition has bettered that of Lipowski (1967), who defined consultation psychiatry as that area of clinical psychiatry which includes all diagnostic, therapeutic, teaching and research activities for psychiatrists in the nonpsychiatric parts of the general hospital. He believes the term liaison psychiatry is rather nondescript and offers little advantages, and that liaison and consultation can be used interchangeably.

The more that attempts are made to distinguish between the two processes, the clearer it becomes that this is a pointless exercise. However, Naylor and Mattson (1973) have made a useful if somewhat personal distinction:

> We tried to disentangle ourselves from being classified as just another group of super specialists whose assigned role was that of consultant, preferring to avoid identification with the prima donna and his individual tour de force. By recognising the disadvantages of this obsolete role, and by adopting the continuum of the liaison position, we feel we can present more effectively the concept of total child care.

For the purposes of this chapter the term paediatric liaison work is used to mean all consultation, diagnostic, therapeutic, teaching, support and research activities carried out by psychiatrists and other mental health professionals in paediatric clinics or on paediatric wards.

THE ILLNESS NETWORK

All professionals involved in the care of sick children need to be aware of the illness network, for not only is an understanding of this network essential to comprehensive assessment and treatment, but also we form an integral part of it. The illness network, illustrated in Figure 58.1, consists of four interacting and interdependent components: (1) the child; (2) the illness; (3) the family; and (4) environmental factors (Lask & Fosson, 1989, pp. 55–67).

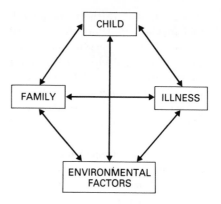

Fig. 58.1 The illness network.

Each component has a number of variables which can affect the balance of the network, and therefore require consideration. Child-related variables include age, temperament, intelligence, understanding of and attitude to the illness, emotional state and coping mechanisms. Illness-related variables include localization, severity, chronicity, prognosis and the relative contribution of physical, social and psychological factors. Family variables include the quality of the marital relationship and of parenting, understanding of and attitudes to the illness, stability, cohesion and communication. Environmental variables include the medical, nursing and other staff involved in the child's care, the child's school and peer group, and friends and neighbours.

The nature of and relationship between each component have the potential for influencing the course of the illness. To give but one example, a doctor's poor communication skills may exacerbate parental anxiety and over-protectiveness, which in turn may contribute to a child's depression and helplessness. In contrast, a doctor who communicates clearly and deals appropriately with parental concerns promotes parental confidence and competence, which in turn can enhance the child's self-image and coping skills.

These factors are considered in more detail in Chapter 42.

THE MULTIDISCIPLINARY TEAM

The multidisciplinary team is central to the concept of paediatric liaison work, and for that matter to good child psychiatric practice. In relation to child protection, the multidisciplinary team has received an official stamp of approval: 'The thrust now must be to ensure that professionals in individual agencies work together on a multidisciplinary basis' (Department of Health, 1988). The multidisciplinary team has been defined as a small, clearly bounded group of people who share a common task, similar values, and who hold distinctive knowledge and skills (Hey, 1979). Each team member will have some specific knowledge and skills distinct from other team members, but also with some overlap.

In paediatric liaison work the multidisciplinary team usually consists of at least one of each of the following: paediatricians, paediatric nurses, play staff, teachers, social worker, psychologist and child psychiatrist. Other disciplines that may be represented include dietetics, speech therapy, physiotherapy, psychotherapy and the chaplaincy. Successful multidisciplinary team work requires clear and accepted leadership, frequent meetings, open communication and regular reviews of the team process. Each team member should be seen as having a special and skilled contribution. The strength of the multidisciplinary team is created by the sharing of these skills and knowledge, leading to a wider understanding of problems and an enhanced potential for solving them (Muir, 1984).

Difficulties may arise if leadership is ineffectual, insensitive or challenged, or when team members find themselves in conflict, either for interpersonal or for ideological reasons, or when pressure of time or lack of commitment leads to irregular and infrequent meetings. (These issues are discussed further in the section entitled 'A model for paediatric liaison work', below.)

In general, given that the paediatrician has ultimate responsibility for the child's overall management, it seems perfectly reasonable for that person to be in charge of the multidisciplinary team, with other specialists acting as consultants. Sometimes the child psychiatrist is perceived, or accepted, as the leader at psychosocial rounds and providing there is general agreement to this there seems to be no contraindication. However it is essential that paediatricians and child psychiatrists have a close working relationship, based on mutual respect and understanding. It is often useful for them to discuss together the nature of their collaboration, laying down the ground rules and sharing expectations. In this way misunderstandings and inappropriate expectations are avoided. Regular reviews of their collaboration will help to ensure a satisfactory working relationship.

Psychiatrists bring to the team a unique background which incorporates training in medicine, paediatrics, adult and child psychiatry. As such they are in a position to advise or coordinate a highly comprehensive programme of assessment and management. To do so they are however dependent on other members of the team.

Social workers are gaining an increasingly high profile in paediatric liaison, especially in relation to child protection work. For social workers to be effective they must have clearly defined roles and be accepted as equals (Bingley *et al.*, 1980). They need to be seen as integral members of multidisciplinary teams, able to offer a social perspective in assessment and treatment, and having a strong and consultative function, as well as their role in liaising with relevant community agencies. The role of the social worker is discussed in full in Chapter 52.

Similar points may be made about psychologists. They bring a particular expertise in regard to standardized psychological assessments, with a focus on the developmental perspective. Communicating with schools and other community-based educational agencies is a significant part of their liaison work. Psychologists can coordinate or supervise the application of behavioural and cognitive techniques in preparation for admission to hospital, and for mastery of fear of procedures

such as venepuncture, catheterization or anaesthesia, as well as for the alleviation of behavioural difficulties, separation anxiety, pain, enuresis, encopresis, vomiting and regurgitation, amongst others. The role of the psychologist has been discussed in detail by Stabler (1979) and Wellisch and Pasnau (1979).

Psychotherapists, although rarely employed on paediatric units, can offer observations of infant behaviour and parent–child interactions, and understanding of worrying behaviour. Their particular expertise is in communicating with distressed children and can be of considerable value to the team. Josse and Challenor (1987) have described the benefits of having a psychotherapist attached to a paediatric diabetic clinic.

Nurses, teachers and play staff have specific roles which are possibly more self-evident than those of other disciplines. Their closer and often more personal contact with children can facilitate crucial observations. Further, their 'lower' position in the ward hierarchy sometimes allows them to become the recipients of important confidentialities from children and parents. Dungar *et al.* (1986) have noted that in the assessment of children who present considerable diagnostic difficulties, the observations by the ward staff prove more important than investigations in elucidating the nature of inexplicable symptoms. Similar points apply to the remaining members of the team.

Clearly, whilst each discipline brings unique expertise to the multidisciplinary team, there is also some overlap. For example, psychiatrists, psychologists and social workers may all be trained in psychotherapy, behaviour therapy or family therapy. The decision as to who does what will depend on specific circumstances, such as the availability of staff and time. This overlap is not a disadvantage but rather allows for the pooling of ideas and experience, hopefully to the advantage of the team and thus to the children and their families. However, at a time of increasing cost-consciousness, the more expensive disciplines such as psychiatry need to give careful consideration to their role in a multidisciplinary team.

Evaluation of multidisciplinary team work as a whole, and of each discipline's contribution, has still to be carried out, and the current emphasis on audit may help us towards this goal.

THE TASKS OF PAEDIATRIC LIAISON WORK

Five main tasks are identifiable: (1) consultation; (2) treatment; (3) support; (4) teaching; and (5) research. Although there can be some considerable overlap between these tasks, each will be considered separately.

Consultation

Lipowski (1974) has noted three trends in the literature dealing with psychiatric consultation:

1 *Patient-oriented*: the patient is the primary focus of the consultant's interest.

2 *Consultee-oriented*: the referrer's motive for requesting a consultation and the related difficulties and expectations are the centre of the consultant's enquiry and advice.

3 *Situation-oriented*: the interpersonal transaction of all the members of the clinical team involved in the care of the patient for whom the consultation has been requested are taken into account to understand the patient's behaviour and the consultee's concern about it.

A good consultant will pay heed to each of these and to the wider aspects of the patient's social context, i.e. the illness network (see the section on the illness network, above).

A number of different conceptualizations of the consultation process have been described. Meyer and Mendelson (1961), for example, have distinguished three main elements of the process: (1) the request for the consultation; (2) the psychiatrist's redefinition of the patient's situation; and (3) the psychiatrist and the operational group. In contrast, Sandt and Leifer (1964) have emphasized the importance of language in the consultation process by describing three different components: (1) the sender; (2) the message; and (3) the receiver. Lipowski (1967) has adopted a more practical approach in viewing the consultation process as having three phases: (1) reception of a consultation request; (2) gathering of information; and (3) communication of the consultant's findings, opinions and advice.

Much has been written about the style and meaning of the requests: for example, whether the request is written or verbal, clear or confused, brief or detailed. Various interpretations can be put on the content and process of the referral request, similar to the hypothesizing so popular in family therapy (Palazzoli *et al.*, 1978), in which an attempt is made to understand the underlying family problems from the information supplied by the referrer. It could be argued that this is a much over-valued technique unless the hypothesizing is followed by a full assessment of the accuracy of the hypothesis, with adjustments being made according to the information obtained. More often than not in clinical practice this does not happen, and the hypothesizing could be seen as simply a pseudointellectual exercise. Much the same could be said about the referral process in paediatric liaison work.

Far more important is the actual information-gathering. In paediatric liaison this can be and usually needs to be a protracted process. Amongst those who can provide useful information are the referrer, other members of the ward or clinic team, the parents, the school, other agencies within the community who may know the child and family, and of course the child. Time is inevitably a constraining factor but every effort should be made to see the child alone, the parents alone, and the family as a group. The more traditional interviews with mother and child may provide useful information, but can fail to reveal the hidden or deeper aspects of a family problem, which become so evident during a family interview. Similarly, careful attention needs to be given to all other aspects of the illness network. Discussions with ward staff and especially the nursing and play staff often reveal diagnostically crucial information. An excellent example has been provided by Apley (1982), who quotes a nurse's report of an 8-year-old

boy admitted for investigations of recurrent abdominal pain. No cause was found and the boy was waiting for his mother to take him home. When he saw her he said: 'There's my mummy — oh my tummy'.

Communicating the results of the consultation is best done both verbally and in writing. The former allows for discussion and questioning and for conveyance of the subtle and complex nuances of the findings, whereas the latter allows for a permanent record. The written report must provide more than a jargon-laden statement of the consultant's opinion. Lask and Fosson (1989, p. 86) have been blunt on this matter:

> A report that states for example: 'this child's denial of his inner reality, with repressed libidinal instincts and unresolved Oedipal fantasies, inevitably impairs his reality adaptation with subsequent dissociation, and loss of use of his limbs' is of no value whatsoever to anyone but its author (and even that is questionable).

At the other extreme is the diagnostically precise but equally unhelpful: 'This child is suffering from a mixed conduct and emotional disorder'. Lask and Fosson emphasize that the written report should include statements about diagnosis or formulation, outlines of aims, advice about therapy and reviews of progress.

No better advice has been given than that of Dean (1963) who recommended that written reports should be conceived to be a guide to action, free from professional jargon and verbiage, and factual rather than speculative, clear in respect of what is speculation or opinion and what is thought to be fact, and organized in an orderly form, stating the problem, its evaluation, and proposed action for its solution. The finer details of the practicalities of consultation are discussed under A Model for Paediatric Liaison Work.

Treatment

Therapeutic interventions are guided by the following principles: (1) clear and prompt definition of therapeutic goals, both immediate and long term, based on comprehensive assessments; (2) choice of treatment tailored to the patient's needs; (3) flexibility in the conduct of the therapy; and (4) incisive intervention by the therapist to achieve the goals expeditiously (Lipowski, 1974). The goal should be beyond treating the immediate crisis but clearly delineated, and therapy should be initiated as quickly as possible. Many different therapeutic techniques can be used in paediatric liaison work. The application of parental counselling and family therapy in paediatric settings has been described by numerous authors (Minuchin *et al.*, 1978; Bingley *et al.*, 1980; Lask, 1987; Gustafsson & Svedin, 1988; John & Bradford, 1991). They have generally claimed favourable results, but evaluation is seldom based on controlled trials (see Chapter 55).

Behavioural techniques are used for a wide variety of paediatric problems, including preparation for hospitalization (Peterson & Mori, 1988), preparation for procedures (Zeltzer *et al.*, 1989), needle and other phobias (Manne *et al.*, 1990), pain (McGrath, 1990), regurgitation and vomiting (Sokel *et al.*, 1990), diabetes (Gilbert *et al.*, 1982), asthma (Lukeman, 1975; Knapp & Wells, 1978), and epilepsy (Lavender, 1981). Specific treatments have included relaxation and hypnotherapy, desensitization, modelling, flooding, reinforcement, shaping and extinction.

The use of individual therapy in paediatric liaison has not been widely reported, and so far the only condition for which it has been shown to be of some — albeit limited — value is childhood asthma (Pinkerton, 1967).

Finally, an interesting treatment model for recurrent abdominal pain, headache, encopresis and enuresis, has been described by Fundingsrud (1988) for use in a paediatric clinic. The model uses a combination of clinical examination, an almost ritualistic documentation of symptoms (symptom registration), and paradoxical intervention. The results were particularly promising for recurrent abdominal pain.

Support

This is an important component of paediatric liaison work that has been underreported, and not as yet evaluated. Bartemeier (1954) has stressed the need to consider the specific problems of the referring physician, but only in so far as they influence the professional relationship with the patient. Lipowski (1967) has said that it is not the consultant's task to offer covert 'psychotherapy' to the referring doctor. Few would disagree with these views but on the other hand the inevitable tensions of working with sick children often go unacknowledged and unresolved. Informal discussion of these issues with ward staff is often perceived as supportive and helpful. Regular meetings, especially with nursing and play staff, can go some way to acknowledging areas of stress, identifying problems, facilitating expressions of distress, and discovering or enhancing strategies for coping. Such groups seem to be particularly valued on neonatal or paediatric intensive care units, and other units where life-and-death issues are everyday events, such as cardiac, renal and oncology wards. Again, however, such groups should aim to be supportive rather than psychotherapeutic.

Teaching

The child psychiatrist has an important educational role in paediatric liaison, and the context provides a valuable opportunity. Those to be educated include consultant and trainee paediatricians, medical students, paediatric nurses and other members of the ward and clinic team. Nor should child psychiatrists forget that every aspect of their paediatric liaison work can and should be educational for themselves. What and how to teach has been the subject of some debate. Work (1978) has stressed the importance of demonstrating the insight phenomenon, rather than imparting concrete knowledge. Williams (1983), in contrast, has argued that this is a mistake given that the career choice of paediatrics reflects in part a preference for didactic learning rather than learning through self-scrutiny. She has made the point that the challenge for psychiatrists is not *how* to teach what is consonant with their craft, but *what* to teach that is consonant with learning styles and with paediatricians' professional requirements. In particular, she argues, they need to learn from psychiatrists when the style and substance of their intervention are insufficient.

With regard to how to teach, there is little doubt that the liaison psychiatrist can teach by providing a conceptual model and example. Liaison teaching can take place at the bedside on joint rounds conducted by the paediatrician and child psychiatrist, but perhaps a more useful forum is the psychosocial round (see A Model for Paediatric Liaison Work), or apprenticeship on particular cases. The advantage of the latter is that the referring paediatrician can follow the progress of the case from the time of referral through to follow-up, having access to the consultant throughout the process. The paediatrician can then learn when and how best to make the referral, and study the liaison psychiatrist in action. Trainee psychiatrists can be taught those skills in a similar manner.

The ideal teaching mode is probably a combination of joint ward rounds, psychosocial rounds and apprenticeship, with seminars for more focused and academic discussion. Liaison psychiatrists whose time is very limited, and who do not have a formal, or even informal, teaching forum can, and indeed should, still take seriously their teaching responsibility, by inviting referrers and trainees to join them for the consultation and if possible any continuing contact.

Research

Not that long ago fewer than 50% of paediatric liaison programmes surveyed reported active ongoing research (Rothenberg, 1979), but liaison child psychiatry has made numerous and varied research contributions on the psychosocial antecedents of illness, and psychological reactions to and coping with a wide range of illness and disability. Many disorders have been the subject of collaborative research and include stillbirth and neonatal death, chromosomal abnormalities, congenital malformations, accidents and injuries, postinfective states, cerebral palsy, epilepsy, spina bifida, muscular dystrophy, metabolic and endocrine disorders, diabetes, blood disorders, malignant disease, asthma, cystic fibrosis, inflammatory bowel disease, peptic ulcer, recurrent abdominal pain, congenital heart disease, skin disease and juvenile arthritis. Further detail is provided by Graham (1991).

There are available many examples of collaborative research in differing paediatric contexts. These include a study by Gath *et al.* (1980), which demonstrated that children with diabetes, compared with healthy controls, have a higher incidence of learning problems, but do not have a higher rate of behavioural disorder. Whitehead *et al.* (1991) have described a detailed study of children with end-stage cystic fibrosis referred for heart—lung transplantation. Psychosocial evaluation demonstrated a 55% incidence of individual and 50% incidence of family morbidity. In a study of childhood asthma, Lask and Matthew (1979) have demonstrated that family therapy as a supplement to conventional medical treatment produced a significant improvement in respiratory function compared with medical treatment alone.

The area in which further information is particularly required is that of evaluation of liaison in general, and specific therapies in particular. Bingley *et al.* (1980), however, have noted that in a group of 95 children referred to a tertiary referral centre and treated by a multidisciplinary team, 57 (60%) were rated as improved at follow-up 12–24 months after discharge. All of these children had previously been unsuccessfully managed elsewhere. Dungar *et al.* (1986) have shown that the use of the multidisciplinary team facilitates the diagnosis of previously unexplained illness.

The methodological problems involved in formal evaluation of such work are complex, but the current emphasis on audit is encouraging attention to this goal.

We need to know if liaison is useful to our colleagues and their patients, whether a liaison service reduces length and frequency of hospitalization and levels of morbidity, whether it raises the standard of psychosocial care and whether it has a positive influence on the practice of paediatric and other members of paediatric teams. Anecdotal reports are encouraging but hard data are needed if paediatric liaison work is to thrive at a time of financial austerity.

PROBLEMS IN PAEDIATRIC LIAISON WORK

Although problems are inevitable, it is possible to recognize and overcome them, thus creating a successful liaison service. A number of potential problems are readily identifiable. For example, there are considerable differences in conceptual emphasis between paediatrics and child psychiatry. Lask and Fosson (1989, p. 86) have compared the stereotypes of medical practice with those of mental health practice: (1) body versus mind; (2) organ or system versus the whole child; (3) individual versus family; (4) immediate versus long-term; (5) life or death versus quality of life; (6) active treatment versus passive involvement; and (7) cure versus care.

The psychiatrist has some additional handicaps with which to contend. In the past, and to some extent still the present, mental health practice has tended to have its own jargon, poor diagnostic precision, an emphasis on long-term therapy taking place behind closed doors, and a lack of systematic evaluation of the efficacy of interventions. On top of this there is still the stigma that may be attached to psychiatry, together with a consequent hostility felt towards it. As other chapters in this book indicate, all of this is changing but it would be unrealistic not to recognize that substantial remnants of these limitations remain.

Although there are obvious variations between individual paediatricians, with some being far more psychologically oriented than others, many will place an emphasis on body rather than mind, organ or system rather than the whole child, the child rather than the family, the present rather than the future, life or death rather than quality of life, active

treatment rather than passive involvement, and cure rather than care. It does need to be reiterated that this is by no means true of all paediatricians, and such generalizations are questionable, but it may be helpful to novices in paediatric liaison work to acknowledge this possibility.

Further problems arise from the traditional style of psychiatric practice. There is a tendency to use a language that is not readily comprehensible to disciplines other than mental health. Linked to this is a tendency to use 'theories, speculations and unsettled controversies which tend to confuse rather than inform' (Rickards, 1978). No amount of psychodynamic speculation is helpful in the immediacy of a crisis when practical advice is sought. Over-reliance on imprecise diagnoses is also unhelpful. Over recent years, research in child psychiatry has done much to demonstrate that certain diagnoses have very important implications for prognosis or treatment or both. For example, that would be the case with autism (Chapter 33), depression (Chapter 19), hyperkinetic disorders (Chapter 17) and obsessive disorders (Chapter 25). However, it has to be admitted that the majority of child psychiatric diagnoses do not carry such clear messages (Chapter 1). Thus, we may take an academic interest in whether a child is suffering from an adjustment reaction, a disturbance of emotion specific to childhood, a mixed disturbance of conduct and emotions or persistent pain, but such a debate is not useful to paediatricians who seek our help.

There are good reasons for the privacy of psychiatric practice, such as respecting confidentiality and encouraging exploration of very personal matters. Equally, however, this can give rise to resentment in paediatric settings, when those staff most intimately involved with the children are not privy to such work. Lourie (1966) has commented on the refusal of some child psychiatrists to send reports to paediatricians because these may be misused by the doctors reading them to parents, other relatives or schools. Such actions do little to promote collaboration. Child psychiatrists should aim, whenever possible, to write reports that can be shared with parents and schools as well as paediatricians. This promotes openness, good communication and respect.

Lewis and Vitulano (1988) have summarized the areas of difficulty in paediatric liaison work as follows: (1) the failure of some child psychiatrists to understand how paediatricians function in practice; (2) a perceived lack of availability of child psychiatrists; (3) professional identity problems in both disciplines; (4) different interviewing techniques; (5) anxiety amongst paediatricians in dealing with problems of children and their families; (7) transference and countertransference issues; (8) time constraints; (9) financial considerations, including inadequate funding for child psychiatry consultation services in paediatrics; (10) ambivalent support for the concept of coordinated multidisciplinary care for the whole child and family; (11) limited opportunity for continuity of care in paediatric training; (12) compartmentalized disease-oriented research rather than collaborative biopsychosocial research; and (13) inadequate outcome studies.

Lewis and Vitulano have raised a number of uncomfortable questions which need to be answered:

1 Do paediatricians really want contact with psychiatrists?
2 If so, exactly what do they want, and how is it to be financed?
3 Do child psychiatrists really want to work with paediatricians, and what exactly do they have to offer that is different?
4 Are they prepared to encourage research and training?

In the next section, some solutions are proposed in the context of a model for paediatric liaison work.

A MODEL FOR PAEDIATRIC LIAISON WORK

A wide variety of models have been described which vary from the provision of a consultation service only through to liaison consultants or staff being full and active members of the paediatric team (Blitzer, 1958; Gardener, 1958; Lourie, 1966; Mattson, 1976; Adams, 1978; Rothenberg, 1979; Stabler, 1979; Bingley *et al.*, 1980; Jellinek *et al.*, 1981; Williams, 1983; Lewis & Vitulano, 1988; Sturge, 1989; Fritz, 1990). In addition, models of liaison in highly specific contexts have been described by Geist (1977) on paediatric surgical wards, Jura and Faguet (1978) in the neonatal intensive care unit and Kasper and Nyamathi (1988) in paediatric intensive care units. Schowalter (1971) and Madow (1988) have reported on liaison programmes for paediatric adolescent units. The principles and the problems are similar whatever the context.

The essence of good paediatric liaison work is to be found in the joint psychosocial round, a regular meeting of the multidisciplinary team. The format of such meetings may differ but the function is to ensure that due consideration is given to the psychosocial aspects of the children and their families. Attention may also be paid to such matters as ward atmosphere and staff tensions and conflicts. Teaching can become an integral part of the meeting. Such meetings are enhanced by the regular attendance of all the paediatricians and senior nursing staff (Bingley *et al.*, 1980) and agreement as to who chairs it. Many such rounds are chaired by the psychiatrist, although it could be argued that they are better chaired by a member of ward staff who is familiar with the key issues and concerns.

It helps if a decision is made in advance of the meeting regarding which cases are to be discussed, so saving time during the meeting. On smaller units it may be possible to discuss all the children in turn. Either way the chairperson should ensure that adequate time is allocated to each case. If it is clear in advance of the psychosocial round that an assessment of a particular child or family will be needed, it is helpful to notify the relevant consultant in advance, so there is a possibility that part at least of the assessment will have been completed by the time the multidisciplinary team meets. At the Hospital for Sick Children, Great Ormond Street, the psychosocial round is standard clinical practice on all the medical and surgical units. Style and format may differ from one unit to another, but the principle is well-accepted.

The well-functioning psychosocial round provides an ethos of psychosocial awareness which can positively influence the general functioning of the unit. Bingley *et al.* (1980), for example, have described how parents are informed in advance, often in the outpatients department, that a psychosocial approach is utilized on the ward, and they and their children are likely to be seen by a social worker, child psychiatrist or psychologist as part of a comprehensive assessment and treatment. This allows for the early introduction of a mental health professional to the family, and the incorporation of psychosocial considerations. The alternative approach, still commonly used, of delaying serious consideration of psychosocial aspects to the end of the assessment period has certain disadvantages. Firstly, such an abrupt change of emphasis may lead parents to reject a psychosocial input, or interpret it as unimportant, or as a criticism of them. Secondly, a delay in assessment may unduly prolong hospital admission, and parents may then for understandable and realistic reasons demand discharge before a therapeutically effective relationship can be established.

This comprehensive approach can also be put into practice by encouraging joint interviewing of the parents or family by the paediatrician and mental health professional. This technique has several advantages (Bingley *et al.*, 1980):

1 It enables both organic and psychosocial factors and their relationships to be discussed with the parents with greater professional expertise.
2 The continuing paediatric involvement emphasizes the importance placed on psychosocial considerations.
3 The combined presence of the paediatrician and mental health professional may help parents appreciate the unity of body and mind.
4 An effective working relationship between paediatrician and mental health professional serves as a useful model of communication.
5 The paediatrician learns techniques of psychosocial assessment.

Whenever possible, the paediatrician should remain involved in continuing treatment for all the above reasons. This joint approach seems to be particularly helpful for the assessment of physical symptoms in which psychosocial factors may be playing a significant part, or in unexplained illness (Dungar *et al.*, 1986). The paediatrician and mental health professional meet together with the parents, and the paediatrician explains the results of the medical assessment. The mental health professional can observe the parental response to the paediatrician's explanation without immediately becoming involved in the discussion. When the paediatrician 'hands over' to the mental health professional, the latter may ask the parents if there is anything else they want to ask the paediatrician or may make an empathic comment about any perceived anxiety, uncertainty or disbelief on their part. This encourages the parents to seek clarification or express doubts or concerns, allowing further exploration as required.

Although many parents are only too ready to explore psychosocial issues some are sceptical or hostile. Lask and Fosson (1989, pp. 80–85) have described a particular technique for working with doubting parents. There are three possible responses to the suggestion that psychosocial assessment or treatment is indicated — (1) acceptance; (2) doubt; and (3) rejection.

It is possible to move straight into assessment and treatment with the acceptance group. For the other two it is necessary to avoid conflict and over-zealous attempts to convince parents that they are wrong. It is preferable to explore their doubts or convictions, which may arise from misunderstanding, lack of trust in doctors or mental health professionals, a history of previous errors, the associated stigma, a sense of guilt or other forms of distress. Misunderstandings are common; parents may assume, for example, that the need to see a psychiatrist implies that the child is mad, malingering or imagining the symptoms. A lack of trust may arise from a suspicion of psychiatry or previous errors. Occasionally an acquaintance or relative has had similar symptoms which have been misdiagnosed. The stigma associated with mental illness still exists and may impede parents' wishes to do what is best for their child. Some parents simply cannot cope with the need for psychiatric help, and others perceive the suggestion as a criticism of their parenting; both groups are likely to reject the offer of such help.

These doubts and concerns are best alleviated by a process of discussion, but still jointly involving the paediatrician and mental health professional. A didactic lecture or statement, or vigorous argument, is not helpful and tends to lead to further rejection. It is better to aim for clarification and normalization. Clarification involves distinguishing between the effects of stress and distress on the one hand and psychiatric illness on the other. Normalization involves discussing common stress reactions such as tension headaches. It can be useful for the paediatrician and mental health professional to discuss with the parents their own stress reactions as a way of conveying the normality of such phenomena. A simple explanation from the paediatrician of psychophysiological processes may also help.

By this stage some parents will have accepted the need for further psychosocial input, whereas others will remain doubtful or determinedly rejecting. It is important to avoid confrontation and a useful step forward is to ask parents what might convince them. If specific answers such as an X-ray or a biopsy are given it is worth advising the paediatrician to carry these out, providing they are not dangerous or in other ways contraindicated. Once completed with normal results, such an approach just might help parents accept a psychosocial input. Those parents who say they don't know what would convince them should be encouraged to explore further this idea, until they can either give a specific answer or realize that nothing would convince them.

A few parents remain determinedly rejecting despite all efforts. Sometimes it is helpful to offer them the chronic illness option. This involves stating that, given the parents' wish not to explore further certain areas it is possible that the current problems will continue indefinitely. An offer is then made to support the parents through what will undoubtedly be a difficult time. Occasionally parents are able to accept this form of help when they are not able to accept an overtly psychological approach.

It is clear that application of this model of liaison depends upon the relationship between the paediatrician and mental health professional being characterized by mutual respect and understanding, a willingness to learn from each other, clear communication and identification and resolution of problems and conflicts. Not all paediatricians would want such close collaboration, and others would have concerns about the time commitment. Lewis and Vitulano (1988) have pointed out that there are wide local variations in needs, wishes and practice, and make a plea for more dialogue at a local level to tackle the issues specific to that agency. A satisfactory compromise can and should be achieved so long as communication channels are kept permanently open.

Sturge (1989) has argued that problems can be avoided by the specialists agreeing on what is required for each separate referral: assessment, consultation, joint work, parallel work or hand-over.

Questions of authority and responsibility also need to be resolved. Mental health professionals must show a willingness to meet paediatricians on their home ground, at their own pace and in their own words (Lourie, 1966). Attending paediatric wards and presentations, showing interest in their work, speaking their language and acceptance of their priorities all help to develop a collaborative relationship.

When there is a shortage of mental health professional time, other priorities must be determined for it may not be possible to provide such a highly elaborate model of liaison. Single-handed psychiatrists will have to decide whether to concentrate their attentions on one particular ward or clinic, or to collaborate with one particular paediatrician, or to offer a more general service by keeping specific times available for consultation. It should not be forgotten that other mental health specialists are available to help psychiatrists with paediatric liaison work, and perhaps the top priority is to develop a paediatric liaison team to share the work.

It is important to be able to offer an emergency consultation service, even if little else is possible. The most likely problems for such an occurrence include a child manifesting violent or self-destructive behaviour, or a parent with a disturbed mental state. Such episodes understandably create considerable anxiety for the ward staff, the other children and their parents. In these circumstances the liaison psychiatrist should visit the ward as quickly as possible, assess the problem and meet with senior members of the ward team to discuss management. When there are issues of child protection, a social worker should be consulted early in the assessment process (see Chapter 52).

Some services have been developed to focus on specific areas, and in an era of increasing technological sophistication it is important to ensure that psychosocial considerations have a high profile. Major and complex surgery for congenital anomalies or life-threatening disease, bone marrow and organ transplantation, renal dialysis, immunosuppressive treatment and isolation are all areas of clinical practice with major psychosocial implications.

CONCLUSIONS

Paediatric liaison work remains a stimulating challenge for child psychiatric practice. It can be costly, demanding and time-consuming. However, when well-conducted, it encourages the promotion of understanding between disciplines, allows for the dissemination of good practice, and is beneficial to children and their families. While much consultation work can be carried out by direct referral to outpatient clinics, the paediatric ward provides the ideal context for effective liaison work. Indications for this joint approach include the following circumstances: (1) children who have obvious disturbances of behaviour or emotions; (2) children who have physical symptoms for which no organic explanation can be found; (3) children with poor adjustment to chronic or recurrent ill health; (4) when there is evidence of significant parental or family pathology; and (5) when abuse or neglect is known or suspected.

Successful collaboration is an achievement, not a gift (Pincus & Minahan, 1973, p. 82) and involves sharing areas or interest, understanding and respecting each other's skills and conceptual frameworks, identifying areas of conflict, exploring ways of resolving them, and developing strategies for building a cohesive and effective team. Rothenberg (1979), having quoted Sperling's triad of attributes to be adopted by the liaison child psychiatrist: 'be available, be practical, and be understandable', adds a fourth and fifth; 'be effective and be able to demonstrate that effectiveness'. Appley's plea for a marriage between paediatricians and child psychiatrists (1984, p. 128) is well-made. But marriages need to be worked at, partners need a home, and the children's needs should always have top priority.

REFERENCES

Adams P. (1978) Techniques for pediatric consultation. In: Faguet R., Fawzy J., Wellisch R. & Pasnau R. (eds) *Contemporary Models in Liaison Psychiatry*, pp. 164–187. Grune & Stratton, New York.

Apley J. (1982) One child. In: Apley J. & Ounsted C. (eds) *One Child*, pp. 23–47. MacKeith Press, London.

Apley J. (1984) If a child cries. Apley J. (ed) Chapter 26, p. 156. Butterworths, London.

Awad G. & Poznanski E. (1975) Psychiatric consultations in a pediatric hospital. *American Journal of Psychiatry*, **132**, 915–918.

Bartemeier L. (1954) Psychiatric consultations. *American Journal of Psychiatry*, **111**, 364–374.

Bingley L., Leonard J., Hensman S., Lask B. & Wolff O. (1980) The comprehensive management of children on a paediatric ward: a family approach. *Archives of Disease in Childhood*, **55**, 555–561.

Blitzer J. (1958) The psychiatrists' job in a children's hospital. *American Journal of Orthopsychiatry*, **28**, 523–539.

Cundall D. (1987) Children and mothers at clinics: who is disturbed? *Archives of Disease in Childhood*, **62**, 820–824.

Dean E. (1963) Writing psychiatric reports. *American Journal of Psychiatry*, **119**, 759–768.

Department of Health (1988) *Working Together: A Guide to Arrangements for the Protection of Children from Abuse*. Her Majesty's Stationery Office, London.

Dulcan M., Costello E., Costello A., Edelbrook C., Brent D. & Janiszewski B. (1990) The pediatrician as gatekeeper to mental health care for children. *Journal of the American Academy of Child and Adolescent Psychiatry*, **29**, 453–458.

Dungar D., Pritchard J., Hensman S., Leonard J., Lask B. & Wolff O. (1986) The investigation of atypical psychosomatic illness: a team approach to diagnosis. *Clinical Pediatrics*, **25**, 341–344.

Fitzgerald M. (1985) Behavioural deviance and maternal depressive symptoms in paediatric outpatients. *Archives of Disease in Childhood*, **60**, 560–562.

Fritz G. (1990) Consultation-liaison in child psychiatry. *Psychosomatics*, **31**, 85–90.

Fundingsrud H. (1988) A consultation model in a paediatric outpatient clinic. *Family Systems Medicine*, **6**, 188–201.

Gardener G. (1958) Psychiatry in a children's hospital. *American Journal of Orthopsychiatry*, **28**, 503–522.

Garralda E. & Bailey D. (1989) Psychiatric disorders in general paediatric referrals. *Archives of Disease in Childhood*, **64**, 1727–1733.

Gath A., Alison-Smith M. & Baum D. (1980) Emotional, behavioural and educational disorders in diabetic children. *Archives of Disease in Childhood*, **55**, 371–375.

Geist R. (1977) Consultation on a pediatric surgical ward. *American Journal of Orthopsychiatry*, **47**, 432–444.

Gilbert B., Johnson S., Spillar R., McCallum M., Silverstain J. & Rossenbloom B. (1982) The effects of a peer-modelling film on children learning to self-inject insulin. *Behavior Therapy*, **13**, 186–193.

Graham P. (1991) *Child Psychiatry — A Developmental Approach*, 2nd edn. Oxford University Press, Oxford.

Greenberg H., Kazak A. & Meadows A. (1989) Psychological functioning in 8–16 year old cancer survivors. *Journal of Paediatrics*, **114**, 488–493.

Gustafsson P. & Svedin C.-G. (1988) Cost effectiveness: family therapy in a pediatric setting. *Family Systems Medicine*, **6**, 162–175.

Hey A. (1979) Organizing teams/alternative patterns. In: Marshall M., Preston Shoot M. & Wincott E. (eds) *Teamwork: For and Against*, p. 27. BASW, Birmingham.

Hoare P. (1984) The development of psychiatric disorder among school children with epilepsy. *Developmental Medicine and Child Neurology*, **26**, 3–13.

Jedlicka-Kohler I. & Gotz M. (1988) Interventional assessment of physical and mental health in children and adolescents with CF. *Scandinavian Journal of Gastroenterology*, **23**, 34–37.

Jellinek M., Herzog D. & Selter F. (1981) A psychiatric consultation service for hospitalized children. *Psychosomatics*, **22**, 27–33.

John A. & Bradford R. (1991) Integrating family therapy into inpatient paediatric settings: a model. *Journal of Family Therapy*, **13**, 207–224.

Josse J. & Challenor J. (1987) Liaison psychotherapy in a hospital, paediatric diabetic clinic. *Archives of Disease in Childhood*, **62**, 518–522.

Jura M. & Faguet R. (1978) The earliest intervention: consultation to the high-risk parent and professional in the neonatal intensive care unit. In: Faguet R., Fawzy J., Wellisch R. & Pasnau R. (eds) *Contemporary Models in Liaison Psychiatry*, pp. 48–63. Grune & Stratton, New York.

Kasper J. & Nyamathi A. (1988) Parents of children in the pediatric intensive care unit: what are their needs? *Heart Lung*, **17**, 574–581.

Knapp T. & Wells L. (1978) Behaviour therapy for asthma — a review. *Behavioural Research and Therapy*, **16**, 103–115.

Lask B. (1987) Physical illness, the family and the setting. In: Bentovim A., Gorell Barnes G. & Cooklin A. (eds) *Family Therapy*, pp. 319–

344. Academic Press, London.

Lask B. & Fosson A. (1989) *Childhood Illness — The Psychosomatic Approach*. John Wiley, Chichester.

Lask B. & Matthew D. (1979) Childhood asthma — a controlled trial of family therapy. *Archives of Disease in Childhood*, **54**, 116–119.

Lavender A. (1981) A behavioral approach to the treatment of epilepsy. *Behavioral Psychotherapy*, **9**, 231–243.

Lewis M. & Vitulano L. (1988) Child, adolescent psychiatry consultation-liaison service in pediatrics. *Developmental and Behavioural Paediatrics*, **9**, 388–390.

Lipowski Z. (1967) Review of consultation psychiatry and psychosomatic medicine. *Psychosomatic Medicine*, **29**, 153–171.

Lipowski Z. (1974) Consultation-liaison psychiatry: an overview. *American Journal of Psychiatry*, **131**, 623–630.

Lourie R. (1966) Problems of diagnosis and treatment: communication between paediatrician and psychiatrist. *Paediatrics*, **37**, 1000–1004.

Lukeman J. (1975) Conditioning methods of treating childhood asthma. *Journal of Child Psychology and Psychiatry*, **16**, 165–168.

McFadyen A., Broster G. & Black D. (1991) The impact of a child psychiatry liaison service on patterns of referral. *British Journal of Psychiatry*, **158**, 93–96.

McGrath P. (1990) *Pain in Children: Nature, Assessment and Treatment*. Guilford Press, New York.

Madow M. (1988) Issues in the diagnosis and treatment of adolescents in a general hospital inpatient unit. *General Hospital Psychiatry*, **10**, 122–128.

Manne S., Redd W. & Jacobson P. (1990) Behavioral intervention to reduce child and parent distress during venepuncture. *Journal of Consulting and Clinical Psychology*, **58**, 562–572.

Mattson A. (1976) Child psychiatry ward rounds on pediatrics. *Journal of the American Academy of Child Psychiatry*, **15**, 357–365.

Meyer E. & Mendelson M. (1961) Psychiatric consultations with patients on medical and surgical wards. *Psychiatry*, **24**, 197–204.

Minuchin S., Rosman B. & Baker L. (1978) *Psychosomatic families*. Harvard Press, Cambridge, MA.

Morris J. & Craft A. (1990) Childhood cancer at what cost? *Archives of Disease in Childhood*, **65**, 638–640.

Muir L. (1984) Teamwork. In: Olsen R. (ed) *Social Work and Mental Health*, pp. 168–176. Tavistock, London.

Mulhern R., Wasserman A., Friedman A. & Fairclough D. (1989) Social competence and behavioral adjustment of children who are long term survivors of cancer. *Paediatrics*, **88**, 18–25.

Naylor K. & Mattson A. (1973) For the sake of the children: trials and tribulations of child psychiatry-liaison service. *Psychiatry in Medicine*, **4**, 389–401.

Palazzoli M., Cecchin G., Prata G. & Boscolo L. (1978) *Paradox and Counterparadox*, pp. 14–15. Jason Aronson, New York.

Palfrey J., Walker D., Builer J. & Singer J. (1989) Patterns of response in families of chronically disabled children. *American Journal of Orthopsychiatry*, **19**, 94–104.

Peterson L. & Mori L. (1988) Preparation for hospitalization. In: Routh D. (ed) *Handbook for Pediatric Psychology*, pp. 460–491. Guilford, New York.

Phipps S., Drotar D., Joseph C., Gees C. & Doershuk C. (1989) Home apnoeic monitoring. *Developmental and Behavioural Paediatrics*, **10**, 7–12.

Pincus A. & Minahan A. (1973) *Social Work Practice: Model and Method*, p. 82. F. E. Peacock, Itaska, IL.

Pinkerton P. (1967) Correlating physiological with psychodynamic data in the study and management of childhood asthma. *Journal of Psychosomatic Research*, **11**, 11–25.

Plant J. (1932) The promise of psychiatry. *American Journal of Disease of Childhood*, **44**, 1308–1320.

Rickards W. (1978) Patterns of collaboration between child psychiatrists and paediatricians. *Australian Paediatric Journal*, **14**, 66–68.

Rothenberg M. (1979) Child psychiatry-pediatrics consultation-liaison services in the hospital setting. *General Hospital Psychiatry*, **1**, 281–286.

Rutter M., Tizard J. & Whitmore K. (eds) (1970) *A Neuropsychiatric Study in Childhood*. Clinics in Developmental Medicine 35/36. Heinemann/Spastics International Medical Publications, London.

Sandt J. & Leifer R. (1964) The psychiatric consultation. *Comprehensive Psychiatry*, **5**, 409–413.

Schowalter J. (1971) Utilization of child psychiatry on a paediatric adolescent ward. *Journal of the American Academy of Child Psychiatry*, **10**, 684–699.

Smithells R. (1982) In praise of outpatients: partnership in paediatrics. In: Apley J. & Ounstead C. (eds) *One Child*, pp. 135–146. MacKeith Press, London.

Sokel B., Devane S., Bentovim A. & Milla P. (1990) Self-hypnotherapeutic treatment of habitual reflex vomiting. *Archives of Disease in Childhood*, **65**, 626–627.

Stabler B. (1979) Emerging models of psychologist-pediatrician liaison. *Journal of Pediatric Psychology*, **4**, 307–313.

Steinberg D. & Yule W. (1986) Consultative work. In: Rutter M. & Hersov L. (eds) *Child and Adolescent Psychiatry: Modern Approaches*, pp. 914–926. Blackwell Scientific Publications, Oxford.

Stocking M., Rothney W., Grosser A. & Goodwin R. (1972) Psychopathology in the pediatric hospital. *American Journal of Public Health*, **62**, 551–556.

Sturge J. (1989) Joint work in paediatrics: a child psychiatry perspective. *Archives of Disease in Childhood*, **64**, 155–158.

Wellisch D. & Pasnau R. (1979) Psychology interns on a consultation-liaison service. *General Hospital Psychiatry*, **1**, 287–294.

Whitehead B., Holms P., Goodwin M., Martin I., Lask B., Serrano E., Scott J., Smyth R., Higenbottom T., Wallwork J., Elliot M. & de Leval M. (1991) Heart–lung transplantation for cystic fibrosis 1: assessment. *Archives of Disease in Childhood*, **66**, 1018–1026.

Williams J. (1983) Teaching how to counsel in a pediatric clinic. *Journal of the American Academy of Child Psychiatry*, **22**, 399–403.

Work H. (1978) The burned-out missionary. *Pediatrics*, **62**, 425–427.

Zeltzer L., Jay S. & Fisher D. (1989) The management of pain associated with paediatric procedures. *Pediatric Clinics of North America*, **36**, 1–24.

Chapter 59
Adolescent Services

Derek Steinberg

INTRODUCTION

Services for psychiatrically disturbed adolescents exist where facilities for children tail off and those for adults begin. It is an area of psychiatric service marked by both gaps and duplication, and the types of problem encountered are coloured by such particularly adolescent issues as the transition from school to work, from the family to successfully or problematically negotiated independence, and youthful experiment, misbehaviour and criminality, as well as the whole range of psychiatric disorder. All of the broad groups of conditions seen in the whole of psychiatry may also be encountered in adolescence; however, the developmental changes of this period result in the clinical phenomena of this age group being sometimes less clear and more variable than those seen in older patients.

Changes in personal responsibility accompany these chronological and maturational changes — not only the degree of responsibility an adolescent is able or willing to take, but those he or she is expected or empowered to take — and of course this includes such decisions as where and with whom to live, and whether to accept or reject treatment or other help. In adolescence questions of authority and consent are particularly complex. Very small children cannot have much formal impact on decisions made in their interest, and in adult psychiatry the patient may generally take or leave what is offered, except in the special and relatively unusual circumstances of being convicted of an offence or being regarded as at risk or dangerous because of mental illness. What is peculiar to adolescence, and the ambiguous and changing position each boy or girl occupies between, say, 10 and 20, is the existence of a moral, legal and social potential space into which any number of people may step and claim authority: one or other parent, if not the two together; the Department of Social Services; various representatives of the law; the adolescent's teachers and the education authority; any other professionals who may be asked to advise or take responsibility; and, not least, 'public opinion', in whatever local or national manifestation; and the adolescent himself or herself.

All these influences have to be taken into account when decisions are made about issues of care and treatment, and they directly affect the development, organization and function of adolescent services. The result is a tension between expectations which tend to be antithetical. On the one hand, services for troubled adolescents need to be clear-cut in terms of aims, methods and clientele; to have coherence and authority in their practice; to have good, well-established working relationships between workers with diverse interests, responsibilities and skills; to be based on well-founded principles; and to be reasonably economical. On the other hand, adolescent services have to meet an extraordinarily wide range of need, are often expected to be extremely adaptable and to incorporate a very wide spectrum of opinions and approaches which are often mutually inconsistent and sometimes not well-founded; and, particularly where residential care is concerned, they tend to be very expensive.

These are some of the organizational issues that challenge the development of adolescent services. They are reflected sharply in the therapeutic relationship too. The adolescent, whether well, ill or something in between, has also to engage in a complex negotiation about authority with adults with whom he or she is involved. This applies whether the issue is doing what his or her parents want, agreeing to a behaviour therapy contract, accepting admission to residential care and the rules that go with it, or engaging in psychotherapy. The balance that has to be achieved between appropriate and sustainable adult authority and the adolescent's autonomy and self-esteem can be a precarious one, yet has to be sustained upon the shifting and uncertain foundations outlined.

Fortunately it can be done, and the literature carries many accounts of how individual practitioners and centres have met these challenges with their own solutions. Not surprisingly, the pattern has tended to be one of clinics and agencies surviving and even flourishing where they have set firm and sometimes quite individualistic limits on their aims and practices, and of serious organizational problems, sometimes resulting in chaos and closure, where they have not. The development of comprehensive networks or even part-networks of services in this field, able to work together and learn from each other, is a challenge of major proportions.

ADOLESCENTS AND THEIR PROBLEMS

The range of needs in a given community may be assessed in terms of the epidemiology of problems, by asking potential users of services what they want, and by looking at the types of request and referral actually made to services for adolescents.

The 1-year period prevalence of psychiatric disorder, broadly defined, is about 10–15% — a rate that rises to 21% or more in the UK when older teenagers, those living in inner cities and self-report studies are included (Graham & Rutter, 1973; Leslie, 1974; Rutter *et al.*, 1976). These levels are similar to those reported from Australia (Krupinski *et al.*, 1967; Henderson *et al.*, 1971), Scandinavia (Lavik, 1977) and the US (Feldman & Stiffman, 1986). This represents a large number of young people, particularly if we bear in mind that, while the adolescent group accounts for some 15% of the population at present in the UK, in many parts of the world the proportion of children and teenagers can rise to 40% or more.

Who is available to attend to the needs of this potentially very large number of young people in difficulty? Help tends to be shared between child and adult psychiatric and psychological services, general practice, paediatric and other health agencies, aspects of the educational and social services, the police and probation services and, often, a number of small, independent helping and counselling agencies. In quite large numbers of individual cases care is often satisfactory and even exemplary; but in terms of the overall provision of services, the general picture in the UK (despite its high reputation in this area) is of patchy, uneven, underfunded and poorly coordinated services with areas of unnecessary overlap and many serious gaps (Health Advisory Service, 1986).

Between 1984 and 1986, the Health Advisory Service of the National Health Service conducted a series of visits and surveys of services for disturbed adolescents in England, Wales and Scotland. The survey was itself patchy and impressionistic, and attracted a good deal of criticism, but many people familiar with the services surveyed would be likely to agree with many of the observations made. For example, there was a lack of basic information and knowledge about existing services for adolescents, even among locally based people who needed to know; funding responsibilities were unclear or disputed; there was a lack of trust between different practitioners and agencies, with working relationships either absent or marked by competitiveness and mutual suspicion; there was unsystematic planning, or no planning at all; there was a lack of sufficient numbers of staff, many of whom lacked basic and/or in-service training and support, a situation that was particularly apparent in many social service department children's homes (which also contained many of the most disturbed and socially deprived young people); and the occasional outstanding service depended on small local initiatives or the leadership of one individual; when such leadership was lost, the facility characteristically collapsed. Inpatient psychiatric units were regarded as expensive and sometimes too inclined to adhere to a single conceptual model of treatment. Eclecticism was recommended. A vivid and recurring impression of the group interviews, for one who was involved in several, was of very large numbers of professionals working with adolescents in a given district getting together, not without interest and anticipation, for the very first time.

There have been a few studies from adolescent psychiatric units themselves of their use by the local community. In one survey of 100 medical and nonmedical referrers (mostly social workers, child and adult psychiatrists and general practitioners) using a regional adolescent unit serving a total population of $3\frac{1}{2}$ million, the most highly preferred service would have been the availability of immediate and direct admission of a boy or girl to the hospital on the basis of a telephoned request. Outpatient facilities were seen as lower priorities by all except general practitioners, and the availability of preliminary consultation about young people's cases was rated low by all except social workers (Steinberg *et al.*, 1981). It is probable that these responses were affected by the fact that the survey was conducted from an inpatient unit in a region reasonably well-served by outpatient child and adolescent clinics.

Pyne and his colleagues (1986), also working from an inpatient unit, surveyed the views of the families using the service. They found that involvement of the family in treatment was generally disliked, and that parents felt there was too much treatment and not enough containment, which were perceived as mutually exclusive. Another study by Jones *et al.* (1978), however, found that family approaches were regarded as helpful by over half the adolescents and parents.

Information from referrals to child and adolescent psychiatric clinics adds to the overall picture. Studies in the US (Rosen *et al.*, 1965) and the UK (Wing & Fryers, 1976) show a rising rate in referrals from childhood, through adolescence and into adulthood. Attempted suicide shows a very great increase during the teenage years (Shaffer & Fisher, 1981; Hawton *et al.*, 1982; McClure, 1986) and this is paralleled by, though not necessarily always related to, an increase in depressive conditions, including manic-depressive illness (Loranger & Levine, 1978; Carlson & Cantwell, 1982; Hawton *et al.*, 1982; Cantwell & Carlson, 1983; Lewinsohn *et al.*, 1986). The studies by Hawton (1987), in particular, have suggested the relatively small part psychiatric disorder and psychiatric treatment play in the understanding and management of drug overdoses in teenagers, for many of whom the origins of the behaviour and the responses needed are largely social (however, see Chapter 23).

The schizophrenic illnesses (Weiner & DelGaudio, 1976), obsessive-compulsive disorder (Rapaport, 1989), social phobias and agoraphobia (Abe & Masui, 1981) and anorexia nervosa and other eating disorders (see Chapter 24) also become noticeably more prominent through older childhood and into adolescence.

Nevertheless, most young people referred to adolescent psychiatric clinics tend to be in the clinical categories of emotional, conduct and mixed emotional and conduct disorders, where family and social influences are particularly strongly marked and the case for individual illness is less clear (Bruggen *et al.*, 1973; Steinberg *et al.*, 1981; Steinberg, 1991b). Many services, recognizing this, have made family and social models of assessment and treatment and crisis intervention the emphasis of their work (Bruggen *et al.*, 1973; Patterson,

1974; Ro-Trock *et al.*, 1977; Wells *et al.*, 1978), sometimes playing down or apparently excluding the making of individual clinical diagnoses. On the other hand, a broadly family-based and problem-oriented assessment, giving a descriptive account of the presenting problem in systemic terms (see Chapter 5), can complement an individually focused clinical diagnosis. Both aspects can contribute to the diagnostic formulation in a way that guides management helpfully, in particular indicating who, or which agency, is in the best position to provide different aspects of help (Steinberg, 1983, 1987, 1989b).

The experience of two adolescent units known by referrers to take this broadly eclectic approach (Steinberg *et al.*, 1981; Steinberg, 1986a) gives a composite picture of the pattern of referrals consistent with that described, with fairly minor variations, elsewhere (Bruggen *et al.*, 1973; Framrose, 1975; Perinpanayagam, 1978; Wells *et al.*, 1978; Lordi, 1979; Novello, 1979; Bedford & Tennant, 1981; Parry-Jones, 1986; Gabel, 1989; Khan, 1990; Hendren & Berlin, 1991b). For example:

1 Many enquiries demonstrate both uncertainty and controversy among those involved so far about how best to approach complex problems in this age group (e.g. serious misbehaviour, sexual abuse, family breakdown), and the part psychiatry in general, and admission to hospital in particular, might play.

2 Anxiety and pressure for immediate action, often to do with removal of adolescents from their current situation, or for an immediate and complete transfer of responsibility and care, are common. There can be heated disagreement about what is needed, e.g. over hospital admission versus reception into local authority care.

3 There is commonly a wider range of problems presenting to a single service than it can deal with. For example, a sequence of referrals may indicate a need for a gentle and supportive psychotherapeutic milieu, a secure setting able to contain violently aggressive behaviour or persistent absconding, and the facilities for the supervision of, say, medication, behaviour therapy and the management of anorexia nervosa. General psychiatric services commonly find they have to specialize in the above areas, but adolescent psychiatric units are usually expected to specialize only in 'adolescence' and to manage most or all of this range of care.

4 The ages of the young people referred may range from children of 11 or 12 to young adults of 19, 20 or more. Nevertheless, it tends to be assumed that the social and educational aspects of the setting will be appropriate for the whole range of their developmental needs.

All of these categories of need are likely to be compounded by the complex issues to do with the family, school and the transition to other forms of education or to work. There will often be interactions between developmental status, educational problems and, sometimes, misbehaviour or delinquency which have not been recognized or met (Rutter & Giller, 1983; Farrington, 1985).

There may be legal, ethical and administrative dilemmas, for example, disagreement between the adults responsible for the adolescent about how to proceed, the refusal of a particular service to admit someone of a particular age or from a particular address, or untested procedures arising from the new Children Act in the UK (Her Majesty's Stationery Office, 1989) and recent legislative developments in the US (Melton & Schmechel, 1989). There can be problems in reaching working agreements between services that operate on different professional and conceptual bases, as Skynner (1974) and Dupont and Dowdney (1990) have reported in the cases of psychotherapists and clinical psychologists, respectively, in their work with schools.

The significance of cultural differences between the staff and culture of a service and the culture and ethnic background of its clientele has tended to be relatively neglected. Burke (1976), Rack (1982), McShane (1988), Lee (1988), Spencer *et al.* (1988), Accharya *et al.* (1989), Littlewood and Lipsedge (1989), Kareem and Littlewood (1992) and Steinberg (1992b) have given accounts of the problems of negotiating cultural differences constructively in work with individuals and families from ethnic minority groups or those who are recent immigrants. Hendren and Berlin (1991b) and Porter and Blackwell (1991) have provided detailed accounts of orientating child and adolescent psychiatric services to multicultural needs in the US. Vargas (1991) has described the evaluation of this work, and Rindner (1991) has discussed it in terms of staff recruitment and training in multicultural settings.

All these things influence consent, which is at the heart of being able to proceed with and sustain assessment and treatment with the necessary confidence and authority. Consent needs to be informed, which means that adolescents and parents need information about the natures of the problem and treatment, both of which may well involve uncertainties, controversies and ambiguities; the only certain factor may be that management may include inconvenience, discomfort and risk and, even, may not help. Authority and decision-making in such circumstances need to be shared, with the clinician taking his or her responsibilities (including the responsibility to explain and inform), and the adolescent and family theirs, which includes the right to decline all or part of what is offered. However, as mentioned earlier, in issues of child care it may not be as simple as that. Firstly, there is the formal age of consent of the adolescent to be taken into account; in the UK it is 16 years. Secondly, an adolescent younger than 16 may also have the maturity and understanding to justify priority being given to his or her views and, further, this will also depend on the degree of invasiveness of the treatment (e.g. medication) or the upheaval in his or her life (e.g. removal from home). Thirdly, to a greater or lesser extent the wider community increasingly expects a right to be involved in what happens to children, whatever parents may wish. The recommendation and use of any aspect of adolescent services require repeated negotiation and consultation (Steinberg, 1992a) between professionals and with the adolescent and the family; clinical decisions can still be taken authoritatively within this context, urgently if necessary, and indeed it may be easier to do so when some clarity has been established about who is properly responsible for what (Steinberg, 1987, 1989b, 1994).

To this rich mixture of problems, wishes, needs and options may be added the findings that at least in some studies adolescents admitted to psychiatric units have a relatively high incidence of all degrees of physical disorder, not always related in obvious ways to their psychiatric problems (Gabel & Hsu, 1986).

Even when accidents, drug abuse and other forms of self-injury are excluded, the adolescent population in general shows a relatively high morbidity rate for blood, central nervous system and bone cancers (Neinstein, 1984); for obesity, skin allergy and respiratory disorders (Garrell, 1965; Shen, 1980); for dental problems (Guthrie & Howell, 1972); and for gynaecological disorders (Neinstein, 1984). Further, adolescent presentations to psychiatrists include a relatively high proportion of psychosomatic conditions, including illness behaviour, pretence of illness, asthma and eating disorders (Ford, 1983; Blum, 1986). For all three reasons — the health and development of the general adolescent population, the frequency of psychosomatic conditions, and the somewhat unexpected findings of a high level of physical disorder coexisting with psychiatric conditions — it seems important that adolescent psychiatric services continue to include a general medical component in their practice and in the training of their staff, despite the advances made in nonmedical psychological and social techniques. Indeed, at least in relation to adolescent psychiatric units, experience at the Bethlem Adolescent Unit suggests that it may be *because* of the appropriate and effective use of community-oriented services that

young people admitted to psychiatric units represent a group with an increasingly high level of psychiatric disturbance and physical morbidity. Adolescent medicine as a separate specialty is far less well-established in the UK than it is in the US, although it is beginning to receive more detailed and systematic attention here too (Brook, 1993). There is the opportunity, now, for adolescent psychiatry and adolescent medicine to share some aspects of the further development that both need, particularly since much that has been said here about authority, autonomy and consent, and the role of the doctor as educator as well as decision-maker, applies as much to general health issues as to psychiatric matters.

This short account of adolescent problems and needs from the perspectives of epidemiology, various professional groups and agencies, and from a number of adolescent psychiatric units, would not be complete without acknowledging that social workers, teachers, housing officers and workers in voluntary and self-help agencies commonly report an undercurrent of troubling difficulties concerning young people which, while not meriting referral to specialist agencies, do appear to call for more counselling, advice and special educational resources than is generally available. An extremely wide spectrum of resources is needed for this complex and heterogeneous range of problems, issues and disorders. What is available?

ADOLESCENT SERVICES: FACILITIES

Coherent and comprehensive plans for model services do not exist. Figure 59.1 outlines the range of facilities and services

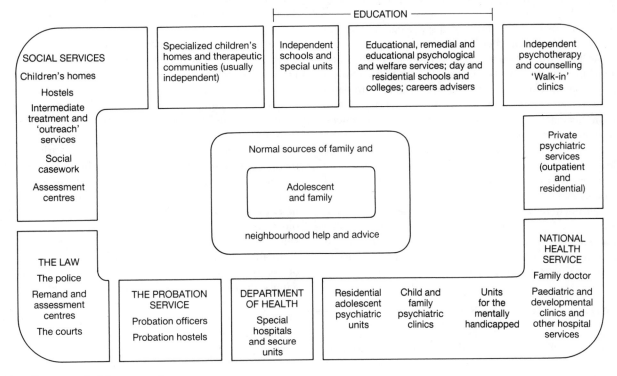

Fig. 59.1 The range of adolescent services.

expected to be available in a developed, but not ideal service. It is based on British provision and uses that terminology, but the principles are common to most countries.

There will be a child and family psychiatric clinic, ordinarily staffed by psychiatrists, psychologists and social workers, often with the services of a specialist psychotherapist, and occasionally with a community psychiatric nurse. The professions will usually have different employers — the area health authority (psychiatrist, and nurse if there is one), the Education Department (the psychologist) and the Department of Social Services (social workers). The psychologist usually attends the clinic in his or her capacity as a member of the Schools Psychological Service. Increasingly, the psychiatrist is likely to have sessions at a hospital Department of Child and Adolescent Psychiatry, although not necessarily at one of the relatively few adolescent inpatient units. In general, there is likely to be a child psychiatric clinic available for child and adolescent outpatients and their families for each total population of about 300 000. The picture is complicated, especially in large cities with university teaching hospitals, by Departments of Child and Adolescent Psychiatry operating hospital outpatient clinics, with broadly similar staffing, teaching and research functions. Occasionally, one will have its own inpatient Children's Unit, admitting boys and girls up to 12 or 13 years of age. In the wider region, serving a total population of perhaps 3–4 million, there is likely to be an inpatient Adolescent Unit, usually located for historical reasons in the local general psychiatric hospital. It may or may not share staff with the child psychiatric clinic and the hospital outpatient clinic, although this is increasingly the trend. It may operate according to any of the models of adolescent psychiatric care described below.

There will also be a range of psychological, psycho-therapeutic, educational, social, forensic and other facilities providing for disturbed adolescents (Sheldrick, 1990). Their relationship with the 'core' of adolescent psychiatric services is likely to be more or less *ad hoc*, though typically with paths beaten between certain agencies because of special mutual needs or personal contacts. For example, different general practitioners may favour the child psychiatric clinic, the hospital Children's Department's outpatient clinic, or the Adolescent Unit. Correspondingly, the Adolescent Unit may have established informal contacts with three or four residential schools and therapeutic communities, and a social service legal department may regularly approach one or two particular psychiatrists or psychologists for Court assessments and reports. These informal and often arbitrary personal contacts make a major contribution to the nature of the network of adolescent services in a given area.

MODELS OF REFERRAL, ASSESSMENT AND TREATMENT

Some of the facilities are characterized by lack of resources in the face of great and increasing demand. For example, it would be hoped that front-line social service workers would

have the time, training and supervision to be able to respond to the needs of families in difficulties, and have ready access to first-rate fostering services or children's homes when family breakdown is irrevocable in a particular adolescent's case. Although adequate and sometimes good resources of this sort widely exist, many children's homes have run into difficulties and closed down because of financial and staffing problems, while social workers in the field often find themselves too over-stretched to provide more than a patchy supervisory function to adolescents and families. Even then, this is often in relation to problems currently generating the most public concern, for example, the sexually abused. Whatever the current picture, however, and despite the problems accompanying the institutionalization of children, it seems that the triad of family casework, short-term and long-term fostering and good children's homes would be an essential component of the network of care for troubled adolescents (see Chapter 15); with the added hope that the more effective the first and second resources, the less will be the need for institutional homes for children.

The complex patterns of deprivation that may result in adolescents going into residential care mean that many such homes have, or aspire to, a broadly therapeutic milieu. That is to say, attention will be paid to understanding and working with the feelings of adolescents; other homes may focus on structure, consistency of handling, limit-setting and social and behavioural training. There may be a visiting psychiatrist or psychologist to help with this work. In practice, many homes find they fall short of these ideals, due to under-funding and lack of staff training and supervision time.

If the function of the children's homes is to provide safety, good care and a constructive, supportive environment that will prevent or minimize emotional injury, the purpose of a therapeutic community is more specifically to provide a total environment designed to treat emotional, behavioural and personality problems and enhance normal social and emotional development. In the words of the title of a classic text on hospitals providing this type of care, their special approach is the 'community as doctor' (Rapoport, 1960). They tend towards long-term care which seeks to repair and replace the deficiencies of the boy's or girl's family and earlier development. Education is usually integral to the milieu, and while contact with families is ordinarily maintained, active family therapy is exceptional. Therapeutic communities are often individualistic, if not idiosyncratic, and their strengths are often rooted in a charismatic and sometimes autocratic leadership which, paradoxically but not necessarily inaccurately, maintains that it fosters full community participation in all decisions. This may include those concerned with the admission and discharge of individuals. The therapeutic communities are not easily categorized, but for the purposes of the clinician dealing with a wide range of adolescent disturbances, fall broadly into three groups: (1) those that operate primarily on the principles of one or other school of group therapy, and tend to expect a reasonably high level of motivation on the part of the young people referred to them;

(2) those that have a more obviously parental, nurturing function, more structure and direction from the staff, and which accept less mature teenagers, including some with pervasive developmental disorders (the communities based on the teachings of Rudolf Steiner come into this category); and (3) more specialized centres for very severely impaired young people with chronic psychotic and severe pervasive personality disorders. Accounts of different types of therapeutic community will be found in Bettelheim (1950, 1960), Rapoport (1960), Whiteley (1970), Clark (1977), Lampen (1978), Rose (1986) and Anthony (1991).

Other medium- to long-term forms of care include the hospitals, homes, day-centres and hostels for those with mental handicap, and secure treatment centres for absconding, offending or dangerous young people who need to be kept safely in one place whilst systematic management is attempted. Some are run by the Department of Health, e.g. the Glenthorne and St Charles Youth Treatment Centres and the Gardener Secure Psychiatric Adolescent Unit, and a small number are in the private sector (Bedford & Tennant, 1981). The Aycliffe Centre in the north of England operates on behavioural and educational lines and copes with severely disturbed young people (Hoghughi, 1978). When such settings are considered for individual adolescents, the referring authority has also to consider the costs, at present of the order of £6000 ($9000) or more per month for several months to several years. More intensively staffed facilities are more expensive. It is an inescapable fact of the residential solution for the problems of developing young people that if the facilities are to be first-rate in terms of safety, staff skills and in the general standard of care, then senior and experienced staff in a high staff-to-resident ratio will be needed. This is costly. The present situation is that there are very few such centres, but they take a small proportion of the young people from less well-endowed services (residential or community-based) when, as happens from time to time, local or national concern for particular adolescents or problems reaches a peak.

It may be added that, in the UK at present, this financial outlay — which may reach £80 000 per year or more per child, for a financially hard-pressed local authority — is in contrast to the use of National Health Service units, for which there is no direct charge. This is bound to be a factor in negotiations about placing adolescents who are on the psychiatric/social deprivation borderline.

The educational system provides another important resource for disturbed teenagers. Identification of educational needs (see Chapter 63) goes hand-in-hand with identification of family issues (see Chapter 5) during the process of making a comprehensive assessment and care plan for adolescents. Schools specializing in educational or behavioural problems, or both, or which operate on therapeutic community lines as outlined above, may be recommended. However, an alternative ordinary school, on a day or residential basis, sometimes meets an adolescent's need for a fresh start in a normal but different atmosphere, away from home if necessary. The British tradition of resorting fairly readily to the notion that

bringing up children away from home can be a good thing has its problems (Millham *et al.*, 1978; Millham, 1981), but it has also left a legacy of a number of good if sometimes idiosyncratic boarding schools up and down the country, in which troubled teenagers can often do well.

The facilities available for young offenders represent another and large area of assessment, management methods and provision (see Chapter 50). Social service departments and clinical teams frequently collaborate with the probation services, the police and the Courts, where minor offences or frank mental illness are concerned, but for the large number of delinquent adolescents, facilities tend to be more self-contained and with their own psychological and psychiatric staff in assessment and treatment centres. Sometimes these are close to the community (Brown, 1985), more often in young people's detention centres and prisons. Overall, the success of various types of detention has remained in doubt, and in recent years more attention has been paid to prevention, and particularly the early recognition of high-risk groups, with training in social competence for parents as well as children (Farrington, 1985).

The literature on walk-in, self-referral services for adolescents is scanty. Accounts of such facilities in North London (Laufer, 1968; London Youth Advisory Centre, 1985, 1987) suggest heavy though fluctuating use, with young women's concerns about contraception, pregnancy and related matters being common, and short-term contact predominating. The London Youth Advisory Centre, in its survey of 1 year's work, reported over 3000 telephone calls, of which just under half were for appointments, most of the rest being by way of general enquiry or requests for information. Over 500 young people were seen, with girls outnumbering boys 2 : 1. Nearly 90% were in the age range 16—25, with true self-referral increasing with age; general practitioners and other doctors referred only 12%, and a similar proportion of close relatives influenced referral, especially in boys. Over half of the referrals were influenced by friends. In a further account of the centre, Rose (1990) discussed the problems of such a service trying to balance swift appointments against having to have a waiting list, with a steady drop-out rate when the wait became longer than a few weeks. These findings are in contrast to surveys of psychiatric unit referrals (Steinberg *et al.*, 1981), where the self-referral rate is extremely low, and problems of sexual relationships and pregnancy as overt issues are relatively unusual. Bearing in mind the dramatic increase of need in this area, from a high level of teenage pregnancies and a high illegitimacy rate to increasing concern about sexually related diseases, there is a formidable preventive problem which individual clinical services acting alone, in a reactive rather than proactive and educational way, will not be able to meet (Peterson, 1980; Her Majesty's Stationery Office, 1982). Other self-referral services based in universities (Ryle, 1973; Newsome *et al.*, 1975) also discuss the issue of accessibility, with the account by Newsome and her colleagues describing the value of a counselling service having among its functions less stigmatizing and less immediately emotive purposes such as, for example, advice about career decisions and academic matters.

Alcohol and drug abuse is widespread internationally, and affects large numbers of young people, and here also there is the problem of specialist services appearing too daunting to approach on a self-help basis. Assistance tends to be sought through informal social networks, with approaches to specialist clinics being made only by a minority, and after considerable delay (Sheehan *et al.*, 1988; see Chapter 3). When services are organized very close to the communities they serve, they tend to be seen as more accessible, and tend also to raise the level of skills among those first likely to be approached for help (Strang, 1991).

Finally, adolescents are regularly treated throughout the general medical services, but only recently has there been recognition of the level and range of morbidity in this age group, and their special needs in terms of availability and accessibility of facilities. Of course, some professional workers have more interest in this age group than others, in the particular biopsychosocial and developmental conceptual models of diagnosis and treatment needed, and in the special problems as well as opportunities involved in working on a multidisciplinary basis with this age group (Neistein, 1984; Steinberg, 1991a,b; Brook, 1993; Tyrer & Steinberg, 1993).

MODELS OF SERVICE

We have seen that conceptions of services for adolescents are marked by complexity, diversity and controversy; this is true at all levels of severity and need, and is at its sharpest where residential provision is concerned (Millham *et al.*, 1978; Bruggen & Westland, 1979; Millham, 1981; Steinberg, 1981). All forms of residential care are also very expensive, largely due to high staffing costs, and unit costs will rise as the need for proper basic and continuing training and in-service supervision is recognized. The blurred boundaries between problems needing psychiatric care and those needing social or educational care, and the enormously different financial implications of short-term and long-term care, and particularly intensive or high-security care, are causing increasing concern to those with funding responsibilities, whether in medical insurance organizations or government departments. In the US, financial pressures have caused a drive towards shorter-term hospitalization and correspondingly towards tighter definitions of disorder and treatment goals and more accurate predictors of outcome (Doherty, 1975; Heinman & Shanfield, 1980; Canton & Gralnic, 1987; Khan, 1990; Hendren & Berlin, 1991a,b). Meanwhile, costs, plus the apparent failure of all sorts of residential institutions to correct the ills for which they were established, have led to a move towards community care, but with little definition of what is entailed, the staff and costs involved, or how it might be evaluated.

Such considerations point to the need for more effective planning in which clinicians, researchers and administrators can share, and for useful measures of performance and outcome, but such joint planning and the establishment of agreed methods of evaluation have so far proved challenging in child and adolescent psychiatry (Wells, 1986, 1992; Thomas & Hardwick, 1989; Hardwick, 1990; Hendren & Berlin, 1991b; Subotsky, 1992). The relative disorganization of services, referred to earlier, not only presents problems for planning and funding facilities, and makes the evaluation of care difficult, but also obstructs access to care. Thus, quite often, professional workers, as well as the community generally, do not know what is available in the way of services, what to expect from them, and how to make choices between them.

CONCEPTS OF CARE FOR ADOLESCENTS

It is possible to start to make sense of this field by beginning with a rough categorization of approaches into treatment, education and training, care, and control (Steinberg, 1981, 1982). Of course they overlap, but the core philosophy of each is fundamentally different. Thus *treatment* concerns the identification and treatment of abnormality; *education* and *training* is about providing the conditions in which individuals achieve as nearly as feasible their full potential; *care* is about adequate safe-guarding and upbringing and the meeting of basic physical, psychological and social needs; *control* concerns the external assertion that some patterns of behaviour will be required or tolerated, and some will be prevented. Thus an adolescent may enter a comprehensive treatment programme, but still needs satisfactory care on the part of his or her parents. This is a separate issue, albeit one which has impact on the treatment plan. He or she is also entitled to appropriate education. Meanwhile, other people, for example, the family, peers and the community at large, have the right to a consensus about behaviour which will or will not be acceptable. Thus the responses to a misbehaving adolescent could be therapeutic (for example, psychotherapy); or focused on the provision of competent care (for example, through the Department of Social Services); or mediated through the provision of remedial education; or by the young person being made the subject of a supervision or probation order, or *in extremis* held in a safe and secure setting; or, usually, a combination of these.

All children and adolescents need care and individually appropriate education and control; not all children and adolescents need treatment. However, treatment is quite often sought for young people in whom the most important needs are in the other three areas, and it is attention to one or other of these that makes the difference. Further, when psychological or psychiatric treatment is needed, it may only be feasible if the other three areas receive proper attention. A brief example will illustrate this.

> A teenage girl is repeatedly absconding from children's homes, and presenting in hospital emergency departments with cut wrists and minor overdoses of drugs. Her family have distanced themselves from her, and she is being moved from children's home to children's home because of the anxiety and disruption she causes. She is presented as someone for whom

psychiatric treatment is the obvious and primary need. Not only is her most obvious need, however, for a consistent, safe, containing and caring environment, with mobilization of the best efforts of her careworkers and her parents, but these things alone are likely to result in her feeling and behaving better. Further, even if it does seem that she might benefit from, for example, psychotherapy or antidepressant medication, she still needs help in the other areas. Indeed, containment (for example, being required to attend for psychotherapy or to live in a therapeutic community) may be an essential precondition for any treatment to be sustained. Detention under the Mental Health Act, other than possibly for a few hours or days, would almost certainly be inappropriate.

Often, in the cases of such young people, even acknowledging the height of the adolescent's distress and the genuine chaos in his or her life, with clarification of who will in future pay consistent attention to the needs which have been exposed by this crisis, is likely to reduce the risk of repetition, and lay the foundations for at least the beginning of progress. What often proves problematic in such situations is not so much the mysteries of the young patient's mind, but the challenge of organizing care. Many emergencies in adolescent psychiatry, even when there is a definite clinical diagnosis to be made, have many of the qualities of the example given here (Steinberg, 1987, 1989b, 1994).

AUTHORITY AND ADOLESCENT SERVICES

The importance of authority and clarity being built into the procedures of adolescent services has already been mentioned. This is partly for practical and organizational reasons, the field being so full of complexities and ambiguities, and also because clarity about who is responsible for what is a precondition of competent and ethical practice, effective therapeutic relationships and adequate instruction and support of staff (Lampen, 1978; Bruggen, 1979; Steinberg, 1983, 1987, 1989b, 1991a).

We have also seen that in the UK there is a spreading band of grey on each side of what was once quite clear — namely, 16 years as the age of consent. It is not crystal clear, neither in law nor according to good practice, that an adolescent under the age of 16 (and his or her doctor) must accept completely the authority of the parents, if he or she has sufficient understanding to contribute to a decision. Under or over the age of 16, the blurred boundaries between medical treatment and proper care (for example, adequate feeding in anorexia nervosa, requirement to live in a therapeutic community, or behavioural management in a structured setting) await clearer legal interpretations and guidelines.

Meanwhile, having stressed the importance of recognizing the adolescent's need for reasonable autonomy and professional needs for reasonable authority, there are very many occasions in family work with adolescents when the authority of the parents, in handling the boy or girl or in making decisions about treatment or the use of services, needs recognition and encouragement too.

MEDICAL AND SOCIAL MODELS OF RESPONSE

The spectrum of problems that young people present includes, at one end, diagnosable disorders, and at the other problems, which, while causing real distress, difficulty and danger, are more likely to be understood and resolved by proper attention to issues of care and control. Between the ends of this spectrum are many combinations of syndrome and circumstance that require the use of both diagnosis of a disorder and the description of a particular constellation of social circumstances. This, of course, is recognized in the principle of multiaxial classification (see Chapter 1).

Many clinics place emphasis on individual clinical diagnosis, while others emphasize family assessment and diagnosis (Wells, 1986; Wells *et al.*, 1978). Many family-oriented clinics will also make clinical diagnoses but nevertheless tend to take an approach that is primarily based on family dynamics or crisis intervention; thus the main descriptions given, and recommendations made, are in terms of family or social management of the young person (Bruggen *et al.*, 1973). There is no doubt that this meets the needs of many adolescent referrals, yet it is not the most appropriate approach for many others, for example, adolescents with mental illnesses. Of course, once any service demonstrates its competence in a particular way, it is likely to attract one type of referral at the expense of others. This reinforces its view of the 'best' way to work, and indeed that team or unit is likely to become particularly skilled at working in that way. On the one hand, the team or unit working with one particular perspective will develop the confidence and expertise needed in work with adolescents; on the other, they may set up a barrier against other referrals (Jaffa & Dezsery, 1989). Wells (1986), meanwhile, has warned against adolescent services that offer to meet the whole range of expectations, and end up meeting few.

TO ADMIT OR NOT TO ADMIT?

Hersov and Bentovim (1985) and Ponton (1989) have suggested, for inpatient services for younger people, that admission to a hospital unit is most appropriate in the following circumstances:

1 When the adolescent's mental state is so bizarre, or his or her distress is so great, that greater containment, supervision and monitoring of treatment is needed than is possible on an outpatient basis.

2 When psychiatric disorder gives rise to dangerous behaviour, such as suicidal attempts or self-neglect.

3 When a complex problem requires a period of continuous observation, using medical, psychological and nursing skills, and perhaps the need for special investigations and assessment, such as electroencephalographic telemetry or functional analysis.

4 When treatment can only be undertaken safely and effectively, at least initially, with 24-hour supervision, and perhaps controlled circumstances, as in a trial of medication or behaviour therapy. This category would also include a trial of psychotherapeutic work with an impulsive, volatile or potentially psychotic adolescent.

5 When a trial period away from an intractably chaotic household may provide guidance about the young person's potential for relating in a more constructive, happier way with adults and with peers, and help make decisions about longer-term care. Hospital units are not ordinarily neutral settings; however, when large and sensitive questions about whether or not the major part of a psychological problem is in the child or intractably in the family, a defined assessment period in a hospital may be perceived as more acceptable to a family than direct admission to a care setting.

PROBLEMS OF ADMISSION TO A GENERAL ADOLESCENT UNIT

Caution about admission should be exercised when: (1) persistently violent behaviour appears to be due to enduring personality characteristics, personal repertoire and lifestyle rather than to treatable psychiatric disorder, unless there is an unusual degree of motivation to change on the part of the adolescent; (2) when a side-effect of admission will be to reinforce an assumption of mental illness and irresponsibility, when therapeutic work requires the opposite; (3) when it may perpetuate and worsen an adolescent's rejection from a family; and (4) in most cases of young people who need admission for treatment of drug abuse, because of the specialised therapeutic environment needed.

Three controversies, in particular, commonly surround admissions to adolescent units. The first is the preference of most units for some degree of planning of an admission, except when the problem is one of acute illness requiring bed rest and medication. The experience of most adolescent psychiatrists is of the necessity for clarity and predictability, not only about treatment plans, but also about authority, responsibility, and the sustainability of treatment. Many an adolescent has been rushed into a unit by a grateful referrer and unwary recipient, only to be discharged a few days later because of a change of mind on the adolescent's or parents' part, or by lack of opportunity for the implications of admission (e.g. the programme, the rules for behaviour, attending the unit's school, family involvement, the requirements of treatment) to have been properly understood and agreed. Unfortunately, such precipitate breakdown of treatment seems most likely to happen when it has already become the pattern, so that the adolescent and family experience yet another failure. Crises in adolescent psychiatry are common, but emergencies needing immediate, direct admission to a hospital ward or any other primarily medical intervention are relatively rare (Steinberg, 1989b). On the other hand, the need for clarification, explanation, goal-setting and negotiation around the question of genuinely informed consent for treatment, by those in a position to give it, applies in every case (Steinberg, 1983, 1987; Khan, 1990) and does not have to be time-consuming (Steinberg, 1989b).

A related controversy concerns the admission of adolescents to adult wards, about which strong feelings prevail. The reasons usually given as to why a particular ward is quite unsuitable for young people often amount to it being unsuitable for anybody. The special advantages of an adolescent psychiatric service are due to its integration of clinical, developmental, educational and family issues, and a unit that attempts to maintain this regime cannot, in general, function as an acute admission ward, with several admissions a week of young people from casualty departments, who may need to stay for only a few days. Although an adolescent unit should offer direct admission of acutely psychotic or severely depressed young people when it can (and such presentations are relatively rare), an adult psychiatric unit should be a reasonable place for a young person to be treated for a few days until an adolescent psychiatric team can contribute to the assessment and arrange a planned transfer if necessary.

The problem for the planning and operation of adolescent services is that the qualities required in an acute, swift admission–swift 'disposal' service, are likely to be different from what is needed in even a short-stay adolescent unit, where symptomatic control and short-term holding are not enough, and developmental issues (such as reactivation of infantile conflicts, ambivalence towards, and conflict with, figures in authority, and atypical psychopathology and response to treatment) require attention (Munoz-Milan, 1986; Khan, 1990). Thus even a short-stay adolescent unit requires, by definition, a specialized approach and milieu that can deal with such issues as family and peer relationships, authority and decisions about care, control and education. This is likely to be an over-specialized resource for the routine admission of large numbers of young people who have, for example, taken overdoses, whose need for admission is very brief, and few of whom need even short-term residential psychiatric care. Thus, Hawton (1987), reviewing a large body of research into the increasing problem of adolescent drug overdoses, concluded that inpatient treatment had a very limited role for these young people, and that problem-oriented outpatient help, preferably home-based and involving the family doctor, was likely to be more helpful — though this approach too, he points out, needs systematic evaluation. The possible relationship between an adolescent psychiatric service and a short-stay acute general ward is discussed further below.

A further problem is that of young people who are hard to place, and who often have a long history of failed family, foster and residential care, abortive attempts at treatment, and who may be violent, self-destructive or frequent absconders (Millham *et al.*, 1978; Millham, 1981). Sometimes they show all three of these patterns of behaviour, are emotionally chaotic and disruptive to the milieu of any establishment that tries to help them — a phenomenon in keeping with the young person's history and psychopathology. The despairing, angry dependence which is often seen, and in which help is at the same time demanded and rejected, may require control, at least at first, rather than an appeal to the adolescent's own responsibility and motivation, and for such reasons many of these young people are often not acceptable to therapeutic communities. Such adolescents may be helped by therapeutic communities which persist despite repeated absconding and rule-breaking; sometimes they are helped by an adolescent service which persists on an outpatient basis, thereby providing some continuity, even though one residential setting after another breaks down. Sometimes physically secure centres are needed. Bruggen and Westland (1979) pointed out the limits of what an inpatient service can offer these young people, and suggested long-term collaboration between psychiatric and social service departments. However, such collaboration can be difficult to sustain, and is often challenged by the more disturbed type of youngster's repeated and forceful insistence that it cannot work.

SUPPLY AND DEMAND

The number of young people in the community causing concern is far greater than the number who could, or probably should, have a comprehensive psychiatric assessment. The question arises how best this potential demand should be responded to. Many would feel, particularly in the UK, that holding back demand by a direct charge to the clientele would be unacceptable. Overly long waiting lists are fundamentally unsound, because either the degree of urgency in the queue becomes an unknown quantity, or the service ends up seeing only urgent cases, while the other children and families wait. Lack of knowledge of the availability of services or how to use them may well be one of the most significant barriers to service use, and is as unsatisfactory as the other obstacles. There would be far less of a problem if the criteria for psychiatric assessment or treatment were clear, and agreed between front-line professionals and secondary and tertiary sources of advice, but they are not. For example, except in the case of severe mental illnesses, there are no broadly shared criteria for referral as there are, say, between general practitioner and general hospital physician or surgeon. Further, different adolescent service specialists have different approaches, for example, some emphasizing family assessment and treatment and others individual work, some focusing on the adolescent's psychodynamic state and others using wider biopsychosocial concepts.

Meanwhile, whatever approach is the best (and it is likely that clientele, referrers and service providers will have different views), the costs of all forms of care and treatment are likely to set an increasing constraint on all aspects of adolescent services. There are continuing financial limits on services, whatever the source of the money, and whether or not widely acceptable clinical and social criteria are developed (Sharfstein & Beigel, 1984; Staton, 1989; Hendren & Berlin, 1991a,b). While studies of costs and cost-effectiveness are being attempted in this field (Parry-Jones, 1990), the ethical, philosophical and political considerations of how much a community should spend, and on what, are complex (Mooney & McGuire, 1988) and not likely to be resolved before economic solutions become imperative, and imposed.

A COMMUNITY-ORIENTED APPROACH BASED ON AN INPATIENT UNIT: AN OUTREACH SERVICE

At the Adolescent Unit at Bethlem Royal Hospital, we are developing a model of responding to referrals in which many of the issues discussed in preceding pages become the key focus of the work of the outreach team. Instead of automatically offering an appointment (or admission), a consultative discussion by telephone, often followed up by a meeting, is offered to referrers. In this consultation, more information is gathered, the nature of problems clarified, and negotiation about what is needed, and who is in a position to do what, is undertaken. The object is to rationalize the use of the adolescent service, clarify goals, time-scales and key staff to be involved, establish lines of liaison, and to facilitate continuing involvement of those (family and professionals) outside the unit. This approach, of course, owes much to the family and crisis models of intervention acknowledged above (Bruggen *et al.*, 1973), but at Bethlem the outreach workers are integral members of the staff of an inpatient unit whose approach is primarily medically and diagnostically oriented (Steinberg, 1986a), and this crucial difference allows management-oriented negotiation and planning about *how much* of the problem is best seen in social and family terms, requiring social and family responses, and *how much* is a question of psychiatric disorder. It also includes the sometimes problematic assumption that every young patient should have a home address outside the hospital, with people outside the hospital collaborating with the inpatient staff throughout admission about, among other things, weekend leave and ultimate discharge. In many countries and communities the question of the home address is often not a controversial issue, but in the UK with its tradition of residential care (Millham, 1981), its complex network of services for young people, and complex laws and expectations about their care, it is not uncommon that on admission to hospital some adolescents risk losing parental and other adult ties, and have no one able or willing to look after them when psychiatric care is judged to be completed.

It is for such reasons that much has been said about the value of care in the community. The outreach experiment at Bethlem is an attempt to deal with the detailed practicalities of the larger question: who really needs psychiatric hospital admission, and how can alternatives be identified and encouraged? This work is currently being evaluated in terms of problem and symptom resolution, consumer satisfaction and referrer satisfaction and is based on an examination of changing referral and service patterns at the Bethlem unit over the past 40 years.

Examples of what the outreach workers actually do include offering telephone information, advice and consultation; attending the conferences of referring agencies, to avoid duplication of history-taking and assessment procedures, except where there is a useful reason for it; working in the home, for example, establishing trust with unwilling families and housebound adolescents; and visiting nonhospital residential settings on a consultative basis, or on a part-consultative basis when some direct work needs to be done with the referred adolescent.

One of our observations is that, as more referred adolescents are helped outside the unit, those who are admitted form a particularly dependent and disturbed group, with major implications for their nursing care. If competent outpatient and community care does develop effectively and on a large scale, and this is certainly a widely held hope, the consequent impact on all forms of residential care needs careful monitoring. The problems currently being encountered in children's homes in the UK, with accusations of the abuse of adolescents' civil rights, or their physical abuse, could emerge in any service trying to contain and help very disturbed young people, particularly if the service becomes over-stretched. This problem needs meeting by meticulous attention to containing and restraint procedures (Khan, 1990), basic training appropriate to the task and a much increased priority for in-service training and supervision. Aspects that deserve attention include appreciation of the importance of effective and focused consultation with colleagues and clientele about matters of consent (Steinberg, 1992a), scrupulous record-keeping, and audit in some form to evaluate and monitor working methods.

Assumptions are frequently made about the best way to help staff work effectively together, for example, by use of staff groups (Foskett, 1986; Steinberg, 1986a,b, 1991a; Khan, 1990). However, while attention to staff communication and relationships is important, the most helpful ways of doing so have yet to be demonstrated.

In the end, all these facets of professional work come down to good training, appropriate supervision and evaluation of effectiveness. This represents an academic dimension to adolescent services that is characteristically given low priority, or none at all, especially outside health facilities. However, recently renewed concern about the size and range of psychosocial problems, and the difficulties and costs of meeting them, has generated new activity in the field of audit and service evaluation, and this may enable administrative questions to be framed and responded to in ways informed by the methods of good training and research.

ISSUES IN THE PLANNING AND DEVELOPMENT OF ADOLESCENT SERVICES

The work undertaken in adolescent services crosses many boundaries, almost every one of them either in dispute or representing a grey area. Social problems shade into psychological and psychiatric conditions; adolescent outpatients are seen at child psychiatric clinics and in the outpatient clinics of inpatient services, which may be nearby; the field of mental handicap and learning impairment overlaps with adolescent psychiatry, and both with aspects of paediatrics; the debate about the integration or separation of child psychiatry and adolescent psychiatry is not complete, particularly at the upper

end of the age range. As Parry-Jones (1992) pointed out, adolescent psychiatric services can be pulled in two directions, towards integrated services for children or towards comprehensive psychiatric services for all age groups. Further, in later childhood and adolescence, the problems of teenagers and young adults with chronic mental illnesses emerge (Looney, 1988; Watts *et al.*, 1989). This highlights not only overlapping services (and the gaps between them), but major differences of emphasis too, for example, in the family and developmental perspective child and adolescent psychiatrists are likely to take, in the case of, say, a 20-year-old with autism or schizophrenia, while adult psychiatric services will often have a different orientation and the facilities and staff skills that go with it.

This very short list of differences in presenting problems, in the client group, in the services likely to be available, and in the approach they take, could be extended many times over. The expectations, skills and services of, say, school psychologists, school counsellors, probation officers, psychotherapists, family doctors, specialist teachers and the staff of the many types of residential centres for children have hardly been touched upon.

It is tempting to wish that adolescent services should be available on a systematic and comprehensive basis. This would help in terms of availability (information and ease of access), in collaboration between facilities, and in evaluating services. It would also enable there to be machinery for developing services and adapting them to changing needs, for example, changes in the population, or in methods of clinical management — even of changes in the availability of funds.

There are, however, four major obstacles to any prospect of bringing about improved coherence in adolescent services in the near future, at least where a number of services are already in place (the situation might be different where a completely new service is being developed).

The first is the need for information about the range and nature of problems in the area, the types of skills available and their usefulness. The logistics and cost of such enquiries can be considerable, and the questions not easy to formulate or answer. For example, to what extent can, say, one professional worker with a special interest in psychotherapy, or behaviour therapy, be regarded as an enduring resource on which long-term planning can be based? Skills and services tend to be in flux.

The second, as mentioned above, is the dual question of fund availability and cost-effectiveness. Both may be hard to establish.

The third is the very different set of priorities likely to be identified by the adolescent service workers consulted. This will be for professional, historical and organizational reasons, with the clientele and problems they see being strongly influential.

Fourthly, least welcome perhaps as factors to be faced, but none the less influential for that, are competition and suspicion between some workers and some agencies, making difficult both the machinery of consultation and planning and the meeting of minds (Steinberg, 1981, 1983; Health Advisory Service, 1986; Parry-Jones, 1986, 1992).

EVALUATION OF SERVICES AND TREATMENTS

Amid the problems, there is a great deal of effective practice, and what is effective needs to be established wherever feasible, identified, funded and encouraged. This cannot always be done in that order; the nature of the field is that individuality and diversity are needed, and working experiments are often set up, on the grounds of what seems right in good faith and in the light of experience. Innovations deserve encouragement and assistance with the building-in of systematic monitoring and evaluation. Under-funded, over-stretched services are characteristically forced to give evaluation, like training, less priority than service delivery. Even though academic centres are themselves often in an equivalent over-committed position, there is room for improved working relationships between the two (Taylor, 1986).

TRAINING

From a longer-term point of view, the training of all potential adolescent service personnel would benefit by teaching on evaluative thinking and methods, and on the issues involved in service development. Although multidisciplinary and multi-agency work has its problems (Steinberg, 1981; Parry-Jones, 1986), it is important for people in training to develop a genuine grasp, as opposed to a nodding acquaintanceship, of what others are doing in the broad field. In this respect, it is important to be conscious of the way in which budgetary machinery can powerfully influence which groups can train and work together, and which are drawn apart.

LIAISON WITH MANAGEMENT

The Health Advisory Service survey (1986) drew attention to the need for joint planning and collaboration at senior administrative levels, particularly where funding and joint funding decisions could be made, rather than only at the practitioner level, where the initiatives often begin. How much the latter 'low-level' joint planning of adolescent services by groups of practitioners can achieve is likely to depend heavily on chance factors like individual drive and creativity, and the local management's flexibility. 'High-level' planning, however, risks drawing up grand designs which, at a clinical level, get priorities wrong and may not work particularly well. For example, formal enquiries into the systematic mishandling of children in institutions in the UK repeatedly demonstrate the obvious — that costly institutions often devote insufficient resources to staff training and supervision. The straightforward question from management to practitioner level: 'What are you trying to do, with what resources, and how is it progressing?' seems not to be asked except after a publicized scandal. However, Thomas and Hardwick (1989) and Hardwick (1990),

have demonstrated imaginative ways involving audit in which clinicians can engage senior administrators' interest in working together. It may be that such consultation within a particular sphere of work is a necessary first step towards wider involvement of clinicians and other practitioners with management. In our present state of knowledge about adolescent problems and the effectiveness of various responses, it does seem that progress needs to be made at this relatively modest level before more elaborate and well-based plans will be feasible.

CONCEPTUAL FRAMEWORKS FOR ADOLESCENT SERVICES

Diversity

The idea of rationalizing adolescent services seems clear enough when a limited view is taken of the facilities to include. Thus, it may be thought that a model service for severely ill young people would consist primarily of outpatient clinics and short- and long-stay psychiatric units and after-care hostels. However, the Bethlem unit's experience, with its clinical focus on work with severely psychiatrically disturbed young people (Steinberg, 1986b,c), is that family and individual psychotherapy, general medical and paediatric services, therapeutic communities of very different types, secure units, forensic and drug services, independent residential schools and departments of social services are all needed — to name a few. These other resources are either part of quite different services, for example general hospitals or education departments, or depend for their strengths and value on their individuality, as in the case of many independent schools and therapeutic communities. This range of facilities cannot logistically be pulled into one network, even if it were a good idea to think in terms of a monolithic service.

The type of resources needed will also depend on the culture of the community served, although it is probably helpful to think in terms of the types of services likely to be needed by a community in, say, an industrialized country or one moving in that direction, for the purposes of this chapter.

Ways of classifying resources

The advantages of valid systems of classification of disorders is well-established (see Chapter 1) and one way of classifying (or planning for) services would be to think primarily in terms of the particular clinical groups to be served. However, the value of thinking in broad terms about the problems of adolescents (e.g. using multiaxial diagnostic systems, family as well as individual assessments, and being problem-focused as well as illness-focused) has led many services and settings for adolescents to take a rather broader approach. For example, a therapeutic community may consider the admission of a boy or girl with a psychotic disorder and on medication, if there has been sufficient explanation and collaboration with the referring psychiatric unit; similarly, an ordinary residential school may consider accepting an adolescent with a psychiatric disorder.

It is therefore appropriate to think of a taxonomy of adolescent services not only in terms of which young people they take on, but of what they do. The coarse classification into *treatment, training, care* and *control* may then be elaborated further as follows.

Treatment

Treatment, or therapy, suggests the treatment of disorder. A treatment unit is one which, within broad and flexible limits, will expect to have an end-point in view, by which time a treatment or range of treatments will have been tried. Diagnosis or assessment will necessarily be part of its function.

The types of treatment facilities needed would include:

1 Acute general medical and acute psychiatric facilities, neither of which can easily be met by a general-purpose, medium-stay adolescent psychiatric unit without seriously compromising its primary functions.

2 A general psychiatric adolescent unit working in liaison with medical and acute psychiatric services, with outpatient and day-patient facilities and with the capacity to work on a consultative, outreach basis with these and any other services.

3 It is likely that a separate service would be needed for the assessment and treatment of young people with severe learning problems, because of the importance, in both settings, of a manageable social milieu in which communication and learning can take place. It is probable that two of these settings (**2** and **3**) could deal with the range of most young people needing short- to medium-term assessment and treatment. Behavioural training represents a specialized component of residential therapy for young people with pervasive developmental or learning problems or persistent conduct disorders and likely to be emphasised in **3**.

4 The above facilities will have outpatient clinics for those who do not need very frequent contact, and day-patient facilities for those who do, but who do not need 5-day or 7-day residential supervision and treatment. Such clinics would see only a minority of the area's patients, however, and most adolescents would be served by the psychological, psychiatric and counselling clinics and centres in the area working with adolescents and families. In some large cities, notably London, referrers may not be clear about the basis on which to use one or other service, and explicit clarification may be needed.

5 Some residential treatment is long-term. In general, this is because it is rehabilitative, dealing with chronic illness in older adolescents and young adults, or long-stay, where the degree of disturbance and the monitoring and adjustment of treatment require a very long period of continuing medical and nursing supervision. However, when such long-term work is needed, there is a corresponding need for detailed attention to wider issues, such as emotional and social development, and education and training. Teenagers with psychoses or pervasive developmental disorders and who need residential treatment will particularly need a setting with specialized

educational and training facilities. Here too, the need for prolonged treatment coexists with and overlaps with two other foci, those of education and training, and care.

6 Finally, therapeutic communities are helpful for young people whose emotional and behavioural problems and dependence needs are such that they require a more prolonged experience of psychotherapy and social therapy than can be met on an outpatient, sessional basis, and of more controlled and monitored relationships than can be found at home, even with family therapy. Here, too, treatment overlaps with care, and to meet particularly immature emotional needs the milieu may be closer to care and nurturing than to treatment as such.

Training

Training may include special education, vocational training and social training, and can help in the rehabilitation of young people with problems of personality development, chronic neurotic or psychotic conditions or learning problems. The combination of attendance at such a centre with family or individual therapy is an ideal arrangement for some young people, especially if there are links with further training, work and housing possibilities. Many areas in the UK have the rudiments of such facilities, but usually they cannot meet the level of need.

Care

Care services are to a variable extent provided by the social service departments, although increasingly in the UK they buy the services of independent residential care settings. When a social service department is active and reasonably well-resourced, it is in the position to make a central and most important contribution to the range of services for young people at every level: emergency protection and care of children at risk, arranging their assessment and, if necessary, fostering or residential care, and providing children's homes which could provide first-rate care or which sometimes have the qualities of therapeutic communities. They may organize self-help services, youth groups and open-access counselling services, sometimes in collaboration with voluntary or paid youth workers. In this enormous range of work they would ideally be able to work closely with psychiatric, psychological, probation and forensic services and the Courts. From time to time and place to place, this job description works in whole or in part. When there is economic and social deprivation, however, the social service departments like their clientele become over-stretched and under-funded, with many gaps and deficiencies.

Control

Control is implicit in good care, and vice versa. Much conduct disorder is treated by behavioural and social learning methods in individual and family work, and as a function of hospital admission. Similar work is attempted for a proportion of young offenders (see Chapter 56), a minority of whom are persistently dangerous, to themselves as well as others.

Many cannot be effectively treated or reliably diagnosed, yet their behaviour cannot be tolerated by the community, and the ethics, legal issues and practicalities of holding and managing these adolescents pose major problems for the adolescent services and the community. The behaviour of such young people and the special characteristics of the services looking after them can mean that both adolescents and staff may risk becoming isolated. The extremes of behaviour of some young people can also risk their individual differences, including their positive qualities, becoming subjugated to the wider need to contain their behaviour effectively. It is important that settings where the priority is for containment continue to be involved with and learn from developments in other fields of adolescent care, and that studies are undertaken into what works best and how it is achieved.

INFORMATION AND ADVICE

We have seen that information on the nature of adolescent problems and the services available for them is incompletely and unevenly distributed. It is also hard to keep information up-to-date, because quite often good practice seems to depend on individual and team initiatives that sooner or later succumb to changes in leadership and personnel; many centres depend on young, ambitious and underpaid staff who soon move on. Nevertheless, often enough the right service or setting for a particular adolescent can be found, given determination, persistence and time. It would be sensible for machinery to be established to collate information about services for adolescents at a number of key and identified centres.

Information, education and advice for the general public are variably available through government publications, the mass media and through special advisory centres, which offer guidance and sometimes counselling on health, sexual employment, transcultural and other matters. It may be that these will always result from *ad hoc* and piecemeal initiatives, for example in response to the public concern of the moment. However, whatever their provenance, such aspects of services for adolescents and families are important.

CONCLUSIONS

It seems inherently unlikely that comprehensive adolescent services could ever be developed on the basis of a grand scheme, even if the extraordinary amount of money this would need were available. The need for good services for young people is as urgent a need as ever, yet at the same time these services and skills need to develop to match the changing needs of the community and advances in our understanding of problems and their management, rather than be set up as a monolithic complex of facilities. I would suggest there are two main ways forward. The first is for more teaching and research to be shared between all relevant services, for more exchange. The obstacles to this are likely to be personal, rather than

financial. To an extent, it is already beginning to happen, particularly, I think it is fair to say, in the less ideologically bound, more enquiring child psychiatric and psychotherapeutic centres.

The second is for specialist services to be more outward-looking, with key staff having consultative skills to complement their specialized technical skills. Specialist expertise in a specialist centre should represent what those making referrals to the service cannot do for themselves. Yet we have seen that such referrals tend to be based on rather arbitrary grounds and incomplete information. Moreover, there are many reasons for maintaining and encouraging the relationships the adolescent already has (e.g. with parents, teachers and other workers outside the specialist service), and for helping to extend these outside relationships and skills when this is indicated, necessary and feasible. Consultative approaches are concerned with maintaining and maximizing what others can do — a process which logically leads to clarification into a sharper focus what the specialist or specialized service needs to do to fill any gaps remaining (Caplan, 1970; Conoley, 1981; Gallesich, 1982; Steinberg & Hughes, 1987; Steinberg 1989a, 1992a,b,c).

The consultative approach represents a process of case-focused, personnel-focused and service-focused enquiry each time it is employed. It involves negotiation, information exchange and clarification about what is wanted, what is needed and what is possible. As a fourth arm of every specialist service, alongside clinical practice, teaching and research, it could help develop links between services on the basis of rationally based collaboration over individual pieces of work.

REFERENCES

Abe K. & Masui T. (1981) Age—sex trends of phobic and anxiety symptoms in adolescents. *British Journal of Psychiatry*, **138**, 297–302.

Accharya S., Moorhouse S., Littlewood R. & Kareem J. (1989) The Nafsiyat Intercultural Therapy Centre. A psychotherapy centre for ethnic minorities. *Psychiatric Bulletin*, **13**(7), 358–360.

Anthony E.J. (1991) The therapeutic matrix in the in-patient treatment of adolescents. In: Hendren R. & Berlin I. (eds) *Psychiatric In-patient Care of Children and Adolescents: A Multicultural Approach*, pp. 194–206. Wiley, New York.

Bedford A. & Tennant G. (1981) Behaviour training with disturbed adolescents. *Newsletter of the Association for Child Psychology and Psychiatry*, **7**, 6–12.

Bettelheim B. (1950) *Love is not Enough*. Free Press, New York.

Bettelheim B. (1960) *The Informed Heart*. Free Press, New York.

Blum R. (1986) Psychosomatic illness in adolescence. In: Feldman R. & Stiffman A. (eds) *Advances in Adolescent Mental Health*, pp. 119–162. JAI Press, Greenwich, CT.

Brook C.G.D. (1993) *The Practice of Medicine in Adolescence*. Edward Arnold, Sevenoaks.

Brown B. (1985) An application of social learning methods in a research programme for young offenders. *Journal of Adolescence*, **8**, 321–331.

Bruggen P. (1979) Authority in work with young adolescents: a personal review. *Journal of Adolescence*, **2**, 345–354.

Bruggen P. & Westland P. (1979) Difficult to place adolescents: are more resources required? *Journal of Adolescence*, **2**, 245–250.

Bruggen P., Byng-Hall J. & Pitt-Aitkens T. (1973) The reason for admission as a focus of work in an adolescent unit. *British Journal of Psychiatry*, **122**, 319–329.

Burke A.W. (1976) Socio-cultural determinants of attempted suicide among West Indians in Birmingham. *British Journal of Psychiatry*, **129**, 261–266.

Canton C. & Gralnic A. (1987) A review of issues surrounding length of psychiatric hospitalization. *Hospital Community Psychiatry*, **38**, 858–863.

Cantwell D. & Carlson G. (eds) (1983) *Affective Disorders in Childhood and Adolescence: An Update.* Spectrum Publications, New York.

Caplan G. (1970) *The Theory and Practice of Mental Health Consultation.* Tavistock Publications, London.

Carlson G. & Cantwell D. (1982) Suicidal behavior and depression in children and adolescents. *Journal of the American Academy of Child Psychiatry*, **21**, 361–368.

Clark D.H. (1977) The therapeutic community. *British Journal of Psychiatry*, **13**, 553–564.

Conoley J.C. (1981) (ed) *Consultation in Schools: Theory, Research, Practice.* Academic Press, New York.

Doherty E. (1975) Length of hospitalization in a short-term therapeutic community. *Archives of General Psychiatry*, **33**, 87–92.

Dupont T.S. & Dowdney L. (1990) Dilemmas in working with schools. *Newsletter of the Association for Child Psychology and Psychiatry*, **12**(1), 13–16.

Farrington D.P. (1985) Delinquency prevention in the 1980s. *Journal of Adolescence*, **8**(1), 3–16.

Feldman R. & Stiffman A. (1986) Mental health disorders in adolescence: issues and prospects. In: Feldman R. & Stiffman A. (eds) *Advances in Adolescent Mental Health*, pp. 1–18. JAI Press, Greenwich, CT.

Ford C. (1983) *The Somatizing Disorders.* Elsevier Biomedical, New York.

Foskett J. (1986) The staff group. In: Steinberg D. (ed) *The Adolescent Unit: Work and Teamwork in Adolescent Psychiatry*, pp. 169–178. Wiley, Chichester.

Framrose R. (1975) The first 70 admissions to an adolescent unit in Edinburgh. General characteristics and treatment outcome. *British Journal of Psychiatry*, **126**, 380–389.

Gabel S. (1989) Medical evaluation. In: Hsu G. & Hersen M. (eds) *Recent Developments in Adolescent Psychiatry*, pp. 51–69, Wiley, New York.

Gabel S. & Hsu L. (1986) Routine laboratory tests in adolescent psychiatric in-patients: their value in making psychiatric diagnoses and in detecting medical disorders. *Journal of the American Academy of Child Psychiatry*, **25**, 113–119.

Gallesich J. (1982) *The Profession and Practice of Consultation. A Handbook for Consultants, Trainers of Consultants and Consumers of Consultation Services.* Jossey-Bass, London.

Garrell D.C. (1965) Adolescent medicine. A survey in the United States and Canada. *American Journal of Diseases of Children*, **109**, 314–321.

Graham P. & Rutter M. (1973) Psychiatric disorder in the young adolescent. *Proceedings of the Royal Society of Medicine*, **66**, 1226–1229.

Guthrie A. & Howell M. (1972) Mobile medical care for alienated youths. *Journal of Pediatrics*, **81**, 1025–1033.

Hardwick P. (1990) Health services review: a commentary on East Dorset. *Newsletter of the Association for Child Psychology and Psychiatry*, **12**(6), 18–19.

Hawton K. (1987) Assessment and aftercare of adolescents who take overdoses. In: Diekstra R. & Hawton K. (eds) *Suicide in Adolescence*, pp. 79–93. Martinus Nijhoff Kluwer, Lancaster.

Hawton K., O'Grady J., Osborne M. & Cole D. (1982) Adolescents who take overdoses: their characteristics, problems and contacts with helping agencies. *British Journal of Psychiatry*, **140**, 118–123.

Health Advisory Service (1986) *Bridges over Troubled Waters.* Department of Health, London.

Heinman E. & Shanfield S. (1980) Length of stay for patients in one city's hospitals with psychiatric units. *Hospital Community Psychiatry*, **31**, 632–634.

Henderson A., Krupinski J. & Stoller A. (1971) Epidemiological aspects of adolescent psychiatry. In: Howells J. (ed) *Modern Perspectives in Adolescent Psychiatry.* Oliver & Boyd, Edinburgh.

Hendren R. & Berlin I. (1991a) Further directions. In: Hendren R. & Berlin I. (eds) *Psychiatric In-patient Care of Children and Adolescents; A Multicultural Approach*, pp. 313–319. Wiley, New York.

Hendren R. & Berlin I. (1991b) *Psychiatric In-patient Care of Children and Adolescents; A Multicultural Approach.* Wiley, New York.

Hendren R. & Berlin I. (1991c) A philosophy of in-patient care. In: Hendren R. & Berlin I. (eds) *Psychiatric In-patient care of Children and Adolescents: A Multicultural Approach*, pp. 3–13. Wiley, New York.

Her Majesty's Stationery Office (1982) *Experience and Participation: Report of the Review Group of Youth Services in England.* HMSO, London.

Her Majesty's Stationery Office (1989) *An Introduction to the Children Act 1989.* HMSO, London.

Hersov L. & Bentovim A. (1985) In-patient and day hospital units. In: Rutter M. & Hersov L. (eds) *Child and Adolescent Psychiatry: Modern Approaches*, 2nd edn, pp. 766–779. Blackwell Scientific Publications, Oxford.

Hoghughi M. (1978) *Troubled and Troublesome: Coping with Severely Disordered Children.* André Deutsch, London.

Hollis C. & Steinberg D. (1992) Changes in referral patterns and admission practice in an adolescent unit over 40 years (in preparation).

Jaffa T. & Dezery A. (1989) Reasons for admission to an adolescent unit. *Journal of Adolescence*, **12**, 187–195.

Jones R., Allen D., Wells P. & Morris A. (1978) An adolescent unit assessed: attitudes to a treatment experience for adolescents and their families. *Journal of Adolescence*, **1**, 371–383.

Kareem J. & Littlewood R. (eds) (1992) *Intercultural Therapy: Theory and Techniques.* Blackwell Scientific Publications, Oxford.

Khan A. (1990) *Short-term Psychiatric Hospitalization of Adolescents.* Year Book Medical Publishers, Chicago.

Krupinski J., Baikie A., Stoller A., Graves J., O'Day D. & Polke P. (1967) A community mental health survey of Heyfield, Victoria. *Medical Journal of Australia*, **1**, 1204–1211.

Lampen J. (1978) Drestin a little brief authority: controls in residential work with adolescents. *Journal of Adolescence*, **1**, 163–175.

Laufer M. (1968) *The Work of the Brent Consultation Centre.* Monograph no. 1. Centre for the Study of Adolescence, London.

Lavik N. (1977) Urban–rural differences in rates of disorder. A comparative psychiatric population study of Norwegian adolescents. In: Graham P. (ed) *Epidemiological Approaches in Child Psychiatry*, pp. 223–251. Academic Press, London.

Lee E. (1988) Cultural factors in working with South East Asian refugee adolescents. *Journal of Adolescence*, **11**(2), 167–179.

Leslie S. (1974) Psychiatric disorder in the young adolescents of an industrial town. *British Journal of Psychiatry*, **125**, 113–124.

Lewinsohn P., Duncan E., Stanton A. & Hautzinger M. (1986) Age at first onset for non-bipolar depression. *Journal of Abnormal Psychology*, **95**, 378–383.

Littlewood R. & Lipsedge M. (1989) *Aliens and Alienists: Ethnic Minorities and Psychiatry*, 2nd edn. Unwin Hyman, London.

London Youth Advisory Centre (1985) *A Statement of its Work, Objectives and Future Planning.* Brandon Centre, London.

London Youth Advisory Centre (1987) *Hampstead Health Authority Review of Family Planning Services and Psychosexual Services*. Brandon Centre, London.

Looney J. (ed) (1988) *Chronic Mental Illness in Children and Adolescents*. American Psychiatric Press, Washington, DC.

Loranger A. & Levine P. (1978) Age of onset of bipolar affective illness. *Archives of General Psychiatry*, **35**, 1345–1348.

Lordi W. (1979) Hospital and residential treatment of adolescents. In: Novello J. (ed) *The Short Course in Adolescent Psychiatry*, pp. 246–262. Brunner/Mazel, New York.

McClure G. (1986) Recent changes in suicide among adolescents in England and Wales. *Journal of Adolescence*, **9**, 135–143.

McShane D. (1988) An analysis of mental health research with American Indian youth. *Journal of Adolescence*, **11**, 87–116.

Melton G. & Schmechel L. (1989) Legal issues. In: Hsu L. & Hersen M. (eds) *Recent Developments in Adolescent Psychiatry*, pp. 135–158. Wiley, New York.

Millham S. (1981) The therapeutic implications of locking up children. *Journal of Adolescence*, **4**, 13–26.

Millham S., Bullock R. & Hosie K. (1978) *Locking up Children: Secure Provision within the Child Care System*. Saxon House, Farnborough.

Mooney G. & McGuire A. (eds) (1988) *Medical Ethics and Economics in Health Care*. Oxford University Press, Oxford.

Munoz-Milan R. (1986) The optimal length of hospitalization of adolescents. *Hospital Community Psychiatry*, **37**, 545.

Neinstein L. (1984) *Adolescent Health Care*. Urban & Schwarzenberg, Baltimore, MD.

Newsome A., Thorne B. & Wyld K. (1975) *Student Counselling in Practice*. University of London Press, London.

Novello J. (ed) (1979) *The Short Course in Adolescent Psychiatry*. Brunner/Mazel, New York.

Parry-Jones W.L. (1986) Multi-disciplinary teamwork: help or hindrance? In: Steinberg D. (ed) *The Adolescent Unit. Work and Teamwork in Adolescent Psychiatry*, pp. 193–200. Wiley, Chichester.

Parry-Jones W.L. (1990) Adolescent psychiatric services: development and expansion. In: Hendrik S.J.H. & Black M. (eds) *Child and Adolescent Psychiatry: into the 1990s*, pp. 83–89. Royal College of Psychiatrists, London.

Parry-Jones W.L. (1992) Management in the National Health Service in relation to children and the provision of child psychiatric services. *Newsletter of the Association for Child Psychology and Psychiatry*, **14**(1), 3–10.

Patterson G.R. (1974) Intervention for boys with conduct problems: multiple settings, treatment and criteria. *Journal of Consulting and Clinical Psychology*, **42**, 471–481.

Perinpanayagam K. (1978) Dynamic approach to adolescence: treatment. *British Medical Journal*, **1**, 563–566.

Peterson E. (1980) *Disturbed Adolescents; The Case for the Integration of Young Peoples' Services*. Origen, London.

Ponton L.E. (1989) In-patient treatment of children and adolescents: policy statement of the Committee on Adolescent Psychiatry and Hospitalization of the American Psychiatric Association and the American Academy of Child and Adolescent Psychiatry, Washington, DC. Quoted in Hendress R. & Berlin I. (1991) (eds) *Psychiatric In-patient Care of Children and Adolescents*, pp. 3–13. Wiley, New York.

Porter N. & Blackwell S. (1991) Working with resistance in families: a cross-cultural perspective. In: Hendress R. & Berlin I. (eds) *Psychiatric In-patient Care of Children and Adolescents: A Multicultural Approach*, pp. 143–160. Wiley, New York.

Pyne N., Morrison R. & Ainsworth P. (1986) *A Consumer Survey of an Adolescent Unit*. *Journal of Adolescence*, **9**(1), 63–72.

Rack P. (1982) *Race, Culture and Mental Disorder*. Tavistock, London.

Rapoport J. (1989) *Obsessive-compulsive Disorder in Children and Adolescents*. American Psychiatric Press, Washington, DC.

Rapoport R.N. (1960) *Community as Doctor. New Perspectives on a Therapeutic Community*. Tavistock, London.

Rindner E. (1991) Recruiting, developing and training staff for work in the multicultural setting of a children's psychiatric hospital. In: Hendress R. & Berlin I. (eds) *Psychiatric In-Patient Care of Children and Adolescents: A Multicultural Approach*, pp. 235–249. Wiley, New York.

Rose J. (1990) *Preliminary Findings from the Waiting List Study*. Brandon Centre, London.

Rose M. (1986) The design of atmosphere: ego-nurture and psychic change in residential treatment. *Journal of Adolescence*, **9**, 49–62.

Rosen B., Bahn A., Shellow R. & Bower E. (1965) Adolescent patients served in outpatient psychiatric clinics. *American Journal of Public Health*, **55**, 1563–1577.

Ro-Trock C., Wellisch D. & Schroder J. (1977) A family therapy outcome study in an inpatient setting. *American Journal of Orthopsychiatry*, **47**, 514–522.

Rutter M. & Giller H. (1983) *Juvenile Delinquency: Trends and Perspectives*. Penguin, Harmondsworth.

Rutter M., Graham P., Chadwick O. & Yule W. (1976) Adolescent turmoil: fact or fiction? *Journal of Child Psychology and Psychiatry*, **17**, 35–56.

Ryle A. (1973) *Student Casualties*. Penguin, Harmondsworth.

Shaffer D. & Fisher P. (1981) The epidemiology of suicide in children and young adolescents. *Journal of the American Academy of Child Psychiatry*, **20**, 545–565.

Sharfstein S. & Beigel A. (1984) Less is more? To-day's economics and its challenge to psychiatry. *American Journal of Psychiatry*, **141**, 1403–1407.

Sheehan M., Oppenheimer E. & Taylor C. (1988) Who comes for treatment: drug misusers at three London agencies. *British Journal of Addiction*, **83**, 311–320.

Shen J.T.Y. (ed) (1980) *Clinical Practice of Adolescent Medicine*. Appleton-Century-Crofts, New York.

Sheldrick C. (1990) Approaches to treatment and facilities. In: Bluglass R. & Bowden P. (eds) *Principles and Practice of Forensic Psychiatry*, pp. 1041–1050. Churchill Livingstone, Edinburgh.

Skynner A.C.R. (1974) An experiment in group consultation with the staff of a comprehensive school. *Group Process*, **6**, 99–114.

Spencer M., Dobbs B. & Swanson D. (1988) African American adolescents: adaptational and socio-economic diversity in behavioural outcomes. *Journal of Adolescence*, **11**, 117–137.

Staton D. (1989) Mental health care economics and the future of psychiatric practice. *Psychiatric Annals*, **19**, 421–427.

Steinberg D. (1981) *Using Child Psychiatry: The Functions and Operations of a Specialty*. Hodder & Stoughton, London.

Steinberg D. (1982) Treatment, training, care or control? The functions of adolescent units. *British Journal of Psychiatry*, **141**, 306–309.

Steinberg D. (1983) *The Clinical Psychiatry of Adolescence. Clinical Work from a Social and Developmental Perspective*. Wiley, Chichester.

Steinberg D. (1986a) *The Adolescent Unit. Work and Teamwork in Adolescent Psychiatry*. Wiley, Chichester.

Steinberg D. (1986b) Developments in a psychiatric service for adolescents. In: Steinberg D. (ed) *The Adolescent Unit. Work and Teamwork in Adolescent Psychiatry*, pp. 209–221. Wiley, Chichester.

Steinberg D. (1986c) The psychiatrist and the adolescent unit. In: Steinberg D. (ed) *The Adolescent Unit. Work and Teamwork in Adolescent Psychiatry*, pp. 121–129. Wiley, Chichester.

Steinberg D. (1987) *Basic Adolescent Psychiatry*. Blackwell Scientific Publications, Oxford.

Steinberg D. (1989a) *Interprofessional Consultation. Innovation and Imagination in Working Relationships*. Blackwell Scientific Publications, Oxford.

Steinberg D. (1989b) Management of crises and emergencies. In: Hsu L.K.G. & Hersen M. (eds) *Recent Developments in Adolescent Psychiatry*, pp. 87–114. Wiley, New York.

Steinberg D. (1991a) Achievement in failure: working with staff in dangerous situations. In: Papadatou D. & Papadatos C. (eds) *Children and Death*, pp. 303–308. Hemisphere, New York.

Steinberg D. (1991b) The concept of adolescent psychiatry. In: Seva A. (ed) *The European Handbook of Psychiatry and Mental Health*, vol. II, pp. 1474–1477. Anthropos, Barcelona.

Steinberg D. (1992a) Informed consent: consultation as a basis for collaboration between disciplines and between professionals and their patients. *Journal of Interprofessional Care*, **6**(1), 43–48.

Steinberg D. (1992b) The imagination in therapy: consultative and creative approaches in therapeutic work across cultures. In: Kareem J. & Littlewood R. (eds) *Intercultural Therapy: Theory and Techniques*, pp. 59–73. Blackwell Scientific Publications, Oxford.

Steinberg D. (1992c) Consultative work in child and adolescent psychiatry. *Archives of Disease in Childhood*, **67**(1), 1302–1305.

Steinberg D. (1994) Crisis work with adolescents: a general strategy for intervention. In: Tsiantis J. (ed) *Basic Child Psychiatry*, vol. 2, Kastaniotis Publications, Athens.

Steinberg D. & Bailey A.J. Physical disorder among adolescent psychiatric in-patients (in preparation).

Steinberg D. & Hughes L. (1987) The emergence of work-centred illness in consultative work. *Journal of Adolescence*, **10**, 309–316.

Steinberg D., Galhenage D.P.C. & Robinson S.C. (1981) Two years referrals to a regional adolescent unit: some implications for psychiatric services. *Social Science and Medicine*, **15E**, 113–122.

Strang J. (1991) Service development and organisation: drugs. In: Glass I.B. (ed) *The International Handbook of Addiction Behaviour*, pp. 283–291. Tavistock/Routledge, London.

Subotsky F. (1992) Psychiatric treatment for children — the organization of services. *Archives of Disease in Childhood*, **67**, 971–975.

Taylor E. (1986) Research and the psychiatric professions. In: Steinberg D. (ed) *The Adolescent Unit. Work and Teamwork in Adolescent Psychiatry*, pp. 147–154. Wiley, Chichester.

Thomas H. & Hardwick P. (1989) An audit of a small child psychiatric clinic. *Newsletter of the Association for Child Psychology and Psychiatry*, **11**(1), 10–14.

Tyrer P. & Steinberg D. (1993) *Models for Mental Disorder: Conceptual Models in Psychiatry*, 2nd edn. Wiley, Chichester.

Vargas L.A. (1991) Evaluating outcome in a multicultural in-patient setting. In: Hendren R. & Berlin I. (eds) *Psychiatric In-patient Care of Children and Adolescents: A Multicultural Approach*, pp. 289–310. Wiley, New York.

Watts E.L., Jenkins M.E. & Richardson G.J.R. (1989) Who cares for the older adolescent? *Psychiatric Bulletin*, **13**(7), 345–346.

Weiner I.B. & DelGaudio A.C. (1976) Psychopathology in adolescence: an epidemiological study. *Archives of General Psychiatry*, **33**, 187–193.

Wells P. (1986) Cut price adolescent units that meet all needs and none? *Bulletin of the Royal College of Psychiatrists*, **10**, 231–232.

Wells P. (1992) Survival in a cold climate. *Psychiatric Bulletin*, **16**, 10–14.

Wells P., Morris A., Jones R.M. & Allen D.J. (1978) An adolescent unit assessed: a consumer survey. *British Journal of Psychiatry*, **132**, 300–308.

Whitely J. (1970) The response of psychopaths to a therapeutic community. *British Journal of Psychiatry*, **116**, 517–529.

Wing J.K. & Fryers T. (1976) *Psychiatric Services in Camberwell and Salford: Statistics from the Camberwell and Salford Psychiatric Registers 1954–1974*. Institute of Psychiatry, London.

Chapter 60
Services for Children and Adolescents with Severe Learning Difficulties (Mental Retardation)

Glynis Murphy

INTRODUCTION

The last two decades have seen enormous changes taking place in services for children and adults with learning difficulties (mental retardation). The normalization movement, which began in the 1960s, has radically changed at least some of the services (and service philosophies) and the trend towards deinstitutionalization has made family and community support a central issue.

The emphasis in this chapter will be on children with severe learning difficulties (or severe mental retardation: see Chapter 35 for explanations of terminology). Such children are likely to need lifelong services and are unlikely to 'disappear' into the ordinary community; but they can lead a relatively normal life with appropriate support. Service requirements tend to be different for severely than for mildly disabled children; but it is important that services recognize a continuum of need and respond to children's individual situations rather than to their categorization.

The terminology of the subject still gives rise to disagreement and confusion. People who have pervasive learning disabilities, when asked, protest about labels. For example, in the report from a self-advocacy conference recently in the US people said: 'We still hate the word "retarded"... Being called retarded hurts. As soon as you are labelled retarded you are treated differently. You get shoved to the back of the line. Others stop talking to you' (InterSev, 1987, quoted in Perske, 1991, p. 19). In the UK, People First, an organization for people with disabilities, say they would prefer not to be labelled at all but that, if labels have to be used, 'people with learning difficulties' is preferred. Increasingly, in the UK, this term or the term learning disabilities is being employed by health authorities, social services departments and education authorities. In the US, the term developmental disabilities is gaining acceptance (Rowitz, 1987), though many still employ the phrase mental retardation.

Such rapid changes in terminology are likely to lead to confusion: people outside the field, when they meet terms like learning difficulty or learning disability tend to assume that it applies to people within the normal range for IQ with specific learning problems (such as in reading or writing). Meanwhile, people who do work in the field find the old terms, such as mental handicap and mental retardation,

pejorative and tend to dismiss professionals who use such phrases. Labels will continue to change and frequent education will be necessary to keep professionals and others up-to-date with their meaning.

NORMALIZATION

One of the major changes to services for children and adults with learning difficulties in the last two or three decades has been the appearance of the normalization movement. According to Wolfensberger (1980a), the concept of normalization can be credited to Bank-Mikkelsen from Denmark. Like many western countries, Denmark began to create institutions for people with learning difficulties in the second half of the 1800s. These institutions became increasingly custodial in orientation and there was a belief, lasting almost until World War II, that the remainder of the community needed protection from people with learning difficulties because of their dangerous criminal tendencies (Bank-Mikkelsen, 1980). Up until 1945 in Denmark, children with learning difficulties were deemed ineducable and were not entitled to schooling (see also the section on education services, below). Changes to the services began largely as a result of parental pressure, and led eventually to a new Danish Act in 1959, which stated the objective of creating 'an existence for the mentally retarded as close to normal living conditions as possible'. Since that time the size of Danish institutions (which were under the direction of psychiatrists) rapidly shrank, the quality of residential settings rose, and there was a rapid increase in the numbers of schools and day-facilities which people with learning difficulties could attend (Bank-Mikkelsen, 1980).

Nirje expanded this principle of normalization and proposed that the crucial components were normal rhythms for each day, each week and each year. For example, children with learning difficulties would attend schools each day like their brothers and sisters, would have weekends off like everyone else and holidays away in the summer. He also proposed that the normal experiences of the life cycle should be available to people with learning difficulties (early childhood, school years, adulthood and leaving home, old age), and that they should be treated with normal respect, live in normal environments and have normal economic assistance (Nirje, 1980). He believed that physical, social, functional and organizational integration were essential for the achievement of normalization (cf. Bank-Mikkelsen who felt that integration was not always essential).

In the US in the 1970s, after visits to northern Europe, Wolfensberger adopted the idea of normalization and turned the principle into a metatheory (Wolfensberger, 1980a,b), applying it to all human services. Initially, he defined normalization as 'the use of culturally valued means in order to enable people to live culturally valued lives' (Wolfensberger, 1980a), and he developed with Glenn what has become a well-known tool, PASS (Program Analysis of Service Systems), for the assessment of services (Wolfensberger & Glenn, 1975). He saw the normalization principle as arising from an understanding of the way that certain groups of people had been devalued by society, and the effect that this had on their behaviour, their living conditions and their expectations.

More recently, Wolfensberger has renamed normalization, partly because he felt that the apparent transparency of the term meant that people erroneously thought they knew what it meant. He considered that some of the criticisms of normalization, by Throne (1975) and Mesibov (1976) for example, arose out of their misunderstanding of the principle (Wolfensberger, 1980b). The new term he suggested was social role valorization (SRV) and he proposed it because he had decided that 'the most explicit and highest goal of normalization must be the creation, support and defence of valued social roles for people who are at risk of social devaluation' (Wolfensberger, 1983). He considered that to achieve SRV it was necessary to enhance people's social image (e.g. through appropriate physical settings and activities) and to enhance their personal competencies (e.g. by addressing clients' needs).

Normalization has been misunderstood at times and Wolfensberger has been at pains to stress that it is not synonymous with humanization or with mainstreaming, nor does it mean that people have to be treated normally nor that they will become 'normal' or be 'cured'. He admits that, at times, corollaries of the principle conflict and he has provided guidelines on how to address such difficulties (Wolfensberger, 1980b). Nevertheless, normalization/SRV has had an enormous influence on the provision of services in the west, as even its critics admit (Mesibov, 1990). Frequently, it is employed as the basic service ideology and the goals of services are often stated in terms of the five accomplishments proposed by O'Brien: (1) community presence; (2) participation; (3) respect; (4) choice; and (5) competence (O'Brien, 1987).

PREVALENCE

The prevalence of mild learning difficulties (IQ more than 2 s.d. below the mean) is approximately 2–3 per 100, as would be expected from a normal distribution (Richardson & Koller, 1985), whereas the prevalence of severe learning difficulties (IQ below 50 or 3.3 s.d. below the mean) is approximately 3–4 per 1000 in western countries (Alberman, 1984; Roberts, 1987).

Studies of prevalence in the developing world have been surprisingly recent. Those that have examined the prevalence of mild learning difficulties have produced misleadingly high figures when they have made inappropriate use of western tests and western means (Reddy, 1987). Of more interest are the studies of severe learning difficulties.

An international pilot study of severe childhood disability conducted an examination of the feasibility of screening for severe 'mental retardation' in nine developing countries, including Bangladesh, Brazil, India, Malaysia, Nepal, Pakistan, Philippines, Sri Lanka and Zambia (Belmont, 1986). In the pilot study, about 1000 house-to-house interviews were completed at each site with families with 3–9-year-old children, using two questionnaires. The most successful one in terms of validity was the short (10-question) yes/no format questionnaire which asked about delays in motor milestones, sensory impairments, motor deficits/abnormalities, seizures, speech and language comprehension and general ability to learn: about 90% of children whom professionals later diagnosed as 'severely mentally retarded' scored positive on the short questionnaire (although it also detected a variety of other conditions without the presence of 'mental retardation'). The percentage of children who scored positive on the short questionnaire varied from 7% (India) to 30% (Brazil) of all the children whose families were interviewed. Whether or not this represents a true difference in prevalence between countries is not yet certain since the samples came from different areas (some rural, some urban) and interviewers may have made somewhat different interpretations of equivocal answers. Belmont (1986) concluded that the prevalence of severe learning difficulties (or severe mental retardation) lay between 5 and 15 per 1000 in all sites save one and that this should be considered 'a first approximation'.

MEDICAL ASPECTS OF PREVENTION

Medical aspects of prevention can be broadly divided into prenatal, perinatal and postnatal measures. *Prenatal measures* include population-based interventions such as maternal inoculations (e.g. for rubella), prenatal testing (blood tests, scans, etc.), and general medical surveillance of pregnancy. Some prenatal services, such as genetic counselling and amniocentesis, are offered only to people considered to be at high risk of giving birth to a child with disabilities. *Perinatal care* is crucial and varies enormously from country to country. Most births in western countries occur in hospitals with trained medical personnel, while the vast majority of births in developing countries occur outside hospitals, often with poorly trained attendants (Mehta, 1987). *Postnatal prevention* includes some highly developed and well-established general programmes, such as inoculations against diseases that carry the risk of sequelae involving brain damage, and routine neonatal testing programmes with medical follow-up (for example, for congenital hypothyroidism and phenylketonuria).

Prenatal services

Infections

In many countries, pregnant women may be tested for rubella antibodies and inoculated after childbirth to prevent later infection and damage to future births. Universal immunization, however, would be more effective and in some countries, for example the US, children are immunized against rubella in infancy (Graham, 1987). In the UK a universal inoculation programme for teenage girls was begun in 1970 with the aim of eliminating rubella embryopathy. By 1986—1987, in the UK, 2—3% of pregnant women still remained susceptible and 60 congenitally infected children were notified that year to the National Congenital Rubella Surveillance Programme (Miller, 1990). The rate was much reduced, but even with national immunization programmes rubella embryopathy had not been eliminated (perhaps partly due to reinfection of some women).

Blood tests and amniocentesis

Routine blood tests for pregnant mothers in the west have for many years included checks on syphilis infection and rhesus antibodies, both of which have long been recognized as potential risks for the fetus. Routine blood tests may also be used to detect neural tube defects in the fetus, since high maternal serum α-fetoprotein levels have been shown to be associated with open lesions (Cuckle, 1987). Maternal serum α-fetoprotein rises early in normal pregnancy so that abnormally high levels can only be judged in the light of true gestational age. Consequently mothers whose levels are high can only be considered to be at risk of carrying a fetus with a neural tube defect if the fetal gestational age is known with some certainty. Routine ultrasound scan allows gestational age to be estimated, and is therefore used in conjunction with serum α-fetoprotein levels to detect at-risk mothers. Certain diagnosis is possible following amniocentesis, offered to at-risk mothers, and detection of an affected fetus at this stage would lead to the mother being offered a termination of pregnancy.

In the UK and a number of other western countries, the knowledge that the risk of having a child with Down's syndrome rose with maternal age led to mothers over 35 years of age being offered amniocentesis. When affected babies were detected the mothers were offered a termination. There have been a number of problems with this approach. Firstly, fewer mothers over 35 years now become pregnant, and the majority of Down's syndrome babies are now born to mothers under 35 years. Only 36% of affected fetuses would have been detected if all mothers over 35 years had been screened in 1985 (Harris & Andrews, 1988). Secondly, not all mothers over 35 years would choose to have the test, on the grounds that they would not want to incur the slightly increased risk of miscarrying, or would not wish to abort an affected fetus. Thirdly, people working with children and adults with Down's syndrome (and other disabling conditions) have argued strongly that offering terminations on the grounds of amniocentesis testing runs counter to normalization philosophy, since it devalues the affected fetus (Williams, 1992, and see below).

More recently, routine maternal blood tests have been employed for the detection of Down's syndrome in the fetus. Maternal age, low levels of maternal serum α-fetoprotein and maternal oestriol concentrations may be combined to estimate the risk of a Down's syndrome fetus and to allow selective offering of amniocentesis (Wald & Cuckle, 1987). Moreover, maternal serum pregnancy-associated plasma protein a (PAPP-A) concentrations, may be an even better marker of a Down's syndrome fetus (Wald et al., 1992).

Genetic counselling

Approximately 60—70% of children with severe learning difficulties have genetic defects (see Chapter 35). Roberts (1987) estimated that 36% of those with severe learning difficulties had a chromosomal defect (e.g. Down's syndrome), 15—20% had a single-gene defect or fragile X chromosome, and 12—15% had complex genetic defects that contributed to their learning difficulty. Genetic counselling may therefore be able to assist parents in reducing the incidence of severe learning difficulties, by providing advice about forms of inheritance of familial disorders (see Chapter 9). Estimating risks for particular parents before conception can be very difficult, although few would argue that it was unethical.

Genetic counselling methods extend to testing the fetus and the selective offer of termination of pregnancy. This raises profound ethical issues, with no easy answer. Some women will refuse to abort their fetus, even if informed of the risk. For example, in one study, 6 of 35 women with relatives with fragile X said they would not abort such a fetus and a further 18 were unsure if they would do so (Meryash, 1992). However, ethical questions arise even over the offer of abortion. Pueschel (1991) noted that those who believe in aborting affected fetuses have argued that it benefits the women and her family, benefits society (by eliminating certain genes and by reducing the financial burden of caring for dependants) and that the fetus has a right to be born healthy. There are, however, alternative viewpoints: many parents of children with learning difficulties report that their disabled children have benefited them and their families (e.g. by teaching caring, patience and empathy). Moreover, Pueschel considered that the oft-quoted economic cost—benefit analyses, comparing the costs of prenatal tests and abortion to the cost of caring for a child and adult, were often biased because they included costs of institutional care which were rarely necessary for (e.g.) people with Down's syndrome. Pueschel (1991) also remarked that offering an abortion to a family implied that the fetus was undesirable or unfit and Williams (1992) argued that this contributed to the devaluation of disabled people.

Postnatal services

Low birth weight

The survival of preterm low birth weight babies has improved enormously in the last few decades: Pearse (1987) estimated that in Sheffield, UK, survival rates for babies weighing between 1000 and 1250 g increased from 59 to 79% between 1980 and 1985, and survival rates for babies of 750–1000 g rose even more, from 14 to 75%. The majority of low birth weight babies survive to become perfectly healthy, normal children but the risk of disability is substantially higher than in children of normal birth weight. For example, Saigal *et al.* (1991) studied a group of 145 babies born in Canada with an extremely low birth weight (ELBW; less than 1001 g). When tested at 8 years, 8–12% scored more than 2 s.d. below the mean on the Wechsler Intelligence Scale for Children (WISC), compared with 1–2% of control comparison children. The WISC IQ score distribution was skewed to the left for ELBW children, there was a significant difference in the mean IQ for the two groups, and the ELBW children were still significantly lighter and had smaller head circumferences, more visual deficits and motor skills deficits. The findings were similar in Australia (Victorian Infant Collaborative Study Group, 1991) in an 8-year follow-up of 88 ELBW infants and in the US for a smaller group of 28 ELBW infants at 6 years (Teplin *et al.*, 1991).

Mental development can to some extent be predicted from the neonatal risk factors of infection, blood pH, seizures, intraventricular haemorrhage, assisted ventilation periventricular leukomalacia and hypoglycaemia (Brazy *et al.*, 1991). The corresponding preventive measures are to reduce these risk factors in the neonatal period and to regard babies who show them as being in need of psychological monitoring and intervention. In spite of all the difficulties that families experience with ELBW and very low birth weight babies, it appears that they still express a preference for such babies to be saved, when asked later (Lee *et al.*, 1991).

Phenylketonuria

In 1964, a neonatal screening programme for phenylketonuria began in the UK. From the early 1970s, this screening involved a heel-prick blood test for all infants a few days old, with follow-up for infants detected as positive for the disorder. The treatment required was provision of a low-phenylalanine diet, which most families seemed to find fairly easy to learn to use, and the programme was very successful in preventing major learning difficulties (Smith, 1987), though children's intelligence was not quite the same as their unaffected siblings (Dobson *et al.*, 1976).

It used to be thought that the low-phenylalanine diet could be discontinued at around 8 years with no deleterious effects, but it has now become clear that blood phenylalanine levels are correlated with both IQ and behaviour (Smith *et al.*, 1988, 1990), and that discontinuation or relaxation of the diet leads to a slowing of cognitive development (Holtzman *et al.*, 1986; Smith *et al.*, 1991). Mothers with phenylketonuria have also been shown to need to keep to strict low-phenylalanine diets while pregnant to avoid the risk of having babies with microcephaly, malformations and low birth weight. If maternal phenylalanine levels are kept low, the infants are born healthy with normal head circumferences and no malformations (Drogari *et al.*, 1987).

Congenital hypothyroidism

From 1982 in the UK, the routine neonatal heelprick blood spots were also analysed to detect raised thyroid-stimulating hormone in order to prevent the relatively common disorder of congenital hypothyroidism (affecting 1 in 3500 children), which was known to lead to severe learning difficulties if untreated or treated late (Raiti & Newns, 1971). Children with raised thyroid-stimulating hormone levels were given thyroxine replacement (Grant, 1987), with the dose titrated against the child's thyroid-stimulating hormone and thyroxine levels, and monitored at intervals of 6 or 12 months. Similar programmes began in the US, Canada and Europe at around the same time. Follow-up by the Congenital Hypothyroidism Register in the UK indicated that the treated children attained IQs in the normal range and were not behaviourally disturbed on average (Murphy *et al.*, 1986a), and similar results were obtained elsewhere (e.g. New England Congenital Hypothyroidism Collaborative, 1985). However, it did appear that those children whose thyroxine levels had been lowest before treatment (often those children who were athyroid) did least well, and it was concluded that there may have been some prenatal damage (Murphy *et al.*, 1990). Nevertheless, both this screening programme and the phenylketonuria screening programme have been accepted as highly effective (and cost-effective) preventive services.

Secondary and associated handicaps

Medical services may be able to assist in the prevention of secondary and associated handicaps as well as the handicaps resulting directly from brain dysfunction. Epilepsy, for example, is common and needs the same kinds of treatment and service as when it occurs in children who do not have learning difficulties (see Chapter 11). Motor problems and sensory impairment are also major causes of morbidity in this group.

It seems likely that hearing impairments have been grossly under-estimated in the past amongst people with learning difficulties. Cunningham and McArthur (1981), for example, found that all of the children in their cohort of children with Down's syndrome had a hearing loss, even though half of them had passed the local authority's screening procedure. A number of British surveys of special schools and adult day-centres have reported that only 2–3% of the children and adults have hearing impairments, while careful surveys that include hearing tests have found that the true figures should be more like 50—60% (Nolan *et al.*, 1980; Hogg & Sebba, 1986).

Similarly, visual impairments have been variously reported as occurring amongst only 7—8%, or over 40% of children and adults with severe learning difficulties, depending on whether staff report or individual testing has been used (Hogg & Sebba, 1986). Particular kinds of visual impairment are typical of specific disorders and certain disorders, such as cerebral palsy and rubella embryopathy, have especially high rates of visual difficulties.

Motor impairments are also common amongst children with learning difficulties. It appears that about 20% of children with severe learning difficulties have cerebral palsy and, amongst children with profound disabilities, such as those in special care classes in British schools, around 50% may be unable to walk as a result of cerebral palsy (Hogg & Sebba, 1986).

The prompt recognition and amelioration of associated problems are an important form of tertiary prevention in the postnatal period. Surgical correction of congenital (e.g. cardiac) defects may enhance the quality of life. It is much more controversial whether services should aim at the surgical correction of facial appearance in Down's syndrome (Pueschel *et al.*, 1986). While it usually improves eating, drooling and respiration (by the reduction in tongue size), it does little to improve speech and articulation, produces equivocal results for appearance, and few changes in social acceptance when studies are carefully designed — i.e. when noninvolved subjects' opinions are asked and controls included (Katz & Kravetz, 1989). This kind of difference of opinion is not unusual in evaluations of the effects of facial surgery, but it is likely to limit the enthusiasm of others for such radical (and risky) interventions.

SOCIAL ASPECTS OF PREVENTION AND EARLY INTERVENTION

Programmes compensating for social deprivation

The aetiological role of a depriving environment (see Chapter 35) has resulted in calls for social and educational approaches to prevention. Early enrichment programmes such as Head Start are described in Chapter 47. Many had short-term effects upon cognitive development, but they were relevant to the prevention of mild learning disability rather than the severe disabilities that are the subject of this chapter. Nevertheless, the experience helps to suggest how social interventions might be applied in the early course of severely disabled children. Overall, it seemed likely that where long-term gains were achieved, the effect was not so much a direct result of the preschool programme as an indirect result of the change in parental attitudes and expectations that some programmes achieved (Clarke & Clarke, 1986), and some concluded that home intervention programmes would be more productive (Bronfenbrenner, 1976).

Programmes for children with special needs

One home intervention project, the Portage Scheme, is essentially a precision teaching programme for mildly disabled children (Shearer & Shearer, 1972). The Portage Scheme involved weekly home visits by a home adviser, who could be a qualified psychologist, nurse or teacher, or unqualified, but had to be specifically trained for the job of adviser. At each visit, the adviser and parent would plan a series of developmental short-term goals and training methods for the week. The parent would then train the child in the coming week, record the outcome and report progress to the home adviser at the following visit.

One of the advantages of the programme was that the package was extremely well-organized, with over 500 behaviours on the developmental checklist, divided into five areas (self-help, socialization, language, cognitive and motor skills); and each of the curriculum cards provided suggested ways for teaching the skill, usually employing simple behavioural methods.

Initial evaluations of the project suggested that it produced impressive gains of an average of 13 months in mental age over an 8-month period for young children with learning difficulties in the US (Shearer & Shearer, 1972), and similar results were demonstrated in Glamorgan, Wales (Revill & Blunden, 1979), though not all programmes showed positive results (Clements *et al.*, 1982).

The Portage Scheme has since been criticized for a number of reasons (Sturmey & Crisp, 1986). It was not designed specifically for children with severe learning difficulties, and the curriculum, which was developmentally based, made assumptions about the order of skill acquisition and effectiveness of social reinforcement that were not always justified for more disabled children. Moreover, research projects evaluating this and other home intervention packages were often poorly designed so that true effects were difficult to ascertain (Dunst & Rheingrover, 1981; Simeonsson *et al.*, 1982). Nevertheless, early intervention based in the home, sometimes including work with parent groups (e.g. Baker, 1977, 1989), grew in popularity in the 1970s and 1980s, and most projects reported high levels of parental satisfaction and positive gains for the children involved, including children with cerebral palsy, cri-du-chat syndrome, Down's syndrome and a variety of other conditions (Cunningham & Sloper, 1985; Rynders & Stealey, 1985).

By 1986, the US legislature was sufficiently convinced about the effects of early intervention programmes to pass a law to assist states in setting up comprehensive early education programmes for children with learning difficulties (the Education of the Handicapped Act Amendments, 1986 — Public Law 99—457). The law mandated states to provide services for 3—5-year-olds with special needs by 1991—1992, and it was estimated by the US Department of Education that already by 1990 over 600 000 children under 5 with special needs were receiving early intervention services (Hebbeler *et al.*, 1991).

Researchers, meanwhile, were becoming increasingly aware

of the complexity of factors determining early intervention outcome. It appeared that severity of disability, for instance, affected the gains in interventions, and two meta-analyses claimed that while effect sizes were as high as 80% for at-risk and disadvantaged children, they were as low as 20% for 'biologically handicapped' children (White & Castro, 1985; Castro & Mastropieri, 1986). In other words, at-risk/disadvantaged children could be expected to gain 80% of a standard deviation, i.e. about 12 IQ points, from early intervention programmes in comparison to those not in intervention programmes, while children with 'biological' handicaps would only be expected to gain 20% of a standard deviation, i.e. 3 IQ points.

A number of studies have indeed shown that the severity of the disability limited the outcome of early intervention (Guralnick, 1991). Gibson and Harris (1988), in pooling findings from 21 studies of early intervention in children with Down's syndrome, concluded that short-term benefits certainly did occur, particularly in fine motor skills, social skills and developmental quotient (though less so in language, cognitive and gross motor domains). The disappointing aspect of all the projects was that of long-term follow-up: all the studies that included such measures concluded that there was little or no discernible long-term effect of early intervention on linguistic or cognitive skills or IQ for children with Down's syndrome (e.g. Cunningham, 1987).

It may of course be that early interventions are just not good enough yet, and that more could be obtained from better programmes. Guralnick (1989) and Woolery (1991) argued that researchers were still unsure precisely what the curriculum ought to be (e.g. whether particular behaviours should be taught or particular functions focused on; whether certain skills were keystone skills, which could or should be taught and, if so, when; what models of development were most appropriate for defining the curriculum), and precisely how children with special needs could be assisted to learn more quickly (e.g. whether teacher-directed programmes produced slower or faster learning; whether natural reinforcers were adequate; how multiple behaviours could be taught at one time). Early intervention programmes have increasingly moved towards more family-centred models and Dunst *et al.* (1991) argued that this is the result of increasing evidence that family-centred interventions result in 'broader-based positive influences on a number of aspects of child, parent and family functioning'. Over the next decade, it should become possible to determine whether or not this is, indeed, true.

EFFECTS ON THE FAMILY

The initial effects

The discovery that a child in the family has a severe learning difficulty or a condition likely to lead to a severe learning difficulty can be devastating. For children with Down's syndrome, the family typically learns very soon after the child's birth and Carr's research showed that mothers recall very accurately over an extremely long period who told them the news, what was said and how it was said (Carr, 1988). For other families, the realization is often more insidious, beginning with suspicions about late attainment of milestones and ending, sometimes years later, with the certainty that the child has a severe learning difficulty (both Quine & Pahl, 1987 and Nursey *et al.*, 1991, found that over 20% of families had their child's condition confirmed after he or she was over 2 years of age). Often families may have to assimilate this knowledge without the biological cause of the disability ever being established, and for western families this may be one of the hardest aspects to bear.

According to Carr (1985), Quine and Pahl (1987) and Nursey *et al.* (1991), parents usually want to be told about their child's disability as soon as possible, and prefer to know the truth. Who tells them appears to be far less important than how the telling is done and most families need the professional involved to take time and trouble over the telling, to be prepared to answer questions and to be available again at later dates for further questions (Cunningham *et al.*, 1984). Considerable knowledge is necessary for an accurate response to all of a parent's questions and referral by the paediatrician to psychologists or others with expertise in later development may be wise. For many parents, for example, questions about later ability and skills arise and both over- and under-optimism by their informant can be extremely upsetting (Carr, 1985). In fact, relatively few good longitudinal studies exist that provide hard evidence on which prognosis can be based, and prediction of ability from early infancy is notoriously imprecise (Berger & Yule, 1985). Many children may attain basic self-help skills by adulthood: in Carr's (1988) longitudinal study of people with Down's syndrome, for example, about 70% could feed themselves, over 70% were clean and dry, nearly 70% could dress and about 60% could bath themselves by the age of 21 years. On the other hand, only about 30% could go out alone and 74% were said by their mothers to be in need of constant or nearly constant supervision (i.e. could not be left for more than 1 hour at a time).

Later family life

Mothers and fathers

When first told of their child's disability, many families go through stages of shock, denial and adaptation (Cunningham & Davis, 1985). In the 1960s, it was often assumed that many families would make a poor adaptation to the task of bringing up a child with a learning difficulty and it was frequently asserted by those who adopted this pathological model that marital disharmony and parental stress would, therefore, be rife. Properly controlled studies in the 1970s and 1980s showed that this was not necessarily the case (Crnic *et al.*, 1983; Byrne & Cunningham, 1985; Carr, 1988; Minnes, 1988a) and that families differed greatly in the effects of a disabled member on their well-being.

The burden of care for parents of children with disabilities is certainly greater than that for parents of other children, and numerous studies have shown that it is the mother on whom the burden of care mainly falls. For example, Holmes and Carr (1991) found that, where adults with Down's syndrome or autism needed assistance in physical care, it was the mother who provided that help in almost all cases: other family members helped the mother in less than 50% of the tasks (except eating, where fathers more often helped). In very few cases (11% and less of tasks) did other family members alone help the disabled adult with physical care, with the exception of shaving (done by someone other than the mother in 37% of cases). Mothers also did most of the caring for the adults at night, though fathers did help with supervision in the evening and at weekends. The majority of studies have shown that these findings are also typical of families with younger disabled members. Some have found that social class did not affect participation by fathers (Hirst, 1985), but that unemployed fathers helped more (Cooke & Lawton, 1984); however others have found the reverse (Ayer & Alaszewski, 1984).

Not surprisingly, faced with this increased burden of care, mothers of disabled children sometimes have been shown to be significantly more stressed and/or depressed than the matched mothers of other young children (Cummings *et al.*, 1966), and so have fathers (Wishart *et al.*, 1981). It appears that a diagnosis of autism, lower levels of adaptive behaviour, increased maladaptive behaviour, lower social responsiveness, a more difficult temperament, more medical child problems and increased age are all important predictors of stress (Holroyd & McArthur, 1976; Beckman, 1983; Gallagher *et al.*, 1983; Friedrich *et al.*, 1985; Minnes, 1988a,b). However, it is clear that not all mothers nor all fathers feel stressed or depressed, even in the face of major stressors (Byrne & Cunningham, 1985). Social support appears to be an important buffer and single mothers report higher stress levels than mothers in two-parent families (Beckman, 1983; Houser & Seligman, 1991). It seems that the social support does not need to include much physical help, and that emotional support is more important. Mothers who rate their marital satisfaction as high, for example, or who rate their family relationships and cohesion as good, show better coping (Friedrich *et al.*, 1985; Minnes, 1988b). Personal characteristics of the mothers, such as locus of control and hardiness, and certain demographic characteristics (e.g. socioeconomic status and employment outside the home) are also predictive of coping (Gallagher *et al.*, 1983; Minnes, 1988b; Gill & Harris, 1991). It seems that similar factors (e.g. social support, child adaptive and maladaptive behaviour) are correlated with coping in families who foster disabled children (Stoneman & Crapps, 1988).

Parent-training programmes that used to concentrate simply on teaching parents the necessary skills for increasing their children's appropriate behaviour and reducing their challenging behaviour (Carr, 1985) have now begun to recognize parental beliefs and attitudes as important (Cunningham, 1987; Baker *et al.*, 1991). There has been a gradual broadening of the perceived task of professionals involved with families (see also the section on early intervention), to include assisting them to build social support networks, altering their perceptions of the child and improving their coping strategies, as well as teaching them specific skills.

Effects on siblings

Siblings may also need advice. Early research into the effects of a disabled child on other children in the family examined the issue, largely through interviewing parents and/or teachers about the children's behaviour at home and/or at school. Some found increased rates of behavioural deviance in the siblings of children with Down's syndrome (Gath, 1974; Lobato *et al.*, 1987; Bagenholm & Gillberg, 1991); others did not (Carr, 1988), with the support of studies of other handicapping conditions (Dyson, 1989; Mates, 1990). Siblings of behaviourally disturbed disabled children tended to show more disturbed behaviour themselves (Gath & Gumley, 1987).

More recent studies have tended to interview siblings themselves, as well as to ask parents and teachers about their behaviour. McHale *et al.* (1986) found no overall mean differences between the siblings of autistic children, of children with learning disability, and controls, in the children's attitudes to their disabled/nondisabled sibling, or in their perception of the sibling's role in the family, or in their perception of their sibling's effect on their own peer relationships. For each of these measures, however, a few children showed more extreme negative feelings towards their disabled sibling than were shown by any children towards nondisabled siblings. These negative feelings appeared to relate mainly to their perception of parental favouritism, and their feelings of rejection of their disabled sibling.

Studies by Lobato *et al.* (1987, 1991) found no differences between siblings of learning-disabled and nondisabled children when the measures involved self-concept, family role-play, empathy and direct observation of behaviour. They did find more deviance in sibs of learning-disabled children when the measure was mothers' rating: the influence may well have been that of mothers' perception.

In later years, as the siblings move into adulthood, it appears that many feel they have a lifelong responsibility for their disabled brother's or sister's care (Wilson *et al.*, 1992). Most relationships in Wilson's study were, however, characterized by warmth, commitment and involvement, though not surprisingly relationships showed less reciprocity when the disabled sibling had lower general competence. It has been suggested by Begun (1989) that siblings do not so much suffer from emotional damage when they have a severely disabled sibling as from affective disengagement so that, although the relationship may still be positive, it tends to be less intimate.

SERVICE NEEDS

Community-based services

Children with severe learning difficulties are likely to have a variety of psychological, educational, social and medical needs during their lives. In many countries, however, there are administrative divisions between educational, social and medical services, such that many parents find they have to interact with a bewildering array of professionals.

Initially, most children with severe learning difficulties and their families are seen by paediatricians. The physical and administrative arrangements of such paediatric services need to be appropriate for families who may find it difficult to travel and wait, especially if their youngsters are hyperactive or show other challenging behaviours. Apart from providing parents with information about their child's diagnosis, paediatricians often need to advise parents about their child's sensory impairments, epilepsy and other medical issues. These additional difficulties vary to some degree with the aetiology of the disability, but all are more common amongst children with profound and multiple impairments. A service will therefore need to call on ophthalmic and audiological services, physiotherapy and orthopaedics, specialist dental resources, and speech and language therapy.

Ideally, the early services that children and their families should be offered should include the six components of Cunningham's service for the Manchester Down's syndrome cohort (Cunningham, 1987): (1) provision of accurate information about the child's condition (including causes, risks, mortality, short- and long-term prospects); (2) emotional support to the family; (3) information on local and national services and agencies of relevance; (4) help with how to use services (e.g. assisting parents to prepare lists of questions for professionals); (5) an advocacy role (when asked), liaising between parents and services; and (6) an intervention service to provide advice on how to foster child development, how to cope with difficult behaviours, and how to help siblings and spouses to deal with their feelings and interrelationships.

Cunningham and his colleagues found that their developmental intervention service did not have a significant effect on the child's developmental quotient, when blindly assessed around 5 years later, but that parents reported that aspects 1–5 of the service were important for them. Other studies have shown similar effects (Davis & Rushton, 1991).

As children come of school age, many families may need little in the way of specialist services apart from those offered by schools (see the section on education services below). Other families need more assistance. One exemplary programme for children with severe learning difficulties in the US provided out-of-home respite care (weekends or 5 days or less); interim residential placement for training, skill development and medical care; cooperative residential care; training and follow-up for parents, teachers and day-care workers; home-bound teaching; day treatment programmes; after-school programmes; consulting services; medication evaluations; foster care and foster parent training; and group home programmes and in-home respite care (Schroeder & Schroeder, 1990). These particular service providers prided themselves on flexibility: the intention was to negotiate with families what their requirements were and then to set up services to suit them, rather than setting up a large bureau-cratic organization running a limited set of services on a 'take it or leave it' basis. Unfortunately, such service flexibility is rare, and family-based services vary enormously, even within relatively small areas, such as single states in the US (Herman & Hazel, 1991).

Some families, while wanting to continue caring for their children, feel the need for short breaks in the form of respite care, and several studies have examined the characteristics of families who use such services. It appears that families who use respite care are characterized by higher perceived stress levels (Factor *et al.*, 1990) and lower social support (Halpern, 1985; Factor *et al.*, 1990). The children for whom the care is required have been shown to have lower functional skill levels (i.e. to be more cognitively, socially and physically disabled), and more often show challenging behaviour (Halpern, 1985; Marc & McDonald, 1988; Factor *et al.*, 1990). All of these factors are also known to be important predictors of a family's likelihood of seeking permanent out-of-home placement (German & Maisto, 1982; Tausig, 1985; Cole, 1986; Cole & Meyer, 1989; Bromley & Blacher, 1991). It seems probable that where families are offered flexible community-based services and/or respite care, they are less likely to be forced by circumstance into seeking long-term residential care (Cole & Meyer, 1989).

In general, families, when asked, have been very positive about respite care, and Botuck and Winsberg (1991) demonstrated that mothers experienced feelings of increased well-being and decreased depression during and soon after periods of respite care. Combining the availability of such care with other community-based facilities for families seems likely to reduce the numbers of children and adults with disabilities who eventually require residential care in the long term.

Residential services

The use of hospitals to provide long-term residential care has declined dramatically in western countries. In the UK, for example, in 1971, it was estimated that over 6000 children resided in mental handicap hospitals, but by 1984 only about 1000 children were so placed (Mittler & Serpell, 1985). Similar changes have occurred in the US and elsewhere in the west (Lakin & Bruininks, 1985; Schopler & Hennike, 1990).

Some of this change comes from increased efforts to provide community-based support for families, so that long-term residential care has been less necessary. Some change stems from changes in the type of residential provision. Children who are unable to live with their family are likely to be fostered in other families or to become resident in homes that are run by private or voluntary bodies (Beyer *et al.*, 1991). The size and organization of such homes vary; increasingly they have adopted normalization or 'ordinary life' principles (Towell, 1985), and have thus become smaller (Beyer *et al.*, 1991) and more modelled on family life.

The need for substitute care arises when the difficulties of caring for a child overwhelm the family resources, or when an intensive form of education or therapy requires a residential basis, or when family life has been unsatisfactory and damaging to the child. Fostering and adoption have steadily increased their scope (see Chapter 15) but not all children can be placed in families. Severely challenging, autistic and hyperactive behaviours, together with uncontrolled seizures and severe motor incapacity, are the major determinants of residential care.

The changes in residential provision have resulted in heated argument at times. Surveys of people with learning disabilities and severely challenging behaviour showed that many of the children lived at home, despite major difficulties (Oliver *et al.*, 1987), and parent interview studies suggested that many families actually received very little help (Qureshi, 1992). As a result there has sometimes been a massive outcry from parents when plans are made to close institutions, because of their fears of extra family burdens with inadequate community services. These fears usually subside when closure has been achieved (Landesman & Butterfield, 1987).

Disputes have also arisen about what forms of residential care are preferable. Frequently, services are planned on the basis of ideology, and much more research is needed to guide rational provision. Landesman and Butterfield (1987), in reviewing research into quality of care in residential placements, argued that there were three major difficulties encountered in drawing general conclusions: firstly, the lack of agreed terminology or categories for describing the kinds of residential placements studied; secondly, the very small number of studies that were able to assign people randomly to placements in an unbiased way; and thirdly, the poor agreement on quality of life measures. They concluded that studies so far (mainly of adult placements) had shown that within one type of residential care, variations were very large (see also Allen, 1989). Even within one house, residents' experiences of quality of care could be very different. They also considered that none of the currently available assessment instruments that measure adaptive behaviour allowed good prediction of successful community adaptation (see also the section on challenging behaviour, below). This means that parents still face difficult decisions in choosing a placement to suit their child or adolescent.

EDUCATION SERVICES

Provision of service

There has been a gradual advance towards the position that schooling should be provided for all children. The milestones in the UK were the Education Act (1944), by which local education authorities were required to make general provision for children with special educational needs (Pritchard, 1963); and the Education (Handicapped Children) Act (1970), by which the responsibility for educating all children, even with the most severe learning difficulties, was passed to the education authorities. In the US, state laws about the education of disabled children culminated in the Education for All Handicapped Children Act, which was passed by the Senate in 1975.

This Act also required that individualized educational programmes be developed for all children with disabilities and that parents be properly consulted as part of this process (Armfield, 1985). Similar provisions in the UK came with the Warnock report and the Education Act, (1981) proposing that all children with learning difficulties should have a detailed, individualized assessment of their needs by multiprofessional teams; and that, wherever possible, special classes and units should be attached to, and function as part of, ordinary schools, rather than being organized separately (Warnock, 1978, p. 345).

China also moved towards the idea of integration, setting up classes for disabled children in ordinary primary schools from 1981, though some provision remained segregated, as in the UK and US (Tao Kuo-Tai, 1988).

The move towards integration was supported both by changing social attitudes and by research suggesting that there might be deleterious effects of segregation. For example, it was well-established that children learnt some social behaviour by modelling on peers, and it had been demonstrated that highly competent peers were more frequently adopted as models than less competent peers (Vaughan & Waters, 1981). Moreover, it had become clear that IQ was not constant (Murphy, 1987), and that children segregated too early on the basis of IQ assessments alone might be trapped unnecessarily in the special school system.

In practice, integration affected younger children more than older children (partly because of the concerns of misclassification) and mildly disabled children more than severely disabled children (Gulliford, 1985). Special resources are often partially and flexibly integrated. By contrast, in Italy, laws were passed which 'abolished all special institutions, and enforced mainstreaming of all handicapped students, irrespective of the type and severity of the handicap' (Meazzini, 1984). It resulted in chaos and frustration, according to Meazzini, because no one was prepared for the sudden change.

The extent to which integration is academically and socially successful is likely to depend upon the way that it is introduced, the appropriateness of the extra teaching support provided and the extent to which the school functions in other respects as an efficient system (see Chapter 63).

The curriculum and teaching methods

The curriculum, for most children in special schools in the UK, was rather traditional until the 1970s. Students attended to table-top tasks for much of their school day. During the 1970s and early 1980s, however, there was growing concern about the goals of education for children with severe learning difficulties. Given that about 25% of children in special schools developed no spoken language (Mittler & Preddy, 1981), the traditional '3Rs' curriculum seemed inappropriate. There were, therefore, increasing moves to reverse the usual core and peripheral subjects in the school curriculum, so that more school time could be spent learning self-help and social skills, particularly for the least able children, who often had multiple and complex deficits (Gulliford, 1985; Hogg & Seba, 1986). The price to be paid was that curricular change made integration into mainstream schools even more problematic. There was also the difficulty of knowing precisely what to teach, in what order, and developmental checklists were often adopted as a guide to curriculum planning for the less able.

There is a growing recognition of the need for specialist methods for teaching children with severe learning difficulties. Behavioural methods have been increasingly adopted, both to promote the precision of teaching (by allowing clear planning of short- and long-term goals, ongoing analysis of outcome and definite techniques for achieving the goals), and to assist teachers in managing challenging behaviour in the classroom.

In the UK, a nationwide training programme in behavioural methods for teachers in special schools, was launched in 1976: the Education of the Developmentally Young (EDY) course (McBrien & Foxen, 1987). During the first phase of the project, teachers, nursery nurses and classroom assistants in special education were successfully trained to employ individual training programmes in classrooms. In the second phase, over 100 educational psychologists and advisers in special education from all over the UK were trained to run the courses themselves, in their own education authorities, with the result that over 2500 people had successfully completed the courses by the end of 1984. As an exercise in pyramid teaching, the EDY project was successful: within a relatively short period the expertise of 'hands-on' staff to run behavioural programmes had greatly increased.

The teaching of communication skills is particularly important because of the frequency and severity of language problems in those with severe learning disabilities (Clements, 1987). Various aspects of language can be taught using operant methods, including the use of rule-governed grammatical forms, such as tenses and plural endings. Generalization, however, is often very poor. Not all children can be taught to speak, and there are some cognitive prerequisites (Cromer, 1981).

Accordingly, there has been a move away from special language training sessions towards incidental learning (Clements, 1987), which can take place in the child's natural environment of home or school, and which is embedded in social interaction. Welding such learning into the school curriculum has been difficult, but Robson (1987) has shown that it is possible to alter teachers' behaviour in order to promote incidental language learning by providing them with a self-instructional pack (TASS). He showed that not only did teachers massively increase their structuring utterances (models, prompts, imitation requests, etc.) after the course, but also this had an effect on the child's use of words — though not on a length–complexity index. Similarly, Dodd and Leahy (1989) have demonstrated that the parents of children with Down's syndrome can be taught to provide daily language practice for their children as part of their normal home environment, and that this results in improvements in phonology over a period of a few months.

It is also possible to teach signing to augment verbal communication. There used to be worries that speech might be more delayed as a consequence. It is now clear that the reverse is true (Lloyd & Karlan, 1984; Clements, 1987). Signing does not delay speech, and it provides the opportunity for communication for many children who might otherwise have no speech at all (Kiernan, 1985). There have been a number of popular signing systems: Makaton is by far the most popular in the UK, while in the US, American sign language is the most widely used (Kiernan, 1985). Ease of use by care staff, parents and teachers is important: the limits of sign-learning by children with learning difficulties are often determined more by how many adults in their environment can and do learn the system, than how easy it is for the children to learn.

Other augmentative communication systems include graphic ones such as the Bliss symbols. In practice, these are most often employed for children with cerebral palsy, for whom the boards may be attached to their wheelchairs. Such systems may also be advantageous for children without motor difficulties, since the symbols impose less memory load, are easier for the uninitiated adult to understand, and require less immediate attention than signing systems.

Recent years have seen an emergence of computer-aided learning and microelectronic aids into the classroom, and these are especially important for children with profound and multiple handicaps (Lovett, 1985). Early experimental studies demonstrated that even the most disabled individuals were able to learn simple responses given appropriate sensory feedback or reinforcement (Murphy, 1982). During the 1970s and 1980s, a number of toys were designed that provided sensory feedback on contact, e.g the Pethna toys of Woods and Parry (1981). Some evaluations of these kinds of toys demonstrated that they were more effective in promoting active toy play and reducing stereotypes amongst children with profound disabilities than were similar toys without sensory feedback, or similar toys that children were trained to play with by operant techniques (Murphy *et al.*, 1985, 1986b).

CHALLENGING BEHAVIOUR

Definition and prevalence

Severely challenging behaviour is 'behaviour of such an intensity, frequency or duration that the physical safety of the person or others, is likely to be placed in serious jeopardy, or behaviour which is likely to limit seriously, or delay access to and use of, ordinary community facilities' (Emerson *et al.*, 1988).

Where services have been set up specifically for the assessment and treatment of challenging behaviour, the most common referrals have been for aggression, damage to the environment, self-injury and noncompliance (Emerson, 1990). Such behaviours are not uncommon; they are generally more prevalent in children with autism or severe learning difficulties than in mild learning difficulties; and they tend to increase in prevalence around the late teenage years and early 20s (Oliver *et al.*, 1987). Some behaviours (e.g. self-injury) are more common amongst children with sensory impairments, and many (e.g. sleep problems, aggression, self-injury) are associated with poor communication skills (Eyman & Call, 1977; Wing & Gould, 1979; Wing, 1981; Oliver *et al.*, 1987; Quine, 1991).

Drug treatment

Treatment of challenging behaviour by the use of medication appears to be relatively ineffective (see Chapter 51). Indeed, the hazards of drugs such as the neuroleptics and sedatives and the uncertainty over their value in those with no clear psychiatric diagnosis raise substantial ethical queries about their use. Nevertheless, medication is widely used. Oliver *et al.* (1987) surveyed a total population of people with learning difficulties and self-injury. They found that 44% of people were receiving psychotropic medication, excluding anticonvulsants. The prescribed medication was usually a neuroleptic (36%), though some were prescribed anxiolytics (10%) and some hypnotics/sedatives (4%). Very few were receiving lithium (2%) or tricyclic antidepressants (2%). It was more common for people in hospital to be receiving medication and less common for children (who also tended to be living at home). Very few children or adults had behavioural programmes (2%), even though this was thought to be the most effective treatment (Murphy & Wilson, 1985b).

Surveys of people with severe learning difficulties in the US have shown similar levels of psychotropic prescribing (35–50%) for those living in institutions (Lipman, 1970; Aman & Singh, 1988; Chadsey-Rusch & Sprague, 1989; Stone *et al.*, 1989). The prescriptions are often provided on a long-term basis. Meanwhile, researchers have argued that the evidence in favour of using psychotropic medication to control behaviour in children and adults with severe learning difficulties is questionable because of the poor methodology of drug trials and the danger of tardive dyskinesia (Chadsey-Rusch & Sprague, 1989). Attempts in the US to reduce psychotropic drug use, mainly as a result of litigation (Beyer, 1988; Rinck *et al.*, 1989), have shown that it is possible to decrease rates to about 20% simply by introducing a review process (Briggs, 1989).

Medication can sometimes be helpful in reducing challenging behaviours (Schroeder, 1988) and certain kinds of medication (e.g. anticonvulsants) are important for maintaining the well-being of children and adults with severe learning difficulties (Stores, 1988; see Chapter 11). The current patterns of prescribing, however, tend to be over-liberal, especially for adults, and are rarely carefully monitored or preceded by placebo-controlled double-blind trials with measures of learning and challenging behaviour. The percentage of children who are receiving medication to control their challenging behaviour is probably of the order of 10% in community samples. While this may not seem alarming, it is likely to increase as the individuals become larger and more difficult to control physically (Aman & Singh, 1988).

Behavioural treatment

In many cases, the treatment of choice for challenging behaviour is behavioural, and this normally involves the cooperation and coordination of carers, teachers and professionals.

Behavioural treatment has become increasingly sophisticated over the last 20 years. In the 1970s, many treatment programmes for severely dangerous behaviour, such as self-injury or aggression, were essentially punitive (Murphy & Wilson, 1985a; Murphy, 1993a), sometimes employing forms of aversive stimulus that many professionals, carers and parents would now find unacceptable, such as contingent shock (Donnellan & LaVigna, 1991; Murphy, 1993b). In the short term, the programmes were often successful (Bruhl *et al.*, 1982), although evidence accumulated that the longer-term outcome was bleak (Murphy & Wilson, 1985b).

One of the difficulties with the early programmes was the lack of proper functional analysis prior to treatment. Theoretically, it was possible for challenging behaviour, however it originated, to be maintained by positive reinforcement (e.g. contingent presentation of food, drink or social attention) or negative reinforcement (e.g. contingent removal of aversive stimuli, such as demands). Very often, in the early days, it was simply assumed that contingent social attention was the important component and treatment programmes were designed accordingly, often employing extinction or punishment (e.g. time out) paradigms. It became clear, however, that incorrect assumptions about the factors in the child's environment that were maintaining the challenging behaviour could lead not only to an ineffective treatment programme, but even to a worsening of the behaviour. If behaviour, reinforced by escape from tasks (negative reinforcement), was followed by time out, for example, it would be expected that the frequency of the behaviour would increase rather than decrease.

The advent of a new method of functional analysis, the use of analogue conditions, during the early 1980s (Iwata *et al.*, 1982) led to a resurgence of interest in this facet of behavioural treatment. Iwata and colleagues applied a standard set of conditions, or brief sessions, each one intended to represent possible real-life situations, and logged the effect on the rates of challenging behaviour (in this case, self-injury) in 9 children (most of whom had profound disabilities). The conditions included social disapproval, academic demand, low stimulation and control settings, each one 15 minutes long. They inferred the function of the self-injury in an individual from the situations in which it most appeared. The commonest functions were sensory stimulation, task avoidance and social attention.

Since Iwata's study appeared, there have been a number of suggested adjustments to the methodology (e.g. Oliver *et al.*, 1993; Oliver, 1991b) and a questionnaire method of functional analysis has also appeared (Durand & Crimmins, 1988), though the validity of this has since been questioned (Oliver, 1991a). Thus, while it would be premature to conclude that the best method of functional analysis has been determined, it can be said that a number of possible methods exist and the hope is that treatment effectiveness will, therefore, improve.

Alongside the increasing interest in functional analysis, there has appeared an emphasis on the constructional approach to treatment which has meant a reduction in punishment-based programmes (Goldiamond, 1974; Cullen & Partridge, 1981; Zarkowska & Clements, 1988; Donnellan *et al.*, 1988). This approach proposes that the best treatment for challenging behaviour is to examine what the person should have been doing (rather than what he or she should not have been doing), and provide skills training and positive reinforcement to promote these prosocial behaviours. Allied to this, there has appeared an increasing concentration on communicative skills with sophisticated analyses of the relationship of such skills to challenging behaviour. Carr and Durand (1985), for example, employed analogue conditions to deduce the function of aggressive, self-injurious and other challenging behaviours in children with autism in a classroom setting. They concluded that for some children contingent social attention appeared to be the crucial reinforcer, while for others demand avoidance was the reinforcer. They proceeded to teach the children specific communicative responses (e.g. 'Am I doing good work?' and 'Help me'), and demonstrated reductions associated with increased use of the communicative phrase which matched the function of each child's behaviour.

In spite of these new approaches, challenging behaviours still remain a major reason for family breakdown and institutionalization (Intagliata & Willer, 1982; Tausig, 1985). Even the most sophisticated approaches sometimes fail to make an impact, especially on very high-rate, entrenched behaviours. Part of the reason for this may be the somewhat simplistic behavioural models adopted in the past, though whether the more advanced models (Oliver & Head, 1990; Murphy, 1993a) are really superior remains to be seen.

From the service point of view, one of the important issues for the next few years will be the extent to which community-based living arrangements will be feasible for children with very severe and intransigent challenging behaviours. In the UK, one innovative service set up by the South-east Thames Regional Health Authority to provide residential services within local districts for the most severely challenging young people in the region demonstrated that it was possible to devise individual service plans for the people to live in ordinary houses with support staff. However, the service costs were very high, staff were highly stressed, the challenging behaviour often remained at a high rate, and the Regional Special Development Team workers found it difficult to reduce their support to these local services (Emerson, 1988; P. McGill, 1992, personal communication). Nevertheless, the project demonstrated that it was possible for even the most severely challenging young people to live in the community, and it is likely that other similar projects will be set up in the next decade.

SERVICES IN DEVELOPING COUNTRIES

Most professionals would agree that the 20th century has seen some major errors perpetrated in service provision for children with learning difficulties. Provision of universal schooling was a clear advance in services (though many would argue that segregation of these educational services was unwise), while the increasing provision of hospital-based accommodation was an enormous mistake. Some developing countries have also fallen into the institution trap, and recent reports from Europe and further east have suggested that this was a particular problem in Greece, Romania (Gath, 1992) and Russia (*Guardian*, 6 March, 1992). China also has some institutions for children, though much of its provision for children in schools appears to be forward-thinking (Tao Kuo-Tai, 1988).

Service development in some places has been exemplary, at least in patches. In Zimbabwe, for instance, Zimcare Trust (a nongovernmental agency) launched a home support service for families with children with learning disabilities, using the World Health Organization strategy of community-based rehabilitation. The programme built on local, already existing, services, employed indigenous support workers and used professionals mainly as trainers. It resulted in a sustainable service which promoted and mobilized resources available in local communities, instead of 'professionalizing' services and reducing community self-sufficiency (McConkey, 1988; Ager, 1990).

CONCLUSIONS

Those involved in services for children with severe learning disabilities, either as professionals or carers, have seen enormous alterations in the last two decades. In the west there have been radical changes to terminology and to ideology, linked to major increases in community-based family support, early intervention and educational services. There have been intense debates about dogma and data in the integration of special education, and in the provision of services in the community for children and adolescents with severe challenging behaviours, together with rapid declines in hospital-based residential places. Some carers in developing countries have certainly seen both the best and the worst of western services, though many will probably have seen no services at all, and will have had to rely on the immediate family, the extended family and community support in attempting to assist those with disabilities to achieve an ordinary life.

REFERENCES

Ager A. (1990) Planning sustainable services: principles for the effective targeting of resources in developed and developing nations. In: Fraser W.I. (ed) *Key Issues in Mental Retardation Research*, pp. 385–394. Routledge, London.

Alberman E. (1984) Epidemiological aspects of severe mental retardation. In: Dobbing J., Clarke A.D.B., Corbett J.A., Hogg J. & Robinson R.O. (eds) *Scientific Studies in Mental Retardation*, pp. 3–23. Royal Society of Medicine, London.

Allen D. (1989) The effects of deinstitutionalization on people with mental handicaps: a review. *Mental Handicap Research*, **2**, 18–37.

Aman M.G. & Singh N.N. (1988) Patterns of drug use: methodological considerations, measurement techniques and future trends. In: Aman M.G. & Singh N.N. (eds) *Psychopharmacology of the Developmental Disabilities*, pp. 1–28. Springer-Verlag, New York.

Armfield A.H. (1985) Special education in the United States. In: Craft M., Bicknell J. & Hollins S. (eds) *Mental Handicap*, pp. 247–257. Baullière-Tindall, London.

Ayer S. & Alaszewski A. (1984) *Community Care and the Mentally Handicapped*. Croom Helm, London.

Bagenholm A. & Gillberg C. (1991) Psychosocial effects on siblings of children with autism and mental retardation: a population-based study. *Journal of Mental Deficiency Research*, **35**, 291–307.

Baker B. (1977) Support systems for the parent therapist. In: Mittler P.J. (ed) *Research to Practice in Mental Retardation*, vol. I. University Park Press, Baltimore, MD.

Baker B.L. (1989) Parent training and developmental disabilities. *Monograph of the American Association on Mental Retardation*, no. 13, American Association on Mental Retardation, Washington DC.

Baker B.L., Landen S.I. & Kashima K.J. (1991) Effects of parent training on families of children with mental retardation: increased burden or generalised benefit? *American Journal of Mental Deficiency*, **96**, 127–136.

Bank-Mikkelsen N.E. (1980) Denmark. In: Flynn R.J. & Nitsch K.E. (eds) *Normalisation, Social Integration and Community Services*. Austin. TX.

Beckman P.J. (1983) Influence of selected child characteristics on stress in families of handicapped infants. *American Journal of Mental Deficiency*, **88**, 150–156.

Begun A.L. (1989) Sibling relationships involving developmentally disabled people. *American Journal on Mental Retardation*, **93**, 566–574.

Belmont L. (1986) Screening for severe mental retardation in developing countries: the International Pilot Study of Severe Childhood Disability. In: Berg F.M. (ed) *Science and Service in Mental Retardation*. Methuen, London.

Berger M. & Yule W. (1985) IQ tests and assessment. In: Clarke A.M., Clarke A.D.B. & Berg J.M. (eds) *Mental Deficiency: The Changing Outlook*, 4th edn., pp. 53–96. Methuen, London.

Beyer H.A. (1988) Litigation and use of psychoactive drugs in developmental disabilities. In: Aman M.G. & Singh N.N. (eds) *Psychopharmacology of the Developmental Disabilities*, pp. 29–58. Springer-Verlag, New York.

Beyer S., Todd S. & Felce D. (1991) The implementation of the All-Wales Mental Handicap Strategy. *Mental Handicap Research*, **4**, 115–140.

Botuck S. & Winsberg B.G. (1991) Effects of respite on mothers of school-age and adult children with severe disabilities. *Mental Retardation*, **29**, 43–47.

Brazy J.E., Eckerman C.O., Oehler J.M., Goldstein R.F. & O'rand A.M. (1991) Nursery Neurobiologic Risk Score: important factors in predicting outcome in very low birthweight infants. *Journal of Pediatrics*, **118**, 783–792.

Briggs R. (1989) Monitoring and evaluating psychotropic drug use for persons with mental retardation: a follow-up report. *American Journal on Mental Retardation*, **93**, 633–639.

Bromley B.E. & Blacher J. (1991) Parental reasons for out-of-home placement of children with severe handicaps. *Mental Retardation*, **29**, 275–280.

Bronfenbrenner U. (1976) Is early intervention effective? Facts and principles of early intervention: a summary. In: Clarke A.M. & Clarke A.D.B. (eds) *Early Experience: Myth and Evidence*, pp. 247–256. Open Books, London.

Bruhl H.H., Fielding L., Joyce M., Peters W. & Wieseler N. (1982) Thirty month demonstration project for treatment of self-injurious behaviour in severely retarded individuals. In: Hollis J.H. & Meyer C.E. (eds) *Life-threatening Behaviour*, pp. 191–275. American Association of Mental Deficiency, Washington DC.

Byrne E.H. & Cunningham C.C. (1985) The effects of mentally handicapped children on families: a conceptual review. *Journal of Child Psychology and Psychiatry*, **26**, 847–864.

Carr J. (1985) The effect on the family of a severely mentally handicapped child. In: Clarke A.M., Clarke A.D.B. & Berg J.M. (eds) *Mental Deficiency: The Changing Outlook*, 4th edn., pp. 512–548. Methuen, London.

Carr J. (1988) Six weeks to 21 years old: a longitudinal study of children with Down's syndrome and their families. *Journal of Child Psychology and Psychiatry*, **29**, 407–431.

Carr E.G. & Durand V.M. (1985) Reducing behaviour problems through functional communication training. *Journal of Applied Behaviour Analysis*, **18**, 111–126.

Castro G. & Mastropieri M.H. (1986) The efficacy of early intervention programs: a meta-analysis. *Exceptional Children*, **52**, 417–424.

Chadsey-Rusch J. & Sprague R.L. (1989) Maladaptive behaviours associated with neuroleptic drug maintenance. *American Journal on Mental Retardation*, **93**, 607–617.

Clarke A.M. & Clarke A.D.B. (1986) Thirty years of child psychology: a selective review. *Journal of Child Psychology and Psychiatry*, **27**, 719–759.

Clements J.C. (1987) Language and communication. In: Clements J.C. (ed) *Severe Learning Disability and Psychological Handicap*, pp. 133–154. John Wiley, London.

Clements J.C., Evans C., Jones C., Osbourne K. & Upton G. (1982) Evaluation of a home-based training programme with severely mentally handicapped children. *Behaviour Research and Therapy*, **20**, 243–249.

Cole D.H. (1986) Out-of-home placement and family adaptation: a theoretical framework. *American Journal of Mental Deficiency*, **91**, 226–236.

Cole D.A. & Meyer L.H. (1989) Impact of needs and resources on family plans to seek out-of-home placement. *American Journal on Mental Retardation*, **93**, 380–387.

Cooke K. & Lawton D. (1984) Informal support for the carers of disabled children. *Child: Care, Health and Development*, **10**, 67–79.

Crnic K.A., Friedrich W.N. & Greenberg M.T. (1983) Adaptation of families with mentally retarded children: a model of stress, coping and family ecology. *American Journal of Mental Deficiency*, **8**, 125–138.

Cromer R.F. (1981) Developmental language disorders: cognitive process semantics, pragmatics, phonology and syntax. *Journal of Autism and Developmental Disorders*, **11**, 57–74.

Cuckle H. (1987) Screening for neural tube defects. In: Hosking G. & Murphy G. (eds) *Prevention of Mental Handicap: A World View*. Royal Society of Medicine, London.

Cullen C. & Partridge K. (1981) The constructional approach: a way of using different data. *Apex: Journal of the British Institute of Mental Handicap*, **8**, 135–136.

Cummings S.T., Bayley H.C. & Rie H.E. (1966) Effects of the child's deficiency on the mother: a study of mothers of mentally retarded, chronically ill and neurotic children. *American Journal of Orthopsychiatry*, **36**, 595–608.

Cunningham C. (1987) Early intervention in Down's syndrome. In: Hosking G. & Murphy G. (eds) *Prevention of Mental Handicap: A World View*, pp. 169–182. Royal Society of Medicine, London.

Cunningham C. & Davis H. (1985) Early parent counselling. In: Craft M., Bicknell J. & Hollins S. (eds) *Mental Handicap: A Multi-disciplinary Approach*, pp. 162–176. Baullière-Tindall, London.

Cunningham C. & McArthur K. (1981) Hearing loss and treatment in young Down syndrome children. *Child: Care, Health and Development,* **7**, 357–374.

Cunningham C. & Sloper P. (1985) Early intervention for the child. In: Craft M., Bicknell J. & Hollins S. (eds) *Mental Handicap: A Multi-disciplinary Approach,* pp. 209–228. Ballière-Tindall, London.

Cunningham C., Morgan P. & McGrucken R.B. (1984) Down syndrome: is dissatisfaction with disclosure of diagnosis inevitable? *Developmental Medicine and Child Neurology,* **26**, 33–39.

Davis H. & Rushton R. (1991) Counselling and supporting parents of children with developmental delay: a research evaluation. *Journal of Mental Deficiency Research,* **35**, 89–112.

Dobson J.C., Kushida E., Williamson M.L. & Freidman E.G. (1976) Intellectual performance of 36 phenylketonuric patients and their non-affected siblings. *Pediatrics,* **58**, 53–58.

Dodd B. & Leahy J. (1989) Phonological disorders and mental handicap. In: Beberidge M., Conti-Ramsden G. & Leudar I. (eds) *Language and Communication in Mentally Handicapped People,* pp. 33–57. Chapman & Hall, London.

Donnellan A.M. & LaVigna G.W. (1991) Myths about punishment. In: Repp A. & Singh N. (eds) *Aversive and Non-aversive Treatment: The Great Debate in Developmental Disabilities.* Sycamore Press, Dekalb, IL.

Donnellan A.M., LaVigna G.W., Negri-Shoultz N. & Fassbender L.L. (1988) *Progress without Punishments.* Teacher's College Press, London.

Drogari E., Smith I., Beasley M. & Lloyd J.K. (1987) Timing of strict diet in relation to fetal damage in maternal phenylketonuria. *Lancet,* **2**, 927–930.

Dunst C.J. & Rheingrover R.M. (1981) An analysis of the efficacy of infant intervention programs with organically handicapped children. *Evaluation and Program Planning,* **4**, 287–323.

Dunst C.J., Johanson C., Trivette C.M. & Hamby D. (1991) Family oriented early intervention policies and practices: family-centred or not? *Exceptional Children,* **58**, 115–126.

Durand V.M. & Crimmins D.B. (1988) Identifying the variables maintaining self-injurious behaviour. *Journal of Autism and Developmental Disorders,* **18**, 99–117.

Dyson L.L. (1989) Adjustment of siblings of handicapped children: a comparison. *Journal of Pediatric Psychology,* **14**, 215–229.

Emerson E. (1990) Designing individualized community-based placements as an alternative to institutions for people with severe mental handicap and severe problem behaviour. In: Fraser W.I. (ed) *Key Issues in Mental Retardation Research.* Routledge London.

Emerson E., Cummings R., Barrett S., Hughes H., McCool C. & Toogood A. (1988) Challenging behaviour and community services. II. Who are the people who challenge services? *Mental Handicap,* **16**, 16–19.

Eyman R.K. & Call T. (1977) Maladaptive behaviour and community placement of mentally retarded persons. *American Journal of Mental Deficiency,* **82**, 137–144.

Factor D.C., Perry A. & Freeman N. (1990) Brief report: stress, social support and respite carers in families with autistic children. *Journal of Autism and Developmental Disorders,* **20**, 139–146.

Friedrich W.N., Wilturner L.T. & Cohen D.S. (1985) Coping resources and parenting mentally retarded children. *American Journal of Mental Deficiency,* **90**, 130–139.

Gallagher J.J., Beckman P. & Cross A.H. (1983) Families of handicapped children: sources of stress and its amelioration. *Exceptional Children,* **50**, 10–19.

Gath A. (1974) Sibling reactions to mental handicap: a comparison of brothers and sisters of mongol children: *Journal of Child Psychology and Psychiatry,* **15**, 187–198.

Gath A. (1992) A visit to Romania in October 1990 and to Leros in May 1991. *Journal of Intellectual Disability Research,* **36**, 3–5.

Gath A. & Gumley D. (1987) Retarded children and their siblings. *Journal of Child Psychology and Psychiatry,* **28**, 715–730.

German M.L. & Maisto A.A. (1982) The relationship of a perceived family support system to the institutional placement of mentally retarded children. *Education and Training of the Mentally Retarded,* **17**, 17–23.

Gibson D. & Harris A. (1988) Aggregated early intervention effects for Down's syndrome persons: patterning and longevity of benefits. *Journal of Mental Deficiency Research,* **32**, 1–17.

Gill M.J. & Harris S.L. (1991) Hardiness and social support as predictors of psychological discomfort in mothers of children with autism. *Journal of Autism and Developmental Disorders,* **21**, 407–416.

Goldiamond I. (1974) Towards a constructional approach to social problems. *Behaviourism,* **2**, 1–84.

Graham A.C. (1987) Immunisation: an overview. In: Hosking G. & Murphy G. (eds) *Prevention of Mental Handicap: A World View.* Royal Society of Medicine, London.

Grant D.B. (1987) Congenital hypothyroidism. In: Hosking G. & Murphy G. (eds) *Prevention of Mental Handicap: A World View.* Royal Society of Medicine, London.

Gulliford R. (1985) Education. In: Clarke A.M., Clarke A.D.B. & Berg J.M. (eds) *Mental Deficiency: The Changing Outlook,* 4th edn., pp. 639–685. Methuen, London.

Guralnick M.J. (1989) Social competence as a future direction for early intervention programs. *Journal of Mental Deficiency Research,* **33**, 275–282.

Guralnick M.J. (1991) The next decade of research on the effectiveness of early intervention. *Exceptional Children,* **58**, 174–183.

Halpern P.L. (1985) Respite care and family functioning in families with retarded children. *Health and Social Work,* **10**, 138–150.

Harris R. & Andrews T. (1988) Pre-natal screening for Down syndrome. *Archives of Disease in Childhood,* **63**, 705–706.

Hebbeler K.M., Smith B.J. & Black T.L. (1991) Federal early childhood special education policy: a model for the improvement of services for children with disabilities. *Exceptional Children,* **58**, 104–111.

Herman S.E. & Hazel K.L. (1991) Evaluation of family support services: changes in availability and accessibility. *Mental Retardation,* **29**, 351–357.

Hirst M. (1985) Dependency and family care of young adults with disabilities. *Child: Care, Health and Development,* **11**, 241–257.

Holmes N. & Carr J. (1991) The pattern of care in families of adults with a mental handicap: a comparison between families of autistic adults and Down syndrome adults. *Journal of Autism and Developmental Disorders,* **21**, 159–176.

Hogg J. & Sebba J. (1986) *Profound Retardation and Multiple Impairment,* vol. I. Croom Helm, London.

Holroyd J. & McArthur D. (1976) Mental retardation and stress on the parents: a contrast between Down syndrome and childhood autism. *American Journal of Mental Deficiency,* **80**, 431–436.

Holtzman N.A., Kronmal R.A., Van Doornick W., Azen C. & Koch R. (1986) Effect of age at loss of dietary control on intellectual performance and behaviour in children with phenylketonuria. *New England Journal of Medicine,* **314**, 593–598.

Houser R. & Seligman M. (1991) A comparison of stress and coping by fathers of adolescents with mental retardation and fathers of adolescents without mental retardation. *Research in Developmental Disabilities,* **12**, 251–260.

Intagliata J. & Willer B. (1982) Reinstitutionalisation of mentally retarded persons successfully placed into family-care and group homes. *American Journal of Mental Deficiency,* **87**, 34–39.

Iwata B.A., Dorsey M.F., Slifer K.J., Ballman K.E. & Richman G.S. (1982) Toward a functional analysis of self-injury. *Analysis and Intervention in Developmental Disability,* **2**, 3–20.

Katz S. & Kravetz S. (1989) Facial plastic surgery for persons with

Down syndrome: research findings and their professional and social implications. *American Journal on Mental Retardation*, **94**, 101–110.

Kiernan C. (1985) Communication. In: Clarke A.M., Clarke A.D.B. & Berg J.M. (eds) *Mental Deficiency: The Changing Outlook*, 4th edn., pp. 584–638. Methuen, London.

Lakin K.C. & Bruninks R.H. (1985) Social integration of developmentally disabled persons. In: Lakin K.C. & Bruninks R.H. (eds) *Strategies for Achieving Community Integration of Developmentally Disabled Citizens*. Paul Brockes, Baltimore, MD.

Landesman S. & Butterfield E.C. (1987) Normalisation and deinstitutionalisation of mentally retarded individuals: controversy and facts. *American Psychologist*, **42**, 809–816.

Lee S.K., Penner P.L. & Cox M. (1991) Impact of very low birthweight infants on the family and its relationship to the parental attitudes. *Pediatrics*, **88**, 105–109.

Lipman R.S. (1970) The use of pharmacological agents in residential facilities for the retarded. In: Menolascino F. (ed) *Psychiatric Approaches to Mental Retardation*, pp. 387–398. Basic Books, New York.

Lloyd L.L. & Karlan G.R. (1984) Non-speech communication symbols & systems: where have we been and where are we going? *Journal of Mental Deficiency Research*, **28**, 3–20.

Lobato D., Barbour L., Hall L.J. & Miller C.T. (1987) Psychosocial characteristics of pre-school children. *Journal of Abnormal Child Psychology*, **15**, 329–338.

Lobato D.J., Miller C.T., Barbour L., Hall L.J. & Pezullo J. (1991) Pre-school siblings of handicapped children: interactions with mothers, brothers and sisters. *Research in Developmental Disabilities*, **12**, 387–399.

Lovett S. (1985) Microelectronic & computer-based technology. In: Clarke A.M., Clarke A.D.B. & Berg J.M. (eds) *Mental Deficiency: The Changing Outlook*, 4th edn., pp. 549–583. Methuen, London.

Marc D.L. & McDonald L. (1988) Respite care — who needs it? *Mental Retardation*, **26**, 93–96.

Mates T.F. (1990) Siblings of autistic children: their adjustment and performance at home and in school. *Journal of Autism and Developmental Disorders*, **20**, 543–553.

McBrien J.A. & Foxen T.H. (1987) A pyramid model of staff training in behavioural methods: the E.D.Y. project. In: Hogg J. & Mittler P. (eds) *Staff Training in Mental Handicap*, pp. 131–147. Croom Helm, Beckenham, Kent.

McConkey R. (1988) Out of Africa: an alternative style of service for people with mental handicap and their families. *Mental Handicap*, **16**, 23–26.

McHale S.M., Sloan J. & Simeonsson R.J. (1986) Sibling relationships of children with autistic, mentally retarded and non-handicapped brothers and sisters. *Journal of Autism and Developmental Disorders*, **16**, 399–413.

Meazzini P. (1984) Mainstreaming handicapped students. In: Dobbing J., Clarke A.D.B., Corbett J., Hogg J. & Robinson R.O. (eds) *Scientific Studies in Mental Retardation*, pp. 527–546. Macmillan Press, London.

Mehta A.C. (1987) Perinatology in the less developed country (India). In: Hosking G.W. & Murphy G.H. (eds) *Prevention of Mental Handicap: A World View*, pp. 117–121. Royal Society of Medicine, London.

Meryash D.L. (1992) Characteristics of fragile-X relatives with different attitudes toward terminating an affected pregnancy. *American Journal on Mental Retardation*, **96**, 528–535.

Mesibov G.B. (1976) Alternatives to the principle of normalisation. *Mental Retardation*, **14**, 30–32.

Mesibov G.B. (1990) Normalisation and its relevance today. *Journal of Autism and Developmental Disorders*, **20**, 379–390.

Miller E. (1990) Rubella reinfection. *Archives of Disease in Childhood*, **65**, 820–821.

Minnes P.M. (1988a) Family stress associated with a developmentally handicapped child. In: Bray N.W. (ed) *International Review of Research in Mental Retardation*, vol. 15. Academic Press, New York.

Minnes P.M. (1988b) Family resources and stress associated with having a mentally retarded child. *American Journal on Mental Retardation*, **93**, 184–192.

Mittler P. & Preddy D. (1981) Mentally handicapped pupils and school leavers: a survey in North West England. In: Cooper B. (ed) *Assessing the Handicaps and Needs of Mentally Retarded Children*, pp. 48–59. Academic Press, London.

Mittler P. & Serpell R. (1985) Services: an international perspective. In: Clarke A.M., Clarke A.D.S. & Berg J.M. (eds) *Mental Deficiency: The Changing Outlook*, 4th edn., pp. 715–787. Methuen, London.

Murphy G. (1982) Sensory reinforcement in the mentally handicapped and autistic child: a review. *Journal of Autism and Developmental Disorders*, **12**, 265–278.

Murphy G. (1987) Are intelligence tests outmoded? *Archives of Disease in Childhood*, **62**, 773–775.

Murphy G. (1993a) The treatment of challenging behaviour in people with learning difficulties. In: Thompson C. & Cowen P. (eds) *Violence: Basic and Clinical Science*. Butterworth-Heinemann, Oxford.

Murphy G. (1993b) The use of aversive stimuli in treatment: technical philosophical and ideological issues. *Journal of Intellectual Disability Research*, **37**, 211–219.

Murphy G. & Wilson B. (1985a) Long-term outcome of contingent shock treatment for self-injurious behaviour. In: Murphy G. & Wilson B. (eds) *Self-injurious Behaviour*, pp. 403–408. British Institute of Mental Handicap, Kidderminster.

Murphy G. & Wilson B. (1985b) *Self-injurious Behaviour*. British Institute of Mental Handicap, Kidderminster.

Murphy G., Callias M. & Carr J. (1985) Increasing simple toy play in the profoundly mentally handicapped: I. Training to play, *Journal of Autism and Developmental Disorders*, **15**, 375–388.

Murphy G., Carr J. & Callias M. (1986b) Increasing simple toy play in the profoundly mentally handicapped. II. Designing special toys. *Journal of Autism and Developmental Disorders*, **16**, 45–58.

Murphy G., Hulse J.A., Jackson D., Tyrer P., Glossop J., Smith I. & Grant D.B. (1986a) Early treated hypothyroidism: development at 3 years. *Archives of Disease in Childhood*, **61**, 761–765.

Murphy G.J., Hulse J.A., Smith I. & Grant D.B. (1990) Congenital hypothyroidism: physiological and psychological factors in early development. *Journal of Child Psychology and Psychiatry*, **31**, 711–725.

New England Congenital Hypothyroidism Collaborative (1985) Neonatal hypothyroidism screening; status of patients at 6 years of age. *Journal of Pediatrics*, **107**, 915–919.

Nirje B. (1980) The normalisation principle. In: Flynn R.J. & Nitsch K.E. (eds) *Normalisation, Social Integration and Community Services*, pp. 31–49. Pro-ed, Austin, TX.

Nolan M., McCartney E., McCarthur K. & Rowson V.J. (1980) A study of the hearing and receptive vocabulary of the trainees of an adult training centre. *Journal of Mental Deficiency Research*, **24**, 271–280.

Nursey A.D., Rohde J.R. & Farmer R.D.T. (1991) Ways of telling new parents about their child and his or her mental handicap: a comparison of doctors' and parents' views. *Journal of Mental Deficiency Research*, **35**, 48–57.

O'Brien J. (1987) A guide to personal futures planning. In: Bellamy G.T. & Wilcox B. (eds) *A Comprehensive Guide to the Activities Catalogue: An Alternative Curriculum For Youth and Adults With Severe Learning Disabilities*. Paul H. Brookes, Baltimore, MD.

Oliver C. (1991a) Self-injurious behaviour in people with mental handicap: prevalence, individual characteristics and functional analysis: Unpublished PhD thesis, University of London.

Oliver C. (1991b) The application of analogue methodology to the functional analysis of challenging behaviour. In: Remington B. (ed) *The Challenge of Severe Mental Handicap: Analytic Approach*, pp. 97–118. Wiley, Chichester.

Oliver C. & Head M. (1990) Self-injurious behaviour in people with learning disabilities: determinants and interventions. *International Review of Psychiatry*, **2**, 99–114.

Oliver C., Murphy G.H. & Corbett J.A. (1987) Self-injurious behaviour in people with mental handicap: a total population study. *Journal of Mental Deficiency Research*, **31**, 147–162.

Oliver C., Murphy G., Crayton L. & Corbett J. (1993) Self-injurious behaviour in Rett's syndrome: interactions between features of Rett's syndrome and operant conditioning. *Journal of Autism and Developmental Disorders*, **23**, 91–109.

Pearse R.G. (1987) Modern neonatalogy and the low birthweight baby. In: Hosking G. & Murphy G. (eds) *Prevention of Mental Handicap: A World View*, pp. 111–116. Royal Society of Medicine, London.

Perske R. (1991) *Unequal Justice*. Abingdon Press, Nashville, TN.

Pritchard D.G. (1963) *Education and the Handicapped, 1760–1960*. Routledge & Kegan Paul, London.

Pueschel S.M. (1991) Ethical considerations relating to prenatal diagnosis of fetuses with Down syndrome. *Mental Retardation*, **29**, 185–190.

Pueschel S.M., Monteiro L.A. & Erickson M. (1986) Parents and physicians' perceptions of facial plastic surgery in children with Down syndrome. *Journal of Mental Deficiency Research*, **30**, 71–79.

Quine L. (1991) Sleep problems in children with mental handicap. *Journal of Mental Deficiency Research*, **35**, 269–290.

Quine L. & Pahl J. (1987) First diagnosis of severe handicap: a study of parental reactions. *Developmental Medicine and Child Neurology*, **29**, 232–242.

Qureshi H. (1992) Parents caring for young adults with mental handicap and challenging behaviour. Paper presented at the Department of Health conference (Challenging Behaviour in People with Learning Disabilities), Manchester, UK.

Raiti S. & Newns G.H. (1971) Cretinism: early diagnosis and its relation to mental prognosis. *Archives of Disease in Childhood*, **46**, 692–694.

Reddy G.N.N. (1987) Prevention of mental handicap — a world view. In: Hosking G. & Murphy G. (eds) *Prevention of Mental Handicap: A World View*, pp. 3–6. Royal Society of Medicine, London.

Revill S. & Blunden R. (1979) A home training service for pre-school developmentally handicapped children. *Behaviour Research and Therapy*, **17**, 207–214.

Richardson S.A. & Koller H. (1985) Epidemiology. In: Clarke A.M., Clarke A.D.B & Berg J.M. (eds) *Mental Deficiency: The Changing Outlook*, 4th edn. Methuen, London.

Rinck C., Guidry J. & Calkins C.F. (1989) Review of states' practices on the use of psychotropic medication. *American Journal on Mental Retardation*, **93**, 657–668.

Roberts D.F. (1987) Population genetics of mental handicap. In: Hosking G. & Murphy G. (eds) *Prevention of Mental Handicap: A World View*. Royal Society of Medicine, London.

Robson C. (1987) Evaluation of a self-instructional package. In: Hogg J. & Mittler P. (eds) *Staff Training in Mental Handicap*. Croom Helm, Beckenham, Kent.

Rowitz L. (1987) The American mental retardation service system. *Journal of Mental Deficiency Research*, **31**, 337–347.

Rynders J.E. & Stealey D.S. (1985) Early education: a strategy for producing a less (least) restrictive environment for young children with severe handicaps. In: Lakin K.C. & Bruininks R.H. (eds) *Strategies for Achieving Community Integration of Developmentally Disabled Citizens*, pp. 129–158. Paul H. Brookes, Baltimore, MD.

Saigal S., Szatmari P., Rosenbaum P., Campbell D. & King S. (1991) Cognitive abilities and school performance of extremely low birth-weight children and matched term control children at age 9 years: a regional study. *Journal of Pediatrics*, **118**, 751–760.

Schopler E. & Hennike J.M. (1990) Past and present trends in residential treatment. *Journal of Autism and Developmental Disorders*, **20**, 291–298.

Schroeder S. (1988) Neuroleptic medications for persons with developmental disabilities. In: Aman M.G. & Singh N.N. (eds) *Psychopharmacology of the Developmental Disabilities*, pp. 82–100. Springer-Verlag, New York.

Schroeder C.S. & Schroeder S.R. (1990) The future of children is now. *Journal of Autism and Developmental Disorders*, **20**, 367–378.

Shearer M. & Shearer D.E. (1972) The Portage project: a model for early childhood education. *Exceptional Children*, **36**, 210–217.

Simeonsson R.J., Cooper D.H. & Sheiner A.P. (1982) A review and analysis of the effectiveness of early intervention programs. *Pediatrics*, **69**, 635–641.

Smith I. (1987) Phenylketonuria. In: Hosking G. & Murphy G. (eds) *Prevention of Mental Handicap: A World View*, pp. 59–61. Royal Society of Medicine, London.

Smith I., Beasley M., Wolff O.H. & Ades A.E. (1988) Behaviour disturbance in 8 year old children with early treated phenylketonuria. *Journal of Pediatrics*, **112**, 403–408.

Smith I., Beasley M.G., & Ades A.E. (1990) Intelligence and quality of dietary treatment in phenylketonuria. *Archives of Disease in Childhood*, **65**, 472–478.

Smith I., Beasley M. & Ades A.E. (1991) Effect on intelligence of relaxing low phenylalanine diet in phenylketonuria. *Archives of Disease in Childhood*, **66**, 311–316.

Stone R.K., Alvarez W.F., Ellman G., Hom A.C. & White J.F. (1989) Prevalence and prediction of psychotropic drug use in California developmental centers. *American Journal on Mental Retardation*, **93**, 627–632.

Stoneman Z. & Crapps J.M. (1988) Correlates of stress, perceived competence and depression among family care providers. *American Journal on Mental Retardation*, **93**, 166–173.

Stores G. (1988) Antiepileptic drugs. In: Aman M.G. & Singh N.N. (eds) *Psychopharmacology of the Developmental Disabilities*, pp. 101–118. Springer-Verlag, New York.

Sturmey P. & Crisp A.G. (1986) Portage guide to early education: a review of research. *Educational Psychology*, **6**, 139–157.

Tao Kuo-Tai (1988) Mentally retarded persons in the People's Republic of China: review of epidemiological studies and services. *American Journal on Mental Retardation*, **93**, 193–199.

Tausig M. (1985) Factors in family decision making about placement for developmentally disabled individuals. *American Journal of Mental Deficiency*, **89**, 352–361.

Teplin S.W., Burchinal M., Johnson-Martin N., Humphry R.A. & Kraybill E.N. (1991) Neurodevelopmental, health and growth status at age 6 years of children with birth weights less than 1001 grams. *Journal of Pediatrics*, **118**, 768–777.

Throne J. (1975) Normalisation through the normalisation principle: right ends, wrong means. *Mental Retardation*, **13**, 23–25.

Towell D. (1985) Residential needs and services. In: Craft M., Bicknell J. & Hollins S. (eds) *Mental Handicap: a Multi-Disciplinary Approach*, pp. 15–23. Ballière-Tindall, London.

Vaughan B.E. & Waters E. (1981) Attention structure, sociometric status and dominance: interrelations, behavioural correlates and relationships to social competence. *Developmental Psychology*, **17**, 275–288.

Victorian Infant Collaborative Study Group (1991) Eight year outcome in infants with birthweight of 500 to 999 grams: continuing regional study of 1979 and 1980 births. *Journal of Pediatrics*, **118**, 761–767.

Wald N.J. & Cuckle H.S. (1987) Recent advances in screening for neural tube defects and Down syndrome. *Ballière's Clinical Obstetrics and Gynaecology*, **1**, 649−676.

Wald N., Stone R., Cuckle H.S., Grudzinskas J.G., Barkai G., Brambati B., Teisner B. & Fuhrmann W. (1992) First trimester concentrations of pregnancy associated plasma protein A and placental protein 14 in Down syndrome. *British Medical Journal*, **305**, 28.

Warnock M.H. (1978) *Special Educational Needs*. HMSO, London.

White K.R. & Castro G. (1985) An integrative review of early intervention efficacy studies with at-risk children: implications for the handicapped. *Analysis and Intervention in Developmental Disabilities*, **5**, 177−201.

Williams P. (1992) Ethical issues in prevention and treatment. *Speak Out* (newsletter of CMHERA), **15**, 2−11.

Wilson C.J., McGillivray J.A. & Zeitlin A.G. (1992) The relationship between attitude to disabled siblings and ratings of behavioural competency. *Journal of Intellectual Disability Research*, **36**, 325−336.

Wing L. (1981) Language, social and cognitive impairments in autism and severe mental retardation. *Journal of Autism and Developmental Disorders*, **11**, 31−44.

Wing L. & Gould J. (1979) Severe impairments of social interaction and associated abnormalities in children: epidemiology and classification. *Journal of Autism and Developmental Disorders*, **9**, 11−19.

Wishart M.C., Bidder R.T. & Gray O.P. (1981) Parents' reports of family life with a developmentally delayed child. *Child: Care, Health and Development*, **7**, 267−279.

Wolfensberger W. (1980a) A brief overview of the principle of normalisation. In: Flynn R.J. & Nitsch K.E. (eds) *Normalisation, Social Integration and Community Services*, pp. 7−30. Pro-ed, Austin, TX.

Wolfensberger W. (1980b) The definition of normalisation: update, problems, disagreements and misunderstandings. In: Flynn R.J. & Nitsch K.E. (eds) *Normalisation, Social Integration and Community Services*, pp. 71−115. Pro-ed, Austin, TX.

Wolfensberger W. (1983) Social role valorisation: a proposed new term for the principle of normalisation. *Mental Retardation*, **21**, 234−239.

Wolfensberger W. & Glenn L. (1975) *Program Analysis of Service Systems (PASS). A Method for the Quantitative Evaluation of Human Services: Handbook*, 3rd edn. National Institute on Mental Retardation, Toronto.

Woods P. & Parry R. (1981) Pethna: tailor-made toys for the severely retarded and multiply handicapped. *Apex: Journal of the British Institute of Mental Handicap*, **9**, 53−54.

Woolery M. (1991) Instruction in early childhood special education: 'seeing through a glass darkly…knowing in part'. *Exceptional Children*, **58**, 127−135.

Zarkowska E. & Clements J. (1988) *Problem Behaviour in People with Severe Learning Disabilities: A Practical Guide to the Constructional Approach*. Croom Helm, Beckenham, Kent.

Chapter 61
Practice in Nonmedical Settings

A.R. Nicol

The hallmarks of a good child psychiatry service include the breadth of expertise that it can bring to bear and the flexibility with which it can respond to children's problems. Two characteristics of the specialty are essential to these ends: the multidisciplinary team and the ability to move in a variety of settings. These should be both medical settings, such as the paediatric ward and the outpatient clinic, and non-medical settings such as schools, children's homes and of course the homes of the families themselves. This chapter focuses on but one component of this essential spread of service. The sceptic may say: Why make life so complicated? Why not stick to the provision of good services in what is basically a clinic setting? Eight answers to this question come to mind.

1 Child and adolescent psychiatric disturbance is very common, whereas the availability of services is limited and costly. It was recognized many years ago in the Court Report (1976) that children's emotional well-being is not the province of child psychiatric teams alone. The worker in non-medical settings can mobilize help from non-medical professionals such as teachers and care workers. It is here that skills in mental health consultation become important, and we return to this later in the chapter.

2 Many children, adolescents and their families who suffer psychological distress are reluctant to attend a clinic, but may, on the other hand, be available in settings such as the school. They may be prepared to be seen at home or to attend more familiar and less potentially stigmatizing settings such as their family doctor or health visitor. In a recent French study, for example, 50% of children identified as disturbed had been seen by one of a wide range of professionals (E. Fombonne, personal communication). Again, a mental health consultation approach could have brought mental health skills to where they might be effective.

3 The problem may be relatively straightforward and the mobilization of the full range of expertise of the clinic base not needed. Again, support for professionals in the field can help.

4 A child psychiatric service is surrounded by continuing changes in the surrounding agencies that can offer opportunities for better service delivery. In recent years, there have been enormous changes in the policies and practices of social agencies for children, principally education and social services agencies. These may be in response to new demands, such as the discovery of the extent and effects of child abuse. At other times the pressure may come from changes in social outlook and political pressures, such as the ebb and flow of formal instructional approaches and self-discovery approaches in educational philosophy. A healthy outreach into nonmedical settings, not only at a front-line level but also at a strategic level (for example, by serving on interagency planning committees), should enable the child psychiatrist to cooperate in providing the best service for children, grasping opportunities in the constantly changing welfare scene.

5 Schools and public arrangements for child care and education give both an opportunity and a responsibility to the community to promote optimum child development and to remedy deviant development where this seems to be occurring. Clinic work tends to be family-centred. In order to participate in this public duty, the child and adolescent psychiatrist must be equipped to work in nonclinic settings. One of my tasks in this chapter is to explore the role of the child psychiatric team in this context.

6 Children's behaviour is very much determined by the environment they are in at the time. The recognition of this is fundamental to child and adolescent psychiatry, for example the presence of peers in the classroom or the sex of the teacher may have a profound effect on behaviour (Prendergast & Prout, 1987). Behaviour and emotions always occur in a social context. When they are exaggerated, self-defeating or giving rise to marked distress, they come to be called 'psychopathology'. If feelings and behaviour are detached from their 'ecological' context, much of the potential for effective intervention may be thrown away. Yet this context is available for study by the professional who is prepared to step outside the clinic. The first task, therefore is to provide a way of describing and understanding the environmental component of behaviour. This is the subject of the next section.

7 The results of treatment may be situation-specific. Many examples can be found of treatment that has been highly successful but has not generalized to environments other than those where the treatment took place. This has proved a most intractable problem but has been confronted by behaviour therapists (Wahler *et al.*, 1979). A partial answer is to take the treatment, and indeed the service, to the environment, be it home or school, where the problem is manifest.

8 Work away from medical settings offers opportunities for primary and secondary prevention. In primary prevention a whole population is targeted. For example, we will see in the section on the school and emotional development that characteristics of the school can have a profound effect on the adjustment of the pupils. Secondary prevention involves action at an early stage in the development of disorders, offering early treatment. The treatment research that is described in the section on the school as a treatment environment offers an example.

CONCEPTS

We need now to turn to some of the concepts and research that are relevant to treatment away from medical settings, in particular the sensitivity of behaviour to the environment of the child or young person.

The development of human ecology

The description of environments and their relationship to behaviour has been the subject of several different lines of enquiry. The most distinguished early work was that of the Midwest Psychological Field Station, University of Kansas (Barker, 1968; see Price, 1976, for a brief and helpful account).

Starting with the field theory of Lewin (Hall & Lindzey, 1970 give an excellent introductory account), Barker and his colleagues (Barker, 1968) developed a classification of behavioural settings of children in an entire small town in Kansas. The idea is that the meaning of behaviour cannot be divorced from the setting in which it occurs. A setting includes a location, a set of people and a function. For example, a football game requires a ground, a referee, two opposing teams, spectators and the joint aim of a competition of skill which constitutes the game. Each of these groups behave in characteristic ways that have more to do with the occasion (or setting) than with the individuals concerned. Settings come and go, for example the football game occurs on Saturday afternoons and next week there will be different teams and probably a partly different crowd; but the setting will be identifiable as being in the same place and bringing forth similar behaviour. When we turn to motivational considerations, the relevance of a description of the environment in this way becomes very clear. Barker developed ideas that help us to understand how behaviour in settings is determined. People share an understanding of a setting and the sense of reward that follows achievement of these goals: a feeling of well-being follows a win by the home team. When considering deviant or disturbed behaviour, the concept of the setting becomes very relevant. Rowdy behaviour that would be normal in the school playground is not be tolerated in the classroom.

This important early work helps us to understand the relationship of the individual to the environment. This environment has a physical and an interpersonal component. It is in the interpersonal world that the main progress has been made in understanding the child with problems. The influence of the notion of behaviour settings in child development has been pervasive and profound, leading to work about the way in which the individual interacts with the environment.

An early example of this focus on relationships and the development of group behaviour in children and adolescent peers helps us to see the importance of the environmental perspective. This is the Robbers' Cave experiment, one of a series conducted in the 1950s (Sherif & Sherif, 1956). A summer camp for boys aged about 11 was set up. They were all well-adjusted, doing well at school and healthy. Two groups of boys were taken to the camp site separately by bus, unaware of the existence of the other. They then unwittingly took part in an experiment.

The experiment took as its starting point the knowledge from previous work that groups are profoundly influenced by social environment and that if two groups are set up, intergroup hostility is liable to develop. This includes the development of stereotypes, an increase in cohesion and alteration in relationships within the groups.

The experiment was to explore how such conflict could be reduced, and how this affected intragroup organization.

In the field, major rancour developed when one of the teams lost a tug-of-war game. This resulted in the burning of the flag of the rival team. Within-group dynamics changed dramatically during this period. Craig, for example, was a peaceful and respected leader of the Eagles gang in the first stage. With the outbreak of hostilities he rapidly lost status to Mason, a more pugnacious youth, as a more combative style became the norm.

Turning to attempts at healing, simple socializing between the two gangs made little difference to the level of enmity. Equally, favourable information and reconciliation between the leaders were ineffective. It was only when a task was set that required a contribution from both the gangs in concert that peace broke out. Several such tasks were arranged within the experiment. In one example, the gangs were taken to a distant picnic site. The idea was that when they got there (in separate transport) a lorry would go and collect provisions for their meals. This ancient lorry then 'broke down' — a situation that could only be rectified by both groups collaborating in pulling it uphill to get it going. Following this joint task, there were many signs of increased friendliness and sharing between the warring gangs. The breaking-down of barriers was confirmed by marked changes in choice on serial sociometry tests conducted before and after the youngsters experienced these healing superordinate tasks.

The Robbers' Cave and similar experiments illustrate several issues. Firstly, they show the profound way in which well-adjusted children's behaviour can be influenced by the social setting. It should be noted that it is mainly the manipulation of the social environment that brought about such profound changes in the boys' behaviour.

A second issue is that of cause and effect. Gorell Barnes (see Chapter 55) argues that the family can be usefully viewed as a social system. This is equally true of non-family environments, such as the summer camp or the school. This does not of course mean that the qualities of the individual child are not important; this is far from the case, as illustrated by the contrasting fates of Craig and Mason. However, these outcomes are the product of social forces which would have been difficult to predict.

A further point is that these experiments show the way in which social psychological phenomena may be put to therapeutic account. The development has come to be called the ecological approach.

Similar forces are at work in establishments that contain disturbed children and young people. Two examples illustrate how this can be for good or ill.

The present author consulted for many years at an establishment for disturbed conduct-disordered boys. Behaviour control and aggression were, not surprisingly, a common problem. At the same time, staff had difficulty establishing an atmosphere of *esprit de corps*. One winter, the house was gutted by a serious fire. This resulted in the boys having to live for many months in arctic weather in a series of temporary huts in the garden. The opportunities and temptations for misbehaviour seemed, on the face of it, never to have been better; for example, the first 2 hours of every morning were spent unfreezing the water pipes! What actually happened was that the boys seemed to respond to the common enemy — in this case the weather. Behaviour was exemplary.

A second more sinister example is Cottage Six (Polsky, 1962). This was a residential establishment where the delinquent teenagers had therapy during the day but were left during evenings and weekends with poorly trained residential staff. From the outside, the establishment seemed to work well. Closer examination, however, showed that a very high price was being paid for the surface calm. Order was maintained by the handing over of authority to a senior group of extremely violent youths who kept order by operating a reign of terror with their younger and weaker peers. This is a phenomenon that can only too easily develop in situations of under-funding, poor staffing and inadequate training that are so common in the much under-valued world of residential child care. At the time of writing, there are a number of scandals associated with residential care of children. These have demonstrated again the consequences of poor training and inadequate inspection of residential establishments.

So far, we have considered relatively short-term and potentially reversible ways in which environments can alter behaviour and social systems. There is also evidence that environments can influence behaviour over long time spans and, indeed, bring about enduring changes in life thereafter. The work on differences in the qualities of schools and their outcomes offers an example.

THE SCHOOL AND EMOTIONAL DEVELOPMENT

The school environment

As a specialized setting for child development, the school long precedes the clinic or indeed a health setting of any sort. Dewey (1916) traces the school as arising from apprenticeship situations where skills were commonly passed down the family. As society became more complex and with industrialization this was no longer possible. The school environment is one where the child spends a large proportion of his or her waking life and where he or she has to learn to cope with many challenges, not only in the sphere of learning but also coping with relationship issues such as cooperation and sharing, competition and authority — all challenges and growth points for the child and opportunities for the perceptive teacher. The learning situation is full of problems: the management of pupils' anxiety, rebelliousness, discouragement and unhappiness is essential to good teaching (Galloway, 1985).

From a common-sense point of view, it is likely that some schools are better able to support the learning and socialization process than others. Parents have always known this and conscientious parents are very particular about the education of their children and, when they have the power to do so, will act to ensure that it is of high quality. Relatively recently, research on the effects of school on child and adolescent development has revealed that there are indeed large differences between schools. In this approach, the behavioural and educational outcome of a number of schools are related to qualities of the environment within the school (Rutter *et al.*, 1979; Galloway *et al.*, 1985; Mortimore *et al.*, 1989).

With their focus on the school as a social entity, the school differences studies use school-wide outcome measures such as attainment, truancy rates, delinquency and behavioural questionnaires to gain a general picture of outcome in the schools under study. The research strategy comprises two stages. In the first stage, the progress of a cohort of pupils is measured in a longitudinal design, comparing a number of schools. The school attainment, adjustment and factors which indicate social disadvantage at the outset are measured and taken into account in the monitoring of progress. When the progress of the children in different schools is compared, there has been a consistent finding of large differences between schools. When the performance of the schools has been identified in this way, the schools can be compared to identify those school qualities that are associated with differences in outcome. Many of the successful qualities showed considerable consistency among different studies.

Positive leadership from the head teacher has consistently been found to be associated with better adjustment and progress of pupils. This leadership style included monitoring pupils' progress, active involvement in curriculum planning and staff training in a way that involved staff in decisions where appropriate. Associated with this was a sense of consistency within the school with low staff turnover and good communication between teachers who were taking the same class. At the class level, a degree of structure to the lessons was associated with good progress, as was a teaching pace and style that challenged the children intellectually. A work-centred environment which concentrated on one or two themes at a time, even if at different levels for different children, seemed to be the key to success. High levels of communication in the shape of good teacher record-keeping and links with children and parents were key ingredients. What results is an accent on rewards and praise, an atmosphere of direction and orderliness which makes the school a comfortable and facilitating place to be. Most of the studies have used a rather limited set of measures to assess these outcomes. One hopes that parents may hope for more than simple school attendance and attainment in basic subjects in their children's education. Those studies that have considered a wider range of indicators have on the whole showed a reasonable degree of correlation among them (Mortimore *et al.*, 1989).

Clinical implications

At this point, it is necessary to take a little time to consider the implications of these findings for the clinician. Any sensitive visitor will quickly recognize the well-run school. Clinicians also need to develop the expertise to recognize that the atmosphere of the individual classroom is important, although it will be necessary to collaborate with educational psychologists and advisers in developing support for the teacher in bringing about change in the classroom. Consultation and collaboration may enable the clinician to pinpoint difficulties between teacher and child and develop ways in which consultation can help. The skills needed are described more fully in the section on interventions that use the environment.

Does the influence of being in a particular social environment, such as the school, affect subsequent adjustment? A follow-up of children attending 12 schools in London offers some interesting possibilities. The schools showed quite wide variation in truancy and behaviour (Rutter *et al.*, 1979). Equally, the postschool prospects of these children showed variation. On the other hand, this variation seemed to be due entirely to the fact that children in the less successful school dropped out earlier and failed to attend school consistently (Gray *et al.*, 1980). This is an illustration of a theme that has emerged in other parts of this book: a depriving experience in one period of life, be it difficult circumstances in the early years, poor school experience or an early pregnancy, puts the child at a disadvantage at subsequent life stages. The clinician with a perspective that extends beyond the clinic has many opportunities to observe the unfolding of transactional processes.

A final optimistic note: the effectiveness of schools can change quite rapidly, over the period of 2−3 years (Reynolds, 1991).

The school as a treatment environment

In the introduction, I underlined the way that children's behaviour is sensitive to the environment (point 6) and the way that therapeutic success in one setting does not necessarily, or even often, extend to another environment (point 7). The implications of this truth have not been lost on the many researchers who have evaluated therapy in schools. Thera-

peutic interventions in the context of ordinary schools may be classroom-based, such as behaviour modification programmes to encourage on-task behaviour (O'Leary & O'Leary, 1976), or may involve removal of children from the class for special sessions with a therapeutic goal. Consultation, social problem-solving training, social skills training or group counselling and crisis intervention have all been used in this way. Maher and Zins (1987) offer an overview of these many approaches. In keeping with the theme of how social settings influence treatment, one particularly comprehensive study will be described in more detail: the 'Help Starts Here' project. This was a controlled comparison of interventions that may be applied to 7- and 11-year-old children. It has given pointers as to which approaches may be the most effective (Kolvin *et al.*, 1981) and some tentative leads about the effects of the environment. In the case of 7-year-olds, the interventions compared were parent counselling−teacher consultation, nurture work (a teacher aid support programme) and play-group therapy, using the technique developed by Axline (1947). Compared with a no-treatment control group, the play-group therapy had the greatest impact on the children's problems, followed by the nurture work. The consultation programme was only marginally effective. At senior level, the programmes compared were group counselling using a Rogerian technique (Rogers, 1952), behaviour modification in the classroom and, again, a parent counselling−teacher consultation approach. The most effective interventions in this case were group therapy and behaviour modification. In short, direct involvement of skilled and trained professionals with the children was associated with effective intervention. The theoretical framework underlying the treatment approach seemed less important.

Several other findings of this study pointed to the importance of intervention in the normal environments of the child, in this case the school. The first point was that the follow-ups were long-term, at 18 months and 3 years. Very interestingly, the therapeutic effects of the study seemed to outlive the treatments in that the improvements compared to the control group continued between the 18-month and 3-year follow-ups. This finding suggests that therapeutic qualities were present in the school that continued to have an effect after the formal intervention was complete. Equally, there was some evidence of generalization in the later follow-ups in that the children who had the more successful interventions also showed changes in home-based measures (Nicol *et al.*, 1985b).

Interventions that use the environment

The Help Starts Here project is an illustration of how techniques developed in the clinic can be successfully applied in the community. To some extent, however, the approaches that were used, especially the group counselling, were a rather direct transfer of clinic techniques. Other approaches have marshalled the resources of the non-medical setting more fully to the services of the intervention, as in the case of bullying.

Bullying has always occurred, but recently, as a result of some highly publicized cases of suicide, there has been considerable alarm about the extent and destructiveness of this behaviour in ordinary schools. That the problem is widespread has been shown in numerous studies using questionnaires, interviews and sociometric tests. These show that at least 10% of children are involved in any one school either as bullies or as victims (Besag, 1989). A special helpline that was set up in the UK in 1990 was besieged by several thousand calls in 3 months (La Fontaine, 1991). Bullying flourishes in an atmosphere of secrecy, fear and vindictiveness. It does not come readily to the attention of the school staff and, when it does, it is all too easy to deny its importance and gravity. Because it is so closely linked to the school setting, it can only be handled within the school with the full cooperation of the school staff.

Many studies have attempted to characterize the bully and the victim. The results are predictable. The bully emerges as relatively socially competent and confident, from a background where aggression in condoned and often with other behaviour problems. Girl bullies are more likely to use indirect methods such as social isolation, malicious rumours and name-calling to persecute the victim. The victim is more likely to be shy, anxious and socially isolated and may have some disability or motor clumsiness. The cycle of teasing and bullying may start relatively innocuously, but can become repetitive and may totally dominate the life of the victim. Symptoms of stress such as bed-wetting or insomnia are likely to develop and add to the miserable vicious cycle. Such interactions can extend over long time periods and etch deeply into the confidence and self-esteem of the victim. The pitiless attacks by the bully are mirrored by indifference and isolation from the other children and often the teachers.

Treatment of the individual can offer no more than a partial answer to the problem. The intervention should start with a review of the school and indeed the education authority's attitude to the problem. There should be an explicit policy that bullying must not be condoned. This should be widely publicized. Architectural considerations are important: bullying flourishes in isolated and unsupervised changing rooms and corridors out of the sight of supervising staff and this should be born in mind in buildings and alterations to the school. Secluded paths and bus stops in the vicinity of the school offer other vulnerable points.

Attention to the ethos of the school, as described in the section on the school environment earlier in this chapter, is crucial to the management of bullying. There should be an atmosphere of autonomy in the context of support and with an overall sense of the school as a community where each is responsible for the self and the other. For their part, pupils need to be told that they have the right to attend school without fear of being bullied. A curriculum relevant to the needs of all pupils is important. Undue attention to 'successful' children and 'failures' acts as a source of frustration and alienation. This is fertile soil for the development of disaffection and macho attitudes.

All these issues point up the central importance of staff morale in the management of bullying. A contented and dedicated staff group means adequate punctuality, good supervision, a well-structured curriculum and attention to the children's needs. Cases of bullying identified early can be quickly discouraged, whereas neglect of warning signs can be taken as permission to continue by the potential bully. Pastoral staff or heads of house can identify and so support isolated children who are likely to be vulnerable. It may be possible to involve more senior and mature children to offer support.

As well as these school-wide considerations, there should be programmes that help the individual child who is coming under pressure from bullies. Advice on self-protection can be given to a larger group, to avoid putting the individual under the spotlight. This could include ways of acting that give an air of confidence, how to insulate oneself from being hurt by taunts, sticking with friends and the importance of letting adults know what is happening. When cases come to light, the teacher should analyse the situation and offer more specific help. The bully should be firmly confronted but not in a punitive way that may simply model vindictiveness.

It is essential to involve parents when major bullying is discovered. Parents of victims may be very distressed to find out what is happening to their child, particularly if the school responds with indifference. Clear advice, support and partnership with parents can be a great help. The parents of bullies may need advice on discipline techniques at home. Besag (1989) gives a full account with many practical hints on how to tackle bullying in school.

A major evaluation of a nationwide campaign against bullying which involved the whole school system has been carried out in Norway. This involved training for both teachers and parents. The results were most encouraging (Olweus, 1991).

PRACTICE

The emphasis placed so far in this chapter on the ecological approach does not mean that the approaches that underlie treatment discussed in the other chapters of this book are not relevant to practice in nonmedical settings. This is far from the case. Modifications of techniques developed in clinic settings are the main contribution that the mental health worker can make to work in nonclinic settings. These will include psychodynamic and behavioural approaches, both of which can be very usefully adapted to settings in school, residential and fostering environments. The only reason why the ecological approach is given such prominence here is that environmental awareness is a key additional perspective that can be brought into play when practice moves into nonclinic settings.

The enthusiastic clinician, keen to move out of the clinic to where the action is, may be bewildered and discouraged when, instead of an equally enthusiastic response, he or she meets polite resistance and even sabotage of carefully prepared ideas. Communication and legitimacy need particular consideration.

Communication

In this section we will distinguish the mental health worker from the colleague who works in the community by calling the latter the community worker. Community workers may be categorized into those who have almost continuous contact with the child, such as foster parents; those who have long periods of contact, such as teachers, nursing staff and care workers; and those with relatively fleeting contact such as a field social worker. All these professionals will meet with a lot of child disturbance, although it is not their sole or even main concern.

The quotation marks around the word psychopathology earlier in the chapter (see point 6) were intended to warn the reader that such terminology may have little currency outside clinic confines. The move from the clinic can be experienced as a liberation, but it has its frightening aspects. Models of behaviour based on descriptive psychiatry are unlikely to be received with sympathy and whereas systems theory, behavioural or psychodynamic theories may be points of contact, there may be differences in terminology, perception and level of training that can become very apparent in community settings. More importantly, there may be other explanatory models, more or less well-formulated and explicit, which form the basis for the management of problems. In the search for points of contact it is vital to try to detect the frame of reference of the other professionals in the field — a process that can only be achieved by listening, by asking tactful questions and by an attitude of humility.

There are several reasons why subtle detective work may be needed. Firstly, community workers may not be fully aware of, and therefore may not easily be able to report, their own set of assumptions. Secondly, the clinician may be part of the assumptive system, cast in a less than complimentary light which the worker may not easily dislose. For example, the mental health worker may be seen as an unwelcome agent of social control on the part of the 'powers that be'. Thirdly, the workers may be reluctant to reveal a working model that they fear may be criticized or ridiculed by the mental health woker. Fourthly, the mental health worker may find it difficult to cope with the assumptions of others because of different underlying political assumptions or because the assumptions of the other worker seem to cast him or her in an unfair light. Most importantly, the mental health worker may be dismissive of the model and belief systems of others and unable to accept that they may have usefulness and validity.

Practice in nonclinic settings is a collaborative exercise. Not to accept the need for this detective work is to run the high risk of communication blocks which are certain to derail cooperative efforts. For this reason, it is worth citing some of the concepts that are commonly found among community workers in child care and education.

Labelling theory

The idea here is that each child is an individual and that the application of labels is damaging, as it tends to depersonalize, to rob individual children of responsibility for their actions, and to push them into a deviant role. Few would deny the importance of all these considerations but empirical evidence for labelling is much more limited than the claims of some professionals would suggest. Two areas come to mind: the first is the process of court appearance in delinquent boys. In a major longitudinal study, Farrington *et al.* (1978) matched boys who appeared before the court with a group who had similar self-report delinquency scores but no court appearance. In the years after the court appearance, the self-report scores of the convicted boys increased, whereas those of the non-convicted controls decreased. However, these differences were not sustained at further follow-up.

The second example comes from research in the classroom. A great deal of research has been carried out about the effect of teachers' preconceptions of children's abilities on academic progress. Some studies have used an experimental approach, giving teachers false information and assessing the effect on the progress of children in their classes. This approach has yielded mixed results, possibly because the attempt to prejudice teachers was unsuccessful (perhaps teachers aren't that gullible). The second strategy has been to find naturalistic differences in teachers' attitudes. For example, teachers' assessment of ability can be compared with those gained from objective tests, or children whose older siblings are known to the teachers can be compared according to whether those siblings were high or low achievers. These studies have been more consistent in showing that teacher expectations can, indeed, have an important effect on pupil progress (Pilling & Kellmer Pringle, 1978). To sum up, it does seem that with some children, in some situations, labelling effects can be important.

Although this is true, to fail to analyse and classify also leads to problems in that without a common language of diagnosis and management, which to some would mean labelling, cooperative progress becomes extremely difficult. A wide variety of ideologically driven practices will be found in nonclinic settings. These may impinge on the work of the psychiatrist in many ways. For example, it is not uncommon for institutions to be operating a total ban on the use of psychotropic drugs, on the grounds that they imply an illness label. To avoid stigmatization is a sensible principle, but should not be a pretext to avoid effective treatment.

Behavioural difficulties and special educational need

These terms are linked to the philosophy of special educational need. In the British system, children who required special education were, in the past, placed in an administrative category that was linked to special educational provision in a segregated environment. Over the last 20 years, searching questions have been asked about the effectiveness of such special provision (see Chapter 63). The situation was radically changed by the influential Warnock Report (1978). This document advanced a concept of special educational need which encompasses everything about the child — abilities as well as disabilities — indeed all the factors that have a bearing on his or her educational progress. Educational need, whether resulting from physical disabilities, learning difficulties or behaviour, must now be more widely and individually defined. This allows for individual educational planning which should be provided for in as ordinary an environment as possible by the provision of special resources in mainstream school. The term learning difficulties is designed to be value-free and non-stigmatizing. It does not, on the other hand, take the place of psychiatric diagnosis and formulation because it is directed at educational need rather than a total view of the child in terms of psychiatric syndrome, development, health and environmental factors.

Challenging behaviour

Challenging behaviour is a common, modern but somewhat ambiguous term used in practical situations. It may reflect the fact that the individual child's challenging behaviour disrupts the well-ordered setting of the school or youth club, or it may be that the child's behaviour is a challenge to the professional skills of those who care for him or her. It is perhaps typical of a number of such terms in that its usage seems implicitly to reject a deeper interpretation of behaviour, including any notion of diagnosis or interpretation. It is a further indication of the deep distrust abroad of any suspicion of labelling or categorization of children. It is the behaviour and emotional problems that need to be categorized, the children should be valued as unique people (see Chapter 1).

The single-problem agency

There are currently many agencies that have a central focus on one type of problem, such as, Rape Crisis Centres and The National Society for the Prevention of Cruelty to Children. It would be extremely unfair to state that such organizations cannot have a broader focus, but collaboration with a mental health service may be both mutually beneficial and serve the needs of children by offering a broad choice of frameworks and approaches.

Panic responses

A panic response can also be a barrier to communication. This often takes the form of an assumption that there is a cut-off point where troublesome problems are seen to change in quality by community workers and become a 'mental illness' that such workers are incompetent to handle. This assumption may be linked to perplexity in the face of disturbed behaviour, to ingrained attitudes in the leadership or to relationship problems in the establishment concerned. The result is a helpless call for 'experts', a belief that drug therapy is needed and that the current environment is unsuitable for the child's needs. Often an undercurrent of hostility hampers collaboration. The clinician who is comfortable in work outside medical settings can at least detect this phenomenon even if, at this stage, a helpful response is often difficult. Mental illnesses such as schizophrenia do present in nonmedical

settings but the same attitude of partnership and collaboration is needed as with other problems, although the details of management will be different from the variety of other problems that may be encountered.

Legitimacy

This edition of this textbook emerges into an environment of increasing managerial control over the delivery of services. This trend is not limited to medical services; indeed line management is far more evident in other major agencies. This means that informal working relationships on the ground are increasingly hard to sustain unless supported by senior management. Resistance to obvious need may be due to the fact that contractual arrangements have not been negotiated at a higher level of management. It is not possible for fieldworkers to respond unless this homework has been done.

CORE SKILLS

There are three core skills that are particularly relevant to work in nonclinic settings: (1) direct work with the client, often called counselling; (2) mental health consultation; and (3) a variety of activities which are commonly called networking.

Counselling

This term is so widely used for so many activities and in so many settings that it is difficult to discuss it at length in the abstract. Community workers may have relevant training to undertake counselling. If not, the clinician may be able to advise on reputable training programmes in the area. An alternative may be to develop the appropriate training courses as an extension of the service offered by the clinic.

Mental health consultation

Clinicians working in nonmedical settings must be prepared to develop skills in mental health consultation. Consultation as a professional activity has the following features: it takes place between a consultant who is available to impart professional expertise and one or a group of consultees who have a problem with clients in that area of expertise. It is a voluntary, nonsupervisory relationship in which the consultant has no responsibility for the client and the consultee is under no obligation to follow the consultant's suggestions. The personal feelings of the consultee are of interest only in so far as they impinge on his or her work with the client or in the workplace (see Chapter 58).

Setting up consultation

This summary draws on the accounts by Caplan (1970) and Gallissich (1982). Among others, Caplan describes, two themes that may characterize any consultation enterprise. In the first type, the consultant's expertise and knowledge are simply brought to bear in the client's problem as related by the consultee. The second type takes us back to the importance of terminology. A key component of consultation is the ability to share a set of concepts and a language. This can be a problem because, as already mentioned, a variety of concepts may be found in nonclinic settings that may not coincide with those of the consultant. For this reason, an in-service session that describes the consultation scheme to potential consultees is very helpful (Curtis *et al.*, 1987). Time constraints must also be seriously considered. Consultation is unlikely to be taken seriously if staff are expected to fit consultation among their other duties without adequate timetabling. A somewhat separate issue is that individual consultees' belief systems or prejudices may intrude into their professional activity.

Although there is no supervisory or managerial relationship between consultant and consultee, both work in the social framework of their agencies and the relationship between them. The consultant must, at an early stage, make contact with senior management in the consultee's agency and learn about the authority structure and communication network of the organization. The consultant must gauge accurately where his or her input is located in this authority structure. If staff members who reach out for help through the consultation process have problems and are isolated in their organization, help can be offered but the consultant needs to relate to the mainstream of the organization and, in particular, to the authority structure. To put it bluntly, identification with a marginal clique in the organization will inhibit progress. Caplan recommends a formal contract, outlining the service to be offered, and also what is not on offer. Of particular importance, therapy for the personal problems of staff members is not part of consultation. Issues of seniority and status between the consultant and consultee also need to be addressed. Problems can arise if differences are too great, such as a head of clinic as consultant and a probationer as consultee. This problem is lessened if several consultees are seen in a group.

The introduction of consultation in a district is often an evolutionary process in which stages can be identified from referrals to the clinic, to a closer relationship involving education of staff, to closer collaboration and consultation with staff. Finally, and far less common, although described by Caplan (1970), can come consultation with the agency administrators.

Relationship-building and diagnostic phase

Having dealt with the organizational issues, we must now turn to the practical matter of consultant–consultee interaction. The starting point must be the problem that is troubling the consultee about the client. With this in mind, the consultant must encourage the consultee to tell the story. Often the consultee will start with something like: 'What do you do with a child who shouts "knickers" in class all the time?' or: 'What do you do with children who keep running away?' or: 'What do you do with a mother who threatens to beat up the

headteacher?' These are the openings of professionals who on the one hand may be feeling a bit worried and defensive, and on the other want to test the mettle of the consultant. Gentle encouragement to move towards describing concrete examples is the best response at this stage. Once this is achieved, the consultant should become quite active, asking about the setting, the people who are typically present when the behaviour occurs, and more details about the child and family. The emphasis of such discussions will be shaped by the theoretical orientation of the consultant.

Even in psychodynamic approaches, the discussion should be centred primarily on what happened (behaviour) and only once this is established should the discussion turn to the feelings of the various parties involved. The following can act as a framework for this stage of the consultation. In behavioural approaches, the discussion will turn in a different direction at this point in a search for reinforcers in the child's natural environment and the development of a functional analysis (see Chapter 50).

Where?

It is helpful to ask about the setting in which the behaviour manifests. Is it in one place or several? If more than one, what do they have in common? Is it to do with an audience? Is it a setting, such as a classroom, where the child may feel unable to cope?

What else has happened?

How does the behaviour relate to possibly significant life events, for example, a home visit or the admission of a new child to the class or foster placement?

Towards or against whom?

One of the stressful aspects of front-line work in nonclinical settings is the intensity with which children develop feelings about members of staff which relate to their experience of parenting and family life (called transference feelings in psychodynamic therapy — see Chapter 54). A common example is the child who behaves particularly badly towards a foster carer or house parent in place of his or her own mother. These relationships can also of course have all the agonizing ambivalence of any disturbed relationship. Examples are children who test limits to the extent that they elicit the rejection that they most fear, or children who seem to develop a relationship of being 'too good' but at the same time show their underlying rage by stealing from the foster family.

What is the pace and intensity?

Behaviour can be diverted into more adaptive channels if these take account of the level of intensity. It is no good asking a hyperactive child to sit quietly reading a book but an opportunity to let off steam in a more constructive way is more likely to help.

Consultees will often be surprised at how much they have observed about the child's life space once they have been helped to put this together in an organized way. The consultee is usually in an ideal situation to make observations and empathic observation is *par excellence* a quality that is invested in individuals, whatever level of training they may have. Thus the consultant will be able to listen to such an account with genuine respect while ideological baggage and speculation are left on one side. Such ego-building and support are an essential component of the work of the consultant.

Only when a reasonable amount of information has been elicited should attention be allowed to turn to speculation and hypothesis-building.

At any time during this consultation process, an issue concerning the consultee may arise. At such times, the consultant must consider whether to move to consultee-centred work. There are four reasons why such a move may be necessary: (1) lack of knowledge; (2) lack of skill; (3) lack of confidence; and (4) lack of professional objectivity. It is this latter that requires the greatest skill in management for the consultant. The problem may reside in the relationship between the consultant and consultee or between the consultee and the client.

Between consultant and consultee, problems can arise from inappropriate over-identification, from an inappropriate attempt by the consultee to develop a relationship with the consultant or from the consultee attempting to seek personal therapy. In the relationship between the consultee and the client, the most common problem is so-called theme interference. Classification is an innate human attribute and one shared by consultees. Such themes, which may be quite unconscious, should become detectable to the consultant and very often can be seen to be getting in the way of the consultee's capacity to help the client. Take the example of a troublesome severely mentally handicapped boy. The problems are of long-standing lack of motivation and a tendency to sink into apathy and self-stimulation. It quickly becomes clear that the teacher's attention is focused firmly on the boy's masturbation, which dominates her attention to the exclusion of other problems. Caplan (1970) advises that the consultant should explore but not confront such prejudices. They will be found to have two components: the initial categorization of the client and an assumed inevitable outcome. The best way of coping with such phenomena is to question the link between the preconception and the assumed outcome (which is usually an extremely gloomy one). For example, the masturbation may indicate to the teacher that the boy has been prematurely sexualized by severe sexual abuse which will lead, inevitably, to him becoming a sexual offender. The best approach is to offer alternative possible outcomes, for example that this is self-stimulation which can be avoided by structuring the boy's time more closely. Another approach is for the consultant to relate a similar case that responded to simple measures and where the supposedly inevitable disaster failed to materialize.

Executive skills

It is essential not only that the consultant is active but also that he or she has clinical skills and techniques relevant to the problem under discussion. The details will differ according to the theoretical orientation of the consultant and the trick is to select areas from one's own experience that may be relevant and simple enough to be applied by someone whose skills are less specialized. A few points apply to all consultations.

As in all clinical work, it is important, according to orientation, to arrive at a behavioural hypothesis or dynamic formulation. This can be shared in simple jargon-free language with the consultee. In the normal way it should inform further work.

It is very important to be optimistic. In behavioural terms, the consultant's main contribution can often be as a reinforcer of the consultee's efforts, which are so often not acknowledged by authoritarian and bureaucratic management structures.

A common put-down for the enthusiastic consultant is: 'it's been tried before' — don't let this put you off.

Don't try to be a guru. This chapter has devoted attention to resistances that the clinician may encounter in nonmedical settings. The obverse of this is dependent over-valuation of the consultant by staff who feel lost and under-trained for the job at hand. To be fêted and worshipped, however discreetly, is a seductive mixture but, of course, the opposite of the sense of independence that the consultant should be trying to instil.

A final word of warning is needed. Some professionals take on the consultation mode of practice as an exclusive way of working, abandoning face-to-face clinical work almost entirely. This carries dangers, for the consultant should be respected as having high-level skills in direct clinical work.

Having described the process of consultation in some detail, it may be helpful to consider one setting where it can be used effectively. Children's homes and assessment centres provide a good example.

Consulting in residential establishments

Residential homes for children are settings where consultation commonly occurs. We will take them as an example of how such work can be organized. The basic principles of the approach are outlined below.

The work should be cleared with the leaders of the service. There should be an agreement that a regular time will be set aside by the staff for consultation. The consultant should not have any other role in the organization (e.g. consultants can be asked to be on the management committee. This is fine but if they do so they should resign as consultant).

In coming to an agreement, preferably in the form of a contract on both sides, the consultant should determine how the establishment works, for example:

What is the underlying philosophy, and how tightly specified is it?

Is there clarity of communication between staff, especially junior and senior staff?

Is there clear integration of the day, with varied activities so that the children are not spending a lot of time idle?

Do the children and the furniture and equipment look well-cared-for?

Is there a sense of order and organization, with the children taking part in activities as a matter of course without confrontations and major outbreaks of oppositional behaviour?

Is there some kind of key worker approach so that children have a named individual to turn to? Such a system is important as a basis for consultation.

What is the level and quality of training of the staff?

Is there a built-in trust system with privileges for conforming behaviour?

Is there a lot of unexplained disturbed behaviour such as absconding, self-mutilation or parasuicide?

Are all the staff invested with power, authority and self-confidence, or are there one or two people on whom the others rely to establish order? At worst, do the staff rely on the older and tougher boys to help keep order?

It is an undeniable truth that consultation can only be helpful to an establishment that is already running reasonably well. Prospective consultants will serve children better by being clear, if tactful, in drawing attention to serious short-comings in the structure of an establishment rather than taking part in a consultation project that has no hope of success.

We will now move on to techniques. The aim here is to arm the potential consultant with some ideas with which to start work. For a fuller account the reader should refer to Redl and Wineman (1957), Trieschman *et al.* (1969) or Bettelheim (1950).

The starting point is the routines of daily living. The change points in such an integrated day are of vital importance to therapy. These are the times when for the individual child, in the context of change and stress, the strength and flexibility of the ego as a mediator between external reality, instinctual impulses and the conscience are tested. It is at these turning points of the day that the youngsters' problems very often become manifest. Key points in the day may include bedtimes, getting up times and mealtimes. Relationships with staff members and other children are likely to lead to stress and breakdown. All children are likely to have trigger points at which they break down or where their maladaptive defence mechanisms lead them into difficulties. For example, the staff member may notice that a child shows continuous reluctance to settle down at the beginning of the school day, unsettling the class with clowning and pranks. Another child may have extreme reluctance to settle at night, terrified of being alone with frightening and unhappy fantasies once the lights are out. We will return to this theme of repetitive maladaption shortly. Firstly it should be added that strengths and interests in whatever field are the building blocks of rehabilitation to at least the same extent as the analysis of difficulties.

Emotional first aid

In establishments that are suffering from high levels of disturbance, the staff have an urgent need to gain behavioural control. In these circumstances it is most important to think of the children as an interacting group. Will a planned intervention result in children gaining an audience for outrageous behaviour? Will it mean that they will lose face in front of their peers? Group awareness is vital. Apter (1982) enumerates some well-established techniques that can be used, or in the case of the consultant, suggested to staff. These are as follows:

Planned ignoring: Don't attend to and thus risk reinforcing behaviours that will extinguish themselves in a short time; intervention may be counterproductive.

Nonverbal techniques can be used to communicate your control and cut into communication channels that are reinforcing the behaviour.

Proximity: Being close to the child, even without tactile contact, can support self-control.

Involvement in an interest relationship: Use the child's interest to focus attention, e.g. in a favourite activity.

Affection: A show of affection at a time of stress can abort a potential rise in tension and outburst of angry behaviour.

Use of humour: A skilful use of humour can relieve tension.

Hurdle help: Assist the child at a frustrating point in an activity sequence by structuring the task into easier stages.

Interpretation as interference: Let the child know that you know how he or she feels, even if the expression of such feelings is inappropriate. This can take the steam out of a situation, if properly handled.

Regrouping: Change the interpersonal environment by moving the child to another group within the establishment.

Direct appeal: To child loyalty, for example. This is a tricky one because you need to be reasonably sure that such loyalty will be forthcoming.

Limitation of choice: Cut down on irrelevant choice, for example of food or play equipment and therefore potential disorganization.

Calming time out: Time out must be achieved with calmness if it is to be genuinely helpful.

Physical restraint: Light holding until the child regains control.

Authoritative forbidding: Staff should be in a position to say no firmly when this is required.

Two topics will be discussed in more detail: the temper tantrum, as a common problem where consultation can be of great help; and the life space interview. This latter technique can be used by residential workers and is of great value.

Management of a temper tantrum

This is a common problem for residential care workers and one, among many, that the consultant may be asked about. Trieschman *et al.* (1969) describe management in a particularly helpful way, as a series of stages. Their conclusions are based on detailed participant observation of disturbed boys aged

7—12 years in a therapeutic residential centre. There are six such stages and each is characterized by characteristic behaviour and underlying feelings and psychodynamics. The first sign of trouble is often a restlessness and irritability. The child seems dissatisfied and often tries to pick a fight or argument. At this stage the worker may wish to try to avert the tantrum; however this is not always possible or even useful at this stage. The next three stages are concerned with various phases of ego disintegration: a violent phase of complete loss of control, followed by marked oppositional behaviour, leading to withdrawal. These phases can tax the therapist's confidence, training and professionalism to the utmost. It is very easy to get caught up in the wild shouting and insults of the decompensated child. The taunts and insults, however crude, seem to be unerringly aimed at the emotional weak point of the worker. Next comes a quiet self-isolating phase. It is sensible to respect the child's withdrawal at this time and await the next phase, which is one of self-doubt and remorse. If this last stage does not materialize, it is often sensible to try and evoke it. This is the time when therapy is likely to have an impact, particularly in the form of the life space interview.

The life space interview

This is the cornerstone of the ego psychology-based therapeutic milieu approach. There is no substitute for reading the original account (Redl, 1966) but a brief summary will be given here. By close contact in the therapeutic milieu, the worker will have noticed a pattern in the child's problems, either through a series of temper tantrums or other maladaptive behaviours. He or she then plans an intervention. This may consist of taking the child aside, for example at the self-doubt and remorse stage of the temper tantrum. The issues surrounding the temper are then raised. The child's view of what happened will always be very distorted and he or she will claim amnesia of this time of high drama and stress. The therapist's first task is to relate the facts of the situation (so-called reality rub-in). The next step, which may take time, is to link the behaviour with underlying feeling. This is particularly difficult with disturbed children whose only defence from inner chaos may be rigid denial of any evidence of an inner emotional life. Time may be needed to tackle the issue of the self-defeating nature and destructiveness of the behaviour under review. Following this, the worker and child will have to work on alternative behaviours that may serve the child better if he or she is to work towards giving up the difficulty. This may be achieved by some level of contract with follow-up interviews.

This is a brief introduction to some of the issues in the practice of consultation. The techniques needed will, of course, vary considerably according to the type of setting where the consultation is taking place. The techniques used may have to vary: for example, the consultant may be very familiar with behaviour therapy or the establishment may be run along behavioural lines, so that a more behavioural approach to consultation will be indicated.

Networking

Enormous numbers of professional workers can become involved in situations of family difficulty. In a recent study of a random sample of teenagers with severe learning difficulties (but not necessarily with behavioural difficulties), Dossetor and Nicol (1991) found an average of six professionals visiting any given family, and this in a district without lavish resources! Coordination of effort is needed if waste of scarce resources is to be avoided. A variety of devices can be useful.

The case conference

This has been the main vehicle for coordination of effort in network situations. It was developed in a major way in relation to work in child abuse, where coordination is of vital importance (HMSO, 1991; see Chapter 64).

Regular network meetings

The fact that professionals serving the same child population are employed in different agencies and management structures does not mean that they cannot collaborate closely. Regular meetings to discuss individual problems can be of great benefit.

Information-gathering

Telephone calls, letters, case note reviews and collection of information from as many sources as possible can enrich assessment work greatly. The present author, along with most clinicians, can remember situations where coordination and simple review of voluminous notes from a variety of agencies could have prevented a disaster.

The life table

This technique was developed by Adolf Meyer (1866—1950) to plot the relationship between life events and illness. It can be of great help in organizing and making sense of historical information where time relationships are complex. The process is very simple. A large sheet of paper is taken and a series of columns are drawn up. Each column is designed to chart the progress of a particular problem area for the child and family. For example, one column might be the times the father was out of work; another might be a record of the child's change of school. The development of such a chart from old and not very legible records is extremely laborious but it does clarify the course of events and can pay big dividends in terms of understanding.

Review and follow-up

The need to follow up and review difficult situations is also a crucial part of the process of networking. A common finding in the tragic cases of child abuse that have come before the

Courts and judicial inquiries is that follow-up has been sloppy and inadequate.

Parent and family organizations

Recent decades have seen the growth of a large number of organizations for different sorts of problems in children. Examples in the mental health field are Mencap, for people with learning difficulties, the Autistic Society and Schizophrenia Fellowship. It would be difficult to over-estimate the importance of these organizations as a source of mutual support and in the struggle for adequate resources for children with difficulties. Compared to families of children with disabilities of physical origin, such organizations are relatively sparse in the field of mental health and there can be little doubt that further development in this area would be a powerful force against stigma and in favour of a voice for children with emotional difficulties and their families.

Knowledge of community agencies

The vast panoply of statutory and voluntary agencies that now exist and that are of potential help to children and families in difficulties is evidence of the health, vigour and altruism of modern society. It is important to know of their existence in the area in which you work.

There are several other techniques that are common in network situations. It is important that the clinician has some knowledge of them.

Life story book

Life story books, which resemble simple life tables, can be used diagnostically and therapeutically (Ryan & Walter, 1985). A good-quality scrapbook or album is used. Information from the notes can be gathered, old photographs can be brought into play and memories evoked to recall people and places that have figured in the child's life. Places that have a key emotional meaning or that are important in the development of the child's identity can be visited. Access to the case notes is now within the child's rights in many countries; this can also play a part. This work can be undertaken by the child's key worker with back-up consultation. Such consultation can be important in helping the key worker use the opportunities which such an exercise affords for counselling and also in identifying points at which the material is likely to put the child under stress.

Geneograms

The geneogram (Lieberman, 1979) is another technique that can be very useful in helping a child make sense of his or her experience (see Chapter 5).

Therapeutic fostering

This is a more ambitious recent development for children with special health needs, for children who need assessment or as a bridge into independent living. The origin was as a direct response to the ineffectiveness of residential treatment of delinquency (Hazel, 1981). Characteristics of this specialized form of fostering include extra payments, special training for the foster parents, a time-limited placement, usually to an outer limit of between 6 months and 2 years, and the development of a contract between carers, the young person and the social services department (Shaw & Hipgrave, 1983). The children concerned are from the category of 'difficult to place' due to emotional disturbance, to the fact that they are adolescent and, at least in the early days of such schemes, the fact that they have spent many years in care. These are factors that Triseliotis (1989) reports as being associated with a high risk of fostering breakdown. Schemes such as these have grown in number and scope in the UK in the last decade (Shaw & Hipgrave, 1989a,b). The topic of fostering is covered in Chapter 15, but the therapeutic aspects merit presentation here.

The concept of fostering contracts is one that derives from task-centred casework. Contracts are a device that is available for citizens of equal status to enter of their free will. As such it can be argued that such a concept is inappropriate for an adolescent in care who essentially has few options. It may be better to call such an arrangement an understanding of the aims and responsibilities of the placement (Shaw & Hipgrave, 1983).

Turning to the content of the training and treatment aspects of therapeutic fostering, this is somewhat different from that of residential care. From anecdotal data, Triseliotis (1989) reports that foster carers find it helpful to have a social worker who listens and shows understanding but who also makes suggestions for problem-solving, including behavioural methods — a process which could well be classified as mental health consultation. Training and support are of central importance. Good preplacement preparation, in general, contributes to better stability and this is also an area where practice has developed considerably, with the use of methods such as life story books and geneograms (Shaw & Hipgrave, 1989b). The best-known pioneer in therapeutic fostering in the UK was the Kent scheme (Hazel, 1981). Here the planners of the scheme saw the main task as bringing the foster carers' experience as parents on to the task. To this end they developed the foster carers' group as the keystone of the scheme in relation to support and training. Attendance was a required condition of entry into the scheme, and it was in the context of these groups that the carers developed their expertise and commitment to the fostering enterprise.

Since the pioneering Kent scheme the scope — if not the staffing levels — of specialist fostering has extended greatly. Training packs from British Agencies of Adoption and Fostering and the Open University have contributed much to training.

Special fostering and residential care were originally seen as alternatives. Special fostering has been shown in one study to offer a higher level of child orientation, more opportunity for community contact, and a richer physical environment (Shaw & Hipgrave, 1989b). Further, the interaction between foster carers and children was found to be more frequent and prolonged than in residential settings and to be marked by more sharing of opinion, information and explanation. The last decade has seen widespread closure of children's homes and this has led to something of a reevaluation of the situation. Special fostering has its own casualties, in particular the danger of fostering breakdown. Residential facilities, although clearly not having the same role as in the past, can serve as a safety net, a resource of support for foster carers and a setting for the preparation of children for fostering (Shaw & Hipgrave, 1989b). There is to date no thoroughgoing study of the outcome of special fostering.

THE ORGANIZATION OF A SERVICE IN NONMEDICAL SETTINGS

It is as well to conclude with a brief account of how a service may be organized. This will vary from country to country according to the organization of the health care system in general. For the purposes of this discussion, it will be assumed that the clinician is attached to a clinic which is capable of providing a wide range of services to the local community, sometimes in medical and sometimes in nonmedical settings. There are some basic principles.

Firstly, there needs to be an agreement, as part of the clinic's operational policy, that work in nonmedical settings is important. It is best if the service as a whole has a statement of aims. This can include direct work in the clinic, in other medical settings such as the paediatric ward, special care baby unit or the child development centre, and in nonmedical settings such as special schools and residential homes. In addition, there should be agreement that consultation is important and appropriate. Teaching activities is another area that should be accepted as part of the clinic's task. A teaching commitment to nonmedical professionals in the local community, either on courses developed by the clinic or as a visiting speaker or tutor, may be one of the most effective ways of helping them to help children.

What are the needs of the community?

Calculations can be made from epidemiological findings which give some guidance, but they do not by themselves identify the wish for services by families and workers in primary care settings. Some attempts have been made to estimate need (Kurtz, 1992). One of the problems is that need is likely to be much greater than the supply of expertise available from the clinic. The simple conclusion must be that the major problems of child unhappiness and maladjustment will not be helped by one profession or in one setting alone. Collaboration with other agencies and professionals is essential. Providers of services are likely to be the only people who can identify gaps in the service and they have a duty to identify these and bring them to the attention of those responsible for funding. One way to identify gaps is to draw up a district profile. This can include all the settings where service should be being provided. Against this list of settings a second column can be filled in, stating whether the need in each setting is being met. In completing this second column it is important to consider other agencies that may be fulfilling the role. It could be that there are areas where collaboration could mean that relatively little input from the child psychiatry service can make a great difference.

What are the needs of the clinician?

The process of collaboration is not for the impatient, nor is it for those whose feelings of insecurity dictate a small set of secure ground rules for practice. Work in nonmedical settings often means that laboriously acquired skills are questioned or ignored. This can be difficult and discouraging. The clinician working in such settings can easily become professionally isolated. The inflated status of being a 'proper doctor' can rub off on the psychiatrist working in a hospital setting in a way that does not happen in community-based work. In fact, it is the community worker who has the harder job and who needs professional companionship and support. There is no place for the isolated child and adolescent psychiatrist working alone.

Who will pay?

This question is becoming increasingly relevant as cost containment of medical services becomes more and more central to government policy. This matter ties up with the need to demonstrate which services are effective. The work in schools described earlier in this chapter has been found effective but the research needed is expensive and difficult to carry out. In individual services there is a need to carry out audit activity and quality control. Audit is no less possible in child and adolescent services than in any other field and a start has been made.

Ethical aspects

The clinician in nonmedical settings may come up against ethical dilemmas and it is most important that these are confronted rather than avoided. Two connected dilemmas come to mind as specific to this field of work: advocacy and whistle-blowing.

The idea that political pressure is sometimes the most helpful intervention one can undertake arises from several strands. Calls from governments for cost containment have coexisted with many statutory changes in provision that, although imaginative and progressive, require resources that have not been forthcoming. The result is unacceptable cuts in staffing and services. In venturing from a clinic setting the clinician may be shocked by the lack of resources and the impossibility of carrying out the job in hand with what is available. He or she may also come under pressure, because of perceived high status and independence, to take on an advocacy role. This is not the place for a detailed treatment of the subject of advocacy, but this should not be taken as a denial of its importance. Careful balance is required, because the cry for more resources can block attempts to do the best with what is available.

Whistle-blowing refers to the professional's right and duty to expose gross abuses or exploitation of sick and handicapped people. The abuse may be an official cover-up of seriously inadequate services or the abuse of helpless people by members of staff. In exposing such injustices, it is important to seek advice and support and to gather firm evidence as far as possible if an allegation is to be made. It must be remembered that what is required is action that is most likely to solve the problem, not a public demonstration. There may be impartial complaints procedures that should be explored or appeal to a higher authority. It may be necessary to consider other options, such as informing and if necessary embarrassing officials whose duty it is to provide better services or seeking legal advice, when other options are ineffective.

In conclusion, it has only been possible to touch on some of the opportunities of work in nonmedical settings in the course of one chapter. Different countries and cultures will be at very different stages along the road to integration of services on the ground. The most basic message of this chapter should be that great benefits can be achieved by breaking down barriers between services and finding common ground in helping children. Child psychiatry services are in a good position to take a lead.

REFERENCES

Apter S.J. (1982) *Troubled Children, Troubled Systems*. Pergamon, New York.

Axline V. (1947) *Play Therapy*. Houghton Mifflin, Boston.

Barker R.G. (1968) *Ecological Psychology: Concepts and Methods for Studying the Environment of Human Behavior*. Stanford University Press, Stanford, CA.

Besag V. (1989) *Bullies and Victims in Schools*. Open University Press, Milton Keynes.

Bettelheim B. (1950) *Love is not Enough. The Treatment of Emotionally Disturbed Children*. Free Press, Glencoe, IL.

Caplan G. (1970) *The Theory and Practice of Mental Health Consultation*. Tavistock, London.

Court Report (1976) *Fit for the Future*. Report of the Committee on Child Health Services. Chairman: Court S.D.M. Her Majesty's Stationery Office, London.

Curtis M.J., Zins J.E. & Graden J.L. (1987) Prereferral intervention programs: enhancing student performance in regular educational settings. In: Maher C.A. & Zins J.E. (eds) *Psychoeducational Interventions in the Schools*, pp. 7–25. Pergamon Press, New York.

Dewey J. (1916) *Democracy and the School*. Macmillan, New York.

Dossetor D. & Nicol A.R. (1991) Community care of adolescents with developmental retardation: problems and proposals. *Health Trends*, **4**, 148–151.

Farrington D.P. (1977) The effects of public labelling. *British Journal of Criminology*, **17**, 112–125.

Farrington D.P., Osborn S. & West D.J. (1978) The persistence of labelling effects. *British Journal of Criminology*, **18**, 277–284.

Gallessich J. (1982) *The Profession and Practice of Consultation: A Handbook for Consultants, Trainees of Consultants and Consumers of Consultation Services*. Jossey-Bass, San Francisco, CA. (UK distributors: Marston Book Services, Oxford.)

Galloway D. (1985) Pastoral care and school effectiveness. In: Reynolds D. (ed) *Studying School Effectiveness*. Falmer Press, Lewes.

Galloway D., Martin R. & Wilcox B. (1985) Persistent absence from school and exclusion from school: the predictive power of school and community variables. *British Journal of Educational Research*, **11**, 51–61.

Gray G., Smith A. & Rutter M. (1980) School attendance and the first year of employment. In: Hersov L. & Berg I. (eds) *Out of School: Modern Perspectives in Truancy and School Refusal*. Wiley, Chichester.

Hall C.S. & Lindzey G. (1970) *Theories of Personality*. Wiley, New York.

Hazel N. (1981) *A Bridge to Independence*. Basil Blackwell, Oxford.

Her Majesty's Stationery Office (1991) *Working Together under the Children Act 1989*. HMSO, London.

Kolvin I., Garside R.F., Nicol A.R., Macmillan A., Wolstenholme F. & Leitch I.M. (1981) *Help Starts Here*. Tavistock, London.

Kurtz Z. (1992) *With Health in Mind. Mental Health Care of Children and Young People*. Action For Sick Children/South West Thames Regional Health Authority, London.

La Fontaine J. (1991) *Bullying: The Child's View*. Calouste Gulbenkian Foundation, London.

Lieberman S. (1979) *Transgenerational Family Therapy*. Croom Helm, London.

Maher C.A. & Zins J.E. (eds) (1987) *Psychoeducational Interventions in the Schools*. Pergamon, New York.

Mortimore P., Sammons P., Stoll L., Lewis D. & Ecob R. (1989) *School Matters. The Junior Years*. Open Books, London.

Nicol A.R., Willcox C. & Hibbert K. (1985a) What sort of children are suspended from school and what can we do for them? In: Nicol A.R. (ed) *Longitudinal Studies in Child Psychology and Psychiatry: Practical Lessons from Research Experience*. Wiley, Chichester.

Nicol A.R., Macmillan A., Kolvin I. & Wolstenholme F. (1985b) What sort of therapy should be given for what sort of problem? In: Nicol A.R. (ed) *Longitudinal Studies in Child Psychology and Psychiatry: Practical Lessons from Research Experience*. Wiley, Chichester.

O'Leary S.G. & O'Leary K.D. (1976) Behavior modification in the school. In: Leitenberg H. (ed) *Handbook of Behavior Modification*. Prentice Hall, Englewood Cliffs, NJ.

Olweus D. (1991) Bully/victim problems among schoolchildren: basic facts and effects of a school based intervention programme. In: Rubin K. & Pepler D. (eds) *The Development and Treatment of Child Aggression*. Erlbaum, Hillsdale, NJ.

Pilling D. & Kellmer Pringle M. (1978) *Controversial Issues in Child Development*. National Children's Bureau/Paul Elek, London.

Polsky H.W. (1962) *Cottage Six. The Social System of Delinquent Boys in Residential Treatment*. Russell Sage Foundation, New York.

Prendergast S. & Prout A. (1987) 'Smile at him when you ask for the books': transmitting sexuality in school. In: Booth T. & Coulby D. (eds) *Producing and Reducing Disaffection*. Open University Press, Milton Keynes.

Price R. (1976) Behaviour setting theory and research. In: Moos R.H. (ed) *The Human Context*. John Wiley, New York.

Redl F. (1966) *When We Deal With Children*. The Free Press, New York.

Redl F. & Wineman D. (1957) *The Aggressive Child*. Free Press, Glencoe, IL.

Reynolds D. (1991) School effectiveness and school improvements in the 1990s. *Newsletter: Association of Child Psychology and Psychiatry*, **13**, 5–9.

Rogers C.R. (1952) *Client Centred Therapy*. Houghton Mifflin, Boston, MA.

Rutter M., Maughn B., Mortimore P. & Ouston J. (1979) *Fifteen Thousand Hours*. Open Books, London.

Ryan T. & Walter R. (1985) *Making Life Story Books*. British Association of Adoption and Fostering, London.

Shaw M. & Hipgrave T. (1983) *Specialist Fostering*. Batsford, London.

Shaw M. & Hipgrave T. (1989a) Young people and their carers in specialist fostering. *Adoption and Fostering*, **13**(4), 11–17.

Shaw M. & Hipgrave T. (1989b) Specialist fostering 1988 — a research study. *Adoption and Fostering*, **13**(3), 17–21.

Sherif M. & Sherif C.W. (1956) *An Outline of Social Psychology*. Harper & Row, New York.

Spivack G. & Shure M.B. (1974) *Social Adjustment of Young Children*. Jossey Bass, San Francisco, CA.

Trieschman A.E., Whittaker J.K. & Brendtro L.K. (1969) *The Other 23 Hours*. Aldine, Chicago, IL.

Triseliotis J. (1989) Foster care outcomes: a review of research findings. *Adoption and Fostering*, **13**(3), 17–21.

Triseliotis J. & Russell J. (1984) *Hard to Place: The Outcome of Adoption and Residential Care*. Heinemann & Gower, London.

Wahler R.G., Berland R.M. & Coe T.D. (1979) Generalization processes in child behaviour change. In: Lahey B.D. & Kazdin A.E. (eds) *Advances in Clinical Child Psychology*. Plenum Press, New York.

Warnock Report (1978) *Special Education Needs. Report of the Committee of Enquiry into the Needs of Children and Young People. The Warnock Report*. Her Majesty's Stationery Office, London.

Chapter 62
Primary Care Psychiatry

M. Elena Garralda

WHY PRIMARY CARE PSYCHIATRY?

Contact with primary health care — also called general practice or family doctor service — is a common experience in childhood. Over the course of 1 year most children are taken by their parents to primary care health services and work with children has been estimated to occupy about a third of the doctor's time (Court Report, 1976; Hart, 1982). There are developmental trends reflecting the differential experience of illness at different ages, and young preschool children are taken to consultations more than older children. Thus, 90% of preschoolers but 64% of 5–14-year-olds will consult at least once a year and the average annual number of consultations of over 4 a year is also higher in preschoolers (Court Report, 1976).

The majority of children's consultations are for physical health problems, but a small proportion are for psychological or developmental problems and, as well as referring to child psychiatric and related services when necessary, attending to psychological and social issues is one of the tasks of the general practitioner.

In recent years there has been an increased emphasis on the importance of mental health problems in the primary care setting and it is now accepted that knowledge and expertise in the psychological and social aspects of child acute and chronic conditions should be part of the paediatric training required by primary care doctors (Joint Working Party, 1976). Child psychiatrists have also recognized a need to work more closely with medical and nursing colleagues, especially in primary care and in paediatrics (Black, 1983). Consultation to other professionals concerned with the care of children such as general practitioners is regarded as a responsibility of child psychiatrists, next to diagnostic assessment and treatment of children and families (Royal College of Psychiatry, 1986). This is in line with the conclusions of a World Health Organization working group, that the crucial question is not how the general practitioner can fit into the mental health services but rather how the psychiatrist can collaborate most effectively with primary medical services and reinforce the effectiveness of the primary physician as a member of the mental health team (Shepherd, 1982).

The role of primary care services is not confined to the treatment of childhood psychiatric morbidity; more ambitiously, they may be in a position to contribute to prevention (Royal College of General Practitioners, 1981). General practitioners tend to be consulted for physical, psychosomatic and psychological complaints at times of life change such as pregnancy, childbirth, the loss of a parent or the occurrence of a serious physical illness in a close relative. At these sensitive periods the behaviour of individuals and families will take a new form, and the general practitioner can have a role in ensuring that the changes that do occur allow as far as possible for subsequent healthy development and adaptation. As it relates to children, preventive action at times of life change include making active efforts to identify situations in which over-close mother–child relationships tend to develop: recognizing families in which children are being reared with little warmth and affection: preparing children for temporary separations to reduce distress; and so preventing potentially longer-term behaviour disturbances.

Epidemiological work in child psychiatry has underlined how important it is that primary care services attend to the psychiatric needs of children. Whilst psychiatric disorders are present in a substantial proportion (10–20%) of children in the general population, the majority of disturbed children are not under the care of psychiatric services (Rutter *et al.*, 1970; Offord *et al.*, 1987). Existing psychiatric services would not be able to attend to their needs without a major and unrealistic expansion. Moreover there are indications that it is the more severely affected children who tend to be referred, predominantly by general practitioners, to psychiatric services (Garralda & Bailey, 1988). The milder nature of the difficulties of nonreferred children makes it plausible that they will respond in the primary care setting to less sophisticated interventions than those provided in specialist child psychiatric services.

Further weight to the argument in favour of an increased role for general practice services in the promotion of mental health services for children comes from recent research findings (Garralda & Bailey, 1986a, 1987; Bowman & Garralda, 1983) showing that over and above those consultations where the presenting symptoms are primarily psychological in nature, psychiatric disorders and psychosomatic issues are of relevance as background or associated factors in a considerable additional number of somatic presentations.

This chapter will review the organization of primary care

services and research showing the contribution of psychiatric disorder to primary care work. Specific issues to be addressed are: how much does psychiatric disorder feature amongst children attending general practice clinics? To what extent is it recognized? How much of it presents somatically, and what is the contribution of life stress to a child's consultation in primary care? What should be done after recognition? What organization and training are needed to support it? What determines referral of children by general practitioners to child psychiatrists?

Consideration will be given to working models for psychiatric and primary care liaison, and to attempts that have been made at evaluating professional interventions in this setting. Primary care interventions for psychiatric problems in adults will be described as well as interventions that have been tested for parents and children, prior to outlining future directions in this area.

PRIMARY CARE SERVICES

Primary care services are delivered to children through three main avenues (Graham, 1982); (1) through general practitioners, family practitioners or general paediatricians; (2) by child health clinics, which often have a preschool as well as school medical service component; and (3) through hospital casualty departments, particularly in big cities (Jackson, 1980).

The organization of services varies from country to country. Graham (1982) reviewed these variations as they apply to European countries. They involve: (1) the degree to which primary services are delivered by family doctors and general practitioners rather than primary care paediatricians; (2) the extent to which preventive work is linked to general practitioner illness service; (3) the proportion of services which is delivered privately, on an insurance basis, or as part of centrally organized and funded national or regional health service; (4) the level of surveillance service provided; and (5) the degree of compulsion or inducement attached to preventive services.

In the UK, general practitioners deliver primary care services for the whole population. Their services are free; they are family services in that they attend to both children and adults; they are involved in assessment and in treatment and also in the prevention of ill health, including mental health. A general practitioner will attend to the needs of about 2000 patients in the local general population but some doctors work together with other doctors in health practices with correspondingly larger populations and with more opportunities for providing a number of primary care services, including the appointment of paramedical staff. Many general practices have nurses attached with a special commitment to supervise the development and health of under-5-year-olds (paediatric nurses or health visitors).

Primary care doctors are the major referring source to many secondary or hospital medical services. In the UK about 10% of attendances will result in such a referral, with variations depending upon the nature of the problem presented (Her Majesty's Stationery Office, 1986). General practitioners are major referring agents to child psychiatric clinics (Gath *et al.*, 1977; Steinberg *et al.*, 1981; Garralda, 1983). Some of these referrals are filtered by the hospital paediatric service and paediatricians also are common referring agents to child psychiatry (McFadyen *et al.*, 1991).

Because in countries other than the UK there is no such sharp differentiation between primary and secondary paediatric care, with many paediatricians providing a primary care-type service, this review, though primarily emphasizing primary care work, will also consider aspects of the psychiatric problems of children as they present in general paediatric clinics in as far as these are likely to represent primary care work in some countries.

CHILD PSYCHIATRIC MORBIDITY IN PRIMARY CARE WORK

The contribution of psychiatric disorders

Until recently there has been little detailed knowledge on the extent and nature of the contribution of psychological problems to children's consultations in primary care and on what determines the referral of children to psychiatric services. It is now becoming clear that child mental health problems are the main reason for consultation in many children presenting to general paediatric and hospital outpatient paediatric clinics and that, moreover, psychiatric disturbance is an associated problem in a considerably larger proportion of children presenting with somatic symptoms.

A number of surveys in various countries have documented that some 2–5% of children attend primary care or general paediatric clinics with child mental health problems as main presenting complaints (for example, anxiety, behavioural problems, overactivity; Coleman *et al.*, 1977; Jonsell, 1977; Bailey *et al.*, 1978; Goldberg *et al.*, 1979, 1984; Jacobson *et al.*, 1980; Starfield *et al.*, 1980; Garralda & Bailey, 1986a,b, 1989). Educational and social problems also feature as reasons for consultation (Curtis Jenkins, 1979; Starfield *et al.*, 1980).

However, Bailey *et al.* (1978) showed that over and above overt mental health presentations, psychosocial factors may contribute to a substantial additional number of consultations. They obtained information from general practitioners on presentations of children under the age of 16 years attending during the course of 1 month. Although the proportion of presenting psychological problems was low (3.5%), in as many as a quarter of attenders doctors identified what may be regarded as psychosomatic issues or psychological problems associated with physical presentations, for example wheezing probably due to stress.

More recently, systematic research interviews comparable to those used with general population epidemiological surveys have been employed to outline the nature of the associated psychological factors. This has involved obtaining information from parents and/or children in interviews separate from the primary care consultation to allow judgements to be made on the presence or absence of childhood psychiatric disturbance. These studies have found high rates of disorder in about a quarter of the children (Giel *et al.*, 1981; Garralda & Bailey, 1986b; Costello *et al.*, 1988) and the rates are probably slightly higher in countries with paediatrically staffed primary care services (Garralda & Bailey, 1989). Most disturbed children present at the surgery with somatic symptoms.

It has been shown that rates of disturbance among consulting children are higher than in the general population — a phenomenon which may be particularly evidenced in surgeries or general practices based in socially advantaged areas — and that disturbed children tend to feature particularly amongst frequent surgery attenders (Ryle, 1967; Garralda & Bailey, 1986a,b; Bowman & Garralda, 1993). In line with these results, general population studies have found disturbed children to be high users of medical services, although this may apply only to urban and not to rural areas (Richman *et al.*, 1982; Offord *et al.*, 1987).

Whilst most of the work above has been carried out on schoolchildren, there is evidence to suggest that emotional distress similarly contributes to somatic presentations of adolescents (Hawton *et al.*, 1982; Choquet & Menke, 1989).

It is of considerable practical and theoretical interest to know whether the increased tendency to consult of many disturbed children is mediated by links with certain physical symptoms. In older children there is little specificity in the range of presenting physical symptoms (Garralda & Bailey, 1986a,b). If not as a presenting symptom, however, a consistent associated feature is the global health indicator of energy level. Disturbed children are not only more commonly described as 'bounding with energy', but more interestingly perhaps, also as tired and lethargic. In line with this, mothers of disturbed school-age children who are frequent attenders to primary care tend to view their children as more lethargic, generally in poorer health and handicapped by their symptoms, when compared with nondisturbed children who are also frequent surgery attenders (Bowman F.M. & Garralda M.E., unpublished data).

There is more specificity in the type of psychiatric disorder than physical disorder in children attending medical settings. Although the range of common psychiatric disorders is seen, in contrast with general population findings, an excess is found of emotional over conduct disorders (Garralda & Bailey, 1986b, 1989; Costello *et al.*, 1988). Symptoms likely to discriminate between disturbed and nondisturbed children, particularly with paediatrically staffed clinics, are worrying, fears, irritability and problems in relationships, restlessness and over-activity. Other less frequently reported clinical features — namely, obsessional traits, worrying about health and school refusal — may be specifically related to a tendency to emphasize somatic or psychological symptoms as a response to stress or difficulty in these children. In general, enquiring about emotional symptomatology and levels of activity should be productive in facilitating the identification of childhood psychiatric disturbance in paediatric primary care settings (Garralda & Bailey, 1989).

Somatic symptoms in children thus appear to become prominent and lead to seeking medical attention more when they are part of frank neurotic disorders than in association with conduct disorders. This is probably linked to characteristic parental attitudes. Increased parent–child emotional closeness or involvement is described in emotional disorders, suggesting greater parent–child mutuality. This might make mothers more attuned to both emotional and physical symptoms, more anxious about them, more nurturing and likely to seek medical help when the child has emotional disorder rather than when he or she has a conduct disorder.

Existing research supports the notion that an important reason for disturbed schoolchildren to be taken to general practitioners is parental stress and concern which becomes focused on parenting and encompasses both health and control issues.

It must be stressed that most ill-health episodes in children, as in adults, do not lead to medical consultations (Wadsworth *et al.*, 1971; Banks *et al.*, 1975; Scambler *et al.*, 1981; Hart, 1982; Cunningham-Burley & Irvine, 1987), nor is the perceived severity of the symptom by the subject necessarily the determinant of consultations (Hannay & Maddox, 1975); social and other factors are of relevance also. Better maternal education is associated with an increased concern about detecting illness in children and taking precautions, with a tendency to perceive them as sick, and with an increased likelihood to consult (Mechanic, 1964; Campion & Gabriel, 1985). A perception of the child as particularly vulnerable, specially fragile or susceptible to physical illness and damage is also linked to early difficulties — for example, several neonatal complications — and to low scores on maternal well-being, marital problems and the presence of behaviour difficulties in the child (Perrin *et al.*, 1989; Bowman F.M. & Garralda M.E., unpublished work). These factors are likely to mediate the increased consultations of disturbed children.

Family stress is related to an increased tendency to consult for children's physical symptoms as well as to childhood psychiatric disturbance. Roghmann and Haggerty (1972) showed an association between stress in the family and over-utilization of the health services — interestingly for the children's but not for the mother's complaints. Tuch (1975) found that paramenstrual women were more apt to bring their children to paediatric clinics than women who were between periods and their children were considered to be less sick and with shorter illnesses. Mechanic (1964, 1979) noted that mothers who were under stress reported more illness symptomatology not only for themselves but also for their children and they were somewhat more likely to telephone the doctor concerning the children's health. Mothers with neurotic disorders report more days unwell in their children and take them to the doctor more than psychologically healthy mothers (Shepherd *et al.*, 1966a) and mothers who have been treated for 'nerves' are over-represented among those taking their children especially frequently to child health clinics (Woodward *et al.*, 1988).

Associations between family stress and childhood psychiatric disorder have similarly long been recognized and are a feature of disturbed children attending medical settings. These families experience psychosocial disadvantage with an excess of broken homes, marital discord and maternal mental health problems. However, it is striking that the stress reported by these mothers about their children appears to be more marked than the stress they feel about other associated problematic psychosocial areas (for example, marriage and finances): the problems these mothers experience in controlling their children seem to be of paramount importance to them. This can contribute to consultations by undermining their sense of confidence in parenting in relation to both the somatic and behavioural problems (Garralda & Bailey, 1986b, 1989).

This phenomenon may be regarded as an illustration of the well-known fact that the complaints that parents bring to clinics often have many and varied underlying motivations. Yudkin (1961) described this graphically in relation to children attending his paediatric clinics with coughs. The underlying concerns ranged from worries by mothers because of arguments with their mother-in-law on whether their children were properly looked after; concern that the children might have tuberculosis, like other members of the family; worry about asthma because of related family deaths; wanting the doctor to prescribe a convalescent holiday to gain some relief from the child; battles over children's feeding habits; and wanting support to keep the child at home in a school-refusing child. More recent work has shown that when mothers are questioned about the reasons for attending paediatric clinics, as many as a third relate fears and worries which become apparent only in detailed enquiry and which cannot be anticipated from the ostensible reason for seeking assistance (Bass & Cohen, 1982).

Psychosomatic problems

The presence of psychiatric disorder, defined as handicapping abnormalities of emotions, behaviour or relationships mostly involving emotional and to a lesser extent conduct disorders, is not sufficient to explain the range of problems presenting to general practitioners and paediatricians where psychosocial factors have a significant part to play. A useful complementary concept to explore these is that of psychosomatic presentations. These can be defined in either a broad or narrow sense. Defined in a broad way, they apply to any physical presentations where the doctor makes a clinical judgement that psychological or social factors are contributing in a significant way, for example aggravating the symptom. This broad definition is in keeping with the commonly held view amongst medical practitioners which assumes that psychological events can be relevant in the aetiology or in the maintenance of virtually any physical condition (Shepherd *et al.*, 1966a). The alternative and narrower definition of psychosomatic problems is that based on the assumption that certain somatic symptoms (for example, abdominal pains, headaches) are often an expression of the somatization of distress, and thus especially sensitive to the presence of psychological and social

stress: in other words, primarily psychosomatic in nature.

There are indications that both the narrow and broad definitions are useful to further our understanding of the contribution of psychological factors to medical help-seeking. Using a narrow definition, Starfield *et al.* (1980) found psychosomatic problems (e.g. children presenting with insomnia, headache, asthma, abdominal pain or other abdominal symptoms) in 8–10% of children attending various primary care facilities in the US. Interestingly, there is suggestive evidence that psychosomatic presentations may be found in excess at psychosocial transitional periods, that is, during the early elementary school years (particularly in boys) and in early adolescence (especially in girls), perhaps reflecting the stress of early learning performance for boys and of puberty in girls (Schor, 1986) and a special link between attendance for some types of psychosomatic symptoms and environmental stress.

Moreover these problems appear to be particularly prominent and persistent among children who are frequent users of school and other medical facilities. Lewis *et al.* (1977) found that about 15% of their sample of schoolchildren were high users of such services. These children tended to complain of headaches or stomachaches and they came from families with high medical service use. There was considerable continuity and when followed into adulthood these children still had a pattern of high use of medical services, an excess of stomach pains and headaches, as well as symptoms of depression and continuing academic problems (Lewis & Lewis, 1989).

The use of a broad psychosomatic definition results, not surprisingly, in higher rates of identification. When doctors are asked to note any physical presentations with associated or contributing psychological factors, for example asthma exacerbated by stress, such presentations are recorded for about a fifth of schoolchildren attending primary care and for as many as half in those countries with paediatrically staffed clinics, indicating a high degree of sensitivity and vigilance by many clinicians to these issues (Bailey *et al.*, 1978; Garralda & Bailey, 1987, 1990).

The presenting symptoms in these cases tend to be those regarded traditionally as having psychosomatic components (for example, aches and pains, incontinence, asthma and blackouts) but virtually any physical complaint is featured. The children do have an excess of emotional and behavioural symptoms, with mood changes and relationship problems; however, most do not suffer from psychiatric disorders and, as with the more narrowly defined psychosomatic problems described before, additional specific psychological issues appear to be relevant. These include child personality factors (fussiness, sensitivity); birth order effects (middle or young children); family ill health, probably sensitizing parents to health problems in the children; suggestions of close parent–child relationships; and family psychosocial stress. A special stress by mothers over parenting and concerns over schooling have particularly been noted in primary care settings, suggesting the relevance of high academic and behavioural expectations.

Different associated factors may be relevant according to

age and developmental level, with indications that behavioural and emotional symptoms have closer associations with psychosomatic presentations in younger children (aged 7–9 years), whereas in older preadolescent children a sensitive personality and high levels of concern about health in the family appear more relevant (Garralda, 1989a).

Addressing the psychosocial concerns of the families of children with psychosomatic presentations may have substantial consequences for medical service use. These children come from families with a high tendency to focus on health issues, as shown by the fact that they are high users of primary care and that the children themselves are given more hospital appointments, more referrals to specialist clinics and more follow-up appointments at the surgery than children with purely physical presentations (Garralda & Bailey, 1987).

Recognition of psychiatric disorders and psychosomatic problems in primary care

The recognition of child psychiatric disorders by physicians is obviously a prerequisite for primary care and paediatric services to become fully involved in the mental health promotion of children and adolescents, but the evidence indicates that recognition is often quite limited. The adult literature shows that between a quarter and a half of medical patients have psychiatric morbidity but the physician recognition rates are between 40 and 50% (Nabarro, 1984). Comparable rates are reported for doctor recognition of actual childhood psychiatric disturbance in primary care settings (Garralda & Bailey, 1986a; Chang et al., 1988; Garralda, 1989b), with indications that they are less likely to identify existing behaviour than somatic concerns by parents (Starfield & Borkowf, 1969). Doctors identify psychological problems associated with somatic presentations in a considerable percentage of children but the majority of these children fail to show psychiatric disturbance from research interviews, and conversely many disturbed children are not identified as such by doctors.

As in adult studies (Goldberg & Huxley, 1980), there is wide variation between doctors, with some not identifying any disturbed children at all. Identification rates are likely to be somewhat higher in paediatrically staffed clinics (Garralda, 1989b). However, considerably lower rates of identification of children's mental health problems by primary care workers (between 10 and 22%) have been reported in surveys carried out in developing countries (Giel et al., 1981).

Doctors' assessments tend to be highly specific but only moderately sensitive: thus they tend not to identify non-disturbed children as disturbed but they miss a considerable percentage of disturbed children. Recognition is higher when children have severe, as opposed to milder, problems and accordingly the more severely affected children are more likely to be referred to psychiatric services (Costello & Edelbrock, 1985; Garralda, 1989b). As well as severity, recognition may partly be linked to the child's age (more 7–14-year-olds), social circumstances (being on welfare, broken

homes) and with presenting symptoms (chronic conditions, digestive problems and ill-defined problems; Goldberg et al., 1979).

Child psychiatry teaching to medical students is still scarce in many medical schools (Cottrell, 1987) and many doctors will not have obtained any substantial teaching in child psychiatry. This is bound to be related to the low identification of the less severe, and therefore less obvious, psychiatric difficulties. At the simplest level, identification could be improved by clinicians systematically asking general questions of parents at the surgery as to the likelihood of the child having any behavioural or emotional problems (Costello et al., 1988), but the motivation for clinicians to recognize these problems should be enhanced by the development of appropriate and effective therapeutic strategies in primary care and in paediatric clinics.

Life changes and medical help-seeking in children

The established relationship between family stress and medical help-seeking raises the issue of the extent to which the presence of recent life changes or stresses overburdens the usual coping strategies by parents and determines consultations. The available data fail to provide an unequivocal answer to this question, perhaps due to the fact that for the most part research in this area has used life events inventories and these, popular as they are because of their simplicity and expediency, have important methodological short-comings.

Beutrais et al. (1982), from a survey study using a maternal life events inventory, concluded that events predicted accident frequency in preschool children and that they increased the risk for medical consultations for problems such as burns, accidental poisoning and gastroenteritis. However the time span for the occurrence of events in these mothers extended to 3 years, thus failing to address the issue of recent acute stresses, and in any case events were more closely linked to hospitalization than to general practice consultation.

Work especially focused on stresses occurring in the 3 months prior to consultation shows that events are increased but only in psychiatrically disturbed children and that a background of psychosocial disadvantage probably mediates the association. Bailey and Garralda (1987, 1990a) failed to find that life events, measured with a modified version of Coddington's Inventory, were increased among most children aged 7–12 years attending primary health care or general paediatric clinics but events were more common among psychiatrically disturbed children attending. Disturbed children had had an excess of life events in the 3 months prior to the consultation, particularly undesirable events with family arguments, and changes in parental financial and work status. Some of these events can be regarded as symptomatic of psychiatric disturbance or as a feature of the disadvantaged psychosocial background, such as broken homes, family discord, low socioeconomic status, known to be associated with childhood disorder.

Methodological problems become particularly limiting when

prepubertal children themselves are asked to report on recent life events, because of immaturities in memory recall involving timing of events, but even so, results are compatible with those obtained from adult inventories. Consistent with their parents' reports, children with psychiatric disorders attending general paediatric clinics report more undesirable and loss events. Intriguingly, attending these clinics is for most children associated with reporting fewer events, particularly few positive happenings — as if these children viewed their lives as less eventful and exciting (Bailey & Garralda, 1990b). The validity and significance of this need further elucidation.

The same applies to the associations between life changes and possible psychosomatic problems. In line with the clinical notion that psychosomatic problems are a reaction to stress, life events have been found to be increased among children presenting with recurrent functional pains (Greene *et al.*, 1985) and there is tentative evidence suggesting that stress involving bereavements or permanent separations is increased amongst children attending primary care clinics with psychosomatic problems (Bailey & Garralda, 1987).

Referrals to child psychiatry by primary care workers and paediatricians

Perhaps the area of clinical activity where there is currently most professional commonality between primary care doctors and child psychiatrists is the point of referral to child psychiatry.

About 1 in 10 children with psychiatric disturbances attending general practice are referred to child psychiatric clinics (Ryle, 1967; Garralda & Bailey, 1988) and a significant proportion of children seen in psychiatric clinics are referred by general practitioners (Steinberg *et al.*, 1981; Garralda, 1983). However, the factors that determine referrals are not well-understood. Whilst doctors' recognition of disturbance is obviously important (Goldberg *et al.*, 1979), so are parental attitudes because parents are usually responsible for seeking help. Earlier surveys emphasized parental attitudes towards the child's problems to such an extent that they made them appear more relevant to the referral than the actual disturbance in the child (Shepherd *et al.*, 1966b; Gath, 1972). More recent work has helped to clarify that both are important.

Most prepubertal schoolchildren referred to child psychiatric clinics by general practitioners have been found to be disturbed, whether from research interviews, general practitioners' estimates, or both (Gath, 1972; Garralda & Bailey, 1988; Bailey & Garralda, 1989). The factors determining referral by general practitioners in this age group are comparable to those that determine referral for the majority of children attending clinics and are therefore probably not specific. Referral is linked to high severity levels of disturbance (Langner *et al.*, 1974; Garralda & Bailey, 1988) and to male sex (Lurie, 1974; Gath *et al.*, 1977; Laclave & Campbell, 1986) and, consistent with the increase of boys among referred children, there is also an excess of antisocial symptoms, suggesting that maternal stress related to ability to control

antisocial disturbance in boys is a prominent factor related to referrals in this age group (Wolff, 1967).

The severity of disturbed referred chidren's difficulties appears often to be part of multiple psychosocial family stress, with unemployment, marital and mental health problems in the mothers, low support from their families, disadvantaged socioeconomic groups and high levels of stress felt by the parents in relation to parenting. The picture that emerges is one of parents distressed about antisocial behaviour in the children and concerned about their ability to control them in difficult socioeconomic circumstances. For primary care as well as for many other referrals, this highlights the clinically well-recognized need that psychiatric clinics identify ways of mobilizing the parents' resources for feeling in control of the children and have expertise in dealing with social problems, over and above providing expert advice on childhood psychiatric disturbance (Garralda & Bailey, 1988).

The link between disadvantaged socioeconomic status and primary care referrals found in recent studies is at variance with earlier reports and may reflect more general changes in child psychiatric practice and availability (Shepherd *et al.*, 1966b; Langner *et al.*, 1974; Gath *et al.*, 1977). Roghmann *et al.* (1982) noted an increase in utilization of child psychiatric services in the 1960s and 1970s in the US, with indications that this may have been more marked in the lower rather than the higher socioeconomic groups.

An interesting minority of children referred by general practitioners to child psychiatry are found not to be sufficiently disturbed to be considered as having psychiatric disorders. A detailed analysis of these children has documented that, contrary to expectations, these parents do not necessarily regard their children as disturbed any more frequently than non-referred psychologically healthy children, nor is the referral a 'ticket' for help with psychiatric morbidity in the parents. It seems likely from this work that, quite specifically, for a number of parents the difficulty they experience in controlling and coping with exuberant activity in somewhat rebellious children in the context of difficult economic and housing circumstances is an important reason for seeking help, but this is a finding needing replication (Garralda & Bailey, 1988).

Children are unlikely to be referred by general practitioners to psychiatric clinics unless they present at the surgery with overt psychological symptoms and it appears that, as well as the length of time the patient is known to the doctor (Goldberg *et al.*, 1979), a maternal request for referral is an important determinant in many cases (Bailey & Garralda, 1989), with the general practitioner's role in the process being often rather passive. On the basis of the little audit work which has been carried out in this area, most parents appear to be satisfied with the part played by the primary care doctor in the referral process, but this only applies to children who have been referred, and there may be many nonreferred children whose parents' attitudes toward general practitioners' helpfulness are more jaundiced.

PSYCHIATRIC INTERVENTIONS IN PRIMARY CARE

Remarkably little is known about the treatments available for psychiatrically disturbed children in primary care and paediatric settings.

Goldberg *et al.* (1984) asked primary care paediatricians in the US to indicate the treatment provided by them to children 7–14 years of age attending with diagnoses of mental health problems. Doctors reported providing some treatment for the majority of detected disturbed children and for nearly a third this was the only known source of care for the problem. More than half the disturbed children had sought help or had been referred to mental health services in the past and over one-third had had some treatment in these settings.

The most frequent treatment provided by paediatricians was supportive therapy or counselling (81%). Suggestions for environmental changes were also quite frequent (provided in half of the presentations). Drugs were prescribed for only 11% of affected children (amphetamines in 4%). Significantly, a diagnosis of attention deficit disorder in some primary care clinics in the US virtually predicts the use of methylphenidate and the lack of use of other treatment forms (Wolraich *et al.*, 1990).

Generally comparable results to those in the US emerged from a similar enquiry in the UK by Bailey *et al.* (1978). Half the families of children identified by general practitioners as having mainly psychological symptoms were provided with an opportunity at the clinic to ventilate the problem. A quarter were offered a psychotherapeutic intervention, defined as an attempt to make the patient or mother aware of motivations of which she was previously unaware. Although this was not documented, it is likely that a number of these children had had some contact with other services and that the general practitioner was not the sole source of help. In surveys of children referred to child psychiatric services, up to half have had the prior contact with other services for the child's mental health problems (for example school, paediatric, social services, or health visitors; Reder & Kraemer, 1980; Bailey Garralda, 1989).

A surprisingly high percentage of children (46%) were prescribed medication in the survey by Bailey *et al.*, when compared with the North American study by Goldberg *et al.* (1984) and with British surveys of children referred to psychiatric services where drugs are prescribed for about 1 in 10. It is possible that general practitioners prescribe more for the children whom they do not refer to child psychiatry, but even though there are suggestions of less prescribing in these cases in the UK (Bailey & Garralda, 1989), it remains common for British primary care doctors to prescribe psychotropic medication for children, particularly hypnotics and anti-depressants for enuresis (Adams, 1991; and see Chapter 51).

There is very little knowledge on the exact nature of the supportive and psychotherapeutic interventions provided by doctors in primary care and the relative importance given by them to reflective or behavioural approaches has not been systematically scrutinized, nor have the benefits in terms of parent satisfaction or symptom reduction. There is, however, some evidence that the style of the intervention affects parent satisfaction. Whilst the adult literature indicates that whether the doctor takes a sharing or a directive approach is of little consequence for psychiatric presentations (Savage & Armstrong, 1990), work with young mothers in health clinics has documented the superiority of statements by doctors reflecting empathy and encouragement over the simple expression of support (Wasserman *et al.*, 1984).

At the most basic level, being able to share the main concern with a doctor is obviously regarded as important by mothers. Early studies showed that this was not always achieved (Korsch & Negrete, 1972), in spite of the fact that patients' rapport and cooperation should thrive on specific instructions, expressions of trust in the mother's care-taking ability and offers of continuing interest. Unquestionably, attention to effective communication should be a priority if primary care services are to be able to attend to the mental health needs of children.

The professional skills additional to the recognition of disorder and family stress required for primary care to expand its mental health role will be similar to those recommended for general paediatrics (Graham & Jenkins, 1985). They include the following: (1) an awareness of relevant psychosocial factors, including an ascertainment of who is chiefly concerned about the child's symptoms, as well as skills in interviewing children with and without their parents; (2) advice on simple behavioural techiques for minor behavioural problems, for example tantrums, oppositional behaviour, sleep problems and bed-wetting; (3) counselling skills for families dealing with stress, which may include maternal depression and/or loss of confidence in the ability to parent, counselling skills over concerns over school, attainments and development; (4) a knowledge of family dynamics and ability to recognize deviations such as those involved in marital breakdown, over-concern and over-protection of the child as a result of family sensitization and worry about health issues; and (5) skills to determine when referral for a psychiatric opinion is called for.

Organization of services for child psychiatry and primary care liaison

There is hardly any published information on ongoing liaison schemes between child psychiatrists and primary care doctors. In contrast, adult psychiatrists have been actively involved in liaison work for several decades and the modes proposed by them provide useful guidance.

The history and current status of these developments have been comprehensively outlined by Mitchell (1983, 1985) and his account will be summarized here. Balint pioneered the field through general practitioner seminars focused on the relationship between the doctor and the patient using a psychodynamic perspective as the primary diagnostic and management tool. The general practitioners participating published subsequently what they had learned from the seminars.

By the 1980s 1 in 5 British psychiatric consultants surveyed indicated that they or their junior staff spent some time in a general practice setting (Strathdee & Williams, 1984) and other members of the psychiatric team have similarly reported attachment liaison schemes in general practice. Recently Subotsky and Brown (1990) have described a *child* psychiatric clinic in general practice.

The model now generally accepted as providing best for the needs of patients and fitting in with the actual organization of services is that of an attachment–liaison philosophy where the psychiatrist's task is to work alongside the general practitioner and other members of the primary care health team. A model where the psychiatrist replaces the family doctor as first-contact doctor may be more appropriate in countries where there is not a well-organized family doctor service and pending their promotion. The purposes of the psychiatric–general practice liaison can be defined as follows: (1) to help general practitioners identify psychiatric morbidity in the practice; (2) to assist them to deal directly with cases within their competence and skill; (3) to help define the best time for specialist referral; (4) for the specialist to take on the assessment and to initiate the joint care of referred patients and their relatives; and (5) to share with the primary care team the continuing burden of chronically sick patients and to explore the limits both of the doctor–family relationship and that of general practitioner and specialist in the setting of general practice.

A number of different ways of working together are discussed by Mitchell (1985) within the attachment–liaison style.

1 *Regular and coordinated home visits.* In children, as in adults, these would be reserved for the very few instances of children who are severely psychiatrically disturbed, with for example acute psychotic or neurotic disorders or severe psychosomatic problems, when attendance by the child to the psychiatric clinic is compromised by the child's or family's attitude or handicap.

2 *Shift of psychiatric clinics to health centres or surgeries.* Unless the psychiatrist has time to meet and talk to members of the primary care team, the advantages of this approach would be limited. However, apparently efficient liaison can be achieved with frequent brief face-to-face contacts between psychiatrists and general practitioners during the course of clinical work in heath centre clinics, and this may reduce the need for referral and admission to hospital (Darling & Tyrer, 1990). In child psychiatry it may lead to improved take-up rates (Cottrell *et al.*, 1988; Subotsky & Brown, 1990).

3 *Visits to health centres or surgeries to see selected patients.* This approach is time-consuming but it may lead to doctors learning how to use each other better.

4 *Regular group discussions* at the health centre or surgery, using either the Balint-type seminars in which the doctor–patient interaction is the focus of the discussion, or the mental health consultation model in which the task of the consultant as to help appreciate all the dimensions of the disorder in the patient.

5 *Conjoint consultations* in the health care centre or surgery to

be used with highly selected and prepared patients. In child psychiatry important links can at the same time be developed with health visitors and community child psychiatric nurses.

These models are not exclusive and have several elements in common which may be important for the success of the venture. These include regular and readily available face-to-face contacts between professionals, time for the growth of understanding of what each wants from the other, a common and acceptable meeting ground, and openness of communication based on mutual respect and trust. In addition, an important way to promote liaison between child and psychiatrists and primary care doctors is the participation of child psychiatrists in the postgraduate training of general practitioners, in order that basic information on assessment, handling and counselling skills can be taught.

A liaison approach appears particularly helpful for the needs of some children, for example those with developmental delays. The general practitioner may be in a good position to act as the coordinator for the high number of separate and sometimes disparate professional agencies involved. Without the opportunity for discussion of mental health aspects the psychiatric needs of these children may be left unmet (Dossetor & Nicol, 1990/1991).

As in adult psychiatry, there must be reservations about the value of these liaison schemes because of practical considerations. The ratio of child psychiatrists to general practitioners is such that only a minority of general practitioners in a health district could be accommodated. Moreover, child psychiatrists also consult with other services, for example education and social services. If such interventions are developed in child psychiatry they must be closely monitored and evaluated to help determine provision, and paramedical professionals from both services should be involved. These schemes will be shown to be worth doing if more children with psychiatric disorders are identified and successfully helped in the general practice setting and if it results in more efficient referrals to specialist clinics.

Sensitization of workers

A handful of reports in the literature describe packages designed to help with the identification or screening of mental health problems in primary care. Their effects remain to be evaluated but they represent first steps in the right direction.

Metz *et al.* (1976) added a psychosocial screening package to a paediatric screening evaluation for 4–16-year-olds in the US. The package yielded nine scores on potential difficulties in areas including the child's behaviour, family stress, cognitive and educational attainment and skills. In 4% of the children problems were identified and the paediatricians were supplied with a computer-printed report outlining the main problems. The authors concluded that screening children for serious psychological problems can be done routinely by paraprofessional personnel and the computerized method of reporting results was found to be popular with the paediatricians. The low identification rates reported, however, make it unlikely that this resulted in substantially increased sensitization by primary care workers to psychiatric difficulty.

More recently, simple, quick, easy-to-complete questionnaires have been developed or adapted to screen children and young people with behaviour problems, depression, and parent–teenager conflict in primary care and paediatric settings (Jellinek *et al.*, 1986; Schubiner & Robin, 1990; Scott Smith *et al.*, 1990). They have proved efficient in their purpose but their contribution towards helping clinicians attend successfully to the needs of disturbed children remains to be demonstrated.

The impersonal nature of questionnaires begs the question of how useful they will turn out to be for face-to-face interventions in paediatric consultations. It seems probable that the use of opening questions during the consultation will prove to be useful as an aid in the identification of psychiatric disorders (Costello *et al.*, 1988) and the exploration of the actual rather than the ostensible reason for seeking paediatric attention. This may well involve behavioural and emotional features in the child.

In Bass and Cohen's survey (1982) the use of opening questions proved productive. Paediatricians asked systematically and regardless of the presenting complaint and degree of anxiety the following questions: 'What are you concerned about?' followed by: 'Is there anything specific about the fever, the cold or infection that causes you concern?' The actual reasons for seeking attention identified for a third of attenders were family history of past similar disease; parents thinking the worst with fears of cancer or leukaemia; and family stress factors, themselves possibly associated with behavioural or emotional difficulties, such as authority figures causing the visit, death in the family, travel or moving, or absent parents.

Interesting initiatives exploring the potential of primary care to respond to mental health problems in children have been carried out in developing countries through World Health Organization-sponsored research. In one survey this involved the development of programmes for training primary care workers in the use of screening questionnaires containing information on growth as well as developmental milestones and home risk factors. This appeared to result in slow, neglected and retarded children being identified earlier and in the start of home stimulation programmes for these children. The use of home risk factors also helped in the identification of children in need and led to useful psychological interventions (Nikapota & Graham, 1986).

Giel *et al.* (1986) showed that with the use of a small set of simple questions it was possible to identify probably disturbed children and to increase awareness on the part of family care workers in various developing countries. Brief training sessions led to improved identification by the carers of severe psychiatric problems (for example, emergencies such as suicidal behaviour, depression or psychosis), neuropsychiatric problems (epilepsy and mental retardation) and in improved attitudes by them towards the management of cases.

Primary care interventions for adult psychiatric patients

Alongside the several decades of experience by adult psychiatry in developing links with primary care, controlled investigations on the effects of psychological intervention have been reported. In so far as psychiatric disorders in parents influence childhood disturbance, these interventions could have beneficial effects on the children's mental health.

Individual case descriptions indicate that brief psychotherapeutic interventions and advice can be successfully employed for patients with psychological problems in primary care. Group studies have also shown that minor affective disorders respond to brief counselling by general practitioners as well as to anxiolytic medication, and that substantial reductions in anxiety can be achieved in general practice with interventions by clinical psychologists using anxiety-management techniques (Gath & Catalan, 1986). These techniques include problem definition, record-keeping and symptom monitoring, setting homework, reducing medication and the identification of helpful strategies and preparation for the future. They also involve learning how to control symptoms by relaxation and distraction; controlling upsetting thoughts and panic management; and dealing with avoidance and increasing confidence. Minor affective disorders with predominant anxiety in adults may therefore become treatable largely by psychological means with little recourse to medication and without excessive demands on the general practitioner's time. Parental mastery in dealing with anxiety situations could influence the children's ability to do so too.

Other techniques have been employed of potential relevance for child mental health. There is, for example, evidence to indicate that supportive care by social workers attached to general practice gives valuable clinical and social benefits to patients with neurotic disorders (Wilkinson, 1982; Corney, 1987). In Corney's study, the social worker's intervention was mainly concerned with practical tasks — counselling alone took up a quarter of her time. Depressed women attending general practice for treatment were shown to benefit if the condition involved acute exacerbations of chronic disorders, if they had poor relations with their partners, and if they had practical problems for which they were motivated to seek help. Women with more acute conditions did not benefit. Maternal health problems and marital discord are linked to childhood psychiatric disturbance and these interventions could be of benefit for children's mental health.

More specifically, the findings that counselling mothers with postnatal depression by health visitors in general practice can lead to substantial improvements should have implications for the mother's ability to respond to the child and to promote his or her health and psychological development (Brown & Davidson, 1978; Cogill *et al.*, 1986; Holden *et al.*, 1989; Puckering, 1989; Murray *et al.*, 1991).

Psychiatric interventions for adults in primary care can be of use not simply for patients presenting with conspicuous or overt psychiatric symptoms but also for those with hidden psychiatric morbidity. Johnstone and Goldberg (1976) showed that case detection and treatment at the surgery for subjects with psychiatric morbidity which had not been manifest to the doctor prior to the study resulted in noticeable symptomatic improvements, particularly in the short term. Replication of this work for a childhood population is called for.

Interventions for parents and children

Controlled studies on the effectiveness of counselling in primary care — whether for interactional, behavioural or emotional disorders in children — or, from the primary prevention perspective, more ambitious efforts such as counselling and education for parenthood in pregnancy around the time of delivery pose formidable technical difficulty and have attracted few investigators.

Most of the work reported so far has important methodological limitations and cannot be regarded as conclusive, but it suggests avenues for future and more systematic exploration.

Interventions with mothers of young children

Primary care paediatric services have an important role in disseminating information about health, child development and behaviours, and this probably becomes most apparent with mothers of young children because of their higher frequency of service use.

In the British study by Cunningham-Burley and Irvine (1987), mothers were found to cope with most episodes of ill health in the children at home. These mothers often said that when attending primary care services it did not worry them if the doctor did not give them a prescription provided that they received assurance and learned from advice provided during the consultation. The authors of the survey felt that plainly some of the mothers' home nursing activities had been taught to them by general practitioners.

This makes it crucial that serious attention is given to primary care workers being taught appropriate techniques to deal with behaviour and developmental problems in children that they can disseminate in clinics. The importance of this is underlined by the fact that different professionals (for example, general practitioners, clinical medical officers and community paediatricians) have been shown to give conflicting advice (Jewel & Bain, 1985), probably reflecting insufficient emphasis in training.

Further reports, mainly from the US, testify to the educational potential of primary care services. McCune *et al.* (1984) enquired from parents attending a child health provision clinic about their knowledge of child development. The main sources parents identified as helpful in relation to child-rearing issues were health professionals (paediatricians and nurses), relatives and printed media (books and magazines). Interestingly, large numbers of parents indicated that they used television as a source of information but gave it as of low ranking in helpfulness. Parents often said that they would welcome discussion with paediatricians on specific aspects of child development by scheduling extra visits to the clinic, and they also indicated that educational pamphlets were useful. When asked what questions about raising the child they would like to talk to the paediatrician about, given the available time, half responded to this question and the majority of the answers were concerned with psychosocial issues. The authors identified differences in mothers' knowledge about child development, which were linked to the age of the parent, educational level and income. This difference needs to be recognized when active steps are taken to promote the educational role of the primary care services.

A handful of reports have documented the effects of educative/supportive interventions. In a controlled study, Gutelius *et al.* (1977) described an intensive child health supervision programme with emphasis on providing counselling and anticipatory guidance to the mothers of 47 normal first-born black infants from low-income families. There was a nonintervention comparison group. The intervention consisted of contact with the mothers by a project nurse starting in the seventh month of pregnancy, with subsequent contact by the nurse and by a paediatrician at well-being clinics. There were also group sessions and the mothers were given direct advice about their personal life. There were behavioural benefits during the first 6 years of life, with positive effects also found in diet and eating habits, toilet training and in child-rearing practices. The results showed that beneficial effects can result from systematic counselling in primary care settings but they are in need of replication.

Cullen (1976), a general practitioner practising in a rural community in Australia, arranged to see the mothers of 124 children for a series of 12 20–30-minute interventions spaced at intervals of 3 months in the first year and at 6 months in the succeeding 4 years of the child's life. Child-rearing concepts and attitudes were explored. When compared with a control nonintervention group of children, those in the index group showed fewer behavioural problems at 6 years of age from mothers' reports and the children themselves expressed more positive feelings towards their mothers. However, a greater number were late for school and boys were more excitable and hard to control. The author wondered whether the confidence of the boys' mothers in the intervention group might have been affected by too cautious an approach to disciplining problems. The study did demonstrate that, through regular supervision, doctors may be able to influence parental actions and their children's behaviour and feelings, and that they may foster a good long-term relationship between physicians and parents, but it also highlighted possible deleterious effects.

Other initiatives have addressed the possibility of influencing special child-rearing practices, for example toilet training, during well visits of mothers with their children, with encouraging but uncontrolled results (Brazelton, 1962).

Over and above primary prevention, especially appropriate in primary care paediatrics are interventions which target presentations combining both physical and behavioural symptoms. Furnell and Dutton (1986) saw 29 children referred to paediatricians with prolonged histories of toddler's diarrhoea and associated behavioural difficulties and offered a treatment consisting of counselling for parental anxiety regarding environmental stress and training and support for parents in consistent and effective management of childhood behaviour, using operant conditioning principles. The diarrhoea stopped in two-thirds of the children with a mean 2 months' treatment and the mothers' ratings on the children's behaviour similarly improved significantly; the improvement was maintained at 6-month follow-up. This was an uncontrolled study but was interesting in showing a reduction in parallel somatic and behavioural symptoms with counselling and behavioural management.

There has been interest in extending the use of behavioural techniques to help parents of preschool children deal with behavioural problems and sleep difficulties in primary care. Unfortunately, attempts at training specialist nurses or health visitors in these techniques, although popular with the health visitors themselves, have had disappointing results in terms of child behaviour change.

A rather different way of approaching the issue of confidence in parenting was documented by Benson and Turk (1988) in their study on the effects of group therapy for mothers who were frequent attenders to primary care services for themselves and for their children. The authors reasoned that the frequency of attendance would be related to maternal anxiety and depression and that both these symptoms and attendance rates would decrease with group therapy aimed at encouraging discussion of feeling and coping strategies. It was not possible for this study — based on a small group of less than 10 index mothers and controls — to provide direct evidence for the effectiveness of group therapy, but whatever the mechanisms, there was a reduction in consultation rates, suggesting better coping strategies.

It can be concluded that generally educative or therapeutic interventions, not necessarily focused on any particular treatment modality but involving ongoing support, advice and guidance with child-rearing in well-being clinics, may lead to favourable behavioural outcomes in young children, but these reports are in clear need of methodological refinement and replication.

Interventions with schoolchildren and adolescents

No adequately controlled studies have been reported of psychiatric intervention for schoolchildren and adolescents but there have been pilot and anecdotal accounts worthy of note.

In a survey already described, Metz *et al.* (1976) screened American children for psychological problems as part of a paediatric evaluation. Although only 4% were identified as at risk psychosocially, the mothers of 15% expressed a wish to speak to a mental health professional. Requests were common for boys, mixed racial groups and for children with established psychiatric disorders.

A psychiatric social worker in the Department of Pediatrics telephoned the parents who had indicated a desire for an appointment and was able to reach a third of them. Half of these appeared for the interview, virtually all with significant problems, but the need or desire for further assistance varied considerably. This could have been due to the fact that further appointments would have entailed an expense for most of the patients under their health plan contract, but the overall take-up rate was disappointing.

More encouraging were the results of a pilot study by Coverley *et al.* (1991) in the UK. The mothers of frequently attending 7–12-year-olds who were found from psychiatric interviews to be psychiatrically disturbed were offered a psychiatric consultation at a primary care centre. One-third of these children had at some point in the past been in contact with psychiatric services but at the time of the study only 3% were under psychiatric care and 6% had had recent contact with general practitioners because of psychological symptoms. The consultations consisted of a single interview with a child psychiatrist and they were structured in such a way that, if successful, they could be taught to and used by general practitioners. They aimed to promote parental confidence in dealing with difficult behaviour through clarification of the problems, empathic and encouraging remarks, and advice on management. Two-thirds of the 26 mothers offered treatment attended for the intervention and of these, a further two-thirds reported it to have been markedly helpful at a 3-month follow-up. The main areas of improvement reported by the parents were in the child's emotional or behavioural problems, in the parents' confidence in managing the problem, and concern about the problem. Even though in this small sample group there was no consistent pattern in behavioural questionnaire score changes, the results are sufficiently encouraging to make future more rigorous investigations of interest.

The possible benefits when general practitioners intervene for educational problems were described by Curtis Jenkins (1979). A general practitioner himself, he assessed 24 children seen over a 14-month period primarily for failing at school. With the aid of a screening test on language and educational skills he was able to clarify the nature of the children's difficulties and to differentiate, for example, problems of deafness from mental handicap. He felt this resulted in reduction of anger and puzzlement in many parents and in remedial help for the children, sometimes after contact between the doctor and the schools. This report probably represents an isolated initiative, but given the link between educational concerns in parents and psychosomatic presentations in preadolescent children, enquiry about educational achievements and aspirations could well reveal stresses related to somatic presentations.

An experimental child-initiated system provided for children aged 5–12 by school nursing services was documented by Lewis *et al.* (1977). Children in school were told that whenever they had a health problem that they could not solve they were to indicate this to the school nurse. The child was then involved in describing ways of coping with the problem and the choice of solutions and, when necessary, assistance was provided in formulating options. Reasonable decisions were reinforced and there was considerable rehearsal and stimulation, for example, 'Next time, what can you do?' The system proved successful in encouraging children to initiate visits to the school nursing service. During a 2-year period most children visited the service and a small percentage of high users (15% of all children) accounted for over half of all visits. High utilization was associated with females, more affluent social class, only or youngest children, and with higher use of paediatric services by the children and of mothers' use of care. Significant reductions in perceived susceptibility by children to illness were found among regular users, and the value of self-care as a means of maintaining health and in the treatment of minor problems increased significantly in most age groups. However, no changes in the patterns of use of medical services were observed and the ultimate usefulness of this intervention remains uncertain.

The primary care setting may prove promising as a resource for promoting mental health in adolescents. In a preliminary investigation, a general practitioner invited youngsters registered at the practice to attend his surgery for a general health discussion. Following a single-letter approach, over half the youngsters attended and this resulted in consultations found by the doctor to be both enjoyable and productive, with effective discussion of general health issues and also of personal problems (Donovan & McCarthy, 1988).

FUTURE DIRECTIONS

The existing evidence indicates that the question is clearly not one of whether, but how, primary care psychiatry should be implemented. Many parents prefer to take their child with emotional behaviour problems to the family doctor or a paediatrician, rather than the psychiatrist (Lurie, 1974). Youngsters with emotional distress may not be ready to discuss their personal problems, but consult doctors and nurses for physical health care more than nondisturbed youngsters (Choquet & Menke, 1989). Doctors usually see themselves as responsible for psychosocial problems, including giving advice to parents on bringing up children, although this is probably more the case for older than for younger doctors (Whitfield & Bucks, 1988).

The future of primary care is most likely to be informed by the development in parallel of educational, clinical and research initiatives.

Education

Changing attitudes and increasing knowledge by primary care workers about mental health problems and services must remain a priority for health educators and child psychiatrists alike, so that disturbed children can be identified, treated and referred when appropriate.

The child psychiatric teaching in medical schools remains variable and often limited. However, academic departments of child psychiatry are now being developed in various countries and this should contribute significantly to increasing and improving the future exposure of medical students to child psychiatry concepts. Many future family doctors will start their training with some degree of sensitization to these problems. Child psychiatrists should be in a position to contribute in an important way to teaching communication skills with parents and children so that parental concerns, stresses and understanding of difficulties can be explored efficiently.

Child psychiatrists may profitably take an active part in postgraduate training programmes for family doctors, not simply to sensitize them but to impart knowledge on strategies to help with difficulties. The development of a positive therapeutic attitude should be complemented by learning specific techniques aimed at promoting optimal parenting and the alleviation of suffering and handicap in children. Child psychiatric involvement in ongoing postgraduate courses and the setting-up of courses for paramedical primary care staff, for example for health visitors, should be further educational target areas.

Liaison and attachment schemes

Promising attachment schemes by child psychiatrists in general practice have now been described. Further extension, generalization and documentation of attachment liaison initiatives similar to those outlined by Mitchell (1983; 1985) for adults should lead to improved mutual understanding between specialists and primary services.

For adult patients, nonpsychiatrist mental health workers (community nurses, social workers, clinical psychologists and counsellors) already provide most mental health care in primary care settings (Wilkinson, 1988). The development of such attachments in relation to child mental health also seems highly desirable.

Work to increase recognition of morbidity by primary care workers

Primary care recognition of psychiatric difficulties in children can be increased by the use of opening questions introducing the possibility that psychiatric symptoms or psychosomatic issues may be playing a part in consultations. The use of questionnaires may also be helpful. Comparative work needs now to be carried out to examine the relative merit and usefulness of different techniques before the use of any one can be widely recommended.

Research into psychiatric morbidity in primary care

Most of the research so far has addressed the problems of school-age children and little is known about the precise way in which psychiatric disturbance contributes to the presentations of young preschoolers and of adolescents. In these age groups the pattern of consultation and of psychiatric morbidity is quite different to that of schoolchildren and it cannot be assumed that the nature of the psychiatric difficulties or of the psychosomatic associations will be comparable. Moreover, the types of interventions to be instituted would be quite different, with primary emphasis on parental advice and support in young children, but work directly with the adolescent in the older age group. Further research in this area is needed to guide future educational and clinical developments.

Psychiatric interventions in primary care

Many of the interventions described in this chapter have consisted of isolated initiatives and have lacked sufficient methodological rigour to allow more than tentative conclusions. It is important that they are replicated and carefully documented. Over and above the use of nonspecific therapeutic techniques such as encouragement, empathy and support, which are particularly appreciated by parents, a number of areas can be highlighted for further development:

1 Primary care as a setting for the promotion of child mental health through educational guidance on emotional and social child development milestones and on the child-rearing and parenting attitudes and techniques that maximize them.

2 Attention to postnatal and other types of maternal depression, taking into account the potential deleterious effects on parenting.

3 Informed discussion with parents of disturbed children on the nature of any existing childhood psychiatric or psychosomatic presentations, as well as empathic encouragement to help parents gain a sense of control over these problems through understanding and through the use of corrective parenting techniques.

4 Setting-up mothers' groups to clarify the nature of the concerns that lead to excessively frequent attendance for children's difficulties.

5 Setting-up of services to provide children with anxiety-management techniques.

6 Counselling for distressed adolescents.

Policy measures may be required for primary care to take a more active role than at present in the promotion of child mental health. However, changes to current practice may not be readily implemented without some supportive clinical and research evidence. Two decades after Shepherd *et al.* (1966a) demonstrated the crucial role of general practitioners in the provision of mental health care for adults, their findings have been consistently replicated, yet there has been slow progress in upgrading psychiatric training for family doctors. Proposals to increase funding for mental health services in primary care are unlikely to be well-received unless they include mechanisms to reduce payments in other sectors of the health service (Eisenberg, 1988), and will prove difficult to implement at times of financial stringency. This makes it the more pressing that increasingly sound research-based arguments which take into account costs as well as the potential influence of psychiatric interventions for medical help-seeking and general physical well-being are used as a stimulus to increase mental health promotion activities in general practice clinics.

An important task for research is that of operationalizing mental health promotion and therapeutic techniques, targeting them appropriately, taking into account developmental aspects in controlled studies, and the examination of both short-term and long-term effects. From a public health perspective this may be one of the most important tasks for child psychiatry research and practice of the future.

REFERENCES

Adams S. (1991) Prescribing of psychotropic drugs to children and adolescents. *British Medical Journal*, **302**, 217.

Bailey D. & Garralda M.E. (1987) Children attending general practice: a study of recent life events. *Journal of the American Academy of Child and Adolescent Psychiatry*, **26**, 858–864.

Bailey D. & Garralda M.E. (1989) Referral to child psychiatry: parent and doctor motives and expectations. *Journal of Child Psychology and Psychiatry*, **30**, 449–458.

Bailey D. & Garralda M.E. (1990a) Psychological screening for the paediatrician. *Journal of the American Academy of Child and Adolescent Psychiatry*, **29**(5), 838–839.

Bailey D. & Garralda M.E. (1990b) Life events: children's reports. *Social Psychiatry and Psychiatric Epidemiology*, **25**, 283–288.

Bailey V., Graham P. & Boniface D. (1978) How much child psychiatry does a general practitioner do? *Journal of the Royal College of General Practitioners*, **28**, 621–626.

Banks M.H., Beresford, S.A.A., Merrell D.C., Waller J.J. & Watkins C.J. (1975) Factors influencing demand for primary medical care in women aged 20–44 years. A preliminary report. *International Journal of Epidemiology*, **4**, 189–195.

Bass L.W. & Cohen R.L. (1982) Ostensible versus actual reasons for seeking pediatric attention: another look at the parental ticket of admission. *Pediatrics*, **70**, 870–874.

Benson P. & Turk T. (1988) Group therapy in a general practice setting for frequent attenders: a controlled study of mothers with pre-school children. *Journal of the Royal College of General Practitioners*, **38**, 539–541.

Beutrais A.I., Fergusson D.M. & Shannon F.T. (1982) Life events and childhood morbidity: a prospective study. *Pediatrics*, **70**, 935–940.

Black D. (1983) Are child guidance clinics an anachronism? *Archives of Disease in Childhood*, **58**, 644–645.

Bowman F.M. & Garralda M.E. (1993) Psychiatric morbidity among children who are frequent attenders in general practice. *British Journal of General Practice*, **43**, 6–9.

Brazelton T.B. (1962) A child-oriented approach to toilet training. *Pediatrics*, **29**, 121–128.

Brown G.W. & Davidson S. (1978) Social class, psychiatric disorder of mother, and accidents to children. *Lancet*, **i**, 378–381.

Campion P. & Gabriel J. (1985) Illness behaviour in mothers with young children. *Social Science and Medicine*, **20**, 325–330.

Chang G., Warner V. & Weissman M.M. (1988) Physicians' recognition of psychiatric disorders in children and adolescents. *American Journal of Diseases in Childhood*, **142**, 736–739.

Choquet M. & Menke H. (1989) Suicidal thoughts during early adolescence: prevalence, associated troubles and help-seeking behavior. *Acta Psychiatrica Scandinavica*, **81**, 170–177.

Cogill S.R., Caplan H.L., Alexandra H., Mordecai Robson K. & Kumar R. (1986) Impact of maternal postnatal depression on cognitive development of young children. *British Medical Journal*, **292**, 1165–1167.

Coleman J.V., Patrick D.L. & Baker S.M. (1977) The mental health of children in an HMO program. *Behavioral Pediatrics*, **91**, 150–153.

Corney R.H. (1987) Marital problems and treatment outcome in depressed women. A clinical trial of social work intervention.

British Journal of Psychiatry, **151**, 652–659.

Costello E.J. & Edelbrock C.S. (1985) Detection of psychiatric disorders in pediatric primary care: a preliminary report. *Journal of the American Academy of Child Psychiatry*, **24**, 771–774.

Costello E.J., Costello A.J. Edelbrok C., Burns B.J., Dulcan M.K., Brent D. & Janiszewski S. (1988) DSM-III disorders in pediatric primary care: prevalence and risk factors. *Archives of General Psychiatry*, **45**, 1105–1116.

Cottrell D. (1987) A survey of undergraduate teaching of child and adolescent psychiatry in the United Kingdom. *Bulletin of the Royal College of Psychiatrists*, **11**, 265–268.

Cottrell D., Hill P., Walk D., Dearnaley J. & Ierotheou A. (1988) Factors influencing non-attendance at child psychiatry out-patient appointments. *British Journal of Psychiatry*, **152**, 201–204.

Court Report (1976) *Fit for the Future*. HMSO, London.

Coverley C.T., Garralda M.E. & Bowman F. (1991) A short psychiatric intervention in general practice: a pilot outcome study. Poster presented at the Spring Meeting of the Child Psychiatry Section of the Royal College of Psychiatrists, London, March 1991.

Cullen K.J. (1976) A six-year controlled trial of prevention of children's behavior disorders. *Journal of Pediatrics*, **88**, 662–666.

Cunningham-Burley S. & Irvine S. (1987) Practice research. 'And have you done anything so far?' An examination of lay treatment of children's symptoms. *British Medical Journal*, **295**, 700–702.

Curtis Jenkins G.H. (1979) The identification of children with learning problems in general practice. *Journal of the Royal College of General Practitioners*, **29**, 647–651.

Darling C. & Tyrer P. (1990) Brief encounters in general practice: liaison in general practice psychiatry clinics. *Psychiatric Bulletin*, **14**, 592–594.

Donovan C.F. & McCarthy S. (1988) Is there a place for adolescent screening in general practice? *Health Trends*, **20**, 64.

Dossetor D. & Nicol R. (1990/1991) Community care for adolescents with developmental retardation: problems and proposals. *Health Trends*, **4**, 148–151.

Eisenberg L. (1988) The relationship between psychiatric research and public policy. *British Journal of Psychiatry*, **153**, 21–29.

Furnell J.R.G. & Dutton P.V. (1986) Alleviation of toddler's diarrhoea by environmental management. *Journal of Psychosomatic Research*, **30**, 283–288.

Garralda M.E. (1983) Child psychiatric emergencies: a research note. *Journal of Child Psychology and Psychiatry*, **24**, 261–267.

Garralda M.E. (1989a) Psychosomatic presentations to general paediatric clinics: developmental aspects. Paper presented at the Child Psychiatry European Research Meeting on Developmental Psychopathology, Marburg, 1989.

Garralda M.E. (1989b) Mental health problems in children referred to general paediatric clinics. Paper presented at the Research Conference on Mental Health Services for Children and Adolescents in Primary Care Settings. Newhaven, CT. June 1989.

Garralda M.E. & Bailey D. (1986a) Psychological deviance in children attending general practice. *Psychological Medicine*, **16**, 423–429.

Garralda M.E. & Bailey D. (1986b) Children with psychiatric disorders in primary care. *Journal of Child Psychology and Psychiatry*, **27**, 611–624.

Garralda M.E. & Bailey D. (1987) Psychosomatic aspects of children's consultations in primary care. *European Archives of Psychiatry and Neurological Sciences*, **236**, 319–322.

Garralda M.E. & Bailey D. (1988) Child and parental factors related to the referral of children to child psychiatry. *British Journal of Psychiatry*, **153**, 81–89.

Garralda M.E. & Bailey D. (1989) Psychiatric disorders in general paediatric referrals. *Archives of Disease in Childhood*, **64**, 1727–1733.

Garralda M.E. & Bailey D. (1990) Paediatric identification of psycho-

logical factors associated with general paediatric consultations. *Journal of Psychosomatic Research*, **34**, 303–312.

Gath D. (1972) Psychiatric services for children. In: Mandelbrote B.M. & Gelder M.G. (eds) *Psychiatric Aspects of Medical Practice*, pp. 138–160. Staple Press, London.

Gath D. & Catalan J. (1986) The treatment of emotional disorders in general practice: psychological methods versus medication. *Journal of Psychosomatic Research*, **30**, 381–386.

Gath D., Cooper B., Gattoni F. & Rockett D. (1977) *Child Guidance and Delinquency in a London Borough*. Oxford University Press, Oxford.

Giel R., de Arango M.V., Climent C.E., Harding T.W., Ibrahim H.H.A., Ladrido-Ignacio L., Srinivasa Murthy R., Salazar M.C., Wig N.N. & Younis Y.O.A. (1981) Childhood mental disorders in primary health care: results of observations in 4 developing countries. *Pediatrics*, **68**, 677–683.

Giel R., Harding T.W., ten Horn G.M.H.H., Ignacio L.L., Srinivasa Murthy R., Sirag A.O., Suleiman M.A. & Wig N.N. (1986) The detection of childhood mental disorders in primary care in some developing countries. In: Henderson A.S. & Burrows G. (eds) *Handbook of Studies on Social Psychiatry*. Oxford University Press, Oxford.

Goldberg D.P. & Huxley P. (1980) *Mental Illness in the Community — The Pathway to Psychiatric Care*. Tavistock, London.

Goldberg I.D., Regier D.A., McInerny T.K., Pless I.B. & Roghmann K.J. (1979) The role of the pediatrician in the delivery of mental services to children. *Pediatrics*, **63**, 898–909.

Goldberg I.D., Roghmann K.J., McInerny T.K. & Burke J.D. (1984) Mental health problems among children seen in pediatric practice: prevalence and management. *Pediatrics*, **73**, 278–292.

Graham P. (1982) Child psychiatry in relation to primary health care. *Social Psychiatry*, **17**, 109–116.

Graham P. & Jenkins S. (1985) Training of paediatricians for psychosocial aspects of their work. *Archives of Disease in Childhood*, **60**, 777–780.

Greene J.D., Walker L.S., Hickson G. & Thompson J. (1985) Stressful life events and somatic complaints in adolescents. *Pediatrics*, **75**, 19–22.

Gutelius M.F., Kirsch A.D., MacDonald S., Brooks M.R. & McErlean T. (1977) Controlled study of child health supervision: behavioral results. *Pediatrics*, **60**, 294–304.

Hannay D.R. & Maddox E.J. (1975) Incongruous referrals. *Lancet*, **ii**, 1195–1196.

Hart C.R. (1982) The quality of child care. In: Hart C.R. (ed) *Child Care in General Practice*, 2nd edn., pp. 3–21. Churchill Livingstone, London.

Hawton K., O'Grady J., Osborn M. & Cole D. (1982) Adolescents who take overdoses: their characteristics, problems and contacts with helping agencies. *British Journal of Psychiatry*, **140**, 118–123.

Her Majesty's Stationery Office (1986) *Morbidity Statistics from General Practice 1981–1982. Third National Study*. Government Statistical Service. HMSO, London.

Holden J.M., Sagovsky R. & Cox J.L. (1989) Counselling in a general practice setting: controlled study of health visitor intervention in treatment of postnatal depression. *British Medical Journal*, **298**, 223–226.

Jackson J. (1980) Paediatric primary care in Inner London. *Journal of the Royal College of General Practitioners*, **30**, 520–528.

Jacobson A.M., Irving D.G., Goldberg I.D., Burns B.J., Hoeper E.W., Hankin J.R. & Hewitt K. (1980) Diagnosed mental disorder in children and use of health services in four organized health care settings. *American Journal of Psychiatry*, **137**, 559–565.

Jellinek M.S., Murphy J.M. & Burn B.J. (1986) Brief psychosocial screening in outpatient pediatric practice. *Journal of Pediatrics*, **109**, 371–378.

Jewell D. & Bain J. (1985) Common childhood problems: variations in management. *British Medical Journal*, **291**, 941–944.

Johnstone A. & Goldberg D. (1976) Psychiatric screening in general practice: a controlled trial. *Lancet*, **i**, 605–608.

Joint Working Party of the British Paediatric Association and the Royal College of General Practitioners (1976) The paediatric training required by the general practitioner. *Journal of the Royal College of General Practitioners*, **26**, 128–136.

Jonsell R. (1977) Patients at a paediatric out-patient clinic. A study with particular reference to psychological and social background factors. *Acta Paediatrica Scandinavica*, **66**, 729–734.

Korsch B.M. & Negrete V.F. (1972) Doctor–patient communication. *Scientific American*, **227**, 66–74.

Laclave L.J. & Campbell J.L. (1986) Psychiatric intervention in children: sex differences in referral rates. *Journal of the American Academy of Child Psychiatry*, **24**, 430–432.

Langner T.S., Gersten J.C., Greene E.L., Eisenberg J.G., Hersow J.H. & McCarthy E.D. (1974) Treatment of psychological disorders amongst urban children. *Journal of Consulting and Clinical Psychology*, **42**, 170–179.

Lewis C.E. & Lewis M.A. (1989) Educational outcomes and illness behaviors of participants in a child-initiated care system: a 12-year follow-up study. *Pediatrics*, **84**, 845–950.

Lewis C.E., Lewis M.A., Lorimer A. & Palmer B.B. (1977) Child-initiated care: the use of school nursing services by children in an 'adult-free' system. *Pediatrics*, **60**, 499–507.

Lurie O. (1974) Parents' attitudes toward children's problems and toward use of mental health services: socioeconomic-differences. *American Journal of Orthopsychiatry*, **44**, 109–119.

McCune Y., Richardson M.M. & Powell J.A. (1984) Psychological health issues in pediatric practices: parents' knowledge and concerns. *Pediatrics*, **74**, 183–190.

McFadyen A., Broster G. & Black D. (1991) The impact of a child psychiatry-liaison service on patterns of referral. *British Journal of Psychiatry*, **158**, 93–96.

Mechanic D. (1964) The influence of mothers on their children's health attitudes and behaviour. *Pediatrics*, **33**, 444–453.

Mechanic D. (1979) Development of psychological distress among young adults. *Archives of General Psychiatry*, **36**, 1233–1239.

Metz J.R., Allen C.M., Barr G. & Shinefield H. (1976) A pediatric screening examination for psychosocial problems. *Pediatrics*, **58**, 595–606.

Mitchell A.K.R. (1983) Liaison psychiatry in general practice. *British Journal of Hospital Medicine*, **30**, 100–106.

Mitchell A.R.K. (1985) Psychiatrists in primary health care settings. *British Journal of Psychiatry*, **147**, 371–379.

Murray L., Cooper P.J. & Stein A. (1991) Postnatal depression and infant development. *British Medical Journal*, **302**, 978–979.

Nabarro J. (1984) Unrecognized psychiatric illness in medical patients. *British Medical Journal*, **289**, 635–636.

Nikapota A. & Graham P. (1986) Child mental health in the year 2000. Paper presented at the 11th International Congress of Child and Adolescent Psychiatry, July 1986, Paris.

Offord D.R., Boyle M.H., Szatmari P., Rae-Grant N.I., Links P.S., Cadman D.T., Byles J.A., Crawford J.W., Munroe Blum H., Byrne C., Thomas H., Woodward C.A. (1987) Ontario Child Health Study. II. Six-month prevalence of disorder and rates of service utilization. *Archives of General Psychiatry*, **44**, 832–836.

Perrin E.C., West P.D. & Culley B.S. (1989) Is my child normal yet? Correlates of vulnerability. *Pediatrics*, **83**, 355–363.

Puckering C. (1989) Maternal depression. *Journal of Child Psychology and Psychiatry*, **30**, 807–817.

Reder P. & Kraemer S. (1980) Dynamic aspects of professional collaborations in child guidance referral. *Journal of Clinical Psychology*, **40**, 372–377.

Richman N., Stevenson J. & Graham P.J. (1982) *Pre-school to School: A Behavioural Study*. Academic Press, London.

Roghmann K.J. & Haggerty R.J. (1972) Family stress and the use of health services. *International Journal of Epidemiology*, **1**, 279–286.

Roghmann K.J., Babigan H.M., Goldberg D. & Zastowny T.R. (1982) The increasing number of children using psychiatric services: analysis of a cumulative psychiatric case register. *Pediatrics*, **70**, 790–801.

Royal College of General Practitioners (1981) *Prevention of Psychiatric Disorders in General Practice. Report from General Practice 20*. Royal College of General Practitioners, London.

Royal College of Psychiatry (1986) The rules, responsibilities and work of the child and adolescent psychiatrist. *Bulletin of the Royal College of Psychiatrists*, **10**, 202–206.

Rutter M., Tizard J. & Whitmore K. (eds) (1970) *Education, Health and Behaviour*. Longmans, London.

Ryle A. (1967) *Neurosis in the Ordinary Family*. Tavistock, London.

Savage R. & Armstrong D. (1990) Effect of a general practitioner's consulting style on patients' satisfaction: a controlled study. *British Medical Journal*, **301**, 968–970.

Scambler A., Scambler G. & Craig D. (1981) Kinship and friendship networks in women's demand for primary care. *Journal of the Royal College of General Practice*, **31**, 746–750.

Schor E.L. (1986) Use of health care services by children and diagnoses received during presumably stressful life transitions. *Pediatrics*, **77**, 834–841.

Schubiner H. & Robin A. (1990) Screening adolescents for depression and parent–teenager conflict in an ambulatory medical setting: a preliminary investigation. *Pediatrics*, **85**, 813–818.

Scott Smith M., Mitchell J., McCauley E.A. & Calderon R. (1990) Screening for anxiety and depression in an adolescent clinic. *Pediatrics*, **85**, 262–266.

Shepherd M. (1982) Psychiatric research and primary care in Britain — past, present and future. *Psychological Medicine*, **12**, 493–499.

Shepherd M., Cooper B., Brown A.C. & Kalton G. (1966a) *Psychiatric Illness in General Practice*. Oxford University Press, London.

Shepherd M., Oppenheimer A.N. & Mitchell S. (1966b) Childhood behaviour disorder and the child guidance clinic: an epidemiological study. *Journal of Child Psychology and Psychiatry*, **7**, 39–52.

Starfield B. & Borkowf S. (1969) Physicians' recognition of complaints made by parents about their children's health. *Pediatrics*, **43**, 168–172.

Starfield B., Gross E., Wood M., Pantell R., Allen C., Gordon B., Moffatt P., Drachman R. & Katz H. (1980) Psychosocial and psychosomatic diagnoses in primary care of children. *Pediatrics*, **66**, 159–167.

Steinberg D., Galhenage D.P.C. & Robinson S.C. (1981) Two years' referrals to a regional adolescent unit: some implications for psychiatric services. *Social Science and Medicine*, **15**, 113–122.

Strathdee G. & Williams P. (1984) A survey of psychiatrists in primary care; the silent growth of a new service. *Journal of the Royal College of General Practitioners*, **34**, 615–618.

Subotsky F. & Brown R.M. (1990) Working alongside the general practitioner: a child psychiatric clinic in the general practice setting. *Child Health Care Development*, **16**, 189–196.

Tuch R.H. (1975) The relationship between a mother's menstrual status and her response to illness in her child. *Psychosomatic Medicine*, **37**, 388–394.

Wadsworth M., Butterfield W.J.H. & Blaney R. (1971) *Health and Sickness: The Choice of Treatment*. Tavistock, London.

Wasserman R.C., Barriatua R.D., Carter W.B. & Lippincott B.A. (1984) Pediatric clinician's support for parents makes a difference: an outcome based on analysis of clinician parent interaction. *Pediatrics*, **74**, 1047–1063.

Whitfield M. & Bucks R. (1988) General practitioners' responsibilities to their patients. *British Medical Journal*, **297**, 398–400.

Wilkinson G. (1982) Social work: effective or affective? *British Medical Journal*, **284**, 1659–1660.

Wilkinson G. (1988) I don't want you to see a psychiatrist. *British Medical Journal*, **279**, 1144–1145.

Wolff S. (1967) Behavioural characteristics of primary school children referred to a psychiatric department. *British Journal of Psychiatry*, **193**, 885–893.

Wolraich M.L., Lindgren S., Stromquist A., Milich R., Davis C. &

Watson D. (1990) Stimulant medication use by primary care physicians in the treatment of attention deficit hyperactivity disorder. *Pediatrics*, **86**, 95–101.

Woodward C.A., Boyle M.H., Offord D.R., Cadman D.T., Links P.S., Munroe-Blum H., Byrne C. & Thomas H. (1988) Ontario Child Health Study: patterns of ambulatory medical care utilization and their correlates. *Pediatrics*, **82**, 425–434.

Yudkin S. (1961) Six children with coughs: the second diagnosis. *Lancet*, **ii**, 561–563.

Chapter 63
Special Educational Treatment

Patricia Howlin

WHAT ARE SPECIAL EDUCATIONAL NEEDS?

The Warnock Committee (Warnock, 1978) estimated that around one-fifth of all school-age children will at some time have difficulties that interfere with learning and for which they will require special educational provision. Although the accuracy of this estimate, and the validity of some of the premises on which it was based, have been questioned (Lewis & Vulliamy, 1981), the Warnock Report nevertheless highlighted the fact that a significant proportion of children in mainstream schools are in need of specialist help. It was also apparent that, for many, no such help was forthcoming. Who, then, are these children with exceptional needs, why should they require additional aid, and what form should this take?

One of the difficulties in interpreting, in practical terms, the requirements of Warnock's '20%' is the great variability of the needs of the children encompassed by this statistic. For some, the extent of their disability will be such that they are unlikely ever to lead independent lives. For others, their difficulties may interfere with schooling but should not, ultimately, reduce their chances of playing a full role in society.

Amongst the former group are children with marked developmental delays or pervasive disorders such as autism, and those with severe and chronically disabling physical conditions. The latter, and by far the largest group, comprises children of many different kinds. Firstly, there are those with mild to moderate delays or those who suffer from specific learning difficulties that limit their opportunities to benefit from the normal curriculum. Such problems may include specific reading retardation or developmental language delays. Secondly, there are children who need special educational treatment because they have sensory or physical disabilities that affect learning or their ability to attend classes, or that require regular medical treatment in the educational setting. This would include those with visual or hearing impairments, or who suffer from physical disability or chronic illness. A third group of needs arises because children's emotional or behavioural disturbance interferes with their learning or their ability to cope with the demands of the normal classroom. Then, there are those children who, because of persisting difficulties within the family, may benefit from schooling away from home, not because it offers special *educational* provision as such but because they require an environment that is more conducive to the child's general developmental needs. Finally, there will be many children who require special educational help because of a combination of these difficulties.

Clearly, different needs have different implications for service. Before any decisions regarding special provision are made, assessments of the child's overall level of development, as well as his or her relative attainments in specific areas such as language and academic skills, will be required. For children with physical or sensory impairments evaluation should take into account not only the severity of these but also the extent to which they may interfere with the child's ability to profit socially and academically from the school environment and curriculum. For those with behavioural or emotional difficulties it will be necessary to ascertain how these obstruct the child's own ability to learn and how they may affect other class members; it will also be necessary to consider possible reasons underlying these problems.

The next, and usually more difficult step, is to find educational provision that can deal adequately with these needs. The following sections will focus separately on provision for children whose special educational needs stem from relatively mild, transient or specific disorders and for those whose disability is profound, global and persisting.

MEETING THE EDUCATIONAL NEEDS OF CHILDREN WITH MILD TO MODERATE LEARNING DIFFICULTIES

Although one of the major debates in educational research during the past two decades has concerned the benefits, or otherwise, of integrated schooling for children with learning disability (Howlin, 1985), the situation seems to have changed remarkably little from that pertaining a century ago. As a local school inspector from West Lambeth then observed: 'Opinion is divided on the subject, but there appears to be amongst the teachers with whom I have spoken rather a general agreement that the children...are as well, if not better, in the ordinary classroom under ordinary environments than they would be if drafted into special classes' (Currey, 1898).

Rich and Ross (1989), although acknowledging the many limitations of studies in this area (no control groups;

nonrandom placements; small sample sizes; and failure to provide details of pupil, teacher or school characteristics), affirm that 'handicapped students assigned to the regular classroom significantly outperformed those students assigned to segregated alternatives, particularly the self contained special class'. The meta-analysis of Carlberg and Kavale (1980) reported, somewhat confusingly, that special classes produced significantly poorer results in terms of social and academic outcomes for students with below-average IQs but were significantly better for learning-disabled children. Unfortunately, no definitions of these categories were presented and sophisticated meta-analyses of this kind are of little value if the basic database is flawed by inadequate experimental designs. Other studies, such as that by Marston (1988), although small in scale, suggest that when adequate analyses are performed, attainments of special needs students are enhanced by special rather than regular educational placements. Most recent reviews, however, conclude that because of methodological deficits there is no convincing evidence to support the integration versus segregation argument one way or another (Bicklen, 1987; Zigler & Hodapp, 1987; Affleck *et al.*, 1988).

Although there is still 'no unambiguous answer to the primitive question of whether segregated or integrated placement is superior' (Meyers *et al.*, 1980), clearly there are strong arguments in favour of integrated schooling for those with mild to moderate disabilities. In principle at least, integration avoids the stigma of labelling and hence should result in better social adjustment and improved self-esteem. The value of imitation and modelling in acquiring academic and social skills is also well-documented (Knoblock, 1982; Bicklen, 1985). Moreover, once children are placed in separate education they are likely to remain there, with chances of reintegration diminishing with age (Walker *et al.*, 1988). The most important consideration, however, must be that if these children are to play a full role in society as they grow older then the earlier this process can begin the better. Thus, offering special help within the normal school system is likely to be of far greater benefit than the removal of the child from that system.

Improving classroom structure

Bickel and Bickel (1986) suggested that rather than concentrating on the issue of special education it is more appropriate to think in terms of powerful effective education for all children and to adapt what is known about good educational practice to meet special needs. Unfortunately, it is clear that many mainstream schools offer a far from optimum environment for their pupils. Hargreaves (1988) found that a quarter of secondary schools inspected between 1982 and 1986 were unsatisfactory and a third of 15 000 lessons observed were less than adequate. Although recent research on the factors that constitute an effective school suggests that the issues involved are extremely complex (Reynolds, 1991), many of the variables identified as important for success in mainstream schools have been replicated in studies of children with learning

difficulties. To maximize the chances of success there must be appropriately individualized and structured teaching programmes (Krupski, 1985; Center *et al.*, 1991), with goals that are clear to both teachers and pupils and which can be modified according to children's skills and needs (Bickel & Bickel, 1986; Fuchs *et al.*, 1989). One of the best indicators of academic gains seems to be the amount of time spent on learning tasks (Sindelar *et al.*, 1986). Rich and Ross (1989) noted that within the normal school day almost half the time involved nonlearning time; if regular classes are to meet the needs of students with disabilities this is obviously an area that could be greatly improved.

Although these goals, in themselves, are not particularly complex, meeting them will present problems when classes are large or if no additional support is made available to teachers. In successful studies, such as those by Guralnick and Groom (1987, 1988), it is evident that the proportion of children with handicaps in the classroom is very low and that overall group size is also small. In their work with integrated play groups the class size was only 8 — hardly representative of most regular play groups. Burstein (1986) and Cooper and Spence (1990) suggested that instruction in small groups is required at least part of the time and Zigmund and Baker (1990), in a follow-up of 13 students with learning disabilities, concluded that such children will not succeed in mainstream education if teachers simply continue with 'business as usual'.

Extra classroom provision

Because of the difficulties faced in meeting the needs of children with learning difficulties when teachers have to cope, at the same time, with the demands of perhaps 30 other children, various alternatives to full-time integration have been explored. These include resource centres, partial integration in special classes on the mainstream site or special support for the child in the regular classes. Hegarty *et al.* (1982a) found that placement on the same site as the normal school was essential to promote integration and was also important in allowing for gradual reassimilation into the normal classroom. The resource room model has become increasingly popular over the last decade but there is as yet little standardization of this type of facility. The extent to which specialist knowledge, based on experimental work in the area of learning difficulties, is actually applied is often limited and evaluations are few. Of those that have been carried out, some have reported better educational achievements for resource room programmes (Rich & Ross, 1989); others have found in favour of integrated classes (Wang & Birch, 1984); still others have found no differences in educational standards (Affleck *et al.*, 1988).

Claims that the time allotted to learning is less in special schools or resource classes than in regular classes (Zabel *et al.*, 1988) have not generally been supported by observational data. Rich and Ross (1989) found that, in general, resource rooms provided more time on teaching than did regular classes. However, there remains the danger that such provision may simply become yet another means of excluding slow or difficult pupils. Resource teachers, too, may face isolation from the rest of the school unless attention is paid to the ways in which their supportive services can be fully assimilated.

The variable results of resource room teaching are reflected in the uneven use of this type of provision. Figures from the US in 1986, for example, indicated that although Massachusetts and many other states favoured resource rooms, in Michigan and Alabama the majority of learning-disabled children were in regular classes whilst in California two-thirds were in special classrooms (Cole, 1989).

Special teaching techniques

A variety of different teaching approaches for this group of children, that may be implemented in regular or special classes, has been assessed, although rarely with conclusive results. Cooperative learning (groups of students working together to achieve mutual goals) has been recommended in a number of studies but there is little evidence that this is more effective than individual learning (Tateyama-Sniezek, 1990). Self-evaluation and self-monitoring programmes have been found to be successful by some authors (Sainato *et al.*, 1990). Research into the 'adaptive learning environments model' (Wang & Walberg, 1988) has produced only equivocal results (Fuchs & Fuchs, 1988), as has evaluation of programmes involving direct instruction versus mediated learning (Dale & Cole, 1988).

Despite their popularity in other settings, the application of behavioural or cognitive-behavioural approaches within academic contexts has tended to decrease over recent years (Sulzer-Azaroff & Gillat, 1990). Ault *et al.* (1989), in a review of 31 studies comparing different educational strategies, suggested that behavioural techniques utilizing stimulus-fading, prompting and shaping procedures were particularly effective but their overall conclusion that 'providing a massive amount of support . . . is more likely to increase the probability of learning than providing smaller amounts of support' is disappointingly vague.

A major difficulty in evaluating special teaching programmes lies in the limited focus of many outcome studies. Cognitive difficulties are frequently associated with a wide range of social, emotional and behavioural problems and these, too, must be considered when assessing the effectiveness of intervention.

Improving social adjustment

Self-perception

The school experience of children with learning difficulties is often very negative and there is considerable evidence of more dissatisfaction and anxiety about peer relations, lower self-esteem and high rates of depressive symptomatology (Taylor *et al.*, 1987; Gurney, 1988; Maag & Behrens, 1989). There is little evidence that educational placement *per se* has

any significant effect on such problems. Although a review by Gurney (1988) concluded that self-esteem is enhanced by segregation, there are many studies suggesting that segregation has negative effects and many others reporting no differences in terms of placement. Smith *et al.* (1977) suggested that partial integration may be more likely to enhance self-esteem, but Jenkins and Heinen (1989), in a study of 337 children with special needs, found that the majority preferred to receive additional help from their own teacher rather than from a specialist, because this made them feel less conspicuous.

Studies by Harter (1984) indicated that placement may be a less important variable than the child's perceived reference group. They found that children with specific learning difficulties tended to compare themselves with regular classroom peers and hence had a negative view of their own competence. More globally 'retarded' children tended to compare themselves with similarly disabled peers, whether or not they were mainstreamed, and their self-esteem was generally more positive. However, in that the IQ of the 'mentally retarded' children ranged from 50 to 100, this finding clearly needs to be further explored.

Acceptance by peers

There is little evidence that contact with children with special needs leads to improved attitudes on the part of peers, no matter how early this begins (Esposito & Reed, 1986). In a very detailed study of the peer relationships of mildly delayed children placed in mainstreamed play groups, Guralnick and Groom (1987, 1988) reported persisting deficits in their social behaviours and found that normal peers continued to perceive them as less competent and of lower social status; few children were able to establish reciprocal friendships. Work by Goodman *et al.* (1972) also suggested that levels of acceptance may decline rather than improve with age. Moreover, although it is often assumed that exposure to normal peers will increase prosocial behaviours (and hence social acceptability), there is only limited evidence to support this. Studies by Apolloni and Cooke (1978), Gresham (1982), Honig and McCarron (1988) and others indicate that modelling is unlikely to occur unless specific intervention takes place. Guralnick and Groom (1987) reported that mildly handicapped children did attempt to play with and interact with their peers, but their efforts received little encouragement. The same authors (1988) found that, although peer-related social behaviours and the frequency of constructive play increased in main-streamed settings, there were no differences in the amount of group play. Similarly, Beckman and Kohl (1987), using children as their own controls, found that the frequency of peer interactions was greater in integrated settings but there were no improvements in the complexity of play. Jenkins *et al.* (1985), in one of the few well-controlled, comparative studies in this area, involving random assignment to class-rooms and careful matching procedures, assessed children across a wide range of measures, including cognitive, language, motor and social behaviour. After 1 year, few differences between groups were found; children in the segregated groups performed better on measures of gross motor skill; and those in integrated groups scored higher only on a social play measure taken in an analogue setting.

It is clear that normal children are remarkably sensitive to differences, whether children with disabilities are labelled or not (Corman & Gottlieb, 1978; Bak *et al.*, 1987). Levels of acceptance are affected by a whole range of factors including behavioural competence, aggressiveness, temperamental characteristics and type and level of handicap (Bak & Siperstein, 1987; Keogh & Burnstein, 1988; Price & Dodge, 1989), but generally acceptance is most likely to occur only if the perceived differences between the handicapped child and his or her peers are slight. Truesdell (1990), for example, noted that mainstreaming often only occurs in low-achieving classes, so that differences between the 'special' students and their peers tend to be minimal.

The involvement of normal peers in intervention

Many studies have suggested that social skills training is crucial if these difficulties are to be minimized. However, successful programmes also involve special training for peers and the manipulation of classroom structure to encourage use of taught skills. Sasso and Rude (1987) and Strain and Odom (1986) found that training normal peers to initiate interactions increased both the frequency and quality of positive social interactions; similar findings have been reported by Donaldson (1980) and Fox (1989). The use of peers as monitors seems to have positive effects on academic attainments and specific, cooperative goal incentives have been used successfully by Cosden *et al.* (1985). Several other studies indicate that cooperative learning strategies, within mainstream classrooms, lead to more positive interactions during lessons and free time, and may result in increased rates of friendships between normal and handicapped children (Johnson & Johnson, 1986; Acton & Zarbatany, 1988; Putnam *et al.*, 1989). Although caution is needed in interpreting the results of much of this research (Topping, 1992), peer tutoring, at least if adequately structured, seems to be far more effective than attempts to change the attitudes of normal peers by indirect methods, such as teaching tapes, stories or simulations, which show little generalization to classroom behaviours (Fiedler & Simpson, 1987; Siperstein *et al.*, 1988).

Although some concern has been expressed about the effects of such programmes on normal peers there is no evidence of any long-term deleterious effects on the progress of other children (Strain *et al.*, 1976; Guralnick, 1978; Price & Goodman, 1980). Indeed, Maheady *et al.* (1988) found that a peer tutoring programme resulted in academic gains for both normal and learning-disabled children. However, again, in all these studies teacher–pupil ratios were generally high and class sizes small, so that their relevance for larger, less well-functioning classrooms remains in question.

Teacher training and support

It is apparent that if children with learning difficulties are to profit from education alongside their peers, modifications to classroom programmes and structure will be needed; these in turn will require special training and support for teachers. Deno *et al.* (1990) reported that staff in special education programmes were more 'data based' and personally knowledgeable about their pupils and that they used this knowledge to tailor programmes to individual needs. Nowacek *et al.* (1990) found that special education teachers were able to exert greater control over their students' behaviour by the use of more directive teaching methods and they made better use of reinforcement, feedback and monitoring techniques. They noted that many of these behaviours paralleled those used by effective teachers in mainstream schools. However, even with special training there may still be room for considerable improvement. Jenkins *et al.* (1988) reported a lack of attention to individual differences in placing children in special education and Algozzine *et al.* (1988) noted few modifications to teacher communication patterns or instructional methods despite the clearly differing needs of the students involved. Carri (1985) also called for better in-service training and the assessment of individual needs rather than assuming a homogeneity of problems, and hence of teaching strategies, as is too often the case.

Nevertheless, training alone is unlikely to be the solution to all problems, nor do general attempts to improve the school environment seem to result in a better outcome (Deno *et al.*, 1990). Instead, more specific changes are needed. Consultation services, by specially trained professionals who can offer continuing help to teachers in mainstream classes, have been found effective in a number of studies and the earlier this help can be obtained the better (Gutkin *et al.*, 1980; Graden *et al.*, 1985; Fuchs *et al.*, 1990). However, there are anxieties that teacher status and independence may, if care is not taken, be reduced rather than enhanced by such intervention (Pugach & Johnson, 1989) and the provision of specialist support teachers, working alongside the class teacher, may be more valuable (Cantrell & Cantrell, 1979). Unfortunately, in practice, the additional help offered to many teachers comprises just an untrained helper; there is little experimental or empirical evidence that such support is likely to be effective.

Altering teacher attitudes

Despite recent changes in legislation, it is hardly surprising that, without adequate help, teachers' attitudes to children with special needs are often less than positive. As Campbell *et al.* (1985) pointed out, regular classroom teachers are now expected to teach students who, 10 years ago, would have been taught in small groups by specially trained teachers. Croll and Moses (1985) noted the difficulties faced by teachers in providing the individual attention required by pupils with special needs and Lowden (1985), in a survey of Welsh primary school teachers, concluded that the results did not suggest a 'generally tolerant attitude towards slow learners'. Moreover, tolerance may well decrease as children grow older and the demands on academic attainments increase. Hanrahan *et al.* (1990) found that, whereas regular class teachers of children under 8 tended to rate academic achievement as less important than did special class teachers, these attitudes were reversed for older children, with the result that teachers in normal schools began to show more negative attitudes towards mainstreaming. There is some evidence, too (Gersten *et al.*, 1988) that effective class teachers in normal schools may be more intolerant of children with handicaps, presumably because of their higher expectations and standards.

Although marked behavioural problems are particularly difficult for mainstream teachers to accept (Chazan *et al.*, 1981), even children with relatively mild handicaps may prove hard to cope with without extra help and better understanding on the part of the teachers. Unless problems of teacher bias are adequately tackled, the quality of teaching for students with learning difficulties is likely to suffer. There is no evidence that simple exposure to handicap has any positive effects. Instead, adequate preparation by teaching colleges, specific training in the skills necessary to promote progress and minimize difficulties, and some degree of ongoing support are all necessary if attitudes and actions are to be improved.

SPECIAL EDUCATION FOR CHILDREN WITH SPECIFIC LEARNING DIFFICULTIES

Data on the effectiveness or otherwise of special education for this group of children are difficult to obtain, because of problems of recognition, wide variability in diagnostic attitudes and even greater variation in provision.

Language disorders

Recognition of early language delays is often poor. Official statistics indicating that 0.02% of school-age children require special education for language disability (Barton & Tomlinson, 1981) fall far short of the 3% of preschool children identified by screening studies in the UK as having significant language delays (Stevenson & Richman, 1976) or the even higher figures of up to 8% reported more recently in New Zealand and Ottawa (Silva, 1980; Beitchman *et al.*, 1986). Provision has clearly not kept pace with recognition and, although a small number of special schools and a larger number of special classrooms, often attached to normal schools, have grown up over recent years, many children with language difficulties still fail to receive any special help. Speech therapy within the regular school system is sparse and the option for most children is either no help at all or segregated teaching in the early school years with virtually no provision at the secondary school stage. Rutter *et al.* (1992) found that even children with very severe early language delays received little specialist help and had frequent changes of school throughout childhood. A long-term follow-up revealed that the secondary and tertiary educational provision for this group was worse, in some respects, than that for a group of autistic individuals of similar IQ. This finding may well be attributable to the fact that the handicaps of the autistic group, being more evident, resulted in their receiving greater help and support than the less obviously handicapped children with specific language delays.

Although many children with early language delays do eventually catch up without sequelae, even in the absence of special services (see Chapter 32), follow-up studies suggest that a significant proportion of those with persisting delays are at risk of developing additional problems (Howlin & Rutter, 1987b; Rutter & Mawhood, 1991). Even if therapy is available initially, this is rarely sustained once the more obvious speech deficits begin to improve; advice and support for regular class teachers are also limited. A meta-analysis of the effects of specialist intervention with linguistically impaired children (Nye *et al.*, 1987) suggested that therapy can be effective in improving language development. Although poor research design limited firm conclusions, it seemed that structured programmes, especially those utilizing a modelling approach, were more successful than those employing general stimulation methods. Outcome was also affected by the nature of the child's difficulties, with syntactic problems proving most amenable to treatment and pragmatic disorders showing least response. Unfortunately, despite the implications of research findings (Bishop & Edmundson, 1987; Nye *et al.*, 1987) there is still a tendency to treat children with language disorders as a homogeneous group and the educational focus remains on the linguistic difficulties rather than encompassing other important areas of development.

Difficulties in reading

The continuing debate over whether specific reading difficulties or dyslexia actually exists has not helped to encourage education authorities either to recognize the extent of the problem or to offer special provision. It is estimated that between 3 and 10% of school-age children have persistent and marked reading disabilities (at least 2 s.d. below predicted levels; Maughan *et al.*, 1985) and the adverse effects on educational progress have been well-documented (see Chapter 36). Nevertheless, most children with such difficulties receive little specialist support. Because of the lack of provision in regular schools, some private schools have been set up for children who are severely disabled in this way but there is little evaluation of this form of provision and effective treatment generally remains elusive. Almost any type of remedial intervention seems to produce short-term gains, but these are rarely maintained (Yule & Rutter, 1985).

Confusion about the causes and correlates of reading difficulties has led to equally confusing notions about treatment. Intervention programmes focusing on perceptual or emotional difficulties have assumed that these problems are primary to the reading failure, rather than a result of it, and have not proved particularly successful (Yule & Rutter, 1985) Similarly, drug treatments designed to reduce attentional problems have failed to produce beneficial effects (Aman, 1980; Gittelman & Feingold, 1983). Recently, focus on improving awareness of rhyme and alliteration has been suggested as a possible treatment technique (Bryant *et al.*, 1989), but although this helps to enhance reading skills in a normal population, its value for children with severe reading difficulties has yet to be assessed. To date, programmes based on reinforcement principles, often combined with systematic phonic teaching, have resulted in the most enduring gains (Gittelman & Feingold, 1983; Yule & Rutter, 1985; Singh & Singh, 1986; O'Connor *et al.*, 1987). However, it is important to be aware that the techniques involved in these experimental studies are rarely implemented to the same extent in regular classrooms and on the whole, unless remedial programmes are sustained, significant gains are rare.

Difficulties in spelling and mathematics

Although spelling difficulties are commonly associated with reading problems, they can also occur on their own. Frith (1983) has used the terms dysgraphic to describe children with poor spelling but adequate reading, and dyslexic for children who are impaired in both. Although her experimental and theoretical work has been influential in highlighting possible causes of reading and spelling difficulties, effective intervention techniques have been slow to emerge. Studies of children with mathematical difficulties are even less advanced and systematic help for such children is virtually non-existent.

The long-term outcome for children with learning disabilities

The vocational outcome for students with mild or specific difficulties, whether placed in special or mainstream schools, seems to be generally poor. Drop-out rates from school before graduation are extremely high (generally between 35 and 50%; de Bettencourt *et al.*, 1989) and although tertiary education facilities are improving, these remain variable in quality (Bursuck *et al.*, 1989). There has been some increase in vocational training programmes, with Zetlin and Murtaugh (1990) reporting 75% participation in postschool educational programmes in the US; nevertheless, few of these were of a high academic or vocational level and many students dropped out before the course was completed. Transition services, to facilitate the move from school or college into employment, are also greatly needed (Fairweather, 1989). Hasazi *et al.* (1985) reported overall employment rates of around 50%, with 62% of resource room students finding jobs as compared with only 36% of special class pupils. However, as severity of impairment was not taken into account, the effects of placement on later outcome could not be determined. Edgar (1985) found that degree of disability was a major factor influencing later employment, with only 38% of mildly retarded students findings jobs, compared with 64% of behaviourally disordered or learning-disabled pupils. It is also important to note that, although superficially rates of employment may seem reason-

ably high, earnings and job status are low, with a large proportion of the groups studied still living with their parents, suggesting a pattern of financial instability and family dependence (Hazasi *et al.*, 1985; Mithaug *et al.*, 1985; de Bettencourt *et al.*, 1989). Zetlin and Murtaugh (1990) recorded a high frequency of drifting from job to job, with two-thirds of jobs lasting less than 3 months. The subjects in this study had all attended special schools or classes, but the authors reported no evidence of better outcome for those attending regular school. Hazasi *et al.* (1985) noted that the majority (82%) of those in jobs had found employment through their own personal network (families, self or friends) rather than through school or other agencies. Lack of suitable jobs was reported by Szivos (1990) who also noted that work experience was often very negative, with many clients expressing feelings of incompetence and low self-esteem. Women's job prospects seem to be even more limited than their male counterparts (Hasazi *et al.*, 1989).

The situation for children with specific learning difficulties appears to be very similar. Maughan and Yule (Chapter 36) noted the poor long-term outcome for many individuals with reading difficulties. Rutter *et al.* (1992) found that only 60% of young adults with early language disorders were in independent employment and, again, the level of jobs held was generally low.

In summary, although children with learning difficulties can and should profit from mainstream education, this is unlikely to prove successful without restructuring the school environment to provide support for teachers and pupils. The most successful integration studies have been conducted in the context of special educational projects and their relevance for teachers coping with classes of 30 or more children with little or no additional help is questionable. In order to facilitate normalization, much greater attention to individual needs and to practical support and adequate training for staff is required. If simply viewed as a cheap option, it will clearly benefit no one. It is regrettable, therefore, that although the specific intention of the Warnock Committee was that only children with the most severe difficulties would require segregated provision, inadequacies in funding and in teacher training have led to many parents using the subsequent legislation to achieve specialist provision rather than attempting to obtain adequate support in a mainstream setting.

SPECIAL EDUCATION FOR CHILDREN WITH BEHAVIOURAL AND EMOTIONAL PROBLEMS

The attention given to this group of children reflects not only the immediate disruption that they may cause within the school but also concerns that, if left untreated, their difficulties may well persist into adult life (see Chapter 18). Very often judgements as to whether a child has behavioural or emotional problems depend more on the attitudes, policies and practices of the school and the tolerance level of individual teachers than on any objective criteria. Thus, Galloway *et al.* (1982)

suggested that it may be more accurate to describe these children as disturbing rather than disturbed. Rutter (1983), Reynolds (1982, 1991) and Hallinger and Murphy (1986) have discussed in detail the roles of schools in maintaining or minimizing disruptive behaviours. In some cases, transfer to a different but well-functioning mainstream school, where teachers are sensitive to the child's needs, may be sufficient significantly to reduce the level of problems. In others, the introduction of special procedures in the classroom or even removal from mainstream education may be required.

Management techniques within the classroom

Strategies based on behavioural principles are used widely to minimize the problems shown by pupils with behavioural, attentional or social difficulties (see Chapter 50). Behavioural approaches to treatment have many advantages in that they do not require the segregation of the child with problems; additional help within the classroom is not necessary, although adequate teacher training clearly is; and the basic techniques are flexible enough to be adapted to the particular needs of an individual child or classroom. Moreover, placing the focus of intervention on positive, on-task behaviours is more desirable (as well as apparently more successful) than concentrating on disruptive behaviours (McNamara & Jolly, 1990). The use of behavioural self-management techniques, too, is growing. (Fantuzzo *et al.*, 1988; Panagopoulou-Stamatelatou, 1990).

Such approaches are not without their critics, however. Galloway and Goodwin (1987) suggested that many behavioural programmes are limited by their failure to take account of factors outside the classroom and that, if such approaches are to make a more extensive contribution to the education of children with special needs, they will need to address themselves to wider aspects of school curriculum, organization and climate than is currently the case (MacAulay, 1990). Moreover, sometimes very simple changes to classroom organization, such as altering the seating arrangements (Wheldall & Lam, 1987), may have a greater and more persisting effect than the introduction of complex behavioural programmes. Nevertheless, if carried out sensitively, behavioural programmes can produce rapid and enduring gains. Unfortunately, there seems to be continuing resistance by colleges of education to incorporate such training into teaching courses (Merrett & Houghton, 1989); lack of cooperation from other staff members and the difficulties in ensuring that peer reinforcement does not maintain undesirable behaviours may also be considerable (Tsoi & Yule, 1976; Moss & Childs, 1981).

Another approach to treatment, that takes account of the links between behavioural disturbance and emotional problems, involves the use of counselling and psychotherapeutic techniques. Most evaluative studies have suggested that the effects of such interventions on behavioural disturbance are minimal (Mitchell & Rosa, 1981) and Galloway *et al.* (1982) noted that counselling is unlikely to make much impact on disruptive behaviours unless all other aspects of a pupil's welfare at school, together with family or other out-of-

school factors affecting progress and adjustment, are taken into account. Nevertheless, follow-up studies by Wright *et al.* (1976) and Kolvin *et al.* (1981) indicate that psychotherapeutic techniques may have some long-term effects on behavioural problems, although not on academic outcome. Certainly, counselling or psychotherapeutic techniques may be of help in raising the low self-esteem of many children with behavioural and learning difficulties. The problem is that most teachers, concerned about *current* levels of disturbance, would consider 2−3 years too long to wait for an improvement. When resources are scarce, attention to children's emotional problems is often limited and hence intervention has tended to focus much more on observable behavioural problems rather than on associated emotional or social difficulties.

This focus on manifest problems, rather than possible underlying factors, has also resulted, particularly in the US, in an ever-increasing dependence on medical treatments to reduce behavioural or attention difficulties (see Chapter 17).

Links between school and home in the treatment of children with disturbing behaviour

The association between behavioural disorders in children and problems within the family has led, in recent years, to greater attempts to involve families in treatment. Positive attitudes to such outreach services have been reported (Harvey *et al.*, 1977; Dowling & Osborne, 1985; Dowling, 1990) but there are few evaluative reports on the effects on the children's behaviour and those that do exist are somewhat equivocal in their findings. Wasik *et al.* (1990) found that a home-based family education programme was not, in itself, effective in improving the cognitive performance on disadvantaged children but needed to be combined with good day-care. Kolvin *et al.* (1981) also found that intervention focusing on the involvement of parents was less effective than direct intervention using either behavioural or psychotherapeutic techniques.

Special schools for 'maladjusted' pupils

Despite the influences of the integration movement, over the past 30 years there has been a steady rise in the numbers of children identified as 'maladjusted', paralleled, until recently, by an increase in special boarding and day-schools. However, the quality of education provided is variable and relatively few children (around 20% or less) subsequently return to mainstream school (Cooling, 1974; Dawson, 1980). The chances of reintegration are further reduced for children attending boarding schools (Marshall, 1971; Atkinson, 1975). In general, follow-up studies of children attending 'maladjusted' schools are difficult to interpret because of many methodological problems (in particular, the failure to take into account differences in intake or spontaneous improvement rates). Galloway and Goodwin (1987) argued that 'both day and residential schools must be considered expensive, inefficient and ill-conceived'. Nevertheless, there may well be a case for residential provision for children whose difficulties stem not so much from their educational needs as from disturbance or inadequacies within the family or a lack of appropriate stimulation in the home. Although noneducational considerations officially play no role in decisions about schooling, placement away from home may offer some children the chance they need to thrive, whilst avoiding the much more extreme step of total removal from the home.

On- and off-site provision

Cave and Maddison (1978), in a detailed review of educational provision, concluded that integration for emotionally and behaviourally disturbed children should be feasible with adequate support, resources and training for teachers. Unfortunately, such provision is frequently lacking (Galloway et al., 1982; Bullock et al., 1985; Stainback & Stainback, 1990) and the meta-analysis of Carlberg and Kavale (1980) suggests that, for this group, special classes may produce better results in terms of both academic and social outcomes.

Reluctance to accept children with disturbing behaviours has been found in even the most progressive areas. Data from Massachusetts and California, for example, indicate that the majority of such children are taught in resource areas, special classes or private schools rather than in regular classes (Cole, 1989). The old notion of 'contagion' (Redl, 1966) has proved hard to dispel in an age of increasing classroom violence and many teachers have no wish to submit other students or themselves to the disruption that a very disturbed child can cause. Little evidence for the concept of contagion exists and, although aggressive children may elicit more aggressive or disruptive behaviours from their peers (Rutter et al., 1979; Lyons et al., 1988), the amount of disturbance seems to be influenced by the effectiveness of the teacher (Saunders, 1971). Hegarty and colleagues (1982a) reported that the presence of behaviourally disturbed children significantly affected teachers' tolerance of integration programmes for other children with learning difficulties. Work by Bullock et al. (1985) also suggests that negative teacher perceptions are more common in public school settings than in special residential schools.

Because of the difficulties in meeting the needs of these children without adequate support for class teachers, recent years have witnessed a rapid growth in on- and off-site provision, including sanctuaries, withdrawal groups, resource rooms, tutorial classes, educational guidance centres and intermediate treatment units. In principle such centres offer small classrooms, remedial teaching and more general support and are designed to enable pupils to be *temporarily* withdrawn from the classroom whilst maintaining links with the main school. However, on the whole, they have tended to become yet another means of segregating pupils with difficult behaviours. Because of the obvious disadvantages of off-site units, in terms of maintaining links with the parent school, on-site

units, generally serving only the host school, have become more popular. There have now been a number of studies of both on- and off-site units in the UK, the US and New Zealand (Galloway et al., 1982; Mortimore et al., 1983; Topping, 1983; Galloway & Barrett, 1984). Concerns about their effectiveness and their appropriateness for pupils with special needs have been expressed on several different fronts. It is evident that there are no clear policies for the admission of pupils to such units and that provision varies widely from area to area, in ways that have little association with possible numbers of disturbed children (Taylor et al., 1979). Schools, too, differ markedly in the frequency with which they refer children. Mortimore et al. (1983) found that the majority of children in these units were from highly disadvantaged backgrounds; there was also apprehension about the disproportionate number of pupils from minority ethnic groups, especially those of Afro-Carribean origin (see report of the Inner London Education Authority (ILEA), 1981). Other concerns have centred on the poor accommodation and the unacceptably narrow curriculum offered in many of these units (Dawson, 1980; Mortimore et al., 1983; Galloway & Goodwin, 1987). Finding appropriately trained and competent staff may also present considerable difficulties.

Problems in the breadth and quality of teaching and the very variable links with the parent school have generally resulted in low rates of return to mainstream education (Wilson & Evans, 1980). Indeed, despite the expressed principle of reintegrating pupils, Galloway and Goodwin (1987) conclude that: 'in the overwhelming majority of units this aim was rapidly, if tacitly abandoned'. There are exceptions to this, with studies by Dain (1977), Lane (1977) and Mickleborough (1980) reporting relatively high rates of return to mainstream schooling. The ILEA study found that only 31% of pupils returned to their parent school, although a further 55% left for other normal reasons — mainly that of reaching school-leaving age. Mortimore et al. (1983) found that only 11% of user schools felt that placement had facilitated a successful return to school and few teachers reported improvements in pupils' behaviour, work or attitudes. In all, 40% of head teachers commented on some adverse effects of the centres, most of these focusing on the problems of reintegration; one-third reported that the attitudes and behaviours of some pupils had become more difficult following their time at special centres. The benefits that are reported seem to be for the children remaining behind, rather than those transferred to the centres. Some 62% of teachers in the Galloway et al. (1982) study thought that such units benefited the rest of the class and 68% of head teachers in the Mortimore study reported improved classroom management, with 35% reporting that the other pupils were now more settled and had better relationships with their teachers. As far as the pupils at the centres were concerned, only 48% expected to return to normal school but 51% felt that the centres had helped with academic progress and 25% considered that the units had helped them to cope with and solve their own problems. Surprisingly few children (7%) actively disliked the centres and attendance tended to be better than it had been at the mainstream school.

The general conclusions from these studies are that such centres are expensive, and in offering a very narrow curriculum may hinder rather than encourage children's return to normal schools. However, unless adequate resources and support are provided within mainstream schools — and there is little evidence of funds being made available for this — segregation of this kind may sometimes be the only practical option.

Children who exclude themselves from school

The greater part of this chapter has been devoted to the problems of children who, for one reason or another, are placed in or excluded from schools, with no consideration of their own views. A significant proportion of secondary-school-age children, however, 'vote with their feet' when it comes to expressing their opinions of school. Truancy rates vary widely between schools, even when the population served is apparently fairly homogeneous (Galloway *et al.*, 1982), and are frequently associated with other factors indicative of ineffective schooling. Whatever the causes, the links between persistent nonattendance at school and low scholastic attainments, high rates of antisocial and aggressive behaviours, poorer employment prospects and increased conviction rates are well-established (Hersov & Berg, 1980; Fogelman, 1992).

Assessments of therapeutic effectiveness are often limited by confusions over diagnosis and causation (Hersov, 1985). Early treatments tended to focus on resolving the separation anxiety, which was considered to be at the basis of the school refusal. Lewis (1980) concluded that psychotherapeutic interventions may be of some value, although lack of adequate controls makes the interpretation of findings difficult. Behavioural treatments (Yule, 1985) seem to be particularly effective when children have only been away from school for a short time so it is crucial that schools recognize the problem within the very early days; it seems essential, too, to establish parents' collaboration in treatment.

The link between truancy and adverse school factors has led other writers to focus on changes in school management style (Galloway *et al.*, 1982). The school's acceptance of contingency contracts and a 'graded change' approach to reentry appear to be particularly important. However, perhaps one of the most effective studies, in terms of returning persistent nonattenders to school, was that of Berg *et al.* (1978). They found that outcome was much better in cases where adjournment, rather than suspension, orders were issued, obliging the child and family to return to the Court to report on progress. Adjournment orders have the advantage of ensuring more participation, not only on the part of the family but also of school welfare officers and social workers. Unfortunately, objections to interfering with British justice in this way led to the cessation of what may have been a swift, cheap and effective way of dealing with this otherwise tenacious problem.

Although finding alternative solutions for dealing with persistent nonattendance has proved difficult, two forms of treatment that are not advisable are the use of home tuition or special truancy groups, either on or off site. Both have the serious disadvantage of isolating the child even further from his or her peer group; they relieve the pressure on the family and the child of facing the problems of returning to school and do virtually nothing to address either the causes or the solution to the problem. Comparing different approaches to the treatment of school refusal, Blagg and Yule (1984) found behavioural treatments to be more effective than hospital treatment or home tuition (only 10% of the home-tutored group returned to school, compared with 37.5% of the hospitalized group and 93.3% of the children receiving behaviour therapy). Whatever the treatment employed, outcome for children of 10 years and below is generally good; outcome for children in the 11–16-year age range is far less predictable. Berg *et al.* (1969) achieved only a 59% favourable outcome and Miller *et al.* (1972) in a study of older children found that neither systematic desensitization with contingency management nor psychotherapy was any more effective than being placed on a waiting list. The Rapid Behavioural Treatment Approach of Blagg produced a more successful long-term outcome with children in the 11–16 years age range than any other reported study (see Blagg, 1987, for further details of treatment and diagnosis of school phobia).

SPECIAL EDUCATION FOR CHILDREN WITH PHYSICAL AND SENSORY HANDICAPS

Physical disabilities

For almost a century the desirability of integrating children with physical handicaps into normal classrooms has been noted (Charity Organization Society, 1893 — cited in Cole, 1989). In practice, this frequently involves simply the provision of physical aids; some, often inadequate, manipulations to the physical environment; and the use of classroom assistants (or even classmates) to augment what the class teacher is able to do. Few mainstream schools have adequate access to trained nursing or physiotherapy help, and little guidance is provided on how to deal with the child's educational, social and emotional problems, particularly those related to teasing, feelings of isolation or low self-esteem.

Cole (1989) noted that there were over 2000 more children in schools for the physically handicapped in 1983 than there had been two decades earlier and, as is the case with other disabilities, tolerance among teachers and peers tends to decrease with age (Hunt, 1981; Anderson & Clarke, 1982). Thus, by secondary school, when access to the normal curriculum becomes most important in terms of future academic progress, possibilities for integration are further reduced.

Because physical handicap is such a broad category, comparative outcome studies of the effects of special or regular schooling are difficult to interpret. On the whole, social adjustment seems to be better in children attending normal schools or special units attached to normal schools than in those in segregated provision (Cope & Anderson, 1977; Carr, 1982). There is also evidence that academic attainments may be higher in the integrated groups (O'Moore, 1978; Carr *et al.*, 1981).

Recently, conductive education methods have been claimed to alleviate or even cure the physical disabilities of children suffering from cerebral palsy but despite these claims no evaluative data are available (Yule, 1992). As the intensity of intervention required effectively excluded the children from participating in normal educational provision, until objective outcome measures are obtained its value as an alternative form of therapy remains highly questionable.

Hearing impairments

Although some authors have argued strongly in favour of integration for all children with hearing impairments (Lynas, 1984), others, such as Gregory (1987) claimed that the immense communication problems of this group of children are generally under-estimated and that they may do much better in the more supportive atmosphere of a special school or unit. Moores (1982) suggested that deaf students in integrated settings appear to do better because they have higher academic potential to start with and are in school settings more appropriate to their needs. However, even when factors such as age, IQ and degree of hearing loss are controlled, findings tend to be contradictory. Kluwin and Moores (1989) have criticized the design of most studies in this area, and concluded that student characteristics are a primary determinant of achievement, with quality of instruction being far more crucial for outcome than type of placement. Further discussion of these issues is given in Chapter 41.

Visual problems

It is estimated that only about 30% of visually impaired children attend mainstream schools in the UK and, although the figure is higher in the US (59%; Cole, 1989), only a third of children were enrolled in regular classes, with 50% based in resource rooms or special classes and 20% in separate schools. Adequate comparative studies of children in these different placements are rare and Jamieson *et al.* (1977) noted that individual aptitudes, the quality of teaching and the availability of resources will all influence outcome. Chapman and Stone (1988) commented on the excellent examination results obtained by many special schools for the blind. Hegarty *et al.* (1982b), on the other hand, noted the success of resource room provision (albeit with careful preparation of staff, sighted pupils and their parents beforehand) in increasing functional integration. (For further discussion, see Chapter 41.)

SPECIAL EDUCATION FOR CHILDREN WITH SEVERE AND PERVASIVE LEARNING DIFFICULTIES

Many children with severe and pervasive handicaps will continue to need special help and support throughout their lives and for them issues of integration during the school years are perhaps less crucial. Certainly, most reviews (Carlberg & Kavale, 1980) indicate that the success of integration is highly dependent on cognitive levels. Ispa and Matz (1978), in a study of preschool integration programmes, found that children with the lowest IQs tended to profit least and, although the large-scale studies of Guralnick and Groom (1987, 1988) are often cited in favour of integrated provision, the mean IQ of the children involved was over 70. Similarly, in the study by Casey *et al.* (1988), although suggesting that Down's syndrome children attending mainstream school made better progress in numeracy, language comprehension and mental age than a segregated control group, integrated children were considerably younger initially and also showed a greater range of competence, some having IQs within the normal range.

Rich and Ross (1989) reported that special schools or classes offered more to children with mild to moderate retardation and they found, in general, that resource rooms provided more time on teaching than did regular classes, with the advantages being greater for those with severe learning difficulties. Deno *et al.* (1990) also found that the more handicapped students did less well in integrated or resource programmes than did those with mild disabilities.

Age is another factor in predicting the success of integrated programmes. A number of studies indicate that, although full- or part-time integration seems to work well during the junior school period, at the secondary school stage there is a drift back towards segregation (Budgell, 1986). Even with very young children, however, acceptance may be limited and Sinson and Wetherick (1986) found that young Down's syndrome children were very clearly rejected by normal playgroup peers.

As with other groups, acceptance by teachers and peers is related to behavioural and temperamental characteristics. In that children with severe or multiple impairments are more likely to show behavioural difficulties and are so clearly 'different' from their normal peers, successful integration will require commensurately greater input. Bullock and Rigg (1980) argued that, unless adequate provision is available, children with more severe problems may receive less individualized instruction in normal classes than in so-called restrictive environments. There is also the danger that special help, even if available in the classroom, may focus less on integration than on the minimization of behavioural difficulties so that the child is tolerated but certainly not assimilated.

Intervention programmes for children with severe learning difficulties

Although curricular content and teaching standards in schools for the severely handicapped have been criticized, comparative evaluations of teaching practices are limited. Behavioural approaches to teaching have been widely employed and have proved effective in minimizing behavioural problems and improving learning skills. Language-training programmes and social skills training packages, also employing behavioural techniques, have been used more recently (Gresham, 1982; Goldstein & Wickstrom, 1986), as have cognitive-behavioural techniques to increase self-control and develop anger-management strategies etc. Modification of peer behaviours may also be required. Work by Strain and Odom (1986) and Goldstein and Ferrell (1987) illustrates how teaching peers to prompt, respond to or initiate social and verbal interactions can significantly improve communication. These effects seem to be enhanced if high-status peers are involved in the training programmes (Sasso & Rude, 1987). The deliberate structuring of collaborative learning activities between handicapped and nonhandicapped children also improves classroom behaviours (Putnam *et al.*, 1989).

Intervention programmes for children with autism

Several authors have reported a degree of success in increasing simple academic skills, play and social behaviours in children with autism placed in mainstream schools (Egel *et al.*, 1980; McHale & Simeonsson, 1980; Lord, 1984; Odom & Strain, 1986; Brady *et al.*, 1987; McEvoy *et al.*, 1988; Schuler, 1989). However, the majority of such programmes have involved very intensive and structured input from highly trained professionals, often on a temporary basis only. Even with considerable incentives for the normal peers there are likely to be problems in maintaining cooperation without considerable environmental restructuring (Schuler, 1989). Moreover, although some studies suggest that academic attainments are enhanced when autistic children are educated in integrated classrooms (again of an experimental nature – Hoyson *et al.*, 1984; Harris *et al.*, 1991), other comparative research suggests that progress in language development is not enhanced in integrated settings (Harris *et al.*, 1990). Certainly, for the more severely handicapped autistic child it is unlikely that integration can be adequately achieved without additional skilled help in the classroom.

The studies of Rutter and Bartak (1973) indicated the importance of structured education, focusing directly on educational goals, in improving both academic and social competence. Behavioural methods, too, have proved successful in decreasing undesirable behaviours and improving skills. Egel *et al.* (1980) concluded that behavioural models resulted in much more effective teaching strategies than those derived from psychoanalytic or sensory-deficit models and highly structured and behaviourally based approaches to teaching, such as are incorporated into the TEACCH programmes of Schopler and his colleagues (see Short, 1984), have produced encouraging results. Communication programmes and social skills training have resulted in limited improvements (Howlin & Rutter, 1987a; Williams, 1989) and, again, progress seems to be enhanced if the programme extends to the training of normal peers (Lord, 1984; Brady *et al.*, 1987; Schuler, 1989). The degree of teacher intervention is also important for success (Meyer *et al.*, 1987).

Well-controlled studies are lacking and, in the absence of comparison groups, claims about the effectiveness of special education programmes may be over-stated. Lovaas (1987) has reported dramatic improvements in a group of autistic children exposed to very intensive behavioural training and education from an early age. It is claimed that many showed significant increases in IQ and were subsequently indistinguishable from their normal peers but problems in group selection and data collection complicate the interpretation of results (Schopler, 1987).

Not all children with autism, of course, are severely retarded. For those of normal IQ, access to the normal school curriculum is crucial if they are to be able to compete academically (and subsequently in terms of job prospects) with their peers. However, unless teaching staff within the mainstream setting have some understanding of these children's very specific difficulties, they may become extremely isolated, lonely and rejected. Once again, adequate training and specialist support for the regular classroom teachers are essential (Russo & Koegel, 1977). The successful programmes reported in the literature are a far cry from the attempts of many education authorities to provide special provision through the medium of a well-meaning but untrained classroom aide. Gilbey and Jones (1988), in a survey of educational provision in England and Wales, found that only 12 education authorities claimed to be educating children with a diagnosis of autism in mainstream school. Only 17 children were involved and it was evident that the majority of their teachers had no prior knowledge of autism or of the problems it might entail. The amount of extra help provided varied from none to full-time, with 11 of the 17 children receiving additional (but rarely specially trained) help for half time or less. Because of this failure to provide teaching staff with adequate training or support to deal with the often very disruptive behaviours of children with autism, it is sometimes preferable for education in the early years to be provided in specialist autistic units. Once major difficulties are brought under control gradual, integration into more normal provision can be undertaken.

Postschool provision

For all children with pervasive learning difficulties, the outlook on leaving school is likely to be bleak. Although special training programmes are being developed to improve integration after school age (Mesibov, 1989; Moon *et al.*, 1990), the number of individuals served by these programmes is still very small. Wehman *et al.* (1989) found that only 11% of individuals in supported employment schemes in the US (71% of whom had a primary disability of mental retardation) were severely or profoundly retarded. Of students labelled moderately, severely or profoundly handicapped, 88% had never worked in the 5-year period since leaving school (Wehman *et al.*, 1985). Other studies in Massachusetts, Oregon and Maryland, Colorado and Virginia (McDonnell *et al.*, 1985; Mithaug *et al.*, 1985) have reported similar findings.

Even in the absence of severe learning difficulties, individuals with autism are likely to face major problems in finding employment unless special training schemes are implemented (Smith, 1990). The follow-up study of Rutter *et al.* (1992) of higher-functioning adults with autism indicated that only

16% were in paid employment of any kind and that the jobs involved were of a much lower level than predicted on the basis of IQ or educational attainments.

Early prevention of learning, emotional and behavioural difficulties

The failure of many intervention approaches, particularly with older children, has led to a heightened awareness of the need to intervene in high-risk groups of children before they even enter school. Although preschool centres for children with severe learning or physical difficulties have become well-established in recent years, provision for children with milder handicaps is more limited. This reluctance to invest significant resources in younger children is perhaps understandable in that follow-up studies of preschool units have generally produced inconsistent, or only very short-term results. Thus, Woolacott et al. (1978) reported no significant improvements in children attending a day-hospital preschool and Barton (1984) found only 25% of children attending a therapeutic preschool unit subsequently went on to normal play group or school.

Nurture work, either in special groups or within the classroom, for children who, because of inadequate stimulation or adverse early experience, are unable to cope with the demands of a normal classroom has also received growing support in recent years. However, evaluative studies are few and, although an early study by Cowen et al. (1971) found beneficial effects on learning and social adjustment, methodological problems limit the reliability of their findings. Kolvin et al. (1981) found that nurture work in the classroom could produce positive short-term gains but follow-up studies suggested that other forms of behavioural or psychotherapeutic intervention were more effective. In that nurture programmes make use of nonprofessional help, potentially they might seem to provide a relatively cheap form of specialized education, but without special training of both teachers and aides the results are likely to be limited (Cowen et al., 1979).

One specific type of intervention that has been more systematically investigated than most is the Portage programme (Shearer & Shearer, 1972), designed specifically for children with early developmental delays. Despite its widespread use in Europe and North America, methodological problems and the lack of long-term follow-up studies mean, again, that the comparative effectiveness of this approach remains unclear (Sturmey & Crisp, 1986).

A much more expensive form of intervention has been the massive growth of brief, compensatory programmes such as Head Start in the US. Such programmes have been widely criticized on theoretical, experimental, statistical and economic grounds (Cave & Maddison, 1978; Ottenbacher, 1989). Rhine (1981) discussed the many problems involved in carrying out large-scale evaluations of this kind of intervention, when programmes often differ in important ways and where involvement of teachers or parents may be extremely variable. Nevertheless, some programmes have been found to have surprisingly persistent effects (Zigler & Valentine, 1980; Rhine, 1981; Lazar & Darlington, 1982; Lee et al., 1990). Changes in overall cognitive levels have been limited but a number of studies have shown continuing gains in reading, arithmetic and other school achievements. Darlington et al. (1980), in an analysis of the results of approximately 2700 children, ranging in age from 9 to 19 years, found that the greatest effects were on general school progress with significantly fewer children who had attended preschool programmes being assigned to special educational classes or being held back a grade.

For children with handicaps the duration, intensity and degree of structure seem to be of particular importance for outcome (Casto & Mastropieri, 1986) but Sigel (1990) noted that there remain many questions to be answered about the goals and structures of these early programmes and the types and ages of children for whom they prove most effective. Attention to wider social issues and the linking of preschool education to later schooling may also be crucial if outcome measures are to be not only statistically significant but of practical value to large numbers of children and their families.

CONCLUSIONS

The major finding to emerge from recent research in special education is that it is not where children are placed but the quality of education they receive that is the crucial factor. Over 20 years ago Dunn (1968) noted: 'any arrangement may be good or bad for a particular child depending on the quality of teaching or type of curriculum offered'. Adherence to assumptions that normalization excludes specialist help, that 'separate' always implies 'unequal', or that the least restrictive environment is always to be preferred will always be inappropriate (Zigler & Hodapp, 1987; Mesibov, 1990). The focus of debate and of experimental research should be not on whether one form of schooling is 'better' than another but on what happens within particular settings; it is also essential to distinguish between different groups of children rather than assuming heterogeneity of needs. At the present time it is clear that the type of teaching received by many children is determined more by national legislation or local provision than by any assessment of individual needs. What is needed is a continuum of facilities, from special day and boarding schools, through special classes and resource centres attached to normal schools, to full-time integration with help, as necessary, provided within the classroom. Diagnosis and assessment of the child should be used to ensure that the school placement is matched to individual needs. It is crucial, too, that teacher support, training and resources are adequate to ensure the implementation and ongoing monitoring of optimum teaching strategies.

Moreover, since all children and most schools change with time, flexibility of provision is important. The continuing effectiveness of placements should be regularly monitored, with opportunities being made available for children to change schools when appropriate. Much of the debate over integration versus segregation has been conducted on the tacit assumption that such provision has to be permanent. For many children, early special provision may help to overcome problems that would otherwise interfere with learning. Once these have been adequately dealt with, gradual introduction into normal schools and the eventual withdrawal of special help may well be possible. The longer-term advantages of specialist intervention on a temporary basis still need greater investigation, as do the procedures required to ensure smooth transition back into the mainstream.

A further need is for closer cooperation between all the professionals involved in the child's care so that medical, social, psychological and psychiatric advice can be incorporated as necessary into special education programmes. The involvement of parents in decisions about placement is also likely to be to the child's advantage.

Finally, the evaluation of specialist provision needs to take into account the effects, not only on a child's educational attainments, but on many other areas of social and emotional functioning, and not only during the school years but in later life as well.

REFERENCES

Acton H.M. & Zarbatany L. (1988) Interaction and performance with co-operative groups: effects on non-handicapped students' attitudes towards their mildly retarded peers. *American Journal of Mental Retardation*, **93**, 16–23.

Affleck J.Q., Madge S., Adams A. & Lowenbraun S. (1988) Integrated classroom vs resource model: academic viability and effectiveness. *Exceptional Children*, **54**, 339–348.

Algozzine K.M., Morsink C.V. & Algozzine B. (1988) What's happening in self-contained special education classrooms? *Exceptional Children*, **55**, 259–265.

Aman M.G. (1980) Psychotropic drugs and learning problems — a selective review. *Journal of Learning Disabilities*, **13**, 87–97.

Anderson E.M. & Clarke L. (with Spain B.) (1982) *Disability in Adolescence*. Methuen, London.

Appolloni T. & Cooke T.P. (1978) Integrated programming at the infant toddler and pre-school levels. In: Guralnick M. (ed) *Early Intervention and the Integration of Handicapped and Non-handicapped Children*. University Park Press, Baltimore, MD.

Atkinson G.C.E. (1975) The Highfield Experiment. *New Behaviour*, July 10, 54–57.

Ault M.J., Wolery M., Doyle P.M. & Gast D.L. (1989) Review of comparative studies in the instruction of students with moderate and severe handicaps. *Exceptional Children*, **55**, 346–356.

Bak J.J. & Siperstein G.N. (1987) Effects of mentally retarded children's behavioural competence as non-retarded peers' behaviours and attitudes towards establishing ecological validity in attitude research. *American Journal of Mental Deficiency*, **92**, 31–39.

Bak J.J., Cooper E.M., Dobroth K.M. & Siperstein G.N. (1987) Special class placements as labels. Effects on children's attitudes toward learning handicapped peers. *Exceptional Children*, **54**, 151–155.

Barton L. (1984) Special children. In: Barton L. & Tomlinson S. (eds) *Special Education and Social Interests*, pp. 72–84. Croom Helm, London.

Barton L. & Tomlinson S. (1981) *Special Education: Policy, Practices and Social Issues*. Harper Row, London.

Beckman P.J. & Kohl F.L. (1987) Interactions of pre-schoolers with and without handicaps in integrated and segregated settings. A longitudinal study. *Mental Retardation*, **25**, 5–11.

Beitchman J.H., Nair R., Clegg M. & Patel P.G. (1986) Prevalence of speech and language disorders in 5 year old kindergarten children in the Ottawa Carlton Region. *Journal of Speech and Hearing Disorders*, **51**, 98–110.

Berg I., Nichols K. & Pritchard C. (1969) School phobia — its classification and relationship to dependency. *Journal of Child Psychology and Psychiatry*, **10**, 23–41.

Berg I., Butler A., Hullin R., Smith R. & Tyrer S. (1978) Features of children taken to Juvenile Court for failure to attend school. *Psychological Medicine*, **8**, 447–453.

Bickel W.E. & Bickel D.D. (1986) Effective schools, classrooms and instruction: implications for special education. *Exceptional Children*, **52**, 489–500.

Bicklen D.S. (1985) *Achieving the Complete School. Effective Strategies for Mainstreaming*. Teachers' College Press, New York.

Bicklen D.S. (1987) The integration question — educational and residential placement issues. In: Cohen D.J. & Donnellan A.M. (eds) *Handbook of Autism and Pervasive Developmental Disorders*, pp. 653–667. Winston-Wiley, New York.

Bishop D.M. & Edmundson A. (1987) Language-impaired 4-year-olds: distinguishing transient from persistent impairment. *Journal of Speech and Hearing Disorders*, **52**, 156–173.

Blagg N. (1987) *School Phobia and its Treatment*. Croom Helm, London.

Blagg N. & Yule W. (1984) The behavioural treatment of school refusal; a comparative study. *Behaviour Research and Therapy*, **22**, 119–127.

Brady M.P., Shores R.E., McEvoy M.A., Ellis D. & Fox J.J. (1987) Increasing social interactions of severely handicapped autistic children. *Journal of Autism and Developmental Disorders*, **17**, 375–390.

Bryant P.E., Bradley L., MacLean M. & Crossland J. (1989) Nursery rhymes, phonological skills and reading. *Journal of Child Language*, **16**, 407–428.

Budgell P. (1986) Drifting towards segregation. *British Journal of Special Education*, **13**, 94–96.

Bullock L.M. & Rigg W.C. (1980) Relationship of individualised instruction to placement of exceptional children. *Exceptional Children*, **47**, 224–225.

Bullock L.M., Zagar E.L., Donahue C.A. & Pelton G.B. (1985) Teachers' perceptions of behaviourally disordered students in a variety of settings. *Exceptional Children*, **52**, 123–130.

Burstein N. (1986) The effects of classroom organization on mainstreamed pre-school children. *Exceptional Children*, **52**, 425–434.

Bursuck W.D., Rose E., Cowen S. & Yahaya M.A. (1989) Nationwide survey of post secondary education services for students with learning disabilities. *Exceptional Children*, **56**, 236–245.

Campbell N.J., Dobson J.E. & Bost J.M. (1985) Educator perceptions of behaviour problems of mainstreamed students. *Exceptional Children*, **51**, 298–303.

Cantrell R.P. & Cantrell M.L. (1979) Preventive mainstreaming: impact of a supportive services program on pupils. *Exceptional Children*, **46**, 381–386.

Carlberg C. & Kavale K. (1980) The efficacy of special versus regular class placement for exceptional children: a meta-analysis. *Journal of Special Education*, **14**, 295–309.

Carr J. (1982) Social relationships amongst spina bifida children attending ordinary or special schools. Report to Inner London Education Authority Research and Statistics Group.

Carr J., Hallwell M. & Pearson A. (1981) Educational attainments of spina bifida children attending ordinary or special schools. *Zeitschrift für Kinderchirurgie*, **34**, 364–370.

Carri L. (1985) In service teachers' assessed needs in behavioural disorders, mental retardation and learning disabilities. Are they similar? *Exceptional Children*, **51**, 411–416.

Casey W., Jones D., Kugler B. & Watkins B. (1988) Integration of Down's syndrome children in the primary school: a longitudinal study of cognitive development and academic attainments. *British Journal of Educational Psychology*, **58**, 279–286.

Casto G. & Mastropieri M.A. (1986) The efficacy of early intervention programs: a meta-analysis. *Exceptional Children*, **52**, 417–424.

Cave C. & Maddison P. (1978) *A Survey of Recent Research in Special Education*. NFER, Oxford.

Center Y., Ward J. & Ferguson C. (1991) Towards an index to evaluate the integration of children with disabilities into regular classrooms. *Educational Psychology*, **11**, 77–95.

Chapman E.K. & Stone J.M. (1988) *The Visually Handicapped Child in Your Classroom*. Cassell, London.

Chazan M., Laing A., Shackleton-Bailey M. & Jones G. (1981) Young children with special needs in ordinary schools. In: Swann W. (ed) *The Practice of Special Education*, pp. 122–136. Blackwell/Open University Press, Guildford.

Cole T. (1989) *Apart or A Part? Integration and the Growth of British Special Education*. Open University Press, Milton Keynes.

Cooling M. (1974) Educational provisions for maladjusted children in boarding schools. MEd Thesis, Birmingham University.

Cooper D.H. & Spence D.L. (1990) Maintaining at risk children in regular education settings; initial effects of individual differences and classroom environments. *Exceptional Children*, **56**, 117–126.

Cope C. & Anderson E. (1977) *Special Units in Ordinary Schools: An Exploratory Study of Special Provision for Disabled Children*. Institute of Education, London.

Corman L. & Gottlieb J. (1978) Mainstreaming mentally retarded children: a review of research. In: Ellis R. (ed) *International Review of Research in Mental Retardation*, vol. 9, pp. 251–276. Academic Press, New York.

Cosden M., Pearl R. & Bryan T.H. (1985) The effects of co-operative and individual goal structures on learning disabled and non-disabled students. *Exceptional Children*, **52**, 103–114.

Cowen E.L., Dorr D., Izzo L.D., Madonia A. & Trost M.A. (1971) The Primary Mental Health Project: a new way to conceptualize and deliver school mental health service. *Psychology in the Schools*, **8**, 216–266.

Cowen E., Orgel A., Gesten E. & Wilson A. (1979) The evaluation of an intervention program for young schoolchildren with acting out problems. *Journal of Abnormal Child Psychology*, **7**, 381–396.

Croll P. & Moses D. (1985) *One in Five*. Routledge & Kegan-Paul, London.

Currey W.E. (1988) In: *Report of the Department Committee on Defective and Epileptic Children (Sharpe Report)*, vol. 2, p. 216. Her Majesty's Stationery Office, London.

Dain P. (1977) Disruptive children and the key centre. *Remedial Education*, **12**, 163–167.

Dale P.S. & Cole K.N. (1988) Comparison of academic and cognitive programs for young handicapped children. *Exceptional Children*, **54**, 439–447.

Darlington R.B., Royce J.M., Snipper A.S., Murray H.W. & Lazar I. (1980) Pre-school programs and later school competence of children from low income families. *Science*, **208**, 202–203.

Dawson R. (1980) *Special Provision for Disturbed People: A Survey*. Macmillan Education, London.

de Bettencourt L.U., Zigmond N. & Thornton H. (1989) Follow up of post-secondary age rural learning disabled graduates and dropouts. *Exceptional Children*, **55**, 40–49.

Deno S., Maruyama G., Espin C. & Cohen C. (1990) Educating students with mild disabilities in general education classrooms: Minnesota alternatives. *Exceptional Children*, **57**, 150–160.

Donaldson P. (1980) Changing attitudes towards handicapped persons: a review and analysis of research. *Exceptional Children*, **46**, 504–514.

Dowling E. (1990) Children's disturbing behaviour — whose problem is it? An account of a school based service for parents and teachers. *Newsletter: Association for Child Psychology and Psychiatry*, **12**, 8–12.

Dowling E. & Osborne E. (1985) *The Family and the School — A Joint Systems Approach*. Routledge & Kegan Paul, London.

Dunn L.M. (1968) Special education for the mildly retarded: is much of it justified? *Exceptional Children*, **35**, 5–22.

Edgar E. (1985) How do special education students fare after they leave school? A response to Hasazi, Gordon & Roe. *Exceptional Children*, **51**, 470–473.

Egel A.L., Koegel R.L. & Schreibman L. (1980) Review of educational treatment procedures for autistic children. In: Mann L. & Sabatino D. (eds) *Fourth Review of Special Education*, pp. 109–149. Grune & Stratton, New York.

Esposito B.G. & Reed T.M. (1986) The effects of contact with handicapped persons on young children's attitudes. *Exceptional Children*, **53**, 224–229.

Fairweather J.S. (1989) Transition and other services for handicapped students in local education agencies. *Exceptional Children*, **55**, 315–320.

Fantuzzo J.W., Polite K., Cook D.M. & Quinn G. (1988) An evaluation of the effectiveness of teachers- vs student-management classroom interventions. *Psychology in the Schools*, **25**, 154–163.

Fiedler C.R. & Simpson R.L. (1987) Modifying the attitudes of non-handicapped high school students towards handicapped peers. *Exceptional Children*, **53**, 342–349.

Fogelman K. (1992) The long term effects of truancy. *Newsletter: Association for Child Psychology and Psychiatry*, **14**, 57–61.

Fox C.L. (1989) Peer acceptance of learning disabled children in the regular classroom. *Exceptional Children*, **56**, 50–59.

Frith U. (1983) The similarities and differences between reading and spelling problems. In: Rutter M. (ed) *Developmental Neuropsychiatry*, pp. 520–541. Guilford Press, New York.

Fuchs D. & Fuchs L.S. (1988) Evaluation of the Adaptive Learning Environment Model. *Exceptional Children*, **55**, 115–127.

Fuchs L.S., Fuchs D. & Hamlett C.L. (1989) Effects of alternative goal structures within curriculum based measures. *Exceptional Children*, **55**, 429–438.

Fuchs D., Fuchs L.S. & Bahr M.W. (1990) Mainstream Assistance Teams — a scientific basis for the art of consultation. *Exceptional Children*, **57**, 128–134.

Galloway D. & Barrett C. (1984) Off site centres for disruptive secondary school pupils in New-Zealand. *Educational Research*, **26**, 106–110.

Galloway D. & Goodwin C. (1987) *The Education of Disturbing Children. Pupils with Learning and Adjustment Difficulties*. Longman, London.

Galloway D., Ball T., Blomfield D. & Seyd R. (1982) *Schools and Disruptive Pupils*. Longman, London.

Gersten R., Walker H. & Darch C. (1988) Relationship between teachers' effectiveness and their tolerance for handicapped students. *Exceptional Children*, **54**, 433–438.

Gilbey K. & Jones G.E. (1988) *Autistic Children in Ordinary Mainstream Schools*. Summary Report. DHSS/DES Research Project. Child Development Research Project. University of Nottingham, Nottingham.

Gittelman R. & Feingold I. (1983) Children with reading disorders. I. Efficacy of reading remediation. *Journal of Child Psychology and Psychiatry*, **24**, 167–193.

Goldstein H. & Ferrell D.R. (1987) Augmenting communicative interactions between handicapped and non-handicapped pre-school children. *Journal of Speech and Hearing Disorders*, **52**, 200–211.

Goldstein H. & Wickstrom S. (1986) Peer intervention effects on communicative interaction among handicapped and non-handicapped pre-schools. *Journal of Applied Behavior Analysis*, **19**, 209–214.

Goodman H., Gottlieb J. & Harrison J. (1972) Social acceptance of EMR's integrated into a non-graded elementary school. *American Journal of Mental Deficiency*, **76**, 412–417.

Graden J.L., Casey A. & Bonstrom O. (1985) Implementing a pre-referral intervention system. Part II: The data. *Exceptional Children*, **51**, 487–496.

Gregory S. (1987) Review of W. Lynas 'Integrating the handicapped into ordinary schools'. *British Deaf News*, **32**, 9.

Gresham F.M. (1982) Misguided mainstreaming. The case for social skills training with handicapped children. *Exceptional Children*, **43**, 422–433.

Guralnick M. (1978) Integrated pre-schools as educational and therapeutic environments. In: Guralnick M.J. (ed) *Early Intervention and the Integration of Handicapped and Non-handicapped Children*, pp. 115–146. University Park Press, Baltimore, MD.

Guralnick M.J. & Groom J.M. (1987) The peer relations of mildly delayed and non-handicapped pre-school children in mainstreamed playgroups. *Child Development*, **52**, 1556–1572.

Guralnick M.J. & Groom J.M. (1988) Friendships of pre-school children in mainstreamed playgroups. *Developmental Psychology*, **24**, 595–604.

Gurney P.W. (1988) *Self Esteem in Children with Special Educational Needs*. Routledge, London.

Gutkin T.B., Singer J.H. & Brown R. (1980) Teacher reactions to school based consultation services. A multivariate analysis. *Journal of School Psychology*, **18**, 126–134.

Hallinger P. & Murphy J. (1986) The social context of effective schools. *American Journal of Education*, **94**, 328–355.

Hanrahan J., Goodman W. & Rapagna S. (1990) Preparing mentally retarded students for mainstreaming: priorities of regular class and special school teachers. *American Journal on Mental Retardation*, **94**, 470–474.

Hargreaves D. (1988) Quoted in Cole T. (1989) *Apart or A Part? Integration and the Growth of British Special Education*. Open University Press, Milton Keynes.

Harris S.L., Handleman J.S., Kristoff B., Bass L. & Gordon R. (1990) Changes in language development among autistic and peer children in segregated and integrated preschool settings. *Journal of Autism and Developmental Disorders*, **20**, 23–32.

Harris S.L., Handleman J.S., Gordon R., Kristoff B., Bass L. & Fuentes F. (1991) Changes in cognitive and language functioning of pre-school children with autism. *Journal of Austism and Developmental Disorders*, **21**, 281–290.

Harter S. (1984) Processes underlying the construction, maintenance and enhancement of the self concept in children. In: Suls J. & Greenwald A. (eds) *Psychological Perspectives on the Self*, vol. 3, pp. 24–58. Lawrence Erlbaum, Hillsdale, NJ.

Harvey L., Kolvin I., McLaren M., Nicol A.R. & Wolstenholme F. (1977) Introducing a school social worker into schools. *British Journal of Guidance and Counselling*, **5**, 26–40.

Hasazi S.B., Gordon L.R. & Roe C.A. (1985) Factors associated with the employment status of handicapped youth exiting high school from 1979–1983. *Exceptional Children*, **51**, 455–469.

Hasazi S.B., Johnson R.E., Hasazi J.E., Gordon L.R. & Hull M. (1989) Employment of youth with and without handicaps following high school: outcomes and correlates. *Journal of Special Education*, **23**, 243–255.

Hegarty S., Pocklington K. & Lucas D. (1982a) *Integration in Action. Case Studies in the Integration of Pupils with Special Needs*. NFER, Oxford.

Hegarty S., Pocklington K. & Lucas D. (1982b) *Educating Pupils with Special Needs in the Ordinary School*. NFER, Oxford.

Hersov L. (1985) School refusal. In: Rutter M. & Hersov L. (eds) *Child and Adolescent Psychiatry: Modern Approaches*, pp. 382–399. Blackwell Scientific Publications, Oxford.

Hersov L. & Berg I. (1980) *Out of School: Modern Perspectives in School Refusal and Truancy*. Wiley, Chichester.

Honig A.S. & McCarron P.A. (1988) Prosocial behaviours of handicapped and typical peers in an integrated pre-school. *Early Child Development and Care*, **33**, 113–125.

Howlin P. (1985) Special educational treatment. In: Rutter M. & Hersov L. (eds) *Child and Adolescent Psychiatry: Modern Approaches*, pp. 851–870. Blackwell Scientific Publications, Oxford.

Howlin P. & Rutter M. (1987a) *Treatment of Autistic Children*. Wiley, Chichester.

Howlin P. & Rutter M. (1987b) The consequences of language delay for other aspects of development. In: Yule W. & Rutter M. (eds) *Language Development and Disorders*. Clinics in Developmental Medicine, pp. 271–294. MacKeith Press/Blackwell, London.

Hoyson M., Jamieson B. & Strain P.S. (1984) Individualized group instruction of normally developing and autistic-like children. *Journal of the Division for Early Childhood*, **8**, 157–172.

Hunt G. (1981) Spina bifida: implications for 100 children at school. *Developmental Medicine and Child Neurology*, **23**, 160–172.

Inner London Education Authority (1981) *Ethnic Census of School Support Centres and Educational Guidance Centres*. RS 784/81. (c)

Ispa J. & Matz R.D. (1978) Integrating handicapped pre-school children within a cognitively-oriented program. In: Guralnick M. (ed) *Early Intervention and the Integration of Handicapped and Non-Handicapped Children*, pp. 167–190. University Park Press, Baltimore, MD.

Jamieson M., Partlett M. & Pocklington K. (1977) *Towards Integration: A Study of Blind and Partially Sighted Children in Ordinary Schools*. NFER, Windsor.

Jenkins J.R. & Heinen A. (1989) Students' preferences for service delivery: pull-outs, in class or integrated models. *Exceptional Children*, **55**, 516–523.

Jenkins J.R., Speltz M.L. & Odom S.L. (1985) Integrating normal and handicapped pre-schoolers: effects on child development and social interaction. *Exceptional Children*, **52**, 7–17.

Jenkins J.R., Pious C.G. & Peterson D.C. (1988) Categorical programs for remedial and handicapped students. *Exceptional Children*, **55**, 147–158.

Johnson D.W. & Johnson R.T. (1986) Mainstreaming and co-operative learning strategies. *Exceptional Children*, **52**, 553–561.

Keogh B.K. & Burnstein N.D. (1988) Relationship of temperament to pre-schoolers' interactions with peers and teachers. *Exceptional Children*, **54**, 456–461.

Kluwin T.M. & Moores D.F. (1989) Mathematics achievement of hearing impaired adolescents in different placements. *Exceptional Children*, **55**, 327–335.

Knoblock P. (1982) *Teaching and Mainstreaming Autistic Children*. Love Publishing, Denver, CO.

Kolvin I., Garside R.F., Nicol A.R., Macmillan A., Wolstenholme F. & Leitch I.M. (1981) *Help Starts Here: The Maladjusted Child in the Ordinary School*. Tavistock, London.

Krupski A. (1985) Variations in attention as a function of classroom task demands in learning handicapped and C.A. matched non-handicapped children. *Exceptional Children*, **52**, 52–56.

Lane D. (1977) Aspects of the use of behaviour modification in secondary schools. *Bulletin of the British Association for Behavioural Psychotherapy*, **5**, 76–79.

Lazar I. & Darlington R. (1982) Lasting effects of early education. *Monographs of the Society for Research in Child Development*, vol. 47, No. 195.

Lee V.E., Brooks-Gunn J., Schnur E. & Liaw F.R. (1990) Are head start effects sustained? A longitudinal follow-up comparison of disadvantaged children attending headstart, no pre-school and other pre-school programs. *Child Development*, **61**, 495–507.

Lewis M. (1980) Psychotherapeutic treatment in school refusal. In: Hersov L. & Berg I. (eds) *Out of School: Modern Perspectives in Truancy and School Refusal*, pp. 251–266. Wiley, Chichester.

Lewis I. & Vulliamy G. (1981) The social context of educational practice: the case of special education. In: Barton L. & Tomlinson S. (eds) *Special Education: Policy, Practices and Social Issues*, pp. 36–52. Harper Row, London.

Lord C. (1984) The development of peer relations in children with autism. *Applied Developmental Psychology*, **1**, 165–230.

Lovaas O.I. (1987) Behavioral treatment and normal educational and intellectual functioning in young autistic children. *Journal of Consulting and Clinical Psychology*, **55**, 3–9.

Lowden G. (1985) The units approach to integration. *British Journal of Special Education*, **12**, 10–12.

Lynas W. (1984) *Integrating the Handicapped into Ordinary Schools*. Croom Helm, London.

Lyons J., Serbin L.A. & Marchessault K. (1988) The social behaviour of peer identified, aggressive, withdrawn and aggressive/withdrawn children. *Journal of Abnormal Child Psychology*, **16**, 539–552.

Maag J.W. & Behrens J.T. (1989) Depression and cognitive self statements of learning disabled and seriously emotionally disturbed adolescents. *Journal of Special Education*, **23**, 17–27.

McDonnell J.J., Wilcox B., Boles S.M. & Bellamy G.T. (1985) Transition issues facing youth with severe disabilities: parents' perspective. *Journal of the Association for Persons with Severe Handicaps*, **II**, 53–60.

McEvoy M.A., Nordquist V.M., Twardosz S., Heckaman K.A., Wehby J.H. & Denny R.K. (1988) Promoting autistic children's peer interaction in an integrated early childhood setting using affection activities. *Journal of Applied Behaviour Analysis*, **21**, 193–200.

McHale S. & Simeonsson R. (1980) Effects of interaction on non-handicapped children's attitudes towards autistic children. *American Journal of Mental Deficiency*, **83**, 18–25.

McNamara E. & Jolly M. (1990) Are disruptive behaviours reduced when levels of on-task behaviours increase? An across settings study of a class of 12 and 13 year old pupils. II. *Behavioural Psychotherapy*, **18**, 239–250.

MacAulay D.A. (1990) Classroom environment: a literature review. *Educational Psychology*, **10**, 239–253.

Maheady L., Sacca M.K. & Harper G.F. (1988) Classwide peer tutoring with mildly handicapped high school students. *Exceptional Children*, **55**, 52–59.

Marshall M. (1971) The effect of special educational treatment of maladjusted pupils in a day school. *Association of Educational Psychologists' Journal*, **2**, 23–25.

Marston D. (1988) The effectiveness of special education. A time series analysis of reading performance in regular and special education settings. *Journal of Special Education*, **21**, 13–26.

Maughan B., Gray G. & Rutter M. (1985) Reading retardation and anti-social behaviour: a follow-up into employment. *Journal of Child Psychology and Psychiatry*, **26**, 741–754.

Merrett F. & Houghton S. (1989) Does it work with the older ones? A review of behavioural studies carried out in British secondary schools since 1981. *Educational Psychology*, **9**, 287–309.

Mesibov G.B. (1989) Supported employment schemes for adults with autism. Lecture given at International Conference on Autism, Aussois, 1989.

Mesibov G.B. (1990) Normalization and its relevance today. *Journal of Autism and Developmental Disorders*, **20**, 379–390.

Meyer L.M., Fox A., Schermer A., Ketelsen D., Montan N., Maley K. & Cole D. (1987) The effects of teacher intrusion on social play interactions between children with autism and their non-

handicapped peers. *Journal of Autism and Developmental Disorders*, **17**, 315–322.

Meyers C., Macmillan D. & Yoshida R. (1980) Regular class placement of EMR students: from efficacy to mainstreaming. A review of issues and research. In: Gottlieb J. (ed) *Educating Mentally Retarded Persons in the Mainstream*. University Park Press, Baltimore, MD.

Mickleborough P.J. (1980) *Atherstone Day Unit: Fifth Annual Report*. Warwickshire LEA, Atherstone.

Miller L.C., Barrett C.L., Hampe E. & Noble M. (1972) Comparison of reciprocal inhibition, psychotherapy and waiting list control for phobic children. *Journal of Abnormal Psychology*, **79**, 269–279.

Mitchell S. & Rosa P. (1981) Boyhood behaviour problems as precursors of criminality: a 15 year follow-up. *Journal of Child Psychology and Psychiatry*, **22**, 19–23.

Mithaug D.E., Horiuchi C.N. & Fanning P.N. (1985) A report of the Colorado Statewide follow-up survey of special education students. *Exceptional Children*, **51**, 397–404.

Moon M.S., Inge K.S., Wehman P., Brooke V. & Barcus J.M. (1990) *Helping Persons with Severe Mental Retardation Get and Keep Employment*. Paul Brookes, Baltimore, MD.

Moores D.F. (1982) *Educating the Deaf: Psychology Principles and Practice*. Houghton Mifflin, Boston, MA.

Mortimore P., Davies J., Varlaam A., West A., Devine P. & Mazza J. (1983) *Behaviour Problems in Schools: An Evaluation of Support Centres*. Croom Helm, London.

Moss G. & Childs J. (1981) In service training for teachers in behavioural psychology: problems of implementation. In: Wheldall K. (ed) *The Behaviourist in the Classroom: Aspects of Applied Behavioural Analysis in British Education Contexts*, pp. 92–97. Educational Review no. 1. Faculty of Education, University of Birmingham.

Nowacek E.J., Mckinney J.D. & Hallahan D.P. (1990) Instructional behaviours of more and less effective beginning regular and special educators. *Exceptional Children*, **57**, 140–147.

Nye C., Foster S.H. & Seaman D. (1987) Effectiveness of language intervention with the language/learning disabled. *Journal of Speech and Hearing Disorders*, **52**, 348–357.

O'Connor G., Glynn T. & Tuck B. (1987) Contexts for remedial reading practice: reading and pause, prompt and praise tutoring. *Educational Psychology*, **7**, 207–211.

Odom S.L. & Strain P.S. (1986) A comparison of peer initiation and teacher antecedent interventions for promoting reciprocal social interaction of autistic pre-schoolers. *Journal of Applied Behaviour Analysis*, **19**, 59–71.

O'Moore M. (1978) The social and emotional adjustment and educational attainments of children with physical handicaps at ordinary and special schools. Paper presented to the Annual Conference, British Psychological Society, York, 1978.

Ottenbacher K.J. (1989) Statistical conclusion validity of early intervention research with handicapped children. *Exceptional Children*, **55**, 534–540.

Panagopoulou-Stamatelatou A. (1990) The use of behavioural self management in primary school settings: a review. *Educational Psychology*, **10**, 207–223.

Price J.M. & Dodge K.A. (1989) Reactive and pro-active aggression in childhood: relations to peer status and social context dimensions. *Journal of Abnormal Child Psychology*, **17**, 455–471.

Price M. & Goodman L. (1980) Individualised education programs: a cost study. *Exceptional Children*, **46**, 446–458.

Pugach M.C. & Johnson W. (1989) The challenge of implementing collaboration between general and special education. *Exceptional Children*, **56**, 232–235.

Putnam J.W., Rynders J.E., Johnson R.T. & Johnson D.W. (1989) Collaborative skill instructions for promoting positive interactions between mentally handicapped and non-handicapped children.

Exceptional Children, **55**, 550–557.

Redl F. (1966) *When We Deal With Children*. Free Press, New York.

Reynolds D. (1982) The search for effective schools. *School Organisation*, **2**, 215–237.

Reynolds D. (1991) School effectiveness and school improvement in the 1990s. *Newsletter of the Association for Child Psychology and Psychiatry*, **13**, 5–9.

Rhine W. (1981) *Making Schools More Effective: New Directions from Follow Through*. Academic Press, New York.

Rich H.L. & Ross S.M. (1989) Students' time on learning tasks in special education. *Exceptional Children*, **55**, 508–515.

Russo D. & Koegel R. (1977) A method of integrating an autistic child into a normal public classroom. *Journal of Applied Behavior Analysis*, **10**, 579–590.

Rutter M. (1983) School effects on pupil progress: research findings and policy implications. *Child Development*, **54**, 1–29.

Rutter M. & Bartak L. (1973) Special education treatment of autistic children: a comparative study. II. Follow-up findings and implications for services. *Journal of Child Psychology and Psychiatry*, **41**, 241–270.

Rutter M. & Mawhood L. (1991) The long term psychosocial sequelae of specific developmental disorders of speech and language. In: Rutter M. & Casaer P. (eds) *Biological Risk Factors for Psychosocial Disorders*, pp. 233–259. Cambridge University Press, Cambridge.

Rutter M., Maughan B., Mortimore P. & Ouston J. (with Smith A.) (1979) *Fifteen Thousand Hours. Secondary Schools and their Effects on Children*. Open Books, London.

Rutter M., Mawhood L. & Howlin P. (1992) Language delay and social development. In: Fletcher P. & Hall D. (eds) *Specific Speech and Language Disorders in Children*, pp. 63–78. Whurr Publishers, London.

Sainato D.M., Strain P.S., Lefebvre D. & Rapp N. (1990) Effects of self evaluation on the independent work skills of pre-school children with disabilities. *Exceptional Children*, **56**, 540–549.

Sasso G.M. & Rude H.A. (1987) Unprogrammed effects of training high status peers to interact with severely handicapped children. *Journal of Applied Behaviour Analysis*, **20**, 35–44.

Saunders B. (1971) The effect of the emotionally disturbed child in the public school classroom. *Psychology in Schools*, **8**, 23–26.

Schopler E. (1987) Letter to the editor. *Autism Research Review*, **1**, 7.

Schuler A. (1989) Socialization. Paper presented at International Conference on Educational Issues in Autism. Mons August, 1980.

Shearer M.S. & Shearer D.E. (1972) The Portage Project: a model for early childhood education. *Exceptional Children*, **36**, 210–217.

Short A. (1984) Short term treatment outcome using parents as therapists for their own autistic children. *Journal of Child Psychology and Psychiatry*, **25**, 443–485.

Sigel I.E. (1990) Psycho-educational intervention; future directors. *Merrill Palmer Quarterly*, **36**, 159–172.

Silva P.A. (1980) The prevalence, stability and significance of developmental language delays in pre-school children. *Developmental Medicine and Child Neurology*, **22**, 768–777.

Sindelar P.T., Smith M.A., Harriman N.E., Hale R.L. & Wilson R.J. (1986) Teacher effectiveness in special education programmes. *Journal of Special Education*, **20**, 195–207.

Singh N.N. & Singh J. (1986) A behavioural remediation program for oral reading: effects on errors and comprehension. *Educational Psychology*, **6**, 105–111.

Sinson J.C. & Wetherick N.E. (1986) Integrating young children with Down's syndrome. *British Journal of Mental Subnormality*, **32**, 93–101.

Siperstein G.P., Bak J. & O'Keefe P. (1988) The relationship between children's attitudes toward and their social acceptance of mentally retarded peers. *American Journal on Mental Retardation*, **93**, 24–27.

Smith M.D. (1990) *Autism and Life in the Community*. Paul Brookes, Baltimore, MD.

Smith M.D., Dorecki D.R. & Davis E.E. (1977) School related factors influencing the self-concepts of children with learning problems. *Peabody Journal of Education*, **54**, 185–195.

Stevenson J. & Richman N. (1976) The prevalence of language delay in a population of 3 year old children and its association with general retardation. *Developmental Medicine and Child Neurology*, **18**, 431–444.

Strain P.S. & Odom S.L. (1986) Peer social initiations: effective intervention for social skills development of exceptional children. *Exceptional Children*, **52**, 543–551.

Strain P.S., Shores R.E. & Kerr M.M. (1976) Direct and 'spillover' effects of social reinforcement on the social interaction of behaviourally handicapped pre-school children. *Journal of Applied Behaviour Analysis*, **9**, 31–40.

Sturmey P. & Crisp A.C. (1986) Portage guide to early education. A review of research. *Educational Psychology*, **6**, 139–155.

Sulzer-Azaroff B. & Gillat A. (1990) Trends in behaviour analysis in education. *Journal of Applied Behaviour Analysis*, **23**, 491–495.

Szivos S.E. (1990) Attitudes to work and their relationship to self esteem and aspirations among young adults with a mild mental handicap. *British Journal of Mental Subnormality*, **36**, 108–117.

Tateyama-Sniezek E. (1990) Co-operative learning: does it improve the academic achievement of students with handicaps? *Exceptional Children*, **56**, 426–437.

Taylor A.R., Asher S.R. & Williams G.A. (1987) The social adaptation of mainstreamed mildly retarded children. *Child Development*, **58**, 1321–1334.

Taylor L., Lacey R. & Bracken D. (1979) *In Whose Best Interests?* Cobden Trust, Surrey.

Topping K. (1983) *Educational Systems for Disruptive Adolescents*. Croom Helm, London.

Topping K. (1992) Peer tutoring and co-operative learning: an overview. *Psychologist*, **5**, 151–157.

Truesdell L.A. (1990) Behavior and achievement of mainstreamed junior high special class students. *Journal of Special Education*, **24**, 234–242.

Tsoi M. & Yule W. (1976) The effects of group reinforcement in classroom behaviour modification. *Educational Studies*, **2**, 129–140.

Walker D.K., Singer J.D., Palfrey J.S., Orza M., Wenger M. & Butler J.A. (1988) Who leaves and who stays in special education: a 2 year follow-up study. *Exceptional Children*, **54**, 393–402.

Wang M.C. & Birch J.S. (1984) Effective special education in regular classes. *Exceptional Children*, **50**, 391–398.

Wang M.C. & Walberg H.J. (1988) Four fallacies of segregationism. *Exceptional Children*, **55**, 128–137.

Warnock H.M. (1978) *Special Educational Needs. Report of the Committee of Enquiry into the Education of Handicapped Children and Young People*. HMSO, London.

Wasik B.H., Ramey C.T., Bryant D.M. & Sparling J.J. (1990) A longitudinal study of two early intervention strategies: project CARE. *Child Development*, **61**, 1682–1696.

Wehman P., Kregel J. & Seyfarth J. (1985) A follow-up of mentally retarded graduates' vocational and independent living skills. *Virginia Rehabilitation Counselling Bulletin*, **29**, 90–99.

Wehman P., Kregel J. & Shafer M.S. (1989) *Emerging Trends in the National Supported Employment Initiative. A Preliminary Analysis of 27 States*. Virginia Commonwealth University Rehabilitation, Research and Training Center, Richmond, VA.

Wheldall K. & Lam Y.Y. (1987) Rows versus tables. II. The effects of classroom seating arrangements in classroom disruption rates on task behaviour and teacher behaviour in three special school classes. *Educational Psychology*, **7**, 303–310.

Williams T.I. (1989) A social skills group for autistic children. *Journal of Autism and Developmental Disorders*, **19**, 143–156.

Wilson M. & Evans M. (1980) *Education of Disturbed Pupils*. Methuen Educational, London.

Woolacott S., Graham P.J. & Stevenson J. (1978) A controlled evaluation of the therapeutic effectiveness of a psychiatric day centre for pre-school children. *British Journal of Psychiatry*, **132**, 349–355.

Wright D.M., Moelis I. & Pollack L.J. (1976) The outcome of individual child psychotherapy: increments at follow-up. *Journal of Child Psychology and Psychiatry*, **17**, 275–285.

Yule W. (1985) Behavioural approaches. In: Rutter M. & Hersov L. (eds) *Child and Adolescent Psychiatry: Modern Approaches*, pp. 794–808. Blackwell Scientific Publications, Oxford.

Yule W. (1992) Review of 'Conductive Education' by Hari M. & Akos K., 1971. *Journal of Child Psychology and Psychiatry*, **33**, 634–635.

Yule W. & Rutter M. (1985) Reading and other learning difficulties. In: Rutter M. & Hersov L. (eds) *Child and Adolescent Psychiatry:*

Modern Approaches, pp. 444–464. Blackwell Scientific Publications, Oxford.

Zabel R.M., Peterson R.L. & Smith C.R. (1988) Use of time by teachers of behaviourally disordered students: a replication. *Behaviour Disorders*, **13**, 89–97.

Zetlin A. & Murtaugh M. (1990) Whatever happened to those with borderline IQs? *American Journal of Mental Retardation*, **94**, 463–469.

Zigler E. & Hodapp R.M. (1987) The developmental implications of integrating autistic children within the public schools. In: Cohen D. & Donnellan A. (eds) *Handbook of Autism and Pervasive Developmental Disorders*, pp. 668–676. Wiley, New York.

Zigler E. & Valentine J. (1980) *Project Head Start: A Legacy of the War on Poverty*. Free Press, New York.

Zigmund N. & Baker J. (1990) Mainstream experiences for learning disabled students (Project MELD): preliminary report. *Exceptional Children*, **54**, 176–185.

Chapter 64
Legal Aspects of Child Care

Stephen Wolkind

The origins of child psychiatry are closely linked to the judicial system. Levy (1951) has described how the Child Guidance movement was founded with the expectation that it would provide a solution to the problem of juvenile delinquency. The assessment of young offenders being brought before the courts has always been, and continues to be, an important part of the work of the child psychiatrist. The type of reports required and the nature of the psychiatric recommendations that can be made are described in Chapter 56.

The last 10 years have however seen a new and growing link between child psychiatry and the law. Before that time child psychiatrists did occasionally become involved in legal issues unconnected with delinquency. On relatively rare occasions they would be asked, possibly by one of the parties involved in a marital dispute, to give evidence when the custody of the child or access arrangements could not be agreed upon. The change has been in the increasing demand for such opinions, the greater acceptance by the judiciary of the usefulness of the opinions and the broadening of the work from marital disputes to include those where the dispute is between the parents and the state, represented generally by a social work agency. This change has not been well-documented but at many meetings of child psychiatrists the increasing workload caused by such cases is a frequent point of discussion. The demands are considered so great that they are influencing the number of child psychiatrists who, it is estimated, will be required in the future (Cox, 1990). The change is also reflected in the literature. There has been a steady increase in the number of articles appearing in professional and scientific journals on the role of the child psychiatrist in legal aspects of child care. In 1990 the *Journal of the American Academy of Child and Adolescent Psychiatry* devoted a special section to this topic (Herman, 1990). In 1989 the first British textbook was published (Black *et al.*, 1989). It is not only psychiatrists who have had to learn to cope with these new demands and acquire the skills necessary to meet them. Richards (1988) has called for developmental psychologists to find ways of using their expertise and knowledge to help the courts.

The speed of these new developments and the technical difficulties in framing and carrying out formal research studies means that there has been very little evaluation of this work, on whether it is justified or whether it and the recommendations it produces actually benefit the children it is supposed to help. This will be a major task for the next 10 years and it is encouraging that a start is being made. Thus, Ash and Guyer (1986) have examined whether courts make appropriate use of the psychiatric advice offered to them, and Wald and colleagues (1988) have examined how different legal decisions affect children.

In this chapter various basic principles underlying this area of practice will be presented. Some of the views will, of necessity, be personal and cannot be supported by research data. What is crucial is that all who undertake this work do so with an open mind, prepared to modify their approach as new empirical data become available. It can be easy for an individual to develop a rigid and possibly idiosyncratic set of practices and viewpoints which is applied to all cases. A major safeguard is for this work to be continuously exposed to peer review and audit in the same way as any other clinical activity in psychiatry (Department of Health, 1990). Case presentations can be made to fellow clinicians who should be asked to comment on the conclusions drawn by the presenter. It can be useful for several professionals to observe a video-taped clinical interview and rate certain key features, such as the quality of the relationship between parent and child or the reliability of a child's description of events. Regular reviews should be made of the proportion of recommendations accepted by the court. A formal 'adverse event' audit should be made of cases where a strongly argued opinion is totally rejected. Peers can help the practitioner understand whether it was the opinion that was at fault or the way it was presented. Courts appear increasingly to value the contributions of child psychiatrists and a condition for future collaboration might be that they agree to formal follow-up studies which will allow us to see whether our predictions are justified and our opinions helpful in the long term.

This chapter will not seek to provide a comprehensive introduction to child-care law. This varies greatly not only between countries but even between states and other components of different countries. It will attempt to examine how present legal thinking has evolved and will describe some of the settings in which a child's future can be decided. Its major task, however, will be to describe how a knowledge of developmental psychopathology can be combined with clinical expertise to provide a written report and an opinion, both of which can be defended in court and hopefully will help the court best meet the needs of the child requiring its protection.

LEGAL AND HISTORICAL BACKGROUND

The recent and rapid rise in the use of child psychiatrists by the court is probably a direct consequence of the growing awareness of child abuse, of the many forms it can take and of its long-term effects (see Chapters 13 and 14). After the general acceptance of Kempe's work on physical abuse (Kempe *et al.*, 1962), social workers and judges could not fail to realize that for many abused children the emotional consequences of the abuse were as, if not more, severe than the physical sequelae. This led to an acceptance that emotional abuse, even in the absence of physical abuse, was a legitimate reason for state intervention (Wolkind, 1988), though this move was opposed by some (Goldstein *et al.*, 1980b). Such a concept is, however, highly complex and experts in child development and the consequences of deviant development were clearly needed to give the courts information on the current state of knowledge (O'Regan, 1990). The growing awareness of the complexity of the issues that had to be decided upon led not only to a greater use of child psychiatrists but also, in the UK, to a greater use by local authorities of the higher courts to deal with the more difficult cases. This can well be seen in the use of wardship, a procedure which makes the child the responsibility of the court and its judges, and in which significant changes in the life of the child can only occur with the permission of the court (White, 1991). In 1971 the Family Division of the High Court dealt with 622 applications for wardship. Of these, only 2.5% were made by local authorities. By 1986 the total figure was 3339: the local authority proportion had risen to over 50% (Waterhouse, 1989).

These recent changes can also be seen, however, as part of a lengthier process which has occurred in almost all western countries. Over the past 60 years there has been a progressive shift in the public and legal view, from seeing the child as virtually the property of its parents to a perception of the child as having needs and rights of its own. This has been paralleled by a move to greater state intervention to ensure those rights (Yates, 1989). Though the ethics and legality of this process are constantly and legitimately being questioned, the point has now been reached where in many countries the basic philosophy underpinning the body of child-care law is that the needs of the child are paramount. An example which well illustrates the magnitude of the change can be seen in custody arrangements made after a divorce. The assumption in the UK until the 1930s was that as the 'senior' partner, the father had virtually automatic right to have the care of the children. From then on custody became ever more likely to be granted to the mother. This owed less to an attempt to grant greater equality to women than to an awareness that the young child might have a greater need for its mother than for its father (Yates, 1989).

The move for the state increasingly to take on an active role as protector of the child, with professionals having the right to intervene in the affairs of a family, increased through the 1970s and early 1980s. This growing interventionist policy was strongly fuelled in the UK by the massive publicity given to a number of appalling abuse cases which resulted in the death of a number of children (Department of Health, 1989). Since then there has been evidence of a retreat. The Children Act (1989) has, as a key principle, the notion that the state should only intervene if it can be clearly demonstrated that any intervention would be better for the child than leaving things as they are. These newer changes probably reflect a disillusioning acceptance of the research evidence (Wald *et al.*, 1988), that very often state care has little more to offer a child than less than adequate parenting in the family of origin. Concern has been expressed that this has led to the pendulum moving back in favour of parents' rights at the expense of children's needs (Eekelaar, 1991). The debate will continue, hopefully increasingly informed by research findings.

However, enormous variations remain between and within different countries. MacPherson (1984) has produced a detailed bibliography giving an account of the legal framework and child-care legislation of virtually every country of the world. In the UK the large number of different laws dealing with child care and protection have been brought together in one simplified and unified structure, the Children Act (1989) (Department of Health, 1989), which was implemented in October 1991. Eekelaar and Dingwall (1990) and Allen (1990) have provided a detailed guide to and analysis of the implications of the act for children, their families and those who work with them. In the US legislation varies from state to state — Freed and Walker (1989) provide an overview of the legal principles involved and the interstate variations. In the European Community attempts are being made to try to harmonize child-care law throughout the member states (Kerckhoff, 1981). De Jonge (1989) describes the situation in Australia. In developing countries a wide range of legal philosophies exists, with in most cases the law reflecting the traditional social values of their communities (MacPherson, 1984). There is some evidence that, here too, changes are occurring if these values conflict with the basic needs of children.

THE KEY QUESTIONS

Any court charged with the responsibility of ensuring the welfare of children will need to decide upon a wide range of disputed issues. These will include financial settlements, matters of religious upbringing or type of schooling. Occasionally the help of a psychiatrist might be required. Thus an opinion might be sought on the suitability of a particular educational regime for a child with a condition such as autism, or of the implications for a child's social development of being entered by one parent into a very extreme religious sect against the wishes of the other parent. The two basic questions, however, which will be most commonly asked of the court are with whom and where the child should live and what contact the child should have with certain individuals with whom he or she is not living.

The first of these questions may arise in a number of ways. Following a divorce or separation each partner may seek custody of the child. It needs to be remembered that in the majority of cases such decisions are arrived at by mutual agreement, possibly with the help of the parents' solicitors. In more difficult cases mediation services, often linked to courts, will help many families resolve their difficulties (Garwood, 1989; Yates, 1990). Those that reach the courts for a decision thus represent the most difficult cases, ones where there is a great deal of bitterness and open hostility or where highly complicated factors of great psychiatric relevance are present. There is rarely a simple answer to the dispute, with one parent being obviously able to meet all the child's needs and the other having nothing to offer. An example might be a conflict between a mother with a past history of alcoholism who has left her husband and is now living in a stable relationship with a lesbian partner, and a father with a history of recurrent depression and previous suicide attempts. On occasion other relatives, such as grandparents who have played a major part in bringing up the child, may seek to have custody. More frequently, however, a social service agency will be arguing in court that the biological family has failed to meet the needs of the child and that alternative care, possibly on a permanent basis, is required. They might argue for a foster family, or adoption or for admission to a residential unit. The court will need to hear from the child psychiatrist the advantages and disadvantages of each of these options as compared to those of keeping the child with its own family. The term custody has an unfortunate legal and possessive ring to it. The British Children Act recognizes this and replaces it with the more neutral term of residence.

The second question involves contact with the child, most often by noncustodial parents, but also by other adults who have been important in its life (Bullock *et al.*, 1991). If the child is living with its mother, should it have contact with its father? Even fewer of these cases will not be dealt with informally or through mediation (Davis & Roberts, 1989). Those that reach the courts are usually marked by quite remarkable levels of conflict. A balance may need to be struck, for example between a child's right to know a father of whom it has fond memories and the indirect effects on the child of the extreme anxieties, felt by the mother at contact continuing with a man who frequently physically assaulted her. A child in foster care with no prospect of being rehabilitated at home may wish to have some contact with its parents. There may, however, be clear evidence that this contact is undermining the stability of the placement and the confidence of the foster parents. Issues of continuing contact with biological parents after adoption are becoming more common (see Chapter 16). The need to maintain contact between siblings in different placements may need to be considered by the court. In the UK the new legislation specifically mentions the right of grandparents to seek contact with their grandchildren who might be in the care of a local authority.

In addition to these two main questions which involve the child psychiatrist, a further one which is very specific to the specialty is that of a child's right and ability to give consent for treatment. Parents of a child who soils at school and is totally

ostracized by other children may see no reason for bringing him to treatment. The family of a child with anorexia nervosa may refuse to allow her to enter hospital. As our knowledge of the efficacy of treatment increases, so the child psychiatrist can help the Court decide where the balance should lie between the child's need for treatment and the danger of weakening parental authority.

THE ROLE OF THE CHILD PSYCHIATRIST

The range of settings and legal philosophies that exist in different countries has been referred to previously. One dimension on which they could all be placed is the extent to which they use an adversarial or an inquisitorial system. Thus in English law, with its adversarial system, though all will be expected to be attempting to obtain the best for the child, the different parties are opposing each other and are seeking to demonstrate to the judge that their solution is the best. Even though judges make it clear that they expect psychiatrists to be independent, lawyers may see the issue in terms of winning and losing. Expert witnesses can easily be seen as the 'property' of their side and will be expected wholeheartedly to support their case. Under the Children Act (1989), although the system remains adversarial, the role of the expert witness should move closer to that seen in an inquisitorial system, such as in the Scottish Family Hearings (Martin & Murray, 1981) or the New Zealand Family Court (Bridge & Hipgrave, 1989), where all parties are expected to work with the Court to determine the best outcome. The expert is expected not to be partisan and is there solely to help the court.

For a child psychiatrist the inquisitorial system is clearly preferable. No matter what the system, however, it is essential that the child psychiatrist makes it clear to all parties that irrespective of who has commissioned his or her involvement, he or she sees the task as solely to represent the child's interests. This can be difficult in an adversarial system where immense psychological pressures can build up in conferences with lawyers during which attempts are made to denigrate evidence and experts produced by the opposing side. One way in which the psychiatrist can distance him- or herself from this process is by insisting from the start that he or she is independent and obtaining an agreement in writing that no matter what opinion he or she gives, this will be made available to all parties. This can prevent the psychiatrist from being seen solely as a hired help of one side and can also prevent the potentially damaging process of a child being taken to a succession of psychiatrists until one produces a report favourable to the commissioning side. One final weapon of the legal profession or of a small unscrupulous part of it, namely to refuse to pay for an unfavourable report, has been firmly rejected as unacceptable by the High Court (Noble, 1983). The pressure on the psychiatrist to take a partisan stance can however be very great.

A second crucial point in examining the role of the child psychiatrist is the absolute need to ensure that personal, political or social views are not presented in the guise of expert evidence. For example, a psychiatrist may have strong views that intercountry adoption represents an unacceptable form of neocolonialism. It is perfectly reasonable to argue for this view as long as it is made clear to the Court that this is a personal view. If, however, the psychiatrist wishes to be genuinely considered as an expert witness, it would also be necessary to point to the evidence that the majority of such adoptions are, from the point of view of the child, highly successful (Tizard, 1991). Unless this sharp differentiation is made between personal views and those based on a body of scientific knowledge, great harm can be done to the profession, as well as to the child whose future is being considered.

When differences of opinion between psychiatrists are present, judges are increasingly likely to ask for these to be discussed out of the court and an explanation given for the discrepancy. In most cases the difference represents a relatively minor disagreement over the weight to be given to a particular factor. A presentation to the court of the reasons behind these different emphases can be very valuable. If, however, one or even both of the opinions cannot be justified on the basis of research findings or generally accepted clinical practice, the psychiatric evidence may lose all credibility.

SOME BASIC PRINCIPLES

Though each case will differ, fundamental to the psychiatric contribution will be a shared body of scientific knowledge and an agreed spectrum of clinical practice and techniques. In addition some general principles will apply to the majority of child-care cases.

Natural justice versus the child's best interests

Most health care professionals, when asked to give evidence in court, will assume and hope that their testimony will help to ensure that natural justice is obtained for those frequently deprived individuals caught up in legal proceedings. In particular, psychiatrists will wish to protect the interests of their mentally ill patients. Usually the child psychiatrist's evidence will coincide with what society would regard as just and fair. The caring parents whose children were removed by an over-zealous welfare agency may be given help and another chance to try and cope with their children. A grossly abusive and violent father may be prevented from doing further harm to his children by having unsupervised access visits stopped. There are occasions, however, when this will not be the case. If there is a choice between trying to right previous wrongs done to a parent and best meeting the current needs of a child, the psychiatrist must pursue the second of these goals. Poor practice by other agencies may be commented on in the court but the child's needs must be the centrepoint of the evidence. Others will argue for justice.

Case study

A mildly mentally impaired mother provided just adequate parenting for her 4- and 6-year-old daughters. Their basic needs were met and their intellectual and social development was within normal limits. A minor head laceration following a fall from a swing by the younger child led to both children being admitted to residential care to assess whether this had been due to neglect. Visits to the unit by the mother involved a long journey and to cope with this she would take alcohol. The visits were a disaster. The girls screamed and clung to her and soiled after she had left. The elder child was sexually abused by an older boy in the home. The mother was considered not to be helping the staff in their work with the children and access was cut to once a month. After 18 months both girls showed severe disturbance with tantrums, enuresis and, in the younger, continuous encopresis. The level of disturbance was such that they had moved way beyond their mother's coping ability. She had moved into a state of chronic depression. Attempts to improve her functioning failed and the girls' needs for stability were so great that eventually placement for adoption had to be recommended. The original decision to remove the girls had been manifestly wrong, but 18 months later this could not be undone by the psychiatrist.

When a parent has a major mental illness, this approach may produce considerable conflict between child and adult psychiatrists. Those who have successfully treated a mother might see no reason why, 2 years after the original illness, her child cannot be restored to her. The child psychiatrist's perspective might be totally different, seeing an infant who has had numerous disruptions and poor development, now settled, progressing and attached to foster parents who after 2 years are making a commitment to offer the child a permanent home. The ability to understand the needs of children of psychiatrically ill parents and explain these to a parent is one of the many reasons why all intending general psychiatrists should obtain training in child development and developmental psychopathology.

Time

An absolute prerogative for any child psychiatrist intending to act as an expert witness in care cases is a thorough knowledge of developmental psychopathology. How this growing body of empirical data can be used to help the courts has been discussed by Wolkind (1984). One factor of enormous practical importance which emerges from it is the crucial element of time. The development of attachment between carer and child is well-documented (Bowlby, 1969; Rutter, 1981). Thus, though signs of differential relationships are seen before the age of 6 months, a move to a new caretaker can, if undertaken with appropriate sensitivity, be made with remarkably little disruption to the child's functioning and well-being. Certainly adoption before that age leads to an outcome, in terms of emotional and social development, virtually identical to that of non-adopted children (Humphrey & Ounstead, 1963). From 6 months to 3 years the selective nature of attachments becomes more obvious, as does the distress shown by a child when an attachment relationship is broken. Though a change of care-takers is not necessarily associated with permanent psycho-logical damage, the child's distress and subsequent withdrawal can be very great — so great that it can lead to real difficulties in a new placement (Rutter, 1981). This may particularly be the case if the child had experienced earlier disruptions (Trasler, 1960). From 3 years onwards, though attachment remains as important as before, the child's growing cognitive skills and consequent ability to understand what is happening help to make moves less overwhelmingly difficult.

Unfortunately legal processes tend to have a time sequence of their own and this may not in any way fit the needs of the child. For a great variety of reasons, court hearings can be delayed for months or even years. A major strength of the British Children Act (1989) is the recognition of this fact and the duty it imposes on courts, lawyers and professional advisers to ensure that no undue delays occur. Such delays may totally change the possibilities available for a child.

Case study

A girl of 15 gave birth to a baby. She came from a family with numerous problems. She and her siblings all had a history of minor delinquency. Her parents took the baby from her and offered to care permanently for him. The local authority were unhappy about this and, at 3 months, requested a report from a child psychiatrist. She was most unhappy about the child's prospects in this family. She felt that, though the care being given was just adequate, the grandparents age, the grand-mother's poor health, the problems they had with their own children and a continuing feud with the child's father all suggested that the baby's best interests would be best met by adoption out of the family. Delays in obtaining a date for a hearing, the need to appoint a guardian-*ad-litem* and to obtain ever more reports led to a first hearing not taking place until the child was aged 19 months. A second psychiatrist, asked to comment at that point, stated that, had he been asked for a report at 3 months he would have produced one identical to that produced by his colleague, but now, 16 months later, he felt that to move the child might be potentially more damaging than leaving him in a loving but highly problematic family. The first psychiatrist agreed with this new view.

The work on attachment, though invaluable, cannot answer all the questions that relate to time in care proceedings. The court will often be looking for guidelines as to how long a child of a particular age should have been with, say, foster parents before it becomes more harmful to move the child again as opposed to allowing it to stay. Goldstein *et al.* (1980a) have pointed out the difficulties in trying to evaluate how the past experiences, emotional state and cognitive development of each child will combine to affect that child's sense of time. They suggest however some general guidelines. Thus, for a child under the age of 5 they consider that parental absence of over 2 months is 'beyond comprehension'; for a young school-age child, 6 months. Though there are no empirical data to

back these particular limits, clinical experience does support them as useful starting points. Other factors, however, which can strengthen the attachment process, such as foster parents nursing a child through a severe illness, might suggest much shorter periods. Time will also be central when the frequency of access is being considered. Though the crucial factor is often the quality of the relationship between the custodial and non-custodial parents, frequency itself may at times be important, with over-frequent contacts having a harmful effect (Johnston *et al.*, 1989). It is however very difficult to decide what is an appropriate level and at what stage any frequency is so limited that no meaningful contact can be maintained, or so great that a child develops unmanageable split loyalties. Usually courts attempt to take a common-sense approach, but this is based on an adult's sense of time. There is an urgent need for research into this whole question. It will clearly be important to link this with research on the development of a child's general sense of time.

Permanence

Until the mid 1970s the vast majority of children coming into state or local authority care were assumed to have been admitted for a temporary period. The assumption was that at some stage they would return to their family of origin. The only exceptions were babies given up at birth and being placed for adoption. In 1973 Rowe and Lambert studied a large sample of children in local authority care in the UK. They found that, if a child had been in care for 6 months or longer, there was in fact only a negligable chance of that child returning to its family. It has since been demonstrated that not only do they not return, but they will very often lose all contact with both the immediate and extended family (Millham *et al.*, 1986). Rowe and Lambert pointed out how these children had been left in a state of limbo, losing their roots and belonging nowhere. Many would have experienced several moves while in the care system. Rowe and Lambert's work was instrumental in producing a change in policy both towards these children 'permanently in temporary care' and towards adoption. It became accepted that if a child could not return home it had to be provided with a permanent home (Thoburn *et al.*, 1986) and that on the whole this was most easily found through adoption. Strong support for the import-ance of permanency in planning for children comes from the comparison between the results of adoption, where its presence is virtually a defining feature, and foster care, where it may well not be an expectation. Children in foster care are far more likely to suffer breakdowns in placement and their rates of psychiatric disorder are far higher than amongst those who are adopted (Wolkind, 1979). Recent work suggests that permanence, however it is provided, is associated not only with better emotional and behavioural functioning but also with improved educational performance (Aldgate, 1990). Rowe has repeated her study 16 years after her original work (Rowe *et al.*, 1989). Her newer findings are depressingly similar to those of 1973, demonstrating that changes in policy are not necessarily followed by changes in practice. She also found that 6 weeks in care predicted that the child would not return home, just as 6 months did.

The concept of permanence must often be discussed in the psychiatric evidence. A sense of belonging seems essential for emotional, social and educational progress. Permanence should not, however, be seen as synonymous with adoption. Some older children may even without physical contact retain a strong psychological link with their family of origin and will request and should have the right to experience permanence in a residential unit. Some children may be permanent members of a foster family which, for various reasons, does not wish to adopt. It is important to stress the principle rather than a rigid policy.

Family structure and adversity

In some western societies the traditional biologically related two-parent nuclear family is now becoming a minority (Rimmer, 1983). By far the commonest 'nontraditional' group are single-parent families, with the vast majority being headed by mothers (Lambert & Streather, 1980). Other common patterns are one biological parent and one nonrelated stepparent or cohabitee. Less usual structures, such as a homosexual couple, may also be seen. Such families will be disproportionately over-represented amongst those involved in the child-care courts. This fact could be taken to suggest that, by their very nature, they cannot truly meet their children's needs. The child psychiatrist may well be asked to comment upon this, and give his or her views on the general acceptability of a certain family structure. It is legitimate for lawyers and judges to consider this, but the responsibility of the child psychiatrist is not to provide moral judgements, but to present to the Courts the evidence on how any particular family configuration might affect its children. If views beyond this are given, it is essential for the psychiatrist to make it plain to the court that in this instance he or she is speaking in a personal capacity and not as an expert witness.

In looking at the known information on family structure the evidence is complex, but the general outlines of the mechanisms by which family structure influences the development and adjustment of children is beginning to emerge. Children living in certain types of family will have above-average rates of psychiatric disorder and other difficulties. These can, to a limited extent, be related to some aspects of the family structure itself but, far more importantly, to certain other factors which are commoner but not universal in such families, and which when present in traditional families are associated there too with problems (Rutter & Madge, 1976). Thus children in one-parent families do less well than the average child (Lambert & Streather, 1980). This is far less due to the single-parent status itself than to the fact that these families are far more likely than most to be living in poverty and in poor housing. In turn it can be demonstrated that it is not these factors in themselves which are causal but that they act through the way they influence the functioning of the family and the relationships within it (Rutter *et al.*, 1975). An example which demonstrates this well is seen from the litera-

ture on divorce. One of the most predictable consequences of divorce is that the mother, who in the vast majority of cases will be the parent who retains custody of the children, will experience a sharp drop in living standards (Zill, 1984). A second predictable consequence is that, at least in the medium term, any involved children will have high rates of disorder. Remarriage will usually lead to a rise in the living standards of the family, but despite this there may be no improvement or even a decline in the children's functioning. The crucial role of the expectations and relationships of the adults following divorce will determine the success or otherwise of arrangements such as joint custody (Steinmen *et al.*, 1985) or access (Hetherington *et al.*, 1979).

This general mechanism appears to apply to all non-traditional families. It is the relationships within them and the way these impinge upon the child which are crucial. As an example, Tasker and Golombok (1991) have reviewed the evidence on this point for a group which may produce strong reactions amongst the general public — children being brought up by lesbian couples. The evidence supports the argument outlined above. Until a short time ago the notion of a homosexual couple rearing children might have seemed an astonishing idea to both child psychiatrists and the general public. In recent years this and other new forms of family structure have reached public awareness. Children are being conceived by artificial insemination by donor, by *in vitro* fertilization or through surrogacy. The legal and ethical dilemmas posed are being increasingly discussed (Peritore, 1988). Psychiatric and psychological knowledge of the effects of these procedures is minimal. Even with lesbian parents, an area thought to be well-studied, it is important to realize the limitations of the existing data. Virtually all the research is confined to children whose earliest years were spent with heterosexual couples. Opinions will be required on a wide range of situations and clearly further research is much needed.

The argument that family structure in itself cannot be taken as a reason for a psychiatrist making a particular recommendation to a court can be expanded to include mental illness and impairment. Children of mentally ill parents will have rates of psychiatric disorder well above the average. Again it is not the illness itself which is crucial but rather the presence of secondary factors such as family disharmony or lack of warmth (Quinton & Rutter, 1984). What is central is how the parental illness impinges on the child — not the illness itself. An identical argument applies to mild mental impairment of a parent. This too is not necessarily a bar to successfully bringing up children. It is only when this is combined with a lack of social support or other family difficulties that a poor outcome is to be expected (Gath, 1988).

The particular child or a child in general

A frequently used term used when looking at children's needs is that of good-enough parenting. Winnicott (1965), its originator, was trying to emphasize that for a child to develop well, adequate rather than superb parenting skills are required. This idea is of course correct and certainly applies to the vast majority of children of all temperamental styles. Unfortunately, in work for the courts we are often dealing with a child who falls well outside the average in terms of temperament, ability or behaviour. One would hesitate to suggest that Winnicott's idea be qualified by the addition of 'if there is a good enough child', but many, if not the majority, of these children will be ones with special needs. This term, defined legally in the Children Act (Department of Health, 1989) and in most American states, implies that the child might well require parenting that is far more than adequate, as well as help from outside the family.

Many children who enter the care system and require the protection of the courts begin life with genetic disadvantages. There may well be a family history of schizophrenia or of mental retardation, parental factors associated with a child being admitted to care (Rice *et al.*, 1971). Those in care, with their deprived backgrounds, are more likely than average to have suffered birth complications with potential adverse consequences for both cognitive and emotional development (Birch & Gussow, 1970). Their physical health may be poorer than average (Bamford & Wolkind, 1988). These vulnerable children may well require a very high level of stimulation, nurturance and care if they are to have any chance of reaching their full potential. They will require parents who can negotiate with, use and possibly demand extensive help from educational and health services. A parent whose capacity successfully to care for an 'average' child is just adequate might not be good enough for this particular child. This deficit may of course not be grounds for removing or failing to rehabilitate a child; professional help may compensate for much. It is however one of the factors which should be presented to the court.

For some children it is the experiences such as abuse or neglect which led to the court proceedings that have directly caused the special need. For others it is factors such as poor institutional care or multiple placements occurring after removal from the family which have caused the difficulty. Such experiences may have produced severe behavioural problems. For some of these children the level of disturbance will be so great that even parenting well above the average will be insufficient. Special arrangements such as professional foster care may be needed (Wolkind, 1978).

The importance of looking in detail at the individual characteristics of the child arises forcefully on those occasions when not all the children in a family have been treated in the same way. It is not uncommon to find that it is only one child in a family who has been chronically abused or neglected or, conversely, given excellent care. This type of pattern may have arisen in a number of ways. In a family on the borders of adequate coping, events occurring around the time of a particular child's entry into the family may lead to that child failing to receive satisfactory care. This may then lead on to an escalating cycle of rejection and neglect. Prematurity and perinatal illness have been particularly implicated in starting this pattern (Martin, 1981). Some parents, for a mixture of social and emotional reasons, may have real difficulties in coping with children of one sex (Korbin, 1987). In other cases a child's difficult temperament may lead to that child becoming the target of all the hostility within a family (Belsky & Vondra, 1989). In all such cases it is essential to consider separately the different needs of each individual child. It is easy to take a judgemental stance and feel that if one child has been seriously neglected the parents do not deserve to keep their other children. This may well do the other children a great disservice.

There is one exception to the rule that any reports should not concentrate on parenting or care in general but only as regards the child or children in question. This applies to those relatively uncommon occasions when a court is asked to decide the future of an unborn child. This involves highly complex legal and ethical issues. The child psychiatrist's report will concentrate on the mother's personality, parenting skills and social supports, predominantly using past behaviour as a predictor for the future. Even here, however, consideration may have to be given to the possible individual characteristics of the child. In many cases there may be no or minimal special needs. On some occasions, however the court may have to be warned that, even before the child is born, this may not be the case. The child may well be born at risk, possibly due to opiate withdrawal (Finnegan, 1981) or the fetal alcohol syndrome (Jones & Smith, 1973).

The least detrimental alternative

This ungrammatical, but important phrase was introduced into legal child-care work by Goldstein *et al.* (1980a). It encapsulates a fundamental truth which underlies virtually all children's legal hearings. In court, great efforts may be made by lawyers to demonstrate that a particular course of action could have potentially serious consequences for a child. Thus, a child psychiatrist might be arguing that a child's needs will be best met by terminating parental access and placing the child for adoption. It may be put in cross-examination that this course would have serious disadvantages; the child needs to have a feeling of belonging to its family of origin to prevent confusion of identity. If adoption is thought to be essential to the child it can be tempting to deny that this is the case and insist that the disadvantages are so insignificant they can be ignored. This is of course not true. The number of adult adoptees who, even though they show no psychiatric disorder, do feel a real sense of loss and need to discover their origins is probably very great. It is essential to acknowledge this, but then to point out that this disadvantage must be weighed against that of leaving the child in a state of psychological limbo, exposed to unhappy and traumatic access visits. Adoption is not the ideal solution — clearly in this case it is the least detrimental.

All involved with children whose future must be decided by the courts should constantly be reminded of the fact that ideal solutions do not exist. The fact that the child's future can only be decided through the courts implies that the child has already experienced a loss. The prime aim of the legal intervention is to try and minimize the harm already done and as far as possible to prevent harm occurring in the future. Courts can be best helped if, rather than speaking of the absolute advantage of one course, the psychiatrist spells out the advantages and disadvantages of every possible course open to the child. The psychiatrist can then more rationally argue for the preferred choice.

THE SPECIFIC TASKS OF THE CHILD PSYCHIATRIST

The court will have before it lawyers, often specialists in family law, arguing for their clients. It will hear from witnesses to fact; these will include professionals such as social workers or community nurses who will describe the work they have done with the child and family. The child's guardian-*ad-litem*, usually a very experienced social worker, will give an opinion on what should be done. Expert witnesses from a variety of disciplines may be called. All of these may well be giving to the court, on the basis of their observations and experience, an opinion on the key question, for example, should an estranged father see his children or should an abused child be permanently removed from its parents? With all these views being presented it is essential that the child psychiatrist clarifies to the court the particular expertise of the specialty and on which points the psychiatrist can truly be regarded as an expert. How the child psychiatric perspective differs from that of other related professions should be presented. Expertise can be claimed in four main areas, each of which may be of help to the court: (1) providing a psychiatric assessment of the child; (2) helping the court understand and evaluate the child's wishes; (3) commenting on a family's functioning and on the parenting skills available within it; and (4) introducing key concepts from developmental psychopathology and explaining their relevance to the case being heard.

Before looking individually at each of these areas, it will be helpful to look at the assessment on which the opinion will be based. Its nature will greatly depend on the questions being asked. For this reason it is important to ask referrers to be as specific as possible. Any referrer who asks merely for a psychiatric assessment should be asked why. A good referral might, after giving details of the case, ask:

1 What is the balance of advantages and disadvantages of the child remaining in foster care or being returned to its parents?
2 If it is to remain in foster care, should contact with parents be maintained and if so, how often should this occur?
3 Is the child showing signs of disturbance and if so, is any treatment required?

These questions will not only focus the thinking of the psychiatrist but will help determine the best way of structuring the assessment. This should in general follow normal good practice. As much available information as possible, such as school and social work reports, should be collected before decisions are made on who should be seen and where. It may become apparent from this that there is no disagreement about the basic facts, such as that a child is well-cared-for and securely attached to a foster mother and that the biological

mother has now fully recovered from a psychiatric illness and is successfully caring for a new baby. In this case it might be possible to give an opinion purely from the papers, spelling out the relative merits for the child of remaining in a relationship with a secure attachment as opposed to being brought up in its family of origin.

In other cases a child needs to be seen with a number of different individuals. Time may not allow every possible combination of individuals to be observed and the information in the reports and their quality and reliability will determine the priorities. The specific questions will also determine the best settings in which the interviews should be conducted. If the main focus is a couple's handling of their children, a home visit may be best, if on an individual's psychiatric state and ability to withstand stress, a formal clinic interview could be preferable. It is essential to ensure that the child is not harmed by the process. If a child has not had contact with a parent for many years it is inappropriate that this should occur in a clinic waiting room. Great care must be taken to minimize any possibilities of the assessment changing a child's perceptions and disturbing its security before a hearing takes place. Thus, after many years of uncertainty a child may have come to see itself as a full member of a foster family. A further attempt may be made by a parent to regain care of the child. The possibility of this parent successfully dealing with the child should be assessed, as should the position of the child within the foster family. What, however, is not justified is to sow in the child's mind the possibility of yet another move, possibly to a setting which it recalls with fear. Every effort should be made to make the assessment a positive experience rather than one that adds to the family's difficulties. Children should not be allowed to have repeated interviews conducted by a series of psychiatrists. If the psychiatrist knows his or her conclusions will not be favourable to the parents' case they should be told this at the time of the interview, explaining the reasoning behind this. Though many parents will be distressed or angry, this may well be the first time a professional has explained why it is felt they cannot meet the needs of their child. Some will be grateful for this and, though they will continue to disagree, they can appreciate that the role of the child psychiatrist is to place the child's current needs as the central issue.

Child psychiatrists are often criticized in court, usually by those whose views they are not supporting, for spending only 1–2 hours or even less with the various individuals involved in the case. It must be argued that these interviews are taking place against a background of experience of having interviewed and observed many similar families and in the context of having read many reports about the family. More prolonged work is only required if the interviews present a picture totally different from that described by others.

In some cases a child psychiatrist may consider that, in addition to the normal process of history-taking and observation, a special but possibly controversial technique, such as the use of anatomically explicit dolls (Yates & Terr, 1988) is required in a particular case. This must never be at the expense of a formal psychiatric assessment, but should be in addition. The reasons for using the technique should be explained with an indication of its validity and acceptance by the profession at large.

Providing a psychiatric assessment of the child

In some centres, particularly those involved predominantly in community work, child psychiatric practice has moved far from its medical origins. This has reached a point where some referrers, either social workers or lawyers, are surprised to be presented with a report whose major finding deals not with family dynamics or matters of social policy but rather with an account of the diagnostic process in child psychiatry, leading on to a formal diagnosis with comments on aetiology and prognosis. In practice, however, this may prove to be the most important and helpful contribution of the psychiatrist. Once introduced to the way in which a diagnostic system such as ICD-10 (World Health Organization, 1992) or DSM-IV (American Psychiatric Association, in press) can be used creatively, nonpsychiatrists can soon appreciate its value. Thus, in giving an opinion, the first statement should be whether a child has a disorder. The absence as well as the presence of a disorder may be of very great significance. It might be argued that a particular lifestyle of a parent is totally unacceptable. This may be true, but if the child shows no disorder this should, at the very least, make those advocating removal of that child think again. If a child who was previously very disturbed is now after 2 years in a foster home showing no disorder, this may be strong grounds for not moving the child on.

If, on the other hand, the child does have a disorder, the diagnosis should be presented to the court with an opinion as to the extent to which it might have been caused or is being maintained by environmental factors. Thus, if a child shows a clear picture of autism, there may remain many reasons why the state should intervene, but the expectation that the disorder will remit should not be one of them. In contrast, it could be argued that conduct disorder is predominantly environmentally induced and maintained. If a young child exhibits many symptoms of conduct disorder, it can be stated that the prognosis will be poor if it remains in its current environment. The court can be advised whether the prognosis may change if the child moves to a different environment. The particular type of environment which would most likely facilitate positive change can be described.

The presentation of a diagnostic formulation should not be confined to axis 1 of ICD-10. It is important to ensure that sufficient information is available to allow the child's functioning on the remaining axes to be described. Children who are in care or come before the courts are amongst the most deprived in any community. Mild learning disorders, developmental delays and physical ill health are common (Bamford & Wolkind, 1988). Too often these are overlooked as problems in their own right and are dismissed as minor parts of a deprivation syndrome that require no specific interventions.

Clinically one sees children with remediable developmental conditions such as enuresis or reading retardation, or physical problems such as poor hearing or a squint, which have been ignored while attention has been devoted to one area, such as the effects of sexual abuse. The use of a full diagnostic formulation can help the court proceedings become a crucial and constructive turning point in the life of the child.

The child's wishes

One of the most difficult tasks facing a court is the weight to be given to the stated wishes of the child. In most legal systems considerable importance is placed on these. They cannot, however, be taken in isolation and in addition it could be harmful for a young child to be left with the feeling that he or she has made the decisions about the future. The guidance to the British Children Act (1989) (Department of Health, 1989) states the dilemma. The act seeks to 'strike a balance between the need to recognize the child as an independent person and the risk of casting upon him the burden of resolving problems caused by his parents'. In this field the psychiatrist may be called on to advise the court in two main areas: the weight to be placed on the child's views in custody and access cases, and the ability of a child or adolescent to give consent to treatment.

The stated wishes of the child

The full wording in the Children Act (1989) relating to this topic is that the court must have regard to 'the ascertainable wishes and feelings of the child considered in the light of his or her age and understanding'. At the extreme ends of the spectrum there is rarely any great dilemma. It would be pointless to try to over-ride the decision of a 16-year-old that she is not prepared to attend access visits with her father. A 2-year-old cannot be expected to state his views as to whether he wishes to remain with his foster parents or be returned to his family of origin. As one moves in from these extremes the picture becomes progressively cloudier. A child will often cling to what she knows. She may be shouldering a deep sense of guilt for her own abuse. An inquiry into the death of a child at the hands of her father — a death which followed years of brutality and maltreatment — heard how her last words before dying were to apologize to him (The Bridge, 1991). There is evidence that some children who have been abused may show excessive attachment behaviours — a pattern not to be confused with a secure attachment — towards their abusive carers (Bowlby, 1969). They may firmly state that all is well and that they do not wish to leave. In evaluating these statements one helpful body of knowledge is that provided by Piaget and Inhelder (1969). It is probable that children need to have reached the stage in early adolescence of formal operations before they can be expected to weigh up the advantages and disadvantages of their current situation against those of a new one, totally unknown to them. It is important in these concepts to use the child's cognitive age rather than a purely chronological one. Not only the child's ability but also the presence of psychiatric disorder will influence the way the child's wishes will be regarded. The psychiatrist may need to point out to the court that the views of a 12-year-old with a mental age of 9 and a serious attention deficit disorder may need to be evaluated differently to the views of most 12-year-olds. In addition, the psychiatrist can help the court see the child's wishes in the context of all else that has been observed and is known about that child. A child seen separately with each parent may state firmly in the presence of both mother and father that this is the parent with whom he wishes to live. With one this may be said in a warm relaxed manner with much eye contact; with the other, in a frozen and stilted way. A child may state that he wishes to leave his foster home but in all his drawings and in play he presents a warm picture of himself as one of the foster family. Great clinical skill is required to determine the significance of such observations: a combination of factual descriptions of what has been observed and an account of the child's emotional and cognitive state can be of great help to the courts.

Consent to treatment

An issue which has grown in prominence in recent years is the ability of a child or, more usually, an adolescent to consent to or refuse treatment. In the US, under common law a minor under the age of 18 (19 in three states) must have parental consent for medical care. There is concern that this may well deter some adolescents from seeking appropriate help, particularly in the fields of sexual medicine or mental health (Robinson, 1991). In some circumstances court hearings may be held to determine whether interventions can be performed without the knowledge or agreement of parents. Quinn (1991) has described the situation in Ohio of the young woman seeking an abortion without involving her parents. If a court has not given permission, any doctor carrying out the procedure would be guilty of a criminal act. It would be normal for medical evidence to be given as to whether the young woman has sufficient maturity to give consent. However, Quinn has reservations as to whether legal or clinical definitions of maturity can really be given to courts.

In the UK an important judgement from the House of Lords is the best guide to current practice (Gillick *v* West Norfolk and Wisbech Health Authority and the Department of Health, 1985). In this well-publicised case a mother sought to obtain an assurance from the courts that no doctor employed in the health service would, without her agreement, be able to give contraceptive advice to her children under the age of 16. The judgement stated that parental powers existed for the protection of the child. These could not, however, be regarded as being dependent upon a fixed age, but rather upon the understanding of the individual child. This judgement makes it clear that young people under the age of 16 may have the right to seek or refuse psychiatric treatment. It is the responsibility of the doctor offering the treatment to form a judgement of the young people's capacity to do so. Black *et al.* (1991,

pp. 113–181) discussed this further in the context of both the Mental Health Act (Department of Health and Social Security, 1983) and the Children Act (Department of Health, 1989).

This task will follow the general technique of evaluating the child's cognitive age and emotional functioning, as well as its chronological age, as described previously. There is, however, evidence that the majority of adolescents are well able to understand the issues concerning consent to treatment. Weithorn and Campbell (1982) gave a series of vignettes describing various treatment dilemmas to groups of subjects aged 9, 14, 18 and 21. The 14-year-olds demonstrated a level of competence identical to that of the two older groups — a finding the authors claim could have been predicted from Piagetan theory. This would suggest that, although every effort should be made to involve parents in treatment issues, if an adolescent disagrees with their views or refuses to allow them to be consulted, he or she will probably be capable of giving informed consent. The psychiatrist faced with this scenario would however be well-advised to seek a legal opinion before proceeding. A related issue coming increasingly into prominence is that of children giving evidence in criminal courts. Very similar principles will apply (Spencer & Flin, 1990).

Parenting

In most centres child psychiatrists will have received during their training considerable experience in adult work. Courts can rightly expect them to comment on parents as well as children. Part of any assessment should include an evaluation of each parent's mental health and personality. What is crucial, however, and what distinguishes child psychiatrists' contribution from that of adult psychiatrists, is that these factors need to be seen less as important in their own right but far more for what they say about the individual as a *parent* (Oates, 1984). The assessment should start with the premise that the best people to bring up a child are its parents. Strengths and the possibility of building on them should be emphasized rather than only searching for weaknesses.

Parents need to be seen with their children. The clinical situation can be used to obtain a rough estimate of the parent's sensitivity to their children's cues and of the quality of attachment between them. The validity of these clinical observations has yet to be established and they must be presented with caution. Asking parents to explain what they told their children about the reason for the interview can reveal a great deal about parental attitudes.

The availability to parents of support from other adults and their ability to use this is of major importance (Rutter *et al.*, 1983), as is their ability or otherwise to use professional help and seek advice. Seeing a couple together may reveal depths of hostility not apparent when they were seen alone. If an initial assessment reveals any difficulties in parenting it is important, if at all possible, to try and see whether the capacity to change exists. Techniques originally designed to help parents deal with noncomplaint children (Patterson, 1971) have been adapted to ascertain whether parents can become more aware of their children's needs and more stimulating and sensitive in their approach (Jenner, 1992).

If a parent has a psychiatric illness the nature and severity of that illness is of less importance than how it directly impinges upon the child (Quinton & Rutter, 1984), the disruptions in the continuity of care it may cause (Rice *et al.*, 1971) and how it can disrupt parenting functions (Mills *et al.*, 1985).

It is important for the child psychiatrist to know when help from colleagues in other branches of the specialty is required. If the dangerousness of a parent is an issue in a case where physical abuse has occurred, it is wise to recommend that a forensic psychiatrist be consulted. If the prognosis of a parent with an unusual pattern of psychiatric disorder is a major point for consideration, an expert in that disorder needs to be involved.

Introducing key developmental concepts to the court

In addition to clinical observations and formulations, the child psychiatrist needs to be able to place these in the context of a body of knowledge in developmental psychopathology (Wolkind, 1984). His or her responsibility is to make the court aware of how its actions fit into this framework and the potential effects they could have on the child. Relevant points need to be presented in an understandable fashion with an indication of the strength of the evidence and how they relate to the particular case being heard. Of particular importance will be the work on attachment referred to above and that detailing how early experiences and behaviour relate to later psychopathology. The possible relationship between a child's behaviour and parental functioning will need to be explained. It may be necessary to explain that this is not a one-way process and that children can strongly influence their parents (Hinde, 1980). Equally, however, the court may have to be told that, at the time of the hearing, it is no longer possible to trace the pathways by which the present situation has been reached and that the important task is not to attribute parental blame, but rather to determine whether at this stage this particular child can be successfully cared for by these particular parents.

The report

The formal written report is the culmination of the psychiatric intervention. It is on the basis of this that the decision will be made as to whether the psychiatrist will need to give evidence directly to the court. The helpfulness of child psychiatry will be largely judged from written reports. Courts vary in the format that they will regard as acceptable. A variety of specimen reports is presented by Black *et al.* (1991).

The following is suggested as a guideline to the structure a report might follow — one which can help the court see how the assessment took place and what led to the final recommendations.

The qualifications of the writer

The report should start with an account of the qualifications and professional post held by the writer. It is not usually necessary to detail one's clinical and academic experience but on occasion this can be helpful. If an unusual diagnosis or family structure is the key issue in the case and the writer has special knowledge of the topic, this should be stated.

The commissioning and scope of the report

A statement should be given describing who commissioned the report and what questions were asked. The attitude of other parties to the involvement of the psychiatrist should be stated, i.e. did they oppose this or agree that this should be a joint approach for an independent opinion? In some cases it is helpful to state the main areas of disagreement between the parties and how many of these are within the expertise of a child psychiatrist.

The organization of the assessment

A factual account should be given of who was seen, when and where. A list should be given of all documents read and whether this was before or after the various interviews.

The interviews

The content of each interview should be given. If the information obtained is identical to that presented in social enquiry or other reports, there is no need to repeat all the detail. A comment such as: 'Mrs *x* gave me a detailed account of her life history and of the events leading to her child being taken into care. This did not differ from that given to the social worker, with the exception of the following points' will suffice. This should be followed by a description of the observations made during the interview. These should be factual descriptions and not interpretations. Thus, when describing the interactions between a child and parent, this should be in terms of what actually occurred and not in terms of the quality of the attachment.

The interpretation of the material

Here all the information gathered and observed should be used to give clinical opinions. Diagnoses, the quality of attachment and other relationships can be presented, together with the data on which they are based. The significance of these both in terms of aetiology and prognosis should be discussed.

The options

The implications for the child of these clinical findings should be described. This should be done in the light of all the different options open to it through the decisions of the court.

Recommendations

On the basis of the last section, a series of recommendations can be made. In many cases it is preferable to point out the relative merits and demerits of each possible option rather than asserting in absolute terms. In some cases there are crucial disputes over matters of factual evidence — matters which the psychiatrist is in no position to resolve. Here recommendations should be qualified by a comment such as: 'If the court decides the mother's account of the events is true, then on the basis of my observations I would see *x* as the preferred option. If, however, the court does not feel this is true, *Y* might be the best outcome'.

The report should be signed and dated.

CONCLUSIONS AND THE WAY FORWARD

Some psychiatrists resent the amount of legal work that arises from child psychiatric practice. A minority will refuse to be involved in any case which might come to court. It is very time-consuming to prepare a report and it can be highly stressful to have to defend one's professional expertise against possibly hostile questioning in court. Greater public exposure of our clinical skills and the body of knowledge that underpin these has, however, enhanced the reputation of the specialty. More importantly, however, a good court decision can be a major positive turning point in the life of a child. It can give the child a chance to move on to a new developmental pathway with a power that can only be matched by purely clinical techniques with great difficulty. A bad decision can, of course, have the reverse effect. It is challenging and humbling that we have the power to influence these decisions. Assessments for the courts must be seen as a central and valuable part of the work of child psychiatrists, not as a nuisance which takes us away from our real tasks.

The questions being asked in court appear to be becoming ever more complex. Politicosocial influences can produce dramatic changes in child-care policy and practice. As an example, views on the desirability or otherwise of transracial adoptions have shifted markedly over the last 10 years. This shift has not been based on data collected from research (Silverman & Feigelman, 1990). It is essential that the child psychiatrist keep up to date on the scientific literature and is in a position to help the courts disentangle what is really known from what is believed. Increasing dissatisfaction with the quality of some of the care offered to children removed from their families is leading to a major rethink (Levy & Kahan, 1991). Here again, a prime task for the child psychiatrist is to ensure that the growing body of knowledge within the specialty is made available, in an understandable form, to those who have the power to make decisions for children.

REFERENCES

Aldgate J. (1990) Foster children at school: success or failure. *Adoption*

and Fostering, **14**, 38–49.

Allen N. (1990) *Making Sense of the Children Act.* Longman, London.

American Psychiatric Association (1994) *Diagnostic and Statistical Manual of Mental Disorders — 4th edition — DSM-IV.* American Psychiatric Association, Washington DC.

Ash P. & Guyer M. (1986) The functions of psychiatric evaluation in contested child custody and visitation cases. *Journal of the American Academy of Child Psychiatry,* **25**, 554–561.

Bamford F. & Wolkind S.N. (1988) *The Physical and Mental Health of Children in Care: Research Needs.* Economic and Social Research Council, London.

Belsky J. & Vondra J. (1989) Lessons from child abuse: the determinants of parenting. In: Cicchetti D. & Carlson V. (eds) *Child Maltreatment,* pp. 153–202. Cambridge University Press, Cambridge.

Birch H.G. & Gussow J.D. (1970) *Disadvantaged Children: Health, Nutrition and School Failure.* Harcourt, Brace and World, New York.

Black D., Wolkind S.R. & Harris-Hendriks J. (eds) (1991) *Child Psychiatry and the Law* (2nd edition). Gaskell & Royal College of Psychiatrists, London.

Bowlby J. (1969) *Attachment and Loss. Vol. I Attachment.* Hogarth Press, London.

Bridge C. & Hipgrave T. (1989) The New Zealand Family Court. *Children and Society,* **3**, 325–338.

Bullock R., Hosie K., Little M. & Millham S. (1991) The research background to the law on parental access to children in care. *Journal of Social Welfare and Family Law,* 85–93.

Cox A. (1990) Regional strategies for child and adolescent psychiatry. In: Harris-Hendriks J. & Black M. (eds) *Child and Adolescent Psychiatry into the 90s.* Occasional Papers 8. Royal College of Psychiatrists, London.

Davis G. & Roberts M. (1989) Mediation in disputes over children. *Children and Society,* **3**, 275–279.

de Jonge A. (1989) Some changing aspects of child rights in Australia — in and out of court. *Journal of Social Welfare and Family Law,* 163–173.

Department of Health (1989) *An Introduction to the Children Act 1989.* Her Majesty's Stationery Office, London.

Department of Health (1990) *The Quality of Medical Care.* Her Majesty's Stationery Office, London.

Department of Health (1991) *Child Abuse: A Study of Enquiry Reports 1980–1989.* Her Majesty's Stationery Office, London.

Department of Health and Social Security (1983) *The Mental Health Act. Memorandum on Parts I-VI, VIII-X.* Her Majesty's Stationery Office, London.

Eekelaar J. (1991) Parental responsibility: state of nature or nature of the state. *Journal of Social Welfare and Family Law,* 37–50.

Eekelaar J. & Dingwall R. (1990) *The Reform of Child Care Law: A Practical Guide to the Children Act 1989.* Routledge, London.

Finnegan L.P. (1981) The effects of narcotics and alcohol on pregnancy and the newborn. In: Millman R.B., Cushman P. Jr & Lowinson J.H. (eds) *Research Developments in Drug and Alcohol Abuse,* pp. 136–157. New York Academy of Science, New York.

Freed D.J. & Walker T.B. (1989) Family law in the 50 states: an overview. *Family Law Quarterly,* **22**, 367–526.

Garwood F. (1989) Involving children in conciliation. *Children and Society,* **3**, 311–324.

Gath A. (1988) Mentally handicapped people as parents. *Journal of Child Psychology and Psychiatry,* **29**, 739–744.

Gillick *versus* West Norfolk and Wisbech Health Authority and the Department of Health (1985) *Weekly Law Reports,* **3**, 830.

Goldstein J., Freud A. & Solnit A.J. (1980a) *Beyond the Best Interests of the Child.* Burnett Books, London.

Goldstein J., Freud A. & Solnit A.J. (1980b) *Before the Best Interests of the Child.* Burnett Books, London.

Hetherington E.M., Cox M. & Cox R. (1979) Family intervention and the social, emotional and cognitive development of children following divorce. In: Vaughn L. & Brazelton T.B. (eds) *The Family Setting Priorities*, pp. 89–128. Science and Medical, New York.

Herman S.P. (1990) Forensic child psychiatry: introduction. *Journal of the American Academy of Child and Adolescent Psychiatry*, **29**, 955–957.

Hinde R.A. (1980) Family influences. In: Rutter M. (ed) *Developmental Psychiatry*, pp. 47–66. William Heinemann, London.

Humphrey M. & Ounstead C. (1963) Adoptive families referred for psychiatric advice. Part 1. The children. *British Journal of Psychiatry*, **109**, 599–608.

Jenner S. (1992) The assessment and treatment of parenting problems.

Johnston J.R., Kline M. & Tschann J.M. (1989) Ongoing postdivorce conflict; effects on children of joint custody and frequent access. *American Journal of Orthopsychiatry*, **59**, 576–592.

Jones K.S. & Smith D.W. (1973) Recognition of the fetal alcohol syndrome in early infancy. *Lancet*, **2**, 999–1001.

Kempe C.H., Silverman F.N., Steele B.F., Droegemuller W. & Silver H.K. (1962) The battered child syndrome. *Journal of the American Medical Association*, **181**, 107–112.

Kerckhoff R.D. (1981) Attempts to harmonize family law: The role of the Council of Europe. *Journal of Comparative Family Studies*, **12**, 275–284.

Korbin J.E. (1987) Child maltreatment in cross-cultural perspective. In: Gelles R.J. & Lancaster J.B. (eds) *Child Abuse and Neglect: Biosocial Dimensions*, pp. 31–56. Aldine De Gruyter, New York.

Lambert L. & Streather J. (1980) *Children in Changing Families*. Macmillan/National Children's Bureau, London.

Levy A. & Kahan B.R. (1991) *The Pindown Experience and the Protection of Children*. Staffordshire County Council, Staffordshire.

Levy D.M. (1951) Critical evaluation of the present state of child psychiatry. *American Journal of Psychiatry*, **108**, 481–490.

MacPherson S. (1984) *Legislation and Child Welfare: An Annotated Bibliography*. World Health Organization, Geneva.

Martin F.M. & Murray K. (1981) *Children Out of Court*. Scottish Academic Press, Edinburgh.

Martin H.P. (1981) The neuropsychodevelopmental aspects of child abuse and neglect. In: Ellerstein N.S. (ed) *Child Abuse and Neglect: A Medical Reference*, pp. 95–119. Wiley, New York.

Millham S., Bullock R., Hosie K. & Haak M. (1986) *Lost in Care*. Gower, Aldershot.

Mills M., Puckering C., Pound A. & Cox A. (1985) What is it about depressed mothers that influences their children's functioning? In: Stevenson J. (ed) *Recent Research in Developmental Psychopathology*, pp. 11–18. Pergamon Press, Oxford.

Noble P. (1983) A case report in relation to access. *Journal of Child Psychology and Psychiatry*, **24**, 297–300.

Oates M. (1984) Assessing fitness to parent. In: *Taking a Stand*. British Agencies for Adoption and Fostering, London.

O'Regan T. (1990) Emotional abuse within a changing legal framework. *Journal of Child Care Law*, **2**, 119–125.

Patterson G. (1971) *Families: Application of Social Learning to Family Life*. Research Press, Champaign, IL.

Peritore L. (1988) A select bibliography on surrogacy. *Family Law Quarterly*, **22**, 213–227.

Piaget J. & Inhelder B. (1969) (Original French edition 1966) *The Psychology of the Child* (translated by Weaver H.) Routledge & Kegan Paul, London.

Quinn K.M. (1991) Competence to have an abortion: adolescent issues. *Newsletter of the American Academy of Psychiatry and the Law*, **16**, 19.

Quinton D. & Rutter M. (1984) Family pathology and child psychiatry disorder; a 4 year prospective study. In: Nicol A.R. (ed) *Longitudinal Studies in Child Psychology and Psychiatry: Lessons from Research Experi-*ence, pp. 91–135. Wiley, Chichester.

Rice E.P., Ekdahl M.C. & Miller L. (1971) *Children of Mentally Ill Parents; Problems in Child Care*. Behavioural Publishers, New York.

Richards M.P.M. (1988) Developmental psychology and family law: a discussion paper. *British Journal of Developmental Psychology*, **6**, 169–182.

Rimmer L. (1983) Changing family patterns: some implications for policy. In: White Franklin A. (ed) *Family Matters, Perspectives on the Family and Social Policy*, pp. 11–18. Pergamon, Oxford.

Robinson R. (1991) Consent and confidentiality for adolescents in US. *British Medical Journal*, **303**, 539.

Rowe J. & Lambert L. (1973) *Children Who Wait*. British Association of British Adoption Agencies, London.

Rowe J., Hundleby M. & Garnett L. (1989) *Child Care Now*. Research Series. British Agencies for Adoption and Fostering, London.

Rutter M. (1981) *Maternal Deprivation Reassessed*, 2nd end. Penguin, Harmondsworth.

Rutter M. & Madge N. (1976) *Cycles of Disadvantage: A Review of Research*. Heinemann Educational, London.

Rutter M., Yule B., Quinton D. & Berger M. (1975) Attainment and adjustment in two geographical areas. III. Some factors accounting for area differences. *British Journal of Psychiatry*, **126**, 520–533.

Rutter M., Quinton D. & Liddle C. (1983) Parenting in two generations: looking backwards and looking forwards. In: Madge N. (ed) *Families at Risk*, pp. 60–98. Heinemann Educational, London.

Silverman A.R. & Feigelman W. (1990) Adjustment in interracial adoptees; an overview. In: Brodzinsky D.M. & Schechter M.D. (eds) *The Psychology of Adoption*, pp. 187–200. Oxford University Press, New York.

Spencer J.R. & Flin R. (1990) *The Evidence of Children: The Law and the Psychology*. Blackstone Press, London.

Steinman S., Zemmelman S.E. & Knoblauch T.M. (1985) A study of parents who sought joint custody after a divorce. *Journal of the American Academy of Child Psychiatry*, **24**, 554–562.

Tasker F.L. & Golombok S. (1991) Children raised by lesbian mothers: the empirical evidence. *Family Law*, **21**, 184–187.

The Bridge (1991) *Sukina: An Evaluation Report of the Circumstances Leading to her Death*. The Bridge Child Care Consultancy Service, London.

Thoburn J., Murdoch A. & O'Brien A. (1986) *Permanence in Child Care*. Basil Blackwell, Oxford.

Tizard B. (1991) Intercountry adoption: a review of the evidence. *Journal of Child Psychology and Psychiatry*, **32**, 743–756.

Trasler G. (1960) *In Place of Parents: A Study of Foster Care*. Routledge & Kegan Paul, London.

Wald M.S., Carlsmith J.M. & Leiderman P.H. (1988) *Protecting Abused and Neglected Children*. Stanford University Press, Stanford, CA.

Waterhouse J. (1989) Allegations of child abuse — the court's approach. In: Levy A. (ed) *Focus on Child Abuse*, pp. 2–17. Hawkesmore, London.

Weithorn L.A. & Campbell S.B. (1982) The competency of children and adolescents to make informed treatment decisions. *Child Development*, **53**, 1589–1598.

White R. (1991) Legal aspects. In: Black D., Wolkind S. & Hendriks-Harris J. (eds) *Child Psychiatry and the Law*, pp. 182–187. Gaskell/Royal College of Psychiatrists, London.

Winnicot D. (1965) *The Maturational Process and the Facilitating Environment*. Hogarth, London.

Wolkind S.N. (1978) Fostering the disturbed child. *Journal of Child Psychology and Psychiatry*, **19**, 393–397.

Wolkind S.N. (1979) Psychological development of the adopted child. In: Wolkind S.N. (ed) *Medical Aspects of Adoption and Foster Care*, pp. 67–73. Heinemann, London.

Wolkind S.N. (1984) A child psychiatrist in court: using the contribution of developmental psychology. In: *Taking a Stand*, pp. 7–17. British Agencies for Adoption and Fostering, London.

Wolkind S.N. (1988) Signs of emotional abuse. *Journal of Social Welfare and Law*, **2**, 82–87.

World Health Organization (1992) *The ICD-10 Classification of Mental and Behavioural Disorders: Clinical Descriptions and Diagnostic Guidelines.* World Health Organization, Geneva.

Yates A. & Terr L. (1988) Debate forum: anatomically correct dolls, should they be used as a basis for expert testimony? *Journal of the American Academy of Child Psychiatry*, **27**, 254–257.

Yates C. (1989) Religious education and upbringing — child right or parent prerogative. *Journal of Child Care Law*, **1**, 89–94.

Yates C. (1990) The conciliation project report: a study of non judicial dispute resolution in family cases. *Journal of Social Welfare and Family Law*, 33–43.

Zill N. (1984) *Happy, Healthy and Insecure*. Doubleday, New York.

Index